Price Guide and Bibliographic Checklist
for
Children's & Illustrated Books
for the years 1880 - 1960

1996 Edition

Compiled by:

E. Lee Baumgarten

Martinsburg, WV

E. Lee Baumgarten Books

First published in hardback and Perfect-bound formats: November 1995

ISBN: 0-9647285-0-8   (Hardback Edition)

             0-9647285-1-6   (Softbound Edition)

Library of Congress Catalog Card Number: 95-96231

INTRODUCTION

Welcome to the first true "book" edition of the *Price Guide & Bibliographic Checklist for Children's & Illustrated Books*. I can state with absolute confidence that you've purchased the most comprehensive single-source reference work of its kind on the market, and one that I believe you'll make good use of in the years to come for both market values and bibliographic information. I recall talking to Mr. Jeff Dykes at his home sometime in 1989 when I purchased a few books, including his own "Fifty Great Western Illustrators". I only met him the one time, but I remember discussing the topic of when to "go to press" with one's work. He informed me (correctly!) that research can easily become an obsession, and there comes a time when you must resist the temptation to continue adding more and more titles and simply print the book. So, with just about 4,700 new titles accumulated as of September 1995, I've (finally!) decided to take his advice and wrap up the research effort for this edition of the guide. I hope you find it beneficial to your business and/or collecting endeavors.

I expanded the date parameters for this new printing to include books published through 1960. The total count for this year's guide is 10,405 titles, sorted three ways within the same volume for your convenience. My research, as usual, focused almost exclusively on trade editions of children's and other illustrated books. With very few exceptions private-press, signed and limited-edition books were purposely excluded from the guide, as these books are typically worth more than their counterpart trade editions, and deserve a more thorough description than space permits here. Moreover, I purposely excluded the majority of "Little Golden Books" published in the 1940's and 1950's. This category of children's books has already been thoroughly covered by Rebecca Greason in her book, "Golden Book Collectibles".

This year I altered the methodology for adding new titles to the guide. In previous years I relied primarily on dealer and auction catalog entries and the corresponding prices contained therein, and afterwards verified bibliographic details as necessary at the Library of Congress (LC). I decided to reverse the process for the latest printing (hence the slight enhancement to the title: "... and Bibliographic Checklist...") by first examining the LC card catalog file, then the deposit copy, and subsequently establishing either a real price range based on recent catalog entries located for that book, or my own "best-guess" range based on a number of factors explained later in the introduction. The earlier method was too dependent on first locating reference to a given book in a dealer or auction catalog, whereas the new method allowed me much greater freedom to make full use of the vast resources at LC to provide you with a reasonably comprehensive listing of available trade edition titles by any given author. I also "back-tracked" to enhance the bibliographic details for books already included in the guide, especially occurrences of "stated" first editions and the presence of illustrated or colored endpapers, among other features.

One of my goals for this new printing was to physically examine each LC deposit copy for all American-published books documented in the guide. As of this writing I have handled slightly over 4,000 American-published LC deposit copy titles contained in the guide, and have accounted for and verified bibliographic details for most of the remaining titles through either the LC card catalog, the National Union Catalog (NUC), or the catalog of books in the British Museum (BM).

Since the vast majority of LC deposit copies are first editions, I thought it would be especially useful to observe the markings and physical characteristics of these books in an effort to determine the general identifying features of the 1st edition. Unfortunately, not all LC deposit copies were available for examination. Over time, more than a few books have been stolen from the collection. Additionally, a significant number were not on the shelf for reasons other than pilfering, and still more have been rebound in standard "library binding", thereby eliminating the opportunity to see the original binding type and endpapers. I did, however, place special emphasis on examining titles that could possibly be "stated" first editions. For some companies, such as Doubleday, it is usually a given that the first edition will be so stated. For others, some of which are notoriously inconsistent with their methods, the only way to know if the first edition should be stated is by examining the LC deposit copy.

Regarding books that I could not physically examine, I verified basic bibliographic information through the LC card catalog files. Unfortunately, for reasons unknown to me, many of the LC catalog cards representing books published in the 1950's contained only minimal information. Unlike entries for the previous 40 or 50 years, features such as pictorial endpapers, type of illustration (color or b/w) and specific page count for unpaginated books were rarely documented, therefore requiring a physical examination of the actual book to determine these and other features. For reasons outlined above, it was not always possible to see a particular book, resulting in a number of entries for which only the catalog card data is currently listed. Also, there were a number of books simply not contained in the Library's collection. I found reference to many such titles in NUC, but for others there is no reference available that I'm aware of other than an occasional offer for sale in dealer or auction catalogs. Interestingly, many titles in the latter category were published by the P.F. Volland company.

Sometime within the past two years I began to *fully* appreciate the enormity of the Library of Congress collection, both in terms of copyright deposit copies and bibliographic reference materials. It seemed as though every time I turned around I discovered more authors, titles and/or illustrators to include in the guide. Throughout my research effort, the need to see any given book prompted a trip to the card catalog room where I first looked up the author and LC call number. Invariably, I found additional titles by that same author, many of which were illustrated by different artists. In some instances, this prompted still another examination of the card catalog for an illustrator name, which would in turn point to yet another author or title. And so on and so forth. The best analogy I can think of is the steel ball inside a pinball machine, continually bouncing from one rubber bumper to another!

This year I've included a new descriptive abbreviation to help identify a first edition: {std} -- representing a stated first edition. This is especially useful for many books published after 1922. Also new for this year's edition are: **pep** (pictorial), **dep** (decorative), and **cep** (colored) endpapers; and **SC** (Scribner Illustrated Classic). See *Key to Descriptive Terms* on page 7 of the introduction for a more thorough explanation of these and other terms. I hope they prove useful to you.

As in previous printings, I have excluded books that typically market for less than $20, although there may be an occasional entry listed out at $15. As a general rule, books that commonly sell below $20 fall into one or both of the following categories: 1) books not widely collected; 2) reprints published by companies such as Grosset/Dunlap, A.L. Burt, Hurst, Sun Dial, Triangle and others, including various book clubs. The principal purpose of this guide is to provide both bibliographic detail and the average retail market price of some of the more collectible children's and illustrated books of the time period, rather than attempting to distinguish between, let's say, a resale value of $7 or $10 for reprints and less desirable titles.

Throughout the next few pages, I write briefly on some important points to consider when using this guide. I urge you to read the entire introduction before proceeding on to the list itself.

Condition:

Condition is of the utmost importance in determining the value of any book. Having said that, I believe the standards are not quite as strict for children's books as they are for modern first editions since, after all, it is commonly understood that children's books typically have been subjected to rough handling over the years by their intended users. Because of this, you should pay close attention to any and all defects, and keep in mind also that the prices listed within this guide are for books in Very Good (VG) condition; that is, books that are free from major defects such as excessive cover soiling, loose or broken hinges, dog-eared, loose or missing pages, crayoned plates and/or text, and any other defect which would significantly detract from the aesthetic value of the book. Generally, a VG book is one with a minimum of wear, the text and covers clean and tight, with no major internal or external faults. Only the rarest books will bring anything more than a few dollars in poor condition. For this reason, *downward pricing adjustments should be made for copies that are below the "VG" standard*. Conversely, books which are in exceptionally fine condition may be worth considerably more than the price listed in this guide.

Book Values:

The prices in this guide represent **retail values** and are given in U.S. dollars. The actual dollar sign has been omitted to avoid redundancy. Most values are based on the examination and cross-referencing of hundreds of recent dealer catalogs and major book auction "prices-realized" slips which I have studied and compared over the last six years. As you are no doubt aware, many factors must be considered in pricing a book, one of the most important being condition. You should also keep in mind that many of the prices in this guide are based on books that receive a broad exposure primarily through nationwide catalog distribution, major antiquarian book fairs and various national trade publications. A book that may sell rather quickly when nationally advertised or offered for sale by a dealer with a large customer base may not sell for a long time or for nearly the same price to a walk-in customer at a shop. Other factors such as geographic location, the customer base, the individual dealer's business philosophy, etc. play a large part in determining the value of any given book. For the above reasons, I've provided a value range for the titles in this guide. In establishing this range, I have attempted to eliminate anomalies (i.e., a one-time auction price that is far outside the value range -- on either end of the scale -- determined by comparing prices in numerous dealer and auction catalogs). Furthermore, pay close attention to entries that are followed by an asterisk {*}. The value range for these titles is strictly "best-guess" on my part. I didn't want to lose the bibliographic entry simply because I couldn't find a price reference of any sort in a recent catalog. One final point on values: the trend seems to continue in the upward direction, especially for titles by highly collected authors and illustrators. However, there is always the possibility that a given author and/or illustrator may diminish in popularity, resulting in a decrease in market value for that individual's works.

First Editions:

Within the context of this price guide, the term **first edition (1st)** should be interpreted to mean: *"the first illustrated edition by the respective artist"*. In many cases the listed book may also be a true first edition, but that is not always the case. To illustrate the point (no pun intended!), the true 1st edition of Kipling's **Brushwood Boy** was published in 1899 and illustrated by Orson Lowell. Less than 10 years later, another edition was published which featured color plates by an artist named Townsend. In this case, the edition by Townsend would accurately be termed a **first thus**; that is, the first edition with Townsend's plates, although not a true 1st. It is, however, listed as a **1st** in this guide. Another good example is Charles Dickens, whose titles have been illustrated by a large number of artists over the years. Numerous editions of his **Christmas Carol** appear in this guide, many of which are listed as a 1st for the corresponding illustrator, according to the above criteria.

As a general rule, if the date on the title page corresponds to that on the copyright page, it is a first, or first thus. Unfortunately though, the determination is rarely quite that simple. Some publishing companies, such as David McKay, Reilly-Britton, Bobbs-Merrill, Doran, Farrar and Harcourt Brace rarely placed a date on the title page, including first editions. Others such as Doran and Farrar/Rinehart used a publisher's design on the copyright page to signify a first edition. And still others stated concisely: "First Edition", or "First Printing", or used letters of the alphabet to signify a first edition. Scribner and Rand/McNally are two examples of companies that used the letter "A" on the copyright page to signify a first edition of a given title. As mentioned earlier, a new designation is included in this year's edition: {std}, and it appears in the title and descriptive field of the guide, signifying a "stated" first edition or first printing.

As if determining the first edition isn't sometimes difficult enough, in more than a few instances you must also determine what characteristics comprise a first "state" of a 1st edition. With children's books, the number of color plates can help to ascertain a first printing. Whether or not any edges are gilt and/or uncut can also play a part in identifying the first printing of a given book. Many of the Scribner Classics (identified as SC in this year's guide) may appear to be first printings, but if the top edge is not gilt, it is in fact a later printing of the 1st. Typographical errors, binding color and presence or absence of pictorial endpapers are other features that can assist in identifying a first state of a first edition. Hopefully I've made it easier for you by including many of these designations in the guide. First edition points of some books, such as the majority of those authored by L. Frank Baum, have already been exhaustively researched by others in the field. In this guide, I simply use the designation: [1] to denote the first state of a first edition, as defined in reference works such as Jacob Blanck's **Bibliography of American Literature**, or Hanff/Greene's **Bibliographia Oziana**. I would also highly recommend obtaining a copy of **First Editions: A Guide to Identification** (ISBN 0-930358-08-2), available from the Spoon River Press, for a more in-depth discussion of each publisher's methods for designating their first editions.

Regarding Reprints:

Early reprints appear to hold value much better than their counterparts in the modern first edition genre of the trade. As an example, books illustrated by Johnny Gruelle, most of which were originally published by the Volland publishing company, were reprinted by Donohue, and from what I've been able to determine, have a value of 60% - 80% of the Volland originals, all else being equal. Likewise, reprints of L. Frank Baum and W. W. Denslow published by Donohue, while nowhere near the value of the originals, are nevertheless valuable in the collector's market, and should not be considered worthless.

I have not included reprints <u>by the same publisher</u> in this guide. I believe no useful purpose is served by listing out numerous later editions of a title by the same publisher/illustrator combination, since the value of such reprints can somewhat be determined by looking up the price range for the first (or first thus) edition, and then subtracting a percentage of that value to determine the price of the later printing. For example, a 1919 reprint of the Scribner Illustrated Classic "Treasure Island", illustrated by N.C. Wyeth, would be worth less than the first edition (published in 1911), and a 1940 printing, although in the same format, would be worth still less.

Dust Jackets:

Many of the prices listed in this guide are for books without dust jackets (DJ). I would estimate that a children's book which includes the original DJ should be worth at least 150% of a copy lacking the DJ, and in some cases the price discrepancy can be far greater, depending on factors such as author, scarcity, age, title or artist. Generally speaking, any collectible book published prior to 1920 that still has its original DJ in acceptable condition is considered exceptionally desirable, and therefore commands a much higher price than a copy lacking it.

Publishers:

Please note the publisher of the books you run across. For your convenience, I have documented specific publishers of the books in this guide, rather than simply stating **New York, London, Boston,** etc. Many of the more popular titles were reprinted by companies such as Grosset & Dunlap, A.L. Burt, Hurst, Sun Dial and others. Books which bear these imprints are worth considerably less than those listed in this price guide. Exceptions to this rule would include the turn-of-the-century "gift books" illustrated by artists such as Harrison Fisher, H.C. Christy, Coles Phillips, etc. This type of book is sought for the color plates, without regard for the publisher.

<u>A Word about Grosset & Dunlap:</u> Although the vast majority of books published by this company are reprints, there are numerous instances in which Grosset & Dunlap published the first edition, and I've tried to list only those titles for which I could not locate (either in the Library of Congress Card Catalog file or the National Union Catalog) the same author/title/illustrator combination published the same year or earlier by another company.

Convention for Publication Dates

The presence, absence, and/or location of a publication date in a given book is, in many instances, an important determining factor for distinguishing between first or later editions. Not all sources make note of the publication date in the same manner, and because of this there may instances in which discrepancies may exist in this guide. This is especially true of books published in Great Britain. In this guide publication date information should be interpreted according to the following example:

1900	=	The date appears on the title page. This includes books that have <u>all</u> publishing information, including copyright notice, on title page only. Many picture books were so designed.
(1900)	=	(Enclosed in parenthesis): Date appears on copyright page only.
[1900]	=	[Enclosed in brackets]: Date does not appear on either the title or copyright page, and "1900" represents either the actual or approximate date of publication. The designations "n.d." and "circa" (or "ca"), used by some dealers, are equivalent terms for this notation.

The "LC" Column

The right-most column (LC) contains, when applicable, either of two designations (in some cases both): 1) the letter "R", signifying a book that the Library of Congress has placed in its Rare Book Division; 2) the asterisk symbol:

(*), highlighting a book I discovered by searching through the LC card catalog file, NUC or other sources and for which I've found no offer for sale in any recent dealer or auction catalogs. This feature should be especially helpful in identifying additional scarce titles by collectible authors and illustrators.

PLEASE NOTE: The price range given for any book with the "*" symbol is admittedly an educated guess on my part, based on factors such as author, illustrator, subject matter, physical appearance, whether or not the book in question is a Caldecott or Newbery award winner, a **Peter Parley to Penrod** title, included in LC Rare Book Division, and so forth. I tried to limit this group to titles that I believe are collectible for one or more of these reasons.

Regarding the "R" designation (for Rare Book Division at LC): I was told by a number of people at the Library that the inclusion of a given title in Rare Books doesn't necessarily indicate a bona fide rarity, even though this is true in many cases. Sometimes a book may have been placed in this division because of a signature, or the result of a donation by a collector, or a dust-jacketed copy that is considered rare as a result thereof. I mention this because I'm sure you'll find examples of books that you think should be considered "rare" (and indeed are), but nevertheless are not included in the LC Rare Book Division. I'll leave you to draw your own conclusions in this matter.

Exceptions & Clarifications

The vast majority of books within this price guide contain either color or black and white plates and/or in-text illustrations by the designated illustrator. The few exceptions are as follows:

Margaret Armstrong	:	Cover Art, textual designs (books are usually illustrated by another artist or not at all)
Frank Hazenplug	:	Cover Art, title-page design
Bruce Rogers	:	Title-page design, devices & designs on cover & spine, typeface design
Unknown	:	Unable to determine specific artist
Various	:	Illustrated by 2 or more artists
Chromos	:	Chromolithographs (undetermined artist). Color reproduction process used mainly before 1900. When known, books illustrated with chromos are listed under the specific artist name.

Special Acknowledgements

This year I would like to express my gratitude to Ms. Victoria Hill of the Humanities and Social Sciences Division at the Library of Congress. Her assistance in providing me with special computer printouts proved instrumental in documenting many new titles for each of the following publishers: Volland, R.H. Russell, W.R. Scott and Holiday House. Without her help, it would have taken many hours and some tiring footwork to accumulate this new information via the card catalog file and other sources. Some of the titles published by these companies (especially Russell) were by authors who wrote only one book and therefore would have been exceptionally difficult to locate by chance in the card catalog file.

I also thank Carolyn Clugston Michaels, author of "Children's Book Collecting", for graciously sending me a listing of titles in her P.F. Volland collection. Thanks also to Lauren Bufferd of the Chicago Public Library for providing me with list of Volland titles in the library collection.

Once again I would like to express thanks to Mr. William H. Mobley of the Collections Development Office at the Library of Congress for separating out catalogs and other material having to do with children's and illustrated books. Since 1989 he has been particularly helpful in guiding me to pertinent reference works and areas of the Library that facilitated my research.

Finally, but in no way least on the list, I thank both the Main Reading Room staff and the Rare Book Division staff in the Library's Jefferson Building. From the Main Reading Room I would like to thank Francine Spraggin-Via, Gwen Latson, Darnell Moses, Margo Rush, Sheleta Slye, Tyrone Smith, James Kee, Willie Hopkin, Tanya Lowery, Rocita Lawson, Reginald Delauder, Jermone Dixon, Michelle Bridges, Jon Moten and Tiffany Corley. At one point, Ms. Spraggin-Via jokingly referred to me as "Mr. PZ", because of the 15 book requests per hour (mostly from the PZ children's fiction section) that I usually submitted on any given day at the Library. I'm sure the staff working in the stacks had other names for me that are best left unprinted! I also thank Anthony Edwards, Charles Kelly, Clark Evans and Rob Shields of the Rare Book Division for retrieving approximately 450 books for me over the past two years.

Enjoy the Guide!

I hope this price guide and bibliographic checklist proves useful to you, and assists you in both saving and making money, building a collection by a specific author/publisher/illustrator, or identifying a previously unknown (or long-forgotten) title. Please feel free to write me for any reason. As always I welcome your opinions (both critical and complimentary!), as well as any reference to other illustrated books not currently included in the guides. One final comment here - the prices in this guide, or any other for that matter, are not "set in stone". Rather, they are meant to function as an "eye-opener" to those not familiar with this field, and as a convenient "reminder" to those who are. Enjoy the guide, and again, don't hesitate to write me for any reason.

By the way, if you are currently making use of this guide in a library or other institution and would like your own personal copy, simply drop me a note at the address listed below and I'll send free ordering details as soon as I receive your correspondence. Also -- a separate publication featuring Library of Congress internal call numbers, card catalog numbers and National Union Catalog reference for most of the American-published books in this guide should be ready by mid-1996. Simply send a post card stating your interest and you'll receive a notice when it's ready to send. See additional information in the back of this book.

E. Lee Baumgarten
P.O. Box 2876
Martinsburg, WV 25401

KEY TO DESCRIPTIVE TERMS (including book sizes):

1-color	=	Single color combined with black/white/grey in the illustrations.
2-color	=	Two different colors combined with black/white/grey in the illustrations.
1st	=	first edition by the respective artist.
[1]	=	a number in brackets indicates the state of the first edition for a given book. It will appear as follows: 1st [1],... or 1st [2],... etc. Books with this designation are predominantly those listed in **Bibliography of American Literature** or books by L. Frank Baum.
1st AM	=	1st American illustrated edition. This term is used when the true 1st was originally published in Britain or elsewhere.
1st UK	=	1st British illustrated edition. Used when the true 1st was originally published in America or elsewhere.
12mo	=	Twelvemo: Book is 7 - 7½" (17.9 - 19.5 cm) tall.
16mo	=	Sixteenmo: Book is 6 - 7" (15.2 - 17.8 cm) tall.
24mo	=	Twentyfourmo: Book is 5 - 6" (12.7 - 15 cm) tall.
4to	=	Quarto: Book is 10.5" - 13" (26 - 33 cm) tall.
8vo	=	Octavo: Book is 8" - 10" (20 - 25.4 cm) tall.
AEG	=	All Edges Gilt.
b/w	=	Black & White illustrations.
box	=	Original publisher's box.
cep	=	Colored endpapers (solid color other than white; no design)
cl (or) cloth	=	Cloth covers.
CM [or] CH	=	Book won the Caldecott Medal [or] Caldecott Honor award
cp	=	Color plates.
color (or) col	=	Color illustrations on pages that are integral parts of the book (as opposed to color <u>plates</u>).
cvr by...	=	The front cover of the book was designed/decorated by <ARTIST NAME>.
dep	=	Designed endpapers (includes lines, marbling and other patterns).
DJ	=	Dust jacket present (also abbreviated DW by some dealers).
folio (or) fol	=	Size reference: Book is 13" (33.1 cm) or taller
fp	=	Full-page (example: fp b/w = full-page black & white illustrations)
frn by...	=	Frontispiece by <ARTIST NAME>.
glt (or) gilt	=	Cover and/or spine is decorated to some extent in gilt
ibds (or) ipcb	=	Illustrated boards or paper-covered boards
lg	=	Large (used with size designations).
ltr (or) later	=	An edition subsequent to the first (a reprint).
NM [or] NH	=	Book won the Newbery Medal [or] Newbery Honor award
ob	=	Oblong -- used with size designations. Book is wider than it is tall.
p-o	=	Paste-on (a pictorial paper label glued (pasted down) to the front cover of the book).
pep	=	Pictorial endpapers (more elaborate than dep or cep)
pl	=	Plates (in the majority of instances, "pl" refers to black & white plates)
PPP [or] PPPa	=	A selection from Jacob Blanck's **Peter Parley to Penrod** reference work. (PPPa = Borderline selection)
p (or) pp	=	Number of pages in the text of the book, not including the ads or index, if any.
sm	=	Small (used with book size designations)
sq	=	Square (used with size designations)
{std}	=	Stated first edition. Used when the first edition of a book specifically states either: "First Edition", or "First Printing". (See section on First Editions for more detail on this designation).
teg	=	Top edge gilt.
{this fmt}	=	this format -- Book was previously published in larger or smaller size.
{this pub}	=	this publisher -- Most often refers to the first edition of a title featuring the work of the same illustrator which was previously released by a different publishing company.
ticp	=	Tipped-in color plates. In most cases, a color sheet is pasted down on one edge onto heavier stock paper in the book.
uncut	=	The foredge and bottom edge of the pages have not been trimmed, creating a rough & uneven look. In some cases, this feature helps to determine a first state of the first edition.
unpag	=	No page numbering in book (variation: [nn]p, where nn = a number enclosed in brackets to denote the page count: [42]pp; [312]p, etc.)
wrps	=	Wraps (soft-covered paper or cardboard binding, much the same as a paperback book).
"/"	=	The slash is used (as infrequently as possible!) in lieu of connecting words or phrases in the title.
<color>/gilt	=	color of cloth and gilt design [or lettering] on cover or spine (red/gilt, aqua/gilt, etc.)

And Now the Listings.....

The data file for the 1996 edition contains exactly 10,405 records, indexed 3 ways to provide you with an easy method for locating any given book. Each section has its own page-numbering scheme, as opposed to an overall page count from beginning to end, and is located at the bottom of each page.

Section 1:   **Author-Sorted Index (full information).** The principal sort column is farthest to the left. Within each author designation, the list is "sub-sorted" first according to title, then date, finally artist. This is especially helpful for titles such as "Alice in Wonderland", allowing you to scan chronologically for this or any other multi-edition title in the guide.

Section 2:   **Illustrator-Sorted Index (full information).** The principal sort column is third from the right -- <ARTIST>. Each artist designation is "sub-sorted" first according to title, and then date.

Section 3:   **Title Cross-Reference (partial information).** This section allows quick lookup of any title in the file for which the author/editor/illustrator is unknown to you. Once you locate the author's name next to a given title, you can then utilize the full information in Sections 1 or 2.

            NOTE: *Section 3 is an abbreviated listing!* Titles that contain obvious reference to author, editor, compiler and/or illustrator have been excluded from this section (i.e., "Fairy Tales by Andersen", "Willy Pogany's Mother Goose", "Canterbury Tales of Chaucer", "Poems by....", and so forth. Such titles can be easily found in either the author- or illustrator-sorted section.

Section 1

Author-Sorted

Index

AUTHOR	TITLE	PUBLISHER	DATE	ARTIST	PRICE	LC
A.E.	Earth Breath (1st, 12mo, 94p, ipcb, uncut, cvr & title pg by...)	J. Lane	(1897)	Bradley, W.	180-225	R
Aanrud, Hans.	Sidsel Longskirt & Solve Suntrap (1st, 8vo, 257p, col frn, pep)	Winston	(1935)	D'Aulaire, I. & E.	30-45	
Abbot, A.B.	Frigate's Namesake (1st, 8vo, 204p, blue cl, 17pl)	Century	1901	Varian, G.	25-40	*
Abbott, C.	Howard Pyle: A Chronicle (1st, sm4to, 249p, grey bds, 6cp)	Harper	1925	Pyle, H.	120-150	
Abbott, C.C.	Freedom of the Fields (1st, 8vo, 233p, frn by...)	Lippincott	1898	Stephens, A.B.	35-50	
Abbott, C.C.	Travels in a Treetop (1st, 12mo, 215p, frn by...)	Lippincott	1898	Stephens, A.B.	35-50	
Abbott, E.H.	Sick-a-Bed-Lady (1st, 8vo, 371p, 9pl)	Century	1911	Greer, B.	25-40	
Abbott, J.	Franconia Stories (1st, 8vo, 321p, p-o, blue/gilt, 12pl, pep)	Putnam	1923	Armstrong, H.M.	30-45	
Abbott, Lyman	Christ's Secret of Happiness (1st, 8vo, bds, gilt)	Crowell	(1907)	Armstrong, M.	45-60	*
Abdullah, Achmed	Cat Had Nine Lives (1st, 8vo, 312p, gilt, b/w)	Farrar/Rine.	(1933)	Berry, E.	25-40	*
Abingdon, Alex	Boners (1st, sq16mo, 102p, b/w)	Viking	1931	Seuss, Dr.	100-130	*
Abingdon, Alex	More Boners (1st, 16mo, 89p, b/w)	Viking	1931	Seuss, Dr.	100-130	*
Abingdon, Alex	Omnibus Boners (1st, 16mo, b/w)	Viking	1931	Seuss, Dr.	90-120	*
About, E.	King of the Mountains (1st, sm8vo, 246p, cvr by...)	Rand/McNally	1897	Denslow, W.W.	25-40	*
Ackerman, A.W.	Price of Peace (1st, sm8vo, 390p, rust/gilt)	McClurg	1894	Armstrong, M.	30-45	*
Adams, A.	Log of a Cowboy (1st, 8vo, 387p, gilt, 6pl, map, PPPa)	Houghton	1903	Smith, E.B.	80-120	
Adams, A.	Texas Matchmaker (1st, 12mo, 355p, 6pl)	Houghton	1904	Smith, E.B.	80-120	
Adams, A.	The Outlet (1st, 8vo, 371p, brown/gilt, 6pl)	Houghton	1905	Smith, E.B.	60-80	
Adams, Darwin	Adventures of Monte & Molly (1st, 4to, blue cl, 152p, cp)	Macaulay	(1938)	Van Zelm, L.F.	75-100	*
Adams, F.U.	John Henry Smith (1st, 8vo, 346p, p-o, b/w)	Doubleday/Page	1905	Frost, A.B.	30-45	*
Adams, J.D.	Mountains are Free (1st {std}, 8vo, gilt, 250p, 10pl, NH)	Dutton	(1930)	Nadejen, T.	50-70	*
Adams, J.D.	Vaino: Boy of New Finland (1st, 8vo, 273p, pep, NH)	Dutton	1929	Ostman, L.	40-65	*
Adams, K.	Book of Enchantment Tales (1st, 4to, 23p, pep, 4cp)	Dodd	1928	Lenski, L.	50-80	
Adams, K.	Book of Princess Stories (1st, 4to, blue/gilt, 223p, 4cp, pep)	Dodd	1927	Lenski, L.	50-80	
Adams, K.	There Were Giants (1st, 8vo, 234p, green cl, 4pl, pep)	Dodd	1929	Lenski, L.	30-45	
Adams, M.M.	Choir Visible (1st, 8vo, 185p, teg, cvr by...)	Way/Williams	1897	Hazenplug, F.	80-130	
Adams, S.H.	Flying Death (1st, 12mo, brown cl, 239p, 4pl)	McClure	1908	Macauley, C.R.	30-45	
Adams, S.W.	Five Little Friends (1st, 12mo, 139p, color)	MacMillan	1922	Petershams	45-65	*
Adams, V.M.	Captain Joe & the Eskimo (1st, lg8vo, ipcb, [40]p, 1-color)	W.R. Scott	1943	Tobey, B.	65-80	*
Adams, W.I.L.	In Nature's Image (1st, lg8vo, gilt)	Baker/Taylor	1898	(Photos)	45-65	
Adams, W.I.L.	Sunlight & Shadow (1st, 8vo, 141p, AEG)	Baker/Taylor	1897	(Photos)	70-120	
Adcock, Marion	Littlest One (1st, 4to, 41p, ibds, 4cp)	L: Harrap	1914	Tarrant, M.	60-80	
Adcock, Marion	Littlest One (1st AM, 8vo, ibds, p-o, 4cp)	Stokes	[1915]	Tarrant, M.	45-70	*
Addington, S.	Boy Who Lived in Pudding Lane (1st, 8vo, 93p, 6cp, pep, p-o)	Atl. Month Pr.	(1922)	Kay, G.A.	50-70	*
Addington, S.	Grammar Town (1st, 8vo, p-o, 79p, 4cp, pep)	McKay	(1927)	Kay, G.A.	25-45	
Addington, S.	Great Adven./Mrs. Santa Claus (1st, 8vo, p-o, 107p, 5cp)	Little/Brown	1923	Kay, G.A.	45-60	
Addington, S.	Jerry Juddikins (1st, 8vo, 65p, p-o, 4cp, pep)	McKay	(1926)	Kay, G.A.	30-45	
Addington, S.	Pied Piper of Pudding Lane (1st, 8vo, p-o, 97p, 4cp, pep)	Atl. Month Pr.	(1923)	Kay, G.A.	30-45	
Addington, S.	Pudding Lane People (1st, lg8vo, p-o, 183p, 4cp, pep)	Little/Brown	1926	Scott, J.L.	25-45	
Addington, S.	Round the Year on Pudding Lane (1st, lg8vo, 231p, p-o, 9pl, pep)	Little/Brown	1924	Kay, G.A.	45-60	*
Addington, S.	Tommy Tingle-Tangle (1st, sq8vo, ibds, 39p, color, pep)	Volland	(1927)	Kay, G.A.	60-85	
Addison, J.	Mrs. John Vernon (1st, 12mo, p-o, 205p, frn by...)	Badger	1909	Gibson, C.D.	20-25	*
Ade, G.	Artie (1st {1st bk.}, 12mo, 192p, teg, blue cl)	H. Stone	1896	McCutcheon, J.T.	50-85	
Ade, G.	In Pastures New (1st, 12mo, 309p, red cl, b/w)	McClure	1906	Levering, A.	25-40	
Ade, G.	Knocking the Neighbors (1st, 12mo, 229p, brown cl, 15pl)	Doubleday/Page	1912	Levering, A.	45-65	R
Ade, G.	More Fables (1st, 12mo, 218p, teg, title page by..)	H. Stone	1900	Hazenplug, F.	30-45	
Ade, G.	People You Know (1st, 12mo, blue cl, 224p, b/w)	R.H. Russell	1903	McCutcheon, J.T.	35-50	
Ade, G.	Pink Marsh (1st, sm8vo, green cl, 197p, teg, uncut)	H. Stone	1897	McCutcheon, J.T.	50-70	
Ade, G.	Sultan of Sulu (1st, 12mo, 127p, b/w)	R.H. Russell	1903	Unknown	45-60	*
Ade, G.	True Bills (1st, 16mo, 154p, b/w)	Harper	1904	Smith, H.L.	30-50	
Adelson, L.	Who Blew that Whistle? (1st, lg8vo, ipcb, 45p, 1-color, pep)	W.R. Scott	(1946)	Fabres, O.	45-65	*
Adrian, M.	Fiddler Crab (1st, 8vo, 40p, aqua cl, 2-color)	Holiday House	(1953)	Martinez, J.	20-25	*
Adrian, M.	Garden Spider (1st, sm8vo, 38p, blue cl, 2-color, pep)	Holiday House	(1951)	Ray, R.	20-25	*
Adrian, M.	Gray Squirrel (1st, 8vo, 46p, rust cl, 2-color, cep)	Holiday House	(1955)	Ferguson, W.	20-25	*
Adshead, Gladys	Brownies - Hush! (1st, ob12mo, [64]p, orang cl, 1-color, cep)	NY: OUP	(1938)	Jones, E.O.	25-40	*
Adshead, Gladys	What Miranda Knew (1st, 12mo, [48]p, beige cl, color)	NY: OUP	(1944)	Jones, E.O.	30-45	*
Aesopus	Aesop for Children (1st, 4to, p-o, 112p, color, pep)	Rand/McNally	(1919)	Winter, M.	65-90	
Aesopus	Aesop's Fables (1st, sm4to, color green/gilt)	L: Chatto	1875	Bennett, C.	200-300	
Aesopus	Aesop's Fables (4to, ibds, 390p, b/w)	NY: Cassell	1884	Griset, E.	180-250	*
Aesopus	Aesop's Fables (1st {1st bk}, 16mo, [60]p, red/gilt, teg, pep)	L: J.M. Dent	1895	Robinson, C.	150-200	
Aesopus	Aesop's Fables (1st, 8vo, 275p, 16cp)	Moffat	1905	Conde, J.M.	70-100	*
Aesopus	Aesop's Fables (1st, lg8vo, p-o, 111p, 12cp)	Stokes	(1908)	Perkins, L.F.	70-110	
Aesopus	Aesop's Fables (1st AM, 16mo, gilt, p-o, 47p, 24cp)	Jack/Dutton	[1910]	Praeger, S.R.	60-80	*
Aesopus	Aesop's Fables (1st, 8vo, 172p, teg, brown/gilt, 6pl)	Century	1911	Smith, E.B.	100-150	
Aesopus	Aesop's Fables (1st, 8vo, 209p, gilt, 12cp)	L: A&C Black	(1912)	Folkard, C.	85-130	
Aesopus	Aesop's Fables (1st AM, sq8vo, 224p, p-o, 13cp)	Doubleday/Page	1912	Rackham, A.	200-300	
Aesopus	Aesop's Fables (1st, sm4to, green/gilt, 223p, 13cp, pep)	L: Heinemann	1912	Rackham, A.	250-400	
Aesopus	Aesop's Fables (1st, 8vo, 259p, cp)	Platt/Peck	(1913)	Conde, J.M.	35-50	*
Aesopus	Aesop's Fables (1st, 8vo, 318p, color)	Lippincott	1916	Opper, F.	45-60	*
Aesopus	Aesop's Fables (1st, 8vo, 340p, green cl, p-o, 48cp, pep)	L: Ward Lock	[1920]	Rountree, H.	120-180	*
Aesopus	Aesop's Fables (8vo, red cl, 340p, 30cp, reprint, pep)	L: Ward Lock	[1924]	Rountree, H.	75-100	
Aesopus	Aesop's Fables (1st, 8vo, 194p, color)	Harper	(1927)	Rhead, L.	25-40	*

AUTHOR	TITLE	PUBLISHER	DATE	ARTIST	PRICE	LC
Aesopus	Aesop's Fables (1st, lg8vo, p-o, 136p, 8cp)	McKay	[1929]	Fry, Nora	60-85	*
Aesopus	Aesop's Fables (1st AM, lg8vo, p-o, 86p, red cl, pep)	Viking	1933	Artzybasheff, B.	50-70	
Aesopus	Aesop's Fables (1st, 4to, 312p, plates)	L: Harrap	1936	Gooden, S.	60-80	*
Aesopus	Aesop's Fables (8vo, gilt, p-o, t.e. red, 13cp)	Garden City	(1939)	Rackham, A.	65-80	
Aesopus	Aesop's Fables (1st, lg4to, brown/gilt, 134p, pep)	Heritage Press	(1941)	Lawson, R.	70-100	*
Aesopus	Aesop's Fables (1st, 4to, 71p, color)	Duell/Sloan	(1944)	Kelen, E.	35-50	*
Aesopus	Aesop's Fables (1st, 8vo, 162p, color)	Lippincott	(1949)	Rounds, G.	35-50	*
Aesopus	Animals of Aesop (1st, lg8vo, 210p, color)	D. Estes	1900	Mora, J.J.	65-80	*
Aesopus	Book of Fables (sm8vo, 32cp)	Am. Book Exch.	1880	Griset, E.	90-130	
Aesopus	Fables of Aesop (1st, 8vo, 222p, gilt, AEG)	L: MacMillan	1894	Heighway, R.	70-100	
Aesopus	Fables of Aesop (1st, lg4to, 152p, brown/gilt, pep, 23 ticp)	L: Hodder	[1909]	Detmold, E.J.	450-600	
Aesopus	Fables of Aesop (1st, 8vo, 254p, color)	Whitman	(1925)	Dash, J.E.	25-40	
Aesopus	Hundred Fables of Aesop (1st, 4to, 201p, yellow cl, b/w)	L: J. Lane	1899	Billinghurst, P.	125-180	
Aesopus	Never-Grow-Old Stories (12mo, 144p, color)	Lyons/Carnahan	(1925)	Billinghurst, P.	30-45	*
Aflalo, F.G.	Fisherman's Weather (1st, 8vo, teg, gilt, 256p, 8cp)	L: A&C Black	1906	Whymper, C.	50-80	
Agnew, G.	Let's Pretend (1st, 12mo, 63p, blue/gilt, teg, pep)	L: J. Saville	1927	Shepard, E.H.	70-85	
Aguilar, G.	Vale of Cedars (1st, 8vo, 428p, uncut, teg, col frn, 11pl, pep)	L: Dent	1902	Robinson, T.H.	50-70	
Aikins, Ruth	Smiling Princess (1st, sq8vo, [31]p, p-o, color, pep)	Norcross	(1922)	Boyle, M.	50-80	*
Ainslie, K.	At Great Aunt Martha's (ob8vo, ibds, [32]p, 16 color, p-o)	L: Castell	[1905]	Ainslie, K.	80-120	
Ainslie, K.	Catharine Susan & Me Goes Abroad (16mo, wraps, color)	L: Castell	[1900]	Ainslie, K.	100-130	
Ainslie, K.	Catharine Susan & Me's Coming Out (16mo, wraps, [32]p, color)	L: Castell	[1910]	Ainslie, K.	80-120	
Ainslie, K.	Catharine Susan in Hot Water (sq16mo, wraps, color)	L: Castell	[1905]	Ainslie, K.	80-120	
Ainslie, K.	Catharine Susan's Little Holiday (12mo, wraps, color)	L: Castell	[1905]	Ainslie, K.	80-100	*
Ainslie, K.	Lady Tabitha and Us (ob8vo, wraps, 14 color)	L: Castell	[1900]	Ainslie, K.	85-100	
Ainslie, K.	Me & Catharine Susan Earns an Honest Penny (sq16mo, wraps, col)	L: Castell	[1905]	Ainslie, K.	70-90	
Ainslie, K.	Me and Catharine Susan (16mo, wraps, [40]p, 20 fp color)	L: Castell	[1903]	Ainslie, K.	70-95	
Ainslie, K.	Mops Versus Tails (ob8vo, [24]p, ibds, color, pep)	L: Castell	[1905]	Ainslie, K.	100-150	
Ainslie, K.	Oh! Poor Amelia Jane! (12mo, [28]p, wraps, color)	L: Castell	[1900]	Ainslie, K.	100-130	
Ainslie, K.	Sammy Goes a Hunting (8vo, ibds, [24]p, 12 fp color, pep)	L: Castell	[1900]	Ainslie, K.	80-100	
Ainslie, K.	Why Was He Late? (8vo, 12cp, wraps)	L: Castell	[1905]	Ainslie, K.	70-100	
Akers, Floyd	Boy Fortune Hunters in Alaska (1st [1], 8vo, 291p, brwn cl, 3pl)	Reilly/Britton	(1908)	Heath, H.	150-220	
Akers, Floyd	Boy Fortune Hunters in China (1st [1], 12mo, brown cl, frn by)	Reilly/Britton	(1909)	Nelson, E.A.	160-220	*
Akers, Floyd	Boy Fortune Hunters in Egypt (1st [1], 12mo, 291p, 3pl)	Reilly/Britton	(1908)	Nelson, E.A.	180-250	
Akers, Floyd	Boy Fortune Hunters in Yucatan (1st, 8vo, 343p, tan cl, frn by)	Reilly/Britton	(1910)	Rieman, G.A.	200-300	
Akers, Floyd	Boy Fortune Hunters/South Seas (1st, 8vo, 263p, tan cl, frn by)	Reilly/Britton	(1911)	Nelson, E.A.	200-300	
Albee, George	Three Young Kings (1st {std}, 4to, 47p, yel cl, 1-color, pep)	Watts	1956	Keats, E.J.	45-60	*
Alcott, L.M.	Candy Country (1st, 12mo, 52p, 3pl)	Little/Brown	(1900)	Unknown	60-80	R*
Alcott, L.M.	Christmas Dream (1st, 12mo, green cl, 55p)	Little/Brown	(1901)	Unknown	50-70	*
Alcott, L.M.	Eight Cousins (1st, sm8vo, 292p, 8pl)	Little/Brown	1904	Richards, H.R.	25-40	
Alcott, L.M.	Eight Cousins (1st, 8vo, 278p, 6cp)	Little/Brown	1927	Price, H.L.	20-35	
Alcott, L.M.	Eight Cousins (1st, 8vo, col frn, 253p, cp)	Winston	(1931)	Burd, C.M.	25-45	
Alcott, L.M.	Frost King (4to, ipcb, color, pep)	Whitman	(1929)	Frobisher, M.S	35-50	
Alcott, L.M.	Garland for Girls (1st, 8vo, 286p, 8pl)	Little/Brown	1908	Atwood, C.E.	25-40	
Alcott, L.M.	Good Wives (1st UK, 12mo, 316p, 8cp)	L: G. Bell	1911	Wheelhouse, M.V.	25-40	
Alcott, L.M.	Jo's Boys... (sm8vo, teg, 358p, 10pl)	Little/Brown	1903	Ahrens, E.W.	40-60	*
Alcott, L.M.	Little Men (sm8vo, 381p, teg, green/gilt, 15pl)	Little/Brown	1901	Birch, R.	30-50	
Alcott, L.M.	Little Men (1st, 8vo, 349p, p-o, 4cp, pep)	Winston	(1928)	Burd, C.M.	20-30	*
Alcott, L.M.	Little Women (8vo, 617p, teg, 15pl)	Little/Brown	1914	Stephens, A.B.	25-45	
Alcott, L.M.	Little Women (1st, 8vo, p-o, 617p, green/gilt, 8cp, pep)	Little/Brown	1915	Smith, J.W.	140-180	
Alcott, L.M.	Little Women (lg8vo, green cl, p-o, 475p, 8cp)	Garden City	1932	Stein, H.	25-40	
Alcott, L.M.	Old-Fashioned Girl (1st, sm8vo, green/gilt, teg, 371p, 12pl)	Little/Brown	1902	Smith, J.W.	90-130	
Alcott, L.M.	Rose In Bloom (1st, 8vo, p-o, 320p, 4cp)	Winston	(1933)	Burd, C.M.	20-30	
Alcott, L.M.	Rose in Bloom (1st, 8vo, teg, 344p, 8pl)	Little/Brown	1904	Richards, H.R.	25-40	
Alcott, L.M.	Silver Pitchers (1st, 8vo, 365p, 8pl)	Little/Brown	1908	Kennedy, J.W.	30-45	
Alcott, L.M.	Under the Lilacs (1st, 8vo, 302p, green cl, teg, 8pl)	Little/Brown	1905	Stephens, A.B.	50-70	*
Alcott, L.M.	Under the Lilacs (1st, 8vo, 284p, col frn, cp)	Little/Brown	1928	Davis, M.	25-40	
Alden, R.M.	Knights/Silver Shield (1st, 4to, tan cl, 149p, 10cp)	Bobbs-Merrill	(1906)	Greenland, K.	75-110	*
Alden, R.M.	Why the Chimes Rang (1st, 8vo, 148p, b/w)	Bobbs-Merrill	(1908)	Greenland, K.	30-45	*
Alden, R.M.	Why the Chimes Rang (sm8vo, olive cl, p-o, [40]p)	Bobbs-Merrill	(1909)	Bunker, M.	20-35	
Alden, R.M.	Why the Chimes Rang (1st, 4to, 148p, orang cl, p-o, 8cp)	Bobbs-Merrill	(1924)	Sturges, K.	45-60	*
Alden, R.M.	Why the Chimes Rang (1st, 4to, red cl, [28]p, color, pep)	Bobbs-Merrill	1954	Busoni, R.	25-40	*
Alden, W.L.	Among the Freaks (1st, 195p, 45 illus)	Longmans	1896	Upton, F.	120-160	
Aldin, C.	Artist's Models (1st, 4to, 80p, grey cl, 20pl)	L: Witherby	(1930)	Aldin, C.	120-165	
Aldin, C.	Artist's Models (1st AM, 4to, blue cl, 80p, 20 fp b/w)	Scribner	1930	Aldin, C.	160-200	
Aldin, C.	Bobtail Puppy Book (1st AM, lg8vo, 37p, ibds, 12 fp color)	NY: Hodder	[1915]	Aldin, C.	75-100	*
Aldin, C.	Bunnyborough (4to, 48p, DJ)	L: Eyre/Spotts	(1946)	Aldin, C.	60-80	
Aldin, C.	Cathedrals & Abbey Churches of England (1st, 4to, 111p, 16cp)	L: Eyre/Spotts	(1924)	Aldin, C.	100-180	
Aldin, C.	Cecil Aldin Book (1st, 4to, cloth, 192p, 15cp)	L: Eyre/Spotts	1932	Aldin, C.	100-140	
Aldin, C.	Dogs of Character (1st, 4to, p-o, gilt, 118p, teg, 2cp)	L: Eyre/Spotts	1927	Aldin, C.	90-130	
Aldin, C.	Farmyard Puppies (1st, sq4to, ibds, 12cp)	L: H. Frowde	(1911)	Aldin, C.	140-185	
Aldin, C.	Gay Dog (1st, 4to, ibds, [50]p, 24cp)	L: Heinemann	1905	Aldin, C.	180-270	
Aldin, C.	Great Adventure (1st, folio, ibds, 16cp, pep)	L: H. Milford	[1920]	Aldin, C.	200-280	

AUTHOR	TITLE	PUBLISHER	DATE	ARTIST	PRICE	LC
Aldin, C.	Happy Annual (sm folio, ibds, 48p, color)	Dutton	(1907)	Aldin/Hassall	220-300	
Aldin, C.	Just Among Friends (1st AM, folio, 28p)	Scribner	1934	Aldin, C.	80-100	
Aldin, C.	Merry & Bright (1st, lg4to, bds, p-o, 24cp, pep)	L: H. Frowde	(1911)	Aldin, C.	180-250	
Aldin, C.	Mrs. Tickler's Caravan (1st AM, sm4to, p-o, 91p, color, pep)	Scribner	1931	Aldin, C.	70-100	
Aldin, C.	Old Inns (1st AM, sm4to, 149p, 16cp)	Doubleday/Page	1921	Aldin, C.	70-90	
Aldin, C.	Old Manor Houses (1st, lg8vo, 108p, grey/gilt, 12cp, pep)	L: Heinemann	(1923)	Aldin, C.	120-160	
Aldin, C.	Red Puppy Book (1st, lg8vo, 48p, 12cp)	L: H. Frowde	[1910]	Aldin, C.	140-185	
Aldin, C.	Romance of the Road (1st, folio, 123p, buckram, 10 ticp)	L: Eyre/Spotts	1928	Aldin, C.	125-150	
Aldin, C.	Rough & Tumble (4to, ibds, p-o, 24cp, pep)	L: H. Frowde	[1912]	Aldin, C.	300-400	
Aldin, C.	Scarlet to M.F.H. (1st AM, 4to, 151p, red/gilt, color)	Scribner	(1933)	Aldin, C.	65-80	*
Aldin, C.	The Widow (1st AM, 12mo, 31p, ibds, p-o, 3 ticp)	Dutton	1909	Aldin, C.	70-90	*
Aldin, C.	Time I Was Dead (1st, lg8vo, 389p, gilt, 9cp)	L: Eyre/Spotts	1934	Aldin, C.	120-160	
Aldin, C.	White Kitten Book (1st, 4to, ibds, unpag, 12cp)	L: H. Frowde	[1909]	Aldin, C.	160-250	
Aldin, C.	White Puppy Book (1st, 4to, ibds, [48]p, 12cp)	L: Hodder	[1909]	Aldin, C.	140-200	
Aldington (tr.)	The Decameron... (1st, lg8vo, black cl, p-o, 576p, 16cp)	Garden City	(1930)	DeBosschere, J.	45-65	
Aldington, R.	All Men are Enemies (1st {std}, 8vo, 574p, b/w, DJ)	Doubleday/Dor.	1933	Kent, R.	50-70	
Aldington, W.	Golden Asse/Lucius Apuleius (8vo, brown/gilt, 8cp)	L: J. Lane	1923	DeBosschere, J.	75-100	
Aldredge, Edna	The Timbertoes (1st, 8vo, pep, p-o, red cl, 117p, color)	Harter	(1932)	Gee, J.	65-80	*
Aldrich, A.R.	Songs about Life, Love & Death (1st, 12mo, 133p)	Scribner	1892	Armstrong, M.	45-60	
Aldrich, T.B.	Judith of Bethulia (1st, 8vo, green/gilt, 98p, teg)	Houghton	1904	Rogers, B.	25-40	
Aldrich, T.B.	Marjorie Daw (1st, 8vo, 123p, gilt)	Houghton	1908	Clay, J.C.	30-45	
Aldrich, T.B.	Sea Turn (1st, 8vo, grey cl, 300p)	Houghton	1902	Rogers, B.	20-35	
Alexander, L.C.	My Five Tigers (1st, 8vo, 118p, green cl, fp b/w)	Crowell	(1956)	Bacon, P.	20-30	*
Alexander, L.M.	Candy (1st, 8vo, cloth, 310p, 5pl, pep, DJ)	Dodd	1934	Kent, R.	60-80	
Alger, Leclaire	Dougal's Wish (1st {std}, 8vo, 244p, rust cl, fp b/w)	Harper	1942	Simont, M.	30-45	*
Alger, Leclaire	Jan & Wonderful Mouth-Organ (1st {std}, 8vo, 177p, col frn, pep)	Harper	1939	Becker, C.	25-40	*
Allan, M.B.	Rhyme Garden (1st, 4to, ipcb, 8cp)	L: Bodley Head	1917	Allan, M.B.	35-50	*
Allee, M.H.	Ann's Surprising Summer (1st, sm8vo, 198p, b/w, pep)	Houghton	1933	DeGogorza, M.	25-40	*
Allee, M.H.	Jane's Island (1st, 8vo, 235p, green cl, fp b/w, pep, NH)	Houghton	1931	DeGogorza, M.	40-60	*
Allee, M.H.	Judith Lankester (1st, sm8vo, 241p, b/w, pep)	Houghton	1930	Price, H.L.	20-30	*
Allee, M.H.	Little American Girl (1st, 8vo, 237p, b/w, pep)	Houghton	1938	Quinn, P.	20-35	*
Allee, M.H.	Susanna & Tristram (1st, sm8vo, 220p, b/w, pep)	Houghton	1929	Price, H.L.	25-40	*
Allen, D.	Birth of the Opal (1st, 4to, p-o, bds, 95p, 12 ticp)	L: Allen	1913	Allen, D.	60-85	
Allen, F.M.	Brayhard (1st, 8vo, teg, 308p, green/gilt, b/w)	L: Ward/Down.	1890	Furniss, H.	50-75	
Allen, F.W.	Golden Road (1st, 8vo, 228p, teg, col frn, pep)	Wessels/Bissel	1910	Hood, G.	35-50	
Allen, G.	British Barbarians (1st, 8vo, olive/gilt, 202p, cvr by...)	L: J. Lane	1895	Beardsley, A.	70-100	
Allen, G.	Miss Cayley's Adventures (1st AM, 8vo, 344p, tan cl, b/w)	Putnam	1899	Browne, G.	40-60	*
Allen, G.	Woman Who Did (8vo, 241p, later, cvr by...)	L: J. Lane	1895	Beardsley, A.	50-80	
Allen, J.L.	Kentucky Cardinal Aftermath (1st AM, 8vo, 276p, teg)	MacMillan	1900	Thomson, H.	60-80	
Allen, Marian	Wind in the Chimney (1st, 4to, 89p, grey cl, 6 ticp)	L: Blackwell	[1931]	Allen, M.	25-40	*
Allen, Phil S.	Begging Bear (1st, lg ob4to, 60p, p-o, 20cp)	Reilly/Lee	(1932)	Moe, L.M.	100-150	
Allen, Phil S.	King Arthur & his Knights (1st, sm4to, 455p, black cl, p-o, 8cp)	Rand/McNally	(1924)	Neill/Schaeffer	50-70	*
Allen, R.B.	Saga of Gisli (1st {std}, lg8vo, 148p, uncut, b/w, DJ)	Harcourt	(1936)	Kent, R.	85-120	
Allen, W.B.	Play Away (1st, 12mo, 171p, tan cl, 6pl)	Estes	(1902)	Bridgman, L.J.	20-35	
Allingham, W.	Rhymes for the Young Folks (1st, 8vo, 75p, 2 illus by...)	L: Cassell	(1887)	Greenaway, K.	150-200	
Allison, J.M.	Five Black Cousins... (1st, sm8vo, white/gilt, uncut, designs)	L: J. Cape	1924	Austen, J.	70-100	*
Almond, Linda S.	Little Glad Heart (1st, sm8vo, 317p, 6pl)	Page	1922	Withington, E.R.	20-25	*
Almond, Linda S.	Mary Redding Takes Charge (1st, sm8vo, 310p, col frn, cp)	Crowell	(1926)	Whittemore, C.	20-25	*
Almond, Linda S.	Peter Rabbit & the Little Girl (1st, 24mo, 58p, col frn)	Altemus	(1930)	Willis, B.G.	30-45	*
Almond, Linda S.	Peter Rabbit & the Tinybits (12mo, cloth, color)	Platt/Munk	(1935)	Hoopes, M.C.	40-65	*
Almond, Linda S.	When Peter Rabbit Went a-Fishing (24mo, bds, p-o, 64p, 25col pep)	Altemus	(1923)	Hoopes, M.C.	25-40	
Almond, Linda S.	When Peter Rabbit Went to School (1st, 16mo, p-o, 58p, 27 col)	Platt/Munk	(1935)	Almond, L.	35-50	
Alsop, Reese F.	George & his Horse (1st, 8vo, 164p, red cl, b/w)	Dodd	1948	Brown, Paul	25-40	*
Altsheler, J.A.	Apache Gold (1st, sm8vo, 382p, cp)	Appleton	1913	Unknown	30-45	*
Altsheler, J.A.	Free Rangers (1st, 8vo, 365p, 4cp)	Appleton	1909	Unknown	25-40	*
Amber	Rosemary & Rue (1st, sm8vo, 303p, cvr by...)	Rand/McNally	1896	Denslow, W.W.	35-50	*
Ambrose, B.A.	Coppa Hamba (1st, 4to, [82]p, orange cl, 3cp, fp b/w, pep)	Suttonhouse	1936	Pogany, W.	100-150	*
Amend, Ottillie	Jolly Jungle Jingles (1st, ob4to, ibds, 30p, color)	Volland	(1929)	Barte, E.	80-130	*
Ames, E.M.	Patsy for Keeps (1st, 4to, ibds, 95p, doll bk., color)	NY: S. Gabriel	(1932)	Hicks, A.L.	65-90	*
Ames, Evelyn	My Brother Bird (1st, 8vo, 125p, red cl, fp b/w, pep)	Dodd	1954	DuBois, W.P.	35-50	*
Ames, Mrs. E.	Really & Truly (1st, ob4to, unpag, color)	L: E. Arnold	[1899]	Ames, E.	180-250	*
Ames, Mrs. E.	Tim & the Dusty Man (ob folio, ibds, 24cp)	L: Richards	[1907]	Ames, E.	180-260	
Ames, Mrs. E.	Tremendous Twins (1st, ob folio, 95p, color)	L: Richards	1900	Ames, E.	200-300	*
Andersen, H.C.	Andersen Fairy Book (1st, lg8vo, 416p, 8cp, pep)	Stokes	(1921)	Choate/Curtis	50-70	*
Andersen, H.C.	Andersen in German (1st, 8vo, 219p, beige cl, b/w)	L: J.M. Dent	1902	Robinson Bros.	200-285	
Andersen, H.C.	Andersen's Best Fairy Tales (1st, 12mo, 200p, color, pep)	Rand/McNally	(1911)	Henderson, W.P.	35-50	*
Andersen, H.C.	Danish Fairy Tales (1st {1st bk.}, 8vo, red/gilt, 332p, 16pl)	L: Bliss Sands	1897	Robinson, W.H.	200-250	
Andersen, H.C.	Emperor's New Clothes (1st, 8vo, 43p, cloth, color)	Houghton	1949	Burton, V.L.	50-80	
Andersen, H.C.	Fairy Stories (1st, sm4to, 340p, blue cl, p-o, 48cp)	L: Ward Lock	1917	Tarrant, M.	140-200	
Andersen, H.C.	Fairy Stories (lg4to, ibds, 8cp)	(London)	[1930]	Anderson, A.	90-135	
Andersen, H.C.	Fairy Tales (8vo, ibds, 4cp)	L: Coker	[n.d.]	Clarke, H.	80-100	
Andersen, H.C.	Fairy Tales (1st, folio, 94p, AEG, green/gilt, 12cp)	L: Sampson	1872	Boyle, E.V.	800-1000	

AUTHOR	TITLE	PUBLISHER	DATE	ARTIST	PRICE	LC
Andersen, H.C.	Fairy Tales (4to, blue bds)	Scribner	1875	Boyle, E.V.	250-350	
Andersen, H.C.	Fairy Tales (lg8vo, AEG, 288p, 6 chromos)	L: Nister	[1890]	Hardy, E.S.	150-185	
Andersen, H.C.	Fairy Tales (1st, lg8vo, 219p, b/w)	L: E. Arnold	1893	Lemann, E.A.	80-100	
Andersen, H.C.	Fairy Tales (1st, 12mo, 539p, col frn, pl)	L: Dent	1899	Robinson Bros.	120-170	*
Andersen, H.C.	Fairy Tales (1st, 4to, white/gilt, AEG, 320p, col frn, b/w)	L: G. Newnes	1899	Stratton, H.	160-220	
Andersen, H.C.	Fairy Tales (1st AM, 4to, blue/gilt, AEG, 320p, b/w, cep)	NY: Truslove	1899	Stratton, H.	130-180	*
Andersen, H.C.	Fairy Tales (1st, 4to, 2 volumes, bds, gilt, b/w)	L: Heinemann	1900	Tegner, H.	300-400	
Andersen, H.C.	Fairy Tales (1st AM, lg4to, 524p, gilt, 85pl)	Century	1900	Tegner, H.	225-300	
Andersen, H.C.	Fairy Tales (1st {this fmt}, 16mo, 312p, 12 b/w)	L: Dent	1901	Robinson Bros.	100-140	*
Andersen, H.C.	Fairy Tales (1st, sm4to, 188p, 24pl)	D. Estes	(1902)	Mora, J.J.	160-220	
Andersen, H.C.	Fairy Tales (1st AM, 8vo, green/gilt, 28cp)	Dodge	[1905]	Stratton, H.	160-200	
Andersen, H.C.	Fairy Tales (4to, ibds, [86]p, 24cp)	L: Blackie	[1905]	Stratton, H.	65-80	*
Andersen, H.C.	Fairy Tales (8vo, 380p, color)	L: Blackie	[1908]	Stratton, H.	70-100	*
Andersen, H.C.	Fairy Tales (sm8vo, 441p, col frn, dep)	Lippincott	(1908)	Stratton, H.	35-60	*
Andersen, H.C.	Fairy Tales (1st, 8vo, 408p, b/w)	L: Seeley	(1909)	Brock, H.M.	65-80	*
Andersen, H.C.	Fairy Tales (4to, 416p, 8cp)	L: Heinemann	1909	Edwards, C.H.	100-130	
Andersen, H.C.	Fairy Tales (1st, sm4to, 392p, gilt, 24cp, pep)	Dent/Dutton	1910	Armfield, M.	120-160	
Andersen, H.C.	Fairy Tales (1st, sm8vo, 324p, cp)	Nister/Dutton	[1910]	Pape, F.	65-90	*
Andersen, H.C.	Fairy Tales (1st, 8vo, 219p, teg, pep, cp)	Lippincott	1911	Kirk, M.L.	100-140	
Andersen, H.C.	Fairy Tales (1st, 4to, black/gilt, teg, 431p, 24cp, pep)	L: Jack	1911	Walton, C.	200-300	
Andersen, H.C.	Fairy Tales (1st AM, sm4to, blue/gilt, teg, 431p, uncut, 24cp)	Stokes	[1911]	Walton, C.	140-220	R*
Andersen, H.C.	Fairy Tales (1st, 12mo, 170p, b/w)	Chi: Flanagan	(1912)	Hodge, H.	30-45	*
Andersen, H.C.	Fairy Tales (1st AM, 4to, red/gilt, 16 ticp)	Holt	1913	Robinson, W.H.	200-250	
Andersen, H.C.	Fairy Tales (4to, 320p, red/gilt, 16 ticp)	L: Hodder	[1913]	Robinson, W.H.	160-200	
Andersen, H.C.	Fairy Tales (1st, 4to, red/gilt, 289p, 16 ticp)	L: Constable	1913	Robinson, W.H.	280-400	
Andersen, H.C.	Fairy Tales (1st, sm4to, 141p, blue/gilt, 12cp)	Tuck/McKay	[1914]	Attwell, M.L.	165-225	
Andersen, H.C.	Fairy Tales (1st UK, lg8vo, 268p, p-o, 12cp, pep)	L: Harrap	(1914)	Walker, D.S.	170-220	
Andersen, H.C.	Fairy Tales (1st, sm4to, p-o, gilt, 267p, 12cp)	Doubleday/Page	1914	Walker, D.S.	140-170	
Andersen, H.C.	Fairy Tales (1st AM, 4to, 319p, grey cl, p-o, teg, 16 ticp)	Brentano's	(1916)	Clarke, H.	500-700	
Andersen, H.C.	Fairy Tales (1st, 4to, 319p, teg, 16 ticp, 24pl)	L: Harrap	1916	Clarke, H.	650-1000	
Andersen, H.C.	Fairy Tales (1st, 4to, 286p, p-o, 15cp, pep)	Rand/McNally	(1916)	Winter, M.	70-120	
Andersen, H.C.	Fairy Tales (1st, sm8vo, 489p, 7cp)	Jacobs	[1917]	Abbott, E.P.	40-65	
Andersen, H.C.	Fairy Tales (1st, 8vo, p-o, 513p, 12cp)	L: Chambers	[1917]	Robinson, G.	120-165	
Andersen, H.C.	Fairy Tales (4to, ibds, 176p, 24cp)	L: Ward Lock	[1920]	Tarrant, M.	80-120	
Andersen, H.C.	Fairy Tales (1st, lg8vo, 349p, grey/gilt, 17 ticp)	L: H. Milford	(1921)	Cramer, Rie	250-300	
Andersen, H.C.	Fairy Tales (1st AM, 4to, blue/gilt, 179p, 12cp, pep)	NY: Nelson	[1922]	Appleton, H.C.	85-120	
Andersen, H.C.	Fairy Tales (1st, lg8vo, p-o, 180p, blue/gilt, 2cp)	Cupples	(1923)	Neill, J.R.	70-90	
Andersen, H.C.	Fairy Tales (1st, 4to, 197p, green/gilt, 12 ticp, pep)	L: Hodder	(1924)	Nielsen, K.	800-1000	
Andersen, H.C.	Fairy Tales (1st AM, 4to, p-o, 281p, pep, 12 ticp)	Doran	(1924)	Nielsen, K.	400-600	
Andersen, H.C.	Fairy Tales (1st, 8vo, [310]p, col frn)	Saalfield	(1925)	Brundage, F.	25-40	*
Andersen, H.C.	Fairy Tales (1st, 8vo, 309p, cream cl, 8cp)	L: Harrap	1925	Orr, M.S.	50-75	*
Andersen, H.C.	Fairy Tales (4to, 245p, 16cp, pep)	Donohue	(1926)	Lee, E.D.	65-80	
Andersen, H.C.	Fairy Tales (1st, 8vo, p-o, 276p, black/gilt, pep, 4cp)	Winston	(1926)	Richardson, F.	40-60	
Andersen, H.C.	Fairy Tales (2nd, 4to, 320p, green cl, 16cp, 24pl)	L: Harrap	(1930)	Clarke, H.	200-300	
Andersen, H.C.	Fairy Tales (2nd AM, 4to, 16cp)	Brentano's	(1930)	Clarke, H.	160-230	
Andersen, H.C.	Fairy Tales (1st, lg8vo, 367p, 24cp)	Penn	(1930)	Kutcher, B.	45-60	*
Andersen, H.C.	Fairy Tales (1st {this pub}, sm4to, 355p, color)	Houghton	1931	Robinson, W.H.	65-80	*
Andersen, H.C.	Fairy Tales (1st {this pub}, 4to, p-o, 272p, 8cp)	Garden City	(1932)	Nielsen, K.	75-100	
Andersen, H.C.	Fairy Tales (1st, 4to, 287p, teg, uncut, 12cp, pep)	L: Harrap	(1932)	Rackham, A.	250-320	
Andersen, H.C.	Fairy Tales (1st AM, lg8vo, teg, 288p, 12cp, pep)	McKay	(1932)	Rackham, A.	185-240	
Andersen, H.C.	Fairy Tales (1st {std}, 4to, 253p, p-o, color, pep, DJ)	Coward	(1933)	MacKinstry, E.	70-100	
Andersen, H.C.	Fairy Tales (1st, sm8vo, 224p, tan cl, 13 fp b/w)	Appleton/Cent.	(1935)	Tenggren, G.	35-50	*
Andersen, H.C.	Fairy Tales (1st, sm8vo, 343p, color)	Grosset/Dunlap	(1945)	Szyk, A.	35-50	*
Andersen, H.C.	Fairy Tales (1st, 8vo, blue cl, 273p, 10 fp color, DJ)	NY: OUP	(1945)	Tudor, T.	145-200	
Andersen, H.C.	Fairy Tales (1st, 4to, 56p, color)	Duell/Sloan	(1946)	Taylor/Day	35-50	*
Andersen, H.C.	Fairy Tales & Legends (1st, 8vo, gilt, 470p, a.e. red, 10 b/w)	L: Cobden	(1935)	Whistler, R.	150-200	R
Andersen, H.C.	Fairy Tales & Legends (1st AM, 8vo, 470p, b/w)	NY: OUP	1936	Whistler, R.	80-120	*
Andersen, H.C.	Fairy Tales & Stories (2nd, 8vo, 512p, 4cp)	L: Routledge	[1905]	Bayes, A.W.	80-100	
Andersen, H.C.	Fairy Tales & Stories (2nd, 8vo, 572p, cvr by...)	L: Routledge	[1905]	King, J.	80-100	
Andersen, H.C.	Fairy Tales & Stories (1st AM, sm8vo, 408p, 8pl)	C.L. Bowman	1909	Brock, H.M.	65-80	*
Andersen, H.C.	Fairy Tales & Stories (1st, 8vo, 214p, gilt, col frn, pep)	L: MacMillan	1921	Pape, Eric	65-80	
Andersen, H.C.	Fairy Tales & Wonder Stories (1st, lg8vo, 442p, b/w, dep)	Harper	1914	Rhead, L.	65-90	*
Andersen, H.C.	Fairy Tales, Stories & Legends (1st, 8vo, 541p, 4pl)	L: Cassell	(1910)	Attwell, M.L.	50-75	*
Andersen, H.C.	Favorite Fairy Tales (1st, lg8vo, [33]p, color)	Wilcox/Follett	(1946)	Stearns, S.	50-80	*
Andersen, H.C.	Fir Tree (1st, 4to, [24]p, color)	Grosset/Dunlap	(1948)	Schlesinger, A.	35-50	*
Andersen, H.C.	Flower Maiden (1st, 8vo, 118p, p-o, pep, 3cp by...)	Jacobs	(1922)	Abbott, E.P.	25-45	*
Andersen, H.C.	It's Perfectly True... (1st, lg8vo, 305p, 29pl, pep, DJ)	Harcourt	(1938)	Bennett, R.	50-70	R
Andersen, H.C.	Little Match Girl (1st, 4to, ibds, [24]p, pep, fp color)	Grosset/Dunlap	(1944)	Tenggren, G.	35-50	*
Andersen, H.C.	Little Mermaid (1st, 12mo, 56p, green/gilt, 1-color, pep)	Holiday House	1935	Bianco, P.	35-50	
Andersen, H.C.	Little Mermaid (1st, 4to, blue/gilt, [48]p, 6 fp col, pep)	MacMillan	1939	Lathrop, D.	120-150	
Andersen, H.C.	Mermaid & other Tales (1st, sm8vo, 127p, p-o, gilt, 8cp)	Dent/Dutton	(1914)	Armfield, M.	70-90	
Andersen, H.C.	Old Man is Always Right (1st {std}, sq8vo, ibds, 28p)	Harper	(1940)	Rojankovsky, F.	40-65	

AUTHOR: 4

AUTHOR	TITLE	PUBLISHER	DATE	ARTIST	PRICE	LC
Andersen, H.C.	Real Princess (1st, 4to, green cl, p-o, [18]p, color)	Whitman	1932	Collin, H.	35-50	
Andersen, H.C.	Seven Tales (1st, 8vo, 128p, blue/gilt, 5cp, fp b/w)	Harper	1959	Sendak, M.	100-160	*
Andersen, H.C.	Snow Queen (1st, lg8vo, 232p, 35 illus, AEG)	L: E. Arnold	1894	Lemann, E.A.	80-100	
Andersen, H.C.	Snow Queen (sq8vo, 32p, ibds, 15 fp color)	L: Blackie	[1910]	Cramer, Rie	60-80	
Andersen, H.C.	Snow Queen (4to, ibds, 31p, 8cp)	L: Nelson	[1919]	Appleton, H.C.	50-70	
Andersen, H.C.	Snow Queen (1st, 8vo, red cl, 209p, col frn, pep)	Dutton	(1929)	Beverly, K.	65-90	
Andersen, H.C.	Snow Queen (1st, 4to, 63p, pep, 6 fp color)	MacMillan	1942	Hauman, G.& D.	45-60	*
Andersen, H.C.	Steadfast Tin Soldier (1st, sq12mo, ibds, unpag, color)	MacMillan	1927	Richards, G.M.	45-65	
Andersen, H.C.	Steadfast Tin Soldier (1st, lg8vo, ibds, [28]p, color, pep)	NY: Maxton	1946	Harriet	35-50	*
Andersen, H.C.	Steadfast Tin Soldier (1st, 4to, unpag, CH)	Scribner	(1953)	Brown, Marcia	65-90	*
Andersen, H.C.	Stories & Fairy Tales (2 vols, 8vo, teg, green/gilt, uncut)	L: G. Allen	1893	Gaskin, A.J.	100-150	
Andersen, H.C.	Stories by... (lg8vo, 159p, 7cp, later)	L: Hodder	[1920]	Dulac, E.	80-100	
Andersen, H.C.	Stories from Andersen (4to, 288p, AEG, grey/gilt, 6 chromos)	L: Nister	[1890]	Hardy, E.S.	100-150	
Andersen, H.C.	Stories from Andersen (lg8vo, blue/gilt, 195p, 14cp, later)	Hodder	[1915]	Dulac, E.	120-175	
Andersen, H.C.	Stories from... (8vo, 159p, 6 ticp, later)	L: Hodder	[1925]	Dulac, E.	80-100	*
Andersen, H.C.	Stories from... (4to, blue cl, 16cp)	Doubleday/Dor.	(1930)	Dulac, E.	75-120	
Andersen, H.C.	Stories... (1st, lg4to, 250p, orange/gilt, 28 ticp)	L: Hodder	(1911)	Dulac, E.	280-450	R
Andersen, H.C.	Tales from Andersen (8vo, 194p)	L: Constable	1896	Stratton, H.	100-130	*
Andersen, H.C.	Tales from Andersen (1st {std}, lg8vo, 78p, color)	Dutton	1946	Paflin, R.	65-80	*
Andersen, H.C.	The Nightingale (1st, 4to, blue/gilt, 125p, 12 ticp)	L: Hodder	(1911)	Dulac, E.	200-260	
Andersen, H.C.	The Nightingale (1st {std}, 12mo, 20p, color, pep)	Harper	1937	Marine, E.	35-50	*
Andersen, H.C.	The Swineherd (folio, ibds, unpag, color, pep)	Knopf	[1924]	Nerman, E.R.	50-65	
Andersen, H.C.	Three Hanses (1st, 8vo, 283p, DJ)	Little/Brown	1942	Chappell, W.	30-45	
Andersen, H.C.	Three Tales/Hans Andersen (lg sq8vo, 79p, blue/gilt, 22 b/w)	L: MacMillan	1910	Sambourne, L.	70-120	
Andersen, H.C.	Thumbelina (1st, 16mo, 79p, fp color, pep)	MacMillan	1928	Nerman, E.R.	35-50	*
Andersen, H.C.	Thumbelina (1st, sq32mo, ipcb, [60]p, color, dep)	Holiday House	(1939)	Scott, H.	50-70	R*
Andersen, H.C.	Thumbelina (1st, 4to, ibds, [48]p, fp color, pep)	Hyperion Press	(1943)	Fabres, O.	50-80	
Andersen, H.C.	Thumbelisa... (1st, lg8vo, [80]p, p-o, 3cp)	Doubleday/Page	1923	Walker, D.S.	65-80	*
Andersen, H.C.	Tumble-Bug (1st, lg8vo, green cl, 166p, pep, fp 1-color)	Harcourt	(1940)	List, H.	30-45	*
Andersen, H.C.	Ugly Duckling (1st, 4to, unpag, color)	L: D. Nutt	1894	Van Hoytems, T.	70-100	*
Andersen, H.C.	Ugly Duckling (1st, sm4to, 24p, ibds, 3 fp color)	Moffat	1905	Squire, M.H.	100-165	R*
Andersen, H.C.	Ugly Duckling (1st, 16mo, bds, p-o, 57p, color)	Reilly/Britton	(1912)	Neill, J.R.	60-80	
Andersen, H.C.	Ugly Duckling (1st, sm8vo, 127p, p-o, 8cp)	L: Dent	(1913)	Armfield, M.	40-65	
Andersen, H.C.	Ugly Duckling (1st, 24mo, [42]p, ibds, color, pep)	MacMillan	1927	Hader, B.& E.	30-50	
Andersen, H.C.	Ugly Duckling (1st, lg8vo, [40]p, ibds, 5cp, pep)	Saalfield	1931	Peat, F.B.	50-80	
Andersen, H.C.	Ugly Duckling (1st, ob4to, [40]p, p-o, color, pep)	Lippincott	(1939)	Disney Studios	180-240	
Andersen, H.C.	Ugly Duckling (1st, 8vo, ibds, [32]p, color)	Grosset/Dunlap	(1945)	Rojankovsky, F.	25-45	
Andersen, H.C.	Ugly Duckling (1st AM, ob4to, ibds, 54p, 24 fp color)	MacMillan	1955	Larsen, J.	50-75	*
Andersen, H.C.	What the Moon Saw (brown/gilt, 6 chromos)	(London)	[1880]	Bayes, A.W.	100-140	*
Andersen, H.C.	Wild Swans (1st, sm8vo, 117p, color, pep)	Jacobs	(1922)	Abbott, E.P.	45-60	*
Andersen, H.C.	Wild Swans... (1st AM, ob4to, 48p, ibds, 14 chromos)	Dutton	[1880]	Havers, A.	170-220	
Anderson, A.	Ann Anderson's Fairy Book (1st AM, 4to, 190p, p-o, 12cp, pep)	Nelson	(1928)	Anderson, A.	100-150	
Anderson, A.	Betty Book (1st, 4to, ibds, 32p, 13cp)	Nelson	[1912]	Anderson, A.	100-150	
Anderson, A.	Golden Story Book (4to, 8cp)	(London)	1933	Anderson, A.	50-70	
Anderson, A.	Nursery Zoo (4to, p-o, red cl, unpag, color)	Nelson	[1925]	Anderson, A.	60-80	
Anderson, A.	Old French Nursery Songs (1st, sm4to, 64p, ibds, 8cp)	L: Harrap	(1920)	Anderson, A.	100-130	
Anderson, A.	Patsy Book (1st, lg4to, ibds, unpag, 12cp, pep)	T. Nelson	[1919]	Anderson, A.	85-130	
Anderson, B.	Topsy Turvey's Pigtails (1st, lg8vo, 91p, color)	Rand/McNally	(1930)	Friend, E.	30-45	
Anderson, C.W.	Big Red (1st, ob4to, tan cl, pep, 64p, b/w)	MacMillan	1943	Anderson, C.W.	30-45	*
Anderson, C.W.	Billy & Blaze (1st, sm4to, orange cl, [56]p, fp b/w)	MacMillan	1936	Anderson, C.W.	35-50	*
Anderson, C.W.	Black Bay & Chestnut (1st, ob folio, [52]p, b/w, pep)	MacMillan	1939	Anderson, C.W.	50-75	*
Anderson, C.W.	Blaze & the Gypsies (1st, sm4to, green cl, [56]p, fp b/w)	MacMillan	1937	Anderson, C.W.	45-60	
Anderson, C.W.	Blaze Finds the Trail (1st {std}, sm4to, cloth, [48]p, b/w, cep)	MacMillan	1950	Anderson, C.W.	45-60	
Anderson, C.W.	Deep Through the Heart (1st, ob4to, [96]p, pep, b/w)	MacMillan	1940	Anderson, C.W.	35-50	*
Anderson, C.W.	Heads Up & Heels Down (1st {std}, 8vo, 144p, green cl, b/w)	MacMillan	1944	Anderson, C.W.	30-45	*
Anderson, C.W.	High Courage (1st, 8vo, red cl, 124p, fp b/w, pep)	MacMillan	1941	Anderson, C.W.	30-50	*
Anderson, C.W.	Horses are Folks (1st, ob4to, ibds, 89p, b/w, pep)	Harper	(1950)	Anderson, C.W.	40-60	
Anderson, C.W.	Salute (1st, sm4to, tan cl, p-o, 63p, b/w, pep)	MacMillan	1940	Anderson, C.W.	35-50	*
Anderson, C.W.	Thoroughbreds (1st, ob4to, 72p, b/w, pep, DJ)	MacMillan	1942	Anderson, C.W.	35-50	
Anderson, C.W.	Tomorrow's Champion (1st, ob4to, [84]p, green/gilt, b/w)	MacMillan	1946	Anderson, C.W.	30-50	
Anderson, C.W.	Touch of Greatness (1st, ob4to, blue cl, 96p, b/w, DJ)	MacMillan	1945	Anderson, C.W.	30-45	
Anderson, I.	Great Sea Horse (1st, 4to, red/gilt, teg, 251p, 24cp, pep)	Little/Brown	1909	Elliott, J.	80-100	
Anderson, R.C.	Animals in Social Captivity (1st, 8vo, gilt, p-o, 96p, 10cp dep)	Stewart/Kidd	(1914)	Herschede, I.N.	45-60	*
Anderson, Rbt. G.	Half-Past Seven Stories (1st, lg8vo, p-o, 251p, 16cp)	Putnam	(1922)	Smith, D.H.	30-45	*
Anderson, Rbt. G.	Seven O'Clock Stories (1st, lg8vo, 180p, gilt, p-o, 20cp, pep)	Putnam	(1920)	Smith, E.B.	130-160	
Andre, R.	Little Blossoms (sm4to, [32]p, ibds, 10 chromos)	L: G. Allen	1885	Andre, R.	320-500	
Andrews, M.S.	Better Treasure (1st, 8vo, red/gilt, 72p, cvr by...)	Bobbs-Merrill	(1908)	Armstrong, M.	25-40	
Andrews, M.S.	Bob & the Guides (1st, 8vo, green/gilt, 351p, teg)	Scribner	1906	Armstrong, M.	20-25	
Andrews, M.S.	Eternal Masculine (1st, 8vo, 430p, green/gilt)	Scribner	1913	Armstrong, M.	35-50	
Andrews, M.S.	The Militants (1st, 12mo, teg, 378p, green/gilt, cvr by...)	Scribner	1907	Armstrong, M.	45-60	
Andrews, M.S.	The Militants (1st, 12mo, 379p, teg, 2pl by...)	Scribner	1907	Wyeth, N.C.	45-60	
Angelo, V.	Bells of Bleeker Street (1st, 8vo, cloth, 185p, pep, b/w)	Viking	1949	Angelo, V.	70-100	R*

AUTHOR	TITLE	PUBLISHER	DATE	ARTIST	PRICE	LC
Angelo, V.	Golden Gate (1st, 8vo, aqua/gilt, 273p, b/w, DJ)	Viking	1939	Angelo, V.	35-50	
Angelo, V.	Marble Fountain (1st, 8vo, 223p, tan cl, b/w, pep)	Viking	1951	Angelo, V.	25-40	*
Angelo, V.	Nino (1st, 8vo, beige cl, 244p, 1-color, pep, DJ, NH)	Viking	1938	Angelo, V.	50-70	
Angelo, V.	Rooster Club (1st, 8vo, 150p, rust/gilt, b/w)	Viking	1944	Angelo, V.	25-40	
Anglund, J.W.	Brave Cowboy (1st {std}, 12mo, cloth, unpag, 2-color)	Harcourt	(1959)	Anglund, J.W.	35-50	*
Anglund, J.W.	Friend is Someone Who Likes You (1st {std}, 12mo, [27]p, color)	Harcourt	(1958)	Anglund, J.W.	35-50	*
Anglund, J.W.	In a Pumpkin Shell (1st {std}, lg8vo, yellow cl, [30]p, color)	Harcourt	(1960)	Anglund, J.W.	60-85	*
Anglund, J.W.	Look Out the Window (1st {std}, 8vo, yellow cl, [36]p, 2-col)	Harcourt	(1959)	Anglund, J.W.	35-50	*
Anglund, J.W.	Love is a Special Way of Feeling (1st {std}, 12mo, [30]p, 2-col)	Harcourt	(1960)	Anglund, J.W.	35-50	*
Annixter, Jane	Buffalo Chief (1st, 8vo, 219p, red cl, pep by...)	Holiday House	(1958)	Wilson, C.B.	25-40	*
Annixter, Jane	The Runner (1st, 8vo, 220p, red cl, pep)	Holiday House	(1956)	Laune, P.	20-30	*
Annixter, Paul	Wilderness Ways (1st, lg8vo, p-o, 313p, col frn, 13pl)	Penn	(1930)	Bull, C.L.	50-65	*
Annixter, Paul	Wilderness Ways (1st UK, 8vo, green/gilt, 313p, 12pl)	L: Harrap	1931	Bull, C.L.	35-50	
Anthony, E. & J.	Fairies Up-to-Date (1st, lg8vo, 189p, red cl, p-o, unpag, col)	Little/Brown	1923	DeBosschere, J.	150-200	
Anthony, Edward	Pussycat Princess (1st, sm4to, red cl, 157p, b/w)	Century	1922	(Photos)	85-130	
Arcambeau, E.	Book of Bridges (1st, 4to, 149p, green cl, p-o, 18cp)	L: Gowans/Gray	1911	King, J.	270-320	
Archer, J.C.	Rosalina (1st, 16mo, 95p, 24cp)	L: Richards	1904	Archer, J.C.	50-70	
Ardizzone, E.	Baggage to the Enemy (1st, 12mo, blue cl, 121p, b/w)	L: J. Murray	1941	Ardizzone, E.	100-150	*
Ardizzone, E.	Little Tim/Brave Sea Captain (1st AM, folio, ibds, color)	L/NY: OUP	1936	Ardizzone, E.	250-400	*
Ardizzone, E.	Lucy Brown & Mr. Grimes (1st AM, sm folio, ibds, 32p, color)	L/NY: OUP	[1937]	Ardizzone, E.	250-350	
Ardizzone, E.	Nicholas & Fast Moving Diesel (1st, lg4to, yel bds, 35p, color)	L: Eyre/Spotts	(1947)	Ardizzone, E.	200-265	
Ardizzone, E.	Paul, Hero of the Fire (1st AM, 8vo, ibds, [40]p, color, pep)	Houghton	(1948)	Ardizzone, E.	100-150	*
Ardizzone, E.	Tim & Charlotte (1st, 4to, ibds, unpag, color)	L/NY: OUP	(1951)	Ardizzone, E.	100-150	*
Ardizzone, E.	Tim & Lucy Go to Sea (1st AM, folio, ibds, [64]p, color)	L/NY: OUP	[1938]	Ardizzone, E.	250-400	
Ardizzone, E.	Tim All Alone (1st, 4to, red cl, unpag, color)	L: OUP	(1957)	Ardizzone, E.	90-130	*
Ardizzone, E.	Tim in Danger (1st, 4to, ipcb, unpag, color)	L/NY: OUP	(1953)	Ardizzone, E.	100-150	*
Ardizzone, E.	Tim to the Rescue (1st, 4to, [48]p, ibds, color)	L/NY: OUP	(1949)	Ardizzone, E.	100-150	*
Ardley, Pat	Advens./Mr. Horace Hedgehog (1st, ob4to, ibds, 56p, 6 fp col)	L: Collins	(1935)	Ardley, E.C.	75-100	*
Aristophanes	Eleven Comedies (1st, 8vo, 2 vols, black/gilt, 16cp)	H. Liveright	1928	DeBosschere, J.	80-120	
Arkwright, R.	Brownikins & Other Fancies (1st, 4to, p-o, [82]p, 5 ticp, pep)	L: Wells/Gard.	[1910]	Robinson, C.	250-350	
Armer, L.A.	Cactus (1st, 8vo, 102p, col frn, b/w)	Stokes	1934	Armer, S.	25-40	*
Armer, L.A.	Forest Pool (1st {std}, 4to, 40p, pep, 8cp, CH)	Longmans	(1938)	Armer, L.A.	70-100	R
Armer, L.A.	Waterless Mountain (1st {std}, lg8vo, 212p, cloth, 16pl, NM)	Longmans	1931	Armer, L.A.	70-110	
Armfield, C.	Armfield's Animal Book (1st, 8vo, 96p, orange cl, 8 ticp)	L: Duckworth	(1922)	Armfield, M.	65-80	
Armfield, C.	Flower Book (lg8vo, teg, bds, uncut, 16cp)	L: Warne	[1910]	Armfield, M.	70-90	
Armfield, C.	Sylvia's Travels (sm4to, 256p, 14cp)	L: Dent	1911	Armfield, M.	50-80	
Armfield, C.	Tales from Timbuktu (1st, lg8vo, 179p)	L: Chatto	(1923)	Armfield, M.	50-80	*
Armfield, C.	Tales from Timbuktu (1st AM, 8vo, 179p, col frn, 11 fp b/w)	Harcourt	[1924]	Armfield, M.	30-45	*
Armfield, M.	Hanging Garden... (1st, 4to, 75p, 8cp)	L: Simpkin	1914	Armfield, M.	45-65	*
Armour, M.	Fall of the Nibelungs (1st, 8vo, 16pl)	L: Dent	1897	MacDougall, W.B.	170-240	
Armour, M.	Shadow of Love (1st, 8vo, 124p)	L: Duckworth	1898	MacDougall, W.B.	65-80	*
Armour, M. (ed.)	Eerie Book (1st, lg8vo, teg, 211p, uncut, 15pl)	L: Shiells	1898	MacDougall, W.B.	150-225	
Armstrong, Leroy	Byrd Flam in Town (1st, 8vo, 139p, cvr & illus by...)	Chi: Bearhope	(1894)	Denslow, W.W.	30-45	*
Armstrong, M.	Fieldbook of Western Wilderness (1st, 12mo, 596p, color)	Putnam	1915	Armstrong, M.	100-160	
Arnold, E.	Adzuma (1st, 12mo, 170p, green/gilt)	Scribner	1893	Armstrong, M.	30-45	*
Arnold, E.	Japonica (1st, 4to, cloth, 128p, b/w pl)	Scribner	1891	Blum, R.	50-75	
Arnold, E.	Light of Asia (1st, 4to, black/silver, p-o, 182p, 12pl)	McKay	(1932)	Pogany, W.	100-150	
Arnold, E.	Potiphar's Wife (1st, 12mo, 127p, green/gilt)	Scribner	1892	Armstrong, M.	25-40	*
Arnold, E.	Song Celestial (1st, 4to, 135p, black/silver, p-o, 18pl)	McKay	(1934)	Pogany, W.	85-120	
Arnold, E.	Voyage of Ithobal (1st, 8vo, teg, blue cl, 8pl)	Dillingham	1901	Lumley, A.	20-25	
Arnold, M.	Poems (1st, 12mo, brown/gilt, 374p, teg, uncut, 18pl)	J. Lane	1900	Ospovat, H.	40-65	
Arnold, M.	Scholar-Gypsy (1st, 4to, gilt, unpag, 10 ticp)	L: Nicholson	1933	Adams, F.	60-80	
Arnold, M.	Scholar-Gypsy & Thyrsis (1st, 4to, 67p, 10cp)	L: P.L. Warner	(1910)	Flint, W.R.	100-145	
Arthur, Lady	Dream of Little Hazy Cream (folio, ibds, p-o, 12cp)	L: Bickers	[1900]	Frere, C.F.	100-165	*
Artzybasheff, B.	As I See (1st, 4to, unpag, col frn, fp b/w)	Dodd	1954	Artzybasheff, B.	50-75	*
Artzybasheff, B.	Busiest Man in Town (1st, sm8vo, 45p, gilt)	Time Inc.	1933	Artzybasheff, B.	65-80	
Artzybasheff, B.	Fairy Shoemaker (1st, lg8vo, bds, b/w, 114p, DJ)	MacMillan	1928	Artzybasheff, B.	75-100	
Artzybasheff, B.	Poor Shaydullah (1st, sq8vo, [59]p, grey cl, 10 fp b/w)	MacMillan	1931	Artzybasheff, B.	40-60	
Artzybasheff, B.	Seven Simeons (1st, 4to, [32]p, green cl, color, dep, CH)	Viking	1937	Artzybasheff, B.	70-115	
Asbjornsen, P.C.	East o/t Sun West o/t Moon (1st, 12mo, 198p, cp)	MacMillan	1928	Collin, H.	35-50	*
Asbjornsen, P.C.	East o/t Sun/West o/t Moon (1st, 12mo, 218p, 9cp)	Row/Peterson	(1912)	Richardson, F.	50-80	*
Asbjornsen, P.C.	East o/t Sun/West o/t Moon (1st, 4to, gilt, 206p, pep, 25 ticp)	L: Hodder	(1914)	Nielsen, K.	600-800	
Asbjornsen, P.C.	East o/t Sun/West o/t Moon (1st AM, 4to, 205p, p-o, 25 ticp pep)	Doran	[1914]	Nielsen, K.	450-600	
Asbjornsen, P.C.	East o/t Sun/West o/t Moon (1st, 8vo, p-o, 289p, green cl, 8cp)	McKay	(1921)	Cooke, E.	65-80	
Asbjornsen, P.C.	East o/t Sun/West o/t Moon (1st, lg8vo, 248p, col frn)	Saalfield	(1924)	Brundage, F.	30-45	*
Asbjornsen, P.C.	East o/t Sun/West o/t Moon (1st, lg8vo, 192p, col, p-o, gilt pep)	Whitman	(1924)	Higgins, V.M.	45-60	*
Asbjornsen, P.C.	East o/t Sun/West o/t Moon (8vo, 204p, p-o, cp, pep, later)	Garden City	[1930]	Nielsen, K.	75-100	
Asbjornsen, P.C.	East o/t Sun/West o/t Moon (1st, 4to, 188p, 22 fp b/w, pep)	Viking	1938	D'Aulaire, I.& E.	40-65	*
Asbjornsen, P.C.	Fairy Tales from the Far North (1st, 8vo, 303p, b/w pl)	L: D. Nutt	1897	Werenskiold, E.	100-150	
Asbjornsen, P.C.	Fairy Tales from the Far North (1st AM, 8vo, 303p, b/w)	A.C. Armstrong	1897	Werenskiold, E.	80-120	*
Asbjornsen, P.C.	Fifteen Norse Tales (1st, 8vo, 180p)	L: Nelson	1931	Pailthorpe, D.	50-65	*
Asbjornsen, P.C.	Norse Fairy Tales (1st, sm8vo, 463p, 8cp, 20pl, pep)	L: Freemantle	1910	Knowles, H.& R.	200-300	

AUTHOR	TITLE	PUBLISHER	DATE	ARTIST	PRICE	LC
Asbjornsen, P.C.	Norse Fairy Tales (16mo, ibds, 8cp)	L: Routledge	[1920]	Knowles, R.L.	160-200	
Asbjornsen, P.C.	Round the Yule Log (1st, lg8vo, 316p)	L: Sampson	1881	Unknown	65-90	*
Asbjornsen, P.C.	Tales from the Field (1st AM, 8vo, 403p, gilt, 11pl)	Putnam	1896	Smith, J. Moyr	50-80	
Asbjornsen, P.C.	Three Billy Goats Gruff (1st {std}, 4to, green cl, unpag)	Harcourt	(1957)	Brown, Marcia	35-50	*
Ash, Fenton	Black Opal (1st, 8vo, 320p, blue cl, 3 color)	L: J.F. Shaw	(1915)	E.S.H.	40-60	*
Ash, Fenton	By Airship to Ophir (1st, 8vo, 320p, red/gilt, 3 color)	L: J.F. Shaw	(1911)	Pearse, A.	70-100	*
Ash, Frank	Trip to Mars (1st AM, 8vo, red/gilt, 318p, 6cp)	Chambers/Lipp.	1909	Groome, W.H.C.	100-150	
Ashford, Daisy	Young Visitors (1st, 8vo, 91p, ibds, b/w)	Doubleday	1951	DuBois, W.P.	35-50	*
Ashley, D.	French Fairy Tales (1st, lg8vo, 136p, cp)	L: R. Tuck	[1917]	Attwell, M.L.	130-180	
Ashley, Fred	Temple of Fire (1st, 8vo, green/gilt, 332p, 8pl)	L: I. Pitman	1905	Daniel, V.S.	50-80	*
Ashmore, M.	Lost, Stolen & Strayed (1st AM, 8vo, 96p, col frn)	Scribner	1931	Aldin, C.	60-85	
Aspden, Don	Barney's Barges (1st, 8vo, 192p, green cl, fp b/w, pep)	Holiday House	(1944)	Pitz, H.C.	20-30	*
Aspden, Don	Mike of Company D. (1st, 8vo, 261p, green cl, b/w)	Scribner	1939	Brown, Paul	25-40	*
Asquith, C. (ed.)	Flying Carpet (1st, 4to, 200p, cloth, 4 ticp)	Scribner	(1925)	Various	30-45	
Asquith, C. (ed.)	Sails of Gold (1st AM, 4to, 166p, ticp)	Scribner	(1927)	Various	30-45	*
Asquith, C. (ed.)	Treasure Cave (1st, 4to, 144p, 5 ticp)	Scribner	(1928)	Various	30-45	
Asquith, C. (ed.)	Treasure Ship (1st, 4to, 198p, 4 ticp)	Scribner	(1926)	Various	30-45	
Astor, J.J.	Journey in Other Worlds (1st, 8vo, blue/silver, 476p, 10pl)	Appleton	1894	Beard, D.	150-200	
Atherton, G.	Gorgeous Isle (1st, 8vo, 223p, orang cl, 4cp, pep)	Doubleday/Page	1908	Phillips, C.	35-50	
Atherton, G.	Splendid Idle Forties (1st, 8vo, 389p, gilt, 8pl)	MacMillan	1902	Fisher, H.	30-45	
Atherton, G.	Valiant Runaways (1st, sm8vo, 276p, 8pl)	Dodd	1898	Greenough, W.C.	25-40	*
Atkey, B.	Easy Money (1st, 8vo, p-o, 311p)	Estes	(1908)	Stampa, G.L.	20-30	
Atkins, E.H.	Pot of Gold (1st, 8vo, p-o, 164p, 4cp, 6pl, pep)	Stokes	1930	LaDow, St. C.	45-60	*
Atkinson, Brooks	Once Around the Sun (1st {std}, 8vo, 376p, blue cl, fp b/w)	Harcourt	(1951)	Freeman, D.	30-45	*
Atkinson, E.	Greyfriars Bobby (1st, 12mo, 291p, frontis, PPPa)	Harper	1912	Unknown	45-60	*
Atkinson, E.	Greyfriars Bobby (1st, lg8vo, red cl, 269p, uncut, 4pl)	Harper	1929	Kirmse, M.	25-40	*
Atkinson, E.	Johnny Apple-Seed (1st, sm8vo, 340p, b/w)	Harper	1915	Merrill, F.	20-30	*
Atkinson, J.C.	Scenes in Fairyland (1st, 8vo, 246p, green cl, 4pl)	L: MacMillan	1892	Brock, C.E.	50-75	*
Attwood, Wm.	Man Who Could Grow Hair (1st {std}, sm8vo, 240p, ipcb, b/w)	Knopf	1949	Duvoisin, R.	30-50	*
Atwater, R.	Doris & the Trolls (1st, 12mo, 124p, blue cl, 1-color)	Rand/McNally	(1931)	Gee, J.	50-80	
Atwater, R.	Mr. Popper's Penguins (1st {std}, 8vo, 138p, 1-col, pep, DJ, NH)	Little/Brown	1938	Lawson, R.	70-100	R
Aubrey, Frank	Devil-Tree of El Dorado (1st, 8vo, brown/gilt, 392p, 8pl)	L: Hutchinson	1896	Hyland/Ellis	150-200	
Aubrey, Frank	Queen of Atlantis... (1st AM, 8vo, red/gilt, 391p, 8pl)	Lippincott	1900	Smith, D.M.	120-165	
Ault, L.& N.	Podgy Book of Tales (1st, 12mo, 223p, pict cl, 16cp)	L: Richards	(1907)	Ault, N.	130-180	*
Ault, L.& N.	Sammy & the Snarlywink (1st, 16mo, 95p, green cl, 24cp)	L: Richards	1904	Ault, N.	100-150	
Ault, N.	Dreamland Shores (1st AM, sm4to, 83p, 6 ticp, pep)	Dodd	(1920)	Ault, N.	100-145	*
Aunt Jo	Jo & Uncle George Kritters (1st, lg8vo, ibds, color)	Little/Brown	1922	Brown, Paul	60-90	
Aunt Jo	Kritters of Kitchen Kingdom (1st, 4to, 39p, ibds, 16 fp color)	Little/Brown	1922	Brown, Paul	70-110	R
Auslander, Jos.	Letters to Women... (1st {std}, 8vo, 85p, frn & b/w illus)	Harper	1929	Leighton, C.	45-60	*
Austen, J.	Emma (1st, 12mo, green/gilt, 504p, teg, b/w)	L: G. Allen	1898	Hammond, C.	45-60	
Austen, J.	Northanger Abbey (1st, 8vo, AEG, red cloth, b/w)	L: MacMillan	1897	Thomson, H.	70-90	
Austen, J.	Northanger Abbey (1st, 8vo, 206p, gilt, 24cp)	L: J.M. Dent	1907	Brock, C.E.	50-75	
Austen, J.	Pride & Prejudice (1st, 12mo, 476p, AEG, grn/gilt, b/w, cep)	L: G. Allen	1894	Thomson, H.	65-90	
Austen, J.	Pride & Prejudice (1st, 8vo, 336p, teg, gilt, uncut, 24 color)	L: J.M. Dent	1907	Brock, C.E.	45-60	
Austen, J.	Rogues in Porcelain (1st, sm4to, pink bds, p-o, 14cp, pep)	L: Chapman	1924	Austen, J.	50-70	
Austen, J.	Rogues in Porcelain (1st AM, lg8vo, 258p, bds, 15cp, pep)	NY: Greenberg	1924	Austen, J.	60-80	
Austen, J.	Sense & Sensibility (1st, 8vo, teg, 389p, gilt, b/w)	L: G. Allen	1899	Hammond, C.	60-80	
Austin, Cyril F.	Advens. of Benjamin & Christabel (1st, ob4to, unpag, color)	Nister/Dutton	(1911)	Austin, H.	50-70	*
Austin, Cyril F.	Edward Buttoneye & his Advens. (sq16mo, ibds, chromos)	L: Nister	[1910]	Austin, H.	65-80	*
Austin, Margot	Archie Angel (1st {std}, 4to, yellow cl, 45p, b/w, pep)	Dutton	1957	Austin, M.	45-65	*
Austin, Margot	Barney's Adventure (1st {std}, sm4to, ibds, [42]p, b/w, pep)	Dutton	(1941)	Austin, M.	30-50	
Austin, Margot	Brave John Henry (1st {std}, sm4to, 43p, b/w)	Dutton	(1955)	Austin, M.	30-45	*
Austin, Margot	Effelli (1st {std}, 4to, ibds, [56]p, fp b/w, pep)	Dutton	1942	Austin, M.	35-50	*
Austin, Margot	First Prize for Danny (1st {std}, sm4to, ibds, 43p, b/w, pep)	Dutton	(1952)	Austin, M.	35-50	*
Austin, Margot	Gabriel Churchkitten (1st {std}, 4to, ipcb, [36]p, pep, b/w)	Dutton	1942	Austin, M.	70-100	*
Austin, Margot	Gabriel Churchkitten & Moths (1st {std}, sm4to, ipcb, [41]p, b/w)	Dutton	1948	Austin, M.	65-90	*
Austin, Margot	Growl Bear (1st {std}, 4to, ipcb, 42p, pep, b/w)	Dutton	(1951)	Austin, M.	45-65	*
Austin, Margot	Lutie (1st {std}, lg8vo, ibds, [42]p, b/w)	Dutton	1944	Austin, M.	35-50	*
Austin, Margot	Manuel's Kite String (1st, sm8vo, 112p, color)	Scribner	1943	Austin, M.	35-50	*
Austin, Margot	Moxie & Hanty & Bunty (1st, 8vo, ipcb, [44]p, 1-color)	Scribner	1939	Austin, M.	45-60	*
Austin, Margot	Once Upon a Springtime (1st, 8vo, 43p, ipcb, fp 1-color)	Scribner	1940	Austin, M.	30-50	*
Austin, Margot	Peter Churchmouse (1st {std}, sm4to, ipcb, [41]p, b/w, pep)	Dutton	1941	Austin, M.	70-100	
Austin, Margot	Poppet (1st {std}, 4to, ibds, [38]p, b/w)	Dutton	(1949)	Austin, M.	30-45	
Austin, Margot	Three Silly Kittens (1st {std}, 4to, ibds, 44p, b/w)	Dutton	(1950)	Austin, M.	30-45	
Austin, Margot	Trumpet (1st {std}, sq4to, ipcb, [40]p, b/w, pep)	Dutton	1943	Austin, M.	35-50	
Austin, Margot	Tumble Bear (1st, sm4to, [44]p, olive cl, fp b/w, cep)	Scribner	(1940)	Austin, M.	35-50	*
Austin, Margot	Willamette Way (1st, sm4to, [44]p, tan cl, fp color)	Scribner	1941	Austin, M.	45-65	*
Austin, Margot	William's Shadow (1st {std}, sm4to, ibds, 43p, b/w, pep)	Dutton	(1954)	Austin, M.	30-50	*
Austin, Mary	Isidro (1st, 8vo, 425p, green/gilt, dep, 4cp)	Houghton	1905	Pape, Eric	50-70	
Austin, Mary	Land of Little Rain (1st, 8vo, green/gilt, 281p, p-o, teg)	Houghton	1903	Smith, E.B.	240-350	
Austin, Mary	The Flock (1st, 8vo, 266p, frn by...)	Houghton	1906	Smith, E.B.	40-60	
Austin, Mary	The Ford (1st, sm8vo, 440p, 4pl)	Houghton	1917	Smith, E.B.	50-70	

AUTHOR	TITLE	PUBLISHER	DATE	ARTIST	PRICE	LC
Austin, Mary	Trail Book (1st, 8vo, 304p)	Houghton	1918	Winter, M.	35-50	
Austin, Mary H.	California: Land of the Sun (1st, lg8vo, 178p, gilt, 32 ticp)	L: A&C Black	1914	Palmer, S.	120-165	
Austin, S.	Story Without an End (1st, 8vo, 40p, AEG, 15cp)	L: Sampson	1868	Boyle, E.V.	600-800	
Auston, C.	Little Blue Rabbit (sq16mo, ibds)	L: Nister	(1905)	Austin, H.	30-50	
Averill, Esther	Daniel Boone (1st AM {std}, 4to, ipcb, 58p, color)	Harper	(1945)	Rojankovsky, F.	60-80	
Averill, Esther	Flash: Story of a Horse (1st AM, narrow 4to, 32p, color, ibds)	Smith/Haas	(1934)	Rojankovsky, F.	70-100	*
Averill, Esther	Flash: Story of a Horse (1st UK, 4to, ibds, 32p, color)	L: Faber	(1934)	Rojankovsky, F.	90-130	*
Averill, Esther	Powder (1st AM, 4to, ibds, 29p, color)	Smith/Haas	(1933)	Rojankovsky, F.	75-110	*
Averill, Naomi	Choochee: Story/Eskimo Boy (1st, sq4to, [40]p, ibds, pep, col)	Grosset/Dunlap	1937	Averill, N.	70-95	*
Averill, Naomi	Whistling-Two-Teeth (1st, lg sq8vo, [24]p, color, pep)	Grosset/Dunlap	1939	Averill, N.	50-80	*
Avery, Kay	Wee Willow Whistle (1st {std}, 4to, ipcb, [32]p, color)	Knopf	(1947)	Bromhall, W.	30-45	*
Aydelotte, Dora	Green Gravel (1st, 12mo, green cl, uncut, 249p, b/w)	Appleton/Cent.	1937	Daugherty, J.	25-40	*
Ayer, Jean	Picnic Book (1st, 12mo, 46p, color, wraps)	MacMillan	1934	Petershams	30-45	*
Ayers, Ray F.	King of Kinkiddie... (1st, sm8vo, 262p, 15pl)	Dutton	1904	Bobbett, Walt.	45-60	*
Ayme, Marcel	Magic Pictures (1st {std}, 8vo, blue cl, 117p, b/w)	Harper	(1954)	Sendak, M.	120-175	
Ayme, Marcel	Wonderful Farm (1st {std}, 8vo, 182p, red cl, b/w)	Harper	(1951)	Sendak, M.	140-180	R
Bacheller, I.	Charge It (1st, 12mo, p-o, 192p, b/w)	Harper	1912	Koerner	20-35	
Bacon, J.D.	Biography of a Boy (1st, 8vo, 322p, blue cl, 14pl)	Harper	1910	O'Neill, R.	50-80	
Bacon, J.D.	Idyll/All Fool's Day (1st, 8vo, 120p, p-o, 10pl)	Dodd	1908	Crosby, R.M.	20-30	*
Bacon, J.D.	In the Border Country (1st, 8vo, 130p, 5cp)	Doubleday/Page	1909	Peck, C.E.	25-40	
Bacon, J.D.	Luck/O'Lady Joan (1st, sm8vo, 58p, frn by)	F.G. Browne	1913	Williams, C.E.	20-30	*
Bacon, J.D.	Ten to Seventeen (1st, sm8vo, 261p, green cl, p-o, 3pl by...)	Harper	1908	Smith, J.W.	35-60	*
Bacon, P.	Animosities (1st {std}, 8vo, 106p, ibds, b/w)	Harcourt	(1931)	Bacon, P.	35-60	
Bacon, P.	Ballad of Tangle Street (1st, ob4to, ibds, 24p, b/w)	MacMillan	1929	Bacon, P.	80-100	
Bacon, P.	Cat Calls (1st {std}, lg8vo, 87p, b/w, DJ)	McBride	(1935)	Bacon, P.	45-60	
Bacon, P.	Lion-Hearted Kitten (1st, 8vo, 102p, 10pl)	MacMillan	1927	Bacon, P.	35-50	*
Bacon, P.	Mercy & the Mouse (1st, 8vo, pink cl, 85p, 7pl, cep)	MacMillan	1928	Bacon, P.	40-60	*
Bacon, P.	Mischief in Mayfield (1st {std}, lg8vo, 177p, 15pl)	Harcourt	(1933)	Bacon, P.	25-40	*
Bacon, P.	Mystery at East Hatchett (1st, 8vo, 170p, b/w)	Viking	1939	Bacon, P.	25-45	*
Bacon, P.	Off With Their Heads! (1st {std}, lg8vo, [89]p, b/w)	McBride	(1934)	Bacon, P.	30-45	
Bacon, P.	Starting from Scratch (1st {spiral}, [48]p, ibds, b/w)	J. Messner	1945	Bacon, P.	50-75	*
Bacon, P.	Terrible Nuisance (1st {std}, 4to, 142p, blue cl, 8pl)	Harcourt	(1931)	Bacon, P.	60-90	R
Bacon, P.	True Philosopher (1st, 12mo, blue cl, 55p, 13pl)	Bos: Four Seas	1919	Bacon, P.	50-70	*
Badger, J.E.	Lost City (1st, 8vo, 326p, blue/gilt, 8pl)	D. Estes	(1898)	Bridgman, L.J.	50-70	
Baer, Howard	Now This, Now That (1st, ob4to, [30]p, tan cl, b/w, cep)	Holiday House	1957	Baer, H.	25-40	*
Bagnold, Enid	Alice & Thomas & Jane (1st AM, 8vo, yellow cl, 173p, b/w)	Knopf	1931	Jones, Laurie	20-30	
Bailey, A.C.	Katrina & Jan (1st, 8vo, ibds, unpag, color, pep)	Volland	(1923)	Rosse, H.	45-60	*
Bailey, A.C.	Kimo (1st, 8vo, ibds, 96p, color, pep)	Volland	(1928)	Holling, L.W.	50-75	*
Bailey, A.C.	Skating Gander (1st, 8vo, ibds, 93p, color, pep)	Volland	(1927)	Myers, M.H.	35-50	
Bailey, A.W.	Roberta and her Brothers (1st, 8vo, 310p, 4pl)	Little/Brown	1906	Richards, H.R.	20-30	*
Bailey, C.S.	Children of the Handcrafts (1st, lg8vo, 192p, b/w, dep)	Viking	1935	Paull, G.	30-45	
Bailey, C.S.	Country-Stop (1st, 8vo, 128p, dep, 8 fp color)	Viking	1942	Paull, G.	35-50	*
Bailey, C.S.	Finnigan II - His Nine Lives (1st, tall 4to, red cl, 95p, pep)	Viking	1953	Seredy, K.	45-60	*
Bailey, C.S.	Firelight Stories (1st, sm8vo, 192p, 9pl)	M. Bradley	1907	Horne, D.W.	20-25	*
Bailey, C.S.	For the Children's Hour (1st, 8vo, 336p, 8pl)	M. Bradley	1906	Breck, G.W.	20-30	*
Bailey, C.S.	Li'l Hannibal (1st, 8vo, [24]p, color, pep)	Platt/Munk	(1938)	Unknown	45-65	*
Bailey, C.S.	Miss Hickory (1st, lg8vo, tan cl, 123p, fp b/w, pep, DJ, NM)	Viking	1946	Gannett, R.C.	75-120	R
Bailey, C.S.	Peter Newell's Mother Goose (1st, 8vo, 265p, 20pl)	Holt	1905	Newell, P.	85-120	
Bailey, C.S.	Read Aloud Stories (1st, 8vo, 215p, red/gilt, 6cp, pep)	M. Bradley	(1929)	Lupprian, H.	25-40	*
Bailey, C.S.	Stories & Rhymes for a Child (1st, 8vo, 194p, col frn, p-o, 5pl)	M. Bradley	1909	Wright, C.	20-30	*
Bailey, C.S.	Tops & Whistles (1st, lg8vo, 193p, 20 fp b/w, pep)	Viking	1937	Paull, G.	25-40	*
Bailey, C.S.	Wonder Stories (1st, 8vo, p-o, 344p, 6cp, pep)	M. Bradley	1920	Burd, C.M.	25-40	*
Bailey, C.S.	Wonderful Days (1st, lg8vo, 254p, col frn)	Whitman	(1929)	Falls, C.B.	35-50	*
Bailey, M.	Seven Peas in the Pod (1st, 8vo, 201p, 4cp)	L: Harrap	(1921)	Nixon, K.	60-80	
Bailey, T.	Star in the Well (1st, sm8vo, 46p, wraps, color decor by...)	Volland	(1928)	Moschcowitz, P.	45-60	*
Bain, R.N.	Russian Fairy Tales (1st, 8vo, 264p, gilt, b/w)	Way/Williams	1895	Gere, C.M.	100-130	*
Bain, R.N.	Russian Fairy Tales (1st, 4to, teg, p-o, 283p, 16pl)	L: Harrap	1915	Nisbet, N.L.	150-200	
Bain, R.N.	Weird Tales from Northern Seas (1st, 8vo, 201p, blue/gilt, 12pl)	L: Kegan Paul	1893	Housman, L.	140-200	
Baity, E.C.	America Before Man (1st, 4to, 224p, pep, maps, b/w)	Viking	1953	Falls, C.B.	45-60	*
Baity, E.C.	Americans Before Columbus (1st, sm4to, 256p, gilt, pep, NH)	Viking	1951	Falls, C.B.	35-50	*
Baker, Augusta	Golden Lynx (1st {std}, 8vo, 160p, red cl, fp b/w)	Lippincott	(1960)	Troyer, J.	40-65	*
Baker, Augusta	Talking Tree (1st {std}, 8vo, 255p, maroon cl, b/w)	Lippincott	(1955)	Troyer, J.	40-65	*
Baker, C.	Coquo & the King's Children (1st, 8vo, 250p, brown/gilt, 6 col)	McClurg	1902	Perkins, L.F.	25-40	
Baker, C.	Court Jester (1st, 8vo, 259p, b/w pl)	Bobbs-Merrill	(1906)	Webb, M.E.	20-30	*
Baker, C.	Magic Image from India (1st, 4to, 163p, 5cp)	Stern	1909	Lachman, H.B.	65-90	*
Baker, C.	Queen's Page (1st, sm8vo, 319p, 12pl)	Bobbs-Merrill	(1905)	Cory, F.	50-65	
Baker, C.	Young People in Old Places (1st, 8vo, green cl, 322p, fp b/w)	Bobbs-Merrill	(1906)	Booth, F.	30-45	*
Baker, Edna D.	Child is Born (1st, folio, ibds, 60p, color, pep)	Reilly/Lee	(1932)	Royt, M.	30-45	*
Baker, Geo.	Point Lace & Diamonds (1st, 4to, 82p, 12cp)	Stokes	1892	Day, F.	90-145	
Baker, K.W.	Garden of the Plynck (1st, 4to, ibds, 112p, col frn, b/w)	Yale U. Press	(1920)	Minard, F.	65-100	*
Baker, M.	Lady Arabella's Birthday Party (1st, 8vo, [95]p, silhouet., pep)	Dodd	1940	Baker, M.	30-50	
Baker, Nina B.	Peter the Great (1st, 8vo, 310p, fp b/w)	Vanguard Pr.	(1943)	Slobodkin, L.	30-45	*

AUTHOR	TITLE	PUBLISHER	DATE	ARTIST	PRICE	LC
Baker, O.	Dusty Star (1st, 8vo, 302p, aqua/gilt, uncut, 4pl, pep)	Dodd	1922	Bransom, P.	25-40	*
Baker, O.	Panther Magic (1st, 8vo, gilt, 312p, 8cp, pep)	Dodd	1928	Wiese, K.	25-40	*
Baker, O.	Shasta of the Wolves (1st, 8vo, 276p, 4cp)	Dodd	1919	Bull, C.L.	20-35	*
Baker, O.	Thunder Boy (1st, 8vo, red cl, 288p, 4pl, pep)	Dodd	1924	Bransom, P.	25-40	*
Balch, F.H.	Bridge of the Gods (1st, 8vo, teg, 280p, 8pl)	McClurg	1902	Dixon, M.	30-45	
Balch, Glenn	Brave Riders (1st {std}, sm8vo, 191p, green cl, b/w)	Crowell	(1959)	Keats, E.J.	25-45	*
Balch, Glenn	Hide-Rack Kidnapped (1st, sm8vo, 302p, dp pl)	Crowell	1939	Mason, G.F.	20-30	*
Baldwin, Clara	Little Tuck (1st {std}, lg8vo, 95p, yellow cl, b/w)	Doubleday	(1959)	Galdone, P.	30-45	*
Baldwin, J.	Story of Roland (1st, sm4to, 347p, p-o, 10cp, pep, SC)	Scribner	(1930)	Hurd, P.	70-90	
Baldwin, J.	Story of Seigfried (1st, 8vo, red/gilt, 306p, teg, PPP)	Scribner	1882	Pyle, H.	150-200	
Baldwin, J.	Story of Siegfried (1st, 4to, p-o, 279p, black cl, 6cp, pep, SC)	Scribner	(1931)	Hurd, P.	70-100	
Baldwin, J.	Story of the Golden Age (1st, 8vo, 286p, uncut, PPP)	Scribner	1887	Pyle, H.	180-230	
Baldwin, J.	The Sampo (1st, 8vo, green cl, 368p, 4cp)	Scribner	1912	Wyeth, N.C.	60-80	
Baldwin, May	Holly House & Ridges Row (1st, 8vo, 339p, red/gilt, 12cp)	L: Chambers	1908	Wheelhouse, M.V.	45-60	
Baldwin, May	That Little Limb (1st, 8vo, 199p, ibds)	L: Chambers	1905	Attwell, M.L.	65-80	*
Ballantyne, Joan	Kidnappers at Coombe (1st, 8vo, 203p, DJ)	L: Nelson	1960	Ardizzone, E.	30-45	
Bancroft, Alberta	Goblins of Haubeck (1st, 12mo, 117p, green/gilt, pep, col frn)	McBride	1925	Sichel, H.	20-30	*
Bancroft, Alberta	Lost Village (1st, 8vo, 130p, green cl, 4 fp color)	Doran	(1927)	Barney, M.W.	45-65	
Bancroft, Hubert H.	New Pacific (1st, 8vo, 738p, map, green/gilt, cvr by...)	Bancroft Co.	1900	Armstrong, M.	45-60	*
Bancroft, L.	Babes in Birdland (1st, lg8vo, green ipcb, 116p, 8cp)	Reilly/Britton	(1911)	Enright, M.W.	350-500	
Bancroft, L.	Bandit Jim Crow (1st, 8vo, [64]p, 15cp)	Reilly/Britton	(1906)	Enright, M.W.	280-400	
Bancroft, L.	Mr. Woodchuck (1st, 8vo, 62p, ibds, color, cep)	Reilly/Britton	(1906)	Enright, M.W.	280-400	
Bancroft, L.	Policeman Blue Jay (1st, 8vo, ibds, 115p, 8cp)	Reilly/Britton	(1907)	Enright, M.W.	400-600	
Bancroft, L.	Prince Mud-Turtle (1st, 12mo, 61p, tan cl, cep, 14 fp color)	Reilly/Britton	(1906)	Enright, M.W.	280-350	
Bancroft, L.	Sugar-Loaf Mountain (1st, 8vo, cloth, 64p, 16cp, cep)	Reilly/Britton	(1906)	Enright, M.W.	280-400	
Bancroft, L.	Twinkle & Chubbins (1st, 8vo, 384p, yellow cl, color)	Reilly/Britton	(1911)	Enright, M.W.	420-600	
Bancroft, L.	Twinkle's Enchantment (1st, 8vo, 64p, 15cp)	Reilly/Britton	(1906)	Enright, M.W.	300-450	
Bangs, J.K.	Alice in Blunderland (1st, 12mo, 124p, brown cl, p-o, b/w)	Doubleday/Page	1907	Levering, A.	45-60	
Bangs, J.K.	Andiron Tales (1st, sm4to, green cl, p-o, 101p, 8cp)	Winston	(1906)	Dwiggins, C.V.	100-150	*
Bangs, J.K.	Autobiography of Methuselah (1st, 12mo, 185p, cp)	Dodge	(1909)	Cooper, F.G.	35-50	*
Bangs, J.K.	Bikey the Skycycle (1st, 8vo, blue/gilt, 321p, col frn, 7pl)	NY: Riggs	1902	Newell, P.	35-50	
Bangs, J.K.	Booming of Acre Hill (1st, 12mo, teg, uncut, 265p, b/w)	Harper	1900	Gibson, C.D.	30-45	
Bangs, J.K.	Dreamers, A Club (1st, 16mo, brown/gilt, 247p, b/w)	Harper	1899	Penfield, E.	30-45	
Bangs, J.K.	Emblemland (1st, 8vo, 164p, blue/gilt, fp b/w)	R.H. Russell	1902	Macauley, C.R.	60-85	*
Bangs, J.K.	Enchanted Typewriter (1st, 12mo, 171p, uncut, 10pl)	Harper	1899	Newell, P.	40-60	
Bangs, J.K.	From Pillar to Post (1st, 8vo, 339p, b/w)	Century	1916	Neill, J.R.	35-50	*
Bangs, J.K.	Ghosts I Have Met (1st, 16mo, 191p, uncut, 23pl)	Harper	1898	Various	40-65	
Bangs, J.K.	Half-Hours with Jimmie-Boy (1st, 8vo, green cl, 212p, b/w)	R.H. Russell	1893	Various	50-65	
Bangs, J.K.	House Boat on the Styx (1st, 16mo, green/gilt, 171p, 23pl)	Harper	1896	Newell, P.	35-50	
Bangs, J.K.	Idiot at Home (1st, 12mo, 314p, teg, uncut)	Harper	1900	Richards, F.T.	35-50	*
Bangs, J.K.	In Camp with a Tin Soldier (1st, 12mo, grey cl, 194p, b/w)	R.H. Russell	1892	Ashe, E.M.	35-50	
Bangs, J.K.	Jack & the Check Book (1st, 8vo, 236p, green cl, b/w)	Harper	1911	Levering, A.	35-50	
Bangs, J.K.	Little Book of Christmas (1st, 8vo, 173p, 4cp)	Little/Brown	1912	Becher, A.E.	30-45	*
Bangs, J.K.	Lohengrin (1st, 4to, green/gilt)	Brentano's	(1891)	Gregory, F.M.	80-100	
Bangs, J.K.	Mantel-Piece Minstrels (1st, 12mo, 84p, pcb)	R.H. Russell	1896	Unknown	35-60	
Bangs, J.K.	Molly & The Unwiseman (1st, 8vo, 198p, 8pl)	Coates	1902	Levering, A.	35-50	*
Bangs, J.K.	Molly & Unwiseman Abroad (1st, 8vo, p-o, 262p, teg, 10cp)	Lippincott	1910	Wiederseim, G.	100-180	
Bangs, J.K.	Mr. Bonaparte of Corsica (1st, 12mo, 265p, gilt)	Harper	1895	McVickar, H.W.	30-45	
Bangs, J.K.	Mr. Munchausen (1st, sm8vo, 180p, tan cl, 15cp)	Noyes	1901	Newell, P.	35-50	
Bangs, J.K.	Olympian Nights (1st, 12mo, red/gilt, 224p, 16pl)	Harper	1902	Levering, A.	45-60	
Bangs, J.K.	Peeps at People (1st, 12mo, 184p, gilt, 36pl)	Harper	1899	Penfield, E.	30-50	
Bangs, J.K.	Pursuit of the House Boat (1st, 12mo, 204p, 24pl)	Harper	1897	Newell, P.	35-50	
Bangs, J.K.	R. Holmes & Co. (1st, 12mo, 230p, blue cl, 6pl)	Harper	1906	Adamson, S.	80-100	
Bangs, J.K.	Real Thing... (1st, sm8vo, 135p, brown/gilt, uncut, 4pl)	Harper	1909	Unknown	25-40	
Bangs, J.K.	Rebellious Heroine (1st, 12mo, yellow/gilt, 8pl)	Harper	1896	Smedley, W.T.	30-45	
Bangs, J.K.	The Bicyclers (1st, 16mo, 176p, blue/gilt, 4pl)	Harper	1896	Penfield, E.	30-50	
Bangs, J.K.	The Idiot (1st, 12mo, 115p, 8pl)	Harper	1895	Richards, F.T.	30-45	
Bangs, J.K.	Tiddledywink Tales (1st, 8vo, red/gilt, 236p, b/w)	R.H. Russell	1891	Johnson, C.H.	80-100	
Bangs, J.K.	Tiddledywink's Poetry Book (1st, sm8vo, [64]p, b/w)	R.H. Russell	1892	Johnson, C.H.	65-80	*
Banks, C.E.	Child of the Sun (1st, lg8vo, tan cl, teg, 166p, 16cp)	H. Stone	1900	Betts, L.	50-75	
Banks, Helen M.	Polly's Garden (1st, sm8vo, 96p, grey cl, 4cp)	MacMillan	1918	Pogany, W.	25-40	*
Banks, Helen W.	Life of Jesus Retold for Children (1st, 4to, 93p, p-o, 5cp)	Stokes	(1922)	Choate/Curtis	30-45	*
Bannerman, H.	All About Little Black Sambo (1st, 16mo, 48p, bds, p-o, color)	Cupples	(1917)	Bannerman, H.	100-145	
Bannerman, H.	Little Black Bobtail (1st AM, 16mo, bds, 115p, p-o, 27cp)	Stokes	(1909)	Bannerman, H.	160-220	
Bannerman, H.	Little Black Mingo (1st, 16mo, 143p, green cl, color)	L: J. Nisbet	(1901)	Bannerman, H.	250-400	
Bannerman, H.	Little Black Quasha (1st AM, 16mo, 110p, cp)	Stokes	(1908)	Bannerman, H.	200-260	
Bannerman, H.	Little Black Quibba (1st, 16mo, 143p, color)	L: J. Nisbet	(1902)	Bannerman, H.	300-450	
Bannerman, H.	Little Black Quibba (1st AM, 16mo, 143p, ibds, p-o, color)	Stokes	1903	Bannerman, H.	250-400	
Bannerman, H.	Little Black Sambo (1st, 16mo, green cl, 57p, 25 fp color)	L: Richards	1899	Bannerman, H.	7000	
Bannerman, H.	Little Black Sambo (1st AM, 16mo, 56p, color)	Stokes	[1900]	Bannerman, H.	500-700	*
Bannerman, H.	Little Black Sambo (1st {large fmt}, sq8vo, AEG, 109p)	L: Richards	1903	Bannerman, H.	1200	
Bannerman, H.	Little Black Sambo (1st, 24mo, ibds, 56p, color)	Reilly/Britton	1905	Bannerman, H.	250-400	

AUTHOR	TITLE	PUBLISHER	DATE	ARTIST	PRICE	LC
Bannerman, H.	Little Black Sambo (sq8vo, ibds, 28p, color)	Reilly/Britton	(1908)	Neill, J.R.	100-165	
Bannerman, H.	Little Black Sambo (sq8vo, ibds, [42]p, color)	Saalfield	[1920]	Williams, F.W.	100-165	*
Bannerman, H.	Little Black Sambo (1st, 8vo, 63p, col frn, color)	Whitman	(1925)	Shinn, C.X.	65-90	
Bannerman, H.	Little Black Sambo (1st, 16mo, ibds, [39]p, color)	MacMillan	1927	Dobias, F.	65-90	
Bannerman, H.	Little Black Sambo (4to, 40p, green bds, p-o, color)	Platt/Munk	(1927)	Eulalie	60-85	
Bannerman, H.	Little Black Sambo (8vo, 59p, ibds, color)	McKay	(1931)	Bannerman, H.	75-100	*
Bannerman, H.	Little Black Sambo (folio, wraps, 8cp)	Harter	(1931)	Peat, F.B.	120-165	
Bannerman, H.	Little Black Sambo (1st {this fmt}, 4to, 59p, blue cl, DJ)	L: Chatto	(1932)	Bannerman, H.	280-400	
Bannerman, H.	Little Black Sambo (1st, 8vo, [20]p, color)	Saalfield	(1932)	Peat, F.B.	100-130	
Bannerman, H.	Little Black Sambo (1st, 16mo, [42]p, ibds, color)	Whitman	(1934)	Jordan, N.	75-100	*
Bannerman, H.	Little Black Sambo (1st, folio, [16]p)	Whitman	(1935)	Ward, Keith	70-100	*
Bannerman, H.	Little Black Sambo (12mo, ibds, color)	McLoughlin	(1938)	Lupprian, H.	90-140	
Bannerman, H.	Little Black Sambo (12mo, 113p, p-o, bds)	L: Chatto	1941	Bannerman, H.	120-165	
Bannerman, H.	Little Black Sambo (lg4to, ipcb)	Saalfield	1942	Hays, Ethel	65-90	
Bannerman, H.	Little Black Sambo (sm4to, [22]p, color)	Grosset/Dunlap	(1942)	Moore, Robert	45-65	*
Bannerman, H.	Little Black Sambo (4to, wraps)	NY: S. Gabriel	1948	Russell, M.L.	60-95	
Bannerman, H.	Little Black Sambo (1st, sm8vo, [42]p, color)	Simon/Schuster	(1948)	Tenggren, G.	50-80	*
Bannerman, H.	Little Black Sambo & Baby Elephant (24mo, 62p, 30 col, pep)	Platt/Munk	1925	VerBeck, F.	50-75	
Bannerman, H.	Little Black Sambo Story Book (1st, sm4to, 63p, col frn)	Altemus	(1930)	VerBeck, F.	130-180	R*
Bannerman, H.	Little Black Sambo Story Book (4to, 63p, ipcb, color)	Platt/Munk	(1935)	VerBeck, F.	120-165	
Bannerman, H.	Little Degchie Head (1st, 16mo, 143p, green cl, p-o)	L: J. Nisbet	1903	Bannerman, H.	320-450	
Bannerman, H.	Little Kettle-Head (1st AM, 16mo, 144p, ibds, col frn, cp)	Stokes	1904	Bannerman, H.	280-400	
Bannerman, H.	New Story/Little Black Sambo (folio, wraps, [12]p, color)	Whitman	1932	Bennett, J.C.	80-120	
Bannerman, H.	Pat & the Spider (1st, 16mo, 143p, color)	L: J. Nisbet	(1904)	Bannerman, H.	275-400	
Bannerman, H.	Pat & the Spider (1st AM, 16mo, ipcb, 143p, color)	Stokes	(1905)	Bannerman, H.	220-300	
Bannerman, H.	Sambo & the Twins (1st, 16mo, 92p, red cl, color)	Stokes	1936	Bannerman, H.	120-165	
Bannerman, H.	Story of Little Black Sambo (ob12mo, 32p, ibds, color)	Winston	(1930)	Stephenson, E.	70-100	*
Bannerman, H.	Story of the Teasing Monkey (1st AM, 16mo, 142p, cp)	Stokes	(1907)	Bannerman, H.	250-350	*
Banning, Kendall	Pirates! (1st {this pub}, 12mo, [31]p, wraps, 13 fp woodcuts)	Chi: Woodworth	1918	Baumann, G.	100-165	
Bannon, L.	Gregorio & the White Llama (1st, sq lg8vo, 44p, pep, p-o, col)	Whitman	1944	Bannon, L.	30-45	
Bannon, L.	Horse on a Houseboat (1st, 8vo, cloth, 94p, pep, b/w, DJ)	Whitman	(1951)	Bannon, L.	20-30	
Bannon, L.	Manuela's Birthday in Old Mexico (1st, sq4to, 46p, p-o, color)	Whitman	1939	Bannon, L.	35-50	
Bannon, L.	Patty Paints a Picture (1st, sq4to, [48]p, p-o, color, pep, DJ)	Whitman	1946	Bannon, L.	30-45	
Bannon, L.	Watchdog (1st, 4to, [48]p, color)	Whitman	1948	Bannon, L.	25-40	*
Banta, N.M.	Brownies & the Goblins (1st, 8vo, 128p, color, pep)	Chi: Flanagan	1915	Benson, A.B.	65-80	*
Banta, N.M.	Four-and-Forty Fairies (1st, 12mo, grey cl, 128p, 1-color, pep)	Chi: Flanagan	1923	Dulin, D.	45-65	*
Barbour, R.H.	Finkler's Field (1st, 8vo, 226p, 4cp)	Appleton	1911	Unknown	35-50	
Barbour, R.H.	Golden Heart (1st, 8vo, 219p, teg, p-o, 5cp, pep)	Lippincott	1910	Underwood, C.F.	20-30	
Barbour, R.H.	Half-Back (1st, 8vo, orange cl, 267p, PPP)	Appleton	1899	Clinedinst, W.	100-145	*
Barbour, R.H.	Hearts Content (1st, 8vo, teg, 204p, p-o, cp)	Lippincott	1915	Holloway, E.	20-30	
Barbour, R.H.	Hitting the Line (1st, sm8vo, 322p, 5cp)	Appleton	1917	Rockwell, N.	75-100	*
Barbour, R.H.	House in the Hedge (1st, sm8vo, 251p, col frn, 3pl)	Moffat	1911	Kay, G.A.	30-50	*
Barbour, R.H.	Lady Laughter (1st, 8vo, 176p, teg, p-o, 4cp)	Lippincott	1913	Hoskins, G.	25-40	*
Barbour, R.H.	Lucky Seventh (1st, sm8vo, 310p, 4cp)	Appleton	1915	Rockwell, N.	70-100	*
Barbour, R.H.	On Your Mark (1st, 8vo, 267p, p-o, 4cp)	Appleton	1904	Relyea, C.M.	20-25	
Barbour, R.H.	Orchard Princess (1st, 8vo, p-o, 219p, 4cp)	Lippincott	1905	Flagg, J.M.	20-30	
Barbour, R.H.	Purple Pennant (1st, sm8vo, 322p, cp)	Appleton	1916	Rockwell, N.	100-150	*
Barbour, R.H.	Secret Play (1st, 8vo, 335p, 4cp)	Appleton	1915	Rockwell, N.	100-150	*
Barbour, R.H.	Story the Dogie Told to Me (1st, sm8vo, p-o, 182p)	Dodd	1914	Rae, J.	30-45	*
Barclay, F.	Following of the Star (1st, lg8vo, teg, cloth, cvr by...)	Putnam	1911	Armstrong, M.	35-50	*
Barclay, F.	Following of the Star (1st, lg8vo, teg, 8pl by...)	Putnam	1911	Townsend, F.H.	35-50	*
Barclay, F.	Mistress of Shenstone (1st, lg8vo, teg, uncut, gilt, 8cp)	Putnam	1910	Armstrong, M.	40-60	
Barclay, F.	The Rosary (1st, lg8vo, 389p, teg, blue/gilt)	Putnam	1910	Armstrong, M.	30-45	
Bare, A.E.	Maui's Summer (1st, 4to, yellow cl, [48]p, color, pep)	Houghton	1952	Bare, A.E.	45-70	*
Barfield, O.	Silver Trumpet (1st, 8vo, green cl, 142p, 8cp)	L: Faber/Gwyen	1925	James, G.	35-50	*
Baring, M.	Glass Mender (1st, 8vo, blue/gilt, 260p, teg, 12cp)	L: J. Nisbet	1910	Baring, M.	50-80	
Baring-Gould, S.	Amazing Adventures (1st, ob folio, 53p, color)	L: Skeffington	[1903]	Neilson, H.B.	140-200	*
Baring-Gould, S.	Book of Fairy Tales (1st, 8vo, teg, 244p, gilt, uncut, 5pl)	L: Methuen	1894	Gaskin, A.J.	95-125	
Baring-Gould, S.	Book of Ghosts (1st, 8vo, 383p)	L: Methuen	1904	Smith, D.M.	50-70	*
Baring-Gould, S.	Book of Nursery Songs & Rhymes (1st, 8vo, teg, 16pl)	L: Methuen	1895	Various	180-240	
Baring-Gould, S.	Book of Nursery Songs & Rhymes (2nd, 8vo, b/w)	L: Methuen	1906	Various	140-200	
Baring-Gould, S.	Book of Pictured Carols (1st, 8vo, uncut, 75p)	L: G. Allen	1893	Various	120-165	
Baring-Gould, S.	Broom-Squire (1st, 8vo, 384p, 12pl)	L: Methuen	1896	Dadd, Frank	50-65	*
Baring-Gould, S.	Crock of Gold (1st AM, 8vo, gilt, teg, 8pl)	L.C. Page	1899	Bedford, F.D.	40-60	
Baring-Gould, S.	Gladys of the Stewponey (1st, 8vo, 319p)	L: Methuen	1897	Townsend/Munns	45-60	*
Baring-Gould, S.	Old English Fairy Tales (1st AM, 8vo, teg, 400p, gilt, b/w)	Way/Williams	1895	Bedford, F.D.	100-150	
Baring-Gould, S.	Siegfried (1st, 8vo, red/gilt, 351p, col frn, 10 fp b/w)	L: Dean	1904	Robinson, C.	120-185	
Barker, C.M.	Book of Flower Fairies (1st, 8vo, green/gilt, 92p, color)	L: Blackie	(1927)	Barker, C.M.	200-250	
Barker, C.M.	Children's Book of Hymns (8vo, 84p, 12 ticp)	L: Blackie	[1925]	Barker, C.M.	70-100	
Barker, C.M.	Flower Fairies of Autumn (12mo, ibds, p-o, 24cp)	L: Blackie	[1927]	Barker, C.M.	70-90	
Barker, C.M.	Flower Fairies of Spring (12mo, bds, p-o, 24cp)	L: Blackie	[1925]	Barker, C.M.	70-90	
Barker, C.M.	Flower Fairies of Summer (1st, 12mo, 25p, 24cp)	L: Blackie	(1923)	Barker, C.M.	70-90	

AUTHOR	TITLE	PUBLISHER	DATE	ARTIST	PRICE	LC
Barker, C.M.	Flower Fairy Alphabet (1st, 12mo, 24p, p-o, 24cp)	L: Blackie	(1934)	Barker, C.M.	70-90	
Barker, C.M.	Flower Songs of the Seasons (4to, ibds, p-o, 12 ticp)	L: Blackie	[1915]	Barker, C.M.	70-90	
Barker, C.M.	Summer Songs with Music (4to, bds, p-o, 12 ticp)	L: Blackie	[1920]	Barker, C.M.	80-100	
Barker, D.O.	He Leadeth Me... (1st, AM, lg8vo, 256p, gilt, 16cp)	NY: M.S. Mill	[1938]	Barker, C.M.	30-45	*
Barker, Mrs. S.	Birthday Book/Children (1st, 16mo, 128p, green/gilt, p-o, 12cp)	L: Routledge	(1880)	Greenaway, K.	180-265	
Barker, Mrs. S.	Feathered & Four-Footed Friends (1st, sq8vo, 96p, 24cp)	L: Routledge	1993	Zwecker, J.B.	70-100	*
Barksdale, L.	First Thanksgiving (1st {std}, sm8vo, 57p, 6cp)	Knopf	1942	Lenski, L.	30-55	
Barlow, J.	Battle of the Frogs & Mice (1st, 8vo, green cl, unpag, 4pl)	L: Methuen	1894	Bedford, F.D.	70-100	
Barlow, J.	End of Elfintown (1st, 8vo, gilt, uncut, 77p, AEG, 8pl)	L: MacMillan	1894	Housman, L.	280-370	
Barlow, J.	Irish Ways (1st, 8vo, 262p, 16cp)	L: G. Allen	(1909)	Goble, W.	185-250	
Barnaby, H.T.	Long-Eared Bat (1st, 4to, ibds, unpag, 4cp)	Saalfield	(1929)	Peat, F.B.	70-90	*
Barnes, J.	Ships & Sailors (1st, ob folio, 124p, ibds, 12cp)	Stokes	1898	Zogbaum, R.F.	140-200	
Barnes, James	Drake & his Yeomen (1st, sm8vo, 415p, col frn, 7pl)	MacMillan	1899	Chapman, C.T.	25-40	*
Barnes, James	Loyal Traitor (1st, 12mo, 306p, 21pl)	Harper	1897	Keller, A.I.	25-40	*
Barnes, James	Son of Light Horse (1st, 12mo, 242p, 8pl)	Harper	1904	Mears, W.E.	20-35	*
Barnes, James	Yankee Ships & Yankee Sailors (1st, sm8vo, 281p, 13pl)	MacMillan	1897	Zogbaum, R.	25-40	*
Barnes, Madeline	Stirabout Stories (1st, 4to, ibds, 80p, 8cp)	L: Blackie	[1929]	Anderson, A.	65-85	
Barnes, Madeline	Tub-Time Tales (1st, 4to, 79p, ibds, p-o, 8cp)	L: Blackie	1920	Anderson, A.	180-220	
Barnes, Nancy	Carlota (1st, 8vo, 214p, uncut, b/w pl)	J. Messner	(1943)	Barber, J.	25-40	*
Barnes, Nancy	Wonderful Year (1st, 8vo, 185p, NH)	J. Messner	(1946)	Seredy, K.	45-60	*
Barnes, Ruth A.	I Hear America Singing (1st, 8vo, 346p, 1-color, pep)	Winston	(1937)	Lawson, R.	35-50	*
Barney, M.W.	Weather Signs & Rhymes (1st {std}, sq8vo, yellw cl, [103]p, pep)	Knopf	1931	Barney, M.W.	80-120	*
Barnum, Jay H.	Little Old Truck (1st, 8vo, 46p, blue cl, color, pep)	Wm. Morrow	1953	Barnum, J.H.	30-45	*
Barnum, Jay H.	Motorcycle Dog (1st, 8vo, blue cl, 48p, 2-color, pep)	Wm. Morrow	1958	Barnum, J.H.	30-45	*
Barnum, Jay H.	New Fire Engine (1st, 8vo, red cl, 47p, 2-color, pep)	Wm. Morrow	1952	Barnum, J.H.	30-45	*
Barr, A.	Knight of the Nets (1st, 8vo, 314p, cvr by...)	Dodd	1896	'AM'	20-25	*
Barr, A.	Song of a Single Note (1st, 8vo, 330p, 4pl)	Dodd	1902	Betts, A.W.	20-25	
Barr, A.	Souls of Passage (1st, sm8vo, 327p, 6pl)	Dodd	1901	McConnell, E.	20-25	*
Barr, A.	Thyra Varrick (1st, sm8vo, green cl, 343p, 12pl)	J.F. Taylor	1903	Ziegler, L.W.	20-30	
Barr, Rbt.	Strong Arm (1st, 8vo, 336p, cvr by...)	Stokes	1899	Edwards, G.W.	20-30	*
Barrie, J.M.	Admirable Crichton (1st, 4to, 235p, gilt, 21 ticp)	L: Hodder	[1914]	Thomson, H.	125-165	
Barrie, J.M.	Little White Bird (1st AM, 8vo, 286p, teg, uncut, 2pl by...)	Scribner	1912	Rackham, A.	140-185	
Barrie, J.M.	Little White Bird (8vo, teg, 242p, 2pl by...)	L: Hodder	1912	Rackham, A.	220-300	
Barrie, J.M.	My Lady Nicotine (1st {this pub}, 8vo, teg, 276p)	J. Knight	1896	Prendergast, M	85-130	
Barrie, J.M.	Peter & Wendy (1st AM, lg8vo, 267p, gilt, 13pl, SC)	Scribner	1911	Bedford, F.D.	150-200	
Barrie, J.M.	Peter & Wendy (1st, 8vo, 267p, green/gilt, 13pl)	L: Hodder	(1911)	Bedford, F.D.	120-140	
Barrie, J.M.	Peter Pan (1st, sq8vo, blue cl, 73p, 16 illus, pep)	S. Burdett	(1916)	Woodward, A.B.	60-80	
Barrie, J.M.	Peter Pan (1st, 8vo, 27p, color)	Grosset/Dunlap	1942	Miss Elliott	25-40	*
Barrie, J.M.	Peter Pan (1st, 8vo, 242p, pink cl, fp b/w)	Scribner	1950	Unwin, N.S.	30-45	*
Barrie, J.M.	Peter Pan (1st UK, 8vo, red/gilt, 23 b/w illus, DJ)	L: Hodder	1951	Unwin, N.S.	45-60	
Barrie, J.M.	Peter Pan & Wendy (1st, lg8vo, 185p, blue/gilt, 12 ticp)	L: Hodder	(1921)	Attwell, M.L.	160-240	
Barrie, J.M.	Peter Pan & Wendy (1st AM, 4to, gilt, p-o, 185p, 12cp, SC)	Scribner	1921	Attwell, M.L.	140-200	
Barrie, J.M.	Peter Pan & Wendy (1st, 4to, 272p, blue/gilt, color)	L: Hodder	[1925]	Hudson, G.	130-185	
Barrie, J.M.	Peter Pan & Wendy (1st AM, sm4to, 216p, gilt, 12cp, pep)	Scribner	1940	Blampied, E.	75-120	
Barrie, J.M.	Peter Pan Picture Book (1st, lg8vo, 62p, p-o, 28cp, pep)	L: G. Bell	1907	Woodward, A.B.	170-240	
Barrie, J.M.	Peter Pan Picture Book (1st, lg4to, ibds, [89]p, 24cp, pep)	Whitman	(1931)	Best, R.	70-100	
Barrie, J.M.	Peter Pan... (1st AM, lg8vo, 125p, green/gilt, 50 ticp)	Scribner	1906	Rackham, A.	350-500	
Barrie, J.M.	Peter Pan... (1st, sm4to, 125p, red/gilt, 50 ticp)	L: Hodder	1906	Rackham, A.	450-600	
Barrie, J.M.	Quality Street (1st, 4to, 198p, blue/gilt, 22 ticp, pep)	L: Hodder	[1913]	Thomson, H.	130-200	
Barrie, J.M.	Sentimental Tommy (1st AM, 8vo, 478p, brown/gilt, cvr by...)	Scribner	1896	Armstrong, M.	25-45	
Barringer, M.	Four & Lena (1st {std}, 8vo, 216p, black cl, 6cp, pep)	Doubleday/Dor.	1938	Petershams	35-50	
Barringer, M.	Martin the Goose Boy (1st {std}, 8vo, 188p, black cl, 8cp, pep)	Doubleday/Dor.	1932	Petershams	45-60	
Barrows, M.	Ezra the Elephant (1st, sq8vo, ibds, [44]p, color, pep)	Grosset/Dunlap	1934	Smock, N.S.	25-40	*
Barrows, M.	Muggins Mouse (1st, folio, ibds, 60p, color)	Reilly/Lee	1932	Ward, Keith	50-90	*
Barrows, M.	Who's Who in the Zoo (1st, folio, 60p, p-o, pep, 25 fp color)	Reilly/Lee	(1932)	Winter, M.	100-140	*
Barske, C.	King Cotton (1st, folio, ipcb, 23p, color)	A.& W. Guild	1938	Wright, G.	65-90	
Barton, O.R.	Cloud Boat Stories (1st, 8vo, 138p, blue cl, p-o, 4cp)	Houghton	1917	Winter, M.	40-70	
Barton, W.E.	Hero in Homespun (1st, 8vo, 393p, 10pl)	Chi: Lamson	1897	Beard, D.	65-80	*
Barton, W.E.	Prairie Schooner (1st, 8vo, 382p, 5pl)	Wilde	(1900)	Burgess, H.	20-30	*
Bartruse, G.	Children in Japan (1st, lg8vo, [32]p, bds, p-o, 16cp)	McBride	1915	Pogany, W.	160-200	
Bartug, C.M.	Mother Goose Etiquette Rhymes (1st, ob8vo, 32p, blue cl, pep)	Whitman	1941	Peters, M.	45-65	*
Baruch, D.W.	Big Fellow at Work (1st {std}, 12mo, 103p, b/w, pep)	Harper	1930	Hader, B.& E.	65-80	
Baruch, D.W.	Blimps & Such (1st, 4to, 80p, ibds, col frn, b/w, DJ)	Harper	1932	Wolcott, E.T.	50-85	
Baruch, D.W.	Bobby Goes Riding (1st, 8vo, [35]p, red cl, color, pep)	Lothrop/Lee	1934	Brann, E.	25-40	*
Baruch, D.W.	Funny Little Boy (1st, sq12mo, [36]p, color, pep)	Lothrop/Lee	1936	Lietta	25-40	*
Baruch, D.W.	I Like Animals (1st {std}, 16mo, ipcb, 48p, b/w, dep)	Harper	1933	Waterall, C.P.	20-35	*
Baruch, D.W.	I Like Automobiles (1st, 8vo, [55]p, color, pep)	NY: J. Day	(1931)	Fujikawa, G.	30-45	*
Barzini, Luigi	Little Match Man (1st, lg8vo, 164p, p-o, 5cp, pep)	Penn	1917	Longstreet, H.	35-50	*
Bascom, L.R.	Bugaboo Men (1st, sq4to, green cl, [72]p, pep, color)	NY: Sully	(1914)	Bascom, L.R.	90-120	*
Basile, G.	Stories from the Pentamerone (1st, 4to, red/gilt, 304p, 32cp)	L: MacMillan	1911	Goble, W.	180-260	
Bates, Clara D.	Doll Rosy's Days (1st, ob12mo, ipcb, [31]p, 12cp)	Lothrop	(1884)	Hassam, F.C.	150-200	
Bates, Clara D.	On the Tree Top (1st, 4to, [90]p, ibds, 4cp)	D. Lothrop	(1891)	Various	80-120	

AUTHOR	TITLE	PUBLISHER	DATE	ARTIST	PRICE	LC
Bates, Clara D.	On the Way to Wonderland (1st, 4to, [38]p, ibds, color, pep)	Lothrop	(1885)	(Chromos)	100-150	
Bates, H.E.	Down the River (1st AM, 4to, 151p, wood engravings, DJ)	Holt	1937	Parker, A.M.	35-50	
Bates, H.E.	My Uncle Silas (1st, 4to, 190p, b/w)	L: J. Cape	(1939)	Ardizzone, E.	150-200	*
Bates, H.E.	Through the Woods (1st AM, 4to, 142p, engravings)	MacMillan	1936	Parker, A.M.	30-50	
Bates, Helen D.	Betsy Ross (1st, 8vo, 127p, b/w, DJ)	Whittlesey	1936	Lawson, R.	30-45	
Bates, Kath. L.	Once Upon a Time (1st, lg4to, p-o, blue cl, 128p, color, pep)	Rand/McNally	(1921)	Price, M.E.	50-70	
Bateson, C.	Man in the Camelot Cloak (1st, 8vo, 320p, teg, 4pl)	Saalfield	1903	Dunton, W.H.	30-45	*
Baum, Frank J.	Laughing Dragon of Oz (1st [Big-Little bk.], sq32mo, 425p, ibds)	Whitman	(1934)	Youngren, M.	200-300	*
Baum, L.F.	American Fairy Tales (1st, 8vo, [205]p, teg, cloth, b/w)	Geo. Hill	1901	Various	700-1000	*
Baum, L.F.	Army Alphabet (1st, lg4to, ibds, 29cp)	Geo. Hill	1900	Kennedy, H.	700-1000	
Baum, L.F.	Baum's American Fairy Tales (1st, 4to, [223]p, p-o, 16cp)	Bobbs-Merrill	(1908)	Kerr, G.F.	600-850	
Baum, L.F.	Daring Twins (1st [1], sm8vo, blue cl, 317p, 4pl)	Reilly/Britton	(1911)	Batchelder, P.M.	200-300	
Baum, L.F.	Daring Twins (1st [1], sm8vo, 317p, blue cl, cvr by...)	Reilly/Britton	(1911)	Hazenplug, F.	200-300	
Baum, L.F.	Dorothy & Wizard of Oz (1st [1], 8vo, p-o, 256p, pep, 16cp)	Reilly/Britton	(1908)	Neill, J.R.	600-800	
Baum, L.F.	Dot & Tot in Merryland (1st [1], 8vo, [226]p, gilt, color, pep)	Geo. Hill	1901	Denslow, W.W.	600-800	R
Baum, L.F.	Dot & Tot in Merryland (2nd, 8vo, [226]p, color)	Bobbs-Merrill	(1903)	Denslow, W.W.	220-400	
Baum, L.F.	Emerald City of Oz (1st [1], 8vo, 296p, p-o, 16 ticp, pep)	Reilly/Britton	(1910)	Neill, J.R.	650-800	R
Baum, L.F.	Enchanted Island of Yew (1st [1], 8vo, 242p, tan cl, 8cp, pep)	Bobbs-Merrill	(1903)	Cory, F.	300-400	
Baum, L.F.	Father Goose's Yearbook (1st, 12mo, [128]p, p-o, buckram)	Reilly/Britton	(1907)	Enright, W.J.	250-350	
Baum, L.F.	Father Goose: His Book (1st [1], 4to, ibds, [106]p)	Geo. Hill	(1899)	Denslow, W.W.	4000	R
Baum, L.F.	Father Goose: His Book (4to, unpag, ibds, color)	Donohue	[1913]	Denslow, W.W.	150-220	
Baum, L.F.	Gingerbread Man (1st, sm4to, ibds, 62p, col frn)	Reilly/Britton	(1917)	Neill, J.R.	200-275	
Baum, L.F.	Glinda of Oz (1st [1], lg8vo, grey cl, p-o, 279p, 12cp, pep)	Reilly/Lee	(1920)	Neill, J.R.	350-500	R
Baum, L.F.	John Dough & the Cherub (1st [1], 8vo, tan cl, 315p, col, pep)	Reilly/Britton	(1906)	Neill, J.R.	600-800	
Baum, L.F.	Last Egyptian (1st, 12mo, blue cl, p-o, 287p, 8cp)	Stern	1908	Wightman, F.P.	200-300	
Baum, L.F.	Life & Advens. of Santa Claus (1st [1], sq8vo, 206p, 20cp, pep)	Bowen-Merrill	1902	Clark, M.C.	600-800	
Baum, L.F.	Little Wizard Stories/Oz (1st [1], 8vo, p-o, 152p, 42cp)	Reilly/Britton	(1914)	Neill, J.R.	350-450	
Baum, L.F.	Lost Princess of Oz (1st [1], 8vo, 312p, p-o, 12cp, pep)	Reilly/Britton	(1917)	Neill, J.R.	700-800	
Baum, L.F.	Lucky Bucky in Oz (1st, 8vo, p-o, blue cl, pep, 289p)	Reilly/Lee	(1942)	Neill, J.R.	165-220	
Baum, L.F.	Magic Cloak... (1st [1], 8vo, 58p, ibds)	Reilly/Britton	(1916)	Neill, J.R.	450-600	
Baum, L.F.	Magic of Oz (1st [1], lg8vo, [266]p, p-o, green cl, 12cp)	Reilly/Lee	(1919)	Neill, J.R.	400-600	
Baum, L.F.	Magical Monarch of Mo (1st [1], lg8vo, [237]p, p-o, 12cp)	Bobbs-Merrill	(1903)	VerBeck, F.	500-750	
Baum, L.F.	Marvelous Land of Oz (1st [1], lg8vo, 287p, green cl, 16cp, pep)	Reilly/Britton	1904	Neill, J.R.	700-850	
Baum, L.F.	Master Key (1st [1], 8vo, 245p, olive/gilt, p-o, 12cp)	Bowen-Merrill	(1901)	Cory, F.	280-350	
Baum, L.F.	Mother Goose in Prose (1st [1], 4to, gilt, 265p, cloth, 12pl)	Way/Williams	(1897)	Parrish, M.	7000	R
Baum, L.F.	Mother Goose in Prose (1st UK, lg4to, tan cl, 265p)	L: Duckworth	(1898)	Parrish, M.	5000	
Baum, L.F.	Mother Goose in Prose (3rd, sq8vo, 265p, 12pl)	Bobbs-Merrill	(1905)	Parrish, M.	500-700	
Baum, L.F.	Navy Alphabet (1st, lg4to, ibds, unpag, color)	Geo. Hill	1900	Kennedy, H.	700-1000	
Baum, L.F.	New Wizard of Oz (2nd, lg8vo, green cl, [261]p, 16cp, pep)	Bobbs-Merrill	(1903)	Denslow, W.W.	1500	
Baum, L.F.	New Wonderland (1st [1], 4to, [189]p, cloth, 16cp, pep)	R.H. Russell	1900	VerBeck, F.	3000	
Baum, L.F.	Ozma of Oz (1st [1], 8vo, 270p, tan cl, color, pep)	Reilly/Britton	(1907)	Neill, J.R.	500-750	
Baum, L.F.	Patchwork Girl of Oz (1st [1], 8vo, 341p, green cl, color, pep)	Reilly/Britton	(1913)	Neill, J.R.	500-750	
Baum, L.F.	Phoebe Daring... (1st, 8vo, 298p, grey cl, 4pl)	Reilly/Britton	(1912)	Nuyttens, J.P.	180-250	
Baum, L.F.	Queen Zixi of Ix (1st [1], 8vo, 303p, green cl, 16cp)	Century	1905	Richardson, F.	400-500	
Baum, L.F.	Rinkitink in Oz (1st [1], 8vo, blue cl, 314p, p-o, 12cp, pep)	Reilly/Britton	(1916)	Neill, J.R.	550-700	
Baum, L.F.	Road to Oz (1st [1], 8vo, green cl, b/w, p-o, 261p, pep)	Reilly/Britton	(1909)	Neill, J.R.	400-600	
Baum, L.F.	Royal Book of Oz (1st [1], 8vo, 312p, grey cl, 12cp, pep)	Reilly/Lee	(1921)	Neill, J.R.	220-300	
Baum, L.F.	Scarecrow of Oz (1st [1], lg8vo, green cl, p-o, 288p, 12cp, pep)	Reilly/Britton	(1915)	Neill, J.R.	400-600	
Baum, L.F.	Sea Fairies (1st [1], 8vo, p-o, 240p, green cl, 12pl, pep)	Reilly/Britton	(1911)	Neill, J.R.	400-550	
Baum, L.F.	Sky Island (1st, lg8vo, blue cl, p-o, [288]p, 12cp, pep)	Reilly/Britton	(1912)	Neill, J.R.	400-600	
Baum, L.F.	Songs of Father Goose (1st, 4to, ibds, 84p, b/w)	Geo. Hill	1900	Denslow, W.W.	350-500	
Baum, L.F.	Songs of Father Goose (2nd, 4to, 83p, ibds)	Bobbs-Merrill	(1909)	Denslow, W.W.	180-240	
Baum, L.F.	Tik-Tok of Oz (1st [1], lg8vo, 272p, blue cl, p-o, pep, 12cp)	Reilly/Britton	(1914)	Neill, J.R.	650-800	
Baum, L.F.	Tin Woodman of Oz (1st [1], 8vo, red cl, 288p, 12cp, pep)	Reilly/Britton	(1918)	Neill, J.R.	400-600	
Baum, L.F.	Wizard of Oz (1st, ob8vo, [56]p, ibds, color, pep)	Grosset/Dunlap	1939	Lebeck, O.	70-125	*
Baum, L.F.	Woggle-Bug Book (1st, folio, [48]p, wraps, color)	Reilly/Britton	1905	Morgan, Ike	2500	
Baum, L.F.	Wonderful Wizard of Oz (1st [1], 8vo, [261]p, 24cp, pep, PPP)	Geo. Hill	1900	Denslow, W.W.	7000	R
Baum, L.F. (intro)	Animal ABC (1st, 24mo, ibds, 124p, color)	Reilly/Britton	1905	Unknown	90-130	
Baxter, Betty	Supposin' (1st, 12mo, 40p, color, pep)	Volland	(1931)	Dudley, C.	45-60	*
Baylor, F.C.	Juan & Juanita (1st, 8vo, green/gilt, 276p, b/w, pep, PPP)	Ticknor	1888	Sandham, H.	180-250	*
Baylor, F.C.	Juan & Juanita (1st, 8vo, 300p, blue cl, p-o, 4cp, pep)	Houghton	1926	Tenggren, G.	60-85	
Bayne, C. (ed.)	My Book/Best Fairy Tales (1st, 4to, blue/gilt, 368p, 16cp)	L: Cassell	(1915)	Rountree, H.	170-220	
Bayne, C. (ed.)	My Book/Best Fairy Tales (1st AM, sm4to, blue/gilt, 368p, 16cp)	Funk/Wagnalls	[1915]	Rountree, H.	85-130	
Beach, R.	Iron Trail (1st, sm8vo, red/gilt, 390p, 8pl)	Harper	1913	Bracker, M.L.	20-30	
Beach, R.	Ne'er-Do-Well (1st, 12mo, 402p, p-o, 8pl)	Harper	1911	Christy, H.C.	25-40	
Beach, R.	Silver Horde (1st, 8vo, red cl, p-o, 389p, 8pl)	Harper	1909	Dunn, H.T.	25-40	
Beach, R.	The Net (1st, 8vo, p-o, 4pl)	Harper	1912	Tittle, W.	20-35	
Beacom, John	How the Buffalo Lost his Crown (1st, ob folio, 7pl)	Forest/Stream	1894	Russell, C.M.	1200	
Bealer, A.W.	Picture-Skin Story (1st, sq8vo, [27]p, pink cl, color, cep)	Holiday House	1957	Bealer, A.W.	35-50	*
Beaman, E.H.	Ozmar the Mystic (1st, 8vo, 378p, blue/gilt, 12pl)	L: Bliss Sands	1896	Smith, Thomas	45-65	*
Beard, D.	Animal Book & Campfire Stories (1st, 8vo, 538p, col frn)	Moffat	1907	Beard, D.	35-50	
Beard, D.	Moonblight (1st, sm8vo, 238p, green/gilt, uncut, b/w)	A. Brandt	1904	Beard, D.	50-80	*

AUTHOR: 12

AUTHOR	TITLE	PUBLISHER	DATE	ARTIST	PRICE	LC
Beard, P.	Marjorie's Little Doll School (1st, 8vo, 208p)	Doran	(1917)	(Photos)	70-100	*
Beard, P.	Pantalette Doll (1st, lg8vo, p-o, 160p, color, pep)	Whitman	(1931)	Hubbard, E.M.	35-60	*
Beard, P.	Pillow-Time Tales (1st, 4to, p-o, 96p, color)	Rand/McNally	(1927)	Eger, R.C.	35-50	*
Beard, P.	Twilight Tales (1st, 8vo, p-o, 96p, 7cp)	Rand/McNally	(1929)	Eger, R.C.	45-60	
Beard, P.	What Happened After Stories (1st, sq4to, 125p, p-o, color, pep)	Whitman	(1929)	Higgins, V.M.	35-50	
Beardsley, Alice	Turn-Around Book (1st, lg8vo, p-o, unpag)	Bobbs-Merrill	(1914)	Beardsley, Alice	80-100	*
Beardsley, Aubrey	Book of 50 Drawings (1st, 4to)	L: Smithers	1897	Beardsley, A.	240-350	
Beardsley, Aubrey	Second Book of 50 Drawings (1st, 4to, red/gilt)	L: Smithers	1899	Beardsley, A.	250-450	
Beardsley, Aubrey	Under The Hill (1st, 4to, teg, blue/gilt, uncut, 15pl)	L: J. Lane	1904	Beardsley, A.	300-500	
Beauclerk, H.	Green Lacquer Pavillion (1st AM, 8vo, 319p, gilt, b/w)	Doran	(1926)	Dulac, E.	60-80	
Beauclerk, H.	Green Lacquer Pavillion (1st, 12mo, tan/gilt, 319p, 10pl)	L: Collins	1926	Dulac, E.	85-120	
Beauclerk, H.	Love of the Foolish Angel (1st, 8vo, blue/gilt, 251p, b/w)	L: Collins	1929	Dulac, E.	85-100	
Beaumont, C.W.	Sea Magic... (1st, 8vo, 120p, pcb, gilt, color)	L: Bodley Head	(1928)	Payne, W.	45-60	*
Beckenbaugh, G.	Cotton Tails (1st, ob4to, [99]p, ipcb, fp b/w)	R.H. Russell	1900	Beckenbaugh, G.	140-200	*
Becker, May L.	Golden Tales of Far West (1st, 8vo, 304p, decor by...)	Dodd	1935	Lenski, L.	35-50	*
Becker, May L.	Golden Tales of Prairie States (1st, sm8vo, 355p, decor by...)	Dodd	1932	Lenski, L.	35-50	*
Becker, May L.	Louisa Alcott's People (1st, 4to, 211p, gilt, p-o, 4cp, pep, SC)	Scribner	1936	Fogarty, T.	70-120	
Bedford, F.D.	Night of Wonders (1st, ob8vo, ibds, 124p, teg, 24cp, pep)	L: Richards	[1906]	Bedford, F.D.	200-270	
Beeching (ed.)	Book/Christmas Verse (1st, sm8vo, 174p, teg, gilt, designs by..)	L: Methuen	1895	Crane, W.	90-135	
Beecroft, John	Rocco Came In (1st, 4to, red cl, [30]p, fp color)	Dodd	1959	Wiese, K.	20-30	*
Beerbohm, M.	50 Caracitures (1st, sm4to, green/gilt, 50 tipl)	L: Heinemann	1913	Beerbohm, M.	120-175	
Beerbohm, M.	A Survey (1st, 4to, gilt, col frn, 51 tipl)	L: Heinemann	1921	Beerbohm, M.	100-165	
Beerbohm, M.	Caricatures of 25 Gentlemen (1st, 4to)	L: Smithers	1896	Beerbohm, M.	120-180	
Beerbohm, M.	Dreadful Dragon of Hay Hill (1st, lg8vo, 113p, ibds, col frn)	L: Heinemann	1928	Beerbohm, M.	50-70	
Beerbohm, M.	Happy Hypocrite (1st, 4to, 70p, white/gilt, uncut, 24cp, dep)	L: J. Lane	(1915)	Sheringham, G.	90-130	
Beerbohm, M.	More (1st, 8vo, green cloth)	L: J. Lane	1899	Beerbohm, M.	145-170	
Beerbohm, M.	Observations (1st, 4to, 52pl, DJ)	L: Heinemann	1925	Beerbohm, M.	70-100	
Beerbohm, M.	Poet's Corner (1st, folio, ibds, 20cp)	L: Heinemann	1904	Beerbohm, M.	150-200	
Beerbohm, M.	Rossetti & his Circle (1st, 4to, blue/gilt, 23 ticp)	L: Heinemann	1922	Beerbohm, M.	120-180	
Beerbohm, M.	Second Childhood of John Bull (1st, folio, bds, 15cp)	L: Swift	(1911)	Beerbohm, M.	150-200	*
Beerbohm, M.	Things New & Old (1st, 4to, col frn, 49pl)	L: Heinemann	1923	Beerbohm, M.	90-130	
Beerbohm, M.	Works of... (1st, 8vo, brown/gilt, 165p, uncut)	Scribner	1896	Armstrong, M.	150-220	
Beerbohm, M.	Zuleika Dobson (1st, 8vo, brown cl, 350p, gilt)	L: Heinemann	1911	Beerbohm, M.	150-200	
Begbie, H.	Great Men (sm4to, 51p, ibds, 24cp)	L: Richards	1901	Gould, F.C.	75-100	
Begbie, H.	Political Struwwelpeter (4to, ipcb, [24]p, color)	L: Richards	1899	Gould, F.C.	150-185	
Begbie, H.	Struwwelpeter Alphabet (1st, 4to, ipcb, [26]p, color)	L: Richards	1900	Gould, F.C.	160-180	
Behn, Harry	All Kinds of Time (1st {std}, 12mo, ibds, [61]p, color, cep)	Harcourt	(1950)	Behn, H.	65-100	R*
Behn, Harry	Little Hill (1st {std}, 12mo, 58p, ipcb, 1-color, cep)	Harcourt	(1949)	Behn, H.	65-100	R*
Behn, Harry	Painted Cave (1st {std}, 8vo, ipcb, 63p, 1-color, cep)	Harcourt	(1957)	Behn, H.	65-100	R*
Behn, Harry	Windy Morning (1st {std}, 12mo, ipcb, 61p, 1-color, cep)	Harcourt	(1953)	Behn, H.	65-100	R*
Behn, Harry	Wizard in the Well (1st {std}, 12mo, ipcb, 62p, 1-color, cep)	Harcourt	(1956)	Behn, H.	65-100	R*
Beim, Lorraine	Gregori's Lamb (1st, 8vo, 92p, ipcb, color, pep)	Saalfield	1948	Busoni, R.	30-45	
Beim, Lorraine	Just Plain Maggie (1st {std}, 8vo, 185p, green cl, fp b/w)	Harcourt	(1950)	Cooney, B.	30-50	*
Beim, Lorraine	Two is a Team (1st, 8vo, [61]p, red cl, fp color, pep)	Harcourt	(1945)	Crichlow, E.	35-60	*
Beistle, A.S.	I Spy (1st, 8vo, spiral-bound ibds, [17]p, color)	McKay	(1944)	Beistle, M.A.	35-50	*
Beistle, A.S.	Just Peggy (1st, sm8vo, 63p, b/w)	McKay	(1939)	Beistle, M.A.	25-40	
Beistle, A.S.	Mr. Heinie (1st {std}, ob8vo, [32]p, ipcb, color, pep)	McKay	(1938)	Beistle, M.A.	35-50	*
Beistle, A.S.	Mr. Heinie & Scroot (1st {std}, ob8vo, [36]p, ibds, color, pep)	McKay	(1939)	Beistle, M.A.	45-60	*
Beistle, A.S.	Open Daily (1st {std}, lg8vo, ibds, 90p, color)	McKay	(1942)	Beistle, M.A.	25-40	*
Belasco, D.	Return of Peter Grimm (1st, 8vo, 344p, p-o, 3cp)	Dodd	1912	Rae, J.	25-40	
Bell, J.J.	Jack of All Trades (1st, 4to, brown cl, 64p, 32cp)	L: J. Lane	1900	Robinson Bros.	245-300	
Bell, J.J.	New Noah's Ark (1st, 4to, brown cl, 64p, color)	L: J. Lane	1899	Robinson, C.	200-240	
Bell, L.	Runaway Equator (1st, 8vo, 118p, p-o, 16pl)	Stokes	(1911)	Newell, P.	130-200	
Bell, L.P.	Kitchen Fun (1st, sm4to, ibds, 27p, cvr by...)	Harter	1932	Smith, J.W.	45-65	
Bell, Thelma H.	Black Face (1st {std}, lg8vo, [48]p, color, pep)	Doubleday/Dor.	1931	Bell, C.	65-90	*
Bellamy, W.	Century of Charades (1st, 16mo, 100p)	Houghton	1901	Rogers, B.	25-40	
Bellew, F.P.	Chip's Dogs (1st, ob4to, ibds, [64]p, b/w)	R.H. Russell	1895	Bellew, F.P.	100-170	*
Belloc, H.	Bad Child's Book of Beasts (1st, sm4to, 47p, grey bds, b/w)	L: Duckworth	(1896)	Blackwood, B.T.	200-300	
Belloc, H.	But Softly - We are Observed (1st, 8vo, 312p, DJ)	L: Arrowsmith	(1928)	Chesterton, G.K.	70-115	
Belloc, H.	Cautionary Tales for Children (1st, sq8vo, ibds, 79p, b/w)	L: E. Nash	(1907)	Blackwood, B.T.	120-165	
Belloc, H.	Haunted House (1st, 8vo, 269p, 37 illus, DJ)	L: Arrowsmith	(1927)	Chesterton, G.K.	60-95	
Belloc, H.	Missing Masterpiece (1st, 8vo, 319p, DJ)	L: Arrowsmith	(1929)	Chesterton, G.K.	70-115	
Belloc, H.	Modern Traveller (1st, 8vo, ibds, 80p, b/w)	L: E. Arnold	1898	Blackwood, B.T.	120-160	
Belloc, H.	Moral Alphabet (1st, 4to, 63p, ibds, b/w)	L: E. Arnold	1899	Blackwood, B.T.	100-150	
Belloc, H.	More Beasts for Worse Children (1st, ob4to, ibds, 48p)	L: Duckworth	1897	Blackwood, B.T.	140-200	
Belloc, H.	New Cautionary Tales (1st AM, 8vo, ibds, 79p, b/w)	Harper	1931	Bentley, N.	30-45	*
Belloc, H.	Postmaster-General (1st, 8vo, 286p, 30 illus, DJ)	L: Arrowsmith	(1932)	Chesterton, G.K.	70-100	
Belloc, H.	Shadowed! (1st AM {std}, 8vo, 312p, 37 illus, DJ)	Harper	1929	Chesterton, G.K.	80-120	
Belloc, H.	Songs from Bad Child's Bk./Beasts (1st, 4to, ibds, b/w)	L: Duckworth	1932	Blackwood, B.T.	50-85	
Belpre, Pura	Perez & Martina (1st, ob4to, 79p, 16cp, pep)	Warne	(1932)	Sanchez, C.M.	70-100	*
Bemelmans, L.	Best of Times (1st, lg4to, 188p, 50 color, DJ)	Simon/Schuster	1948	Bemelmans, L.	120-165	
Bemelmans, L.	Blue Danube (1st, 8vo, blue cl, 153p, 14cp, pep, DJ)	Viking	1945	Bemelmans, L.	65-90	

AUTHOR	TITLE	PUBLISHER	DATE	ARTIST	PRICE	LC
Bemelmans, L.	Castle Number Nine (1st, 4to, [48]p, grn/gilt, color, pep, DJ)	Viking	1937	Bemelmans, L.	120-165	
Bemelmans, L.	Donkey Inside (1st, 8vo, 224p, 4 dp color, DJ)	Viking	1941	Bemelmans, L.	65-100	
Bemelmans, L.	Fifi (1st, lg4to, [46]p, color)	Simon/Schuster	1940	Bemelmans, L.	90-140	R*
Bemelmans, L.	Golden Basket (1st, 4to, 96p, pink cl, color, dep, NH)	Viking	1936	Bemelmans, L.	120-160	R
Bemelmans, L.	Hansi (1st {1st book}, 4to, ibds, [64]p, color, pep, DJ)	Viking	1934	Bemelmans, L.	180-240	
Bemelmans, L.	Happy Place (1st {std}, 8vo, 59p, 3 dp color, DJ)	Little/Brown	(1952)	Bemelmans, L.	60-80	
Bemelmans, L.	Life Class (1st, 8vo, 260p, red cl, p-o, DJ)	Viking	1938	Bemelmans, L.	80-120	
Bemelmans, L.	Madeline (1st, lg4to, [48]p, ibds, color, pep, CH)	Simon/Schuster	1939	Bemelmans, L.	125-160	
Bemelmans, L.	Madeline & the Bad Hat (1st, red cl, lg4to, 54p, pep, col)	Viking	(1956)	Bemelmans, L.	160-200	
Bemelmans, L.	Madeline & the Gypsies (1st, 4to, 56p, ibds, pep, color)	Viking	(1958)	Bemelmans, L.	130-165	R
Bemelmans, L.	Madeline's Rescue (1st, lg4to, 56p, red cl, color, pep, CM)	Viking	1953	Bemelmans, L.	120-165	R
Bemelmans, L.	Parsley (1st, lg ob4to, 46p, green cl, color)	Harper	(1955)	Bemelmans, L.	70-110	R
Bemelmans, L.	Quito Express (1st, ob8vo, 47p, ibds, 1-color)	Viking	1938	Bemelmans, L.	90-140	
Bemelmans, L.	Rosebud (1st, 4to, ibds, 32p, color, pep, DJ)	Random	1942	Bemelmans, L.	120-165	
Bemelmans, L.	Small Bear (1st, 8vo, 186p, col frn, b/w, pep)	Viking	1939	Bemelmans, L.	70-100	*
Bemelmans, L.	Sunshine... (1st, lg4to, [44]p, ibds, color, pep, DJ)	Simon/Schuster	(1950)	Bemelmans, L.	140-180	
Bemelmans, L.	Tale of Two Glimps (1st, ob4to, [48]p, ibds, color)	NY: CBS	(1947)	Bemelmans, L.	120-180	
Bemelmans, L.	The Highworld (1st, lg8vo, red cl, 113p, pep, fp color)	Harper	(1954)	Bemelmans, L.	50-75	*
Bemelmans, L.	World of Bemelmans (1st, 8vo, 503p)	Viking	1955	Bemelmans, L.	40-70	*
Benet, Laura	Caleb's Luck (1st, lg8vo, [28]p, ibds, pep, color)	Grosset/Dunlap	1942	Credle, E.	65-80	R*
Benet, W.R.	Flying King of Kurio (1st, 8vo, 289p, 4cp, pep)	Doran	(1926)	Smalley, J.	30-50	
Benet, W.R.	Timothy's Angels (1st, sm4to, ipcb, [24]p, fp color, pep)	Crowell	(1947)	Alajalov	45-60	
Bennet, H.	Round the Hearth (4to, ibds)	Dutton	(1880)	13 Chromos	80-100	
Bennett, A.	Old Wives' Tale (1st, lg8vo, 729p, 20 color)	Heritage Press	1947	Austen, J.	40-60	
Bennett, Anna E.	Little Witch (1st {std}, [1st bk.], 8vo, 127p, grn cl, b/w, DJ)	Lippincott	(1953)	Stone, H.	45-60	
Bennett, John	Barnaby Lee (1st, 12mo, 454p, blue/gilt, 34pl, PPP)	Century	1902	DeLand, C.O.	100-120	*
Bennett, John	Master Skylark (1st, 8vo, brown cl, 380p, b/w, PPP)	Century	1897	Birch, R.	90-125	
Bennett, John	Master Skylark (1st, 4to, blue cl, 322p, p-o, 8cp, pep)	Century	1922	Pitz, H.C.	25-40	
Bennett, John	Pigtail/Ah Lee Ben Loo (1st, 8vo, 298p, orange cl, b/w, pep, NH)	Longmans	1928	Bennett, J.C.	65-90	
Bennett, R.	Skookum & Sandy (1st {std}, sm4to, ipcb, [71]p, b/w, pep)	Doubleday/Dor.	1935	Bennett, R.	20-35	*
Bennett, R.A.	For the White Christ (1st, 8vo, p-o, 474p, 4cp)	McClurg	1906	Kinneys	20-30	
Bennett, R.A.	Thyra: Romance of the Polar Pit (1st, 8vo, 258p, gilt, 5pl)	Holt	1901	Blumenschein, E.	25-40	*
Bennett, Rowena B.	Around a Toadstool Table (1st, 8vo, ibds, 109p, fp b/w)	Chi: Rockwell	1930	Holling, L.W.	65-90	*
Benoit, C.F.	Children's Stories that Never Grow Old (12mo, 312p, yellow cl)	Reilly/Britton	(1908)	Neill, J.R.	65-80	
Benson, A.B.	Brownie Primer (1st, sm sq8vo, 98p, color)	Chi: Flanagan	(1905)	Gilbert, J.D.	50-75	
Benstead, V. (adap)	Three Little Pigs (1st, 8vo, ibds, [28]p, color, pep)	Random	1942	Cameron, M.	25-40	*
Benton, T.H.	Europe After 8:15 (1st, 8vo, 222p, 8pl)	J. Lane	1914	Benton, T.H.	80-110	
Bergengren, R.W.	David the Dreamer (1st, ob4to, green cl, p-o, gilt, 10 fp col)	Atl. Month Pr.	(1922)	Freud, Tom	450-600	*
Bergengren, R.W.	Gentlemen & All Merry Companions (1st, 12mo, 247p)	Bos: Brimmer	1922	Sloan, J.	35-50	*
Bergengren, R.W.	Jane, Joseph & John (1st, 4to, ibds, 62p, 6cp)	Atl. Month Pr.	(1918)	Day, M.	35-50	*
Bergengren, R.W.	Susan & the Butterbees (1st {std}, sm8vo, 175p, b/w, pep)	Longmans	1947	Vaughan, A.	25-40	*
Berlic-Mazuranic	Croation Tales of Long Ago (1st, 8vo, 259p, 10 ticp)	L: T.F. Unwin	1924	Kirin, V.	150-185	
Berlyn, F.	Sunrise-Land (1st, 8vo, 345p, grey cloth)	L: Jarrolds	1894	Rackham, A.	200-300	
Bernard, F.S.	Through Cloud Mountain (1st, 4to, 215p, gilt, p-o, 8cp, pep)	Lippincott	1922	Kay, G.A.	45-65	
Berry, E.	Black Folk Tales (1st {std}, 8vo, 80p, 1-color)	Harper	1928	Berry, E.	40-60	
Berry, E.	Careers of Cynthia (1st, sm8vo, red cl, 320p, 9 fp b/w)	Harcourt	(1932)	King, R.	25-40	*
Berry, E.	Girls in Africa (1st, 8vo, 128p, col frn, fp b/w, pep)	MacMillan	1928	Berry, E.	40-60	*
Berry, E.	Humbo the Hippo (1st {std}, sm8vo, ipcb, [41]p, color, pep)	Harper	1932	Berry, E.	30-50	*
Berry, E.	Humbo the Hippo (8vo, ibds, [18]p, color, pep)	Grosset/Dunlap	1938	Berry, E.	25-40	
Berry, E.	Illustrations of Cynthia (1st {std}, 8vo, 205p, 8 fp b/w)	Harcourt	(1931)	King, R.	20-30	*
Berry, E.	Juma of the Hills (1st, 8vo, 260p, b/w, pep)	Harcourt	(1932)	Berry, E.	25-40	*
Berry, E.	Mom Du Jos... (1st {std}, 8vo, 116p, col frn, cep, DJ)	Doubleday/Dor.	1931	Berry, E.	70-100	
Berry, E.	One-String Fiddle (1st, [64]p, peach cl, pep, color)	Winston	(1939)	Berry, E.	25-40	*
Berry, E.	Penny-Whistle (1st, 8vo, [40]p, yellow cl, color)	MacMillan	1930	Berry, E.	30-45	*
Berry, E.	Strings to Adventure (1st, 8vo, 221p, 7pl, pep)	Lothrop/Lee	1935	Berry, E.	25-40	*
Berry, E.	Sunhelmet Sue (1st, sm8vo, 239p, yellow cl, fp b/w)	Lothrop	1936	Berry, E.	20-30	*
Berry, E.	Winged Girl of Knossos (1st {std}, 8vo, 253p, b/w, pep, NH)	Appleton/Cent.	1933	Berry, E.	30-50	*
Beskow, E.	Adventures of Peter & Lotta (1st AM, ob4to, ibds, 15 color)	Harper	[1931]	Beskow, E.	80-100	
Beskow, E.	Aunt Brown's Birthday (1st AM, lg ob4to, [23]p, ibds, 16cp)	Harper	1930	Beskow, E.	80-100	
Beskow, E.	Aunt Green.../Aunt Lavender (1st AM, lg ob4to, 30p, bds, 15cp)	Harper	1930	Beskow, E.	90-130	*
Beskow, E.	Buddy's Advens. in the Blueberry Patch (1st, ob folio, ibds)	Harper	[1931]	Beskow, E.	100-145	*
Beskow, E.	Elf Children of the Woods (1st, ob folio, [32]p, color)	Harper	1932	Beskow, E.	120-150	*
Beskow, E.	Hat House (1st, ob4to, ibds, unpag, fp color)	Harper	1931	Beskow, E.	90-130	
Beskow, E.	Ollie's Ski Trip (1st AM, lg4to, [29]p, ibds, 14 fp color)	Harper	[1928]	Beskow, E.	120-150	
Beskow, E.	Sun-Egg (1st, ob4to, [26]p, ibds, 12cp, DJ)	Harper	1933	Beskow, E.	85-110	
Beskow, E.	Tale of Wee Little Old Woman (1st AM, sq4to, ibds, unpag, color)	Harper	1930	Beskow, E.	100-130	
Best, A.	Sojo: Story of Little Lazy Bones (1st, 8vo, ibds, unpag, pep)	Harter	(1934)	Berry, E.	40-60	*
Best, H.	Garram the Hunter (1st {std}, sm8vo, 332p, 6pl, pep, NH)	Doubleday/Dor.	1930	Berry, E.	30-50	*
Best, H.	Son of the White Man (1st {std}, 8vo, orang cl, 315p, b/w, pep)	Doubleday/Dor.	1931	Berry, E.	25-45	*
Beston, Henry	Tree that Ran Away (1st, sm8vo, 69p, green cl, cep, b/w)	MacMillan	1941	Eichenberg, F.	25-40	*
Bialk, Elisa	Ride 'Em Peggy! (1st, 8vo, red cl, 196p, doub pg illus)	Houghton	1950	Brown, Paul	30-45	
Bialk, Elisa	Silver Purse (1st {std}, sm8vo, 169p, orange cl, b/w)	World	(1952)	Galdone, P.	20-30	*

AUTHOR	TITLE	PUBLISHER	DATE	ARTIST	PRICE	LC
Bianco, M.W.	Adventures of Andy (1st, sm4to, 227p, 8cp, pep)	Doran	(1927)	Underwood, L.	50-80	*
Bianco, M.W.	Apple Tree (1st, 8vo, bds, p-o, 47p, b/w, dep)	Doran	(1926)	Artzybasheff, B.	30-45	*
Bianco, M.W.	Bright Morning (1st, 8vo, 143p, b/w, dep, DJ)	Viking	1942	Platt, M.	25-40	
Bianco, M.W.	Franzi & Gizi (1st, 4to, p-o, [56]p, fp color, pep)	J. Messner	1941	Loeffler, G.	30-45	*
Bianco, M.W.	House that Grew Smaller (1st, 12mo, 40p, p-o, color, cep, DJ)	MacMillan	1931	Field, R.	35-50	
Bianco, M.W.	Hurdy-Gurdy Man (1st, sq12mo, 56p, ibds, cep, b/w, DJ)	OUP	(1933)	Lawson, R.	80-110	
Bianco, M.W.	Little Wooden Doll (1st, 8vo, 65p, blue cl, pep, 6cp)	MacMillan	1925	Bianco, P.	35-50	
Bianco, M.W.	Poor Cecco (1st AM, 4to, blue/gilt, 175p, 7 ticp, pep)	Doran	(1925)	Rackham, A.	100-150	R
Bianco, M.W.	Skin Horse (1st, 8vo, ibds, 42p, pep, 5cp, DJ)	Doran	(1927)	Bianco, P.	100-165	
Bianco, M.W.	Street of Little Shops (1st {std}, 8vo, 111p, uncut, cep, 8cp)	Doubleday/Dor.	1932	Paull, G.	50-85	R*
Bianco, M.W.	Winterbound (1st, 8vo, blue cl, 234p, pep, NH)	Viking	1936	Unknown	45-60	*
Bianco, M.W. (ed.)	Rufus the Fox (1st, folio, ibds, [44]p, color)	Harper	1937	Samivel	65-80	*
Bianco, P.	Doll in the Window (1st, sq8vo, 32p, blue cl, color)	NY: OUP	1953	Bianco, P.	30-45	*
Bianco, P.	Joy & the Christmas Angel (1st, 8vo, green bds, pep, 40p, col)	NY: OUP	1949	Bianco, P.	35-50	*
Bianco, P.	Look-Inside Easter Egg (1st, sq12mo, pink bds, dep, 8fp col)	NY: OUP	1952	Bianco, P.	50-70	R*
Bianco, P.	Paradise Square (1st sm8vo, 94p, yel cl, 12 fp 1-color, dep)	OUP	1950	Bianco, P.	30-50	*
Bianco, P.	Starlit Journey (1st, 8vo, 47p, blue cl, col frn, pep, DJ)	MacMillan	1933	Bianco, P.	45-60	
Bibbins, R.M.	Mammy 'mongst the Wild Nations (1st, sm8vo, 305p, 8pl)	Stokes	(1904)	Wightman, F.P.	50-80	*
Bickley, F.L.	Adventures of Harlequin (1st, 8vo, 119p, bds, p-o, 20 col, pep)	L: Selwyn	1923	Austen, J.	45-65	
Bicknell, A.G.	Flower Folk (1st, 4to, 71p, fp color)	Putnam	(1936)	Grenwis, M.	80-100	*
Biddle, A.	Second Froggy Fairy Book (1st, 8vo, 90p, col frn, 11 fp b/w)	Drexel Biddle	1898	Pennock, A.	80-120	
Bigelow, P.	Borderland of Czar & Kaiser (1st, 8vo, 343p, gilt, 50pl)	Harper	1895	Remington, F.	60-80	
Bigelow, P.	White Man's Africa (1st, 8vo, 271p, 3pl by…)	Harper	1900	Remington, F.	50-80	
Biggers, E.D.	Agony Column (1st, 8vo, 193p, brown cl, 9pl)	Bobbs-Merrill	(1916)	Grefe, W.	35-50	
Biggers, E.D.	Love Insurance (1st, 12mo, 402p, brown cl, 8pl)	Bobbs-Merrill	(1914)	Snapp, F.	35-60	
Biggers, E.D.	Seven Keys to Baldpate (1st, 8vo, blue/gilt, b/w)	Bobbs-Merrill	(1913)	Snapp, F.	50-75	
Bigham, M.A.	Bad Little Rabbit (1st, sq12mo, 155p, color)	Little/Brown	1927	Young, F.L.	25-40	*
Bigham, M.A.	Blackie, His Friends & Enemies (1st, sm8vo, 200p, 5pl)	Little/Brown	1906	Atwood, C.E.	25-40	*
Bigham, M.A.	Goober Village (1st, sm8vo, 184p, color)	Rand/McNally	(1936)	Winter, M.	25-40	*
Bigham, M.A.	More Mother Goose Village Stories (1st, 8vo, 274p, color)	Rand/McNally	(1922)	Brock, Emma	40-65	
Bigham, M.A.	Mother Goose Village (1st, sq8vo, 196p, color, pep)	Rand/McNally	(1903)	Brison, E.S.	50-70	
Bigham, M.A.	Overheard in Fairyland (1st, 8vo, 237p, col frn, cp)	Little/Brown	(1909)	Clements, R.S.	35-50	*
Bigham, M.A.	Sonny Elephant (1st, sm8vo, 201p, cloth, col frn, b/w)	Little/Brown	1930	Hader, B.& E.	35-50	*
Bigham, M.A.	Wishing Fairies (1st, blue cl, 37p, 8cp)	Dodd	1905	Cory, F.	65-80	
Bilibin, I.	Russian Wonder Tales (1st AM, 8vo, 323p, tan cl, 12cp)	Century	1912	Bilibin, I.	200-320	
Bindloss, H.	Lorimer of the Northwest (1st, 12mo, 384p, cvr by…)	Stokes	(1909)	Hood, G.	30-45	
Bindloss, H.	Masters of the Wheat-Lands (1st, 8vo, 354p)	Stokes	(1910)	Cuneo, C.	25-40	*
Bindloss, H.	Winston of the Prairie (1st, sm8vo, p-o, 340p, 3cp)	Stokes	(1907)	Dunton, W.H.	30-45	
Bingham, C.	Airship in Animal Land (ob4to, ibds, 8 chromos)	L: Nister	[1910]	Thompson, G.H.	250-400	*
Bingham, C.	Dandy Lion (4to, ibds, t-i col frn, b/w)	L: Nister	[1900]	Wain, L.	100-140	
Bingham, C.	Funny Favorites (1st, sm4to, [44]p, ibds, tip-in col frn)	L: Nister	[1907]	Wain, L.	200-300	
Bingham, C.	Jingles, Jokes & Funny Folks (sm4to, wraps, b/w)	McLoughlin	[1910]	Wain, L.	75-120	*
Bingham, C.	Kittenland (sm folio, ipcb, 8cp)	L: Collins	(1903)	Wain, L.	300-400	
Bingham, C.	Ping Pong (ob narrow 4to, wraps, 6cp)	L: R. Tuck	[1903]	Wain, L.	350-500	
Bingham, C.	Pretty Pets (4to {enlarged ed.}, [20]p, 4 chromos)	L: Nister	[1910]	Foster, W.	80-100	
Bingham, C.	To Nursery Land (4to, 56p, 16 color, green cl)	L: R. Tuck	[1900]	Wain, L.	250-350	
Bingham, D.	The Bastille (1st AM, 8vo, 2 volumes, blue/gilt)	J. Pott	1901	Armstrong, M.	90-120	
Binney, I.	Boppet, Please Stop It (1st, 8vo, ipcb, 48p, 1-color)	W.R. Scott	1946	Binney, I.	35-50	*
Birch, V.	Green-Faced Toad (1st, lg8vo, 107p, green cl, 8cp)	Stokes	1923	Lenski, L.	70-100	
Bird, M.H.	Snow Man's Christmas (1st, 16mo, p-o, grn cl, 87p, 24 col, pep)	Stern	1908	Claghorn, J.C.	45-65	
Birdsall, K.N.	Jacks of All Trades (1st, 8vo, 236p, 6cp)	Appleton	1902	Russell, W.	25-40	*
Birnbaum, A.	Green Eyes (1st, sq4to, [40]p, pep, color, CH)	Capitol Pub.	(1953)	Birnbaum, A.	70-100	R*
Bischoff, Ilse	Wonderful Poodle (1st, sm4to, 79p, pep, b/w)	Crowell	(1949)	Bischoff, I.	25-40	*
Bishop, C.H.	All Alone (1st, 4to, unpag, b/w, pep, NH)	Viking	1953	Rojankovsky, F.	45-60	
Bishop, C.H.	Augustus (1st, sm4to, [32]p, ipcb, color, pep)	Viking	1945	Paull, G.	25-45	*
Bishop, C.H.	Big Loop (1st, 8vo, tan cl, 221p, fp b/w, pep)	Viking	1955	Fontsere, C.	25-40	*
Bishop, C.H.	Ferryman (1st, ob lg8vo, [64]p, ipcb, 1-color, pep)	Coward	1941	Wiese, K.	35-50	*
Bishop, C.H.	Five Chinese Brothers (1st, lg ob8vo, ipcb, [52]p, 1-col, pep)	Coward	(1938)	Wiese, K.	35-50	
Bishop, C.H.	King's Day (1st, lg8vo, [47]p, ipcb, fp b/w, cep)	Coward	1940	Spiegel, D.	25-45	*
Bishop, C.H.	Man Who Lost his Head (1st, ob4to, ibds, pep, [53]p, b/w)	Viking	1942	McCloskey, R.	35-60	*
Bishop, C.H.	Martin DePorres, Hero (1st, 8vo, 120p, beige cl, fp b/w, pep)	Houghton	1954	Charlot, J.	45-65	*
Bishop, C.H.	Pancakes-Paris (1st sm4to, 63p, grey cl, pep, NH)	Viking	1947	Schreiber, G.	45-65	
Bishop, C.H.	Twenty & Ten (1st, lg8vo, 76p, pep, b/w)	Viking	1952	DuBois, W.P.	35-50	*
Bjornson, B.	Pastor Sang (1st, 8vo, teg, uncut, frn by…)	L: Longmans	1893	Beardsley, A.	70-90	
Black, Dorothy	Magic Egg (1st, 4to, 111p)	L: A&C Black	1922	Folkard, C.	85-100	*
Black, I.S.	Barbara's Birthday (1st, 8vo, 44p, color)	W.R. Scott	1946	Takis, N.	45-65	*
Black, I.S.	Big Puppy & Little Puppy (1st, 8vo, yellow cl, [33]p, b/w, pep)	Holiday House	1960	Sherman, T.	20-30	*
Black, I.S.	Dog Doctor (1st, lg ob8vo, ipcb, [40]p, 1-color)	W.R. Scott	(1947)	Fischetti, J.R.	45-75	*
Black, I.S.	Dusty & his Friends (1st, sm8vo, [56]p)	Holiday House	(1950)	Latham, B.	20-30	*
Black, I.S.	Flipper: Sea Lion (1st, sm8vo, [50]p, color, pep)	Holiday House	1940	Rounds, G.	30-45	*
Black, I.S.	Kip: Young Rooster (1st, 12mo, [68]p, purple cl, b/w)	Holiday House	(1939)	Wiese, K.	25-45	*
Black, I.S.	Maggie, Mischievous Magpie (1st, sm8vo, [61]p, grn cl, b/w, cep)	Holiday House	(1949)	Latham, B.	35-60	R*

AUTHOR	TITLE	PUBLISHER	DATE	ARTIST	PRICE	LC
Black, I.S.	Night Cat (1st, lg ob8vo, [32]p, black cl, cep, b/w)	Holiday House	1957	Galdone, P.	30-45	*
Black, I.S.	Spoodles, Puppy Who Learned (1st, ob8vo, [48]p, ipcb, 1-color)	W.R. Scott	(1948)	Whistle, J.	35-50	*
Black, I.S.	This is the Bread that Betsy Ate (1st, ob4to, [26]p, color)	W.R. Scott	1945	Ullman, A.	40-65	*
Black, I.S.	Toby: A Curious Cat (1st, 8vo, rust cl, [63]p, b/w, cep)	Holiday House	1948	Wiese, K.	25-45	*
Black, Marg.	Three Brothers & a Lady (1st, 4to, 62p, color, DJ)	L: Acorn Press	1947	Ardizzone, E.	85-120	
Blackburn, H.	Breton Folk (1st, lg8vo, gilt, 200p, AEG, cep)	L: Sampson	1880	Caldecott, R.	120-150	
Blackmore, R.D.	Fringilla (1st, 8vo, 128p, 8pl)	L: Matthews	1895	Muckley, L.F.	350	
Blackmore, R.D.	Lorna Doone (1st, lg8vo, p-o, 351p, black cl, color)	M. Bradley	(1921)	Brett, H.M.	50-70	
Blackmore, R.D.	Lorna Doone (1st, 8vo, p-o, 646p, black/gilt, 8cp, pep)	Dodd	(1930)	Schaeffer, M.	30-50	
Blackmore, R.D.	Lorna Doone (1st, lg4to, 520p, teg, gilt, 16 ticp)	L: Boots	[1931]	Brock/Brittan	85-130	
Blackmore, R.D.	Lorna Doone (1st, 4to, blue cl, col frn)	L: J. Lane	1933	Pape, F.	65-80	
Blaisdell, E.W.	Animals at the Fair (1st, ob4to, [47]p, color)	R.H. Russell	(1902)	Blaisdell, E.W.	150-225	*
Blaisdell, M.F.	Pretty Polly Flinders (1st, sm sq8vo, green cl, 188p, 4cp)	Little/Brown	1914	Wireman, K.	25-40	*
Blake, A.H.	China (1st, sm4to, 138p, blue/gilt, 16cp)	L: A&C Black	1909	Menpes, M.	60-90	
Blake, Wm.	Art of William Blake (1st, 4to, green/gilt, 56p, 51pl)	Moffat	1907	Blake, Wm.	65-80	
Blake, Wm.	Land of Dreams (1st, 8vo, 42p, gilt, b/w, pep, DJ)	MacMillan	1928	Bianco, P.	45-60	
Blake, Wm.	Songs of Experience (1st, 8vo, 83p, green cl, uncut)	L: D. Nutt	1899	Levetus, C.	80-100	
Blake, Wm.	Songs of Innocence (1st, 24mo, 118p, designs by…)	L: Wells/Gard.	1899	Levetus, C.	70-90	*
Blake, Wm.	Songs of Innocence (1st, 8vo, 31p, p-o, 4cp)	L: Jack	[1905]	Allen, O.	45-70	*
Blake, Wm.	Songs of Innocence (1st, 8vo, green/gilt, p-o, 49p, 12cp)	L: H. Daniel	(1911)	Appleton, H.C.	90-120	*
Blake, Wm.	Songs of Innocence (1st, 12mo, 56p, teg, gilt, 7cp)	L: Dent	(1911)	Robinson, C.	180-200	
Blake, Wm.	Songs of Innocence (lg8vo, green/gilt, 12cp)	L: Simpkin	(1922)	Appleton, H.C.	65-80	
Blake, Wm.	Songs of Innocence (1st, 4to, 42p, 12cp)	L: Medici	1927	Parsons, J.	60-80	
Blakeley, E.S.	Fairy Starlight (1st, 12mo, lavender cl, 213p, b/w)	McClurg	1896	Perkins, L.F.	65-90	*
Blanchard, A.E.	Bonny Bairns (1st, 4to, 48p, ibds, 25cp)	Worthington	(1888)	Waugh, Ida	165-220	
Blanchard, A.E.	Four Corners (1st, sm8vo, 387p, green cl, 5pl)	Jacobs	(1906)	Smith, Wuanita	25-45	*
Blanchard, A.E.	Janet's College Career (1st, 8vo, 365p, 5pl)	Jacobs	(1904)	Waugh, Ida	20-30	*
Blanchard, A.E.	Journey of Joy (1st, 8vo, 305p, 7pl)	Estes	(1908)	Bridgman, L.J.	20-35	*
Blanchard, A.E.	Little Girl's Summer Holidays (1st, sm8vo, 5cp)	Jacobs	(1911)	Otis, E.	25-40	*
Blanchard, A.E.	Little Miss Mouse (1st, sm8vo, 230p, p-o, 5cp, pep)	Jacobs	(1906)	Unknown	25-40	
Blanchard, A.E.	Mammy's Baby (4to, [16]p, ipcb, chromos)	Worthington	(1890)	Waugh, Ida	120-165	
Blanchard, A.E.	My Own Dolly (1st, 8vo, ipcb, 64p, 15cp)	Dutton	1882	Waugh, Ida	100-150	
Blanchard, A.E.	Tangles & Curls (1st, 4to, [16]p, ibds, 9pl)	Worthington	1888	Waugh, Ida	100-120	
Blanchard, A.E.	Tell Me a Story (1st, lg sq8vo, [15]p, ibds, 10 fp color)	Worthington	1888	Waugh, Ida	120-165	
Blanchard, A.E.	Three Pretty Maids (1st, 12mo, 243p, b/w plates)	Lippincott	1897	Stephens, A.B.	25-40	*
Blanchard, A.E.	Twenty Little Maidens (1st, lg8vo, 160p, 18pl)	Lippincott	1893	Waugh, Ida	45-65	*
Blanchard, A.E.	Wee Babies (1st, 4to, ibds, unpag, color)	Dutton	1882	Waugh, Ida	85-100	
Blanck, Jacob	Jonathan & the Rainbow (1st, 4to, ibds, 48p, color)	Houghton	1948	Slobodkin, L.	45-65	*
Blanck, Jacob	King & Noble Blacksmith (1st, sm4to, yellow cl, 48p, color)	Houghton	1950	Slobodkin, L.	45-60	
Blichfeldt, E.H.	Mexican Journey (1st, 8vo, 280p, orange cl, map, cvr by…)	Crowell	(1912)	Armstrong, M.	30-45	*
Blodgett, M.F.	At the Queen's Mercy (1st, 8vo, 261p, teg, uncut, 5pl)	Chi: Lamson	1897	Sandham, H.	60-80	*
Blodgett, M.F.	Fairy Tales (1st, sm4to, yellow cl, 204p, teg, 12pl, pep)	Chi: Lamson	1896	Reed, E.	375-500	
Blodgett, M.F.	Giant's Ruby (1st, 8vo, 292p, blue cl, 6pl)	Little/Brown	1903	Pyle, Kath.	70-100	
Blodgett, M.F.	Magic Slippers (1st, 12mo, 90p, 4cp)	Little/Brown	1917	Blodgett, M.	30-45	
Blodgett, M.F.	Peasblossom (1st, 8vo, 177p, p-o, 5cp)	Doran	(1917)	Blodgett, M.	30-45	*
Blodgett, M.F.	When Christmas Came Too Early (1st, 12mo, 107p, 6cp)	Little/Brown	1912	McClellan, R.	30-45	*
Blumberg, F.B.	Rowena Teena Tot & Blackberries (1st, 4to, ibds, p-o, 32p, col)	Whitman	(1934)	Grosjean, M.	85-140	*
Blyton, E.	Silver & Gold (1st, sq8vo, p-o, 128p, 8cp)	NY: Nelson	(1928)	Everett, E.	40-65	
Bock, Geo. E.	What Makes the Wheels Go 'Round (1st, 4to, 76p, pep, dp color)	MacMillan	1931	Artzybasheff, B.	100-160	*
Boggs, R.S.	Three Golden Oranges (1st {std}, sm8vo, 137p, 6pl, pep)	Longmans	1936	Brock, Emma	35-50	*
Bolton, C.K.	Love Story/Ursula Wolcott (1st, 12mo, 31p, designs by..)	Chi: Lamson	1895	Reed, E.	100-165	*
Bond, Gladys B.	Blue Chimney (1st, sm8vo, 164p, red cl, b/w, pep)	Holiday House	(1959)	Shortall, L.	25-40	*
Bone, Gertrude	Children's Children (1st, 4to, 271p, brown bds, gilt)	L: Duckworth	1908	Bone, M.	50-75	
Bone, Gertrude	This Old Man (1st, lg8vo, 131p, blue bds, gilt, frn by…)	L: MacMillan	1925	Bone, M.	30-45	
Bonner, G.	The Pioneer (1st, 8vo, 392p, blue/gilt, cvr by…)	Bobbs-Merrill	(1905)	Armstrong, M.	30-45	*
Bonner, G.	The Pioneer (1st, 8vo, 392p, 6pl)	Bobbs-Merrill	(1905)	Fisher, H.	25-45	*
Bonner, M.G.	365 Bedtime Stories (1st, 4to, p-o, 20cp)	Stokes	1923	Choate, F.	30-45	
Bonner, M.G.	Daddy's Bedtime Fairy Stories (1st, 12mo, 120p, color)	Stokes	(1916)	Choate/Curtis	35-50	*
Bonner, M.G.	Hundred Trips to Storyland (1st, 8vo, 327p, orang cl, 7cp, pep)	Macaulay	(1930)	Lupprian, H.	45-65	*
Bonner, M.G.	Magic Clock (1st, 8vo, yellow cl, 187p, 8cp)	Macaulay	(1931)	Price, L.	50-75	
Bonner, M.G.	Magic Journeys (1st, 4to, orange cl, 286p, 16cp)	Macaulay	(1928)	Price, L.	60-80	
Bonner, M.G.	Magic Map (1st, 4to, 238p, 17cp)	Macaulay	(1927)	Price, L.	60-80	
Bonner, M.G.	Magic Music Shop (1st, folio, orang cl, 95p, color, pep)	Macaulay	(1929)	Price, L.	70-100	
Bonner, M.G.	Miss Angelina Adorable (1st, 8vo, cloth, [102]p, color)	M. Bradley	(1928)	Scott, J.L.	30-45	
Bonner, M.G.	Mrs. Cucumber Green (1st, 8vo, 108p, pep, color)	M. Bradley	(1927)	Scott, J.L.	20-30	*
Bonner, M.G.	Story Teller's Holiday (1st, lg4to, [64]p, red cl, p-o)	McLoughlin	(1938)	Scott, J.L.	85-130	
Bonney, T.G.	The Mediterranean (1st, 8vo, blue/gilt)	J. Pott	1902	Armstrong, M.	40-60	
Bonte, W.	Christmas Stocking Rhymes (4to, tan cl, p-o, 38p, 17 color)	Caldwell	(1904)	Bridgman, L.J.	70-100	
Bonte, W.	Fun & Nonsense (1st, 4to, p-o, [40]p, color)	Caldwell	(1904)	Bonte, W.	65-100	*
Bontemps, A.	Drums at Dusk (1st {std}, sm8vo, 226p, black cl, b/w, cep)	MacMillan	1939	Margenta	50-70	*
Bontemps, A.	Fast Sooner Hound (1st, sq8vo, beige cl, 28p, color, pep)	Houghton	(1942)	Burton, V.L.	65-90	*
Bontemps, A.	Golden Slippers (1st {std}, 8vo, 220p, b/w pl)	Harper	(1941)	Sharon, H.B.	45-65	*

AUTHOR	TITLE	PUBLISHER	DATE	ARTIST	PRICE	LC
Bontemps, A.	Lonesome Boy (1st, 8vo, blue cl, 28p, fp b/w, cep)	Houghton	1955	Topolski, F.	45-65	*
Bontemps, A.	Popo & Fifina (1st, 8vo, 100p, orange cl, 6pl)	MacMillan	1932	Campbell, E.S.	80-120	R*
Bontemps, A.	Sad-Faced Boy (1st, 8vo, 118p, col frn, 7pl, pep)	Houghton	1937	Burton, V.L.	35-50	*
Bontemps, A.	Sam Patch... (1st, sq8vo, yellow cl, 32p, color, pep)	Houghton	1951	Brown, Paul	65-80	*
Bontemps, A.	Slappy Hooper... (1st, ob8vo, 44p, color, pep)	Houghton	1946	Koering, U.	45-70	*
Bontemps, A.	Story of the Negro (1st, 8vo, 239p, b/w, NH)	Knopf	1948	Lufkin, R.	70-100	*
Bontemps, A.	We Have Tomorrow (1st, sm8vo, 131p, photos by...)	Houghton	1945	Palfi, M.	45-70	*
Bontemps, A.	You Can't Eat a Possum (1st, sm8vo, 120p, red cl, 4cp)	Wm. Morrow	1934	Bischoff, I.	50-80	*
Booth, M.B.	Sleepy-Time Stories (1st, 12mo, 177p, teg, gilt, 17pl)	Putnam	1899	Humphrey, M.	140-170	
Booth, M.B.	Twilight Fairy Tales (1st, 8vo, 273p, gilt, teg, 16cp)	Putnam	1906	Rand, Amy	65-95	
Borrow, G.	Lavengro (1st, 8vo, teg, green/gilt, 655p, 12 ticp, cep)	L: Foulis	(1914)	Sullivan, E.J.	45-60	
Boston, Lucy	Children of the Green Knowe (1st, sm8vo, 157p, cloth, 6pl)	L: Faber	(1954)	Boston, Peter	65-90	
Boston, Lucy	Children of the Green Knowe (1st AM {std}, 8vo, 157p, pcb, b/w)	Harcourt	(1955)	Boston, Peter	50-85	R
Boston, Lucy	River at Green Knowe (1st {std}, 8vo, 153p, green cl, b/w)	Harcourt	(1959)	Boston, Peter	65-80	
Boston, Lucy	Treasure of Green Knowe (1st AM {std}, 8vo, 185p, cloth, b/w)	Harcourt	(1958)	Boston, Peter	50-80	*
Boswell, H.	French Canada (1st, ob8vo, 82p, 25cp, DJ)	Viking	1938	Boswell, H.	35-50	
Boult, E.M.	Romance of Cinderella (1st, 4to, 146p, color)	R.H. Russell	1902	Stevens, B.	160-250	*
Boult, K.F.	Heroes of the Norselands (1st, 8vo, 211p, 9pl)	L: Dent	1903	Robinson, T.H.	45-60	*
Bourget, P.	Antigone (1st, 8vo, red/gilt, uncut, 297p)	Scribner	1898	Armstrong, M.	30-45	*
Bourget, P.	Monica (1st, 12mo, 289p, red cl, cvr by...)	Scribner	1902	Armstrong, M.	25-40	*
Bourget, P.	Tragic Idyll (1st, 8vo, red/gilt, 452p, uncut)	Scribner	1896	Armstrong, M.	30-45	*
Bourke, S.T.E.	Fables in Feathers (1st, sq8vo, 114p, 9pl)	Crowell	(1907)	Conde, J.M.	35-50	*
Bourman, C.	The Bridge (1st, 4to, green/gilt, 249p, uncut, 24cp)	J. Lane	1926	Brangwyn, F.	60-80	
Bouten, E.G.	Grandmother's Doll (1st, lg8vo, 106p, gilt, color)	Duffield/Green	(1931)	Carter, H.	45-60	*
Bouve, E.T.	Centuries Apart (1st, 8vo, grey/gilt, 6pl, maps, 347p)	Little/Brown	1894	Harper, W. St. J.	35-50	
Bouvet, M.	Little House in Pimlico (1st, 8vo, blue cl, 245p, b/w, cep)	McClurg	1897	Armstrong, M.	20-30	
Bouvet, M.	Little Marjorie's Love Story (1st, 8vo, 124p, 16pl)	McClurg	1891	Armstrong, H.M.	25-45	
Bouvet, M.	My Lady (1st, 12mo, beige/silver, 284p, 12pl)	McClurg	1894	Armstrong, H.M.	35-50	
Bouvet, M.	Prince Tip-Top (1st, sm8vo, 134p, olive/white)	McClurg	1892	Armstrong, H.M.	45-60	*
Bouvet, M.	Sweet William (1st, 8vo, 209p, blue cl, 16 b/w, cep)	McClurg	1890	Armstrong, M.	30-50	
Bouvet, M.	Tales of an Old Chateau (1st, 12mo, 235p, gilt)	McClurg	1899	Armstrong, M.	40-60	
Bowen, W.A.	Enchanted Forest (1st, 12mo, 197p, color, pep)	MacMillan	1920	Petershams	45-60	*
Bowen, W.A.	Merrimeg (1st, 12mo, 166p, green/gilt, 7cp, pep)	MacMillan	1923	Brock, Emma	25-40	*
Bowen, Wm.	Old Tobacco Shop (1st, 8vo, 236p, green/gilt cl, p-o, NH)	MacMillan	1921	Unknown	50-70	
Bower, B.M.	Chip of the Flying-U (1st, 12mo, 264p, red cl, 3cp)	Dillingham	(1906)	Russell, C.M.	35-50	
Bower, B.M.	Lure of the Dim Trails (1st, 8vo, red cl, 210p, 3cp)	Dillingham	(1907)	Russell, C.M.	35-50	
Bower, B.M.	Range Dwellers (1st, 12mo, 356p, 3cp)	Street & Smith	(1907)	Russell, C.M.	150-200	*
Bower, B.M.	Uphill Climb (1st, 8vo, 283p, 4pl)	Little/Brown	1913	Russell, C.M.	60-85	*
Bowie, W.R.	Story of Jesus for Young People (1st, 8vo, 125p, blue cl, 6cp)	Scribner	1937	Lawson, R.	50-70	
Bowie, W.R.	When Jesus was Born (1st, sq12mo, ibds, color)	Harper	1928	Falls, C.B.	45-60	
Bowman, J.	Happy all Day Through (1st, lg ob4to, ibds, color)	Volland	(1917)	Scott, J.L.	60-80	
Bowman, J.C.	John Henry... (1st, 8vo, t.e. red, 288p, 2cp, 12pl)	Whitman	1942	LaGrone, R.	30-45	
Bowman, J.C.	Mystery Mountain (1st, 8vo, 293p, blue cl, 4cp, 10pl, pep)	Whitman	1940	Wallower, L.	30-45	*
Bowman, J.C.	Pecos Bill (1st, lg8vo, 296p, 6cp, 15pl, pep, NH)	Whitman	1937	Bannon, L.	80-120	*
Bowman, J.C.	Tales from a Finnish Tupa (1st, 8vo, grey cl, 273p, pep, 6cp)	Whitman	1936	Bannon, L.	35-50	*
Bowman, J.C.	Winabojo (1st, 8vo, 296p, orang cl, col frn, 12pl, pep)	Whitman	1941	Sperry, A.	30-45	*
Boyajian, Z.C.	Armenian Legends & Poems (folio, cloth, 196p, ticp)	Dent/Dutton	[1915]	Boyajian, Z.C.	130-185	*
Boyajian, Z.C.	Gilgamesh: Dream of Eternal Quest (1st, lg4to, 110p, gilt 15ticp)	L: G.W. Jones	1924	Boyajian, Z.C.	100-150	*
Boyd, Eliz. M.	All About David (1st, lg8vo, 117p, pep, b/w)	Winston	(1940)	Sarg, T.	25-40	*
Boyd, J.	Drums (1st, 4to, p-o, 409p, 17cp, pep, SC)	Scribner	1928	Wyeth, N.C.	100-165	
Boylan, G.D.	Kids of Many Colors (1st, 8vo, tan cl, 156p, color)	Chi: Jamieson	(1901)	Morgan, Ike	100-150	*
Boylan, G.D.	Kiss of Glory (1st, sm8vo, 298p, col frn & cvr by...)	Dillingham	(1902)	Leyendecker, J.C.	35-50	*
Boylan, G.D.	Old House (1st, 12mo, 112p, cvr by...)	E.R. Herrick	(1897)	Denslow, W.W.	40-65	*
Boylan, G.D.	Pipes of Clovis (1st, sm8vo, 258p, green cl, 4cp)	Little/Brown	1913	Chamberlin, E.H.	20-25	*
Boylan, G.D.	Steps to Nowhere (1st, 4to, 230p, p-o, blue cl, 8cp)	Baker/Taylor	1910	Morgan, Ike	100-150	
Boylan, G.D.	Yama Yama Land (1st, sq8vo, 200p, p-o, color)	Reilly/Britton	(1909)	Keller, E.	80-100	
Boylan, G.D.	Young Folks Uncle Tom's Cabin (1st, 4to, ipcb, 166p, 16 fp b/w)	Jamieson	1901	Morgan, Ike	165-220	*
Boyle, E.	Scrap Basket Sam (12mo, 4cp)	Rand/McNally	(1923)	Gregory, D.L.	25-40	
Boyle, Kay	Youngest Camel (1st {std}, 8vo, 96p, beige cl, 6cp)	Little/Brown	1939	Kredel, F.	20-35	
Boyle, V.F.	Devil Tales (1st, 8vo, 211p, 28pl)	Harper	1900	Frost, A.B.	70-90	
Boyles, K.	Langford of the Three Bars (1st, 8vo, 278p, 4cp)	McClurg	1907	Wyeth, N.C.	50-70	
Boyles, K.	Spirit Trail (1st, 8vo, 416p, ibds, 4cp)	McClurg	1910	Dixon, M.	35-50	
Bradford, Marg.	Keep Singing, Keep Humming (1st, lg ob 8vo, 66p, color)	W.R. Scott	1953	Bloch, B.	35-50	*
Bradley, A.G.	Highways & Byways/North Wales (1st, 8vo, 474p, b/w)	L: MacMillan	1898	Thomson/Pennell	65-80	*
Bradley, Mary H.	Alice in Elephantland (1st, sm8vo, 187p, pep, b/w)	Appleton	1929	Bradley, A.H.	45-60	*
Bradley, Mary H.	Alice in Jungleland (1st, 8vo, 170p, green cl, b/w, pep)	Appleton	1927	(Photos)	80-100	*
Bradley, Mary H.	Wine of Astonishment (1st, 8vo, pcb, 313p, cvr by...)	Appleton	1919	Armstrong, M.	30-45	*
Bradley, W.	Peter Poodle... (1st, sq4to, 166p, ibds, 26 fp color, pep)	Dodd	1906	Bradley, W.	650-900	
Bradley, W.	Wonderbox Stories (1st, 8vo, 154p, gold cl, fp b/w)	Century	1916	Bradley, W.	300-500	
Bradley-Birt, F.	Bengal Fairy Tales (1st, lg8vo, 209p, 6 color)	L: J. Lane	1920	Tagore, A.N.	80-100	
Brady, C.T.	And Thus He Came (1st, sm8vo, teg, 6cp)	Putnam	1916	Everett, W.	20-25	*
Brady, C.T.	Little Angel/Canyon Creek (1st, 8vo, 292p, 6pl)	Revell	1914	Hoskins, G.	25-40	*

AUTHOR	TITLE	PUBLISHER	DATE	ARTIST	PRICE	LC
Brady, C.T.	My Lady's Slipper (1st, teg, 245p, 4pl)	Dodd	1905	Ditzler, C.W.	20-25	*
Brady, C.T.	Reuben James (1st, 8vo, 158p, pict cl, b/w)	Appleton	1900	Various	20-30	*
Brady, C.T.	West Wind (1st, 8vo, 389p, 4cp)	McClurg	1910	Dixon, M.	25-45	
Brady, L.E.	Green Forest Fairy Book (1st, 8vo, 271p, 8cp)	Little/Brown	1920	Preston, A.B.	65-100	
Bragdon, Elspeth	That Jud! (1st, 8vo, ivory cl, 126p, fp b/w)	Viking	(1957)	Schreiber, G.	30-45	*
Brailsford, M.	Making of William Penn (1st, 8vo, 367p, t-i frn by...)	Longmans	1930	Leighton, C.	30-45	
Braine, S.E.	Princess of Hearts (1st, 8vo, AEG, 172p, green/gilt, col frn)	L: Blackie	1899	Woodward, A.B.	120-165	
Braine, S.E.	To Tell the King the Sky is Falling (1st, 8vo, 171p, b/w)	L: Blackie	(1896)	Woodward, A.B.	45-60	
Braine/Floyd	In Nurseryland (1st, 4to, ibds, [48]p, color)	L: R. Tuck	[1900]	Wain, L.	450-600	
Brainerd, E.H.	For Love of Mary Ellen (1st, 12mo, 43p, tan cl, 4pl)	Harper	1912	O'Neill, R.	30-45	
Brainerd, E.H.	How Could You, Jean? (1st, 8vo, 337p, 4pl)	Doubleday/Page	1917	Flagg, J.M.	20-30	*
Brainerd, E.S.	Millicent in Dreamland (1st, 12mo, 94p)	Page	1902	Barry, E.B.	20-35	*
Branley, Frank	Mickey's Magnet (1st, sm8vo, [48]p, yellow cl, color, dep)	Crowell	1956	Johnson, C.	30-50	*
Breakenridge, W.	Helldorado (1st, lg8vo, brown cl, 256p, DJ)	Houghton	1928	(Photos)	65-80	
Brennan, G.H.	Bill Truetell... (1st, 8vo, col frn & cvr by...)	McClurg	1909	Flagg, J.M.	20-25	
Brenner, A.	Boy Who Could Do Anything (1st, 4to, 136p, cep)	W.R. Scott	(1942)	Charlot, J.	50-75	
Brenner, A.	Dumb Juan & the Bandits (1st, 8vo, green cl, [47]p, 1-color)	W.R. Scott	(1957)	Charlot, J.	40-65	*
Brenner, A.	Hero by Mistake (1st, 8vo, 43p, ipcb, pep, 1-color)	W.R. Scott	(1953)	Charlot, J.	35-50	*
Brenner, A.	I Want to Fly (1st, lg8vo, [34]p, ipcb, color, pep)	W.R. Scott	1943	Bloch, L.	35-50	*
Brentano, C.M.	Fairy Tales from Brentano (1st, 8vo, 252p, gilt, b/w)	(London)	1885	Gould, F.C.	150-200	*
Brentano, C.M.	Fairy Tales from Brentano (sm8vo, 326p, col frn, 8pl)	Stokes	(1925)	Gould, F.C.	30-50	*
Brereton, F.S.	Boy of the Dominion (1st, 8vo, 367p, gilt, 6cp)	L: Blackie	1913	Rainey, W.	35-50	
Brereton, F.S.	Indian & Scout (1st, 8vo, 368p, gilt, 6pl)	L: Blackie	1911	Cuneo, C.	30-45	
Brett, Edna P.	Circus Day... (1st, 12mo, 64p, 8 fp color, ibds)	Rand/McNally	1922	Riley, G.C.	20-30	
Brewton, John	Gaily We Parade (1st, sm4to, 218p, pep, b/w)	MacMillan	1940	Lawson, R.	45-65	*
Brickdale, E.	Golden Book of Famous Women (4to, blue/gilt, 200p, 16 ticp)	L: Hodder	[1916]	Brickdale, E.F.	100-130	
Bridges, Wm.	Toco Toucan (1st {std}, 8vo, [32]p, color)	Harper	(1940)	Wiese, K.	20-40	*
Bridgman, Betty	Lullaby for Eggs (1st {std}, 8vo, ibds, unpag, fp color)	MacMillan	1955	Jones, E.O.	25-40	*
Bridgman, Clare	Bairn's Coronation Book (24mo, 120p, 44cp)	L: Dent	[1902]	Robinson, C.	80-120	
Bridgman, Clare	Book of Days for Little Ones (1st, 12mo, 3cp)	L: Dent	1901	Robinson, C.	100-140	
Bridgman, Clare	Book of Shops (1st, sq12mo, 120p, color)	L: Dent	1902	Robinson, C.	120-170	
Bridgman, Clare	Shopping Day (1st, 16mo, 120p)	Dent/Dutton	1902	Robinson, C.	65-80	*
Bridgman, L.J.	Bridgman's Kewts (1st, 4to, [94]p, color, pep)	Caldwell	(1902)	Bridgman, L.J.	70-100	*
Bridgman, L.J.	Farmer Fox (1st, 4to, [36]p, ibds, p-o, color)	Caldwell	(1900)	Bridgman, L.J.	45-70	
Bridgman, L.J.	Guess (1st, 4to, ibds, [104]p, color, pep)	Caldwell	(1901)	Bridgman, L.J.	70-100	
Bridgman, L.J.	Guess Again (1st, lg4to, ibds, [104]p, color)	Caldwell	(1902)	Bridgman, L.J.	70-100	
Bridgman, L.J.	Mother Goose/Wild Beast Show (1st, lg4to, ibds, [104]p, col)	Caldwell	(1900)	Bridgman, L.J.	200-300	
Bridgman, L.J.	Mother Wild Beast/Wild Beast Show (1st, lg4to, ibds, color)	Caldwell	(1900)	Bridgman, L.J.	200-300	*
Bridgman, L.J.	Seem-So's (1st, 8vo, p-o, [80]p, silhouettes, col frn)	Caldwell	(1906)	Bridgman, L.J.	65-80	*
Brigham, S.J.	Under Blue Skies (4to, bds)	Worthington	1886	(Chromos)	80-110	
Bright, Rbt.	Travels of Ching (1st, sm ob8vo, ipcb, [65]p, 1-color, pep)	W.R. Scott	1943	Bright, R.	30-45	*
Brill, Geo. R.	Rhymes of the Golden Age (1st, lg8vo, 121p, p-o, pep, 12 col)	Stern	1908	Brill, G.R.	65-80	*
Brine, M.D.	Funnyland Boys (1st, sm8vo, 54p, ipcb, col frn, b/w)	Drexel Biddle	1903	Unknown	60-100	*
Brine, M.D.	Little Miss Toodledums (1st, 8vo, b/w pl)	Dutton	1893	Upton, F.	60-85	*
Brine, M.D.	Mother & Baby (1st, 4to, uncut, 48p, 14pl)	R.H. Russell	1901	Various	160-200	*
Brine, M.D.	Poor Sally/her Christmas (1st, 8vo, 182p, b/w pl)	Dutton	1898	Upton, F.	80-120	*
Brinig, M.	Flutter of an Eyelid (1st, 12mo, 310p)	Farrar/Rine.	1933	Ward, L.	30-45	*
Brininstool, E.A.	Trail Dust of a Maverick (1st, sm8vo, p-o, 249p)	Dodd	1914	(Photos)	30-45	
Brink, C.R.	Anything Can Happen on a River (1st, sm8vo, 224p, blue cl, b/w)	MacMillan	1934	Berger, W.W.	25-40	*
Brink, C.R.	Baby Island (1st, sm8vo, 172p, pep, 6cp)	MacMillan	1937	Sewell, H.	30-45	*
Brink, C.R.	Caddie Woodlawn (1st, 8vo, 270p, b/w, cep, DJ, NM)	MacMillan	1935	Seredy, K.	70-95	
Brink, C.R.	Lad with a Whistle (1st, 8vo, 235p, fp b/w, pep)	MacMillan	1941	Ball, Rbt.	25-40	*
Brink, C.R.	Mademoiselle Misfortune (1st, 8vo, 267p, 12 fp b/w, cep)	MacMillan	1936	Seredy, K.	30-50	*
Brink, C.R.	Magical Melons (1st, 8vo, 193p, grey cloth, b/w)	MacMillan	1944	Davis, M.	20-30	*
Brisley, J.L.	Further Doings/Milly-Molly-Mandy (1st AM, 12mo, 95p, color)	G. Sully	1932	Brisley, J.	25-40	*
Bro, Marguerite	Su-Mei's Golden Year (1st {std}, 8vo, 246p, beige cl, b/w)	Doubleday	1950	Wiese, K.	30-45	*
Bro, Marguerite	Three & Domingo (1st {std}, sm8vo, 127p)	Doubleday	1953	Weisgard, L.	30-45	*
Broadbent, H.	Sing-A-Song (1st, ob folio, ibds, unpag, 8cp)	L: M. Goshen	1912	Dowdall, N.	130-180	*
Broadwood, Lucy	English Nursery Rhymes (lg4to, color)	L: A&C Black	(1916)	Wheeler, D.M.	100-150	
Broadwood, Lucy	Songs/Alice in Wonderland (4to, blue/gilt, 48p, p-o, 12 ticp)	L: A&C Black	1921	Folkard, C.	100-140	
Brock, Emma	Hen that Kept House (1st {std}, ob4to, [40]p, color, dep)	Knopf	1933	Brock, Emma	35-50	*
Brock, Emma	Present for Auntie (1st {std}, sm8vo, [96]p, cloth)	Knopf	1939	Brock, Emma	25-40	
Brock, Emma	To Market! To Market! (1st, ob8vo, [41]p, color)	Knopf	1930	Brock, Emma	25-45	*
Bronson, E.B.	Red Blooded (1st, 8vo, 342p, 10pl)	McClurg	1910	Dixon, M.	35-50	
Bronson, E.B.	Reminiscences of a Ranchman (1st, 8vo, p-o, 369p, 8cp)	McClurg	(1910)	Dixon, M.	50-65	
Bronson, W.S.	Children of the Sea (1st, lg8vo, 264p, col frn, pep, b/w)	Harcourt	(1940)	Bronson, W.S.	40-60	*
Bronson, W.S.	Water People (1st, lg8vo, 119p, color, pep)	Wise-Parlow	(1935)	Bronson, W.S.	45-60	*
Bronte, C.	Shirley (1st, 8vo, 2 volumes, teg)	L: Dent	1905	Dulac, E.	120-165	
Bronte, E.J.	Wuthering Heights (1st {std}, 4to, 325p, 12pl, DJ)	Random	1931	Leighton, C.	60-85	
Brook, Arthur	Witch's Hollow (1st, 8vo, 211p, 8cp)	L: A&C Black	1920	Folkard, C.	120-140	*
Brooke, L.L.	Johnny Crow's Garden (1st, ibds, 48p, p-o, 8cp)	L: Warne	1903	Brooke, L.L.	130-165	
Brooke, L.L.	Johnny Crow's New Garden (1st, 8vo, blue bds, p-o, 8cp)	L: Warne	1935	Brooke, L.L.	65-90	

AUTHOR	TITLE	PUBLISHER	DATE	ARTIST	PRICE	LC
Brooke, L.L.	Johnny Crow's Party (1st, sq8vo, green bds, p-o, 48p, 8cp)	L: Warne	1907	Brooke, L.L.	130-165	
Brooke, L.L.	Ring O' Roses (lg8vo, [59]p, blue/gilt, pep, 32cp)	L: Warne	[1901]	Brooke, L.L.	50-80	
Brooke, L.L.	Tailor & the Crow (1st, sq8vo, gilt, p-o, 40p, 6cp, pep)	L: Warne	(1911)	Brooke, L.L.	90-140	
Brookfield, A.	Aesop's Fables for Little Readers (1st, 4to, red/gilt, 71p, b/w)	L: T.F. Unwin	(1888)	Ford, H.J.	180-220	
Brooks, C.S.	Journeys to Baghdad (1st, 8vo, bds, p-o, 140p, teg, 27 woodcuts)	Yale U. Press	1915	Lewis, A.	35-50	*
Brooks, E.C.	Francisco... (1st, sm8vo, 152p, 6pl)	Page	1910	Goss, J.	25-40	*
Brooks, E.S.	Master of Strong Hearts (1st, 8vo, 314p, 10pl)	Dutton	1898	Cary, W.M.	30-50	
Brooks, E.S.	Storied Holidays (1st, 8vo, 271p, cloth)	Lothrop	[1887]	Pyle, H.	150-180	
Brooks, Edward	Story of King Arthur (1st AM, 12mo, 383p, 13pl)	Penn	1900	Beardsley, A.	70-120	*
Brooks, Gwen.	Bronzeville Boys & Girls (1st, 8vo, grey cl, 40p, b/w, cep)	Harper	(1956)	Solbert, R.	100-160	R*
Brooks, Noah	Boy Emigrants (1st, 4to, brown cl, 381p, teg, 10cp, pep, SC)	Scribner	1914	Dunn, H.T.	65-80	
Brooks, W.R.	Clockwork Twin (1st {std}, 8vo, 241p, 7 fp b/w, pep)	Knopf	1937	Wiese, K.	75-90	
Brooks, W.R.	Freddy & Men from Mars (1st {std}, 8vo, 246p, pep, b/w)	Knopf	1954	Wiese, K.	60-80	*
Brooks, W.R.	Freddy & Mr. Camphor (1st {std}, 8vo, 244p, green cl, b/w, pep)	Knopf	1944	Wiese, K.	50-70	
Brooks, W.R.	Freddy the Magician (1st {std}, 8vo, red cl, 258p, b/w)	Knopf	1947	Wiese, K.	50-70	
Brooks, W.R.	Freddy the Pied Piper (1st {std}, 8vo, 253p, b/w)	Knopf	1946	Wiese, K.	50-70	*
Brooks, W.R.	Freddy's Cousin Weedly (1st {std}, sm8vo, 283p, b/w, pep)	Knopf	1940	Wiese, K.	45-65	*
Brooks, W.R.	Story of Freginald (1st, 4to, 249p, pep, beige cl, 10 fp b/w)	Knopf	1936	Wiese, K.	50-70	*
Broughton, P.	Pandy (1st, 12mo, ibds, 40p, 5 fp color, pep)	Volland	(1930)	Barney, M.W.	40-65	*
Brown, A.F.	Book of Saints & Friendly Beasts (1st, 12mo, 225p, b/w)	Houghton	1900	Cory, F.	65-80	*
Brown, A.F.	Curious Book of Birds (1st, 8vo, gilt, 191p, 8pl)	Houghton	1903	Smith, E.B.	45-70	
Brown, A.F.	Fresh Posies (1st, sq8vo, p-o, 4cp)	Houghton	1908	Upjohn, A.M.	35-50	*
Brown, A.F.	In the Days of Giants (1st, 12mo, 259p, 6pl)	Houghton	1902	Smith, E.B.	80-100	
Brown, A.F.	John of the Woods (1st, sm8vo, 189p, 15pl)	Houghton	1909	Smith, E.B.	35-50	
Brown, A.F.	Kisington Town (1st, 8vo, p-o, 213p, 5pl)	Houghton	1915	Winckler, R.	25-40	*
Brown, A.F.	Lonesomest Doll (1st, sm8vo, ibds, 76p, 4pl)	Houghton	1901	Pollak, E.	30-50	*
Brown, A.F.	Lonesomest Doll (1st, 8vo, 81p, tan cl, 4pl)	Houghton	(1928)	Rackham, A.	200-260	
Brown, A.F.	Pocket Full of Posies (1st, 8vo, 169p, tan cl, 5pl)	Houghton	1902	Cory, F.	30-45	
Brown, A.F.	Star Jewels... (1st, 8vo, green/gilt, 133p, 5pl)	Houghton	1905	Brown, E.C.	20-30	*
Brown, A.F.	Tales of the Red Children (1st, sm8vo, 125p, tan cl, b/w)	Appleton	1909	Unknown	25-40	*
Brown, A.F.	Under the Rowan Tree (1st, 8vo, p-o, 189p, col frn, pep)	Houghton	1926	Day, M.	20-35	*
Brown, A.G.	Fireside Battles (1st, 8vo, teg, 327p, 8pl)	Laird & Lee	1900	Leyendecker, J.C.	65-80	*
Brown, Alice	Day of His Youth (1st, 12mo, green/gilt, 143p)	Houghton	1897	Rogers, B.	35-50	R
Brown, Alice	Meadow Grass (1st, 12mo, olive cl, 315p, cvr by...)	Copeland & Day	1895	Rhead, L.	65-90	
Brown, Alice	Merry Links (1st, ob4to, ipcb, p-o, [91]p, fp b/w)	McClure	1903	Clarke, L.	80-120	*
Brown, Alice	One-Footed Fairy (1st, 8vo, p-o, yellow cl, 182p, 12pl)	Houghton	1911	Various	50-80	*
Brown, Alice	Secret of the Clan (1st, 8vo, blue/gilt, 314p, 12pl)	MacMillan	1912	Smith, S.K.	25-40	
Brown, Alice	Story of Thyrza (1st, 8vo, gilt, 326p, col frn)	Houghton	1909	Stephens, A.B.	25-40	
Brown, Alice	Tiverton Tales (1st, 8vo, green/gilt, 339p, designs by..)	Houghton	1899	Rogers, B.	20-25	
Brown, Anna R.	Wine-Press (1st, 8vo, 390p, rust cl)	Appleton	1905	Armstrong, M.	30-45	*
Brown, C.	Bold Robin (1st, 8vo, gilt, 200p, uncut, teg, p-o, 7cp)	Dutton	(1905)	Bennett, F.I.	30-45	*
Brown, Dr. John	Jeems the Door Keeper (1st, 16mo, teg, uncut, 105p, 8 ticp)	L: Foulis	1912	MacGoun, H.C.P.	50-65	
Brown, Dr. John	Little Book of Children (12mo, 57p, ibds, teg, gilt, 8cp)	L: Foulis	1923	MacGoun, H.C.P.	30-45	*
Brown, E.P.	Ciderville Folks (1st, 4to, tan/gilt, 496p, b/w)	Date Pub. Co.	(1898)	Beard, F.	45-65	*
Brown, Gladys	Two-Bow Bill (1st, 8vo, 46p, blue cl, color, pep)	Wm. Morrow	1955	Barnum, J.H.	25-45	*
Brown, J.	Enchanted Peacock (1st, 4to, p-o, 4cp, 4pl)	Rand/McNally	(1911)	Perkins, L.F.	65-80	
Brown, J.	Mermaid's Gift (1st, 8vo, blue/gilt, p-o, 168p, 8cp)	Rand/McNally	(1912)	Enright, M.W.	90-130	
Brown, K.	Putter Perkins (1st, 12mo, green cl, 121p, 10pl)	Houghton	1923	Kemble, E.W.	30-50	*
Brown, K.H.	Hallowell Partnership (1st, 8vo, 241p, 4pl)	Scribner	1912	Peck, C.E.	20-30	*
Brown, M.	Surprising Advens. of Tuppy & Tue (1st, sm8vo, 190p, 4cp)	L: Cassell	1904	Rackham, A.	350-420	
Brown, M.W.	Baby Animals (1st, lg8vo, ipcb, [48]p, color, pep)	Random	(1941)	Cameron, M.	40-65	*
Brown, M.W.	Bad Little Duckhunter (1st, ob4to, ipcb, [30]p, color)	W.R. Scott	(1947)	Hurd, C.	65-80	
Brown, M.W.	Big Red Barn (1st, ob8vo, unpag)	W.R. Scott	1956	Hartman, R.	35-50	*
Brown, M.W.	Black and White (1st, 4to, ibds, [32]p, fp b/w)	Harper	1944	Shaw, C.G.	85-100	
Brown, M.W.	Bumble Bugs & Elephants (1st, sq4to, ibds, unpag, color)	W.R. Scott	1938	Hurd, C.	80-120	
Brown, M.W.	Child's Good Morning (1st, sq4to, ibds, unpag, color)	W.R. Scott	1952	Charlot, J.	70-100	
Brown, M.W.	Child's Good Night Book (1st, 12mo, [24]p, color, CH)	W.R. Scott	1943	Charlot, J.	70-110	*
Brown, M.W.	Children's Year (1st {std}, ob12mo, [26]p, ipcb, pep, color)	Harper	1937	Rojankovsky, F.	40-70	*
Brown, M.W.	Christmas in the Barn (1st, ob8vo, red cl, [32]p, color, pep)	Crowell	(1952)	Cooney, B.	60-90	*
Brown, M.W.	Country Noisy Book (1st, 8vo, [44]p, bds, color, pep)	W.R. Scott	(1940)	Weisgard, L.	65-90	
Brown, M.W.	Dark Wood o/t Golden Birds (1st, 8vo, ibds, unpag, 2-color, pep)	Harper	(1950)	Weisgard, L.	75-110	R*
Brown, M.W.	David's Little Indian (1st, 16mo, blue cl, [48]p, fp color)	W.R. Scott	(1956)	Charlip, R.	80-120	R*
Brown, M.W.	Dead Bird (1st, ob8vo, blue cl, [48]p, color)	W.R. Scott	(1958)	Charlip, R.	80-120	R*
Brown, M.W.	Diggers (1st, ob8vo, unpag, ibds, color)	Harper	(1960)	Hurd, C.	45-60	
Brown, M.W.	Don't Frighten the Lion (1st {std}, sq4to, [26]p, p-o, 1-col)	Harper	(1942)	Rey, H.A.	70-100	*
Brown, M.W.	Dream Book (1st, sm4to, [24]p, color)	Random	(1950)	Floethe, R.	45-60	*
Brown, M.W.	First Story (1st, 4to, [31]p, ibds, 1-color, pep)	Harper	(1947)	Simont, M.	50-85	
Brown, M.W.	Fish with a Deep Sea Smile (1st {std}, 8vo, 128p, color, cep)	Dutton	(1938)	Rauch, R.	45-65	
Brown, M.W.	Fox Eyes (1st, 8vo, unpag)	Pantheon	1951	Charlot, J.	60-90	*
Brown, M.W.	Golden Bunny (1st, folio, ibds, [25]p, color, pep, GGB)	Simon/Schuster	(1953)	Weisgard, L.	35-60	R*
Brown, M.W.	Golden Egg Book (1st, folio, ibds, [28]p, color, GGB)	Simon/Schuster	(1947)	Weisgard, L.	35-50	
Brown, M.W.	Goodnight Moon (1st, ob8vo, [31]p, color)	Harper	1947	Hurd, C.	70-100	

AUTHOR	TITLE	PUBLISHER	DATE	ARTIST	PRICE	LC
Brown, M.W.	Hidden House (1st {std}, sq8vo, ibds, unpag, color)	Holt	(1953)	Fine, A.	30-50	*
Brown, M.W.	Important Book (1st, 4to, [21]p, color)	Harper	1949	Weisgard, L.	70-100	*
Brown, M.W.	Indoor Noisy Book (1st, 8vo, ipcb, [44]p, color)	W.R. Scott	(1942)	Weisgard, L.	50-80	*
Brown, M.W.	Little Brass Band (1st, ob8vo, [25]p, ipcb, dep, color)	Harper	(1955)	Hurd, C.	50-70	*
Brown, M.W.	Little Chicken (1st {std}, ob8vo, cloth, [39]p, color)	Harper	(1943)	Weisgard, L.	30-50	
Brown, M.W.	Little Cowboy (1st, lg8vo, ipcb, [33]p, color, pep)	W.R. Scott	(1948)	Slobodkina, E.	50-80	*
Brown, M.W.	Little Farmer (1st, sm4to, [38]p, ipcb, color)	W.R. Scott	1948	Slobodkina, E.	50-80	*
Brown, M.W.	Little Fir Tree (1st, ob8vo, unpag, orange cl, color, dep)	Crowell	1954	Cooney, B.	50-75	*
Brown, M.W.	Little Fireman (1st, 8vo, ibds, [34]p, color, cep, p-o)	W.R. Scott	(1938)	Slobodkina, E.	60-80	*
Brown, M.W.	Little Fisherman (1st, lg8vo, ibds, [34]p, color)	W.R. Scott	1945	Ipcar, D.	60-85	*
Brown, M.W.	Little Frightened Tiger (1st {std}, ob4to, ibds, unpag, color)	Doubleday	1953	Weisgard, L.	50-70	
Brown, M.W.	Little Fur Family (1st {this format}, 8vo, [37]p, b/w)	Harper	1946	Williams, Garth	80-130	
Brown, M.W.	Little Pig's Picnic... (1st, 8vo, 102p, cloth, color, dep)	Heath	(1939)	Disney Studios	45-70	*
Brown, M.W.	Mister Dog (1st, sm8vo, unpag, ibds, color, LGB)	Simon/Schuster	(1952)	Williams, Garth	20-30	*
Brown, M.W.	My World (1st, ob8vo, [34]p, ibds, color, cep)	Harper	1949	Hurd, C.	50-80	
Brown, M.W.	Nibble Nibble (1st, 4to, [64]p, 1-color)	W.R. Scott	1959	Weisgard, L.	45-60	*
Brown, M.W.	Night and Day (1st {std}, 4to, cloth, [32]p, color)	Harper	(1942)	Weisgard, L.	65-90	
Brown, M.W.	Noisy Bird Book (1st, 8vo, ibds, [41]p, color)	W.R. Scott	1943	Weisgard, L.	50-80	*
Brown, M.W.	Noisy Book (1st, sq8vo, [42]p, ibds, color, pep)	W.R. Scott	(1939)	Weisgard, L.	60-80	
Brown, M.W.	Noon Balloon (1st, 4to, ibds, unpag, color, pep)	Harper	1952	Weisgard, L.	45-60	
Brown, M.W.	Peppermint Family (1st, ob8vo, [32]p, ipcb, fp 2-color, dep)	Harper	(1950)	Hurd, C.	60-90	*
Brown, M.W.	Polite Penguin (1st {std}, sm4to, green cl, 31p, 2-color, pep)	Harper	(1941)	Rey, H.A.	50-80	*
Brown, M.W.	Poodle & the Sheep (1st {std}, ob8vo, [55]p, ibds, 1-color, pep)	Dutton	1941	Weisgard, L.	45-70	
Brown, M.W.	Pussy Willow (1st, lg4to, [25]p, color, pep, GGB)	Simon/Schuster	1951	Weisgard, L.	35-55	
Brown, M.W.	Pussycat's Christmas (1st, sq8vo, yellow cl, [32]p, color, dep)	Crowell	1949	Stone, H.	50-70	*
Brown, M.W.	Quiet Noisy Book (1st, 4to, ipcb, [34]p, pep, color)	Harper	1950	Weisgard, L.	70-100	R*
Brown, M.W.	Runaway Bunny (1st {std}, ob8vo, [40]p, color, pep)	Harper	(1942)	Hurd, C.	70-100	R*
Brown, M.W.	SHHhhh... Bang! (1st {std}, sm4to, ipcb, [32]p, fp 2-col, cep)	Harper	(1943)	DeVeyrac, R.	65-100	*
Brown, M.W.	Seashore Noisy Book (1st, 8vo, ibds, [42]p, color, pep)	W.R. Scott	(1941)	Weisgard, L.	40-65	
Brown, M.W.	Sleepy ABC (1st, lg8vo, ibds, unpag, color, dep)	Lothrop/Lee	1953	Slobodkina, E.	50-80	*
Brown, M.W.	Sneakers (1st, sm8vo, 144p, blue cl, b/w)	W.R. Scott	(1955)	Charlot, J.	45-70	*
Brown, M.W.	Streamlined Pig (1st {std}, ob4to, [32]p, color, pep)	Harper	1938	Wiese, K.	50-80	
Brown, M.W.	Summer Noisy Book (1st, 4to, ibds, color)	Harper	1951	Weisgard, L.	80-120	
Brown, M.W.	Three Little Animals (1st, 4to, ibds, [30]p, color)	Harper	(1956)	Williams, Garth	80-130	R*
Brown, M.W.	Two Little Trains (1st, sm sq4to, ipcb, [32]p, pep, color)	W.R. Scott	1949	Charlot, J.	100-145	R*
Brown, M.W.	Wait Till the Moon is Full (1st, sm4to, ibds, [32]p, 1-color)	Harper	(1948)	Williams, Garth	65-100	*
Brown, M.W.	Wheel on the Chimney (1st, 4to, [28]p, tan cl, color, CH)	Lippincott	(1954)	Gergely, T.	70-120	R*
Brown, M.W.	When the Wind Blew (1st {std}-[1st Bk], lg8vo, unpag, ibds, col)	Harper	1937	Slocum, R.	80-130	*
Brown, M.W.	Where Have You Been? (1st, ob16mo, orang cl, [29]p, 1-col, dep)	Crowell	1952	Cooney, B.	70-100	R*
Brown, M.W.	Willie's Adventures (1st, sm8vo, grey cl, 68p, b/w)	W.R. Scott	(1954)	Johnson, C.	60-100	R*
Brown, M.W.	Willie's Walk to Grandmama (1st, sm8vo, ipcb, [26]p, color)	W.R. Scott	1944	Bloch, L.	45-60	
Brown, M.W.	Winter Noisy Book (1st, sm4to, [42]p, ipcb, pep, color)	W.R. Scott	1947	Shaw, C.G.	45-60	
Brown, M.W.	Wonderful Story (1st, 4to, ibds, 92p, color, pep, BGB)	Simon/Schuster	(1948)	Miller, J.P.	35-50	*
Brown, M.W.	Young Kangaroo (1st, 8vo, 42p, color)	W.R. Scott	(1955)	Shimin, S.	45-70	*
Brown, M.W. (ed.)	Fables of La Fontaine (1st {std}, 4to, ibds, 39p, color, pep)	Harper	(1940)	Helle, A.	60-80	
Brown, Marcia	Felice (1st, 4to, [32]p, color, pep)	Scribner	(1958)	Brown, Marcia	70-110	R*
Brown, Marcia	Henry Fisherman (1st, ob4to, [32]p, color, pep, CH)	Scribner	1949	Brown, Marcia	65-100	*
Brown, Marcia	Little Carousel (1st {1st Bk}, 4to, [32]p, ipcb, color)	Scribner	1946	Brown, Marcia	65-90	
Brown, Marcia	Peter Piper's Alphabet (1st, ob4to, ibds, [32]p, color, pep)	Scribner	(1959)	Brown, Marcia	75-125	*
Brown, Marcia	Skipper John's Cook (1st, 4to, unpag, blue cl, pep, CH)	Scribner	1951	Brown, Marcia	70-100	*
Brown, Marcia	Stone Soup (1st, 4to, [48]p, 2-color, pep, CH)	Scribner	1947	Brown, Marcia	70-115	*
Brown, Marcia	Tamarindo! (1st, 4to, tan cl, [32]p, color)	Scribner	(1960)	Brown, Marcia	45-60	*
Brown, Palmer	Beyond the Pawpaw Trees (1st {1st bk}, sm8vo, grey cl, 121p, b/w)	Harper	(1954)	Brown, Palmer	65-95	R*
Brown, Palmer	Cheerful (1st, 16mo, beige cl, 58p, color)	Harper	(1957)	Brown, Palmer	50-80	R*
Brown, Palmer	Silver Nutmeg (1st, sm8vo, green cl, 137p, b/w)	Harper	(1956)	Brown, Palmer	45-60	*
Brown, Palmer	Something for Christmas (1st, 12mo, white cl, 32p, color)	Harper	(1958)	Brown, Palmer	50-80	R*
Brown, Paul	Black & White (1st, ob4to, [62]p, b/w)	Scribner	1939	Brown, Paul	50-85	*
Brown, Paul	Circus School (1st, 4to, [64]p, color)	Scribner	1946	Brown, Paul	55-80	*
Brown, Paul	Crazy Quilt (1st, ob4to, ipcb, [120]p, fp b/w, pep)	Scribner	1934	Brown, Paul	65-90	*
Brown, Paul	Daffy Taffy (1st, 4to, [32]p, color, cep)	Scribner	1955	Brown, Paul	45-65	*
Brown, Paul	Draw Horses: It's Fun & Easy (1st, 8vo, 60p, b/w)	Scribner	1949	Brown, Paul	45-70	*
Brown, Paul	Fire! The Mascot (1st, 4to, red cl, [96]p, b/w, DJ)	Scribner	1939	Brown, Paul	50-85	
Brown, Paul	Hi Guy the Cinderella Horse (1st, 4to, [62]p, cloth, b/w)	Scribner	(1944)	Brown, Paul	45-60	*
Brown, Paul	Merrylegs (1st, sm8vo, [64]p, grey cl, 1-color, pep)	Scribner	1946	Brown, Paul	40-65	*
Brown, Paul	Mick & Mac (1st, 4to, ibds, [96]p, b/w, pep)	Scribner	1937	Brown, Paul	75-120	
Brown, Paul	No Trouble at All (1st, 8vo, 126p)	Scribner	1940	Brown, Paul	30-50	*
Brown, Paul	Piper's Pony (1st, ob4to, ipcb, [120]p, fp b/w, pep)	Scribner	1935	Brown, Paul	65-80	*
Brown, Paul	Polo (1st, lg8vo, 88p, b/w)	Scribner	1949	Brown, Paul	35-50	*
Brown, Paul	Pony Farm (1st, 8vo, [92]p, ibds, b/w, pep)	Scribner	(1948)	Brown, Paul	30-45	
Brown, Paul	Puff Ball (1st, 12mo, blue cl, [32]p, color, cep)	Scribner	1942	Brown, Paul	40-60	*
Brown, Paul	Sparkie & Puff Ball (1st, 4to, [32]p, red cl, color)	Scribner	1954	Brown, Paul	50-80	*
Brown, Paul	Three Rings: A Circus Book (1st, 4to, ibds, [76]p, color, pep)	Scribner	1938	Brown, Paul	50-85	

AUTHOR	TITLE	PUBLISHER	DATE	ARTIST	PRICE	LC
Brown, Paul	War Paint: An Indian Pony (1st, 4to, [96]p, b/w, DJ)	Scribner	1936	Brown, Paul	60-80	
Brown, V.	My Brother (1st, 12mo, 176p, beige cl, frn by...)	L: J. Lane	1896	Beardsley, A.	85-110	
Browne, E.G.	Magic Whistle (1st, lg8vo, 221p, color)	Dodd	1920	Anderson, F.	45-70	*
Browne, E.G.	Puck's Broom (1st AM, sm8vo, 237p, red/gilt, 4cp)	Moffat	1923	Nixon, K.I.	25-45	*
Browne, Edgar G.	Nutcracker & Mouse King (1st, lg8vo, pink bds, 92p, p-o, 4cp)	Dodd	1916	Anderson, F.	60-80	
Browne, Frances	Granny's Wonderful Chair (1st, 8vo, gilt, 213p, 8cp)	McClure	1904	Truman, Edith	30-50	
Browne, Frances	Granny's Wonderful Chair (24mo, gilt, 166p, AEG, 12cp)	L: H. Frowde	1908	Margetson, W.H.	85-140	
Browne, Frances	Granny's Wonderful Chair (1st, 4to, 211p, red/gilt, 6cp, pep)	Dutton	(1916)	Pyle, Kath.	80-100	
Browne, Frances	Granny's Wonderful Chair (1st, sm8vo, 184p, cp)	MacMillan	1924	Brock, Emma	25-40	*
Browne, Maggie	Book of Betty Barber (1st, 8vo, brown cl, teg, p-o, 129p, 6cp)	L: Duckworth	(1910)	Rackham, A.	280-400	*
Browne, Maggie	Book of Betty Barber (1st AM, sq8vo, teg, p-o, 130p, 6cp)	Badger	[1910]	Rackham, A.	300-400	
Browne, Maggie	Wanted - A King (1st, 12mo, 193p, green/gilt, teg, pep)	L: Cassell	1890	Furniss, H.	120-180	*
Browne, P.E.	Peace at any Price (1st, 8vo, brown pcb, 70p, p-o, 6pl)	Appleton	1916	Newell, P.	70-100	*
Browne, P.E.	Scars & Stripes (1st, 8vo, gilt, 208p, frn by..)	Doran	(1917)	Newell, P.	25-45	*
Brownell, Eliz.	Really Babies (1st, 4to, p-o, gilt, 63p)	Rand/McNally	(1908)	(Photos)	90-140	*
Browning, E.B.	Rhyme of the Duchess May (1st, 12mo, p-o, wraps, uncut, 5cp)	L: Foulis	[1907]	Cameron, K.	60-80	
Browning, E.B.	Sonnetts from the Portuguese (1st, 12mo, AEG, gilt, [98]p, col)	Putman	(1902)	Armstrong, M.	50-75	
Browning, E.B.	Sonnetts from the Portuguese (1st, 8vo, 96p, 8 ticp)	Crowell	(1936)	Pogany, W.	50-65	
Browning, R.	Dramatis Personae... (1st, sm4to, teg, green/gilt, 10cp)	L: Chatto	1909	Brickdale, E.F.	65-80	
Browning, R.	Last Ride Together (1st, 8vo, AEG, unpag)	Putnam	1906	Armstrong, M.	50-85	
Browning, R.	Men and Women (1st, sm8vo, green/gilt, teg, 312p, 15pl)	L: Dent	1903	Ospovat, H.	60-80	
Browning, R.	Pied Piper of Hamelin (1st, 4to, orang ibds, 64p, ae blue, col)	L: Routledge	[1888]	Greenaway, K.	170-225	
Browning, R.	Pied Piper of Hamelin (1st, 8vo, 64p, uncut, 12pl)	L: Heinemann	1893	Thomson, H.	80-120	
Browning, R.	Pied Piper of Hamelin (1st, folio, red/gilt, unpag, b/w)	L: Quilter	1898	Quilter, H.	130-165	
Browning, R.	Pied Piper of Hamelin (1st, sm4to, p-o, gilt, 56p, pep, color)	Rand/McNally	(1910)	Dunlap, H.	70-100	
Browning, R.	Pied Piper of Hamelin (1st, 8vo, green/gilt, teg, 8cp)	L: J.M. Dent	1912	Tarrant, M.	50-80	
Browning, R.	Pied Piper of Hamelin (1st, sm4to, p-o, [64]p, color, pep)	Whitman	1927	McCracken, J.	45-70	
Browning, R.	Pied Piper of Hamelin (1st AM, 8vo, 45p, p-o, 4cp, pep, DJ)	Lippincott	[1934]	Rackham, A.	140-185	
Browning, R.	Pied Piper of Hamelin (1st, 8vo, wraps, 4cp, pep, DJ)	L: Harrap	(1934)	Rackham, A.	230-285	
Browning, R.	Pied Piper of Hamelin (1st, folio, ibds, unpag, color, pep)	Grosset/Dunlap	(1936)	Duvoisin, R.	70-110	*
Browning, R.	Pippa Passes (1st, 8vo, green cl, 72p, 7pl)	L: Duckworth	1898	Brooke, L.L.	65-80	
Browning, R.	Pippa Passes (1st, 8vo, teg, uncut, green/gilt, unpag)	Dodd	1900	Armstrong, M.	65-80	
Browning, R.	Pippa Passes (1st, 8vo, 254p, gilt, teg, uncut, 10cp)	L: Chatto	1908	Brickdale, E.F.	70-90	
Browning, R.	Pippa Passes (1st AM, 8vo, 254p, grey/gilt, 10cp)	Lippincott	1909	Brickdale, E.F.	60-80	
Browning, R.	Rabbi Ben Ezra (1st, 16mo, 16p, pcb, p-o)	(Concord)	(1902)	Bradley, W.	65-80	
Browning, R.	Rabbi Ben Ezra... (1st, 4to, 84p, 12 ticp)	L: Hodder	(1915)	Partridge, B.	80-100	
Bruce, J.	School Days (1st, 4to, 165p, ipcb, 11cp, pep)	Brentano's	1907	Bruce, J.	60-90	
Bruce, M.	Kris & Kristina (1st {std}, 8vo, ibds, 60p, color, pep)	Doubleday/Dor.	(1927)	Daugherty, J.	30-45	
Brummitt, S.W.	Brother Van (1st, sm8vo, 171p, pict cl, 2 illus by...)	(NY)	(1919)	Russell, C.M.	40-65	*
Brunefille, G.	Topo... (1st, 12mo, AEG, 140p, green/gilt)	L: Marcus Ward	1878	Greenaway, K.	200-250	
Bryant, B.M.	Yammy Buys a Bicycle (1st, 8vo, 168p, pep, 5cp)	Whitman	1940	Woodward, H.	30-45	*
Bryant, S.C.	Best Stories to Tell Children (1st, blue/gilt, 181p, 16cp)	Houghton	1912	Beard, P.	40-60	
Bryant, S.C.	Brother Rabbit (12mo, p-o, 59p, 4cp, later)	L: Harrap	1926	Appleton, H.C.	55-80	
Bryant, S.C.	Epaminondas & his Auntie (1st, sq8vo, 16p, color, pep)	Houghton	1938	Hogan, I.	50-80	R
Bryant, S.C.	Stories to Tell the Littlest Ones (1st, 12mo, 178p, 6cp)	L: Harrap	1918	Pogany, W.	80-130	
Bryson, C.L.	Tan & Teckle (1st, 8vo, grey cl, 238p, 8pl)	Revell	(1908)	Bull, C.L.	30-45	
Buchan, J.	Lake of Gold (1st AM, 8vo, 189p, green cl, b/w, pep, DJ)	Houghton	1941	Levenson, S.	40-60	
Buchan, J.	Magic Walking Stick (1st, 8vo, red/gilt, 176p, b/w, pep)	Houghton	1932	Becher, A.E.	35-50	
Buchanan, G.	Jeptha (1st {1st illus bk.}, 8vo, blue/gilt, 130p, 5pl)	L: A. Gardner	[1903]	King, J.	220-350	
Buchanan, T.	Castle Comedy (1st, 8vo, lavender cl, teg, 235p, 4cp, pep)	Harper	1904	Green, E.S.	40-60	
Buck, Pearl S.	Johnny Jack & his Beginnings (1st, 8vo, 47p, green cl, 1-color)	NY: J. Day	(1954)	Werth, K.	40-65	*
Buck, Pearl S.	Stories for Little Children (1st, ob8vo, [48]p, 10 fp 2-color)	NY: J. Day	(1940)	Yap, W.	70-100	R*
Buck, Pearl S.	Water-Buffalo Children (1st, 8vo, ipcb, 59p)	NY: J. Day	(1943)	Smith, Wm. A.	45-70	*
Buckland, J.	Two Little Runaways (1st, 8vo, 358p, tan/gilt, b/w)	L: Longmans	1898	Aldin, C.	140-185	
Buckley, E.F.	Children of the Dawn (1st, 8vo, 348p, gilt, 24pl)	L: Wells/Gard.	1908	Pape, F.	70-120	
Buckley, E.F.	Children of the Dawn (1st AM, 8vo, 348p)	Stokes	(1909)	Pape, F.	45-65	*
Buff, M. & C.	Apple and the Arrow (1st, sm4to, 75p, gilt, color, pep, NH)	Houghton	1951	Buff, M.& C.	45-65	
Buff, M. & C.	Elf Owl (1st, 4to, 72p, 1-color, pep)	Viking	(1958)	Buff, M.& C.	65-90	R*
Buff, M. & C.	Hah-Nee of the Cliff Dwellers (1st, 4to, 68p, color)	Houghton	1956	Buff, M.& C.	60-90	R
Buff, M. & C.	Hurry, Scurry & Flurry (1st, 4to, 73p, pep, 1-color)	Viking	1954	Buff, M.& C.	65-80	R*
Buff, M. & C.	Kobi, a Boy of Switzerland (1st, lg8vo, 128p, dp col, dep)	Viking	1939	Buff, C.	30-50	*
Buff, Mary	Big Tree (1st, 4to, 79p, grey cl, 1-color, DJ, NH)	Viking	1946	Buff, M.& C.	50-80	
Buff, Mary	Dancing Cloud (1st, ob4to, ipcb, 80p, fp color, cep)	Viking	1937	Buff, C.	65-90	*
Buff, Mary	Dash and Dart (1st, 4to, 73p, 4 dp cp, dep, CH)	Viking	1942	Buff, M.& C.	60-100	*
Buff, Mary	Magic Maize (1st, 4to, 76p, pep, 9 fp color, NH)	Houghton	1953	Buff, M.& C.	50-80	*
Buffano, R.	Magic Strings... (1st, 8vo, 182p, 11 b/w)	MacMillan	1939	Artzybasheff, B.	35-50	*
Bulfinch, T.	Book of Myths (1st, lg8vo, 126p, color, DJ)	MacMillan	1942	Sewell, H.	50-75	
Bulfinch, T.	Legends of Charlemagne (1st, 4to, teg, p-o, 273p, 8cp, pep)	Cosmopolitan	1924	Wyeth, N.C.	180-220	
Bull, C.L.	Under the Roof of the Jungle (1st, 8vo, green cl, 271p, 4cp)	Page	1911	Bull, C.L.	30-45	*
Bulla, Clyde R.	Donkey Cart (1st, 8vo, yellow cl, 89p, b/w, pep)	Crowell	(1946)	Lenski, L.	35-50	*
Bulla, Clyde R.	Ghost Town Treasure (1st, 8vo, yellow cl, 86p, b/w, pep)	Crowell	(1957)	Freeman, D.	25-45	*
Bulla, Clyde R.	Old Charlie (1st, sm8vo, 80p, b/w)	Crowell	1957	Galdone, P.	25-40	*

AUTHOR	TITLE	PUBLISHER	DATE	ARTIST	PRICE	LC
Bulla, Clyde R.	Poppy Seeds (1st, 8vo, unpag)	Crowell	(1955)	Charlot, J.	40-70	*
Bulla, Clyde R.	Songs of Mr. Small (1st, 4to, 40p, color, DJ)	NY: OUP	1954	Lenski, L.	40-60	
Bulla, Clyde R.	Sword in the Tree (1st {std}, 8vo, 113p, red cl, b/w)	Crowell	1956	Galdone, P.	25-45	*
Bulla, Clyde R.	Valentine Cat (1st, 4to, unpag, pink cl, 2-color)	Crowell	(1959)	Weisgard, L.	30-45	*
Bulla, Clyde R.	We Are thy Children (1st {std}, ob4to, [32]p)	Crowell	1952	Lenski, L.	65-80	*
Bullard, Marion	Somersaulting Rabbit (1st, ob4to, 45p, ibds, 12pl)	Dutton	(1927)	Bullard, M.	85-130	*
Bullen, F.T.	Cruise of the Cachalot (1st, lg8vo, 301p, 8cp, pep)	Dodd	1926	Schaeffer, M.	30-50	
Bunner, H.C.	Jersey Street & Jersey Lane (1st, 8vo, blue/gilt, teg, 201p)	Scribner	1896	Armstrong, M.	35-50	R
Bunner, H.C.	Love in Old Cloathes (1st, 8vo, teg, uncut, 217p)	Scribner	1896	Armstrong, M.	30-45	
Bunner, H.C.	Three Operettas (1st, ob4to, 163p)	Harper	1897	Weldon/Taylor	100-165	*
Buntain, R.J.	Birthday Story (1st, sm8vo, unpag)	Holiday House	(1953)	Wilkin, E.	20-30	*
Bunyan, J.	Life & Death of Mr. Badman (1st UK, folio, 143p, teg, 12pl)	L: Heinemann	1900	Rhead Bros.	100-150	
Bunyan, J.	Life & Death of Mr. Badman (1st, folio, ibds, teg, 12pl)	R.H. Russell	1900	Rhead Bros.	120-160	
Bunyan, J.	Pilgrim's Progress (1st, 4to, teg, uncut, black/gilt)	L: Nimmo	1895	Strang, W.	80-100	
Bunyan, J.	Pilgrim's Progress (1st, 8vo, 284p, red cl, 24pl)	L: Bliss Sands	1897	Robinson, W.H.	125-165	*
Bunyan, J.	Pilgrim's Progress (1st, folio, 184p, ibds, b/w)	Century	1898	Rhead Bros.	100-150	
Bunyan, J.	Pilgrim's Progress (1st UK, folio, gilt, 201p)	L: A. Pearson	[1898]	Rhead Bros.	120-160	
Bunyan, J.	Pilgrim's Progress (1st, lg8vo, 315p, green/gilt, 12cp)	L: J.M. Dent	1910	Pape, F.	90-140	
Bunyan, J.	Pilgrim's Progress (sm4to, gilt, 393p, teg, 29cp)	L: Jack	[1910]	Shaw, B.	45-60	
Burdette, R.J.	Smiles Yoked with Sighs (1st, 8vo, 180p, green/gilt)	Bowen-Merrill	(1901)	Vawter, J.W.	20-30	
Burgess, G.	Blue Goops & Red (1st, sm4to, green cl, 81p, b/w, pep)	Stokes	(1909)	Burgess, G.	160-220	
Burgess, G.	Burgess Nonsense Book (1st, 8vo, teg, 239p, gilt)	Stokes	(1901)	Burgess, G.	150-200	
Burgess, G.	Cat's Elegy (1st, 12mo, tan ipcb, [43]p, 1-color)	McClurg	1913	Burgess, G.	70-120	R*
Burgess, G.	Goop Directory/Juvenile Offenders (1st, 12mo, 79p, ibds)	Stokes	(1913)	Burgess, G.	80-120	
Burgess, G.	Goop Tales Alphabetically Told (1st, sq4to, 106p, b/w)	Stokes	(1904)	Burgess, G.	120-160	
Burgess, G.	Goops & How to be Them (1st UK, 8vo, unpag, b/w)	L: Methuen	1900	Burgess, G.	180-250	
Burgess, G.	Goops & How to be Them (1st, sq4to, [96]p, ibds, PPP)	Stokes	(1900)	Burgess, G.	200-300	
Burgess, G.	Heart Line (1st, sm8vo, 584p, p-o, b/w)	Bobbs-Merrill	(1907)	Ralph, L.	35-50	
Burgess, G.	Lady Mechante (1st, 8vo, 393p, lavender cl, 8pl)	Stokes	(1909)	Burgess, G.	40-60	
Burgess, G.	Lively City O'Ligg (1st, sm4to, 219p, ibds, 8cp)	Stokes	(1899)	Burgess, G.	120-150	
Burgess, G.	Maxims of Methuselah (1st, 12mo, ibds, 108p)	Stokes	(1907)	Fancher, L.	25-40	
Burgess, G.	Why Be a Goop? (1st, sq8vo, p-o, red cl, 159p)	Stokes	1924	Burgess, G.	100-140	
Burgess, T.	Advens. of Uncle Billy Possum (1st, 12mo, 117p, grey cl, 6pl)	Little/Brown	1914	Cady, H.	60-80	
Burgess, T.	Adventures of Bobby Coon (1st, 16mo, 117p, 6pl)	Little/Brown	1918	Cady, H.	50-70	
Burgess, T.	Adventures of Buster Bear (1st, sm8vo, tan cl, 6pl)	Little/Brown	1916	Cady, H.	45-60	
Burgess, T.	Adventures of Chatterer the Red Squirrel (1st, 16mo, 120p)	Little/Brown	1915	Cady, H.	60-85	
Burgess, T.	Adventures of Grandfather Frog (1st, 12mo, 120p, 6pl)	Little/Brown	1915	Cady, H.	50-70	
Burgess, T.	Adventures of Jerry Muskrat (1st, 12mo, 120p, 6pl)	Little/Brown	1914	Cady, H.	65-90	
Burgess, T.	Adventures of Jimmy Skunk (1st, 12mo, 118p, grey cl, 6pl)	Little/Brown	1918	Cady, H.	50-70	
Burgess, T.	Adventures of Johnny Chuck (1st, 12mo, 120p, 6pl)	Little/Brown	1913	Cady, H.	60-75	
Burgess, T.	Adventures of Mr. Mocker (1st, 8vo, cloth, 120p, 6pl)	Little/Brown	1914	Cady, H.	70-90	
Burgess, T.	Adventures of Ol' Mistah Buzzard (1st, 12mo, 119p)	Little/Brown	1919	Cady, H.	60-85	
Burgess, T.	Adventures of Old Mr. Toad (1st, 12mo, 120p, 6pl)	Little/Brown	1916	Cady, H.	65-80	
Burgess, T.	Adventures of Peter Cottontail (1st, 12mo, 120p, 6pl)	Little/Brown	1914	Cady, H.	65-80	*
Burgess, T.	Adventures of Poor Mrs. Quack (1st, 12mo, 119p, cloth, 6pl)	Little/Brown	1917	Cady, H.	60-75	
Burgess, T.	Adventures of Prickly Porky (1st, 12mo, grey cl, 116p, 6pl)	Little/Brown	1916	Cady, H.	65-80	
Burgess, T.	Adventures of Reddy Fox (1st, 16mo, grey cl, 120p, 6pl)	Little/Brown	1913	Cady, H.	65-80	
Burgess, T.	Adventures of Sammy Jay (1st, 12mo, 119p, 6pl)	Little/Brown	1915	Cady, H.	65-80	
Burgess, T.	At the Smiling Pool (1st {std}, sq8vo, 185p, red cl, DJ)	Little/Brown	1945	Cady, H.	70-90	
Burgess, T.	Billy Mink (1st, 8vo, p-o, 196p, 8cp)	Little/Brown	1924	Cady, H.	70-100	
Burgess, T.	Blacky the Crow (1st, sm8vo, 206p, p-o, 8cp)	Little/Brown	1922	Cady, H.	70-100	
Burgess, T.	Bowser the Hound (1st, 8vo, p-o, 206p, 8cp)	Little/Brown	1920	Cady, H.	65-90	
Burgess, T.	Boy Scouts in a Trappers' Camp (1st, sm8vo, 362p, 5pl)	Penn	1915	Anderson, F.A.	60-80	*
Burgess, T.	Boy Scouts in a Woodcraft Camp (1st, sm8vo, p-o, 345p, 5pl)	Penn	1912	Corson, C.S.	65-90	*
Burgess, T.	Bride's Primer (1st, lg4to, ipcb, [62]p, 24 fp color)	NY: Phelps	(1905)	Strothmann, F.	250-450	R*
Burgess, T.	Burgess Animal Book for Children (1st, 8vo, green cl, p-o, cp)	Little/Brown	1920	Fuertes, L.A.	65-90	
Burgess, T.	Burgess Animal Paint Book (ob folio, [24]p, wraps, 7 fp color)	Saalfield	1925	Cady, H.	85-125	
Burgess, T.	Burgess Animal Stories (1st, sq8vo, cloth, color)	Platt/Munk	(1942)	Cady, H.	45-60	
Burgess, T.	Burgess Bird Book for Children (1st, 8vo, p-o, 351p, 32cp)	Little/Brown	1919	Fuertes, L.A.	60-85	
Burgess, T.	Buster Bear's Twins (1st, 8vo, p-o, 207p, 8cp)	Little/Brown	1923	Cady, H.	60-80	
Burgess, T.	Christmas Reindeer (1st, 12mo, 139p, red/gilt, 7pl, pep)	MacMillan	1926	Chase, R.	35-50	
Burgess, T.	Cubby Finds an Open Door (ob24mo, ibds, [24]p, color)	Whitman	1929	Jordan, N.	35-50	
Burgess, T.	Farmer Brown's Boy Becomes Curious (ob24mo, ibds, 24p, color)	Whitman	1929	Jordan, N.	35-50	
Burgess, T.	Grandfather Frog Gets a Ride (1st, 12mo, ibds, 29p, color)	Stoll/Edwards	(1928)	Cady, H.	65-80	
Burgess, T.	Great Joke on Jimmy Skunk (1st, 12mo, ibds, 29p, color)	Stoll/Edwards	(1928)	Cady, H.	65-80	
Burgess, T.	Happy Jack (1st, 8vo, 204p, p-o, 8cp)	Little/Brown	1918	Cady, H.	50-75	
Burgess, T.	Jerry Muskrat Wins Respect (4to, wraps, color)	NY: J. Eggers	(1928)	Cady, H.	60-80	
Burgess, T.	Jerry Muskrat at Home (1st, 8vo, 206p, p-o, 8cp)	Little/Brown	1926	Cady, H.	50-80	*
Burgess, T.	Lightfoot the Deer (1st, 8vo, p-o, blue cl, 205p, 8cp)	Little/Brown	1921	Cady, H.	60-75	
Burgess, T.	Little Joe Otter (1st, 8vo, olive cl, p-o, 198p, 8cp)	Little/Brown	1925	Cady, H.	70-90	
Burgess, T.	Longlegs the Heron (1st, 8vo, olive cl, p-o, 207p, 8cp)	Little/Brown	1927	Cady, H.	65-90	
Burgess, T.	Mother West Wind Why Stories (1st, 12mo, 230p, 8pl)	Little/Brown	1915	Cady, H.	65-90	*

AUTHOR	TITLE	PUBLISHER	DATE	ARTIST	PRICE	LC
Burgess, T.	Mother West Wind's Animal Friends (1st, 12mo, 221p, 6pl)	Little/Brown	1912	Kerr, G.F.	100-135	
Burgess, T.	Mother West Wind's Children (1st, 12mo, 243p, 7pl)	Little/Brown	1911	Kerr, G.	70-110	*
Burgess, T.	Mother West Wind's Neighbors (1st, 12mo, tan cl, 223p, 6pl)	Little/Brown	1913	Kerr, G.	70-110	
Burgess, T.	Mrs. Peter Rabbit (1st, 8vo, 205p, p-o, 8cp)	Little/Brown	1919	Cady, H.	70-85	
Burgess, T.	Neatness of Bobby Coon (1st, 12mo, ibds, 29p, color)	Stoll/Edwards	(1927)	Cady, H.	65-80	
Burgess, T.	Old Granny Fox (1st, 8vo, p-o, green cl, 202p, 8cp)	Little/Brown	1920	Cady, H.	65-80	
Burgess, T.	Old Mother West Wind (1st, 12mo, 169p, 7pl, PPP)	Little/Brown	(1910)	Kerr, G.F.	150-200	
Burgess, T.	On the Green Meadows (1st {std}, 8vo, 182p, red cl, color)	Little/Brown	1944	Cady, H.	40-65	
Burgess, T.	Tales from Storyteller's House (1st {std}, sq8vo, 195p, 8cp)	Little/Brown	1937	Palmer, L.	60-75	
Burgess, T.	Tommy & the Wishing Stone (1st, 12mo, 290p, gilt, b/w pl)	Century	1915	Cady, H.	85-120	*
Burgess, T.	While the Story Log Burns (1st {std}, 8vo, 195p, 8cp, DJ)	Little/Brown	1938	Palmer, L.	60-90	
Burgess, T.	Whitefoot the Wood Mouse (1st, sm8vo, p-o, blue cl, 181p, 8cp)	Little/Brown	1922	Cady, H.	75-100	
Burglon, N.	Children of the Soil (1st {std}, 8vo, 272p, pep, col frn, NH)	Doubleday/Dor.	1932	D'Aulaire, E.P.	65-80	*
Burglon, N.	Cuckoo Calls (1st, 8vo, 280p, col frn, pep)	Winston	(1940)	D'Aulaire, I.& E.	25-40	*
Burglon, N.	Deep Silver (1st, 8vo, 215p, blue cl, 12pl)	Houghton	1938	Hurd, P.	50-75	*
Burglon, N.	Gate Swings In (1st {std}, 8vo, 208p, pep, b/w)	Little/Brown	1937	Floethe, R.	30-45	*
Burglon, N.	Ghost Ship (1st, sm8vo, 275p, blue cl, 8pl, pep)	Little/Brown	1936	Nelson, A.R.	20-30	*
Burglon, N.	Shark Hole (1st, sm8vo, 244p, fp b/w)	Holiday House	(1943)	Baldridge, C.L.	20-25	*
Burglon, N.	Sticks Across the Chimney (1st, sm8vo, 256p)	Holiday House	(1938)	Eichenberg, F.	30-50	*
Burke, Thos. (ed.)	Children in Verse (1st, lg8vo, 135p, blue cl, 8cp)	L: Duckworth	1913	Appleton, H.C.	65-80	*
Burke, Thos. (ed.)	Children in Verse (1st AM, 8vo, 135p, teg, 8 ticp)	(Boston)	1914	Appleton, H.C.	50-70	
Burlingame, E.W.	Grateful Elephant (1st, 4to, 172p, col frn, 10pl)	Yale U. Press	1923	Lathrop, D.	85-120	
Burn, J.H.	Mother's Book of Song (1st, 8vo, 216p, blue/gilt, teg, b/w)	L: Wells/Gard.	[1902]	Robinson, C.	130-180	
Burnand (ed.)	Incompleat Angler (1st, 8vo, 94p, b/w)	L: Bradbury	1887	Furniss, H.	80-130	
Burne-Jones, E.	Beginning of the World (lg4to, ibds, 25 illus)	L: Longmans	1902	Burne-Jones, E.	100-150	
Burnett, F.H.	Cozy Lion (1st, 12mo, 104p, blue cl, 20cp)	Century	1907	Cady, H.	60-85	
Burnett, F.H.	Dawn of To-Morrow (1st, 12mo, brown/gilt, 156p, 8cp)	Scribner	1906	Yohn, F.C.	25-40	
Burnett, F.H.	Editha's Burglar (1st [2], 12mo, blue/gilt, 64p, 13pl)	J. Marsh	1888	Sandham, H.	50-70	
Burnett, F.H.	Giovanni & the Other (1st, lg8vo, 193p, olive/gilt, 9pl, cep)	Scribner	1892	Birch, R.	65-80	
Burnett, F.H.	Good Wolf (1st, 8vo, 125p, 5cp)	Moffat	1908	Sichel, H.	30-45	
Burnett, F.H.	In the Closed Room (1st, 8vo, green/gilt, teg, 130p, 8cp, dep)	McClurg	1904	Smith, J.W.	70-100	
Burnett, F.H.	Lady of Quality (1st, sm8vo, 363p, buckram/gilt, b/w)	Scribner	1896	Armstrong, M.	35-50	*
Burnett, F.H.	Land of the Blue Flower (1st, 8vo, gilt, 67p, teg)	Moffat	1909	Ivanowski, S.	35-50	
Burnett, F.H.	Little Hunchback Zia (1st, 12mo, p-o, 55p, 5pl, pep)	Stokes	(1916)	Benda, W.T.	30-50	
Burnett, F.H.	Little Lord Fauntleroy (1st [1], 8vo, 209p, gilt, 26 b/w, PPP)	Scribner	1886	Birch, R.	140-200	
Burnett, F.H.	Little Lord Fauntleroy (1st [new ed.], 4to, teg, p-o, 12cp, SC)	Scribner	1911	Birch, R.	80-120	
Burnett, F.H.	Little Princess (1st, sm4to, blue/gilt, teg, p-o, 12cp, SC)	Scribner	1905	Betts, E.F.	100-150	
Burnett, F.H.	Little Princess (1st UK, 8vo, 302p, p-o, 8cp)	L: Warne	(1905)	Piffard, H.	80-125	
Burnett, F.H.	Little St. Elizabeth (1st AM, sm4to, 146p, 12 b/w)	Scribner	1890	Birch, R.	45-65	
Burnett, F.H.	Lost Prince (1st, 8vo, 415p, blue/gilt, 16pl)	Century	1915	Bower, M.L.	25-40	*
Burnett, F.H.	My Robin (1st, 16mo, green/gilt, 42p, col frn)	Stokes	(1912)	Brennan, A.	30-45	
Burnett, F.H.	One I Knew Best of All (1st, 12mo, 325p, gilt, teg, b/w)	Scribner	1893	Birch, R.	70-85	
Burnett, F.H.	Piccino... (1st, sq8vo, olive/gilt, 203p, 15pl)	Scribner	1894	Birch, R.	65-80	
Burnett, F.H.	Pretty Sister of Jose (1st [1], 12mo, 127p, gilt, 12pl)	Scribner	1889	Reinhart, C.S.	80-120	
Burnett, F.H.	Queen Silver-Bell (1st, 16mo, p-o, 132p, 20cp)	Century	1906	Cady, H.	125-165	
Burnett, F.H.	Racketty-Packetty House (1st, 12mo, 130p, p-o, 24cp)	Century	1906	Cady, H.	100-145	
Burnett, F.H.	Sara Crew... (1st [1], 8vo, 83p, gilt, 6pl)	Scribner	1888	Birch, R.	100-150	
Burnett, F.H.	Secret Garden (1st, 8vo, p-o, teg, 375p, gilt, 4cp)	Stokes	(1911)	Kirk, M.L.	300-500	
Burnett, F.H.	Secret Garden (1st, 8vo, green/gilt, 306p, 8cp, pep)	L: Heinemann	1911	Robinson, C.	400-600	
Burnett, F.H.	Spring Cleaning (1st, 12mo, p-o, 100p, 20cp)	Century	1908	Cady, H.	100-150	
Burnett, F.H.	Two Little Pilgrim's Progress (1st, sq8vo, 191p, gilt, 12pl)	Scribner	1895	Birch, R.	65-80	R
Burnett, F.H.	Way to the House of Santa Claus (1st, ob lg4to, p-o, [25]p, col)	Harper	1916	Unknown	80-120	*
Burnett, F.H.	White People (1st, 12mo, 112p, grey/gilt, 4pl)	Harper	(1917)	Green, E.S.	30-45	
Burney, Fanny	Evelina... (3rd ed., sm8vo, teg, 2 vols, uncut, gilt)	L: J.M. Dent	1893	Beardsley, A.	280-400	
Burney, Fanny	Evelina... (1st, sm8vo, teg, blue cl, 16 b/w, 416p)	L: Newnes	1898	Rackham, A.	175-230	
Burney, Fanny	Evelina... (1st, 8vo, 477p, gilt, b/w)	L: MacMillan	(1903)	Thomson, H.	50-75	
Burnham, C.L.	Clever Betsy (1st, 8vo, red/gilt, 402p, 3pl)	Houghton	1910	O'Neill, R.	25-45	
Burnham, C.L.	Jewel's Story Book (1st, 12mo, 343p, green cl, 6pl, pep)	Houghton	1904	Schmitt, A.	20-25	
Burnham, C.L.	Quest Flower (1st, 8vo, red/gilt, 4cp)	Houghton	1908	Upjohn, A.M.	45-60	
Burns, Rbt.	Cotter's Saturday Night (1st, 12mo, ibds, 17p, frn by..)	L: Hewetson	(1908)	Rackham, A.	120-165	
Burns, Rbt.	Songs & Lyrics of... (1st, 8vo, uncut, teg, 12cp)	L: P.L. Warner	1911	Flint, W.R.	75-100	
Burroughs, E.R.	Tarzan Twins (1st, 8vo, 126p, ibds, 14 fp color)	Volland	(1927)	Grant, Doug	150-220	*
Burroughs, Marg.	Jasper the Drummin' Boy (1st, lg8vo, 63p, fp b/w)	Viking	1947	Lewin, T.	70-95	*
Burrows, Eliz.	Irene of Tundra Towers (1st {std}, sm8vo, 311p, col frn)	Doubleday/Dor.	1928	Daugherty, J.	30-45	*
Burt, Mary E.	Odysseus, Hero of Ithaca (1st, 12mo, 223p, red cl, cvr by...)	Scribner	1898	Armstrong, M.	30-45	*
Burton, Earl	Exciting Adventures of Waldo (1st, sm4to, 64p, grey cl, fp col)	Whittlesey	(1945)	Stone, H.	45-60	*
Burton, Earl & L.	Taffy & Joe (1st, sm4to, green cl, 60p, dp col frn, b/w)	Whittlesey	1947	Stone, H.	40-60	*
Burton, J.B.	Across the Salt Seas (1st, 12mo, teg, 446p, cvr by...)	H. Stone	1897	Hazenplug, F.	45-70	
Burton, R.	Kasidah of Haji Abdu El-Yezdi (1st, lg4to, p-o, 129p, 12pl)	McKay	(1931)	Pogany, W.	65-100	
Burton, V.L.	Calico the Wonder Horse (1st, narrow ob8vo, color, [58]p, DJ)	Houghton	1941	Burton, V.L.	45-65	
Burton, V.L.	Choo-Choo (1st, lg4to, red cl, [48]p, b/w, pep)	Houghton	(1937)	Burton, V.L.	80-120	R*
Burton, V.L.	Katy & the Big Snow (1st, ob4to, 32p, blue cl, color, pep, DJ)	Houghton	1943	Burton, V.L.	100-130	

AUTHOR	TITLE	PUBLISHER	DATE	ARTIST	PRICE	LC
Burton, V.L.	Little House (1st, ob4to, 40p, green cl, color, pep, DJ, CM)	Houghton	1942	Burton, V.L.	85-130	R
Burton, V.L.	Maybelle the Cable Car (1st, sq lg8vo, 42p, pep, color)	Houghton	1952	Burton, V.L.	65-100	R
Burton, V.L.	Mike Mulligan & his Steam Shovel (1st, sq8vo, [48]p, color, pep)	Houghton	1939	Burton, V.L.	70-120	R
Butler, Chas.	Pigs is Pigs (1st, 12mo, 37p, 5pl)	McClure	1906	Crawford, W.	25-40	
Butler, E.C.	Little Mexican Cousin (1st, 8vo, 100p, 10pl)	Page	1905	(Photos)	25-45	*
Butler, E.P.	Confessions of a Daddy (1st, 8vo, red cl, 107p, 9 b/w)	Century	1907	Cory, F.	40-65	*
Butler, E.P.	Incubator Baby (1st, 12mo, 111p, 4cp)	Funk/Wagnalls	1906	Preston, M.W.	20-30	
Butt, G.	Esther... (8vo, green cl, 4 ticp)	L: Marcus Ward	1878	Greenaway, K.	185-230	
Byington, Eloise	Mother Goose Fun (1st, sm8vo, p-o, gilt, 128p, color, pep)	Whitman	(1931)	Frantz, K.	45-60	*
Byington, Eloise	Pancake Brownies (1st, 8vo, p-o, 96p, color, pep)	Whitman	(1928)	Jones, M.	30-45	*
Byington, Eloise	Wishbone Children (1st, 12mo, blue cl, p-o, 64p, pep, color)	Whitman	(1934)	Frantz, K.	25-40	*
Byng, Douglas	Byng Ballads (1st, 8vo, ibds, unpag, 8 fp color)	L: J. Lane	[1932]	Hutton, C.	30-45	*
Bynner, E.L.	Chase of the Meteor... (1st, 8vo, 209p, gilt, 10b/w)	Little/Brown	1891	Merrill, F.	50-70	
Byrne, D.	Messer. Marco Polo (1st, sm8vo, 147p, 4pl, DJ)	Century	1921	Falls, C.B.	50-80	
Byrne, M.	House of the Red Fox (1st, sq12mo, 116p, 8pl)	Stokes	(1907)	Upjohn, A.M.	30-45	*
Byrne, M.	Would-Be Witch (1st, sq12mo, 127p, 8pl)	Stokes	(1906)	Upjohn, A.M.	30-45	*
Byrne, M.A.	One Too Many (1st, 8vo, green cl, 191p, 4pl)	Saalfield	(1912)	Smith, Wuanita	30-45	*
Byron	Don Juan (1st, lg8vo, 17 woodcuts, 408p, buckram)	L: J. Lane	(1926)	Austen, J.	50-70	
Byron, May	Adventures of Trooper Peek-A-Boo (1st, 8vo, unpag)	L: Hodder	[1916]	Preston, C.	50-70	*
Byron, May	Animal Frolics (1st, 4to, unpag)	L: Hodder	[1916]	Aldin, C.	80-100	*
Byron, May	Barbara Peek-A-Boo's Holiday (1st, 4to, unpag)	L: Hodder	[1914]	Preston, C.	80-100	*
Byron, May	Cat's Cradle (1st, sm4to, ibds, [48]p, color)	L: Blackie	[1908]	Wain, L.	350-500	
Byron, May	Cecil Aldin's Happy Family (1st, 4to, teg, p-o, 36cp)	L: H. Frowde	[1912]	Aldin, C.	200-300	
Byron, May	Cecil Aldin's Merry Party (1st, 4to, ibds, gilt, teg, 36cp)	L: H. Frowde	1913	Aldin, C.	250-450	
Byron, May	Friday & Saturday... (1st, ob4to, ibds, unpag, 12 fp color)	L: H. Frowde	[1910]	Hassall, J.	150-200	
Byron, May	Little Brown Rooster (1st, 4to, p-o, orange cl, 6cp)	Nelson	1928	Robinson, G.	50-80	
Byron, May	Peek-a-Boos at the Zoo (1st, sq4to, ibds, unpag, p-o, 12cp)	L: H. Frowde	[1915]	Preston, C.	165-225	
Byron, May	Peek-a-Boos in Town (1st, ob folio, ibds, unpag, 12 fp col)	L: H. Frowde	[1915]	Preston, C.	180-250	
Byron, May	Peek-a-Boos in Winter (ob folio, ibds, 18cp)	L: H. Frowde	[1910]	Preston, C.	280-400	
Byron, May	Sambo & Susanna (ob4to, ibds, 24 color, [french fold paper])	L: Blackie	[1905]	Parkinson, E.	300-500	
Byron, May	Teddy Bear Book (sq8vo, ibds, 12cp)	L: H. Frowde	[1911]	Petherick, R.	200-300	
Byron, May	Teddy Bearoplane (sm4to, ibds, 12cp)	NY: Hodder	[1909]	Sinclair, J.R.	130-200	
Byron, May	William & Woggs (sq8vo, bds, p-o, 6cp)	L: H. Frowde	[1910]	Preston, C.	100-130	*
Cabell, J.B.	Chivalry (1st, 8vo, red cl, teg, 224p, 12cp, dep)	Harper	1909	Pyle, H.	90-125	
Cabell, J.B.	Eagle's Shadow (1st, 8vo, red cl, 256p, 8pl)	Doubleday/Page	1904	Grefe, W.	80-120	
Cabell, J.B.	Gallantry (1st, 8vo, teg, grey cl, 334p, 4 ticp, pep)	Harper	1907	Pyle, H.	100-145	
Cabell, J.B.	Line of Love (1st, 8vo, p-o, teg, 291p, uncut, 10cp)	Harper	1905	Pyle, H.	85-120	
Cabell, J.B.	Soul of Melicent (1st, 8vo, 216p, gilt, p-o, 4cp)	Stokes	(1913)	Pyle, H.	90-130	
Cable, G.W.	Bonaventure (1st, 8vo, 314p, olive/gilt, teg)	Scribner	1902	Armstrong, M.	35-50	
Cable, G.W.	By Low Hill (1st, 8vo, teg, uncut, red cl, 209p, cvr by...)	Scribner	1902	Armstrong, M.	30-45	
Cable, G.W.	Doctor Seiver (8vo, 473p, teg, olive/gilt)	Scribner	1898	Armstrong, M.	25-40	
Cable, G.W.	John March, Southerner (1st, 12mo, green/gilt, 513p)	Scribner	1894	Armstrong, M.	85-100	R*
Cable, G.W.	Kincaid's Battery (1st, 8vo, 396p, 7pl, cvr by...)	Scribner	1908	Armstrong, M.	35-50	
Cable, G.W.	Old Creole Days (1st, 4to, 234p, grey cl, teg, 8pl)	Scribner	1897	Herter, A.	70-90	
Cable, G.W.	Posson Jane... (1st, 12mo, teg, blue/gilt, 162p, uncut)	Scribner	1909	Armstrong, M.	35-50	
Cable, G.W.	Strong Hearts (1st, 12mo, 214p, olive/gilt)	Scribner	1899	Armstrong, M.	35-50	*
Cable, G.W.	The Cavalier (1st [1], 8vo, red/gilt, 311p, b/w)	Scribner	1901	Christy, H.C.	50-65	
Cable, G.W.	The Grandissimes (8vo, 448p, teg, olive/gilt)	Scribner	1898	Armstrong, M.	25-40	
Cabot, C.S.	Football Grandma (1st, 8vo, 79p, tan cl, b/w, pep by...)	Small	1905	Reed, E.	35-50	*
Cabot, E.	Balloon Moon (1st, 8vo, 99p, blue/gilt, col frn, fp b/w)	Holt	(1927)	Lathrop, D.	50-80	
Cadby, C.	Brownies in Switzerland (1st AM, lg8vo, p-o, 127p, 6cp)	Macaulay	(1924)	Stephensons	45-75	*
Cadman, S.P.	Parables of Jesus (1st, 4to, p-o, 163p, purple cl, pep, 8cp)	McKay	(1931)	Wyeth, N.C.	450-600	
Cady, H.	Caleb Cottontail (1st, 8vo, 127p, color, pep)	Houghton	1921	Cady, H.	80-100	
Cady, H.	Holiday Time on Butternut Hill (1st, 24mo, ibds, unpag, 12 col)	Whitman	(1929)	Cady, H.	65-80	
Cady, H.	Time to Get Up (4to, ibds)	Stoll/Edwards	1928	Cady, H.	70-100	*
Cain, Neville	Fairies' Circus (1st, lg4to, ibds, [16]p, calligraphy, color)	R.H. Russell	1903	Unknown	100-160	*
Cain, Neville	Fairies' Menagerie (1st, lg4to, ibds, [16]p, color)	R.H. Russell	1903	Unknown	100-150	*
Caldecott, R.	Fox Jumps Over the Parson's Gate (ob8vo, wraps, 24p, 6cp)	L: Routledge	1883	Caldecott, R.	100-150	*
Caldecott, R.	Gleanings from the Graphic (1st, ob4to, ibds, gilt, 84p, 32 col)	L: Routledge	1889	Caldecott, R.	120-165	
Caldecott, R.	Graphic Pictures (1st, ob folio, 93p, color)	L: Routledge	1883	Caldecott, R.	150-220	
Caldecott, R.	Last Graphic Pictures (1st, ob folio, ipcb, [71]p, color)	L: Routledge	1888	Caldecott, R.	135-170	
Caldecott, R.	More Graphic Pictures (1st, ob folio, ibds, 32cp)	L: Routledge	1887	Caldecott, R.	120-165	
Caldecott, R.	Panjandrum Picture Book (ob. sm4to, [98]p, color)	L: Warne	[1890]	Caldecott, R.	100-140	
Caldecott, R.	Queen of Hearts (1st, sm4to, wraps, 30p, 9cp)	L: Routledge	(1881)	Caldecott, R.	80-120	
Caldecott, R.	Sketch Book (1st, ob4to, 48p, color)	L: Routledge	1883	Caldecott, R.	150-185	
Caldecott, R.	Three Jovial Huntsmen (1st, ob8vo, 7 ticp, p-o, later)	L: Warne	[1908]	Caldecott, R.	80-100	*
Calhoun, M.E.	Dorothy's Rabbit Stories (1st, sq8vo, 115p, grey cl, 10pl)	Crowell	(1907)	Blaisdell, E.W.	45-65	*
Calhoun, Mary	Sweet Papootie Doll (1st, lg8vo, yellow cl, [32]p, 3-color)	Wm. Morrow	1957	Duvoisin, R.	35-50	*
Calkins, E.	Franklin Booth (1st, 4to, 60pl)	R. Frank	1925	Booth, F.	75-90	
Calmour, A.C.	Rumbo Rhymes... (1st, lg8vo, green ibds, 101p, 23cp)	L: Harper	1911	Crane, W.	135-160	
Cammack, K.	Spartan Primer (1st, 4to, ipcb, fp color)	Duffield	1913	Drayton, G.	140-200	
Camp, Ruth O.	Story of the Markets (1st {std}, sm8vo, 128p, col frn, b/w)	Harper	1929	Hader, E.	45-60	*

AUTHOR	TITLE	PUBLISHER	DATE	ARTIST	PRICE	LC
Campbell, A.M.	Fairy Flights in Cloudland (4to, ibds, 16cp)	L: A. Cooke	[1915]	Cook/Christie	140-200	
Campbell, J.	Celtic Dragon Myth (1st, 8vo, 172p, gilt, p-o, 5cp)	J. Grant	1911	Duff, R.	100-130	
Campbell, L.	Funnyfeathers (1st, 4to, 86p, tan cl, 6cp, pep)	Dutton	(1917)	Campbell, L.	55-80	
Campbell, Lang	Dinky Ducklings (1st, 12mo, ibds, 39p, color, pep)	Volland	(1928)	Campbell, L.	50-80	
Campbell, Ruth	Cat Whose Whiskers Slipped (1st, 8vo, ibds, color)	Volland	(1925)	Cadie, V.E.	35-50	
Campbell, Ruth	Runaway Smalls (1st, 4to, ibds, 73p, b/w)	Penn	1923	Price, H.L.	25-40	
Campbell, Ruth	Small Fry/Winged Horse (1st, 8vo, ibds, 28p, 10cp, pep)	Volland	(1927)	Tenggren, G.	50-85	
Campbell, Ruth	Turtle Whose Snap Unfastened (1st, 4to, 93p, ibds, color, pep)	Volland	(1927)	Cadie, V.E.	35-50	
Campbell, W.D.	Beyond the Border (1st AM, 8vo, AEG, 456p)	R.H. Russell	1898	Stratton, H.	75-120	
Canfield, D.	Understood Betsy (1st, 8vo, 271p, green cl, 11pl, PPP)	Holt	1917	Williamson, A.C.	70-100	
Canfield, Dorothy	Made-to-Order Stories (1st, sm8vo, 263p, col frn)	Harcourt	(1925)	Lathrop, D.	35-50	*
Canton, Wm.	Child's Book of Saints (1st [new ed.], 8vo, 257p, 19pl)	L: J.M. Dent	1902	Robinson, T.H.	50-75	*
Canton, Wm.	Child's Book of Warriors (1st, sm8vo, green cl, teg, 319p, 3cp)	L: J.M. Dent	(1912)	Cole, H.	70-100	
Canton, Wm.	Reign of King Herla (1st, 8vo, AEG, 367p, col frn)	L: J.M. Dent	(1900)	Robinson, C.	100-150	
Capes, B.	Romance of Lohengrin (1st, 8vo, blue/gilt, 271p, 14pl)	L: Dean	1905	Pogany, W.	160-220	
Capuana, L.	Golden-Feather (1st {std}, 8vo, 205p, col frn)	Dutton	(1930)	Freeman, M.	30-50	*
Carden, Priscilla	Vanilla Village (1st {std}, lg8vo, 58p, tan cl, pep, color)	Ariel	(1952)	Barnum, J.H.	30-50	*
Carleton, H.G.	Thompson Street Poker Club (1st, 8vo, 48p, ibds, 11 fp b/w)	White & Allen	1888	Kemble, E.W.	80-100	*
Carleton, K.	Dorothy/Motor Girl (1st, 8vo, 386p, 33pl)	Century	1911	Various	20-25	
Carlson, N.S.	Alphonse, that Bearded One (1st {std}, 8vo, blue cl, 78p, b/w)	Harcourt	(1954)	Mordvinoff, N.	50-80	R*
Carlson, N.S.	Evangeline, Pigeon of Paris (1st {std}, 8vo, red cl, 70p fp b/w)	Harcourt	(1960)	Mordvinoff, N.	35-50	*
Carlson, N.S.	Family Under the Bridge (1st, 8vo, 99p, green cl, 11 fp b/w, NH)	Harper	(1958)	Williams, Garth	65-100	R*
Carlson, N.S.	Happy Orpheline (1st, sm4to, blue cl, 96p, fp b/w)	Harper	(1957)	Williams, Garth	30-45	*
Carlson, N.S.	Talking Cat... (1st, sq8vo, 87p, red cl, 15 fp b/w, DJ)	Harper	(1952)	Duvoisin, R.	45-70	
Carlton, M.	Tumble Down Pictures (1st, 4to, ibds, unpag, 6 chromos)	Nister/Dutton	[1898]	Hardy, E.S.	160-220	
Carlyle, T.	Sartor Resartus (1st, sm8vo, AEG, 352p, blue/gilt, b/w, dep)	L: G. Bell	1898	Sullivan, E.J.	85-120	
Carman, B.	Low Tide/Grand Pre (2nd, 12mo, gilt, 132p, teg)	Stone/Kimball	1894	Hallowell, G.H.	50-80	
Carman, B.	Winter Holiday (1st, 12mo, 43p, cvr by...)	Small/Maynard	1899	Meteyard, T.B.	45-60	
Carmer, Carl	Too Many Cherries (1st, 4to, 62p, ipcb, 2-color, pep)	Viking	1949	Barnum, J.H.	45-70	*
Carmichael, Phil	Man from the Moon (1st, 8vo, 296p, blue cl, 8cp)	L: Richards	1909	Watkins, F.	90-135	*
Carpenter, Frances	Tales of a Chinese Grandmother (1st, 8vo, 261p, 9cp)	L: Harrap	(1938)	Hasselriis, M.	30-45	
Carpenter, Frances	Tales/Russian Grandmother (1st AM {std}, 8vo, 292p, 8cp, dep)	Doubleday/Dor.	1933	Bilibin, I.	75-100	
Carpenter, Frances	Wonder Tales of Dogs & Cats (1st, 8vo, yellow cl, 255p, fp b/w)	Doubleday	(1955)	Keats, E.J.	35-50	*
Carpenter, John	Improving Songs/Anxious Children (lg ob4to, 50p, ibds, 19 col)	Schirmer	(1913)	Carpenter, J.& R.	100-140	*
Carpenter, John	When Little Boys Sing (1st, ob folio, cloth, color)	McClurg	(1904)	Carpenter, J.& R.	90-145	
Carr, A.V.	Fairy of the Rhone (1st, 12mo, 69p, woodcuts)	Page	1901	Smith, Winifred	30-45	*
Carr, Mary J.	Peggy & Paul & Laddy (1st, sm8vo, 207p, brown cl, b/w, pep)	Crowell	(1936)	Voute, Kathleen	20-25	*
Carr, Mary J.	Young Mac/Fort Vancouver (1st, 8vo, 238p, blue cl, p-o, col, NH)	Crowell	1940	Holberg, R.	45-65	*
Carr, R.V.	Cowboy Lyrics (1st, sm8vo, 229p, teg)	Small	(1908)	Elwell, R.F.	35-50	
Carroll, L.	Alice... & Through... (1st [combined], 12mo, 383p, green cl)	L: MacMillan	1887	Tenniel, J.	200-300	
Carroll, L.	Alice... & Through... (8vo, teg, 351p, b/w)	Altemus	1895	Tenniel, J.	85-135	*
Carroll, L.	Alice... & Through... (8vo, 255p, beige cl, 16 fp color)	Platt/Peck	(1900)	McManus, B.	100-165	*
Carroll, L.	Alice... & Through... (1st, lg8vo, 255p, yellow cl, 12cp)	A. Wessels	(1900)	McManus, B.	120-170	*
Carroll, L.	Alice... & Through... (1st {this pub}, sm8vo, 317p, col frn)	Collier	1903	Tenniel/Stevens	65-90	*
Carroll, L.	Alice... & Through... (4to, blue/gilt, col frn, b/w)	McLoughlin	[1910]	Tenniel, J.	100-160	*
Carroll, L.	Alice... & Through... (1st [color ed.], 8vo, 292p, gilt, 16cp)	L: MacMillan	1911	Tenniel, J.	160-250	
Carroll, L.	Alice... & Through... (8vo, brown cl, p-o, 335p, 7cp)	Jacobs	[1912]	Abbott, E.P.	120-150	
Carroll, L.	Alice... & Through... (1st, lg8vo, 242p, p-o, 14cp, pep)	Rand/McNally	(1916)	Winter, M.	130-200	
Carroll, L.	Alice... & Through... (lg8vo, 297p, grey cl, col frn)	Grosset/Dunlap	[1919]	(Photos)	70-100	*
Carroll, L.	Alice... & Through... (1st, 8vo, 319p, gilt, p-o, 4cp, pep)	Winston	(1923)	Prittie, E.J.	50-85	
Carroll, L.	Alice... & Through... (8vo, blue/gilt, p-o, 335p, 7cp)	Macrae-Smith	[1925]	Abbott, E.P.	65-90	*
Carroll, L.	Alice... & Through... (1st, 4to, 236p, gilt, p-o, col frn)	Sears	(1926)	Welling, G.	100-165	*
Carroll, L.	Alice... & Through... (4to, 143p, green/gilt, 8 ticp)	L: Collins	[1928]	Rountree, H.	200-265	
Carroll, L.	Alice... & Through... (1st, 8vo, yellow cl, 317p, col frn, 8pl)	L: Clowes	[1935]	Morton-Sale, J.	35-50	*
Carroll, L.	Alice... & Through... (1st {this pub}, 4to, p-o, 59p, cep, col)	Platt/Munk	(1938)	Tenniel, J.	85-120	*
Carroll, L.	Alice... & Through... (1st, sm8vo, ibds, 234p, b/w, pep)	Whitman	(1945)	Card, L.	45-60	*
Carroll, L.	Alice... & Through... (1st, 4to, 159p, ibds, 24 fp color, pep)	Harper	(1949)	Weisgard, L.	75-120	*
Carroll, L.	Alice... & Through... (1st, 8vo, 246p, 8 color)	Dutton	(1954)	Stanley, D.	35-50	*
Carroll, L.	Alice... & Through... (1st, 8vo, ibds, 284p, 2-color, pep)	Whitman	(1955)	Paflin, R.	30-50	*
Carroll, L.	Alice... Through... & Hunting (1st, 8vo, 351p, teg, uncut, b/w)	Boni/Liveright	1925	Tenniel, J.	100-150	*
Carroll, L.	Alice/Wonderland (sm4to, tan cl, 160p, 4cp)	Altemus	(1897)	Tenniel, J.	65-90	*
Carroll, L.	Alice/Wonderland (1st, 4to, 255p, yellow/gilt, 16cp)	Wessels	(1899)	McManus, B.	120-165	R
Carroll, L.	Alice/Wonderland (1st, 12mo, 179p, color)	NY: McKibbin	1899	Tenniel, J.	70-100	*
Carroll, L.	Alice/Wonderland (16mo, ibds, p-o, 126p, 30cp, pep)	Altemus	[1900]	Tenniel, J.	70-100	
Carroll, L.	Alice/Wonderland (sm8vo, green/gilt, 8pl)	L: Ward Lock	[1901]	McManus, B.	60-90	
Carroll, L.	Alice/Wonderland (1st, 8vo, vellum/gilt, 193p, teg, 40pl)	Harper	1901	Newell, P.	120-160	
Carroll, L.	Alice/Wonderland (1st, 12mo, brown cl, 192p, 12pl)	Rand/McNally	(1902)	Cory, F.	35-50	*
Carroll, L.	Alice/Wonderland (32mo, 127p, 32 color)	L: MacMillan	1903	Tenniel, J.	70-120	*
Carroll, L.	Alice/Wonderland (1st, 8vo, 247p, grey/gilt, 12cp)	Stokes	(1904)	Kirk, M.L.	140-200	
Carroll, L.	Alice/Wonderland (sm8vo, ibds, 202p, pep)	Caldwell	[1904]	Tenniel, J.	70-120	*
Carroll, L.	Alice/Wonderland (1st, 8vo, 165p, blue cl, 10cp, pep)	Dodge	1907	Gutmann, B.P.	160-200	
Carroll, L.	Alice/Wonderland (1st, 12mo, 198p, col frn, gilt)	L: Routledge	[1907]	Maybank, T.	100-145	

AUTHOR	TITLE	PUBLISHER	DATE	ARTIST	PRICE	LC
Carroll, L.	Alice/Wonderland (1st, 8vo, green/gilt, 161p, 13cp, pep)	L: Heinemann	(1907)	Rackham, A.	200-300	
Carroll, L.	Alice/Wonderland (1st AM, 8vo, p-o, 162p, 13cp, pep)	Doubleday/Page	[1907]	Rackham, A.	200-300	
Carroll, L.	Alice/Wonderland (1st, sm4to, teg, gilt, 179p, 8cp)	L: Cassell	(1907)	Robinson, C.	400-600	
Carroll, L.	Alice/Wonderland (1st, 8vo, teg, p-o, gilt, 166p, 12cp, pep)	L: Chatto	1907	Sowerby, M.	200-300	
Carroll, L.	Alice/Wonderland (1st, 8vo, blue/gilt, AEG, p-o, 152p, 8cp)	L: J. Lane	(1907)	Walker, W.H.	180-220	
Carroll, L.	Alice/Wonderland (1st Canadian, blue bds, 8 color)	Musson	1908	Pease, B.C.	200-300	
Carroll, L.	Alice/Wonderland (1st, sq12mo, 160p, gilt, p-o, 8cp)	L: Nelson	1908	Rountree, H.	70-100	*
Carroll, L.	Alice/Wonderland (1st AM, 8vo, p-o, 165p, 12cp)	Duffield	1908	Sowerby, M.	180-240	
Carroll, L.	Alice/Wonderland (1st, 4to, ibds, 148p, AEG, 12cp, pep)	L: R. Tuck	(1910)	Attwell, M.L.	165-220	
Carroll, L.	Alice/Wonderland (8vo, 190p, red/gilt, 30pl by...)	L: Collins	[1910]	Robinson, T.H.	100-135	
Carroll, L.	Alice/Wonderland (1st, 8vo, 48p, color)	Barse/Hopkins	[1910]	Von Hofsten, H.	45-80	*
Carroll, L.	Alice/Wonderland (lg8vo, 192p, red cl, 6 ticp)	Small	[1911]	Soper, G.	80-125	
Carroll, L.	Alice/Wonderland (1st, sq8vo, 192p, red cl, 6 ticp)	L: Headley	(1911)	Soper, G.	100-150	
Carroll, L.	Alice/Wonderland (1st AM, sq8vo, 192p, teg, 192p, 6 ticp, pep)	Baker/Taylor	(1911)	Soper, G.	90-140	
Carroll, L.	Alice/Wonderland (sm8vo, uncut, 152p, 8cp)	L/NY: J. Lane	[1911]	Walker, W.H.	75-100	*
Carroll, L.	Alice/Wonderland (1st {this fmt}, sq12mo, 157p, p-o, 8cp)	L: H. Frowde	1913	Sowerby, M.	65-90	
Carroll, L.	Alice/Wonderland (1st, 8vo, 161p, 8cp)	L: Bell	1914	Woodward, A.B.	70-100	
Carroll, L.	Alice/Wonderland (1st AM, lg8vo, 232p, 16 ticp, pep)	Doran	[1915]	Jackson, A.E.	120-180	*
Carroll, L.	Alice/Wonderland (1st, 4to, grn/gilt, teg, 199p, pep, 16 ticp)	L: H. Frowde	[1915]	Jackson, A.E.	180-220	
Carroll, L.	Alice/Wonderland (1st {this pub}, 4to, p-o, ibds, 164p, 8cp)	L: Coker	[1915]	Pease, B.C.	100-140	
Carroll, L.	Alice/Wonderland (1st, 4to, gilt, teg, 6cp)	McClurg	1915	St. John, J.A.	150-200	
Carroll, L.	Alice/Wonderland (1st AM, lg8vo, p-o, 48p, 4cp)	NY: S. Gabriel	(1916)	Robinson, G.	90-140	*
Carroll, L.	Alice/Wonderland (1st, 8vo, 201p, blue/gilt, 6cp)	L: C.H. Kelly	(1916)	Robinson, G.	120-170	
Carroll, L.	Alice/Wonderland (1st, sm4to, p-o, 340p, blue/gilt, 48cp, pep)	L: Ward Lock	1916	Tarrant, M.	180-250	
Carroll, L.	Alice/Wonderland (1st AM, lg8vo, p-o, 332p, 48cp, pep)	Platt/Peck	1916	Tarrant, M.	150-200	
Carroll, L.	Alice/Wonderland (1st, sm8vo, 224p, blue/red, b/w)	Ginn & Co.	(1917)	Herford, O.	80-100	
Carroll, L.	Alice/Wonderland (sm8vo, tan cl, 126p, 4cp, pep)	L: Blackie	[1920]	Adams, F.	70-100	
Carroll, L.	Alice/Wonderland (1st AM, 8vo, 181p, 12cp, pep)	Dodd	(1922)	Hudson, G.	130-175	
Carroll, L.	Alice/Wonderland (1st, 4to, red/gilt, 180p, 12 ticp, pep)	L: Hodder	[1922]	Hudson, G.	240-320	
Carroll, L.	Alice/Wonderland (1st, sq8vo, 241p, p-o, gilt, 8cp, pep)	Lippincott	1923	Kay, G.A.	120-165	
Carroll, L.	Alice/Wonderland (lg8vo, [new ed.], 8cp)	L: Cassell	1928	Robinson, C.	120-165	
Carroll, L.	Alice/Wonderland (1st, 8vo, 174p, blue cl, 6cp)	L: A&C Black	(1929)	Folkard, C.	120-165	
Carroll, L.	Alice/Wonderland (1st, 8vo, purple/gilt, 192p, pep, b/w)	Dutton	(1929)	Pogany, W.	140-200	
Carroll, L.	Alice/Wonderland (4to, 175p, ibds, 24cp, later)	L: Ward Lock	[1929]	Tarrant, M.	140-180	
Carroll, L.	Alice/Wonderland (1st {this pub}, 8vo, 216p, 8cp, pep)	Garden City	(1930)	Jackson, A.E.	50-80	*
Carroll, L.	Alice/Wonderland (lg8vo, ibds, 8cp, later)	L: H. Milford	[1933]	Jackson, A.E.	60-80	
Carroll, L.	Alice/Wonderland (lg ob8vo, unpag, [movie ed.], b/w)	Whitman	(1934)	(Photos)	80-120	*
Carroll, L.	Alice/Wonderland (1st, 12mo, ipcb, [56]p, 8 fp color)	McLoughlin	(1940)	Tenniel, J.	70-100	*
Carroll, L.	Alice/Wonderland (1st, 8vo, 150p, color)	Random	(1946)	Kredel F.	45-70	*
Carroll, L.	Alice/Wonderland (1st, sq8vo, ibds, [32]p, color, pep)	Rand/McNally	1951	Holland, J.	30-50	*
Carroll, L.	Alice/Wonderland (1st, 4to, green cl, 64p, p-o, 15 fp col, pep)	Random	1955	Torrey, M.	65-80	*
Carroll, L.	Further Nonsense Prose... (1st, 4to, 127p, yellow bds)	L: T.F. Unwin	1926	Bateman, H.M.	70-90	
Carroll, L.	Further Nonsense Prose... (1st AM, lg8vo, ipcb, p-o, 118p)	Appleton	1926	Bateman, H.M.	65-90	
Carroll, L.	Hunting of the Snark (1st, lg8vo, ibds, teg, 248p, 40pl)	Harper	1903	Newell, P.	120-160	
Carroll, L.	Hunting of the Snark (1st, 8vo, red cl, 46p, b/w)	L: Chatto	1941	Peake, M.	130-200	*
Carroll, L.	Nursery Alice (1st, 4to, ibds, 56p, 20 color, cep)	L: MacMillan	1890	Tenniel, J.	600-800	
Carroll, L.	Rhyme? And Reason? (1st, 8vo, 214p, green/gilt, b/w)	L: MacMillan	1883	Frost/Holiday	220-285	
Carroll, L.	Sylvie & Bruno (1st, 8vo, AEG, 400p, gilt, 46 illus)	L: MacMillan	1889	Furniss, H.	120-160	
Carroll, L.	Sylvie & Bruno Concluded (1st, 8vo, red/gilt, AEG, 423p)	L: MacMillan	1893	Furniss, H.	140-220	
Carroll, L.	Tangled Tale (1st, 8vo, 152p, AEG, red/gilt, 6pl)	L: MacMillan	1885	Frost, A.B.	300-500	
Carroll, L.	Three Sunsets... (1st, sq8vo, green/gilt, AEG, 68p, 12 fp b/w)	L: MacMillan	1898	Thomson, E.G.	280-350	*
Carroll, L.	Through the Looking Glass (12mo, 175p, grey/gilt, 4 chromos)	DeWolfe/Fiske	1898	Tenniel, J.	130-180	
Carroll, L.	Through the Looking Glass (1st, lg8vo, 139p, grey/gilt, 12cp)	Mansfield/Wes.	1899	McManus, B.	120-160	
Carroll, L.	Through the Looking Glass (1st, lg8vo, bds, teg, 211p, 40pl)	Harper	1902	Newell, P.	100-145	
Carroll, L.	Through the Looking Glass (1st, 8vo, gilt, p-o, 271p, 12cp)	Stokes	(1905)	Kirk, M.L.	200-300	
Carroll, L.	Through the Looking Glass (1st, 8vo, blue cl, 185p, 10cp)	Dodge	(1909)	Gutmann, B.P.	120-185	
Carroll, L.	Through the Looking Glass (1st, 12mo, 218p, tan cl, b/w)	Rand/McNally	(1917)	Cory, F.	30-60	*
Carroll, L.	Through the Looking Glass (1st, 8vo, 235p, red/gilt, 8cp, pep)	Lippincott	(1929)	Kay, G.A.	30-50	*
Carroll, L.	Through the Looking Glass (1st {this pub}, 4to, 96p, color)	Whittlesey	(1946)	Tenniel, J.	35-50	*
Carroll, L.	Through the Looking Glass (1st, sm4to, [30]p, ipcb, color, pep)	NY: Maxton	1947	Collison, M.	35-65	*
Carruth, F.W.	Those Dale Girls (1st, sm8vo, 318p, cvr by...)	McClurg	1899	Hazenplug, F.	40-60	*
Carruth, H.	Mr. Milo Bush (1st, 12mo, green cl, 217p, 4pl)	Harper	1899	Frost, A.B.	30-50	
Carruth, H.	Track's End (1st, 12mo, blue cl, 230p, 9pl, pep)	Harper	1911	Carleton, C.	35-50	
Carruth, H.	Voyage of the Rattletrap (1st, 12mo, gilt, 207p, b/w, PPPa)	Harper	1897	Wilder, H.M.	65-90	*
Carryl, C.E.	Admiral's Caravan (1st, sq8vo, 140p, gilt, b/w, PPP)	Century	1892	Birch, R.	90-120	R
Carryl, G.W.	Fables for the Frivolous (1st, 8vo, 120p, teg, gilt, 6pl)	Harper	1898	Newell, P.	60-85	
Carryl, G.W.	Far from Maddening Girls (1st, 8vo, 185p, 8pl)	McClure	1904	Newell, P.	45-70	
Carryl, G.W.	Garden of Years (1st, 8vo, 129p, uncut, teg, dep, frn by...)	Putnam	1904	Parrish, M.	60-85	R
Carryl, G.W.	Grimm's Tales Made Gay (1st, sq8vo, green cl, 142p, b/w)	Houghton	(1902)	Levering, A.	100-145	R
Carryl, G.W.	Mother Goose for Grownups (1st, lg8vo, teg, 125p, 3pl by...)	Harper	1900	Newell, P.	100-125	
Carse, R.	Monarchs of Merry England (1st, 4to, 52p, p-o, 10cp)	L: T.F. Unwin	1904	Robinson, W.H.	250-300	
Carson, Norma B.	Children's Own Story Book (1st, sm4to, yellow cl, 160p, col)	Reilly/Britton	(1916)	Sewsmith, H.	45-60	*

AUTHOR	TITLE	PUBLISHER	DATE	ARTIST	PRICE	LC
Carson, Thos.	Ranching Sport/Travel (1st AM, 8vo, 319p, teg)	Scribner	(1912)	Various	65	
Carter, C.F.	Katooticut (1st, 4to, ipcb, 153p, fp b/w)	R.H. Russell	1899	Conde, J.M.	140-200	*
Carter, R.G.	White Plume of Navarre (1st, 8vo, p-o, 192p, color)	Volland	(1928)	Stevens, B.	45-75	*
Carter, Russell	Brothers of the Frontier (1st, sm8vo, 205p, tan cl, b/w)	Appleton/Cent.	1938	Sperry, A.	25-40	*
Carter, Russell	Crimson Cutlass (1st, 8vo, 302p, col frn, pep)	Penn	(1933)	Schoonover, F.	20-30	*
Carus, Helena	Metten of Tyre (1st {std}, 8vo, 171p, col frn, fp b/w, pep)	Doubleday/Dor.	1930	Bock, V.	25-40	*
Cary, E.L.	Emerson, Poet & Thinker (1st, lg8vo, blue/gilt, 284p)	Putnam	1904	Armstrong, M.	45-65	
Cary, E.L.	Tennyson (1st, lg8vo, blue/gilt, 213p, teg)	Putnam	1906	Armstrong, M.	30-45	
Cary, E.L.	The Rossettis (2nd, lg8vo, teg, uncut, gilt)	Putnam	1902	Armstrong, M.	50-65	
Cary, E.L.	William Morris (1st, 4to, teg, blue/gilt, 296p, uncut)	Putnam	1902	Armstrong, M.	35-50	
Cary, E.L.	Works of J.M. Whistler (1st, lg8vo, bds, 302p, uncut, 31pl)	Moffat	1907	Whistler, J.M.	85-110	
Casserley, A.T.	Roseen (1st {std}, 8vo, green cl, 152p, b/w, cep)	Harper	1929	Casserley, A.T.	20-25	*
Castle, A.	Heart of Lady Ann (1st, 12mo, 263p, lavender/gilt, 4cp, pep)	Harper	1905	Betts, E.F.	30-45	
Castle, A.& E.	Our Sentimental Garden (1st AM, 8vo, gilt, 304p, 8 ticp, pep)	Lippincott	1914	Robinson, C.	100-165	
Castle, A.& E.	Our Sentimental Garden (1st, lg8vo, 304p, gilt, 8 ticp, pep)	L: Heinemann	(1914)	Robinson, C.	140-200	
Castle, E.	Marshfield the Observer (1st, 8vo, grey ipcb, cvr by…)	H. Stone	1900	Hazenplug, F.	45-60	
Castle, Jane	Peep-Lo (1st, 8vo, 34p, blue cl, b/w, pep)	Holiday House	1959	Castle, J.	20-30	*
Cather, W.	My Antonia (1st, sm8vo, 418p, brown cl, 6pl)	Houghton	1918	Benda, W.T.	200-350	
Catherwood, Mary	Lazarre (1st, 8vo, 436p, gilt)	Bowen-Merrill	1901	Castaigne, A.	25-40	
Catherwood, Mary	Spanish Peggy (1st, 8vo, uncut, teg, 85p, red cl, p-o, b/w)	H. Stone	1899	Leyendecker, J.C.	80-100	
Catrevas, C.	Fairy Tales for Little People (1st, 4to, 246p, p-o, col frn, pep)	Sears	(1927)	Becker, C.	30-45	
Caudill, R.	Tree of Freedom (1st, 8vo, 279p, green cl, pep, DJ, NH)	Viking	1949	Morse, D.B.	35-50	
Cautley, Marg.	Building a House in Sweeden (1st, sq8vo, 40p, fp brown illus)	MacMillan	1931	Sewell, H.	30-50	
Cavally, Fred. L.	Mother Goose's Teddy Bears (1st, 4to, red cl, [64]p, p-o, 32cp)	Bobbs-Merrill	1907	Cavally, F.L.	280-450	
Cavanah, F.	Boyhood Adventures of Our Presidents (1st, 8vo, 256p, fp b/w)	Rand/McNally	(1938)	Foster, G.	30-45	*
Cavanah, F.	Louis of New Orleans (1st, lg8vo, ipcb, 36p, color, pep)	McKay	(1941)	Weisgard, L.	35-50	*
Cavanah, F.	Pedro of Santa Fe (1st, lg8vo, ipcb, [35]p, 3-color, pep)	McKay	(1941)	Weisgard, L.	30-45	*
Cawein, M.J.	Message of the Lilies (1st, narrow 8vo, pcb, color, pep)	Volland	(1913)	Unknown	65-90	R*
Cawein, M.J.	So Many Ways (1st, 12mo, pcb, gilt, [12]p, color)	Volland	(1911)	Unknown	65-90	R*
Celli, Rose	Wild Animals/Little Ones (1st AM, 4to, [16]p, wraps, 12 color)	A.& W. Guild	(1933)	Rojankovsky, F.	35-50	
Cellini, B.	Autobiography of Benvenuto Cellini (1st, sm4to, 442p, 15cp)	Doubleday	1946	Dali, S.	120-165	
Cervantes	Adventures of Don Quixote (1st, 8vo, 532p, teg, uncut, b/w, pep)	Dent/Dutton	1902	Robinson, W.H.	100-140	
Cervantes	Adventures of Don Quixote (1st, sm4to, 287p, color)	Houghton	1928	Bacharach, H.I.	30-45	*
Cervantes	Don Quixote (1st AM, lg8vo, 11cp)	J. Lane	1900	Crane, W.	85-120	
Cervantes	Don Quixote (1st, lg8vo, 245p, uncut, 11cp)	L: Blackie	1900	Crane, W.	170-220	
Cervantes	Don Quixote (1st, lg8vo, 340p, 48cp)	L: Ward Lock	[1910]	Theaker, H.G.	50-75	*
Cervantes	Don Quixote (1st, 341p, p-o)	Stokes	1922	Choate/Curtis	25-40	
Cervantes	Don Quixote (1st, lg4to, 311p, black/gilt, 25 color)	L: Constable	1922	DeBosschere, J.	100-160	
Cervantes	Don Quixote (8vo, red/gilt, 614p, 16 b/w)	Dodd	1925	Robinson, W.H.	70-90	
Cervantes	History of Don Quixote… (1st, 4to, gilt, 25cp)	(London)	1922	DeBosschere, J.	80-120	
Cesaresco, E.	Fairies' Fountain (1st, 8vo, 268p, blue/gilt, col frn, 15pl)	L: Fairbanks	1908	Robinson, C.	180-225	
Chabot, Adrien	Dancing-Master (1st, 12mo, teg, green cl, 139p, 4pl)	Lippincott	1901	Smith, J.W.	120-170	*
Chaffee, Allen	Brownie: Engineer of Beaver Brook (1st, lg8vo, 99p, 4cp)	M. Bradley	(1925)	Bransom, P.	30-50	
Chaffee, Allen	Wild Folk (1st, 8vo, 94p, pep, col frn by…)	M. Bradley	(1930)	Bull, C.L.	20-25	*
Chalmers, Mary	Come for a Walk with Me (1st, 16mo, [30]p, ipcb, 3-color)	Harper	(1955)	Chalmers, M.	25-45	*
Chalmers, Patrick	Cricket in the Cage (1st, 8vo, 77p, gilt)	L: A&C Black	1933	Shepard, E.H.	35-50	*
Chalmers, Patrick	Dozen Dogs or So (1st, 4to, 47p, brown cl, 13cp)	L: Eyre/Spotts	1928	Aldin, C.	75-100	
Chalmers, Patrick	Last Muster (1st, 8vo, 127p, 24 illus)	L: Eyre/Spotts	1939	Aldin, C.	35-50	
Chamberlain, Esth.	Coast of Chance (1st, 8vo, tan/gilt, 465p, 4pl)	Bobbs-Merrill	(1908)	Underwood, C.F.	20-25	*
Chamberlin, E.C.	Omar the Discontented Cat (1st, 12mo, [39]p, ipcb, pep, color)	Volland	(1925)	Sturges, K.	35-50	*
Chamberlin, E.C.	Shoes, Ships & Sealing Wax (1st, 8vo, 123p, ibds, color)	Saalfield	(1928)	Scott, J.L.	20-30	
Chambers, M.C.	Boy Heroes of Chapultepec (1st {std}, 8vo, 182p, 1-color, pep)	Winston	(1953)	Krush, J.	25-40	*
Chambers, M.C.	Water-Carrier's Secrets (1st, 8vo, 157p, 29 fp 1-color, pep)	OUP	(1942)	Weisgard, L.	25-40	*
Chambers, Rbt.	Anne's Bridge (1st, 8vo, 161p, green/gilt)	Appleton	1914	Hutt, H.	25-40	
Chambers, Rbt.	Ashes of Empire (1st, 8vo, 342p, cvr by…)	Stokes	(1898)	Bradley, W.	70-90	
Chambers, Rbt.	Barbarians (1st, 8vo, 353p, 4pl)	Appleton	1917	Keller, A.I.	20-30	
Chambers, Rbt.	Forest-Land (1st, 4to, ipcb, 118p, 8cp, pep)	Appleton	1905	Knipe, E.B.	70-100	
Chambers, Rbt.	Garden-Land (1st, sm4to, 129p, ipcb, 8cp, pep)	Appleton	1907	Cady, H.	150-200	
Chambers, Rbt.	Gay Rebellion (1st, 8vo, 299p, b/w)	Appleton	1913	Frederick, E.	20-30	
Chambers, Rbt.	Green Mouse (1st, 8vo, 281p, p-o, 6cp, pep)	Appleton	1910	Frederick, E.	20-30	
Chambers, Rbt.	Iole (1st, sm8vo, 142p, p-o, 2pl by…)	Appleton	1905	Leyendeckers	25-40	
Chambers, Rbt.	Japonette (1st, 8vo, 384p, p-o, 21 b/w)	Appleton	1912	Gibson, C.D.	20-35	
Chambers, Rbt.	Maid-at-Arms (1st, 8vo, green/gilt)	Harper	1902	Christy, H.C.	25-40	
Chambers, Rbt.	Maker of Moons (1st, 8vo, blue cl, 401p)	Putnam	1896	Unknown	75-100	
Chambers, Rbt.	Mountain-Land (1st, lg8vo, ibds, 122p, 8cp)	Appleton	1906	Richardson, F.	70-100	
Chambers, Rbt.	Orchard-Land (1st, sm4to, 112p, 7cp)	Harper	1903	Birch, R.	85-120	
Chambers, Rbt.	Outdoorland (1st, sm4to, 105p, 7cp)	Harper	1902	Birch, R.	70-90	
Chambers, Rbt.	Outdoorland (1st, sm4to, green cl, 311p, 22cp)	Appleton	1931	Green/Birch	80-100	
Chambers, Rbt.	Police! (1st, 8vo, 292p, gilt, p-o, cp)	Appleton	1915	Hutt, H.	20-35	
Chambers, Rbt.	River-Land (1st, sm4to, gilt, 92p, 8cp)	Harper	1904	Green, E.S.	90-140	
Chambers, Rbt.	Streets of Ascalon (1st, 8vo, 440p, gilt, 14 double pg pl)	Appleton	1912	Gibson, C.D.	20-30	
Chamisso, A.	Peter Schlemihl (1st, sm4to, 104p, green/gilt, 35 woodcuts)	McKay	(1929)	Gincano, John	35-50	*

AUTHOR	TITLE	PUBLISHER	DATE	ARTIST	PRICE	LC
Champney, E.W.	Romance of Old Japan (1st, 8vo, 444p, teg, 96pl)	Putnam	1917	Champney, F.	40-60	
Chan, Chih-Yi	Good-Luck Horse (1st, ob8vo, grn cl, [47]p, pep, 10 fp col, CH)	Whittlesey	(1943)	Chan, P.	70-90	*
Channing, Blanche	Zodiac Stories (1st, sm8vo, 311p, gilt, b/w)	Dutton	1899	Channing B.M.	30-45	*
Chapin, A.A.	Everyday & Nowaday Fairy Book (lg4to, 160p, ibds, 8cp)	L: Coker	[1920]	Smith, J.W.	180-250	
Chapin, A.A.	Everyday Fairy Book (1st, 4to, 160p, p-o, 7cp)	Dodd	1915	Smith, J.W.	250-320	
Chapin, A.A.	Everyday Fairy Book (1st UK, 4to, 160p, p-o, 7cp)	L: Harrap	1917	Smith, J.W.	185-250	
Chapin, A.A.	Humpty Dumpty (1st, 4to, 206p, p-o, 6cp, pep)	Dodd	1905	Betts, E.F.	140-185	
Chapin, A.A.	Nowadays Fairy Book (1st, lg4to, ibds, 159p, 6 ticp)	Dodd	1911	Smith, J.W.	280-400	
Chapin, A.A.	True Story of Humpty Dumpty (1st, 4to, 205p, p-o, pep, 6cp)	Dodd	1905	Betts, E.F.	100-140	
Chapin, F.	Pinkey & the Plumed Knight (1st, 4to, tan cl, 207p, 8cp, cep)	Saalfield	(1909)	Johnson, Merle	65-80	*
Chapman, W.G.	Green Timber Trails (1st, 8vo, green cl, 283p, 8pl)	Century	1919	Bransom/Bull	30-45	*
Chappell, G.S.	Basket of Poses (1st, 4to, pcb, p-o, 109p, b/w)	A.& C. Boni	1924	Kent, R.	80-100	
Chappell, G.S.	Rollo in Society (1st, 16mo, p-o, 178p)	Putnam	1922	Kent, R.	60-85	R
Charles, R.H.	Roundabout Turn (1st, sq8vo, [54]p, orange/gilt, pep, 4cp)	L: Warne	1930	Brooke, L.L.	75-120	
Charlip, R.	Dress Up/Let's Have a Party (1st, ob8vo, ipcb [25]p, 3-col, pep)	W.R. Scott	1956	Charlip, R.	50-70	*
Charlip, R.	Where is Everybody? (1st, lg ob8vo, yellow cl, [50]p, 1-color)	W.R. Scott	1957	Charlip, R.	50-70	*
Charlot, J.	Dance of Death (1st, ob8vo, black/silver, [102]p, fp b/w)	Sheed/Ward	(1951)	Charlot, J.	65-100	*
Charskaya, L.A.	Little Princess Nina (1st, sm8vo, 288p, col frn by…)	Holt	1924	Artzybasheff, B.	35-50	*
Chater, M.	Bubble Ballads (1st, 4to, p-o, 148p, 16pl)	Century	1914	Kay, G.A.	50-75	
Chaucer, G.	Canterbury Pilgrims (1st, 4to, p-o, 310p, 12cp)	Stokes	(1914)	Kirk, M.L.	65-80	
Chaucer, G.	Canterbury Tales (1st, lg8vo, 235p, teg, gilt, 6cp)	Fox Duffield	1904	Clark, W.A.	45-60	
Chaucer, G.	Canterbury Tales (1st, 4to, 637p, teg, 24cp, DJ)	L: Medici	1928	Flint, W.R.	120-180	
Chaucer, G.	Canterbury Tales (1st AM, 8vo, 245p, 12cp)	Cape/Smith	1930	Flint, W.R.	60-85	*
Chaucer, G.	Canterbury Tales (1st, lg8vo, 627p, b/w, DJ)	Garden City	1934	Kent, R.	60-80	
Chaucer, G.	Chanticleer & the Fox (1st, 4to, [36]p, red cl, color, dep, CM)	Crowell	(1958)	Cooney, B.	70-100	*
Chaucer, G.	Complete Poetical Works of… (1st, 4to, blue/gilt, teg, 32cp)	L: MacMillan	1912	Goble, W.	200-240	
Chaucer, G.	Gateway to Chaucer (1st, sm8vo, blue/gilt, 269p, teg, 15cp)	L: Nelson	[1915]	Anderson, A.	130-165	*
Chaundler, C.	Arthur & His Knights (1st AM, lg8vo, 311p, 8 ticp, pep)	Stokes	[1923]	Mackenzie, T.	100-165	
Chaundler, C.	Thirteenth Orphan (1st, 8vo, 255p, col frn, 6pl)	L: J. Nisbet	[1920]	Appleton, H.C.	35-50	*
Cheatham, G.	Nursery Garland (1st, lg4to, ibds, 171p, 14cp)	Schirmer	(1917)	Robertson, W.G.	130-165	
Cheever, H.A.	Little Mr. Van Vere of China (1st, sq8vo, 243p, col frn, b/w)	Estes	(1898)	Barry, E.B.	35-50	*
Cheney, Cora	Key of Gold (1st {std}, 8vo, 127p)	Holt	(1955)	Galdone, P.	20-30	*
Cheney, Cora	Peg-Legged Pirate of Sulu (1st {std}, sm8vo, 109p, b/w, cep)	Knopf	1960	Keats, E.J.	30-50	*
Cheney, Cora	Rocking Chair Buck (1st {std}, 8vo, 128p, b/w)	Holt	(1956)	Galdone, P.	20-30	*
Cheney, W.	The Challenge (1st, 12mo, 386p, red cl, 4pl)	Bobbs-Merrill	(1906)	Wyeth, N.C.	20-35	
Cherr, Pat	My Dog is Lost! (1st, lg8vo, beige cl, [48]p, 1-color)	Crowell	(1960)	Keats, E.J.	35-50	*
Chesson	Tales from Tennyson (4to, ibds, 4 chromos)	L: R. Tuck	[1890]	Brundage, F.	90-120	
Chester, Geo. R.	Little Prince Toofat (1st, sq4to, 71p, col frn, cp)	McCann	(1922)	Lawson, R.	160-200	R
Chester, Geo. R.	The Jingo (1st, 8vo, grey/gilt, 394p, 10pl)	Bobbs-Merrill	(1912)	Wilson, F.V.	30-45	*
Chesterton, G.K.	Club of Queer Trades (1st, 8vo, 270p, 6pl)	Harper	1905	Various	45-60	*
Chesterton, G.K.	Coloured Lands (1st, lg8vo, 238p, yellow cl, DJ)	L: Sheed/Ward	1938	Chesterton, G.K.	70-100	
Chesterton, G.K.	Innocence of Father Brown (1st AM, 8vo, red cl, 334p, 7pl)	NY: J. Lane	1911	Foster, W.L.	45-60	*
Chesterton, G.K.	Innocence of Father Brown (1st, 8vo, 334p, red/gilt, 8pl)	L: Cassell	1911	Lucas, S.S.	180-220	
Chesterton, G.K.	Napoleon of Notting Hill (1st, 8vo, uncut, 301p, 8pl)	L: J. Lane	1904	Robertson, W.G.	150-185	
Chesterton, G.K.	St. Francis of Assissi (1st, sm8vo, 185p, brwn/gilt, p-o, 7 ticp)	L: Hodder	[1926]	Robinson, F.C.	70-100	
Chestnutt, Charles	Conjure Woman (1st, sm8vo, 229p, green cl, designs by…)	Houghton	1899	Rogers, B.	300-400	
Chestnutt, Charles	Wife of His Youth (1st, 8vo, 323p, pink/gilt)	Houghton	1899	DeLand, C.O.	230-300	
Chidsey, A.	Rustam Lion of Persia (1st, 8vo, 271p, blue cl, b/w, pep)	Minton Balch	1930	Lenski, L.	30-45	
Childs, M.F.	De Namin ob De Twins (1st, 8vo, teg, 139p, 7pl)	Dodge	1908	Potthast, E.	70-110	
Chilvers, H.A.	Out of the Crucible (1st, 8vo, 273p, 16 illus)	L: Cassell	1929	Timlin, W.M.	100-130	*
Chisholm, A.M.	Boss of Wind River (1st, 12mo, blue cl, 341p, 4cp)	Doubleday/Page	1911	Johnson, F.T.	20-25	
Chisholm, L.	Enchanted Land (1st, sm4to, 211p, p-o, white/gilt, teg, 30cp)	L: Jack	(1906)	Cameron, K.	150-180	
Chisholm, L.	Enchanted Land (1st AM, 4to, 211p, AEG, green/gilt, 30cp)	Putnam	(1906)	Cameron, K.	125-165	
Chisholm, L.	Golden Staircase (1st, lg8vo, 361p, uncut, gilt, teg, 16cp)	L: Jack	(1906)	Spooner, M.D.	65-80	
Chisholm, L.	In Fairyland (1st, lg8vo, p-o, AEG, 30cp, pep)	Putnam/Jack	(1904)	Cameron, K.	120-165	
Chisholm, L.	Staircase of Stories (1st, sm4to, 527p, p-o, 31cp)	L: Jack	(1919)	Various	75-120	*
Chittenden, W.L.	Bermuda Verses (1st, 8vo, 68p, green cl, 29pl)	Putnam	1909	(Photos)	40-65	
Chittenden, W.L.	Ranch Verses (1st, 8vo, 189p, 14pl)	Putnam	1893	(Photos)	80-120	
Choate, F.	Abby in the Gobi (1st, ob4to, ibds, 63p, color, pep)	McBride	(1929)	Choate/Curtis	50-75	*
Choate, F.	Dance of the Hours (1st, 8vo, 242p, pep, fp b/w)	Harcourt	(1934)	Choate/Curtis	20-30	*
Choate, F.	Little People of the Hills (1st, 8vo, 234p, fp b/w)	Harcourt	(1928)	Choate/Curtis	25-40	*
Choate, F.	Pinafores & Pantalets (1st, 8vo, 207p, uncut, pep, 8 fp 2-col)	Harcourt	(1931)	Choate/Curtis	25-40	*
Cholmondeley, M.	Red Pottage (1st, 8vo, 202p, tan wraps, 8pl)	L: Newnes	1904	Rackham, A.	375-550	
Chrisman, A.B.	Shen of the Sea (1st, 8vo, 252p, red/gilt, pep, NM)	Dutton	(1925)	Hasselriis, E.	40-70	
Chrisman, A.B.	Treasures Long Hidden (1st {std}, 8vo, blue cl, 302p, b/w, pep)	Dutton	1941	Yap, W.	25-45	*
Chrisman, A.B.	Wind that Wouldn't Blow (1st, sm8vo, 355p, uncut, b/w, pep)	Dutton	(1927)	Hasselriis, E.	30-45	*
Christie, E.R.	Fairy Tales from England (1st, 8vo, 232p, 6pl)	L: T.F. Unwin	1896	Holland, A.	50-70	
Christie, E.R.	Fairy Tales from Finland (1st, 12mo, 232p, teg, uncut, b/w)	L: T.F. Unwin	1896	Holland, A.	50-85	*
Christie, G.F.	Round De Ole Plantation (1st, 4to, ibds, unpag, 24 fp color)	L: Blackie	[1906]	Christie, G.F.	350-500	*
Christopher, Anne	Monkey Twins (1st, ob8vo, [31]p, pep, ipcb, color)	Whitman	(1935)	Hogan, I.	50-70	*
Christopher, Anne	Petunia Be Keerful (1st, 8vo, ibds, [41]p, color)	Whitman	(1934)	Hogan, I.	60-80	
Christy, H.C.	American Girl (1st, lg8vo, 157p, p-o, 16cp)	Moffat	1906	Christy, H.C.	70-100	

AUTHOR: 28

AUTHOR	TITLE	PUBLISHER	DATE	ARTIST	PRICE	LC
Christy, H.C.	Christy Girl (1st, lg8vo, [48]p, p-o, 16cp)	Bobbs-Merrill	(1906)	Christy, H.C.	70-100	
Christy, H.C.	Drawings (1st, ob folio, [58]p, ibds, 28pl)	Moffat	1905	Christy, H.C.	100-150	
Christy, H.C.	Our Girls (1st, lg8vo, 159p, p-o, 16cp)	Moffat	1907	Christy, H.C.	70-120	
Christy, H.C.	Songs of Sentiment (1st, 8vo, grey/gilt, p-o, 12cp)	Moffat	1910	Christy, H.C.	70-120	
Churchill, W.	The Crossing... (1st, 8vo, green/gilt, 296p, 10pl)	MacMillan	1930	Rae, J.	30-45	
Chute, Marchette	Rhymes About the City (1st, sm8vo, 57p, cloth, DJ)	MacMillan	1946	Chute, M.	45-60	
Chute, Marchette	Rhymes About the Country (1st, 4to, tan cl, 74p, b/w, pep)	MacMillan	1941	Chute, M.	50-65	
Ciardi, John	Reason for the Pelican (1st, lg8vo, 64p, blue cl, b/w)	Lippincott	(1959)	Gekiere, M.	35-50	*
Ciardi, John	Scrappy the Pup (1st {std}, 4to, blue cl, unpag, 1-color, cep)	Lippincott	(1960)	Miller, Jane	65-80	*
Clark, A.N.	Blue Canyon Horse (1st, sm4to, 54p, fp color, pep)	Viking	1954	Hauser, A.	65-80	R*
Clark, A.N.	In My Mother's House (1st, 4to, 56p, brown cl, pep, color, CH)	Viking	1941	Herrera, V.	65-90	R
Clark, A.N.	Little Navajo Bluebird (1st, 8vo, 143p)	Viking	1943	Lantz, P.	30-45	*
Clark, A.N.	Looking for Something (1st, 8vo, 53p, dp color, pep)	Viking	1952	Politi, L.	25-40	
Clark, A.N.	Magic Money (1st, sm4to, 121p, red cl, pep, fp 1-color)	Viking	1950	Politi, L.	25-45	*
Clark, A.N.	Santiago (1st, 8vo, 189p, color, pep, DJ)	Viking	1955	Ward, L.	25-40	
Clark, A.N.	Secret of the Andes (1st, 4to, 131p, grey cl, col frn, pep, NM)	Viking	1952	Charlot, J.	75-100	R
Clark, A.N.	Third Monkey (1st, 4to, 44p, color, pep)	Viking	1956	Freeman, D.	30-50	*
Clark, G.O	Nightmare Land (1st, lg4to, [105]p, color)	R.H. Russell	1901	Goodwin, C.L.	180-270	*
Clark, G.O.	Moon Babies (1st, ob4to, ibds, 48p, color)	R.H. Russell	1900	Hyde, Helen	150-200	
Clark, J.M.	Legends/King Arthur & his Knights (8vo, 307p, AEG, 6cp, pep)	L: Nister	[1899]	Margetson, W.H.	70-100	*
Clark, M.	Poppy Seed Cakes (1st {std}, sm sq8vo, 154p, 16cp, pep)	Doubleday/Page	1924	Petershams	70-120	R*
Clark, Mary S.	Lost Legends/Nursery Songs (1st, 12mo, 278p, red cl, uncut, 8cp)	L: G. Bell	1920	Woodward, A.B.	70-90	
Clark, Mary S.	Turnaside Cottage (8vo, [new ed.], green/gilt, 191p, col frn)	L: Marcus Ward	[1880]	Greenaway, K.	150-200	
Clarkson, L.	Buttercup's Visit... (folio, cloth, chromos)	Dutton	1881	Clarkson, L.	75-100	
Clarkson, L.	Fly-Away Fairies (1st, 4to, ibds, unpag, 16cp)	Dutton	1882	Clarkson, L.	120-165	
Clarkson, L.	Gathering of the Lillies (1st, 4to, AEG, cloth)	Sibole	(1870)	Clarkson, L.	160-230	
Clarkson, L.	Heartsease & Happy Days (folio, AEG, chromos)	Dutton	1883	Clarkson, L.	120-165	
Clarkson, L.	Indian Summer (1st, folio, AEG, gilt, 12cp)	Dutton	1881	Clarkson, L.	100-150	
Clarkson, L.	Violet Among the Lilies (4to, silver/gilt, AEG)	Dutton	1885	Clarkson, L.	85-100	
Clarkson, L.	Violet with Eyes of Blue (4to, gilt, 9 chromos)	(Phila)	(1876)	Clarkson, L.	90-120	
Claudy, C.H.	Tell Me Why Stories (1st, lg8vo, tan cl, 154p, 8cp)	McBride	1912	Rockwell, N.	600-800	*
Claudy, C.H.	Tell Me Why Stories (1st {this fmt}, 8vo, blue cl, 209p, 8cp)	McBride	1914	Wrenn, T.	20-30	*
Clay, Beatrice	Stories of King Arthur (1st, 8vo, 322p)	L: Dent	1905	Curtis, D.	25-40	*
Clay, J.C.	Lovers' Mother Goose (1st, 4to, 92p, gilt, color)	Bobbs-Merrill	(1905)	Clay, J.C.	50-80	
Clay/Herford	Cupid's Cyclopedia (1st, 12mo, ibds)	Scribner	1910	Clay/Herford	60-85	
Clayton, J.	Bunny Brothers (8vo, pcb, 96p)	L: Sully	(1915)	Clayton, M.	30-45	
Clayton, John	Dot in Dreamland (8vo, green cl, p-o, 10cp)	Whitman	(1916)	Clayton, M.	65-85	
Clemens, W.M.	Ken of Kipling (1st, 12mo, 141p, orange cl)	New Amsterdam	1899	McManus, B.	40-70	
Clement, Marg.	Flowers of Chivalry (1st {std}, 4to, ipcb, 72p, color, cep)	Doubleday/Dor.	1934	L'Hardy, G.& P.	50-85	*
Clement, Marg.	In France (1st, 8vo, blue cl, 151p, dp b/w, pep)	Viking	1956	DuBois, W.P.	25-40	*
Clement, Marg.	Where Was Bobby? (1st {std}, 8vo, 151p, 19cp, pep)	Doubleday/Dor.	1928	Petershams	35-50	*
Clinton, A.L.	Treasure Book/Best Stories (1st, 4to, 92p, ibds, 10cp)	Saalfield	(1933)	Peat, F.B.	45-60	
Cloud, V.W.	Down Durley Land (1st, 4to, 95p, teg, green/gilt, 1-color)	Century	1898	Birch, R.	50-75	
Clymer, E.L.	Chester (1st, sm8vo, 141p, red cl, fp b/w)	Dodd	1954	Keats, E.J.	30-45	*
Clymer, E.L.	Grocery Mouse (1st, 8vo, 94p, color)	McBride	1945	Bendick, J.	20-25	*
Coatsworth, E.	Alice-All-by-Herself (1st, 8vo, 181p, col frn, 7pl, pep, DJ)	MacMillan	1937	DeAngeli, M.	50-70	
Coatsworth, E.	Atlas & Beyond (1st {std}, 12mo, 61p, p-o, dep, woodcuts by...)	Harper	1924	Cimino, H.	35-50	*
Coatsworth, E.	Away Goes Sally (1st, lg8vo, 122p, p-o, b/w, pep)	MacMillan	1934	Sewell, H.	45-70	R
Coatsworth, E.	Big Green Umbrella (1st, sq8vo, ibds, [28]p, color, pep)	Grosset/Dunlap	(1944)	Sewell, H.	45-60	*
Coatsworth, E.	Boy with a Parrot (1st, 8vo, green cl, 101p, dp color, cep)	MacMillan	1930	Bronson, W.A.	25-45	*
Coatsworth, E.	Cat & the Captain (1st, 16mo, 95p, green cl, 3cp, pep)	MacMillan	1927	Kaye, G.	35-50	*
Coatsworth, E.	Cat Who Went to Heaven (1st, lg8vo, red cl, 57p, b/w, NM)	MacMillan	1930	Ward, L.	65-80	R
Coatsworth, E.	Country Neighborhood (1st {std} 8vo, 181p, decor by...)	MacMillan	1944	Woodward, H.	25-40	*
Coatsworth, E.	Cricket & the Emperor's Son (1st, sq8vo, dep, 112p, b/w)	MacMillan	1932	Yap, W.	45-60	*
Coatsworth, E.	Dancing Tom (1st, sq12mo, tan cl, [49]p, 1-color)	MacMillan	1938	Paull, G.	30-45	*
Coatsworth, E.	Desert Dan (1st, lg8vo, 61p, fp b/w)	Viking	(1960)	Johnson, H.	25-45	*
Coatsworth, E.	Door to the North (1st {std}, 8vo, 246p)	Winston	(1950)	Chapman, F.T.	25-40	*
Coatsworth, E.	Fair American (1st, 8vo, 132p, p-o, pep, 14pl)	MacMillan	1940	Sewell, H.	30-50	
Coatsworth, E.	Five Bushel Farm (1st, lg8vo, 152p, pep, p-o, b/w, DJ)	MacMillan	1939	Sewell, H.	35-50	*
Coatsworth, E.	Forgotten Island (1st, sm8vo, 65p, tan cl, b/w)	Grosset/Dunlap	(1942)	Paull, G.	25-45	*
Coatsworth, E.	Golden Horseshoe (1st, 8vo, 151p, gilt, pep, 14pl)	MacMillan	1935	Lawson, R.	45-60	
Coatsworth, E.	House-Boat Summer (1st, 8vo, 191p, p-o, 1-color, pep, DJ)	MacMillan	1942	Davis, M.	25-45	
Coatsworth, E.	Kitten Stand (1st, 8vo, ipcb, [28]p, color, pep)	Grosset/Dunlap	(1945)	Keeler, K.	35-50	*
Coatsworth, E.	Knock at the Door (1st, ob8vo, 73p, gilt, col frn, b/w)	MacMillan	1931	Bedford, F.D.	35-50	
Coatsworth, E.	Little Haymakers (1st {std}, sm8vo, tan cl, 79p, fp b/w)	MacMillan	1949	Paull, G.	25-40	*
Coatsworth, E.	Littlest House (1st, 8vo, p-o, 152p, 1-color, pep)	MacMillan	1940	Davis, M.	25-40	
Coatsworth, E.	Lonely Maria (1st, 8vo, yellow cl, [38]p, 2-color)	Pantheon	(1960)	Ness, E.M.	45-60	*
Coatsworth, E.	Night & the Cat (1st, 4to, blue cl, 55p, 10pl)	MacMillan	1950	Foujita	45-60	*
Coatsworth, E.	Peaceable Kingdom (1st, lg ob8vo, [39]p, 2-color, pep)	Pantheon	(1958)	Eichenberg, F.	35-50	*
Coatsworth, E.	Plum Daffy Adventure (1st {std}, 8vo, 161p, blue cl, b/w, pep)	MacMillan	1947	Davis, M.	35-50	*
Coatsworth, E.	Sun's Diary (1st, sq8vo, ibds, [98]p, b/w, cep)	MacMillan	1929	McIntosh, F.	65-80	R
Coatsworth, E.	Sword of the Wilderness (1st, 8vo, 160p, b/w, pep)	MacMillan	1936	Stein, H.	20-35	*

AUTHOR	TITLE	PUBLISHER	DATE	ARTIST	PRICE	LC
Coatsworth, E.	Toast to the King (1st, 8vo, 159p, pep)	Coward	(1940)	Orr, F.	25-40	*
Coatsworth, E.	Tonio & the Stranger (1st, 8vo, 69p, b/w)	Grosset/Dunlap	(1941)	Bronson, W.S.	25-40	*
Coatsworth, E.	Toutou in Bondage (1st, 8vo, 56p, dp illus, pep)	MacMillan	1929	Handforth, T.	35-50	*
Coatsworth, E.	White Horse (1st {std}, 8vo, 164p, p-o, 14 fp b/w, pep, DJ)	MacMillan	1942	Sewell, H.	40-65	
Coatsworth, E.	Wonderful Day (1st {std}, 8vo, yellow cl, 126p, pep)	MacMillan	1946	Sewell, H.	35-60	*
Coatsworth, E.	You Shall Have a Carriage (1st {std}, 8vo, 138p, pep)	MacMillan	1941	Pitz, H.C.	25-40	*
Cobb, I.	Back Home (1st, 8vo, cloth, 348p, 10pl)	Doran	(1912)	Unknown	45-60	
Cobb, I.	Cobb's Anatomy (1st, 8vo, tan pcb, 141p, 17pl, pep)	Doran	(1912)	Newell, P.	35-50	
Cobb, I.	Cobb's Bill of Fare (1st, 8vo, tan, pcb, 148p, 15pl, pep)	Doran	(1913)	Newell, P.	35-50	
Cobb, I.	Fibble, D.D. (1st, 8vo, 279p, blue cl, p-o, b/w, pep)	Doran	(1916)	Sarg, T.	30-50	
Cobb, L.M.	Animal Tales/Old North State (1st, 8vo, 200p, uncut, b/w, pep)	Dutton	1938	Hogan, I.	30-50	*
Coblentz, C.C.	Animal Pioneers (1st, 8vo, green cl, 241p, b/w)	Little/Brown	1936	Wiese, K.	25-45	*
Coblentz, C.C.	Beggar's Penny (1st {std}, 8vo, 269p, map)	Longmans	1943	Van Stockum, H.	25-45	*
Coblentz, C.C.	Bells of Leyden Sing (1st {std}, 8vo, 259p, pep, b/w)	Longmans	1944	Van Stockum, H.	25-45	*
Coblentz, C.C.	Blue & Silver Necklace (1st {std}, 8vo, 242p, blue cl, 6pl)	Little/Brown	1937	Earle, E.	20-35	*
Coblentz, C.C.	Blue Cat of Castle Town (1st {std}, 8vo blue cl, 123p, b/w, pep)	Longmans	1949	Holland, J.	40-70	R
Coblentz, C.C.	Falcon of Eric the Red (1st {std}, 8vo, 211p, dp pl)	Longmans	1942	Pitz, H.C.	30-45	*
Coblentz, C.C.	Sequoya (1st {std}, sm8vo, 199p, decor by...)	Longmans	1946	Ray, R.	25-45	*
Coburn, Grace	Heroes & Wizards (1st, 8vo, 246p, col frn, 8 fp b/w)	L: Nelson	1939	Parsons, J.	25-40	*
Coburn, W.D.	Rhymes of the Roundup Camp (1st, 12mo, 138p, 7 b/w)	Ridgley Pr.	1899	Russell, C.M.	200-300	
Coburn, W.D.	Rhymes of the Roundup Camp (sm8vo, teg, 137p, 7pl)	Putnam	1903	Russell, C.M.	100-140	*
Cocke, Sarah J.	Bypaths in Dixie (1st, 8vo, blue/gilt, 317p, 7pl)	Dutton	(1911)	Smith, Duncan	45-60	*
Coffin, J.H.	Vendor of Dreams (1st, 4to, 108p, blue/gilt, teg, 3cp)	Dodd	1917	Coffin, H.	45-60	*
Coggins, Herbert	Busby & Co. (1st, 8vo, 96p, rust cl, fp b/w, pep)	Whittlesey	(1952)	Duvoisin, R.	30-45	
Colby, J.P.	Jim the Cat (1st {std}, lg8vo, yellow cl, 46p, fp b/w)	Little/Brown	(1957)	Nichols, M.C.	30-45	
Colby, J.P.	Peter Paints the U.S.A. (1st, 4to, 47p, red cl, color, pep)	Houghton	1948	Bare, A.E.	45-65	*
Colcock, A.T.	Margaret Tudor (12mo, 169p, green cl)	Stokes	(1901)	Gilbert, W.	20-30	
Cole, Frank (ed.)	Picture Birthday Book/Boys & Girls (16mo, gilt, 12cp)	L: Harrap	(1915)	Tarrant, M.	50-75	
Coleman, O.	Successful Houses (lg8vo, tan cl, cvr by...)	H. Stone	1899	Hazenplug, F.	65-90	
Coleridge, C.R.	Minstrel Dick (1st, 8vo, 288p, 3pl)	L: Wells/Gard.	1896	Robinson, C.	50-80	*
Coleridge, S.T.	Kubla Kahn (1st {std}, 4to, unpag, gilt, 13 fp brown illus)	Dutton	1933	Vassos, J.	100-140	
Coleridge, S.T.	Rime of the Ancient Mariner (1st, lg4to, gilt, teg, pep, 20 ticp)	L: Harrap	(1910)	Pogany, W.	250-400	
Coleridge, S.T.	Rime of the Ancient Mariner (1st AM, lg4to, gilt, 20 ticp, pep)	Crowell	(1910)	Pogany, W.	200-300	
Coleridge, S.T.	Rime/Ancient Mariner (1st {this fmt}, sm4to, teg, gilt, 20 ticp)	Doran	[1915]	Pogany, W.	120-165	
Collins, C.	All Round the Farm (4to, ibds)	L: Nister	[1880]	(Chromos)	70-100	
Collins, Dale	Shipmates Down Under (1st, sm8vo, green cl, 188p, b/w, cep)	Holiday House	(1950)	Busoni, R.	20-30	*
Collis, Maurice	Quest for Sita (1st AM, 8vo, blue/gilt, uncut, 31 fp b/w)	NY: J. Day	1947	Peake, M.	80-100	*
Collodi, C.	Adventures Every Child Should Know (1st, 12mo, 241p, 8cp)	Doubleday/Page	1909	Chamberlin, E.H.	40-60	*
Collodi, C.	Adventures of Pinocchio (8vo, 259p, p-o, 8cp)	Winston	(1920)	Richardson, F.	40-65	
Collodi, C.	Adventures of Pinocchio (1st AM, lg4to, 404p, cp, DJ)	MacMillan	(1925)	Mussino, A.	180-250	
Collodi, C.	Adventures of Pinocchio (1st {std}, sm8vo, 280p, col frn)	Doubleday/Dor.	1930	Liddell, M.	50-80	*
Collodi, C.	Adventures of Pinocchio (1st {this fmt}, lg8vo, 254p, p-o, 5cp)	Rand/McNally	(1939)	Friend, E.	60-85	
Collodi, C.	Pinocchio (1st, 12mo, 212p, gilt, 12cp, pep)	Ginn	(1904)	Copeland, C.	45-65	
Collodi, C.	Pinocchio (1st, sq8vo, p-o, ibds, 268p, 13cp)	Dent/Dutton	1911	Folkard, C.	80-100	
Collodi, C.	Pinocchio (1st, lg8vo, 205p, p-o, 8cp)	Whitman	(1917)	Carsey, A.	50-65	
Collodi, C.	Pinocchio (1st {Gift ed.}, lg8vo, 234p, p-o, teg, 14 ticp)	Lippincott	1920	Kirk, M.L.	100-140	
Collodi, C.	Pinocchio (1st, 8vo, 167p, gilt, p-o, 21cp, pep)	Winston	(1923)	Richardson, F.	70-120	*
Collodi, C.	Pinocchio (1st, lg8vo, 247p, p-o, col frn, b/w)	Saalfield	(1924)	Brundage, F.	50-80	
Collodi, C.	Pinocchio (1st {this pub.}, 8vo, p-o, DJ)	McKay	(1925)	Folkard, C.	65-80	
Collodi, C.	Pinocchio (1st, lg8vo, 255p, pep, p-o, fp color)	Whitman	(1926)	Higgins, V.M.	50-65	*
Collodi, C.	Pinocchio (1st, sm4to, 236p, p-o, orange cl, pep)	Sears	(1926)	Rule, C.	35-50	*
Collodi, C.	Pinocchio (1st, 8vo, p-o, 213p, 5cp, pep)	Houghton	1927	Bacharach, H.I.	65-100	
Collodi, C.	Pinocchio (1st, 8vo, red/gilt, p-o, 239p, 6cp, pep)	T. Nelson	1928	Wiese, K.	50-75	*
Collodi, C.	Pinocchio (1st [Gift ed.], 4to, 284p, 10cp)	Lippincott	(1930)	Tinker, J.H.	65-80	*
Collodi, C.	Pinocchio (1st, 8vo, p-o, blue cl, 323p, 4cp, pep)	Garden City	1932	Petershams	65-90	
Collodi, C.	Pinocchio (1st, sm8vo, rust cl, 282p, 13 fp b/w)	Appleton/Cent.	(1935)	Sewell, H.	30-50	*
Collodi, C.	Pinocchio (1st [Movie ed.], sm ob4to, ibds, [50]p)	Grosset/Dunlap	1939	(Photos)	60-80	*
Collodi, C.	Pinocchio (1st, 4to, ibds, 96p, cvr & col frn by...)	Saalfield	(1939)	Madsen, E.	75-100	*
Collodi, C.	Pinocchio (1st, 4to, red cl, 122p, pep, 6cp)	Platt/Munk	(1940)	Sarg, T.	80-120	
Collodi, C.	Pinocchio (1st, 8vo, 239p, pep, fp color)	World	(1946)	Floethe, R.	30-45	*
Collodi, C.	Pinocchio (1st, 4to, yellow bds, [65]p, 7 fp color)	Random	(1946)	Lenski, L.	65-100	
Collodi, C.	Pinocchio in Africa (1st AM, 12mo, green cl, 152p)	Ginn	(1911)	Copeland, C.	80-130	
Collodi, C.	Pinocchio's Advens. in Wonderland (12mo, 212p, 4cp)	J. Marsh	(1898)	Quentin, R.	180-250	
Collodi, C.	Pinocchio's Advens/Wonderland (1st AM, sm8vo, green/gilt, 212p)	J. Marsh	(1898)	Unknown	300-400	R*
Collodi, C.	Story of a Puppet (1st {Engl.trans.}, 8vo, grn/gilt, 232p, teg)	L: T. F. Unwin	1892	Mazzanti, C.	800-1000	
Colmont, Marie	Down the River (1st {std}, lg4to, [24]p, pep, 5 dp color)	Harper	1940	Exter, A.	35-60	*
Colt, Terry S.	Knights, Goats & Battleships (1st {std}, 12mo, 316p, col, pep)	Doubleday/Dor.	1930	Flack, M.	25-40	*
Colum, P.	Adventures of Odysseus (1st, 8vo, 254p, 8cp, pep)	MacMillan	1918	Pogany, W.	50-70	
Colum, P.	At the Gateways of the Day (1st, 8vo, 217p, fp b/w)	Yale U. Press	1924	Fraser, J.M.	25-40	
Colum, P.	Big Tree of Bunlahy (1st, 8vo, 166p, col frn, DJ, NH)	MacMillan	1933	Yeats, J.B.	80-100	
Colum, P.	Boy Apprenticed to an Enchanter (1st, sm8vo, 168p, b/w)	MacMillan	1920	Walker, D.S.	30-50	
Colum, P.	Boy Who Knew what the Birds Said (1st, 12mo, 178p, b/w)	MacMillan	1918	Walker, D.S.	30-45	

AUTHOR	TITLE	PUBLISHER	DATE	ARTIST	PRICE	LC
Colum, P.	Boy in Eirinn (1st, 8vo, 255p, blue/gilt, col frn, 4pl)	Dutton	(1913)	Yeats, J.B.	100-140	*
Colum, P.	Boy in Eirinn (1st UK, bds, 255p, 6pl)	L: Dent	1915	Yeats, J.B.	150-185	
Colum, P.	Bright Islands (1st, 8vo, 233p, gilt, pep, b/w)	Yale U. Press	1925	Fraser, J.M.	35-50	
Colum, P.	Children Who Followed/Piper (1st, sm8vo, 152p, col frn)	MacMillan	1922	Walker, D.S.	45-60	
Colum, P.	Children of Odin (1st, sm8vo, 282p, 4cp)	MacMillan	1920	Pogany, W.	30-45	
Colum, P.	Creatures (1st, 8vo, bds, 56p, 10 illus, pep)	MacMillan	1927	Artzybasheff, B.	50-70	
Colum, P.	Forge in the Forest (1st, 8vo, 149p, black/gilt, pep, 9cp)	MacMillan	1925	Artzybasheff, B.	50-80	
Colum, P.	Frenzied Prince (1st {std}, sm4to, 196p, 10 fp color, pep, DJ)	McKay	(1943)	Pogany, W.	65-80	
Colum, P.	Girl Who Sat by the Ashes (1st, 8vo, 175p, col frn)	MacMillan	1919	Walker, D.S.	30-45	
Colum, P.	Golden Fleece (1st, sq8vo, 290p, gilt, 8cp, pep, NH)	MacMillan	1921	Pogany, W.	45-60	
Colum, P.	Island of the Mighty (1st, 8vo, 265p, gilt, 3cp, 19pl)	MacMillan	1924	Jones, W.	30-45	
Colum, P.	King of Ireland's Son (1st, 8vo, green/gilt, 316p, 4cp)	Holt	1916	Pogany, W.	70-100	*
Colum, P.	King of Ireland's Son (1st UK, 8vo, 316p, 4cp)	L: Harrap	1920	Pogany, W.	70-100	
Colum, P.	King of Ireland's Son (1st {this pub.}, sq8vo, 316p, 4cp)	MacMillan	1921	Pogany, W.	25-40	
Colum, P.	Legend of St. Columbia (1st, lg8vo, green cl, 156p, b/w)	MacMillan	1935	MacKinstry, E.	40-65	
Colum, P.	Orpheus: Myths of the World (1st, 4to, 327p, grey cl, 20pl)	MacMillan	1930	Artzybasheff, B.	35-50	
Colum, P.	Peep-Show Man (1st, 12mo, blue cl, 65p, 4cp, pep)	MacMillan	1924	Lenski, L.	40-60	
Colum, P.	Six Who were Left in a Shoe (1st, sq8vo, ibds, unpag, col, pep)	Volland	(1923)	Walker, D.S.	50-65	
Colum, P.	The Voyagers (1st, sm8vo, 188p, 3cp, fp b/w, NH)	MacMillan	1925	Jones, W.	40-60	*
Colum, P.	White Sparrow (1st, sq8vo, 46p, grey cl, pep, DJ)	MacMillan	1933	Ward, L.	45-60	
Colvile, Kath.	Jason & the Princess (1st AM, sm8vo, blue cl, 86p, 4cp)	Houghton	(1926)	Rutherston, A.	30-45	*
Compton, M.	Snow Bird & Water Tiger... (1st UK, 8vo, 201p, teg, gilt, b/w)	L: Lawrence	1895	Greenough, W.C.	70-85	
Comstock, E.B.	Fairy Frolics (1st, 4to, [64]p, p-o, 6cp)	Rand/McNally	(1913)	Comstock, E.B.	160-220	
Comstock, E.B.	Tuck-Me-In Stories (1st, lg8vo, 76p, color)	Moffat	1917	Comstock, E.B.	65-80	*
Comstock, H.T.	Princess Rags & Tatters (1st, 12mo, grey cl, 112p, 4cp)	Doubleday/Page	1912	Thayer, L.	30-45	
Cone, H.G.	Baby Sweethearts (1st, folio, ipcb, 12cp)	Stokes	1890	Humphrey, M.	380-500	R
Cone, H.G.	Bonnie Little People (1st, lg4to, 12p, 6cp)	Stokes	1890	Humphrey, M.	400-550	
Cone, H.G.	One, Two, Three, Four (1st, 4to, ibds, unpag, 4cp)	Stokes	1889	Humphrey, M.	200-250	
Conger, Marion	Circus Time (1st, sm8vo, [42]p, ibds, color, LGB)	Simon/Schuster	(1948)	Gergely, T.	45-60	*
Conklin, Gladys	I Like Caterpillars (1st, sm4to, yellow cl, [26]p, color)	Holiday House	(1958)	Latham, B.	25-45	*
Conkling, H.	Silverhorn (1st, 8vo, p-o, 159p, col frn, fp b/w, pep)	Stokes	1924	Lathrop, D.	70-90	
Conner, Ralph	Black Rock (1st, 8vo, tan cl, 322p, cvr by...)	Revell	1900	Hazenplug, F.	20-35	
Conner, Ralph	Black Rock (1st, tan cl, 8vo, 322p, 8pl by...)	Revell	1900	Rhead, L.	20-35	
Connolly, J.	Story of an Old Fashioned Doll (1st, 8vo, 107p)	L: D. Nutt	1905	Ault, N.	50-70	
Connolly, J.B.	Crested Seas (1st, 8vo, 311p, gilt, teg, 2pl by..)	Scribner	1907	Wyeth, N.C.	30-45	
Connolly, J.B.	Hiker Joy (1st, 12mo, red/gilt, uncut, 244p, 4pl)	Scribner	1920	Wyeth, N.C.	25-40	
Conrad, J.	Romance (1st AM, 8vo, 428p, 8pl)	McClure	1904	Macauley, C.R.	120-165	
Converse, F.	House of Prayer (1st, 12mo, 276p, teg, uncut, 8pl)	L: Dent	1908	Webb, M.E.	25-40	
Cook, Bernadine	Curious Little Kitten (1st, ob4to, green cl, unpag, 1-color)	W.R. Scott	1956	Charlip, R.	50-80	*
Cook, Bernadine	Little Fish that Got Away (1st, sm8vo, unpag, 2-color)	W.R. Scott	1956	Johnson, C.	35-50	*
Cook, Hartley K.	Over the Hills & Far Away (1st, 8vo, 263p, pep by...)	L: Allen/Unwin	1947	Ardizzone, E.	35-50	
Cook, W.	Peggy's Travels (1st, 4to, 98p, brown bds, 15cp)	L: Blackie	[1908]	Cook, A.M.	100-150	
Cook, W.W.	Wilby's Dan (1st, 12mo, 325p, 8cp)	Dodd	1904	Falls, C.B.	60-80	*
Cooke, Alistair	Christmas Eve (1st AM {std}, 8vo, 56p, bds, 1-color)	Knopf	(1952)	Simont, M.	35-50	
Cooke, E.V.	Biography of Our Baby (1st, lg8vo, white/gilt, [60]p, color)	Dodge	(1906)	Pease, B.C.	165-200	
Cooke, E.V.	Chronicles of a Little Tot (1st, 8vo, 119p, 3cp)	Dodge	(1905)	Pease, B.C.	160-220	
Cooke, E.V.	Impertinent Poems (1st, 8vo, p-o, teg, uncut, 103p, 11cp)	Dodge	(1907)	Ross, G.	30-50	
Cooke, E.V.	Story Club (1st, 8vo, p-o, 210p, cp)	Dodge	(1912)	Curtis, E.	25-40	*
Cooke, E.V.	Told to the Little Tot (1st, 8vo, 132p, p-o, teg, 10cp)	Dodge	(1906)	Pease, B.C.	160-200	*
Cooke, G.M.	Doings of the Dollivers (1st, 12mo, 174p, 7pl)	Sturgis	1910	Linnell, H.	35-50	*
Cooke, G.M.	Huldah (1st, 8vo, 316p, cvr by...)	Bobbs-Merrill	(1904)	Armstrong, M.	30-50	
Cooke, G.M.	Huldah (1st, 8vo, 316p, 8pl by...)	Bobbs-Merrill	(1904)	Cory, F.	30-50	
Cooke, G.M.	Their First Formal Call (1st, 8vo, 55p, p-o, gilt, 14pl)	Harper	1906	Newell, P.	65-90	
Cooke, M.B.	Dual Alliance (1st, 8vo, 165p, blue cl, 4cp, dep)	Doubleday/Page	1915	Blumenschein, M.	25-40	*
Coolidge, D.	Hidden Water (1st, 8vo, ibds, 483p, 4cp)	McClurg	1910	Dixon, M.	35-60	
Coolidge, D.	The Texican (1st, lg8vo, beige cl, 369p, 5cp)	McClurg	1911	Dixon, M.	45-70	
Coolidge, F.	Little Ugly Face (1st, sm8vo, 181p, 2-color)	MacMillan	1925	Petershams	25-45	*
Coolidge, S.	Guernsey Lily (lg sq8vo, brown/gilt, 238p, 10 illus)	Roberts	1881	Greenaway, K.	100-165	
Coolidge, S.	What Katy Did (1st, 8vo, p-o, 271p, 5cp, pep)	Little/Brown	1924	Coleman, R.P.	25-40	
Cooney, Barbara	Captain Pottle's House (1st, sm8vo, 172p, green cl, b/w)	Farrar/Rine.	(1943)	Cooney, B.	30-45	*
Cooney, Barbara	King of Wreck Island (1st {1st bk}, 8vo, blue cl, 91p, fp b/w)	Farrar/Rine.	(1941)	Cooney, B.	35-60	*
Cooney, Barbara	The Kellyhorns (1st, 8vo, red cl, 259p, b/w)	Farrar/Rine.	(1942)	Cooney, B.	30-45	*
Coonley, L.A.	Singing Verses for Children (1st, ob4to, 80p, gilt)	MacMillan	1897	Tyler, A.K.	65-100	
Cooper, F.T.	Argosy of Fables (1st, 4to, 485p, blue cl, 24 ticp, pep)	Stokes	(1921)	Bransom, P.	120-150	
Cooper, J.F	Last of the Mohicans (1st, 4to, 370p, p-o, 14cp, pep, SC)	Scribner	1919	Wyeth, N.C.	150-200	
Cooper, J.F.	Last of the Mohicans (1st, 8vo, p-o, 523p, 8cp)	Holt	(1910)	Smith, E.B.	65-90	
Cooper, J.F.	Last of the Mohicans (1st, sm8vo, p-o, 437p, 8cp, pep)	McKay	(1928)	Hurd, P.	45-60	*
Cooper, J.F.	The Deerslayer (1st, 4to, p-o, 462p, 9cp, pep, SC)	Scribner	1925	Wyeth, N.C.	140-200	
Cooper, J.F.	The Deerslayer (1st, 8vo, black cl, p-o, 556p, 4cp)	Harper	(1926)	Rhead, L.	35-50	
Cooper, J.F.	The Pathfinder (1st, 12mo, 516p, b/w pl)	Macrae Smith	(1926)	Humphreys, D.S.	20-30	*
Cooper, J.F.	The Pathfinder (1st, sm8vo, 540p, blue/gilt, p-o, 8cp, pep)	NY: Nelson	(1928)	Boog, C.M.	25-40	*
Cooper, J.F.	The Pathfinder (1st, 8vo, blue cl, p-o, 430p, 6cp, pep)	Minton Balch	1928	Ward, E.F.	35-50	

AUTHOR	TITLE	PUBLISHER	DATE	ARTIST	PRICE	LC
Cooper, J.F.	The Spy (1st, 4to, blue cl, 389p, p-o, 8cp, pep)	Minton Balch	1924	Baldridge, C.L.	30-45	
Cooper, J.F.	The Spy (1st, 8vo, 415p, p-o, 8cp)	Houghton	1924	Brett, H.M.	25-40	
Cooper, Page	Amigo, Circus Horse (1st {std}, 8vo, 238p, yel cl, uncut, b/w)	World Pub. Co.	(1955)	Pitz, H.C.	30-45	*
Cooper, Page	Great Horse Stories (1st {std}, 8vo, 366p, maroon cl, fp b/w)	Doubleday	1946	Brown, Paul	25-45	*
Copeland, W.	Awful Airship (1st, ob16mo, 62p, 30cp)	L: Blackie	[1906]	Robinson, C.	200-280	
Copeland, W.	Babes & Blossoms (1st AM, sm8vo, ipcb, 16cp)	Caldwell	[1908]	Robinson, C.	165-230	
Copeland, W.	Babes & Blossoms (1st, 8vo, ibds, [66]p, 16cp, pep)	L: Blackie	(1908)	Robinson, C.	180-275	
Copeland, W.	Black Cat Book (1st, 8vo, unpag)	L: Blackie	[1905]	Robinson, C.	100-140	*
Copeland, W.	Book of the Zoo (1st, 16mo, 120p)	L: Dent	1902	Robinson, C.	75-100	*
Copeland, W.	Farm Book (1st, 16mo, 120p)	Dent/Dutton	1901	Robinson, C.	65-80	*
Copeland, W.	Mad Motor (1st, ob24mo, ibds, color)	L: Blackie	(1906)	Robinson, C.	170-200	
Copley, F.B.	Impeachment/President Israels (1st, 12mo, blue/gilt, 124p, 3pl)	NY: MacMillan	1913	Unknown	25-45	
Corbet, K.& S.	Animal Land Where there are No People (1st AM, ob8vo)	Dutton	1897	Corbet, K.	80-100	*
Corbett, B.	Baby Days (1st, 4to, grey cloth, color)	Rand/McNally	(1910)	Corbett, B.L.	100-160	
Corbett, E.T.	3 Wise Old Couples (1st, 4to, ipcb, unpag, 15 chromos)	L: Cassell	(1881)	Hopkins, E.	80-100	*
Corbett, Scott	Sauce for the Gander (1st AM, sm8vo, yellow cl, 238p, fp b/w)	Crowell	1951	Freeman, D.	30-45	*
Corelli, M.	Devil's Motor (1st, 4to, 42p, red/gilt, 6 ticp)	L: Hodder	[1910]	Severn, A.	90-135	
Corkey, E.	Magic Circle (1st, lg8vo, gilt, 256p, b/w)	L: Blackie	[1924]	Brock, C.E.	40-60	
Cormack, M.	Wind of the Vikings (1st, 8vo, 259p, tan cl, 6 fp b/w, pep)	Appleton/Cen.	1937	Lawson, R.	30-50	*
Corrin, S.	Plucky Sailor & Postage Stamp (1st, 8vo, ibds, unpag, color)	L: Faber	1954	Ardizzone, E.	50-70	*
Cory, F.	Little Me (1st {std}, sm8vo, ipcb, [56]p, fp b/w)	Dutton	(1936)	Cory, F.	30-50	*
Cory, F.	Our Baby Book (lg4to, pink cl, [89]p, p-o, color)	Bobbs-Merrill	(1907)	Cory, F.	80-100	
Cory, F.	Sonny Sayings (1st, ob4to, ibds, 112p, b/w)	Dutton	(1929)	Cory, F.	50-70	
Coryell, Hubert	Klondike Gold (1st, 8vo, 319p, blue cl, pep, b/w)	MacMillan	1938	Sperry, A.	35-50	*
Cosgrove, R.R.	Hidden Valley of Oz (1st, lg8vo, blue cl, p-o, 313p, b/w, pep)	Reilly/Lee	(1951)	Dirk	180-220	
Costantino, Joan	Pepito at Capistrano (1st, lg8vo, p-o, 32p, color)	Whitman	1943	Patton, L.	20-30	*
Costello, C.J.	Old Mother Hubbard (4to, pict cl, color)	Chi: Jamieson	(1902)	Kennedy, H.O.	100-160	
Costello, F.H.	Nelson's Yankee Boy (1st, 12mo, 293p, 6pl)	Holt	1904	Dunton, W.H.	30-45	*
Courlander, H.	Cow-Tail Switch (1st, sm4to, brown cl, 143p, b/w, NH)	Holt	(1947)	Chastain, M.L.	40-65	*
Courlander, H.	Ride with the Sun (1st, sm8vo, 296p, green cl, b/w)	Whittlesey	(1955)	Duvoisin, R.	25-40	*
Courlander, H.	Terrapin's Pot of Sense (1st {std}, lg8vo, 125p, b/w)	Holt	(1957)	Fax, E.	25-40	*
Courlander, H.	Tiger's Whisper (1st {std}, sm8vo, blue cl, 152p, fp b/w)	Harcourt	(1959)	Arno, E.	25-40	*
Courlander, H.	Uncle Bouqui of Haiti (1st, 8vo, 126p, 1-color, pep)	Wm. Morrow	1942	Crockett, L.H.	25-45	*
Coussens, P.W.	Child's Book of Stories (1st, lg8vo, gilt, p-o, 463p, 10cp, pep)	Duffield	1911	Smith, J.W.	260-320	
Cowan, James	Daybreak... (1st, sm8vo, gilt, 399p, teg, b/w)	NY: Richmond	1896	Greenough, W.C.	70-100	
Cowen, Wm. J.	Man with Four Lives (1st, sm8vo, 277p, b/w pl)	Farrar/Rine.	(1934)	Ward, L.	30-45	*
Cowham, Hilda	Blacklegs.... (1st, 4to, 76p, teg, gilt, color)	L: Kegan Paul	1911	Cowham, H.	100-150	
Cowham, Hilda	Somebody's Baby (4to, ibds, 16 fp color)	L: R. Tuck	[1915]	Cowham, H.	100-165	
Cowie, John	Alliterative Anomalies/Infants & Invalids (ob4to, ibds, color)	Dodd	[1900]	Hammond, Wm.	160-220	*
Cowper, Wm.	Diverting History/John Gilpin (1st, ob4to [36]p, gilt, bds, 8cp)	L: Routledge	[1888]	Rosa, H.	100-150	
Cowper, Wm.	Diverting History/John Gilpin (1st, 8vo, 50p, blue cl, 12pl)	L: Aldine Hse.	1898	Brock, C.E.	50-75	*
Cox, F.T.	Chronicles of Rhoda (1st, 12mo, 289p, red/gilt, 2cp)	Small	(1909)	Smith, J.W.	80-120	
Cox, F.T.	Epic of Ebenezer (1st, 12mo, ibds, 72p)	Dodd	1912	Rae, J.	20-30	
Cox, P.	Another Brownie Book (1st, 4to, 144p, ibds)	Century	(1890)	Cox, P.	180-220	
Cox, P.	Brownie Clown of Brownie Town (ob8vo, 103p, ibds)	Century	[1908]	Cox, P.	170-240	*
Cox, P.	Brownie Year Book (lg4to, [26]p, ibds, 12cp)	McLoughlin	[1895]	Cox, P.	280-350	
Cox, P.	Brownies & Prince Florimel (1st, lg8vo, tan cl, 246p, p-o)	Century	1918	Cox, P.	100-130	
Cox, P.	Brownies Abroad (1st UK, 4to, 14p, red cl)	L: T.F. Unwin	(1899)	Cox, P.	160-200	
Cox, P.	Brownies Abroad (1st, 4to, 144p, ibds)	Century	(1899)	Cox, P.	200-250	
Cox, P.	Brownies Around the World (1st, 4to, ibds, 144p)	Century	(1894)	Cox, P.	160-200	
Cox, P.	Brownies Through the Union (1st, 4to, ibds, 144p)	Century	(1895)	Cox, P.	120-180	
Cox, P.	Brownies Through the Union (1st UK, 4to, 144p, cloth)	L: T.F. Unwin	1895	Cox, P.	250-350	
Cox, P.	Brownies at Home (1st, 4to, ibds, 144p)	Century	(1893)	Cox, P.	170-220	
Cox, P.	Brownies in Fairyland (1st, 8vo, 118p, cloth, b/w)	Century	(1925)	Cox, P.	150-185	
Cox, P.	Brownies in the Philippines (1st, 4to, ibds, 144p)	Century	(1904)	Cox, P.	160-200	
Cox, P.	Brownies: Their Book (1st, 4to, grn ipcb, 144p, b/w, cep, PPP)	Century	(1887)	Cox, P.	240-300	R
Cox, P.	Brownies: Their Book (1st UK, 4to, green ibds, 144p)	L: T.F. Unwin	1888	Cox, P.	180-250	
Cox, P.	Children's Funny Book (8vo, pcb, 30p)	Lothrop	(1879)	Cox, P.	85-100	
Cox, P.	Comic Yarns (1st, 8vo, 517p, blue/gilt, b/w, dep)	Hubbard	1889	Cox, P.	100-165	
Cox, P.	Frontier Humor (1st, 24mo, 343p, b/w)	Hubbard	(1895)	Cox, P.	60-85	
Cox, P.	Jolly Chinee (1st, thin 4to, p-o)	Conkey	(1900)	Cox, P.	90-130	
Cox, P.	Palmer Cox Brownie Primer (1st, 12mo, 108p, yel bds)	Century	1906	Cox, P.	100-165	
Cox, P.	Queer People (1st UK, sq4to, cloth)	L: T.F. Unwin	1896	Cox, P.	130-175	
Cox, P.	Queer People/Paws & Claws (1st, 4to, ibds, [119]p)	Hubbard	(1888)	Cox, P.	140-180	
Cox, P.	Queerie Queers with Hands, Wings & Claws (lg8vo, ibds, b/w)	Larkin	(1887)	Cox, P.	100-150	
Cox-McCormack, N.	Peeps: Really Truly Sunshine Fairy (1st, 8vo, [37]p, ibds, col)	Volland	(1918)	Dodge, K.S.	65-80	
Coybee, E.	Flower Book (1st, 16mo, green cl, color)	L: Richards	1901	Benson, N.	100-150	
Coyle, Kath.	Josephine (1st {std}, sm8vo, blue cl, 174p, b/w)	Harper	(1942)	Bacon, P.	35-50	*
Craddock, Harry	Savoy Cocktail Book (1st, 8vo, 287p, pcb, gilt, color)	L: Constable	1930	Rumbold, G.	160-200	
Craddock, C.E.	Phantoms of the Foot-Bridge (1st, 8vo, 353p, grn/gilt, 14pl)	Harper	1895	Frost, A.B.	40-65	
Craddock, C.E.	Young Mountaineers (1st, 8vo, 262p, green/gilt, 4pl)	Houghton	1897	Fraser, M.	35-50	
Craddock, H.C.	Best Teddy Bear in the World (1st, 8vo, 96p)	L: Nelson	(1926)	Appleton, H.C.	50-80	*

AUTHOR	TITLE	PUBLISHER	DATE	ARTIST	PRICE	LC
Cradock, H.C.	House of Fancy (1st, 4to, 32p)	L: O'Connor	1922	Appleton, H.C.	50-75	*
Cradock, H.C.	Josephine & Her Dolls (1st, 4to, ibds, 47p, 12 ticp)	L: Blackie	1916	Appleton, H.C.	240-300	
Cradock, H.C.	Josephine Dolly Book (4to, ibds, p-o, 8cp)	L: Blackie	[1920]	Appleton, H.C.	70-100	
Cradock, H.C.	Josephine Keeps House (1st, lg8vo, bds, p-o, 64p, 8cp)	L: Blackie	1931	Appleton, H.C.	100-140	*
Cradock, H.C.	Josephine Keeps School (1st, 4to, p-o, 64p, 8cp)	L: Blackie	[1925]	Appleton, H.C.	65-100	
Cradock, H.C.	Josephine is Busy (1st, lg8vo, 63p, color)	L: Blackie	1918	Appleton, H.C.	100-140	*
Cradock, H.C.	Josephine's Birthday (1st, 4to, 64p, p-o, ibds, 8cp)	L: Blackie	(1920)	Appleton, H.C.	65-100	
Cradock, H.C.	Josephine's Happy Family (1st AM, 4to, 63p, p-o, 8cp)	Stokes	[1920]	Appleton, H.C.	50-80	
Cradock, H.C.	Josephine's Pantomime (1st, lg8vo, bds, p-o, 64p, 8cp)	L: Blackie	(1939)	Appleton, H.C.	50-80	
Cradock, H.C.	Peggy & Joan (1st, 4to, 96p, 8cp, p-o)	L: Blackie	(1922)	Appleton, H.C.	65-90	
Craig, Alexander	Ionia... (1st, 8vo, grey buckram, 301p, 6pl)	E.A. Weeks	1898	Leyendecker, J.C.	85-130	
Craig, E.G.	Nothing... (1st, sm4to, bds, 26pl)	L: Chatto	1925	Craig, E.G.	100-160	
Craig, E.G.	Woodcuts & Some Words (1st, 4to, 122p, blue cl, 59pl)	L: Dent	1924	Craig, E.G.	80-135	
Craik, D.	Adventures of a Brownie (4to, ipcb)	Crowell	(1893)	Bridgman, C.	50-70	
Craik, D.	Adventures of a Brownie (1st, 16mo, 57p, p-o)	Reilly/Britton	(1912)	Neill, J.R.	35-60	
Craik, D.	Adventures of a Brownie (sm4to, grey cl, p-o, 12cp)	Whitman	[1920]	Carsey, A.	30-45	*
Craik, D.	Adventures of a Brownie (1st, 4to, teg, 281p, p-o, 14 ticp)	Lippincott	1922	Kirk, M.L.	80-100	
Craik, D.	Adventures of a Brownie (1st, 8vo, p-o, 128p, color)	Rand/McNally	(1923)	Winter, M.	50-65	
Craik, D.	Fairy Book (1st, 4to, 379p, teg, green/gilt, 32cp)	L: MacMillan	1913	Goble, W.	300-450	
Craik, D.	Fairy Book (1st, 8vo, 416p, gilt, teg, 32cp)	L: Nelson	(1913)	Various	160-185	
Craik, D.	Fairy Book (1st, 8vo, 403p, col frn)	Harper	(1922)	Rhead, L.	35-50	*
Craik, D.	Fairy Book (1st {this format}, 8vo, 232p, red/gilt, 16cp)	L: MacMillan	1923	Goble, W.	100-150	
Craik, D.	Little Lame Prince (1st, 4to, p-o, 121p, gilt, color)	Rand/McNally	(1909)	Dunlap, H.	65-80	
Craik, D.	Little Lame Prince (1st, 8vo, 128p, green/gilt, p-o, 9cp, pep)	Whitman	(1927)	Higgins, V.M.	40-60	
Cramer, M.	Diamond Princess (ob8vo, 56p, 5cp)	NY: Warne	(1931)	Cramer, Rie	50-80	
Crane, S.	Great Battles of the World (1st, 8vo, red/gilt, 278p, 7pl)	Lippincott	1901	Sloan, J.	180-250	
Crane, S.	The Monster... (1st, 8vo, 188p, orange/gilt, 25pl)	Harper	1899	Newell, P.	170-220	
Crane, S.	War is Kind (1st, tall 8vo, 6 woodcuts, 96p, uncut)	Stokes	1899	Bradley, W.	350-500	
Crane, S.	Whilomville Stories (1st, 8vo, green/gilt, 198p, 34pl)	Harper	1900	Newell, P.	180-230	
Crane, Thos.	Abroad (sq8vo, ipcb, 56p, color)	L: Marcus Ward	(1882)	(Chromos)	80-125	
Crane, W.	Aladdin's Picture Book (4to, unpag, ipcb, 24 color)	L: Routledge	[1880]	Crane, W.	250-400	
Crane, W.	Baby's Bouquet (1st, ob8vo, ipcb, 56p, 11cp)	L: Routledge	[1878]	Crane, W.	200-300	
Crane, W.	Baby's Opera (1st AM, sq8vo, 54p, ipcb, color)	McLoughlin	[1877]	Crane, W.	185-265	
Crane, W.	Baby's Own Aesop (1st, 12mo, ipcb, 56p, color)	L: Routledge	1887	Crane, W.	200-300	
Crane, W.	Bases of Design (1st, 8vo, teg, blue/gilt, 365p)	L: G. Bell	1898	Crane, W.	145-180	
Crane, W.	Blue Beard's Picture Book (1st, 4to, color)	L: Routledge	[1875]	Crane, W.	180-250	
Crane, W.	Columbia's Courtship (1st, 4to, [12]p, blue/gilt, 12cp)	Prang Co.	[1893]	Crane, W.	250-400	
Crane, W.	Flora's Feast... (1st, 4to, ibds, 40cp, dep)	L: Cassell	1889	Crane, W.	200-300	
Crane, W.	Floral Fantasy (1st, 4to, 48p, cloth, 44cp)	L: Harper	1899	Crane, W.	185-260	
Crane, W.	Flower Wedding (1st, lg8vo, ipcb, 40cp)	L: Cassell	1905	Crane, W.	220-300	
Crane, W.	Flowers/Shakespeare's Garden (1st, 4to, ibds, uncut, 40cp)	L: Cassell	1906	Crane, W.	200-300	
Crane, W.	Goody Two Shoes... (4to, red cl, 18cp)	J. Lane	(1901)	Crane, W.	180-240	
Crane, W.	Ideals in Art (1st, 8vo, teg, 287p, gilt, b/w, cvr by...)	L: G. Bell	1905	Crane, W.	100-165	
Crane, W.	India Impressions (1st, lg8vo, green/gilt, 325p, 16pl)	MacMillan	1907	Crane, W.	125-170	
Crane, W.	Legends for Lionel (1st, 4to, ibds, 40p, color)	L: Cassell	1887	Crane, W.	150-220	
Crane, W.	Line & Form (1st, 8vo, 282p, teg, blue/gilt)	L: G. Bell	1900	Crane, W.	140-220	
Crane, W.	Masque of Days (1st, 4to, [40]p, ipcb, color, pep)	L: Cassell	1901	Crane, W.	200-300	
Crane, W.	Pothooks & Perseverance (1st, sq8vo, ibds, [24]p, color, pep)	L: Marcus Ward	1886	Crane, W.	200-300	
Crane, W.	Queen Summer (1st, lg4to, ibds, teg, 40p, color, pep)	L: Cassell	1891	Crane, W.	250-300	
Crane, W.	Romance of the Three R's (1st, sq4to, ibds, [80]p, color, pep)	L: Marcus Ward	1886	Crane, W.	250-400	
Crane, W.	Sirens Three (1st, 4to, grey bds)	L: MacMillan	1886	Crane, W.	180-220	
Crane, W.	Slateandpencilvania (1st, sq8vo, ibds, 24p, color)	L: Marcus Ward	1885	Crane, W.	150-200	
Crane, W.	Triplets (1st, lg4to, 1/500 signed)	L: Routledge	1899	Crane, W.	350-450	
Crane, W.	Valentine & Orson (4to, wraps, 8cp)	L: Routledge	[1873]	Crane, W.	140-200	
Crane, W.	Walter Crane's Picture Book (4to, ibds, [145]p, color)	Cupples	(1903)	Crane, W.	90-150	
Crane, W.	William Morris to Whistler (1st, 12mo, 277p, blue cl)	L: G. Bell	1911	Crane, W.	80-100	
Crary, M.	Daughter of the Stars (1st, 4to, 190p, 2cp by...)	L: Hatchard	1939	Dulac, E.	120-180	R
Crawford, F.M.	Diva's Ruby (1st, 8vo, 430p, 12pl)	MacMillan	1908	Flagg, J.M.	25-40	*
Crawford, F.M.	Little City of Hope (1st, 8vo, 209p, grey cl, 8pl)	MacMillan	1907	Benda, W.T.	20-30	
Crawford, F.M.	Salve Venetia (1st, 8vo, 2 volumes, gilt)	MacMillan	1905	Pennell, J.	45-60	
Crawford, M.	Constantinople (1st, 8vo, teg)	Scribner	1895	Armstrong, M.	35-50	
Crawford, P.	Blot: Little City Cat (1st, ob4to, ibds, 56p, b/w)	Cape/Smith	1930	Holling, H.C.	70-100	
Crawford, P.	Blot: Little City Cat (1st {this pub}, sq8vo, 56p, dep, b/w)	Holt	(1946)	Cooney, B.	30-50	*
Crawford, P.	Hello, the Boat! (1st, 8vo, 227p, tan cl, pep, NH)	Holt	(1938)	Laning, E.	45-65	*
Crawford, P.	Let's Go! (1st, sm8vo, 73p, b/w)	Holt	(1949)	Guerin, T.	25-40	*
Crawford, P.	Second Shift (1st, sm8vo, blue cl, 211p, 1-color)	Holt	(1943)	Bernbach, G.	20-30	*
Crawford, P.	Secret Brother (1st, sm8vo, 238p, b/w)	Holt	(1941)	Woodbury, M.J.	20-35	*
Crawford, P.	Walking on Gold (1st, sm8vo, 284p, dp b/w, pep)	J. Messner	(1940)	Sherman, R.	20-30	*
Credle, Ellis	Across the Cotton Patch (1st, ob4to, green cl, [59]p, b/w)	Nelson	1935	Credle, E.	50-80	*
Credle, Ellis	Big Doin's on Razorback Ridge (1st, 8vo, orange cl, 125p, b/w)	Nelson	(1956)	Credle, E.	25-40	*
Credle, Ellis	Down, Down the Mountain (1st, 4to, [47]p, 2-color)	Nelson	1934	Credle, E.	60-80	*
Credle, Ellis	Flop-Eared Hound (1st, 8vo, [61]p, b/w)	NY: OUP	(1938)	(Photos)	50-80	*

AUTHOR	TITLE	PUBLISHER	DATE	ARTIST	PRICE	LC
Credle, Ellis	Goat that Went to School (1st, 8vo, [28]p, ipcb, color, pep)	Grosset/Dunlap	(1940)	Credle, E.	35-50	*
Credle, Ellis	Johnny & his Mule (1st, sq12mo, [44]p, b/w)	NY: OUP	1946	(Photos)	45-70	*
Credle, Ellis	Little Jeems Henry (1st, sq8vo, 44p, b/w)	Nelson	1936	Credle, E.	50-70	*
Credle, Ellis	My Pet Peepelo (1st, lg8vo, green cl, 62p, b/w)	NY: OUP	1948	(Photos)	30-45	*
Credle, Ellis	Pig-O-Wee (1st, lg8vo, ibds, [44]p, color)	Rand/McNally	(1936)	Credle, E.	35-50	*
Cregan, M.	Old John (1st, 8vo, 183p, 11pl, pep, DJ)	MacMillan	1936	Sewell, H.	35-50	
Crespi, P.	170 Cats (1st {std}, ob4to, ibds, unpag, 1-color)	Random	(1939)	Gay, Z.	50-85	
Crespi, P.	Manuelito of Costa Rica (1st, 4to, [40]p, color, pep)	J. Messner	(1940)	Gay, Z.	40-60	*
Cresswell, B.	Royal Progress/King Pepito (1st, 4to, tan ibds, 48p, 12cp)	L: SPCK	[1889]	Greenaway, K.	150-200	
Creswick, Paul	Greypaws... (1st, 8vo, 64p, 5pl)	L: Partridge	[1909]	Lucas, K.	50-65	*
Creswick, Paul	Hastings the Pirate (1st, 8vo, 303p)	Nister/Dutton	(1902)	Robinson, T.H.	45-60	*
Creswick, Paul	In Alfred's Days (sm8vo, teg, uncut, 304p, 18pl)	L: Nister	[1900]	Robinson, T.H.	40-60	
Creswick, Paul	Robin Hood & his Adventures (1st, 8vo, 312p, 4cp)	Nister/Dutton	(1902)	Robinson, T.H.	50-70	
Creswick, Paul	Under the Black Raven (1st, 8vo, 303p, teg, b/w pl)	Nister/Dutton	(1901)	Robinson, T.H.	45-60	*
Crew, A.	Mary & her Kitchen Garden (1st, lg8vo, 52p, p-o, 9cp, pep)	Doran	(1917)	Stanley, L.W.	35-50	
Criss, Mildred	Malou (1st {std}, 8vo, blue cl, 280p, uncut, col frn, 4 fp b/w)	Doubleday/Dor.	1929	Lederer, C.	20-35	*
Crissey, F.	Country Boy (1st, 8vo, 300p, gilt, uncut, cvr by...)	Revell	(1903)	Hazenplug, F.	65-80	
Crissey, F.	Country Boy (1st, 8vo, 300p, uncut, gilt, 14pl by...)	Revell	(1903)	McClure, G.M.	40-60	*
Crissey, F.	Tattlings of a Retired Politician (1st, lg8vo, teg, 487p)	Chi: Thompson	1904	McCutcheon, J.T.	25-40	
Crockett, D.	Adventures of Davy Crockett (1st, 8vo, black cl, 258p, p-o, 3cp)	Scribner	1934	Thomason, J.	45-70	*
Crockett, S.R.	Loves of Miss Ann (1st, 12mo, blue cl, 421p)	Dodd	1904	Armstrong, M.	35-50	*
Crockett, S.R.	Red Axe (1st, 8vo, 421p)	L: Smith Elder	1898	Richards, F.	25-40	*
Crockett, S.R.	Sir Toady Crusoe (1st, 8vo, 406p, blue cl, b/w)	L: Wells/Gard.	1905	Browne, G.	45-70	
Crockett, S.R.	Sir Toady Crusoe (1st AM, 12mo, 356p, b/w)	Stokes	(1905)	Browne, G.	35-50	
Crockett, S.R.	Surprising Advens. of Sir Toady Lion (1st AM, 8vo, 314p, b/w)	Stokes	(1897)	Browne, G.	45-65	
Crockett, S.R.	Sweetheart Travellers (1st AM, lg8vo, 310p, ibds, teg, b/w)	Stokes	(1895)	Browne/Groome	50-75	*
Crockett, S.R.	Tales of Our Coast (1st AM, 8vo, 203p, red buckram, teg, uncut)	Dodd	1896	Brangwyn, F.	60-80	*
Croll, Pauline	Just for You (1st, 12mo, 37p, color)	Volland	(1918)	Basset, M.	35-50	*
Cromie, Rbt.	From the Cliffs of Croaghaun (1st AM, 8vo, blue/gilt, 343p, 2pl)	Saalfield	1904	Praut, V.	30-45	
Crommelin, May	Little Soldiers (1st, 4to, 94p, 39 color)	L: Hutchinson	[1916]	Wain, L.	300-500	*
Crosby, E.	Captain Jinks, Hero (1st, sm8vo, tan cl, 393p, 9pl)	Funk/Wagnalls	1902	Beard, D.	20-35	
Crosby, P.	Dear Sooky (1st, 8vo, ipcb, 124p, 7 ticp, dep)	Putnam	1929	Crosby, P.L.	35-50	
Cross, L.	Book of Old Sun Dials (1st, 8vo, ibds, 102p)	L: Foulis	(1915)	Rawlings, A.	50-85	
Crothers, S.M.	Children of Dickens (1st, 4to, p-o, 259p, 10cp, pep, SC)	Scribner	1925	Smith, J.W.	85-120	
Crothers, S.M.	Gentle Reader (1st, 12mo, 321p)	Houghton	1903	Rogers, B.	20-30	
Crothers, S.M.	Miss Muffet's Christmas Party (1st, 8vo, blue/gilt, 106p, pep)	Houghton	1902	Long, O.M.	30-45	
Crothers, S.M.	Pardoner's Wallet (1st, 12mo, 287p, teg)	Houghton	1905	Rogers, B.	20-30	
Crowley, Mary C.	Daughter of New France (1st, 8vo, 409p, blue/gilt, 6pl)	Little/Brown	1901	DeLand, C.O.	25-40	
Crowley, Maude	Azor (1st, sm8vo, 54p, b/w)	NY: OUP	1948	Sewell, H.	30-45	*
Crowley, Maude	Azor & the Haddock (1st, sm8vo, 63p, grey cl, b/w)	NY: OUP	1949	Sewell, H.	30-45	*
Crownfield, Gertrude	Little Tailor of Windy Way (1st, sm8vo, 132p, 4cp)	MacMillan	1917	Pogany, W.	25-40	*
Crowninshield, Mrs.	Lattitude 19 (1st, 8vo, 418p, red cl, 7pl)	Appleton	1898	Gibbs, G.	35-50	*
Crowninshield, Mrs.	Light-House Children Abroad (1st, 8vo, 446p, 38 b/w, gilt)	D. Lothrop	1889	Bridgman, L.J.	30-45	*
Crowninshield, Mrs.	San Isidro (1st, 8vo, 312p, yellow cl, cvr by...)	H. Stone	1900	Hazenplug, F.	45-65	
Culbertson, A.V.	At the Big House (1st, sm8vo, blue cl, p-o, 348p, b/w)	Bobbs-Merrill	(1904)	Blaisdell, E.W.	45-60	
Culbertson, A.V.	Banjo Talks (1st, 8vo, 171p, 23pl)	Bobbs-Merrill	(1905)	(Photos)	70-120	*
Culbertson, P.	Bear Facts (1st {std}, 8vo, ibds, color)	Winston	(1948)	Fennell, P.	30-45	*
Cullen, Countee	Lost Zoo (1st {std}, 8vo, 72p, yellow cl, 16cp, pep)	Harper	(1940)	Sebree, C.	100-165	*
Cullen, Countee	My Lives & How I Lost Them (1st {std}, 8vo, orang cl, 160p, b/w)	Harper	(1942)	Macguire, R.R.	80-120	*
Culver, H.	Book of Old Ships (1st {this pub}, 4to, 306p, ibds, 5cp)	Garden City	(1935)	Grant, G.	30-45	
Cuming, E.W.D.	Three Jovial Puppies (1st, lg4to, bds, 36p, p-o, color)	L: Blackie	[1908]	Shepherd, J.A.	85-120	
Cuming, E.W.D.	Wonders in Monsterland (1st, 12mo, 257p, col frn, cp)	Longmans/Allen	1902	Shepherd, J.A.	100-150	*
Cummings, E.	Marmaduke of Tennessee (1st, 8vo, 371p, 5pl)	McClurg	1914	Schoonover, F.	25-40	
Cunnington, S.	Stories from Dante (1st, p-o, 8vo, 355p, gilt, 16cp)	L: Harrap	1911	Paul, E.	75-90	
Cuppy, Will	How to Become Extinct (1st, sm8vo, 181p, cream cl, b/w)	Farrar/Rine.	(1941)	Steig, Wm.	30-45	*
Curtin, J.S.	Fairy Tales of Eastern Europe (1st, 8vo, 259p, 4cp)	McBride	1914	Hood, G.	50-70	
Curtis, A.T.	Grandpa's Little Girls & Friends (1st 12mo, p-o, 190p, 5pl, pep)	Penn	1910	Smith, Wuanita	25-40	
Curtis, A.T.	Grandpa's Little Girls at School (1st, 12mo, 195p, p-o, 5pl)	Penn	1908	Smith, Wuanita	25-40	
Curtis, G.W.	Prue & I (8vo, teg, 234p)	Crowell	1899	Edwards, H.C.	20-30	
Custer, E.B.	Following The Guidon (1st, 8vo, 341p, 2pl by...)	Harper	1890	Remington, F.	50-75	
Custer, E.B.	Tenting on the Plains (1st, 702p, 11 b/w, gilt)	Webster	1887	Remington, F.	135-160	
Cutler, Carl	Greyhounds of the Sea (1st {std}, 4to, 592p, 8cp, photos)	Putnam	1930	Unknown	35-50	
Cutler, U.W.	Stories of King Arthur (1st, 8vo, 308p, dp cp, pep)	Crowell	(1941)	Blaisdell, E.	25-45	*
Cutting, M.S.	Suburban Whirl (1st, 12mo, green cl, uncut, 202p, 7pl)	McClure	1907	Stephens, A.B.	20-30	
Cutting, M.S.	The Wayfarers (1st, 8vo, 374p, 16pl)	McClure	1908	Stephens, A.B.	20-35	
D'Arcy, Ella	Monochromes (1st, 8vo, 260p, green cl, cvr & ti page by...)	L: J. Lane	1895	Beardsley, A.	65-80	*
D'Aulaire, I.& E.	Abraham Lincoln (1st {std}, folio, 55p, ibds, 5 fp color, CM)	Doubleday/Dor.	1939	D'Aulaire, I.& E.	80-120	
D'Aulaire, I.& E.	Animals Everywhere (1st, 4to, yel bds, [29]p, color, pep, DJ)	Doubleday	1954	D'Aulaire, I.& E.	60-85	
D'Aulaire, I.& E.	Benjamin Franklin (1st {std}, 4to, ibds, [48]p, color, DJ)	Doubleday	(1950)	D'Aulaire, I.& E.	50-70	
D'Aulaire, I.& E.	Buffalo Bill (1st {std}, 4to, ibds, [40]p, color)	Doubleday	1952	D'Aulaire, I.& E.	50-80	
D'Aulaire, I.& E.	Children o/t North Lights (1st lg4to, ibds, [40]p, color, pep)	Viking	1935	D'Aulaire, I.& E.	65-80	
D'Aulaire, I.& E.	Columbus (1st {std}, 4to, ibds, 57p, pep, color)	Doubleday	1955	D'Aulaire, I.& E.	70-110	R*

AUTHOR	TITLE	PUBLISHER	DATE	ARTIST	PRICE	LC
D'Aulaire, I.& E.	Conquest of the Atlantic (1st, lg4to, ibds, 55p, color, DJ)	Viking	1933	D'Aulaire, I.& E.	80-120	
D'Aulaire, I.& E.	Don't Count Your Chicks (1st {std} folio, [40]p, ibds, col, pep)	Doubleday/Dor.	1943	D'Aulaire, I.& E.	80-120	R
D'Aulaire, I.& E.	Foxie (1st {std}, ob4to, red cl, [40]p, b/w, pep, DJ)	Doubleday	1949	D'Aulaire, I.& E.	65-85	
D'Aulaire, I.& E.	George Washington (1st {std}, 4to, ibds, [55]p, 13 fp color)	Doubleday/Dor.	(1936)	D'Aulaire, I.& E.	30-45	
D'Aulaire, I.& E.	Leif the Lucky (1st {std}, lg4to, ibds, [56]p, color, pep, DJ)	Doubleday/Dor.	1941	D'Aulaire, I.& E.	70-100	
D'Aulaire, I.& E.	Lord's Prayer (1st {std}, lg4to, [32]p, ibds, color, pep)	Doubleday/Dor.	1934	D'Aulaire, I.& E.	60-80	
D'Aulaire, I.& E.	Magic Meadow (1st {std}, lg4to, ibds, 55p, pep, 25 color)	Doubleday	1958	D'Aulaire, I.& E.	50-70	*
D'Aulaire, I.& E.	Magic Rug (1st {std}, ob4to, [63]p, ibds, pep, color)	Doubleday/Dor.	1931	D'Aulaire, I.& E.	70-100	
D'Aulaire, I.& E.	Nils (1st {std}, 4to, ibds, [40]p, color, pep, DJ)	Doubleday	(1948)	D'Aulaire, I.& E.	65-90	
D'Aulaire, I.& E.	Ola (1st {std}, 4to, ibds, [55]p, color, pep, DJ)	Doubleday/Dor.	1932	D'Aulaire, I.& E.	75-120	R
D'Aulaire, I.& E.	Ola & Blakken & Line... (1st {std}, folio, [39]p, ibds, color)	Doubleday/Dor.	1933	D'Aulaire, I.& E.	65-80	
D'Aulaire, I.& E.	Pocahantas (1st {std}, 4to, ibds, [40]p, b/w)	Doubleday	1946	D'Aulaire, I.& E.	50-80	
D'Aulaire, I.& E.	Star Spangled Banner (1st {std}, lg4to, ibds, [38]p, col, pep)	Doubleday/Dor.	1942	D'Aulaire, I.& E.	60-90	
D'Aulaire, I.& E.	Too Big (1st {std}, sq8vo, ibds, [32]p, color, pep)	Doubleday/Dor.	1945	D'Aulaire, I.& E.	45-70	
D'Aulaire, I.& E.	Wings for Per (1st {std}, lg4to, ibds, [40]p, color, pep, DJ)	Doubleday/Dor.	(1944)	D'Aulaire, I.& E.	70-100	
D'Aulnoy	D'Aulnoy's Fairy Tales (1st, 4to, gilt, teg, p-o, 457p, 9cp pep)	McKay	1923	Tenggren, G.	120-170	
D'Aulnoy	Fairy Tales (1st, 8vo, 535p, teg, cvr by...)	L: Lawrence	1892	Crane, W.	180-250	
D'Aulnoy	Fairy Tales (1st, 8vo, 535p, teg, gilt, b/w by...)	L: Lawrence	1892	Peters, C.	180-250	
D'Aulnoy	White Cat... (1st, 4to, ibds, p-o, 8cp, pep, DJ)	MacMillan	1928	MacKinstry, E.	85-110	
D'Harnoncourt, R.	Mexicana (1st {std}, 4to, ipcb, fp b/w, dep)	Knopf	1931	D'Harnoncourt, R.	65-90	*
Daglish, A. (ed.)	Land of Nursery Rhyme (1st, 8vo, 240p, fp color, pep)	Dutton	(1932)	Folkard, C.	60-80	*
Dahl, Ronald	Gremlins (1st, 4to, ibds, [48]p, fp color)	Random	(1943)	Disney Studios	250-400	
Daldorne, Evan	Wooing of the Water-Witch (1st, 8vo, gilt, 132p, AEG)	Holt	1880	Smith, J. Moyr	90-145	*
Daley, C.F.	Skating Party (1st, 4to, ibds)	Worthington	(1891)	6 Chromos	75-120	
Daley, C.F.	Sundials (1st, 4to, ibds, 12cp)	Worthington	(1891)	Shepley, A.B.	100-150	
Dalgliesh, A.	Adam & the Golden Cock (1st, sm8vo, 64p, grey cl, 1-color)	Scribner	(1959)	Weisgard, L.	30-50	*
Dalgliesh, A.	Along Janet's Road (1st, sm8vo, 208p, gilt, pep, decor by...)	Scribner	1946	Milhous, K.	30-45	*
Dalgliesh, A.	America Builds Homes (1st, sq8vo, ibds, [84]p, color, DJ)	Scribner	(1938)	Maloy, L.	30-45	
Dalgliesh, A.	Bears on Hemlock Mountain (1st, 8vo, unpag, 1-color, NH)	Scribner	(1952)	Sewell, H.	50-85	*
Dalgliesh, A.	Blue Teapot (1st, 8vo, 73p, col frn, pep)	MacMillan	1931	Woodward, H.	30-45	
Dalgliesh, A.	Book for Jennifer (1st, 8vo, 114p, uncut, 10cp)	Scribner	1940	Milhous, K.	50-70	
Dalgliesh, A.	Choosing Book (1st, 16mo, [56]p, red cl, color)	MacMillan	1932	Wilkin, E.B.	30-45	*
Dalgli^Esh, A.	Christmas (1st, 8vo, 232p, col frn, b/w, pep)	Scribner	1934	Woodward, H.	35-50	
Dalgliesh, A.	Columbus Story (1st, 4to, [30]p, dp color)	Scribner	(1955)	Politi, L.	70-100	R*
Dalgliesh, A.	Courage of Sarah Noble (1st, 8vo, 52p, 7 fp illus, NH)	Scribner	(1954)	Weisgard, L.	45-60	*
Dalgliesh, A.	Davenports & Cherry Pie (1st, 8vo, 196p, grey cl, fp b/w)	Scribner	(1949)	Gag, Flavia	35-50	*
Dalgliesh, A.	Davenports are at Dinner (1st, 8vo, ivory cl, 182p, b/w)	Scribner	1948	Gag, Flavia	30-50	*
Dalgliesh, A.	Enchanted Book (1st, 8vo, 246p, blue/gilt, pep, fp color)	Scribner	(1947)	Cacciola, C.	45-60	*
Dalgliesh, A.	Fourth of July Story (1st, 4to, [30]p, fp color)	Scribner	(1956)	Nonnast, M.	30-50	*
Dalgliesh, A.	Gulliver Joins the Army (1st, sm8vo, 96p, b/w)	Scribner	1942	Segner, E.	20-30	*
Dalgliesh, A.	Happily Ever After (1st, 4to, 60p, 7 fp color, DJ)	Scribner	(1939)	Milhous, K.	70-90	
Dalgliesh, A.	Happy School Year (1st, sm8vo, 141p, color)	Rand/McNally	(1924)	Brand, M.S.	20-30	*
Dalgliesh, A.	Little Angel (1st, 8vo, 70p, color, pep, DJ)	Scribner	1943	Milhous, K.	35-50	
Dalgliesh, A.	Little Wooden Farmer (1st, ob8vo, green cl, [43]p, color, pep)	MacMillan	1930	Baumeister, T.	35-50	*
Dalgliesh, A.	Long Live the King! (1st, sq8vo, ipcb, 76p, color, dep)	Scribner	1937	Maloy, L.	25-40	
Dalgliesh, A.	Once On a Time (1st, sm4to, 70p, 10 fp color)	Scribner	(1938)	Milhous, K.	30-45	*
Dalgliesh, A.	Relief's Rocker (1st, 8vo, 62p)	MacMillan	1932	Woodward, H.	20-35	*
Dalgliesh, A.	Reuben & his Red Wheelbarrow (1st, 8vo, ibds, [28]p, pep, col)	Grosset/Dunlap	1946	Bischoff, I.	25-40	*
Dalgliesh, A.	Roundabout (1st, 8vo, 64p, b/w, pep)	MacMillan	1934	Woodward, H.	30-45	*
Dalgliesh, A.	Sailor Sam (1st, sq12mo, ipcb, [38]p, cep, color)	Scribner	1935	Dalgliesh, A.	30-45	
Dalgliesh, A.	Silver Pencil (1st, 8vo, 235p, blue/gilt, pep, NH)	Scribner	1944	Milhous, K.	50-70	
Dalgliesh, A.	Smiths & Rusty (1st, 8vo, 118p, b/w)	Scribner	1936	Hader, B.& E.	30-50	*
Dalgliesh, A.	Thanksgiving Story (1st, 4to, red cl, unpag, fp color, CH)	Scribner	(1954)	Sewell, H.	65-80	R*
Dalgliesh, A.	The Hollyberrys (1st, sq12mo, 59p, 12 fp color, cep)	Scribner	(1939)	Herric, Pru	30-45	
Dalgliesh, A.	Three from Greenways (1st, sm8vo, 63p)	Scribner	1941	Howe, G.	25-40	*
Dalgliesh, A.	West Indian Play Days (1st, 12mo, 174p, col frn, b/w, pep)	Rand/McNally	(1926)	Price, M.E.	30-45	*
Dalgliesh, A.	Wings Around South America (1st, 4to, 158p, fp color, cep)	Scribner	1941	Milhous, K.	30-45	
Dalgliesh, A.	Wings for the Smiths (1st, 8vo, blue cl, 89p, 3cp, cep)	Scribner	1937	Hader, B.& E.	30-45	
Dalgliesh, A.	Young Aunts (1st, 8vo, 116p, red cl, color)	Scribner	1939	Becker, C.	20-25	*
Dali, S.	50 Secrets... (1st, 8vo, DJ)	Dial	1948	Dali, S.	100-145	
Dali, S.	Hidden Faces (1st, 8vo, black cl, 413p, b/w frn, DJ)	Dial	1944	Dali, S.	165-220	
Dali, S.	Secret Life of... (1st AM, 4to, p-o, 400p, buckram, 3cp)	Dial	1942	Dali, S.	130-165	
Dall, A.R.	Scamper... (1st, sq8vo, 72p, 5cp, fp b/w)	MacMillan	(1934)	Flack, M.	50-80	*
Dalrymple, Leona	Uncle Noah's Christmas Inspiration (1st, 12mo, 124p, pep, 4cp)	McBride	1912	Yohn, F.C.	30-50	*
Dalton, Agnes M.	From Sioux to Susan (1st, 8vo, 342p, 22 b/w illus)	Century	1905	Gutmann, B.P.	65-80	*
Daly, T.A.	Madrigali (1st, sm8vo, 169p, gilt, frn by...)	McKay	(1912)	Sloan, J.	30-45	*
Dana, M.P.	Jingle Book (1st, sm4to, [32]p, color)	W.R. Scott	1940	Dana, M.	40-60	*
Dana, R.H.	Two Years Before the Mast (1st, lg8vo, 553p, p-o, 10cp, pep)	Houghton	1911	Smith, E.B.	70-90	
Dana, R.H.	Two Years Before the Mast (1st, 8vo, 415p, 15cp)	L: MacMillan	1915	Pears, Charles	25-40	*
Danks, B.M.	Janet & the Fairies (sm8vo, 64p, 4cp)	L: A&C Black	(1937)	Outhwaite, I.R.	160-200	
Dante	Ad Astra (1st, lg4to, ipcb, unpag, b/w)	R.H. Russell	1902	Armstrong, M.	150-200	
Dante	New Life (1st, 4to, 168p, teg, color)	L: Harrap	[1916]	Paul, E.	80-120	

AUTHOR	TITLE	PUBLISHER	DATE	ARTIST	PRICE	LC
Daringer, H.F.	Adopted Jane (1st, sm8vo, 225p, fp b/w)	Harcourt	(1947)	Seredy, K.	25-45	*
Daringer, H.F.	Mary Montgomery, Rebel (1st, 8vo, green cl, 222p, b/w, DJ)	Harcourt	(1948)	Seredy, K.	35-50	
Darling, E.B.	Baldy of Nome (1st, 8vo, blue cl, 301p, 15pl)	Penn	1916	(Photos)	40-65	
Darling, E.B.	Luck of the Trail (1st {std}, 8vo, uncut, 309p, col frn, pep)	Doubleday/Dor.	1933	Dennis, M.	25-40	*
Darling, E.B.	Navarre of the North (1st {std}, 8vo, 268p, pep, frn by...)	Doubleday/Dor.	1930	Bull, C.L.	45-60	
Darton (ed.)	Seven Champions of Christendom (8vo, blue/gilt, teg, 416p)	L: Wells/Gard.	(1913)	Ault, N.	65-80	
Darton, F.J.	Wonder Book of Beasts (1st, 8vo, 403p, gilt, teg, 22pl)	L: Wells/Gard.	(1909)	Clayton, M.	85-125	
Darton, H.	Story o/t Canterbury Pilgrims (1st, 4to, p-o, 310p, pep, 10cp)	Stokes	(1914)	Kirk, M.L.	80-120	
Darwin, Bernard	Elves & Princes (1st, 8vo, 199p)	L: Duckworth	1913	Monsell, J.R.	120-165	*
Darwin, Bernard	Mr. Tootleoo & Co. (1st AM, ob 4to, [45]p, ibds, 22 fp color)	Harper	(1936)	Darwin, E.	250-400	*
Daskam, J.	Her Fiance (1st, 12mo, 164p, 5pl)	Altemus	(1904)	Green, E.S.	40-60	
Daskam, J.	Imp & The Angel (1st, 8vo, 168p, tan cl, 8pl)	Scribner	1901	Rosenmeyer, B.J.	30-50	*
Daskam, J.	Memoirs of a Baby (1st, 8vo, 272p, blue cl, b/w)	Harper	1904	Cory, F.	25-40	
Daskam, J.	Whom the Gods Destroyed (1st, sm8vo, 236p, red/gilt)	Scribner	1902	Armstrong, M.	35-50	
Daskein, Tarella	Chimney Town (1st, lg8vo, 238p, blue cl, color)	L: A&C Black	1934	Outhwaite, I.R.	100-140	*
Daudet, A.	Letters from my Mill (1st, 8vo, 236p, tan/gilt, 10cp)	Dodd	1893	Lemaire, M.	30-45	
Daugherty, J.	Abraham Lincoln (1st, 4to, 216p, fp 1-color, DJ)	Viking	1943	Daugherty, J.	45-60	
Daugherty, J.	Andy & the Lion (1st, sm4to, ipcb, [79]p, color, pep, DJ, CH)	Viking	1938	Daugherty, J.	90-120	R
Daugherty, J.	Daniel Boone (1st {this pub}, 4to, 95p, color, pep, NM)	Viking	1939	Daugherty, J.	65-90	
Daugherty, J.	Lincoln's Gettysburg Address (1st {std}, lg4to, ibds, [40]p, col)	Whitman	(1947)	Daugherty, J.	45-70	
Daugherty, J.	Of Courage Undaunted... (1st, sm4to, 168p, b/w, DJ)	Viking	1951	Daugherty, J.	35-60	
Daugherty, J.	Poor Richard (1st, 4to, brown cl, 158p, 2-color, pep, DJ)	Viking	1941	Daugherty, J.	40-60	
Daugherty, J.	West of Boston (1st, 4to, 94p, yellow cl)	Viking	1956	Daugherty, J.	20-30	*
Daugherty, J.	Wild Wild West (1st, 4to, ibds, [34]p, color, pep)	McKay	(1948)	Daugherty, J.	30-50	
Daugherty, Sonia	All Things New (1st, sm8vo, 296p, orange cl, b/w)	Nelson	1936	Daugherty, J.	25-40	*
Daugherty, Sonia	Broken Song (1st, sm8vo, 270p, b/w)	Nelson	1934	Seredy, K.	25-45	*
Daugherty, Sonia	Mashinka's Secret (1st, 12mo, 276p, 28 b/w)	Stokes	1932	Daugherty, J.	20-30	*
Daugherty, Sonia	Vanka's Donkey (1st, 8vo, ivory cl, 62p, 1-color, pep)	Stokes	1940	Daugherty, J.	45-60	*
Daugherty, Sonia	Way of an Eagle (1st, 8vo, 352p, fp b/w)	NY: OUP	(1941)	Daugherty, J.	25-45	*
Daugherty, Sonia	Wings of Glory (1st, 8vo, 236p, gilt, color)	NY: OUP	(1940)	Daugherty, J.	25-40	*
Dauzet, M.	Forest Friends (1st, sq4to, 18p, ibds, fp color, pep)	Saalfield	1940	Peat, F.B.	40-60	
Dauzet, M.	One Happy Day (lg sq4to, ibds, [16]p, color, pep)	Saalfield	1939	Scott, J.L.	30-45	*
Davidson (ed.)	Ali Baba & the Forty Thieves (folio, ibds, 9 fp color)	L: Blackie	[1900]	Stratton, H.	60-80	
Davidson, G.	Arabian Nights Retold for Children (8vo, 352p, red cl, 16cp)	L: Blackie	[1925]	Bull, Rene	65-80	*
Davidson, G.	Gyp's Hour of Bliss (1st, 4to, ibds, 48p, 15cp, pep)	L: Collins	(1919)	Aldin, C.	175-220	
Davidson, G.	Helpers Without Hands (sm4to, p-o, bds, 118p, 32cp)	L: Wells/Gard.	(1914)	Noble, E.	150-200	
Davidson, John	Plays by... (1st, 8vo, gilt, 294p, uncut, cvr by...)	L: Matthews	1894	Beardsley, A.	80-120	
Davidson, John	Wonderful Mission/Earl Lavender (1st, 8vo, gilt, uncut, cvr by..)	L: Ward/Down.	1895	Beardsley, A.	70-90	*
Davies, M.C.	Little Freckled Person (1st, 8vo, 104p, 8pl)	Houghton	1919	Cue, H.	20-30	*
Davies, Maria T.	Rose of Old Harpeth (1st, sm8vo, 312p, blue cl, cvr by...)	Bobbs-Merrill	(1911)	Armstrong, M.	35-50	*
Davies, W.B.	Hour of Magic (1st, 12mo, pcb, 34p)	L: J. Cape	(1922)	Nicholson, W.	100-150	
Davies, W.H.	True Travellers (1st, 8vo, 53p, grey bds)	L: J. Cape	1923	Nicholson, W.	120-160	
Davis, Duke	Flashlights from Mountain & Plain (1st, sm8vo, 266p, 4cp)	(New Jersey)	1911	Russell, C.M.	100-150	
Davis, F.H.	Myths & Legends of Japan (1st, 432p, gilt, 32cp)	L: Harrap	1912	Paul, E.	70-90	
Davis, L.R.	Americans Every One (1st {std}, sm8vo, 123p, color)	Doubleday/Dor.	1942	Weisgard, L.	30-45	*
Davis, L.R.	Buttonwood Island (1st {std}, sm8vo, 299p, b/w, pep)	Doubleday/Dor.	1940	Brown, Paul	25-40	*
Davis, L.R.	Danny's Luck (1st, ob4to, ipcb, 43p, 2-color, pep)	Doubleday	1953	Woodward, H.	45-60	*
Davis, L.R.	Grab Bag (1st {std}, sm8vo, 312p, b/w, pep)	Doubleday/Dor.	1941	Weisgard, L.	20-35	*
Davis, L.R.	Hobby Horse Hill (1st {std}, 8vo, 270p, uncut, b/w, pep)	Doubleday/Dor.	1939	Brown, Paul	25-40	*
Davis, L.R.	Melody, Mutton, Bone & Slam (1st, 8vo, 245p, brown cl, b/w)	Doubleday	1947	Brown, Paul	20-35	*
Davis, L.R.	Plow Penny Mystery (1st {std}, 8vo, 275p, b/w)	Doubleday/Dor.	1942	Brown, Paul	20-35	*
Davis, L.R.	Roger & the Fox (1st {std}, ob4to, [43]p, ipcb, dep, color, CH)	Doubleday	1947	Woodward, H.	60-100	*
Davis, L.R.	Round Robin (1st, 8vo, 147p, b/w)	Scribner	1943	Woodward, H.	20-35	*
Davis, L.R.	Summer is Fun (1st {std}, sm ob4to, ibds, 48p, color)	Doubleday	1951	Woodward, H.	30-45	*
Davis, L.R.	Very Special Pet (1st, 8vo, ibds, [28]p, color)	Grosset/Dunlap	1944	Wiese, K.	30-45	*
Davis, L.R.	Wild Birthday Cake (1st {std}, ob4to, [50]p, ibds, pep, col, CH)	Doubleday	1949	Woodward, H.	70-120	*
Davis, M.E.M.	Moons of Balbanca (1st, 8vo, 180p, 6pl)	Houghton	1908	Rand, A.	40-65	
Davis, M.G.	Baker's Dozen (1st {std}, 8vo, 207p, orang cl, dep)	Harcourt	(1930)	Brock, Emma	25-40	*
Davis, M.G.	Handsome Donkey (1st, lg8vo, yellow cl, 67p, 3-color, pep)	Harcourt	(1933)	Brock, Emma	30-45	*
Davis, M.G.	Sandy's Kingdom (1st, lg8vo, green cl, 79p, b/w, pep)	Harcourt	(1935)	Brock, Emma	25-40	*
Davis, M.G.	Truce of the Wolf (1st, sm4to, uncut, 125p, fp b/w, dep, NH)	Harcourt	(1931)	Van Everan, J.	35-50	*
Davis, M.G.	Wakaima & the Clay Man (1st {std}, 8vo, 145p, uncut, b/w, pep)	Longmans	(1946)	Johnson, Avery	45-70	*
Davis, M.G.	With Cap & Bells (1st, sm8vo, 246p, b/w, pep)	Harcourt	(1937)	Bennett, R.	25-40	*
Davis, R.H.	About Paris (1st, 12mo, 219p, 30pl)	Harper	1895	Gibson, C.D.	25-40	
Davis, R.H.	Bar Sinister (1st, 8vo, teg, uncut, 108p, 7cp)	Scribner	1903	Ashe, E.M.	25-40	
Davis, R.H.	Captain Macklin (1st, sm8vo, teg, uncut, 328p, 7pl)	Scribner	1902	Clark, W.A.	25-45	
Davis, R.H.	Congo & Coasts of Africa (1st, 8vo, teg, 220p, 32pl)	Scribner	1907	(Photos)	30-45	*
Davis, R.H.	Cuba in War Time (1st, 12mo, 143p, brown bds, 24pl)	R.H. Russell	1897	Remington, F.	180-220	
Davis, R.H.	Lion & the Unicorn (1st [1], 8vo, 204p, green/gilt, 6pl)	Scribner	1899	Christy, H.C.	30-45	
Davis, R.H.	Ranson's Folly (1st, 8vo, red/gilt, teg, 345p, uncut, 16pl)	Scribner	1902	Various	30-50	
Davis, R.H.	Scarlet Car (1st, 8vo, tan cl, 166p, uncut, 12pl)	Scribner	1907	Steele, F.D.	25-40	
Davis, R.H.	Soldiers of Fortune (1st, 12mo, 364p, 6pl, yellow/gilt)	Scribner	1897	Gibson, C.D.	20-30	

AUTHOR	TITLE	PUBLISHER	DATE	ARTIST	PRICE	LC
Davis, R.H.	Van Bibber & Others (1st, 12mo, 249p, gilt, 4pl)	Harper	1892	Gibson, C.D.	25-40	
Davis, R.H.	West From a Car Window (1st, 8vo, blue cl, 242p)	Harper	1892	Remington, F.	90-135	
Davis, Rbt.	Gid Granger (1st, sm8vo, 179p, tan cl, fp b/w)	Holiday House	(1945)	Wilson, C.B.	20-35	*
Davis, Rbt.	Hudson Bay Express (1st, 8vo, 262p, blue cl, b/w)	Holiday House	(1942)	Pitz, H.C.	20-30	*
Davis, Rbt.	Padre Porko (1st, sm8vo, 165p, grey cl, fp b/w, cep)	Holiday House	(1939)	Eichenberg, F.	30-45	R*
Davis, Rbt.	Partners of Powder Hole (1st, 8vo, 167p)	Holiday House	(1947)	Davis, M.	20-30	*
Davis, Rbt.	Pepperfoot of Thursday Market (1st, sm8vo, 187p, b/w, pep)	Holiday House	(1941)	Baldridge, C.L.	35-60	R*
Davis, Rbt.	That Girl of Pierre's (1st, 8vo, 230p, rust cl, b/w, pep)	Holiday House	(1948)	Goff, L.L.	20-30	*
Davis, Rbt.	Tree Toad (1st, 8vo, 276p, b/w)	Stokes	1942	McCloskey, R.	30-50	*
Davis, Reb. H.	Kent Hampden (1st, 8vo, 152p, 4pl)	Scribner	1892	Zogbaum, R.F.	30-45	*
Dawe, W.C.	Yellow & White (1st, 8vo, yellow cl, cvr & ti page by)	L: J. Lane	1895	Beardsley, A.	80-100	
Dawson, A.J.	The Message (1st, 8vo, 386p, black/gilt, 4cp)	L: Richards	1907	Brock, H.M.	65-90	*
Dawson, Carley	Dragon Run (1st, 8vo, 282p)	Houghton	1955	Ward, L.	30-45	*
Dawson, Carley	Mr. Wicker's Window (1st, 8vo, 272p)	Houghton	1952	Ward, L.	25-40	*
Dawson, Coningsby	Little House (1st, 8vo, pcb, p-o, 127p, 8pl, pep)	NY: J. Lane	1920	Langdale, S.	25-40	*
Dawson, Forbes	Sensational Trance (1st, 8vo, 178p, red cl, 20pl)	L: Downey	1895	Mackenzie, F.	80-100	
Dawson, L.H. (ed.)	Stories from Faerie Queen (1st, 8vo, 234p)	L: Harrap	1909	Hammond, G.D.	40-65	*
Day, L.B.	Folk Tales of Bengal (1st, 4to, red/gilt, [274]p, 32cp)	L: MacMillan	1912	Goble, W.	200-250	
Day, L.G.	In Shadow Town (1st, lg4to, p-o, unpag)	Saalfield	(1907)	(Photos)	100-140	*
Day, M.	Tell 'Em Again Tales (1st, sq4to, ibds, 48p, 3 fp color, pep)	Duffield	1924	Glackens, L.M.	70-120	*
De La Mare, W.	Bells & Grass (1st AM, 8vo, p-o, 144p, b/w, pep, DJ)	Viking	1942	Lathrop, D.	60-85	
De La Mare, W.	Broomsticks & other Fairy Tales (1st, 8vo, 378p, woodcuts)	L: Constable	1925	Bold	60-80	*
De La Mare, W.	Child's Day (1st, lg8vo, 56p, ti-pl)	L: Constable	1912	(Photos)	150-200	*
De La Mare, W.	Come Hither (1st, 8vo, 696p, green cl, b/w)	L: Constable	1923	Buckels, A.	50-65	*
De La Mare, W.	Come Hither (1st AM, 8vo, gilt, 696p, b/w)	Knopf	(1923)	Buckels, A.	40-60	
De La Mare, W.	Crossings... (1st, lg8vo, 170p, teg, blue/gilt, col frn)	Knopf	1923	Lathrop, D.	70-120	
De La Mare, W.	Desert Islands & Robinson Crusoe (1st AM, lg8vo, 299p, b/w)	Farrar/Rine.	1930	Whistler, R.	50-80	*
De La Mare, W.	Desert Islands & Robinson Crusoe (1st {std}, 4to, 285p, b/w)	L: Faber	1930	Whistler, R.	70-100	*
De La Mare, W.	Down-Adown-Derry (1st, 4to, 190p, blue/gilt, teg, 3cp, 32pl)	L: Constable	(1922)	Lathrop, D.	100-145	
De La Mare, W.	Down-Adown-Derry (1st AM, 8vo, 195p, gilt, uncut, col frn)	Holt	1922	Lathrop, D.	70-100	R
De La Mare, W.	Dutch Cheese (1st {std}, 4to, 75p, green/gilt, 4cp)	Knopf	1931	Lathrop, D.	70-100	
De La Mare, W.	Dutch Cheese (1st, 8vo, 143p, gilt)	L: Faber	(1946)	Hawkins, I.	50-80	
De La Mare, W.	Flora: A Book of Drawings (1st, 4to, 45p, ibds, 8cp)	L: Heinemann	(1919)	Bianco, P.	80-100	*
De La Mare, W.	Flora: A Book of Drawings (1st AM, 4to, 45p, uncut, 8cp)	Lippincott	[1919]	Bianco, P.	75-90	*
De La Mare, W.	Lord Fish (1st, 8vo, mauve/gilt, 289p, 3cp, pep)	L: Faber	[1933]	Whistler, R.	60-80	
De La Mare, W.	Love (1st, 8vo, 592p, grey/gilt, col frn, 24 b/w)	L: Faber	1943	Freedman, B.	45-70	
De La Mare, W.	Lucy (1st, 8vo, 40p, ipcb, p-o, b/w)	L: Blackwell	(1927)	Miller, H.T.	45-65	R*
De La Mare, W.	Magic Jacket (1st, sm8vo, 146p)	L: Faber	(1943)	Hawkins, I.	30-50	*
De La Mare, W.	Miss Jemima (1st, sm8vo, ipcb, 36p, col frn, 3 fp b/w)	L: Blackwell	[1925]	Buckels, A.	70-120	R*
De La Mare, W.	Mr. Bumps & His Monkey (1st, sq8vo, 69p, 7 fp color, DJ)	Winston	(1942)	Lathrop, D.	80-120	
De La Mare, W.	Old Lion (1st, sm8vo, 155p)	L: Faber	(1942)	Hawkins, I.	30-50	*
De La Mare, W.	Peacock Pie (1st, 8vo, 178p, green/gilt, col frn)	L: Constable	(1916)	Robinson, W.H.	100-130	
De La Mare, W.	Peacock Pie (1st AM, 8vo, green/gilt, 178p, col frn)	Holt	[1917]	Robinson, W.H.	70-120	
De La Mare, W.	Peacock Pie (1st, 4to, teg, 127p, blue/gilt, 16cp)	L: Constable	1924	Fraser, C.L.	85-125	
De La Mare, W.	Peacock Pie (1st AM, lg8vo, 128p, blue/gilt, 16cp)	Holt	[1924]	Fraser, C.L.	60-80	
De La Mare, W.	Peacock Pie (1st AM, 8vo, 111p, blue/gilt, 2-color)	Holt	1936	Crowe, J.	30-50	*
De La Mare, W.	Peacock Pie (1st, 8vo, 107p, yellow cl, b/w)	L: Faber	(1946)	Ardizzone, E.	70-100	R*
De La Mare, W.	Rhymes & Verses (1st {std}, 8vo, 344p, pl)	Holt	(1947)	Blaisdell, E.	25-45	*
De La Mare, W.	Songs of Childhood (1st, sm8vo, 173p, gilt, teg, 8cp)	L: Longmans	1923	Canziani, E.	60-80	
De La Mare, W.	Stories from the Bible (1st, lg8vo, 393p, pep, 9cp)	Cosmopolitan	1929	Nadejen, T.	45-60	*
De La Mare, W.	Story of Miss Jemima (1st {this fmt}, 8vo, 55p, color, pep)	Grosset/Dunlap	(1940)	Farnam, N.H.	60-90	*
De La Mare, W.	Stuff & Nonsense (1st, 12mo, green/gilt, 110p, teg)	L: Constable	1927	Bold	60-90	
De La Mare, W.	This Year: Next Year (1st AM, sm4to, ibds, [64]p, color, pep)	Holt	(1937)	Jones, H.	70-120	*
De La Mare, W.	Three Mulla Mulgars (1st, 8vo, teg, green/gilt, 312p, 2cp)	L: Duckworth	1910	Monsell, J.R.	160-220	
De La Mare, W.	Three Mulla Mulgars (1st, 8vo, blue/gilt, 275p, 8cp, pep)	Knopf	1919	Lathrop, D.	120-165	
De La Mare, W.	Three Mulla Mulgars (1st UK, 4to, 12pl)	L: Duckworth	1921	Lathrop, D.	80-120	
De La Mare, W.	Three Royal Monkeys (1st, 8vo, 272p, purple cl, 1-color)	L: Faber	(1946)	Eldridge, M.E.	45-70	*
De La Mare, W.	Told Again (1st AM, 8vo, 248p, color)	Knopf	1927	Watson, A.H.	35-65	*
De La Mare, W.	Told Again (1st, 8vo, 320p, blue/gilt, 8cp)	L: Blackwell	1927	Watson, A.H.	60-80	
De La Rame, L.	Bimbi (1st AM, 8vo, 303p, 8pl)	Lippincott	1892	Garrett, E.H.	50-85	*
De La Rame, L.	Bimbi (1st, 8vo, 212p, red/gilt, 8cp)	Lippincott	1910	Kirk, M.L.	35-50	*
De La Rame, M.	Nurnberg Stove (1st, 12mo, 96p, 4cp)	Lippincott	1916	Kirk, M.L.	20-35	
DeAngeli, M.	Black Fox of Lorne (1st {std}, 4to, 191p, 11 fp b/w, NH)	Doubleday	1956	DeAngeli, M.	45-60	*
DeAngeli, M.	Bright April (1st {std}, sq4to, 86p, color, pep, DJ)	Doubleday	(1946)	DeAngeli, M.	45-65	
DeAngeli, M.	Copper-Toed Boots (1st {std}, sm4to, ibds, [92]p, color, pep)	Doubleday/Dor.	1938	DeAngeli, M.	40-65	
DeAngeli, M.	Door in the Wall (1st {std}, 8vo, brown cl, 112p, pep, DJ, NM)	Doubleday	(1949)	DeAngeli, M.	70-110	R
DeAngeli, M.	Elin's Amerika (1st {std}, sq8vo, tan cl, [96]p, color, pep, DJ)	Doubleday/Dor.	1941	DeAngeli, M.	45-65	
DeAngeli, M.	Henner's Lydia (1st {std}, sq8vo, ibds, [70]p, color)	Doubleday/Dor.	1936	DeAngeli, M.	45-60	
DeAngeli, M.	Jared's Island (1st {std}, sm4to, blue/gilt, 95p, col frn, DJ)	Doubleday	1947	DeAngeli, M.	50-65	
DeAngeli, M.	Just Like David (1st {std}, 8vo, green cl, 122p, color, pep)	Doubleday	(1951)	DeAngeli, M.	35-50	
DeAngeli, M.	Nursery & Mother Goose Rhymes (1st {std}, folio, 192p, col, CH)	Doubleday	1954	DeAngeli, M.	70-100	
DeAngeli, M.	Petite Suzanne (1st {std}, sq4to, ibds, [88]p, color, pep, DJ)	Doubleday/Dor.	1937	DeAngeli, M.	50-70	

AUTHOR	TITLE	PUBLISHER	DATE	ARTIST	PRICE	LC
DeAngeli, M.	Skippack School (1st {std}, sq8vo, [88]p, color, pep, DJ)	Doubleday/Dor.	1939	DeAngeli, M.	50-65	
DeAngeli, M.	Summer Day with Ted & Nina (1st {std}, 8vo, ibds, [32]p, color)	Doubleday/Dor.	1940	DeAngeli, M.	65-80	
DeAngeli, M.	Ted & Nina Go/Grocery Store (1st {std}, ob12mo ibds, color, pep)	Doubleday/Dor.	1935	DeAngeli, M.	45-60	
DeAngeli, M.	Ted & Nina Have/Happy Rainy Day (1st {std}, ob12mo, ibds, col)	Doubleday/Dor.	1936	DeAngeli, M.	45-60	
DeAngeli, M.	Thee, Hannah! (1st {std}, sq8vo, unpag, color, DJ)	Doubleday/Dor.	1940	DeAngeli, M.	60-90	R
DeAngeli, M.	Up the Hill (1st {std}, sq8vo, tan cl, 88p, color, pep, DJ)	Doubleday/Dor.	1942	DeAngeli, M.	40-60	
DeAngeli, M.	Yonie Wondernose (1st {std}, sq4to, ibds, color, pep, DJ, CH)	Doubleday/Dor.	1944	DeAngeli, M.	65-90	
DeBosschere, J.	Beasts & Men (4to, 179p, green cl, 12cp, pep)	L: Heinemann	(1918)	DeBosschere, J.	150-200	
DeBosschere, J.	Christmas Tales of Flanders (1st AM, 4to, 144p, gilt, 12cp, pep)	Dodd	1917	DeBosschere, J.	160-200	
DeBosschere, J.	City Curious (1st, lg8vo, [179]p, 8cp, pep)	L: Heinemann	(1920)	DeBosschere, J.	160-200	
DeBosschere, J.	City Curious (1st AM, sq8vo, yellow cl, [179]p, 8cp, pep)	Dodd/Hein.	1920	DeBosschere, J.	160-200	
DeBosschere, J.	Closed Door (1st, 8vo, 131p, 16pl)	L: J. Lane	1917	DeBosschere, J.	100-140	
DeBosschere, J.	Folk Tales/Flanders (1st AM, 4to, 179p, teg, gilt, 12cp)	Dodd	1918	DeBosschere, J.	140-185	
DeBosschere, J.	Gulliver's Travels/Lilliput (1st, 4to, 135p, 4cp, pink cl)	L: Heinemann	(1920)	DeBosschere, J.	150-200	
DeBosschere, J.	Love Books of Ovid (1st, lg8vo, blue/gilt, 16cp)	L: J. Lane	1930	DeBosschere, J.	35-50	*
DeBosschere, J.	Weird Islands (1st, sm4to, 210p, blue cl)	L: Chapman	1921	DeBosschere, J.	100-145	*
DeBrunhoff, J.	ABC of Babar (1st AM, sq8vo, ibds, [60]p, color, pep)	Random	(1936)	DeBrunhoff, J.	180-300	
DeBrunhoff, J.	Babar & Father Christmas (1st AM, lg4to, ibds, [40]p, color)	Random	(1940)	DeBrunhoff, J.	280-400	
DeBrunhoff, J.	Babar & His Children (1st AM, folio, ibds, [40]p, color, pep)	Random	(1938)	DeBrunhoff, J.	250-400	R
DeBrunhoff, J.	Babar & Zephir (1st, 4to, ibds, 39p, color)	Random	(1942)	DeBrunhoff, J.	100-140	
DeBrunhoff, J.	Babar the King (1st AM, lg folio, 48p, ibds, color, pep)	Smith/Haas	1935	DeBrunhoff, J.	280-400	R
DeBrunhoff, J.	Babar the King (1st {this format}, sq8vo, ibds, 48p, color)	Random	(1935)	DeBrunhoff, J.	100-140	*
DeBrunhoff, J.	Babar the King (1st UK, folio, ibds, color)	L: Methuen	1936	DeBrunhoff, J.	250-400	
DeBrunhoff, J.	Babar's Friend Zephir (1st UK, folio, ibds, color)	L: Methuen	1937	DeBrunhoff, J.	200-300	
DeBrunhoff, J.	Story of Babar (1st {this format}, sq8vo, ibds, 48p, color)	Random	(1933)	DeBrunhoff, J.	100-140	*
DeBrunhoff, J.	Story of Babar (1st AM, folio, 47p, ibds, color, pep)	Smith/Haas	1933	DeBrunhoff, J.	350-500	
DeBrunhoff, J.	Travels of Babar (1st AM, folio, ibds, 47p, color, pep)	Smith/Haas	1934	DeBrunhoff, J.	300-450	
DeBrunhoff, J.	Travels of Babar (1st {this format}, sq8vo, 48p, ibds, col)	Random	(1934)	DeBrunhoff, J.	100-140	*
DeBrunhoff, J.	Zephir's Holidays (1st AM, folio, [40]p, ibds, color, pep)	Random	(1937)	DeBrunhoff, J.	250-400	R
DeBrunhoff, L.	Babar's Cousin that Rascal Arthur (1st, folio, 47p, ibds, col)	Random	(1948)	DeBrunhoff, L.	220-350	
DeBrunhoff, L.	Babar's Picnic (1st AM, folio, 39p, ibds, color)	Random	(1949)	DeBrunhoff, L.	280-400	
DeBrunhoff, L.	Babar's Visit to Bird Island (1st UK, sm folio, ibds, color)	L: Methuen	(1952)	DeBrunhoff, L.	280-400	
DeBrunhoff, L.	Picnic at Babar's (1st UK, folio, 40p, ibds, color)	L: Methuen	(1950)	DeBrunhoff, L.	200-280	*
DeJong, Meindert	Along Came a Dog (1st, 8vo, 172p, b/w, NH)	Harper	(1958)	Sendak, M.	120-170	R*
DeJong, Meindert	Bells of the Harbor (1st {std}, 8vo, 289p, pep, b/w)	Harper	1941	Wiese, K.	25-40	*
DeJong, Meindert	Big Goose & Little White Duck (1st {std}, 8vo, 160p, 8cp, pep)	Harper	1938	Potter, E.	30-55	*
DeJong, Meindert	Billy & the Unhappy Bull (1st {std}, 8vo, 206p, brown cl, b/w)	Harper	(1946)	Simont, M.	35-50	*
DeJong, Meindert	Cat that Walked a Week (1st {std}, 8vo, grey cl, 148p, 13 fp bw)	Harper	1943	Robinson, J.	30-45	*
DeJong, Meindert	Dirk's Dog Bello (1st {std}, 8vo, 296p, color, pep)	Harper	1939	Wiese, K.	35-50	
DeJong, Meindert	Good Luck Duck (1st, lg8vo, yellow cl, 57p, color, pep)	Harper	(1950)	Simont, M.	35-50	*
DeJong, Meindert	House of Sixty Fathers (1st, 8vo, 189p, tan cl, b/w, NH)	Harper	(1956)	Sendak, M.	120-165	R*
DeJong, Meindert	Hurry Home, Candy (1st, 8vo, 244p, green cl, b/w, NH)	Harper	(1953)	Sendak, M.	120-165	R*
DeJong, Meindert	Little Cow & the Turtle (1st, 8vo, 178p, b/w, DJ)	Harper	(1955)	Sendak, M.	180-250	
DeJong, Meindert	Little Stray Dog (1st {std}, 8vo, 51p, b/w)	Harper	(1943)	Shenton, E.	30-50	*
DeJong, Meindert	Shadrach (1st {std}, 8vo, rust cl, 182p, b/w, NH)	Harper	(1953)	Sendak, M.	100-165	R*
DeJong, Meindert	Singing Hill (1st, 8vo, 180p, b/w, DJ)	Harper	(1962)	Sendak, M.	65-80	
DeJong, Meindert	Wheel on the School (1st, 8vo, 298p, b/w, uncut, DJ, NM)	Harper	(1954)	Sendak, M.	145-200	R
DeJong, Meindert	Wheels Over the Bridge (1st {std}, 8vo, 219p, pep, 10pl)	Harper	(1941)	Watson, A.A.	25-40	*
DeKoven, R.	Sawdust Doll (1st, 12mo, 237p, blue/gilt, teg)	Stone/Kimball	1895	Hazenplug, F.	100-140	*
DeLeeuw, Hendrik	Java Jungle Tales (1st {std}, 8vo, 311p, col frn, pep)	Doubleday/Dor.	1933	Wiese, K.	30-45	*
DeLeeuw, Hendrik	Peewee the Mousedeer (1st {std}, lg ob8vo, 71p, color)	McKay	1943	Gergely, T.	45-60	*
DeMille, W.M.C.	Forest Ring (1st, lg8vo, 180p, gilt, p-o, 10cp)	Doran	(1914)	Sichel, H.	50-70	*
DeMontaigne	Essays (1st, 8vo, cp)	Garden City	1947	Dali, S.	160-230	
DeMonvel, M.B.	Good Children & Bad (1st AM, ob4to, 48p, gilt, color)	Cassell	(1890)	DeMonvel, M.B.	150-180	
DeMonvel, M.B.	Jeanne d' Arc (1st, ob4to, white cl, 47p, color)	(Paris)	[1896]	DeMonvel, M.B.	160-220	
DeMonvel, M.B.	Joan of Arc (1st AM, ob4to, 47p, purple cl, color)	Century	1907	DeMonvel, M.B.	100-140	
DeMonvel, M.B.	Joan of Arc (1st {this pub}, ob4to, tan cl, p-o, [25]p, 10 col)	McKay	1918	DeMonvel, M.B.	50-70	*
DeMorgan, M.	Necklace of Princess Fiorimonde (1st, 12mo, gilt, 184p, AEG, dep)	L: MacMillan	1880	Crane, W.	175-220	
DeMorgan, M.	Windfairies... (1st, 8vo, 236p, gilt, AEG, 8 fp color)	L: Seeley	1900	Cockerell, O.	80-100	
DeMusset, Paul	Mr. Wind & Madam Rain (lg8vo, 150p, red/gilt, AEG, 25pl)	Putnam	1904	Bennett, C.	70-100	*
DeRegniers, B.S.	Giant Story (1st, 4to, unpag, grey cl, color)	Harper	(1953)	Sendak, M.	130-200	*
DeRegniers, B.S.	Snow Party (1st {std}, sm4to, unpag)	Pantheon	(1959)	Zimnik, R.	65-100	R*
DeRegniers, B.S.	Was It a Good Trade? (1st {std}, narrow ob8vo, [29]p, ibds col)	Harcourt	1956	Haas, I.	50-90	R*
DeRegniers, B.S.	What Can You Do with a Shoe? (1st, ob4to, ipcb, unpag, 1-color)	Harper	(1955)	Sendak, M.	160-220	*
DeSegur, S.	Memoirs of a Donkey (1st, 16mo, blue cl, 238p, fp b/w, pep)	MacMillan	1924	Ford, L.	30-50	*
DeSegur, S.	Old French Fairy Tales (1st, lg4to, 279p, gilt, p-o, 8cp, pep)	Penn	(1920)	Sterrett, V.	200-280	
DeSegur, S.	Sophie... (1st, 8vo, 157p, b/w, dep)	Knopf	1929	Barney, M.W.	20-35	*
DeSegur, S.	Wise Little Donkey (1st, lg8vo, p-o, 191p, pep, 4cp)	Whitman	(1931)	Brock, Emma	25-40	*
DeSelincourt, Hugh	Oxford From Within (1st, 4to, 180p, blue/gilt, 12cp)	L: Chatto	1910	Markino, Y.	80-100	
DeVries, P.J.C.	Princess Who Grew (1st, 8vo, 112p, p-o, col frn, 5pl)	Stokes	1927	Cramer, Rie	25-45	*
DeWolf, W.L.	Mardo's Animal Rhymes (1st, sq8vo, 44p, 4cp)	Rand/McNally	(1916)	Winter, M.	45-65	
Dean, G.M.	Riders of the Gabilans (1st, 8vo, 191p)	Viking	1944	Dennis, W.	20-30	*

AUTHOR	TITLE	PUBLISHER	DATE	ARTIST	PRICE	LC
Deardon, H.	Wonderful Adventure (1st, sm8vo, 115p, p-o, b/w)	Cosmopolitan	1928	Blood, W.C.	20-30	*
Deardon, H.	Wonderful Adventure (1st UK, 4to, ibds, 52p, b/w)	L: Heinemann	1929	Rountree, H.	35-50	*
Dearmer, M.	Book of Penny Toys (1st, 4to, ibds, 94p, 14 color)	L: MacMillan	1899	Dearmer, M.	250-400	*
Dearmer, M.	Child's Life of Christ (1st, 8vo, 290p, 8cp)	L: Methuen	1906	Brickdale, E.F.	50-80	*
Dearmer, M.	Cockyolly Bird (1st, 4to, 221p)	L: Hodder	(1914)	Dearmer, M.	150-200	*
Dearmer, M.	Playmate, A Christmas Mystery (1st, 8vo, 31p, 4 illus)	L: A. Mowbray	1910	Stratton, H.	65-90	*
Dearmer, P.	Little Lives of the Saints (1st, 12mo, 144p, green cl, dep)	L: Wells/Gard.	1900	Robinson, C.	70-100	*
Debenham, M.H.	Whispering Winds & Tales they Told (1st, 8vo, 195p, gilt, 25pl)	L: Blackie	1895	Hardy, P.	50-75	*
Decker, K.	Evangelina Cisneros (1st, 8vo, teg, uncut, 257p, 4pl by...)	Continental	1898	Remington, F.	40-60	
Defoe, D.	Moll Flanders (1st, 4to, 333p, black/gilt, 16pl, pep)	L: J. Lane	(1929)	Austen, J.	50-85	
Defoe, D.	Robinson Crusoe (4to, A.E. Red)	L: Nister	(1890)	6 Chromos	80-125	
Defoe, D.	Robinson Crusoe (1st, 8vo, blue/gilt, 435p, p-o, 12cp)	Houghton	1909	Smith, E.B.	60-80	
Defoe, D.	Robinson Crusoe (lg8vo, 352p, tan cl, 24 ticp)	L: Hodder	[1910]	Pocock, N.	70-100	
Defoe, D.	Robinson Crusoe (1st, lg8vo, 382p, p-o, 16cp, pep)	Rand/McNally	(1914)	Winter, M.	45-70	
Defoe, D.	Robinson Crusoe (1st, 4to, ibds, 80p, col frn, 6 color)	L: Blackie	[1916]	Hassall, J.	80-120	
Defoe, D.	Robinson Crusoe (1st, 4to, teg, p-o, 368p, 13cp, pep)	Cosmopolitan	1920	Wyeth, N.C.	145-200	
Defoe, D.	Robinson Crusoe (1st, 8vo, blue cl, 320p, 6cp)	L: Harrap	1933	Abbott, E.P.	65-80	
Defoe, D.	Robinson Crusoe (8vo, 472p, teg, bds, 16 fp color)	L: J.M. Dent	(1945)	Symington, J.A.	85-130	*
Defoe, D.	Robinson Crusoe (1st, 8vo, pcb, pep, 4 fp col)	NY: World	(1946)	Duvoisin, R.	35-50	*
Deihl, E.G.	Mother Brown Earth's Children (1st, 8vo, 111p, pep, p-o by...)	Whitman	(1927)	Winter, M.	30-45	*
Deihl, E.G.	Teddy Bear that Prowled the Night (4to, ibds, 24p, color)	NY: S. Gabriel	(1924)	Russell, L.M.	70-100	*
Del Rio, A.M.	Sun, Moon & a Rabbit (1st, ob4to, 191p, color)	Sheed/Ward	1935	Charlot, J.	95-160	R*
Deland, E.D.	Oakleigh (1st, 12mo, green cl, 233p, 19pl)	Harper	1896	Stephens, A.B.	30-45	
Deland, M.	An Encore (1st {std}, 8vo, teg, 79p, 3pl)	Harper	1907	Stephens, A.B.	30-45	
Deland, M.	Around Old Chester (1st, 8vo, p-o, 6pl)	Harper	1915	Stephens, A.B.	30-50	
Deland, M.	Awakening of Helena Richie (1st, 8vo, 357p, col frn, 7pl)	Harper	1906	Clark, W.A.	20-30	
Deland, M.	Dr. Lavendar's People (1st, 12mo, 370p, 12pl)	Harper	1903	Hitchcock, L.	25-40	
Deland, M.	Old Chester Tales (1st [1], 12mo, 360p, green cl, 16pl)	Harper	1899	Pyle, H.	65-80	
Deland, M.	Old Garden (1st, 8vo, 114p, color, cvr by...)	L: McIlvaine	1893	Crane, W.	120-160	
Deland, M.	Old Garden (1st AM, 8vo, 114p, uncut, color, dep)	Houghton	1894	Crane, W.	85-100	
Deland, M.	Way to Peace (1st, 8vo, grey cl, teg, uncut, 93p, 7pl, dep)	Harper	1910	Stephens, A.B.	30-45	
Deland, M.	Where Laborers are Few (1st, 8vo, 86p, 3pl)	Harper	1909	Stephens, A.B.	30-45	
Deming, T.O.	American Animal Life (1st, ob4to, [74]p, 24cp)	Stokes	1916	Deming, E.W.	130-175	
Deming, T.O.	Animal Folk of Wood & Plain (1st, ob4to, [38]p, p-o, 12cp)	Stokes	(1916)	Deming, E.W.	120-150	
Deming, T.O.	Children of the Wild (1st, 4to, [26]p, 6cp)	Stokes	(1902)	Deming, E.W.	75-100	
Deming, T.O.	Cosel: With Geronimo on His Last Raid (1st, 8vo, 125p, 6cp)	Davis Co.	1938	Deming, E.W.	45-60	*
Deming, T.O.	Four-Footed Wilderness People (1st, ob4to, ibds, 38p, 12cp)	Stokes	1916	Deming, E.W.	100-170	*
Deming, T.O.	Indian Child Life (1st, ob4to, ibds, [74]p, 18cp)	Stokes	1899	Deming, E.W.	150-185	
Deming, T.O.	Indians of the Wigwams (1st, sm8vo, 239p, 31 fp color)	Whitman	1938	Deming, E.W.	50-80	*
Deming, T.O.	Little Braves (1st, ob4to, [48]p, 9 fp color)	Stokes	1929	Deming, E.W.	70-100	*
Deming, T.O.	Little Brothers of the West (1st, 4to, p-o, [26]p, 6cp)	Stokes	(1902)	Deming, E.W.	80-120	
Deming, T.O.	Little Indian Folk (1st, ob4to, [38]p, 9cp)	Stokes	1899	Deming, E.W.	150-175	*
Deming, T.O.	Little Red People (1st, ob4to, [38]p, 9cp)	Stokes	1899	Deming, E.W.	140-175	*
Deming, T.O.	Many Snows Ago (1st, ob4to, [96]p, 18 fp color)	Stokes	1929	Deming, E.W.	75-130	
Deming, T.O.	Red Folk & Wild Folk (1st, 4to, [51]p, p-o, 12cp)	Stokes	(1902)	Deming, E.W.	100-160	
Deming, T.O.	Red People of the Wooded Country (1st, 12mo, 191p, fp color)	Whitman	(1932)	Deming, E.W.	30-45	*
Deming, T.O.	Wigwam Children (1st, ob4to, [48]p, 9cp)	Stokes	1929	Deming, E.W.	70-130	
Demuth, Averil	Trudi and Hansel (1st, 8vo, silver cl, 174p, fp color, pep)	Winston	(1938)	Lavrin, Nora	25-40	
Denslow, W.W.	Billy Bounce (1st, lg8vo, orange cl, 279p, p-o, 16cp)	Dillingham	(1906)	Denslow, W.W.	350-450	
Denslow, W.W.	Denslow's 5 Little Pigs (1st, 4to, wraps, [12]p, color, pep)	Dillingham	(1903)	Denslow, W.W.	145-220	
Denslow, W.W.	Denslow's Animal Fair (1st, 4to, wraps, unpag, color)	Dillingham	(1904)	Denslow, W.W.	150-200	
Denslow, W.W.	Denslow's Humpty Dumpty (1st, 4to, grey cl, p-o, 74p, fp color)	Dillingham	(1903)	Denslow, W.W.	260-400	R
Denslow, W.W.	Denslow's One Ring Circus (1st, 4to, wraps, [12]p, color, pep)	Dillingham	(1903)	Denslow, W.W.	180-250	
Denslow, W.W.	Denslow's Tom Thumb (1st, 4to, wraps, [12]p, color, pep)	Dillingham	(1903)	Denslow, W.W.	150-200	
Denslow, W.W.	Denslow's Zoo (1st, 4to, [12]p, wraps, color, pep)	Dillingham	(1903)	Denslow, W.W.	180-250	
Denslow, W.W.	House that Jack Built (1st, 4to, [12]p, wraps, color, pep)	Dillingham	(1903)	Denslow, W.W.	170-230	
Denslow, W.W.	Jack & the Bean Stalk (1st, 4to, wraps, [12]p, color)	Dillingham	(1903)	Denslow, W.W.	150-225	
Denslow, W.W.	Little Red Riding Hood (1st, 4to, [12]p, wraps, color)	Dillingham	(1903)	Denslow, W.W.	150-200	
Denslow, W.W.	Mary Had a Little Lamb (1st, 4to, wraps, [12]p, color)	Dillingham	(1903)	Denslow, W.W.	120-165	
Denslow, W.W.	Night Before Christmas (1st, 4to, ibds, p-o, 64p, color)	Dillingham	(1902)	Denslow, W.W.	300-350	
Denslow, W.W.	Night Before Christmas (lg8vo, p-o, [32]p, color, later)	Donohue	[1915]	Denslow, W.W.	150-185	
Denslow, W.W.	Old Mother Hubbard (1st, 4to, wraps, [12]p, color)	Dillingham	(1903)	Denslow, W.W.	180-225	
Denslow, W.W.	Scarecrow & the Tin Man (1st, 4to, [74]p, p-o, color)	Dillingham	(1904)	Denslow, W.W.	500-700	
Denslow, W.W.	Scarecrow & the Tin Man (4to, red cl, p-o, [74]p, color)	Donohue	[1913]	Denslow, W.W.	200-300	
Denslow, W.W.	Simple Simon (1st, 4to, wraps, unpag, color)	Dillingham	(1904)	Denslow, W.W.	100-135	
Denslow, W.W.	Tom Thumb (1st, 4to, [12]p, wraps, color)	Dillingham	(1903)	Denslow, W.W.	200-300	
Denslow, W.W.	When I Grow Up (1st, 4to, 104p, 24 color, tan cl)	Century	1909	Denslow, W.W.	150-200	
Denton, C.J.	Daisy Dells (1st, lg8vo, 222p, p-o, color)	Whitman	(1927)	Cheney, G.	30-45	*
Derrick, Freda	Ark Book (1st, ob sm4to, ibds, unpag, p-o, color)	L: Blackie	[1920]	Derrick, Freda	120-165	
Deutsch, B.	Heroes of the Kalevala (1st, lg8vo, 238p, blue cl, 12pl, cep)	J. Messner	(1940)	Eichenberg, F.	45-60	*
Deutsch, B.	It's a Secret! (1st {std}, sq12mo, 47p, 2-color, pep)	Harper	(1941)	Bayley, D.	50-80	R*
Deutsch, B.	Tales of Faraway Folk (1st, 8vo, yellow cl, 68p, b/w, pep)	Harper	(1952)	Lorentowicz, I.	25-45	*

AUTHOR	TITLE	PUBLISHER	DATE	ARTIST	PRICE	LC
Deutsch, B.	The Welcome (1st {std}, sm8vo, 197p, blue cl, 9 fp b/w)	Harper	(1942)	Simont, M.	45-60	R*
Deutsch, B. (tr.)	Crocodile (1st AM, ob4to, 31p, b/w)	Lippincott	(1931)	Chukovsky, K.	130-170	*
Dewar, G.A.B.	Wild Life/Hampshire Highlands (1st, 8vo, teg, grn/gilt, b/w, pep)	L: J.M. Dent	1899	Rackham, A.	200-350	
Dewey, K.F.	Star People (1st, 8vo, 232p, pict cl, fp b/w)	L: Longmans	1910	Comstock, F.B.	65-80	
Dickens, C.	Battle of Life (1st, 12mo, gilt, 165p, teg, 8cp)	L: J.M. Dent	1907	Brock, C.E.	35-50	
Dickens, C.	Boots of the Holly Tree Inn (8vo, red/gilt, pep, 44p, col frn)	Harper	1928	Lawson, M.A.	30-45	*
Dickens, C.	Christmas Carol (1st, 4to, 121p, t-i frn, 23pl)	S.E. Cassino	1887	Gaugengigl, I.M.	80-120	*
Dickens, C.	Christmas Carol (1st, sm8vo, 157p, teg, b/w pl)	Putnam	1900	Coburn, F.S.	25-40	*
Dickens, C.	Christmas Carol (1st, 12mo, 158p, teg, color)	Dent/Dutton	(1905)	Brock, C.E.	30-50	
Dickens, C.	Christmas Carol (1st, sm4to, 198p, col frn, 9pl)	Baker/Taylor	(1905)	Williams, G.A.	60-85	*
Dickens, C.	Christmas Carol (8vo, AEG, blue cl)	Putnam	1907	Merrill, F.	30-50	
Dickens, C.	Christmas Carol (1st, sm8vo, 48p, 6cp, pep)	Brewer/Barse	(1907)	Von Hofsten, H.	25-40	*
Dickens, C.	Christmas Carol (1st, 4to, red/gilt, 116p, pep, 9 ticp)	L: Hodder	[1911]	Michael, A.C.	80-140	R
Dickens, C.	Christmas Carol (1st, 12mo, 157p, tan cl, 12pl)	Rand/McNally	(1912)	Winter, M.	35-50	*
Dickens, C.	Christmas Carol (1st, 12mo, 113p, b/w)	Page	1913	Boog, C.M.	25-40	
Dickens, C.	Christmas Carol (1st AM, 8vo, 78p, 4cp)	Stokes	[1913]	Nichols, S.B.	35-50	*
Dickens, C.	Christmas Carol (1st, 8vo, p-o, 153p, 8cp)	L: Simpkin	1914	Appleton, H.C.	50-75	
Dickens, C.	Christmas Carol (1st, 8vo, 130p, blue/gilt, teg, 8cp)	McKay	(1914)	Keller, A.I.	30-45	
Dickens, C.	Christmas Carol (8vo, bds, p-o, 168p, 13 ticp)	Crowell	[1915]	Everett, E.	65-90	
Dickens, C.	Christmas Carol (12mo, ipcb, p-o)	Reilly/Britton	1915	Neill, J.R.	50-65	
Dickens, C.	Christmas Carol (1st, 8vo, olive/gilt, 147p, 12cp, pep)	L: Heinemann	(1915)	Rackham, A.	120-165	
Dickens, C.	Christmas Carol (1st AM, 8vo, 146p, purple/gilt, 12cp, pep)	Lippincott	(1915)	Rackham, A.	90-140	
Dickens, C.	Christmas Carol (1st, 8vo, 166p, gilt, 4cp, 15pl, pep)	MacMillan	1923	Bedford, F.D.	50-70	
Dickens, C.	Christmas Carol (1st, 8vo, 249p, blue/gilt, 7cp)	Saalfield	(1929)	Peat, F.B.	50-70	
Dickens, C.	Christmas Carol (1st AM, 8vo, red/gilt, 77p, 4cp)	Dodd	(1935)	Brock, H.M.	50-70	*
Dickens, C.	Christmas Carol (1st {std}, sm4to, red/gilt, teg, pep, 12 col)	Winston	1938	Shinn, E.	90-120	R*
Dickens, C.	Christmas Carol (1st, 4to, ibds, 74p, 11 fp color, pep)	Grosset/Dunlap	(1939)	Young, W.M.	35-50	
Dickens, C.	Christmas Carol (1st, 12mo, [60]p, color)	McLoughlin	(1940)	Graef, R.A.	25-40	*
Dickens, C.	Christmas Carol (1st, 12mo, 148p, ipcb, uncut, color)	Holiday House	(1940)	Reed, P.	45-60	*
Dickens, C.	Christmas Stories from Dickens (4to, AEG, gilt, 12cp)	L: R. Tuck	[1898]	Brundage, F.	160-200	
Dickens, C.	Cricket o/t Hearth (1st, sm8vo, teg, uncut, 174p, dep, cvr by..)	Putnam	1900	Armstrong, M.	25-40	
Dickens, C.	Cricket on the Hearth (1st AM, 8vo, 182p, red/gilt, color, DJ)	Harper	1927	Bedford, F.D.	75-110	
Dickens, C.	David Copperfield (1st, 4to, gilt, 572p, 20 ticp, pep)	Westminster Pr	(1911)	Reynolds, F.	160-225	
Dickens, C.	David Copperfield (1st, 12mo, 506p, b/w pl)	MacMillan	1925	Smith, H.S.	25-40	*
Dickens, C.	David Copperfield (1st {std}, 8vo, 423p, color)	Winston	(1948)	Shinn, E.	35-50	*
Dickens, C.	Dickens' Children (1st, lg8vo, [48]p, gilt, p-o, teg, 10cp)	Scribner	1912	Smith, J.W.	150-200	
Dickens, C.	Great Expectations (1st, lg8vo, 457p, col frn, cp)	Heritage Press	(1939)	Ardizzone, E.	80-100	*
Dickens, C.	Haunted Man (8vo, vellum, 8cp)	L: Dent	1907	Brock, C.E.	60-95	
Dickens, C.	Holly Tree Inn (1st, sm4to, 139p, 9pl, col frn)	Baker/Taylor	(1907)	Williams, G.A.	40-65	
Dickens, C.	Holly Tree... (1st AM, sm4to, green cloth, 192p, 30pl)	Scribner	(1925)	Shepard, E.H.	45-65	
Dickens, C.	Life of Nicholas Nickleby (lg8vo, 711p, color)	Dodd	1931	Brock, C.E.	35-50	
Dickens, C.	Life of Our Lord (1st, sm4to, 125p, gilt, 12 color)	Garden City	(1939)	Shinn, E.	30-45	
Dickens, C.	Magic Fishbone (1st, ob8vo, [40]p, ibds, 7cp, pep)	L: Warne	(1922)	Bedford, F.D.	60-85	
Dickens, C.	Magic Fishbone (1st, 4to, ibds, 36p, color)	Vanguard Pr.	(1953)	Slobodkin, L.	50-80	R
Dickens, C.	Mr. Pickwick's Christmas (1st, 4to, p-o, AEG, 149p, 6cp)	Baker/Taylor	(1906)	Williams, G.A.	45-65	
Dickens, C.	Mr. Pickwick... (4to, red/gilt, 21 ticp)	(NY & Lon)	[1911]	Reynolds, F.	165-200	
Dickens, C.	Old Curiosity Shop (1st, 4to, 359p, teg, red/gilt, 21 ticp)	L: Hodder	[1912]	Reynolds, F.	165-220	
Dickens, C.	Old Curiosity Shop (12mo, 618p, col frn, 23 b/w)	Macrae Smith	(1925)	Green, C.	20-35	*
Dickens, C.	Posthumous Papers/Pickwick Club (1st, 2 vols, 4to, bds, color)	L: Chapman	1910	Aldin, C.	140-200	
Dickens, C.	Posthumous Papers/Pickwick Club (1st, 4to, gilt, 534p, 20 ticp)	Westminster Pr	(1912)	Reynolds, F.	150-200	
Dickens, C.	Posthumous Papers/Pickwick Club (1st AM, lg8vo, 687p, 16cp, pep)	Dodd	1930	Brock, C.E.	45-60	
Dickens, C.	Tale of Two Cities (1st, lg8vo, teg, p-o, 362p, 10cp, pep)	Cosmopolitan	1921	Dunn, H.T.	60-90	
Dickens, C.	The Chimes (1st, 12mo, gilt, 167p, 8cp)	L: J.M. Dent	1906	Brock, C.E.	35-50	*
Dickens, C.	The Chimes (1st, lg8vo, p-o, 210p, col frn, 9pl)	Baker/Taylor	(1908)	Williams, G.A.	35-50	*
Dickens, C.	The Chimes (1st, 12mo, 189p, AEG, grey/gilt, 4cp, 11pl)	Putnam	1911	Coburn, F.S.	45-60	
Dickens, C.	The Chimes (1st, 8vo, 137p, red/gilt, 7 ticp, pep)	L: Hodder	[1912]	Thomson, H.	140-180	
Dickerson	Wonderful Wishes of Jackie & Jean (1st, 4to, 146p, 6cp)	Wessels	(1905)	Falls, C.B.	90-130	*
Dike, H.	Stories of Great Metropolitan Operas (1st, lg8vo, 247p, 12cp)	Random	(1943)	Tenggren, G.	30-45	
Dimmick, R.C.	Bogie Man (1st, lg8vo, ibds, [71]p, fp b/w)	Winston	(1906)	Neale, M.B.	55-85	*
Disney, W.	40 Big Pages of Mickey Mouse (folio, wraps, color)	Whitman	(1936)	Disney Studios	120-170	*
Disney, W.	ABC Mickey Mouse Alphabet Bk. (1st, 8vo, [32]p, color, pep)	Whitman	(1936)	Disney Studios	150-200	*
Disney, W.	Advens./Mickey Mouse Bk. # 2 (1st, 8vo, [32]p, ibds, pep, col)	McKay	(1932)	Disney Studios	250-400	
Disney, W.	Ave Maria (1st, 4to, blue/gilt, [32]p, color, pep)	Random	(1940)	Disney Studios	80-125	
Disney, W.	Big Bad Wolf & Little Red Riding Hood (1st, 4to, ipcb, 60p, col)	Blue Ribbon	(1934)	Disney Studios	140-200	*
Disney, W.	Bongo (1st {std}, folio, [26]p, ibds, color, GGB)	Simon/Schuster	(1947)	Starr, E.	70-100	*
Disney, W.	Cold-Blooded Penguin (1st {std}, sm8vo, ibds, unpag, pep, col)	Simon/Schuster	1944	Disney Studios	80-120	*
Disney, W.	Come Play with Donald Duck (1st, 8vo, [32]p, color)	Grosset/Dunlap	(1948)	Disney Studios	65-80	*
Disney, W.	Come Play with Mickey Mouse (1st, 8vo, [32]p, color)	Grosset/Dunlap	(1948)	Disney Studios	65-90	*
Disney, W.	Country Cousin (1st, 4to, ibds, [20]p, color)	McKay	1937	Disney Studios	90-130	*
Disney, W.	Dance of the Hours (1st, lg8vo, [36]p, color, pep)	Harper	(1940)	Disney Studios	120-160	*
Disney, W.	Disney's Bambi (1st, 4to, [52]p, ibds, color)	Simon/Schuster	(1941)	Disney Studios	70-120	*
Deutsny, W.	Disney's Bambi (8vo, [32]p, color, pep)	Grosset/Dunlap	(1942)	Disney Studios	65-80	

AUTHOR: 40

AUTHOR	TITLE	PUBLISHER	DATE	ARTIST	PRICE	LC
Disney, W.	Disney's Bambi (8vo, 101p, color)	D.C. Heath	(1944)	Disney Studios	40-60	*
Disney, W.	Disney's Cinderella (1st, folio, ibds, [26]p, color, GGB)	Simon/Schuster	(1950)	Disney Studios	70-120	
Disney, W.	Disney's Cinderella (8vo, [34]p, color)	Whitman	1950	Disney Studios	65-100	*
Disney, W.	Disney's Davy Crockett (1st, lg4to, ibds, 48p, color, BGB)	Simon/Schuster	(1955)	Disney Studios	45-70	*
Disney, W.	Disney's Dumbo (1st, lg ob8vo, wraps, [12]p, color)	Disney Prod.	1941	Disney Studios	150-200	*
Disney, W.	Disney's Dumbo (1st {this pub}, 8vo, [42]p, color)	Simon/Schuster	(1947)	Disney Studios	70-100	*
Disney, W.	Disney's Forest Friends (8vo, [28]p, ibds, color, pep)	Grosset/Dunlap	(1938)	Disney Studios	80-130	*
Disney, W.	Disney's Lady & the Tramp (1st, folio, unpag, ipcb, color, BGB)	Simon/Schuster	(1955)	Disney Studios	90-140	*
				Studios	65-90	*
					100-140	*
					80-120	*
					125-170	R
					70-100	*
				Studios	100-150	*
				Studios	90-145	
				Studios	80-125	*
Disney, W.	Disney's Tonka (1st, 8vo, ipcb, 66p, color, pep)	Golden Press	(1959)	...ene, H.	70-120	*
Disney, W.	Disney's Version of Pinocchio (ob8vo, [48]p, color, pep)	Grosset/Dunlap	1939	Disney Studios	90-130	*
Disney, W.	Disney's Version of Pinocchio (sq12mo, [24]p, color)	Whitman	(1940)	Disney Studios	75-115	*
Disney, W.	Donald Duck (1st, folio, [14]p, color)	Whitman	1935	Disney Studios	250-400	R*
Disney, W.	Donald Duck (4to, ibds, [33]p, color, pep)	Grosset/Dunlap	(1936)	Disney Studios	250-400	
Disney, W.	Donald Duck & his Friends (1st, 4to, ipcb, 45p, b/w, pep)	Whitman	1937	Disney Studios	150-200	*
Disney, W.	Donald Duck & his Friends (8vo, 102p, pep, color)	Heath	(1939)	Disney Studios	150-200	*
Disney, W.	Donald Duck & his Nephews (1st, 8vo, cloth, 66p, pep, color)	Heath	(1940)	Disney Studios	45-60	
Disney, W.	Donald Duck Off the Beam (1st [Big-Little], 32mo, 425p, ibds)	Whitman	(1943)	Disney Studios	100-140	*
Disney, W.	Donald Duck Sees South America (8vo, 138p, maps, color)	Heath	(1945)	Disney Studios	50-80	
Disney, W.	Donald Duck Treasury (1st, lg8vo, 116p)	Golden Press	1960	Disney Studios	70-100	*
Disney, W.	Donald Duck has Ups & Downs (1st, sm4to, 24p, color)	Whitman	1937	Disney Studios	150-200	*
Disney, W.	Donald Duck his Story Book (1st, 4to, ipcb, 46p, pep, b/w)	Whitman	1937	Disney Studios	100-150	*
Disney, W.	Donald Duck in High Andes (1st, 8vo, [32]p, color)	A.& W. Guild	1943	Disney Studios	100-160	*
Disney, W.	Donald's Lucky Day (1st, ob4to, [20]p, color)	Whitman	(1939)	Disney Studios	100-150	*
Disney, W.	Donald's Penguin (1st, sm4to, ibds, [24]p, pep, color)	Garden City	1940	Disney Studios	65-80	*
Disney, W.	Dopey: He Don't Talk None (sm folio, wraps, [12]p, color)	Whitman	1938	Disney Studios	130-165	
Disney, W.	Dumbo of the Circus (1st, sq4to, ibds, [52]p, color, pep)	Garden City	(1941)	Disney Studios	100-140	*
Disney, W.	Dumbo of the Circus (1st {this pub}, 8vo, 90p, color, pep)	Heath	(1948)	Disney Studios	65-80	*
Disney, W.	Elmer Elephant (1st, 8vo, ibds, 46p, color)	McKay	(1936)	Disney Studios	65-100	*
Disney, W.	Elmer Elephant (folio, wraps, [10]p, fp color, linen)	Whitman	1938	Disney Studios	120-165	
Disney, W.	Figaro and Cleo (1st, 8vo, ibds, [27]p, color, pep)	Random	1940	Disney Studios	100-160	
Disney, W.	Golden Touch (1st, 8vo, ibds, 212p, 6cp, pep)	Whitman	(1937)	Disney Studios	80-120	
Disney, W.	Hiawatha (1st, 4to, ibds, [20]p, fp color, pep)	McKay	1937	Disney Studios	120-170	
Disney, W.	Honest John & Giddy (1st, 8vo, [24]p, ibds, color, pep)	Random	1940	Disney Studios	80-120	*
Disney, W.	Jiminy Cricket (1st, 8vo, ibds, [24]p, color, pep)	Random	1940	Disney Studios	90-140	
Disney, W.	Little Pigs' Picnic (8vo, 102p, color, pep)	Heath	(1939)	Disney Studios	65-90	*
Disney, W.	Little Wise Hen (1st, ob4to, 48p, ibds, 9 fp color)	Whitman	(1934)	Disney Studios	150-200	
Disney, W.	Magnificent Mr. Toad (1st, 4to, [32]p, color)	Grosset/Dunlap	(1949)	Disney Studios	100-170	*
Disney, W.	Mickey & the Beanstalk (1st, 8vo, ipcb, [32]p, color, pep)	Grosset/Dunlap	(1947)	Disney Studios	80-120	*
Disney, W.	Mickey Mouse (1st {Big-Little}, 32mo, ibds, 316p, b/w)	Whitman	1933	Disney Studios	100-160	*
Disney, W.	Mickey Mouse & Mail Pilot (1st {Big-Little}, 32mo, ibds, 296p)	Whitman	1933	Disney Studios	100-160	*
Disney, W.	Mickey Mouse & Pluto (1st, lg8vo, [66]p, color, pep)	Whitman	1936	Disney Studios	120-170	*
Disney, W.	Mickey Mouse & his Friends (1st, folio, wraps, linen, 8cp)	Whitman	(1936)	Disney Studios	150-200	
Disney, W.	Mickey Mouse & his Friends (1st {this pub}, 8vo, 102p, color)	NY: Nelson	1937	Disney Studios	70-100	*
Disney, W.	Mickey Mouse & his Horse Tanglefoot (1st, 8vo, ibds, 60p, color)	McKay	(1936)	Disney Studios	250-350	
Disney, W.	Mickey Mouse ABC Story (1st, 8vo, ipcb, [31]p, color, pep)	Whitman	(1937)	Disney Studios	250-400	*
Disney, W.	Mickey Mouse Alphabet A to Z (4to, ibds, [32]p, 1-color)	L: Collins	[1936]	Disney Studios	180-235	
Disney, W.	Mickey Mouse Alphabet from A to Z (4to, ibds, [32]p)	Whitman	(1936)	Disney Studios	140-200	
Disney, W.	Mickey Mouse Birthday Book (1st, 4to, ibds, 64p, color, BGB)	Simon/Schuster	(1953)	Disney Studios	50-80	*
Disney, W.	Mickey Mouse Crusoe (1st, 8vo, wraps, 71p, col frn, b/w)	Whitman	(1936)	Disney Studios	100-130	*
Disney, W.	Mickey Mouse Fire Brigade (1st UK, ibds, 77p, b/w)	L: Collins	1936	Disney Studios	150-220	
Disney, W.	Mickey Mouse Fire Brigade (1st, 4to, ibds, color)	Whitman	1936	Disney Studios	140-200	
Disney, W.	Mickey Mouse Has a Busy Day (1st, sq4to, wraps, 16p, color)	Whitman	(1937)	Disney Studios	120-200	*
Disney, W.	Mickey Mouse Movie Stories (8vo, ibds, 197p)	L: Dean	[1931]	Disney Studios	250-375	
Disney, W.	Mickey Mouse Movie Stories (1st, 8vo, gilt, 190p, p-o)	McKay	(1931)	Disney Studios	250-350	R
Disney, W.	Mickey Mouse Story Book (1st, 8vo, 62p, wraps, b/w)	McKay	(1931)	Disney Studios	250-400	
Disney, W.	Mickey Mouse at the Circus (1st UK, 4to, ibds, color)	L: Birn Bros.	(1937)	Disney Studios	180-260	
Disney, W.	Mickey Mouse has a Party (1st, lg8vo, wraps, 48p, 2-color)	Whitman	1938	Disney Studios	160-220	*
Disney, W.	Mickey Mouse in Giantland (1st, 8vo, 45p, p-o, fp color, pep)	McKay	(1934)	Disney Studios	270-500	*
Disney, W.	Mickey Mouse in Giantland (1st UK, 8vo, 93p, ibds)	L: Collins	(1934)	Disney Studios	230-350	
Disney, W.	Mickey Mouse in Pigmey Land (1st, 4to, ipcb, 71p, col frn)	Whitman	1936	Disney Studios	150-200	*
Disney, W.	Mickey Mouse the Boat-Builder (1st, ob8vo, [28]p, ibds, col, pep)	Grosset/Dunlap	1938	Disney Studios	120-160	*
Disney, W.	Nursery Stories/Silly Symphony (1st, 8vo, 212p, ibds, 6cp, pep)	Whitman	(1937)	Disney Studios	140-200	
Disney, W.	Nutcracker Suite (1st, lg sq4to, ibds, [72]p, color, pep)	Little/Brown	1940	Disney Studios	120-165	
Disney, W.	Our Friend the Atom (1st, 4to, 166p, pep, color, GGB)	Simon/Schuster	(1956)	Disney Studios	90-135	

AUTHOR	TITLE	PUBLISHER	DATE	ARTIST	PRICE	LC
Disney, W.	Pastoral (1st {std}, lg8vo, [36]p, color, pep)	Harper	(1940)	Disney Studios	100-150	*
Disney, W.	Peculiar Penguins (1st, 8vo, 45p, red cl, p-o, color, pep)	McKay	(1934)	Disney Studios	130-200	
Disney, W.	Pinocchio Picture Book (lg4to, [14]p, wraps, color)	Grosset/Dunlap	(1940)	Disney Studios	120-180	R*
Disney, W.	Pinocchio Picture Book (lg4to, wraps, color, shape bk.)	Whitman	1940	Disney Studios	150-200	*
Disney, W.	Pluto & the Puppy (1st, 4to, ibds, [36]p, color, pep)	Grosset/Dunlap	(1937)	Disney Studios	140-200	
Disney, W.	Practical Pig (1st, lg sq8vo, ibds, [24]p, color, pep)	Garden City	1940	Disney Studios	90-150	*
Disney, W.	Princess Elizabeth Gift Book (1st, lg8vo, white cl, 224p, color)	L: Hodder	[1933]	Disney Studios	85-100	
Disney, W.	Robber Kitten (1st, ob4to, ipcb, 46p, 9 fp color)	McKay	(1935)	Disney Studios	180-300	
Disney, W.	Runaway Lamb at County Fair (1st, sm4to, ipcb, [31]p, color)	Grosset/Dunlap	(1949)	Disney Studios	70-100	*
Disney, W.	Snow White & Seven Dwarfs (1st {this pub}, sq4to, ibds, color)	McKay	1937	Disney Studios	120-170	
Disney, W.	Snow White & Seven Dwarfs (lg4to, ibds, 80p, color)	Grosset/Dunlap	(1937)	Disney Studios	85-100	
Disney, W.	Snow White & Seven Dwarfs (1st, 12mo, 63p, ibds, 14 color)	Whitman	(1938)	Disney Studios	120-170	*
Disney, W.	Snow White & Seven Dwarfs (ob8vo, ipcb, unpag, color)	Grosset/Dunlap	(1938)	Disney Studios	120-165	
Disney, W.	Snow White & Seven Dwarfs (folio, 12p, wraps, color)	Whitman	1938	Disney Studios	250-300	R
Disney, W.	Sorcerer's Apprentice (1st, ob8vo, 34p, color, pep)	Grosset/Dunlap	(1940)	Disney Studios	120-165	*
Disney, W.	Stories from Fantasia (narrow 4to, [movie ed.], 72p, ibds, col)	Random	(1940)	Disney Studios	85-140	
Disney, W.	Story of Casey Jr. (1st, lg8vo, ibds, [26]p, 4 fp color, pep)	Garden City	(1941)	Disney Studios	80-120	*
Disney, W.	Story of Minnie Mouse (ibds, 34pl)	Whitman	(1938)	Disney Studios	70-100	*
Disney, W.	Story of Timothy's House (1st, sm4to, ibds, [28]p, color)	Garden City	(1941)	Disney Studios	80-120	*
Disney, W.	Three Little Pigs (1st, sm4to, ibds, 62p, 12 color, pep)	Blue Ribbon	(1933)	Disney Studios	160-200	
Disney, W.	Three Orphan Kittens (1st, ob4to, ibds, [46]p, 9 color)	McKay	(1935)	Disney Studios	140-200	
Disney, W.	Through the Picture Frame (1st, sq8vo, [24]p, ibds, col)	Simon/Schuster	1944	Disney Studios	60-80	*
Disney, W.	Timid Elmer (1st, sq12mo, ipcb, 64p, b/w)	Whitman	1939	Disney Studios	90-130	*
Disney, W.	Tortoise & the Hare (1st, ob4to, ibds, 48p, 9 fp color)	McKay	(1935)	Disney Studios	180-250	*
Disney, W.	Walt Disney Parade (1st, 4to, 176p, color, pep)	Garden City	(1940)	Disney Studios	90-145	*
Disney, W.	Water Babies' Circus (8vo, 78p, color pep)	Heath	(1940)	Disney Studios	50-85	*
Disney, W.	Wise Little Hen (1st, ob4to, 48p, fp color)	McKay	(1934)	Disney Studios	180-220	*
Disney, W.	Wise Little Hen (1st {this fmt}, folio, [8]p, wraps, color)	Disney Prod.	(1937)	Disney Studios	180-250	*
Disney, W.	Wonderful Tar Baby (1st, 8vo, ipcb, [32]p, color, pep)	Grosset/Dunlap	(1946)	Disney Studios	70-120	*
Dix, B.M.	Hugh Gwyeth: Roundhead Cavalier (1st, 12mo, pep, b/w)	MacMillan	1928	Daugherty, J.	30-45	*
Dix, B.M.	Merrylips (1st, 8vo, 307p, 8pl, PPPa)	MacMillan	1906	Merrill, F.	35-50	*
Dix, D.	Fables of the Elite (1st, 12mo, teg, 261p, b/w pl)	Fenno	1902	Swinnerton	40-65	*
Dix, D.	Mirandy (1st, 8vo, brown cl, 256p, 21pl)	Hearst	1914	Kemble, E.W.	35-50	
Dixon (ed.)	Fairy Tales/Arabian Nights (1st, 8vo, 477p, col frn, 16pl)	L: Dent	1907	Batten, J.D.	85-130	
Dixon, Charles	Fifteen Hundred Miles an Hour (1st, 8vo, blue/gilt, AEG, 6pl)	L: Bliss Sands	1895	Layard, A.	50-75	
Dixon, E. (ed.)	Fairy Tales/Arabian Nights (1st, sm4to, 267p, gilt, teg, 5pl)	L: J.M. Dent	1893	Batten, J.D.	100-135	
Dixon, Maynard	Injun Babies (1st, 8vo, 72p, p-o, 7cp, pep)	Putnam	1923	Dixon, M.	50-80	*
Dixon, Thomas	Fall of a Nation (1st, 8vo, red/gilt, 362p, 6pl)	Appleton	1916	Wrenn, Chas.	20-30	
Dixon, Thomas	Leopard's Spots (1st, 8vo, red cl, 465p, 8pl)	Doubleday/Page	1902	Williams, C.D.	30-45	
Dixon, Thomas	Life Worth Living (1st, 8vo, 140p, teg)	Doubleday/Page	1905	(Photos)	25-40	
Dixon, Thomas	The Clansman (1st, 8vo, 374p, red cl, b/w)	Doubleday/Page	1905	Keller, A.I.	30-45	
Dixon, Thomas	The One Woman (1st, 8vo, 350p, red cl, 8pl)	Doubleday/Page	1903	Clinedinst, W.	25-40	
Dixon, Thomas	The Traitor (1st, 8vo, red cl, 331p, 4cp)	Doubleday/Page	1907	Williams, C.D.	25-40	
Djurklou, Baron G.	Fairy Tales from Sweedish (1st UK, 8vo, gilt, 178p, 20 fp b/w)	L: Heinemann	1901	Various	120-170	
Dobbs, Rose	No Room (1st, sm8vo, [48]p)	Coward	(1944)	Eichenberg, F.	30-45	*
Dobias, D.F.	Casey Joins the Circus (1st, sq8vo, [33]p, color, pep)	Grosset/Dunlap	(1936)	Dobias, D.F.	45-60	*
Dobson, Austin	Ballad of Beau Brocade (1st, 8vo, 89p, uncut, gilt, teg, b/w)	L: Kegan Paul	1892	Thomson, H.	60-85	
Dobson, Austin	Proverbs in Porcelain (1st, sq8vo, teg, 112p, uncut, b/w)	L: Kegan Paul	1893	Partridge, B.	50-75	
Dobson, Austin	Story of Rosina (1st, sm8vo, AEG, 120p, gilt, 28pl, cep)	L: Kegan Paul	1895	Thomson, H.	65-80	
Dobson, L.	Poems by Dobson, Locker & Praed (lg4to, p-o, gilt, 6cp)	Stokes	1892	Humphrey, M.	300-450	
Dodge, Louis	Everychild (1st, 4to, 284p, 6cp, pep, uncut, SC)	Scribner	1921	Laite, B.F.	50-70	*
Dodge, Louis	Sandman's Forest (1st, 8vo, 293p, p-o, grn/gilt, pep, 6cp, SC)	Scribner	1918	Bransom, P.	70-100	
Dodge, Louis	Sandman's Mountain (1st, 8vo, 278p, grn/gilt, pep, 6cp, SC)	Scribner	1920	Bransom, P.	70-100	
Dodge, M.M.	Hans Brinker (1st, 8vo, blue cl, cvr by...)	Scribner	1896	Armstrong, M.	30-45	
Dodge, M.M.	Hans Brinker (1st, 4to, p-o, teg, 8cp, pep, SC)	Scribner	1915	Edwards, G.W.	50-65	
Dodge, M.M.	Hans Brinker (1st, 4to, p-o, teg, 345p, 8cp, pep)	McKay	1918	Enright, M.W.	60-85	
Dodge, M.M.	Hans Brinker (1st, 8vo, blue cl, 305p, p-o, 4cp)	Garden City	1932	Hurd, P.	30-45	
Dodge, M.M.	Land of Pluck (1st, 8vo, 313p, gilt, teg, b/w)	Century	1894	Various	45-60	
Dodge, M.M.	Rhymes & Jingles (1st, 8vo, gilt, teg, uncut, 222p, b/w)	Scribner	1904	Stilwell, S.	75-100	
Dodge, M.M.	When Life is Young (1st, 12mo, teg, 255p)	Century	1894	Various	30-45	
Dodge, T.A.	Riders/Many Lands (1st, 8vo, brown/gilt, teg, 406p)	Harper	1894	Remington, F.	100-130	
Dodworth, D.	Mrs. Doodlepunk Trades Work (1st, ob8vo, red cl, [48]p, 1-color)	W.R. Scott	1957	Dodworth, D.	30-50	*
Dolbier, Maurice	Jenny: Bus that Nobody Loved (1st, 4to, 43p, ipcb, color, pep)	Random	1944	Gergely, T.	45-70	*
Dolbier, Maurice	Magic Bus (1st, lg8vo, 43p, color)	Wonder	1948	Gergely, T.	30-45	*
Dolbier, Maurice	Magic Shop (1st, 8vo, 74p, ipcb, 1-color)	Random	(1946)	Eichenberg, F.	45-70	*
Dole, N.H.	Russian Fairy Book (1st UK, lg8vo, 126p, 16cp)	L: Richards	1908	Bilibin, I.	375-450	
Dolson, Hildegarde	Sorry to Be So Cheerful (1st {std}, sm8vo, 207p, b/w)	Random	(1955)	Galdone, P.	25-40	*
Donahey, M.D.	Adventure of a Happy Dolly (4to, p-o, 123p, 5cp)	Barse	(1914)	Evans, G.	65-80	
Donahey, M.D.	Castle of Grumpy Grouch (1st, sm4to, 150p, color)	Stern	1908	Clay, J.R.	70-100	*
Donahey, M.D.	Down Spider Web Lane (1st, 4to, p-o, 130p, 6cp)	Stern	1909	Kay, G.A.	80-100	
Donahey, M.D.	Magical House of Zur (1st, 4to, 124p, p-o, 6cp)	Barse	(1914)	Wireman, E.	50-70	
Donahey, M.D.	Peter & Prue... (1st, sm8vo, 258p, p-o, 5cp, pep)	Rand/McNally	(1924)	Gaze, H.	140-185	

AUTHOR: 42

AUTHOR	TITLE	PUBLISHER	DATE	ARTIST	PRICE	LC
Donahey, M.D.	Prince Without a Country (1st, 4to, p-o, 125p, 6cp)	Barse	(1916)	Carlson, G.	40-60	
Donahey, M.D.	Talking Bird & Wonderful Wishes (1st, lg8vo, p-o, 146p, 6cp, pep)	Whitman	(1920)	Falls, C.B.	70-100	*
Donahey, M.D.	Through the Little Green Door (8vo, 176p, p-o, 3cp)	Barse	(1910)	Kay, G.A.	50-65	
Donahey, Wm.	Adventures of the Teenie Weenies (1st, lg4to, 128p, p-o, 9cp)	Reilly/Lee	(1920)	Donahey, Wm.	130-170	
Donahey, Wm.	Alice & the Teenie Weenies (1st, lg8vo, 105p, p-o, color)	Reilly/Lee	(1927)	Donahey, Wm.	70-100	*
Donahey, Wm.	Down the River with/Teenie Weenies (4to, p-o, 128p, 8cp)	Reilly/Lee	(1921)	Donahey, Wm.	140-200	
Donahey, Wm.	Teenie Weenie Days (1st, lg8vo, 65p, 4 fp color, pep)	Whittlesey	(1944)	Donahey, Wm.	65-100	
Donahey, Wm.	Teenie Weenie Neighbors (1st {std}, 8vo, 68p, 5 color, pep)	Whittlesey	(1945)	Donahey, Wm.	70-100	
Donahey, Wm.	Teenie Weenie Town (1st, 8vo, 71p, red cl, p-o, color, pep)	Whittlesey	(1942)	Donahey, Wm.	50-70	*
Donahey, Wm.	Teenie Weenies Under the Rose Bush (1st, 4to, p-o, 120p, 8cp)	Reilly/Lee	(1922)	Donahey, Wm.	150-200	
Donahey, Wm.	Teenie Weenies in Wonderland (1st, 4to, 120p, color)	Reilly/Lee	(1923)	Donahey, Wm.	70-100	*
Donaldson, J.W.	Arthur Pendragon of Britain (1st, 8vo, 542p, uncut, 4pl, pep)	Putnam	(1943)	Wyeth, Andrew	70-100	*
Donaldson, Lois	Runzel-Punzel (1st, 8vo, yellow cl, p-o, 16p, color, cep)	Whitman	1933	Ritter, M.	45-60	
Donnell, A.H.	Rebecca Mary (1st, 12mo, blue cl, 194p, p-o, 9pl)	Harper	1905	Green, E.S.	35-50	
Donnell, A.H.	Very Small Person (1st, 8vo, p-o, 193p, 8cp)	Harper	1906	Green, E.S.	35-60	
Dooley, Mrs.	Dem Good Ole Times (1st, 8vo, 151p, teg, 16 ticp)	Doubleday/Page	1906	Gutherz, S.	85-130	
Dopp, K.E.	Story of the Early Sea People (1st, 8vo, 224p, b/w)	Rand/McNally	(1912)	Unknown	25-40	*
Dorey, J.	Three & the Moon (1st, 4to, blue/silver, 103p, 8cp)	Knopf	1929	Artzybasheff, B.	50-70	
Dorrington, A.	Our Lady of Darkness (1st, 12mo, 371p, red/gilt, 4pl)	Macaulay	1910	Rae, J.	45-60	*
Dorrington, A.	Radium Terrors (1st, sm8vo, red/gilt, 361p, 4pl)	Doubleday/Page	1912	Michael, A.C.	30-50	
Dostoievsky, F.	Poor Folk (1st, 8vo, title pg & cvr by...)	L: Matthews	1894	Beardsley, A.	100-150	
Doubleday, R.	From Cattle-Ranch To College (1st, 8vo, blue cl, 24pl)	Doub./McClure	1899	(Photos)	65-80	
Doucet, J.	Tales of the Spinner (1st, lg8vo, [121]p, teg, uncut, gilt, b/w)	R.H. Russell	1902	Jones, A.G.	130-200	R*
Douglas, A.M.	Clover's Princess (1st, 16mo, p-o, 95p, blue/gilt, 6pl)	Altemus	(1904)	Neill, J.R.	50-70	
Douglas, B.	Favorite French Fairy Tales (1st AM, 8vo, 255p, 7cp)	Dodd	(1921)	Cramer, Rie	75-100	
Douglas, N.	South Wind (1st, 8vo, 2 volumes, 15cp)	Argus Books	1929	Austen, J.	75-100	
Douglas, R.B.	Life & Times of Madame Du Barry (1st, 4to, 386p, cvr by...)	L: Smithers	1896	Beardsley, A.	120-160	
Dow, E.C.	Diary of a Birthday Doll (1st, 8vo, 88p, 6cp)	Stern	1908	Nosworthy, F.	70-100	
Dow, E.C.	Proud Roxana (1st, lg8vo, 130p, p-o, 6cp)	Stern	1909	Wireman, E.	80-125	
Dowd, E.	Doodles (1st, sm8vo, 347p, grey cl, col frn)	Houghton	1915	Kirk, M.L.	35-50	
Downer, M.L.	The Flower (1st, ob8vo, brown cl, [32]p, 3-color)	W.R. Scott	1955	Downer, M.L.	25-40	*
Downey, Fairfax	Army Mule (1st, sm8vo, 192p, b/w)	Dodd	1945	Brown, Paul	20-30	*
Downey, Fairfax	Cats of Destiny (1st, 8vo, blue cl, 170p, 39 fp b/w)	Scribner	1950	Brown, Paul	25-45	*
Downey, Fairfax	Dogs of Destiny (1st, 8vo, 196p, b/w, DJ)	Scribner	1949	Brown, Paul	40-60	
Downey, Fairfax	Horses of Destiny (1st, 8vo, 186p, rust cl, fp b/w)	Scribner	1949	Brown, Paul	25-40	*
Downey, Fairfax	Jezebel the Jeep (1st, 8vo, 150p, grey cl, uncut, b/w)	Dodd	1944	Brown, Paul	25-45	*
Downey, Fairfax	Portrait of an Era (1st, 4to, 391p, DJ)	Scribner	(1936)	Gibson, C.D.	40-60	
Dowson, Ernest	Beauty & the Beast (1st, lg4to, green/gilt, teg, uncut, 4cp)	L: J. Lane	1908	Condor, C.	160-200	
Dowson, Ernest	Poems of E. Dowson (1st, green/gilt, teg, 4pl, cvr by...)	L: J. Lane	1905	Beardsley, A.	100-125	
Doyle, A.C.	Adventures of Gerard (1st AM, 8vo, 297p, uncut, 16pl)	McClure	1903	Wollen, W.B.	60-85	
Doyle, A.C.	Desert Drama (1st AM, 8vo, 277p, tan cl, 32pl)	Lippincott	1898	Paget, S.	70-100	
Doyle, A.C.	Last Galley (1st AM, 12mo, red cl, 321p, col frn by...)	Doubleday/Page	1911	Wyeth, N.C.	100-160	
Doyle, A.C.	Memoirs of Sherlock Holmes (1st, 8vo, AEG, blue cl, 279p)	L: G. Newnes	1904	Paget, S.	350-500	
Doyle, A.C.	Poison Belt (1st, 8vo, 199p, blue/gilt, uncut, 16pl)	L: Hodder	(1913)	Rountree, H.	165-220	*
Doyle, A.C.	Sir Nigel (1st AM, 8vo, 346p, 6pl)	McClure	1906	Kinneys	70-90	
Doyle, A.C.	The Parasite (1st AM, 12mo, 143p, 4pl)	Harper	1895	Pyle, H.	70-100	
Doyle, A.C.	White Company (1st, 4to, 363p, teg, p-o, 13cp, pep)	Cosmopolitan	1922	Wyeth, N.C.	160-200	
Doyle, A.C.	White Company (1st, 8vo, 403p, col frn, 2 dp pl, 7pl)	Harper	1928	Daugherty, J.	35-50	*
Drachman, Holger	Paul & Virginia/Northern Zone (1st, 8vo, gilt, teg, cvr by...)	Way/Williams	1896	Rogers, B.	90-120	
Drayton, G.	Baby Bears & their Wishing Rings (1st, lg ob8vo, 167p, color)	Century	(1914)	Drayton, G.	150-200	*
Drayton, G.	Let's Go to the Zoo (1st, ob4to, 44p, ibds, shape bk., 6cp)	Duffield	(1914)	Drayton, G.	130-185	
Drayton, Michael	Court of Faery (8vo, teg, gilt, 8pl)	L: Routledge	1906	Maybank, T.	80-135	*
Dreiser, T.	Hoosier Holiday (1st [1], lg8vo, olive bds, gilt, 513p)	NY: J. Lane	1916	Booth, F.	70-90	
Drinkwater, J.	All About Me (1st, 8vo, 103p, teg, gilt, 9pl, pep)	L: Collins	1928	Brock, H.M.	35-50	
Drinkwater, J.	Christmas Poems (1st, sq8vo, orange wraps, uncut, 6 b/w)	L: Sidgwick	1931	Shepard, E.H.	60-85	
Drinkwater, J.	Cotswold Characters (1st, 12mo, bds, 54p, DJ)	Yale U. Press	1921	Nash, P.	140-200	R
Drinkwater, J.	More About Me (1st AM, 8vo, 110p, orange cl, b/w)	Houghton	1930	Brock, H.M.	30-50	*
Drummond, F.	Fringes of Paradise (1st, 12mo, ipcb, 48p, 4cp)	L: F. Muller	(1935)	King, J.	50-65	
Drummond, Henry	Monkey that Would Not Kill (1st AM, 12mo, 115p, cloth, 16pl)	Dodd	1898	Wain, L.	180-250	*
Drummond, Henry	Monkey that Would Not Kill (1st, 8vo, 115p, gilt, 16 fp b/w)	L: Hodder	1898	Wain, L.	180-250	*
Drury, W.P.	Peradventure of Private Pagett (1st, 12mo, orang cl, 242p, 8pl)	L: Chapman	1904	Rackham, A.	200-300	*
DuBois, Theodora	Banjo the Crow (1st, sm4to, 142p, pep, b/w)	Houghton	1943	Torrey, H.	30-45	*
DuBois, Theodora	Travelling Toys (1st, lg8vo, 201p, p-o, 4cp, pep)	Penn	1934	Peat, F.B.	50-85	
DuBois, W.E.B.	Quest of the Silver Fleece (1st, 8vo, 434p, grey cl)	McClurg	1911	DeLay, H.S.	200-280	
DuBois, W.P.	Bear Party (1st, sm8vo, ibds, unpag, color, CH)	Viking	1951	DuBois, W.P.	65-100	
DuBois, W.P.	Elisabeth the Cow Ghost (1st, sq12mo, [47]p, color)	NY: Nelson	1936	DuBois, W.P.	35-50	*
DuBois, W.P.	Flying Locomotive (1st, ob8vo, ibds, 47p, color)	Viking	1941	DuBois, W.P.	65-80	
DuBois, W.P.	Giant Otto (1st, sq16mo, [40]p, ibds, 17cp, pep)	Viking	1936	DuBois, W.P.	80-130	
DuBois, W.P.	Great Geppy (1st, 4to, 92p, 22 fp color, dep)	Viking	1940	DuBois, W.P.	100-150	R
DuBois, W.P.	Lion (1st, 4to, 36p, color, pep, CH)	Viking	1956	DuBois, W.P.	90-140	R*
DuBois, W.P.	Otto at Sea (1st, sq16mo, ibds, [40]p, color, pep)	Viking	1936	DuBois, W.P.	120-165	
DuBois, W.P.	Otto in Texas (1st, sm4to, 45p, color, pep)	Viking	(1959)	DuBois, W.P.	70-120	R*

AUTHOR	TITLE	PUBLISHER	DATE	ARTIST	PRICE	LC
DuBois, W.P.	Peter Graves (1st, lg8vo, ibds, 168p, dep, b/w)	Viking	1950	DuBois, W.P.	45-60	*
DuBois, W.P.	Squirrel Hotel (1st, lg8vo, red cl, ... w)	Viking	1952	DuBois, W.P.	40-65	*
DuBois, W.P.	The Giant (1st, lg8vo, ...	Viking	1954	DuBois, W.P.	50-90	R*
	... r, DJ)	Viking	1938	DuBois, W.P.	70-100	
	... DJ, NM)	Viking	1947	DuBois, W.P.	80-110	R
	...	L: R. Hale	1949	DuBois, W.P.	45-60	*
	...	Harper	1928	Berry, E.	20-40	*
	...	...er	1928	Berry, E.	25-45	*
	...		1928	Berry, E.	25-40	*
	...		1898	DuMaurier, G.	100-145	
	...		1897	DuMaurier, G.	45-70	
	...	Harper	1894	Armstrong, M.	30-45	
	...	Lothrop/Lee	(1907)	Copeland, C.	20-25	
	...[120]p, 19cp)	NY: Hodder	[1912]	Detmold, E.J.	230-300	
	... 120p, pcb, p-o, 19 ticp)	L: Hodder	[1912]	Detmold, E.J.	200-300	
	...st, 4to, bds, 120p, p-o, 19 ticp)	L: H. Frowde	(1914)	Detmold, E.J.	220-320	
	...y Dogs (1st AM, 4to, 120p, ibds, p-o, 19 ticp)	NY: Hodder	[1914]	Detmold, E.J.	250-300	
	...ook of Baby Pets (1st, lg4to, ibds, [120]p, p-o, 19 ticp)	L: Hodder	(1913)	Detmold, E.J.	280-400	
Dulac, E.	Edmund Dulac's Fairy Book (1st AM, 4to, p-o, gilt 174p, 16 ticp)	Doran	(1916)	Dulac, E.	230-280	
Dulac, E.	Fairy Garland (1st, lg8vo, 251p, 12 ticp)	L: Cassell	(1928)	Dulac, E.	150-200	
Dulac, E.	Fairy Garland (1st AM, lg8vo, blue/gilt, 251p, p-o, 12 ticp)	Scribner	(1929)	Dulac, E.	130-180	
Dulac, E.	Fairy Tales of Allied Nations (1st, 4to, 174p, gilt, 16 ticp)	L: Hodder	[1916]	Dulac, E.	250-350	
Dulac, E.	Lyrics Pathetic & Humorous... (1st, 4to, ibds, [49]p, color, pep)	L: Warne	1908	Dulac, E.	300-450	
Dulac, E.	Picture Book/French Red Cross (1st, 4to, 135p, 19 ticp)	L: Hodder	(1915)	Dulac, E.	240-300	R
Dumas, A.	Count of Monte Cristo (4to, black/gilt, p-o, 8cp, pep)	Dodd	(1920)	Schaeffer, M.	35-50	
Dumas, A.	Dumas Fairy Tale Book (8vo, 290p, grey cl, 4cp)	L: Warne	1924	Rountree, H.	65-80	*
Dumas, A.	Nutcracker of Nuremberg (1st, 8vo, black/gilt, 154p, b/w)	McBride	1930	Hasselriis, E.	30-45	
Dumas, A.	Three Musketeers (1st, 8vo, 545p, p-o, 8cp)	Rand/McNally	(1923)	Winter, M.	50-80	
Dumas, A.	Three Musketeers (1st, lg8vo, black/gilt, 555p, 8cp)	Dodd	(1929)	Schaeffer, M.	40-60	
Dumas, A.	Three Musketeers (1st, 8vo, 459p, pep)	Winston	(1931)	Higgins, E.R.	25-40	*
Dunbar, A.	Once There was a Prince (1st, 8vo, 302p, blue cl, pep, col frn)	Little/Brown	1928	Day, M.	35-50	*
Dunbar, J.	Young Hopeful (1st, 8vo, 78p, blue/gilt, b/w)	L: H. Jenkins	1932	Robinson, C.	80-100	*
Dunbar, P.L.	Candle-Lightin' Time (1st, 8vo, teg, 127p, green cl, uncut)	Dodd	1901	Armstrong, M.	140-180	
Dunbar, P.L.	Folks from Dixie (1st, 12mo, 263p, 8pl)	Dodd	1898	Kemble, E.W.	150-185	
Dunbar, P.L.	Heart of Happy Hollow (1st, sm8vo, 309p, 6pl)	Dodd	1904	Kemble, E.W.	150-180	
Dunbar, P.L.	Li'L' Gal (1st, 8vo, teg, green cl, cvr by...)	Dodd	1904	Armstrong, M.	100-165	
Dunbar, P.L.	Poems of Cabin & Field (1st, 8vo, teg, 125p, uncut, green/gilt)	Dodd	1899	(Photos)	135-160	
Dunbar, P.L.	Strength of Gideon (1st, 8vo, 362p, gilt, 6pl)	Dodd	1900	Kemble, E.W.	180-265	
Dunbar, P.L.	When Malindy Sings (1st, 8vo, 144p, teg, cvr by...)	Dodd	1903	Armstrong, M.	130-170	
Duncan, Eula G.	Big Road Walker (1st, 8vo, 121p, cep, 17 fp b/w)	Stokes	1940	Eichenberg, F.	70-100	*
Duncan, N.	Suitable Child (1st, 8vo, ipcb, teg, 96p, pep, 5 ticp)	Revell	1909	Green, E.S.	45-60	
Dunham, Curtis	Bobbie in Bugaboo Land (1st, lg8vo, grey cl, 215p, 11 pl)	Bobbs-Merrill	(1907)	Kerr, G.F.	90-120	*
Dunham, Curtis	Golden Goblin (1st, lg8vo, ipcb, 190p, 8cp)	Bobbs-Merrill	(1906)	Kerr, G.F.	80-100	
Dunham, E.	Diary of a Mouse (1st, 8vo, p-o)	Dodge	(1907)	Gutmann, B.P.	80-120	
Dunne, F.P.	Mr. Dooley's Philosophy (1st, 12mo, red cl, 263p, b/w by...)	R.H. Russell	1900	Kemble, E.W.	25-40	
Dunne, F.P.	Mr. Dooley's Philosophy (1st, 8vo, red cl, col frn by...)	R.H. Russell	1900	Nicholson, W.	25-40	
Duplaix, G.	Gaston & Josephine (1st, 4to, ibds, color)	NY: OUP	1933	Duplaix, G.	80-120	
Duplaix, G.	Gaston & Josephine (1st {this pub.}, lg4to, 48p, color)	Harper	1936	Duplaix, G.	70-100	*
Duplaix, G.	Merry Shipwreck (1st {std}, 4to, ibds, [34]p, color, dep)	Harper	(1942)	Gergely, T.	70-100	*
Duplaix, G.	Pee-Gloo (1st, 4to, [40]p, ibds, pep, color)	Harper	1935	Duplaix, G.	70-120	*
Duplaix, G.	Popo the Hippopotamus (1st, ob12mo, ibds, [28]p, color)	Whitman	(1935)	Duplaix, G.	70-120	
Duplaix, G.	Topsy Turvey Circus (1st {std}, 4to, [40]p, ibds, color, pep)	Harper	(1940)	Gergely, T.	65-100	*
Duplaix, L.	Pedro, Nina & Perrito (1st, lg4to, [48]p, ibds, fp color, pep)	Harper	1939	Latham, B.	80-100	*
Duppa, C.M.	Stories of a Lowly Life (1st, lg8vo, 95p, uncut, red/gilt)	L: MacMillan	1898	Wain, L.	100-140	
Durant, Nancy M.	Oliver & the Crying Chip (1st, 12mo, 79p, blue cl, 10 b/w)	Sherman French	1915	Betacourt, A.B.	25-40	*
Durston, G.R.	Candle Light (1st, 4to, ibds, 116p, color, pep)	Saalfield	(1906)	Greenland, K.	70-100	*
Duvoisin, R.	All Aboard! (1st, folio, 44p, ibds, color)	Grosset/Dunlap	(1935)	Duvoisin, R.	90-130	*
Duvoisin, R.	Christmas Cake (1st, ob12mo, [29]p, b/w, ibds, pep)	A.A. Group	(1941)	Duvoisin, R.	30-50	*
Duvoisin, R.	Christmas Whale (1st {std}, ob8vo, [45]p, ibds, color)	Knopf	(1945)	Duvoisin, R.	35-50	
Duvoisin, R.	Donkey-Donkey (1st, 8vo, ibds, [46]p, color, pep)	Whitman	(1933)	Duvoisin, R.	100-150	
Duvoisin, R.	Donkey-Donkey (1st {this pub}, lg8vo, ipcb, pep, 39p, color)	Grosset/Dunlap	(1940)	Duvoisin, R.	50-70	*
Duvoisin, R.	Easter Treat (1st {std}, sm4to, [16]p, 1-color)	Knopf	(1954)	Duvoisin, R.	45-60	*
Duvoisin, R.	Little Boy Who was Drawing (1st, sm4to, [56]p, color)	Scribner	1932	Duvoisin, R.	60-85	*
Duvoisin, R.	One Thousand Christmas Beards (1st, lg8vo, unpag, ibds, col, DJ)	Knopf	(1955)	Duvoisin, R.	70-100	
Duvoisin, R.	Petunia (1st {std}, lg8vo, [32]p, color)	Knopf	(1950)	Duvoisin, R.	40-65	*
Duvoisin, R.	Petunia & the Song (1st {std}, sm4to, unpag, color)	Knopf	(1951)	Duvoisin, R.	40-65	*
Duvoisin, R.	Petunia Takes a Trip (1st {std}, 4to, unpag, color, pep)	Knopf	(1953)	Duvoisin, R.	50-70	R
Duvoisin, R.	Petunia's Christmas (1st {std}, lg8vo, unpag, color, pep)	Knopf	(1952)	Duvoisin, R.	40-65	*
Duvoisin, R.	They Put Out to Sea (1st {std}, 4to, 171p, 8 dp color, pep)	Knopf	1943	Duvoisin, R.	40-65	R*
Dwiggins, W.	Marionette in Motion (1st, 8vo, 25p, b/w, DJ)	(Detroit)	1939	Dwiggins, W.A.	120-160	
Dwight, G.	Yellow Cat & Friends (1st, 4to, ipcb, 88p, 14cp)	Appleton	1905	Dimock, E.	50-75	
Dyer, Kate G.	Turky Trott & Black Santa (1st, 4to, [39]p, orang cl, col frn)	Platt/Munk	(1942)	Robson, J.	70-100	

AUTHOR: 44

AUTHOR	TITLE	PUBLISHER	DATE	ARTIST	PRICE	LC
Dyer, R.O.	Daytime Story Book (1st, sm8vo, 152p, col frn)	Lothrop/Lee	(1917)	Inglis, A.	20-35	*
Dyer, R.O.	Sleepy-Time Story Book (1st, sm8vo, 147p, gilt, pep, col frn)	Lothrop/Lee	(1915)	Stephens, A.B.	30-45	*
Dyer, W.A.	All Around Robin Hood's Barn (1st {std}, lg8vo, 204p, p-o, 24cp)	Doubleday/Page	1926	Bull, C.L.	45-65	
Dyer, W.A.	Country Cousins (1st {std}, lg8vo, 164p, col frn, 11pl, pep)	Doubleday/Dor.	1927	Bull, C.L.	30-45	
Eager, E.M.	Mouse Manor (1st {1st bk}, 8vo, blue cl, [57]p, 10 fp col, pep)	Ariel	(1952)	Bailey-Jones, B.	35-50	*
Eager, E.M.	Playing Possum (1st, lg8vo, [32]p, green cl, 1-color, pep)	Putnam	1955	Galdone, P.	35-50	*
Eames, G.T.	Ghost Town Cowboy (1st, 8vo, 176p, beige cl, uncut, b/w, pep)	J. Messner	(1951)	Brown, Paul	25-45	*
Eames, G.T.	Good Luck Colt (1st, 8vo, 191p, red cl, fp b/w, pep)	J. Messner	(1953)	Brown, Paul	30-45	*
Eames, G.T.	Horse to Remember (1st, 8vo, 146p, b/w, pep)	J. Messner	(1947)	Brown, Paul	30-45	*
Earl of Birkenhead	World in 2030 (1st, lg8vo, 215p, black cl, 9pl)	L: Hodder	(1930)	Kauffer, E.M.	45-65	
Earle, A.M.	Child Life in Colonial Days (1st, 8vo, 418p, gilt, teg)	MacMillan	1899	(Photos)	35-50	
Earle, A.M.	Colonial Days in Old New York (1st, sm8vo, 312p, gilt)	Scribner	1896	Armstrong, M.	25-40	
Earle, A.M.	Costumes of Colonial Times (1st, 8vo, blue/gilt, 264p)	Scribner	1894	Armstrong, M.	50-75	
Earle, A.M.	Curious Punishments... (1st, 8vo, 149p, teg)	H. Stone	1896	Hazenplug, F.	50-85	
Earle, A.M.	Home Life in Colonial Days (1st, 8vo, teg, 470p)	MacMillan	1898	(Photos)	30-45	
Earle, A.M.	Stage Coach & Tavern Days (1st, sm8vo, uncut, 449p, teg, b/w)	MacMillan	1900	(Photos)	35-50	
Eastman, C.A.	Indian Boyhood (1st, teg, 289p, 4pl)	McClure	1902	Blumenschien, M.	30-45	
Eastman, C.A.	Old Indian Days (1st, 8vo, p-o, 279p)	McClure	1907	Groesbeck, D.	30-45	
Eastman, C.A.	Wigwam Evenings (1st, 8vo, 253p, 18pl)	Little/Brown	1909	Deming, E.W.	70-90	
Eastman, Charlotte	Evolution of Dodd's Sister (1st, sm8vo, 230p, cvr by...)	Rand/McNally	1897	Denslow, W.W.	25-40	*
Eastwick, I.O.	Fairies & Suchlike (1st {std}, sq8vo, 63p, ipcb, 1-color, pep)	Dutton	1946	Merwin, D.	35-50	*
Eaton, A.T.	Animal's Christmas (1st, sm8vo, grey cl, 124p, 1-color, dep)	Viking	1944	Angelo, V.	45-70	R*
Eaton, J.	Betsy's Napoleon (1st, 8vo, 274p, bds, color, pep, DJ)	Wm. Morrow	1936	Brissaud, P.	25-40	
Eaton, J.	Daughter of the Seine (1st {std}, lg8vo, blue cl, 324p, pep, NH)	Harper	1929	(Photos)	50-70	*
Eaton, J.	Leader by Destiny (1st, 8vo, 402p, blue/gilt, 19pl, DJ, NH)	Harcourt	(1938)	Rose, J.M.	40-65	
Eaton, J.	Lone Journey (1st, 8vo, 266p, map, b/w, NH)	Harcourt	(1944)	Ishmael, W.	35-50	
Eaton, S.	More about Teddy B. & Teddy G. (1st, 4to, ibds, p-o, 186p)	Stern	1907	Culver, R.K.	250-350	
Eaton, S.	Prince Domino & Muffles (1st, sq8vo, p-o, 146p, 7cp)	Stern	1910	Twelvetrees, C.	100-150	
Eaton, S.	Roosevelt Bears (1st, 4to, 180p, bds, p-o, 16cp)	Stern	1906	Campbell, V.F.	300-450	R
Eaton, S.	Roosevelt Bears Abroad (1st, 4to, ibds, p-o, 178p, 12cp)	Stern	1908	Culver, R.K.	280-400	
Eaton, S.	Teddy-B & Teddy-G/Bear Detectives (4to, ipcb, 152p, p-o, 15cp)	Barse	(1909)	Wightman, F.P.	180-250	
Eaton, S.	Teddy-B & Teddy-G/Bear Detectives (1st, 4to, bds, p-o, 15cp)	Stern	1909	Wightman, F.P.	250-325	
Eaton, S.	Travelling Bears at Play (1st, 4to, 62p, color)	Barse	(1916)	Campbell, V.F.	150-220	*
Eaton, S.	Travelling Bears in New York (1st, 4to, 60p, color)	Barse	(1915)	Campbell, V.F.	150-220	*
Eaton, S.	Travelling Bears/East & West (1st, 4to, bds, 63p, p-o, cp)	Barse	(1915)	Campbell, V.F.	150-220	
Eaton, S.	Travelling Bears/Outdoor Sports (1st, 4to, 60p, col frn)	Barse	(1915)	Campbell, V.F.	150-220	
Eberle, I.	Evie & Cooky (1st, 8vo, 122p, 1-color, pep)	Knopf	(1957)	Slobodkin, L.	20-30	*
Eberle, I.	Evie & Wonderful Kangaroo (1st, 8vo, 128p, 1-color, pep)	Knopf	(1955)	Slobodkin, L.	20-30	*
Eberle, I.	Grasses (1st, 8vo, green cl, 56p, brown illus)	Walck	1960	Keats, E.J.	35-60	*
Eberle, I.	Hop, Skip & Fly (1st, 8vo, 70p, grey cl, 2-color)	Holiday House	(1937)	Bostelmann, E.	20-30	*
Eberle, I.	Our Oldest Friends (1st, sm8vo, 146p, 1-color)	Holiday House	(1942)	Kirmse, M.	20-30	*
Eberle, I.	Phoebe-Belle (1st, 8vo, 63p, 1-color, pep)	Greystone Pr.	(1941)	Eichenberg, F.	35-50	*
Eberle, I.	Sea-Horse Adventure (1st, 8vo, [55]p, blue cl, 2-color)	Holiday House	(1937)	Bostelmann, E.	20-30	*
Eberle, I.	Spice on the Wind (1st, 8vo, 56p, brown cl, 2-color, pep)	Holiday House	(1940)	Jones, R.C.	50-80	R*
Eberle, I.	Through the Harbor from Everywhere (1st {std}, 8vo, 158p, pep)	Bobbs-Merrill	(1938)	Weisgard, L.	30-45	*
Eberle, I.	Wide Fields (1st, 8vo, 193p, green cl, 8pl)	Crowell	1943	Eichenberg, F.	30-45	*
Eddison, E.R.	Worm Ouroboros (1st AM, 8vo, 445p, b/w)	A.& C. Boni	1926	Henderson, K.	30-50	*
Edey, B.O.	Six Giants & a Griffin (1st, 4to, 46p, 6pl)	R.H. Russell	1903	Ruyl, B.B.	140-200	*
Edgar, M.G.	Treasury of Verse... (1st AM, lg8vo, 261p, teg, gilt, pep, 8cp)	Crowell	(1908)	Pogany, W.	100-150	
Edgar, M.G.	Treasury of Verse/School & Home (1st, 8vo, 523p, col frn, pep)	Crowell	(1926)	Appleton, H.C.	35-50	*
Edgeworth, M.	Helen (1st, 12mo, blue/gilt, 490p, AEG, b/w, dep)	L: MacMillan	1896	Hammond, C.	60-80	
Edgeworth, M.	Tales from.... (1st AM, 8vo, brown/gilt, teg, 412p, uncut, b/w)	Stokes	(1903)	Thomson, H.	85-100	
Edmonds, W.D.	Matchlock Gun (1st {std}, sm4to, 50p, dp color, pep, NM)	Dodd	1941	Lantz, P.	65-110	
Edmonds, W.D.	Two Logs Crossing (1st 8vo, 82p, green/gilt, fp b/w, pep)	Dodd	1943	Gergely, T.	35-50	*
Edmondson, N.M.	Lavender Garden (1st, 8vo, 158p, lavender/gilt, 4cp, pep)	L: Warne	1929	Howard, C.T.	30-50	
Edwards, G.W.	Alsace-Lorraine (1st AM, 4to, 344p, blue/gilt, 35pl)	Penn	(1918)	Edwards, G.W.	75-100	
Edwards, G.W.	Book of Old English Love Songs (1st, gilt)	NY: MacMillan	1897	Edwards, G.W.	35-50	*
Edwards, G.W.	Forest of Arden (1st, 4to, red/gilt, 213p, teg, 6cp)	Stokes	(1914)	Edwards, G.W.	30-45	
Edwards, G.W.	Thus Think and Smoke Tobacco (1st, sm4to, red/gilt, AEG)	Stokes	1891	Edwards, G.W.	100-140	
Edwards, Harry S.	Marbeau Cousins (1st, sm8vo, 294p, cvr by....)	Rand/McNally	(1898)	Denslow, W.W.	30-45	*
Edwards, Harry S.	Two Runaways (1st, 8vo, 246p, b/w pl)	Century	(1889)	Kemble, E.W.	45-65	*
Eells, E.S.	Brazilian Fairy Book (1st, 8vo, 193p, gilt, 6cp, pep)	Stokes	1926	Hood, G.	60-80	
Eells, E.S.	Magic Tooth (1st, 8vo, orange cl, 243p, col frn, 10 fp b/w)	Little/Brown	1927	Choate/Curtis	35-50	*
Egan, Constance	Epaminondas & the Lettuces (1st, 16mo, 62p, brown bds)	L: Collins	[1938]	Kennedy, A.E.	50-70	*
Egan, Constance	Epaminondas & the Puppy (1st, 12mo, unpag, pep, color)	L: Collins	1959	Kennedy, A.E.	90-130	*
Egan, Constance	Epaminondas Helps in the Garden (1st, 16mo, 62p, blue bds)	L: Collins	[1937]	Kennedy, A.E.	50-70	*
Egan, M.F.	Everybody's Saint Francis (1st, 8vo, grn/gilt, teg, 191p, 8cp)	Century	1912	DeMonvel, M.B.	50-70	
Eggleston, E.	Hoosier Schoolboy (1st [1], 8vo, 181p, 5pl, PPP)	Scribner	1883	Bush, G.D.	100-140	
Eggleston, G.C.	Last of the Flatboats (1st, 8vo, green/gilt, 382p, 4pl)	Lothrop	(1900)	Harding, C.	25-40	
Ehrlich, Bettina	Cocolo Comes to America (1st, folio, ibds, [32]p, color)	Harper	1949	Ehrlich, B.	50-85	*
Ehrlich, Bettina	Cocolo's Home (1st, folio, ibds, [32]p, color)	Harper	1950	Ehrlich, B.	50-75	*
Eichenberg, Fritz	Ape in a Cape (1st {std}, 4to, [32]p, color, pep, CH)	Harcourt	(1952)	Eichenberg, F.	70-110	R*

AUTHOR	TITLE	PUBLISHER	DATE	ARTIST	PRICE	LC
Eichenberg, Fritz	Dancing in the Moon (1st {std}, 4to, red cl, [21]p, color, pep)	Harcourt	(1955)	Eichenberg, F.	70-120	R*
Eickemeyer, R.	Down South (1st, folio, ibds, [47]p, p-o, b/w)	R.H. Russell	1900	(Photos)	350-400	
Eidinoff, M.L.	Atomics for the Millions (1st, 8vo, 281p, blue cl, b/w, DJ)	Whittlesey	(1947)	Sendak, M.	380-500	
Eldridge, E.J.	Yen-Foh, a Chinese Boy (1st, 8vo, 29p, color, pep)	Whitman	1935	Wiese, K.	30-50	*
Elias, E. (ed.)	Cinderella (1st, sm4to, red bds, p-o, 8 dp color)	McBride	1915	Pogany, W.	160-230	
Eliot, E.C.	Wind Boy (1st {std}, sm8vo, 238p, col frn, b/w)	Doubleday/Page	1923	Bromhall, W.	20-30	
Eliot, Geo.	Adam Bede (1st, 4to, 523p, p-o, teg, gilt, 16cp)	L: Chambers	[1900]	Browne, G.	70-100	
Eliot, Geo.	Scenes from Clerical Life (1st, 12mo, 429p, grn/gilt, AEG, 16cp)	L: MacMillan	1906	Thomson, H.	50-90	
Eliot, Geo.	Silas Marner (1st, sm8vo, green/gilt, 262p, teg, 24cp, dep)	L: Dent	1905	Brock, C.E.	30-45	
Eliot, T.S.	Old Possum's Book of Practical Cats (1st, 8vo, 50p, color)	L: Faber	(1940)	Bentley, N.	65-100	*
Elkin, Ben	Gillespie & the Guards (1st, 4to, 62p, fp 1-color, CH)	Viking	1956	Daugherty, J.	50-90	*
Elkin, R.H.	Children's Corner (1st AM, ob8vo, p-o, gilt, 15 ticp)	McKay	[1915]	LeMair, H.W.	160-200	
Elkin, R.H.	Little People (ob4to, red/gilt, p-o, 16 fp color)	McKay/Augener	[1920]	LeMair, H.W.	140-220	
Elkin, R.H.	Old Dutch Nursery Rhymes (1st, ob4to, p-o, 31p, color)	L: Augener	(1917)	LeMair, H.W.	160-200	
Elliott, H.	Alliterative Alphabet... (1st, 4to, [55]p, blue bds, color)	McKay	(1947)	Green, E.S.	85-120	*
Elliott, K.M.	Jo-Yo's Idea (1st {std}, 8vo, 114p, cloth, fp color, cep)	Knopf	1939	Duvoisin, R.	35-50	*
Elliott, K.M.	Riema... (1st {std}, 8vo, 54p, ibds, color, pep, DJ)	Knopf	1937	Duvoisin, R.	40-60	
Elliott, K.M.	Soomoon, Boy of Bali (1st {std}, 8vo, 88p, ibds, pep, color)	Knopf	1938	Duvoisin, R.	70-100	R
Elliott, K.M.	Three Sneezes... (1st {std}, 8vo, 244p, color, pep, DJ)	Knopf	1941	Duvoisin, R.	35-50	
Ellis, F.S.	History of Reynard the Fox (1st, 8vo, 289p, uncut, designs)	L: D. Nutt	1897	Crane, W.	80-100	
Elmslie, T.C.	His Lordship's Puppy (1st, sm8vo, 205p, 4pl)	Penn	1901	Waugh, Ida	25-40	
Ely, H.R.	Another Hardy Garden Book (1st, 8vo, teg, uncut, 232p, cvr by)	MacMillan	1905	Armstrong, M.	30-45	
Emanuel, W.	Conceited Puppy... (1st AM, 12mo, ibds, p-o, color)	Dutton	(1905)	Aldin, C.	80-120	
Emanuel, W.	Dog Day (1st AM, lg4to, [59]p, ibds, 28cp)	R.H. Russell	1902	Aldin, C.	140-200	
Emanuel, W.	Dog Day (1st, lg4to, ibds, unpag, 28cp)	L: Heinemann	1902	Aldin, C.	165-220	
Emanuel, W.	Dog Day (24mo, 55p, ibds, 28cp)	Dutton	(1907)	Aldin, C.	100-130	*
Emanuel, W.	Dogs of War (1st, lg8vo, tan cl, 243p, 12cp)	L: Bradbury/Ag	(1906)	Aldin, C.	90-125	
Emblen, Don L.	Palomino Boy (1st, 8vo, blue cl, 189p, pep, decor by...)	Viking	1948	Ward, L.	25-40	*
Embry, Margaret	Blue-Nosed Witch (1st, 8vo, 45p, yellow cl, b/w, pep)	Holiday House	(1955)	Rose, C.	20-30	*
Embry, Margaret	Kid Sister (1st, sm8vo, 165p, yellow cl, fp b/w, pep)	Holiday House	(1958)	Freeman, D.	20-30	*
Emerson, C.	Hat Tub Tale... (1st {std}, 8vo, 185p, blue cl, uncut, b/w, pep)	Dutton	1928	Lenski, L.	30-45	*
Emerson, C.	Mr. Nip & Mr. Tuck (1st {std}, 8vo, 173p, aqua/gilt, b/w, dep)	Dutton	1930	Lenski, L.	30-45	*
Emerson, C.D.	Little Green Car (1st, 8vo, ipcb, [28]p, color, pep)	Grosset/Dunlap	(1946)	Galdone, P.	35-50	*
Emerson, C.D.	School Days in Disneyville (1st, 8vo, 102p, color, pep)	Heath	(1939)	Disney Studios	45-60	*
Emerson, W.G.	Smoky God (1st, 8vo, 186p, blue cl, 11pl)	Chi: Forbes	1908	Williams, J.A.	35-50	*
Emery, Carlyle	Polly Through the Crystal (1st, 16mo, ipcb)	Whitman	1932	Bennett, J.C.	20-30	
Emery, Carlyle	Polly Through the Mountains (1st, 16mo, ipcb)	Whitman	1932	Bennett, J.C.	20-30	
Emmet, R.	Pretty Peggy... (lg sq8vo, ibds, 64p, chromos)	Dodd	1880	Emmet, R.	80-100	
Endres, Ernest	Day with The Gnomes (1st, 24mo, [54]p, ibds, pep, 19 color)	L: Nister	[1910]	Endres, E.	100-130	
England, G.A.	Air Trust (8vo, red/gilt, 4pl)	P. Wagner	(1915)	Sloan, J.	130-165	
England, G.A.	Flying Legion (1st, 8vo, 394p, frn by...)	McClurg	1920	Monahan, P.J.	35-60	*
England, G.A.	Golden Blight (1st, 8vo, 350p, brown/gilt, 5pl)	H.K. Fly	(1916)	Sloan, J.	65-80	*
English, Doug	Book of Nimble Beasts (1st, 8vo, green/gilt, 318p)	L: E. Nash	1910	(Photos)	35-50	*
English, James W.	Tailbone Patrol (1st, 8vo, 186p, grey cl, fp b/w, pep)	Holiday House	(1955)	Wells, P.	20-30	*
English, T.D.	Little Giant... (1st, 4to, 150p, t.e. yellow, 4 fp b/w)	McClurg	1904	Perkins, L.F.	65-80	
Enright, E.	Christmas Tree for Lydia (1st, 24mo, ipcb, 38p, 6cp, dep)	Rinehart	(1951)	Enright, E.	35-50	*
Enright, E.	Four-Story Mistake (1st, 8vo, 177p, 9 fp 1-color, pep)	Farrar/Rine.	(1942)	Enright, E.	30-45	*
Enright, E.	Gone-Away Lake (1st {std}, 8vo, 192p, green cl, b/w, NH)	Harcourt	(1957)	Krush, B.& J.	45-60	*
Enright, E.	Kintu: A Congo Adventure (1st, 8vo, p-o, 54p, color, DJ)	Farrar/Rine.	1935	Enright, E.	45-75	
Enright, E.	Sea is All Around (1st, lg8vo, 124p, green cl, 6cp, pep, DJ)	Farrar/Rine.	(1940)	Enright, E.	50-70	*
Enright, E.	The Saturdays (1st, sm8vo, red cl, 175p, fp 1-color, pep)	Farrar/Rine.	(1941)	Enright, E.	30-45	*
Enright, E.	Then There were Five (1st, 8vo, blue cl, 241p, uncut, b/w)	Farrar/Rine.	(1944)	Enright, E.	30-45	*
Enright, E.	Thimble Summer (1st, 8vo, 124p, color, pep, DJ, NM)	Farrar/Rine.	1938	Enright, E.	65-90	
Erskine, P.	Iona (1st, 8vo, blue cl)	Dibble	1891	Armstrong, M.	45-70	
Ervin, M.C.	As Told by the Typewriter Girl (1st, 8vo, 245p)	Herrick	(1898)	McManus, B.	50-75	
Estes, Eleanor	Ginger Pye (1st {std}, 8vo, 250p, yellow cl, b/w, NM)	Harcourt	(1951)	Estes, E.	60-90	R*
Estes, Eleanor	Hundred Dresses (1st, sm4to, 80p, red cl, color, NH)	Harcourt	(1944)	Slobodkin, L.	65-90	
Estes, Eleanor	Middle Moffat (1st, 8vo, 317p, p-o, b/w, pep, NH)	Harcourt	(1942)	Slobodkin, L.	60-85	
Estes, Eleanor	Pinkey Pye (1st {std}, sm8vo, 192p, pink cl, b/w)	Harcourt	(1958)	Ardizzone, E.	50-80	R*
Estes, Eleanor	Rufus M. (1st, 8vo, 320p, red cl, b/w, pep, NH)	Harcourt	(1943)	Slobodkin, L.	60-80	
Estes, Eleanor	Sleeping Giant (1st, 8vo, 101p, green cl, fp color)	Harcourt	(1948)	Estes, E.	35-50	*
Estes, Eleanor	Sun, Wind & Mr. Todd (1st, 4to, [92]p, brown cl, 1-color, pep)	Harcourt	(1943)	Slobodkin, L.	40-60	*
Estes, Eleanor	The Moffats (1st [1st bk.], 8vo, pink cl, 290p, b/w, pep)	Harcourt	(1941)	Slobodkin, L.	50-80	R*
Estes, Eleanor	Witch Family (1st {std}, 8vo, green cl, 86p, b/w)	Harcourt	(1960)	Ardizzone, E.	35-50	*
Ets, Marie H.	Another Day (1st, ob4to, 40p, pep, b/w)	Viking	1953	Ets, M.H.	50-80	R*
Ets, Marie H.	Beasts & Nonsense (1st, 8vo, 64p)	Viking	1952	Ets, M.H.	35-50	*
Ets, Marie H.	In the Forest (1st, ob4to, ipcb, [45]p, b/w, CH)	Viking	1944	Ets, M.H.	65-100	R*
Ets, Marie H.	Little Old Automobile (1st, 4to, ipcb, [32]p, b/w, pep)	Viking	1948	Ets, M.H.	40-65	*
Ets, Marie H.	Mister Penny (1st {1st book}, ob4to, ibds, 48p, b/w, pep)	Viking	1935	Ets, M.H.	120-165	
Ets, Marie H.	Mr. Penny's Race Horse (1st, 4to, 63p, CH)	Viking	1956	Ets, M.H.	65-100	R
Ets, Marie H.	Mr. T.W. Anthony Woo (1st, ob4to, ibds, 54p, pep, b/w, CH)	Viking	1951	Ets, M.H.	70-100	*
Ets, Marie H.	Nine Days to Christmas (1st, 4to, 48p, color, CM)	Viking	(1959)	Ets, M.H.	80-120	*

AUTHOR	TITLE	PUBLISHER	DATE	ARTIST	PRICE	LC
Ets, Marie H.	Oley, the Sea Monster (1st, 4to, ipcb, [32]p, b/w, pep)	Viking	1947	Ets, M.H.	45-70	*
Ets, Marie H.	Play with Me (1st, sm4to, 31p, color, CH)	Viking	(1955)	Ets, M.H.	70-100	*
Ets, Marie H.	Story of a Baby (1st, lg4to, 63p, blue cl, pep, b/w)	Viking	1939	Ets, M.H.	50-80	*
Eustis, C.	Cooking in Old Creole Days (1st, 8vo, ipcb, 112p, 8pl)	R.H. Russell	1903	Pennington, H.	80-120	R*
Evans, C.S.	Cinderella (1st, 4to, 110p, cream bds, ti-col frn, dp b/w, pep)	L: Heinemann	(1919)	Rackham, A.	225-280	
Evans, C.S.	Sleeping Beauty (1st, 4to, ibds, 110p, 1 ticp, 4 dp color)	L: Heinemann	(1920)	Rackham, A.	180-250	
Evans, Eva K.	Jerome Anthony (1st, 8vo, blue cl, 88p, b/w)	Putnam	(1936)	Berry, E.	35-50	*
Evans, Eva K.	Key Corner (1st, sm8vo, 206p, tan cl, pep, fp b/w)	Putnam	(1938)	Berry, E.	25-45	*
Evans, Eva K.	Mr. Jones & Mr. Finnigan (1st, 4to, [32]p, tan cl, 2-col, dep)	NY: OUP	(1941)	Berry, E.	30-45	*
Evans, F.A.	Alice's Adventures in Pictureland (1st, sm4to, 192p, b/w pl)	Dodge	(1900)	Wheelan, A.R.	100-165	*
Evans, F.A.	Jewel Story Book (1st, 12mo, 102p, green cl, 4pl)	Saalfield	1903	Fry, W.H.	20-30	
Evans, F.G.	Puffin, Puma & Co. (1st AM, sm4to, ibds, 96p)	MacMillan	1929	Morrow, G.	20-25	
Evans, Lawton	America First (1st, 8vo, 447p, p-o, pep, col frn, 9pl)	M. Bradley	1920	Winter, M.	35-50	*
Evans, Lawton	Once to Every Man (1st, 8vo, 317p, 4pl)	H.K. Fly	(1914)	Fischer, A.O.	30-45	
Evans, Myfanwy	No Rubbish Here (1st, 4to, green ibds, 34p, color)	L: Collins	(1936)	Tempest, M.	70-100	*
Evans, S.	High History of the Holy Grail (1st, 8vo, gilt, teg, 379p, 22pl)	L: Dent	1903	King, J.	450-600	
Evarts, Hal G.	Bald Face & other Animal Stories (1st, 8vo, 317p, 8pl, pep)	Knopf	1921	Bull, C.L.	20-30	*
Evarts, Hal G.	Passing of the Old West (1st, 8vo, 234p, 8pl)	Little/Brown	1921	Bull, C.L.	20-30	*
Evers, Alf	Colonel's Squad (1st {std}, 8vo, blue/gilt, 200p, b/w)	MacMillan	1952	Sewell, H.	25-40	*
Evers, Alf	In the Beginning (1st, 8vo, aqua cl, [30]p, 2-color, dep)	MacMillan	1954	Sewell, H.	45-60	R*
Evers, Helen	This Little Pig (1st, ob4to, [32]p, ibds, color, pep)	Farrar/Rine.	(1932)	Unknown	40-60	*
Everson, Dale	Different Dog (1st, 4to, blue cl, 31p, 2-color, pep)	Wm. Morrow	1960	Galdone, P.	30-45	*
Everson, Howard	Coming o/t Dragon Ships (1st {std}, 8vo, 128p, col frn, 9pl pep)	Dutton	1931	D'Aulaire, E.P.	45-60	*
Ewing, J.H.	Blue & Red…. (4to, ibds, 32p, chromos)	L: SPCK	[1881]	Andre, R.	145-200	
Ewing, J.H.	Daddy Darwin's Dovecoat (1st, 8vo, 52p, ibds, gilt, teg, col frn)	L: SPCK	[1884]	Caldecott, R.	70-100	
Ewing, J.H.	Daddy Darwin's Dovecoat (1st AM, 12mo, 62p, ibds)	Roberts	1886	Caldecott, R.	60-80	
Ewing, J.H.	Daddy Darwin's Dovecoat (1st, 12mo, 78p, grey cl, 6pl)	D. Estes	1898	Barry, E.B.	30-45	*
Ewing, J.H.	Flat Iron for a Farthing (1st, 12mo, 235p, 8cp)	L: G. Bell	1908	Wheelhouse, M.V.	30-45	*
Ewing, J.H.	Great Emergency (1st, 12mo, 166p, b/w pl)	L.C. Page	1897	Barry, E.B.	25-40	*
Ewing, J.H.	Jacanapes (1st, lg8vo, ibds, 184p, teg, col frn)	L: SPCK	1884	Caldecott, R.	120-160	
Ewing, J.H.	Jacanapes (1st, 8vo, 80p, gilt, AEG, 7pl)	Dutton	1893	Gordon, F.C.	35-50	*
Ewing, J.H.	Jacanapes (1st, 12mo, 60p, blue cl, b/w)	J. Knight	1895	Sacker, A.	30-45	*
Ewing, J.H.	Jacanapes (1st {this pub}, 12mo, 71p, rust cl, 6pl)	D. Estes	(1902)	Bruce, J.	20-30	*
Ewing, J.H.	Jacanapes (1st, 12mo, 72p, col frn, 4 fp b/w, dep)	McLoughlin	(1906)	Noble-Ives, S.	30-45	*
Ewing, J.H.	Jacanapes (1st, 8vo, 196p, 8cp)	L: Bell	1913	Brock, H.M.	40-60	
Ewing, J.H.	Jacanapes (1st, sm8vo, green cl, 62p, color, pep)	OUP	1948	Tudor, T.	100-130	
Ewing, J.H.	Jan of the Windmill (1st, 12mo, 307p, 8cp, pep)	L: G. Bell	1917	Wheelhouse, M.V.	35-50	*
Ewing, J.H.	Lob Lie-by-the-Fire (1st, 8vo, 72p, ibds)	L: SPCK	(1885)	Caldecott, R.	70-90	
Ewing, J.H.	Lob Lie-by-the-Fire (1st, sq8vo, teg, 189p, 8cp)	L: Bell	1909	Woodward, A.B.	40-60	
Ewing, J.H.	Lob Lie-by-the-Fire (1st, 8vo, 144p, b/w)	NY: OUP	(1937)	Ivins, F.W.	20-30	*
Ewing, J.H.	Master Fritz (1st, ob8vo, 32p, ibds, color)	L: SPCK	[1883]	Andre, R.	120-165	*
Ewing, J.H.	Mrs. Overtheway's Rememberances (sq8vo)	L: H. Frowde	(1915)	Brock, C.E.	25-40	
Ewing, J.H.	Mrs. Overtheway's Rememberances… (1st, 8vo, teg, 8cp)	L: G. Bell	1909	Wheelhouse, M.V.	30-45	
Ewing, J.H.	Old Fashioned Fairy Tales (1st, 12mo, 125p, 8cp, pep)	L: G. Bell	(1919)	Robertson, W.G.	120-160	
Ewing, J.H.	Our Garden (1st, ob8vo, ibds, 32p, color)	L: SPCK	[1883]	Andre, R.	100-140	*
Ewing, J.H.	Six to Sixteen (1st, 12mo, green cl, 237p, teg, 8cp)	L: G. Bell	1910	Wheelhouse, M.V.	25-40	
Ewing, J.H.	Soldier's Children (ob8vo, 32p, ibds, chromos)	L: SPCK	[1883]	Andre, R.	75-100	
Ewing, J.H.	Stories by J.H. Ewing (1st, lg8vo, blue cl, p-o, 426p, 8cp)	Duffield	1920	Cooke, E.	50-75	
Ewing, J.H.	The Brownies (1st, 12mo, ibds, 50p, color, DJ)	Scribner	1946	Milhous, K.	30-45	
Ewing, J.H.	Three Christmas Trees (1st, 12mo, green/gilt, 88p, col frn, dep)	MacMillan	1930	Bianco, P.	30-45	
Ewing, J.H.	We & the World (1st, 12mo, rust cl, 315p, teg, 8cp)	L: G. Allen	1910	Wheelhouse, M.V.	25-40	
Ewing, J.H.	Week Spent in a Glass Pond (4to, ibds, 32p, chromos)	L: Wells/Gard.	[1883]	Andre, R.	180-265	
Fable, L.	Gingerbread Man (1st, 4to, [32]p, p-o, bds, 8cp)	McBride	1915	Pogany, W.	100-130	
Fabre	Fabre's Book of Insects (1st, lg4to, white/gilt, 12 ticp)	L: Hodder	(1921)	Detmold, E.J.	220-300	
Fairmont, E.	Rhymes for Kindly Children (4to, [127]p, color)	Wise-Parlow	(1937)	Gruelle, J.	35-50	
Falkberget, J.	Broomstick & Snowflake (1st, 8vo, blue cl, 88p, b/w, cep)	MacMillan	1933	Sewell, H.	35-50	*
Fallon, Sara W.	Animal-Alphabet Book (1st, ob4to, [54]p, color)	L: G. Allen	1899	Fallon, S.W.	100-165	*
Falls, C.B.	ABC Book (1st, lg4to, [30]p, ibds, 26cp)	Doubleday/Page	1923	Falls, C.B.	150-200	
Falls, C.B.	ABC Book (lg4to, orang ibds, unpag, fp color)	Doubleday/Dor.	1939	Falls, C.B.	120-165	R*
Falls, C.B.	Modern ABC Book (1st, lg4to, [32]p, 26 color)	NY: J. Day	1930	Falls, C.B.	140-200	*
Farjeon, B.L.	Lucy & their Majesties (1st, 8vo, 332p, tan cl, 20pl)	Century	1904	Cory/Varian	25-40	
Farjeon, B.L.	Lucy & their Majesties (1st, 8vo, 332p, tan cl, 20pl)	Century	1904	Varian/Cory	30-45	
Farjeon, E.	Alphabet of Magic (1st, 8vo, 57p)	L: Medici	1928	Tarrant, M.	45-65	*
Farjeon, E.	Ameliaranne/Magic Ring (1st AM, 8vo, [63]p, p-o, color, pep)	McKay	[1933]	Pearse, S.B.	40-60	
Farjeon, E.	Cherrystones (1st AM {std}, 12mo, red/gilt, 58p, fp b/w)	Lippincott	(1944)	Morton-Sale, J.	25-40	
Farjeon, E.	Come Christmas (1st, sm8vo, ipcb, 62p, color)	Stokes	1928	Field, R.	30-45	*
Farjeon, E.	Fair of St. James (1st, 8vo, 310p, green/gilt, b/w)	Stokes	1932	Lathrop, D.	50-80	
Farjeon, E.	Glass Slipper (1st, 8vo, 175p, b/w, DJ)	L: OUP	1955	Shepard, E.H.	45-60	
Farjeon, E.	Glass Slipper (1st AM, 8vo, 187p, red cl, b/w, DJ)	Viking	1956	Shepard, E.H.	30-45	
Farjeon, E.	Heroes & Heroines (1st AM, lg8vo, 79p, ibds, fp color, DJ)	Dutton	[1933]	Thornycroft, R.	45-65	
Farjeon, E.	Italian Peepshow (1st, 8vo, p-o, 146p, 12 fp color, pep)	Stokes	1926	Thornycroft, R.	30-45	*
Farjeon, E.	Joan's Door (1st, 8vo, 127p)	L: Collins	(1926)	Townsend, W.	30-45	*

AUTHOR	TITLE	PUBLISHER	DATE	ARTIST	PRICE	LC
Farjeon, E.	Kings & Queens (1st AM, 8vo, 79p, color, DJ)	Dutton	1932	Thornycroft, R.	45-60	
Farjeon, E.	Kings & Queens (1st, 8vo, 79p, ibds, 38cp, DJ)	L: Gollancz	(1932)	Thornycroft, R.	50-65	
Farjeon, E.	Kings & Queens (sm4to, ibds, 86p, 40 color, DJ)	Lippincott	[1940]	Thornycroft, R.	30-50	
Farjeon, E.	Kings & Queens (sm4to, red cl, 86p, 40 fp color)	Dent/Dutton	(1940)	Thornycroft, R.	30-50	*
Farjeon, E.	Little Bookroom (1st AM, 8vo, 302p, red cl, DJ)	NY: OUP	1956	Ardizzone, E.	70-90	R*
Farjeon, E.	Martin Pippin/Apple Orchard (1st, 8vo, brown cl, 369p, 5 ticp)	L: Collins	(1921)	Brock, C.E.	50-70	
Farjeon, E.	Martin Pippin/Daisy-Field (1st AM {std}, 8vo, 320p, col frn)	Stokes	1938	Morton-Sale, J.	50-65	*
Farjeon, E.	Nursery Rhymes/London Town (1st, 8vo, [64]p, blue/gilt, col frn)	L: Duckworth	(1916)	Gill, M.	70-90	*
Farjeon, E.	Nuts & May (1st, 4to, p-o, 263p, color)	L: Collins	1926	Thornycroft, R.	70-120	*
Farjeon, E.	Old Nurse's Stocking Basket (1st AM, 8vo, 154p, col frn, b/w)	Stokes	1931	Whydale, E.H.	30-45	
Farjeon, E.	One Foot in Fairyland (1st, 8vo, 261p, gilt, b/w, cep, DJ)	Stokes	1938	Lawson, R.	80-100	
Farjeon, E.	Perfect Zoo (1st, ob4to, red cl, p-o, 31p, 12cp)	McKay	(1929)	Kruse, K.	120-160	
Farjeon, E.	Perfect Zoo (1st {this pub.}, 4to, color)	L: Harrap	1947	Burrell, K.	40-65	*
Farjeon, E.	Perkin the Pedlar (1st, sm4to, blue cl, 205p, 8cp)	L: Faber	(1932)	Leighton, C.	65-80	*
Farjeon, E.	Prayer for Little Things (1st, 8vo, [13]p, color, dep, DJ)	Houghton	1945	Jones, E.O.	30-45	
Farjeon, E.	Silver Curlew (1st, 8vo, 192p, b/w)	L: OUP	1953	Shepard, E.H.	45-60	*
Farjeon, E.	Singing Games for Children (1st, 8vo, 71p)	Dent/Dutton	[1919]	Littlejohns, J.	45-60	*
Farjeon, E.	Songs for Music.... (1st, sm8vo, 61p, frn by...)	L: Selwyn	(1922)	Austen, J.	45-65	
Farjeon, E.	Tale of Tom Tiddler (1st, 8vo, 191p)	L: Collins	(1929)	Brock, H.M.	65-80	*
Farjeon, E.	Tales from Chaucer (1st, 8vo, 244p, 12cp)	L: J. Cape	1930	Flint, W.R.	70-85	
Farjeon, E.	Ten Saints (1st AM {std}, 8vo, 124p, 10 fp color, pep)	NY: OUP	1936	Sewell, H.	50-75	
Farjeon, E.	Westwoods (1st, sm8vo, ibds, [44]p, b/w, pep)	A.& W. Guild	(1935)	Smith, M.	25-40	
Farjeon, E.	Wonders of Herodotus (1st, 8vo, 176p)	L: Nelson	1937	Nelson, E.	35-50	*
Farley, Walter	Blood Bay Colt (1st {std}, 8vo, 307p, fp b/w)	Random	(1950)	Menasco, M.	25-40	*
Farmer, J.E.	The Grenadier (1st, 8vo, 328p, red cl, cvr by...)	Dodd	1898	Edwards, G.W.	20-30	
Farmiloe, Edith	Mr. Biddle & the Dragon (4to, red cl, 47p, 20pl)	L: Skeffington	1904	Farmiloe, E.	50-80	
Farnol, J.	Amateur Gentleman (1st UK, 8vo, blue/gilt, 599p, teg, 21cp)	L: Sampson	(1916)	Brock, C.E.	65-80	*
Farnol, J.	Broad Highway (1st, lg8vo, 493p, blue/gilt, p-o, 24cp)	L: Sampson	1910	Brock, C.E.	50-75	
Farnol, J.	Broad Highway (1st AM, lg8vo, 518p, p-o, teg, 24cp)	Little/Brown	1912	Brock, C.E.	45-60	
Farnol, J.	Honorable Mr. Tawnish (1st AM, sm8vo, 165p, lavender/gilt, 4cp)	Little/Brown	1913	Brock, C.E.	20-30	
Farnol, J.	Honorable Mr. Tawnish (1st, 8vo, 118p, gilt, teg, 8cp)	L: Sampson	1913	Brock, C.E.	45-60	
Farnol, J.	Money Moon (1st, 4to, p-o, teg, 385p, 22pl)	Dodd	1911	Keller, A.I.	40-60	
Farnol, J.	My Lady Caprice (1st, 8vo, teg, p-o, 289p)	Dodd	1907	Ditzler, C.W.	20-25	
Farr, Florence	Dancing Faun (1st, 8vo, 149p, ti-page & cvr by...)	L: E. Matthews	1894	Beardsley, A.	45-60	*
Farrar, Evelyn	Stories from the Bible (1st, sm4to, 243p, gilt, 12pl)	L: Henry	1896	Hallward, R.	35-50	*
Farrow, D.P.	Little Brown Hen (1st, sq12mo, [48]p, orange cl, color, cep)	MacMillan	1941	Dobias, F.	35-50	*
Farrow, G.E.	Absurd Ditties (1st, 8vo, blue/gilt, AEG, 224p, b/w)	L: Routledge	1903	Hassall, J.	65-90	
Farrow, G.E.	Adventures in Wallypug-Land (1st, AEG, 8vo, gilt, 186p, 17pl)	L: Methuen	1898	Wright, A.	100-140	
Farrow, G.E.	Adventures in Wallypug-Land (1st AM, 8vo, blue cl, AEG, b/w)	New Amsterdam	1899	Wright, A.	70-100	*
Farrow, G.E.	Adventures of a Dodo (1st, 8vo, gilt, 245p, 70 b/w, pep)	L: T.F. Unwin	(1907)	Pogany, W.	180-260	
Farrow, G.E.	All About the Wallypug (1st, folio, unpag)	L: R. Tuck	[1904]	Unknown	100-150	*
Farrow, G.E.	Baker Minor & Dragon (1st, lg8vo, blue/gilt, AEG, 210p, b/w)	L: A. Pearson	1902	Wright, A.	90-110	*
Farrow, G.E.	Dwindleberry Zoo (1st, lg8vo, 208p)	L: Blackie	1909	Browne, G.	120-165	*
Farrow, G.E.	Escape of the Mullingong (1st, 12mo, AEG, 148p, gilt)	L: Blackie	1907	Browne, G.	100-150	
Farrow, G.E.	King's Gardens (1st, 8vo, 43p)	L: Hutchinson	1896	Bowley, A.L.	65-80	*
Farrow, G.E.	Little Panjandrum's Dodo (1st, 8vo, 210p, gilt, b/w)	L: Skeffington	1899	Wright, A.	60-80	
Farrow, G.E.	Mandarin's Kite (1st, 8vo, 154p)	L: Skeffington	1900	Wright, A.	50-75	*
Farrow, G.E.	Missing Prince (1st, lg8vo, 197p, green/gilt, AEG, b/w)	L: Hutchinson	1896	Furniss, H.& D.	90-120	
Farrow, G.E.	Missing Prince (1st AM, 8vo, 198p, pict cl, b/w)	Dodd	1897	Furniss, H.& D.	70-100	*
Farrow, G.E.	Mysterious Voyage (1st, 8vo, 160p, 32 illus)	L: Partridge	[1910]	Roberts, K.M.	45-60	*
Farrow, G.E.	New Panjandrum (1st, 8vo, 199p, gilt, AEG, b/w)	L: A. Pearson	1902	Wright, A.	80-100	
Farrow, G.E.	Pixie Pickles (1st, lg4to, ibds, 46p, 20 pl)	L: Skeffington	[1908]	Neilson, H.B.	145-200	
Farrow, G.E.	Professor Philanderpan (1st, 8vo, 216p, green/gilt, AEG, b/w)	L: A. Pearson	1904	Wright, A.	50-80	*
Farrow, G.E.	Round the World ABC (1st, 4to, [54]p, ibds, 26 color)	L: Nister	[1904]	Hassall, J.	180-250	
Farrow, G.E.	Wallypug Birthday Book (1st, sq8vo, gilt, AEG, 143p, 12cp)	L: Routledge	1904	Wright, A.	150-220	
Farrow, G.E.	Wallypug Tales (1st, sm folio, grey ibds, unpag, color)	L: R. Tuck	[1904]	Wright, A.	200-260	
Farrow, G.E.	Wallypug at Play (folio, ibds, 12 chromos)	L: R. Tuck	[1895]	Wright, A.	350-500	
Farrow, G.E.	Wallypug in Fogland (1st, 8vo, 207p, blue/gilt, AEG, b/w)	L: A. Pearson	1904	Wright, A.	100-160	*
Farrow, G.E.	Wallypug in London (1st, 8vo, 174p, b/w)	L: Methuen	1898	Wright, A.	80-120	
Farrow, G.E.	Wallypug in the Moon (1st AM, 8vo, 256p, AEG, blue/gilt, b/w)	Lippincott	1905	Wright, A.	100-130	
Farrow, G.E.	Wallypug in the Moon (1st, 8vo, AEG, 256p, grey/gilt)	L: A. Pearson	1905	Wright, A.	100-150	*
Farrow, G.E.	Wallypug of Why (1st, 8vo, green/gilt, 201p, AEG, 15pl)	L: Hutchinson	(1895)	Furniss, H.& D.	130-175	
Farrow, G.E.	Wallypug of Why (1st AM, lg8vo, 201p, b/w illus)	Dodd	1896	Furniss, H.	120-160	*
Farrow, G.E.	Zoo Babies (4to, green bds, 24 color)	L: H. Frowde	[1905]	Aldin, C.	250-350	*
Father Tuck	Pa Cats, Ma Cats... (1st, lg4to, gilt, 12cp)	L: R. Tuck	[1901]	Wain, L.	300-400	
Fatio, Louise	Anna the Horse (1st {std}, 8vo, ipcb, [48]p, 3-color, pep)	Aladdin	(1951)	Duvoisin, R.	35-50	*
Fatio, Louise	Christmas Forest (1st, 8vo, ibds, [44]p, pep, color)	Aladdin	(1950)	Duvoisin, R.	45-65	*
Fatio, Louise	Happy Lion (1st, sm4to, [30]p, yellow cl, 2-color)	Whittlesey	(1954)	Duvoisin, R.	50-80	R*
Fatio, Louise	Happy Lion in Africa (1st, sm4to, green cl, 30p, 2-color)	Whittlesey	(1955)	Duvoisin, R.	35-50	*
Faulkner, Georgene	Little Peachling... (1st, 4to, 91p, orange cl, color, pep)	Volland	(1928)	Richardson, F.	60-80	
Faulkner, Georgene	Road to Enchantment (1st, 8vo, 312p, p-o, 8cp)	Sears	(1929)	Richardson, F.	80-120	
Faulkner, Georgene	Squeaky & the Scare Box (1st, 8vo, [32]p, ibds, 4cp, pep)	Grosset/Dunlap	(1931)	Richardson, F.	50-80	

AUTHOR	TITLE	PUBLISHER	DATE	ARTIST	PRICE	LC
Faulkner, Georgene	Story Lady's Christmas Stories (1st, 8vo, 93p, red cl, 5cp, pep)	Sears	(1927)	Richardson, F.	30-45	*
Faulkner, Georgene	Story Lady's Italian Tales (1st, 8vo, 95p, gilt, uncut, pep, 5cp)	Chi: Daughaday	(1916)	Richardson, F.	65-80	*
Faulkner, Georgene	Story Lady's Nursery Tales (1st, 8vo, 241p, p-o, 8cp, pep)	Sears	(1927)	Winter, M.	65-80	*
Faulkner, Georgene	White Elephant (1st, 8vo, ibds, 92p, 10 fp color, pep)	Volland	(1929)	Richardson, F.	65-85	R
Faulkner, John	Chooky (1st {std}, 8vo, 250p, beige cl, b/w)	Norton	(1950)	Busoni, R.	25-40	*
Faulkner, Wm.	Green Bough (1st, 8vo, green cl, 67p, title page by...)	Smith/Haas	1933	Ward, L.	150-250	*
Faure, G.	Gardens of Rome (lg4to, p-o, 100p, cp)	Brentano's	1920	Vignal, P.	70-100	
Fay, E.	Road to Fairyland (1st AM, 8vo, grey cl, 218p, col frn by..)	Putnam	(1926)	Rackham, A.	145-200	
Fenner, P.R.	Circus Parade (1st {std}, lg8vo, beige cl, 174p, uncut, fp b/w)	Knopf	1954	Ames, L.	30-45	*
Fenner, P.R.	Demons & Dervishes (1st {std}, 8vo, red cl, 183p, fp b/w, pep)	Knopf	(1946)	Pitz, H.C.	30-45	*
Fenner, P.R.	Giants & Witches (1st {std}, 8vo, red cl, 208p, fp b/w, pep)	Knopf	1943	Pitz, H.C.	35-50	*
Fenner, P.R.	Giggle Box (1st {std}, lg8vo, yellow cl, 144p, uncut, b/w, pep)	Knopf	1950	Steig, W.	35-60	*
Fenner, P.R.	Princesses & Peasant Boys (1st {std}, 8vo, 188p, b/w, pep)	Knopf	1944	Pitz, H.C.	25-40	*
Fenner, P.R.	Stories of the Sea (1st {std}, lg8vo, beige cl, 178p, b/w)	Knopf	1953	Werth, K.	25-40	*
Fenner, P.R.	Yankee Doodle (1st {std}, 8vo, red cl, 214p, uncut, fp b/w)	Knopf	1951	Pitz, H.C.	25-45	*
Fenton, Edward	Nine Lives (1st, 4to, ipcb, 62p, pep, b/w)	Pantheon	(1951)	Galdone, P.	45-60	*
Ferrer, Melchor	Tito's Hats (1st, sq4to, [28]p, ibds, dep)	Garden City	(1940)	Charlot, J.	45-60	
Fesenden, L.D.	Colonial Dame (1st, 8vo, 116p, cvr by...)	Rand/McNally	1897	Denslow, W.W.	35-50	
Feuillet, O.	Story of Mr. Punch (1st, 8vo, 139p, p-o, col frn, fp b/w, pep)	Dutton	(1929)	Hader, B.& E.	30-45	
Fezandie, Clement	Through the Earth (1st, 8vo, tan cl, 238p, 15pl by...)	Century	1898	MacKay, W.A.	60-85	
Fezandie, Clement	Through the Earth (1st, 8vo, tan cl, 238p, cvr by...)	Century	1898	McManus, B.	60-85	
Fiedler, Jean	Big Brother Danny (1st, sm8vo, unpag, blue cl, fp b/w)	Holiday House	1953	Fiedler, H.	20-25	*
Fiedler, Jean	Green Thumb Story (1st, sm8vo, 38p, red cl, 2-color, pep)	Holiday House	1952	Latham, B.	20-25	*
Field, E.	Christmas Tales/Christmas Verse (1st, 4to, 119p, gilt, 8cp, SC)	Scribner	1912	Storer, F.	70-100	
Field, E.	Lullaby Land (1st, 8vo, teg, 229p, gilt)	Scribner	1897	Robinson, C.	120-180	
Field, E.	Lullaby Land (1st UK, sm8vo, 229p, gilt, AEG)	L: J. Lane	1898	Robinson, C.	120-160	
Field, E.	Poems of Childhood (1st UK, 8vo, 199p, red/gilt, teg, pep, 8cp)	L: J. Lane	1904	Parrish, M.	140-185	
Field, E.	Poems of Childhood (1st, 4to, p-o, teg, 199p, 8cp, pep, SC)	Scribner	1904	Parrish, M.	140-200	
Field, E.	Songs by Eugene Field (1st, 4to, 112p)	Scribner	1914	Armstrong, M.	80-100	
Field, E.	Sugar-Plum Tree (1st, 4to, ipcb, 34p, 12cp)	Saalfield	1930	Peat, F.B.	50-65	
Field, E.	With Trumpet & Drum (1st, 8vo, 126p, blue/white, cvr by...)	Scribner	1892	Armstrong, M.	35-50	
Field, E.	Wynken, Blynken & Nod (1st, folio, wraps, 12p, color)	Saalfield	1930	Peat, F.B.	40-60	
Field, H.	Our Western Archipelago (1st, 8vo, beige cl, cvr by...)	Scribner	1895	Armstrong, M.	100-135	
Field, L.A.	Peter Rabbit & his Pa (8vo, 56p, color)	Saalfield	(1916)	Albert, V.	45-65	*
Field, M.	Tragic Mary (1st, 8vo, 261p, ipcb, cvr by...)	L: G. Bell	1890	Image, S.	180-250	
Field, R.	All Through the Night (1st, 24mo, ibds, [40]p, 1-color)	MacMillan	1940	Field, R.	30-50	
Field, R.	Alphabet for Boys & Girls (1st, 16mo, red cl, [59]p, color)	Doubleday/Page	1926	Field, R.	25-45	*
Field, R.	American Folk & Fairy Tales (1st, 8vo, 302p, green cl, 8cp)	Scribner	1929	Freeman, M.	50-65	
Field, R.	Bird Began to Sing (1st, 8vo, 64p, p-o, 4cp, pep)	Wm. Morrow	(1932)	Bischoff, I.	25-45	*
Field, R.	Branches Green (1st, 8vo, green cl, 66p, 12 b/w, DJ)	MacMillan	1934	Lathrop, D.	70-90	
Field, R.	Calico Bush (1st, lg8vo, 213p, p-o, color, DJ, NH)	MacMillan	1931	Lewis, A.	45-70	
Field, R.	Christmas Time (1st, 24mo, [32]p, white pcb, col frn, pep)	MacMillan	1941	Field, R.	20-35	*
Field, R.	Eliza & the Elves (1st, 8vo, green/gilt, 96p, 2cp, pep)	MacMillan	1926	MacKinstry, E.	65-85	
Field, R.	Hepatica Hawks (1st, 8vo, 239p, blue cl, 6pl, NH)	MacMillan	1932	Lewis, A.	40-65	
Field, R.	Hitty... (1st, sq8vo, 207p, p-o, 3cp, NM, PPPa)	MacMillan	1929	Lathrop, D.	100-135	
Field, R.	Little Book of Days (1st {std}, 16mo, green cl, [59]p, col, cep)	Garden City	1927	Field, R.	30-45	
Field, R.	Little Dog Toby (1st, 12mo, blue cl, 118p, 4cp, pep)	MacMillan	1928	Field, R.	25-40	
Field, R.	Magic Pawnshop (1st, 8vo, ibds, 125p, color, DJ)	Dutton	(1927)	MacKinstry, E.	50-80	
Field, R.	Patchwork Plays (1st {std}, 8vo, 139p, blue cl, b/w, DJ)	Doubleday/Dor.	1930	Field, R.	35-50	
Field, R.	People from Dickens (1st, sm4to, p-o, 208p, 8cp, pep, SC)	Scribner	1935	Fogarty, T.	65-100	
Field, R.	Pocket-Handerchief Park (1st {std}, 16mo, 61p, color, cep)	Doubleday/Dor.	1929	Field, R.	30-45	
Field, R.	Pointed People (1st, sm8vo, 98p, orange cl, b/w, DJ)	Yale U. Press	1924	Field, R.	35-50	
Field, R.	Polly Patchwork (1st {std}, 16mo, 56p, color)	Doubleday/Dor.	1928	Field, R.	30-45	
Field, R.	Prayer for a Child (1st, sq8vo, [31]p, color, cep, DJ, CM)	MacMillan	1944	Jones, E.O.	65-100	R
Field, R.	Susanna B. & William C. (1st, 24mo, 62p, yellow cl, cep, color)	Wm. Morrow	1934	Field, R.	35-50	*
Field, R.	Taxis & Toadstools (1st {std}, 8vo, 129p, green cl, color, cep)	Doubleday/Page	1926	Field, R.	50-75	R
Field, R.	Yellow Ship (1st {std}, 16mo, 62p, tan cl, color, dep, DJ)	Doubleday/Dor.	1931	Field, R.	30-50	
Fielding-Hall, H.	Margaret's Book (1st, 4to, AEG, red/gilt, 283p, 12 ticp)	L: Hutchinson	(1913)	Robinson, C.	240-350	
Fielding-Hall, H.	Margaret's Book (1st AM, 4to, 283p, teg, gilt, 12 ticp)	Stokes	(1913)	Robinson, C.	180-260	
Fillebrown, R.H.	Rhymes/Happy Childhood (1st, lg8vo, 119p, p-o, 3cp, pep)	Winston	(1908)	Prittie, E.J.	40-65	
Fillmore, P.H.	Hickory Limb (1st, 8vo, green cl, 70p, p-o, 4pl)	J. Lane	1910	O'Neill, R.	45-60	
Fillmore, P.H.	Little Question of Ladies' Rights (1st, 12mo, 79p, p-o, b/w)	J. Lane	1916	O'Neill, R.	35-50	
Finger, C.J.	Adventure Under Sapphire Skies (1st, 12mo, 293p, uncut, b/w)	Wm. Morrow	1931	Finger, H.	20-30	*
Finger, C.J.	Bushrangers (1st, 8vo, 216p, color, pep)	McBride	1924	Honore, P.	40-65	*
Finger, C.J.	Courageous Companions (1st {std}, lg8vo, 304p, gilt, pep, 10pl)	Longmans	(1929)	Daugherty, J.	30-50	
Finger, C.J.	Dog at His Heel (1st, 8vo, 304p, orange cl, dp color, pep)	Winston	(1936)	Pitz, H.C.	30-45	*
Finger, C.J.	Frontier Ballads (1st {std}, lg8vo, 181p, 3cp, b/w)	Doubleday/Dor.	1927	Honore, P.	45-70	*
Finger, C.J.	Golden Tales from Far Away (1st, 8vo, 233p, col frn, pep)	Winston	(1940)	Finger, H.	30-45	*
Finger, C.J.	Highwaymen... (1st, 8vo, 258p, tan cl, uncut, 8cp, pep)	McBride	1923	Honore, P.	40-70	*
Finger, C.J.	Romantic Rascals (1st, lg8vo, 251p, uncut, 8cp, pep)	McBride	1927	Honore, P.	40-65	*
Finger, C.J.	Spreading Stain (1st {std}, sm8vo, 245p, col frn by...)	Doubleday/Page	1927	Honore, P.	30-45	*
Finger, C.J.	Tales Worth Telling (1st, lg8vo, 250p, orang cl, pep, 10cp)	Century	1927	Honore, P.	40-70	*

AUTHOR	TITLE	PUBLISHER	DATE	ARTIST	PRICE	LC
Finger, C.J.	Tales from Silver Lands (1st {std}, sm4to, 225p, 10cp, pep, NM)	Doubleday/Page	1924	Honore, P.	70-100	R*
Finney, C.	Circus of Dr. Lao (1st, 8vo, red cl, 154p, p-o, 8pl)	Viking	1935	Artzybasheff, B.	50-75	
Finta, Alex.	My Brothers & I (1st, 8vo, tan cl, 185p, b/w)	Holiday House	(1940)	Finta, A.	20-35	*
Fischer, Hans	Pitschi (1st, ob folio, ibds, [32]p, color, pep)	Harcourt	1953	Fischer, H.	100-160	R*
Fischer, Marj.	All on a Summer's Day (1st {std}, 8vo, 157p, grn cl, b/w, pep)	Random	(1941)	Eichenberg, F.	30-45	*
Fischer, Marj.	Dog Cantbark (1st {std}, 4to, [32]p, gilt, color, cep, DJ)	Random	(1940)	Duvoisin, R.	45-60	
Fischer, Marj.	Street Fair (1st, 8vo, blue/gilt, 216p, 18cp, pep)	Smith/Haas	(1935)	Floethe, R.	30-50	*
Fish	Noah's Ark Book (4to, ibds, color)	L: Bodley Head	[1915]	Fish, A.H.	100-160	
Fish, H.D.	Animals of the Bible (1st, 4to, [65]p, gilt, CM)	Stokes	1937	Lathrop, D.	120-165	
Fish, H.D.	Animals of the Bible (1st UK, 4to, aqua/gilt, [66]p, pep)	L: OUP	1938	Lathrop, D.	100-135	
Fish, H.D.	Butterfly Land (1st AM, ob4to, [15]p, p-o, 7cp)	Stokes	1931	Olfers, S.	130-180	
Fish, H.D.	Four & Twenty Blackbirds (1st, 4to, 104p, 1-color, pep, CH)	Stokes	1937	Lawson, R.	100-150	
Fish, H.D.	When the Root Children Wake Up (1st AM, 4to, [22]p, 9cp, pep)	Stokes	1930	Olfers, S.	100-150	
Fisher, H.	American Beauties (1st, 4to, 93p, red/gilt, 21cp)	Bobbs-Merrill	(1909)	Fisher, H.	220-300	
Fisher, H.	American Beauties (4to, p-o, 94p, reprint, 21cp)	Grosset/Dunlap	(1909)	Fisher, H.	140-200	
Fisher, H.	American Girl (1st, folio, brown bds, p-o, 12 ticp)	Scribner	1909	Fisher, H.	400-600	
Fisher, H.	American Girls in Miniature (1st, 12mo, ibds, p-o, 32cp)	Scribner	1912	Fisher, H.	150-220	
Fisher, H.	Bachelor Belles (1st, 4to, [134]p, p-o, grey/gilt, 22cp)	Dodd	1908	Fisher, H.	200-300	
Fisher, H.	Fair Americans (1st, 4to, [100]p, p-o, 22cp)	Scribner	1911	Fisher, H.	180-220	
Fisher, H.	Garden of Girls (1st Canadian, lg4to, 16 ticp)	(Toronto)	1910	Fisher, H.	350-500	
Fisher, H.	Garden of Girls (1st, folio, p-o, ibds, 16 ticp)	Dodd	1910	Fisher, H.	350-500	
Fisher, H.	Harrison Fisher Book (1st, 4to, p-o, 9cp)	Scribner	1907	Fisher, H.	170-250	
Fisher, H.	Little Gift Book (1st, lg8vo, ibds, 32cp)	Scribner	1913	Fisher, H.	180-260	
Fisher, H.	Maidens Fair (1st, folio, grey bds, p-o, 16 ticp)	Dodd	1912	Fisher, H.	300-450	
Fisher, H.	Pictures in Color (1st, lg4to, p-o, bds, 16cp)	Scribner	1910	Fisher, H.	350-500	
Fisher, Murray	Golliwogg's Dream... Little Folks (1st, sm4to, unpag, ibds, col)	L: Cassell	[1910]	Hart, Frank	80-130	*
Fiske, J.	Life Everlasting (1st, 12mo, 87p)	Houghton	1901	Rogers, B.	20-30	
Fitch, Wm. C.	Knighting of the Twins (1st {1st bk}, 8vo, tan cl, 275p, b/w)	Bos: Roberts	(1891)	Gerson, V.	80-100	*
Fitzgerald, Hugh	Sam Steele's Advens. in Panama (1st, 8vo, green cl, 5pl)	Reilly/Britton	(1907)	Heath, H.	650-800	*
Fitzgerald, Hugh	Sam Steele's Advens. on Land & Sea (1st, 8vo, gilt, p-o, 5pl)	Reilly/Britton	(1906)	Heath, H.	450-600	*
Fitzgerald, J.	Bixby of Boston (1st, 12mo, uncut, 83p, 20pl)	Broadway	1906	Fitzgerald, J.	20-30	*
Fitzgerald, S.	Zankiwank & Bletherwitch (1st AM, 8vo, 188p, gilt, b/w)	Stokes	(1896)	Rackham, A.	450-600	
Fitzgerald, S.	Zankiwank & Bletherwitch (1st, 8vo, teg, green/gilt, 188p)	L: J.M. Dent	1896	Rackham, A.	600-800	
Fitzhugh, P.K.	Boy's Book of Scouts (1st, 8vo, 317p, 3pl by...)	Crowell	(1917)	Remington, F.	65-90	*
Fitzhugh, P.K.	King Time (1st, 8vo, green/gilt, 233p, 8cp, pep)	Caldwell	(1908)	Bridgman, L.J.	60-85	
Flack, M.	All Around Town (1st {std}, 8vo, bds, 283p, col frn)	Doubleday/Dor.	1929	Flack, M.	30-45	
Flack, M.	Angus & the Cat (1st {std}, lg ob8vo, [32]p, ibds, color)	Doubleday/Dor.	1931	Flack, M.	65-80	
Flack, M.	Angus & the Ducks (1st {std}, lg ob8vo, [32]p, ibds, col, pep)	Doubleday/Dor.	1930	Flack, M.	60-80	
Flack, M.	Angus Lost (1st {std}, ob4to, [32]p, ibds, color, pep)	Doubleday/Dor.	1932	Flack, M.	50-80	*
Flack, M.	Ask Mr. Bear (1st, sq8vo, [32]p, color, pep, DJ)	MacMillan	1932	Flack, M.	65-80	
Flack, M.	Boats on the River (1st, ob4to, 31p, ibds, color, CH)	Viking	1946	Barnum, J.H.	65-110	
Flack, M.	Humphrey (1st {std}, 4to, ibds, [80]p, color, pep)	Doubleday/Dor.	1934	Flack, M.	45-60	*
Flack, M.	I See a Kitty (1st, sq12mo, ibds, [16]p, color)	Garden City	1943	Larsson, K.	25-40	*
Flack, M.	New Pet (1st {std}, 4to, ibds, [32]p, color, DJ)	Doubleday/Dor.	(1943)	Flack, M.	45-60	
Flack, M.	Pedro (1st, 8vo, blue cl, 96p, dp color, pep, DJ)	MacMillan	1940	Larsson, K.	45-60	
Flack, M.	Restless Robin (1st, sm ob4to, [48]p, green cl, color, pep)	Houghton	1937	Flack, M.	45-60	
Flack, M.	Story about Ping (1st, lg8vo, ipcb, [32]p, color)	Viking	1933	Wiese, K.	120-160	R
Flack, M.	Tatuk, Arctic Boy (1st {std}, 8vo, 139p, uncut, col frn, pep)	Doubleday/Dor.	1928	Flack, M.	25-40	*
Flack, M.	Tim Tadpole... (1st {std}, 8vo, [32]p, ibds, p-o, color, pep)	Doubleday/Dor.	1934	Flack, M.	35-50	
Flack, M.	Up in The Air (1st, lg8vo, blue cl, [40]p, color)	MacMillan	1935	Larsson, K.	25-40	
Flack, M.	Walter the Lazy Mouse (1st {std}, 4to, [80]p, color, cep)	Doubleday/Dor.	1937	Flack, M.	35-50	
Flack, M.	William & his Kitten (1st, ob8vo, ibds, [32]p, color, pep)	Houghton	1938	Flack, M.	30-45	
Flack, M.	Willy Nilly (1st, 4to, ibds, [32]p, color, pep)	MacMillan	1936	Flack, M.	30-50	
Flagg, J.M.	Adventures of Kitty Cobb (1st, lg sq4to, ibds, [67]p, b/w, pep)	Doran	(1912)	Flagg, J.M.	90-120	
Flagg, J.M.	All in the Same Boat (1st, 12mo, 105p)	Life Pub. Co.	1908	Flagg, J.M.	25-40	*
Flagg, J.M.	City People (1st, folio, ibds, [84]p, b/w)	Scribner	1909	Flagg, J.M.	75-120	
Flagg, J.M.	I Should Say So (1st, sm8vo, 202p, b/w pl)	Doran	(1914)	Flagg, J.M.	25-40	*
Flagg, J.M.	Why they Married (1st, lg4to, 107p, ibds)	Life Pub. Co.	1906	Flagg, J.M.	85-120	
Flanders, H.H.	Looking Out of Jimmie (1st, 8vo, 94p, gilt, pep, uncut, b/w)	Dutton	(1927)	Pogany, W.	40-60	*
Flaubert, G.	Madame Bovary (lg8vo, 416p, grey cl, 13pl)	L: J. Lane	(1928)	Austen, J.	50-75	
Flaubert, G.	Temptation of St. Anthony (1st, sm8vo, 360p, teg, gilt, 8pl)	L: Nichols	1895	Gorski, S.	45-60	
Fleckenstein, A.	Prince of Gravas... (1st, 8vo, 270p, grey/gilt, 3pl)	Jacobs	1898	Waugh, J.	35-65	
Flecker, J.E.	Hassan (1st, 4to, 155p, teg, red/gilt, 12 ticp, pep)	L: Heinemann	1924	Mackenzie, T.	100-150	
Flemwell, G.	Alpine Flowers & Gardens (1st, 8vo, 167p, gilt, teg, 20cp)	L: A&C Black	1910	Flemwell, G.	70-120	
Fletcher, J.S.	Life in Arcadia (1st, sm8vo, 265p, green/gilt, cvr by...)	L: J. Lane	1896	Wilson, P.	50-70	
Fletcher, J.S.	Making of Matthais (1st, sm8vo, AEG, 141p, blue/gilt, b/w)	L: J. Lane	1898	Kemp-Welch, L.	30-50	
Fleuron, S.	Grim: Story of a Pike (1st, sm8vo, green cl, 186p, 4pl)	Knopf	1921	Lathrop, D.	45-65	
Fleuron, S.	Wild Horses of Iceland (1st, 8vo, 234p, red cl, 15 fp b/w)	L: Eyre/Spotts	[1933]	Aldin, C.	50-70	*
Flint, W.R.	Watercolors of... (1st, ob. folio, 8 ticp)	L: Studio	(1920)	Flint, W.R.	100-130	
Flower, Esther	Nurse Nora... (1st, 12mo, 163p, 9pl)	J. Pott	1903	Cory/Graef	25-40	*
Foley, James W.	Christmas Prayer (1st, 16mo, ibds, [24]p, color)	Volland	(1915)	Foley, J.W.	45-60	LC
Foley, James W.	Some One Like You (1st, 16mo, ibds, color, pep)	Volland	(1916)	Unknown	65-80	*

AUTHOR	TITLE	PUBLISHER	DATE	ARTIST	PRICE	LC
Foley, James W.	Through All the Years (1st, sq16mo, pep, unpag, color)	Volland	(1920)	Unknown	30-45	*
Folkard, C.	Teddy Tail of the Daily Mail (4to, ibds, color)	L: A&C Black	[1915]	Folkard, C.	70-100	
Follett, H.T.	House Afire! (1st, 8vo, 102p, pep)	Scribner	1941	Sperry, A.	30-45	*
Follett, H.T.	Magic Portholes (1st, lg8vo, 321p, orange cl, fp b/w, pep)	MacMillan	1932	Sperry, A.	30-45	*
Follett, H.T.	Ocean Outposts (1st, 4to, 133p, maps by...)	Scribner	1942	Sperry, A.	30-45	*
Follett, H.T.	Stars to Steer By (1st, sm8vo, blue cl, 257p, fp b/w)	MacMillan	1934	Sperry, A.	30-45	*
Forbes, Eliz. S.	King Arthur's Wood (1st, ob folio, 120p, buckram, 14cp)	L: Simpkin	1904	Forbes, E.S.	850-1000	
Forbes, Esther	America's Paul Revere (1st, 4to, 46p, color, red cl, DJ)	Houghton	1946	Ward, L.	45-60	
Forbes, Esther	Johnny Tremain (1st, 8vo, 256p, cloth, col frn, pep, DJ, NM)	Houghton	1943	Ward, L.	70-100	R
Forbes, Helen	Mario's Castle (1st, 12mo, 198p, col frn, pep, 3pl)	MacMillan	1928	DeAngeli, M.	35-50	*
Forbush, Wm. B.	Wonder Book/Myths & Legends (lg8vo, blue cl, p-o, 3cp, 11 b/w)	Winston	(1928)	Richardson, F.	20-30	*
Ford, Julia E.	Imagina (1st, lg8vo, 178p, blue/gilt, 2 fp color)	Duffield	1914	Rackham, A.	150-200	
Ford, Julia E.	Snickerty Nick (1st, lg8vo, 78p, blue cl, 3cp)	Moffat	1919	Rackham, A.	165-250	
Ford, Lauren	Ageless Story (1st, sq4to, blue/gilt, [40]p, color, CH)	Dodd	1939	Suba, S.	65-80	*
Ford, P.L.	Checked Love Affair (1st, 8vo, 112p, teg, gilt, 5pl)	Dodd	1903	Fisher, H.	30-45	
Ford, P.L.	His Version of It (1st, 8vo, teg, 109p)	Dodd	1905	Hutt, H.	25-40	
Ford, P.L.	Love Finds the Way (1st, 8vo, teg, 108p, uncut, cvr by...)	Dodd	1904	Armstrong, M.	30-45	
Ford, P.L.	Wanted a Chaperone (1st, 8vo, 109p, teg, uncut, cvr by...)	Dodd	1902	Armstrong, M.	30-50	*
Ford, P.L.	Wanted a Chaperone (1st, 8vo, 109p, teg, uncut, 6cp)	Dodd	1902	Christy, H.C.	30-50	
Ford, P.L.	Wanted a Matchmaker (1st, 8vo, teg, 112p, cvr by...)	Dodd	1900	Armstrong, M.	30-45	
Ford, P.L.	Wanted a Matchmaker (1st, 8vo, 112p, teg, green/gilt, 5pl by...)	Dodd	1900	Christy, H.C.	35-50	
Forester, C.S.	Poo Poo & the Dragons (1st {std}, 8vo, 142p, green cl, b/w, pep)	Little/Brown	1942	Lawson, R.	165-220	
Forestier, A.	Belgium (1st, sm4to, brown bds, 77cp)	L: A&C Black	1908	Forestier, A.	60-85	
Forman, J.M.	Island of Enchantment (1st, 8vo, blue/gilt, teg, 106p, 4cp, dep)	Harper	1905	Pyle, H.	70-95	
Forrest, A.S.	Morocco (1st, lg8vo, gilt, 231p, teg, 74cp)	L: A&C Black	1904	Forrest, A.S.	70-100	
Forrester, I.L.	Us Fellers (1st, 4to, blue cl, p-o, 150p, 7cp)	Jacobs	(1907)	Kilvert, C.	45-60	*
Forster, F.J.	On the Road to Make-Believe (1st, 4to, 128p, p-o, color)	Rand/McNally	(1924)	Trippe, U.	45-65	*
Forster, F.J.	Tippytoes... (1st, 4to, 96p, color)	Rand/McNally	(1926)	Trippe, U.	35-50	*
Forsyth, G.A.	Thrilling Days/Army Life (1st, sm8vo, 196p, 16pl)	Harper	1900	Zogbaum, R.F.	50-75	*
Forsythe, C.	Old Songs for Young Americans (1st, ob4to, green cl, color)	Doubleday/Page	1901	Ostertag, B.	80-120	
Fort, Chas.	LO! (1st, 8vo, 411p, 12 illus, DJ)	NY: Kendall	(1931)	King, Alex.	100-150	
Fortesque, J.W.	Drummer's Coat (1st, sq8vo, 184p red/gilt, 4pl)	L: MacMillan	1899	Brock, H.M.	70-85	
Foster, Genevieve	Abraham Lincoln's World (1st, sm4to, 347p, b/w, cep, NH)	Scribner	1944	Foster, G.	65-90	R*
Foster, Genevieve	Birthdays of Freedom (1st, 4to, [59]p, color, NH)	Scribner	(1952)	Foster, G.	50-80	*
Foster, Genevieve	George Washington (1st, 8vo, 93p, dp color, NH)	Scribner	(1949)	Foster, G.	50-80	*
Foster, Genevieve	George Washington's World (1st, 4to, 348p, 1-color, cep, NH)	Scribner	1942	Foster, G.	50-85	R*
Foster, M.B.	Day in a Child's Life (1st, 4to, 29p, ibds, color)	L: Routledge	[1881]	Greenaway, K.	180-250	
Fouque, La Motte	Sintram and his Companions (1st, 12mo, 12pl)	L: Dent	1900	Robinson, C.	140-200	
Fouque, La Motte	Sintram and his Companions (1st, 8vo, 193p, olive cl, teg, 20pl)	L: Methuen	(1908)	Sullivan, E.J.	70-90	
Fouque, La Motte	Undine (1st, 8vo, blue/gilt, 204p, teg, 19pl)	L: MacMillan	1897	Pitman, R.M.M.	70-100	
Fouque, La Motte	Undine (1st AM, 4to, 136p, grey/gilt, 15 ticp, pep)	Doubleday/Page	1909	Rackham, A.	185-225	
Fouque, La Motte	Undine (1st, sm4to, 136p, blue/gilt, 15 ticp, pep)	L: Heinemann	1909	Rackham, A.	265-320	
Fox, F.M.	Adventures of Sonny Bear (1st, sm8vo, 80p, 15cp)	Rand/McNally	(1916)	Carr, W.	45-60	*
Fox, F.M.	Angeline Goes Traveling (1st, 12mo, p-o, 256p, 5cp)	Rand/McNally	(1927)	Gregory, D.L.	25-40	*
Fox, F.M.	Betty of Mackinaw (1st, 12mo, 109p, b/w)	Page	1901	Barry, E.B.	20-25	*
Fox, F.M.	County Christmas (1st, 12mo, 111p, 10pl)	Page	1907	Barry, E.B.	20-35	*
Fox, F.M.	Janey (1st, 8vo, 121p, blue cl, p-o, 4cp)	Rand/McNally	(1925)	Gregory, D.L.	20-25	
Fox, F.M.	Little Cat/Could Not Sleep (1st {std}, ob4to, [31]p, pep, color)	Dutton	1941	Suba, S.	65-80	*
Fox, F.M.	Little Giant's Neighbours (1st, 12mo, 132p, b/w)	L.C. Page	1903	Dodge, F.E.	20-30	*
Fox, F.M.	Mother Nature's Little Ones (1st, 12mo, 92p, fp b/w)	L.C. Page	1904	Barry, E.B.	20-30	*
Fox, F.M.	Nancy Davenport (1st, 12mo, 261p, p-o, 5cp)	Rand/McNally	(1928)	Eger, R.C.	20-30	*
Fox, F.M.	Nannette (1st, 8vo, 80p, red/gilt, color, pep)	Volland	(1929)	Gruelle, Justin	40-60	
Fox, F.M.	Seven Christmas Candles (1st, 8vo, 192p, 6cp)	Page	1909	Barry, E.B.	30-45	*
Fox, F.M.	Sister Sally (1st, 8vo, 105p, gilt, p-o, 4cp)	Rand/McNally	(1925)	Gregory, D.L.	20-30	
Fox, F.M.	True Monkey Stories (1st, lg8vo, 55p, green cl, fp color, pep)	Lothrop/Lee	(1941)	Gergely, T.	35-50	*
Fox, F.M.	What Gladys Saw (1st, 12mo, green cl, 318p, 5pl)	W.A. Wilde	(1902)	Copeland, C.	25-40	
Fox, F.M.	Wildling Princess (1st, 8vo, 79p, gilt, pep, 10cp)	Volland	(1929)	Perkins, J.E.	70-100	
Fox, John Jr.	Blue Grass & Rhododendron (1st, 8vo, teg, 294p, uncut)	Scribner	1901	Armstrong, M.	65-90	
Fox, John Jr.	Christmas Eve on Lonesome (1st, sm8vo, 234p, teg, 8cp)	Scribner	1904	Various	20-30	
Fox, John Jr.	Heart of the Hills (1st, 8vo, red/gilt, 396p, 7pl)	Scribner	1913	Yohn, F.C.	20-30	
Fox, John Jr.	In Happy Valley (1st, 8vo, 229p, red/gilt, 8pl)	Scribner	1917	Yohn, F.C.	25-40	
Fox, John Jr.	Little Shepherd of Kingdom Come (1st, 4to, 322p, p-o, 14cp, SC)	Scribner	1931	Wyeth, N.C.	180-225	
Fox, John Jr.	Trail of the Lonesome Pine (1st, 12mo, teg, uncut, 422p)	Scribner	1908	Yohn, F.C.	25-40	
France, A.	At the Sign o/t Reine Padauque (1st, 4to, 275p, gilt, 12pl, pep)	L: J. Lane	1922	Pape, F.	35-50	
France, A.	Bee... (1st, 8vo, grey bds, [128]p, teg, 17 ticp)	L: Dent	1912	Robinson, C.	200-300	
France, A.	CLIO (1st sm8vo, teg, 7 color illus.)	Paris: Calmann	1900	Mucha, A.	450-600	
France, A.	Girls & Boys (1st AM, 4to, 25p, ipcb, 12cp)	Duffield	1913	DeMonvel, M.B.	100-135	
France, A.	Gods are Athirst (1st, lg8vo, 285p, black/gilt, 12cp)	L: J. Lane	(1927)	Austen, J.	45-65	
France, A.	Golden Tales of Anatole France (1st {this fmt}, 4to, 352p)	Dodd	1927	Patterson, M.	40-65	
France, A.	Honey-Bee (1st, lg8vo, red cl, 172p, uncut, teg, 12cp, pep)	L: J. Lane	1911	Lundborg, F.	45-60	
France, A.	In ALL France (1st, 8vo, p-o, 110p, color)	Whitman	(1930)	Enders, L.	25-40	*
France, A.	Little Sea-Dogs (1st, 8vo, 149p, 8cp)	L: Bodley Head	1925	Foster, M.L.	35-50	*

AUTHOR	TITLE	PUBLISHER	DATE	ARTIST	PRICE	LC
France, A.	Our Children (1st AM, lg4to, ibds, 25p, 12cp)	Duffield	1917	DeMonvel, M.B.	80-120	
France, A.	Revolt of the Angels (1st, 8vo, 357p, 12 tipl)	L: J. Lane	1924	Pape, F.	80-100	
France, A.	Revolt of the Angels (1st AM, 8vo, 357p, black/gilt, 12 tipl)	Dodd/Lane	1924	Pape, F.	50-65	
France, A.	Thais (1st, 4to, black/gilt, 247p, 12pl, pep)	L: Bodley Head	1926	Pape, F.	50-70	
France, A.	Well of St. Clare (1st, 8vo, black bds, 302p, gilt, 12pl)	L: J. Lane	(1928)	Pape, F.	45-65	
Franchi, A.	Little Lead Soldier (1st, lg8vo, p-o, 186p, 5cp)	Penn	1919	Price, H.L.	35-50	
Franchot, A.W.	Bobs, King of Fortunate Isle (1st, 8vo, 210p, blue cl, col frn)	Dutton	(1928)	Smith, J.W.	35-50	*
Franchot, A.W.	Bugs, Wings & other Things (1st, 8vo, 99p, green/gilt, pep, 7cp)	Dutton	(1918)	Cady/Smith	150-180	
Franchot, A.W.	Bugs, Wings & other Things (1st, 8vo, 99p, green/gilt, 7cp, pep)	Dutton	(1918)	Smith/Cady	150-180	
Franchot, A.W.	White Giant & Black Giant (1st, lg8vo, ipcb, 72p, fp b/w)	Dutton	(1924)	Gamble, J.	35-50	*
Francis, J.G.	Book of Cheerful Cats (1st, ob8vo, 37p, b/w, PPPa)	Century	1892	Francis, J.G.	80-135	*
Francis, J.G.	Joyous Aztecs (1st {std}, ob8vo, 42p, b/w)	Century	(1929)	Francis, J.G.	50-80	*
Francis, P.W.	Remarkable Advens/Little Boy Pip (1st, 8vo, ibds, 60p, col, pep)	Paul Elder	(1907)	Johnson, M.	65-80	*
Francoise	Fanchette & Jeannot (1st AM, sm4to, ibds, [24]p, color)	Grosset/Dunlap	1937	Francoise	45-60	*
Francoise	Gay ABC (1st, lg8vo, grey cl, [55]p, fp color)	Scribner	(1939)	Francoise	120-165	*
Francoise	Jeanne-Marie Counts her Sheep (1st, sm4to, [32]p, color)	Scribner	1951	Francoise	50-85	R*
Francoise	Mr. & Mrs. So and So (1st, 4to, [36]p, color, pep)	OUP	(1939)	Francoise	35-50	*
Francoise	Story of Colette (1st, lg8vo, ibds, fp color)	Scribner	(1940)	Francoise	50-85	*
Frank, Mabel L.	Child's Day in Song (1st, lg4to, ibds, 31p, 12cp)	Schirmer	(1916)	Whitelaw, N.	65-80	*
Franklin, B.	Bird in the Hand (1st {std}, 4to, blue cl, [36]p, color, cep)	MacMillan	(1951)	Petershams	35-50	*
Frasconi, Antonio	See & Say (1st {std}, 4to, yellow cl, [32]p, color, pep)	Harcourt	(1955)	Frasconi, A.	65-90	R*
Fraser, C.L.	Lute of Love (1st, 16mo, wraps, 66p)	L: Selwyn	(1920)	Fraser, C.L.	50-65	
Fraser, C.L.	Nursery Rhymes (1st AM, 8vo, 46p, cp)	Knopf	1920	Fraser, C.L.	70-100	
Fraser, C.L.	Pirates (1st AM {std}, 4to, ibds, 159p, 8pl)	McBride	1922	Fraser, C.L.	85-120	
Fraser, W.A.	Blood Lilies (1st, 8vo, 262p, 6pl)	Scribner	1903	Schoonover, F.	25-40	
Fraser, W.A.	Sazada Tales (1st, 8vo, 231p, green/gilt, 24 b/w illus)	Scribner	1905	Heming, A.	25-40	*
Fraser, W.A.	The Outcasts (1st, 8vo, green/gilt, 138p, teg, 8pl, pep)	Scribner	1901	Heming, A.	40-60	
Fraser-Simson, H.	Hums of Pooh (1st AM, lg4to, 67p)	Dutton	(1930)	Shepard, E.H.	65-80	*
Frazer, Lilly	Leaves from The Golden Bough (1st, 8vo, 248p, gilt, teg, b/w)	L: MacMillan	1924	Brock, H.M.	35-50	
Frederic, H.	Market Place (1st, 12mo, 401p, 8pl)	Stokes	1899	Fisher, H.	25-40	
Freeman, Don	Beady Bear (1st, lg ob8vo, red cl, 48p, fp b/w)	Viking	1954	Freeman, D.	30-45	*
Freeman, Don	Chuggy & Blue Caboose (1st, ob4to, 48p, red cl, color)	Viking	1951	Freeman, D.	35-50	*
Freeman, Don	Cyrano the Crow (1st, 4to, [47]p, ibds, color)	Viking	(1960)	Freeman, D.	40-65	*
Freeman, Don	Fly High, Fly Low (1st, 4to, blue cl, 56p, pep, CH)	Viking	(1957)	Freeman, D.	50-80	*
Freeman, Don	It Shouldn't Happen (1st {std}, sm8vo, [212]p, b/w)	Harcourt	(1945)	Freeman, D.	25-40	*
Freeman, Don	Mop Top (1st, sm4to, beige cl, 48p, 1-color, pep)	Viking	1955	Freeman, D.	30-45	*
Freeman, Don	Night the Lights Went Out (1st, lg8vo, 48p, blue cl, 1-color)	Viking	1958	Freeman, D.	25-45	*
Freeman, Don	Norman the Doorman (1st, sm ob4to, yellow cl, 64p, color, pep)	Viking	(1959)	Freeman, D.	35-60	*
Freeman, Don	Space Witch (1st, sm4to, blue cl, 47p, 1-color)	Viking	(1959)	Freeman, D.	35-50	*
Freeman, H.C.	Brief History of Butte Montana (1st, 123p, 4 illus by..)	(Chicago)	1900	Russell, C.M.	100-120	*
Freeman, L.C.	Nip & Tuck (1st, 4to, orange cl, p-o, 156p, 8cp, pep)	Sears	(1926)	Freeman, L.C.	70-100	
Freeman, L.C.	Nip & Tuck in Toyland (1st, 4to, p-o, 8cp, pep)	Sears	(1927)	Freeman, L.C.	70-100	
Freeman, Lydia	Pet of the Met (1st, sm ob4to, 63p, pep, color)	Viking	1953	Freeman, D.	65-110	R
Freeman, M.E.	Fair Lavina... (1st, 12mo, 308p, lavender/gilt, 8pl)	Harper	1907	Various	20-35	
Frees, Harry W.	Little Folks of Animal Land (1st, 8vo, 252p, blue/gilt, p-o)	Lothrop/Lee	(1915)	(Photos)	90-130	*
Frees, Harry W.	Sandman: His Animal Stories (1st, 8vo, 273p, b/w)	Page	1916	(Photos)	70-100	
Frey, N.A.	River Horse (1st, 8vo, 150p, green cl, b/w)	W.R. Scott	(1953)	George, R.	25-40	*
Friedlander, G.	Jewish Fairy Book (1st, 8vo, 188p, gilt, 8cp, pep)	Stokes	(1920)	Hood, G.	45-70	
Friedrich, Priscilla	Easter Bunny that Overslept (1st, 4to, yellow cl, [33]p, color)	Lothrop	1957	Adams, A.	45-65	*
Frisbie, W.A.	ABC Mother Goose (1st, 4to, [52]p, beige cl, color)	Rand/McNally	(1905)	Bartholomew, F.	165-200	
Frisbie, W.A.	Pirate Frog... (1st, 4to, [94]p, ibds, color)	Rand/McNally	(1901)	Bartholomew, F.	130-180	
Frith, Henry	King Arthur & his Knights (1st, 8vo, black cl, p-o, 406p, 4cp)	Garden City	1932	Schoonover, F.	40-65	
Fritz, Jean	Cabin Faced West (1st, 8vo, blue cl, 124p, b/w)	Coward	(1958)	Rojankovsky, F.	25-40	*
Fritz, Jean	Fish Head (1st, sm4to, tan cl, [38]p, fp 3-color, pep)	Coward	(1954)	Simont, M.	45-70	*
Frost, A.B.	Book of Drawings (1st, folio, p-o, ibds, 39pl)	Collier	(1904)	Frost, A.B.	100-150	
Frost, A.B.	Bull Calf (1st, ob4to, 112p, 105pl)	Scribner	1892	Frost, A.B.	120-185	
Frost, A.B.	Carlo (1st, ob8vo, 109p, b/w)	Doubleday/Page	1913	Frost, A.B.	60-80	
Frost, A.B.	Stuff & Nonsense (1st, 4to, ipcb, 92p, b/w)	Scribner	(1884)	Frost, A.B.	100-130	*
Frost, F.	Little Whistler (1st, 8vo, green cl, 48p, fp color, DJ)	Whittlesey	(1949)	Duvoisin, R.	35-50	
Frost, W.H.	Court of King Arthur (1st, 8vo, red/gilt, 320p, 6pl)	Scribner	1896	Burleigh, S.R.	65-80	
Fry, J.H.	Revolt Against Beauty (1st, 8vo, 212p, designs by...)	Putnam	1934	Richardson, F.	25-40	*
Fryer, Alfred C.	Fairy Tales/Harz Mountains (1st, lg8vo, 206p, gilt, b/w)	L: D. Nutt	1908	Ogders, A.M.	65-80	*
Fryer, J.E.	Bible Story Book (1st, lg8vo, blue cl, p-o, 352p, 4cp)	Winston	(1924)	Prittie, E.J.	50-70	
Fryer, J.E.	Mary Frances Cook Book (1st, lg8vo, blue cl, 175p)	Winston	(1912)	Hayes, M.H.	120-185	
Fryer, J.E.	Mary Frances First Aid Book (1st, lg8vo, p-o, 144p, gilt)	Winston	(1916)	Boyer, J.A.	120-185	
Fryer, J.E.	Mary Frances Garden Book (1st, lg8vo, p-o, gilt, 378p, col, pep)	Winston	(1916)	Zwirner, W.	120-185	
Fryer, J.E.	Mary Frances Housekeeper (1st, sm4to, p-o, 253p)	Winston	(1914)	Greene, J.	120-185	*
Fryer, J.E.	Mary Frances Knitting & Crocheting Bk. (1st, 4to, 270p, p-o)	Winston	(1918)	Boyer, J.A.	130-185	
Fryer, J.E.	Mary Frances Sewing Book (1st, 8vo, p-o, 280p, blue cl, pep)	Winston	(1913)	Boyer, J.A.	130-185	
Fryer, J.E.	Mary Frances Story Book (1st, lg8vo, p-o, 328p, pep)	Winston	(1921)	Prittie, E.J.	120-185	
Fuller, O.M.	Book of Dragons (1st, 4to, green cl, 181p, 4cp, DJ)	McBride	1931	Key, A.	65-80	
Fullylove, J.	Edinburgh (1st, 8vo, 176p, teg, blue/gilt, 21cp)	L: A&C Black	1904	Fullylove, J.	65-90	

AUTHOR	TITLE	PUBLISHER	DATE	ARTIST	PRICE	LC
Futrelle, J.	Chase o/t Golden Plate (1st, sm8vo, 220p, green cl, p-o)	Dodd	1906	Grefe, W.	40-60	
Fyleman, R.	40 Good-Night Tales (1st AM, 8vo, 131p, p-o, 4cp)	Doran	(1924)	Grosvenor, T.	30-45	*
Fyleman, R.	Adventure Club (1st, 8vo, 80p, blue/gilt, 10 b/w)	L: Methuen	1925	Watson, A.H.	35-50	*
Fyleman, R.	Adventure Club (1st AM, 8vo, p-o, 138p, col frn, b/w)	Doran	(1926)	Watson, A.H.	25-40	*
Fyleman, R.	Fairies & Chimneys (1st, 8vo, 62p, col frn, silhouettes)	Doran	(1920)	Grosvenor, T.	30-50	
Fyleman, R.	Fairy Queen (1st, 8vo, 64p, cloth, col frn, pep)	Doran	(1923)	Fyleman, R.	65-80	*
Fyleman, R.	Garland of Roses (1st, 8vo, blue/gilt, 129p, 17pl)	L: Methuen	1928	Bull, Rene	100-145	
Fyleman, R.	Katy Kruse Dolly Book (1st AM, ob4to, ibds, 32p, 12cp)	Doran	(1927)	(Photos)	120-150	
Fyleman, R.	Katy Kruse Play Book (1st AM, 4to, p-o, 32p, 12cp)	McKay	(1930)	Kruse, K.	120-165	*
Fyleman, R.	Katy Kruse Play Book (1st, 4to, ibds, p-o, 32p, 12cp)	L: Harrap	(1930)	Kruse, K.	120-165	*
Fyleman, R.	Little Christmas Book (1st, 8vo, orang ibds, pep, 41p, 2-color)	Doran	(1927)	Hummel, L.	20-35	
Fyleman, R.	Old Fashioned Girls (1st, 8vo, 33p, 12pl)	L: Methuen	1928	Everett, E.	30-50	*
Fyleman, R.	Princess Comes to Our Town (1st {std}, sm8vo, 158p col frn, pep)	Doubleday/Dor.	1928	Berry, E.	30-45	*
Fyleman, R.	Rainbow Cat (1st, 8vo, 117p, p-o, col frn)	Doran	(1923)	Grosvenor, T.	25-40	*
Fyleman, R.	Rose Fyleman Fairy Book (1st, 4to, 102p, blue/gilt, 12 ticp)	L: Methuen	1923	Miller, H.T.	120-160	
Fyleman, R.	Round the Mulberry Bush (1st, 4to, 192p, red cl, 6cp)	Dodd	(1928)	Various	40-65	
Fyleman, R.	Widdy-Widdy-Wurkey (1st, 8vo, 70p, beige cl, b/w)	L: Blackwell	1934	Carrick, V.	35-50	*
Gaboriau, Emile	Within an Inch of His Life (1st AM, 8vo, teg, 608p, gilt, 4pl)	Scribner	1913	Sloan, J.	70-100	*
Gag, Asta	Sue & Sew-and-Sew (1st, 8vo, 63p, ibds, b/w, pep)	Coward	(1931)	Gag, Flavia	35-50	*
Gag, Flavia	Sing a Song of Seasons (1st, 4to, ibds, 29p)	Coward	(1936)	Gag, Flavia	45-65	*
Gag, W.	ABC Bunny (1st {std}, lg4to, ibds, [32]p, pep, NH)	Coward	1933	Gag, W.	170-220	R
Gag, W.	Funny Thing (1st, ob8vo, yellow ipcb, unpag, b/w, pep)	Coward	1929	Gag, W.	160-220	
Gag, W.	Gone is Gone (1st, 12mo, yellow cl, unpag, col frn)	Coward	(1935)	Gag, W.	130-170	
Gag, W.	Growing Pains (1st, lg8vo, 479p, blue ibds, b/w)	Coward	1940	Gag, W.	130-165	
Gag, W.	Millions of Cats (1st, ob8vo, ipcb, [32]p, b/w, pep, NH)	Coward	1928	Gag, W.	200-300	R
Gag, W.	Nothing at All (1st, lg ob8vo, ibds, [32]p, color, pep, CH)	Coward	(1941)	Gag, W.	180-240	
Gag, W.	Snippy & Snappy (1st, ob8vo, yellow ibds, [48]p, b/w, pep)	Coward	1931	Gag, W.	140-200	
Gag, W.	Three Gay Tales from Grimm (1st, ipcb, 63p, b/w)	Coward	(1943)	Gag, W.	100-165	
Gag, W.	Wanda Gag's Story Book (1st, ob16mo, [112]p, yel bds, pep, p-o)	Coward	(1932)	Gag, W.	150-200	
Gaggin, E.R.	Down Ryton Water (1st, 8vo, green/silver, 369p, b/w, pep, NH)	Viking	1941	Hader, E.	35-50	*
Gaggin, E.R.	Ear for Uncle Emil (1st, 8vo, 238p, 83 b/w, pep)	Viking	1939	Seredy, K.	25-40	*
Gaggin, E.R.	Jolly Animals (1st, sq4to, p-o, 110p, 7 fp color, pep)	Rand/McNally	(1930)	Ward, Keith	80-120	*
Gail, Otto W.	By Rocket to the Moon (1st AM, 8vo, black cl, 303p, te red, 8pl)	Sears	(1931)	Von Grunberg, R.	60-85	
Gaines, M.L.	I Heah de Voices Callin' (1st, 12mo, 91p, 11pl)	(Atlanta)	1916	(Photos)	65-80	
Gale, Eliz.	Katrina Van Ost & Silver Rose (1st, sm8vo, 294p, fp b/w)	Putnam	(1934)	DeAngeli, M.	20-30	*
Gale, Eliz.	Seven Beads of Wampum (1st, 8vo, 298p, pep)	Putnam	(1936)	Lawson, R.	50-85	*
Gale, N.	June Romance (1st, 12mo, teg, blue cl, 193p, b/w)	Stone/Kimball	1899	Oakley, V.	75-90	
Gale, N.	Songs for Little People (1st, 8vo, teg, 110p, uncut, gilt, 8pl)	L: Constable	1896	Stratton, H.	100-165	
Gall, Alice	Each in his Way (1st {std}, 8vo, 180p, brown bds, p-o, b/w, pep)	OUP	(1937)	Wiese, K.	25-40	
Gall, Alice	Little Black Ant (1st, 8vo, 128p, pep)	OUP	(1936)	Torrey, H.	25-40	*
Galsworthy, J.	Memories (1st, 4to, green/gilt, 69p, teg, 4 ticp, 24pl)	Scribner	(1914)	Earl, M.	70-110	
Galt, J.	Annals of the Parish (1st, 12mo, gilt, 334p, AEG, 40pl, pep)	L: MacMillan	1896	Brock, C.E.	50-65	
Galt, Tom	Seven Days from Sunday (1st {std}, 8vo, rust cl, 215p, b/w)	Crowell	(1956)	Freeman, D.	30-50	*
Gannett, R.S.	Dragons of Blueland (1st, sm8vo, 87p, blue/gilt, pep, b/w)	Random	(1951)	Gannett, R.C.	35-50	*
Gannett, R.S.	Elmer & the Dragon (1st, sm8vo, 86p, red/gilt, pep, b/w)	Random	(1950)	Gannett, R.C.	35-50	*
Gannett, R.S.	My Father's Dragon (1st, 8vo, 86p, pep, NH)	Random	(1948)	Gannett, R.C.	50-80	R*
Gannett, R.S.	Wonderful House-Boat-Train (1st {std}, 8vo, 63p, pep, b/w)	Random	(1949)	Eichenberg, F.	45-65	*
Gardiner, A.	Father's Gone A-Whaling (1st {std}, 8vo, 198p, col frn, DJ)	Doubleday/Page	1926	Berry, E.	30-50	
Gardiner, Linda	Sylvia in Flowerland (8vo, grey bds, gilt, 16 b/w)	L: Seeley	1899	Butler, H.E.	65-80	*
Garelick, M.	What's Inside? (1st, ob8vo, unpag, beige cl, b/w)	W.R. Scott	(1955)	(Photos)	30-50	*
Garis, H.	Rick & Ruddy (1st, sm8vo, p-o, 282p, 6pl)	M. Bradley	1920	Goss, J.	25-45	
Garis, H.	Rick & Ruddy in Camp (1st, sm8vo, 254p, tan cl, 4pl)	M. Bradley	1921	Winter, M.	25-40	*
Garis, H.	Tuftoo the Clown (1st, sm8vo, 283p, 10 b/w, pep)	Appleton	1928	Daugherty, J.	30-45	*
Garis, H.	Uncle Wiggily & Alice/Wonderland (4to, gilt, 361p, 8cp, pep, p-o)	Fenno	(1918)	Bloomfield, E.	40-65	*
Garis, H.	Uncle Wiggily & Mother Goose (1st, lg8vo, 175p, p-o, 6cp)	Fenno	(1916)	Bloomfield, E.	45-65	*
Garis, H.	Uncle Wiggily & his Flying Rug (1st {this pub}, 12mo, 33p, bds)	Whitman	(1940)	Campbell, L.	30-45	*
Garis, H.	Uncle Wiggily & the Pirates (sq12mo, 33p, ibds, color)	Whitman	(1940)	Campbell, L.	30-45	*
Garis, H.	Uncle Wiggily Goes Camping (sq12mo, ibds, 33p, color)	Whitman	(1940)	Campbell, L.	30-45	
Garis, H.	Uncle Wiggily Plays Indian Hunter (1st, 12mo, bds, 33p, color)	Whitman	(1940)	Campbell, L.	30-45	*
Garis, H.	Uncle Wiggily on Roller Skates (1st {this pub}, 12mo, 33p, col)	Whitman	(1940)	Campbell, L.	30-45	*
Garis, H.	Uncle Wiggily's Apple Roast (1st, 8vo, red cloth, p-o, color)	Graham	(1924)	Campbell, L.	30-45	
Garis, H.	Uncle Wiggily's Arabian Nights (1st, 4to, 8cp)	Fenno	(1917)	Bloomfield, E.	35-50	
Garis, H.	Uncle Wiggily's Automobile (8vo, 184p, color)	Platt/Munk	(1939)	Rache, A.	20-30	*
Garis, H.	Uncle Wiggily's Happy Days (1st, sm4to, 211p, col frn)	Platt/Munk	(1947)	Rache, A.	30-45	
Garis, H.	Uncle Wiggily's Visit to the Farm (1st, sq12mo, 33p, p-o, col)	Graham	(1927)	Campbell, L.	30-45	
Garis, H.	Uncle Wiggily's Woodland Games (1st, sq12mo, [32]p, p-o, color)	Graham	(1922)	Campbell, L.	30-45	
Garis, H.	White Crystals (1st, 8vo, tan cl, 243p, 6pl)	Little/Brown	1904	Day, B.C.	35-50	
Garland, H.	Book of American Indian (1st {std}, 4to, bds, 274p, p-o, 4cp)	Harper	1923	Remington, F.	160-200	
Garland, H.	Boy Life on the Prairie (1st, 12mo, brown/gilt, 423p, teg, 8pl)	MacMillan	1899	Deming, E.W.	45-60	
Garland, H.	Money Magic (1st, 8vo, pcb, 354p, 8pl)	Harper	1907	Marchand, J.	30-45	
Garland, H.	Prairie Songs... (1st, sm8vo, green/gilt, 164p, teg, uncut)	Stone/Kimball	1893	Carpenter, H.T.	50-80	R
Garland, H.	Tyranny of the Dark (1st, 8vo, blue/gilt, 438p, 8pl)	Harper	1905	Mears, W.E.	25-40	

AUTHOR	TITLE	PUBLISHER	DATE	ARTIST	PRICE	LC
Garner, Elvira	Ezekiel (1st [1st bk.], sm4to, ibds, [44]p, color)	Holt	(1937)	Garner, E.	80-120	
Garner, Elvira	Ezekiel Travels (1st, lg8vo, [46]p, ibds, color)	Holt	(1938)	Garner, E.	90-130	
Garner, Elvira	Little Cat Lost (1st, sq4to, [28]p, 2-color, pep)	J. Messner	(1943)	Thorne, D.	35-50	*
Garner, Elvira	Sarah Faith Anderson (1st, sm8vo, [106]p, color)	J. Messner	(1939)	Garner, E.	35-50	*
Garner, Elvira	Way Down in Tennessee (1st, 8vo, [96]p, ibds, color, pep)	J. Messner	1941	Garner, E.	90-130	
Garnett (ed.)	Poems by Robert Browning (1st, 8vo, 377p, gilt, b/w)	L: Bell	1900	Shaw, B.	60-80	
Garnett, L.A.	Creature Songs (1st, lg4to, 30p, p-o, green/gilt, 10pl)	NY: Ditson	(1912)	Newell, P.	140-200	
Garnett, L.A.	Muffin Shop (1st, folio, p-o, 79p, color)	Rand/McNally	(1908)	Dunlap, H.	100-165	
Garnett, L.A.	The Merrymakers (1st, sm4to, ipcb, 80p, 8 fp color)	Rand/McNally	(1918)	McCracken, J.	45-65	
Garnett, L.M.	Ottoman Wonder Tales (1st, sq8vo, 266p, teg, 12cp)	L: A&C Black	1915	Folkard, C.	70-115	
Garrard, P.	Running Away with Nebby (1st {std}, sm4to, 144p, 6cp, 11pl, pep)	McKay	(1944)	Pogany, W.	65-80	
Garrett, H.	Angelo, the Naughty One (1st, 4to, ipcb, 40p, color, pep)	Viking	1944	Politi, L.	50-85	
Garrott, H.	Snythergen (1st, 8vo, blue/gilt, 157p, 4cp, 16pl, pep)	McBride	1923	Walker, D.S.	50-80	
Garrott, H.	Squiffer (1st {std}, 8vo, 226p, green/gilt, uncut, 4cp, pep)	McBride	1924	Walker, D.S.	70-90	
Garstin, N.	Suitors of Aprille (1st, 8vo, teg, 212p, 19pl)	L: J. Lane	1900	Robinson, C.	100-160	
Garth, Mary	What Happened to Hannah (4to, p-o, color)	L: Goschen	1913	Payne, Irene	50-70	*
Gask, Lilian	Fairies & Christmas Child (1st AM, lg8vo, p-o, 261p, 8cp, pep)	Crowell	(1912)	Pogany, W.	180-240	
Gask, Lilian	Fairies & the Christmas Child (1st, 8vo, 260p)	L: Harrap	[1912]	Pogany, W.	65-80	*
Gask, Lilian	Folk Tales of Many Lands (1st AM, 8vo, p-o, uncut, 8cp)	Crowell	(1910)	Pogany, W.	100-150	
Gask, Lilian	Folk Tales of Many Lands (1st, 8vo, red/gilt, 287p, p-o, 8cp)	L: Harrap	1910	Pogany, W.	125-165	
Gask, Lilian	Legends of our Little Brothers (1st AM, 8vo, p-o, 268p, 15pl)	Crowell	(1912)	Wilson, P.	35-50	
Gask, Lilian	Legends of our Little Brothers (1st, 8vo, 268p, 15pl)	L: Harrap	1912	Wilson, P.	45-60	*
Gask, Lilian	Pig Tales (1st, 8vo, 64p)	Nister/Dutton	[1906]	Heatly, E.	35-50	*
Gask, Lilian	True Stories/Big Game & Jungles (1st, 8vo, 235p, 16cp)	L: Harrap	1933	Cameron, W.F.	50-65	*
Gaskell, C.M.	Lady Anne's Fairy Tales (1st, 4to, teg, 258p, white/gilt, 12cp)	L: Richards	1914	Atkinson, M.T.	140-200	
Gaskell, Mrs.	Cranford (1st, 8vo, 316p, b/w)	L: Bliss Sands	1896	Robinson, T.H.	35-50	*
Gaskell, Mrs.	Cranford (1st {color ed.}, 12mo, teg, gilt, 298p, 40cp)	L: MacMillan	1898	Thomson, H.	65-90	
Gaskell, Mrs.	Cranford (1st, 8vo, 313p, red/gilt, teg, 16 illus)	L: J. Nisbet	1900	Brock, H.M.	50-65	
Gaskell, Mrs.	Cranford (1st AM, sm8vo, teg, green/gilt, 255p, 24cp)	Dent/Dutton	1904	Brock, C.E.	35-50	
Gaskell, Mrs.	Cranford (1st, sm8vo, 247p, teg, 24cp)	L: Chapman	[1911]	Paul, E.	40-60	
Gasquet, A.	Greater Abbeys of England (1st, lg8vo, 378p, teg, 60cp)	L: Chatto	1908	Goble, W.	160-200	
Gasquet, A.	Greater Abbeys of England (1st AM, 8vo, 378p, teg, 60cp)	Dodd	1908	Goble, W.	130-180	
Gaster, Moses	Rumanian Legends & Fairy Tales (1st, 4to, ibds, 12cp)	L: R. Tuck	(1923)	Brock, C.E.	80-135	
Gate, E.M.	Punch & Robinetta (1st, sm8vo, 118p, brown cl, 8pl)	Yale U. Press	1923	Field, R.	30-45	*
Gate, E.M.	Tales from the Secret Kingdom (1st, 8vo, ibds, silhouettes)	Yale U. Press	1919	Buffam, K.G.	30-45	
Gate, E.M.	Tales/Enchanted Isles (1st, sq8vo, 118p, green cl, col frn, b/w)	Yale U. Press	1926	Lathrop, D.	60-80	
Gates, Doris	Blue Willow (1st, 8vo, 172p, blue cl, 10pl, pep, DJ, NH)	Viking	1940	Lantz, P.	50-80	
Gates, Doris	Little Vic (1st, 8vo, 160p, tan cl, b/w, pep)	Viking	1951	Seredy, K.	25-40	*
Gates, Doris	Sarah's Idea (1st, 8vo, orange cl, 146p, fp b/w, pep)	Viking	1938	Torrey, M.	20-35	*
Gates, Doris	Sensible Kate (1st, 8vo, yellow cl, 189p, b/w, pep, DJ)	Viking	1943	Torrey, M.	30-45	
Gates, Doris	Trouble for Jerry (1st, 8vo, 179p, rust cl, fp b/w, pep)	Viking	1944	Torrey, M.	25-40	*
Gates, Eleanor	Cupid the Cowpunch (1st, sm8vo, 316p, p-o, 8pl)	McClure	1907	Various	35-60	
Gates, Eleanor	Good Night (1st, 8vo, 53p, bds, 5cp)	Crowell	(1907)	Rackham, A.	350-500	
Gates, J.S.	April Fool Doll (1st, 4to, 152p, red cl, p-o)	Bobbs-Merrill	(1909)	Keep, V.	50-70	
Gates, J.S.	Land of Delight (1st, lg8vo, green cl, 115p, 16pl)	Houghton	1915	(Photos)	30-45	*
Gates, J.S.	Little Girl Blue Lives in the Woods... (1st, 16mo, 53p, 4cp)	Houghton	1910	Keep, V.	45-70	
Gates, J.S.	Little Girl Blue Plays I-Spy (1st, 16mo, 61p, color)	Houghton	1913	Keep, V.	45-60	*
Gates, J.S.	Little Red, White, Blue (1st, 4to, 118p, 9pl)	Bobbs-Merrill	(1906)	Keep, V.	50-65	
Gates, J.S.	Live Doll's House Party (1st, sm4to, red cl, 102p, p-o, 8pl)	Bobbs-Merrill	(1906)	Keep, V.	60-75	
Gates, J.S.	Live Doll's Play Days (1st, sm4to, p-o, red cl, 109p)	Bobbs-Merrill	(1908)	Keep, V.	60-75	
Gates, J.S.	Live Dolls in Fairyland (1st, 4to, p-o, 136p, 6cp)	Bobbs-Merrill	(1911)	Keep, V.	60-80	
Gates, J.S.	Live Dolls in Wonderland (1st, 8vo, 149p, p-o, 5pl)	Bobbs-Merrill	(1912)	Keep, V.	60-75	
Gates, J.S.	Nanette Goes to Visit Grandmother (1st, 16mo, ibds, 53p, 6cp)	Houghton	1915	(Photos)	50-65	*
Gates, J.S.	One Day in Betty's Life (1st, ob4to, [56]p, 2-color)	Bobbs-Merrill	(1913)	Unknown	90-130	*
Gates, J.S.	Story of the Live Dolls (1st, sm4to, 103p, p-o, b/w)	Bowen-Merrill	1901	Keep, V.	60-80	
Gates, J.S.	Story of the Lost Doll (1st, sm4to, red cl, p-o, 10pl)	Bobbs-Merrill	(1905)	Keep, V.	50-70	
Gates, J.S.	Story of the Mince Pie (1st, 8vo, 164p, p-o, 16cp)	Dodd	1916	Rae, J.	65-80	*
Gates, J.S.	Story of the Three Dolls (1st, sm4to, red cl, 148p, p-o, 9pl)	Bobbs-Merrill	(1905)	Keep, V.	70-100	
Gates, J.S.	Sunshine Annie (1st, 8vo, 148p, red cl, p-o, 15cp, pep)	Bobbs-Merrill	(1910)	Cory, F.	75-100	
Gates, J.S.	Tommy Sweet Tooth (1st, sq16mo, ibds, 64p, color, pep)	Houghton	1911	Churbuck, E.V.	30-45	
Gatti, Attilio	Wrath of Moto (1st, lg8vo, 160p, b/w)	Scribner	1941	Bransom, P.	25-40	*
Gatty, M.	Parables from Nature (1st, 8vo, green cl, 210p, 8pl)	L: G. Bell	1910	Woodward, A.B.	50-65	
Gay, J.	Beggar's Opera (1st, 4to, 93p, bds, p-o, 8cp)	L: Heinemann	1921	Fraser, C.L.	65-90	
Gay, J.	Polly: An Opera (1st, lg8vo, blue bds, 107p, 8cp)	L: Heinemann	1923	Nicholson, W.	70-100	
Gay, J.	Shire Colt (1st {std}, 4to, ibds, [62]p, lithos, DJ)	Doubleday/Dor.	1931	Gay, Z.	65-95	R
Gay, Romney	Five Little Playmates (1st, 12mo, ibds, [61]p, color)	Grosset/Dunlap	(1941)	Gay, R.	25-40	*
Gay, Romney	Peter's Adventure (1st, sq12mo, ibds, [34]p, color)	Whitman	1936	Gay, R.	25-40	
Gay, Romney	Toby & Sue (1st, sq8vo, ibds, [34]p, color)	Grosset/Dunlap	1937	Gay, R.	35-50	*
Gay, Romney	Tommy Grows Wise (1st, sq12mo, ibds, [30]p, color)	Grosset/Dunlap	1939	Gay, R.	25-40	
Gay, Zhenya	Pancho & His Burro (1st, sm4to, ibds, pep, [29]p, color)	Wm. Morrow	1930	Gay, Z.	45-60	
Gay, Zhenya	Sakimura (1st, 8vo, ibds, [42]p, color)	Viking	1937	Gay, Z.	45-70	
Gay, Zhenya	Town Cats (1st {std}, 4to, ipcb, 110p, fp b/w)	Knopf	1932	Gay, Z.	35-50	*

AUTHOR	TITLE	PUBLISHER	DATE	ARTIST	PRICE	LC
Gay, Zhenya	Wonderful Things! (1st, 4to, tan cl, 62p, fp b/w)	Viking	1954	Gay, Z.	25-40	*
Gaze, H.	Coppertop (1st AM, lg8vo, 338p, blue/gilt, 12cp)	Harper	(1924)	Gaze, H.	120-160	
Gaze, H.	Goblin's Glen (1st, 8vo, 242p, red/gilt, 6cp)	Little/Brown	1924	Gaze, H.	140-200	
Gaze, H.	Merry Piper (1st UK, lg8vo, 247p, 8cp, 12pl)	L: Longmans	1925	Gaze, H.	140-200	
Gaze, H.	Merry Piper (1st AM, 8vo, yellow cl, 247p, 8cp, 12pl, pep)	Little/Brown	1925	Gaze, H.	120-170	
Gee, John	Bunnie Bear (1st, 8vo, ibds, color)	Volland	(1928)	Gee, J.	35-50	*
Geister, E.	What Shall We Play? (1st, lg8vo, 175p, ibds, p-o, col frn, cep)	Doran	(1924)	MacKinstry, E.	40-65	
Geller, J.J.	Grandfather's Follies (1st, sq4to, 218p, b/w)	Macaulay	(1934)	Held, J.	40-65	
Gellibrand, E.	J. Cole (1st, 8vo, 86p, beige cl, 4cp)	Lippincott	1917	Kirk, M.L.	30-45	
Gemmill, J.	Joan Wanted a Kitty (1st, 8vo, blue cl, 150p, pep, color, DJ)	Winston	(1937)	DeAngeli, M.	50-75	
Gendel, Evelyn	Tortoise & Turtle (1st {std}, 4to, ibds, [64]p, color, pep)	Simon/Schuster	1960	Knight, H.	35-50	*
Genevoix, M.	Last Hunt (1st {std}, 8vo, p-o, 281p, 10 fp brown illus, pep)	Random	(1940)	Ward, L.	30-50	
George, Jean C.	My Side of the Mountain (1st {std}, 8vo, 178p, pep, b/w, NH)	Dutton	1959	George, J.C.	45-65	*
Gere, Frances K.	Once Upon a Time in Egypt (1st, ob4to, ibds, 71p, color, pep)	Longmans	1937	Gere, F.K.	70-100	R
Gerry, M.S.	The Flowers (1st, 8vo, 40p, green cl, p-o, 3cp)	Harper	1910	Green, E.S.	30-45	
Gerson, V.	Happy Heart Family (1st, lg8vo, 35p, p-o, color)	Fox Duffield	1904	Gerson, V.	100-130	
Gerson, V.	Little Dignity (1st {1st bk.}, sm4to, 64p, ibds, chromos)	NY: Routledge	1881	Gerson, V.	100-120	
Gerson, V.	More Advens/Happy Heart Family (1st, 4to, 47p, p-o, 4cp)	Fox Duffield	1905	Gerson, V.	120-150	
Gianakoulis, T.P.	Fairy Tales of Modern Greece (1st {std}, 8vo, 126p, pep)	Dutton	1930	Reiss, H.	45-65	*
Gibbings, Rbt.	Iorana! (1st AM, 8vo, 157p, uncut, p-o, gilt, b/w, pep)	Houghton	1932	Gibbings, R.	45-70	R
Gibbings, Rbt.	Lovely is The Lee (1st AM {std}, 8vo, 199p, green/gilt, DJ)	Dutton	1945	Gibbings, R.	35-50	
Gibbings, Rbt.	Over the Reefs (1st, 8vo, 240p, gilt, wood engravings)	L: Dent	1948	Gibbings, R.	25-40	
Gibbon, J.M.	Reign of Old King Cole (8vo, pict cl, 338p)	Dutton	(1911)	Robinson, C.	140-170	
Gibbons, Mary	Story of Ophelia (1st {std}, 4to, ibds, [32]p, color)	Doubleday	1954	Ness, E.M.	50-70	*
Gibbs, Geo.	American Sea Fights (1st, elephant folio, 12 ticp)	R.H. Russell	1902	Gibbs, G.	200-350	*
Gibson, C.D.	Americans (1st, ob folio, ipcb, [88]p, teg, fp b/w)	R.H. Russell	1900	Gibson, C.D.	150-200	
Gibson, C.D.	Drawings (1st, ob folio, [88]p, ibds, teg, b/w)	R.H. Russell	1897	Gibson, C.D.	140-200	
Gibson, C.D.	Education of Mr. Pipp (1st, ob folio, ibds, [78]p, b/w)	R.H. Russell	1899	Gibson, C.D.	150-200	
Gibson, C.D.	Eighty Drawings including Weaker Sex (1st, ob folio, ibds, b/w)	Scribner/Lane	1903	Gibson, C.D.	130-200	
Gibson, C.D.	Everyday People (1st, ob folio, b/w pl)	Scribner	1904	Gibson, C.D.	130-180	
Gibson, C.D.	Gibson Book (1st, ob folio, 2 volumes, red cl, teg)	Scribner	1906	Gibson, C.D.	220-300	
Gibson, C.D.	Our Neighbors (1st, ob folio, [68]p, b/w)	Scribner	1905	Gibson, C.D.	140-180	
Gibson, C.D.	Pictures of People (1st, ob folio, ibds, b/w)	R.H. Russell	1896	Gibson, C.D.	130-165	
Gibson, C.D.	Sketches in Egypt (1st, lg8vo, 115p, b/w)	Doub./McClure	1899	Gibson, C.D.	120-165	
Gibson, C.D.	Social Ladder (1st, ob. folio, [79]p, teg, b/w)	R.H. Russell	1902	Gibson, C.D.	160-200	
Gibson, C.D.	Widow & Her Friends (1st, ob folio, [79]p, bds, b/w)	R.H. Russell	1901	Gibson, C.D.	120-150	
Gibson, Katherine	Zauberlinda: Wise Witch (1st, 4to, 256p, blue cl, 1-color, pep)	Chi: R. Smith	(1901)	Tibbitts, M.	100-150	*
Gibson, Lydia	Teacup Whale (1st, ob8vo, ipcb, dep, 23p, b/w)	Farrar/Rine.	(1934)	Gibson, L.	30-45	*
Gielow, M.S.	Old Plantation Days (1st, sm8vo, 183p, b/w)	R.H. Russell	1902	Unknown	100-150	*
Gilbert, Henry	King Arthur's Knights (1st AM, 4to, 367p, gilt, teg, 16cp, dep)	Stokes	1911	Crane, W.	140-200	
Gilbert, Henry	King Arthur's Knights (1st, 8vo, teg, 367p, 16cp)	L: Jack	1911	Crane, W.	165-200	R
Gilbert, Henry	Robin Hood... (1st AM, 8vo, teg, gilt, 16cp)	Stokes	(1912)	Crane, W.	90-120	
Gilbert, P.T.	Egbert & his Marvelous Adventures (1st {std}, sm8vo, 103p, b/w)	Harper	(1944)	Rey, H.A.	35-50	*
Gilbert, P.T.	Elmer Buys a Circus (1st, 8vo, ibds, 71p, b/w)	Grosset/Dunlap	(1941)	Stossel, A.	20-25	*
Gilbert, W.S.	Bab Ballads (1st AM, 16mo, 184p, grey bds, uncut)	R.H. Russell	1906	Gilbert, W.S.	30-50	
Gilbert, W.S.	Iolanthe... (1st, 4to, green/gilt, teg, 224p, uncut, 32cp)	L: Bell	1910	Flint, W.R.	130-165	
Gilbert, W.S.	Pinafore Picture Book (1st, 4to, 131p, blue cl, 16cp)	L: G. Bell	1908	Woodward, A.B.	70-120	
Gilbert, W.S.	Princess Ida (1st, lg8vo, 150p, green/gilt, color)	L: G. Bell	1912	Flint, W.R.	70-115	
Gilbert, W.S.	Savoy Operas (1st, 4to, 208p, gilt, teg, 32cp)	L: G. Bell	1909	Flint, W.R.	100-165	
Gilbert, W.S.	Story of the Mikado (1st, sm4to, ibds, 114p, 6cp)	L: O'Conner	1921	Woodward, A.B.	45-60	
Gilbert, W.S.	The Mikado (1st, 8vo, 96p, 8cp)	L: MacMillan	1928	Flint, W.R.	60-80	
Gilbert, W.S.	Yoeman of the Guard (1st, 8vo, 102p, gilt, 8cp)	L: MacMillan	1929	Flint, W.R.	50-70	
Gilbert, Wm.	Magic Mirror (1st, 8vo, 253p, purple/gilt, p-o, teg, 20cp)	L: MacLaren	1908	Menzies, J.	65-90	
Gilby/Cuming	George Moorland... (1st, 8vo, 290p, teg, 50cp)	L: A&C Black	1907	Moorland, G.	70-100	
Gilchrist, Marie	Story of the Great Lakes (1st {std}, 4to, [32]p, ibds, color)	Harper	(1942)	DeWitt, C.H.	25-40	
Gilfillan, A.B.	Sheep (1st, 8vo, 272p, b/w)	Little/Brown	1929	Wiese, K.	20-35	
Gill, Frances	Little Days (1st, 8vo, ibds, [51]p, col frn)	Houghton	1917	Winter, M.	65-80	
Gillilan, S.	Danny & Fanny (1st, lg8vo, p-o, 96p, color, pep)	Rand/McNally	(1928)	Eger, R.C.	30-45	*
Gillmore, Inez H.	Angel Island (1st, 8vo, blue cl, 351p, 2pl)	Holt	1914	Rae, J.	100-120	
Gilly Bear	Adventures of Peterkin (1st, lg8vo, 153p, brown/gilt, 12cp)	NY: S. Gabriel	(1916)	Ohrenschall, H.	65-80	
Gilly Bear	Tom Tit Tales (1st, 4to, 155p, purple/gilt, 12cp)	NY: S. Gabriel	(1915)	Ohrenschall, H.	60-80	
Gilman, Eliz. L.	Picnic Adventures (1st, sm8vo, green cl, 192p, 12 dp 1-color)	Farrar/Rine.	(1940)	Cosgrave, J.O.	45-70	*
Gilmour, Marg.	Ameliaranne Gives a Concert (1st, 8vo, unpag)	L: Harrap	1944	Pearse, S.B.	50-70	*
Gilmour, Marg.	Ameliaranne at the Circus (1st, 12mo, p-o, [63]p, color)	L: Harrap	(1931)	Pearse, S.B.	40-65	*
Gilmour, Marg.	Ameliaranne at the Seaside (1st, 8vo, unpag)	L: Harrap	1935	Pearse, S.B.	50-65	*
Gilmour, Marg.	Seven Little Spillikins (ob8vo, p-o, color)	McKay	[1930]	Govey, L.	60-75	
Gilson, R.R.	In the Morning Glow (1st, 8vo, p-o, 16pl)	Harper	1904	Stephens, A.B.	30-50	
Gilson, R.R.	Katrina (1st, 8vo, green cl, 316p, teg, 6cp)	Baker/Taylor	(1906)	Stephens, A.B.	30-45	
Gilson, R.R.	Mother & Father (1st, 8vo, teg, 63p, green cl, b/w)	Harper	1903	Stephens, A.B.	45-65	
Gimmage, Peter	Picture Book of Ships (1st, 4to, 64p, fp color, pep)	MacMillan	1930	Craig, H.	35-65	*
Gipson, Fred B.	Old Yeller (1st, 8vo, ibds, 158p, 6 fp b/w, NH)	Harper	(1956)	Burger, C.	45-70	*
Gipson, Fred B.	Trail-Driving Rooster (1st, 8vo, grey cl, 79p, b/w)	Harper	(1955)	Simont, M.	30-45	*

AUTHOR	TITLE	PUBLISHER	DATE	ARTIST	PRICE	LC
Gipson, M.	Hello Peter (1st {std}, ob8vo, [31]p, color, dep)	Doubleday	(1948)	Hurd, C.	45-60	*
Girvin, B.	Alice & the White Rabbit (1st, 8vo, 160p, 33 illus)	L: Partridge	(1909)	Unknown	65-80	*
Girvin, B.	Girl Scout (1st, 8vo, 319p, color)	L: H. Frowde	1913	Tenison, N.	25-45	*
Girvin, B.	Good Queen Bees (1st, ob4to, ibds, unpag, 23cp)	L: D. Nutt	1907	Hassall, J.	80-135	*
Girvin, B.	Mr. Piccolo (1st, 8vo, 247p)	L: G. Allen	1911	Quick, H.	25-45	*
Girvin, B.	Pam & Billy (1st, 8vo, 209p, col frn, 12pl)	L: G. Allen	1910	Quick, H.	35-50	*
Girvin, B.	Queer Cousin Claude (1st, 8vo, 280p)	L: G. Allen	1912	Hardy, E.S.	30-45	*
Girvin, B.	Round Fairyland with Alice (1st, 8vo, brown/gilt)	L: Wells/Gard.	(1948)	Cable, W.L.	65-80	*
Girvin, B.	Round Fairyland/Alice & White Rabbit (1st, 8vo, 312p)	L: Wells/Gard.	1916	Furniss, D.	70-100	*
Girvin/Cosens	Wee Men (1st, 12mo, p-o, 160p, 4cp)	L: Hutchinson	[1923]	Robinson, C.	140-180	
Glasgow, E.	The Deliverance (1st, 8vo, 543p, red/gilt, 4cp)	Doubleday/Page	1904	Schoonover, F.	30-45	
Glave, E.J.	In Savage Africa (1st, lg8vo, 247p, grey cl, b/w)	R.H. Russell	(1892)	Various	100-160	*
Gleaves, Suzanne	Tip & Dip (1st, lg8vo, rust cl, [62]p, 1-color)	Lippincott	(1960)	Adams, A.	45-60	*
Glendon, George	Emperor of the Air (1st, 8vo, 311p, red/gilt, 8pl)	L: Methuen	1910	Buckland, A.H.	45-60	*
Glover, C.	British Fairy & Folk Tales (1st, sq8vo, 281p, 8cp)	L: A&C Black	1920	Folkard, C.	85-120	
Godden, Rumer	Candy Floss (1st, lg8vo, pink cl, 63p, color, dep)	Viking	(1960)	Adams, A.	65-100	R*
Godden, Rumer	Doll's House (1st AM, sm8vo, 125p, yellow, cl, 4cp, DJ)	Viking	1948	Saintsbury, Dana	45-70	
Godden, Rumer	Fairy Doll (1st, 8vo, grey cl, 67p, 2-color, pep)	Viking	1956	Adams, A.	45-70	*
Godden, Rumer	Impunity Jane (1st, 8vo, 48p, color, pep)	Viking	1954	Adams, A.	65-100	R*
Godden, Rumer	Mouse House (1st, lg8vo, tan cl, 63p, color, pep)	Viking	1957	Adams, A.	65-100	R*
Godden, Rumer	Mousewife (1st, 8vo, 46p, b/w)	Viking	1951	DuBois, W.P.	35-50	*
Godden, Rumer	Story of Holly & Ivy (1st, lg8vo, 64p, ibds, 2-color, pep)	Viking	(1958)	Adams, A.	50-70	*
Godfrey, Hollis	Man Who Ended War (1st, 8vo, blue/gilt, 301p, p-o, 4pl)	Little/Brown	1898	Grunwald, C.	50-70	
Godolphin, M.	Pilgrims' Progress (1st, 4to, red cl, b/w, 120p, DJ)	Stokes	1939	Lawson, R.	65-80	
Goethe	Faust (1st, 4to, red/gilt, teg, 205p, 31 ticp)	L: Hutchinson	1908	Pogany, W.	200-300	
Goethe	Faust (1st, 8vo, 262p, 6pl, DJ)	Cape/Smith	(1930)	Ward, L.	80-100	
Goldberg, M.	Lunch Box Story (1st, sm8vo, red cl, [30]p, b/w)	Holiday House	1951	Tobias, B.	20-30	*
Goldberg, M.	Twirly Skirt (1st, 8vo, 45p, green cl, fp b/w, pep)	Holiday House	1954	Stone, H.	40-65	R*
Goldberg, M.	Wait for the Rain (1st, sm8vo, [43]p, blue cl, b/w, cep)	Holiday House	(1952)	Price, C.	20-25	*
Golding, Harry	Book of the Clock (1st, 8vo, p-o, 140p, 27cp)	L: Ward Lock	1920	Tarrant, M.	75-100	
Golding, Harry	Our Animal Friends (4to, ibds, 176p, 24cp)	L: Ward Lock	[1920]	Tarrant, M.	65-80	*
Golding, Harry	Willie Winkie... (16mo, 96p, ibds, 24 fp color)	L: Ward Lock	[1920]	Tarrant, M.	65-80	
Golding, Harry	Zoo Days (2nd, lg8vo, p-o, 48cp)	L: Ward Lock	[1920]	Tarrant, M.	30-50	
Goldman, J.M.	School in Our Village (1st, 8vo, DJ)	L: Batsford	1957	Ardizzone, E.	25-40	*
Goldoni, C.	The Liar (1st, sm4to, ibds, 93p, p-o, col frn)	L: Selwyn	1922	Fraser, C.L.	45-60	*
Goldoni, C.	The Liar (1st AM, 8vo, 93p, bds, DJ)	Knopf	1922	Fraser, C.L.	65-80	
Goldsmith, Milton	Dorothy's Dolls... (1st, 8vo, 59p, ibds, 14cp)	NY: Ullman	(1908)	Hermony, N.	65-80	*
Goldsmith, O.	Comedies of... (1st, 8vo, AEG, 310p, b/w)	L: G. Allen	1896	Hammond, C.	65-80	
Goldsmith, O.	Deserted Village (1st, 4to, 59p, AEG, 119p)	Harper	1902	Abbey, E.A.	85-100	
Goldsmith, O.	Deserted Village (1st, ob4to, 59p, vellum/gilt, 14cp, pep)	L: Gowans/Gray	1907	Reid, S.	100-160	
Goldsmith, O.	Deserted Village (1st, 4to, 99p, teg, 40 ticp)	L: Constable	1909	Hankey, W.L.	90-120	
Goldsmith, O.	Elegy/Glory of Her Sex... (1st, ob4to, wraps, [24]p, 6cp)	L: Routledge	(1885)	Caldecott, R.	70-95	
Goldsmith, O.	Little Goody Two-Shoes (1st, 8vo, [40]p, ibds, pep, color)	Saalfield	(1929)	Peat, F.B.	45-60	
Goldsmith, O.	Mrs. Mary Blaize (1st, 24p, wraps, 6cp)	L: Routledge	(1885)	Caldecott, R.	65-90	
Goldsmith, O.	She Stoops to Conquer (1st, folio, AEG)	Harper	1887	Abbey, E.A.	100-160	
Goldsmith, O.	She Stoops to Conquer (1st, 4to, 198p, gilt, 25 ticp)	L: Hodder	(1912)	Thomson, H.	120-160	
Goldsmith, O.	Vicar of Wakefield (1st, 8vo, 305p, AEG, gilt, b/w)	L: MacMillan	1890	Thomson, H.	60-80	
Goldsmith, O.	Vicar of Wakefield (1st, 8vo, 222p, green/gilt, uncut, 12cp)	L: Dent	1898	Bedford, F.D.	65-90	
Goldsmith, O.	Vicar of Wakefield (1st, 8vo, AEG, 224p, green cl)	L: Nister	[1898]	Paget, H.M.	50-70	
Goldsmith, O.	Vicar of Wakefield (1st, 8vo, green/gilt, 260p, teg, 13cp)	L: A&C Black	1903	Wright, J.M.	80-120	*
Goldsmith, O.	Vicar of Wakefield (1st, 8vo, 242p, teg, uncut, 25cp, dep)	L: Dent	1904	Brock, C.E.	30-50	
Goldsmith, O.	Vicar of Wakefield (1st AM, 8vo, blue/gilt, teg, 7cp)	Lippincott	1912	Brock, H.M.	50-70	
Goldsmith, O.	Vicar of Wakefield (1st AM, 4to, 345p, blue/gilt, 16cp)	Holt	1914	Sullivan, E.J.	90-140	
Goldsmith, O.	Vicar of Wakefield (1st, 4to, 345p, green/gilt, teg, 16cp)	L: Constable	1914	Sullivan, E.J.	120-165	
Goldsmith, O.	Vicar of Wakefield (1st, 4to, teg, uncut, gilt, 232p, 12cp, pep)	L: Harrap	(1929)	Rackham, A.	220-260	
Goldsmith, O.	Vicar of Wakefield (1st AM, 4to, gilt, 232p, teg, 12cp, pep)	McKay	[1929]	Rackham, A.	100-130	
Gomme, Alice B.	Children's Singing Games (1st, ob4to, ibds, b/w)	L: D. Nutt	1894	Smith, Winifred	100-165	*
Gomme, G.L.	Princess's Story Book (1st, sm8vo, gilt, teg, 443p, 23pl)	L: Constable	1901	Stratton, H.	75-125	*
Goodloe, A.C.	College Girls (1st, 8vo, 288p, 11pl)	Scribner	1895	Gibson, C.D.	30-45	
Goodrich, A.	Gleam O'Dawn (1st, 8vo, 308p, 4pl)	Appleton	1908	Hutchinson	20-25	
Goodwin, M.W.	Head of a Hundred (1st, 12mo, green/gilt, 225p, teg, 2pl by...)	Little/Brown	1897	Smith, J.W.	70-90	
Goodwin, M.W.	Head of a Hundred (1st {new ed}, 12mo, 221p, red/glt, 2pl)	Little/Brown	1900	Smith, J.W.	75-100	
Goodwin, M.W.	Sir Christopher... (1st, 12mo, 411p, frn by...)	Little/Brown	1901	Pyle, H.	25-40	
Gordon, A.C.	Maje: A Love Story (1st, 12mo, ipcb, uncut, 119p, 4pl)	Scribner	1914	Unknown	35-50	*
Gordon, A.L.	Racing Rhymes (1st, 12mo, 146p, uncut, b/w)	R.H. Russell	1901	Unknown	65-80	*
Gordon, Eliz.	Billy Bunny's Fortune (1st, 12mo, [40]p, ibds, color, pep)	Volland	(1919)	Enright, M.W.	50-70	
Gordon, Eliz.	Bird Children (1st, lg8vo, 96p, ibds, color, pep)	Volland	(1912)	Ross, M.T.	85-140	
Gordon, Eliz.	Buddy Jim... (1st, 8vo, ibds, [93]p, color)	Volland	(1922)	Rae, J.	40-65	
Gordon, Eliz.	Butterfly Babies' Book (1st, 8vo, 78p, ibds, color)	Rand/McNally	(1914)	Ross, M.T.	70-100	
Gordon, Eliz.	Dolly & Molly at Seashore (1st, 16mo, 32p, color)	Rand/McNally	(1914)	Beem, F.	35-60	*
Gordon, Eliz.	Dolly & Molly at the Circus (1st, 16mo, 32p, color)	Rand/McNally	(1914)	Beem, F.	35-60	*
Gordon, Eliz.	Flower Children (1st, 8vo, ibds, [92]p, color, pep)	Volland	(1910)	Ross, M.T.	100-140	

AUTHOR	TITLE	PUBLISHER	DATE	ARTIST	PRICE	LC
Gordon, Eliz.	Happy Home Children (1st, 12mo, [34]p, ibds, pep, color)	Volland	(1924)	Foster, M.L.	50-70	
Gordon, Eliz.	I Wonder Why? (1st, sm8vo, 72p, color)	Rand/McNally	(1916)	Ross, M.T.	40-65	
Gordon, Eliz.	Just You (1st, sq16mo, ipcb, color, pep)	Volland	(1920)	Unknown	50-70	*
Gordon, Eliz.	King Gumdrop... (1st, lg8vo, 112p, p-o, fp color)	Whitman	(1916)	Frazee, H.	55-70	
Gordon, Eliz.	Lorraine & Little People of Spring (1st, sm8vo, 64p, color)	Rand/McNally	(1918)	Lee, E.D.	30-45	*
Gordon, Eliz.	Lorraine & Little People of Summer (1st, sm8vo, 64p, color)	Rand/McNally	(1920)	McCracken, J.	30-45	*
Gordon, Eliz.	Lorraine & the Little People (1st, 12mo, 73p, color)	Rand/McNally	(1915)	Ross, M.T.	70-90	
Gordon, Eliz.	More Really So Stories (1st, 8vo, ibds, 95p, color, pep)	Volland	(1929)	Rae, J.	65-85	
Gordon, Eliz.	Mother Earth's Children (1st, 8vo, 95p, ibds, color, pep)	Volland	(1914)	Ross, M.T.	70-100	
Gordon, Eliz.	Really So Stories (1st, lg8vo, ibds, 96p, 11cp, pep)	Volland	(1924)	Rae, J.	60-85	
Gordon, Eliz.	Sheaf of Roses (1st, 8vo, [72]p, ipcb, color)	Rand/McNally	(1915)	Martin, F.W.	35-50	*
Gordon, Eliz.	Some Smiles (1st, 12mo, ibds, [29]p, color)	Wilde	(1911)	Ross, M.T.	35-50	
Gordon, Eliz.	Tale of Johnny Mouse (1st, 8vo, ibds, color)	Volland	(1920)	Enright, M.W.	70-100	
Gordon, Eliz.	Turned-Intos (1st, 8vo, ipcb, unpag, color, pep)	Volland	(1920)	Scott, J.L.	65-80	
Gordon, Eliz.	Wild Flower Children (1st, 8vo, ibds, [84]p, color, pep)	Volland	(1918)	Scott, J.L.	100-150	
Gordon, H.C.	Flower Name Fancies (1st, 4to, green cl, 31 fp b/w)	L: J. Lane	1918	Fauconnet, G.R.	45-65	*
Gordon, H.C.	Golden Key (1st, 8vo, 223p, col frn, 5 fp b/w)	L: J. Murray	(1932)	Oldfield, M.	30-45	*
Gordon, H.C.	Lost Princess (1st, 8vo, 159p)	L: J. Murray	(1933)	Dixon, G.S.	35-50	*
Gordon, H.C.	Paradoc to the Rescue (1st, 8vo, 206p)	L: J. Murray	(1939)	Tozer, K.	30-45	*
Gordon, H.C.	Rhymes/Red Triangle (1st, 8vo, ibds, [60]p, chromos)	J. Lane	[1918]	Dennys, J.	100-150	
Gordon, Pat	Boy Jones (1st, 8vo, red cl, 158p, 10pl, pep)	Viking	1943	Adams, A.	45-60	*
Gordon, Pat	Witch of Scrapfaggot Green (1st, 4to, 78p, 10 fp b/w, DJ)	Viking	1948	DuBois, W.P.	65-80	
Gorey, Edward	Bug Book (1st {std}, 16mo, wraps, unpag, color)	Looking Glass	(1959)	Gorey, E.	70-100	R*
Gorey, Edward	Doubtful Guest (1st {std}, ob8vo, ibds, [30]p, b/w)	Doubleday	1957	Gorey, E.	50-70	*
Gorey, Edward	Listing Attic (1st {std}, sm8vo, ibds, unpag, b/w)	Duell/Sloan	(1954)	Gorey, E.	45-60	*
Gorey, Edward	Object Lesson (1st {std}, ob8vo, tan bds, b/w, DJ)	Doubleday	1958	Gorey, E.	70-90	*
Gorey, Edward	Unstrung Harp (1st {std}-[1st bk.], 8vo, ibds, unpag, DJ)	Duell/Sloan	(1953)	Gorey, E.	90-130	*
Gorham, Maurice	Back to the Local (1st, 8vo, 126p, red/gilt, 21 b/w)	L: P. Marshall	1949	Ardizzone, E.	70-100	
Gorham, Maurice	Londoners (1st, 8vo, 158p, brown bds, 24 b/w)	L: P. Marshall	(1951)	Ardizzone, E.	50-65	
Gorham, Maurice	Showmen & Suckers (1st, 8vo, 262p, red bds, 35 b/w)	L: P. Marshall	(1951)	Ardizzone, E.	65-80	
Gorham, Maurice	The Local (1st, 8vo, 51p)	L: Cassell	1939	Ardizzone, E.	75-100	*
Goss, F.C.	Little St. Sunshine (1st, 8vo, green/gilt, 153p)	Bowen-Merrill	1902	Keep, V.	30-45	*
Gosse (intro)	Allies' Fairy Book (1st, 8vo, blue/gilt, 12cp)	L: Heinemann	(1916)	Rackham, A.	240-320	
Gosse, E.	In Russet & Silver (1st, 12mo, 159p, tan cl, cvr by...)	Stone/Kimball	1894	Bradley, W.	100-130	*
Goudey, Alice E.	Houses from the Sea (1st, 4to, unpag, color, CH)	Scribner	(1959)	Adams, A.	65-90	*
Goudge, Eliz.	Little White Horse (1st AM {std}, 8vo, 280p, blue cl, b/w, pep)	Coward	(1947)	Hodges, C.W.	45-60	
Goudge, Eliz.	Reward of Faith (1st AM, 8vo, blue cl, 186p, b/w)	Coward	(1950)	Unwin, N.S.	30-45	*
Goudge, Eliz.	Sister of the Angels (1st AM, 8vo, blue/gilt, 154p, fp b/w)	Coward	(1939)	Hodges, C.W.	25-40	*
Goudge, Eliz.	Smoky House (1st AM, 8vo, 286p, 6pl)	Coward	(1940)	Floethe, R.	30-50	*
Gould, E.L.	Little Polly Prentiss (1st, sm8vo, 192p, 5pl)	Penn	1902	Waugh, Ida	25-40	
Gould, F.C.	Tales Told in the Zoo (1st, lg8vo, 136p, col frn, 5pl)	L: T.F. Unwin	1900	Gould, F.C.	45-65	
Gould, F.J.	Children's Plutarch (1st, 8vo, 171p, 3pl)	Harper	1910	Crane, W.	100-150	
Goulden, S.	Royal Reflections (1st, 8vo, ibds, b/w, DJ)	L: Methuen	1936	Shepard, E.H.	45-60	
Gowans, Adam I.	Treasury of English Verse (1st, 8vo, 303p, green cl, 50pl)	L: Gowans/Gray	1907	Reid, S.	70-100	*
Gower, M.L.	Fighting Six (1st, 8vo, 250p, b/w)	Harcourt	(1929)	Millar, H.R.	25-40	*
Grabo, C.H.	Peter & the Princess (1st, sm4to, teg, gilt, p-o, 243p, 8cp pep)	Reilly/Lee	(1920)	Neill, J.R.	200-300	
Graham, Al	Mouse with a Small Guitar (1st, 8vo, 35p, grey cl, color, pep)	Welch Pub. Co.	(1947)	Palazzo, T.	35-60	*
Graham, Al	Timothy Turtle (1st, lg4to, [30]p, pep, CH)	Welch Pub. Co.	(1946)	Palazzo, T.	70-100	*
Graham, E.	Night Adventures of Alexis (sm4to, 34p, 9cp)	L: Faber/Gwyer	1925	Langlands, W.	40-65	*
Graham, H.	Deportmental Ditties (1st, 4to, 127p)	L: Mills/Boom	(1909)	Baumer, L.	30-50	
Graham, H.	Deportmental Ditties (1st AM, 16mo, 134p, 3pl)	Duffield	1909	Grant, G.	25-45	*
Graham, H.	Misrepresentative Women (1st, 8vo, ibds, 120p, 12pl)	Duffield	1906	Groesbeck, D.	20-35	
Graham, Mary N.	Fifty Songs for Boys & Girls (1st, ob4to, 60p, color)	Whitman	(1935)	Scott, J.L.	70-100	*
Graham, Stephen	New York Nights (1st, 8vo, 288p, bds, 14 b/w)	Doran	(1927)	Wiese, K.	35-50	*
Graham, T.	Hike & the Aeroplane (1st, sm8vo, 275p, 4pl)	Stokes	(1912)	Hutchins, A.	500-650	
Grahame, K.	Bertie's Escapade (1st, sm8vo, 41p, grey cl, b/w)	Lippincott	(1949)	Shepard, E.H.	45-70	R
Grahame, K.	Dream Days (1st, sq8vo, teg, 228p, gilt, 9pl, pep)	L: J. Lane	(1902)	Parrish, M.	130-170	
Grahame, K.	Dream Days (1st, 8vo, 192p, color, pep)	L: J. Lane	1922	Lenski, L.	70-100	*
Grahame, K.	Dream Days (1st AM, 8vo, 172p, gilt, pep)	Dodd	1931	Shepard, E.H.	35-50	
Grahame, K.	Golden Age (1st, 8vo, red/gilt, 252p, teg, 19pl, pep)	J. Lane	1900	Parrish, M.	120-165	
Grahame, K.	Golden Age (2nd, 8vo, 252p, 18pl)	J. Lane	1904	Parrish, M.	65-85	
Grahame, K.	Golden Age (1st, sm4to, 243p, uncut, 19cp)	L: J. Lane	1914	Moony, R.J.E.	90-135	
Grahame, K.	Golden Age (1st [1st bk.], 8vo, uncut, 199p, 4 ticp)	L: J. Lane	1921	Lenski, L.	75-100	
Grahame, K.	Golden Age (1st, 12mo, 166p, beige/gilt, t.e. pink, b/w, DJ)	L: J. Lane	(1928)	Shepard, E.H.	100-150	
Grahame, K.	Golden Age (1st AM, sm8vo, 170p, b/w, pep)	Dodd	1929	Shepard, E.H.	65-80	
Grahame, K.	Pagan Papers (1st, 12mo, bds, 165p, teg, title page by...)	H. Stone	1894	Beardsley, A.	100-150	R
Grahame, K.	Reluctant Dragon (1st, 8vo, [57]p, cloth, b/w, DJ)	Holiday House	(1938)	Shepard, E.H.	50-80	
Grahame, K.	Reluctant Dragon (1st, lg4to, [72]p, ibds, color, pep)	Garden City	(1941)	Disney Studios	165-200	*
Grahame, K.	The Headswoman (1st AM, 8vo, 53p, 7cp, DJ)	Dodd	1922	Foster, M.L.	60-85	
Grahame, K.	Wind in the Willows (1st, 8vo, 302p, teg, blue/gilt, frn by)	L: Methuen	(1908)	Robertson, W.G.	500-700	
Grahame, K.	Wind in the Willows (1st AM, 8vo, grn/glt, 302p, teg, frn by...)	Scribner	1908	Robertson, W.G.	350-500	
Grahame, K.	Wind in the Willows (1st, 8vo, blue/gilt, teg, 351p, 10cp, pep)	Scribner	1913	Bransom, P.	140-185	

AUTHOR	TITLE	PUBLISHER	DATE	ARTIST	PRICE	LC
Grahame, K.	Wind in the Willows (1st, 8vo, gilt, 302p, p-o, 12cp, pep)	Scribner	1922	Barnhart, N.	100-145	
Grahame, K.	Wind in the Willows (1st, 8vo, 247p, blue/gilt, teg, color)	L: Methuen	(1927)	Payne, W.	100-145	
Grahame, K.	Wind in the Willows (1st, 8vo, green/gilt, 312p, b/w, pep)	L: Methuen	(1931)	Shepard, E.H.	150-200	
Grahame, K.	Wind in the Willows (1st AM, 8vo, blue/gilt, b/w, pep)	Scribner	1933	Shepard, E.H.	85-100	
Grahame, K.	Wind in the Willows (1st {this pub}, lg8vo, 190p, 12cp, box)	Heritage Press	(1940)	Rackham, A.	100-130	
Gramatky, H.	Creeper's Jeep (1st, 4to, [64]p, color)	Putnam	(1948)	Gramatky, H.	45-60	
Gramatky, H.	Hercules (1st, 4to, [72]p, red cl, color, pep)	Putnam	(1940)	Gramatky, H.	70-100	*
Gramatky, H.	Homer & the Circus Train (1st, 4to, unpag, pep, color)	Putnam	(1957)	Gramatky, H.	35-50	*
Gramatky, H.	Little Toot (1st, sq8vo, unpag, pep, color)	Putnam	1939	Gramatky, H.	120-165	R*
Gramatky, H.	Loopy (1st, 4to, [72]p, color, pep)	Putnam	(1941)	Gramatky, H.	45-60	*
Grant, Gordon	Greasy Luck (1st, 4to, white cl, 128p, pep)	Payson	(1932)	Grant, G.	35-50	
Grant, Gordon	Secret Voyage (1st, lg8vo, 63p, b/w)	Wm. Morrow	1942	Grant, G.	30-45	
Grant, Gordon	Ships Under Sail (1st, lg4to, ibds, 25p, color)	Garden City	(1939)	Grant, G.	30-50	
Grant, Gordon	Story of the Ship (1st, folio, ipcb, [48]p, color, pep)	McLoughlin	(1919)	Grant, G.	45-70	
Grant, J.C.	Baby Weems (1st {std}, lg8vo, [64]p, blue cl, 2-color, pep)	Doubleday/Dor.	1941	Disney Studios	70-100	*
Grant, Rbt.	Art of Living (1st, 8vo, 353p, green/gilt, teg)	Scribner	1895	Armstrong, M.	25-40	
Grant, Rbt.	Bachelor's Christmas (1st, 8vo, olive/gilt, teg, 309p)	Scribner	1895	Armstrong, M.	30-45	
Grant, Rbt.	Jack Hall (1st, 8vo, blue/gilt, 294p, PPP)	Jordan Marsh	1888	Attwood, F.G.	80-100	*
Grant, Rbt.	The Undercurrent (1st, 8vo, blue cl, 480p, cvr by...)	Scribner	1904	Armstrong, M.	25-45	
Grant, Rbt.	Unleavened Bread (1st, 8vo, green/gilt, 431p)	Scribner	1900	Armstrong, M.	25-40	
Grant, V.	Tinker Tim the Toy Maker (1st, lg4to, ibds, 29p, color, pep)	Whitman	1934	Grant, V.	75-115	R
Granville, A.	Fallen Race (1st, 8vo, blue/gilt, 352p, 5pl)	F.T. Neely	(1892)	Mason, E.	200-250	
Gratacap, L.P.	Mayor of New York (1st, 8vo, red/gilt, 471p, 4pl)	Dillingham	(1910)	Chase, J.C.	50-65	
Gratacap, L.P.	New Northland (1st, sm8vo, 391p, blue/gilt, 16pl)	NY: T. Benton	1915	Operti, A.	45-60	*
Graves, A.P.	Irish Fairy Book (1st, 8vo, 410p, col frn, 11pl, pep)	L: T.F. Unwin	(1909)	Denham, G.	65-80	
Graves, A.P.	Irish Fairy Book (1st AM, gilt, 310p, col frn, 13pl, pep)	Stokes	[1910]	Denham, G.	65-90	*
Graves, Rbt.	Penny Fiddle (1st, sm4to, green bds, color, DJ)	L: Cassell	(1960)	Ardizzone, E.	65-80	
Graves, Rbt.	Penny Fiddle (1st AM {std}, 8vo, 62p, green cl, fp 2-color)	Doubleday	1960	Ardizzone, E.	35-50	*
Gray, Eliz. J.	Adam of the Road (1st, lg8vo, 317p, green cl, 23pl, pep, NM)	Viking	1942	Lawson, R.	65-100	R
Gray, Eliz. J.	Adam of the Road (1st UK, 8vo, 174p, b/w)	L: A&C Black	1943	Lawson, R.	30-45	*
Gray, Eliz. J.	Beppy Marlowe of Charles Town (1st, sm8vo, 281p, color, pep)	Viking	1936	Barton, L.	25-40	*
Gray, Eliz. J.	Fair Adventure (1st, sm8vo, 298p, pep)	Viking	1940	Reischer, A.K.	20-30	*
Gray, Eliz. J.	Meggy McIntosh (1st {std}, 8vo, 274p, col frn, pep, NH)	Doubleday/Dor.	1930	DeAngeli, M.	50-75	*
Gray, Eliz. J.	Meredith's Ann (1st {std}, sm8vo, yellow cl, 267p, col frn, pep)	Doubleday/Page	1927	Cutts, G.B.	20-30	*
Gray, Eliz. J.	Penn (1st, 8vo, red cl, 298p, maps, b/w, pep, DJ, NH)	Viking	1938	Whitney, G.G.	45-60	
Gray, Eliz. J.	Sandy (1st, sm8vo, 233p, col frn by...)	Viking	1945	Hallock, R.M.	20-30	*
Gray, Eliz. J.	Tangle Garden (1st {std}, sm8vo, 327p, pep, col frn by...)	Doubleday/Dor.	1928	Cutts, G.B.	20-30	*
Gray, Eliz. J.	Tilly-Tod (1st {std}, sm8vo, 173p, blue cl, col frn, b/w, pep)	Doubleday/Dor.	1929	Frye, M.H.	30-45	*
Gray, Eliz. J.	Young Walter Scott (1st, 8vo, 239p, pep, port. frn, NH)	Viking	1935	Seredy, K.	50-70	*
Gray, Maxwell	Great Refusal (1st, 8vo, brown cl)	Appleton	1906	Armstrong, M.	25-40	*
Gray, P.L.	In a Car of Gold (1st, 8vo, 156p, brown/gilt, 6pl)	Saalfield	1902	Gutman, Bernard	25-40	*
Gray, T.	Elegy in a Country Church Yard (4to, teg, uncut, 8 ticp)	L: Medici	(1931)	Adams, F.	50-65	
Gray, T.	Elegy in a Country Church Yard (1st, 4to, 75p, ibds, 18pl)	Dutton	(1931)	Vassos, J.	65-80	
Gray, W.C.	Musings/Campfire & Wayside (1st, 8vo, 337p, black/gilt)	Revell	1902	Hazenplug, F.	35-50	*
Green, A.K.	Mayor's Wife (1st, sm8vo, 389p, p-o)	Bobbs-Merrill	(1907)	Stephens, A.B.	20-30	
Green, A.K.	Woman in the Alcove (1st, 12mo, beige/gilt, 372p, 5pl)	Bobbs-Merrill	(1906)	Keller, A.I.	20-35	
Green, Allen A.	Good Fairy & the Bunnies (1st, ob4to, ibds, 140p, 11cp)	McClurg	1906	Richardson, F.	200-300	
Green, L.M.	Brother of the Birds (1st AM, lg4to, 123p, purple/gilt, 21 tipl)	McKay	(1929)	DeMonvel, M.B.	120-165	
Green, M.M.	Everybody Eats (1st, lg8vo, [20]p, color)	W.R. Scott	1946	Glannon, E.J.	35-50	*
Green, M.M.	Everybody has a House (1st, lg8vo, spiral-bnd, [20]p, color)	W.R. Scott	1944	Bendick, J.	35-50	*
Green, M.M.	Is it Hard? Is it Easy? (1st, sq8vo, [20]p, color)	W.R. Scott	1948	Bloch, L.	35-50	*
Green, Roger L.	Modern Fairy Stories (1st {std}, 8vo, 270p, 8cp)	Dutton	(1955)	Shepard, E.H.	65-80	*
Greenaway, K.	A Apple Pie (1st, ob4to, green ibds, [44]p, A.E. Red)	L: Routledge	[1886]	Greenaway, K.	180-250	
Greenaway, K.	English Spelling Book (1st, 12mo, grey bds, 108p)	L: Routledge	1885	Greenaway, K.	175-230	
Greenaway, K.	Greenaway's Babies (12mo, linen, 12p, color)	Saalfield	1907	Greenaway, K.	100-135	
Greenaway, K.	K. Greenaway's Alphabet (1st, 48mo, ibds, [32]p, color)	L: Routledge	[1885]	Greenaway, K.	140-180	
Greenaway, K.	K. Greenaway's Book of Games (1st, sm4to, ipcb, 64p, 24cp)	L: Routledge	[1889]	Greenaway, K.	175-220	
Greenaway, K.	Kate Greenaway's Birthday Book (1st, 24mo, beige cl, color)	L: Routledge	[1880]	Greenaway, K.	175-250	
Greenaway, K.	Language of Flowers (1st, 16mo, green ibds, 80p, color)	L: Routledge	[1884]	Greenaway, K.	120-185	
Greenaway, K.	Marigold Garden (1st, 4to, green ibds, 60p, color)	L: Routledge	[1885]	Greenaway, K.	160-220	
Greenaway, K.	Painting Book (1st, lg8vo, 80p, wraps)	L: Routledge	[1884]	Greenaway, K.	200-280	
Greenaway, K.	Queen Victoria's Jubilee Garland (1st, ob8vo, wraps, AEG, col)	L: Routledge	1887	Greenaway, K.	280-320	
Greenaway, K.	Trot's Journey (1st, p-o, 8vo, 79p)	Worthington	(1882)	Greenaway, K.	100-160	
Greenaway, K.	Under the Window (1st, lg8vo, green ibds, 64p, color, cep)	L: Routledge	[1878]	Greenaway, K.	220-300	
Greenaway, K.	Under the Window (sq8vo, green ibds, 63p, color)	McLoughlin	[1879]	Greenaway, K.	200-250	
Greene, G.	Little Horse Bus (1st, sq8vo, 35p, gilt, color, DJ)	L: Parrish	1952	Craigie, D.	200-300	
Greene, G.	Little Steam Roller (1st, sq8vo, 33p, DJ)	L: Parrish	1953	Craigie, D.	200-300	
Greene, G.	Little Train (1st, ob8vo, 42p, DJ)	L: Eyre/Spotts	1946	Craigie, D.	200-300	
Greene, H.P.	Pilot & Other Stories (1st, 8vo, 227p, 8cp)	MacMillan	1916	Ford, H.J.	100-150	
Greene, Jean	Forgetful Elephant (1st {std}, 4to, ipcb, [32]p, color, pep)	McKay	(1945)	Gergely, T.	60-85	*
Greene, Mrs.	Grey House on the Hill (1st, sm8vo, red cl, 205p, 8cp)	L: Nelson	[1903]	Rackham, A.	180-225	
Greene, S.P.M.	Deacon Lysander (1st, 12mo, teg, 223p, red/gilt, 4pl)	Baker/Taylor	(1904)	Peck, H.J.	25-40	

AUTHOR: 58

AUTHOR	TITLE	PUBLISHER	DATE	ARTIST	PRICE	LC
Greene, S.P.M.	Power Lot (1st, 8vo, teg, 396p, 5pl)	Baker/Taylor	1906	Levy, A.O.	20-25	
Greener, Leslie	Moon Ahead (1st, 8vo, green cl, 256p, fp b/w, pep)	Viking	1951	DuBois, W.P.	30-50	*
Greenslet, F.	Quest of the Holy Grail (1st, 4to, 78p, gilt, teg, uncut, 26pl)	Curtis/Cameron	1902	Abbey, E.A.	120-150	
Greer, Blanche	Thunder's Tail (1st, 4to, ipcb, [24]p, 1-color)	Coward	1944	Greer, B.	40-65	
Grego, J.	Cruikshank's Water Colours (1st, 4to, gilt, teg, 326p, 67cp)	L: A&C Black	1903	Cruikshank, G.	90-145	
Gregory, L.F.	Mama Nelly & I (1st, 4to, p-o, 167p, green cl, 5cp)	Stern	1908	Evans, G.	100-140	
Gregory, Lady	Golden Apple (1st, sm8vo, 117p, tan cl, 8cp)	Putnam	1916	Gregory, M.	30-45	*
Grey, Sydney	Story-Land (sq8vo, 111p, ibds, 32 color)	L: R.T.S.	(1884)	Barnes, R.	85-120	
Grey, Zane	Desert Gold (1st, 12mo, 325p, gilt, p-o, 4pl)	Harper	1913	Duer, D.	120-165	*
Grey, Zane	Don: Story of Lion Dog (1st {std}, 12mo, 69p, col frn, 4pl, pep)	Harper	1928	Wiese, K.	45-60	*
Grey, Zane	Riders of the Purple Sage (1st, 12mo, 335p, p-o, 4pl)	Harper	1912	Duer, D.	150-200	
Grey, Zane	Wolf-Tracker (1st, 12mo, orange cl, 98p, col frn, b/w, pep)	Harper	1930	Wiese, K.	50-80	*
Grierson, E.W.	Children's Tales/Scottish Ballads (1st, 4to, 326p, teg, 12cp)	L: A&C Black	1906	Stewart, A.	120-160	*
Griggs, Mary	Yellow Cat (1st, 8vo, 110p, yellow cl, 6 doub pg cp)	L: H. Milford	(1936)	Morton-Sale, J.	65-80	*
Grimalkin	Cats! Cats! Cats! (4to, blue cl, 47p, color)	L: Sands	[1901]	Wain, L.	350-500	
Grimm Bros.	Fairy Tales (1st, 4to, ibds)	Worthington	(1888)	Crane, W.	140-200	
Grimm Bros.	Fairy Tales (1st, sm8vo, 464p, col frn, pep)	L: Freemantle	1900	Rackham, A.	100-170	*
Grimm Bros.	Fairy Tales (1st, lg8vo, 305p, 12 illus)	L: Sands	1902	Hassall, J.	65-80	*
Grimm Bros.	Fairy Tales (1st, 8vo, 511p, cvr by....)	L: Routledge	(1904)	King, J.	100-120	
Grimm Bros.	Fairy Tales (1st, 8vo, 511p, red cl, 4cp)	L: Routledge	(1904)	Wehnert, E.H.	100-120	
Grimm Bros.	Fairy Tales (1st, 8vo, 336p, 20cp)	L: Blackie	1905	Stratton, H.	100-150	
Grimm Bros.	Fairy Tales (1st, 24mo, 127p, ibds, color)	Reilly/Britton	1905	Unknown	60-85	
Grimm Bros.	Fairy Tales (1st, 8vo, 408p)	L: J. Nisbet	1906	Dudley, A.	70-90	*
Grimm Bros.	Fairy Tales (8vo, 340p, ibds, teg, later)	L: Wells/Gard.	1908	Browne, G.	65-80	
Grimm Bros.	Fairy Tales (1st, 8vo, 336p, 16cp)	L: Cassell	1908	Monsell, J.R.	80-120	*
Grimm Bros.	Fairy Tales (1st, 4to, 117p, p-o, brown cl, 6cp)	Stern	1909	Betts, E.F.	180-220	
Grimm Bros.	Fairy Tales (1st, sm4to, 325p, gilt, 40 ticp, pep)	L: Constable	1909	Rackham, A.	750-1000	
Grimm Bros.	Fairy Tales (1st AM, 4to, ibds, gilt, 325p, 40 ticp)	Doubleday/Page	1909	Rackham, A.	480-700	
Grimm Bros.	Fairy Tales (1st, 4to, 255p, 12cp)	L: Richards	1909	Sowerby, M.	100-135	*
Grimm Bros.	Fairy Tales (1st AM, 4to, 136p, blue/gilt, 12cp)	McKay	[1910]	Attwell, M.L.	160-250	
Grimm Bros.	Fairy Tales (1st, 8vo, 356p, gilt, p-o, pep, 4cp)	L: Nister	[1910]	Robinson, C.	190-265	
Grimm Bros.	Fairy Tales (1st AM, 8vo, 255p, 12cp, dep)	Stokes	(1910)	Sowerby, M.	80-120	*
Grimm Bros.	Fairy Tales (1st, 8vo, 331p, cream cl, 12cp)	L: A&C Black	(1911)	Folkard, C.	70-100	*
Grimm Bros.	Fairy Tales (1st, sm sq4to, 275p, p-o, 11cp, 7pl, pep)	Rand/McNally	(1913)	Dunlap, H.	65-80	
Grimm Bros.	Fairy Tales (1st, lg8vo, 346p, 23 ticp)	L: Hodder	(1913)	Pocock, N.	100-165	*
Grimm Bros.	Fairy Tales (1st AM, 4to, blue/gilt, 346p, 23 ticp)	Doran	[1913]	Pocock, N.	80-125	
Grimm Bros.	Fairy Tales (1st, 8vo, 275p, p-o, 12cp)	Rand/McNally	(1913)	Winter, M.	50-70	
Grimm Bros.	Fairy Tales (1st, lg8vo, 419p, p-o, gilt, 11cp)	Cupples	(1914)	Gruelle, J.	170-230	
Grimm Bros.	Fairy Tales (1st, 8vo, 333p)	L: Harrap	1914	Orr, M.S.	65-80	*
Grimm Bros.	Fairy Tales (1st, 8vo, 443p, b/w)	Harper	(1917)	Rhead, L.	35-50	*
Grimm Bros.	Fairy Tales (1st, lg8vo, 308p, p-o, 12cp, pep, SC)	Scribner	1920	Abbott, E.P.	100-160	
Grimm Bros.	Fairy Tales (1st, 8vo, ibds, 6cp)	Donohue	(1920)	Burd, C.M.	30-45	
Grimm Bros.	Fairy Tales (4to, 229p, p-o, 24cp, pep)	Donohue	(1920)	Lee, E.D.	85-120	*
Grimm Bros.	Fairy Tales (1st, sm4to, 344p, 48cp)	L: Ward Lock	1920	Theaker, H.G.	70-100	*
Grimm Bros.	Fairy Tales (1st UK, 8vo, 308p, gilt, 12cp, pep)	L: Hodder	1921	Abbott, E.P.	140-200	
Grimm Bros.	Fairy Tales (1st, 4to, p-o, 367p, 23cp)	Penn	1922	Cramer, Rie	100-145	
Grimm Bros.	Fairy Tales (1st, 8vo, 310p, cp)	Winston	(1922)	Prittie, E.J.	50-75	*
Grimm Bros.	Fairy Tales (1st AM, 8vo, 278p, cp)	Doran	(1924)	Soper, G.	45-60	*
Grimm Bros.	Fairy Tales (sm4to, ibds, 175p, 16cp, reprint)	L: Ward Lock	[1925]	Theaker, H.G.	65-80	
Grimm Bros.	Fairy Tales (1st, lg8vo, 244p, col frn)	Sears	(1926)	Combs, L.	25-40	*
Grimm Bros.	Fairy Tales (8vo, green cl, 337p, 8cp, pep, rprnt)	Garden City	[1930]	Pocock, N.	45-60	
Grimm Bros.	Fairy Tales (lg4to, 128p, gilt, 8cp)	L: Collins	[1931]	Anderson, A.	75-100	*
Grimm Bros.	Fairy Tales (1st, sm4to, 253p, color)	Whitman	(1941)	Young, Goldy	30-45	*
Grimm Bros.	Fairy Tales (1st, 8vo, 363p, 10cp, cep)	Grosset/Dunlap	(1945)	Kredel, F.	60-90	R*
Grimm Bros.	Fairy Tales (1st, 8vo, 382p, color)	World Pub. Co.	(1947)	Becker, M.L.	25-45	*
Grimm Bros.	Favorite Fairy Tales told in Germany (1st {std}, lg8vo, 83p)	Little/Brown	(1959)	Suba, S.	45-60	*
Grimm Bros.	Golden Bird (1st, sm8vo, 116p, color, pep)	Jacobs	(1922)	Smith, Wuanita	50-70	*
Grimm Bros.	Golden Goose (1st, sm8vo, 23p, tan cl, 2-color, pep)	Houghton	1947	Bare, A.E.	50-80	
Grimm Bros.	Goose Girl (1st, 16mo, tan cl, 165p, 3cp, 10 fp b/w, dep)	MacMillan	1929	Nerman, E.R.	45-60	*
Grimm Bros.	Grimm's & Andersen's Fairy Tales (1st, folio, [176]p, col, cep)	L: Blackie	[1906]	Stratton, H.	180-250	R*
Grimm Bros.	Grimm's Animal Stories (1st, 4to, green cl, p-o, 9cp)	Duffield	(1911)	Rae, J.	185-300	
Grimm Bros.	Hansel & Gretel (1st, 12mo, red bds, 58p, p-o, color)	Reilly/Britton	(1908)	Neill, J.R.	70-100	
Grimm Bros.	Hansel & Gretel (folio, shape bk, [12]p, wraps, color)	Stecher	1916	Price, M.E.	40-65	
Grimm Bros.	Hansel & Gretel (1st, lg8vo, blue/gilt, 159p, 20 ticp)	L: Constable	(1920)	Rackham, A.	185-250	
Grimm Bros.	Hansel & Gretel (1st AM, lg8vo, 159p, 20 ticp)	Dutton	(1920)	Rackham, A.	160-240	R
Grimm Bros.	Hansel & Gretel (1st AM, 4to, red cl, p-o, gilt, 310p, 12cp)	Doran	(1925)	Nielsen, K.	250-350	
Grimm Bros.	Hansel & Gretel (folio, wraps, color)	Harter	1932	Peat, F.B.	45-60	
Grimm Bros.	Hansel & Gretel (1st, 12mo, [32]p, color)	Rand/McNally	1937	Livings, B.	30-45	*
Grimm Bros.	Hansel & Gretel (1st, sq12mo, [60]p, color)	McLoughlin	(1943)	Rice, A.	30-50	*
Grimm Bros.	Hansel & Gretel (1st {std}, sm4to, [32]p, color, pep, DJ)	Knopf	1944	Chappell, W.	35-50	
Grimm Bros.	Household Stories (1st, 12mo, 269p, AEG, 11pl, pep)	L: MacMillan	1882	Crane, W.	240-300	
Grimm Bros.	Household Tales (1st, sm8vo, 400p, b/w, pep)	L: Dent	1901	Bell, R.A.	120-200	*

AUTHOR	TITLE	PUBLISHER	DATE	ARTIST	PRICE	LC
Grimm Bros.	Household Tales (1st, sm4to, 303p, yellow cl, 6 fp color)	L: Eyre/Spotts	(1946)	Peake, M.	125-185	
Grimm Bros.	Little Brother/Little Sister (1st AM, 4to, 251p, 12 ticp)	Dodd	(1917)	Rackham, A.	200-265	
Grimm Bros.	Little Brother/Little Sister (1st, 4to, gilt 251p, 12 ticp, pep)	L: Constable	(1917)	Rackham, A.	260-400	
Grimm Bros.	More Tales from Grimm (1st, sm8vo, 257p, blue cl, col frn)	Coward	(1947)	Gag, W.	100-150	R
Grimm Bros.	Robber Bridegroom (1st, lg4to, p-o, 39p, pep, 8 ticp)	L: A&C Black	1922	Owen, H.S.	120-175	
Grimm Bros.	Snow White & Seven Dwarfs (sm4to, 236p, green cl, p-o, 12cp, pep)	Dodd	1913	Falls, C.B.	100-140	
Grimm Bros.	Snow White... (1st, sm8vo, 115p, col frn, cp, pep)	Jacobs	(1922)	Smith, Wuanita	45-60	*
Grimm Bros.	Snow White... (1st, 8vo, green ibds, 43p, CH)	Coward	(1938)	Gag, W.	140-170	
Grimm Bros.	Snowdrop... (1st, lg8vo, 165p, blue/gilt, 20 ticp)	L: Constable	(1920)	Rackham, A.	180-220	
Grimm Bros.	Snowdrop.... (1st AM, lg8vo, 165p, teg, 20 ticp)	Dutton	(1920)	Rackham, A.	150-180	
Grimm Bros.	Tales from Grimm (1st, 8vo, blue cl, 237p, col frn, 6pl)	Coward	(1936)	Gag, W.	140-180	R
Grimm Bros.	Tales from Grimm (1st {std}, lg8vo, 78p, color)	Dutton	1945	Paflin, R.	65-80	*
Grimm Bros.	Three Tales from Grimm (1st AM, sm4to, pink cl, color)	MacMillan	1938	Schlotter, B.	90-140	
Grinnell, G.B.	Jack Among the Indians (1st, sm8vo, 301p, 8pl)	Stokes	(1900)	Deming, E.W.	40-65	
Grinnell, G.B.	Jack in the Rockies (1st, 12mo, 272p, green cl, 8pl)	Stokes	(1904)	Deming, E.W.	30-45	
Grinnell, G.B.	Jack/Young Ranchman (1st, 8vo, 304p, 8pl)	Stokes	1899	Deming, E.W.	45-60	
Grinnell, G.B.	Trail & Camp Fire (1st, 8vo, 353p, b/w)	Forest/Stream	1897	Seton, E.T.	180-250	
Grishina, N.G.	Gresha/Clay Pig (1st, 8vo, p-o, color)	Stokes	1930	Grishina, N.G.	65-80	*
Grishina, N.G.	Magic Squirrel (1st, 8vo, 142p, p-o, 3cp, 7pl)	Stokes	1934	Grishina, N.G.	45-65	*
Grishina, N.G.	Peter-Pea (1st, 8vo, p-o, 95p, cp)	Stokes	1926	Grishina, N.G.	40-65	*
Grishina, N.G.	Sparrow House (1st, 8vo, p-o, 175p, 5cp)	Stokes	1928	Grishina, N.G.	40-65	*
Groesbeck, T.	The Incas (1st, 4to, green/gilt, 71p, teg, uncut, 14pl)	Putnam	1896	Pape, Eric	65-80	*
Gropper, Wm.	Little Tailor (1st, 8vo, brown illus, pep, unpag)	Dodd	1955	Gropper, W.	65-80	*
Groth, Eleanor	Adventures in a Dishpan (1st, sm4to, ibds, 31p, color, pep)	Grosset/Dunlap	(1936)	Groth, M.	25-40	
Grove, F.	Story Without an End (1st, 8vo, 165p, teg, gilt, 8 ticp)	L: Duckworth	(1912)	Pape, F.	65-80	
Grover, E.O.	Kittens & Cats (1st, 8vo, yellow cl, 78p, 39pl, dep)	Houghton	1911	(Photos)	100-180	*
Grover, E.O.	Overall Boys (1st, sq8vo, 123p, pict cl, color pep)	Rand/McNally	(1905)	Corbett, B.L.	70-100	
Grover, E.O.	Overall Boys in Switzerland (1st, 8vo, beige cl, 160p, pep)	Rand/McNally	(1916)	Melcher, B.C.	65-80	
Grover, E.O.	Sonbonnet Babies in Holland (1st, 8vo, map, 150p, color, pep)	Rand/McNally	(1915)	Melcher, B.C.	65-100	
Grover, E.O.	Sunbonnet Babies ABC Book... (1st, 4to, p-o, 64p, pep, color)	Rand/McNally	(1929)	Melcher, B.C.	75-100	
Grover, E.O.	Sunbonnet Babies in Holland (1st, sq8vo, 150p, color, pep)	Rand/McNally	(1915)	Corbett, B.L.	70-100	
Grover, E.O.	Sunbonnet Babies in Italy (1st, 8vo, 187p, color, pep)	Rand/McNally	(1922)	Melcher/McCracken	60-100	*
Grover, E.O.	Sunbonnet Babies in Mother Goose Land (1st, lg8vo, 115p, color)	Rand/McNally	(1927)	Melcher, B.C.	80-120	
Grover, E.O.	Sunbonnet Babies' Book (1st, sq8vo, 106p, color, pep)	Rand/McNally	(1902)	Corbett, B.L.	75-100	
Gruelle, J.	All About Cinderella (1st, 12mo, brown bds, p-o)	Cupples	(1916)	Gruelle, J.	70-100	
Gruelle, J.	All About Mother Goose (sq16mo, 48p, color)	Cupples	(1916)	Gruelle, J.	100-140	*
Gruelle, J.	Beloved Belindy (1st, 8vo, ibds, [95]p, color, pep)	Volland	(1926)	Gruelle, J.	80-125	
Gruelle, J.	Beloved Belindy (8vo, [94]p, color, pep)	Donohue	(1926)	Gruelle, J.	45-60	*
Gruelle, J.	Camel with Wrinkled Knees (8vo, [44]p, color)	McLoughlin	1943	Gruelle, J.	35-50	*
Gruelle, J.	Cheery Scarcrow (1st, 12mo, ibds, [39]p, pep, 6cp)	Volland	(1929)	Gruelle, J.	80-120	
Gruelle, J.	Eddie Elephant (1st, 12mo, ibds, [39]p, color, pep)	Volland	(1921)	Gruelle, J.	80-120	
Gruelle, J.	Friendly Fairies (1st, lg8vo, [86]p, ibds, color, pep)	Volland	(1919)	Gruelle, J.	120-185	
Gruelle, J.	Funny Little Book (1st, 12mo, ibds, [40]p, pep, color)	Volland	(1917)	Gruelle, J.	120-165	
Gruelle, J.	Johnny Mouse & Wishing Stick (1st, lg8vo, ipcb, 89p, color, pep)	Bobbs-Merrill	(1922)	Gruelle, J.	80-120	R
Gruelle, J.	Little Brown Bear (1st, 12mo, ibds, [40]p, color, pep)	Volland	(1920)	Gruelle, J.	70-100	
Gruelle, J.	Little Sunny Stories (1st, 12mo, [40]p, color)	Volland	(1919)	Gruelle, J.	70-120	*
Gruelle, J.	Magical Land of Noom (1st, 4to, ibds, 157p, 12cp, pep)	Volland	(1922)	Gruelle, J.	200-300	
Gruelle, J.	Marcella Stories (1st, 8vo, ibds, 94p, color, pep)	Volland	(1929)	Gruelle, J.	80-120	
Gruelle, J.	My Very Own Fairy Stories (1st, 12mo, ibds, [95]p, color, pep)	Volland	(1917)	Gruelle, J.	130-180	
Gruelle, J.	Orphant Annie Story Book (1st, 8vo, 85p, p-o, color, pep)	Bobbs-Merrill	(1921)	Gruelle, J.	75-120	
Gruelle, J.	Paper Dragon (1st, 8vo, ibds, [96]p, color, pep)	Volland	(1926)	Gruelle, J.	80-125	
Gruelle, J.	Raggedy Andy Goes Sailing (1st, 12mo, [59]p, ipcb, 10 fp color)	McLoughlin	(1941)	Gruelle, J.	45-65	*
Gruelle, J.	Raggedy Andy Stories (1st, lg8vo, ibds, unpag, color, pep)	Volland	(1920)	Gruelle, J.	100-130	
Gruelle, J.	Raggedy Ann & Betsy Bonnet String (1st, 8vo, 95p, ibds, color)	Gruelle Co.	(1943)	Gruelle, J.	45-60	
Gruelle, J.	Raggedy Ann & Golden Butterfly (1st, lg8vo, 95p, ibds, col, cep)	Gruelle Co.	(1940)	Gruelle, J.	50-80	*
Gruelle, J.	Raggedy Ann & Happy Toad (1st, 12mo, ibds, [50]p, color)	McLoughlin	1940	Gruelle, J.	45-65	*
Gruelle, J.	Raggedy Ann & Laughing Brook (1st, 12mo, ibds, [59]p, color)	McLoughlin	1940	Gruelle, J.	45-65	*
Gruelle, J.	Raggedy Ann & Left-Handed Safety Pin (1st, 12mo, 45p, col, pep)	Whitman	(1935)	Gruelle, J.	35-50	*
Gruelle, J.	Raggedy Ann Helps Grandpa Hoppergrass (1st, 12mo, [50]p, color)	McLoughlin	1940	Gruelle, J.	35-50	*
Gruelle, J.	Raggedy Ann Stories (1st, 8vo, ibds, [95]p, color, pep)	Volland	(1918)	Gruelle, J.	100-140	
Gruelle, J.	Raggedy Ann Stories (1st {this pub}, lg8vo, 95p, color)	Gruelle Co.	(1947)	Gruelle, J.	45-65	*
Gruelle, J.	Raggedy Ann in Cookie Land (1st, lg8vo, ibds, 95p, color, pep)	Volland	(1931)	Gruelle, J.	70-120	
Gruelle, J.	Raggedy Ann in Deep Deep Woods (1st, 8vo, ibds, [95]p, col, pep)	Volland	(1930)	Gruelle, J.	80-120	
Gruelle, J.	Raggedy Ann in Magic Book (1st, lg8vo, [91]p, ibds, color)	Gruelle Co.	(1939)	Gruelle, Worth	70-100	
Gruelle, J.	Raggedy Ann in Snow White Castle (1st, 8vo, ibds, 95p, color)	Gruelle Co.	(1946)	Gruelle, Justin	60-80	
Gruelle, J.	Raggedy Ann in the Garden (1st, 12mo, [61]p, ipcb, 10 fp color)	McLoughlin	1940	Gruelle, J.	45-65	*
Gruelle, J.	Raggedy Ann's Alphabet Book (1st, 8vo, [38]p, ibds, color)	Volland	(1925)	Gruelle, J.	90-125	
Gruelle, J.	Raggedy Ann's Lucky Pennies (1st, 8vo, ibds, 94p, color, pep)	Volland	(1932)	Gruelle, J.	70-100	
Gruelle, J.	Raggedy Ann's Magical Wishes (1st, lg8vo, 94p, ibds, color, pep)	Volland	(1928)	Gruelle, J.	100-165	
Gruelle, J.	Raggedy Ann's Wishing Pebble (1st, lg8vo, ibds, unpag, col, pep)	Volland	(1925)	Gruelle, J.	80-120	
Gruelle, J.	Raggedy Ann.../Camel/Wrinkled Knees (8vo, ibds, [95]p, pep, col)	Volland	(1924)	Gruelle, J.	70-100	
Gruelle, J.	Raggedy Ann/Golden Meadow (1st, lg4to, ibds, 56p, 14 color, pep)	Whitman	1935	Gruelle, J.	80-130	

AUTHOR	TITLE	PUBLISHER	DATE	ARTIST	PRICE	LC
Gruelle, J.	Wooden Willie (1st, 8vo, ibds, 95p, color, pep)	Volland	(1927)	Gruelle, J.	90-130	
Gruelle, Justin	Camel with Wrinkled Knees (1st {this pub}, 12mo, ibds, [59]p col)	McLoughlin	(1941)	Gruelle, Justin	45-60	*
Gruelle, Justin	Mother Goose Parade (1st, lg4to, ibds, [31]p, color, pep)	Volland	(1929)	Gruelle, Justin	65-100	
Gugu	Mother Duck's Children (sq4to, 48p, ibds, color)	R.H. Russell	1900	Unknown	150-200	
Guizow, P.	Animals in the Ark (1st, ob8vo, p-o, 31p, 7cp)	Duffield	(1909)	Vimar, A.	65-90	
Gullick, M.E.	Teddy's Year with the Fairies (1st, lg8vo, 176p, ibds, 3cp, pep)	L: R.T.S.	(1920)	Robinson, C.	120-170	*
Gulliver, L.	Gulliver's Bird Book (1st, folio, 103p, color)	Page	1902	Bridgman, L.J.	100-145	
Gulliver, L.	Over the Nonsense Road (1st, 8vo, 234p, orang cl, 8cp)	Appleton	1910	Strothmann, F.	50-80	
Gurko, Leo	Tom Paine, Freedom's Apostle (1st {std}, 8vo, 213p, b/w, NH)	Crowell	(1957)	Kredel, F.	45-60	*
Gury, Jeremy	Wonderful World of Aunt Tuddy (1st {std}, 4to, ibds, color)	Random	(1958)	Knight, H.	45-70	*
Gwynn, S.L.	Fair Hills of Ireland (1st, 8vo, 416p)	L: MacMillan	1906	Thomson, H.	50-70	*
Habberton, J.	Tiger & the Insect (1st, 8vo, ipcb, 235p, uncut, 9pl)	R.H. Russell	1902	Russell, W.	30-45	
Habberton, J.	With the Dream Maker (1st, 8vo, 112p, 5pl)	Jacobs	1898	Claghorn, J.C.	25-40	*
Hadden, C.	Operas of Richard Wagner (1st, 8vo, gilt, teg, 246p, 24cp)	L: Jack	1908	Shaw, B.	60-75	
Hader, B.	Story of Pancho (1st, sm4to, cloth, [56]p, color)	MacMillan	1942	Hader, B.& E.	35-50	
Hader, B.	Whiffy McMann (1st, sq12mo, [56]p, ipcb, 1-color)	NY: OUP	(1933)	Hader, B.	50-70	*
Hader, B.& E.	Banana Tree House (1st, lg8vo, 108p, color, pep)	Coward	(1938)	Hader, B.& E.	45-60	*
Hader, B.& E.	Big City (1st, 4to, cloth, [80]p, fp color, pep)	MacMillan	1947	Hader, B.& E.	40-65	
Hader, B.& E.	Big Snow (1st, 4to, blue cl, [48]p, color, dep, DJ, CM)	MacMillan	1948	Hader, B.& E.	80-120	R
Hader, B.& E.	Billy Butter (1st, ob8vo, cloth, 92p, color, pep, DJ)	MacMillan	1936	Hader, B.& E.	45-70	
Hader, B.& E.	Cat & the Kitten (1st, 8vo, 98p, green cl, color, pep)	MacMillan	1940	Hader, B.& E.	35-50	
Hader, B.& E.	Chuck-a-Luck & his Reindeer (1st, ob8vo, ipcb, 28p, color)	Houghton	1933	Hader, B.& E.	65-90	*
Hader, B.& E.	Cock-a-Doodle-Doo (1st, 4to, [56]p, fp color, CH)	MacMillan	(1939)	Hader, B.& E.	75-110	*
Hader, B.& E.	Cricket (1st, 8vo, p-o, red cl, 160p, color, pep)	MacMillan	1938	Hader, B.& E.	40-60	
Hader, B.& E.	Ding Dong Bell (1st {std}, lg8vo, ipcb, 45p, fp color)	MacMillan	1957	Hader, B.& E.	35-50	*
Hader, B.& E.	Farmer in the Dell (1st, sm4to, green cl, [90]p, color, pep)	MacMillan	1931	Hader, B.& E.	45-60	*
Hader, B.& E.	Friendly Phoebe (1st {std}, 8vo, 45p, color)	MacMillan	1953	Hader, B.& E.	30-50	
Hader, B.& E.	Green & Gold... (1st, 8vo, 48p, color, pep)	MacMillan	1936	Hader, B.& E.	35-50	
Hader, B.& E.	Jamaica Johnny (1st, sq8vo, 90p, green cl, 6 fp color, pep, DJ)	MacMillan	1935	Hader, B.& E.	70-90	
Hader, B.& E.	Lions/Tigers/Elephants Too (1st {std}, ob8vo, ibds, [61]p, col)	Longmans	1930	Hader, B.& E.	65-80	*
Hader, B.& E.	Little Appaloosa (1st {std}, sq4to, [43]p, color)	MacMillan	(1949)	Hader, B.& E.	50-75	
Hader, B.& E.	Little Stone House (1st, sm4to, green cl, [63]p, color)	MacMillan	(1944)	Hader, B.& E.	45-70	*
Hader, B.& E.	Little Town (1st, 4to, [87]p, orang cl, pep, color)	MacMillan	1941	Hader, B.& E.	65-80	*
Hader, B.& E.	Little White Foot (1st {std}, 8vo, blue cl, unpag, color, cep)	MacMillan	1952	Hader, B.& E.	35-50	*
Hader, B.& E.	Midget & Bridget (1st, lg ob8vo, 90p, orang cl, color, color)	MacMillan	1934	Hader, B.& E.	45-60	
Hader, B.& E.	Mighty Hunter (1st, 4to, [49]p, color, pep, DJ, CH)	MacMillan	(1943)	Hader, B.& E.	60-90	
Hader, B.& E.	Mr. Billy's Gun (1st {std}, 4to, unpag, color)	MacMillan	1960	Hader, B.& E.	30-45	*
Hader, B.& E.	Old Woman & Crooked Sixpence (1st, 16mo, [42]p, color)	MacMillan	1928	Hader, B.& E.	50-70	*
Hader, B.& E.	Picture Bk. o/t States (1st {std}, ob folio, color, [60]p, pep)	Harper	1928	Hader, B.& E.	100-160	*
Hader, B.& E.	Picture Book of Travel (1st, 4to, p-o, 63p, color, pep)	MacMillan	1928	Hader, B.& E.	60-85	
Hader, B.& E.	Rainbow's End (1st, sq8vo, 168p, 4 fp color, DJ)	MacMillan	1945	Hader, B.& E.	35-50	
Hader, B.& E.	Reindeer Trail (1st {std}, sm4to, blue cl, unpag, color)	MacMillan	(1959)	Hader, B.& E.	35-50	*
Hader, B.& E.	Spunky (1st, ob8vo, blue cl, 90p, color, pep)	MacMillan	1933	Hader, B.& E.	45-60	*
Hader, B.& E.	Squirrely of Willow Hill (1st {std}, 8vo, [47]p, color, cep)	MacMillan	1950	Hader, B.& E.	40-60	
Hader, B.& E.	Stop, Look & Listen (1st, sq12mo, ipcb, 48p, 2-color, pep)	Longmans	(1936)	Hader, B.& E.	45-70	*
Hader, B.& E.	Story of the Three Bears (1st, sq8vo, ibds, color, pep)	MacMillan	1928	Hader, B.& E.	45-65	*
Hader, B.& E.	The Runaways (1st {std}, 4to, green cl, 38p, color)	MacMillan	1956	Hader, B.& E.	25-40	*
Hader, B.& E.	The Skyrocket (1st, lg8vo, 148p, grey/red, 4 fp color, cep)	MacMillan	1946	Hader, B.& E.	25-40	
Hader, B.& E.	Tommy Thatcher Goes to Sea (1st, 8vo, 95p, 6 fp color, pep)	MacMillan	1937	Hader, B.& E.	35-50	
Hader, B.& E.	Tooky... (1st {std}, ob8vo, ibds, [61]p, color, pep)	Longmans	1931	Hader, B.& E.	65-80	*
Hader, B.& E.	Two Funny Clowns (1st, ob8vo, [52]p, color)	Coward	(1929)	Hader, B.& E.	35-50	
Hader, B.& E.	What'll You Do When You Grow Up? (1st, sq12mo, [63]p, col, pep)	Longmans	1929	Hader, B.& E.	65-80	*
Hader, B.& E.	Wish on the Moon (1st {std}, sq4to, 40p, dep, color)	MacMillan	1954	Hader, B.& E.	25-40	*
Haggard, H.R.	Child of the Storm (1st AM, 8vo, red cl, 335p, 3pl)	NY: Longmans	1913	Michael, A.C.	50-70	*
Haggard, H.R.	Ivory Child (1st, 8vo, 344p, col frn, 3pl)	L: Cassell	(1916)	Michael, A.C.	70-95	
Haggard, H.R.	Mahatma & the Hare (1st, 8vo, 165p, red cl, 12pl)	L: Longmans	1911	Brock/Horton	85-130	
Haggard, H.R.	Montezuma's Daughter (1st, 8vo, green/gilt, uncut, 24pl)	L: Longmans	1893	Greiffenhagen, M.	75-100	
Haggard, H.R.	People of the Mist (1st, 8vo, 343p, blue/gilt, 16pl)	L: Longmans	1894	Layard, A.	70-120	
Haggard, H.R.	Winter Pilgrimmage (1st, 8vo, 335p, 31pl)	L: Longmans	1901	(Photos)	75-100	*
Hahn, E.	Picture Story of China (1st, 4to, 52p, DJ)	Reynal/Hitch.	(1946)	Wiese, K.	40-60	
Haines, Alice C.	Boys (1st, lg ob4to, ibds, 8cp)	Stokes	(1905)	Knipe, E.B.	80-120	
Haines, Alice C.	Girls (1st, lg4to, ipcb, 4cp)	Stokes	(1905)	Knipe, E.B.	80-100	
Haines, Alice C.	Indian Boys & Girls (1st, sm4to, 47p, 4cp)	Stokes	(1906)	Deming, E.W.	65-80	*
Haines, Alice C.	Little Japs at Home (1st, lg4to, ibds, [26]p, 4cp)	Stokes	(1905)	Mar, Alice	170-240	
Haines, Wm.	Slim (1st, 8vo, 414p, 6 fp b/w, pep)	Little/Brown	1934	Lawson, R.	35-50	
Hains, T.J.	Black Barque (1st, 8vo, 322p, 5pl)	Page	1905	Dunton, W.H.	30-45	*
Haldane, W.A.	Dream Bag (1st, 8vo, 131p, 6cp)	Laird & Lee	(1904)	Heath, H.	70-100	*
Halkett, S.	Elf King's Flowers (1st, 4to, 79p, ibds, col frn, pep)	Dutton	(1924)	Pyle, Kath.	35-50	
Hall, A.G.	Nansen (1st, 8vo, 165p, 10pl, pep, NH)	Viking	1940	Artzybasheff, B.	50-70	
Hall, A.N.	Wonder Hill (1st, 4to, p-o, 271p, 10cp, pep)	Rand/McNally	(1914)	Hall, N.	120-165	
Hall, A.V.	Poems of a South African (1st, 8vo, 313p, gilt, 6cp)	L: Longmans	1931	Detmold, E.J.	100-165	
Hall, A.V.	Rainbow Houses for Boys & Girls (1st, 8vo, blue cl, 92p, 6cp)	L: J. Cape	1923	Detmold, E.J.	140-185	

AUTHOR	TITLE	PUBLISHER	DATE	ARTIST	PRICE	LC
Hall, A.W. (ed.)	Icelandic Fairy Tales (1st, 12mo, 317p, gilt, 8pl)	L: Warne	1897	Mason, E.A.	70-110	
Hall, E.C.	Aunt Jane of Kentucky (1st, 12mo, 283p)	Little/Brown	1907	Strong, B.	20-30	
Hall, E.G.	College on Horseback (1st, 12mo, 319p, pep)	Random	1933	Brown, Paul	20-30	*
Hall, G.	Allegretto (1st, sq8vo, beige/gilt, 111p, teg, b/w)	Roberts	1894	Herford, O.	50-80	
Hall, G.	Monkey Shines (lg8vo, ipcb, 10cp)	Wessels	(1904)	Jones, L.F.	25-40	
Hall, Rosalys	Animals to Africa (1st, sq8vo, [27]p, fp color, dep)	Holiday House	(1939)	Eichenberg, F.	45-65	*
Hall, Tom	When Cupid Calls (1st, sm8vo, teg, 116p)	Herrick	1898	McManus, B.	20-35	*
Hall, Tom	When Hearts are Trumps (1st, 12mo, teg, ti. page by)	Stone/Kimball	1894	Bradley, W.	45-60	*
Hall, Wm.	Christmas Pony (1st {std}, sm4to, ipcb, unpag, color)	Knopf	(1948)	Duvoisin, R.	45-65	*
Hall, Wm.	Shoelace Robin (1st, 8vo, ipcb, [20]p, 1-color, pep)	Crowell	1945	Lawson, R.	45-60	*
Hall, Wm.	Walking Hat (1st {std}, 4to, ibds, [32]p, color)	Knopf	(1950)	Wiese, K.	40-65	
Halle, L.J.	Birds Against Men (1st, 8vo, 228p, b/w)	Viking	1938	Ward, L.	35-50	*
Hallock, G.T.	Bird in the Bush (1st, 12mo, 47p, pep)	Dutton	1930	Hallock, G.T.	25-45	*
Hallock, G.T.	Boy Who Was (1st {std}, sm4to, 153p, ipcb, 10cp, pep, NH)	Dutton	(1928)	Wood, H.	45-70	*
Hallock, G.T.	Petersham's Hill (1st, sm8vo, green cl, 132p, 5 fp b/w, pep)	Dutton	(1927)	Wood, H.	30-45	*
Halstead	Story of the Philippines (1st, sm4to, 400p, cvr by...)	(Chicago)	(1898)	Denslow, W.W.	75-100	*
Hamblen, H.E.	Story of a Yankee Boy (1st, 12mo, 339p, 4pl)	Scribner	1898	Edwards, H.C.	25-40	
Hamer, S.H.	Enchanted Wood (1st, 8vo, 100p, 8cp)	L: Duckworth	1909	Rountree, H.	65-80	*
Hamer, S.H.	Enchanted Wood (1st AM, 12mo, 101p, p-o, 8cp)	Estes	[1910]	Rountree, H.	50-70	
Hamer, S.H.	Forest Foundling (1st AM, sm4to, p-o, 109p, 8cp)	Estes	[1909]	Rountree, H.	70-90	R
Hamer, S.H.	Forest Foundling (1st, sm4to, 109p, 8cp)	L: Duckworth	1909	Rountree, H.	80-100	*
Hamer, S.H.	Four Glass Balls (1st, 8vo, 109p, color)	L: Duckworth	1911	Rountree, H.	65-80	*
Hamer, S.H.	Jungle School (1st, 4to, 64p, color)	L: Cassell	1900	Neilson, H.B.	50-70	*
Hamer, S.H.	Magic Wand (lg8vo, 88p, cloth, 12cp)	Estes	[1908]	Rountree, H.	70-100	
Hamer, S.H.	Micky Magee's Menagerie (1st, lg8vo, 100p)	L: Cassell	1897	Neilson, H.B.	45-60	*
Hamer, S.H.	Princess & the Dragon (1st, 8vo, p-o, 78p, 12cp)	L: Duckworth	(1908)	Hassall, J.	60-80	
Hamer, S.H.	Princess & the Dragon (1st AM, 8vo, green cl, p-o, 78p, 12cp)	Estes	[1908]	Hassall, J.	50-70	
Hamer, S.H.	Quackles Junior (1st, sm4to, ibds, 4cp)	L: Cassell	1903	Rountree, H.	40-65	
Hamer, S.H.	Story of the Ring (1st AM, 8vo, 53p, 4cp)	Dodd	1907	Rountree, H.	50-70	*
Hamer, S.H.	Story of the Ring (1st, 8vo, 53p, 4cp)	L: Cassell	1907	Rountree, H.	60-80	*
Hamer, S.H.	The Dolomites (1st, lg8vo, 305p, 16cp)	L: Methuen	1910	Rountree, H.	90-120	*
Hamer, S.H.	The Dolomites (1st AM, sm4to, 305p, 16cp)	NY: J. Lane	1910	Rountree, H.	85-110	*
Hamer, S.H.	Transformations of the Truefitts (1st, 4to, 77p, 4cp)	L: Cassell	1908	Rountree, H.	70-100	*
Hamer, S.H.	Wonderful Isles (1st, sm4to, 107p, 8cp)	L: Duckworth	1908	Rountree, H.	65-80	*
Hamer, S.H.	Wonderful Isles (1st AM, sm4to, p-o, 107p, 8cp)	Estes	[1908]	Rountree, H.	40-60	
Hamill, K.F.	Rhymes for Wee Sweethearts (1st, lg8vo, 181p, p-o, 5cp)	Jacobs	(1906)	Wager-Smith	40-70	*
Hamilton, Eliz.	P-Zoo (1st, ob4to, ipcb, [32]p, 1-color, pep)	Coward	(1945)	Hurd, P.	100-165	*
Hamilton, M.	Kingdoms Curious (1st, 8vo, 248p, tan/gilt, 8pl)	L: Heinemann	1905	Various	120-160	
Hamilton, W.	Sixty Years on the Plains (1st, 8vo, 244p, p-o, 6pl)	Forest/Stream	1905	Russell, C.M.	150-200	
Hamlin, M.S.	Nan in the City (1st, 12mo, 251p, red cl, 3pl)	Roberts	1897	Bridgman, L.J.	30-45	
Hamlin, M.S.	Nan's Chicopee Children (1st, sm8vo, 223p, 5pl)	Little/Brown	1900	Bridgman, L.J.	20-35	*
Hammond, H.	Further Fortunes of Pinkey Perkins (1st, sm8vo, 391p, 22pl)	Century	1906	Varian, G.	30-45	
Hammond, H.	Pinkey Perkins, Just a Boy (1st, 8vo, 327p, b/w, PPPa)	Century	1905	Varian, G.	80-130	*
Hamp, S.F.	Coco Bolo (1st, 12mo, 145p, 12pl)	Badger	1911	Hopp, O.	30-45	*
Hancock, H.I.	Chuggins (1st, sm8vo, 96p, col frn, 4pl)	Altemus	(1904)	Neill, J.R.	30-50	*
Handasyde	Four Gardens (1st AM, 8vo, 161p, purple/gilt, 8cp, pep)	Lippincott	1912	Robinson, C.	80-100	
Handforth, T.	Faraway Meadow (1st {std}, ob4to, [32]p, color, pep)	Doubleday/Dor.	1939	Handforth, T.	50-80	*
Handforth, T.	Mei Li (1st {std}, 4to, [58]p, orange/gilt, b/w, pep, CM)	Doubleday/Dor.	1938	Handforth, T.	70-120	R
Hanemann, H.W.	As Is (1st, 8vo, ipcb, 190p, uncut, b/w)	Harcourt	(1923)	Held, J.	45-60	
Hankins, Maude M.	Daddy Gander (1st, 12mo, ibds, [40]p, color)	Volland	(1928)	Cadie, V.E.	60-80	*
Hankins, Maude M.	Fermentations of Eliza (1st, 12mo, 203p, 4pl)	Crowell	(1915)	Hankins, C.	45-70	*
Hanson, J.M.	Frontier Ballads (1st, 8vo, ibds, 92p, 7cp)	McClurg	1910	Dixon, M.	45-60	
Harben, Wm. N.	Mam' Linda (1st, 12mo, 387p, green/gilt, 8pl)	Harper	1907	Masters, F.B.	30-45	
Harbour, H.	Where Flies the Flag (1st, 12mo, 286p, gilt, 6cp)	L: Collins	[1904]	Rackham, A.	160-220	*
Hardy, A.S.	Aurelie (1st, 8vo, 31p, blue pcb, p-o, 2cp)	Harper	1912	Green, E.S.	45-60	
Hardy, M.E.	Girl of the Forest (1st, lg8vo, p-o, 222p, color)	Whitman	1927	Cady, C.J.	25-40	*
Hardy, M.E.	Little King/Princess True (1st, 8vo, 182p, 4pl)	Rand/McNally	(1912)	Winter, M.	65-80	
Hardy, T.	Jude the Obscure (1st AM, 8vo, 488p)	Harper	1896	Unknown	150	
Hardy, T.	Return of the Native (1st, 8vo, 484p)	L: ^EacMillan	1929	Leighton, C.	45-60	*
Hardy, T.	Selected Poems of... (pcb, teg, frn by...)	L: P.L. Warner	1926	Nicholson, W.	140-200	
Hare, C.	Story of Bayard (1st, 8vo, 256p, color)	L: Dent	1911	Cole, H.	50-70	
Hare, K.	Roads & Vagabonds (1st, lg4to, 189p, red/gilt, 2cp)	L: Eyre/Spotts	(1930)	Aldin, C.	100-140	
Harland, H.	Cardinal's Snuff-Box (1st, 8vo, red/gilt, 263p, teg)	J. Lane	1903	Wilmshurst, G.	25-40	
Harland, M.	When Grandmamma Was 14 (1st, 8vo, 399p, 4pl)	Lothrop	1905	Barry, E.B.	20-30	*
Harland, M.	Where Ghosts Walk (1st, 8vo, green cl, teg, 305p)	Putnam	1898	Armstrong, M.	40-65	
Harmon, M.	How Santa Found the Cobbler's Shop (1st, 4to, [46]p, color, pep)	Suttonhouse	1936	Pogany, W.	90-150	*
Harper, T.A.	His Excellency & Peter (1st {std}, 8vo, 313p, col frn, pep uncut)	Doubleday/Dor.	1930	Wiese, K.	20-30	
Harper, T.A.	Mushroom Boy (1st, 8vo, 215p, 4cp, pep)	Penn	1924	Clark, F.	25-40	
Harper, T.A.	Siberian Gold (1st {std}, 8vo, brown cl, 335p, col frn, pep)	Doubleday/Page	1927	Artzybasheff, B.	30-45	
Harper, Vincent	Mortgage on the Brain (1st, 8vo, brown/gilt, 293p, 4pl)	Doubleday/Page	1905	Macauley, C.R.	25-40	*
Harper, Wilhelmina	Brownie of the Circus (1st {std}, 8vo, 107p, color, pep)	McKay	(1941)	Neville, V.	35-50	*
Harper, Wilhelmina	Flying Hoofs (1st, 8vo, 282p, red cl, 3 dp cp, b/w)	Houghton	1939	Brown, Paul	25-40	*

AUTHOR	TITLE	PUBLISHER	DATE	ARTIST	PRICE	LC
Harper, Wilhelmina	Gunniwolf... (1st {std}, 8vo, green/gilt, 104p, fp color, pep)	McKay	(1936)	Seredy, K.	65-80	*
Harper, Wilhelmina	Harvest Feast (1st {std}, sm8vo, 308p, orange cl, b/w, pep)	Dutton	(1938)	Jones, W.	20-30	*
Harper, Wilhelmina	Selfish Giant... (1st {std}, lg8vo, 86p, 6cp, DJ)	McKay	(1935)	Seredy, K.	50-65	
Harper, Wilhelmina	Uncle Sam's Story Book (1st {std}, lg8vo, 144p, color)	McKay	(1944)	Paull, G.	30-45	*
Harraden, B.	New Book of the Fairies (1st, 8vo, 190p, gilt, 10pl)	L: Griffith	[1891]	Lupton, E.D.	65-80	*
Harraden, B.	Untold Tales of the Past (1st, 8vo, 273p, teg, gilt, b/w)	L: Blackwood	1897	Millar, H.R.	60-75	
Harrington, J.W.	Adventures of Admiral Frog (1st, lg8vo, ipcb, fp 1-color)	R.H. Russell	1902	Price, W.B.	100-180	*
Harris, A.V.	Favorites from Fairyland (1st, 8vo, blue cl, 130p, 6pl)	Harper	1911	Newell, P.	100-165	
Harris, Credo	Where Souls of Men are Calling (1st, 12mo, 298p, col frn by...)	Britton	(1918)	Neill, J.R.	30-50	*
Harris, Isobel	Little Boy Brown (1st, 4to, 44p, tan cl, 1-color, cep)	Lippincott	1949	Francoise, A.	65-90	R*
Harris, J.C.	Aaron in the Wildwoods (1st [1], lg8vo, yellow cl, 270p, 24pl)	Houghton	1897	Herford, O.	130-180	
Harris, J.C.	Bishop & Boogerman (1st, 8vo, green cl, 184p, 8cp)	Doubleday/Page	1909	Harding, C.	80-120	
Harris, J.C.	Children's Uncle Remus (1st, 12mo, 64p)	L: Harrap	1942	Appleton, H.C.	50-65	*
Harris, J.C.	Chronicles/Aunt Minervy Ann (1st [1], 8vo, teg, uncut 210p, 31pl)	Scribner	1899	Frost, A.B.	100-140	R
Harris, J.C.	Daddy Jake the Runaway (1st, 8vo, 145p, cream bds, 19 b/w, cep)	Century	(1889)	Kemble, E.W.	120-165	*
Harris, J.C.	Daddy Jake the Runaway (1st UK, sq4to, 145p, b/w)	L: T.F. Unwin	1890	Kemble, E.W.	100-150	
Harris, J.C.	Free Joe... (1st, 8vo, uncut, 236p, 1st cvr by...)	Scribner	1887	Armstrong, M.	150-200	
Harris, J.C.	Little Mr. Thimblefinger (1st, lg8vo, 230p, ae green, 32pl, cep)	Houghton	1894	Herford, O.	120-165	R
Harris, J.C.	Little Union Scout (1st, 8vo, green/gilt, 181p, 8pl)	McClure	1904	Gibbs, G.	100-140	
Harris, J.C.	Mr. Rabbit at Home (1st, 8vo, 304p, tan cl, ae green, 25pl, cep)	Houghton	1895	Herford, O.	120-150	R
Harris, J.C.	Nights with Uncle Remus (1st, 8vo, 416p, blue/gilt, 20pl, cep)	Bos: Osgood	1883	Church/Beard	200-300	
Harris, J.C.	Nights with Uncle Remus (1st, 8vo, 367p, b/w)	L: A. Moring	[1907]	Shepherd, J.A.	180-250	*
Harris, J.C.	Nights with Uncle Remus (1st, lg8vo, gilt, p-o, 328p, 12cp)	Houghton	(1917)	Winter, M.	100-165	
Harris, J.C.	On the Plantation (1st, 8vo, orange/gilt, 233p, b/w)	Appleton	1892	Kemble, E.W.	140-185	
Harris, J.C.	Plantation Pageants (1st, sq8vo, green cl, 247p, 20pl, cep)	Houghton	1899	Smith, E.B.	140-200	R
Harris, J.C.	Plantation Pageants (1st UK, 12mo, 247p, 20 fp b/w)	L: Constable	1899	Smith, E.B.	80-120	
Harris, J.C.	Shadow Between his Shoulder Blades (1st, 12mo, 132p, 4pl)	Small	(1909)	Harding, G.	85-120	
Harris, J.C.	Story of Aaron (1st, lg8vo, tan/gilt, 198p, 25pl)	Houghton	1896	Herford, O.	130-170	R
Harris, J.C.	Tales of Home Folks/Peace & War (1st, 8vo, 417p, 4pl, cep)	Houghton	1898	Smith, E.B.	80-100	
Harris, J.C.	Tar-Baby (1st, lg8vo, 190p, teg, uncut, 9pl)	Appleton	1904	Frost/Kemble	150-185	
Harris, J.C.	Told by Uncle Remus (1st, 12mo, gilt, p-o, teg, 295p, uncut)	McClure	1905	Various	160-220	
Harris, J.C.	Uncle Remus (1st [1], 8vo, 231p, gilt, 8pl, dep, PPP)	Appleton	1881	Church/Moser	600-900	
Harris, J.C.	Uncle Remus (1st, folio, [111]p, 12cp)	L: Nelson	[1906]	Rountree, H.	350-500	
Harris, J.C.	Uncle Remus & Brer Rabbit (1st, ob4to, [63]p, grn cl, p-o, col)	Stokes	1907	Conde, J.M.	250-350	
Harris, J.C.	Uncle Remus & Little Boy (1st, 8vo, 173p, brown cl, p-o, 8cp)	Small	(1910)	Conde, J.M.	130-180	R
Harris, J.C.	Uncle Remus & his Friends (1st, 8vo, 357p, green cl)	Houghton	1892	Frost, A.B.	120-165	
Harris, J.C.	Uncle Remus Returns (1st, 12mo, 175p, col frn, 7pl)	Houghton	(1918)	Frost/Conde	125-170	R
Harris, J.C.	Uncle Remus Stories (1st, sm folio, ibds, 92p, color, GGB)	Simon/Schuster	(1947)	Disney Studios	70-100	*
Harris, J.C.	Uncle Remus... (sm8vo, 8cp, later)	L: Nelson	[1930]	Rountree, H.	80-120	
Harris, J.C.	Wally Wandroon... (1st, lg8vo, 294p, 31pl)	McClure	1903	Mosley, K.	120-160	
Harris, J.C.	Witch Wolf... (1st {std}, 12mo, 30p, tan pcb, b/w)	Bacon/Brown	1921	Dwiggins, W.A.	130-165	R
Harris, Leila	Blackfellow Bundi... (1st, lg8vo, 63p, pep, p-o, color)	Whitman	1939	Wiese, K.	35-50	
Harris, M.V.	Carnival Time (1st, 4to, p-o, 64p)	Whitman	1938	Wiese, K.	30-45	*
Harris-Burland, J.	Gold Worshipers (1st, 8vo, brown cl, 6pl)	Dillingham	(1906)	Grunwald, C.	40-60	
Harris-Burland, J.	Princess Thora (1st, 8vo, 360p, blue/gilt, 4pl)	Little/Brown	1904	Cuneo, C.	80-130	
Harrison, Ada	Lucy's Village (1st, 8vo, unpag, 8cp)	L: OUP	[1933]	Austin, R.	35-50	*
Harrison, B.	Bric-a-Brac Stories (1st, 8vo, 24 illus, 299p)	Scribner	1885	Crane, W.	125-165	
Harrison, E.O.	Flaming Sword... (1st, 4to, blue/silver, 133p, 4cp)	McClurg	1908	Perkins, L.F.	50-80	
Harrison, E.O.	Glittering Festival (1st, 4to, 176p, gilt, p-o, 4cp)	McClurg	1911	Wilson, C.P.	70-90	
Harrison, E.O.	Moon Princess (1st, 4to, blue cl, 6cp)	McClurg	1905	Perkins, L.F.	70-85	
Harrison, E.O.	Prince Silverwings... (1st, 4to, blue/silver, 313p, 4cp)	McClurg	1902	Perkins, L.F.	65-90	
Harrison, E.O.	Star Fairies (1st, 4to, 128p, 6cp)	McClurg	1903	Perkins, L.F.	70-90	
Harrison, Eliz.	In the Story World (1st, 12mo, 204p, gilt, dep, fp b/w)	M. Bradley	(1931)	Lupprian, H.	25-40	
Harrison, F.	Elfin Song (1st AM, sm4to, teg, gilt, 142p, pep, 12 ticp)	Caldwell	[1912]	Harrison, F.	250-350	
Harrison, F.	Elfin Song (1st, sm4to, teg, 142p, 12 ticp, pep)	L: Blackie	(1912)	Harrison, F.	280-450	
Harrison, F.	In the Fairy Ring (1st, lg4to, 63p, AEG, gilt, pep, 25cp)	L: Blackie	(1908)	Harrison, F.	250-300	
Harrison, F.	Pixy Book (lg8vo, ibds, p-o, 12cp)	L: Blackie	[1918]	Harrison, F.	260-350	
Harrison, F.	Rhyme of a Run... (1st, ob4to, green/gilt, 20 ticp, pep)	L: Blackie	[1907]	Harrison, F.	200-250	
Harrison, G.	Bird Diary (1st, sq8vo, 151p, p-o, 20pl, DJ)	L: Dent	1936	Gibbings, R.	65-80	
Harrison, Mrs. B.	The Carlyles (1st, 8vo, 283, brown cl, cvr by...)	Appleton	1905	Armstrong, M.	25-40	*
Harrison, T.M.	Modern Arms and a Feudal Throne (1st, 8vo, 376p, green cl, 4pl)	Fenno	1904	Starkweather, W.	35-50	*
Harshberger, K.	Zoological Soliloquies (1st, lg4to, ibds, [44]p, color)	A.& C. Boni	1926	Harshberger, K.	90-120	
Hart, Ruby	In the Woods (1st, sm sq4to, wraps, color)	Volland	(1931)	Hart, R.	45-60	*
Harte, Bret	Her Letter (1st, lg8vo, p-o, green/gilt, teg, unpag, col, pep)	Houghton	1905	Keller, A.I.	35-50	
Harte, Bret	Queen of Pirate Isle (1st, sm4to, tan cl, 58p, AEG, color)	L: Chatto	[1886]	Greenaway, K.	200-300	
Harte, Bret	Queen of Pirate Isle (1st AM, sm4to, 58p, AEG, color)	Houghton	1887	Greenaway, K.	180-260	
Harte, Bret	Salomy Jane (1st, 8vo, p-o, blue cl, 78p, color)	Houghton	1910	Fisher, H.	50-75	
Hartland, Edwin	English Fairy & Folk Tales (1st, sm8vo, 282p, AEG, 13pl)	L: W. Scott	1893	Brock, C.E.	65-80	*
Hartog, C.	Barbara's Song Book (ob4to, ibds, p-o, 8cp)	L: G. Allen	1900	Hassall, J.	130-200	
Hartwell (ed.)	Magic Bed (1st, 12mo, 109p, b/w pl)	Altemus	(1906)	Neill, J.R.	60-90	*
Harwood, E.	Old English Sing-Games (1st, ob4to, 56p, ibds, color)	L: Allen	1900	Harwood, E.	120-200	
Haskell, H.	Nadya Makes her Bow (1st, 8vo, green cl, uncut, 349p, b/w)	Dutton	1938	Artzybasheff, B.	30-45	*

AUTHOR	TITLE	PUBLISHER	DATE	ARTIST	PRICE	LC
Haskell, H.E.	O-Heart-San (1st, 8vo, cloth, 6cp)	Page	1908	Fairbanks, F.	20-30	*
Haslewood, C.	Dear Old Nursery Rhymes (1st, 4to, ibds, 48p, 8 chromos)	NY: Warne	[1896]	Haslewood, C.	75-120	
Hauff, Wilhelm	Dwarf Long-Nose (1st, sq8vo, ipcb, 61p, 2-color, pep)	Random	(1960)	Sendak, M.	130-170	R*
Hauff, Wilhelm	Fairy Tales (1st, 8vo, 344p, gilt, pep, 6cp, 12pl)	Nister/Dutton	[1910]	Dixon, A.A.	60-85	*
Hauser, Heinrich	Folding Father (1st, lg ob8vo, ipcb, [24]p, 2-color, pep)	Lothrop	1942	Gergely, T.	45-65	*
Havighurst, Walt.	Song of the Pines (1st {std}, 8vo, 205p, maps, dep, b/w, NH)	Winston	(1949)	Floethe, R.	70-100	*
Hawes, C.B.	Dark Frigate (1st, 8vo, yellow cl, 247p, b/w, PPP, NM)	Atl. Month Pr.	(1923)	Ripley, A.L.	65-95	
Hawes, C.B.	Great Quest (1st, 8vo, 359p, 5pl, NH)	Little/Brown	(1921)	Varian, G.	40-65	*
Hawes, Eliz.	Men Can Take It (1st {std}, 8vo, blue cl, 275p, 14pl)	Random	(1939)	Thurber, J.	65-80	*
Hawkes, Clarence	Field & Forest Friends (1st, 12mo, 207p, pep, 4pl)	F.G. Browne	1913	Copeland, C.	25-40	
Hawkes, Clarence	Silversheene: King of Sled Dogs (1st, 8vo, 234p, 4pl)	M. Bradley	(1924)	Bull, C.L.	20-25	*
Hawkes, Clarence	White Czar... (1st, 8vo, 202p, b/w pl)	M. Bradley	1923	Bull, C.L.	20-25	*
Hawkins, A.H.	Dolly Dialogues (1st, sm sq8vo, 111p, wraps)	(London)	1894	Rackham, A.	175-250	
Hawkins, Q.	Aunt-Sitter (1st, 8vo, 35p, yellow cl, b/w, pep)	Holiday House	(1958)	Turkle, B.	20-30	*
Hawkins, Q.	Don't Run, Apple! (1st, 8vo, ipcb, [36]p, b/w, pep)	Holiday House	(1944)	Cote, P.	25-40	
Hawkins, Q.	Mark, Mark, Shut the Door! (1st, 8vo, [31]p, ipcb, 2-color)	Holiday House	(1947)	Busoni, R.	30-45	*
Hawkins, Q.	Prayers & Graces/Small Children (1st, sq8vo, [32]p, ibds, color)	Grosset/Dunlap	(1941)	DeAngeli, M.	30-50	*
Hawkins, Q.	Puppy for Keeps (1st, 8vo, [28]p, b/w, pep)	Holiday House	(1943)	Wiese, K.	20-25	*
Hawkins, Q.	Too Many Dogs (1st, 8vo, [57]p, olive cl, fp b/w, pep)	Holiday House	(1946)	Wiese, K.	20-25	*
Hawkins, Q.	Who Wants an Apple (1st, 8vo, [39]p, ipcb, b/w, pep)	Holiday House	(1942)	Granahan, L.& D.	20-30	*
Hawksley, E.D.	Charles Dickens Birthday Book (1st, sm4to, cloth, 12pl)	L: Faber	(1948)	Ardizzone, E.	65-80	*
Hawley, H.E.	Story of a Little Tin Soldier (1st, 4to, p-o, 64p, 6cp)	Cupples	(1914)	Low, L.	50-70	
Hawley, H.E.	Timothy Toddlekin (1st, 4to, red cl, 64p, p-o, 6cp, 6pl)	Cupples	(1914)	Low, L.	40-65	
Hawley, H.E.	Woodland Party (1st, 4to, p-o, 49p, 6cp)	Cupples	(1913)	Low, L.	50-70	
Hawthorne, H.	Lure of the Garden (1st, 4to, uncut, 259p, teg, dep, 6cp by...)	Century	1911	Betts, A.W.	120-140	
Hawthorne, H.	Lure of the Garden (1st, 4to, teg, uncut, 259p, dep, 1cp by...)	Century	1911	Parrish, M.	100-140	
Hawthorne, H.	Romantic Rebel (1st {std}, 8vo, 231p, b/w, NH)	Century	(1932)	Berger, W.M.	35-50	*
Hawthorne, J.	Rumpty-Dudget's Tower (1st, 8vo, 72p, col frn)	Stokes	1924	Hood, G.	30-50	*
Hawthorne, N.	Golden Touch (1st, 8vo, orange cl, 61p, fp 2-color, dep)	Whittlesey	(1959)	Galdone, P.	35-50	*
Hawthorne, N.	In Colonial Days (1st, 8vo, 104p, red/gilt, cvr by...)	Page	1906	McManus, B.	20-35	
Hawthorne, N.	In Colonial Days (1st, 8vo, 104p, beige/gilt, cp)	Page	1906	Merrill, F.	20-35	
Hawthorne, N.	Scarlet Letter (1st, 8vo, AEG, blue bds, 8pl)	L: Bliss Sands	1897	Robinson, T.H.	65-90	
Hawthorne, N.	Scarlet Letter (1st, 4to, uncut, 296p, gilt, teg, 31 ticp)	L: Methuen	(1920)	Thomson, H.	160-220	
Hawthorne, N.	Scarlet Letter (1st AM, 4to, ibds, 31 ticp)	Doran	(1920)	Thomson, H.	150-200	
Hawthorne, N.	Snow Image (1st, 16mo, blue cl, 69p, dp color, pep)	MacMillan	1930	Lathrop, D.	40-60	
Hawthorne, N.	Tanglewood Tales (1st, sm4to, 190p, b/w pl)	Houghton	1887	Edwards, G.W.	80-120	*
Hawthorne, N.	Tanglewood Tales (1st UK, 4to, 190p, b/w)	L: Chatto	1888	Edwards, G.W.	85-100	
Hawthorne, N.	Tanglewood Tales (sm8vo, uncut, 12cp)	L: Dent	1903	Fell, H.G.	80-120	
Hawthorne, N.	Tanglewood Tales (16mo, 107p, gilt, p-o, uncut, 8cp)	Jack/Dutton	[1908]	Allen, O.	35-50	*
Hawthorne, N.	Tanglewood Tales (12mo, red cl, 320p, 4cp, 24pl, pep)	L: T.F. Unwin	[1910]	Pogany, W.	100-130	
Hawthorne, N.	Tanglewood Tales (1st, 8vo, 242p, 6cp, pep)	L: G. Allen	1912	Soper, G.	100-140	
Hawthorne, N.	Tanglewood Tales (1st, lg8vo, p-o, gilt, 283p, 10cp, pep)	Rand/McNally	(1913)	Winter, M.	70-120	
Hawthorne, N.	Tanglewood Tales (1st UK, lg8vo, 283p, blue/gilt, 10cp)	L: Duckworth	1914	Winter, M.	70-100	
Hawthorne, N.	Tanglewood Tales (1st, 4to, 245p, gilt, 14 ticp, pep)	L: Hodder	[1919]	Dulac, E.	165-220	
Hawthorne, N.	Tanglewood Tales (1st, lg4to, p-o, 261p, gilt, pep, 10cp)	Penn	(1921)	Sterrett, V.	200-280	
Hawthorne, N.	Wonder Book (1st sm8vo, 201p, color, by...)	Macrae Smith	(1925)	Abbott, E.P.	25-40	
Hawthorne, N.	Wonder Book (1st, lg8vo, 232p, col frn, pep)	Sears	(1928)	Chuse, A.	25-40	*
Hawthorne, N.	Wonder Book (1st, 12mo, 234p, color)	Saalfield	(1929)	Peat, F.B.	30-45	*
Hawthorne, N.	Wonder Book & Tanglewood Tales (1st, 8vo, teg, 421p)	Houghton	1898	Crane/Edwards	200-265	
Hawthorne, N.	Wonder Book... (1st, lg8vo, 210p, cloth, 19cp)	L: McIlvaine	1892	Crane, W.	170-220	
Hawthorne, N.	Wonder Book... (1st AM, 4to, 210p, 19cp)	Houghton	1893	Crane, W.	140-180	
Hawthorne, N.	Wonder Book... (1st, lg8vo, p-o, 125p, 12cp)	Stokes	(1908)	Perkins, L.F.	60-80	
Hawthorne, N.	Wonder Book... (1st AM, lg8vo, gilt, 320p, 4cp, pep)	Jacobs	(1909)	Pogany, W.	100-165	
Hawthorne, N.	Wonder Book... (1st, 8vo, teg, ibds, gilt, 24cp)	L: Dent	1910	Fell, H.G.	80-120	
Hawthorne, N.	Wonder Book... (1st, 4to, p-o, 358p, blue/gilt, pep, 10cp)	Duffield	1910	Parrish, M.	160-200	
Hawthorne, N.	Wonder Book... (1st, lg8vo, p-o, 254p, 8cp)	Rand/McNally	(1913)	Winter, M.	70-110	
Hawthorne, N.	Wonder Book... (1st, 4to, 207p, red/gilt, 16 ticp, 8cp, pep)	L: Hodder	[1922]	Rackham, A.	240-300	
Hawthorne, N.	Wonder Book... (1st AM, 4to, red/gilt, 16 ticp, 8cp)	Doran	[1922]	Rackham, A.	200-260	
Hawthorne, N.	Wonder Book... (1st, 8vo, p-o, gilt, 421p, 4cp)	Houghton	1923	Tenggren, G.	30-50	
Hawthorne, N.	Wonder Book... (1st, 8vo, p-o, 403p, red/gilt, 4cp, pep)	Winston	(1930)	Richardson, F.	35-50	
Hawthorne, N.	Wonder Tales (1st, 12mo, 62p, b/w)	Penn	1908	LeFanu, B.	20-30	*
Hawtrey	Life of St. Mary Magdalen (1st, 12mo, gilt, 285p, cvr by...)	L: J. Lane	1904	King, J.	80-120	
Hay, Helen	Beasts & Birds (1st, lg4to, ibds, 15 fp illus)	R.H. Russell	1900	VerBeck, F.	200-300	
Hay, Helen	Verses/Jock & Joan (1st, lg sq4to, 32p, ibds, 6cp)	Fox Duffield	1905	Harding, C.	170-225	
Hay, I.	Lighter Side of School Life (1st, 8vo, 226p, teg, 12pl)	L: Foulis	(1914)	Baumer, L.	25-40	
Hay, J.	Castilion Days (1st, 8vo, teg, green cl)	Houghton	1903	Pennell, J.	40-60	
Hay, J.	Pike County Ballads (1st, 8vo, p-o, 47p, 6cp, pep)	Houghton	(1912)	Wyeth, N.C.	90-140	
Hay, Timothy	Horses (1st {std}, sm ob4to, [32]p, ipcb, fp b/w)	Harper	(1944)	Wag	70-110	*
Haydon, A.L.	Book of Robin Hood (8vo, green cl, 263p, 12cp)	L: Warne	[1931]	Robinson, T.H.	45-60	
Haydon, A.L.	Stories of King Arthur (1st, 12mo, 94p, p-o, red/gilt, 4cp by)	L: Cassell	1910	Rackham, A.	140-200	*
Hayes, Nancy M.	Book of Games (1st, 8vo, ibds, 144p, p-o, dep, 24cp)	L: Ward Lock	1920	Tarrant, M.	125-200	
Hayman, D. (ed.)	Tales of Longfellow (cloth, cp)	L: R. Tuck	(1910)	Brundage, F.	50-70	*

AUTHOR	TITLE	PUBLISHER	DATE	ARTIST	PRICE	LC
Haynes, L.M.	Over the Rainbow Bridge (1st, sq8vo, [42]p, ibds, color)	Volland	(1920)	Browne, C.L.	65-100	
Hays, M.G.	Kaptin Kiddo & Puppo (ob4to, ibds, color)	L: Chambers	1910	Wiederseim, G.	600-800	
Hays, M.G.	Kiddie Land (1st, 4to, [52]p, tan bds, p-o, 6cp, pep)	Jacobs	(1910)	Wiederseim, G.	250-350	
Hays, M.G.	Kiddie Rhymes (1st, 4to, [52]p, ibds, p-o, 7cp, pep)	Jacobs	(1911)	Wiederseim, G.	250-350	*
Hays, M.G.	Little Pets Book (1st, 4to, ibds, 6cp)	Jacobs	(1911)	Wiederseim, G.	200-300	
Hays, M.G.	Rag Animals ABC (lg4to, stiff wrps, 30p, color)	Donohue	(1913)	Hays, M.G.	150-200	*
Hays, M.G.	Rosy Childhood (1st, 4to, ibds, 6 fp color, pep)	Jacobs	(1911)	Wiederseim, G.	160-240	*
Hays, M.G.	Vegetable Verselets (1st, 12mo, 60p, ibds, 20 fp 1-color)	Lippincott	1911	Wiederseim, G.	150-220	R*
Hazard, R.H.	House on Stilts (1st, 8vo, red cl, 346p, 4pl)	Dillingham	(1910)	Lemon, J.A.	25-40	
Hazelton, Mary	Our Little African Cousin (1st, 12mo, 98p, b/w)	L.C. Page	1902	Bridgman, L.J.	25-40	
Headland, I.T.	Chinese Boy & Girl (1st, 8vo, ibds, 176p)	Revell	(1901)	(Photos)	85-120	
Headland, I.T.	Chinese Mother Goose Rhymes (1st, 8vo, 160p, ibds)	Revell	(1900)	(Photos)	85-120	
Heal, Edith	Dogie Boy (1st, sm4to, 79p, brown cl, pep, 11 fp color)	Whitman	1943	Sperry, A.	30-45	
Hearn, L.	Kwaidan.... (1st, 12mo, 240p, teg, uncut, designs by..)	Houghton	1904	Rogers, B.	100-120	
Hearn, L.	Romance of the Milky Way (1st, 12mo, 209p, t.e. yellow)	Houghton	1905	Rogers, B.	85-100	
Heath, J.F.	Built-Upon House (1st, lg8vo, 126p, p-o, color)	Whitman	(1929)	Dotterer, L.J.	30-45	*
Heath, J.F.	Mooky & Tooky (1st, lg8vo, ipcb, [45]p, 1-color, pep)	Howell/Soskin	(1946)	Bare, A.E.	35-50	*
Heaton, J.L.	Book of Lies (1st, 12mo, black/silver, 175p, b/w)	NY: Morse	1896	VerBeck, F.	70-100	*
Hecht, Ben	Cat/Jumped Out of the Story (1st {std}, 8vo, bds, p-o, pep, col)	Winston	(1947)	Bacon, P.	35-50	*
Heilberg, N.	White-Ear & Peter (1st, 8vo, 222p, red/gilt, 16cp)	L: MacMillan	1912	Aldin, C.	100-130	
Heine, H.	Atta Troll (1st, 12mo, 185p, grey bds, gilt, pep, b/w)	L: Sidgwick	1913	Pogany, W.	120-165	
Heine, H.	Atta Troll (1st AM, 12mo, 185p, bds, gilt, 3pl)	Huebsch	(1914)	Pogany, W.	100-130	
Held, John	Danny Decoy (1st, sq8vo, ibds, [83]p, 2-color, pep)	A.S. Barnes	(1942)	Held, J.	70-100	*
Helle, A.	Big Beasts & Little Beasts (1st, ob12mo, p-o, 80p, 20cp)	Stokes	1924	Helle, A.	120-150	
Hellman, Sam	Low Bridge & Punk Pungs (1st, 12mo, 111p, b/w pl)	Little/Brown	1924	Sarg, T.	30-45	*
Helm, C.	Cecily (1st, 4to, p-o, 298p, 8cp, pep)	Lippincott	(1924)	Kay, G.A.	75-120	
Henderson, B.	Wonder Tales of Ancient Wales (1st, 8vo, gilt, 166p, teg, 8cp)	L: P. Allan	(1921)	Williamson, D.	80-130	*
Henderson, D.	Danny the Dream Man (1st, sq8vo, ibds, [48]p, color, pep)	Volland	(1928)	Henderson, D.	70-100	
Henderson, G.	Ring of the Nibelung (1st, 8vo, 218p, beige cl, col frn, b/w)	Knopf	1932	Tenggren, G.	40-65	
Henderson, J.	Jamaica (1st, 8vo, blue/gilt, teg, 24cp)	L: A&C Black	1906	Forrest, A.S.	70-120	
Henderson, L.L.	Resolute (1st, sq8vo, 64p, ipcb, fp b/w)	McKay	(1940)	Beistle, M.A.	35-60	*
Henderson, L.R.	Magic Aeroplane (1st, lg4to, ibds, 96p, 6cp)	Reilly/Britton	(1911)	Nelson, E.A.	160-220	
Hendrich, Paula	Trudy's First Day at Camp (1st, sm4to, yellow cl, unpag, color)	Lothrop	(1959)	Adams, A.	45-60	*
Hendry, Hamish	Holidays & Happy Days (1st, 8vo, teg, 120p, 24cp)	L: Richards	1901	Mason, E.F.	85-130	
Hendry, Hamish	Red Apple & Silver Bells (1st, 8vo, 151p, AEG, red/silver, 20pl)	L: Blackie	[1897]	Woodward, A.B.	50-75	*
Henius, F.	Stories from the Americas (1st, lg8vo, orang cl, 115p, fp b/w)	Scribner	1944	Politi, L.	45-60	*
Henry, A.H.	By Order of the Prophet (1st, 8vo, orang cl, 402p, 5pl)	Revell	1902	Paxon, E.S.	25-40	
Henry, M.	Born to Trot (1st {A}, lg8vo, 219p, gilt, pep, color)	Rand/McNally	(1950)	Dennis, W.	30-50	
Henry, M.	Boy & a Dog (1st, sm4to, [42]p, 2-color, pep)	Wilcox/Follett	1944	Thorne, D.	30-50	*
Henry, M.	Brighty of the Grand Canyon (1st {A}, 4to, 224p, pep, 4 fp col)	Rand/McNally	(1953)	Dennis, W.	30-45	*
Henry, M.	Cinnabar: One O'Clock Fox (1st {A}, lg8vo, 154p, pep)	Rand/McNally	(1956)	Dennis, W.	30-45	
Henry, M.	Dilly-Dally Sally (1st, sq4to, ipcb, [16]p, pep, color)	Saalfield	1940	Blackwood, G.R.	45-60	*
Henry, M.	Gaudenzia (1st {A}, sm4to, 237p, red/gilt, 7 fp color, pep)	Rand/McNally	(1960)	Ward, L.	30-50	*
Henry, M.	Justin Morgan had a Horse (1st, 4to, [89], pep, NH)	Wilcox/Follett	1945	Dennis, W.	50-70	*
Henry, M.	King of the Wind (1st {A}, 4to, red cl, 175p, color, pep, NM)	Rand/McNally	(1948)	Dennis, W.	50-85	R
Henry, M.	Little Fellow (1st, 4to, [64]p, color)	Winston	(1945)	Thorne, D.	35-50	
Henry, M.	Misty of Chincoteague (1st {A}, sm4to, 173p, color, pep, DJ, NH)	Rand/McNally	(1947)	Dennis, W.	50-80	
Henry, M.	Sea Star: Orphan of Chincoteague (1st, lg8vo, 172p, color, pep)	Rand/McNally	(1949)	Dennis, W.	30-50	
Henry, M.	Wagging Tails (1st {A}, 4to, brown cl, 64p, 24 fp color, pep)	Rand/McNally	(1955)	Dennis, W.	35-50	*
Henry, O.	Gift of the Magi (1st, blue bds, b/w, DJ)	L: Harrap	1939	Gooden, S.	65-90	
Henry, O.	Trimmed Lamp (1st, 12mo, 260p, frn by...)	McClure	1907	Stephens, A.B.	65-80	
Henty, G.A.	Treasure of the Incas (1st, 8vo, green/gilt, 8pl)	L: Blackie	1903	Paget, W.	35-50	*
Henty, G.A.	Yuletide Yarns (1st AM, sm8vo, beige cl, 370p, teg)	Longmans	1899	Unknown	45-60	*
Herben, B.S.	Jack O'Health, Peg O'Joy (1st, 12mo, 39p, 10cp)	Scribner	(1921)	Richardson, F.	65-85	
Herbertson, A.	Be-Wee the Gnome... (1st AM, 8vo, p-o, ibds, 116p, pep, 20cp)	Cupples	(1921)	Govey, L.	80-125	
Herbertson, A.	Book of Happy Gnomes (1st, 8vo, 191p)	L: H. Milford	(1924)	Govey, L.	65-80	*
Herbertson, A.	Busy Broom (1st, 4to, unpag, color)	L: Cassell	[1910]	Monsell, J.R.	65-80	
Herbertson, A.	Dolly Book (1st, 4to, 62p)	L: H. Milford	1920	Govey, L.	65-80	*
Herbertson, A.	Heroic Legends (1st, 8vo, 253p, AEG, gilt, 16cp, cep)	L: Blackie	1908	Stratton, H.	100-145	
Herbertson, A.	Lucy-Mary (1st, 8vo, 203p)	L: Blackie	1910	Tarrant, M.	45-60	*
Herbertson, A.	Sing Song Stories (4to, ibds, 111p, p-o, 3cp by...)	L: H. Milford	[1922]	Wright, A.	85-130	
Herbertson, A.	Teddy & Trots in Wonderland (1st, 8vo, 254p, 27 illus)	L: Ward Lock	1910	Maybank, T.	70-100	*
Herbertson, A.	Tinkler Johnny (sm8vo, green cl, p-o, 4cp)	L: Blackie	[1915]	Harrison, F.	35-50	
Herford, B.	Monologues (1st, 8vo, 139p, grey cl, 18 b/w)	Scribner	1908	Herford, O.	45-65	
Herford, O.	Alphabet of Celebrities (1st, lg 8vo, [58]p, ibds, 26 fp b/w)	Small	1899	Herford, O.	100-160	
Herford, O.	Artful Antics (1st, sq8vo, tan cl, 100p, b/w)	Century	1894	Herford, O.	70-100	*
Herford, O.	Artful Antics (1st UK, sm8vo, yellow cl, 100p, b/w)	L: Gay & Bird	1894	Herford, O.	50-75	
Herford, O.	Astonishing Tale/Pen & Ink Puppet (1st, ob4to, [62]p, ibds)	Scribner	1907	Herford, O.	65-80	*
Herford, O.	Bashful Earthquake (1st, 12mo, teg, uncut, ipcb, 126p)	Scribner	1898	Herford, O.	45-70	R
Herford, O.	Child's Primer/Natural History (1st UK, sq4to, b/w)	L: J. Lane	1900	Herford, O.	65-90	
Herford, O.	Confessions of a Caricaturist (1st, 12mo, 65p, 9pl)	Scribner	1917	Herford, O.	30-45	*
Herford, O.	Cupid's Almanac (1st, narrow 4to, [58]p, ipcb, col frn, pep)	Houghton	1908	Clay/Herford	35-50	*

AUTHOR	TITLE	PUBLISHER	DATE	ARTIST	PRICE	LC
Herford, O.	Cupid's Almanac (1st, narrow 4to, [58]p, ipcb, col frn, pep)	Houghton	1908	Herford/Clay	35-50	*
Herford, O.	Deb's Dictionary (1st, 8vo, [151]p, cloth, b/w)	Lippincott	1931	Herford, O.	30-45	
Herford, O.	Excuse it Please (1st {std}, sm8vo, 171p, ipcb, DJ)	Lippincott	(1929)	Herford, O.	30-45	
Herford, O.	Happy Days (1st, 16mo, ipcb, [44]p, color, pep)	Kennerley	1917	Clay/Herford	30-45	
Herford, O.	Happy Days (1st, 16mo, ipcb, [44]p, color, pep)	Kennerley	1917	Herford/Clay	30-45	
Herford, O.	Herford Aesop (1st, 8vo, 90p, col frn)	Ginn & Co.	(1921)	Herford, O.	65-80	
Herford, O.	Kitten's Garden of Verses (1st, 12mo, 59p, 25pl)	Scribner	1911	Herford, O.	50-70	
Herford, O.	Laughing Willow (1st, sm8vo, ipcb, 134p, col frn)	Doran	(1918)	Herford, O.	35-50	*
Herford, O.	More Animals (1st, sq8vo, ibds, 99p, 24pl)	Scribner	1901	Herford, O.	80-100	R
Herford, O.	Mythological Zoo (1st, sq8vo, ibds, 45p, 22pl)	Scribner	1912	Herford, O.	50-70	
Herford, O.	Overheard in a Garden (1st, sm8vo, ibds, teg, 104p, col frn)	Scribner	1900	Herford, O.	60-85	
Herford, O.	Pen & Inklings (1st [1st bk.], 12mo, tan cl, b/w)	L: G. Allen	1893	Herford, O.	80-100	
Herford, O.	Peter Pan Alphabet (1st, sq8vo, ibds, [57]p, fp b/w)	Scribner	1907	Herford, O.	85-120	*
Herford, O.	Rubaiyat of a Persian Kitten (1st, sm8vo, [76]p, ibds, 35pl)	Scribner	1904	Herford, O.	40-70	
Herford, O.	Sea Legs (1st, ob12mo, [55]p, ibds, p-o, 23 fp 2-color)	Lippincott	(1931)	Herford, O.	40-60	
Herford, O.	Simple Jography (1st, 8vo, ibds, [100]p, b/w)	Luce	(1908)	Herford, O.	30-45	*
Herford, O.	Smoker's Yearbook (1st, lg8vo, [28]p, 12cp)	Moffat	1908	Collins, S.	65-90	*
Herford, O.	This Giddy Globe (1st, 12mo, 138p, tan cl, b/w)	Doran	(1919)	Herford, O.	20-30	
Herr, Charlotte	Unselfish Pig (1st, 12mo, ibds, color)	Volland	(1913)	Beem, F.	40-65	*
Herr, Charlotte	Wise Mamma Goose (1st, 12mo, ibds, 21p, color)	Volland	(1913)	Beem, F.	40-60	*
Herr, Charoltte	Brownie Robinson Crusoe (1st, 8vo, 163p, p-o, 8cp)	Dodd	1920	White, O.A.	30-45	*
Herrick, F.H.	Home Life/Wild Birds (1st, sm4to, 148p, brown/gilt)	Putnam	1901	Armstrong, M.	45-70	
Herrick, R.	Flower Poems (8vo, 93p, p-o, teg, 12cp)	L: Routledge	[n.d.]	Castle, F.	50-80	
Herrick, R.	Herrick's Poems (lg4to, 188p, green cl)	Harper	1899	Abbey, E.A.	100-135	
Herrick, R.	Love's Dilemmas (1st, 8vo, 193p, cvr by...)	H. Stone	1898	Bradley, W.	85-100	
Herrick, R.	Poetry of... (4to, uncut, dec cl)	Harper	1899	Abbey, E.A.	100-150	
Herzog, E.	Tinkers of Turntable (1st, 8vo, grey cl, 125p, b/w)	W.R. Scott	(1940)	Suba, S.	30-45	*
Heward, C.	Ameliaranne & Green Umbrella (1st AM, 8vo, 109p, p-o, col, pep)	Jacobs	(1920)	Pearse, S.B.	60-80	
Heward, C.	Ameliaranne & the Monkey (1st AM, 8vo, p-o, [63]p, color, pep)	McKay	(1929)	Pearse, S.B.	50-65	
Heward, C.	Ameliaranne Camps Out (1st, 4to, ibds, unpag)	L: Harrap	(1939)	Pearse, S.B.	50-75	
Heward, C.	Ameliaranne Cinema Star (1st, 12mo, tan bds, p-o, unpag)	L: Harrap	(1929)	Pearse, S.B.	50-75	
Heward, C.	Ameliaranne Gives a Party (1st, 8vo, ibds, pep, 28 color)	L: Harrap	(1938)	Pearse, S.B.	50-75	
Heward, C.	Ameliaranne Goes Touring (1st, 4to, ibds, unpag, pep, color)	L: Harrap	(1941)	Pearse, S.B.	50-75	
Heward, C.	Ameliaranne Keeps Shop (1st, 8vo, ibds, [128]p, color, pep)	McKay	(1928)	Pearse, S.B.	45-60	
Heward, C.	Ameliaranne at the Farm (1st, 8vo, [58]p, ibds, pep)	L: Harrap	1937	Pearse, S.B.	45-60	
Heward, C.	Ameliaranne at the Farm (1st AM, 8vo, [58]p, p-o, color)	McKay	(1937)	Pearse, S.B.	45-70	
Heward, C.	Grandpa & the Tiger (1st, 8vo, 109p, orange cl, p-o, color pep)	Jacobs	(1924)	Govey, L.	55-80	*
Heward, C.	Pillow Stories (1st, sm8vo, 150p, b/w)	L: Richards	1901	Bradley, G.M.	85-100	
Heward, C.	Twins & Tabiffa (1st, 8vo, 121p, p-o, blue cl, color, pep)	Jacobs	(1923)	Pearse, S.B.	40-60	
Hewes, A.D.	Boy of the Lost Crusade (1st, 8vo, p-o, 279p, gilt, 4cp, pep)	Houghton	1923	Tenggren, G.	30-50	
Hewes, A.D.	Codfish Musket (1st {std}, 8vo, 390p, pep, NH)	Doubleday/Dor.	1936	Sperry, A.	40-65	
Hewes, A.D.	Glory of the Seas (1st {std}, 8vo, 315p, blue cl, col frn, NH)	Knopf	1933	Wyeth, N.C.	35-50	*
Hewes, A.D.	Spice & Devil's Cave (1st, sm8vo, 331p, gilt, pep, DJ, NH)	Knopf	1930	Ward, L.	60-80	
Hewes, A.D.	Sword of Roland Arnot (1st, 8vo, red cl, 206p, 4cp, DJ)	Houghton	1939	Strayer, P.	30-45	
Hewes, A.D.	Swords on the Sea (1st, sm8vo, 272p, col frn, pep, 7pl)	Knopf	1928	Bloch, L.	20-30	*
Hewlett, M.	Forest Lovers (1st AM, lg8vo, 384p, teg, uncut, 16 ticp)	Scribner	1909	Hartrick, A.S.	40-65	
Hewlett, M.	Masque of Dead Florentines (1st, ob8vo, uncut, teg, 51p, 4pl)	L: J.M. Dent	1895	Batten, J.D.	75-100	
Hewlett, P.	Grandmother's Fairy Tales (1st, 4to, 116p, 8cp)	L: Heinemann	1915	Lalan, M.	100-140	
Heyward, DuBose	Country Bunny & Little Gold Shoes (1st, sm4to, [48]p, color)	Houghton	1939	Flack, M.	80-120	*
Hiatt, C.	Picture Posters (1st, 8vo, 367p, 151pl)	L: G. Bell	1895	Various	350-450	
Hichens, R.	Flames (1st, 8vo, 523p, pcb, cvr by...)	H. Stone	1897	Kimbrough, F.R.	45-60	
Hichens, R.	Holy Land (1st, 4to, 302p, uncut, teg, 18cp)	Century	1910	Guerin, J.	70-85	
Hichens, R.	Near East (1st, 4to, teg, blue/gilt, 50pl)	Century	1913	Guerin, J.	65-80	
Hicks, G.	One of Us (1st, 8vo, [64]p, 30 b/w illus, DJ)	Equinox	(1935)	Ward, L.	50-70	
Higgins, A.C.	Dream Blocks (1st, lg8vo, p-o, 47p, beige cl, 15cp, pep)	Duffield	1908	Smith, J.W.	300-450	
Higgins, Alice	Runaway Rhymes (1st, 8vo, 127p, red bds, gilt, pep, 14 fp col)	Volland	(1931)	Lamb, T.	65-80	
Higgins, V.M.	Endless Story (1st, 8vo, 71p, color, pep)	Whitman	(1916)	Higgins, V.M.	45-65	*
Higgins, V.M.	Magic Circus (8vo, ibds, doll bk.)	Chi: Stanton	1918	Higgins, V.M.	40-65	
Higgins, V.M.	Real Story of a Real Doll (1st, 8vo, 116p, pep, 4cp)	McBride	(1929)	Higgins, V.M.	30-45	*
Higgins, V.M.	Woodcutter's Son (1st, lg8vo, 68p, 4cp)	Whitman	1917	Higgins, V.M.	35-50	
Hill, F.T.	Washington: Man of Action (1st, lg4to, green/gilt, 329p, 27cp)	Appleton	(1914)	Job	135-200	
Hill, W.E.	Among Us Cats (1st {std}, lg8vo, p-o, 128p, col frn, 61pl, pep)	Harper	1926	Hill, W.E.	70-90	*
Hill, Wm.	Jackie Boy in Rainbowland (1st, 8vo, p-o, 84p, color)	Rand/McNally	(1911)	Cory, F.	70-90	
Hinkle, T.C.	Dr. Rabbit & Ki-Yi Coyote (1st, sm8vo, 106p, yellow bds, color)	Rand/McNally	(1918)	Winter, M.	40-65	*
Hinkle, T.C.	Snowy Tail: Champion Jack Rabbit (1st, 12mo, ibds, 64p)	Rand/McNally	(1921)	Winter, M.	40-65	*
Hinkson, H.A.	King's Liege (1st, 8vo, 224p, blue cl, col frn, 3pl)	L: Blackie	1910	Dixon, A.A.	45-60	*
Hinkson, H.A.	Splendid Knight (1st, 8vo, 262p, grey cl, b/w)	L: F.V. White	1905	Wood, Lawson	75-120	*
Hinkson, K.T.	Cuckoo Songs (1st, 12mo, brown/gilt, cvr & ti page by....)	L: Matthews	1894	Housman, L.	100-135	
Hoban, Russell	Bedtime for Frances (1st, 4to, unpag)	Harper	(1960)	Williams, Garth	65-80	*
Hobart, G.V.	Li'l Verses for Li'l Fellers (1st, 4to, 121p, 7cp, 8pl)	R.H. Russell	1903	Mars/Squire	80-130	*
Hobbes, J.O.	Dream & the Business (1st, 8vo, blue cl, teg, cvr by...)	L: T.F. Unwin	1906	Beardsley, A.	75-120	
Hobbes, J.O.	School for Saints (1st, 8vo, 405p, grey/gilt, cvr by...)	Stokes	(1897)	Bradley, W.	65-85	

AUTHOR	TITLE	PUBLISHER	DATE	ARTIST	PRICE	LC
Hodder, W.R.	Daughter of the Dawn (1st, 8vo, green cl, 333p, 12pl)	L: Jarrold	1903	Piffard, H.	45-65	*
Hoffman, A.S.	Book of the Sagas (1st, 8vo, 320p, gilt, 6cp)	L: Nister	[1913]	Browne, G.	85-120	
Hoffman, A.S.	Children's Shakespeare (1st, sq8vo, 472p, 21cp)	L: Dent	1911	Folkard, C.	80-120	
Hoffman, H.	Nutcracker & Mouse King (sm4to, 123p, orang cl, p-o, color)	Whitman	(1930)	Brock, Emma	45-60	*
Hoffman, H.	Slovenly Peter (1st {std}, lg8vo, ibds, [30]p, color)	Harper	1935	Kredel, F.	100-140	*
Hoffmann, Eleanor	Cat of Paris (1st, sm8vo, 145p, blue cl, b/w, pep)	Stokes	1940	Gay, Z.	25-40	*
Hoffmann, Eleanor	Lion of Barbary (1st, 8vo, 217p, blue cl, b/w)	Holiday House	(1946)	Coggins, J.	20-30	*
Hoffmann, Eleanor	Mischief in Fez (1st, lg8vo, 109p, blue cl, 8 fp 1-color, dep)	Holiday House	(1943)	Eichenberg, F.	45-70	*
Hofman, Caroline	All Around the Sun-Dial (1st, 4to, 79p, col frn)	Dutton	(1917)	Elmer, R.R.	25-40	*
Hofman, Caroline	Little Red Balloon (1st, 12mo, ibds, [39]p, color)	Volland	(1918)	Elmer, R.R.	50-75	
Hofman, Caroline	Princess Finds a Playmate (1st, 12mo, ibds, unpag, color)	Volland	(1918)	Elmer, R.R.	50-90	*
Hofman, Caroline	Wise Gray Cat (1st, 12mo, unpag, color)	Volland	(1918)	Elmer, R.R.	70-100	*
Hogan, Erlin	Four Funny Men (1st {std}, 12mo, ibds, [55]p, 1-color, pep)	Dutton	(1939)	Hogan, I.	30-50	*
Hogan, Inez	Bear Twins (1st {std}, sm8vo, [45]p, ipcb, 1-color, pep)	Dutton	(1935)	Hogan, I.	35-50	*
Hogan, Inez	Big Ones (1st {std}, 4to, yellow cl, unpag, b/w, pep)	Dutton	(1957)	Hogan, I.	40-60	*
Hogan, Inez	Elephant Twins (1st {std}, 8vo, ipcb, [45]p, pep)	Dutton	(1936)	Hogan, I.	35-50	*
Hogan, Inez	Giraffe Twins (1st {std}, 8vo, [48]p, ipcb, 1-color, pep)	Dutton	(1948)	Hogan, I.	30-50	*
Hogan, Inez	Kangaroo Twins (1st {std}, 8vo, [49]p, ibds, color, pep)	Dutton	(1938)	Hogan, I.	50-70	
Hogan, Inez	Little Black & White Lamb (1st, sm8vo, [103]p, color)	Macrae-Smith	(1927)	Hogan, I.	50-70	*
Hogan, Inez	Little Toy Airplane (1st, ob8vo, [57]p, color, pep)	Macrae-Smith	(1930)	Hogan, I.	55-80	*
Hogan, Inez	Monkey Twins, They Saw it All (1st {std}, sm8vo, ipcb, b/w, pep)	Dutton	(1943)	Hogan, I.	30-50	
Hogan, Inez	Mule Twins (1st {std}, 8vo, ibds, [49]p, b/w, pep)	Dutton	(1939)	Hogan, I.	50-80	
Hogan, Inez	Nappy Chooses a Pet (1st {std}, 8vo, [48]p, ipcb, b/w, pep)	Dutton	1946	Hogan, I.	30-45	*
Hogan, Inez	Nicodemus & his Little Sister (1st {std} 12mo, ibds, [47]p, col)	Dutton	1932	Hogan, I.	70-100	
Hogan, Inez	Nicodemus & the Goose (1st {std}, 8vo, ibds, [47]p, color pep)	Dutton	(1945)	Hogan, I.	50-65	
Hogan, Inez	Nicodemus & the Houn' Dog (1st {std}, 8vo, [52]p, ibds, color)	Dutton	(1933)	Hogan, I.	40-65	
Hogan, Inez	Nicodemus Laughs (1st {std}, 8vo, ibds, [40]p, color, pep)	Dutton	(1941)	Hogan, I.	50-65	
Hogan, Inez	Runaway Toys (1st {std}, lg8vo, [40]p, pep, color)	Dutton	(1950)	Hogan, I.	30-50	
Hogan, Inez	Sandy, Skip & Man in the Moon (1st, sm8vo, gilt, 93p, color)	Macrae-Smith	(1928)	Hogan, I.	45-65	*
Hogan, Inez	Twin Kids (1st, 8vo, 50p, ipcb, 1-color, pep)	Dutton	(1937)	Hogan, I.	45-60	
Hogan, Inez	We are a Family (1st {std}, sq4to, 93p, b/w, pep)	Dutton	(1952)	Hogan, I.	30-50	*
Hogan, Inez	World Round (1st {std}, 4to, [64]p, blue cl, b/w, pep)	Dutton	(1949)	Hogan, I.	30-45	*
Hogate, E.C.	Sunbonnets & Overalls... (1st, 8vo, 83p, color, pep)	Rand/McNally	(1914)	Corbett, B.L.	85-100	
Hogg, J.	Kilmeny (1st, 16mo, 31p, 5cp)	L: Foulis	1911	King, J.	130-160	
Hogg, J.	Songs of Ettrick Shepherd (1st, 12mo, 151p, teg, 7 ticp)	L: Foulis	(1912)	King, J.	100-150	
Holberg, R.	Mitty on Mr. Syrup's Farm (1st {std} 4to, ibds, [32]p, col, pep)	Doubleday/Dor.	1936	Holberg, R.	25-45	
Holbrook, Florence	Hiawatha Alphabet (1st, 4to, 30p, p-o, fp color)	Rand/McNally	(1910)	Pohl, H.D.	65-90	*
Holbrook, Florence	Hiawatha Primer (1st, 8vo, green cl, 148p, 8cp)	Houghton	1898	Smith, E.B.	70-85	
Holbrook, S.	America's Ethan Allen (1st, lg8vo, 95p, color, DJ, CH)	Houghton	1949	Ward, L.	55-80	
Holder, Charles F.	Treasure Divers (1st, sm8vo, 207p, blue/silver, 13pl)	Dodd	1898	Greenough, W.C.	30-45	
Holdridge, Betty	Island Boy (1st, 8vo, 110p, green cl, 1-color, pep)	Holiday House	(1942)	Lantz, P.	20-35	*
Hole, Christina	Witchcraft in England (1st, 8vo, 167p, maroon/gilt, fp b/w)	L: Batsford	1945	Peake, M.	90-125	*
Hole, Christina	Witchcraft in England (1st AM, lg8vo, 168p, fp b/w)	Scribner	1947	Peake, M.	70-100	*
Holland, Josiah G.	Arthur Bonnicastle (12mo, green/gilt, 422p, cvr by...)	Scribner	1896	Armstrong, M.	30-50	*
Holland, R. (ed.)	King Arthur & Knights of Rountable (1st, 8vo, 360p, p-o, 7cp pep)	Jacobs	(1919)	Speed, L.	50-65	
Holland, R.S.	Yankee Ships in Pirate Waters (1st, lg8vo, p-o, 317p, 5cp, pep)	Macrae-Smith	(1931)	Schoonover, F.	35-50	
Holling, H.C.	Book of Cowboys (1st, 4to, orang cl, pep, 126p, color, DJ)	Platt/Munk	(1936)	Holling, H.C.	35-50	
Holling, H.C.	Book of Indians (1st, 4to, 125p, pep, 6cp)	Platt/Munk	(1935)	Holling, H.C.	35-50	
Holling, H.C.	Choo-Me-Shoo (1st {std}, 8vo, ibds, color, pep)	Volland	(1928)	Holling, H.C.	65-80	*
Holling, H.C.	Claws of the Thunderbird (1st, 8vo, 128p, gilt, color, pep)	Volland	(1928)	Holling, H.C.	35-50	
Holling, H.C.	Little Big-Bye-and-Bye (1st, 12mo, [40]p, ibds, color, pep)	Volland	(1926)	Holling, H.C.	45-60	
Holling, H.C.	Little Buffalo Boy (1st, sq8vo, ibds, [42]p, color, pep)	Garden City	(1939)	Holling, H.C.	60-90	
Holling, H.C.	Minn of the Mississippi (1st, 4to, 88p, yel cl, col, pep, NH)	Houghton	1951	Holling, H.C.	50-80	
Holling, H.C.	Paddle to the Sea (1st, 4to, beige cl, unpag, color, pep, CH)	Houghton	1941	Holling, H.C.	60-85	R
Holling, H.C.	Pagoo (1st, 4to, 86p, green cl, pep, color)	Houghton	1957	Holling, H.C.	25-40	*
Holling, H.C.	Rocky Billy (1st, 8vo, blue cl, 148p, color, pep)	MacMillan	1928	Holling, H.C.	45-60	
Holling, H.C.	Rum-Tum-Tummy... (sq8vo, ibds, color)	Saalfield	1936	Holling, H.C.	50-80	
Holling, H.C.	Seabird (1st, 4to, 58p, blue cl, color, pep, DJ, NH)	Houghton	1948	Holling, H.C.	50-80	
Holling, H.C.	Tree in the Trail (1st, 4to, [70]p, 35 fp color, pep)	Houghton	1942	Holling, H.C.	30-45	
Holling, H.C.	Twins Who Flew Around the World (1st, folio, gilt, 67p, color)	Platt/Munk	(1931)	Holling, H.C.	50-75	
Holloway, J.	At Flower Farm (1st, 4to, ibds, p-o, 4cp)	Stern	1909	Beard/Kay	80-110	
Holme, C.	Trumpet in the Dust (1st, 8vo, 255p, 6 woodcuts)	L: Nicholson	1934	Leighton, C.	65-80	*
Holmes, Mabel D.	Joan of Arc (1st, sm4to, 300p, gilt, p-o, 4cp, pep)	Winston	(1930)	Prittie, E.J.	30-50	
Holmes, O.W.	Autocrat at Breakfast Table (1st, 8vo, teg, 2vols, gilt, 15pl)	Houghton	1894	Pyle, H.	120-165	
Holmes, O.W.	Bunker Hill Battle (4to, blue cl, 32p)	Dodd	(1890)	32 Chromos	90-140	
Holmes, O.W.	Dorothy Q. (1st, 8vo, grey cl, t.e. silver, 131p, b/w)	Houghton	1893	Pyle, H.	70-90	
Holmes, O.W.	Grandmother's Story/Bunker Hill Battle (1st, 8vo, 32p, col, dep)	Dodd	(1883)	McVickar, H.W.	45-70	*
Holmes, O.W.	One-Hoss Shay (1st [new ed.], 12mo, teg, gilt, 12cp)	Houghton	1905	Pyle, H.	85-120	
Holt, Ardern	Fancy Dresses Described (2nd, 12mo, 105p, 48pl)	L: Debenham	[1881]	Greenaway, K.	140-170	
Holton, Priscila	Blue Junk (1st {std}, sm8vo, 178p, blue cl, b/w, pep)	Longmans	1931	Wiese, K.	45-65	*
Homer, A.N.	Hernani the Jew (1st, 8vo, 332p, cvr by...)	Rand/McNally	(1897)	Denslow, W.W.	30-45	*
Hood, Thos.	Haunted House (1st, 12mo, AEG, green/gilt, b/w)	L: Lawrence	1896	Railton, H.	35-50	

AUTHOR	TITLE	PUBLISHER	DATE	ARTIST	PRICE	LC
Hood, Thos.	Humerous Poems (1st, sm8vo, AEG, 236p, gilt, b/w, cep)	L: MacMillan	1893	Brock, C.E.	50-70	
Hood, Thos.	Tucker/Little Bo Peep (4to)	L: Cassell	1891	Adams, A.W.	65-80	
Hooker, F.	Garden of the Lost Key (1st {std}, 8vo, 288p, col frn, pep)	Doubleday/Dor.	1929	Hader, E.	65-80	*
Hoover, B.R.	Pa Flickinger's Folks (1st, 12mo, grey cl, 274p, 10pl)	Harper	1909	Strothmann, F.	40-60	
Hope, A.	Advens. of Lady Ursula (1st, 8vo, grey/gilt, 125p, teg, uncut)	R.H. Russell	1898	(Photos)	30-45	*
Hope, A.	Comedies of Courtship (1st, sm8vo, 377p, buckram/gilt)	Scribner	1896	Armstrong, M.	30-45	*
Hope, A.	Dolly Dialogues (1st, AM, 12mo, 195p, uncut, teg, frn by...)	Holt	1894	Rackham, A.	80-100	
Hope, A.	Dolly Dialogues (1st, 8vo, 202p, p-o, teg, 18pl)	R.H. Russell	1901	Christy, H.C.	45-65	R
Hope, A.R.	Tales For Toby (1st, 8vo, 207p, 5pl)	L: Dent	1900	Robinson, W.H.	100-130	
Hope, E.	Alice in the Delighted States (1st AM, 8vo, 303p, 12pl, cep)	MacVeagh/Dial	1928	Irvin, Rea	70-90	
Hope, L.	India's Love Lyrics (1st, lg8vo, 181p, 8cp)	Dodd	1902	Shaw, B.	75-100	
Hopkins, H.C.	Moon-Boat (1st, lg4to, tan/gilt, [27]p, p-o, 11cp)	McKay	(1918)	Clayton, W.P.	125-160	
Hopkins, H.M.	Flight of Rosy Dawn (1st, 12mo, 98p, b/w)	Page	1903	Bruce, J.	25-40	*
Hopkins, N.M.	Racoon Lake Mystery (1st, sm8vo, blue cl, 319p, 4cp)	Lippincott	1917	Hoskins, G.	25-40	
Horgan, Paul	Habit of Empire (1st {this pub}, 8vo, 114p, 8 dp b/w)	Harper	(1939)	Hurd, P.	35-50	*
Horgan, Paul	Return of the Weed (1st {std}, 8vo, 97p, 7 fp b/w)	Harper	1936	Hurd, P.	30-45	*
Horn, M.D.	Farm on the Hill (1st, 4to, 78p, blue cl, 8cp, pep, DJ)	Scribner	1936	Wood, Grant	125-160	
Horne, Richard H.	King Penguin (1st, 12mo, tan cl, 95p, 4cp, pep)	MacMillan	1925	Daugherty, J.	25-40	*
Horne, Richard H.	Memoirs of a London Doll (1st UK, blue cl, 2cp)	L: Harrap	1923	Brock, E.	50-70	*
Hornibrook, I.	Scout of Today (1st, 8vo, 290p, 5pl)	Houghton	1913	Reading, J.	20-30	*
Hornung, E.W.	Shadow of the Rope (1st, 8vo, teg, 377p, 3pl)	Scribner	1906	Dunn, H.T.	35-50	
Horton, George	Edge of Hazard (1st, 8vo, 429p, aqua cl, cvr by...)	Bobbs-Merrill	(1906)	Armstrong, M.	30-45	*
Horwitz, C.N.	Fairy-Lure (1st, 12mo, 345p, 1-color decor by...)	Lothrop	(1891)	Bridgman, L.J.	45-60	*
Hough, E.	King of Gee Whiz (1st, lg8vo, 210p, green cl, 8cp)	Bobbs-Merrill	(1906)	Cesare, O.E.	125-200	R
Hough, E.	Law of the Land (1st, 8vo, 416p, tan cl, 5pl)	Bobbs-Merrill	(1904)	Keller, A.I.	25-40	
Hough, E.	Singing Mouse Stories (1st [1st bk], 12mo, [182]p teg)	Forest/Stream	1895	Bradley, W.	95-120	
Hough, E.	Singing Mouse Stories (1st, 12mo, 235p, green/gilt)	Bobbs-Merrill	(1910)	Bunker, M.	30-45	
Hough, E.	Story of the Cowboy (1st UK, 8vo)	(London)	1897	Russell, C.M.	100-150	
Hough, E.	Story of the Cowboy (1st, 8vo, 349p, 6pl by...)	Appleton	1897	Russell, C.M.	120-165	
Hough, E.	Way to the West (1st, sm8vo, grey cl, 446p, 6pl)	Bobbs-Merrill	(1903)	Remington, F.	60-80	
Hough, E.	Young Alaskans (1st, 8vo, orang cl, 292p, 4pl, PPP)	Harper	1908	Carpenter, D.	140-180	*
Housman, C.	Were-Wolf (1st, sq8vo, 124p, pink cl, uncut, 6pl)	L: J. Lane	1896	Housman, L.	180-300	
Housman, L.	All-Fellows & Cloak of Friendship (1st, 8vo, 192p, grn cl, 7pl)	L: J. Cape	(1923)	Housman, L.	65-85	
Housman, L.	All-Fellows... (1st, sq8vo, 138p, green/gilt, uncut, 8pl)	L: Kegan Paul	1896	Housman, L.	85-120	
Housman, L.	Angels & Ministers (1st, 8vo, 139p)	L: J. Cape	1922	Rutherston, A.	30-45	*
Housman, L.	Bethlehem (1st, 8vo, green/gilt, 85p, cvr by...)	L: MacMillan	1902	Housman, L.	80-110	
Housman, L.	Blue Moon (1st, 8vo, 210p, teg, blue/gilt, 8pl)	L: J. Murray	1904	Housman, L.	100-150	
Housman, L.	Cloak of Friendship (1st, 8vo, 192p, cvr by...)	L: J. Murray	1905	Housman, L.	75-100	
Housman, L.	Cotton Woolleena (1st, 8vo, 36p, wraps, p-o)	L: Blackwell	[1933]	Allen, M.	65-80	*
Housman, L.	Doorway in Fairyland (1st, 8vo, 220p, 14pl)	L: J. Cape	(1922)	Housman, L.	120-170	
Housman, L.	Farm in Fairyland (1st AM, 8vo, teg, 160p, 12pl)	Dodd	1894	Housman, L.	160-200	
Housman, L.	Farm in Fairyland (1st [1st bk.], 8vo, gilt, 160p, 12pl)	L: Kegan Paul	1894	Housman, L.	200-250	
Housman, L.	Field of Clover (1st, 12mo, green/gilt, 148p, 11pl)	L: Kegan Paul	1898	Housman, L.	180-220	
Housman, L.	Field of Clover (1st AM, sm8vo, 148p, teg, 11pl)	J. Lane	1902	Housman, L.	100-135	
Housman, L.	Golden Sovereign (1st, 8vo, green/gilt, 349p)	L: J. Cape	1937	Shepard, E.H.	50-65	
Housman, L.	Gracious Majesty (1st, 8vo, 222p)	L: J. Cape	1941	Shepard, E.H.	45-60	*
Housman, L.	Green Arras (1st, 8vo, green/gilt, 90p, uncut, 5pl)	L: J. Lane	1896	Housman, L.	125-165	
Housman, L.	House of Joy (1st, 8vo, 181p, gilt, uncut, 9pl)	L: Kegan Paul	1895	Housman, L.	140-170	
Housman, L.	Little Land (1st, 8vo, 97p, ipcb, gilt, 4pl)	L: Richards	1899	Housman, L.	160-225	
Housman, L.	Magic Horse (1st, smsq8vo, [58]p, gilt, 12cp)	L: Hodder	(1911)	Dulac, E.	180-250	
Housman, L.	Moonshine & Clover (1st, 8vo, 220p, blue/silver)	L: J. Cape	(1922)	Housman, L.	70-100	
Housman, L.	Princess Badoura (1st, 4to, teg, 113p, gilt, 10 ticp)	L: Hodder	[1913]	Dulac, E.	250-320	
Housman, L.	Sabrina Warham (1st AM, 8vo, teg, brown/gilt)	MacMillan	1904	Housman, L.	70-90	
Housman, L.	Spikenard (1st AM, 8vo, 53p, brown pcb, gilt)	Badger	1898	Housman, L.	80-100	
Housman, L.	Story of the Seven Young Goslings (1st, 4to, ibds, [32]p, 6cp)	L: Blackie	1899	Dearmer, M.	250-400	
Housman, L.	What-O'Clock Tales (1st, 8vo, 225p, 14 fp b/w)	L: Blackwell	(1932)	Monsell, J.R.	45-60	*
Housman, L. (ed.)	Stories from Arabian Nights (1st, 4to, 133p, 50 ticp)	L: Hodder	(1907)	Dulac, E.	300-400	
Housman, L. (ed.)	Stories from Arabian Nights (1st AM, 4to, 133p, gilt, 50 ticp)	Scribner	(1907)	Dulac, E.	300-450	
Housman, L. (ed.)	Stories from Arabian Nights (8vo, 24 ticp, later)	L: Hodder	[1911]	Dulac, E.	100-140	
Hovey, R.	Marriage of Guenevere (1st, 8vo, 179p, cvr by...)	H. Stone	1895	Meteyard, T.B.	65-90	R
Howard, A.W.	Ching-Li & the Dragons (1st, 4to, blue/silver, 55p, 10pl)	MacMillan	1931	Ward, L.	45-65	
Howard, Eliz.	Dorinda (1st, sm8vo, 303p, beige cl, fp b/w, pep)	Lothrop/Lee	(1944)	Weisgard, L.	20 5-40	
Howard, F.M.	Porpoise of Pirate Bay (1st, 8vo, 152p, 8 fp b/w, pep)	Random	(1938)	Ward, L.	30-45	
Howard, H.	Doings of the Dollymites (1st, 24mo, red cl, 94p, 23cp)	L: Sands	(1905)	Billinghurst, P.	80-120	
Howard, Janet	Jumpy the Kangaroo (1st, sq12mo, [42]p, ibds, color, pep)	Lothrop/Lee	(1944)	Duvoisin, R.	50-80	*
Howells, W.D.	Boy's Town (1st, 8vo, aqua/gilt, 247p, 23pl, PPP)	Harper	1890	Farney, H.F.	170-200	
Howells, W.D.	Christmas Every Day... (1st, 8vo, 150p, rust cl, 14 b/w)	Harper	1893	Unknown	35-50	R*
Howells, W.D.	Coast of Bohemia (1st, 12mo, red cl, 340p, 8pl)	Harper	1893	Small, F.O.	45-60	
Howells, W.D.	Fennel & Rue (1st, 8vo, 130p, green/gilt, 4pl)	Harper	1908	Harding, C.	25-40	
Howells, W.D.	Flight of Pony Baker (1st, sm8vo, red/silver, 223p, 8pl, PPP)	Harper	1902	Shinn, F.S.	100-165	R
Howells, W.D.	Stops of Various Quills (1st, 8vo, teg, gilt, designs by...)	Harper	1895	Pyle, H.	60-85	
Howes, E.	Long Bright Land (1st, 8vo, 207p, grn/gilt, col frn, 12pl, pep)	Little/Brown	1929	Lathrop, D.	65-80	

AUTHOR	TITLE	PUBLISHER	DATE	ARTIST	PRICE	LC
Howes, E.	Mrs. Kindbush (1st, 8vo, 160p, 4cp)	L: Cassell	1933	Anderson, A.	80-110	
Howland, E.	Scary-Ann/Cookie Man (1st, 8vo, ibds, 100p, color, pep)	Suttonhouse	1932	Eulalie	50-80	
Howlett, E.	Driving Lessons (1st, sm4to, 159p, 20pl)	R.H. Russell	1894	(Photos)	100-160	*
Hoyt, E.	Nancy's Country Christmas (1st, 8vo, teg, 224p, uncut, col frn)	Doubleday/Page	1904	Betts, A.W.	30-45	
Hubbard, R.	Queer Person (1st {std}, 8vo, 336p, doub. plates, pep, NH)	Doubleday/Dor.	1930	Von Schmidt, H.	50-85	*
Hubbell, R.S.	If I Could Fly (1st, 8vo, teg, 113p, 5cp, pep)	Putnam	1917	Gaze, H.	90-140	
Hubbell, R.S.	Quacky Doodles... (1st, 8vo, ibds, [88]p, color)	Volland	(1916)	Gruelle, J.	60-75	
Hudson, Alma	Peter Rabbit & the Fairies (sq12mo, 48p, red bds, p-o, 8cp)	Cupples	(1921)	Hudson, R.	60-80	
Hudson, Alma	Peter Rabbit/Mother Goose Land (16mo, red bds, p-o, 48p, color)	Cupples	(1921)	Hudson, R.	45-75	*
Hudson, C.	Crimson Conquest (1st, 8vo, 454p, cvr by...)	McClurg	1907	Leyendecker, J.C.	40-60	
Hudson, W.H.	Birds in Town & Village (1st, 323p, green/gilt, 8cp)	L: Dent	1919	Detmold, E.J.	100-135	
Hudson, W.H.	Birds in Town & Village (1st AM, blue/gilt, 323p, 8cp)	Dutton	(1920)	Detmold, E.J.	80-130	
Hudson, W.H.	Disappointed Squirrel (1st, 4to, p-o, 144p, 8 ticp, pep)	Doran	(1925)	Kirmse, M.	50-75	
Hudson, W.H.	Green Mansions (1st, lg8vo, 325p, ibds, woodcuts)	L: Duckworth	1926	Henderson, K.	40-60	
Hudson, W.H.	Little Boy Lost (1st, 8vo, buckram, 201p, b/w pl)	L: Duckworth	1905	McCormick, A.D.	140-185	
Hudson, W.H.	Little Boy Lost (1st, 4to, teg, 187p, gilt, uncut, pep, 8cp)	Knopf	1920	Lathrop, D.	120-160	
Hudson, W.H.	Purple Land (1st, lg8vo, red/gilt, 368p)	L: Duckworth	1929	Henderson, K.	35-50	
Hudson, W.H.	Tales of the Pampas (1st, 8vo, beige cl, 245p, 6pl)	Knopf	1939	Duvoisin, R.	30-50	*
Hueffer, F.M.	Cinque Ports... (1st, 4to, 403p, buckram, 14pl)	L: Blackwood	1900	Hyde, W.	350-500	
Huffard, G.T.	My Poetry Book (1st, lg8vo, blue cl, 6cp)	(London)	1934	Pogany, W.	45-60	
Huffard, G.T.	My Poetry Book (1st AM, lg8vo, 504p, blue/gilt, 6cp, pep)	Winston	(1934)	Pogany, W.	30-50	
Hughes, Langston	Dream Keeper (1st {std}, 8vo, 77p, blue/silver, b/w)	Knopf	1932	Sewell, H.	380-500	R
Hughes, R.	Colonel Crockett's Cooperative Christmas (1st, sm8vo, 66p, 6cp)	Jacobs	(1906)	Unknown	20-30	
Hughes, Rich. A.	Don't Blame Me! (1st {std}, sm8vo, 159p, b/w)	Harper	(1940)	Eichenberg, F.	40-65	*
Hughes, Rupert	Fairy Detective (1st, 12mo, 72p, tan cl, p-o, 5pl)	Harper	(1919)	Chase, R.	25-45	*
Hughes, Rupert	Lakerim Athletic Club (1st, sm8vo, 286p, 20pl, PPPa)	Century	1898	Relyea, C.M.	70-100	*
Hughes, Shirley	Lucy & Tom's Day (1st, ob4to, tan cl, [27]p, fp color)	W.R. Scott	(1960)	Hughes, S.	30-50	*
Hughes, Thos.	Tom Brown's School Days (1st, 8vo, 376p, pict cl)	Harper	1911	Rhead, L.	50-65	
Hugo, V.	Les Miserables (sm4to, black cl, 585p, 11cp)	Dodd	[1925]	Schaeffer, M.	40-60	
Hugo, V.	Story of the Bold Pecopin (1st, sm4to, 92p, gilt, 8pl)	L: Smith Elder	1902	Millar, H.R.	65-80	*
Hulbert, H.B.	Omjee, The Wizard... (1st, lg8vo, 156p, black cl, color, pep)	M. Bradley	(1925)	Lupprian, H.	35-50	
Hume, F.	Chronicles of Fairy-Land (1st, 8vo, 191p, teg, gilt, pep, 8cp)	Lippincott	1911	Kirk, M.L.	90-145	
Humphrey, M.	Babes of the Year (1st, sq8vo, ibds, 25p, 12cp)	Stokes	1888	Humphrey, M.	250-400	
Humphrey, M.	Book of Fairy Tales (1st, 4to, ipcb, [30]p, 12cp)	Stokes	1892	Humphrey, M.	450-600	
Humphrey, M.	Children of the Revolution (1st, 4to, ibds, [24]p, 12cp)	Stokes	1900	Humphrey, M.	400-500	
Humphrey, M.	Gallant Little Patriots (1st, 4to, ipcb, 12cp)	Stokes	1899	Humphrey, M.	450-650	
Humphrey, M.	Golf Girl (1st, 4to, ibds, color)	Stokes	(1899)	Humphrey, M.	300-400	
Humphrey, M.	Little Heroes & Heroines (1st, 4to, ibds, 6cp)	Stokes	1899	Humphrey, M.	200-350	
Humphrey, M.	Little Soldiers & Sailors (1st, 4to, ibds, [19]p, 6cp)	Stokes	(1899)	Humphrey, M.	250-300	
Humphrey, M.	Rosebud Stories (1st, 8vo, 24p, ipcb, 6cp)	Holiday Pub.	1906	Humphrey, M.	150-200	
Humphrey, M.	Tiny Toddlers (folio, color, ibds)	Stokes	1890	Humphrey, M.	650-800	*
Humphrey, Mabel	Book of the Child (1st, folio, ibds, 4cp by...)	Stokes	(1903)	Green, E.S.	600-750	
Humphrey, Mabel	Book of the Child (1st, folio, ibds, 3cp by...)	Stokes	(1903)	Smith, J.W.	600-750	
Humphrey, Mabel	Bright Days... (lg4to, 36p, ibds, 12cp)	Stokes	1901	Spiegle, F.	125-180	
Humphrey, Mabel	Little Continentals (1st, lg4to, ibds, 6cp)	Stokes	1900	Humphrey, M.	350-500	
Hunt, B.S.	Stories of Little Brown Koko (1st, 4to, bds, 96p)	Am. Colortype	1940	Wagstaff, D.	65-100	
Hunt, Clara W.	About Harriet (1st, 8vo, 150p, p-o, fp color)	Houghton	1916	Enright, M.W.	35-50	*
Hunt, Enid	Fine Lady Upon a White Horse (4to, gilt, 120p, 8cp)	Dodge	[1929]	Peto, G.	70-100	
Hunt, M.L.	Benjie's Hat (1st, 8vo, 119p, orange cl, pep, b/w)	Stokes	1938	Paull, G.	20-30	*
Hunt, M.L.	Better Known as Johnny Appleseed (1st {std}, 8vo, 212p, cep, NH)	Lippincott	(1950)	Daugherty, J.	45-70	R*
Hunt, M.L.	Billy Button's Buttered Biscuit (1st, 12mo, 56p, color, cep)	Stokes	1941	Milhous, K.	20-35	*
Hunt, M.L.	Boy Who Had no Birthday (1st, 8vo, orange cl, 259p, fp b/w)	Stokes	1935	Wright, C.	20-30	*
Hunt, M.L.	Corn-Belt Billy (1st, lg8vo, ibds, [26]p, pep, color)	Grosset/Dunlap	(1942)	Wiese, K.	30-45	*
Hunt, M.L.	Double Birthday Present (1st {std}, sm8vo, 52p, red cl, col frn)	Lippincott	(1947)	Blaisdell, E.	20-30	*
Hunt, M.L.	Have You Seen Tom Thumb? (1st, sm8vo, blue cl, 259p, dep, NH)	Stokes	1942	Eichenberg, F.	45-65	*
Hunt, M.L.	John of Pudding Lane (1st, 8vo, 161p, color, pep)	Stokes	(1941)	Funk, C.E.	25-40	*
Hunt, M.L.	Little Girl with Seven Names (1st, 8vo, 63p, b/w, pep)	Stokes	1936	Paull, G.	25-40	*
Hunt, M.L.	Lucinda: Little Girl of 1860 (1st, sm8vo, 233p, blue cl, b/w)	Stokes	1934	Wright, C.	20-30	*
Hunt, M.L.	Michel's Island (1st, sm4to, 265p, pep, b/w)	Stokes	1940	Seredy, K.	25-40	*
Hunt, M.L.	Peddler's Clock (1st, sq8vo, ipcb, [28]p, pep, color)	Grosset/Dunlap	(1943)	Jones, E.O.	30-45	*
Hunt, M.L.	Peter Piper's Pickled Peppers (1st, 16mo, 62p, cep, 4cp)	Stokes	1942	Milhous, K.	25-40	*
Hunt, M.L.	Sibby Botherbox (1st {std}, 8vo, 174p, blue cl, pep, b/w)	Lippincott	(1945)	Collison, M.	25-45	*
Hunt, M.L.	Such a Kind World (1st, sq8vo, [28]p, color)	Grosset/Dunlap	1947	Potter, E.	25-40	*
Hunt, M.L.	Susan Beware! (1st, 8vo, 243p, green cl, b/w, pep)	Stokes	1937	Boyle, M.	20-30	*
Hunt, M.L.	Wonderful Baker (1st {std}, 8vo, blue cl, 47p, b/w, dep)	Lippincott	(1950)	Paull, G.	25-40	*
Hunt, M.L.	Young Man of the House (1st {std}, 8vo, 171p, 10 fp b/w)	Lippincott	(1944)	Slobodkin, L.	25-40	*
Hunt, Marigold	Hester & the Gnomes (1st, 8vo, 124p, blue cl, fp b/w, pep)	Whittlesey	(1955)	Charlot, J.	45-60	*
Hunter, N.	Incredible Advens/Professor Brawnestawm (1st, lg8vo, col frn)	L: Bodley Head	1933	Robinson, W.H.	150-250	
Hunter, Richard	Dollies (1st, 24mo, olive cl)	L: Richards	1902	Cobb/Hunter	100-150	*
Hunter, Richard	Little Pickles (sm4to, ibds, 44p, color)	L: Blackie	[1900]	Cobb, Ruth	150-200	
Hunter, Richard	Silver Bubbles... (lg4to, 20cp)	L: Nelson	[1915]	Cobb, Ruth	150-200	
Huntington, I.M.	Christmas Party for Santa Claus (1st, 8vo, 102p, 6cp)	Rand/McNally	(1912)	Unknown	65-90	*

AUTHOR	TITLE	PUBLISHER	DATE	ARTIST	PRICE	LC
Huntington, I.M.	Garden of Hearts' Delight (1st, sm4to, p-o, gile, 167p, 15cp)	Rand/McNally	(1911)	Enright, M.W.	80-120	
Huntington, I.M.	Peter Pumpkin/Wonderland (1st, sq4to, 264p, 15pl)	Rand/McNally	(1908)	Hunt, M.I.	70-100	
Hurd, C.	Merry Chase (1st {std}, lg8vo, [25]p, yellow cl, pep, color)	Random	(1941)	Hurd, C.	35-60	*
Hurd, C.	The Race (1st {std}, lg8vo, [27]p, yellow cl, color, pep)	Random	(1940)	Hurd, C.	35-60	*
Hurd, E.T.	Annie Moran (1st, ob4to, ibds, [32]p, color, pep)	Lothrop/Lee	1942	Hurd, C.	45-60	*
Hurd, E.T.	Benny the Bulldozer (1st, ob4to, [33]p, ibds, 1-color, pep)	Lothrop/Lee	1947	Hurd, C.	45-60	*
Hurd, E.T.	Caboose (1st, ob4to, [33]p, ibds, 1-color)	Lothrop/Lee	1950	Hurd, C.	45-60	
Hurd, E.T.	Cat from Telegraph Hill (1st, sm4to, unpag, ipcb, pep, color)	Lothrop/Lee	(1955)	Hurd, C.	35-50	*
Hurd, E.T.	Devil's Tail (1st {std}, 8vo, 216p, t.e. red, fp b/w)	Doubleday	(1954)	Hurd, C.	25-40	*
Hurd, E.T.	Engine, Engine No. 9 (1st, ob8vo, [34]p, ibds, color, pep)	Lothrop/Lee	1940	Hurd, C.	60-80	
Hurd, E.T.	Faraway Christmas (1st, 8vo, blue cl, [33]p, 1-color, pep)	Lothrop/Lee	1958	Hurd, C.	30-45	*
Hurd, E.T.	Fox in a Box (1st {std}, lg8vo, ibds, unpag, pep, color)	Doubleday	(1957)	Hurd, C.	45-60	
Hurd, E.T.	Hurry Hurry (1st, 8vo, ipcb, 45p, 1-color, cep)	W.R. Scott	(1938)	Shipman, M.D.	35-50	*
Hurd, E.T.	It's Snowing (1st, 4to, silver cl, unpag, dep, b/w)	NY: Sterling	(1957)	Hurd, C.	40-65	*
Hurd, E.T.	Jerry the Jeep (1st, ob4to, [32]p, ipcb, 1-color, pep)	Lothrop/Lee	(1945)	Friday, T.	35-60	*
Hurd, E.T.	Johnny Littlejohn (1st, narrow ob8vo, unpag, yellow cl, 1-color)	Lothrop/Lee	(1957)	Hurd, C.	30-45	*
Hurd, E.T.	Nino & his Fish (1st, lg8vo, unpag, ipcb, color, pep)	Lothrop/Lee	(1954)	Hurd, C.	25-40	*
Hurd, E.T.	Old Silversides (1st, ob4to, [30]p, ibds, 1-color, pep)	Lothrop/Lee	1951	Hurd, C.	45-60	
Hurd, E.T.	Sky High (1st, lg ob8vo, [34]p, color, pep)	Lothrop/Lee	(1941)	Hurd, C.	30-50	*
Hurd, E.T.	Speedy... (1st, lg ob8vo, ibds, [36]p, 1-color, pep)	Lothrop/Lee	1942	Hurd, C.	35-50	*
Hurd, E.T.	Toughy & his Trailer Truck (1st, ob8vo, ibds, [34]p, pep, 1-col)	Lothrop/Lee	1948	Hurd, C.	45-65	*
Hurd, E.T.	Willy's Farm (1st, 4to, 64p, ipcb, color, pep)	Lothrop/Lee	(1949)	Hurd, C.	45-65	*
Hurd, Marian K.	Miss Billy: Neighborhood Story (1st, sm8vo, 349p, 6pl)	Lothrop	(1905)	Copeland, C.	30-45	*
Hurd, Marian K.	When She Came Home from College (1st, 12mo, 272p, 7pl)	Houghton	1909	Gibbs, G.	20-35	
Hurrell, M.I.	Adventures of Friskers & His Friends (1st, 12mo, 159p, 16cp)	L: R. Culley	[1907]	Wain, L.	100-160	*
Hurst, Edward H.	Mystery Island (1st, 8vo, 313p, uncut, gilt, col frn by...)	Page	1907	Tyng, G.	20-25	*
Hutchinson, V.	Candle-Light Stories (1st, 4to, 146p, 6cp, pep)	Minton Balch	1928	Lenski, L.	70-100	
Hutchinson, V.	Chimney Corner Fairy Tales (1st, 4to, 183p, 6cp, pep)	Minton Balch	1926	Lenski, L.	70-100	
Hutchinson, V.	Circus Comes to Town (1st, 4to, [66]p, color, pep)	Minton Balch	(1932)	Berry, E.	35-50	*
Hutchinson, V.	Fireside Poems (1st, 4to, 147p, 5cp, pep)	Minton Balch	1930	Lenski, L.	65-90	
Hutchinson, V.	Fireside Stories (1st, 8vo, 150p, 6cp, pep)	Minton Balch	1927	Lenski, L.	60-90	
Hutchinson, W.M.L.	Golden Porch (1st, 8vo, 302p, purple cl, pep, col frn, fp b/w)	NY: Longmans	1925	Walker, D.S.	50-70	
Hutchinson, W.M.L.	Orpheus with his Lute (1st, 8vo, 300p, col frn, b/w, pep)	NY: Longmans	1926	Walker, D.S.	50-75	*
Hutchinson, W.M.L.	Sunset of the Heroes (8vo, 281p, green/gilt, pep, teg, 8cp)	L: J.M. Dent	[1910]	Cole, H.	65-90	*
Hutt, H.	Girls (1st, 4to, [38]p, blue cl, p-o, 16cp)	Scribner	1910	Hutt, H.	100-130	
Hutt, H.	Henry Hutt Picture Book (1st, 4to, [84]p, p-o, 10cp)	Century	1908	Hutt, H.	85-120	
Hutt, H.	Rosebuds (1st, 4to, 27p, 11 ticp)	Bobbs-Merrill	(1912)	Hutt, H.	130-170	*
Hutt, H.	She Loves Me (1st, 4to, p-o, unpag, 8cp)	Bobbs-Merrill	(1911)	Hutt, H.	100-130	
Hutton, W.H.	Hampton Court (1st, sm4to, 244p, blue bds, gilt, b/w)	L: Nimmo	1897	Railton, H.	50-70	
Hyde, Eliz.	Little Brothers to the Scouts (12mo, blu cl, p-o, 72p, 10cp)	Rand/McNally	(1917)	Hyde, Eliz.	25-40	
Hyde, F.	Ritz Carltons (1st, 8vo, 157p, pcb, b/w)	NY: Macy	1927	Irvin, Rea	30-45	*
Inayat, N.	Twenty Jakata Tales (1st AM, lg8vo, 138p, gilt, col frn, 19pl)	McKay	(1939)	LeMair, H.W.	80-120	
Inayat, N.	Twenty Jataka Tales (1st, 8vo, blue cl, 138p, col frn, 19pl)	L: Harrap	(1939)	LeMair, H.W.	120-165	
Ingelow, J.	Mopsa the Fairy (1st, lg8vo, teg, 257p, 10cp, pep)	Lippincott	1910	Kirk, M.L.	80-100	
Ingelow, J.	Mopsa the Fairy (1st, 8vo, p-o, 259p, uncut, col frn, 12pl pep)	Harper	1927	Lathrop, D.	75-120	
Ingelow, J.	Mopsa the Fairy (1st, 8vo, 259p, blue cl, col frn, pep)	MacMillan	1927	Walker, D.S.	80-120	
Ingold, John	Glimpses from Wonderland (1st, 8vo, 287p, blue/gilt, 5pl)	L: J. Long	1900	Bauerle, A.	30-50	*
Ingoldsby, T.	Ingoldsby Legends (1st, 8vo, teg, 638p, green/gilt, 12cp, pep)	L: Dent	1898	Rackham, A.	165-220	
Ingoldsby, T.	Ingoldsby Legends (1st, 8vo, 640p)	L/NY: J. Lane	1903	Cole, H.	45-60	*
Ingoldsby, T.	Ingoldsby Legends (1st AM, 4to, teg, green/gilt, 24 ticp, pep)	Dent/Dutton	1907	Rackham, A.	250-400	
Ingoldsby, T.	Ingoldsby Legends (1st, 8vo, a.e. blue, 546p, 16cp)	L: MacMillan	1911	Theaker, H.G.	80-120	
Ingoldsby, T.	Jackdaw of Rheims (1st, folio, unpag, white/gilt, teg, 12 ticp)	L: Gay/Hancock	1913	Folkard, C.	120-180	*
Ingoldsby, T.	Jackdaw of Rheims (1st AM, lg4to, purple cl, 12 ticp)	Winston	1914	Folkard, C.	70-100	*
Ingoldsby, T.	Misadventures at Margate (folio, ibds, 18p, fp color)	L: Eyre/Spotts	[1885]	Jessop, E.M.	70-90	*
Ingpen, R.	1000 Poems for Children (1st, sm4to, 563p, 8cp)	Jacobs	(1923)	Betts, E.F.	100-135	
Ingraham, C.	Cottontail & Wishing-Fairy (1st, lg8vo, pcb, 39p, p-o, 2cp, pep)	Brentano's	(1921)	Walker, D.S.	80-120	*
Ingraham, C.	Elephant & Wishing Fairy (1st, lg8vo, bds, unpag, p-o, 2cp, pep)	Brentano's	(1921)	Walker, D.S.	80-120	
Ingraham, C.	Peacock & Wishing-Fairy (1st, lg8vo, p-o, pcb, [42]p, 2cp, pep)	Brentano's	(1921)	Walker, D.S.	85-140	*
Ingraham, C.	Wishing Fairy's Animal Friends (1st, lg8vo, 141p, p-o, 8cp, pep)	Brentano's	(1921)	Walker, D.S.	100-160	
Ingraham, C.	Zebra & the Wishing Fairy (1st, lg8vo, [45]p, color, pep)	Brentano's	(1921)	Walker, D.S.	85-140	*
Inman, H.E.	Gobbo Bobo (1st, 8vo, 477p, gilt, AEG, b/w)	L: Warne	1900	Mason, E.A.	85-110	*
Inman, H.E.	Old Santa Fe Trail (1st, 8vo, 493p, teg, 8pl)	MacMillan	1897	Remington, F.	150-185	
Inman, H.E.	One-Eyed Griffin... (1st, 12mo, 353p, teg, gilt, 4pl, dep)	L: Warne	1897	Mason, E.A.	100-130	
Inman, H.E.	Owl King... (1st, 12mo, 353p, teg, 4pl, dep)	L: Warne	1897	Mason, E.A.	100-130	
Iogolevitch, Paul	Young Russian Corporal (1st, sm8vo, 327p, frn & b/w by...)	Harper	1919	Neill, J.R.	45-60	*
Ipcar, D.	Animal Hide & Seek (1st, lg8vo, [36]p, ipcb, color, pep)	W.R. Scott	(1947)	Ipcar, D.	50-80	*
Irving, W.	Bold Dragon (1st, 8vo, 240p, blue cl, b/w, pep, DJ)	Knopf	1930	Daugherty, J.	35-50	
Irving, W.	Bracebridge Hall (1st, 12mo, 284p, gilt, AEG)	L: MacMillan	1877	Caldecott, R.	145-200	
Irving, W.	Bracebridge Hall (1st, 2 vols, 8vo, teg, 5pl by...)	Putnam	1896	Rackham, A.	120-160	
Irving, W.	Child's Rip Van Winkle (1st, 8vo, 39p, red cl, p-o, 12cp)	Stokes	(1908)	Kirk, M.L.	70-100	
Irving, W.	Christmas Day (sm8vo, bds, p-o, 6 ticp)	L: Hodder	(1915)	Aldin, C.	65-80	
Irving, W.	Christmas Dinner (1st, 8vo, ipcb, 22p, b/w)	W. Rudge	1929	Ross, G.	45-75	R

AUTHOR	TITLE	PUBLISHER	DATE	ARTIST	PRICE	LC
Irving, W.	Christmas at Bracebridge Hall (1st, 12mo, 267p, teg, 24cp, dep)	L: Dent	1906	Brock, C.E.	40-65	
Irving, W.	History of New York (1st, lg4to, bds, teg, p-o, 299p, 8pl)	R.H. Russell	1900	Parrish, M.	250-350	
Irving, W.	History of New York (1st {this format}, 4to, 299p, bds, 8 ticp)	Dodd	1915	Parrish, M.	200-250	
Irving, W.	History of New York (1st {std}, 4to, 427p, uncut, pep, DJ)	Doran	1928	Daugherty, J.	65-90	R
Irving, W.	Keeping of Christmas... (1st, 12mo, teg, gilt, 24cp)	Dutton	1906	Brock, C.E.	45-60	
Irving, W.	Legend of Sleepy Hollow (1st, 12mo, 61p, ibds, p-o, cvr by...)	R.H. Russell	(1897)	Bradley, W.	120-150	
Irving, W.	Legend of Sleepy Hollow (1st, 8vo, teg, 191p, red/gilt)	Putnam	1899	Armstrong, M.	80-100	
Irving, W.	Legend of Sleepy Hollow (1st, sm4to, 92p, p-o, pep, 14pl)	Bobbs-Merrill	(1906)	Keller, A.I.	75-100	
Irving, W.	Legend of Sleepy Hollow (1st AM sm4to, 102p, teg, p-o, 8cp, pep)	McKay	(1928)	Rackham, A.	145-200	
Irving, W.	Legend of Sleepy Hollow (1st, 4to, gilt, teg, 102p, 8cp, pep)	L: Harrap	(1928)	Rackham, A.	240-300	
Irving, W.	Legends of the Alhambra (1st, 4to, 229p, teg, p-o, 8cp)	Lippincott	1909	Hood, G.	50-70	
Irving, W.	Old Christmas (8vo, gilt, 165p, b/w, AEG)	L: MacMillan	1894	Caldecott, R.	70-100	
Irving, W.	Old Christmas (1st AM, 8vo, [176]p, p-o, red/gilt, 27cp)	NY: Sully	1908	Aldin, C.	120-160	
Irving, W.	Old Christmas (1st AM, 8vo, 176p, color)	Dodd	(1908)	Aldin, C.	80-130	*
Irving, W.	Old Christmas (1st, 8vo, 115p, gilt, p-o, teg, 2cp, 16pl, pep)	Putnam	(1916)	Dadd, Frank	35-50	*
Irving, W.	Old Christmas (1st, 8vo, 284p, color)	L: Constable	1918	Baumer, L.	45-60	*
Irving, W.	Old Christmas (1st AM, 8vo, 284p, color)	Houghton	1919	Baumer, L.	35-50	*
Irving, W.	Old Christmas & Bracebridge Hall (8vo, red cl, 285p, 8 color)	L: Constable	1918	Baumer, L.	30-45	
Irving, W.	Old Christmas Day (12mo, 34p, p-o, 5cp)	L: Foulis	[1912]	Brock, H.M.	40-60	
Irving, W.	Old English Christmas (1st, 12mo, 124p, blue/gilt, 17 ticp)	L: Foulis	[1910]	Brock, H.M.	60-85	
Irving, W.	Old English Christmas (1st AM, 12mo, 123p, ibds, p-o, 17 ticp)	Jacobs	(1910)	Brock, H.M.	45-60	
Irving, W.	Old Fashioned Christmas Day (sm8vo, ibds, p-o, 6 ticp)	L: Hodder	[1910]	Aldin, C.	100-135	*
Irving, W.	Rip Van Winkle (sq4to, [11]p, wraps, 6 chromos)	McLoughlin	[1880]	Nast, Thos.	180-265	
Irving, W.	Rip Van Winkle (1st, lg4to, 49p, b/w pl)	S.E. Cassino	1888	Merrill, F.	90-140	*
Irving, W.	Rip Van Winkle (1st, sm8vo, bds, 35p, frn & cvr by...)	R.H. Russell	(1897)	Bradley, W.	180-250	
Irving, W.	Rip Van Winkle (1st, sm8vo, teg, uncut, red/gilt, 115p, cvr by)	Putnam	1899	Armstrong, M.	50-70	
Irving, W.	Rip Van Winkle (1st, 4to, 57p, green/gilt, 51 ticp, dep)	L: Heinemann	1905	Rackham, A.	350-450	
Irving, W.	Rip Van Winkle (1st AM, 4to, green/gilt, 51 ticp)	Doubleday/Page	1905	Rackham, A.	250-350	
Irving, W.	Rip Van Winkle (1st, 12mo, 218p, b/w pl)	L: MacMillan	1908	Boughton, G.H.	45-65	*
Irving, W.	Rip Van Winkle (lg8vo, 68p, col frn, cp)	Stokes	[1915]	Robinson, C.	90-160	*
Irving, W.	Rip Van Winkle (1st, lg8vo, 86p, teg, gilt, p-o, 8cp, pep)	McKay	(1921)	Wyeth, N.C.	160-220	
Irving, W.	Rip Van Winkle (1st, 12mo, 69p, beige cl, 4cp)	Lippincott	(1923)	Cooke, E.	35-50	*
Irving, W.	Rip Van Winkle (1st, 12mo, blue cl, 183p, 4cp, fp b/w, pep)	MacMillan	1925	Pape, Eric	35-50	*
Irving, W.	Rip Van Winkle (1st, sm8vo, 92p, col frn, b/w)	Saalfield	(1927)	Brundage, F.	25-40	*
Irving, W.	Rip Van Winkle (1st, 8vo, 127p, b/w)	Stokes	1933	Perard, V.	20-35	*
Irving, W.	Rip Van Winkle (1st, lg4to, [40]p, color, pep)	Garden City	(1939)	Shinn, E.	65-90	*
Irving, W.	Rip Van Winkle (1st, 12mo, [60]p, color)	McLoughlin	(1941)	Graef, R.A.	25-45	*
Irving, W.	Rip Van Winkle & Sleepy Hollow (sm8vo, 148p, red cl, 8cp)	Lippincott	(1924)	Cooke, E.	25-40	
Irving, W.	Rip Van Winkle & Sleepy Hollow (1st, 8vo, 105p, 1-color, pep)	MacMillan	(1951)	Petershams	50-85	*
Irving, W.	Tales of a Traveller (1st, 2vols, lg8vo, white/gilt, 5pl by...)	Putnam	1895	Rackham, A.	100-135	
Irving, W.	The Alhambra (1st, 12mo, green/gilt, AEG, 436p, b/w, cep)	L: MacMillan	1896	Pennell, J.	45-65	
Irving, W.	The Alhambra (1st, 8vo, blue cl, 3cp)	L: MacMillan	1926	Goble, W.	85-110	
Irwin, V.	Mountain of Jade (1st, 8vo, 236p, cloth)	MacMillan	1926	Daugherty, J.	25-40	
Irwin, W.	Nautical Lays of a Landsman (1st, sm8vo, 135p, 5pl, dep)	Dodd	1904	Newell, P.	45-60	
Isben, H.	Peer Gynt (1st {std}, 4to, green bds, p-o, 286p, pep, 10cp)	Doubleday/Dor.	1929	MacKinstry, E.	60-80	
Isben, H.	Peer Gynt (1st AM, 4to, 255p, orange cl, 12cp)	Lippincott	[1936]	Rackham, A.	120-180	
Isben, H.	Peer Gynt (1st, 4to, brown/gilt, 12cp, pep)	(London)	(1936)	Rackham, A.	150-200	
Isham, F.S.	Black Friday (1st, 8vo, 409p, 6pl)	Bobbs-Merrill	(1904)	Fisher, H.	25-40	
Isham, F.S.	Under the Rose (1st, 12mo, 427p, green cl, cvr by...)	Bobbs-Merrill	(1903)	Armstrong, M.	20-25	
Isham, F.S.	Under the Rose (1st, 12mo, 427p, green cl, 4cp by...)	Bobbs-Merrill	(1903)	Christy, H.C.	20-25	
Jacberns, R.	Attic Boarders (1st, 8vo, 298p, 6cp)	L: Chambers	1909	Earnshaw, H.C.	35-50	*
Jacberns, R.	Boy and a Secret (1st, 8vo, 304p, 10pl)	L: Chambers	1908	Attwell, M.L.	65-100	
Jacberns, R.	Crab Cottage (1st, 12mo, 285p, 6pl, cep)	L: Chambers	1905	Menzies, J.	50-70	
Jacberns, R.	Poor Uncle Harry (1st, 8vo, 275p, red cl, 6cp)	L: Chambers	1910	Cowham, H.	45-60	*
Jacberns, R.	Tabitha Smallways, Schoolgirl (1st, 8vo, 304p, 6cp)	L: Chambers	1912	Attwell, M.L.	50-80	*
Jacberns, R.	Troublesome Dog (1st, 8vo, 297p, 6cp)	L: Chambers	(1911)	Attwell, M.L.	45-65	*
Jackson, Charlotte	Round the Afternoon (1st, 4to, blue cl, [63]p, pep, color)	Dodd	1946	Weisgard, L.	30-45	*
Jackson, Charlotte	Sarah Deborah's Day (1st, lg8vo, ipcb, 74p, 2-color, pep)	Dodd	1941	Simont, M.	35-50	*
Jackson, G.E.	By Love's Sweet Rule (1st, 12mo, 320p, b/w)	Winston	1906	Smith, Wuanita	25-45	*
Jackson, G.E.	Maid of Middies' Haven (1st, 12mo, 299p, 4pl)	McBride	1912	Rockwell, N.	150-200	*
Jackson, G.E.	Peterkin (1st, lg8vo, p-o, 75p, col frn by...)	Duffield	1912	Parrish, M.	120-165	*
Jackson, G.E.	Wee Winkles & her Friends (1st, 8vo, 155p, 8pl)	Harper	1907	Robinson, R.	35-50	*
Jackson, G.E.	Wee Winkles/Snowball (1st, 8vo, 147p, 8pl)	Harper	1906	Hart, M.T.	30-45	*
Jackson, G.E.	Wee Winkles/Wideawake (1st, 8vo, p-o, 153p, 8pl)	Harper	1905	Hart, M.T.	50-75	*
Jackson, H.H.	Father Junipero... (1st, sm8vo, 159p, b/w)	Little/Brown	1902	Sandham, H.	30-45	
Jackson, H.H.	Ramona (1st, 8vo, col frn, 447p, b/w)	Little/Brown	1932	Stoops, H.M.	25-40	
Jackson, Jesse	Anchor Man (1st {std}, 8vo, 142p, red cl, fp b/w)	Harper	1947	Spiegel, D.	50-80	*
Jackson, Jesse	Call Me Charley (1st {std}, 8vo, 156p, b/w)	Harper	(1945)	Spiegel, D.	45-60	*
Jackson, Joseph	Christmas Flower (1st {std}, 8vo, 31p, ibds, 1-color, pep)	Harcourt	(1951)	Lea, Tom	30-50	*
Jackson, K.& B.	Farm Stories (1st {std}, folio, ibds, 91p, color, GGB)	Simon/Schuster	(1946)	Tenggren, G.	70-100	
Jackson, L.F.	Peter Patter Book (1st, 4to, 110p, color)	Rand/McNally	(1918)	Wright, B.F.	45-75	
Jackson, L.F.	Rimskittle's Book (1st, folio, p-o, unpag, color, pep)	Rand/McNally	(1926)	Eger, R.C.	65-85	

AUTHOR	TITLE	PUBLISHER	DATE	ARTIST	PRICE	LC
Jacobs (ed.)	Tales/Boccaccio (1st, sq8vo, teg, 117p, 20pl)	L: G. Allen	1899	Shaw, B.	80-100	
Jacobs, H.	Hindu Fairy Tales (1st, 8vo, 186p, 4cp)	L: Harrap	1919	Jacobs, H.	40-60	
Jacobs, J.	Book of Wonder Voyages (1st, 8vo, 224p, uncut, 7pl)	L: D. Nutt	1896	Batten, J.D.	160-200	
Jacobs, J.	Celtic Fairy Tales (1st, lg8vo, 267p, green cl, 8pl)	L: D. Nutt	1892	Batten, J.D.	140-185	
Jacobs, J.	English Fairy Tales (1st, 8vo, 253p, AEG, 8pl)	L: D. Nutt	1890	Batten, J.D.	70-100	*
Jacobs, J.	English Fairy Tales (1st AM, 8vo, 253p, 8pl)	Putnam	1891	Batten, J.D.	65-80	
Jacobs, J.	More Celtic Fairy Tales (1st, 8vo, 234p, 8pl)	L: D. Nutt	1894	Batten, J.D.	100-130	
Jacobs, J.	More English Fairy Tales (1st, 8vo, blue cl, 243p, 8pl)	L: D. Nutt	1894	Batten, J.D.	70-100	
Jacobs, J. (ed.)	Indian Fairy Tales (1st AM, 8vo, 255p, 8pl)	Putnam	1892	Batten, J.D.	100-145	*
Jacobs, J. (ed.)	Indian Fairy Tales (1st, 8vo, 255p, uncut, 9pl)	L: D. Nutt	1892	Batten, J.D.	70-90	*
Jacobs, Joseph	Molly Whuppie (1st AM, 8vo, tan cl, [46]p, fp 3-color)	OUP	[1939]	Doane, P.	30-50	*
Jacobs, Violet	Golden Heart (1st AM, 8vo, 171p, green/gilt, p-o, 16pl)	Doubleday/Page	1905	Sandheim, M.	45-60	*
Jacobs-Bond, C.	Tales of Little Cats (1st, 12mo, ibds, [38]p, color, pep)	Volland	(1918)	Dodge, K.S.	50-70	
Jacobs-Bond, C.	Tales of Little Dogs (1st, smsq8vo, ibds, [35]p, color, pep)	Volland	(1921)	Dodge, K.S.	65-80	*
Jahn, Mary L.	Yelly (1st, lg ob4to, [32]p, color, pep)	NY: OUP	(1941)	Scott, H.	45-60	*
James, G.	Green Willow... (1st, sm4to, blue/gilt, 281p, 40 ticp)	L: MacMillan	1910	Goble, W.	350-465	
James, G.	Green Willow... (1st {this format}, 8vo, gilt, 281p, 16cp)	L: MacMillan	1912	Goble, W.	130-180	
James, G.W.	California, Romantic & Beautiful (1st, 8vo, teg, 433p, gilt)	Page	1914	(Photos)	45-65	
James, Hart.	Magic Jaw Bone (1st, 12mo, 107p, 2-color)	Altemus	(1906)	Neill, J.R.	50-70	
James, Henry	Daisy Miller (1st, 8vo, stripe cl, 133p, b/w)	Harper	1892	McVickar, H.W.	90-130	
James, Henry	English Hours (1st AM, lg8vo, cloth, 336p)	Houghton	1905	Pennell, J.	60-80	
James, Henry	English Hours (1st AM, lg8vo, 336p, design by...)	Houghton	1905	Rogers, B.	125-150	
James, Henry	Italian Hours (1st AM, 8vo, 504p, teg, uncut, 32cp)	Houghton	1909	Pennell, J.	80-130	
James, Henry	Julia Bride (1st, 8vo, 83p, teg, 4pl)	Harper	1909	Smedley, W.T.	80-100	
James, Henry	Little Tour in France (1st, 8vo, teg, 345p, b/w)	Houghton	1900	Pennell, J.	80-120	
James, Henry	Question of Our Speech (1st, 8vo, gilt, teg, 115p, uncut)	Houghton	1905	Rogers, B.	100-140	
James, Henry	What Maisie Knew (1st AM, sm8vo, 470p, grey/gilt, cvr by...)	H. Stone	1897	Hazenplug, F.	100-140	
James, Will	All in the Day's Riding (1st, 8vo, 251p, DJ)	Scribner	1933	James, W.	120-160	
James, Will	Big-Enough (1st, 8vo, 314p, cloth, b/w, DJ)	Scribner	1931	James, W.	100-120	
James, Will	Cow Country (1st, lg8vo, 242p, brown cl, 28pl, DJ)	Scribner	1927	James, W.	120-160	
James, Will	Cowboys North & South (1st, lg8vo, 217p, 51 fp b/w)	Scribner	1924	James, W.	70-100	
James, Will	Dark Horse (1st, 8vo, green cl, col frn, 306p, DJ)	Scribner	1939	James, W.	120-165	
James, Will	Drifting Cowboy (1st, lg8vo, 241p, 36 fp b/w)	Scribner	1925	James, W.	80-100	
James, Will	Flint Spears (1st, 8vo, 272p, cloth, col frn, DJ)	Scribner	1938	James, W.	100-120	
James, Will	Horses I've Known (1st, 8vo, 280p, 29pl, col frn, DJ)	Scribner	1940	James, W.	85-130	
James, Will	In the Saddle with Uncle Bill (1st, 8vo, 289p, 33pl)	Scribner	1935	James, W.	120-165	
James, Will	Lone Cowboy... (1st, 8vo, gilt, uncut, 431p, fp b/w, DJ)	Scribner	1930	James, W.	100-135	
James, Will	Look-See with Uncle Bill (1st, 8vo, 253p, col frn, DJ)	Scribner	1938	James, W.	100-140	
James, Will	My First Horse (1st, ob8vo, blue cl, [45]p, fp color)	Scribner	1940	James, W.	90-120	
James, Will	Sand (1st, 8vo, 328p, green cl, fp b/w, DJ)	Scribner	1929	James, W.	120-165	
James, Will	Scorpion: Good Bad Horse (1st, 8vo, 312p, col frn, b/w, DJ)	Scribner	1936	James, W.	70-115	
James, Will	Smoky the Cow Horse (1st, 8vo, 310p, b/w, PPP, NM)	Scribner	1926	James, W.	100-150	
James, Will	Smoky the Cow Horse (1st {thus}, 4to, p-o, 263p, 6cp, pep, SC)	Scribner	(1929)	James, W.	65-100	
James, Will	Sun Up, Tales of the Cow Camps (1st, lg8vo, p-o, 342p, b/w)	Scribner	1931	James, W.	70-100	
James, Will	Three Mustangeers (1st, 8vo, 338p, green cl, fp b/w)	Scribner	1933	James, W.	80-100	
James, Will	Uncle Bill... (1st, 8vo, 241p, DJ)	Scribner	1932	James, W.	70-85	
James, Will	Young Cowboy (1st, ob sm4to, 72p, p-o, 5cp)	Scribner	1935	James, W.	120-180	
Jameson, Anna	Shakespeare's Heroines (lg8vo, 308p, gilt, AEG, 6cp, pep)	L: Nister	[1900]	Paget, W.	65-90	
Jamieson, M.M.	Little Redskins (sq12mo, ibds, chromos)	L: Nister	[1910]	Jamieson, M.M.	65-90	
Jamison, C.V.	Lady Jane (1st, lg8vo, 233p, b/w)	Century	1891	Birch, R.	40-65	
Janvier, T.A.	Aztec Treasure House (1st, 8vo, 446p, grey/gilt, 19pl, PPPa)	Harper	1890	Remington, F.	80-125	
Janvier, T.A.	In Old New York (1st, 12mo, 285p, rust/gilt, cvr by...)	Harper	1894	Armstrong, M.	40-65	*
Janvier, T.A.	In Old New York (1st, 12mo, 285p, rust/gilt, b/w by...)	Harper	1894	Pyle, H.	40-65	
Janvier, T.A.	Legends/City of Mexico (1st, 8vo, 164p, 6pl)	Harper	1910	Clark, W.A.	25-40	
Janvier, T.A.	Santa Fe's Partner (1st, 8vo, 237p, teg, green/gilt, 8pl)	Harper	1907	Arthurs, S.	20-30	
Jaufre	Jaufre the Knight & Fair Brunissende (1st, 8vo, 124p, decor by)	Holiday House	1935	Atherton, J.	25-40	*
Jefferson, C.E.	World's Christmas Tree (1st, sm8vo, 44p, green/gilt, cvr by...)	Crowell	(1906)	Armstrong, M.	35-50	*
Jeffries, R.	Bevis... (1st, 8vo, ibds, 8cp)	L: Duckworth	1913	Rountree, H.	65-90	
Jeffries, R.	Bevis... (1st, 8vo, 519p, DJ)	L: J. Cape	1932	Shepard, E.H.	45-60	
Jenks, Tudor	Magician for One Day (1st, 24mo, brown ipcb, 107p, color)	Altemus	(1905)	Neill, J.R.	50-85	*
Jenks, Tudor	Rescue Syndicate (1st, 24mo, ipcb, 110p, b/w, pep)	Altemus	(1905)	Neill, J.R.	50-80	*
Jenks, Tudor	Timothy's Magical Afternoon (1st, 24mo, ipcb, 98p, b/w, pep)	Altemus	(1905)	Neill, J.R.	65-80	
Jenkyn-Thomas, W.	Welsh Fairy Book (1st AM, 8vo, blue/gilt, col frn, 303p)	Stokes	[1907]	Pogany, W.	90-145	*
Jenkyn-Thomas, W.	Welsh Fairy Book (1st, 8vo, 312p, blue cl, col frn, 9pl)	L: T.F. Unwin	(1907)	Pogany, W.	180-275	
Jennings, A.	Beating Back (1st, 8vo, 355p, 3pl by...)	Appleton	1914	Russell, C.M.	60-80	*
Jepson, Edgar	Garden at 19 (1st AM, 8vo, 299p, green cl, 4pl)	Wessels	1910	Boehm, H.B.	70-100	
Jepson, Edgar	Happy Pollyooly (1st, sm8vo, 314p, 5pl)	Bobbs-Merrill	(1915)	Birch, R.	40-60	*
Jerome, J.K.	Tea-Table Talk (1st, 8vo, 153p, blue cl, cvr by...)	Dodd	1903	Falls, C.B.	25-40	
Jerome, J.K.	Three Men on Wheels (1st AM, 8vo, 301p, green cl)	Dodd	1900	Fisher, H.	35-50	
Jerome, J.K.	Told After Supper (1st, 12mo, 169p, teg, uncut)	Field & Tuer	1891	Skeaping, K.M.	65-90	
Jerrold, A.	Cruise in the Acorn (1st, 8vo, 140p, p-o, gilt, 6 ticp)	L: Marcus Ward	1875	Greenaway, K.	260-320	
Jerrold, D.	Fireside Saints (1st, 12mo, teg, 109p, gilt, col frn, b/w, pep)	L: Blackie	1903	Robinson, C.	70-100	

AUTHOR	TITLE	PUBLISHER	DATE	ARTIST	PRICE	LC
Jerrold, W.C.	Big Book of Fables (1st, lg8vo, 293p, teg, red cl, 28cp, pep)	L: Blackie	1912	Robinson, C.	265-340	
Jerrold, W.C.	Big Book of Fairy Tales (1st AM, 4to, 344p, 12cp)	Caldwell	(1911)	Robinson, C.	200-300	
Jerrold, W.C.	Big Book of Fairy Tales (1st, 4to, 344p, gilt, AEG, 12cp)	L: Blackie	1911	Robinson, C.	280-350	
Jerrold, W.C.	Big Book of Nursery Rhymes (1st, 4to, red/gilt, 320p, AEG, 18cp)	L: Blackie	[1903]	Robinson, C.	275-400	
Jerrold, W.C.	Bon-Mots... (1st, 24mo, 192p, gilt, teg, cvr by...)	L: J.M. Dent	1893	Beardsley, A.	75-100	
Jerrold, W.C.	Bon-Mots/Eighteenth Century (1st, 16mo, 195p)	L: Dent	1897	Woodward, A.B.	35-50	*
Jerrold, W.C.	Nonsense Nonsense! (1st, 4to, [68]p, ibds, 30cp)	L: Blackie	1902	Robinson, C.	275-400	
Jerrold, W.C.	Road, Rail & Sea (1st, 4to, ibds, unpag, 10cp)	L: Blackie	[1906]	Robinson, C.	180-250	
Jewett, E.M.	Egyptian Tales of Magic (1st, sm8vo, 257p, color)	Little/Brown	1924	Day, M.	25-40	*
Jewett, E.M.	Hidden Treasure of Glaston (1st, 8vo, grn cl 307p, b/w, pep, NH)	Viking	1946	Chapman, F.T.	35-50	*
Jewett, E.M.	Mystery at Boulder Point (1st, 8vo, 281p, grey cl, fp b/w)	Viking	1949	Barnum, J.H.	20-35	*
Jewett, E.M.	Told on the King's Highway (1st, 8vo, 246p, b/w, pep)	Viking	1943	Lawson, M.A.	30-45	*
Jewett, E.M.	Which was Witch? (1st, sm8vo, 160p, yellow cl, b/w, pep)	Viking	1953	Yashima, T.	50-90	R*
Jewett, E.M.	Wonder Tales from Tibet (1st, sm8vo, 183p, green cl, 8cp)	Little/Brown	1922	Day, M.	25-40	*
Jewett, J.H.	Bunny Stories (1st, sq8vo, 210p, b/w)	Stokes	1892	Barnes, C.	65-80	
Jewett, J.H.	Con the Wizard (1st AM, narrow 12mo, 123p, ibds, 8cp)	Stokes	(1905)	Little, E.R.	45-60	
Jewett, J.H.	Little Christmas (1st, 8vo, 113p, ibds, 8cp)	Stokes	(1906)	Upjohn, A.M.	35-50	*
Jewett, J.H.	Little Governor/Fableland (1st, narrow 8vo, 104p, ibds, 5cp)	Stokes	(1907)	Farnsworth, E.N.	60-80	
Jewett, J.H.	Snuggy Bedtime Stories (1st, ob12mo, 126p, ibds, 8cp)	Stokes	(1906)	Upjohn, A.M.	45-70	
Jewett, S.O.	Betty Leicester's Christmas (1st, 12mo, 68p, ibds, 8cp)	Houghton	1899	Betts, A.W.	45-60	*
Jewett, S.O.	Deephaven (1st, 8vo, 305p, teg)	Houghton	1894	Woodbury, C.& M.	70-90	
Joan, Natalie	Ameliaranne in Town (1st, 12mo, unpag, color)	L: Harrap	1930	Pearse, S.B.	35-50	*
Joan, Natalie	Cosy-Time Tales (1st, 4to, ibds, 8cp)	L: T. Nelson	(1922)	Anderson, A.	130-200	
Joan, Natalie	Glad Book (1st, 8vo, ibds, 12 fp color)	L: H. Milford	(1921)	Sowerby, M.	80-120	
Joan, Natalie	Lie-Down Stories (1st, lg8vo, p-o, 77p, grey bds, 8cp)	L: Blackie	(1919)	Anderson, A.	140-200	
Joan, Natalie	Little Mothers (ob8vo, ibds, p-o, 12 fp color)	L: H. Milford	[1908]	Cramer, Rie	100-140	
Johns, Rowland	Jock the King's Pony (1st {std}, 8vo, ibds, 60p, b/w, pep)	Dutton	(1936)	Brown, Paul	45-75	*
Johnson, A.E.	Below Zero (lg4to, cloth, 12cp)	L: Hodder	[1910]	Pocock, N.	50-80	
Johnson, A.E.	John Hassall, R.I. (1st, 8vo, 44p, 7cp, 28pl)	L: A&C Black	1907	Hassall, J.	60-90	
Johnson, A.E.	Russian Ballet (1st AM, 4to, gilt, 240p, ipcb, 12cp)	Houghton	1913	Bull, Rene	165-200	
Johnson, A.E.	Russian Ballet (1st, lg4to, 240p, teg, gilt, uncut, 12cp)	L: Constable	1913	Bull, Rene	225-300	
Johnson, Ben	His Volpone (1st, 4to, blue/gilt, 74p)	L: Smithers	1898	Beardsley, A.	200-300	
Johnson, Burgess	Bashful Ballads (1st, 8vo, teg, 145p, b/w)	Harper	1911	Walker, A.B.	20-35	
Johnson, Burgess	Little Book/Necessary Nonsense (1st {std}, 16mo, 81p, b/w, dep)	Harper	1929	MacKinstry, E.	25-40	*
Johnson, Burgess	Pleasant Tragedies of Childhood (1st, 4to, gilt, 119p, 30pl, pep)	Harper	1905	Cory, F.	80-120	
Johnson, C.	Fir-Tree Fairy Book (1st, 8vo, 333p, color, pep)	Little/Brown	1912	Popini, A.	45-60	*
Johnson, Clifton	Parson's Devil (1st, 8vo, 296p, green cl, 4pl)	Crowell	(1927)	Newell, P.	65-90	
Johnson, Crockett	Barnaby (1st, 12mo, 361p, blue cl, b/w)	Holt	1943	Johnson, C.	45-60	*
Johnson, Crockett	Barnaby & Mr. O'Malley (1st, 12mo, 328p, b/w)	Holt	(1944)	Johnson, C.	45-65	*
Johnson, Crockett	Blue Ribbon Puppies (1st, 16mo, ibds, 31p, 2-color)	Harper	1958	Johnson, C.	45-70	
Johnson, Crockett	Harold & the Purple Crayon (1st, 16mo, ibds, unpag, 1-color)	Harper	1955	Johnson, C.	50-80	R*
Johnson, Crockett	Harold's Circus (1st, 16mo, ibds, unpag, 1-color)	Harper	1959	Johnson, C.	50-75	*
Johnson, Crockett	Terrible Terrifying Toby (1st, lg8vo, unpag)	Harper	1957	Johnson, C.	50-70	*
Johnson, Crockett	Who's Upside Down? (1st, lg8vo, [24]p, ipcb, b/w)	W.R. Scott	1952	Johnson, C.	45-70	*
Johnson, E.F.	Little Book of Prayers (1st, 12mo, unpag, 1-color, pep, DJ)	Viking	1941	Petershams	45-65	
Johnson, E.G.	Private Memoirs of Madame Roland (1st, teg)	McClurg	1900	Armstrong, M.	30-45	
Johnson, Gerald W.	America is Born (1st, 4to, 254p, red cl, b/w, NH)	Wm. Morrow	1959	Fisher, L.E.	50-80	R*
Johnson, J.P.	20 Years of Hus'ling (1st, 8vo, 664p, tan cl, 48 b/w)	Chi: Thompson	1900	Denslow, W.W.	100-150	
Johnson, J.W.	God's Trombones (1st, 8vo, bds, gilt, 56p, 8pl, DJ)	Viking	1927	Douglas, A.	180-240	
Johnson, L.R.	Teddy-Bear ABC (1st, sq8vo, [55]p, color, pep)	Caldwell	(1907)	Sanford, M.L.	180-300	*
Johnson, M.	Cat's Fairy Land... (1st, 12mo, 184p, gilt)	H. Carter	1900	(Photos)	100-160	
Johnson, Margaret	Polly & the Wishing Ring (1st, 12mo, 123p, 4cp)	MacMillan	1918	Pogany, W.	30-45	*
Johnson, Margaret	What O'Clock Jingles (1st, ob8vo, ibds, [30]p, 27 b/w)	D. Lothrop	(1887)	Johnson, M.	60-85	*
Johnson, O.	Tennessee Shad (1st, 8vo, red cl, 307p, 8pl, PPP)	Baker/Taylor	1911	Gruger, F.R.	120-165	
Johnson, O.	The Varmint (1st, 8vo, 396p, green cl, 6pl, PPP)	Baker/Taylor	1910	Gruger, F.R.	120-150	
Johnson, R.M.	Widow Guthrie (1st, sm8vo, blue/gilt, 309p, 6pl, cep)	Appleton	1890	Kemble, E.W.	30-45	*
Johnson, Richard	Saint George & the Dragon (1st, lg8vo, [30]p, pep)	Scribner	1941	Maloy, L.	25-40	*
Johnston, A.F.	Georgina of the Rainbows (1st, sm8vo, 348p, b/w pl)	NY: Britton	(1916)	Neill, J.R.	40-60	*
Johnston, A.F.	Giant Scissors (1st, 8vo, 201p, blue/gilt, teg, 8cp)	Page	1906	Merrill, F.	25-40	
Johnston, A.F.	It Was the Road to Jericho (1st {std}, 8vo, [41]p, gilt, pep)	Britton	(1919)	Neill, J.R.	40-60	
Johnston, A.F.	Little Colonel (1st, 8vo, 102p, green/gilt, b/w, PPP)	J. Knight	1896	Barry, E.B.	130-200	
Johnston, A.F.	Little Colonel's Knight Comes Riding (1st, 8vo, 318p, b/w)	Page	1907	Barry, E.B.	25-40	
Johnston, A.F.	Mary Ware of Texas (1st, 8vo, pict cl, 8pl)	Page	1910	Merrill, F.	25-40	
Johnston, A.F.	May Ware, Little Colonel's Chum (1st, 12mo, 305p, tan cl, 8pl)	Page	1908	Barry, E.B.	25-40	
Johnston, A.F.	Mildred's Inheritance (1st, 12mo, 74p, 10pl)	Page	1906	Horne, D.W.	20-35	*
Johnston, A.F.	Miss Santa Claus o/t Pullman (1st, 8vo, 172p, gilt, colfrn, 8pl)	Century	1913	Birch, R.	25-40	
Johnston, A.F.	Ole Mammy's Torment (1st, 12mo, 118p, fp b/w)	Page	1897	Johnston/Sacker	30-50	
Johnston, A.F.	Road of the Loving Heart (1st, sm8vo, 77p, pep, b/w)	Page	1922	Bromhall, W.	20-30	
Johnston, A.F.	Story of Dago (1st, 12mo, 101p, 10pl)	Page	1900	Barry, E.B.	25-40	*
Johnston, A.F.	Two Little Knights of Kentucky (1st, 8vo, 203p, blue/gilt, 8cp)	Page	1907	Brett, H.M.	25-40	
Johnston, H.	Pioneers in Canada (1st, 8vo, 328p, gilt, 8cp)	L: Blackie	1912	Wall-Cousins, E.	30-50	
Johnston, I.M.	Jeweled Toad (1st, sm4to, 211p, ibds, 8cp)	Bobbs-Merrill	(1907)	Denslow, W.W.	200-260	

AUTHOR	TITLE	PUBLISHER	DATE	ARTIST	PRICE	LC
Johnston, M.	Long Roll (1st, 8vo, 683p, grey cl, 4cp, pep)	Houghton	1911	Wyeth, N.C.	30-45	
Johnston, M.	Prisoners of Hope (1st, 8vo, 378p)	Houghton	1899	Rogers, B.	30-45	
Johnston, M.	To Have & to Hold (1st, 8vo, green cl, 403p, 8pl)	Houghton	1900	Various	30-50	
Johnston, M.	To Have & to Hold (1st {this format}, lg8vo, 331p, 5cp)	Houghton	1931	Schoonover, F.	45-60	
Johnston, R.M.	Pearce Amerson's Will (1st, 12mo, teg, 275p, cvr by...)	Way/Williams	1898	Hazenplug, F.	75-120	
Jones, E.O.	Big Susan (1st, sq8vo, ibds, 83p, color, pep, DJ)	MacMillan	1947	Jones, E.O.	45-60	
Jones, E.O.	David: Bible Story with Pictures (1st, 4to, ibds, color)	MacMillan	1937	Jones, E.O.	35-50	*
Jones, E.O.	Minnie the Mermaid (1st, sq12mo, [48]p, red cl, color)	NY: OUP	(1939)	Jones, E.O.	30-45	
Jones, H.	Prince Boo Hoo & Little Smuts (1st, sq8vo, 319p, teg, uncut)	L: Wells/Gard.	(1896)	Browne, G.	100-165	
Jones, Idwal	Chef's Holiday (1st {std}, sm8vo, 210p, b/w)	Longmans	1952	Duvoisin, R.	20-35	*
Jones, Idwal	Whistler's Van (1st, 8vo, 235p, b/w, pep, NH)	Viking	1936	Gay, Z.	50-70	*
Jones, J.O.	Little Child (1st, ob4to, ibds, 40p, pep, fp color)	Viking	1946	Jones, E.O.	30-45	*
Jones, J.O.	Secrets (1st, 8vo, 24p, fp color, DJ)	Viking	1945	Jones, E.O.	30-45	
Jones, J.O.	Small Rain (1st, ob8vo, ibds, [40]p, 1-color, pep, DJ, CH)	Viking	1943	Jones, E.O.	60-90	
Jones, J.O. (ed.)	Many Mansions... (1st, lg8vo, 134p, color, DJ)	Viking	1947	Ward, L.	30-45	
Jones, J.O. (ed.)	This is the Way (1st, sm ob4to, 62p, 2-color, pep)	Viking	1951	Jones, E.O.	25-40	*
Jones, Paul	Alphabet of Aviation (1st, 4to, blue cl, 28 fp color)	Macrae-Smith	(1928)	Shenton, E.	130-165	*
Jones, V.M.	Peter & Gretchen/Old Nuremberg (1st, 4to, p-o, 96p, color, pep)	Whitman	1935	Sewell, H.	35-50	
Jones, W.	How the Derrick Works (1st, 4to, black cl, 43p, 1-color, cep)	MacMillan	(1930)	Jones, W.	50-80	
Jordan, E.	May Iverson... (1st, 8vo, blue cl, 282p, p-o, 8pl)	Harper	1904	Harding, C.	40-60	
Jordan, N.	Mother Goose Handicraft (1st, sm8vo, 149p, fp b/w)	Harcourt	(1945)	Jordan, N.	45-70	*
Joseph, A.W.	Sondo: A Liberian Boy (1st, 4to, ibds, pep, 32p, fp b/w)	Whitman	(1936)	Magnie, B.	50-70	
Joslin, Sesyle	What Do You Say, Dear? (1st, ob8vo, unpag, CH)	W.R. Scott	1958	Sendak, M.	120-170	*
Judah, Aaron	Pot of Gold (1st, 8vo, 62p, red cloth, b/w)	L: Faber	1959	Peake, M.	45-60	*
Judson, C.I.	Boat Builder (1st, 8vo, tan cl, 121p, fp b/w, pep)	Scribner	1940	Sperry, A.	30-45	*
Judson, C.I.	Flower Fairies (1st, lg8vo, p-o, pep, 93p, 6cp)	Rand/McNally	(1915)	Enright, M.W.	65-80	*
Judson, C.I.	Garden Adventures of Tommy Tittlemouse (1st, sm8vo, 64p, color)	Rand/McNally	(1922)	Beem, F.	20-30	*
Judson, C.I.	Good-Night Stories (1st, 12mo, pict cl, 131p, b/w)	McClurg	1916	Wilson, C.P.	20-35	*
Judson, C.I.	Green Ginger Jar (1st, 8vo, green cl, 210p, fp b/w, pep)	Houghton	1949	Brown, Paul	35-50	*
Judson, C.I.	Mr. Justice Holmes (1st, sm4to, 192p, NH)	Follett	(1956)	Todd, R.	65-80	*
Judson, C.I.	People Who Work Near our House (1st, sm8vo, 48p, color)	Rand/McNally	(1942)	Ward, Keith	35-50	*
Judson, C.I.	People Who Work in Country & City (1st, sm4to, 94p, color)	Rand/McNally	(1943)	Ward, Keith	35-50	*
Judson, C.I.	Pioneer Girl (1st, sm8vo, ipcb, 80p, fp 1-color, pep)	Rand/McNally	(1939)	Foster, G.	25-40	*
Judson, C.I.	Railway Engineer (1st, 8vo, 171p, b/w pl, pep)	Scribner	(1941)	Simon, E.M.	25-40	*
Judson, C.I.	Reaper Man (1st, 8vo, 156p, b/w)	Houghton	1948	Brown, Paul	25-40	*
Judson, C.I.	They Came from France (1st, 8vo, red cl, 245p, fp b/w, pep)	Houghton	1943	Lenski, L.	30-45	*
Jungman, B.	Holland (1st, lg8vo, teg, 212p, 75cp)	L: A&C Black	1904	Jungman, N.	65-100	
Justus, May	At the Foot of Windy Low (1st, 8vo, green cl, 80p, 10cp, pep)	Volland	(1930)	Dudley, C.	50-70	
Justus, May	Gabby Gaffer (1st, 8vo, green/gilt, 80p, 10cp, pep)	Volland	(1929)	Dudley, C.	45-65	
Justus, May	House in No-End Hollow (1st {std}, sm8vo, 286p, col frn, pep)	Doubleday/Dor.	1938	Berry, E.	25-40	*
Justus, May	Sammy (1st, 4to, cloth, 47p, color)	Whitman	1946	Chisholm, C.	20-30	*
Kaberry, C.J.	Our Little Neighbors (4to, pcb, 105p, 11 ticp)	L: OUP	(1921)	Detmold, E.J.	200-320	
Kahl, V.	Away Went Wolfgang (1st, ob4to, beige cl, [32]p, color)	Scribner	1954	Kahl, V.	50-80	R*
Kahmann, C.	Jasper the Gypsy Dog (1st, 8vo, yellow cl, 93p, b/w, pep)	J. Messner	(1938)	Wiese, K.	30-45	*
Kalashnikoff, N.	Jumper (1st, 8vo, blue/silver, 224p, b/w)	Scribner	1944	Shenton, E.	25-40	*
Kalashnikoff, N.	My Friend Yakub (1st, sm8vo, 249p, fp b/w)	Scribner	(1953)	Rojankovsky, F.	25-40	
Kalashnikoff, N.	The Defender (1st, 8vo, 136p, tan cl, 8 fp b/w, NH)	Scribner	1951	Shenton, E.	60-85	*
Kalashnikoff, N.	Toyon: Dog of the North (1st {std}, 8vo, 246p, uncut, b/w)	Harper	(1950)	Markovia, A.	20-30	*
Kalnay, Francis	Chucaro, Wild Pony of Pampa (1st {std}, 8vo, 126p, b/w, NH)	Harcourt	(1958)	DeMiskey, J.	45-60	*
Kalnay, Francis	Richest Boy in the World (1st {std}, 8vo, 92p, grn cl, fp b/w)	Harcourt	(1959)	Mars, W.T.	30-45	*
Kaplan, A.O.	Baby's Biography (1st, 4to, AEG, 67p, gilt, color)	Brentano's	1891	Brundage, F.	130-165	
Kastner, Erich	Animal's Conference (1st AM, 4to, ibds, [62]p, color)	McKay	(1949)	Trier, W.	65-90	*
Kastner, Erich	Emil & the Detectives (1st {std}, 8vo, 224p, yellow cl, color)	Doubleday/Dor.	1930	Trier, W.	80-100	*
Kastner, Erich	Emil & the Three Twins (1st UK, 8vo, 251p, ibds, 8 illus)	L: Cape	1935	Trier, W.	65-80	
Kastner, Erich	Flying Classroom (1st UK, 8vo, 223p, ibds, 10 illus)	L: Cape	1934	Trier, W.	65-80	
Kastner, Erich	Puss in Boots (1st AM, 4to, ibds, 66p, color)	J. Messner	1957	Trier, W.	25-40	*
Kato, N. (tr.)	Children's Stories/Japanese Fairy Tales... (1st, 4to, ibds, 10cp)	L: R. Tuck	[1918]	Theaker, H.G.	80-125	
Kauffmann, R.	Barbary Bo... (1st, 8vo, p-o, 261p, 5pl)	Penn	1929	Schoonover, F.	25-45	
Kauffmann, R.	Spanish Dollars (1st, 8vo, p-o, 7pl)	Penn	1925	Lee, M.V.	20-30	
Kay, G.A.	Adventures in Geography (1st, 4to, orang cl, color)	Volland	(1930)	Kay, G.A.	35-50	
Kay, G.A.	Adventures on our Street (1st, sm4to, p-o, 130p, 4cp, pep)	McKay	(1925)	Kay, G.A.	50-70	
Kay, G.A.	Book of Seven Wishes (1st, 8vo, 224p, blue cl, 4cp, pep)	Moffat	1917	Kay, G.A.	50-85	
Kay, G.A.	Fairy Who Believed in Human Beings (1st, 8vo, 169p, 4cp)	Moffat	1918	Kay, G.A.	70-100	
Kay, G.A.	Friends of Jimmy (1st, lg8vo, ibds, [95]p, color, pep)	Volland	(1926)	Kay, G.A.	50-80	
Kay, G.A.	Helping the Weatherman (1st, 8vo, ibds, unpag, color, pep)	Volland	(1920)	Kay, G.A.	50-70	
Kay, G.A.	Jolly Old Shadow Man (1st, 12mo, ibds, [39]p, color, pep)	Volland	(1920)	Kay, G.A.	50-70	
Kay, G.A.	Peter, Patter & Pixie (1st, lg4to, ibds, 22p, 5cp)	McBride	1931	Kay, G.A.	65-90	
Kay, G.A.	Us Kids at the Circus (1st, 8vo, ibds, 120p, color, pep)	Volland	(1927)	Kay, G.A.	60-80	*
Kay, G.A.	When the Sandman Comes (1st, 8vo, 183p, p-o, pep, 4cp)	Moffat	1916	Kay, G.A.	50-70	
Kay, Helen	One Mitten Lewis (1st, 4to, ibds, [32]p, color)	Lothrop/Lee	(1955)	Werth, K.	40-60	
Kaye, M.	Potter Pinner Meadow (1st, sq4to, 40p, ibds)	L: Collins	(1930)	Tempest, M.	50-70	
Keats, J.	Isabella... (1st, 4to, teg, gilt, 8pl)	L: Kegan Paul	1898	MacDougall, W.B.	150-200	

AUTHOR	TITLE	PUBLISHER	DATE	ARTIST	PRICE	LC
Keats, J.	Isabella... (1st, 12mo, 42p, wraps, uncut, 5cp)	L: Foulis	1907	King, J.	70-100	
Keats, Mark	Sancho & Stubborn Mule (1st, ob12mo, ipcb, [41]p, 2-color, pep)	W.R. Scott	(1944)	Eichenberg, F.	50-80	*
Keeler, D.B.	Memoirs of Simple Simon (1st, 4to, [56]p, color)	R.H. Russell	(1901)	Vandevort, C.S.	120-170	*
Keen, R.H.	Little Ape... (1st [1st bk.], 8vo, yellow cl, 68p, 4pl)	L: Hendersons	1921	Austen, J.	145-200	
Keiser, M.	God Returns to Vuelta Abajo (1st, lg8vo, 149p, rust cl, p-o)	W.R. Scott	(1936)	Low, J.	70-100	R*
Kellock, Harold	Down in the Grass (1st, 12mo, 247p, uncut, col frn, 25 fp b/w)	Coward	1929	Wiese, K.	30-45	*
Kellogg, V.	Nuova or the New Bee (1st, 8vo, 150p, col frn, 14pl, pep)	Houghton	1920	Winter, M.	50-70	
Kelly, A.	The Rosebud.... (1st, 4to, 78p, 20 ticp)	L: T.F. Unwin	1909	Crane, W.	180-225	
Kelly, E.M.	When I was Little (1st, 8vo, p-o, 96p, color)	Rand/McNally	(1915)	Squire, M.H.	50-75	
Kelly, Eric P.	At the Sign/Golden Compass (1st, 8vo, grn/gilt, 195p, 11pl, pep)	MacMillan	1938	Lufkin, R.	20-30	*
Kelly, Eric P.	Blacksmith of Vilno (1st, 8vo, 184p, green cl, 3cp)	MacMillan	1930	Pruszynska, A.	30-45	*
Kelly, Eric P.	Christmas Nightingale (1st, 8vo, red cl, 73p, 4 b/w)	MacMillan	1932	DeAngeli, M.	25-40	*
Kelly, Eric P.	Girl Who Would Be Queen (1st, 8vo, 201p)	McClurg	1939	Bock, V.	20-30	*
Kelly, Eric P.	Gold Star of Halich (1st, 8vo, green cl, 215p, 3cp, fp b/w)	MacMillan	1931	Pruszynska, A.	35-50	*
Kelly, Eric P.	In Clean Hay (1st {std}, 8vo, ibds, 31p, color, cep)	MacMillan	1953	Petershams	25-40	*
Kelly, Eric P.	Three Sides of Agiochook (1st, 8vo, 211p, b/w, pep)	MacMillan	1935	Appleton, LeRoy	25-45	*
Kelly, Eric P.	Treasure Mountain (1st, 8vo, 211p, green cl, pep, b/w)	MacMillan	1937	Lufkin, R.	25-40	*
Kelly, Eric P.	Trumpeter of Krakow (1st, 8vo, 218p, blue cl, 3cp, NM)	MacMillan	1928	Pruszynska, A.	65-90	*
Kelly, F.	Delafield Affair (1st, 8vo, ibds, 422p, 4cp)	McClurg	1909	Dixon, M.	35-50	
Kelly, James P.	Prince Izon (1st, 8vo, 399p, brown cl, p-o, 5cp)	McClurg	1910	Betts, H.& E.	30-50	*
Kelly, R.T.	Egypt (1st, 8vo, gilt, teg, 246p, 75cp)	L: A&C Black	1902	Kelly, R.T.	65-90	
Kelman, J.H.	Stories from Chaucer (1st, 12mo, 114p, p-o, gilt, 8cp)	L: Jack	[1906]	Robinson, W.H.	120-165	
Kelsey, A.	Once the Hodja (1st {std}, 12mo, 170p)	Longmans	1943	Dobias, F.	25-40	*
Kemble, E.W.	Comical Coons (1st UK, ob4to, ibds, unpag, b/w)	L: Kegan Paul	1898	Kemble, E.W.	280-350	
Kemble, E.W.	Coon Alphabet (1st, sm4to, ibds, b/w)	R.H. Russell	1898	Kemble, E.W.	250-400	
Kemble, E.W.	Kemble's Coons (1st, ob4to, ibds, 31pl, b/w)	R.H. Russell	1896	Kemble, E.W.	225-350	
Kemble, E.W.	Kemble's Pickaninnies (1st, lg ob4to, 31pl, b/w)	R.H. Russell	1901	Kemble, E.W.	250-400	*
Kemble, E.W.	Kemble's Sketch Book (1st, lg ob8vo, tan buckram, 30pl)	R.H. Russell	1899	Kemble, E.W.	180-240	
Kemble, E.W.	Life's Book of Animals (1st, ob4to, 80p, buckram, b/w)	Doub./McClure	1898	Various	75-100	
Kemble, E.W.	The Blackberries... (1st, ob4to, ibds, [36]p, 16cp)	R.H. Russell	1897	Kemble, E.W.	280-450	
Kempis	Imitation of Christ (sm4to, 274p, 8cp)	L: Chatto	1908	Flint, W.R.	60-85	
Kempson, F.C.	Sad Fate of Erica's Blackamoor (1st, ob folio, ibds, [40]p)	L: E. Arnold	1903	Kempson, F.C.	140-175	
Kendall, Carol	Gammage Cup (1st {std}, 8vo, 221p, blue cl, b/w, NH)	Harcourt	(1959)	Blegvad^E E.	30-50	*
Kennan, G.	Tragedy of Pelee (1st, 8vo, 257p, 7pl)	Outlook	1902	Varian, G.	30-45	
Kennedy, H.A.	New World Fairy Book (1st, 8vo, 354p, gilt, teg, uncut, b/w)	L: Dent	1904	Millar, H.R.	70-100	*
Kennedy, M.	Forest Beyond the Woodlands (1st, 8vo, 152p, pcb, 14pl)	Knopf	1921	Knowlton, V.	30-45	*
Kennedy, M.	Surprise to the Children (1st {std}, sq4to, ibds, 6cp)	Doubleday/Dor.	1933	Dowd, J.H.	30-45	
Kennedy, Mary	Jenny (1st, 8vo, 153p, green cl, 11 fp b/w)	Lothrop/Lee	(1954)	Adams, A.	25-40	*
Kennedy, Mary	Violets are Blue (1st, 8vo, 154p, blue cl, fp b/w)	Lothrop/Lee	(1951)	Stone, H.	25-40	*
Kent, Louise A.	Red Rajah (1st, sm8vo, 290p, blue cl, 6 fp b/w, pep)	Houghton	1933	Wiese, K.	25-40	*
Kent, R.	It's Me O Lord... (1st, lg8vo, gilt, 617p, b/w)	Dodd	(1955)	Kent, R.	35-50	*
Kent, R.	N by E (1st, 8vo, white cl, 281p, DJ)	Brewer/Warren	1930	Kent, R.	80-100	
Kent, R.	Northern Christmas (1st, 12mo, [32]p, ipcb, 1-color, DJ)	A.A. Group	(1941)	Kent, R.	50-70	
Kent, R.	On Earth Peace... (1st, 12mo, [24]p, ibds, 1-color)	A.A. Group	(1942)	Kent, R.	35-50	
Kent, R.	Rockwellkentiana (1st {std}, 4to, col frn, blue cl, DJ)	Harcourt	1933	Kent, R.	75-100	
Kent, R.	Salamina (1st {std}, 8vo, blue/silver, 336p, 23pl)	Harcourt	1935	Kent, R.	80-130	R
Kent, R.	This is my Own (1st {std}, 8vo, cream cl, 393p, DJ)	Duell/Sloan	(1940)	Kent, R.	100-140	
Kent, R.	Voyaging: Southward... (1st, 4to, yellow cl, 184p, pep)	Putnam	1924	Kent, R.	70-100	
Kent, R.	Wilderness (1st, 4to, teg, 217p, grey/gilt, pep)	Putnam	1920	Kent, R.	100-165	
Kenward, James	Suburban Child (1st, 8vo, 140p, white ipcb, 11 b/w, DJ)	L: Cambridge	1955	Ardizzone, E.	50-70	
Kenyon, C.R.	Argonauts of the Amazon (1st, 8vo, blue/gilt, 305p, 6pl)	L: Chambers	1901	Rackham, A.	200-250	
Kepes, J.A.	Five Little Monkeys (1st {1st bk}, lg sq8vo, 32p, col, pep, CH)	Houghton	1952	Kepes, J.A.	70-100	*
Kepes, J.A.	Two Little Birds & Three (1st, 8vo, 62p, blue cl, fp 1-color)	Houghton	1960	Kepes, J.A.	60-90	R*
Ketchum, J.	Stick-in-the-Mud (1st, sm8vo, unpag, green cl, pep, 1-color)	W.R. Scott	(1953)	Ketchum, F.	30-50	*
Key, A.	Red Eagle (1st, 4to, 95p, ibds, pep, color)	Volland	(1930)	Key, A.	70-90	
Keyes, A.M.	Five Senses (1st, 8vo, ivory cl, 252p, 5cp)	Moffat	1911	Smith, J.W.	250-320	
Keys, Leonora	Happy Dollies (lg8vo, [46]p, color, cloth)	Whitman	(1914)	Lee, E.D.	80-100	
Keys, Leonora	Play Dollies (sm4to, 38p, ibds, color)	Whitman	(1927)	Lee, E.D.	75-100	*
Kidd, Dudley	Bull of the Kraal (1st, lg8vo, teg, uncut, 12cp)	L: A&C Black	1908	Goodall, A.M.	120-160	*
Kidd, Will	Dickydidos (1st, folio, 94p, ibds, 22cp)	L: Richards	[1903]	Kidd, Will	250-400	*
Kilbourne, C.E.	Baby Elephant & Zoo Man (1st, 8vo, p-o, color, pep)	Penn	1911	Longstreet, H.	70-110	*
Kilbourne, C.E.	Baby Ostrich & Mr. Wise Owl (1st, 16mo, ipcb, p-o, 82p, col, pep)	Penn	1915	Longstreet, H.	80-120	R*
Kilbourne, C.E.	Baby Reindeer & Silver Fox (1st, 16mo, ipcb, p-o, 82p, col, pep)	Penn	1916	Longstreet, H.	70-100	R*
Kilmer, J.	Trees (1st, 8vo, [24]p, ipcb, color, DJ)	Doran	(1925)	MacKinstry, E.	45-65	
King, B.	Ruffs & Pompons (1st, 8vo, 256p, col frn, 6pl, pep)	Little/Brown	1924	Day, M.	25-40	
King, Ben	Ben King's Southland Melodies (1st, 8vo, green cl, 128p, b/w)	Chi: Forbes	1911	(Photos)	80-130	
King, Ben	Jane Jones.... (1st, 8vo, 94p, 16cp)	Chi: Forbes	1909	Williams, J.A.	65-100	*
King, C.	Apache Princess (1st, 12mo, 328p, p-o, teg, 6pl)	Hobart	1903	Deming/Remington	35-50	
King, C.	Apache Princess (1st, 12mo, 328p, p-o, teg, 6pl)	Hobart	1903	Remington/Deming	35-50	
King, C.	Cadet Days (1st, sm8vo, 293p, blue/gilt, PPP)	Harper	1894	Zogbaum, R.F.	90-120	
King, C.	Daughter of the Sioux (1st, 8vo, 306p, teg, p-o, 4pl)	Hobart	1903	Remington, F.	50-70	
King, C.	From School to Battlefield (1st, 8vo, beige cl, 322p, 6pl)	Lippincott	1899	Oakley, V.	90-120	

AUTHOR	TITLE	PUBLISHER	DATE	ARTIST	PRICE	LC
King, C.	Medal of Honor (1st, 8vo, p-o, teg, 348p, 3pl by...)	Hobart	1905	Deming, E.W.	30-50	*
King, C.	To the Front (1st, 8vo, ibds, 260p, 4pl)	Harper	1908	Remington, F.	60-80	*
King, C.	Tonio, Son of Sierras (1st, 12mo, 338p, 4cp, 4pl)	Dillingham	(1906)	Post, C.J.	20-30	
King, Eliz.	New House that Jack Built (1st, 4to, ibds, [31]p, color)	McBride	1932	Dennis, A.	35-50	*
King, G.	Herodotus (1st {std}, 8vo, 274p, 14pl, map, pep, DJ)	Doubleday/Dor.	1929	Artzybasheff, B.	65-80	
King, J.M.	City of the West (1st, 8vo, wraps, 27p, 24 ticp)	L: Foulis	1910	King, J.	150-200	*
King, J.M.	Dwellings/Old World Town (8vo, 51p, wraps, 24 b/w)	L: Gowans/Gray	1909	King, J.	100-160	
King, J.M.	Grey City of the North (1st, 8vo, 51p, wraps, 26pl)	L: Foulis	(1910)	King, J.	130-200	
King, J.M.	How Cinderella/Go to the Ball (1st, 8vo, 57p, teg, 16 ticp)	L: Foulis	(1924)	King, J.	300-500	
King, J.M.	Legends of Flowers (1st, sm8vo, teg, p-o, 168p)	L: Foulis	1909	King, J.	100-140	
King, J.M.	Little White Town of Never Weary (1st, 4to, 155p, 4 ticp, cep)	L: Harrap	(1917)	King, J.	300-450	
King, Marian	Amnon, Lad of Palestine (1st, sm8vo, 96p, color, pep)	Houghton	1931	Enright, E.	25-50	*
King, Marian	Kees (1st, 4to, 79p, ibds, color, pep)	Harper	1930	Enright, E.	35-50	
King, Marian	Kees & Kleintje (1st, 4to, 80p, p-o, color, pep)	Whitman	(1934)	Enright, E.	45-60	
King, Marian	Sean & Sheela (1st, lg8vo, p-o, 135p, dp color, pep)	Whitman	1937	Brock, Emma	25-40	
King-Hall, E.	Adventures in Toyland (1st, 4to, blue/gilt, AEG, 152p, 8cp)	L: Blackie	[1897]	Woodward, A.B.	150-200	
Kinglake, A.W.	Eothen (1st, sm8vo, 341p, teg, uncut, blue cl, b/w)	L: Newnes	1898	Millar, H.R.	60-80	
Kingman, Lee	Best Christmas (1st {std}, sm8vo, 95p, b/w, cep)	Doubleday	(1949)	Cooney, B.	25-45	*
Kingman, Lee	Ilenka (1st, 4to, red cl, [48]p, color)	Houghton/JLG	1945	Bare, A.E.	45-70	*
Kingman, Lee	Mikko's Fortune (1st {std}, ob4to, blue cl, 46p, color, pep)	Farrar/Rine.	(1955)	Bare, A.E.	50-75	*
Kingman, Lee	Peter's Long Walk (1st {std}, ob lg8vo, 47p, ibds, color)	Doubleday	1953	Cooney, B.	65-100	R*
Kingman, Lee	Pierre Pidgeon (1st, 4to, unpag, color, CH)	Houghton	1943	Bare, A.E.	65-95	*
Kingman, Lee	Rocky Summer (1st, 8vo, 209p, blue cl, b/w)	Houghton	1948	Cooney, B.	25-45	*
Kingsbury, H.O.	All Aboard for Wonderland (1st, 4to, 190p, 4cp)	Moffat	1917	Kay, G.A.	70-115	*
Kingsley, C.	Hereward the Wake (1st, 8vo, 196p, pcb, p-o, 8cp)	L: Jack	[1910]	Orr, M.S.	65-80	*
Kingsley, C.	Heroes/Greek Fairy Tales (1st, 8vo, 166p, 9 ticp)	L: Medici	1928	Flint, W.R.	85-100	
Kingsley, C.	The Heroes (1st, 8vo, AEG, 296p, 6cp, pep)	L: Nister	[1899]	Robinson, T.H.	70-100	
Kingsley, C.	The Heroes (1st, sm4to, blue cl, 186p, uncut, 24cp)	R.H. Russell	1901	Mars/Squire	180-225	R*
Kingsley, C.	The Heroes (12mo, grey cl, p-o, 157p, 4cp, dep)	L: Blackie	[1907]	Dixon, A.A.	45-60	
Kingsley, C.	The Heroes (1st, 8vo, 166p, gilt, teg, 12 ticp)	L: P.L. Warner	1914	Flint, W.R.	70-100	*
Kingsley, C.	The Heroes (1st, 8vo, 221p, 8cp)	L: A&C Black	1915	Tawse, S.	35-50	*
Kingsley, C.	The Heroes (sm4to, 6cp)	Doran	(1920)	Soper, G.	35-50	
Kingsley, C.	The Heroes (1st, 8vo, 212p, 16cp)	L: MacMillan	1928	Brock, H.M.	50-70	*
Kingsley, C.	Water Babies (1st, 8vo, 371p, blue/gilt, AEG, b/w, cep)	L: MacMillan	1885	Sambourne, L.	75-120	
Kingsley, C.	Water Babies (1st, sm8vo, 308p, gilt, b/w)	Stokes	1891	Gordon, F.C.	90-125	
Kingsley, C.	Water Babies (1st [new ed.], 8vo, blue/gilt, 330p, b/w)	L: MacMillan	1894	Sambourne, L.	85-120	
Kingsley, C.	Water Babies (1st, 12mo, 295p, b/w)	Rand/McNally	(1900)	Phillips, M.E.	25-45	*
Kingsley, C.	Water Babies (1st, lg8vo, 231p, cp, pep)	A. Wessels	1900	Wright, G.	65-90	*
Kingsley, C.	Water Babies (1st, 8vo, 104p, b/w)	Saalfield	(1905)	Williams, C.B.	30-45	*
Kingsley, C.	Water Babies (1st, 24mo, 117p, green cl, uncut, 8 ticp)	Jack/Dutton	[1906]	Cameron, K.	35-50	*
Kingsley, C.	Water Babies (1st, 8vo, green/gilt, AEG, 336p, 6cp)	Nister/Dutton	[1908]	Dixon, A.A.	160-220	
Kingsley, C.	Water Babies (1st, 8vo, 284p, p-o, teg, 12cp)	L: Dent	1908	Tarrant, M.	70-100	
Kingsley, C.	Water Babies (1st, 4to, AEG, green/gilt, 32 ticp)	L: MacMillan	1909	Goble, W.	285-400	
Kingsley, C.	Water Babies (1st, 8vo, 256p)	L: Blackie	1909	Woodward, A.B.	50-75	*
Kingsley, C.	Water Babies (1st {this format}, 8vo, 273p, gilt, 16cp)	L: MacMillan	1910	Goble, W.	120-160	*
Kingsley, C.	Water Babies (lg8vo, teg, 4cp)	Baker/Taylor	(1910)	Soper, G.	35-50	
Kingsley, C.	Water Babies (1st AM, 4to, p-o, teg, 246p, 8 ticp)	Stokes	[1911]	Cameron, K.	90-120	
Kingsley, C.	Water Babies (1st, 12mo, 208p, b/w)	D.C. Heath	(1914)	Babbitt/Blossom	30-45	*
Kingsley, C.	Water Babies (1st, sm4to, 115p, red cl, 12cp)	L: R. Tuck	[1915]	Attwell, M.L.	145-200	
Kingsley, C.	Water Babies (1st AM, 8vo, green cl, p-o, 320p, 8cp)	Houghton	(1915)	Robinson, W.H.	240-300	
Kingsley, C.	Water Babies (1st, 8vo, 319p, green/gilt, 8cp)	L: Constable	1915	Robinson, W.H.	350-500	
Kingsley, C.	Water Babies (1st, sm4to, p-o, gilt, 362p, 12cp, pep)	Dodd	(1916)	Smith, J.W.	300-400	
Kingsley, C.	Water Babies (1st {this format}, 12mo, 270p, p-o, 8cp, pep)	Dodd	1916	Smith, J.W.	120-165	*
Kingsley, C.	Water Babies (1st, 8vo, 340p, grey cl, p-o, 48cp, pep)	L: Ward Lock	1916	Theaker, H.G.	90-140	
Kingsley, C.	Water Babies (1st, 12mo, 280p)	Ginn & Co.	(1916)	Young, F.L.	25-40	*
Kingsley, C.	Water Babies (1st, 8vo, teg, 316p, 8cp, pep)	Lippincott	1917	Kirk, M.L.	70-100	
Kingsley, C.	Water Babies (1st UK, 4to, 240p, gilt, 12 ticp)	L: Boots	[1918]	Smith, J.W.	250-300	
Kingsley, C.	Water Babies (1st, 4to, teg, blue/gilt, 252p, pep, 16 ticp)	L: OUP	[1920]	Jackson, A.E.	180-250	
Kingsley, C.	Water Babies (1st AM, lg8vo, blue/gilt, p-o, 180p, 12cp, pep)	Nelson	[1924]	Anderson, A.	130-180	
Kingsley, C.	Water Babies (1st, lg8vo, yellow cl, p-o, 12cp)	L: Jack	(1924)	Anderson, A.	160-220	
Kingsley, C.	Water Babies (1st, 8vo, 282p, p-o, 7cp)	Winston	(1930)	Everett, E.	35-65	
Kingsley, C.	Water Babies (1st, 4to, 56p, color)	Duell/Sloan	(1946)	Collison, M.	35-50	*
Kingsley, C.	Westward Ho! (16mo, 2 volumes, teg, uncut, b/w)	L: MacMillan	1896	Brock, C.E.	50-75	
Kingsley, C.	Westward Ho! (12mo, 589p, 15pl)	L: J. Long	1904	Copping, H.	45-65	*
Kingsley, C.	Westward Ho! (1st, lg8vo, 604p, p-o, 14cp, pep)	Jacobs	[1920]	Oakley, T.	60-80	
Kingsley, C.	Westward Ho! (1st, 4to, 413p, p-o, 14cp, pep, SC)	Scribner	1920	Wyeth, N.C.	150-220	
Kingsley, C.	Westward Ho! (1st, 12mo, 342p, col frn, b/w)	MacMillan	1930	Pitz, H.C.	35-50	*
Kingsley, F.M.	Glass House (1st, sm8vo, 312p, 4pl)	Dodd	1909	Stephens, A.B.	25-40	*
Kingsley, F.M.	Those Brewster Children (1st, 12mo, tan cl, 214p, 3pl)	Dodd	1910	Chamberlin, E.H.	20-25	*
Kingsley, F.M.	Transfiguration of Miss Philura (1st, 16mo, 81p, beige cl)	Funk/Wagnalls	(1901)	Armstrong, M.	35-50	
Kinney, T.& M.	Dance: Its Place in Art & Life (1st, 8vo, 334p, col frn)	Stokes	1914	Kinneys	30-45	
Kipling, R.	Almanac of 12 Sports (1st AM, 4to, ipcb, 12cp)	R.H. Russell	1898	Nicholson, W.	200-300	

AUTHOR	TITLE	PUBLISHER	DATE	ARTIST	PRICE	LC
Kipling, R.	Almanac of 12 Sports (1st, 4to, ibds, unpag, 12cp)	L: Heinemann	1898	Nicholson, W.	350-450	
Kipling, R.	Brushwood Boy (1st, 8vo, blue cl, teg, uncut, 119p, b/w, pep)	Doub./McClure	1899	Lowell, O.	100-165	
Kipling, R.	Brushwood Boy (1st AM {this artist}, 8vo, 73p, p-o, teg, 12cp)	Doubleday/Page	1907	Townsend, F.H.	50-80	
Kipling, R.	Brushwood Boy (1st, 8vo, 91p, grey/gilt, teg, 12cp)	L: MacMillan	1907	Townsend, F.H.	60-95	
Kipling, R.	Captains Courageous (1st AM, 8vo, grn/gilt, 323p, teg, b/w)	Century	1897	Taber, I.W.	140-170	
Kipling, R.	Collected Verse of... (1st, 4to, red/gilt, 392p, teg, 17 ticp)	Doubleday/Page	1910	Robinson, W.H.	180-260	
Kipling, R.	Dead King (1st, 8vo, 48p, wraps, designs by...)	L: Hodder	[1910]	Robinson, W.H.	120-170	
Kipling, R.	East of Suez (1st, 4to, 72p, blue/gilt, 10cp)	L: MacMillan	1931	Maxwell, D.	80-100	
Kipling, R.	Elephant's Child (1st, 8vo, ibds, [28]p, color)	Garden City	(1942)	Rojankovsky, F.	25-40	*
Kipling, R.	How the Leopard Got his Spots (1st, lg8vo, ibds, [28]p, color)	Garden City	(1942)	Rojankovsky, F.	35-50	*
Kipling, R.	How the Rhinoceros Got his Skin (1st, lg8vo, ibds, [31]p, col)	Garden City	(1942)	Rojankovsky, F.	35-50	*
Kipling, R.	Indian Tales (1st AM, 8vo, 750p, 16pl)	Caldwell	(1899)	Various	80-120	
Kipling, R.	Jungle Book (1st, 8vo, 314p, red/gilt, teg, 16cp)	L: MacMillan	1908	Detmold, E.J.	240-350	
Kipling, R.	Jungle Book (1st AM, 8vo, green/gilt, teg, 351p, 16cp, pep)	Century	1913	Detmold, E.J.	180-240	
Kipling, R.	Just So Stories... (1st, sq4to, red cl, 249p, 22pl)	L: MacMillan	1902	Kipling, R.	200-250	
Kipling, R.	Just So Stories... (1st AM, lg8vo, green cl, 249p, b/w)	Doubleday/Page	1902	Kipling, R.	180-250	R
Kipling, R.	Kim (1st AM, 4to, teg, 460p, uncut, 10 tipl)	Doubleday/Page	1901	Kipling, J.L.	180-220	
Kipling, R.	Puck of Pook's Hill (1st, 8vo, 306p, gilt, b/w pl)	L: MacMillan	1906	Millar, H.R.	100-145	
Kipling, R.	Puck of Pook's Hill (1st AM, 8vo, grn/gilt, teg, 277p, 4cp)	Doubleday/Page	1906	Rackham, A.	100-140	
Kipling, R.	Rewards & Fairies (1st, 8vo, red/gilt, teg, 338p, 4pl)	L: MacMillan	1910	Craig, F.	85-100	
Kipling, R.	Sea & Sussex (1st AM {std}, sm4to, 94p, teg, blue cl, 24 ticp)	Doubleday/Page	1926	Maxwell, D.	80-120	
Kipling, R.	Sea & Sussex (1st, 4to, 94p, blue/gilt, teg, 24 ticp)	L: MacMillan	1926	Maxwell, D.	120-165	
Kipling, R.	Second Jungle Book (1st, 8vo, 238p, blue/gilt, AEG)	L: MacMillan	1895	Kipling, J.L.	180-250	
Kipling, R.	Seven Seas (1st {illus ed}, 8vo, teg, uncut, 209p, 8pl)	Appleton	1905	Unknown	45-70	*
Kipling, R.	Soldier Tales (1st, 8vo, AEG, 172p, blue/gilt, 21pl)	L: MacMillan	1896	Unknown	100-140	
Kipling, R.	Song of the English (1st, lg4to, 91p, 30 ticp)	L: Hodder	(1909)	Robinson, W.H.	250-400	
Kipling, R.	Song of the English (1st AM, 4to, red/gilt, 30 ticp)	Doubleday/Page	(1909)	Robinson, W.H.	250-350	
Kipling, R.	Songs of the Sea (1st, 4to, 99p, blue cl, 12cp)	L: MacMillan	1927	Maxwell, D.	65-80	
Kipling, R.	Tales of India (1st, lg8vo, p-o, 320p, black cl, 5cp)	Rand/McNally	(1935)	Strayer, P.	40-65	
Kipling, R.	Tales of the Punjab (1st, 8vo, 359p, black/gilt, 5pl)	L: MacMillan	1894	Kipling, J.L.	160-220	
Kipling, R.	They (1st AM, 8vo, 80p, p-o, teg, uncut, 15cp)	Doubleday/Page	1906	Townsend, F.H.	60-80	
Kipling, R.	They (1st {this format}, red/gilt, teg, 27cp)	L: MacMillan	1925	Townsend, F.H.	35-50	
Kipling, R.	Wee Willie Winkie (1st, 12mo, ibds, color)	MacMillan	1927	Hader, B.& E.	50-80	
Kipling, R.	With the Night Mail (1st, 8vo, teg, blue cl, 77p, pep, 4cp)	Doubleday/Page	1909	Leyendecker, F.X.	150-180	
Kirk, V.	Mickey & the Monkeys (1st, 4to, 175p, col frn, b/w, pep)	Viking	1927	Rule, C.	35-50	
Kirkwood, E.B.	Animal Children (1st, 8vo, yellow ipcb, p-o, 96p, pep, color)	Volland	(1913)	Ross, M.T.	90-140	
Kiser, S.E.	Love Sonnets/Office Boy (1st, 16mo, ibds, 42p)	Chi: Forbes	1902	McCutcheon, J.T.	25-40	*
Kissin, Rita	Pete the Pelican (1st, 8vo, 31p, p-o, b/w, pep)	Lippincott	(1937)	Stolper, J.	45-65	*
Kiviat, Esther	Paji (1st {std}, sm4to, 56p, color, DJ)	McGraw-Hill	(1946)	Price, H.	45-60	
Kjelgaard, J.A.	Big Red (1st, 8vo, 231p, tan cl, b/w, pep)	Holiday House	(1945)	Kuhn, B.	20-30	*
Kjelgaard, J.A.	Buckskin Brigade (1st, 8vo, 310p)	Holiday House	(1947)	Ray, R.	20-25	*
Kjelgaard, J.A.	Chip the Dam Builder (1st, sm8vo, 233p, b/w, pep)	Holiday House	(1950)	Ray, R.	20-25	*
Kjelgaard, J.A.	Fire-Hunter (1st, 8vo, 217p, tan cl, b/w, pep)	Holiday House	(1951)	Ray, R.	20-25	*
Kjelgaard, J.A.	Forest Patrol (1st, sm8vo, 293p, rust cl, fp b/w)	Holiday House	(1941)	Palazzo, T.	30-45	*
Kjelgaard, J.A.	Haunt Fox (1st, sm8vo, 220p, brown cl, b/w, pep)	Holiday House	(1954)	Rounds, G.	45-60	R*
Kjelgaard, J.A.	Rebel Siege (1st, 8vo, 221p)	Holiday House	(1943)	Wilson, C.B.	20-25	*
Kjelgaard, J.A.	Snow Dog (1st, 8vo, 236p, olive cl, b/w, pep)	Holiday House	(1948)	Landau, J.	20-25	*
Kjelgaard, J.A.	Stormy (1st, 8vo, 190p, grey cl, pep)	Holiday House	(1959)	Unknown	20-25	*
Klein, C.	Music Master (1st, 8vo, 341p, p-o, 4cp)	Dodd	1909	Rae, J.	30-45	
Knatchbull-Hugessen	Princess with Pea-Green Nose (1st, 12mo, 114p, col frn, pep)	Harper	1927	Cocks, Myra	20-35	
Kneeland, C.A.	Smuggler's Island (1st, sm8vo, red cl, 356p, b/w, PPPa)	Houghton	1915	Goldsmith, W.	60-100	R*
Knevels, G.	Wonderful Bed (1st, 8vo, 229p, 4cp)	Bobbs-Merrill	(1912)	Chamberlin, E.H.	35-50	*
Knibbs, H.H.	Tang of Life (1st, sm8vo, 393p, 4cp)	Houghton	1918	Smith, E.B.	35-50	
Knight, R.A.	Brave Companions (1st {std}, 8vo, blue cl, 215p, col frn)	Doubleday	1945	Ward, L.	30-45	*
Knipe, A.A.	Cavalier Maid (1st, 8vo, 255p, 6pl)	MacMillan	1919	Knipe, E.B.	25-40	
Knipe, A.A.	Everybody's Washington (1st, 4to, 282p, uncut, p-o, 7cp, pep)	Dodd	1931	Schaeffer, M.	30-45	
Knipe, A.A.	Luck of Denewood (1st, 8vo, brown cl, b/w)	Century	1921	Knipe, E.B.	30-45	
Knipe, A.A.	Remember Rhymes (1st, 4to, brown/gilt, 80p, 4cp, pep)	Penn	1914	Knipe, E.B.	75-100	
Knipe, E.& A.	Lucky Sixpence (1st, 8vo, 378p, 4pl, PPPa)	Century	(1912)	Becher, A.E.	200-300	
Knipe, E.B.	May Flower Maid (1st, 8vo, 297p, blue cl, 4pl)	Century	1920	Knipe, E.B.	30-45	
Knobel, E.	When Little Thoughts Go Rhyming (1st, 8vo, p-o, 96p, 10cp)	Rand/McNally	(1916)	Enright, M.W.	50-65	
Knott, M.O.	Gone Away with O'Malley (1st {std}, 8vo, red cl, 280p, b/w, pep)	Doubleday/Dor.	1944	Brown, Paul	25-40	
Knowles, H.	Peeps into Fairyland (1st, lg4to, 89p, tan/gilt, 6cp, pep)	L: Butterworth	(1924)	Knowles, H.J.	500-700	
Knowles, J. (arr.)	King Arthur & his Knights (1st, 8vo, 340p, 8cp)	L: Warne	(1912)	Speed, L.	65-80	
Knowles, R.E.	Dawn at Shanty Bay (1st, 8vo, green/gilt, 156p, col frn, dep)	Revell	(1907)	McClure, G.M.	30-45	
Koch, Dorothy	Gone is My Goose (1st, lg8vo, green cl, [27]p, 1-color, cep)	Holiday House	(1956)	Lee, Doris	25-40	*
Koch, Dorothy	I Play at the Beach (1st, lg8vo, blue cl, [28]p, color, pep)	Holiday House	1955	Rojankovsky, F.	35-50	*
Koch, Dorothy	Let it Rain (1st, 4to, [27]p, green cl, color, cep)	Holiday House	(1959)	Stone, H.	30-50	*
Konody, P.G.	Art of Walter Crane (1st, folio, teg, 147p, 16cp)	L: G. Bell	1902	Crane, W.	300-400	
Kossak-Szczucka	Troubles of a Gnome (1st, 4to, ibds, 102p, 8cp)	L: A&C Black	1928	Folkard, C.	130-180	
Kozisek, Josef	Forest Story (1st, 4to, ibds, [58]p, color, pep)	MacMillan	1929	Mates, R.	120-165	*
Kozisek, Josef	Magic Flutes (1st, ob folio, [56]p, ibds, color)	L: Longmans	1929	Mates, R.	200-300	

AUTHOR	TITLE	PUBLISHER	DATE	ARTIST	PRICE	LC
Krag, M.A.	Martha-Jane: Nursery Nonsense (1st, ob4to, [24]p)	Bowen-Merrill	1897	Keep, V.	120-170	
Kramer, N. (ed.)	Cozy Hour Story Book (1st, 4to, 63p, yellow cl, color, pep)	Random	1960	Weisgard, L.	30-50	*
Kramer, N. (ed.)	Storybook (1st, lg8vo, 160p, b/w, cep)	J. Messner	(1955)	Krush, B.& J.	30-45	*
Krasilovsky, P.	Man Who Didn't Wash his Dishes (1st {std}, lg8vo, [33]p)	Doubleday	(1950)	Cooney, B.	30-50	*
Kraus, Robert	I, Mouse (1st, 12mo, ibds, 32p, b/w)	Harper	(1958)	Kraus, R.	30-50	*
Krauss, Ruth	Backward Day (1st, 8vo, [31]p, color)	Harper	1950	Simont, M.	25-45	*
Krauss, Ruth	Bears (1st, 4to, [23]p, ibds, 2-color)	Harper	(1948)	Rowand, P.	40-60	*
Krauss, Ruth	Big World & Little House (1st, 4to, ibds, [41]p, color, pep)	NY: Schuman	1949	Simont, M.	50-70	R
Krauss, Ruth	Birthday Party (1st, ob12mo, ipcb, [23]p, dep, color)	Harper	1957	Sendak, M.	130-180	R*
Krauss, Ruth	Bundle Book (1st, lg ob8vo, ipcb, unpag, pep, color, DJ)	Harper	(1951)	Stone, H.	35-50	
Krauss, Ruth	Carrot Seed (1st, sm8vo, olive cl, [25]p, fp 2-color, cep)	Harper	1945	Johnson, C.	45-60	*
Krauss, Ruth	Charlotte & White Horse (1st, 16mo, ibds, [20]p, color, dep)	Harper	(1955)	Sendak, M.	120-170	
Krauss, Ruth	Good Man & his Good Wife (1st, 8vo, [32]p, fp 2-color)	Harper	1944	Reinhardt, A.	30-45	*
Krauss, Ruth	Great Duffy (1st, sm4to, [32]p, color)	Harper	(1946)	Richter	30-45	*
Krauss, Ruth	Growing Story (1st, 4to, [32]p, color)	Harper	(1947)	Rowand, P.	45-60	*
Krauss, Ruth	Happy Day (1st, lg4to, [33]p, CH)	Harper	1949	Simont, M.	70-110	
Krauss, Ruth	Hole is to Dig (1st, 12mo, ibds, green pep, DJ)	Harper	(1952)	Sendak, M.	200-300	R
Krauss, Ruth	How to Make an Earthquake (1st, 8vo, 28p, ipcb, 1-color)	Harper	(1954)	Johnson, C.	45-65	*
Krauss, Ruth	I Want to Paint My Bathroom Blue (1st, 8vo, ibds, [22]p col, cep)	Harper	1956	Sendak, M.	120-170	R*
Krauss, Ruth	I'll Be You and You Be Me (1st, 4to, ibds, pep, [38]p, b/w)	Harper	(1954)	Sendak, M.	130-170	R
Krauss, Ruth	Is This You? (1st, 12mo, ipcb, [40]p, cep)	W.R. Scott	1955	Johnson, C.	50-85	R*
Krauss, Ruth	Monkey Day (1st, lg4to, ibds, [26]p, fp 1-color)	Harper	(1957)	Rowand, P.	40-65	
Krauss, Ruth	Open House for Butterflies (1st, 16mo, ibds, [46]p, pep, b/w)	Harper	(1960)	Sendak, M.	130-170	R
Krauss, Ruth	Somebody Else's Nut Tree (1st, 4to, ibds, 43p, fp b/w)	Harper	(1958)	Sendak, M.	120-165	*
Krauss, Ruth	Very Special House (1st, 4to, ibds, [22]p, 1-color, CH)	Harper	(1953)	Sendak, M.	140-200	R*
Krehbiel, H.	How to Listen to Music (1st, 12mo, 361p)	Scribner	1897	Armstrong, M.	45-60	
Kreymborg, A.	Funnybone Alley (1st, 4to, teg, 269p, gilt, 7 ticp, pep)	Macaulay	(1927)	Artzybasheff, B.	80-120	
Kristoffersen, E.M.	Hans Christian Elsinore (1st, sq4to, 80p, pep, color)	Whitman	1937	Collin, H.	45-60	
Kristoffersen, E.M.	Bee in Her Bonnet (1st, 8vo, 168p, b/w, pep)	Crowell	1944	Sewell, H.	20-35	
Krumgold, Joseph	And Now Miguel (1st {std}, 8vo, 245p, b/w, pep, DJ, NM)	Crowell	(1953)	Charlot, J.	80-125	
Krumgold, Joseph	Onion John (1st {std}, 8vo, 248p, b/w, NM)	Crowell	(1959)	Shimin, S.	50-90	*
Kubota, H.	Golden Footprints (1st {std}, 8vo, 50p, blue cl, 1-color, pep)	World Pub. Co.	(1960)	Yashima, T.	80-120	R*
Kuh, Charlotte	The Deliveryman (1st, 16mo, ibds, [42]p, color)	MacMillan	1929	Wiese, K.	30-50	*
Kuh, Charlotte	The Engineer (1st, 16mo, [42]p, ibds, color)	MacMillan	1929	Wiese, K.	30-50	*
Kuh, Charlotte	The Fireman (1st, 16mo, [42]p, ibds, color)	MacMillan	1929	Wiese, K.	30-50	
Kuh, Charlotte	The Motorman (1st, 16mo, [42]p, ibds, color)	MacMillan	1929	Wiese, K.	35-50	*
Kuh, Charlotte	The Policeman (1st, 16mo, [42]p, ibds, color)	MacMillan	1929	Wiese, K.	45-60	*
Kuh, Charlotte	Train, a Boat & an Island (1st, sq8vo, 89p, col frn, b/w)	MacMillan	1932	Dobias, F.	25-40	*
Kuhns, O.	Switzerland (2nd, 8vo, blue/gilt, 294p)	Crowell	(1910)	Armstrong, M.	35-50	
Kunhardt, D.	Junket is Nice (1st, sm ob4to, ibds, [63]p, 1-color)	Harcourt	1933	Kunhardt, D.	65-100	*
Kunhardt, D.	Little Ones (1st, sm4to, red cl, 78p, color, DJ)	Viking	1935	Wiese, K.	35-50	
Kunhardt, D.	Lucky Mrs. Ticklefeather (1st, sm ob4to, ibds, [63]p, 1-color)	Harcourt	1935	Kunhardt, D.	65-100	*
Kunhardt, D.	Now Open the Box (1st, sm ob4to, [61]p, ipcb, color)	Harcourt	1934	Kunhardt, D.	65-100	*
Kunhardt, D.	Once there was a Little Boy (1st, lg8vo, 66p, color)	Viking	1946	Sewell, H.	30-50	*
Kunhardt, D.	Wise Old Aard-Vark (1st, ob4to, ibds, 62p, 1-color)	Viking	1936	Kunhardt, D.	100-150	
Kunos, I	Turkish Fairy Tales… (1st, lg8vo, 275p, teg, 9pl)	L: Lawrence	1896	Levetus, C.	70-90	
Kunos, I.	Forty-Four Turkish Tales (1st, 4to, tan cl, teg, 363p, 16 ticp)	L: Harrap	(1913)	Pogany, W.	180-260	
Kyle, Anne D.	Apprentice of Florence (1st, 8vo, 276p, b/w, pep, NH)	Houghton	1933	Berry, E.	35-50	*
Kyle, Anne D.	Prince of the Pale Mountains (1st, sm8vo, 250p, col frn, pep)	Houghton	1929	Barney, M.W.	25-40	*
Kyle, Anne D.	Red Sky over Rome (1st, 8vo, 260p, 8pl)	Houghton	1938	DeAngeli, M.	35-50	*
Kyne, P.B.	Three Godfathers (1st, 8vo, 95p, 5pl)	Doran	(1913)	Dixon, M.	25-40	*
Kyser, Halsa A.	Little Cumsee in Dixie (1st {std}, sm8vo, 158p, b/w, pep)	Longmans	1938	Berry, E.	40-60	*
L'Hommedieu, D.	Scampy the Little Black Cocker (1st, sm4to, ibds, 62p, pep, col)	Lippincott	(1939)	Kirmse, M.	60-90	*
LaFontaine, J.	Fables in Rhyme for Little Folks (1st, 8vo, ibds, color)	Volland	(1918)	Rae, J.	70-100	
LaFontaine, J.	Fables of Jean De La Fontaine (1st, 8vo, 469p, 12pl)	L: Heinemann	1933	Gooden, S.	75-120	
LaFontaine, J.	Fables of La Fontaine (1st, 4to, 304p, teg, gilt, 24pl)	L: Nimmo	1884	Delierre, A.	100-145	*
LaFontaine, J.	Hundred Fables of La Fontaine (1st, 4to, green cl, 202p, b/w)	L: J. Lane	1900	Billinghurst, P.	80-100	
LaPrade, E.	Alice in Orchestralia (1st, sm8vo, 171p, b/w)	Doubleday/Page	1925	Snell, C.	25-40	
LaRue, M.G.	Billy Bang Book (1st, 12mo, 176p, 2-color)	MacMillan	1927	Petershams	30-55	*
LaRue, M.G.	Cats for the Tooseys (1st, lg4to, 40p, ipcb, b/w)	Nelson	1939	Wiese, K.	50-80	*
LaRue, M.G.	Good-Time Book (1st, 12mo, 111p, 2-color, cep)	MacMillan	1931	Peck, A.G.	25-40	*
LaRue, M.G.	Hoot-Owl (1st, 12mo, blue cl, 207p, 2-color, pep)	MacMillan	1936	Seredy, K.	30-45	*
LaRue, M.G.	Letter to Popsey (1st, sq8vo, [28]p, ibds, color, pep)	Grosset/Dunlap	1942	Lenski, L.	35-50	*
LaRue, M.G.	Little Indians (1st, sm8vo, 170p, color)	MacMillan	1930	Petershams	40-60	*
LaRue, M.G.	Under the Story Tree (1st, 12mo, 139p, color)	MacMillan	1923	Petershams	40-60	*
LaRue, M.G.	Zip the Toy Mule (1st, sm4to, 46p, 6cp, pep)	MacMillan	1932	Petershams	40-60	
Laboulaye, E.R.	Laboulaye's Fairy Book (1st, lg8vo, 199p, p-o, 12cp, DJ)	Harper	(1920)	McCandlish, E.	60-80	
Laboulaye, E.R.	Laboulaye's Fairy Book (1st, sm8vo, 363p, black cl, p-o, b/w)	Harper	(1925)	Potter, E.E.	30-50	*
Lacey, Marion	Picture Book of Musical Instruments (1st, 4to, ibds, 55p, b/w)	Lothrop/Lee	(1942)	Weisgard, L.	35-60	*
Ladas, Alexis	Seal that Couldn't Swim (1st {std}, lg8vo, 55p, blue cl, 3-col)	Little/Brown	(1959)	Simont, M.	25-45	*
Lady Frazer	Singing Wood (1st, 8vo, 144p, col frn)	L: A&C Black	1931	Brock, H.M.	35-50	*
Lagerlof, Selma	Christ Legends (1st, 8vo, 244p, blue cl, b/w)	L: E. Matthews	1930	Knowles, H.J.	45-60	*

AUTHOR	TITLE	PUBLISHER	DATE	ARTIST	PRICE	LC
Lagerlof, Selma	Further Adventures of Nils (1st {Engl lang.}, 12mo, 339p, 15pl)	Doubleday/Page	1911	Heiberg, A.	80-100	*
Lagerlof, Selma	Wonderful Adventures of Nils (1st AM, 8vo, 430p, 8pl, pep)	Doubleday/Page	1907	Heartt, H.	90-140	
Lagerlof, Selma	Wonderful Adventures of Nils (1st, sq8vo, 263p, 24cp, pep)	Doubleday/Page	1913	Frye, M.H.	100-150	
Laing, A.K.	Haunted Omnibus (1st, 8vo, 848p, fp b/w)	Farrar/Rine.	(1937)	Ward, L.	40-65	*
Laing, Allan M.	Prayers & Graces (1st, sq12mo, 64p, blue/gilt, 30 b/w)	L: Gollancz	1944	Peake, M.	70-100	
Laird, Rowena	Stuffy (1st, sm4to, [32]p, p-o, color)	Wm. Morrow	1945	Laird, R.	25-40	
Lamb, C.	Adventures of Ulysses (1st, 4to, 117p, uncut, 16cp, cep)	R.H. Russell	1902	Mars/Squire	140-185	*
Lamb, C.	Dissertation Upon a Roast Pig (1st, 12mo, pcb, p-o)	(Concord)	(1904)	Bradley, W.	75-100	
Lamb, C.	Essays of Elia (8vo, green/gilt, teg, uncut, 310p)	L: Methuen	1902	Jones, G.	35-50	
Lamb, C.	Last Essays of Elia (1st, 12mo, 254p, teg, uncut)	L: Dent	1900	Brock, C.E.	40-60	
Lamb, C.	Mrs. Leicester's School (1st, sq8vo, 128p, ibds, 20cp)	L: Dent	1899	Green, Winifred	75-100	
Lamb, C.	Tales from Shakespeare (1st, 8vo, 362p, blue/gilt, teg, 15pl)	L: Freemantle	1899	Bell, R.A.	60-85	
Lamb, C.	Tales from Shakespeare (lg8vo, AEG, 319p, gilt, 6cp, pep)	L: Nister	[1901]	Paget, W.	80-100	
Lamb, C.	Tales from Shakespeare (1st, 8vo, red cl, 296p, 16pl)	L: Sands	[1902]	Robinson, W.H.	130-170	*
Lamb, C.	Tales from Shakespeare (1st, sm8vo, 363p, gilt, teg, 24pl)	L: G. Bell	1903	Shaw, B.	50-70	
Lamb, C.	Tales from Shakespeare (1st AM, 4to, 324p, gilt, teg, 20cp)	Scribner	[1905]	Price, N.M.	70-95	
Lamb, C.	Tales from Shakespeare (1st, 8vo, 304p, gilt, teg, 12cp, pep)	L: Dent	1909	Rackham, A.	250-320	
Lamb, C.	Tales from Shakespeare (1st AM, 8vo, 304p, teg, 12cp, pep)	Dutton	1909	Rackham, A.	200-260	
Lamb, C.	Tales from Shakespeare (1st, 8vo, 242p, ticp)	L: Scott	1915	Mulliner, M.	100-130	
Lamb, C.	Tales from Shakespeare (1st, 8vo, 366p, b/w)	Harper	(1918)	Rhead, L.	25-45	*
Lamb, C.	Tales from Shakespeare (1st, 8vo, 472p, blue cl, p-o, 48cp)	L: Ward Lock	1919	Jackson, A.E.	50-70	
Lamb, C.	Tales from Shakespeare (1st, lg8vo, teg, 377p, p-o, pep, 11cp)	McKay	1922	Green, E.S.	60-85	
Lamb, C.	Tales from Shakespeare (1st, 8vo, 308p, teg, gilt, 12cp)	L: Warne	1923	Pape, F.	70-85	
Lamb, C.	Tales from Shakespeare (1st, sm8vo, 375p, blue cl, 4cp, pep)	MacMillan	1923	Petershams	45-60	
Lamb, C.	Tales from Shakespeare (1st, 8vo, p-o, 323p, 12pl)	Winston	(1924)	Godwin, F.	30-45	
Lamb, C.	Tales from Shakespeare (lg8vo, 14cp, DJ)	Doran	[1924]	Soper, G.	45-70	
Lamb, C.	Tales from Shakespeare (1st, 8vo, 346p, 6cp)	Houghton	1925	Elwell, R.F.	25-40	
Lamb, C.	Tales from Shakespeare (1st, 8vo, 296p, color, pep)	Garden City	1939	Kredel, F.	25-45	*
Lamb, Dean I.	Incurable Filibuster (1st, 8vo, 298p, uncut, b/w, pep)	Farrar/Rine.	(1934)	Brown, Paul	35-50	*
Lamb, Harold	Kirdy (1st {std}, sm8vo, red cl, uncut, 276p, frn & pep by...)	Doubleday/Dor.	1933	Artzybasheff, B.	35-60	*
Lamb, Tom	Jolly Kid Alphabet (1st, lg ob4to, ibds, color)	Volland	[1930]	Lamb, T.	200-300	
Lamb, Tom	Tale of Bingo (1st, 8vo, ibds, 120p, color)	Volland	(1927)	Lamb, T.	65-80	*
Lambert, C.	Story of Alaska (1st {std}, sq4to, ibds, [40]p, color, pep)	Harper	(1940)	DeWitt, C.H.	25-40	
Lambert, H.G.C.	Peter Pixie at Play (4to, ibds, p-o, 6cp, pep)	L: Gale	[1910]	Lambert, M.	165-220	*
Lamprey, L.	Children of Ancient Britain (1st, 12mo, 222p, fp b/w)	Little/Brown	1921	Petershams	35-50	*
Lamprey, L.	Long Ago People (1st, 12mo, 222p, fp b/w)	Little/Brown	1921	Petershams	35-50	*
Lamprey, L.	Treasure Valley (1st, 8vo, 337p, yellow cl, p-o, 4cp, pep)	Wm. Morrow	(1928)	Freeman, M.	25-40	*
Lane, Marg.	Tale of Beatrix Potter (1st, 8vo, 162p, 4cp, 16 b/w)	Warne	(1946)	Potter, B.	85-100	
Lang, A.	Animal Story Book (1st, 12mo, AEG, 400p, blue/gilt, cep)	L: Longmans	1896	Ford, H.J.	100-150	
Lang, A.	Blue Fairy Book (1st, 8vo, blue/gilt, AEG, b/w)	L: Longmans	1889	Ford/Hood	750-1100	
Lang, A.	Blue Fairy Book (1st, 4to, teg, p-o, blue cl, 8cp)	McKay	(1921)	Godwin, F.	60-85	
Lang, A.	Blue Poetry Book (1st, 12mo, blue/gilt, AEG, 243p, 12pl, cep)	L: Longmans	1891	Ford, H.J.	150-200	
Lang, A.	Book of Dreams & Ghosts (1st, 8vo, 303p, gilt, teg, cvr by...)	L: Longmans	1897	Woodroffe, P.	50-70	
Lang, A.	Book of Princes & Princesses (1st, 8vo, gilt, 361p, AEG, 8cp)	L: Longmans	1908	Ford, H.J.	160-200	
Lang, A.	Book of Romance (1st, sm8vo, AEG, 384p, gilt, 8cp, pep)	L: Longmans	1902	Ford, H.J.	160-200	
Lang, A.	Brown Fairy Book (1st, 8vo, AEG, 350p, 8cp, 22pl, pep)	L: Longmans	1904	Ford, H.J.	180-250	
Lang, A.	Crimson Fairy Book (1st, 8vo, AEG, 371p, 8cp, pep)	L: Longmans	1903	Ford, H.J.	200-265	
Lang, A.	Disentanglers (1st, sm8vo, 418p, AEG, 7pl)	L: Longmans	1902	Ford, H.J.	100-150	
Lang, A.	Gold of Fairnilee (1st, 4to, teg, 86p, uncut, 13cp)	L: Arrowsmith	(1888)	Leamann, E.A.	100-150	*
Lang, A.	Green Fairy Book (1st, 8vo, AEG, 366p, gilt, b/w, cep)	L: Longmans	1892	Ford, H.J.	200-280	
Lang, A.	Grey Fairy Book (1st, 8vo, AEG, 387p, 32pl, cep)	L: Longmans	1900	Ford, H.J.	200-260	
Lang, A.	Lilac Fairy Book (1st, 8vo, 369p, gilt, AEG, 6cp)	L: Longmans	1910	Ford, H.J.	220-280	
Lang, A.	Little Wildrose (1st, 12mo, 258p, blu/glt, col frn, 19 b/w, pep)	L: Longmans	1906	Ford, H.J.	80-130	
Lang, A.	My Own Fairy Book (1st, 8vo, 402p, rust cl, p-o, pep, 4cp)	McKay	(1927)	Kay, G.A.	30-45	*
Lang, A.	Nursery Rhyme Book (1st, 8vo, AEG, 288p, green/gilt, pep)	L: Warne	1897	Brooke, L.L.	120-170	
Lang, A.	Olive Fairy Book (1st, 8vo, AEG, 336p, 8cp, pep)	L: Longmans	1907	Ford, H.J.	200-300	
Lang, A.	Orange Fairy Book (1st, 8vo, orang/gilt, 358p, AEG, 8cp)	L: Longmans	1906	Ford, H.J.	180-260	
Lang, A.	Pink Fairy Book (1st, 8vo, AEG, 360p, b/w, cep)	L: Longmans	1897	Ford, H.J.	240-300	
Lang, A.	Prince Prigio (1st {std}, sq8vo, green cl, 108p, b/w, pep, DJ)	Little/Brown	1942	Lawson, R.	65-80	
Lang, A.	Prince Ricardo of Pantouflia (1st, 8vo, 204p, gilt, 12pl)	L: Arrowsmith	(1893)	Browne, G.	125-170	
Lang, A.	Princess Nobody (1st, 4to, ibds, 56p, color)	L: Longmans	(1884)	Doyle, R.	350-500	
Lang, A.	Red Book of Animal Stories (1st, 8vo, gilt, AEG, 379p, 33pl)	L: Longmans	1899	Ford, H.J.	140-200	
Lang, A.	Red Fairy Book (1st, 8vo, red/gilt, AEG, 367p, b/w)	L: Longmans	1890	Ford/Speed	350-500	
Lang, A.	Red Fairy Book (1st, 4to, 285p, p-o, teg, red cl, 8cp, pep)	McKay	(1924)	Tenggren, G.	160-220	
Lang, A.	Red Fairy Book (1st, 8vo, 399p, p-o, 7cp)	Macrae-Smith	[1925]	Lee, M.V.	50-70	
Lang, A.	Red Fairy Book (1st, 8vo, 386p, gilt, p-o, 4cp)	Winston	(1930)	Richardson, F.	35-50	
Lang, A.	Red Romance Book (1st, 8vo, 366p, AEG, 8cp, 28pl, pep)	L: Longmans	1905	Ford, H.J.	130-170	
Lang, A.	Red True Story Book (1st, 12mo, 419p, AEG, 19pl, cep)	L: Longmans	1895	Ford, H.J.	140-200	
Lang, A.	Story of the Golden Fleece (1st, 8vo, 93p, 6pl)	Altemus	(1903)	Thompson, M.	65-80	*
Lang, A.	Strange Story Book (1st, lg8vo, teg, gilt, 312p, 12cp)	L: Longmans	1913	Ford, H.J.	145-180	
Lang, A.	Tales of Troy & Greece (1st, 8vo, 302p, teg, uncut, 16pl)	L: Longmans	1907	Ford, H.J.	145-180	*
Lang, A.	Tales/Fairy Court (1st, 8vo, 108p, gilt, AEG, 12cp)	L: Collins	(1907)	Dixon, A.A.	150-200	

AUTHOR	TITLE	PUBLISHER	DATE	ARTIST	PRICE	LC
Lang, A.	Tartan Tales (1st {std}, 8vo, 301p, black cl, 8pl, DJ)	Longmans	1928	Blaine, M.	50-75	
Lang, A.	True Story Book (1st, 8vo, blue/gilt, 337p, AEG, 9pl, cep)	L: Longmans	1893	Various	150-220	
Lang, A.	Trusty John... (1st, sm8vo, maroon/gilt, 258p, col frn, 14pl)	L: Longmans	1906	Ford, H.J.	100-150	
Lang, A.	Violet Fairy Book (1st, 12mo, 388p, AEG, 8cp, cep)	L: Longmans	1901	Ford, H.J.	220-320	
Lang, A.	Yellow Fairy Book (1st, 12mo, AEG, 321p, 22pl, cep)	L: Longmans	1894	Ford, H.J.	200-275	
Lang, A. (tr.)	Johnny Nut & Golden Goose (1st, 4to, 45p, teg, blu/glt, b/w, cep)	L: Longmans	1887	Lynen, A.	80-120	
Lang, Don	Tramp: The Sheep Dog (1st, sq8vo, [28]p, ibds, color, pep)	Grosset/Dunlap	1943	Wiese, K.	25-45	*
Lang, Jean	Book of Myths (1st, 8vo, 340p, 20cp)	L: Jack	1914	Stratton, H.	80-120	
Lang, L.B.	All Sorts of Stories Book (1st, 12mo, AEG, 377p, gilt, 5cp)	L: Longmans	1911	Ford, H.J.	140-180	
Lang, L.B.	Book of Saints & Heroes (1st, 8vo, blue/gilt, teg, 351p, 12cp)	L: Longmans	1912	Ford, H.J.	120-160	
Lang, L.B.	Red Book of Heroes (1st, 8vo, 368p, red/gilt, AEG, 8cp)	L: Longmans	1909	Mills, A.W.	120-180	
Langer, S.K.	Cruise of the Little Dipper (1st, 12mo, 176p, gilt, 5cp, pep)	NY: Norcross	(1923)	Sewell, H.	90-140	
Langford, George	Stories/First American Animals (1st, lg8vo, p-o, 242p, 5cp)	Boni/Liveright	(1923)	Mahon, Ty	45-60	*
Langley, Noel	Tale/Land of Green Ginger (1st AM, lg4to, 143p, green cl, col)	Wm. Morrow	1938	Langley, N.	140-175	*
Langstaff, John	Frog Went A-Courtin' (1st {std}, lg4to, [32]p, color, pep, CM)	Harcourt	(1955)	Rojankovsky, F.	80-130	R*
Lanier, S.	Boy's King Arthur (1st UK, 4to, 321p, 14cp)	L: Hodder	[1918]	Wyeth, N.C.	130-180	*
Lanier, S.	Boy's Mabinogian (1st, 8vo, 361p, gilt, 12pl, cep, PPPa)	Scribner	1881	Fredericks, A.	70-100	*
Lansdale, M.	Chateaus of Touraine (1st, 4to, 363p, uncut, teg, gilt, 16cp)	Century	1906	Guerin, J.	65-80	
Lansing, Eliz.	Jubilant for Sure (1st {std}, 8vo, green cl, 148p, fp b/w)	Crowell	(1954)	Keats, E.J.	65-90	R*
Lansing, Eliz.	Pony that Ran Away (1st {std}, sm8vo, 149p, red cl, b/w, dep)	Crowell	(1951)	Cooney, B.	30-45	*
Lansing, Eliz.	Sure Thing for Shep (1st {std}, sm8vo, red cl, 177p, b/w)	Coward	(1956)	Keats, E.J.	35-50	*
Lapen, F.	Brownyboo (4to, ibds, cp)	Saalfield	(1908)	Miller, H.L.	75-100	
Lardner, R.	Bib Ballads (1st {1st bk.}, 8vo, teg, brown/gilt, [63]p)	Volland	(1915)	Fox, F.	180-240	R
Lardner, R.	Big Town (1st, sm8vo, 244p, green cl, b/w pl)	Bobbs-Merrill	(1921)	Preston, M.W.	80-100	
Lardner, R.	Gullible's Travels (1st, sm8vo, blue cl, 255p, col frn)	Bobbs-Merrill	(1917)	Preston, M.W.	100-125	
Larken, E.P.	Sea-Prince (1st, 12mo, blue/gilt, teg, 340p, b/w, dep)	L: Jarrolds	1899	Bayes, J.M.	45-60	
Larned, W.T.	American Indian Fairy Tales (1st, 8vo, ibds, [88]p, color, pep)	Volland	(1921)	Rae, J.	85-120	
Larned, W.T.	Fairy Tales From France (1st, lg8vo, ibds, [93]p, color, pep)	Volland	(1920)	Rae, J.	70-90	
Larrimore, L.	Blossoming of Patricia-The-Less (1st, lg8vo, 253p, p-o, 4cp)	Penn	1924	Price, H.L.	45-60	
Latham, Jean L.	Carry On, Mr. Bowditch (1st, 8vo, green cl, 251p, fp b/w, NM)	Houghton	1955	Cosgrave, J.O.	60-85	
Lathbury, M.A.	April Skies (1st, 4to, ibds, 12 chromos)	Worthington	1889	Lathbury, M.A.	100-145	
Lathbury, M.A.	Idyls of the Months (4to, ibds, AEG)	L: Routledge	(1885)	14 Chromos	120-160	
Lathrop, D.	Angel in the Woods (1st {std}, 8vo, red cl, [48]p, fp b/w, cep)	MacMillan	1947	Lathrop, D.	40-60	
Lathrop, D.	Bouncing Betsy (1st, ob4to, [41]p, 16pl, DJ)	MacMillan	1936	Lathrop, D.	60-80	
Lathrop, D.	Colt from Moon Mountain (1st, 8vo, [62]p, b/w, pep, DJ)	MacMillan	1941	Lathrop, D.	140-175	
Lathrop, D.	Dog in the Tapestry Garden (1st, sm4to, red cl, b/w)	MacMillan	1942	Lathrop, D.	30-55	*
Lathrop, D.	Fairy Circus (1st {1st bk.}, ob8vo, gilt, 67p, 8cp, 12pl, NH)	MacMillan	1931	Lathrop, D.	140-200	
Lathrop, D.	Follow the Brook (1st {std}, sm4to, blue cl, 40p, fp b/w)	MacMillan	(1960)	Lathrop, D.	35-60	*
Lathrop, D.	Hide and Go Seek (1st, 4to, grey cl, unpag, fp b/w, pep, DJ)	MacMillan	1938	Lathrop, D.	65-90	
Lathrop, D.	Let Them Live (1st {std}, 8vo, orang cl, 80p, b/w, cep, DJ)	MacMillan	1951	Lathrop, D.	45-60	
Lathrop, D.	Little White Goat (1st, ob4to, 59p, col frn, 15pl, pep)	MacMillan	1933	Lathrop, D.	80-120	
Lathrop, D.	Littlest Mouse (1st {std}, sm8vo, ibds, 32p, b/w)	MacMillan	(1955)	Lathrop, D.	25-45	*
Lathrop, D.	Lost Merry-Go-Round (1st, sq8vo, 104p, col frn, 10pl, pep)	MacMillan	1934	Lathrop, D.	80-100	
Lathrop, D.	Presents for Lupe (1st, sq4to, orang cl, [40]p, color, dep, DJ)	MacMillan	1940	Lathrop, D.	50-75	
Lathrop, D.	Puffy & Seven Leaf Clover (1st {std}, 8vo, 34p, 2-color, cep)	MacMillan	(1954)	Lathrop, D.	35-50	*
Lathrop, D.	Puppies for Keeps (1st {std}, ob4to, brown cl, [40]p, color, DJ)	MacMillan	1943	Lathrop, D.	75-90	
Lathrop, D.	Skittle-Skattle Monkey (1st, lg8vo, red cl, [48]p, b/w, DJ)	MacMillan	1945	Lathrop, D.	70-100	
Lathrop, D.	Snail Who Ran (1st, 16mo, green cl, 57p, col frn)	Stokes	1934	Lathrop, D.	45-60	
Lathrop, D.	Who Goes There? (1st, ob4to, [40]p, 16 fp b/w, pep)	MacMillan	1935	Lathrop, D.	65-100	
Lattimore, Eleanor	Lost Leopard (1st, ob8vo, orange cl, 104p, 8cp, pep)	Harcourt	(1935)	Lattimore, E.	30-45	
Lau, Josephine	Cheeky: A Prairie Dog (1st, 8vo, 62p, color, pep)	Whitman	1937	Wiese, K.	25-40	*
Laughlin, C.E.	Felicity (1st, 8vo, green/gilt, 426p, 4cp)	Scribner	1907	Stephens, A.B.	25-40	
Laughlin, E.O.	Johnnie (1st, 12mo, 227p, teg, uncut)	Bowen-Merrill	1899	(Photos)	25-40	*
Lawless, E.	Book of Gilly (1st, 8vo, 298p, 4pl)	L: Smith Elder	1906	Brooke, L.L.	50-70	
Lawrence, C.H.	Santa Claus in Toyland (1st, 4to, 96p, ibds, 8cp, 12pl)	Reilly/Britton	(1915)	Lawrence, C.H.	120-175	
Lawrence, J.	Man in the Moon Stories... (1st, 4to, 121p, gilt, p-o, 8cp, pep)	Cupples	(1922)	Gruelle, J.	165-220	
Lawson, L.	Christmas Roses (lg8vo, [31]p, ibds, 10 chromos, pep)	Nister/Dutton	[1880]	Lawson, L.	145-200	
Lawson, Marie A.	Dragon John (1st, 8vo, 51p, green cl, 2-color, dep)	Viking	1943	Lawson, M.A.	25-45	*
Lawson, Marie A.	Hail Columbia (1st {std}, 4to, 387p, 7cp, 14 2-color, pep)	Doubleday/Dor.	1931	Lawson, M.A.	35-50	*
Lawson, Marie A.	Sea is Blue (1st, 8vo, 126p, pep, 11pl)	Viking	1946	Lawson, M.A.	30-45	*
Lawson, R.	At that Time (1st, 8vo, 127p, b/w, DJ)	Viking	1947	Lawson, R.	40-60	
Lawson, R.	Ben & Me (1st {std}, sq8vo, 114p, brown cl, pep, DJ)	Little/Brown	1939	Lawson, R.	100-140	
Lawson, R.	Captain Kidd's Cat (1st {std}, 8vo, 151p, green cl, b/w, DJ)	Little/Brown	(1956)	Lawson, R.	50-75	
Lawson, R.	Country Colic (1st {std}, sq8vo, 70p, beige cl, b/w, pep)	Little/Brown	1944	Lawson, R.	30-50	
Lawson, R.	Edward, Hoppy & Joe (1st {std}, 8vo, 122p, fp b/w, pep)	Knopf	(1952)	Lawson, R.	50-75	
Lawson, R.	Fabulous Flight (1st {std}, 8vo, 152p, green cl, b/w, pep)	Little/Brown	1949	Lawson, R.	40-60	
Lawson, R.	Great Wheel (1st, 8vo, 188p, pep, b/w, green cl, DJ, NH)	Viking	(1957)	Lawson, R.	70-100	*
Lawson, R.	I Discover Columbus (1st {std}, 8vo, blue cl, 113p, pep, DJ)	Little/Brown	1941	Lawson, R.	50-65	
Lawson, R.	McWhinney's Jaunt (1st {std}, sq8vo, 77p, cloth, b/w, DJ)	Little/Brown	1951	Lawson, R.	45-70	
Lawson, R.	Mr. Revere & I (1st {std}, 8vo, 152p, b/w, pep)	Little/Brown	(1953)	Lawson, R.	70-90	R
Lawson, R.	Mr. Twigg's Mistake (1st {std}, 8vo, 143p, aqua cl, pep, DJ)	Little/Brown	1947	Lawson, R.	65-80	
Lawson, R.	Mr. Wilmer (1st {std}, 8vo, 218p, beige cl, b/w, DJ)	Little/Brown	1945	Lawson, R.	50-80	

AUTHOR	TITLE	PUBLISHER	DATE	ARTIST	PRICE	LC
Lawson, R.	Rabbit Hill (1st, 8vo, 128p, pep, DJ, NM)	Viking	1944	Lawson, R.	90-130	R
Lawson, R.	Robbut: Tale of Tails (1st, 4to, ibds, 94p, pep, DJ)	Viking	1948	Lawson, R.	75-100	
Lawson, R.	Smeller Martin (1st, sm4to, green cl, 157p, fp b/w, DJ)	Viking	1950	Lawson, R.	40-60	
Lawson, R.	They Were Strong & Good (1st, lg4to, unpag, fp b/w, pep, CM)	Viking	1940	Lawson, R.	80-120	
Lawson, R.	Tough Winter (1st, 8vo, 128p, blue/silver, pep, DJ)	Viking	1954	Lawson, R.	65-80	
Lawson, R.	Watchwords of Liberty (1st {std}, 4to, 115p, b/w, pep, DJ)	Little/Brown	1943	Lawson, R.	50-65	
Layard, George S.	Cruikshank's Portraits of Himself (1st, 8vo, 98p, 17pl)	L: Spencer	1897	Cruikshank, G.	100-165	*
Layard, George S.	Suppressed Plates... (1st, 8vo, 254p, gilt, b/w)	L: A&C Black	1907	Various	130-165	
LeBaron, G.	Twixt You & Me (1st, 8vo, 296p, decorations by...)	Little/Brown	1898	Pyle, Kath.	35-50	*
LeBaron, G.	Twixt You & Me (1st, 8vo, 296p, 5pl by...)	Little/Brown	1898	Thompson, E.B.	35-50	*
LeBlanc, G.	Children's Blue Bird (1st, sq8vo, 172p, 12cp)	L: Methuen	1913	Rothenstein, A.	70-100	
LeFanu, J.S.	In a Glass Darkly (1st {1st illus bk.}, 8vo, 382p, b/w)	L: P. Davies	1929	Ardizzone, E.	120-180	*
LeFevre, A.	Odd One (1st, sq8vo, uncut, 142p)	Revell	1898	Lathbury, M.	30-45	*
LeFevre, A.	Puzzling Pair (1st, sq8vo, 144p, b/w)	Revell	1898	Lance, E.	20-30	*
LeGallienne, Eva	Flossie & Bossie (1st {std}, sm8vo, 210p, 30 fp b/w, DJ)	Harper	(1949)	Williams, Garth	50-85	R
LeGallienne, R.	Maker of Rainbows (1st, 8vo, 104p, teg, p-o, 2cp, 3pl)	Harper	1912	Green, E.S.	65-90	R
LeGallienne, R.	Mr. Sun & Mrs. Moon (1st, folio, bds, [62]p, 12pl)	R.H. Russell	1902	Unknown	185-230	R
LeGallienne, R.	October Vagabonds (1st, 8vo, ipcb, gilt, 201p, col frn, pep)	Kennerley	1910	Fogarty, T.	45-70	R
LeGallienne, R.	Old Country House (1st, lg4to, bds, teg, 144p, 6pl)	Harper	1902	Green, E.S.	100-150	
LeGallienne, R.	Perseus & Andromeda (1st, 8vo, teg, gilt, p-o, uncut, 53p, 6pl)	R.H. Russell	1902	Various	80-130	R*
LeGallienne, R.	Prose Fancies (1st AM, 12mo, gilt, 201p, cvr by...)	H. Stone	1896	Hazenplug, F.	60-80	
LeGallienne, R.	Quest of the Golden Girl (1st, 8vo, green/gilt, 308p, teg)	J. Lane	1896	Bradley, W.	75-100	
LeGallienne, R.	Romance of Perfume (1st, sm4to, ipcb, 8cp)	R. Hadnut	1928	Barbier, G.	70-85	
LeGallienne, R.	Romance of Zion Chapel (1st {std}, 8vo, 297p, teg, cvr by...)	J. Lane	1898	Bradley, W.	90-130	
LeGallienne, R.	Wagner's Tristan & Isolde (1st, 4to, black/gilt, 7cp)	Stokes	(1909)	Williams, G.A.	100-130	
LeGallienne, R.	Young Lives (1st, 8vo, teg, 386p, cvr by...)	J. Lane	1899	Bradley, W.	85-120	
LeMair, H.W.	Auntie's Little Rhyme Book (ob12mo, ibds, 26p, 10 color)	Augener/McKay	[1918]	LeMair, H.W.	120-165	
LeMair, H.W.	Baby's Little Rhyme Book (ob 12mo, ibds, 10 color)	L: Augener	[1920]	LeMair, H.W.	130-165	
LeMair, H.W.	Daddy's Little Rhyme Book (ob 12mo, ibds, 10 color)	L: Augener	[1920]	LeMair, H.W.	130-165	
LeMair, H.W.	Granny's Little Rhyme Book (ob12mo, 26p, ibds, 12 color)	L: Augener	(1912)	LeMair, H.W.	120-165	
LeMair, H.W.	Mother's Little Rhyme Book (ob 16mo, ibds)	McKay	[n.d.]	LeMair, H.W.	100-130	
LeMair, H.W.	Nursie's Little Rhyme Book. (ob12mo, ibds, 26p, 10 color)	Augener/McKay	[1915]	LeMair, H.W.	120-165	
LeWitt, J.	The Vegetabull (1st {std}, 4to, ibds, [32]p)	Harcourt	1956	LeWitt, J.	30-50	*
Lea, John	Willie Wimple's Adventures (1st, 4to, ibds, 16cp)	L: T.F. Unwin	(1908)	Cowham, H.	200-300	
Leach, Maria	Rainbow Bk./American Folk Tales (1st {std}, 4to, 318p, color)	World Pub. Co.	(1958)	Simont, M.	30-50	*
Leacock, S.B.	Nonsense Novels (1st, 8vo, 176p, grey bds, gilt, 8 color)	L: Bodley Head	1921	Kettelwell, J.	65-90	
Leaf, M.	Ferdinand the Bull (4to, wraps, 31p, color)	Whitman	(1936)	Disney Studios	80-100	
Leaf, M.	Ferdinand the Bull (1st, 4to, [8]p, stiff wraps, color)	Whitman	(1938)	Disney Studios	100-145	
Leaf, M.	Ferdinand the Bull (1st {this pub}, ob8vo, [14]p, wraps, 6 col)	Dell	1938	Disney Studios	65-90	*
Leaf, M.	Gordon the Goat (1st {std}, 8vo, green cl, 48p, color)	Lippincott	(1944)	Leaf, M.	30-45	*
Leaf, M.	Noodle (1st, ob8vo, brown cl, [48]p, fp 1-color, pep)	Stokes	1937	Bemelmans, L.	85-100	
Leaf, M.	Story of Ferdinand (1st, 8vo, ibds, [68]p, b/w, pep, DJ)	Viking	1936	Lawson, R.	380-550	R
Leaf, M.	Story of Simpson & Sampson (1st, sq4to, [64]p, blue cl, b/w pep)	Viking	1941	Lawson, R.	65-100	*
Leaf, M.	Wee Gillis (1st, 4to, ipcb, [76]p, 33 fp b/w, pep, CH)	Viking	1938	Lawson, R.	70-100	R
Leamy, Edmund	Fairy Minstrel of Glenmalure (1st, 8vo, p-o, 4cp)	D. Fitzgerald	(1913)	Casseau, V.	35-50	*
Leamy, Edmund	Fairy Minstrel of Glenmalure (1st {this pub}, sm8vo, 92p, b/w)	Longmans	1937	Bennett, R.	25-40	*
Lear, E.	Alphabet Book (1st, ob8vo, ibds, [55]p, color)	Reilly/Britton	(1915)	Richardson, F.	75-120	
Lear, E.	Duck & the Kangaroo (1st, 12mo, [56]p, pep, color)	Western Prntg.	(1932)	Ward, Keith	45-60	*
Lear, E.	Nonsense Songs (1st, 8vo, AEG, [148]p, gilt, 14cp, pep)	L: Warne	[1900]	Brooke, L.L.	145-200	
Lear, E.	Owl & the Pussycat (1st, ob8vo, [56]p, color, pep)	Whitman	(1932)	Ward, Keith	30-45	*
Lear, E.	Pelican Chorus (sq8vo, ibds, p-o, [80]p, 7cp)	L: Warne	(1900)	Brooke, L.L.	60-75	
Lear, E.	The Jumblies (sm4to, ibds, p-o, 6cp)	L: Warne	[1905]	Brooke, L.L.	80-100	
Lebeck, O.	Diary of Terwilliger Jellico (1st, lg8vo, ibds, [48]p, col, pep)	Grosset/Dunlap	1935	Lebeck, O.	35-50	
Lecky, E.	Here, There, Everywhere (1st, 4to, unpag)	L: R. Tuck	(1890)	(Chromos)	70-110	
Lederer, J.	Fafan in China (1st, 8vo, 137p, green cl, b/w, pep)	Holiday House	(1939)	Sanderson, W.	20-25	*
Lee, A.	Round Rabbit (1st, 12mo, brown cl, 52p, 6pl)	Copeland & Day	1898	O'Neill, R.	200-300	
Lee, Al	Tommy Toodles (1st, 8vo, p-o, blue cl, 192p, 26pl)	Harper	1896	Newell, P.	160-200	
Lee, E.D.	Ever Living Fairy Tales (lg8vo, green cl, p-o, 18cp)	(NY)	1924	Lee, E.D.	40-60	*
Lee, Frank H.	Children's King Arthur (1st, 8vo, 77p)	L: Harrap	1935	Appleton, H.C.	45-60	*
Lee, H.	Legends from Fairyland (1st, 8vo, 276p, blue/gilt, 17pl, pep)	L: Chatto	1907	Knowles, R.L.	180-240	
Lee, J.	Happy Island (1st, 8vo, 330p, frn by...)	Century	1910	Schoonover, F.	20-25	
Lee, M.	Marcos... (1st, 4to, p-o, 79p, color)	Whitman	1937	Hader, B.& E.	35-50	
Lee, V.	Ballet of the Nations (1st AM, 4to, ibds, 24p, uncut, 1-color)	Putnam	1915	Armfield, M.	90-140	R*
Leet, F.R.	Animal Caravan (1st, lg4to, 60p, ibds, 12 fp color)	Saalfield	(1930)	Peat, F.B.	40-65	
Leet, F.R.	Hop, Skip & Jump (4to, ibds, 34p, 6cp, DJ)	Saalfield	1936	Peat, F.B.	65-80	
Leet, F.R.	Purr & Meow (1st, 4to, ibds, 60p, 12cp)	Saalfield	(1931)	Peat, F.B.	50-70	
Leet, F.R.	To the Circus the Children Go (ob folio, wraps, color)	Saalfield	1931	Kay, G.A.	35-50	*
Lefevre, F.	Cock, Mouse & Little Red Hen (1st, 8vo, 103p, 24cp)	L: Richards	1907	Sarg, T.	200-300	
Lefevre, F.	Cock, Mouse & Little Red Hen (1st AM, 8vo, 103p, 24cp)	Jacobs	(1907)	Sarg, T.	145-220	
Lefevre, F.	Cock, Mouse & Little Red Hen (ob folio, wraps, color)	Saalfield	1931	Peat, F.B.	50-80	
Lefevre, F.	Fiddle Diddle Dee (1st, sm8vo, orang cl, [63]p, fp color, pep)	Greenberg	(1928)	Barney, M.W.	60-90	*
Lefevre, F.	Soldier Boy (1st, sm8vo, [64]p, orang cl, color, pep)	Greenberg	(1926)	Sarg, T.	50-70	

AUTHOR	TITLE	PUBLISHER	DATE	ARTIST	PRICE	LC
Lefferts, S.T.	Mr. Cinnamon Bear (1st, sq16mo, ibds, 85p, color)	Bossette Co.	(1907)	Bacquet, L.	160-220	*
Lefferts, S.T.	Pansy Wedding (1st, sq16mo, 86p, color, pep)	Cupples	(1909)	Smith, Wuanita	50-80	*
Lefferts, S.T.	Patriotic Jubilee (1st, sq16mo, 84p, color, pep)	Cupples	(1910)	Smith, Wuanita	50-80	*
Leigh, M.C.	Love Songs & Verses (1st, sm4to, 65p, teg, 4pl)	L: Humphreys	1913	Robinson, G.	50-90	
Leighton (ed.)	Fleur & Blanchefleur (1st, 4to, 61p, 37 color illus)	L: O'Connor	(1922)	Brickdale, E.F.	50-70	
Leighton, C.	Country Matters (1st, 4to, 159p, 70 wood engravings)	MacMillan	1937	Leighton, C.	50-80	R*
Leighton, C.	Farmer's Year... (1st, ob folio, 54p, pep, 12 fp woodcuts)	L: Collins	1933	Leighton, C.	120-165	*
Leighton, C.	Four Hedges... (1st, lg8vo, 167p, blue cl, wood engravings)	MacMillan	1935	Leighton, C.	35-50	
Leighton, C.	Sometime Never (1st, lg8vo, 178p, b/w, DJ)	MacMillan	1939	Leighton, C.	45-60	
Leighton, C.	Southern Harvest (1st UK, 4to, 123p)	L: Gollancz	1943	Leighton, C.	45-70	*
Leighton, C.	Where Land Meets Sea (1st, 4to, 202p, 4 fp b/w)	Rinehart	(1954)	Leighton, C.	30-50	
Leighton, Rbt.	Wreck of the Golden Fleece (1st, 8vo, 352p, green cl, 6pl)	L: Blackie	(1893)	Brangwyn, F.	45-60	*
Lemonnier	Birds & Beasts (1st, 8vo, teg, 196p, 6cp)	L: G. Allen	(1911)	Detmold, E.J.	150-200	
Lenotre, Therese	Mystery of Dog Flip (1st, sm8vo, 190p, cloth, b/w, dep)	Stokes	1939	Eichenberg, F.	25-45	*
Lenski, L.	A-Going to the Westward (1st, 8vo, 370p, uncut, b/w, pep)	Stokes	1937	Lenski, L.	45-60	*
Lenski, L.	Alphabet People (1st {std}, lg8vo, 104p, p-o, blue cl, col, pep)	Harper	1928	Lenski, L.	60-90	
Lenski, L.	Arabella & Her Aunts (1st, sq12mo, p-o, 115p, 5cp, cep, DJ)	Stokes	1932	Lenski, L.	100-135	
Lenski, L.	Bayou Suzette (1st {std}, 8vo, 207p, map, fp b/w, pep)	Stokes	1943	Lenski, L.	45-60	*
Lenski, L.	Benny & His Penny (1st, ob4to, blue cl, [32]p, color)	Knopf	1931	Lenski, L.	65-80	*
Lenski, L.	Blue Ridge Billy (1st {std}, 8vo, 203p, b/w, pep)	Lippincott	(1946)	Lenski, L.	30-45	
Lenski, L.	Blueberry Corners (1st, 8vo, blue/gilt, 209p, b/w, pep)	Stokes	1940	Lenski, L.	35-50	*
Lenski, L.	Bound Girl of Cobble Hill (1st, 8vo, 292p, uncut, b/w, dep)	Stokes	1938	Lenski, L.	30-45	
Lenski, L.	Cotton in My Sack (1st {std}, lg8vo, 191p, dp b/w, pep)	Lippincott	(1949)	Lenski, L.	35-50	
Lenski, L.	Cowboy Small (1st, 8vo, tan cl, [48]p, color, pep)	OUP	(1949)	Lenski, L.	45-65	
Lenski, L.	Easter Rabbit's Parade (1st, lg8vo, ipcb, [31]p, color, pep)	OUP	(1936)	Lenski, L.	50-75	
Lenski, L.	Gooseberry Garden (1st {std}, ob8vo, ipcb, [32]p, color)	Harper	1934	Lenski, L.	60-80	*
Lenski, L.	Grandmother Tippytoe (1st, sm4to, p-o, 104p, 8cp)	Stokes	1931	Lenski, L.	45-60	
Lenski, L.	Indian Captive (1st, 8vo, 269p, pep, color, DJ, NH)	Stokes	1941	Lenski, L.	50-85	
Lenski, L.	Jack Horner's Pie (1st, lg8vo, 83p, color)	Harper	1927	Lenski, L.	45-60	
Lenski, L.	Johnny Goes to the Fair (1st, 8vo, [32]p, yellow cl, color)	Minton Balch	1932	Lenski, L.	40-60	*
Lenski, L.	Judy's Journey (1st {std}, 8vo, 212p, b/w, pep)	Lippincott	1947	Lenski, L.	30-45	
Lenski, L.	Little Airplane (1st, sq8vo, [48]p, 1-color, pep)	OUP	(1938)	Lenski, L.	35-50	
Lenski, L.	Little Family (1st {std}, sq12mo, ibds, unpag, color, dep)	Doubleday/Dor.	1932	Lenski, L.	30-50	
Lenski, L.	Little Fire Engine (1st, ob8vo, red/gilt, [46]p, 1-color)	OUP	1946	Lenski, L.	45-60	
Lenski, L.	Little Girl of 1900 (1st, 8vo, 218p, p-o, col frn, 9pl, pep)	Stokes	1928	Lenski, L.	65-90	R*
Lenski, L.	Mamma Hattie's Girl (1st {std}, 8vo, 182p, pep, b/w, DJ)	Lippincott	(1953)	Lenski, L.	35-50	
Lenski, L.	Now It's Fall (1st, ob12mo, [48]p, color, DJ)	OUP	(1948)	Lenski, L.	40-60	
Lenski, L.	Ocean-Born Mary (1st, sm8vo, 388p, pep, b/w)	Stokes	1939	Lenski, L.	45-60	*
Lenski, L.	Phebe Fairchild... (1st, 8vo, 316p, rust/gilt, b/w, dep, NH)	Stokes	1936	Lenski, L.	45-65	
Lenski, L.	Prairie School (1st {std}, 8vo, 196p, b/w)	Lippincott	(1951)	Lenski, L.	30-45	*
Lenski, L.	Puritan Adventure (1st {std}, 8vo, 223p, color, DJ)	Lippincott	1944	Lenski, L.	30-45	*
Lenski, L.	Skipping Village (1st, 4to, 179p, blue cl, 4cp, 3pl, pep)	Stokes	1927	Lenski, L.	50-75	
Lenski, L.	Spinach-Boy (1st, 12mo, 91p, p-o, 6cp, pep, DJ)	Stokes	1930	Lenski, L.	50-65	
Lenski, L.	Spring is Here (1st, ob12mo, [48]p, yellow cl, color, cep, DJ)	OUP	(1945)	Lenski, L.	50-80	
Lenski, L.	Strawberry Girl (1st {std}, 8vo, 194p, green/gilt, dep, DJ, NM)	Lippincott	(1945)	Lenski, L.	65-90	R
Lenski, L.	Sugarplum House (1st {std}, ob8vo, ipcb, [91]p, color)	Harper	1935	Lenski, L.	50-70	
Lenski, L.	Surprise for Mother (1st, sq12mo, 91p, yellow cl, col frn, b/w)	Stokes	1934	Lenski, L.	35-50	
Lenski, L.	Susie Mauiar (1st, ob8vo, unpag, color, dep)	NY: OUP	(1939)	Lenski, L.	45-60	*
Lenski, L.	Texas Tomboy (1st {std}, 4to, 180p)	Lippincott	(1950)	Lenski, L.	45-65	*
Lenski, L.	Two Brothers/Animal Friends (1st, ob12mo, 122p, p-o, col, pep)	Stokes	1929	Lenski, L.	80-120	*
Lenski, L.	Two Brothers/Baby Sister (1st, ob12mo, 121p, p-o, 12cp, pep)	Stokes	1930	Lenski, L.	80-120	
Lenski, L.	Washington Picture Book (1st, ob4to, ibds, [32]p, color, pep)	Coward	1930	Lenski, L.	70-120	
Lent, Henry B.	Air Pilot (1st, sq16mo, [42]p, color, pep)	MacMillan	1937	Hauman, G.& D.	30-45	
Lent, Henry B.	Bus Driver (1st, sq16mo, [42]p, color, pep)	MacMillan	1937	Winslow, E.	30-45	*
Lent, Henry B.	The Captain (1st, sq16mo, [42]p, color, pep)	MacMillan	1937	Winslow, E.	30-45	*
Lent, Henry B.	The Farmer (1st, sq16mo, ipcb, [42]p, color, pep)	MacMillan	1937	Hader, B.& E.	35-50	
Lent, Henry B.	The Storekeeper (1st, sq16mo, [42]p, color, pep)	MacMillan	1937	Hauman, G.& D.	30-45	
Leonard, M.F.	How the Two Ends Met (1st, 8vo, 97p, 4pl)	Crowell	(1903)	Falls, C.B.	45-60	*
Leonard, M.F.	Susan Grows Up (1st, 8vo, 307p, 8pl)	Crowell	(1914)	Elmer, R.R.	20-30	*
Leonard, Nellie	Graymouse Family (1st, 8vo, 209p, b/w)	Crowell	(1950)	Cooney, B.	45-70	R*
Lever, Chas.	Charles O'Malley... (1st, 8vo, 628p, uncut, red/gilt, 16pl)	L: Service	1897	Rackham, A.	140-170	
Lever, Chas.	Templelogue Lever (1st, 4to, AEG, green cl, 631p, 32cp)	NY: Pollard	1880	Browne, H.K.	135-160	
Levy, N.	Opera Guyed (1st, 8vo, 87p, b/w, DJ)	Knopf	1923	Irvin, Rea	35-60	
Lewis, A.H.	Black Lion Inn (1st, 8vo, 380p, 16pl)	R.H. Russell	1903	Remington, F.	70-85	
Lewis, A.H.	Peggy O'Neal (1st, 8vo, uncut, 494p, 4cp)	Drexel/Biddle	1903	Hutt, H.	30-45	
Lewis, A.H.	Sandburrs (1st, 8vo, 318p, 16pl)	Stokes	(1900)	Taylor, H.W.	40-65	
Lewis, A.H.	The Throwback (1st, 12mo, 347p, green cl, 4cp)	Outing	1906	Wyeth, N.C.	35-50	
Lewis, A.H.	Wolfville (1st, 12mo, red cl, 337p, 18pl)	Stokes	(1897)	Remington, F.	90-130	
Lewis, A.H.	Wolfville Days (1st, 8vo, 311p, frn by...)	Stokes	(1902)	Remington, F.	50-70	
Lewis, A.H.	Wolfville Folks (1st, 8vo, 321p, frn by...)	Appleton	1908	Dunton, W.H.	30-45	
Lewis, B.	Blue Mountain (1st {std}, lg8vo, blue cl, 59p, fp b/w, dep)	Knopf	1956	Adams, A.	35-50	*
Lewis, C.S.	Horse & his Boy (1st, 8vo, grey/silver, 199p)	L: G. Bles	(1954)	Baynes, P.D.	250-400	*

AUTHOR	TITLE	PUBLISHER	DATE	ARTIST	PRICE	LC
Lewis, C.S.	Last Battle (1st AM {std}, sm8vo, 174p, blue cl, b/w)	MacMillan	(1956)	Baynes, P.D.	160-200	R*
Lewis, C.S.	Last Battle (1st, 8vo, blue cl, 184p, b/w, DJ)	L: Bodley Head	1956	Baynes, P.D.	350-500	*
Lewis, C.S.	Lion, Witch & the Wardrobe (1st AM, 8vo, 154p, b/w, DJ)	MacMillan	1950	Baynes, P.D.	200-300	
Lewis, C.S.	Magician's Nephew (1st AM {std}, sm8vo, 167p, green cl, b/w)	MacMillan	(1955)	Baynes, P.D.	130-170	
Lewis, C.S.	Prince Caspian (1st AM {std}, sm8vo, 186p, green cl, 4 fp b/w)	MacMillan	1951	Baynes, P.D.	150-200	
Lewis, C.S.	Silver Chair (1st AM {std}, sm8vo, 208p, blue cl, 4 fp b/w)	MacMillan	(1953)	Baynes, P.D.	90-140	*
Lewis, C.S.	Voyage o/t Dawn Treader (1st AM {std}, sm8vo, 210p, blue cl, b/w)	MacMillan	1952	Baynes, P.D.	100-160	
Lewis, Cecil D.	Christmas Eve (1st, sm8vo, unpag, wraps, col frn)	L: Faber	1954	Ardizzone, E.	45-60	*
Lewis, Cecil D.	Otterbury Incident (1st, 8vo, 148p, red cl, b/w, DJ)	L: Putnam	1948	Ardizzone, E.	75-100	*
Lewis, Cecil D.	Otterbury Incident (1st AM, 8vo, cloth, 160p, b/w, DJ)	Viking	1949	Ardizzone, E.	85-100	
Lewis, Claudia	Straps the Cat (1st, 12mo, 141p, rust cl, fp b/w)	W.R. Scott	(1957)	Ruhtenberg, C.	35-50	*
Lewis, E.W.	Next-Door Morelands (1st, 8vo, 342p, 4pl)	Little/Brown	1907	Aherns, E.W.	20-25	*
Lewis, Eliz. F.	Ho-Ming, Girl of New China (1st, 8vo, 266p, gilt, pep, 4cp)	Winston	1934	Wiese, K.	20-25	*
Lewis, Eliz. F.	When the Typhoon Blows (1st, 8vo, 273p, orange cl, col frn, pep)	Winston	(1942)	Wiese, K.	25-40	*
Lewis, Eliz. F.	Young Fu/Upper Yangtze (1st, 8vo, 265p, black cl, 4cp, pep, NM)	Winston	1932	Wiese, K.	50-85	R
Lida	Bruin the Brown Bear (1st {std}, 4to, ibds, [32]p, color, pep)	Harper	1937	Rojankovsky, F.	35-50	
Lida	Cuckoo (1st {std}, sm sq4to, ibds, [32]p, pep, color)	Harper	1942	Rojankovsky, F.	45-60	*
Lida	Little French Farm (1st {std}, 4to, ibds, [26]p, color, pep)	Harper	1939	Guertik, H.	80-120	*
Lida	Plouf the Little Wild Duck (1st, sq4to, ibds, [40]p, color, pep)	Harper	1936	Rojankovsky, F.	45-60	*
Lida	Pompom (1st, sq4to, ibds, [38]p, color, pep, DJ)	Harper	1936	Rojankovsky, F.	50-70	
Lida	Scuff the Seal (1st {std}, sq4to, ibds, [32]p, color, pep)	Harper	1937	Rojankovsky, F.	45-70	*
Lida	Spiky the Hedgehog (1st {std}, 4to, ibds, unpag, color, pep)	Harper	1938	Rojankovsky, F.	50-70	
Lida	The Kingfisher (1st {std}, sm sq4to, ibds, [32]p, pep, color)	Harper	1940	Rojankovsky, F.	45-60	
Liddell, Mary	Little Machinery (1st, 4to, 62p, ibds, color)	Doubleday/Page	(1926)	Liddell, M.	90-130	
Lide, A.A.	Aztec Drums (1st {std}, sm8vo, 142p, blue cl, fp b/w, pep)	Longmans	1931	Sanchez, C.M.	20-30	*
Lide, A.A.	Inemak: Little Greenlander (1st, sm8vo, 148p, blue cl, fp b/w)	Rand/McNally	(1927)	Clarke, W.W.	20-35	*
Lide, A.A.	Ood-Le-Uk: Wanderer (1st, sm8vo, 265p, col frn, pep, NH)	Little/Brown	1930	Lufkin, R.	30-55	*
Lide, A.A.	Pearls of Fortune (1st, sm8vo, 276p, col frn, 11 fp b/w, dep)	Little/Brown	1931	Cheney, P.	20-30	*
Lide, A.A.	Princess of Yucatan (1st {std}, 12mo, tan cl, 187p, b/w, pep)	Longmans	1939	Sanchez, C.M.	25-40	*
Lide, A.A.	Yinka-Tu the Yak (1st, 4to, ibds, 63p, color, pep)	Viking	1938	Wiese, K.	35-50	
Liers, Emil	Otter's Story (1st, 8vo, blue cl, 191p, fp b/w)	Viking	1953	Palazzo, T.	45-65	R*
Liggett, Thos.	Pigeon, Fly Home! (1st, 8vo, 189p, tan cl, b/w, pep)	Holiday House	(1956)	Simont, M.	20-30	*
Lightfoot, B.H.	Jolly Jack Horner (1st, 8vo, p-o, 4 color)	Whitman	(1916)	Rosenkrans, E.	30-50	
Lilly, Jean	Hundred Tuftys (1st {std}, 4to, [32]p, ipcb, 2-color, pep)	Dutton	(1940)	Gergely, T.	70-90	*
Lincoln, J.	Cape Cod Ballads (1st [1st bk.], 8vo, yellow/gilt, 198p)	NJ: Brandt	1902	Kemble, E.W.	100-150	
Linderman, F.B.	Blackfeet Indians (1st, lg4to, 65p, ibds, 49 color)	(St. Paul)	1935	Reiss, W.	140-200	
Linderman, F.B.	How It Came About Stories (1st, sm4to, 221p, 6cp, p-o, SC)	Scribner	1921	Boog, C.M.	75-120	*
Linderman, F.B.	Indian Old-Man Stories (1st, sm4to, p-o, 169p, 9cp, SC)	Scribner	1920	Russell, C.M.	140-200	
Linderman, F.B.	Indian Why Stories (1st, 8vo, maroon cl, p-o, 236p, 8cp, SC)	Scribner	1915	Russell, C.M.	150-200	
Linderman, F.B.	Kootenai Why Stories (1st, 8vo, 166p, color)	Scribner	1926	Bull, C.L.	65-80	*
Lindgren, Astrid	Bill Bergson Lives Dangerously (1st, sm8vo, 214p, b/w, pep)	Viking	1954	Freeman, D.	25-45	*
Lindquist, Jennie	Golden Name Day (1st, 8vo, blue cl, 247p, pep, b/w, NH)	Harper	(1955)	Williams, Garth	65-90	R*
Lindquist, Jennie	Little Silver House (1st, sm8vo, 213p, green cl, b/w)	Harper	(1959)	Williams, Garth	35-50	*
Lindsay, M.M.	Bobby & the Big Road (1st, sm8vo, 112p, blue cl, 16cp)	Lothrop/Lee	(1920)	Young, F.L.	25-45	*
Lindsay, M.M.	Joyous Guests (1st, lg8vo, 208p, 13cp)	Lothrop/Lee	(1921)	Berger, W.M.	35-50	
Lindsay, M.M.	Joyous Travelers (1st, 8vo, 157p, blue/gilt, col frn)	Lothrop/Lee	(1919)	Berger, W.M.	25-40	
Lindsay, M.M.	Little Missy (1st, sq8vo, 188p, 8cp)	Lothrop/Lee	(1922)	Young, F.L.	30-45	*
Lindsay, M.M.	Posey & the Pedlar (1st, sm8vo, tan cl, 186p, fp b/w)	Lothrop/Lee	1938	Credle, E.	30-45	*
Lindsay, M.M.	Story-Teller (1st, sm sq8vo, 117p, 12cp)	Lothrop/Lee	(1915)	Young, F.L.	30-45	*
Lindsay, N.	Magic Pudding (1st AM, 12mo, orange cl, [159]p, b/w)	Farrar/Rine.	[1936]	Lindsay, N.	40-60	
Lindsay, V.	Johnny Appleseed (1st, 12mo, green cl, 144p, color)	MacMillan	1928	Richards, G.	45-70	
Lindsey, Wm.	Curtain of Forgetfulness (1st, lg8vo, 31p, 11 ticp)	Houghton	1923	Paul, E.	65-100	
Lindsey, Wm.	Severed Mantle (1st, lg8vo, 452p, 7cp)	Houghton	1909	Keller, A.I.	20-35	
Linnell, O.	Autumn Songs with Music (4to, bds, p-o, 12 ticp)	L: Blackie	[1920]	Barker, C.M.	85-100	
Linnell, O.	Spring Songs with Music (4to, bds, p-o, 12 ticp)	L: Blackie	[1920]	Barker, C.M.	80-100	
Lionni, L.	Inch by Inch (1st, sq4to, ipcb, unpag, color, pep, CH)	Obolensky	(1960)	Lionni, L.	70-110	R*
Lionni, L.	Little Blue & Little Yellow (1st, sq8vo, ibds, unpag, color)	Obolensky	(1959)	Lionni, L.	70-100	R*
Lipkind, Wm.	Christmas Bunny (1st {std}, 4to, [49]p, green cl, color, pep)	Harcourt	(1953)	Mordvinoff, N.	65-90	R*
Lipkind, Wm.	Finders Keepers (1st {std}, 4to, [32]p, pep, 28 color, CM)	Harcourt	(1951)	Mordvinoff, N.	80-100	*
Lipkind, Wm.	Sleepyhead (1st {std}, 4to, green cl, [38]p, 2-color, pep)	Harcourt	(1957)	Mordvinoff, N.	45-65	*
Lipkind, Wm.	Two Reds (1st {std}, 4to, [48]p, color, pep, CH)	Harcourt	(1950)	Mordvinoff, N.	80-120	R*
Lipman, M.	The Chatterlings (1st, lg8vo, 96p, ibds, color, pep)	Volland	(1928)	Lipman, M.	50-80	R
Lippincott, J.W.	Black Wings (1st {std}, sm8vo, 143p, blue cl, col frn, pep)	Lippincott	(1947)	Hunt, L.B.	45-60	*
Lippincott, J.W.	Bun, a Wild Rabbit (1st, 12mo, 124p, p-o, 12pl)	Penn	1918	(Photos)	20-40	*
Lippincott, J.W.	Gray Squirrel (1st, 12mo, 144p, p-o, 7pl)	Penn	1921	(Photos)	20-40	*
Lippincott, J.W.	Phantom Deer (1st {std}, sm8vo, blue cl, 192p, 1 dpcp, 4pl)	Lippincott	(1954)	Bransom, P.	30-45	*
Lippincott, J.W.	Red Roan Pony (1st, 8vo, 320p, red cl, col frn, 4pl, pep)	Penn	(1934)	Hunt, L.B.	45-60	*
Lippincott, J.W.	Red Roan Pony (1st {new ed}, sm8vo, 218p, red cl, 1 dp col, 6pl)	Lippincott	(1951)	Anderson, C.W.	25-40	*
Lippincott, J.W.	Wahoo Bobcat (1st {std}, 8vo, 207p, 1 dp color, 4 dp b/w)	Lippincott	(1950)	Bransom, P.	30-45	*
Lippincott, J.W.	Wilderness Champion (1st {std}, 8vo, 195p, 6 dp b/w, 5pl, cep)	Lippincott	(1944)	Bransom, P.	30-45	*
Lippincott, J.W.	Wolf King (1st, 8vo, 316p, col frn, 4pl, pep)	Penn	(1933)	Bransom, P.	25-40	*
Lippmann, J.M.	Dearie Dot/The Dog (1st, sm8vo, 194p, 5pl)	Penn	1903	Winner, M.F.	20-30	*

AUTHOR	TITLE	PUBLISHER	DATE	ARTIST	PRICE	LC
Lippmann, J.M.	Dreamland (1st, 8vo, green/gilt, 211p, 5pl, dep)	Penn	1901	Betts, A.W.	30-45	
Lippmann, J.M.	Jock O'Dreams (1st, 8vo, 211p, gilt, b/w)	Roberts	1891	McDermott, J.	30-45	*
Lippmann, J.M.	Sweet P's (1st, 8vo, 192p, 5pl, pep)	Penn	1902	Waugh, Ida	25-40	
Litsey, E.C.	Race of the Swift (1st, sm8vo, 151p, 4pl)	Little/Brown	1905	Bull, C.L.	20-30	*
Little, F.	Little Sister Snow (1st, 12mo, 141p, p-o, 12cp)	Century	1909	Kataoka, G.	20-35	
Littlewood, L.	Bower Book of Simple Poems.... (1st, 8vo, 267p, red cl, 10cp)	L: O'Connor	(1922)	Appleton, H.C.	75-90	
Littlewood, S.R.	Child of the Sea (1st, 8vo, 196p, 8cp)	L: Simpkin	1915	Appleton, H.C.	35-50	*
Littlewood, S.R.	Valentine & Orson (1st, 4to, 143p, p-o, 8cp)	L: Simpkin	1919	Anderson, F.	80-125	
Lloyd, J.U.	Red-Head (1st, 8vo, teg, 208p)	Dodd	1903	Birch, R.	30-45	
Lloyd, J.U.	Right Side of the Car (1st, 12mo, 59p, teg, green/gilt)	Badger	1897	Hapgood, T.B.	30-50	
Lloyd, J.U.	Stringtown on the Pike (1st, 8vo, 414p, tan cl, p-o, b/w)	Dodd	1900	(Photos)	20-25	
Lloyd, N.	Soldier of the Valley (1st, 8vo, red/gilt, 325p, 34 fp b/w)	Scribner	1904	Frost, A.B.	50-75	
Locke, A.	New Negro (1st, 8vo, 445p, col frn, b/w, DJ)	A.& C. Boni	1925	Reiss, W.	180-250	
Locke, Wm. J.	Beloved Vagabond (1st, sm4to, 267p, 16cp)	L: J. Lane	1922	Dulac, Jean	80-120	
Locke, Wm. J.	Christmas Mystery (1st, 8vo, 54p, green/gilt, 4pl, dep)	NY: J. Lane	1910	Campbell, B.	65-80	*
Locke, Wm. J.	Christmas Mystery (1st, 8vo, 35p, orang cl, 6cp)	L: J. Lane	1922	Lendon, W.W.	30-50	*
Locke, Wm. J.	Fortunate Youth (1st, sm8vo, 352p, green/gilt, cvr by...)	NY: J. Lane	1914	Hazenplug, F.	30-45	*
Locke, Wm. J.	Fortunate Youth (1st, sm8vo, 352p, green/gilt, 8pl by...)	NY: J. Lane	1914	Keller, A.I.	30-45	*
Locke, Wm. J.	Golden Journey/Mr. Paradyne (1st AM, 8vo, ibds, 53p, 8cp, pep)	Dodd	1924	Foster, M.L.	45-65	*
Locke, Wm. J.	Story of the Three Wise Men (1st, 8vo, 38p, gilt, 6cp)	L: J. Lane	1922	Lendon, W.W.	35-50	
Locker, Mrs. F.	What the Blackbird Said (1st, sq8vo, 187p, gilt, b/w)	L: Routledge	1881	Caldecott, R.	85-130	
Lockhart, C.	Lady Doc (1st, 8vo, tan cloth, 339p, 4pl)	Lippincott	1912	Hoskins, G.	25-40	
Lockhart, C.	Man from Bitter Roots (1st, 8vo, red/gilt, 3cp)	Lippincott	1915	Hoskins, G.	25-40	
Lockridge, Frances	Cat Who Rode Cows (1st {std}, sm8vo, yellow cl, 36p, b/w)	Lippincott	(1955)	Bacon, P.	30-45	*
Lockridge, Frances	Cats & People (1st {std}, 8vo, 286p, b/w)	Lippincott	(1950)	Stone, H.	25-45	*
Lofting, H.	Dr. Dolittle & Green Canary (1st {std}, 8vo, 276p, col frn, pep)	Lippincott	(1950)	Lofting, H.	70-100	
Lofting, H.	Dr. Dolittle & Secret Lake (1st {std}, 8vo, 366p p-o colfrn)	Lippincott	(1948)	Lofting, H.	70-100	
Lofting, H.	Dr. Dolittle in the Moon (1st, 8vo, p-o, 307p, col frn, pep)	Stokes	(1928)	Lofting, H.	65-100	
Lofting, H.	Dr. Dolittle in the Moon (1st UK, 8vo, 319p, 2cp, pep)	L: J. Cape	(1929)	Lofting, H.	60-90	
Lofting, H.	Dr. Dolittle's Birthday Book (1st, sq12mo, gilt, col frn, dep)	Stokes	(1935)	Lofting, H.	60-90	
Lofting, H.	Dr. Dolittle's Caravan (1st {std}, 8vo, p-o, col frn, pep)	Stokes	(1926)	Lofting, H.	70-100	
Lofting, H.	Dr. Dolittle's Circus (1st, 8vo, 379p, p-o, col frn, pep)	Stokes	1924	Lofting, H.	70-100	
Lofting, H.	Dr. Dolittle's Garden (1st, 8vo, 327p, p-o, col frn, pep)	Stokes	(1927)	Lofting, H.	70-90	
Lofting, H.	Dr. Dolittle's Post Office (1st, 8vo, 359p, col frn, pep)	Stokes	(1923)	Lofting, H.	70-100	
Lofting, H.	Dr. Dolittle's Puddleby Advens (1st {std} 8vo, 241p, pep, colfrn)	Lippincott	(1952)	Lofting, H.	50-70	*
Lofting, H.	Dr. Dolittle's Return (1st, 8vo, p-o, 273p, col frn, b/w, pep)	Stokes	1933	Lofting, H.	65-90	
Lofting, H.	Dr. Dolittle's Zoo (1st, 8vo, grey cl, p-o, 338p, col frn, pep)	Stokes	(1925)	Lofting, H.	70-100	
Lofting, H.	Gub Gub's Book (1st, 8vo, 185p, p-o, 2cp, 6pl, pep)	Stokes	(1932)	Lofting, H.	70-120	
Lofting, H.	Noisy Nora (1st, 16mo, [53]p, pink cl, p-o, pep, color)	Stokes	(1929)	Lofting, H.	90-135	*
Lofting, H.	Porridge Poetry (1st, ob8vo, [96]p, p-o, yellow cl)	Stokes	(1924)	Lofting, H.	80-120	
Lofting, H.	Story of Dr. Dolittle (1st, 8vo, p-o, 180p, col frn, PPP)	Stokes	1920	Lofting, H.	85-120	
Lofting, H.	Story of Mrs. Tubbs (1st, sm ob8vo, p-o, [95]p, color)	Stokes	(1923)	Lofting, H.	85-125	
Lofting, H.	Tommy, Tilly & Mrs. Tubbs (1st UK, ob12mo, 72p, ibds, 2 col)	L: J. Cape	(1937)	Lofting, H.	85-120	
Lofting, H.	Twilight of Magic (1st, 8vo, p-o, 303p, col frn, b/w, pep)	Stokes	1930	Lenski, L.	60-90	
Lofting, H.	Voyages of Doctor Dolittle (1st, 12mo, p-o, 364p, 2cp, pep, NM)	Stokes	1922	Lofting, H.	100-170	
London, J.	Before Adam (1st, 8vo, brown cl, 242p, uncut, 8cp)	MacMillan	1907	Bull, C.L.	120-165	
London, J.	Call of the Wild (1st, 8vo, teg, 231p, green/gilt, pep, PPP)	MacMillan	1903	Bull, C.L.	150-200	
London, J.	Call of the Wild (1st, 8vo, 254p, p-o, blue cl, 16cp)	MacMillan	1912	Bransom, P.	180-250	
London, J.	Children of the Frost (1st, sm8vo, 261p, blue cl, 8pl)	MacMillan	1902	Reay, R.M.	350-500	
London, J.	Cruise of the Snark (1st, 8vo, 340p, teg, p-o, blue cl)	MacMillan	1911	(Photos)	220-350	
London, J.	Daughter of the Snows (1st, 12mo, 334p, 4cp)	Lippincott	1902	Yohn, F.C.	200-300	
London, J.	John Barleycorn (1st, 8vo, 343p, 8pl)	Century	1913	Dunn, H.T.	140-175	
London, J.	People of the Abyss (1st, lg8vo, 319p, teg, uncut, 9pl)	MacMillan	1903	(Photos)	200-300	
London, J.	Scarlet Plague (1st, 8vo, 181p, b/w, pep)	MacMillan	1915	Grant, G.	150-200	
London, J.	Sea Wolf (1st, 8vo, blue cl, teg, 366p, 6pl)	MacMillan	1904	Aylward, W.J.	180-230	
London, J.	Smoke Bellew (1st, 8vo, blue cl, 385p, 8pl)	Century	1912	Monahan, P.J.	165-220	
London, J.	Son of the Sun (1st, 8vo, blue cl, 333p, 3pl)	Doubleday/Page	1912	Fischer, A.O.	150-185	
London, J.	Tales/Fish Patrol (1st, 8vo, teg, 243p, map, 7pl)	MacMillan	1905	Varian, G.	220-280	
London, J.	The Game (1st, 8vo, 182p, teg, uncut, col frn, 5pl)	MacMillan	1905	Hutt, H.	180-220	
London, J.	The Road (1st, 8vo, grey/gilt, teg, 224p)	MacMillan	1907	(Photos)	250-320	
London, J.	Valley of the Moon (1st, orang cl, 530p, col frn by...)	MacMillan	1913	Harper, G.	180-225	
London, J.	White Fang (1st, 8vo, blue cl, 328p, 8cp, PPP)	MacMillan	1906	Bull, C.L.	150-180	
Long, J.L.	Billy Boy (1st, 8vo, blue cl, 74p, teg, p-o, uncut, 4pl, pep)	Dodd	1906	Smith, J.W.	160-220	
Long, J.L.	Felice (1st, sm8vo, 156p, frn by...)	Moffat	1908	Flagg, J.M.	20-25	*
Long, J.L.	Madame Butterfly (1st, 8vo, teg, gilt, 152p, uncut, 16pl)	Century	1903	Abbott, C.Y.	20-25	
Long, J.L.	Seffy (1st, sm8vo, 144p, green/gilt, 8cp)	Bobbs-Merrill	(1905)	Williams, C.D.	25-40	
Long, J.L.	War (1st, 12mo, red cl, 371p, 4cp)	Bobbs-Merrill	(1913)	Wyeth, N.C.	50-85	
Long, O.M.	The Lollipops (1st, ob8vo, ipcb, [28]p, b/w)	R.H. Russell	1901	Long, O.M.	100-140	*
Long, W.J.	Brier-Patch Philosophy (1st, 12mo, 296p, teg, col frn, 4pl)	Ginn	1906	Copeland, C.	30-45	
Long, W.J.	How Animals Talk (1st, 4to, 301p, 8cp)	Harper	(1919)	Copeland, C.	30-45	
Long, W.J.	Mother Nature (1st {std}, sm4to, green/gilt, 330p, 8cp)	Harper	(1923)	Bull, C.L.	35-50	
Long, W.J.	Northern Trails (1st, 8vo, teg, 390p, gilt, b/w)	Ginn	1905	Copeland, C.	25-40	

AUTHOR	TITLE	PUBLISHER	DATE	ARTIST	PRICE	LC
Long, W.J.	Wood-Folk Comedies (1st, lg8vo, green/gilt, 307p, 8cp)	Harper	(1920)	Bull, C.L.	25-40	
Longfellow, H.W.	Children's Longfellow (1st, 4to, 324p, p-o, 8cp)	Houghton	1908	Various	40-65	*
Longfellow, H.W.	Courtship of Miles Standish (1st, lg8vo, 152p, 8cp)	Bobbs-Merrill	(1903)	Christy, H.C.	40-60	
Longfellow, H.W.	Courtship of Miles Standish (1st, sm4to, 148p, p-o, 8cp, pep)	Houghton	1920	Wyeth, N.C.	145-200	
Longfellow, H.W.	Evangeline (1st, 8vo, 143p, teg, gilt, 5cp by...)	Houghton	1897	Oakley, V.	180-230	
Longfellow, H.W.	Evangeline (1st, 8vo, 143p, teg, gilt, 5cp by...)	Houghton	1897	Smith, J.W.	180-230	
Longfellow, H.W.	Evangeline (1st, 4to, red/gilt, 132p, 6cp)	Bobbs-Merrill	(1905)	Christy, H.C.	30-50	
Longfellow, H.W.	Evangeline (1st, 8vo, teg, p-o, 172p)	Reilly/Britton	(1909)	Neill, J.R.	70-95	
Longfellow, H.W.	Golden Legend (1st, 4to, green/gilt, teg, 153p, 25 ticp)	L: Hodder	[1910]	Meteyard, S.	120-165	
Longfellow, H.W.	Golden Legend (1st AM, 4to, 153p, gilt, 25 ticp)	Doran	[1912]	Meteyard, S.	100-140	
Longfellow, H.W.	Hanging of the Crane (1st, 8vo, teg, p-o, 10cp)	Houghton	1907	Keller, A.I.	35-50	
Longfellow, H.W.	Hiawatha (1st, 8vo, suede/gilt, 242p, teg, 23pl)	Houghton	1891	Remington, F.	220-300	
Longfellow, H.W.	Hiawatha (1st, sm4to, p-o, gilt, 189p, 16cp)	Bobbs-Merrill	(1906)	Fisher, H.	80-120	
Longfellow, H.W.	Hiawatha (lg8vo, p-o, 193p, 9pl by...)	Riverside	1908	Remington, F.	100-140	
Longfellow, H.W.	Hiawatha (1st, 8vo, p-o, b/w pl)	Reilly/Britton	(1909)	Neill, J.R.	70-100	
Longfellow, H.W.	Hiawatha (1st, sm4to, 313p, p-o, 11cp)	Stokes	(1910)	Kirk, M.L.	70-100	
Longfellow, H.W.	Hiawatha (1st, 8vo, 245p, buckram)	Rand/McNally	(1911)	(Photos)	100-130	
Longfellow, H.W.	Hiawatha (1st, red/gilt, 8vo, teg, 242p, p-o by...)	Houghton	1911	Parrish, M.	300-500	
Longfellow, H.W.	Hiawatha (1st, 8vo, teg, red cl, 242p, b/w illus by...)	Houghton	1911	Remington, F.	300-500	
Longfellow, H.W.	Hiawatha (1st, 8vo, red/gilt, teg, 242p, frn by...)	Houghton	1911	Wyeth, N.C.	300-500	
Longfellow, H.W.	Story of Evangeline (1st, 4to, p-o, 260p, 11cp)	Stokes	(1913)	Kirk, M.L.	100-140	*
Longfellow, H.W.	Story of Hiawatha (1st, 4to, ibds, [68]p, color)	Random	(1951)	Sperry, A.	35-50	*
Loomis, C.B.	Just Rhymes (1st, sm8vo, ibds, 70p, b/w)	R.H. Russell	1899	Cory, F.	65-80	
Loomis, C.B.	Little Maud & her Mama (1st, 16mo, 43p, brown cl, 4pl)	Doubleday/Page	1909	Loomis, C.B.	30-45	*
Loomis, C.B.	More Cheerful Americans (1st, 8vo, green cl, 284p)	Holt	1904	Various	25-40	
Loomis, C.B.	Yankee Enchantments (1st, 8vo, 328p, gilt, 20 fp b/w, pep)	McClure	1900	Cory, F.	45-65	
Lord Brabourne	Friends & Foes from Fairy Land (1st AM, yellow cl)	Little/Brown	1886	Sambourne, L.	90-135	
Lord Dunsany	Book of Wonder (1st, 8vo, 98p, brown pcb, p-o, 10pl)	L: Heinemann	1912	Sime, S.H.	60-85	*
Lord Dunsany	Gods of Pegana (1st, 8vo, 94p, grey bds, uncut, 8pl)	L: E. Matthews	1905	Sime, S.H.	50-80	*
Lord Dunsany	Sword of Welleran (1st, 4to, 243p, green/gilt, teg, 10pl)	L: G. Allen	1908	Sime, S.H.	70-90	
Lord Dunsany	Time & the Gods (1st AM, 8vo, bds, 179p, p-o, 10pl)	J.W. Luce	1913	Sime, S.H.	50-75	
Lorimer, G.H.	False Gods (1st, 8vo, p-o, 91p, 4pl)	Appleton	1906	Leyendecker, J.C.	50-65	
Loti, P.	Romance of a Child (1st, 8vo, cvr by...)	Rand/McNally	1897	Denslow, W.W.	45-60	
Loud, Marian V.	Picnic on a Pyramid (1st, 8vo, 114p, grey cl, 4pl)	Saalfield	1904	Loud, M.V.	30-45	*
Lounsberry, A.	Frank & Bessie's Forester (1st, sm8vo, 191p, p-o & frn by...)	Stokes	(1912)	Kirk, M.L.	30-45	
Love, E.	Rocking Island (1st, lg8vo, p-o, 182p, purple cl, 6cp)	Nelson	(1927)	Love, E.	30-45	
Lovelace, M.H.	Betsy-Tacy (1st, 8vo, 112p, pink cl, b/w, pep)	Crowell	1940	Lenski, L.	30-45	*
Lovelace, M.H.	Over the Big Hill (1st, 8vo, 171p, b/w, pep)	Crowell	1942	Lenski, L.	25-40	
Lovelace, R.	Songs & Sonnets (1st, 8vo, 57p, uncut, 1-color)	R.H. Russell	1901	Unknown	65-100	*
Loveland, Mrs. S.	Illustrated Bible Story Book (1st, lg4to, 126p, p-o, 12cp, pep)	Rand/McNally	(1923)	Winter, M.	45-70	
Lovell, Dorothy A.	Silvanus Goes to Sea (1st, ob4to, blue ibds, unpag, 12 color)	L: Faber	[1943]	Bentley, N.	25-40	
Lovell, L.	Walcott Twins (1st, 8vo, 211p, 5pl)	Penn	1900	Waugh, Ida	25-40	
Lover, S.	Handy Andy (1st, 12mo, 523p, blue/gilt, AEG, pep, 40pl)	L: MacMillan	1896	Brock, H.M.	60-80	
Low, Frances H.	Little Men in Scarlet (1st, 8vo, 237p, green/gilt, b/w)	L: Jarrold	1896	Guthrie, J.J.	25-40	*
Low, Frances H.	Queen Victoria's Dolls (1st, 4to, [86]p, gilt, ae yellow, 34cp)	L: Newnes	1894	Wright, A.	100-165	
Lowe, S.E.	New Story of Peter Rabbit (16mo, tan bds, 8cp)	Whitman	1926	Wright, A.	70-100	*
Lowell, J.R.	Biglow Papers (8vo, blue/gilt, title page by...)	Hennebery	[1900]	Hazenplug, F.	30-45	
Lowell, J.R.	The Courtin' (1st, 8vo, teg, bds/gilt, unpag, color, pep)	Houghton	1909	Keller, A.I.	30-45	
Lowell, Joan	Cradle of the Deep (1st, 8vo, 261p, pep, b/w)	Simon/Schuster	1929	Wiese, K.	30-50	*
Lownsbery, Eloise	Out of the Flame (1st {std}, sm8vo, 352p, pep, b/w, NH)	NY: Longmans	1931	Wolcott, E.T.	30-45	*
Lowrey, J.S.	Day in the Jungle (1st, sm8vo, ibds, [42]p, color, pep, LGB)	A.& W. Guild	1943	Gergely, T.	25-45	*
Lowrey, J.S.	Poky Little Puppy (1st, 12mo, [42]p, ibds, color, LGB)	Simon/Schuster	1942	Tenggren, G.	35-50	
Lowry, H.D.	Make-Believe (1st, 8vo, 177p, teg, green/gilt)	L: J. Lane	1896	Robinson, C.	90-140	
Lucas, E.V.	All the World Over (1st, ob4to, 30ff, ibds, 30cp)	L: Richards	1898	Farmiloe, E.	100-165	
Lucas, E.V.	Another Book of Verses for Children (1st AM, 8vo, 431p, 18pl)	MacMillan	1907	Bedford, F.D.	50-75	
Lucas, E.V.	As the Bee Sucks (1st, 8vo, 169p, pink cl, b/w)	L: Methuen	(1937)	Shepard, E.H.	40-65	*
Lucas, E.V.	Book of Shops (ob4to, ipcb, 24cp)	L: Richards	1900	Bedford, F.D.	170-220	
Lucas, E.V.	Edwin A. Abbey (8vo, 2 vols, pcb)	Scribner	1921	Abbey, E.A.	100-160	
Lucas, E.V.	Forgotten Tales of Long Ago (1st, 8vo, 424p, teg, 23pl)	L: Wells/Gard.	1906	Bedford, F.D.	60-80	
Lucas, E.V.	Four & Twenty Toilers (1st AM, ob4to, blue cl, p-o, 24cp)	McDevitt/Wilsn	[1900]	Bedford, F.D.	160-220	
Lucas, E.V.	Mr. Punch's Country Songs (1st, lg4to, 92p, ibds, b/w)	L: Methuen	1928	Shepard, E.H.	65-90	*
Lucas, E.V.	Old Fashioned Tales (1st, 8vo, teg, 389p, gilt, col frn)	L: Wells/Gard.	[1905]	Bedford, F.D.	70-100	
Lucas, E.V.	Playtime & Company (1st, 4to, ibds, b/w, 95p, pep, DJ)	L: Methuen	(1925)	Shepard, E.H.	100-165	
Lucas, E.V.	The Slowcoach (1st AM, 8vo, 367p, p-o, frn by...)	MacMillan	1910	Hood, G.	35-50	
Lucas, E.V.	The Slowcoach (1st, 8vo, brown cl, 284p, 16cp, pep)	L: Wells/Gard.	[1912]	Wheelhouse, M.V.	35-60	
Lucas, E.V.	Visit to London (1st, 4to, ipcb, 118p, 24cp)	L: Methuen	1902	Bedford, F.D.	100-165	
Lucas, E.V.	Visit to London (1st AM, 4to, ibds, 118p, 24cp)	Brentano's	[1902]	Bedford, F.D.	90-140	
Ludins, Ryah	Wonder Rock (1st, ob8vo, [40]p, ibds, 2-color)	Coward	1931	Ludins, R.	35-50	*
Ludmann, Oscar	Hansi the Stork (1st, ob8vo, 62p, fp color)	Whitman	(1932)	Brock, Emma	25-45	*
Lummis, C.F.	Enchanted Burro (1st, 8vo, 277p, teg, 15pl)	Way/Williams	1897	Corwin, C.A.	50-80	
Lummis, C.F.	Gold Fish of Gran Chimu (1st, 12mo, gilt, 126p, teg, 7pl)	Bos: Lamson	1896	Sandham, H.	90-140	
Lummis, C.F.	King of the Broncos (1st, 8vo, 254p, red/gilt, photos, cvr by)	Scribner	1897	Armstrong, M.	65-80	

AUTHOR	TITLE	PUBLISHER	DATE	ARTIST	PRICE	LC
Lummis, C.F.	Land of Poco Tiempo (1st, 8vo, 310p, orange/gilt, cvr by...)	Scribner	1893	Armstrong, M.	25-40	*
Lupprian, H.	Honey Land (1st, 4to, [30]p, ibds, color)	McLoughlin	1927	Lupprian, H.	80-120	
Lustig, Sonia	Roses of the Winds (1st {std}, sm8vo, 275p, col frn, pep, b/w)	Doubleday/Page	1926	Artzybasheff, B.	30-45	*
Lyall, Edna	Autobiography of a Slander (1st, 8vo, blue/gilt, 146p, AEG)	L: Longmans	1892	Speed, L.	50-80	
Lyall, M.M.	Cubies' ABC (1st, ob8vo, p-o, 56p, color)	Putnam	1913	Lyall, E.H.	170-230	
Lyle, E.P.	Lone Star (1st, 8vo, p-o, 431p, 4pl)	Doubleday/Page	1907	Goodwin, P.R.	30-45	
Lyle, E.P.	The Missourian (1st, 8vo, 519p, 8pl)	Doubleday/Page	1905	Haskell, J.	25-45	
Lyle, G.M.	Little Travellers in Wales (1st, 8vo, p-o, 127p, b/w, pep)	Whitman	1929	Frazee, H.	25-40	*
Lyman, Betty K.	Peter-Pan Twins are Glad to Help (sm4to, ibds, 12p)	Whitman	1928	Chase, R.	30-50	
Lyman, E.B.	Me'ow Jones (1st, 8vo, p-o, 91p, 5cp, pep)	Doran	(1917)	Daniels, J.	25-40	
Lynch, M.B.	Henry the Navigator (1st, 8vo, yellow cl, 72p, 4 fp b/w, pep)	NY: Nelson	1935	Artzybasheff, B.	30-45	*
Lynch, Patricia	Turf-Cutter's Donkey (1st, sm8vo, green cl, 245p, 5cp, dep)	Dutton	1935	Yeats, J.B.	80-120	*
Lynde, F.	Taming/Red Butte Western (1st, 8vo, 410p, 4pl)	Scribner	1910	Dixon, M.	30-45	
Lyons, A. Neil	Simple Simon... (1st, 8vo, 344p, red/gilt, 8pl)	L: J. Lane	1914	Peto, G.	35-50	
Lyons, A. Neil	Tom, Dick & Harriet (1st, 8vo, 254p, green cl, b/w)	L: Cresset Pr.	(1937)	Ardizzone, E.	80-120	
Lytton, E.B.	Last Days of Pompeii (1st, 4to, p-o, 425p, 9cp, pep, SC)	Scribner	1926	Yohn, F.C.	60-75	
Mabie, H.W.	Book of Christmas (1st, 12mo, 369p, gilt, 12pl)	MacMillan	1909	Edwards, G.W.	30-45	*
Mabie, H.W.	In Arcady (1st, 8vo, 128p, teg, green/gilt, 4pl, pep)	Dodd	1903	Low, W.H.	30-45	
Mabie, H.W.	Myths Every Child Should Know (1st, 4to, p-o, 224p, 11cp)	Doubleday/Page	1914	Frye, M.H.	50-70	
Mabie, H.W.	Norse Stories (1st, 8vo, green/gilt, 250p, 10cp)	Dodd	1901	Wright, G.	65-90	
Mabie, H.W.	Under The Trees (1st, 8vo, teg, 165p, green/gilt, 6pl, pep)	Dodd	1902	Hinton, C.L.	35-50	
MacDonald, Betty	Hello, Mrs. Piggle-Wiggle (1st {std}, 8vo, green cl, 119p, col)	Lippincott	(1957)	Knight, H.	60-110	*
MacDonald, Betty	Mrs. Piggle-Wiggle (1st {std}, sm8vo, 119p, blue cl, 8 fp col)	Lippincott	(1947)	Bennett, R.	70-120	*
MacDonald, Betty	Mrs. Piggle-Wiggle's Farm (1st {std}, 8vo, 128p, b/w)	Lippincott	(1954)	Sendak, M.	120-180	
MacDonald, E.R.	Little Canadian Cousin (1st, 8vo, 129p, 6pl)	Page	1904	Bridgman, L.J.	20-35	*
MacDonald, Geo.	Back of the North Wind (1st, 8vo, 378p, gilt, frn & cvr by...)	L: Blackie	(1899)	Housman, L.	130-165	
MacDonald, Geo.	Back of the North Wind (1st, 8vo, 352p, gilt, pep, teg, 12cp)	Lippincott	1909	Kirk, M.L.	75-100	
MacDonald, Geo.	Back of the North Wind (1st, 8vo, 391p, p-o, 12cp)	L: Blackie	1911	Pape, F.	95-130	
MacDonald, Geo.	Back of the North Wind (1st AM, 8vo, blue cl, p-o, 12 fp color)	Caldwell	[1911]	Pape, F.	65-90	*
MacDonald, Geo.	Back of the North Wind (1st, 4to, p-o, teg, 342p, 8cp, pep)	McKay	1919	Smith, J.W.	130-180	
MacDonald, Geo.	Back of the North Wind (1st AM, 8vo, 376p, 12pl, col frn, pep)	NY: MacMillan	(1924)	Bedford, F.D.	65-80	
MacDonald, Geo.	Back of the North Wind (1st, 8vo, p-o, 326p, 4cp)	McKay	(1926)	Kay, G.A.	50-70	
MacDonald, Geo.	Dealings with Fairies (1st AM, 8vo, 284p, gilt)	Routledge	1890	Brooke, L.L.	80-120	
MacDonald, Geo.	Fairy Fleet (1st, 8vo, [52]p, pattern cl, 1-color)	Holiday House	1936	Van Veen, S.	50-85	R*
MacDonald, Geo.	Fairy Tales (1st [new ed.], lg8vo, 435p, gilt, 12 b/w)	L: Fifield	1904	Hughes, A.	140-200	
MacDonald, Geo.	Gutta-Percha Willie (1st, 12mo, 212p, blue/gilt, cvr by...)	L: Blackie	(1900)	Housman, L.	70-90	
MacDonald, Geo.	Gutta-Percha Willie (1st, 12mo, blue cl, 212p, 8pl by...)	L: Blackie	(1900)	Hughes, A.	70-90	
MacDonald, Geo.	Light Princess (1st, sm8vo, 192p, cloth, 3pl)	L: Blackie	(1891)	Brooke, L.L.	120-160	
MacDonald, Geo.	Light Princess (1st, 8vo, 305p, tan cl, 7 fp b/w)	Putnam	(1893)	Humphrey, M.	160-220	
MacDonald, Geo.	Light Princess (1st, 12mo, 133p, col frn, 12pl, pep)	MacMillan	1926	Lathrop, D.	85-100	
MacDonald, Geo.	Lost Princess (1st, 8vo, 258p, blue/gilt, 6pl)	L: Wells/Gard.	(1895)	Walker, A.G.	125-160	
MacDonald, Geo.	Magic Crook (1st, 8vo, 273p, b/w)	L: Fifield	1911	Hughes, A.	100-145	
MacDonald, Geo.	Phantastes (1st, sm8vo, 280p, aqua cloth, 25 illus)	L: Chatto	1894	Bell, J.	145-220	
MacDonald, Geo.	Phantastes (1st, 8vo, 320p, blue/gilt, uncut, teg, 33 b/w)	L: A. Fifield	1905	Hughes, A.	170-250	
MacDonald, Geo.	Phantastes (8vo, 320p, blue/gilt, uncut, teg, b/w)	L: Dent	[1910]	Hughes, A.	160-220	
MacDonald, Geo.	Princess & Curdie (1st, 8vo, 304p, blue/gilt, 31 b/w, cep)	L: Blackie	1900	Stratton, H.	120-150	
MacDonald, Geo.	Princess & Curdie (1st, 8vo, 305p, gilt, 12cp)	Lippincott	1908	Kirk, M.L.	70-100	
MacDonald, Geo.	Princess & Curdie (1st, 8vo, p-o, cloth, 274p, 4cp, pep)	McKay	[1926]	Kay, G.A.	40-60	
MacDonald, Geo.	Princess & Curdie (1st, 8vo, p-o, 265p, gilt, col frn, 12pl pep)	MacMillan	1927	Lathrop, D.	85-130	
MacDonald, Geo.	Princess & Curdie (1st, 8vo, 240p)	MacMillan	(1954)	Unwin, N.S.	25-45	*
MacDonald, Geo.	Princess & Goblin (1st, 8vo, 313p, aqua/gilt, cep, cvr by..)	L: Blackie	1900	Housman, L.	130-170	
MacDonald, Geo.	Princess & Goblin (1st, 8vo, 313p, aqua/gilt, cep, 30 b/w by..)	L: Blackie	1900	Hughes, A.	130-170	
MacDonald, Geo.	Princess & Goblin (1st, 8vo, red/gilt, 305p, teg, pep, 12cp)	Lippincott	1907	Kirk, M.L.	80-120	
MacDonald, Geo.	Princess & Goblin (1st AM, 8vo, 308p, teg, blue/gilt, p-o, 12cp)	Caldwell	[1911]	Stratton, H.	135-180	
MacDonald, Geo.	Princess & Goblin (1st, 8vo, teg, 308p, p-o, gilt, 12cp)	L: Blackie	1911	Stratton, H.	165-200	
MacDonald, Geo.	Princess & Goblin (1st, 4to, gilt, p-o, teg, 203p, 8cp, pep)	McKay	1920	Smith, J.W.	140-200	
MacDonald, Geo.	Princess & Goblin (1st, 12mo, 267p, blue/gilt, col frn)	MacMillan	1926	Bedford, F.D.	70-100	
MacDonald, Geo.	Princess & Goblin (1st, 8vo, 251p, col frn)	Saalfield	(1927)	Brundage, F.	25-40	
MacDonald, Geo.	Princess & Goblin (1st, lg8vo, 271p, 4cp)	Doubleday/Dor.	1928	MacKinstry, E.	60-85	
MacDonald, Geo.	Princess & Goblin (1st, 8vo, olive cl, 249p, 1-color, pep)	MacMillan	(1951)	Unwin, N.S.	30-45	*
MacDonald, Geo.	Ronald Bannerman's Boyhood (12mo, 335p, teg, p-o, gilt, 12cp)	L: Blackie	[1910]	Wheelhouse, M.V.	85-120	
MacDonald, Golden	Big Dog, Little Dog (1st, lg sq8vo, [36]p, red cl, b/w, dep)	Doubleday/Dor.	(1943)	Weisgard, L.	35-50	*
MacDonald, Golden	Little Island (1st {std}, ob4to, [42]p, ibds, color, pep, CM)	Doubleday	1946	Weisgard, L.	100-150	R*
MacDonald, Golden	Little Lost Lamb (1st {std}, 4to, 48p, ibds, color, pep, CH)	Doubleday	1945	Weisgard, L.	70-120	
MacDonald, Golden	Red Light Green Light (1st {std}, ob4to, ibds, [40]p, col, cep)	Doubleday/Dor.	(1944)	Weisgard, L.	70-100	R*
MacDonald, Greville	Billy Barnicoat (1st AM, 8vo, 230p, fp b/w)	Dutton	1923	Bedford, F.D.	35-50	*
MacDonald, Greville	Count Billy (1st {std}, 8vo, 246p, gilt, uncut, col frn, 6pl)	Dutton	1928	Bedford, F.D.	30-45	*
MacDonald, L.	Babies' Classics (1st, 4to, 79p, blue/gilt, b/w)	L: Longmans	1904	Hughes, A.	90-140	
MacDonald, Ray	Mad Scientist (1st, 8vo, blue cl, 242p, 8pl)	NY: Cochrane	1908	Bunnell, C.B.	65-80	*
MacDonald, Zillah	Eileen's Adventures in Wonderland (1st, 8vo, p-o, 241p, col frn)	Stokes	(1920)	Hay, S.	75-125	*
MacDonell, Anne	Italian Fairy Book (8vo, gilt, 307p, col frn, 17 fp b/w, pep)	Stokes	[1911]	Williams, M.M.	65-80	
MacDonough, G.	Babes in Toyland (1st, sm4to, 180p, tan cloth, 7cp, pep)	Fox Duffield	1904	Betts, E.F.	150-220	

AUTHOR	TITLE	PUBLISHER	DATE	ARTIST	PRICE	LC
MacDonough, G.	Babes in Toyland (2nd, 8vo, aqua cl, 180p, p-o, 7cp)	Macaulay	(1924)	Betts, E.F.	80-125	
MacFall, H.	Book of Lovat (1st, 4to, ipcb, 183p, 8cp)	L: Dent	1923	Fraser, C.L.	75-100	
MacGrath, H.	Best Man (1st, 8vo, 207p, green/gilt, p-o, 8pl)	Bobbs-Merrill	(1907)	Grefe, W.	20-30	
MacGrath, H.	Half a Rogue (1st, 8vo, red cl, 449p, p-o, 4pl)	Bobbs-Merrill	(1906)	Fisher, H.	20-30	
MacGrath, H.	Man on the Box (1st, 8vo, 361p, aqua cloth)	Bobbs-Merrill	(1904)	Armstrong, M.	20-30	
MacGregor, B.	King Longbeard (1st, 8vo, 262p, blue/gilt, 12pl)	L: J. Lane	1898	Robinson, C.	180-220	
MacGregor, Ellen	Miss Pickerell Goes to Mars (1st, sm8vo, red cl, 128p, fp b/w)	Whittlesey	(1951)	Galdone, P.	25-45	*
MacGregor, Ellen	Theodore Turtle (1st, 4to, green cl, 32p, color, pep)	Whittlesey	1955	Galdone, P.	45-60	*
MacGregor, M.	King Arthur's Knights (12mo, 155p, 8cp)	L: Jack	(1909)	Cameron, K.	50-80	
MacGregor, M.	Pilgrim's Progress told to Children (24mo, p-o, 8cp)	L: Jack	[1910]	Shaw, B.	25-40	
MacGregor, M.	Romance of the Netherlands (1st, 8vo, teg, 344p, uncut, 12cp)	Jack/Stokes	[1910]	McCormick, A.D.	50-65	
MacGregor, M.	Story of France (1st AM, lg8vo, 508p, 20cp)	Stokes	[1920]	Rainey, W.	35-50	
MacHarg, Wm. B.	Let's Pretend... (1st, 8vo, 80p, color)	Volland	1914	Butler, B.	30-45	*
MacKay, H.	Stories for Pictures (1st, 8vo, ibds, uncut, teg, 168p, 8cp pep)	Duffield	1912	Walker, D.S.	70-100	
MacKay, M.	Cow Range & Hunting Trail (1st, 8vo, gilt, 243p, 3pl by...)	Putnam	1925	Russell, C.M.	85-100	
MacKaye, P.	Tall Tales/Kentucky Mountains (1st, 8vo, ipcb, p-o, col frn 185p)	Doran	(1926)	MacKinstry, E.	30-45	*
MacKenzie, C.	Kensington Rhymes (1st, 4to, pcb, 9cp)	(London)	(1913)	Monsell, J.R.	80-100	
MacKenzie, D.A.	Indian Fairy Stories (1st, 8vo, 200p, 8pl)	L: Blackie	1915	Armfield, M.	40-65	
MacKinstry, E.	Fairy Alphabet (1st, lg8vo, 59p, ibds, 26pl, DJ)	Viking	1933	MacKinstry, E.	80-120	
MacKinstry, E.	Puck in Pasture (1st {std}, 8vo, ibds, 79p, pep, b/w)	Doubleday/Page	1925	MacKinstry, E.	35-50	
MacLaren, Ian	Doctor o/t Old School (1st {this fmt.}, green bds, AEG, b/w)	Hodder	1895	Gordon, F.C.	60-80	*
MacLeod	Mountain Lovers (8vo, 241p, blue/white, cvr by...)	L: J. Lane	1895	Beardsley, A.	30-50	
MacManus, Seumas	Donegal Fairy Stories (1st, sm8vo, 256p, 34pl)	McClure	1900	VerBeck, F.	45-60	*
MacMillan, C.	Canadian Wonder Tales (1st, 4to, 199p, 17cp, pep)	L: J. Lane	1918	Sheringham, G.	70-100	
MacMunn, G.F.	Armies of India (1st, 8vo, blue/gilt, 224p, teg, 72cp)	L: A&C Black	1911	Lovett, A.C.	60-100	
MacPherson, J.F.	Children For Ever (1st, 8vo, 352p, 16 color)	L: J. Long	1908	Sarg, T.	100-145	*
Macaulay, T.B.	Lays of Ancient Rome (1st AM, black/gilt, teg, 180p, 12 ticp)	Longmans	1929	Cox, E.A.	50-75	
Macauley, C.R.	Fantasma Land (1st, brown/gilt, 8vo, 204p, b/w)	Bobbs-Merrill	(1904)	Macauley, C.R.	60-85	
Machen, Arthur	Great God Pan/Inmost Light (1st AM, 8vo, 234p, gilt, cvr by...)	Roberts	1894	Beardsley, A.	150-200	
Machray, R.	Night Side of London (1st, 8vo, yellow cl, 300p, b/w)	Lippincott	1902	Browne, T.	30-45	
Mack, R.E.	All-Around the Clock (lg8vo, ibds, 64p)	Dutton	[1885]	23 Chromos	100-160	
Mack, R.E.	Old Father Santa Claus (4to, ibds, [40]p, 14 chromos)	Nister/Dutton	[1885]	Lawson, L.	180-265	
Mack, R.E.	Queen of the Meadow (lg8vo, ipcb)	Dutton	(1885)	16 Chromos	100-165	
Mack, R.E.	Under the Mistletoe (lg8vo, ibds, [40]p, 14 chromos)	Nister/Dutton	(1890)	Lawson, L.	100-160	
Mackall, L.	Poodle-Oodle on Doodle Farm (1st, ob12mo, p-o, 137p, color, pep)	Stokes	1929	Wiese, K.	35-50	
Mackenzie, D.	Indian Myth & Legend (1st, 8vo, 463p, gilt, 8cp, 32pl)	L: Gresham	[1910]	Goble, W.	150-200	
Macleod, F.	Hills of Ruel (1st AM, 4to, teg, 92p, pep, 8 ticp)	Duffield	1921	Lawrence, M.H.	80-100	
Macleod, Mary	Book of King Arthur (1st AM, 8vo, 417p, pl)	Stokes	[1900]	Walker, A.G.	65-90	*
Macleod, Mary	Book of King Arthur (1st {std}, 8vo, blue cl, 324p, color)	Lippincott	(1949)	Pitz, H.C.	30-50	*
Macleod, Mary	King Arthur & Noble Knights (1st, 8vo, 418p, gilt, 35 fp b/w)	L: Wells/Gard.	(1900)	Walker, A.G.	100-140	
Macleod, Mary	Red Cross Knight & Sir Guyan (1st, 8vo, 128p)	L: Wells/Gard.	1908	Walker, A.G.	35-50	*
Macvane, E.	Adventures of Joujou (1st, sq8vo, 302p, teg, p-o, 15cp, pep)	Lippincott	1906	VerBeck, F.	50-65	
Macy, S.B.	Book of the Kingdom (1st, 4to, 388p, col frn)	L: Longmans	1912	Robinson, T.H.	70-100	*
Macy, S.B.	From Slavery to Freedom (4to, 299p, green/gilt, 8cp, pep)	L: Longmans	1910	Robinson/Sarg	160-220	
Macy, S.B.	From Slavery to Freedom (4to, 299p, green/gilt, 8cp, pep)	L: Longmans	1910	Sarg/Robinson	160-220	
Madariaga, S.	Sir Bob (1st {std}, 8vo, 202p, b/w)	Harcourt	(1930)	Ward, L.	30-45	*
Madison, J.	Sweethearts Always (1st, 8vo, 232p, grey/gilt, teg, uncut, 12pl)	Reilly/Britton	1906	Hall, H.P.	85-120	
Madison, J.	Sweethearts Always (2nd, 8vo, 210p, green/gilt, 8cp)	Reilly/Britton	1907	Manning, F.S.	65-80	
Madison, L.F.	Captain Kitty Colonial (1st, 8vo, blue cl, 309p, p-o, col frn)	Penn	1923	Davis, M.	20-40	*
Madison, L.F.	Joan of Arc (1st, 4to, 389p, p-o, blue/gilt, 8cp, pep)	Penn	1918	Schoonover, F.	45-70	
Madison, L.F.	Lafayette (1st, 4to, p-o, 371p, blue cl, 8cp, pep)	Penn	1921	Schoonover, F.	50-75	
Madison, L.F.	Lincoln (1st, tall 8vo, p-o, 368p, 8cp, pep)	Penn	1928	Schoonover, F.	50-70	
Madison, L.F.	Washington (1st, 4to, blue/gilt, p-o, 399p, 8cp, pep)	Penn	1925	Schoonover, F.	50-70	
Maeterlinck, M.	Blue Bird (1st AM, 4to, teg, blue/gilt, 211p, 25 ticp)	Dodd	1911	Robinson, F.C.	120-165	
Maeterlinck, M.	Children's Blue Bird (1st, 4to, p-o, 182p, teg, 19pl)	Dodd	1913	Paus, H.	60-85	
Maeterlinck, M.	Hours of Gladness (1st, 4to, 181p, white/gilt, 20 ticp)	L: G. Allen	(1912)	Detmold, E.J.	280-350	
Maeterlinck, M.	Life of the Bee (1st, 4to, 232p, teg, 13 ticp)	L: G. Allen	1911	Detmold, E.J.	250-350	
Maeterlinck, M.	Life of the Bee (1st AM, 4to, 262p, teg, green/gilt, 13 ticp)	Dodd	1912	Detmold, E.J.	150-200	
Maeterlinck, M.	My Dog (1st, sm8vo, p-o, 6cp)	L: Allen	1913	Aldin, C.	100-150	
Maeterlinck, M.	News of Spring (1st AM, 4to, green/gilt, 213p, teg, 20 ticp)	Dodd	1913	Detmold, E.J.	220-300	
Maeterlinck, M.	Old Fashioned Flowers (1st, sm8vo, 105p, 6cp)	Dodd	1905	Falls, C.B.	50-70	
Maeterlinck, M.	Our Friend the Dog (1st AM, 8vo, 67p, gilt, 6cp)	Dodd	1913	Aldin, C.	85-120	
Maeterlinck, M.	The Swarm (1st, 8vo, green cl, p-o, 113p, frn by...)	Dodd	1906	Euwer, A.	25-40	
Maeterlinck, M.	Tyltyl (1st, 4to, blue/gilt, p-o, 159p, 8 ticp, pep)	Dodd	1920	Paus, H.	90-135	
Maeterlinck, M.	Tyltyl (1st UK, sm4to, p-o, 159p, blue/gilt, 8 ticp)	L: Methuen	(1921)	Paus, H.	70-100	
Maeterlinck, M.	Visions of Spring... (1st, 4to, teg, 213p, gilt, 20 ticp)	Dodd	1913	Detmold, E.J.	320-400	
Magruder, Julia	Child Amy (1st, 8vo, 302p, red/gilt, 7pl)	Lothrop	(1894)	Armstrong, H.M.	30-50	*
Magruder, Julia	Miss Ayr of Virginia (1st, 8vo, green cl, 395p, cvr by..)	H. Stone	1896	Kimbrough, F.R.	60-80	
Magruder, Julia	Princess Sonia (1st, 12mo, 225p, 17pl)	Century	1895	Gibson, C.D.	25-40	*
Magruder, Julia	Sunny Southerner (1st, 12mo, 194p, teg, b/w pl)	Page	1901	Hubbell, H.	20-30	
Magruder, Julia	The Violet (1st, sm8vo, 210p, 11pl)	Longmans	1896	Gibson, C.D.	25-40	*
Major, C.	Dorothy Vernon/Haddon Hall (1st, 8vo, 369p, blue/gilt, col frn)	MacMillan	1902	Christy, H.C.	25-40	

AUTHOR	TITLE	PUBLISHER	DATE	ARTIST	PRICE	LC
Major, C.	Forest Hearth (1st, sm8vo, teg, green/gilt, 354p, 8pl)	MacMillan	1903	DeLand, C.O.	25-40	
Makower, S.	Mirror of Music (1st, 8vo, 179p, uncut, cvr by...)	L: J. Lane	1895	Beardsley, A.	70-100	
Malcolm, F.	My Fairyland (1st, 4to, 85p, grey ibds, 4 ticp)	L: Harrap	1916	Anderson, F.	100-150	
Malcolmson, A.	Song of Robin Hood (1st, lg4to, 123p, color, DJ, CH)	Houghton	1947	Burton, V.L.	100-145	
Malcolmson, A.	Yankee Doodle's Cousins (1st, 4to, 267p, red cl, fp b/w, pep)	Houghton	1941	McCloskey, R.	75-120	R*
Malet, Lucas	Little Peter (1st, 8vo, grey/gilt, 168p, 9pl)	L: Kegan Paul	1888	Hardy, P.	50-70	*
Malet, Lucas	Little Peter (1st {new ed.}, sm4to, 175p, white cl, 8 ticp)	L: H. Frowde	1909	Brock, C.E.	45-60	*
Malkus, A.S.	Caravans to Sante Fe (1st {std}, 12mo, 289p, b/w)	Harper	1928	Lawson, M.A.	30-45	*
Malkus, A.S.	Dark Star of Itza (1st {std}, 8vo, 217p, brown cl, 6 fp b/w, NH)	Harcourt	(1930)	Houser, L.	40-60	
Malkus, A.S.	Dragon Fly of Zuni (1st, 8vo, 213p, uncut, fp b/w, pep)	Harcourt	(1928)	Berry, E.	25-45	*
Malkus, A.S.	Spindle Imp (1st, sm8vo, pink cl, 176p, uncut, fp b/w, pep)	Harcourt	(1931)	Berry, E.	30-45	*
Mallison, C.	Wooster-Poosters (1st, ob4to, p-o, 88p, 15cp, pep)	Stokes	(1931)	Mallison, C.	90-140	
Malloch, D.	Little Hop Skipper (1st, 8vo, 99p, blue cl, col frn)	Doran	(1926)	Green, E.S.	30-45	
Malloch, D.	Someone to Care (1st, sq16mo, color, ibds)	Volland	(1920)	Unknown	30-45	*
Malmberg, Bertil	Ake & his World (1st, 8vo, red/gilt, uncut, b/w)	Farrar/Rine.	(1940)	Cooney, B.	35-50	*
Malone, H.	Lost Fairy Tales (1st, 8vo, gilt, 288p, 8cp)	L: C.H. Kelly	(1915)	Robinson, G.	65-85	
Malory, T.	Boy's King Arthur (1st, 8vo, 403p, gilt, 12pl, cep)	Scribner	1880	Kappes, A.	90-135	
Malory, T.	Boy's King Arthur (1st, 4to, p-o, teg, 321p, 14cp, pep, SC)	Scribner	1917	Wyeth, N.C.	140-200	*
Malory, T.	Death of King Arthur (1st, 8vo, 51p)	L: MacMillan	1928	Donaldson, C.	35-50	*
Malory, T.	King Arthur & his Knights (1st, 8vo, pep, 4cp)	Winston	(1927)	Godwin, F.	25-45	*
Malory, T.	King Arthur... (1st, 12mo, 64p, green wraps, fp b/w)	Penn	1908	LeFanu, B.	35-50	*
Malory, T.	King Arthur... (1st, 12mo, 335p, cp)	MacMillan	1916	Thomson, R.	35-50	*
Malory, T.	Le Morte D'Arthur (1st, lg8vo, teg, 2 volumes, 36cp)	L: P.L Warner	(1920)	Flint, W.R.	160-220	
Malory, T.	Le Morte D'Arthur (lg8vo, 531p, red/gilt, teg, 24cp)	Hale/Cushman	(1927)	Flint, W.R.	100-140	*
Malory, T.	Malory's King Arthur (1st, 8vo, 421p, cp, pep)	Baker/Taylor	(1911)	Birch, R.	65-90	*
Malory, T.	Women of Morte Darthur (1st, 8vo, 251p)	L: Methuen	1927	Alexander, A.D.	50-65	*
Malot, H.	Adventures of Perrine (1st, lg8vo, 284p, black cl, p-o 5cp, pep)	Rand/McNally	(1932)	Winter, M.	45-65	
Malot, H.	Adventures of Remi (1st, lg8vo, p-o, 492p, gilt, pep, 8cp)	Rand/McNally	(1925)	Schaeffer, M.	30-45	*
Malot, H.	Nobody's Boy (1st AM, 8vo, 372p, green cl, p-o, 4cp)	Cupples	1916	Gruelle, J.	45-70	
Malot, H.	Nobody's Boy (1st, sm4to, p-o, 308p, 8cp, pep)	Cupples	(1930)	Gooch, T.	25-40	*
Maloy, L.	Arabella of the Merry-Go-Round (1st, sm ob4to, 64p, color)	Scribner	1935	Maloy, L.	25-40	
Maloy, L.	Tea Party in Plumpudding Street (1st, lg8vo, ibds, [54]p, 1-col)	Grosset/Dunlap	(1946)	Maloy, L.	25-40	
Maloy, L.	Wooden Shoes in America (1st, ob4to, [72]p, color)	Scribner	(1940)	Maloy, L.	35-50	*
Mandal, S.R.	Happy Flute (1st, lg8vo, 54p, tan cl, 10 fp b/w, pep, DJ)	Stokes	1939	Lathrop, D.	80-100	
Manners, R.	Cuba & other Verse (1st, 8vo, 155p, teg)	Way/Williams	1898	Hazenplug, F.	120-170	
Manning, A.	Household/Sir Thomas Moore (1st, 12mo, 185p, teg, 24 color, dep)	L: J.M. Dent	1906	Brock, C.E.	35-65	*
Manning, W.	Child's Dream of the Zoo (sq4to, 24p, wraps)	L: Routledge	1889	Griset, E.	80-100	
Mansfield, R.	Blown Away (1st, 8vo, 180p, cvr by...)	Page	1897	McManus, B.	50-80	
Mansion, Horace	Old English Nursery Songs (1st, 4to, ibds, p-o, 6cp)	L: Harrap	[1915]	Anderson, A.	100-165	
Mansion, Horace	Old English Nursery Songs (1st AM, 4to, ibds, p-o, 6cp)	Brentano's	[1915]	Anderson, A.	130-175	
Marais, Josef	Koos the Hottentot (1st {std}, 8vo, ibds, 182p, color)	Knopf	1945	Stahlhut, H.	60-80	R
Marc, E.	Doris & David All Alone (1st, 8vo, 259p, red cl, 4cp, pep)	L: Hutchinson	(1922)	Robinson, C.	80-100	
March, Eleanor	Little White Barbara (1st, 24mo, green cl, [91]p, color)	L: Richards	1902	March, E.	180-220	
March, Eleanor	Three Naughty Elves (1st, ob4to, 37p, ibds, color)	L: Liberty	[1903]	Evans, E.	180-250	*
March, Mary E.	Rhymes of Early Jungle Folk (1st, lg8vo, 124p, woocuts, pep)	Chi: Kerr	1922	Esherick, W.H.	30-45	
Marcher, M.W.	Monarch Butterfly (1st, 8vo, 42p, green cl, 2-color)	Holiday House	(1954)	Latham, B.	30-50	R*
Marchioness/London	Magic Ink Spot (1st, 8vo, 208p, 16cp)	L: MacMillan	1928	Brock, E./Stewart	80-100	*
Marino, Josef	Hi! Ho! Pinocchio (1st, 4to, 127p, col frn, p-o, b/w, cep)	Reilly/Lee	(1940)	Donahey, Wm.	80-130	*
Marion	Mummy's Bedtime Story Book (1st, lg4to, ibds, 56p, pep, 12cp)	L: C. Palmer	(1920)	King, J.	400-600	
Markham, E.	Man With the Hoe... (1st, 12mo, 114p, gilt, teg, b/w)	Doub./McClure	1900	Pyle, H.	80-100	
Marks, J.	Cheerful Cricket... (1st, 4to, [124]p, green cl, dep, color)	Small	1907	Brown, E.	80-130	
Marks, J.	Through Welsh Doorways (1st, 8vo, 244p, rust/gilt, 4pl)	Houghton	1909	Betts, A.W.	30-45	
Marquand, John	Haven's End (1st, 8vo, 341p, uncut, b/w)	Little/Brown	1933	Lawson, R.	45-60	*
Marquis, Don	Archy Does His Part (1st {std}, 12mo, p-o, 269p, b/w, pep)	Doubleday/Dor.	1935	Herriman, G.	20-35	*
Marquis, Don	Danny's Own Story (1st, 8vo, green cl, 333p, p-o, 16pl)	Doubleday/Page	1912	Kemble, E.W.	100-150	
Marriott, C.	Sally Castleton, Southerner (1st, 8vo, uncut 312p, col frn, 5pl)	Lippincott	1913	Wyeth, N.C.	65-80	
Marryat, Fred.	Children o/t New Forest (1st, 4to, black cl, p-o, 9cp, pep, SC)	Scribner	1927	Good, S.	70-100	
Marryat, Fred.	Children of the New Forest (1st, 8vo, 397p, p-o, 8cp)	Holt	1911	Smith, E.B.	65-80	
Marryat, Fred.	Children of the New Forest (8vo, p-o, 8cp)	L: Constable	1914	Smith, E.B.	45-60	
Marryat, Fred.	Children of the New Forest (1st, 8vo, 322p, green cl, 10 fp b/w)	MacMillan	1930	Ward, L.	35-50	
Marryat, Fred.	Jacob Faithful (1st, 8vo, blue/gilt, 416p, AEG, b/w, dep)	L: MacMillan	1895	Brock, H.M.	50-75	
Marryat, Fred.	Japhet... (1st, 12mo, blue/gilt, 401p, AEG, 13pl, pep)	L: MacMillan	1895	Brock, H.M.	70-90	
Marryat, Fred.	King's Own (1st, 12mo, AEG, 429p, 40pl, pep)	L: MacMillan	1896	Townsend, F.H.	45-65	
Marryat, Fred.	King's Own (1st, 8vo, 451p, 6pl)	L: OUP	1907	Goble, W.	90-120	*
Marryat, Fred.	Masterman Ready (1st, sm4to, 403p, p-o, 6cp)	Harper	1928	Rae, J.	30-45	
Marryat, Fred.	Newton Foster (1st, 12mo, 393p, blue/gilt, 40 b/w, pep)	L: MacMillan	1897	Sullivan, E.J.	45-60	
Marryat, Fred.	Snarleyyow (1st, sm8vo, 405p, blue/gilt, AEG)	L: MacMillan	1897	Millar, H.R.	45-60	
Marsh, Geo.	Sled Trails/White Waters (1st, 8vo, 298p, p-o, 10pl)	Penn	1929	Schoonover, F.	25-40	
Marsh, Geo.	Toilers of the Trails (1st, sm4to, p-o, 245p, col frn, 8pl)	Penn	1921	Schoonover, F.	30-50	
Marsh, Lewis	Tales of the Fairies (1st, 8vo, 5cp, 7 b/w, gilt)	L: Hodder	[1912]	Govey, L.	130-175	
Marsh, Lewis	Tales of the Homeland (1st, 8vo, buckram, 199p, 6cp)	L: Hodder	[1911]	Robinson, T.H.	65-80	*
Marshall, A.	Peggy in Toyland (1st, 8vo, ipcb, 277p, b/w)	Dodd	1920	Barton, H.M.	35-50	*

AUTHOR	TITLE	PUBLISHER	DATE	ARTIST	PRICE	LC
Marshall, B.G.	Cedric the Forester (1st, 8vo, 278p, 18pl, NH)	Appleton	1921	Williams, J.S.	30-55	*
Marshall, C.	Two Wyoming Girls (1st, 12mo, 329p)	Penn	1899	Waugh, Ida	25-40	*
Marshall, H.	Scenery of London (1st, 8vo, 223p, gilt, teg, 75cp)	L: A&C Black	1905	Marshall, H.	50-90	
Marshall, H.E.	Empire Story (8vo, 493p, 8cp, maps)	Stokes	(1908)	Skelton, J.R.	40-60	
Marshall, Helen L.	New Mexican Boy (1st, 8vo, 85p, 9 fp color, cep)	Holiday House	(1940)	Rush, O.	20-25	*
Marshall, Mrs.	Girl Ranchers of San Coulee (1st, 12mo, 322p, 4pl)	Penn	1897	Waugh, Ida	30-50	
Marshall, Peter	Let's Keep Christmas (1st, 12mo, ibds, [32]p, 2-color, pep)	McGraw/Hill	1953	Cooney, B.	30-50	
Martens, F.	Fairy Tales from Orient (1st, 8vo, 293p, blue cl, 4cp, pep)	McBride	1923	Hood, G.	50-70	
Martin, Chas. M.	Orphans of the Range (1st, 8vo, 192p, blue cl, fp b/w)	Viking	1950	Barnum, J.H.	30-45	*
Martin, E.S.	Cousin Anthony & I (1st, 8vo, 255p, green cl, cvr by...)	Scribner	1895	Armstrong, M.	25-45	
Martin, E.S.	Lucid Intervals (1st, 8vo, 263p, teg, blue cl, 6pl)	Harper	1900	Stilwell, S.	45-60	
Martin, E.S.	Luxury of Children (1st, 8vo, 213p, green/gilt, p-o, teg, 8cp)	Harper	1904	Stilwell, S.	60-80	
Martin, H.R.	His Courtship (1st, 8vo, uncut, 322p, 4pl)	McClure	1907	Stephens, A.B.	25-40	*
Martin, J.	Children's Munchausen (1st, lg8vo, p-o, 8cp)	Houghton	1921	Ross, G.	30-45	
Martin, J.	Prayers for Little Men & Women (1st, 8vo, 96p, gilt, 6 ticp)	Harper	1912	Rae, J.	50-65	
Martin, Pat. M.	Pointed Brush (1st, 4to, red cl, unpag, color, pep)	Lothrop	1959	Duvoisin, R.	25-45	*
Martin, Pat. M.	Sylvester Jones & Voice in the Forest (1st, 4to, [32]p, 2-color)	Lothrop/Lee	(1958)	Weisgard, L.	30-45	*
Martineau, H.	Feats on the Fiord (1st, 8vo, 301p, blue/gilt, col frn)	MacMillan	1924	Artzybasheff, B.	35-50	
Martineau, H.	Feats on the Fjord (1st, 16mo, blue cl, teg, 237p, col frn)	L: Dent	1899	Rackham, A.	150-200	
Martineau, H.	Feats on the Fjord (1st AM, 12mo, p-o, 128p, 8cp)	Dutton	[1914]	Rackham, A.	80-120	
Marvel, I.	Reveries of a Bachelor (1st, 8vo, 338p, blue cl, 15cp)	Bobbs-Merrill	(1906)	Ashe, E.M.	20-25	
Marzials	Pan Pipes (1st, ob4to, tan ibds, 51p, dep, color)	L: Routledge	1883	Crane, W.	170-230	
Masefield, J.	Book of Discoveries (1st, 8vo, 354p, teg, 53 b/w)	L: Wells/Gard.	1910	Browne, G.	50-70	
Masefield, J.	Jim Davis (1st, 8vo, blue/gilt, p-o, 226p, 8cp)	Stokes	1924	Schaeffer, M.	30-45	*
Masefield, J.	Martin Hyde (1st, 8vo, 303p, green cl, 16pl)	L: Wells/Gard.	1910	Dugdale, T.C.	35-50	*
Masefield, J.	Midnight Folk (1st, 4to, 282p, blue cl, 6cp)	L: Heinemann	(1931)	Hilder, R.	70-100	
Masefield, J.	Reynard the Fox (1st, 4to, 116p, 4cp)	L: Heinemann	1921	Armour, G.D.	80-100	
Masefield, J.	Reynard the Fox (1st AM, 4to, 339p, 4cp)	MacMillan	1921	Armour, G.D.	60-85	
Masefield, J.	Reynard the Fox (1st, lg8vo, ibds, [94]p, color, pep)	Volland	(1925)	Rae, J.	65-80	
Masefield, J.	Right Royal (1st AM, 8vo, black/gilt, 116p, 4cp)	MacMillan	1922	Aldin, C.	60-80	
Mason, A.	From the Horn of the Moon (1st {std}, 8vo, 259p, blue cl, b/w)	Doubleday/Dor.	1931	Lawson, R.	35-50	
Mason, A.	Roving Lobster (1st {std}, 8vo, 132p, green cl, 10 fp b/w, cep)	Doubleday/Dor.	1931	Lawson, R.	65-100	
Mason, A.	Wee Men of Ballywooden (1st {std}, lg8vo, 266p, pep, 4pl)	Doubleday/Dor.	1930	Lawson, R.	100-145	
Mason, A.	Wee Men of Ballywooden (1st {this pub}, 8vo, p-o, 266p, 4pl pep)	Garden City	(1937)	Lawson, R.	45-65	
Mason, E.	Old-World Love Stories (1st, 8vo, 282p, gilt, teg, 8 ticp)	L: J.M. Dent	1913	Knowles, R.L.	150-200	
Mason, Edith H.	Great Plan (1st, 8vo, green/white, 308p, 5pl)	McClurg	1913	St. John, J.A.	60-80	
Mason, Francis E.	Daddy Gander (1st, 4to, ibds, [90]p, color)	F.E. Mason	(1900)	Spedon	50-70	*
Mason, Miriam E.	Miss Posy Longlegs (1st {std}, 8vo, 54p, 1-color, DJ)	MacMillan	(1955)	Petershams	30-45	*
Mason, Miriam E.	Smiling Hill Farm (1st, 8vo, 311p, pep, b/w)	Ginn	(1937)	Seredy, K.	25-45	*
Mason, Miriam E.	Susannah: Pioneer Cow (1st, 8vo, yellow cl, 151p, 1-color, cep)	MacMillan	1941	Petershams	45-60	*
Mason, Miriam E.	Timothy has Ideas (1st {std}, 8vo, 127p, blue cl, fp b/w)	MacMillan	1943	Hader, B.& E.	45-60	*
Mason, W.	Uncle Walt (1st, 8vo, brown cl, teg, 189p, cvr by...)	Chi: Adams	1910	Bradley, W.	70-85	
Massey, Jeanne	Littlest Witch (1st, sm ob4to, [33]p, orange cl, 2-color)	Knopf	(1959)	Adams, A.	40-60	*
Masson, T.	Corner In Women (1st, 8vo, teg, ipcb, gilt, 332p, b/w)	Moffat	1905	Various	30-50	
Masson, T.	Corner in Women (1st, 8vo, teg, ipcb, gilt, 332p, cvr by...)	Moffat	1905	Gibson, C.D.	30-50	
Matheson, Annie	Songs of Love & Praise (1st, 8vo, unpag, designs by...)	L: J.M. Dent	1907	Robinson, C.	65-80	*
Mathews, F.A.	My Lady Peggy Goes to Town (1st, 8vo, teg, 338p, b/w)	Bowen-Merrill	1901	Fisher, H.	20-35	
Mathews, J.	Belle's Pink Boots (1st, AEG, green/gilt, 16cp)	Dutton	1881	Waugh, Ida	100-165	
Mattheson, J.	Needle in the Haystack (1st, sq8vo, 189p, blue cl, 8cp, pep)	Wm. Morrow	1930	D'Aulaire, E.P.	35-50	
Matthews, B.	Poems of American Patriotism (1st, 4to, p-o, 14cp, pep, SC)	Scribner	1922	Wyeth, N.C.	200-300	
Maud, C.	Wagner's Heroes (1st, 8vo, 285p, black/silver, 7pl)	L: E. Arnold	1896	Maud, W.T.	45-65	
Maud, C.	Wagner's Heroes (1st, 12mo, blue buckram, 284p, uncut, 8pl)	L: E. Arnold	(1897)	Fell, H.G.	60-80	
Maugham, W.S.	Princess September & Nightingale (1st, lg8vo, [31]p, col, pep)	OUP	(1939)	Jones, R.C.	45-60	*
Maunder, I.	Plain Princess (1st, 4to, 95p, brown cl, 14pl, dep)	L: Longmans	1905	Taylor/Baxter	80-120	
Maunder, I.	Songs of Happy Children (12mo, 110p, teg, b/w)	L: Clark	[1908]	Robinson, C.	50-70	
Maurois, Andre	Fatapoufs & Thinifers (1st, lg4to, pep, blue cl, 92p, color)	Holt	(1940)	Bruller, Jean	35-50	*
Maxwell, D.	Excursions in Color (1st, lg8vo, 89 illus, 118p)	L: Cassell	1927	Maxwell, D.	70-120	
Maxwell, D.	New Lights O'London (1st, lg8vo, 65 illus)	L: H. Jenkins	1926	Maxwell, D.	65-90	
Maxwell, D.	Wembley in Colour (1st, 4to, bds, 112p, 37cp)	L: Longmans	1924	Maxwell, D.	65-80	
Maxwell, G.S.	Just Beyond London (1st, 8vo, 18pl)	L: Methuen	1927	Maxwell, D.	70-100	
Maxwell, Wm.	Heavenly Tenants (1st, 8vo, blue cl, 56p, 1-color, pep, NH)	Harper	(1946)	Karasz, I.	65-90	R*
May, Charles P.	Box Turtle Lives in Armor (1st, sm8vo, 42p, 2-color, cep)	Holiday House	(1960)	Castle, J.	20-25	*
May, Eliz.	Flower Babies (1st, 4to, [100]p, ibds, color)	Saalfield	(1905)	Rockwell, I.M.	145-200	*
May, Rbt.	Benny the Bunny Liked Beans (1st {std}, 8vo, [25]p, ibds, color)	Knopf	(1940)	Hubbell, H.W.	30-45	*
Mayer, Henry	Adventures of a Japanese Doll (1st, ob4to, 127p, ibds, 30cp)	L: Richards	1901	Mayer, H.	200-300	
Mayer, Henry	In Laughland (1st, folio, [58]p)	R.H. Russell	1899	Mayer, H.	250-400	*
Mayer, Henry	Trip to Toyland (lg ob4to, ibds, 127p, 30 fp color)	L: Richards	1900	Mayer, H.	200-300	
Mayol, L.B.	Jiji Lou (1st, 4to, p-o, 142p, blue cl, 8 fp color, dep)	Saalfield	1928	Peat, F.B.	50-65	
Mayol, L.B.	Story of a Happy Doll (4to, ibds, 142p, 1cp, DJ)	Saalfield	1928	Peat, F.B.	35-50	
McBride, Mary M.	How Dear to My Heart (1st {std}, 8vo, 196p, b/w)	MacMillan	1940	Hader, E.	35-60	*
McCabe, O.	Rose Fairies (1st, 8vo, 159p, p-o, green cl, 12cp, pep)	Rand/McNally	(1911)	Dunlap, H.	65-90	
McCall, S.	Truth Dexter (1st, 8vo, 375p, blue cloth, frn by...)	Little/Brown	1903	Smith, J.W.	30-50	

|--------|-------|-----------|------|--------|-------|-----|
McCleery, Wm.	Wolf Story (1st {std}, 12mo, 82p, red cl, p-o, col frn)	Knopf	1947	Chappell, W.	50-85	R
McClintock, M.	Story of New England (1st {std}, 4to, ibds, 39p, col, pep)	Harper	1941	DeWitt, C.H.	35-50	
McClintock, M.	Story of the Mississippi (1st {std}, 4to, ibds, 39p, col, pep)	Harper	1941	DeWitt, C.H.	30-50	
McCloskey, R.	Blueberries for Sal (1st, ob4to, 54p, fp 1-color, CH)	Viking	1948	McCloskey, R.	60-90	*
McCloskey, R.	Homer Price (1st, lg8vo, 149p, blue cloth, sepia)	Viking	1943	McCloskey, R.	60-100	R*
McCloskey, R.	Lentil (1st {1st bk.}, lg4to, beige cl, fp b/w, [61]p, pep)	Viking	1940	McCloskey, R.	85-130	R
McCloskey, R.	Make Way for Ducklings (1st, lg4to, [70]p, 1-color, pep, CM)	Viking	1941	McCloskey, R.	100-170	R
McCloskey, R.	One Morning in Maine (1st, lg4to, 64p, grey cl, pep, DJ, CH)	Viking	1952	McCloskey, R.	100-140	
McCloskey, R.	Time of Wonder (1st, lg4to, 63p, blue cl, color, CM)	Viking	(1957)	McCloskey, R.	70-100	*
McConnell, Marg.	Bobo the Barrage Balloon (1st, lg8vo, 36p, ipcb, 1-color, pep)	Lothrop/Lee	1943	Gergely, T.	45-60	*
McCook, Henry C.	Old Farm Fairies (1st, 8vo, 392p, woodcuts)	L: Hodder	1895	Various	65-90	*
McCoy, N.	Jupie the Wise Old Owl (1st, 8vo, cloth, 95p, 3cp, pep)	MacMillan	1931	McCoy, N.	20-35	
McCracken, H.	Biggest Bear on Earth (1st, sm4to, 114p, col frn, 6pl, cep)	Stokes	(1943)	Bransom, P.	35-50	*
McCready, T.L.	Biggity Bantam (1st, 8vo, yellow cl, 49p, color, cep)	Ariel	(1954)	Tudor, T.	70-110	
McCready, T.L.	Increase Rabbit (1st, sm8vo, yellow cl, unpag, color, pep)	Ariel	(1958)	Tudor, T.	70-110	*
McCready, T.L.	Mr. Stubbs (1st, sm8vo, 48p, red cl, color, pep)	Ariel	(1956)	Tudor, T.	70-110	*
McCready, T.L.	Pekin White (1st, sm8vo, green cl, 49p, color, pep)	Ariel	(1955)	Tudor, T.	70-110	*
McCullough, J.G.	At Our House (1st, sm4to, [41]p)	W.R. Scott	1943	Duvoisin, R.	35-50	*
McCullough, J.G.	Dark is Dark (1st, lg8vo, [34]p, ibds, color, cep)	W.R. Scott	1947	Shaw, C.G.	35-50	*
McCutcheon, G.B.	Beverly of Graustark (1st, 8vo, blue cl, 357p, 5cp)	Dodd	1904	Fisher, H.	20-30	
McCutcheon, G.B.	Butterfly Man (1st, 8vo, teg, 121p, lavender cl, 4cp)	Dodd	1910	Fisher, H.	20-30	
McCutcheon, G.B.	Daughter of Anderson Crow (1st, 8vo, 346p, col frn)	Dodd	1907	Justice, B.M.	20-35	
McCutcheon, G.B.	Day of the Dog (1st, 8vo, red/gilt, 137p, 5cp, pep)	Dodd	1904	Fisher, H.	35-50	
McCutcheon, G.B.	Husbands of Edith (1st, 12mo, 126p, 5cp)	Dodd	1908	Fisher, H.	25-40	
McCutcheon, G.B.	In the Bishop's Carriage (1st, 8vo, 280p, red cl)	Bobbs-Merrill	(1904)	Armstrong, M.	25-40	
McCutcheon, G.B.	Jane Cable (1st, 8vo, 336p, 5cp)	Dodd	1906	Fisher, H.	20-25	
McCutcheon, G.B.	Man from Brodneys (1st, 8vo, p-o, 355p, 4cp)	Dodd	1908	Fisher, H.	20-35	
McCutcheon, G.B.	Nedra (1st, sm8vo, 343p, 5cp, p-o)	Dodd	1905	Fisher, H.	20-35	
McCutcheon, G.B.	Purple Parasol (1st, 8vo, green/gilt, 108p, 5cp)	Dodd	1905	Fisher, H.	25-40	
McCutcheon, G.B.	The Alternative (1st, 8vo, p-o, 119p, cp)	Dodd	1909	Fisher, H.	25-40	
McCutcheon, G.B.	The Sherrods (1st, sm8vo, 343p, cvr by...)	Dodd	1903	Armstrong, M.	25-40	
McCutcheon, J.T.	Congressman Pumphrey (1st, 8vo, 126p, b/w)	Bobbs-Merrill	(1907)	McCutcheon, J.T.	20-30	*
McDougall, Walt	Rambillicus Book (1st, lg8vo, 239p, 20pl)	Jacobs	(1903)	McDougall, W.H.	65-80	*
McElhone, N.K.	Secrets of the Elves (green cloth, p-o)	Devin-Adair	1913	Wheelan, A.R.	120-180	
McElhone, N.K.	Surprise Book (1st, lg ob4to, yellow cl, 33pl)	Stokes	1901	Wheelan, A.R.	120-180	
McElrath, F.	The Rustler (1st, 8vo, 425p, 7pl)	Funk/Wagnalls	1902	Deming, E.W.	45-60	
McElravy, May F.	Tortilla Girl (1st, 4to, 28p, p-o, 46p, pep, color, DJ)	Whitman	1946	Bannon, L.	35-50	
McEvoy, Joseph P.	Bam Bam Clock (1st, sq12mo, ibds, [38]p, color, pep)	Volland	(1920)	Gruelle, J.	70-100	
McEvoy, Joseph P.	Slams of Life... (1st, sm4to, 127p, uncut, 10 fp b/w)	Volland	(1919)	King, Frank	65-80	*
McFarlane, A.E.	Great Bear Island (1st, 8vo, 290p, 8pl)	Houghton	1911	Fogarty, T.	25-40	
McGaw, Jessie B.	How Medicine Man Cured Paleface Women (1st, ob4to, [62]p, 1-col)	W.R. Scott	(1956)	McGaw, J.B.	35-50	*
McGinley, Phyllis	All Around the Town (1st {std}, 4to, [63]p, fp color, CH)	Lippincott	(1948)	Stone, H.	60-85	*
McGinley, Phyllis	Blunderbus (1st {std}, 4to, 47p, yellow cl, 1-color)	Lippincott	(1951)	Wiesner, Wm.	30-45	*
McGinley, Phyllis	Horse Who Lived Upstairs (1st {std}, sm4to, [48]p, color)	Lippincott	(1944)	Stone, H.	40-70	*
McGinley, Phyllis	Lucy McLockett (1st, sm4to, [32]p, color)	Lippincott	(1959)	Stone, H.	45-70	*
McGinley, Phyllis	Merry Christmas, Happy New Year (1st, 8vo, bds, 48p, color)	Viking	(1958)	Karasz, I.	20-35	*
McGinley, Phyllis	Most Wonderful Doll in the World (1st, 8vo, 61p, color, CH)	Lippincott	(1950)	Stone, H.	50-90	*
McGinley, Phyllis	Name for Kitty (1st, sm8vo, ibds, [28]p, color, LGB)	Simon/Schuster	(1948)	Rojankovsky, F.	20-30	*
McGinley, Phyllis	On the Contrary (1st {std}, sm8vo, 119p, b/w)	Doubleday/Dor.	1934	McGinley, P.	25-40	*
McGinley, Phyllis	Plain Princess (1st {std}, sm8vo, 62p, color)	Lippincott	(1945)	Stone, H.	30-45	*
McGinley, Phyllis	Year Without a Santa Claus (1st, sm4to, tan cl, [32]p, color)	Lippincott	1957	Werth, K.	25-40	*
McGovern, Mary H.	Fifty Famous Fairy Tales (1st, sm4to, 254p, cp)	Whitman	(1917)	Lee, E.D.	50-85	*
McIlwraith, J.N.	Curious Career of Roderick Campbell (1st, 8vo, 287p, 4pl)	Houghton	1901	Schoonover, F.	20-35	
McIntyre, J.T.	In the Rockies with Kit Carson (1st, 8vo, p-o, 220p, b/w)	Penn	1913	Boyer, R.L.	25-40	
McKay (ed.)	Tale of the Cauldron (1st, ob8vo, 64p, ibds, 16cp)	MacLeod	1927	Browne, G.	60-85	
McKenna, Dolores	Adventures of a Wee Mouse (1st, 8vo, [30]p, p-o, 6cp, pep)	Stokes	(1921)	Bennett, R.H.	25-40	
McKenney, John	Tackroom Tattles (1st, 8vo, 230p, beige cl, fp b/w, cep)	Scribner	1934	Brown, Paul	35-50	*
McKinley, C.F.	Harriett (1st, lg8vo, 44p, 1-color)	Viking	1946	DuBois, W.P.	65-90	R
McKown, G.	All the Days Were Antonia's (1st, 8vo, 268p, fp b/w, pep)	Viking	1939	Gay, Z.	20-35	*
McLeod, Emilie	Seven Remarkable Bears (1st, sq8vo, 46p, blue cl, fp 2-col, pep)	Houghton	1954	Kepes, J.A.	45-70	*
McMahon, J.	Deenie Folks/Friends of Theirs (1st, 8vo, color, ibds)	Volland	(1925)	Gee, J.	50-70	*
McManus, B.	Bachelor Ballads (1st, 8vo, beige cl, 159p, color)	New Amsterdam	1898	McManus, B.	50-75	
McManus, B.	Calendar of Omar Khayaam (4to, ibds, dep, color)	Page	1904	McManus, B.	70-100	*
McManus, B.	Little Dutch Cousin (1st, 12mo, 99p, 6pl)	Page	1906	McManus, B.	20-35	*
McManus, B.	Little French Cousin (1st, sm8vo, 116p, 6pl)	Page	1905	McManus, B.	20-35	*
McManus, B.	Little Hindu Cousin (1st, sm8vo, 103p, 6pl)	Page	1907	McManus, B.	20-35	*
McManus, B.	Little Scotish Cousin (1st, sm8vo, 95p, 6pl)	Page	1906	McManus, B.	20-35	*
McNagny, B.	Noah's Nightmare (1st, 4to, p-o, [67]p, 30cp)	Bobbs-Merrill	(1926)	McNagny, B.	50-80	
McNeely, M.H.	Jumping-Off Place (1st {std}, sm8vo, 308p, b/w, pep, NH)	Longmans	1929	Siegel, W.	45-60	*
McNeely, M.H.	Rusty Ruston (1st {std}, 12mo, grn cl, 293p, col frn, 5pl, dep)	Longmans	1928	Burns, E.	25-45	*
McNeely, M.H.	Way to Glory (1st {std}, 12mo, 240p, b/w)	Longmans	1932	Esley, J.	30-45	*
McNeely, M.H.	Winning Out (1st {std}, 12mo, 308p, b/w)	Longmans	1931	Price, H.L.	30-45	*

AUTHOR	TITLE	PUBLISHER	DATE	ARTIST	PRICE	LC
McNeer, May	Golden Flash (1st, 8vo, 227p, pep, color)	Viking	1947	Ward, L.	30-45	
McNeer, May	John Wesley (1st, lg8vo, 96p, color, DJ)	Abingdon	(1951)	Ward, L.	25-40	
McNeer, May	Martin Luther (1st, lg8vo, 95p, rust cl, pep, color, DJ)	Abingdon	(1953)	Ward, L.	45-65	R
McNeer, May	Prince Bantam (1st, sm4to, 229p, aqua cl, col frn, 15 fp b/w)	MacMillan	1929	Ward, L.	35-50	
McNeer, May	Stop Tim! (1st, ob8vo, ibds, [39], 2-color, pep)	Farrar/Rine.	1930	Ward, L.	45-60	
McNeer, May	Story of California (1st {std}, 4to, [32]p, ibds, color, pep)	Harper	1944	DeWitt, C.H.	45-60	*
McNeer, May	Story of the South-West (1st, sq4to, ibds, [32]p, col, pep, DJ)	Harper	(1948)	DeWitt, C.H.	25-40	*
McNeer, May	Tales/Crescent Moon (1st, lg8vo, 306p, blue/silver, color, pep)	Farrar/Rine.	(1930)	Lederer, C.	35-50	
McNeer, May	Tinka Minka & Linka (1st, 8vo, 30p, yellow cl, cep, fp color)	Knopf	1931	Lederer, C.	30-45	*
McNeer, May	Waif Maid (1st, 8vo, p-o, 212p, col frn, woodcuts, cep)	MacMillan	1930	Ward, L.	35-50	
McNeil, E.	Dickon Bend-The-Bow (1st, sm4to, 126p, color, pep)	Saalfield	1903	Wagner, Rob.	65-80	*
McNeil, E.	Lost Treasure Cave (1st, 8vo, tan cl, 352p, 8pl)	Dutton	1905	Cary, W.M.	30-50	
McNeil, E.	With Kit Carson in the Rockies (1st, 8vo, 333p, 5pl)	Dutton	(1909)	Hutchinson	25-40	
McNeil, Marion	Little Green Cart (1st, 4to, ibds, [38]p, color, pep)	Saalfield	(1931)	Francoise	45-60	
McNeil, Marion	Round the Mulberry Bush (1st, 4to, ibds, 32p, 8cp)	Saalfield	1933	Peat, F.B.	50-70	
McSpadden, J.W.	Robin Hood & his Merry Outlaws (1st, 8vo, 285p)	World	1946	Slobodkin, L.	45-60	*
McSpadden, J.W.	Robin Hood/his Merry Outlaws (1st, 8vo, grn cl, 320p, teg, 12cp)	Crowell	(1923)	Stewart, A.	35-50	*
McSpadden, J.W.	Stories From Wagner (8vo, [new ed.], 282p, cvr by...)	Crowell	(1914)	Armstrong, M.	30-45	
Meader, S.W.	Black Bucaneer (1st, lg8vo, black/gilt, 269p, 8cp)	Harcourt	(1920)	Schaeffer, M.	30-45	*
Meader, S.W.	Boy with a Pack (1st, 8vo, 297p, brown cl, b/w, pep, NH)	Harcourt	(1939)	Shenton, E.	30-50	*
Means, F.C.	Assorted Sisters (1st, sm8vo, 250p, color)	Houghton	1947	Blair, H.	20-35	*
Means, F.C.	At the End of Nowhere (1st, 8vo, 232p, white cl, 12pl)	Houghton	1940	Hendrickson, D.	25-40	*
Means, F.C.	Borrowed Brother (1st, 8vo, blue cl, 239p, b/w)	Houghton	1958	Morse, D.B.	25-40	*
Means, F.C.	Bowlful of Stars (1st, 8vo, green cl, 247p, b/w, pep)	Houghton	1934	Pitz, H.C.	25-40	*
Means, F.C.	Candle in the Mist (1st, sm8vo, 252p, blue cl, pep, 4pl)	Houghton	1931	DeAngeli, M.	30-50	*
Means, F.C.	Emmy & the Blue Door (1st, 8vo, yellow cl, 217p, b/w)	Houghton	1959	Nicholas, F.	20-30	*
Means, F.C.	Great Day in the Morning (1st, 8vo, red cl, 182p, 6cp, pep)	Houghton	1946	Blair, H.	35-50	*
Means, F.C.	Hetty of the Grande Deluxe (1st, 8vo, grey cl, 188p, 8cp, pep)	Houghton	1951	Blair, H.	25-40	*
Means, F.C.	House Under the Hill (1st, 8vo, 184p, green cl, 8cp, pep)	Houghton	1949	Blair, H.	25-45	*
Means, F.C.	Knock at the Door, Emmy (1st, 8vo, 240p, tan cl, b/w)	Houghton	1956	Lantz, P.	30-45	*
Means, F.C.	Moved-Outers (1st, 12mo, 154p, orang cl, 5cp, pep, NH)	Houghton	1945	Blair, H.	40-65	*
Means, F.C.	Rains Will Come (1st, 8vo, 241p, green cl, b/w)	Houghton	1954	Kabotie, F.	25-45	*
Means, F.C.	Ranch and Ring (1st, sm8vo, tan cl, 260p, fp b/w, pep)	Houghton	1932	Peck, H.J.	20-35	*
Means, F.C.	Shadow Over Wide Ruin (1st, 8vo, 227p, 6 fp 1-color, pep)	Houghton	1942	Bjorklund, L.F.	25-45	*
Means, F.C.	Shuttered Windows (1st, 8vo, 206p, 8pl)	Houghton	1938	Sperry, A.	45-60	*
Means, F.C.	Tangled Waters (1st, sm8vo, 212p, col frn)	Houghton	1936	Stoops, H.M.	20-35	*
Means, F.C.	Whispering Girl (1st, sm8vo, 225p, col frn, pep)	Houghton	1941	Howard, O.	20-35	*
Medary, Marj.	Joan & the Three Deer (1st {std}, 8vo, 160p, b/w)	Random	(1939)	Wiese, K.	30-45	*
Medary, Marj.	Topgallant: A Herring Gull (1st {std}, 8vo, 159p, p-o, pep, b/w)	Smith/Haas	(1935)	Ward, L.	30-50	*
Mee, J.	Three Little Frogs (1st, 8vo, ibds, color)	Volland	(1924)	Rae, J.	50-75	
Meigs, C.	Clearing Weather (1st, 8vo, blue cl, 312p, 3cp, pep, NH)	Little/Brown	1928	Dobias, F.	35-50	*
Meigs, C.	Covered Bridge (1st, sq8vo, 145p, blue cl, col frn, b/w)	MacMillan	1936	DeAngeli, M.	35-50	
Meigs, C.	Invincible Louisa (1st, sm8vo, 260p, red cl, 16pl, NM)	Little/Brown	1933	(Photos)	60-90	R*
Meigs, C.	Kingdom of the Winding Road (1st, sm8vo, blue cl, 238p, 6cp)	MacMillan	1915	White, F.	40-65	
Meigs, C.	Master Simon's Garden (1st, 8vo, 320p, blue cl, col frn, pep)	MacMillan	1929	Rae, J.	50-70	R
Meigs, C.	Mother Makes Christmas (1st, sq8vo, ibds, [28]p, pep, 14 color)	Grosset/Dunlap	1940	Lenski, L.	45-60	*
Meigs, C.	New Moon (1st, 8vo, blue/gilt, 251p, col frn)	MacMillan	1924	DeAngeli, M.	35-50	*
Meigs, C.	Pool of Stars (1st, 8vo, 203p, blue cl, pep, col frn)	MacMillan	1929	Rae, J.	20-30	*
Meigs, C.	Scarlet Oak (1st, 8vo, 198p, col frn, pep, 8pl, DJ)	MacMillan	1938	Jones, E.O.	30-45	
Meigs, C.	Swift Rivers (1st, 8vo, black cl, p-o, 269p, 6cp, pep)	Little/Brown	1937	Hurd, P.	35-50	*
Meigs, C.	Trade Wind (1st, 8vo, 309p, black cl, p-o, 8cp, pep)	Little/Brown	1927	Pitz, H.C.	30-45	*
Meigs, C.	Willow Whistle (1st, ob4to, 144p, yellow cl, col frn, 10pl)	MacMillan	1931	Smith, E.B.	65-90	R
Meigs, C.	Wind in the Chimney (1st, 8vo, 144p, blue cl, col frn, 8pl, cep)	MacMillan	1934	Mansfield, L.	20-30	
Meigs, C.	Windy Hill (1st, 8vo, 210p, frontis, NH)	MacMillan	1921	Unknown	30-45	*
Meigs, C.	Wonderful Locomotive (1st, ob8vo, gilt, 104p, 3cp, pep, DJ)	MacMillan	1928	Hader, B.& E.	85-100	
Melville, Herman	Moby Dick (1st, lg8vo, p-o, 540p, black/gilt, teg, 12cp, pep)	Dodd	1922	Schaeffer, M.	45-60	
Melville, Herman	Moby Dick (1st, sm8vo, 822p, black/silver, DJ)	Random	1930	Kent, R.	90-120	
Melville, Herman	Moby Dick (1st, lg8vo, 414p, black/gilt, p-o, 15cp, pep)	Winston	(1931)	Fischer, A.O.	30-50	
Melville, Herman	Omoo (1st, 4to, teg, 299p, black cl, 8cp, pep)	Dodd	1924	Schaeffer, M.	35-50	
Melville, Herman	Typee (sm4to, black cl, 283p, 8cp, pep)	Dodd	(1923)	Schaeffer, M.	35-50	
Mencken, H.L.	Christmas Story (1st {std}, sq12mo, [31]p, p-o, pep, color)	Knopf	1946	Crawford, Bill	65-80	*
Mendel, F.E.	Little Polish Cousin (1st, 12mo, 147p, 6pl)	Page	1912	O'Brien, H.	25-40	*
Mendes, C.	Fairy Spinning Wheel (1st, sq8vo, 146p, 14 fp b/w)	Badger	1898	Peabody, M.L.	100-130	*
Menotti, G-C.	Amahl & Night Visitors (1st, 8vo, [89]p, bds, 17 color, pep)	Whittlesey	(1952)	Duvoisin, R.	35-50	
Menpes, D.	World Pictures (1st AM, 8vo, 332p, color)	R.H. Russell	1902	Menpes, M.	70-100	*
Menpes, M.	Brittany (1st, 8vo, gilt, 254p, teg, 75cp)	L: A&C Black	1912	Menpes, M.	65-100	
Menpes, M.	Japan (1st, lg8vo, 207p, teg, blue/gilt, 75cp)	L: A&C Black	1905	Menpes, M.	65-100	
Menpes, M.	Rembrandt (1st, 4to, 50p, teg, gilt, 16cp)	L: A&C Black	1905	Menpes, M.	70-110	
Menpes, M.	World's Children (1st, 8vo, teg, 246p, blue/gilt, 100cp)	L: A&C Black	1903	Menpes, M.	80-130	
Meredith, G.	Jump to Glory Jane (1st, 8vo, ipcb, teg, designs by...)	L: Swan	1892	Housman, L.	100-150	
Meredith, O.	Lucille (1st, 8vo, teg, cvr by...)	Stokes	(1897)	Bradley, W.	60-85	
Meredith, O.	Lucille (1st, 8vo, teg, 12cp by...)	Stokes	(1897)	Lemaire, M.	60-85	

AUTHOR	TITLE	PUBLISHER	DATE	ARTIST	PRICE	LC
Merimee, P.	Carmen (1st AM, 4to, teg, red/gilt, 16cp)	Hearst	1915	Bull, Rene	100-140	
Merimee, P.	Carmen (1st, lg4to, 203p, red/gilt, teg, pep, 18cp)	L: Hutchinson	(1915)	Bull, Rene	140-200	
Merington, M.	Captain Lettarblair (1st, 8vo, aqua/gilt, 212p, cvr by…)	Bobbs-Merrill	(1906)	Armstrong, M.	30-45	
Meriwether, L.	Afloat & Ashore on the Mediterranean (1st, 8vo, brown/gilt)	Scribner	1892	Armstrong, M.	30-45	
Merriam, Eve	Gaggle of Geese (1st, 4to, yellow cl, unpag, color, pep)	Knopf	(1960)	Galdone, P.	40-60	*
Merrill, Jean	Shan's Lucky Knife (1st, sm4to, [48]p, 2-color)	W.R. Scott	1960	Solbert, R.	25-40	
Merriman, H.S.	Grey Lady (1st, 8vo, blue/gilt, 342p, 12pl)	L: Smith Elder	1897	Rackham, A.	160-225	
Merriman, H.S.	Money Spinner (1st, sm8vo, 242p, gilt, 12pl)	L: Smith Elder	1896	Rackham, A.	200-300	
Merryman, M.P.	Daddy Domino (1st {std}, 8vo, ibds, 6 fp color)	Volland	(1929)	Scott, J.L.	65-100	
Merryman, M.P.	Mr. Wubbles Bubbles (1st, 12mo, [44]p, color)	Saalfield	1936	Cadie, V.E.	35-50	*
Merryman, M.P.	Quack! Said Jerusha (1st, 8vo, ibds, [50]p, 1-color, pep)	Sears	(1930)	Phipps, M.	45-60	
Merwin, S.	Road Builders (1st, 8vo, 313p, 10pl)	MacMillan	1905	Masters, F.B.	25-40	
Merwin, S.	Silk (1st, 12mo, 266p, red/gilt, pep, col frn by…)	Houghton	1923	Wyeth, N.C.	35-50	
Messer, C.J.	Next-Night Stories (1st, 12mo, 261p, 8pl)	Lothrop/Lee	1912	Bridgman, L.J.	30-45	*
Metcalf, S.	Annabel (1st [1], 8vo, 231p, grey/gilt, p^Eo, 6pl)	Reilly/Britton	(1906)	Hall, H.P.	475-700	
Metcalf, S.	Annabel (2nd, 8vo, 213p, green cl, 3pl)	Reilly/Britton	(1912)	Nuyttens, J.P.	170-240	
Metcalfe, F.	Side Show Studies (1st, 12mo, 232p)	Outing	1906	Herford, O.	35-50	*
Meyer, Edith P.	Tim Chick (1st, sm sq4to, 42p, p-o, color)	Rand/McNally	1932	Ward, Keith	35-50	*
Meyer, L.R.	Mary North (1st, 8vo, 339p, cvr by…)	Revell	(1903)	Hazenplug, F.	45-60	*
Meynell, A.	Flower of the Mind (sm8vo, green/gilt, 348p, cvr by…)	L: Richards	1897	Housman, L.	60-85	
Meynell, A.	The Children (1st, 12mo, gilt, 96p, title page by…)	L: J. Lane	1897	Robinson, C.	70-100	
Michael, A.C.	Artist in Spain (1st, 4to, rust cl, 205p, 20 ticp)	L: Hodder	[1920]	Michael, A.C.	50-70	
Michelson, M.	Anthony Overman (1st, 8vo, 330p, 5pl)	Doubleday/Page	1906	Clay, J.C.	20-30	*
Michelson, M.	In The Bishop's Carriage (1st, 8vo, red cl, 280p, 6pl)	Bobbs-Merrill	(1904)	Fisher, H.	20-30	
Michelson, M.	Michael Thwaites's Wife (1st, 8vo, red cl, 402p, 3cp)	Doubleday/Page	1909	Phillips, C.	20-25	
Miers, E.S.	Rainbow Book/American History (1st {std}, 4to, 319p, color, DJ)	World	(1955)	Daugherty, J.	35-50	*
Mighels, P.V.	Chatwit the Man-Talk Bird (1st, 8vo, blue cl, 265p, b/w)	Harper	1906	Mighels, P.	20-35	
Mighels, P.V.	Furnace of Gold (1st, sm8vo, 402p, p-o, 12pl)	D. Fitzgerald	(1910)	Marchand, J.	20-30	
Mijatovich, M.	Serbian Fairy Tales (1st, 8vo, gilt, 204p, 8cp)	L: Heinemann	(1917)	Stanley, S.	70-90	
Mijatovich, M.	Serbian Fairy Tales (1st AM, 8vo, black cl, 204p, 8cp)	McBride	1918	Stanley, S.	65-80	
Milhous, Kath.	Appolonia's Valentine (1st, 4to, red cl, [32]p, color, DJ)	Scribner	(1954)	Milhous, K.	70-120	R*
Milhous, Kath.	Corporal Keeperupper (1st, sm8vo, 62p, ipcb, color)	Scribner	1943	Milhous, K.	25-40	*
Milhous, Kath.	Egg Tree (1st, sm4to, [32]p, aqua cl, color, DJ, CM)	Scribner	(1950)	Milhous, K.	100-135	
Milhous, Kath.	First Christmas Crib (1st, 12mo, ibds, 47p, color)	Scribner	1944	Milhous, K.	20-25	*
Milhous, Kath.	Herodia the Lovely Puppet (1st, 8vo, 193p, red cl, pep, 7cp)	Scribner	1942	Milhous, K.	60-100	R*
Milhous, Kath.	Lovina (1st, ob4to, [48]p, red cl, color)	Scribner	(1940)	Milhous, K.	30-45	*
Milhous, Kath.	Snow Over Bethlehem (1st, 8vo, 98p, pep, 3 dp color)	Scribner	1945	Milhous, K.	25-40	*
Milius, W.	Here Comes Daddy (1st, ob8vo, ipcb, [22]p, color)	W.R. Scott	1944	Milius, W.	35-50	*
Millar, H.R.	Dreamland Express (1st AM, ob4to, 56p, ibds, 14cp)	Dodd	(1927)	Millar, H.R.	85-125	
Millay, Edna St. V.	Princess Marries the Page (1st {std}, lg8vo, 50p, bds, col frn)	Harper	1932	Paget-Fredericks	70-100	R*
Miller, A.D.	Calderon's Prisoner (1st, 8vo, olive/gilt, 294p, cvr by…)	Scribner	1903	Armstrong, M.	20-30	
Miller, A.D.	Modern Obstacle (1st, 8vo, 273p, blue cl, cvr by…)	Scribner	1903	Armstrong, M.	35-50	
Miller, E.	The Yoke (1st, 12mo, 616p, blue/gilt, cvr by…)	Bobbs-Merrill	(1904)	Armstrong, M.	30-45	
Miller, E.C.	Children of Mountain Eagle (1st {std}, sm8vo, 328p, 3cp, pep)	Doubleday/Dor.	1927	Petershams	30-45	*
Miller, E.C.	Pran of Albania (1st {std}, 8vo, 257p, col frn, pep, NH)	Doubleday/Dor.	1929	Petershams	60-95	
Miller, E.C.	Young Trajan (1st {std}, 8vo, 232p, black cl, pep, col frn)	Doubleday/Dor.	1931	Petershams	25-40	*
Miller, J.R.	Glimpses of Heavenly Life (1st, 32p)	Crowell	(1908)	Armstrong, M.	30-45	
Miller, Jane	Jimmy the Groceryman (1st, sm8vo, 88p, blue cl, color, pep)	Houghton	(1934)	Hader, B.& E.	45-60	*
Miller, Leo E.	Adrift on the Amazon (1st, 8vo, 263p, olive cl, 4pl)	Scribner	1923	Rogers, W.A.	25-40	*
Miller, Leo E.	Hidden People (1st, 8vo, 321p, 8pl)	Scribner	1920	Bransom, P.	25-40	*
Miller, Leo E.	In the Tiger's Lair (1st, 8vo, 252p, 4pl)	Scribner	1921	Bransom, P.	25-40	*
Miller, M.B.	Menagerie (1st, sq8vo, 124p, col frn, 8pl, pep)	MacMillan	1928	Sewell, H.	30-50	
Miller, Mary B.	Give a Guess (1st, 8vo, blue cl, [32]p, 1-color, dep)	Pantheon	1957	Kepes, J.A.	50-80	R*
Miller, O.B.	Come Play with Me (1st, sm8vo, ibds, [38]p, color, pep)	Volland	(1918)	Browne, C.L.	80-120	*
Miller, O.B.	Little Pictures of Japan (1st, 4to, 191p, p-o, pep, color)	Book House	(1925)	Sturges, K.	40-60	
Miller, O.B.	Nursery Friends from France (1st, 4to, 190p, p-o, color)	Book House	(1925)	Petershams	35-50	
Miller, O.B.	Sunny Rhymes/Happy Children (1st, 8vo, ibds, [40]p, pep, color)	Volland	(1917)	Browne, C.L.	50-70	*
Miller, O.B.	Tales Told in Holland (1st, 4to, 190p, p-o, pep, gilt, color)	Book House	(1926)	Petershams	45-60	
Miller, O.B.	Whisk Away on a Sunbeam (1st, tall 8vo, [93]p, pep, ibds, col)	Volland	(1919)	Enright, M.W.	70-110	
Miller, O.T.	Kristy's Rainy Day Picnic (1st, 12mo, 235p, p-o, 4cp, pep)	Houghton	1906	Farnsworth, E.N.	25-40	
Miller, Warren	Goings on at Little Wishful (1st {std}, ob4to, [30]p, 2-col, cep)	Little/Brown	(1959)	Sorel, E.	50-80	R*
Miller, Warren	King Carlo of Capri (1st {std}, lg8vo, [32]p, 2-color, pep)	Harcourt	(1958)	Sorel, E.	50-80	R*
Miller, Warren	Pablo Paints a Picture (1st {std}, ob4to, [28]p, 1-color, pep)	Little/Brown	(1959)	Sorel, E.	45-70	*
Mills, E.A.	Animal Trainer (1st, ob8vo, 31p, p-o, 6cp)	Duffield	1910	Vimar, A.	60-85	
Mills, E.A.	In Beaver World (1st, 8vo, 221p, olive cl, 19pl, pep)	Houghton	1913	(Photos)	60-80	
Mills, G.R.	Talking Dolls (1st, 4to, [96]p, color, pep)	Greenberg	(1930)	Sarg, T.	65-80	*
Mills, W.H.	Marionettes, Masks & Shadows (1st {std}, 8vo, 270p, col frn)	Doubleday/Page	1927	Bell, C.	35-50	*
Mills, W.J.	Caroline of Courtlandt Street (1st, lg8vo, 291p, gilt, teg, 6cp)	Harper	1905	Betts, A.W.	50-65	
Mills, W.J.	Girl I Left Behind Me (1st, 4to, 90p, teg, p-o, 11cp, pep)	Dodd	1910	Rae, J.	70-90	
Mills, W.J.	Through the Gates of Old Romance (1st, sm8vo, 283p, teg, b/w)	Lippincott	1903	Rae, J.	30-45	
Mills, W.J.	Van Rensselaers of Old Manhattan (1st, 8vo, p-o, 215p, 5cp)	Stokes	(1907)	Rae, J.	30-45	
Milne (intro)	Fun & Fantasy (1st, lg4to, ibds, color)	L: Methuen	1927	Shepard, E.H.	120-170	

AUTHOR	TITLE	PUBLISHER	DATE	ARTIST	PRICE	LC
Milne, A.A.	Christopher Robin Birthday Bk. (1st, 16mo, 215p, orang/gilt, b/w)	L: Methuen	(1930)	Shepard, E.H.	180-240	
Milne, A.A.	Christopher Robin Story Book (1st AM, 8vo, 171p, b/w)	Dutton	(1929)	Shepard, E.H.	120-180	
Milne, A.A.	Christopher Robin Verses (1st, 8vo, 210p, blue/gilt, 12cp)	L: Methuen	(1932)	Shepard, E.H.	160-220	
Milne, A.A.	Christopher Robin Verses (1st AM {std}, 8vo, 210p, 12cp)	Dutton	(1932)	Shepard, E.H.	130-185	*
Milne, A.A.	Gallery of Children (1st AM, 4to, 105p, p-o, gilt, 12cp)	McKay	(1925)	LeMair, H.W.	120-165	
Milne, A.A.	Gallery of Children (1st, lg4to, p-o, 105p, 12cp)	L: Stan. Paul	(1925)	LeMair, H.W.	180-265	
Milne, A.A.	Gallery of Children (1st AM {this fmt}, 12mo, 125p, b/w, DJ)	McKay	[1939]	Watson, A.H.	65-100	
Milne, A.A.	House at Pooh Corner (1st [1], 12mo, 178p, teg, pink/gilt, pep)	L: Methuen	(1928)	Shepard, E.H.	280-400	
Milne, A.A.	King's Breakfast (1st, lg8vo, bds, 17p, b/w, DJ)	L: Methuen	(1925)	Shepard, E.H.	120-160	
Milne, A.A.	Magic Hill (1st {this pub}, 4to, 40p, ibds, 8 fp color)	Grosset/Dunlap	(1937)	Sewell, H.	70-120	
Milne, A.A.	More Very Young Songs (1st, folio, 40p, bds, b/w)	L: Methuen	(1928)	Shepard, E.H.	130-180	
Milne, A.A.	Now We Are Six (1st, 12mo, 103p, maroon/gilt, teg, pep)	L: Methuen	(1927)	Shepard, E.H.	250-350	
Milne, A.A.	Now We Are Six (1st AM, 8vo, buckram, 103p, gilt)	Dutton	(1927)	Shepard, E.H.	180-250	
Milne, A.A.	Old Sailor (1st AM, lg8vo, ipcb, [23]p, 1-color, pep)	Dutton	(1947)	Shepard, E.H.	80-120	*
Milne, A.A.	Once On a Time (1st, 8vo, 316p, blue cl, p-o, col frn, 3pl)	L: Hodder	(1917)	Brock, H.M.	130-165	*
Milne, A.A.	Once On a Time (1st, 12mo, gilt, 269p, col frn, pep)	L: Hodder	[1922]	Robinson, C.	150-180	
Milne, A.A.	Once On a Time (1st AM, 8vo, 358, col frn, pep)	Putnam	1922	Robinson, C.	100-140	
Milne, A.A.	Princess & the Apple Tree (1st, 4to, 40p, 8 fp color)	Grosset/Dunlap	(1937)	Sewell, H.	65-100	*
Milne, A.A.	Sneezles (1st AM, lg sq8vo, ibds, [23]p, pep)	Dutton	(1947)	Shepard, E.H.	70-100	*
Milne, A.A.	Songs from Now We are Six (1st, sm folio, 33p, bds, p-o, b/w)	L: Methuen	(1927)	Shepard, E.H.	150-200	
Milne, A.A.	Teddy Bear... (1st AM, lg4to, bds, p-o, 43p)	Dutton	(1926)	Shepard, E.H.	130-165	
Milne, A.A.	Teddy Bear... (1st, lg4to, bds, p-o, 43p)	L: Methuen	(1926)	Shepard, E.H.	120-165	
Milne, A.A.	Very Young Verses (1st, sm8vo, 88p, blue cl, 6pl)	L: Methuen	(1929)	Shepard, E.H.	100-140	*
Milne, A.A.	When We Were Very Young (1st AM, 12mo, 100p, gilt)	Dutton	(1924)	Shepard, E.H.	140-195	*
Milne, A.A.	When We Were Very Young (1st, 12mo, 100p, gilt, AEG)	L: Methuen	(1924)	Shepard, E.H.	420-600	
Milne, A.A.	Winnie-the-Pooh (1st, 12mo, 158p, gilt, teg, pep)	L: Methuen	(1926)	Shepard, E.H.	250-400	
Milne, A.A.	Winnie-the-Pooh (1st AM, 12mo, 158p, b/w)	Dutton	(1926)	Shepard, E.H.	200-280	
Milne, J.	Travels in Hope (1st, 4to, 190p, blue cl, 22cp)	L: Hodder	[1926]	Maxwell, D.	75-110	
Milne-Home, M.P.	Mama's Black Nurse Stories (1st, 8vo, 131p, grey/gilt, 6 fp b/w)	L: Blackwood	1890	Milne-Home, M.P.	65-80	
Milton, J.	Comus (1st, 12mo, 83p, teg, gilt, 9pl)	L: Routledge	1906	King, J.	240-320	
Milton, J.	Comus (1st AM, 4to, teg, green/gilt, 76p, 24 ticp, pep)	Doubleday/Page	[1921]	Rackham, A.	175-235	
Miltoun, F.	Automobilist Abroad (1st, 8vo, 381p, p-o, col frn)	Page	1907	McManus, B.	25-40	
Miltoun, F.	Castles & Chateaux of Touraine (1st, 8vo, 347p, 39pl)	Page	1906	McManus, B.	35-50	
Miltoun, F.	Rambles on the Riviera (1st, 8vo, teg, 434p, 32pl)	Page	1906	McManus, B.	30-45	
Minarik, E.H.	Father Bear Comes Home (1st, 8vo, ibds, 62p, color)	Harper	(1959)	Sendak, M.	100-160	*
Minarik, E.H.	Little Bear (1st, 8vo, 63p, ibds, color)	Harper	(1957)	Sendak, M.	120-170	R
Minarik, E.H.	No Fighting! No Biting! (1st, 8vo, 62p, b/w)	Harper	1958	Sendak, M.	120-165	*
Minnion, W.J.	Topsy Turvey (1st, 4to, 72p)	L: Connoisseur	1913	Robinson, C.	140-200	*
Mirza, Y.B.	Children of the Housetops (1st {std}, sm8vo, 248p, col frn)	Doubleday/Dor.	1931	Dobias, F.	20-30	*
Mirza, Y.B.	Myself when Young (1st {std}, 8vo, 260p, col frn)	Doubleday/Dor.	1929	Nadejen, T.	30-45	*
Mirza, Y.B.	Son of the Sword (1st, 8vo, black cl, 211p, pep, designs by...)	Viking	1934	Artzybasheff, B.	30-45	*
Misch, Rbt. J.	At Daddy's Office (1st {std}, sm4to, ibds, [32]p, color)	Knopf	(1946)	Duvoisin, R.	35-50	*
Mitchell G.W.	Kernel Cob & Little Miss Sweetclover (1st, 8vo, [96]p, col, pep)	Volland	(1918)	Sarg, T.	80-120	*
Mitchell, E.	Chickabiddy Stories (1st, 8vo, 110p, 4 ticp)	L: Wells/Gard.	(1899)	Barham, S.	100-140	
Mitchell, Edith	Betty, Bobby & Bubbles (1st, 12mo, ibds, [40]p, pep, color)	Volland	(1921)	Scott, J.L.	40-60	*
Mitchell, G.W.	Little Babs (1st, 12mo, ibds, color)	Volland	(1919)	Henderson, A.	50-70	
Mitchell, J.A.	Amos Judd (1st, 8vo, teg, 252p, 8cp)	Scribner	1901	Keller, A.I.	20-25	
Mitchell, J.A.	Drowsy (1st [1], 8vo, blue/gilt, 301p, 19pl)	Stokes	(1917)	Macdonall, A.	30-45	
Mitchell, L.S.	Guess What's in the Grass (1st, ob4to, ibds, [30]p, 2-col, pep)	W.R. Scott	1945	Glannon, E.J.	60-90	*
Mitchell, L.S.	Red, White & Blue Auto (1st, ob8vo, [33]p, color)	W.R. Scott	1943	Gergely, T.	50-80	*
Mitchell, Lebbeus	Bobby in Search of/Birthday (1st, 8vo, pcb, 64p, p-o, gilt, b/w)	Volland	1916	Nuyttens, J.P.	35-50	
Mitchell, Muriel M.	Adventures of Nip & Tuck (1st, 8vo, 40p, pep, ipcb, color)	Volland	(1927)	Ellsworth, M.	65-80	*
Mitchell, S.W.	Adventures of Francois (1st, 8vo, 321p, orange cl, 15pl)	Century	1898	Castaigne, A.	35-50	
Mitchell, S.W.	Mr. Kris Kringle (1st, 8vo, teg, 105p, 5cp)	Jacobs	1893	DeLand, C.O.	75-120	R
Mitchell, S.W.	Red City (1st, 8vo, 421p, p-o, 10pl)	Century	1908	Keller, A.I.	20-30	
Mitchison, Naomi	Rib of the Green Umbrella (1st, 8vo, 160p)	L: Collins	1960	Ardizzone, E.	25-40	*
Mitford, M.R.	Our Village (1st, sm8vo, AEG, green/gilt, b/w, cep)	L: MacMillan	1893	Thomson, H.	50-65	
Mitford, M.R.	Our Village (1st, lg8vo, green/gilt, 256p, teg, 16 ticp)	L: MacMillan	1910	Rawlings, A.	80-100	
Mockler, G.	Little Girl from Next Door (1st, 8vo, 160p, 2pl by...)	L: Blackie	1896	Brooke, L.L.	50-70	*
Mockler, G.	Spring Fairies & Sea Fairies (1st, sm8vo, 192p, red/gilt, b/w)	L: G. Allen	1897	Benson, N.	90-125	
Moe, Louis M.	Kylle Kluk (1st AM, ob4to, [24]p, orang cl, 11 fp color)	NY: Laidlaw	[1931]	Moe, L.M.	120-185	*
Moe, Louis M.	Peter Kroak (1st AM, ob4to, [17]p, p-o, 8 fp color, cep)	Whitman	1932	Moe, L.M.	130-180	*
Moe, Louis M.	Vain Pussy Cat (1st, ob4to, ipcb, [32]p, b/w, pep)	Coward	(1929)	Moe, L.M.	120-185	*
Moerleim, G.	Trip Around the World (1st, 4to, AEG, red/gilt, 100 chromos)	Burgheim	1880	Unknown	150-200	
Moeschlin, Elsa	Little Boy with Big Apples (1st, 4to, ibds, [23]p, color)	Coward	[1932]	Moeschlin, E.	85-120	
Moeschlin, Elsa	Red Horse (1st AM, 4to, ibds, [20]p, color, cep)	Coward	[1929]	Moeschlin, E.	70-100	
Moffat, A.	Little Songs/Long Ago (1st, ob4to, 64p, p-o, 32 fp color)	L: Augener	(1912)	LeMair, H.W.	140-170	
Moffat, A.	Our Old Nursery Rhymes (1st, ob4to, 63p, p-o, 30 fp color)	L: Augener	1911	LeMair, H.W.	150-200	
Molesworth, M.	Adventures of Herr Baby (1st, sm4to, red/gilt, 171p, 13pl, dep)	L: MacMillan	1881	Crane, W.	100-160	*
Molesworth, M.	Christmas Child (1st, 12mo, 223p, gilt, 7pl, cep)	L: MacMillan	1880	Crane, W.	100-150	
Molesworth, M.	Christmas-Tree Land (1st, 12mo, 223p, red cl, 7pl)	L: MacMillan	1884	Crane, W.	85-100	
Molesworth, M.	Cozy Corner Stories (1st, sm4to, ibds, 12 chromos)	L: Nister	(1895)	Bennett, H.M.	100-160	

AUTHOR	TITLE	PUBLISHER	DATE	ARTIST	PRICE	LC
Molesworth, M.	Cuckoo Clock (1st, 8vo, teg, red/gilt, 283p, pep, 8cp)	Lippincott	1914	Kirk, M.L.	35-50	*
Molesworth, M.	Enchanted Garden: Fairy Stories (1st, 12mo, 221p, teg, b/w)	L: T.F. Unwin	1892	Hennessey, W.J.	50-70	
Molesworth, M.	Fairies Afield (1st, 8vo, 252p)	L: MacMillan	1911	Hammond, G.D.	50-80	*
Molesworth, M.	Fairies of Sorts (1st, 8vo, gilt, 249p, AEG, 8pl)	L: MacMillan	1908	Hammond, G.D.	80-110	*
Molesworth, M.	February Boys (1st, 8vo, 266p, 8cp)	L: Chambers	1909	Attwell, M.L.	50-80	*
Molesworth, M.	February Boys (1st AM, 8vo, 265p, 8cp)	Dutton	[1910]	Attwell, M.L.	45-65	
Molesworth, M.	Four Winds Farm (1st, 8vo, blue cl, 180p, 6pl)	L: MacMillan	1886	Crane, W.	80-125	
Molesworth, M.	Girls & I (1st, 12mo, orange cl, 192p, 7pl, cep)	L: MacMillan	1892	Brooke, L.L.	70-100	
Molesworth, M.	Grim House (1st, 8vo, 289p)	L: J. Nisbet	1899	Goble, W.	70-100	*
Molesworth, M.	House that Grew (1st, 12mo, 206p, orange/gilt, 7pl)	L: MacMillan	1900	Woodward, A.B.	65-80	
Molesworth, M.	Little Miss Peggy (1st, 12mo, red cl, 195p, 12pl)	L: MacMillan	1887	Crane, W.	85-100	
Molesworth, M.	Magic Nuts (1st, 8vo, 194p, orange/gilt, 7pl)	L: MacMillan	1898	Pitman, R.M.M.	45-60	
Molesworth, M.	Mary (1st, 8vo, 180p)	L: MacMillan	1893	Brooke, L.L.	65-80	*
Molesworth, M.	Miss Mouse & her Boys (1st, 8vo, green/gilt, 198p, 7pl)	L: MacMillan	1897	Brooke, L.L.	35-50	
Molesworth, M.	Next-Door House (1st, 8vo, 226p, grey cl, 6pl)	L: Chambers	1893	Hatherell, W.	35-50	*
Molesworth, M.	Nurse Heatherdale's Story (1st, 12mo, 202p, red cl, cep, 7pl)	L: MacMillan	1891	Brooke, L.L.	70-100	*
Molesworth, M.	Old Pincushion (1st AM, 8vo, 271p, brown cl, 8cp)	Dutton	[1910]	Attwell, M.L.	40-65	
Molesworth, M.	Old Pincushion (1st, 8vo, 271p, 8cp)	L: Chambers	1910	Attwell, M.L.	65-80	*
Molesworth, M.	Oriel Window (1st, 8vo, 182p, 7pl)	MacMillan	1896	Brooke, L.L.	60-80	
Molesworth, M.	Palace in the Garden (1st, 8vo, 298p)	L: Hatchards	1887	Bennett, H.M.	65-80	*
Molesworth, M.	Peterkin (1st, sm8vo, 198p, orange cloth, 8pl)	L: MacMillan	1902	Millar, H.R.	35-50	
Molesworth, M.	Rectory Children (1st, 8vo, 212p, 7pl)	L: MacMillan	1889	Crane, W.	70-90	*
Molesworth, M.	Rosy (1st, sm8vo, red/gilt, 204p, 8pl, cep)	L: MacMillan	1882	Crane, W.	80-100	
Molesworth, M.	Ruby Ring (1st, 8vo, 213p, orange cl, 8pl)	L: MacMillan	1904	Pitman, R.M.M.	35-50	
Molesworth, M.	Stories by Mrs. Molesworth (1st, 4to, p-o, green cl, 353p, 8cp)	Duffield	1922	Cooke, E.	60-80	
Molesworth, M.	Studies & Stories (1st, 8vo, 256p, gilt, uncut, pep, frn by...)	L: A.D. Innes	1893	Crane, W.	125-160	
Molesworth, M.	Tales Told in the Twilight (1st, 8vo, 152p, color)	Nister/Dutton	[1911]	Various	65-80	*
Molesworth, M.	Tapestry Room (1st, 8vo, red cl, unpag, 7pl)	L: MacMillan	1879	Crane, W.	100-145	
Molesworth, M.	This & That (1st, 12mo, 212p, orange/gilt, 8pl)	L: MacMillan	1899	Thomson, H.	50-65	
Molesworth, M.	Three Witches (1st, 8vo, 278p, blue cl, 13pl)	L: Chambers	1900	Baumer, L.	35-50	*
Molesworth, M.	Two Little Waifs (1st, 8vo, 216p, 7pl)	L: MacMillan	(1883)	Crane, W.	100-140	
Molesworth, M.	US: An Old Fashioned Story (1st, 8vo, red/gilt, 240p, 7pl)	L: MacMillan	1886	Crane, W.	70-100	
Molesworth, O.	Sunny Land Stories (sm4to, ibds, 6cp)	L: Nister	(1890)	Bennett, H.M.	75-110	
Molloy, Anne	Lucy's Christmas (1st, 8vo, 46p, red cl, color)	Houghton	1950	Cosgrave, J.O.	20-35	*
Molloy, Anne	Shooting Star Farm (1st, 8vo, 231p, b/w, dep)	Houghton	1946	Cooney, B.	30-45	*
Molloy, Anne	The Pigeoneers (1st, 4to, 180p, grey cl, woodcuts, dep, DJ)	Houghton	1947	Converse, E.	45-60	
Molnar, F.	Blue-Eyed Lady (1st, 4to, blue cl, 46p, color, pep, DJ)	Viking	1942	Sewell, H.	35-50	
Monrad, Jean	How Many Kisses Good Night? (1st, ob8vo, [20]p, color)	W.R. Scott	1949	Bloch, L.	25-45	*
Monro, W.D.	India's Gods & Heroes (1st AM, 8vo, uncut, 237p, 16cp)	Crowell	(1910)	Paul, E.	60-80	
Monroe, H.	Dance of the Seasons (1st, 8vo, 20p, wraps, cvr & ti page by..)	R.F. Seymour	1911	Bradley, W.	80-130	R
Monsell, J.R.	Hooded Crow (1st, 8vo, unpag, yellow cl, color)	L: Blackwell	(1926)	Monsell, J.R.	60-80	*
Monsell, J.R.	Pink Knight (1st, 16mo, 95p, 24cp)	L: Richards	1901	Monsell, J.R.	85-120	
Montefiore	Friend & Foe (8vo, ipcb, 107p)	Dutton	(1898)	5 Chromos	80-130	
Montgomery, F.T.	Billy Whiskers at the Fair (1st, 4to, ibds, 163p, cp)	Saalfield	(1909)	DeBebian, A.	30-50	*
Montgomery, F.T.	Billy Whiskers in the South (1st, 4to, 148p, 6cp)	Saalfield	(1917)	Fitzgerald, W.	65-80	
Montgomery, F.T.	Billy Whiskers' Kids (1st, 8vo, 134p, 6cp)	Saalfield	(1903)	Fry, W.H.	45-60	*
Montgomery, F.T.	Cats & Kitts (1st, 8vo, 63p, p-o, 6cp)	Brewer/Barse	(1908)	Von Hofsten, H.	60-80	*
Montgomery, F.T.	Horses & Colts (1st, 8vo, red cl, p-o)	Barse	(1911)	Von Hofsten, H.	30-45	*
Montgomery, F.T.	On a Lark to the Planets (1st, 12mo, blue/silver, 180p, 7cp)	Saalfield	1904	Elrod, W.D.	180-260	
Montgomery, F.T.	Wonderful Electric Elephant (1st, 8vo, 253p, 50pl)	Saalfield	1903	Coolidge, C.M.	60-85	*
Montgomery, F.T.	Zip: Advens. of a Frisky Fox Terrier (1st, 8vo, 77p, ipcb, 4cp)	Saalfield	(1917)	Higgins, V.M.	50-80	*
Montgomery, L.M.	Anne of Avonlea (1st, sm8vo, 367p, p-o, green cl, col frn)	Page	1909	Gibbs, G.	100-165	
Montgomery, L.M.	Anne of Green Gables (1st, sm8vo, 429p, p-o, gilt, 8pl, PPP)	Page	1907	Claus, M.A.	120-160	
Montgomery, L.M.	Anne of Ingleside (1st, 12mo, 323p, col frn)	Stokes	1939	John, C.V.	45-60	*
Montgomery, L.M.	Anne of the Island (1st, sm8vo, 326p, col frn & p-o)	Page	1915	Taylor, H.W.	90-140	*
Montgomery, L.M.	Anne's House of Dreams (1st, 8vo, 346p, p-o, col frn)	Stokes	(1917)	Kirk, M.L.	90-140	
Montgomery, L.M.	Chronicles of Avonlea (1st, 8vo, 306p, p-o, gilt, col frn)	Page	1912	Gibbs, G.	100-165	
Montgomery, L.M.	Emily Climbs (1st, sm8vo, green cl, 312p, col frn & p-o by)	Stokes	1925	Kirk, M.L.	70-100	
Montgomery, L.M.	Emily of New Moon (1st, sm8vo, 351p, col frn & p-o by...)	Stokes	1923	Kirk, M.L.	70-100	
Montgomery, L.M.	Emily's Quest (1st, sm8vo, 310p, green cl, p-o & col frn by...)	Stokes	1927	Kirk, M.L.	65-80	*
Montgomery, L.M.	Further Chronicles of Avonlea (1st, sm8vo, 301p, 6pl)	Page	1920	Goss, J.	65-90	*
Montgomery, L.M.	Golden Road (1st, sm8vo, 369p, p-o, gilt, col frn)	Page	1913	Gibbs, G.	100-140	
Montgomery, L.M.	Jane of Lantern Hill (1st, sm8vo, 297p, col frn)	Stokes	1937	Costello, L.	65-90	*
Montgomery, L.M.	Kilmeny of the Orchard (1st, sm8vo, 256p, p-o, 4cp)	Page	1910	Gibbs, G.	100-165	
Montgomery, L.M.	Magic for Marigold (1st, sm8vo, 328p, p-o, col frn)	Stokes	1929	Shoemaker, E.C.	65-90	
Montgomery, L.M.	Mistress Pat (1st, 12mo, 338p, col frn)	Stokes	1935	Lawson, M.A.	45-65	*
Montgomery, L.M.	Pat of Silver Bush (1st, sm8vo, 329p, col frn)	Stokes	1933	Cooke, E.	60-80	*
Montgomery, L.M.	Rainbow Valley (1st, sm8vo, 341p, col frn & p-o by...)	Stokes	1919	Kirk, M.L.	70-100	
Montgomery, L.M.	Rilla of Ingleside (1st, sm8vo, 370p, col frn)	Stokes	(1921)	Kirk, M.L.	80-100	
Montgomery, L.M.	Story Girl (1st, sm8vo, 365p, gilt, p-o, col frn)	Page	1911	Gibbs, G.	90-135	
Montgomery, L.M.	Story Girl (1st UK, 8vo, red cl, 365p, p-o, col frn by...)	L: I. Pitman	1911	Gibbs, G.	70-90	*
Montgomery, R.G.	Broken Fang (1st, 8vo, red cl, 186p, 10cp, pep)	Donahue	(1935)	Hunt, L.B.	50-80	*

AUTHOR	TITLE	PUBLISHER	DATE	ARTIST	PRICE	LC
Montgomery, R.G.	Hill Ranch (1st {std}, 8vo, green cl, 200p, uncut, b/w)	Doubleday	(1951)	Cooney, B.	30-50	*
Montgomery, R.G.	Kildee House (1st {std}, 8vo, 209p, gilt, b/w, NH)	Doubleday	(1949)	Cooney, B.	45-70	R*
Montgomery, R.G.	Mister Jim (1st {std}, 8vo, cloth, 219p, b/w)	World	(1957)	Galdone, P.	30-50	*
Montgomery, R.G.	Troopers Three (1st {std}, sm8vo, 233p, col frn, pep)	Doubleday/Dor.	1932	Gay, Z.	20-30	*
Moodey, M.M.	Here Comes the Peddler! (1st, lg8vo, ipcb, [32]p, b/w, cep)	Holiday House	(1947)	Markham, K.	20-30	*
Moodie, S.	Roughing It in the Bush (1st, 8vo, 568p, uncut, teg, ticp)	L: G. Bell	1913	Stewart, R.	50-70	
Moon, C.	Painted Moccasins (1st, 8vo, 318p, green/gilt, col frn, pep)	Stokes	1931	Moon, C.	30-45	
Moon, G.	Arrow of Tee-May (1st {std}, sm8vo, 284p, col frn, b/w, pep)	Doubleday/Dor.	1931	Moon, C.	30-45	
Moon, G.	Book of Nah-Wee (1st {std}, sm sq4to, 59p, ibds, color, pep)	Doubleday/Dor.	1932	Moon, C.	30-45	
Moon, G.	Chi-Wee and Loki (1st {std}, 8vo, 208p, tan cl, col frn, 18pl)	Doubleday/Page	1926	Moon, C.	30-45	
Moon, G.	Daughter of Thunder (1st, sm8vo, 184p, col frn, pep)	MacMillan	1942	Moon, C.	25-40	
Moon, G.	Far-Away Desert (1st {std}, sm8vo, 261p, color, pep)	Doubleday/Dor.	1932	Moon, C.	30-45	
Moon, G.	Indian Legends in Rhyme (1st, sm4to, p-o, 54p, cp)	Stokes	(1917)	Moon, C.	100-130	
Moon, G.	Lost Indian Magic (1st, sm8vo, 301p, p-o, 8cp, pep)	Stokes	1918	Moon, C.	30-50	*
Moon, G.	Magic Trail (1st {std}, sm8vo, 234p, col frn, 13pl, pep)	Doubleday/Dor.	1929	Moon, C.	40-60	
Moon, G.	Missing Katchina (1st {std}, 8vo, 286p, col frn, b/w, pep)	Doubleday/Dor.	1930	Moon, C.	30-45	*
Moon, G.	Nadita (1st {std}, 8vo, 274p, col frn, 16pl, pep)	Doubleday/Dor.	1927	Moon, C.	30-45	
Moon, G.	Runaway Papoose (1st {std}, 8vo, 264p, col frn, b/w, pep, NH)	Doubleday/Dor.	1928	Moon, C.	35-50	
Moon, G.	Singing Sands (1st {std}, 8vo, 245p, col frn, b/w)	Doubleday/Dor.	1936	Moon, C.	25-40	
Moon, G.	Solita (1st {std}, 8vo, tan cl, 241p, col frn, b/w, pep)	Doubleday/Dor.	1938	Moon, C.	30-45	
Moon, G.	Tita of Mexico (1st, sm8vo, 213p, col frn, 4pl, pep)	Stokes	1934	Moon, C.	30-45	*
Moon, G.	White Indian (1st {std}, sm8vo, 221p, col frn, b/w, pep)	Doubleday/Dor.	1937	Moon, C.	25-45	*
Moon, G.	Wongo & the Wise Old Crow (1st, 8vo, 188p, pep, gilt, col frn)	Reilly/Lee	(1923)	Moon, C.	45-60	*
Moorat, Joseph	Thirty Old-Time Nursery Songs (1st, lg4to, 32p, ibds, col, pep)	L: Jack	[1895]	Woodroffe, P.	165-250	
Moorat, Joseph	Ye Booke of Nursery Rhymes (1st, lg ob4to, [47]p, ipcb, b/w)	L: G. Bell	(1895)	Woodroffe, P.	140-200	
Moorat, Joseph	Ye Second Book of Nursery Rhymes (1st, ob4to, ipcb, 54p, b/w)	L: G. Allen	1896	Woodroffe, P.	100-150	
Moore, Ann C.	Nicholas (1st, 12mo, red/gilt, 331p, col frn, pep, NH)	Putnam	1924	Van Everan, J.	60-80	
Moore, Ann C.	Nicholas & Golden Goose (1st, 12mo, 259p, blue/gilt, color, pep)	Putnam	1932	Van Everan, J.	25-40	*
Moore, C.C.	Night Before Christmas (8vo, [24]p, pep, 12 chromos)	L: Nister	[1885]	Lawson, L.	100-150	*
Moore, C.C.	Night Before Christmas (4to, ibds)	McLoughlin	[1888]	16 Chromos	120-160	
Moore, C.C.	Night Before Christmas (1st, ob8vo, [32]p, ibds, 12cp, pep)	Houghton	(1912)	Smith, J.W.	185-250	
Moore, C.C.	Night Before Christmas (folio, wraps, color)	Saalfield	[1915]	Brundage, F.	35-50	*
Moore, C.C.	Night Before Christmas (folio, wraps {shape bk}, color)	NY: Stecher	(1917)	Price, M.E.	35-50	
Moore, C.C.	Night Before Christmas (1st, 4to, ibds, [26]p, color)	Dutton	1928	MacKinstry, E.	80-130	R
Moore, C.C.	Night Before Christmas (1st AM, 8vo, p-o, 37p, 4cp, pep)	Lippincott	[1931]	Rackham, A.	140-185	
Moore, C.C.	Night Before Christmas (folio, wraps, unpag, color)	Saalfield	(1932)	Peat, F.B.	45-70	
Moore, C.C.	Night Before Christmas (4to, [16]p, wraps, color)	Whitman	(1935)	Ward, Keith	35-50	*
Moore, C.C.	Night Before Christmas (1st {std}, lg8vo, ibds, [43]p, col, DJ)	Harcourt	(1937)	Birch, R.	70-120	R
Moore, C.C.	Night Before Christmas (1st, 24mo, ibds, [37]p, color)	Holiday House	(1937)	Bischoff, I.	65-95	R*
Moore, C.C.	Night Before Christmas (1st, lg4to, [24]p, ipcb, color, pep)	Grosset/Dunlap	1937	Gooch, T.	65-80	R*
Moore, C.C.	Night Before Christmas (16mo, ibds, 62p, color)	Rand/McNally	(1938)	Biers, C.	20-30	
Moore, C.C.	Night Before Christmas (1st, 4to, ipcb, [18]p, color)	Whitman	1940	Masden, E.	25-45	*
Moore, C.C.	Night Before Christmas (1st, 4to, [24]p, ibds, color)	Winston	(1942)	Shinn, E.	35-50	
Moore, C.C.	Night Before Christmas (1st, 8vo, ibds, [16]p, color)	Dutton	(1944)	Paflin, R.	25-40	
Moore, C.C.	Night Before Christmas (1st, 4to, ibds, [25]p, color, pep)	Wilcox/Follett	1949	Friend, E.	30-50	*
Moore, C.C.	Night Before Christmas (1st, lg4to, ibds, [28]p, color, pep)	Grosset/Dunlap	1949	Weisgard, L.	65-90	*
Moore, C.C.	Visit from Saint Nicholas (1st, 16mo, 53p, gilt, pep, color)	MacMillan	1925	Whittemore, C.	40-65	R*
Moore, C.C.	Visit from Saint Nicholas (1st, 24mo, [42]p, ibds, pep, color)	MacMillan	1937	Hader, B.& E.	25-40	*
Moore, C.C.	Visit from Santa Claus (4to, ibds, 12cp, 24p)	Stokes/Allen	1887	Gerson, V.	170-220	
Moore, Colleen	Enchanted Castle (1st, 4to, 63p, ibds, 6 fp 1-color, cep)	Garden City	1935	Lawson, M.A.	30-50	
Moore, F.F.	Impudent Comedian (1st, 8vo, green cl, 274p, 10pl)	H. Stone	1897	Sauber, R.	45-70	
Moore, M.	Illegitimate Sonnets (1st {1st illus}, 8vo, gilt, 125p, pep)	NY: Twayne	(1950)	Gorey, E.	50-85	*
Moore, N.H.	Deeds of Daring... (1st, sm8vo, 300p, 6cp)	Stokes	(1906)	Gunn, Archie	20-30	*
Moore, T.	Lalla Rookh (1st, 4to, 179p, red/gilt, uncut, 16pl, pep)	MacVeagh/Dial	1930	Kutcher, B.	45-60	
Moorepark, C.	Alphabet of Animals (1st, 4to, ibds, 105p, b/w)	L: Blackie	1899	Moorepark, C.	160-200	
Moran, Jim	Sophocles the Hyena (1st, sm4to, red cl, 48p, 2-color)	Whittlesey	(1954)	Duvoisin, R.	45-65	*
Mord, W.	Four Champions/Great Britain & Ireland (1st, 4to, ibds, 16cp)	L: T.F. Unwin	[1905]	Robinson, C.	220-300	
Morgan, H.	Island Impossible (1st, 12mo, 206p, 5pl)	Little/Brown	1899	Pyle, Kath.	50-80	*
Morgenstern, Eliz.	Little Gardeners (1st AM, sm sq4to, 14p, color, p-o)	Whitman	1933	Bantzer, M.	45-60	*
Morier, J.	Hajji Baba of Ispahan (1st, 2volumes, tan/gilt, cvr by..)	Stone/Kimball	1895	Hazenplug, F.	60-80	
Morier, J.	Hajji Baba of Ispahan (1st, 4to, 403p, gilt, color, DJ)	Random	1937	Baldridge, C.L.	35-50	
Morley, C.	Don't Open Until Christmas (1st {std}, sm8vo, ibds, 26p, b/w)	Doubleday/Dor.	1931	Willard, H.	20-35	*
Morley, C.	Goldfish Under the Ice (1st {std}, sm8vo, 69p, 14 b/w, cep)	Doubleday/Dor.	1932	Wiese, K.	30-45	
Morley, C.	Where the Blue Begins (1st AM, 4to, blue/gilt, teg, 227p, 4cp)	Doubleday/Page	(1925)	Rackham, A.	125-160	
Morley, Charles	Peter, a Cat O' One Tail (1st AM, 8vo, 110p, ibds, b/w)	Putnam	1892	Wain, L.	200-300	
Morris, A.A.	Digging in Yucatan (1st {std}, 8vo, 279p, pep)	Doubleday/Dor.	1931	Charlot, J.	45-60	*
Morris, Alice T.	Child's Book of Empire (1st, 4to, unpag)	L: Blackie	[1914]	Robinson, C.	150-200	*
Morris, Alice T.	Elephant's Apology (1st, sm8vo, AEG, 152p, blue/gilt, b/w, cep)	L: Blackie	1899	Woodward, A.B.	80-120	
Morris, Alice T.	Old Friends/New Fables (1st AM, 4to, p-o, 52p, 21 ticp)	Dodge	[1916]	Moorepark, C.	150-180	
Morris, Alice T.	Old Friends/New Fables (1st, 4to, 51p, p-o, 21 ticp)	L: Blackie	1916	Moorepark, C.	165-180	
Morris, Alice T.	Troubles of Tatters (1st, lg8vo, 155p, b/w)	L: Blackie	1898	Woodward, A.B.	70-100	
Morris, C.	Trouble Woman (1st, 12mo, 58p)	Funk/Wagnalls	1904	Armstrong, M.	35-50	*

AUTHOR	TITLE	PUBLISHER	DATE	ARTIST	PRICE	LC
Morris, C.L.	Behind Moroccan Walls (1st, lg4to, 239p, 20pl)	MacMillan	1931	Artzybasheff, B.	65-80	
Morris, Ethel.	Ameliaranne Bridesmaid (1st, 8vo, ibds, unpag, p-o, color)	L: Harrap	(1946)	Pearse, S.B.	30-45	
Morris, Ethel.	Ameliaranne's Moving-Day (1st, 8vo, unpag)	L: Harrap	1950	Pearse, S.B.	45-60	*
Morris, F.	Deal in Wheat... (1st, 12mo, red/gilt, teg, 272p)	Doubleday/Page	1903	Remington, F.	45-70	
Morris, G.	Voice in the Rice (1st, 12mo, 158p, 6cp)	Dodd	1910	Leyendecker, J.C.	50-65	
Morris, K.	Book of Three Dragons (1st {std}, 4to, gilt, 206p, 8pl, pep)	Longmans	(1930)	Horvath, F.H.	75-100	R
Morris, M.	Bryn Mawr Stories (1st, 8vo, teg, green/gilt, illus by...)	Jacobs	(1901)	Green, E.S.	100-135	
Morris, M.	Bryn Mawr Stories (1st, 8vo, teg, green/gilt, cvr by...)	Jacobs	(1901)	Leyendecker, J.C.	100-135	
Morris, Wm.	Defense of Guenevere (1st, 8vo, teg, 310p, red/gilt, 24pl)	L: J. Lane	1904	King, J.	280-350	
Morris, Wm.	Doom of King Acrisius (1st, 8vo, teg, uncut, 82p, 11pl)	R.H. Russell	1902	Burne-Jones, E.	80-120	
Morris, Wm.	Early Poems of... (1st AM, 4to, 194p, teg, 16 ticp)	Dodge	(1914)	Harrison, F.	120-165	
Morris, Wm.	Early Poems of... (1st, 4to, blue/gilt, teg, 194p, 16 ticp, pep)	L: Blackie	1914	Harrison, F.	175-220	
Morris, Wm.	History of Over Sea (1st, 4to, 28p, ipcb)	R.H. Russell	1902	Rhead, L.	120-160	
Morris, Wm.	Life & Death of Jason (1st, 8vo, 332p, blue cl, 6cp)	Swarthmore Pr.	(1915)	Armfield, M.	75-90	
Morris, Wm.	Pygmalion & the Image (1st, 8vo, white/gilt, teg, 34p, 5pl)	R.H. Russell	1903	Burne-Jones, E.	70-100	*
Morris, Wm.	Wolf's Head & the Queen (1st, lg8vo, 243p, p-o, col frn, 13pl)	Scribner	1931	Grofe, N.	40-60	
Morrison, M.W.	Stories True & Fancies New (1st, 8vo, 208p, 11pl)	Estes & Laur.	(1898)	Bridgman, L.J.	60-80	*
Morrow, Eliz.	Beast, Bird & Fish (1st {std}, 4to, [59]p, pep)	Knopf	1933	D'Harnoncourt, R.	80-130	*
Morrow, Eliz.	My Favorite Age (1st, sm8vo, 220p, green cl, fp b/w, cep)	MacMillan	1943	Suba, S.	25-40	*
Morrow, Eliz.	Painted Pig (1st, 4to, ipcb, 32p, fp color, pep)	Knopf	1930	D'Harnoncourt, R.	80-120	R
Morrow, Eliz.	Pint of Judgment (1st {std}, 24mo, ibds, 43p, dep)	Knopf	(1939)	Suba, S.	25-40	*
Morrow, Eliz.	Rabbit's Nest (1st {std}, 24mo, 43p, ipcb, 1-color, pep)	MacMillan	1940	Willard, H.	35-50	*
Morrow, Eliz.	Shannon (1st {std}, 24mo, ipcb, 68p, fp b/w)	MacMillan	1941	Torrey, H.	25-45	*
Morrow, Honore	Ship's Monkey (1st, 8vo, 188p, color, pep, DJ)	Wm. Morrow	1933	Grant, G.	20-25	
Morrow, W.C.	Lentala/South Seas (1st, 8vo, grey cl, 278p, p-o, 7cp)	Stokes	(1908)	Dixon, M.	30-45	*
Morse, Eliz.	Chang of the Siamese Jungle (1st {std}, sm8vo, 195p, pep)	Dutton	(1930)	Berry, E.	20-40	*
Morse, Eliz.	Siamese Cat (1st, sm8vo, 62p, b/w)	Dutton	(1929)	Seymour, Ruth	25-40	*
Morse, L.B.	Road to Nowhere (1st, sm8vo, 236p)	Harper	1900	Morse, E.	45-60	*
Morton, J.B.	Who's Who in the Zoo (1st, 4to, 173p, 3cp)	L: Eyre/Spotts	1933	Aldin, C.	80-100	
Moses, H.S.	Here Comes the Circus (1st, lg8vo, 47p, color)	Houghton	1941	Suba, S.	45-60	*
Moses, M. (ed)	Treasury of Plays/Children (1st, 8vo, 550p, col frn, 8pl, pep)	Little/Brown	1921	Sarg, T.	50-80	
Mother Goose	Animal Mother Goose... (1st, 8vo, 168p, grey cl, b/w, pep)	Lothrop/Lee	(1921)	(Photos)	100-130	*
Mother Goose	Baby's Mother Goose (1st, sq16mo, [16]p, color, pep)	Grosset/Dunlap	1938	Stearns, S.	45-65	*
Mother Goose	Boyd Smith Mother Goose (1st, 4to, red/gilt, 223p, 20cp)	Putnam	(1919)	Smith, E.B.	180-220	
Mother Goose	Children's Mother Goose (1st, 4to, 120p, color, pep)	Reilly/Lee	(1921)	Donahey, Wm.	90-145	*
Mother Goose	Complete Mother Goose (1st, lg8vo, 227p, 11cp)	Stokes	(1909)	Betts, E.F.	165-230	
Mother Goose	Crooked Man (1st {std}, 12mo, [56]p, pep)	Longmans	(1940)	Barto, E.	25-40	*
Mother Goose	Denslow's Mother Goose (1st [1], 4to, ibds, [96]p, color, pep)	McClure	1901	Denslow, W.W.	375-500	R
Mother Goose	Denslow's Mother Goose (1st UK, 4to, unpag, color)	L: Chambers	1902	Denslow, W.W.	280-400	
Mother Goose	Disney's Mother Goose (1st, folio, ibds, [28]p, color, GGB)	Simon/Schuster	(1949)	Disney Studios	80-130	*
Mother Goose	Ella D. Lee Mother Goose (1st, 4to, 280p, 24cp, pep)	Donohue	(1918)	Lee, E.D.	100-145	
Mother Goose	Everychild's Mother Goose (1st, 12mo, 308p, 64 fp 1-color)	MacMillan	1918	Wilson, E.R.	50-80	*
Mother Goose	Familiar Rhymes of Mother Goose (1st, 8vo, 30cp, pcb)	L: Nister	1888	Loomis, C.B.	180-260	
Mother Goose	Family Mother Goose (1st, 12mo)	Harper	(1951)	Weisgard, L.	65-80	*
Mother Goose	Fanny Cory Mother Goose (1st, 4to, gilt, p-o, 74p, 12cp, pep)	Bobbs-Merrill	(1913)	Cory, F.	150-220	
Mother Goose	Favorite Mother Goose Rhymes (4to, ibds, color)	Platt/Munk	(1937)	Eulalie	45-65	*
Mother Goose	Favorite Nursery Rhymes (1st, 4to, 47p, 6cp)	Stokes	(1906)	Betts, E.F.	120-165	*
Mother Goose	Gay Mother Goose (1st, 4to, beige cl, 63p, fp color)	Scribner	(1938)	Francoise	50-80	*
Mother Goose	Golden Mother Goose (1st, folio, ibds, 96p, color, GGB)	Simon/Schuster	(1948)	Provensen, A.& M.	70-120	*
Mother Goose	J.W. Smith Mother Goose (1st, ob4to, 173p, p-o, 12cp, 5pl, pep)	Dodd	(1914)	Smith, J.W.	280-450	
Mother Goose	Jolly Mother Goose (1st, folio, [66]p, p-o, 19cp)	Rand/McNally	(1916)	Wright, B.F.	80-125	
Mother Goose	Little Mother Goose (1st, sm4to, bds, p-o, [30]p, 16cp)	McBride	1915	Pogany, W.	180-250	
Mother Goose	Little Mother Goose (1st, ob8vo, p-o, 176p, gilt, 12cp)	Dodd	(1918)	Smith, J.W.	180-225	
Mother Goose	Littlefolks' Mother Goose (1st, lg4to, 158p, p-o, b/w, pep)	Sears	(1926)	Rule, C.	35-50	*
Mother Goose	Lois Lenski's Mother Goose (1st, sm8vo, 83p, 2-color)	Harper	(1936)	Lenski, L.	80-120	*
Mother Goose	Masha's Stuffed Mother Goose (1st {std}, 4to, 64p, color)	Garden City	1946	Masha	50-70	*
Mother Goose	Mickey Mouse & Mother Goose (1st, 8vo, ibds, 136p, color, pep)	Whitman	(1937)	Disney Studios	70-90	*
Mother Goose	Most Popular Mother Goose Songs (1st, ob4to, 44p, ipcb, 39cp)	NY: Hinds	(1915)	Hill, M.B.	100-165	
Mother Goose	Mother Goose (1st, 12mo, yellow ibds, 48p, color)	L: Routledge	[1881]	Greenaway, K.	220-300	
Mother Goose	Mother Goose (4to, ibds, [48]p, color)	McLoughlin	[1882]	Greenaway, K.	180-250	
Mother Goose	Mother Goose (1st, 4to, ibds, 24cp)	Stokes	1891	Humphrey, M.	400-500	
Mother Goose	Mother Goose (1st, sm8vo, [64]p, color)	McLoughlin	(1909)	Bennett, C.H.	65-80	*
Mother Goose	Mother Goose (1st AM, 4to, p-o, 262p, 13cp)	Century	1913	Rackham, A.	220-300	R
Mother Goose	Mother Goose (1st, sm4to, grey cl, 159p, 13 ticp, pep)	L: Heinemann	(1913)	Rackham, A.	300-400	R
Mother Goose	Mother Goose (1st, 12mo, 173p, black cl, p-o, 12cp)	Dodd	1914	Smith, J.W.	400-600	
Mother Goose	Mother Goose (1st AM, 8vo, 255p, 16cp)	McKay	(1915)	Orr, M.S.	80-120	*
Mother Goose	Mother Goose (1st, 4to, teg, 255p, 16cp)	L: Harrap	(1915)	Orr, M.S.	160-200	
Mother Goose	Mother Goose (1st, lg4to, grey/gilt, [119]p, p-o, color)	Volland	(1915)	Richardson, F.	130-185	
Mother Goose	Mother Goose (4to, 108p, cp)	Donohue	(1915)	Richardson, F.	70-85	
Mother Goose	Mother Goose (1st, 4to, 16cp, DJ)	L: Coker	(1920)	Tarrant, M.	100-120	
Mother Goose	Mother Goose (sm4to, p-o, color)	Volland	(1921)	Eulalie	65-80	
Mother Goose	Mother Goose (1st, folio, ibds, color)	Volland	(1921)	Richardson, F.	100-150	

AUTHOR	TITLE	PUBLISHER	DATE	ARTIST	PRICE	LC
Mother Goose	Mother Goose (1st {std}, lg4to, 96p, black cl, color, pep)	Doubleday/Page	1924	Falls, C.B.	125-170	
Mother Goose	Mother Goose (1st AM, 12mo, 125p, 8cp)	Dent/Dutton	[1927]	Chadburn, M.	40-65	*
Mother Goose	Mother Goose (1st, lg4to, ipcb, [60]p, p-o, 8cp)	Saalfield	(1929)	Peat, F.B.	85-100	
Mother Goose	Mother Goose (1st AM, 8vo, 340p, 8cp)	Dutton	(1932)	Folkard, C.	100-140	
Mother Goose	Mother Goose (1st, 4to, 224p, ibds, 12pl)	L: Harrap	1932	Tawse, S.	80-100	
Mother Goose	Mother Goose (1st, lg4to, [28]p, 12 fp color, pep)	Whitman	(1934)	Newton/Horn	80-100	*
Mother Goose	Mother Goose (1st, folio, 144p, yellow cl, color, pep)	Heritage Press	(1936)	Duvoisin, R.	80-120	R*
Mother Goose	Mother Goose (1st, lg4to, 113p, color, pep)	Saalfield	(1938)	Lohman, F.D.	65-80	*
Mother Goose	Mother Goose (1st, 32mo, [41]p, color, pep)	Holiday House	(1939)	Ives, R.	45-65	*
Mother Goose	Mother Goose (1st, lg8vo, ibds, [52]p, color, pep)	Random	(1940)	Doane, P.	35-60	*
Mother Goose	Mother Goose (1st, 4to, 136p, color, pep)	Little/Brown	1940	Tenggren, G.	65-80	
Mother Goose	Mother Goose (1st, 4to, 380p, color, pep)	Whitman	(1941)	Snow, D.J.	30-45	*
Mother Goose	Mother Goose (1st {new ed}, 4to, ipcb, 112p, color, pep)	Heritage Press	(1943)	Duvoisin, R.	50-70	*
Mother Goose	Mother Goose (1st, sm sq8vo, green cl, 87p, color, pep, CH)	NY: OUP	(1944)	Tudor, T.	200-350	
Mother Goose	Mother Goose (1st, 12mo, [53]p, wraps, color)	Whitman	1944	Weihs, E.	30-50	*
Mother Goose	Mother Goose (1st, lg8vo, [40]p, color)	Wonder	(1946)	Hirsch, J.	45-65	*
Mother Goose	Mother Goose (1st, 12mo, [52]p, 2-color)	Whitman	1950	Vaughn, E.F.	30-50	*
Mother Goose	Mother Goose & her Goslings (1st, 8vo, 125p, color)	Chi: Stanton	(1918)	Higgins, V.M.	65-80	*
Mother Goose	Mother Goose ABC (4to, 14p, wraps, color)	Donohue	(1913)	Brundage, F.	65-80	*
Mother Goose	Mother Goose Bk. of Rhymes (narrow folio, wraps, color)	Stecher	1927	Price, M.E.	45-60	
Mother Goose	Mother Goose Book (ob4to, red cl, p-o, 11cp)	Whitman	(1915)	Perkins, L.F.	85-125	
Mother Goose	Mother Goose Jungle Book (1st, 4to, 63p, color)	Madison Co.	1903	Von Hofsten, H.	60-100	*
Mother Goose	Mother Goose Melodies (1st, lg8vo, 186p, 8cp)	Houghton	1879	Kappes, A.	220-300	
Mother Goose	Mother Goose Nursery Almanac (1st {std}, folio, ibds, 88p, col)	Garden City	1960	Palazzo, T.	70-120	*
Mother Goose	Mother Goose Nursery Rhymes (1st AM, 8vo, 363p, 24pl)	Dodge	(1909)	Hassall, J.	70-120	*
Mother Goose	Mother Goose Nursery Rhymes (4to, ibds, 16 fp color)	L: R. Tuck	[1910]	Attwell, M.L.	150-200	*
Mother Goose	Mother Goose Nursery Rhymes (1st {this pub}, sq8vo, 136p, b/w)	Platt/Peck	(1912)	McManus, B.	70-90	
Mother Goose	Mother Goose Nursery Rhymes (4to, ibds, 128p, 16cp)	L: Jack	[1915]	Orr, J.	150-180	
Mother Goose	Mother Goose Nursery Rhymes (1st, sm8vo, 256p, color, pep)	Winston	(1928)	Greene, J.	30-45	*
Mother Goose	Mother Goose Nursery Rhymes (1st, 8vo, 159p)	L: Collins	[1928]	Robinson, C.	70-100	*
Mother Goose	Mother Goose Nursery Rhymes (1st, 4to, 176p, 24cp)	L: Ward Lock	[1929]	Tarrant, M.	80-100	*
Mother Goose	Mother Goose Nursery Rhymes (1st, 8vo, red/gilt 385p, 11cp, pep)	Cupples	(1930)	Cooke, E.	75-130	
Mother Goose	Mother Goose Nursery Tales (12mo, 91p, green cl, p-o, color)	Altemus	(1904)	Neill, J.R.	75-90	*
Mother Goose	Mother Goose Picture Book (1st, 12mo, 119p, color, pep)	S. Gabriel	(1939)	Deane, E.	45-60	*
Mother Goose	Mother Goose Rhymes (1st, 8vo, 199p, b/w)	Baker/Tayler	1911	Knowles, M.	80-120	*
Mother Goose	Mother Goose Rhymes (1st, 8vo, 206p, cp)	NY: Noble	1917	Knowles, M.	70-110	R*
Mother Goose	Mother Goose Rhymes (1st, 4to, p-o, [120]p, 8cp, pep)	Platt/Munk	(1931)	Lenski/Eulalie	40-65	
Mother Goose	Mother Goose Rhymes (1st, 4to, red cl, [83]p, color, pep)	Platt/Munk	(1940)	Austin, M.	65-100	*
Mother Goose	Mother Goose Rhymes (1st, 12mo, [62]p, color)	Rand/McNally	(1942)	Wedde, J.	35-50	*
Mother Goose	Mother Goose Song Book (folio, ibds)	A.& C. Boni	(1926)	Harshberger, K.	70-100	
Mother Goose	Mother Goose Song Book (1st, ob4to, 100p, color)	Garden City	(1948)	Smith, Marion F.	70-120	*
Mother Goose	Mother Goose Stories (folio, ibds, 76p, 14 fp color)	L: Collins	[1928]	Newton, Ruth	50-70	
Mother Goose	Mother Goose in Holland (1st, 4to, 90p, color, pep)	Jacobs	(1912)	Post, M.A.	70-100	*
Mother Goose	Mother Goose in Silhouettes (1st, sq16mo, 78p, b/w)	Houghton	1907	Buffam, K.G.	65-90	*
Mother Goose	Mother Goose in Song & Rhyme (1st, 4to, 87p, 2-color, pep)	Graham	(1930)	Burd, C.M.	35-50	*
Mother Goose	Mother Goose's Nursery Rhymes (1st, sm8vo, 320p, col frn, b/w)	Lippincott	1900	Opper, F.	50-80	*
Mother Goose	Mother Goose's Nursery Rhymes (1st, 8vo, 364p)	L: Blackie	1909	Hassall, J.	65-80	*
Mother Goose	Mother Goose's Nursery Rhymes (1st, 8vo, 159p, ibds, color)	L: A&C Black	(1919)	Folkard, C.	100-145	
Mother Goose	Mother Goose: Best Known Rhymes (1st, lg4to, ibds, [34]p, color)	Saalfield	1933	Peat, F.B.	70-100	
Mother Goose	Mother Goose: Her Book (1st, lg8vo, 48p, color, pep)	Duffield	(1906)	Smith, H.L.	50-80	*
Mother Goose	Mother Goose: Her Own Book (1st, folio, [55]p, color, pep)	Reilly/Lee	(1932)	Royt, M.	100-160	*
Mother Goose	Mother Goose: Her Rhymes (lg8vo, blue cl, 142p, 6 ticp, pep)	Saalfield	(1915)	Matthews, H.B.	90-120	
Mother Goose	Mother Goose: Her Rhymes & Riddles (1st, 4to, [16]p, color)	Saalfield	1939	Peat, F.B.	65-80	*
Mother Goose	My First Mother Goose (1st, 8vo, ipcb, [32]p, color, pep)	Wilcox/Follett	(1946)	Gehr, M.	40-60	*
Mother Goose	Nursery Rhymes from Mother Goose (1st, lg4to, [48]p, color)	Scribner	1907	Wiederseim, G.	150-200	*
Mother Goose	Nursery Rhymes from Mother Goose (sm8vo, 111p, color)	Scribner	1916	Drayton, G.	140-200	*
Mother Goose	Old Mother Goose Nurs. Rhyme Bk. (16mo, 96p, 24 color, ibds)	T. Nelson	[1920]	Anderson, A.	70-100	
Mother Goose	Old Mother Goose in a New Dress (1st, ob4to, [45]p, color, pep)	NY: Laidlaw	1932	Hall, D.	100-150	*
Mother Goose	Old Mother Goose... (lg4to, p-o, 144p, red cl, 24cp, pep)	T. Nelson	[1926]	Anderson, A.	150-200	
Mother Goose	Original Melodies from... (1st, lg8vo, green cl, 96p, color, cep)	Phi: Davis Co.	(1938)	Deming, K.O.	65-90	*
Mother Goose	Picture Book Mother Goose (1st, sq8vo, [151]p, color)	Coward	(1930)	Hader, B.& E.	140-200	
Mother Goose	Piper's Son (1st {std}, 16mo, blue cl, [56]p, fp b/w, pep)	Longmans	(1942)	Barto, E.	30-50	*
Mother Goose	Pogany's Mother Goose (1st, 4to, [152]p, teg, gilt, col, pep)	Nelson	(1928)	Pogany, W.	140-200	
Mother Goose	Rainbow Mother Goose (1st, 8vo, 160p, 8cp, pep)	World	(1947)	Cassel, L.	70-100	R*
Mother Goose	Real Mother Goose (1st, lg4to, [132]p, color, pep)	Rand/McNally	(1916)	Wright, B.F.	80-130	*
Mother Goose	Real Mother Goose (4to, p-o, 33cp)	Rand/McNally	(1928)	Winter, M.	75-90	
Mother Goose	Real Mother Goose (lg4to, 134p, color)	Rand/McNally	(1941)	Wright, B.F.	45-65	*
Mother Goose	Romney Gay Mother Goose (1st, sq4to, ipcb, 56p, color, pep)	Grosset/Dunlap	(1936)	Gay, R.	65-90	*
Mother Goose	Songs from Mother Goose (1st, 4to, 83p, color)	MacMillan	1920	Enright, M.W.	100-150	*
Mother Goose	Stokes Wonder Bk. of Mother Goose (1st, 4to, 240p, 24cp, pep)	Stokes	(1919)	Choate/Curtis	60-85	*
Mother Goose	Tall Bk./Mother Goose (1st {std}, lg4to, 120p, ibds, color, pep)	Harper	(1942)	Rojankovsky, F.	65-90	*
Mother Goose	Teenie Weenie Man's Mother Goose (1st, 4to, 126p, 12cp, pep)	Reilly/Lee	(1921)	Donahey, Wm.	165-220	

AUTHOR	TITLE	PUBLISHER	DATE	ARTIST	PRICE	LC
Mother Goose	Tiny Book of Nursery Rhymes (1st, 12mo, ipcb, 61p, color, pep)	Harter	(1934)	Van Nortwick, C.	35-50	*
Mother Goose	True Mother Goose (1st, lg8vo, 138p)	Chi: Lamson	1896	McManus, B.	100-165	R*
Mother Goose	True Mother Goose (1st, lg8vo, 138p, b/w)	Mansfield/Wes.	1899	McManus, B.	80-150	*
Mother Goose	True Mother Goose (1st {this pub.}, 4to, 136p)	Wessels	1901	McManus, B.	80-100	
Mott, L.	White Darkness (1st, sm8vo, blue cl, 308p, 3pl by...)	Outing	1907	Schoonover, F.	30-45	
Moulton, L.C.	Arthur O'Shaughnessy (1st, 12mo, cvr by...)	Stone/Kimball	1894	Hallowell, G.H.	70-90	
Moulton, L.C.	In Childhood's Country (1st, 8vo, tan cl, 69p, uncut, 9pl, pep)	Copeland & Day	1896	Reed, E.	180-250	
Mourat, Joseph	Humpty Dumpty & other Songs (1st, sq4to, ibds, 32p, 7 fp b/w)	L: Blackwell	1920	Woodroffe, P.	180-220	
Mowbray, John	Dismal Jimmy of the Fourth (1st, 8vo, 215p, p-o, col frn, 3pl)	L: Cassell	1928	Brock, H.M.	25-40	*
Muehl, L.B.	My Name Is... (1st, sm8vo, tan cl, [55]p, 2-color)	Holiday House	(1959)	Watson, A.A.	20-35	*
Muir, J.	Stickeen... (1st, 12mo, tan cl, [73]p, designs, PPPa)	Houghton	1909	Rogers, B.	100-165	
Mukerji, D.G.	Chief of the Herd (1st {std}, 8vo, 168p, pep)	Dutton	(1929)	Blaine, M.	20-30	*
Mukerji, D.G.	Fierce Face (1st {std}, 8vo, 77p, green cl, pep, DJ)	Dutton	1936	Lathrop, D.	80-115	
Mukerji, D.G.	Gay Neck (1st, 8vo, 197p, t.e. blue, gilt, b/w, pep, DJ, NM)	Dutton	(1927)	Artzybasheff, B.	70-95	R
Mukerji, D.G.	Ghond the Hunter (1st {std}, 8vo, gilt, 204p, 3 dp pl)	Dutton	(1928)	Artzybasheff, B.	45-65	
Mukerji, D.G.	Master Monkey (1st {std}, 8vo, aqua/gilt, 261p, pep, 5pl)	Dutton	(1932)	Weber, F.	30-50	*
Mukerji, D.G.	Rama, Hero of India (1st {std}, 8vo, red/gilt, 219p, dep)	Dutton	(1930)	D'Aulaire, E.P.	45-60	*
Mulford, C.	Bar 20 (1st, 8vo, 382p, 2pl by...)	Outing	1907	Wyeth, N.C.	45-60	
Mulford, C.	Buck Peters, Ranchman (1st, 8vo, 367p, 4cp)	McClurg	1912	Dixon, M.	35-50	
Mulford, C.	Coming of Cassidy (1st, 12mo, 438p, 5cp)	McClurg	1913	Dixon, M.	50-65	
Mulford, C.	Hopalong Cassidy (1st, 8vo, 392p, 5pl)	McClurg	1910	Dixon, M.	50-70	
Muller, C.	How they Carried the Goods (1st, 4to, 318p, 4cp, 9pl)	Sears	(1932)	Tenggren, G.	35-50	
Muller, M.	Memories... (1st, 8vo, 135p, teg, gilt, p-o, 8pl)	McClurg	1902	Ostertag, B.	35-50	
Muller, M.	Memories... (2nd, lg8vo, blue/gilt, teg, cvr by...)	McClurg	1906	Armstrong, M.	80-125	
Munkittrick, R.K.	Farming (1st, 8vo, green pcb, [102]p, 1-color)	Harper	1891	Frost, A.B.	75-100	R
Munkittrick, R.K.	Moon Prince & Other Nabobs (1st, sm8vo, 340p, aqua/gilt, b/w)	Harper	1893	Various	45-65	*
Munro, E.S.	Topsy-Turvey Tales (1st, lg8vo, 180p, 6cp, 16 b/w)	L: J. Lane	1923	Robinson, W.H.	150-220	
Munroe, K.	Blue Dragon (1st, 12mo, 268p, grey cl, 7pl)	Harper	1904	Mears, W.E.	30-45	
Munroe, K.	Copper Princess (1st, 12mo, 237p, 12pl)	Harper	1898	Rogers, W.A.	30-50	*
Munroe, K.	Flamingo Feather (1st, lg8vo, p-o, 222p, 10cp)	Harper	(1915)	Schoonover, F.	45-70	
Munroe, K.	Forward March (1st, 8vo, 254p, 20pl)	Harper	1899	(Photos)	40-60	*
Munroe, K.	Fur-Seal's Tooth (1st, 12mo, 267p, green cl, b/w)	Harper	1894	Rogers, W.A.	60-80	
Munroe, K.	Ready Rangers (1st, 8vo, 334p, red cl, 6pl)	Lothrop	(1897)	Rogers, W.A.	35-50	*
Munroe, K.	Son of Satsuma (1st, 8vo, 306p, 8pl)	Scribner	1901	Zogbaum, R.F.	30-55	
Munroe, K.	Under the Great Bear (1st, 12mo, 313p, 12pl)	Doubleday/Page	1900	Giles, H.	30-45	*
Munroe, K.	White Conquerors (1st, 12mo, 326p, uncut, gilt, 8pl)	Harper	1893	Stacey, W.S.	35-50	
Murai, G.	Kibun Daizin (1st, sm8vo, 164p, 12pl)	Century	1904	Varian, G.	30-45	*
Murphey, E.A.	Nihal (1st, lg8vo, aqua cl, 39p, fp 2-color)	Crowell	(1960)	Keats, E.J.	45-65	*
Murphy, Ruby B.	Who's Who in Mother Goose Land (1st, 12mo, [31]p, ibds, 1-color)	Rand/McNally	1935	Combet, F.	30-45	
Murray, Gilbert	Airplane Spider (1st, 12mo, grey cl, 86p, p-o, 7cp)	Little/Brown	1920	Cady, H.	100-150	*
Murray, Gilbert	Airplane Spider (1st UK, 8vo, tan bds, p-o, 7cp)	L: A&C Black	1921	Cady, H.	100-150	
Murray, Hilda	Flower Legends for Children (1st, ob4to, ibds, 63p, 14cp, pep)	L: Longmans	1901	Eland, J.S.	100-140	*
Musselman, M.M.	I Married a Redhead (1st, sm8vo, 244p, b/w)	Crowell	(1949)	Galdone, P.	25-40	*
Musson, B.	Maisie & her Dog Skip in Fairyland (1st, 8vo, 165p, 8cp)	Harper	1903	Cory, F.	45-70	
Muter, Gladys N.	Duck's Adventure (1st, sm sq4to, color)	Volland	(1927)	Unknown	45-60	*
Muter, Gladys N.	Little Bim the Circus Boy (1st, ob folio, color)	Volland	(1924)	Scott, J.L.	120-175	*
Muter, Gladys N.	Mother Let Me Do It (1st {std}, 12mo, ibds, [36]p, color)	Volland	(1925)	Barney, M.W.	45-65	*
Muter, Gladys N.	Told in Our Neighborhood (1st, sm8vo, ibds, color)	Volland	(1925)	Foster, M.L.	35-50	*
Mutt, E.	Fairy Tales from Baltic Shores (1st, lg8vo, p-o, 382p, pep, 8cp)	Penn	(1930)	Berkowitz, J.	50-65	
Myers, Grace	Fishing Line (1st, ob8vo, yellow cl, [24]p, 1-color, pep)	Abingdon	1953	Galdone, P.	35-50	*
N/A	100 Best Fairy Tales (folio, ibds, 123p, 8cp, DJ)	Whitman	(1937)	Anderson, A.	100-140	
N/A	A Carol: Good King Wenceslas (4to, [26]p, wraps, p-o, 12 ticp)	L: L.B. Hill	[1920]	King, J.	300-450	
N/A	ABC Dogs (folio, ibds, [32]p, color, pep)	NY: W. Funk	1940	Tice, C.	120-180	
N/A	Adventures of Jack (narrow folio, wraps, [16]p, color)	Stecher	1921	Brundage, F.	40-60	
N/A	Aladdin (1st, 16mo, 61p, pep)	L: J.M. Dent	1895	Heath, S.H.	35-60	*
N/A	Aladdin (1st, sq4to, wraps, [15]p, chromos)	McLoughlin	1898	Unknown	35-60	*
N/A	Aladdin (1st, lg8vo, red cl, 39p, 8cp)	L: J. Lane	1924	Beaman, S.G.H.	25-40	*
N/A	Aladdin (1st AM, sm4to, 39p, 8cp)	McBride	1925	Beaman, S.G.H.	35-65	*
N/A	Aladdin & his Wonderful Lamp (12mo, 38p, color, pep)	NY: Nelson	1928	Anderson, A.	45-60	
N/A	Aladdin & his Wonderful Lamp (1st, 4to, [17]p, cloth, color, DJ)	MacMillan	1935	MacKinstry, E.	70-100	
N/A	Ali Baba & Aladdin (1st, 4to, 128p, ibds, 8cp)	L: Harrap	1918	Mackenzie, T.	160-200	
N/A	Ali Baba & the Forty Thieves (12mo, ibds, 4cp)	Nelson	[1920]	Anderson, A.	55-70	
N/A	All About Hansel & Gretel (sq16mo, ibds, p-o, 48p, 8cp)	Cupples	(1917)	Gruelle, J.	100-140	*
N/A	All About Red Riding Hood (sq16mo, ibds, p-o, 48p, color)	Cupples	(1916)	Gruelle, J.	100-140	*
N/A	All About Story Book (1st, sq4to, 63p, orange/gilt, color)	Cupples	(1929)	Various	70-100	*
N/A	All Shakespeare's Tales (1st, lg8vo, p-o, 453p, 11cp)	Stokes	(1911)	Kirk, M.L.	70-100	
N/A	American Stage of Today (1st, folio, ipcb, designs by...)	Collier	(1910)	Bradley, W.	120-165	
N/A	Animal Alphabet (4to, 24p, color, wraps, pep)	Whitman	[1930]	Cady, H.	100-160	*
N/A	Animals on the Farm (1st, 4to, linen, [20]p, 8cp)	Saalfield	1936	Burd, C.M.	25-40	
N/A	Arabian Nights (1st, 12mo, 424p, AEG, blue/gilt, b/w, cep)	L: Longmans	1898	Ford, H.J.	180-220	
N/A	Arabian Nights (1st, 4to, 472p, green cl, b/w)	L: Newnes	1899	Various	100-120	*
N/A	Arabian Nights (1st, 8vo, 501p, 4cp by...)	L: Routledge	1904	Cooper, A.W.	120-160	

AUTHOR	TITLE	PUBLISHER	DATE	ARTIST	PRICE	LC
N/A	Arabian Nights (1st, 8vo, 501p, cvr by...)	L: Routledge	1904	King, J.	120-160	
N/A	Arabian Nights (folio, unpag)	L: Blackie	(1906)	Stratton, H.	70-100	*
N/A	Arabian Nights (1st, 8vo, 328p, 5cp)	Nister/Dutton	[1907]	Paget, W.	65-90	*
N/A	Arabian Nights (1st, lg8vo, 435p)	L: Constable	(1908)	Various	65-80	*
N/A	Arabian Nights (1st, lg8vo, 339p, teg, p-o, 12cp, pep, SC)	Scribner	1909	Parrish, M.	160-200	R
N/A	Arabian Nights (1st, 12mo, 318p, cp)	Baker/Taylor	1910	Emerson/D'Emo	25-40	*
N/A	Arabian Nights (8vo, 352p, 29cp)	L: Blackie	[1910]	Stratton, H.	45-75	*
N/A	Arabian Nights (8vo, 435p, col frn)	Dodge	(1910)	Various	20-35	*
N/A	Arabian Nights (1st AM, sm4to, p-o, 299p, teg, 20 ticp)	Dodd	1912	Bull, Rene	225-300	
N/A	Arabian Nights (1st, sm4to, 299p, p-o, gilt, 20 ticp)	L: Constable	1912	Bull, Rene	250-400	
N/A	Arabian Nights (1st, 8vo, 412p, teg, gilt, 12cp)	L: A&C Black	(1913)	Folkard, C.	130-180	
N/A	Arabian Nights (1st, lg8vo, teg, 294p, gilt, 15cp)	L: Harrap	1913	Orr, M.S.	80-100	
N/A	Arabian Nights (1st AM, 8vo, 294p, 15cp)	Holt	1913	Orr, M.S.	65-80	
N/A	Arabian Nights (1st, 8vo, 295p, 6cp)	L: Allen/Unwin	(1913)	Soper, G.	60-80	
N/A	Arabian Nights (1st, lg8vo, 293p, p-o, 16cp, pep)	Rand/McNally	(1914)	Winter, M.	60-80	
N/A	Arabian Nights (8vo, 299p, green cl, p-o, 7 ticp, later)	L: Constable	[1917]	Bull, Rene	130-180	
N/A	Arabian Nights (1st, sm8vo, 420p, cp)	Jacobs	(1918)	Lister, W.H.	20-30	*
N/A	Arabian Nights (1st, sm8vo, 371p, col frn, b/w)	MacMillan	1923	Pape, Eric	30-50	
N/A	Arabian Nights (1st, 8vo, 257p, cp)	Winston	(1924)	Bolton, A.H.	20-30	*
N/A	Arabian Nights (1st, 4to, 240p, teg, white/gilt, 12 ticp)	L: Hodder	(1924)	Detmold, E.J.	250-400	
N/A	Arabian Nights (1st AM, lg8vo, blue/gilt, 297p, p-o, 12 ticp)	Dodd	(1925)	Detmold, E.J.	180-265	
N/A	Arabian Nights (1st, lg8vo, 242p, col frn, pep)	Sears	(1928)	Becker, C.	25-40	
N/A	Arabian Nights (1st, 4to, 308p, black cl, p-o, 16cp, pep)	Penn	(1928)	Sterrett, V.	200-280	
N/A	Arabian Nights (1st, 12mo, grey cl, 402p, 11 fp b/w)	Appleton/Cent.	(1936)	Artzybasheff, B.	40-65	*
N/A	Arabian Nights (1st, 8vo, 308p)	Longmans	1946	Bock, V.	30-45	*
N/A	Arabian Nights (1st, 8vo, 327p, color)	Grosset/Dunlap	(1946)	Goodenow, E.	25-40	*
N/A	Arabian Nights' Entertainment (1st, 8vo, 430p, p-o, 4cp, pep)	Harper	(1916)	Rhead, L.	35-60	
N/A	Around the House (1st, 4to, ibds, 96p, 63 illus)	Worthington	1888	Greenaway, K.	80-120	
N/A	At Home (sq8vo, 56p, ipcb)	L: Marcus Ward	(1880)	(Chromos)	70-100	
N/A	Aucassin & Nicolette (1st, 12mo, teg, vellum, 4pl)	L: J. Murray	1902	Housman, L.	120-160	
N/A	Aucassin & Nicolette (1st, 8vo, 91p, teg, 12pl, vellum)	L: Routledge	1905	James, G.	70-85	
N/A	Aucassin & Nicolette (1st, 8vo, 72p, color)	Dent/Dutton	1910	Armfield, M.	50-65	*
N/A	Aucassin & Nicolette (1st, lg8vo, 131p, teg, 6cp)	L: A&C Black	1911	Anderson, A.	70-120	
N/A	Aucassin & Nicolette (1st, lg4to, 69p, gilt, 17pl)	L: Melrose	1914	Smith, E.L.	100-150	
N/A	Aucassin & Nicolette (1st AM, 4to, p-o, unpag, 13 ticp)	Brentano's	[1917]	Paul, E.	90-130	
N/A	Aucassin & Nicolette (1st, 4to, 120p, p-o, teg, 13 ticp)	L: Harrap	[1917]	Paul, E.	120-170	
N/A	Aucassin & Nicolette (1st, narrow 12mo, 106p, color)	Holiday House	1936	Simpson, M.	60-85	R*
N/A	Aunt Louisa's Choice Present (sq4to, AEG)	Warne	(1880)	24 Chromos	90-140	
N/A	Baby's Animal Book (sm8vo, ibds, 10cp)	Platt/Munk	1929	Eulalie	45-60	
N/A	Baby's Birthday Book (sq16mo, ibds, A.E. pink, color)	L: Marcus Ward	[1885]	Greenaway, K.	150-200	
N/A	Baby's Record (1st, 4to, green/silver, 12cp)	Stokes	1898	Humphrey, M.	450-600	
N/A	Banbury Cross... (1st, 8vo, unpag, red cl, 29pl)	L: Dent	1893	Woodward, A.B.	45-65	*
N/A	Beauty & the Beast (1st, 4to, 57p, gilt, 10cp)	L: Sampson	[1875]	Boyle, E.V.	400-600	
N/A	Beauty & the Beast (4to, wraps, 6cp)	L: Warne	[1895]	Brock, H.M.	80-120	
N/A	Beauty & the Beast Pict. Book (4to, yel cl, 24cp)	Dodd	[1915]	Crane, W.	100-150	*
N/A	Bedtime Story Book (lg4to, wraps, 16cp)	L: Birn Bros.	(1943)	Wood, Lawson	60-80	
N/A	Bettina's Bonnet (sq12mo, ibds, 10 fp color)	Hearst	1915	Drayton, G.	85-100	*
N/A	Black Doggies (16mo, red cloth, silhouttes)	L: Blackie	[1907]	Robinson, C.	250-350	
N/A	Book for Little People (4to, ibds, 16 chromos)	L: Nister	[1890]	Hardy, E.S.	200-300	
N/A	Book of Fairy Tales (1st, 4to, gilt, unpag, pep, 24cp)	L: Warne	[1914]	Brock, H.M.	200-285	
N/A	Book of Job (1st, sm4to, teg, gilt, 103p, uncut, 16pl)	L: Dent	1895	Fell, H.G.	100-150	
N/A	Book of Job (1st, 4to, teg, 102p, gilt, 8 ticp)	L: C. Palmer	1916	Tongue, M.C.	85-130	
N/A	Book of New Fairy Tales (4to, grey bds, p-o, [72]p, 7cp by...)	Dodge	[1910]	Dixon, A.A.	70-100	
N/A	Book of Nursery Rhymes (1st AM, lg8vo, 91p, cp)	Doub./McClure	1897	Bedford, F.D.	100-140	
N/A	Book of Nursery Rhymes (1st, 4to, ibds, 91p, 21cp)	L: Methuen	1897	Bedford, F.D.	165-220	
N/A	Book of Pets (lg4to, ibds, 12cp by...)	L: Gardner	1897	Humphrey, M.	350-500	
N/A	Book of Pets (lg4to, ibds, 12cp by...)	Gardner/Dar.	1897	Tucker, E.S.	350-500	
N/A	Book of Psalms (1st, sm folio, teg, gilt, 282p, 24cp)	L: Hutchinson	(1912)	Pape, F.	100-150	
N/A	Book of Ruth (1st AM, 4to, tan/gilt, 16 designs by...)	Dodd	1896	MacDougall, W.B.	150-200	
N/A	Breman Band (1st, 16mo, [42]p, ibds, color, pep)	MacMillan	1927	Dobias, F.	30-45	*
N/A	Briar Rose Book of Old Fairy Tales (4to, p-o, 159p, cp)	L: Jack	[1915]	Anderson, A.	80-120	
N/A	Bumps & Thumps (sq4to, pict tan cloth, color)	Caldwell	(1903)	Bridgman, L.J.	85-110	
N/A	Chicken Little & Little Half Chick (1st, sq12mo, ibds, color)	MacMillan	1927	Hader, B.& E.	45-60	*
N/A	Children All (4to, ibds)	Lothrop	(1898)	6 Chromos	100-140	
N/A	Children at Play in Many Lands (1st, lg ob4to, [16]p, color)	Volland	1922	Rae, J.	100-150	*
N/A	Children's Bible (1st, 4to, black cl, p-o, 15cp)	Scribner	1922	Various	60-80	
N/A	Children's Story Garden (1st, 8vo, 247p, blue cl, col frn, 9pl)	Lippincott	1920	Wireman, K.	30-50	
N/A	Christmas Card (8vo, wraps, 8cp)	Dutton	1883	Waugh, Ida	60-90	
N/A	Christmas Story from Saint Mark (1st, 24mo, ibds, unpag, color)	Volland	(1921)	Rae, J.	45-60	*
N/A	Cinderella (sm4to, ipcb)	Dutton	(1890)	5 Chromos	70-95	
N/A	Cinderella (16mo, ibds, cp)	Reilly/Britton	1907	Bell, R.A.	65-80	
N/A	Cinderella (16mo, ibds, p-o)	Reilly/Britton	1908	Neill, J.R.	80-100	

AUTHOR	TITLE	PUBLISHER	DATE	ARTIST	PRICE	LC
N/A	Cinderella (4to, ipcb, teg, 62p, gilt, 12 ticp)	L: Hodder	[1915]	Sowerby, M.	90-120	
N/A	Cinderella (1st AM, 4to, ibds, 100p, DJ)	Lippincott	(1919)	Rackham, A.	200-250	
N/A	Cinderella (sm folio, 16p, wraps, 8cp)	Harter	(1931)	Peat, F.B.	40-55	
N/A	Cinderella (1st, 4to, blue cl, [17]p, color, DJ)	MacMillan	1934	Sewell, H.	85-100	R
N/A	Cinderella (folio, [22]p, color)	Whitman	1935	Bennett, J.C.	35-50	*
N/A	Cinderella (1st, 24mo, [41]p, ipcb, 2-color)	Holiday House	[1938]	Scott, H.	45-60	*
N/A	Cinderella (1st, 4to, ibds, [32]p, color, pep)	Garden City	1938	Weisgard, L.	65-80	*
N/A	Cinderella (1st, lg8vo, [16]p, color, pep)	Grosset/Dunlap	(1939)	Stenberg-Masolle	35-50	*
N/A	Cinderella (1st, ob4to, [14]p, color)	McLoughlin	1943	McKean, E.C.	45-60	*
N/A	Cinderella (lg8vo, [33]p, color)	Wilcox/Follett	(1948)	Stolberg, D.	30-45	*
N/A	Cinderella's Picture Book (1st, 4to, 8cp)	J. Lane	(1897)	Crane, W.	120-160	
N/A	Comin' Thro the Rye (1st, lg8vo, p-o, 6cp)	Bobbs-Merrill	(1909)	Underwood, C.F.	30-45	
N/A	Coridon's Song (1st, 12mo, green/gilt, AEG, 163p, b/w, cep)	L: MacMillan	1894	Thomson, H.	90-135	
N/A	Daisy Days (4to, ipcb)	Fiske Co.	1890	(Chromos)	65-90	
N/A	Dandy-Andy Book (lg8vo, 24p, p-o, 12cp)	Nelson	[1907]	Anderson, A.	65-90	
N/A	Daniel in the Lion's Den (1st, 16mo, brown cl, 100p, 19cp)	L: Richards	1903	Wilson, P.	70-100	
N/A	Death & Burial of Poor Cock Robin (4to)	McLoughlin	(1880)	(Lithos)	75-120	
N/A	Diamond Fairy Book (1st, 8vo, 310p, gilt, AEG, b/w, dep)	L: Hutchinson	(1897)	Millar, H.R.	100-165	
N/A	Diamonds & Toads (4to, linen wraps, 6cp)	McLoughlin	[1875]	Greenaway, K.	165-220	
N/A	Dick Whittington & his Cat (4to, ibds, color)	L: Hodder	[1910]	Hassall, J.	80-120	
N/A	Dick Whittington & his Cat (1st, 24mo, ipcb, [38]p, 2-color)	Holiday House	1937	Eichenberg, F.	65-80	R*
N/A	Dick Whittington & his Cat (1st, 4to, ibds, [32]p, color, CH)	Scribner	1950	Brown, Marcia	65-100	*
N/A	Droll Doings (1st, 4to, [64]p, red cl, 40 color)	L: Blackie	[1905]	Neilson, H.B.	120-170	*
N/A	Early Work of Aubrey Beardsley (1st, lg4to)	L: J. Lane	1899	Beardsley, A.	200-300	
N/A	Ecclesiasticus... (1st, 4to, black/gilt, 165p, teg, 16cp)	L: J. Lane	1927	Brunton, V.	70-120	
N/A	Everyman & other Plays (1st, 4to, black cl, 201p, 18cp)	L: Chapman	1925	Austen, J.	100-135	
N/A	Fair Women from Vogue (4to, 28p, tan buckram)	Fashion Co.	1894	Armstrong, M.	120-175	
N/A	Fairy Ship (lg sq4to, wraps, 12p)	J. Lane	(1890)	Crane, W.	80-120	
N/A	Fairy Tale Omnibus (1st, 4to, red cl, col frn, 4cp)	L: Collins	[1915]	Anderson, A.	65-80	*
N/A	Fairy Tales in Other Lands (1st, 12mo, 96p, ibds, 4cp)	L: Cassell	[1925]	Folkard, C.	70-100	
N/A	Fairy Tales/Arabian Nights (1st, 12mo, 287p, col frn, 12pl)	L: Dent	1899	Robinson, T.H.	65-80	*
N/A	Faithful Friends (4to, pict red cl, 6pl by...)	L: Blackie	[1913]	Rackham, A.	250-300	
N/A	Famous Animal Tales (1st, lg8vo, 158p, 8cp, pep)	L: Harrap	(1935)	Aris, E.	70-100	
N/A	Famous Love Songs (1st, lg8vo, blue cl, p-o, 17cp)	Bobbs-Merrill	(1909)	Underwood, C.F.	50-65	
N/A	Father Tuck's Bird ABC (4to, wraps, [14]p, 4cp)	L: R. Tuck	1895	Unknown	70-100	
N/A	Favorite Fairy Tales (1st, 8vo, 355p, gilt, teg, 16pl)	Harper	1907	Newell, P.	170-220	
N/A	Favorite Fairy Tales (1st, folio, ibds, [28]p, color, GGB)	Simon/Schuster	(1949)	Rojankovsky, F.	45-60	*
N/A	Favourite Fairy Tales (lg4to, ibds, 16 color)	L: Nelson	[1929]	Anderson, A.	70-100	
N/A	First Graces (1st, 16mo, blue cl, 47p, p-o, color, pep)	NY: OUP	1955	Tudor, T.	100-140	
N/A	First Prayers (1st, 16mo, 48p, blue cl, p-o, color)	NY: OUP	(1952)	Tudor, T.	90-130	
N/A	Foolish Fox (1st, 16mo, ibds, p-o, 92p, color)	Altemus	(1904)	Neill, J.R.	40-60	R
N/A	Four Feet by Two (lg8vo, ibds)	L: Nister	[1890]	8 Chromos	70-120	
N/A	Funny Bunny ABC (1st AM, folio, p-o, color)	NY: Sully	[1912]	Anderson, A.	80-100	
N/A	Funny Little Darkies (1st, sq4to, wraps, 6cp)	McLoughlin	[1890]	(Lithos)	200-300	
N/A	Gingerbread Boy (ob12mo, 32p, bds, p-o)	Winston	(1918)	Richardson, F.	35-50	
N/A	Gingerbread Boy (folio, wraps, 16 color)	Whitman	(1941)	Peat, F.B.	40-60	
N/A	Golden Book/Songs & Ballads (4to, 198p, green/gilt, 24 ticp)	L: Hodder	[1915]	Brickdale, E.F.	85-130	
N/A	Golden Fairy Book (1st, lg8vo, 312p, AEG, b/w, gilt)	L: Hutchinson	[1890]	Millar, H.R.	100-150	
N/A	Golden Goose (1st, sq16mo, ibds, [42]p, color)	MacMillan	1928	Seaman, M.L.	50-80	
N/A	Golden Goose Book (1st, sq4to, green cl, unpag, 8cp)	L: Warne	(1905)	Brooke, L.L.	70-100	*
N/A	Golden Ship... (1st, 8vo, 98p, green bds, gilt, b/w)	(London)	1900	Woodward/Bell	120-160	*
N/A	Goldilocks (folio, wraps, color)	Saalfield	1919	Brundage, F.	45-60	
N/A	Goldilocks & Three Bears (1st, ob4to, [14]p, color)	McLoughlin	1943	McKean, E.C.	35-65	*
N/A	Good Dog Book (1st, 8vo, blue cl, 264p, p-o, 5cp)	Houghton	1924	Tenggren, G.	40-60	
N/A	Great Big Animal Book (1st, folio, ibds, color, GGB)	Simon/Schuster	1950	Rojankovsky, F.	35-50	
N/A	Happy Day Begins (lg sq4to, wraps, [12]p, color)	Saalfield	1931	Scott, J.L.	45-60	
N/A	Hind in the Wood (1st, 4to, wraps, 5cp)	L: Routledge	[1875]	Crane, W.	100-140	
N/A	History of Ali Baba (1st, 24mo, 63p, b/w)	L: Dent	1895	Fell, H.G.	65-80	*
N/A	History of Cinderella (1st, 24mo, 63p, gilt, teg, uncut, 14pl)	L: Dent	1894	Fell, H.G.	80-120	
N/A	Holly Berries (1st, 4to, 48p, ibds)	Dutton	(1881)	Waugh, Ida	70-100	
N/A	Homes in the Wilderness (1st, 8vo, 74p, p-o, maps)	W.R. Scott	(1939)	Stewart, M.W.	35-50	*
N/A	Hop O' My Thumb (4to, wraps, 8cp)	L: Warne	[1910]	Brock, H.M.	60-90	
N/A	House that Jack Built (1st {std}, 4to, [32]p, 3-color, dep, CH)	Harcourt	(1958)	Frasconi, A.	75-110	R*
N/A	Humpty-Dumpty (4to, wraps, fp color)	L: Blackie	[1910]	Hassall, J.	60-80	
N/A	Hunchback of Notre-Dame (1st, 424p, 16cp)	Dodd	1928	Wheelwright, R.	45-60	*
N/A	Ideal Heads (1st, folio, brown/gilt, AEG, 20cp)	Sunshine	1890	Various	250-400	
N/A	In Cat & Dog Land (lg4to, 36p, ibds, 12pl)	L: R. Tuck	[1900]	Wain, L.	200-275	
N/A	In the Beginning... (1st, 4to, cloth, color, DJ)	NY: OUP	(1941)	Daugherty, J.	45-60	
N/A	Indian Fairy Book (1st, 8vo, 303p, 8cp, pep)	Stokes	(1916)	Choate/Curtis	65-100	
N/A	Indian Fairy Book (8vo, 303p, 8cp)	L: Richards	[1920]	Choate/Curtis	70-90	
N/A	Intimations of Immortality... (4to, 12cp)	L: J.M. Dent	[1913]	Neilson-Gray	100-150	
N/A	Irish Fairy Tales (1st, 12mo, 236p, 2pl)	L: T.F. Unwin	1892	Yeats, J.B.	250-320	

AUTHOR: 100

AUTHOR	TITLE	PUBLISHER	DATE	ARTIST	PRICE	LC
N/A	Jack & the Beanstalk (1st, 12mo, [31]p, color)	NY: Sully	(1920)	Stecher, W.F.	30-50	*
N/A	Jack & the Beanstalk (1st, sq16mo, ibds, color, pep)	MacMillan	1927	Dobias, F.	35-50	
N/A	Jack & the Beanstalk (1st, 24mo, ibds, [39]p, decor by...)	Holiday House	(1935)	Parker, Arvilla	60-90	R*
N/A	Jack Frost Arrives on Butternut Hill (1st, 12mo, color)	Whitman	1929	Cady, H.	50-65	
N/A	Jack the Giant Killer (1st, 24mo, 82p, teg, uncut, 12pl, pep)	L: J.M. Dent	1894	Bell, R.A.	65-85	
N/A	Jolly Old Sports (folio, ibds, p-o, 36cp)	L: Blackie	[1912]	Adams, F.	150-200	
N/A	Just Because of You (1st, 12mo, ibds, color)	Volland	(1925)	Myers, M.H.	35-50	*
N/A	King Albert's Book (1st, 4to, 187p, pcb, 17 ticp)	L: Hodder	(1914)	Various	100-165	
N/A	King Arthur & His Knights (1st, lg8vo, 256p, p-o, 4cp)	Winston	(1927)	Godwin, F.	30-45	
N/A	Kingdom & Power & Glory (1st, 4to, 170p, brown cl, DJ)	Knopf	1929	Daugherty, J.	40-65	
N/A	Kittens (1st, folio, [12]p, wraps, 6cp)	Saalfield	1937	Peat, F.B.	45-60	
N/A	Land of Don't-Want-To (lg8vo, 212p, blue cl, p-o, 10cp)	Rand/McNally	(1923)	Winter, M.	45-60	
N/A	Land of Enchantment (1st, 4to, 144p, olive/gilt, 14pl)	L: Cassell	1907	Rackham, A.	220-265	
N/A	Liberty Belles (1st, folio, brown/gilt, 8cp)	Bobbs-Merrill	(1912)	Christy, H.C.	130-170	
N/A	Little Book of Bores (1st, 12mo, 52p, b/w)	Scribner	1906	Herford, O.	45-65	
N/A	Little Bright Eyes (1st, sm4to, unpag, ipcb)	Juvenile Pub.	1890	Various	40-60	
N/A	Little Housekeepers (folio, wraps, 8cp)	Saalfield	1934	Peat, F.B.	45-60	
N/A	Little Red Riding Hood (12mo, ibds, 57p, fp color)	Reilly/Britton	(1908)	Neill, J.R.	80-100	*
N/A	Love Songs Old & New (1st, sm4to, p-o, unpag, 18cp)	Bobbs-Merrill	(1909)	Underwood, C.F.	70-90	
N/A	Lovely Woman (1st, 4to, p-o, 9cp)	Bobbs-Merrill	(1910)	Various	100-150	
N/A	Maisie-Daisie Book (lg8vo, 24p, p-o, 12cp)	Nelson	[1918]	Anderson, A.	50-75	
N/A	Man in the Moon (1st, 4to, bds, 31p, p-o, 12cp, pep)	L: Blackie	[1918]	Harrison, F.	120-165	
N/A	May & November Correspondence (1st, bds, p-o & frn by...)	Houghton	1928	Green, E.S.	35-50	
N/A	Merry Children's Nursery Rhymes (1st, 4to, ipcb, t-i frn)	L: Nister	[1890]	Various	75-100	
N/A	Merry Times (4to, ipcb, AEG)	Fiske Co.	1890	8 Chromos	80-120	
N/A	Merry Times (sm folio, 14p, wraps, 12 fp color)	L: R. Tuck	[1900]	Wain, L.	150-200	*
N/A	My High School Days (8vo, teg, green/gilt, color)	Caldwell	(1908)	Bridgman, L.J.	50-65	
N/A	My Picture Scrap Book (folio, ibds)	L: Nister	(1880)	(Chromos)	130-165	
N/A	Night Before Christmas & Jingles (sq8vo, 48p, p-o, 12cp by...)	Hurst	(1908)	Morgan, Ike	130-165	*
N/A	No Place Like Home (ob. folio, ibds)	J. Knight	1891	6 Chromos	60-100	
N/A	Nursery Rhyme Picture Book (1st, ipcb, [32]p, p-o, 15cp, pep)	L: Warne	[1905]	Brooke, L.L.	130-165	
N/A	Nursery Rhymes (1st, 16mo, grey bds, 48p, p-o, 8cp, pep)	L: Warne	[1917]	Brooke, L.L.	60-80	
N/A	Nursery Rhymes (1st, 4to, 46p, ibds, 23 color)	L: Jack	(1919)	Fraser, C.L.	80-120	
N/A	Nursery Rhymes (1st, 8vo, 340p, blue/gilt, p-o, 44cp, pep)	L: Ward Lock	[1920]	Tarrant, M.	100-140	*
N/A	Oaktree Fairy Book (1st, 8vo, p-o)	Little/Brown	1905	Bonte, W.	50-70	
N/A	Odyssey of Homer (1st, sm4to, 332p, teg, gilt, 20cp)	Hale-Cushman	(1930)	Flint, W.R.	80-120	*
N/A	Old English Songs (1st, sm8vo, 163p, AEG, green/gilt)	L: MacMillan	1894	Thomson, H.	50-75	
N/A	Old English Songs & Ballads (1st, lg4to, 198p, 24 ticp)	L: Hodder	[1915]	Brickdale, E.F.	160-235	
N/A	Old English Songs & Dances (1st, sm folio, [62]p, ibds, color)	L: Longmans	1902	Robertson, W.G.	250-450	
N/A	Old English Songs & Dances (folio, ibds, color)	L: Hamish	[1910]	Robertson, W.G.	200-300	
N/A	Old Fairy Tales (1st, 4to, gilt, 11cp)	L: Warne	(1914)	Brock, H.M.	100-150	
N/A	Old Mother Hubbard (4to, ibds, 12cp)	L: Blackie	(1900)	Adams, F.	100-140	
N/A	Old Nursery Rhymes (4to, 142p, beige cl, 24cp)	L: Nelson	[1931]	Wood, Lawson	150-200	
N/A	Old Songs/French & English (1st, 4to, p-o, 63p, 24cp)	Penn	1923	Cramer, Rie	100-150	
N/A	Old Time Rhymes (1st, lg4to, gilt, 36 ticp, pep)	L: Blackie	1913	Adams, F.	300-350	
N/A	Old Woman & her Pig (1st, 24mo, [41]p)	Holiday House	[1937]	Tinker, J.H.	25-40	*
N/A	Oranges & Lemons (1st, 4to, [26]p, wraps, 8cp)	L: Warne	[1913]	Brooke, L.L.	100-145	
N/A	Oriental Fairy Tales (1st, 8vo, p-o, 627p, gilt, 16 ticp)	Duffield	1923	Cramer, Rie	85-120	
N/A	Our Amateur Circus (1st, ob8vo, black/gilt, color)	Harper	1892	McVickar, H.W.	120-165	
N/A	Peter Pan's ABC (4to, ibds, p-o, gilt, 25cp)	L: H. Frowde	[1912]	White, F.	180-260	
N/A	Peter Rabbit Story Book (lg8vo, 62p, col frn)	Platt/Munk	(1935)	Willis, B.G.	70-100	*
N/A	Picture & Rhyme Book (folio, wraps, 20 color)	Saalfield	1941	Peat, F.B.	60-80	
N/A	Picture Story Book (folio, [18]p, wraps, shape bk., 12 color)	Saalfield	1929	Peat, F.B.	40-60	
N/A	Prince Ahmed/Fairy Perie Banou (1st, 8vo, 118p, bds, p-o, 5cp)	L: Gay/Hancock	(1915)	Robinson, C.	125-160	
N/A	Psalms of David (1st, lg8vo, red cl, 16pl)	Revell	1900	Rhead, L.	65-100	
N/A	Puss In Boots (4to, cloth, p-o, 8cp)	Warne	[1900]	Brock, H.M.	60-85	
N/A	Puss in Boots (lg4to, 8cp)	Warne	[1907]	Brock, H.M.	35-50	*
N/A	Puss in Boots (1st, 24mo, [38]p)	Holiday House	1936	Eichenberg, F.	35-50	*
N/A	Puss in Boots (1st, sq16mo, [41]p, color, pep)	MacMillan	1937	Dobias, F.	65-90	*
N/A	Puss in Boots (1st, 16mo, [59]p, fp color)	McLoughlin	(1941)	Sari	20-30	*
N/A	Queen Mab's Fairy Realm (1st, 8vo, AEG, 310p, gilt, 27pl, pep)	L: G. Newnes	1901	Various	170-220	
N/A	Quiver of Love (1st, sq8vo, 152p, green cl, 8 ticp)	L: Marcus Ward	1876	Crane/Greenaway	250-350	
N/A	Quiver of Love (1st, sq8vo, 152p, green cl, 8 ticp)	L: Marcus Ward	1876	Greenaway/Crane	250-350	
N/A	Reign of King Oberon (1st, 8vo, 338p, col frn, pep)	L: Dent	(1902)	Robinson, C.	100-140	
N/A	Rhymes of Old Times (1st, 8vo, 107p, teg, 16 ticp)	L: Medici	1925	Tarrant, M.	50-70	
N/A	Rhymes without Reason (1st, sm4to, yellow cl, 16 fp color)	L: Eyre/Spotts	1944	Peake, M.	90-130	*
N/A	Ride a Cock-Horse (1st, 4to, 29p, ibds, color)	L: Chatto	1940	Peake, M.	300-450	
N/A	Robber Kitten (1st, 16mo, 96p, gilt, color)	Altemus	(1904)	Neill, J.R.	65-80	
N/A	Robin Hood (1st, lg8vo, olive cl, 115p, 12cp)	Stokes	(1906)	Perkins, L.F.	75-90	
N/A	Robin Hood (1st, lg8vo, green/gilt, p-o, teg, 362p, 8cp, pep)	McKay	1917	Wyeth, N.C.	140-200	
N/A	Romance of Tristam & Isoude (4to, color)	Brentano's	[1910]	Paul, E.	50-75	*
N/A	Rosie-Posie Book (4to, p-o, blue cl, 12cp)	T. Nelson	[1917]	Anderson, A.	50-80	

AUTHOR	TITLE	PUBLISHER	DATE	ARTIST	PRICE	LC
N/A	Sermon on the Mount (1st, 4to, unpag, 18cp, DJ)	Winston	1946	Shinn, E.	25-40	
N/A	Seven Voyages of Sinbad (1st, 12mo, 71p, ipcb, color)	Holiday House	1939	Reed, P.	60-90	R*
N/A	Seven Voyages of Sinbad the Sailor (1st AM, 4to, 71p, 8cp)	McBride	1926	Beaman, S.G.H.	50-80	*
N/A	Silly Hare (sm4to, ipcb)	McLoughlin	[1893]	4 Chromos	65-80	
N/A	Simple Addition (lg8vo, p-o, blue cl, unpag)	McLoughlin	[1880]	21 Chromos	100-150	
N/A	Sinbad the Sailor (1st, 8vo, 279p)	L: Lawrence	1896	Strang/Clark	50-75	*
N/A	Sinbad the Sailor (1st, lg4to, 223p, gilt, bds, p-o, 23 ticp)	L: Hodder	(1914)	Dulac, E.	450-600	
N/A	Sleeping Beauty (1st, 12mo, ibds, 40p, color, pep)	NY: Nelson	1928	Anderson, A.	50-75	
N/A	Sleeping Beauty Picture Book (4to, 24cp)	Dodd	[1915]	Evans, E.	100-150	
N/A	Sleeping Partners (1st, 4to, blue bds, 20cp)	L: Eyre/Spotts	1929	Aldin, C.	180-220	
N/A	Snow White & Rose Red (sq4to, wraps, [16]p, color)	Stecher	1929	Brundage, F.	35-50	
N/A	Some British Ballads (1st, 4to, 170p, blue/gilt, 16 ticp, pep)	L: Constable	1919	^Eackham, A.	160-200	
N/A	Some Old Nursery Tales (lg8vo, ibds, 98p, 12cp)	L: Blackie	[1920]	Adams, F.	100-150	
N/A	Song of Songs... (1st, 4to, 16p, gilt, teg, buckram, 12pl)	L: Chapman	1897	Fell, H.G.	120-145	
N/A	Song of Songs... (1st AM, narrow 4to, [21]p, 6pl)	R.H. Russell	1902	Burne-Jones, E.	80-120	*
N/A	Song of Songs... (1st, sm4to, 66p, teg, brown/gilt, 10 ticp)	L: P.L. Warner	1913	Flint, W.R.	65-80	
N/A	Songs of Bryn Mawr College (1st, ob4to, 137p, p-o, ibds)	C.W. Beck	1903	Green, E.S.	100-165	
N/A	Spin Top Spin (1st AM, 4to, ibds, [32]p, color)	MacMillan	1929	Eisgruber, E.	75-100	
N/A	Stories Merry & Wise (4to, ibds)	McLoughlin	[1898]	6 Chromos	70-100	
N/A	Stories from Arabian Nights (lg8vo, 205p, 8cp, pep, later)	Garden City	[1932]	Dulac, E.	65-80	
N/A	Stories from Aunt Judy (8vo, teg, 268p, 8cp, pep)	L: Bell	1913	Everett, E.	65-90	
N/A	Stories from the Odyssey (16mo, 118p, brown/gilt, p-o)	L: Jack	[1910]	Robinson, W.H.	70-100	*
N/A	Story Book (4to, ibds, 248p, 6cp)	Whitman	[1930]	Attwell, M.L.	85-130	
N/A	Story of Little Red Hen (1st, folio, red ipcb, [16]p, b/w)	Whitman	(1935)	Ward, Keith	85-120	*
N/A	Story of Noah's Ark (1st, 4to, ibds, [88]p, color)	Garden City	(1955)	Palazzo, T.	40-65	*
N/A	Story of Simple Simon (4to, ibds, 12cp)	L: Blackie	[1920]	Adams, F.	90-150	
N/A	Story of the Firemen (4to, wraps)	McLoughlin	[1908]	(Chromos)	70-100	
N/A	Stuffed Owl (1st AM, sm8vo, bds, p-o, 236p, 6pl, pep)	Coward	(1930)	Beerbohm, M.	30-45	*
N/A	Tales & Talks About Animals (4to, 29cp, pcb, p-o)	Caldwell	[1901]	Unknown	50-80	*
N/A	Tales from Arabian Nights (1st, 8vo, 128p, p-o, 8cp)	L: Dent	(1914)	Robinson/Curtis	100-130	*
N/A	Tales from Arabian Nights (sm4to, 190p, gilt, 20 ticp, later)	L: Hodder	[1920]	Dulac, E.	150-180	
N/A	Tales from Arabian Nights (1st, lg8vo, 340p, 48cp)	L: Ward Lock	1920	Jackson, A.E.	70-100	*
N/A	Tales of Hoffman (4to, 207p, 10cp)	L: Harrap	(1932)	Laboccetta, M.	120-160	
N/A	Tall Book of Nursery Tales (1st, 8vo, ibds, color, DJ)	A.& W. Guild	(1944)	Rojankovsky, F.	60-80	*
N/A	Three Bears (8vo, [16]p, linen, color)	McLoughlin	1888	Andre, R.	80-120	*
N/A	Three Bears (4to, wraps, 8cp)	L: Warne	[1900]	Brooke, L.L.	45-70	
N/A	Three Bears (12mo, 63p, color)	Rand/McNally	(1937)	Price, M.E.	30-45	*
N/A	Three Bears (1st, sm4to, [18]p, color, pep)	Grosset/Dunlap	(1938)	Tedder, E.	25-40	*
N/A	Three Billy Goats Gruff (1st, sq16mo, ibds, color)	MacMillan	1927	Dobias, F.	20-30	*
N/A	Three Little Kittens (4to, wraps)	McLoughlin	[1880]	6 Chromos	120-165	
N/A	Three Little Kittens (lg4to, ibds)	L: Nister	[1890]	5 Chromos	50-75	
N/A	Three Little Kittens (1st, 16mo, [42]p, ibds, color)	MacMillan	1928	Wiese, K.	35-50	
N/A	Three Little Kittens (1st, 12mo, [32]p, color)	Rand/McNally	1938	Brice, Tony	20-30	*
N/A	Three Little Kittens (1st, 4to, ipcb, [16]p, color, dep)	Saalfield	1940	Peat, F.B.	35-60	*
N/A	Three Little Pigs (tall 4to, ibds, color)	L: Blackie	[1925]	Adams, F.	75-100	
N/A	Three Little Pigs (1st, ob8vo, [48]p, color, pep)	Whitman	(1933)	Jordan, S.	25-45	*
N/A	Three Little Pigs (folio, wraps, 16p, color)	Saalfield	1933	Peat, F.B.	40-65	
N/A	Three Little Pigs (1st, 12mo, [47]p, color)	Rand/McNally	1941	Brice, T.	20-35	*
N/A	Told in the Twilight (1st, 8vo, tan cloth, 9pl)	Herrick	(1898)	McManus, B.	65-80	
N/A	Tom/Piper's Son (4to, ibds, [32]p, 12cp, pep)	L: Blackie	[1920]	Adams, F.	75-100	
N/A	Two Jolly Mariners (ob4to, ibds, 24cp)	L: Blackie	[1917]	Orr, S.	150-185	
N/A	Wedding Bells (4to, blue/silver, AE silver, 4 chromos)	L: R. Tuck	[1900]	Brundage, F.	100-150	
N/A	Whose Little Kitty are You? (folio, ibds, color)	NY: S. Gabriel	1913	Brundage, F.	40-60	
N/A	Wonder Stories of Herodotus (1st, 8vo, 12cp)	Harper	1900	Fell, H.G.	80-110	
N/A	Wonderful Kittens (sq4to, ibds, 5cp)	Worthington	1883	Weir, H.	130-180	
N/A	World's Fairy Book (1st, lg8vo, 256p, 12cp)	L: Harrap	(1930)	Orr, M.S.	100-130	
N/A	Yankee Doodle (4to, wraps, 6 chromos by...)	McLoughlin	[1872]	Nast, Thos.	150-200	
N/A	Young Folks Birthday Book (sq12mo, 188p, fp color)	L: Hills & Co.	[1905]	Aldin, C.	100-130	*
N/A	Yours Truly (ob folio, ibds, b/w)	(NY)	1907	Various	80-130	
N/A	Zig Zag Fables (1st, ob4to, 36p, ibds, color)	L: Wells/Gard.	1897	Shepherd, J.A.	150-200	
Nash, Dorothy	Moon Baby (4to, ibds, p-o, 87p, 9 ticp)	L: Jarrolds	[1905]	Nash/Rudge	100-150	*
Nash, Ogden	Bad Parents' Garden of Verse (1st, 8vo, 132p, b/w)	Simon/Schuster	1936	Birch, R.	45-60	*
Nash, Ogden	Christmas that Almost Wasn't (1st {std}, 8vo, 63p, 8 fp color)	Little/Brown	(1957)	Nash, L.	40-65	*
Nash, Ogden	Cricket of Carador (1st {std}-{1st bk}, 8vo, 165p, col frn, pep)	Doubleday/Page	1925	Rule, C.	50-75	
Nash, Ogden	Happy Days (1st, 8vo, 161p, p-o, b/w)	Simon/Schuster	1933	Soglow, Otto	70-100	*
Nash, Ogden	Musical Zoo (1st {std}, 4to, 47p, cloth, b/w, DJ)	Little/Brown	1947	Owen, Frank	40-65	
Nash, Ogden	You Can't Get There from Here (1st {std}, 12mo, gilt, 190p, b/w)	Little/Brown	(1957)	Sendak, M.	90-140	
Nast, Thomas	Christmas Drawings/Human Race (1st, 4to, [67]p, fp b/w)	Harper	1890	Nast, Thos.	180-260	*
Nathan, J.	Ameliaranne/Big Treasure (1st AM, 8vo, red cl, p-o, color)	McKay	[1932]	Pearse, S.B.	45-60	
Nathan, Rbt.	Fiddler in Barly (1st, 8vo, 137p, 6 woodcuts)	L: Heinemann	1927	Leighton, C.	50-75	*
Nathan, Rbt.	Jonah... (1st, 8vo, 212p, 5 engravings)	Knopf	1934	Artzybasheff, B.	30-45	*
Nathan, Robert	Snowflake & the Starfish (1st {std}, 8vo, 68p, fp 2-color)	Knopf	(1959)	Weisgard, L.	30-45	

AUTHOR: 102

AUTHOR	TITLE	PUBLISHER	DATE	ARTIST	PRICE	LC
Naylor, James B.	Witch Crow & Barney Bylow (1st, sm4to, ipcb, 118p, 6cp)	Saalfield	1906	Williams, C.B.	35-50	*
Neally, A.	Baby Days... (1st, 4to, bds)	Dutton	1890	Waugh, Ida	150-200	
Neidlinger, W.H.	Small Songs for Small Singers (1st, lg4to, 57p, ibds, color)	NY: Schirmer	1896	Bobbett, Walt.	35-50	*
Nella	Prince Babillon (1st, 8vo, 131p, uncut, gilt, color)	Kennerley	[1910]	Robinson, C.	120-165	
Nelson, M.W.	Pinky Finds a Home (1st, 12mo, 118p, col frn)	Holiday House	(1940)	Heyneman, A.	20-30	*
Nesbit, E.	As Happy as a King (1st, ob8vo, unpag)	L: Marcus Ward	[1896]	Praeger, S.R.	80-100	*
Nesbit, E.	Bastable Children (1st {this fmt}, 8vo, 293p, col frn)	Coward	(1929)	Browne/Blam	45-60	*
Nesbit, E.	Book of Dogs (1st, obsm4to, 55p, b/w)	Dutton	1898	Austen, W.	160-220	*
Nesbit, E.	Book of Dragons (1st, 8vo, 290p, gilt, teg, 8 fp color by...)	L: Harper	1901	Fell, H.G.	400-500	
Nesbit, E.	Book of Dragons (1st, 8vo, teg, 290p, blue/gilt, 16 b/w by...)	L: Harper	1901	Millar, H.R.	400-500	
Nesbit, E.	Cat Tales (1st, 12mo, 62p, grey cl, cp)	Nister/Dutton	[1904]	Watkin, I.	120-160	*
Nesbit, E.	Children's Shakespeare (1st AM, 8vo, gilt, 76p, ibds, 11 fp b/w)	Altemus	(1900)	Brundage, F.	65-80	
Nesbit, E.	Daphne of Fitzroy Street (1st AM, 12mo, 417p, col frn by..)	Doubleday/Page	1909	Cootes, F.G.	65-90	
Nesbit, E.	Enchanted Castle (1st AM, 12mo, 297p, 8pl)	Harper	1908	Millar, H.R.	180-220	*
Nesbit, E.	Enchanted Castle (1st, 8vo, 352p, red/gilt, 46pl)	L: T.F. Unwin	1908	Millar, H.R.	160-250	
Nesbit, E.	Five Children (1st, 8vo, 306p, col frn)	Coward	1930	Millar/Blam	70-100	*
Nesbit, E.	Five Children and It (1st, 8vo, 301p, teg, red/gilt, 46pl)	L: T.F. Unwin	1902	Millar, H.R.	120-200	*
Nesbit, E.	Five of Us & Madeline (1st, 8vo, 310p, red cl)	L: T.F. Unwin	1925	Unwin, N.S.	100-150	
Nesbit, E.	Harding's Luck (1st, 8vo, gilt, 16 b/w, teg)	L: Hodder	1909	Millar, H.R.	200-300	
Nesbit, E.	Harding's Luck (1st AM, 12mo, green cl, 308p, 16pl)	Stokes	(1910)	Millar, H.R.	150-230	
Nesbit, E.	House of Arden (1st, 8vo, 349p, teg, red/gilt, 33pl)	L: T.F. Unwin	1908	Millar, H.R.	250-320	
Nesbit, E.	House of Arden (1st AM, 12mo, 349p, gilt, 33pl)	Dutton	1909	Millar, H.R.	180-250	
Nesbit, E.	Incomplete Amorist (1st AM, 12mo, p-o, 356p, 8pl)	Doubleday/Page	1906	Underwood, C.F.	70-100	*
Nesbit, E.	Magic City (1st, 12mo, red/gilt, teg, 333p, 26pl)	L: MacMillan	1910	Millar, H.R.	200-300	
Nesbit, E.	Magic World (1st, 12mo, teg, 280p, red/gilt, 24pl)	L: MacMillan	1912	Millar, H.R.	250-350	
Nesbit, E.	New Treasure Seekers (1st, 8vo, red/gilt, 328p, teg, 33pl)	L: T.F. Unwin	1904	Browne/Baumer	160-200	
Nesbit, E.	Nine Unlikely Tales for Children (8vo, gilt, 279p)	L: T.F. Unwin	1901	Bowley/Millar	140-180	*
Nesbit, E.	Oswald Bastable & Others (1st, 12mo, teg, 369p, gilt, 22pl)	L: Wells/Gard.	(1905)	Brock/Millar	200-300	
Nesbit, E.	Phoenix & the Carpet (1st, lg8vo, blue/gilt, 321p, col frn, teg)	L: Newnes	(1904)	Millar, H.R.	250-350	
Nesbit, E.	Pomander of Verse (1st, sm8vo, gilt, teg, 88p, cvr by..)	J. Lane	1895	Housman, L.	130-165	
Nesbit, E.	Pug Peter (1st, 4to, 64p, teg, blue cloth, color)	L: A. Cooke	(1905)	Rountree, H.	200-260	
Nesbit, E.	Pussy & Doggy Tales (1st, 12mo, 132p, b/w)	L: J.M. Dent	1899	Kemp-Welch, L.	140-200	*
Nesbit, E.	Railway Children (1st, 8vo, 309p, uncut, teg, gilt, 20pl)	L: Wells/Gard.	(1906)	Brock, C.E.	250-400	
Nesbit, E.	Red House (1st AM, 12mo, 274p, green cl)	Harper	1902	Keller, A.I.	70-110	
Nesbit, E.	Royal Children of English History (1st, 4to, 94p, 10cp)	L: R. Tuck	(1896)	Brundage/Bowley	180-260	*
Nesbit, E.	Story of Five Rebellious Dolls (1st, ob folio, ibds, 8cp, pep)	L: Nister	(1904)	Hardy, E.S.	250-375	
Nesbit, E.	Story of the Amulet (1st, 12mo, teg, 374p, red/gilt, 48pl)	L: T.F. Unwin	1906	Millar, H.R.	140-180	
Nesbit, E.	Story of the Treasure Seekers (1st, 8vo, 296p, AEG, 17pl)	L: T.F. Unwin	1899	Browne/Baumer	250-300	
Nesbit, E.	The Wouldbegoods (1st AM, sm8vo, 313p, 16pl)	Harper	1901	Birch, R.	160-220	
Nesbit, E.	These Little Ones (1st, 8vo, 210p, teg, 10pl)	L: G. Allen	1909	Pryse, S.	140-200	
Nesbit, E.	Wet Magic (1st, 12mo, teg, red/gilt, 274p, 12pl)	L: T. Laurie	(1913)	Millar, H.R.	135-180	
Nesbit, E.	Wonderful Garden... (1st, 8vo, teg, 402p, red/gilt, 26 b/w)	L: MacMillan	1911	Millar, H.R.	200-250	
Nesbit, W.D.	A Friend or Two (1st, 16mo, ibds, color)	Volland	(1915)	Unknown	65-80	*
Nesbit, W.D.	As Children Do (1st, 12mo, 96p, decor by...)	Volland	(1929)	Friend, E.	45-60	*
Nesbit, W.D.	Friend O'Mine (1st, 12mo)	Volland	(1912)	Unknown	35-60	*
Nesbit, W.D.	In Tumbledown Town (1st, sm8vo, ibds, color)	Volland	(1926)	Gee, J.	50-80	*
Nesbit, W.D.	Jolly Kid Book (1st, ob4to, ibds, [12]p, color)	Volland	(1926)	Meyers, M.H.	120-170	
Nesbit, W.D.	Land of Make-Believe (1st, 8vo, green cl, 98p, 5pl)	Harper	1907	Unknown	30-50	*
Nesbit, W.D.	Oh Skin-nay! (1st, ob folio, [125]p, illus)	Volland	(1913)	Briggs, C.A.	70-90	*
Nesbit, W.D.	Sermons in Song (1st, 12mo, 96p)	Volland	(1929)	Unknown	30-50	*
Nesbit, W.D.	Trail to Boyland (1st, 8vo, tan/gilt, uncut, 163p, 5pl)	Bobbs-Merrill	(1904)	Vawter, W.	30-45	*
Nesbit, W.D.	When a Feller Needs a Friend (1st, lg4to, ibds, [96]p, 3-color)	Volland	(1914)	Briggs, C.A.	90-135	*
New, C.M.	Woman Reigns (1st, 16mo, 112p, teg, cvr by...)	Bowen-Merrill	1895	Rogers, B.	20-30	*
Newberry, C.T.	April's Kittens (1st {std}, 4to, [32]p, gilt, color, pep, CH)	Harper	1940	Newberry, C.T.	70-115	*
Newberry, C.T.	Babette (1st {std}, lg8vo, 32p, pep, color)	Harper	1937	Newberry, C.T.	50-70	*
Newberry, C.T.	Barkis (1st {std}, sm ob4to, 31p, color, pep, CH)	Harper	1938	Newberry, C.T.	70-120	*
Newberry, C.T.	Cousin Toby (1st {std}, 8vo, [32]p, yellow bds, pep)	Harper	1939	Newberry, C.T.	70-100	
Newberry, C.T.	Herbert the Lion (1st, ob4to, [41]p, pep, color)	Brewer/Warren	1931	Newberry, C.T.	80-120	*
Newberry, C.T.	Herbert the Lion (1st {thus}-{std}, ob4to, ibds 64]p, pep, col)	Harper	1939	Newberry, C.T.	70-100	*
Newberry, C.T.	Kitten's ABC (1st {std}, lg4to, ibds, [36]p, color, DJ)	Harper	(1946)	Newberry, C.T.	70-100	
Newberry, C.T.	Lambert's Bargain (1st {std}, 4to, 31p, b/w, pep, DJ)	Harper	1941	Newberry, C.T.	50-80	
Newberry, C.T.	Marshmallow (1st {std}, lg ob4to, [31]p, color, CH)	Harper	(1942)	Newberry, C.T.	70-120	
Newberry, C.T.	Mittens (1st {std}, sm4to, ibds, [28]p, pep, 12cp)	Harper	1936	Newberry, C.T.	40-60	*
Newberry, C.T.	Pandora (1st {std}, folio, ibds, p-o, [35]p, b/w)	Harper	(1944)	Newberry, C.T.	70-100	
Newberry, C.T.	T-Bone the Baby-Sitter (1st, ob4to, [30]p, color, CH)	Harper	1950	Newberry, C.T.	65-100	*
Newbery, F.E.	Everyday Honor (1st, 12mo, 429p, b/w)	Jacobs	1898	Waugh, Ida	20-35	*
Newbolt, H.	Book of the Happy Warrior (1st, 8vo, 284p, 8cp)	L: Longmans	1917	Ford, H.J.	65-80	*
Newbolt, H.	Drake's Drum... (1st, 4to, green cl, 143p, 12cp)	L: Hodder	[1914]	McCormick, A.D.	65-100	
Newbolt, H.	Taken From the Enemy (1st, 8vo, teg, 170p, p-o, 8cp)	L: Chatto	1911	Leake, G.	25-45	
Newell, D.	American Animals (1st, 8vo, blue cl, 80p, 10cp, pep)	Volland	(1929)	Newell, D.	60-80	
Newell, Hope	Steppin & Family (1st, 8vo, 198p, color, pep)	NY: OUP	(1942)	Peck, A.M.	65-80	*
Newell, P.	Hole Book (1st, 4to, p-o, [51]p, blue cloth, 24 fp color, PPP)	Harper	(1908)	Newell, P.	200-300	R

AUTHOR	TITLE	PUBLISHER	DATE	ARTIST	PRICE	LC
Newell, P.	Peter Newell's Pictures & Rhymes (1st, ob8vo, tan cl, p-o, 50pl)	Harper	1899	Newell, P.	170-250	
Newell, P.	Rocket Book (1st, lg8vo, [48]p, p-o, 23 fp color)	Harper	(1912)	Newell, P.	180-260	R
Newell, P.	Shadow Show (1st, ob8vo, ipcb, 72p, color)	Century	1896	Newell, P.	250-300	
Newell, P.	Slant Book (1st, 8vo, [47]p, ibds, 22 fp color)	Harper	(1910)	Newell, P.	200-300	R
Newell, P.	Topsys & Turveys (1st, ob4to, bds, p-o, 31cp)	Century	1893	Newell, P.	250-350	
Newell, P.	Topsys & Turvys Number 2 (1st, oblg8vo, ipcb)	Century	(1894)	Newell, P.	200-300	
Newman, I.	Fairy Flowers (1st AM, 8vo, ibds, 196p, 15 ticp, pep)	Holt	(1926)	Pogany, W.	130-180	
Newman, I.	Fairy Flowers (1st, 4to, ibds, 160p, 15 ticp, pep)	L: H. Milford	(1926)	Pogany, W.	160-200	
Newman, I.	Fairy Flowers (sm4to, 160p, bds, 15 ticp)	NY: OUP	1929	Pogany, W.	100-130	
Newman, I.	Flowers Facts & Fables (1st, 4to, 141p, ibds, 7cp, cep)	NY: Snellgrove	1937	Pogany, W.	80-100	
Newman, I.	Legend of the Lilac (1st, 4to, ibds, [23]p, 4cp)	Whitman	1926	Pogany, W.	45-60	
Newman, I.	Legend of the Tulip... (1st, 4to, [24]p, ibds, 5cp)	Whitman	(1926)	Pogany, W.	45-70	
Newman, I.	Shades of Blue (8vo, blue/silver, 96p, 16cp)	NY: Harrison	(1927)	Fouts, H.E.	65-90	
Newman, I.	Wee Miss Violet... (1st, 4to, ibds, unpag, 4cp)	Whitman	(1926)	Pogany, W.	35-60	*
Neyhart, L.	Henry's Lincoln (1st, lg8vo, 49p, ipcb, 9 fp b/w, pep)	Holiday House	(1945)	Wilson, C.B.	35-50	R*
Nichols, B.	Book of Old Ballads (1st, 4to, 279p, brown/gilt, 16cp)	L: Hutchinson	1934	Brock, H.M.	65-80	
Nicholson, M.	Hoosier Chronicle (1st, 8vo, 606p, brown/gilt, 4cp)	Houghton	1912	Yohn, F.C.	20-30	
Nicholson, M.	House of a Thousand Candles (1st, 8vo, 382p, 7cp)	Bobbs-Merrill	(1905)	Christy, H.C.	20-30	
Nicholson, M.	Little Brown Jug at Kildare (1st, 8vo, blue cl, 422p, 5pl)	Bobbs-Merrill	(1908)	Flagg, J.M.	20-30	
Nicholson, M.	Lords of High Decision (1st, 8vo, 503p, 4cp)	Doubleday/Page	1909	Keller, A.I.	20-30	*
Nicholson, M.	Reversible Santa Claus (1st, 8vo, blue cl, 176p, 4cp, dep)	Houghton	1917	Minard, F.H.	20-35	*
Nicholson, M.	Siege of the Seven Suitors (1st, 8vo, green cl, 401p, col frn)	Houghton	1910	Phillips, C.	20-25	
Nicholson, M.	The Poet (1st, 8vo, teg, 190p, blue/gilt, cep, 4cp)	Houghton	1914	Booth, F.	35-50	
Nicholson, M.	The Poet (1st, 8vo, teg, 190p, 4cp & designs by...)	Houghton	1914	Dwiggins, W.A.	30-45	
Nicholson, M.	Zelda Dameron (1st, 8vo, 411p, cvr by...)	Bobbs-Merrill	(1904)	Armstrong, M.	30-45	
Nicholson, M.	Zelda Dameron (1st, 8vo, 411p, 8cp by...)	Bobbs-Merrill	(1904)	Clay, J.C.	30-45	
Nicholson, Wm.	An Alphabet (1st AM, 4to, ibds, 26cp)	R.H. Russell	1898	Nicholson, W.	400-550	
Nicholson, Wm.	An Alphabet (1st, lg4to, ipcb, 26cp)	L: Heinemann	1898	Nicholson, W.	400-600	
Nicholson, Wm.	Book of Blokes (1st, sm8vo, 30p, green/gilt)	L: Faber	[1929]	Nicholson, W.	350-500	
Nicholson, Wm.	Clever Bill (1st, ob4to, yellow ipcb, 21cp)	L: Heinemann	[1926]	Nicholson, W.	400-600	
Nicholson, Wm.	Clever Bill (1st AM, ob sm4to, yel bds, 23p, color)	Doubleday/Dor.	[1927]	Nicholson, W.	350-500	
Nicholson, Wm.	London Types (1st AM, lg4to, ibds, 28p, 12cp)	R.H. Russell	1898	Nicholson, W.	220-300	
Nicholson, Wm.	London Types (1st, folio, ipcb, 12cp)	L: Heinemann	1898	Nicholson, W.	350-400	
Nicholson, Wm.	Pirate Twins (1st, ob4to, ibds, 32p, color)	L: Faber	(1929)	Nicholson, W.	300-500	
Nicholson, Wm.	Pirate Twins (1st AM, ob8vo, 28p, ibds, color)	Coward	(1929)	Nicholson, W.	250-400	
Niebuhr	Greek Heroes (12mo, p-o, teg, blue/gilt, 4cp)	L: Cassell	1910	Rackham, A.	250	
Nightingale, M.	Tony-O'-Dreams (lg8vo, p-o, 160p, 8cp)	L: Simpkin	1919	Nightingale, M.	60-90	*
Nisbet, J.	Our Forests & Woodlands (1st, 8vo, teg, gilt, 340p, pep)	L: J.M. Dent	1900	Rackham, A.	140-180	
Nixon-Roulet	Little Spanish Cousin (1st, sm8vo, 125p, 6pl)	Page	1906	McManus, B.	20-35	*
Noble, T.T.	Round of Carols (1st {std}, 4to, red/gilt, 72p, b/w, pep, DJ)	OUP	1935	Sewell, H.	35-50	
Noble-Ives, S.	Key to Betsy's Heart (1st, 12mo, 225p, green cl, 4pl)	MacMillan	1916	Noble-Ives, S.	20-30	
Noble-Ives, S.	Songs of the Shining Way (1st, 8vo, tan ipcb, 45p, fp b/w)	R.H. Russell	1899	Noble-Ives, S.	65-80	*
Noble-Ives, S.	Story of the Teddy the Bear (1st, lg4to, [42]p, ibds, 5cp)	McLoughlin	[1907]	Noble-Ives, S.	80-130	
Nodier, C.	Luck of the Bean Rows (1st, sm4to, 60p, ibds, 28 color)	L: O'Connor	(1921)	Fraser, C.L.	50-70	
Nodier, C.	Woodcutter's Dog (1st, lg8vo, 18p, bds, 12 color)	L: O'Connor	1921	Fraser, C.L.	50-65	
Norman	Elfin Rhymes (1st AM, sm4to, unpag, 40 color)	Stokes	(1900)	Moorepark, C.	120-200	
Norman	Elfin Rhymes (1st, 4to, unpag, 40 color)	L: Gay & Bird	1900	Moorepark, C.	150-240	*
Norman	Ten Little Boer Boys (ob4to, ibds, 14cp)	L: Dean	[1900]	Forrest, A.S.	145-200	
Norris, C.G.	Zest (1st {std}, 8vo, 445p, pict cl, frn by...)	Doubleday/Dor.	1933	Kent, R.	35-50	
Norris, June	Dotzie the Dancey Duck (1st, sq8vo, ibds, color)	Volland	(1927)	Tower, L.	45-60	*
Norris, June	Katherine the Komical Kow (1st, 12mo, ibds, color, pep)	Volland	(1926)	Tower, L.	50-70	*
North, S.	Birthday of Little Jesus (1st {std}, 4to, ipcb, 1-color, pep)	Grosset/Dunlap	(1952)	Angelo, V.	65-80	*
North, S.	Five Little Bears (1st, 8vo, ipcb, [32]p, 1-color, pep)	Rand/McNally	(1935)	Frazee, H.	30-50	*
North, S.	Greased Lightning (1st, 4to, [93]p, color, pep)	Winston	(1940)	Wiese, K.	35-50	*
North, S.	Midnight & Jeremiah (1st {std}, 8vo, 125p, tan cl, color, pep)	Winston	(1943)	Wiese, K.	35-50	*
North, S.	So Red the Nose (1st, sm8vo, pink cl, [72]p, fp b/w)	Farrar/Rine.	(1935)	Nelson, R.C.	25-40	*
North, S.	Zipper ABC Book (1st, 12mo, ipcb, [59]p, 2-color)	Rand/McNally	(1937)	Ward, Keith	50-70	*
Norton, A.	Sword is Drawn (1st, 12mo, 180p, col frn, 4 fp b/w, pep, DJ)	Houghton	1944	Coburn, D.	180-265	
Norton, Mary	Bed-Knob & Broomstick (1st AM {std}, sm8vo, blue cl, 189p, b/w)	Harcourt	(1957)	Blegvad, E.	65-80	*
Norton, Mary	Bonfires & Broomsticks (1st, 8vo, 119p, pep, b/w)	L: Dent	(1947)	Adshead, M.	45-60	
Norton, Mary	Borrowers Afield (1st AM {std}, 8vo, 215p, green cl, b/w, DJ)	Harcourt	(1955)	Krush, B.& J.	50-80	
Norton, Mary	Borrowers Afloat (1st AM {std}, 8vo, 191p, b/w, DJ)	Harcourt	(1959)	Krush, B.& J.	50-80	
Norton, Mary	Borrowers Afloat (1st, sm8vo, 176p, blue cl, col frn, DJ)	L: Dent	(1959)	Stanley, Diana	70-90	
Norton, Mary	Magic Bed-Knob (1st {1st bk}, 4to, ibds, [48]p, fp color, pep)	Hyperion Press	(1943)	Peirce, W.	65-90	*
Norton, Mary	The Borrowers (1st AM {std}, 8vo, 180p, blue cl, b/w, DJ)	Harcourt	(1953)	Krush, B.& J.	50-80	
Norwood, Edwin P.	Adventures of Diggeldy Dan (1st, 8vo, p-o, 240p, 8cp)	Little/Brown	1922	Peyton, A.C.	20-35	*
Norwood, Edwin P.	Davy Winkle in Circusland (1st, 8vo, 202p, tan cl, col frn)	Little/Brown	1926	Peyton, A.C.	25-40	
Norwood, Edwin P.	In the Land of Diggeldy Dan (1st, 8vo, p-o, 226p, 8cp)	Little/Brown	1923	Peyton, A.C.	20-35	*
Noseworthy, F.	Land of Play (1st, 4to, 128p, p-o, blue cl, 10cp)	Cupples	(1911)	Kirk, M.L.	70-100	
Noyes, A.	Forty Singing Seamen (1st, 8vo, ipcb, 124p, 6cp, pep)	Stokes	(1930)	MacKinstry, E.	45-60	
Noyes, A. (ed.)	Magic Casement (1st, 8vo, 391p, gilt, b/w)	L: Chapman	(1908)	Reid, S.	35-50	
Noyes, Alfred	Sherwood (1st, 8vo, 225p, black/gilt, p-o, 4cp)	Stokes	1911	Nichols, S.B.	30-45	*

AUTHOR	TITLE	PUBLISHER	DATE	ARTIST	PRICE	LC
Nuckel, O.	Destiny... (1st AM, sm4to, 190p, red cl, woodcuts)	Farrar/Rine.	(1930)	Nuckel, O.	45-70	
Nulets, L.E.	Stories of the Little Fishes (1st, 8vo, 288p, 6pl)	Page	1905	Schneider, S.	20-30	*
Nyce, Vera	Adventures of Greyfur Family (1st, 16mo, 76p, 24cp)	Lippincott	(1917)	Nyce, Helen	45-60	*
Nyce, Vera	Greyfur's Neighbors (1st, 16mo, 76p, 24cp)	Lippincott	(1917)	Nyce, Helen	45-60	*
Nye, Edgar W.	Guest at the Ludlow (1st, 8vo, red/gilt, 262p, teg, 21pl)	Bowen-Merrill	1897	Braunhold, L.	25-40	
Nye, Harry	Home is If You Find It (1st {std}, 12mo, 251p)	Doubleday	1947	Galdone, P.	30-45	*
O'Brien, Jack	Corporal Corey (1st, lg8vo, gilt, 276p, col frn)	Winston	(1936)	Wiese, K.	25-40	*
O'Brien, Jack	Silver Chief (1st, 8vo, 218p, col frn)	Winston	(1933)	Wiese, K.	20-30	
O'Brien, Jack	Silver Chief to the Rescue (1st, 8vo, silver cl, 235p, col frn)	Winston	(1937)	Wiese, K.	25-40	
O'Cluny, Thomas	Merry Multifleet/Mounting Multicorps (1st, 8vo, 206p, 16 illus)	L: J.M. Dent	1904	Robinson, W.H.	100-130	*
O'Day, James	Daddy Long Legs Fun Songs (lg4to, ibds, color)	Chi: Witmark	1900	Keller, E.	120-180	
O'Donnell, T.C.	Ladder of Ricketty Rungs (1st, 8vo, ibds, unpag, color, pep)	Volland	(1923)	Scott, J.L.	50-70	
O'Dyer, Ruth	Adventures of the Ink Spots (1st, 8vo, orang cl, 158p, col frn)	Lothrop/Lee	(1923)	Bridgman, L.J.	70-100	
O'Hara, Mary	My Friend Flicka (1st, 8vo, 285p, col frn, 14pl, DJ)	Lippincott	1941	Curry, J.S.	45-60	
O'Malley, F.W.	War-Whirl in Washington (1st, 8vo, 298p, grey cl, 16pl)	Century	1918	Sarg, T.	35-50	
O'Neill, G.	Tomorrow's House (1st, sq8vo, purple cl, 159p, b/w, pep)	Dutton	1930	O'Neill, R.	65-90	
O'Neill, M.	Elf-Errant (1st, 8vo, teg, 109p, pink/gilt, 7pl)	Lawrence	1895	Britten, W.E.	70-95	
O'Neill, Rose	Garda (1st {std}, 8vo, blue cloth, 305p, pep, DJ)	Doubleday/Dor.	1929	O'Neill, R.	35-50	
O'Neill, Rose	Goblin Woman (1st {std}, 8vo, 345p, b/w, pep)	Doubleday/Dor.	1930	O'Neill, R.	40-60	
O'Neill, Rose	Kewpie Kutouts (1st, 4to, bds, p-o, 48p, pep, color)	Stokes	(1914)	O'Neill, R.	700-1000	*
O'Neill, Rose	Kewpie Primer (1st, sq8vo, pict cloth, 118p, color, cep)	Stokes	(1916)	O'Neill, R.	280-400	
O'Neill, Rose	Kewpies & Dotty Darling (1st, 4to, p-o, tan bds, 88p, pep)	Stokes	(1912)	O'Neill, R.	250-400	
O'Neill, Rose	Kewpies & Runaway Baby (1st {std}, 8vo, 111p, red cl, col, cep)	Doubleday/Dor.	1928	O'Neill, R.	180-250	
O'Neill, Rose	Kewpies: Their Book (1st, lg4to, tan bds, p-o, 80p, dep)	Stokes	(1913)	O'Neill, R.	300-450	
O'Neill, Rose	Lady in the White Veil (1st, 12mo, blue cl, 350p, 5pl)	Harper	1909	O'Neill, R.	50-80	*
O'Neill, Rose	Loves of Edwy (1st, sm8vo, tan cl, 432p, b/w)	Lothrop	(1904)	O'Neill, R.	50-70	
O'Neill, Rose	Master-Mistress (1st, 8vo, maroon bds, 227p, 9pl)	Knopf	1922	O'Neill, R.	50-75	
O'Sullivan, V.	Book of Bargains (1st, 8vo, 185p, frn by...)	L: Smithers	1896	Beardsley, A.	70-85	
Ogburn, Charlton	The Bridge (1st, 8vo, cloth, 68p, fp 2-color)	Houghton	1957	Ness, E.M.	50-80	*
Ogburn, Charlton	White Falcon (1st, 8vo, tan/silver, 51p, b/w, pep)	Houghton	1955	Bryson, B.	65-80	R*
Ogden, Ruth	Little Homespun (1st, 127p, 15pl)	Stokes	(1897)	Humphrey, M.	100-140	
Ogden, Ruth	Little Pierre & Big Peter (1st, 8vo, p-o, 367p, 5cp, pep)	Stokes	(1915)	Kirk, M.L.	50-75	
Ogden, Ruth	Little Queen of Hearts (1st, 8vo, 232p, 15 fp b/w, gilt)	Stokes	(1893)	Ogden, H.A.	35-50	*
Ogden, Ruth	Loyal Little Redcoat (1st, 4to, 217p, gilt, b/w, PPPa)	Stokes	1890	Ogden, H.A.	65-80	
Olcott, F.J.	Bible Stories to Read & Tell (1st, 8vo, blue cl, 465p, 8cp)	Houghton	1916	Pogany, W.	45-65	
Olcott, F.J.	Book of Elves & Fairies (1st, 8vo, 303p, p-o, 3cp by...)	Houghton	1918	Winter, M.	75-100	
Olcott, F.J.	Book of Elves & Fairies (1st UK, 8vo, 303p, 3cp by...)	L: Harrap	1919	Winter, M.	70-100	*
Olcott, F.J.	Go! Champions of Light (1st, 8vo, 226p, b/w, pep, DJ)	Revell	(1933)	Walker, D.S.	40-60	
Olcott, F.J.	Red Indian Fairy Book (1st, 8vo, 338p, col frn, 5pl)	Houghton	1917	Richardson, F.	65-80	
Olcott, F.J.	Wonder Tales/Baltic Wizards (1st {std}, 8vo, 234p col frn, pep)	Longmans	1928	Candell, V.G.	30-45	
Olcott, F.J.	Wonder Tales/Windmill Lands (1st, 8vo, 238p, col frn, pep, DJ)	L: Longmans	1926	Rosse, H.	45-70	
Olcott, F.J.	Wonderful Garden (1st, 12mo, 483p, p-o, 4cp)	Houghton	1919	Winter, M.	40-65	
Olcott, F.J. (ed.)	Adventures of Haroun Er Raschid (1st, 8vo, 363p, gilt, col frn)	Holt	1923	Pogany, W.	45-60	*
Olcott, F.J. (ed.)	More Tales/Arabian Nights (1st, sm8vo, 274p, red/gilt, 12cp)	Holt	1915	Pogany, W.	100-135	
Olcott, F.J. (ed.)	Tales of the Persian Genii (1st, 8vo, gilt, pep, 225p, 4cp)	Houghton	(1917)	Pogany, W.	45-70	
Olcott, F.J. (ed.)	Tales of the Persian Genii (1st UK, 8vo, grey cl, 225p, 4cp)	L: Harrap	1919	Pogany, W.	70-90	
Olcott, F.J. (ed.)	Wonder Tales/Goblin Hills (1st {std}, 12mo, 268p, col frn, pep)	NY: Longmans	1930	Sichel, H.	35-50	*
Olcott, F.J. (ed.)	Wonder Tales/Pirate Isles (1st, 12mo, 256p, orang cl, col frn)	NY: Longmans	1927	Rosse, H.	35-50	*
Olds, Eliz.	Big Fire (1st, ob8vo, red cl, [32]p, color, pep)	Houghton	1945	Olds, E.	35-50	*
Olds, Eliz.	Feather Mountain (1st, lg ob8vo, aqua cl, 27p, color, pep, CH)	Houghton	1951	Olds, E.	65-90	*
Olds, Eliz.	Riding the Rails (1st, ob8vo, 43p, color, dep)	Houghton	1948	Olds, E.	35-50	*
Olmstead, M.	Land of Never Was (1st, sm4to, p-o, 148p, 12cp, pep)	Jacobs	(1908)	Knipe, H.A.	60-90	
Olmstead, M.	Land of Really True (1st, sm4to, p-o, 187p, 12cp, pep)	Jacobs	(1909)	Knipe, H.A.	40-65	
Omar Khayyam	Rubaiyat... (folio, brown/gilt, unpag, 56pl)	Houghton	1884	Vedder, E.	300-450	
Omar Khayyam	Rubaiyat... (1st, 16mo, green ipcb, 61p)	R.H. Russell	(1897)	Bradley, W.	80-130	
Omar Khayyam	Rubaiyat... (1st, 4to, uncut, green/gilt, 43p, b/w)	L: MacMillan	1898	MacDougall, W.B.	100-165	
Omar Khayyam	Rubaiyat... (1st, 8vo, 65p)	L: J. Lane	1901	Cole, H.	70-100	*
Omar Khayyam	Rubaiyat... (1st, 8vo, 33p)	L: G. Bell	1902	Bell, R.A.	65-80	*
Omar Khayyam	Rubaiyat... (1st, 8vo, 25p, 12 illus)	L: A. Moring	1903	McManus, B.	65-90	*
Omar Khayyam	Rubaiyat... (1st, 4to, unpag)	Dodge	[1905]	(Photos)	75-120	
Omar Khayyam	Rubaiyat... (1st, sm4to, 135p, grey cl, cp)	L: Gibbings	1906	Brangwyn, F.	90-160	*
Omar Khayyam	Rubaiyat... (1st {this pub}, 12mo, 159p, color)	Page	1907	McManus, B.	35-50	*
Omar Khayyam	Rubaiyat... (1st, 8vo, 147p, AEG, grey cl, color)	Nister/Dutton	[1907]	Robinson, T.H.	70-100	
Omar Khayyam	Rubaiyat... (1st AM, 4to, teg, blue/gilt, ticp)	Dodge	[1908]	Hanscom, A.	100-125	
Omar Khayyam	Rubaiyat... (1st, lg4to, white/gilt, unpag, 20 ticp)	L: Hodder	[1909]	Dulac, E.	250-350	
Omar Khayyam	Rubaiyat... (8vo, teg, 160p, 12pl)	Elder	1909	James, G.	35-50	
Omar Khayyam	Rubaiyat... (1st, 4to, 203p, teg, 16cp)	L: A&C Black	1909	James, G.	100-150	
Omar Khayyam	Rubaiyat... (1st, 4to, ibds, teg, gilt, 24 ticp)	L: Harrap	(1909)	Pogany, W.	250-320	
Omar Khayyam	Rubaiyat... (1st AM, 4to, ibds, teg, 96p, 24 ticp)	Crowell	(1909)	Pogany, W.	165-220	
Omar Khayyam	Rubaiyat... (1st, 12mo, beige/gilt, teg, 69p, 8 ticp, pep)	L: Foulis	(1910)	Brangwyn, F.	80-120	
Omar Khayyam	Rubaiyat... (32mo, leather, teg, 86p, 3 ticp)	L: Collins	[1910]	Robinson, C.	65-80	
Omar Khayyam	Rubaiyat... (1st, 4to, [38]p)	L: A. Harriman	1911	Hall, I.H.	70-90	*

AUTHOR	TITLE	PUBLISHER	DATE	ARTIST	PRICE	LC
Omar Khayyam	Rubaiyat... (1st, 4to, blue/gilt, [88]p, 10 ticp)	L: Hodder	[1913]	Bull, Rene	350-500	
Omar Khayyam	Rubaiyat... (1st, 4to, red/gilt, unpag, teg, uncut, col frn)	L: Methuen	1913	Sullivan, E.J.	100-140	
Omar Khayyam	Rubaiyat... (1st AM, 4to, red/gilt, unpag, teg, col frn)	Dutton	(1913)	Sullivan, E.J.	80-130	
Omar Khayyam	Rubaiyat... (4to, uncut, buckram, 15 ticp)	L: Foulis	(1919)	Brangwyn, F.	120-165	
Omar Khayyam	Rubaiyat... (1st AM, 4to, p-o, gilt, 6 ticp, 32 tipl)	Dodd	[1920]	Balfour, R.	270-350	
Omar Khayyam	Rubaiyat... (1st, 4to, bds, p-o, 6 ticp, 32 tipl)	L: Constable	1920	Balfour, R.	300-400	
Omar Khayyam	Rubaiyat... (lg8vo, green/gilt, 4 color, pep)	L: Sampson	[1920]	Brangwyn, F.	45-60	
Omar Khayyam	Rubaiyat... (lg8vo, 20 ticp, later)	Doran	[1920]	Dulac, E.	100-130	
Omar Khayyam	Rubaiyat... (lg8vo, 96p, green/gilt, 12 ticp, reprint)	Crowell	[1920]	Pogany, W.	70-100	
Omar Khayyam	Rubaiyat... (1st, 8vo, 63p, 7 ticp)	L: L.B. Hill	(1920)	Tagore, A.N.	100-130	*
Omar Khayyam	Rubaiyat... (1st, 12mo, 86p, color)	Harper	1921	Jones, W.J.	35-50	*
Omar Khayyam	Rubaiyat... (1st, 4to, 108p, ibds, 18pl)	L: Bodley Head	(1922)	Fish, A.H.	150-200	
Omar Khayyam	Rubaiyat... (1st, 8vo, 159p, 8cp)	L: Kegan Paul	(1923)	Weston, H.	45-65	*
Omar Khayyam	Rubaiyat... (1st, 4to, 128p, gilt, 12 ticp)	L: L.B. Hill	[1925]	Palmer, D.M.	145-200	
Omar Khayyam	Rubaiyat... (1st, 4to, 56p, 4 ticp)	L: Collins	(1929)	Robinson, C.	100-160	*
Omar Khayyam	Rubaiyat... (1st {this pub.}, lg8vo, 197p, cp)	Doubleday/Dor.	1930	Dulac, E.	40-65	
Omar Khayyam	Rubaiyat... (4to, 171p, later ed.)	L: Harrap	(1930)	Pogany, W.	70-100	*
Omar Khayyam	Rubaiyat... (sm4to, blue ibds, [40]p, 8cp)	Heritage Press	1946	Szyk, A.	45-70	
Orcutt, Wm. D.	Princess Kallisto (1st, 4to, 138p, ibds, 6 fp color)	Little/Brown	1902	Amsden, H.	150-200	*
Orcutt, Wm. D.	Princess Kallisto... (1st UK, 4to, 139p, 12 color)	L: Jack	1905	Amsden, H.	140-220	*
Orr, Aileen	Miss Manners (1st, 8vo, AEG, blue cl, 26cp)	L: A. Melrose	1909	Hassall, J.	180-250	
Orr, M.S.	The Alphabet (1st, 4to, ibds, 60p, 26cp)	L: J.M. Dent	1931	Orr, M.S.	140-185	
Ort, Jane	Mr. Mogo Mouse (1st, sm8vo, ibds, 39p, color, pep)	Volland	(1930)	Ort, J.	35-50	
Orton, Ruth	Pepitó the Colt (1st, ob4to, ibds, 36p, b/w, pep)	Houghton	1933	Thorne, D.	40-65	*
Osborne, N.C.	Good Wind & Good Water (1st, sm8vo, 248p, red cl, b/w, pep)	Viking	1934	Wiese, K.	25-40	*
Osbourne, M. (ed.)	Favorite Fairy Tales (1st, sm4to, 365p, p-o, b/w & pep by...)	Penn	(1930)	Berkowitz, J.	50-70	
Osbourne, M. (ed.)	Favorite Fairy Tales (1st, sm4to, 365p, p-o, 20cp by...)	Penn	(1930)	Cramer, Rie	50-70	
Ostrander, Fannie	Baby Goose: His Adventures (1st, lg8vo, ibds, unpag, color)	Laird & Lee	(1900)	Hirchert, R.W.	70-100	*
Ostrander, Fannie	Gift of the Magic Staff (1st, 8vo, 221p, green cl, 8pl)	Revell	(1902)	Dwiggens, Will	40-65	
Ostrander, Fannie	Goose Family Tales (1st, sq8vo, 87p, gilt, color)	Conkey	(1905)	Carqueville, W.	80-120	
Otis, James	Boy's Revolt (1st, 8vo, 193p, 16pl)	Estes	(1894)	Hooper, W.P.	35-50	
Otis, James	Fighting for the Empire (1st, 8vo, 466p, 8pl)	Estes	(1900)	Merrill, F.	35-50	
Otis, James	Jenny Wren's Boarding House (1st, 8vo, blue cl, 173p, PPP)	Estes	(1893)	Rogers, W.A.	130-170	
Otis, James	Old Ben (1st, 12mo, ipcb, 188p, 7pl)	Harper	1911	Noble-Ives, S.	25-40	
Otis, James	Princess & Joe Potter (1st, sq8vo, 249p, 7pl)	Estes	(1898)	Oakley, V.	100-150	
Otis, James	Tim & Tip (1st, 16mo, 179p, 13 fp b/w, dep)	Harper	1883	Rogers, W.A.	70-100	R*
Otis, James	Toby Tyler... (1st, sq8vo, 265p, brown/gilt, 21 fp b/w, PPP)	Harper	1881	Rogers, W.A.	140-200	
Otto, M.G.	Great Aunt Victoria's House (1st {std}, 8vo, yel cl, 120p, b/w)	Holt	(1957)	Adams, A.	35-50	*
Otto, M.G.	Man in the Moon (1st {std}, sm8vo, green cl, 128p, fp b/w)	Holt	(1957)	Galdone, P.	35-60	*
Otto, M.G.	Pumpkin, Ginger & Spice (1st {std}, sm8vo, 116p, yellow cl, b/w)	Holt	(1954)	Cooney, B.	35-50	*
Otto, M.G.	Roly-Poly Snowman (1st {std}, 8vo, blue cl, 83p, fp b/w)	Holt	(1954)	Suba, S.	30-50	*
Oursler, Fulton	String of Blue Beads (1st {std}, 12mo, ibds, [32]p, color)	Doubleday	1956	Lonette, R.	25-40	*
Outhwaite, G.	Enchanted Forest (1st, 4to, 93p, gilt, pep, 16 ticp)	L: A&C Black	1921	Outhwaite, I.R.	500-700	
Outhwaite, I.	Blossom: A Fairy Story (1st, 4to, p-o, blue cl, 94p, 8cp, pep)	L: A&C Black	(1928)	Outhwaite, I.R.	500-700	
Outhwaite, I.	Bunny & Brownie (1st UK, 4to, 99p, blue cl, 8 color, p-o, pep)	L: A&C Black	(1930)	Outhwaite, I.R.	450-600	
Outhwaite, I.	Fairyland (1st, lg4to, blue cl, 128p, 15cp, pep)	L: A&C Black	(1931)	Outhwaite, I.R.	650-900	
Outhwaite, I.	Little Fairy Sister (2nd, 4to, 91p, 8cp, pep)	L: A&C Black	1929	Outhwaite, I.R.	180-260	
Outhwaite, I.	Sixpence to Spend (4to, bds, 5 ticp)	(Sydney)	1935	Outhwaite, I.R.	350-500	
Outhwaite, I. & A.	Little Green Road to Fairyland (1st, 4to, 103p, bds, p-o, 8cp)	L: A&C Black	1922	Outhwaite, I.R.	300-450	
Outhwaite, I. & A.	Little Green Road to Fairyland (1st AM, 4to, pep, 102p, 8cp)	Dutton	[1922]	Outhwaite, I.R.	200-300	
Overton, G.	Anne Carmel (1st, sm8vo, 335p, teg, 6pl)	MacMillan	1903	Keller, A.I.	20-35	*
Ovington, Mary W.	Hazel (1st, sm8vo, 162p, b/w)	NY: Crisis Pub	(1913)	Roseland, H.	80-100	*
Ovington, Mary W.	Zeke (1st, sm8vo, blue cl, 205p, uncut, b/w)	Harcourt	(1931)	Davis, N.H.	80-120	*
Owen, C.D.	Seth Way (1st, sm8vo, 413p, col frn)	Houghton	1917	Booth, F.	35-50	*
Owen, Dora	Book of Fairy Poetry (1st, 4to, 180p, grey cl, 16 ticp, pep)	L: Longmans	1920	Goble, W.	250-300	
Owen, M.A.	Old Rabbit the Voodoo (1st, 8vo, blue cl)	L: T.F. Unwin	1893	Wain, L.	60-85	
Owen, Ruth	Castle in Silver Wood (1st, 8vo, 181p, blue cl, col frn, pep)	Dodd	1939	Simont, M.	30-45	*
Oxenham, E.J.	Goblin Island (1st, 8vo, 316p, p-o, col frn)	L: Collins	[1907]	Robinson, T.H.	50-80	*
Oxley, J.M.	Family on Wheels (1st AM, sm8vo, 219p, 4pl)	Crowell	(1905)	Smith, E.B.	30-45	*
Oxley, J.M.	Fife & Drum/Louisburg (1st, 8vo, 307p, 4pl)	Little/Brown	1899	DeLand, C.O.	25-40	
Pace, Mildred M.	Friend of Animals (1st, 8vo, 125p, pink cl, fp b/w)	Scribner	1942	Brown, Paul	20-35	*
Page, Marg.	In Childhood Land (lg4to, ibds, color)	Saalfield	1903	Greenland, K.	100-165	
Page, T.N.	Bred in the Bone (1st, 8vo, 274p, teg, 8pl)	Scribner	1904	Fisher, H.	25-40	
Page, T.N.	Captured Santa Claus (1st, 12mo, 81p, teg, 4cp)	Scribner	1902	Jacobs, W.L.	30-45	
Page, T.N.	Gordon Keith (1st, 8vo, blue/gilt, 548p)	Scribner	1903	Armstrong, M.	30-45	
Page, T.N.	John Marvel, Assistant (1st, 12mo, green cl, 8pl)	Scribner	1909	Flagg, J.M.	20-30	
Page, T.N.	Old Gentlemen of the Black Stock (1st, 12mo, 170p, teg, 7cp)	Scribner	1900	Christy, H.C.	30-45	
Page, T.N.	On Newfound River (1st, 8vo, 286p, blue/gilt, teg, 4cp)	Scribner	1906	Jackson, J.E.	20-35	
Page, T.N.	Passtime Stories (1st, sm8vo, grey cl, 220p, 21pl)	Harper	1898	Frost, A.B.	35-50	
Page, T.N.	Santa Claus' Partner (1st, 8vo, red/gilt, 177p, teg, 8cp)	Scribner	1899	Glackens, W.	30-45	
Page, T.N.	Social Life in Old Virginia (1st, 8vo, teg, 109p, green/gilt)	Scribner	1897	Armstrong, M.	45-60	
Page, T.N.	Tommy Trot's Visit to Santa Claus (1st, 8vo, 98p, uncut, 6cp)	Scribner	1908	Anderson, V.C.	20-35	

AUTHOR	TITLE	PUBLISHER	DATE	ARTIST	PRICE	LC
Page, T.N.	Two Little Confederates (1st, sm4to, 189p, gilt, p-o, col frn)	Scribner	1932	Thomason, J.W.	60-85	
Page, T.N.	Two Prisoners (1st, 8vo, 82p, teg, gilt, 5cp)	R.H. Russell	1903	Keep, V.	25-40	
Page, T.N.	Under the Crust (1st, 8vo, 307p, green/gilt)	Scribner	1907	Armstrong, M.	25-40	
Paget-Fredericks, J.	Green-Pipes (1st {1st bk.}, folio, 50p, green/gilt, 6cp)	MacMillan	1929	Paget-Fredericks	80-100	
Paget-Fredericks, J.	Miss Pert's Christmas Tree (1st, lg4to, red/gilt, 24p, 6cp, pep)	MacMillan	1929	Paget-Fredericks	60-85	*
Paine, A.B.	Arkansas Bear (1st, 8vo, 118p, b/w)	R.H. Russell	1898	VerBeck, F.	230-400	*
Paine, A.B.	Beacon Prize Medals (1st, 12mo, 325p, 6pl)	Baker/Taylor	1899	Wright/Huestis	35-50	*
Paine, A.B.	Great White Way (1st, 8vo, blue cl, teg, 327p, 6pl)	J.F. Taylor	1901	Rosenmeyer, B.J.	80-100	
Paine, A.B.	Hollow Tree (1st, 8vo, 128p, ibds, PPP)	R.H. Russell	1898	Conde, J.M.	100-150	
Paine, A.B.	Hollow Tree (1st UK, 4to, 128p, ibds)	L: Constable	1898	Conde, J.M.	80-100	
Paine, A.B.	Hollow Tree Snowed-In Book (1st, 8vo, cloth, 285p)	Harper	1910	Conde, J.M.	45-60	
Paine, A.B.	In the Deep Woods (1st, sm4to, 134p, ipcb, 52pl)	R.H. Russell	1899	Conde, J.M.	120-165	*
Paine, A.B.	Mr. Crow & the Whitewash (1st, 8vo, 120p, p-o, gilt)	Harper	(1917)	Conde, J.M.	50-70	
Paine, A.B.	Mr. Rabbit's Wedding (1st, sm8vo, gilt, p-o, 123p, fp b/w)	Harper	(1917)	Conde, J.M.	50-70	
Paine, A.B.	Tent Dwellers (1st, 8vo, uncut, 272p, b/w)	Outing	1908	Watson, H.	30-45	
Paine, R.D.	Blackbeard Buccaneer (1st, 8vo, 309p, p-o, 6pl)	Penn	1922	Schoonover, F.	30-45	
Palazzo, T.	Charley the Horse (1st, sq4to, 56p, color, pep)	Viking	1950	Palazzo, T.	45-60	*
Palazzo, T.	Federico the Flying Squirrel (1st, 4to, 54p, ipcb, color, pep)	Viking	1951	Palazzo, T.	45-60	*
Palazzo, T.	Giant Nursery Book (1st, lg4to, 188p)	Garden City	1957	Palazzo, T.	45-65	*
Palazzo, T.	Great Othello (1st, ob4to, 48p, blue cl, 1-color)	Viking	1952	Palazzo, T.	40-65	*
Palazzo, T.	Susie the Cat (1st, 4to, 50p, ipcb, color, pep)	Viking	1949	Palazzo, T.	35-50	*
Palgrave, F.	Golden Treasury of Songs & Lyrics (1st, 8vo, teg, uncut, 24cp)	L: Dent	1907	Bell, R.A.	80-120	
Palgrave, F.	Golden Treasury of Songs & Lyrics (8vo, yel cl, 459p, 12 ticp)	Hodder	[1915]	Brickdale, E.F.	80-100	
Palgrave, F.	Golden Treasury/Songs & Lyrics (1st, 4to, p-o, 373p, pep, 8cp)	Duffield	1911	Parrish, M.	160-200	
Palmer, Eliz.	Good Old Clipsy (1st, 8vo, 194p, tan cl, fp 1-color)	Scribner	1941	Brown, Paul	45-70	*
Palmer, G. (tr)	Odyssey of Homer (1st, 4to, red/gilt, 314p, p-o, 16cp, pep)	Houghton	1929	Wyeth, N.C.	160-220	
Palmer, S.	Surrey (1st, 8vo, blue/gilt, 252p, teg, 75p)	L: A&C Black	1906	Palmer, S.	70-100	
Palmer, Winthrop	American Songs for Children (1st, ob4to, 64p, b/w)	MacMillan	1931	Cady, H.	45-65	*
Paltenghi, M.	Honey on a Raft (1st, 4to, ibds, [36]p, 15 fp b/w, pep)	Garden City	(1941)	Anderson, C.W.	35-50	
Paltenghi, M.	Honey the City Bear (1st, 4to, 31p, ipcb, 14 fp b/w)	Grosset/Dunlap	1937	Anderson, C.W.	50-80	*
Paltenghi, M.	Remus Goes to Town (1st, 4to, 29p, ipcb, 15 fp b/w)	Grosset/Dunlap	1938	Anderson, C.W.	50-80	*
Paltenghi, M.	Rumpus Rabbit (1st {std}, narrow 4to, 25p, green cl, b/w)	Harper	1939	Anderson, C.W.	50-70	*
Pancoast, M.H.	Rejuvenation/Mama & Papa Goose (1st, lg4to, ipcb, [84]p, color)	NY: Britton	(1916)	Pancoast, M.H.	150-230	*
Paquin, S.S.	Garden Fairies (1st, sm4to, 179p, p-o, 4cp)	Moffat	1908	Chamberlin, E.H.	65-80	*
Pardee, L.C.	Folk of the Woods (1st, lg8vo, p-o, 129p, teg, 10cp)	Doubleday/Page	1913	Bull, C.L.	30-45	
Parish, Helen R.	At the Palace Gates (1st, sm4to, ipcb, 64p, fp 2-color, pep)	Viking	1949	Politi, L.	45-70	*
Parish, Helen R.	Our Lady of Guadalupe (1st, 4to, 48p, 6 dp color)	Viking	1955	Charlot, J.	65-90	
Parker, A.C.	Skunny Wundy (1st, 4to, p-o, 262p, 6 ticp)	Doran	(1926)	Crawford, W.	65-90	
Parker, B.	Arctic Orphans (ob folio, ibds, color, pep)	L: Chambers	[1910]	Parker, N.	400-600	
Parker, B.	Cinderella at the Zoo (4to, ibds, 16 chromos)	L: Chambers	[1900]	Parker, B.	300-450	
Parker, B.	Funny Bunnies (ob folio, ibds, 12cp)	L: Chambers	[1905]	Parker, N.	250-400	*
Parker, B.	History of the Hoppers (lg4to, ibds, color)	Chambers/Stoke	[1908]	Parker, N.	250-350	
Parker, B.	Lays of the Grays (ob 4to, ibds, color)	L: Chambers	[1910]	Parker, B.	250-400	
Parker, B.& N.	Larder Lodge (lg ob4to, ibds, 14 fp color)	L: Chambers	[1910]	Parker, N.	240-350	
Parker, D.	High Society (1st, lg4to, ipcb, 65p, pep)	Putnam	(1920)	Fish, A.H.	60-90	
Parker, F.	Hope Hathaway (1st, 8vo, 408p, green cl, 9pl)	C.M. Clark	1904	Russell, C.M.	80-100	
Parker, Gilbert	Lane that Had No Turning (1st, lg8vo, 215p, teg, uncut, 5pl)	Doubleday/Page	1902	Schoonover, F.	30-50	
Parker, Gilbert	March of the White Guard (1st, 12mo, 133p, b/w)	Fenno	1902	Starkweather, W.	20-30	
Parker, Gilbert	Money Master (1st, 8vo, green/gilt, 360p, 6pl)	Harper	1915	Castaigne, A.	20-35	*
Parker, Gilbert	Northern Lights (1st, 12mo, green/gilt, 352p, 16pl)	Harper	1909	Various	30-45	
Parker, Gilbert	The Weavers (1st, 8vo, 530p, olive/gilt, 8pl)	Harper	1907	Castaigne, A.	20-25	
Parker, Gilbert	When Valmond Came to Pontiac (1st, 12mo, teg, green/gilt, 222p)	Stone/Kimball	1895	Rogers, B.	60-90	
Parker, L.N.	Pomander Walk (1st, lg8vo, 267p, 16pl)	J. Lane	1911	Williams, J.A.	45-70	*
Parkes, W.T.	Spook Ballads (1st, 12mo, 246p, brown/gilt, b/w, cep)	L: Simpkin	1895	Parkes, W.T.	50-65	
Parkman, F.	Oregon Trail (1st, 8vo, 411p, 10pl)	Little/Brown	1892	Remington, F.	140-200	
Parkman, F.	Oregon Trail (1st, 8vo, 364p, p-o, 5cp, pep)	Little/Brown	1925	Wyeth, N.C.	125-165	
Parkman, F.	Oregon Trail (1st, 8vo, 388p, black cl, p-o, 4cp)	Winston	(1931)	Jackson, W.H.	35-60	
Parks, G.T.	Here Comes Daddy (1st, ob8vo, ibds, unpag, color)	W.R. Scott	1951	Gropper, W.	45-65	*
Parrish, A.& D.	Dream Coach (1st, 8vo, 143p, blue/gilt, fp b/w, pep, NH)	MacMillan	1924	Parrish, A.& D.	45-65	
Parrish, A.& D.	Floating Island (1st {std}, lg8vo, p-o, 265p, 13pl, NH)	Harper	(1930)	Parrish, A.	60-85	R
Parrish, A.& D.	Knee-High to a Grasshopper (1st, 8vo, yellow cl, 209p, b/w, pep)	MacMillan	1923	Parrish, A.& D.	35-50	
Parrish, Anne	Story of Appleby Capple (1st, lg4to, 184p, pep, b/w, NH)	Harper	(1950)	Parrish, A.	50-80	*
Parrish, R.	Air Pilot (1st, 8vo, 318p, 3cp)	McClurg	1913	Underwood, C.F.	25-45	
Parrish, R.	Beth Norvell (1st, 8vo, 341p, tan cl, col frn by...)	McClurg	1907	Wyeth, N.C.	30-45	
Parrish, R.	Bob Hampton of Placer (1st, 8vo, 383p, 4cp)	McClurg	1906	Keller, A.I.	20-30	
Parrish, R.	Don MacGrath (1st, 8vo, 269p, b/w pl)	McClurg	1910	Norton, J.W.	25-40	
Parrish, R.	Great Plains (1st, 8vo, 399p, 32pl)	McClurg	1907	(Engravings)	45-70	
Parrish, R.	Keith of the Border (1st, 8vo, 362p, 4cp)	McClurg	1910	Dunton, W.H.	30-45	
Parrish, R.	Last Voyage of the Donna Isabel (1st, 8vo, blue cl, 366p, 4cp)	McClurg	1908	True, A.	20-35	
Parrish, R.	Love Under Fire (1st, 8vo, 400p, 5cp)	McClurg	1911	Kimball, A.	20-30	*
Parrish, R.	Maid of the Forest (1st, 8vo, 427p, 5cp)	McClurg	1913	Schoonover, F.	25-40	
Parrish, R.	My Lady of the South (1st, 8vo, 360p, tan cl, 4cp)	McClurg	1909	Kimball, A.	20-25	

AUTHOR	TITLE	PUBLISHER	DATE	ARTIST	PRICE	LC
Parrish, R.	Prisoners of Chance (1st, 8vo, yellow cl, 423p, 4cp)	McClurg	1908	Kinneys	25-40	
Parrish, R.	Sword of the Old Frontier (1st, 8vo, 407p, tan cl, 4cp)	McClurg	1905	Yohn, F.C.	20-35	
Parrish, R.	When Wilderness was King (1st, 8vo, 388p, uncut, 6cp, dep)	McClurg	1904	Kinneys	20-30	
Parry, David M.	Scarlet Empire (1st, 8vo, red/gilt, 400p, 10pl)	Bobbs-Merrill	(1906)	Wall, H.C.	65-90	
Parry, E.A.	Butterscotia... (1st, 8vo, blue/gilt, uncut, 170p, map, 6pl)	L: D. Nutt	1896	MacGregor, A.	150-220	
Parry, E.A.	First Book of Krab (1st, lg8vo, green cl, 132p, uncut)	L: D. Nutt	1897	MacGregor, A.	120-170	
Parry, E.A.	Gamble Gold (1st, sq8vo, ibds, 248p, AEG, gilt, 15pl)	L: Hutchinson	1907	Furniss, H.	50-65	
Parry, E.A.	Katawampus: Its Treatment & Cure (1st, 8vo, green cl, 96p, b/w)	L: D. Nutt	1895	MacGregor, A.	100-145	
Parry, E.A.	Scarlet Herring (1st, 8vo, 253p, uncut, green/gilt, b/w, AEG)	L: Smith Elder	1899	Rusden, A.D.	65-80	
Parsons, F.T.	According to Season... (1st, 8vo, 197p, green/gilt, cvr by...)	Scribner	1902	Armstrong, M.	30-45	*
Parsons, F.T.	How to Know the Ferns (1st, 8vo, brown/gilt, 215p)	Scribner	1899	Armstrong, M.	45-60	
Parsons, G.	Stream of History (1st, lg8vo, 590p, gilt, b/w, pep)	Scribner	1928	Daugherty, J.	30-45	
Patch, E.M.	Holiday Hill (1st, sq8vo, 135p, pep)	MacMillan	1931	(Photos)	25-40	
Patri, Angelo	Pinocchio in America (1st {std}, 8vo, 255p, col frn, 17pl, pep)	Doubleday/Dor.	1928	Liddell, M.	50-75	
Pattee, F.L.	House/Black Ring (1st, 8vo, 324p, cvr by...)	Holt	1905	Stuart, B.	20-25	*
Pauli, Hertha	Most Beautiful House... (1st {std}, 8vo, 114p, color, DJ)	Knopf	1949	Wiese, K.	20-30	
Payne, E.	Katy No-Pocket (1st, 4to, [32]p, color, pep)	Houghton	1944	Rey, H.A.	45-65	*
Peabody, J.	Book of the Little Past (1st, sm4to, 50p, p-o, pcb, 6cp)	Houghton	1908	Green, E.S.	70-100	
Peacock, T.L.	Gryll Grange (1st, sm8vo, 292p, AEG, b/w)	L: MacMillan	1896	Townsend, F.H.	45-65	
Peacock, T.L.	Maid Marian.... (1st, AEG, 12mo, 321p, blue bds, dep)	L: MacMillan	1895	Thomson, H.	60-80	
Peacock, T.L.	Maid Marian/Crotchet Castle (1st, 12mo, AEG, gilt, 321p, dep)	L: MacMillan	1895	Townsend, F.H.	65-80	
Peacock, T.L.	Melincourt... (1st, 8vo, 326p, AEG, blue bds, 40 illus)	L: MacMillan	1896	Townsend, F.H.	65-80	
Peacock, T.L.	Misfortunes of Elphin & Rhododaphne (1st, 8vo, 262p)	L: MacMillan	1897	Townsend, F.H.	50-75	*
Peacocke, I.M.	My Friend Phil (1st, 8vo, p-o, 320p, 6cp)	L: Ward Lock	1915	Tarrant, M.	50-70	*
Peake, Elmore E.	House of Hawley (1st, 8vo, 341p, cvr by...)	Appleton	1905	Armstrong, M.	30-45	*
Peake, M.	Shapes & Sounds (1st, 8vo, 23p, ibds)	L: Chatto	1941	Peake, M.	200-300	
Pearson, E.L.	Voyage of the Hoppergrass (1st, 8vo, 348p, b/w, PPPa)	MacMillan	1913	Fogarty, T.	85-100	R*
Peary, J.	Children of the Arctic (1st, 4to, cloth, 120p)	Stokes	(1903)	(Photos)	70-90	
Peary, J.	Snow Baby (1st, 4to, p-o, 84p, PPP)	Stokes	(1901)	(Photos)	100-140	
Peary, M.A.	Little Tooktoo (1st, 8vo, ibds, 62p, pep, 5cp)	Wm. Morrow	(1930)	Wiese, K.	40-65	*
Pease, E.F.	Gay Pippo (1st, 4to, p-o, 80p, color, pep)	Whitman	1936	Wiese, K.	30-50	
Pease, E.F.	Jolly Little Clown (1st, lg8vo, p-o, 126p, pep)	Whitman	(1927)	Hetherington	35-50	*
Pease, Howard	Jungle River (1st {std}, sm8vo, 295p, col frn, pep)	Doubleday/Dor.	1938	Sperry, A.	30-45	*
Pease, Howard	Thunderbolt House (1st {std}, sm8vo, 287p, b/w, pep)	Doubleday/Dor.	1944	Sperry, A.	20-40	*
Pease, J.V.D.	Nimbo (1st, 8vo, p-o, 64p, cp)	Whitman	(1934)	Young, E.M.	30-45	*
Pease, L.	Child You Used to Be (1st, 8vo, 198p, 10pl)	McClurg	1909	Perkins, L.F.	45-65	*
Pease, L.	Dollies in Happy-Land (1st, lg8vo, pict cl, [45]p, color)	Whitman	(1914)	Lee, E.D.	80-120	
Pease, L.	Four & Twenty Dollies (1st, sm sq4to, 94p, ibds, color)	Hamming	(1914)	Lee, E.D.	65-80	
Peat, F.B.	Magnificent Squeak (1st, 8vo, ibds, 42p, color)	Saalfield	(1929)	Peat, F.B.	45-60	
Peat, F.B.	Rags (1st, lg4to, [12]p, wraps, color)	Saalfield	1929	Peat, F.B.	50-65	
Peat, F.B.	Stories Children Like (1st, lg4to, [34]p, ibds, 8cp)	Saalfield	1933	Peat, F.B.	45-60	
Peat, F.E.	Christmas Carols (1st, folio, ibds, 45p, gilt, pep)	Saalfield	(1937)	Peat, F.B.	45-60	
Peattie, D.C.	Book of Hours (1st, 8vo, 246p, 202p, b/w, cvr by...)	Putnam	1937	Ward, L.	35-50	*
Peattie, D.C.	Child's Story of the World (1st, sq8vo, [148]p, color, pep)	Simon/Schuster	1937	Averill, N.	70-90	*
Peattie, D.C.	Journey into America (1st, 8vo, 276p, color, pep)	Houghton	1943	Ward, L.	25-40	*
Peattie, D.C.	Story of America (1st, sq8vo, [24]p, ibds, color, pep)	Grosset/Dunlap	1937	Averill, N.	35-50	*
Peattie, D.C.	Story of Ancient Civilization (1st, sq8vo, [24]p ibds, col, pep)	Grosset/Dunlap	1937	Averill, N.	35-50	*
Peattie, D.C.	Story of the First Men (1st, sq8vo, ibds, [24]p, color, pep)	Grosset/Dunlap	1937	Averill, N.	35-50	*
Peattie, E.W.	Azalea at Sunset Gap (1st, sm8vo, tan cl, 286p, 4pl)	Reilly/Britton	(1914)	Nuyttens, J.P.	25-40	*
Peattie, E.W.	Edda & the Oak (1st, sq8vo, 134p, p-o)	Rand/McNally	(1911)	Merrill, K.	30-45	*
Peattie, E.W.	Mountain Woman (1st, 12mo, 251p, teg, cvr by...)	Way/Williams	1896	Rogers, B.	85-125	
Peck, H.T.	Hilda and the Wishes (1st, sm8vo, 240p, 8pl)	Dodd	1907	Leonard, M.E.	30-50	*
Peck, Leigh	Don Coyote (1st, sm4to, 78p, color, cep, DJ)	Houghton	1942	Burton, V.L.	45-60	
Peck, Leigh	Pecos Bill & Lightning (1st, sm4to, 68p, color)	Houghton	1940	Wiese, K.	25-40	*
Peck, T.A.	Sword of Dundee (1st, sm8vo, 398p, p-o, 7pl)	Duffield	1908	Rae, J.	30-45	*
Pedley, M.	Land of Goodness Knows Where (1st, 8vo, 117p, col frn, b/w)	L: Newnes	(1923)	Knowles, H.J.	90-135	
Peedie, J.M.	Donald in Numberland (1st, 8vo, ipcb, [64]p, color, dep)	R.D. Henkle	(1927)	Hader, B.& E.	70-100	*
Peirce, G.	How Percival Caught the Python (1st, sq24mo, [89]p, color)	Holiday House	(1937)	Unknown	30-50	*
Peirce, G.	How Percival Caught the Tiger (1st, sq24mo, [89]p, color)	Holiday House	(1936)	Unknown	30-50	*
Peltier, F.	Through the Rainbow (1st, 8vo, blue cl, p-o, 117p, 7cp)	Revell	(1917)	Wilson, C.P.	25-40	
Pemberton, Max	House Under the Sea (1st AM, 8vo, 346p, brown/gilt, 8pl)	Appleton	1902	Forestier, A.	30-45	
Pemberton, Max	Pro Patria (1st, 8vo, red/gilt, 16pl)	L: Ward Lock	1904	Forestier, A.	40-65	
Penfield, E.	Big Book of Horses & Goats (1st, ob folio, [24]p, color)	R.H. Russell	1901	Penfield, E.	200-300	*
Penfield, E.	Holland Sketches (1st, sm4to, 147p, ibds, 34 ticp, pep)	Scribner	1907	Penfield, E.	120-165	
Penfield, E.	Spanish Sketches (1st, sm4to, 146p, yellow bds, 27 ticp, pep)	Scribner	1911	Penfield, E.	120-160	
Pennell, E.R.	Life of J.M. Whistler (4to, 2 volumes, bds, b/w)	Lippincott	1909	Whistler, J.M.	70-90	
Pennell, E.R.	Our House (1st, 8vo, ipcb, 373p, 10pl)	Houghton	1912	Pennell, J.	35-65	*
Pennell, E.R.	To Gypsyland (1st UK, sm8vo, pink cl, 240p, b/w)	L: T.F. Unwin	1893	Pennell, J.	35-50	
Pennell, J.	Adventures of an Illustrator (1st, folio, buckram, 372p)	Little/Brown	1925	Pennell, J.	65-80	
Pennell, J.	French Cathedrals (1st, 4to, 424p)	Century	1910	Pennell, J.	45-65	
Pennell, J.	Jew at Home (1st, 12mo, red cl, 105p, b/w)	Appleton	1892	Pennell, J.	80-125	
Pennell, J.	Our Philadelphia (1st, 4to, red/gilt, 552p, teg)	Lippincott	1914	Pennell, J.	50-80	

AUTHOR	TITLE	PUBLISHER	DATE	ARTIST	PRICE	LC
Pennell, J.	Pictures of Panama Canal (1st, 4to, brown cl, p-o, 28pl)	Lippincott	1912	Pennell, J.	50-80	
Pennell, J.	Play in Provence (1st, 8vo, tan cl, teg, uncut, 202p, b/w)	Century	1892	Pennell, J.	35-50	
Pennell, J.	Wonder of Work (1st, 4to, brown cl, p-o, 52pl)	Lippincott	1916	Pennell, J.	65-90	
Perera, Lydia	Frisky (1st, sm8vo, [46]p, red cl, color, cep)	Holiday House	1955	Liebman, O.	20-30	*
Perez, Luis	El Coyote the Rebel (1st {std}, sm8vo, orange cl, 233p, b/w)	Holt	(1947)	Politi, L.	35-50	*
Perez-Guerra, A.	Poppy, Adventures of a Fairy (1st, lg8vo, ibds, 80p, pep, b/w)	Rand/McNally	(1931)	West, B.	80-120	*
Perez-Guerra, A.	Poppy, Adventures of a Fairy (16mo, [62]p, ibds, 16 color)	Rand/McNally	(1942)	Barclay, B.	35-50	*
Perkins, E.E.	News from Notown (1st, 4to, 108p, b/w)	Houghton	1919	Perkins, L.F.	35-50	
Perkins, L.F.	American Twins of the Revolution (1st, 8vo, 208p, pep, b/w)	Houghton	1926	Perkins, L.F.	30-45	*
Perkins, L.F.	Belgian Twins (1st, 8vo, brown cl, 198p, b/w)	Houghton	1917	Perkins, L.F.	25-45	
Perkins, L.F.	Book of Joys (1st, lg8vo, 212p, green cl, uncut, p-o, 5cp)	McClurg	1907	Perkins, L.F.	50-75	
Perkins, L.F.	Cave Twins (1st, 8vo, 164p, b/w)	Houghton	1916	Perkins, L.F.	35-50	*
Perkins, L.F.	Chinese Twins (1st, 8vo, yellow cl, 166p, col frn, b/w)	Houghton	1935	Perkins, L.F.	25-40	
Perkins, L.F.	Cornelia (1st, sm8vo, 202p, 8pl)	Houghton	1919	Perkins, L.F.	30-45	*
Perkins, L.F.	Dutch Twins (1st, 8vo, 190p, b/w, PPPa)	Houghton	1911	Perkins, L.F.	45-60	
Perkins, L.F.	Filipino Twins (1st, 8vo, 150p, b/w)	Houghton	1923	Perkins, L.F.	30-45	
Perkins, L.F.	French Twins (1st, 8vo, blue cl, 202p, b/w)	Houghton	1918	Perkins, L.F.	35-50	
Perkins, L.F.	Indian Twins (1st, 8vo, 203p, b/w)	Houghton	1930	Perkins, L.F.	35-50	*
Perkins, L.F.	Irish Twins (1st, 8vo, 206p, b/w)	Houghton	1913	Perkins, L.F.	35-50	*
Perkins, L.F.	Italian Twins (1st, lg8vo, green cl, 149p, b/w, pep)	Houghton	1920	Perkins, L.F.	30-45	
Perkins, L.F.	Japanese Twins (1st, 8vo, 178p, beige cl, b/w, pep)	Houghton	1912	Perkins, L.F.	30-45	
Perkins, L.F.	Mexican Twins (1st, 8vo, 186p, b/w)	Houghton	1915	Perkins, L.F.	30-45	
Perkins, L.F.	Mr. Chick... (1st, ob4to, 117p, p-o, orange cl, fp b/w)	Houghton	1926	Perkins, L.F.	35-55	
Perkins, L.F.	Pickaninny Twins (1st, 8vo, 152p, tan cl, b/w, pep)	Houghton	1931	Perkins, L.F.	90-140	
Perkins, L.F.	Puritan Twins (1st, 8vo, 179p, pep, b/w)	Houghton	1921	Perkins, L.F.	25-40	
Perkins, L.F.	Spartan Twins (1st, 12mo, 161p, b/w)	Houghton	1920	Perkins, L.F.	30-45	
Perkins, L.F.	Swiss Twins (1st, 8vo, 132p, brown cl, b/w, pep)	Houghton	1922	Perkins, L.F.	30-45	
Perkins, Marlin	Zooparade (1st {A}, 4to, beige cl, 94p, 16 fp color, pep)	Rand/McNally	(1954)	Bransom, P.	45-60	
Perrault, C.	Cinderella (1st, lg8vo, unpag, color, CM)	Scribner	1954	Brown, Marcia	70-100	*
Perrault, C.	Fairy Tales (1st, sm4to, p-o, 107p, 12cp)	L: Simpkin	(1911)	Appleton, H.C.	80-100	
Perrault, C.	Fairy Tales (1st, 12mo, p-o, 128p, 8cp)	L: Dent	(1913)	Robinson, C.	90-125	
Perrault, C.	Fairy Tales (1st, sm4to, blue bds, p-o, color)	L: Selwyn	1922	Austen, J.	45-60	*
Perrault, C.	Fairy Tales (1st, 4to, blue/gilt, 160p, 12cp, 12pl)	L: Harrap	(1922)	Clarke, H.	350-500	
Perrault, C.	Fairy Tales (1st AM, 4to, blue/gilt, 160p, 12cp, 12pl)	Dodge	[1922]	Clarke, H.	300-450	
Perrault, C.	Old Time Stories (1st AM, 4to, 200p, p-o, gilt, 6 ticp)	Dodd	(1921)	Robinson, W.H.	200-300	
Perrault, C.	Old-Time Stories (1st, 4to, red/gilt, 200p, 6 ticp)	L: Constable	1921	Robinson, W.H.	280-400	
Perrault, C.	Once Upon a Time (1st, 4to, 115p)	L: O'Connor	1922	Sinclair, H.	70-120	*
Perrault, C.	Puss in Boots (1st, 4to, [30]p, color, pep, CH)	Scribner	(1952)	Brown, Marcia	70-100	R*
Perrault, C.	Sleeping Beauty (1st, 4to, teg, blue/gilt, 12cp)	Dodge	[1922]	Clarke, H.	275-400	
Perrault, C.	Story of Blue-Beard (1st, 8vo, green cl, 61p)	L: Lawrence	1895	Southall, J.E.	65-80	*
Perrault, C.	Tales of Past Times... (1st, sq8vo, blue bds, 63p, p-o, color)	L: Selwyn	(1922)	Austen, J.	80-100	
Perry, Bliss	Plated City (1st, sm8vo, brown cl, 397p)	Scribner	1895	Armstrong, M.	25-40	*
Perry, Bliss	Salem Kittredge... (1st, 8vo, 291p, yellow cl)	Scribner	1894	Armstrong, M.	20-35	
Perry, F.F.	Their Hearts' Desire (1st, lg8vo, teg, 152p, 6cp, dep)	Dodd	1909	Fisher, H.	65-80	
Perry, Nora	Another Flock of Girls (1st, sq8vo, 194p, green/gilt)	Little/Brown	1890	Birch/Copeland	45-60	*
Perry, Nora	Flock of Girls & Boys (1st, sm8vo, 323p, grey/gilt, 9pl)	Little/Brown	1895	Parker, C.T.	30-45	
Perry, S.G.	Angel of Christmas (1st, 12mo, p-o, 4cp)	Stokes	1917	Kirk, M.L.	25-40	
Perry, S.G.	Kind Adventure (1st, 12mo, 318p, green cl, p-o, 4cp)	Stokes	(1914)	Kirk, M.L.	45-60	
Peterkin, Julia	Plantation Christmas (1st, sm8vo, red cl, 26p, p-o, 1-color)	Houghton	1934	Hendrickson, D.	20-30	
Petersen, H.	Dulcibel (1st, 12mo, grey cl, 402p, teg, p-o, 3cp)	Winston	1907	Pyle, H.	40-65	
Petersham, M.	American ABC (1st, lg8vo, [56]p, gilt, color, cep, CH)	MacMillan	1941	Petershams	80-120	
Petersham, M.	Auntie & Celia Jane & Miki (1st {std}, 4to, ibds, [64]p, col, NH)	Doubleday/Dor.	1932	Petershams	80-120	*
Petersham, M.	Box with Red Wheels (1st, sm4to, [32]p, color)	MacMillan	(1949)	Petershams	50-80	*
Petersham, M.	Christ Child (1st {std}, 4to, ibds, [62]p, color, pep)	Doubleday/Dor.	(1931)	Petershams	45-70	
Petersham, M.	Circus Baby (1st, 4to, ibds, [32]p, color)	MacMillan	(1950)	Petershams	65-100	
Petersham, M.	Get-A-Way & Harry Janos (1st, 4to, ibds, p-o, [64]p, 14cp)	Viking	1933	Petershams	70-100	
Petersham, M.	Miki (1st {std}, 4to, [63]p, ibds, color, pep)	Doubleday/Dor.	1929	Petershams	50-80	
Petersham, M.	Miki & Mary... (1st, 4to, ibds, [64]p, color, pep, DJ)	Viking	1934	Petershams	70-100	
Petersham, M.	Moses (1st, lg8vo, blue cl, [32]p, color, pep, DJ)	Winston	1938	Petershams	50-70	
Petersham, M.	Rooster Crows (1st, sm4to, [64]p, tan cl, color, cep, CM)	MacMillan	1945	Petershams	75-110	R
Petersham, M.	Ruth (1st, sm4to, blue/gilt, [32]p, pep, 8 fp color)	Winston	1938	Petershams	35-50	
Petersham, M.	Stories from the Old Testament (1st, lg8vo, [128]p, color, pep)	Winston	1938	Petershams	35-50	
Petersham, M.	Story Book of Clothes (1st, 12mo, 31p, p-o, yellow cl, color)	Winston	1933	Petershams	25-40	
Petersham, M.	Story Book of Cotton (1st, sq8vo, [32]p, p-o, color)	Winston	1939	Petershams	25-40	
Petershams	America's Stamps... (1st, 4to, 144p, 3 fp color, DJ)	MacMillan	1947	Petershams	30-45	
Petershams	Ark/Father Noah & Mother Noah (1st {std}, sq4to, ibds, col, pep)	Doubleday/Dor.	1930	Petershams	70-100	R*
Petershams	Boy Who Had no Heart (1st {std}, sm4to, red cl, [30]p, color)	MacMillan	(1955)	Petershams	45-60	
Petershams	Jesus' Story (1st, sm8vo, 119p, 6 fp color, cep, DJ)	MacMillan	1942	Petershams	40-60	
Petershams	Silver Mace (1st {std}, 4to, ibds, 38p, fp color)	MacMillan	(1956)	Petershams	45-60	
Peterson, Barbara	Whitefoot Mouse (1st, 8vo, 52p, red cl, 2-color, pep)	Holiday House	(1959)	Peterson, R.F.	20-25	*
Peto, Gladys	China Cow (1st, 4to, p-o, 129p, black/gilt, 8cp)	Houghton	[1926]	Peto, G.	70-100	
Peto, Gladys	Gladys Peto's Children's Book (lg8vo, ibds, 7cp)	L: Routledge	[1930]	Peto, G.	65-90	*

AUTHOR	TITLE	PUBLISHER	DATE	ARTIST	PRICE	LC
Peto, Gladys	Twilight Stories (1st, 4to, ibds, unpag, 8cp)	L: J.F. Shaw	[1932]	Peto, G.	85-120	*
Petrovitch, W.	Heroes & Legends of Serbians (1st, 4to, 394p, teg, 32cp)	L: Harrap	1914	James, G.	65-90	
Petry, Ann	Drugstore Cat (1st, lg8vo, 87p, red cl, fp b/w, pep)	Crowell	1949	Suba, S.	50-75	*
Pezet, A.W.	Aristokia (1st, 8vo, 214p, blue/gilt, 8pl)	Century	1919	Sarg, T.	25-45	*
Phelps, E.S.	Avery... (1st, 12mo, 238p)	Houghton	1902	Rogers, B.	20-30	
Phelps, E.S.	Supply at St. Agatha's (1st, 8vo, 38p, uncut, teg, 2pl by...)	Houghton	1896	Smith, E.B.	30-50	
Philbrook, Eliz.	Far From Marlborough Street (1st, sm8vo, 302p, b/w)	Viking	1944	Torrey, M.	30-45	*
Phillips, C.	Gallery of Girls (1st, 4to, p-o, unpag, green cl, 39cp)	Century	1911	Phillips, C.	250-350	
Phillips, C.	Young Man's Fancy (1st, 4to, unpag, gilt, 19cp)	Bobbs-Merrill	(1912)	Phillips, C.	200-300	
Phillips, D.G.	The Cost (1st, 8vo, 402p, grey cl, 16 b/w illus)	Bobbs-Merrill	(1904)	Fisher, H.	20-35	
Phillips, E.C.	Little Rag Doll (1st, 8vo, p-o, 173p, 4cp, pep)	Houghton	1930	Lenski, L.	50-70	
Phillips, E.C.	Name for Obed (1st, lg8vo, 117p, 1-color, pep, DJ)	Houghton	1941	Lenski, L.	50-70	
Phillips, E.C.	Peter Peppercorn (1st, sm4to, 148p, pep, color, DJ)	Houghton	1939	Bischoff, I.	25-40	
Phillips, E.C.	Wee Ann (1st, 12mo, 134p, 4cp, pep)	Houghton	1919	Butler, E.F.	20-30	*
Phillips, H.W.	The Pets (1st, 12mo, 47p, tan cl, 5pl)	McClure	1906	Frost, A.B.	25-40	
Phillips, J.	Trip to Fairyland (1st, sq8vo, [53]p, gilt)	Conkey	(1905)	Carqueville, W.	80-120	
Phillips, J.C.	Plantation Sketches (1st, ob folio, brown ibds, b/w)	R.H. Russell	1899	Phillips, J.C.	200-300	
Phillips, M.E.	Tommy Tregennis (lg8vo, teg, 209p, 7cp)	L: Constable	1914	Wheelhouse, M.V.	50-85	*
Phillpotts, E.	Dish of Apples (1st, sm4to, lavender cl, 75p, 3 ticp, pep)	Hodder	[1921]	Rackham, A.	180-220	
Phillpotts, E.	Flint Heart (1st, 8vo, 310p, teg, gilt, 16cp)	L: Smith Elder	1910	Folkard, C.	90-120	
Phillpotts, E.	Flint Heart (1st AM, 8vo, 334p, 16cp)	Dutton	(1910)	Folkard, C.	65-100	
Phillpotts, E.	Girl & The Faun (1st, sm4to, 78p, 4cp)	L: A&C Black	1916	Brangwyn, F.	100-130	
Phillpotts, E.	Girl & The Faun (1st AM, sm4to, pict cl, 78p, 4cp)	Lippincott	1917	Brangwyn, F.	80-120	
Phipps, Mary	All About Patsy (1st {std}, 8vo, red cl, 136p, 16cp, 38pl, pep)	Doubleday/Dor.	1930	Phipps, M.	85-135	
Phipps, Mary	Liza Jane & the Kinkies (1st, 4to, ibds, [90]p, color, pep)	Sears	(1929)	Phipps, M.	150-220	*
Phleger, Fred	Whales Go By (1st {std}, lg8vo, ipcb, 62p, p-o, pep, color)	Random	(1959)	Galdone, P.	30-45	*
Pickard, W.B.	Adventures of Alcassin (1st, 8vo, 352p, red/gilt)	L: J. Cape	1936	DeBosschere, J.	35-50	
Pickett, G.E.	Heart of a Soldier (1st, sm4to, 215p, pcb)	NY: Moyle	(1913)	Booth, F.	50-70	
Pidgin, C.F.	Blennerhassett (1st, 8vo, blue cl, teg, 12pl)	C.M. Clark	1901	Stephens, C.H.	20-30	
Pier, A.S.	Boys of St. Timothy's (1st, 12mo, 284p, 3pl, PPPa)	Scribner	1904	Wyeth, N.C.	65-90	
Pierson, C.D.	Among the Farmyard People (1st, sm8vo, teg, uncut, 245p, 11pl)	Dutton	1899	Gordon, F.C.	35-50	*
Pierson, C.D.	Among the Forest People (1st, 12mo, teg, 219p, gilt)	Dutton	(1898)	Gordon, F.C.	35-50	
Pierson, C.D.	Among the Meadow People (1st, 12mo, 127p, gilt, teg, b/w, uncut)	Dutton	1897	Gordon, F.C.	35-50	*
Pierson, C.D.	Among the Night People (1st, 8vo, 221p)	Dutton	(1902)	Gordon, F.C.	35-50	*
Pierson, C.D.	Among the Pond People (1st, 12mo, 210p, teg, 12 b/w)	Dutton	1901	Gordon, F.C.	30-50	*
Pierson, C.D.	Plucky Allens (1st, sm8vo, green/gilt, 327p, 5 fp b/w)	Dutton	(1925)	Daugherty, J.	25-45	*
Pierson, C.D.	Tales of a Poultry Farm (1st, 8vo, 195p, gilt, 9pl)	L: J. Murray	1904	Pierson, C.D.	45-60	*
Pine, F.W. (ed.)	Franklin's Autobiography (1st, lg8vo, green cl, 341p, 10cp)	Holt	1916	Smith, E.B.	50-70	
Pine, Tillie S.	Indians Knew (1st, sm4to, teal cl, 32p, 2-color, pep)	Whittlesey	(1957)	Keats, E.J.	65-90	*
Piper, W.	Brimful Book (1st, 4to, [74]p, p-o, color)	Platt/Munk	(1929)	Eulalie	40-60	
Piper, W.	Children of Other Lands (1st, lg4to, [85]p, p-o, orang cl, 5cp)	Platt/Munk	(1933)	Holling, H.C.	50-70	
Piper, W.	Little Folks/Other Lands (1st, lg4to, [80]p, gilt, p-o, color)	Platt/Munk	(1929)	Holling, H.C.	60-80	*
Piper, W. (ed.)	Famous Rhymes/Mother Goose (4to, blue/gilt, p-o, color)	Platt/Munk	(1923)	Various	35-60	*
Piper, W. (ed.)	Jolly Rhymes of Mother Goose (1st, 12mo, [118]p, col frn)	Platt/Munk	(1932)	Lenski, L.	45-60	*
Piper, W. (ed.)	Little Engine that Could (1st, sm8vo, unpag, p-o, color, pep)	Platt/Munk	(1930)	Lenski, L.	50-70	
Piper, W. (ed.)	Stories Children Love (lg4to, green cl, p-o, [71]p, color)	Platt/Munk	(1932)	Lenski/Eulalie	45-60	
Piper, W. (ed.)	Tales from Storyland (1st, lg4to, p-o, [80]p, color)	Platt/Munk	(1941)	Hauman, G.& D.	35-60	*
Plimpton, Geo.	Rabbit's Umbrella (1st, 8vo, 159p, yellow cl, b/w, pep)	Viking	1955	DuBois, W.P.	35-50	*
Plummer, M.W.	Chronicles of the Cid (1st, 12mo, 155p, 10pl)	Holt	1910	McVickar, H.W.	50-80	*
Poe, E.A.	Poetical Works of... (1st AM, 4to, bds, 28cp)	Doran	[1921]	Dulac, E.	200-280	
Poe, E.A.	Selected Tales of Mystery (1st AM, 4to, 334p, teg, 16cp)	Lippincott	1909	Shaw, B.	70-125	*
Poe, E.A.	Tales of Mystery... (1st, 8vo, 416p)	L: A. Pearson	1905	McCormick, A.D.	65-80	*
Poe, E.A.	Tales of Mystery... (1st, 4to, 383p, p-o, teg, 8 ticp, 24pl)	L: Harrap	1919	Clarke, H.	450-600	
Poe, E.A.	Tales of Mystery... (1st AM, 4to, p-o, 8 ticp, 24pl)	Brentano's	[1919]	Clarke, H.	350-500	
Poe, E.A.	Tales of Mystery... (1st {this pub}, 4to, p-o, 412p, 8 ticp)	Tudor	1933	Clarke, H.	125-165	
Poe, E.A.	Tales of Mystery... (1st AM, 4to, gilt, 318p, 12cp, pep)	Lippincott	[1935]	Rackham, A.	200-280	
Poe, E.A.	Tales of Mystery... (1st, 4to, 318p, gilt, 12cp, pep)	L: Harrap	(1935)	Rackham, A.	240-300	
Poe, E.A.	Tales of Mystery... (4to, black cl, cp, later)	Lippincott	1940	Clarke, H.	80-100	
Poe, E.A.	The Bells... (1st, 4to, teg, green/gilt, pep, 28 ticp)	L: Hodder	(1912)	Dulac, E.	280-400	
Poe, E.A.	The Raven (1st, sm8vo, 110p, b/w pl, pep)	Reilly/Britton	(1910)	Neill, J.R.	80-120	*
Pogany, Elaine	Peterkin (1st, 4to, ibds, [75]p, 14 fp color, pep)	McKay	1940	Pogany, W.	100-165	
Pogany, Nebby	Hungarian Fairy Book (1st, 8vo, 287p, blue/gilt, col frn)	L: T.F. Unwin	(1913)	Pogany, W.	130-165	
Pogany, Nebby	Magyar Fairy Tales (1st {std}, 8vo, green/gilt, 268p, b/w, pep)	Dutton	(1930)	Pogany, W.	100-150	R
Politi, L.	Boat for Peppe (1st, 4to, cloth, [38]p, color, DJ)	Scribner	1950	Politi, L.	65-80	
Politi, L.	Butterflies Come (1st, sm4to, yellow cl, unpag, color)	Scribner	(1957)	Politi, L.	30-50	*
Politi, L.	Juanita (1st, sm4to, [31]p, color, CH)	Scribner	1948	Politi, L.	65-100	*
Politi, L.	Little Leo (1st, 4to, [30]p, color, DJ)	Scribner	1951	Politi, L.	75-100	
Politi, L.	Little Pancho (1st {1st book}, 16mo, [40]p, ibds, color, pep)	Viking	1938	Politi, L.	65-100	
Politi, L.	Mission Bell (1st, ob8vo, [32]p, blue cl, color)	Scribner	1953	Politi, L.	30-45	*
Politi, L.	Pedro, Angel of Olvera Street (1st, 8vo, [32]p, color, CH)	Scribner	1946	Politi, L.	60-95	*
Politi, L.	Song of the Swallows (1st, 4to, [32]p, color, CM)	Scribner	1949	Politi, L.	70-100	R
Politi, L.	St. Francis & the Animals (1st, 8vo, beige cl, unpag, color)	Scribner	1957	Politi, L.	25-40	*

AUTHOR	TITLE	PUBLISHER	DATE	ARTIST	PRICE	LC
Pollard, A.	Romance of King Arthur (1st AM, lg8vo, 517p, green/gilt, 16cp)	MacMillan	1917	Rackham, A.	170-240	
Pollard, E.F.	Little Chief (1st, sm8vo, teg, uncut, 236p, 6pl)	L: Nister	(1901)	Robinson, T.H.	30-45	
Pollard, J.	Boston Tea Party (1st, 8vo, ipcb, [32]p, color)	Dodd	1882	McVickar, H.W.	75-90	
Pollard, J.	Elfin-Land (1st, lg ob4to, [40]p, ibds, chromos, dep)	G.W. Harlan	(1882)	Saterlee, W.	140-200	
Pollard, Percival	Posters in Miniature (1st, 8vo, [255]p, 250pl)	R.H. Russell	1896	Various	200-300	
Ponsat, Georges	Romance of the River (1st AM, 8vo, green/gilt, 290p, col frn)	Dodd	(1924)	Detmold, E.J.	30-45	*
Ponset, Marie	Fairy Tale Book (1st, folio, ibds, 156p, color, GGB)	Simon/Schuster	(1958)	Segur, A.	120-180	*
Pool, M.L.	Chums (1st, 8vo, 241p, 4pl)	Page	1900	Bridgman, L.J.	25-40	*
Pool, M.L.	Little Bermuda (1st, 8vo, 163p, 4pl)	Page	1899	Bridgman, L.J.	20-35	*
Pool, M.L.	Mrs. Gerald (1st, 8vo, 339p, orange/silver, 13pl)	Harper	1896	Rogers, W.A.	20-40	
Pool, M.L.	Red-Bridge Neighborhood (1st, 8vo, 369p, 13pl)	Harper	1898	Carleton, C.	20-35	
Pope, A.	Rape of the Lock (1st, 12mo, AEG, 11 illus)	L: Smithers	1896	Beardsley, A.	175-220	
Pope, Eliz. M.	Sherwood Ring (1st, 8vo, tan cl, 266p, fp b/w)	Houghton	1958	Ness, E.M.	50-80	R*
Pope, J.	Babes & Beasts (1st, 8vo, ibds, unpag, color)	L: Blackie	[1912]	Robinson, C.	150-220	*
Pope, J.	Babes & Birds (1st AM, 8vo, ibds, 17cp)	Caldwell	[1910]	Robinson, C.	150-220	
Pope, J.	Babes & Birds (1st, 8vo, ibds, unpag, 17cp)	L: Blackie	[1910]	Robinson, C.	170-240	
Pope, J.	Baby Scouts (1st, ob 16mo, unpag)	L: Blackie	[1911]	Robinson, C.	125-160	*
Pope, J.	Bobbity Flop (1st, ob8vo, unpag)	L: Blackie	[1912]	Macgregor, A.J.	50-70	*
Pope, J.	Bunny Book (1st, 4to, [36]p, ibds, color)	L: Blackie	(1909)	Macgregor, A.J.	50-70	*
Pope, J.	Cat Scouts (1st, sm4to, ibds, [48]p, p-o, 6cp)	L: Blackie	[1912]	Wain, L.	350-500	
Porter, E.	Pollyanna (1st, 8vo, 310p, pink/gilt, 8pl, PPP)	Page	1913	Mulford, S.	100-160	
Porter, E.	Pollyanna (1st UK, 8vo, 310p, 8pl)	L: I. Pitman	1913	Mulford, S.	90-120	
Porter, E.	Pollyanna (1st {this pub.}, 8vo, 255p, 8pl)	L: Harrap	1938	Tawse, S.	45-60	*
Porter, E.	Pollyanna Grows Up (1st, 8vo, 308p, 8pl)	L.C. Page	1915	Taylor, H.W.	60-100	*
Porter, G.S.	At the Foot of the Rainbow (1st, 8vo, 258p, yellow cl, 4cp)	Outing	1907	Kemp, O.	400-600	
Porter, G.S.	Birds of the Bible (1st, lg8vo, 469p, 81 illus, pep)	Jennings	(1909)	(Photos)	185-250	
Porter, G.S.	Daughter of the Land (1st, 8vo, 475p, green cl, col frn)	Doubleday/Page	1918	Rogers, F.	30-45	
Porter, G.S.	Fire Bird (1st {std}, 8vo, 71p, tan bds, pep, 3cp by...)	Doubleday/Page	1922	Grant, G.	240-300	
Porter, G.S.	Freckles (1st, 8vo, teg, 433p, uncut, 6pl, PPPa)	Doubleday/Page	1904	Crawford, E.S.	400-600	
Porter, G.S.	Friends In Feathers (1st, lg8vo, teg, 335p, b/w)	Doubleday/Page	1917	(Photos)	160-200	
Porter, G.S.	Girl of the Limberlost (1st, 8vo, 485p, 4pl, pep)	Doubleday/Page	1909	Benda, W.T.	50-70	
Porter, G.S.	Her Father's Daughter (1st, 8vo, 486p, pep, col frn by...)	Doubleday/Page	1921	Summers, D.G.	45-70	
Porter, G.S.	Homing With Birds (1st, 8vo, 381p)	Doubleday/Page	1919	(Photos)	120-150	
Porter, G.S.	Jesus of the Emerald (1st, lg8vo, [44]p, white bds, col frn)	Doubleday/Page	1923	Winchell, E.	350-500	
Porter, G.S.	Keeper of the Bees (1st {std}, 8vo, 515p, 3pl)	Doubleday/Page	1925	Grant, G.	50-70	
Porter, G.S.	Laddie (1st, 8vo, 602p, blue cl, col frn, 3pl)	Doubleday/Page	1913	Pfeifer	35-50	
Porter, G.S.	Magic Garden (1st {std}, sm8vo, 272p, pep, designs by...)	Doubleday/Page	1927	Thayer, L.	100-130	
Porter, G.S.	Michael O'Halloran (1st, 8vo, 560p, green cl, 4pl, pep)	Doubleday/Page	1915	Rogers, F.	45-60	
Porter, G.S.	Morning Face (1st, sm4to, 127p, blue/gilt, color)	Doubleday/Page	(1916)	(Photos)	200-260	
Porter, G.S.	Moths of the Limberlost (1st, 4to, tan cl, 370p, color)	Doubleday/Page	1912	(Photos)	185-250	
Porter, G.S.	Music of the Wild (1st, 8vo, 430p, green/gilt)	Jennings	(1910)	(Photos)	165-220	
Porter, G.S.	Song of the Cardinal (1st {1st bk.}, 8vo, red cl, 163p, 17pl)	Bobbs-Merrill	(1903)	(Photos)	130-165	
Porter, G.S.	Tales You Won't Believe (1st {std}, 8vo, 327p, grey cl, 23pl)	Doubleday/Page	1925	(Photos)	150-175	
Porter, G.S.	The Harvester (1st, 8vo, 564p, 4cp)	Doubleday/Page	1911	Jacobs, W.L.	35-50	
Porter, G.S.	What I Have Done with Birds (1st, 4to, 258p, green cl, p-o)	Bobbs-Merrill	(1907)	(Photos)	180-250	
Porter, Jane	Biffy Buffalo (1st, 8vo, 63p, color, pep)	Wm. Morrow	1942	Smalley, J.	35-50	*
Porter, Rose	Charm of Birds (1st, 12mo, 206p, teg, cvr by...)	Herrick	(1897)	McManus, B.	35-50	
Potter, B.	All About Peter Rabbit (16mo, 47p, bds, p-o, 8cp)	Cupples	(1914)	Hartley, D.	65-90	
Potter, B.	Appley Dapply's Nursery Rhymes (1st, 16mo, p-o [52]p, ibds, 15cp)	L: Warne	[1917]	Potter, B.	450-600	
Potter, B.	Cecily Parsley's Nursery Rhymes (1st, 16mo orang bds, p-o, 15cp)	L: Warne	(1922)	Potter, B.	400-600	
Potter, B.	Fairy Caravan (1st, 8vo, green/gilt, p-o, 225p, 6cp)	McKay	(1929)	Potter, B.	280-400	
Potter, B.	Ginger & Pickles (1st, 8vo, 52p, bds, p-o, 10cp, pep)	L: Warne	1909	Potter, B.	450-600	
Potter, B.	Pie & Patty Pan (1st, 12mo, 52p, p-o, bds, 10cp)	L: Warne	1905	Potter, B.	385-500	
Potter, B.	Roly Poly Pudding (1st, lg8vo, 69p, p-o, 18cp)	L: Warne	1908	Potter, B.	375-500	
Potter, B.	Story of Miss Moppet (1st, 16mo, bds, p-o, 14cp)	L: Warne	1906	Potter, B.	400-600	
Potter, B.	Story of Peter Rabbit (1st, 24mo, p-o, ibds)	Reilly/Britton	(1911)	Neill, J.R.	75-100	
Potter, B.	Story of Peter Rabbit (16mo, ibds, [58]p, color)	Whitman	(1932)	Jordan, N.	45-65	
Potter, B.	Tailor of Gloucester (1st, 16mo, green bds, 85p, p-o, 27cp)	L: Warne	1903	Potter, B.	500-650	
Potter, B.	Tale of Benjamin Bunny (1st, 16mo, 85p, p-o, tan bds, col, pep)	L: Warne	1904	Potter, B.	400-500	
Potter, B.	Tale of Flopsy Bunnies (1st, sm8vo, 85p, bds, p-o, 27cp, pep)	L: Warne	1909	Potter, B.	450-600	
Potter, B.	Tale of Jemima Puddle Duck (1st, sq16mo, grey bds, p-o, 85p)	L: Warne	1908	Potter, B.	450-600	
Potter, B.	Tale of Johnny Town Mouse (1st, 16mo, 85p, bds, p-o)	L: Warne	1918	Potter, B.	380-500	
Potter, B.	Tale of Little Pig Robinson (1st, sq8vo, 141p, p-o, gilt, 6cp)	L: Warne	(1930)	Potter, B.	250-400	
Potter, B.	Tale of Little Pig Robinson (1st AM, 8vo, p-o, 141p, 6cp, pep)	McKay	(1930)	Potter, B.	200-300	
Potter, B.	Tale of Mr. Jeremy Fisher (1st, 24mo, red bds, 85p, p-o, color)	L: Warne	1906	Potter, B.	400-650	
Potter, B.	Tale of Mr. Tod (1st, 16mo, grey bds, p-o, 94p, color)	L: Warne	1912	Potter, B.	400-600	
Potter, B.	Tale of Mrs. Tiggy-Winkle (1st, 16mo, grey bds, 85p, p-o, col)	L: Warne	1905	Potter, B.	450-600	
Potter, B.	Tale of Mrs. Tittlemouse (1st, 24mo, bds, 85p, p-o, 27p)	L: Warne	1910	Potter, B.	380-550	
Potter, B.	Tale of Peter Rabbit (1st {trade}, 16mo, 97p, grey bds, p-o 31cp)	L: Warne	(1902)	Potter, B.	600-800	
Potter, B.	Tale of Peter Rabbit (1st {this pub}, 16mo, 127p, grn cl, 31cp)	Altemus	1904	Potter, B.	200-300	R*
Potter, B.	Tale of Peter Rabbit (12mo, yellow cl, p-o, color)	Hurst	(1908)	Anderson, S.W.	70-100	*
Potter, B.	Tale of Peter Rabbit (lg4to, wraps, 8 color)	Harter	1931	Peat, F.B.	70-90	

AUTHOR	TITLE	PUBLISHER	DATE	ARTIST	PRICE	LC
Potter, B.	Tale of Pigling Bland (1st, 16mo, 94p, bds, p-o, 15cp, pep)	L: Warne	1913	Potter, B.	380-500	
Potter, B.	Tale of Squirrel Nutkin (1st, 16mo, grey bds, p-o, 27cp)	L: Warne	1903	Potter, B.	350-500	
Potter, B.	Tale of Timmy Tiptoes (1st, sq16mo, 85p, brown bds, p-o, color)	L: Warne	1911	Potter, B.	350-500	
Potter, B.	Tale of Tom Kitten (1st, 16mo, green bds, 85p, p-o, pep, color)	L: Warne	1907	Potter, B.	400-550	
Potter, B.	Tale of Two Bad Mice (1st, 16mo, bds, p-o, 85p, color, pep)	L: Warne	1904	Potter, B.	450-650	
Potter, B.	Wag by Wall (1st {std}, 12mo, [30]p, buckram, p-o, t-i frn)	Horn Book	1944	Lankes, J.J.	100-165	
Potter, M.C.	Sally Gabble & the Fairies (1st, 12mo, 87p, col frn, b/w, DJ)	MacMillan	1929	Sewell, H.	70-90	
Potter, M.C.	The Gigglequicks (1st, 12mo, ibds, color)	Volland	(1918)	Sarg, T.	85-120	*
Potter, M.K.	Love in Art (1st, 12mo, 260p, teg, cvr by…)	Page	1898	Armstrong, M.	30-45	
Potter, M.K.	Peggy's Trial (1st, 12mo, 97p, b/w)	Page	1901	Barry, E.B.	20-35	*
Poulsson, E.	Finger Plays/Nursery & Kindergarten (1st, 8vo, [80]p)	Lothrop	1893	Bridgman, L.J.	35-50	
Poulsson, E.	In the Child's World (1st, sq8vo, 443p, b/w)	M. Bradley	1893	Bridgman, L.J.	35-50	
Poulsson, E.	What Happened to Inger Johanne (1st, 8vo, grey cl, 283p, color)	Lothrop/Lee	(1919)	Young, F.L.	25-40	*
Pourrat, Henry	Treasury of French Tales (1st, 8vo, 239p, bds, 9 fp b/w)	Houghton	1953	Baynes, P.D.	70-100	*
Powell, Miriam	Jareb (1st {std}, sm8vo, grey cl, 241p, b/w, cep)	Crowell	(1952)	Simont, M.	30-45	*
Powell, R.S.	Phyllis in Bohemia (1st, 12mo, 233p, teg, cvr by…)	H. Stone	1897	Hazenplug, F.	40-70	
Powell, R.S.	Phyllis in Bohemia (1st, 12mo, teg, 233p, 3pl)	H. Stone	1897	Lowell, O.	45-60	
Power, Rhoda	How it Happened (1st, 8vo, beige cl, 188p, 12pl)	(Cambridge)	1930	Parker, A.M.	45-60	*
Powers, Tom	Scotch Circus (1st, 8vo, [96]p, 7 fp color)	Houghton	1934	Lenski, L.	45-60	
Powers, Tom	Virgin with Butterflies (1st {std}, 8vo, 188p, black cl, b/w)	Bobbs-Merrill	(1945)	Duvoisin, R.	35-50	*
Powys, L.	Impassioned Clay (1st {std}, 8vo, bds, 120p, tp-in frn, DJ)	Longmans	1931	Ward, L.	100-130	
Powys, L.	The Twelve Months (1st UK, 4to, 88p)	L: J. Lane	(1936)	Gibbings, R.	60-80	
Praeger, S.R.	Adventures of Three Bold Bears (ob4to, ibds, 48p)	L: Longmans	1897	Praeger, S.R.	100-165	
Praeger, S.R.	Little Twin Dragon (1st, 60p, ob4to, ibds)	L: Longmans	1900	Praeger, S.R.	100-165	
Pratt, C.S.	Bye O' Baby Ballads (lg8vo, [61]p, ipcb, 14 chromos)	Lothrop	(1886)	Hassam, F.C.	250-320	
Pratt, Ella	Happy Children (1st, lg4to, 64p, ibds, 8cp)	Crowell	(1896)	McCullough, Wm.	130-165	*
Pratt, L.	Ezekiel Expands (1st, 8vo, 228p)	Houghton	1914	Kemble, E.W.	50-85	
Pratt, Marg.	Flash of Washington Square (1st, 4to, green cl, [29]p, dp col)	Lothrop/Lee	1954	Duvoisin, R.	45-70	*
Pratt, Marg.	Successful Secretary (1st, sm8vo, 144p, p-o, 15 fp b/w)	Lothrop/Lee	(1946)	Duvoisin, R.	35-50	*
Pratt, Marg.	Talking Typewriter (1st {std}, sm4to, ibds, 38p, color, pep)	Lothrop/Lee	(1940)	Gergely, T.	35-50	
Prentiss, L.E.	Dickens' Year Book (1st, 8vo, tan bds, p-o, unpag)	McClurg	1913	Groesbeck, D.	25-40	
Preston, Hayter	House of Vanities (1st, 12mo, 59p, bds, b/w)	J. Lane	1922	Fraser, C.L.	50-75	
Preston, Hayter	Windmills (1st, 4to, yellow cl, 125p, uncut, 16cp)	Lane/Dodd	(1923)	Brangwyn, F.	70-100	
Preston, Tom	Peek-A-Boo Twins (1st, 4to, tan bds, p-o, 12cp)	L: H. Frowde	(1915)	Preston, C.	200-300	
Price, Eleanor C.	Adventures of King Arthur (1st, 8vo, 153p, 6cp, p-o)	L: Coker	1931	Wheelwright, R.	35-50	*
Price, Luxor	The Quoks (1st UK, lg4to, 62p, ibds, color)	L: Chambers	(1924)	Price, L.	180-300	
Price, Luxor	The Quoks (1st, 4to, [63]p, p-o, red cl, color)	Stokes	1924	Price, L.	150-220	
Price, M.E.	Angora Twinnies (4to, wraps, [12]p, shape book, color)	Stecher	1919	Price, M.E.	45-60	
Price, M.E.	Betty Fairy Book (folio, [14]p, wraps, shape book, color)	Stecher	1915	Price, M.E.	65-80	
Price, M.E.	Child's Book of Myths (1st, 4to, blue cl, p-o, 112p, 6cp)	Rand/McNally	(1924)	Price, M.E.	50-80	
Price, M.E.	Down Comes the Wilderness (1st {std}, sm8vo, 212p, b/w, pep)	Harper	1937	Price, M.E.	20-35	*
Price, M.E.	Enchantment Tales for Children (1st, 4to, 118p, p-o, col, pep)	Rand/McNally	(1926)	Price, M.E.	50-80	
Price, M.E.	Land of Nod (folio, wraps, [12]p, shape book, color)	Stecher	1916	Price, M.E.	45-60	
Price, M.E.	Legends o/t Seven Seas (1st {std}, 8vo, 168p, gilt col frn, pep)	Harper	1929	Price, M.E.	30-45	
Price, M.E.	Manger Babe (folio, [14]p, wraps, shape bk., color)	Stecher	1916	Price, M.E.	45-60	
Price, M.E.	Monkey-Do (1st {std}, 8vo, 149p, b/w, pep)	Harper	1934	Price, M.E.	20-35	*
Price, M.E.	Mota & the Monkey Tree (1st {std}, 8vo, 146p, pep)	Harper	1935	Price, M.E.	25-40	*
Price, M.E.	Myths & Enchantment Tales (1st, 8vo, 100p, color)	Rand/McNally	(1935)	Price, M.E.	30-45	*
Price, M.E.	Visit to Santa Claus (sm4to, wraps, color)	Stecher	[1915]	Price, M.E.	35-50	
Price, M.E.	Windy Shore (1st {std}, 4to, brown cl, 181p, col frn, 18pl, pep)	Harper	1930	Price, M.E.	35-50	
Prishvin, M.	Treasure Trove of the Sun (1st, 4to, 80p, color, pep)	Viking	1952	Rojankovsky, F.	50-80	R*
Pritchard, M.T.	Upward Path (1st, sm8vo, 255p)	Harcourt	(1920)	Unknown	65-80	*
Procter, E.H.	Rabbit's Day in Town (1st, 4to, ibds, unpag, 20 fp color)	L: Blackie	[1908]	Corbould, W.	120-175	*
Prokofieff, S.	Peter & the Wolf (1st {std}, ob4to, [32]p, p-o, color, DJ)	Knopf	(1940)	Chappell, W.	30-50	
Proudfit, I.B.	Treasure Hunter (1st, lg8vo, 206p, dep)	J. Messner	(1939)	Gramatky, H.	65-80	*
Pugh, E.	Tony Drum (1st, sm8vo, 225p, tan cl, 10cp)	Holt	1898	Nicholson, W.	70-100	
Puner, Helen	Sitter Who Didn't Sit (1st, sm4to, [26]p, color)	Lothrop/Lee	1949	Duvoisin, R.	35-50	*
Pushkin, A.	Ballad of Yukon Jake (1st, 12mo, 36p, 2pl, pcb)	Coward	1928	Kent, R.	60-75	
Pushkin, A.	Golden Cockerel (1st, folio, red/gilt, 46p, 12cp, pep, DJ)	NY: Nelson	1938	Pogany, W.	100-145	
Putnam, Nina W.	Adventures in the Open (1st, sm8vo, ibds, color)	Volland	(1918)	Dodge, K.S.	45-65	*
Putnam, Nina W.	Sunny Bunny (1st, 8vo, ibds, [42]p, color, pep)	Volland	(1918)	Gruelle, J.	85-130	
Putnam, Nina W.	Winkle, Twinkle & Lollypop (1st, 8vo, ibds, color)	Volland	(1918)	Dodge, K.S.	60-80	*
Pycraft, W.P.	Animal Why Book (1st AM, sm4to, 90p, p-o, 31 ticp)	Stokes	[1910]	Noble, E.	150-200	*
Pycraft, W.P.	Pads, Paws & Claws (1st, 4to, ibds, 123p, p-o, 32 ticp)	L: Wells/Gard.	(1911)	Noble, E.	150-185	
Pyle, H.	Book of American Spirit (1st {std}, lg4to, 344p, ibds, p-o, 23cp)	Harper	1923	Pyle, H.	140-200	
Pyle, H.	Book of Pirates (1st, lg4to, 247p, bds, gilt, p-o, 11cp, 25pl)	Harper	1921	Pyle, H.	150-200	
Pyle, H.	Champions of the Round Table (1st, lg8vo, tan/gilt, 328p, b/w)	Scribner	1905	Pyle, H.	180-220	
Pyle, H.	Garden Behind the Moon (1st, 12mo, green/gilt, 192p, 10pl)	Scribner	1895	Pyle, H.	130-170	
Pyle, H.	Men of Iron (1st, 8vo, 328p, red cl, teg, 15pl)	Harper	1892	Pyle, H.	140-200	
Pyle, H.	Merry Advens./Robin Hood (1st 4to, leather/gilt, 296p, 23fp b/w)	Scribner	1883	Pyle, H.	600-850	
Pyle, H.	Modern Aladdin (1st, 8vo, 205p, blue/gilt, b/w)	Harper	1892	Pyle, H.	100-130	
Pyle, H.	Otto of the Silver Hand (1st, lg8vo, olive/gilt, 173p, PPP)	Scribner	1888	Pyle, H.	180-250	

AUTHOR	TITLE	PUBLISHER	DATE	ARTIST	PRICE	LC
Pyle, H.	Pepper and Salt (1st, 4to, tan/gilt, 121p, b/w)	Harper	1886	Pyle, H.	280-400	
Pyle, H.	Price of Blood (1st, 12mo, ipcb, 98p, 6cp, A.E. red)	Badger	1899	Pyle, H.	150-220	
Pyle, H.	Rose of Paradise (1st, 12mo, green/gilt, 231p, 8pl)	Harper	1888	Pyle, H.	100-150	
Pyle, H.	Ruby of Kishmoor (1st, 8vo, teg, 74p, gilt, 10cp)	Harper	1908	Pyle, H.	80-120	
Pyle, H.	Stolen Treasure (1st, 12mo, 253p, orange cl, p-o, 8pl)	Harper	1907	Pyle, H.	90-120	
Pyle, H.	Story of Jack Ballister's Fortunes (1st, 8vo, 420p, 14pl)	Century	1895	Pyle, H.	150-200	
Pyle, H.	Story of King Arthur... (1st, lg8vo, tan/gilt, 313p, b/w, cep)	Scribner	1903	Pyle, H.	140-200	
Pyle, H.	Story of Sir Lancelot (1st, lg8vo, 340p, tan/gilt, b/w)	Scribner	1907	Pyle, H.	160-200	
Pyle, H.	Story of the Grail (1st, sm4to, 258p, tan/gilt, b/w)	Scribner	1910	Pyle, H.	150-200	R
Pyle, H.	Twilight Land (1st, 8vo, 438p, gilt, b/w)	Harper	1895	Pyle, H.	120-165	
Pyle, H.	Wonder Clock (1st, tall 8vo, grey cl, 318p, b/w)	Harper	1888	Pyle, H.	200-300	
Pyle, H.	Yankee Doodle (1st, 4to, 31p, ibds, 8 fp color)	Dodd	1881	Pyle, H.	350-500	
Pyle, Kath.	As the Goose Flies (1st, 8vo, 183p, gilt, 6pl)	Little/Brown	1901	Pyle, Kath.	40-60	
Pyle, Kath.	Black-Eyed Puppy (1st, 8vo, 89p, p-o, 12cp)	Dutton	1923	Pyle, Kath.	45-60	
Pyle, Kath.	Careless Jane (1st, sm8vo, green cl, 110p, b/w)	Dutton	(1902)	Pyle, Kath.	45-65	*
Pyle, Kath.	Charlemagne & his Knights (1st, sm4to, gilt, 302p, col frn, 7pl)	Lippincott	(1932)	Pyle, Kath.	45-60	
Pyle, Kath.	Childhood (1st, sm4to, ibds, 46p, 21cp)	Dutton	(1904)	Stilwell, S.	140-200	
Pyle, Kath.	Christmas Angel (1st, 12mo, green/gilt, teg, 136p, 6pl)	Little/Brown	1900	Pyle, Kath.	65-85	
Pyle, Kath.	Counterpane Fairy (1st, 8vo, green/gilt, uncut, teg, 191p)	Dutton	1898	Pyle, Kath.	70-90	*
Pyle, Kath.	Fairy Tales from Far & Near (1st, 8vo, green cl, 274p, 7cp)	Little/Brown	1922	Pyle, Kath.	50-80	
Pyle, Kath.	Fairy Tales from India (1st, 4to, 229p, red/gilt, 12cp, pep)	Lippincott	1926	Pyle, Kath.	60-85	
Pyle, Kath.	Fairy Tales from Many Lands (1st, 8vo, 316p, col frn)	Dutton	(1911)	Pyle, Kath.	60-80	*
Pyle, Kath.	In the Green Forest (1st, lg8vo, green cl, 171p, 5pl)	Little/Brown	1902	Pyle, Kath.	50-70	
Pyle, Kath.	Katherine Pyle's Bk/Fairy Tales (1st, 8vo, 338p, col frn, 28pl)	Dutton	(1925)	Pyle, Kath.	100-150	
Pyle, Kath.	Lazy Matilda... (1st, 8vo, 173p, blue cl, b/w)	Dutton	(1921)	Pyle, Kath.	30-45	*
Pyle, Kath.	Mother's Nursery Tales (1st, 8vo, gilt, 376p, 7cp)	Dutton	(1918)	Pyle, Kath.	100-145	
Pyle, Kath.	Nancy Rutledge (1st, 8vo, 206p, 6pl)	Little/Brown	1906	Pyle, Kath.	45-60	
Pyle, Kath.	Rabbit Witch (1st, ob4to, 81p, cloth)	Dutton	(1895)	Pyle, Kath.	100-135	
Pyle, Kath.	Six Little Ducklings (1st, 8vo, green cl, p-o, 99p, 24pl, pep)	Dodd	1915	Pyle, Kath.	85-120	
Pyle, Kath.	Tales from Greek Mythology (1st, 8vo, blue cl, 312p, 12pl)	Lippincott	1928	Pyle, Kath.	50-70	
Pyle, Kath.	Tales from Norse Mythology (1st, sm4to, 256p, 8cp, pep)	Lippincott	1930	Pyle, Kath.	45-65	
Pyle, Kath.	Tales of Folk & Fairies (1st, 8vo, blue cl, 288p, 6cp)	Little/Brown	1919	Pyle, Kath.	60-80	
Pyle, Kath.	Tales of Two Bunnies (1st, 8vo, 87p, red cl, b/w, pep)	Dutton	(1913)	Pyle, Kath.	65-100	
Pyle, Kath.	Tales of Wonder & Magic (1st, 8vo, green cl, 314p, 8cp)	Little/Brown	1920	Pyle, Kath.	65-80	*
Pyle, Kath.	Two Little Mice (1st, 8vo, 108p, 16pl)	Dodd	1917	Pyle, Kath.	50-70	
Pyle, Kath.	Where the Wind Blows (1st, 4to, 120p, p-o, 11cp)	R.H. Russell	1902	Day, B.C.	200-250	
Pyle, Kath.	Where the Wind Blows (1st {this pub.}, 8vo, 295p, 10pl)	Dutton	(1910)	Day, B.C.	70-100	*
Pyle, Kath.	Wonder Tales Retold (1st, 8vo, green/gilt, 322p, 8cp)	Little/Brown	1916	Pyle, Kath.	50-70	
Pyle/Porter	Theodora (1st, 12mo, 271p, 4pl)	Little/Brown	1907	McCullough, Wm.	30-45	*
Pyrnelle, L.C.	Diddie, Dumps & Tot (1st, 12mo, green cl, 217p, 12pl, PPP)	Harper	1882	Unknown	250-320	
Pyrnelle, L.C.	Diddie, Dumps & Tot (1st, 8vo, 214p, col frn, cp)	Harper	1930	Kay, G.A.	60-80	*
Queen Marie	Dreamer of Dreams (1st, lg8vo, 181p, grey/gilt, 6 ticp)	L: Hodder	[1915]	Dulac, E.	250-300	
Queen Marie	Lost Princess (sm4to, red cl, 159p, 6 ticp, pep)	L: Warne	[1915]	Attwell, M.L.	70-90	
Queen Marie	Magic Doll of Roumania (1st, 8vo, p-o, 319p, 10cp)	Stokes	1929	Petershams	85-120	
Quick, Herbert	In the Fairyland of America (1st, 8vo, green cl, p-o, 190p)	Stokes	(1901)	Deming, E.W.	100-150	
Quick, Herbert	Vandemark's Folly (1st, 12mo, 420p, 8pl)	Bobbs-Merrill	(1922)	Wyeth, N.C.	30-50	
Quick, Herbert	Virginia of the Air Lanes (1st, 8vo, blue cl, 424p, 5pl)	Bobbs-Merrill	(1909)	Leigh, W.R.	45-60	*
Quigg, Jane	Fun for Freddy (1st, 8vo, 106p, green cl, b/w)	NY: OUP	(1953)	Cooney, B.	25-45	*
Quiller-Couch, A.	Fairy Tales from Far & Near (1st, 12mo, teg, 192p)	L: Cassell	1895	Millar, H.R.	100-140	*
Quiller-Couch, A.	In Powder & Crinoline (1st, 4to, 164p, ibds, teg, gilt, 24 ticp)	L: Hodder	[1913]	Nielsen, K.	650-850	
Quiller-Couch, A.	Roll Call of Honor (1st, lg8vo, p-o, 348p, 9cp)	Nelson	1911	Almond, W.D.	45-60	
Quiller-Couch, A.	Sleeping Beauty... (4to, red cl, 16 ticp, later)	Doran	[1910]	Dulac, E.	150-200	
Quiller-Couch, A.	Sleeping Beauty... (1st, 4to, 129p, gilt, 30 ticp)	L: Hodder	(1910)	Dulac, E.	350-450	
Quiller-Couch, A.	Sleeping Beauty... (1st AM, lg4to, 129p, maroon/gilt, 30 ticp)	NY: Hodder	[1910]	Dulac, E.	250-350	
Quiller-Couch, A.	Sleeping Beauty... (8vo, 196p, black cl, p-o, 8cp, pep)	Garden City	[1932]	Dulac, E.	45-60	*
Quiller-Couch, A.	Splendid Spur (1st, 4to, orange cl, 274p, p-o, 15cp)	Doran	(1927)	Daugherty, J.	35-50	*
Quiller-Couch, A.	Splendid Spur (1st {this pub.}, lg8vo, p-o, 274p, 4cp, pep)	Garden City	1937	Daugherty, J.	30-45	*
Quiller-Couch, A.	Treasure Book of Children's Verse (4to, 336p, gilt, 20 ticp)	L: Hodder	[1915]	Gray, M.E.	80-125	
Quiller-Couch, A.	Troublesome Ursula (1st, p-o, 8pl)	L: Chambers	[1915]	Attwell, M.L.	45-65	
Quiller-Couch, A.	Twelve Dancing Princesses (1st AM, 8vo, 244p, 16 ticp, pep)	Doran	[1913]	Nielsen, K.	320-400	
Quiller-Couch, A.	Twelve Dancing Princesses (sm4to, 244p, col frn, cp)	Doubleday/Dor.	1930	Nielsen, K.	85-100	
Quilp, J.	Baron Verdigris (1st, 8vo, 214p, cvr by...)	L: Henry Co.	1894	Beardsley, A.	60-85	
Rackham, A.	Arthur Rackham Fairy Book (1st, lg8vo, red cl, 287p, 8cp, pep)	L: Harrap	(1933)	Rackham, A.	170-250	
Rackham, A.	Fairy Book (1st, 8vo, 111p, blue/gilt, 11cp)	Doubleday/Page	1923	Rackham, A.	140-180	
Rackham, A.	Rackham's Book of Pictures (1st, 4to, grey/gilt, 44 ticp)	L: Heinemann	(1913)	Rackham, A.	300-400	
Radcliffe, W.	Saint's Garden (1st, sm8vo, 150p, green/gilt, 8pl)	L: SPCK	1927	Robinson, C.	100-140	
Rae, J.	Big Family (1st, ob4to, p-o, 50p)	Dodd	1916	Rae, J.	50-70	*
Rae, J.	Granny Goose (1st, lg4to, 44p, ibds, 21 fp color, pep)	Volland	(1926)	Rae, J.	160-220	
Rae, J.	Grasshopper Green/Meadow Mice (1st, 12mo, ibds, [40]p, color)	Volland	(1922)	Rae, J.	65-80	
Rae, J.	Lucy Locket... (1st, 8vo, 120p, ibds, color)	Volland	(1928)	Rae, J.	65-80	
Rae, J.	New Adventures of Alice (1st, lg8vo, ibds, 158p gilt, 12cp, pep)	Volland	(1917)	Rae, J.	120-165	
Rae, J.	Why: Reflections for Children (1st, 4to, blue cl, p-o)	Dodd	1910	Rae, J.	85-100	

AUTHOR	TITLE	PUBLISHER	DATE	ARTIST	PRICE	LC
Rahr, Ruth	Journey of the Toys (1st, 4to, 87p, p-o, blue cl, pep, color)	(Wisconsin)	(1934)	Ertz, Bruno	65-80	
Raiker, A.M.	Dulcibella & the Fairies (1st, 4to, green bds, 54p, p-o, 13cp)	L: C. Faulkner	(1919)	Miller, H.T.	180-250	
Raine, W.M.	Daughter of Raasay (1st [1st bk.], 12mo, 311p, cvr by...)	Stokes	(1902)	Bradley, W.	100-150	*
Raine, W.M.	Daughter of Raasay (1st [1st bk.], 12mo, 311p, b/w pl)	Stokes	(1902)	Travis, S.	100-150	*
Raine, W.M.	Wyoming (1st, sm8vo, 353p, 4pl)	Dillingham	1908	Rowe, C.	35-50	
Ralph, J.	Dixie... (1st, 4to, 411p, gilt, b/w)	Harper	1896	Various	50-70	
Ralph, J.	On Canada's Frontier (1st, 8vo, 325p, 60 illus by...)	Harper	1892	Remington, F.	70-100	
Ramal, W.	Songs of Childhood (1st, 12mo, teg, gilt, frn by...)	L: Longmans	1902	Doyle, R.	300-400	
Ramsden, G.	Smile Within a Tear (1st, sm8vo, 251p, blue/gilt, 8pl)	L: Hutchinson	1897	Newcombe, B.	50-80	
Rand, Ann	Little River (1st {std}, ob4to, ibds, [32]p, color, pep)	Harcourt	(1959)	Rojankovsky, F.	40-65	
Rand, Ann	Sparkle & Spin (1st {std}, sm4to, blue cl, [30]p, color, dep)	Harcourt	(1957)	Rand, P.	60-85	R*
Rand, W.B.	Lilliput Lyrics (1st, 8vo, 330p, gilt, col frn, b/w)	L: J. Lane	1899	Robinson, C.	70-100	
Randolph, Althea	Bouquet of Rhymes for Children (1st, folio, ibds, 6cp)	Bonnell/Silver	(1909)	Whitney, I.	120-180	*
Randolph, Jane	Circus in Peter's Closet (1st, 8vo, blue cl, 48p, 3-color, pep)	Crowell	(1955)	Freeman, D.	35-50	*
Rankin, L.S.	Daughter of the Mountains (1st, lg8vo, 191p, fp b/w, pep, NH)	Viking	1948	Wiese, K.	50-70	R
Rankin, L.S.	Gentling of Jonathan (1st, 8vo, 223p, green cl, b/w, pep)	Viking	1950	Townsend, L.	30-50	*
Ranking, B.M.	Flowers & Fancies (1st, 24mo, 186p, 4 color)	L: Marcus Ward	1882	Greenaway, K.	180-230	
Ransom, Will	Little Dutchy... (1st, 4to, ibds, 12 ticp)	L: Harrap	(1925)	Cramer, Rie	130-180	
Ransome, A.	Aladdin & his Wonderful Lamp (1st, 4to, [128]p, cloth, 12 ticp)	L: J. Nisbet	[1919]	Mackenzie, T.	280-400	
Ransome, A.	Aladdin & his Wonderful Lamp (1st AM, sm4to, [128]p, 12ticp pep)	Brentano's	[1920]	Mackenzie, T.	120-165	
Ransome, A.	Bohemia in London (1st AM, 8vo, 284p, teg, uncut, 16pl)	Dodd	1907	Taylor, F.	40-60	*
Ransome, A.	Old Peter's Russian Tales (1st {this pub}, 8vo, 309p, 7cp)	L: Nelson	1935	Mitrokhin, D.	65-80	*
Rasmussen, K.	People of the Frozen North (1st UK, 4to, 358p, 12cp)	L: Trubner	1908	Moltke, H.	100-140	
Ratzesberger, A.	Ali Hassan of Hamadan (1st, 8vo, 95p, p-o, 12cp, pep)	Whitman	(1933)	Akbar, A.	30-45	*
Ratzesberger, A.	Camel Bells (1st, 4to, ipcb, 80p, color, pep)	Whitman	1935	Wiese, K.	30-50	*
Ratzesberger, A.	Donkey Beads (1st, lg8vo, 62p, p-o, pep, color)	Whitman	1938	Wiese, K.	30-45	*
Rawlings, M.K.	Secret River (1st, 8vo, [57]p, b/w, brown pages, NH)	Scribner	(1955)	Weisgard, L.	70-100	R*
Rawlings, M.K.	The Yearling (1st {Pulitzer ed.}, sm4to, 400p, 14cp, DJ)	Scribner	1939	Wyeth, N.C.	100-140	
Rawlings, M.K.	The Yearling (1st {this fmt}, 4to, 400p, p-o, 12cp, pep, SC)	Scribner	1940	Wyeth, N.C.	140-200	
Ray, A.C.	Hearts & Creeds (1st, 8vo, 320p, 4pl)	Little/Brown	1906	Stephens, A.B.	25-40	
Ray, A.C.	Janet: Her Winter in Quebec (1st, 12mo, 370p, 4pl)	Little/Brown	1914	Stephens, A.B.	20-30	*
Ray, A.C.	Nathalie's Chum (1st, 8vo, 289p, 6pl)	Little/Brown	1902	Thompson, E.B.	30-50	
Ray, A.C.	Nathalie's Sister (1st, 12mo, 290p, 6pl)	Little/Brown	1904	Stephens, A.B.	30-45	*
Ray, A.C.	Playground Toni (1st, 8vo, ipcb, 136p, 4pl)	Crowell	(1900)	(Photos)	20-30	
Ray, A.C.	Sidney: Summer on St. Lawrence (1st, 12mo, 332p, blue/gilt, 4pl)	Little/Brown	1905	Stephens, A.B.	30-45	
Raymond, E.	Boys & Girls of Brantham (1st, sm8vo, 283p, grey/gilt, 6pl)	Little/Brown	1899	Barry, E.B.	25-40	*
Raymond, E.	The Whirligig (1st, 12mo, 351p, 6pl)	Penn	1905	Rollins, R.	30-50	*
Raymond, M.T.	Roberta Goes Adventuring (1st, 8vo, ibds, 96p, color, pep)	Volland	(1931)	Campbell, E.	50-70	
Raymond, W.	Charity Chance (1st, 12mo, 256p, cvr by..)	Dodd	1896	McManus, B.	20-25	*
Raymond, W.	Tryphena In Love... (1st, 12mo, teg, 295p, col frn, 12pl)	L: Dent	1912	Brock, C.E.	40-60	
Raymond, W.M.	Rebels of the New South (1st, 8vo, 294p, b/w pl)	C.H. Kerr	1905	Ball, P.B.	20-35	*
Rayner, E.	Free to Serve (2nd, 8vo, 434p, cover art by..)	Copeland & Day	1897	Parrish, M.	125-165	
Read, Opie	Arkansas Planter (1st, 8vo, teg, 315p, cvr by...)	Rand/McNally	(1896)	Denslow, W.W.	60-85	
Read, Opie	Bolanyo (1st, 12mo, tan cl, teg, 309p, uncut, cvr by...)	Way/Williams	1897	Parrish, M.	200-320	
Read, Opie	Waters of Caney Fork (1st, 8vo, 287p, cvr by...)	Rand/McNally	1898	Denslow, W.W.	45-60	
Reade, C.	Cloister & Hearth (1st, 4to, 663p, violet/gilt, teg, 20cp)	L: Chatto	1909	Shaw, B.	50-70	
Reade, C.	Peg Woffington (1st, 12mo, 298p, green/gilt, AEG, b/w)	L: G. Allen	1899	Thomson, H.	65-80	
Reade, C.	Peg Woffington (1st AM, 12mo, green/gilt, 298p, AEG)	Doub./McClure	1899	Thomson, H.	50-70	
Reed, H.L.	Amy in Acadia (1st, 8vo, 344p, blue cl, 6pl)	Little/Brown	1905	Pyle, Kath.	35-50	
Reed, H.L.	Brenda's Bargain (1st, 8vo, 251p, 6pl)	Little/Brown	1903	Thompson, E.B.	30-45	
Reed, H.L.	Brenda's Cousin at Radcliffe (1st, 8vo, 318p, 5pl)	Little/Brown	1902	Stephens, A.B.	30-45	*
Reed, H.L.	Brenda's Summer at Rockley (1st, 8vo, blue/gilt, 376p, 5pl)	Little/Brown	1901	Smith, J.W.	180-220	
Reed, H.L.	Brenda's Ward (1st, 8vo, 340p, 6pl)	Little/Brown	1906	Merrill, F.	20-30	
Reed, H.L.	Brenda, Her School & her Club (1st, sm8vo, 328p, gilt, 5pl)	Little/Brown	1900	Smith, J.W.	140-180	
Reed, L.	Sausages & Sundials (1st, 4to, 131p, ibds, b/w)	L: Jarrolds	[1927]	Stimpson, M.	30-45	
Reed, Myrtle	Book of Clever Beasts (1st, 8vo, p-o, 231p, col frn, 8pl)	Putnam	1904	Newell, P.	70-100	
Reed, Myrtle	Old Rose and Silver (1st, 8vo, 364p, teg, lavender cl)	Putnam	1909	Armstrong, M.	30-50	
Reed, Myrtle	Pickaback Songs (1st, 4to, [70]p, ibds, pep, color)	Putnam	1903	Morgan, Ike	300-400	
Reed, Myrtle	Weaver of Dreams (1st, 8vo, teg, 374p, blue/gilt)	Putnam	1911	Armstrong, M.	30-50	
Reed, Myrtle	White Shield (1st, 8vo, 343p, lavender/gilt, teg)	Putnam	1912	Armstrong, M.	30-45	
Reely, Mary	Blue Mittens (1st, 8vo, 153p, green cl, b/w, pep)	E.M. Hale	1935	Wiese, K.	30-45	*
Reeves, James	Titus in Trouble (1st, 4to, ibds, unpag, 46 color)	L: Bodley Head	(1959)	Ardizzone, E.	100-140	*
Reid, K.E.J.	Book of Wedding Days (1st, 4to, red/silver, te silver, [108]p)	L: Longmans	1889	Crane, W.	250-300	
Reid, Sydney	How Sing Found the World is Round (1st, 12mo, [40]p, ibds, col)	Volland	(1921)	Dodge, K.S.	70-100	*
Reid, Sydney	Josey & the Chipmunk (1st, sm8vo, 301p, 17pl)	Century	1900	Cory, F.	45-60	*
Remington, F.	Crooked Trails (1st, sm4to, 150p, tan cloth)	Harper	1898	Remington, F.	180-250	
Remington, F.	Done in the Open (1st, folio, [90]p, ibds, 70 b/w)	R.H. Russell	1902	Remington, F.	250-400	
Remington, F.	Drawings (1st, ob folio, ibds, 60pl)	R.H. Russell	1897	Remington, F.	650-900	
Remington, F.	Frontier Sketches (1st, ob4to, pcb, 15pl)	Werner	1898	Remington, F.	350-500	
Remington, F.	John Ermine/Yellowstone (1st, 8vo, 271p, teg, 7pl)	MacMillan	1902	Remington, F.	120-165	
Remington, F.	Men with The Bark On (1st, sm8vo, 209p, tan cl, 32pl)	Harper	1900	Remington, F.	130-165	
Remington, F.	Pony Tracks (1st {1st bk.}, 8vo, tan/gilt, 269p, 70 illus)	Harper	1895	Remington, F.	350-500	

AUTHOR	TITLE	PUBLISHER	DATE	ARTIST	PRICE	LC
Remington, F.	Stories of Peace & War (1st, 12mo, blue cl, 98p, 2pl)	Harper	1899	Remington, F.	80-120	
Remington, F.	Sundown Leflare (1st, 12mo, brown/gilt, 115p, 12pl)	Harper	1899	Remington, F.	130-170	
Remington, F.	Way of an Indian (1st, 12mo, red cl, 251p, p-o, 14pl)	Fox Duffield	1906	Remington, F.	100-150	
Reno, E.W.	Pick the Vegetables (1st, 4to, wraps, unpag)	Lothrop/Lee	1944	Weisgard, L.	65-90	*
Reno, E.W.	Pup Called Cinderella (1st {std}, 8vo, [32]p, ibds, 1-col, b/w)	Bobbs-Merrill	(1939)	Weisgard, L.	30-45	*
Repplier, A.	Fireside Sphinx (1st, 12mo, teg, 305p, gilt, b/w)	Houghton	1901	Bonsall, E.F.	20-30	
Retner, Beth	Tired Trolly Car (1st {std}, 8vo, 158p, green cl, 4cp, dep)	Doubleday/Page	1926	Millard, C.E.	20-30	*
Rey, H.A.	Anybody at Home? (1st, ob8vo, [24]p, color)	Houghton	1942	Rey, H.A.	50-85	*
Rey, H.A.	Cecily G. & the 9 Monkeys (1st AM, lg4to, 31p, color)	Houghton	1942	Rey, H.A.	70-100	*
Rey, H.A.	Curious George (1st, lg8vo, [55]p, color, pep)	Houghton	1941	Rey, H.A.	80-120	*
Rey, H.A.	Curious George Takes a Job (1st, 4to, 47p, color, pep)	Houghton	1947	Rey, H.A.	75-100	*
Rey, H.A.	Elizabeth (1st {std}, sq4to, ipcb, [32]p, color)	Harper	(1942)	Rey, H.A.	60-90	*
Rey, H.A.	Humpty Dumpty... (1st {std}, ob4to, [23]p, color)	Harper	(1943)	Rey, H.A.	80-120	*
Rey, H.A.	Raffy & the 9 Monkeys (1st, lg4to, 31p, ibds, color)	L: Chatto	1939	Rey, H.A.	90-135	*
Rey, H.A.	Tit for Tat (1st {std}, sq4to, ipcb, [30]p, color)	Harper	(1942)	Rey, H.A.	60-100	*
Rey, M.E.	Billy's Picture (1st, sm4to, ibds, [22]p, color)	Harper	(1948)	Rey, H.A.	65-90	*
Rey, M.E.	Pretzel (1st {std}-[1st bk.], 4to, [30]p, cloth, color)	Harper	(1944)	Rey-H.A.	70-100	*
Rey, M.E.	Pretzel & the Puppies (1st, lg8vo, ibds, [30]p, color)	Harper	(1946)	Rey, H.A.	35-60	*
Rey, M.E.	Spotty (1st, sm4to, [30]p, ibds, p-o, color)	Harper	(1945)	Rey, H.A.	35-50	*
Reynier, M.	Wild Animals at Home (sq4to, wraps, [16]p, color)	A.& W. Guild	(1934)	Rojankovsky, F.	30-45	
Reynolds, B.L.	Pepper (1st, 8vo, grey cl, 169p, fp b/w)	Scribner	(1952)	Cooney, B.	30-45	*
Rhead, G.W.	Treatment of Drapery in Art (1st, 8vo, 119p, 32pl, cvr by...)	L: G. Bell	1904	Crane, W.	95-130	
Rhead, Louis	Robin Hood (1st, 4to, p-o, b/w)	Harper	1912	Rhead, L.	65-80	
Rhoads, Dorothy	Bright Feather (1st {std}, 8vo, 196p, uncut, pep, col frn, b/w)	Doubleday/Dor.	1932	Houser, L.	25-40	*
Rhoads, Dorothy	Corn Grows Ripe (1st, lg8vo, 88p, pep, 1-color, DJ, NH)	Viking	1956	Charlot, J.	60-90	
Rhoads, Dorothy	Story of Chan Yuc (1st {std}, sq4to, [45]p, ibds, color)	Doubleday/Dor.	1941	Charlot, J.	65-80	
Rhodes, E.M.	Desire of the Moth (1st, 8vo, 149p, 2pl)	Holt	1916	Dunn, H.T.	35-50	
Rhodes, E.M.	West is West (1st, 8vo, 304p, black cloth, frn by...)	H.K. Fly	(1917)	Dunn, H.T.	65-80	
Rhys, E. (ed.)	English Fairy Book (1st, 8vo, 318p)	L: T.F. Unwin	1912	Whitney, F.C.	50-75	*
Rhys, E. (ed.)	English Fairy Tales (12mo, p-o, 128p, gilt, 8cp)	Dutton	(1906)	Cole, H.	50-75	
Rhys, E. (ed.)	Fairy-Gold (1st, 8vo, 474p, 12cp)	L: Dent	1906	Cole, H.	60-100	
Rhys, Grace (ed.)	Children's Garland of Verse (8vo, 296p, 8cp)	L: J.M. Dent	1921	Robinson, C.	130-180	*
Rhys, Grace (ed.)	Fairy Gifts (1st, 12mo, 61p, uncut, teg, gilt, 16pl)	L: J.M. Dent	1895	Fell, H.G.	75-90	
Rhys, Grace (ed.)	Magic Wood Beyond the World (8vo, ibds, 4cp)	L: Harrap	1931	Tarrant, M.	40-65	
Rhys, Mimpsy	Mr. Hermit Crab (1st, 8vo, green cl, 190p, col frn, 6pl, pep)	MacMillan	1929	Sewell, H.	30-45	*
Rice, Alice H.	Captain June (1st, 8vo, blue cl, 120p, 8pl)	Century	1907	Weldon, C.D.	20-35	
Rice, Alice H.	Lovey Mary (1st, 8vo, teg, uncut, 236p, 24pl)	Century	1903	Shinn, F.S.	20-30	
Rice, Alice H.	Romance of Billy-Goat Hill (1st, 12mo, green/gilt, 404p, 8pl)	Century	1912	Wright, G.	20-30	
Rice, Ethel	Wiggle & Waggle (1st, 4to, bds, [28]p, p-o, color, pep)	NY: S. Gabriel	(1939)	Kay, A.	45-60	
Rich, Edwin G.	Hans the Eskimo (1st, 8vo, 287p, blue cl, p-o, b/w)	Houghton	1934	Kent, R.	25-40	*
Rich, Edwin G.	Who-So Stories (1st, sm8vo, 207p, col frn)	Small/Maynard	(1918)	Copeland, C.	25-40	*
Richards, A.M.	New Alice/Old Wonderland (1st, 8vo, 309p, teg, red/gilt, b/w)	Lippincott	1895	Richards, A.M.	120-180	
Richards, Dorothy	Adventures in an Old Shoe House (1st, 12mo, ibds, 6cp)	L: Faber	(1948)	Thomas, E.	35-50	
Richards, Dorothy	Roma Rabbit's Picnic (1st, 12mo, ibds, 6cp)	L: Faber	(1947)	Thomas, E.	35-50	
Richards, L.E.	Captain January (1st, sq8vo, teg, 133p, gilt, b/w)	Estes	1893	Merrill, F.	45-65	*
Richards, L.E.	Fairy Operettas (1st, 12mo, 119p, col frn)	Little/Brown	1916	Basset, M.R.	35-60	*
Richards, L.E.	Golden Windows (1st, 8vo, 123p, green/gilt, teg, 5pl)	Little/Brown	1903	Becher, A.E.	20-35	
Richards, L.E.	Merry-Go-Round (1st, 8vo, 113p, bds, p-o, b/w)	Appleton/Cent.	1935	Lefferts, W.E.	25-40	*
Richards, L.E.	Silver Crown (1st, 8vo, 105p, teg, grey/gilt, cvr by...)	Little/Brown	1906	Smith, J.W.	45-60	
Richards, L.E.	The Piccolo (1st, lg8vo, 121p, pict cl)	Estes	(1906)	Unknown	25-40	*
Richards, L.E.	Tirra Lirra (1st, 8vo, 194p, col frn, pep, NH)	Little/Brown	1932	Davis, M.	35-50	*
Richardson, E.	Doors... (1st, 8vo, 160p, 12cp)	L: Headley	[1909]	Richardson, E.	120-160	*
Richardson, E.	Songs of Near & Far Away (1st, 4to, tan cl, 80p, color)	L: Cassell	1900	Richardson, E.	100-150	*
Richardson, E.	Sun-Moon & Stars... (1st, 4to, green cl, unpag, b/w)	L: Bodley Head	1899	Richardson, E.	100-150	
Richardson, F.	Book for Children (1st, ob4to, 107p, pep, p-o, 35cp)	Donohue	(1938)	Richardson, F.	80-100	
Richardson, F.	Book of Drawings (1st, sm folio, [106]p, b/w, grey bds)	Lakeside Pr.	1899	Richardson, F.	350-500	
Richardson, W.C.F.	India Rubber Jack (1st, 16mo, blue cl, [124]p, 28 color)	L: Swan/Sonn.	[1902]	Sichel, G.	100-140	
Richmond, Grace S.	On Christmas Day in the Evening (1st, 8vo, 76p, white bds, 4cp)	Doubleday/Page	1910	Relyea, C.M.	25-40	*
Rickert, Edith	Blacksmith & the Birds (1st {std}, 12mo, 46p orang cl, pep, b/w)	Doubleday/Dor.	1928	Daugherty, J.	30-45	*
Rideout, H.	Lola the Bear (1st, 8vo, 159p, gilt, col frn, 3pl, DJ)	Duffield	1928	Ward, L.	40-60	
Rigby, D.	Moustachio (1st, 4to, [31]p, ibds, 1-color, DJ)	Harper	(1947)	Duvoisin, R.	35-50	
Rihbany, A.M.	Christ Story for Boys & Girls (1st, 8vo, gilt, p-o, 239p, 4cp)	Houghton	(1923)	Tenggren, G.	45-60	
Riis, J.A.	Children of the Tenements (1st, 8vo, green cl, 387p, 8pl)	MacMillan	1903	Various	65-80	
Riley, A.	Voyage of the Wishbone Boat (lg8vo, ipcb, 205p, fp color, pep)	Caldwell	(1907)	Bridgman, L.J.	75-110	
Riley, J.W.	All the Year Round (1st, 4to, gilt, ibds, [30]p, p-o, 12cp)	Bobbs-Merrill	(1912)	Baumann, G.	250-400	R
Riley, J.W.	Book of Joyous Children (1st, 8vo, teg, 176p, uncut)	Scribner	1902	Vawter, J.W.	30-50	
Riley, J.W.	Boy Lives on our Farm (1st, sq4to, p-o, [18]p, 5cp)	Bobbs-Merrill	(1908)	Betts, E.F.	100-145	
Riley, J.W.	Boys of the Old Glee Club (1st, tall 8vo, unpag, 13pl)	Bobbs-Merrill	(1907)	Vawter, J.W.	50-80	R
Riley, J.W.	Defective Santa Claus (1st, 12mo, green/gilt, 77p, cvr by...)	Bobbs-Merrill	(1904)	Armstrong, M.	50-80	R
Riley, J.W.	Defective Santa Claus (1st, 12mo, green/gilt, 77p, b/w)	Bobbs-Merrill	(1904)	Vawter, J.W.	50-80	R
Riley, J.W.	Discouraging Model (1st, lg8vo, ipcb, [12]p, color)	Bobbs-Merrill	(1914)	Christy, H.C.	80-100	R*
Riley, J.W.	Flying Islands o/t Night (1st, 4to, bds, 124p, gilt, 16 ticp pep)	Bobbs-Merrill	(1913)	Booth, F.	130-170	R

AUTHOR	TITLE	PUBLISHER	DATE	ARTIST	PRICE	LC
Riley, J.W.	Good-Bye Jim (1st, sq8vo, 56p, 11cp)	Bobbs-Merrill	(1913)	Christy, H.C.	45-70	*
Riley, J.W.	Host of Children (1st, 4to, p-o, 189p, brown/gilt, 16cp, pep)	Bobbs-Merrill	(1920)	Betts, E.F.	100-145	R
Riley, J.W.	Old Sweetheart of Mine (1st, ob4to, AEG, color)	Bowen-Merrill	1891	(Chromos)	120-165	
Riley, J.W.	Old Sweetheart of Mine (1st, 8vo, p-o, 19pl)	Bobbs-Merrill	(1902)	Christy, H.C.	35-50	
Riley, J.W.	Orphant Annie Book (1st, sq folio, [30]p, ibds, 8cp)	Bobbs-Merrill	(1908)	Betts, E.F.	150-200	
Riley, J.W.	Poems Here at Home (1st, 8vo, green cl, 187p, teg, b/w)	Century	1893	Kemble, E.W.	50-80	
Riley, J.W.	Raggedy Man (1st, lg4to, [30]p, p-o, 9cp)	Bobbs-Merrill	(1907)	Betts, E.F.	160-200	R
Riley, J.W.	Riley Baby Book (1st, 8vo, red/gilt, unpag, t-i col frn)	Bobbs-Merrill	(1913)	Cotton, W.	100-140	R
Riley, J.W.	Riley Child Verse (1st, sm4to, p-o, 58p, 8cp)	Bobbs-Merrill	(1906)	Betts, E.F.	120-165	R
Riley, J.W.	Riley Fairy Tales (1st, sm4to, [33]p, p-o, color)	Bobbs-Merrill	(1923)	Vawter, W.	50-75	*
Riley, J.W.	Riley Roses (1st, sm4to, [30]p, green/gilt, 8cp)	Bobbs-Merrill	(1909)	Christy, H.C.	65-80	
Riley, J.W.	Rubaiyat of Doc Sifers (1st, 12mo, teg, 211p, green/gilt, b/w)	Century	1897	Relyea, C.M.	45-70	R
Riley, J.W.	Runaway Boy (1st, lg8vo, p-o, red cl, [40]p, pep, 8cp)	Bobbs-Merrill	(1906)	Betts, E.F.	100-150	
Riley, J.W.	The Rose (1st, sm4to, ibds, [16]p)	Bobbs-Merrill	(1916)	Christy, H.C.	45-60	
Riley, J.W.	While the Heart Beats Young (1st, lg8vo, 110p, p-o, 16cp, dep)	Bobbs-Merrill	(1906)	Betts, E.F.	100-160	
Rinder, F.	Old World Japan (1st, 8vo, blue cl, teg, uncut, 195p, 15pl)	L: G. Allen	1895	Robinson, T.H.	65-90	
Rinehart, M.R.	Man in the Lower Ten (1st, 8vo, 372p, cp)	Bobbs-Merrill	(1909)	Christy, H.C.	50-75	
Rinehart, M.R.	When a Man Marries (1st, 12mo, 353p, 5cp)	Bobbs-Merrill	(1909)	Fisher, H.	25-40	*
Ring, B.	Peik (1st, 8vo, cloth, 268p, 15 fp b/w, cep)	Little/Brown	1932	Lawson, R.	50-70	
Rion, H.	Smiling Road (1st, 8vo, green cl, 191p, 10pl)	E.J. Clode	(1910)	VerBeck, F.	25-40	*
Rippey, Sarah C.	Goody-Naughty Book (1st, 12mo, tan cl, p-o, [62]p, color)	Rand/McNally	(1913)	Wright, B.F.	30-45	
Rippey, Sarah C.	Raggedies in Fairy Land (1st, 4to, 96p, p-o, pep, 3cp)	Rand/McNally	(1930)	Cady, H.	100-130	
Rippey, Sarah C.	Sunny-Sulky Book (1st, sm8vo, p-o, 12cp)	Rand/McNally	(1915)	Wright, B.F.	35-60	
Ritchie, Jean	Singing Family of the Cumberlands (1st, 8vo, grn cl, 282p, b/w)	NY: OUP	1955	Sendak, M.	120-170	*
Rives, A.	Athelwold (1st, 8vo, 118p, 8pl)	Harper	1893	Gow, M.	70-100	
Rives, A.	Damsel Errant (1st, 12mo, teg, 211p, uncut, 4pl)	Lippincott	1898	Oakley, V.	80-100	*
Rives, H.E.	Valiants of Virginia (1st, 8vo, red/gilt, 432p)	Bobbs-Merrill	(1912)	Armstrong, M.	20-35	
Rix, H.	Prince Pimpernel (1st, 8vo, 141p, 8cp)	L: Duckworth	1909	Pape, F.	80-120	
Robbins, Louis	Dutch Doll Ditties (1st, 4to, 23p, grey bds, p-o, b/w)	L: Longmans	1904	(Photos)	80-100	
Robbins, Ruth	Baboushka & Three Kings (1st, sq12mo, ipcb, [28]p, col, pep, CM)	Parnassus Pr.	(1960)	Sidjakov, N.	65-100	R*
Roberts, C.G.D.	Earth's Enigmas (1st, 12mo, 285p, red cl, 10pl)	Page	1903	Bull, C.L.	40-60	
Roberts, C.G.D.	Kindred of the Wild (1st, 8vo, 374p, green/gilt, teg, 50pl)	Page	1902	Bull, C.L.	40-65	
Roberts, C.G.D.	Red Fox (1st, 8vo, uncut, 340p, teg, 48pl)	Page	1905	Bull, C.L.	40-60	
Roberts, C.G.D.	Secret Trails (1st, 12mo, 212p, green/gilt, 8pl)	MacMillan	1916	Bransom, P.	35-50	*
Roberts, C.G.D.	Watchers of the Trails (1st, sm8vo, uncut, 361p, 48pl, pep)	Page	1904	Bull, C.L.	30-45	
Roberts, C.G.D.	Watchers of the Trails (1st UK, green bds, 361p, gilt, 48pl)	L: Duckworth	1904	Bull, C.L.	35-50	
Roberts, C.G.D.	Young Acadian (1st, 12mo, 139p, 6pl)	Page	1907	McManus, B.	25-40	*
Roberts, E.M.	Time of Man (1st, 8vo, 397p, p-o)	Viking	1945	Leighton, C.	35-50	
Roberts, G.E.	Flying Plover (1st, 8vo, 125p, tan cl, 6pl, cvr by...)	Page	1909	Bull, C.L.	35-50	
Roberts, K.	Trending into Maine (1st, lg8vo, 382p, tan cl, 14cp, pep)	Little/Brown	1938	Wyeth, N.C.	70-100	
Roberts, Theodore	Red Feathers (1st, 8vo, p-o, 325p, col frn, 9pl)	Page	1907	Bull, C.L.	30-45	
Robertson, Keith	Henry Reed, Inc. (1st, 8vo, 239p, b/w)	Viking	(1958)	McCloskey, R.	30-60	R*
Robertson, Keith	Missing Brother (1st, 8vo, 220p, orange cl, b/w)	Viking	1950	Busoni, R.	25-40	*
Robertson, W.G.	Baby's Day Book (1st, lg8vo, 127p, grey cl, col frn, b/w)	L: J. Lane	1908	Robertson, W.G.	145-200	
Robertson, W.G.	Gold, Frankincense & Myrrh (1st, 4to, blue cl, 152p, 12cp)	L: J. Lane	1907	Robertson, W.G.	185-265	
Robertson, W.G.	Golden Book of Sonnets (1st, 8vo, vellum)	L: Harrap	1903	Pogany, W.	130-180	
Robertson, W.G.	Masque of May Morning (1st, 4to, green cl, 62p, 12cp)	L: J. Lane	1904	Robertson, W.G.	180-250	
Robertson, W.G.	Pinkie & the Fairies (1st, 12mo, 146p, 6 fp b/w)	L: Heinemann	1909	Robertson, W.G.	120-160	
Robertson, W.G.	Yen of Songs/Baby in a Garden (1st, 8vo, 111p)	L: J. Lane	1906	Robertson, W.G.	130-165	*
Robida, A.	Treasure of Corcassone (1st {std}, 8vo, 213p, col frn, 7pl, pep)	Longmans	1928	Lathrop, D.	40-60	
Robins, E.	Prudence & Peter... (1st, sm8vo, 244p, grey cl, p-o)	Wm. Morrow	(1928)	Lenski, L.	35-50	
Robins, E.	Under the Southern Cross (1st, 8vo, teg, p-o, 234p, 4cp, pep)	Stokes	(1907)	Rae, J.	30-45	
Robinson, C.	Black Bunnies (1st, 16mo, blue/gilt, silhouettes)	L: Blackie	(1907)	Robinson, C.	250-400	*
Robinson, C.	Silly Submarine (1st, ob16mo, ibds, 30 color, pep)	L: Blackie	(1906)	Robinson, C.	170-220	
Robinson, E.	Captain of the Old School (1st, 8vo, grey cl, 15pl)	Little/Brown	1901	Stephens, A.B.	30-45	
Robinson, E.	Loyal Little Maid (12mo, 79p, b/w illus)	J. Knight	1897	Sacker, A.	20-30	
Robinson, E.A.	Children of the Night (1st, sm8vo, 123p, tan cl, cvr by...)	Badger	1897	Hapgood, T.B.	200-300	
Robinson, Gertrude	Chee-Chee's Brother (1st {std}, sm4to, grn cl, 40p, fp b/w, pep)	Dutton	(1937)	Latimer, G.M.	25-45	*
Robinson, Gertrude	White Heron Feather (1st {std}, 12mo, orang cl, 299p, pep)	Harper	(1930)	Berry, E.	25-45	*
Robinson, M.L.	All by Ourselves (1st, sm8vo, 254p, decor by...)	Dutton	(1924)	Wright, M.S.	20-30	*
Robinson, M.L.	Bright Island (1st, 8vo, 268p, silver cl, b/w, pep, DJ, NH)	Random	(1937)	Ward, L.	50-70	
Robinson, M.L.	Little Lucia's School (1st, 12mo, 138p)	Dutton	(1926)	Balcom, S.T.	20-30	*
Robinson, M.L.	Robin & Angus (1st, 8vo, green cl, 186p, col frn, fp b/w)	MacMillan	1931	Wilkin, E.B.	20-35	*
Robinson, M.L.	Robin & Tito (1st, 8vo, 192p, col frn)	MacMillan	1930	Burns, E.	20-25	*
Robinson, M.L.	Runner of the Mountain Tops (1st {std}, 8vo, blue/gilt, DJ, NH)	Random	(1939)	Ward, L.	50-85	
Robinson, M.L.	Sarah's Daikin (1st, sm8vo, 271p, green/gilt, uncut, b/w)	Dutton	(1927)	Brown, Julie	20-30	*
Robinson, M.L.	Skipper Riley: Terrier Dog (1st, 8vo, blue cl, 90p, b/w)	Random	(1955)	Shortall, L.	25-40	*
Robinson, M.L.	Strong Wings (1st {std}, 8vo, 249p, blue cl, b/w)	Random	(1951)	Ward, L.	25-40	*
Robinson, S.	City Child (1st, 12mo, red/gilt, 64p, DJ)	Farrar/Rine.	1931	Kent, R.	65-80	
Robinson, Tom P.	Buttons (1st, lg4to, [63]p, red cl, p-o, b/w, DJ)	Viking	1938	Bacon, P.	30-45	
Robinson, Tom P.	Greylock & the Robins (1st, sm4to, 32p, ibds, color)	Viking	1946	Lawson, R.	70-100	
Robinson, Tom P.	In & Out (1st, lg8vo, 140p, color, DJ)	Viking	1943	DeAngeli, M.	35-60	

AUTHOR	TITLE	PUBLISHER	DATE	ARTIST	PRICE	LC
Robinson, Tom P.	Mr. Red Squirrel (1st, sm4to, ibds, [32]p, color, pep)	Viking	1943	Wiese, K.	30-45	*
Robinson, Tom P.	Trigger John's Son (1st, 8vo, 284p, b/w, DJ)	Viking	1949	McCloskey, R.	45-60	
Robinson, W.	Golden Palace/Neverland (1st, sm8vo, green cl, 307p, 6cp)	Dutton	1907	Davidson, C.D.	50-70	*
Robinson, W.H.	Absurdities (1st, lg4to, ibds, fp b/w illus)	L: Hutchinson	[1934]	Robinson, W.H.	120-165	
Robinson, W.H.	Adventures of Uncle Lubin (1st, sm4to, 117p, col frn)	L: Richards	1902	Robinson, W.H.	450-600	
Robinson, W.H.	Adventures of Uncle Lubin (sm4to, ibds, 7 b/w, later, DJ)	L: Chatto	(1934)	Robinson, W.H.	150-200	
Robinson, W.H.	Bill the Minder (1st AM, 4to, p-o, 254p, gilt, 16 ticp)	Holt	1912	Robinson, W.H.	300-450	
Robinson, W.H.	Bill the Minder (1st, 4to, green/gilt, 255p, p-o, 16 ticp)	L: Constable	1912	Robinson, W.H.	400-600	
Robinson, W.H.	Book of Goblins (1st, 4to, 239p, blue/gilt, 7cp)	L: Hutchinson	(1934)	Robinson, W.H.	300-425	
Robinson, W.H.	Child's Arabian Nights (2nd, 4to, ibds, 84p, 12cp)	L: Richards	1904	Robinson, W.H.	500-700	
Robinson, W.H.	Humours of Golf (1st AM, 4to, ibds, 50p, b/w)	Dodd	1923	Robinson, W.H.	100-165	
Robinson, W.H.	Hunlikely! (1st, 4to, ibds, 24pl)	L: Duckworth	(1916)	Robinson, W.H.	130-170	
Robinson, W.H.	Jamboree of Laughter (4to, 24p, wraps)	Jones	(1920)	Robinson, W.H.	100-125	
Robinson, W.H.	Railway Ribaldry (1st, 4to, [96]p, wraps, 88 fp b/w)	G.W. Railway	1935	Robinson, W.H.	160-200	
Robinson, W.H.	Some Frightful War Pictures (1st, folio, [54]p, 24 fp b/w, pep)	L: Duckworth	(1915)	Robinson, W.H.	180-250	
Robinson, W.H.	Uncle Lubin (1st AM, 8vo, green cl, b/w)	Brentano's	1902	Robinson, W.H.	450-600	*
Roche, J.J.	Her Majesty the King (1st, sm8vo, 149p, 8cp)	R.H. Russell	1902	Herford, O.	65-90	*
Roche, J.J.	Sorrows of Sap'ed (1st, 8vo, uncut, 195p, p-o, 8cp)	Harper	1904	Mears, W.E.	20-30	
Rockwood, Roy	Through Space to Mars (1st, sm8vo, 248p, blue cl, 4pl)	Cupples	(1910)	Kuser, G.M.	65-90	*
Rodgers, C.	Pirate's Loot (1st, 8vo, yellow cl, 282p, 30 fp 1-color)	Sears	(1931)	Tenggren, G.	45-65	
Rogers, Cameron	Drake's Quest (1st, sm8vo, 284p, col frn)	Doubleday/Page	1927	Daugherty, J.	25-45	*
Rogers, Eliz.	Angela of Angel Court (1st {std}, 8vo, 116p, grn cl, b/w, pep)	Crowell	(1954)	Adams, A.	25-40	*
Rogerson, Sidney	Both Sides of the Road (1st, 4to, red cl, 183p, 23cp)	L: Collins	1949	Tunnicliffe, C.F.	45-60	
Rollins P.A.	Gone Haywire (1st, 8vo, 269p, 4 dp b/w, pep)	Scribner	1939	Hurd, P.	30-50	*
Rollins, P.A.	Jinglebob (1st, 4to, black cl, 263p, p-o, 4cp, pep, SC)	Scribner	1930	Wyeth, N.C.	200-300	
Rook, Clarence	Hooligan Nights (1st, 8vo, 289p, rust cl, col frn by...)	L: Richards	1899	Nicholson, W.	50-80	*
Roosevelt, Eleanor	Christmas (1st {std}, 24mo, ibds, 42p, 8 fp b/w, dep)	Knopf	1940	Kredel, F.	30-45	
Roosevelt, T.	Ranch Life... (1st, 4to, tan/gilt, 180p, AEG, b/w)	Century	(1888)	Remington, F.	165-200	
Root, Charlet	Feast of Lamps (1st, lg8vo, 75p, p-o, color)	Whitman	1938	Duvoisin, R.	60-90	*
Rosenthal, L.	Kingdom of the Pearl (1st AM, 4to, bds, p-o, 10 ticp)	Brentano's	[1920]	Dulac, E.	350-450	
Rosman, A.G.	Jock the Scot (1st, 4to, 204p, p-o, 7cp, pep)	Minton Balch	(1930)	Esley, H.	25-45	
Ross, M.I.	Back of Time (1st {std}, sm8vo, 271p, pep, b/w)	Harper	1932	Wiese, K.	25-45	*
Ross, M.I.	Morgan's Fourth Son (1st {std}, 8vo, 252p, uncut, 6pl)	Harper	(1940)	Daugherty, J.	25-40	
Ross, R.	Aubrey Beardsley (1st, 12mo, 112p, teg, gilt, 16pl)	L: J. Lane	1909	Beardsley, A.	50-75	
Rosseau, Victor	Messiah of the Cylinder (1st, 8vo, green/gilt, 319p, 11pl)	McClurg	1917	Coll, J.C.	35-50	*
Rossetti, C.	Goblin Market (1st, 8vo, AEG, 63p, olive/gilt, 12pl)	L: MacMillan	1893	Housman, L.	260-350	
Rossetti, C.	Goblin Market (1st, lg8vo, ibds, 79p, 8cp)	L: Blackie	1923	Harrison, F.	130-180	
Rossetti, C.	Goblin Market (1st, 8vo, wraps, 43p, 4cp, pep)	L: Harrap	(1933)	Rackham, A.	180-250	
Rossetti, C.	Goblin Market (1st AM, 8vo, p-o, red cl, 4cp, pep)	Lippincott	[1933]	Rackham, A.	100-140	
Rossetti, C.	Maude: Prose & Verse (1st, 12mo, red pcb, title pg by..)	H. Stone	1897	Hazenplug, F.	40-65	
Rossetti, C.	Pageant & other Poems (1st, 8vo, 198p, blue/gilt)	MacMillan	1881	Rossetti, D.G.	90-130	
Rossetti, C.	Poems by... (1st AM, 4to, teg, 369p, 36 ticp)	Estes	(1910)	Harrison, F.	200-300	
Rossetti, C.	Poems by... (1st, 4to, white/gilt, teg, 369p, 36 ticp, pep)	L: Blackie	(1910)	Harrison, F.	250-380	
Rossetti, C.	Prince's Progress (1st, 8vo, 146p, teg, b/w)	L: A. Melrose	[1900]	Sandheim, M.	75-90	
Rossetti, C.	Shorter Poems of... (1st, 4to, ibds, 6cp)	L: Blackie	[1920]	Harrison, F.	70-90	
Rossetti, C.	Sing Song (1st [new ed.], 12mo, AEG, 135p, gilt, b/w)	L: MacMillan	1893	Hughes, A.	100-165	
Rossetti, C.	Sing-Song (1st, 16mo, green cl, 122p, b/w, pep)	MacMillan	1924	Davis, M.	25-40	
Rossetti, D.G.	Blessed Damozel (1st, 8vo, 54p, gilt, teg, uncut)	L: Duckworth	1898	MacDougall, W.B.	85-120	
Rossetti, D.G.	Pictures & Poems (1st, folio, [54]p, 13 tipl)	R.H. Russell	1899	Unknown	250-375	*
Rostand, E.	Story of Chanticleer (1st AM, 8vo, 144p, 12cp)	Stokes	(1913)	Shepherd, J.A.	50-70	
Rostand, E.	Story of Chanticleer (1st, 8vo, 144p, cloth, 12cp)	L: Heinemann	1913	Shepherd, J.A.	65-80	
Rosvall, T.D.	Very Stupid Folk (1st {std}, 12mo, cloth, 52p, b/w)	Dutton	1938	Gergely, T.	25-40	
Rounds, Glen	Blind Colt (1st, lg8vo, blue cl, [80]p, color)	Holiday House	(1941)	Rounds, G.	35-50	*
Rounds, Glen	Lumbercamp (1st, sm8vo, wood bds, 116p, b/w, pep)	Holiday House	1937	Rounds, G.	25-40	*
Rounds, Glen	Ol' Paul, Mighty Logger (1st, 12mo, beige cl, 132p, b/w, pep)	Holiday House	1936	Rounds, G.	45-65	R*
Rounds, Glen	Whitey & Jinglebob (1st, sq8vo, [28]p, ibds, pep, color)	Grosset/Dunlap	(1946)	Rounds, G.	35-50	*
Rounds, Glen	Whitey & the Blizzard (1st, sm8vo, blue cl, 31p, b/w, cep)	Holiday House	(1952)	Rounds, G.	25-45	*
Rounds, Glen	Whitey Looks for a Job (1st, lg8vo, [28]p, ibds, color)	Grosset/Dunlap	(1944)	Rounds, G.	35-50	*
Rounds, Glen	Whitey's First Roundup (1st, lg8vo, [28]p, ibds, color)	Grosset/Dunlap	(1942)	Rounds, G.	35-50	*
Rounds, Glen	Whitey's Sunday Horse (1st, lg8vo, [28]p, ibds, color)	Grosset/Dunlap	1943	Rounds, G.	45-60	*
Rountree, H.	Adventures of Mabel (1st AM, sm4to, 223p, 8cp)	Dodd	1916	Rountree, H.	50-70	
Rountree, H.	Peter Pink-Eye (1st AM, 8vo, p-o, 85p, 8cp)	Estes	(1908)	Rountree, H.	45-70	
Rountree, H.	Sonny Jim (4to, ibds, unpag, 14 color)	L: A. Cooke	[n.d.]	Rountree, H.	150-200	
Rourke, C.	Davy Crockett (1st, 8vo, green cl, 276p, 8pl, NH)	Harcourt	(1934)	MacDonald, J.	40-65	*
Rouse, W.H.D.	Giant Crab (1st, 8vo, 134p, 7pl)	L: D. Nutt	1897	Robinson, W.H.	180-240	
Rouse, W.H.D.	Talking Thrush (8vo, 8pl, cvr by...)	L: Dent	1902	Robinson, W.H.	170-230	
Routledge, Wm.	Children's Musical Cinderella (1st, 4to, [30]p, wraps, 8cp)	L: Routledge	1879	Crane, W.	120-160	
Rowand, Phyllis	Cats Who Stayed for Dinner (1st, 8vo, ipcb, [41]p, color, pep)	Wonder Books	(1951)	Burchard, P.	35-50	*
Rowand, Phyllis	Day After Yesterday (1st {std}, 8vo, 54p, green cl, fp 2-color)	Little/Brown	(1953)	Rowand, P.	30-45	*
Rowand, Phyllis	Watch the Birdie! (1st, lg8vo, ipcb, [40]p, 1-color)	W.R. Scott	1947	Rowand, P.	30-50	*
Rowe, Dorothy	Begging Dear (1st, sm8vo, 109p, tan cl, 8cp, pep)	MacMillan	1928	Ward, L.	30-50	*
Rowe, Dorothy	Traveling Shops (1st, sm8vo, yellow cl, 109p, col frn, pep)	MacMillan	1929	Ward, L.	25-45	*

AUTHOR	TITLE	PUBLISHER	DATE	ARTIST	PRICE	LC
Rowe, Nellie	Crystal Locket (1st, 8vo, 143p, ipcb, 10cp, pep)	Whitman	1935	Enright, E.	35-50	*
Rowland, E.E.	In & Out of the Nursery (1st, ob folio, [62]p)	R.H. Russell	(1900)	Eickmeyer, R.	300-450	*
Rowland, H.	Countess Diane (1st, 8vo, 149p, uncut, p-o, 5cp, pep)	Dodd	1908	Rae, J.	35-50	
Rowsell, M.	Pedlar & His Dog (8vo, green cl, p-o, 156p, 4cp)	L: Blackie	[1912]	Pape, F.	40-60	
Ruding, W.	Evil Motherhood (1st, 8vo, blue/gilt, 99p, uncut, frn by...)	L: Matthews	1895	Beardsley, A.	100-160	
Rumbold, G.	Wayside Book... (1st, 8vo, 175p, ibds, color)	L: Methuen	1934	Rumbold, G.	65-80	*
Ruskin, J.	King of the Golden River (1st AM, 8vo, red cl, 47p, p-o, 4cp)	Lippincott	(1932)	Rackham, A.	120-180	
Ruskin, J.	King of the Golden River (1st, 8vo, wraps, 47p, 4cp, pep)	L: Harrap	(1932)	Rackham, A.	165-220	
Ruskin, John (ed.)	Dame Wiggin of Lee (1st, 12mo, 20p, gilt)	L: G. Allen	1885	Greenaway, K.	125-160	
Russell, Arthur	Snowy for Luck (1st, 8vo, p-o, 128p, col frn, pep)	Whitman	1934	Wiese, K.	20-35	*
Russell, C.M.	Good Medicine (1st, 4to, 162p, tan cl, col frn)	Doubleday/Dor.	(1930)	Russell, C.M.	100-150	
Russell, C.M.	Trails Plowed Under (1st {std}, 4to, 210p, 5 dp cp)	Doubleday/Page	1927	Russell, C.M.	100-160	
Russell, D.	Betty's Diary (1st, 8vo, 261p, p-o, 5cp)	L: Blackie	[1914]	Appleton, H.C.	40-60	
Russell, M.	April Baby's Book of Tunes (1st, sq8vo, tan cl, 75p, 16cp)	L: MacMillan	1900	Greenaway, K.	200-300	
Russell, R.H.	Delft Cat (1st, 16mo, 71p, uncut, b/w)	R.H. Russell	1896	Smith, F.B.	65-100	*
Russell, W.	Bending of the Twig (1st, 297p, p-o, cvr by...)	Dodd	1903	Richards, A.M.	20-35	
Russell, W.C.	Lady Maud (8vo, 312p, b/w pl)	Fenno	(1896)	Shute, A.B.	20-30	*
Russell, W.C.	Rose Island (1st, 8vo, 359p, cvr by...)	H. Stone	1899	Hazenplug, F.	45-65	
Russell, W.C.	Tragedy of Ida Noble (1st UK, 8vo, 315p, blue buckram, b/w)	L: Hutchinson	1893	Hopkins, E.	70-90	
Russell, W.C.	Two Captains (1st UK, 8vo, 372p, cloth, b/w)	L: Sampson	1897	Rosenmeyer, B.J.	65-80	
Ryan, M.E.	Flute of the Gods (1st, 8vo, 333p, p-o, 24pl)	Stokes	(1909)	Curtis, E.	30-45	
Ryan, M.E.	House of the Dawn (1st, 8vo, 407p, 4pl)	McClurg	1914	Booth, H.	20-30	*
Ryder, Arthur	Twenty-Two Goblins (1st, 8vo, 220p, 20cp)	L: Dent	1917	Nahl, Perham	65-90	*
Sabatini, Rafael	Captain Blood (1st, 12mo, black cl, 356p, col frn by...)	Houghton	1922	Wyeth, N.C.	25-40	*
Sabin, E.H.	Magical Man of Mirth (1st, 8vo, p-o, 233p, 8cp, pep)	Jacobs	(1910)	Knipe, H.A.	50-65	
Sabin, E.H.	Queen of the City of Mirth (1st, 8vo, p-o, 164p, 8cp)	Jacobs	(1911)	Knipe, H.A.	50-80	
Sabin, E.H.	Stella's Adventure in Starland (1st, 8vo, 210p, 9pl)	Small	1907	Brown, E.	60-80	*
Sabin, E.L.	Gold Seekers of '49 (1st, sm8vo, 335p, tan cl, col frn, 4pl by)	Lippincott	1915	Stephens, C.H.	50-80	R*
Sabin, E.L.	Range & Trail (1st, 8vo, 445p, 8pl)	Crowell	(1910)	Rowe, C.	35-60	
Sacher-Masoch, L.	Jewish Tales (1st, 12mo, 317p, beige/gilt, cvr by...)	McClurg	1894	Armstrong, M.	50-80	*
Sackett, Rose M.	Cousin from Clare (1st, 8vo, 270p, green cl, 4pl)	MacMillan	1932	DeAngeli, M.	30-45	
Sackville, M.	Dream Pedlar (1st, sm4to, 184p, blue/gilt, 16 ticp)	L: Simpkin	(1914)	Anderson, F.	130-170	
Sackville, M.	Travelling Companions... (1st, 8vo, 132p, blue/gilt, 12cp)	L: Simpkin	(1915)	Anderson, F.	100-150	
Sage, A.C.	Little Colonial Dame (1st, sm4to, 197p, 16pl)	Stokes	(1898)	Humphrey, M.	50-70	
Sage, A.C.	Two Girls/Old New Jersey (1st, lg8vo, 195p, 16pl)	Stokes	(1912)	Connah, D.J.	20-35	*
Sage, B.	Rhymes of If & Why (1st, 4to, 31p, ibds, 4cp)	Duffield	1927	Robinson, B.	70-90	
Sage, B.	Rhymes of Real Children (1st, sq4to, 32p, ibds, 6cp)	Fox/Duffield	1903	Smith, J.W.	275-400	
Sage, J.	Man in the Manhole & Fix-It-Men (1st, lg8vo, ipcb, [40]p, col)	W.R. Scott	1946	Ballantine, B.	30-45	*
Saint, L.B.	Knight of the Cross (1st, 8vo, 220p, uncut, p-o, teg, 7 ticp)	Jacobs	(1914)	Saint, L.B.	20-30	
Saint-Exupery, A.	Flight to Arras (1st AM, 8vo, 255p, 13pl, pep)	Reynal/Hitch.	(1942)	Lamotte, B.	65-80	*
Saint-Exupery, A.	Little Prince (1st AM, sq8vo, 91p, color)	Reynal/Hitch.	(1943)	Saint-Exupery, A.	100-145	*
Saint-Exupery, A.	Southern Mail (1st AM, sm8vo, 253p, 1-color lithos by...)	Smith/Haas	1933	Ward, L.	65-85	*
Saint-Exupery, A.	Wind, Sand & Stars (1st AM, 8vo, 306p, pep, 1-color designs)	Reynal/Hitch.	(1939)	Cosgrave, J.O.	65-85	*
Salten, Felix	Bambi... (1st AM {std}, 12mo, 293p, green/gilt, b/w, pep)	Simon/Schuster	1928	Wiese, K.	85-125	R
Salten, Felix	Favorite Animal Stories (1st, 8vo, orange cl, 243p, b/w)	J. Messner	(1948)	Eichenberg, F.	35-50	*
Salten, Felix	Rennie the Rescuer (1st {std}, 8vo, 326p, cloth, b/w)	Bobbs-Merrill	1940	Thorne, D.	35-50	
Sampson, Martin	Good Giant (1st, 8vo, 218p, col frn, 10pl, pep)	Houghton	1928	Hilton	35-50	*
Sandburg, C.	Early Moon (1st {std}, lg8vo, 136p, b/w)	Harcourt	(1930)	Daugherty, J.	70-90	*
Sandburg, C.	Rootabaga Country (1st, 4to, 259p, col frn, 16 b/w, pep)	Harcourt	(1929)	Bacon, P.	65-90	
Sandburg, C.	Rootabaga Pigeons (1st, 8vo, blue cl, 218p, col frn)	Harcourt	(1923)	Petershams	70-100	
Sandburg, C.	Rootabaga Stories (1st, 8vo, 230p, blue cl, col frn, PPP)	Harcourt	(1922)	Petershams	70-110	
Sandler, M.C.	Mamma's Angel Child (1st, 8vo, ibds, p-o, 115p, color)	Rand/McNally	(1915)	Ross, M.T.	90-140	
Sandoz, M.	House Without Windows (1st, 8vo, DJ)	(London)	1950	Dali, S.	100-165	
Sandoz, M.	On the Verge (1st {std}, 4to, 127p, col frn, cep, DJ)	Doubleday	1950	Dali, S.	150-200	
Sandoz, M.	The Maze (1st {std}, 8vo, bds, 110p, uncut, 13pl, DJ)	Doubleday	1945	Dali, S.	160-220	
Sandwell, H.B.	Valley of Color Days (1st, 8vo, tan cl, 299p, 6cp, pep)	Little/Brown	1924	Preston, A.B.	45-60	
Sandys, Ruth	Numerous Names Nimbly Narrated (1st, lg4to, ibds, unpag, col)	L: H. Milford	(1930)	Sandys, R.	150-200	
Santos-Dumont	My Air-Ships (1st, sm8vo, 356p, blue cl, b/w)	Century	1904	(Photos)	70-90	
Sarg, Tony	Tony Sarg's Alphabet (1st UK, sm4to, [30]p, ibds, color, DJ)	(London)	(1930)	Sarg, T.	80-120	
Sarg, Tony	Tony Sarg's Book of Animals (4to, green ibds, color)	Greenberg	(1925)	Sarg, T.	75-110	
Sarg, Tony	Tony Sarg's Book of Tricks (1st, 4to, ibds, [96]p, color, pep)	Greenberg	(1928)	Sarg, T.	70-100	
Sarg, Tony	Tony Sarg's New York (1st, lg4to, [60]p, 24cp)	Greenberg	1926	Sarg, T.	70-120	
Sarg, Tony	Where is Tommy? (1st, ob4to, [20]p, ipcb, color)	Greenberg	(1932)	Sarg, T.	35-50	
Sargant, Alice	Crystal Ball (1st, 8vo, 119p)	L: G. Bell	(1894)	Florence, M.S.	100-160	*
Sassoon, S.	Memoirs of a Fox Hunting Man (1st AM, lg8vo, 296p, 7pl)	Coward	1929	Nicholson, W.	80-110	
Sauer, J.L.	Fog Magic (1st, 8vo, grey cl, 107p, pep, NH)	Viking	1943	Ward, L.	60-100	R*
Sauer, J.L.	Light at Tern Rock (1st, 4to, 62p, pep, brown illus, NH)	Viking	1951	Schreiber, G.	65-100	R*
Sauer, J.L.	Mike's House (1st, sm4to, red cl, 31p, 2-color, pep)	Viking	1954	Freeman, D.	45-65	*
Saunders, L.	Knave of Hearts (1st {hardback}, folio, 46p, p-o, color, pep)	Scribner	1925	Parrish, M.	800-1000	
Saunders, M.	Alpatok (1st, 12mo, tan cl, 51p, b/w)	Page	1906	Horne, D.W.	20-30	*
Saunders, M.	Beautiful Joe's Paradise (1st, 8vo, red/gilt, p-o, 365p, 15pl)	L.C. Page	1902	Bull, C.L.	20-30	
Saunders, M.	Nita (1st, 12mo, 77p)	Page	1904	Barry, E.B.	20-30	*

AUTHOR	TITLE	PUBLISHER	DATE	ARTIST	PRICE	LC
Saunders, Phyllis	Flame Flower (1st, lg8vo, purple cl, 127p, p-o, 4cp)	L: Butterworth	1922	Miller, H.T.	100-150	
Sautriax [Rabelais]	Gargantua (1st, ob folio, 52p, ibds, 6cp)	Duffield	1921	Leroy, Adrien	120-170	*
Sawyer, E.A.	Christmas Maker's Club (1st, 8vo, 275p, 6pl)	Page	1908	Williamson	20-30	*
Sawyer, E.A.	Elsa's Gift Home (1st, 8vo, 229p, 6pl)	Page	1911	Nosworthy, F.	20-30	*
Sawyer, R.S.	Christmas Anna Angel (1st, 8vo, 48p, color, pep, CH)	Viking	1944	Seredy, K.	65-90	
Sawyer, R.S.	Doctor Danny (1st, sm8vo, 410p, ibds, pep, 8pl)	Harper	1918	Williams, J.S.	20-40	*
Sawyer, R.S.	Enchanted Schoolhouse (1st, lg8vo, green cl, 128p, fp b/w, pep)	Viking	1956	Troy, H.	20-35	*
Sawyer, R.S.	Journey Cake, Ho! (1st, 4to, 45p, 2-color, pep, DJ, CH)	Viking	1953	McCloskey, R.	65-100	R
Sawyer, R.S.	Least One (1st, lg8vo, 89p, 2-color, pep, DJ)	Viking	1936	Politi, L.	35-50	
Sawyer, R.S.	Leerie (1st, 12mo, 309p, 4pl)	Harper	(1920)	Balmer, C.	20-35	*
Sawyer, R.S.	Little Red Horse (1st, sm8vo, 108p, brown cl, pep, color, DJ)	Viking	1950	Barnum, J.H.	40-65	
Sawyer, R.S.	Long Christmas (1st, 4to, 200p, cloth, dep, DJ)	Viking	1941	Angelo, V.	35-50	
Sawyer, R.S.	Maggie Rose: Her Birthday Christmas (1st {std}, 12mo, 151p, b/w)	Harper	1952	Sendak, M.	130-175	*
Sawyer, R.S.	Primrose Ring (1st, 12mo, 186p, b/w, pl)	Harper	(1915)	Munsell, F.	20-35	*
Sawyer, R.S.	Roller Skates (1st, 8vo, 186p, 1-color, pep, DJ, NM)	Viking	1936	Angelo, V.	50-80	R
Sawyer, R.S.	Silver Sixpence (1st, 12mo, 331p, 4pl)	Harper	1921	Crank, J.H.	20-30	*
Sawyer, R.S.	This Way to Christmas (1st, 12mo, 165p, gilt, frn by...)	Harper	(1916)	Rockwell, N.	45-60	*
Sawyer, R.S.	This Way to Christmas (1st, lg8vo, 175p, 10cp)	Harper	1924	Barney, M.W.	45-60	
Sawyer, R.S.	Tonio Antonia (1st, 8vo, 132p, red/gilt, 8 fp b/w, pep)	Viking	1934	Mora, L.	25-40	*
Sawyer, R.S.	Year of the Christmas Dragon (1st, lg8vo, red cl, 88p, b/w, pep)	Viking	(1960)	Troy, H.	25-45	*
Sayers, F.C.	Blue Bonnets for Lucinda (1st, sq8vo, ibds, [30]p, color, pep)	Viking	1934	Sewell, H.	35-50	
Sayers, F.C.	Mr. Tidy Paws (1st, sm4to, ibds, 64p, b/w, pep, DJ)	Viking	1935	Gay, Z.	45-60	
Sayers, F.C.	Tag-Along Tooloo (1st, 8vo, 87p, pep, 8 fp color)	Viking	1941	Sewell, H.	25-40	*
Schackne, S.	Rowena the Skating Cow (1st, 4to, [61]p, tan cl, 28 fp color)	Scribner	1940	Eichenberg, F.	65-100	*
Schauffer, R.H.	Romantic America (1st, 4to, 339p, gilt, teg, col frn by...)	Century	1913	Parrish, M.	80-125	
Schlein, M.	Big Cheese (1st, sm4to, white cl, [48]p, 2-color)	W.R. Scott	1958	Low, J.	30-45	*
Schlein, M.	Big Talk (1st, sq8vo, olive cl, [36]p, 2-color, pep)	W.R. Scott	1955	Weiss, H.	30-50	*
Schlein, M.	Elephant Herd (1st, lg8vo, ipcb, [40]p, 1-color, cep)	W.R. Scott	1954	Shimin, S.	30-50	*
Schlein, M.	Fast is Not a Ladybug (1st, sm8vo, ipcb, [34]p, 1-color, pep)	W.R. Scott	(1953)	Kessler, L.	30-45	*
Schlein, M.	Four Little Foxes (1st, sm4to, ipcb, unpag, color, pep)	W.R. Scott	1953	Quintanilla, L.	45-70	*
Schlein, M.	Heavy is a Hippopotamus (1st, sm8vo, ipcb, unpag, 1-color, pep)	W.R. Scott	1954	Kessler, L.	50-80	R*
Schlein, M.	It's About Time (1st, sm8vo, [41]p)	W.R. Scott	1955	Kessler, L.	30-45	*
Schlein, M.	Kittens, Cubs & Babies (1st, sm4to, green cl, unpag, color)	W.R. Scott	1959	Charlot, J.	60-90	*
Schlein, M.	Little Rabbit the High Jumper (1st, 8vo, [46]p, 2-color)	W.R. Scott	1957	Sherman, T.	30-50	*
Schlein, M.	Shapes (1st, 8vo, ibds, [33]p, color)	W.R. Scott	1952	Berman, S.	25-40	*
Schlein, M.	When Will the World be Mine? (1st, 4to, unpag, pep, color, CH)	W.R. Scott	(1953)	Charlot, J.	70-120	*
Schmidt, S.L.	New Land (1st, sm8vo, 317p, brown cl, 9 fp b/w, pep, NH)	McBride	1933	Dobias, F.	30-55	*
Schmidt, S.L.	Ranching on Eagle Eye (1st {std}, 12mo, 374p, pep)	McBride	(1936)	Laune, P.	25-40	*
Schmidt, S.L.	Secret of Silver Peak (1st, sm8vo, 334p, rust cl, b/w)	Random	(1938)	Kreis, H.	25-40	*
Schmidt, S.L.	Shadow over Winding Ranch (1st, 8vo, 298p, beige cl, b/w)	Random	(1940)	Busoni, R.	30-45	*
Schneider, H.	Follow the Sunset (1st {std}, 4to, ibds, 43p, color, cep)	Doubleday	(1952)	Corcos, L.	50-85	R*
Schneider, H.	How Big is Big? (1st {this fmt.}, 4to, [40]p, color)	W.R. Scott	1950	Shimin, S.	25-45	*
Schneider, H.	Let's Look Under the City (1st, sm8vo, grey cl, 70p, 1-color)	W.R. Scott	(1954)	Ballantine, B.	20-30	*
Schneider, N.	Let's Find Out (1st, lg8vo, 38p, color)	W.R. Scott	(1946)	Bendick, J.	35-50	*
Schneider, N.	Let's Look Inside your House (1st, lg8vo, 39p, color)	W.R. Scott	(1948)	Ivins, B.	45-60	*
Schneider, N.	While Susie Sleeps (1st, sm4to, [32]p, color)	W.R. Scott	(1948)	Wilson, D.	45-60	*
Schrank, J.	Seldom & the Golden Cheese (1st, 8vo, blue cl, uncut, 8pl, pep)	Dodd	1933	Tenggren, G.	45-65	
Schreiber, G.	Bambino the Clown (1st, 4to, 30p, ipcb, color, pep, CH)	Viking	1947	Schreiber, G.	70-100	
Schultz, J.W.	Gold Dust (1st, 8vo, 243p, b/w, DJ)	Houghton	1934	Mulford, S.	35-50	
Schultz, J.W.	In the Great Apache Forest (1st, 8vo, 225p, green cl, 4pl)	Houghton	1920	Cue, H.	25-40	*
Schultz, J.W.	Lone Bull's Mistake (1st, 8vo, 207p, p-o, 4pl)	Houghton	1918	Varian, G.	35-50	
Schultz, J.W.	Plumed Snake Medicine (1st, 8vo, 244p, p-o, 4pl)	Houghton	1924	Varian, G.	40-60	*
Schultz, J.W.	Quest of the Fish-Dog Skin (1st, 8vo, tan cl, p-o, 4pl)	Houghton	1913	Varian, G.	45-60	
Schultz, J.W.	Seizer of Eagles (1st, 8vo, 230p, brown cl, 4pl)	Houghton	1922	Schoonover, F.	25-40	*
Schultz, J.W.	Skull Head the Terrible (1st, 8vo, 208p, brown cl, 4pl, pep)	Houghton	1929	Schoonover, F.	25-40	*
Schultz, J.W.	With the Indians in the Rockies (1st, 8vo, p-o, 227p, 6pl)	Houghton	1912	Varian, G.	40-60	*
Schultz, J.W.	With the Indians in the Rockies (1st, lg8vo, 252p, p-o, 4cp)	Houghton	1925	Brett, H.M.	25-40	*
Schwartz, Eliz. R.	Cottontail Rabbit (1st, 8vo, 45p, olive cl, 2-color, cep)	Holiday House	(1957)	Schwartz, C.	25-40	*
Schwatka, Fred	Children of the Cold (1st, 12mo, 212p, b/w)	NY: Cassell	(1886)	Bobbett, Walt.	70-90	*
Schwimmer, R.	Tisza Tales (1st {std}, 8vo, 225p, blue/gilt, 8cp, pep, DJ)	Doubleday/Dor.	1928	Pogany, W.	85-100	
Scott, A.M.	Flower Babies' Book (8vo, 78p, ibds, color)	Rand/McNally	(1914)	Ross, M.T.	60-80	
Scott, A.M.	Year with the Fairies (1st, lg4to, ibds, [100]p, color, pep)	Volland	(1914)	Ross, M.T.	120-145	
Scott, F.E.	Kindergarten Limericks (1st, 4to, [59]p, 27cp)	Hurst	(1915)	Scott, A.O.	140-200	*
Scott, Gabriel	Kari (1st {std}, 8vo, 242p, blue cl, uncut, col frn, 7pl, pep)	Doubleday/Dor.	1931	D'Aulaire, E.P.	30-45	*
Scott, J.L.	Round the World We Sail (1st, sq4to, ibds, [16]p, color, pep)	Saalfield	1939	Scott, J.L.	35-50	
Scott, Michael	Tom Cringle's Log (1st, 8vo, 569p, AEG, blue/gilt, 42 b/w)	L: MacMillan	1895	Symington, J.A.	35-50	
Scott, Michael	Tom Cringle's Log (1st, 4to, black/gilt, 384p, p-o, 7cp, pep)	Dodd	1927	Schaeffer, M.	40-60	
Scott, Sally	Benjie & his Family (1st {std}, 8vo, yellow cl, [62]p, fp b/w)	Harcourt	(1952)	Krush, B.	25-40	*
Scott, Sally	Chica (1st {std}, 8vo, 114p, rust cl, fp b/w)	Harcourt	(1954)	Krush, J.	25-45	*
Scott, Sally	Rip & Royal (1st {std}, 8vo, 58p, tan cl, b/w)	Harcourt	(1950)	Krush, B.	25-45	*
Scott, Sally	What Susan Wanted (1st {std}, sm8vo, pink cl, 36p, fp b/w)	Harcourt	(1956)	Krush, B.	30-50	*
Scott, Walter	Ivanhoe (1st, 8vo, blue/gilt, 523p, teg, uncut, 12cp, pep)	L: Dent	1899	Brock, C.E.	65-90	

AUTHOR	TITLE	PUBLISHER	DATE	ARTIST	PRICE	LC
Scott, Walter	Ivanhoe (1st, sm8vo, 346p, 4cp)	Appleton	1910	Unknown	20-35	*
Scott, Walter	Ivanhoe (1st, 8vo, red cl, 676p, teg, 16cp)	Houghton	1913	Smith, E.B.	75-120	
Scott, Walter	Ivanhoe (1st, 12mo, 336p, cp)	Row/Peterson	(1914)	Cole, C.L.	25-40	*
Scott, Walter	Ivanhoe (1st AM, 8vo, 563p, 12cp)	Lipp./Jack	[1915]	Greiffenhagen, M.	35-60	*
Scott, Walter	Ivanhoe (1st, lg8vo, p-o, 637p, blue/gilt, 14cp, pep)	Rand/McNally	(1918)	Winter, M.	45-70	
Scott, Walter	Ivanhoe (1st, 4to, 515p, p-o, blue/gilt, 10cp, pep)	Harper	1922	Schoonover, F.	50-70	
Scott, Walter	Ivanhoe (1st, 8vo, red cl, 469p, uncut, 6pl)	Sears	(1928)	Pitz, H.C.	25-40	*
Scott, Walter	Kenilworth (1st, 4to, teg, red/gilt, 551p, uncut, 12cp)	L: Jack	(1920)	Ford, H.J.	100-160	
Scott, Walter	Lady of the Lake (1st, 4to, green/gilt, 13cp)	Bobbs-Merrill	(1910)	Christy, H.C.	60-90	
Scott, Walter	Quentin Durward (1st, sm8vo, 348p, 4cp)	Appleton	1910	Varian, G.	20-35	*
Scott, Walter	Quentin Durward (1st, 4to, 422p, gilt, p-o, 13cp, pep, SC)	Scribner	1923	Chambers, C.B.	65-100	
Scott, Walter	Quentin Durward (1st, lg8vo, uncut, 499p, 16cp)	Dodd	1923	Tarrant, P.	30-45	*
Scott, Wm. R.	Apple that Jack Ate (1st, sm ob4to, ipcb, [25]p, color, dep)	W.R. Scott	1951	Shaw, C.G.	30-45	*
Scott, Wm. R.	This is the Milk that Jack Drank (1st, ob4to, ipcb, [24]p, col)	W.R. Scott	1944	Shaw, C.G.	45-65	*
Scott, Wm. R.	Water that Jack Drank (1st, ob4to, ipcb, [24]p, color, pep)	W.R. Scott	1950	Shaw, C.G.	50-65	*
Scott-Gatty	I Wonder Why? (lg4to, 72p, bds, p-o, 16 ticp)	L: Collins	1920	Robertson, W.G.	130-170	
Scoville, S.	Lords of the Wild (1st, 8vo, green cl, 246p, 4pl, pep)	Wm. Morrow	1928	Bull, C.L.	20-35	
Scribner, Grace	American Pilgrimage (1st, 12mo, 89p, 4 woodcuts)	Vanguard Pr.	(1927)	Ward, L.	45-60	*
Scripps, H.J.	Little Handfull (1st, 8vo, 224p, ibds, 4pl)	L: Blackie	(1894)	Brooke, L.L.	70-90	
Scudder, Horace E.	Children's Book (8vo, p-o by…)	Houghton	1909	Parrish, M.	50-70	*
Seabrook, Katie	Colette & Baba in Timbuctoo (1st {std}, 8vo, 168p, frn by…)	Coward	(1933)	Berry, E.	20-30	*
Seabrook, Katie	Gao of the Ivory Coast (1st, 8vo, 121p, col frn, 4pl)	Coward	(1931)	D'Aulaire, E.P.	45-65	*
Seaman, Louise	Brave Bantam (1st, 8vo, green cl, 48p, b/w, pep)	MacMillan	1946	Sewell, H.	25-40	*
Seaman, Louise	Mr. Peck's Pets (1st {std}, 8vo, 96p, b/w, pep)	MacMillan	1947	Hader, B.& E.	25-40	*
Sears, P.M.	Barn Swallow (1st, 8vo, 45p, fp 2-color, cep)	Holiday House	(1955)	Ferguson, W.	20-25	*
Sears, P.M.	Downy Woodpecker (1st, 8vo, 43p, 2-color, cep)	Holiday House	(1953)	Latham, B.	25-40	*
Sears, P.M.	Firefly (1st, sm8vo, 37p, green cl, 2-color, pep)	Holiday House	1956	Rounds, G.	25-40	*
Sears, P.M.	Tree Frog (1st, 8vo, 45p, green cl, 2-color)	Holiday House	(1954)	Latham, B.	35-50	R*
Seawell, M.E.	Betty at Fort Blizzard (1st, 8vo, 224p, teg, p-o, 4cp)	Lippincott	1916	Frederick, E.	20-25	
Seawell, M.E.	Chateau of Montplaisir (1st, 8vo, uncut, 245p, blue cl, cvr by)	Appleton	1906	Armstrong, M.	30-45	
Seawell, M.E.	Fortunes of Fifi (1st, 8vo, 239p)	Bobbs-Merrill	(1903)	Armstrong, M.	25-40	
Seawell, M.E.	Francezka (1st, 8vo, 466p, green/gilt, cvr by…)	Bobbs-Merrill	(1902)	Armstrong, M.	30-45	
Seawell, M.E.	Francezka (1st, 8vo, 466p, green/gilt, 7pl)	Bobbs-Merrill	(1902)	Fisher, H.	30-45	
Seawell, M.E.	House of Egremont (1st, 8vo, 515p)	Scribner	1900	Relyea, C.M.	15-20	
Seawell, M.E.	Loves of Lady Arabella (1st, 8vo, p-o, 244p, 12cp)	Bobbs-Merrill	(1906)	Underwood, C.F.	20-25	
Seawell, M.E.	Midshipman Paulding (1st, 8vo, 133p)	Appleton	1891	Edwards, G.W.	35-50	
Seawell, M.E.	Papa Bouchard (1st, 12mo, 261p, uncut, teg)	Scribner	1901	Glackens, W.	20-30	
Seccombe, Lieut.	Good Old Story/Cinderella (1st AM, sm4to, 48p, gilt, 12cp)	NY: Armstrong	(1882)	Seccombe, Lieut.	100-150	*
Sechrist, Eliz. H.	Rufie Had a Monkey! (1st, lg8vo, [46]p, red cl, b/w, cep)	McKay	(1939)	Janeway, H.	80-130	*
Sedberry, J.H.	Under the Flag of the Cross (1st, 8vo, blue/gilt, 10pl)	C.M. Clark	1908	Kirkpatrick, W.	65-90	
Sedgwick, Anne D.	Dull Miss Archinard (1st, 12mo, 287p, beige/gilt)	Scribner	1898	Armstrong, M.	30-45	*
Sedlacek, H.	Nursery Rhymes/Bohemia (1st AM, lg4to, [24]p, ibds, color, pep)	McBride	1929	Mates, R.	75-100	
Seeger, E.	Pageant of Chinese History (1st {std}, 8vo, 386p, b/w, pep, NH)	Longmans	1934	Watkins, B.	45-60	*
Seeger, Ruth C.	Animal Folk Songs for Children (1st {std}, 4to, 80p)	Doubleday	1950	Cooney, B.	35-50	*
Seegmiller, W.	Hand Clasp (1st, narrow 16mo)	Volland	(1911)	Unknown	40-65	*
Seegmiller, W.	Journeys in Storyland (1st, sm8vo, [120]p, pep, color)	Houghton	1922	Enright, M.W.	45-60	*
Seegmiller, W.	Little Rhymes for Little Readers (1st, lg4to, 81p, pep)	Rand/McNally	(1903)	Hallock, R.M.	65-80	*
Sefton, H.L.	Dream Imp & Others (1st, 4to, 96p, red/gilt, 10cp)	L: Bickers	[1912]	MacQuigg, G.E.	120-180	
Seitz, D.	The Bucaneers (1st, 8vo, p-o, teg, 52p, frn by…)	Harper	1912	Pyle, H.	50-80	
Selden, George	Cricket in Times Square (1st, lg8vo, 151p, fp b/w, NH)	Ariel	(1960)	Williams, Garth	45-65	*
Selden, George	Dog that Could Swim Underwater (1st, 8vo, grey cl, 126p, b/w)	Viking	1956	Dennis, M.	25-45	*
Selsam, M.E.	A Time for Sleep (1st, sm8vo, [57]p)	W.R. Scott	1953	Ludwig, H.	25-40	*
Selsam, M.E.	All About Eggs (1st, sm8vo, [62]p, 3-color)	W.R. Scott	1952	Ludwig, H.	30-45	*
Selsam, M.E.	Nature Detective (1st, ob8vo, [48]p, color)	W.R. Scott	1958	Sherman, T.	25-40	*
Selsam, M.E.	Seeds & More Seeds (1st, 8vo, ibds, 60p, 2-color)	Harper	(1959)	Ungerer, T.	25-40	*
Seltzer, C.A.	Range Boss (1st, 8vo, 333p, 4pl)	McClurg	1916	Schoonover, F.	25-40	
Seltzer, C.A.	Range Riders (1st, 8vo, 310p)	Outing	1911	Rowe, C.	30-45	
Semple, D.	Tommy & Jane & the Birds (1st, 8vo, p-o, 94p, color, pep)	Saalfield	(1929)	Peat, F.B.	45-75	
Sendak, Jack	Circus Girl (1st, lg8vo, beige cl, [30]p, color)	Harper	1957	Sendak, M.	120-165	R*
Sendak, Jack	Happy Rain (1st, sm4to, 40p, blue cl, 8 fp b/w)	Harper	(1956)	Sendak, M.	160-250	R*
Sendak, M.	Kenny's Window (1st, lg sq8vo, tan cl, 1-color, unpag)	Harper	(1956)	Sendak, M.	130-170	R*
Sendak, M.	Sign on Rosie's Door (1st, 8vo, grey cl, 47p, color)	Harper	(1960)	Sendak, M.	120-165	*
Sendak, M.	Very Far Away (1st, 8vo, green cl, cep, 52p, color)	Harper	(1957)	Sendak, M.	120-165	R*
Seredy, K.	Chestry Oak (1st, 8vo, 236p, red cl, fp b/w)	Viking	1948	Seredy, K.	30-50	*
Seredy, K.	Good Master (1st, sq8vo, 211p, b/w, pep, DJ, NH)	Viking	1935	Seredy, K.	65-90	R
Seredy, K.	Gypsy (1st, lg4to, 62p, cloth, 29pl, DJ)	Viking	1951	Seredy, K.	85-100	
Seredy, K.	Listening (1st, 8vo, gilt, 157p, pep, 18pl)	Viking	1936	Seredy, K.	30-45	*
Seredy, K.	Open Gate (1st, 8vo, blue cl, 280p, fp b/w, pep, DJ)	Viking	1943	Seredy, K.	35-50	
Seredy, K.	Philomena (1st, tall 8vo, 95p, cloth, b/w, pep)	Viking	1955	Seredy, K.	30-45	
Seredy, K.	Singing Tree (1st, 8vo, 247p, color, 32 fp b/w, pep, NH)	Viking	1939	Seredy, K.	45-65	*
Seredy, K.	Tree for Peter (1st, lg8vo, 102p, cloth, brown illus)	Viking	1941	Seredy, K.	35-50	*
Seredy, K.	White Stag (1st, lg8vo, 95p, gilt, b/w, pep, DJ, NM)	Viking	1937	Seredy, K.	100-145	

AUTHOR	TITLE	PUBLISHER	DATE	ARTIST	PRICE	LC
Seredy, K.	White Stag (1st UK, 4to, cloth, 94p, b/w, DJ)	L: Harrap	(1938)	Seredy, K.	35-50	
Service, Rbt.	Trail of Ninety-Eight (1st, 8vo, 514p, 4pl)	Dodd	1911	Dixon, M.	30-45	
Serviss, G.P.	Columbus of Space (1st, 8vo, 298p, green cl, 4pl)	Appleton	1911	Heath, H.	120-200	
Serviss, G.P.	Second Deluge (1st, sm8vo, 399p, aqua cl, 4pl)	McBride	1912	Varian, G.	150-200	
Seton, E.T.	Animal Heroes (1st, 8vo, green/gilt, 362p, teg, 19pl)	Scribner	1905	Seton, E.T.	50-80	
Seton, E.T.	Arctic Prairies (1st, lg8vo, 415p, green/gilt, uncut)	Scribner	1911	(Photos)	70-110	R
Seton, E.T.	Biography of a Grizzly (1st, sq8vo, 167p, 12 tipl, cep)	Century	1900	Seton, E.T.	70-90	
Seton, E.T.	Biography of a Silver Fox (1st, sm8vo, blue cl, 209p, 10pl)	Century	1909	Seton, E.T.	50-65	
Seton, E.T.	Bird Portraits (1st, lg4to, 40p, green cl, 20pl)	Ginn	1901	Seton, E.T.	120-160	
Seton, E.T.	Book of Woodcraft (1st, lg8vo, 567p, green/gilt, b/w)	Doubleday/Page	1912	Seton, E.T.	30-45	
Seton, E.T.	Krag & Johnny Bear (1st, sm8vo, 141p, b/w pl)	Scribner	1902	Seton, E.T.	60-90	
Seton, E.T.	Lives of the Hunted (1st, 8vo, 360p, green/gilt, teg, b/w)	Scribner	1901	Seton, E.T.	65-80	
Seton, E.T.	Monarch the Big Bear... (1st, 8vo, 214p, blue cl, p-o)	Scribner	1904	Seton, E.T.	40-60	
Seton, E.T.	Preacher of Cedar Mountain (1st, 8vo, 426p, gilt, frn by...)	Doubleday/Page	1917	Rowe, C.	25-40	*
Seton, E.T.	Rolf in the Woods (1st, lg8vo, 437p, green/gilt, 12pl)	Doubleday/Page	1911	Seton, E.T.	35-50	
Seton, E.T.	Studies/Art Anatomy/Animals (1st, folio, green/gilt, 49pl)	L: MacMillan	1896	Seton, E.T.	350-500	
Seton, E.T.	Trail of the Sandhill Stag (1st, 8vo, teg, 93p, gilt, col frn)	Scribner	1899	Seton, E.T.	70-90	
Seton, E.T.	Two Little Savages (1st, 8vo, grey/gilt, 552p, 29pl)	Doubleday/Page	1903	Seton, E.T.	65-80	
Seton, E.T.	Wild Animal Play for Children (1st, sm8vo, green cl, 79p, b/w)	Doubleday/Page	1900	Seton, E.T.	90-120	
Seton, E.T.	Wild Animals I Have Known (1st, 8vo, teg, 359p, PPP)	Scribner	1898	Seton, E.T.	90-130	
Seton, E.T.	Wild Animals at Home (1st, 8vo, 226p, gilt, b/w)	Doubleday/Page	1913	Seton, E.T.	50-70	
Seton, E.T.	Woodmyth & Fable (1st, 8vo, 181p, red/gilt)	Century	1905	Seton, E.T.	70-100	
Seton, G.	Nimrod's Wife (1st, 8vo, 406p, 18pl)	Doubleday/Page	1907	Seton, E.T.	45-70	
Seton, G.	Woman Tenderfoot (1st, 8vo, 361p, teg, b/w)	Doubleday/Page	1900	Seton, E.T.	50-70	
Setoun, G.	Child World (1st, 8vo, AEG, 174p, uncut, 14pl)	L: J. Lane	1896	Robinson, C.	130-180	
Seuss, Dr.	500 Hats/Bartholomew Cubbins (1st, 4to, ibds, [47]p, pep, col)	Vanguard Pr.	(1938)	Seuss, Dr.	130-185	
Seuss, Dr.	And to Think/I Saw It/Mulberry Street (1st, 4to, [32]p, ibds pep)	Vanguard Pr.	1937	Seuss, Dr.	250-350	R*
Seuss, Dr.	Bartholomew & the Oobleck (1st, lg4to, [48]p, red ibds, CH)	Random	(1950)	Seuss, Dr.	200-300	*
Seuss, Dr.	Cat in the Hat (1st, sm4to, 61p, ipcb, color, pep)	Random	(1957)	Seuss, Dr.	250-400	R*
Seuss, Dr.	Cat in the Hat Comes Back (1st {std}, 4to, 61p, color, pep)	Random	(1958)	Seuss, Dr.	250-350	
Seuss, Dr.	Green Eggs & Ham (1st, lg8vo, 62p)	Random	1960	Seuss, Dr.	120-170	*
Seuss, Dr.	Happy Birthday to You! (1st, lg4to, [57]p, ibds, color)	Random	(1959)	Seuss, Dr.	200-300	*
Seuss, Dr.	Horton Hatches the Egg (1st {std}, sq4to, [55]p, ibds, color)	Random	(1940)	Seuss, Dr.	180-240	*
Seuss, Dr.	Horton Hears a Who! (1st, 4to, unpag, ibds, color, pep)	Random	(1954)	Seuss, Dr.	150-200	*
Seuss, Dr.	How the Grinch Stole Christmas (1st, lg4to, ibds, unpag, color)	Random	1957	Seuss, Dr.	250-350	
Seuss, Dr.	If I Ran the Circus (1st, lg4to, ibds, pep, unpag)	Random	(1956)	Seuss, Dr.	200-350	*
Seuss, Dr.	If I Ran the Zoo (1st, lg4to, ibds, [56]p, color, pep, CH)	Random	(1950)	Seuss, Dr.	200-300	*
Seuss, Dr.	King's Stilts (1st, lg4to, [48]p, red epps, color)	Random	(1939)	Seuss, Dr.	300-400	*
Seuss, Dr.	McElligot's Pool (1st, 4to, [56]p, green cl, color, CH)	Random	(1947)	Seuss, Dr.	220-300	
Seuss, Dr.	On Beyond Zebra (1st, 4to, unpag)	Random	(1955)	Seuss, Dr.	200-250	*
Seuss, Dr.	One Fish Two Fish Red Fish Blue Fish (1st, lg8vo, 62p, ipcb, col)	Random	1960	Seuss, Dr.	120-180	*
Seuss, Dr.	Scrambled Eggs Supper (1st, lg4to, ibds, [52]p, color, pep)	Random	(1953)	Seuss, Dr.	200-300	
Seuss, Dr.	Seven Lady Godivas (1st {std}, 4to, [80]p, 1-color, pep, DJ)	Random	(1939)	Seuss, Dr.	240-350	
Seuss, Dr.	Thidwick/Big-Hearted Moose (1st, 4to, blue cl, [40]p, color)	Random	(1948)	Seuss, Dr.	220-320	
Seuss, Dr.	Yertle the Turtle (1st, 4to, ibds, unpag, 2-color, pep)	Random	(1958)	Seuss, Dr.	200-250	*
Sewell, A.A.	Ballad of the Prince (1st, lg4to, unpag, 12pl)	R.H. Russell	1900	Sewell, A.A.	180-250	*
Sewell, Anna	Black Beauty (1st, sm8vo, 200p, 22 illus)	Hovendon	1894	Toaspern, H.	45-60	*
Sewell, Anna	Black Beauty (1st, sm8vo, 262p, b/w pl)	Page	1902	Austin/Toaspern	25-40	*
Sewell, Anna	Black Beauty (1st, 12mo, 319p, b/w)	Rand/McNally	(1904)	Copeland, C.	25-40	*
Sewell, Anna	Black Beauty (1st, 8vo, 96p)	Saalfield	(1905)	Miller, H.L.	30-45	*
Sewell, Anna	Black Beauty (1st, 8vo, p-o, 261p, color)	Dodge	(1907)	Pancoast, C.W.	35-50	*
Sewell, Anna	Black Beauty (1st, sm8vo, 45p, 6cp, pep)	Brewer/Barse	(1907)	Von Hofsten, H.	25-40	*
Sewell, Anna	Black Beauty (sm8vo, red cl, 58p, p-o, color)	Reilly/Britton	1908	Neill, J.R.	65-90	
Sewell, Anna	Black Beauty (1st, 8vo, 295p, 12cp)	Jacobs	(1910)	Scrivener, M.	45-65	*
Sewell, Anna	Black Beauty (8vo, p-o, 357p, 20 fp color)	Platt/Peck	(1911)	Burke, J.M.	35-50	
Sewell, Anna	Black Beauty (1st, lg8vo, 278p, teg, p-o, 12cp)	Barse	(1911)	Dickey, R.L.	35-50	*
Sewell, Anna	Black Beauty (1st, 4to, blue/gilt, 291p, 18 ticp, pep)	L: Jarrolds	[1912]	Aldin, C.	140-200	
Sewell, Anna	Black Beauty (1st AM, 8vo, 291p, 18 ticp, pep)	Stokes	[1913]	Aldin, C.	120-165	*
Sewell, Anna	Black Beauty (1st, 8vo, 224p, blue/gilt, 24cp)	L: J.M. Dent	1915	Kemp-Welch, L.	100-130	
Sewell, Anna	Black Beauty (1st, lg8vo, p-o, 239p, 4cp, 13pl, pep)	Dodd	1923	Pyle, Kath.	80-120	
Sewell, Anna	Black Beauty (1st, 4to, 244p, p-o, gilt, col frn)	Sears	(1926)	McMann, J.S.	35-50	*
Sewell, Anna	Black Beauty (1st, lg8vo, green/gilt, p-o, 293p, 4cp, pep)	Winston	(1927)	Prittie, E.J.	30-45	
Sewell, Anna	Black Beauty (1st, 8vo, 234p, col frn)	Saalfield	(1930)	Williams, F.W.	20-35	*
Sewell, Anna	Black Beauty (1st, 8vo, 224p, 8cp)	L: Bell	1931	Woodward, A.B.	45-60	
Sewell, Anna	Black Beauty (1st, sm8vo, 288p, 45p, pep, 10cp)	Grosset/Dunlap	(1945)	Eichenberg, F.	35-50	*
Sewell, Anna	Black Beauty (1st, 8vo, 315p, color)	World Pub. Co.	(1946)	Dennis, W.	35-50	*
Sewell, Anna	Black Beauty (1st, 4to, 62p, color)	Random	1949	Erickson, P.	35-50	*
Sewell, Anna	Black Beauty (1st, lg ob8vo, unpag, b/w)	Scribner	(1952)	Brown, Paul	70-90	*
Sewell, Daisy	About Fairies.... (1st, sq8vo, ibds, 76p, 5cp)	L: Allenson	[1930]	McConnell, J.	100-140	
Sewell, Daisy	Visions in Fairyland (1st, sq8vo, ibds, 69p, 3cp)	L: Allenson	[1930]	McConnell, J.	100-150	
Sewell, H.	ABC for Everyday (1st, 4to, ipcb, [28]p, pep, 2-color)	MacMillan	1930	Sewell, H.	100-140	R*
Sewell, H.	Belinda the Mouse (1st, sq12mo, grey cl, [61]p, color, DJ)	OUP	(1944)	Sewell, H.	35-50	

AUTHOR	TITLE	PUBLISHER	DATE	ARTIST	PRICE	LC
Sewell, H.	Birthdays for Robin (1st, sq12mo, [46]p, grey cl, fp 3-color)	MacMillan	1943	Sewell, H.	30-45	*
Sewell, H.	Blue Barns (1st, sq4to, [46]p, DJ)	MacMillan	1933	Sewell, H.	65-100	R
Sewell, H.	First Bible (1st, 4to, blue/gilt, 110p, 13pl, pep)	OUP	1934	Sewell, H.	70-120	
Sewell, H.	Head for Happy (1st, ob4to, [56]p, cloth, p-o, pep, DJ)	MacMillan	1931	Sewell, H.	70-100	
Sewell, H.	Jimmy & Jemima (1st, 8vo, [47]p, cloth, p-o, color)	MacMillan	1940	Sewell, H.	35-50	
Sewell, H.	Ming & Mehitable (1st, 16mo, yellow cl, [60]p, dep, color)	MacMillan	1936	Sewell, H.	35-50	*
Sewell, H.	Peggy & the Pony (1st, sq8vo, blue cl, [47]p, 2-color, DJ)	OUP	(1936)	Sewell, H.	45-70	
Sewell, H.	Peggy & the Pup (1st, sq8vo, [46]p, beige cl, fp 2-color)	OUP	(1941)	Sewell, H.	30-50	*
Sewell, H.	Three Tall Tales (1st, sq4to, ibds, [40]p, color)	MacMillan	1947	Sewell, H.	50-80	*
Sewell, H.	Words to the Wise (1st, ob8vo, [64]p, 1-color, tan cl, dep)	Dodd	(1932)	Sewell, H.	30-50	*
Shakespeare, Wm.	As You Like It (1st, 4to, ibds, 143p, gilt, 40 ticp)	L: Hodder	[1909]	Thomson, H.	130-165	
Shakespeare, Wm.	As You Like It (1st, 4to, red cl, p-o, 6 ticp)	L: Jackson	1930	Austen, J.	70-100	
Shakespeare, Wm.	Comedy of the Twelfth Night (1st, 4to, green/gilt, 40 ticp)	L: Hodder	[1908]	Robinson, W.H.	200-300	
Shakespeare, Wm.	Hamlet (1st, lg4to, 165p, gilt, 30 ticp)	L: Hodder	[1900]	Simmonds, W.G.	125-160	
Shakespeare, Wm.	Hamlet (1st, 4to, black bds, gilt, 35 b/w)	L: Selwyn	(1922)	Austen, J.	185-245	
Shakespeare, Wm.	Hamlet (1st AM, 4to, black bds, b/w)	Dutton	(1922)	Austen, J.	120-145	
Shakespeare, Wm.	Macbeth (black bds, 125p)	Garden City	1936	Dali, S.	170-230	
Shakespeare, Wm.	Merchant of Venice (sm4to, cloth, gilt, 143p, 16 ticp)	L: Hodder	[1920]	Linton, J.	60-85	
Shakespeare, Wm.	Merry Wives of Windsor (1st AM, 4to, red/gilt, teg, 40 ticp)	Stokes	(1910)	Thomson, H.	160-220	
Shakespeare, Wm.	Merry Wives of Windsor (1st, 4to, teg, gilt, 172p, 40 ticp)	L: Heinemann	1910	Thomson, H.	180-250	
Shakespeare, Wm.	MidSummer Night's Dream (1st, sq8vo, green/gilt, teg, 128p, pep)	L: Dent	1895	Bell, R.A.	80-120	
Shakespeare, Wm.	MidSummer Night's Dream (1st, 4to, p-o, 93p, 12cp, pep)	Stokes	(1907)	Perkins, L.F.	100-165	
Shakespeare, Wm.	MidSummer Night's Dream (1st, lg8vo, 134p, grey/gilt, 40 ticp)	L: Heinemann	1908	Rackham, A.	350-500	
Shakespeare, Wm.	MidSummer Night's Dream (1st AM, 4to, 187p, teg, gilt, 12 ticp)	Holt	1914	Robinson, W.H.	280-360	
Shakespeare, Wm.	MidSummer Night's Dream (1st, lg4to, 187p, gilt, 12 ticp)	L: Constable	1914	Robinson, W.H.	320-450	
Shakespeare, Wm.	Romeo & Juliet (1st, 4to, purple cl, 8 ticp)	L: Batsford	1936	Messel, O.	70-100	*
Shakespeare, Wm.	Songs (1st, 12mo, 140p, uncut, green/gilt, teg, 11pl)	J. Lane	1901	Ospovat, H.	50-65	
Shakespeare, Wm.	Songs & Sonnets (1st AM, 4to, 240p, blue/gilt, 12 ticp, pep)	McKay	[1915]	Robinson, C.	180-275	
Shakespeare, Wm.	Songs & Sonnets (1st, lg8vo, 240p, blue/gilt, 12 ticp, pep)	L: Duckworth	(1915)	Robinson, C.	240-320	
Shakespeare, Wm.	The Tempest (4to, teg, 106p, uncut)	L: Freemantle	1901	Bell, R.A.	70-90	
Shakespeare, Wm.	The Tempest (1st, 4to, blue/gilt, 144p, 40 ticp)	L: Hodder	[1908]	Dulac, E.	300-400	
Shakespeare, Wm.	The Tempest (1st, 4to, gilt, teg, 130p, 20 ticp, pep)	L: Chapman	1908	Woodroffe, P.	150-200	
Shakespeare, Wm.	The Tempest (1st, sm4to, olive/gilt, 185p, 20 ticp)	L: Heinemann	1926	Rackham, A.	250-400	
Shakespeare, Wm.	Under the Greenwood Tree (1st, 8vo, 270p, green cl, 10cp)	L: Chatto	1913	Henderson, K.	45-60	*
Shakespeare, Wm.	Under the Greenwood Tree (1st, 4to, 236p, wood engravings)	L: MacMillan	1940	Leighton, C.	45-60	*
Shakespeare, Wm.	Under the Greenwood Tree (4to, black/gilt, 51p, color)	NY: OUP	[1940]	Weisgard, L.	45-65	*
Shakespeare, Wm.	Venus & Adonis (1st, 4to, red cl, 112p, pep, 12cp)	Macveagh/Dial	1930	Kutcher, B.	30-45	*
Shakespeare, Wm.	Winter's Tale (1st, sm4to, 98p, gilt, 12cp, DJ)	L: Dent	(1922)	Armfield, M.	85-120	
Shankland, Frank	Bird Book (1st, 4to, ibds, 8 fp color)	Saalfield	(1931)	Peat, F.B.	40-60	
Shannon, Monica	California Fairy Tales (1st {std}, sm8vo, 298p, cp)	Doubleday/Page	1926	Millard, C.E.	45-60	*
Shannon, Monica	Dobry (1st, 8vo, 176p, grey cl, col frn, pep, DJ, NM)	Viking	1934	Katchamakoff, A.	75-100	
Shannon, Monica	Eyes for the Dark (1st {std}, 8vo, 311p, 4cp, 15pl)	Doubleday/Dor.	1928	Millard, C.E.	30-45	*
Shannon, Monica	Goose Grass Rhymes (1st {std}, sm8vo, 155p, col frn, pep)	Doubleday/Dor.	1930	Brown, N.K.	35-50	*
Shannon, Monica	Tawnymore (1st {std}, sm8vo, 254p, col frn, fp b/w, pep)	Doubleday/Dor.	1931	Charlot, J.	45-60	*
Shapiro, I.	Yankee Thunder (1st, 8vo, 205p, cloth, DJ)	J. Messner	(1944)	Daugherty, J.	30-45	
Sharp, D.L.	Roof & Meadow (1st, 8vo, green cl, b/w, 281p)	Century	1904	Horsfall, B.	20-35	
Sharp, E.	All the Way to Fairyland (1st, 8vo, 196p, 8cp & cvr by...)	Longmans	1898	Dearmer, P.	85-120	*
Sharp, E.	At the Relton Arms (1st, 12mo, 182p, uncut, design by..)	L: J. Lane	1895	Beardsley, A.	60-80	
Sharp, E.	Child's Christmas (1st, lg8vo, 227p, orang/gilt, AEG, 38 color)	L: Blackie	(1906)	Robinson, C.	180-245	
Sharp, E.	Child's Christmas (1st AM, lg8vo, 227p, color, pep)	Caldwell	[1907]	Robinson, C.	165-220	
Sharp, E.	Hill that Fell Down (1st, 8vo, 275p)	L: Blackie	1909	Browne, G.	45-60	*
Sharp, E.	Micky... (1st, 8vo, 240p)	L: MacMillan	1905	Brock, H.M.	35-50	*
Sharp, E.	Round the World to Wympland (1st, 8vo, 235p, 8pl)	L: J. Lane	1902	Woodward, A.B.	70-100	*
Sharp, E.	Story o/t Weathercock (1st, 4to, 258p, red/gilt, AEG, 16cp, pep)	L: Blackie	(1907)	Robinson, C.	200-280	
Sharp, E.	Story o/t Weathercock (1st AM, 4to, 258p, teg, red/gilt, 16cp)	Caldwell	[1907]	Robinson, C.	160-225	
Sharp, E.	What Happened at Christmas (1st, 4to, unpag)	L: Blackie	[1915]	Robinson, C.	130-170	*
Sharp, E.	Wymps & other Fairy Tales (1st, 8vo, 190p, 8cp)	NY: J. Lane	1897	Dearmer, M.	250-320	
Sharp, E.	Youngest Girl in the School (1st, 8vo, 326p)	L: MacMillan	1901	Brock, C.E.	35-50	*
Sharp, M.	Rescuers: A Fantasy (1st {std}, 8vo, blue cl, 149p, b/w, DJ)	Little/Brown	(1959)	Williams, Garth	100-165	*
Shaw, C.G.	Blue Guess Book (1st, 8vo, ipcb, [48]p, color)	W.R. Scott	(1942)	Shaw, C.G.	45-65	
Shaw, C.G.	Giant of Central Park (1st, lg8vo, ipcb, [64]p, fp b/w)	W.R. Scott	(1940)	Shaw, C.G.	35-50	*
Shaw, C.G.	Guess Book (1st, 8vo, [48]p, ipcb, color)	W.R. Scott	(1941)	Shaw, C.G.	35-50	*
Shaw, G.B.	St. Joan (1st, folio, ibds, 182p, p-o, teg, 16 ticp)	L: Constable	(1924)	Ricketts, C.	180-250	
Shay, F.	Drawn from the Wood (1st, 8vo, 186p, b/w)	Macaulay	(1929)	Held, J.	45-60	
Shay, F.	More Pious Friends (1st, 8vo, 192p, b/w)	Macaulay	(1927)	Held, J.	50-65	
Shelby, A.B.	Lullaby Book (1st, 8vo, blue/gilt, 183p, col frn by...)	Duffield	1921	Smith, J.W.	50-75	
Sheldon, Chas.	Crucifixion of Philip Strong (1st, 8vo, 267p, gray/gilt, cvr)	McClurg	1894	Armstrong, M.	25-40	*
Shelley	Poems of Shelley (1st, 16mo, 244p, teg, purple/gilt, 8cp)	L: Jack	(1907)	King, J.	80-120	
Shelley, M.W.	Frankenstein... (1st, 8vo, 259p, 15 b/w)	Smith/Haas	1934	Ward, L.	120-165	
Shelley, P.B.	Sensitive Plant (1st, 8vo, 60p, teg, uncut, 12pl)	L: Aldine Hse.	1898	Housman, L.	130-180	
Shelley, P.B.	Sensitive Plant (1st AM, 4to, 127p, gilt, teg, 18 ticp)	Heinn/Lipp.	(1911)	Robinson, C.	220-350	
Shelley, P.B.	Sensitive Plant (1st, 4to, teg, 127p, gilt, 18 ticp)	L: Heinemann	(1911)	Robinson, C.	280-400	

AUTHOR: 122

AUTHOR	TITLE	PUBLISHER	DATE	ARTIST	PRICE	LC
Shepard, O.	Pedlar's Progress (1st, 8vo, 546p, 5pl, DJ)	Little/Brown	1937	Alcott, B.	35-50	
Shephard, E.	Paul Bunyon (1st, 8vo, 234p, fp b/w)	Harcourt	(1924)	Kent, R.	80-100	
Shepperd, E.	Plantation Songs for My Lady's Banjo (1st, lg8vo, 150p, 25pl)	R.H. Russell	1901	(Photos)	160-250	
Sheridan, R.B.	School for Scandal (1st, 4to, gilt, teg, 196p, 25 ticp)	L: Hodder	(1911)	Thomson, H.	140-200	
Sheridan, R.B.	The Duenna (1st, lg8vo, 105p, grey cl, 12cp)	L: Constable	1925	Sheringham, G.	50-70	
Sheridan, R.B.	The Rivals (1st, 8vo, 365p, b/w)	(London)	1896	Sullivan, E.J.	60-90	
Sheridan, R.B.	The Rivals (1st, 8vo, 131p, 17pl, cvr by...)	Crowell	(1907)	Armstrong, M.	35-50	
Sherlock, Philip	Anansi the Spider Man (1st {std}, 8vo, green cl, 112p, b/w)	Crowell	(1954)	Brown, Marcia	45-70	R*
Sherman, F.D.	Little Folk Lyrics (1st, 8vo, 140p)	Houghton	1897	Rogers, B.	30-45	
Sherman, Fanny J.	Admiral Wags of USS Lexington (1st {std}, 4to, 84p, 1-color)	Dodd	1943	Brown, Paul	25-40	*
Sherman, S.	Critical Woodcuts (1st, 8vo, 348p, 15 fp b/w, DJ)	Scribner	1926	Zadig, B.	45-60	
Sherratt, J.L.	Goblin Gobblers (1st, ob8vo, 64p, bds, p-o, 10cp)	L: Warne	(1910)	Crombie, C.E.	130-185	
Sherwood, E.H.	Bobbie Bubbles (1st, sq8vo, 78p, ibds, color)	Rand/McNally	(1916)	Sherwood, E.H.	70-90	*
Sherwood, E.H.	Jack Jingling in Jungleland (1st, sm ob4to, 80p, ibds, fp color)	Rand/McNally	(1918)	Sherwood, E.H.	80-125	
Sherwood, L.	Old Abe, American Eagle (1st, 8vo, 60p, ibds, color, DJ)	Scribner	1946	Milhous, K.	25-40	
Sherwood, M.	Fairchild Family (sq8vo, 111p, gilt, p-o, 8cp)	Dutton	(1908)	Beale, E.	45-60	
Sherwood, M.	Prince Por Quoi (1st, 12mo, 211p)	Houghton	1907	Rogers, B.	20-35	
Shetter, S.C.	When Grandma Was a Little Girl (1st, 12mo, 250p, p-o, 4cp)	Rand/McNally	(1926)	Gregory, D.L.	20-25	
Shiel, M.P.	Lord of the Sea (1st AM, 8vo, 474p, blue cl, frn by...)	Stokes	(1901)	Russell, W.	100-150	
Shiel, M.P.	Shapes in the Fire (1st AM, 8vo, blue cl, cvr & ti page by..)	Roberts	1896	Beardsley, A.	160-200	
Shimer, E.D.	Fairy Stories... (1st, sm8vo, 277p, b/w)	L.A. & N.	1920	Perkins, L.F.	45-60	*
Shipman, Neil	Kurly Kew & Tree-Princess (1st, 8vo, 200p, orang cl, 6cp, pep)	MacVeagh/Dial	1930	Ellender, E.	30-45	*
Shippen, K.B.	Big Mose (1st {std}, 8vo, grey cl, 90p, b/w)	Harper	(1953)	Graham, M.B.	30-45	*
Shippen, K.B.	Great Heritage (1st, 8vo, 230p, yellow cl, pep)	Viking	1947	Falls, C.B.	35-50	*
Shippen, K.B.	Men, Microscopes & Living Things (1st, 8vo, grn cl, fp b/w, NH)	Viking	1955	Ravielli, A.	50-80	R*
Shippen, K.B.	Moses (1st, 8vo, blue cl, 132p, frn by...)	Harper	(1949)	Cassel, L.	30-45	*
Shippen, K.B.	Mr. Bell Invents the Telephone (1st, 8vo, 183p, 2-color)	Random	(1952)	Floethe, R.	30-50	*
Shippen, K.B.	New Found World (1st, lg8vo, 262p, blue cl, b/w, pep, NH)	Viking	1945	Falls, C.B.	45-70	*
Shirk, J.C.	Bela the Juggler (1st {std}, lg8vo, grn cl, 66p, 2-color, pep)	Suttonhouse	(1936)	Finger, H.	30-45	*
Shirk, J.C.	Mr. Baxter's Dandelion Garden (1st {std}, 4to, 58p, fp b/w, dep)	Dutton	1940	Shirk, J.C.	25-40	*
Shirley (ed.)	La Fontaine's Fables (1st, sm ob4to, 64p, color)	L: T. Nelson	1905	Bull/Park	140-200	
Shirley, E.	The Twins (4to, 63p, ibds, 24cp)	L: Nelson	[1905]	Hassall, J.	140-200	
Sholl, A.	Faery Tales of Weir (1st, 8vo, 172p, purple/gilt, col frn, pep)	Dutton	(1918)	Pyle, Kath.	65-90	
Shuldham, E.	Pictures from Birdland (1st {1st bk.}, 4to, ibds, 24cp)	L: Dent	1899	Detmold, E.J.	400-600	
Shute, H.A.	Farming It (1st, 12mo, 248p, gilt, 16pl)	Houghton	1909	Birch, R.	25-40	
Siberiak, M.	Verotchka's Tales (1st, 8vo, pink/gilt, uncut, 190p, 10pl, dep)	Dutton	(1922)	Artzybasheff, B.	50-80	
Sidgwick (ed.)	Ballads & Lyrics of Love (1st, lg8vo, teg, 178p, uncut, 10cp)	L: Chatto	1908	Shaw, B.	65-90	
Sidgwick (ed.)	Legendary Ballads (1st, lg8vo, 180p, red/gilt, teg, 10cp)	L: Chatto	1908	Shaw, B.	60-90	
Sidney, Marg.	Ballad of the Lost Hare (1st, ob4to, ibds, [44]p, color)	D. Lothrop	1882	9 Chromos	100-150	R*
Sidney, Marg.	Five Little Peppers Midway (1st, 16mo, 512p, gilt, 20pl)	D. Lothrop	(1890)	Taylor, W.L.	60-80	
Sidney, Marg.	Our Davie Pepper (1st, 16mo, 492p, green/gilt, 6pl)	Lothrop/Lee	(1916)	Stephens, A.B.	25-45	
Siebe, Josephine	Kasperle's Adventures (1st, sq8vo, pink cl, 199p, 6cp, pep)	MacMillan	1929	Dobias, F.	30-45	*
Siegel, Wm.	Around the World in a Mailbag (1st, 4to, ibds, [30]p, col, pep)	McBride	1932	Siegel, W.	35-50	*
Sill, L.M.	Sunnyfield (1st, 8vo, 228p, 4pl)	Harper	1909	Robinson, R.	25-40	
Sill, S.C.	Reminiscences/Chest of Drawers (1st, sm8vo, [40]p, AEG, 6pl)	Lippincott	1900	Smith, J.W.	70-110	
Sime, Sidney H.	Bogey Beasts (1st, 4to, ibds)	L: Goodwin	(1923)	Sime, S.H.	250-400	
Simmons, H.B.	Jingle Jangle Rhyme Book (1st, ob4to, ibds, 18cp)	Stokes	1898	Simmons, H.B.	150-220	*
Simon, Ellen	Critter Book (1st, ob4to, [48]p, color)	Holiday House	(1940)	Simon, E.	35-60	*
Simon, Norma	Baby House (1st, lg8vo, mauve cl, [25]p, 1-color, dep)	Lippincott	1955	Adams, A.	30-50	*
Simon, Norma	Tree For Me (1st, 8vo, green cl, [26]p, 1-color, dep)	Lippincott	(1956)	Stone, H.	30-45	*
Simont, M.	Lovely Summer (1st, sm4to, blue cl, [46]p, b/w)	Harper	(1952)	Simont, M.	25-40	*
Simont, M.	Mimi (1st, 8vo, beige cl, 55p, b/w)	Harper	(1954)	Simont, M.	45-60	*
Simont, M.	Plumber Out of the Sea (1st, lg8vo, ipcb, 39p, 2-color, pep)	Harper	(1955)	Simont, M.	35-50	*
Simont, M.	Polly's Oats (1st, sm4to, [46]p, fp b/w)	Harper	(1951)	Simont, M.	30-45	*
Sinclair, B.W.	North of Fifty-Three (1st, sm8vo, 345p, 4pl)	Little/Brown	1914	Fischer, A.O.	20-35	
Sinclair, B.W.	Raw Gold (1st, sm8vo, 311p, 4pl)	Dillingham	1908	Rowe, C.	35-50	
Sinclair, M.	Immortal Moment (1st, 8vo, 315p, white cl, 4pl)	Doubleday/Page	1908	Phillips, C.	30-45	
Sinclair, M.	Judgement of Eve (1st, 8vo, 122p, uncut, 8pl)	Harper	1908	Adams, J.W.	20-30	*
Sinclair, M.	Uncanny Stories (1st, 8vo, red/gilt, 362p, 21pl)	MacMillan	1923	DeBosschere, J.	80-120	
Singer, Caroline	Ali Lives in Iran (1st, 4to, 71p, color, pep)	Holiday House	1937	Baldridge, C.L.	20-35	*
Singer, Caroline	Boomba Lives in Africa (1st, 4to, ibds, [64]p, color, pep)	Holiday House	1935	Baldridge, C.L.	30-50	*
Singer, Caroline	Half the World is Isfahan (1st, lg4to, ibds, 153p, 6 fp color)	NY: OUP	1936	Baldridge, C.L.	70-120	R*
Singer, Caroline	Santa Claus Comes to America (1st {std}, 4to, unpag, ibds, col)	Knopf	1942	Baldridge, C.L.	30-45	*
Singleton, E.	Goldenrod Fairy Book (1st, 8vo, blue/gilt, 342p, pep, 16cp)	Dodd	1903	Falls, C.B.	100-125	
Singleton, E.	Wildflower Fairy Book (1st, lg8vo, gilt, 354p, teg, pep, 16cp)	Dodd	1905	Falls, C.B.	100-130	
Singmaster, Elsie	Bred in the Bone (1st, 8vo, green/gilt, 300p, 6pl)	Houghton	1925	Green, E.S.	30-45	
Singmaster, Elsie	Isle of Que (1st {std}, 8vo, 152p, designs by...)	Longmans	(1948)	Hader, E.	45-65	*
Singmaster, Elsie	Swords of Steel (1st, 8vo, 262p, b/w, pep, NH)	Houghton	1933	Hendrickson, D.	35-50	*
Singmaster, Elsie	When Sarah Saved the Day (1st, 12mo, 135p, pink cl, 4pl)	Houghton	1909	Becher, A.E.	20-30	
Singmaster, Elsie	Young Ravenals (1st, 12mo, 214p, blue cl, 9pl)	Houghton	1932	Price, H.L.	20-35	*
Skaar, G.M.	All About Dogs, Dogs, Dogs (1st, sq8vo, wraps, unpag, color)	W.R. Scott	1947	Skaar, G.M.	45-60	*
Skaar, G.M.	Nothing But Cats, Cats, Cats (1st, ob8vo, wraps, [20]p, color)	W.R. Scott	1947	Skaar, G.M.	45-60	*

AUTHOR	TITLE	PUBLISHER	DATE	ARTIST	PRICE	LC
Skaar, G.M.	Very Little Dog (1st, ob8vo, [20]p, ipcb, 2-color)	W.R. Scott	1949	Skaar, G.M.	35-50	*
Skaar, G.M.	What Do they Say! (1st, ob8vo, ibds, [20]p, color)	W.R. Scott	1950	Skaar, G.M.	30-50	*
Skariatina, I.	Little Era in Old Russia (1st {std}, 8vo, 392p, b/w, pep)	Bobbs-Merrill	(1934)	Baldridge, C.L.	25-40	*
Skelding, S.	Flowers of Dell & Bower	Stokes	1886	12 Chromos	90-120	
Skelding, S.	Flowers of Glade & Garden (1st, 4to, AEG, gilt)	Stokes	1884	12 Chromos	100-130	
Skinner, A.M.	Child's Book of Country Stories (1st, lg8vo, 265p, p-o, 4cp)	Duffield	1925	Smith, J.W.	165-200	
Skinner, A.M.	Child's Book of Country Stories (1st {this pub}, 8vo, p-o, 4cp)	Dial	1935	Smith, J.W.	80-100	
Skinner, A.M.	Child's Book of Modern Stories (1st, lg8vo, gilt p-o, 340p, 8cp)	Duffield	1920	Smith, J.W.	140-185	
Skinner, A.M.	Child's Book of Modern Stories (4to, gilt, 341p, p-o, 8cp)	Dial	1935	Smith, J.W.	70-100	
Skinner, A.M.	Little Child's Book of Stories (1st, lg8vo, 258p, gilt 8cp, pep)	Duffield	1922	Smith, J.W.	150-220	*
Skinner, A.M.	Topaz Story Book (1st, 12mo, 381p, col frn by…)	Duffield	1917	Parrish, M.	100-150	*
Skinner, A.M.	Turquoise Story Book (1st, sm8vo, blue cl, frn by…)	Duffield	1918	Parrish, M.	100-140	
Skinner, A.W.	Very Little Child's Bk. of Stories (1st, lg8vo, 232p, gilt, 8cp)	Duffield	1923	Smith, J.W.	150-220	*
Skinner, C.M.	Do-Nothing Days (1st, 12mo, 219p, teg, frn by…)	Lippincott	1899	Oakley, V.	80-100	
Skinner, C.M.	With Feet to the Earth (1st, 12mo, 231p, teg, frn by…)	Lippincott	1899	Oakley, V.	90-120	
Sleight, C.L.	Prince of the Pin Elves (1st, 8vo, 159p, b/w)	Page	1897	Sacker, A.	50-65	
Slobodkin, L.	Adventures of Arab (1st, lg8vo, 128p, color, cep)	MacMillan	1946	Slobodkin, L.	30-45	
Slobodkin, L.	Big Circus April 1st (1st {std}, sm8vo, 90p, cep, DJ)	MacMillan	(1953)	Slobodkin, L.	25-40	
Slobodkin, L.	Bixxy & the Secret Message (1st {std}, 8vo, 94p, b/w, pep)	MacMillan	1949	Slobodkin, L.	20-30	*
Slobodkin, L.	Dinny & Danny (1st {std}, 4to, [30]p, color, pep)	MacMillan	(1951)	Slobodkin, L.	30-45	*
Slobodkin, L.	Gogo: French Seagull (1st {std}, 4to, [46]p, fp color)	MacMillan	(1960)	Slobodkin, L.	35-50	*
Slobodkin, L.	Hustle & Bustle (1st, ob lg8vo, [36]p, 1-color)	MacMillan	1948	Slobodkin, L.	25-45	*
Slobodkin, L.	Magic Michael (1st, ob8vo, red cl, unpag, color, cep)	MacMillan	(1944)	Slobodkin, L.	25-40	*
Slobodkin, L.	Mr. Mushroom (1st {std}, sq16mo, ipcb, [32]p, color)	MacMillan	(1950)	Slobodkin, L.	25-40	*
Slobodkin, L.	Mr. Petersand's Cats & Kittens (1st {std}, 8vo, 63p, col, cep)	MacMillan	(1954)	Slobodkin, L.	25-40	*
Slobodkin, L.	Seaweed Hat (1st, 8vo, [48]p, color)	MacMillan	1947	Slobodkin, L.	30-45	*
Slobodkin, L.	Space Ship Returns to Apple Tree (1st {std}, 8vo, 128p, b/w)	MacMillan	(1958)	Slobodkin, L.	25-45	*
Slobodkin, L.	Space Ship Under Apple Tree (1st {std}, 8vo, 116p, blue cl, b/w)	MacMillan	(1952)	Slobodkin, L.	25-45	*
Slobodkina, E.	Caps for Sale (1st, 8vo, [43]p, color, pep)	W.R. Scott	1940	Slobodkina, E.	35-50	*
Slobodkina, E.	Wonderful Feast (1st, sq8vo, ipcb, [26]p, color)	Lothrop/Lee	1955	Slobodkina, E.	40-60	*
Smalley, J.	Do You Know about Fishes? (1st, ob8vo, 45p, color, pep)	Wm. Morrow	(1936)	Smalley, J.	50-70	*
Smalley, J.	Do You Know? (1st, ob8vo, 44p, color, pep)	Wm. Morrow	(1934)	Smalley, J.	50-70	*
Smalley, J.	How It All Began (1st, 8vo, ibds, 94p, color)	Wm. Morrow	(1932)	Smalley, J.	50-80	
Smalley, J.	Now and Then… (1st, 8vo, 91p, ibds, color, pep)	Wm. Morrow	(1931)	Smalley, J.	65-110	
Smalley, J.	Plum to Plum Jam (1st, 8vo, 87p, ibds, color, pep)	Wm. Morrow	(1929)	Smalley, J.	70-100	
Smalley, J.	Rice to Rice Pudding (1st, smsq8vo, 85p, ibds, color, pep)	Wm. Morrow	(1928)	Smalley, J.	70-90	
Smeaton, O.	Mystery of the Pacific (1st, 8vo, 335p, red/gilt, 8pl)	L: Blackie	1899	Paget, W.	60-85	
Smedley, C.	Wizards of Ryetown (1st, 12mo, gilt, 273p, b/w)	Holt	1905	MacGregor, A.	50-70	
Smith, A.C.	Turquoise Cup (1st, 8vo, blue bds, 209p, frn by…)	Scribner	1903	Parrish, M.	70-100	
Smith, C.M.	Queen Bee (1st, 8vo, gilt, 2cp by…)	L: Nelson	1907	Dulac, E.	100-150	
Smith, E.	Song Devices & Jingles (1st, lgsq8vo, 65p, 6cp)	Lothrop/Lee	(1920)	Young, F.L.	25-40	*
Smith, E.B.	After they Came Out of the Ark (1st, ob4to, ibds, 48p, 22cp)	Putnam	(1918)	Smith, E.B.	150-200	
Smith, E.B.	Chicken World (1st, ob4to, ibds, [28]p, color)	Putnam	1910	Smith, E.B.	130-170	
Smith, E.B.	Circus & All About It (1st, 4to, p-o, 62p, 16cp, pep)	Stokes	(1909)	Smith, E.B.	180-240	
Smith, E.B.	Early Life of Mr. Man… (1st, ob4to, ibds, 56p, 23cp, pep)	Houghton	1914	Smith, E.B.	140-200	
Smith, E.B.	Fun in the Radio World (1st, ob4to, [30]p, p-o, 12cp, pep)	Stokes	1923	Smith, E.B.	140-200	
Smith, E.B.	In the Land of Make-Believe (1st, ob4to, ibds, [28]p, 12cp, pep)	Holt	(1916)	Smith, E.B.	180-250	R*
Smith, E.B.	Lions 'n' Elephants & Everything (1st, ob4to, [32]p, ibds, 12cp)	Putnam	(1929)	Smith, E.B.	185-250	
Smith, E.B.	My Village (1st [1st bk], 12mo, teg, 325p)	Scribner	1896	Smith, E.B.	80-100	
Smith, E.B.	Pocahontas & Captain Smith (1st, ob4to, ibds, unpag, color, pep)	Houghton	1906	Smith, E.B.	140-200	
Smith, E.B.	Railroad Book (1st, ob4to, [28]p, p-o, 12cp, pep)	Houghton	1913	Smith, E.B.	160-225	R
Smith, E.B.	Seashore Book (1st, ob4to, [30]p, ibds, 12cp, pep)	Houghton	1912	Smith, E.B.	150-200	R
Smith, E.B.	So Long Ago (1st, lg4to, green cl, 36p, 17cp, DJ)	Houghton	1944	Smith, E.B.	70-100	
Smith, E.B.	Story of Noah's Ark (1st, ob4to, ibds, [56]p, p-o, 26cp, pep)	Houghton	1905	Smith, E.B.	140-200	
Smith, F.B.	Real Latin Quarter (1st, 8vo, 204p, b/w)	Funk/Wagnalls	1901	Smith, F.B.	30-45	
Smith, F.H.	Arm-Chair at the Inn (1st, sm8vo, green cl, uncut, 357p)	Scribner	1912	Various	25-40	
Smith, F.H.	Caleb West, Master Diver (1st, 8vo, green cl, 378p, 6pl by…)	Houghton	1898	Keller, A.I.	25-45	
Smith, F.H.	Charcoals of New & Old New York (1st, 4to, 142p, bds, 23 tipl)	Doubleday/Page	1912	Smith, F.H.	80-100	
Smith, F.H.	Colonel Carter's Christmas (1st, 8vo, teg, gilt, 159p, 8cp)	Scribner	1903	Yohn, F.C.	20-30	
Smith, F.H.	Day at Laguerre's… (1st, 8vo, tan cl, 190p)	Houghton	1892	Smith, F.H.	85-100	
Smith, F.H.	Fortunes of Oliver Horn (1st, 8vo, green cl, uncut, 552p)	Scribner	1902	Clark, W.A.	20-30	
Smith, F.H.	Gondola Days (1st, 12mo, 205p, red/gilt)	Houghton	1897	Rogers, B.	25-40	
Smith, F.H.	In Dickens' London (1st, 4to, bds, 199p, teg, 22 tipl)	Scribner	1914	Smith, F.H.	65-80	
Smith, F.H.	Old Lines & New in Black & White (1st, ob folio, p-o, 12pl)	Houghton	1886	Smith, F.H.	80-100	
Smith, F.H.	Other Fellow (1st, 8vo, teg, 218p)	Houghton	1899	Rogers, B.	25-40	
Smith, F.H.	Outdoor Sketching (1st, sm8vo, pcb, 145p, 3pl)	Scribner	1915	Smith, F.H.	25-45	
Smith, F.H.	Romance of an Old Fashioned Gentleman (1st, 8vo, 213p, teg, 5cp)	Scribner	1907	Keller, A.I.	20-30	
Smith, F.H.	Tom Grogan (1st, 12mo, 246p, teg, 19pl)	Houghton	1896	Reinhart, C.S.	25-40	
Smith, F.H.	Wood Fire in No.3 (1st, sm8vo, 298p, teg, uncut, 9cp)	Scribner	1905	Kimball, A.	20-30	
Smith, G.	Arabella & Araminta Stories (1st, sq8vo, 103p, 15pl, PPPa)	(Boston)	1895	Reed, E.	350-500	*
Smith, G.	Arabella & Araminta Stories (8vo, 103p, 15pl, pep, later)	Small	1903	Reed, E.	90-140	
Smith, G.	Boys of Marmiton Prairie (1st, sm8vo, 262p, 5pl)	Little/Brown	1899	Day, B.C.	25-40	*

AUTHOR	TITLE	PUBLISHER	DATE	ARTIST	PRICE	LC
Smith, G.	Doris & Julie (1st, lg sq8vo, 167p, 14cp)	Harper	1901	Mears, W.E.	65-80	*
Smith, G.	Jolly Polly Stories (1st, lg sq8vo, 99p, b/w)	Small	1918	Drake, E.D.	30-45	*
Smith, G.	Little Girl & Phillip (1st, lg sq8vo, 187p, 8cp)	Harper	1902	Robinson, R.	40-65	*
Smith, G.	Little Mother & Georgie (1st, sq8vo, beige cl, 150p, 12cp)	Harper	1905	'DD'	50-70	*
Smith, G.	Little Precious (1st, 8vo, 146p, 15cp)	Harper	1904	'DD'	45-60	
Smith, G.	Loveable Tales/Janey, Josey & Joe (1st, 4to, grn cl, 157p, 16cp)	Harper	1902	Mars, E.	65-100	
Smith, G.	Peter & Ellen (1st, lgsq8vo, 15cp)	Harper	1903	Mars, E.	65-80	*
Smith, G.	Roggie & Reggie Stories (1st, lgsq8vo, 15cp)	Harper	1900	Mars, E.	65-80	*
Smith, G.	Wonderful Stories of Jane & John (1st, 8vo, 74p, 10cp)	H. Stone	1899	Woods, A.	100-150	*
Smith, Harriet L.	Pollyanna of the Orange Blossoms (1st, 8vo, p-o, 313p, 6pl)	Page	1924	Taylor, H.W.	25-40	*
Smith, Harriet L.	Pollyanna's Jewels (1st, 8vo, 328p, blue cl, p-o, 6pl)	Page	(1925)	Taylor, H.W.	25-40	*
Smith, J.W.	Child's Book of Old Verses (1st, lg8vo, p-o, teg, 124p, 10cp)	Duffield	1910	Smith, J.W.	160-240	
Smith, Laura R.	Good-Night Stories (1st, tall 8vo, 120p, ipcb, 8cp)	Chi: Stanton	(1921)	Burd, C.M.	40-60	*
Smith, Laura R.	Pixie in the House (1st, sm8vo, 123p, pep)	McClurg	1915	Wilson, C.P.	25-40	*
Smith, Laura R.	Runaway Bunny (1st, sm8vo, 128p, pep, color)	Chi: Flanagan	1923	Dulin, D.	30-45	
Smith, Lawrence B.	Fur or Feather (1st, 4to, 144p, b/w, DJ)	Scribner	1946	Brown, Paul	50-70	
Smith, M.P.W.	Young Puritans in Captivity (1st, 8vo, grey cl, 323p, 6pl, dep)	Little/Brown	1899	Smith, J.W.	100-160	
Smith, M.P.W.	Young Puritans/Old Hadley (1st, 12mo, 345p, gilt, 5pl, dep)	Roberts	1897	Bridgman, L.J.	25-45	*
Smith, M.S.	Twenty Centuries of Paris (1st, 8vo, blue/gilt, 400p, cvr by...)	Crowell	(1913)	Armstrong, M.	30-45	*
Smith, N.A.	Boys & Girls of Bookland (1st, lg4to, p-o, 100p, 11cp, cep)	Cosmopolitan	1923	Smith, J.W.	130-165	
Smith, N.A.	Boys & Girls of Bookland (lg4to, 100p, brown pcb, 11cp, later)	McKay	(1924)	Smith, J.W.	100-150	
Smith, Pamela C.	Annancy Stories (1st, folio)	R.H. Russell	1899	Smith, Pamela	150-200	*
Smith, Pamela C.	Golden Vanity & Green Bed (1st, folio, p-o, green cl, 12cp)	Doub./McClure	1899	Smith, Pamela	200-270	
Smith, R.G.	Ancient Tales/Japan (1st, 8vo, teg, 361p, color)	L: A&C Black	1908	Smith, R.G.	70-120	
Smith, Susan C.	Christmas Tree in the Woods (1st, sq12mo, [38]p, color, pep)	Minton Balch	(1932)	Sewell, H.	30-50	*
Smith, Susan C.	Tranquilina's Paradise (1st, lg4to, 34p, color, pep)	Minton Balch	(1930)	Handforth, T.	65-90	*
Smith, Thorne	Lazy Bear Lane (1st {std}, 8vo, 240p, green cl, pep, b/w, DJ)	Doubleday/Dor.	1931	Shanks, G.	120-165	
Smith, Wallace	Little Tigress (1st, 8vo, 209p, teg, 15pl)	Putnam	1923	Smith, Wallace	25-40	*
Smith, Wm. J.	Boy Blue's Book of Beasts (1st {std}, 8vo, 58p, fp 1-color, cep)	Little/Brown	(1957)	Kepes, J.A.	65-80	R*
Smith, Wm. J.	Laughing Time (1st {std}, 8vo, 54p, yellow cl, fp 1-color, cep)	Little/Brown	(1955)	Kepes, J.A.	65-80	R*
Smith, Wm. J.	Puptents & Pebbles (1st {std}, 4to, yellow cl, 32p, color, pep)	Little/Brown	(1959)	Kepes, J.A.	60-90	R*
Snedeker, C.D.	Downright Dencey (1st {std}, 8vo, 314p, col frn, pep, NH)	Doubleday/Dor.	1927	Barney, M.W.	45-70	
Snedeker, C.D.	Forgotten Daughter (1st {std}, 8vo, 309p, col frn, 3pl, pep, NH)	Doubleday/Dor.	1933	Lathrop, D.	60-85	
Snedeker, C.D.	Luke's Quest (1st {std}, sm8vo, blue cl, 208p, uncut, b/w)	Doubleday	1947	Unwin, N.S.	25-40	*
Snedeker, C.D.	Theras & his Town (1st {std}, sm8vo, 252p, pep, 4pl)	Doubleday/Page	1924	Harting, M.W.	25-45	*
Snedeker, C.D.	White Isle (1st {std}, sm8vo, 271p, pep, b/w pl)	Doubleday/Dor.	1940	Kredel, F.	20-35	*
Snell, Roy	Eskimo Island & Penguin Land (1st, 8vo, 128p, cloth, p-o by...)	Whitman	1928	Winter, M.	20-30	
Snow, Jack	Magical Mimics in Oz (1st, 8vo, grey cl, p-o, 243p)	Reilly/Lee	(1946)	Kramer, F.	260-400	
Snow, Jack	Shaggy Man of Oz (1st, 4to, grey cl, p-o, 254p)	Reilly/Lee	(1949)	Kramer, F.	280-400	
Snowden, J.H.	Wonderful Night (1st, 12mo, blue cl, 95p, p-o, designs by...)	MacMillan	1919	Petershams	20-30	*
Snyder, F.	Lovely Garden (1st, 12mo, ibds, [38]p, color)	Volland	(1919)	Rae, J.	65-80	
Snyder, F.	Rhymes for Kindly Children (1st, 8vo, ibds, [95]p, color)	Volland	(1916)	Gruelle, J.	80-120	
Somervell, A.	Singing Time (1st, 4to, ibds, p-o, 48p, b/w)	L: Constable	1899	Brooke, L.L.	100-130	
Somerville, Wm.	The Chase (1st, lg sq8vo, 87p, gilt, teg, b/w)	L: Redway	1896	Thomson, H.	65-85	
Sorensen, Virginia	Curious Missie (1st {std}, 8vo, 208p)	Harcourt	(1953)	Miller, M.	30-45	*
Sorensen, Virginia	Miracles on Maple Hill (1st {std}, 8vo, 180p, b/w, NM)	Harcourt	(1956)	Krush, B.& J.	50-85	R*
Sorensen, Virginia	Plain Girl (1st {std}, 8vo, 151p)	Harcourt	(1955)	Geer, G.	25-45	*
Sousa, J.P.	Fifth String (1st, 8vo, green cl, 124p, teg, b/w pl)	Bowen-Merrill	(1902)	Christy, H.C.	25-40	
Sousa, J.P.	Pipetown Sandy (1st, 8vo, brown/gilt, 383p, cvr by...)	Bobbs-Merrill	(1905)	Armstrong, M.	25-40	
Southwart, Eliz.	Password to Fairyland (1st, 4to, 186p, tan cl, 8cp)	L: Simpkin	[1920]	Anderson, F.	220-320	
Southwold, S.	Book of Animal Tales (1st, sm4to, 286p, ibds, 8cp)	L: Harrap	1929	Appleton, H.C.	65-90	*
Southwold, S.	Book of Animal Tales (1st AM, lg8vo, ibds, 286p, 8cp)	Crowell	(1929)	Appleton, H.C.	55-80	
Southwold, S.	Three by Candlelight (sm8vo, 128p, blue/gilt, 2cp)	L: Collins	[1920]	Anderson, A.	40-65	
Sowerby, Githa	Bonnie Book (1st, 8vo, p-o, 12cp)	L: OUP	(1919)	Sowerby, M.	65-100	
Sowerby, Githa	Dainty Book (1st, sq8vo, ibds, unpag, 12cp)	Hodder	[1915]	Sowerby, M.	65-80	*
Sowerby, Githa	Gay Book (1st {this pub.}, 8vo, [29]p, ibds, 12 fp color)	A.& W. Guild	(1935)	Sowerby, M.	30-45	
Sowerby, Githa	Glad Book (1st {this pub}, 8vo, [29]p, ibds, 12 fp color)	A.& W. Guild	(1935)	Sowerby, M.	30-45	
Sowerby, Githa	Little Stories/Little People (1st, lg8vo, 72p)	L: H. Frowde	[1910]	Sowerby, M.	65-80	*
Sowerby, Githa	Merry Book (smsq4to, white bds, 12cp)	L: Hodder	[1908]	Sowerby, M.	60-85	
Sowerby, Githa	Poems of Childhood (1st, 4to, teg, ibds, gilt, 12 ticp)	L: H. Frowde	(1912)	Sowerby, M.	130-165	
Sowerby, Githa	The Bumbletoes (1st, 12mo, ibds, 60p, 12cp)	L: Chatto	1907	Sowerby, M.	70-100	*
Sowerby, Githa	Wise Book (1st AM, 12mo, ipcb, 13cp)	Dent/Dutton	1906	Sowerby, M.	65-80	
Sowerby, Githa	Yesterday's Children (1st, 4to, p-o, 12cp)	Duffield	1909	Sowerby, M.	70-100	
Sowerby, M.	Childhood (1st AM, lg8vo, 44p, p-o, 12cp)	Duffield	1907	Sowerby, M.	90-125	
Sowers, P.A.	Dhan of the Pearl Country (1st, lg8vo, p-o, 125p, color)	Whitman	1939	Ayer, M.	25-40	*
Sowers, P.A.	Sons of the Dragon (1st, 8vo, 285p, yellow cl, 4cp)	Whitman	1942	Ayer, M.	20-30	*
Sparrow, W.S.	Book of Bridges (1st, 4to, 415p, cloth, cp)	L: J. Lane	1915	Brangwyn, F.	90-130	
Sparrow, W.S.	Frank Brangwyn: His Work (1st, sm4to, 258p, teg, 20cp)	L: Kegan Paul	1910	Brangwyn, F.	75-100	
Sparrow, W.S.	Prints & Drawings of Frank Brangwyn (1st, 4to, 287p, gilt, 50pl)	L: J. Lane	1919	Brangwyn, F.	100-150	
Speare, Eliz. G.	Calico Captive (1st, 8vo, red cl, 274p, b/w)	Houghton	1957	Mars, W.T.	25-40	*
Spearman, Frank	Nan of Music Mountain (1st, 12mo, green cl, 430p, 4cp)	Scribner	1916	Wyeth, N.C.	30-45	
Spearman, Frank	Robert Kimberly (1st, 8vo, 437p, gilt, 4cp)	Scribner	1911	Flagg, J.M.	20-25	

AUTHOR	TITLE	PUBLISHER	DATE	ARTIST	PRICE	LC
Spearman, Frank	Whispering Smith (1st, 12mo, red cl, 421p, 4cp)	Scribner	1906	Wyeth, N.C.	30-45	
Spence, L.	Myths of Babylonia & Assyria (1st AM, 4to, teg, 411p, 8cp)	Stokes	[1915]	Paul, E.	75-100	
Spencer, W.	Poems of Spencer (1st, 16mo, purple/gilt, 290p, teg, 8cp)	L: Jack	(1906)	King, J.	100-150	
Spenser, Edmund	Shepheard's Calander (1st, 8vo, ibds, [118]p, 12pl)	L: Harper	1898	Crane, W.	150-200	
Spenser, Edmund	Una & Red Cross Knight (1st, 8vo, 264p)	L: J.M. Dent	1905	Robinson, T.H.	50-65	*
Sperry, A.	All Sail Set (1st, sm4to, 175p, pep, b/w, NH)	Winston	(1935)	Sperry, A.	45-60	*
Sperry, A.	Call it Courage (1st, lg8vo, 95p, beige cl, 1-color, pep, NM)	MacMillan	1940	Sperry, A.	50-85	R*
Sperry, A.	Coconut: Wonder Tree (1st, 8vo, blue cl, [47]p, 1-color, pep)	MacMillan	1942	Sperry, A.	25-40	*
Sperry, A.	Frozen Fire (1st {std}, 8vo, 192p, green cl, b/w)	Doubleday	(1956)	Sperry, A.	20-30	*
Sperry, A.	Little Eagle: A Navaho Boy (1st, 4to, 102p, color, pep, DJ)	Winston	(1938)	Sperry, A.	35-50	
Sperry, A.	One Day with Manu (1st [1st bk.], 4to, ibds, [64]p, color, pep)	Winston	(1933)	Sperry, A.	50-80	*
Sperry, A.	One Day with Tuktu (1st, sm4to, blue/gilt, 10 dp color, pep)	Winston	1935	Sperry, A.	25-40	
Sperry, A.	Rain Forest (1st, 8vo, 190p, green cl, pep, 1-color)	MacMillan	1947	Sperry, A.	30-45	*
Sperry, A.	Storm Canvas (1st {std}, 8vo, pep, 301p, col frn)	Winston	(1944)	Sperry, A.	25-40	
Sperry, A.	Wagons Westward (1st, 8vo, 276p, orang cl, pep, b/w)	Winston	1936	Sperry, A.	30-45	*
Spicer, M.D.	Rainbows (1st, 8vo, 44p, white cl, p-o, b/w)	L: A. Melrose	1913	Robinson, C.	80-100	
Spiegelberg, F.	Princess Goldenhair... (1st, 8vo, 176p, p-o, color)	Rand/McNally	(1915)	Winter, M.	65-80	*
Spiegelberg, F.	Princess Goldenhair... (8vo, 176p, green cl, p-o, 8cp)	World	(1932)	Winter, M.	50-70	
Spielmann, M.H.	Child of the Air (1st, 8vo, blue cl, 125p, pep)	L: Duckworth	1910	Wilhelm, C.	50-80	
Spielmann, M.H.	Hugh Thomson: His Art (1st, lg8vo, 269p, gilt, 12cp)	L: A&C Black	1931	Thomson, H.	85-125	
Spielmann, M.H.	Kate Greenaway (1st, lg8vo, blue cl, cp)	L: A&C Black	1905	Greenaway, K.	80-120	
Spielmann, M.H.	Littledom Castle (1st, sm8vo, 377p, gilt, col & b/w, teg)	L: Routledge	1903	Various	400-550	
Spielmann, M.H.	Love Family (1st, 8vo, ibds, 63p, 12cp)	L: G. Allen	(1908)	Park, C.M.	90-130	*
Spielmann, M.H.	My Son & I (1st, 8vo, red/gilt, teg, 307p, uncut, col frn, 9pl)	L: G. Allen	1908	Thomson, H.	60-85	
Spielmann, M.H.	Rainbow Book (1st, 8vo, 289p, teg, red/gilt, 16pl)	L: Chatto	1909	Various	140-180	
Spilka, A.	Whom Shall I Marry? (1st, 8vo, pink cl, [33]p, 1-color)	Holiday House	1960	Spilka, A.	25-40	*
Spofford, H.P.	Fairy Changeling (1st, 8vo, 75p, 20pl)	Badger	1911	Cory, F.	70-110	
Spofford, H.P.	Maid He Married (1st, 8vo, blue cl, 210p, teg)	Stone/Kimball	1899	Oakley, V.	80-95	
Spurr, H.A.	Bachelor Ballads (1st, sm8vo, 194p, teg, green cl)	L: Greening	1899	Hassall, J.	45-60	
Spyri, J.	Cornelli... (1st {Gift ed.}, 4to, teg, 275p, p-o, pep, 14 ticp)	Lippincott	1921	Kirk, M.L.	65-90	
Spyri, J.	Dora (1st, 8vo, red/gilt, 216p, 8cp)	Lippincott	(1924)	Kirk, M.L.	30-45	*
Spyri, J.	Eveli (1st, 8vo, red ibds, 272p, 8cp)	Lippincott	1926	Greer, B.	20-40	*
Spyri, J.	Gritli's Chldren (1st {Gift ed.}, 4to, 264p, p-o, teg, 14cp pep)	Lippincott	(1924)	Kirk, M.L.	70-100	
Spyri, J.	Heidi (1st {this pub}, 12mo, red cl, 338p, b/w pl)	Crowell	(1902)	Unknown	25-40	*
Spyri, J.	Heidi (1st, 8vo, 219p, color)	Dent/Dutton	(1909)	Lawson, L.	25-40	*
Spyri, J.	Heidi (1st, 8vo, 318p, 8cp)	Lippincott	1915	Kirk, M.L.	25-40	*
Spyri, J.	Heidi (1st {Gift ed.}, sm4to, gilt, 318p, teg, 14 ticp, pep)	Lippincott	1919	Kirk, M.L.	80-120	
Spyri, J.	Heidi (1st, lg8vo, 368p, p-o, gilt, pep, 8cp)	Rand/McNally	(1921)	Enright, M.W.	45-60	*
Spyri, J.	Heidi (1st, lg8vo, 380p, teg, p-o, blue cl, 10cp, pep)	McKay	1922	Smith, J.W.	120-160	
Spyri, J.	Heidi (1st, 8vo, 356p, blue cl, p-o, 4cp)	Houghton	1923	Tenggren, G.	50-90	
Spyri, J.	Heidi (1st, 8vo, 328p, 8cp)	L: Harrap	1924	Anderson, A.	65-80	*
Spyri, J.	Heidi (1st, 8vo, 307p, col frn)	Saalfield	(1924)	Brundage, F.	20-30	
Spyri, J.	Heidi (1st, 8vo, blue cl, p-o, 290p, 4cp)	Winston	(1924)	Burd, C.M.	25-40	
Spyri, J.	Heidi (1st, 8vo, 284p, p-o, 1-color, pep)	Whitman	(1924)	Higgins, V.M.	30-50	*
Spyri, J.	Heidi (1st, lg8vo, 333p, col frn, 23pl, p-o)	Harper	(1925)	Rhead, L.	25-40	*
Spyri, J.	Heidi (1st, 12mo, 305p, p-o, gilt, 7 fp color)	Macrae-Smith	(1925)	Shoemaker, E.C.	20-30	
Spyri, J.	Heidi (1st, 4to, 243p, col frn, 1-color)	Sears	(1926)	Welling, G.	20-30	*
Spyri, J.	Heidi (1st, 8vo, 433p, pep, 12cp)	Crowell	(1927)	Whittemore, C.	25-40	*
Spyri, J.	Heidi (1st, 8vo, blue cl, p-o, 319p, 4cp, pep)	Garden City	1932	Petershams	35-50	
Spyri, J.	Heidi (1st, lg4to, 284p, ibds, col frn)	Whitman	(1934)	Vernon, E.	30-45	*
Spyri, J.	Heidi (8vo, 285p)	NY: Nelson	(1938)	Clere, V.	25-40	*
Spyri, J.	Mazli (1st {Gift ed.}, sm4to, 320p, teg, p-o, 14cp, pep)	Lippincott	(1923)	Kirk, M.L.	80-100	
Spyri, J.	Moni the Goat Boy (1st, 12mo, 43p, 3pl)	Crowell	(1914)	Unknown	20-30	*
Spyri, J.	Moni the Goat Boy (1st, 12mo, red cl, 72p, 4cp)	Lippincott	1916	Kirk, M.L.	35-50	*
Spyri, J.	New Year's Carol (1st, 12mo, 34p, col frn)	Houghton	(1924)	Wesson, G.E.	25-40	*
Spyri, J.	Peppino (1st, 12mo, 114p, red cl, 4cp)	Lippincott	(1926)	Greer, B.	30-45	*
Spyri, J.	Shirley Temple in Heidi (1st, sm8vo, 404p, photos)	Saalfield	(1937)	(Photos)	65-80	*
Spyri, J.	Story of Rico (1st, 8vo, 163p, blue cl, 3cp)	Beacon Press	(1921)	Greene, J.	30-45	*
Spyri, J.	Tiss - A Little Alpine Waif (1st, 8vo, 78p, col frn, pep)	Crowell	(1921)	Carlson, G.	20-30	*
Spyri, J.	Vinzi (1st, 8vo, 296p, red cl, 8cp)	Lippincott	1923	Kirk, M.L.	20-30	*
Squier, E-L.	Wild Heart (1st, 8vo, green cl, 220p, b/w)	Cosmopolitan	1922	Bransom, P.	25-45	
Squire, C.	Celtic Myth & Legend (1st, 8vo, 450p, gilt, 4cp)	L: Gresham	[1910]	Various	80-135	
Squires, F.	Architec-tonics (1st {1st bk.}, 12mo, gilt, 172p, col frn)	Comstock Co.	1914	Kent, R.	160-200	R
St. Francis/Assisi	Song of the Sun (1st {std}, [32]p, sq8vo, 11 fp color, pep, DJ)	MacMillan	1952	Jones, E.O.	35-50	
St. John, J.A.	Face in the Pool (1st, lg4to, 156p, grey/gilt, 4cp)	McClurg	1905	St. John, J.A.	100-145	
St. Mars, F.	Pinion & Paw (1st, sm8vo, green cl, 296p, 12pl)	L: Chambers	1919	Rountree, H.	45-60	*
Stables, Gordon	Boy's Book of Battleships (lg4to, ibds, 16 color)	L: Blackie	[1909]	Robinson, C.	120-165	
Stables, Gordon	City at the Pole (1st, 8vo, blue cl, 8pl)	L: J. Nisbet	1906	Pearse, A.	50-75	
Stables, Wm. G.	Young Peggy McQueen (1st, 8vo, 152p, 4cp)	L: Collins	1903	Goble, W.	80-100	*
Stacpoole, H.D.	Blue Lagoon (1st, 8vo, blue/gilt, 326p, 13 ticp)	L: T.F. Unwin	1910	Pogany, W.	150-180	
Stacpoole, H.D.	Pierrette (1st, 8vo, 294p, teg, b/w)	L: J. Lane	1900	Robinson, C.	80-100	
Stacpoole, H.D.	Pierrot! (1st, 8vo, red cl, uncut, pep, cvr & title page by...)	L: J. Lane	1896	Beardsley, A.	65-80	*

AUTHOR	TITLE	PUBLISHER	DATE	ARTIST	PRICE	LC
Stacpoole, H.D.	Poppyland (1st, 4to, 219p, blue/gilt, 17cp, pep)	L: Bodley Head	1914	Pearce, L.	120-180	
Stafford, M.A.	Muskox: Little Tootoo's Friend (1st, 8vo, 64p, color, pep)	Wm. Morrow	(1931)	Wiese, K.	45-65	*
Stanley, H.M.	London Street Arabs (1st, 4to, green cl, 28pl)	L: Cassell	1890	Tennant, D.	40-65	
Stapp, E.B.	Bread & Lasses (1st, 8vo, 94p, 6pl)	(DeMoines)	1902	Monahan, P.J.	25-45	
Stapp, E.B.	Uncle Peter-Heathen (1st, 8vo, 285p, 10cp)	McKay	(1912)	Macy, H.	20-30	
Starkie, Walter	Spanish Raggle-Taggle (1st, 8vo, 488p, red/gilt, frn by...)	L: J. Murray	(1934)	Rackham, A.	35-50	
Staunton, S.	Daughters of Destiny (1st [1], 8vo, p-o, gilt, 319p, 8cp)	Reilly/Britton	(1906)	Peirce/DeLay	170-220	
Staunton, S.	Fate of a Crown (1st, 8vo, 306p, red/gilt, 6pl)	Reilly/Britton	(1905)	Sheffer, G.C.	300-400	*
Staver, M.W.	New & True (1st, sm4to, 136p, green/gilt, 4pl, dep)	Lee & Shepard	1892	Various	180-230	*
Stawell, Mrs. R.	Fairies I Have Met (1st, 8vo, green cl, 117p, 8cp)	L: J. Lane	[1907]	Dulac, E.	265-320	
Stawell, Mrs. R.	Fairies I Have Met (8vo, 117p, 8cp)	L: Hodder	[1910]	Dulac, E.	185-260	
Stawell, Mrs. R.	Fairy of Old Spain... (1st AM, 8vo, beige/gilt, 134p, 6cp)	Dutton	1912	Pape, F.	65-110	
Stawell, Mrs. R.	My Days with the Fairies (1st, 4to, 169p, red/gilt, 8 ticp)	L: Hodder	(1913)	Dulac, E.	300-450	
Stawell, R. (ed.)	Fabre's Book of Insects (1st AM, 4to, 271p, grn/gilt, 12 ticp)	Dodd	1921	Detmold, E.J.	180-240	
Stawell, R. (ed.)	Fabre's Book of Insects (1st {this pub.}, 4to, 271p, 12 ticp)	Tudor	1936	Detmold, E.J.	70-90	
Steedman, Amy	Apple Pie... (8vo, grey cl, p-o, 8cp)	L: Jack	[1908]	Beale, E.	30-45	*
Steedman, Amy	Legends/Stories of Italy... (1st, lg8vo, teg ibds, gilt, 12 ticp)	L: Jack	[1907]	Cameron, K.	100-150	
Steedman, Amy	Madonna of the Goldfinch (1st, 8vo, 194p, uncut, 8 ticp)	L: Jack	[1917]	Steedman, E.M.	50-75	
Steedman, Amy	Margot/Golden Fish (8vo, 96p, AEG, p-o, 8cp)	L: Jack	(1911)	Spooner, M.D.	40-65	
Steedman, Amy	Our Island Saints (1st AM, 8vo, teg, 178p, 8 ticp)	Putnam	(1912)	Spooner, M.D.	40-70	
Steedman, Amy	Stories from Grimm... (16mo, 116p, p-o, 8cp)	Jack/Dutton	[1908]	Rountree, H.	50-75	
Steedman, C.	Bucking the Sagebrush (1st, 8vo, 270p, map, teg, 9pl)	Putnam	1904	Russell, C.M.	130-170	
Steele, F.A.	Adventures of Akbar (1st AM, 8vo, 204p, gilt, 8cp)	Stokes	(1913)	Shaw, B.	50-70	
Steele, F.A.	Adventures of Akbar (1st, 8vo, 204p, gilt, 8cp)	L: Heinemann	1913	Shaw, B.	60-80	
Steele, F.A.	English Fairy Tales (1st AM, 8vo, red/gilt, 363p, 16cp, pep)	MacMillan	1918	Rackham, A.	180-260	
Steele, R.	Perverse Widow (1st AM, 12mo, ibds, p-o, 3 ticp)	Dutton	1909	Aldin, C.	85-120	
Steele, R.	Perverse Widow (1st, 16mo, 31p, bds, p-o, teg, 3 ticp)	L: Heinemann	1909	Aldin, C.	100-130	
Steele, R.	Story of Alexander (1st, 8vo, 226p, uncut, 6pl)	L: D. Nutt	1894	Mason, F.	60-80	
Steele, R. (tr.)	Renaud of Montauban (1st, 8vo, 284p, gilt, uncut 10 fp b/w)	L: G. Allen	1897	Mason, F.	70-95	
Steele, Wm. O.	Buffalo Knife (1st {std}, 8vo, 177p, b/w, DJ)	Harcourt	(1952)	Galdone, P.	20-30	*
Steele, Wm. O.	Flaming Arrows (1st {std}, sm8vo, 178p)	Harcourt	(1957)	Galdone, P.	25-45	*
Steele, Wm. O.	Golden Root (1st {std}, sm8vo, 76p)	Aladdin	1951	Kredel, F.	25-40	*
Steele, Wm. O.	Perilous Road (1st {std}, 8vo, 191p, blue cl, b/w, NH)	Harcourt	1958	Galdone, P.	65-80	*
Steele, Wm. O.	Wilderness Journey (1st {std}, sm8vo, aqua cl, 209p, b/w)	Harcourt	(1953)	Galdone, P.	25-40	*
Steig, Wm.	About People (1st {std}, 8vo, 105p, b/w)	Random	(1939)	Steig, W.	65-90	*
Steig, Wm.	Agony in the Kindergarten (1st {std}, lg8vo, b/w)	Duell/Sloan	(1950)	Steig, W.	70-100	*
Steig, Wm.	All Embarrassed (1st {std}, 8vo, 101p, b/w)	Duell/Sloan	(1944)	Steig, Wm.	40-65	*
Steig, Wm.	Dreams of Glory (1st {std}, lg8vo, 147p, b/w)	Knopf	(1953)	Steig, Wm.	35-50	*
Steig, Wm.	Lonely Ones (1st {std}, 8vo, 102p, ibds, fp b/w)	Duell/Sloan	(1942)	Steig, W.	50-85	*
Steig, Wm.	Persistent Faces (1st {std}, 8vo, brown cl, [186]p, b/w)	Duell/Sloan	(1945)	Steig, W.	45-60	*
Steig, Wm.	Rejected Lovers (1st {std}, 8vo, 152p, b/w)	Knopf	1951	Steig, Wm.	40-65	*
Steig, Wm.	Small Fry (1st, ob12mo, [128]p, b/w)	Duell/Sloan	(1944)	Steig, Wm.	45-70	*
Steig, Wm.	Till Death Do Us Part (1st {std}, 8vo, [128]p, b/w)	Duell/Sloan	(1947)	Steig, Wm.	45-70	*
Stein, E.	Child Songs of Cheer (1st, 8vo, 120p, gilt, 4cp, pep)	Lothrop/Lee	(1918)	Inglis, A.	25-40	*
Stein, E.	Troubadour Tales (1st, sm8vo, 165p, gilt, frn by...)	Bobbs-Merrill	(1903)	Parrish, M.	85-120	
Stein, Gertrude	The World's Round (1st, 4to, 67p, blue bds)	W.R. Scott	1939	Hurd, C.	120-165	
Steiner, C.	Kiki & Muffy (1st {std}, ob8vo, ibds, [26]p, 2-color, cep)	Doubleday/Dor.	1943	Steiner, C.	35-50	
Steiner, C.	Kiki Dances (1st {std}, sm4to, ibds, [32]p, color)	Doubleday	(1949)	Steiner, C.	45-70	
Steiner, C.	Patsy's Pet (1st {std}, sm ob4to, ibds, [30]p, color)	Doubleday	1955	Steiner, C.	35-50	
Stephan, A.C.	Fairy Tales of a Parrot (1st, 8vo, ibds, [90]p, 6 ticp, dep)	Nister/Dutton	(1892)	Ellis, T.	130-165	
Stephens, J.	Crock of Gold (1st, 8vo, 298p, green/gilt, 6 fp 2-color, pep)	MacMillan	1922	Jones, W.	30-45	*
Stephens, J.	Crock of Gold (1st, sm4to, 227p, red/gilt, 12cp)	L: MacMillan	1926	Mackenzie, T.	80-100	
Stephens, J.	Irish Fairy Tales (1st, 8vo, 318p, green/gilt, 16cp)	L: MacMillan	1920	Rackham, A.	200-300	
Stephens, R.N.	Captain Ravenshaw (1st, 12mo, teg, blue/gilt, 369p)	Page	1901	Various	30-45	
Sterling, M.B.	Story of Sir Galahad (1st, 8vo, 223p, tan cl, 7cp, pep)	Dutton	(1908)	Chapman, W.E.	35-55	*
Sterling, S.H.	Lady of King Arthur's Court (1st, 8vo, teg, 262p, p-o, 5cp)	Jacobs	(1907)	Peck, C.E.	45-70	
Sterling, S.H.	Robin Hood & his Merry Men (8vo, brown cl, 118p, 7cp)	L: Coker	[1933]	Wheelwright, R.	30-45	*
Sterling, S.H.	Shakespeare's Sweetheart (1st, 8vo, p-o, teg, 282p, 5pl)	Jacobs	(1905)	Peck, C.E.	25-45	
Sterne, Emma G.	All About Little Boy Blue (1st, 24mo, ibds, p-o, 48p, color)	Cupples	(1924)	Gooch, T.	35-50	*
Sterne, Emma G.	All About Peter Pan (1st, 24mo, tan bds, 48p, p-o, 8cp)	Cupples	(1924)	Gooch, T.	45-60	*
Sterne, Emma G.	Drums of Monmouth (1st, 8vo, 287p, aqua cl, uncut, b/w, pep)	Dodd	1935	Lawson, R.	30-45	*
Sterne, Emma G.	Miranda is a Princess (1st, 8vo, 221p, yellow cl, b/w, pep)	Dodd	1937	Lawson, R.	45-65	*
Sterne, Emma G.	Pirate of Chatham Square (1st, 8vo, 213p, b/w, pep)	Dodd	1939	Simont, M.	20-30	*
Sterne, Laurence	Sentimental Journey.... (1st, lg8vo, 253p, black/gilt, 12 b/w)	Dodd	1929	Angelo, V.	40-60	
Sterne, Laurence	Sentimental Journey/France & Italy (1st, 12mo, blue/gilt, AEG)	L: Bliss Sands	1897	Robinson, T.H.	65-80	
Sterne, Laurence	Sentimental Journey/France & Italy (1st, 4to, teg, 12cp)	Putnam	1910	Hopkins, E.	75-100	
Stevens, D.K.	Ballads of the Be-Ba-Boes (1st, 4to, yellow cl, 100p)	Houghton	1913	Daland, K.M.	80-100	
Stevens, F.	Adventures in Hiveland (1st, 8vo, 227p, green/gilt, b/w)	L: Hutchinson	1903	Sargent, L.A.	120-180	
Stevens, F.	Through Merrie England (1st, 8vo, grn/gilt, teg, 214p, 12cp, pep)	L: Warne	(1928)	Bedford, F.D.	45-60	
Stevens, J.	Paul Bunyon (1st, 8vo, 245p, woodcuts)	Knopf	(1925)	Lewis, A.	25-40	
Stevens, Thos.	Children of the World from A to Z (1st, 4to, [58]p, 26cp)	R.H. Russell	1903	Collins, A.H.	180-300	*
Stevenson, A.M.	Bridget's Fairies (1st, sm8vo, p-o, 131p, b/w)	L: R.T.S.	(1919)	Robinson, C.	130-200	

AUTHOR	TITLE	PUBLISHER	DATE	ARTIST	PRICE	LC
Stevenson, R.L.	Black Arrow (1st, 4to, teg, p-o, 328p, 14cp, pep, SC)	Scribner	1916	Wyeth, N.C.	150-200	
Stevenson, R.L.	Catriona (1st, 8vo, 357p, 4cp)	L: Cassell	(1915)	Michael, A.C.	45-60	*
Stevenson, R.L.	Child's Garden of Verses (1st, 8vo, teg, uncut, gilt, 137p)	Scribner	1895	Robinson, C.	220-260	R
Stevenson, R.L.	Child's Garden of Verses (1st UK, 8vo, 136p, AEG, gilt, b/w)	L: J. Lane	1895	Robinson, C.	150-185	
Stevenson, R.L.	Child's Garden of Verses (1st, 12mo, 107p b/w)	Page	1900	Barry, E.B.	25-40	*
Stevenson, R.L.	Child's Garden of Verses (1st, lg sq4to, ibds, 115p, 12cp)	R.H. Russell	(1900)	Mars/Squire	165-220	
Stevenson, R.L.	Child's Garden of Verses (1st {this pub.}, 8vo, 94p, cp)	Rand/McNally	(1902)	Mars/Squire	65-80	
Stevenson, R.L.	Child's Garden of Verses (1st, 8vo, blue cl, 110p, 21pl)	Dodge	(1905)	Pease, B.C.	90-130	
Stevenson, R.L.	Child's Garden of Verses (1st, sm8vo, 131p, cp, pep)	Chi: Flanagan	(1908)	O'Reilly, E.D.	40-65	*
Stevenson, R.L.	Child's Garden of Verses (1st {col ed}, 8vo, glt, teg, 8cp, pep)	L: Bodley Head	(1908)	Robinson, C.	180-220	
Stevenson, R.L.	Child's Garden of Verses (1st, 4to, blue/gilt, teg, 12ticp, pep)	L: Chatto	1908	Sowerby, M.	140-170	
Stevenson, R.L.	Child's Garden of Verses (1st AM, 4to, 125p, teg, 12cp, pep)	Scribner	1908	Sowerby, M.	120-160	
Stevenson, R.L.	Child's Garden of Verses (1st, sm4to, 91p, color)	McLoughlin	(1909)	Comstock, E.B.	45-70	*
Stevenson, R.L.	Child's Garden of Verses (1st, 8vo, 115p, 8cp)	Scribner	1909	Storer, E.	40-65	
Stevenson, R.L.	Child's Garden of Verses (12mo, ibds, 92p)	Barse	(1910)	Von Hofsten, H.	35-50	
Stevenson, R.L.	Child's Garden of Verses (12mo, 96p, cloth)	Donohue	(1916)	Sheldon, M.	35-50	
Stevenson, R.L.	Child's Garden of Verses (1st, 4to, p-o, 140p, color, pep)	Whitman	(1917)	Weage, J.W.	50-70	*
Stevenson, R.L.	Child's Garden of Verses (1st, 4to, 96p, p-o, 8cp, pep)	Rand/McNally	(1919)	Hallock, R.M.	50-70	
Stevenson, R.L.	Child's Garden of Verses (1st, 8vo, 191p, teg, gilt, 8cp)	Lippincott	1919	Kirk, M.L.	80-120	
Stevenson, R.L.	Child's Garden of Verses (1st, 8vo, [306]p, col frn)	Saalfield	(1924)	Brundage, F.	30-45	*
Stevenson, R.L.	Child's Garden of Verses (1st, ob4to, p-o, 89p, gilt, 12cp, pep)	McKay	(1926)	LeMair, H.W.	200-300	
Stevenson, R.L.	Child's Garden of Ve^Eses (1st, lg8vo, 243p, col frn, b/w, pep)	Sears	(1926)	Noe, Eva	25-40	*
Stevenson, R.L.	Child's Garden of Verses (1st, 16mo, 121p, col frn, b/w)	MacMillan	1927	Davis, M.	20-35	*
Stevenson, R.L.	Child's Garden of Verses (1st, 4to, 85p, p-o, 11 fp color, pep)	Platt/Munk	(1929)	Eulalie	45-65	
Stevenson, R.L.	Child's Garden of Verses (1st, 4to, ibds, [36]p, 8 fp color)	Saalfield	(1930)	Burd, C.M.	25-45	
Stevenson, R.L.	Child's Garden of Verses (1st, 8vo, 127p, color)	Whitman	(1930)	McCracken, J.	25-40	*
Stevenson, R.L.	Child's Garden of Verses (1st, 4to, 76p, color, pep)	Graham	(1930)	Pratt, J.C.	30-50	
Stevenson, R.L.	Child's Garden of Verses (1st, 12mo, 91p, b/w, pep)	Whitman	(1931)	Good, P.R.	20-35	*
Stevenson, R.L.	Child's Garden of Verses (1st UK, ob4to, ibds, pep, 71p, 12cp)	L: Harrap	(1931)	LeMair, H.W.	200-275	
Stevenson, R.L.	Child's Garden of Verses (folio, ibds, 60p, color, pep)	Whitman	1932	Bennett, J.C.	40-65	
Stevenson, R.L.	Child's Garden of Verses (1st {this fmt} ob8vo, [24]p, col, pep)	Grosset/Dunlap	1938	Bennett, J.C.	35-50	*
Stevenson, R.L.	Child's Garden of Verses (4to, ibds, 89p, 7cp, pep)	Saalfield	(1940)	Peat, F.B.	40-60	
Stevenson, R.L.	Child's Garden of Verses (1st, 12mo, 68p, color)	Rand/McNally	(1942)	Brice, T.	25-40	*
Stevenson, R.L.	Child's Garden of Verses (1st, sq4to, ibds, [30]p, fp col, pep)	Garden City	1942	Doane, P.	40-65	
Stevenson, R.L.	Child's Garden of Verses (1st, 4to, 112p, ibds, color)	Heritage Press	1944	Duvoisin, R.	35-50	*
Stevenson, R.L.	Child's Garden of Verses (1st, 12mo, ipcb, [52]p, color, pep)	Whitman	1947	Scott, J.L.	25-40	*
Stevenson, R.L.	Child's Garden of Verses (1st, 8vo 118p, grn cl, p-o, 15cp, pep)	OUP	1947	Tudor, T.	150-180	
Stevenson, R.L.	Child's Garden/Verses (1st, 4to, p-o, 125p, teg uncut, 12cp, SC)	Scribner	1905	Smith, J.W.	160-230	
Stevenson, R.L.	David Balfour (1st, 4to, p-o, 356p, 12cp, pep, SC)	Scribner	1924	Wyeth, N.C.	100-150	
Stevenson, R.L.	Dr. Jekyll & Mr. Hyde (1st, lg8vo, gilt, teg, 189p, 8pl)	Scott-Thaw	1904	Macauley, C.R.	70-100	*
Stevenson, R.L.	Dr. Jekyll & Mr. Hyde (1st, 8vo, gilt, 12 fp b/w)	Folio Society	1948	Peake, M.	70-100	
Stevenson, R.L.	Ebb-Tide (1st, 16mo, 204p, gilt, cvr by...)	Stone/Kimball	1894	Meteyard, T.B.	70-110	
Stevenson, R.L.	Fables (1st AM, 4to, maroon/gilt, teg, 83p, 20pl)	Scribner	1914	Herman, E.R.	90-140	
Stevenson, R.L.	Kidnapped (1st, 12mo, 319p, 16pl)	L: Cassell	1907	Hole, W.B.	35-55	*
Stevenson, R.L.	Kidnapped (1st, 8vo, 343p, 8cp)	L: Cassell	1913	Stott, W.R.S.	45-60	*
Stevenson, R.L.	Kidnapped (1st UK, 4to, green cl, p-o, 14cp)	L: Cassell	(1913)	Wyeth, N.C.	160-200	
Stevenson, R.L.	Kidnapped (1st, 4to, map, teg, 289p, 14cp, pep, SC)	Scribner	1913	Wyeth, N.C.	180-300	
Stevenson, R.L.	Kidnapped (1st, 8vo, p-o, 332p, 7cp, pep)	Jacobs	(1915)	Abbott, E.P.	40-60	
Stevenson, R.L.	Kidnapped (1st, sm8vo, 262p, cp)	Rand/McNally	(1916)	Winter, M.	65-90	*
Stevenson, R.L.	Kidnapped (1st, 8vo, 301p, col frn, b/w, pep)	Harper	(1921)	Rhead, L.	25-45	*
Stevenson, R.L.	Kidnapped (1st AM, 8vo, 327p, blue cl, 16pl)	MacMillan	1925	Goble, W.	140-180	
Stevenson, R.L.	Kidnapped (1st, 8vo, 348p, p-o, 4cp, pep)	Winston	(1925)	Godwin, F.	25-40	*
Stevenson, R.L.	Kidnapped (1st, 8vo, 251p)	L: MacMillan	1928	Brock, C.E.	45-60	*
Stevenson, R.L.	Kidnapped (1st, 4to, 290p)	L: OUP	1930	Hilder, R.	35-50	*
Stevenson, R.L.	Kidnapped (1st, 12mo, 387p, b/w)	MacMillan	(1930)	Rowe, C.	25-40	*
Stevenson, R.L.	Master of Ballantrae (1st, 8vo, 349p, 12cp)	L: Cassell	1911	Paget, W.	35-50	*
Stevenson, R.L.	Master of Ballantrae (1st, 8vo, 259p)	L: MacMillan	1928	Brock, H.M.	35-50	*
Stevenson, R.L.	Merry Men (1st, 8vo, 266p)	L: MacMillan	1928	Millar, H.R.	30-45	*
Stevenson, R.L.	Pavilion on the Links (1st, 8vo, 96p, 24cp)	L: Chatto	1913	Browne, G.	65-80	*
Stevenson, R.L.	Songs with Music/Child's Garden/Verses (1st, 4to, 55p, pcb, 12cp)	L: Jack	[1915]	Tarrant, M.	75-100	
Stevenson, R.L.	St. Ives (1st, 8vo, 438p, brown cl)	Scribner	1897	Armstrong, M.	50-80	
Stevenson, R.L.	Stevenson Song Book (1st, 4to, ibds, 119p)	Scribner	1897	Armstrong, M.	70-100	
Stevenson, R.L.	Travels with a Donkey in the Cevennes (1st, 8vo, 189p, gilt, 8pl)	L: J. Lane	1931	Blampied, E.	80-100	
Stevenson, R.L.	Treasure Island (1st, 12mo, 388p)	Scribner	1900	Paget, W.	45-60	*
Stevenson, R.L.	Treasure Island (1st, sm8vo, 292p, cp, pep)	Jacobs	(1911)	Abbott, E.P.	35-60	*
Stevenson, R.L.	Treasure Island (1st, 8vo, 339p, 12cp)	L: Cassell	1911	Cameron, J.	65-80	*
Stevenson, R.L.	Treasure Island (1st, 4to, p-o, gilt, teg, 273p, 14cp, pep, SC)	Scribner	1911	Wyeth, N.C.	220-300	
Stevenson, R.L.	Treasure Island (1st, 8vo, 288p, 35pl, pep)	Harper	(1915)	Rhead, L.	35-50	*
Stevenson, R.L.	Treasure Island (1st, 8vo, 258p, p-o, cp, pep)	Rand/McNally	(1915)	Winter, M.	65-90	*
Stevenson, R.L.	Treasure Island (1st, sm8vo, 306p, 7cp, fp b/w)	Scribner	1918	Varian, G.	50-85	*
Stevenson, R.L.	Treasure Island (1st, sm8vo, 312p, blue cl, pep, 4cp)	L: MacMillan	1923	Goble, W.	85-125	
Stevenson, R.L.	Treasure Island (1st, 8vo, 230p, col frn)	Saalfield	(1924)	Brundage, F.	25-40	*

AUTHOR	TITLE	PUBLISHER	DATE	ARTIST	PRICE	LC
Stevenson, R.L.	Treasure Island (1st, 8vo, 304p, p-o, 3cp)	Winston	(1924)	Godwin, F.	25-40	*
Stevenson, R.L.	Treasure Island (1st, lg8vo, 241p, col frn)	Sears	(1926)	Kelsey, C.W.	25-40	*
Stevenson, R.L.	Treasure Island (1st AM, lg8vo, 287p, green/gilt, 12 ticp)	Doran	[1927]	Dulac, E.	120-170	
Stevenson, R.L.	Treasure Island (1st {this pub}, 8vo, green cl, 287p, 8cp)	Garden City	[1930]	Dulac, E.	80-120	*
Stevenson, R.L.	Treasure Island (1st, sm4to, 228p, color, pep)	Grosset/Dunlap	(1930)	Justis, L.	35-50	*
Stevenson, R.L.	Treasure Island (1st, 8vo, red/gilt, 252p, 10cp)	L: Muller	1934	Orr, M.S.	80-120	
Stevenson, R.L.	Treasure Island (1st, 8vo, 287p, color, pep)	World Pub. Co.	(1946)	Becker, M.L.	25-40	*
Stevenson, R.L.	Treasure Island (1st, 8vo, 342p, color)	Grosset/Dunlap	(1947)	Price, N.	25-45	*
Stevenson, R.L.	Treasure Island (1st, 8vo, gilt, 20 fp b/w)	L: Eyre/Spotts	1949	Peake, M.	80-120	*
Stevenson, R.L.	Weir of Hermiston (1st AM, 8vo, teg, gilt, 266p)	Scribner	1896	Armstrong, M.	45-60	
Steward, R.	Surprising Advens of Man in the Moon (1st, 4to, 142p, 12cp)	Lee & Shepard	(1903)	Bridgman, L.J.	100-120	*
Stewart, Anna B.	Gentlest Giant (1st {1st bk.}, 4to, 142p, blue bds, color)	NY: Wayne	1915	Walker, D.S.	100-120	
Stewart, Anna B.	Gentlest Giant (1st {this pub}, 8vo, blue cl, 148p, uncut, dep)	McBride	1929	Walker, D.S.	30-50	*
Stewart, Anna B.	Young Miss Burney (1st {std}, 8vo, green/gilt, 270p, b/w)	Lippincott	1947	Stone, H.	25-40	*
Stewart, E.P.	Letters of a Woman Homesteader (1st, 12mo, 282p, 6pl)	Houghton	1914	Wyeth, N.C.	55-85	
Stewart, M.	Way to Wonderland (1st, lg8vo, 144p, gilt, 194p, p-o, 6cp, pep)	Dodd	(1917)	Smith, J.W.	170-240	
Stewart, M.	Way to Wonderland (1st UK, lg8vo, 144p, blue/gilt, 6 ticp, pep)	L: Hodder	[1918]	Smith, J.W.	220-300	
Stewart, Mary	Once Upon a Time Tales (1st, 8vo, 275p, pep, 8cp)	Revell	(1912)	McClure, G.M.	40-60	*
Stickney, J.H.	Bird World (1st, 8vo, 214p, green cl, 10pl by...)	Ginn & Co.	1898	Seton, E.T.	80-120	*
Stigand, C.H.	Black Tales/White Children (1st, 8vo, 200p, b/w, DJ)	L: Constable	(1914)	Hargrave, J.	120-170	
Stilwell, Alison	Chin Ling & Chinese Cricket (1st, lg8vo, [48]p, color)	MacMillan	1947	Enright, M.W.	45-60	
Stilwell, S.	Musical Tree (1st, 4to, tan cloth, color)	Penn	1925	Stilwell, S.	65-85	
Stimson, F.J.	Mrs. Knollys... (1st, 8vo, green/gilt, teg, 207p)	Scribner	1897	Armstrong, M.	25-45	*
Stirling, Monica	Little Ballet Dancer (1st, lg8vo, ipcb, 61p, 2-color, pep)	Lothrop	1952	Stone, H.	25-40	*
Stockton, Frank	Adventures of Captain Horn (1st, 8vo, green/gilt, 404p)	Scribner	1895	Armstrong, M.	25-40	
Stockton, Frank	Afield & Afloat (1st, 8vo, teg, 422p, 12pl)	Scribner	1900	Newell, P.	35-50	
Stockton, Frank	Associate Hermits (1st, 12mo, green/gilt, 257p, 9pl)	Harper	1899	Frost, A.B.	40-65	R
Stockton, Frank	Bicycle of Cathay (1st, sm8vo, 240p, 32pl)	Harper	1900	Lowell, O.	30-45	
Stockton, Frank	Captain Chap (1st, sm8vo, 298p, tan cl, 6pl)	Lippincott	1897	Stephens, C.H.	35-50	
Stockton, Frank	Fanciful Tales (1st, 12mo, maroon cl, 135p)	Scribner	1894	Armstrong, M.	65-80	*
Stockton, Frank	Floating Prince... (1st, 8vo, 199p, PPP, b/w)	Scribner	1881	Unknown	100-165	*
Stockton, Frank	Girl at Cobhurst (1st, 8vo, green/gilt, 408p)	Scribner	1898	Armstrong, M.	20-35	
Stockton, Frank	Great Stone of Sardis (1st, 8vo, 230p, teg, uncut, gilt, 52pl)	Harper	1898	Newell, P.	60-85	R
Stockton, Frank	John Gayther's Garden... (1st, 8vo, grn/gilt, uncut, teg, 365p)	Scribner	1902	Armstrong, M.	40-65	R
Stockton, Frank	Kate Bonnet (1st, 8vo, 420p, b/w pl)	Appleton	1902	Keller/Potter	30-45	
Stockton, Frank	Mrs. Cliff's Yacht (1st, 8vo, 341p, 8pl, cvr by...)	Scribner	1896	Armstrong, M.	25-45	
Stockton, Frank	Pomona's Travels (1st [1], 8vo, 275p, teg, gilt, 10pl)	Scribner	(1894)	Frost, A.B.	60-80	
Stockton, Frank	Queen's Museum (1st, 4to, 219p, gilt, p-o, teg, 10cp, pep, SC)	Scribner	1906	Richardson, F.	130-180	
Stockton, Frank	Squirrel Inn (1st, sm8vo, 222p, teg, b/w)	Century	1891	Frost, A.B.	45-60	
Stockton, Frank	Storyteller's Pack (1st, 8vo, 380p, gilt, 16pl, teg, cvr by...)	Scribner	1897	Armstrong, M.	45-60	
Stockton, Frank	Ting-a-Ling (1st [1st bk.], 8vo, 187p, green/gilt, PPP)	Hurd/Houghton	1870	Bensell, E.B.	285-400	R
Stoddard, Ann	Good Little Dog (1st {std}, 8vo, [55]p, 16cp)	Century	(1930)	Hader, B.& E.	45-65	
Stoddard, Ann	Here Bingo! (1st {std}, sq8vo, ibds, [61]p, 16 fp color)	Century	(1932)	Hader, B.& E.	35-60	
Stoddard, C.W.	Cruise Under the Crescent (1st, 8vo, 358p, cvr by...)	Rand/McNally	(1898)	Denslow, W.W.	40-60	*
Stoddard, W.O.	Little Smoke (1st, sm8vo, blue/silver, 295p, 14pl, PPP)	Appleton	1891	Dellenbaugh, F.	160-250	*
Stokely, E.K.	Pantaloon (1st, sm4to, 168p, orang cl, 6cp, pep)	Doran	(1927)	Kay, G.A.	45-65	*
Stokes, H.	Belgium (1st, lg4to, black cl, 390p, 52 b/w illus)	L: Kegan Paul	1916	Brangwyn, F.	100-140	
Stokes, Vernon	Blobbs at the Sea Side (folio, ibds, 11 chromos)	L: Chambers	[1908]	Stokes, V.	240-300	
Stokley, E.	Bubbleloon (1st, sm4to, 201p, blue/gilt, 6 ticp, pep)	Doran	(1926)	Porter, J.E.	65-90	
Stolz, Mary S.	Emmett's Pig (1st, 8vo, ibds, 61p, 2-color)	Harper	(1959)	Williams, Garth	40-65	*
Stolz, Mary S.	Leftover Elf (1st, 8vo, 57p, green cl, fp b/w)	Harper	(1952)	Bacon, P.	25-40	*
Stone, Amy	Here's Juggins (1st, sm8vo, 162p, blue cl, 6cp, pep)	Lothrop/Lee	1936	Woodward, H.	25-45	*
Stone, Amy	P-Penny & his Little Red Cart (1st, sm8vo, 165p, color, pep)	Lothrop/Lee	1934	Woodward, H.	30-45	*
Stone, C.R.	Inga of Porcupine Mine (1st, sm8vo, 212p, blue cl, b/w)	Holiday House	(1942)	Simon, E.	20-25	*
Stone, Eugenia	Secret of the Bog (1st, sm8vo, 217p, b/w, cep)	Holiday House	(1948)	Price, C.	20-30	*
Stone, S.B.	Kingdom of Why (1st, 8vo, green cl, 275p, p-o, 9pl)	Bobbs-Merrill	(1913)	Newell, P.	120-150	
Stone, Wm. S.	Pepe was the Saddest Bird (1st {std}, 8vo, [62]p, ipcb, b/w)	Knopf	1944	Mordvinoff, N.	65-90	R*
Stone, Wm. S.	Ship of Flame (1st {std}, lg4to, 164p, bds, col frn, b/w)	Knopf	1945	Mordvinoff, N.	70-120	R*
Stone, Wm. S.	Teri Taro from Bora Bora (1st {std}, sm8vo, 133p, 8cp, pep)	Knopf	1940	Sperry, A.	30-45	*
Stone, Wm. S.	Thunder Island (1st {std}, sm8vo, 194p, 7cp)	Knopf	(1942)	Mordvinoff, N.	30-50	*
Stong, Phil	Cowhand Goes to Town (1st {std}, 4to, ibds, 85p, color)	Dodd	1939	Wiese, K.	30-45	
Stong, Phil	Edgar: The 7:58 (1st, sm8vo, 101p, pep, b/w)	Farrar/Rine.	1938	Lenski, L.	35-50	*
Stong, Phil	Farm Boy... (1st {std}, 4to, col frn, 80p, pep)	Doubleday/Dor.	1934	Wiese, K.	30-45	*
Stong, Phil	High Water (1st {std}, 4to, ibds, 79p, color, pep)	Dodd	1937	Wiese, K.	35-50	*
Stong, Phil	Hired Man's Elephant (1st, 8vo, 149p, beige cl, b/w)	Dodd	1939	Lee, Doris	25-40	*
Stong, Phil	Honk! the Moose (1st {std}, sm4to, ibds, 80p, color, pep, NH)	Dodd	1935	Wiese, K.	65-90	R*
Stong, Phil	Positive Pete (1st, sm4to, ibds, 64p, color, pep, DJ)	Dodd	1947	Wiese, K.	35-50	
Stong, Phil	Young Settler (1st {std}, sm4to, ibds, 80p, 20 fp color, pep)	Dodd	1938	Wiese, K.	30-60	*
Stonier, G.W.	Pictures on the Pavement (1st, 8vo, 214p, brown cl)	L: M. Joseph	1955	Ardizzone, E.	50-65	
Storm, T.	Immensee (1st, 8vo, olive cl, 9cp)	McClurg	1907	Armstrong, M.	80-120	
Stowe, H.B.	Uncle Tom's Cabin (1st, 8vo, 529p, gilt, cvr by...)	L: Routledge	1904	King, J.	145-180	
Stowe, H.B.	Uncle Tom's Cabin (1st, 8vo, 529p, gilt, illus by...)	L: Routledge	1904	Thomas, G.	145-180	

AUTHOR	TITLE	PUBLISHER	DATE	ARTIST	PRICE	LC
Stowe, H.B.	Uncle Tom's Cabin (1st, 8vo, 508p, 8cp)	L: A&C Black	1904	Vedder, S.H.	70-100	*
Stowe, H.B.	Uncle Tom's Cabin (16mo, p-o, gilt, 115p, 8cp)	Jack/Dutton	[1908]	Forrest, A.S.	45-60	*
Stowe, H.B.	Uncle Tom's Cabin (brown cl, p-o, 12mo, 46p, 6 color)	Barse	[1915]	Von Hofsten, H.	50-70	*
Stowe, H.B.	Uncle Tom's Cabin (1st, 8vo, 446p, pep)	E. McCann	(1929)	Daugherty, J.	35-50	*
Strahorn, C.A.	15 Thousand Miles by Stage (1st, 8vo, 673p, teg, 4cp)	Putnam	1911	Russell, C.M.	130-170	
Strain, E.H.	School in Fairyland (1st, 8vo, green cl, 186p, 7pl)	L: T.F. Unwin	1896	Brooke, L.L.	100-150	
Stranathan, May	Silhouette Stories (1st, 8vo, 198p, brown cl, 14 fp bw)	Moffat	1921	Taylor, E.C.	30-45	*
Strang, H.	Big Book of Fairy Stories (1st, 8vo, 191p, ibds, 4cp, pep)	L: H. Milford	(1929)	Watson, A.H.	70-100	
Strang, H.	Old Man of the Mountain (1st, 8vo, 322p, b/w)	L: H. Frowde	(1916)	Bull, Rene	65-80	*
Strang, H.	Rose Book of the Fairies (4to, ibds, 6cp)	L: H. Milford	(1922)	Govey, L.	65-80	
Strang, H.	Rose Fairy Book (1st, 4to, 303p, p-o, pep, 12 ticp)	L: Hodder	[1912]	Govey, L.	180-230	
Strang, H.	What Baby Reads (1st AM, 12mo, bds, gilt, p-o, [32]p, 6cp)	NY: Hodder	[1910]	Sowerby, M.	50-70	*
Strang, W.	Book of Giants (1st, 8vo, 56p, 12pl)	(London)	1898	Strang, W.	150-200	
Stratton, Clarence	Swords & Statues (1st, 8vo, 254p, col frn, gilt, 7 b/w)	Winston	(1937)	Lawson, R.	65-80	*
Streamer, Col. D.	Baby's Baedeker (1st, 8vo, 56p, uncut, ibds, 9pl)	R.H. Russell	1902	Unknown	70-100	*
Streamer, Col. D.	Ruthless Rhymes for Heartless Homes (1st, sm8vo, ibds, b/w, pep)	R.H. Russell	1901	J.W.A.	80-100	
Streatfield, N.	Ballet Shoes (1st, 8vo, 294p, color)	Random	(1937)	Floethe, R.	25-40	*
Streatfield, N.	Circus Shoes (1st {std}, 8vo, 401p, color)	Random	(1939)	Floethe, R.	30-45	
Streatfield, N.	Party Shoes (1st AM {std}, 8vo, 333p, grey cl, fp b/w)	Random	(1947)	Zinkeisen, A.	25-40	
Streatfield, N.	Stranger in Primrose Lane (1st {std}, 8vo, 338p, p-o, 7cp)	Random	(1941)	Floethe, R.	35-50	*
Streatfield, N.	Theater Shoes (1st {std}, 8vo, 282p, color)	Random	(1945)	Floethe, R.	25-40	*
Strettell, A.	Lullabies of Many Lands (1st, 4to, 127p, gilt, teg, uncut, dep)	L: G. Allen	1894	Harding, E.J.	65-80	
Stringer, A.J.	Loom of Destiny (1st, 12mo, 208p, blue/silver, cvr by...)	Small	1899	Peabody, M.L.	45-75	*
Stroebe, C. (ed.)	Danish Fairy Book (1st, 8vo, blue cl, 218p, 6cp, pep)	Stokes	(1922)	Hood, G.	40-70	*
Stroebe, C. (ed.)	Norwegian Fairy Book (1st, 8vo, 304p, 6cp, pep)	Stokes	(1922)	Hood, G.	40-70	
Strong, R.	Yoyo's Animal Friends (4to, 170p, teg, 3cp)	Dent/Dutton	1913	Flower, N.	40-70	
Struther, J.	Modern Struwwelpeter (1st, 8vo, bds, color)	L: Methuen	1936	Shepard, E.H.	70-90	
Struther, J.	Sycamore Square... (1st, 8vo, green/gilt, 63p, b/w)	L: Methuen	(1932)	Shepard, E.H.	45-60	
Stuart, Ruth M.	Aunt Amity's Silver Wedding (1st, 8vo, green/gilt, 228p, b/w)	Century	1909	Frost, A.B.	30-50	
Stuart, Ruth M.	Daddy' Do-Funny's Wisdom Jingles (1st, sm8vo, 95p, b/w, pep)	Century	1913	Clements, G.H.	50-80	*
Stuart, Ruth M.	George Washington Jones (1st, 12mo, 147p, 5pl)	Altemus	(1903)	Potthast, E.	30-50	
Stuart, Ruth M.	Gobolinks (1st, ob8vo, ibds, 73p, b/w)	Century	1896	Unknown	80-120	
Stuart, Ruth M.	Haunted Photograph (1st, 12mo, gilt, 168p, 10pl)	Century	1911	Various	50-80	
Stuart, Ruth M.	Holly & Pizen (1st, 12mo, 216p, 7pl)	Century	1899	Potthast, E.	50-70	*
Stuart, Ruth M.	In Simkinsville (1st, 8vo, 244p, 8pl)	Harper	1897	Various	30-50	
Stuart, Ruth M.	Moriah's Mourning (1st, 12mo, 218p, 8pl)	Harper	1898	Frost/Kemble	40-65	*
Stuart, Ruth M.	Napoleon Jackson (1st, sm8vo, 132p, red/gilt, 8pl)	Century	1902	Potthast, E.	40-60	
Stuart, Ruth M.	River's Children (1st, 16mo, 179p, green/gilt, 5pl)	Century	1904	Edwards, H.C.	30-45	
Stuart, Ruth M.	Second Wooing of Salina Sue (1st, 12mo, 236p, 12pl)	Harper	1905	Frost/Kemble	40-65	*
Stuart, Ruth M.	Solomon Crow's Christmas Pockets (1st, 12mo, gilt, 201p, 14pl)	Harper	1897	Frost, A.B.	45-60	*
Stuart, Ruth M.	Sonny's Father (1st, 12mo, teg, 240p, uncut, 2pl by...)	Century	1910	Smith, J.W.	60-90	
Stuart, Ruth M.	Sonny, A Christmas Guest (1st, sm8vo, 135p, teg, gilt, 13pl)	Century	1904	Cory, F.	30-45	
Stuart, Ruth M.	Story of Babette (1st, sm8vo, 209p, beige/gilt, cvr by...)	Harper	1894	Armstrong, M.	35-50	*
Sturges, L.B.	Runaway Toys (1st, 12mo, [64]p, black cl, p-o, color)	Rand/McNally	(1920)	Sturges, L.B.	70-100	*
Sturges, L.B.	Toys of Nuremberg (1st, sm8vo, p-o, [80]p, color)	Rand/McNally	(1915)	Sturges, L.B.	50-70	
Sturgis, E.B.	My Busy Days (1st, lg4to, 50p, ibds, 8cp)	Appleton	1908	Hinchman, M.	100-160	*
Sudermann, H.	Magda (1st, 12mo, 161p, red/gilt, cvr by...)	Chi: Lamson	1896	Rhead, L.	70-100	
Sullivan, Frank	In One Ear (1st, 8vo, red/gilt, 169p, frn by...)	Viking	1933	Seuss, Dr.	65-90	*
Surtees, R.S.	Jorrock's on 'Unting (1st, 16mo, teg, bds, 32p, p-o, 3 ticp)	L: Heinemann	1909	Aldin, C.	100-135	
Sutton, Adah L.	Mr. Bunny - His Book (4to, ipcb, 106p, color)	Saalfield	(1900)	Fry, W.H.	200-250	*
Sutton, Adah L.	Teddy Bears (1st, 4to, 154p, ibds, 6cp)	Saalfield	1907	Unknown	220-350	
Swan, O.	Deep Water Days (1st, lg8vo, 506p, p-o, 11cp, pep)	Macrae-Smith	(1929)	Various	50-70	
Swan, O.	Frontier Days (1st, 4to, 512p, 3cp by...)	Macrae-Smith	(1928)	Schoonover, F.	50-70	
Sweetser, K.D.	Book of Indian Braves (1st, lg8vo, 183p, p-o, col frn)	Harper	1913	Williams, G.A.	45-60	
Sweetser, K.D.	Boys & Girls from George Eliot (1st, lg8vo, 212p, 8pl)	Duffield	1906	Williams, G.A.	45-60	*
Sweetser, K.D.	Ten Boys from Dickens (1st, lg8vo, 223p, uncut, b/w pl)	R.H. Russell	1901	Williams, G.A.	50-80	
Sweetser, K.D.	Ten Girls from Dickens (1st, 8vo, 236p, p-o, uncut, 11pl)	Baker/Taylor	1902	Williams, G.A.	45-65	
Swift, H.H.	House by the Sea (1st, 8vo, 245p, blue cl, 8pl, pep, DJ)	Harcourt	(1938)	Ward, L.	35-50	
Swift, H.H.	Little Blacknose (1st, 8vo, 149p, color, pep, DJ, NH)	Harcourt	1929	Ward, L.	40-65	
Swift, H.H.	North Star Shining (1st, 4to, 44p, 8 fp color)	Wm. Morrow	(1947)	Ward, L.	70-90	*
Swift, H.H.	Railroad to Freedom (1st, 8vo, 364p, pep, NH)	Harcourt	(1932)	Daugherty, J.	45-60	*
Swift, J.	Gulliver's Travels (1st, 12mo, 381p, b/w)	MacMillan	1894	Brock, C.E.	45-60	*
Swift, J.	Gulliver's Travels (1st, 8vo, 414p, 12cp)	L: Routledge	1895	Wheeler, E.J.	35-60	*
Swift, J.	Gulliver's Travels (1st, sm8vo, 355p, pl)	J. Lane	1900	Cole, H.	30-45	*
Swift, J.	Gulliver's Travels (8vo, brown cl, AEG, 6cp)	L: Nister	[1900]	Jacobs, E.A.	65-90	
Swift, J.	Gulliver's Travels (1st AM, 8vo, teg, 291p, 12 ticp, pep)	Dent/Dutton	1909	Rackham, A.	180-240	
Swift, J.	Gulliver's Travels (1st, 8vo, 291p, gilt, teg, 12 ticp, pep)	L: Dent	1909	Rackham, A.	250-300	
Swift, J.	Gulliver's Travels (1st, 8vo, blue/gilt, AEG, 332p, 6cp, pep)	Nister/Dutton	[1910]	Jackson, A.E.	70-100	
Swift, J.	Gulliver's Travels (1st, sm8vo, 304p, cp, pep)	Doubleday/Page	1912	Groesbeck, D.S.	20-35	*
Swift, J.	Gulliver's Travels (1st, 8vo, 235p, 8cp, pep)	L: Sidgwick	(1912)	Staynes, P.A.	30-50	*
Swift, J.	Gulliver's Travels (1st AM, 8vo, 235p, 8cp, pep)	Holt	(1912)	Staynes, P.A.	30-45	*
Swift, J.	Gulliver's Travels (1st, lg8vo, 344p, gilt, p-o, 12cp, pep)	Rand/McNally	(1912)	Winter, M.	65-100	

AUTHOR	TITLE	PUBLISHER	DATE	ARTIST	PRICE	LC
Swift, J.	Gulliver's Travels (1st, 8vo, 350p, b/w, pep)	Harper	1913	Rhead, L.	30-45	*
Swift, J.	Gulliver's Travels (1st, 8vo, 296p, blue/gilt, 12cp, pep)	MacMillan	1917	Pogany, W.	80-100	
Swift, J.	Gulliver's Travels (1st, 8vo, 221p, col frn, cp)	Lippincott	1918	Kirk, M.L.	60-75	*
Swift, J.	Gulliver's Travels (1st AM, 4to, 135p, blue/gilt, 4cp)	Dodd/Hein.	[1920]	DeBosschere, J.	85-130	
Swift, J.	Gulliver's Travels (1st, sm8vo, 370p, cp)	Jacobs	[1923]	Smith, Wuanita	25-40	*
Swift, J.	Gulliver's Travels (1st, 8vo, 274p, cp, pep)	Winston	(1930)	Prittie, E.J.	25-40	
Swift, J.	Gulliver's Travels (1st, lg8vo, 309p, cp)	Houghton	1931	Bacharach, H.I.	25-40	*
Swift, J.	Gulliver's Travels (1st, sm8vo, 64p)	Chi: Rockwell	1931	Stahl, B.	45-65	*
Swift, J.	Gulliver's Travels (1st, lg8vo, 343p, b/w)	Heritage Press	1940	Eichenberg, F.	35-60	*
Swift, J.	Gulliver's Travels (1st, smvo, 306p, color)	Grosset/Dunlap	(1947)	Watson, A.	35-50	*
Swinburne, A.C.	Selected Poems... (1st, 4to, black/gilt, 217p, 10pl, pep)	Lane/Dodd	(1928)	Clarke, H.	200-250	
Swinburne, A.C.	Springtide of Life (1st, 4to, green/gilt, 133p, 8cp, pep)	L: Heinemann	(1918)	Rackham, A.	200-250	
Swinburne, A.C.	Springtide of Life (1st AM, 4to, 132p, green cl, 8cp, pep)	Lippincott	1918	Rackham, A.	165-220	
Swinburne, A.C.	Tale of Balen (1st AM, 8vo, 132p, olive/gilt, cvr by...)	Scribner	1896	Armstrong, M.	70-90	*
Sykes, M.	Poe's Run.... (1st, 8vo, teg, green cl, 84p, b/w)	Cannon Pr.	1904	Tarkington, B.	35-50	
Sylva, C.	Lily of Life (1st, 4to, gilt, teg, 146p, p-o, 18 ticp)	L: Hodder	[1910]	Stratton, H.	350-450	
Sylva, C.	Peeping Pansy (1st, 4to, red/gilt, 312p, 8 ticp)	L: Hodder	(1918)	Attwell, M.L.	100-130	
Sylvester, C.	Manny & Co. (1st, 8vo, [40]p, color)	Volland	1913	Dodge, K.S.	45-70	*
Symington, E.H.	By Light of Sun (1st, 8vo, 196p, fp woodcuts by...)	Putnam	1941	Leighton, C.	35-50	*
Symonds, J.A.	In the Key of Blue (1st, 8vo, 302p, blue/gilt, cvr by...)	L: Matthews	1893	Ricketts, C.	125-200	
Symons, A.	Aubrey Beardsley (1st, 8vo, bds, gilt, 6 b/w)	L: Unicorn Pr.	1898	Beardsley, A.	150-200	
Syrett, Netta	Godmother's Garden (1st, 8vo, 222p)	L: Blackie	[1918]	Harrison, F.	50-70	*
Syrett, Netta	Rachel & the Seven Wonders (1st, 8vo, 172p, p-o, 5cp, pep)	Stokes	(1923)	Mercer, J.	70-90	
Syrett, Netta	Tinkelly Winkle (1st, 8vo, 157p, green cl, 8cp)	Dodd	1923	Foster, M.L.	30-45	*
Syrett, Netta	Toby & the Odd Beasts (8vo, blue cl, p-o, 5cp)	(London)	1921	Govey, L.	100-135	
Syrett, Netta	Vanishing Princess (1st, 8vo, 93p)	L: D. Nutt	[1910]	Robinson, C.	90-130	*
Szyk, Arthur	New Order (1st, 4to, 8 fp color, DJ)	Putnam	(1941)	Szyk, A.	100-165	
Taggart, M.A.	Pussy-Cat Town (1st, 8vo, 245p, green/gilt, color, pep)	Page	1906	Chase, R.	35-50	
Tagore, R.	Stray Birds (1st, 8vo, 84p, col frn by...)	L: MacMillan	1917	Pogany, W.	30-50	
Tappan, E.M.	House with the Silver Door (1st, sm8vo, grn cl, 184p, p-o, 4cp)	Houghton	1913	Chamberlin, E.H.	25-40	*
Tappan, E.M.	Prince from Nowhere... (1st, sm8vo, 206p, blue cl, 8cp)	Houghton	1928	Nystrom, J.	25-40	*
Tappan, E.M.	Robin Hood: His Book (1st, 8vo, tan cl, 267p, 6cp)	Little/Brown	1903	Harding, C.	50-70	
Tarbell, Ida M.	Madame Roland (1st, sm8vo, 328p, blue/gilt, cvr by...)	Scribner	1896	Armstrong, M.	30-45	*
Tarkington, B.	Beasley's Christmas Party (1st, 8vo, 100p, gilt, color)	Harper	1909	Clements, R.S.	40-60	
Tarkington, B.	Man from Home (1st, 8vo, 175p, tan cl, 7pl)	Harper	1908	(Photos)	50-70	
Tarkington, B.	Penrod (1st [1], 8vo, p-o, 345p, blue cl, PPP)	Doubleday/Page	1914	Grant, G.	200-250	
Tarkington, B.	Penrod & Sam (1st, 8vo, 356p, green cl, 8pl, PPP)	Doubleday/Page	1916	Brehm, W.	70-100	
Tarkington, B.	Penrod Jashper (1st {std}, 8vo, blue cl, 321p, b/w)	Doubleday/Dor.	1929	Grant, G.	35-50	
Tarkington, B.	Seventeen (1st, sm8vo, 328p, orange cl)	Harper	(1916)	Brown, A.W.	60-90	
Tarkington, B.	Two Vanrevels (1st, 8vo, 351p, green/gilt, teg, 7pl)	McClure	1902	Hutt, H.	30-50	
Tarn, W.W.	Treasure of Isle of Mist (1st, 8vo, grn/gilt, 163p, fp 1-color)	L: P. Allan	1919	Macdonald, S.	45-65	
Tarn, W.W.	Treasure of Isle of Mist (1st, 8vo, 184p, pep, b/w)	Putnam	(1934)	Lawson, R.	30-45	*
Tarrant, M.	Joan in Flowerland (1st, 8vo, 60p, blue cl, 16cp, DJ)	L: Warne	(1935)	Tarrant, M.	85-120	
Tarrant, M.	Margaret Tarrant's Christmas Garland (1st, sq8vo, 125p, 19 ticp)	Hale-Cushman	(1942)	Tarrant, M.	45-60	*
Tarry, Ellen	Hezekiah Horton (1st, lg8vo, 39p, color)	Viking	1942	Harrington, O.	50-85	*
Tarry, Ellen	Janie Belle (1st, 4to, [30]p, ibds, fp brown illus)	Garden City	1940	Sheldon, M.	70-100	
Tarry, Ellen	My Dog Rinty (1st, lg8vo, [48]p, tan cl, b/w photos by...)	Viking	1946	Alland, A.& A.	65-80	R*
Tarry, Ellen	Runaway Elephant (1st, lg8vo, ipcb, 37p, fp 1-color, pep)	Viking	1950	Harrington, O.	70-120	R*
Tate, Eliz.	Little Flower Girl (1st, lg8vo, aqua cl, [40]p, 3-color, pep)	Lothrop/Lee	(1956)	Stone, H.	45-60	*
Taylor, A.& J.	Original Poems (2nd AM, 8vo, 415p, gilt, teg, tan cl, col frn)	Stokes	(1905)	Bedford, F.D.	45-65	
Taylor, A.& J.	Original Poems... (2nd, 8vo, teg, uncut, col frn)	L: Wells/Gard.	1905	Bedford, F.D.	90-130	*
Taylor, B.	Boys of Other Countries (1st, 8vo, 263p, col frn)	Putnam	1912	Coburn, F.S.	20-30	
Taylor, B.L.	Well in the Wood (1st, 8vo, 191p, blue cl, 8pl)	Bobbs-Merrill	(1904)	Cory, F.	35-50	
Taylor, C.B.	Nicanor, Teller of Tales (1st, 8vo, p-o, 422p, pep, 5cp)	McClurg	1906	Kinneys	20-30	
Taylor, Deems	Fantasia (1st, lg4to, tan cloth, 158p, 17cp, pep)	Simon/Schuster	1940	Disney Studios	150-220	
Taylor, I.S.	Baby's Book (sm4to, AEG, 4cp)	L: R. Tuck	[1904]	Brundage, F.	80-100	
Taylor, Jane	Little Ann... (1st, lg8vo, ibds, 64p, color, cep)	L: Routledge	[1883]	Greenaway, K.	160-220	
Taylor, M.I.	Little Mistress Goodhope (1st, 12mo, gilt, p-o, 186p, col frn)	McClurg	1902	Smith, J.W.	180-260	
Taylor, Paul B.	Tippletappleteven Town (1st, sq8vo, [12]p, ibds, color, pep)	Holt	(1931)	Taylor, P.B.	65-90	*
Taylor, S.	Story of a Little Poet (1st, 8vo, green cl, 8pl)	Little/Brown	1901	Stephens, A.B.	25-40	
Taylor, Una	Early Italian Love Stories (1st, 4to, 144p)	L: Longmans	1899	Ford, H.J.	100-160	
Teal, Val	Little Woman Wanted Noise (1st, 8vo, [40]p, orang cl, b/w, pep)	Rand/McNally	(1943)	Lawson, R.	80-120	*
Teasdale, S.	Rainbow Gold (1st, 8vo, 267p, blue/gilt, col frn, b/w, pep)	MacMillan	1922	Walker, D.S.	45-60	
Teasdale, S.	Stars Tonight (1st, 8vo, blue cl, 49p, col frn, 14 fp b/w)	MacMillan	1930	Lathrop, D.	45-60	
Teilhet, Darwin	Skwee-Gee (1st {std}, 4to, ibds, [40]p, color)	Doubleday/Dor.	1940	Gramatky, H.	45-60	*
Tempski, Armine	Bright Spurs (1st, 8vo, 283p, peach cl, uncut, b/w)	Dodd	1946	Brown, Paul	30-50	*
Tempski, Armine	Pam's Paradise Ranch (1st, 8vo, 333p, orang cl, uncut, pep, b/w)	Dodd	1940	Brown, Paul	25-40	*
Tenggren, G.	Tenggren's Story Book (1st {std}, lg4to, ibds, color, pep, GGB)	Simon/Schuster	1944	Tenggren, G.	75-110	
Tennyson, A.	Dream of Fair Women (1st AM, lg8vo, 197p, gilt, b/w)	Page/Richards	1900	Sullivan, E.J.	65-90	
Tennyson, A.	Dream of Fair Women (1st, lg8vo, [96]p, p-o, 22cp)	Bobbs-Merrill	(1907)	Fisher, H.	200-270	
Tennyson, A.	Dream of Fair Women (lg8vo, p-o, 148p, 21cp)	Grosset/Dunlap	(1907)	Fisher, H.	160-200	
Tennyson, A.	Dream of Fair Women (8vo, grey bds, 79p, 8cp, pep)	L: Blackie	[1915]	Harrison, F.	50-70	

AUTHOR	TITLE	PUBLISHER	DATE	ARTIST	PRICE	LC
Tennyson, A.	Geraint & Enid (1st, 16mo, blue/gilt, 4cp)	L: Jack	[n.d.]	Shaw, B.	70-90	
Tennyson, A.	Guinevere... (1st, 4to, teg, 156p, gilt, 24 ticp)	L: Blackie	1912	Harrison, F.	200-265	
Tennyson, A.	Guinevere... (1st AM, 4to, 156p, gilt, teg, 24 ticp)	D. Estes	1912	Harrison, F.	140-200	
Tennyson, A.	Idylls of the King (1st, lg4to, [114]p, uncut, 24 woodcuts)	R.H. Russell	1898	Rhead, L.	100-145	
Tennyson, A.	Idylls of the King (1st, 4to, 174p, gilt, 21 ticp)	L: Hodder	(1911)	Brickdale, E.F.	160-225	
Tennyson, A.	Idylls of the King (1st, 4to, black cl, p-o, 394p, 12 ticp, pep)	Stokes	(1912)	Kirk, M.L.	80-120	
Tennyson, A.	Lady of Shalott (1st, lg8vo, [64]p, blue/gilt, AEG, color, dep)	Dodd	(1881)	Pyle, H.	350-450	
Tennyson, A.	Maud (1st, 8vo, teg, uncut, 107p, green/gilt, dep, 10cp)	Dodd	1905	Armstrong, M.	35-50	
Tennyson, A.	Maud (1st, sm4to, 103p, uncut, 8cp, DJ)	L: MacMillan	1922	Sullivan, E.J.	60-75	
Tennyson, A.	The Princess (1st, 4to, brown/gilt, 14cp)	Bobbs-Merrill	(1911)	Christy, H.C.	75-100	
Tennyson, H.	Jack & the Bean Stalk (1st, sq8vo, 70p, green cl, b/w)	L: MacMillan	1886	Caldecott, R.	150-200	
Terhune, A.P.	Book of Famous Dogs (1st {std}, 8vo, 300p, b/w pl)	Doubleday/Dor.	1937	Dickey, R.L.	25-40	*
Terhune, A.P.	Columbia Stories (1st {1st bk.}, sm8vo, 214p, b/w)	Dillingham	1897	Thornburgh, F.	35-60	*
Terhune, A.P.	Dogs (1st, 4to, ipcb, 60p, col frn, fp b/w)	Saalfield	(1940)	Wiese, K.	30-45	*
Terhune, A.P.	Further Adventures of Lad (1st, sm8vo, 341p, col frn)	Doran	(1922)	Bull, C.L.	30-45	
Terhune, A.P.	Heart of a Dog (1st, 8vo, 249p, 8 ticp)	Doran	(1924)	Kirmse, M.	25-40	
Terhune, A.P.	My Friend the Dog (1st {std}, lg8vo, gilt, 317p, 8 ticp, pep)	Harper	1926	Kirmse, M.	25-45	*
Terhune, A.P.	Real Tales of Real Dogs (1st, lg4to, 92p, b/w)	Saalfield	(1935)	Thorne, D.	30-45	*
Terhune, A.P.	Story of Damon & Pythias (1st, 12mo, 307p, 14pl)	Grosset/Dunlap	(1915)	(Photos)	25-40	*
Terhune, A.P.	The Woman (1st, 12mo, 341p, b/w pl)	Bobbs-Merrill	(1912)	King, W.B.	25-40	*
Terhune, A.P.	True Dog Stories (1st, 12mo, 60p, b/w)	Saalfield	1936	Thorne, D.	25-40	*
Terhune, Anice	Chinese Child's Day (1st, lg4to, 33p, ibds, 15 color)	NY: Schirmer	[1910]	Wheelan, A.R.	100-150	
Terhune, Anice	Dutch Ditties for Children (1st, lg4to, 31p, ibds, 15 color)	NY: Schirmer	[1910]	Wheelan, A.R.	80-125	
Terry, R.R.	Old Rhymes with New Tunes (1st, 4to, ibds, 32p, b/w)	Longmans	1912	Pippet, G.	45-60	*
Thacher, L.W.	Listening Child (1st, sm8vo, 405p, blue cl, col frn, 11pl, pep)	MacMillan	1924	Barnhart, N.	25-40	*
Thackeray, L.	Light Side of Egypt (1st, ob4to, ibds, unpag, 36cp)	L: A&C Black	1908	Thackeray, L.	80-125	
Thackeray, Wm.	Ballads & Songs (1st, 12mo, AEG, 276p, red/gilt)	L: Cassell	1896	Brock, H.M.	65-80	
Thackeray, Wm.	Chronicle of the Drum (1st, 4to, AEG, 70p, brown cl, 32pl)	Scribner	1882	Various	125-165	
Thackeray, Wm.	History of Henry Esmond (1st, AEG, 50 illus)	L: MacMillan	1905	Thomson, H.	50-80	
Thackeray, Wm.	Rose & the Ring (lg8vo, 159p, green cl, col frn, 12pl, pep)	Stokes	[1910]	Browne, G.	45-70	
Thackeray, Wm.	Rose & the Ring (1st AM, 4to, red/gilt, 128p, 12 ticp, pep)	Crowell	[1911]	Monsell, J.R.	80-115	
Thackeray, Wm.	Rose & the Ring (1st, sq8vo, 128p, gilt, teg, 12 ticp, pep)	L: Kegan Paul	1911	Monsell, J.R.	100-145	
Thackeray, Wm.	Rose & the Ring (4to, 161p, p-o, color)	Brentano's	[1920]	Tinker, J.H.	65-80	
Thackeray, Wm.	Vanity Fair (1st, 4to, p-o, teg, gilt, 20 ticp)	L: Hodder	(1913)	Baumer, L.	100-140	*
Thanet, O.	Adventure in Photography (1st, 12mo, photos, cvr by...)	Scribner	1893	Armstrong, M.	60-80	
Thanet, O.	Heart of Toil (1st, 8vo, teg, 215p, cvr by...)	Scribner	1898	Armstrong, M.	35-50	*
Thanet, O.	Heart of Toil (1st, 8vo, teg, 215p, 24pl by...)	Scribner	1898	Frost, A.B.	35-50	*
Thanet, O.	Man of the Hour (1st, 12mo, green/gilt, 477p)	Bobbs-Merrill	(1905)	Armstrong, M.	25-40	
Thanet, O.	Missionary Sheriff (1st, 12mo, 248p, blue/gilt, 15pl)	Harper	1897	Frost/Carleton	30-45	
Thanet, O.	Slave to Duty (1st, 12mo, 221p, teg, frn by...)	H. Stone	1898	Oakley, V.	60-80	
Thaxter, Cellia	Idyls and Pastorals (1st, 8vo, AEG, 58p, gilt, 24pl)	D. Lothrop	(1886)	Various	80-100	*
Thaxter, Cellia	Island Garden (1st, lg8vo, 126p, white/gilt, teg, col frn, b/w)	Houghton	1894	Hassam, C.	280-400	
Thayer, Jane	Mrs. Perrywinkle's Pets (1st, sm8vo, yell cl, 45p, 2-color, dep)	Wm. Morrow	1955	Galdone, P.	25-40	*
Thomas, Dorothy	Hi-Po the Hippo (1st {std}, folio, [48]p, ibds, color)	Random	(1942)	Gannett, R.C.	90-130	*
Thomas, E.M.	Babes of the Nations (1st, lg8vo, ibds, 12cp)	Stokes	1889	Humphrey, M.	400-600	
Thomas, E.M.	Children of Spring (4to, wraps, 3 chromos)	Stokes	1888	Humphrey, M.	300-450	*
Thomas, E.M.	In Sunshine Land (1st, 8vo, tan/silver, 152p, b/w pl, cep)	Houghton	1894	Pyle, Kath.	50-70	
Thomas, E.M.	Songs/Jingles/Rhymes (1st, 4to, p-o, 251p, b/w)	Stokes	(1894)	Humphrey, M.	250-350	
Thomas, E.M.	Tiny Folk of Sunny Days (1st, lg8vo, unpag, 6cp)	Stokes	1889	Humphrey, M.	250-400	*
Thomas, E.M.	Tiny Folk of Wintery Days (1st, lg8vo, cloth, unpag, 6cp)	Stokes	1889	Humphrey, M.	350-500	
Thomas, E.M.	Winter Swallow... (1st, 8vo, 120p, p-o, green/gilt, cvr by...)	Scribner	1896	Armstrong, M.	30-45	*
Thomas, Marg. L.	Geo. Washington Lincoln Goes Around/World (1st, 8vo, p-o, 205p)	NY: T. Nelson	(1927)	Pogany, W.	65-100	*
Thomason, J.W.	Fix Bayonets (1st, lg8vo, 245p, bds, col frn)	Scribner	1926	Thomason, J.W.	35-60	
Thompson, B.J.	Bible Children... (1st {std}, sm4to, ibds, [32]p, color, DJ)	Dodd	(1937)	Seredy, K.	35-50	
Thompson, B.J.	Candle Burns for France (1st, 12mo, 80p, col frn, DJ)	Bruce	(1946)	Seredy, K.	35-50	
Thompson, B.J.	Golden Trumpets (1st, sm8vo, 163p, blue/gilt, 2-color)	MacMillan	1927	Torrey, H.M.	25-40	
Thompson, C.M.	Calico Cat (1st, 12mo, green/gilt, 228p, 8pl)	Houghton	1908	Gruger, F.R.	25-40	*
Thompson, Dorothy	Once on Christmas (1st, 16mo, ipcb, [44]p, pep, b/w)	NY: OUP	1938	Lenski, L.	20-30	
Thompson, J.M.	Over Indian/Animal Trails (1st, 8vo, gilt, p-o, 263p, 8cp)	Stokes	(1918)	Bransom, P.	35-50	*
Thompson, K.L.	Ameliaranne at the Zoo (1st AM, 8vo, p-o)	McKay	[1920]	Pearse, S.B.	45-60	
Thompson, Kay	Eloise (1st {std}, 4to, 65p, white cloth, color, pep)	Simon/Schuster	1955	Knight, H.	100-150	*
Thompson, Kay	Eloise at Christmastime (1st {std}, 4to, red ibds, [52]p, col)	Random	(1958)	Knight, H.	120-160	
Thompson, Kay	Eloise in Moscow (1st {std}, 4to, [66]p, ibds, pep, color)	Simon/Schuster	1959	Knight, H.	120-165	
Thompson, Kay	Eloise in Paris (1st {std}, 4to, red pcb, [65]p, pep)	Simon/Schuster	1957	Knight, H.	130-165	
Thompson, Mary W.	Blueberry Muffin (1st {std}, sm8vo, 248p, b/w)	Longmans	(1942)	Berry, E.	20-40	*
Thompson, Maurice	Alice of Old Vincennes (1st [1], 8vo, 419p, green/gilt, 6pl)	Bobbs-Merrill	(1900)	Yohn, F.C.	25-40	
Thompson, Maurice	Rosalynde's Lovers (1st, 8vo, p-o, 249p, 11pl, dep)	Bowen-Merrill	1901	Peirson, G.	20-25	
Thompson, R.P.	Captain Salt in Oz (1st, 8vo, 306p, blue cl, p-o, b/w, pep)	Reilly/Lee	(1936)	Neill, J.R.	230-300	
Thompson, R.P.	Cowardly Lion of Oz (1st [1], lg8vo, 291p, p-o, pep, 12cp)	Reilly/Lee	(1923)	Neill, J.R.	250-400	
Thompson, R.P.	Curious Cruise of Captain Santa (1st, sq8vo, 124p, p-o, color)	Reilly/Lee	(1926)	Neill, J.R.	250-350	
Thompson, R.P.	Giant Horse of Oz (1st, lg8vo, 283p, p-o, brown cl, pep, 12cp)	Reilly/Lee	(1928)	Neill, J.R.	240-320	
Thompson, R.P.	Gnome King of Oz (1st, lg8vo, 282p, p-o, green cl, pep, 12cp)	Reilly/Lee	(1927)	Neill, J.R.	250-400	

AUTHOR: 132

AUTHOR	TITLE	PUBLISHER	DATE	ARTIST	PRICE	LC
Thompson, R.P.	Grampa in Oz (1st, lg8vo, 271p, 12cp, p-o)	Reilly/Lee	(1924)	Neill, J.R.	200-300	
Thompson, R.P.	Handy Mandy in Oz (1st, 4to, 246p, blue cl, p-o, pep)	Reilly/Lee	(1937)	Neill, J.R.	280-400	
Thompson, R.P.	Hungry Tiger of Oz (1st, 8vo, p-o, 261p, 12cp, pep)	Reilly/Lee	(1926)	Neill, J.R.	230-300	
Thompson, R.P.	Jack Pumpkinhead of Oz (1st, 8vo, 252p p-o, 12cp, pep)	Reilly/Lee	(1929)	Neill, J.R.	260-320	
Thompson, R.P.	Kabumpo in Oz (1st, lg8vo, blue cl, 297p, p-o, 12cp, pep)	Reilly/Lee	(1922)	Neill, J.R.	250-400	
Thompson, R.P.	King Kojo (1st, 8vo, red cl, p-o, 239p, 8cp, pep)	McKay	(1938)	Marge	170-250	*
Thompson, R.P.	Lost King of Oz (1st, 8vo, p-o, 280p, 12cp, pep)	Reilly/Lee	(1925)	Neill, J.R.	200-240	
Thompson, R.P.	Ojo in Oz (1st, 8vo, p-o, 304p, red cl, 12cp, pep)	Reilly/Lee	(1933)	Neill, J.R.	200-265	
Thompson, R.P.	Ozoplanning/Wizard of Oz (1st, lg8vo, 272p, p-o, yellow cl, pep)	Reilly/Lee	(1939)	Neill, J.R.	250-350	
Thompson, R.P.	Perhappsy Chaps (1st [1st bk.], tall 8vo, ibds, color, pep)	Volland	(1918)	Henderson, A.	350-500	
Thompson, R.P.	Pirates in Oz (1st [1], 8vo, green cl, p-o, 280p, 12cp, pep)	Reilly/Lee	(1931)	Neill, J.R.	280-400	
Thompson, R.P.	Princess of Cozytown (1st, lg8vo, ibds, [96]p, color, pep)	Volland	(1922)	Scott, J.L.	130-180	
Thompson, R.P.	Purple Prince of Oz (1st [1], lg8vo, p-o, 281p, 12cp, pep)	Reilly/Lee	(1932)	Neill, J.R.	320-450	
Thompson, R.P.	Silver Princess of Oz (1st, lg8vo, 255p, orang cl, p-o, b/w, pep)	Reilly/Lee	(1938)	Neill, J.R.	300-400	
Thompson, R.P.	Speedy in Oz (1st, lg8vo, p-o, 298p, blue cl, 12cp, pep)	Reilly/Lee	(1934)	Neill, J.R.	280-400	
Thompson, R.P.	Wishing Horse of Oz (1st, 4to, grey cl, 298p, p-o, 12cp)	Reilly/Lee	(1935)	Neill, J.R.	275-400	
Thompson, R.P.	Wonder Book (1st, 4to, green cl, 217p, p-o, 7cp)	Reilly/Lee	(1929)	Donahey, Wm.	180-250	
Thompson, R.P.	Yellow Knight of Oz (1st, 8vo, 275p, grey cl, p-o, 12cp, pep)	Reilly/Lee	(1930)	Neill, J.R.	220-285	
Thomson, C.L.	Celtic Wonder World (1st, 8vo, 150p, b/w)	L: H. Marshall	1902	Conner, E.	60-80	
Thomson, C.L.	Selections from LeMorte Darthur (1st, 8vo, 240p)	L: H. Marshall	1902	Stratton, H.	50-75	*
Thomson, Hugh	Jack the Giant Killer (1st, sq8vo, [32]p, wraps, 16 color)	L: MacMillan	1898	Thomson, H.	170-300	
Thoreau, H.D.	Cape Cod (1st, 8vo, gilt, teg, 319p, cvr by...)	Crowell	(1908)	Armstrong, M.	50-75	
Thoreau, H.D.	Maine Woods (1st, 8vo, teg, 423p, green/gilt)	Crowell	(1909)	Armstrong, M.	45-65	*
Thoreau, H.D.	Men of Concord (1st, 4to, 255p, green/silver, 10cp, pep, DJ)	Houghton	1936	Wyeth, N.C.	145-180	
Thoreau, H.D.	Week Along/Concord & Merrimack Rivers (1st, 8vo, gilt)	Crowell	(1911)	Armstrong, M.	35-50	
Thornley (tr.)	Daphnis & Chloe (1st, 4to, 200p, gilt, buckram, 12cp)	L: G. Bles	1925	Austen, J.	90-135	
Thurber, J.	Further Fables/Our Time (1st {std}, 8vo, 174p, bds, gilt, b/w)	Simon/Schuster	1956	Thurber, J.	45-65	*
Thurber, J.	Great Quillow (1st, lg sq8vo, 54p, p-o, yellow cl, color, DJ)	Harcourt	(1944)	Lee, Doris	70-120	
Thurber, J.	Many Moons (1st, 4to, red cl, [47]p, color, pep, DJ, CM)	Harcourt	(1943)	Slobodkin, L.	125-160	R
Thurber, J.	Owl in the Attic (1st {std}, 8vo, 151p, yellow cl, b/w)	Harper	1931	Thurber, J.	100-130	R*
Thurber, J.	Thirteen Clocks (1st, 8vo, ibds, 124p, color, pep)	Simon/Schuster	(1950)	Simont, M.	65-80	R
Thurber, J.	White Deer (1st, 8vo, green cl, 115p, color, DJ)	Harcourt	(1945)	Freeman, D.	70-100	
Thurber, J.	Wonderful O. (1st {std}, 8vo, bds, 72p, 2-color, dep, DJ)	Simon/Schuster	(1957)	Simont, M.	50-70	
Thurston, C.B.	Discontented Stuffed Cat (1st, 4to, ibds, b/w)	Saalfield	(1910)	Thurston, C.B.	65-80	*
Thurston, C.B.	Jingle of a Jap (1st, lg8vo, [64]p, p-o, color, pep)	Caldwell	(1906)	Thurston, C.B.	70-120	*
Thurston, E.T.	Open Window (1st, lg8vo, 287p, blue/gilt, 4cp)	L: Chapman	1913	Robinson, C.	85-130	*
Thurston, K.C.	The Mystics (1st, sm8vo, black/gilt, 191p, 8pl)	Harper	1907	Gibbs, G.	20-25	*
Thwaites, R.G.	Down Historic Waterways (1st, sm8vo, 300p, cvr by...)	McClurg	1902	Hazenplug, F.	60-80	*
Tietjens, E.	Boy of the Desert (1st, 8vo, 182p, green cl, dep, fp b/w)	Coward	1928	Hollingsworth, W.	25-40	*
Tietjens, E.	Boy of the South Seas (1st, 8vo, 193p, 20 fp b/w, pep, NH)	Coward	(1931)	Sheldon, M.	45-60	*
Tietjens, E.	Gingerbread Boy (1st, 16mo, ipcb, [57]p, color, pep)	Whitman	(1932)	Jordan, N.	30-45	*
Tietjens, E.& J.	Jaw Breaker's Alphabet (1st, ob4to, ibds, [111]p, b/w, dep)	A.& C. Boni	1930	Post, H.	60-80	*
Tileston, M.W.	Chiquita (1st, 12mo, orange cl, 306p, col frn, 7pl)	Merrill	1902	(Photos)	25-45	
Tileston, M.W.	Sugar & Spice/All That's Nice (1st, 8vo, red/gilt, 220p, 4cp)	Little/Brown	1928	Davis, M.	30-45	
Tileston, M.W.	Sugar & Spice/All that's Nice (1st, 12mo, red/gilt, 239p, b/w)	Little/Brown	(1910)	Various	30-45	*
Tilney, F.C.	Robin Hood & his Merry Outlaws (12mo, grn/gilt, 128p, p-o, 8cp)	Dent/Dutton	[1899]	Railton, I.	30-50	*
Tilton, D.	Miss Petticoats (1st, 8vo, tan cl, teg, 7cp)	C.M. Clark	1902	Stephens, C.H.	15-25	
Timlin, W.M.	Ship that Sailed to Mars (1st, lg4to, 48p, ibds, 48 ticp)	L: Harrap	(1923)	Timlin, W.M.	900-1100	
Tippett, James S.	Christmas Magic (1st, 16mo, ibds, [40]p, fp color, pep)	Grosset/Dunlap	(1944)	Sewell, H.	30-50	*
Tittle, W.	Colonial Holidays (1st, sm4to, 73p, p-o, 22cp)	Doubleday/Page	1910	Tittle, W.	60-80	
Tittle, W.	First Nantuckett Tea-Party (1st, 4to, tan cl, p-o, 23cp)	Doubleday/Page	1907	Tittle, W.	45-70	
Tittle, W.	My Country (1st, lg4to, ipcb, color)	Tandy-Thomas	(1909)	Tittle, W.	65-100	*
Titus, Eve	Anatole & the Cat (1st, 4to, 32p, red cl, color, CH)	Whittlesey	(1957)	Galdone, P.	70-100	*
Titus, Eve	Basil of Baker Street (1st, 8vo, beige cl, 96p, b/w)	Whittlesey	(1958)	Galdone, P.	25-40	*
Todd, M.L.	Corona & Coronet (1st, 8vo, teg, 383p)	Houghton	1898	Rogers, B.	30-45	
Todd, Ruthven	Space Cat (1st, sm8vo, 69p, blue cl, fp b/w)	Scribner	(1952)	Galdone, P.	30-45	*
Todd, Ruthven	Space Cat Visits Venus (1st, sm8vo, 87p, fp b/w)	Scribner	(1955)	Galdone, P.	30-45	*
Toland, M.B.M.	Legend Laymone (1st, 4to, 61p, gilt, teg, 10pl, dep)	Lippincott	1890	Various	65-80	*
Tolkien, J.R.R.	Farmer Giles of Ham (1st, 8vo, 78p, orange cl, 2 fp color, pep)	L: Allen/Unwin	1949	Baynes, P.D.	150-200	
Tolkien, J.R.R.	Farmer Giles of Ham (1st AM, 8vo, blue cl, 79p, color)	Houghton	1950	Baynes, P.D.	130-180	*
Tolkien, J.R.R.	The Hobbit (1st AM, sm8vo, 310p, beige cl, 4cp, pep, DJ)	Houghton	1938	Tolkien, J.R.R.	350-500	
Tomkins, J.	Polar Bear Twins (1st, 8vo, 106p, cloth, b/w)	Stokes	1937	Wiese, K.	25-40	
Tomlins, W.	Child's Garden of Song (1st, lg8vo, 72p, red/gilt, color)	McClurg	1895	Ricketts, E.	100-150	
Tomlinson, E.	Jersey Boy in the Revolution (1st, 8vo, 428p, 4pl)	Houghton	1899	Schoonover, F.	30-45	
Tomlinson, E.	Scouting with Daniel Boone (1st, 8vo, 303p, green cl, 8pl)	Doubleday/Page	1914	Rockwell, N.	100-140	
Tomlinson, H.M.	Sea & the Jungle (1st, 8vo, 343p, green ipcb, woodcuts)	L: Duckworth	1930	Leighton, C.	45-60	*
Tompkins, Jane	Moo-Wee: The Musk-Ox (1st, 8vo, blue cl, 103p, 11 fp b/w, pep)	Stokes	1938	Wiese, K.	25-40	
Tompkins, Jane	Raccoon Twins (1st, 8vo, 126p, orange cl, b/w, pep)	Stokes	1942	Wiese, K.	25-45	*
Tompkins, Jane	Red Squirrel Twins (1st {std}, 8vo, tan cl, 123p, b/w)	Stokes	(1950)	Wiese, K.	25-40	*
Tompkins, Jane	Storks Fly Home (1st {std}, sm8vo, [58]p, col frn, b/w)	Stokes	(1943)	Gergely, T.	35-50	*
Toogood, C.C.	Child's Prayer (1st, lg8vo, [16]p, blue/gilt, col frn)	McKay	(1925)	Smith, J.W.	35-50	*
Toon, G.E.	Animal Story Book (1st, folio, 63p, ibds, 12cp)	Saalfield	(1928)	Burd, C.M.	30-50	

AUTHOR	TITLE	PUBLISHER	DATE	ARTIST	PRICE	LC
Toon, G.E.	Ducky Dee (4to, ibds, 8cp)	Saalfield	1928	Burd, C.M.	30-45	*
Tooze, Ruth	America (1st, lg8vo, 31p, cloth, color)	Viking	1953	Angelo, V.	35-50	*
Topelius, Z.	Canute Whistlewinks... (1st {std}, 8vo, 272p, orang cl, 5cp, dep)	NY: Longmans	1927	McIntosh, F.	40-60	
Torjesen, Eliz.	Captain Ramsay's Daughter (1st, 8vo, 223p, blue cl, fp b/w, pep)	Lothrop/Lee	(1953)	Adams, A.	30-50	*
Torrey, M.	Artie & the Princess (1st, lg8vo, 107p, green cl, 5cp, pep)	Howell/Soskin	(1945)	Torrey, M.	20-35	*
Torrey, M.	Merriweathers (1st, 8vo, 254p)	Viking	1949	Torrey, M.	30-45	*
Torrey, M.	Penny (1st, tall 8vo, 126p, color)	Howell/Soskin	1944	Torrey, M.	25-40	
Torrey, M.	Three Little Chipmunks (1st, 4to, ipcb, [40]p, color, pep)	Grosset/Dunlap	(1947)	Torrey, M.	30-45	*
Totheroh, D.	David Hotfoot (1st, 8vo, p-o, 246p, col frn, 4pl)	Doran	(1926)	Day, M.	25-40	
Tousey, S.	Bob & the Railroad (1st {std}, 8vo, ibds, 53p, pep, color)	Doubleday/Dor.	1941	Tousey, S.	30-45	*
Tousey, S.	Buffalo Bill (1st, 8vo, [36]p, map, ibds, color, pep)	Rand/McNally	1938	Tousey, S.	25-40	
Tousey, S.	Chinky Joins the Circus (1st {std}, lg ob8vo, [56]p, ibds, col)	Doubleday/Dor.	1938	Tousey, S.	25-40	
Tousey, S.	Chinky: Banker Pony (1st {std}, ob8vo, ibds, [56]p, color, pep)	Doubleday/Dor.	1937	Tousey, S.	35-50	
Tousey, S.	Cowboy Tommy (1st {std}, ob8vo, ibds, [56]p, pep, color)	Doubleday/Dor.	1932	Tousey, S.	30-45	
Tousey, S.	Cowboy Tommy's Roundup (1st {std}, ob8vo, [56]p, pep, color)	Doubleday/Dor.	1934	Tousey, S.	35-50	*
Tousey, S.	Cowboys of America (1st, 8vo, [36]p, ibds, color)	Rand/McNally	1937	Tousey, S.	25-40	
Tousey, S.	Daniel Boone (1st, 8vo, [36]p, map, color)	Rand/McNally	1939	Tousey, S.	30-45	*
Tousey, S.	Davy Crockett (1st, sm4to, 48p, cloth, p-o, color)	Whitman	1948	Tousey, S.	25-40	
Tousey, S.	Dick & the Canal Boat (1st {std}, lg8vo, [41]p, ipcb, color)	Doubleday/Dor.	1943	Tousey, S.	25-40	
Tousey, S.	Fisherman Tommy (1st, 4to, 47p, pep, color)	Houghton	1940	Tousey, S.	30-45	*
Tousey, S.	Indians & Cowboys (1st, 8vo, [76]p, color, pep)	Rand/McNally	(1940)	Tousey, S.	25-40	
Tousey, S.	Indians of the Plains (1st, 8vo, ipcb, [36]p, 1-color)	Rand/McNally	1940	Tousey, S.	30-45	*
Tousey, S.	Jerry & Pony Express (1st {std}, ob8vo, [56]p, pep, color)	Doubleday/Dor.	1936	Tousey, S.	30-45	*
Tousey, S.	Little Bear's Pinto Pony (1st, lg8vo, 29p, p-o, col frn)	Whitman	1943	Tousey, S.	25-40	
Tousey, S.	Lumberjack Bill (1st, 4to, blue cl, 47p, color, pep)	Houghton	1943	Tousey, S.	35-50	*
Tousey, S.	Steamboat Billy (1st {std}, ob8vo, ibds, [56]p, color, pep)	Doubleday/Dor.	1935	Tousey, S.	45-60	
Towers, Alton	Billy Bunce... (1st, 4to, ibds, unpag, 17cp)	L: A. Cooke	(1907)	Rountree, H.	200-300	
Towers, Alton	Bunny & Bobbie (1st, 4to, unpag)	Cooke/Stokes	[1907]	Various	70-100	*
Towers, Alton	Child's Aesop (1st AM, 16mo, red cl, 117p, color)	Stokes	[1902]	Billinghurst, P.	65-100	*
Towne, C.H.	Rise & Fall of Prohibition (1st, sm8vo, blue/gilt, 220p, 4pl)	MacMillan	1923	Newell, P.	50-80	
Towne, Rbt. D.	Teddy Bears Come to Life (1st, 12mo, ibds, unpag, color)	Reilly/Britton	(1907)	Bray, J.R.	70-100	*
Towne, Rbt. D.	Teddy Bears in Hot Water (1st, sm8vo, ibds, unpag, color)	Reilly/Britton	(1907)	Sieber, C.A.	70-100	
Towne, Rbt. D.	Teddy Bears in a Smashup (1st, 12mo, [16]p, color)	Reilly/Britton	(1907)	Sieber, C.A.	65-90	*
Towne, Rbt. D.	Teddy Bears on a Lark (1st, 12mo, [16]p, color)	Reilly/Britton	(1907)	Sieber, C.A.	65-80	
Towne, Rbt. D.	Teddy Bears on a Tobaggon (1st, 12mo, [12]p, color)	Reilly/Britton	(1907)	Bray, J.R.	65-90	*
Townsend, R.	Journey to the Garden Gate (1st, 4to, p-o, gilt, 127p, 8cp, pep)	Houghton	1919	Winter, M.	50-80	
Tracy, Edward B.	King of the Stallions (1st, 8vo, orange cl, 241p, b/w, DJ)	Dodd	1947	Brown, Paul	35-50	
Tracy, Louis	American Emperor (1st AM, 8vo, tan/gilt, 16pl)	Putnam	1897	Hope, E.S.	60-75	
Tracy, Louis	Final War (1st, sq8vo, 372p, grey/gilt, 16pl)	L: C. Pearson	1896	Sherie, E.F.	25-40	*
Tracy, Louis	Lost Provinces (1st, 8vo, 380p, olive/gilt, 12pl)	L: C. Pearson	1898	Piffard, H.	45-60	*
Tracy, Louis	The Invaders (1st, 8vo, maroon cl, 428p, 4pl)	L: C. Pearson	1901	Wood, Lawson	65-80	*
Tracy, Louis	Wings of the Morning (1st, lg8vo, black/gilt, 320p, teg, 12cp)	E.J. Clode	(1924)	Schaeffer, M.	30-45	
Tracy, Louis	Wings of the Morning (lg8vo, 319p, cp)	Winston	[1927]	Schaeffer, M.	30-45	
Travers, Georgia	Wily Woodchucks (1st, ob4to, [32]p, color, DJ)	Coward	(1946)	Gag, Flavia	30-50	
Travers, P.L.	Fox at the Manger (1st, 8vo, blue cl)	L: Collins	1942	Bewick, T.	50-65	*
Travers, P.L.	Mary Poppins (1st AM, 12mo, 206p, blue cl, b/w, pep, DJ)	Reynal/Hitch.	(1934)	Shepard, M.	200-320	R
Travers, P.L.	Mary Poppins Comes Back (1st AM, 12mo, 268p, green cl, b/w, pep)	Reynal/Hitch.	(1935)	Shepard, M.	130-165	
Travers, P.L.	Mary Poppins Comes Back (1st, sm8vo, 303p, beige cl, b/w, DJ)	L: Lovat/Dicks	(1935)	Shepard, M.	250-350	
Travers, P.L.	Mary Poppins Opens the Door (1st AM, sm8vo, 239p, grey cl, b/w)	Reynal/Hitch.	(1943)	Shepard/Sims	70-115	*
Travers, P.L.	Mary Poppins in the Park (1st AM {std}, 12mo, 235p, b/w, dep)	Harcourt	(1952)	Shepard, M.	70-100	*
Trease, G.	Secret Fiord (1st AM {std}, sm8vo, 241p)	Harcourt	(1950)	Krush, J.	25-45	*
Trease, G.	Trumpets in the West (1st AM {std}, sm8vo, 239p)	Harcourt	(1947)	Krush, J.	30-45	*
Treffinger, C.	Jimmy's Shoes (1st, 12mo, red cl, 219p, pep, 3pl)	Penn	(1934)	Collings, R.C.	30-45	*
Treffinger, C.	Li Lun: Lad of Courage (1st, 8vo, 93p, grn cl, 1-color, pep, NH)	Abingdon/Coke.	(1947)	Wiese, K.	40-65	*
Treffinger, C.	Rag Doll Jane (1st, lg4to, ibds, 12cp)	Saalfield	(1930)	Peat, F.B.	65-80	
Tregarthen, Enys	Doll Who Came Alive (1st, sq12mo, 75p, fp 3-color)	NY: J. Day	(1942)	Unwin, N.S.	45-65	*
Trent, R.	First Christmas (1st, 12mo, ipcb, [32]p, color, pep)	Harper	1948	Simont, M.	35-50	*
Trent, R.	To Church We Go (1st, sm4to, [28]p, color)	Wilcox/Follett	1948	Anglund, J.W.	70-100	*
Trent, R.	To Church We Go (1st {this artist}, 4to, [32]p, ibds, 1-color)	Follett	(1956)	Jones, E.O.	25-45	*
Tresselt, A.R.	Autumn Harvest (1st, sm4to, ipcb, [25]p, color, pep)	Lothrop/Lee	1951	Duvoisin, R.	20-35	*
Tresselt, A.R.	Follow the Road (1st, 4to, unpag, color)	Lothrop/Lee	1953	Duvoisin, R.	35-50	*
Tresselt, A.R.	Follow the Wind (1st, 4to, color, [26]p)	Lothrop/Lee	(1950)	Duvoisin, R.	35-50	*
Tresselt, A.R.	Frog in the Well (1st, sm4to, green cl, [32]p, color, pep)	Lothrop/Lee	1958	Duvoisin, R.	35-50	*
Tresselt, A.R.	Rain Drop Splash (1st, 4to, [29]p, ipcb, color, pep, CH)	Lothrop/Lee	(1946)	Weisgard, L.	60-90	*
Tresselt, A.R.	Sun Up (1st, 4to, ibds, pep, [25]p, color)	Lothrop/Lee	1949	Duvoisin, R.	45-60	*
Tresselt, A.R.	White Snow, Bright Snow (1st, 4to, 33p, color, DJ, CM)	Lothrop/Lee	(1947)	Duvoisin, R.	75-100	
Trimpey, Alice	Story of My Dolls (1st, 4to, 76p, ibds, b/w, pep)	Whitman	1935	Scott, J.L.	60-85	*
Trine, Ralph W.	In Tune with the Infinite (1st, 8vo, ibds, 254p, 8 ticp)	L: Foulis	(1926)	Robinson, F.C.	70-100	*
Tripp, E.	Tin Fiddle (1st, ob4to, pink cl, unpag, brown illus, cep)	NY: OUP	1954	Sendak, M.	160-200	R
Tripp, Paul	Tale of Tubby the Tuba (1st, ob8vo, ibds, [26]p, color, pep)	Vanguard Pr.	(1948)	Maas, G.	65-90	*
Tschiffely, A.F.	Tale of Two Horses (1st AM, 8vo, 220p, pep, b/w)	Simon/Schuster	1935	Wiese, K.	30-45	*
Tucker, E.S.	Baby Folk (1st, 4to, [26]p, ibds, 6cp)	Stokes	(1898)	Humphrey, M.	180-250	*

AUTHOR	TITLE	PUBLISHER	DATE	ARTIST	PRICE	LC
Tucker, E.S.	Baby and Me! (4to, [13]p, ibds)	Worthington	[1890]	6 Chromos	80-130	*
Tucker, E.S.	Bubbles (4to, 12p, ibds, 6cp)	Worthington	(1892)	Tucker, E.S.	75-120	
Tucker, E.S.	Cats & Kittens (1st, lg4to, ibds, 6cp)	Stokes	1895	Boston, F.J.	120-180	*
Tucker, E.S.	Children of Colonial Days (1st, lg4to, [50]p, 12cp)	Stokes	1894	Moran, E.P.	150-220	*
Tucker, E.S.	Cup of Tea (ob4to, 22p, ibds, chromos)	Worthington	1892	Tucker, E.S.	120-165	
Tucker, E.S.	Favorite Pets (1st, 4to, ibds, 12cp)	Stokes	1893	Tucker, E.S.	100-130	
Tucker, E.S.	Little Belles & Beaux (1st, lg4to, ibds, 6cp)	Stokes	1896	Brundage, F.	140-220	
Tucker, E.S.	Little Grown-Ups (1st, 4to, ibds, 12cp)	Stokes	1897	Humphrey, M.	400-600	
Tucker, E.S.	Little Grown-Ups (1st UK, 4to, ibds, 12cp)	L: Wells/Gard.	1897	Humphrey, M.	300-450	*
Tucker, E.S.	Little Men & Maids (1st, 4to, ibds, [26]p, 6cp)	Stokes	1898	Brundage, F.	150-240	*
Tucker, E.S.	Littlest Ones (1st, lg4to, ibds, 12cp)	Stokes	1898	Humphrey, M.	350-500	
Tucker, E.S.	Make-Believe Men & Women (1st, 4to, [26]p, ibds, 6cp)	Stokes	1897	Humphrey, M.	380-500	
Tucker, E.S.	Old Youngsters (1st, lg4to, ibds, unpag, 6cp)	Stokes	1897	Humphrey, M.	300-400	
Tucker, E.S.	Rhymes & Stories of Olden Times (1st, lg4to, ibds, [26]p, 6cp)	Stokes	1894	Moran, E.P.	120-165	*
Tucker, E.S.	Royal Little People (1st, 4to, unpag, ibds, 12cp)	Stokes	(1895)	Tucker, E.S.	100-150	
Tudor, T.	1 Is One (1st, ob4to, unpag, pep, pink cl, color, CH)	NY: OUP	1956	Tudor, T.	100-145	*
Tudor, T.	A is for Annabelle (1st, ob4to, unpag, grn/gilt, 27 color, pep)	NY: OUP	1954	Tudor, T.	100-150	*
Tudor, T.	Alexander the Gander (1st, 24mo, green cl, [47]p, color, pep)	OUP	(1939)	Tudor, T.	150-200	*
Tudor, T.	Amanda & the Bear (1st, 12mo, unpag, p-o, blue cl, color, dep)	NY: OUP	1951	Tudor, T.	90-135	*
Tudor, T.	Around the Year (1st, lg ob8vo, [54]p, cloth, color)	NY: OUP	1957	Tudor, T.	100-150	
Tudor, T.	Becky's Birthday (1st, 4to, yellow cl, color)	Viking	(1960)	Tudor, T.	120-165	*
Tudor, T.	County Fair (1st, 24mo, [47]p, red/white, pep, color, DJ)	L: OUP	1940	Tudor, T.	120-150	
Tudor, T.	Doll's Christmas (1st, sq12mo, red cl, [29]p, pep, p-o, color)	NY: OUP	1950	Tudor, T.	120-160	
Tudor, T.	Dorcas Porcas (1st, 24mo, [35]p, orang cl, color, DJ)	NY: OUP	(1942)	Tudor, T.	250-400	
Tudor, T.	Edgar Allan Crow (1st, sq12mo, p-o, unpag, fp color, DJ)	OUP	1953	Tudor, T.	180-220	
Tudor, T.	Linsey Woolsey (1st, sq24mo, [43]p, yellow bds, color)	NY: OUP	1946	Tudor, T.	160-200	*
Tudor, T.	Pumpkin Moonshine (1st, 24mo, blue cl, [41]p, color, pep)	OUP	(1938)	Tudor, T.	160-240	*
Tudor, T.	Snow Before Christmas (1st, sq12mo, [37]p, pep, p-o, color)	NY: OUP	(1941)	Tudor, T.	100-165	
Tudor, T.	Tale for Easter (1st, sq12mo, [33]p, dep, p-o, color)	NY: OUP	(1941)	Tudor, T.	90-130	*
Tudor, T.	Thistly B. (1st, sq12mo, [27]p, red bds, p-o, color)	NY: OUP	1949	Tudor, T.	130-165	*
Tudor, T.	White Goose (1st, sq12mo, grey cl, p-o, [27]p, color)	OUP	(1943)	Tudor, T.	140-175	
Tunis, Edwin	Oars & Sails (1st {std}, lg4to, 78p, ivory cl, b/w)	World Pub. Co.	(1952)	Tunis, E.	80-130	R*
Tunis, John R.	World Series (1st, sm8vo, 318p, blue cl, 24pl, pep)	Harcourt	(1941)	Barnum, J.H.	25-40	*
Turner, Josie	Elsie Dinsmore on the Loose (1st, sm8vo, 166p)	Cape/Smith	(1930)	Kelley, E.	30-45	*
Turner, N.B.	Magpie Lane (1st, sm8vo, 88p, orang cl, silhouettes, dep)	Harcourt	(1927)	Merwin, D.	25-45	*
Turner, N.B.	Ray Coon to the Rescue (1st, 8vo, 80p, ipcb, b/w, pep)	Rand/McNally	(1931)	Ward, Keith	45-70	*
Turner, N.B.	When it Rained Cats & Dogs (1st {std}, 4to, ibds, [32]p, color)	Lippincott	(1946)	Gergely, T.	65-80	R
Turner, N.B.	Zodiac Town (1st, 8vo, 131p, gilt, 13 b/w, pep)	Atl. Month Pr.	(1921)	Bromhall, W.	35-50	
Turner, Thyra	Christmas House... (1st, 12mo, ibds, 25p, 14 color, DJ)	Scribner	1943	Gag, Flavia	70-100	
Turpin, Edna	Littling of Gaywood (1st, 12mo, 265p, pep, b/w)	Random	(1939)	Eichenberg, F.	30-45	*
Twain, M.	$30000 Bequest (1st, sm8vo, 522p, red cl, 8pl)	Harper	1906	Unknown	100-140	
Twain, M.	Adventures of Huckleberry Finn (1st, 4to, 346p, 8 ticp, box)	Heritage Press	(1940)	Rockwell, N.	80-100	
Twain, M.	Adventures of Tom Sawyer (1st, 8vo, 264p, p-o, 4cp, pep)	Winston	(1931)	Hurd, P.	35-50	*
Twain, M.	Adventures of Tom Sawyer (1st, 4to, 284p, 8 ticp, box)	Heritage Press	(1937)	Rockwell, N.	80-100	
Twain, M.	American Claimant (1st, 8vo, 279p, green/gilt)	Webster	1892	Beard, D.	180-230	
Twain, M.	Dog's Tale (1st AM, 8vo, 36p, 4cp)	Harper	1904	Smedley, W.T.	100-140	
Twain, M.	Double-Barrelled Detective Story (1st, 8vo, teg, uncut, 7pl)	Harper	1902	Hitchcock, L.	130-165	
Twain, M.	Eve's Diary (1st, 8vo, 109p, red cloth, b/w)	Harper	1906	Ralph, L.	100-150	
Twain, M.	Extracts from Adam's Diary (1st, 8vo, red cl, 89p)	Harper	1904	Strothmann, F.	80-110	
Twain, M.	Horse's Tale (1st, 8vo, red cl, 153p, 5pl)	Harper	1907	Hitchcock, L.	100-135	
Twain, M.	Huckleberry Finn (1st, 8vo, p-o, 421p, cp)	Harper	(1923)	Brehm, W.	25-45	*
Twain, M.	Jumping Frog (1st, 8vo, 65p, 11pl)	Harper	1903	Strothmann, F.	70-100	
Twain, M.	Mysterious Stranger (1st, 4to, 151p, gilt, teg, p-o, 7cp)	Harper	(1916)	Wyeth, N.C.	100-150	
Twain, M.	Prince & the Pauper (1st, 8vo, 296p, 7cp)	Harper	1909	Hatherell, W.	35-50	*
Twain, M.	Prince & the Pauper (1st, lg8vo, 284p, p-o, cp)	Harper	(1917)	Booth, F.	50-75	
Twain, M.	Prince & the Pauper (1st, 8vo, 274p, p-o, gilt, color, pep)	Winston	(1937)	Lawson, R.	45-65	
Twain, M.	St. Joan of Arc (1st, lg8vo, black/gilt, 32p, p-o, 4 ticp, pep)	Harper	(1919)	Pyle, H.	70-100	
Twain, M.	Tom Sawyer Abroad (1st, 8vo, 219p, white cl)	NY: Webster	1894	Beard, D.	375-450	
Tyler, Anna C.	Twenty-Four Unusual Stories (1st, 12mo, 328p, fp b/w)	Harcourt	1921	Petershams	45-60	*
Tyman, Loretta	Julio (1st, 8vo, beige cl, 176p, fp b/w)	Abelard	(1955)	Charlot, J.	45-65	*
Tynan, Kath.	Little Book of Courtesies (1st, 12mo, teg, 57p, gilt, col frn)	L: Dent	1906	Robinson, C.	70-100	
Tyrell, Eleanor	How I Tamed the Wild Squirrels (1st, sq8vo, 111p, pep, p-o, 6cp)	L: Nelson	[1918]	Appleton, H.C.	55-90	
Tyrell, Eleanor	More About the Squirrels (1st, sq8vo, 111p, pep, p-o, 6cp)	L: Nelson	[1918]	Appleton, H.C.	55-90	
Udry, J.M.	Moon Jumpers (1st, 4to, ibds, [31]p, 7 dp color, CH)	Harper	(1959)	Sendak, M.	250-400	*
Udry, J.M.	Theodore's Parents (1st, 4to, [30]p, green cl, color)	Lothrop/Lee	(1958)	Adams, A.	45-60	*
Udry, J.M.	Tree is Nice (1st, 4to, ibds, [30]p, fp color, CM)	Harper	1956	Simont, M.	70-100	R*
Uncle Frank	Uncle Frank's Visit to Fairy-Land (1st, 12mo, 244p, b/w)	Doub./McClure	1897	Stevens, W.D.	70-100	*
Uncle Milton	Bennie & Jennie (obsm4to, ibds, cp)	Cupples	1907	Wall, B.	65-80	
Underdown, E.	Gateway to Romance (1st, 4to, 299p, teg, 16cp)	L: Nelson	[1909]	Various	80-100	
Underdown, E.	Gateway to Spenser (1st, 8vo, 399p, 16cp)	L: Nelson	[1911]	Pape, F.	65-80	*
Underdown, E.	Stories from Chaucer (1st, 12mo, p-o, 157p, 8cp)	T. Nelson	1913	Anderson, A.	45-65	
Underhill (ed.)	Dwarf's Tailor... (1st, lg8vo, 260p, p-o by...)	Harper	(1924)	Gaze, H.	40-60	

AUTHOR	TITLE	PUBLISHER	DATE	ARTIST	PRICE	LC
Underhill, A.F.	Goochy Goggles... (1st, sm4to, [93]p, ibds, color)	McLoughlin	(1926)	Sturges, K.	50-80	*
Underwood, C.F.	American Types (1st, 4to, p-o, red cl, 16cp)	Stokes	(1912)	Underwood, C.F.	70-100	
Underwood, P.	When Christmas Comes Around (1st, 4to, ipcb, 26p, 6cp, pep)	Duffield	1915	Smith, J.W.	500-800	
Ungerer, Tomi	Crictor (1st, 4to, green ibds, 32p, 2-color)	Harper	(1958)	Ungerer, T.	65-90	R*
Ungerer, Tomi	Emile (1st, 4to, 32p, ibds, 2-color)	Harper	(1960)	Ungerer, T.	60-80	*
Ungerer, Tomi	Mellops Go Diving for Treasure (1st, 8vo, ibds, unpag, 2-color)	Harper	(1957)	Ungerer, T.	50-80	*
Ungerer, Tomi	Mellops Go Flying (1st, ob8vo, ibds, [32]p, 2-color)	Harper	(1957)	Ungerer, T.	60-100	R*
Unknown	Christmas Letter (1st, 12mo, 85p, 13pl)	Cupples	1902	Smith, Wuanita	40-60	
Unknown	Eric Prince of Lorlonia (1st, 8vo, gilt, AEG, 182p, 8cp)	L: MacMillan	1895	Woodward, A.B.	100-145	
Unknown	Infernal Marriage (1st, 85p, lg8vo, 5cp)	L: Jackson	1929	Austen, J.	140-170	
Unknown	Leather Bottel (1st, 16mo, pcb, 14p, uncut)	(Concord)	(1903)	Bradley, W.	80-100	
Unknown	Rule Britannia (4to, ibds, 66p, 8 fp color)	L: Hodder	[1916]	Robinson, C.	200-300	
Unknown	Soldiers of the King (4to, 66p, ibds, 8cp)	L: Hodder	[1916]	Robinson, C.	200-300	
Unknown	Stealers of Light (1st, 4to, blue/gilt, 190p, 2 ticp)	L: Hodder	1916	Dulac, E.	100-145	
Unknown	Wonders of Wilmington (lg4to, ibds, 5pl)	Hull	[n.d.]	Robinson, W.H.	300	
Untermeyer, L.	Book of Noble Thoughts (1st, 8vo, 121p, ibds, 1-color, dep)	A.A. Group	(1946)	Kent, R.	30-50	
Untermeyer, L.	Magic Circle (1st, sm8vo, 288p, fp b/w)	Harcourt	(1952)	Krush, B.& J.	30-45	*
Untermeyer, L.	New Songs for New Voices (1st, lg4to, 258p, pep)	Harcourt	(1928)	Bacon, P.	25-40	*
Unwin, Nora S.	Lucy & Little Red Horse (1st, 4to, bds, p-o, gilt, 8 fp color)	L: A. Moring	(1943)	Unwin, N.S.	45-60	
Upham, Eliz.	Little Brown Bear (1st, 4to, [58]p, 8 fp color, pep)	Platt/Munk	(1942)	Hartwell, M.	50-70	*
Upham, Eliz.	Little Brown Bear & His Friends (1st, 4to, unpag, col, pep, DJ)	Platt/Munk	(1952)	Hartwell, M.	40-60	
Upham, Eliz.	Little Brown Monkey (1st, 4to, [56]p, color, pep)	Platt/Munk	(1949)	Hartwell, M.	40-60	*
Upton, B.	Adventures of Two Dutch Dolls (1st, ob4to, 64p, ibds, 29cp)	Longmans	1898	Upton, F.	300-400	
Upton, B.	Golliwogg in Holland (1st, ob4to, ibds, 31 fp color, dep)	L: Longmans	1904	Upton, F.	250-350	R
Upton, B.	Golliwogg in War! (1st, ob4to, 65p, ibds, color)	L: Longmans	1899	Upton, F.	280-400	
Upton, B.	Golliwogg's Bicycle Club (1st, ob4to, ibds)	L: Longmans	1896	Upton, F.	240-285	
Upton, B.	Golliwogg's Christmas (1st, ob4to, 62p, ipcb, 31 fp color)	L: Longmans	1907	Upton, F.	185-225	
Upton, B.	Golliwogg's Circus (1st, ob4to, ibds, 31 fp color)	L: McLoughlin	1903	Upton, F.	250-350	R
Upton, B.	Golliwogg's Desert Island (1st, ob4to, ibds, 64p, color)	L: Longmans	1906	Upton, F.	180-230	
Upton, B.	Golliwogg's Fox Hunt (1st, ob4to, ipcb, 32 fp color)	Longmans	1905	Upton, F.	200-240	
Upton, B.	Golliwogg's Polar Advens. (ob4to, 63p, ibds, color)	L: Longmans	1900	Upton, F.	160-200	
Upton, B.	Two Dutch Dolls & Golliwogg (1st, ob4to, ibds, 64p, dep)	Longmans	1895	Upton, F.	240-320	
Upton, F.	Adventures of Borbee & Wisp (1st, sq4to, ibds, [67]p, 31 color)	L: Longmans	1908	Upton, F.	250-350	
Upton, F.	Golliwogg at Sea-Side (1st, ob4to, ibds, 63p)	L: Longmans	1898	Upton, F.	240-320	
Upton, F.	Golliwogg's Air-Ship (ob4to, ipcb, 65p)	L: Longmans	1902	Upton, F.	230-320	
Upton, F.	Golliwogg's Auto Go Cart (1st, ob4to, ibds, 66p)	L: Longmans	1901	Upton, F.	200-300	
Upton, F.	Vege-Men's Revenge (1st, ob4to, ibds, 63p, color)	L: Longmans	1897	Upton, F.	280-375	
Uttley, Alison	Adventures of Peter & Judy in Bunnyland (4to, ibds, 39p, 8cp)	L: Collins	[1935]	Young, L.	130-200	*
Uttley, Alison	Hare & the Easter Egg (1st, sq12mo, 80p, grn bds, 16 fp color)	L: Collins	(1952)	Tempest, M.	35-50	
Uttley, Alison	Knot Squirrel Tied (1st, 8vo, 101p, grey pcb, p-o, 23 col)	L: Collins	1937	Tempest, M.	45-60	
Uttley, Alison	Little Grey Rabbit & Weasels (1st, 80p, pcb, p-o, color, pep)	L: Collins	1947	Tempest, M.	45-60	
Uttley, Alison	Little Grey Rabbit's Christmas (1st, sq8vo, 104p, ibds, color)	L: Collins	1939	Tempest, M.	50-70	
Uttley, Alison	Moonshine & Magic (1st, 8vo, 208p, cloth, 8cp)	L: Faber	1932	Townshend, W.	30-45	
Uttley, Alison	Story of Fuzzypeg the Hedgehog (1st, 8vo, 98p, 23cp, pep)	L: Heinemann	1932	Tempest, M.	65-80	*
Uttley, Alison	Wise Owl's Story (1st, sm8vo, 108p, ipcb, p-o, pep)	L: Collins	1935	Tempest, M.	45-65	
Vaile, C.M.	Orcutt Girls (8vo, 316p, green cl)	Wilde	(1896)	Merrill, F.	20-25	
Van Deeser	How to Find Happyland (1st, p-o, AEG, 122p)	Putnam	1907	Storer, F.	45-60	
Van Derveer, H.	Little Slam Bang (1st, 8vo, 38p, color)	Volland	(1928)	Ransom, F.C.	35-50	*
Van Doren, M.	Transparent Tree (1st, 4to, ipcb, 87p, 2-color, pep)	Holt	(1940)	Van Doren, M.	65-90	R*
Van Dresser, J.	Jimsey (1st, 8vo, 90p, p-o, color)	Rand/McNally	(1925)	Gregory, D.L.	60-80	
Van Dyke, H.	Blue Flower (1st, 8vo, 298p, blue/gilt, teg, 3cp by...)	Scribner	1909	Pyle, H.	20-35	
Van Dyke, H.	Broken Soldier & Maid of France (1st, 8vo, 66p, blu/gilt, 2 ticp)	Harper	(1919)	Schoonover, F.	30-45	
Van Dyke, H.	Companionable Books (1st, 8vo, blue/gilt, 391p)	Scribner	1922	Armstrong, M.	20-40	
Van Dyke, H.	Days Off (1st, 12mo, teg, 322p, uncut)	Scribner	1907	Armstrong, M.	20-30	
Van Dyke, H.	First Christmas Tree (1st, 8vo, olive/gilt, 76p, teg, 4pl)	Scribner	1897	Pyle, H.	60-95	
Van Dyke, H.	Fisherman's Luck (1st [new ed.], 12mo, 285p, cvr by...)	Scribner	1905	Armstrong, M.	20-30	
Van Dyke, H.	Little Rivers (1st, 12mo, teg, 348p, uncut, blue/gilt)	Scribner	1903	Armstrong, M.	20-25	
Van Dyke, H.	Lost Boy (1st, 16mo, 69p, green/gilt, 3pl by...)	Harper	1914	Wyeth, N.C.	20-30	
Van Dyke, H.	Spirit of Christmas (1st, 8vo, 59p)	Scribner	1905	Armstrong, M.	45-60	
Van Dyke, H.	Story of the Other Wise Man (8vo, gold cl, 87p, designs by...)	Harper	(1907)	Monetti, E.	70-100	
Van Dyke, H.	Story of the Other Wise Man (1st, lg8vo, 72p, uncut, 8cp)	Harper	(1920)	Flannagan	45-60	
Van Dyke, H.	The Mansion (1st, 8vo, 45p, green/gilt, 2 ticp, pep)	Harper	1911	Green, E.S.	30-45	
Van Dyke, H.	Through South America (1st, 8vo, blue/gilt, 428p)	Crowell	(1912)	Armstrong, M.	50-70	
Van Dyke, H.	Unknown Quantity (1st, 12mo, teg, 370p, uncut)	Scribner	1912	Armstrong, M.	20-30	
Van Dyke, J.C.	Opal Sea (1st, sm8vo, 262p, green/gilt, cvr by...)	Scribner	1906	Armstrong, M.	30-45	*
Van Dyke, J.C.	Studies in Pictures (1st, 12mo, 136p, maroon/gilt)	Scribner	1907	Armstrong, M.	20-30	
Van Dyne, Edith	Aunt Jane's Nieces (1st, 12mo, p-o, 325p, 6pl)	Reilly/Britton	(1906)	Nelson, E.A.	200-300	
Van Dyne, Edith	Aunt Jane's Nieces Abroad (1st, 12mo, green cl, p-o, 5pl)	Reilly/Britton	(1906)	Nelson, E.A.	160-220	
Van Dyne, Edith	Flying Girl (1st [1], sm8vo, red cl, 232p, 4pl)	Reilly/Britton	(1911)	Nuyttens, J.P.	200-265	
Van Dyne, Edith	Flying Girl & her Chum (1st, 12mo, 313p, red cl, 4pl)	Reilly/Britton	(1912)	Nuyttens, J.P.	180-220	
Van Housen, Nita	Poogie & Sibella (1st, 8vo, green cl, 81p, 8 fp color)	Whitman	(1932)	Brock, Emma	25-40	*
Van Loon, H.W.	Elephant Up a Tree (1st, 8vo, 206p, 3cp)	Simon/Schuster	1933	Van Loon, H.	25-40	

AUTHOR	TITLE	PUBLISHER	DATE	ARTIST	PRICE	LC
Van Loon, H.W.	Folk Songs of Many Lands (1st, 4to, ibds, 96p)	Simon/Schuster	1938	Van Loon, H.	25-45	*
Van Loon, H.W.	History with a Match (1st, 4to, 126p, p-o, color)	McKay	1917	Van Loon, H.	45-70	*
Van Loon, H.W.	Message of the Bells (1st, 12mo, ibds, gilt, pep, 16p, color)	(Garden City)	(1942)	Van Loon, H.	45-60	*
Van Loon, H.W.	Story of Mankind (1st, lg8vo, 479p, p-o, NM, PPPa)	Boni/Liveright	(1921)	Van Loon, H.	50-80	
Van Loon, H.W.	Wilbur the Hat (1st, 4to, ibds, 110p, p-o, color, pep)	H.B. Liveright	(1925)	Van Loon, H.	80-100	
Van Millingen	Constantinople (1st, 4to, 282p, teg, tan/gilt, 63cp)	L: A&C Black	1906	Goble, W.	120-185	
Van Sickle, J.H.	Magic Key (1st, 12mo, blue cl, 270p, 10 fp b/w)	Houghton	(1931)	Perkins, L.F.	25-40	*
Van Sinderen, A.	Peter Makebelieve (1st, lg8vo, 65p, 5 fp color)	Yale U. Press	1945	Bacon, P.	50-70	*
Van Stockum, H.	Andries (1st, 8vo, 192p, grey cl, 1 dp color, fp b/w)	Viking	1942	Van Stockum, H.	30-45	*
Van Stockum, H.	Angel's Alphabet (1st, lg8vo, [64]p, ipcb, fp b/w)	Viking	1948	Van Stockum, H.	30-45	*
Van Stockum, H.	Cottage at Bantry Bay (1st, 8vo, 252p, pep)	Viking	1938	Van Stockum, H.	25-40	*
Van Stockum, H.	Day on Skates (1st {std}, ob4to, 40p, 8cp, pep, NH)	Harper	1934	Van Stockum, H.	50-80	*
Van Stockum, H.	France on the Run (1st, 8vo, 303p, pep)	Viking	1939	Van Stockum, H.	30-45	*
Van Stockum, H.	Gerrit & the Organ (1st, 8vo, 178p, col frn, fp b/w)	Viking	1943	Van Stockum, H.	25-40	*
Van Stockum, H.	Pageen (1st, 8vo, 268p, b/w, pep)	Viking	1941	Van Stockum, H.	30-45	*
Van Stockum, H.	Patsy & the Pup (1st, sm8vo, 82p, ipcb, fp b/w)	Viking	1950	Van Stockum, H.	30-45	*
Van Stockum, H.	The Mitchells (1st, 8vo, 246p)	Viking	1945	Van Stockum, H.	25-40	*
Van Sutphen, W.	Golfer's Alphabet (1st, 4to, ibds, 128p, 28pl)	Harper	1898	Frost, A.B.	250-400	
Van Valkenburgh, H.	Myself & I (1st, 12mo, [36]p, color)	Volland	(1918)	Unknown	30-50	*
Van Vrooman, M.	Shine (1st {std}, 12mo, 50p, ibds, b/w, pep)	Dutton	(1939)	Hogan, I.	50-80	*
Vance, Louis J.	Bronze Bell (1st, sm8vo, 361p, 4cp)	Dodd	1909	Fisher, H.	25-40	*
Vance, Marguerite	Paula (1st, 8vo, 223p, green cl, uncut, b/w, dep)	Dodd	1939	Angelo, V.	20-35	*
Various	Adventures of Odysseus (1st, 8vo, 227p, green/gilt, teg, 13pl)	Dutton	(1900)	Robinson, C.	165-220	
Various	Book of Modern Ballads (sm4to, AEG, gilt, 6 chromos)	Hildesheimer	[1890]	Havers, A.	85-120	*
Various	Brains & Bravery (1st, 8vo, 398p, green/gilt, 8pl)	L: Chambers	1903	Rackham, A.	150-200	*
Various	Legends from River & Mountain (1st, 8vo, 328p, b/w)	L: G. Allen	1896	Robinson, T.H.	75-100	
Various	Old Old Tales Retold (1st, ob4to, [108]p, blue/gilt, color, pep)	Volland	(1923)	Richardson, F.	100-170	
Various	Peep into Cat-Land (sq8vo, 32p, ibds)	L: Warne	1890	Howell, C.E.	70-100	
Various	Ruby Fairy Book (1st, 8vo, gilt, b/w)	L: Hutchinson	(1900)	Millar, H.R.	70-100	
Various	Sleepy-Song Book (1st AM, 4to, blue cl, p-o, 12cp, pep)	McBride	1915	Anderson, A.	100-165	
Various	Sleepy-Song Book (1st, 4to, ibds, p-o, 12cp, pep)	L: Harrap	(1915)	Anderson, A.	90-120	
Various	Sung Under the Silver Umbrella (1st, lg8vo, 211p, red cl, b/w)	MacMillan	1935	Lathrop, D.	35-50	*
Various	Told Under the Blue Umbrella (1st, 8vo, 161p, b/w)	MacMillan	1933	Davis, M.	25-40	*
Various	Told Under the Christmas Tree (1st {std}, 8vo, 304p, b/w)	MacMillan	1948	Petershams	35-50	*
Various	Told Under the Magic Umbrella (1st, lg8vo, 248p, b/w)	MacMillan	1939	Jones, E.O.	25-45	*
Various	Wayfarer's Love (1st, 8vo, green/gilt, uncut, cvr by...)	L: Constable	1904	Crane, W.	60-80	
Various	Whole Family (1st, 8vo, blue/gilt, 12pl)	Harper	1908	Stephens, A.B.	50-70	
Various	Wimp & the Woodle (1st, 4to, blue/gilt bds, 180p, 7cp, pep)	Suttonhouse	1935	Pogany, W.	130-180	R
Vassos, R.	Contempo (1st, lg4to, [50]p, woodcuts)	Dutton	1929	Vassos, J.	100-140	
Vassos, R.	Humanities (1st, lg4to, 140p, 24 fp b/w)	Dutton	1935	Vassos, J.	85-120	
Vassos, R.	Ultimo (1st, lg8vo, [52]p, ibds, 22pl)	Dutton	1930	Vassos, J.	90-130	
Vaughn, R.	Then & Now (1st, 8vo, 461p, black/gilt, 8pl)	(Minneap)	1900	Russell, C.M.	200-250	
Veale, E.	Bonny Birds (8vo, wraps, 16p, b/w)	Hubbard	(1896)	Cox, P.	35-60	*
Veale, E.	Captivating Stories/Animals (1st, 4to, yel cl, [96]p, 2-color)	Juvenile Pub.	(1908)	Cox, P.	150-225	
Veale, E.	Christmas Pudding (sm8vo, blue cl, p-o, 320p, b/w)	Caldwell	(1900)	Cox, P.	65-100	*
Veale, E.	Funny Foxes (8vo, 32p, wraps, b/w)	Hubbard	(1896)	Cox, P.	50	*
Velvin, E.	Rataplan.... (1st, sm8vo, red/gilt, 328p, p-o, 12cp)	Altemus	(1902)	Verbeek, G.	50-85	*
VerBeck, F.	Acrobatic Animals (1st, lg ob4to, ibds, [58]p, b/w)	R.H. Russell	1899	VerBeck, F.	160-200	
VerBeck, F.	Book of Bears (1st, lg4to, ibds, [85]p, color)	Lippincott	1906	VerBeck, F.	180-240	
VerBeck, F.	Hand-Book of Golf for Bears (1st, lg8vo, ipcb, [59]p, 1-color)	R.H. Russell	1900	VerBeck, F.	350-500	*
VerBeck, F.	The Dumpies (1st, ob4to, 119p)	R.H. Russell	1897	VerBeck, F.	100-150	
VerBeck, F.	Three Bears (1st, sm folio, [60]p)	R.H. Russell	(1899)	VerBeck, F.	300-500	*
VerBeck, F.	VerBeck's Bears in Mother Goose-Land (4to, gilt, bds, 3cp)	L: H. Milford	[1900]	VerBeck, F.	200-300	
Verne, Jules	20 Thousand Leagues... (1st, 4to, black cl, p-o, 4cp, pep, SC)	Scribner	1925	Aylward, W.J.	65-90	
Verne, Jules	Antarctic Mystery (1st AM, 8vo, 336p, red/silver, 17pl)	Lippincott	1899	Roux, G.	350-400	R
Verne, Jules	Michael Strogoff (1st, 4to, p-o, 397p, 9cp, pep, SC)	Scribner	1927	Wyeth, N.C.	150-200	
Verne, Jules	Mysterious Island (1st, sm4to, 493p, gilt, p-o, 14cp, pep, SC)	Scribner	1918	Wyeth, N.C.	165-220	
Vernede, R.E.	Fair Dominion (1st, 8vo, blue cl, teg, 293p, uncut, 12cp)	J. Pott	1911	Cuneo, C.	25-45	
Vetsch, Earnest	New Story/Little Black Sambo (12mo, grey bds, color)	Whitman	1926	Thurston, C.B.	90-120	
Vickers, V.C.	Google Book (1st, lg4to, p-o, 24cp)	L: Medici	(1931)	Vickers, V.C.	130-180	
Viele, H.K.	Heartbreak Hill (1st, 12mo, 330p, grey cl, p-o, 6cp, pep)	Duffield	1908	Rae, J.	25-40	*
Vincent, Kitty	Gin & Ginger (1st, 8vo, col frn, 19 fp b/w)	L: Bodley Head	1927	Fish, A.H.	65-80	*
Vinton, Iris	Flying Ebony (1st, sm8vo, 289p, olive cl, b/w)	Dodd	1947	Simont, M.	30-45	*
Voight, V.F.	Apple Tree Cottage (1st, sm8vo, green cl, b/w, cep)	Holiday House	(1949)	Wilkin, E.	20-25	*
Voight, V.F.	House in Robin Lane (1st, sm8vo, 220p, yellow, cl, b/w)	Holiday House	(1951)	Martinez, J.	20-25	*
Voight, V.F.	Lions in the Barn (1st, sm8vo, 95p, yellow cl, b/w, pep)	Holiday House	1955	Wiese, K.	20-30	*
Voight, V.F.	Rolling Show (1st, 8vo, 188p, red cl, b/w, cep)	Holiday House	1956	Wiese, K.	20-30	*
Voight, V.F.	Zeke & the Fisher-Cat (1st, 8vo, 201p, red cl, b/w, pep)	Holiday House	(1953)	McChesney, H.	20-30	*
Voltaire, J.F.	Candide (1st, 8vo, 111p, maroon/gilt)	Random	1930	Kent, R.	45-60	*
Von Gottschalck, O.	Innocent Industries (1st, lg4to, ibds, [50]p, b/w)	R.H. Russell	1903	Von Gottschalck	145-200	*
Von Hutten, B.	One Way Out (1st, 8vo, p-o, lavender cl, 4cp)	Dodd	1906	Fisher, H.	30-45	
Vorse, M.E.	Grubby Gets Clean (1st, 8vo, ipcb, [41]p, 1-color, cep)	W.R. Scott	1943	Blaisdell, E.W.	30-45	*

AUTHOR	TITLE	PUBLISHER	DATE	ARTIST	PRICE	LC
Vorse, M.E.	Skinny Gets Fat (1st, 8vo, ipcb, [41]p, 1-color, pep)	W.R. Scott	1940	Hogan, I.	45-60	*
Vorse, M.E.	Wakey Goes to Bed (1st, 8vo, ipcb, [41]p, brown illus, cep)	W.R. Scott	1941	Hogan, I.	45-60	*
Vorse, M.H.	Very Little Person (1st, 8vo, 163p, green/gilt, 8pl)	Houghton	1911	O'Neill, R.	35-50	*
Voss, R.	Sigurd Eckdel's Bride (1st, 8vo, 235p, 4pl)	Little/Brown	1900	Schoonover, F.	25-40	
Vredenberg, E.	Old Fairy Tales (4to, ibds, 104p, 8cp)	L: R. Tuck	[1912]	Brundage/Bowley	130-200	
Vredenburg, E.	Golden Locks & Pretty Frocks (8vo, ibds, p-o, 12cp)	L: R. Tuck	(1914)	Richardson, A.	160-200	*
Waddell, H.	Beasts & Saints (1st, 8vo, 151p, red cl, 6pl)	L: Constable	1934	Gibbings, R.	80-100	*
Wade, B.E.	Ant Ventures (1st, 8vo, green cl, p-o, 246p, 5cp, pep)	Rand/McNally	(1924)	Cady, H.	75-100	
Wade, B.E.	Garden in Pink (1st, lg8vo, p-o, blue cl, 12pl)	McClurg	1905	Perkins, L.F.	30-50	
Wade, B.E.	Magic Stone (1st, lg8vo, 254p, p-o, gilt, 7cp)	NY: Sully	1917	Carlson, G.	40-60	
Wadsworth, W.	Modern Story Book (1st, folio, 124p, color)	Rand/McNally	(1931)	Eger, R.C.	90-130	*
Wagner, R.	Parsifal (1st, 4to, [192]p, grey/gilt, 16 ticp, pep)	L: Harrap	(1912)	Pogany, W.	200-300	
Wagner, R.	Parsifal (1st AM, 4to, maroon/gilt, teg, 16 ticp, pep)	Crowell	(1912)	Pogany, W.	220-300	
Wagner, R.	Rhinegold & the Valkyrie (1st AM, lg8vo, 160p, 34 ticp, pep)	Doubleday/Page	1910	Rackham, A.	240-300	
Wagner, R.	Rhinegold & the Valkyrie (1st, 4to, 160p, gilt, 34 ticp, pep)	L: Heinemann	1910	Rackham, A.	300-400	
Wagner, R.	Seigfried... (1st, sm4to, 182p, tan/gilt, 30 ticp, pep)	L: Heinemann	1911	Rackham, A.	260-320	
Wagner, R.	Siegfried... (1st AM, sm4to, 182p, blue/gilt bds, 30 ticp)	Doubleday/Page	1911	Rackham, A.	220-275	
Wagner, R.	Tale of Lohengrin (1st, 4to, brown/gilt, 8 ticp, pep)	L: Harrap	(1913)	Pogany, W.	240-350	
Wagner, R.	Tale of Lohengrin (1st AM, grey/gilt, 4to, teg, 8 ticp)	Crowell	(1913)	Pogany, W.	200-350	
Wagner, R.	Tannhauser (1st, 4to, unpag, grey/gilt, 22 ticp)	L: Harrap	(1911)	Pogany, W.	180-240	
Wagner, R.	Tannhauser (1st AM, 4to, black/gilt, unpag, 22 ticp)	Brentano's	[1911]	Pogany, W.	140-200	
Wahlenberg, A.	Old Sweedish Fairy Tales (1st, lg8vo, p-o, 296p, pep, 8cp)	Penn	1925	Berkowitz, J.	60-80	
Wahlenberg, A.	Sweedish Fairy Tales (1st, sm8vo, 158p, 14pl)	McClurg	1901	Armstrong, H.M.	50-75	*
Wahn, J.& G.	Edgar, Runaway Elephant (1st, 4to, ipcb, [38]p, color)	W.R. Scott	(1941)	Wahn, J.& G.	65-80	*
Wain, L.	Big Dogs, Little Dogs, Cats & Kittens (1st, folio, color, gilt)	L/NY: R. Tuck	[1900]	Wain, L.	250-400	*
Wain, L.	Daddy Cat (1st AM, sm4to, 36p, ibds, color)	Dodge	[1915]	Wain, L.	250-400	*
Wain, L.	Funny Frolics (sm4to, [32]p, ibds, color frn)	L: Nister	[1900]	Wain, L.	140-175	
Wain, L.	Louis Wain's Baby Picture Book (1st, 4to, ibds, unpag, b/w)	L: Clarke	1903	Wain, L.	200-300	
Wain, L.	Louis Wain's Cats & Dogs (1st, lg4to, ibds)	L: R. Tuck	(1903)	Wain, L.	500-600	*
Wain, L.	Louis Wain's Children's Book (1st, 4to, ibds, 17pl)	L: Hutchinson	(1923)	Wain, L.	300-500	
Wain, L.	Louis Wain's Father Christmas (8vo, ibds, p-o, 5 ticp)	L: J.F. Shaw	(1912)	Wain, L.	350-500	
Wain, L.	Pussies & Puppies (1st, 4to, ibds, 96p, color & b/w)	L: Partridge	[1899]	Wain, L.	280-400	
Wain, L.	Somebody's Pussies (4to, ibds, 13cp)	L: R. Tuck	[1920]	Wain, L.	800-1000	
Walcott, E.A.	Blindfolded (1st, 8vo, tan cl, 400p, 8pl)	Bobbs-Merrill	(1906)	Stephens, A.B.	20-35	
Waldeck, T.	Jamba the Elephant (1st, 8vo, 224p, b/w)	Viking	1942	Wiese, K.	20-25	*
Waldstein, H.F.	We Three Kings (1st {std}, ob4to, [23]p, color)	Harper	(1944)	Rey, H.A.	80-120	*
Walford, L.B	Little Legacy (1st, 12mo, blue cl, 344p, teg, frn by...)	H. Stone	1899	Oakley, V.	70-90	
Walker, D.S.	Dream Boats (1st, lg8vo, 219p, 4cp, 16pl, pep, DJ)	Doubleday/Page	1918	Walker, D.S.	120-165	
Walker, D.S.	Sally's ABC (1st, 4to, [58]p, buckram, 2-color, pep, DJ)	Harcourt	1929	Walker, D.S.	120-160	
Walker, M.	Lady Hollyhock & her Friends (1st, sm4to, 153p, color)	Baker/Taylor	(1906)	Hunt, M.I.	70-100	*
Wallace, D.	Fur Trail Adventures (1st, 8vo, 320p, 7pl)	McClurg	1915	Deming, E.W.	30-45	
Wallace, E.K.	Quest of the Dream (1st, 12mo, teg, 292p, blue/gilt)	Putnam	1913	Armstrong, M.	20-30	
Wallace, Lew	Chariot Race of Ben-Hur (1st, lg8vo, 133p, uncut, teg, 4cp)	Harper	1908	Ivanowski, S.	25-40	
Wallace, Lew	First Christmas (1st, 8vo, 108p, teg, lavender/gilt, 4 tipl)	Harper	1902	(Photos)	30-50	
Wallace, Lew	Wooing of Malkatoon (1st, lg8vo, green/gilt, 168p, teg)	Harper	1898	DuMond	30-45	
Wallace, Susan A.	Along the Bosphorus (1st, 8vo, teg, uncut, 383p, cvr by...)	Rand/McNally	1898	Denslow, W.W.	30-45	*
Waller, M.E.	Daughter of the Rich (1st, 8vo, p-o, 296p, 5cp, pep)	Little/Brown	1924	Green, E.S.	30-45	*
Wallis, I.H.	Cloud Kingdom (1st, 12mo, green/gilt, 174p, teg, 18pl)	L: J. Lane	(1905)	Robinson, C.	165-250	
Walpole, H.	Jeremy (1st AM, 8vo, 304p, col frn, b/w, pep)	Doran	(1919)	Shepard, E.H.	35-50	*
Walsh, Chad	Nellie & her Flying Crocodile (1st {std}, 8vo, 179p, b/w)	Harper	(1956)	Simont, M.	30-45	*
Walter, E.D.	Bugs (1st, lg4to, wraps, [16]p, color)	Whitman	1931	Roberts, H.M.	35-50	
Walters, L.	Year's at the Spring (1st AM, 4to, 128p, 12cp, 12pl)	Brentano's	(1920)	Clarke, H.	185-235	
Walters, L.	Year's at the Spring (1st, sm4to, green/gilt, 12cp, 12pl, cep)	L: Harrap	1920	Clarke, H.	250-300	
Walton, Isaac	Complete Angler (4to, 25pl)	L: Hodder	[1911]	Thorpe, J.	130-170	
Walton, Isaac	Complete Angler (1st, 4to, teg, 12cp)	L: Harrap	(1931)	Rackham, A.	220-265	
Walton, Isaac	Complete Angler (1st AM, sm4to, 224p, gilt, teg, 12cp, pep)	McKay	[1931]	Rackham, A.	140-200	
Ward, G.	In the Miz (1st, 4to, blue cl, p-o, 159p, 8cp)	Little/Brown	1904	Atwood, C.E.	70-120	
Ward, H.F.	In Place of Profit (1st, 8vo, green cl, 460p, gilt, woodcuts)	Scribner	1933	Ward, L.	35-50	
Ward, Lynd	Biggest Bear (1st, 4to, 84p, beige cl, b/w, CM)	Houghton	1952	Ward, L.	70-115	*
Ward, Lynd	God's Man (1st, 8vo, woodcuts, ipcb, 293p, cep)	Cape/Smith	(1929)	Ward, L.	100-140	
Ward, Lynd	Mad-Man's Drum (1st, 8vo, ipcb, [257]p, woodcuts, cep)	Cape/Smith	(1930)	Ward, L.	120-160	
Ward, Lynd	Vertigo (1st, 8vo, 231p, woodcuts)	Random	1937	Ward, L.	85-120	
Ward, Lynd	Wild Pilgrimage (1st, lg8vo, [95]p, p-o, woodcuts)	Smith/Haas	1932	Ward, L.	130-160	
Ward, Marion	Boat Children of Canton (1st {std}, 4to, 92p, color, pep)	McKay	(1944)	Sewell, H.	20-35	*
Ward, Mrs. H.	Coryston Family (1st, 8vo, red/gilt, 328p, 8pl)	Harper	1913	Green, E.S.	40-65	
Ward, Mrs. H.	Milly & Olly (1st, 8vo, 302p, p-o, 8pl, pep)	Doubleday/Page	1907	Hallock, R.M.	25-40	*
Warde, M.	Holiday Book (1st, 8vo, 208p, 5pl)	Little/Brown	1925	Peck, A.M.	20-30	
Ware, R.D.	In the Woods/On the Shore (1st, 8vo, 279p, photos, frn by...)	Page	1908	Bull, C.L.	35-50	*
Warner, A.	Susan Clegg... (1st, 12mo, 279p, grey cl, 4pl)	Little/Brown	1907	Stephens, A.B.	20-30	
Warner, A.	The Panther (1st, 8vo, teg, uncut, 91p)	Small	1908	Thomas, P.K.	20-25	*
Warner, A.	When Woman Proposes (1st, 8vo, 158p, teg, purple cl, color)	Little/Brown	1911	Ditzler, C.W.	20-25	
Warner, C.D.	Backlog Studies (1st, 12mo, 257p, title page by...)	Houghton	1899	Rogers, B.	25-40	

AUTHOR	TITLE	PUBLISHER	DATE	ARTIST	PRICE	LC
Warner, J. (ed.)	Golden Book of Poetry (1st, lg4to, 97p, ibds, color, GGB)	Simon/Schuster	1947	Elliot, Gertrude	30-45	
Warner, S.	Wide, Wide World (1st, 8vo, 592p, 6pl)	Fenno	(1904)	Dunton, H.	30-45	*
Warren, C.	Girl of the Governor (1st, 8vo, 407p, 9pl, cvr by...)	Scribner	1900	Armstrong, M.	30-45	
Warren, C.	Little Betty Marigold (1st, 12mo, 107p, 14 color)	C.M. Clark	1907	Goldsmith, W.	20-30	*
Warren, I.R.	In Cupid's Court (1st, 12mo, 79p, white/gilt, fp b/w)	R.H. Russell	1900	Unknown	65-80	*
Warren, I.R.	Mother Love (1st, 8vo, 166p, teg, p-o, col frn)	Jacobs	(1911)	Boyer, J.A.	25-40	
Warren, M.R.	Mother Goose & her Friends (1st, sm4to, 305p, p-o, pep, 12 ticp)	Doran	(1922)	Federer, C.A.	65-90	*
Warren, M.R.	Tales Told by Gander (8vo, green/gilt, 305p, p-o, 12 ticp, pep)	Doran	(1922)	Federer, C.A.	60-95	
Warren, Maude L.	Little Pioneers (1st, 12mo, 253p, b/w, pep)	Rand/McNally	(1916)	Perkins, L.F.	25-40	*
Warwick, Charles	Mirabeau & the French Revolution (1st, 8vo, 483p, 15pl)	Lippincott	1905	Neill, J.R.	45-60	*
Washburn, C.C.	Pages/Book of Paris (1st, 8vo, pcb, p-o, 276p, b/w)	Houghton	1910	Hornby, L.G.	25-40	*
Washburne, Heluiz	Rhaman: Boy of Kashmir (1st, lg8vo, 127p, red cl, color, pep)	Whitman	1939	Duvoisin, R.	45-65	*
Washburne, M.F.	Old Fashioned Fairy Tales (1st, 8vo, brown/gilt, 102p, 3cp, pep)	Rand/McNally	(1909)	Webb, M.E.	65-90	*
Wasson, V.P.	Chosen Baby (1st {A}, ob8vo, blue cl, [48]p, color, pep)	Carrick/Evans	(1939)	Woodward, H.	45-60	*
Wasson, V.P.	Chosen Baby (1st {this pub.}, 8vo, 46p, color)	Lippincott	(1950)	Woodward, H.	30-45	*
Watanna, O.	Japanese Blossom (1st, 8vo, 263p, uncut, teg, 4cp, dep)	Harper	1906	Ziegler, L.W.	25-40	
Watanna, O.	Tama (1st, 8vo, 244p, uncut, gilt, teg, 4cp, dep)	Harper	1910	Kataoka, G.	25-40	
Waterloo, S.	Story of AB (1st, 8vo, black cl, 351p, PPPa)	Way/Williams	1897	Bradley, W.	120-165	
Waterloo, S.	The Seekers (1st, 8vo, red cloth, cvr by...)	H. Stone	1900	Bradley, W.	75-90	
Waterman (ed.)	Ben King's Verse (1st, 8vo, 1 illus by...)	Chi: Forbes	1894	Denslow, W.W.	80-95	
Waters, R.J.	El Estranjero (1st, lg8vo, 298p, b/w)	Rand/McNally	1910	Chapin, W.E.	25-40	*
Waterstone, S.S.	Short Stories of Musical Melodies (1st, 4to, ibds, gilt)	Volland	(1915)	Dodge, K.S.	140-200	*
Watson, E.	Lament of Billy Villy (lg sq8vo, wraps, 8cp)	L: R. Tuck	[1890]	Wain, L.	200-300	
Watson, Eliz.	Story of Bread (1st {std}, 12mo, 48p, 4cp, pep)	Harper	1927	Daugherty, J.	25-45	*
Watson, H.B.M.	Chloris of the Island (1st, 8vo, 281p, 32pl)	Harper	1900	Brock, C.& H.	40-60	*
Watson, H.B.M.	The Adventurers (1st, sm8vo, 298p, 20pl)	Harper	1899	Keller, A.I.	30-45	*
Watson, N.D.	Fairy Tale Picture Book (1st {std}, lg4to, 91p, color)	Garden City	1957	Watson, A.A.	50-80	*
Watson, V.	Princess Pocahontas (1st, lg8vo, 306p, blue/gilt, p-o, 9cp)	Penn	1916	Edwards, G.W.	60-80	
Watson, V.	With Cortes the Conqueror (1st, 4to, p-o, 332p, 8cp, pep)	Penn	1917	Schoonover, F.	50-80	
Watson, Virginia	Trail of Courage (1st, 8vo, grey cl, 181p, fp b/w)	Crowell	(1948)	Brown, Marcia	30-45	*
Wattles, W.D.	Hell-Fire Harrison (1st, sm8vo, green cl, 6cp)	Page	1910	Merrill, F.	20-25	
Watts, Isaac	Childhood Songs of Long Ago (1st, 8vo, 87p, 20pl, pep)	Herrick	(1897)	McManus, B.	60-80	
Watts, Isaac	Divine & Moral Songs for Children (16mo, bds, 12 fp color)	L: Matthews	(1897)	Gaskin, A.J.	90-130	*
Waugh, A.	Hot Countries (1st, 8vo, 304p, gilt, b/w)	Farrar/Rine.	(1930)	Ward, L.	45-60	
Waugh, A.	Most Women (1st, 8vo, gilt, 323p, woodcuts)	Farrar/Rine.	(1931)	Ward, L.	30-50	*
Waugh, A.	Square Book of Animals (1st, sq4to, [14]p, ibds, 12cp)	L: Heinemann	1900	Nicholson, W.	350-500	
Waugh, A.	Square Book of Animals (1st AM, sq4to, [14]p, ibds, 12cp)	R.H. Russell	1900	Nicholson, W.	280-400	R
Waugh, D.	Among the Leaves & Grasses (1st, sm4to, orang cl, 93p, color)	Holt	1931	Waugh, D.	65-100	
Waugh, F.	Clan of Munes (1st, ob4to, blue cl, 58p, 8 fp color)	Scribner	1916	Waugh, F.	250-400	R
Waugh, Ida	Becky Longnose... (4to, wraps, 8cp)	McLoughlin	(1882)	Waugh, Ida	50-65	
Waugh, Ida	Ida Waugh's Alphabet Book (1st, 4to, ibds, 26 illus)	Lippincott	1888	Waugh, Ida	100-145	
Waugh, Ida	Ideal Heads (1st, folio, brown/gilt, [51]p, AEG, 20 chromos)	Sunshine Co.	1890	Waugh, I.	150-230	*
Waugh, Ida	Little Chicks/Baby Tricks (1st, 4to, ibds, 44p)	Dutton	1885	Waugh, Ida	100-120	
Waugh, Ida	Over the Hills (1st, 4to, ibds, [48]p, color)	McLoughlin	(1882)	Waugh, Ida	120-165	
Waylett, Richard	Mixed Pickles (1st, 12mo, ibds, 48p, p-o, 10cp)	L: Gale	[1916]	Various	30-50	
Waylett, Richard	Puppy Tales (1st, 4to, ibds, 16cp)	L: Lawrence	[1915]	Aldin, C.	160-200	
Weatherly, F.E.	Book of Gnomes (1st, ob4to, [25]p, ibds, 8 chromos, pep)	L: Nister	[1900]	Hardy, E.S.	250-400	
Weatherly, F.E.	Out of Town (1st, 8vo, 64p, ibds, 12 chromos)	Dutton	(1884)	Watt, L.	70-130	
Weatherly, F.E.	Told in the Twilight (1st, 8vo, 64p, ibds)	Dutton	(1883)	27 Chromos	100-140	
Weaver, A.V.	Frawg (1st, ob12mo, p-o, 128p, color, pep)	Stokes	1930	Weaver, A.V.	100-165	*
Webb, E. & D.	Littlest Fairy (1st, sm4to, ibds, 158p, p-o, 8cp, pep)	Dodge	(1910)	Clements, R.S.	150-200	
Webb, M. St. John	Littlest One Again (1st, 4to, p-o, bds, 4cp)	L: Harrap	1926	Tarrant, M.	65-90	
Webb, M. St. John	Magic Lamplighter (1st, 8vo, 167p, 7cp, pep)	L: Medici	1926	Tarrant, M.	45-60	
Webb, M. St. John	Sea-Shore Fairies (1st, 16mo, tan bds, p-o, 6 fp color)	L: Mod.Art.Soc	(1925)	Tarrant, M.	85-120	
Webb, M. St. John	Seed Fairies (1st, 12mo, 39p, bds, p-o, 6 ticp, pep)	L: Mod.Art Soc	[1923]	Tarrant, M.	100-140	
Webb, M. St. John	Wild Fruit Fairies (1st, 12mo, 41p, ibds, 6cp)	L: Medici	1932	Tarrant, M.	65-80	
Webb, R.	Me & Lawson (1st, sm8vo, 78p, 4pl, cvr by...)	Dillingham	(1905)	Denslow, W.W.	85-100	
Webb, W.P.	Uncle Swithin's Inventions (1st, lg8vo, 114p, fp b/w, pep)	Holiday House	(1947)	Rounds, G.	20-35	*
Webber, Frank M.	Peter Painter's Merry-Go-Round (1st {std}, sm4to, ibds, [32]p)	McKay	(1946)	Neville, V.	40-65	*
Webber, I.E.	Anywhere in the World (1st, sm8vo, ipcb, 64p, color)	W.R. Scott	(1947)	Webber, I.E.	30-45	*
Webber, I.E.	Bits that Grow Big (1st, sm8vo, ipcb, 64p, 2-color)	W.R. Scott	(1949)	Webber, I.E.	30-50	*
Webber, I.E.	It Looks Like This (1st, 8vo, [40]p, b/w)	W.R. Scott	1949	Webber, I.E.	25-40	*
Webber, I.E.	Thanks to Trees (1st, sm8vo, grey cl, 60p, 3-color, pep)	W.R. Scott	(1952)	Webber, I.E.	30-45	*
Webber, I.E.	Travelers All (1st, sm8vo, [32]p, color)	W.R. Scott	1944	Webber, I.E.	30-50	*
Webber, I.E.	Up Above & Down Below (1st, sm8vo, ibds, [31]p, color)	W.R. Scott	(1943)	Webber, I.E.	30-50	*
Weber, Lenora M.	Wind on the Prairie (1st, 8vo, 276p, pep, col frn, b/w)	Little/Brown	1929	Wiese, K.	25-40	*
Webling, P.	Saints & their Stories (1st, 8vo, grey cl, 312p, 7 ticp, pep)	L: J. Nisbet	[1914]	Robinson, F.C.	70-100	
Webster, J.	Daddy Long Legs (1st, 12mo, blue cl, 304p, b/w, PPP)	Century	1912	Webster, J.	45-60	
Webster, J.	Jerry Junior (1st, 8vo, green cl, p-o, 282p, 15pl)	Century	1907	Lowell, O.	20-25	
Wedgwood, Henry A.	Bird Talisman (1st, 8vo, 70p, geilt, pep, 8cp)	L: Faber	1939	Raverat, G.	45-60	*
Weeden, Mrs. H.	Bandanna Ballads (1st, 8vo, green/gilt, uncut, 90p, 24pl)	Doub./McClure	1899	Weeden, H.	70-120	
Weedon, L.L.	Child Characters/Dickens (1st, 8vo, 320p, AEG, 6cp)	L: Nister	(1905)	Dixon, A.A.	75-100	

AUTHOR	TITLE	PUBLISHER	DATE	ARTIST	PRICE	LC
Weedon, L.L.	Model Menagerie (ob folio, pop-up, ipcb, 24p)	L: Nister	[1880]	6 Chromos	300-400	
Weil, Ann	Red Sails to Capri (1st, 8vo, 156p, pep, NH)	Viking	1952	Falls, C.B.	30-45	*
Weil, Ann	Silver Fawn (1st {std}, 8vo, 228p, 1-color, pep)	Bobbs-Merrill	(1939)	Leon, E.	25-45	*
Weil, Ann	Very First Day (1st, sm8vo, red cl, [32]p, 1-color)	Appleton/Cent.	(1946)	Robinson, J.	25-40	*
Weisgard, L.	Clean Pig (1st, ob4to, [34]p, fp brown illus, pep)	Scribner	1952	Weisgard, L.	30-45	*
Weisgard, L.	Mr. Peaceable Paints (1st, ob4to, [32]p, cloth, dp color)	Scribner	1956	Weisgard, L.	35-50	
Weisgard, L.	Pelican Here, Pelican There (1st, 4to, [30]p, 6 dp color, pep)	Scribner	1948	Weisgard, L.	35-50	R*
Weisgard, L.	Silly Willy Nilly (1st, sm4to, [32]p, 8 fp color)	Scribner	1953	Weisgard, L.	50-80	R*
Weisgard, L.	Suki/Siamese Pussy (1st, sm4to, [32]p, color, DJ)	NY: Nelson	1937	Weisgard, L.	50-70	
Weisgard, L.	Treasures to See (1st {std}, sm4to, [32]p, rust cl, color)	Harcourt	(1956)	Weisgard, L.	50-85	R*
Weisgard, L.	Who Dreams of Cheese? (1st, 4to, black cl, [32]p, color)	Scribner	1950	Weisgard, L.	60-85	R*
Weiss, Edna S.	Sally Saucer (1st, 8vo, 179p, yellow cl, b/w)	Houghton	1956	Stone, H.	20-30	*
Welch, C.	Stories Children Love (1st, sm8vo, 439p, cp)	Dodge	(1909)	Grimball, M.	35-60	*
Welch, D.	Story of Louise (1st, 12mo, tan cl, uncut, 194p, cvr by...)	(NY)	1901	Denslow, W.W.	45-60	
Welles, W.	Skipping Along (1st, 8vo, green cl, 52p, b/w)	MacMillan	1931	Davis, M.	20-30	*
Wellman, M.W.	Rebel Mail Runner (1st, sm8vo, 221p, red cl, b/w, pep)	Holiday House	(1954)	Van Veen, S.	20-30	*
Wellman, M.W.	To Unknown Lands (1st, 8vo, 202p, black cl, b/w, pep)	Holiday House	(1956)	Fisher, L.E.	20-25	*
Wells, A.R.	Rollicking Rhymes for Youngsters (1st, 8vo, 157p, 26 fp color)	Revell	(1902)	Bridgman, L.J.	45-60	
Wells, A.R.	Witchery Ways (1st, 12mo, 189p, 8pl)	Altemus	(1904)	Bridgman, L.J.	20-35	*
Wells, Carolyn	Beauties (1st, lg4to, ibds, p-o, 16 ticp)	Dodd	1913	Fisher, H.	300-450	
Wells, Carolyn	Folly for the Wise (1st, 8vo, 170p, blue/gilt)	Bobbs-Merrill	(1904)	Armstrong, M.	45-70	
Wells, Carolyn	Folly in Fairyland (1st, sm8vo, 261p, 12pl)	Altemus	(1901)	Morgan, W.	45-60	
Wells, Carolyn	Folly in the Forest (1st, 8vo, 282p, olive cl, 12pl)	Altemus	(1902)	Birch, R.	30-45	
Wells, Carolyn	Happychaps (1st, 4to, 135p, brown cl, color)	Century	1908	Cady, H.	100-145	
Wells, Carolyn	Idle Idyls (1st, 8vo, green/gilt, teg, 155p, b/w pl)	Dodd	1900	Herford, O.	30-50	
Wells, Carolyn	In the Reign of Queen Dick (1st, 8vo, tan cl, 229p, 8pl)	Appleton	1904	Strothmann, F.	30-50	
Wells, Carolyn	Jingle Book (1st, sm8vo, 124p, blue cl, teg, b/w)	MacMillan	1899	Herford, O.	70-100	
Wells, Carolyn	Jingle Book (8vo {new ed.}, green cl, p-o, 124p, b/w)	Donohue	(1906)	Herford, O.	35-50	*
Wells, Carolyn	Merry-Go-Round (1st, sm8vo, gilt, 152p, 11pl)	R.H. Russell	1901	Newell, P.	150-180	
Wells, Carolyn	Mother Goose's Menagerie (1st, 8vo, tan cl, 111p, 12cp)	Noyes/Platt	1901	Newell, P.	170-225	
Wells, Carolyn	Pete & Polly Stories (1st, lg8vo, green cl, 229p, 6pl)	McClurg	1902	Cory, F.	70-85	
Wells, Carolyn	Phenomenal Fauna (1st, sq8vo, [90]p, ibds, 21cp)	R.H. Russell	1902	Herford, O.	60-90	
Wells, Carolyn	Rubaiyat of a Motor Car (1st, 12mo, [60]p, ibds, 14cp)	Dodd	1906	Strothmann, F.	45-60	*
Wells, Carolyn	Seven Ages of Childhood (1st, sm4to, gilt, 56p, p-o, 7cp, pep)	Moffat	1909	Smith, J.W.	280-400	
Wells, Carolyn	Story of Betty (1st {1st bk.}, sm8vo, red cl, 260p, 32pl)	Century	1899	Birch, R.	50-70	*
Wells, Carveth	Jungle Man & his Animals (1st {this pub}, 4to, 68p, ibds, 7cp)	McBride	(1925)	Sarg, T.	150-200	
Wells, Carveth	Jungle Man & his Animals (1st, lg4to, ibds, 68p, 12cp)	Duffield	1925	Sarg, T.	160-200	*
Wells, H.G.	Adventures of Tommy (1st, lg4to, 45p, bds, color)	L: Harrap	(1929)	Wells, H.G.	180-220	
Wells, H.G.	Adventures of Tommy (1st AM, 4to, red cl, [46]p, p-o, color)	Stokes	1929	Wells, H.G.	100-145	
Wells, H.G.	First Men in the Moon (1st AM, 8vo, 312p, blue/gilt, 12pl)	Bowen-Merrill	(1901)	Hering, E.	160-220	*
Wells, H.G.	First Men in the Moon (1st AM, 8vo, gilt, 12pl)	Stokes	(1901)	Hering, E.	180-250	
Wells, H.G.	First Men in the Moon (1st UK, 8vo, 342p, blue/gilt, 14pl)	L: G. Newnes	1901	Shepperson, C.	300-450	*
Wells, H.G.	Little Wars (1st AM, sm4to, p-o, blue cl, 16l)	Small/Maynard	(1913)	(Photos)	140-200	*
Wells, H.G.	Modern Utopia (1st, 8vo, red/gilt, teg, 393p, 7pl)	L: Chapman	1905	Sullivan, E.J.	170-250	
Wells, H.G.	Time Machine (1st {this pub}, sm4to, 86p, bds, color designs)	Random	1931	Dwiggins, W.A.	65-80	*
Wells, H.G.	War in the Air (1st, 8vo, blue/gilt, 389p, uncut, 16pl)	L: G. Bell	1908	Michael, A.C.	260-350	
Wells, H.G.	War in the Air (1st AM, 8vo, 395p, grey/gilt, uncut, 20pl)	MacMillan	1908	Pape, Eric	240-300	
Wells, H.G.	War of the Worlds (1st AM, 8vo, green cl, 291p, 16pl)	Harper	1898	Goble, W.	250-320	
Wells, H.G.	When the Sleeper Wakes (1st AM, 8vo, red/gilt, 328p, 3pl)	Harper	1899	Lanos, H.	180-220	
Wells, Rhea	Beppo the Donkey (1st {std}, 12mo, 135p, color, pep)	Doubleday/Dor.	1930	Wells, Rhea	30-45	*
Wells, Rhea	Coco the Goat (1st {std}, sm8vo, 135p, dp color, pep)	Doubleday/Dor.	1929	Wells, Rhea	25-40	*
Wells, Rhea	Zeke the Raccoon (1st, sm8vo, green cl, 159p, 8cp, pep)	Viking	1933	Wells, Rhea	25-40	*
Welsh, Richard	Kiddie-Kar Book (lg ob4to, ibds, p-o, 9cp)	Lippincott	(1920)	Stilwell, S.	180-250	*
Werner, Elsa	Golden Bible (1st {std}, folio, 124p, ibds, color, GGB)	Simon/Schuster	(1946)	Rojankovsky, F.	25-40	
Werner, Jane	Elves & Fairies (1st, sm folio, ibds, 76p, color, pep, GGB)	Simon/Schuster	(1951)	Williams, Garth	160-200	
Werner, Jane	Tall Book of Make-Believe (1st, narrow 4to, ibds, 92p, col, pep)	Harper	(1950)	Williams, Garth	60-100	*
Wesselhoeft, Lily	Diamond King.... (1st, 12mo, tan cl, 255p, 4pl)	Little/Brown	1907	Atwood, C.E.	20-35	*
Wesselhoeft, Lily	Fairy-Folk of Blue Hill (1st, 8vo, 240p, b/w)	Page	1898	Eastman, A.L.	30-50	
Wesselhoeft, Lily	Madam Mary of the Zoo (1st, 12mo, 248p, blue/silver, 3pl by...)	Little/Brown	1899	Bridgman, L.J.	20-35	
West, M.	Clair De Lune (1st, lg4to, 140p, teg, brown/gilt, 8 ticp, pep)	L: Harrap	[1913]	Paul, E.	140-180	
West, Paul	Pearl & Pumpkin (1st [1], lg8vo, grn cl, 240p, p-o, 16cp, pep)	Dillingham	(1904)	Denslow, W.W.	300-400	
West, Paul	Pearl & Pumpkin (lg8vo, 239p, p-o, 16cp, later)	Donohue	[1911]	Denslow, W.W.	200-280	
Westerman, J.M.E.	Fairy Tales/Wonderland (1st, 4to, 160p, orange cl, 3cp, 14pl)	L: Blackie	[1932]	Hassall, J.	100-145	*
Weston, C.	Bhimsa the Dancing Bear (1st, sm8vo, 120p, 2-color, cep, NH)	Scribner	1945	Duvoisin, R.	60-85	
Weston, C.	There & Then (1st, sm8vo, 176p, green/gilt, fp b/w)	Scribner	1947	DeGoutiere, G.	30-45	*
Weston, J.L.	Sir Gleges/Sir Libeaus Desconus (1st AM, 12mo, 77p)	New Amsterdam	1902	Watts, C.	40-60	
Wetmore, C.H.	Bedtime Stories (1st, 4to, p-o, 120p, color)	Macaulay	1914	Bailey, M.L.	65-80	*
Wetmore, C.H.	Queen Tiny's Little People (1st, 4to, 105p, color, p-o)	Macaulay	1914	Bailey, M.L.	65-80	*
Weyman, S.J.	Castle Inn (1st, 8vo, blue/gilt, 371p, frn by...)	L: Smith Elder	1898	Rackham, A.	120-145	
Wharton, A.H.	Heirlooms in Miniatures (1st, 8vo, 259p, uncut, teg)	Lippincott	1898	Unknown	20-30	
Wharton, A.H.	Social Life/Early Republic (1st, 8vo, 346p, teg, uncut)	Lippincott	1902	Unknown	25-40	
Wharton, E.	Book of the Homeless (1st, 4to, 155p, bds, 8cp, 13pl)	Scribner	1916	Various	120-165	

AUTHOR	TITLE	PUBLISHER	DATE	ARTIST	PRICE	LC
Wharton, E.	Fruit of the Tree (1st, 12mo, 633p, red/gilt, 3pl)	Scribner	1907	Kimball, A.	90-120	
Wharton, E.	House of Mirth (1st, 8vo, teg, uncut, 533p, 8pl)	Scribner	1905	Wenzell, A.B.	90-120	
Wharton, E.	Italian Backgrounds (1st, 8vo, green/gilt, 214p, cvr by...)	Scribner	1905	Armstrong, M.	75-100	
Wharton, E.	Italian Backgrounds (1st, 8vo, 214p, 12pl by...)	Scribner	1905	Peixotto, E.C.	75-100	
Wharton, E.	Italian Villas... (1st, 4to, teg, 270p, gilt, 15cp)	Scribner	1904	Parrish, M.	300-450	
Wharton, E.	Motor-Flight through France (1st, 8vo, teg, 201p, 48pl)	Scribner	1908	(Photos)	65-80	
Wharton, E.	Sanctuary (1st, 8vo, 184p, green/gilt, uncut, col frn, 10pl)	Scribner	1903	Clark, W.A.	100-135	
Wharton, T.I.	Bobbo and other Fancies (1st, 8vo, 182p, uncut, b/w)	Harper	1897	Various	25-40	
Wheeler, Candace	Doubledarling & Dreamspinner (1st, 8vo, 167p blue cl, p-o, 11cp)	Fox Duffield	1905	Keith, D.W.	70-100	
Wheeler, Opal	H.M.S. Pinafore (1st {std}, 4to, 96p, color, DJ)	Dutton	1946	Kredel, F.	25-40	
Wheeler, Opal	Sing Mother Goose (1st {std}, 4to, 102p, ibds, color, CH)	Dutton	1945	Torrey, M.	65-90	*
Wheeler, Opal	Sing for America (1st {std}, 4to, 127p, ibds, color, pep)	Dutton	(1944)	Tenggren, G.	40-65	
Wheeler, Opal	Sing for Christmas (1st {std}, 4to, ibds, 127p, 12cp, pep, DJ)	Dutton	1943	Tenggren, G.	70-100	
Wheeler, Opal	Sing in Praise (1st {std}, 4to, 94p, ibds, color, pep, CH)	Dutton	1946	Torrey, M.	50-85	*
Wheeler, P.	Albanian Wonder Tales (1st {std}, 8vo, 282p, col frn, b/w, pep)	Doubleday/Dor.	1936	Petershams	65-80	*
Wheeler, P.	Hathoo of the Elephants (1st, sm8vo, orang cl, 333p, pep by...)	Viking	1943	Falls, C.B.	30-45	*
Wheelwright, J.	Bad Penny (1st, 8vo, teg, 162p)	Chi: Lamson	1896	Attwood, F.G.	50-70	*
Whishaw, F.	Emperor's Englishman (1st, 8vo, 342p)	L: Hutchinson	1896	Goble, W.	80-100	*
White, Anne H.	Junket (1st, 8vo, 184p, b/w, DJ)	Viking	1955	McCloskey, R.	40-65	*
White, Anne H.	Story of Seraphina (1st, 4to, 128p, orang cl, b/w)	Viking	1951	Palazzo, T.	30-50	*
White, Anne H.	Uninvited Donkey (1st, 8vo, 223p, blue cl, b/w)	Viking	(1957)	Freeman, D.	30-45	*
White, C.	Flip Flop Show (folio, bds, color)	Donohue	(1909)	White, C.	65-80	
White, E.B.	Charlotte's Web (1st {std}, 8vo, 184p, b/w, pep, NH)	Harper	(1952)	Williams, Garth	85-100	R
White, E.B.	Stuart Little (1st {std}, 8vo, tan cl, b/w, 131p, pep, DJ)	Harper	(1945)	Williams, Garth	100-135	R
White, E.O.	Ann Frances (1st, 8vo, 126p, blue cl, 7cp, cep)	Houghton	1935	Sewell, H.	30-45	
White, E.O.	Blue Aunt (1st, 8vo, 144p, col frn & cvr by...)	Houghton	1918	Pyle, Kath.	30-50	
White, E.O.	Borrowed Sister (1st, 8vo, 150p, green cl, p-o, 4pl)	Houghton	1906	Pyle, Kath.	50-70	
White, E.O.	Green Door (1st, 8vo, 212p, silhouettes, DJ)	Houghton	1930	Hummel, L.	50-65	
White, E.O.	Only Child (1st, 8vo, 167p, grey cl, p-o, 4pl)	Houghton	1905	Pyle, Kath.	30-50	
White, E.O.	When Molly was Six (1st, 8vo, 133p, cloth, 3pl)	Houghton	1894	Pyle, Kath.	35-50	
White, E.O.	Where is Adelaide? (1st, 8vo, 155p, orange cl, b/w, dep)	Houghton	1933	Sewell, H.	20-30	
White, Hervey	Snake Gold (1st, 12mo, 220p, decor by...)	MacMillan	1926	MacKinstry, E.	25-40	*
White, Richardson	Aesop's Fables in Rhyme (1st, lg4to, ibds, [100]p, 50pl, pep)	Saalfield	1903	Bull, C.L.	120-200	*
White, Roma	Brownies & Rose-Leaves (1st, 12mo, 200p, tan cl, b/w, dep)	L: Innes	1892	Brooke, L.L.	65-80	
White, Roma	Moonbeams/Brownies (1st, sq12mo, 5pl)	L: A.D. Innes	1894	Brooke, L.L.	75-100	
White, S.E.	Arizona Nights (1st, 8vo, gilt, p-o, 351p, 7cp)	McClure	1907	Wyeth, N.C.	45-70	
White, S.E.	Camp & Trail (1st, 8vo, 236p, col frn, 11pl)	Outing	1907	(Photos)	30-50	
White, S.E.	Conjuror's House (1st, 8vo, uncut, 260p, 6pl)	McClure	1903	Chapman, C.S.	30-45	
White, S.E.	Daniel Boone (1st {std}, 8vo, 308p, blue cl, p-o, 5pl, PPP)	Doubleday/Page	1922	Schuyler, R.	75-100	R
White, S.E.	Daniel Boone (1st, 8vo, 274p, p-o, 4cp, 10pl, DJ)	Doubleday/Page	1926	Daugherty, J.	50-65	
White, S.E.	Gold (1st, 12mo, green cl, 437p, pep, 4cp)	Doubleday/Page	1913	Fogarty, T.	25-40	
White, S.E.	Rules of the Game (1st, 8vo, 644p, 4cp)	Doubleday/Page	1910	Hiller, L.A.	25-40	
White, S.E.	The Forest (1st, 8vo, green cl, teg, 276p, 17pl)	Outlook	1903	Fogarty, T.	25-40	
White, S.E.	The Mountains (1st, 8vo, 282p, teg, col frn, 15pl)	McClure	1904	Lungren, F.H.	30-45	
White, S.E.	The Pass (1st, 8vo, 194p, blue cl, 15pl)	Outing	1906	Lungren, F.H.	25-40	
White, S.E.	The Riverman (1st, 8vo, p-o, 368p, 12pl)	McClure	1908	Wyeth, N.C.	50-70	
White, T.H.	Mistress Masham's Repose (1st, 8vo, 225p, gilt, fp b/w, pep)	Putnam	(1946)	Eichenberg, F.	30-50	*
White, T.H.	Sword in the Stone (1st, 8vo, 339p, black cl, b/w)	L: Collins	1938	White, T.H.	120-160	
White, T.H.	Sword in the Stone (1st AM, sm8vo, 311p, gilt, pep by....)	Putnam	1939	Lawson, R.	80-130	*
White, T.H.	Sword in the Stone (1st AM, sm8vo, 311p, blue/gilt, b/w)	Putnam	1939	White, T.H.	80-130	*
White, T.H.	Witch in the Wood (1st AM, 8vo, blue/gilt bds, 270p, b/w)	Putnam	1939	White, T.H.	100-150	
White, W.A.	Court of Boyville (1st, 8vo, 358p, buckram, PPP)	Doub./McClure	1899	Lowell, O.	120-160	
White, W.A.	Martial Advens. of Henry & Me (1st, 8vo, 340p, red cl, 25 b/w)	MacMillan	1918	Sarg, T.	20-30	*
Whitehead, R.	Five & Ten (1st, 8vo, red cl, [41]p, color, pep)	Houghton	1943	Lenski, L.	45-60	
Whitehorn, A.L.	Wonder Tales of Old Japan (1st, 8vo, 173p, p-o, 12cp)	L: Jack	1911	Obata, S.	70-90	*
Whitehorn, A.L.	Wonder Tales of Old Japan (1st AM, 8vo, 173p, teg, p-o, 12cp)	Stokes	(1912)	Obata, S.	60-90	*
Whiteing, R.	Paris of Today (1st, 4to, 249p, teg, b/w)	Century	1900	Castaigne, A.	50-70	
Whitlock, Brand	Happy Average (1st, sm8vo, 347p, green/gilt, cvr by...)	Bobbs-Merrill	(1904)	Armstrong, M.	25-40	*
Whitman, W.	Poems of Leaves & Grass (1st, 4to, teg, gilt, 24 ticp)	L: J.M. Dent	1913	Cook, M.	100-130	
Whitman, W.	There was a Child Went Forth (1st {std}, 4to, ipcb, [32]p, col)	Harper	(1943)	Gay, Z.	45-70	*
Whitney, A.D.T.	Mother Goose for Grown Folks (1st {new ed}, 12mo, 204p)	Houghton	1898	Hoppin, A.	45-60	*
Whitney, Casper	On Snow-Shoes/Barren Grounds (1st, 8vo, teg, 324p, blue cl, b/w)	Harper	1896	Remington, F.	75-115	
Whitney, Casper	Sporting Pilgrimage (1st, lg8vo, red cl, 379p)	Harper	1894	Remington, F.	50-70	
Whitney, Elinor	Timothy & the Blue Cart (1st, 8vo, 168p, p-o, col frn, pep)	Stokes	1930	Hader, B.& E.	35-50	*
Whitney, Elinor	Tod of the Fens (1st, 8vo, 239p, red cl, col frn, pep, NH)	MacMillan	1928	Goble, W.	45-60	*
Whitney, H.H.	Bed-Time Book (1st, lg4to, ipcb, 31p, 6cp, pep)	Duffield	1907	Smith, J.W.	280-400	
Whitson, J.H.	Barbara, Woman of the West (1st, sm8vo, green cl, 314p, 5pl)	Little/Brown	1903	Emerson, C.	20-35	
Whittemore	Flower Fairies (4to, ibds)	L: Cassell	(1886)	(Chromos)	130-180	
Whittier, J.G.	Jack in the Pulpit (1st, sq8vo, color)	NY: S. Tilton	1883	Unknown	70-90	*
Whittier, J.G.	Snowbound (lg8vo, teg, 96p)	Houghton	1906	Various	25-50	
Whittier, J.G.	Snowbound (1st, 8vo, p-o, 123p, green cl, 12pl, pep)	Reilly/Britton	(1909)	Neill, J.R.	50-70	
Whittier, J.G.	Tent on the Beach (1st, 8vo, green/gilt, 110p, teg)	Houghton	1899	Armstrong, M.	45-60	

AUTHOR	TITLE	PUBLISHER	DATE	ARTIST	PRICE	LC
Whyte, A.G.	Christabel's Fairyland (1st, 4to, ibds, 183p, color)	L: Chapman	1926	Gautier, P.	80-120	
Widdemer, M.	Binkie and Bell Dolls (1st, 8vo, tan cl, 146p, p-o, 8cp, pep)	Penn	1923	Price, H.L.	45-70	*
Wiederseim, G.	Baby's Day (1st, 4to, ibds, 11 fp color)	Stokes	1910	Wiederseim, G.	140-200	
Wiederseim, G.	Dolly Drake (1st, 4to, ibds, [16]p, color, shape bk.)	Stokes	(1909)	Wiederseim, G.	100-150	*
Wiederseim, G.	Ducky Daddles (folio, shape bk, 16p, ibds, color)	Stokes	(1911)	Wiederseim, G.	120-200	
Wiederseim, G.	Fido (shape book, folio, ibds, 16p, color)	Stokes	(1910)	Wiederseim, G.	130-200	
Wiederseim, G.	Little Sunbeam's Book (wraps)	Hurst	(1918)	Wiederseim, G.	50-70	
Wiese, K.	Buddy the Bear (1st, 4to, ibds, color, [32]p, pep, DJ)	Coward	1936	Wiese, K.	70-90	
Wiese, K.	Chinese Ink Stick (1st {std}, 8vo, 199p, 4cp, pep, DJ)	Doubleday/Dor.	1929	Wiese, K.	50-65	
Wiese, K.	Ella the Elephant (1st, 4to, p-o, [31]p, 2-color, pep)	Coward	1931	Wiese, K.	35-50	
Wiese, K.	Fish in the Air (1st, ob4to, ipcb, [32]p, color, pep, CH)	Viking	1948	Wiese, K.	65-110	R*
Wiese, K.	Joe Buys Nails (1st {std}, ob8vo, ibds, [54]p, color)	Doubleday/Dor.	1931	Wiese, K.	45-60	
Wiese, K.	Karoo the Kangaroo (1st {1st bk.}, sm4to, [35]p, color, pep)	Coward	1929	Wiese, K.	45-65	
Wiese, K.	Liang & Lo (1st {std}, ob4to, ibds, [56]p, color, pep)	Doubleday/Dor.	1930	Wiese, K.	45-65	*
Wiese, K.	Parrot Dealer (1st {std}, 8vo, 239p, pep)	Coward	(1932)	Wiese, K.	30-45	*
Wiese, K.	You Can Write Chinese (1st, ob4to, ibds, [64]p, color, CH)	Viking	1945	Wiese, K.	80-120	*
Wiggin & Smith	Talking Beasts... (1st, 8vo, 391p, p-o, col frn, pl)	Doubleday/Page	1911	Nelson, H.	25-40	*
Wiggin, K.D.	Affair at the Inn (1st, 8vo, 220p, 6pl)	Houghton	1904	Justice, M.	25-40	
Wiggin, K.D.	Birds' Christmas Carol (1st, 8vo, 91p, green cl, col frn)	Houghton	1912	Wireman, K.	35-50	
Wiggin, K.D.	Cathedral Courtship (1st, 8vo, 104p, teg, 6pl)	Houghton	1901	Brock, C.E.	30-45	*
Wiggin, K.D.	Diary of a Goose Girl (1st, 12mo, 117p, tan cl, b/w)	Houghton	1902	Shepperson, C.	25-40	
Wiggin, K.D.	Mother Carey's Chickens (1st, 8vo, green cl, 356p, 10pl)	Houghton	1911	Stephens, A.B.	40-65	
Wiggin, K.D.	Mother Carey's Chickens (1st, 8vo, 289p, p-o, 4cp, 10 b/w)	Houghton	1930	Green, E.S.	35-50	
Wiggin, K.D.	New Chronicles of Rebecca (1st, 12mo, p-o, 278p, 8pl)	Houghton	1907	Yohn, F.C.	25-40	
Wiggin, K.D.	Old Peabody Pew (1st, 8vo, grey cl, teg, 143p, 6pl, pep)	Houghton	1907	Stephens, A.B.	30-45	
Wiggin, K.D.	Penelope's Irish Experiences (1st, 8vo, gilt, AEG, 335p, b/w)	L: Gay & Bird	1902	Brock, C.E.	40-60	
Wiggin, K.D.	Romance of a Christmas Card (1st, 8vo, 123p, teg, p-o, pep, 5cp)	Houghton	1916	Hunt, E.A.	35-60	
Wiggin, K.D.	Scottish Chiefs (1st, 4to, p-o, gilt, 503p, 17cp, pep, SC)	Scribner	1921	Wyeth, N.C.	150-200	
Wiggin, K.D.	Susanna & Sue (1st, 8vo, 225p, teg, p-o, color, dep)	Houghton	1909	Wyeth, N.C.	60-80	
Wiggin, K.D.	Tales of Laughter (1st, lg8vo, 331p, black cl, 8cp)	Doubleday/Page	1926	MacKinstry, E.	60-85	
Wightman, F.P.	Jingle Jangle Jumbly Lays... (1st, lg4to, [26]p, color)	NY: Blanchard	1899	Wightman, F.P.	200-300	*
Wightman, F.P.	Little Leather Breeches (1st, 4to, wraps, [48]p, color)	J.F. Taylor	1899	Wightman, F.P.	85-125	*
Wiig, Hanna	Tale of Tiny Tutak (1st AM, 16mo, unpag, color, pep)	Lippincott	[1957]	Skauge, S.	25-40	*
Wilde, O.	Ballad of Redding Gaol (1st, 4to, bds, 124p, 16pl)	Dutton	1928	Vassos, J.	70-100	
Wilde, O.	Birthday of the Infanta (1st, 8vo, 58p, blue cl, 3 dp color)	MacMillan	1929	Bianco, P.	35-50	
Wilde, O.	Canterville Ghost (1st, 16mo, 123p, blue cl, pl)	Bos: J.W. Luce	1906	Goldsmith, W.	150-200	*
Wilde, O.	Fisherman & his Soul (1st, 4to, 212p, gilt, 15 ticp)	Farrar/Rine.	(1929)	Nadejen, T.	100-165	
Wilde, O.	Happy Prince (1st AM, 8vo, grey cl, 116p, 3pl)	Roberts	1888	Crane, W.	280-400	
Wilde, O.	Happy Prince (1st, 8vo, p-o, 204p, gilt, 8cp)	Stokes	(1913)	Nichols, S.B.	60-80	
Wilde, O.	Happy Prince (1st AM, 4to, 134p, gilt, teg, 12 ticp, pep)	Putnam	(1913)	Robinson, C.	400-600	
Wilde, O.	Happy Prince (1st, 4to, teg, gilt, 134p, 12 ticp, dep)	L: Duckworth	(1913)	Robinson, C.	600-800	
Wilde, O.	Happy Prince (1st, 4to, blue/gilt, teg, 148p, pep, 12cp)	Winston	(1940)	Shinn, E.	50-80	*
Wilde, O.	Harlot's House (1st, sm4to, ibds, 105p, 16pl, DJ)	Dutton	1929	Vassos, J.	100-140	
Wilde, O.	House of Pomegranates (1st, lg8vo, gilt, 158p, uncut)	L: Osgood	1891	Ricketts, C.	400-600	
Wilde, O.	House of Pomegranates (1st, 8vo, 158p, gilt, uncut, dep, 4pl)	L: McIlvanie	1891	Shannon, C.	650-900	
Wilde, O.	House of Pomegranates (1st, 4to, teg, 162p, gilt, 16 ticp, pep)	L: Methuen	(1915)	King, J.	600-800	
Wilde, O.	House of Pomegranates (1st AM, 4to, teg, 162p, gilt 16ticp, pep)	Brentano's	[1915]	King, J.	550-750	
Wilde, O.	House of Pomegranates (1st, 8vo, black/gilt, 180p, 16pl, pep)	Dodd	1925	Kutcher, B.	45-60	
Wilde, O.	Salome... (1st, 8vo, blue/gilt, 10pl)	L: Matthews	1894	Beardsley, A.	900-1200	
Wilde, O.	Salome... (2nd, sm4to, gilt, 66p, teg, 16pl)	L: J. Lane	1907	Beardsley, A.	300-450	
Wilde, O.	Salome... (sm8vo, 36p, black/gilt, 16pl)	Bos: J.W. Luce	1907	Beardsley, A.	100-160	
Wilde, O.	Salome... (1st, 8vo, bds, 57p, 13pl)	Dutton	(1927)	Vassos, J.	100-140	
Wilde, O.	The Spinx (4to, teg, 10pl)	J. Lane	1920	Alastair	200-300	
Wilde, O.	Woman of No Importance (1st, pink/gilt, cvr by...)	L: J. Lane	1894	Ricketts, C.	260	
Wilder, L.I.	By the Shores of Silver Lake (1st {std}, 8vo, 260p, col frn, NH)	Harper	1939	Sewell/Boyle	100-140	R*
Wilder, L.I.	Farmer Boy (1st {std}, 8vo, 230p, col frn, b/w, dep)	Harper	1933	Sewell, H.	70-100	R*
Wilder, L.I.	Little House in Big Woods (1st {1st bk}, 8vo, 176p, col frn, NH)	Harper	1932	Sewell/Boyle	100-135	*
Wilder, L.I.	Little House o/t Prairie (1st {std}, sq8vo, 200p, col frn, dep)	Harper	1935	Sewell/Boyle	150-200	R*
Wilder, L.I.	Little House on the Prairie (1st, 8vo, DJ)	Harper	(1953)	Williams, Garth	50-80	R*
Wilder, L.I.	Little Town o/t Prairie (1st {std}, 8vo, 288p, col frn, dep, NH)	Harper	(1941)	Sewell/Boyle	100-140	R*
Wilder, L.I.	Long Winter (1st {std}, 8vo, 325p, col frn, dep, NH)	Harper	1940	Sewell/Boyle	100-140	R*
Wilder, L.I.	On the Banks of Plum Creek (1st {std}, 8vo, 239p, col frn, NH)	Harper	1937	Sewell/Boyle	100-145	*
Wilder, L.I.	These Happy Golden Years (1st {std}, 8vo, 299p, col frn, NH)	Harper	(1943)	Sewell/Boyle	100-150	R*
Wilder, T.N.	Bridge/San Luis Rey (1st, 8vo, 139p, red cl, color)	Longmans	(1935)	Leighton, C.	70-100	
Wilhelmson, C.	Midsummer Night (1st, 8vo, uncut, 305p, 10pl)	Farrar/Rine.	1930	Ward, L.	70-90	
Wilkins, M.E.	Decorative Plaques (1st, sq12mo, [32]p, ibds, designs by...)	Lothrop	(1883)	Barnes, G.F.	350-500	
Wilkins, M.E.	Heart's Highway (1st [1], 8vo, green cl, 308p, 8pl)	Doubleday/Page	1900	DuMond	30-45	
Wilkins, M.E.	Jerome, A Poor Man (1st, 12mo, 506p)	Harper	1897	Keller, A.I.	30-45	
Wilkins, M.E.	Six Trees (1st, 12mo, green cl, 206p, 16pl)	Harper	1903	Broughton, C.	30-45	
Wilkins, M.E.	Wind in the Rose Bush (1st, 8vo, green/gilt, 237p, 8pl)	Doubleday/Page	1903	Newell, P.	50-70	
Wilkinson, F.	Kings & Queens (1st, 8vo, tan cl, uncut, 6pl)	McClure	1903	Betts, E.F.	30-45	
Wilkinson, F.	Lady of the Flag-Flowers (1st, 12mo, 364p, cvr by...)	H. Stone	1899	Hazenplug, F.	45-70	

AUTHOR	TITLE	PUBLISHER	DATE	ARTIST	PRICE	LC
Willard, C.D.	Fall of Ulysses (1st, 8vo, grey pcb, gilt, unpag, 4cp, dep)	Doran	1912	VerBeck, F.	60-85	*
Willard, F.E.	Wheel Within a Wheel (1st, 12mo, 75p, tan buckram, 7pl)	Revell	1895	(Photos)	80-100	
Willcox, L.C.	Torch: Book of Poems for Boys (1st, sm4to, 514p, gilt, 7cp)	Harper	1924	Various	50-75	
Willett, Edward	Cat's Cradle Rhymes for Children (sm4to, ibds, 60p, fp color)	Worthington	1881	Kendrick, C.	75-130	*
Williams, C.A.	ABC of Animals (1st, 4to, 17p, color, cep)	Stokes	(1911)	Williams, G.A.	80-130	*
Williams, C.A.	Bettijak Book (4to, p-o, color)	Stokes	(1914)	Williams, G.A.	180-220	
Williams, C.A.	Magic Book (1st, 4to, 64p, color)	Stokes	(1912)	Williams, G.A.	80-120	*
Williams, C.A.	Mammy's Lil'l Chillums (1st, sm4to, [63]p, ibds, fp color)	Stokes	(1904)	Williams, G.A.	160-200	R
Williams, C.A.	Stories that Glue Told (1st, ob folio, [36]p, ibds, color)	Stokes	1907	Williams, G.A.	100-150	*
Williams, C.A.	Story Book of Silhouettes (ob folio, ibds, b/w)	Stokes	(1914)	Williams, G.A.	130-200	
Williams, E.	Ridolfo (1st, 8vo, p-o, 406p, 4cp)	McClurg	1906	Leyendecker, J.C.	60-80	
Williams, Eleanor	And a Good Fat Hen (1st, lg8vo, red cl, [47]p, lettering by…)	Putnam	(1939)	Gag, Flavia	30-50	*
Williams, Emery	Alphabet of Indians (1st, folio, ipcb, [57]p, fp 1-color)	R.H. Russell	1900	Williams, E.	250-400	*
Williams, G.A.	Boy's Book of Indians & Wild West (1st, ob4to, p-o, 47p, 11cp)	Stokes	1911	Williams, G.A.	70-100	
Williams, Garth	Adventures of Benjamin Pink (1st, 8vo, 151p, green cl, b/w)	Harper	(1951)	Williams, Garth	30-45	*
Williams, Garth	Chicken Book (1st, ob8vo, [31]p, color)	Howell/Soskin	(1946)	Williams, Garth	65-80	*
Williams, Garth	Rabbit's Wedding (1st, 4to, ibds, unpag, color)	Harper	(1958)	Williams, Garth	75-120	
Williams, Gwen M.	Timid Timothy… (1st, sm ob8vo, ibds, [68]p, color)	W.R. Scott	1944	Weisgard, L.	25-40	*
Williams, Herschel	Children of the Clouds (1st, lg8vo, 224p, col frn, 10 b/w, pep)	NY: Nelson	1929	Wiese, K.	30-45	
Williams, Herschel	Jolly Old Whistle (1st, lg8vo, 187p, purple cl, col frn)	Nelson	1927	Wiese, K.	30-45	
Williams, I.A.	Where the Bee Sucks (4to, blue/gilt, 87p, teg, 12 ticp)	L: Medici	[1915]	Cameron, K.	65-80	
Williams, Jay	Tournament of the Lions (1st, 8vo, black/gilt, 120p, 5 fp b/w)	Walck	1960	Keats, E.J.	35-50	*
Williams, M.	Velveteen Rabbit (1st, lg8vo, 19p, ipcb, 7cp, pep)	L: Heinemann	1922	Nicholson, W.	450-600	
Williams, M.	Velveteen Rabbit (1st AM, 8vo, ibds, 33p, 7cp, pep)	Doran	[1922]	Nicholson, W.	350-500	
Williams, Michael	Little Brother Francis of Assisi (1st, sm8vo, 188p, 4pl, dep)	MacMillan	1926	Artzybasheff, B.	30-50	*
Williams, Orlando	Three Naughty Children (1st, 4to, 110p)	L: Duckworth	1922	Monsell, J.R.	50-70	*
Williams, W.H.	Fairy Tales from Folk Lore (1st, 12mo, 288p, b/w)	Moffat	1908	Squire, M.H.	35-50	
Williamson, C.& N.	Princess Passes (1st, 12mo, green cl, 369p, 12 pl by…)	Holt	1905	Penfield, E.	25-40	
Williamson, H.	Baby Bear (1st {std}, 8vo, [55]p, green ibds, color)	Doubleday/Dor.	(1930)	Hader, B.& E.	50-70	
Williamson, H.	Gods & Mortals in Love (9cp, cloth)	L:Country Life	(1935)	Dulac, E.	75-100	
Williamson, H.	Humpy, Son of the Sands (1st {std}, 8vo, [47]p, color, pep)	Doubleday/Dor.	1937	Hader, B.& E.	60-90	*
Williamson, H.	Lion Cub: Jungle Tale (1st {std}, 8vo, ipcb, [51]p, color, pep)	Doubleday/Dor.	(1931)	Hader, B.& E.	50-80	*
Williamson, H.	Little Elephant (1st {std}, sq8vo, ibds, [55]p, 4cp, DJ)	Doubleday/Dor.	(1930)	Hader, B.& E.	45-60	
Williamson, H.	Monkey Tale (1st {std}, 8vo, [49]p, pep, color)	Doubleday/Dor.	(1929)	Hader, B.& E.	45-60	*
Williamson, H.	Stripey (1st {std}, sm4to, ibds, [47]p, color, pep, DJ)	Doubleday/Dor.	1939	Hader, B.& E.	50-70	
Williston, T.P.	Hindu Stories (1st, 8vo, 111p, p-o, brown cl, color, pep)	Rand/McNally	(1925)	Squire, M.H.	35-50	*
Williston, T.P.	Japanese Fairy Tales (1st, sm8vo, blue cl, 88p, 8 fp color, pep)	Rand/McNally	(1904)	Ogawa, S.	45-65	
Willoughby, Rachel	Tunes for Tiny Troubadours (1st, lg4to, ibds, 31p, color)	Putnam	(1936)	Willoughby, W.	65-80	*
Willson, Dixie	Circus ABC (1st, sm4to, 97p, brown cl)	Stokes	1924	Berry, E.	40-65	
Willson, Dixie	Clown Town (1st {std}, 8vo, [62]p, color)	Doubleday/Page	1924	Berry, E.	25-45	*
Willson, Dixie	Empty Elephant (1st, 4to, ibds, [39]p, color)	Volland	(1923)	Berry, E.	80-130	
Willson, Dixie	Honey Bear (1st, sm8vo, ibds, [36]p, pep, color)	Volland	(1923)	Barney, M.W.	65-90	
Willson, Dixie	Once Upon a Monday (1st, 8vo, ibds, 40p, color)	Volland	(1931)	Berry, E.	65-90	*
Willson, Dixie	Pinky-Pup & Empty Elephant (1st, lg4to, ibds, 60p, color)	Volland	(1922)	Berry, E.	75-120	
Willson, Dixie	Pinky-Pup & Empty Elephant (1st [new ed], sq8vo, ibds, col, pep)	Volland	(1928)	Berry, E.	65-80	*
Willson, Dixie	Tuffy Good Luck (1st, sq12mo, ipcb, pep, 39p, color)	Volland	(1927)	DeKarekjarto, I.	70-100	
Willson, J.	Lucian's Wonderland… (1st, 8vo, brown/gilt, 163p, 15pl)	L: Blackwood	1899	Garnett, A.P.	90-145	
Wilson, A.E.	Devota (1st, 8vo, teg, p-o, 122p, red/gilt, dep)	Dillingham	(1907)	Travis, S.	20-30	
Wilson, E.	Undertaker's Garland (1st, 12mo, 192p, uncut, p-o, 5pl)	Knopf	1922	Artzybasheff, B.	45-65	R
Wilson, E.H.	About Ricco (1st, 4to, pep, 123p, p-o, color, DJ)	Whitman	1937	Gag, W.	50-85	
Wilson, E.H.	Flyaway Flippety (1st {std}, lg8vo, 104p, pep, 14cp)	Harper	1932	Wilson, E.H.	25-40	*
Wilson, Edward A.	Pirate's Treasure (1st, 8vo, ibds, color)	Volland	(1926)	Wilson, E.H.	35-50	*
Wilson, H.L.	Boss of the Little Arcady (1st, 8vo, green cl, 371p, 4pl)	Lothrop/Lee	1905	O'Neill, R.	30-50	
Wilson, H.L.	Lions of the Lord (1st, 8vo, p-o, 520p, 6pl)	Lothrop	(1903)	O'Neill, R.	30-45	
Wilson, H.L.	The Seeker (1st, 8vo, green cl, 341p, b/w)	Doubleday/Page	1904	O'Neill, R.	25-40	
Wilson, R.	Indian Story Book (1st, 8vo, 272p, blue/gilt, 16cp)	L: MacMillan	1914	Pape, F.	90-110	
Wilson, R.	Russian Story Book (1st, 8vo, 307p, gilt, 16cp)	L: Methuen	1916	Pape, F.	60-80	
Wilson, Romer	Red Magic… (1st, sm8vo, red/gilt, 368p, 8cp)	L: J. Cape	(1930)	Nielsen, K.	400-600	
Wilson, Romer	Red Magic… (1st AM, 8vo, 368p, black cl, uncut, 8cp)	Harcourt	(1931)	Nielsen, K.	350-500	
Wilson, Romer	Silver Magic (1st, 8vo, 432p, 8cp)	L: J. Cape	(1929)	Brunton, V.	80-130	
Wilson, W.	George Washington (1st, 8vo, 333p, teg, 20pl)	Harper	1897	Pyle, H.	65-100	
Winder, Blanche	King Arthur & his Knights (8vo, 128p, 48cp)	L: Ward Lock	[1910]	Theaker, H.G.	70-100	*
Winfrey, Guy	Bunny Bearskin (1st, 8vo, ibds, color, pep)	M. Bradley	(1926)	Tessin, L.	70-100	
Winfrey, Guy	Pussy Purr-Mew (1st, 8vo, [126]p, ibds, color, pep)	M. Bradley	(1927)	Tessin, L.	80-120	
Wing, Paul	Unsuccessful Elf (1st, ob4to, ibds, [44]p, 6 fp color, pep)	Rinehart	(1947)	Irvin, Rea	60-80	
Winlow, Clara V.	Kitten that Grew Too Fat (1st, lg ob8vo, 93p, 24 fp color)	Macrae-Smith	(1929)	Hogan, I.	45-70	*
Winsor, F.	Space Child's Mother Goose (1st {std}, 8vo, [88]p, b/w, pep)	Simon/Schuster	1958	Parry, M.	30-45	*
Winter, A.A.	Jewel Weed (1st, 12mo, p-o, 434p, 5pl)	Bobbs-Merrill	(1910)	Fisher, H.	25-40	*
Winter, B. (ed.)	Stories of King Arthur (1st, 8vo, green cl, p-o, 340p, 48cp)	L: Ward Lock	[1925]	Theaker, H.G.	65-80	
Winter, M.	Billy Popgun (1st, 4to, ibds, p-o, 61p, 8cp, pep)	Houghton	1912	Winter, M.	150-200	
Wister, A.L.	Happy-Go-Lucky (1st, 8vo, green/gilt, 115p, teg, 4cp)	Lippincott	1906	Johann, P.G.	30-45	*
Wister, O.	Dragon of Wantley (1st, 8vo, teg, blue/gilt, 149p, b/w)	Lippincott	1892	Stewardson, J.	80-125	R

AUTHOR	TITLE	PUBLISHER	DATE	ARTIST	PRICE	LC
Wister, O.	Jimmyjohn Boss (1st, 8vo, 333p, 5pl by...)	Harper	1900	Remington, F.	50-70	
Wister, O.	Journey in Search of Christmas (1st Canadian, 8vo, 93p)	(Toronto)	1904	Remington, F.	50-75	
Wister, O.	Journey in Search of Christmas (1st, 8vo, teg, gilt, 93p, 3pl)	Harper	1904	Remington, F.	70-85	
Wister, O.	Members of the Family (1st, 317p, 12pl)	MacMillan	1911	Dunn, H.T.	25-40	
Wister, O.	Mother (1st, 8vo, 95p, p-o, uncut, 3cp, 4pl, dep)	Dodd	1907	Rae, J.	30-45	
Wister, O.	Padre Ignacio (1st, 8vo, ibds, 65p, col frn)	Harper	1925	Hogg, Z.	25-40	
Wister, O.	Red Men & White (1st, 8vo, 280p, 17 illus)	Harper	1896	Remington, F.	60-80	
Wister, O.	The Virginian (1st, 8vo, 504p, tan cloth, 8pl)	MacMillan	1902	Keller, A.I.	150-200	
Wister, O.	The Virginian (1st, red cl, p-o, 506p, teg, 10pl by...)	MacMillan	1911	Remington, F.	250-300	*
Wister, O.	The Virginian (1st, red cl, p-o, 506p, teg, 42 illus by...)	MacMillan	1911	Russell, C.M.	250-300	*
Wither, G.	Love Song (1st, 16mo, blue pcb, p-o, 14p, uncut)	(Concord)	(1903)	Bradley, W.	70-90	
Wodehouse, P.G.	Intrusion of Jimmy (1st, sm8vo, 314p, black/gilt, p-o, col frn)	NY: Watt	(1910)	Unknown	300-400	
Wodehouse, P.G.	Mike (1st, 8vo, 339p, olive cl, 12pl)	L: A&C Black	1909	Whitwell, T.M.R.	1000	
Wodehouse, P.G.	Piccadilly Jim (1st, sm8vo, 363p, orange cl, 8cp)	Dodd	1917	Preston, M.W.	250-400	
Wodehouse, P.G.	Prince & Betty (1st AM, sm8vo, 300p, black/gilt, p-o)	NY: Watt	(1912)	Grefe, W.	350-500	
Wodehouse, P.G.	Psmith in the City (1st, 8vo, 266p, blue cl, 12pl)	L: A&C Black	1910	Whitwell, T.M.R.	800-1000	
Wolf, A.S.	House of Cards (1st, 8vo, black/gilt, cvr by...)	Stone/Kimball	1896	Hazenplug, F.	50-80	
Wood, E.	Back Home (1st, 8vo, 8pl)	McClure	1905	Frost, A.B.	40-65	R*
Wood, Esther	Great Sweeping Day (1st {std}, 12mo, 158p, pep)	Longmans	1936	Wood, E.	20-35	*
Wood, Esther	Pedro's Coconut Skates (1st {std}, sm8vo, 191p, pep)	Longmans	1938	Wood, E.	20-35	*
Wood, J.S.	Yale Yarns (1st, 12mo, 307p, buckram)	Putnam	1895	Armstrong, M.	45-65	
Wood, M. & H.	Something Perfectly Silly (1st, sq8vo, ibds, [66]p, color, pep)	Knopf	1930	Wood, M.& H.	80-120	*
Woodcock, L.	This is the Way the Animals Walk (1st, ob8vo, [20]p, color)	W.R. Scott	1946	Binney, I.	35-50	*
Woodhouse, S.C.	Cats at School (1st, 4to, french fold, 21cp)	L: Routledge	[1911]	Wain, L.	375-550	*
Woodhouse, S.C.	Crude Ditties (1st, 16mo, 103p, tan cl, 24 fp color)	Swan/Dutton	1903	Macgregor, A.J.	80-100	*
Woodhouse, S.C.	Two Cats at Large (1st, 4to, ibds, 24 fp color)	L: Routledge	[1910]	Wain, L.	500-700	*
Woodruff, E.	Dickey Bird (1st, lg4to, black cl, 146p, 6 ticp, pep)	M. Bradley	(1928)	Tenggren, G.	250-320	
Woodruff, E.	Stories from the Magic World (4to, 130p, color)	McLoughlin	(1938)	Tenggren, G.	140-220	
Woodruff, H.S.	Mis' Beauty (1st, 12mo, 163p, p-o, 5cp)	A. Harriman	1911	Woodruff, H.	70-100	*
Woods, M.	Come Unto these Yellow Sands (1st, 4to, ibds, 234p, 16cp)	L: J. Lane	1915	Hancock, J.	70-100	
Woodward, C.S.	Dreams & Fables (1st, 8vo, 110p, green cl)	L: Longmans	1929	Everett, E.	25-40	*
Woodward, H.	Everyday Children (1st, sq12mo, ipcb, [48]p, 1-color, pep)	NY: OUP	(1935)	Woodward, H.	25-45	*
Woodward, H.	Time Was (1st, 4to, [48]p, color)	Scribner	(1941)	Gag, Flavia	30-50	
Woole, R.	Animal Legends of Many Lands (4to, gilt, 144p, 12cp)	Tuck/McKay	[1915]	Noble, E.	85-140	
Woolf, Rose	Children's Stories/Arabian Nights (1st, lg8vo, 144p, 10cp)	L: R. Tuck	[1914]	Theaker, H.G.	65-90	*
Worm, Piet	3 Little Horses (1st, narrow 4to, red bds, 62p, pep)	Random	(1954)	Worm, P.	65-80	*
Worth, Kath.	They Loved to Laugh (1st {std}, sm8vo, grey cl, 269p, b/w, pep)	Doubleday/Dor.	1942	DeAngeli, M.	25-45	*
Worthington, Eliz.	Lullabies of Many Lands (ibds, 24 color)	Caldwell	(1908)	Worthington, E.	70-100	
Wright, E.B.	Saturday Flight (1st, ob8vo, [20]p, color)	W.R. Scott	1944	Rose, R.	30-45	*
Wright, F.	New Zealand (1st, 8vo, gilt, teg, 241p, 75cp)	L: A&C Black	1908	Wright, F.	70-120	
Wright, H.B.	Uncrowned King (1st, 16mo, green cl, 118p, 5pl)	Book Supp. Co.	1910	Neill, J.R.	60-80	
Wright, Henrietta	Princess Liliwinkins (1st, 8vo, 220p, 9pl)	Harper	1889	Unknown	50-65	*
Wright, Isa L.	Having Fun (1st, 12mo, 124p, color)	Houghton	(1929)	Woodward, H.	30-45	*
Wright, Isa L.	Remarkable Tale of a Whale (1st, 8vo, ibds, color)	Volland	(1920)	Held, J.	65-90	*
Wright, M.O.	Four-Footed Americans... (1st, sm8vo, 432p, b/w)	MacMillan	1898	Seton, E.T.	65-80	
Wright, M.O.	Wabeno the Magician (1st, 8vo, 344p, green/gilt, b/w)	MacMillan	1899	Gleeson, J.M.	30-50	
Wurth, A.	Rag Doll Susie... (1st, lg sq8vo, [16]p, ibds, 6 color, pep)	Saalfield	1939	Peat, F.B.	65-80	
Wyatt, Horace	Malice in Kulturland (1st AM, 12mo, 84p, b/w)	Dutton	(1917)	Tell, W.	50-80	*
Wynne, Annette	Treasure Things (1st, 12mo, [39]p, ibds, pep, color)	Volland	(1922)	Merritt, E.	45-70	*
Wyss, J.D.	Swiss Family Robinson (8vo, green bds, 291p, gilt, 6cp, 8pl)	Nister/Dutton	[1900]	Kley, H.	65-80	
Wyss, J.D.	Swiss Family Robinson (1st, 8vo, 307p, grey/gilt, 12cp)	L: A&C Black	(1907)	Rountree, H.	65-90	*
Wyss, J.D.	Swiss Family Robinson (1st, lg8vo, 602p, red cl, b/w)	Harper	1909	Rhead, L.	45-65	*
Wyss, J.D.	Swiss Family Robinson (1st, 8vo, 454p, beige cl, 12cp)	L: J.M. Dent	1910	Folkard, C.	70-100	
Wyss, J.D.	Swiss Family Robinson (1st AM, 4to, red cl, 25 ticp)	Hodder	[1913]	Robinson, T.H.	80-120	
Wyss, J.D.	Swiss Family Robinson (1st, sm4to, 431p, teg, red/gilt, 25 ticp)	L: H. Milford	[1913]	Robinson, T.H.	100-150	
Wyss, J.D.	Swiss Family Robinson (1st, 8vo, 441p, 14cp, pep)	Rand/McNally	(1916)	Winter, M.	45-80	*
Wyss, J.D.	Swiss Family Robinson (1st AM, 12mo, 307p, cp)	MacMillan	1926	Rountree, H.	30-50	*
Wyss, J.D.	Swiss Family Robinson (8vo, 436p, color, pep)	Garden City	(1931)	Robinson, T.H.	30-50	*
Wyss, J.D.	Swiss Family Robinson (1st, sm8vo, 237p)	Whitman	(1935)	Bennett, J.C.	25-45	*
Wyss, J.D.	Swiss Family Robinson (lg4to, 96p, color)	Saalfield	(1940)	Muheim, H.	25-50	*
Wyss, J.D.	Swiss Family Robinson (1st, 8vo, 388p, 9cp)	Grosset/Dunlap	(1949)	Ward, L.	40-65	*
Yashima, M. & T.	Plenty to Watch (1st, sm4to, 39p, color)	Viking	1954	Yashima, T.	70-110	R*
Yashima, Taro	Crow Boy (1st, lg4to, 37p, brown cl, color, DJ, CH)	Viking	1955	Yashima, T.	75-100	
Yashima, Taro	Umbrella (1st, ob4to, 32p, pep, fp color, CH)	Viking	(1958)	Yashima, T.	70-100	R*
Yashima, Taro	Village Tree (1st, 4to, grey cl, 34p, fp color, dep)	Viking	1953	Yashima, T.	65-100	R*
Yates, Eliz.	Amos Fortune, Free Man (1st {std}, 8vo, 181p, b/w, NM)	Aladdin	1950	Unwin, N.S.	80-120	R*
Yates, Eliz.	Mountain Born (1st, 8vo, 118p, brown cl, b/w, pep, NH)	Coward	(1943)	Unwin, N.S.	40-65	*
Yates, Eliz.	Once in the Year (1st, 8vo, red cl, p-o, [64]p, 1-color)	Coward	(1947)	Unwin, N.S.	30-45	
Yeats, W.B.	Four Plays for Dancers (1st AM, 8vo, bds, 138p, b/w)	MacMillan	1921	Dulac, E.	100-140	
Yeats, W.B.	Land of Hearts Desire (1st AM, 16mo, pcb, frn by...)	H. Stone	1894	Beardsley, A.	100-130	
Yeats, W.B.	Plays/Irish Theatre (8vo, 224p, brown bds, uncut, 4cp)	L: Bullen	1911	Craig, E.G.	100-140	
Yeats, W.B.	Poems (1st, 8vo, 286p, beige/gilt, uncut, ti page by....)	L: T.F. Unwin	1895	Fell, H.G.	120-165	

AUTHOR	TITLE	PUBLISHER	DATE	ARTIST	PRICE	LC
Yonge, C.M.	Dove in the Eagle's Nest (1st, 8vo, 294p, 3cp, 8pl, pep, DJ)	MacMillan	1926	DeAngeli, M.	50-70	
Yonge, C.M.	Heir of Redclyffe (1st, 8vo, blue/gilt, 524p, 4 illus by)	L: MacMillan	1881	Greenaway, K.	50-80	
Yonge, C.M.	Lances of Lynwood (1st, 12mo, green cl, 217p, col frn, 6pl, pep)	MacMillan	1929	DeAngeli, M.	25-40	*
Yonge, C.M.	Little Duke (1st, 8vo, 240p, red/gilt, 4cp)	Duffield	1923	Stevens, B.	30-45	
Yonge, C.M.	Little Duke (1st, 8vo, blue cl, 3cp, 7pl, pep)	MacMillan	1927	DeAngeli, M.	35-50	*
Yonge, C.M.	Prince & the Page (1st, 8vo, 246p, blue cl, 3cp, 8pl, pep)	MacMillan	1925	DeAngeli, M.	45-60	*
Young, C.	Night-Caps for the Babies (1st, 8vo, 126p, 8cp)	L: J. Lane	(1907)	Walker, W.H.	60-85	
Young, Ella	Tangle-Coated Horse (1st {std}, 8vo, blck cl, 186p, b/w, pep, NH)	Longmans	1929	Bock, V.	30-55	*
Young, Ella	Unicorn with Silver Shoes (1st {std}, 8vo, gilt, 214p, 9pl, pep)	Longmans	1932	Lawson, R.	50-75	R
Young, Ella	Wonder Smith & His Son (1st, 8vo, grn/gilt, 191p, b/w, dep, NH)	Longmans	1927	Artzybasheff, B.	65-80	R
Young, Evelyn	Wu & Lu & Li (1st, sq12mo, [31]p, green cl, color)	NY: OUP	(1939)	Young, E.	35-50	
Young, Gerald	Witches' Kitchen (1st, sm4to, p-o, 223p, gilt, 8cp)	L: Harrap	(1910)	Pogany, W.	150-200	
Young, Gerald	Witches' Kitchen (1st AM, 8vo, 223p, teg, p-o, 8cp, pep)	Crowell	(1911)	Pogany, W.	100-165	*
Young, Lillian E.	Advens. of Tommy Cat the Sailor (1st, sm4to, 165p, 20 fp color)	Sears	(1928)	Young, L.E.	35-50	*
Young, Lillian E.	Pussy Willow's Naughty Kittens (1st, 4to, p-o, 54p)	Funk/Wagnalls	(1924)	Young, L.E.	35-50	*
Young, Martha	Behind the Dark Pines (1st, 8vo, 287p, tan cl, 27pl)	Appleton	1912	Conde, J.M.	30-50	
Young, Martha	Plantation Bird Legends (1st, 8vo, 249p, 28pl)	Appleton	1916	Conde, J.M.	75-100	*
Young, Percy	Ding Dong Bell (1st, 4to, ibds, 141p, b/w)	L: Dobson	(1957)	Ardizzone, E.	50-70	*
Zeitlin, I.	Gessar-Khan (1st, 4to, 203p, gilt, 40 color)	Doran	(1927)	Nadejen, T.	40-70	
Zeitlin, I.	King's Pleasure (1st {std}, lg8vo, 230p, blue/gilt, 17cp, cep)	Harper	1929	Nadejen, T.	50-70	
Zeitlin, I.	Skazki (1st, 4to, 335p, black/gilt, teg, pep, 24 ticp)	Doran	(1926)	Nadejen, T.	65-90	
Zion, Gene	All Falling Down (1st, 4to, ipcb, [31]p, color, CH)	Harper	(1951)	Graham, M.B.	60-90	R*
Zion, Gene	Dear Garbage Man (1st, 4to, ibds, unpag, color)	Harper	(1957)	Graham, M.B.	45-70	*
Zion, Gene	Harry the Dirty Dog (1st, 4to, ibds, [30]p, color)	Harper	(1956)	Graham, M.B.	65-80	R*
Zion, Gene	Really Spring (1st, lg4to, ipcb, [30]p, 3-color)	Harper	(1956)	Graham, M.B.	65-85	*
Zion, Gene	Summer Snowman (1st, narrow 4to, unpag, yellow, cl, color, cep)	Harper	(1955)	Graham, M.B.	50-80	*
Zistel, E.	Treasury of Cat Stories (1st, sm8vo, grey cl, 278p, 12pl)	Greenberg	(1944)	Bacon, P.	40-60	*
Zogbaum, R.F.	Horse, Foot & Dragons (1st, sm4to, 176p, teg, b/w)	Harper	1888	Zogbaum, R.F.	180-250	
Zogbaum, R.F.	Junior Officer o/t Watch (1st, 8vo, 311p, 4pl)	Appleton	1908	Zogbaum, R.F.	25-40	*
Zolotow, C.	In My Garden (1st, sm4to, unpag, blue cl, fp color)	Lothrop/Lee	1960	Duvoisin, R.	40-65	*
Zolotow, C.	Indian, Indian (1st, sm8vo, ibds, unpag, color, LGB)	Simon/Schuster	(1952)	Weisgard, L.	20-35	*
Zolotow, C.	Not a Little Monkey (1st, sm4to, green cl, unpag, pep, color)	Lothrop/Lee	1957	Duvoisin, R.	40-60	*
Zolotow, C.	One Step, Two (1st, sm4to, unpag, color)	Lothrop/Lee	1954	Duvoisin, R.	40-65	*
Zolotow, C.	Park Book (1st {std}, sm ob4to, [32]p, color, pep)	Harper	(1944)	Rey, H.A.	100-150	R*
Zolotow, C.	Sleepy Book (1st, sm4to, blue cl, [36]p, color, dep)	Lothrop/Lee	1958	Bobri, V.	35-50	*
Zolotow, C.	Storm Book (1st, 4to, ipcb, unpag, 7 fp color, cep, CH)	Harper	(1952)	Graham, M.B.	70-100	*
Zwilgmeyer, D.	Johnny Blossom (1st, 8vo, yellow cl, 157p, pep, 10 fp b/w)	Pilgrim Press	(1948)	D'Aulaire, I.& E.	45-65	*

Section 2

Illustrator-Sorted

Index

AUTHOR	TITLE	PUBLISHER	DATE	ARTIST	PRICE	LC
Barr, A.	Knight of the Nets (1st, 8vo, 314p, cvr by...)	Dodd	1896	'AM'	20-25	*
Smith, G.	Little Mother & Georgie (1st, sq8vo, beige cl, 150p, 12cp)	Harper	1905	'DD'	50-70	*
Smith, G.	Little Precious (1st, 8vo, 146p, 15cp)	Harper	1904	'DD'	45-60	
Crane, Thos.	Abroad (sq8vo, ipcb, 56p, color)	L: Marcus Ward	(1882)	(Chromos)	80-125	
Collins, C.	All Round the Farm (4to, ibds)	L: Nister	[1880]	(Chromos)	70-100	
N/A	At Home (sq8vo, 56p, ipcb)	L: Marcus Ward	(1880)	(Chromos)	70-100	
N/A	Daisy Days (4to, ipcb)	Fiske Co.	1890	(Chromos)	65-90	
Whittemore	Flower Fairies (4to, ibds)	L: Cassell	(1886)	(Chromos)	130-180	
Lecky, E.	Here, There, Everywhere (1st, 4to, unpag)	L: R. Tuck	(1890)	(Chromos)	70-110	
N/A	My Picture Scrap Book (folio, ibds)	L: Nister	(1880)	(Chromos)	130-165	
Riley, J.W.	Old Sweetheart of Mine (1st, ob4to, AEG, color)	Bowen-Merrill	1891	(Chromos)	120-165	
Bates, Clara D.	On the Way to Wonderland (1st, 4to, [38]p, ibds, color, pep)	Lothrop	(1885)	(Chromos)	100-150	
N/A	Story of the Firemen (4to, wraps)	McLoughlin	[1908]	(Chromos)	70-100	
Brigham, S.J.	Under Blue Skies (4to, bds)	Worthington	1886	(Chromos)	80-110	
Parrish, R.	Great Plains (1st, 8vo, 399p, 32pl)	McClurg	1907	(Engravings)	45-70	
N/A	Death & Burial of Poor Cock Robin (4to)	McLoughlin	(1880)	(Lithos)	75-120	
N/A	Funny Little Darkies (1st, sq4to, wraps, 6cp)	McLoughlin	[1890]	(Lithos)	200-300	
Hope, A.	Advens. of Lady Ursula (1st, 8vo, grey/gilt, 125p, teg, uncut)	R.H. Russell	1898	(Photos)	30-45	*
Bradley, Mary H.	Alice in Jungleland (1st, 8vo, 170p, green cl, b/w, pep)	Appleton	1927	(Photos)	80-100	*
Carroll, L.	Alice... & Through... (lg8vo, 297p, grey cl, col frn)	Grosset/Dunlap	[1919]	(Photos)	70-100	*
Carroll, L.	Alice/Wonderland (lg ob8vo, unpag, [movie ed.], b/w)	Whitman	(1934)	(Photos)	80-120	*
Mother Goose	Animal Mother Goose... (1st, 8vo, 168p, grey cl, b/w, pep)	Lothrop/Lee	(1921)	(Photos)	100-130	*
Seton, E.T.	Arctic Prairies (1st, lg8vo, 415p, green/gilt, uncut)	Scribner	1911	(Photos)	70-110	R
Darling, E.B.	Baldy of Nome (1st, 8vo, blue cl, 301p, 15pl)	Penn	1916	(Photos)	40-65	
Culbertson, A.V.	Banjo Talks (1st, 8vo, 171p, 23pl)	Bobbs-Merrill	(1905)	(Photos)	70-120	*
King, Ben	Ben King's Southland Melodies (1st, 8vo, green cl, 128p, b/w)	Chi: Forbes	1911	(Photos)	80-130	
Chittenden, W.L.	Bermuda Verses (1st, 8vo, 68p, green cl, 29pl)	Putnam	1909	(Photos)	40-65	
Porter, G.S.	Birds of the Bible (1st, lg8vo, 469p, 81 illus, pep)	Jennings	(1909)	(Photos)	185-250	
English, Doug	Book of Nimble Beasts (1st, 8vo, green/gilt, 318p)	L: E. Nash	1910	(Photos)	35-50	*
Lippincott, J.W.	Bun, a Wild Rabbit (1st, 12mo, 124p, p-o, 12pl)	Penn	1918	(Photos)	20-40	*
James, G.W.	California, Romantic & Beautiful (1st, 8vo, teg, 433p, gilt)	Page	1914	(Photos)	45-65	
White, S.E.	Camp & Trail (1st, 8vo, 236p, col frn, 11pl)	Outing	1907	(Photos)	30-50	
Johnson, M.	Cat's Fairy Land... (1st, 12mo, 184p, gilt)	H. Carter	1900	(Photos)	100-160	
Earle, A.M.	Child Life in Colonial Days (1st, 8vo, 418p, gilt, teg)	MacMillan	1899	(Photos)	35-50	
De La Mare, W.	Child's Day (1st, lg8vo, 56p, ti-pl)	L: Constable	1912	(Photos)	150-200	*
Peary, J.	Children of the Arctic (1st, 4to, cloth, 120p)	Stokes	(1903)	(Photos)	70-90	
Headland, I.T.	Chinese Boy & Girl (1st, 8vo, ibds, 176p)	Revell	(1901)	(Photos)	85-120	
Headland, I.T.	Chinese Mother Goose Rhymes (1st, 8vo, 160p, ibds)	Revell	(1900)	(Photos)	85-120	
Tileston, M.W.	Chiquita (1st, 12mo, orange cl, 306p, col frn, 7pl)	Merrill	1902	(Photos)	25-45	
Davis, R.H.	Congo & Coasts of Africa (1st, 8vo, teg, 220p, 32pl)	Scribner	1907	(Photos)	30-45	*
London, J.	Cruise of the Snark (1st, 8vo, 340p, teg, p-o, blue cl)	MacMillan	1911	(Photos)	220-350	
Eaton, J.	Daughter of the Seine (1st {std}, lg8vo, blue cl, 324p, pep, NH)	Harper	1929	(Photos)	50-70	*
Eickemeyer, R.	Down South (1st, folio, ibds, [47]p, p-o, b/w)	R.H. Russell	1900	(Photos)	350-400	
Howlett, E.	Driving Lessons (1st, sm4to, 159p, 20pl)	R.H. Russell	1894	(Photos)	100-160	*
Robbins, Louis	Dutch Doll Ditties (1st, 4to, 23p, grey bds, p-o, b/w)	L: Longmans	1904	(Photos)	80-100	
Wallace, Lew	First Christmas (1st, 8vo, 108p, teg, lavender/gilt, 4 tipl)	Harper	1902	(Photos)	30-50	
Credle, Ellis	Flop-Eared Hound (1st, 8vo, [61]p, b/w)	NY: OUP	(1938)	(Photos)	50-80	*
Munroe, K.	Forward March (1st, 8vo, 254p, 20pl)	Harper	1899	(Photos)	40-60	*
Porter, G.S.	Friends In Feathers (1st, lg8vo, teg, 335p, b/w)	Doubleday/Page	1917	(Photos)	160-200	
Doubleday, R.	From Cattle-Ranch To College (1st, 8vo, blue cl, 24p)	Doub./McClure	1899	(Photos)	65-80	
Lippincott, J.W.	Gray Squirrel (1st, 12mo, 144p, p-o, 7pl)	Penn	1921	(Photos)	20-40	*
Breakenridge, W.	Helldorado (1st, lg8vo, brown cl, 256p, DJ)	Houghton	1928	(Photos)	65-80	
Longfellow, H.W.	Hiawatha (1st, 8vo, 245p, buckram)	Rand/McNally	(1911)	(Photos)	100-130	
Patch, E.M.	Holiday Hill (1st, sq8vo, 135p, pep)	MacMillan	1931	(Photos)	25-40	
Earle, A.M.	Home Life in Colonial Days (1st, 8vo, teg, 470p)	MacMillan	1898	(Photos)	30-45	
Porter, G.S.	Homing With Birds (1st, 8vo, 381p)	Doubleday/Page	1919	(Photos)	120-150	
Gaines, M.L.	I Heah de Voices Callin' (1st, 12mo, 91p, 11pl)	(Atlanta)	1916	(Photos)	65-80	
Mills, E.A.	In Beaver World (1st, 8vo, 221p, olive cl, 19pl, pep)	Houghton	1913	(Photos)	60-80	
Adams, W.I.L.	In Nature's Image (1st, lg8vo, gilt)	Baker/Taylor	1898	(Photos)	45-65	
Day, L.G.	In Shadow Town (1st, lg4to, p-o, unpag)	Saalfield	(1907)	(Photos)	100-140	*
Meigs, C.	Invincible Louisa (1st, sm8vo, 260p, red cl, 16pl, NM)	Little/Brown	1933	(Photos)	60-90	R*
Laughlin, E.O.	Johnnie (1st, 12mo, 227p, teg, uncut)	Bowen-Merrill	1899	(Photos)	25-40	*
Credle, Ellis	Johnny & his Mule (1st, sq12mo, [44]p, b/w)	NY: OUP	1946	(Photos)	45-70	*
Fyleman, R.	Katy Kruse Dolly Book (1st AM, ob4to, ibds, 32p, 12cp)	Doran	(1927)	(Photos)	120-150	
Grover, E.O.	Kittens & Cats (1st, 8vo, yellow cl, 78p, 39pl, dep)	Houghton	1911	(Photos)	100-180	*
Gates, J.S.	Land of Delight (1st, lg8vo, green cl, 115p, 16pl)	Houghton	1915	(Photos)	30-45	*
Dixon, Thomas	Life Worth Living (1st, 8vo, 140p, teg)	Doubleday/Page	1905	(Photos)	25-40	
Frees, Harry W.	Little Folks of Animal Land (1st, 8vo, 252p, blue/gilt, p-o)	Lothrop/Lee	(1915)	(Photos)	90-130	*
Butler, E.C.	Little Mexican Cousin (1st, 8vo, 100p, 10pl)	Page	1905	(Photos)	25-45	*
Wells, H.G.	Little Wars (1st AM, sm4to, p-o, blue cl, 16pl)	Small/Maynard	(1913)	(Photos)	140-200	*
Tarkington, B.	Man from Home (1st, 8vo, 175p, tan cl, 7pl)	Harper	1908	(Photos)	50-70	
Beard, P.	Marjorie's Little Doll School (1st, 8vo, 208p)	Doran	(1917)	(Photos)	70-100	*

AUTHOR	TITLE	PUBLISHER	DATE	ARTIST	PRICE	LC
Porter, G.S.	Morning Face (1st, sm4to, 127p, blue/gilt, color)	Doubleday/Page	(1916)	(Photos)	200-260	
Porter, G.S.	Moths of the Limberlost (1st, 4to, tan cl, 370p, color)	Doubleday/Page	1912	(Photos)	185-250	
Wharton, E.	Motor-Flight through France (1st, 8vo, teg, 201p, 48pl)	Scribner	1908	(Photos)	65-80	
Porter, G.S.	Music of the Wild (1st, 8vo, 430p, green/gilt)	Jennings	(1910)	(Photos)	165-220	
Santos-Dumont	My Air-Ships (1st, sm8vo, 356p, blue cl, b/w)	Century	1904	(Photos)	70-90	
Credle, Ellis	My Pet Peepelo (1st, lg8vo, green cl, 62p, b/w)	NY: OUP	1948	(Photos)	30-45	*
Gates, J.S.	Nanette Goes to Visit Grandmother (1st, 16mo, ibds, 53p, 6cp)	Houghton	1915	(Photos)	50-65	*
London, J.	People of the Abyss (1st, lg8vo, 319p, teg, uncut, 9pl)	MacMillan	1903	(Photos)	200-300	
Collodi, C.	Pinocchio (1st [Movie ed.], sm ob4to, ibds, [50]p)	Grosset/Dunlap	1939	(Photos)	60-80	*
Shepperd, E.	Plantation Songs for My Lady's Banjo (1st, lg8vo, 150p, 25pl)	R.H. Russell	1901	(Photos)	160-250	
Ray, A.C.	Playground Toni (1st, 8vo, ipcb, 136p, 4pl)	Crowell	(1900)	(Photos)	20-30	
Dunbar, P.L.	Poems of Cabin & Field (1st, 8vo, teg, 125p, uncut, green/gilt)	Dodd	1899	(Photos)	135-160	
Anthony, Edward	Pussycat Princess (1st, sm4to, red cl, 157p, b/w)	Century	1922	(Photos)	85-130	
Chittenden, W.L.	Ranch Verses (1st, 8vo, 189p, 14pl)	Putnam	1893	(Photos)	80-120	
Brownell, Eliz.	Really Babies (1st, 4to, p-o, gilt, 63p)	Rand/McNally	(1908)	(Photos)	90-140	*
Omar Khayyam	Rubaiyat... (1st, 4to, unpag)	Dodge	[1905]	(Photos)	75-120	
Frees, Harry W.	Sandman: His Animal Stories (1st, 8vo, 273p, b/w)	Page	1916	(Photos)	70-100	
Spyri, J.	Shirley Temple in Heidi (1st, sm8vo, 404p, photos)	Saalfield	(1937)	(Photos)	65-80	*
Peary, J.	Snow Baby (1st, 4to, p-o, 84p, PPP)	Stokes	(1901)	(Photos)	100-140	
Porter, G.S.	Song of the Cardinal (1st {1st bk.}, 8vo, red cl, 163p, 17pl)	Bobbs-Merrill	(1903)	(Photos)	130-165	
Earle, A.M.	Stage Coach & Tavern Days (1st, sm8vo, uncut, 449p, teg, b/w)	MacMillan	1900	(Photos)	35-50	
Terhune, A.P.	Story of Damon & Pythias (1st, 12mo, 307p, 14pl)	Grosset/Dunlap	(1915)	(Photos)	25-40	*
Lloyd, J.U.	Stringtown on the Pike (1st, 8vo, 414p, tan cl, p-o, b/w)	Dodd	1900	(Photos)	20-25	
Adams, W.I.L.	Sunlight & Shadow (1st, 8vo, 141p, AEG)	Baker/Taylor	1897	(Photos)	70-120	
Porter, G.S.	Tales You Won't Believe (1st {std}, 8vo, 327p, grey cl, 23pl)	Doubleday/Page	1925	(Photos)	150-175	
London, J.	The Road (1st, 8vo, grey/gilt, teg, 224p)	MacMillan	1907	(Photos)	250-320	
Brininstool, E.A.	Trail Dust of a Maverick (1st, sm8vo, p-o, 249p)	Dodd	1914	(Photos)	30-45	
Porter, G.S.	What I Have Done with Birds (1st, 4to, 258p, green cl, p-o)	Bobbs-Merrill	(1907)	(Photos)	180-250	
Garelick, M.	What's Inside? (1st, ob8vo, unpag, beige cl, b/w)	W.R. Scott	(1955)	(Photos)	30-50	*
Willard, F.E.	Wheel Within a Wheel (1st, 12mo, 75p, tan buckram, 7pl)	Revell	1895	(Photos)	80-100	
Haggard, H.R.	Winter Pilgrimmage (1st, 8vo, 335p, 31pl)	L: Longmans	1901	(Photos)	75-100	*
Skelding, S.	Flowers of Dell & Bower (1st, lg8vo, AEG)	Stokes	1886	12 Chromos	90-120	
Skelding, S.	Flowers of Glade & Garden (1st, 4to, AEG, gilt)	Stokes	1884	12 Chromos	100-130	
Bennet, H.	Round the Hearth (4to, ibds)	Dutton	(1880)	13 Chromos	80-100	
Lathbury, M.A.	Idyls of the Months (4to, ibds, AEG)	L: Routledge	(1885)	14 Chromos	120-160	
Moore, C.C.	Night Before Christmas (4to, ibds)	McLoughlin	[1888]	16 Chromos	120-160	
Mack, R.E.	Queen of the Meadow (lg8vo, ipcb)	Dutton	(1885)	16 Chromos	100-165	
N/A	Simple Addition (lg8vo, p-o, blue cl, unpag)	McLoughlin	[1880]	21 Chromos	100-150	
Mack, R.E.	All-Around the Clock (lg8vo, ibds, 64p)	Dutton	[1885]	23 Chromos	100-160	
N/A	Aunt Louisa's Choice Present (sq4to, AEG)	Warne	(1880)	24 Chromos	90-140	
Weatherly, F.E.	Told in the Twilight (1st, 8vo, 64p, ibds)	Dutton	(1883)	27 Chromos	100-140	
Holmes, O.W.	Bunker Hill Battle (4to, blue cl, 32p)	Dodd	(1890)	32 Chromos	90-140	
N/A	Silly Hare (sm4to, ipcb)	McLoughlin	[1893]	4 Chromos	65-80	
N/A	Cinderella (sm4to, ipcb)	Dutton	(1890)	5 Chromos	70-95	
Montefiore	Friend & Foe (8vo, ipcb, 107p)	Dutton	(1898)	5 Chromos	80-130	
N/A	Three Little Kittens (lg4to, ibds)	L: Nister	[1890]	5 Chromos	50-75	
Tucker, E.S.	Baby and Me! (4to, [13]p, ibds)	Worthington	[1890]	6 Chromos	80-130	*
N/A	Children All (4to, ibds)	Lothrop	(1898)	6 Chromos	100-140	
Weedon, L.L.	Model Menagerie (ob folio, pop-up, ipcb, 24p)	L: Nister	[1880]	6 Chromos	300-400	
N/A	No Place Like Home (ob. folio, ibds)	J. Knight	1891	6 Chromos	60-100	
Defoe, D.	Robinson Crusoe (4to, A.E. Red)	L: Nister	(1890)	6 Chromos	80-125	
Daley, C.F.	Skating Party (1st, 4to, ibds)	Worthington	(1891)	6 Chromos	75-120	
N/A	Stories Merry & Wise (4to, ibds)	McLoughlin	(1898)	6 Chromos	70-100	
N/A	Three Little Kittens (4to, wraps)	McLoughlin	[1880]	6 Chromos	120-165	
N/A	Four Feet by Two (lg8vo, ibds)	L: Nister	[1890]	8 Chromos	70-120	
N/A	Merry Times (4to, ipcb, AEG)	Fiske Co.	1890	8 Chromos	80-120	
Sidney, Marg.	Ballad of the Lost Hare (1st, ob4to, ibds, [44]p, color)	D. Lothrop	1882	9 Chromos	100-150	R*
Goldsmith, O.	Deserted Village (1st, 4to, 59p, AEG, 119p)	Harper	1902	Abbey, E.A.	85-100	
Lucas, E.V.	Edwin A. Abbey (8vo, 2 vols, pcb)	Scribner	1921	Abbey, E.A.	100-160	
Herrick, R.	Herrick's Poems (lg4to, 188p, green cl)	Harper	1899	Abbey, E.A.	100-135	
Herrick, R.	Poetry of... (4to, uncut, dec cl)	Harper	1899	Abbey, E.A.	100-150	
Greenslet, F.	Quest of the Holy Grail (1st, 4to, 78p, gilt, teg, uncut, 26pl)	Curtis/Cameron	1902	Abbey, E.A.	120-150	
Goldsmith, O.	She Stoops to Conquer (1st, folio, AEG)	Harper	1887	Abbey, E.A.	100-160	
Long, J.L.	Madame Butterfly (1st, 8vo, teg, gilt, 152p, uncut, 16pl)	Century	1903	Abbott, C.Y.	20-25	
Carroll, L.	Alice... & Through... (8vo, brown cl, p-o, 335p, 7cp)	Jacobs	[1912]	Abbott, E.P.	120-150	
Carroll, L.	Alice... & Through... (8vo, blue/gilt, p-o, 335p, 7cp)	Macrae-Smith	[1925]	Abbott, E.P.	65-90	*
Andersen, H.C.	Fairy Tales (1st, sm8vo, 489p, 7cp)	Jacobs	[1917]	Abbott, E.P.	40-65	
Grimm Bros.	Fairy Tales (1st, lg8vo, 308p, p-o, 12cp, pep, SC)	Scribner	1920	Abbott, E.P.	100-160	
Grimm Bros.	Fairy Tales (1st UK, 8vo, 308p, gilt, 12cp, pep)	L: Hodder	1921	Abbott, E.P.	140-200	
Andersen, H.C.	Flower Maiden (1st, 8vo, 118p, p-o, pep, 3cp by...)	Jacobs	(1922)	Abbott, E.P.	25-45	*
Stevenson, R.L.	Kidnapped (1st, 8vo, p-o, 332p, 7cp, pep)	Jacobs	(1915)	Abbott, E.P.	40-60	
Defoe, D.	Robinson Crusoe (1st, 8vo, blue cl, 320p, 6cp)	L: Harrap	1933	Abbott, E.P.	65-80	

AUTHOR	TITLE	PUBLISHER	DATE	ARTIST	PRICE	LC
Stevenson, R.L.	Treasure Island (1st, sm8vo, 292p, cp, pep)	Jacobs	(1911)	Abbott, E.P.	35-60	*
Andersen, H.C.	Wild Swans (1st, sm8vo, 117p, color, pep)	Jacobs	(1922)	Abbott, E.P.	45-60	*
Hawthorne, N.	Wonder Book (1st sm8vo, 201p, color, by...)	Macrae Smith	(1925)	Abbott, E.P.	25-40	
Rogers, Eliz.	Angela of Angel Court (1st {std}, 8vo, 116p, grn cl, b/w, pep)	Crowell	(1954)	Adams, A.	25-40	*
Simon, Norma	Baby House (1st, lg8vo, mauve cl, [25]p, 1-color, dep)	Lippincott	1955	Adams, A.	30-50	*
Lewis, B.	Blue Mountain (1st {std}, lg8vo, blue cl, 59p, fp b/w, dep)	Knopf	1956	Adams, A.	35-50	*
Gordon, Pat	Boy Jones (1st, 8vo, red cl, 158p, 10pl, pep)	Viking	1943	Adams, A.	45-60	*
Godden, Rumer	Candy Floss (1st, lg8vo, pink cl, 63p, color, dep)	Viking	(1960)	Adams, A.	65-100	R*
Torjesen, Eliz.	Captain Ramsay's Daughter (1st, 8vo, 223p, blue cl, fp b/w, pep)	Lothrop/Lee	(1953)	Adams, A.	30-50	*
Friedrich, Priscilla	Easter Bunny that Overslept (1st, 4to, yellow cl, [33]p, color)	Lothrop	1957	Adams, A.	45-65	*
Godden, Rumer	Fairy Doll (1st, 8vo, grey cl, 67p, 2-color, pep)	Viking	1956	Adams, A.	45-70	*
Otto, M.G.	Great Aunt Victoria's House (1st {std}, 8vo, yel cl, 120p, b/w)	Holt	(1957)	Adams, A.	35-50	*
Goudey, Alice E.	Houses from the Sea (1st, 4to, unpag, color, CH)	Scribner	(1959)	Adams, A.	65-90	*
Godden, Rumer	Impunity Jane (1st, 8vo, 48p, color, pep)	Viking	1954	Adams, A.	65-100	R*
Kennedy, Mary	Jenny (1st, 8vo, 153p, green cl, 11 fp b/w)	Lothrop/Lee	(1954)	Adams, A.	25-40	*
Massey, Jeanne	Littlest Witch (1st, sm ob4to, [33]p, orange cl, 2-color)	Knopf	(1959)	Adams, A.	40-60	*
Godden, Rumer	Mouse House (1st, lg8vo, tan cl, 63p, color, pep)	Viking	1957	Adams, A.	65-100	R*
Godden, Rumer	Story of Holly & Ivy (1st, lg8vo, 64p, ibds, 2-color, pep)	Viking	(1958)	Adams, A.	50-70	*
Udry, J.M.	Theodore's Parents (1st, 4to, [30]p, green cl, color)	Lothrop/Lee	(1958)	Adams, A.	45-60	*
Gleaves, Suzanne	Tip & Dip (1st, lg8vo, rust cl, [62]p, 1-color)	Lippincott	(1960)	Adams, A.	45-60	*
Hendrich, Paula	Trudy's First Day at Camp (1st, sm4to, yellow cl, unpag, color)	Lothrop	(1959)	Adams, A.	45-60	*
Hood, Thos.	Tucker/Little Bo Peep (4to)	L: Cassell	1891	Adams, A.W.	65-80	
Carroll, L.	Alice/Wonderland (sm8vo, tan cl, 126p, 4cp, pep)	L: Blackie	[1920]	Adams, F.	70-100	
Gray, T.	Elegy in a Country Church Yard (4to, teg, uncut, 8 ticp)	L: Medici	(1931)	Adams, F.	50-65	
N/A	Jolly Old Sports (folio, ibds, p-o, 36cp)	L: Blackie	[1912]	Adams, F.	150-200	
N/A	Old Mother Hubbard (4to, ibds, 12cp)	L: Blackie	[1900]	Adams, F.	100-140	
N/A	Old Time Rhymes (1st, lg4to, gilt, 36 ticp, pep)	L: Blackie	1913	Adams, F.	300-350	
Arnold, M.	Scholar-Gypsy (1st, 4to, gilt, unpag, 10 ticp)	L: Nicholson	1933	Adams, F.	60-80	
N/A	Some Old Nursery Tales (lg8vo, ibds, 98p, 12cp)	L: Blackie	[1920]	Adams, F.	100-150	
N/A	Story of Simple Simon (4to, ibds, 12cp)	L: Blackie	[1920]	Adams, F.	90-150	
N/A	Three Little Pigs (tall 4to, ibds, color)	L: Blackie	[1925]	Adams, F.	75-100	
N/A	Tom/Piper's Son (4to, ibds, [32]p, 12cp, pep)	L: Blackie	[1920]	Adams, F.	75-100	
Sinclair, M.	Judgement of Eve (1st, 8vo, 122p, uncut, 8pl)	Harper	1908	Adams, J.W.	20-30	*
Bangs, J.K.	R. Holmes & Co. (1st, 12mo, 230p, blue cl, 6pl)	Harper	1906	Adamson, S.	80-100	
Norton, Mary	Bonfires & Broomsticks (1st, 8vo, 119p, pep, b/w)	L: Dent	(1947)	Adshead, M.	45-60	
Lewis, E.W.	Next-Door Morelands (1st, 8vo, 342p, 4pl)	Little/Brown	1907	Aherns, E.W.	20-25	*
Alcott, L.M.	Jo's Boys... (sm8vo, teg, 358p, 10pl)	Little/Brown	1903	Ahrens, E.W.	40-60	*
Ainslie, K.	At Great Aunt Martha's (ob8vo, ibds, [32]p, 16 color, p-o)	L: Castell	[1905]	Ainslie, K.	80-120	
Ainslie, K.	Catharine Susan & Me Goes Abroad (16mo, wraps, color)	L: Castell	[1900]	Ainslie, K.	100-130	
Ainslie, K.	Catharine Susan & Me's Coming Out (16mo, wraps, [32]p, color)	L: Castell	[1910]	Ainslie, K.	80-120	
Ainslie, K.	Catharine Susan in Hot Water (sq16mo, wraps, color)	L: Castell	[1905]	Ainslie, K.	80-120	
Ainslie, K.	Catharine Susan's Little Holiday (12mo, wraps, color)	L: Castell	[1905]	Ainslie, K.	80-100	*
Ainslie, K.	Lady Tabitha and Us (ob8vo, wraps, 14 color)	L: Castell	[1900]	Ainslie, K.	85-100	
Ainslie, K.	Me & Catharine Susan Earns an Honest Penny (sq16mo, wraps, col)	L: Castell	[1905]	Ainslie, K.	70-90	
Ainslie, K.	Me and Catharine Susan (16mo, wraps, [40]p, 20 fp color)	L: Castell	[1903]	Ainslie, K.	70-95	
Ainslie, K.	Mops Versus Tails (ob8vo, [24]p, ibds, color, pep)	L: Castell	[1905]	Ainslie, K.	100-150	
Ainslie, K.	Oh! Poor Amelia Jane! (12mo, [28]p, wraps, color)	L: Castell	[1900]	Ainslie, K.	100-130	
Ainslie, K.	Sammy Goes a Hunting (8vo, ibds, [24]p, 12 fp color, pep)	L: Castell	[1900]	Ainslie, K.	80-100	
Ainslie, K.	Why Was He Late? (8vo, 12cp, wraps)	L: Castell	[1905]	Ainslie, K.	70-100	
Ratzesberger, A.	Ali Hassan of Hamadan (1st, 8vo, 95p, p-o, 12cp, pep)	Whitman	(1933)	Akbar, A.	30-45	*
Benet, W.R.	Timothy's Angels (1st, sm4to, ipcb, [24]p, fp color, pep)	Crowell	(1947)	Alajalov	45-60	
Wilde, O.	The Spinx (4to, teg, 10pl)	J. Lane	1920	Alastair	200-300	
Field, L.A.	Peter Rabbit & his Pa (8vo, 56p, color)	Saalfield	(1916)	Albert, V.	45-65	*
Shepard, O.	Pedlar's Progress (1st, 8vo, 546p, 5pl, DJ)	Little/Brown	1937	Alcott, B.	35-50	
Byron, May	Animal Frolics (1st, 4to, unpag)	L: Hodder	[1916]	Aldin, C.	80-100	*
Aldin, C.	Artist's Models (1st, 4to, 80p, grey cl, 20pl)	L: Witherby	(1930)	Aldin, C.	120-165	
Aldin, C.	Artist's Models (1st AM, 4to, blue cl, 80p, 20 fp b/w)	Scribner	1930	Aldin, C.	160-200	
Sewell, Anna	Black Beauty (1st, 4to, blue/gilt, 291p, 18 ticp, pep)	L: Jarrolds	[1912]	Aldin, C.	140-200	
Sewell, Anna	Black Beauty (1st AM, 8vo, 291p, 18 ticp, pep)	Stokes	[1913]	Aldin, C.	120-165	*
Aldin, C.	Bobtail Puppy Book (1st AM, lg8vo, 37p, ibds, 12 fp color)	NY: Hodder	[1915]	Aldin, C.	75-100	*
Aldin, C.	Bunnyborough (4to, 48p, DJ)	L: Eyre/Spotts	(1946)	Aldin, C.	60-80	
Aldin, C.	Cathedrals & Abbey Churches of England (1st, 4to, 111p, 16cp)	L: Eyre/Spotts	(1924)	Aldin, C.	100-180	
Aldin, C.	Cecil Aldin Book (1st, 4to, cloth, 192p, 15cp)	L: Eyre/Spotts	1932	Aldin, C.	100-140	
Byron, May	Cecil Aldin's Happy Family (1st, 4to, teg, p-o, 36cp)	L: H. Frowde	[1912]	Aldin, C.	200-300	
Byron, May	Cecil Aldin's Merry Party (1st, 4to, ibds, gilt, teg, 36cp)	L: H. Frowde	1913	Aldin, C.	250-450	
Irving, W.	Christmas Day (sm8vo, bds, p-o, 6 ticp)	L: Hodder	[1915]	Aldin, C.	65-80	
Emanuel, W.	Conceited Puppy... (1st AM, 12mo, ibds, p-o, color)	Dutton	(1905)	Aldin, C.	80-120	
Emanuel, W.	Dog Day (1st, lg4to, ibds, unpag, 28cp)	L: Heinemann	1902	Aldin, C.	165-220	
Emanuel, W.	Dog Day (1st AM, lg4to, [59]p, ibds, 28cp)	R.H. Russell	1902	Aldin, C.	140-200	
Emanuel, W.	Dog Day (24mo, 55p, ibds, 28cp)	Dutton	(1907)	Aldin, C.	100-130	*
Aldin, C.	Dogs of Character (1st, 4to, p-o, gilt, 118p, teg, 2cp)	L: Eyre/Spotts	1927	Aldin, C.	90-130	
Emanuel, W.	Dogs of War (1st, lg8vo, tan cl, 243p, 12cp)	L: Bradbury/Ag	(1906)	Aldin, C.	90-125	

AUTHOR	TITLE	PUBLISHER	DATE	ARTIST	PRICE	LC
Chalmers, Patrick	Dozen Dogs or So (1st, 4to, 47p, brown cl, 13cp)	L: Eyre/Spotts	1928	Aldin, C.	75-100	
Aldin, C.	Farmyard Puppies (1st, sq4to, ibds, 12cp)	L: H. Frowde	(1911)	Aldin, C.	140-185	
Aldin, C.	Gay Dog (1st, 4to, ibds, [50]p, 24cp)	L: Heinemann	1905	Aldin, C.	180-270	
Aldin, C.	Great Adventure (1st, folio, ibds, 16cp, pep)	L: H. Milford	[1920]	Aldin, C.	200-280	
Davidson, G.	Gyp's Hour of Bliss (1st, 4to, ibds, 48p, 15cp, pep)	L: Collins	(1919)	Aldin, C.	175-220	
Surtees, R.S.	Jorrock's on 'Unting (1st, 16mo, teg, bds, 32p, p-o, 3 ticp)	L: Heinemann	1909	Aldin, C.	100-135	
Aldin, C.	Just Among Friends (1st AM, folio, 28p)	Scribner	1934	Aldin, C.	80-100	
Chalmers, Patrick	Last Muster (1st, 8vo, 127p, 24 illus)	L: Eyre/Spotts	1939	Aldin, C.	35-50	
Ashmore, M.	Lost, Stolen & Strayed (1st AM, 8vo, 96p, col frn)	Scribner	1931	Aldin, C.	60-85	
Aldin, C.	Merry & Bright (1st, lg4to, bds, p-o, 24cp, pep)	L: H. Frowde	(1911)	Aldin, C.	180-250	
Aldin, C.	Mrs. Tickler's Caravan (1st AM, sm4to, p-o, 91p, color, pep)	Scribner	1931	Aldin, C.	70-100	
Maeterlinck, M.	My Dog (1st, sm8vo, p-o, 6cp)	L: Allen	1913	Aldin, C.	100-150	
Irving, W.	Old Christmas (1st AM, 8vo, [176]p, p-o, red/gilt, 27cp)	NY: Sully	1908	Aldin, C.	120-160	
Irving, W.	Old Christmas (1st AM, 8vo, 176p, color)	Dodd	(1908)	Aldin, C.	80-130	*
Irving, W.	Old Fashioned Christmas Day (sm8vo, ibds, p-o, 6 ticp)	L: Hodder	[1910]	Aldin, C.	100-135	*
Aldin, C.	Old Inns (1st AM, sm4to, 149p, 16cp)	Doubleday/Page	1921	Aldin, C.	70-90	
Aldin, C.	Old Manor Houses (1st AM, lg8vo, 108p, grey/gilt, 12cp, pep)	L: Heinemann	(1923)	Aldin, C.	120-160	
Maeterlinck, M.	Our Friend the Dog (1st AM, 8vo, 67p, gilt, 6cp)	Dodd	1913	Aldin, C.	85-120	
Steele, R.	Perverse Widow (1st, 16mo, 31p, bds, p-o, teg, 3 ticp)	L: Heinemann	1909	Aldin, C.	100-130	
Steele, R.	Perverse Widow (1st AM, 12mo, ibds, p-o, 3 ticp)	Dutton	1909	Aldin, C.	85-120	
Dickens, C.	Posthumous Papers/Pickwick Club (1st, 2 vols, 4to, bds, color)	L: Chapman	1910	Aldin, C.	140-200	
Waylett, Richard	Puppy Tales (1st, 4to, ibds, 16cp)	L: Lawrence	[1915]	Aldin, C.	160-200	
Aldin, C.	Red Puppy Book (1st, lg8vo, 48p, 12cp)	L: H. Frowde	[1910]	Aldin, C.	140-185	
Masefield, J.	Right Royal (1st AM, 8vo, black/gilt, 116p, 4cp)	MacMillan	1922	Aldin, C.	60-80	
Hare, K.	Roads & Vagabonds (1st, lg4to, 189p, red/gilt, 2cp)	L: Eyre/Spotts	(1930)	Aldin, C.	100-140	
Aldin, C.	Romance of the Road (1st, folio, 123p, buckram, 10 ticp)	L: Eyre/Spotts	1928	Aldin, C.	125-150	
Aldin, C.	Rough & Tumble (4to, ibds, p-o, 24cp, pep)	L: H. Frowde	[1912]	Aldin, C.	300-400	
Aldin, C.	Scarlet to M.F.H. (1st AM, 4to, 151p, red/gilt, color)	Scribner	(1933)	Aldin, C.	65-80	*
N/A	Sleeping Partners (1st, 4to, blue bds, 20cp)	L: Eyre/Spotts	1929	Aldin, C.	180-220	
Aldin, C.	The Widow (1st AM, 12mo, 31p, ibds, p-o, 3 ticp)	Dutton	1909	Aldin, C.	70-90	*
Aldin, C.	Time I Was Dead (1st, lg8vo, 389p, gilt, 9cp)	L: Eyre/Spotts	1934	Aldin, C.	120-160	
Buckland, J.	Two Little Runaways (1st, 8vo, 358p, teg, tan/gilt, b/w)	L: Longmans	1898	Aldin, C.	140-185	
Aldin, C.	White Kitten Book (1st, 4to, ibds, unpag, 12cp)	L: H. Frowde	[1909]	Aldin, C.	160-250	
Aldin, C.	White Puppy Book (1st, 4to, ibds, [48]p, 12cp)	L: Hodder	[1909]	Aldin, C.	140-200	
Heilberg, N.	White-Ear & Peter (1st, 8vo, 222p, red/gilt, 16cp)	L: MacMillan	1912	Aldin, C.	100-130	
Morton, J.B.	Who's Who in the Zoo (1st, 4to, 173p, 3cp)	L: Eyre/Spotts	1933	Aldin, C.	80-100	
Fleuron, S.	Wild Horses of Iceland (1st, 8vo, 234p, red cl, 15 fp b/w)	L: Eyre/Spotts	[1933]	Aldin, C.	50-70	*
N/A	Young Folks Birthday Book (sq12mo, 188p, fp color)	L: Hills & Co.	[1905]	Aldin, C.	100-130	*
Farrow, G.E.	Zoo Babies (4to, green bds, 24 color)	L: H. Frowde	[1905]	Aldin, C.	250-350	*
Aldin, C.	Happy Annual (sm folio, ibds, 48p, color)	Dutton	(1907)	Aldin/Hassall	220-300	
Malory, T.	Women of Morte Darthur (1st, 8vo, 251p)	L: Methuen	1927	Alexander, A.D.	50-65	*
Allan, M.B.	Rhyme Garden (1st, 4to, ipcb, 8cp)	L: Bodley Head	1917	Allan, M.B.	35-50	*
Tarry, Ellen	My Dog Rinty (1st, lg8vo, [48]p, tan cl, b/w photos by...)	Viking	1946	Alland, A.& A.	65-80	R*
Allen, D.	Birth of the Opal (1st, 4to, p-o, bds, 95p, 12 ticp)	L: Allen	1913	Allen, D.	60-85	
Housman, L.	Cotton Woolleena (1st, 8vo, 36p, wraps, p-o)	L: Blackwell	[1933]	Allen, M.	65-80	*
Allen, Marian	Wind in the Chimney (1st, 4to, 89p, grey cl, 6 ticp)	L: Blackwell	[1931]	Allen, M.	25-40	*
Blake, Wm.	Songs of Innocence (1st, 8vo, 31p, p-o, 4cp)	L: Jack	[1905]	Allen, O.	45-70	*
Hawthorne, N.	Tanglewood Tales (16mo, 107p, gilt, p-o, uncut, 8cp)	Jack/Dutton	[1908]	Allen, O.	35-50	*
Almond, Linda S.	When Peter Rabbit Went to School (1st, 16mo, p-o, 58p, 27 col)	Platt/Munk	(1935)	Almond, L.	35-50	
Quiller-Couch, A.	Roll Call of Honor (1st, lg8vo, p-o, 348p, 9cp)	Nelson	[1911]	Almond, W.D.	45-60	
Ames, Mrs. E.	Really & Truly (1st, ob4to, unpag, color)	L: E. Arnold	[1899]	Ames, E.	180-250	*
Ames, Mrs. E.	Tim & the Dusty Man (ob folio, ibds, 24cp)	L: Richards	[1907]	Ames, E.	180-260	
Ames, Mrs. E.	Tremendous Twins (1st, ob folio, 95p, color)	L: Richards	1900	Ames, E.	200-300	*
Fenner, P.R.	Circus Parade (1st {std}, lg8vo, beige cl, 174p, uncut, fp b/w)	Knopf	1954	Ames, L.	30-45	*
Orcutt, Wm. D.	Princess Kallisto (1st, 4to, 138p, bds, 6 fp color)	Little/Brown	1902	Amsden, H.	150-200	*
Orcutt, Wm. D.	Princess Kallisto... (1st UK, 4to, 139p, 12 color)	L: Jack	1905	Amsden, H.	140-220	*
N/A	100 Best Fairy Tales (folio, ibds, 123p, 8cp, DJ)	Whitman	(1937)	Anderson, A.	100-140	
N/A	Aladdin & his Wonderful Lamp (12mo, 38p, color, pep)	NY: Nelson	1928	Anderson, A.	45-60	
N/A	Ali Baba & the Forty Thieves (12mo, ibds, 4cp)	Nelson	[1920]	Anderson, A.	55-70	
Anderson, A.	Ann Anderson's Fairy Book (1st AM, 4to, 190p, p-o, 12cp, pep)	Nelson	(1928)	Anderson, A.	100-150	
N/A	Aucassin & Nicolette (1st, lg8vo, 131p, teg, 6cp)	L: A&C Black	1911	Anderson, A.	70-120	
Anderson, A.	Betty Book (1st, 4to, ibds, 32p, 13cp)	Nelson	[1912]	Anderson, A.	100-150	
N/A	Briar Rose Book of Old Fairy Tales (4to, p-o, 159p, cp)	L: Jack	[1915]	Anderson, A.	80-120	
Joan, Natalie	Cosy-Time Tales (1st, 4to, ibds, 8cp)	L: T. Nelson	(1922)	Anderson, A.	130-200	
N/A	Dandy-Andy Book (lg8vo, 24p, p-o, 12cp)	Nelson	[1907]	Anderson, A.	65-90	
Andersen, H.C.	Fairy Stories (lg4to, ibds, 8cp)	(London)	[1930]	Anderson, H.	90-135	
N/A	Fairy Tale Omnibus (1st, 4to, red cl, col frn, 4cp)	L: Collins	[1915]	Anderson, A.	65-80	*
Grimm Bros.	Fairy Tales (lg4to, 128p, gilt, 8cp)	L: Collins	[1931]	Anderson, A.	75-100	*
N/A	Favourite Fairy Tales (lg4to, ibds, 16 color)	L: Nelson	[1929]	Anderson, A.	70-100	
N/A	Funny Bunny ABC (1st AM, folio, p-o, color)	NY: Sully	[1912]	Anderson, A.	80-100	
Chaucer, G.	Gateway to Chaucer (1st, sm8vo, blue/gilt, 269p, teg, 15cp)	L: Nelson	[1915]	Anderson, A.	130-165	*
Anderson, A.	Golden Story Book (4to, 8cp)	(London)	1933	Anderson, A.	50-70	

AUTHOR	TITLE	PUBLISHER	DATE	ARTIST	PRICE	LC
Spyri, J.	Heidi (1st, 8vo, 328p, 8cp)	L: Harrap	1924	Anderson, A.	65-80	*
Joan, Natalie	Lie-Down Stories (1st, lg8vo, p-o, 77p, grey bds, 8cp)	L: Blackie	(1919)	Anderson, A.	140-200	
N/A	Maisie-Daisie Book (lg8vo, 24p, p-o, 12cp)	Nelson	[1918]	Anderson, A.	50-75	
Howes, E.	Mrs. Kindbush (1st, 8vo, 160p, 4cp)	L: Cassell	1933	Anderson, A.	80-110	
Anderson, A.	Nursery Zoo (4to, p-o, red cl, unpag, color)	Nelson	[1925]	Anderson, A.	60-80	
Mansion, Horace	Old English Nursery Songs (1st, 4to, ibds, p-o, 6cp)	L: Harrap	[1915]	Anderson, A.	100-165	
Mansion, Horace	Old English Nursery Songs (1st AM, 4to, ibds, p-o, 6cp)	Brentano's	[1915]	Anderson, A.	130-175	
Anderson, A.	Old French Nursery Songs (1st, sm4to, 64p, ibds, 8cp)	L: Harrap	(1920)	Anderson, A.	100-130	
Mother Goose	Old Mother Goose Nurs. Rhyme Bk. (16mo, 96p, 24 color, ibds)	T. Nelson	[1920]	Anderson, A.	70-100	
Mother Goose	Old Mother Goose... (lg4to, p-o, 144p, red cl, 24cp, pep)	T. Nelson	[1926]	Anderson, A.	150-200	
Anderson, A.	Patsy Book (1st, lg4to, ibds, unpag, 12cp, pep)	T. Nelson	[1919]	Anderson, A.	85-130	
N/A	Rosie-Posie Book (4to, p-o, blue cl, 12cp)	T. Nelson	[1917]	Anderson, A.	50-80	
N/A	Sleeping Beauty (1st, 12mo, ibds, 40p, color, pep)	NY: Nelson	1928	Anderson, A.	50-75	
Various	Sleepy-Song Book (1st, 4to, ibds, p-o, 12cp, pep)	L: Harrap	(1915)	Anderson, A.	90-120	
Various	Sleepy-Song Book (1st AM, 4to, blue cl, p-o, 12cp, pep)	McBride	1915	Anderson, A.	100-165	
Barnes, Madeline	Stirabout Stories (1st, 4to, ibds, 80p, 8cp)	L: Blackie	[1929]	Anderson, A.	65-85	
Underdown, E.	Stories from Chaucer (1st, 12mo, p-o, 157p, 8cp)	T. Nelson	1913	Anderson, A.	45-65	
Southwold, S.	Three by Candlelight (sm8vo, 128p, blue/gilt, 2cp)	L: Collins	[1920]	Anderson, A.	40-65	
Barnes, Madeline	Tub-Time Tales (1st, 4to, 79p, ibds, 8cp)	L: Blackie	1920	Anderson, A.	180-220	
Kingsley, C.	Water Babies (1st AM, lg8vo, blue/gilt, p-o, 180p, 12cp, pep)	Nelson	[1924]	Anderson, A.	130-180	
Kingsley, C.	Water Babies (1st, lg8vo, yellow cl, p-o, 12cp)	L: Jack	(1924)	Anderson, A.	160-220	
Anderson, C.W.	Big Red (1st, ob4to, tan cl, pep, 64p, b/w)	MacMillan	1943	Anderson, C.W.	30-45	*
Anderson, C.W.	Billy & Blaze (1st, sm4to, orange cl, [56]p, fp b/w)	MacMillan	1936	Anderson, C.W.	35-50	*
Anderson, C.W.	Black Bay & Chestnut (1st, ob folio, [52]p, b/w, pep)	MacMillan	1939	Anderson, C.W.	50-75	*
Anderson, C.W.	Blaze & the Gypsies (1st, sm4to, green cl, [56]p, fp b/w)	MacMillan	1937	Anderson, C.W.	45-60	
Anderson, C.W.	Blaze Finds the Trail (1st {std}, sm4to, cloth, [48]p, b/w, cep)	MacMillan	1950	Anderson, C.W.	45-60	
Anderson, C.W.	Deep Through the Heart (1st, ob4to, [96]p, pep, b/w)	MacMillan	1940	Anderson, C.W.	35-50	
Anderson, C.W.	Heads Up & Heels Down (1st {std}, 8vo, 144p, green cl, b/w)	MacMillan	1944	Anderson, C.W.	30-45	*
Anderson, C.W.	High Courage (1st, 8vo, red cl, 124p, fp b/w, pep)	MacMillan	1941	Anderson, C.W.	30-50	*
Paltenghi, M.	Honey on a Raft (1st, 4to, ibds, [36]p, 15 fp b/w, pep)	Garden City	(1941)	Anderson, C.W.	35-50	
Paltenghi, M.	Honey the City Bear (1st, 4to, 31p, ipcb, 14 fp b/w)	Grosset/Dunlap	1937	Anderson, C.W.	50-80	*
Anderson, C.W.	Horses are Folks (1st, ob4to, ibds, 89p, b/w, pep)	Harper	(1950)	Anderson, C.W.	40-60	
Lippincott, J.W.	Red Roan Pony (1st {new ed}, sm8vo, 218p, red cl, 1 dp col, 6pl)	Lippincott	(1951)	Anderson, C.W.	25-40	*
Paltenghi, M.	Remus Goes to Town (1st, 4to, 29p, ipcb, 15 fp b/w)	Grosset/Dunlap	1938	Anderson, C.W.	50-80	*
Paltenghi, M.	Rumpus Rabbit (1st {std}, narrow 4to, 25p, green cl, b/w)	Harper	1939	Anderson, C.W.	50-70	*
Anderson, C.W.	Salute (1st, sm4to, tan cl, p-o, 63p, b/w, pep)	MacMillan	1940	Anderson, C.W.	35-50	*
Anderson, C.W.	Thoroughbreds (1st, ob4to, 72p, b/w, pep, DJ)	MacMillan	1942	Anderson, C.W.	35-50	
Anderson, C.W.	Tomorrow's Champion (1st, ob4to, [84]p, green/gilt, b/w)	MacMillan	1946	Anderson, C.W.	30-50	
Anderson, C.W.	Touch of Greatness (1st, ob4to, blue cl, 96p, b/w, DJ)	MacMillan	1945	Anderson, C.W.	30-45	
Sackville, M.	Dream Pedlar (1st, sm4to, 184p, blue/gilt, 16 ticp)	L: Simpkin	(1914)	Anderson, F.	130-170	
Browne, E.G.	Magic Whistle (1st, lg8vo, 221p, color)	Dodd	1920	Anderson, F.	45-70	*
Malcolm, F.	My Fairyland (1st, 4to, 85p, grey ibds, 4 ticp)	L: Harrap	1916	Anderson, F.	100-150	
Browne, Edgar G.	Nutcracker & Mouse King (1st, lg8vo, pink bds, 92p, p-o, 4cp)	Dodd	1916	Anderson, F.	60-80	
Southwart, Eliz.	Password to Fairyland (1st, 4to, 186p, tan cl, 8cp)	L: Simpkin	[1920]	Anderson, F.	220-320	
Sackville, M.	Travelling Companions... (1st, 8vo, 132p, blue/gilt, 12cp)	L: Simpkin	(1915)	Anderson, F.	100-150	
Littlewood, S.R.	Valentine & Orson (1st, 4to, 143p, p-o, 8cp)	L: Simpkin	1919	Anderson, F.	80-125	
Burgess, T.	Boy Scouts in a Trappers' Camp (1st, sm8vo, 362p, 5pl)	Penn	1915	Anderson, F.A.	60-80	*
Potter, B.	Tale of Peter Rabbit (12mo, yellow cl, p-o, color)	Hurst	(1908)	Anderson, S.W.	70-100	*
Page, T.N.	Tommy Trot's Visit to Santa Claus (1st, 8vo, 98p, uncut, 6cp)	Scribner	1908	Anderson, V.C.	20-35	
Ewing, J.H.	Blue & Red.... (4to, ibds, 32p, chromos)	L: SPCK	[1881]	Andre, R.	145-200	
Andre, R.	Little Blossoms (sm4to, [32]p, ibds, 10 chromos)	L: G. Allen	1885	Andre, R.	320-500	
Ewing, J.H.	Master Fritz (1st, ob8vo, 32p, ibds, color)	L: SPCK	[1883]	Andre, R.	120-165	*
Ewing, J.H.	Our Garden (1st, ob8vo, ibds, 32p, color)	L: SPCK	[1883]	Andre, R.	100-140	*
Ewing, J.H.	Soldier's Children (ob8vo, 32p, ibds, chromos)	L: SPCK	[1883]	Andre, R.	75-100	
N/A	Three Bears (8vo, [16]p, linen, color)	McLoughlin	1888	Andre, R.	80-120	*
Ewing, J.H.	Week Spent in a Glass Pond (4to, ibds, 32p, chromos)	L: Wells/Gard.	[1883]	Andre, R.	180-265	
Tooze, Ruth	America (1st, lg8vo, 31p, cloth, color)	Viking	1953	Angelo, V.	35-50	
Eaton, A.T.	Animal's Christmas (1st, sm8vo, grey cl, 124p, 1-color, dep)	Viking	1944	Angelo, V.	45-70	R*
Angelo, V.	Bells of Bleeker Street (1st, 8vo, cloth, 185p, pep, b/w)	Viking	1949	Angelo, V.	70-100	R*
North, S.	Birthday of Little Jesus (1st {std}, 4to, ipcb, 1-color, pep)	Grosset/Dunlap	(1952)	Angelo, V.	65-80	*
Angelo, V.	Golden Gate (1st, 8vo, aqua/gilt, 273p, b/w, DJ)	Viking	1939	Angelo, V.	35-50	
Sawyer, R.S.	Long Christmas (1st, 4to, 200p, cloth, dep, DJ)	Viking	1941	Angelo, V.	35-50	
Angelo, V.	Marble Fountain (1st, 8vo, 223p, tan cl, b/w, pep)	Viking	1951	Angelo, V.	25-40	*
Angelo, V.	Nino (1st, 8vo, beige cl, 244p, 1-color, pep, DJ, NH)	Viking	1938	Angelo, V.	50-70	
Vance, Marguerite	Paula (1st, 8vo, 223p, green cl, uncut, b/w, dep)	Dodd	1939	Angelo, V.	20-35	*
Sawyer, R.S.	Roller Skates (1st, 8vo, 186p, 1-color, pep, DJ, NM)	Viking	1936	Angelo, V.	50-80	R
Angelo, V.	Rooster Club (1st, 8vo, 150p, rust/gilt, b/w)	Viking	1944	Angelo, V.	25-40	
Sterne, Laurence	Sentimental Journey.... (1st, lg8vo, 253p, black/gilt, 12 b/w)	Dodd	1929	Angelo, V.	40-60	
Anglund, J.W.	Brave Cowboy (1st {std}, 12mo, cloth, unpag, 2-color)	Harcourt	(1959)	Anglund, J.W.	35-50	*
Anglund, J.W.	Friend is Someone Who Likes You (1st {std}, 12mo, [27]p, color)	Harcourt	(1958)	Anglund, J.W.	35-50	*
Anglund, J.W.	In a Pumpkin Shell (1st {std}, lg8vo, yellow cl, [30]p, color)	Harcourt	(1960)	Anglund, J.W.	60-85	LC
Anglund, J.W.	Look Out the Window (1st {std}, 8vo, yellow cl, [36]p, 2-col)	Harcourt	(1959)	Anglund, J.W.	35-50	*

AUTHOR	TITLE	PUBLISHER	DATE	ARTIST	PRICE	LC
Anglund, J.W.	Love is a Special Way of Feeling (1st {std}, 12mo, [30]p, 2-col)	Harcourt	(1960)	Anglund, J.W.	35-50	*
Trent, R.	To Church We Go (1st, sm4to, [28]p, color)	Wilcox/Follett	1948	Anglund, J.W.	70-100	*
Cradock, H.C.	Best Teddy Bear in the World (1st, 8vo, 96p)	L: Nelson	(1926)	Appleton, H.C.	50-80	*
Russell, D.	Betty's Diary (1st, 8vo, 261p, p-o, 5cp)	L: Blackie	[1914]	Appleton, H.C.	40-60	
Southwold, S.	Book of Animal Tales (1st AM, lg8vo, ibds, 286p, 8cp)	Crowell	(1929)	Appleton, H.C.	55-80	
Southwold, S.	Book of Animal Tales (1st, sm4to, 286p, ibds, 8cp)	L: Harrap	1929	Appleton, H.C.	65-90	*
Littlewood, L.	Bower Book of Simple Poems.... (1st, 8vo, 267p, red cl, 10cp)	L: O'Connor	(1922)	Appleton, H.C.	75-90	
Bryant, S.C.	Brother Rabbit (12mo, p-o, 59p, 4cp, later)	L: Harrap	1926	Appleton, H.C.	55-80	
Littlewood, S.R.	Child of the Sea (1st, 8vo, 196p, 8cp)	L: Simpkin	1915	Appleton, H.C.	35-50	*
Burke, Thos. (ed.)	Children in Verse (1st, lg8vo, 135p, blue cl, 8cp)	L: Duckworth	1913	Appleton, H.C.	65-80	*
Burke, Thos. (ed.)	Children in Verse (1st AM, 8vo, 135p, teg, 8 ticp)	(Boston)	1914	Appleton, H.C.	50-70	
Lee, Frank H.	Children's King Arthur (1st, 8vo, 77p)	L: Harrap	1935	Appleton, H.C.	45-60	*
Harris, J.C.	Children's Uncle Remus (1st, 12mo, 64p)	L: Harrap	1942	Appleton, H.C.	50-65	*
Dickens, C.	Christmas Carol (1st, 8vo, p-o, 153p, 8cp)	L: Simpkin	1914	Appleton, H.C.	50-75	
Perrault, C.	Fairy Tales (1st, sm4to, p-o, 107p, 12cp)	L: Simpkin	(1911)	Appleton, H.C.	80-100	
Andersen, H.C.	Fairy Tales (1st AM, 4to, blue/gilt, 179p, 12cp, pep)	NY: Nelson	[1922]	Appleton, H.C.	85-120	
Cradock, H.C.	House of Fancy (1st, 4to, 32p)	L: O'Connor	1922	Appleton, H.C.	50-75	*
Tyrell, Eleanor	How I Tamed the Wild Squirrels (1st, sq8vo, 111p, pep, p-o, 6cp)	L: Nelson	[1918]	Appleton, H.C.	55-90	
Cradock, H.C.	Josephine & Her Dolls (1st, 4to, ibds, 47p, 12 ticp)	L: Blackie	1916	Appleton, H.C.	240-300	
Cradock, H.C.	Josephine Dolly Book (4to, ibds, p-o, 8cp)	L: Blackie	[1920]	Appleton, H.C.	70-100	
Cradock, H.C.	Josephine Keeps House (1st, lg8vo, bds, p-o, 64p, 8cp)	L: Blackie	1931	Appleton, H.C.	100-140	*
Cradock, H.C.	Josephine Keeps School (1st, 4to, bds, p-o, 64p, 8cp)	L: Blackie	[1925]	Appleton, H.C.	65-100	
Cradock, H.C.	Josephine is Busy (1st, lg8vo, 63p, color)	L: Blackie	1918	Appleton, H.C.	100-140	*
Cradock, H.C.	Josephine's Birthday (1st, 4to, 64p, p-o, ibds, 8cp)	L: Blackie	(1920)	Appleton, H.C.	65-100	
Cradock, H.C.	Josephine's Happy Family (1st AM, 4to, 63p, p-o, 8cp)	Stokes	[1920]	Appleton, H.C.	50-80	
Cradock, H.C.	Josephine's Pantomime (1st, lg8vo, bds, p-o, 64p, 8cp)	L: Blackie	(1939)	Appleton, H.C.	50-80	
Tyrell, Eleanor	More About the Squirrels (1st, sq8vo, 111p, pep, p-o, 6cp)	L: Nelson	[1918]	Appleton, H.C.	55-90	
Cradock, H.C.	Peggy & Joan (1st, 4to, 96p, 8cp, p-o)	L: Blackie	(1922)	Appleton, H.C.	65-90	
Andersen, H.C.	Snow Queen (4to, ibds, 31p, 8cp)	L: Nelson	[1919]	Appleton, H.C.	50-70	
Blake, Wm.	Songs of Innocence (1st, 8vo, green/gilt, p-o, 49p, 12cp)	L: H. Daniel	(1911)	Appleton, H.C.	90-120	*
Blake, Wm.	Songs of Innocence (lg8vo, green/gilt, 12cp)	L: Simpkin	(1922)	Appleton, H.C.	65-80	
Chaundler, C.	Thirteenth Orphan (1st, 8vo, 255p, col frn, 6pl)	L: J. Nisbet	[1920]	Appleton, H.C.	35-50	*
Edgar, M.G.	Treasury of Verse/School & Home (1st, 8vo, 523p, col frn, pep)	Crowell	(1926)	Appleton, H.C.	35-50	*
Kelly, Eric P.	Three Sides of Agiochook (1st, 8vo, 211p, b/w, pep)	MacMillan	1935	Appleton, LeRoy	25-45	*
Archer, J.C.	Rosalina (1st, 16mo, 95p, 24cp)	L: Richards	1904	Archer, J.C.	50-70	
Gorham, Maurice	Back to the Local (1st, 8vo, 126p, red/gilt, 21 b/w)	L: P. Marshall	1949	Ardizzone, E.	70-100	
Ardizzone, E.	Baggage to the Enemy (1st, 12mo, blue cl, 121p, b/w)	L: J. Murray	1941	Ardizzone, E.	100-150	*
Hawksley, E.D.	Charles Dickens Birthday Book (1st, sm4to, cloth, 12pl)	L: Faber	(1948)	Ardizzone, E.	65-80	*
Lewis, Cecil D.	Christmas Eve (1st, sm8vo, unpag, wraps, col frn)	L: Faber	1954	Ardizzone, E.	45-60	*
Young, Percy	Ding Dong Bell (1st, 4to, ibds, 141p, b/w)	L: Dobson	(1957)	Ardizzone, E.	50-70	*
Dickens, C.	Great Expectations (1st, lg8vo, 457p, col frn, cp)	Heritage Press	(1939)	Ardizzone, E.	80-100	*
LeFanu, J.S.	In a Glass Darkly (1st {1st illus bk.}, 8vo, 382p, b/w)	L: P. Davies	1929	Ardizzone, E.	120-180	*
Ballantyne, Joan	Kidnappers at Coombe (1st, 8vo, 203p, DJ)	L: Nelson	1960	Ardizzone, E.	30-45	
Farjeon, E.	Little Bookroom (1st AM, 8vo, 302p, red cl, b/w)	NY: OUP	1956	Ardizzone, E.	70-90	R*
Ardizzone, E.	Little Tim/Brave Sea Captain (1st AM, folio, ibds, color)	L/NY: OUP	1936	Ardizzone, E.	250-400	*
Gorham, Maurice	Londoners (1st, 8vo, 158p, brown bds, 24 b/w)	L: P. Marshall	(1951)	Ardizzone, E.	50-65	
Ardizzone, E.	Lucy Brown & Mr. Grimes (1st AM, sm folio, ibds, 32p, color)	L/NY: OUP	[1937]	Ardizzone, E.	250-350	
Bates, H.E.	My Uncle Silas (1st, 4to, 190p, b/w)	L: J. Cape	(1939)	Ardizzone, E.	150-200	*
Ardizzone, E.	Nicholas & Fast Moving Diesel (1st, lg4to, yel bds, 35p, color)	L: Eyre/Spotts	(1947)	Ardizzone, E.	200-265	
Lewis, Cecil D.	Otterbury Incident (1st, 8vo, 148p, red cl, b/w, DJ)	L: Putnam	1948	Ardizzone, E.	75-100	*
Lewis, Cecil D.	Otterbury Incident (1st AM, 8vo, cloth, 160p, b/w, DJ)	Viking	1949	Ardizzone, E.	85-100	
Cook, Hartley K.	Over the Hills & Far Away (1st, 8vo, 263p, pep by...)	L: Allen/Unwin	1947	Ardizzone, E.	35-50	
Ardizzone, E.	Paul, Hero of the Fire (1st AM, 8vo, ibds, [40]p, color, pep)	Houghton	(1948)	Ardizzone, E.	100-150	*
De La Mare, W.	Peacock Pie (1st, 8vo, 107p, yellow cl, b/w)	L: Faber	(1946)	Ardizzone, E.	70-100	R*
Graves, Rbt.	Penny Fiddle (1st, sm4to, green bds, color, DJ)	L: Cassell	(1960)	Ardizzone, E.	65-80	
Graves, Rbt.	Penny Fiddle (1st AM {std}, 8vo, 62p, green cl, fp 2-color)	Doubleday	1960	Ardizzone, E.	35-50	*
Stonier, G.W.	Pictures on the Pavement (1st, 8vo, 214p, brown cl)	L: M. Joseph	1955	Ardizzone, E.	50-65	
Estes, Eleanor	Pinkey Pye (1st {std}, sm8vo, 192p, pink cl, b/w)	Harcourt	(1958)	Ardizzone, E.	50-80	R*
Corrin, S.	Plucky Sailor & Postage Stamp (1st, 8vo, ibds, unpag, color)	L: Faber	1954	Ardizzone, E.	50-70	*
Mitchison, Naomi	Rib of the Green Umbrella (1st, 8vo, 160p)	L: Collins	1960	Ardizzone, E.	25-40	*
Goldman, J.M.	School in Our Village (1st, 8vo, DJ)	L: Batsford	1957	Ardizzone, E.	25-40	*
Gorham, Maurice	Showmen & Suckers (1st, 8vo, 262p, red bds, 35 b/w)	L: P. Marshall	(1951)	Ardizzone, E.	65-80	
Kenward, James	Suburban Child (1st, 8vo, 140p, white ipcb, 11 b/w, DJ)	L: Cambridge	1955	Ardizzone, E.	50-70	
Gorham, Maurice	The Local (1st, 8vo, 51p)	L: Cassell	1939	Ardizzone, E.	75-100	*
Black, Marg.	Three Brothers & a Lady (1st, 4to, ibds, 62p, color, DJ)	L: Acorn Press	1947	Ardizzone, E.	85-120	
Ardizzone, E.	Tim & Charlotte (1st, 4to, ibds, unpag, color)	L/NY: OUP	(1951)	Ardizzone, E.	100-150	*
Ardizzone, E.	Tim & Lucy Go to Sea (1st AM, folio, ibds, [64]p, color)	L/NY: OUP	[1938]	Ardizzone, E.	250-400	
Ardizzone, E.	Tim All Alone (1st, 4to, red cl, unpag, color)	L: OUP	(1957)	Ardizzone, E.	90-130	*
Ardizzone, E.	Tim in Danger (1st, 4to, ipcb, unpag, color)	L/NY: OUP	(1953)	Ardizzone, E.	100-150	*
Ardizzone, E.	Tim to the Rescue (1st, 4to, [48]p, ibds, color)	L/NY: OUP	(1949)	Ardizzone, E.	100-150	*
Reeves, James	Titus in Trouble (1st, 4to, ibds, unpag, 46 color)	L: Bodley Head	(1959)	Ardizzone, E.	100-140	*
Lyons, A. Neil	Tom, Dick & Harriet (1st, 8vo, 254p, green cl, b/w)	L: Cresset Pr.	(1937)	Ardizzone, E.	80-120	

AUTHOR	TITLE	PUBLISHER	DATE	ARTIST	PRICE	LC
Estes, Eleanor	Witch Family (1st {std}, 8vo, green cl, 86p, b/w)	Harcourt	(1960)	Ardizzone, E.	35-50	*
Ardley, Pat	Advens./Mr. Horace Hedgehog (1st, ob4to, ibds, 56p, 6 fp col)	L: Collins	(1935)	Ardley, E.C.	75-100	*
N/A	Famous Animal Tales (1st, lg8vo, 158p, 8cp, pep)	L: Harrap	(1935)	Aris, E.	70-100	
Armer, L.A.	Forest Pool (1st {std}, 4to, 40p, pep, 8cp, CH)	Longmans	(1938)	Armer, L.A.	70-100	R
Armer, L.A.	Waterless Mountain (1st {std}, lg8vo, 212p, cloth, 16pl, NM)	Longmans	1931	Armer, L.A.	70-110	
Armer, L.A.	Cactus (1st, 8vo, 102p, col frn, b/w)	Stokes	1934	Armer, S.	25-40	*
Armfield, C.	Armfield's Animal Book (1st, 8vo, 96p, orange cl, 8 ticp)	L: Duckworth	(1922)	Armfield, M.	65-80	
N/A	Aucassin & Nicolette (1st, 8vo, 72p, color)	Dent/Dutton	1910	Armfield, M.	50-65	*
Lee, V.	Ballet of the Nations (1st AM, 4to, ibds, 24p, uncut, 1-color)	Putnam	1915	Armfield, M.	90-140	R*
Andersen, H.C.	Fairy Tales (1st, sm4to, 392p, gilt, 24cp, pep)	Dent/Dutton	1910	Armfield, M.	120-160	
Armfield, C.	Flower Book (lg8vo, teg, bds, uncut, 16cp)	L: Warne	[1910]	Armfield, M.	70-90	
Armfield, M.	Hanging Garden... (1st, 4to, 75p, 8cp)	L: Simpkin	1914	Armfield, M.	45-65	*
MacKenzie, D.A.	Indian Fairy Stories (1st, 8vo, 200p, 8pl)	L: Blackie	1915	Armfield, M.	40-65	
Morris, Wm.	Life & Death of Jason (1st, 8vo, 332p, blue cl, 6cp)	Swarthmore Pr.	(1915)	Armfield, M.	75-90	
Andersen, H.C.	Mermaid & other Tales (1st, sm8vo, 127p, p-o, gilt, 8cp)	Dent/Dutton	(1914)	Armfield, M.	70-90	
Armfield, C.	Sylvia's Travels (sm4to, 256p, 14cp)	L: Dent	1911	Armfield, M.	50-80	
Armfield, C.	Tales from Timbuktu (1st, lg8vo, 179p)	L: Chatto	(1923)	Armfield, M.	50-80	*
Armfield, C.	Tales from Timbuktu (1st AM, 8vo, 179p, col frn, 11 fp b/w)	Harcourt	[1924]	Armfield, M.	30-45	*
Andersen, H.C.	Ugly Duckling (1st, sm8vo, 127p, p-o, 8cp)	L: Dent	(1913)	Armfield, M.	40-65	
Shakespeare, Wm.	Winter's Tale (1st, sm4to, 98p, gilt, 12cp, DJ)	L: Dent	(1922)	Armfield, M.	85-120	
Masefield, J.	Reynard the Fox (1st, 4to, 116p, 4cp)	L: Heinemann	1921	Armour, G.D.	80-100	
Masefield, J.	Reynard the Fox (1st AM, 4to, 339p, 4cp)	MacMillan	1921	Armour, G.D.	60-85	
Magruder, Julia	Child Amy (1st, 8vo, 302p, red/gilt, 7pl)	Lothrop	(1894)	Armstrong, H.M.	30-50	*
Abbott, J.	Franconia Stories (1st, 8vo, 321p, p-o, blue/gilt, 12pl, pep)	Putnam	1923	Armstrong, H.M.	30-45	
Bouvet, M.	Little Marjorie's Love Story (1st, 8vo, 124p, 16pl)	McClurg	1891	Armstrong, H.M.	25-45	
Bouvet, M.	My Lady (1st, 12mo, beige/silver, 284p, 12pl)	McClurg	1894	Armstrong, H.M.	35-50	
Bouvet, M.	Prince Tip-Top (1st, sm8vo, 134p, olive/white)	McClurg	1892	Armstrong, H.M.	45-60	*
Wahlenberg, A.	Sweedish Fairy Tales (1st, sm8vo, 158p, 14pl)	McClurg	1901	Armstrong, H.M.	50-75	*
Parsons, F.T.	According to Season... (1st, 8vo, 197p, green/gilt, cvr by...)	Scribner	1902	Armstrong, M.	30-45	*
Dante	Ad Astra (1st, lg4to, ipcb, unpag, b/w)	R.H. Russell	1902	Armstrong, M.	150-200	
Thanet, O.	Adventure in Photography (1st, 12mo, photos, cvr by...)	Scribner	1893	Armstrong, M.	60-80	
Stockton, Frank	Adventures of Captain Horn (1st, 8vo, green/gilt, 404p)	Scribner	1895	Armstrong, M.	25-40	
Arnold, E.	Adzuma (1st, 12mo, 170p, green/gilt)	Scribner	1893	Armstrong, M.	30-45	*
Meriwether, L.	Afloat & Ashore on the Mediterranean (1st, 8vo, brown/gilt)	Scribner	1892	Armstrong, M.	30-45	
Ely, H.R.	Another Hardy Garden Book (1st, 8vo, teg, uncut, 232p, cvr by)	MacMillan	1905	Armstrong, M.	30-45	
Bourget, P.	Antigone (1st, 8vo, red/gilt, uncut, 297p)	Scribner	1898	Armstrong, M.	30-45	*
Grant, Rbt.	Art of Living (1st, 8vo, 353p, green/gilt, teg)	Scribner	1895	Armstrong, M.	25-40	
Holland, Josiah G.	Arthur Bonnicastle (12mo, green/gilt, 422p, cvr by...)	Scribner	1896	Armstrong, M.	30-50	*
Grant, Rbt.	Bachelor's Christmas (1st, 8vo, olive/gilt, teg, 309p)	Scribner	1895	Armstrong, M.	30-45	
Andrews, M.S.	Better Treasure (1st, 8vo, red/gilt, 72p, cvr by...)	Bobbs-Merrill	(1908)	Armstrong, M.	25-40	
Fox, John Jr.	Blue Grass & Rhododendron (1st, 8vo, teg, 294p, uncut)	Scribner	1901	Armstrong, M.	65-90	
Andrews, M.S.	Bob & the Guides (1st, 8vo, green/gilt, 351p, teg)	Scribner	1906	Armstrong, M.	20-25	
Cable, G.W.	Bonaventure (1st, 8vo, 314p, olive/gilt, teg)	Scribner	1902	Armstrong, M.	35-50	
Cable, G.W.	By Low Hill (1st, 8vo, teg, uncut, red cl, 209p, cvr by...)	Scribner	1902	Armstrong, M.	30-45	
Miller, A.D.	Calderon's Prisoner (1st, 8vo, olive/gilt, 294p, cvr by...)	Scribner	1903	Armstrong, M.	20-30	
Dunbar, P.L.	Candle-Lightin' Time (1st, 8vo, teg, 127p, green cl, uncut)	Dodd	1901	Armstrong, M.	140-180	
Thoreau, H.D.	Cape Cod (1st, 8vo, gilt, teg, 319p, cvr by...)	Crowell	(1908)	Armstrong, M.	50-75	
Merington, M.	Captain Lettarblair (1st, 8vo, aqua/gilt, 212p, cvr by...)	Bobbs-Merrill	(1906)	Armstrong, M.	30-45	
Seawell, M.E.	Chateau of Montplaisir (1st, 8vo, uncut, 245p, blue cl, cvr by)	Appleton	1906	Armstrong, M.	30-45	
Abbott, Lyman	Christ's Secret of Happiness (1st, 8vo, bds, gilt)	Crowell	(1907)	Armstrong, M.	45-60	*
Earle, A.M.	Colonial Days in Old New York (1st, sm8vo, 312p, gilt)	Scribner	1896	Armstrong, M.	25-40	
Hope, A.	Comedies of Courtship (1st, sm8vo, 377p, buckram/gilt)	Scribner	1896	Armstrong, M.	30-45	*
Van Dyke, H.	Companionable Books (1st, 8vo, blue/gilt, 391p)	Scribner	1922	Armstrong, M.	20-40	
Crawford, M.	Constantinople (1st, 8vo, teg)	Scribner	1895	Armstrong, M.	35-50	
Earle, A.M.	Costumes of Colonial Times (1st, 8vo, blue/gilt, 264p)	Scribner	1894	Armstrong, M.	50-75	
Martin, E.S.	Cousin Anthony & I (1st, 8vo, 255p, green cl, cvr by...)	Scribner	1895	Armstrong, M.	25-45	
Dickens, C.	Cricket o/t Hearth (1st, sm8vo, teg, uncut, 174p, dep, cvr by..)	Putnam	1900	Armstrong, M.	25-40	
Sheldon, Chas.	Crucifixion of Philip Strong (1st, 8vo, 267p, gray/gilt, cvr)	McClurg	1894	Armstrong, M.	25-40	*
Van Dyke, H.	Days Off (1st, 12mo, teg, 322p, uncut)	Scribner	1907	Armstrong, M.	20-30	
Riley, J.W.	Defective Santa Claus (1st, 12mo, green/gilt, 77p, cvr by...)	Bobbs-Merrill	(1904)	Armstrong, M.	50-80	R
Cable, G.W.	Doctor Seiver (8vo, 473p, teg, olive/gilt)	Scribner	1898	Armstrong, M.	25-40	
Sedgwick, Anne D.	Dull Miss Archinard (1st, 12mo, 287p, beige/gilt)	Scribner	1898	Armstrong, M.	30-45	*
Horton, George	Edge of Hazard (1st, 8vo, 429p, aqua cl, cvr by...)	Bobbs-Merrill	(1906)	Armstrong, M.	30-45	*
Cary, E.L.	Emerson, Poet & Thinker (1st, lg8vo, blue/gilt, 284p)	Putnam	1904	Armstrong, M.	45-65	
Andrews, M.S.	Eternal Masculine (1st, 8vo, 430p, green/gilt)	Scribner	1913	Armstrong, M.	35-50	
N/A	Fair Women from Vogue (4to, 28p, tan buckram)	Fashion Co.	1894	Armstrong, M.	120-175	
Stockton, Frank	Fanciful Tales (1st, 12mo, maroon cl, 135p)	Scribner	1894	Armstrong, M.	65-80	*
Armstrong, M.	Fieldbook of Western Wilderness (1st, 12mo, 596p, color)	Putnam	1915	Armstrong, M.	100-160	
Van Dyke, H.	Fisherman's Luck (1st [new ed.], 12mo, 285p, cvr by...)	Scribner	1905	Armstrong, M.	20-30	
Barclay, F.	Following of the Star (1st, lg8vo, teg, cloth, cvr by...)	Putnam	1911	Armstrong, M.	35-50	*
Wells, Carolyn	Folly for the Wise (1st, 8vo, 170p, blue/gilt)	Bobbs-Merrill	(1904)	Armstrong, M.	45-70	
Seawell, M.E.	Fortunes of Fifi (1st, 8vo, 239p)	Bobbs-Merrill	(1903)	Armstrong, M.	25-40	

AUTHOR	TITLE	PUBLISHER	DATE	ARTIST	PRICE	LC
Seawell, M.E.	Francezka (1st, 8vo, 466p, green/gilt, cvr by...)	Bobbs-Merrill	(1902)	Armstrong, M.	30-45	
Harris, J.C.	Free Joe... (1st, 8vo, uncut, 236p, 1st cvr by...)	Scribner	1887	Armstrong, M.	150-200	
Stockton, Frank	Girl at Cobhurst (1st, 8vo, green/gilt, 408p)	Scribner	1898	Armstrong, M.	20-35	
Warren, C.	Girl of the Governor (1st, 8vo, 407p, 9pl, cvr by...)	Scribner	1900	Armstrong, M.	30-45	
Miller, J.R.	Glimpses of Heavenly Life (1st, 32p)	Crowell	(1908)	Armstrong, M.	30-45	
Page, T.N.	Gordon Keith (1st, 8vo, blue/gilt, 548p)	Scribner	1903	Armstrong, M.	30-45	
Gray, Maxwell	Great Refusal (1st, 8vo, brown cl)	Appleton	1906	Armstrong, M.	25-40	*
Dodge, M.M.	Hans Brinker (1st, 8vo, blue cl, cvr by...)	Scribner	1896	Armstrong, M.	30-45	
Whitlock, Brand	Happy Average (1st, sm8vo, 347p, green/gilt, cvr by...)	Bobbs-Merrill	(1904)	Armstrong, M.	25-40	*
Thanet, O.	Heart of Toil (1st, 8vo, teg, 215p, cvr by...)	Scribner	1898	Armstrong, M.	35-50	*
Herrick, F.H.	Home Life/Wild Birds (1st, sm4to, 148p, brown/gilt)	Putnam	1901	Armstrong, M.	45-70	
Peake, Elmore E.	House of Hawley (1st, 8vo, 341p, cvr by...)	Appleton	1905	Armstrong, M.	30-45	*
Parsons, F.T.	How to Know the Ferns (1st, 8vo, brown/gilt, 215p)	Scribner	1899	Armstrong, M.	45-60	
Krehbiel, H.	How to Listen to Music (1st, 12mo, 361p)	Scribner	1897	Armstrong, M.	45-60	
Cooke, G.M.	Huldah (1st, 8vo, 316p, cvr by...)	Bobbs-Merrill	(1904)	Armstrong, M.	30-50	
Storm, T.	Immensee (1st, 8vo, olive cl, 9cp)	McClurg	1907	Armstrong, M.	80-120	
Janvier, T.A.	In Old New York (1st, 12mo, 285p, rust/gilt, cvr by...)	Harper	1894	Armstrong, M.	40-65	*
McCutcheon, G.B.	In the Bishop's Carriage (1st, 8vo, 280p, red cl)	Bobbs-Merrill	(1904)	Armstrong, M.	25-40	
Erskine, P.	Iona (1st, 8vo, blue cl)	Dibble	1891	Armstrong, M.	45-70	
Wharton, E.	Italian Backgrounds (1st, 8vo, green/gilt, 214p, cvr by...)	Scribner	1905	Armstrong, M.	75-100	
Bunner, H.C.	Jersey Street & Jersey Lane (1st, 8vo, blue/gilt, teg, 201p)	Scribner	1896	Armstrong, M.	35-50	R
Sacher-Masoch, L.	Jewish Tales (1st, 12mo, 317p, beige/gilt, cvr by...)	McClurg	1894	Armstrong, M.	50-80	*
Stockton, Frank	John Gayther's Garden... (1st, 8vo, grn/gilt, uncut, teg, 365p)	Scribner	1902	Armstrong, M.	40-65	R
Cable, G.W.	John March, Southerner (1st, 12mo, green/gilt, 513p)	Scribner	1894	Armstrong, M.	85-100	R*
Cable, G.W.	Kincaid's Battery (1st, 8vo, 396p, 7pl, cvr by...)	Scribner	1908	Armstrong, M.	35-50	
Lummis, C.F.	King of the Broncos (1st, 8vo, 254p, red/gilt, photos, cvr by)	Scribner	1897	Armstrong, M.	65-80	
Burnett, F.H.	Lady of Quality (1st, sm8vo, 363p, buckram/gilt, b/w)	Scribner	1896	Armstrong, M.	35-50	*
Lummis, C.F.	Land of Poco Tiempo (1st, 8vo, 310p, orange/gilt, cvr by...)	Scribner	1893	Armstrong, M.	25-40	*
Browning, R.	Last Ride Together (1st, 8vo, AEG, unpag)	Putnam	1906	Armstrong, M.	50-85	
Irving, W.	Legend of Sleepy Hollow (1st, 8vo, teg, 191p, red/gilt)	Putnam	1899	Armstrong, M.	80-100	
Dunbar, P.L.	Li'L' Gal (1st, 8vo, teg, green cl, cvr by...)	Dodd	1904	Armstrong, M.	100-165	
Bouvet, M.	Little House in Pimlico (1st, 8vo, blue cl, 245p, b/w, cep)	McClurg	1897	Armstrong, M.	20-30	
Van Dyke, H.	Little Rivers (1st, 12mo, teg, 348p, uncut, blue/gilt)	Scribner	1903	Armstrong, M.	20-25	
Ford, P.L.	Love Finds the Way (1st, 8vo, teg, 108p, uncut, cvr by...)	Dodd	1904	Armstrong, M.	30-45	
Potter, M.K.	Love in Art (1st, 12mo, 260p, teg, cvr by...)	Page	1898	Armstrong, M.	30-45	
Bunner, H.C.	Love in Old Cloathes (1st, 8vo, teg, uncut, 217p)	Scribner	1896	Armstrong, M.	30-45	
Crockett, S.R.	Loves of Miss Ann (1st, 12mo, blue cl, 421p)	Dodd	1904	Armstrong, M.	35-50	*
Tarbell, Ida M.	Madame Roland (1st, sm8vo, 328p, blue/gilt, cvr by...)	Scribner	1896	Armstrong, M.	30-45	*
Thoreau, H.D.	Maine Woods (1st, 8vo, teg, 423p, green/gilt)	Crowell	(1909)	Armstrong, M.	45-65	*
Thanet, O.	Man of the Hour (1st, 12mo, green/gilt, 477p)	Bobbs-Merrill	(1905)	Armstrong, M.	25-40	
MacGrath, H.	Man on the Box (1st, 8vo, 361p, aqua cloth)	Bobbs-Merrill	(1904)	Armstrong, M.	20-30	
Tennyson, A.	Maud (1st, 8vo, teg, uncut, 107p, green/gilt, dep, 10cp)	Dodd	1905	Armstrong, M.	35-50	
Muller, M.	Memories... (2nd, lg8vo, blue/gilt, teg, cvr by...)	McClurg	1906	Armstrong, M.	80-125	
Blichfeldt, E.H.	Mexican Journey (1st, 8vo, 280p, orange cl, map, cvr by...)	Crowell	(1912)	Armstrong, M.	30-45	*
Barclay, F.	Mistress of Shenstone (1st, lg8vo, teg, uncut, gilt, 8cp)	Putnam	1910	Armstrong, M.	40-60	
Miller, A.D.	Modern Obstacle (1st, 8vo, 273p, blue cl, cvr by...)	Scribner	1903	Armstrong, M.	35-50	
Bourget, P.	Monica (1st, 12mo, 289p, red cl, cvr by...)	Scribner	1902	Armstrong, M.	25-40	*
Stockton, Frank	Mrs. Cliff's Yacht (1st, 8vo, 341p, 8pl, cvr by...)	Scribner	1896	Armstrong, M.	25-45	
Stimson, F.J.	Mrs. Knollys... (1st, 8vo, green/gilt, teg, 207p)	Scribner	1897	Armstrong, M.	25-45	*
Bancroft, Hubert H.	New Pacific (1st, 8vo, 738p, map, green/gilt, cvr by...)	Bancroft Co.	1900	Armstrong, M.	45-60	*
Burt, Mary E.	Odysseus, Hero of Ithaca (1st, 12mo, 223p, red cl, cvr by...)	Scribner	1898	Armstrong, M.	30-45	*
Reed, Myrtle	Old Rose and Silver (1st, 8vo, 364p, teg, lavender cl)	Putnam	1909	Armstrong, M.	30-50	
Van Dyke, J.C.	Opal Sea (1st, sm8vo, 262p, green/gilt, cvr by...)	Scribner	1906	Armstrong, M.	30-45	*
Field, H.	Our Western Archipelago (1st, 8vo, beige cl, cvr by...)	Scribner	1895	Armstrong, M.	100-135	
Sousa, J.P.	Pipetown Sandy (1st, 8vo, brown/gilt, 383p, cvr by...)	Bobbs-Merrill	(1905)	Armstrong, M.	25-40	
Browning, R.	Pippa Passes (1st, 8vo, teg, uncut, green/gilt, unpag)	Dodd	1900	Armstrong, M.	65-80	
Perry, Bliss	Plated City (1st, sm8vo, brown cl, 397p)	Scribner	1895	Armstrong, M.	25-40	*
Cable, G.W.	Posson Jane... (1st, 12mo, teg, blue/gilt, 162p, uncut)	Scribner	1909	Armstrong, M.	35-50	
Arnold, E.	Potiphar's Wife (1st, 12mo, 127p, green/gilt)	Scribner	1892	Armstrong, M.	25-40	*
Ackerman, A.W.	Price of Peace (1st, sm8vo, 390p, rust/gilt)	McClurg	1894	Armstrong, M.	30-45	*
Johnson, E.G.	Private Memoirs of Madame Roland (1st, teg)	McClurg	1900	Armstrong, M.	30-45	
Wallace, E.K.	Quest of the Dream (1st, 12mo, teg, 292p, blue/gilt)	Putnam	1913	Armstrong, M.	20-30	
Irving, W.	Rip Van Winkle (1st, sm8vo, teg, uncut, red/gilt, 115p, cvr by)	Putnam	1899	Armstrong, M.	50-70	
Davies, Maria T.	Rose of Old Harpeth (1st, sm8vo, 312p, blue cl, cvr by...)	Bobbs-Merrill	(1911)	Armstrong, M.	35-50	*
Perry, Bliss	Salem Kittredge... (1st, 8vo, 291p, yellow cl)	Scribner	1894	Armstrong, M.	20-35	
Barrie, J.M.	Sentimental Tommy (1st AM, 8vo, 478p, brown/gilt, cvr by...)	Scribner	1896	Armstrong, M.	25-45	
Page, T.N.	Social Life in Old Virginia (1st, 8vo, teg, 109p, green/gilt)	Scribner	1897	Armstrong, M.	45-60	
Aldrich, A.R.	Songs about Life, Love & Death (1st, 12mo, 133p)	Scribner	1892	Armstrong, M.	45-60	
Field, E.	Songs by Eugene Field (1st, 4to, ipcb, 112p)	Scribner	1914	Armstrong, M.	80-100	
Browning, E.B.	Sonnetts from the Portuguese (1st, 12mo, AEG, gilt, [98]p, col)	Putnam	(1902)	Armstrong, M.	50-75	
Van Dyke, H.	Spirit of Christmas (1st, 8vo, 59p)	Scribner	1905	Armstrong, M.	45-60	
Stevenson, R.L.	St. Ives (1st, 8vo, 438p, brown cl)	Scribner	1897	Armstrong, M.	50-80	

ILLUSTRATOR: 8

AUTHOR	TITLE	PUBLISHER	DATE	ARTIST	PRICE	LC
Stevenson, R.L.	Stevenson Song Book (1st, 4to, ibds, 119p)	Scribner	1897	Armstrong, M.	70-100	
McSpadden, J.W.	Stories From Wagner (8vo, [new ed.], 282p, cvr by...)	Crowell	(1914)	Armstrong, M.	30-45	
Stuart, Ruth M.	Story of Babette (1st, sm8vo, 209p, beige/gilt, cvr by...)	Harper	1894	Armstrong, M.	35-50	*
Stockton, Frank	Storyteller's Pack (1st, 8vo, 380p, gilt, 16pl, teg, cvr by...)	Scribner	1897	Armstrong, M.	45-60	
Cable, G.W.	Strong Hearts (1st, 12mo, 214p, olive/gilt)	Scribner	1899	Armstrong, M.	35-50	*
Van Dyke, J.C.	Studies in Pictures (1st, 12mo, 136p, maroon/gilt)	Scribner	1907	Armstrong, M.	20-30	
Bouvet, M.	Sweet William (1st, 8vo, 209p, blue cl, 16 b/w, cep)	McClurg	1890	Armstrong, M.	30-50	
Kuhns, O.	Switzerland (2nd, 8vo, blue/gilt, 294p)	Crowell	(1910)	Armstrong, M.	35-50	
Swinburne, A.C.	Tale of Balen (1st AM, 8vo, 132p, olive/gilt, cvr by...)	Scribner	1896	Armstrong, M.	70-90	*
Bouvet, M.	Tales of an Old Chateau (1st, 12mo, 235p, gilt)	McClurg	1899	Armstrong, M.	40-60	
Cary, E.L.	Tennyson (1st, lg8vo, blue/gilt, 213p, teg)	Putnam	1906	Armstrong, M.	30-45	
Whittier, J.G.	Tent on the Beach (1st, 8vo, green/gilt, 110p, teg)	Houghton	1899	Armstrong, M.	45-60	
Bingham, D.	The Bastille (1st AM, 8vo, 2 volumes, blue/gilt)	J. Pott	1901	Armstrong, M.	90-120	
Harrison, Mrs. B.	The Carlyles (1st, 8vo, 283, brown cl, cvr by...)	Appleton	1905	Armstrong, M.	25-40	*
Cable, G.W.	The Grandissimes (8vo, 448p, teg, olive/gilt)	Scribner	1898	Armstrong, M.	25-40	
Bonney, T.G.	The Mediterranean (1st, 8vo, blue/gilt)	J. Pott	1902	Armstrong, M.	40-60	
Andrews, M.S.	The Militants (1st, 12mo, teg, 378p, green/gilt, cvr by...)	Scribner	1907	Armstrong, M.	45-60	
Bonner, G.	The Pioneer (1st, 8vo, 392p, blue/gilt, cvr by...)	Bobbs-Merrill	(1905)	Armstrong, M.	30-45	*
Sheridan, R.B.	The Rivals (1st, 8vo, 131p, 17pl, cvr by...)	Crowell	(1907)	Armstrong, M.	35-50	
Barclay, F.	The Rosary (1st, lg8vo, 389p, teg, blue/gilt)	Putnam	1910	Armstrong, M.	30-45	
Cary, E.L.	The Rossettis (2nd, lg8vo, teg, uncut, gilt)	Putnam	1902	Armstrong, M.	50-65	
McCutcheon, G.B.	The Sherrods (1st, sm8vo, 343p, cvr by...)	Dodd	1903	Armstrong, M.	25-40	
Grant, Rbt.	The Undercurrent (1st, 8vo, blue cl, 480p, cvr by...)	Scribner	1904	Armstrong, M.	25-45	
Miller, E.	The Yoke (1st, 12mo, 616p, blue/gilt, cvr by...)	Bobbs-Merrill	(1904)	Armstrong, M.	30-45	
Van Dyke, H.	Through South America (1st, 8vo, blue/gilt, 428p)	Crowell	(1912)	Armstrong, M.	50-70	
Bourget, P.	Tragic Idyll (1st, 8vo, red/gilt, 452p, uncut)	Scribner	1896	Armstrong, M.	30-45	*
Kingsley, F.M.	Transfiguration of Miss Philura (1st, 16mo, 81p, beige cl)	Funk/Wagnalls	(1901)	Armstrong, M.	35-50	
DuMaurier, G.	Trilby (1st, sm8vo, 464p, beige/gilt, b/w, cvr by...)	Harper	1894	Armstrong, M.	30-45	
Morris, C.	Trouble Woman (1st, 12mo, 58p)	Funk/Wagnalls	1904	Armstrong, M.	35-50	*
Smith, M.S.	Twenty Centuries of Paris (1st, 8vo, blue/gilt, 400p, cvr by...)	Crowell	(1913)	Armstrong, M.	30-45	*
Page, T.N.	Under the Crust (1st, 8vo, 307p, green/gilt)	Scribner	1907	Armstrong, M.	25-40	
Isham, F.S.	Under the Rose (1st, 12mo, 427p, green cl, cvr by...)	Bobbs-Merrill	(1903)	Armstrong, M.	20-25	
Van Dyke, H.	Unknown Quantity (1st, 12mo, teg, 370p, uncut)	Scribner	1912	Armstrong, M.	20-30	
Grant, Rbt.	Unleavened Bread (1st, 8vo, green/gilt, 431p)	Scribner	1900	Armstrong, M.	25-40	
Rives, H.E.	Valiants of Virginia (1st, 8vo, red/gilt, 432p)	Bobbs-Merrill	(1912)	Armstrong, M.	20-35	
Ford, P.L.	Wanted a Chaperone (1st, 8vo, 109p, teg, uncut, cvr by...)	Dodd	1902	Armstrong, M.	30-50	*
Ford, P.L.	Wanted a Matchmaker (1st, 8vo, teg, 112p, cvr by...)	Dodd	1900	Armstrong, M.	30-45	
Reed, Myrtle	Weaver of Dreams (1st, 8vo, teg, 374p, blue/gilt)	Putnam	1911	Armstrong, M.	30-50	
Thoreau, H.D.	Week Along/Concord & Merrimack Rivers (1st, 8vo, gilt)	Crowell	(1911)	Armstrong, M.	35-50	
Stevenson, R.L.	Weir of Hermiston (1st AM, 8vo, teg, gilt, 266p)	Scribner	1896	Armstrong, M.	45-60	
Dunbar, P.L.	When Malindy Sings (1st, 8vo, 144p, teg, cvr by...)	Dodd	1903	Armstrong, M.	130-170	
Harland, M.	Where Ghosts Walk (1st, 8vo, green cl, teg, 305p)	Putnam	1898	Armstrong, M.	40-65	
Reed, Myrtle	White Shield (1st, 8vo, 343p, lavender/gilt, teg)	Putnam	1912	Armstrong, M.	30-45	
Daskam, J.	Whom the Gods Destroyed (1st, sm8vo, 236p, red/gilt)	Scribner	1902	Armstrong, M.	35-50	
Cary, E.L.	William Morris (1st, 4to, teg, blue/gilt, 296p, uncut)	Putnam	1902	Armstrong, M.	35-50	
Bradley, Mary H.	Wine of Astonishment (1st, 8vo, pcb, 313p, cvr by...)	Appleton	1919	Armstrong, M.	30-45	*
Brown, Anna R.	Wine-Press (1st, 8vo, 390p, rust cl)	Appleton	1905	Armstrong, M.	30-45	*
Thomas, E.M.	Winter Swallow... (1st, 8vo, 120p, p-o, green/gilt, cvr by...)	Scribner	1896	Armstrong, M.	30-45	*
Field, E.	With Trumpet & Drum (1st, 8vo, 126p, blue/white, cvr by...)	Scribner	1892	Armstrong, M.	35-50	
Beerbohm, M.	Works of... (1st, 8vo, brown/gilt, 165p, uncut)	Scribner	1896	Armstrong, M.	150-220	
Jefferson, C.E.	World's Christmas Tree (1st, sm8vo, 44p, green/gilt, cvr by...)	Crowell	(1906)	Armstrong, M.	35-50	*
Wood, J.S.	Yale Yarns (1st, 12mo, 307p, buckram)	Putnam	1895	Armstrong, M.	45-65	
Nicholson, M.	Zelda Dameron (1st, 8vo, 411p, cvr by...)	Bobbs-Merrill	(1904)	Armstrong, M.	30-45	
Courlander, H.	Tiger's Whisper (1st {std}, sm8vo, blue cl, 152p, fp b/w)	Harcourt	(1959)	Arno, E.	25-40	*
Janvier, T.A.	Santa Fe's Partner (1st, 8vo, 237p, teg, green/gilt, 8pl)	Harper	1907	Arthurs, S.	20-30	
Aesopus	Aesop's Fables (1st AM, lg8vo, p-o, 86p, red cl, pep)	Viking	1933	Artzybasheff, B.	50-70	
Bianco, M.W.	Apple Tree (1st, 8vo, bds, p-o, 47p, b/w, dep)	Doran	(1926)	Artzybasheff, B.	30-45	*
N/A	Arabian Nights (1st, 12mo, grey cl, 402p, 11 fp b/w)	Appleton/Cent.	(1936)	Artzybasheff, B.	40-65	*
Artzybasheff, B.	As I See (1st, 4to, unpag, col frn, fp b/w)	Dodd	1954	Artzybasheff, B.	50-75	*
Morris, C.L.	Behind Moroccan Walls (1st, lg4to, 239p, 20pl)	MacMillan	1931	Artzybasheff, B.	65-80	
Artzybasheff, B.	Busiest Man in Town (1st, sm8vo, 45p, gilt)	Time Inc.	1933	Artzybasheff, B.	65-80	
Finney, C.	Circus of Dr. Lao (1st, 8vo, red cl, 154p, p-o, 8pl)	Viking	1935	Artzybasheff, B.	50-75	
Colum, P.	Creatures (1st, 8vo, bds, 56p, 10 illus, pep)	MacMillan	1927	Artzybasheff, B.	50-70	
Artzybasheff, B.	Fairy Shoemaker (1st, lg8vo, bds, b/w, 114p, DJ)	MacMillan	1928	Artzybasheff, B.	75-100	
Martineau, H.	Feats on the Fiord (1st, 8vo, 301p, blue/gilt, col frn, pep)	MacMillan	1924	Artzybasheff, B.	35-50	
Colum, P.	Forge in the Forest (1st, 8vo, 149p, black/gilt, pep, 9cp)	MacMillan	1925	Artzybasheff, B.	50-80	
Kreymborg, A.	Funnybone Alley (1st, 4to, teg, 269p, gilt, 7 ticp, pep)	Macaulay	(1927)	Artzybasheff, B.	80-120	
Mukerji, D.G.	Gay Neck (1st, 8vo, 197p, t.e. blue, gilt, b/w, pep, DJ, NM)	Dutton	(1927)	Artzybasheff, B.	70-95	R
Mukerji, D.G.	Ghond the Hunter (1st {std}, 8vo, gilt, 204p, 3 dp pl)	Dutton	(1928)	Artzybasheff, B.	45-65	
Lynch, M.B.	Henry the Navigator (1st, 8vo, yellow cl, 72p, 4 fp b/w, pep)	NY: Nelson	1935	Artzybasheff, B.	30-45	*
King, G.	Herodotus (1st {std}, 8vo, 274p, 14pl, map, pep, DJ)	Doubleday/Dor.	1929	Artzybasheff, B.	65-80	
Nathan, Rbt.	Jonah... (1st, 8vo, 212p, 5 engravings)	Knopf	1934	Artzybasheff, B.	30-45	*

AUTHOR	TITLE	PUBLISHER	DATE	ARTIST	PRICE	LC
Lamb, Harold	Kirdy (1st {std}, sm8vo, red cl, uncut, 276p, frn & pep by...)	Doubleday/Dor.	1933	Artzybasheff, B.	35-60	*
Williams, Michael	Little Brother Francis of Assisi (1st, sm8vo, 188p, 4pl, dep)	MacMillan	1926	Artzybasheff, B.	30-50	*
Charskaya, L.A.	Little Princess Nina (1st, sm8vo, 288p, col frn by...)	Holt	1924	Artzybasheff, B.	35-50	*
Buffano, R.	Magic Strings... (1st, 8vo, 182p, 11 b/w)	MacMillan	1939	Artzybasheff, B.	35-50	*
Haskell, H.	Nadya Makes her Bow (1st, 8vo, green cl, uncut, 349p, b/w)	Dutton	1938	Artzybasheff, B.	30-45	*
Hall, A.G.	Nansen (1st, 8vo, 165p, 10pl, pep, NH)	Viking	1940	Artzybasheff, B.	50-70	
Colum, P.	Orpheus: Myths of the World (1st, 4to, 327p, grey cl, 20pl)	MacMillan	1930	Artzybasheff, B.	35-50	
Artzybasheff, B.	Poor Shaydullah (1st, sq8vo, [59]p, grey cl, 10 fp b/w)	MacMillan	1931	Artzybasheff, B.	40-60	
Lustig, Sonia	Roses of the Winds (1st {std}, sm8vo, 275p, col frn, pep, b/w)	Doubleday/Page	1926	Artzybasheff, B.	30-45	*
Artzybasheff, B.	Seven Simeons (1st, 4to, [32]p, green cl, color, dep, CH)	Viking	1937	Artzybasheff, B.	70-115	
Harper, T.A.	Siberian Gold (1st {std}, 8vo, brown cl, 335p, col frn, pep)	Doubleday/Page	1927	Artzybasheff, B.	30-45	
Mirza, Y.B.	Son of the Sword (1st, 8vo, black cl, 211p, pep, designs by...)	Viking	1934	Artzybasheff, B.	30-45	*
Dorey, J.	Three & the Moon (1st, 4to, blue/silver, 103p, 8cp)	Knopf	1929	Artzybasheff, B.	50-70	
Wilson, E.	Undertaker's Garland (1st, 12mo, 192p, uncut, p-o, 5pl)	Knopf	1922	Artzybasheff, B.	45-65	R
Siberiak, M.	Verotchka's Tales (1st, 8vo, pink/gilt, uncut, 190p, 10pl, dep)	Dutton	(1922)	Artzybasheff, B.	50-80	
Bock, Geo. E.	What Makes the Wheels Go 'Round (1st, 4to, 76p, pep, dp color)	MacMillan	1931	Artzybasheff, B.	100-160	*
Young, Ella	Wonder Smith & His Son (1st, 8vo, grn/gilt, 191p, b/w, dep, NH)	Longmans	1927	Artzybasheff, B.	65-80	R
Davis, R.H.	Bar Sinister (1st, 8vo, teg, uncut, 108p, 7cp)	Scribner	1903	Ashe, E.M.	25-40	
Bangs, J.K.	In Camp with a Tin Soldier (1st, 12mo, grey cl, 194p, b/w)	R.H. Russell	1892	Ashe, E.M.	35-50	
Marvel, I.	Reveries of a Bachelor (1st, 8vo, 338p, blue cl, 15cp)	Bobbs-Merrill	(1906)	Ashe, E.M.	20-25	
Jaufre	Jaufre the Knight & Fair Brunissende (1st, 8vo, 124p, decor by)	Holiday House	1935	Atherton, J.	25-40	*
Gaskell, C.M.	Lady Anne's Fairy Tales (1st, 4to, teg, 258p, white/gilt, 12cp)	L: Richards	1914	Atkinson, M.T.	140-200	
Carroll, L.	Alice/Wonderland (1st, 4to, ibds, 148p, AEG, 12cp, pep)	L: R. Tuck	(1910)	Attwell, M.L.	165-220	
Jacberns, R.	Boy and a Secret (1st, 8vo, 304p, 10pl)	L: Chambers	1908	Attwell, M.L.	65-100	
Grimm Bros.	Fairy Tales (1st AM, 4to, 136p, blue/gilt, 12cp)	McKay	[1910]	Attwell, M.L.	160-250	
Andersen, H.C.	Fairy Tales (1st, sm4to, 141p, blue/gilt, 12cp)	Tuck/McKay	[1914]	Attwell, M.L.	165-225	
Andersen, H.C.	Fairy Tales, Stories & Legends (1st, 8vo, 541p, 4pl)	L: Cassell	(1910)	Attwell, M.L.	50-75	*
Molesworth, M.	February Boys (1st, 8vo, 266p, 8cp)	L: Chambers	1909	Attwell, M.L.	50-80	*
Molesworth, M.	February Boys (1st AM, 8vo, 265p, 8cp)	Dutton	[1910]	Attwell, M.L.	45-65	
Ashley, D.	French Fairy Tales (1st, lg8vo, 136p, cp)	L: R. Tuck	[1917]	Attwell, M.L.	130-180	
Queen Marie	Lost Princess (sm4to, red cl, 159p, 6 ticp, pep)	L: Warne	[1915]	Attwell, M.L.	70-90	
Mother Goose	Mother Goose Nursery Rhymes (4to, ibds, 16 fp color)	L: R. Tuck	[1910]	Attwell, M.L.	150-200	*
Molesworth, M.	Old Pincushion (1st, 8vo, 271p, 8cp)	L: Chambers	1910	Attwell, M.L.	65-80	*
Molesworth, M.	Old Pincushion (1st AM, 8vo, 271p, brown cl, 8cp)	Dutton	[1910]	Attwell, M.L.	40-65	
Sylva, C.	Peeping Pansy (1st, 4to, red/gilt, 312p, 8 ticp)	L: Hodder	(1918)	Attwell, M.L.	100-130	
Barrie, J.M.	Peter Pan & Wendy (1st AM, 4to, gilt, p-o, 185p, 12cp, SC)	Scribner	1921	Attwell, M.L.	140-200	
Barrie, J.M.	Peter Pan & Wendy (1st, lg8vo, 185p, blue/gilt, 12 ticp)	L: Hodder	(1921)	Attwell, M.L.	160-240	
N/A	Story Book (4to, ibds, 248p, 6cp)	Whitman	[1930]	Attwell, M.L.	85-130	
Jacberns, R.	Tabitha Smallways, Schoolgirl (1st, 8vo, 304p, 6cp)	L: Chambers	1912	Attwell, M.L.	50-80	*
Baldwin, May	That Little Limb (1st, 8vo, 199p, ibds)	L: Chambers	1905	Attwell, M.L.	65-80	*
Jacberns, R.	Troublesome Dog (1st, 8vo, 297p, 6cp)	L: Chambers	(1911)	Attwell, M.L.	45-65	*
Quiller-Couch, A.	Troublesome Ursula (1st, p-o, 8pl)	L: Chambers	[1915]	Attwell, M.L.	45-65	
Kingsley, C.	Water Babies (1st, sm4to, 115p, red cl, 12cp)	L: R. Tuck	[1915]	Attwell, M.L.	145-200	
Wheelwright, J.	Bad Penny (1st, 8vo, teg, 162p)	Chi: Lamson	1896	Attwood, F.G.	50-70	*
Grant, Rbt.	Jack Hall (1st, 8vo, blue/gilt, 294p, PPP)	Jordan Marsh	1888	Attwood, F.G.	80-100	*
Bigham, M.A.	Blackie, His Friends & Enemies (1st, sm8vo, 200p, 5pl)	Little/Brown	1906	Atwood, C.E.	25-40	*
Wesselhoeft, Lily	Diamond King.... (1st, 12mo, tan cl, 255p, 4pl)	Little/Brown	1907	Atwood, C.E.	20-35	*
Alcott, L.M.	Garland for Girls (1st, 8vo, 286p, 8pl)	Little/Brown	1908	Atwood, C.E.	25-40	
Ward, G.	In the Miz (1st, 4to, blue cl, p-o, 159p, 8cp)	Little/Brown	1904	Atwood, C.E.	70-120	
Ault, N.	Dreamland Shores (1st AM, sm4to, 83p, 6 ticp, pep)	Dodd	(1920)	Ault, N.	100-145	
Ault, L.& N.	Podgy Book of Tales (1st, 12mo, 223p, pict cl, 16cp)	L: Richards	(1907)	Ault, N.	130-180	*
Ault, L.& N.	Sammy & the Snarlywink (1st, 16mo, 95p, green cl, 24cp)	L: Richards	1904	Ault, N.	100-150	
Darton (ed.)	Seven Champions of Christendom (8vo, blue/gilt, teg, 416p)	L: Wells/Gard.	(1913)	Ault, N.	65-80	
Connolly, J.	Story of an Old Fashioned Doll (1st, 8vo, 107p)	L: D. Nutt	1905	Ault, N.	50-70	
Bickley, F.L.	Adventures of Harlequin (1st, 8vo, 119p, bds, p-o, 20 col, pep)	L: Selwyn	1923	Austen, J.	45-65	
Shakespeare, Wm.	As You Like It (1st, 4to, red cl, p-o, 6 ticp)	L: Jackson	1930	Austen, J.	70-100	
Thornley (tr.)	Daphnis & Chloe (1st, 4to, 200p, gilt, buckram, 12cp)	L: G. Bles	1925	Austen, J.	90-135	
Byron	Don Juan (1st, lg8vo, 17 woodcuts, 408p, buckram)	L: J. Lane	(1926)	Austen, J.	50-70	
N/A	Everyman & other Plays (1st, 4to, black cl, 201p, 18cp)	L: Chapman	1925	Austen, J.	100-135	
Perrault, C.	Fairy Tales (1st, sm4to, blue bds, p-o, color)	L: Selwyn	1922	Austen, J.	45-60	*
Allison, J.M.	Five Black Cousins... (1st, sm8vo, white/gilt, uncut, designs)	L: J. Cape	1924	Austen, J.	70-100	*
France, A.	Gods are Athirst (1st, lg8vo, 285p, black/gilt, 12cp)	L: J. Lane	(1927)	Austen, J.	45-65	
Shakespeare, Wm.	Hamlet (1st AM, 4to, black bds, b/w)	Dutton	(1922)	Austen, J.	120-145	
Shakespeare, Wm.	Hamlet (1st, 4to, black bds, gilt, 35 b/w)	L: Selwyn	(1922)	Austen, J.	185-245	
Unknown	Infernal Marriage (1st, 85p, lg8vo, 5cp)	L: Jackson	1929	Austen, J.	140-170	
Keen, R.H.	Little Ape... (1st [1st bk.], 8vo, yellow cl, 68p, 4pl)	L: Hendersons	(1921)	Austen, J.	145-200	
Flaubert, G.	Madame Bovary (lg8vo, 416p, grey cl, 13pl)	L: J. Lane	(1928)	Austen, J.	50-75	
Defoe, D.	Moll Flanders (1st, 4to, 333p, black/gilt, 16pl, pep)	L: J. Lane	(1929)	Austen, J.	50-85	
Bennett, A.	Old Wives' Tale (1st, lg8vo, 729p, 20 color)	Heritage Press	1947	Austen, J.	40-60	
Austen, J.	Rogues in Porcelain (1st AM, lg8vo, 258p, bds, 15cp, pep)	NY: Greenberg	1924	Austen, J.	60-80	
Austen, J.	Rogues in Porcelain (1st, sm4to, pink bds, p-o, 14cp, pep)	L: Chapman	1924	Austen, J.	50-70	
Farjeon, E.	Songs for Music.... (1st, sm8vo, 61p, frn by...)	L: Selwyn	(1922)	Austen, J.	45-65	

ILLUSTRATOR: 10

AUTHOR	TITLE	PUBLISHER	DATE	ARTIST	PRICE	LC
Douglas, N.	South Wind (1st, 8vo, 2 volumes, 15cp)	Argus Books	1929	Austen, J.	75-100	
Perrault, C.	Tales of Past Times... (1st, sq8vo, blue bds, 63p, p-o, color)	L: Selwyn	(1922)	Austen, J.	80-100	
Nesbit, E.	Book of Dogs (1st, obsm4to, 55p, b/w)	Dutton	1898	Austen, W.	160-220	*
Austin, Cyril F.	Advens. of Benjamin & Christabel (1st, ob4to, unpag, color)	Nister/Dutton	(1911)	Austin, H.	50-70	*
Austin, Cyril F.	Edward Buttoneye & his Advens. (sq16mo, ibds, chromos)	L: Nister	[1910]	Austin, H.	65-80	*
Auston, C.	Little Blue Rabbit (sq16mo, ibds)	L: Nister	(1905)	Austin, H.	30-50	
Austin, Margot	Archie Angel (1st {std}, 4to, yellow cl, 45p, b/w, pep)	Dutton	1957	Austin, M.	45-65	*
Austin, Margot	Barney's Adventure (1st {std}, sm4to, ibds, [42]p, b/w, pep)	Dutton	(1941)	Austin, M.	30-50	
Austin, Margot	Brave John Henry (1st {std}, sm4to, 43p, b/w)	Dutton	(1955)	Austin, M.	30-45	*
Austin, Margot	Effelli (1st {std}, 4to, ibds, [56]p, fp b/w, pep)	Dutton	1942	Austin, M.	35-50	*
Austin, Margot	First Prize for Danny (1st {std}, sm4to, ibds, 43p, b/w, pep)	Dutton	(1952)	Austin, M.	35-50	*
Austin, Margot	Gabriel Churchkitten (1st {std}, 4to, ipcb, [36]p, pep, b/w)	Dutton	1942	Austin, M.	70-100	*
Austin, Margot	Gabriel Churchkitten & Moths (1st {std}, sm4to, ipcb, [41]p, b/w)	Dutton	1948	Austin, M.	65-90	*
Austin, Margot	Growl Bear (1st {std}, 4to, ipcb, 42p, pep, b/w)	Dutton	(1951)	Austin, M.	45-65	*
Austin, Margot	Lutie (1st {std}, lg8vo, ibds, [42]p, b/w)	Dutton	1944	Austin, M.	35-50	*
Austin, Margot	Manuel's Kite String (1st, sm8vo, 112p, color)	Scribner	1943	Austin, M.	35-50	*
Mother Goose	Mother Goose Rhymes (1st, 4to, red cl, [83]p, color, pep)	Platt/Munk	(1940)	Austin, M.	65-100	*
Austin, Margot	Moxie & Hanty & Bunty (1st, 8vo, ipcb, [44]p, 1-color)	Scribner	1939	Austin, M.	45-60	*
Austin, Margot	Once Upon a Springtime (1st, 8vo, 43p, ipcb, fp 1-color)	Scribner	1940	Austin, M.	30-50	*
Austin, Margot	Peter Churchmouse (1st {std}, sm4to, ipcb, [41]p, b/w, pep)	Dutton	1941	Austin, M.	70-100	
Austin, Margot	Poppet (1st {std}, 4to, ibds, [38]p, b/w)	Dutton	(1949)	Austin, M.	30-45	
Austin, Margot	Three Silly Kittens (1st {std}, 4to, ibds, 44p, b/w)	Dutton	(1950)	Austin, M.	30-45	
Austin, Margot	Trumpet (1st {std}, sq4to, ipcb, [40]p, b/w, pep)	Dutton	1943	Austin, M.	35-50	
Austin, Margot	Tumble Bear (1st, sm4to, [44]p, olive cl, fp b/w, cep)	Scribner	(1940)	Austin, M.	35-50	*
Austin, Margot	Willamette Way (1st, sm4to, [44]p, tan cl, fp color)	Scribner	1941	Austin, M.	45-65	*
Austin, Margot	William's Shadow (1st {std}, sm4to, ibds, 43p, b/w, pep)	Dutton	(1954)	Austin, M.	30-50	*
Harrison, Ada	Lucy's Village (1st, 8vo, unpag, 8cp)	L: OUP	[1933]	Austin, R.	35-50	*
Sewell, Anna	Black Beauty (1st, sm8vo, 262p, b/w pl)	Page	1902	Austin/Toaspern	25-40	*
Peattie, D.C.	Child's Story of the World (1st, sq8vo, [148]p, color, pep)	Simon/Schuster	1937	Averill, N.	70-90	*
Averill, Naomi	Choochee: Story/Eskimo Boy (1st, sq4to, [40]p, ibds, pep, col)	Grosset/Dunlap	1937	Averill, N.	70-95	*
Peattie, D.C.	Story of America (1st, sq8vo, [24]p, ibds, color, pep)	Grosset/Dunlap	1937	Averill, N.	35-50	*
Peattie, D.C.	Story of Ancient Civilization (1st, sq8vo, [24]p ibds, col, pep)	Grosset/Dunlap	1937	Averill, N.	35-50	*
Peattie, D.C.	Story of the First Men (1st, sq8vo, ibds, [24]p, color, pep)	Grosset/Dunlap	1937	Averill, N.	35-50	*
Averill, Naomi	Whistling-Two-Teeth (1st, lg sq8vo, [24]p, color, pep)	Grosset/Dunlap	1939	Averill, N.	50-80	*
Sowers, P.A.	Dhan of the Pearl Country (1st, lg8vo, p-o, 125p, color)	Whitman	1939	Ayer, M.	25-40	*
Sowers, P.A.	Sons of the Dragon (1st, 8vo, 285p, yellow cl, 4cp)	Whitman	1942	Ayer, M.	20-30	*
Verne, Jules	20 Thousand Leagues... (1st, 4to, black cl, p-o, 4cp, pep, SC)	Scribner	1925	Aylward, W.J.	65-90	
London, J.	Sea Wolf (1st, 8vo, blue cl, teg, 366p, 6pl)	MacMillan	1904	Aylward, W.J.	180-230	
Kingsley, C.	Water Babies (1st, 12mo, 208p, b/w)	D.C. Heath	(1914)	Babbitt/Blossom	30-45	*
Cervantes	Adventures of Don Quixote (1st, sm4to, 287p, color)	Houghton	1928	Bacharach, H.I.	30-45	*
Swift, J.	Gulliver's Travels (1st, lg8vo, 309p, cp)	Houghton	1931	Bacharach, H.I.	25-40	*
Collodi, C.	Pinocchio (1st, 8vo, p-o, 213p, 5cp, pep)	Houghton	1927	Bacharach, H.I.	65-100	
Bacon, P.	Animosities (1st {std}, 8vo, 106p, ibds, b/w)	Harcourt	(1931)	Bacon, P.	35-60	
Bacon, P.	Ballad of Tangle Street (1st, ob4to, ibds, 24p, b/w)	MacMillan	1929	Bacon, P.	80-100	
Robinson, Tom P.	Buttons (1st, lg4to, [63]p, red cl, p-o, b/w, DJ)	Viking	1938	Bacon, P.	30-45	
Bacon, P.	Cat Calls (1st {std}, lg8vo, 87p, b/w, DJ)	McBride	(1935)	Bacon, P.	45-60	
Lockridge, Frances	Cat Who Rode Cows (1st {std}, sm8vo, yellow cl, 36p, b/w)	Lippincott	(1955)	Bacon, P.	30-45	*
Hecht, Ben	Cat/Jumped Out of the Story (1st {std}, 8vo, bds, p-o, pep, col)	Winston	(1947)	Bacon, P.	35-50	*
Coyle, Kath.	Josephine (1st {std}, sm8vo, blue cl, 174p, b/w)	Harper	(1942)	Bacon, P.	35-50	*
Stolz, Mary S.	Leftover Elf (1st, 8vo, 57p, green cl, fp b/w)	Harper	(1952)	Bacon, P.	25-40	*
Bacon, P.	Lion-Hearted Kitten (1st, 8vo, 102p, 10pl)	MacMillan	1927	Bacon, P.	35-50	*
Bacon, P.	Mercy & the Mouse (1st, 8vo, pink cl, 85p, 7pl, cep)	MacMillan	1928	Bacon, P.	40-60	*
Bacon, P.	Mischief in Mayfield (1st {std}, lg8vo, 177p, 15pl)	Harcourt	(1933)	Bacon, P.	25-40	*
Alexander, L.C.	My Five Tigers (1st, 8vo, 118p, green cl, fp b/w)	Crowell	(1956)	Bacon, P.	20-30	*
Bacon, P.	Mystery at East Hatchett (1st, 8vo, 170p, b/w)	Viking	1939	Bacon, P.	25-45	*
Untermeyer, L.	New Songs for New Voices (1st, lg4to, 258p, pep)	Harcourt	(1928)	Bacon, P.	25-40	*
Bacon, P.	Off With Their Heads! (1st {std}, lg4to, [89]p, b/w)	McBride	(1934)	Bacon, P.	30-45	
Van Sinderen, A.	Peter Makebelieve (1st, lg8vo, 65p, 5 fp color)	Yale U. Press	1945	Bacon, P.	50-70	*
Sandburg, C.	Rootabaga Country (1st, 4to, 259p, col frn, 16 b/w, pep)	Harcourt	(1929)	Bacon, P.	65-90	
Bacon, P.	Starting from Scratch (1st {spiral}, [48]p, ibds, b/w)	J. Messner	1945	Bacon, P.	50-75	*
Bacon, P.	Terrible Nuisance (1st {std}, 4to, 142p, blue cl, 8pl)	Harcourt	(1931)	Bacon, P.	60-90	R
Zistel, E.	Treasury of Cat Stories (1st, sm8vo, grey cl, 278p, 12pl)	Greenberg	(1944)	Bacon, P.	40-60	*
Bacon, P.	True Philosopher (1st, 12mo, blue cl, 55p, 13pl)	Bos: Four Seas	1919	Bacon, P.	50-70	*
Lefferts, S.T.	Mr. Cinnamon Bear (1st, sq16mo, ibds, 85p, color)	Bossette Co.	(1907)	Bacquet, L.	160-220	*
Baer, Howard	Now This, Now That (1st, ob4to, [30]p, tan cl, b/w, cep)	Holiday House	1957	Baer, H.	25-40	*
Wetmore, C.H.	Bedtime Stories (1st, 4to, p-o, 120p, color)	Macaulay	1914	Bailey, M.L.	65-80	*
Wetmore, C.H.	Queen Tiny's Little People (1st, 4to, 105p, color, p-o)	Macaulay	1914	Bailey, M.L.	65-80	*
Eager, E.M.	Mouse Manor (1st {1st bk}, 8vo, blue cl, [57]p, 10 fp col, pep)	Ariel	(1952)	Bailey-Jones, B.	35-50	*
Baker, M.	Lady Arabella's Birthday Party (1st, 8vo, [95]p, silhouet., pep)	Dodd	1940	Baker, M.	30-50	
Robinson, M.L.	Little Lucia's School (1st, 12mo, 138p)	Dutton	(1926)	Balcom, S.T.	20-30	*
Singer, Caroline	Ali Lives in Iran (1st, 4to, 71p, color, pep)	Holiday House	1937	Baldridge, C.L.	20-35	*
Singer, Caroline	Boomba Lives in Africa (1st, 4to, ibds, [64]p, color, pep)	Holiday House	1935	Baldridge, C.L.	30-50	*

AUTHOR	TITLE	PUBLISHER	DATE	ARTIST	PRICE	LC
Morier, J.	Hajji Baba of Ispahan (1st, 4to, 403p, gilt, color, DJ)	Random	1937	Baldridge, C.L.	35-50	
Singer, Caroline	Half the World is Isfahan (1st, lg4to, ibds, 153p, 6 fp color)	NY: OUP	1936	Baldridge, C.L.	70-120	R*
Skariatina, I.	Little Era in Old Russia (1st {std}, 8vo, 392p, b/w, pep)	Bobbs-Merrill	(1934)	Baldridge, C.L.	25-40	*
Davis, Rbt.	Pepperfoot of Thursday Market (1st, sm8vo, 187p, b/w, pep)	Holiday House	(1941)	Baldridge, C.L.	35-60	R*
Singer, Caroline	Santa Claus Comes to America (1st {std}, 4to, unpag, ibds, col)	Knopf	1942	Baldridge, C.L.	30-45	*
Burglon, N.	Shark Hole (1st, sm8vo, 244p, fp b/w)	Holiday House	(1943)	Baldridge, C.L.	20-25	*
Cooper, J.F.	The Spy (1st, 4to, blue cl, 389p, p-o, 8cp, pep)	Minton Balch	1924	Baldridge, C.L.	30-45	
Omar Khayyam	Rubaiyat... (1st AM, 4to, p-o, gilt, 6 ticp, 32 tipl)	Dodd	[1920]	Balfour, R.	270-350	
Omar Khayyam	Rubaiyat... (1st, 4to, bds, p-o, 6 ticp, 32 tipl)	L: Constable	1920	Balfour, R.	300-400	
Raymond, W.M.	Rebels of the New South (1st, 8vo, 294p, b/w pl)	C.H. Kerr	1905	Ball, P.B.	20-35	*
Brink, C.R.	Lad with a Whistle (1st, 8vo, 235p, fp b/w, pep)	MacMillan	1941	Ball, Rbt.	25-40	*
Schneider, H.	Let's Look Under the City (1st, sm8vo, grey cl, 70p, 1-color)	W.R. Scott	(1954)	Ballantine, B.	20-30	*
Sage, J.	Man in the Manhole & Fix-It-Men (1st, lg8vo, ipcb, [40]p, col)	W.R. Scott	1946	Ballantine, B.	30-45	*
Sawyer, R.S.	Leerie (1st, 12mo, 309p, 4pl)	Harper	(1920)	Balmer, C.	20-35	*
Bannerman, H.	All About Little Black Sambo (1st, 16mo, 48p, bds, p-o, color)	Cupples	(1917)	Bannerman, H.	100-145	
Bannerman, H.	Little Black Bobtail (1st AM, 16mo, bds, 115p, p-o, 27cp)	Stokes	(1909)	Bannerman, H.	160-220	
Bannerman, H.	Little Black Mingo (1st, 16mo, 143p, green cl, color)	L: J. Nisbet	(1901)	Bannerman, H.	250-400	
Bannerman, H.	Little Black Quasha (1st AM, 16mo, 110p, cp)	Stokes	(1908)	Bannerman, H.	200-260	
Bannerman, H.	Little Black Quibba (1st, 16mo, 143p, color)	L: J. Nisbet	(1902)	Bannerman, H.	300-450	
Bannerman, H.	Little Black Quibba (1st AM, 16mo, 143p, ibds, p-o, color)	Stokes	1903	Bannerman, H.	250-400	
Bannerman, H.	Little Black Sambo (1st, 16mo, green cl, 57p, 25 fp color)	L: Richards	1899	Bannerman, H.	7000	
Bannerman, H.	Little Black Sambo (1st AM, 16mo, 56p, color)	Stokes	[1900]	Bannerman, H.	500-700	*
Bannerman, H.	Little Black Sambo (1st {large fmt}, sq8vo, AEG, 109p)	L: Richards	1903	Bannerman, H.	1200	
Bannerman, H.	Little Black Sambo (1st, 24mo, ibds, 56p, color)	Reilly/Britton	1905	Bannerman, H.	250-400	
Bannerman, H.	Little Black Sambo (8vo, 59p, ibds, color)	McKay	(1931)	Bannerman, H.	75-100	*
Bannerman, H.	Little Black Sambo (1st {this fmt}, 4to, 59p, blue cl, DJ)	L: Chatto	(1932)	Bannerman, H.	280-400	
Bannerman, H.	Little Black Sambo (12mo, 113p, p-o, bds)	L: Chatto	1941	Bannerman, H.	120-165	
Bannerman, H.	Little Degchie Head (1st, 16mo, 143p, green cl, p-o)	L: J. Nisbet	1903	Bannerman, H.	320-450	
Bannerman, H.	Little Kettle-Head (1st AM, 16mo, 144p, ibds, col frn, cp)	Stokes	1904	Bannerman, H.	280-400	
Bannerman, H.	Pat & the Spider (1st, 16mo, 143p, color)	L: J. Nisbet	(1904)	Bannerman, H.	275-400	
Bannerman, H.	Pat & the Spider (1st AM, 16mo, ipcb, 143p, color)	Stokes	(1905)	Bannerman, H.	220-300	
Bannerman, H.	Sambo & the Twins (1st, 16mo, 92p, red cl, color)	Stokes	1936	Bannerman, H.	120-165	
Bannerman, H.	Story of the Teasing Monkey (1st AM, 16mo, 142p, cp)	Stokes	(1907)	Bannerman, H.	250-350	*
Bannon, L.	Gregorio & the White Llama (1st, sq lg8vo, 44p, pep, p-o, col)	Whitman	1944	Bannon, L.	30-45	
Bannon, L.	Horse on a Houseboat (1st, 8vo, cloth, 94p, pep, b/w, DJ)	Whitman	(1951)	Bannon, L.	20-30	
Bannon, L.	Manuela's Birthday in Old Mexico (1st, sq4to, 46p, p-o, color)	Whitman	1939	Bannon, L.	35-50	
Bannon, L.	Patty Paints a Picture (1st, sq4to, [48]p, p-o, color, pep, DJ)	Whitman	1946	Bannon, L.	30-45	
Bowman, J.C.	Pecos Bill (1st, lg8vo, 296p, 6cp, 15pl, pep, NH)	Whitman	1937	Bannon, L.	80-120	*
Bowman, J.C.	Tales from a Finnish Tupa (1st, 8vo, grey cl, 273p, pep, 6cp)	Whitman	1936	Bannon, L.	35-50	*
McElravy, May F.	Tortilla Girl (1st, 4to, 28p, p-o, 46p, pep, color, DJ)	Whitman	1946	Bannon, L.	35-50	
Bannon, L.	Watchdog (1st, 4to, [48]p, color)	Whitman	1948	Bannon, L.	25-40	*
Morgenstern, Eliz.	Little Gardeners (1st AM, sm sq4to, 14p, color, p-o)	Whitman	1933	Bantzer, M.	45-60	*
Barnes, Nancy	Carlota (1st, 8vo, 214p, uncut, b/w pl)	J. Messner	(1943)	Barber, J.	25-40	*
LeGallienne, R.	Romance of Perfume (1st, sm4to, ipcb, 8cp)	R. Hadnut	1928	Barbier, G.	70-85	
Perez-Guerra, A.	Poppy, Adventures of a Fairy (16mo, [62]p, ibds, 16 color)	Rand/McNally	(1942)	Barclay, B.	35-50	*
Grimm Bros.	Golden Goose (1st, sm8vo, 23p, tan cl, 2-color, pep)	Houghton	1947	Bare, A.E.	50-80	
Kingman, Lee	Ilenka (1st, 4to, red cl, [48]p, color)	Houghton/JLG	1945	Bare, A.E.	45-70	*
Bare, A.E.	Maui's Summer (1st, 4to, yellow cl, [48]p, color, pep)	Houghton	1952	Bare, A.E.	45-70	*
Kingman, Lee	Mikko's Fortune (1st {std}, ob4to, blue cl, 46p, color, pep)	Farrar/Rine.	(1955)	Bare, A.E.	50-75	*
Heath, J.F.	Mooky & Tooky (1st, lg8vo, ipcb, [45]p, 1-color, pep)	Howell/Soskin	(1946)	Bare, A.E.	35-50	
Colby, J.P.	Peter Paints the U.S.A. (1st, 4to, 47p, red cl, color, pep)	Houghton	1948	Bare, A.E.	45-65	*
Kingman, Lee	Pierre Pidgeon (1st, 4to, unpag, color, CH)	Houghton	1943	Bare, A.E.	65-95	*
Mitchell, E.	Chickabiddy Stories (1st, 8vo, 110p, 4 ticp)	L: Wells/Gard.	(1899)	Barham, S.	100-140	
Baring, M.	Glass Mender (1st, 8vo, blue/gilt, 260p, teg, 12cp)	L: J. Nisbet	1910	Baring, M.	50-80	
Linnell, O.	Autumn Songs with Music (4to, bds, p-o, 12 ticp)	L: Blackie	[1920]	Barker, C.M.	85-100	
Barker, C.M.	Book of Flower Fairies (1st, 8vo, green/gilt, 92p, color)	L: Blackie	(1927)	Barker, C.M.	200-250	
Barker, C.M.	Children's Book of Hymns (8vo, 84p, 12 ticp)	L: Blackie	[1925]	Barker, C.M.	70-100	
Barker, C.M.	Flower Fairies of Autumn (12mo, ibds, p-o, 24cp)	L: Blackie	[1927]	Barker, C.M.	70-90	
Barker, C.M.	Flower Fairies of Spring (12mo, bds, p-o, 24cp)	L: Blackie	[1925]	Barker, C.M.	70-90	
Barker, C.M.	Flower Fairies of Summer (1st, 12mo, 25p, 24cp)	L: Blackie	(1923)	Barker, C.M.	70-90	
Barker, C.M.	Flower Fairy Alphabet (1st, 12mo, 24p, p-o, 24cp)	L: Blackie	(1934)	Barker, C.M.	70-90	
Barker, C.M.	Flower Songs of the Seasons (4to, ibds, p-o, 12 ticp)	L: Blackie	[1915]	Barker, C.M.	70-90	
Barker, D.O.	He Leadeth Me... (1st, AM, lg8vo, 256p, gilt, 16cp)	NY: M.S. Mill	[1938]	Barker, C.M.	30-45	*
Linnell, O.	Spring Songs with Music (4to, bds, p-o, 12 ticp)	L: Blackie	[1920]	Barker, C.M.	80-100	
Barker, C.M.	Summer Songs with Music (4to, bds, p-o, 12 ticp)	L: Blackie	[1920]	Barker, C.M.	80-100	
Jewett, J.H.	Bunny Stories (1st, sq8vo, 210p, b/w)	Stokes	1892	Barnes, C.	65-80	
Wilkins, M.E.	Decorative Plaques (1st, sq12mo, [32]p, ibds, designs by...)	Lothrop	(1883)	Barnes, G.F.	350-500	
Grey, Sydney	Story-Land (sq8vo, 111p, ibds, 32 color)	L: R.T.S.	(1884)	Barnes, R.	85-120	
Snedeker, C.D.	Downright Dencey (1st {std}, 8vo, 314p, col frn, pep, NH)	Doubleday/Dor.	1927	Barney, M.W.	45-70	
Lefevre, F.	Fiddle Diddle Dee (1st, sm8vo, orang cl, [63]p, fp color, pep)	Greenberg	(1928)	Barney, M.W.	60-90	*
Willson, Dixie	Honey Bear (1st, sm8vo, ibds, [36]p, pep, color)	Volland	(1923)	Barney, M.W.	65-90	
Bancroft, Alberta	Lost Village (1st, 8vo, 130p, green cl, 4 fp color)	Doran	(1927)	Barney, M.W.	45-65	

ILLUSTRATOR: 12

AUTHOR	TITLE	PUBLISHER	DATE	ARTIST	PRICE	LC
Muter, Gladys N.	Mother Let Me Do It (1st {std}, 12mo, ibds, [36]p, color)	Volland	(1925)	Barney, M.W.	45-65	*
Broughton, P.	Pandy (1st, 12mo, ibds, 40p, 5 fp color, pep)	Volland	(1930)	Barney, M.W.	40-65	*
Kyle, Anne D.	Prince of the Pale Mountains (1st, sm8vo, 250p, col frn, pep)	Houghton	1929	Barney, M.W.	25-40	*
DeSegur, S.	Sophie... (1st, 8vo, 157p, b/w, dep)	Knopf	1929	Barney, M.W.	20-35	*
Sawyer, R.S.	This Way to Christmas (1st, lg8vo, 175p, 10cp)	Harper	1924	Barney, M.W.	45-60	
Barney, M.W.	Weather Signs & Rhymes (1st {std}, sq8vo, yellw cl, [103]p, pep)	Knopf	1931	Barney, M.W.	80-120	*
Thacher, L.W.	Listening Child (1st, sm8vo, 405p, blue cl, col frn, 11pl, pep)	MacMillan	1924	Barnhart, N.	25-40	*
Grahame, K.	Wind in the Willows (1st, 8vo, gilt, 302p, p-o, 12cp, pep)	Scribner	1922	Barnhart, N.	100-145	
Flack, M.	Boats on the River (1st, ob4to, 31p, ibds, color, CH)	Viking	1946	Barnum, J.H.	65-110	
Barnum, Jay H.	Little Old Truck (1st, 8vo, 46p, blue cl, color, pep)	Wm. Morrow	1953	Barnum, J.H.	30-45	*
Sawyer, R.S.	Little Red Horse (1st, sm8vo, 108p, brown cl, pep, color, DJ)	Viking	1950	Barnum, J.H.	40-65	
Barnum, Jay H.	Motorcycle Dog (1st, 8vo, blue cl, 48p, 2-color, pep)	Wm. Morrow	1958	Barnum, J.H.	30-45	*
Jewett, E.M.	Mystery at Boulder Point (1st, 8vo, 281p, grey cl, fp b/w)	Viking	1949	Barnum, J.H.	20-35	*
Barnum, Jay H.	New Fire Engine (1st, 8vo, red cl, 47p, 2-color, pep)	Wm. Morrow	1952	Barnum, J.H.	30-45	*
Martin, Chas. M.	Orphans of the Range (1st, 8vo, 192p, blue cl, fp b/w)	Viking	1950	Barnum, J.H.	30-45	*
Carmer, Carl	Too Many Cherries (1st, 4to, 62p, ipcb, 2-color, pep)	Viking	1949	Barnum, J.H.	45-70	*
Brown, Gladys	Two-Bow Bill (1st, 8vo, 46p, blue cl, color, pep)	Wm. Morrow	1955	Barnum, J.H.	25-45	*
Carden, Priscilla	Vanilla Village (1st {std}, lg8vo, 58p, tan cl, pep, color)	Ariel	(1952)	Barnum, J.H.	30-50	*
Tunis, John R.	World Series (1st, sm8vo, 318p, blue cl, 24pl, pep)	Harcourt	(1941)	Barnum, J.H.	25-40	*
Fox, F.M.	Betty of Mackinaw (1st, 12mo, 109p, b/w)	Page	1901	Barry, E.B.	20-25	*
Raymond, E.	Boys & Girls of Brantham (1st, sm8vo, 283p, grey/gilt, 6pl)	Little/Brown	1899	Barry, E.B.	25-40	*
Stevenson, R.L.	Child's Garden of Verses (1st, 12mo, 107p b/w)	Page	1900	Barry, E.B.	25-40	*
Fox, F.M.	County Christmas (1st, 12mo, 111p, 10pl)	Page	1907	Barry, E.B.	20-35	*
Ewing, J.H.	Daddy Darwin's Dovecoat (1st, 12mo, 78p, grey cl, 6pl)	D. Estes	1898	Barry, E.B.	30-45	*
Ewing, J.H.	Great Emergency (1st, 12mo, 166p, b/w pl)	L.C. Page	1897	Barry, E.B.	25-40	*
Johnston, A.F.	Little Colonel (1st, 8vo, 102p, green/gilt, b/w, PPP)	J. Knight	1896	Barry, E.B.	130-200	
Johnston, A.F.	Little Colonel's Knight Comes Riding (1st, 8vo, 318p, b/w)	Page	1907	Barry, E.B.	25-40	
Cheever, H.A.	Little Mr. Van Vere of China (1st, sq8vo, 243p, col frn, b/w)	Estes	(1898)	Barry, E.B.	35-50	*
Johnston, A.F.	May Ware, Little Colonel's Chum (1st, 12mo, 305p, tan cl, 8pl)	Page	1908	Barry, E.B.	25-40	
Brainerd, E.S.	Millicent in Dreamland (1st, 12mo, 94p)	Page	1902	Barry, E.B.	20-35	*
Fox, F.M.	Mother Nature's Little Ones (1st, 12mo, 92p, fp b/w)	L.C. Page	1904	Barry, E.B.	20-30	*
Saunders, M.	Nita (1st, 12mo, 77p)	Page	1904	Barry, E.B.	20-30	*
Potter, M.K.	Peggy's Trial (1st, 12mo, 97p, b/w)	Page	1901	Barry, E.B.	20-35	*
Fox, F.M.	Seven Christmas Candles (1st, 8vo, 192p, 6cp)	Page	1909	Barry, E.B.	30-45	*
Johnston, A.F.	Story of Dago (1st, 12mo, 101p, 10pl)	Page	1900	Barry, E.B.	25-40	*
Harland, M.	When Grandmamma Was 14 (1st, 8vo, 399p, 4pl)	Lothrop	1905	Barry, E.B.	20-30	*
Amend, Ottillie	Jolly Jungle Jingles (1st, ob4to, ibds, 30p, color)	Volland	(1929)	Barte, E.	80-130	*
Frisbie, W.A.	ABC Mother Goose (1st, 4to, [52]p, beige cl, color)	Rand/McNally	(1905)	Bartholomew, F.	165-200	
Frisbie, W.A.	Pirate Frog... (1st, 4to, [94]p, ibds, color)	Rand/McNally	(1901)	Bartholomew, F.	130-180	
Mother Goose	Crooked Man (1st {std}, 12mo, [56]p, pep)	Longmans	(1940)	Barto, E.	25-40	*
Mother Goose	Piper's Son (1st {std}, 16mo, blue cl, [56]p, fp b/w, pep)	Longmans	(1942)	Barto, E.	30-50	*
Marshall, A.	Peggy in Toyland (1st, 8vo, ipcb, 277p, b/w)	Dodd	1920	Barton, H.M.	35-50	*
Gray, Eliz. J.	Beppy Marlowe of Charles Town (1st, sm8vo, 281p, color, pep)	Viking	1936	Barton, L.	25-40	*
Bascom, L.R.	Bugaboo Men (1st, sq4to, green cl, [72]p, pep, color)	NY: Sully	(1914)	Bascom, L.R.	90-120	*
Croll, Pauline	Just for You (1st, 12mo, 37p, color)	Volland	(1918)	Basset, M.	35-50	*
Richards, L.E.	Fairy Operettas (1st, 12mo, 119p, col frn)	Little/Brown	1916	Basset, M.R.	35-60	*
Baum, L.F.	Daring Twins (1st [1], sm8vo, blue cl, 317p, 4pl)	Reilly/Britton	(1911)	Batchelder, P.M.	200-300	
Carroll, L.	Further Nonsense Prose... (1st AM, lg8vo, ipcb, p-o, 118p)	Appleton	1926	Bateman, H.M.	65-90	
Carroll, L.	Further Nonsense Prose... (1st, 4to, 127p, yellow bds)	L: T.F. Unwin	1926	Bateman, H.M.	70-90	
Jacobs, J.	Book of Wonder Voyages (1st, 8vo, 224p, uncut, 7pl)	L: D. Nutt	1896	Batten, J.D.	160-200	
Jacobs, J.	Celtic Fairy Tales (1st, lg8vo, 267p, green cl, 8pl)	L: D. Nutt	1892	Batten, J.D.	140-185	
Jacobs, J.	English Fairy Tales (1st, 8vo, 253p, AEG, 8pl)	L: D. Nutt	1890	Batten, J.D.	70-100	*
Jacobs, J.	English Fairy Tales (1st AM, 8vo, 253p, 8pl)	Putnam	1891	Batten, J.D.	65-80	
Dixon, E. (ed.)	Fairy Tales/Arabian Nights (1st, sm4to, 267p, gilt, teg, 5pl)	L: J.M. Dent	1893	Batten, J.D.	100-135	
Dixon (ed.)	Fairy Tales/Arabian Nights (1st, 8vo, 477p, col frn, 16pl)	L: Dent	1907	Batten, J.D.	85-130	
Jacobs, J. (ed.)	Indian Fairy Tales (1st AM, 8vo, 255p, 8pl)	Putnam	1892	Batten, J.D.	100-145	*
Jacobs, J. (ed.)	Indian Fairy Tales (1st, 8vo, 255p, uncut, 9pl)	L: D. Nutt	1892	Batten, J.D.	70-90	*
Hewlett, M.	Masque of Dead Florentines (1st, ob8vo, uncut, teg, 51p, 4pl)	L: J.M. Dent	1895	Batten, J.D.	75-100	
Jacobs, J.	More Celtic Fairy Tales (1st, 8vo, 234p, 8pl)	L: D. Nutt	1894	Batten, J.D.	100-130	
Jacobs, J.	More English Fairy Tales (1st, 8vo, blue cl, 243p, 8pl)	L: D. Nutt	1894	Batten, J.D.	70-100	
Ingold, John	Glimpses from Wonderland (1st, 8vo, 287p, blue/gilt, 5pl)	L: J. Long	1900	Bauerle, A.	30-50	*
Riley, J.W.	All the Year Round (1st, 4to, gilt, ibds, [30]p, p-o, 12cp)	Bobbs-Merrill	(1912)	Baumann, G.	250-400	R
Banning, Kendall	Pirates! (1st {this pub}, 12mo, [31]p, wraps, 13 fp woodcuts)	Chi: Woodworth	1918	Baumann, G.	100-165	
Dalgliesh, A.	Little Wooden Farmer (1st, ob8vo, green cl, [43]p, color, pep)	MacMillan	1930	Baumeister, T.	35-50	*
Graham, H.	Deportmental Ditties (1st, 4to, 127p)	L: Mills/Boom	(1909)	Baumer, L.	30-50	
Hay, I.	Lighter Side of School Life (1st, 8vo, 226p, teg, 12pl)	L: Foulis	(1914)	Baumer, L.	25-40	
Irving, W.	Old Christmas (1st, 8vo, 284p, color)	L: Constable	1918	Baumer, L.	45-60	*
Irving, W.	Old Christmas (1st AM, 8vo, 284p, color)	Houghton	1919	Baumer, L.	35-50	*
Irving, W.	Old Christmas & Bracebridge Hall (8vo, red cl, 285p, 8 color)	L: Constable	1918	Baumer, L.	30-45	
Molesworth, M.	Three Witches (1st, 8vo, 278p, blue cl, 13pl)	L: Chambers	1900	Baumer, L.	35-50	*
Thackeray, Wm.	Vanity Fair (1st, 4to, p-o, teg, gilt, 20 ticp)	L: Hodder	(1913)	Baumer, L.	100-140	*
Andersen, H.C.	Fairy Tales & Stories (2nd, 8vo, 512p, 4cp)	L: Routledge	[1905]	Bayes, A.W.	80-100	

AUTHOR	TITLE	PUBLISHER	DATE	ARTIST	PRICE	LC
Andersen, H.C.	What the Moon Saw (brown/gilt, 6 chromos)	(London)	[1880]	Bayes, A.W.	100-140	*
Larken, E.P.	Sea-Prince (1st, 12mo, blue/gilt, teg, 340p, b/w, dep)	L: Jarrolds	1899	Bayes, J.M.	45-60	
Deutsch, B.	It's a Secret! (1st {std}, sq12mo, 47p, 2-color, pep)	Harper	(1941)	Bayley, D.	50-80	R*
Tolkien, J.R.R.	Farmer Giles of Ham (1st, 8vo, 78p, orange cl, 2 fp color, pep)	L: Allen/Unwin	1949	Baynes, P.D.	150-200	
Tolkien, J.R.R.	Farmer Giles of Ham (1st AM, 8vo, blue cl, 79p, color)	Houghton	1950	Baynes, P.D.	130-180	*
Lewis, C.S.	Horse & his Boy (1st, 8vo, grey/silver, 199p)	L: G. Bles	(1954)	Baynes, P.D.	250-400	*
Lewis, C.S.	Last Battle (1st, 8vo, blue cl, 184p, b/w, DJ)	L: Bodley Head	1956	Baynes, P.D.	350-500	*
Lewis, C.S.	Last Battle (1st AM {std}, sm8vo, 174p, blue cl, b/w)	MacMillan	(1956)	Baynes, P.D.	160-200	R*
Lewis, C.S.	Lion, Witch & the Wardrobe (1st AM, 8vo, 154p, b/w, DJ)	MacMillan	1950	Baynes, P.D.	200-300	
Lewis, C.S.	Magician's Nephew (1st AM {std}, sm8vo, 167p, green cl, b/w)	MacMillan	(1955)	Baynes, P.D.	130-170	
Lewis, C.S.	Prince Caspian (1st AM {std}, sm8vo, 186p, green cl, 4 fp b/w)	MacMillan	1951	Baynes, P.D.	150-200	
Lewis, C.S.	Silver Chair (1st AM {std}, sm8vo, 208p, blue cl, 4 fp b/w)	MacMillan	(1953)	Baynes, P.D.	90-140	*
Pourrat, Henry	Treasury of French Tales (1st, 8vo, 239p, bds, 9 fp b/w)	Houghton	1953	Baynes, P.D.	70-100	*
Lewis, C.S.	Voyage o/t Dawn Treader (1st AM {std}, sm8vo, 210p, blue cl, b/w)	MacMillan	1952	Baynes, P.D.	100-160	
Steedman, Amy	Apple Pie... (8vo, grey cl, p-o, 8cp)	L: Jack	[1908]	Beale, E.	30-45	*
Sherwood, M.	Fairchild Family (sq8vo, 111p, gilt, p-o, 8cp)	Dutton	(1908)	Beale, E.	45-60	
Bealer, A.W.	Picture-Skin Story (1st, sq8vo, [27]p, pink cl, color, cep)	Holiday House	1957	Bealer, A.W.	35-50	*
N/A	Aladdin (1st, lg8vo, red cl, 39p, 8cp)	L: J. Lane	1924	Beaman, S.G.H.	25-40	*
N/A	Aladdin (1st AM, sm4to, 39p, 8cp)	McBride	1925	Beaman, S.G.H.	35-65	*
N/A	Seven Voyages of Sinbad the Sailor (1st AM, 4to, 71p, 8cp)	McBride	1926	Beaman, S.G.H.	50-80	*
Twain, M.	American Claimant (1st, 8vo, 279p, green/gilt)	Webster	1892	Beard, D.	180-230	
Beard, D.	Animal Book & Campfire Stories (1st, 8vo, 538p, col frn)	Moffat	1907	Beard, D.	35-50	
Crosby, E.	Captain Jinks, Hero (1st, sm8vo, tan cl, 393p, 9pl)	Funk/Wagnalls	1902	Beard, D.	20-35	
Barton, W.E.	Hero in Homespun (1st, 8vo, 393p, 10pl)	Chi: Lamson	1897	Beard, D.	65-80	*
Astor, J.J.	Journey in Other Worlds (1st, 8vo, blue/silver, 476p, 10pl)	Appleton	1894	Beard, D.	150-200	
Beard, D.	Moonblight (1st, sm8vo, 238p, green/gilt, uncut, b/w)	A. Brandt	1904	Beard, D.	50-80	
Twain, M.	Tom Sawyer Abroad (1st, 8vo, 219p, white cl)	NY: Webster	1894	Beard, D.	375-450	
Brown, E.P.	Ciderville Folks (1st, 4to, tan/gilt, 496p, b/w)	Date Pub. Co.	(1898)	Beard, F.	45-65	*
Bryant, S.C.	Best Stories to Tell Children (1st, blue/gilt, 181p, 16cp)	Houghton	1912	Beard, P.	40-60	
Holloway, J.	At Flower Farm (1st, 4to, ibds, p-o, 4cp)	Stern	1909	Beard/Kay	80-110	
Sharp, E.	At the Relton Arms (1st, 12mo, 182p, uncut, design by..)	L: J. Lane	1895	Beardsley, A.	60-80	
Symons, A.	Aubrey Beardsley (1st, 8vo, bds, gilt, 6 b/w)	L: Unicorn Pr.	1898	Beardsley, A.	150-200	
Ross, R.	Aubrey Beardsley (1st, 12mo, 112p, teg, gilt, 16pl)	L: J. Lane	1909	Beardsley, A.	50-75	
Quilp, J.	Baron Verdigris (1st, 8vo, 214p, cvr by...)	L: Henry Co.	1894	Beardsley, A.	60-85	
Jerrold, W.C.	Bon-Mots... (1st, 24mo, 192p, gilt, teg, cvr by...)	L: J.M. Dent	1893	Beardsley, A.	75-100	
Beardsley, Aubrey	Book of 50 Drawings (1st, 4to)	L: Smithers	1897	Beardsley, A.	240-350	
O'Sullivan, V.	Book of Bargains (1st, 8vo, 185p, frn by...)	L: Smithers	1896	Beardsley, A.	70-85	
Allen, G.	British Barbarians (1st, 8vo, olive/gilt, 202p, cvr by...)	L: J. Lane	1895	Beardsley, A.	70-100	
Farr, Florence	Dancing Faun (1st, 8vo, 149p, ti-page & cvr by...)	L: E. Matthews	1894	Beardsley, A.	45-60	*
Hobbes, J.O.	Dream & the Business (1st, 8vo, blue cl, teg, cvr by...)	L: T.F. Unwin	1906	Beardsley, A.	75-120	
N/A	Early Work of Aubrey Beardsley (1st, lg4to)	L: J. Lane	1899	Beardsley, A.	200-300	
Burney, Fanny	Evelina... (3rd ed., sm8vo, teg, 2 vols, uncut, gilt)	L: J.M. Dent	1893	Beardsley, A.	280-400	
Ruding, W.	Evil Motherhood (1st, 8vo, blue/gilt, 99p, uncut, frn by...)	L: Matthews	1895	Beardsley, A.	100-160	
Machen, Arthur	Great God Pan/Inmost Light (1st AM, 8vo, 234p, gilt, cvr by...)	Roberts	1894	Beardsley, A.	150-200	
Johnson, Ben	His Volpone (1st, 4to, blue/gilt, 7pl)	L: Smithers	1898	Beardsley, A.	200-300	
Yeats, W.B.	Land of Hearts Desire (1st AM, 16mo, pcb, frn by...)	H. Stone	1894	Beardsley, A.	100-130	
Douglas, R.B.	Life & Times of Madame Du Barry (1st, 4to, 386p, cvr by...)	L: Smithers	1896	Beardsley, A.	120-160	
Makower, S.	Mirror of Music (1st, 8vo, 179p, uncut, cvr by...)	L: J. Lane	1895	Beardsley, A.	70-100	
D'Arcy, Ella	Monochromes (1st, 8vo, 260p, green cl, cvr & ti page by...)	L: J. Lane	1895	Beardsley, A.	65-80	*
MacLeod	Mountain Lovers (8vo, 241p, blue/white, cvr by...)	L: J. Lane	1895	Beardsley, A.	30-50	
Brown, V.	My Brother (1st, 12mo, 176p, beige cl, frn by...)	L: J. Lane	1896	Beardsley, A.	85-110	
Grahame, K.	Pagan Papers (1st, 12mo, bds, 165p, teg, title page by...)	H. Stone	1894	Beardsley, A.	100-150	R
Bjornson, B.	Pastor Sang (1st, 8vo, teg, uncut, frn by...)	L: Longmans	1893	Beardsley, A.	70-90	
Stacpoole, H.D.	Pierrot! (1st, 8vo, red cl, uncut, pep, cvr & title page by...)	L: J. Lane	1896	Beardsley, A.	65-80	*
Davidson, John	Plays by... (1st, 8vo, gilt, 294p, uncut, cvr by...)	L: Matthews	1894	Beardsley, A.	80-120	
Dowson, Ernest	Poems of E. Dowson (1st, green/gilt, teg, 4pl, cvr by...)	L: J. Lane	1905	Beardsley, A.	100-125	
Dostoievsky, F.	Poor Folk (1st, 8vo, title pg & cvr by...)	L: Matthews	1894	Beardsley, A.	100-150	
Pope, A.	Rape of the Lock (1st, 12mo, AEG, 11 illus)	L: Smithers	1896	Beardsley, A.	175-220	
Wilde, O.	Salome... (1st, 8vo, blue/gilt, 10pl)	L: Matthews	1894	Beardsley, A.	900-1200	
Wilde, O.	Salome... (sm8vo, 36p, black/gilt, 16pl)	Bos: J.W. Luce	1907	Beardsley, A.	100-160	
Wilde, O.	Salome... (2nd, sm4to, gilt, 66p, teg, 16pl)	L: J. Lane	1907	Beardsley, A.	300-450	
Beardsley, Aubrey	Second Book of 50 Drawings (1st, 4to, red/gilt)	L: Smithers	1899	Beardsley, A.	250-450	
Shiel, M.P.	Shapes in the Fire (1st AM, 8vo, blue cl, cvr & ti page by..)	Roberts	1896	Beardsley, A.	160-200	
Brooks, Edward	Story of King Arthur (1st AM, 12mo, 383p, 13pl)	Penn	1900	Beardsley, A.	70-120	*
Beardsley, Aubrey	Under The Hill (1st, 4to, teg, blue/gilt, uncut, 15pl)	L: J. Lane	1904	Beardsley, A.	300-500	
Allen, G.	Woman Who Did (8vo, 241p, later, cvr by...)	L: J. Lane	1895	Beardsley, A.	50-80	
Davidson, John	Wonderful Mission/Earl Lavender (1st, 8vo, gilt, uncut, cvr by..)	L: Ward/Down.	1895	Beardsley, A.	70-90	*
Dawe, W.C.	Yellow & White (1st, 8vo, yellow cl, cvr & ti page by)	L: J. Lane	1895	Beardsley, A.	80-100	
Beardsley, Alice	Turn-Around Book (1st, lg8vo, p-o, unpag)	Bobbs-Merrill	(1914)	Beardsley, Alice	80-100	*
Richards, L.E.	Golden Windows (1st, 8vo, 123p, green/gilt, teg, 5pl)	Little/Brown	1903	Becher, A.E.	20-35	
Bangs, J.K.	Little Book of Christmas (1st, 8vo, 173p, 4cp)	Little/Brown	1912	Becher, A.E.	30-45	*
Knipe, E.& A.	Lucky Sixpence (1st, 8vo, 378p, 4pl, PPPa)	Century	(1912)	Becher, A.E.	200-300	

AUTHOR	TITLE	PUBLISHER	DATE	ARTIST	PRICE	LC
Buchan, J.	Magic Walking Stick (1st, 8vo, red/gilt, 176p, b/w, pep)	Houghton	1932	Becher, A.E.	35-50	
Singmaster, Elsie	When Sarah Saved the Day (1st, 12mo, 135p, pink cl, 4pl)	Houghton	1909	Becher, A.E.	20-30	
Beckenbaugh, G.	Cotton Tails (1st, ob4to, [99]p, ipcb, fp b/w)	R.H. Russell	1900	Beckenbaugh, G.	140-200	*
N/A	Arabian Nights (1st, lg8vo, 242p, col frn, pep)	Sears	(1928)	Becker, C.	25-40	
Catrevas, C.	Fairy Tales for Little People (1st, 4to, 246p, p-o, col frn, pep)	Sears	(1927)	Becker, C.	30-45	
Alger, Leclaire	Jan & Wonderful Mouth-Organ (1st {std}, 8vo, 177p, col frn, pep)	Harper	1939	Becker, C.	25-40	*
Dalgliesh, A.	Young Aunts (1st, 8vo, 116p, red cl, color)	Scribner	1939	Becker, C.	20-25	*
Grimm Bros.	Fairy Tales (1st, 8vo, 382p, color)	World Pub. Co.	(1947)	Becker, M.L.	25-45	*
Stevenson, R.L.	Treasure Island (1st, 8vo, 287p, color, pep)	World Pub. Co.	(1946)	Becker, M.L.	25-40	*
Lucas, E.V.	Another Book of Verses for Children (1st AM, 8vo, 431p, 18pl)	MacMillan	1907	Bedford, F.D.	50-75	
MacDonald, Geo.	Back of the North Wind (1st AM, 8vo, 376p, 12pl, col frn, pep)	NY: MacMillan	(1924)	Bedford, F.D.	65-80	
Barlow, J.	Battle of the Frogs & Mice (1st, 8vo, green cl, unpag, 4pl)	L: Methuen	1894	Bedford, F.D.	70-100	
MacDonald, Greville	Billy Barnicoat (1st AM, 8vo, 230p, fp b/w)	Dutton	1923	Bedford, F.D.	35-50	*
N/A	Book of Nursery Rhymes (1st, 4to, ibds, 91p, 21cp)	L: Methuen	1897	Bedford, F.D.	165-220	
N/A	Book of Nursery Rhymes (1st AM, lg8vo, 91p, cp)	Doub./McClure	1897	Bedford, F.D.	100-140	
Lucas, E.V.	Book of Shops (ob4to, ipcb, 24cp)	L: Richards	1900	Bedford, F.D.	170-220	
Dickens, C.	Christmas Carol (1st, 8vo, 166p, gilt, 4cp, 15pl, pep)	MacMillan	1923	Bedford, F.D.	50-70	
MacDonald, Greville	Count Billy (1st {std}, 8vo, 246p, gilt, uncut, col frn, 6pl)	Dutton	1928	Bedford, F.D.	30-45	*
Dickens, C.	Cricket on the Hearth (1st AM, 8vo, 182p, red/gilt, color, DJ)	Harper	(1927)	Bedford, F.D.	75-110	
Baring-Gould, S.	Crock of Gold (1st AM, 8vo, gilt, teg, 8pl)	L.C. Page	1899	Bedford, F.D.	40-60	
Lucas, E.V.	Forgotten Tales of Long Ago (1st, 8vo, 424p, teg, 23pl)	L: Wells/Gard.	1906	Bedford, F.D.	60-80	
Lucas, E.V.	Four & Twenty Toilers (1st AM, ob4to, blue cl, p-o, 24cp)	McDevitt/Wilsn	[1900]	Bedford, F.D.	160-220	
Coatsworth, E.	Knock at the Door (1st, ob8vo, 73p, gilt, col frn, b/w)	MacMillan	1931	Bedford, F.D.	35-50	
Dickens, C.	Magic Fishbone (1st, ob8vo, [40]p, ibds, 7cp, pep)	L: Warne	(1922)	Bedford, F.D.	60-85	
Bedford, F.D.	Night of Wonders (1st, ob8vo, ibds, 124p, teg, 24cp, pep)	L: Richards	[1906]	Bedford, F.D.	200-270	
Baring-Gould, S.	Old English Fairy Tales (1st AM, 8vo, teg, 400p, gilt, b/w)	Way/Williams	1895	Bedford, F.D.	100-150	
Lucas, E.V.	Old Fashioned Tales (1st, 8vo, teg, 389p, gilt, col frn)	L: Wells/Gard.	[1905]	Bedford, F.D.	70-100	
Taylor, A.& J.	Original Poems (2nd AM, 8vo, 415p, gilt, teg, tan cl, col frn)	Stokes	(1905)	Bedford, F.D.	45-65	
Taylor, A.& J.	Original Poems... (2nd, 8vo, teg, uncut, col frn)	L: Wells/Gard.	1905	Bedford, F.D.	90-130	*
Barrie, J.M.	Peter & Wendy (1st AM, lg8vo, 267p, gilt, 13pl, SC)	Scribner	1911	Bedford, F.D.	150-200	
Barrie, J.M.	Peter & Wendy (1st, 8vo, 267p, green/gilt, 13pl)	L: Hodder	(1911)	Bedford, F.D.	120-140	
MacDonald, Geo.	Princess & Goblin (1st, 12mo, 267p, blue/gilt, col frn)	MacMillan	1926	Bedford, F.D.	70-100	
Stevens, F.	Through Merrie England (1st, 8vo, grn/gilt, teg, 214p, 12cp, pep)	L: Warne	(1928)	Bedford, F.D.	45-60	
Goldsmith, O.	Vicar of Wakefield (1st, 8vo, 222p, green/gilt, uncut, 12cp)	L: Dent	1898	Bedford, F.D.	65-90	
Lucas, E.V.	Visit to London (1st AM, 4to, ibds, 118p, 24cp)	Brentano's	[1902]	Bedford, F.D.	90-140	
Lucas, E.V.	Visit to London (1st, 4to, ipcb, 118p, 24cp)	L: Methuen	1902	Bedford, F.D.	100-165	
Gordon, Eliz.	Dolly & Molly at Seashore (1st, 16mo, 32p, color)	Rand/McNally	(1914)	Beem, F.	35-60	*
Gordon, Eliz.	Dolly & Molly at the Circus (1st, 16mo, 32p, color)	Rand/McNally	(1914)	Beem, F.	35-60	*
Judson, C.I.	Garden Adventures of Tommy Tittlemouse (1st, sm8vo, 64p, color)	Rand/McNally	(1922)	Beem, F.	20-30	*
Herr, Charlotte	Unselfish Pig (1st, 12mo, ibds, color)	Volland	(1913)	Beem, F.	40-65	*
Herr, Charlotte	Wise Mamma Goose (1st, 12mo, ibds, 21p, color)	Volland	(1913)	Beem, F.	40-60	*
Beerbohm, M.	50 Caracitures (1st, sm4to, green/gilt, 50 tipl)	L: Heinemann	1913	Beerbohm, M.	120-175	
Beerbohm, M.	A Survey (1st, 4to, gilt, col frn, 51 tipl)	L: Heinemann	1921	Beerbohm, M.	100-165	
Beerbohm, M.	Caricatures of 25 Gentlemen (1st, 4to)	L: Smithers	1896	Beerbohm, M.	120-180	
Beerbohm, M.	Dreadful Dragon of Hay Hill (1st, lg8vo, 113p, ibds, col frn)	L: Heinemann	1928	Beerbohm, M.	50-70	
Beerbohm, M.	More (1st, 8vo, green cloth)	L: J. Lane	1899	Beerbohm, M.	145-170	
Beerbohm, M.	Observations (1st, 4to, 52pl, DJ)	L: Heinemann	1925	Beerbohm, M.	70-100	
Beerbohm, M.	Poet's Corner (1st, folio, ibds, 20cp)	L: Heinemann	1904	Beerbohm, M.	150-200	
Beerbohm, M.	Rossetti & his Circle (1st, 4to, blue/gilt, 23 ticp)	L: Heinemann	1922	Beerbohm, M.	120-180	
Beerbohm, M.	Second Childhood of John Bull (1st, folio, bds, 15cp)	L: Swift	(1911)	Beerbohm, M.	150-200	*
N/A	Stuffed Owl (1st AM, sm8vo, bds, p-o, 236p, 6pl, pep)	Coward	(1930)	Beerbohm, M.	30-45	*
Beerbohm, M.	Things New & Old (1st, 4to, col frn, 49pl)	L: Heinemann	1923	Beerbohm, M.	90-130	
Beerbohm, M.	Zuleika Dobson (1st, 8vo, brown cl, 350p, gilt)	L: Heinemann	1911	Beerbohm, M.	150-200	
Behn, Harry	All Kinds of Time (1st {std}, 12mo, ibds, [61]p, color, cep)	Harcourt	(1950)	Behn, H.	65-100	R*
Behn, Harry	Little Hill (1st {std}, 12mo, 58p, ipcb, 1-color, cep)	Harcourt	(1949)	Behn, H.	65-100	R*
Behn, Harry	Painted Cave (1st {std}, 8vo, ipcb, 63p, 1-color, cep)	Harcourt	(1957)	Behn, H.	65-100	R*
Behn, Harry	Windy Morning (1st {std}, 12mo, ipcb, 61p, 1-color, cep)	Harcourt	(1953)	Behn, H.	65-100	R*
Behn, Harry	Wizard in the Well (1st {std}, 12mo, ipcb, 62p, 1-color, cep)	Harcourt	(1956)	Behn, H.	65-100	R*
Beistle, A.S.	I Spy (1st, 8vo, spiral-bound ibds, [17]p, color)	McKay	(1944)	Beistle, M.A.	35-50	*
Beistle, A.S.	Just Peggy (1st, sm8vo, 63p, b/w)	McKay	(1939)	Beistle, M.A.	25-40	
Beistle, A.S.	Mr. Heinie (1st {std}, ob8vo, [32]p, ipcb, color, pep)	McKay	(1938)	Beistle, M.A.	35-50	*
Beistle, A.S.	Mr. Heinie & Scroot (1st {std}, ob8vo, [36]p, ibds, color, pep)	McKay	(1939)	Beistle, M.A.	45-60	*
Beistle, A.S.	Open Daily (1st {std}, lg8vo, ibds, 90p, color)	McKay	(1942)	Beistle, M.A.	25-40	*
Henderson, L.L.	Resolute (1st, sq8vo, 64p, ipcb, fp b/w)	McKay	(1940)	Beistle, M.A.	35-60	*
Bell, Thelma H.	Black Face (1st {std}, lg8vo, [48]p, color, pep)	Doubleday/Dor.	1931	Bell, C.	65-90	*
Mills, W.H.	Marionettes, Masks & Shadows (1st {std}, 8vo, 270p, col frn)	Doubleday/Page	1927	Bell, C.	35-50	*
MacDonald, Geo.	Phantastes (1st, sm8vo, 280p, aqua cloth, 25 illus)	L: Chatto	1894	Bell, J.	145-220	
N/A	Cinderella (16mo, ibds, cp)	Reilly/Britton	1907	Bell, R.A.	65-80	
Palgrave, F.	Golden Treasury of Songs & Lyrics (1st, 8vo, teg, uncut, 24cp)	L: Dent	1907	Bell, R.A.	80-120	
Grimm Bros.	Household Tales (1st, sm8vo, 400p, b/w, pep)	L: Dent	1901	Bell, R.A.	120-200	*
N/A	Jack the Giant Killer (1st, 24mo, 82p, teg, uncut, 12pl, pep)	L: J.M. Dent	1894	Bell, R.A.	65-85	
Shakespeare, Wm.	MidSummer Night's Dream (1st, sq8vo, green/gilt, teg, 128p, pep)	L: Dent	1895	Bell, R.A.	80-120	

AUTHOR	TITLE	PUBLISHER	DATE	ARTIST	PRICE	LC
Omar Khayyam	Rubaiyat... (1st, 8vo, 33p)	L: G. Bell	1902	Bell, R.A.	65-80	*
Lamb, C.	Tales from Shakespeare (1st, 8vo, 362p, blue/gilt, teg, 15pl)	L: Freemantle	1899	Bell, R.A.	60-85	
Shakespeare, Wm.	The Tempest (4to, teg, 106p, uncut)	L: Freemantle	1901	Bell, R.A.	70-90	
Bellew, F.P.	Chip's Dogs (1st, ob4to, ibds, [64]p, b/w)	R.H. Russell	1895	Bellew, F.P.	100-170	*
Bemelmans, L.	Best of Times (1st, lg4to, 188p, 50 color, DJ)	Simon/Schuster	1948	Bemelmans, L.	120-165	
Bemelmans, L.	Blue Danube (1st, 8vo, blue cl, 153p, 14cp, pep, DJ)	Viking	1945	Bemelmans, L.	65-90	
Bemelmans, L.	Castle Number Nine (1st, 4to, [48]p, grn/gilt, color, pep, DJ)	Viking	1937	Bemelmans, L.	120-165	
Bemelmans, L.	Donkey Inside (1st, 8vo, 224p, 4 dp color, DJ)	Viking	1941	Bemelmans, L.	65-100	
Bemelmans, L.	Fifi (1st, lg4to, [46]p, color)	Simon/Schuster	1940	Bemelmans, L.	90-140	R*
Bemelmans, L.	Golden Basket (1st, 4to, 96p, pink cl, color, dep, NH)	Viking	1936	Bemelmans, L.	120-160	R
Bemelmans, L.	Hansi (1st {1st book}, 4to, ibds, [64]p, color, pep, DJ)	Viking	1934	Bemelmans, L.	180-240	
Bemelmans, L.	Happy Place (1st {std}, 8vo, 59p, 3 dp color, DJ)	Little/Brown	(1952)	Bemelmans, L.	60-80	
Bemelmans, L.	Life Class (1st, 8vo, 260p, red cl, p-o, DJ)	Viking	1938	Bemelmans, L.	80-120	
Bemelmans, L.	Madeline (1st, lg4to, [48]p, ibds, color, pep, CH)	Simon/Schuster	1939	Bemelmans, L.	125-160	
Bemelmans, L.	Madeline & the Bad Hat (1st, red cl, lg4to, 54p, pep, col)	Viking	(1956)	Bemelmans, L.	160-200	
Bemelmans, L.	Madeline & the Gypsies (1st, 4to, 56p, ibds, pep, color)	Viking	(1958)	Bemelmans, L.	130-165	R
Bemelmans, L.	Madeline's Rescue (1st, lg4to, 56p, red cl, color, pep, CM)	Viking	1953	Bemelmans, L.	120-165	R
Leaf, M.	Noodle (1st, ob8vo, brown cl, [48]p, fp 1-color, pep)	Stokes	1937	Bemelmans, L.	85-100	
Bemelmans, L.	Parsley (1st, lg ob4to, 46p, green cl, color)	Harper	(1955)	Bemelmans, L.	70-110	R
Bemelmans, L.	Quito Express (1st, ob8vo, 47p, ibds, 1-color)	Viking	1938	Bemelmans, L.	90-140	
Bemelmans, L.	Rosebud (1st, 4to, ibds, 32p, color, pep, DJ)	Random	1942	Bemelmans, L.	120-165	
Bemelmans, L.	Small Bear (1st, 8vo, 186p, col frn, b/w, pep)	Viking	1939	Bemelmans, L.	70-100	*
Bemelmans, L.	Sunshine... (1st, lg4to, [44]p, ibds, color, pep, DJ)	Simon/Schuster	(1950)	Bemelmans, L.	140-180	
Bemelmans, L.	Tale of Two Glimps (1st, ob4to, [48]p, ibds, color)	NY: CBS	(1947)	Bemelmans, L.	120-180	
Bemelmans, L.	The Highworld (1st, lg8vo, red cl, 113p, pep, fp color)	Harper	(1954)	Bemelmans, L.	50-75	*
Bemelmans, L.	World of Bemelmans (1st, 8vo, 503p)	Viking	1955	Bemelmans, L.	40-70	*
Porter, G.S.	Girl of the Limberlost (1st, 8vo, 485p, 4pl, pep)	Doubleday/Page	1909	Benda, W.T.	50-70	
Crawford, F.M.	Little City of Hope (1st, 8vo, 209p, grey cl, 8pl)	MacMillan	1907	Benda, W.T.	20-30	
Burnett, F.H.	Little Hunchback Zia (1st, 12mo, p-o, 55p, 5pl, pep)	Stokes	(1916)	Benda, W.T.	30-50	
Cather, W.	My Antonia (1st, sm8vo, 418p, brown cl, 6pl)	Houghton	1918	Benda, W.T.	200-350	
Green, M.M.	Everybody has a House (1st, lg8vo, spiral-bnd, [20]p, color)	W.R. Scott	1944	Bendick, J.	35-50	*
Clymer, E.L.	Grocery Mouse (1st, 8vo, 94p, color)	McBride	1945	Bendick, J.	20-25	*
Schneider, N.	Let's Find Out (1st, lg8vo, 38p, color)	W.R. Scott	(1946)	Bendick, J.	35-50	*
Aesopus	Aesop's Fables (1st, sm4to, color green/gilt)	L: Chatto	1875	Bennett, C.	200-300	
DeMusset, Paul	Mr. Wind & Madam Rain (lg8vo, 150p, red/gilt, AEG, 25pl)	Putnam	1904	Bennett, C.	70-100	*
Mother Goose	Mother Goose (1st, sm8vo, [64]p, color)	McLoughlin	(1909)	Bennett, C.H.	65-80	*
Brown, C.	Bold Robin (1st, 8vo, gilt, 200p, uncut, teg, p-o, 7cp)	Dutton	(1905)	Bennett, F.I.	30-45	*
Molesworth, M.	Cozy Corner Stories (1st, sm4to, ibds, 12 chromos)	L: Nister	(1895)	Bennett, H.M.	100-160	
Molesworth, M.	Palace in the Garden (1st, 8vo, 298p)	L: Hatchards	1887	Bennett, H.M.	65-80	*
Molesworth, O.	Sunny Land Stories (sm4to, ibds, 6cp)	L: Nister	(1890)	Bennett, H.M.	75-110	
Stevenson, R.L.	Child's Garden of Verses (folio, ibds, 60p, color, pep)	Whitman	1932	Bennett, J.C.	40-65	
Stevenson, R.L.	Child's Garden of Verses (1st {this fmt} ob8vo, [24]p, col, pep)	Grosset/Dunlap	1938	Bennett, J.C.	35-50	*
N/A	Cinderella (folio, [22]p, color)	Whitman	1935	Bennett, J.C.	35-50	*
Bannerman, H.	New Story/Little Black Sambo (folio, wraps, [12]p, color)	Whitman	1932	Bennett, J.C.	80-120	
Bennett, John	Pigtail/Ah Lee Ben Loo (1st, 8vo, 298p, orange cl, b/w, pep, NH)	Longmans	1928	Bennett, J.C.	65-90	
Emery, Carlyle	Polly Through the Crystal (1st, 16mo, ipcb)	Whitman	1932	Bennett, J.C.	20-30	
Emery, Carlyle	Polly Through the Mountains (1st, 16mo, ipcb)	Whitman	1932	Bennett, J.C.	20-30	
Wyss, J.D.	Swiss Family Robinson (1st, sm8vo, 237p)	Whitman	(1935)	Bennett, J.C.	25-45	*
Leamy, Edmund	Fairy Minstrel of Glenmalure (1st {this pub}, sm8vo, 92p, b/w)	Longmans	1937	Bennett, R.	25-40	*
Andersen, H.C.	It's Perfectly True... (1st, lg8vo, 305p, 29pl, pep, DJ)	Harcourt	(1938)	Bennett, R.	50-70	R
MacDonald, Betty	Mrs. Piggle-Wiggle (1st {std}, sm8vo, 119p, blue cl, 8 fp col)	Lippincott	(1947)	Bennett, R.	70-120	*
Bennett, R.	Skookum & Sandy (1st {std}, sm4to, ipcb, [71]p, b/w, pep)	Doubleday/Dor.	1935	Bennett, R.	20-35	*
Davis, M.G.	With Cap & Bells (1st, sm8vo, 246p, b/w, pep)	Harcourt	(1937)	Bennett, R.	25-40	*
McKenna, Dolores	Adventures of a Wee Mouse (1st, 8vo, [30]p, p-o, 6cp, pep)	Stokes	(1921)	Bennett, R.H.	25-40	
Stockton, Frank	Ting-a-Ling (1st [1st bk.], 8vo, 187p, green/gilt, PPP)	Hurd/Houghton	1870	Bensell, E.B.	285-400	R
Banta, N.M.	Brownies & the Goblins (1st, 8vo, 128p, color, pep)	Chi: Flanagan	1915	Benson, A.B.	65-80	*
Coybee, E.	Flower Book (1st, 16mo, green cl, color)	L: Richards	1901	Benson, N.	100-150	
Mockler, G.	Spring Fairies & Sea Fairies (1st, sm8vo, 192p, red/gilt, b/w)	L: G. Allen	1897	Benson, N.	90-125	
Belloc, H.	New Cautionary Tales (1st AM, 8vo, ibds, 79p, b/w)	Harper	1931	Bentley, N.	30-45	*
Eliot, T.S.	Old Possum's Book of Practical Cats (1st, 8vo, 50p, color)	L: Faber	(1940)	Bentley, N.	65-100	*
Lovell, Dorothy A.	Silvanus Goes to Sea (1st, ob4to, blue ibds, unpag, 12 color)	L: Faber	[1943]	Bentley, N.	25-40	
Benton, T.H.	Europe After 8:15 (1st, 8vo, 222p, 8pl)	J. Lane	1914	Benton, T.H.	80-110	
Lindsay, M.M.	Joyous Guests (1st, lg8vo, 208p, 13cp)	Lothrop/Lee	(1921)	Berger, W.M.	35-50	
Lindsay, M.M.	Joyous Travelers (1st, 8vo, 157p, blue/gilt, col frn)	Lothrop/Lee	(1919)	Berger, W.M.	25-40	
Hawthorne, H.	Romantic Rebel (1st {std}, 8vo, 231p, b/w, NH)	Century	(1932)	Berger, W.M.	35-50	*
Brink, C.R.	Anything Can Happen on a River (1st, sm8vo, 224p, blue cl, b/w)	MacMillan	1934	Berger, W.W.	25-40	*
Mutt, E.	Fairy Tales from Baltic Shores (1st, lg8vo, p-o, 382p, pep, 8cp)	Penn	(1930)	Berkowitz, J.	50-65	
Osbourne, M. (ed.)	Favorite Fairy Tales (1st, sm4to, 365p, p-o, b/w & pep by...)	Penn	(1930)	Berkowitz, J.	50-70	
Wahlenberg, A.	Old Sweedish Fairy Tales (1st, lg8vo, p-o, 296p, pep, 8cp)	Penn	1925	Berkowitz, J.	60-80	
Schlein, M.	Shapes (1st, 8vo, ibds, [33]p, color)	W.R. Scott	1952	Berman, S.	25-40	*
Crawford, P.	Second Shift (1st, sm8vo, blue cl, 211p, 1-color)	Holt	(1943)	Bernbach, G.	20-30	LC
Kyle, Anne D.	Apprentice of Florence (1st, 8vo, 276p, b/w, pep, NH)	Houghton	1933	Berry, E.	35-50	*

AUTHOR	TITLE	PUBLISHER	DATE	ARTIST	PRICE	LC
Berry, E.	Black Folk Tales (1st {std}, 8vo, 80p, 1-color)	Harper	1928	Berry, E.	40-60	
Thompson, Mary W.	Blueberry Muffin (1st {std}, sm8vo, 248p, b/w)	Longmans	(1942)	Berry, E.	20-40	*
Abdullah, Achmed	Cat Had Nine Lives (1st, 8vo, 312p, gilt, b/w)	Farrar/Rine.	(1933)	Berry, E.	25-40	*
Morse, Eliz.	Chang of the Siamese Jungle (1st {std}, sm8vo, 195p, pep)	Dutton	(1930)	Berry, E.	20-40	*
Willson, Dixie	Circus ABC (1st, sm4to, 97p, brown cl)	Stokes	1924	Berry, E.	40-65	
Hutchinson, V.	Circus Comes to Town (1st, 4to, [66]p, color, pep)	Minton Balch	(1932)	Berry, E.	35-50	*
Willson, Dixie	Clown Town (1st {std}, 8vo, [62]p, color)	Doubleday/Page	1924	Berry, E.	25-45	*
Seabrook, Katie	Colette & Baba in Timbuctoo (1st {std}, 8vo, 168p, frn by...)	Coward	(1933)	Berry, E.	20-30	*
DuChaillu, Paul	Country of the Dwarfs (1st, 12mo, 261p)	Harper	1928	Berry, E.	20-40	*
Malkus, A.S.	Dragon Fly of Zuni (1st, 8vo, 213p, uncut, fp b/w, pep)	Harcourt	(1928)	Berry, E.	25-45	*
Willson, Dixie	Empty Elephant (1st, 4to, ibds, [39]p, color)	Volland	(1923)	Berry, E.	80-130	
Gardiner, A.	Father's Gone A-Whaling (1st {std}, 8vo, 198p, col frn, DJ)	Doubleday/Page	1926	Berry, E.	30-50	
Best, H.	Garram the Hunter (1st {std}, sm8vo, 332p, 6pl, pep, NH)	Doubleday/Dor.	1930	Berry, E.	30-50	*
Berry, E.	Girls in Africa (1st, 8vo, 128p, col frn, fp b/w, pep)	MacMillan	1928	Berry, E.	40-60	*
Justus, May	House in No-End Hollow (1st {std}, sm8vo, 286p, col frn, pep)	Doubleday/Dor.	1938	Berry, E.	25-40	*
Berry, E.	Humbo the Hippo (1st {std}, sm8vo, ipcb, [41]p, color, pep)	Harper	1932	Berry, E.	30-50	*
Berry, E.	Humbo the Hippo (8vo, ibds, [18]p, color, pep)	Grosset/Dunlap	1938	Berry, E.	25-40	
Evans, Eva K.	Jerome Anthony (1st, 8vo, blue cl, 88p, b/w)	Putnam	(1936)	Berry, E.	35-50	*
Berry, E.	Juma of the Hills (1st, 8vo, 260p, b/w, pep)	Harcourt	(1932)	Berry, E.	25-40	*
Evans, Eva K.	Key Corner (1st, sm8vo, 206p, tan cl, pep, fp b/w)	Putnam	(1938)	Berry, E.	25-45	*
Kyser, Halsa A.	Little Cumsee in Dixie (1st {std}, sm8vo, 158p, b/w, pep)	Longmans	1938	Berry, E.	40-60	*
DuChaillu, Paul	Lost in the Jungle (1st, 12mo, 269p)	Harper	1928	Berry, E.	25-45	*
Berry, E.	Mom Du Jos... (1st {std}, 8vo, 116p, col frn, cep, DJ)	Doubleday/Dor.	1931	Berry, E.	70-100	
Evans, Eva K.	Mr. Jones & Mr. Finnigan (1st, 4to, [32]p, tan cl, 2-col, dep)	NY: OUP	(1941)	Berry, E.	30-45	*
DuChaillu, Paul	My Apingi Kingdom (1st, 12mo, 263p, pep)	Harper	1928	Berry, E.	25-40	*
Willson, Dixie	Once Upon a Monday (1st, 8vo, ibds, 40p, color)	Volland	(1931)	Berry, E.	65-90	*
Berry, E.	One-String Fiddle (1st, [64]p, peach cl, pep, color)	Winston	(1939)	Berry, E.	25-40	*
Berry, E.	Penny-Whistle (1st, 8vo, [40]p, yellow cl, color)	MacMillan	1930	Berry, E.	30-45	*
Willson, Dixie	Pinky-Pup & Empty Elephant (1st, lg4to, ibds, 60p, color)	Volland	(1922)	Berry, E.	75-120	*
Willson, Dixie	Pinky-Pup & Empty Elephant (1st [new ed], sq8vo, ibds, col, pep)	Volland	(1928)	Berry, E.	65-80	*
Fyleman, R.	Princess Comes to Our Town (1st {std}, sm8vo, 158p col frn, pep)	Doubleday/Dor.	1928	Berry, E.	30-45	*
Best, A.	Sojo: Story of Little Lazy Bones (1st, 8vo, ibds, unpag, pep)	Harter	(1934)	Berry, E.	40-60	*
Best, H.	Son of the White Man (1st {std}, 8vo, orang cl, 315p, b/w, pep)	Doubleday/Dor.	1931	Berry, E.	25-45	*
Malkus, A.S.	Spindle Imp (1st, sm8vo, pink cl, 176p, uncut, fp b/w, pep)	Harcourt	(1931)	Berry, E.	30-45	*
Berry, E.	Strings to Adventure (1st, 8vo, 221p, 7pl, pep)	Lothrop/Lee	1935	Berry, E.	25-40	*
Berry, E.	Sunhelmet Sue (1st, sm8vo, 239p, yellow cl, fp b/w)	Lothrop	1936	Berry, E.	20-30	*
Robinson, Gertrude	White Heron Feather (1st {std}, 12mo, orang cl, 299p, pep)	Harper	(1930)	Berry, E.	25-45	*
Berry, E.	Winged Girl of Knossos (1st {std}, 8vo, 253p, b/w, pep, NH)	Appleton/Cent.	1933	Berry, E.	30-50	*
Beskow, E.	Adventures of Peter & Lotta (1st AM, ob4to, ibds, 15 color)	Harper	[1931]	Beskow, E.	80-100	
Beskow, E.	Aunt Brown's Birthday (1st AM, lg ob4to, [23]p, ibds, 16cp)	Harper	1930	Beskow, E.	80-100	
Beskow, E.	Aunt Green.../Aunt Lavender (1st AM, lg ob4to, 30p, bds, 15cp)	Harper	1930	Beskow, E.	90-130	*
Beskow, E.	Buddy's Advens. in the Blueberry Patch (1st, ob folio, ibds)	Harper	[1931]	Beskow, E.	100-145	*
Beskow, E.	Elf Children of the Woods (1st, ob folio, [32]p, color)	Harper	1932	Beskow, E.	120-150	*
Beskow, E.	Hat House (1st, ob4to, ibds, unpag, fp color)	Harper	1931	Beskow, E.	90-130	
Beskow, E.	Ollie's Ski Trip (1st AM, lg4to, [29]p, ibds, 14 fp color)	Harper	[1928]	Beskow, E.	120-150	
Beskow, E.	Sun-Egg (1st, ob4to, [26]p, ibds, 12cp, DJ)	Harper	1933	Beskow, E.	85-110	
Beskow, E.	Tale of Wee Little Old Woman (1st AM, sq4to, ibds, unpag, color)	Harper	1930	Beskow, E.	100-130	
Barrie, J.M.	Peter Pan Picture Book (1st, lg4to, ibds, [89]p, 24cp, pep)	Whitman	(1931)	Best, R.	70-100	
Durant, Nancy M.	Oliver & the Crying Chip (1st, 12mo, 79p, blue cl, 10 b/w)	Sherman French	1915	Betacourt, A.B.	25-40	*
Jewett, S.O.	Betty Leicester's Christmas (1st, 12mo, 68p, ibds, 8cp)	Houghton	1899	Betts, A.W.	45-60	*
Mills, W.J.	Caroline of Courtlandt Street (1st, lg8vo, 291p, gilt, teg, 6cp)	Harper	1905	Betts, A.W.	50-65	
Lippmann, J.M.	Dreamland (1st, 8vo, green/gilt, 211p, 5pl, dep)	Penn	1901	Betts, A.W.	30-45	
Hawthorne, H.	Lure of the Garden (1st, 4to, uncut, 259p, teg, dep, 6cp by...)	Century	1911	Betts, A.W.	120-140	
Hoyt, E.	Nancy's Country Christmas (1st, 8vo, teg, 224p, uncut, col frn)	Doubleday/Page	1904	Betts, A.W.	30-45	
Barr, A.	Song of a Single Note (1st, 8vo, 330p, 4pl)	Dodd	1902	Betts, A.W.	20-25	
Marks, J.	Through Welsh Doorways (1st, 8vo, 244p, rust/gilt, 4pl)	Houghton	1909	Betts, A.W.	30-45	
Ingpen, R.	1000 Poems for Children (1st, sm4to, 563p, 8cp)	Jacobs	(1923)	Betts, E.F.	100-135	
MacDonough, G.	Babes in Toyland (1st, sm4to, 180p, tan cloth, 7cp, pep)	Fox Duffield	1904	Betts, E.F.	150-220	
MacDonough, G.	Babes in Toyland (2nd, 8vo, aqua cl, 180p, p-o, 7cp)	Macaulay	(1924)	Betts, E.F.	80-125	
Riley, J.W.	Boy Lives on our Farm (1st, sq4to, p-o, [18]p, 5cp)	Bobbs-Merrill	(1908)	Betts, E.F.	100-145	
Mother Goose	Complete Mother Goose (1st, lg8vo, 227p, 11cp)	Stokes	(1909)	Betts, E.F.	165-230	
Grimm Bros.	Fairy Tales (1st, 4to, 117p, p-o, brown cl, 6cp)	Stern	1909	Betts, E.F.	180-220	
Mother Goose	Favorite Nursery Rhymes (1st, 4to, 47p, 6cp)	Stokes	(1906)	Betts, E.F.	120-165	*
Castle, A.	Heart of Lady Ann (1st, 12mo, 263p, lavender/gilt, 4cp, pep)	Harper	1905	Betts, E.F.	30-45	
Riley, J.W.	Host of Children (1st, 4to, p-o, 189p, brown/gilt, 16cp, pep)	Bobbs-Merrill	(1920)	Betts, E.F.	100-145	R
Chapin, A.A.	Humpty Dumpty (1st, 4to, 206p, p-o, 6cp, pep)	Dodd	1905	Betts, E.F.	140-185	
Wilkinson, F.	Kings & Queens (1st, 8vo, tan cl, uncut, 6pl)	McClure	1903	Betts, E.F.	30-45	
Burnett, F.H.	Little Princess (1st, sm4to, blue/gilt, teg, p-o, 12cp, SC)	Scribner	1905	Betts, E.F.	100-150	
Riley, J.W.	Orphant Annie Book (1st, sq folio, [30]p, ibds, 8cp)	Bobbs-Merrill	(1908)	Betts, E.F.	150-200	
Riley, J.W.	Raggedy Man (1st, lg4to, [30]p, p-o, 9cp)	Bobbs-Merrill	(1907)	Betts, E.F.	160-200	R
Riley, J.W.	Riley Child Verse (1st, sm4to, p-o, 58p, 8cp)	Bobbs-Merrill	(1906)	Betts, E.F.	120-165	R
Riley, J.W.	Runaway Boy (1st, lg8vo, p-o, red cl, [40]p, pep, 8cp)	Bobbs-Merrill	(1906)	Betts, E.F.	100-150	

AUTHOR	TITLE	PUBLISHER	DATE	ARTIST	PRICE	LC
Chapin, A.A.	True Story of Humpty Dumpty (1st, 4to, 205p, p-o, pep, 6cp)	Dodd	1905	Betts, E.F.	100-140	
Riley, J.W.	While the Heart Beats Young (1st, lg8vo, 110p, p-o, 16cp, dep)	Bobbs-Merrill	(1906)	Betts, E.F.	100-160	
Kelly, James P.	Prince Izon (1st, 8vo, 399p, brown cl, p-o, 5cp)	McClurg	1910	Betts, H.& E.	30-50	*
Banks, C.E.	Child of the Sun (1st, lg8vo, tan cl, teg, 166p, 16cp)	H. Stone	1900	Betts, L.	50-75	
Andersen, H.C.	Snow Queen (1st, 8vo, red cl, 209p, col frn, pep)	Dutton	(1929)	Beverly, K.	65-90	
Travers, P.L.	Fox at the Manger (1st, 8vo, blue cl)	L: Collins	1942	Bewick, T.	50-65	*
Wilde, O.	Birthday of the Infanta (1st, 8vo, 58p, blue cl, 3 dp color)	MacMillan	1929	Bianco, P.	35-50	
Bianco, P.	Doll in the Window (1st, sq8vo, 32p, blue cl, color)	NY: OUP	1953	Bianco, P.	30-45	*
De La Mare, W.	Flora: A Book of Drawings (1st, 4to, 45p, ibds, 8cp)	L: Heinemann	(1919)	Bianco, P.	80-100	
De La Mare, W.	Flora: A Book of Drawings (1st AM, 4to, 45p, uncut, 8cp)	Lippincott	[1919]	Bianco, P.	75-90	
Bianco, P.	Joy & the Christmas Angel (1st, 8vo, green bds, pep, 40p, col)	NY: OUP	1949	Bianco, P.	35-50	*
Blake, Wm.	Land of Dreams (1st, 8vo, 42p, gilt, b/w, pep, DJ)	MacMillan	1928	Bianco, P.	45-60	
Andersen, H.C.	Little Mermaid (1st, 12mo, 56p, green/gilt, 1-color, pep)	Holiday House	1935	Bianco, P.	35-50	
Bianco, M.W.	Little Wooden Doll (1st, 8vo, 65p, blue cl, pep, 6cp)	MacMillan	1925	Bianco, P.	35-50	
Bianco, P.	Look-Inside Easter Egg (1st, sq12mo, 38p, pink bds, dep, 8fp col)	NY: OUP	1952	Bianco, P.	50-70	R*
Bianco, P.	Paradise Square (1st, sm8vo, 94p, yel cl, 12 fp 1-color, dep)	OUP	1950	Bianco, P.	30-50	*
Bianco, M.W.	Skin Horse (1st, 8vo, ibds, 42p, pep, 5cp, DJ)	Doran	(1927)	Bianco, P.	100-165	
Bianco, P.	Starlit Journey (1st, 8vo, 47p, blue cl, col frn, pep, DJ)	MacMillan	1933	Bianco, P.	45-60	
Ewing, J.H.	Three Christmas Trees (1st, 12mo, green/gilt, 88p, col frn, dep)	MacMillan	1930	Bianco, P.	30-45	
Moore, C.C.	Night Before Christmas (16mo, ibds, 62p, color)	Rand/McNally	(1938)	Biers, C.	20-30	
Dole, N.H.	Russian Fairy Book (1st UK, lg8vo, 126p, pep, 16cp)	L: Richards	1908	Bilibin, I.	375-450	
Bilibin, I.	Russian Wonder Tales (1st AM, 8vo, 323p, tan cl, 12cp)	Century	1912	Bilibin, I.	200-320	
Carpenter, Frances	Tales/Russian Grandmother (1st AM {std}, 8vo, 292p, 8cp, dep)	Doubleday/Dor.	1933	Bilibin, I.	75-100	
Towers, Alton	Child's Aesop (1st AM, 16mo, red cl, 117p, color)	Stokes	[1902]	Billinghurst, P.	65-100	*
Howard, H.	Doings of the Dollymites (1st, 24mo, red cl, 94p, 23cp)	L: Sands	(1905)	Billinghurst, P.	80-120	
Aesopus	Hundred Fables of Aesop (1st, 4to, 201p, yellow cl, b/w)	L: J. Lane	1899	Billinghurst, P.	125-180	
LaFontaine, J.	Hundred Fables of La Fontaine (1st, 4to, green cl, 202p, b/w)	L: J. Lane	1900	Billinghurst, P.	80-100	
Aesopus	Never-Grow-Old Stories (12mo, 144p, color)	Lyons/Carnahan	(1925)	Billinghurst, P.	30-45	*
Binney, I.	Boppet, Please Stop It (1st, 8vo, ipcb, 48p, 1-color)	W.R. Scott	1946	Binney, I.	35-50	*
Woodcock, L.	This is the Way the Animals Walk (1st, ob8vo, [20]p, color)	W.R. Scott	1946	Binney, I.	35-50	*
Carryl, C.E.	Admiral's Caravan (1st, sq8vo, 140p, gilt, b/w, PPP)	Century	1892	Birch, R.	90-120	R
Nash, Ogden	Bad Parents' Garden of Verse (1st, 8vo, 132p, b/w)	Simon/Schuster	1936	Birch, R.	45-60	*
Cloud, V.W.	Down Durley Land (1st, 4to, 95p, teg, green/gilt, 1-color)	Century	1898	Birch, R.	50-75	
Shute, H.A.	Farming It (1st, 12mo, 248p, gilt, 16pl)	Houghton	1909	Birch, R.	25-40	
Wells, Carolyn	Folly in the Forest (1st, 8vo, 282p, olive cl, 12pl)	Altemus	(1902)	Birch, R.	30-45	
Burnett, F.H.	Giovanni & the Other (1st, lg8vo, 193p, olive/gilt, 9pl, cep)	Scribner	1892	Birch, R.	65-80	
Jepson, Edgar	Happy Pollyooly (1st, sm8vo, 314p, 5pl)	Bobbs-Merrill	(1915)	Birch, R.	40-60	*
Jamison, C.V.	Lady Jane (1st, lg8vo, 233p, b/w)	Century	1891	Birch, R.	40-65	
Burnett, F.H.	Little Lord Fauntleroy (1st [1], 8vo, 209p, gilt, 26 b/w, PPP)	Scribner	1886	Birch, R.	140-200	
Burnett, F.H.	Little Lord Fauntleroy (1st [new ed.], 4to, teg, p-o, 12cp, SC)	Scribner	1911	Birch, R.	80-120	
Alcott, L.M.	Little Men (sm8vo, 381p, teg, green/gilt, 15pl)	Little/Brown	1901	Birch, R.	30-50	
Burnett, F.H.	Little St. Elizabeth (1st AM, sm4to, 146p, 12 b/w)	Scribner	1890	Birch, R.	45-65	
Malory, T.	Malory's King Arthur (1st, 8vo, 421p, cp, pep)	Baker/Taylor	(1911)	Birch, R.	65-90	*
Bennett, John	Master Skylark (1st, 8vo, brown cl, 380p, b/w, PPP)	Century	1897	Birch, R.	90-125	
Johnston, A.F.	Miss Santa Claus o/t Pullman (1st, 8vo, 172p, gilt, colfrn, 8pl)	Century	1913	Birch, R.	25-40	
Moore, C.C.	Night Before Christmas (1st {std}, lg8vo, ibds, [43]p, col, DJ)	Harcourt	(1937)	Birch, R.	70-120	R
Burnett, F.H.	One I Knew Best of All (1st, 12mo, 325p, gilt, teg, b/w)	Scribner	1893	Birch, R.	70-85	
Chambers, Rbt.	Orchard-Land (1st, sm4to, 112p, 7cp)	Harper	1903	Birch, R.	85-120	
Chambers, Rbt.	Outdoorland (1st, sm4to, 105p, 7cp)	Harper	1902	Birch, R.	70-90	
Burnett, F.H.	Piccino... (1st, sq8vo, olive/gilt, 203p, 15pl)	Scribner	1894	Birch, R.	65-80	
Lloyd, J.U.	Red-Head (1st, 8vo, teg, 208p)	Dodd	1903	Birch, R.	30-45	
Burnett, F.H.	Sara Crew... (1st [1], 8vo, 83p, gilt, 6pl)	Scribner	1888	Birch, R.	100-150	
Wells, Carolyn	Story of Betty (1st {1st bk.}, sm8vo, red cl, 260p, 32pl)	Century	1899	Birch, R.	50-70	*
Nesbit, E.	The Wouldbegoods (1st AM, sm8vo, 313p, 16pl)	Harper	1901	Birch, R.	160-220	
Burnett, F.H.	Two Little Pilgrim's Progress (1st, sq8vo, 191p, gilt, 12pl)	Scribner	1895	Birch, R.	65-80	R
Perry, Nora	Another Flock of Girls (1st, sq8vo, 194p, green/gilt)	Little/Brown	1890	Birch/Copeland	45-60	*
Birnbaum, A.	Green Eyes (1st, sq4to, [40]p, pep, color, CH)	Capitol Pub.	(1953)	Birnbaum, A.	70-100	R*
Field, R.	Bird Began to Sing (1st, 8vo, 64p, p-o, 4cp, pep)	Wm. Morrow	(1932)	Bischoff, I.	25-45	*
Moore, C.C.	Night Before Christmas (1st, 24mo, ibds, [37]p, color)	Holiday House	(1937)	Bischoff, I.	65-95	R*
Phillips, E.C.	Peter Peppercorn (1st, sm4to, 148p, pep, color, DJ)	Houghton	1939	Bischoff, I.	25-40	
Dalgliesh, A.	Reuben & his Red Wheelbarrow (1st, 8vo, ibds, [28]p, pep, col)	Grosset/Dunlap	1946	Bischoff, I.	25-40	*
Bischoff, Ilse	Wonderful Poodle (1st, sm4to, 79p, pep, b/w)	Crowell	(1949)	Bischoff, I.	25-40	*
Bontemps, A.	You Can't Eat a Possum (1st, sm8vo, 120p, red cl, 4cp)	Wm. Morrow	1934	Bischoff, I.	50-80	*
Means, F.C.	Shadow Over Wide Ruin (1st, 8vo, 227p, 6 fp 1-color, pep)	Houghton	1942	Bjorklund, L.F.	25-45	*
Belloc, H.	Bad Child's Book of Beasts (1st, sm4to, 47p, grey bds, b/w)	L: Duckworth	(1896)	Blackwood, B.T.	200-300	
Belloc, H.	Cautionary Tales for Children (1st, sq8vo, ibds, 79p, b/w)	L: E. Nash	(1907)	Blackwood, B.T.	120-165	
Belloc, H.	Modern Traveller (1st, 8vo, ibds, 80p, b/w)	L: E. Arnold	1898	Blackwood, B.T.	120-160	
Belloc, H.	Moral Alphabet (1st, 4to, 63p, ibds, b/w)	L: E. Arnold	1899	Blackwood, B.T.	100-150	
Belloc, H.	More Beasts for Worse Children (1st, ob4to, ibds, 48p)	L: Duckworth	1897	Blackwood, B.T.	140-200	
Belloc, H.	Songs from Bad Child's Bk./Beasts (1st, 4to, ibds, b/w)	L: Duckworth	1932	Blackwood, B.T.	50-85	
Henry, M.	Dilly-Dally Sally (1st, sq4to, ipcb, [16]p, pep, color)	Saalfield	1940	Blackwood, G.R.	45-60	*
Mukerji, D.G.	Chief of the Herd (1st {std}, 8vo, 168p, pep)	Dutton	(1929)	Blaine, M.	20-30	*

AUTHOR	TITLE	PUBLISHER	DATE	ARTIST	PRICE	LC
Lang, A.	Tartan Tales (1st {std}, 8vo, 301p, black cl, 8pl, DJ)	Longmans	1928	Blaine, M.	50-75	
Means, F.C.	Assorted Sisters (1st, sm8vo, 250p, color)	Houghton	1947	Blair, H.	20-35	*
Means, F.C.	Great Day in the Morning (1st, 8vo, red cl, 182p, 6cp, pep)	Houghton	1946	Blair, H.	35-50	*
Means, F.C.	Hetty of the Grande Deluxe (1st, 8vo, grey cl, 188p, 8cp, pep)	Houghton	1951	Blair, H.	25-40	*
Means, F.C.	House Under the Hill (1st, 8vo, 184p, green cl, 8cp, pep)	Houghton	1949	Blair, H.	25-45	*
Means, F.C.	Moved-Outers (1st, 12mo, 154p, orang cl, 5cp, pep, NH)	Houghton	1945	Blair, H.	40-65	*
Hunt, M.L.	Double Birthday Present (1st {std}, sm8vo, 52p, red cl, col frn)	Lippincott	(1947)	Blaisdell, E.	20-30	*
De La Mare, W.	Rhymes & Verses (1st {std}, 8vo, 344p, pl)	Holt	(1947)	Blaisdell, E.	25-45	*
Cutler, U.W.	Stories of King Arthur (1st, 8vo, 308p, dp cp, pep)	Crowell	(1941)	Blaisdell, E.	25-45	*
Blaisdell, E.W.	Animals at the Fair (1st, ob4to, [47]p, color)	R.H. Russell	(1902)	Blaisdell, E.W.	150-225	*
Culbertson, A.V.	At the Big House (1st, sm8vo, blue cl, p-o, 348p, b/w)	Bobbs-Merrill	(1904)	Blaisdell, E.W.	45-60	
Calhoun, M.E.	Dorothy's Rabbit Stories (1st, sq8vo, 115p, grey cl, 10pl)	Crowell	(1907)	Blaisdell, E.W.	45-65	*
Vorse, M.E.	Grubby Gets Clean (1st, 8vo, ipcb, [41]p, 1-color, cep)	W.R. Scott	1943	Blaisdell, E.W.	30-45	*
Blake, Wm.	Art of William Blake (1st, 4to, green/gilt, 56p, 51pl)	Moffat	1907	Blake, Wm.	65-80	
Barrie, J.M.	Peter Pan & Wendy (1st AM, sm4to, 216p, gilt, 12cp, pep)	Scribner	1940	Blampied, E.	75-120	
Stevenson, R.L.	Travels with a Donkey in the Cevennes (1st, 8vo, 189p, gilt, 8pl)	L: J. Lane	1931	Blampied, E.	80-100	
Norton, Mary	Bed-Knob & Broomstick (1st AM {std}, sm8vo, blue cl, 189p, b/w)	Harcourt	(1957)	Blegvad, E.	65-80	*
Kendall, Carol	Gammage Cup (1st {std}, 8vo, 221p, blue cl, b/w, NH)	Harcourt	(1959)	Blegvad, E.	30-50	*
Bradford, Marg.	Keep Singing, Keep Humming (1st, lg ob8vo, 66p, color)	W.R. Scott	1953	Bloch, B.	35-50	*
Monrad, Jean	How Many Kisses Good Night? (1st, ob8vo, [20]p, color)	W.R. Scott	1949	Bloch, L.	25-45	*
Brenner, A.	I Want to Fly (1st, lg8vo, [34]p, ipcb, color, pep)	W.R. Scott	1943	Bloch, L.	35-50	*
Green, M.M.	Is it Hard? Is it Easy? (1st, sq8vo, [20]p, color)	W.R. Scott	1948	Bloch, L.	35-50	*
Hewes, A.D.	Swords on the Sea (1st, sm8vo, 272p, col frn, pep, 7pl)	Knopf	1928	Bloch, L.	20-30	*
Brown, M.W.	Willie's Walk to Grandmama (1st, sm8vo, ipcb, [26]p, color)	W.R. Scott	1944	Bloch, L.	45-60	
Blodgett, M.F.	Magic Slippers (1st, 12mo, 90p, 4cp)	Little/Brown	1917	Blodgett, M.	30-45	
Blodgett, M.F.	Peasblossom (1st, 8vo, 177p, p-o, 5cp)	Doran	(1917)	Blodgett, M.	30-45	*
Deardon, H.	Wonderful Adventure (1st, sm8vo, 115p, p-o, b/w)	Cosmopolitan	1928	Blood, W.C.	20-30	*
Garis, H.	Uncle Wiggily & Alice/Wonderland (4to, gilt, 361p, 8cp, pep, p-o)	Fenno	(1918)	Bloomfield, E.	40-65	*
Garis, H.	Uncle Wiggily & Mother Goose (1st, lg8vo, 175p, p-o, 6cp)	Fenno	(1916)	Bloomfield, E.	45-65	*
Garis, H.	Uncle Wiggily's Arabian Nights (1st, 4to, 8cp)	Fenno	(1917)	Bloomfield, E.	35-50	
Arnold, E.	Japonica (1st, 4to, cloth, 128p, b/w pl)	Scribner	1891	Blum, R.	50-75	
Bennett, R.A.	Thyra: Romance of the Polar Pit (1st, 8vo, 258p, gilt, 5pl)	Holt	1901	Blumenschein, E.	25-40	*
Cooke, M.B.	Dual Alliance (1st, 8vo, 165p, blue cl, 4cp, dep)	Doubleday/Page	1915	Blumenschein, M.	25-40	*
Eastman, C.A.	Indian Boyhood (1st, teg, 289p, 4pl)	McClure	1902	Blumenschien, M.	30-45	
Schwatka, Fred	Children of the Cold (1st, 12mo, 212p, b/w)	NY: Cassell	(1886)	Bobbett, Walt.	70-90	*
Ayers, Ray F.	King of Kinkiddie... (1st, sm8vo, 262p, 15pl)	Dutton	1904	Bobbett, Walt.	45-60	*
Neidlinger, W.H.	Small Songs for Small Singers (1st, lg4to, 57p, ibds, color)	NY: Schirmer	1896	Bobbett, Walt.	35-50	*
Zolotow, C.	Sleepy Book (1st, sm4to, blue cl, [36]p, color, dep)	Lothrop/Lee	1958	Bobri, V.	35-50	*
N/A	Arabian Nights (1st, 8vo, 308p)	Longmans	1946	Bock, V.	30-45	*
Kelly, Eric P.	Girl Who Would Be Queen (1st, 8vo, 201p)	McClurg	1939	Bock, V.	20-30	*
Carus, Helena	Metten of Tyre (1st {std}, 8vo, 171p, col frn, fp b/w, pep)	Doubleday/Dor.	1930	Bock, V.	25-40	*
Young, Ella	Tangle-Coated Horse (1st {std}, 8vo, blck cl, 186p, b/w, pep, NH)	Longmans	1929	Bock, V.	30-55	*
Jepson, Edgar	Garden at 19 (1st AM, 8vo, 299p, green cl, 4pl)	Wessels	1910	Boehm, H.B.	70-100	
De La Mare, W.	Broomsticks & other Fairy Tales (1st, 8vo, 378p, woodcuts)	L: Constable	1925	Bold	60-80	*
De La Mare, W.	Stuff & Nonsense (1st, 12mo, green/gilt, 110p, teg)	L: Constable	1927	Bold	60-90	
N/A	Arabian Nights (1st, 8vo, 257p, cp)	Winston	(1924)	Bolton, A.H.	20-30	*
Bone, Gertrude	Children's Children (1st, 4to, 271p, brown bds, gilt)	L: Duckworth	1908	Bone, M.	50-75	
Bone, Gertrude	This Old Man (1st, lg8vo, 131p, blue bds, gilt, frn by...)	L: MacMillan	1925	Bone, M.	30-45	
Repplier, A.	Fireside Sphinx (1st, 12mo, teg, 305p, gilt, b/w)	Houghton	1901	Bonsall, E.F.	20-30	
Bonte, W.	Fun & Nonsense (1st, 4to, p-o, [40]p, color)	Caldwell	(1904)	Bonte, W.	65-100	*
N/A	Oaktree Fairy Book (1st, 8vo, p-o)	Little/Brown	1905	Bonte, W.	50-70	
Dickens, C.	Christmas Carol (1st, 12mo, 113p, b/w)	Page	1913	Boog, C.M.	25-40	
Linderman, F.B.	How It Came About Stories (1st, sm4to, 221p, 6cp, p-o, SC)	Scribner	1921	Boog, C.M.	75-120	*
Cooper, J.F.	The Pathfinder (1st, sm8vo, 540p, blue/gilt, p-o, 8cp, pep)	NY: Nelson	(1928)	Boog, C.M.	25-40	*
Riley, J.W.	Flying Islands o/t Night (1st, 4to, bds, 124p, gilt, 16 ticp pep)	Bobbs-Merrill	(1913)	Booth, F.	130-170	R
Calkins, E.	Franklin Booth (1st, 4to, 60pl)	R. Frank	1925	Booth, F.	75-90	
Pickett, G.E.	Heart of a Soldier (1st, sm4to, 215p, pcb)	NY: Moyle	(1913)	Booth, F.	50-70	
Dreiser, T.	Hoosier Holiday (1st [1], lg8vo, olive bds, gilt, 513p)	NY: J. Lane	1916	Booth, F.	70-90	
Twain, M.	Prince & the Pauper (1st, lg8vo, 284p, p-o, cp)	Harper	(1917)	Booth, F.	50-75	
Owen, C.D.	Seth Way (1st, sm8vo, 413p, col frn)	Houghton	1917	Booth, F.	35-50	*
Nicholson, M.	The Poet (1st, 8vo, teg, 190p, blue/gilt, cep, 4cp)	Houghton	1914	Booth, F.	35-50	
Baker, C.	Young People in Old Places (1st, 8vo, green cl, 322p, fp b/w)	Bobbs-Merrill	(1906)	Booth, F.	30-45	*
Ryan, M.E.	House of the Dawn (1st, 8vo, 407p, 4pl)	McClurg	1914	Booth, H.	20-30	*
Eberle, I.	Hop, Skip & Fly (1st, 8vo, 70p, grey cl, 2-color)	Holiday House	(1937)	Bostelmann, E.	20-30	*
Eberle, I.	Sea-Horse Adventure (1st, 8vo, [55]p, blue cl, 2-color)	Holiday House	(1937)	Bostelmann, E.	20-30	*
Tucker, E.S.	Cats & Kittens (1st, lg4to, ibds, [26]p, 6 chromos)	Stokes	1895	Boston, F.J.	120-180	*
Boston, Lucy	Children of the Green Knowe (1st, sm8vo, 157p, cloth, 6pl)	L: Faber	(1954)	Boston, Peter	65-90	
Boston, Lucy	Children of the Green Knowe (1st AM {std}, 8vo, 157p, pcb, b/w)	Harcourt	(1955)	Boston, Peter	50-85	R
Boston, Lucy	River at Green Knowe (1st {std}, 8vo, 153p, green cl, b/w)	Harcourt	(1959)	Boston, Peter	65-80	
Boston, Lucy	Treasure of Green Knowe (1st AM {std}, 8vo, 185p, cloth, b/w)	Harcourt	(1958)	Boston, Peter	50-80	*
Boswell, H.	French Canada (1st, ob8vo, 82p, 25cp, DJ)	Viking	1938	Boswell, H.	35-50	
Irving, W.	Rip Van Winkle (1st, 12mo, 218p, b/w pl)	L: MacMillan	1908	Boughton, G.H.	45-65	*

AUTHOR	TITLE	PUBLISHER	DATE	ARTIST	PRICE	LC
Burnett, F.H.	Lost Prince (1st, 8vo, 415p, blue/gilt, 16pl)	Century	1915	Bower, M.L.	25-40	*
Farrow, G.E.	King's Gardens (1st, 8vo, 43p)	L: Hutchinson	1896	Bowley, A.L.	65-80	*
Nesbit, E.	Nine Unlikely Tales for Children (8vo, gilt, 279p)	L: T.F. Unwin	1901	Bowley/Millar	140-180	*
Boyajian, Z.C.	Armenian Legends & Poems (folio, cloth, 196p, ticp)	Dent/Dutton	[1915]	Boyajian, Z.C.	130-185	*
Boyajian, Z.C.	Gilgamesh: Dream of Eternal Quest (1st, lg4to, 110p, gilt 15ticp)	L: G.W. Jones	1924	Boyajian, Z.C.	100-150	*
Fryer, J.E.	Mary Frances First Aid Book (1st, lg8vo, p-o, 144p, gilt)	Winston	(1916)	Boyer, J.A.	120-185	
Fryer, J.E.	Mary Frances Knitting & Crocheting Bk. (1st, 4to, 270p, p-o)	Winston	(1918)	Boyer, J.A.	130-185	
Fryer, J.E.	Mary Frances Sewing Book (1st, 8vo, p-o, 280p, blue cl, pep)	Winston	(1913)	Boyer, J.A.	130-185	
Warren, I.R.	Mother Love (1st, 8vo, 166p, teg, p-o, col frn)	Jacobs	(1911)	Boyer, J.A.	25-40	
McIntyre, J.T.	In the Rockies with Kit Carson (1st, 8vo, p-o, 220p, b/w)	Penn	1913	Boyer, R.L.	25-40	
N/A	Beauty & the Beast (1st, 4to, 57p, gilt, 10cp)	L: Sampson	[1875]	Boyle, E.V.	400-600	
Andersen, H.C.	Fairy Tales (1st, folio, 94p, AEG, green/gilt, 12cp)	L: Sampson	1872	Boyle, E.V.	800-1000	
Andersen, H.C.	Fairy Tales (4to, blue bds)	Scribner	1875	Boyle, E.V.	250-350	
Austin, S.	Story Without an End (1st, 8vo, 40p, AEG, 15cp)	L: Sampson	1868	Boyle, E.V.	600-800	
Aikins, Ruth	Smiling Princess (1st, sq8vo, [31]p, p-o, color, pep)	Norcross	(1922)	Boyle, M.	50-80	*
Hunt, M.L.	Susan Beware! (1st, 8vo, 243p, green cl, b/w, pep)	Stokes	1937	Boyle, M.	20-30	*
Beach, R.	Iron Trail (1st, sm8vo, red/gilt, 390p, 8pl)	Harper	1913	Bracker, M.L.	20-30	
Bradley, Mary H.	Alice in Elephantland (1st, sm8vo, 187p, pep, b/w)	Appleton	1929	Bradley, A.H.	45-60	*
Heward, C.	Pillow Stories (1st, sm8vo, 150p, b/w)	L: Richards	1901	Bradley, G.M.	85-100	
N/A	American Stage of Today (1st, folio, ipcb, designs by...)	Collier	(1910)	Bradley, W.	120-165	
Chambers, Rbt.	Ashes of Empire (1st, 8vo, 342p, cvr by...)	Stokes	(1898)	Bradley, W.	70-90	
Monroe, H.	Dance of the Seasons (1st, 8vo, 20p, wraps, cvr & ti page by..)	R.F. Seymour	1911	Bradley, W.	80-130	R
Raine, W.M.	Daughter of Raasay (1st [1st bk.], 12mo, 311p, cvr by...)	Stokes	(1902)	Bradley, W.	100-150	*
Lamb, C.	Dissertation Upon a Roast Pig (1st, 12mo, pcb, p-o)	(Concord)	(1904)	Bradley, W.	75-100	
A.E.	Earth Breath (1st, 12mo, 94p, ipcb, uncut, cvr & title pg by...)	J. Lane	(1897)	Bradley, W.	180-225	R
Gosse, E.	In Russet & Silver (1st, 12mo, 159p, tan cl, cvr by...)	Stone/Kimball	1894	Bradley, W.	100-130	*
Unknown	Leather Bottel (1st, 16mo, pcb, 14p, uncut)	(Concord)	(1903)	Bradley, W.	80-100	
Irving, W.	Legend of Sleepy Hollow (1st, 12mo, 61p, ibds, p-o, cvr by...)	R.H. Russell	(1897)	Bradley, W.	120-150	
Wither, G.	Love Song (1st, 16mo, blue pcb, p-o, 14p, uncut)	(Concord)	(1903)	Bradley, W.	70-90	
Herrick, R.	Love's Dilemmas (1st, 8vo, 193p, cvr by...)	H. Stone	1898	Bradley, W.	85-100	
Meredith, O.	Lucille (1st, 8vo, teg, cvr by...)	Stokes	(1897)	Bradley, W.	60-85	
Bradley, W.	Peter Poodle... (1st, sq4to, 166p, ibds, 26 fp color, pep)	Dodd	1906	Bradley, W.	650-900	
LeGallienne, R.	Quest of the Golden Girl (1st, 8vo, green/gilt, 308p, teg)	J. Lane	1896	Bradley, W.	75-100	
Browning, R.	Rabbi Ben Ezra (1st, 16mo, 16p, pcb, p-o)	(Concord)	(1902)	Bradley, W.	65-80	
Irving, W.	Rip Van Winkle (1st, sm8vo, bds, 35p, frn & cvr by...)	R.H. Russell	(1897)	Bradley, W.	180-250	
LeGallienne, R.	Romance of Zion Chapel (1st {std}, 8vo, 297p, teg, cvr by...)	J. Lane	1898	Bradley, W.	90-130	
Omar Khayyam	Rubaiyat... (1st, 16mo, green ipcb, 61p)	R.H. Russell	(1897)	Bradley, W.	80-130	
Hobbes, J.O.	School for Saints (1st, 8vo, 405p, grey/gilt, cvr by...)	Stokes	(1897)	Bradley, W.	65-85	
Hough, E.	Singing Mouse Stories (1st [1st bk], 12mo, [182]p teg)	Forest/Stream	1895	Bradley, W.	95-120	
Waterloo, S.	Story of AB (1st, 8vo, black cl, 351p, PPPa)	Way/Williams	1897	Bradley, W.	120-165	
Waterloo, S.	The Seekers (1st, 8vo, red cloth, cvr by...)	H. Stone	1900	Bradley, W.	75-90	
Mason, W.	Uncle Walt (1st, 8vo, brown cl, teg, 189p, cvr by...)	Chi: Adams	1910	Bradley, W.	70-85	
Crane, S.	War is Kind (1st, tall 8vo, 6 woodcuts, 96p, uncut)	Stokes	1899	Bradley, W.	350-500	
Hall, Tom	When Hearts are Trumps (1st, 12mo, teg, ti. page by)	Stone/Kimball	1894	Bradley, W.	45-60	*
Bradley, W.	Wonderbox Stories (1st, 8vo, 154p, gold cl, fp b/w)	Century	1916	Bradley, W.	300-500	
LeGallienne, R.	Young Lives (1st, 8vo, teg, 386p, cvr by...)	J. Lane	1899	Bradley, W.	85-120	
Dalgliesh, A.	Happy School Year (1st, sm8vo, 141p, color)	Rand/McNally	(1924)	Brand, M.S.	20-30	*
Stokes, H.	Belgium (1st, lg4to, black cl, 390p, 52 b/w illus)	L: Kegan Paul	1916	Brangwyn, F.	100-140	
Sparrow, W.S.	Book of Bridges (1st, 4to, 415p, cloth, cp)	L: J. Lane	1915	Brangwyn, F.	90-130	
Sparrow, W.S.	Frank Brangwyn: His Work (1st, sm4to, 258p, teg, 20cp)	L: Kegan Paul	1910	Brangwyn, F.	75-100	
Phillpotts, E.	Girl & The Faun (1st, sm4to, 78p, 4cp)	L: A&C Black	1916	Brangwyn, F.	100-130	
Phillpotts, E.	Girl & The Faun (1st AM, sm4to, pict cl, 78p, 4cp)	Lippincott	1917	Brangwyn, F.	80-120	
Sparrow, W.S.	Prints & Drawings of Frank Brangwyn (1st, 4to, 287p, gilt, 50pl)	L: J. Lane	1919	Brangwyn, F.	100-150	
Omar Khayyam	Rubaiyat... (1st, sm4to, 135p, grey cl, cp)	L: Gibbings	1906	Brangwyn, F.	90-160	*
Omar Khayyam	Rubaiyat... (1st, 12mo, beige/gilt, teg, 69p, 8 ticp, pep)	L: Foulis	(1910)	Brangwyn, F.	80-120	
Omar Khayyam	Rubaiyat... (4to, uncut, buckram, 15 ticp)	L: Foulis	(1919)	Brangwyn, F.	120-165	
Omar Khayyam	Rubaiyat... (lg8vo, green/gilt, 4 color, pep)	L: Sampson	[1920]	Brangwyn, F.	45-60	
Crockett, S.R.	Tales of Our Coast (1st AM, 8vo, 203p, red buckram, teg, uncut)	Dodd	1896	Brangwyn, F.	60-80	*
Bourman, C.	The Bridge (1st, 4to, green/gilt, 249p, uncut, 24cp)	J. Lane	1926	Brangwyn, F.	60-80	
Preston, Hayter	Windmills (1st, 4to, yellow cl, 125p, uncut, 16cp)	Lane/Dodd	(1923)	Brangwyn, F.	70-100	
Leighton, Rbt.	Wreck of the Golden Fleece (1st, 8vo, 352p, green cl, 6pl)	L: Blackie	(1893)	Brangwyn, F.	45-60	*
Baruch, D.W.	Bobby Goes Riding (1st, 8vo, [35]p, red cl, color, pep)	Lothrop/Lee	1934	Brann, E.	25-40	*
Cooper, F.T.	Argosy of Fables (1st, 4to, 485p, blue cl, 24 ticp, pep)	Stokes	(1921)	Bransom, P.	120-150	
McCracken, H.	Biggest Bear on Earth (1st, sm4to, 114p, col frn, 6pl, cep)	Stokes	(1943)	Bransom, P.	35-50	*
Chaffee, Allen	Brownie: Engineer of Beaver Brook (1st, lg8vo, 99p, 4cp)	M. Bradley	(1925)	Bransom, P.	30-50	
London, J.	Call of the Wild (1st, 8vo, 254p, p-o, blue cl, 16cp)	MacMillan	1912	Bransom, P.	180-250	
Baker, O.	Dusty Star (1st, 8vo, 302p, aqua/gilt, uncut, 4pl, pep)	Dodd	1922	Bransom, P.	25-40	*
Miller, Leo E.	Hidden People (1st, 8vo, 321p, 8pl)	Scribner	1920	Bransom, P.	25-40	*
Miller, Leo E.	In the Tiger's Lair (1st, 8vo, 252p, 4pl)	Scribner	1921	Bransom, P.	25-40	*
Thompson, J.M.	Over Indian/Animal Trails (1st, 8vo, gilt, p-o, 263p, 8cp)	Stokes	(1918)	Bransom, P.	35-50	*
Lippincott, J.W.	Phantom Deer (1st {std}, sm8vo, blue cl, 192p, 1 dpcp, 4pl)	Lippincott	(1954)	Bransom, P.	30-45	*
Dodge, Louis	Sandman's Forest (1st, 8vo, 293p, p-o, grn/gilt, pep, 6cp, SC)	Scribner	1918	Bransom, P.	70-100	

AUTHOR	TITLE	PUBLISHER	DATE	ARTIST	PRICE	LC
Dodge, Louis	Sandman's Mountain (1st, 8vo, 278p, grn/gilt, pep, 6cp, SC)	Scribner	1920	Bransom, P.	70-100	
Roberts, C.G.D.	Secret Trails (1st, 12mo, 212p, green/gilt, 8pl)	MacMillan	1916	Bransom, P.	35-50	*
Baker, O.	Thunder Boy (1st, 8vo, red cl, 288p, 4pl, pep)	Dodd	1924	Bransom, P.	25-40	*
Lippincott, J.W.	Wahoo Bobcat (1st {std}, 8vo, 207p, 1 dp color, 4 dp b/w)	Lippincott	(1950)	Bransom, P.	30-45	*
Squier, E-L.	Wild Heart (1st, 8vo, green cl, 220p, b/w)	Cosmopolitan	1922	Bransom, P.	25-45	
Lippincott, J.W.	Wilderness Champion (1st {std}, 8vo, 195p, 6 dp b/w, 5pl, cep)	Lippincott	(1944)	Bransom, P.	30-45	*
Grahame, K.	Wind in the Willows (1st, 8vo, blue/gilt, teg, 351p, 10cp, pep)	Scribner	1913	Bransom, P.	140-185	
Lippincott, J.W.	Wolf King (1st, 8vo, 316p, col frn, 4pl, pep)	Penn	(1933)	Bransom, P.	25-40	*
Gatti, Attilio	Wrath of Moto (1st, lg8vo, 160p, b/w)	Scribner	1941	Bransom, P.	25-40	*
Perkins, Marlin	Zooparade (1st {A}, 4to, beige cl, 94p, 16 fp color, pep)	Rand/McNally	(1954)	Bransom, P.	45-60	
Chapman, W.G.	Green Timber Trails (1st, 8vo, green cl, 283p, 8pl)	Century	1919	Bransom/Bull	30-45	*
Nye, Edgar W.	Guest at the Ludlow (1st, 8vo, red/gilt, 262p, teg, 21pl)	Bowen-Merrill	1897	Braunhold, L.	25-40	
Towne, Rbt. D.	Teddy Bears Come to Life (1st, 12mo, ibds, unpag, color)	Reilly/Britton	(1907)	Bray, J.R.	70-100	*
Towne, Rbt. D.	Teddy Bears on a Tobaggon (1st, 12mo, [12]p, color)	Reilly/Britton	(1907)	Bray, J.R.	65-90	*
Bailey, C.S.	For the Children's Hour (1st, 8vo, 336p, 8pl)	M. Bradley	1906	Breck, G.W.	20-30	*
Twain, M.	Huckleberry Finn (1st, 8vo, p-o, 421p, cp)	Harper	(1923)	Brehm, W.	25-45	*
Tarkington, B.	Penrod & Sam (1st, 8vo, 356p, green cl, 8pl, PPP)	Doubleday/Page	1916	Brehm, W.	70-100	
Burnett, F.H.	My Robin (1st, 16mo, green/gilt, 42p, col frn)	Stokes	(1912)	Brennan, A.	30-45	
Blackmore, R.D.	Lorna Doone (1st, lg8vo, p-o, 351p, black cl, color)	M. Bradley	(1921)	Brett, H.M.	50-70	
Cooper, J.F.	The Spy (1st, 8vo, 415p, p-o, 8cp)	Houghton	1924	Brett, H.M.	25-40	
Johnston, A.F.	Two Little Knights of Kentucky (1st, 8vo, 203p, blue/gilt, 8cp)	Page	1907	Brett, H.M.	25-40	
Schultz, J.W.	With the Indians in the Rockies (1st, lg8vo, 252p, p-o, 4cp)	Houghton	1925	Brett, H.M.	25-40	*
Stevenson, R.L.	Child's Garden of Verses (1st, 12mo, 68p, color)	Rand/McNally	(1942)	Brice, T.	25-40	*
N/A	Three Little Pigs (1st, 12mo, [47]p, color)	Rand/McNally	1941	Brice, T.	20-35	*
N/A	Three Little Kittens (1st, 12mo, [32]p, color)	Rand/McNally	1938	Brice, Tony	20-30	*
Dearmer, M.	Child's Life of Christ (1st, 8vo, 290p, 8cp)	L: Methuen	1906	Brickdale, E.F.	50-80	*
Browning, R.	Dramatis Personae... (1st, sm4to, teg, green/gilt, 10cp)	L: Chatto	1909	Brickdale, E.F.	65-80	
Leighton (ed.)	Fleur & Blanchefleur (1st, 4to, 61p, 37 color illus)	L: O'Connor	(1922)	Brickdale, E.F.	50-70	
Brickdale, E.	Golden Book of Famous Women (4to, blue/gilt, 200p, 16 ticp)	L: Hodder	[1916]	Brickdale, E.F.	100-130	
N/A	Golden Book/Songs & Ballads (4to, 198p, green/gilt, 24 ticp)	L: Hodder	[1915]	Brickdale, E.F.	85-130	
Palgrave, F.	Golden Treasury of Songs & Lyrics (8vo, yel cl, 459p, 12 ticp)	Hodder	[1915]	Brickdale, E.F.	80-100	
Tennyson, A.	Idylls of the King (1st, 4to, 174p, gilt, 21 ticp)	L: Hodder	(1911)	Brickdale, E.F.	160-225	
N/A	Old English Songs & Ballads (1st, lg4to, 198p, 24 ticp)	L: Hodder	[1915]	Brickdale, E.F.	160-235	
Browning, R.	Pippa Passes (1st, 8vo, 254p, gilt, teg, uncut, 10cp)	L: Chatto	1908	Brickdale, E.F.	70-90	
Browning, R.	Pippa Passes (1st AM, 8vo, 254p, grey/gilt, 10cp)	Lippincott	1909	Brickdale, E.F.	60-80	
Craik, D.	Adventures of a Brownie (4to, ipcb)	Crowell	(1893)	Bridgman, C.	50-70	
O'Dyer, Ruth	Adventures of the Ink Spots (1st, 8vo, orang cl, 158p, col frn)	Lothrop/Lee	(1923)	Bridgman, L.J.	70-100	
Bridgman, L.J.	Bridgman's Kewts (1st, 4to, [94]p, color, pep)	Caldwell	(1902)	Bridgman, L.J.	70-100	*
N/A	Bumps & Thumps (sq4to, pict tan cloth, color)	Caldwell	(1903)	Bridgman, L.J.	85-110	
Bonte, W.	Christmas Stocking Rhymes (4to, tan cl, p-o, 38p, 17 color)	Caldwell	(1904)	Bridgman, L.J.	70-100	
Pool, M.L.	Chums (1st, 8vo, 241p, 4pl)	Page	1900	Bridgman, L.J.	25-40	*
Horwitz, C.N.	Fairy-Lure (1st, 12mo, 345p, 1-color decor by...)	Lothrop	(1891)	Bridgman, L.J.	45-60	*
Bridgman, L.J.	Farmer Fox (1st, 4to, [36]p, ibds, p-o, color)	Caldwell	(1900)	Bridgman, L.J.	45-70	
Poulsson, E.	Finger Plays/Nursery & Kindergarten (1st, 8vo, [80]p)	Lothrop	1893	Bridgman, L.J.	35-50	
Bridgman, L.J.	Guess (1st, 4to, ibds, [104]p, color, pep)	Caldwell	(1901)	Bridgman, L.J.	70-100	
Bridgman, L.J.	Guess Again (1st, lg4to, ibds, [104]p, color)	Caldwell	(1902)	Bridgman, L.J.	70-100	
Gulliver, L.	Gulliver's Bird Book (1st, folio, 103p, color)	Page	1902	Bridgman, L.J.	100-145	
Poulsson, E.	In the Child's World (1st, sq8vo, 443p, b/w)	M. Bradley	1893	Bridgman, L.J.	35-50	
Blanchard, A.E.	Journey of Joy (1st, 8vo, 305p, 7pl)	Estes	(1908)	Bridgman, L.J.	20-35	*
Fitzhugh, P.K.	King Time (1st, 8vo, green/gilt, 233p, 8cp, pep)	Caldwell	(1908)	Bridgman, L.J.	60-85	
Crowninshield, Mrs.	Light-House Children Abroad (1st, 8vo, 446p, 38 b/w, gilt)	D. Lothrop	1889	Bridgman, L.J.	30-45	*
Pool, M.L.	Little Bermuda (1st, 8vo, 163p, 4pl)	Page	1899	Bridgman, L.J.	20-35	*
MacDonald, E.R.	Little Canadian Cousin (1st, 8vo, 129p, 6pl)	Page	1904	Bridgman, L.J.	20-35	*
Badger, J.E.	Lost City (1st, 8vo, 326p, blue/gilt, 8pl)	D. Estes	(1898)	Bridgman, L.J.	50-70	
Wesselhoeft, Lily	Madam Mary of the Zoo (1st, 12mo, 248p, blue/silver, 3pl by...)	Little/Brown	1899	Bridgman, L.J.	20-35	
Bridgman, L.J.	Mother Goose/Wild Beast Show (1st, lg4to, ibds, [104]p, col)	Caldwell	(1900)	Bridgman, L.J.	200-300	
Bridgman, L.J.	Mother Wild Beast/Wild Beast Show (1st, lg4to, ibds, color)	Caldwell	(1900)	Bridgman, L.J.	200-300	
N/A	My High School Days (8vo, teg, green/gilt, color)	Caldwell	(1908)	Bridgman, L.J.	50-65	
Hamlin, M.S.	Nan in the City (1st, 12mo, 251p, red cl, 3pl)	Roberts	1897	Bridgman, L.J.	30-45	
Hamlin, M.S.	Nan's Chicopee Children (1st, sm8vo, 223p, 5pl)	Little/Brown	1900	Bridgman, L.J.	20-35	*
Messer, C.J.	Next-Night Stories (1st, 12mo, 261p, 8pl)	Lothrop/Lee	1912	Bridgman, L.J.	30-45	*
Hazelton, Mary	Our Little African Cousin (1st, 12mo, 98p, b/w)	L.C. Page	1902	Bridgman, L.J.	25-40	
Allen, W.B.	Play Away (1st, 12mo, 171p, tan cl, 6pl)	Estes	(1902)	Bridgman, L.J.	20-35	
Wells, A.R.	Rollicking Rhymes for Youngsters (1st, 8vo, 157p, 26 fp color)	Revell	(1902)	Bridgman, L.J.	45-60	
Bridgman, L.J.	Seem-So's (1st, 8vo, p-o, [80]p, silhouettes, col frn)	Caldwell	(1906)	Bridgman, L.J.	65-80	*
Morrison, M.W.	Stories True & Fancies New (1st, 8vo, 208p, 11pl)	Estes & Laur.	(1898)	Bridgman, L.J.	60-80	*
Steward, R.	Surprising Advens of Man in the Moon (1st, 4to, 142p, 12cp)	Lee & Shepard	(1903)	Bridgman, L.J.	100-120	*
Riley, A.	Voyage of the Wishbone Boat (lg8vo, ipcb, 205p, fp color, pep)	Caldwell	(1907)	Bridgman, L.J.	75-110	
Wells, A.R.	Witchery Ways (1st, 12mo, 189p, 8pl)	Altemus	(1904)	Bridgman, L.J.	20-35	*
Smith, M.P.W.	Young Puritans/Old Hadley (1st, 12mo, 345p, gilt, 5pl, dep)	Roberts	1897	Bridgman, L.J.	25-45	*
Nesbit, W.D.	Oh Skin-nay! (1st, ob folio, [125]p, illus)	Volland	(1913)	Briggs, C.A.	70-90	*
Nesbit, W.D.	When a Feller Needs a Friend (1st, lg4to, ibds, [96]p, 3-color)	Volland	(1914)	Briggs, C.A.	90-135	*

AUTHOR	TITLE	PUBLISHER	DATE	ARTIST	PRICE	LC
Bright, Rbt.	Travels of Ching (1st, sm ob8vo, ipcb, [65]p, 1-color, pep)	W.R. Scott	1943	Bright, R.	30-45	*
Brill, Geo. R.	Rhymes of the Golden Age (1st, lg8vo, 121p, p-o, pep, 12 col)	Stern	1908	Brill, G.R.	65-80	*
Brisley, J.L.	Further Doings/Milly-Molly-Mandy (1st AM, 12mo, 95p, color)	G. Sully	1932	Brisley, J.	25-40	*
Bigham, M.A.	Mother Goose Village (1st, sq8vo, 196p, color, pep)	Rand/McNally	(1903)	Brison, E.S.	50-70	
Eaton, J.	Betsy's Napoleon (1st, 8vo, 274p, bds, color, pep, DJ)	Wm. Morrow	1936	Brissaud, P.	25-40	
O'Neill, M.	Elf-Errant (1st, 8vo, teg, 109p, pink/gilt, 7pl)	Lawrence	1895	Britten, W.E.	70-95	
Watson, H.B.M.	Chloris of the Island (1st, 8vo, 281p, 32pl)	Harper	1900	Brock, C.& H.	40-60	*
Farnol, J.	Amateur Gentleman (1st UK, 8vo, blue/gilt, 599p, teg, 21cp)	L: Sampson	(1916)	Brock, C.E.	65-80	*
Galt, J.	Annals of the Parish (1st, 12mo, gilt, 334p, AEG, 40pl, pep)	L: MacMillan	1896	Brock, C.E.	50-65	
Dickens, C.	Battle of Life (1st, 12mo, gilt, 165p, teg, 8cp)	L: J.M. Dent	1907	Brock, C.E.	35-50	
Farnol, J.	Broad Highway (1st, lg8vo, 493p, blue/gilt, p-o, 24cp)	L: Sampson	1910	Brock, C.E.	50-75	
Farnol, J.	Broad Highway (1st AM, lg8vo, 518p, p-o, teg, 24cp)	Little/Brown	1912	Brock, C.E.	45-60	
Wiggin, K.D.	Cathedral Courtship (1st, 8vo, 104p, teg, 6pl)	Houghton	1901	Brock, C.E.	30-45	*
Dickens, C.	Christmas Carol (1st, 12mo, 158p, teg, color)	Dent/Dutton	(1905)	Brock, C.E.	30-50	
Irving, W.	Christmas at Bracebridge Hall (1st, 12mo, 267p, teg, 24cp, dep)	L: Dent	1906	Brock, C.E.	40-65	
Gaskell, Mrs.	Cranford (1st AM, sm8vo, teg, green/gilt, 255p, 24cp)	Dent/Dutton	1904	Brock, C.E.	35-50	
Cowper, Wm.	Diverting History/John Gilpin (1st, 8vo, 50p, blue cl, 12pl)	L: Aldine Hse.	1898	Brock, C.E.	50-75	*
Hartland, Edwin	English Fairy & Folk Tales (1st, sm8vo, 282p, AEG, 13pl)	L: W. Scott	1893	Brock, C.E.	65-80	*
Swift, J.	Gulliver's Travels (1st, 12mo, 381p, b/w)	MacMillan	1894	Brock, C.E.	45-60	*
Dickens, C.	Haunted Man (8vo, vellum, 8cp)	L: Dent	1907	Brock, C.E.	60-95	
Farnol, J.	Honorable Mr. Tawnish (1st AM, sm8vo, 165p, lavender/gilt, 4cp)	Little/Brown	1913	Brock, C.E.	20-30	
Farnol, J.	Honorable Mr. Tawnish (1st, 8vo, 118p, gilt, teg, 8cp)	L: Sampson	1913	Brock, C.E.	45-60	
Manning, A.	Household/Sir Thomas Moore (1st, 12mo, 185p, teg, 24 color, dep)	L: J.M. Dent	1906	Brock, C.E.	35-65	*
Hood, Thos.	Humerous Poems (1st, sm8vo, AEG, 236p, gilt, b/w, cep)	L: MacMillan	1893	Brock, C.E.	50-70	
Scott, Walter	Ivanhoe (1st, 8vo, blue/gilt, 523p, teg, uncut, 12cp, pep)	L: Dent	1899	Brock, C.E.	65-90	
Irving, W.	Keeping of Christmas... (1st, 12mo, teg, gilt, 24cp)	Dutton	1906	Brock, C.E.	45-60	
Stevenson, R.L.	Kidnapped (1st, 8vo, 251p)	L: MacMillan	1928	Brock, C.E.	45-60	*
Lamb, C.	Last Essays of Elia (1st, 12mo, 254p, teg, uncut)	L: Dent	1900	Brock, C.E.	40-60	
Dickens, C.	Life of Nicholas Nickleby (lg8vo, 711p, color)	Dodd	1931	Brock, C.E.	35-50	
Malet, Lucas	Little Peter (1st {new ed.}, sm4to, 175p, white cl, 8 ticp)	L: H. Frowde	1909	Brock, C.E.	45-60	*
Corkey, E.	Magic Circle (1st, lg8vo, gilt, 256p, b/w)	L: Blackie	[1924]	Brock, C.E.	40-60	
Farjeon, E.	Martin Pippin/Apple Orchard (1st, 8vo, brown cl, 369p, 5 ticp)	L: Collins	(1921)	Brock, C.E.	50-70	
Ewing, J.H.	Mrs. Overtheway's Remembrances (sq8vo)	L: H. Frowde	(1915)	Brock, C.E.	25-40	
Austen, J.	Northanger Abbey (1st, 8vo, 206p, gilt, 24cp)	L: J.M. Dent	1907	Brock, C.E.	50-75	
Wiggin, K.D.	Penelope's Irish Experiences (1st, 8vo, gilt, AEG, 335p, b/w)	L: Gay & Bird	1902	Brock, C.E.	40-60	
Dickens, C.	Posthumous Papers/Pickwick Club (1st AM, lg8vo, 687p, 16cp, pep)	Dodd	1930	Brock, C.E.	45-60	
Austen, J.	Pride & Prejudice (1st, 8vo, 336p, teg, gilt, uncut, 24 color)	L: J.M. Dent	1907	Brock, C.E.	45-60	
Nesbit, E.	Railway Children (1st, 8vo, 309p, uncut, teg, gilt, 20pl)	L: Wells/Gard.	(1906)	Brock, C.E.	250-400	
Gaster, Moses	Rumanian Legends & Fairy Tales (1st, 4to, ibds, 12cp)	L: R. Tuck	(1923)	Brock, C.E.	80-135	
Atkinson, J.C.	Scenes in Fairyland (1st, 8vo, 246p, green cl, 4pl)	L: MacMillan	1892	Brock, C.E.	50-75	*
Eliot, Geo.	Silas Marner (1st, sm8vo, green/gilt, 262p, teg, 24cp, dep)	L: Dent	1905	Brock, C.E.	30-45	
Dickens, C.	The Chimes (1st, 12mo, gilt, 167p, 8cp)	L: J.M. Dent	1906	Brock, C.E.	35-50	*
Raymond, W.	Tryphena In Love... (1st, 12mo, teg, 295p, col frn, 12pl)	L: Dent	1912	Brock, C.E.	40-60	
Goldsmith, O.	Vicar of Wakefield (1st, 8vo, 242p, teg, uncut, 25cp, dep)	L: Dent	1904	Brock, C.E.	30-50	
Kingsley, C.	Westward Ho! (16mo, 2 volumes, teg, uncut, b/w)	L: MacMillan	1896	Brock, C.E.	50-75	
Sharp, E.	Youngest Girl in the School (1st, 8vo, 326p)	L: MacMillan	1901	Brock, C.E.	35-50	*
Horne, Richard H.	Memoirs of a London Doll (1st UK, blue cl, 2cp)	L: Harrap	1923	Brock, E.	50-70	*
Marchioness/London	Magic Ink Spot (1st, 8vo, 208p, 16cp)	L: MacMillan	1928	Brock, E./Stewart	80-100	*
Davis, M.G.	Baker's Dozen (1st {std}, 8vo, 207p, orang cl, dep)	Harcourt	(1930)	Brock, Emma	25-40	*
Browne, Frances	Granny's Wonderful Chair (1st, sm8vo, 184p, cp)	MacMillan	1924	Brock, Emma	25-40	*
Davis, M.G.	Handsome Donkey (1st, lg8vo, yellow cl, 67p, 3-color, pep)	Harcourt	(1933)	Brock, Emma	30-45	*
Ludmann, Oscar	Hansi the Stork (1st, ob8vo, 62p, fp color)	Whitman	(1932)	Brock, Emma	25-45	*
Brock, Emma	Hen that Kept House (1st {std}, ob4to, [40]p, color, dep)	Knopf	1933	Brock, Emma	35-50	*
Bowen, W.A.	Merrimeg (1st, 12mo, 166p, green/gilt, 7cp, pep)	MacMillan	1923	Brock, Emma	25-40	*
Bigham, M.A.	More Mother Goose Village Stories (1st, 8vo, 274p, color)	Rand/McNally	(1922)	Brock, Emma	40-65	
Hoffman, H.	Nutcracker & Mouse King (sm4to, 123p, orang cl, p-o, color)	Whitman	(1930)	Brock, Emma	45-60	*
Van Housen, Nita	Poogie & Sibella (1st, 8vo, green cl, 81p, 8 fp color)	Whitman	(1932)	Brock, Emma	25-40	*
Brock, Emma	Present for Auntie (1st {std}, sm8vo, [96]p, cloth)	Knopf	1939	Brock, Emma	25-40	
Davis, M.G.	Sandy's Kingdom (1st, lg8vo, green cl, 79p, b/w, pep)	Harcourt	(1935)	Brock, Emma	25-40	*
King, Marian	Sean & Sheela (1st, lg8vo, p-o, 135p, dp color, pep)	Whitman	1937	Brock, Emma	25-40	
Boggs, R.S.	Three Golden Oranges (1st {std}, sm8vo, 137p, 6pl, pep)	Longmans	1936	Brock, Emma	35-50	*
Brock, Emma	To Market! To Market! (1st, ob8vo, [41]p, color)	Knopf	1930	Brock, Emma	25-45	*
DeSegur, S.	Wise Little Donkey (1st, lg8vo, p-o, 191p, pep, 4cp)	Whitman	(1931)	Brock, Emma	25-40	*
Drinkwater, J.	All About Me (1st, 8vo, 103p, teg, gilt, 9pl, pep)	L: Collins	1928	Brock, H.M.	35-50	
Thackeray, Wm.	Ballads & Songs (1st, 12mo, AEG, 276p, red/gilt)	L: Cassell	1896	Brock, H.M.	65-80	
N/A	Beauty & the Beast (4to, wraps, 6cp)	L: Warne	[1895]	Brock, H.M.	80-120	
N/A	Book of Fairy Tales (1st, 4to, gilt, unpag, pep, 24cp)	L: Warne	[1914]	Brock, H.M.	200-285	
Nichols, B.	Book of Old Ballads (1st, 4to, 279p, brown/gilt, 16cp)	L: Hutchinson	1934	Brock, H.M.	65-80	
Dickens, C.	Christmas Carol (1st AM, 8vo, red/gilt, 77p, 4cp)	Dodd	(1935)	Brock, H.M.	50-70	*
Gaskell, Mrs.	Cranford (1st, 8vo, 313p, red/gilt, teg, 16 illus)	L: J. Nisbet	1900	Brock, H.M.	50-65	
Mowbray, John	Dismal Jimmy of the Fourth (1st, 8vo, 215p, p-o, col frn, 3pl)	L: Cassell	1928	Brock, H.M.	25-40	*
Fortesque, J.W.	Drummer's Coat (1st, sq8vo, 184p red/gilt, 4pl)	L: MacMillan	1899	Brock, H.M.	70-85	

ILLUSTRATOR: 22

AUTHOR	TITLE	PUBLISHER	DATE	ARTIST	PRICE	LC
Andersen, H.C.	Fairy Tales (1st, 8vo, 408p, b/w)	L: Seeley	(1909)	Brock, H.M.	65-80	*
Andersen, H.C.	Fairy Tales & Stories (1st AM, sm8vo, 408p, 8pl)	C.L. Bowman	1909	Brock, H.M.	65-80	*
Lover, S.	Handy Andy (1st, 12mo, 523p, blue/gilt, AEG, pep, 40pl)	L: MacMillan	1896	Brock, H.M.	60-80	
N/A	Hop O' My Thumb (4to, wraps, 8cp)	L: Warne	[1910]	Brock, H.M.	60-90	
Ewing, J.H.	Jacanapes (1st, 8vo, 196p, 8cp)	L: Bell	1913	Brock, H.M.	40-60	
Marryat, Fred.	Jacob Faithful (1st, 8vo, blue/gilt, 416p, AEG, b/w, dep)	L: MacMillan	1895	Brock, H.M.	50-75	
Marryat, Fred.	Japhet... (1st, 12mo, blue/gilt, 401p, AEG, 13pl, pep)	L: MacMillan	1895	Brock, H.M.	70-90	
Frazer, Lilly	Leaves from The Golden Bough (1st, 8vo, 248p, gilt, teg, b/w)	L: MacMillan	1924	Brock, H.M.	35-50	
Stevenson, R.L.	Master of Ballantrae (1st, 8vo, 259p)	L: MacMillan	1928	Brock, H.M.	35-50	*
Sharp, E.	Micky... (1st, 8vo, 240p)	L: MacMillan	1905	Brock, H.M.	35-50	*
Drinkwater, J.	More About Me (1st AM, 8vo, 110p, orange cl, b/w)	Houghton	1930	Brock, H.M.	30-50	*
Irving, W.	Old Christmas Day (12mo, 34p, p-o, 5cp)	L: Foulis	[1912]	Brock, H.M.	40-60	
Irving, W.	Old English Christmas (1st, 12mo, 124p, blue/gilt, 17 ticp)	L: Foulis	[1910]	Brock, H.M.	60-85	
Irving, W.	Old English Christmas (1st AM, 12mo, 123p, ibds, p-o, 17 ticp)	Jacobs	(1910)	Brock, H.M.	45-60	
N/A	Old Fairy Tales (1st, 4to, gilt, 11cp)	L: Warne	(1914)	Brock, H.M.	100-150	
Milne, A.A.	Once On a Time (1st, 8vo, 316p, blue cl, p-o, col frn, 3pl)	L: Hodder	(1917)	Brock, H.M.	130-165	*
N/A	Puss In Boots (4to, cloth, p-o, 8cp)	Warne	[1900]	Brock, H.M.	60-85	
N/A	Puss in Boots (lg4to, 8cp)	Warne	[1907]	Brock, H.M.	35-50	*
Lady Frazer	Singing Wood (1st, 8vo, 144p, col frn)	L: A&C Black	1931	Brock, H.M.	35-50	*
Farjeon, E.	Tale of Tom Tiddler (1st, 8vo, 191p)	L: Collins	(1929)	Brock, H.M.	65-80	*
Kingsley, C.	The Heroes (1st, 8vo, 212p, 16cp)	L: MacMillan	1928	Brock, H.M.	50-70	*
Dawson, A.J.	The Message (1st, 8vo, 386p, black/gilt, 4cp)	L: Richards	1907	Brock, H.M.	65-90	*
Goldsmith, O.	Vicar of Wakefield (1st AM, 8vo, blue/gilt, teg, 7cp)	Lippincott	1912	Brock, H.M.	50-70	
Blackmore, R.D.	Lorna Doone (1st, lg4to, 520p, teg, gilt, 16 ticp)	L: Boots	[1931]	Brock/Brittan	85-130	
Haggard, H.R.	Mahatma & the Hare (1st, 8vo, 165p, red cl, 12pl)	L: Longmans	1911	Brock/Horton	85-130	
Nesbit, E.	Oswald Bastable & Others (1st, 12mo, teg, 369p, gilt, 22pl)	L: Wells/Gard.	(1905)	Brock/Millar	200-300	
Johnston, A.F.	Road of the Loving Heart (1st, sm8vo, 77p, pep, b/w)	Page	1922	Bromhall, W.	20-30	
Avery, Kay	Wee Willow Whistle (1st {std}, 4to, ipcb, [32]p, color)	Knopf	(1947)	Bromhall, W.	30-45	*
Eliot, E.C.	Wind Boy (1st {std}, sm8vo, 238p, col frn, b/w)	Doubleday/Page	1923	Bromhall, W.	20-30	
Turner, N.B.	Zodiac Town (1st, 8vo, 131p, gilt, 13 b/w, pep)	Atl. Month Pr.	(1921)	Bromhall, W.	35-50	
Coatsworth, E.	Boy with a Parrot (1st, 8vo, green cl, 101p, dp color, cep)	MacMillan	1930	Bronson, W.A.	25-45	*
Bronson, W.S.	Children of the Sea (1st, lg8vo, 264p, col frn, pep, b/w)	Harcourt	(1940)	Bronson, W.S.	40-60	*
Coatsworth, E.	Tonio & the Stranger (1st, 8vo, 69p, b/w)	Grosset/Dunlap	(1941)	Bronson, W.S.	25-40	*
Bronson, W.S.	Water People (1st, lg8vo, 119p, color, pep)	Wise-Parlow	(1935)	Bronson, W.S.	45-60	*
Lawless, E.	Book of Gilly (1st, 8vo, 298p, 4pl)	L: Smith Elder	1906	Brooke, L.L.	50-70	
White, Roma	Brownies & Rose-Leaves (1st, 12mo, 200p, tan cl, b/w, dep)	L: Innes	1892	Brooke, L.L.	65-80	
MacDonald, Geo.	Dealings with Fairies (1st AM, 8vo, 284p, gilt)	Routledge	1890	Brooke, L.L.	80-120	
Molesworth, M.	Girls & I (1st, 12mo, orange cl, 192p, 7pl, cep)	L: MacMillan	1892	Brooke, L.L.	70-100	
N/A	Golden Goose Book (1st, sq4to, green cl, unpag, 8cp)	L: Warne	(1905)	Brooke, L.L.	70-100	*
Brooke, L.L.	Johnny Crow's Garden (1st, ibds, 48p, p-o, 8cp)	L: Warne	1903	Brooke, L.L.	130-165	
Brooke, L.L.	Johnny Crow's New Garden (1st, 8vo, blue bds, p-o, 8cp)	L: Warne	1935	Brooke, L.L.	65-90	
Brooke, L.L.	Johnny Crow's Party (1st, sq8vo, green bds, p-o, 48p, 8cp)	L: Warne	1907	Brooke, L.L.	130-165	
MacDonald, Geo.	Light Princess (1st, sm8vo, 192p, cloth, 3pl)	L: Blackie	(1891)	Brooke, L.L.	120-160	
Mockler, G.	Little Girl from Next Door (1st, 8vo, 160p, 2pl by...)	L: Blackie	1896	Brooke, L.L.	50-70	*
Scripps, H.J.	Little Handfull (1st, 8vo, 224p, ibds, 4pl)	L: Blackie	(1894)	Brooke, L.L.	70-90	
Molesworth, M.	Mary (1st, 8vo, 180p)	L: MacMillan	1893	Brooke, L.L.	65-80	*
Molesworth, M.	Miss Mouse & her Boys (1st, 8vo, green/gilt, 198p, 7pl)	L: MacMillan	1897	Brooke, L.L.	35-50	
White, Roma	Moonbeams/Brownies (1st, sq12mo, 5pl)	L: A.D. Innes	1894	Brooke, L.L.	75-100	
Lear, E.	Nonsense Songs (1st, 8vo, AEG, [148]p, gilt, 14cp, pep)	L: Warne	[1900]	Brooke, L.L.	145-200	
Molesworth, M.	Nurse Heatherdale's Story (1st, 12mo, 202p, red cl, cep, 7pl)	L: MacMillan	1891	Brooke, L.L.	70-100	*
Lang, A.	Nursery Rhyme Book (1st, 8vo, AEG, 288p, green/gilt, pep)	L: Warne	1897	Brooke, L.L.	120-170	
N/A	Nursery Rhyme Picture Book (1st, ipcb, [32]p, p-o, 15cp, pep)	L: Warne	[1905]	Brooke, L.L.	130-165	
N/A	Nursery Rhymes (1st, 16mo, grey bds, 48p, p-o, 8cp, pep)	L: Warne	[1917]	Brooke, L.L.	60-80	
N/A	Oranges & Lemons (1st, 4to, [26]p, wraps, 8cp)	L: Warne	[1913]	Brooke, L.L.	100-145	
Molesworth, M.	Oriel Window (1st, 8vo, 182p, 7pl)	MacMillan	1896	Brooke, L.L.	60-80	
Lear, E.	Pelican Chorus (sq8vo, ibds, p-o, [80]p, 7cp)	L: Warne	(1900)	Brooke, L.L.	60-75	
Browning, R.	Pippa Passes (1st, 8vo, green cl, 72p, 7pl)	L: Duckworth	1898	Brooke, L.L.	65-80	
Brooke, L.L.	Ring O' Roses (lg8vo, [59]p, blue/gilt, pep, 32cp)	L: Warne	[1901]	Brooke, L.L.	50-80	
Charles, R.H.	Roundabout Turn (1st, sq8vo, [54]p, orange/gilt, pep, 4cp)	L: Warne	1930	Brooke, L.L.	75-120	
Strain, E.H.	School in Fairyland (1st, 8vo, green cl, 186p, 7pl)	L: T.F. Unwin	1896	Brooke, L.L.	100-150	
Somervell, A.	Singing Time (1st, 4to, ibds, p-o, 48p, b/w)	L: Constable	1899	Brooke, L.L.	100-130	
Brooke, L.L.	Tailor & the Crow (1st, sq8vo, gilt, p-o, 40p, 6cp, pep)	L: Warne	(1911)	Brooke, L.L.	90-140	
Lear, E.	The Jumblies (sm4to, ibds, p-o, 6cp)	L: Warne	[1905]	Brooke, L.L.	80-100	
N/A	Three Bears (4to, wraps, 8cp)	L: Warne	[1900]	Brooke, L.L.	45-70	
Wilkins, M.E.	Six Trees (1st, 12mo, green cl, 206p, 16pl)	Harper	1903	Broughton, C.	30-45	
Tarkington, B.	Seventeen (1st, sm8vo, 328p, orange cl)	Harper	(1916)	Brown, A.W.	60-90	
Marks, J.	Cheerful Cricket... (1st, 4to, [124]p, green cl, dep, color)	Small	1907	Brown, E.	80-130	
Sabin, E.H.	Stella's Adventure in Starland (1st, 8vo, 210p, 9pl)	Small	1907	Brown, E.	60-80	*
Brown, A.F.	Star Jewels... (1st, 8vo, green/gilt, 133p, 5pl)	Houghton	1905	Brown, E.C.	20-30	*
Robinson, M.L.	Sarah's Daikin (1st, sm8vo, 271p, green/gilt, uncut, b/w)	Dutton	(1927)	Brown, Julie	20-30	*
Sherlock, Philip	Anansi the Spider Man (1st {std}, 8vo, green cl, 112p, b/w)	Crowell	(1954)	Brown, Marcia	45-70	R*
Perrault, C.	Cinderella (1st, lg8vo, unpag, color, CM)	Scribner	1954	Brown, Marcia	70-100	*

AUTHOR	TITLE	PUBLISHER	DATE	ARTIST	PRICE	LC
N/A	Dick Whittington & his Cat (1st, 4to, ibds, [32]p, color, CH)	Scribner	1950	Brown, Marcia	65-100	*
Brown, Marcia	Felice (1st, 4to, [32]p, color, pep)	Scribner	(1958)	Brown, Marcia	70-110	R*
Brown, Marcia	Henry Fisherman (1st, 4to, [32]p, color, pep, CH)	Scribner	1949	Brown, Marcia	65-100	*
Brown, Marcia	Little Carousel (1st {1st Bk}, 4to, [32]p, ipcb, color)	Scribner	1946	Brown, Marcia	65-90	
Brown, Marcia	Peter Piper's Alphabet (1st, ob4to, ibds, [32]p, color, pep)	Scribner	(1959)	Brown, Marcia	75-125	*
Perrault, C.	Puss in Boots (1st, 4to, [30]p, color, pep, CH)	Scribner	(1952)	Brown, Marcia	70-100	R*
Brown, Marcia	Skipper John's Cook (1st, 4to, unpag, blue cl, pep, CH)	Scribner	1951	Brown, Marcia	70-100	*
Andersen, H.C.	Steadfast Tin Soldier (1st, 4to, unpag, CH)	Scribner	(1953)	Brown, Marcia	65-90	*
Brown, Marcia	Stone Soup (1st, 4to, [48]p, 2-color, pep, CH)	Scribner	1947	Brown, Marcia	70-115	*
Brown, Marcia	Tamarindo! (1st, 4to, tan cl, [32]p, color)	Scribner	(1960)	Brown, Marcia	45-60	*
Asbjornsen, P.C.	Three Billy Goats Gruff (1st {std}, 4to, green cl, unpag)	Harcourt	(1957)	Brown, Marcia	35-50	*
Watson, Virginia	Trail of Courage (1st, 8vo, grey cl, 181p, fp b/w)	Crowell	(1948)	Brown, Marcia	30-45	*
Shannon, Monica	Goose Grass Rhymes (1st {std}, sm8vo, 155p, col frn, pep)	Doubleday/Dor.	1930	Brown, N.K.	35-50	*
Brown, Palmer	Beyond the Pawpaw Trees (1st {1st bk}, sm8vo, grey cl, 121p, b/w)	Harper	(1954)	Brown, Palmer	65-95	R*
Brown, Palmer	Cheerful (1st, 16mo, beige cl, 58p, color)	Harper	(1957)	Brown, Palmer	50-80	R*
Brown, Palmer	Silver Nutmeg (1st, sm8vo, green cl, 137p, b/w)	Harper	(1956)	Brown, Palmer	45-60	*
Brown, Palmer	Something for Christmas (1st, 12mo, white cl, 32p, color)	Harper	(1958)	Brown, Palmer	50-80	R*
Sherman, Fanny J.	Admiral Wags of USS Lexington (1st {std}, 4to, 84p, 1-color)	Dodd	1943	Brown, Paul	25-40	*
Downey, Fairfax	Army Mule (1st, sm8vo, 192p, b/w)	Dodd	1945	Brown, Paul	20-30	*
Brown, Paul	Black & White (1st, ob4to, [62]p, b/w)	Scribner	1939	Brown, Paul	50-85	*
Sewell, Anna	Black Beauty (1st, lg ob8vo, unpag, b/w)	Scribner	(1952)	Brown, Paul	70-90	*
Tempski, Armine	Bright Spurs (1st, 8vo, 283p, peach cl, uncut, b/w)	Dodd	1946	Brown, Paul	30-50	*
Davis, L.R.	Buttonwood Island (1st {std}, sm8vo, 299p, b/w, pep)	Doubleday/Dor.	1940	Brown, Paul	25-40	*
Downey, Fairfax	Cats of Destiny (1st, 8vo, blue cl, 170p, 39 fp b/w)	Scribner	1950	Brown, Paul	25-45	*
Brown, Paul	Circus School (1st, 4to, [64]p, color)	Scribner	1946	Brown, Paul	55-80	*
Hall, E.G.	College on Horseback (1st, 12mo, 319p, pep)	Random	1933	Brown, Paul	20-30	*
Brown, Paul	Crazy Quilt (1st, ob4to, ipcb, [120]p, fp b/w, pep)	Scribner	1934	Brown, Paul	65-90	*
Brown, Paul	Daffy Taffy (1st, 4to, [32]p, color, cep)	Scribner	1955	Brown, Paul	45-65	*
Downey, Fairfax	Dogs of Destiny (1st, 8vo, 196p, b/w, DJ)	Scribner	1949	Brown, Paul	40-60	
Brown, Paul	Draw Horses: It's Fun & Easy (1st, 8vo, 60p, b/w)	Scribner	1949	Brown, Paul	45-70	*
Brown, Paul	Fire! The Mascot (1st, 4to, red cl, [96]p, b/w, DJ)	Scribner	1939	Brown, Paul	50-85	
Harper, Wilhelmina	Flying Hoofs (1st, 8vo, 282p, red cl, 3 dp cp, b/w)	Houghton	1939	Brown, Paul	25-40	*
Pace, Mildred M.	Friend of Animals (1st, 8vo, 125p, pink cl, fp b/w)	Scribner	1942	Brown, Paul	20-35	*
Smith, Lawrence B.	Fur or Feather (1st, 4to, 144p, b/w, DJ)	Scribner	1946	Brown, Paul	50-70	*
Alsop, Reese F.	George & his Horse (1st, 8vo, 164p, red cl, b/w)	Dodd	1948	Brown, Paul	25-40	*
Eames, G.T.	Ghost Town Cowboy (1st, 8vo, 176p, beige cl, uncut, b/w, pep)	J. Messner	(1951)	Brown, Paul	25-45	*
Knott, M.O.	Gone Away with O'Malley (1st {std}, 8vo, red cl, 280p, b/w, pep)	Doubleday/Dor.	1944	Brown, Paul	25-40	
Eames, G.T.	Good Luck Colt (1st, 8vo, 191p, red cl, fp b/w, pep)	J. Messner	(1953)	Brown, Paul	30-45	*
Palmer, Eliz.	Good Old Clipsy (1st, 8vo, 194p, tan cl, fp 1-color)	Scribner	1941	Brown, Paul	45-70	*
Cooper, Page	Great Horse Stories (1st {std}, 8vo, 366p, maroon cl, fp b/w)	Doubleday	1946	Brown, Paul	25-45	*
Judson, C.I.	Green Ginger Jar (1st, 8vo, green cl, 210p, fp b/w, pep)	Houghton	1949	Brown, Paul	35-50	*
Brown, Paul	Hi Guy the Cinderella Horse (1st, 4to, [62]p, cloth, b/w)	Scribner	(1944)	Brown, Paul	45-60	*
Davis, L.R.	Hobby Horse Hill (1st {std}, 8vo, 270p, uncut, b/w, pep)	Doubleday/Dor.	1939	Brown, Paul	25-40	*
Eames, G.T.	Horse to Remember (1st, 8vo, 146p, b/w, pep)	J. Messner	(1947)	Brown, Paul	30-45	*
Downey, Fairfax	Horses of Destiny (1st, 8vo, 186p, rust cl, fp b/w)	Scribner	1949	Brown, Paul	25-40	*
Lamb, Dean I.	Incurable Filibuster (1st, 8vo, 298p, uncut, b/w, pep)	Farrar/Rine.	(1934)	Brown, Paul	35-50	*
Downey, Fairfax	Jezebel the Jeep (1st, 8vo, 150p, grey cl, uncut, b/w)	Dodd	1944	Brown, Paul	25-45	*
Aunt Jo	Jo & Uncle George Kritters (1st, lg8vo, ibds, color)	Little/Brown	1922	Brown, Paul	60-90	
Johns, Rowland	Jock the King's Pony (1st {std}, 8vo, ibds, 60p, b/w, pep)	Dutton	(1936)	Brown, Paul	45-75	*
Tracy, Edward B.	King of the Stallions (1st, 8vo, orange cl, 241p, b/w, DJ)	Dodd	1947	Brown, Paul	35-50	
Aunt Jo	Kritters of Kitchen Kingdom (1st, 4to, 39p, ibds, 16 fp color)	Little/Brown	1922	Brown, Paul	70-110	R
Davis, L.R.	Melody, Mutton, Bone & Slam (1st, 8vo, 245p, brown cl, b/w)	Doubleday	1947	Brown, Paul	20-35	*
Brown, Paul	Merrylegs (1st, sm8vo, [64]p, grey cl, 1-color, pep)	Scribner	1946	Brown, Paul	40-65	*
Brown, Paul	Mick & Mac (1st, 4to, ibds, [96]p, b/w, pep)	Scribner	1937	Brown, Paul	75-120	
Aspden, Don	Mike of Company D. (1st, 8vo, 261p, green cl, b/w)	Scribner	1939	Brown, Paul	25-40	*
Brown, Paul	No Trouble at All (1st, 8vo, 126p)	Scribner	1940	Brown, Paul	30-50	*
Tempski, Armine	Pam's Paradise Ranch (1st, 8vo, 333p, orang cl, uncut, pep, b/w)	Dodd	1940	Brown, Paul	25-40	*
Brown, Paul	Piper's Pony (1st, ob4to, ipcb, [120]p, fp b/w, pep)	Scribner	1935	Brown, Paul	65-80	*
Davis, L.R.	Plow Penny Mystery (1st {std}, 8vo, 275p, b/w)	Doubleday/Dor.	1942	Brown, Paul	20-35	*
Brown, Paul	Polo (1st, lg8vo, 88p, b/w)	Scribner	1949	Brown, Paul	35-50	*
Brown, Paul	Pony Farm (1st, 8vo, [92]p, ibds, b/w, pep)	Scribner	(1948)	Brown, Paul	30-45	
Brown, Paul	Puff Ball (1st, 12mo, blue cl, [32]p, color, cep)	Scribner	1942	Brown, Paul	40-60	*
Judson, C.I.	Reaper Man (1st, 8vo, 156p, b/w)	Houghton	1948	Brown, Paul	25-40	*
Bialk, Elisa	Ride 'Em Peggy! (1st, 8vo, red cl, 196p, doub pg illus)	Houghton	1950	Brown, Paul	30-45	
Bontemps, A.	Sam Patch... (1st, sq8vo, yellow cl, 32p, color, pep)	Houghton	1951	Brown, Paul	65-80	*
Brown, Paul	Sparkie & Puff Ball (1st, 4to, [32]p, red cl, color)	Scribner	1954	Brown, Paul	50-80	*
McKenney, John	Tackroom Tattles (1st, 8vo, 230p, beige cl, fp b/w, cep)	Scribner	1934	Brown, Paul	35-50	*
Brown, Paul	Three Rings: A Circus Book (1st, 4to, ibds, [76]p, color, pep)	Scribner	1938	Brown, Paul	50-85	
Brown, Paul	War Paint: An Indian Pony (1st, 4to, [96]p, b/w, DJ)	Scribner	1936	Brown, Paul	60-80	
Miller, O.B.	Come Play with Me (1st, sm8vo, ibds, [38]p, color, pep)	Volland	(1918)	Browne, C.L.	80-120	*
Haynes, L.M.	Over the Rainbow Bridge (1st, sq8vo, [42]p, ibds, color)	Volland	(1920)	Browne, C.L.	65-100	
Miller, O.B.	Sunny Rhymes/Happy Children (1st, 8vo, ibds, [40]p, pep, color)	Volland	(1917)	Browne, C.L.	50-70	*

ILLUSTRATOR: 24

AUTHOR	TITLE	PUBLISHER	DATE	ARTIST	PRICE	LC
Eliot, Geo.	Adam Bede (1st, 4to, 523p, p-o, teg, gilt, 16cp)	L: Chambers	[1900]	Browne, G.	70-100	
Masefield, J.	Book of Discoveries (1st, 8vo, 354p, teg, 53 b/w)	L: Wells/Gard.	1910	Browne, G.	50-70	
Hoffman, A.S.	Book of the Sagas (1st, 8vo, 320p, gilt, 6cp)	L: Nister	[1913]	Browne, G.	85-120	
Farrow, G.E.	Dwindleberry Zoo (1st, lg8vo, 208p)	L: Blackie	1909	Browne, G.	120-165	*
Farrow, G.E.	Escape of the Mullingong (1st, 12mo, AEG, 148p, gilt)	L: Blackie	1907	Browne, G.	100-150	
Grimm Bros.	Fairy Tales (8vo, 340p, ibds, teg, later)	L: Wells/Gard.	1908	Browne, G.	65-80	
Sharp, E.	Hill that Fell Down (1st, 8vo, 275p)	L: Blackie	1909	Browne, G.	45-60	*
Allen, G.	Miss Cayley's Adventures (1st AM, 8vo, 344p, tan cl, b/w)	Putnam	1899	Browne, G.	40-60	*
Stevenson, R.L.	Pavilion on the Links (1st, 8vo, 96p, 24cp)	L: Chatto	1913	Browne, G.	65-80	*
Jones, H.	Prince Boo Hoo & Little Smuts (1st, sq8vo, 319p, teg, uncut)	L: Wells/Gard.	(1896)	Browne, G.	100-165	
Lang, A.	Prince Ricardo of Pantouflia (1st, 8vo, 204p, gilt, 12pl)	L: Arrowsmith	(1893)	Browne, G.	125-170	
Thackeray, Wm.	Rose & the Ring (lg8vo, 159p, green cl, col frn, 12pl, pep)	Stokes	[1910]	Browne, G.	45-70	
Crockett, S.R.	Sir Toady Crusoe (1st, 8vo, 406p, blue cl, b/w)	L: Wells/Gard.	1905	Browne, G.	45-70	
Crockett, S.R.	Sir Toady Crusoe (1st AM, 12mo, 356p, b/w)	Stokes	(1905)	Browne, G.	35-50	
Crockett, S.R.	Surprising Advens. of Sir Toady Lion (1st AM, 8vo, 314p, b/w)	Stokes	(1897)	Browne, G.	45-65	
McKay (ed.)	Tale of the Cauldron (1st, ob8vo, 64p, ibds, 16cp)	MacLeod	1927	Browne, G.	60-85	
Lever, Chas.	Templelogue Lever (1st, 4to, AEG, green cl, 631p, 32cp)	NY: Pollard	1880	Browne, H.K.	135-160	
Machray, R.	Night Side of London (1st, 8vo, yellow cl, 300p, b/w)	Lippincott	1902	Browne, T.	30-45	
Nesbit, E.	New Treasure Seekers (1st, 8vo, red/gilt, 328p, teg, 33pl)	L: T.F. Unwin	1904	Browne/Baumer	160-200	
Nesbit, E.	Story of the Treasure Seekers (1st, 8vo, 296p, AEG, 17pl)	L: T.F. Unwin	1899	Browne/Baumer	250-300	
Nesbit, E.	Bastable Children (1st {this fmt}, 8vo, 293p, col frn)	Coward	(1929)	Browne/Blam	45-60	*
Crockett, S.R.	Sweetheart Travellers (1st AM, lg8vo, 310p, ibds, teg, b/w)	Stokes	(1895)	Browne/Groome	50-75	*
Hopkins, H.M.	Flight of Rosy Dawn (1st, 12mo, 98p, b/w)	Page	1903	Bruce, J.	25-40	*
Ewing, J.H.	Jacanapes (1st {this pub}, 12mo, 71p, rust cl, 6pl)	D. Estes	(1902)	Bruce, J.	20-30	*
Bruce, J.	School Days (1st, 4to, 165p, ipcb, 11cp, pep)	Brentano's	1907	Bruce, J.	60-90	
Maurois, Andre	Fatapoufs & Thinifers (1st, lg4to, pep, blue cl, 92p, color)	Holt	(1940)	Bruller, Jean	35-50	*
N/A	Adventures of Jack (narrow folio, wraps, [16]p, color)	Stecher	1921	Brundage, F.	40-60	
Kaplan, A.O.	Baby's Biography (1st, 4to, AEG, 67p, gilt, color)	Brentano's	1891	Brundage, F.	130-165	
Taylor, I.S.	Baby's Book (sm4to, AEG, 4cp)	L: R. Tuck	[1904]	Brundage, F.	80-100	
Stevenson, R.L.	Child's Garden of Verses (1st, 8vo, [306]p, col frn)	Saalfield	(1924)	Brundage, F.	30-45	*
Nesbit, E.	Children's Shakespeare (1st AM, 8vo, gilt, 76p, ibds, 11 fp b/w)	Altemus	(1900)	Brundage, F.	65-80	
Dickens, C.	Christmas Stories from Dickens (4to, AEG, gilt, 12cp)	L: R. Tuck	[1898]	Brundage, F.	160-200	
Asbjornsen, P.C.	East o/t Sun/West o/t Moon (1st, lg8vo, 248p, col frn)	Saalfield	(1924)	Brundage, F.	30-45	*
Andersen, H.C.	Fairy Tales (1st, 8vo, [310]p, col frn)	Saalfield	(1925)	Brundage, F.	25-40	*
N/A	Goldilocks (folio, wraps, color)	Saalfield	1919	Brundage, F.	45-60	
Spyri, J.	Heidi (1st, 8vo, 307p, col frn)	Saalfield	(1924)	Brundage, F.	20-30	
Tucker, E.S.	Little Belles & Beaux (1st, lg4to, ibds, 6cp)	Stokes	1896	Brundage, F.	140-220	
Tucker, E.S.	Little Men & Maids (1st, 4to, ibds, [26]p, 6cp)	Stokes	1898	Brundage, F.	150-240	*
Mother Goose	Mother Goose ABC (4to, 14p, wraps, color)	Donohue	(1913)	Brundage, F.	65-80	*
Moore, C.C.	Night Before Christmas (folio, wraps, color)	Saalfield	(1915)	Brundage, F.	35-50	*
Collodi, C.	Pinocchio (1st, lg8vo, 247p, p-o, col frn, b/w)	Saalfield	(1924)	Brundage, F.	50-80	
MacDonald, Geo.	Princess & Goblin (1st, 8vo, 251p, col frn)	Saalfield	(1927)	Brundage, F.	25-40	
Irving, W.	Rip Van Winkle (1st, sm8vo, 92p, col frn, b/w)	Saalfield	(1927)	Brundage, F.	25-40	*
N/A	Snow White & Rose Red (sq4to, wraps, [16]p, color)	Stecher	1929	Brundage, F.	35-50	
Chesson	Tales from Tennyson (4to, ibds, 4 chromos)	L: R. Tuck	[1890]	Brundage, F.	90-120	
Hayman, D. (ed.)	Tales of Longfellow (cloth, cp)	L: R. Tuck	(1910)	Brundage, F.	50-70	*
Stevenson, R.L.	Treasure Island (1st, 8vo, 230p, col frn)	Saalfield	(1924)	Brundage, F.	25-40	*
N/A	Wedding Bells (4to, blue/silver, AE silver, 4 chromos)	L: R. Tuck	[1900]	Brundage, F.	100-150	
N/A	Whose Little Kitty are You? (folio, ibds, color)	NY: S. Gabriel	1913	Brundage, F.	40-60	
Vredenberg, E.	Old Fairy Tales (4to, ibds, 104p, 8cp)	L: R. Tuck	[1912]	Brundage/Bowley	130-200	
Nesbit, E.	Royal Children of English History (1st, 4to, 94p, 10cp)	L: R. Tuck	(1896)	Brundage/Bowley	180-260	*
N/A	Ecclesiasticus… (1st, 4to, black/gilt, 165p, teg, 16cp)	L: J. Lane	1927	Brunton, V.	70-120	
Wilson, Romer	Silver Magic (1st, 8vo, 432p, 8cp)	L: J. Cape	(1929)	Brunton, V.	80-130	
Ogburn, Charlton	White Falcon (1st, 8vo, tan/silver, 51p, b/w, pep)	Houghton	1955	Bryson, B.	65-80	R*
De La Mare, W.	Come Hither (1st, 8vo, 696p, green cl, b/w)	L: Constable	1923	Buckels, A.	50-65	*
De La Mare, W.	Come Hither (1st AM, 8vo, gilt, 696p, b/w)	Knopf	(1923)	Buckels, A.	40-60	
De La Mare, W.	Miss Jemima (1st, sm8vo, ipcb, 36p, col frn, 3 fp b/w)	L: Blackwell	[1925]	Buckels, A.	70-120	R*
Glendon, George	Emperor of the Air (1st, 8vo, 311p, red/gilt, 8pl)	L: Methuen	1910	Buckland, A.H.	45-60	*
Buff, Mary	Dancing Cloud (1st, ob4to, ipcb, 80p, fp color, cep)	Viking	1937	Buff, C.	65-90	*
Buff, M. & C.	Kobi, a Boy of Switzerland (1st, lg8vo, 128p, dp col, dep)	Viking	1939	Buff, C.	30-50	*
Buff, M. & C.	Apple and the Arrow (1st, sm4to, 75p, gilt, color, pep, NH)	Houghton	1951	Buff, M.& C.	45-65	
Buff, Mary	Big Tree (1st, 4to, 79p, grey cl, 1-color, DJ, NH)	Viking	1946	Buff, M.& C.	50-80	
Buff, Mary	Dash and Dart (1st, 4to, 73p, 4 dp cp, dep, CH)	Viking	1942	Buff, M.& C.	60-100	*
Buff, M. & C.	Elf Owl (1st, 4to, 72p, 1-color, pep)	Viking	(1958)	Buff, M.& C.	65-90	R*
Buff, M. & C.	Hah-Nee of the Cliff Dwellers (1st, 4to, 68p, color)	Houghton	1956	Buff, M.& C.	60-90	R
Buff, M. & C.	Hurry, Scurry & Flurry (1st, 4to, 73p, pep, 1-color)	Viking	1954	Buff, M.& C.	65-80	R*
Buff, Mary	Magic Maize (1st, 4to, 76p, pep, 9 fp color, NH)	Houghton	1953	Buff, M.& C.	50-80	*
Mother Goose	Mother Goose in Silhouettes (1st, sq16mo, 78p, b/w)	Houghton	1907	Buffam, K.G.	65-90	*
Gate, E.M.	Tales from the Secret Kingdom (1st, 8vo, ibds, silhouettes)	Yale U. Press	1919	Buffam, K.G.	30-45	
White, Richardson	Aesop's Fables in Rhyme (1st, lg4to, ibds, [100]p, 50pl, pep)	Saalfield	1903	Bull, C.L.	120-200	*
Dyer, W.A.	All Around Robin Hood's Barn (1st {std}, lg8vo, 204p, p-o, 24cp)	Doubleday/Page	1926	Bull, C.L.	45-65	
Evarts, Hal G.	Bald Face & other Animal Stories (1st, 8vo, 317p, 8pl, pep)	Knopf	1921	Bull, C.L.	20-30	*

AUTHOR	TITLE	PUBLISHER	DATE	ARTIST	PRICE	LC
Saunders, M.	Beautiful Joe's Paradise (1st, 8vo, red/gilt, p-o, 365p, 15pl)	L.C. Page	1902	Bull, C.L.	20-30	
London, J.	Before Adam (1st, 8vo, brown cl, 242p, uncut, 8cp)	MacMillan	1907	Bull, C.L.	120-165	
London, J.	Call of the Wild (1st, 8vo, teg, 231p, green/gilt, pep, PPP)	MacMillan	1903	Bull, C.L.	150-200	
Dyer, W.A.	Country Cousins (1st {std}, lg8vo, 164p, col frn, 11pl, pep)	Doubleday/Dor.	1927	Bull, C.L.	30-45	
Roberts, C.G.D.	Earth's Enigmas (1st, 12mo, 285p, red cl, 10pl)	Page	1903	Bull, C.L.	40-60	
Roberts, G.E.	Flying Plover (1st, 8vo, 125p, tan cl, 6pl, cvr by...)	Page	1909	Bull, C.L.	35-50	
Pardee, L.C.	Folk of the Woods (1st, lg8vo, p-o, 129p, teg, 10cp)	Doubleday/Page	1913	Bull, C.L.	30-45	
Terhune, A.P.	Further Adventures of Lad (1st, sm8vo, 341p, col frn)	Doran	(1922)	Bull, C.L.	30-45	
Ware, R.D.	In the Woods/On the Shore (1st, 8vo, 279p, photos, frn by...)	Page	1908	Bull, C.L.	35-50	*
Roberts, C.G.D.	Kindred of the Wild (1st, 8vo, 374p, green/gilt, teg, 50pl)	Page	1902	Bull, C.L.	40-65	
Linderman, F.B.	Kootenai Why Stories (1st, 8vo, 166p, color)	Scribner	1926	Bull, C.L.	65-80	*
Scoville, S.	Lords of the Wild (1st, 8vo, green cl, 246p, 4pl, pep)	Wm. Morrow	1928	Bull, C.L.	20-35	
Long, W.J.	Mother Nature (1st {std}, sm4to, green/gilt, 330p, 8cp)	Harper	(1923)	Bull, C.L.	35-50	
Darling, E.B.	Navarre of the North (1st {std}, 8vo, 268p, pep, frn by...)	Doubleday/Dor.	1930	Bull, C.L.	45-60	
Evarts, Hal G.	Passing of the Old West (1st, 8vo, 234p, 8pl)	Little/Brown	1921	Bull, C.L.	20-30	*
Litsey, E.C.	Race of the Swift (1st, sm8vo, 151p, 4pl)	Little/Brown	1905	Bull, C.L.	20-30	*
Roberts, Theodore	Red Feathers (1st, 8vo, p-o, 325p, col frn, 9pl)	Page	1907	Bull, C.L.	30-45	
Roberts, C.G.D.	Red Fox (1st, 8vo, uncut, 340p, teg, 48pl)	Page	1905	Bull, C.L.	40-60	
Baker, O.	Shasta of the Wolves (1st, 8vo, 276p, 4cp)	Dodd	1919	Bull, C.L.	20-35	*
Hawkes, Clarence	Silversheene: King of Sled Dogs (1st, 8vo, 234p, 4pl)	M. Bradley	(1924)	Bull, C.L.	20-25	*
Bryson, C.L.	Tan & Teckle (1st, 8vo, grey cl, 238p, 8pl)	Revell	(1908)	Bull, C.L.	30-45	
Bull, C.L.	Under the Roof of the Jungle (1st, 8vo, green cl, 271p, 4cp)	Page	1911	Bull, C.L.	30-45	*
Roberts, C.G.D.	Watchers of the Trails (1st, sm8vo, uncut, 361p, 48pl, pep)	Page	1904	Bull, C.L.	30-45	
Roberts, C.G.D.	Watchers of the Trails (1st UK, green bds, 361p, gilt, 48pl)	L: Duckworth	1904	Bull, C.L.	35-50	
Hawkes, Clarence	White Czar... (1st, 8vo, 202p, b/w pl)	M. Bradley	1923	Bull, C.L.	20-25	*
London, J.	White Fang (1st, 8vo, blue cl, 328p, 8cp, PPP)	MacMillan	1906	Bull, C.L.	150-180	
Chaffee, Allen	Wild Folk (1st, 8vo, 94p, pep, col frn by...)	M. Bradley	(1930)	Bull, C.L.	20-25	*
Annixter, Paul	Wilderness Ways (1st, lg8vo, p-o, 313p, col frn, 13pl)	Penn	(1930)	Bull, C.L.	50-65	*
Annixter, Paul	Wilderness Ways (1st UK, 8vo, green/gilt, 313p, 12pl)	L: Harrap	1931	Bull, C.L.	35-50	
Long, W.J.	Wood-Folk Comedies (1st, lg8vo, green/gilt, 307p, 8cp)	Harper	(1920)	Bull, C.L.	25-40	
N/A	Arabian Nights (1st AM, sm4to, p-o, 299p, teg, 20 ticp)	Dodd	1912	Bull, Rene	225-300	
N/A	Arabian Nights (1st, sm4to, 299p, p-o, gilt, 20 ticp)	L: Constable	1912	Bull, Rene	250-400	
N/A	Arabian Nights (8vo, 299p, green cl, p-o, 7 ticp, later)	L: Constable	[1917]	Bull, Rene	130-180	
Davidson, G.	Arabian Nights Retold for Children (8vo, 352p, red cl, 16cp)	L: Blackie	[1925]	Bull, Rene	65-80	*
Merimee, P.	Carmen (1st, lg4to, 203p, red/gilt, teg, pep, 18cp)	L: Hutchinson	(1915)	Bull, Rene	140-200	
Merimee, P.	Carmen (1st AM, 4to, teg, red/gilt, 16cp)	Hearst	1915	Bull, Rene	100-140	
Fyleman, R.	Garland of Roses (1st, 8vo, blue/gilt, 129p, 17pl)	L: Methuen	1928	Bull, Rene	100-145	
Strang, H.	Old Man of the Mountain (1st, 8vo, 322p, b/w)	L: H. Frowde	(1916)	Bull, Rene	65-80	*
Omar Khayyam	Rubaiyat... (1st, 4to, blue/gilt, [88]p, 10 ticp)	L: Hodder	[1913]	Bull, Rene	350-500	
Johnson, A.E.	Russian Ballet (1st AM, 4to, gilt, 240p, ipcb, 12cp)	Houghton	1913	Bull, Rene	165-200	
Johnson, A.E.	Russian Ballet (1st, lg4to, 240p, teg, gilt, uncut, 12cp)	L: Constable	1913	Bull, Rene	225-300	
Shirley (ed.)	La Fontaine's Fables (1st, sm ob4to, 64p, color)	L: T. Nelson	1905	Bull/Park	140-200	
Bullard, Marion	Somersaulting Rabbit (1st, ob4to, 45p, ibds, 12pl)	Dutton	(1927)	Bullard, M.	85-130	*
Hough, E.	Singing Mouse Stories (1st, 12mo, 235p, green/gilt)	Bobbs-Merrill	(1910)	Bunker, M.	30-45	
Alden, R.M.	Why the Chimes Rang (sm8vo, olive cl, p-o, [40]p)	Bobbs-Merrill	(1909)	Bunker, M.	20-35	
MacDonald, Ray	Mad Scientist (1st, 8vo, blue cl, 242p, 8pl)	NY: Cochrane	1908	Bunnell, C.B.	65-80	*
Rowand, Phyllis	Cats Who Stayed for Dinner (1st, 8vo, ipcb, [41]p, color, pep)	Wonder Books	(1951)	Burchard, P.	35-50	*
Toon, G.E.	Animal Story Book (1st, folio, 63p, ibds, 12cp)	Saalfield	(1928)	Burd, C.M.	30-50	
N/A	Animals on the Farm (1st, 4to, linen, [20]p, 8cp)	Saalfield	1936	Burd, C.M.	25-40	
Stevenson, R.L.	Child's Garden of Verses (1st, 4to, ibds, [36]p, 8 fp color)	Saalfield	(1930)	Burd, C.M.	25-45	
Toon, G.E.	Ducky Dee (4to, ibds, 8cp)	Saalfield	1928	Burd, C.M.	30-45	*
Alcott, L.M.	Eight Cousins (1st, 8vo, col frn, 253p, cp)	Winston	(1931)	Burd, C.M.	25-45	
Grimm Bros.	Fairy Tales (1st, 8vo, ibds, 6cp)	Donohue	(1920)	Burd, C.M.	30-45	
Smith, Laura R.	Good-Night Stories (1st, tall 8vo, 120p, ipcb, 8cp)	Chi: Stanton	(1921)	Burd, C.M.	40-60	*
Spyri, J.	Heidi (1st, 8vo, blue cl, p-o, 290p, 4cp)	Winston	(1924)	Burd, C.M.	25-40	
Alcott, L.M.	Little Men (1st, 8vo, 349p, p-o, 4cp, pep)	Winston	(1928)	Burd, C.M.	20-30	*
Mother Goose	Mother Goose in Song & Rhyme (1st, 4to, 87p, 2-color, pep)	Graham	(1930)	Burd, C.M.	35-50	*
Alcott, L.M.	Rose In Bloom (1st, 8vo, p-o, 320p, 4cp)	Winston	(1933)	Burd, C.M.	20-30	
Bailey, C.S.	Wonder Stories (1st, 8vo, p-o, 344p, 6cp, pep)	M. Bradley	1920	Burd, C.M.	25-40	*
Gipson, Fred B.	Old Yeller (1st, 8vo, ibds, 158p, 6 fp b/w, NH)	Harper	(1956)	Burger, C.	45-70	*
Burgess, G.	Blue Goops & Red (1st, sm4to, green cl, 81p, b/w, pep)	Stokes	(1909)	Burgess, G.	160-220	
Burgess, G.	Burgess Nonsense Book (1st, 8vo, teg, 239p, gilt)	Stokes	(1901)	Burgess, G.	150-200	
Burgess, G.	Cat's Elegy (1st, 12mo, tan ipcb, [43]p, 1-color)	McClurg	1913	Burgess, G.	70-120	R*
Burgess, G.	Goop Directory/Juvenile Offenders (1st, 12mo, 79p, ibds)	Stokes	(1913)	Burgess, G.	80-120	
Burgess, G.	Goop Tales Alphabetically Told (1st, sq4to, 106p, ibds)	Stokes	(1904)	Burgess, G.	120-160	
Burgess, G.	Goops & How to be Them (1st, sq4to, [96]p, ibds, PPP)	Stokes	(1900)	Burgess, G.	200-300	
Burgess, G.	Goops & How to be Them (1st UK, 8vo, unpag, b/w)	L: Methuen	1900	Burgess, G.	180-250	
Burgess, G.	Lady Mechante (1st, 8vo, 393p, lavender cl, 8pl)	Stokes	(1909)	Burgess, G.	40-60	
Burgess, G.	Lively City O'Ligg (1st, sm4to, 219p, ibds, 8cp)	Stokes	(1899)	Burgess, G.	120-150	
Burgess, G.	Why Be a Goop? (1st, sq8vo, p-o, red cl, 159p)	Stokes	1924	Burgess, G.	100-140	
Barton, W.E.	Prairie Schooner (1st, 8vo, 382p, 5pl)	Wilde	(1900)	Burgess, H.	20-30	*
Sewell, Anna	Black Beauty (8vo, p-o, 357p, 20 fp color)	Platt/Peck	(1911)	Burke, J.M.	35-50	

AUTHOR	TITLE	PUBLISHER	DATE	ARTIST	PRICE	LC
Frost, W.H.	Court of King Arthur (1st, 8vo, red/gilt, 320p, 6pl)	Scribner	1896	Burleigh, S.R.	65-80	
Burne-Jones, E.	Beginning of the World (lg4to, ibds, 25 illus)	L: Longmans	1902	Burne-Jones, E.	100-150	
Morris, Wm.	Doom of King Acrisius (1st, 8vo, teg, uncut, 82p, 11pl)	R.H. Russell	1902	Burne-Jones, E.	80-120	
Morris, Wm.	Pygmalion & the Image (1st, 8vo, white/gilt, teg, 34p, 5pl)	R.H. Russell	1903	Burne-Jones, E.	70-100	*
N/A	Song of Songs... (1st AM, narrow 4to, [21]p, 6pl)	R.H. Russell	1902	Burne-Jones, E.	80-120	*
Robinson, M.L.	Robin & Tito (1st, 8vo, 192p, col frn)	MacMillan	1930	Burns, E.	20-25	*
McNeely, M.H.	Rusty Ruston (1st {std}, 12mo, grn cl, 293p, col frn, 5pl, dep)	Longmans	1928	Burns, E.	25-45	*
Farjeon, E.	Perfect Zoo (1st {this pub.}, 4to, color)	L: Harrap	1947	Burrell, K.	40-65	*
Burton, V.L.	Calico the Wonder Horse (1st, narrow ob8vo, color, [58]p, DJ)	Houghton	1941	Burton, V.L.	45-65	
Burton, V.L.	Choo-Choo (1st, lg4to, red cl, [48]p, b/w, pep)	Houghton	(1937)	Burton, V.L.	80-120	R*
Peck, Leigh	Don Coyote (1st, sm4to, 78p, color, cep, DJ)	Houghton	1942	Burton, V.L.	45-60	
Andersen, H.C.	Emperor's New Clothes (1st, 8vo, 43p, cloth, color)	Houghton	1949	Burton, V.L.	50-80	
Bontemps, A.	Fast Sooner Hound (1st, sq8vo, beige cl, 28p, color, pep)	Houghton	(1942)	Burton, V.L.	65-90	*
Burton, V.L.	Katy & the Big Snow (1st, ob4to, 32p, blue cl, color, pep, DJ)	Houghton	1943	Burton, V.L.	100-130	
Burton, V.L.	Little House (1st, ob4to, 40p, green cl, color, pep, DJ, CM)	Houghton	1942	Burton, V.L.	85-130	R
Burton, V.L.	Maybelle the Cable Car (1st, sq lg8vo, 42p, pep, color)	Houghton	1952	Burton, V.L.	65-100	R
Burton, V.L.	Mike Mulligan & his Steam Shovel (1st, sq8vo, [48]p, color, pep)	Houghton	1939	Burton, V.L.	70-120	R
Bontemps, A.	Sad-Faced Boy (1st, 8vo, 118p, col frn, 7pl, pep)	Houghton	1937	Burton, V.L.	35-50	*
Malcolmson, A.	Song of Robin Hood (1st, lg4to, 123p, color, DJ, CH)	Houghton	1947	Burton, V.L.	100-145	
Eggleston, E.	Hoosier Schoolboy (1st [1], 8vo, 181p, 5pl, PPP)	Scribner	1883	Bush, G.D.	100-140	*
Faulkner, John	Chooky (1st {std}, 8vo, 250p, beige cl, b/w)	Norton	(1950)	Busoni, R.	25-40	*
Beim, Lorraine	Gregori's Lamb (1st, 8vo, 92p, ipcb, color, pep)	Saalfield	1948	Busoni, R.	30-45	
Hawkins, Q.	Mark, Mark, Shut the Door! (1st, 8vo, [31]p, ipcb, 2-color)	Holiday House	(1947)	Busoni, R.	30-45	*
Robertson, Keith	Missing Brother (1st, 8vo, 220p, orange cl, b/w)	Viking	1950	Busoni, R.	25-40	*
Schmidt, S.L.	Shadow over Winding Ranch (1st, 8vo, 298p, beige cl, b/w)	Random	(1940)	Busoni, R.	30-45	*
Collins, Dale	Shipmates Down Under (1st, sm8vo, green cl, 188p, b/w, cep)	Holiday House	(1950)	Busoni, R.	20-30	*
Alden, R.M.	Why the Chimes Rang (1st, 4to, red cl, [28]p, color, pep)	Bobbs-Merrill	1954	Busoni, R.	25-40	*
MacHarg, Wm. B.	Let's Pretend... (1st, 8vo, 80p, color)	Volland	1914	Butler, B.	30-45	*
Phillips, E.C.	Wee Ann (1st, 12mo, 134p, 4cp, pep)	Houghton	1919	Butler, E.F.	20-30	*
Gardiner, Linda	Sylvia in Flowerland (8vo, grey bds, gilt, 16 b/w)	L: Seeley	1899	Butler, H.E.	65-80	*
Girvin, B.	Round Fairyland with Alice (1st, 8vo, brown/gilt)	L: Wells/Gard.	(1948)	Cable, W.L.	65-80	*
Dalgliesh, A.	Enchanted Book (1st, 8vo, 246p, blue/gilt, pep, fp color)	Scribner	(1947)	Cacciola, C.	45-60	*
Campbell, Ruth	Cat Whose Whiskers Slipped (1st, 8vo, ibds, color)	Volland	(1925)	Cadie, V.E.	35-50	
Hankins, Maude M.	Daddy Gander (1st, 12mo, ibds, [40]p, color)	Volland	(1928)	Cadie, V.E.	60-80	*
Merryman, M.P.	Mr. Wubbles Bubbles (1st, 12mo, [44]p, color)	Saalfield	1936	Cadie, V.E.	35-50	*
Campbell, Ruth	Turtle Whose Snap Unfastened (1st, 4to, 93p, ibds, color, pep)	Volland	(1927)	Cadie, V.E.	35-50	
Hardy, M.E.	Girl of the Forest (1st, lg8vo, p-o, 222p, color)	Whitman	1927	Cady, C.J.	25-40	*
Burgess, T.	Advens. of Uncle Billy Possum (1st, 12mo, 117p, grey cl, 6pl)	Little/Brown	1914	Cady, H.	60-80	
Burgess, T.	Adventures of Bobby Coon (1st, 16mo, 117p, 6pl)	Little/Brown	1918	Cady, H.	50-70	
Burgess, T.	Adventures of Buster Bear (1st, sm8vo, tan cl, 6pl)	Little/Brown	1916	Cady, H.	45-60	
Burgess, T.	Adventures of Chatterer the Red Squirrel (1st, 16mo, 120p)	Little/Brown	1915	Cady, H.	60-85	
Burgess, T.	Adventures of Grandfather Frog (1st, 12mo, 120p, 6pl)	Little/Brown	1915	Cady, H.	50-70	
Burgess, T.	Adventures of Jerry Muskrat (1st, 12mo, 120p, 6pl)	Little/Brown	1914	Cady, H.	65-90	
Burgess, T.	Adventures of Jimmy Skunk (1st, 12mo, 118p, grey cl, 6pl)	Little/Brown	1918	Cady, H.	50-70	
Burgess, T.	Adventures of Johnny Chuck (1st, 12mo, 120p, 6pl)	Little/Brown	1913	Cady, H.	60-75	
Burgess, T.	Adventures of Mr. Mocker (1st, 8vo, cloth, 120p, 6pl)	Little/Brown	1914	Cady, H.	70-90	
Burgess, T.	Adventures of Ol' Mistah Buzzard (1st, 12mo, 119p)	Little/Brown	1919	Cady, H.	60-85	
Burgess, T.	Adventures of Old Mr. Toad (1st, 12mo, 120p, 6pl)	Little/Brown	1916	Cady, H.	65-80	
Burgess, T.	Adventures of Peter Cottontail (1st, 12mo, 120p, 6pl)	Little/Brown	1914	Cady, H.	65-80	*
Burgess, T.	Adventures of Poor Mrs. Quack (1st, 12mo, 119p, cloth, 6pl)	Little/Brown	1917	Cady, H.	60-75	
Burgess, T.	Adventures of Prickly Porky (1st, 12mo, grey cl, 116p, 6pl)	Little/Brown	1916	Cady, H.	65-80	
Burgess, T.	Adventures of Reddy Fox (1st, 16mo, grey cl, 120p, 6pl)	Little/Brown	1913	Cady, H.	65-80	
Burgess, T.	Adventures of Sammy Jay (1st, 12mo, 119p, 6pl)	Little/Brown	1915	Cady, H.	65-80	
Murray, Gilbert	Airplane Spider (1st, 12mo, grey cl, 86p, p-o, 7cp)	Little/Brown	1920	Cady, H.	100-150	*
Murray, Gilbert	Airplane Spider (1st UK, 8vo, tan bds, p-o, 7cp)	L: A&C Black	1921	Cady, H.	100-150	
Palmer, Winthrop	American Songs for Children (1st, ob4to, 64p, b/w)	MacMillan	1931	Cady, H.	45-65	*
N/A	Animal Alphabet (4to, 24p, color, wraps, pep)	Whitman	[1930]	Cady, H.	100-160	*
Wade, B.E.	Ant Ventures (1st, 8vo, green cl, p-o, 246p, 5cp, pep)	Rand/McNally	(1924)	Cady, H.	75-100	
Burgess, T.	At the Smiling Pool (1st {std}, sq8vo, 185p, red cl, DJ)	Little/Brown	1945	Cady, H.	70-90	
Burgess, T.	Billy Mink (1st, 8vo, p-o, 196p, 8cp)	Little/Brown	1924	Cady, H.	70-100	
Burgess, T.	Blacky the Crow (1st, sm8vo, 206p, p-o, 8cp)	Little/Brown	1922	Cady, H.	70-100	
Burgess, T.	Bowser the Hound (1st, 8vo, p-o, 206p, 8cp)	Little/Brown	1920	Cady, H.	65-90	
Burgess, T.	Burgess Animal Paint Book (ob folio, [24]p, wraps, 7 fp color)	Saalfield	1925	Cady, H.	85-125	
Burgess, T.	Burgess Animal Stories (1st, sq8vo, cloth, color)	Platt/Munk	(1942)	Cady, H.	45-60	
Burgess, T.	Buster Bear's Twins (1st, 8vo, p-o, 207p, 8cp)	Little/Brown	1923	Cady, H.	60-80	
Cady, H.	Caleb Cottontail (1st, 8vo, 127p, color, pep)	Houghton	1921	Cady, H.	80-100	
Burnett, F.H.	Cozy Lion (1st, 12mo, 104p, blue cl, 20cp)	Century	1907	Cady, H.	60-85	
Chambers, Rbt.	Garden-Land (1st, sm4to, 129p, ipcb, 8cp, pep)	Appleton	1907	Cady, H.	150-200	
Burgess, T.	Grandfather Frog Gets a Ride (1st, 12mo, ibds, 29p, color)	Stoll/Edwards	(1928)	Cady, H.	65-80	
Burgess, T.	Great Joke on Jimmy Skunk (1st, 12mo, ibds, 29p, color)	Stoll/Edwards	(1928)	Cady, H.	65-80	
Burgess, T.	Happy Jack (1st, 8vo, 204p, p-o, 8cp)	Little/Brown	1918	Cady, H.	50-75	
Wells, Carolyn	Happychaps (1st, 4to, 135p, brown cl, color)	Century	1908	Cady, H.	100-145	

AUTHOR	TITLE	PUBLISHER	DATE	ARTIST	PRICE	LC
Cady, H.	Holiday Time on Butternut Hill (1st, 24mo, ibds, unpag, 12 col)	Whitman	(1929)	Cady, H.	65-80	
N/A	Jack Frost Arrives on Butternut Hill (1st, 12mo, color)	Whitman	1929	Cady, H.	50-65	
Burgess, T.	Jerry Muskrat Wins Respect (4to, wraps, color)	NY: J. Eggers	(1928)	Cady, H.	60-80	
Burgess, T.	Jerry Muskrat at Home (1st, 8vo, 206p, p-o, 8cp)	Little/Brown	1926	Cady, H.	50-80	*
Burgess, T.	Lightfoot the Deer (1st, 8vo, p-o, blue cl, 205p, 8cp)	Little/Brown	1921	Cady, H.	60-75	
Burgess, T.	Little Joe Otter (1st, 8vo, olive cl, p-o, 198p, 8cp)	Little/Brown	1925	Cady, H.	70-90	
Burgess, T.	Longlegs the Heron (1st, 8vo, olive cl, p-o, 207p, 8cp)	Little/Brown	1927	Cady, H.	65-90	
Burgess, T.	Mother West Wind Why Stories (1st, 12mo, 230p, 8pl)	Little/Brown	1915	Cady, H.	65-90	*
Burgess, T.	Mrs. Peter Rabbit (1st, 8vo, 205p, p-o, 8cp)	Little/Brown	1919	Cady, H.	70-85	
Burgess, T.	Neatness of Bobby Coon (1st, 12mo, ibds, 29p, color)	Stoll/Edwards	(1927)	Cady, H.	65-80	
Burgess, T.	Old Granny Fox (1st, 8vo, p-o, green cl, 202p, 8cp)	Little/Brown	1920	Cady, H.	65-80	
Burgess, T.	On the Green Meadows (1st {std}, 8vo, 182p, red cl, color)	Little/Brown	1944	Cady, H.	40-65	
Burnett, F.H.	Queen Silver-Bell (1st, 16mo, p-o, 132p, 20cp)	Century	1906	Cady, H.	125-165	
Burnett, F.H.	Racketty-Packetty House (1st, 12mo, 130p, p-o, 24cp)	Century	1906	Cady, H.	100-145	
Rippey, Sarah C.	Raggedies in Fairy Land (1st, 4to, 96p, p-o, pep, 3cp)	Rand/McNally	(1930)	Cady, H.	100-130	
Burnett, F.H.	Spring Cleaning (1st, 12mo, p-o, 100p, 20cp)	Century	1908	Cady, H.	100-150	
Cady, H.	Time to Get Up (4to, ibds)	Stoll/Edwards	1928	Cady, H.	70-100	*
Burgess, T.	Tommy & the Wishing Stone (1st, 12mo, 290p, gilt, b/w pl)	Century	1915	Cady, H.	85-120	*
Burgess, T.	Whitefoot the Wood Mouse (1st, sm8vo, p-o, blue cl, 181p, 8cp)	Little/Brown	1922	Cady, H.	75-100	
Franchot, A.W.	Bugs, Wings & other Things (1st, 8vo, 99p, green/gilt, pep, 7cp)	Dutton	(1918)	Cady/Smith	150-180	
Irving, W.	Bracebridge Hall (1st, 12mo, 284p, gilt, AEG)	L: MacMillan	1877	Caldecott, R.	145-200	
Blackburn, H.	Breton Folk (1st, lg8vo, gilt, 200p, AEG, cep)	L: Sampson	1880	Caldecott, R.	120-150	
Ewing, J.H.	Daddy Darwin's Dovecoat (1st, 8vo, 52p, ibds, gilt, teg, col frn)	L: SPCK	[1884]	Caldecott, R.	70-100	
Ewing, J.H.	Daddy Darwin's Dovecoat (1st AM, 12mo, 62p, ibds)	Roberts	1886	Caldecott, R.	60-80	
Goldsmith, O.	Elegy/Glory of Her Sex... (1st, ob4to, wraps, [24]p, 6cp)	L: Routledge	(1885)	Caldecott, R.	70-95	
Caldecott, R.	Fox Jumps Over the Parson's Gate (ob8vo, wraps, 24p, 6cp)	L: Routledge	1883	Caldecott, R.	100-150	*
Caldecott, R.	Gleanings from the Graphic (1st, ob4to, ibds, gilt, 84p, 32 col)	L: Routledge	1889	Caldecott, R.	120-165	
Caldecott, R.	Graphic Pictures (1st, ob folio, 93p, color)	L: Routledge	1883	Caldecott, R.	150-220	
Ewing, J.H.	Jacanapes (1st, lg8vo, ibds, 184p, teg, col frn)	L: SPCK	1884	Caldecott, R.	120-160	
Tennyson, H.	Jack & the Bean Stalk (1st, sq8vo, 70p, green cl, b/w)	L: MacMillan	1886	Caldecott, R.	150-200	
Caldecott, R.	Last Graphic Pictures (1st, ob folio, ipcb, [71]p, color)	L: Routledge	1888	Caldecott, R.	135-170	
Ewing, J.H.	Lob Lie-by-the-Fire (1st, 8vo, 72p, ibds)	L: SPCK	(1885)	Caldecott, R.	70-90	
Caldecott, R.	More Graphic Pictures (1st, ob folio, ibds, 32cp)	L: Routledge	1887	Caldecott, R.	120-165	
Goldsmith, O.	Mrs. Mary Blaize (1st, 24p, wraps, 6cp)	L: Routledge	(1885)	Caldecott, R.	65-90	
Irving, W.	Old Christmas (8vo, gilt, 165p, b/w, AEG)	L: MacMillan	1894	Caldecott, R.	70-100	
Caldecott, R.	Panjandrum Picture Book (ob. sm4to, [98]p, color)	L: Warne	[1890]	Caldecott, R.	100-140	
Caldecott, R.	Queen of Hearts (1st, sm4to, wraps, 30p, 9cp)	L: Routledge	(1881)	Caldecott, R.	80-120	
Caldecott, R.	Sketch Book (1st, ob4to, 48p, color)	L: Routledge	1883	Caldecott, R.	150-185	
Caldecott, R.	Three Jovial Huntsmen (1st, ob8vo, 7 ticp, p-o, later)	L: Warne	[1908]	Caldecott, R.	80-100	*
Locker, Mrs. F.	What the Blackbird Said (1st, sq8vo, 187p, gilt, b/w)	L: Routledge	1881	Caldecott, R.	85-130	
Stevenson, R.L.	Treasure Island (1st, 8vo, 339p, 12cp)	L: Cassell	1911	Cameron, J.	65-80	*
Chisholm, L.	Enchanted Land (1st, sm4to, 211p, p-o, white/gilt, teg, 30cp)	L: Jack	(1906)	Cameron, K.	150-180	
Chisholm, L.	Enchanted Land (1st AM, 4to, 211p, AEG, green/gilt, 30cp)	Putnam	(1906)	Cameron, K.	125-165	
Chisholm, L.	In Fairyland (1st, lg8vo, p-o, AEG, 30cp, pep)	Putnam/Jack	(1904)	Cameron, K.	120-165	
MacGregor, M.	King Arthur's Knights (12mo, 155p, 8cp)	L: Jack	(1909)	Cameron, K.	50-80	
Steedman, Amy	Legends/Stories of Italy... (1st, lg8vo, teg ibds, gilt, 12 ticp)	L: Jack	(1907)	Cameron, K.	100-150	
Browning, E.B.	Rhyme of the Duchess May (1st, 12mo, p-o, wraps, uncut, 5cp)	L: Foulis	[1907]	Cameron, K.	60-80	
Kingsley, C.	Water Babies (1st, 24mo, 117p, green cl, uncut, 8 ticp)	Jack/Dutton	[1906]	Cameron, K.	35-50	*
Kingsley, C.	Water Babies (1st AM, 4to, p-o, teg, 246p, 8 ticp)	Stokes	[1911]	Cameron, K.	90-120	
Williams, I.A.	Where the Bee Sucks (4to, blue/gilt, 87p, teg, 12 ticp)	L: Medici	[1915]	Cameron, K.	65-80	
Brown, M.W.	Baby Animals (1st, lg8vo, ipcb, [48]p, color, pep)	Random	(1941)	Cameron, M.	40-65	*
Benstead, V. (adap)	Three Little Pigs (1st, 8vo, ibds, [28]p, color, pep)	Random	1942	Cameron, M.	25-40	*
Gask, Lilian	True Stories/Big Game & Jungles (1st, 8vo, 235p, 16cp)	L: Harrap	1933	Cameron, W.F.	50-65	*
Locke, Wm. J.	Christmas Mystery (1st, 8vo, 54p, green/gilt, 4pl, dep)	NY: J. Lane	1910	Campbell, B.	65-80	*
Raymond, M.T.	Roberta Goes Adventuring (1st, 8vo, ibds, 96p, color, pep)	Volland	(1931)	Campbell, E.	50-70	
Bontemps, A.	Popo & Fifina (1st, 8vo, 100p, orange cl, 6pl)	MacMillan	1932	Campbell, E.S.	80-120	R*
Campbell, Lang	Dinky Ducklings (1st, 12mo, ibds, 39p, color, pep)	Volland	(1928)	Campbell, L.	50-80	
Campbell, L.	Funnyfeathers (1st, 4to, 86p, tan cl, 6cp, pep)	Dutton	(1917)	Campbell, L.	55-80	
Garis, H.	Uncle Wiggily & his Flying Rug (1st {this pub}, 12mo, 33p, bds)	Whitman	(1940)	Campbell, L.	30-45	*
Garis, H.	Uncle Wiggily & the Pirates (sq12mo, 33p, ibds, color)	Whitman	(1940)	Campbell, L.	30-45	*
Garis, H.	Uncle Wiggily Goes Camping (sq12mo, ibds, 33p, color)	Whitman	(1940)	Campbell, L.	30-45	
Garis, H.	Uncle Wiggily Plays Indian Hunter (1st, 12mo, bds, 33p, color)	Whitman	(1940)	Campbell, L.	30-45	*
Garis, H.	Uncle Wiggily on Roller Skates (1st {this pub}, 12mo, 33p, col)	Whitman	(1940)	Campbell, L.	30-45	*
Garis, H.	Uncle Wiggily's Apple Roast (1st, 8vo, red cloth, p-o, color)	Graham	(1924)	Campbell, L.	30-45	
Garis, H.	Uncle Wiggily's Visit to the Farm (1st, sq12mo, 33p, p-o, col)	Graham	(1927)	Campbell, L.	30-45	
Garis, H.	Uncle Wiggily's Woodland Games (1st, sq12mo, [32]p, p-o, color)	Graham	(1922)	Campbell, L.	30-45	
Eaton, S.	Roosevelt Bears (1st, 4to, 180p, bds, p-o, 16cp)	Stern	1906	Campbell, V.F.	300-450	R
Eaton, S.	Travelling Bears at Play (1st, 4to, 62p, color)	Barse	(1916)	Campbell, V.F.	150-220	*
Eaton, S.	Travelling Bears in New York (1st, 4to, 60p, color)	Barse	(1915)	Campbell, V.F.	150-220	*
Eaton, S.	Travelling Bears/East & West (1st, 4to, bds, 63p, p-o, cp)	Barse	(1915)	Campbell, V.F.	150-220	
Eaton, S.	Travelling Bears/Outdoor Sports (1st, 4to, 60p, col frn)	Barse	(1915)	Campbell, V.F.	150-220	
Olcott, F.J.	Wonder Tales/Baltic Wizards (1st {std}, 8vo, 234p col frn, pep)	Longmans	1928	Candell, V.G.	30-45	

AUTHOR	TITLE	PUBLISHER	DATE	ARTIST	PRICE	LC
De La Mare, W.	Songs of Childhood (1st, sm8vo, 173p, gilt, teg, 8cp)	L: Longmans	1923	Canziani, E.	60-80	
Carroll, L.	Alice... & Through... (1st, sm8vo, ibds, 234p, b/w, pep)	Whitman	(1945)	Card, L.	45-60	*
Pool, M.L.	Red-Bridge Neighborhood (1st, 8vo, 369p, 13pl)	Harper	1898	Carleton, C.	20-35	
Carruth, H.	Track's End (1st, 12mo, blue cl, 230p, 9pl, pep)	Harper	1911	Carleton, C.	35-50	
Wade, B.E.	Magic Stone (1st, lg8vo, 254p, p-o, gilt, 7cp)	NY: Sully	1917	Carlson, G.	40-60	
Donahey, M.D.	Prince Without a Country (1st, 4to, p-o, 125p, 6cp)	Barse	(1916)	Carlson, G.	40-60	
Spyri, J.	Tiss - A Little Alpine Waif (1st, 8vo, 78p, col frn, pep)	Crowell	(1921)	Carlson, G.	20-30	*
Hough, E.	Young Alaskans (1st, 8vo, orang cl, 292p, 4pl, PPP)	Harper	1908	Carpenter, D.	140-180	*
Garland, H.	Prairie Songs... (1st, sm8vo, green/gilt, 164p, teg, uncut)	Stone/Kimball	1893	Carpenter, H.T.	50-80	R
Carpenter, John	Improving Songs/Anxious Children (lg ob4to, 50p, ibds, 19 col)	Schirmer	(1913)	Carpenter, J.& R.	100-140	*
Carpenter, John	When Little Boys Sing (1st, ob folio, cloth, color)	McClurg	(1904)	Carpenter, J.& R.	90-145	
Ostrander, Fannie	Goose Family Tales (1st, sq8vo, 87p, gilt, color)	Conkey	(1905)	Carqueville, W.	80-120	
Phillips, J.	Trip to Fairyland (1st, sq8vo, [53]p, gilt)	Conkey	(1905)	Carqueville, W.	80-120	
Fox, F.M.	Adventures of Sonny Bear (1st, sm8vo, 80p, 15cp)	Rand/McNally	(1916)	Carr, W.	45-60	*
Fyleman, R.	Widdy-Widdy-Wurkey (1st, 8vo, 70p, beige cl, b/w)	L: Blackwell	1934	Carrick, V.	35-50	*
Craik, D.M.	Adventures of a Brownie (sm4to, grey cl, p-o, 12cp)	Whitman	[1920]	Carsey, A.	30-45	*
Collodi, C.	Pinocchio (1st, lg8vo, 205p, p-o, 8cp)	Whitman	(1917)	Carsey, A.	50-65	
Bouten, E.G.	Grandmother's Doll (1st, lg8vo, 106p, gilt, color)	Duffield/Green	(1931)	Carter, H.	45-60	*
McNeil, E.	Lost Treasure Cave (1st, 8vo, tan cl, 352p, 8pl)	Dutton	1905	Cary, W.M.	30-50	
Brooks, E.S.	Master of Strong Hearts (1st, 8vo, 314p, 10pl)	Dutton	1898	Cary, W.M.	30-50	
Leamy, Edmund	Fairy Minstrel of Glenmalure (1st, 8vo, p-o, 4cp)	D. Fitzgerald	(1913)	Casseau, V.	35-50	*
Shippen, K.B.	Moses (1st, 8vo, blue cl, 132p, frn by...)	Harper	(1949)	Cassel, L.	30-45	
Mother Goose	Rainbow Mother Goose (1st, 8vo, 160p, 8cp, pep)	World	(1947)	Cassel, L.	70-100	R*
Casserley, A.T.	Roseen (1st {std}, 8vo, green cl, 152p, b/w, cep)	Harper	1929	Casserley, A.T.	20-25	*
Mitchell, S.W.	Adventures of Francois (1st, 8vo, 321p, orange cl, 15pl)	Century	1898	Castaigne, A.	35-50	
Catherwood, Mary	Lazarre (1st, 8vo, 436p, gilt)	Bowen-Merrill	1901	Castaigne, A.	25-40	
Parker, Gilbert	Money Master (1st, 8vo, green/gilt, 360p, 6pl)	Harper	1915	Castaigne, A.	20-35	*
Whiteing, R.	Paris of Today (1st, 4to, 249p, teg, b/w)	Century	1900	Castaigne, A.	50-70	
Parker, Gilbert	The Weavers (1st, 8vo, 530p, olive/gilt, 8pl)	Harper	1907	Castaigne, A.	20-25	
Herrick, R.	Flower Poems (8vo, 93p, p-o, teg, 12cp)	L: Routledge	[n.d.]	Castle, F.	50-80	
May, Charles P.	Box Turtle Lives in Armor (1st, sm8vo, 42p, 2-color, cep)	Holiday House	(1960)	Castle, J.	20-25	*
Castle, Jane	Peep-Lo (1st, 8vo, 34p, blue cl, b/w, pep)	Holiday House	1959	Castle, J.	20-30	*
Cavally, Fred. L.	Mother Goose's Teddy Bears (1st, 4to, red cl, [64]p, p-o, 32cp)	Bobbs-Merrill	1907	Cavally, F.L.	280-450	
Hough, E.	King of Gee Whiz (1st, lg8vo, 210p, green cl, 8cp)	Bobbs-Merrill	(1906)	Cesare, O.E.	125-200	R
Mother Goose	Mother Goose (1st AM, 12mo, 125p, 8cp)	Dent/Dutton	[1927]	Chadburn, M.	40-65	*
Chalmers, Mary	Come for a Walk with Me (1st, 16mo, [30]p, ipcb, 3-color)	Harper	(1955)	Chalmers, M.	25-45	*
Collodi, C.	Adventures Every Child Should Know (1st, 12mo, 241p, 8cp)	Doubleday/Page	1909	Chamberlin, E.H.	40-60	*
Paquin, S.S.	Garden Fairies (1st, sm4to, 179p, p-o, 4cp)	Moffat	1908	Chamberlin, E.H.	65-80	*
Tappan, E.M.	House with the Silver Door (1st, sm8vo, grn cl, 184p, p-o, 4cp)	Houghton	1913	Chamberlin, E.H.	25-40	*
Boylan, G.D.	Pipes of Clovis (1st, sm8vo, 258p, green cl, 4cp)	Little/Brown	1913	Chamberlin, E.H.	20-25	*
Kingsley, F.M.	Those Brewster Children (1st, 12mo, tan cl, 214p, 3pl)	Dodd	1910	Chamberlin, E.H.	20-25	*
Knevels, G.	Wonderful Bed (1st, 8vo, 229p, 4cp)	Bobbs-Merrill	(1912)	Chamberlin, E.H.	35-50	*
Scott, Walter	Quentin Durward (1st, 4to, 422p, gilt, p-o, 13cp, pep, SC)	Scribner	1923	Chambers, C.B.	65-100	
Champney, E.W.	Romance of Old Japan (1st, 8vo, 444p, teg, 96pl)	Putnam	1917	Champney, F.	40-60	
Chan, Chih-Yi	Good-Luck Horse (1st, ob8vo, grn cl, [47]p, pep, 10 fp col, CH)	Whittlesey	(1943)	Chan, P.	70-90	*
Channing, Blanche	Zodiac Stories (1st, sm8vo, 311p, gilt, b/w)	Dutton	1899	Channing B.M.	30-45	*
Waters, R.J.	El Estranjero (1st, lg8vo, 298p, b/w)	Rand/McNally	1910	Chapin, W.E.	25-40	*
White, S.E.	Conjuror's House (1st, 8vo, uncut, 260p, 6pl)	McClure	1903	Chapman, C.S.	30-45	
Barnes, James	Drake & his Yeomen (1st, sm8vo, 415p, col frn, 7pl)	MacMillan	1899	Chapman, C.T.	25-40	*
Coatsworth, E.	Door to the North (1st {std}, 8vo, 246p)	Winston	(1950)	Chapman, F.T.	25-40	*
Jewett, E.M.	Hidden Treasure of Glaston (1st, 8vo, grn cl 307p, b/w, pep, NH)	Viking	1946	Chapman, F.T.	35-50	*
Sterling, M.B.	Story of Sir Galahad (1st, 8vo, 223p, tan cl, 7cp, pep)	Dutton	(1908)	Chapman, W.E.	35-55	*
Grimm Bros.	Hansel & Gretel (1st {std}, sm4to, [32]p, color, pep, DJ)	Knopf	1944	Chappell, W.	35-50	
Prokofieff, S.	Peter & the Wolf (1st {std}, ob4to, [32]p, p-o, color, DJ)	Knopf	(1940)	Chappell, W.	30-50	
Andersen, H.C.	Three Hanses (1st, 8vo, 283p, DJ)	Little/Brown	1942	Chappell, W.	30-45	
McCleery, Wm.	Wolf Story (1st {std}, 12mo, 82p, red cl, p-o, col frn)	Knopf	1947	Chappell, W.	50-85	R
Cook, Bernadine	Curious Little Kitten (1st, ob4to, green cl, unpag, 1-color)	W.R. Scott	1956	Charlip, R.	50-80	*
Brown, M.W.	David's Little Indian (1st, 16mo, blue cl, [48]p, fp color)	W.R. Scott	(1956)	Charlip, R.	80-120	R*
Brown, M.W.	Dead Bird (1st, ob8vo, blue cl, [48]p, color)	W.R. Scott	(1958)	Charlip, R.	80-120	R*
Charlip, R.	Dress Up/Let's Have a Party (1st, ob8vo, ipcb [25]p, 3-col, pep)	W.R. Scott	1956	Charlip, R.	50-70	*
Charlip, R.	Where is Everybody? (1st, lg ob8vo, yellow cl, [50]p, 1-color)	W.R. Scott	1957	Charlip, R.	50-70	*
Krumgold, Joseph	And Now Miguel (1st {std}, 8vo, 245p, b/w, pep, DJ, NM)	Crowell	(1953)	Charlot, J.	80-125	
Brenner, A.	Boy Who Could Do Anything (1st, 4to, 136p, fp color, cep)	W.R. Scott	(1942)	Charlot, J.	50-75	
Brown, M.W.	Child's Good Morning (1st, sq4to, ibds, gilt/color)	W.R. Scott	1952	Charlot, J.	70-100	
Brown, M.W.	Child's Good Night Book (1st, 12mo, [24]p, color, CH)	W.R. Scott	1943	Charlot, J.	70-110	*
Rhoads, Dorothy	Corn Grows Ripe (1st, lg8vo, 88p, pep, 1-color, DJ, NH)	Viking	1956	Charlot, J.	60-90	
Charlot, J.	Dance of Death (1st, ob8vo, black/silver, [102]p, fp b/w)	Sheed/Ward	(1951)	Charlot, J.	65-100	*
Morris, A.A.	Digging in Yucatan (1st {std}, 8vo, 279p, pep)	Doubleday/Dor.	1931	Charlot, J.	45-60	*
Brenner, A.	Dumb Juan & the Bandits (1st, 8vo, green cl, [47]p, 1-color)	W.R. Scott	(1957)	Charlot, J.	40-65	*
Brown, M.W.	Fox Eyes (1st, 8vo, unpag)	Pantheon	1951	Charlot, J.	60-90	*
Brenner, A.	Hero by Mistake (1st, 8vo, 43p, ipcb, pep, 1-color)	W.R. Scott	(1953)	Charlot, J.	35-50	*
Hunt, Marigold	Hester & the Gnomes (1st, 8vo, 124p, blue cl, fp b/w, pep)	Whittlesey	(1955)	Charlot, J.	45-60	*

AUTHOR	TITLE	PUBLISHER	DATE	ARTIST	PRICE	LC
Tyman, Loretta	Julio (1st, 8vo, beige cl, 176p, fp b/w)	Abelard	(1955)	Charlot, J.	45-65	*
Schlein, M.	Kittens, Cubs & Babies (1st, sm4to, green cl, unpag, color)	W.R. Scott	1959	Charlot, J.	60-90	*
Bishop, C.H.	Martin DePorres, Hero (1st, 8vo, 120p, beige cl, fp b/w, pep)	Houghton	1954	Charlot, J.	45-65	*
Parish, Helen R.	Our Lady of Guadalupe (1st, 4to, 48p, 6 dp color)	Viking	1955	Charlot, J.	65-90	
Bulla, Clyde R.	Poppy Seeds (1st, 8vo, unpag)	Crowell	(1955)	Charlot, J.	40-70	*
Clark, A.N.	Secret of the Andes (1st, 4to, 131p, grey cl, col frn, pep, NM)	Viking	1952	Charlot, J.	75-100	R
Brown, M.W.	Sneakers (1st, sm8vo, 144p, blue cl, b/w)	W.R. Scott	(1955)	Charlot, J.	45-70	*
Rhoads, Dorothy	Story of Chan Yuc (1st {std}, sq4to, [45]p, ibds, color)	Doubleday/Dor.	1941	Charlot, J.	65-80	
Del Rio, A.M.	Sun, Moon & a Rabbit (1st, ob4to, 191p, color)	Sheed/Ward	1935	Charlot, J.	95-160	R*
Shannon, Monica	Tawnymore (1st {std}, sm8vo, 254p, col frn, fp b/w, pep)	Doubleday/Dor.	1931	Charlot, J.	45-60	*
Ferrer, Melchor	Tito's Hats (1st, sq4to, [28]p, ibds, dep)	Garden City	(1940)	Charlot, J.	45-60	
Brown, M.W.	Two Little Trains (1st, sm sq4to, ipcb, [32]p, pep, color)	W.R. Scott	1949	Charlot, J.	100-145	R*
Schlein, M.	When Will the World be Mine? (1st, 4to, unpag, pep, color, CH)	W.R. Scott	(1953)	Charlot, J.	70-120	*
Gratacap, L.P.	Mayor of New York (1st, 8vo, red/gilt, 471p, 4pl)	Dillingham	(1910)	Chase, J.C.	50-65	
Burgess, T.	Christmas Reindeer (1st, 12mo, 139p, red/gilt, 7pl, pep)	MacMillan	1926	Chase, R.	35-50	
Hughes, Rupert	Fairy Detective (1st, 12mo, 72p, tan cl, p-o, 5pl)	Harper	(1919)	Chase, R.	25-45	*
Lyman, Betty K.	Peter-Pan Twins are Glad to Help (sm4to, ibds, 12p)	Whitman	1928	Chase, R.	30-50	
Taggart, M.A.	Pussy-Cat Town (1st, 8vo, 245p, green/gilt, color, pep)	Page	1906	Chase, R.	35-50	
Courlander, H.	Cow-Tail Switch (1st, sm4to, brown cl, 143p, b/w, NH)	Holt	(1947)	Chastain, M.L.	40-65	*
Denton, C.J.	Daisy Dells (1st, lg8vo, 222p, p-o, color)	Whitman	(1927)	Cheney, G.	30-45	*
Lide, A.A.	Pearls of Fortune (1st, sm8vo, 276p, col frn, 11 fp b/w, dep)	Little/Brown	1931	Cheney, P.	20-30	*
Belloc, H.	But Softly - We are Observed (1st, 8vo, 312p, DJ)	L: Arrowsmith	(1928)	Chesterton, G.K.	70-115	
Chesterton, G.K.	Coloured Lands (1st, lg8vo, 238p, yellow cl, DJ)	L: Sheed/Ward	1938	Chesterton, G.K.	70-100	
Belloc, H.	Haunted House (1st, 8vo, 269p, 37 illus, DJ)	L: Arrowsmith	(1927)	Chesterton, G.K.	60-95	
Belloc, H.	Missing Masterpiece (1st, 8vo, 319p, DJ)	L: Arrowsmith	(1929)	Chesterton, G.K.	70-115	
Belloc, H.	Postmaster-General (1st, 8vo, 286p, 30 illus, DJ)	L: Arrowsmith	(1932)	Chesterton, G.K.	70-100	
Belloc, H.	Shadowed! (1st AM {std}, 8vo, 312p, 37 illus, DJ)	Harper	1929	Chesterton, G.K.	80-120	
Justus, May	Sammy (1st, 4to, cloth, 47p, color)	Whitman	1946	Chisholm, C.	20-30	*
Bonner, M.G.	365 Bedtime Stories (1st, 4to, p-o, 20cp)	Stokes	1923	Choate, F.	30-45	
Choate, F.	Abby in the Gobi (1st, ob4to, ibds, 63p, color, pep)	McBride	(1929)	Choate/Curtis	50-75	*
Andersen, H.C.	Andersen Fairy Book (1st, lg8vo, 416p, 8cp, pep)	Stokes	(1921)	Choate/Curtis	50-70	*
Bonner, M.G.	Daddy's Bedtime Fairy Stories (1st, 12mo, 120p, color)	Stokes	(1916)	Choate/Curtis	35-50	*
Choate, F.	Dance of the Hours (1st, 8vo, 242p, pep, fp b/w)	Harcourt	(1934)	Choate/Curtis	20-30	*
Cervantes	Don Quixote (1st, 341p, p-o)	Stokes	1922	Choate/Curtis	25-40	
N/A	Indian Fairy Book (1st, 8vo, 303p, 8cp, pep)	Stokes	(1916)	Choate/Curtis	65-100	
N/A	Indian Fairy Book (8vo, 303p, 8cp)	L: Richards	[1920]	Choate/Curtis	70-90	
Banks, Helen W.	Life of Jesus Retold for Children (1st, 4to, 93p, p-o, 5cp)	Stokes	(1922)	Choate/Curtis	30-45	*
Choate, F.	Little People of the Hills (1st, 8vo, 234p, fp b/w)	Harcourt	(1928)	Choate/Curtis	25-40	*
Eells, E.S.	Magic Tooth (1st, 8vo, orange cl, 243p, col frn, 10 fp b/w)	Little/Brown	1927	Choate/Curtis	35-50	*
Choate, F.	Pinafores & Pantalets (1st, 8vo, 207p, uncut, pep, 8 fp 2-col)	Harcourt	(1931)	Choate/Curtis	25-40	*
Mother Goose	Stokes Wonder Bk. of Mother Goose (1st, 4to, 240p, 24cp, pep)	Stokes	(1919)	Choate/Curtis	60-85	*
Christie, G.F.	Round De Ole Plantation (1st, 4to, ibds, unpag, 24 fp color)	L: Blackie	[1906]	Christie, G.F.	350-500	*
Christy, H.C.	American Girl (1st, lg8vo, 157p, p-o, 16cp)	Moffat	1906	Christy, H.C.	70-100	
Christy, H.C.	Christy Girl (1st, lg8vo, [48]p, p-o, 16cp)	Bobbs-Merrill	(1906)	Christy, H.C.	70-100	
Longfellow, H.W.	Courtship of Miles Standish (1st, lg8vo, 152p, 8cp)	Bobbs-Merrill	(1903)	Christy, H.C.	40-60	
Riley, J.W.	Discouraging Model (1st, lg8vo, ipcb, [12]p, color)	Bobbs-Merrill	(1914)	Christy, H.C.	80-100	R*
Hope, A.	Dolly Dialogues (1st, 8vo, 202p, p-o, teg, 18pl)	R.H. Russell	1901	Christy, H.C.	45-65	R
Major, C.	Dorothy Vernon/Haddon Hall (1st, 8vo, 369p, blue/gilt, col frn)	MacMillan	1902	Christy, H.C.	25-40	
Christy, H.C.	Drawings (1st, ob folio, [58]p, ibds, 28pl)	Moffat	1905	Christy, H.C.	100-150	
Longfellow, H.W.	Evangeline (1st, 4to, red/gilt, 132p, 6cp)	Bobbs-Merrill	(1905)	Christy, H.C.	30-50	
Sousa, J.P.	Fifth String (1st, 8vo, green cl, 124p, teg, b/w pl)	Bowen-Merrill	(1902)	Christy, H.C.	25-40	
Riley, J.W.	Good-Bye Jim (1st, sq8vo, 56p, 11cp)	Bobbs-Merrill	(1913)	Christy, H.C.	45-70	*
Nicholson, M.	House of a Thousand Candles (1st, 8vo, 382p, 7cp)	Bobbs-Merrill	(1905)	Christy, H.C.	20-30	
Scott, Walter	Lady of the Lake (1st, 4to, green/gilt, 13cp)	Bobbs-Merrill	1910	Christy, H.C.	60-90	
N/A	Liberty Belles (1st, folio, brown/gilt, 8cp)	Bobbs-Merrill	(1912)	Christy, H.C.	130-170	
Davis, R.H.	Lion & the Unicorn (1st [1], 8vo, 204p, green/gilt, 6pl)	Scribner	1899	Christy, H.C.	30-45	
Chambers, Rbt.	Maid-at-Arms (1st, 8vo, green/gilt)	Harper	1902	Christy, H.C.	25-40	
Rinehart, M.R.	Man in the Lower Ten (1st, 8vo, 372p, cp)	Bobbs-Merrill	(1909)	Christy, H.C.	50-75	
Beach, R.	Ne'er-Do-Well (1st, 12mo, 402p, p-o, 8pl)	Harper	1911	Christy, H.C.	25-40	
Page, T.N.	Old Gentlemen of the Black Stock (1st, 12mo, 170p, teg, 7cp)	Scribner	1900	Christy, H.C.	30-45	
Riley, J.W.	Old Sweetheart of Mine (1st, 8vo, p-o, 19pl)	Bobbs-Merrill	(1902)	Christy, H.C.	35-50	
Christy, H.C.	Our Girls (1st, lg8vo, 159p, p-o, 16cp)	Moffat	1907	Christy, H.C.	70-120	
Riley, J.W.	Riley Roses (1st, sm4to, [30]p, green/gilt, 8cp)	Bobbs-Merrill	(1909)	Christy, H.C.	65-80	
Christy, H.C.	Songs of Sentiment (1st, 8vo, grey/gilt, p-o, 12cp)	Moffat	1910	Christy, H.C.	70-120	
Cable, G.W.	The Cavalier (1st [1], 8vo, red/gilt, 311p, b/w)	Scribner	1901	Christy, H.C.	50-65	
Tennyson, A.	The Princess (1st, 4to, brown/gilt, 14cp)	Bobbs-Merrill	(1911)	Christy, H.C.	75-100	
Riley, J.W.	The Rose (1st, sm4to, ibds, [16]p)	Bobbs-Merrill	(1916)	Christy, H.C.	45-60	
Isham, F.S.	Under the Rose (1st, 12mo, 427p, green cl, 4cp by...)	Bobbs-Merrill	(1903)	Christy, H.C.	20-25	
Ford, P.L.	Wanted a Chaperone (1st, 8vo, 109p, teg, uncut, 6cp)	Dodd	1902	Christy, H.C.	30-50	
Ford, P.L.	Wanted a Matchmaker (1st, 8vo, 112p, teg, green/gilt, 5pl by...)	Dodd	1900	Christy, H.C.	35-50	
Deutsch, B. (tr.)	Crocodile (1st AM, ob4to, 31p, b/w)	Lippincott	(1931)	Chukovsky, K.	130-170	*
Gates, J.S.	Tommy Sweet Tooth (1st, sq16mo, ibds, 64p, color, pep)	Houghton	1911	Churbuck, E.V.	30-45	

AUTHOR	TITLE	PUBLISHER	DATE	ARTIST	PRICE	LC
Harris, J.C.	Nights with Uncle Remus (1st, 8vo, 416p, blue/gilt, 20pl, cep)	Bos: Osgood	1883	Church/Beard	200-300	
Harris, J.C.	Uncle Remus (1st [1], 8vo, 231p, gilt, 8pl, dep, PPP)	Appleton	1881	Church/Moser	600-900	
Hawthorne, N.	Wonder Book (1st, lg8vo, 232p, col frn, pep)	Sears	(1928)	Chuse, A.	25-40	*
Chute, Marchette	Rhymes About the City (1st, sm8vo, 57p, cloth, DJ)	MacMillan	1946	Chute, M.	45-60	
Chute, Marchette	Rhymes About the Country (1st, 4to, tan cl, 74p, b/w, pep)	MacMillan	1941	Chute, M.	50-65	
Coatsworth, E.	Atlas & Beyond (1st {std}, 12mo, 61p, p-o, dep, woodcuts by...)	Harper	1924	Cimino, H.	35-50	*
Bird, M.H.	Snow Man's Christmas (1st, 16mo, p-o, grn cl, 87p, 24 col, pep)	Stern	1908	Claghorn, J.C.	45-65	
Habberton, J.	With the Dream Maker (1st, 8vo, 112p, 5pl)	Jacobs	1898	Claghorn, J.C.	25-40	*
Harper, T.A.	Mushroom Boy (1st, 8vo, 215p, 4cp, pep)	Penn	1924	Clark, F.	25-40	
Baum, L.F.	Life & Advens. of Santa Claus (1st [1], sq8vo, 206p, 20cp, pep)	Bowen-Merrill	1902	Clark, M.C.	600-800	
Deland, M.	Awakening of Helena Richie (1st, 8vo, 357p, col frn, 7pl)	Harper	1906	Clark, W.A.	20-30	
Chaucer, G.	Canterbury Tales (1st, lg8vo, 235p, teg, gilt, 6cp)	Fox Duffield	1904	Clark, W.A.	45-60	
Davis, R.H.	Captain Macklin (1st, sm8vo, teg, uncut, 328p, 7pl)	Scribner	1902	Clark, W.A.	25-45	
Smith, F.H.	Fortunes of Oliver Horn (1st, 8vo, green cl, uncut, 552p)	Scribner	1902	Clark, W.A.	20-30	
Janvier, T.A.	Legends/City of Mexico (1st, 8vo, 164p, 6pl)	Harper	1910	Clark, W.A.	25-40	
Wharton, E.	Sanctuary (1st, 8vo, 184p, green/gilt, uncut, col frn, 10pl)	Scribner	1903	Clark, W.A.	100-135	
Andersen, H.C.	Fairy Tales (8vo, ibds, 4cp)	L: Coker	[n.d.]	Clarke, H.	80-100	
Andersen, H.C.	Fairy Tales (1st AM, 4to, 319p, grey cl, p-o, teg, 16 ticp)	Brentano's	(1916)	Clarke, H.	500-700	
Andersen, H.C.	Fairy Tales (1st, 4to, 319p, teg, 16 ticp, 24pl)	L: Harrap	1916	Clarke, H.	650-1000	
Perrault, C.	Fairy Tales (1st AM, 4to, blue/gilt, 160p, 12cp, 12pl)	Dodge	[1922]	Clarke, H.	300-450	
Perrault, C.	Fairy Tales (1st, 4to, blue/gilt, 160p, 12cp, 12pl)	L: Harrap	(1922)	Clarke, H.	350-500	
Andersen, H.C.	Fairy Tales (2nd AM, 4to, 16cp)	Brentano's	(1930)	Clarke, H.	160-230	
Andersen, H.C.	Fairy Tales (2nd, 4to, 320p, green cl, 16cp, 24pl)	L: Harrap	(1930)	Clarke, H.	200-300	
Swinburne, A.C.	Selected Poems... (1st, 4to, black/gilt, 217p, 10pl, pep)	Lane/Dodd	(1928)	Clarke, H.	200-250	
Perrault, C.	Sleeping Beauty (1st, 4to, teg, blue/gilt, 12cp)	Dodge	[1922]	Clarke, H.	275-400	
Poe, E.A.	Tales of Mystery... (1st, 4to, 383p, p-o, teg, 8 ticp, 24pl)	L: Harrap	1919	Clarke, H.	450-600	
Poe, E.A.	Tales of Mystery... (1st AM, 4to, p-o, 8 ticp, 24pl)	Brentano's	[1919]	Clarke, H.	350-500	
Poe, E.A.	Tales of Mystery... (1st {this pub}, 4to, p-o, 412p, 8 ticp)	Tudor	1933	Clarke, H.	125-165	
Poe, E.A.	Tales of Mystery... (4to, black cl, cp, later)	Lippincott	1940	Clarke, H.	80-100	
Walters, L.	Year's at the Spring (1st, sm4to, green/gilt, 12cp, 12pl, cep)	L: Harrap	1920	Clarke, H.	250-300	
Walters, L.	Year's at the Spring (1st AM, 4to, 128p, 12cp, 12pl)	Brentano's	(1920)	Clarke, H.	185-235	
Brown, Alice	Merry Links (1st, ob4to, ipcb, p-o, [91]p, fp b/w)	McClure	1903	Clarke, L.	80-120	*
Lide, A.A.	Inemak: Little Greenlander (1st, sm8vo, 148p, blue cl, fp b/w)	Rand/McNally	(1927)	Clarke, W.W.	20-35	*
Clarkson, L.	Buttercup's Visit... (folio, cloth, chromos)	Dutton	1881	Clarkson, L.	75-100	
Clarkson, L.	Fly-Away Fairies (1st, 4to, ibds, unpag, 16cp)	Dutton	1882	Clarkson, L.	120-165	
Clarkson, L.	Gathering of the Lillies (1st, 4to, AEG, cloth)	Sibole	(1870)	Clarkson, L.	160-230	
Clarkson, L.	Heartsease & Happy Days (folio, AEG, chromos)	Dutton	1883	Clarkson, L.	120-165	
Clarkson, L.	Indian Summer (1st, folio, AEG, gilt, 12cp)	Dutton	1881	Clarkson, L.	100-150	
Clarkson, L.	Violet Among the Lilies (4to, silver/gilt, AEG)	Dutton	1885	Clarkson, L.	85-100	
Clarkson, L.	Violet with Eyes of Blue (4to, gilt, 9 chromos)	(Phila)	(1876)	Clarkson, L.	90-120	
Montgomery, L.M.	Anne of Green Gables (1st, sm8vo, 429p, p-o, gilt, 8pl, PPP)	Page	1907	Claus, M.A.	120-160	
Michelson, M.	Anthony Overman (1st, 8vo, 330p, 5pl)	Doubleday/Page	1906	Clay, J.C.	20-30	*
Clay, J.C.	Lovers' Mother Goose (1st, 4to, 92p, gilt, color)	Bobbs-Merrill	(1905)	Clay, J.C.	50-80	
Aldrich, T.B.	Marjorie Daw (1st, 8vo, 123p, gilt)	Houghton	1908	Clay, J.C.	30-45	
Nicholson, M.	Zelda Dameron (1st, 8vo, 411p, 8cp by...)	Bobbs-Merrill	(1904)	Clay, J.C.	30-45	
Donahey, M.D.	Castle of Grumpy Grouch (1st, sm4to, 150p, color)	Stern	1908	Clay, J.R.	70-100	*
Herford, O.	Cupid's Almanac (1st, narrow 4to, [58]p, ipcb, col frn, pep)	Houghton	1908	Clay/Herford	35-50	*
Clay/Herford	Cupid's Cyclopedia (1st, 12mo, ibds)	Scribner	1910	Clay/Herford	60-85	
Herford, O.	Happy Days (1st, 16mo, ipcb, [44]p, color, pep)	Kennerley	1917	Clay/Herford	30-45	
Clayton, J.	Bunny Brothers (8vo, pcb, 96p)	L: Sully	(1915)	Clayton, M.	30-45	
Clayton, John	Dot in Dreamland (8vo, green cl, p-o, 10cp)	Whitman	(1916)	Clayton, M.	65-85	
Darton, F.J.	Wonder Book of Beasts (1st, 8vo, 403p, gilt, teg, 22pl)	L: Wells/Gard.	(1909)	Clayton, M.	85-125	
Hopkins, H.C.	Moon-Boat (1st, lg4to, tan/gilt, [27]p, p-o, 11cp)	McKay	(1918)	Clayton, W.P.	125-160	
Stuart, Ruth M.	Daddy'Do-Funny's Wisdom Jingles (1st, sm8vo, 95p, b/w, pep)	Century	1913	Clements, G.H.	50-80	*
Tarkington, B.	Beasley's Christmas Party (1st, 8vo, 100p, gilt, color)	Harper	1909	Clements, R.S.	40-60	
Webb, E. & D.	Littlest Fairy (1st, sm4to, ibds, 158p, p-o, 8cp, pep)	Dodge	(1910)	Clements, R.S.	150-200	
Bigham, M.A.	Overheard in Fairyland (1st, 8vo, 237p, col frn, cp)	Little/Brown	(1909)	Clements, R.S.	35-50	*
Spyri, J.	Heidi (8vo, 285p)	NY: Nelson	(1938)	Clere, V.	25-40	*
Barbour, R.H.	Half-Back (1st, 8vo, orange cl, 267p, PPP)	Appleton	1899	Clinedinst, W.	100-145	*
Dixon, Thomas	The One Woman (1st, 8vo, 350p, red cl, 8pl)	Doubleday/Page	1903	Clinedinst, W.	25-40	
Hunter, Richard	Little Pickles (sm4to, ibds, 44p, color)	L: Blackie	[1900]	Cobb, Ruth	150-200	
Hunter, Richard	Silver Bubbles... (lg4to, 20cp)	L: Nelson	[1915]	Cobb, Ruth	150-200	
Hunter, Richard	Dollies (1st, 24mo, olive cl)	L: Richards	1902	Cobb/Hunter	100-150	*
Norton, A.	Sword is Drawn (1st, 12mo, 180p, col frn, 4 fp b/w, pep, DJ)	Houghton	1944	Coburn, D.	180-265	
Taylor, B.	Boys of Other Countries (1st, 8vo, 263p, col frn)	Putnam	1912	Coburn, F.S.	20-30	
Dickens, C.	Christmas Carol (1st, sm8vo, 157p, teg, b/w pl)	Putnam	1900	Coburn, F.S.	25-40	*
Dickens, C.	The Chimes (1st, 12mo, 189p, AEG, grey/gilt, 4cp, 11pl)	Putnam	1911	Coburn, F.S.	45-60	
DeMorgan, M.	Windfairies... (1st, 8vo, 236p, gilt, AEG, 8 fp color)	L: Seeley	1900	Cockerell, O.	80-100	
Knatchbull-Hugessen	Princess with Pea-Green Nose (1st, 12mo, 114p, col frn, pep)	Harper	1927	Cocks, Myra	20-35	
Coffin, J.H.	Vendor of Dreams (1st, 4to, 108p, blue/gilt, teg, 3cp)	Dodd	1917	Coffin, H.	45-60	*
Hoffmann, Eleanor	Lion of Barbary (1st, 8vo, 217p, blue cl, b/w)	Holiday House	(1946)	Coggins, J.	20-30	LC
Scott, Walter	Ivanhoe (1st, 12mo, 336p, cp)	Row/Peterson	(1914)	Cole, C.L.	25-40	*

AUTHOR	TITLE	PUBLISHER	DATE	ARTIST	PRICE	LC
Canton, Wm.	Child's Book of Warriors (1st, sm8vo, green cl, teg, 319p, 3cp)	L: J.M. Dent	(1912)	Cole, H.	70-100	
Rhys, E. (ed.)	English Fairy Tales (12mo, p-o, 128p, gilt, 8cp)	Dutton	(1906)	Cole, H.	50-75	
Rhys, E. (ed.)	Fairy-Gold (1st, 8vo, 474p, 12cp)	L: Dent	1906	Cole, H.	60-100	
Swift, J.	Gulliver's Travels (1st, sm8vo, 355p, pl)	J. Lane	1900	Cole, H.	30-45	*
Ingoldsby, T.	Ingoldsby Legends (1st, 8vo, 640p)	L/NY: J. Lane	1903	Cole, H.	45-60	*
Omar Khayyam	Rubaiyat... (1st, 8vo, 65p)	L: J. Lane	1901	Cole, H.	70-100	*
Hare, C.	Story of Bayard (1st, 8vo, 256p, color)	L: Dent	1911	Cole, H.	50-70	
Hutchinson, W.M.L.	Sunset of the Heroes (8vo, 281p, green/gilt, pep, teg, 8cp)	L: J.M. Dent	[1910]	Cole, H.	65-90	*
Coolidge, S.	What Katy Did (1st, 8vo, p-o, 271p, 5cp, pep)	Little/Brown	1924	Coleman, R.P.	25-40	
Rosseau, Victor	Messiah of the Cylinder (1st, 8vo, green/gilt, 319p, 11pl)	McClurg	1917	Coll, J.C.	35-50	*
Asbjornsen, P.C.	East o/t Sun West o/t Moon (1st, 12mo, 198p, cp)	MacMillan	1928	Collin, H.	35-50	*
Kristoffersen, E.M.	Hans Christian Elsinore (1st, sq4to, 80p, pep, color)	Whitman	1937	Collin, H.	45-60	
Andersen, H.C.	Real Princess (1st, 4to, green cl, p-o, [18]p, color)	Whitman	1932	Collin, H.	35-50	
Treffinger, C.	Jimmy's Shoes (1st, 12mo, red cl, 219p, pep, 3pl)	Penn	(1934)	Collings, R.C.	30-45	*
Stevens, Thos.	Children of the World from A to Z (1st, 4to, [58]p, 26cp)	R.H. Russell	1903	Collins, A.H.	180-300	*
Herford, O.	Smoker's Yearbook (1st, lg8vo, [28]p, 12cp)	Moffat	1908	Collins, S.	65-90	
Hunt, M.L.	Sibby Botherbox (1st {std}, 8vo, 174p, blue cl, pep, b/w)	Lippincott	(1945)	Collison, M.	25-45	*
Carroll, L.	Through the Looking Glass (1st, sm4to, [30]p, ipcb, color, pep)	NY: Maxton	1947	Collison, M.	35-65	*
Kingsley, C.	Water Babies (1st, 4to, 56p, color)	Duell/Sloan	(1946)	Collison, M.	35-50	*
Murphy, Ruby B.	Who's Who in Mother Goose Land (1st, 12mo, [31]p, ibds, 1-color)	Rand/McNally	1935	Combet, F.	30-45	
Grimm Bros.	Fairy Tales (1st, lg8vo, 244p, col frn)	Sears	(1926)	Combs, L.	25-40	*
Stevenson, R.L.	Child's Garden of Verses (1st, sm4to, 91p, color)	McLoughlin	(1909)	Comstock, E.B.	45-70	*
Comstock, E.B.	Fairy Frolics (1st, 4to, [64]p, p-o, 6cp)	Rand/McNally	(1913)	Comstock, E.B.	160-220	
Comstock, E.B.	Tuck-Me-In Stories (1st, lg8vo, 76p, color)	Moffat	1917	Comstock, E.B.	65-80	*
Dewey, K.F.	Star People (1st, 8vo, 232p, pict cl, fp b/w)	L: Longmans	1910	Comstock, F.B.	65-80	
Aesopus	Aesop's Fables (1st, 8vo, 275p, 16cp)	Moffat	1905	Conde, J.M.	70-100	*
Aesopus	Aesop's Fables (1st, 8vo, 259p, cp)	Platt/Peck	(1913)	Conde, J.M.	35-50	*
Young, Martha	Behind the Dark Pines (1st, 8vo, 287p, tan cl, 27pl)	Appleton	1912	Conde, J.M.	30-50	
Bourke, S.T.E.	Fables in Feathers (1st, sq8vo, 114p, 9pl)	Crowell	(1907)	Conde, J.M.	35-50	*
Paine, A.B.	Hollow Tree (1st, 8vo, 128p, ibds, PPP)	R.H. Russell	1898	Conde, J.M.	100-150	
Paine, A.B.	Hollow Tree (1st UK, 4to, 128p, ibds)	L: Constable	1898	Conde, J.M.	80-100	
Paine, A.B.	Hollow Tree Snowed-In Book (1st, 8vo, cloth, 285p)	Harper	1910	Conde, J.M.	45-60	
Paine, A.B.	In the Deep Woods (1st, sm4to, 134p, ipcb, 52pl)	R.H. Russell	1899	Conde, J.M.	120-165	*
Carter, C.F.	Katooticut (1st, 4to, ipcb, 153p, fp b/w)	R.H. Russell	1899	Conde, J.M.	140-200	*
Paine, A.B.	Mr. Crow & the Whitewash (1st, 8vo, 120p, p-o, gilt)	Harper	(1917)	Conde, J.M.	50-70	
Paine, A.B.	Mr. Rabbit's Wedding (1st, sm8vo, gilt, p-o, 123p, fp b/w)	Harper	(1917)	Conde, J.M.	50-70	
Young, Martha	Plantation Bird Legends (1st, 8vo, 249p, 28pl)	Appleton	1916	Conde, J.M.	75-100	*
Harris, J.C.	Uncle Remus & Brer Rabbit (1st, ob4to, [63]p, grn cl, p-o, col)	Stokes	1907	Conde, J.M.	250-350	
Harris, J.C.	Uncle Remus & Little Boy (1st, 8vo, 173p, brown cl, p-o, 8cp)	Small	(1910)	Conde, J.M.	130-180	R
Dowson, Ernest	Beauty & the Beast (1st, lg4to, green/gilt, teg, uncut, 4cp)	L: J. Lane	1908	Condor, C.	160-200	
Sage, A.C.	Two Girls/Old New Jersey (1st, lg8vo, 195p, 16pl)	Stokes	(1912)	Connah, D.J.	20-35	*
Thomson, C.L.	Celtic Wonder World (1st, 8vo, 150p, b/w)	L: H. Marshall	1902	Conner, E.	60-80	
Molloy, Anne	The Pigeoneers (1st, 4to, 180p, grey cl, woodcuts, dep, DJ)	Houghton	1947	Converse, E.	45-60	
Cook, W.	Peggy's Travels (1st, 4to, 98p, brown bds, 15cp)	L: Blackie	[1908]	Cook, A.M.	100-150	
Whitman, W.	Poems of Leaves & Grass (1st, 4to, teg, gilt, 24 ticp)	L: J.M. Dent	1913	Cook, M.	100-130	
Campbell, A.M.	Fairy Flights in Cloudland (4to, ibds, 16cp)	L: A. Cooke	[1915]	Cook/Christie	140-200	
Asbjornsen, P.C.	East o/t Sun/West o/t Moon (1st, 8vo, p-o, 289p, green cl, 8cp)	McKay	(1921)	Cooke, E.	65-80	
Mother Goose	Mother Goose Nursery Rhymes (1st, 8vo, red/gilt 385p, 11cp, pep)	Cupples	(1930)	Cooke, E.	75-130	
Montgomery, L.M.	Pat of Silver Bush (1st, sm8vo, 329p, col frn)	Stokes	1933	Cooke, E.	60-80	*
Irving, W.	Rip Van Winkle (1st, 12mo, 69p, beige cl, 4cp)	Lippincott	(1923)	Cooke, E.	35-50	*
Irving, W.	Rip Van Winkle & Sleepy Hollow (sm8vo, 148p, red cl, 8cp)	Lippincott	(1924)	Cooke, E.	25-40	
Ewing, J.H.	Stories by J.H. Ewing (1st, lg8vo, blue cl, p-o, 426p, 8cp)	Duffield	1920	Cooke, E.	50-75	
Molesworth, M.	Stories by Mrs. Molesworth (1st, 4to, p-o, green cl, 353p, 8cp)	Duffield	1922	Cooke, E.	60-80	
Montgomery, F.T.	Wonderful Electric Elephant (1st, 8vo, 253p, 50pl)	Saalfield	1903	Coolidge, C.M.	60-85	*
Malmberg, Bertil	Ake & his World (1st, 8vo, red/gilt, uncut, b/w)	Farrar/Rine.	(1940)	Cooney, B.	35-50	*
Seeger, Ruth C.	Animal Folk Songs for Children (1st {std}, 4to, 80p)	Doubleday	1950	Cooney, B.	35-50	
Kingman, Lee	Best Christmas (1st {std}, sm8vo, 95p, b/w, cep)	Doubleday	(1949)	Cooney, B.	25-45	*
Crawford, P.	Blot: Little City Cat (1st {this pub}, sq8vo, 56p, dep, b/w)	Holt	(1946)	Cooney, B.	30-50	*
Cooney, Barbara	Captain Pottle's House (1st, sm8vo, 172p, green cl, b/w)	Farrar/Rine.	(1943)	Cooney, B.	30-45	*
Chaucer, G.	Chanticleer & the Fox (1st, 4to, [36]p, red cl, color, dep, CM)	Crowell	(1958)	Cooney, B.	70-100	*
Brown, M.W.	Christmas in the Barn (1st, ob8vo, red cl, [32]p, color, pep)	Crowell	(1952)	Cooney, B.	60-90	*
Quigg, Jane	Fun for Freddy (1st, 8vo, 106p, green cl, b/w)	NY: OUP	(1953)	Cooney, B.	25-45	*
Leonard, Nellie	Graymouse Family (1st, 8vo, 209p, b/w)	Crowell	(1950)	Cooney, B.	45-70	R*
Montgomery, R.G.	Hill Ranch (1st {std}, 8vo, green cl, 200p, uncut, b/w)	Doubleday	(1951)	Cooney, B.	30-50	*
Beim, Lorraine	Just Plain Maggie (1st {std}, 8vo, 185p, green cl, fp b/w)	Harcourt	(1950)	Cooney, B.	30-50	*
Montgomery, R.G.	Kildee House (1st {std}, 8vo, 209p, gilt, b/w, NH)	Doubleday	(1949)	Cooney, B.	45-70	R*
Cooney, Barbara	King of Wreck Island (1st {1st bk}, 8vo, blue cl, 91p, fp b/w)	Farrar/Rine.	(1941)	Cooney, B.	35-60	*
Marshall, Peter	Let's Keep Christmas (1st, 12mo, ibds, [32]p, 2-color, pep)	McGraw/Hill	1953	Cooney, B.	30-50	
Brown, M.W.	Little Fir Tree (1st, ob8vo, unpag, orange cl, color, dep)	Crowell	1954	Cooney, B.	50-75	*
Krasilovsky, P.	Man Who Didn't Wash his Dishes (1st {std}, lg8vo, [33]p)	Doubleday	(1950)	Cooney, B.	30-50	*
Reynolds, B.L.	Pepper (1st, 8vo, grey cl, 169p, fp b/w)	Scribner	(1952)	Cooney, B.	30-45	*
Kingman, Lee	Peter's Long Walk (1st {std}, ob lg8vo, 47p, ibds, color)	Doubleday	1953	Cooney, B.	65-100	R*

AUTHOR	TITLE	PUBLISHER	DATE	ARTIST	PRICE	LC
Lansing, Eliz.	Pony that Ran Away (1st {std}, sm8vo, 149p, red cl, b/w, dep)	Crowell	(1951)	Cooney, B.	30-45	*
Otto, M.G.	Pumpkin, Ginger & Spice (1st {std}, sm8vo, 116p, yellow cl, b/w)	Holt	(1954)	Cooney, B.	35-50	*
Kingman, Lee	Rocky Summer (1st, 8vo, 209p, blue cl, b/w)	Houghton	1948	Cooney, B.	25-45	*
Molloy, Anne	Shooting Star Farm (1st, 8vo, 231p, b/w, dep)	Houghton	1946	Cooney, B.	30-45	*
Cooney, Barbara	The Kellyhorns (1st, 8vo, red cl, 259p, b/w)	Farrar/Rine.	(1942)	Cooney, B.	30-45	*
Brown, M.W.	Where Have You Been? (1st, ob16mo, orang cl, [29]p, 1-col, dep)	Crowell	1952	Cooney, B.	70-100	R*
N/A	Arabian Nights (1st, 8vo, 501p, 4cp by...)	L: Routledge	1904	Cooper, A.W.	120-160	
Bangs, J.K.	Autobiography of Methuselah (1st, 12mo, 185p, cp)	Dodge	(1909)	Cooper, F.G.	35-50	*
Nesbit, E.	Daphne of Fitzroy Street (1st AM, 12mo, 417p, col frn by..)	Doubleday/Page	1909	Cootes, F.G.	65-90	
Sewell, Anna	Black Beauty (1st, 12mo, 319p, b/w)	Rand/McNally	(1904)	Copeland, C.	25-40	*
Long, W.J.	Brier-Patch Philosophy (1st, 12mo, 296p, teg, col frn, 4pl)	Ginn	1906	Copeland, C.	30-45	
Hawkes, Clarence	Field & Forest Friends (1st, 12mo, 207p, pep, 4pl)	F.G. Browne	1913	Copeland, C.	25-40	
Dudley, A.T.	Great Year (1st, sm8vo, 302p, 6pl)	Lothrop/Lee	(1907)	Copeland, C.	20-25	
Long, W.J.	How Animals Talk (1st, 4to, 301p, 8cp)	Harper	(1919)	Copeland, C.	30-45	
Hurd, Marian K.	Miss Billy: Neighborhood Story (1st, sm8vo, 349p, 6pl)	Lothrop	(1905)	Copeland, C.	30-45	*
Long, W.J.	Northern Trails (1st, 8vo, teg, 390p, gilt, b/w)	Ginn	1905	Copeland, C.	25-40	
Collodi, C.	Pinocchio (1st, 12mo, 212p, gilt, 12cp, pep)	Ginn	(1904)	Copeland, C.	45-65	
Collodi, C.	Pinocchio in Africa (1st AM, 12mo, green cl, 152p)	Ginn	(1911)	Copeland, C.	80-130	
Fox, F.M.	What Gladys Saw (1st, 12mo, green cl, 318p, 5pl)	W.A. Wilde	(1902)	Copeland, C.	25-40	
Rich, Edwin G.	Who-So Stories (1st, sm8vo, 207p, col frn)	Small/Maynard	(1918)	Copeland, C.	25-40	*
Kingsley, C.	Westward Ho! (12mo, 589p, 15pl)	L: J. Long	1904	Copping, H.	45-65	*
Corbet, K.& S.	Animal Land Where there are No People (1st AM, ob8vo)	Dutton	1897	Corbet, K.	80-100	*
Corbett, B.	Baby Days (1st, 4to, grey cloth, color)	Rand/McNally	(1910)	Corbett, B.L.	100-160	
Grover, E.O.	Overall Boys (1st, sq8vo, 123p, pict cl, color pep)	Rand/McNally	(1905)	Corbett, B.L.	70-100	
Grover, E.O.	Sunbonnet Babies in Holland (1st, sq8vo, 150p, color, pep)	Rand/McNally	(1915)	Corbett, B.L.	70-100	
Grover, E.O.	Sunbonnet Babies' Book (1st, sq8vo, 106p, color, pep)	Rand/McNally	(1902)	Corbett, B.L.	75-100	
Hogate, E.C.	Sunbonnets & Overalls... (1st, 8vo, 83p, color, pep)	Rand/McNally	(1914)	Corbett, B.L.	85-100	
Procter, E.H.	Rabbit's Day in Town (1st, 4to, ibds, unpag, 20 fp color)	L: Blackie	[1908]	Corbould, W.	120-175	*
Schneider, H.	Follow the Sunset (1st {std}, 4to, ibds, 43p, color, cep)	Doubleday	(1952)	Corcos, L.	50-85	R*
Burgess, T.	Boy Scouts in a Woodcraft Camp (1st, sm8vo, p-o, 345p, 5pl)	Penn	1912	Corson, C.S.	65-90	*
Lummis, C.F.	Enchanted Burro (1st, 8vo, 277p, teg, 15pl)	Way/Williams	1897	Corwin, C.A.	50-80	
Carroll, L.	Alice/Wonderland (1st, 12mo, brown cl, 192p, 12pl)	Rand/McNally	(1902)	Cory, F.	35-50	*
Brown, A.F.	Book of Saints & Friendly Beasts (1st, 12mo, 225p, b/w)	Houghton	1900	Cory, F.	65-80	*
Butler, E.P.	Confessions of a Daddy (1st, 8vo, red cl, 107p, 9 b/w)	Century	1907	Cory, F.	40-65	*
Baum, L.F.	Enchanted Island of Yew (1st [1], 8vo, 242p, tan cl, 8cp, pep)	Bobbs-Merrill	(1903)	Cory, F.	300-400	
Spofford, H.P.	Fairy Changeling (1st, 8vo, 75p, 20pl)	Badger	1911	Cory, F.	70-110	
Mother Goose	Fanny Cory Mother Goose (1st, 4to, gilt, p-o, 74p, 12cp, pep)	Bobbs-Merrill	(1913)	Cory, F.	150-220	
Cooke, G.M.	Huldah (1st, 8vo, 316p, 8pl by...)	Bobbs-Merrill	(1904)	Cory, F.	30-50	
Hill, Wm.	Jackie Boy in Rainbowland (1st, 8vo, p-o, 84p, color)	Rand/McNally	(1911)	Cory, F.	70-90	
Reid, Sydney	Josey & the Chipmunk (1st, sm8vo, 301p, 17pl)	Century	1900	Cory, F.	45-60	*
Loomis, C.B.	Just Rhymes (1st, ibds, 70p, b/w)	R.H. Russell	1899	Cory, F.	65-80	
Cory, F.	Little Me (1st {std}, sm8vo, ipcb, [56]p, fp b/w)	Dutton	(1936)	Cory, F.	30-50	*
Musson, B.	Maisie & her Dog Skip in Fairyland (1st, 8vo, 165p, 8cp)	Harper	1903	Cory, F.	45-70	
Baum, L.F.	Master Key (1st [1], 8vo, 245p, olive/gilt, p-o, 12cp)	Bowen-Merrill	(1901)	Cory, F.	280-350	
Daskam, J.	Memoirs of a Baby (1st, 8vo, 272p, blue cl, b/w)	Harper	1904	Cory, F.	25-40	
Cory, F.	Our Baby Book (lg4to, pink cl, [89]p, p-o, color)	Bobbs-Merrill	(1907)	Cory, F.	80-100	
Wells, Carolyn	Pete & Polly Stories (1st, lg8vo, green cl, 229p, 6pl)	McClurg	1902	Cory, F.	70-85	
Johnson, Burgess	Pleasant Tragedies of Childhood (1st, 4to, gilt, 119p, 30pl, pep)	Harper	1905	Cory, F.	80-120	
Brown, A.F.	Pocket Full of Posies (1st, 8vo, 169p, tan cl, 5pl)	Houghton	1902	Cory, F.	30-45	
Baker, C.	Queen's Page (1st, sm8vo, 319p, 12pl)	Bobbs-Merrill	(1905)	Cory, F.	50-65	
Cory, F.	Sonny Sayings (1st, ob4to, ibds, 112p, b/w)	Dutton	(1929)	Cory, F.	50-70	
Stuart, Ruth M.	Sonny, A Christmas Guest (1st, sm8vo, 135p, teg, gilt, 13pl)	Century	1904	Cory, F.	30-45	
Gates, J.S.	Sunshine Annie (1st, 8vo, 148p, red cl, p-o, 15cp, pep)	Bobbs-Merrill	(1910)	Cory, F.	75-100	
Carroll, L.	Through the Looking Glass (1st, 12mo, 218p, tan cl, b/w)	Rand/McNally	(1917)	Cory, F.	30-60	*
Taylor, B.L.	Well in the Wood (1st, 8vo, 191p, blue cl, 8pl)	Bobbs-Merrill	(1904)	Cory, F.	35-50	
Bigham, M.A.	Wishing Fairies (1st, 8vo, blue cl, 37p, 8cp)	Dodd	1905	Cory, F.	65-80	
Loomis, C.B.	Yankee Enchantments (1st, 8vo, 328p, gilt, 20 fp b/w, pep)	McClure	1900	Cory, F.	45-65	
Flower, Esther	Nurse Nora... (1st, 12mo, 163p, 9pl)	J. Pott	1903	Cory/Graef	25-40	*
Farjeon, B.L.	Lucy & their Majesties (1st, 8vo, 332p, tan cl, 20pl)	Century	1904	Cory/Varian	25-40	
Latham, Jean L.	Carry On, Mr. Bowditch (1st, 8vo, green cl, 251p, fp b/w, NM)	Houghton	1955	Cosgrave, J.O.	60-85	
Molloy, Anne	Lucy's Christmas (1st, 8vo, 46p, red cl, color)	Houghton	1950	Cosgrave, J.O.	20-35	*
Gilman, Eliz. L.	Picnic Adventures (1st, sm8vo, green cl, 192p, 12 dp 1-color)	Farrar/Rine.	(1940)	Cosgrave, J.O.	45-70	*
Saint-Exupery, A.	Wind, Sand & Stars (1st AM, 8vo, 306p, pep, 1-color designs)	Reynal/Hitch.	(1939)	Cosgrave, J.O.	65-85	*
Montgomery, L.M.	Jane of Lantern Hill (1st, sm8vo, 297p, col frn)	Stokes	1937	Costello, L.	65-90	*
Hawkins, Q.	Don't Run, Apple! (1st, 8vo, ipcb, [36]p, b/w, pep)	Holiday House	(1944)	Cote, P.	25-40	
Riley, J.W.	Riley Baby Book (1st, 8vo, red/gilt, unpag, t-i col frn)	Bobbs-Merrill	(1913)	Cotton, W.	100-140	R
Cowham, Hilda	Blacklegs.... (1st, 4to, 76p, teg, gilt, color)	L: Kegan Paul	1911	Cowham, H.	100-150	
Jacberns, R.	Poor Uncle Harry (1st, 8vo, 275p, red cl, 6cp)	L: Chambers	1910	Cowham, H.	45-60	*
Cowham, Hilda	Somebody's Baby (4to, ibds, 16 fp color)	L: R. Tuck	[1915]	Cowham, H.	100-165	
Lea, John	Willie Wimple's Adventures (1st, 4to, ibds, 16cp)	L: T.F. Unwin	(1908)	Cowham, H.	200-300	
Macaulay, T.B.	Lays of Ancient Rome (1st AM, black/gilt, teg, 180p, 12 ticp)	Longmans	1929	Cox, E.A.	50-75	
Cox, P.	Another Brownie Book (1st, 4to, 144p, ibds)	Century	(1890)	Cox, P.	180-220	

AUTHOR	TITLE	PUBLISHER	DATE	ARTIST	PRICE	LC
Veale, E.	Bonny Birds (8vo, wraps, 16p, b/w)	Hubbard	(1896)	Cox, P.	35-60	*
Cox, P.	Brownie Clown of Brownie Town (ob8vo, 103p, ibds)	Century	[1908]	Cox, P.	170-240	*
Cox, P.	Brownie Year Book (lg4to, [26]p, ibds, 12cp)	McLoughlin	[1895]	Cox, P.	280-350	
Cox, P.	Brownies & Prince Florimel (1st, lg8vo, tan cl, 246p, p-o)	Century	1918	Cox, P.	100-130	
Cox, P.	Brownies Abroad (1st UK, 4to, 14p, red cl)	L: T.F. Unwin	(1899)	Cox, P.	160-200	
Cox, P.	Brownies Abroad (1st, 4to, 144p, ibds)	Century	(1899)	Cox, P.	200-250	
Cox, P.	Brownies Around the World (1st, 4to, ibds, 144p)	Century	(1894)	Cox, P.	160-200	
Cox, P.	Brownies Through the Union (1st, 4to, ibds, 144p)	Century	(1895)	Cox, P.	120-180	
Cox, P.	Brownies Through the Union (1st UK, 4to, 144p, cloth)	L: T.F. Unwin	1895	Cox, P.	250-350	
Cox, P.	Brownies at Home (1st, 4to, ibds, 144p)	Century	(1893)	Cox, P.	170-220	
Cox, P.	Brownies in Fairyland (1st, 8vo, 118p, cloth, b/w)	Century	(1925)	Cox, P.	150-185	
Cox, P.	Brownies in the Philippines (1st, 4to, ibds, 144p)	Century	(1904)	Cox, P.	160-200	
Cox, P.	Brownies: Their Book (1st, 4to, grn ipcb, 144p, b/w, cep, PPP)	Century	(1887)	Cox, P.	240-300	R
Cox, P.	Brownies: Their Book (1st UK, 4to, green ibds, 144p)	L: T.F. Unwin	1888	Cox, P.	180-250	
Veale, E.	Captivating Stories/Animals (1st, 4to, yel cl, [96]p, 2-color)	Juvenile Pub.	(1908)	Cox, P.	150-225	
Cox, P.	Children's Funny Book (8vo, pcb, 30p)	Lothrop	(1879)	Cox, P.	85-100	
Veale, E.	Christmas Pudding (sm8vo, blue cl, p-o, 320p, b/w)	Caldwell	(1900)	Cox, P.	65-100	*
Cox, P.	Comic Yarns (1st, 8vo, 517p, blue/gilt, b/w, dep)	Hubbard	1889	Cox, P.	100-165	
Cox, P.	Frontier Humor (1st, 24mo, 343p, b/w)	Hubbard	(1895)	Cox, P.	60-85	
Veale, E.	Funny Foxes (8vo, 32p, wraps, b/w)	Hubbard	(1896)	Cox, P.	50	*
Cox, P.	Jolly Chinee (1st, thin 4to, p-o)	Conkey	(1900)	Cox, P.	90-130	
Cox, P.	Palmer Cox Brownie Primer (1st, 12mo, 108p, yel bds)	Century	1906	Cox, P.	100-165	
Cox, P.	Queer People (1st UK, sq4to, cloth)	L: T.F. Unwin	1896	Cox, P.	130-175	
Cox, P.	Queer People/Paws & Claws (1st, 4to, ibds, [119]p)	Hubbard	(1888)	Cox, P.	140-180	
Cox, P.	Queerie Queers with Hands, Wings & Claws (lg8vo, ibds, b/w)	Larkin	(1887)	Cox, P.	100-150	
Craig, E.G.	Nothing... (1st, sm4to, bds, 26pl)	L: Chatto	1925	Craig, E.G.	100-160	
Yeats, W.B.	Plays/Irish Theatre (8vo, 224p, brown bds, uncut, 4cp)	L: Bullen	1911	Craig, E.G.	100-140	
Craig, E.G.	Woodcuts & Some Words (1st, 4to, 122p, blue cl, 59pl)	L: Dent	1924	Craig, E.G.	80-135	
Kipling, R.	Rewards & Fairies (1st, 8vo, red/gilt, teg, 338p, 4pl)	L: MacMillan	1910	Craig, F.	85-100	
Gimmage, Peter	Picture Book of Ships (1st, 4to, 64p, fp color, pep)	MacMillan	1930	Craig, H.	35-65	*
Greene, G.	Little Horse Bus (1st, sq8vo, 35p, gilt, color, DJ)	L: Parrish	1952	Craigie, D.	200-300	
Greene, G.	Little Steam Roller (1st, sq8vo, 33p, DJ)	L: Parrish	1953	Craigie, D.	200-300	
Greene, G.	Little Train (1st, ob8vo, 42p, DJ)	L: Eyre/Spotts	1946	Craigie, D.	200-300	
Cramer, M.	Diamond Princess (ob8vo, 56p, 5cp)	NY: Warne	(1931)	Cramer, Rie	50-80	
Andersen, H.C.	Fairy Tales (1st, lg8vo, 349p, grey/gilt, 17 ticp)	L: H. Milford	(1921)	Cramer, Rie	250-300	
Grimm Bros.	Fairy Tales (1st, 4to, p-o, 367p, 23cp)	Penn	1922	Cramer, Rie	100-145	
Osbourne, M. (ed.)	Favorite Fairy Tales (1st, sm4to, 365p, p-o, 20cp by...)	Penn	(1930)	Cramer, Rie	50-70	
Douglas, B.	Favorite French Fairy Tales (1st AM, 8vo, 255p, 7cp)	Dodd	(1921)	Cramer, Rie	75-100	
Ransom, Will	Little Dutchy... (1st, 4to, ibds, 12 ticp)	L: Harrap	(1925)	Cramer, Rie	130-180	
Joan, Natalie	Little Mothers (ob8vo, ibds, p-o, 12 fp color)	L: H. Milford	[1908]	Cramer, Rie	100-140	
N/A	Old Songs/French & English (1st, 4to, p-o, 63p, 24cp)	Penn	1923	Cramer, Rie	100-150	
N/A	Oriental Fairy Tales (1st, 8vo, p-o, 627p, gilt, 16 ticp)	Duffield	1923	Cramer, Rie	85-120	
DeVries, P.J.C.	Princess Who Grew (1st, 8vo, 112p, p-o, col frn, 5pl)	Stokes	1927	Cramer, Rie	25-45	*
Andersen, H.C.	Snow Queen (sq8vo, 32p, ibds, 15 fp color)	L: Blackie	[1910]	Cramer, Rie	60-80	
Molesworth, M.	Adventures of Herr Baby (1st, sm4to, red/gilt, 171p, 13pl, dep)	L: MacMillan	1881	Crane, W.	100-160	*
Crane, W.	Aladdin's Picture Book (4to, unpag, ipcb, 24 color)	L: Routledge	[1880]	Crane, W.	250-400	
Konody, P.G.	Art of Walter Crane (1st, folio, teg, 147p, 16cp)	L: G. Bell	1902	Crane, W.	300-400	
Crane, W.	Baby's Bouquet (1st, ob8vo, ipcb, 56p, 11cp)	L: Routledge	[1878]	Crane, W.	200-300	
Crane, W.	Baby's Opera (1st AM, sq8vo, 54p, ipcb, color)	McLoughlin	[1877]	Crane, W.	185-265	
Crane, W.	Baby's Own Aesop (1st, 12mo, ipcb, 56p, color)	L: Routledge	1887	Crane, W.	200-300	
Crane, W.	Bases of Design (1st, 8vo, teg, blue/gilt, 365p)	L: G. Bell	1898	Crane, W.	145-180	
N/A	Beauty & the Beast Pict. Book (4to, yel cl, 24cp)	Dodd	[1915]	Crane, W.	100-150	*
Crane, W.	Blue Beard's Picture Book (1st, 4to, color)	L: Routledge	[1875]	Crane, W.	180-250	
Reid, K.E.J.	Book of Wedding Days (1st, 4to, red/silver, te silver, [108]p)	L: Longmans	1889	Crane, W.	250-300	
Beeching (ed.)	Book/Christmas Verse (1st, sm8vo, 174p, teg, gilt, designs by..)	L: Methuen	1895	Crane, W.	90-135	
Harrison, B.	Bric-a-Brac Stories (1st, 8vo, 24 illus, 299p)	Scribner	1885	Crane, W.	125-165	
Routledge, Wm.	Children's Musical Cinderella (1st, 4to, [30]p, wraps, 8cp)	L: Routledge	1879	Crane, W.	120-160	
Gould, F.J.	Children's Plutarch (1st, 8vo, 171p, 3pl)	Harper	1910	Crane, W.	100-150	
Molesworth, M.	Christmas Child (1st, 12mo, 223p, gilt, 7pl, cep)	L: MacMillan	1880	Crane, W.	100-150	
Molesworth, M.	Christmas-Tree Land (1st, 12mo, 223p, red cl, 7pl)	L: MacMillan	1884	Crane, W.	85-100	
N/A	Cinderella's Picture Book (1st, 4to, 8cp)	J. Lane	(1897)	Crane, W.	120-160	
Crane, W.	Columbia's Courtship (1st, 4to, [12]p, blue/gilt, 12cp)	Prang Co.	[1893]	Crane, W.	250-400	
Cervantes	Don Quixote (1st AM, lg8vo, 11cp)	J. Lane	1900	Crane, W.	85-120	
Cervantes	Don Quixote (1st, lg8vo, 245p, uncut, 11cp)	L: Blackie	1900	Crane, W.	170-220	
N/A	Fairy Ship (lg sq4to, wraps, 12p)	J. Lane	(1890)	Crane, W.	80-120	
Grimm Bros.	Fairy Tales (1st, 4to, ibds)	Worthington	(1888)	Crane, W.	140-200	
D'Aulnoy	Fairy Tales (1st, 8vo, 535p, teg, cvr by...)	L: Lawrence	1892	Crane, W.	180-250	
Crane, W.	Flora's Feast... (1st, 4to, ibds, 40cp, dep)	L: Cassell	1889	Crane, W.	200-300	
Crane, W.	Floral Fantasy (1st, 4to, 48p, cloth, 44cp)	L: Harper	1899	Crane, W.	185-260	
Crane, W.	Flower Wedding (1st, lg8vo, ipcb, 40cp)	L: Cassell	1905	Crane, W.	220-300	
Crane, W.	Flowers/Shakespeare's Garden (1st, 4to, ibds, uncut, 40cp)	L: Cassell	1906	Crane, W.	200-300	
Molesworth, M.	Four Winds Farm (1st, 8vo, blue cl, 180p, 6pl)	L: MacMillan	1886	Crane, W.	80-125	

AUTHOR	TITLE	PUBLISHER	DATE	ARTIST	PRICE	LC
Crane, W.	Goody Two Shoes... (4to, red cl, 18cp)	J. Lane	(1901)	Crane, W.	180-240	
Wilde, O.	Happy Prince (1st AM, 8vo, grey cl, 116p, 3pl)	Roberts	1888	Crane, W.	280-400	
N/A	Hind in the Wood (1st, 4to, wraps, 5cp)	L: Routledge	[1875]	Crane, W.	100-140	
Ellis, F.S.	History of Reynard the Fox (1st, 8vo, 289p, uncut, designs)	L: D. Nutt	1897	Crane, W.	80-100	
Grimm Bros.	Household Stories (1st, 12mo, 269p, AEG, 11pl, pep)	L: MacMillan	1882	Crane, W.	240-300	
Crane, W.	Ideals in Art (1st, 8vo, teg, 287p, gilt, b/w, cvr by...)	L: G. Bell	1905	Crane, W.	100-165	
Crane, W.	India Impressions (1st, lg8vo, green/gilt, 325p, 16p)	MacMillan	1907	Crane, W.	125-170	
Gilbert, Henry	King Arthur's Knights (1st, 8vo, teg, 367p, 16cp)	L: Jack	1911	Crane, W.	165-200	R
Gilbert, Henry	King Arthur's Knights (1st AM, 4to, 367p, gilt, teg, 16cp, dep)	Stokes	1911	Crane, W.	140-200	
Crane, W.	Legends for Lionel (1st, 4to, ibds, 40p, color)	L: Cassell	1887	Crane, W.	150-220	
Crane, W.	Line & Form (1st, 8vo, 282p, teg, blue/gilt)	L: G. Bell	1900	Crane, W.	140-220	
Molesworth, M.	Little Miss Peggy (1st, 12mo, red cl, 195p, 12pl)	L: MacMillan	1887	Crane, W.	85-100	
Crane, W.	Masque of Days (1st, 4to, [40]p, color, pep)	L: Cassell	1901	Crane, W.	200-300	
DeMorgan, M.	Necklace of Princess Fiorimonde (1st, 12mo, gilt, 184p, AEG, dep)	L: MacMillan	1880	Crane, W.	175-220	
Deland, M.	Old Garden (1st, 8vo, 114p, color, cvr by...)	L: McIlvaine	1893	Crane, W.	120-160	
Deland, M.	Old Garden (1st AM, 8vo, 114p, uncut, color, dep)	Houghton	1894	Crane, W.	85-100	
Marzials	Pan Pipes (1st, ob4to, tan ibds, 51p, dep, color)	L: Routl^Edge	1883	Crane, W.	170-230	
Crane, W.	Pothooks & Perseverance (1st, sq8vo, ibds, [24]p, color, pep)	L: Marcus Ward	1886	Crane, W.	200-300	
Crane, W.	Queen Summer (1st, lg4to, ibds, teg, 40p, color, pep)	L: Cassell	1891	Crane, W.	250-300	
Molesworth, M.	Rectory Children (1st, 8vo, 212p, 7pl)	L: MacMillan	1889	Crane, W.	70-90	*
Gilbert, Henry	Robin Hood... (1st AM, 8vo, teg, gilt, 16cp)	Stokes	(1912)	Crane, W.	90-120	
Crane, W.	Romance of the Three R's (1st, sq4to, ibds, [80]p, color, pep)	L: Marcus Ward	1886	Crane, W.	250-400	
Molesworth, M.	Rosy (1st, sm8vo, red/gilt, 204p, 8pl, cep)	L: MacMillan	1882	Crane, W.	80-100	
Calmour, A.C.	Rumbo Rhymes... (1st, lg8vo, green ibds, 101p, 23cp)	L: Harper	1911	Crane, W.	135-160	
Spenser, Edmund	Shepheard's Calander (1st, 8vo, ibds, [118]p, 12pl)	L: Harper	1898	Crane, W.	150-200	
Crane, W.	Sirens Three (1st, 4to, grey bds)	L: MacMillan	1886	Crane, W.	180-220	
Crane, W.	Slateandpencilvania (1st, sq8vo, ibds, 24p, color)	L: Marcus Ward	1885	Crane, W.	150-200	
Molesworth, M.	Studies & Stories (1st, 8vo, 256p, gilt, uncut, pep, frn by...)	L: A.D. Innes	1893	Crane, W.	125-160	
Molesworth, M.	Tapestry Room (1st, 8vo, red cl, unpag, 7pl)	L: MacMillan	1879	Crane, W.	100-145	
Kelly, A.	The Rosebud.... (1st, 4to, 78p, 20 ticp)	L: T.F. Unwin	1909	Crane, W.	180-225	
Rhead, G.W.	Treatment of Drapery in Art (1st, 8vo, 119p, 32pl, cvr by...)	L: G. Bell	1904	Crane, W.	95-130	
Crane, W.	Triplets (1st, lg4to, 1/500 signed)	L: Routledge	1899	Crane, W.	350-450	
Molesworth, M.	Two Little Waifs (1st, 8vo, 216p, 7pl)	L: MacMillan	(1883)	Crane, W.	100-140	
Molesworth, M.	US: An Old Fashioned Story (1st, 8vo, red/gilt, 240p, 7pl)	L: MacMillan	1886	Crane, W.	70-100	
Crane, W.	Valentine & Orson (4to, wraps, 8cp)	L: Routledge	[1873]	Crane, W.	140-200	
Crane, W.	Walter Crane's Picture Book (4to, ibds, [145]p, color)	Cupples	(1903)	Crane, W.	90-150	
Various	Wayfarer's Love (1st, 8vo, green/gilt, uncut, cvr by...)	L: Constable	1904	Crane, W.	60-80	
Crane, W.	William Morris to Whistler (1st, 12mo, 277p, blue cl)	L: G. Bell	1911	Crane, W.	80-100	
Hawthorne, N.	Wonder Book... (1st, lg8vo, 210p, cloth, 19cp)	L: McIlvaine	1892	Crane, W.	170-220	
Hawthorne, N.	Wonder Book... (1st AM, 4to, 210p, 19cp)	Houghton	1893	Crane, W.	140-180	
Hawthorne, N.	Wonder Book & Tanglewood Tales (1st, 8vo, teg, 421p)	Houghton	1898	Crane/Edwards	200-265	
N/A	Quiver of Love (1st, sq8vo, 152p, green cl, 8 ticp)	L: Marcus Ward	1876	Crane/Greenaway	250-350	
Sawyer, R.S.	Silver Sixpence (1st, 12mo, 331p, 4pl)	Harper	1921	Crank, J.H.	20-30	*
Mencken, H.L.	Christmas Story (1st {std}, sq12mo, [31]p, p-o, pep, color)	Knopf	1946	Crawford, Bill	65-80	*
Porter, G.S.	Freckles (1st, 8vo, teg, 433p, uncut, 6pl, PPPa)	Doubleday/Page	1904	Crawford, E.S.	400-600	
Butler, Chas.	Pigs is Pigs (1st, 12mo, 37p, 5pl)	McClure	1906	Crawford, W.	25-40	
Parker, A.C.	Skunny Wundy (1st, 4to, p-o, 262p, 6 ticp)	Doran	(1926)	Crawford, W.	65-90	
Credle, Ellis	Across the Cotton Patch (1st, ob4to, green cl, [59]p, b/w)	Nelson	1935	Credle, E.	50-80	*
Credle, Ellis	Big Doin's on Razorback Ridge (1st, 8vo, orange cl, 125p, b/w)	Nelson	(1956)	Credle, E.	25-40	*
Benet, Laura	Caleb's Luck (1st, lg8vo, [28]p, ibds, pep, color)	Grosset/Dunlap	1942	Credle, E.	65-80	R*
Credle, Ellis	Down, Down the Mountain (1st, 4to, [47]p, 2-color)	Nelson	1934	Credle, E.	60-80	*
Credle, Ellis	Goat that Went to School (1st, 8vo, [28]p, ipcb, color, pep)	Grosset/Dunlap	(1940)	Credle, E.	35-50	*
Credle, Ellis	Little Jeems Henry (1st, sq8vo, 44p, b/w)	Nelson	1936	Credle, E.	50-70	*
Credle, Ellis	Pig-O-Wee (1st, lg8vo, ibds, [44]p, color)	Rand/McNally	(1936)	Credle, E.	35-50	*
Lindsay, M.M.	Posey & the Pedlar (1st, sm8vo, tan cl, 186p, fp b/w)	Lothrop/Lee	1938	Credle, E.	30-45	*
Beim, Lorraine	Two is a Team (1st, 8vo, [61]p, red cl, fp color, pep)	Harcourt	(1945)	Crichlow, E.	35-60	*
Courlander, H.	Uncle Bouqui of Haiti (1st, 8vo, 126p, 1-color, pep)	Wm. Morrow	1942	Crockett, L.H.	25-45	*
Sherratt, J.L.	Goblin Gobblers (1st, ob8vo, 64p, bds, p-o, 10cp)	L: Warne	(1910)	Crombie, C.E.	130-185	
Crosby, P.	Dear Sooky (1st, 8vo, ipcb, 124p, 7 ticp, dep)	Putnam	1929	Crosby, P.L.	35-50	
Bacon, J.D.	Idyll/All Fool's Day (1st, 8vo, 120p, p-o, 10pl)	Dodd	1908	Crosby, R.M.	20-30	*
De La Mare, W.	Peacock Pie (1st AM, 8vo, 111p, blue/gilt, 2-color)	Holt	1936	Crowe, J.	30-50	*
Layard, George S.	Cruikshank's Portraits of Himself (1st, 8vo, 98p, 17pl)	L: Spencer	1897	Cruikshank, G.	100-165	*
Grego, J.	Cruikshank's Water Colours (1st, 4to, gilt, teg, 326p, 67cp)	L: A&C Black	1903	Cruikshank, G.	90-145	
Schultz, J.W.	In the Great Apache Forest (1st, 8vo, 225p, green cl, 4pl)	Houghton	1920	Cue, H.	25-40	*
Davies, M.C.	Little Freckled Person (1st, 8vo, 104p, 8pl)	Houghton	1919	Cue, H.	20-30	*
Eaton, S.	More about Teddy B. & Teddy G. (1st, 4to, ibds, p-o, 186p)	Stern	1907	Culver, R.K.	250-350	
Eaton, S.	Roosevelt Bears Abroad (1st, 4to, ibds, p-o, 178p, 12cp)	Stern	1908	Culver, R.K.	280-400	
Vernede, R.E.	Fair Dominion (1st, 8vo, blue cl, teg, 293p, uncut, 12cp)	J. Pott	1911	Cuneo, C.	25-45	
Brereton, F.S.	Indian & Scout (1st, 8vo, 368p, gilt, 6pl)	L: Blackie	1911	Cuneo, C.	30-45	
Bindloss, H.	Masters of the Wheat-Lands (1st, 8vo, 354p)	Stokes	(1910)	Cuneo, C.	25-40	*
Harris-Burland, J.	Princess Thora (1st, 8vo, 360p, blue/gilt, 4pl)	Little/Brown	1904	Cuneo, C.	80-130	
O'Hara, Mary	My Friend Flicka (1st, 8vo, 285p, col frn, 14pl, DJ)	Lippincott	1941	Curry, J.S.	45-60	

AUTHOR	TITLE	PUBLISHER	DATE	ARTIST	PRICE	LC
Clay, Beatrice	Stories of King Arthur (1st, 8vo, 322p)	L: Dent	1905	Curtis, D.	25-40	*
Ryan, M.E.	Flute of the Gods (1st, 8vo, 333p, p-o, 24pl)	Stokes	(1909)	Curtis, E.	30-45	
Cooke, E.V.	Story Club (1st, 8vo, p-o, 210p, cp)	Dodge	(1912)	Curtis, E.	25-40	*
Gray, Eliz. J.	Meredith's Ann (1st {std}, sm8vo, yellow cl, 267p, col frn, pep)	Doubleday/Page	1927	Cutts, G.B.	20-30	*
Gray, Eliz. J.	Tangle Garden (1st {std}, sm8vo, 327p, pep, col frn by...)	Doubleday/Dor.	1928	Cutts, G.B.	20-30	*
Burglon, N.	Children of the Soil (1st {std}, 8vo, 272p, pep, col frn, NH)	Doubleday/Dor.	1932	D'Aulaire, E.P.	65-80	*
Everson, Howard	Coming o/t Dragon Ships (1st {std}, 8vo, 128p, col frn, 9pl pep)	Dutton	1931	D'Aulaire, E.P.	45-60	*
Seabrook, Katie	Gao of the Ivory Coast (1st, 8vo, 121p, col frn, 4pl)	Coward	(1931)	D'Aulaire, E.P.	45-65	*
Scott, Gabriel	Kari (1st {std}, 8vo, 242p, blue cl, uncut, col frn, 7pl, pep)	Doubleday/Dor.	1931	D'Aulaire, E.P.	30-45	*
Mattheson, J.	Needle in the Haystack (1st, sq8vo, 189p, blue cl, 8cp, pep)	Wm. Morrow	1930	D'Aulaire, E.P.	35-50	
Mukerji, D.G.	Rama, Hero of India (1st {std}, 8vo, red/gilt, 219p, dep)	Dutton	(1930)	D'Aulaire, E.P.	45-60	*
D'Aulaire, I.& E.	Abraham Lincoln (1st {std}, folio, 55p, ibds, 5 fp color, CM)	Doubleday/Dor.	1939	D'Aulaire, I.& E.	80-120	*
D'Aulaire, I.& E.	Animals Everywhere (1st, 4to, yel bds, [29]p, color, pep, DJ)	Doubleday	1954	D'Aulaire, I.& E.	60-85	*
D'Aulaire, I.& E.	Benjamin Franklin (1st {std}, 4to, ibds, [48]p, color, DJ)	Doubleday	(1950)	D'Aulaire, I.& E.	50-70	*
D'Aulaire, I.& E.	Buffalo Bill (1st {std}, 4to, ibds, [40]p, color)	Doubleday	1952	D'Aulaire, I.& E.	50-80	
D'Aulaire, I.& E.	Children o/t North Lights (1st {std}, lg4to, ibds, [40]p, color, pep)	Viking	1935	D'Aulaire, I.& E.	65-80	
D'Aulaire, I.& E.	Columbus (1st {std}, 4to, ibds, 57p, pep, color)	Doubleday	1955	D'Aulaire, I.& E.	70-110	R*
D'Aulaire, I.& E.	Conquest of the Atlantic (1st, lg4to, ibds, 55p, color, DJ)	Viking	1933	D'Aulaire, I.& E.	80-120	
Burglon, N.	Cuckoo Calls (1st, 8vo, 280p, col frn, pep)	Winston	(1940)	D'Aulaire, I.& E.	25-40	*
D'Aulaire, I.& E.	Don't Count Your Chicks (1st {std} folio, [40]p, ibds, col, pep)	Doubleday/Dor.	1943	D'Aulaire, I.& E.	80-120	R
Asbjornsen, P.C.	East o/t Sun/West o/t Moon (1st, 4to, 188p, 22 fp b/w, pep)	Viking	1938	D'Aulaire, I.& E.	40-65	*
D'Aulaire, I.& E.	Foxie (1st {std}, ob4to, red cl, [40]p, b/w, pep, DJ)	Doubleday	1949	D'Aulaire, I.& E.	65-85	
D'Aulaire, I.& E.	George Washington (1st {std}, 4to, ibds, [55]p, 13 fp color)	Doubleday/Dor.	(1936)	D'Aulaire, I.& E.	30-45	
Zwilgmeyer, D.	Johnny Blossom (1st, 8vo, yellow cl, 157p, pep, 10 fp b/w)	Pilgrim Press	(1948)	D'Aulaire, I.& E.	45-65	*
D'Aulaire, I.& E.	Leif the Lucky (1st {std}, lg4to, ibds, [56]p, color, pep, DJ)	Doubleday/Dor.	1941	D'Aulaire, I.& E.	70-100	
D'Aulaire, I.& E.	Lord's Prayer (1st {std}, lg4to, [32]p, ibds, color, pep)	Doubleday/Dor.	1934	D'Aulaire, I.& E.	60-80	
D'Aulaire, I.& E.	Magic Meadow (1st {std}, lg4to, ibds, 55p, pep, 25 color)	Doubleday	1958	D'Aulaire, I.& E.	50-70	*
D'Aulaire, I.& E.	Magic Rug (1st {std}, ob4to, [63]p, ibds, pep, color)	Doubleday/Dor.	1931	D'Aulaire, I.& E.	70-100	
D'Aulaire, I.& E.	Nils (1st {std}, 4to, ibds, [40]p, color, pep, DJ)	Doubleday	(1948)	D'Aulaire, I.& E.	65-90	
D'Aulaire, I.& E.	Ola (1st {std}, 4to, ibds, [55]p, color, pep, DJ)	Doubleday/Dor.	1932	D'Aulaire, I.& E.	75-120	R
D'Aulaire, I.& E.	Ola & Blakken & Line... (1st {std}, folio, [39]p, ibds, color)	Doubleday/Dor.	1933	D'Aulaire, I.& E.	65-80	
D'Aulaire, I.& E.	Pocahantas (1st {std}, 4to, ibds, [40]p, b/w)	Doubleday	1946	D'Aulaire, I.& E.	50-80	
Aanrud, Hans.	Sidsel Longskirt & Solve Suntrap (1st, 8vo, 257p, col frn, pep)	Winston	(1935)	D'Aulaire, I.& E.	30-45	
D'Aulaire, I.& E.	Star Spangled Banner (1st {std}, lg4to, ibds, [38]p, col, pep)	Doubleday/Dor.	1942	D'Aulaire, I.& E.	60-90	
D'Aulaire, I.& E.	Too Big (1st {std}, sq8vo, ibds, [32]p, color, pep)	Doubleday/Dor.	1945	D'Aulaire, I.& E.	45-70	
D'Aulaire, I.& E.	Wings for Per (1st {std}, lg4to, ibds, [40]p, color, pep, DJ)	Doubleday/Dor.	(1944)	D'Aulaire, I.& E.	70-100	
Morrow, Eliz.	Beast, Bird & Fish (1st {std}, 4to, [59]p, color, pep)	Knopf	1933	D'Harnoncourt, R.	80-130	*
D'Harnoncourt, R.	Mexicana (1st {std}, 4to, ipcb, fp b/w, dep)	Knopf	1931	D'Harnoncourt, R.	65-90	*
Morrow, Eliz.	Painted Pig (1st, 4to, ipcb, 32p, fp color, pep)	Knopf	1930	D'Harnoncourt, R.	80-120	R
Baring-Gould, S.	Broom-Squire (1st, 8vo, 384p, 12pl)	L: Methuen	1896	Dadd, Frank	50-65	*
Irving, W.	Old Christmas (1st, 8vo, 115p, gilt, p-o, teg, 2cp, 16pl)	Putnam	(1916)	Dadd, Frank	35-50	*
Stevens, D.K.	Ballads of the Be-Ba-Boes (1st, 4to, yellow cl, 100p)	Houghton	1913	Daland, K.M.	80-100	
Dalgliesh, A.	Sailor Sam (1st, sq12mo, ipcb, [38]p, cep, color)	Scribner	1935	Dalgliesh, A.	30-45	
Dali, S.	50 Secrets... (1st, 8vo, DJ)	Dial	1948	Dali, S.	100-145	
Cellini, B.	Autobiography of Benvenuto Cellini (1st, sm4to, 442p, 15cp)	Doubleday	1946	Dali, S.	120-165	
DeMontaigne	Essays (1st, 8vo, cp)	Garden City	1947	Dali, S.	160-230	
Dali, S.	Hidden Faces (1st, 8vo, black cl, 413p, b/w frn, DJ)	Dial	1944	Dali, S.	165-220	
Sandoz, M.	House Without Windows (1st, 8vo, DJ)	(London)	1950	Dali, S.	100-165	
Shakespeare, Wm.	Macbeth (black bds, 125p)	Garden City	1936	Dali, S.	170-230	
Sandoz, M.	On the Verge (1st {std}, 4to, 127p, col frn, cep, DJ)	Doubleday	1950	Dali, S.	150-200	
Dali, S.	Secret Life of... (1st AM, 4to, p-o, 400p, buckram, 3cp)	Dial	1942	Dali, S.	130-165	
Sandoz, M.	The Maze (1st {std}, 8vo, bds, 110p, uncut, 13pl, DJ)	Doubleday	1945	Dali, S.	160-220	
Dana, M.P.	Jingle Book (1st, sm4to, [32]p, color)	W.R. Scott	1940	Dana, M.	40-60	*
Ashley, Fred	Temple of Fire (1st, 8vo, green/gilt, 332p, 8pl)	L: I. Pitman	1905	Daniel, V.S.	50-80	*
Lyman, E.B.	Me'ow Jones (1st, 8vo, p-o, 91p, 5cp, pep)	Doran	(1917)	Daniels, J.	25-40	
Darwin, Bernard	Mr. Tootleoo & Co. (1st AM, ob 4to, [45]p, ibds, 22 fp color)	Harper	(1936)	Darwin, E.	250-400	*
Aesopus	Fables of Aesop (1st, 8vo, 254p, color)	Whitman	(1925)	Dash, J.E.	25-40	
Daugherty, J.	Abraham Lincoln (1st, 4to, 216p, fp 1-color, DJ)	Viking	1943	Daugherty, J.	45-60	
Daugherty, Sonia	All Things New (1st, sm8vo, 296p, orange cl, b/w)	Nelson	1936	Daugherty, J.	25-40	*
Daugherty, J.	Andy & the Lion (1st, sm4to, ipcb, [79]p, color, pep, DJ, CH)	Viking	1938	Daugherty, J.	90-120	R
Hunt, M.L.	Better Known as Johnny Appleseed (1st {std}, 8vo, 212p, cep, NH)	Lippincott	(1950)	Daugherty, J.	45-70	R*
Rickert, Edith	Blacksmith & the Birds (1st {std}, 12mo, 46p orang cl, pep, b/w)	Doubleday/Dor.	1928	Daugherty, J.	30-45	*
Irving, W.	Bold Dragon (1st, 8vo, 240p, blue cl, b/w, pep, DJ)	Knopf	1930	Daugherty, J.	35-50	
Finger, C.J.	Courageous Companions (1st {std}, lg8vo, 304p, gilt, pep, 10pl)	Longmans	(1929)	Daugherty, J.	30-50	
White, S.E.	Daniel Boone (1st, 8vo, 274p, p-o, 4cp, 10pl, DJ)	Doubleday/Page	1926	Daugherty, J.	50-65	
Daugherty, J.	Daniel Boone (1st {this pub}, 4to, 95p, color, pep, NM)	Viking	1939	Daugherty, J.	65-90	
Rogers, Cameron	Drake's Quest (1st, sm8vo, 284p, col frn)	Doubleday/Page	1927	Daugherty, J.	25-45	*
Sandburg, C.	Early Moon (1st {std}, lg8vo, 136p, b/w)	Harcourt	(1930)	Daugherty, J.	70-90	*
Elkin, Ben	Gillespie & the Guards (1st, 4to, 62p, fp 1-color, CH)	Viking	1956	Daugherty, J.	50-90	*
Aydelotte, Dora	Green Gravel (1st, 12mo, green cl, uncut, 249p, b/w)	Appleton/Cent.	1937	Daugherty, J.	25-40	*
Irving, W.	History of New York (1st {std}, 4to, 427p, uncut, pep, DJ)	Doran	1928	Daugherty, J.	65-90	R
Dix, B.M.	Hugh Gwyeth: Roundhead Cavalier (1st, 12mo, pep, b/w)	MacMillan	1928	Daugherty, J.	30-45	*

AUTHOR	TITLE	PUBLISHER	DATE	ARTIST	PRICE	LC
N/A	In the Beginning... (1st, 4to, cloth, color, DJ)	NY: OUP	(1941)	Daugherty, J.	45-60	
Burrows, Eliz.	Irene of Tundra Towers (1st {std}, sm8vo, 311p, col frn)	Doubleday/Dor.	1928	Daugherty, J.	30-45	*
Horne, Richard H.	King Penguin (1st, 12mo, tan cl, 95p, 4cp, pep)	MacMillan	1925	Daugherty, J.	25-40	*
N/A	Kingdom & Power & Glory (1st, 4to, 170p, brown cl, DJ)	Knopf	1929	Daugherty, J.	40-65	
Bruce, M.	Kris & Kristina (1st {std}, 8vo, ibds, 60p, color, pep)	Doubleday/Dor.	(1927)	Daugherty, J.	30-45	
Daugherty, J.	Lincoln's Gettysburg Address (1st {std}, lg4to, ibds, [40]p, col)	Whitman	(1947)	Daugherty, J.	45-70	
Daugherty, Sonia	Mashinka's Secret (1st, 12mo, 276p, 28 b/w)	Stokes	1932	Daugherty, J.	20-30	*
Ross, M.I.	Morgan's Fourth Son (1st {std}, 8vo, 252p, uncut, 6pl)	Harper	(1940)	Daugherty, J.	25-40	
Irwin, V.	Mountain of Jade (1st, 8vo, 236p, cloth)	MacMillan	1926	Daugherty, J.	25-40	
Daugherty, J.	Of Courage Undaunted... (1st, sm4to, 168p, b/w, DJ)	Viking	1951	Daugherty, J.	35-60	
Pierson, C.D.	Plucky Allens (1st, sm8vo, green/gilt, 327p, 5 fp b/w)	Dutton	(1925)	Daugherty, J.	25-45	*
Daugherty, J.	Poor Richard (1st, 4to, brown cl, 158p, 2-color, pep, DJ)	Viking	1941	Daugherty, J.	40-60	
Swift, H.H.	Railroad to Freedom (1st, 8vo, 364p, pep, NH)	Harcourt	(1932)	Daugherty, J.	45-60	*
Miers, E.S.	Rainbow Book/American History (1st {std}, 4to, 319p, color, DJ)	World	(1955)	Daugherty, J.	35-50	*
Quiller-Couch, A.	Splendid Spur (1st, 4to, orange cl, 274p, p-o, 15cp)	Doran	(1927)	Daugherty, J.	35-50	*
Quiller-Couch, A.	Splendid Spur (1st {this pub.}, lg8vo, p-o, 274p, 4cp, pep)	Garden City	1937	Daugherty, J.	30-45	
Watson, Eliz.	Story of Bread (1st {std}, 12mo, 48p, 4cp, pep)	Harper	1927	Daugherty, J.	25-45	*
Parsons, G.	Stream of History (1st, lg8vo, 590p, gilt, b/w, pep)	Scribner	1928	Daugherty, J.	30-45	
Garis, H.	Tuftoo the Clown (1st, sm8vo, 283p, 10 b/w, pep)	Appleton	1928	Daugherty, J.	30-45	*
Stowe, H.B.	Uncle Tom's Cabin (1st, 8vo, 446p, pep)	E. McCann	(1929)	Daugherty, J.	35-50	*
Daugherty, Sonia	Vanka's Donkey (1st, 8vo, ivory cl, 62p, 1-color, pep)	Stokes	1940	Daugherty, J.	45-60	*
Daugherty, Sonia	Way of an Eagle (1st, 8vo, 352p, fp b/w)	NY: OUP	(1941)	Daugherty, J.	25-45	*
Daugherty, J.	West of Boston (1st, 4to, 94p, yellow cl)	Viking	1956	Daugherty, J.	20-30	*
Doyle, A.C.	White Company (1st, 8vo, 403p, col frn, 2 dp pl, 7pl)	Harper	1928	Daugherty, J.	35-50	*
Daugherty, J.	Wild Wild West (1st, 4to, ibds, [34]p, color, pep)	McKay	(1948)	Daugherty, J.	30-50	
Daugherty, Sonia	Wings of Glory (1st, 8vo, 236p, gilt, color)	NY: OUP	(1940)	Daugherty, J.	25-40	*
Shapiro, I.	Yankee Thunder (1st, 8vo, 205p, cloth, DJ)	J. Messner	(1944)	Daugherty, J.	30-45	
Robinson, W.	Golden Palace/Neverland (1st, sm8vo, green cl, 307p, 6cp)	Dutton	1907	Davidson, C.D.	50-70	*
Madison, L.F.	Captain Kitty Colonial (1st, 8vo, blue cl, 309p, p-o, col frn)	Penn	1923	Davis, M.	20-40	*
Stevenson, R.L.	Child's Garden of Verses (1st, 16mo, 121p, col frn, b/w)	MacMillan	1927	Davis, M.	20-35	*
Coatsworth, E.	House-Boat Summer (1st, 8vo, 191p, p-o, 1-color, pep, DJ)	MacMillan	1942	Davis, M.	25-45	
Coatsworth, E.	Littlest House (1st, 8vo, p-o, 152p, 1-color, pep)	MacMillan	1940	Davis, M.	25-40	
Brink, C.R.	Magical Melons (1st, 8vo, 193p, grey cloth, b/w)	MacMillan	1944	Davis, M.	20-30	*
Davis, Rbt.	Partners of Powder Hole (1st, 8vo, 167p)	Holiday House	(1947)	Davis, M.	20-30	*
Coatsworth, E.	Plum Daffy Adventure (1st {std}, 8vo, 161p, blue cl, b/w, pep)	MacMillan	1947	Davis, M.	35-50	*
Rossetti, C.	Sing-Song (1st, 16mo, green cl, 122p, b/w, pep)	MacMillan	1924	Davis, M.	25-40	
Welles, W.	Skipping Along (1st, 8vo, green cl, 52p, b/w)	MacMillan	1931	Davis, M.	20-30	*
Tileston, M.W.	Sugar & Spice/All That's Nice (1st, 8vo, red/gilt, 220p, 4cp)	Little/Brown	1928	Davis, M.	30-45	
Richards, L.E.	Tirra Lirra (1st, 8vo, 194p, col frn, pep, NH)	Little/Brown	1932	Davis, M.	35-50	*
Various	Told Under the Blue Umbrella (1st, 8vo, 161p, b/w)	MacMillan	1933	Davis, M.	25-40	*
Alcott, L.M.	Under the Lilacs (1st, 8vo, 284p, col frn, cp)	Little/Brown	1928	Davis, M.	25-40	
Ovington, Mary W.	Zeke (1st, sm8vo, blue cl, 205p, uncut, b/w)	Harcourt	(1931)	Davis, N.H.	80-120	*
Smith, G.	Boys of Marmiton Prairie (1st, sm8vo, 262p, 5pl)	Little/Brown	1899	Day, B.C.	25-40	*
Pyle, Kath.	Where the Wind Blows (1st, 4to, 120p, p-o, 11cp)	R.H. Russell	1902	Day, B.C.	200-250	
Pyle, Kath.	Where the Wind Blows (1st {this pub.}, 8vo, 295p, 10pl)	Dutton	(1910)	Day, B.C.	70-100	*
Garis, H.	White Crystals (1st, 8vo, tan cl, 243p, 6pl)	Little/Brown	1904	Day, B.C.	35-50	
Baker, Geo.	Point Lace & Diamonds (1st, 4to, 82p, 12cp)	Stokes	1892	Day, F.	90-145	
Totheroh, D.	David Hotfoot (1st, 8vo, p-o, 246p, col frn, 4pl)	Doran	(1926)	Day, M.	25-40	
Jewett, E.M.	Egyptian Tales of Magic (1st, sm8vo, 257p, color)	Little/Brown	1924	Day, M.	25-40	*
Bergengren, R.W.	Jane, Joseph & John (1st, 4to, ibds, 62p, 6cp)	Atl. Month Pr.	(1918)	Day, M.	35-50	*
Dunbar, A.	Once There was a Prince (1st, 8vo, 302p, blue cl, pep, col frn)	Little/Brown	1928	Day, M.	35-50	*
King, B.	Ruffs & Pompons (1st, 8vo, 256p, col frn, 6pl, pep)	Little/Brown	1924	Day, M.	25-40	
Brown, A.F.	Under the Rowan Tree (1st, 8vo, p-o, 189p, col frn, pep)	Houghton	1926	Day, M.	20-35	*
Jewett, E.M.	Wonder Tales from Tibet (1st, sm8vo, 183p, green cl, 8cp)	Little/Brown	1922	Day, M.	25-40	*
Coatsworth, E.	Alice-All-by-Herself (1st, 8vo, 181p, col frn, 7pl, pep, DJ)	MacMillan	1937	DeAngeli, M.	50-70	
DeAngeli, M.	Black Fox of Lorne (1st {std}, 4to, 191p, 11 fp b/w, NH)	Doubleday	1956	DeAngeli, M.	45-60	*
DeAngeli, M.	Bright April (1st {std}, sq4to, 86p, color, pep, DJ)	Doubleday	(1946)	DeAngeli, M.	45-65	
Means, F.C.	Candle in the Mist (1st, sm8vo, 252p, blue cl, pep, 4pl)	Houghton	1931	DeAngeli, M.	30-50	*
Kelly, Eric P.	Christmas Nightingale (1st, 8vo, red cl, 73p, 4 b/w)	MacMillan	1932	DeAngeli, M.	25-40	
DeAngeli, M.	Copper-Toed Boots (1st {std}, sm4to, ibds, [92]p, color, pep)	Doubleday/Dor.	1938	DeAngeli, M.	40-65	
Sackett, Rose M.	Cousin from Clare (1st, 8vo, 270p, green cl, 4pl)	MacMillan	1932	DeAngeli, M.	30-45	
Meigs, C.	Covered Bridge (1st, sq8vo, 145p, blue cl, col frn, b/w)	MacMillan	1936	DeAngeli, M.	35-50	
DeAngeli, M.	Door in the Wall (1st {std}, 8vo, brown cl, 112p, pep, DJ, NM)	Doubleday	(1949)	DeAngeli, M.	70-110	R
Yonge, C.M.	Dove in the Eagle's Nest (1st, 8vo, 294p, 3cp, 8pl, pep, DJ)	MacMillan	1926	DeAngeli, M.	50-70	
DeAngeli, M.	Elin's Amerika (1st {std}, sq8vo, tan cl, [96]p, color, pep, DJ)	Doubleday/Dor.	1941	DeAngeli, M.	45-65	
DeAngeli, M.	Henner's Lydia (1st {std}, sq8vo, ibds, [70]p, color)	Doubleday/Dor.	1936	DeAngeli, M.	45-60	
Robinson, Tom P.	In & Out (1st, lg8vo, 140p, color, DJ)	Viking	1943	DeAngeli, M.	35-60	
DeAngeli, M.	Jared's Island (1st {std}, sm4to, blue/gilt, 95p, col frn, DJ)	Doubleday	1947	DeAngeli, M.	50-65	
Gemmill, J.	Joan Wanted a Kitty (1st, 8vo, blue cl, 150p, pep, color, DJ)	Winston	(1937)	DeAngeli, M.	50-75	
DeAngeli, M.	Just Like David (1st {std}, 8vo, green cl, 122p, color, pep)	Doubleday	(1951)	DeAngeli, M.	35-50	
Gale, Eliz.	Katrina Van Ost & Silver Rose (1st, sm8vo, 294p, fp b/w)	Putnam	(1934)	DeAngeli, M.	20-30	*
Yonge, C.M.	Lances of Lynwood (1st, 12mo, green cl, 217p, col frn, 6pl, pep)	MacMillan	1929	DeAngeli, M.	25-40	*

AUTHOR	TITLE	PUBLISHER	DATE	ARTIST	PRICE	LC
Yonge, C.M.	Little Duke (1st, 8vo, blue cl, 3cp, 7pl, pep)	MacMillan	1927	DeAngeli, M.	35-50	*
Forbes, Helen	Mario's Castle (1st, 12mo, 198p, col frn, pep, 3pl)	MacMillan	1928	DeAngeli, M.	35-50	*
Gray, Eliz. J.	Meggy McIntosh (1st {std}, 8vo, 274p, col frn, pep, NH)	Doubleday/Dor.	1930	DeAngeli, M.	50-75	*
Meigs, C.	New Moon (1st, 8vo, blue/gilt, 251p, col frn)	MacMillan	1924	DeAngeli, M.	35-50	*
DeAngeli, M.	Nursery & Mother Goose Rhymes (1st {std}, folio, 192p, col, CH)	Doubleday	1954	DeAngeli, M.	70-100	
DeAngeli, M.	Petite Suzanne (1st {std}, sq4to, ibds, [88]p, color, pep, DJ)	Doubleday/Dor.	1937	DeAngeli, M.	50-70	
Hawkins, Q.	Prayers & Graces/Small Children (1st, sq8vo, [32]p, ibds, color)	Grosset/Dunlap	(1941)	DeAngeli, M.	30-50	*
Yonge, C.M.	Prince & the Page (1st, 8vo, 246p, blue cl, 3cp, 8pl, pep)	MacMillan	1925	DeAngeli, M.	45-60	*
Kyle, Anne D.	Red Sky over Rome (1st, 8vo, 260p, 8pl)	Houghton	1938	DeAngeli, M.	35-50	*
DeAngeli, M.	Skippack School (1st {std}, sq8vo, [88]p, color, pep, DJ)	Doubleday/Dor.	1939	DeAngeli, M.	50-65	
DeAngeli, M.	Summer Day with Ted & Nina (1st {std}, 8vo, ibds, [32]p, color)	Doubleday/Dor.	1940	DeAngeli, M.	65-80	
DeAngeli, M.	Ted & Nina Go/Grocery Store (1st {std}, ob12mo ibds, color, pep)	Doubleday/Dor.	1935	DeAngeli, M.	45-60	
DeAngeli, M.	Ted & Nina Have/Happy Rainy Day (1st {std}, ob12mo, ibds, col)	Doubleday/Dor.	1936	DeAngeli, M.	45-60	
DeAngeli, M.	Thee, Hannah! (1st {std}, sq8vo, unpag, color, DJ)	Doubleday/Dor.	1940	DeAngeli, M.	60-90	R
Worth, Kath.	They Loved to Laugh (1st {std}, sm8vo, grey cl, 269p, b/w, pep)	Doubleday/Dor.	1942	DeAngeli, M.	25-45	*
DeAngeli, M.	Up the Hill (1st {std}, sq8vo, tan cl, 88p, color, pep, DJ)	Doubleday/Dor.	1942	DeAngeli, M.	40-60	
DeAngeli, M.	Yonie Wondernose (1st {std}, sq4to, ibds, color, pep, DJ, CH)	Doubleday/Dor.	1944	DeAngeli, M.	65-90	
Montgomery, F.T.	Billy Whiskers at the Fair (1st, 4to, ibds, 163p, cp)	Saalfield	(1909)	DeBebian, A.	30-50	*
Pickard, W.B.	Adventures of Alcassin (1st, 8vo, 352p, red/gilt)	L: J. Cape	1936	DeBosschere, J.	35-50	
DeBosschere, J.	Beasts & Men (4to, 179p, green cl, 12cp, pep)	L: Heinemann	(1918)	DeBosschere, J.	150-200	
DeBosschere, J.	Christmas Tales of Flanders (1st AM, 4to, 144p, gilt, 12cp, pep)	Dodd	1917	DeBosschere, J.	160-200	
DeBosschere, J.	City Curious (1st, lg8vo, [179]p, 8cp, pep)	L: Heinemann	(1920)	DeBosschere, J.	160-200	
DeBosschere, J.	City Curious (1st AM, sq8vo, yellow cl, [179]p, 8cp, pep)	Dodd/Hein.	1920	DeBosschere, J.	160-200	
DeBosschere, J.	Closed Door (1st, 8vo, 131p, 16pl)	L: J. Lane	1917	DeBosschere, J.	100-140	
Cervantes	Don Quixote (1st, lg4to, 311p, black/gilt, 25 color)	L: Constable	1922	DeBosschere, J.	100-160	
Aristophanes	Eleven Comedies (1st, 8vo, 2 vols, black/gilt, 16cp)	H. Liveright	1928	DeBosschere, J.	80-120	
Anthony, E. & J.	Fairies Up-to-Date (1st, lg8vo, 189p, red cl, p-o, unpag, col)	Little/Brown	1923	DeBosschere, J.	150-200	
DeBosschere, J.	Folk Tales/Flanders (1st AM, 4to, 179p, teg, gilt, 12cp)	Dodd	1918	DeBosschere, J.	140-185	
Aldington, W.	Golden Asse/Lucius Apuleius (8vo, brown/gilt, 8cp)	L: J. Lane	1923	DeBosschere, J.	75-100	
Swift, J.	Gulliver's Travels (1st AM, 4to, 135p, blue/gilt, 4cp)	Dodd/Hein.	[1920]	DeBosschere, J.	85-130	
DeBosschere, J.	Gulliver's Travels/Lilliput (1st, 4to, 135p, 4cp, pink cl)	L: Heinemann	(1920)	DeBosschere, J.	150-200	
Cervantes	History of Don Quixote... (1st, 4to, gilt, 25cp)	(London)	1922	DeBosschere, J.	80-120	
DeBosschere, J.	Love Books of Ovid (1st, lg8vo, blue/gilt, 16cp)	L: J. Lane	1930	DeBosschere, J.	35-50	*
Aldington (tr.)	The Decameron... (1st, lg8vo, black cl, p-o, 576p, 16cp)	Garden City	(1930)	DeBosschere, J.	45-65	
Sinclair, M.	Uncanny Stories (1st, 8vo, red/gilt, 362p, 21pl)	MacMillan	1923	DeBosschere, J.	80-120	
DeBosschere, J.	Weird Islands (1st, sm4to, 210p, blue cl)	L: Chapman	1921	DeBosschere, J.	100-145	*
DeBrunhoff, J.	ABC of Babar (1st AM, sq8vo, ibds, [60]p, color, pep)	Random	(1936)	DeBrunhoff, J.	180-300	
DeBrunhoff, J.	Babar & Father Christmas (1st AM, lg4to, ibds, [40]p, color)	Random	(1940)	DeBrunhoff, J.	280-400	
DeBrunhoff, J.	Babar & His Children (1st AM, folio, ibds, [40]p, color, pep)	Random	(1938)	DeBrunhoff, J.	250-400	R
DeBrunhoff, J.	Babar & Zephir (1st, 4to, ibds, 39p, color)	Random	(1942)	DeBrunhoff, J.	100-140	*
DeBrunhoff, J.	Babar the King (1st AM, lg folio, 48p, ibds, color, pep)	Smith/Haas	1935	DeBrunhoff, J.	280-400	R
DeBrunhoff, J.	Babar the King (1st {this format}, sq8vo, ibds, 48p, color)	Random	(1935)	DeBrunhoff, J.	100-140	*
DeBrunhoff, J.	Babar the King (1st UK, folio, ibds, color)	L: Methuen	1936	DeBrunhoff, J.	250-400	
DeBrunhoff, J.	Babar's Friend Zephir (1st UK, folio, ibds, color)	L: Methuen	1937	DeBrunhoff, J.	200-300	
DeBrunhoff, J.	Story of Babar (1st {this format}, sq8vo, ibds, 48p, color)	Random	(1933)	DeBrunhoff, J.	100-140	*
DeBrunhoff, J.	Story of Babar (1st AM, folio, 47p, ibds, color, pep)	Smith/Haas	1933	DeBrunhoff, J.	350-500	
DeBrunhoff, J.	Travels of Babar (1st AM, folio, ibds, 47p, color, pep)	Smith/Haas	1934	DeBrunhoff, J.	300-450	
DeBrunhoff, J.	Travels of Babar (1st {this format}, sq8vo, 48p, ibds, col)	Random	(1934)	DeBrunhoff, J.	100-140	*
DeBrunhoff, J.	Zephir's Holidays (1st AM, folio, [40]p, ibds, color, pep)	Random	(1937)	DeBrunhoff, J.	250-400	R
DeBrunhoff, L.	Babar's Cousin that Rascal Arthur (1st, folio, 47p, ibds, col)	Random	(1948)	DeBrunhoff, L.	220-350	
DeBrunhoff, L.	Babar's Picnic (1st AM, folio, 39p, ibds, color)	Random	(1949)	DeBrunhoff, L.	280-400	
DeBrunhoff, L.	Babar's Visit to Bird Island (1st UK, sm folio, ibds, color)	L: Methuen	(1952)	DeBrunhoff, L.	280-400	
DeBrunhoff, L.	Picnic at Babar's (1st UK, folio, 40p, ibds, color)	L: Methuen	(1950)	DeBrunhoff, L.	200-280	*
Allee, M.H.	Ann's Surprising Summer (1st, sm8vo, 198p, b/w, pep)	Houghton	1933	DeGogorza, M.	25-40	*
Allee, M.H.	Jane's Island (1st, 8vo, 235p, green cl, fp b/w, pep, NH)	Houghton	1931	DeGogorza, M.	40-60	*
Weston, C.	There & Then (1st, sm8vo, 176p, green/gilt, fp b/w)	Scribner	1947	DeGoutiere, G.	30-45	*
Willson, Dixie	Tuffy Good Luck (1st, sq12mo, ipcb, pep, 39p, color)	Volland	(1927)	DeKarekjarto, I.	70-100	
Bennett, John	Barnaby Lee (1st, 12mo, 454p, blue/gilt, 34pl, PPP)	Century	1902	DeLand, C.O.	100-120	*
Crowley, Mary C.	Daughter of New France (1st, 8vo, 409p, blue/gilt, 6pl)	Little/Brown	1901	DeLand, C.O.	25-40	
Oxley, J.M.	Fife & Drum/Louisburg (1st, 8vo, 307p, 4pl)	Little/Brown	1899	DeLand, C.O.	25-40	
Major, C.	Forest Hearth (1st, sm8vo, teg, green/gilt, 354p, 8pl)	MacMillan	1903	DeLand, C.O.	25-40	
Mitchell, S.W.	Mr. Kris Kringle (1st, 8vo, teg, 105p, 5cp)	Jacobs	1893	DeLand, C.O.	75-120	R
Chestnutt, Charles	Wife of His Youth (1st, 8vo, 323p, pink/gilt)	Houghton	1899	DeLand, C.O.	230-300	
DuBois, W.E.B.	Quest of the Silver Fleece (1st, 8vo, 434p, grey cl)	McClurg	1911	DeLay, H.S.	200-280	
Kalnay, Francis	Chucaro, Wild Pony of Pampa (1st {std}, 8vo, 126p, b/w, NH)	Harcourt	(1958)	DeMiskey, J.	45-60	*
Green, L.M.	Brother of the Birds (1st AM, lg4to, 123p, purple/gilt, 21 tipl)	McKay	(1929)	DeMonvel, M.B.	120-165	
Egan, M.F.	Everybody's Saint Francis (1st, 8vo, grn/gilt, teg, 191p, 8cp)	Century	1912	DeMonvel, M.B.	50-70	
France, A.	Girls & Boys (1st AM, 4to, 25p, ipcb, 12cp)	Duffield	1913	DeMonvel, M.B.	100-135	
DeMonvel, M.B.	Good Children & Bad (1st AM, ob4to, 48p, gilt, color)	Cassell	(1890)	DeMonvel, M.B.	150-180	
DeMonvel, M.B.	Jeanne d' Arc (1st, ob4to, white cl, 47p, color)	(Paris)	[1896]	DeMonvel, M.B.	160-220	
DeMonvel, M.B.	Joan of Arc (1st AM, ob4to, 47p, purple cl, color)	Century	1907	DeMonvel, M.B.	100-140	
DeMonvel, M.B.	Joan of Arc (1st {this pub}, ob4to, tan cl, p-o, [25]p, 10 col)	McKay	1918	DeMonvel, M.B.	50-70	*

AUTHOR	TITLE	PUBLISHER	DATE	ARTIST	PRICE	LC
France, A.	Our Children (1st AM, lg4to, ibds, 25p, 12cp)	Duffield	1917	DeMonvel, M.B.	80-120	
Brown, M.W.	SHHhhh... Bang! (1st {std}, sm4to, ipcb, [32]p, fp 2-col, cep)	Harper	(1943)	DeVeyrac, R.	65-100	*
Lambert, C.	Story of Alaska (1st {std}, sq4to, ibds, [40]p, color, pep)	Harper	(1940)	DeWitt, C.H.	25-40	
McNeer, May	Story of California (1st {std}, 4to, [32]p, ibds, color, pep)	Harper	1944	DeWitt, C.H.	45-60	*
McClintock, M.	Story of New England (1st {std}, 4to, ibds, 39p, col, pep)	Harper	1941	DeWitt, C.H.	35-50	
Gilchrist, Marie	Story of the Great Lakes (1st {std}, 4to, [32]p, ibds, color)	Harper	(1942)	DeWitt, C.H.	25-40	
McClintock, M.	Story of the Mississippi (1st {std}, 4to, ibds, 39p, col, pep)	Harper	1941	DeWitt, C.H.	30-50	
McNeer, May	Story of the South-West (1st, sq4to, ibds, [32]p, col, pep, DJ)	Harper	(1948)	DeWitt, C.H.	25-40	*
Mother Goose	Mother Goose Picture Book (1st, 12mo, 119p, color, pep)	S. Gabriel	(1939)	Deane, E.	45-60	*
Dearmer, M.	Book of Penny Toys (1st, 4to, ibds, 94p, 14 color)	L: MacMillan	1899	Dearmer, M.	250-400	*
Dearmer, M.	Cockyolly Bird (1st, 4to, 221p)	L: Hodder	(1914)	Dearmer, M.	150-200	*
Housman, L.	Story of the Seven Young Goslings (1st, 4to, ibds, [32]p, 6cp)	L: Blackie	1899	Dearmer, M.	250-400	
Sharp, E.	Wymps & other Fairy Tales (1st, 8vo, 190p, 8cp)	NY: J. Lane	1897	Dearmer, M.	250-320	
Sharp, E.	All the Way to Fairyland (1st, 8vo, 196p, 8cp & cvr by...)	Longmans	1898	Dearmer, P.	85-120	*
LaFontaine, J.	Fables of La Fontaine (1st, 4to, 304p, teg, gilt, 24pl)	L: Nimmo	1884	Delierre, A.	100-145	*
Stoddard, W.O.	Little Smoke (1st, sm8vo, blue/silver, 295p, 14pl, PPP)	Appleton	1891	Dellenbaugh, F.	160-250	*
Deming, T.O.	American Animal Life (1st, ob4to, [74]p, 24cp)	Stokes	1916	Deming, E.W.	130-175	
Deming, T.O.	Animal Folk of Wood & Plain (1st, ob4to, [38]p, p-o, 12cp)	Stokes	(1916)	Deming, E.W.	120-150	
Garland, H.	Boy Life on the Prairie (1st, 12mo, brown/gilt, 423p, teg, 8pl)	MacMillan	1899	Deming, E.W.	45-60	
Deming, T.O.	Children of the Wild (1st, 4to, [26]p, 6cp)	Stokes	(1902)	Deming, E.W.	75-100	
Deming, T.O.	Cosel: With Geronimo on His Last Raid (1st, 8vo, 125p, 6cp)	Davis Co.	1938	Deming, E.W.	45-60	*
Deming, T.O.	Four-Footed Wilderness People (1st, ob4to, ibds, 38p, 12cp)	Stokes	1916	Deming, E.W.	100-170	*
Wallace, D.	Fur Trail Adventures (1st, 8vo, 320p, 7pl)	McClurg	1915	Deming, E.W.	30-45	
Quick, Herbert	In the Fairyland of America (1st, 8vo, green cl, p-o, 190p)	Stokes	(1901)	Deming, E.W.	100-150	
Haines, Alice C.	Indian Boys & Girls (1st, sm4to, 47p, 4cp)	Stokes	(1906)	Deming, E.W.	65-80	*
Deming, T.O.	Indian Child Life (1st, ob4to, ibds, [74]p, 18cp)	Stokes	1899	Deming, E.W.	150-185	
Deming, T.O.	Indians of the Wigwams (1st, sm8vo, 239p, 31 fp color)	Whitman	1938	Deming, E.W.	50-80	*
Grinnell, G.B.	Jack Among the Indians (1st, sm8vo, 301p, 8pl)	Stokes	(1900)	Deming, E.W.	40-65	
Grinnell, G.B.	Jack in the Rockies (1st, 12mo, 272p, green cl, 8pl)	Stokes	(1904)	Deming, E.W.	30-45	
Grinnell, G.B.	Jack/Young Ranchman (1st, 8vo, 304p, 8pl)	Stokes	1899	Deming, E.W.	45-60	
Deming, T.O.	Little Braves (1st, ob4to, [48]p, 9 fp color)	Stokes	1929	Deming, E.W.	70-100	*
Deming, T.O.	Little Brothers of the West (1st, 4to, p-o, [26]p, 6cp)	Stokes	(1902)	Deming, E.W.	80-120	
Deming, T.O.	Little Indian Folk (1st, ob4to, [38]p, 9cp)	Stokes	1899	Deming, E.W.	150-175	*
Deming, T.O.	Little Red People (1st, ob4to, [38]p, 9cp)	Stokes	1899	Deming, E.W.	140-175	*
Deming, T.O.	Many Snows Ago (1st, ob4to, [96]p, 18 fp color)	Stokes	1929	Deming, E.W.	75-130	
King, C.	Medal of Honor (1st, 8vo, p-o, teg, 348p, 3pl by...)	Hobart	1905	Deming, E.W.	30-50	*
Deming, T.O.	Red Folk & Wild Folk (1st, 4to, [51]p, p-o, 12cp)	Stokes	(1902)	Deming, E.W.	100-160	
Deming, T.O.	Red People of the Wooded Country (1st, 12mo, 191p, fp color)	Whitman	(1932)	Deming, E.W.	30-45	*
McElrath, F.	The Rustler (1st, 8vo, 425p, 7pl)	Funk/Wagnalls	1902	Deming, E.W.	45-60	
Deming, T.O.	Wigwam Children (1st, ob4to, [48]p, 9cp)	Stokes	1929	Deming, E.W.	70-130	
Eastman, C.A.	Wigwam Evenings (1st, 8vo, 253p, 18pl)	Little/Brown	1909	Deming, E.W.	70-90	
Mother Goose	Original Melodies from... (1st, lg8vo, green cl, 96p, color, cep)	Phi: Davis Co.	(1938)	Deming, K.O.	65-90	*
King, C.	Apache Princess (1st, 12mo, 328p, p-o, teg, 6pl)	Hobart	1903	Deming/Remington	35-50	
Graves, A.P.	Irish Fairy Book (1st, 8vo, 410p, col frn, 11pl, pep)	L: T.F. Unwin	(1909)	Denham, G.	65-80	
Graves, A.P.	Irish Fairy Book (1st AM, gilt, 410p, col frn, 13pl, pep)	Stokes	[1910]	Denham, G.	65-90	*
King, Eliz.	New House that Jack Built (1st, 4to, ibds, [31]p, color)	McBride	1932	Dennis, A.	35-50	*
Selden, George	Dog that Could Swim Underwater (1st, 8vo, grey cl, 126p, b/w)	Viking	1956	Dennis, M.	25-45	*
Darling, E.B.	Luck of the Trail (1st {std}, 8vo, uncut, 309p, col frn, pep)	Doubleday/Dor.	1933	Dennis, M.	25-40	*
Sewell, Anna	Black Beauty (1st, 8vo, 315p, color)	World Pub. Co.	(1946)	Dennis, W.	35-50	*
Henry, M.	Born to Trot (1st {A}, lg8vo, 219p, gilt, pep, color)	Rand/McNally	(1950)	Dennis, W.	30-50	
Henry, M.	Brighty of the Grand Canyon (1st {A}, 4to, 224p, pep, 4 fp col)	Rand/McNally	(1953)	Dennis, W.	30-45	*
Henry, M.	Cinnabar: One O'Clock Fox (1st {A}, lg8vo, 154p, pep)	Rand/McNally	(1956)	Dennis, W.	30-45	
Henry, M.	Justin Morgan had a Horse (1st, 4to, [89], pep, NH)	Wilcox/Follett	1945	Dennis, W.	50-70	*
Henry, M.	King of the Wind (1st {A}, 4to, red cl, 175p, color, pep, NM)	Rand/McNally	(1948)	Dennis, W.	50-85	R
Henry, M.	Misty of Chincoteague (1st {A}, sm4to, 173p, color, pep, DJ, NH)	Rand/McNally	(1947)	Dennis, W.	50-80	
Dean, G.M.	Riders of the Gabilans (1st, 8vo, 191p)	Viking	1944	Dennis, W.	20-30	*
Henry, M.	Sea Star: Orphan of Chincoteague (1st, lg8vo, 172p, color, pep)	Rand/McNally	(1949)	Dennis, W.	30-50	
Henry, M.	Wagging Tails (1st {A}, 4to, brown cl, 64p, 24 fp color, pep)	Rand/McNally	(1955)	Dennis, W.	35-50	*
Gordon, H.C.	Rhymes/Red Triangle (1st, 8vo, ibds, [60]p, chromos)	J. Lane	[1918]	Dennys, J.	100-150	
Johnson, J.P.	20 Years of Hus'ling (1st, 8vo, 664p, tan cl, 48 b/w)	Chi: Thompson	1900	Denslow, W.W.	100-150	
Wallace, Susan A.	Along the Bosphorus (1st, 8vo, teg, uncut, 383p, cvr by...)	Rand/McNally	1898	Denslow, W.W.	30-45	*
Read, Opie	Arkansas Planter (1st, 8vo, teg, 315p, cvr by...)	Rand/McNally	(1896)	Denslow, W.W.	60-85	
Waterman (ed.)	Ben King's Verse (1st, 8vo, 1 illus by...)	Chi: Forbes	1894	Denslow, W.W.	80-95	
Denslow, W.W.	Billy Bounce (1st, lg8vo, orange cl, 279p, p-o, 16cp)	Dillingham	(1906)	Denslow, W.W.	350-450	
Armstrong, Leroy	Byrd Flam in Town (1st, 8vo, 139p, cvr & illus by...)	Chi: Bearhope	(1894)	Denslow, W.W.	30-45	*
Fesenden, L.D.	Colonial Dame (1st, 8vo, 116p, cvr by...)	Rand/McNally	1897	Denslow, W.W.	35-50	
Stoddard, C.W.	Cruise Under the Crescent (1st, 8vo, 358p, cvr by...)	Rand/McNally	(1898)	Denslow, W.W.	40-60	*
Denslow, W.W.	Denslow's 5 Little Pigs (1st, 4to, wraps, [12]p, color, pep)	Dillingham	(1903)	Denslow, W.W.	145-220	
Denslow, W.W.	Denslow's Animal Fair (1st, 4to, wraps, unpag, color)	Dillingham	(1904)	Denslow, W.W.	150-200	
Denslow, W.W.	Denslow's Humpty Dumpty (1st, 4to, grey cl, p-o, 74p, fp color)	Dillingham	(1903)	Denslow, W.W.	260-400	R
Mother Goose	Denslow's Mother Goose (1st [1], 4to, ibds, [96]p, color, pep)	McClure	1901	Denslow, W.W.	375-500	R
Mother Goose	Denslow's Mother Goose (1st UK, 4to, unpag, color)	L: Chambers	1902	Denslow, W.W.	280-400	

AUTHOR	TITLE	PUBLISHER	DATE	ARTIST	PRICE	LC
Denslow, W.W.	Denslow's One Ring Circus (1st, 4to, wraps, [12]p, color, pep)	Dillingham	(1903)	Denslow, W.W.	180-250	
Denslow, W.W.	Denslow's Tom Thumb (1st, 4to, wraps, [12]p, color, pep)	Dillingham	(1903)	Denslow, W.W.	150-200	
Denslow, W.W.	Denslow's Zoo (1st, 4to, [12]p, wraps, color, pep)	Dillingham	(1903)	Denslow, W.W.	180-250	
Baum, L.F.	Dot & Tot in Merryland (1st [1], 8vo, [226]p, gilt, color, pep)	Geo. Hill	1901	Denslow, W.W.	600-800	R
Baum, L.F.	Dot & Tot in Merryland (2nd, 8vo, [226]p, color)	Bobbs-Merrill	(1903)	Denslow, W.W.	220-400	
Eastman, Charlotte	Evolution of Dodd's Sister (1st, sm8vo, 230p, cvr by...)	Rand/McNally	1897	Denslow, W.W.	25-40	*
Baum, L.F.	Father Goose: His Book (1st [1], 4to, ibds, [106]p)	Geo. Hill	(1899)	Denslow, W.W.	4000	R
Baum, L.F.	Father Goose: His Book (4to, unpag, ibds, color)	Donohue	[1913]	Denslow, W.W.	150-220	
Homer, A.N.	Hernani the Jew (1st, 8vo, 332p, cvr by...)	Rand/McNally	(1897)	Denslow, W.W.	30-45	*
Denslow, W.W.	House that Jack Built (1st, 4to, [12]p, wraps, color, pep)	Dillingham	(1903)	Denslow, W.W.	170-230	
Denslow, W.W.	Jack & the Bean Stalk (1st, 4to, wraps, [12]p, color)	Dillingham	(1903)	Denslow, W.W.	150-225	
Johnston, I.M.	Jeweled Toad (1st, sm4to, 211p, ibds, 8cp)	Bobbs-Merrill	(1907)	Denslow, W.W.	200-260	
About, E.	King of the Mountains (1st, sm8vo, 246p, cvr by...)	Rand/McNally	1897	Denslow, W.W.	25-40	*
Denslow, W.W.	Little Red Riding Hood (1st, 4to, [12]p, wraps, color)	Dillingham	(1903)	Denslow, W.W.	150-200	
Edwards, Harry S.	Marbeau Cousins (1st, sm8vo, 294p, cvr by....)	Rand/McNally	(1898)	Denslow, W.W.	30-45	*
Denslow, W.W.	Mary Had a Little Lamb (1st, 4to, wraps, [12]p, color)	Dillingham	(1903)	Denslow, W.W.	120-165	
Webb, R.	Me & Lawson (1st, sm8vo, 78p, 4pl, cvr by...)	Dillingham	(1905)	Denslow, W.W.	85-100	
Baum, L.F.	New Wizard of Oz (2nd, lg8vo, green cl, [261]p, 16cp, pep)	Bobbs-Merrill	(1903)	Denslow, W.W.	1500	
Denslow, W.W.	Night Before Christmas (1st, 4to, ibds, p-o, 64p, color)	Dillingham	(1902)	Denslow, W.W.	300-350	
Denslow, W.W.	Night Before Christmas (lg8vo, p-o, [32]p, color, later)	Donohue	[1915]	Denslow, W.W.	150-185	
Boylan, G.D.	Old House (1st, 12mo, 112p, cvr by...)	E.R. Herrick	(1897)	Denslow, W.W.	40-65	*
Denslow, W.W.	Old Mother Hubbard (1st, 4to, wraps, [12]p, color)	Dillingham	(1903)	Denslow, W.W.	180-225	
West, Paul	Pearl & Pumpkin (1st [1], lg8vo, grn cl, 240p, p-o, 16cp, pep)	Dillingham	(1904)	Denslow, W.W.	300-400	
West, Paul	Pearl & Pumpkin (lg8vo, 239p, p-o, 16cp, later)	Donohue	[1911]	Denslow, W.W.	200-280	
Loti, P.	Romance of a Child (1st, 8vo, cvr by...)	Rand/McNally	1897	Denslow, W.W.	45-60	
Amber	Rosemary & Rue (1st, sm8vo, 303p, cvr by...)	Rand/McNally	1896	Denslow, W.W.	35-50	*
Denslow, W.W.	Scarecrow & the Tin Man (1st, 4to, [74]p, p-o, color)	Dillingham	(1904)	Denslow, W.W.	500-700	
Denslow, W.W.	Scarecrow & the Tin Man (4to, red cl, p-o, [74]p, color)	Donohue	[1913]	Denslow, W.W.	200-300	
Denslow, W.W.	Simple Simon (1st, 4to, wraps, unpag, color)	Dillingham	(1904)	Denslow, W.W.	100-135	
Baum, L.F.	Songs of Father Goose (1st, 4to, ibds, 84p, b/w)	Geo. Hill	1900	Denslow, W.W.	350-500	
Baum, L.F.	Songs of Father Goose (2nd, 4to, 83p, ibds)	Bobbs-Merrill	(1909)	Denslow, W.W.	180-240	
Welch, D.	Story of Louise (1st, 12mo, tan cl, uncut, 194p, cvr by...)	(NY)	1901	Denslow, W.W.	45-60	
Halstead	Story of the Philippines (1st, sm4to, 400p, cvr by...)	(Chicago)	(1898)	Denslow, W.W.	75-100	*
Denslow, W.W.	Tom Thumb (1st, 4to, [12]p, wraps, color)	Dillingham	(1903)	Denslow, W.W.	200-300	
Read, Opie	Waters of Caney Fork (1st, 8vo, 287p, cvr by...)	Rand/McNally	1898	Denslow, W.W.	45-60	
Denslow, W.W.	When I Grow Up (1st, 4to, 104p, 24 color, tan cl)	Century	1909	Denslow, W.W.	150-200	
Baum, L.F.	Wonderful Wizard of Oz (1st [1], 8vo, [261]p, 24cp, pep, PPP)	Geo. Hill	1900	Denslow, W.W.	7000	R
Derrick, Freda	Ark Book (1st, ob sm4to, ibds, unpag, p-o, color)	L: Blackie	[1920]	Derrick, Freda	120-165	
N/A	Arabian Nights (1st, 4to, 240p, teg, white/gilt, 12 ticp)	L: Hodder	(1924)	Detmold, E.J.	250-400	
N/A	Arabian Nights (1st AM, lg8vo, blue/gilt, 297p, p-o, 12 ticp)	Dodd	(1925)	Detmold, E.J.	180-265	
Lemonnier	Birds & Beasts (1st, 8vo, teg, 196p, 6cp)	L: G. Allen	(1911)	Detmold, E.J.	150-200	
Hudson, W.H.	Birds in Town & Village (1st, 323p, green/gilt, 8cp)	L: Dent	1919	Detmold, E.J.	100-135	
Hudson, W.H.	Birds in Town & Village (1st AM, blue/gilt, 323p, 8cp)	Dutton	(1920)	Detmold, E.J.	80-130	
Dugdale, F.E.	Book of Baby Beasts (4to, ibds, p-o, [120]p, 19cp)	NY: Hodder	[1912]	Detmold, E.J.	230-300	
Dugdale, F.E.	Book of Baby Birds (1st, sm4to, 120p, pcb, p-o, 19 ticp)	L: Hodder	[1912]	Detmold, E.J.	200-300	
Dugdale, F.E.	Book of Baby Dogs (1st AM, 4to, 120p, ibds, p-o, 19 ticp)	NY: Hodder	[1914]	Detmold, E.J.	250-300	
Dugdale, F.E.	Book of Baby Dogs (1st, 4to, bds, 120p, p-o, 19 ticp)	L: H. Frowde	(1914)	Detmold, E.J.	220-320	
Dugdale, F.E.	Book of Baby Pets (1st, lg4to, ibds, [120]p, p-o, 19 ticp)	L: Hodder	(1913)	Detmold, E.J.	280-400	
Aesopus	Fables of Aesop (1st, lg4to, 152p, brown/gilt, pep, 23 ticp)	L: Hodder	[1909]	Detmold, E.J.	450-600	
Stawell, R. (ed.)	Fabre's Book of Insects (1st AM, 4to, 271p, grn/gilt, 12 ticp)	Dodd	1921	Detmold, E.J.	180-240	
Fabre	Fabre's Book of Insects (1st, lg4to, white/gilt, 12 ticp)	L: Hodder	(1921)	Detmold, E.J.	220-300	
Stawell, R. (ed.)	Fabre's Book of Insects (1st {this pub.}, 4to, 271p, 12 ticp)	Tudor	1936	Detmold, E.J.	70-90	
Maeterlinck, M.	Hours of Gladness (1st, 4to, 181p, white/gilt, 20 ticp)	L: G. Allen	(1912)	Detmold, E.J.	280-350	
Kipling, R.	Jungle Book (1st, 8vo, 314p, red/gilt, teg, 16cp)	L: MacMillan	1908	Detmold, E.J.	240-350	
Kipling, R.	Jungle Book (1st AM, 8vo, green/gilt, teg, 351p, 16cp, pep)	Century	1913	Detmold, E.J.	180-240	
Maeterlinck, M.	Life of the Bee (1st, 4to, 232p, teg, 13 ticp)	L: G. Allen	1911	Detmold, E.J.	250-350	
Maeterlinck, M.	Life of the Bee (1st AM, 4to, 262p, teg, green/gilt, 13 ticp)	Dodd	1912	Detmold, E.J.	150-200	
Maeterlinck, M.	News of Spring (1st AM, 4to, green/gilt, 213p, teg, 20 ticp)	Dodd	1913	Detmold, E.J.	220-300	
Kaberry, C.J.	Our Little Neighbors (4to, pcb, 105p, 11 ticp)	L: OUP	(1921)	Detmold, E.J.	200-320	
Shuldham, E.	Pictures from Birdland (1st {1st bk.}, 4to, ibds, 24cp)	L: Dent	1899	Detmold, E.J.	400-600	
Hall, A.V.	Poems of a South African (1st, 8vo, 313p, gilt, 6cp)	L: Longmans	1931	Detmold, E.J.	100-165	
Hall, A.V.	Rainbow Houses for Boys & Girls (1st, 8vo, blue cl, 92p, 6cp)	L: J. Cape	1923	Detmold, E.J.	140-185	
Ponsat, Georges	Romance of the River (1st AM, 8vo, green/gilt, 290p, col frn)	Dodd	(1924)	Detmold, E.J.	30-45	*
Maeterlinck, M.	Visions of Spring... (1st, 4to, teg, 213p, gilt, 20 ticp)	Dodd	1913	Detmold, E.J.	320-400	
Sewell, Anna	Black Beauty (1st, lg8vo, 278p, teg, p-o, 12cp)	Barse	(1911)	Dickey, R.L.	35-50	*
Terhune, A.P.	Book of Famous Dogs (1st {std}, 8vo, 300p, b/w pl)	Doubleday/Dor.	1937	Dickey, R.L.	25-40	*
Dwight, G.	Yellow Cat & Friends (1st, 4to, ipcb, 88p, 14cp)	Appleton	1905	Dimock, E.	50-75	
Cosgrove, R.R.	Hidden Valley of Oz (1st, lg8vo, blue cl, p-o, 313p, b/w, pep)	Reilly/Lee	(1951)	Dirk	180-220	
Disney, W.	40 Big Pages of Mickey Mouse (folio, wraps, color)	Whitman	(1936)	Disney Studios	120-170	*
Disney, W.	ABC Mickey Mouse Alphabet Bk. (1st, 8vo, [32]p, color, pep)	Whitman	(1936)	Disney Studios	150-200	*
Disney, W.	Advens./Mickey Mouse Bk. # 2 (1st, 8vo, [32]p, ibds, pep, col)	McKay	(1932)	Disney Studios	250-400	
Disney, W.	Ave Maria (1st, 4to, blue/gilt, [32]p, color, pep)	Random	(1940)	Disney Studios	80-125	

AUTHOR	TITLE	PUBLISHER	DATE	ARTIST	PRICE	LC
Grant, J.C.	Baby Weems (1st {std}, lg8vo, [64]p, blue cl, 2-color, pep)	Doubleday/Dor.	1941	Disney Studios	70-100	*
Disney, W.	Big Bad Wolf & Little Red Riding Hood (1st, 4to, ipcb, 60p, col)	Blue Ribbon	(1934)	Disney Studios	140-200	*
Disney, W.	Cold-Blooded Penguin (1st {std}, sm8vo, ibds, unpag, pep, col)	Simon/Schuster	1944	Disney Studios	80-120	*
Disney, W.	Come Play with Donald Duck (1st, 8vo, [32]p, color)	Grosset/Dunlap	(1948)	Disney Studios	65-90	*
Disney, W.	Come Play with Mickey Mouse (1st, 8vo, [32]p, color)	Grosset/Dunlap	(1948)	Disney Studios	65-90	*
Disney, W.	Country Cousin (1st, 4to, ibds, [20]p, color)	McKay	1937	Disney Studios	90-130	*
Disney, W.	Dance of the Hours (1st {std}, lg8vo, [36]p, color, pep)	Harper	(1940)	Disney Studios	120-160	*
Disney, W.	Disney's Bambi (1st, 4to, [52]p, ibds, color)	Simon/Schuster	(1941)	Disney Studios	70-120	*
Disney, W.	Disney's Bambi (8vo, [32]p, color, pep)	Grosset/Dunlap	(1942)	Disney Studios	65-80	
Disney, W.	Disney's Bambi (8vo, 101p, color)	D.C. Heath	(1944)	Disney Studios	40-60	*
Disney, W.	Disney's Cinderella (8vo, [34]p, color)	Whitman	1950	Disney Studios	65-100	*
Disney, W.	Disney's Cinderella (1st, folio, ibds, [26]p, color, GGB)	Simon/Schuster	(1950)	Disney Studios	70-120	
Disney, W.	Disney's Davy Crockett (1st, lg4to, ibds, 48p, color, BGB)	Simon/Schuster	(1955)	Disney Studios	45-70	*
Disney, W.	Disney's Dumbo (1st, lg ob8vo, wraps, [12]p, color)	Disney Prod.	1941	Disney Studios	150-200	*
Disney, W.	Disney's Dumbo (1st {this pub}, 8vo, [42]p, color)	Simon/Schuster	(1947)	Disney Studios	70-100	*
Disney, W.	Disney's Forest Friends (8vo, [28]p, ibds, color, pep)	Grosset/Dunlap	(1938)	Disney Studios	80-130	*
Disney, W.	Disney's Lady & the Tramp (1st, folio, unpag, ipcb, color, BGB)	Simon/Schuster	(1955)	Disney Studios	90-140	*
Mother Goose	Disney's Mother Goose (1st, folio, ibds, [28]p, color, GGB)	Simon/Schuster	(1949)	Disney Studios	80-130	*
Disney, W.	Disney's Pedro (1st, sm8vo, [32]p, ipcb, color, pep)	A.& W. Guild	1943	Disney Studios	65-90	*
Disney, W.	Disney's Peter Pan (1st, folio, ipcb, unpag, color, GGB)	Simon/Schuster	1952	Disney Studios	80-120	*
Disney, W.	Disney's Pinocchio (1st, 4to, ibds, [76]p, color, pep)	Random	1939	Disney Studios	125-170	R
Disney, W.	Disney's Pinocchio (folio, [12]p, color)	Whitman	(1940)	Disney Studios	70-100	*
Disney, W.	Disney's Pinocchio (1st {this pub}, folio, ipcb, color, BGB)	Simon/Schuster	(1954)	Disney Studios	100-150	*
Disney, W.	Disney's Surprise Package (1st, 4to, ibds, 92p, color, pep, GGB)	Simon/Schuster	1944	Disney Studios	90-145	
Disney, W.	Disney's Thumper (1st, 8vo, [32]p, ipcb, color, pep)	Grosset/Dunlap	(1942)	Disney Studios	80-125	*
Disney, W.	Disney's Version of Pinocchio (ob8vo, [48]p, color, pep)	Grosset/Dunlap	1939	Disney Studios	90-130	*
Disney, W.	Disney's Version of Pinocchio (sq12mo, [24]p, color)	Whitman	(1940)	Disney Studios	75-115	*
Disney, W.	Donald Duck (1st, folio, [14]p, color)	Whitman	1935	Disney Studios	250-400	R*
Disney, W.	Donald Duck (4to, ibds, [33]p, color, pep)	Grosset/Dunlap	(1936)	Disney Studios	250-400	*
Disney, W.	Donald Duck & his Friends (1st, 4to, ipcb, 45p, b/w, pep)	Whitman	1937	Disney Studios	150-200	*
Disney, W.	Donald Duck & his Friends (8vo, 102p, pep, color)	Heath	(1939)	Disney Studios	150-200	*
Disney, W.	Donald Duck & his Nephews (1st, 8vo, cloth, 66p, pep, color)	Heath	(1940)	Disney Studios	45-60	
Disney, W.	Donald Duck Off the Beam (1st [Big-Little], 32mo, 425p, ibds)	Whitman	(1943)	Disney Studios	100-140	*
Disney, W.	Donald Duck Sees South America (8vo, 138p, maps, color)	Heath	(1945)	Disney Studios	50-80	
Disney, W.	Donald Duck Treasury (1st, lg8vo, 116p)	Golden Press	1960	Disney Studios	70-100	*
Disney, W.	Donald Duck has Ups & Downs (1st, sm4to, 24p, color)	Whitman	1937	Disney Studios	150-200	*
Disney, W.	Donald Duck his Story Book (1st, 4to, ipcb, 46p, pep, b/w)	Whitman	1937	Disney Studios	100-150	*
Disney, W.	Donald Duck in High Andes (1st, 8vo, [32]p, color)	A.& W. Guild	1943	Disney Studios	100-160	*
Disney, W.	Donald's Lucky Day (1st, ob4to, [20]p, color)	Whitman	(1939)	Disney Studios	100-150	*
Disney, W.	Donald's Penguin (1st, sm4to, ibds, [24]p, pep, color)	Garden City	1940	Disney Studios	65-80	*
Disney, W.	Dopey: He Don't Talk None (sm folio, wraps, [12]p, color)	Whitman	1938	Disney Studios	130-165	
Disney, W.	Dumbo of the Circus (1st, sq4to, ibds, [52]p, color, pep)	Garden City	(1941)	Disney Studios	100-140	*
Disney, W.	Dumbo of the Circus (1st {this pub}, 8vo, 90p, color, pep)	Heath	(1948)	Disney Studios	65-80	*
Disney, W.	Elmer Elephant (1st, 8vo, ibds, 46p, color)	McKay	(1936)	Disney Studios	65-100	*
Disney, W.	Elmer Elephant (folio, wraps, [10]p, fp color, linen)	Whitman	1938	Disney Studios	120-165	
Taylor, Deems	Fantasia (1st, lg4to, tan cloth, 158p, 17cp, pep)	Simon/Schuster	1940	Disney Studios	150-220	
Leaf, M.	Ferdinand the Bull (4to, wraps, 31p, color)	Whitman	(1936)	Disney Studios	80-100	
Leaf, M.	Ferdinand the Bull (1st {this pub}, ob8vo, [14]p, wraps, 6 col)	Dell	1938	Disney Studios	65-90	*
Leaf, M.	Ferdinand the Bull (1st, 4to, [8]p, stiff wraps, color)	Whitman	(1938)	Disney Studios	100-145	
Disney, W.	Figaro and Cleo (1st, 8vo, ibds, [27]p, color, pep)	Random	1940	Disney Studios	100-160	
Disney, W.	Golden Touch (1st, 8vo, ibds, 212p, 6cp, pep)	Whitman	(1937)	Disney Studios	80-120	
Dahl, Ronald	Gremlins (1st, 4to, ibds, [48]p, fp color)	Random	(1943)	Disney Studios	250-400	
Disney, W.	Hiawatha (1st, 4to, ibds, [20]p, fp color, pep)	McKay	1937	Disney Studios	120-170	
Disney, W.	Honest John & Giddy (1st, 8vo, [24]p, ibds, color, pep)	Random	1940	Disney Studios	80-120	*
Disney, W.	Jiminy Cricket (1st, 8vo, ibds, [24]p, color, pep)	Random	1940	Disney Studios	90-140	
Brown, M.W.	Little Pig's Picnic... (1st, 8vo, 102p, cloth, color, dep)	Heath	(1939)	Disney Studios	45-70	*
Disney, W.	Little Pigs' Picnic (8vo, 102p, color, pep)	Heath	(1939)	Disney Studios	65-90	*
Disney, W.	Little Wise Hen (1st, ob4to, 48p, ibds, 9 fp color)	Whitman	(1934)	Disney Studios	150-200	
Disney, W.	Magnificent Mr. Toad (1st, 4to, [32]p, color)	Grosset/Dunlap	(1949)	Disney Studios	100-170	*
Disney, W.	Mickey & the Beanstalk (1st, 8vo, ipcb, [32]p, color, pep)	Grosset/Dunlap	(1947)	Disney Studios	80-120	*
Disney, W.	Mickey Mouse (1st {Big-Little}, 32mo, ibds, 316p, b/w)	Whitman	1933	Disney Studios	100-160	*
Disney, W.	Mickey Mouse & Mail Pilot (1st {Big-Little}, 32mo, ibds, 296p)	Whitman	1933	Disney Studios	100-160	*
Mother Goose	Mickey Mouse & Mother Goose (1st, 8vo, ibds, 136p, color, pep)	Whitman	(1937)	Disney Studios	70-90	*
Disney, W.	Mickey Mouse & Pluto (1st, lg8vo, [66]p, color, pep)	Whitman	1936	Disney Studios	120-170	*
Disney, W.	Mickey Mouse & his Friends (1st, folio, wraps, linen, 8cp)	Whitman	(1936)	Disney Studios	150-200	
Disney, W.	Mickey Mouse & his Friends (1st {this pub}, 8vo, 102p, color)	NY: Nelson	1937	Disney Studios	70-100	*
Disney, W.	Mickey Mouse & his Horse Tanglefoot (1st, 8vo, ibds, 60p, color)	McKay	(1936)	Disney Studios	250-350	*
Disney, W.	Mickey Mouse ABC Story (1st, 8vo, ipcb, [31]p, color, pep)	Whitman	(1937)	Disney Studios	250-400	*
Disney, W.	Mickey Mouse Alphabet A to Z (4to, ibds, [32]p, 1-color)	L: Collins	[1936]	Disney Studios	180-235	
Disney, W.	Mickey Mouse Alphabet from A to Z (4to, ibds, [32]p)	Whitman	(1936)	Disney Studios	140-200	
Disney, W.	Mickey Mouse Birthday Book (1st, 4to, ibds, 64p, color, BGB)	Simon/Schuster	(1953)	Disney Studios	50-80	*
Disney, W.	Mickey Mouse Crusoe (1st, 8vo, wraps, 71p, col frn, b/w)	Whitman	(1936)	Disney Studios	100-130	*

AUTHOR	TITLE	PUBLISHER	DATE	ARTIST	PRICE	LC
Disney, W.	Mickey Mouse Fire Brigade (1st, 4to, ibds, color)	Whitman	1936	Disney Studios	140-200	
Disney, W.	Mickey Mouse Fire Brigade (1st UK, ibds, 77p, b/w)	L: Collins	1936	Disney Studios	150-220	
Disney, W.	Mickey Mouse Has a Busy Day (1st, sq4to, wraps, 16p, color)	Whitman	(1937)	Disney Studios	120-200	*
Disney, W.	Mickey Mouse Movie Stories (8vo, ibds, 197p)	L: Dean	[1931]	Disney Studios	250-375	
Disney, W.	Mickey Mouse Movie Stories (1st, 8vo, gilt, 190p, p-o)	McKay	(1931)	Disney Studios	250-350	R
Disney, W.	Mickey Mouse Story Book (1st, 8vo, 62p, wraps, b/w)	McKay	(1931)	Disney Studios	250-400	
Disney, W.	Mickey Mouse at the Circus (1st UK, 4to, ibds, color)	L: Birn Bros.	(1937)	Disney Studios	180-260	
Disney, W.	Mickey Mouse has a Party (1st, lg8vo, wraps, 48p, 2-color)	Whitman	1938	Disney Studios	160-220	*
Disney, W.	Mickey Mouse in Giantland (1st, 8vo, 45p, p-o, fp color, pep)	McKay	(1934)	Disney Studios	270-500	*
Disney, W.	Mickey Mouse in Giantland (1st UK, 8vo, 93p, ibds)	L: Collins	(1934)	Disney Studios	230-350	
Disney, W.	Mickey Mouse in Pigmey Land (1st, 4to, ipcb, 71p, col frn)	Whitman	1936	Disney Studios	150-200	*
Disney, W.	Mickey Mouse the Boat-Builder (1st, ob8vo, [28]p, ibds, col, pep)	Grosset/Dunlap	1938	Disney Studios	120-160	*
Disney, W.	Nursery Stories/Silly Symphony (1st, 8vo, 212p, ibds, 6cp, pep)	Whitman	(1937)	Disney Studios	140-200	
Disney, W.	Nutcracker Suite (1st, lg sq4to, ibds, [72]p, color, pep)	Little/Brown	1940	Disney Studios	120-165	
Disney, W.	Our Friend the Atom (1st, 4to, 166p, pep, color, GGB)	Simon/Schuster	(1956)	Disney Studios	90-135	
Disney, W.	Pastoral (1st {std}, lg8vo, [36]p, color, pep)	Harper	(1940)	Disney Studios	100-150	*
Disney, W.	Peculiar Penguins (1st, 8vo, 45p, red cl, p-o, color, pep)	McKay	(1934)	Disney Studios	130-200	
Disney, W.	Pinocchio Picture Book (lg4to, [14]p, wraps, color)	Grosset/Dunlap	(1940)	Disney Studios	120-180	R*
Disney, W.	Pinocchio Picture Book (lg4to, wraps, color, shape bk.)	Whitman	1940	Disney Studios	150-200	*
Disney, W.	Pluto & the Puppy (1st, 4to, ibds, [36]p, color, pep)	Grosset/Dunlap	(1937)	Disney Studios	140-200	
Disney, W.	Practical Pig (1st, lg sq8vo, ibds, [24]p, color, pep)	Garden City	1940	Disney Studios	90-150	*
Disney, W.	Princess Elizabeth Gift Book (1st, lg8vo, white cl, 224p, color)	L: Hodder	[1933]	Disney Studios	85-100	
Grahame, K.	Reluctant Dragon (1st, lg4to, [72]p, ibds, color, pep)	Garden City	(1941)	Disney Studios	165-200	*
Disney, W.	Robber Kitten (1st, ob4to, ipcb, 46p, 9 fp color)	McKay	(1935)	Disney Studios	180-300	
Disney, W.	Runaway Lamb at County Fair (1st, sm4to, ipcb, [31]p, color)	Grosset/Dunlap	(1949)	Disney Studios	70-100	*
Emerson, C.D.	School Days in Disneyville (1st, 8vo, 102p, color, pep)	Heath	(1939)	Disney Studios	45-60	*
Disney, W.	Snow White & Seven Dwarfs (lg4to, ibds, 80p, color)	Grosset/Dunlap	(1937)	Disney Studios	85-100	
Disney, W.	Snow White & Seven Dwarfs (1st {this pub}, sq4to, ibds, color)	McKay	1937	Disney Studios	120-170	
Disney, W.	Snow White & Seven Dwarfs (folio, 12p, wraps, color)	Whitman	1938	Disney Studios	250-300	R
Disney, W.	Snow White & Seven Dwarfs (ob8vo, ipcb, unpag, color)	Grosset/Dunlap	(1938)	Disney Studios	120-165	
Disney, W.	Snow White & Seven Dwarfs (1st, 12mo, 63p, ibds, 14 color)	Whitman	(1938)	Disney Studios	120-170	*
Disney, W.	Sorcerer's Apprentice (1st, ob8vo, 34p, color, pep)	Grosset/Dunlap	(1940)	Disney Studios	120-165	*
Disney, W.	Stories from Fantasia (narrow 4to, [movie ed.], 72p, ibds, col)	Random	(1940)	Disney Studios	85-140	
Disney, W.	Story of Casey Jr. (1st, lg8vo, ibds, [26]p, 4 fp color, pep)	Garden City	(1941)	Disney Studios	80-120	*
Disney, W.	Story of Minnie Mouse (ibds, 34pl)	Whitman	(1938)	Disney Studios	70-100	*
Disney, W.	Story of Timothy's House (1st, sm4to, ibds, [28]p, color)	Garden City	(1941)	Disney Studios	80-120	*
Disney, W.	Three Little Pigs (1st, sm4to, ibds, 62p, 12 color, pep)	Blue Ribbon	(1933)	Disney Studios	160-200	
Disney, W.	Three Orphan Kittens (1st, ob4to, ibds, [46]p, 9 color)	McKay	(1935)	Disney Studios	140-200	
Disney, W.	Through the Picture Frame (1st, sq8vo, [24]p, ibds, col)	Simon/Schuster	1944	Disney Studios	60-80	*
Disney, W.	Timid Elmer (1st, sq12mo, ipcb, 64p, b/w)	Whitman	1939	Disney Studios	90-130	*
Disney, W.	Tortoise & the Hare (1st, ob4to, ibds, 48p, 9 fp color)	McKay	(1935)	Disney Studios	180-250	*
Andersen, H.C.	Ugly Duckling (1st, ob4to, [40]p, p-o, color, pep)	Lippincott	(1939)	Disney Studios	180-240	
Harris, J.C.	Uncle Remus Stories (1st, sm folio, ibds, 92p, color, GGB)	Simon/Schuster	(1947)	Disney Studios	70-100	*
Disney, W.	Walt Disney Parade (1st, 4to, 176p, color, pep)	Garden City	(1940)	Disney Studios	90-145	*
Disney, W.	Water Babies' Circus (8vo, 78p, color pep)	Heath	(1940)	Disney Studios	50-85	*
Disney, W.	Wise Little Hen (1st, ob4to, 48p, fp color)	McKay	(1934)	Disney Studios	180-220	*
Disney, W.	Wise Little Hen (1st {this fmt}, folio, [8]p, wraps, color)	Disney Prod.	(1937)	Disney Studios	180-250	*
Disney, W.	Wonderful Tar Baby (1st, 8vo, ipcb, [32]p, color, pep)	Grosset/Dunlap	(1946)	Disney Studios	70-120	*
Farnol, J.	My Lady Caprice (1st, 8vo, teg, p-o, 289p)	Dodd	1907	Ditzler, C.W.	20-25	
Brady, C.T.	My Lady's Slipper (1st, teg, 245p, 4pl)	Dodd	1905	Ditzler, C.W.	20-25	*
Warner, A.	When Woman Proposes (1st, 8vo, 158p, teg, purple cl, color)	Little/Brown	1911	Ditzler, C.W.	20-25	
N/A	Book of New Fairy Tales (4to, grey bds, p-o, [72]p, 7cp by…)	Dodge	[1910]	Dixon, A.A.	70-100	
Weedon, L.L.	Child Characters/Dickens (1st, 8vo, 320p, AEG, 6cp)	L: Nister	(1905)	Dixon, A.A.	75-100	
Hauff, Wilhelm	Fairy Tales (1st, 8vo, 344p, gilt, pep, 6cp, 12pl)	Nister/Dutton	[1910]	Dixon, A.A.	60-85	*
Hinkson, H.A.	King's Liege (1st, 8vo, 224p, blue cl, col frn, 3pl)	L: Blackie	1910	Dixon, A.A.	45-60	*
Lang, A.	Tales/Fairy Court (1st, 8vo, 108p, gilt, AEG, 12cp)	L: Collins	(1907)	Dixon, A.A.	150-200	
Kingsley, C.	The Heroes (12mo, grey cl, p-o, 157p, 4cp, dep)	L: Blackie	[1907]	Dixon, A.A.	45-60	
Kingsley, C.	Water Babies (1st, 8vo, green/gilt, AEG, 336p, 6cp)	Nister/Dutton	[1908]	Dixon, A.A.	160-220	
Gordon, H.C.	Lost Princess (1st, 8vo, 159p)	L: J. Murray	(1933)	Dixon, G.S.	35-50	*
Balch, F.H.	Bridge of the Gods (1st, 8vo, teg, 280p, 8pl)	McClurg	1902	Dixon, M.	30-45	
Mulford, C.	Buck Peters, Ranchman (1st, 8vo, 367p, 4cp)	McClurg	1912	Dixon, M.	35-50	
Mulford, C.	Coming of Cassidy (1st, 12mo, 438p, 5cp)	McClurg	1913	Dixon, M.	50-65	
Kelly, F.	Delafield Affair (1st, 8vo, ibds, 422p, 4cp)	McClurg	1909	Dixon, M.	35-50	
Hanson, J.M.	Frontier Ballads (1st, 8vo, ibds, 92p, 7cp)	McClurg	1910	Dixon, M.	45-60	
Coolidge, D.	Hidden Water (1st, 8vo, ibds, 483p, 4cp)	McClurg	1910	Dixon, M.	35-60	
Mulford, C.	Hopalong Cassidy (1st, 8vo, 392p, 5pl)	McClurg	1910	Dixon, M.	50-70	
Dixon, Maynard	Injun Babies (1st, 8vo, 72p, p-o, 7cp, pep)	Putnam	1923	Dixon, M.	50-80	*
Morrow, W.C.	Lentala/South Seas (1st, 8vo, grey cl, 278p, p-o, 7cp)	Stokes	(1908)	Dixon, M.	30-45	*
Bronson, E.B.	Red Blooded (1st, 8vo, 342p, 10pl)	McClurg	1910	Dixon, M.	35-50	
Bronson, E.B.	Reminiscences of a Ranchman (1st, 8vo, p-o, 369p, 8cp)	McClurg	(1910)	Dixon, M.	50-65	
Boyles, K.	Spirit Trail (1st, 8vo, 416p, ibds, 4cp)	McClurg	1910	Dixon, M.	35-50	
Lynde, F.	Taming/Red Butte Western (1st, 8vo, 410p, 4pl)	Scribner	1910	Dixon, M.	30-45	

ILLUSTRATOR: 42

AUTHOR	TITLE	PUBLISHER	DATE	ARTIST	PRICE	LC
Coolidge, D.	The Texican (1st, lg8vo, beige cl, 369p, 5cp)	McClurg	1911	Dixon, M.	45-70	
Kyne, P.B.	Three Godfathers (1st, 8vo, 95p, 5pl)	Doran	(1913)	Dixon, M.	25-40	*
Service, Rbt.	Trail of Ninety-Eight (1st, 8vo, 514p, 4pl)	Dodd	1911	Dixon, M.	30-45	
Brady, C.T.	West Wind (1st, 8vo, 389p, 4cp)	McClurg	1910	Dixon, M.	25-45	
Stevenson, R.L.	Child's Garden of Verses (1st, sq4to, ibds, [30]p, fp col, pep)	Garden City	1942	Doane, P.	40-65	
Jacobs, Joseph	Molly Whuppie (1st AM, 8vo, tan cl, [46]p, fp 3-color)	OUP	[1939]	Doane, P.	30-50	*
Mother Goose	Mother Goose (1st, lg8vo, ibds, [52]p, color, pep)	Random	(1940)	Doane, P.	35-60	*
Dobias, D.F.	Casey Joins the Circus (1st, sq8vo, [33]p, color, pep)	Grosset/Dunlap	(1936)	Dobias, D.F.	45-60	*
N/A	Breman Band (1st, 16mo, [42]p, ibds, color, pep)	MacMillan	1927	Dobias, F.	30-45	*
Mirza, Y.B.	Children of the Housetops (1st {std}, sm8vo, 248p, col frn)	Doubleday/Dor.	1931	Dobias, F.	20-30	*
Meigs, C.	Clearing Weather (1st, 8vo, blue cl, 312p, 3cp, pep, NH)	Little/Brown	1928	Dobias, F.	35-50	*
N/A	Jack & the Beanstalk (1st, sq16mo, ibds, color, pep)	MacMillan	1927	Dobias, F.	35-50	
Siebe, Josephine	Kasperle's Adventures (1st, sq8vo, pink cl, 199p, 6cp, pep)	MacMillan	1929	Dobias, F.	30-45	*
Bannerman, H.	Little Black Sambo (1st, 16mo, ibds, [39]p, color)	MacMillan	1927	Dobias, F.	65-90	
Farrow, D.P.	Little Brown Hen (1st, sq12mo, [48]p, orange cl, color, cep)	MacMillan	1941	Dobias, F.	35-50	*
Schmidt, S.L.	New Land (1st, sm8vo, 317p, brown cl, 9 fp b/w, pep, NH)	McBride	1933	Dobias, F.	30-55	*
Kelsey, A.	Once the Hodja (1st {std}, 12mo, 170p)	Longmans	1943	Dobias, F.	25-40	*
N/A	Puss in Boots (1st, sq16mo, [41]p, color, pep)	MacMillan	1937	Dobias, F.	65-90	*
N/A	Three Billy Goats Gruff (1st, sq16mo, ibds, color)	MacMillan	1927	Dobias, F.	20-30	*
Kuh, Charlotte	Train, a Boat & an Island (1st, sq8vo, 89p, col frn, b/w)	MacMillan	1932	Dobias, F.	25-40	*
Fox, F.M.	Little Giant's Neighbours (1st, 12mo, 132p, b/w)	L.C. Page	1903	Dodge, F.E.	20-30	*
Putnam, Nina W.	Adventures in the Open (1st, sm8vo, ibds, color)	Volland	(1918)	Dodge, K.S.	45-65	*
Reid, Sydney	How Sing Found the World is Round (1st, 12mo, [40]p, ibds, col)	Volland	(1921)	Dodge, K.S.	70-100	*
Sylvester, C.	Manny & Co. (1st, 8vo, [40]p, color)	Volland	1913	Dodge, K.S.	45-70	*
Cox-McCormack, N.	Peeps: Really Truly Sunshine Fairy (1st, 8vo, [37]p, ibds, col)	Volland	(1918)	Dodge, K.S.	65-80	
Waterstone, S.S.	Short Stories of Musical Melodies (1st, 4to, ibds, gilt)	Volland	(1915)	Dodge, K.S.	140-200	*
Jacobs-Bond, C.	Tales of Little Cats (1st, 12mo, ibds, [38]p, color, pep)	Volland	(1918)	Dodge, K.S.	50-70	
Jacobs-Bond, C.	Tales of Little Dogs (1st, smsq8vo, ibds, [35]p, color, pep)	Volland	(1921)	Dodge, K.S.	65-80	*
Putnam, Nina W.	Winkle, Twinkle & Lollypop (1st, 8vo, ibds, color)	Volland	(1918)	Dodge, K.S.	60-80	*
Dodworth, D.	Mrs. Doodlepunk Trades Work (1st, ob8vo, red cl, [48]p, 1-color)	W.R. Scott	1957	Dodworth, D.	30-50	*
Donahey, Wm.	Adventures of the Teenie Weenies (1st, lg4to, 128p, p-o, 9cp)	Reilly/Lee	(1920)	Donahey, Wm.	130-170	
Donahey, Wm.	Alice & the Teenie Weenies (1st, lg8vo, 105p, p-o, color)	Reilly/Lee	(1927)	Donahey, Wm.	70-100	*
Mother Goose	Children's Mother Goose (1st, 4to, 120p, color, pep)	Reilly/Lee	(1921)	Donahey, Wm.	90-145	*
Donahey, Wm.	Down the River with/Teenie Weenies (4to, p-o, 128p, 8cp)	Reilly/Lee	(1921)	Donahey, Wm.	140-200	
Marino, Josef	Hi! Ho! Pinocchio (1st, 4to, 127p, col frn, p-o, b/w, cep)	Reilly/Lee	(1940)	Donahey, Wm.	80-130	*
Donahey, Wm.	Teenie Weenie Days (1st, lg8vo, 65p, 4 fp color, pep)	Whittlesey	(1944)	Donahey, Wm.	65-100	
Mother Goose	Teenie Weenie Man's Mother Goose (1st, 4to, 126p, 12cp, pep)	Reilly/Lee	(1921)	Donahey, Wm.	165-220	
Donahey, Wm.	Teenie Weenie Neighbors (1st {std}, 8vo, 68p, 5 color, pep)	Whittlesey	(1945)	Donahey, Wm.	70-100	
Donahey, Wm.	Teenie Weenie Town (1st, 8vo, 71p, red cl, p-o, color, pep)	Whittlesey	(1942)	Donahey, Wm.	50-70	*
Donahey, Wm.	Teenie Weenies Under the Rose Bush (1st, 4to, p-o, 120p, 8cp)	Reilly/Lee	(1922)	Donahey, Wm.	150-200	
Donahey, Wm.	Teenie Weenies in Wonderland (1st, 4to, 120p, color)	Reilly/Lee	(1923)	Donahey, Wm.	70-100	*
Thompson, R.P.	Wonder Book (1st, 4to, green cl, 217p, p-o, 7cp)	Reilly/Lee	(1929)	Donahey, Wm.	180-250	
Malory, T.	Death of King Arthur (1st, 8vo, 51p)	L: MacMillan	1928	Donaldson, C.	35-50	*
Heath, J.F.	Built-Upon House (1st, lg8vo, 126p, p-o, color)	Whitman	(1929)	Dotterer, L.J.	30-45	*
Johnson, J.W.	God's Trombones (1st, 8vo, bds, gilt, 56p, 8pl, DJ)	Viking	1927	Douglas, A.	180-240	
Kennedy, M.	Surprise to the Children (1st {std}, sq4to, ibds, 6cp)	Doubleday/Dor.	1933	Dowd, J.H.	30-45	
Broadbent, H.	Sing-A-Song (1st, ob folio, ibds, unpag, 8cp)	L: M. Goshen	1912	Dowdall, N.	130-180	*
Downer, M.L.	The Flower (1st, ob8vo, brown cl, [32]p, 3-color)	W.R. Scott	1955	Downer, M.L.	25-40	*
Lang, A.	Princess Nobody (1st, 4to, ibds, 56p, color)	L: Longmans	(1884)	Doyle, R.	350-500	
Ramal, W.	Songs of Childhood (1st, 12mo, teg, gilt, frn by...)	L: Longmans	1902	Doyle, R.	300-400	
Smith, G.	Jolly Polly Stories (1st, lg sq8vo, 99p, b/w)	Small	1918	Drake, E.D.	30-45	*
Drayton, G.	Baby Bears & their Wishing Rings (1st, lg ob8vo, 167p, color)	Century	(1914)	Drayton, G.	150-200	*
N/A	Bettina's Bonnet (sq12mo, ibds, 10 fp color)	Hearst	1915	Drayton, G.	85-100	*
Drayton, G.	Let's Go to the Zoo (1st, ob4to, 44p, ibds, shape bk., 6cp)	Duffield	(1914)	Drayton, G.	130-185	
Mother Goose	Nursery Rhymes from Mother Goose (sm8vo, 111p, color)	Scribner	1916	Drayton, G.	140-200	*
Cammack, K.	Spartan Primer (1st, 4to, ipcb, fp color)	Duffield	1913	Drayton, G.	140-200	
DuBois, W.P.	Bear Party (1st, sm8vo, ibds, unpag, color, CH)	Viking	1951	DuBois, W.P.	65-100	
DuBois, W.P.	Elisabeth the Cow Ghost (1st, sq12mo, [47]p, color)	NY: Nelson	1936	DuBois, W.P.	35-50	*
DuBois, W.P.	Flying Locomotive (1st, ob8vo, ibds, 47p, color)	Viking	1941	DuBois, W.P.	65-80	
DuBois, W.P.	Giant Otto (1st, sq16mo, [40]p, ibds, 17cp, pep)	Viking	1936	DuBois, W.P.	80-130	
DuBois, W.P.	Great Geppy (1st, 4to, 92p, 22 fp color, dep)	Viking	1940	DuBois, W.P.	100-150	R
McKinley, C.F.	Harriett (1st, lg8vo, 44p, 1-color)	Viking	1946	DuBois, W.P.	65-90	R
Clement, Marg.	In France (1st, 8vo, blue cl, 151p, dp b/w, pep)	Viking	1956	DuBois, W.P.	25-40	*
DuBois, W.P.	Lion (1st, 4to, 36p, color, pep, CH)	Viking	1956	DuBois, W.P.	90-140	R*
Greener, Leslie	Moon Ahead (1st, 8vo, green cl, 256p, fp b/w, pep)	Viking	1951	DuBois, W.P.	30-50	*
Godden, Rumer	Mousewife (1st, 8vo, 46p, b/w)	Viking	1951	DuBois, W.P.	35-50	*
Ames, Evelyn	My Brother Bird (1st, 8vo, 125p, red cl, fp b/w, pep)	Dodd	1954	DuBois, W.P.	35-50	*
DuBois, W.P.	Otto at Sea (1st, sq16mo, ibds, [40]p, color, pep)	Viking	1936	DuBois, W.P.	120-165	
DuBois, W.P.	Otto in Texas (1st, sm4to, 45p, color, pep)	Viking	(1959)	DuBois, W.P.	70-120	R*
DuBois, W.P.	Peter Graves (1st, lg8vo, ibds, 168p, dep, b/w)	Viking	1950	DuBois, W.P.	45-60	*
Plimpton, Geo.	Rabbit's Umbrella (1st, 8vo, 159p, yellow cl, b/w, pep)	Viking	1955	DuBois, W.P.	35-50	*
DuBois, W.P.	Squirrel Hotel (1st, lg8vo, red cl, 48p, pep, b/w)	Viking	1952	DuBois, W.P.	40-65	*

AUTHOR	TITLE	PUBLISHER	DATE	ARTIST	PRICE	LC
DuBois, W.P.	The Giant (1st, lg8vo, 124p, grey cl, fp b/w)	Viking	1954	DuBois, W.P.	50-90	R*
DuBois, W.P.	Three Policemen (1st, lg8vo, blue cl, 92p, 16 color, DJ)	Viking	1938	DuBois, W.P.	70-100	
Bishop, C.H.	Twenty & Ten (1st, lg8vo, 76p, pep, b/w)	Viking	1952	DuBois, W.P.	35-50	*
DuBois, W.P.	Twenty-One Balloons (1st, tall 8vo, ibds, 179p, b/w, DJ, NM)	Viking	1947	DuBois, W.P.	80-110	R
DuBois, W.P.	Twenty-One Balloons (1st UK, sm4to, 179p, red cl, b/w)	L: R. Hale	1949	DuBois, W.P.	45-60	*
Gordon, Pat	Witch of Scrapfaggot Green (1st, 4to, 78p, 10 fp b/w, DJ)	Viking	1948	DuBois, W.P.	65-80	
Ashford, Daisy	Young Visitors (1st, 8vo, 91p, ibds, b/w)	Doubleday	1951	DuBois, W.P.	35-50	*
DuMaurier, G.	Legend of Camelot (1st, ob4to, ibds, 95p, b/w)	Harper	1898	DuMaurier, G.	100-145	
DuMaurier, G.	The Martian (1st, 8vo, orange/gilt, b/w, 471p)	Harper	1897	DuMaurier, G.	45-70	
Wilkins, M.E.	Heart's Highway (1st [1], 8vo, green cl, 308p, 8pl)	Doubleday/Page	1900	DuMond	30-45	
Wallace, Lew	Wooing of Malkatoon (1st, lg8vo, green/gilt, 168p, teg)	Harper	1898	DuMond	30-45	
Grimm Bros.	Fairy Tales (1st, 8vo, 408p)	L: J. Nisbet	1906	Dudley, A.	70-90	*
Justus, May	At the Foot of Windy Low (1st, 8vo, green cl, 80p, 10cp, pep)	Volland	(1930)	Dudley, C.	50-70	
Justus, May	Gabby Gaffer (1st, 8vo, green/gilt, 80p, 10cp, pep)	Volland	(1929)	Dudley, C.	45-65	
Baxter, Betty	Supposin' (1st, 12mo, 40p, color, pep)	Volland	(1931)	Dudley, C.	45-60	*
Grey, Zane	Desert Gold (1st, 12mo, 325p, gilt, p-o, 4pl)	Harper	1913	Duer, D.	120-165	*
Grey, Zane	Riders of the Purple Sage (1st, 12mo, 335p, p-o, 4pl)	Harper	1912	Duer, D.	150-200	
Campbell, J.	Celtic Dragon Myth (1st, 8vo, 172p, gilt, p-o, 5cp)	J. Grant	1911	Duff, R.	100-130	
Masefield, J.	Martin Hyde (1st, 8vo, 303p, green cl, 16pl)	L: Wells/Gard.	1910	Dugdale, T.C.	35-50	*
Crary, M.	Daughter of the Stars (1st, 4to, 190p, 2cp by...)	L: Hatchard	1939	Dulac, E.	120-180	R
Queen Marie	Dreamer of Dreams (1st, lg8vo, 181p, grey/gilt, 6 ticp)	L: Hodder	[1915]	Dulac, E.	250-300	
Dulac, E.	Edmund Dulac's Fairy Book (1st AM, 4to, p-o, gilt 174p, 16 ticp)	Doran	(1916)	Dulac, E.	230-280	
Stawell, Mrs. R.	Fairies I Have Met (1st, 8vo, green cl, 117p, 8cp)	L: J. Lane	[1907]	Dulac, E.	265-320	
Stawell, Mrs. R.	Fairies I Have Met (8vo, 117p, 8cp)	L: Hodder	[1910]	Dulac, E.	185-260	
Dulac, E.	Fairy Garland (1st, lg8vo, 251p, 12 ticp)	L: Cassell	(1928)	Dulac, E.	150-200	
Dulac, E.	Fairy Garland (1st AM, lg8vo, blue/gilt, 251p, p-o, 12 ticp)	Scribner	(1929)	Dulac, E.	130-180	
Dulac, E.	Fairy Tales of Allied Nations (1st, 4to, 174p, gilt, 16 ticp)	L: Hodder	[1916]	Dulac, E.	250-350	
Yeats, W.B.	Four Plays for Dancers (1st AM, 8vo, bds, 138p, b/w)	MacMillan	1921	Dulac, E.	100-140	
Williamson, H.	Gods & Mortals in Love (9cp, cloth)	L:Country Life	(1935)	Dulac, E.	75-100	
Beauclerk, H.	Green Lacquer Pavillion (1st AM, 8vo, 319p, gilt, b/w)	Doran	(1926)	Dulac, E.	60-80	
Beauclerk, H.	Green Lacquer Pavillion (1st, 12mo, tan/gilt, 319p, 10pl)	L: Collins	1926	Dulac, E.	85-120	
Rosenthal, L.	Kingdom of the Pearl (1st AM, 4to, bds, p-o, 10 ticp)	Brentano's	[1920]	Dulac, E.	350-450	
Beauclerk, H.	Love of the Foolish Angel (1st, 8vo, blue/gilt, 251p, b/w)	L: Collins	1929	Dulac, E.	85-100	
Dulac, E.	Lyrics Pathetic & Humorous... (1st, 4to, ibds, [49]p, color, pep)	L: Warne	1908	Dulac, E.	300-450	
Housman, L.	Magic Horse (1st, smsq8vo, [58]p, gilt, 12cp)	L: Hodder	(1911)	Dulac, E.	180-250	
Stawell, Mrs. R.	My Days with the Fairies (1st, 4to, 169p, red/gilt, 8 ticp)	L: Hodder	(1913)	Dulac, E.	300-450	
Dulac, E.	Picture Book/French Red Cross (1st, 4to, 135p, 19 ticp)	L: Hodder	(1915)	Dulac, E.	240-300	R
Poe, E.A.	Poetical Works of... (1st AM, 4to, bds, 28cp)	Doran	[1921]	Dulac, E.	200-280	
Housman, L.	Princess Badoura (1st, 4to, teg, 113p, gilt, 10 ticp)	L: Hodder	[1913]	Dulac, E.	250-320	
Smith, C.M.	Queen Bee (1st, 8vo, gilt, 2cp by...)	L: Nelson	1907	Dulac, E.	100-150	
Omar Khayyam	Rubaiyat... (1st, lg4to, white/gilt, unpag, 20 ticp)	L: Hodder	[1909]	Dulac, E.	250-350	
Omar Khayyam	Rubaiyat... (lg8vo, 20 ticp, later)	Doran	[1920]	Dulac, E.	100-130	
Omar Khayyam	Rubaiyat... (1st {this pub.}, lg8vo, 197p, cp)	Doubleday/Dor.	1930	Dulac, E.	40-65	
Bronte, C.	Shirley (1st, 8vo, 2 volumes, teg)	L: Dent	1905	Dulac, E.	120-165	
N/A	Sinbad the Sailor (1st, lg4to, 223p, gilt, bds, p-o, 23 ticp)	L: Hodder	(1914)	Dulac, E.	450-600	
Quiller-Couch, A.	Sleeping Beauty... (1st, 4to, 129p, gilt, 30 ticp)	L: Hodder	(1910)	Dulac, E.	350-450	
Quiller-Couch, A.	Sleeping Beauty... (4to, red cl, 16 ticp, later)	Doran	[1910]	Dulac, E.	150-200	
Quiller-Couch, A.	Sleeping Beauty... (1st AM, lg4to, 129p, maroon/gilt, 30 ticp)	NY: Hodder	[1910]	Dulac, E.	250-350	
Quiller-Couch, A.	Sleeping Beauty... (8vo, 196p, black cl, p-o, 8cp, pep)	Garden City	[1932]	Dulac, E.	45-60	*
Unknown	Stealers of Light (1st, 4to, blue/gilt, 190p, 2 ticp)	L: Hodder	1916	Dulac, E.	100-145	
Andersen, H.C.	Stories by... (lg8vo, 159p, 7cp, later)	L: Hodder	[1920]	Dulac, E.	80-100	
Andersen, H.C.	Stories from Andersen (lg8vo, blue/gilt, 195p, 14cp, later)	Hodder	[1915]	Dulac, E.	120-175	
Housman, L. (ed.)	Stories from Arabian Nights (1st, 4to, 133p, 50 ticp)	L: Hodder	(1907)	Dulac, E.	300-400	
Housman, L. (ed.)	Stories from Arabian Nights (1st AM, 4to, 133p, gilt, 50 ticp)	Scribner	(1907)	Dulac, E.	300-450	
Housman, L. (ed.)	Stories from Arabian Nights (8vo, 24 ticp, later)	L: Hodder	[1911]	Dulac, E.	100-140	
N/A	Stories from Arabian Nights (lg8vo, 205p, 8cp, pep, later)	Garden City	[1932]	Dulac, E.	65-80	
Andersen, H.C.	Stories from... (8vo, 159p, 6 ticp, later)	L: Hodder	[1925]	Dulac, E.	80-100	*
Andersen, H.C.	Stories from... (4to, blue cl, 16cp)	Doubleday/Dor.	(1930)	Dulac, E.	75-120	
Andersen, H.C.	Stories... (1st, lg4to, 250p, orange/gilt, 28 ticp)	L: Hodder	(1911)	Dulac, E.	280-450	R
N/A	Tales from Arabian Nights (sm4to, 190p, gilt, 20 ticp, later)	L: Hodder	[1920]	Dulac, E.	150-180	
Hawthorne, N.	Tanglewood Tales (1st, 4to, 245p, gilt, 14 ticp, pep)	L: Hodder	[1919]	Dulac, E.	165-220	
Poe, E.A.	The Bells... (1st, 4to, teg, green/gilt, pep, 28 ticp)	L: Hodder	(1912)	Dulac, E.	280-400	
Andersen, H.C.	The Nightingale (1st, 4to, blue/gilt, 125p, 12 ticp)	L: Hodder	[1911]	Dulac, E.	200-260	
Shakespeare, Wm.	The Tempest (1st, 4to, blue/gilt, 144p, 40 ticp)	L: Hodder	[1908]	Dulac, E.	300-400	
Stevenson, R.L.	Treasure Island (1st AM, lg8vo, 287p, green/gilt, 12 ticp)	Doran	[1927]	Dulac, E.	120-170	
Stevenson, R.L.	Treasure Island (1st {this pub}, 8vo, green cl, 287p, 8cp)	Garden City	[1930]	Dulac, E.	80-120	*
Locke, Wm. J.	Beloved Vagabond (1st, sm4to, 267p, 16cp)	L: J. Lane	1922	Dulac, Jean	80-120	
Banta, N.M.	Four-and-Forty Fairies (1st, 12mo, grey cl, 128p, 1-color, pep)	Chi: Flanagan	1923	Dulin, D.	45-65	*
Smith, Laura R.	Runaway Bunny (1st, sm8vo, 128p, pep, color)	Chi: Flanagan	1923	Dulin, D.	30-45	
Grimm Bros.	Fairy Tales (1st, sm sq4to, 275p, p-o, 11cp, 7pl, pep)	Rand/McNally	(1913)	Dunlap, H.	65-80	
Craik, D.	Little Lame Prince (1st, 4to, p-o, 121p, gilt, color)	Rand/McNally	(1909)	Dunlap, H.	65-80	
Garnett, L.A.	Muffin Shop (1st, folio, p-o, 79p, color)	Rand/McNally	(1908)	Dunlap, H.	100-165	

AUTHOR	TITLE	PUBLISHER	DATE	ARTIST	PRICE	LC
Browning, R.	Pied Piper of Hamelin (1st, sm4to, p-o, gilt, 56p, pep, color)	Rand/McNally	(1910)	Dunlap, H.	70-100	
McCabe, O.	Rose Fairies (1st, 8vo, 159p, p-o, green cl, 12cp, pep)	Rand/McNally	(1911)	Dunlap, H.	65-90	
Brooks, Noah	Boy Emigrants (1st, 4to, brown cl, 381p, teg, 10cp, pep, SC)	Scribner	1914	Dunn, H.T.	65-80	
Rhodes, E.M.	Desire of the Moth (1st, 8vo, 149p, 2pl)	Holt	1916	Dunn, H.T.	35-50	
London, J.	John Barleycorn (1st, 8vo, 343p, 8pl)	Century	1913	Dunn, H.T.	140-175	
Wister, O.	Members of the Family (1st, 317p, 12pl)	MacMillan	1911	Dunn, H.T.	25-40	
Hornung, E.W.	Shadow of the Rope (1st, 8vo, teg, 377p, 3pl)	Scribner	1906	Dunn, H.T.	35-50	
Beach, R.	Silver Horde (1st, 8vo, red cl, p-o, 389p, 8pl)	Harper	1909	Dunn, H.T.	25-40	
Dickens, C.	Tale of Two Cities (1st, lg8vo, teg, p-o, 362p, 10cp, pep)	Cosmopolitan	1921	Dunn, H.T.	60-90	
Rhodes, E.M.	West is West (1st, 8vo, 304p, black cloth, frn by...)	H.K. Fly	(1917)	Dunn, H.T.	65-80	
Warner, S.	Wide, Wide World (1st, 8vo, 592p, 6pl)	Fenno	(1904)	Dunton, H.	30-45	*
Hains, T.J.	Black Barque (1st, 8vo, 322p, 5pl)	Page	1905	Dunton, W.H.	30-45	*
Parrish, R.	Keith of the Border (1st, 8vo, 362p, 4cp)	McClurg	1910	Dunton, W.H.	30-45	
Bateson, C.	Man in the Camelot Cloak (1st, 8vo, 320p, teg, 4pl)	Saalfield	1903	Dunton, W.H.	30-45	*
Costello, F.H.	Nelson's Yankee Boy (1st, 12mo, 293p, 6pl)	Holt	1904	Dunton, W.H.	30-45	*
Bindloss, H.	Winston of the Prairie (1st, sm8vo, p-o, 340p, 3cp)	Stokes	(1907)	Dunton, W.H.	30-45	
Lewis, A.H.	Wolfville Folks (1st, 8vo, 321p, frn by...)	Appleton	1908	Dunton, W.H.	30-45	
Duplaix, G.	Gaston & Josephine (1st, 4to, ibds, color)	NY: OUP	1933	Duplaix, G.	80-120	*
Duplaix, G.	Gaston & Josephine (1st {this pub.}, lg4to, 48p, color)	Harper	1936	Duplaix, G.	70-100	*
Duplaix, G.	Pee-Gloo (1st, 4to, [40]p, ibds, pep, color)	Harper	1935	Duplaix, G.	70-120	*
Duplaix, G.	Popo the Hippopotamus (1st, ob12mo, ibds, [28]p, color)	Whitman	(1935)	Duplaix, G.	70-120	
Duvoisin, R.	All Aboard! (1st, folio, 44p, ibds, color)	Grosset/Dunlap	(1935)	Duvoisin, R.	90-130	*
Menotti, G-C.	Amahl & Night Visitors (1st, 8vo, [89]p, bds, 17 color, pep)	Whittlesey	(1952)	Duvoisin, R.	35-50	
Fatio, Louise	Anna the Horse (1st {std}, 8vo, ipcb, [48]p, 3-color, pep)	Aladdin	(1951)	Duvoisin, R.	35-50	*
Misch, Rbt. J.	At Daddy's Office (1st {std}, sm4to, ibds, [32]p, color)	Knopf	(1946)	Duvoisin, R.	35-50	*
McCullough, J.G.	At Our House (1st, sm4to, [41]p)	W.R. Scott	1943	Duvoisin, R.	35-50	*
Tresselt, A.R.	Autumn Harvest (1st, sm4to, ipcb, [25]p, color, pep)	Lothrop/Lee	1951	Duvoisin, R.	20-35	*
Weston, C.	Bhimsa the Dancing Bear (1st, sm8vo, 120p, 2-color, cep, NH)	Scribner	1945	Duvoisin, R.	60-85	
Coggins, Herbert	Busby & Co. (1st, 8vo, 96p, rust cl, fp b/w, pep)	Whittlesey	(1952)	Duvoisin, R.	30-45	*
Jones, Idwal	Chef's Holiday (1st {std}, sm8vo, 210p, b/w)	Longmans	1952	Duvoisin, R.	20-35	*
Stevenson, R.L.	Child's Garden of Verses (1st, 4to, 112p, ibds, color)	Heritage Press	1944	Duvoisin, R.	35-50	*
Duvoisin, R.	Christmas Cake (1st, ob12mo, [29]p, b/w, ibds, pep)	A.A. Group	(1941)	Duvoisin, R.	30-50	*
Fatio, Louise	Christmas Forest (1st, 8vo, ibds, [44]p, pep, color)	Aladdin	(1950)	Duvoisin, R.	45-65	*
Hall, Wm.	Christmas Pony (1st {std}, sm4to, ipcb, unpag, color)	Knopf	(1948)	Duvoisin, R.	45-65	*
Duvoisin, R.	Christmas Whale (1st {std}, ob8vo, [45]p, ibds, color)	Knopf	(1945)	Duvoisin, R.	35-50	
Fischer, Marj.	Dog Cantbark (1st {std}, 4to, [32]p, gilt, color, cep, DJ)	Random	(1940)	Duvoisin, R.	45-60	
Duvoisin, R.	Donkey-Donkey (1st, 8vo, ibds, [46]p, color, pep)	Whitman	(1933)	Duvoisin, R.	100-150	
Duvoisin, R.	Donkey-Donkey (1st {this pub}, lg8vo, ipcb, pep, 39p, color)	Grosset/Dunlap	(1940)	Duvoisin, R.	50-70	*
Duvoisin, R.	Easter Treat (1st {std}, sm4to, [16]p, 1-color)	Knopf	(1954)	Duvoisin, R.	45-60	*
Root, Charlet	Feast of Lamps (1st, lg8vo, 75p, p-o, pep, color)	Whitman	1938	Duvoisin, R.	60-90	*
Pratt, Marg.	Flash of Washington Square (1st, 4to, green cl, [29]p, dp col)	Lothrop/Lee	1954	Duvoisin, R.	45-70	*
Tresselt, A.R.	Follow the Road (1st, 4to, unpag, color)	Lothrop/Lee	1953	Duvoisin, R.	35-50	*
Tresselt, A.R.	Follow the Wind (1st, 4to, color, [26]p)	Lothrop/Lee	(1950)	Duvoisin, R.	35-50	*
Tresselt, A.R.	Frog in the Well (1st, sm4to, green cl, [32]p, color, pep)	Lothrop/Lee	1958	Duvoisin, R.	35-50	*
Fatio, Louise	Happy Lion (1st, sm4to, [30]p, yellow cl, 2-color)	Whittlesey	(1954)	Duvoisin, R.	50-80	R*
Fatio, Louise	Happy Lion in Africa (1st, sm4to, green cl, 30p, 2-color)	Whittlesey	(1955)	Duvoisin, R.	35-50	*
Zolotow, C.	In My Garden (1st, sm4to, unpag, blue cl, fp color)	Lothrop/Lee	1960	Duvoisin, R.	40-65	*
Elliott, K.M.	Jo-Yo's Idea (1st {std}, 8vo, 114p, cloth, fp color, cep)	Knopf	1939	Duvoisin, R.	35-50	*
Howard, Janet	Jumpy the Kangaroo (1st, sq12mo, [42]p, ibds, color, pep)	Lothrop/Lee	(1944)	Duvoisin, R.	50-80	*
Duvoisin, R.	Little Boy Who was Drawing (1st, sm4to, [56]p, color)	Scribner	1932	Duvoisin, R.	60-85	*
Frost, F.	Little Whistler (1st, 8vo, green cl, 48p, fp color, DJ)	Whittlesey	(1949)	Duvoisin, R.	35-50	
Attwood, Wm.	Man Who Could Grow Hair (1st {std}, sm8vo, 240p, ipcb, b/w)	Knopf	1949	Duvoisin, R.	30-50	*
Mother Goose	Mother Goose (1st, folio, 144p, yellow cl, color, pep)	Heritage Press	(1936)	Duvoisin, R.	80-120	R*
Mother Goose	Mother Goose (1st {new ed}, 4to, ipcb, 112p, color, pep)	Heritage Press	(1943)	Duvoisin, R.	50-70	*
Rigby, D.	Moustachio (1st, 4to, [31]p, ibds, 1-color, DJ)	Harper	(1947)	Duvoisin, R.	35-50	
Zolotow, C.	Not a Little Monkey (1st, sm4to, green cl, unpag, pep, color)	Lothrop/Lee	1957	Duvoisin, R.	40-60	*
Zolotow, C.	One Step, Two (1st, sm4to, unpag, color)	Lothrop/Lee	1954	Duvoisin, R.	40-65	*
Duvoisin, R.	One Thousand Christmas Beards (1st, lg8vo, unpag, ibds, col, DJ)	Knopf	(1955)	Duvoisin, R.	70-100	
Duvoisin, R.	Petunia (1st {std}, lg8vo, [32]p, color)	Knopf	(1950)	Duvoisin, R.	40-65	*
Duvoisin, R.	Petunia & the Song (1st {std}, sm4to, unpag, color)	Knopf	(1951)	Duvoisin, R.	40-65	*
Duvoisin, R.	Petunia Takes a Trip (1st {std}, 4to, unpag, color, pep)	Knopf	(1953)	Duvoisin, R.	50-70	R
Duvoisin, R.	Petunia's Christmas (1st {std}, lg8vo, unpag, color, pep)	Knopf	(1952)	Duvoisin, R.	40-65	*
Browning, R.	Pied Piper of Hamelin (1st, folio, ibds, unpag, color, pep)	Grosset/Dunlap	(1936)	Duvoisin, R.	70-110	*
Martin, Pat. M.	Pointed Brush (1st, 4to, red cl, unpag, color, pep)	Lothrop	1959	Duvoisin, R.	25-45	*
Washburne, Heluiz	Rhaman: Boy of Kashmir (1st, lg8vo, 127p, red cl, color, pep)	Whitman	1939	Duvoisin, R.	45-65	*
Courlander, H.	Ride with the Sun (1st, sm8vo, 296p, green cl, b/w)	Whittlesey	(1955)	Duvoisin, R.	25-40	*
Elliott, K.M.	Riema... (1st {std}, 8vo, 54p, ibds, color, pep, DJ)	Knopf	1937	Duvoisin, R.	40-60	
Defoe, D.	Robinson Crusoe (1st, 8vo, pcb, pep, 4 fp col)	NY: World	(1946)	Duvoisin, R.	35-50	*
Puner, Helen	Sitter Who Didn't Sit (1st, sm4to, [26]p, color)	Lothrop/Lee	1949	Duvoisin, R.	35-50	*
Elliott, K.M.	Soomoon, Boy of Bali (1st {std}, 8vo, 88p, ibds, pep, color)	Knopf	1938	Duvoisin, R.	70-100	R
Moran, Jim	Sophocles the Hyena (1st, sm4to, red cl, 48p, 2-color)	Whittlesey	(1954)	Duvoisin, R.	45-65	*
Pratt, Marg.	Successful Secretary (1st, sm8vo, 144p, p-o, 15 fp b/w)	Lothrop/Lee	(1946)	Duvoisin, R.	35-50	*

AUTHOR	TITLE	PUBLISHER	DATE	ARTIST	PRICE	LC
Tresselt, A.R.	Sun Up (1st, 4to, ibds, pep, [25]p, color)	Lothrop/Lee	1949	Duvoisin, R.	45-60	*
Calhoun, Mary	Sweet Papootie Doll (1st, lg8vo, yellow cl, [32]p, 3-color)	Wm. Morrow	1957	Duvoisin, R.	35-50	*
Hudson, W.H.	Tales of the Pampas (1st, 8vo, beige cl, 245p, 6pl)	Knopf	1939	Duvoisin, R.	30-50	*
Carlson, N.S.	Talking Cat... (1st, sq8vo, 87p, red cl, 15 fp b/w, DJ)	Harper	(1952)	Duvoisin, R.	45-70	
Duvoisin, R.	They Put Out to Sea (1st {std}, 4to, 171p, 8 dp color, pep)	Knopf	1943	Duvoisin, R.	40-65	R*
Elliott, K.M.	Three Sneezes... (1st {std}, 8vo, 244p, color, pep, DJ)	Knopf	1941	Duvoisin, R.	35-50	
Powers, Tom	Virgin with Butterflies (1st {std}, 8vo, 188p, black cl, b/w)	Bobbs-Merrill	(1945)	Duvoisin, R.	35-50	*
Tresselt, A.R.	White Snow, Bright Snow (1st, 4to, 33p, color, DJ, CM)	Lothrop/Lee	(1947)	Duvoisin, R.	75-100	
Ostrander, Fannie	Gift of the Magic Staff (1st, 8vo, 221p, green cl, 8pl)	Revell	(1902)	Dwiggens, Will	40-65	
Bangs, J.K.	Andiron Tales (1st, sm4to, green cl, p-o, 101p, 8cp)	Winston	(1906)	Dwiggins, C.V.	100-150	*
Dwiggins, W.	Marionette in Motion (1st, 8vo, 25p, b/w, DJ)	(Detroit)	1939	Dwiggins, W.A.	120-160	
Nicholson, M.	The Poet (1st, 8vo, teg, 190p, 4cp & designs by...)	Houghton	1914	Dwiggins, W.A.	30-45	
Wells, H.G.	Time Machine (1st {this pub}, sm4to, 86p, bds, color designs)	Random	1931	Dwiggins, W.A.	65-80	*
Harris, J.C.	Witch Wolf... (1st {std}, 12mo, 30p, tan pcb, b/w)	Bacon/Brown	1921	Dwiggins, W.A.	130-165	R
Ash, Fenton	Black Opal (1st, 8vo, 320p, blue cl, 3 color)	L: J.F. Shaw	(1915)	E.S.H.	40-60	*
Galsworthy, J.	Memories (1st, 4to, green/gilt, 69p, teg, 4 ticp, 24pl)	Scribner	(1914)	Earl, M.	70-110	
Coblentz, C.C.	Blue & Silver Necklace (1st {std}, 8vo, 242p, blue cl, 6pl)	Little/Brown	1937	Earle, E.	20-35	*
Jacberns, R.	Attic Boarders (1st, 8vo, 298p, 6cp)	L: Chambers	1909	Earnshaw, H.C.	35-50	*
Wesselhoeft, Lily	Fairy-Folk of Blue Hill (1st, 8vo, 240p, b/w)	Page	1898	Eastman, A.L.	30-50	
Andersen, H.C.	Fairy Tales (4to, 416p, 8cp)	L: Heinemann	1909	Edwards, C.H.	100-130	
Edwards, G.W.	Alsace-Lorraine (1st AM, 4to, 344p, blue/gilt, 35pl)	Penn	(1918)	Edwards, G.W.	75-100	
Mabie, H.W.	Book of Christmas (1st, 12mo, 369p, gilt, 12pl)	MacMillan	1909	Edwards, G.W.	30-45	*
Edwards, G.W.	Book of Old English Love Songs (1st, gilt)	NY: MacMillan	1897	Edwards, G.W.	35-50	*
Edwards, G.W.	Forest of Arden (1st, 4to, red/gilt, 213p, teg, 6cp)	Stokes	(1914)	Edwards, G.W.	30-45	
Dodge, M.M.	Hans Brinker (1st, 4to, p-o, teg, 8cp, pep, SC)	Scribner	1915	Edwards, G.W.	50-65	
Seawell, M.E.	Midshipman Paulding (1st, 8vo, 133p)	Appleton	1891	Edwards, G.W.	35-50	
Watson, V.	Princess Pocahontas (1st, lg8vo, 306p, blue/gilt, p-o, 9cp)	Penn	1916	Edwards, G.W.	60-80	
Barr, Rbt.	Strong Arm (1st, 8vo, 336p, cvr by...)	Stokes	1899	Edwards, G.W.	20-30	*
Hawthorne, N.	Tanglewood Tales (1st, sm4to, 190p, b/w pl)	Houghton	1887	Edwards, G.W.	80-120	*
Hawthorne, N.	Tanglewood Tales (1st UK, 4to, 190p, b/w)	L: Chatto	1888	Edwards, G.W.	85-100	
Farmer, J.E.	The Grenadier (1st, 8vo, 328p, red cl, cvr by...)	Dodd	1898	Edwards, G.W.	20-30	
Edwards, G.W.	Thus Think and Smoke Tobacco (1st, sm4to, red/gilt, AEG)	Stokes	1891	Edwards, G.W.	100-140	
Curtis, G.W.	Prue & I (8vo, teg, 234p)	Crowell	1899	Edwards, H.C.	20-30	
Stuart, Ruth M.	River's Children (1st, 16mo, 179p, green/gilt, 5pl)	Century	1904	Edwards, H.C.	30-45	
Hamblen, H.E.	Story of a Yankee Boy (1st, 12mo, 339p, 4pl)	Scribner	1898	Edwards, H.C.	25-40	
Gillilan, S.	Danny & Fanny (1st, lg8vo, p-o, 96p, color, pep)	Rand/McNally	(1928)	Eger, R.C.	30-45	*
Wadsworth, W.	Modern Story Book (1st, folio, 124p, p-o, color)	Rand/McNally	(1931)	Eger, R.C.	90-130	*
Fox, F.M.	Nancy Davenport (1st, 12mo, 261p, p-o, 5cp)	Rand/McNally	(1928)	Eger, R.C.	20-30	*
Beard, P.	Pillow-Time Tales (1st, 4to, p-o, 96p, color)	Rand/McNally	(1927)	Eger, R.C.	35-50	*
Jackson, L.F.	Rimskittle's Book (1st, folio, p-o, unpag, color, pep)	Rand/McNally	(1926)	Eger, R.C.	65-85	
Beard, P.	Twilight Tales (1st, 8vo, p-o, 96p, 7cp)	Rand/McNally	(1929)	Eger, R.C.	45-60	
Ehrlich, Bettina	Cocolo Comes to America (1st, folio, ibds, [32]p, color)	Harper	1949	Ehrlich, B.	50-85	*
Ehrlich, Bettina	Cocolo's Home (1st, folio, ibds, [32]p, color)	Harper	1950	Ehrlich, B.	50-75	*
Fischer, Marj.	All on a Summer's Day (1st {std}, 8vo, 157p, grn cl, b/w, pep)	Random	(1941)	Eichenberg, F.	30-45	*
Hall, Rosalys	Animals to Africa (1st, sq8vo, [27]p, fp color, dep)	Holiday House	(1939)	Eichenberg, F.	45-65	*
Eichenberg, Fritz	Ape in a Cape (1st {std}, 4to, [32]p, color, pep, CH)	Harcourt	(1952)	Eichenberg, F.	70-110	R*
Duncan, Eula G.	Big Road Walker (1st, 8vo, 121p, cep, 17 fp b/w)	Stokes	1940	Eichenberg, F.	70-100	*
Sewell, Anna	Black Beauty (1st, sm8vo, 288p, 45p, pep, 10cp)	Grosset/Dunlap	(1945)	Eichenberg, F.	35-50	*
Eichenberg, Fritz	Dancing in the Moon (1st {std}, 4to, red cl, [21]p, color, pep)	Harcourt	(1955)	Eichenberg, F.	70-120	R*
N/A	Dick Whittington & his Cat (1st, 24mo, ipcb, [38]p, 2-color)	Holiday House	1937	Eichenberg, F.	65-80	R*
Hughes, Rich. A.	Don't Blame Me! (1st {std}, sm8vo, 159p, b/w)	Harper	(1940)	Eichenberg, F.	40-65	*
Salten, Felix	Favorite Animal Stories (1st, 8vo, orange cl, 243p, b/w)	J. Messner	(1948)	Eichenberg, F.	35-50	*
Swift, J.	Gulliver's Travels (1st, lg8vo, 343p, b/w)	Heritage Press	1940	Eichenberg, F.	35-60	*
Hunt, M.L.	Have You Seen Tom Thumb? (1st, sm8vo, blue cl, 259p, dep, NH)	Stokes	1942	Eichenberg, F.	45-65	*
Deutsch, B.	Heroes of the Kalevala (1st, lg8vo, 238p, blue cl, 12pl, cep)	J. Messner	(1940)	Eichenberg, F.	45-60	*
Turpin, Edna	Littling of Gaywood (1st, 12mo, 265p, pep, b/w)	Random	(1939)	Eichenberg, F.	30-45	*
Dolbier, Maurice	Magic Shop (1st, 8vo, 74p, ipcb, 1-color)	Random	(1946)	Eichenberg, F.	45-70	*
Hoffmann, Eleanor	Mischief in Fez (1st, lg8vo, 109p, blue cl, 8 fp 1-color, dep)	Holiday House	(1943)	Eichenberg, F.	45-70	*
White, T.H.	Mistress Masham's Repose (1st, 8vo, 225p, gilt, fp b/w, pep)	Putnam	(1946)	Eichenberg, F.	30-50	*
Lenotre, Therese	Mystery of Dog Flip (1st, sm8vo, 190p, cloth, b/w, dep)	Stokes	1939	Eichenberg, F.	25-45	*
Dobbs, Rose	No Room (1st, sm8vo, [48]p)	Coward	(1944)	Eichenberg, F.	30-45	*
Davis, Rbt.	Padre Porko (1st, sm8vo, 165p, grey cl, fp b/w, cep)	Holiday House	(1939)	Eichenberg, F.	30-45	R*
Coatsworth, E.	Peaceable Kingdom (1st, lg ob8vo, [39]p, 2-color, pep)	Pantheon	(1958)	Eichenberg, F.	35-50	*
Eberle, I.	Phoebe-Belle (1st, 8vo, 63p, 1-color, pep)	Greystone Pr.	(1941)	Eichenberg, F.	35-50	*
N/A	Puss in Boots (1st, 24mo, [38]p)	Holiday House	1936	Eichenberg, F.	35-50	*
Schackne, S.	Rowena the Skating Cow (1st, 4to, [61]p, tan cl, 28 fp color)	Scribner	1940	Eichenberg, F.	65-100	*
Keats, Mark	Sancho & Stubborn Mule (1st, ob12mo, ipcb, [41]p, 2-color, pep)	W.R. Scott	(1944)	Eichenberg, F.	50-80	*
Burglon, N.	Sticks Across the Chimney (1st, sm8vo, 256p)	Holiday House	(1938)	Eichenberg, F.	30-50	*
Beston, Henry	Tree that Ran Away (1st, sm8vo, 69p, green cl, cep, b/w)	MacMillan	1941	Eichenberg, F.	25-40	*
Eberle, I.	Wide Fields (1st, 8vo, 193p, green cl, 8pl)	Crowell	1943	Eichenberg, F.	30-45	*
Gannett, R.S.	Wonderful House-Boat-Train (1st {std}, 8vo, 63p, pep, b/w)	Random	(1949)	Eichenberg, F.	45-65	LC
Rowland, E.E.	In & Out of the Nursery (1st, ob folio, [62]p)	R.H. Russell	(1900)	Eickmeyer, R.	300-450	*

AUTHOR	TITLE	PUBLISHER	DATE	ARTIST	PRICE	LC
N/A	Spin Top Spin (1st AM, 4to, ibds, [32]p, color)	MacMillan	1929	Eisgruber, E.	75-100	
Murray, Hilda	Flower Legends for Children (1st, ob4to, ibds, 63p, 14cp, pep)	L: Longmans	1901	Eland, J.S.	100-140	*
De La Mare, W.	Three Royal Monkeys (1st, 8vo, 272p, purple cl, 1-color)	L: Faber	(1946)	Eldridge, M.E.	45-70	*
Shipman, Neil	Kurly Kew & Tree-Princess (1st, 8vo, 200p, orang cl, 6cp, pep)	MacVeagh/Dial	1930	Ellender, E.	30-45	*
Warner, J. (ed.)	Golden Book of Poetry (1st, lg4to, 97p, ibds, color, GGB)	Simon/Schuster	1947	Elliot, Gertrude	30-45	
Anderson, I.	Great Sea Horse (1st, 4to, red/gilt, teg, 251p, 24cp, pep)	Little/Brown	1909	Elliott, J.	80-100	
Stephan, A.C.	Fairy Tales of a Parrot (1st, 8vo, ibds, [90]p, 6 ticp, dep)	Nister/Dutton	(1892)	Ellis, T.	130-165	
Mitchell, Muriel M.	Adventures of Nip & Tuck (1st, 8vo, 40p, pep, ipcb, color)	Volland	(1927)	Ellsworth, M.	65-80	*
Hofman, Caroline	All Around the Sun-Dial (1st, 4to, 79p, col frn)	Dutton	(1917)	Elmer, R.R.	25-40	*
Hofman, Caroline	Little Red Balloon (1st, 12mo, ibds, [39]p, color)	Volland	(1918)	Elmer, R.R.	50-75	
Hofman, Caroline	Princess Finds a Playmate (1st, 12mo, ibds, unpag, color)	Volland	(1918)	Elmer, R.R.	50-90	*
Leonard, M.F.	Susan Grows Up (1st, 8vo, 307p, 8pl)	Crowell	(1914)	Elmer, R.R.	20-30	*
Hofman, Caroline	Wise Gray Cat (1st, 12mo, unpag, color)	Volland	(1918)	Elmer, R.R.	70-100	*
Montgomery, F.T.	On a Lark to the Planets (1st, 12mo, blue/silver, 180p, 7cp)	Saalfield	1904	Elrod, W.D.	180-260	
Carr, R.V.	Cowboy Lyrics (1st, sm8vo, 229p, teg)	Small	(1908)	Elwell, R.F.	35-50	
Lamb, C.	Tales from Shakespeare (1st, 8vo, 346p, 6cp)	Houghton	1925	Elwell, R.F.	25-40	
Whitson, J.H.	Barbara, Woman of the West (1st, sm8vo, green cl, 314p, 5pl)	Little/Brown	1903	Emerson, C.	20-35	
N/A	Arabian Nights (1st, 12mo, 318p, cp)	Baker/Taylor	1910	Emerson/D'Emo	25-40	*
Emmet, R.	Pretty Peggy… (lg sq8vo, ibds, 64p, chromos)	Dodd	1880	Emmet, R.	80-100	
France, A.	In ALL France (1st, 8vo, p-o, 110p, color)	Whitman	(1930)	Enders, L.	25-40	*
Endres, Ernest	Day with The Gnomes (1st, 24mo, [54]p, ibds, pep, 19 color)	L: Nister	[1910]	Endres, E.	100-130	
King, Marian	Amnon, Lad of Palestine (1st, sm8vo, 96p, color, pep)	Houghton	1931	Enright, E.	25-50	*
Enright, E.	Christmas Tree for Lydia (1st, 24mo, ipcb, 38p, 6cp, dep)	Rinehart	(1951)	Enright, E.	35-50	*
Rowe, Nellie	Crystal Locket (1st, 8vo, 143p, ipcb, 10cp, pep)	Whitman	1935	Enright, E.	35-50	*
Enright, E.	Four-Story Mistake (1st, 8vo, 177p, 9 fp 1-color, pep)	Farrar/Rine.	(1942)	Enright, E.	30-45	*
King, Marian	Kees (1st, 4to, 79p, ibds, color, pep)	Harper	1930	Enright, E.	35-50	
King, Marian	Kees & Kleintje (1st, 4to, 80p, p-o, color, pep)	Whitman	(1934)	Enright, E.	45-60	
Enright, E.	Kintu: A Congo Adventure (1st, 8vo, p-o, 54p, color, DJ)	Farrar/Rine.	1935	Enright, E.	45-75	
Enright, E.	Sea is All Around (1st, lg8vo, 124p, green cl, 6cp, pep, DJ)	Farrar/Rine.	(1940)	Enright, E.	50-70	*
Enright, E.	The Saturdays (1st, sm8vo, red cl, 175p, fp 1-color, pep)	Farrar/Rine.	(1941)	Enright, E.	30-45	*
Enright, E.	Then There were Five (1st, 8vo, blue cl, 241p, uncut, b/w)	Farrar/Rine.	(1944)	Enright, E.	30-45	*
Enright, E.	Thimble Summer (1st, 8vo, 124p, color, pep, DJ, NM)	Farrar/Rine.	1938	Enright, E.	65-90	
Hunt, Clara W.	About Harriet (1st, 8vo, 150p, p-o, fp color)	Houghton	1916	Enright, M.W.	35-50	*
Bancroft, L.	Babes in Birdland (1st, lg8vo, green ipcb, 116p, 8cp)	Reilly/Britton	(1911)	Enright, M.W.	350-500	
Bancroft, L.	Bandit Jim Crow (1st, 8vo, [64]p, 15cp)	Reilly/Britton	(1906)	Enright, M.W.	280-400	
Gordon, Eliz.	Billy Bunny's Fortune (1st, 12mo, [40]p, ibds, color, pep)	Volland	(1919)	Enright, M.W.	50-70	
Stilwell, Alison	Chin Ling & Chinese Cricket (1st, lg8vo, [48]p, color)	MacMillan	1947	Enright, M.W.	45-60	
Judson, C.I.	Flower Fairies (1st, lg8vo, p-o, pep, 93p, 6cp)	Rand/McNally	(1915)	Enright, M.W.	65-80	*
Huntington, I.M.	Garden of Hearts' Delight (1st, sm4to, p-o, gile, 167p, 15cp)	Rand/McNally	(1911)	Enright, M.W.	80-120	
Dodge, M.M.	Hans Brinker (1st, 4to, p-o, teg, 345p, 8cp, pep)	McKay	1918	Enright, M.W.	60-85	
Spyri, J.	Heidi (1st, lg8vo, 368p, p-o, gilt, pep, 8cp)	Rand/McNally	(1921)	Enright, M.W.	45-60	*
Seegmiller, W.	Journeys in Storyland (1st, sm8vo, [120]p, pep, color)	Houghton	1922	Enright, M.W.	45-60	*
Brown, J.	Mermaid's Gift (1st, 8vo, blue/gilt, p-o, 168p, 8cp)	Rand/McNally	(1912)	Enright, M.W.	90-130	
Bancroft, L.	Mr. Woodchuck (1st, 8vo, 62p, ibds, color, cep)	Reilly/Britton	(1906)	Enright, M.W.	280-400	
Bancroft, L.	Policeman Blue Jay (1st, 8vo, ibds, 115p, 8cp)	Reilly/Britton	(1907)	Enright, M.W.	400-600	
Bancroft, L.	Prince Mud-Turtle (1st, 12mo, 61p, tan cl, cep, 14 fp color)	Reilly/Britton	(1906)	Enright, M.W.	280-350	
Mother Goose	Songs from Mother Goose (1st, 4to, 83p, color)	MacMillan	1920	Enright, M.W.	100-150	*
Bancroft, L.	Sugar-Loaf Mountain (1st, 8vo, cloth, 64p, 16cp, cep)	Reilly/Britton	(1906)	Enright, M.W.	280-400	
Gordon, Eliz.	Tale of Johnny Mouse (1st, 8vo, ibds, color)	Volland	(1920)	Enright, M.W.	70-100	
Bancroft, L.	Twinkle & Chubbins (1st, 8vo, 384p, yellow cl, color)	Reilly/Britton	(1911)	Enright, M.W.	420-600	
Bancroft, L.	Twinkle's Enchantment (1st, 8vo, 64p, 15cp)	Reilly/Britton	(1906)	Enright, M.W.	300-450	
Knobel, E.	When Little Thoughts Go Rhyming (1st, 8vo, p-o, 96p, 10cp)	Rand/McNally	(1916)	Enright, M.W.	50-65	
Miller, O.B.	Whisk Away on a Sunbeam (1st, tall 8vo, [93]p, pep, ibds, col)	Volland	(1919)	Enright, M.W.	70-110	
Baum, L.F.	Father Goose's Yearbook (1st, 12mo, [128]p, p-o, buckram)	Reilly/Britton	(1907)	Enright, W.J.	250-350	
Sewell, Anna	Black Beauty (1st, 4to, 62p, color)	Random	1949	Erickson, P.	35-50	*
Rahr, Ruth	Journey of the Toys (1st, 4to, 87p, p-o, blue cl, pep, color)	(Wisconsin)	(1934)	Ertz, Bruno	65-80	
March, Mary E.	Rhymes of Early Jungle Folk (1st, lg8vo, 124p, woocuts, pep)	Chi: Kerr	1922	Esherick, W.H.	30-45	
Rosman, A.G.	Jock the Scot (1st, 4to, 204p, p-o, 7cp, pep)	Minton Balch	(1930)	Esley, H.	25-45	
McNeely, M.H.	Way to Glory (1st {std}, 12mo, 240p, b/w)	Longmans	1932	Esley, J.	30-45	*
Estes, Eleanor	Ginger Pye (1st {std}, 8vo, 250p, yellow cl, b/w, NM)	Harcourt	(1951)	Estes, E.	60-90	R*
Estes, Eleanor	Sleeping Giant (1st, 8vo, 101p, green cl, fp color)	Harcourt	(1948)	Estes, E.	35-50	*
Ets, Marie H.	Another Day (1st, ob4to, 40p, pep, b/w)	Viking	1953	Ets, M.H.	50-80	R*
Ets, Marie H.	Beasts & Nonsense (1st, 8vo, 64p)	Viking	1952	Ets, M.H.	35-50	*
Ets, Marie H.	In the Forest (1st, ob4to, ipcb, [45]p, b/w, CH)	Viking	1944	Ets, M.H.	65-100	R*
Ets, Marie H.	Little Old Automobile (1st, 4to, ipcb, [32]p, b/w, pep)	Viking	1948	Ets, M.H.	40-65	*
Ets, Marie H.	Mister Penny (1st {1st book}, ob4to, ibds, 48p, b/w, pep)	Viking	1935	Ets, M.H.	120-165	
Ets, Marie H.	Mr. Penny's Race Horse (1st, 4to, 63p, CH)	Viking	1956	Ets, M.H.	65-100	R
Ets, Marie H.	Mr. T.W. Anthony Woo (1st, 4to, ibds, 54p, pep, b/w, CH)	Viking	1951	Ets, M.H.	70-100	*
Ets, Marie H.	Nine Days to Christmas (1st, 4to, 48p, color, CM)	Viking	(1959)	Ets, M.H.	80-120	*
Ets, Marie H.	Oley, the Sea Monster (1st, 4to, ipcb, [32]p, b/w, pep)	Viking	1947	Ets, M.H.	45-70	*
Ets, Marie H.	Play with Me (1st, sm4to, 31p, color, CH)	Viking	(1955)	Ets, M.H.	70-100	*
Ets, Marie H.	Story of a Baby (1st, lg4to, 63p, blue cl, pep, b/w)	Viking	1939	Ets, M.H.	50-80	*

AUTHOR	TITLE	PUBLISHER	DATE	ARTIST	PRICE	LC
N/A	Baby's Animal Book (sm8vo, ibds, 10cp)	Platt/Munk	1929	Eulalie	45-60	
Piper, W.	Brimful Book (1st, 4to, [74]p, p-o, color)	Platt/Munk	(1929)	Eulalie	40-60	
Stevenson, R.L.	Child's Garden of Verses (1st, 4to, 85p, p-o, 11 fp color, pep)	Platt/Munk	(1929)	Eulalie	45-65	
Mother Goose	Favorite Mother Goose Rhymes (4to, ibds, color)	Platt/Munk	(1937)	Eulalie	45-65	*
Bannerman, H.	Little Black Sambo (4to, 40p, green bds, p-o, color)	Platt/Munk	(1927)	Eulalie	60-85	
Mother Goose	Mother Goose (sm4to, p-o, color)	Volland	(1921)	Eulalie	65-80	
Howland, E.	Scary-Ann/Cookie Man (1st, 8vo, ibds, 100p, color, pep)	Suttonhouse	1932	Eulalie	50-80	
Maeterlinck, M.	The Swarm (1st, 8vo, green cl, p-o, 113p, frn by...)	Dodd	1906	Euwer, A.	25-40	
N/A	Sleeping Beauty Picture Book (4to, 24cp)	Dodd	[1915]	Evans, E.	100-150	
March, Eleanor	Three Naughty Elves (1st, ob4to, 37p, ibds, color)	L: Liberty	[1903]	Evans, E.	180-250	*
Donahey, M.D.	Adventure of a Happy Dolly (4to, p-o, 123p, 5cp)	Barse	(1914)	Evans, G.	65-80	
Gregory, L.F.	Mama Nelly & I (1st, 4to, p-o, 167p, green cl, 5cp)	Stern	1908	Evans, G.	100-140	
Dickens, C.	Christmas Carol (8vo, bds, p-o, 168p, 13 ticp)	Crowell	[1915]	Everett, E.	65-90	
Woodward, C.S.	Dreams & Fables (1st, 8vo, 110p, green cl)	L: Longmans	1929	Everett, E.	25-40	*
Fyleman, R.	Old Fashioned Girls (1st, 8vo, 33p, 12pl)	L: Methuen	1928	Everett, E.	30-50	*
Blyton, E.	Silver & Gold (1st, sq8vo, p-o, 128p, 8cp)	NY: Nelson	(1928)	Everett, E.	40-65	
N/A	Stories from Aunt Judy (8vo, teg, 268p, 8cp, pep)	L: Bell	1913	Everett, E.	65-90	
Kingsley, C.	Water Babies (1st, 8vo, 282p, p-o, 7cp)	Winston	(1930)	Everett, E.	35-65	
Brady, C.T.	And Thus He Came (1st, sm8vo, teg, 6cp)	Putnam	1916	Everett, W.	20-25	*
Colmont, Marie	Down the River (1st {std}, lg4to, [24]p, pep, 5 dp color)	Harper	1940	Exter, A.	35-60	*
Andersen, H.C.	Thumbelina (1st, 4to, ibds, [48]p, fp color, pep)	Hyperion Press	(1943)	Fabres, O.	50-80	*
Adelson, L.	Who Blew that Whistle? (1st, lg8vo, ipcb, 45p, 1-color, pep)	W.R. Scott	(1946)	Fabres, O.	45-65	*
Haskell, H.E.	O-Heart-San (1st, 8vo, cloth, 6cp)	Page	1908	Fairbanks, F.	20-30	*
Fallon, Sara W.	Animal-Alphabet Book (1st, ob4to, [54]p, color)	L: G. Allen	1899	Fallon, S.W.	100-165	*
Falls, C.B.	ABC Book (1st, lg4to, [30]p, ibds, 26cp)	Doubleday/Page	1923	Falls, C.B.	150-200	
Falls, C.B.	ABC Book (lg4to, orang ibds, unpag, fp color)	Doubleday/Dor.	1939	Falls, C.B.	120-165	R*
Baity, E.C.	America Before Man (1st, 4to, 224p, pep, maps, b/w)	Viking	1953	Falls, C.B.	45-60	*
Baity, E.C.	Americans Before Columbus (1st, sm4to, 256p, gilt, pep, NH)	Viking	1951	Falls, C.B.	35-50	*
Singleton, E.	Goldenrod Fairy Book (1st, 8vo, blue/gilt, 342p, pep, 16cp)	Dodd	1903	Falls, C.B.	100-125	
Shippen, K.B.	Great Heritage (1st, 8vo, 230p, yellow cl, pep)	Viking	1947	Falls, C.B.	35-50	*
Wheeler, P.	Hathoo of the Elephants (1st, sm8vo, orang cl, 333p, pep by...)	Viking	1943	Falls, C.B.	30-45	*
Leonard, M.F.	How the Two Ends Met (1st, 8vo, 97p, 4pl)	Crowell	(1903)	Falls, C.B.	45-60	*
Byrne, D.	Messer. Marco Polo (1st, sm8vo, 147p, 4pl, DJ)	Century	1921	Falls, C.B.	50-80	
Falls, C.B.	Modern ABC Book (1st, lg4to, [32]p, 26 color)	NY: J. Day	1930	Falls, C.B.	140-200	*
Mother Goose	Mother Goose (1st {std}, lg4to, 96p, black cl, color, pep)	Doubleday/Page	1924	Falls, C.B.	125-170	
Shippen, K.B.	New Found World (1st, lg8vo, 262p, blue cl, b/w, pep, NH)	Viking	1945	Falls, C.B.	45-70	*
Maeterlinck, M.	Old Fashioned Flowers (1st, sm8vo, 105p, 6cp)	Dodd	1905	Falls, C.B.	50-70	
Weil, Ann	Red Sails to Capri (1st, 8vo, 156p, pep, NH)	Viking	1952	Falls, C.B.	30-45	*
Grimm Bros.	Snow White & Seven Dwarfs (sm4to, 236p, green cl, p-o, 12cp, pep)	Dodd	1913	Falls, C.B.	100-140	
Donahey, M.D.	Talking Bird & Wonderful Wishes (1st, lg8vo, p-o, 146p, 6cp, pep)	Whitman	(1920)	Falls, C.B.	70-100	*
Jerome, J.K.	Tea-Table Talk (1st, 8vo, 153p, blue cl, cvr by...)	Dodd	1903	Falls, C.B.	25-40	
Bowie, W.R.	When Jesus was Born (1st, sq12mo, ibds, color)	Harper	1928	Falls, C.B.	45-60	
Cook, W.W.	Wilby's Dan (1st, 12mo, 325p, 8cp)	Dodd	1904	Falls, C.B.	60-80	*
Singleton, E.	Wildflower Fairy Book (1st, lg8vo, gilt, 354p, teg, pep, 16cp)	Dodd	1905	Falls, C.B.	100-130	
Bailey, C.S.	Wonderful Days (1st, lg8vo, 254p, col frn)	Whitman	(1929)	Falls, C.B.	35-50	*
Dickerson	Wonderful Wishes of Jackie & Jean (1st, 4to, 146p, 6cp)	Wessels	(1905)	Falls, C.B.	90-130	*
Burgess, G.	Maxims of Methuselah (1st, 12mo, ibds, 108p)	Stokes	(1907)	Fancher, L.	25-40	
Lucas, E.V.	All the World Over (1st, ob4to, 30ff, ibds, 30cp)	L: Richards	1898	Farmiloe, E.	100-165	
Farmiloe, Edith	Mr. Biddle & the Dragon (4to, red cl, 47p, 20pl)	L: Skeffington	1904	Farmiloe, E.	50-80	
De La Mare, W.	Story of Miss Jemima (1st {this fmt}, 8vo, 55p, color, pep)	Grosset/Dunlap	(1940)	Farnam, N.H.	60-90	*
Howells, W.D.	Boy's Town (1st, 8vo, aqua/gilt, 247p, 23pl, PPP)	Harper	1890	Farney, H.F.	170-200	
Miller, O.T.	Kristy's Rainy Day Picnic (1st, 12mo, 235p, p-o, 4cp, pep)	Houghton	1906	Farnsworth, E.N.	25-40	
Jewett, J.H.	Little Governor/Fableland (1st, narrow 8vo, 104p, ibds, 5cp)	Stokes	(1907)	Farnsworth, E.N.	60-80	
Gordon, H.C.	Flower Name Fancies (1st, 4to, green cl, 31 fp b/w)	L: J. Lane	1918	Fauconnet, G.R.	45-65	*
Courlander, H.	Terrapin's Pot of Sense (1st {std}, lg8vo, 125p, b/w)	Holt	(1957)	Fax, E.	25-40	*
Warren, M.R.	Mother Goose & her Friends (1st, sm4to, 305p, p-o, pep, 12 ticp)	Doran	(1922)	Federer, C.A.	65-90	*
Warren, M.R.	Tales Told by Gander (8vo, green/gilt, 305p, p-o, 12 ticp, pep)	Doran	(1922)	Federer, C.A.	60-95	
Nesbit, E.	Book of Dragons (1st, 8vo, 290p, gilt, teg, 8 fp color by...)	L: Harper	1901	Fell, H.G.	400-500	
N/A	Book of Job (1st, sm4to, teg, gilt, 103p, uncut, 16pl)	L: Dent	1895	Fell, H.G.	100-150	
Rhys, Grace (ed.)	Fairy Gifts (1st, 12mo, 61p, uncut, teg, gilt, 16pl)	L: J.M. Dent	1895	Fell, H.G.	75-90	
N/A	History of Ali Baba (1st, 24mo, 63p, b/w)	L: Dent	1895	Fell, H.G.	65-80	*
N/A	History of Cinderella (1st, 24mo, 63p, gilt, teg, uncut, 14pl)	L: Dent	1894	Fell, H.G.	80-120	
Yeats, W.B.	Poems (1st, 8vo, 286p, beige/gilt, uncut, ti page by....)	L: T.F. Unwin	1895	Fell, H.G.	120-165	
N/A	Song of Songs... (1st, 4to, 16p, gilt, teg, buckram, 12pl)	L: Chapman	1897	Fell, H.G.	120-145	
Hawthorne, N.	Tanglewood Tales (sm8vo, uncut, 12cp)	L: Dent	1903	Fell, H.G.	80-120	
Maud, C.	Wagner's Heroes (1st, 12mo, blue buckram, 284p, uncut, 8pl)	L: E. Arnold	(1897)	Fell, H.G.	60-80	
Hawthorne, N.	Wonder Book... (1st, 8vo, teg, ibds, gilt, 24cp)	L: Dent	1910	Fell, H.G.	80-120	
N/A	Wonder Stories of Herodotus (1st, 8vo, 12cp)	Harper	1900	Fell, H.G.	80-110	
Culbertson, P.	Bear Facts (1st {std}, 8vo, ibds, color)	Winston	(1948)	Fennell, P.	30-45	*
Sears, P.M.	Barn Swallow (1st, 8vo, 45p, fp 2-color, cep)	Holiday House	(1955)	Ferguson, W.	20-25	*
Adrian, M.	Gray Squirrel (1st, 8vo, 46p, rust cl, 2-color, cep)	Holiday House	(1955)	Ferguson, W.	20-25	*
Fiedler, Jean	Big Brother Danny (1st, sm8vo, unpag, blue cl, fp b/w)	Holiday House	1953	Fiedler, H.	20-25	*

AUTHOR	TITLE	PUBLISHER	DATE	ARTIST	PRICE	LC
Field, R.	All Through the Night (1st, 24mo, ibds, [40]p, 1-color)	MacMillan	1940	Field, R.	30-50	
Field, R.	Alphabet for Boys & Girls (1st, 16mo, red cl, [59]p, color)	Doubleday/Page	1926	Field, R.	25-45	*
Field, R.	Christmas Time (1st, 24mo, [32]p, white pcb, col frn, cep)	MacMillan	1941	Field, R.	20-35	*
Farjeon, E.	Come Christmas (1st, sm8vo, ipcb, 62p, color)	Stokes	1928	Field, R.	30-45	*
Bianco, M.W.	House that Grew Smaller (1st, 12mo, 40p, p-o, color, cep, DJ)	MacMillan	1931	Field, R.	35-50	
Field, R.	Little Book of Days (1st {std}, 16mo, green cl, [59]p, col, cep)	Garden City	1927	Field, R.	30-45	
Field, R.	Little Dog Toby (1st, 12mo, blue cl, 118p, 4cp, pep)	MacMillan	1928	Field, R.	25-40	
Field, R.	Patchwork Plays (1st {std}, 8vo, 139p, blue cl, b/w, DJ)	Doubleday/Dor.	1930	Field, R.	35-50	
Field, R.	Pocket-Handerchief Park (1st {std}, 16mo, 61p, color, cep)	Doubleday/Dor.	1929	Field, R.	30-45	
Field, R.	Pointed People (1st, sm8vo, 98p, orange cl, b/w, DJ)	Yale U. Press	1924	Field, R.	35-50	
Field, R.	Polly Patchwork (1st {std}, 16mo, 56p, color)	Doubleday/Dor.	1928	Field, R.	30-45	
Gate, E.M.	Punch & Robinetta (1st, sm8vo, 118p, brown cl, 8pl)	Yale U. Press	1923	Field, R.	30-45	*
Field, R.	Susanna B. & William C. (1st, 24mo, 62p, yellow cl, cep, color)	Wm. Morrow	1934	Field, R.	35-50	*
Field, R.	Taxis & Toadstools (1st {std}, 8vo, 129p, green cl, color, cep)	Doubleday/Page	1926	Field, R.	50-75	R
Field, R.	Yellow Ship (1st {std}, 16mo, 62p, tan cl, color, dep, DJ)	Doubleday/Dor.	1931	Field, R.	30-50	
Brown, M.W.	Hidden House (1st {std}, sq8vo, ibds, unpag, color)	Holt	(1953)	Fine, A.	30-50	*
Finger, C.J.	Adventure Under Sapphire Skies (1st, 12mo, 293p, uncut, b/w)	Wm. Morrow	1931	Finger, H.	20-30	*
Shirk, J.C.	Bela the Juggler (1st {std}, lg8vo, grn cl, 66p, 2-color, pep)	Suttonhouse	(1936)	Finger, H.	30-45	*
Finger, C.J.	Golden Tales from Far Away (1st, 8vo, 233p, col frn, pep)	Winston	(1940)	Finger, H.	30-45	*
Finta, Alex.	My Brothers & I (1st, 8vo, tan cl, 185p, b/w)	Holiday House	(1940)	Finta, A.	20-35	*
Melville, Herman	Moby Dick (1st, lg8vo, 414p, black/gilt, p-o, 15cp, pep)	Winston	(1931)	Fischer, A.O.	30-50	
Sinclair, B.W.	North of Fifty-Three (1st, sm8vo, 345p, 4pl)	Little/Brown	1914	Fischer, A.O.	20-35	
Evans, Lawton	Once to Every Man (1st, 8vo, 317p, 4pl)	H.K. Fly	(1914)	Fischer, A.O.	30-45	
London, J.	Son of the Sun (1st, 8vo, blue cl, 333p, 3pl)	Doubleday/Page	1912	Fischer, A.O.	150-185	
Fischer, Hans	Pitschi (1st, ob folio, ibds, [32]p, color, pep)	Harcourt	1953	Fischer, H.	100-160	R*
Black, I.S.	Dog Doctor (1st, lg ob8vo, ipcb, [40]p, 1-color)	W.R. Scott	(1947)	Fischetti, J.R.	45-75	*
Vincent, Kitty	Gin & Ginger (1st, 8vo, col frn, 19 fp b/w)	L: Bodley Head	1927	Fish, A.H.	65-80	*
Parker, D.	High Society (1st, lg4to, ipcb, 65p, pep)	Putnam	(1920)	Fish, A.H.	60-90	
Fish	Noah's Ark Book (4to, ibds, color)	L: Bodley Head	[1915]	Fish, A.H.	100-160	
Omar Khayyam	Rubaiyat... (1st, 4to, 108p, ibds, 18pl)	L: Bodley Head	(1922)	Fish, A.H.	150-200	
Fisher, H.	American Beauties (1st, 4to, 93p, red/gilt, 21cp)	Bobbs-Merrill	(1909)	Fisher, H.	220-300	
Fisher, H.	American Beauties (4to, p-o, 94p, reprint, 21cp)	Grosset/Dunlap	(1909)	Fisher, H.	140-200	
Fisher, H.	American Girl (1st, folio, brown bds, p-o, 12 ticp)	Scribner	1909	Fisher, H.	400-600	
Fisher, H.	American Girls in Miniature (1st, 12mo, ibds, p-o, 32cp)	Scribner	1912	Fisher, H.	150-220	
Fisher, H.	Bachelor Belles (1st, 4to, [134]p, p-o, grey/gilt, 22cp)	Dodd	1908	Fisher, H.	200-300	
Wells, Carolyn	Beauties (1st, lg4to, ibds, p-o, 16 ticp)	Dodd	1913	Fisher, H.	300-450	
McCutcheon, G.B.	Beverly of Graustark (1st, 8vo, blue cl, 357p, 5cp)	Dodd	1904	Fisher, H.	20-30	
Isham, F.S.	Black Friday (1st, 8vo, 409p, 6pl)	Bobbs-Merrill	(1904)	Fisher, H.	25-40	
Page, T.N.	Bred in the Bone (1st, 8vo, 274p, teg, 8pl)	Scribner	1904	Fisher, H.	25-40	
Vance, Louis J.	Bronze Bell (1st, sm8vo, 361p, 4cp)	Dodd	1909	Fisher, H.	25-40	*
McCutcheon, G.B.	Butterfly Man (1st, 8vo, teg, 121p, lavender cl, 4cp)	Dodd	1910	Fisher, H.	20-30	
Ford, P.L.	Checked Love Affair (1st, 8vo, 112p, teg, gilt, 5pl)	Dodd	1903	Fisher, H.	30-45	
McCutcheon, G.B.	Day of the Dog (1st, 8vo, red/gilt, 137p, 5cp, pep)	Dodd	1904	Fisher, H.	35-50	
Tennyson, A.	Dream of Fair Women (lg8vo, p-o, 148p, 21cp)	Grosset/Dunlap	(1907)	Fisher, H.	160-200	
Tennyson, A.	Dream of Fair Women (1st, lg8vo, [96]p, p-o, 22cp)	Bobbs-Merrill	(1907)	Fisher, H.	200-270	
Fisher, H.	Fair Americans (1st, 4to, [100]p, p-o, 22cp)	Scribner	1911	Fisher, H.	180-220	
Seawell, M.E.	Francezka (1st, 8vo, 466p, green/gilt, 7pl)	Bobbs-Merrill	(1902)	Fisher, H.	30-45	
Fisher, H.	Garden of Girls (1st, folio, p-o, ibds, 16 ticp)	Dodd	1910	Fisher, H.	350-500	
Fisher, H.	Garden of Girls (1st Canadian, lg4to, 16 ticp)	(Toronto)	1910	Fisher, H.	350-500	
MacGrath, H.	Half a Rogue (1st, 8vo, red cl, 449p, p-o, 4pl)	Bobbs-Merrill	(1906)	Fisher, H.	20-30	
Fisher, H.	Harrison Fisher Book (1st, 4to, p-o, 9cp)	Scribner	1907	Fisher, H.	170-250	
Longfellow, H.W.	Hiawatha (1st, sm4to, p-o, gilt, 189p, 16cp)	Bobbs-Merrill	(1906)	Fisher, H.	80-120	
McCutcheon, G.B.	Husbands of Edith (1st, 12mo, 126p, 5cp)	Dodd	1908	Fisher, H.	25-40	
Michelson, M.	In The Bishop's Carriage (1st, 8vo, red cl, 280p, 6pl)	Bobbs-Merrill	(1904)	Fisher, H.	20-30	
McCutcheon, G.B.	Jane Cable (1st, 8vo, 336p, 5cp)	Dodd	1906	Fisher, H.	20-25	
Winter, A.A.	Jewel Weed (1st, 12mo, p-o, 434p, 5pl)	Bobbs-Merrill	(1910)	Fisher, H.	25-40	*
Fisher, H.	Little Gift Book (1st, lg8vo, ibds, 32cp)	Scribner	1913	Fisher, H.	180-260	
Fisher, H.	Maidens Fair (1st, folio, grey bds, p-o, 16 ticp)	Dodd	1912	Fisher, H.	300-450	
McCutcheon, G.B.	Man from Brodneys (1st, 8vo, p-o, 355p, 4cp)	Dodd	1908	Fisher, H.	20-35	
Frederic, H.	Market Place (1st, 12mo, 401p, 8pl)	Stokes	1899	Fisher, H.	25-40	
Mathews, F.A.	My Lady Peggy Goes to Town (1st, 8vo, teg, 338p, b/w)	Bowen-Merrill	1901	Fisher, H.	20-35	
McCutcheon, G.B.	Nedra (1st, sm8vo, 343p, 5cp, p-o)	Dodd	1905	Fisher, H.	20-35	
Von Hutten, B.	One Way Out (1st, 8vo, p-o, lavender cl, 4cp)	Dodd	1906	Fisher, H.	30-45	
Fisher, H.	Pictures in Color (1st, lg4to, p-o, bds, 16cp)	Scribner	1910	Fisher, H.	350-500	
McCutcheon, G.B.	Purple Parasol (1st, 8vo, green/gilt, 108p, 5cp)	Dodd	1905	Fisher, H.	25-40	
Harte, Bret	Salomy Jane (1st, 8vo, p-o, blue cl, 78p, color)	Houghton	1910	Fisher, H.	50-75	
Atherton, G.	Splendid Idle Forties (1st, 8vo, 389p, gilt, 8pl)	MacMillan	1902	Fisher, H.	30-45	
McCutcheon, G.B.	The Alternative (1st, 8vo, p-o, 119p, cp)	Dodd	1909	Fisher, H.	25-40	
Phillips, D.G.	The Cost (1st, 8vo, 402p, grey cl, 16 b/w illus)	Bobbs-Merrill	(1904)	Fisher, H.	20-35	
Bonner, G.	The Pioneer (1st, 8vo, 392p, 6pl)	Bobbs-Merrill	(1905)	Fisher, H.	25-45	*
Perry, F.F.	Their Hearts' Desire (1st, lg8vo, teg, 152p, 6cp, dep)	Dodd	1909	Fisher, H.	65-80	
Jerome, J.K.	Three Men on Wheels (1st AM, 8vo, 301p, green cl)	Dodd	1900	Fisher, H.	35-50	

AUTHOR	TITLE	PUBLISHER	DATE	ARTIST	PRICE	LC
Rinehart, M.R.	When a Man Marries (1st, 12mo, 353p, 5cp)	Bobbs-Merrill	(1909)	Fisher, H.	25-40	*
Johnson, Gerald W.	America is Born (1st, 4to, 254p, red cl, b/w, NH)	Wm. Morrow	1959	Fisher, L.E.	50-80	R*
Wellman, M.W.	To Unknown Lands (1st, 8vo, 202p, black cl, b/w, pep)	Holiday House	(1956)	Fisher, L.E.	20-25	*
Fitzgerald, J.	Bixby of Boston (1st, 12mo, uncut, 83p, 20pl)	Broadway	1906	Fitzgerald, J.	20-30	*
Montgomery, F.T.	Billy Whiskers in the South (1st, 4to, 148p, 6cp)	Saalfield	(1917)	Fitzgerald, W.	65-80	
Flack, M.	All Around Town (1st {std}, 8vo, bds, 283p, col frn)	Doubleday/Dor.	1929	Flack, M.	30-45	
Flack, M.	Angus & the Cat (1st {std}, lg ob8vo, [32]p, ibds, color)	Doubleday/Dor.	1931	Flack, M.	65-80	
Flack, M.	Angus & the Ducks (1st {std}, lg ob8vo, [32]p, ibds, col, pep)	Doubleday/Dor.	1930	Flack, M.	60-80	
Flack, M.	Angus Lost (1st {std}, ob4to, [32]p, ibds, color, pep)	Doubleday/Dor.	1932	Flack, M.	50-80	*
Flack, M.	Ask Mr. Bear (1st, sq8vo, [32]p, color, pep, DJ)	MacMillan	1932	Flack, M.	65-80	
Heyward, DuBose	Country Bunny & Little Gold Shoes (1st, sm4to, [48]p, color)	Houghton	1939	Flack, M.	80-120	*
Flack, M.	Humphrey (1st {std}, 4to, ibds, [80]p, color, pep)	Doubleday/Dor.	1934	Flack, M.	45-60	*
Colt, Terry S.	Knights, Goats & Battleships (1st {std}, 12mo, 316p, col, pep)	Doubleday/Dor.	1930	Flack, M.	25-40	*
Flack, M.	New Pet (1st {std}, 4to, ibds, [32]p, color, DJ)	Doubleday/Dor.	(1943)	Flack, M.	45-60	
Flack, M.	Restless Robin (1st, sm ob4to, [48]p, green cl, color, pep)	Houghton	1937	Flack, M.	45-60	
Dall, A.R.	Scamper... (1st, sq8vo, 72p, 5cp, fp b/w)	MacMillan	(1934)	Flack, M.	50-80	*
Flack, M.	Tatuk, Arctic Boy (1st {std}, 8vo, 139p, uncut, col frn, pep)	Doubleday/Dor.	1928	Flack, M.	25-40	*
Flack, M.	Tim Tadpole... (1st {std}, 8vo, [32]p, ibds, p-o, color, pep)	Doubleday/Dor.	1934	Flack, M.	35-50	
Flack, M.	Walter the Lazy Mouse (1st {std}, 4to, [80]p, color, cep)	Doubleday/Dor.	1937	Flack, M.	35-50	
Flack, M.	William & his Kitten (1st, ob8vo, ibds, [32]p, color, pep)	Houghton	1938	Flack, M.	30-45	
Flack, M.	Willy Nilly (1st, 4to, ibds, [32]p, color, pep)	MacMillan	1936	Flack, M.	30-50	
Flagg, J.M.	Adventures of Kitty Cobb (1st, lg sq4to, ibds, [67]p, b/w, pep)	Doran	(1912)	Flagg, J.M.	90-120	
Flagg, J.M.	All in the Same Boat (1st, 12mo, 105p)	Life Pub. Co.	1908	Flagg, J.M.	25-40	*
Brennan, G.H.	Bill Truetell... (1st, 8vo, col frn & cvr by...)	McClurg	1909	Flagg, J.M.	20-25	
Flagg, J.M.	City People (1st, folio, ibds, [84]p, b/w)	Scribner	1909	Flagg, J.M.	75-120	
Crawford, F.M.	Diva's Ruby (1st, 8vo, 430p, 12pl)	MacMillan	1908	Flagg, J.M.	25-40	*
Long, J.L.	Felice (1st, sm8vo, 156p, frn by...)	Moffat	1908	Flagg, J.M.	20-25	*
Brainerd, E.H.	How Could You, Jean? (1st, 8vo, 337p, 4pl)	Doubleday/Page	1917	Flagg, J.M.	20-30	*
Flagg, J.M.	I Should Say So (1st, sm8vo, 202p, b/w pl)	Doran	(1914)	Flagg, J.M.	25-40	*
Page, T.N.	John Marvel, Assistant (1st, 12mo, green cl, 8pl)	Scribner	1909	Flagg, J.M.	20-30	
Nicholson, M.	Little Brown Jug at Kildare (1st, 8vo, blue cl, 422p, 5pl)	Bobbs-Merrill	(1908)	Flagg, J.M.	20-30	
Barbour, R.H.	Orchard Princess (1st, 8vo, p-o, 219p, 4cp)	Lippincott	1905	Flagg, J.M.	20-30	
Spearman, Frank	Robert Kimberly (1st, 8vo, 437p, gilt, 4cp)	Scribner	1911	Flagg, J.M.	20-25	
Flagg, J.M.	Why they Married (1st, lg4to, 107p, ibds)	Life Pub. Co.	1906	Flagg, J.M.	85-120	
Van Dyke, H.	Story of the Other Wise Man (1st, lg8vo, 72p, uncut, 8cp)	Harper	(1920)	Flannagan	45-60	
Flemwell, G.	Alpine Flowers & Gardens (1st, 8vo, 167p, gilt, teg, 20cp)	L: A&C Black	1910	Flemwell, G.	70-120	
Chaucer, G.	Canterbury Tales (1st, 4to, 637p, teg, 24cp, DJ)	L: Medici	1928	Flint, W.R.	120-180	
Chaucer, G.	Canterbury Tales (1st AM, 8vo, 245p, 12cp)	Cape/Smith	1930	Flint, W.R.	60-85	*
Kingsley, C.	Heroes/Greek Fairy Tales (1st, 8vo, 166p, 9 ticp)	L: Medici	1928	Flint, W.R.	85-100	
Kempis	Imitation of Christ (sm4to, 274p, 8cp)	L: Chatto	1908	Flint, W.R.	60-85	
Gilbert, W.S.	Iolanthe... (1st, 4to, green/gilt, teg, 224p, uncut, 32cp)	L: Bell	1910	Flint, W.R.	130-165	
Malory, T.	Le Morte D'Arthur (1st, lg8vo, teg, 2 volumes, 36cp)	L: P.L Warner	(1920)	Flint, W.R.	160-220	
Malory, T.	Le Morte D'Arthur (lg8vo, 531p, red/gilt, teg, 24cp)	Hale/Cushman	(1927)	Flint, W.R.	100-140	*
N/A	Odyssey of Homer (1st, sm4to, 332p, teg, gilt, 20cp)	Hale/Cushman	(1930)	Flint, W.R.	80-120	*
Gilbert, W.S.	Princess Ida (1st, lg8vo, 150p, green/gilt, color)	L: G. Bell	1912	Flint, W.R.	70-115	
Gilbert, W.S.	Savoy Operas (1st, 4to, 208p, gilt, teg, 32cp)	L: G. Bell	1909	Flint, W.R.	100-165	
Arnold, M.	Scholar-Gypsy & Thyrsis (1st, 4to, 67p, 10cp)	L: P.L. Warner	(1910)	Flint, W.R.	100-145	
N/A	Song of Songs... (1st, sm4to, 66p, teg, brown/gilt, 10 ticp)	L: P.L. Warner	1913	Flint, W.R.	65-80	
Burns, Rbt.	Songs & Lyrics of... (1st, 8vo, uncut, teg, 12cp)	L: P.L. Warner	1911	Flint, W.R.	75-100	
Farjeon, E.	Tales from Chaucer (1st, 8vo, 244p, 12cp)	L: J. Cape	1930	Flint, W.R.	70-85	
Kingsley, C.	The Heroes (1st, 8vo, 166p, gilt, teg, 12 ticp)	L: P.L. Warner	1914	Flint, W.R.	70-100	*
Gilbert, W.S.	The Mikado (1st, 8vo, 96p, 8cp)	L: MacMillan	1928	Flint, W.R.	60-80	
Flint, W.R.	Watercolors of... (1st, ob. folio, 8 ticp)	L: Studio	(1920)	Flint, W.R.	100-130	
Gilbert, W.S.	Yoeman of the Guard (1st, 8vo, 102p, gilt, 8cp)	L: MacMillan	1929	Flint, W.R.	50-70	
Streatfield, N.	Ballet Shoes (1st, 8vo, 294p, color)	Random	(1937)	Floethe, R.	25-40	*
Streatfield, N.	Circus Shoes (1st {std}, 8vo, 401p, color)	Random	(1939)	Floethe, R.	30-45	
Brown, M.W.	Dream Book (1st, sm4to, [24]p, color)	Random	(1950)	Floethe, R.	45-60	*
Burglon, N.	Gate Swings In (1st {std}, 8vo, 208p, pep, b/w)	Little/Brown	1937	Floethe, R.	30-45	*
Shippen, K.B.	Mr. Bell Invents the Telephone (1st, 8vo, 183p, 2-color)	Random	(1952)	Floethe, R.	30-50	*
Collodi, C.	Pinocchio (1st, 8vo, 239p, pep, fp color)	World	(1946)	Floethe, R.	30-45	*
Goudge, Eliz.	Smoky House (1st AM, 8vo, 286p, 6pl)	Coward	(1940)	Floethe, R.	30-50	*
Havighurst, Walt.	Song of the Pines (1st {std}, 8vo, 205p, maps, dep, b/w, NH)	Winston	(1949)	Floethe, R.	70-100	*
Streatfield, N.	Stranger in Primrose Lane (1st {std}, 8vo, 338p, p-o, 7cp)	Random	(1941)	Floethe, R.	35-50	*
Fischer, Marj.	Street Fair (1st, 8vo, blue/gilt, 216p, 18cp, pep)	Smith/Haas	(1935)	Floethe, R.	30-50	*
Streatfield, N.	Theater Shoes (1st {std}, 8vo, 282p, color)	Random	(1945)	Floethe, R.	25-40	*
Sargant, Alice	Crystal Ball (1st, 8vo, 119p)	L: G. Bell	(1894)	Florence, M.S.	100-160	*
Strong, R.	Yoyo's Animal Friends (4to, 170p, teg, 3cp)	Dent/Dutton	1913	Flower, N.	40-70	
White, S.E.	Gold (1st, 12mo, green cl, 437p, pep, 4cp)	Doubleday/Page	1913	Fogarty, T.	25-40	
McFarlane, A.E.	Great Bear Island (1st, 8vo, 290p, pep)	Houghton	1911	Fogarty, T.	25-40	
Becker, May L.	Louisa Alcott's People (1st, 4to, 211p, gilt, p-o, 4cp, pep, SC)	Scribner	1936	Fogarty, T.	70-120	
LeGallienne, R.	October Vagabonds (1st, 8vo, ipcb, gilt, 201p, col frn, pep)	Kennerley	1910	Fogarty, T.	45-70	R
Field, R.	People from Dickens (1st, sm4to, p-o, 208p, 8cp, pep, SC)	Scribner	1935	Fogarty, T.	65-100	

AUTHOR	TITLE	PUBLISHER	DATE	ARTIST	PRICE	LC
White, S.E.	The Forest (1st, 8vo, green cl, teg, 276p, 17pl)	Outlook	1903	Fogarty, T.	25-40	
Pearson, E.L.	Voyage of the Hoppergrass (1st, 8vo, 348p, b/w, PPPa)	MacMillan	1913	Fogarty, T.	85-100	R*
Foley, James W.	Christmas Prayer (1st, 16mo, ibds, [24]p, color)	Volland	(1915)	Foley, J.W.	45-60	*
Aesopus	Aesop's Fables (1st, 8vo, 209p, gilt, 12cp)	L: A&C Black	(1912)	Folkard, C.	85-130	
Carroll, L.	Alice/Wonderland (1st, 8vo, 174p, blue cl, 6cp)	L: A&C Black	(1929)	Folkard, C.	120-165	
N/A	Arabian Nights (1st, 8vo, 412p, teg, gilt, 12cp)	L: A&C Black	(1913)	Folkard, C.	130-180	
Glover, C.	British Fairy & Folk Tales (1st, sq8vo, 281p, 8cp)	L: A&C Black	1920	Folkard, C.	85-120	
Hoffman, A.S.	Children's Shakespeare (1st, sq8vo, 472p, 21cp)	L: Dent	1911	Folkard, C.	80-120	
Grimm Bros.	Fairy Tales (1st, 8vo, 331p, cream cl, 12cp)	L: A&C Black	(1911)	Folkard, C.	70-100	*
N/A	Fairy Tales in Other Lands (1st, 12mo, 96p, ibds, 4cp)	L: Cassell	[1925]	Folkard, C.	70-100	
Phillpotts, E.	Flint Heart (1st AM, 8vo, 334p, 16cp)	Dutton	(1910)	Folkard, C.	65-100	
Phillpotts, E.	Flint Heart (1st, 8vo, 310p, teg, gilt, 16cp)	L: Smith Elder	1910	Folkard, C.	90-120	
Ingoldsby, T.	Jackdaw of Rheims (1st, folio, unpag, white/gilt, teg, 12 ticp)	L: Gay/Hancock	1913	Folkard, C.	120-180	
Ingoldsby, T.	Jackdaw of Rheims (1st AM, lg4to, purple cl, 12 ticp)	Winston	1914	Folkard, C.	70-100	*
Daglish, A. (ed.)	Land of Nursery Rhyme (1st, 8vo, 240p, fp color, pep)	Dutton	(1932)	Folkard, C.	60-80	*
Black, Dorothy	Magic Egg (1st, 4to, 111p)	L: A&C Black	1922	Folkard, C.	85-100	*
Mother Goose	Mother Goose (1st AM, 8vo, 340p, 8cp)	Dutton	(1932)	Folkard, C.	100-140	
Mother Goose	Mother Goose's Nursery Rhymes (1st, 8vo, 159p, ibds, color)	L: A&C Black	(1919)	Folkard, C.	100-145	
Garnett, L.M.	Ottoman Wonder Tales (1st, sq8vo, 266p, teg, 12cp)	L: A&C Black	1915	Folkard, C.	70-115	
Collodi, C.	Pinocchio (1st, sq8vo, p-o, ibds, 268p, 13cp)	Dent/Dutton	1911	Folkard, C.	80-100	
Collodi, C.	Pinocchio (1st {this pub.}, 8vo, p-o, DJ)	McKay	(1925)	Folkard, C.	65-80	
Broadwood, Lucy	Songs/Alice in Wonderland (4to, blue/gilt, 48p, p-o, 12 ticp)	L: A&C Black	1921	Folkard, C.	100-140	
Wyss, J.D.	Swiss Family Robinson (1st, 8vo, 454p, beige cl, 12cp)	L: J.M. Dent	1910	Folkard, C.	70-100	
Folkard, C.	Teddy Tail of the Daily Mail (4to, ibds, color)	L: A&C Black	[1915]	Folkard, C.	70-100	
Kossak-Szczucka	Troubles of a Gnome (1st, 4to, ibds, 102p, 8cp)	L: A&C Black	1928	Folkard, C.	130-180	
Brook, Arthur	Witch's Hollow (1st, 8vo, 211p, 8cp)	L: A&C Black	1920	Folkard, C.	120-140	*
Bishop, C.H.	Big Loop (1st, 8vo, tan cl, 221p, fp b/w, pep)	Viking	1955	Fontsere, C.	25-40	*
Forbes, Eliz. S.	King Arthur's Wood (1st, ob folio, 120p, buckram, 14cp)	L: Simpkin	1904	Forbes, E.S.	850-1000	
Brookfield, A.	Aesop's Fables for Little Readers (1st, 4to, red/gilt, 71p, b/w)	L: T.F. Unwin	(1888)	Ford, H.J.	180-220	
Lang, L.B.	All Sorts of Stories Book (1st, 12mo, AEG, 377p, gilt, 5cp)	L: Longmans	1911	Ford, H.J.	140-180	
Lang, A.	Animal Story Book (1st, 12mo, AEG, 400p, blue/gilt, cep)	L: Longmans	1896	Ford, H.J.	100-150	
N/A	Arabian Nights (1st, 12mo, 424p, AEG, blue/gilt, b/w, cep)	L: Longmans	1898	Ford, H.J.	180-220	
Lang, A.	Blue Poetry Book (1st, 12mo, blue/gilt, AEG, 243p, 12pl, cep)	L: Longmans	1891	Ford, H.J.	150-200	
Lang, A.	Book of Princes & Princesses (1st, 8vo, gilt, 361p, AEG, 8cp)	L: Longmans	1908	Ford, H.J.	160-200	
Lang, A.	Book of Romance (1st, sm8vo, AEG, 384p, gilt, 8cp, pep)	L: Longmans	1902	Ford, H.J.	160-200	
Lang, L.B.	Book of Saints & Heroes (1st, 8vo, blue/gilt, teg, 351p, 12cp)	L: Longmans	1912	Ford, H.J.	120-160	
Newbolt, H.	Book of the Happy Warrior (1st, 8vo, 284p, 8cp)	L: Longmans	1917	Ford, H.J.	65-80	*
Lang, A.	Brown Fairy Book (1st, 8vo, AEG, 350p, 8cp, 22pl, pep)	L: Longmans	1904	Ford, H.J.	180-250	
Lang, A.	Crimson Fairy Book (1st, 8vo, AEG, 371p, 8cp, pep)	L: Longmans	1903	Ford, H.J.	200-265	
Lang, A.	Disentanglers (1st, sm8vo, 418p, AEG, 7pl)	L: Longmans	1902	Ford, H.J.	100-150	
Taylor, Una	Early Italian Love Stories (1st, 4to, 144p)	L: Longmans	1899	Ford, H.J.	100-160	
Lang, A.	Green Fairy Book (1st, 8vo, AEG, 366p, gilt, b/w, cep)	L: Longmans	1892	Ford, H.J.	200-280	
Lang, A.	Grey Fairy Book (1st, 8vo, AEG, 387p, 32pl, cep)	L: Longmans	1900	Ford, H.J.	200-260	
Scott, Walter	Kenilworth (1st, 4to, teg, red/gilt, 551p, uncut, 12cp)	L: Jack	(1920)	Ford, H.J.	100-160	
Lang, A.	Lilac Fairy Book (1st, 8vo, 369p, gilt, AEG, 6cp)	L: Longmans	1910	Fogarty, H.J.	220-280	
Lang, A.	Little Wildrose (1st, 12mo, 258p, blu/glt, col frn, 19 b/w, pep)	L: Longmans	1906	Ford, H.J.	80-130	
Lang, A.	Olive Fairy Book (1st, 8vo, AEG, 336p, 8cp, pep)	L: Longmans	1907	Ford, H.J.	200-300	
Lang, A.	Orange Fairy Book (1st, 8vo, orang/gilt, 358p, AEG, 8cp)	L: Longmans	1906	Ford, H.J.	180-260	
Greene, H.P.	Pilot & Other Stories (1st, 8vo, 227p, 8cp)	MacMillan	1916	Ford, H.J.	100-150	
Lang, A.	Pink Fairy Book (1st, 8vo, AEG, 360p, b/w, cep)	L: Longmans	1897	Ford, H.J.	240-300	
Lang, A.	Red Book of Animal Stories (1st, 8vo, gilt, AEG, 379p, 33pl)	L: Longmans	1899	Ford, H.J.	140-200	
Lang, A.	Red Romance Book (1st, 8vo, 366p, AEG, 8cp, 28pl, pep)	L: Longmans	1905	Ford, H.J.	130-170	
Lang, A.	Red True Story Book (1st, 12mo, 419p, AEG, 19pl, cep)	L: Longmans	1895	Ford, H.J.	140-200	
Lang, A.	Strange Story Book (1st, lg8vo, teg, gilt, 312p, 12cp)	L: Longmans	1913	Ford, H.J.	145-180	
Lang, A.	Tales of Troy & Greece (1st, 8vo, 302p, teg, uncut, 16pl)	L: Longmans	1907	Ford, H.J.	145-180	*
Lang, A.	Trusty John... (1st, sm8vo, maroon/gilt, 258p, col frn, 14pl)	L: Longmans	1906	Ford, H.J.	100-150	
Lang, A.	Violet Fairy Book (1st, 12mo, 388p, AEG, 8cp, cep)	L: Longmans	1901	Ford, H.J.	220-320	
Lang, A.	Yellow Fairy Book (1st, 12mo, AEG, 321p, 22pl, cep)	L: Longmans	1894	Ford, H.J.	200-275	
DeSegur, S.	Memoirs of a Donkey (1st, 16mo, blue cl, 238p, fp b/w, pep)	MacMillan	1924	Ford, L.	30-50	*
Lang, A.	Blue Fairy Book (1st, 8vo, blue/gilt, AEG, b/w)	L: Longmans	1889	Ford/Hood	750-1100	
Lang, A.	Red Fairy Book (1st, 8vo, red/gilt, AEG, 367p, b/w)	L: Longmans	1890	Ford/Speed	350-500	
Forestier, A.	Belgium (1st, sm4to, brown bds, 77cp)	L: A&C Black	1908	Forestier, A.	60-85	
Pemberton, Max	House Under the Sea (1st AM, 8vo, 346p, brown/gilt, 8pl)	Appleton	1902	Forestier, A.	30-45	
Pemberton, Max	Pro Patria (1st, 8vo, red/gilt, 16pl)	L: Ward Lock	1904	Forestier, A.	40-65	
Henderson, J.	Jamaica (1st, 8vo, blue/gilt, teg, 24cp)	L: A&C Black	1906	Forrest, A.S.	70-120	
Forrest, A.S.	Morocco (1st, lg8vo, gilt, 231p, teg, 74cp)	L: A&C Black	1904	Forrest, A.S.	70-100	
Norman	Ten Little Boer Boys (ob4to, ibds, 14cp)	L: Dean	[1900]	Forrest, A.S.	145-200	
Stowe, H.B.	Uncle Tom's Cabin (16mo, p-o, gilt, 115p, 8cp)	Jack/Dutton	[1908]	Forrest, A.S.	45-60	*
Foster, Genevieve	Abraham Lincoln's World (1st, sm4to, 347p, b/w, cep, NH)	Scribner	1944	Foster, G.	65-90	R*
Foster, Genevieve	Birthdays of Freedom (1st, 4to, [59]p, color, NH)	Scribner	(1952)	Foster, G.	50-80	*
Cavanah, F.	Boyhood Adventures of Our Presidents (1st, 8vo, 256p, fp b/w)	Rand/McNally	(1938)	Foster, G.	30-45	*
Foster, Genevieve	George Washington (1st, 8vo, 93p, dp color, NH)	Scribner	(1949)	Foster, G.	50-80	*

AUTHOR	TITLE	PUBLISHER	DATE	ARTIST	PRICE	LC
Foster, Genevieve	George Washington's World (1st, 4to, 348p, 1-color, cep, NH)	Scribner	1942	Foster, G.	50-85	R*
Judson, C.I.	Pioneer Girl (1st, sm8vo, ipcb, 80p, fp 1-color, pep)	Rand/McNally	(1939)	Foster, G.	25-40	*
Locke, Wm. J.	Golden Journey/Mr. Paradyne (1st AM, 8vo, ibds, 53p, 8cp, pep)	Dodd	1924	Foster, M.L.	45-65	*
Gordon, Eliz.	Happy Home Children (1st, 12mo, [34]p, ibds, pep, color)	Volland	(1924)	Foster, M.L.	50-70	
France, A.	Little Sea-Dogs (1st, 8vo, 149p, 8cp)	L: Bodley Head	1925	Foster, M.L.	35-50	*
Grahame, K.	The Headswoman (1st AM, 8vo, 53p, 7cp, DJ)	Dodd	1922	Foster, M.L.	60-85	
Syrett, Netta	Tinkelly Winkle (1st, 8vo, 157p, green cl, 8cp)	Dodd	1923	Foster, M.L.	30-45	*
Muter, Gladys N.	Told in Our Neighborhood (1st, sm8vo, ibds, color)	Volland	(1925)	Foster, M.L.	35-50	*
Bingham, C.	Pretty Pets (4to {enlarged ed.}, [20]p, 4 chromos)	L: Nister	[1910]	Foster, W.	80-100	
Chesterton, G.K.	Innocence of Father Brown (1st AM, 8vo, red cl, 334p, 7pl)	NY: J. Lane	1911	Foster, W.L.	45-60	*
Coatsworth, E.	Night & the Cat (1st, 4to, blue cl, 55p, 10pl)	MacMillan	1950	Foujita	45-60	*
Newman, I.	Shades of Blue (8vo, blue/silver, 96p, 16cp)	NY: Harrison	(1927)	Fouts, H.E.	65-90	
Lardner, R.	Bib Ballads (1st {1st bk.}, 8vo, teg, brown/gilt, [63]p)	Volland	(1915)	Fox, F.	180-240	R
Francis, J.G.	Book of Cheerful Cats (1st, ob8vo, 37p, b/w, PPPa)	Century	1892	Francis, J.G.	80-135	*
Francis, J.G.	Joyous Aztecs (1st {std}, ob8vo, 42p, b/w)	Century	(1929)	Francis, J.G.	50-80	*
Francoise	Fanchette & Jeannot (1st AM, sm4to, ibds, [24]p, color)	Grosset/Dunlap	1937	Francoise	45-60	*
Francoise	Gay ABC (1st, lg8vo, grey cl, [55]p, fp color)	Scribner	(1939)	Francoise	120-165	*
Mother Goose	Gay Mother Goose (1st, 4to, beige cl, 63p, fp color)	Scribner	(1938)	Francoise	50-80	*
Francoise	Jeanne-Marie Counts her Sheep (1st, sm4to, [32]p, color)	Scribner	1951	Francoise	50-85	R*
McNeil, Marion	Little Green Cart (1st, 4to, ibds, [38]p, color, pep)	Saalfield	(1931)	Francoise	45-60	
Francoise	Mr. & Mrs. So and So (1st, 4to, [36]p, color, pep)	OUP	(1939)	Francoise	35-50	*
Francoise	Story of Colette (1st, lg8vo, ibds, fp color)	Scribner	(1940)	Francoise	50-85	*
Harris, Isobel	Little Boy Brown (1st, 4to, 44p, tan cl, 1-color, cep)	Lippincott	1949	Francoise, A.	65-90	R*
Byington, Eloise	Mother Goose Fun (1st, sm8vo, p-o, gilt, 128p, color, pep)	Whitman	(1931)	Frantz, K.	45-60	*
Byington, Eloise	Wishbone Children (1st, 12mo, blue cl, p-o, 64p, pep, color)	Whitman	(1934)	Frantz, K.	25-40	
N/A	House that Jack Built (1st {std}, 4to, [32]p, 3-color, dep, CH)	Harcourt	(1958)	Frasconi, A.	75-110	R*
Frasconi, Antonio	See & Say (1st {std}, 4to, yellow cl, [32]p, color, pep)	Harcourt	(1955)	Frasconi, A.	65-90	R*
Gay, J.	Beggar's Opera (1st, 4to, 93p, bds, p-o, 8cp)	L: Heinemann	1921	Fraser, C.L.	65-90	
MacFall, H.	Book of Lovat (1st, 4to, ipcb, 183p, 8cp)	L: Dent	1923	Fraser, C.L.	75-100	
Preston, Hayter	House of Vanities (1st, 12mo, 59p, bds, b/w)	J. Lane	1922	Fraser, C.L.	50-75	
Nodier, C.	Luck of the Bean Rows (1st, sm4to, 60p, ibds, 28 color)	L: O'Connor	(1921)	Fraser, C.L.	50-70	
Fraser, C.L.	Lute of Love (1st, 16mo, wraps, 66p)	L: Selwyn	(1920)	Fraser, C.L.	50-65	
N/A	Nursery Rhymes (1st, 4to, 46p, ibds, 23 color)	L: Jack	(1919)	Fraser, C.L.	80-120	
Fraser, C.L.	Nursery Rhymes (1st AM, 8vo, 46p, cp)	Knopf	1920	Fraser, C.L.	70-100	
De La Mare, W.	Peacock Pie (1st AM, lg8vo, 128p, blue/gilt, 16cp)	Holt	(1924)	Fraser, C.L.	60-80	
De La Mare, W.	Peacock Pie (1st, 4to, teg, 127p, blue/gilt, 16cp)	L: Constable	(1924)	Fraser, C.L.	85-125	
Fraser, C.L.	Pirates (1st AM {std}, 4to, ibds, 159p, 8pl)	McBride	1922	Fraser, C.L.	85-120	
Goldoni, C.	The Liar (1st AM, 8vo, 93p, bds, DJ)	Knopf	1922	Fraser, C.L.	65-80	
Goldoni, C.	The Liar (1st, sm4to, ibds, 93p, p-o, col frn)	L: Selwyn	1922	Fraser, C.L.	45-60	*
Nodier, C.	Woodcutter's Dog (1st, lg8vo, 18p, bds, 12 color)	L: O'Connor	1921	Fraser, C.L.	50-65	
Colum, P.	At the Gateways of the Day (1st, 8vo, 217p, fp b/w)	Yale U. Press	1924	Fraser, J.M.	25-40	
Colum, P.	Bright Islands (1st, 8vo, 233p, gilt, pep, b/w)	Yale U. Press	1925	Fraser, J.M.	35-50	
Cradock, C.E.	Young Mountaineers (1st, 8vo, 262p, green/gilt, 4pl)	Houghton	1897	Fraser, W.	35-50	
North, S.	Five Little Bears (1st, 8vo, ipcb, [32]p, 1-color, pep)	Rand/McNally	(1935)	Frazee, H.	30-50	*
Gordon, Eliz.	King Gumdrop... (1st, lg8vo, 112p, p-o, fp color)	Whitman	(1916)	Frazee, H.	55-70	
Lyle, G.M.	Little Travellers in Wales (1st, 8vo, p-o, 127p, b/w, pep)	Whitman	1929	Frazee, H.	25-40	*
Seawell, M.E.	Betty at Fort Blizzard (1st, 8vo, 224p, teg, p-o, 4cp)	Lippincott	1916	Frederick, E.	20-25	
Chambers, Rbt.	Gay Rebellion (1st, 8vo, 299p, b/w)	Appleton	1913	Frederick, E.	20-30	
Chambers, Rbt.	Green Mouse (1st, 8vo, 281p, p-o, 6cp, pep)	Appleton	1910	Frederick, E.	20-30	
Lanier, S.	Boy's Mabinogian (1st, 8vo, 361p, gilt, 12pl, cep, PPPa)	Scribner	1881	Fredericks, A.	70-100	*
De La Mare, W.	Love (1st, 8vo, 592p, grey/gilt, col frn, 24 b/w)	L: Faber	1943	Freedman, B.	45-70	
Freeman, Don	Beady Bear (1st, lg ob8vo, red cl, 48p, fp b/w)	Viking	1954	Freeman, D.	30-45	*
Lindgren, Astrid	Bill Bergson Lives Dangerously (1st, sm8vo, 214p, b/w, pep)	Viking	1954	Freeman, D.	25-45	*
Freeman, Don	Chuggy & Blue Caboose (1st, ob4to, 48p, red cl, color)	Viking	1951	Freeman, D.	35-50	*
Randolph, Jane	Circus in Peter's Closet (1st, 8vo, blue cl, 48p, 3-color, pep)	Crowell	(1955)	Freeman, D.	35-50	*
Freeman, Don	Cyrano the Crow (1st, 4to, [47]p, ibds, color)	Viking	(1960)	Freeman, D.	40-65	*
Freeman, Don	Fly High, Fly Low (1st, 4to, blue cl, 56p, pep, CH)	Viking	(1957)	Freeman, D.	50-80	*
Bulla, Clyde R.	Ghost Town Treasure (1st, 8vo, yellow cl, 86p, b/w, pep)	Crowell	(1957)	Freeman, D.	25-45	*
Freeman, Don	It Shouldn't Happen (1st {std}, sm8vo, [212]p, b/w)	Harcourt	(1945)	Freeman, D.	25-40	*
Embry, Margaret	Kid Sister (1st, sm8vo, 165p, yellow cl, fp b/w, pep)	Holiday House	(1958)	Freeman, D.	20-30	*
Sauer, J.L.	Mike's House (1st, sm4to, red cl, 31p, 2-color, pep)	Viking	1954	Freeman, D.	45-65	*
Freeman, Don	Mop Top (1st, sm4to, beige cl, 48p, 1-color, pep)	Viking	1955	Freeman, D.	30-45	*
Freeman, Don	Night the Lights Went Out (1st, lg8vo, 48p, blue cl, 1-color)	Viking	1958	Freeman, D.	25-45	*
Freeman, Don	Norman the Doorman (1st, sm ob4to, yellow cl, 64p, color, pep)	Viking	(1959)	Freeman, D.	35-60	*
Atkinson, Brooks	Once Around the Sun (1st {std}, 8vo, 376p, blue cl, fp b/w)	Harcourt	(1951)	Freeman, D.	30-45	*
Freeman, Lydia	Pet of the Met (1st, sm ob4to, 63p, pep, color)	Viking	1953	Freeman, D.	65-110	R
Corbett, Scott	Sauce for the Gander (1st AM, sm8vo, yellow cl, 238p, fp b/w)	Crowell	(1951)	Freeman, D.	30-45	*
Galt, Tom	Seven Days from Sunday (1st {std}, 8vo, rust cl, 215p, b/w)	Crowell	(1956)	Freeman, D.	30-50	*
Freeman, Don	Space Witch (1st, sm4to, blue cl, 47p, 1-color)	Viking	(1959)	Freeman, D.	35-50	*
Clark, A.N.	Third Monkey (1st, 4to, 44p, color, pep)	Viking	1956	Freeman, D.	30-50	*
White, Anne H.	Uninvited Donkey (1st, 8vo, 223p, blue cl, b/w)	Viking	(1957)	Freeman, D.	30-45	*
Thurber, J.	White Deer (1st, 8vo, green cl, 115p, color, DJ)	Harcourt	(1945)	Freeman, D.	70-100	

ILLUSTRATOR: 52

AUTHOR	TITLE	PUBLISHER	DATE	ARTIST	PRICE	LC
Freeman, L.C.	Nip & Tuck (1st, 4to, orange cl, p-o, 156p, 8cp, pep)	Sears	(1926)	Freeman, L.C.	70-100	
Freeman, L.C.	Nip & Tuck in Toyland (1st, 4to, p-o, 8cp, pep)	Sears	(1927)	Freeman, L.C.	70-100	
Field, R.	American Folk & Fairy Tales (1st, 8vo, 302p, green cl, 8cp)	Scribner	1929	Freeman, M.	50-65	
Capuana, L.	Golden-Feather (1st {std}, 8vo, 205p, col frn)	Dutton	(1930)	Freeman, M.	30-50	*
Lamprey, L.	Treasure Valley (1st, 8vo, 337p, yellow cl, p-o, 4cp, pep)	Wm. Morrow	(1928)	Freeman, M.	25-40	*
Arthur, Lady	Dream of Little Hazy Cream (folio, ibds, p-o, 12cp)	L: Bickers	[1900]	Frere, C.F.	100-165	*
Bergengren, R.W.	David the Dreamer (1st, ob4to, green cl, p-o, gilt, 10 fp col)	Atl. Month Pr.	(1922)	Freud, Tom	450-600	*
Hurd, E.T.	Jerry the Jeep (1st, ob4to, [32]p, ipcb, 1-color, pep)	Lothrop/Lee	(1945)	Friday, T.	35-60	*
Collodi, C.	Adventures of Pinocchio (1st {this fmt}, lg8vo, 254p, p-o, 5cp)	Rand/McNally	(1939)	Friend, E.	60-85	
Nesbit, W.D.	As Children Do (1st, 12mo, 96p, decor by...)	Volland	(1929)	Friend, E.	45-60	*
Moore, C.C.	Night Before Christmas (1st, 4to, ibds, [25]p, color, pep)	Wilcox/Follett	1949	Friend, E.	30-50	*
Anderson, B.	Topsy Turvey's Pigtails (1st, lg8vo, 91p, color)	Rand/McNally	(1930)	Friend, E.	30-45	
Alcott, L.M.	Frost King (4to, ipcb, color, pep)	Whitman	(1929)	Frobisher, M.S	35-50	
Stockton, Frank	Associate Hermits (1st, 12mo, green/gilt, 257p, 9pl)	Harper	1899	Frost, A.B.	40-65	R
Stuart, Ruth M.	Aunt Amity's Silver Wedding (1st, 8vo, green/gilt, 228p, b/w)	Century	1909	Frost, A.B.	30-50	
Wood, E.	Back Home (1st, 8vo, 8pl)	McClure	1905	Frost, A.B.	40-65	R*
Frost, A.B.	Book of Drawings (1st, folio, p-o, ibds, 39pl)	Collier	(1904)	Frost, A.B.	100-150	
Frost, A.B.	Bull Calf (1st, ob4to, 112p, 105pl)	Scribner	1892	Frost, A.B.	120-185	
Frost, A.B.	Carlo (1st, ob8vo, 109p, b/w)	Doubleday/Page	1913	Frost, A.B.	60-80	
Harris, J.C.	Chronicles/Aunt Minervy Ann (1st [1], 8vo, teg, uncut 210p, 31pl)	Scribner	1899	Frost, A.B.	100-140	R
Boyle, V.F.	Devil Tales (1st, 8vo, 211p, 28pl)	Harper	1900	Frost, A.B.	70-90	
Munkittrick, R.K.	Farming (1st, 8vo, green pcb, [102]p, 1-color)	Harper	1891	Frost, A.B.	75-100	R
Van Sutphen, W.	Golfer's Alphabet (1st, 4to, ibds, 128p, 28pl)	Harper	1898	Frost, A.B.	250-400	
Thanet, O.	Heart of Toil (1st, 8vo, teg, 215p, 24pl by...)	Scribner	1898	Frost, A.B.	35-50	*
Adams, F.U.	John Henry Smith (1st, 8vo, 346p, p-o, b/w)	Doubleday/Page	1905	Frost, A.B.	30-45	*
Carruth, H.	Mr. Milo Bush (1st, 12mo, green cl, 217p, 4pl)	Harper	1899	Frost, A.B.	30-50	
Page, T.N.	Passtime Stories (1st, sm8vo, grey cl, 220p, 21pl)	Harper	1898	Frost, A.B.	35-50	
Cradock, C.E.	Phantoms of the Foot-Bridge (1st, 8vo, 353p, grn/gilt, 14pl)	Harper	1895	Frost, A.B.	40-65	
Stockton, Frank	Pomona's Travels (1st [1], 8vo, 275p, teg, gilt, 10pl)	Scribner	(1894)	Frost, A.B.	60-80	
Lloyd, N.	Soldier of the Valley (1st, 8vo, red/gilt, 325p, 34 fp b/w)	Scribner	1904	Frost, A.B.	50-75	
Stuart, Ruth M.	Solomon Crow's Christmas Pockets (1st, 12mo, gilt, 201p, 14pl)	Harper	1897	Frost, A.B.	45-60	*
Stockton, Frank	Squirrel Inn (1st, sm8vo, 222p, teg, b/w)	Century	1891	Frost, A.B.	45-60	
Frost, A.B.	Stuff & Nonsense (1st, 4to, ipcb, 92p, b/w)	Scribner	(1884)	Frost, A.B.	100-130	*
Carroll, L.	Tangled Tale (1st, 8vo, 152p, AEG, red/gilt, 6pl)	L: MacMillan	1885	Frost, A.B.	300-500	
Phillips, H.W.	The Pets (1st, 12mo, 47p, tan cl, 5pl)	McClure	1906	Frost, A.B.	25-40	
Harris, J.C.	Uncle Remus & his Friends (1st, 8vo, 357p, green cl)	Houghton	1892	Frost, A.B.	120-165	
Thanet, O.	Missionary Sheriff (1st, 12mo, 248p, blue/gilt, 15pl)	Harper	1897	Frost/Carleton	30-45	
Harris, J.C.	Uncle Remus Returns (1st, 12mo, 175p, col frn, 7pl)	Houghton	(1918)	Frost/Conde	125-170	R
Carroll, L.	Rhyme? And Reason? (1st, 8vo, 214p, green/gilt, b/w)	L: MacMillan	1883	Frost/Holiday	220-285	
Stuart, Ruth M.	Moriah's Mourning (1st, 12mo, 218p, 8pl)	Harper	1898	Frost/Kemble	40-65	*
Stuart, Ruth M.	Second Wooing of Salina Sue (1st, 12mo, 236p, 12pl)	Harper	1905	Frost/Kemble	40-65	*
Harris, J.C.	Tar-Baby (1st, lg8vo, 190p, teg, uncut, 9pl)	Appleton	1904	Frost/Kemble	150-185	
Aesopus	Aesop's Fables (1st, lg8vo, p-o, 136p, 8cp)	McKay	[1929]	Fry, Nora	60-85	*
Montgomery, F.T.	Billy Whiskers' Kids (1st, 8vo, 134p, 6cp)	Saalfield	(1903)	Fry, W.H.	45-60	*
Evans, F.A.	Jewel Story Book (1st, 12mo, 102p, green cl, 4pl)	Saalfield	1903	Fry, W.H.	20-30	
Sutton, Adah L.	Mr. Bunny - His Book (4to, ipcb, 106p, color)	Saalfield	(1900)	Fry, W.H.	200-250	*
Mabie, H.W.	Myths Every Child Should Know (1st, 4to, p-o, 224p, 11cp)	Doubleday/Page	1914	Frye, M.H.	50-70	
Gray, Eliz. J.	Tilly-Tod (1st {std}, sm8vo, 173p, blue cl, col frn, b/w, pep)	Doubleday/Dor.	1929	Frye, M.H.	30-45	*
Lagerlof, Selma	Wonderful Adventures of Nils (1st, sq8vo, 263p, 24cp, pep)	Doubleday/Page	1913	Frye, M.H.	100-150	
Burgess, T.	Burgess Animal Book for Children (1st, 8vo, green cl, p-o, cp)	Little/Brown	1920	Fuertes, L.A.	65-90	
Burgess, T.	Burgess Bird Book for Children (1st, 8vo, p-o, 351p, 32cp)	Little/Brown	1919	Fuertes, L.A.	60-85	
Baruch, D.W.	I Like Automobiles (1st, 8vo, [55]p, color, pep)	NY: J. Day	(1931)	Fujikawa, G.	30-45	*
Fullylove, J.	Edinburgh (1st, 8vo, 176p, teg, blue/gilt, 21cp)	L: A&C Black	1904	Fullylove, J.	65-90	
Hunt, M.L.	John of Pudding Lane (1st, 8vo, 161p, color, pep)	Stokes	(1941)	Funk, C.E.	25-40	*
Girvin, B.	Round Fairyland/Alice & White Rabbit (1st, 8vo, 312p)	L: Wells/Gard.	1916	Furniss, D.	70-100	*
Allen, F.M.	Brayhard (1st, 8vo, teg, 308p, green/gilt, b/w)	L: Ward/Down.	1890	Furniss, H.	50-75	
Parry, E.A.	Gamble Gold (1st, sq8vo, ibds, 248p, AEG, gilt, 15pl)	L: Hutchinson	1907	Furniss, H.	50-65	
Burnand (ed.)	Incompleat Angler (1st, 8vo, 94p, b/w)	L: Bradbury	1887	Furniss, H.	80-130	
Carroll, L.	Sylvie & Bruno (1st, 8vo, AEG, 400p, gilt, 46 illus)	L: MacMillan	1889	Furniss, H.	120-160	
Carroll, L.	Sylvie & Bruno Concluded (1st, 8vo, red/gilt, AEG, 423p)	L: MacMillan	1893	Furniss, H.	140-220	
Farrow, G.E.	Wallypug of Why (1st AM, lg8vo, 201p, b/w illus)	Dodd	1896	Furniss, H.	120-160	*
Browne, Maggie	Wanted - A King (1st, 12mo, 193p, green/gilt, teg, pep)	L: Cassell	1890	Furniss, H.	120-180	*
Farrow, G.E.	Missing Prince (1st, lg8vo, 197p, green/gilt, AEG, b/w)	L: Hutchinson	1896	Furniss, H.& D.	90-120	
Farrow, G.E.	Missing Prince (1st AM, 8vo, 198p, pict cl, b/w)	Dodd	1897	Furniss, H.& D.	70-100	*
Farrow, G.E.	Wallypug of Why (1st, 8vo, green/gilt, 201p, AEG, 15pl)	L: Hutchinson	(1895)	Furniss, H.& D.	130-175	
Fyleman, R.	Fairy Queen (1st, 8vo, 64p, cloth, col frn, pep)	Doran	(1923)	Fyleman, R.	65-80	*
Williams, Eleanor	And a Good Fat Hen (1st, lg8vo, red cl, [47]p, lettering by...)	Putnam	(1939)	Gag, Flavia	30-50	*
Turner, Thyra	Christmas House... (1st, 12mo, ibds, 25p, 14 color, DJ)	Scribner	1943	Gag, Flavia	70-100	
Dalgliesh, A.	Davenports & Cherry Pie (1st, 8vo, 196p, grey cl, fp b/w)	Scribner	(1949)	Gag, Flavia	35-50	*
Dalgliesh, A.	Davenports at Dinner (1st, 8vo, ivory cl, 182p, b/w)	Scribner	1948	Gag, Flavia	30-50	*
Gag, Flavia	Sing a Song of Seasons (1st, 4to, ibds, 29p)	Coward	(1936)	Gag, Flavia	45-65	*
Gag, Asta	Sue & Sew-and-Sew (1st, 8vo, 63p, ibds, b/w, pep)	Coward	(1931)	Gag, Flavia	35-50	*

AUTHOR	TITLE	PUBLISHER	DATE	ARTIST	PRICE	LC
Woodward, H.	Time Was (1st, 4to, [48]p, color)	Scribner	(1941)	Gag, Flavia	30-50	
Travers, Georgia	Wily Woodchucks (1st, ob4to, [32]p, color, DJ)	Coward	(1946)	Gag, Flavia	30-50	
Gag, W.	ABC Bunny (1st {std}, lg4to, ibds, [32]p, pep, NH)	Coward	1933	Gag, W.	170-220	R
Wilson, E.H.	About Ricco (1st, 4to, pep, 123p, p-o, color, DJ)	Whitman	1937	Gag, W.	50-85	
Gag, W.	Funny Thing (1st, ob8vo, yellow ipcb, unpag, b/w, pep)	Coward	1929	Gag, W.	160-220	
Gag, W.	Gone is Gone (1st, 12mo, yellow cl, unpag, col frn)	Coward	(1935)	Gag, W.	130-170	
Gag, W.	Growing Pains (1st, lg8vo, 479p, blue ibds, b/w)	Coward	1940	Gag, W.	130-165	
Gag, W.	Millions of Cats (1st, ob8vo, ipcb, [32]p, b/w, pep, NH)	Coward	1928	Gag, W.	200-300	R
Grimm Bros.	More Tales from Grimm (1st, sm8vo, 257p, blue cl, col frn)	Coward	(1947)	Gag, W.	100-150	R
Gag, W.	Nothing at All (1st, lg ob8vo, ibds, [32]p, color, pep, CH)	Coward	(1941)	Gag, W.	180-240	
Gag, W.	Snippy & Snappy (1st, ob8vo, yellow ibds, [48]p, b/w, pep)	Coward	1931	Gag, W.	140-200	
Grimm Bros.	Snow White... (1st, 8vo, green ibds, 43p, CH)	Coward	(1938)	Gag, W.	140-170	
Grimm Bros.	Tales from Grimm (1st, 8vo, blue cl, 237p, col frn, 6pl)	Coward	(1936)	Gag, W.	140-180	R
Gag, W.	Three Gay Tales from Grimm (1st, ipcb, 63p, b/w)	Coward	(1943)	Gag, W.	100-165	
Gag, W.	Wanda Gag's Story Book (1st, ob16mo, [112]p, yel bds, pep, p-o)	Coward	(1932)	Gag, W.	150-200	
Titus, Eve	Anatole & the Cat (1st, 4to, 32p, red cl, color, CH)	Whittlesey	(1957)	Galdone, P.	70-100	*
Titus, Eve	Basil of Baker Street (1st, 8vo, beige cl, 96p, b/w)	Whittlesey	(1958)	Galdone, P.	25-40	*
Steele, Wm. O.	Buffalo Knife (1st {std}, 8vo, 177p, b/w, DJ)	Harcourt	(1952)	Galdone, P.	20-30	*
Everson, Dale	Different Dog (1st, 4to, blue cl, 31p, 2-color, pep)	Wm. Morrow	1960	Galdone, P.	30-45	*
Myers, Grace	Fishing Cat (1st, ob8vo, yellow cl, [24]p, 1-color, pep)	Abingdon	1953	Galdone, P.	35-50	*
Steele, Wm. O.	Flaming Arrows (1st {std}, sm8vo, 178p)	Harcourt	(1957)	Galdone, P.	25-45	*
Merriam, Eve	Gaggle of Geese (1st, 4to, yellow cl, unpag, color, pep)	Knopf	(1960)	Galdone, P.	40-60	*
Hawthorne, N.	Golden Touch (1st, 8vo, orange cl, 61p, fp 2-color, dep)	Whittlesey	(1959)	Galdone, P.	35-50	*
Nye, Harry	Home is If You Find It (1st {std}, 12mo, 251p)	Doubleday	1947	Galdone, P.	30-45	*
Musselman, M.M.	I Married a Redhead (1st, sm8vo, 244p, b/w)	Crowell	(1949)	Galdone, P.	25-40	*
Cheney, Cora	Key of Gold (1st {std}, 8vo, 127p)	Holt	(1955)	Galdone, P.	20-30	*
Emerson, C.D.	Little Green Car (1st, 8vo, ipcb, [28]p, color, pep)	Grosset/Dunlap	(1946)	Galdone, P.	35-50	*
Baldwin, Clara	Little Tuck (1st {std}, lg8vo, 95p, yellow cl, b/w)	Doubleday	(1959)	Galdone, P.	30-45	*
Otto, M.G.	Man in the Moon (1st {std}, sm8vo, green cl, 128p, fp b/w)	Holt	(1957)	Galdone, P.	35-60	*
MacGregor, Ellen	Miss Pickerell Goes to Mars (1st, sm8vo, red cl, 128p, fp b/w)	Whittlesey	(1951)	Galdone, P.	25-45	*
Montgomery, R.G.	Mister Jim (1st {std}, 8vo, cloth, 219p, b/w)	World	(1957)	Galdone, P.	30-50	*
Thayer, Jane	Mrs. Perrywinkle's Pets (1st, sm8vo, yell cl, 45p, 2-color, dep)	Wm. Morrow	1955	Galdone, P.	25-40	*
Black, I.S.	Night Cat (1st, lg ob8vo, [32]p, black cl, cep, b/w)	Holiday House	1957	Galdone, P.	30-45	*
Fenton, Edward	Nine Lives (1st, 4to, ipcb, 62p, pep, b/w)	Pantheon	(1951)	Galdone, P.	45-60	*
Bulla, Clyde R.	Old Charlie (1st, sm8vo, 80p, b/w)	Crowell	1957	Galdone, P.	25-40	*
Steele, Wm. O.	Perilous Road (1st {std}, 8vo, 191p, blue cl, b/w, NH)	Harcourt	1958	Galdone, P.	65-80	*
Eager, E.M.	Playing Possum (1st, lg8vo, [32]p, green cl, 1-color, pep)	Putnam	1955	Galdone, P.	35-50	*
Cheney, Cora	Rocking Chair Buck (1st {std}, 8vo, 128p, b/w)	Holt	(1956)	Galdone, P.	20-30	*
Bialk, Elisa	Silver Purse (1st {std}, sm8vo, 169p, orange cl, b/w)	World	(1952)	Galdone, P.	20-30	*
Dolson, Hildegarde	Sorry to Be So Cheerful (1st {std}, sm8vo, 207p, b/w)	Random	(1955)	Galdone, P.	25-40	*
Todd, Ruthven	Space Cat (1st, sm8vo, 69p, blue cl, fp b/w)	Scribner	(1952)	Galdone, P.	30-45	*
Todd, Ruthven	Space Cat Visits Venus (1st, sm8vo, 87p, fp b/w)	Scribner	(1955)	Galdone, P.	30-45	*
Bulla, Clyde R.	Sword in the Tree (1st {std}, 8vo, 113p, red cl, b/w)	Crowell	1956	Galdone, P.	25-45	*
MacGregor, Ellen	Theodore Turtle (1st, 4to, green cl, 32p, color, pep)	Whittlesey	1955	Galdone, P.	45-60	*
Phleger, Fred	Whales Go By (1st {std}, lg8vo, ipcb, 62p, p-o, pep, color)	Random	(1959)	Galdone, P.	30-45	*
Steele, Wm. O.	Wilderness Journey (1st {std}, sm8vo, aqua cl, 209p, b/w)	Harcourt	(1953)	Galdone, P.	25-40	*
Franchot, A.W.	White Giant & Black Giant (1st, lg8vo, ipcb, 72p, fp b/w)	Dutton	(1924)	Gamble, J.	35-50	*
Gannett, R.S.	Dragons of Blueland (1st, sm8vo, 87p, blue/gilt, pep, b/w)	Random	(1951)	Gannett, R.C.	35-50	*
Gannett, R.S.	Elmer & the Dragon (1st, sm8vo, 86p, red/gilt, pep, b/w)	Random	(1950)	Gannett, R.C.	35-50	*
Thomas, Dorothy	Hi-Po the Hippo (1st {std}, folio, [48]p, ibds, color)	Random	(1942)	Gannett, R.C.	90-130	*
Bailey, C.S.	Miss Hickory (1st, lg8vo, tan cl, 123p, fp b/w, pep, DJ, NM)	Viking	1946	Gannett, R.C.	75-120	R
Gannett, R.S.	My Father's Dragon (1st, 8vo, 86p, pep, NH)	Random	(1948)	Gannett, R.C.	50-80	R*
Garner, Elvira	Ezekiel (1st [1st bk.], sm4to, ibds, [44]p, color)	Holt	(1937)	Garner, E.	80-120	
Garner, Elvira	Ezekiel Travels (1st, lg8vo, [46]p, ibds, color)	Holt	(1938)	Garner, E.	90-130	
Garner, Elvira	Sarah Faith Anderson (1st, sm8vo, [106]p, color)	J. Messner	(1939)	Garner, E.	35-50	*
Garner, Elvira	Way Down in Tennessee (1st, 8vo, [96]p, ibds, color, pep)	J. Messner	1941	Garner, E.	90-130	
Willson, J.	Lucian's Wonderland... (1st, 8vo, brown/gilt, 163p, 15pl)	L: Blackwood	1899	Garnett, A.P.	90-145	
De La Rame, L.	Bimbi (1st AM, 8vo, 303p, 8pl)	Lippincott	1892	Garrett, E.H.	50-85	*
Baring-Gould, S.	Book of Fairy Tales (1st, 8vo, teg, 244p, gilt, uncut, 5pl)	L: Methuen	1894	Gaskin, A.J.	95-125	
Watts, Isaac	Divine & Moral Songs for Children (16mo, bds, 12 fp color)	L: Matthews	(1897)	Gaskin, A.J.	90-130	*
Andersen, H.C.	Stories & Fairy Tales (2 vols, 8vo, teg, green/gilt, uncut)	L: G. Allen	1893	Gaskin, A.J.	100-150	
Dickens, C.	Christmas Carol (1st, 4to, 121p, t-i frn, 23pl)	S.E. Cassino	1887	Gaugengigl, I.M.	80-120	*
Whyte, A.G.	Christabel's Fairyland (1st, 4to, ibds, 183p, color)	L: Chapman	1926	Gautier, P.	80-120	
Gay, Romney	Five Little Playmates (1st, 12mo, ibds, [61]p, color)	Grosset/Dunlap	(1941)	Gay, R.	25-40	*
Gay, Romney	Peter's Adventure (1st, sq12mo, ibds, [34]p, color)	Whitman	1936	Gay, R.	25-40	
Mother Goose	Romney Gay Mother Goose (1st, sq4to, ipcb, 56p, color, pep)	Grosset/Dunlap	(1936)	Gay, R.	65-90	*
Gay, Romney	Toby & Sue (1st, sq8vo, ibds, [34]p, color)	Grosset/Dunlap	1937	Gay, R.	35-50	*
Gay, Romney	Tommy Grows Wise (1st, sq12mo, ibds, [30]p, color)	Grosset/Dunlap	1939	Gay, R.	25-40	
Crespi, P.	170 Cats (1st {std}, ob4to, ibds, unpag, 1-color)	Random	(1939)	Gay, Z.	50-85	
McKown, G.	All the Days Were Antonia's (1st, 8vo, 268p, fp b/w, pep)	Viking	1939	Gay, Z.	20-35	*
Hoffmann, Eleanor	Cat of Paris (1st, sm8vo, 145p, blue cl, b/w, pep)	Stokes	1940	Gay, Z.	25-40	*
Crespi, P.	Manuelito of Costa Rica (1st, 4to, [40]p, color, pep)	J. Messner	(1940)	Gay, Z.	40-60	*

AUTHOR	TITLE	PUBLISHER	DATE	ARTIST	PRICE	LC
Sayers, F.C.	Mr. Tidy Paws (1st, sm4to, ibds, 64p, b/w, pep, DJ)	Viking	1935	Gay, Z.	45-60	
Gay, Zhenya	Pancho & His Burro (1st, sm4to, ibds, pep, [29]p, color)	Wm. Morrow	1930	Gay, Z.	45-60	
Gay, Zhenya	Sakimura (1st, 8vo, ibds, [42]p, color)	Viking	1937	Gay, Z.	45-70	
Gay, J.	Shire Colt (1st {std}, 4to, ibds, [62]p, lithos, DJ)	Doubleday/Dor.	1931	Gay, Z.	65-95	R
Whitman, W.	There was a Child Went Forth (1st {std}, 4to, ipcb, [32]p, col)	Harper	(1943)	Gay, Z.	45-70	*
Gay, Zhenya	Town Cats (1st {std}, 4to, ipcb, 110p, fp b/w)	Knopf	1932	Gay, Z.	35-50	*
Montgomery, R.G.	Troopers Three (1st {std}, sm8vo, 233p, col frn, pep)	Doubleday/Dor.	1932	Gay, Z.	20-30	*
Jones, Idwal	Whistler's Van (1st, 8vo, 235p, b/w, pep, NH)	Viking	1936	Gay, Z.	50-70	*
Gay, Zhenya	Wonderful Things! (1st, 4to, tan cl, 62p, fp b/w)	Viking	1954	Gay, Z.	25-40	*
Gaze, H.	Coppertop (1st AM, lg8vo, 338p, blue/gilt, 12cp)	Harper	(1924)	Gaze, H.	120-160	
Underhill (ed.)	Dwarf's Tailor… (1st, lg8vo, 260p, p-o by…)	Harper	(1924)	Gaze, H.	40-60	
Gaze, H.	Goblin's Glen (1st, 8vo, 242p, red/gilt, 6cp)	Little/Brown	1924	Gaze, H.	140-200	
Hubbell, R.S.	If I Could Fly (1st, 8vo, teg, 113p, 5cp, pep)	Putnam	1917	Gaze, H.	90-140	
Gaze, H.	Merry Piper (1st UK, lg8vo, 247p, 8cp, 12pl)	L: Longmans	1925	Gaze, H.	140-200	
Gaze, H.	Merry Piper (1st AM, 8vo, yellow cl, 247p, 8cp, 12pl, pep)	Little/Brown	1925	Gaze, H.	120-170	
Donahey, M.D.	Peter & Prue… (1st, sm8vo, 258p, p-o, 5cp, pep)	Rand/McNally	(1924)	Gaze, H.	140-185	
Gee, John	Bunnie Bear (1st, 8vo, ibds, color)	Volland	(1928)	Gee, J.	35-50	*
McMahon, J.	Deenie Folks/Friends of Theirs (1st, 8vo, color, ibds)	Volland	(1925)	Gee, J.	50-70	*
Atwater, R.	Doris & the Trolls (1st, 12mo, 124p, blue cl, 1-color)	Rand/McNally	(1931)	Gee, J.	50-80	
Nesbit, W.D.	In Tumbledown Town (1st, sm8vo, ibds, color)	Volland	(1926)	Gee, J.	50-80	*
Aldredge, Edna	The Timbertoes (1st, 8vo, pep, p-o, red cl, 117p, color)	Harter	(1932)	Gee, J.	65-80	*
Sorensen, Virginia	Plain Girl (1st {std}, 8vo, 151p)	Harcourt	(1955)	Geer, G.	25-45	*
Mother Goose	My First Mother Goose (1st, 8vo, ipcb, [32]p, color, pep)	Wilcox/Follett	(1946)	Gehr, M.	40-60	*
Ciardi, John	Reason for the Pelican (1st, lg8vo, 64p, blue cl, b/w)	Lippincott	(1959)	Gekiere, M.	35-50	*
George, Jean C.	My Side of the Mountain (1st {std}, 8vo, 178p, pep, b/w, NH)	Dutton	1959	George, J.C.	45-65	*
Frey, N.A.	River Horse (1st, 8vo, 150p, green cl, b/w)	W.R. Scott	(1953)	George, R.	25-40	*
Bain, R.N.	Russian Fairy Tales (1st, 8vo, 264p, gilt, b/w)	Way/Williams	1895	Gere, C.M.	100-130	*
Gere, Frances K.	Once Upon a Time in Egypt (1st, ob4to, ibds, 71p, color, pep)	Longmans	1937	Gere, F.K.	70-100	R
McConnell, Marg.	Bobo the Barrage Balloon (1st, lg8vo, 36p, ipcb, 1-color, pep)	Lothrop/Lee	1943	Gergely, T.	45-60	*
Conger, Marion	Circus Time (1st sm8vo, [42]p, ibds, color, LGB)	Simon/Schuster	(1948)	Gergely, T.	45-60	*
Lowrey, J.S.	Day in the Jungle (1st sm8vo, ibds, [42]p, color, pep, LGB)	A.& W. Guild	1943	Gergely, T.	25-45	*
Hauser, Heinrich	Folding Father (1st, lg ob8vo, ipcb, [24]p, 2-color, pep)	Lothrop	1942	Gergely, T.	45-65	*
Greene, Jean	Forgetful Elephant (1st {std}, 4to, ipcb, [32]p, color, pep)	McKay	(1945)	Gergely, T.	60-85	*
Lilly, Jean	Hundred Tuftys (1st {std}, 4to, [32]p, ipcb, 2-color, pep)	Dutton	(1940)	Gergely, T.	70-90	*
Dolbier, Maurice	Jenny: Bus that Nobody Loved (1st, 4to, 43p, ipcb, color, pep)	Random	1944	Gergely, T.	45-70	*
Dolbier, Maurice	Magic Bus (1st, lg8vo, 43p, color)	Wonder	1948	Gergely, T.	30-45	*
Duplaix, G.	Merry Shipwreck (1st {std}, 4to, ibds, [34]p, color, dep)	Harper	(1942)	Gergely, T.	70-100	*
DeLeeuw, Hendrik	Peewee the Mousedeer (1st {std}, lg ob8vo, 71p, color)	McKay	1943	Gergely, T.	45-60	*
Mitchell, L.S.	Red, White & Blue Auto (1st, ob8vo, [33]p, color)	W.R. Scott	1943	Gergely, T.	50-80	*
Tompkins, Jane	Storks Fly Home (1st {std}, sm8vo, [58]p, col frn, b/w)	Stokes	(1943)	Gergely, T.	35-50	*
Pratt, Marg.	Talking Typewriter (1st {std}, sm4to, ibds, 38p, color, pep)	Lothrop/Lee	(1940)	Gergely, T.	35-50	
Duplaix, G.	Topsy Turvey Circus (1st {std}, 4to, [40]p, ibds, color, pep)	Harper	(1940)	Gergely, T.	65-100	*
Fox, F.M.	True Monkey Stories (1st, lg8vo, 55p, green cl, fp color, pep)	Lothrop/Lee	(1941)	Gergely, T.	35-50	*
Edmonds, W.D.	Two Logs Crossing (1st 8vo, 82p, green/gilt, fp b/w, pep)	Dodd	1943	Gergely, T.	35-50	*
Rosvall, T.D.	Very Stupid Folk (1st {std}, 12mo, cloth, 52p, b/w)	Dutton	1938	Gergely, T.	25-40	
Brown, M.W.	Wheel on the Chimney (1st, 4to, [28]p, tan cl, color, CH)	Lippincott	(1954)	Gergely, T.	70-120	R*
Turner, N.B.	When it Rained Cats & Dogs (1st {std}, 4to, ibds, [32]p, color)	Lippincott	(1946)	Gergely, T.	65-80	R
Gerson, V.	Happy Heart Family (1st, lg8vo, 35p, p-o, color)	Fox Duffield	1904	Gerson, V.	100-130	
Fitch, Wm. C.	Knighting of the Twins (1st {1st bk}, 8vo, tan cl, 275p, b/w)	Bos: Roberts	(1891)	Gerson, V.	80-100	*
Gerson, V.	Little Dignity (1st {1st bk.}, sm4to, 64p, ibds, chromos)	NY: Routledge	1881	Gerson, V.	100-120	
Gerson, V.	More Advens/Happy Heart Family (1st, 4to, 47p, p-o, 4cp)	Fox Duffield	1905	Gerson, V.	120-150	
Moore, C.C.	Visit from Santa Claus (4to, ibds, 12cp, 24p)	Stokes/Allen	1887	Gerson, V.	170-220	
Waddell, H.	Beasts & Saints (1st, 8vo, 151p, red cl, 6pl)	L: Constable	1934	Gibbings, R.	80-100	*
Harrison, G.	Bird Diary (1st, sq8vo, 151p, p-o, 20pl, DJ)	L: Dent	1936	Gibbings, R.	65-80	
Gibbings, Rbt.	Iorana! (1st AM, 8vo, 157p, uncut, p-o, gilt, b/w, pep)	Houghton	1932	Gibbings, R.	45-70	R
Gibbings, Rbt.	Lovely is The Lee (1st AM {std}, 8vo, 199p, green/gilt, DJ)	Dutton	1945	Gibbings, R.	35-50	
Gibbings, Rbt.	Over the Reefs (1st, 8vo, 240p, gilt, wood engravings)	L: Dent	1948	Gibbings, R.	25-40	
Powys, L.	The Twelve Months (1st UK, 4to, 88p)	L: J. Lane	(1936)	Gibbings, R.	60-80	
Gibbs, Geo.	American Sea Fights (1st, elephant folio, 12 ticp)	R.H. Russell	1902	Gibbs, G.	200-350	*
Montgomery, L.M.	Anne of Avonlea (1st, sm8vo, 367p, p-o, green cl, col frn)	Page	1909	Gibbs, G.	100-165	
Montgomery, L.M.	Chronicles of Avonlea (1st, 8vo, 306p, p-o, gilt, col frn)	Page	1912	Gibbs, G.	100-165	
Montgomery, L.M.	Golden Road (1st, sm8vo, 369p, p-o, gilt, col frn)	Page	1913	Gibbs, G.	100-140	
Montgomery, L.M.	Kilmeny of the Orchard (1st, sm8vo, 256p, p-o, 4cp)	Page	1910	Gibbs, G.	100-165	
Crowninshield, Mrs.	Lattitude 19 (1st, 8vo, 418p, red cl, 7pl)	Appleton	1898	Gibbs, G.	35-50	*
Harris, J.C.	Little Union Scout (1st, 8vo, green/gilt, 181p, 8pl)	McClure	1904	Gibbs, G.	100-140	
Montgomery, L.M.	Story Girl (1st, sm8vo, 365p, gilt, p-o, col frn)	Page	1911	Gibbs, G.	90-135	
Montgomery, L.M.	Story Girl (1st UK, 8vo, red cl, 365p, p-o, col frn by…)	L: I. Pitman	1911	Gibbs, G.	70-90	*
Thurston, K.C.	The Mystics (1st, sm8vo, black/gilt, 191p, 8pl)	Harper	1907	Gibbs, G.	20-25	*
Hurd, Marian K.	When She Came Home from College (1st, 12mo, 272p, 7pl)	Houghton	1909	Gibbs, G.	20-35	*
Davis, R.H.	About Paris (1st, 12mo, 219p, 30pl)	Harper	1895	Gibson, C.D.	25-40	
Gibson, C.D.	Americans (1st, ob folio, ipcb, [88]p, teg, fp b/w)	R.H. Russell	1900	Gibson, C.D.	150-200	
Bangs, J.K.	Booming of Acre Hill (1st, 12mo, teg, uncut, 265p, b/w)	Harper	1900	Gibson, C.D.	30-45	

AUTHOR	TITLE	PUBLISHER	DATE	ARTIST	PRICE	LC
Goodloe, A.C.	College Girls (1st, 8vo, 288p, 11pl)	Scribner	1895	Gibson, C.D.	30-45	
Masson, T.	Corner in Women (1st, 8vo, teg, ipcb, gilt, 332p, cvr by...)	Moffat	1905	Gibson, C.D.	30-50	
Gibson, C.D.	Drawings (1st, ob folio, [88]p, ibds, teg, b/w)	R.H. Russell	1897	Gibson, C.D.	140-200	
Gibson, C.D.	Education of Mr. Pipp (1st, ob folio, ibds, [78]p, b/w)	R.H. Russell	1899	Gibson, C.D.	150-200	
Gibson, C.D.	Eighty Drawings including Weaker Sex (1st, ob folio, ibds, b/w)	Scribner/Lane	1903	Gibson, C.D.	130-200	
Gibson, C.D.	Everyday People (1st, ob folio, b/w pl)	Scribner	1904	Gibson, C.D.	130-180	
Gibson, C.D.	Gibson Book (1st, ob folio, 2 volumes, red cl, teg)	Scribner	1906	Gibson, C.D.	220-300	
Chambers, Rbt.	Japonette (1st, 8vo, 384p, p-o, 21 b/w)	Appleton	1912	Gibson, C.D.	20-35	
Addison, J.	Mrs. John Vernon (1st, 12mo, p-o, 205p, frn by...)	Badger	1909	Gibson, C.D.	20-25	*
Gibson, C.D.	Our Neighbors (1st, ob folio, [68]p, b/w)	Scribner	1905	Gibson, C.D.	140-180	
Gibson, C.D.	Pictures of People (1st, ob folio, ibds, b/w)	R.H. Russell	1896	Gibson, C.D.	130-165	
Downey, Fairfax	Portrait of an Era (1st, 4to, 391p, DJ)	Scribner	(1936)	Gibson, C.D.	40-60	
Magruder, Julia	Princess Sonia (1st, 12mo, 225p, 17pl)	Century	1895	Gibson, C.D.	25-40	*
Gibson, C.D.	Sketches in Egypt (1st, lg8vo, 115p, b/w)	Doub./McClure	1899	Gibson, C.D.	120-165	
Gibson, C.D.	Social Ladder (1st, ob. folio, [79]p, teg, b/w)	R.H. Russell	1902	Gibson, C.D.	160-200	
Davis, R.H.	Soldiers of Fortune (1st, 12mo, 364p, 6pl, yellow/gilt)	Scribner	1897	Gibson, C.D.	20-30	
Chambers, Rbt.	Streets of Ascalon (1st, 8vo, 440p, gilt, 14 double pg pl)	Appleton	1912	Gibson, C.D.	20-30	
Magruder, Julia	The Violet (1st, sm8vo, 210p, 11pl)	Longmans	1896	Gibson, C.D.	25-40	*
Davis, R.H.	Van Bibber & Others (1st, 12mo, 249p, gilt, 4pl)	Harper	1892	Gibson, C.D.	25-40	
Gibson, C.D.	Widow & Her Friends (1st, ob folio, [79]p, bds, b/w)	R.H. Russell	1901	Gibson, C.D.	120-150	
Gibson, Lydia	Teacup Whale (1st, ob8vo, ipcb, dep, 23p, b/w)	Farrar/Rine.	(1934)	Gibson, L.	30-45	*
Benson, A.B.	Brownie Primer (1st, sm sq8vo, 98p, color)	Chi: Flanagan	(1905)	Gilbert, J.D.	50-75	
Colcock, A.T.	Margaret Tudor (12mo, 169p, green cl)	Stokes	(1901)	Gilbert, W.	20-30	
Gilbert, W.S.	Bab Ballads (1st AM, 16mo, 184p, grey bds, uncut)	R.H. Russell	1906	Gilbert, W.S.	30-50	
Munroe, K.	Under the Great Bear (1st, 12mo, 313p, 12pl)	Doubleday/Page	1900	Giles, H.	30-45	*
Farjeon, E.	Nursery Rhymes/London Town (1st, 8vo, [64]p, blue/gilt, col frn)	L: Duckworth	(1916)	Gill, M.	70-90	*
Chamisso, A.	Peter Schlemihl (1st, sm4to, 104p, green/gilt, 35 woodcuts)	McKay	(1929)	Gincano, John	35-50	*
Day, M.	Tell 'Em Again Tales (1st, sq4to, ibds, 48p, 3 fp color, pep)	Duffield	1924	Glackens, L.M.	70-120	*
Seawell, M.E.	Papa Bouchard (1st, 12mo, 261p, uncut, teg)	Scribner	1901	Glackens, W.	20-30	
Page, T.N.	Santa Claus' Partner (1st, 8vo, red/gilt, 177p, teg, 8cp)	Scribner	1899	Glackens, W.	30-45	
Green, M.M.	Everybody Eats (1st, lg8vo, [20]p, color)	W.R. Scott	1946	Glannon, E.J.	35-50	*
Mitchell, L.S.	Guess What's in the Grass (1st, ob4to, ibds, [30]p, 2-col, pep)	W.R. Scott	1945	Glannon, E.J.	60-90	*
Wright, M.O.	Wabeno the Magician (1st, 8vo, 344p, green/gilt, b/w)	MacMillan	1899	Gleeson, J.M.	30-50	
Owen, Dora	Book of Fairy Poetry (1st, 4to, 180p, grey cl, 16 ticp, pep)	L: Longmans	1920	Goble, W.	250-300	
Chaucer, G.	Complete Poetical Works of... (1st, 4to, blue/gilt, teg, 32cp)	L: MacMillan	1912	Goble, W.	200-240	
Van Millingen	Constantinople (1st, 4to, 282p, teg, tan/gilt, 63cp)	L: A&C Black	1906	Goble, W.	120-185	
Whishaw, F.	Emperor's Englishman (1st, 8vo, 342p)	L: Hutchinson	1896	Goble, W.	80-100	*
Craik, D.	Fairy Book (1st, 4to, 379p, teg, green/gilt, 32cp)	L: MacMillan	1913	Goble, W.	300-450	
Craik, D.	Fairy Book (1st {this format}, 8vo, 232p, red/gilt, 16cp)	L: MacMillan	1923	Goble, W.	100-150	
Day, L.B.	Folk Tales of Bengal (1st, 4to, red/gilt, [274]p, 32cp)	L: MacMillan	1912	Goble, W.	200-250	
Gasquet, A.	Greater Abbeys of England (1st AM, 8vo, 378p, teg, 60cp)	Dodd	1908	Goble, W.	130-180	
Gasquet, A.	Greater Abbeys of England (1st, lg8vo, 378p, teg, 60cp)	L: Chatto	1908	Goble, W.	160-200	
James, G.	Green Willow... (1st, sm4to, blue/gilt, 281p, 40 ticp)	L: MacMillan	1910	Goble, W.	350-465	
James, G.	Green Willow... (1st {this format}, 8vo, gilt, 281p, 16cp)	L: MacMillan	1912	Goble, W.	130-180	
Molesworth, M.	Grim House (1st, 8vo, 289p)	L: J. Nisbet	1899	Goble, W.	70-100	*
Mackenzie, D.	Indian Myth & Legend (1st, 8vo, 463p, gilt, 8cp, 32pl)	L: Gresham	[1910]	Goble, W.	150-200	
Barlow, J.	Irish Ways (1st, 8vo, 262p, 16cp)	L: G. Allen	(1909)	Goble, W.	185-250	
Stevenson, R.L.	Kidnapped (1st AM, 8vo, 327p, blue cl, 16pl)	MacMillan	1925	Goble, W.	140-180	
Marryat, Fred.	King's Own (1st, 8vo, 451p, 6pl)	L: OUP	1907	Goble, W.	90-120	*
Basile, G.	Stories from the Pentamerone (1st, 4to, red/gilt, 304p, 32cp)	L: MacMillan	1911	Goble, W.	180-260	
Irving, W.	The Alhambra (1st, 8vo, blue cl, 3cp)	L: MacMillan	1926	Goble, W.	85-110	
Whitney, Elinor	Tod of the Fens (1st, 8vo, 239p, red cl, col frn, pep, NH)	MacMillan	1928	Goble, W.	45-60	*
Stevenson, R.L.	Treasure Island (1st, sm8vo, 312p, blue cl, pep, 4cp)	L: MacMillan	1923	Goble, W.	85-125	
Wells, H.G.	War of the Worlds (1st AM, 8vo, green cl, 291p, 16pl)	Harper	1898	Goble, W.	250-320	
Kingsley, C.	Water Babies (1st, 4to, AEG, green/gilt, 32 ticp)	L: MacMillan	1909	Goble, W.	285-400	
Kingsley, C.	Water Babies (1st {this format}, 8vo, 273p, gilt, 16cp)	L: MacMillan	1910	Goble, W.	120-160	*
Stables, Wm. G.	Young Peggy McQueen (1st, 8vo, 152p, pl)	L: Collins	1903	Goble, W.	80-100	*
Lang, A.	Blue Fairy Book (1st, 4to, teg, p-o, blue cl, 8cp)	McKay	(1921)	Godwin, F.	60-85	
Stevenson, R.L.	Kidnapped (1st, 8vo, 348p, p-o, 4cp, pep)	Winston	(1925)	Godwin, F.	25-40	*
N/A	King Arthur & His Knights (1st, lg8vo, 256p, p-o, 4cp)	Winston	(1927)	Godwin, F.	30-45	
Malory, T.	King Arthur & his Knights (1st, 8vo, pep, 4cp)	Winston	(1927)	Godwin, F.	25-45	*
Lamb, C.	Tales from Shakespeare (1st, 8vo, p-o, 323p, 12pl)	Winston	(1924)	Godwin, F.	30-45	
Stevenson, R.L.	Treasure Island (1st, 8vo, 304p, p-o, 3cp)	Winston	(1924)	Godwin, F.	25-40	*
Davis, Rbt.	That Girl of Pierre's (1st, 8vo, 230p, rust cl, b/w, pep)	Holiday House	(1948)	Goff, L.L.	20-30	*
Wilde, O.	Canterville Ghost (1st, 16mo, 123p, blue cl, pl)	Bos: J.W. Luce	1906	Goldsmith, W.	150-200	*
Warren, C.	Little Betty Marigold... (1st, 12mo, 107p, 14 color)	C.M. Clark	1907	Goldsmith, W.	20-30	*
Kneeland, C.A.	Smuggler's Island (1st, sm8vo, red cl, 356p, b/w, PPPa)	Houghton	1915	Goldsmith, W.	60-100	R*
Sterne, Emma G.	All About Little Boy Blue (1st, 24mo, ibds, p-o, 48p, color)	Cupples	(1924)	Gooch, T.	35-50	*
Sterne, Emma G.	All About Peter Pan (1st, 24mo, tan bds, 48p, p-o, 8cp)	Cupples	(1924)	Gooch, T.	45-60	*
Moore, C.C.	Night Before Christmas (1st, lg4to, [24]p, ipcb, color, pep)	Grosset/Dunlap	1937	Gooch, T.	65-80	R*
Malot, H.	Nobody's Boy (1st, sm4to, p-o, 308p, 8cp, pep)	Cupples	(1930)	Gooch, T.	25-40	*
Stevenson, R.L.	Child's Garden of Verses (1st, 12mo, 91p, b/w, pep)	Whitman	(1931)	Good, P.R.	20-35	*

AUTHOR	TITLE	PUBLISHER	DATE	ARTIST	PRICE	LC
Marryat, Fred.	Children o/t New Forest (1st, 4to, black cl, p-o, 9cp, pep, SC)	Scribner	1927	Good, S.	70-100	
Kidd, Dudley	Bull of the Kraal (1st, lg8vo, teg, uncut, 12cp)	L: A&C Black	1908	Goodall, A.M.	120-160	*
Aesopus	Aesop's Fables (1st, 4to, 312p, plates)	L: Harrap	1936	Gooden, S.	60-80	*
LaFontaine, J.	Fables of Jean De La Fontaine (1st, 8vo, 469p, 12pl)	L: Heinemann	1933	Gooden, S.	75-120	
Henry, O.	Gift of the Magi (1st, blue bds, b/w, DJ)	L: Harrap	1939	Gooden, S.	65-90	
N/A	Arabian Nights (1st, 8vo, 327p, color)	Grosset/Dunlap	(1946)	Goodenow, E.	25-40	*
Clark, G.O	Nightmare Land (1st, lg4to, [105]p, color)	R.H. Russell	1901	Goodwin, C.L.	180-270	*
Lyle, E.P.	Lone Star (1st, 8vo, p-o, 431p, 4pl)	Doubleday/Page	1907	Goodwin, P.R.	30-45	
Pierson, C.D.	Among the Farmyard People (1st, sm8vo, teg, uncut, 245p, 11pl)	Dutton	1899	Gordon, F.C.	35-50	*
Pierson, C.D.	Among the Forest People (1st, 12mo, teg, 219p, gilt)	Dutton	(1898)	Gordon, F.C.	35-50	
Pierson, C.D.	Among the Meadow People (1st, 12mo, 127p, gilt, teg, b/w, uncut)	Dutton	1897	Gordon, F.C.	35-50	*
Pierson, C.D.	Among the Night People (1st, 8vo, 221p)	Dutton	(1902)	Gordon, F.C.	35-50	*
Pierson, C.D.	Among the Pond People (1st, 12mo, 210p, teg, 12 b/w)	Dutton	1901	Gordon, F.C.	30-50	*
MacLaren, Ian	Doctor o/t Old School (1st {this fmt.}, green bds, AEG, b/w)	Hodder	1895	Gordon, F.C.	60-80	*
Ewing, J.H.	Jacanapes (1st, 8vo, 80p, gilt, AEG, 7pl)	Dutton	1893	Gordon, F.C.	35-50	*
Kingsley, C.	Water Babies (1st, sm8vo, 308p, gilt, b/w)	Stokes	1891	Gordon, F.C.	90-125	
Gorey, Edward	Bug Book (1st {std}, 16mo, wraps, unpag, color)	Looking Glass	(1959)	Gorey, E.	70-100	R*
Gorey, Edward	Doubtful Guest (1st {std}, ob8vo, ibds, [30]p, b/w)	Doubleday	1957	Gorey, E.	50-70	*
Moore, M.	Illegitimate Sonnets (1st {1st illus}, 8vo, gilt, 125p, pep)	NY: Twayne	(1950)	Gorey, E.	50-85	*
Gorey, Edward	Listing Attic (1st {std}, sm8vo, ibds, unpag, b/w)	Duell/Sloan	(1954)	Gorey, E.	45-60	*
Gorey, Edward	Object Lesson (1st {std}, ob8vo, tan bds, b/w, DJ)	Doubleday	1958	Gorey, E.	70-90	*
Gorey, Edward	Unstrung Harp (1st {std}-[1st bk.], 8vo, ibds, unpag, DJ)	Duell/Sloan	(1953)	Gorey, E.	90-130	*
Flaubert, G.	Temptation of St. Anthony (1st, sm8vo, 360p, teg, gilt, 8pl)	L: Nichols	1895	Gorski, S.	45-60	
Brooks, E.C.	Francisco... (1st, sm8vo, 152p, 6pl)	Page	1910	Goss, J.	25-40	*
Montgomery, L.M.	Further Chronicles of Avonlea (1st, sm8vo, 301p, 6pl)	Page	1920	Goss, J.	65-90	*
Garis, H.	Rick & Ruddy (1st, sm8vo, p-o, 282p, 6pl)	M. Bradley	1920	Goss, J.	25-45	
Brentano, C.M.	Fairy Tales from Brentano (1st, 8vo, 252p, gilt, b/w)	(London)	1885	Gould, F.C.	150-200	*
Brentano, C.M.	Fairy Tales from Brentano (sm8vo, 326p, col frn, 8pl)	Stokes	(1925)	Gould, F.C.	30-50	*
Begbie, H.	Great Men (sm4to, 51p, ibds, 24cp)	L: Richards	1901	Gould, F.C.	75-100	
Begbie, H.	Political Struwwelpeter (4to, ipcb, [24]p, color)	L: Richards	1899	Gould, F.C.	150-185	
Begbie, H.	Struwwelpeter Alphabet (1st, 4to, ipcb, [26]p, color)	L: Richards	1900	Gould, F.C.	160-180	
Gould, F.C.	Tales Told in the Zoo (1st, lg8vo, 136p, col frn, 5pl)	L: T.F. Unwin	1900	Gould, F.C.	45-65	
Herbertson, A.	Be-Wee the Gnome... (1st AM, 8vo, p-o, ibds, 116p, pep, 20cp)	Cupples	(1921)	Govey, L.	80-125	
Herbertson, A.	Book of Happy Gnomes (1st, 8vo, 191p)	L: H. Milford	(1924)	Govey, L.	65-80	*
Herbertson, A.	Dolly Book (1st, 4to, 62p)	L: H. Milford	1920	Govey, L.	65-80	*
Heward, C.	Grandpa & the Tiger (1st, 8vo, 109p, orange cl, p-o, color pep)	Jacobs	(1924)	Govey, L.	55-80	*
Strang, H.	Rose Book of the Fairies (4to, ibds, 6cp)	L: H. Milford	(1922)	Govey, L.	65-80	
Strang, H.	Rose Fairy Book (1st, 4to, 303p, p-o, pep, 12 ticp)	L: Hodder	[1912]	Govey, L.	180-230	
Gilmour, Marg.	Seven Little Spillikins (ob8vo, p-o, color)	McKay	[1930]	Govey, L.	60-75	
Marsh, Lewis	Tales of the Fairies (1st, 8vo, 5cp, 7 b/w, gilt)	L: Hodder	[1912]	Govey, L.	130-175	
Syrett, Netta	Toby & the Odd Beasts (8vo, blue cl, p-o, 5cp)	(London)	1921	Govey, L.	100-135	
Rives, A.	Athelwold (1st, 8vo, 118p, 8pl)	Harper	1893	Gow, M.	70-100	
Dickens, C.	Christmas Carol (1st, 12mo, [60]p, color)	McLoughlin	(1940)	Graef, R.A.	25-40	*
Irving, W.	Rip Van Winkle (1st, 12mo, [60]p, color)	McLoughlin	(1941)	Graef, R.A.	25-45	*
Zion, Gene	All Falling Down (1st, 4to, ipcb, [31]p, color, CH)	Harper	(1951)	Graham, M.B.	60-90	R*
Shippen, K.B.	Big Mose (1st {std}, 8vo, grey cl, 90p, b/w)	Harper	(1953)	Graham, M.B.	30-45	*
Zion, Gene	Dear Garbage Man (1st, 4to, ibds, unpag, color)	Harper	(1957)	Graham, M.B.	45-70	*
Zion, Gene	Harry the Dirty Dog (1st, 4to, ibds, [30]p, color)	Harper	(1956)	Graham, M.B.	65-80	R*
Zion, Gene	Really Spring (1st, lg4to, ipcb, [30]p, 3-color)	Harper	(1956)	Graham, M.B.	65-85	*
Zolotow, C.	Storm Book (1st, 4to, ipcb, unpag, 7 fp color, cep, CH)	Harper	(1952)	Graham, M.B.	70-100	*
Zion, Gene	Summer Snowman (1st, narrow 4to, unpag, yellow, cl, color, cep)	Harper	(1955)	Graham, M.B.	50-80	*
Gramatky, H.	Creeper's Jeep (1st, 4to, [64]p, color)	Putnam	(1948)	Gramatky, H.	45-60	
Gramatky, H.	Hercules (1st, 4to, [72]p, red cl, color, pep)	Putnam	(1940)	Gramatky, H.	70-100	*
Gramatky, H.	Homer & the Circus Train (1st, 4to, unpag, pep, color)	Putnam	(1957)	Gramatky, H.	35-50	*
Gramatky, H.	Little Toot (1st, sq8vo, unpag, pep, color)	Putnam	1939	Gramatky, H.	120-165	R*
Gramatky, H.	Loopy (1st, 4to, [72]p, color, pep)	Putnam	(1941)	Gramatky, H.	45-60	*
Teilhet, Darwin	Skwee-Gee (1st {std}, 4to, ibds, [40]p, color)	Doubleday/Dor.	1940	Gramatky, H.	45-60	*
Proudfit, I.B.	Treasure Hunter (1st, lg8vo, 206p, dep)	J. Messner	(1939)	Gramatky, H.	65-80	*
Hawkins, Q.	Who Wants an Apple (1st, 8vo, [39]p, ipcb, b/w, pep)	Holiday House	(1942)	Granahan, L.& D.	20-30	*
Burroughs, E.R.	Tarzan Twins (1st, 8vo, 126p, ibds, 14 fp color)	Volland	(1927)	Grant, Doug	150-220	*
Culver, H.	Book of Old Ships (1st {this pub}, 4to, 306p, ibds, 5cp)	Garden City	(1935)	Grant, G.	30-45	
Graham, H.	Deportmental Ditties (1st AM, 16mo, 134p, 3pl)	Duffield	1909	Grant, G.	25-45	*
Porter, G.S.	Fire Bird (1st {std}, 8vo, 71p, tan bds, pep, 3cp by...)	Doubleday/Page	1922	Grant, G.	240-300	
Grant, Gordon	Greasy Luck (1st, 4to, white cl, 128p, pep)	Payson	(1932)	Grant, G.	35-50	
Porter, G.S.	Keeper of the Bees (1st {std}, 8vo, 515p, 3pl)	Doubleday/Page	1925	Grant, G.	50-70	
Tarkington, B.	Penrod (1st [1], 8vo, p-o, 345p, blue cl, PPP)	Doubleday/Page	1914	Grant, G.	200-250	
Tarkington, B.	Penrod Jashper (1st {std}, 8vo, blue cl, 321p, b/w)	Doubleday/Dor.	1929	Grant, G.	35-50	
London, J.	Scarlet Plague (1st, 8vo, 181p, b/w, pep)	MacMillan	1915	Grant, G.	150-200	
Grant, Gordon	Secret Voyage (1st, lg8vo, 63p, b/w)	Wm. Morrow	1942	Grant, G.	30-45	
Morrow, Honore	Ship's Monkey (1st, 8vo, 188p, color, pep, DJ)	Wm. Morrow	1933	Grant, G.	20-25	
Grant, Gordon	Ships Under Sail (1st, lg4to, ibds, 25p, color)	Garden City	(1939)	Grant, G.	30-50	
Grant, Gordon	Story of the Ship (1st, folio, ipcb, [48]p, color, pep)	McLoughlin	(1919)	Grant, G.	45-70	

AUTHOR	TITLE	PUBLISHER	DATE	ARTIST	PRICE	LC
Grant, V.	Tinker Tim the Toy Maker (1st, lg4to, ibds, 29p, color, pep)	Whitman	1934	Grant, V.	75-115	R
Quiller-Couch, A.	Treasure Book of Children's Verse (4to, 336p, gilt, 20 ticp)	L: Hodder	[1915]	Gray, M.E.	80-125	
Dickens, C.	Old Curiosity Shop (12mo, 618p, col frn, 23 b/w)	Macrae Smith	(1925)	Green, C.	20-35	*
Elliott, H.	Alliterative Alphabet... (1st, 4to, [55]p, blue bds, color)	McKay	(1947)	Green, E.S.	85-120	*
Hardy, A.S.	Aurelie (1st, 8vo, 31p, blue pcb, p-o, 2cp)	Harper	1912	Green, E.S.	45-60	
Humphrey, Mabel	Book of the Child (1st, folio, ibds, 4cp by...)	Stokes	(1903)	Green, E.S.	600-750	
Peabody, J.	Book of the Little Past (1st, sm4to, 50p, p-o, pcb, 6cp)	Houghton	1908	Green, E.S.	70-100	
Singmaster, Elsie	Bred in the Bone (1st, 8vo, green/gilt, 300p, 6pl)	Houghton	1925	Green, E.S.	30-45	
Morris, M.	Bryn Mawr Stories (1st, 8vo, teg, green/gilt, illus by...)	Jacobs	(1901)	Green, E.S.	100-135	
Buchanan, T.	Castle Comedy (1st, 8vo, lavender cl, teg, 235p, 4cp, pep)	Harper	1904	Green, E.S.	40-60	
Ward, Mrs. H.	Coryston Family (1st, 8vo, red/gilt, 328p, 8pl)	Harper	1913	Green, E.S.	40-65	
Waller, M.E.	Daughter of the Rich (1st, 8vo, p-o, 296p, 5cp, pep)	Little/Brown	1924	Green, E.S.	30-45	*
Daskam, J.	Her Fiance (1st, 12mo, 164p, 5pl)	Altemus	(1904)	Green, E.S.	40-60	
Malloch, D.	Little Hop Skipper (1st, 8vo, 99p, blue cl, col frn)	Doran	(1926)	Green, E.S.	30-45	
LeGallienne, R.	Maker of Rainbows (1st, 8vo, 104p, teg, p-o, 2cp, 3pl)	Harper	1912	Green, E.S.	65-90	R
N/A	May & November Correspondence (1st, bds, p-o & frn by...)	Houghton	1928	Green, E.S.	35-50	
Wiggin, K.D.	Mother Carey's Chickens (1st, 8vo, 289p, p-o, 4cp, 10 b/w)	Houghton	1930	Green, E.S.	35-50	
LeGallienne, R.	Old Country House (1st, lg4to, bds, teg, 144p, 6pl)	Harper	1902	Green, E.S.	100-150	
Donnell, A.H.	Rebecca Mary (1st, 12mo, blue cl, 194p, p-o, 9pl)	Harper	1905	Green, E.S.	35-50	
Chambers, Rbt.	River-Land (1st, sm4to, gilt, 92p, 8cp)	Harper	1904	Green, E.S.	90-140	
N/A	Songs of Bryn Mawr College (1st, ob4to, 137p, p-o, ibds)	C.W. Beck	1903	Green, E.S.	100-165	
Duncan, N.	Suitable Child (1st, 8vo, ipcb, teg, 96p, pep, 5 ticp)	Revell	1909	Green, E.S.	45-60	
Lamb, C.	Tales from Shakespeare (1st, lg8vo, teg, 377p, p-o, pep, 11cp)	McKay	1922	Green, E.S.	60-85	
Gerry, M.S.	The Flowers (1st, 8vo, 40p, green cl, p-o, 3cp)	Harper	1910	Green, E.S.	30-45	
Van Dyke, H.	The Mansion (1st, 8vo, 45p, green/gilt, 2 ticp, pep)	Harper	1911	Green, E.S.	30-45	
Donnell, A.H.	Very Small Person (1st, 8vo, p-o, 193p, 8cp)	Harper	1906	Green, E.S.	35-60	
Burnett, F.H.	White People (1st, 12mo, 112p, grey/gilt, 4pl)	Harper	(1917)	Green, E.S.	30-45	
Lamb, C.	Mrs. Leicester's School (1st, sq8vo, 128p, ibds, 20cp)	L: Dent	1899	Green, Winifred	75-100	
Chambers, Rbt.	Outdoorland (1st, sm4to, green cl, 311p, 22cp)	Appleton	1931	Green/Birch	80-100	
Greenaway, K.	A Apple Pie (1st, ob4to, green ibds, [44]p, A.E. Red)	L: Routledge	[1886]	Greenaway, K.	180-250	
Russell, M.	April Baby's Book of Tunes (1st, sq8vo, tan cl, 75p, 16cp)	L: MacMillan	1900	Greenaway, K.	200-300	
N/A	Around the House (1st, 4to, ibds, 96p, 63 illus)	Worthington	1888	Greenaway, K.	80-120	
N/A	Baby's Birthday Book (sq16mo, ibds, A.E. pink, color)	L: Marcus Ward	[1885]	Greenaway, K.	150-200	
Barker, Mrs. S.	Birthday Book/Children (1st, 16mo, 128p, green/gilt, p-o, 12cp)	L: Routledge	(1880)	Greenaway, K.	180-265	
Jerrold, A.	Cruise in the Acorn (1st, 8vo, 140p, p-o, gilt, 6 ticp)	L: Marcus Ward	1875	Greenaway, K.	260-320	
Ruskin, John (ed.)	Dame Wiggin of Lee (1st, 12mo, 20p, gilt)	L: G. Allen	1885	Greenaway, K.	125-160	
Foster, M.B.	Day in a Child's Life (1st, 4to, 29p, ibds, color)	L: Routledge	[1881]	Greenaway, K.	180-250	
N/A	Diamonds & Toads (4to, linen wraps, 6cp)	McLoughlin	[1875]	Greenaway, K.	165-220	
Greenaway, K.	English Spelling Book (1st, 12mo, grey bds, 108p)	L: Routledge	1885	Greenaway, K.	175-230	
Butt, G.	Esther... (8vo, green cl, 4 ticp)	L: Marcus Ward	1878	Greenaway, K.	185-230	
Holt, Ardern	Fancy Dresses Described (2nd, 12mo, 105p, 48pl)	L: Debenham	[1881]	Greenaway, K.	140-170	
Ranking, B.M.	Flowers & Fancies (1st, 24mo, 186p, 4 color)	L: Marcus Ward	1882	Greenaway, K.	180-230	
Greenaway, K.	Greenaway's Babies (12mo, linen, 12p, color)	Saalfield	1907	Greenaway, K.	100-135	
Coolidge, S.	Guernsey Lily (lg sq8vo, brown/gilt, 238p, 10 illus)	Roberts	1881	Greenaway, K.	100-165	
Yonge, C.M.	Heir of Redclyffe (1st, 8vo, blue/gilt, 524p, 4 illus by)	L: MacMillan	1881	Greenaway, K.	50-80	
Greenaway, K.	K. Greenaway's Alphabet (1st, 48mo, ibds, [32]p, color)	L: Routledge	[1885]	Greenaway, K.	140-180	
Greenaway, K.	K. Greenaway's Book of Games (1st, sm4to, ipcb, 64p, 24cp)	L: Routledge	[1889]	Greenaway, K.	175-220	
Spielmann, M.H.	Kate Greenaway (1st, lg8vo, blue cl, cp)	L: A&C Black	1905	Greenaway, K.	80-120	
Greenaway, K.	Kate Greenaway's Birthday Book (1st, 24mo, beige cl, color)	L: Routledge	[1880]	Greenaway, K.	175-250	
Greenaway, K.	Language of Flowers (1st, 16mo, green ibds, 80p, color)	L: Routledge	[1884]	Greenaway, K.	120-185	
Taylor, Jane	Little Ann... (1st, lg8vo, ibds, 64p, color, cep)	L: Routledge	[1883]	Greenaway, K.	160-220	
Greenaway, K.	Marigold Garden (1st, 4to, green ibds, 60p, color)	L: Routledge	[1885]	Greenaway, K.	160-220	
Mother Goose	Mother Goose (1st, 12mo, yellow ibds, 48p, color)	L: Routledge	[1881]	Greenaway, K.	220-300	
Mother Goose	Mother Goose (4to, ibds, [48]p, color)	McLoughlin	[1882]	Greenaway, K.	180-250	
Greenaway, K.	Painting Book (1st, lg8vo, 80p, wraps)	L: Routledge	[1884]	Greenaway, K.	200-280	
Browning, R.	Pied Piper of Hamelin (1st, 4to, orang ibds, 64p, ae blue, col)	L: Routledge	[1888]	Greenaway, K.	170-225	
Greenaway, K.	Queen Victoria's Jubilee Garland (1st, ob8vo, wraps, AEG, col)	L: Routledge	1887	Greenaway, K.	280-320	
Harte, Bret	Queen of Pirate Isle (1st, sm4to, tan cl, 58p, AEG, color)	L: Chatto	[1886]	Greenaway, K.	200-300	
Harte, Bret	Queen of Pirate Isle (1st AM, sm4to, 58p, AEG, color)	Houghton	1887	Greenaway, K.	180-260	
Allingham, W.	Rhymes for the Young Folks (1st, 8vo, 75p, 2 illus by...)	L: Cassell	(1887)	Greenaway, K.	150-200	
Cresswell, B.	Royal Progress/King Pepito (1st, 4to, tan ibds, 48p, 12cp)	L: SPCK	[1889]	Greenaway, K.	150-200	
Brunefille, G.	Topo... (1st, 12mo, AEG, 140p, green/gilt)	L: Marcus Ward	1878	Greenaway, K.	200-250	
Greenaway, K.	Trot's Journey (1st, p-o, 8vo, 79p)	Worthington	(1882)	Greenaway, K.	100-160	
Clark, Mary S.	Turnaside Cottage (8vo, [new ed.], green/gilt, 191p, col frn)	L: Marcus Ward	[1880]	Greenaway, K.	150-200	
Greenaway, K.	Under the Window (1st, lg8vo, green ibds, 64p, color, cep)	L: Routledge	[1878]	Greenaway, K.	220-300	
Greenaway, K.	Under the Window (sq8vo, green ibds, 63p, color)	McLoughlin	[1879]	Greenaway, K.	200-250	
N/A	Quiver of Love (1st, sq8vo, 152p, green cl, 8 ticp)	L: Marcus Ward	1876	Greenaway/Crane	250-350	
Disney, W.	Disney's Tonka (1st, 8vo, ipcb, 60p, color, pep)	Golden Press	(1959)	Greene, H.	70-120	*
Fryer, J.E.	Mary Frances Housekeeper (1st, sm4to, p-o, 253p)	Winston	(1914)	Greene, J.	120-185	*
Mother Goose	Mother Goose Nursery Rhymes (1st, sm8vo, 256p, color, pep)	Winston	(1928)	Greene, J.	30-45	*
Spyri, J.	Story of Rico (1st, 8vo, 163p, blue cl, 3cp)	Beacon Press	(1921)	Greene, J.	30-45	*
Durston, G.R.	Candle Light (1st, 4to, ibds, 116p, color, pep)	Saalfield	(1906)	Greenland, K.	70-100	*

AUTHOR	TITLE	PUBLISHER	DATE	ARTIST	PRICE	LC
Page, Marg.	In Childhood Land (lg4to, ibds, color)	Saalfield	1903	Greenland, K.	100-165	
Alden, R.M.	Knights/Silver Shield (1st, 4to, tan cl, 149p, 10cp)	Bobbs-Merrill	(1906)	Greenland, K.	75-110	*
Alden, R.M.	Why the Chimes Rang (1st, 8vo, 148p, b/w)	Bobbs-Merrill	(1908)	Greenland, K.	30-45	*
Cowan, James	Daybreak... (1st, sm8vo, gilt, 399p, teg, b/w)	NY: Richmond	1896	Greenough, W.C.	70-100	
Compton, M.	Snow Bird & Water Tiger... (1st UK, 8vo, 201p, teg, gilt, b/w)	L: Lawrence	1895	Greenough, W.C.	70-85	
Holder, Charles F.	Treasure Divers (1st, sm8vo, 207p, blue/silver, 13pl)	Dodd	1898	Greenough, W.C.	30-45	
Atherton, G.	Valiant Runaways (1st, sm8vo, 276p, 8pl)	Dodd	1898	Greenough, W.C.	25-40	*
Spyri, J.	Eveli (1st, 8vo, red ibds, 272p, 8cp)	Lippincott	1926	Greer, B.	20-40	*
Spyri, J.	Peppino (1st, 12mo, 114p, red cl, 4cp)	Lippincott	(1926)	Greer, B.	30-45	*
Abbott, E.H.	Sick-a-Bed-Lady (1st, 8vo, 371p, 9pl)	Century	1911	Greer, B.	25-40	
Greer, Blanche	Thunder's Tail (1st, 4to, ipcb, [24]p, 1-color)	Coward	1944	Greer, B.	40-65	
Biggers, E.D.	Agony Column (1st, 8vo, 193p, brown cl, 9pl)	Bobbs-Merrill	(1916)	Grefe, W.	35-50	
MacGrath, H.	Best Man (1st, 8vo, 207p, green/gilt, p-o, 8pl)	Bobbs-Merrill	(1907)	Grefe, W.	20-30	
Futrelle, J.	Chase o/t Golden Plate (1st, sm8vo, 220p, green cl, p-o)	Dodd	1906	Grefe, W.	40-60	
Cabell, J.B.	Eagle's Shadow (1st, 8vo, red cl, 256p, 8pl)	Doubleday/Page	1904	Grefe, W.	80-120	
Wodehouse, P.G.	Prince & Betty (1st AM, sm8vo, 300p, black/gilt, p-o)	NY: Watt	(1912)	Grefe, W.	350-500	
Fox, F.M.	Angeline Goes Traveling (1st, 12mo, p-o, 256p, 5cp)	Rand/McNally	(1927)	Gregory, D.L.	25-40	*
Fox, F.M.	Janey (1st, 8vo, 121p, blue cl, p-o, 4cp)	Rand/McNally	(1925)	Gregory, D.L.	20-25	
Van Dresser, J.	Jimsey (1st, 8vo, 90p, p-o, color)	Rand/McNally	(1925)	Gregory, D.L.	60-80	
Boyle, E.	Scrap Basket Sam (12mo, 4cp)	Rand/McNally	(1923)	Gregory, D.L.	25-40	
Fox, F.M.	Sister Sally (1st, 8vo, 105p, gilt, p-o, 4cp)	Rand/McNally	(1925)	Gregory, D.L.	20-30	
Shetter, S.C.	When Grandma Was a Little Girl (1st, 12mo, 250p, p-o, 4cp)	Rand/McNally	(1926)	Gregory, D.L.	20-25	
Bangs, J.K.	Lohengrin (1st, 4to, green/gilt)	Brentano's	(1891)	Gregory, F.M.	80-100	
Gregory, Lady	Golden Apple (1st, sm8vo, 117p, tan cl, 8cp)	Putnam	1916	Gregory, M.	30-45	*
Scott, Walter	Ivanhoe (1st AM, 8vo, 563p, 12cp)	Lipp./Jack	[1915]	Greiffenhagen, M.	35-60	*
Haggard, H.R.	Montezuma's Daughter (1st, 8vo, green/gilt, uncut, 24pl)	L: Longmans	1893	Greiffenhagen, M.	75-100	
Bicknell, A.G.	Flower Folk (1st, 4to, 71p, fp color)	Putnam	(1936)	Grenwis, M.	80-100	*
Welch, C.	Stories Children Love (1st, sm8vo, 439p, cp)	Dodge	(1909)	Grimball, M.	35-60	*
Aesopus	Aesop's Fables (4to, ibds, 390p, b/w)	NY: Cassell	1884	Griset, E.	180-250	*
Aesopus	Book of Fables (sm8vo, 32cp)	Am. Book Exch.	1880	Griset, E.	90-130	
Manning, W.	Child's Dream of the Zoo (sq4to, 24p, wraps)	L: Routledge	1889	Griset, E.	80-100	
Grishina, N.G.	Gresha/Clay Pig (1st, 8vo, p-o, color)	Stokes	1930	Grishina, N.G.	65-80	*
Grishina, N.G.	Magic Squirrel (1st, 8vo, 142p, p-o, 3cp, 7pl)	Stokes	1934	Grishina, N.G.	45-65	*
Grishina, N.G.	Peter-Pea (1st, 8vo, p-o, 95p, cp)	Stokes	1926	Grishina, N.G.	40-65	*
Grishina, N.G.	Sparrow House (1st, 8vo, p-o, 175p, 5cp)	Stokes	1928	Grishina, N.G.	40-65	*
Prentiss, L.E.	Dickens' Year Book (1st, 8vo, tan bds, p-o, unpag)	McClurg	1913	Groesbeck, D.	25-40	
Graham, H.	Misrepresentative Women (1st, 8vo, ibds, 120p, 12pl)	Duffield	1906	Groesbeck, D.	20-35	
Eastman, C.A.	Old Indian Days (1st, 8vo, p-o, 279p)	McClure	1907	Groesbeck, D.	30-45	
Swift, J.	Gulliver's Travels (1st, sm8vo, 304p, cp, pep)	Doubleday/Page	1912	Groesbeck, D.S.	20-35	*
Morris, Wm.	Wolf's Head & the Queen (1st, lg8vo, 243p, p-o, col frn, 13pl)	Scribner	1931	Grofe, N.	40-60	
Ash, Frank	Trip to Mars (1st AM, 8vo, red/gilt, 318p, 6cp)	Chambers/Lipp.	1909	Groome, W.H.C.	100-150	
Parks, G.T.	Here Comes Daddy (1st, ob8vo, ibds, unpag, color)	W.R. Scott	1951	Gropper, W.	45-65	*
Gropper, Wm.	Little Tailor (1st, 8vo, brown illus, pep, unpag)	Dodd	1955	Gropper, W.	65-80	*
Blumberg, F.B.	Rowena Teena Tot & Blackberries (1st, 4to, ibds, p-o, 32p, col)	Whitman	(1934)	Grosjean, M.	85-140	*
Fyleman, R.	40 Good-Night Tales (1st AM, 8vo, 131p, p-o, 4cp)	Doran	(1924)	Grosvenor, T.	30-45	*
Fyleman, R.	Fairies & Chimneys (1st, 8vo, 62p, col frn, silhouettes)	Doran	(1920)	Grosvenor, T.	30-50	
Fyleman, R.	Rainbow Cat (1st, 8vo, 117p, p-o, col frn)	Doran	(1923)	Grosvenor, T.	25-40	*
Groth, Eleanor	Adventures in a Dishpan (1st, sm4to, ibds, 31p, color, pep)	Grosset/Dunlap	(1936)	Groth, M.	25-40	
Gruelle, J.	All About Cinderella (1st, 12mo, brown bds, p-o)	Cupples	(1916)	Gruelle, J.	70-100	
N/A	All About Hansel & Gretel (sq16mo, ibds, p-o, 48p, 8cp)	Cupples	(1917)	Gruelle, J.	100-140	*
Gruelle, J.	All About Mother Goose (sq16mo, 48p, color)	Cupples	(1916)	Gruelle, J.	100-140	*
N/A	All About Red Riding Hood (sq16mo, ibds, p-o, 48p, color)	Cupples	(1916)	Gruelle, J.	100-140	*
McEvoy, Joseph P.	Bam Bam Clock (1st, sq12mo, ibds, [38]p, color, pep)	Volland	(1920)	Gruelle, J.	70-100	
Gruelle, J.	Beloved Belindy (1st, 8vo, ibds, [95]p, color, pep)	Volland	(1926)	Gruelle, J.	80-125	
Gruelle, J.	Beloved Belindy (8vo, [94]p, color, pep)	Donohue	(1926)	Gruelle, J.	45-60	*
Gruelle, J.	Camel with Wrinkled Knees (8vo, [44]p, color)	McLoughlin	1943	Gruelle, J.	35-50	*
Gruelle, J.	Cheery Scarcrow (1st, 12mo, ibds, [39]p, pep, 6cp)	Volland	(1929)	Gruelle, J.	80-120	
Gruelle, J.	Eddie Elephant (1st, 12mo, ibds, [39]p, color, pep)	Volland	(1921)	Gruelle, J.	80-120	
Grimm Bros.	Fairy Tales (1st, lg8vo, 419p, p-o, gilt, 11cp)	Cupples	(1914)	Gruelle, J.	170-230	
Gruelle, J.	Friendly Fairies (1st, lg8vo, [86]p, ibds, color, pep)	Volland	(1919)	Gruelle, J.	120-185	
Gruelle, J.	Funny Little Book (1st, 12mo, ibds, [40]p, pep, color)	Volland	(1917)	Gruelle, J.	120-165	
Gruelle, J.	Johnny Mouse & Wishing Stick (1st, lg8vo, ipcb, 89p, color, pep)	Bobbs-Merrill	(1922)	Gruelle, J.	80-120	R
Gruelle, J.	Little Brown Bear (1st, 12mo, ibds, [40]p, color, pep)	Volland	(1920)	Gruelle, J.	70-100	
Gruelle, J.	Little Sunny Stories (1st, 12mo, [40]p, color)	Volland	(1919)	Gruelle, J.	70-120	*
Gruelle, J.	Magical Land of Noom (1st, 4to, ibds, 157p, 12cp, pep)	Volland	(1922)	Gruelle, J.	200-300	
Lawrence, J.	Man in the Moon Stories... (1st, 4to, 121p, gilt, p-o, 8cp, pep)	Cupples	(1922)	Gruelle, J.	165-220	
Gruelle, J.	Marcella Stories (1st, 8vo, ibds, 94p, color, pep)	Volland	(1929)	Gruelle, J.	80-120	
Gruelle, J.	My Very Own Fairy Stories (1st, 12mo, ibds, [95]p, color, pep)	Volland	(1917)	Gruelle, J.	130-180	
Malot, H.	Nobody's Boy (1st AM, 8vo, 372p, green cl, p-o, 4cp)	Cupples	1916	Gruelle, J.	45-70	
Gruelle, J.	Orphant Annie Story Book (1st, 8vo, 85p, p-o, color, pep)	Bobbs-Merrill	(1921)	Gruelle, J.	75-120	
Gruelle, J.	Paper Dragon (1st, 8vo, ibds, [96]p, color, pep)	Volland	(1926)	Gruelle, J.	80-125	
Hubbell, R.S.	Quacky Doodles... (1st, 8vo, ibds, [88]p, color)	Volland	(1916)	Gruelle, J.	60-75	

AUTHOR	TITLE	PUBLISHER	DATE	ARTIST	PRICE	LC
Gruelle, J.	Raggedy Andy Goes Sailing (1st, 12mo, [59]p, ipcb, 10 fp color)	McLoughlin	(1941)	Gruelle, J.	45-65	*
Gruelle, J.	Raggedy Andy Stories (1st, lg8vo, ibds, unpag, color, pep)	Volland	(1920)	Gruelle, J.	100-130	
Gruelle, J.	Raggedy Ann & Betsy Bonnet String (1st, 8vo, 95p, ibds, color)	Gruelle Co.	(1943)	Gruelle, J.	45-60	
Gruelle, J.	Raggedy Ann & Golden Butterfly (1st, lg8vo, 95p, ibds, col, cep)	Gruelle Co.	(1940)	Gruelle, J.	50-80	*
Gruelle, J.	Raggedy Ann & Happy Toad (1st, 12mo, ibds, [50]p, color)	McLoughlin	1940	Gruelle, J.	45-65	*
Gruelle, J.	Raggedy Ann & Laughing Brook (1st, 12mo, ibds, [59]p, color)	McLoughlin	1940	Gruelle, J.	45-65	*
Gruelle, J.	Raggedy Ann & Left-Handed Safety Pin (1st, 12mo, 45p, col, pep)	Whitman	(1935)	Gruelle, J.	35-50	*
Gruelle, J.	Raggedy Ann Helps Grandpa Hoppergrass (1st, 12mo, [50]p, color)	McLoughlin	1940	Gruelle, J.	35-50	*
Gruelle, J.	Raggedy Ann Stories (1st, 8vo, ibds, [95]p, color, pep)	Volland	(1918)	Gruelle, J.	100-140	
Gruelle, J.	Raggedy Ann Stories (1st {this pub}, lg8vo, 95p, color)	Gruelle Co.	(1947)	Gruelle, J.	45-65	*
Gruelle, J.	Raggedy Ann in Cookie Land (1st, lg8vo, ibds, 95p, color, pep)	Volland	(1931)	Gruelle, J.	70-120	
Gruelle, J.	Raggedy Ann in Deep Deep Woods (1st, 8vo, ibds, [95]p, col, pep)	Volland	(1930)	Gruelle, J.	80-120	
Gruelle, J.	Raggedy Ann in the Garden (1st, 12mo, [61]p, ipcb, 10 fp color)	McLoughlin	1940	Gruelle, J.	45-65	*
Gruelle, J.	Raggedy Ann's Alphabet Book (1st, 8vo, [38]p, ibds, pep, color)	Volland	(1925)	Gruelle, J.	90-125	
Gruelle, J.	Raggedy Ann's Lucky Pennies (1st, 8vo, ibds, 94p, color, pep)	Volland	(1932)	Gruelle, J.	70-100	
Gruelle, J.	Raggedy Ann's Magical Wishes (1st, lg8vo, 94p, ibds, color, pep)	Volland	(1928)	Gruelle, J.	100-165	
Gruelle, J.	Raggedy Ann's Wishing Pebble (1st, lg8vo, ibds, unpag, col, pep)	Volland	(1925)	Gruelle, J.	80-120	
Gruelle, J.	Raggedy Ann.../Camel/Wrinkled Knees (8vo, ibds, [95]p, pep, col)	Volland	(1924)	Gruelle, J.	70-100	
Gruelle, J.	Raggedy Ann/Golden Meadow (1st, lg4to, ibds, 56p, 14 color, pep)	Whitman	1935	Gruelle, J.	80-130	
Snyder, F.	Rhymes for Kindly Children (1st, lg8vo, ibds, [95]p, color)	Volland	(1916)	Gruelle, J.	80-120	
Fairmont, E.	Rhymes for Kindly Children (4to, [127]p, color, pep)	Wise-Parlow	(1937)	Gruelle, J.	35-50	
Putnam, Nina W.	Sunny Bunny (1st, 8vo, ibds, [42]p, color, pep)	Volland	(1918)	Gruelle, J.	85-130	
Gruelle, J.	Wooden Willie (1st, 8vo, ibds, 95p, color, pep)	Volland	(1927)	Gruelle, J.	90-130	
Gruelle, Justin	Camel with Wrinkled Knees (1st {this pub}, 12mo, ibds, [59]p col)	McLoughlin	(1941)	Gruelle, Justin	45-60	*
Gruelle, Justin	Mother Goose Parade (1st, lg4to, ibds, [31]p, color, pep)	Volland	(1929)	Gruelle, Justin	65-100	
Fox, F.M.	Nannette (1st, 8vo, 80p, red/gilt, color, pep)	Volland	(1929)	Gruelle, Justin	40-60	
Gruelle, J.	Raggedy Ann in Snow White Castle (1st, 8vo, ibds, 95p, color)	Gruelle Co.	(1946)	Gruelle, J.	60-80	
Gruelle, J.	Raggedy Ann in Magic Book (1st, lg8vo, [91]p, ibds, color)	Gruelle Co.	(1939)	Gruelle, Worth	70-100	
Thompson, C.M.	Calico Cat (1st, 12mo, green/gilt, 228p, 8pl)	Houghton	1908	Gruger, F.R.	25-40	*
Johnson, O.	Tennessee Shad (1st, 8vo, red cl, 307p, 8pl, PPP)	Baker/Taylor	1911	Gruger, F.R.	120-165	
Johnson, O.	The Varmint (1st, 8vo, 396p, green cl, 6pl, PPP)	Baker/Taylor	1910	Gruger, F.R.	120-150	
Harris-Burland, J.	Gold Worshipers (1st, 8vo, brown cl, 6pl)	Dillingham	(1906)	Grunwald, C.	40-60	
Godfrey, Hollis	Man Who Ended War (1st, 8vo, blue/gilt, 301p, p-o, 4pl)	Little/Brown	1898	Grunwald, C.	50-70	
Lansdale, M.	Chateaux of Touraine (1st, 4to, 363p, uncut, teg, gilt, 16cp)	Century	1906	Guerin, J.	65-80	*
Hichens, R.	Holy Land (1st, 4to, 302p, uncut, teg, 18cp)	Century	1910	Guerin, J.	70-85	
Hichens, R.	Near East (1st, 4to, teg, blue/gilt, 50pl)	Century	1913	Guerin, J.	65-80	
Crawford, P.	Let's Go! (1st, sm8vo, 73p, b/w)	Holt	(1949)	Guerin, T.	25-40	*
Lida	Little French Farm (1st {std}, 4to, ibds, [26]p, color, pep)	Harper	1939	Guertik, H.	80-120	*
Moore, N.H.	Deeds of Daring... (1st, sm8vo, 300p, 6cp)	Stokes	(1906)	Gunn, Archie	20-30	*
Dooley, Mrs.	Dem Good Ole Times (1st, 8vo, 151p, teg, 16 ticp)	Doubleday/Page	1906	Gutherz, S.	85-130	
Low, Frances H.	Little Men in Scarlet (1st, 8vo, 237p, green/gilt, b/w)	L: Jarrold	1896	Guthrie, J.J.	25-40	*
Gray, P.L.	In a Car of Gold (1st, 8vo, 156p, brown/gilt, 6pl)	Saalfield	1902	Gutman, Bernard	25-40	*
Carroll, L.	Alice/Wonderland (1st, 8vo, 165p, blue cl, 10cp, pep)	Dodge	1907	Gutmann, B.P.	160-200	
Dunham, E.	Diary of a Mouse (1st, 8vo, p-o)	Dodge	(1907)	Gutmann, B.P.	80-120	
Dalton, Agnes M.	From Sioux to Susan (1st, 8vo, 342p, 22 b/w illus)	Century	1905	Gutmann, B.P.	65-80	*
Carroll, L.	Through the Looking Glass (1st, 8vo, blue cl, 185p, 10cp)	Dodge	(1909)	Gutmann, B.P.	120-185	
DeRegniers, B.S.	Was It a Good Trade? (1st {std}, narrow ob8vo, [29]p, ibds col)	Harcourt	1956	Haas, I.	50-90	R*
Hader, B.	Whiffy McMann (1st, sq12mo, [56]p, ipcb, 1-color)	NY: OUP	(1933)	Hader, B.	50-70	*
Williamson, H.	Baby Bear (1st {std}, 8vo, [55]p, green ibds, color)	Doubleday/Dor.	(1930)	Hader, B.& E.	50-70	
Hader, B.& E.	Banana Tree House (1st, lg8vo, 108p, color, pep)	Coward	(1938)	Hader, B.& E.	45-60	*
Hader, B.& E.	Big City (1st, 4to, cloth, [80]p, fp color, cep)	MacMillan	1947	Hader, B.& E.	40-65	
Baruch, D.W.	Big Fellow at Work (1st {std}, 12mo, 103p, b/w, pep)	Harper	1930	Hader, B.& E.	65-80	
Hader, B.& E.	Big Snow (1st, 4to, blue cl, [48]p, color, dep, DJ, CM)	MacMillan	1948	Hader, B.& E.	80-120	R
Hader, B.& E.	Billy Butter (1st, ob8vo, cloth, 92p, color, pep, DJ)	MacMillan	1936	Hader, B.& E.	45-70	
Hader, B.& E.	Cat & the Kitten (1st, 8vo, 98p, green cl, color, pep)	MacMillan	1940	Hader, B.& E.	35-50	
N/A	Chicken Little & Little Half Chick (1st, sq12mo, ibds, color)	MacMillan	1927	Hader, B.& E.	45-60	*
Hader, B.& E.	Chuck-a-Luck & his Reindeer (1st, ob8vo, ipcb, 28p, color)	Houghton	1933	Hader, B.& E.	65-90	*
Hader, B.& E.	Cock-a-Doodle-Doo (1st, 4to, [56]p, fp color, CH)	MacMillan	(1939)	Hader, B.& E.	75-110	*
Hader, B.& E.	Cricket (1st, 8vo, p-o, red cl, 160p, color, pep)	MacMillan	1938	Hader, B.& E.	40-60	
Hader, B.& E.	Ding Dong Bell (1st {std}, lg8vo, ipcb, 45p, fp color)	MacMillan	1957	Hader, B.& E.	35-50	*
Peedie, J.M.	Donald in Numberland (1st, 8vo, ipcb, [64]p, color, dep)	R.D. Henkle	(1927)	Hader, B.& E.	70-100	*
Hader, B.& E.	Farmer in the Dell (1st, sm4to, green cl, [90]p, color, pep)	MacMillan	1931	Hader, B.& E.	45-60	*
Hader, B.& E.	Friendly Phoebe (1st {std}, 8vo, 45p, color)	MacMillan	1953	Hader, B.& E.	30-50	
Stoddard, Ann	Good Little Dog (1st {std}, 8vo, [55]p, 16cp)	Century	(1930)	Hader, B.& E.	45-65	
Hader, B.& E.	Green & Gold... (1st, 8vo, 48p, color, pep)	MacMillan	1936	Hader, B.& E.	35-50	
Stoddard, Ann	Here Bingo! (1st {std}, sq8vo, ibds, [61]p, 16 fp color)	Century	(1932)	Hader, B.& E.	35-60	
Williamson, H.	Humpy, Son of the Sands (1st {std}, 8vo, [47]p, color, pep)	Doubleday/Dor.	1937	Hader, B.& E.	60-90	*
Hader, B.& E.	Jamaica Johnny (1st, sq8vo, 90p, green cl, 6 fp color, pep, DJ)	MacMillan	1935	Hader, B.& E.	70-90	
Miller, Jane	Jimmy the Groceryman (1st, sm8vo, 88p, blue cl, color, pep)	Houghton	(1934)	Hader, B.& E.	45-60	*
Williamson, H.	Lion Cub: Jungle Tale (1st {std}, 8vo, ipcb, [51]p, color, pep)	Doubleday/Dor.	(1931)	Hader, B.& E.	50-80	*
Hader, B.& E.	Lions/Tigers/Elephants Too (1st {std}, ob8vo, ibds, [61]p, col)	Longmans	1930	Hader, B.& E.	65-80	*
Hader, B.& E.	Little Appaloosa (1st {std}, sq4to, [43]p, color)	MacMillan	(1949)	Hader, B.& E.	50-75	

AUTHOR	TITLE	PUBLISHER	DATE	ARTIST	PRICE	LC
Williamson, H.	Little Elephant (1st {std}, sq8vo, ibds, [55]p, 4cp, DJ)	Doubleday/Dor.	(1930)	Hader, B.& E.	45-60	
Hader, B.& E.	Little Stone House (1st, sm4to, green cl, [63]p, color)	MacMillan	(1944)	Hader, B.& E.	45-70	*
Hader, B.& E.	Little Town (1st, 4to, [87]p, orang cl, pep, color)	MacMillan	1941	Hader, B.& E.	65-80	*
Hader, B.& E.	Little White Foot (1st {std}, 8vo, blue cl, unpag, color, cep)	MacMillan	1952	Hader, B.& E.	35-50	*
Lee, M.	Marcos... (1st, 4to, p-o, 79p, color)	Whitman	1937	Hader, B.& E.	35-50	
Hader, B.& E.	Midget & Bridget (1st, lg o8vo, 90p, orang cl, color, color)	MacMillan	1934	Hader, B.& E.	45-60	
Hader, B.& E.	Mighty Hunter (1st, 4to, [49]p, color, pep, DJ, CH)	MacMillan	(1943)	Hader, B.& E.	60-90	
Williamson, H.	Monkey Tale (1st {std}, 8vo, [49]p, pep, color)	Doubleday/Dor.	(1929)	Hader, B.& E.	45-60	*
Hader, B.& E.	Mr. Billy's Gun (1st {std}, 4to, unpag, color)	MacMillan	1960	Hader, B.& E.	30-45	*
Seaman, Louise	Mr. Peck's Pets (1st {std}, 8vo, 96p, b/w, pep)	MacMillan	1947	Hader, B.& E.	25-40	*
Hader, B.& E.	Old Woman & Crooked Sixp^Ence (1st, 16mo, [42]p, color)	MacMillan	1928	Hader, B.& E.	50-70	*
Hader, B.& E.	Picture Bk. o/t States (1st {std}, ob folio, color, [60]p, pep)	Harper	1928	Hader, B.& E.	100-160	*
Mother Goose	Picture Book Mother Goose (1st, sq8vo, [151]p, color)	Coward	(1930)	Hader, B.& E.	140-200	
Hader, B.& E.	Picture Book of Travel (1st, 4to, p-o, 63p, color, pep)	MacMillan	1928	Hader, B.& E.	60-85	
Hader, B.& E.	Rainbow's End (1st, sq8vo, 168p, 4 fp color, DJ)	MacMillan	1945	Hader, B.& E.	35-50	
Hader, B.& E.	Reindeer Trail (1st, sm4to, blue cl, unpag, color)	MacMillan	(1959)	Hader, B.& E.	35-50	*
Dalgliesh, A.	Smiths & Rusty (1st, 8vo, 118p, b/w)	Scribner	1936	Hader, B.& E.	30-50	*
Bigham, M.A.	Sonny Elephant (1st, sm8vo, 201p, cloth, col frn, b/w)	Little/Brown	1930	Hader, B.& E.	35-50	*
Hader, B.& E.	Spunky (1st, ob8vo, blue cl, 90p, color, pep)	MacMillan	1933	Hader, B.& E.	45-60	*
Hader, B.& E.	Squirrely of Willow Hill (1st {std}, 8vo, [47]p, color, cep)	MacMillan	1950	Hader, B.& E.	40-60	
Hader, B.& E.	Stop, Look & Listen (1st, sq12mo, ipcb, 48p, 2-color, pep)	Longmans	(1936)	Hader, B.& E.	45-70	*
Feuillet, O.	Story of Mr. Punch (1st, 8vo, 139p, p-o, col frn, fp b/w, pep)	Dutton	(1929)	Hader, B.& E.	30-45	
Hader, B.	Story of Pancho (1st, sm4to, cloth, [56]p, color)	MacMillan	1942	Hader, B.& E.	35-50	
Hader, B.& E.	Story of the Three Bears (1st, sq8vo, ibds, color, pep)	MacMillan	1928	Hader, B.& E.	45-65	*
Williamson, H.	Stripey (1st {std}, sm4to, ibds, [47]p, color, pep, DJ)	Doubleday/Dor.	1939	Hader, B.& E.	50-70	
Lent, Henry B.	The Farmer (1st, sq16mo, ipcb, [42]p, color, pep)	MacMillan	1937	Hader, B.& E.	35-50	
Hader, B.& E.	The Runaways (1st {std}, 4to, green cl, 38p, color)	MacMillan	1956	Hader, B.& E.	25-40	*
Hader, B.& E.	The Skyrocket (1st, lg8vo, 148p, grey/red, 4 fp color, cep)	MacMillan	1946	Hader, B.& E.	25-40	
Whitney, Elinor	Timothy & the Blue Cart (1st, 8vo, 168p, p-o, col frn, pep)	Stokes	1930	Hader, B.& E.	35-50	*
Mason, Miriam E.	Timothy has Ideas (1st {std}, 8vo, 127p, blue cl, fp b/w)	MacMillan	1943	Hader, B.& E.	45-60	*
Hader, B.& E.	Tommy Thatcher Goes to Sea (1st, 8vo, 95p, 6 fp color, pep)	MacMillan	1937	Hader, B.& E.	35-50	
Hader, B.& E.	Tooky... (1st {std}, ob8vo, ibds, [61]p, color, pep)	Longmans	1931	Hader, B.& E.	65-80	*
Hader, B.& E.	Two Funny Clowns (1st, ob8vo, [52]p, color)	Coward	(1929)	Hader, B.& E.	35-50	*
Andersen, H.C.	Ugly Duckling (1st, 24mo, [42]p, ibds, color, pep)	MacMillan	1927	Hader, B.& E.	30-50	*
Moore, C.C.	Visit from Saint Nicholas (1st, 24mo, [42]p, ibds, pep, color)	MacMillan	1937	Hader, B.& E.	25-40	*
Kipling, R.	Wee Willie Winkie (1st, 12mo, ibds, color)	MacMillan	1927	Hader, B.& E.	50-80	
Hader, B.& E.	What'll You Do When You Grow Up? (1st, sq12mo, [63]p, col, pep)	Longmans	1929	Hader, B.& E.	65-80	*
Dalgliesh, A.	Wings for the Smiths (1st, 8vo, blue cl, 89p, 3cp, cep)	Scribner	1937	Hader, B.& E.	30-45	
Hader, B.& E.	Wish on the Moon (1st {std}, sq4to, 40p, dep, color)	MacMillan	1954	Hader, B.& E.	25-40	*
Meigs, C.	Wonderful Locomotive (1st, ob8vo, gilt, 104p, 3cp, pep, DJ)	MacMillan	1928	Hader, B.& E.	85-100	
Gaggin, E.R.	Down Ryton Water (1st, 8vo, green/silver, 369p, b/w, pep, NH)	Viking	1941	Hader, E.	35-50	*
Hooker, F.	Garden of the Lost Key (1st {std}, 8vo, 288p, col frn, pep)	Doubleday/Dor.	1929	Hader, E.	65-80	*
McBride, Mary M.	How Dear to My Heart (1st {std}, 8vo, 196p, b/w)	MacMillan	1940	Hader, E.	35-60	*
Singmaster, Elsie	Isle of Que (1st {std}, 8vo, 152p, designs by...)	Longmans	(1948)	Hader, E.	45-65	*
Camp, Ruth O.	Story of the Markets (1st {std}, sm8vo, 128p, col frn, b/w)	Harper	1929	Hader, E.	45-60	*
Mother Goose	Old Mother Goose in a New Dress (1st, ob4to, [45]p, color, pep)	NY: Laidlaw	1932	Hall, D.	100-150	*
Metcalf, S.	Annabel (1st [1], 8vo, 231p, grey/gilt, p-o, 6pl)	Reilly/Britton	(1906)	Hall, H.P.	475-700	
Madison, J.	Sweethearts Always (1st, 8vo, 232p, grey/gilt, teg, uncut, 12pl)	Reilly/Britton	1906	Hall, H.P.	85-120	
Omar Khayyam	Rubaiyat... (1st, 4to, [38]p)	L: A. Harriman	1911	Hall, I.H.	70-90	*
Hall, A.N.	Wonder Hill (1st, 4to, p-o, 271p, 10cp, pep)	Rand/McNally	(1914)	Hall, N.	120-165	
Hallock, G.T.	Bird in the Bush (1st, 12mo, 47p, pep)	Dutton	1930	Hallock, G.T.	25-45	*
Stevenson, R.L.	Child's Garden of Verses (1st, 4to, 96p, p-o, 8cp, pep)	Rand/McNally	(1919)	Hallock, R.M.	50-70	
Seegmiller, W.	Little Rhymes for Little Readers (1st, lg4to, 81p, pep)	Rand/McNally	(1903)	Hallock, R.M.	65-80	*
Ward, Mrs. H.	Milly & Olly (1st, 8vo, 302p, p-o, 8pl, pep)	Doubleday/Page	1907	Hallock, R.M.	25-40	*
Gray, Eliz. J.	Sandy (1st, sm8vo, 233p, col frn by...)	Viking	1945	Hallock, R.M.	20-30	*
Moulton, L.C.	Arthur O'Shaughnessy (1st, 12mo, cvr by...)	Stone/Kimball	1894	Hallowell, G.H.	70-90	
Carman, B.	Low Tide/Grand Pre (2nd, 12mo, gilt, 132p, teg)	Stone/Kimball	1894	Hallowell, G.H.	50-80	
Farrar, Evelyn	Stories from the Bible (1st, sm4to, 243p, gilt, 12pl)	L: Henry	1896	Hallward, R.	35-50	*
Goldsmith, O.	Comedies of... (1st, 8vo, AEG, 310p, b/w)	L: G. Allen	1896	Hammond, C.	65-80	
Austen, J.	Emma (1st, 12mo, green/gilt, 504p, teg, b/w)	L: G. Allen	1898	Hammond, C.	45-60	
Edgeworth, M.	Helen (1st, 12mo, blue/gilt, 490p, AEG, b/w, dep)	L: MacMillan	1896	Hammond, C.	60-80	
Austen, J.	Sense & Sensibility (1st, 8vo, teg, 389p, gilt, b/w)	L: G. Allen	1899	Hammond, C.	60-80	
Molesworth, M.	Fairies Afield (1st, 8vo, 252p)	L: MacMillan	1911	Hammond, G.D.	50-80	*
Molesworth, M.	Fairies of Sorts (1st, 8vo, gilt, 249p, AEG, 8pl)	L: MacMillan	1908	Hammond, G.D.	80-110	*
Dawson, L.H. (ed.)	Stories from Faerie Queen (1st, 8vo, 234p)	L: Harrap	1909	Hammond, G.D.	40-65	*
Cowie, John	Alliterative Anomalies/Infants & Invalids (ob4to, ibds, color)	Dodd	[1900]	Hammond, Wm.	160-220	*
Woods, M.	Come Unto these Yellow Sands (1st, 4to, ibds, 234p, 16cp)	L: J. Lane	1915	Hancock, J.	70-100	
Handforth, T.	Faraway Meadow (1st {std}, ob4to, [32]p, color, pep)	Doubleday/Dor.	1939	Handforth, T.	50-80	*
Handforth, T.	Mei Li (1st {std}, 4to, [58]p, orange/gilt, b/w, pep, CM)	Doubleday/Dor.	1938	Handforth, T.	70-120	R
Coatsworth, E.	Toutou in Bondage (1st, 8vo, 56p, dp illus, pep)	MacMillan	1929	Handforth, T.	35-50	*
Smith, Susan C.	Tranquilina's Paradise (1st, lg4to, 34p, color, pep)	Minton Balch	(1930)	Handforth, T.	65-90	*
Goldsmith, O.	Deserted Village (1st, 4to, 99p, teg, 40 ticp)	L: Constable	1909	Hankey, W.L.	90-120	

AUTHOR	TITLE	PUBLISHER	DATE	ARTIST	PRICE	LC
Hankins, Maude M.	Fermentations of Eliza (1st, 12mo, 203p, 4pl)	Crowell	(1915)	Hankins, C.	45-70	*
Omar Khayyam	Rubaiyat... (1st AM, 4to, teg, blue/gilt, ticp)	Dodge	[1908]	Hanscom, A.	100-125	
Robinson, E.A.	Children of the Night (1st, sm8vo, 123p, tan cl, cvr by...)	Badger	1897	Hapgood, T.B.	200-300	
Lloyd, J.U.	Right Side of the Car (1st, 12mo, 59p, teg, green/gilt)	Badger	1897	Hapgood, T.B.	30-50	
Harris, J.C.	Bishop & Boogerman (1st, 8vo, green cl, 184p, 8cp)	Doubleday/Page	1909	Harding, C.	80-120	
Howells, W.D.	Fennel & Rue (1st, 8vo, 130p, green/gilt, 4pl)	Harper	1908	Harding, C.	25-40	
Eggleston, G.C.	Last of the Flatboats (1st, 8vo, green/gilt, 382p, 4pl)	Lothrop	(1900)	Harding, C.	25-40	
Jordan, E.	May Iverson... (1st, 8vo, blue cl, 282p, p-o, 8pl)	Harper	1904	Harding, C.	40-60	
Tappan, E.M.	Robin Hood: His Book (1st, 8vo, tan cl, 267p, 6cp)	Little/Brown	1903	Harding, C.	50-70	
Hay, Helen	Verses/Jock & Joan (1st, lg sq4to, 32p, ibds, 6cp)	Fox Duffield	1905	Harding, C.	170-225	
Strettell, A.	Lullabies of Many Lands (1st, 4to, 127p, gilt, teg, uncut, dep)	L: G. Allen	1894	Harding, E.J.	65-80	
Harris, J.C.	Shadow Between his Shoulder Blades (1st, 12mo, 132p, 4pl)	Small	(1909)	Harding, G.	85-120	
N/A	Book for Little People (4to, ibds, 16 chromos)	L: Nister	[1890]	Hardy, E.S.	200-300	
Weatherly, F.E.	Book of Gnomes (1st, ob4to, [25]p, ibds, 8 chromos, pep)	L: Nister	[1900]	Hardy, E.S.	250-400	
Andersen, H.C.	Fairy Tales (lg8vo, AEG, 288p, 6 chromos)	L: Nister	[1890]	Hardy, E.S.	150-185	
Girvin, B.	Queer Cousin Claude (1st, 8vo, 280p)	L: G. Allen	1912	Hardy, E.S.	30-45	*
Andersen, H.C.	Stories from Andersen (4to, 288p, AEG, grey/gilt, 6 chromos)	L: Nister	[1890]	Hardy, E.S.	100-150	
Nesbit, E.	Story of Five Rebellious Dolls (1st, ob folio, ibds, 8cp, pep)	L: Nister	(1904)	Hardy, E.S.	250-375	
Carlton, M.	Tumble Down Pictures (1st, 4to, ibds, unpag, 6 chromos)	Nister/Dutton	[1898]	Hardy, E.S.	160-220	
Malet, Lucas	Little Peter (1st, 8vo, grey/gilt, 168p, pep, 9pl)	L: Kegan Paul	1888	Hardy, P.	50-70	*
Debenham, M.H.	Whispering Winds & Tales they Told (1st, 8vo, 195p, gilt, 25pl)	L: Blackie	1895	Hardy, P.	50-75	*
Stigand, C.H.	Black Tales/White Children (1st, 8vo, 200p, b/w, DJ)	L: Constable	(1914)	Hargrave, J.	120-170	
London, J.	Valley of the Moon (1st, orang cl, 530p, col frn by...)	MacMillan	1913	Harper, G.	180-225	
Bouve, E.T.	Centuries Apart (1st, 8vo, grey/gilt, 6pl, maps, 347p)	Little/Brown	1894	Harper, W. St. J.	35-50	
Andersen, H.C.	Steadfast Tin Soldier (1st, lg8vo, ibds, [28]p, color, pep)	NY: Maxton	1946	Harriet	35-50	*
Tarry, Ellen	Hezekiah Horton (1st, lg8vo, 39p, color)	Viking	1942	Harrington, O.	50-85	*
Tarry, Ellen	Runaway Elephant (1st, lg8vo, ipcb, 37p, fp 1-color, pep)	Viking	1950	Harrington, O.	70-120	R*
Tennyson, A.	Dream of Fair Women (8vo, grey bds, 79p, 8cp)	L: Blackie	[1915]	Harrison, F.	50-70	
Morris, Wm.	Early Poems of... (1st, 4to, blue/gilt, teg, 194p, 16 ticp, pep)	L: Blackie	1914	Harrison, F.	175-220	
Morris, Wm.	Early Poems of... (1st AM, 4to, 194p, teg, 16 ticp)	Dodge	(1914)	Harrison, F.	120-165	
Harrison, F.	Elfin Song (1st AM, sm4to, teg, gilt, 142p, pep, 12 ticp)	Caldwell	[1912]	Harrison, F.	250-350	
Harrison, F.	Elfin Song (1st, sm4to, teg, 142p, 12 ticp, pep)	L: Blackie	(1912)	Harrison, F.	280-450	
Rossetti, C.	Goblin Market (1st, lg8vo, ibds, 79p, 8cp)	L: Blackie	1923	Harrison, F.	130-180	
Syrett, Netta	Godmother's Garden (1st, 8vo, 222p)	L: Blackie	[1918]	Harrison, F.	50-70	*
Tennyson, A.	Guinevere... (1st AM, 4to, 156p, gilt, teg, 24 ticp)	D. Estes	1912	Harrison, F.	140-200	
Tennyson, A.	Guinevere... (1st, 4to, teg, 156p, gilt, 24 ticp)	L: Blackie	1912	Harrison, F.	200-265	
Harrison, F.	In the Fairy Ring (1st, lg4to, 63p, AEG, gilt, pep, 25cp)	L: Blackie	(1908)	Harrison, F.	250-300	
N/A	Man in the Moon (1st, 4to, bds, 31p, p-o, 12cp, pep)	L: Blackie	[1918]	Harrison, F.	120-165	
Harrison, F.	Pixy Book (lg8vo, ibds, p-o, 12cp)	L: Blackie	[1918]	Harrison, F.	260-350	
Rossetti, C.	Poems by... (1st, 4to, white/gilt, teg, 369p, 36 ticp, pep)	L: Blackie	(1910)	Harrison, F.	250-380	
Rossetti, C.	Poems by... (1st AM, 4to, teg, 369p, 36 ticp)	Estes	(1910)	Harrison, F.	200-300	
Harrison, F.	Rhyme of a Run... (1st, ob4to, green/gilt, 20 ticp, pep)	L: Blackie	[1907]	Harrison, F.	200-250	
Rossetti, C.	Shorter Poems of... (1st, 4to, ibds, 6cp)	L: Blackie	[1920]	Harrison, F.	70-90	
Herbertson, A.	Tinkler Johnny (sm8vo, green cl, p-o, 4cp)	L: Blackie	[1915]	Harrison, F.	35-50	
Mother Goose	Mother Goose Song Book (folio, ibds)	A.& C. Boni	(1926)	Harshberger, K.	70-100	
Harshberger, K.	Zoological Soliloquies (1st, lg4to, ibds, [44]p, color)	A.& C. Boni	1926	Harshberger, K.	90-120	
Fisher, Murray	Golliwogg's Dream... Little Folks (1st, sm4to, unpag, ibds, col)	L: Cassell	[1910]	Hart, Frank	80-130	*
Jackson, G.E.	Wee Winkles/Snowball (1st, 8vo, 147p, 8pl)	Harper	1906	Hart, M.T.	30-45	*
Jackson, G.E.	Wee Winkles/Wideawake (1st, 8vo, p-o, 153p, 8pl)	Harper	1905	Hart, M.T.	50-75	*
Hart, Ruby	In the Woods (1st, sm sq4to, wraps, color)	Volland	(1931)	Hart, R.	45-60	*
Snedeker, C.D.	Theras & his Town (1st {std}, sm8vo, 252p, pep, 4pl)	Doubleday/Page	1924	Harting, M.W.	25-45	*
Potter, B.	All About Peter Rabbit (16mo, 47p, bds, p-o, 8cp)	Cupples	(1914)	Hartley, D.	65-90	
Brown, M.W.	Big Red Barn (1st, ob8vo, unpag)	W.R. Scott	1956	Hartman, R.	35-50	*
Hewlett, M.	Forest Lovers (1st AM, lg8vo, 384p, teg, uncut, 16 ticp)	Scribner	1909	Hartrick, A.S.	40-65	
Upham, Eliz.	Little Brown Bear (1st, 4to, [58]p, 8 fp color, pep)	Platt/Munk	(1942)	Hartwell, M.	50-70	*
Upham, Eliz.	Little Brown Bear & His Friends (1st, 4to, unpag, col, pep, DJ)	Platt/Munk	(1952)	Hartwell, M.	40-60	
Upham, Eliz.	Little Brown Monkey (1st, 4to, [56]p, color, pep)	Platt/Munk	(1949)	Hartwell, M.	40-60	*
Harwood, E.	Old English Sing-Games (1st, ob4to, 56p, ibds, color)	L: Allen	1900	Harwood, E.	120-200	
Lyle, E.P.	The Missourian (1st, 8vo, 519p, 8pl)	Doubleday/Page	1905	Haskell, J.	25-45	
Haslewood, C.	Dear Old Nursery Rhymes (1st, 4to, ibds, 48p, 8 chromos)	NY: Warne	[1896]	Haslewood, C.	75-120	
Farrow, G.E.	Absurd Ditties (1st, 8vo, blue/gilt, AEG, 224p, b/w)	L: Routledge	1903	Hassall, J.	65-90	
Spurr, H.A.	Bachelor Ballads (1st, sm8vo, 194p, teg, green cl)	L: Greening	1899	Hassall, J.	45-60	
Hartog, C.	Barbara's Song Book (ob4to, ibds, p-o, 8cp)	L: G. Allen	1900	Hassall, J.	130-200	
N/A	Dick Whittington & his Cat (4to, ibds, color)	L: Hodder	[1910]	Hassall, J.	80-120	
Grimm Bros.	Fairy Tales (1st, lg8vo, 305p, 12 illus)	L: Sands	1902	Hassall, J.	65-80	*
Westerman, J.M.E.	Fairy Tales/Wonderland (1st, 4to, 160p, orange cl, 3cp, 14pl)	L: Blackie	[1932]	Hassall, J.	100-145	*
Byron, May	Friday & Saturday... (1st, ob4to, ibds, unpag, 12 fp color)	L: H. Frowde	[1910]	Hassall, J.	150-200	
Girvin, B.	Good Queen Bees (1st, ob4to, ibds, unpag, 23cp)	L: D. Nutt	1907	Hassall, J.	80-135	
N/A	Humpty-Dumpty (4to, wraps, fp color)	L: Blackie	[1910]	Hassall, J.	60-80	
Johnson, A.E.	John Hassall, R.I. (1st, 8vo, 44p, 7cp, 28pl)	L: A&C Black	1907	Hassall, J.	60-90	
Orr, Aileen	Miss Manners (1st, 8vo, AEG, blue cl, 26cp)	L: A. Melrose	1909	Hassall, J.	180-250	
Mother Goose	Mother Goose Nursery Rhymes (1st AM, 8vo, 363p, 24pl)	Dodge	(1909)	Hassall, J.	70-120	*

AUTHOR	TITLE	PUBLISHER	DATE	ARTIST	PRICE	LC
Mother Goose	Mother Goose's Nursery Rhymes (1st, 8vo, 364p)	L: Blackie	1909	Hassall, J.	65-80	*
Hamer, S.H.	Princess & the Dragon (1st AM, 8vo, green cl, p-o, 78p, 12cp)	Estes	[1908]	Hassall, J.	50-70	
Hamer, S.H.	Princess & the Dragon (1st, 8vo, p-o, 78p, 12cp)	L: Duckworth	(1908)	Hassall, J.	60-80	
Defoe, D.	Robinson Crusoe (1st, 4to, ibds, 80p, col frn, 6 color)	L: Blackie	[1916]	Hassall, J.	80-120	
Farrow, G.E.	Round the World ABC (1st, 4to, [54]p, ibds, 26 color)	L: Nister	[1904]	Hassall, J.	180-250	
Shirley, E.	The Twins (4to, 63p, ibds, 24cp)	L: Nelson	[1905]	Hassall, J.	140-200	
Thaxter, Cellia	Island Garden (1st, lg8vo, 126p, white/gilt, teg, col frn, b/w)	Houghton	1894	Hassam, C.	280-400	
Pratt, C.S.	Bye O' Baby Ballads (lg8vo, [61]p, ipcb, 14 chromos)	Lothrop	(1886)	Hassam, F.C.	250-320	
Bates, Clara D.	Doll Rosy's Days (1st, ob12mo, ipcb, [31]p, 12cp)	Lothrop	(1884)	Hassam, F.C.	150-200	
Dumas, A.	Nutcracker of Nuremberg (1st, 8vo, black/gilt, 154p, b/w)	McBride	1930	Hasselriis, E.	30-45	
Chrisman, A.B.	Shen of the Sea (1st, 8vo, 252p, red/gilt, pep, NM)	Dutton	(1925)	Hasselriis, E.	40-70	
Chrisman, A.B.	Wind that Wouldn't Blow (1st, sm8vo, 355p, uncut, b/w, pep)	Dutton	(1927)	Hasselriis, E.	30-45	*
Carpenter, Frances	Tales of a Chinese Grandmother (1st, 8vo, 261p, 9cp)	L: Harrap	(1938)	Hasselriis, M.	30-45	
Molesworth, M.	Next-Door House (1st, 8vo, 226p, grey cl, 6pl)	L: Chambers	1893	Hatherell, W.	35-50	*
Twain, M.	Prince & the Pauper (1st, 8vo, 296p, 7cp)	Harper	1909	Hatherell, W.	35-50	*
Lent, Henry B.	Air Pilot (1st, sq16mo, [42]p, color, pep)	MacMillan	1937	Hauman, G.& D.	30-45	
Andersen, H.C.	Snow Queen (1st, 4to, 63p, pep, 6 fp color)	MacMillan	1942	Hauman, G.& D.	45-60	*
Piper, W. (ed.)	Tales from Storyland (1st, lg4to, p-o, [80]p, color)	Platt/Munk	(1941)	Hauman, G.& D.	35-60	*
Lent, Henry B.	The Storekeeper (1st, sq16mo, [42]p, color, pep)	MacMillan	1937	Hauman, G.& D.	30-45	
Clark, A.N.	Blue Canyon Horse (1st, sm4to, 54p, fp color, pep)	Viking	1954	Hauser, A.	65-80	R*
Various	Book of Modern Ballads (sm4to, AEG, gilt, 6 chromos)	Hildesheimer	[1890]	Havers, A.	85-120	*
Andersen, H.C.	Wild Swans... (1st AM, ob4to, 48p, ibds, 14 chromos)	Dutton	[1880]	Havers, A.	170-220	
De La Mare, W.	Dutch Cheese (1st, 8vo, 143p, gilt)	L: Faber	(1946)	Hawkins, I.	50-80	
De La Mare, W.	Magic Jacket (1st, sm8vo, 146p)	L: Faber	(1943)	Hawkins, I.	30-50	*
De La Mare, W.	Old Lion (1st, sm8vo, 155p)	L: Faber	(1942)	Hawkins, I.	30-50	*
MacDonald, Zillah	Eileen's Adventures in Wonderland (1st, 8vo, p-o, 241p, col frn)	Stokes	(1920)	Hay, S.	75-125	*
Fryer, J.E.	Mary Frances Cook Book (1st, lg8vo, blue cl, p-o, 175p)	Winston	(1912)	Hayes, M.H.	120-185	
Bannerman, H.	Little Black Sambo (lg4to, ipcb)	Saalfield	1942	Hays, Ethel	65-90	
Hays, M.G.	Rag Animals ABC (lg4to, stiff wrps, 30p, color)	Donohue	(1913)	Hays, M.G.	150-200	*
Burton, J.B.	Across the Salt Seas (1st, 12mo, teg, 446p, cvr by...)	H. Stone	1897	Hazenplug, F.	45-70	
Lowell, J.R.	Biglow Papers (8vo, blue/gilt, title page by...)	Hennebery	[1900]	Hazenplug, F.	30-45	
Conner, Ralph	Black Rock (1st, 8vo, tan cl, 322p, cvr by...)	Revell	1900	Hazenplug, F.	20-35	
Adams, M.M.	Choir Visible (1st, 8vo, 185p, teg, cvr by...)	Way/Williams	1897	Hazenplug, F.	80-130	
Crissey, F.	Country Boy (1st, 8vo, 300p, gilt, uncut, cvr by...)	Revell	(1903)	Hazenplug, F.	65-80	
Manners, R.	Cuba & other Verse (1st, 8vo, 155p, teg)	Way/Williams	1898	Hazenplug, F.	120-170	
Earle, A.M.	Curious Punishments... (1st, 8vo, 149p, teg)	H. Stone	1896	Hazenplug, F.	50-85	
Baum, L.F.	Daring Twins (1st [1], sm8vo, 317p, blue cl, cvr by...)	Reilly/Britton	(1911)	Hazenplug, F.	200-300	
Thwaites, R.G.	Down Historic Waterways (1st, sm8vo, 300p, cvr by...)	McClurg	1902	Hazenplug, F.	60-80	*
Locke, Wm. J.	Fortunate Youth (1st, sm8vo, 352p, green/gilt, cvr by...)	NY: J. Lane	1914	Hazenplug, F.	30-45	*
Morier, J.	Hajji Baba of Ispahan (1st, 2volumes, tan/gilt, cvr by..)	Stone/Kimball	1895	Hazenplug, F.	60-80	
Wolf, A.S.	House of Cards (1st, 8vo, black/gilt, cvr by...)	Stone/Kimball	1896	Hazenplug, F.	50-80	
Wilkinson, F.	Lady of the Flag-Flowers (1st, 12mo, 364p, cvr by...)	H. Stone	1899	Hazenplug, F.	45-70	
Castle, E.	Marshfield the Observer (1st, 8vo, grey ipcb, cvr by...)	H. Stone	1900	Hazenplug, F.	45-60	
Meyer, L.R.	Mary North (1st, 8vo, 339p, cvr by...)	Revell	(1903)	Hazenplug, F.	45-60	*
Rossetti, C.	Maude: Prose & Verse (1st, 12mo, red pcb, title pg by..)	H. Stone	1897	Hazenplug, F.	40-65	
Ade, G.	More Fables (1st, 12mo, 218p, teg, title page by..)	H. Stone	1900	Hazenplug, F.	30-45	
Gray, W.C.	Musings/Campfire & Wayside (1st, 8vo, 337p, black/gilt)	Revell	1902	Hazenplug, F.	35-50	*
Johnston, R.M.	Pearce Amerson's Will (1st, 12mo, teg, 275p, cvr by...)	Way/Williams	1898	Hazenplug, F.	75-120	
Powell, R.S.	Phyllis in Bohemia (1st, 12mo, 233p, teg, cvr by...)	H. Stone	1897	Hazenplug, F.	40-70	
LeGallienne, R.	Prose Fancies (1st AM, 12mo, gilt, 201p, cvr by...)	H. Stone	1896	Hazenplug, F.	60-80	
Russell, W.C.	Rose Island (1st, 8vo, 359p, cvr by...)	H. Stone	1899	Hazenplug, F.	45-65	
Crowninshield, Mrs.	San Isidro (1st, 8vo, 312p, yellow cl, cvr by...)	H. Stone	1900	Hazenplug, F.	45-65	
DeKoven, R.	Sawdust Doll (1st, 12mo, 237p, blue/gilt, teg)	Stone/Kimball	1895	Hazenplug, F.	100-140	*
Coleman, O.	Successful Houses (lg8vo, tan cl, cvr by...)	H. Stone	1899	Hazenplug, F.	65-90	
Carruth, F.W.	Those Dale Girls (1st, sm8vo, 318p, cvr by...)	McClurg	1899	Hazenplug, F.	40-60	*
James, Henry	What Maisie Knew (1st AM, sm8vo, 470p, grey/gilt, cvr by...)	H. Stone	1897	Hazenplug, F.	100-140	
Lagerlof, Selma	Wonderful Adventures of Nils (1st AM, 8vo, 430p, 8pl, pep)	Doubleday/Page	1907	Heartt, H.	90-140	
Akers, Floyd	Boy Fortune Hunters in Alaska (1st [1], 8vo, 291p, brwn cl, 3pl)	Reilly/Britton	(1908)	Heath, H.	150-220	
Serviss, G.P.	Columbus of Space (1st, 8vo, 298p, green cl, 4pl)	Appleton	1911	Heath, H.	120-200	
Haldane, W.A.	Dream Bag (1st, 8vo, 131p, 6cp)	Laird & Lee	(1904)	Heath, H.	70-100	*
Fitzgerald, Hugh	Sam Steele's Advens. in Panama (1st, 8vo, green cl, 5pl)	Reilly/Britton	(1907)	Heath, H.	650-800	*
Fitzgerald, Hugh	Sam Steele's Advens. on Land & Sea (1st, 8vo, gilt, p-o, 5pl)	Reilly/Britton	(1906)	Heath, H.	450-600	*
N/A	Aladdin (1st, 16mo, 61p, pep)	L: J.M. Dent	1895	Heath, S.H.	35-60	*
Gask, Lilian	Pig Tales (1st, 8vo, 64p)	Nister/Dutton	[1906]	Heatly, E.	35-50	*
Lagerlof, Selma	Further Adventures of Nils (1st {Engl lang.}, 12mo, 339p, 15pl)	Doubleday/Page	1911	Heiberg, A.	80-100	*
Aesopus	Fables of Aesop (1st, 8vo, 222p, gilt, AEG)	L: MacMillan	1894	Heighway, R.	70-100	
Hanemann, H.W.	As Is (1st, 8vo, ipcb, 190p, uncut, b/w)	Harcourt	(1923)	Held, J.	45-60	
Held, John	Danny Decoy (1st, sq8vo, ibds, [83]p, 2-color, pep)	A.S. Barnes	(1942)	Held, J.	70-100	*
Shay, F.	Drawn from the Wood (1st, 8vo, 186p, b/w)	Macaulay	(1929)	Held, J.	45-60	
Geller, J.J.	Grandfather's Follies (1st, sq4to, 218p, b/w)	Macaulay	(1934)	Held, J.	40-65	
Shay, F.	More Pious Friends (1st, 8vo, 192p, b/w)	Macaulay	(1927)	Held, J.	50-65	
Wright, Isa L.	Remarkable Tale of a Whale (1st, 8vo, ibds, color)	Volland	(1920)	Held, J.	65-90	*

AUTHOR	TITLE	PUBLISHER	DATE	ARTIST	PRICE	LC
Helle, A.	Big Beasts & Little Beasts (1st, ob12mo, p-o, 80p, 20cp)	Stokes	1924	Helle, A.	120-150	
Brown, M.W. (ed.)	Fables of La Fontaine (1st {std}, 4to, ibds, 39p, color, pep)	Harper	(1940)	Helle, A.	60-80	
Fraser, W.A.	Sazada Tales (1st, 8vo, 231p, green/gilt, 24 b/w illus)	Scribner	1905	Heming, A.	25-40	*
Fraser, W.A.	The Outcasts (1st, 8vo, green/gilt, 138p, teg, 8pl, pep)	Scribner	1901	Heming, A.	40-60	
Mitchell, G.W.	Little Babs (1st, 12mo, ibds, color)	Volland	(1919)	Henderson, A.	50-70	
Thompson, R.P.	Perhappsy Chaps (1st [1st bk.], tall 8vo, ibds, color, pep)	Volland	(1918)	Henderson, A.	350-500	
Henderson, D.	Danny the Dream Man (1st, sq8vo, ibds, [48]p, color, pep)	Volland	(1928)	Henderson, D.	70-100	
Hudson, W.H.	Green Mansions (1st, lg8vo, 325p, ibds, woodcuts)	L: Duckworth	1926	Henderson, K.	40-60	
Hudson, W.H.	Purple Land (1st, lg8vo, red/gilt, 368p)	L: Duckworth	1929	Henderson, K.	35-50	
Shakespeare, Wm.	Under the Greenwood Tree (1st, 8vo, 270p, green cl, 10cp)	L: Chatto	1913	Henderson, K.	45-60	*
Eddison, E.R.	Worm Ouroboros (1st AM, 8vo, 445p, b/w)	A.& C. Boni	1926	Henderson, K.	30-50	*
Andersen, H.C.	Andersen's Best Fairy Tales (1st, 12mo, 200p, color, pep)	Rand/McNally	(1911)	Henderson, W.P.	35-50	*
Means, F.C.	At the End of Nowhere (1st, 8vo, 232p, white cl, 12pl)	Houghton	1940	Hendrickson, D.	25-40	*
Peterkin, Julia	Plantation Christmas (1st, sm8vo, red cl, 26p, p-o, 1-color)	Houghton	1934	Hendrickson, D.	20-30	
Singmaster, Elsie	Swords of Steel (1st, 8vo, 262p, b/w, pep, NH)	Houghton	1933	Hendrickson, D.	35-50	*
Molesworth, M.	Enchanted Garden: Fairy Stories (1st, 12mo, 221p, teg, b/w)	L: T.F. Unwin	1892	Hennessey, W.J.	50-70	
Harris, J.C.	Aaron in the Wildwoods (1st [1], lg8vo, yellow cl, 270p, 24pl)	Houghton	1897	Herford, O.	130-180	
Carroll, L.	Alice/Wonderland (1st, sm8vo, 224p, blue/red, b/w)	Ginn & Co.	(1917)	Herford, O.	80-100	
Hall, G.	Allegretto (1st, sq8vo, beige/gilt, 111p, teg, b/w)	Roberts	1894	Herford, O.	50-80	
Herford, O.	Alphabet of Celebrities (1st, lg sq8vo, [58]p, ibds, 26 fp b/w)	Small	1899	Herford, O.	100-160	
Herford, O.	Artful Antics (1st, sq8vo, tan cl, 100p, b/w)	Century	1894	Herford, O.	70-100	*
Herford, O.	Artful Antics (1st UK, sm8vo, yellow cl, 100p, b/w)	L: Gay & Bird	1894	Herford, O.	50-75	
Herford, O.	Astonishing Tale/Pen & Ink Puppet (1st, ob4to, [62]p, ibds)	Scribner	1907	Herford, O.	65-80	*
Herford, O.	Bashful Earthquake (1st, 12mo, teg, uncut, ipcb, 126p)	Scribner	1898	Herford, O.	45-70	R
Herford, O.	Child's Primer/Natural History (1st UK, sq4to, b/w)	L: J. Lane	1900	Herford, O.	65-90	
Herford, O.	Confessions of a Caricaturist (1st, 12mo, 65p, 9pl)	Scribner	1917	Herford, O.	30-45	*
Herford, O.	Deb's Dictionary (1st, 8vo, [151]p, cloth, b/w)	Lippincott	1931	Herford, O.	30-45	
Herford, O.	Excuse it Please (1st {std}, sm8vo, 171p, ipcb, DJ)	Lippincott	(1929)	Herford, O.	30-45	
Roche, J.J.	Her Majesty the King (1st, sm8vo, 149p, 8cp)	R.H. Russell	1902	Herford, O.	65-90	*
Herford, O.	Herford Aesop (1st, 8vo, 90p, col frn)	Ginn & Co.	(1921)	Herford, O.	65-80	
Wells, Carolyn	Idle Idyls (1st, 8vo, green/gilt, teg, 155p, b/w pl)	Dodd	1900	Herford, O.	30-50	
Wells, Carolyn	Jingle Book (1st, sm8vo, 124p, blue cl, teg, b/w)	MacMillan	1899	Herford, O.	70-100	
Wells, Carolyn	Jingle Book (8vo {new ed.}, green cl, p-o, 124p, b/w)	Donohue	(1906)	Herford, O.	35-50	*
Herford, O.	Kitten's Garden of Verses (1st, 12mo, 59p, 25pl)	Scribner	1911	Herford, O.	50-70	
Herford, O.	Laughing Willow (1st, sm8vo, ipcb, 134p, col frn)	Doran	(1918)	Herford, O.	35-50	*
N/A	Little Book of Bores (1st, 12mo, 52p, b/w)	Scribner	1906	Herford, O.	45-65	
Harris, J.C.	Little Mr. Thimblefinger (1st, lg8vo, 230p, ae green, 32pl, cep)	Houghton	1894	Herford, O.	120-165	R
Herford, B.	Monologues (1st, 8vo, 139p, grey cl, 18 b/w)	Scribner	1908	Herford, O.	45-65	
Herford, O.	More Animals (1st, sq8vo, ibds, 99p, 24pl)	Scribner	1901	Herford, O.	80-100	R
Harris, J.C.	Mr. Rabbit at Home (1st, 8vo, 304p, tan cl, ae green, 25pl, cep)	Houghton	1895	Herford, O.	120-150	R
Herford, O.	Mythological Zoo (1st, sq8vo, ibds, 45p, 22pl)	Scribner	1912	Herford, O.	50-70	
Herford, O.	Overheard in a Garden (1st, sm8vo, ibds, teg, 104p, col frn)	Scribner	1900	Herford, O.	60-85	
Herford, O.	Pen & Inklings (1st [1st bk.], 12mo, tan cl, b/w)	L: G. Allen	1893	Herford, O.	80-100	
Herford, O.	Peter Pan Alphabet (1st, sq8vo, ibds, [57]p, fp b/w)	Scribner	1907	Herford, O.	85-120	*
Wells, Carolyn	Phenomenal Fauna (1st, sq8vo, [90]p, ibds, 21cp)	R.H. Russell	1902	Herford, O.	60-90	
Herford, O.	Rubaiyat of a Persian Kitten (1st, sm8vo, [76]p, ibds, 35pl)	Scribner	1904	Herford, O.	40-70	
Herford, O.	Sea Legs (1st, ob12mo, [55]p, ibds, p-o, 23 fp 2-color)	Lippincott	(1931)	Herford, O.	40-60	
Metcalfe, F.	Side Show Studies (1st, 12mo, 232p)	Outing	1906	Herford, O.	35-50	*
Herford, O.	Simple Jography (1st, 8vo, ibds, [100]p, b/w)	Luce	(1908)	Herford, O.	30-45	*
Harris, J.C.	Story of Aaron (1st, lg8vo, tan/gilt, 198p, 25pl)	Houghton	1896	Herford, O.	130-170	R
Herford, O.	This Giddy Globe (1st, 12mo, 138p, tan cl, b/w)	Doran	(1919)	Herford, O.	20-30	
Herford, O.	Cupid's Almanac (1st, narrow 4to, [58]p, ipcb, col frn, pep)	Houghton	1908	Herford/Clay	35-50	*
Herford, O.	Happy Days (1st, 16mo, ipcb, [44]p, color, pep)	Kennerley	1917	Herford/Clay	30-45	
Wells, H.G.	First Men in the Moon (1st AM, 8vo, gilt, 12pl)	Stokes	(1901)	Hering, E.	180-250	
Wells, H.G.	First Men in the Moon (1st AM, 8vo, 312p, blue/gilt, 12pl)	Bowen-Merrill	(1901)	Hering, E.	160-220	*
Stevenson, R.L.	Fables (1st AM, 4to, maroon/gilt, teg, 83p, 20pl)	Scribner	1914	Herman, E.R.	90-140	
Goldsmith, Milton	Dorothy's Dolls... (1st, 8vo, 59p, ibds, 14cp)	NY: Ullman	(1908)	Hermony, N.	65-80	*
Clark, A.N.	In My Mother's House (1st, 4to, 56p, brown cl, pep, color, CH)	Viking	1941	Herrera, V.	65-90	R
Dalgliesh, A.	The Hollyberrys (1st, sq12mo, 59p, 12 fp color, cep)	Scribner	(1939)	Herric, Pru	30-45	
Marquis, Don	Archy Does His Part (1st {std}, 12mo, p-o, 269p, b/w, pep)	Doubleday/Dor.	1935	Herriman, G.	20-35	*
Anderson, R.C.	Animals in Social Captivity (1st, 8vo, gilt, p-o, 96p, 10cp dep)	Stewart/Kidd	(1914)	Herschede, I.N.	45-60	*
Cable, G.W.	Old Creole Days (1st, 4to, 234p, grey cl, teg, 8pl)	Scribner	1897	Herter, A.	70-90	
Pease, E.F.	Jolly Little Clown (1st, lg8vo, p-o, 126p, pep)	Whitman	(1927)	Hetherington	35-50	*
Nelson, M.W.	Pinky Finds a Home (1st, 12mo, 118p, col frn)	Holiday House	(1940)	Heyneman, A.	20-30	*
Ames, E.M.	Patsy for Keeps (1st, 4to, ibds, 95p, doll bk., color)	NY: S. Gabriel	(1932)	Hicks, A.L.	65-90	*
Dumas, A.	Three Musketeers (1st, 8vo, 459p, pep)	Winston	(1931)	Higgins, E.R.	25-40	*
Asbjornsen, P.C.	East o/t Sun/West o/t Moon (1st, lg8vo, 192p, col, p-o, gilt pep)	Whitman	(1924)	Higgins, V.M.	45-60	*
Higgins, V.M.	Endless Story (1st, 8vo, 71p, color, pep)	Whitman	(1916)	Higgins, V.M.	45-65	*
Spyri, J.	Heidi (1st, 8vo, 284p, p-o, 1-color, pep)	Whitman	(1924)	Higgins, V.M.	30-50	*
Craik, D.	Little Lame Prince (1st, 8vo, 128p, green/gilt, p-o, 9cp, pep)	Whitman	(1927)	Higgins, V.M.	40-60	
Higgins, V.M.	Magic Circus (8vo, ibds, doll bk.)	Chi: Stanton	1918	Higgins, V.M.	40-65	
Mother Goose	Mother Goose & her Goslings (1st, 8vo, 125p, color)	Chi: Stanton	(1918)	Higgins, V.M.	65-80	*

AUTHOR	TITLE	PUBLISHER	DATE	ARTIST	PRICE	LC
Collodi, C.	Pinocchio (1st, lg8vo, 255p, pep, p-o, fp color)	Whitman	(1926)	Higgins, V.M.	50-65	*
Higgins, V.M.	Real Story of a Real Doll (1st, 8vo, 116p, pep, 4cp)	McBride	(1929)	Higgins, V.M.	30-45	*
Beard, P.	What Happened After Stories (1st, sq4to, 125p, p-o, color, pep)	Whitman	(1929)	Higgins, V.M.	35-50	
Higgins, V.M.	Woodcutter's Son (1st, lg8vo, 68p, 4cp)	Whitman	1917	Higgins, V.M.	35-50	
Montgomery, F.T.	Zip: Advens. of a Frisky Fox Terrier (1st, 8vo, 77p, ipcb, 4cp)	Saalfield	(1917)	Higgins, V.M.	50-80	*
Stevenson, R.L.	Kidnapped (1st, 4to, 290p)	L: OUP	1930	Hilder, R.	35-50	*
Masefield, J.	Midnight Folk (1st, 4to, 282p, blue cl, 6cp)	L: Heinemann	(1931)	Hilder, R.	70-100	
Mother Goose	Most Popular Mother Goose Songs (1st, ob4to, 44p, ipcb, 39cp)	NY: Hinds	(1915)	Hill, M.B.	100-165	
Hill, W.E.	Among Us Cats (1st {std}, lg8vo, p-o, 128p, col frn, 61pl, pep)	Harper	1926	Hill, W.E.	70-90	*
White, S.E.	Rules of the Game (1st, 8vo, 644p, 4cp)	Doubleday/Page	1910	Hiller, L.A.	25-40	
Sampson, Martin	Good Giant (1st, 8vo, 218p, col frn, 10pl, pep)	Houghton	1928	Hilton	35-50	*
Sturgis, E.B.	My Busy Days (1st, lg4to, 50p, ibds, 8cp)	Appleton	1908	Hinchman, M.	100-160	*
Mabie, H.W.	Under The Trees (1st, 8vo, teg, 165p, green/gilt, 6pl, pep)	Dodd	1902	Hinton, C.L.	35-50	
Ostrander, Fannie	Baby Goose: His Adventures (1st, lg8vo, ibds, unpag, color)	Laird & Lee	(1900)	Hirchert, R.W.	70-100	*
Mother Goose	Mother Goose (1st, lg8vo, [40]p, color)	Wonder	(1946)	Hirsch, J.	45-65	*
Twain, M.	Double-Barrelled Detective Story (1st, 8vo, teg, uncut, 7pl)	Harper	1902	Hitchcock, L.	130-165	
Deland, M.	Dr. Lavendar's People (1st, 12mo, 370p, 12pl)	Harper	1903	Hitchcock, L.	25-40	
Twain, M.	Horse's Tale (1st, 8vo, red cl, 153p, 5pl)	Harper	1907	Hitchcock, L.	100-135	
Andersen, H.C.	Fairy Tales (1st, 12mo, 170p, b/w)	Chi: Flanagan	(1912)	Hodge, H.	30-45	*
Goudge, Eliz.	Little White Horse (1st AM {std}, 8vo, 280p, blue cl, b/w, pep)	Coward	(1947)	Hodges, C.W.	45-60	
Goudge, Eliz.	Sister of the Angels (1st AM, 8vo, blue/gilt, 154p, fp b/w)	Coward	(1939)	Hodges, C.W.	25-40	*
Cobb, L.M.	Animal Tales/Old North State (1st, 8vo, 200p, uncut, b/w, pep)	Dutton	1938	Hogan, I.	30-50	*
Hogan, Inez	Bear Twins (1st {std}, sm8vo, [45]p, ipcb, 1-color, pep)	Dutton	(1935)	Hogan, I.	35-50	*
Hogan, Inez	Big Ones (1st {std}, 4to, yellow cl, unpag, b/w, pep)	Dutton	(1957)	Hogan, I.	40-60	*
Hogan, Inez	Elephant Twins (1st {std}, 8vo, ipcb, [45]p, pep)	Dutton	(1936)	Hogan, I.	35-50	*
Bryant, S.C.	Epaminondas & his Auntie (1st, sq8vo, 16p, color, pep)	Houghton	1938	Hogan, I.	50-80	R
Hogan, Erlin	Four Funny Men (1st {std}, 12mo, ibds, [55]p, 1-color, pep)	Dutton	(1939)	Hogan, I.	30-50	*
Hogan, Inez	Giraffe Twins (1st {std}, 8vo, [48]p, ipcb, 1-color, pep)	Dutton	(1948)	Hogan, I.	30-50	*
Hogan, Inez	Kangaroo Twins (1st {std}, 8vo, [49]p, ibds, color, pep)	Dutton	(1938)	Hogan, I.	50-70	
Winlow, Clara V.	Kitten that Grew Too Fat (1st, lg ob8vo, 93p, 24 fp color)	Macrae-Smith	(1929)	Hogan, I.	45-70	*
Hogan, Inez	Little Black & White Lamb (1st, sm8vo, [103]p, color)	Macrae-Smith	(1927)	Hogan, I.	50-70	*
Hogan, Inez	Little Toy Airplane (1st, ob8vo, [57]p, color, pep)	Macrae-Smith	(1930)	Hogan, I.	55-80	*
Christopher, Anne	Monkey Twins (1st, ob8vo, [31]p, pep, ipcb, color)	Whitman	(1935)	Hogan, I.	50-70	*
Hogan, Inez	Monkey Twins, They Saw it All (1st {std}, sm8vo, ipcb, b/w, pep)	Dutton	(1943)	Hogan, I.	30-50	
Hogan, Inez	Mule Twins (1st {std}, 8vo, ibds, [49]p, b/w, pep)	Dutton	(1939)	Hogan, I.	50-80	
Hogan, Inez	Nappy Chooses a Pet (1st {std}, 8vo, [48]p, ipcb, b/w, pep)	Dutton	1946	Hogan, I.	30-45	*
Hogan, Inez	Nicodemus & his Little Sister (1st {std} 12mo, ibds, [47]p, col)	Dutton	1932	Hogan, I.	70-100	
Hogan, Inez	Nicodemus & the Goose (1st {std}, 8vo, ibds, [47]p, color pep)	Dutton	(1945)	Hogan, I.	50-65	
Hogan, Inez	Nicodemus & the Houn' Dog (1st {std}, 8vo, [52]p, ibds, color)	Dutton	(1933)	Hogan, I.	40-65	
Hogan, Inez	Nicodemus Laughs (1st {std}, 8vo, ibds, [40]p, color, pep)	Dutton	(1941)	Hogan, I.	50-65	
Christopher, Anne	Petunia Be Keerful (1st, 8vo, ibds, [41]p, color)	Whitman	(1934)	Hogan, I.	60-80	
Hogan, Inez	Runaway Toys (1st {std}, lg8vo, [40]p, pep, color)	Dutton	(1950)	Hogan, I.	30-50	
Hogan, Inez	Sandy, Skip & Man in the Moon (1st, sm8vo, gilt, 93p, color)	Macrae-Smith	(1928)	Hogan, I.	45-65	*
Van Vrooman, M.	Shine (1st {std}, 12mo, 50p, ibds, b/w, pep)	Dutton	(1939)	Hogan, I.	50-80	*
Vorse, M.E.	Skinny Gets Fat (1st, 8vo, ipcb, [41]p, 1-color, pep)	W.R. Scott	1940	Hogan, I.	45-60	*
Hogan, Inez	Twin Kids (1st, 8vo, 50p, ipcb, 1-color, pep)	Dutton	(1937)	Hogan, I.	45-60	
Vorse, M.E.	Wakey Goes to Bed (1st, 8vo, ipcb, [41]p, brown illus, cep)	W.R. Scott	1941	Hogan, I.	45-60	*
Hogan, Inez	We are a Family (1st {std}, sq4to, 93p, b/w, pep)	Dutton	(1952)	Hogan, I.	30-50	*
Hogan, Inez	World Round (1st {std}, 4to, [64]p, blue cl, b/w, pep)	Dutton	(1949)	Hogan, I.	30-45	*
Wister, O.	Padre Ignacio (1st, 8vo, ibds, 65p, col frn)	Harper	1925	Hogg, Z.	25-40	
Holberg, R.	Mitty on Mr. Syrup's Farm (1st {std} 4to, ibds, [32]p, col, pep)	Doubleday/Dor.	1936	Holberg, R.	25-45	
Carr, Mary J.	Young Mac/Fort Vancouver (1st, 8vo, 238p, blue cl, p-o, col, NH)	Crowell	1940	Holberg, R.	45-65	*
Stevenson, R.L.	Kidnapped (1st, 12mo, 319p, 16pl)	L: Cassell	1907	Hole, W.B.	35-55	*
Christie, E.R.	Fairy Tales from England (1st, 8vo, 232p, 6pl)	L: T.F. Unwin	1896	Holland, A.	50-70	
Christie, E.R.	Fairy Tales from Finland (1st, 12mo, 232p, teg, uncut, b/w)	L: T.F. Unwin	1896	Holland, A.	50-85	*
Carroll, L.	Alice/Wonderland (1st, sq8vo, ibds, [32]p, color, pep)	Rand/McNally	1951	Holland, J.	30-50	*
Coblentz, C.C.	Blue Cat of Castle Town (1st {std}, 8vo blue cl, 123p, b/w, pep)	Longmans	1949	Holland, J.	40-70	R
Crawford, P.	Blot: Little City Cat (1st, ob4to, ibds, 56p, b/w)	Cape/Smith	1930	Holling, H.C.	70-100	
Holling, H.C.	Book of Cowboys (1st, 4to, orang cl, pep, 126p, color, DJ)	Platt/Munk	(1936)	Holling, H.C.	35-50	
Holling, H.C.	Book of Indians (1st, 4to, 125p, pep, 6cp)	Platt/Munk	(1935)	Holling, H.C.	35-50	
Piper, W.	Children of Other Lands (1st, lg4to, [85]p, p-o, orang cl, 5cp)	Platt/Munk	(1933)	Holling, H.C.	50-70	
Holling, H.C.	Choo-Me-Shoo (1st {std}, 8vo, ibds, color, pep)	Volland	(1928)	Holling, H.C.	65-80	*
Holling, H.C.	Claws of the Thunderbird (1st, 8vo, 128p, gilt, color, pep)	Volland	(1928)	Holling, H.C.	35-50	
Holling, H.C.	Little Big-Bye-and-Bye (1st, 12mo, [40]p, ibds, color, pep)	Volland	(1926)	Holling, H.C.	45-60	
Holling, H.C.	Little Buffalo Boy (1st, sq8vo, ibds, [42]p, color, pep)	Garden City	(1939)	Holling, H.C.	60-90	
Piper, W.	Little Folks/Other Lands (1st, lg4to, [80]p, gilt, p-o, color)	Platt/Munk	(1929)	Holling, H.C.	60-80	*
Holling, H.C.	Minn of the Mississippi (1st, 4to, 88p, yel cl, col, pep, NH)	Houghton	1951	Holling, H.C.	50-80	
Holling, H.C.	Paddle to the Sea (1st, 4to, beige cl, unpag, color, pep, CH)	Houghton	1941	Holling, H.C.	60-85	R
Holling, H.C.	Pagoo (1st, 4to, 86p, green cl, pep, color)	Houghton	1957	Holling, H.C.	25-40	*
Holling, H.C.	Rocky Billy (1st, 8vo, blue cl, 148p, color, pep)	MacMillan	1928	Holling, H.C.	45-60	
Holling, H.C.	Rum-Tum-Tummy... (sq8vo, ibds, color)	Saalfield	1936	Holling, H.C.	50-80	
Holling, H.C.	Seabird (1st, 4to, 58p, blue cl, color, pep, DJ, NH)	Houghton	1948	Holling, H.C.	50-80	

AUTHOR	TITLE	PUBLISHER	DATE	ARTIST	PRICE	LC
Holling, H.C.	Tree in the Trail (1st, 4to, [70]p, 35 fp color, pep)	Houghton	1942	Holling, H.C.	30-45	
Holling, H.C.	Twins Who Flew Around the World (1st, folio, gilt, 67p, color)	Platt/Munk	(1931)	Holling, H.C.	50-75	
Bennett, Rowena B.	Around a Toadstool Table (1st, 8vo, ibds, 109p, fp b/w)	Chi: Rockwell	1930	Holling, L.W.	65-90	*
Bailey, A.C.	Kimo (1st, 8vo, ibds, 96p, color, pep)	Volland	(1928)	Holling, L.W.	50-75	*
Tietjens, E.	Boy of the Desert (1st, 8vo, 182p, green cl, dep, fp b/w)	Coward	1928	Hollingsworth, W.	25-40	*
Barbour, R.H.	Hearts Content (1st, 8vo, teg, 204p, p-o, cp)	Lippincott	1915	Holloway, E.	20-30	
Finger, C.J.	Bushrangers (1st, 8vo, 216p, color, pep)	McBride	1924	Honore, P.	40-65	*
Finger, C.J.	Frontier Ballads (1st {std}, lg8vo, 181p, 3cp, b/w)	Doubleday/Dor.	1927	Honore, P.	45-70	*
Finger, C.J.	Highwaymen... (1st, 8vo, 258p, tan cl, uncut, 8cp, pep)	McBride	1923	Honore, P.	40-70	*
Finger, C.J.	Romantic Rascals (1st, lg8vo, 251p, uncut, 8cp, pep)	McBride	1927	Honore, P.	40-65	*
Finger, C.J.	Spreading Stain (1st {std}, sm8vo, 245p, col frn by...)	Doubleday/Page	1927	Honore, P.	30-45	*
Finger, C.J.	Tales Worth Telling (1st, lg8vo, 250p, orang cl, pep, 10cp)	Century	1927	Honore, P.	40-70	*
Finger, C.J.	Tales from Silver Lands (1st {std}, sm4to, 225p, 10cp, pep, NM)	Doubleday/Page	1924	Honore, P.	70-100	R*
Eells, E.S.	Brazilian Fairy Book (1st, 8vo, 193p, gilt, 6cp, pep)	Stokes	1926	Hood, G.	60-80	
Stroebe, C. (ed.)	Danish Fairy Book (1st, 8vo, blue cl, 218p, 6cp, pep)	Stokes	(1922)	Hood, G.	40-70	*
Martens, F.	Fairy Tales from Orient (1st, 8vo, 293p, blue cl, 4cp, pep)	McBride	1923	Hood, G.	50-70	
Curtin, J.S.	Fairy Tales of Eastern Europe (1st, 8vo, 259p, 4cp)	McBride	1914	Hood, G.	50-70	
Allen, F.W.	Golden Road (1st, 8vo, 228p, teg, col frn, pep)	Wessels/Bissel	1910	Hood, G.	35-50	
Friedlander, G.	Jewish Fairy Book (1st, 8vo, 188p, gilt, 8cp, pep)	Stokes	(1920)	Hood, G.	45-70	
Irving, W.	Legends of the Alhambra (1st, 4to, 229p, teg, p-o, 8cp)	Lippincott	1909	Hood, G.	50-70	
Bindloss, H.	Lorimer of the Northwest (1st, 12mo, 384p, cvr by...)	Stokes	(1909)	Hood, G.	30-45	
Stroebe, C. (ed.)	Norwegian Fairy Book (1st, 8vo, 304p, 6cp, pep)	Stokes	(1922)	Hood, G.	40-70	
Hawthorne, J.	Rumpty-Dudget's Tower (1st, 8vo, 72p, col frn)	Stokes	1924	Hood, G.	30-50	*
Lucas, E.V.	The Slowcoach (1st AM, 8vo, 367p, p-o, frn by...)	MacMillan	1910	Hood, G.	35-50	
Otis, James	Boy's Revolt (1st, 8vo, 193p, 16pl)	Estes	(1894)	Hooper, W.P.	35-50	
Almond, Linda S.	Peter Rabbit & the Tinybits (12mo, cloth, color)	Platt/Munk	(1935)	Hoopes, M.C.	40-65	*
Almond, Linda S.	When Peter Rabbit Went a-Fishing (24mo, bds, p-o, 64p, 25col pep)	Altemus	(1923)	Hoopes, M.C.	25-40	
Tracy, Louis	American Emperor (1st AM, 8vo, tan/gilt, 16pl)	Putnam	1897	Hope, E.S.	60-75	
Corbett, E.T.	3 Wise Old Couples (1st, 4to, ipcb, unpag, 15 chromos)	L: Cassell	(1881)	Hopkins, E.	80-100	*
Sterne, Laurence	Sentimental Journey/France & Italy (1st, 4to, teg, 12cp)	Putnam	1910	Hopkins, E.	75-100	
Russell, W.C.	Tragedy of Ida Noble (1st UK, 8vo, 315p, blue buckram, b/w)	L: Hutchinson	1893	Hopkins, E.	70-90	
Hamp, S.F.	Coco Bolo (1st, 12mo, 145p, 12pl)	Badger	1911	Hopp, O.	30-45	*
Whitney, A.D.T.	Mother Goose for Grown Folks (1st {new ed}, 12mo, 204p)	Houghton	1898	Hoppin, A.	45-60	*
Washburn, C.C.	Pages/Book of Paris (1st, 8vo, pcb, p-o, 276p, b/w)	Houghton	1910	Hornby, L.G.	25-40	*
Saunders, M.	Alpatok (1st, 12mo, tan cl, 51p, b/w)	Page	1906	Horne, D.W.	20-30	*
Bailey, C.S.	Firelight Stories (1st, sm8vo, 192p, 9pl)	M. Bradley	1907	Horne, D.W.	20-25	*
Johnston, A.F.	Mildred's Inheritance (1st, 12mo, 74p, 10pl)	Page	1906	Horne, D.W.	20-35	*
Sharp, D.L.	Roof & Meadow (1st, 8vo, green cl, b/w, 281p)	Century	1904	Horsfall, B.	20-35	
Morris, K.	Book of Three Dragons (1st {std}, 4to, gilt, 206p, 8pl, pep)	Longmans	(1930)	Horvath, F.H.	75-100	R
Lockhart, C.	Lady Doc (1st, 8vo, tan cloth, 339p, 4pl)	Lippincott	1912	Hoskins, G.	25-40	
Barbour, R.H.	Lady Laughter (1st, 8vo, 176p, teg, p-o, 4cp)	Lippincott	1913	Hoskins, G.	25-40	*
Brady, C.T.	Little Angel/Canyon Creek (1st, 8vo, 292p, 6pl)	Revell	1914	Hoskins, G.	25-40	*
Lockhart, C.	Man from Bitter Roots (1st, 8vo, red/gilt, 3cp)	Lippincott	1915	Hoskins, G.	25-40	
Hopkins, N.M.	Racoon Lake Mystery (1st, sm8vo, blue cl, 319p, 4cp)	Lippincott	1917	Hoskins, G.	25-40	
Rhoads, Dorothy	Bright Feather (1st {std}, 8vo, 196p, uncut, pep, col frn, b/w)	Doubleday/Dor.	1932	Houser, L.	25-40	*
Malkus, A.S.	Dark Star of Itza (1st {std}, 8vo, 217p, brown cl, 6 fp b/w, NH)	Harcourt	(1930)	Houser, L.	40-60	
Housman, L.	All-Fellows & Cloak of Friendship (1st, 8vo, 192p, grn cl, 7pl)	L: J. Cape	(1923)	Housman, L.	65-85	
Housman, L.	All-Fellows... (1st, sq8vo, 138p, green/gilt, uncut, 8pl)	L: Kegan Paul	1896	Housman, L.	85-120	
N/A	Aucassin & Nicolette (1st, 12mo, teg, vellum, 4pl)	L: J. Murray	1902	Housman, L.	120-160	
MacDonald, Geo.	Back of the North Wind (1st, 8vo, 378p, gilt, frn & cvr by...)	L: Blackie	(1899)	Housman, L.	130-165	
Housman, L.	Bethlehem (1st, 8vo, green/gilt, 85p, cvr by...)	L: MacMillan	1902	Housman, L.	80-110	
Housman, L.	Blue Moon (1st, 8vo, 210p, teg, blue/gilt, 8pl)	L: J. Murray	1904	Housman, L.	100-150	
Housman, L.	Cloak of Friendship (1st, 8vo, 192p, cvr by...)	L: J. Murray	1905	Housman, L.	75-100	
Hinkson, K.T.	Cuckoo Songs (1st, 12mo, brown/gilt, cvr & ti page by....)	L: Matthews	1894	Housman, L.	100-135	
Housman, L.	Doorway in Fairyland (1st, 8vo, 220p, 14pl)	L: J. Cape	(1922)	Housman, L.	120-170	
Barlow, J.	End of Elfintown (1st, 8vo, gilt, uncut, 77p, AEG, 8pl)	L: MacMillan	1894	Housman, L.	280-370	
Housman, L.	Farm in Fairyland (1st [1st bk.], 8vo, gilt, 160p, 12pl)	L: Kegan Paul	1894	Housman, L.	200-250	
Housman, L.	Farm in Fairyland (1st AM, 8vo, teg, 160p, 12pl)	Dodd	1894	Housman, L.	160-200	
Housman, L.	Field of Clover (1st, 12mo, green/gilt, 148p, 11pl)	L: Kegan Paul	1898	Housman, L.	180-220	
Housman, L.	Field of Clover (1st AM, sm8vo, 148p, teg, 11pl)	J. Lane	1902	Housman, L.	100-135	
Meynell, A.	Flower of the Mind (sm8vo, green/gilt, 348p, cvr by...)	L: Richards	1897	Housman, L.	60-85	
Rossetti, C.	Goblin Market (1st, 8vo, AEG, 63p, olive/gilt, 12pl)	L: MacMillan	1893	Housman, L.	260-350	
Housman, L.	Green Arras (1st, 8vo, green/gilt, 90p, uncut, 5pl)	L: J. Lane	1896	Housman, L.	125-165	
MacDonald, Geo.	Gutta-Percha Willie (1st, 12mo, 212p, blue/gilt, cvr by...)	L: Blackie	(1900)	Housman, L.	70-90	
Housman, L.	House of Joy (1st, 8vo, 181p, gilt, uncut, 9pl)	L: Kegan Paul	1895	Housman, L.	140-170	
Meredith, G.	Jump to Glory Jane (1st, 8vo, ipcb, teg, designs by...)	L: Swan	1892	Housman, L.	100-150	
Housman, L.	Little Land (1st, 8vo, 97p, ipcb, gilt, 4pl)	L: Richards	1899	Housman, L.	160-225	
Housman, L.	Moonshine & Clover (1st, 8vo, 220p, blue/silver)	L: J. Cape	(1922)	Housman, L.	70-100	
Nesbit, E.	Pomander of Verse (1st, sm8vo, gilt, teg, 88p, cvr by..)	J. Lane	1895	Housman, L.	130-165	
MacDonald, Geo.	Princess & Goblin (1st, 8vo, 313p, aqua/gilt, cep, cvr by..)	L: Blackie	1900	Housman, L.	130-170	
Housman, L.	Sabrina Warham (1st AM, 8vo, teg, brown/gilt)	MacMillan	1904	Housman, L.	70-90	
Shelley, P.B.	Sensitive Plant (1st, 8vo, 60p, teg, uncut, 12pl)	L: Aldine Hse.	1898	Housman, L.	130-180	

AUTHOR	TITLE	PUBLISHER	DATE	ARTIST	PRICE	LC
Housman, L.	Spikenard (1st AM, 8vo, 53p, brown pcb, gilt)	Badger	1898	Housman, L.	80-100	
Bain, R.N.	Weird Tales from Northern Seas (1st, 8vo, 201p, blue/gilt, 12pl)	L: Kegan Paul	1893	Housman, L.	140-200	
Housman, C.	Were-Wolf (1st, sq8vo, 124p, pink cl, uncut, 6pl)	L: J. Lane	1896	Housman, L.	180-300	
Edmondson, N.M.	Lavender Garden (1st, 8vo, 158p, lavender/gilt, 4cp, pep)	L: Warne	1929	Howard, C.T.	30-50	
Means, F.C.	Whispering Girl (1st, sm8vo, 225p, col frn, pep)	Houghton	1941	Howard, O.	20-35	*
Dalgliesh, A.	Three from Greenways (1st, sm8vo, 63p)	Scribner	1941	Howe, G.	25-40	*
Various	Peep into Cat-Land (sq8vo, 32p, ibds)	L: Warne	1890	Howell, C.E.	70-100	
Beard, P.	Pantalette Doll (1st, lg8vo, p-o, 160p, color, pep)	Whitman	(1931)	Hubbard, E.M.	35-60	*
Magruder, Julia	Sunny Southerner (1st, 12mo, 194p, teg, b/w pl)	Page	1901	Hubbell, H.	20-30	
May, Rbt.	Benny the Bunny Liked Beans (1st {std}, 8vo, [25]p, ibds, color)	Knopf	(1940)	Hubbell, H.W.	30-45	*
Carroll, L.	Alice/Wonderland (1st AM, 8vo, 181p, 12cp, pep)	Dodd	(1922)	Hudson, G.	130-175	
Carroll, L.	Alice/Wonderland (1st, 4to, red/gilt, 180p, 12 ticp, pep)	L: Hodder	[1922]	Hudson, G.	240-320	
Barrie, J.M.	Peter Pan & Wendy (1st, 4to, 272p, blue/gilt, color)	L: Hodder	[1925]	Hudson, G.	130-185	
Hudson, Alma	Peter Rabbit & the Fairies (sq12mo, 48p, red bds, p-o, 8cp)	Cupples	(1921)	Hudson, R.	60-80	
Hudson, Alma	Peter Rabbit/Mother Goose Land (16mo, red bds, p-o, 48p, color)	Cupples	(1921)	Hudson, R.	45-75	*
MacDonald, L.	Babies' Classics (1st, 4to, 79p, blue/gilt, b/w)	L: Longmans	1904	Hughes, A.	90-140	
MacDonald, Geo.	Fairy Tales (1st [new ed.], lg8vo, 435p, gilt, 12 b/w)	L: Fifield	1904	Hughes, A.	140-200	
MacDonald, Geo.	Gutta-Percha Willie (1st, 12mo, blue cl, 212p, 8pl by...)	L: Blackie	(1900)	Hughes, A.	70-90	
MacDonald, Geo.	Magic Crook (1st, 8vo, 273p, b/w)	L: Fifield	1911	Hughes, A.	100-145	
MacDonald, Geo.	Phantastes (1st, 8vo, 320p, blue/gilt, uncut, teg, 33 b/w)	L: A. Fifield	1905	Hughes, A.	170-250	
MacDonald, Geo.	Phantastes (8vo, 320p, blue/gilt, uncut, teg, b/w)	L: Dent	[1910]	Hughes, A.	160-220	
MacDonald, Geo.	Princess & Goblin (1st, 8vo, 313p, aqua/gilt, cep, 30 b/w by..)	L: Blackie	1900	Hughes, A.	130-170	
Rossetti, C.	Sing Song (1st [new ed.], 12mo, AEG, 135p, gilt, b/w)	L: MacMillan	1893	Hughes, A.	100-165	
Hughes, Shirley	Lucy & Tom's Day (1st, ob4to, tan cl, [27]p, fp color)	W.R. Scott	(1960)	Hughes, S.	30-50	*
White, E.O.	Green Door (1st, 8vo, 212p, silhouettes, DJ)	Houghton	1930	Hummel, L.	50-65	
Fyleman, R.	Little Christmas Book (1st, 8vo, orang ibds, pep, 41p, 2-color)	Doran	(1927)	Hummel, L.	20-35	
Thomas, E.M.	Babes of the Nations (1st, lg8vo, ibds, 12cp)	Stokes	1889	Humphrey, M.	400-600	
Humphrey, M.	Babes of the Year (1st, sq8vo, ibds, 25p, 12cp)	Stokes	1888	Humphrey, M.	250-400	
Tucker, E.S.	Baby Folk (1st, 4to, [26]p, ibds, 6cp)	Stokes	(1898)	Humphrey, M.	180-250	*
Cone, H.G.	Baby Sweethearts (1st, folio, ibds, 12cp)	Stokes	1890	Humphrey, M.	380-500	R
N/A	Baby's Record (1st, 4to, green/silver, 12cp)	Stokes	1898	Humphrey, M.	450-600	
Cone, H.G.	Bonnie Little People (1st, lg4to, 12p, 6cp)	Stokes	1890	Humphrey, M.	400-550	
Humphrey, M.	Book of Fairy Tales (1st, 4to, ipcb, [30]p, 12cp)	Stokes	1892	Humphrey, M.	450-600	
N/A	Book of Pets (lg4to, ibds, 12cp by...)	L: Gardner	1897	Humphrey, M.	350-500	
Thomas, E.M.	Children of Spring (4to, wraps, 3 chromos)	Stokes	1888	Humphrey, M.	300-450	*
Humphrey, M.	Children of the Revolution (1st, 4to, ibds, [24]p, 12cp)	Stokes	1900	Humphrey, M.	400-500	
Humphrey, M.	Gallant Little Patriots (1st, 4to, ipcb, 12cp)	Stokes	1899	Humphrey, M.	450-650	
Humphrey, M.	Golf Girl (1st, 4to, ibds, color)	Stokes	(1899)	Humphrey, M.	300-400	
MacDonald, Geo.	Light Princess (1st, 8vo, 305p, tan cl, 7 fp b/w)	Putnam	(1893)	Humphrey, M.	160-220	
Sage, A.C.	Little Colonial Dame (1st, sm4to, 197p, 16pl)	Stokes	(1898)	Humphrey, M.	50-70	
Humphrey, Mabel	Little Continentals (1st, lg4to, ibds, 6cp)	Stokes	1900	Humphrey, M.	350-500	
Tucker, E.S.	Little Grown-Ups (1st UK, 4to, ibds, 12cp)	L: Wells/Gard.	1897	Humphrey, M.	300-450	*
Tucker, E.S.	Little Grown-Ups (1st, 4to, ibds, 12cp)	Stokes	1897	Humphrey, M.	400-600	
Humphrey, M.	Little Heroes & Heroines (1st, 4to, ibds, 6cp)	Stokes	1899	Humphrey, M.	200-350	
Ogden, Ruth	Little Homespun (1st, 127p, 15pl)	Stokes	(1897)	Humphrey, M.	100-140	
Humphrey, M.	Little Soldiers & Sailors (1st, 4to, ibds, [19]p, 6cp)	Stokes	(1899)	Humphrey, M.	250-300	
Tucker, E.S.	Littlest Ones (1st, lg4to, ibds, 12cp)	Stokes	1898	Humphrey, M.	350-500	
Tucker, E.S.	Make-Believe Men & Women (1st, 4to, [26]p, ibds, 6cp)	Stokes	1897	Humphrey, M.	380-500	
Mother Goose	Mother Goose (1st, 4to, ibds, 24cp)	Stokes	1891	Humphrey, M.	400-500	
Tucker, E.S.	Old Youngsters (1st, lg4to, ibds, unpag, 6cp)	Stokes	1897	Humphrey, M.	300-400	
Cone, H.G.	One, Two, Three, Four (1st, 4to, ibds, unpag, 4cp)	Stokes	1889	Humphrey, M.	200-250	
Dobson, L.	Poems by Dobson, Locker & Praed (lg4to, p-o, gilt, 6cp)	Stokes	1892	Humphrey, M.	300-450	
Humphrey, M.	Rosebud Stories (1st, 8vo, 24p, ipcb, 6cp)	Holiday Pub.	1906	Humphrey, M.	150-200	
Booth, M.B.	Sleepy-Time Stories (1st, 12mo, 177p, teg, gilt, 17pl)	Putnam	1899	Humphrey, M.	140-170	
Thomas, E.M.	Songs/Jingles/Rhymes (1st, 4to, p-o, 251p, b/w)	Stokes	(1894)	Humphrey, M.	250-350	
Thomas, E.M.	Tiny Folk of Sunny Days (1st, lg8vo, unpag, 6cp)	Stokes	1889	Humphrey, M.	250-400	*
Thomas, E.M.	Tiny Folk of Wintery Days (1st, lg8vo, cloth, unpag, 6cp)	Stokes	1889	Humphrey, M.	350-500	
Humphrey, M.	Tiny Toddlers (folio, color, ibds)	Stokes	1890	Humphrey, M.	650-800	*
Cooper, J.F.	The Pathfinder (1st, 12mo, 516p, b/w pl)	Macrae Smith	(1926)	Humphreys, D.S.	20-30	*
Wiggin, K.D.	Romance of a Christmas Card (1st, 8vo, 123p, teg, p-o, pep, 5cp)	Houghton	1916	Hunt, E.A.	35-60	
Lippincott, J.W.	Black Wings (1st {std}, sm8vo, 143p, blue cl, col frn, pep)	Lippincott	(1947)	Hunt, L.B.	45-60	*
Montgomery, R.G.	Broken Fang (1st, 8vo, red cl, 186p, 10cp, pep)	Donahue	(1935)	Hunt, L.B.	50-80	*
Lippincott, J.W.	Red Roan Pony (1st, 8vo, 320p, red cl, col frn, 4pl, pep)	Penn	(1934)	Hunt, L.B.	45-60	*
Walker, M.	Lady Hollyhock & her Friends (1st, sm4to, 153p, color)	Baker/Taylor	(1906)	Hunt, M.I.	70-100	*
Huntington, I.M.	Peter Pumpkin/Wonderland (1st, sq4to, 264p, 15pl)	Rand/McNally	(1908)	Hunt, M.I.	70-100	
Hurd, E.T.	Annie Moran (1st, ob4to, ibds, [32]p, color, pep)	Lothrop/Lee	1942	Hurd, C.	45-60	*
Brown, M.W.	Bad Little Duckhunter (1st, ob4to, ipcb, [30]p, color)	W.R. Scott	(1947)	Hurd, C.	65-80	
Hurd, E.T.	Benny the Bulldozer (1st, ob4to, [33]p, ibds, 1-color, pep)	Lothrop/Lee	1947	Hurd, C.	45-60	*
Brown, M.W.	Bumble Bugs & Elephants (1st, sq4to, ibds, unpag, color)	W.R. Scott	1938	Hurd, C.	80-120	
Hurd, E.T.	Caboose (1st, ob4to, [33]p, ibds, 1-color)	Lothrop/Lee	1950	Hurd, C.	45-60	
Hurd, E.T.	Cat from Telegraph Hill (1st, sm4to, unpag, ipcb, pep, color)	Lothrop/Lee	(1955)	Hurd, C.	35-50	*
Hurd, E.T.	Devil's Tail (1st {std}, 8vo, 216p, t.e. red, fp b/w)	Doubleday	(1954)	Hurd, C.	25-40	*

AUTHOR	TITLE	PUBLISHER	DATE	ARTIST	PRICE	LC
Brown, M.W.	Diggers (1st, ob8vo, unpag, ibds, color)	Harper	(1960)	Hurd, C.	45-60	
Hurd, E.T.	Engine, Engine No. 9 (1st, ob8vo, [34]p, ibds, color, pep)	Lothrop/Lee	1940	Hurd, C.	60-80	
Hurd, E.T.	Faraway Christmas (1st, 8vo, ^Eblue cl, [33]p, 1-color, pep)	Lothrop/Lee	1958	Hurd, C.	30-45	*
Hurd, E.T.	Fox in a Box (1st {std}, lg8vo, ibds, unpag, pep, color)	Doubleday	(1957)	Hurd, C.	45-60	
Brown, M.W.	Goodnight Moon (1st, ob8vo, [31]p, color)	Harper	1947	Hurd, C.	70-100	
Gipson, M.	Hello Peter (1st {std}, ob8vo, [31]p, color, dep)	Doubleday	(1948)	Hurd, C.	45-60	*
Hurd, E.T.	It's Snowing (1st, 4to, silver cl, unpag, dep, b/w)	NY: Sterling	(1957)	Hurd, C.	40-65	*
Hurd, E.T.	Johnny Littlejohn (1st, narrow ob8vo, unpag, yellow cl, 1-color)	Lothrop/Lee	(1957)	Hurd, C.	30-45	*
Brown, M.W.	Little Brass Band (1st, ob8vo, [25]p, ipcb, dep, color)	Harper	(1955)	Hurd, C.	50-70	*
Hurd, C.	Merry Chase (1st {std}, lg8vo, [25]p, yellow cl, pep, color)	Random	(1941)	Hurd, C.	35-60	*
Brown, M.W.	My World (1st, ob8vo, [34]p, ibds, color, cep)	Harper	1949	Hurd, C.	50-80	*
Hurd, E.T.	Nino & his Fish (1st, lg8vo, unpag, ipcb, color, pep)	Lothrop/Lee	(1954)	Hurd, C.	25-40	*
Hurd, E.T.	Old Silversides (1st, ob4to, [30]p, ibds, 1-color, pep)	Lothrop/Lee	1951	Hurd, C.	45-60	
Brown, M.W.	Peppermint Family (1st, ob8vo, [32]p, ipcb, fp 2-color, dep)	Harper	(1950)	Hurd, C.	60-90	*
Brown, M.W.	Runaway Bunny (1st {std}, ob8vo, [40]p, color, pep)	Harper	(1942)	Hurd, C.	70-100	R*
Hurd, E.T.	Sky High (1st, lg ob8vo, [34]p, color, pep)	Lothrop/Lee	(1941)	Hurd, C.	30-50	*
Hurd, E.T.	Speedy... (1st, lg ob8vo, ibds, [36]p, 1-color, pep)	Lothrop/Lee	1942	Hurd, C.	35-50	*
Hurd, C.	The Race (1st {std}, lg8vo, [27]p, yellow cl, color, pep)	Random	(1940)	Hurd, C.	35-60	*
Stein, Gertrude	The World's Round (1st, 4to, 67p, blue bds)	W.R. Scott	1939	Hurd, C.	120-165	
Hurd, E.T.	Toughy & his Trailer Truck (1st, ob8vo, ibds, [34]p, pep, 1-col)	Lothrop/Lee	1948	Hurd, C.	45-65	*
Hurd, E.T.	Willy's Farm (1st, 4to, 64p, ipcb, color, pep)	Lothrop/Lee	(1949)	Hurd, C.	45-65	*
Twain, M.	Adventures of Tom Sawyer (1st, 8vo, 264p, p-o, 4cp, pep)	Winston	(1931)	Hurd, P.	35-50	*
Burglon, N.	Deep Silver (1st, 8vo, 215p, blue cl, 12pl)	Houghton	1938	Hurd, P.	50-75	*
Rollins P.A.	Gone Haywire (1st, 8vo, 269p, 4 dp b/w, pep)	Scribner	1939	Hurd, P.	30-50	*
Horgan, Paul	Habit of Empire (1st {this pub}, 8vo, 114p, 8 dp b/w)	Harper	(1939)	Hurd, P.	35-50	*
Dodge, M.M.	Hans Brinker (1st, 8vo, blue cl, 305p, p-o, 4cp)	Garden City	1932	Hurd, P.	30-45	
Cooper, J.F.	Last of the Mohicans (1st, sm8vo, p-o, 437p, 8cp, pep)	McKay	(1928)	Hurd, P.	45-60	*
Hamilton, Eliz.	P-Zoo (1st, ob4to, ipcb, [32]p, 1-color, pep)	Coward	(1945)	Hurd, P.	100-165	*
Horgan, Paul	Return of the Weed (1st {std}, 8vo, 97p, 7 fp b/w)	Harper	1936	Hurd, P.	30-45	*
Baldwin, J.	Story of Roland (1st, sm4to, 347p, p-o, 10cp, pep, SC)	Scribner	(1930)	Hurd, P.	70-90	
Baldwin, J.	Story of Siegfried (1st, 4to, p-o, 279p, black cl, 6cp, pep, SC)	Scribner	(1931)	Hurd, P.	70-100	
Meigs, C.	Swift Rivers (1st, 8vo, black cl, p-o, 269p, 6cp, pep)	Little/Brown	1937	Hurd, P.	35-50	*
Graham, T.	Hike & the Aeroplane (1st, sm8vo, 275p, 4pl)	Stokes	(1912)	Hutchins, A.	500-650	
Goodrich, A.	Gleam O'Dawn (1st, 8vo, 308p, 4pl)	Appleton	1908	Hutchinson	20-25	
McNeil, E.	With Kit Carson in the Rockies (1st, 8vo, 333p, 5pl)	Dutton	(1909)	Hutchinson	25-40	
Chambers, Rbt.	Anne's Bridge (1st, 8vo, 161p, green/gilt)	Appleton	1914	Hutt, H.	25-40	
Hutt, H.	Girls (1st, 4to, [38]p, blue cl, p-o, 16cp)	Scribner	1910	Hutt, H.	100-130	
Hutt, H.	Henry Hutt Picture Book (1st, 4to, [84]p, p-o, 10cp)	Century	1908	Hutt, H.	85-120	
Ford, P.L.	His Version of It (1st, 8vo, teg, 109p)	Dodd	1905	Hutt, H.	25-40	
Lewis, A.H.	Peggy O'Neal (1st, 8vo, uncut, 494p, 4cp)	Drexel/Biddle	1903	Hutt, H.	30-45	
Chambers, Rbt.	Police! (1st, 8vo, 292p, gilt, p-o, cp)	Appleton	1915	Hutt, H.	20-35	
Hutt, H.	Rosebuds (1st, 4to, 27p, 11 ticp)	Bobbs-Merrill	(1912)	Hutt, H.	130-170	*
Hutt, H.	She Loves Me (1st, 4to, p-o, unpag, 8cp)	Bobbs-Merrill	(1911)	Hutt, H.	100-130	
London, J.	The Game (1st, 8vo, 182p, teg, uncut, col frn, 5pl)	MacMillan	1905	Hutt, H.	180-220	
Tarkington, B.	Two Vanrevels (1st, 8vo, 351p, green/gilt, teg, 7pl)	McClure	1902	Hutt, H.	30-50	
Byng, Douglas	Byng Ballads (1st, 8vo, ibds, unpag, 8 fp color)	L: J. Lane	[1932]	Hutton, C.	30-45	*
Hyde, Eliz.	Little Brothers to the Scouts (12mo, blu cl, p-o, 72p, 10cp)	Rand/McNally	(1917)	Hyde, Eliz.	25-40	
Clark, G.O.	Moon Babies (1st, ob4to, ibds, 48p, color)	R.H. Russell	1900	Hyde, Helen	150-200	
Hueffer, F.M.	Cinque Ports... (1st, 4to, 403p, buckram, 14pl)	L: Blackwood	1900	Hyde, W.	350-500	
Aubrey, Frank	Devil-Tree of El Dorado (1st, 8vo, brown/gilt, 392p, 8pl)	L: Hutchinson	1896	Hyland/Ellis	150-200	
Field, M.	Tragic Mary (1st, 8vo, 261p, ipcb, cvr by...)	L: G. Bell	1890	Image, S.	180-250	
Stein, E.	Child Songs of Cheer (1st, 8vo, 120p, gilt, 4cp, pep)	Lothrop/Lee	(1918)	Inglis, A.	25-40	*
Dyer, R.O.	Daytime Story Book (1st, sm8vo, 152p, col frn)	Lothrop/Lee	(1917)	Inglis, A.	20-35	*
Ipcar, D.	Animal Hide & Seek (1st, lg8vo, [36]p, ipcb, color, pep)	W.R. Scott	(1947)	Ipcar, D.	50-80	*
Brown, M.W.	Little Fisherman (1st, lg8vo, ibds, [34]p, color, pep)	W.R. Scott	1945	Ipcar, D.	60-85	*
Hope, E.	Alice in the Delighted States (1st AM, 8vo, 303p, 12pl, cep)	MacVeagh/Dial	1928	Irvin, Rea	70-90	
Levy, N.	Opera Guyed (1st, 8vo, 87p, b/w, DJ)	Knopf	1923	Irvin, Rea	35-60	
Hyde, F.	Ritz Carltons (1st, 8vo, 157p, pcb, b/w)	NY: Macy	1927	Irvin, Rea	30-45	*
Wing, Paul	Unsuccessful Elf (1st, ob4to, ibds, [44]p, 6 fp color, pep)	Rinehart	(1947)	Irvin, Rea	60-80	
Eaton, J.	Lone Journey (1st, 8vo, 266p, map, b/w, NH)	Harcourt	(1944)	Ishmael, W.	35-50	
Wallace, Lew	Chariot Race of Ben-Hur (1st, lg8vo, 133p, uncut, teg, 4cp)	Harper	1908	Ivanowski, S.	25-40	
Burnett, F.H.	Land of the Blue Flower (1st, 8vo, gilt, 67p, teg)	Moffat	1909	Ivanowski, S.	35-50	
Mother Goose	Mother Goose (1st, 32mo, [41]p, color, pep)	Holiday House	(1939)	Ives, R.	45-65	*
Schneider, N.	Let's Look Inside your House (1st, lg8vo, 39p, color)	W.R. Scott	(1948)	Ivins, B.	45-60	*
Ewing, J.H.	Lob Lie-by-the-Fire (1st, 8vo, 144p, b/w)	NY: OUP	(1937)	Ivins, F.W.	20-30	*
Streamer, Col. D.	Ruthless Rhymes for Heartless Homes (1st, sm8vo, ibds, b/w, pep)	R.H. Russell	1901	J.W.A.	80-100	
Carroll, L.	Alice/Wonderland (1st AM, 4to, 232p, 16 ticp, pep)	Doran	[1915]	Jackson, A.E.	120-180	*
Carroll, L.	Alice/Wonderland (1st, 4to, grn/gilt, teg, 199p, pep, 16 ticp)	L: H. Frowde	[1915]	Jackson, A.E.	180-220	
Carroll, L.	Alice/Wonderland (1st {this pub}, 8vo, 216p, 8cp, pep)	Garden City	(1930)	Jackson, A.E.	50-80	*
Carroll, L.	Alice/Wonderland (lg8vo, ibds, 8cp, later)	L: H. Milford	[1933]	Jackson, A.E.	60-80	
Swift, J.	Gulliver's Travels (1st, 8vo, blue/gilt, AEG, 332p, 6cp, pep)	Nister/Dutton	[1910]	Jackson, A.E.	70-100	
N/A	Tales from Arabian Nights (1st, lg8vo, 340p, 48cp)	L: Ward Lock	1920	Jackson, A.E.	70-100	*

AUTHOR	TITLE	PUBLISHER	DATE	ARTIST	PRICE	LC
Lamb, C.	Tales from Shakespeare (1st, 8vo, 472p, blue cl, p-o, 48cp)	L: Ward Lock	1919	Jackson, A.E.	50-70	
Kingsley, C.	Water Babies (1st, 4to, teg, blue/gilt, 252p, pep, 16 ticp)	L: OUP	[1920]	Jackson, A.E.	180-250	
Page, T.N.	On Newfound River (1st, 8vo, 286p, blue/gilt, teg, 4cp)	Scribner	1906	Jackson, J.E.	20-35	
Parkman, F.	Oregon Trail (1st, 8vo, 388p, black cl, p-o, 4cp)	Winston	(1931)	Jackson, W.H.	35-60	
Swift, J.	Gulliver's Travels (8vo, brown cl, AEG, 6cp)	L: Nister	[1900]	Jacobs, E.A.	65-90	
Jacobs, H.	Hindu Fairy Tales (1st, 8vo, 186p, 4cp)	L: Harrap	1919	Jacobs, H.	40-60	
Page, T.N.	Captured Santa Claus (1st, 12mo, 81p, teg, 4cp)	Scribner	1902	Jacobs, W.L.	30-45	
Porter, G.S.	The Harvester (1st, 8vo, 564p, 4cp)	Doubleday/Page	1911	Jacobs, W.L.	35-50	
N/A	Aucassin & Nicolette (1st, 8vo, 91p, teg, 12pl, vellum)	L: Routledge	1905	James, G.	70-85	
Petrovitch, W.	Heroes & Legends of Serbians (1st, 4to, 394p, teg, 32cp)	L: Harrap	1914	James, G.	65-90	
Omar Khayyam	Rubaiyat... (8vo, teg, 160p, 12pl)	Elder	1909	James, G.	35-50	
Omar Khayyam	Rubaiyat... (1st, 4to, 203p, teg, 16cp)	L: A&C Black	1909	James, G.	100-150	
Barfield, O.	Silver Trumpet (1st, 8vo, green cl, 142p, 8cp)	L: Faber/Gwyen	1925	James, G.	35-50	*
James, Will	All in the Day's Riding (1st, 8vo, 251p, DJ)	Scribner	1933	James, W.	120-160	
James, Will	Big-Enough (1st, 8vo, 314p, cloth, b/w, DJ)	Scribner	1931	James, W.	100-120	
James, Will	Cow Country (1st, lg8vo, 242p, brown cl, 28pl, DJ)	Scribner	1927	James, W.	120-160	
James, Will	Cowboys North & South (1st, lg8vo, 217p, 51 fp b/w)	Scribner	1924	James, W.	70-100	
James, Will	Dark Horse (1st, 8vo, green cl, col frn, 306p, DJ)	Scribner	1939	James, W.	120-165	
James, Will	Drifting Cowboy (1st, lg8vo, 241p, 36 fp b/w)	Scribner	1925	James, W.	80-100	
James, Will	Flint Spears (1st, 8vo, 272p, cloth, col frn, DJ)	Scribner	1938	James, W.	100-120	
James, Will	Horses I've Known (1st, 8vo, 280p, 29pl, col frn, DJ)	Scribner	1940	James, W.	85-130	
James, Will	In the Saddle with Uncle Bill (1st, 8vo, 289p, 33pl)	Scribner	1935	James, W.	120-165	
James, Will	Lone Cowboy... (1st, 8vo, gilt, uncut, 431p, fp b/w, DJ)	Scribner	1930	James, W.	100-135	
James, Will	Look-See with Uncle Bill (1st, 8vo, 253p, col frn, DJ)	Scribner	1938	James, W.	100-140	
James, Will	My First Horse (1st, ob8vo, blue cl, [45]p, fp color)	Scribner	1940	James, W.	90-120	
James, Will	Sand (1st, 8vo, 328p, green cl, fp b/w, DJ)	Scribner	1929	James, W.	120-165	
James, Will	Scorpion: Good Bad Horse (1st, 8vo, 312p, col frn, b/w, DJ)	Scribner	1936	James, W.	70-115	
James, Will	Smoky the Cow Horse (1st, 8vo, 310p, b/w, PPP, NM)	Scribner	1926	James, W.	100-150	
James, Will	Smoky the Cow Horse (1st {thus}, 4to, p-o, 263p, 6cp, pep, SC)	Scribner	(1929)	James, W.	65-100	
James, Will	Sun Up, Tales of the Cow Camps (1st, lg8vo, p-o, 342p, b/w)	Scribner	1931	James, W.	70-100	
James, Will	Three Mustangeers (1st, 8vo, 338p, green cl, fp b/w)	Scribner	1933	James, W.	80-100	
James, Will	Uncle Bill... (1st, 8vo, 241p, DJ)	Scribner	1932	James, W.	70-85	
James, Will	Young Cowboy (1st, ob sm4to, 72p, p-o, 5cp)	Scribner	1935	James, W.	120-180	
Jamieson, M.M.	Little Redskins (sq12mo, ibds, chromos)	L: Nister	[1910]	Jamieson, M.M.	65-90	
Sechrist, Eliz. H.	Rufie Had a Monkey! (1st, lg8vo, [46]p, red cl, b/w, cep)	McKay	(1939)	Janeway, H.	80-130	*
Ingoldsby, T.	Misadventures at Margate (folio, ibds, 18p, fp color)	L: Eyre/Spotts	[1885]	Jessop, E.M.	70-90	*
Hill, F.T.	Washington: Man of Action (1st, lg4to, green/gilt, 329p, 27cp)	Appleton	(1914)	Job	135-200	
Wister, A.L.	Happy-Go-Lucky (1st, 8vo, green/gilt, 115p, teg, 4cp)	Lippincott	1906	Johann, P.G.	30-45	*
Montgomery, L.M.	Anne of Ingleside (1st, 12mo, 323p, col frn)	Stokes	1939	John, C.V.	45-60	*
Davis, M.G.	Wakaima & the Clay Man (1st {std}, 8vo, 145p, uncut, b/w, pep)	Longmans	(1946)	Johnson, Avery	45-70	*
Johnson, Crockett	Barnaby (1st, 12mo, 361p, blue cl, b/w)	Holt	1943	Johnson, C.	45-60	*
Johnson, Crockett	Barnaby & Mr. O'Malley (1st, 12mo, 328p, b/w)	Holt	(1944)	Johnson, C.	45-65	*
Johnson, Crockett	Blue Ribbon Puppies (1st, 16mo, ibds, 31p, 2-color)	Harper	1958	Johnson, C.	45-70	
Krauss, Ruth	Carrot Seed (1st, sm8vo, olive cl, [25]p, fp 2-color, cep)	Harper	1945	Johnson, C.	45-60	*
Johnson, Crockett	Harold & the Purple Crayon (1st, 16mo, ibds, unpag, 1-color)	Harper	1955	Johnson, C.	50-80	R*
Johnson, Crockett	Harold's Circus (1st, 16mo, ibds, unpag, 1-color)	Harper	1959	Johnson, C.	50-75	*
Krauss, Ruth	How to Make an Earthquake (1st, 8vo, 28p, ipcb, 1-color)	Harper	(1954)	Johnson, C.	45-65	*
Krauss, Ruth	Is This You? (1st, 12mo, ipcb, [40]p, cep)	W.R. Scott	1955	Johnson, C.	50-85	R*
Cook, Bernadine	Little Fish that Got Away (1st, sm8vo, unpag, 2-color)	W.R. Scott	1956	Johnson, C.	35-50	*
Branley, Frank	Mickey's Magnet (1st, sm8vo, [48]p, yellow cl, color, dep)	Crowell	1956	Johnson, C.	30-50	*
Johnson, Crockett	Terrible Terrifying Toby (1st, lg8vo, unpag)	Harper	1957	Johnson, C.	50-70	*
Johnson, Crockett	Who's Upside Down? (1st, lg8vo, [24]p, ipcb, b/w)	W.R. Scott	1952	Johnson, C.	45-70	*
Brown, M.W.	Willie's Adventures (1st, sm8vo, grey cl, 68p, b/w)	W.R. Scott	(1954)	Johnson, C.	60-100	R*
Bangs, J.K.	Tiddledywink Tales (1st, 8vo, red/gilt, 236p, b/w)	R.H. Russell	1891	Johnson, C.H.	80-100	
Bangs, J.K.	Tiddledywink's Poetry Book (1st, 8vo, red/gilt, [64]p, b/w)	R.H. Russell	1892	Johnson, C.H.	65-80	*
Chisholm, A.M.	Boss of Wind River (1st, 12mo, blue cl, 341p, 4cp)	Doubleday/Page	1911	Johnson, F.T.	20-25	
Coatsworth, E.	Desert Dan (1st, lg8vo, 61p, fp b/w)	Viking	(1960)	Johnson, H.	25-45	*
Francis, P.W.	Remarkable Advens/Little Boy Pip (1st, 8vo, ibds, 60p, col, pep)	Paul Elder	(1907)	Johnson, M.	65-80	*
Johnson, Margaret	What O'Clock Jingles (1st, ob8vo, ibds, [30]p, 27 b/w)	D. Lothrop	(1887)	Johnson, M.	60-85	*
Chapin, F.	Pinkey & the Plumed Knight (1st, 4to, tan cl, 207p, 8cp, cep)	Saalfield	(1909)	Johnson, Merle	65-80	*
Johnston, A.F.	Ole Mammy's Torment (1st, 12mo, 118p, fp b/w)	Page	1897	Johnston/Sacker	30-50	
Doucet, J.	Tales of the Spinner (1st, lg8vo, [121]p, teg, uncut, gilt, b/w)	R.H. Russell	1902	Jones, A.G.	130-200	R*
Jones, E.O.	Big Susan (1st, sq8vo, ibds, 83p, color, pep, DJ)	MacMillan	1947	Jones, E.O.	45-60	
Adshead, Gladys	Brownies - Hush! (1st, ob12mo, [64]p, orang cl, 1-color, cep)	NY: OUP	(1938)	Jones, E.O.	25-40	*
Jones, E.O.	David: Bible Story with Pictures (1st, 4to, ibds, color)	MacMillan	1937	Jones, E.O.	35-50	*
Jones, J.O.	Little Child (1st, ob4to, ibds, 40p, pep, fp color)	Viking	1946	Jones, E.O.	30-45	*
Bridgman, Betty	Lullaby for Eggs (1st {std}, 8vo, ibds, unpag, fp color)	MacMillan	1955	Jones, E.O.	25-40	*
Jones, E.O.	Minnie the Mermaid (1st, sq12mo, [48]p, red cl, color)	NY: OUP	(1939)	Jones, E.O.	30-45	
Hunt, M.L.	Peddler's Clock (1st, sq8vo, ipcb, [28]p, pep, color)	Grosset/Dunlap	(1943)	Jones, E.O.	30-45	*
Farjeon, E.	Prayer for Little Things (1st, 8vo, [13]p, color, dep, DJ)	Houghton	1945	Jones, E.O.	30-45	
Field, R.	Prayer for a Child (1st, sq8vo, [31]p, color, cep, DJ, CM)	MacMillan	1944	Jones, E.O.	65-100	R
Meigs, C.	Scarlet Oak (1st, 8vo, 198p, col frn, pep, 8pl, DJ)	MacMillan	1938	Jones, E.O.	30-45	

AUTHOR	TITLE	PUBLISHER	DATE	ARTIST	PRICE	LC
Jones, J.O.	Secrets (1st, 8vo, 24p, fp color, DJ)	Viking	1945	Jones, E.O.	30-45	
Jones, J.O.	Small Rain (1st, ob8vo, ibds, [40]p, 1-color, pep, DJ, CH)	Viking	1943	Jones, E.O.	60-90	
St. Francis/Assisi	Song of the Sun (1st {std}, [32]p, sq8vo, 11 fp color, pep, DJ)	MacMillan	1952	Jones, E.O.	35-50	
Jones, J.O. (ed.)	This is the Way (1st, sm ob4to, 62p, 2-color, pep)	Viking	1951	Jones, E.O.	25-40	*
Trent, R.	To Church We Go (1st {this artist}, 4to, [32]p, ibds, 1-color)	Follett	(1956)	Jones, E.O.	25-45	*
Various	Told Under the Magic Umbrella (1st, lg8vo, 248p, b/w)	MacMillan	1939	Jones, E.O.	25-45	*
Adshead, Gladys	What Miranda Knew (1st, 12mo, [48]p, beige cl, color)	NY: OUP	(1944)	Jones, E.O.	30-45	*
Lamb, C.	Essays of Elia (8vo, green/gilt, teg, uncut, 310p)	L: Methuen	1902	Jones, G.	35-50	
De La Mare, W.	This Year: Next Year (1st AM, sm4to, ibds, [64]p, color, pep)	Holt	(1937)	Jones, H.	70-120	*
Hall, G.	Monkey Shines (lg8vo, ipcb, 10cp)	Wessels	(1904)	Jones, L.F.	25-40	
Bagnold, Enid	Alice & Thomas & Jane (1st AM, 8vo, yellow cl, 173p, b/w)	Knopf	1931	Jones, Laurie	20-30	
Byington, Eloise	Pancake Brownies (1st, 8vo, p-o, 96p, color, pep)	Whitman	(1928)	Jones, M.	30-45	*
Maugham, W.S.	Princess September & Nightingale (1st, lg8vo, [31]p, col, pep)	OUP	(1939)	Jones, R.C.	45-60	*
Eberle, I.	Spice on the Wind (1st, 8vo, 56p, brown cl, 2-color, pep)	Holiday House	(1940)	Jones, R.C.	50-80	R*
Stephens, J.	Crock of Gold (1st, 8vo, 298p, green/gilt, 6 fp 2-color, pep)	MacMillan	1922	Jones, W.	30-45	*
Harper, Wilhelmina	Harvest Feast (1st {std}, sm8vo, 308p, orange cl, b/w, pep)	Dutton	(1938)	Jones, W.	20-30	*
Jones, W.	How the Derrick Works (1st, 4to, black cl, 43p, 1-color, cep)	MacMillan	(1930)	Jones, W.	50-80	
Colum, P.	Island of the Mighty (1st, 8vo, 265p, gilt, 3cp, 19pl)	MacMillan	1924	Jones, W.	30-45	
Colum, P.	The Voyagers (1st, sm8vo, 188p, 3cp, fp b/w, NH)	MacMillan	1925	Jones, W.	40-60	*
Omar Khayyam	Rubaiyat... (1st, 12mo, 86p, color)	Harper	1921	Jones, W.J.	35-50	*
Burgess, T.	Cubby Finds an Open Door (ob24mo, ibds, [24]p, color)	Whitman	1929	Jordan, N.	35-50	
Burgess, T.	Farmer Brown's Boy Becomes Curious (ob24mo, ibds, 24p, color)	Whitman	1929	Jordan, N.	35-50	
Tietjens, E.	Gingerbread Boy (1st, 16mo, ipcb, [57]p, color, pep)	Whitman	(1932)	Jordan, N.	30-45	*
Bannerman, H.	Little Black Sambo (1st, 16mo, [42]p, ibds, color)	Whitman	(1934)	Jordan, N.	75-100	*
Jordan, N.	Mother Goose Handicraft (1st, sm8vo, 149p, fp b/w)	Harcourt	(1945)	Jordan, N.	45-70	*
Potter, B.	Story of Peter Rabbit (16mo, ibds, [58]p, color)	Whitman	(1932)	Jordan, N.	45-65	
N/A	Three Little Pigs (1st, ob8vo, [48]p, color, pep)	Whitman	(1933)	Jordan, S.	25-45	*
Jungman, B.	Holland (1st, lg8vo, teg, 212p, 75cp)	L: A&C Black	1904	Jungman, N.	65-100	
McCutcheon, G.B.	Daughter of Anderson Crow (1st, 8vo, 346p, col frn)	Dodd	1907	Justice, B.M.	20-35	
Wiggin, K.D.	Affair at the Inn (1st, 8vo, 220p, 6pl)	Houghton	1904	Justice, M.	25-40	
Stevenson, R.L.	Treasure Island (1st, sm4to, 228p, color, pep)	Grosset/Dunlap	(1930)	Justis, L.	35-50	*
Means, F.C.	Rains Will Come (1st, 8vo, 241p, green cl, b/w)	Houghton	1954	Kabotie, F.	25-45	*
Kahl, V.	Away Went Wolfgang (1st, ob4to, beige cl, [32]p, color)	Scribner	1954	Kahl, V.	50-80	R*
Malory, T.	Boy's King Arthur (1st, 8vo, 403p, gilt, 12pl, cep)	Scribner	1880	Kappes, A.	90-135	
Mother Goose	Mother Goose Melodies (1st, lg8vo, 186p, 8cp)	Houghton	1879	Kappes, A.	220-300	
Maxwell, Wm.	Heavenly Tenants (1st, 8vo, blue cl, 56p, 1-color, pep, NH)	Harper	(1946)	Karasz, I.	65-90	R*
McGinley, Phyllis	Merry Christmas, Happy New Year (1st, 8vo, bds, 48p, color)	Viking	(1958)	Karasz, I.	20-35	*
Little, F.	Little Sister Snow (1st, 12mo, 141p, p-o, 12cp)	Century	1909	Kataoka, G.	20-35	
Watanna, O.	Tama (1st, 8vo, 244p, uncut, gilt, teg, 4cp, dep)	Harper	1910	Kataoka, G.	25-40	
Shannon, Monica	Dobry (1st, 8vo, 176p, grey cl, col frn, pep, DJ, NM)	Viking	1934	Katchamakoff, A.	75-100	
Earl of Birkenhead	World in 2030 (1st, lg8vo, 215p, black cl, 9pl)	L: Hodder	(1930)	Kauffer, E.M.	45-65	
Rice, Ethel	Wiggle & Waggle (1st, 4to, bds, [28]p, p-o, color, pep)	NY: S. Gabriel	(1939)	Kay, A.	45-60	
Kay, G.A.	Adventures in Geography (1st, 4to, orang cl, color)	Volland	(1930)	Kay, G.A.	35-50	
Kay, G.A.	Adventures on our Street (1st, sm4to, p-o, 130p, 4cp, pep)	McKay	(1925)	Kay, G.A.	50-70	
Carroll, L.	Alice/Wonderland (1st, sq8vo, 241p, p-o, gilt, 8cp, pep)	Lippincott	1923	Kay, G.A.	120-165	
Kingsbury, H.O.	All Aboard for Wonderland (1st, 4to, 190p, 4cp)	Moffat	1917	Kay, G.A.	70-115	*
MacDonald, Geo.	Back of the North Wind (1st, 8vo, p-o, 326p, 4cp)	McKay	(1926)	Kay, G.A.	50-70	
Kay, G.A.	Book of Seven Wishes (1st, 8vo, 224p, blue cl, 4cp, pep)	Moffat	1917	Kay, G.A.	50-85	
Addington, S.	Boy Who Lived in Pudding Lane (1st, 8vo, 93p, 6cp, pep, p-o)	Atl. Month Pr.	(1922)	Kay, G.A.	50-70	*
Chater, M.	Bubble Ballads (1st, 4to, p-o, 148p, 16pl)	Century	1914	Kay, G.A.	50-75	
Helm, C.	Cecily (1st, 4to, p-o, 298p, 8cp, pep)	Lippincott	(1924)	Kay, G.A.	75-120	
Pyrnelle, L.C.	Diddie, Dumps & Tot (1st, 8vo, 214p, col frn, cp)	Harper	1930	Kay, G.A.	60-80	*
Donahey, M.D.	Down Spider Web Lane (1st, 4to, p-o, 130p, 6cp)	Stern	1909	Kay, G.A.	80-100	
Kay, G.A.	Fairy Who Believed in Human Beings (1st, 8vo, 169p, 4cp)	Moffat	1918	Kay, G.A.	70-100	
Kay, G.A.	Friends of Jimmy (1st, lg8vo, ibds, [95]p, color, pep)	Volland	(1926)	Kay, G.A.	50-80	
Addington, S.	Grammar Town (1st, 8vo, p-o, 79p, 4cp, pep)	McKay	(1927)	Kay, G.A.	25-45	
Addington, S.	Great Adven./Mrs. Santa Claus (1st, 8vo, p-o, 107p, 5cp)	Little/Brown	1923	Kay, G.A.	45-60	
Kay, G.A.	Helping the Weatherman (1st, 8vo, ibds, unpag, color, pep)	Volland	(1920)	Kay, G.A.	50-70	
Barbour, R.H.	House in the Hedge (1st, sm8vo, 251p, col frn, 3pl)	Moffat	1911	Kay, G.A.	30-50	*
Addington, S.	Jerry Juddikins (1st, 8vo, 65p, p-o, 4cp, pep)	McKay	(1926)	Kay, G.A.	30-45	
Kay, G.A.	Jolly Old Shadow Man (1st, 12mo, ibds, [39]p, color, pep)	Volland	(1920)	Kay, G.A.	50-70	
Lang, A.	My Own Fairy Book (1st, 8vo, 402p, rust cl, p-o, pep, 4cp)	McKay	(1927)	Kay, G.A.	30-45	*
Stokely, E.K.	Pantaloon (1st, sm4to, 168p, orang cl, 6cp, pep)	Doran	(1927)	Kay, G.A.	45-65	*
Kay, G.A.	Peter, Patter & Pixie (1st, lg4to, ibds, 22p, 5cp)	McBride	1931	Kay, G.A.	65-90	
Addington, S.	Pied Piper of Pudding Lane (1st, 8vo, p-o, 97p, 4cp, pep)	Atl. Month Pr.	(1923)	Kay, G.A.	30-45	
MacDonald, Geo.	Princess & Curdie (1st, 8vo, p-o, cloth, 274p, 4cp, pep)	McKay	[1926]	Kay, G.A.	40-60	
Addington, S.	Round the Year on Pudding Lane (1st, lg8vo, 231p, p-o, 9pl, pep)	Little/Brown	1924	Kay, G.A.	45-60	*
Bernard, F.S.	Through Cloud Mountain (1st, 4to, 215p, gilt, 8cp, pep)	Lippincott	1922	Kay, G.A.	45-65	
Donahey, M.D.	Through the Little Green Door (8vo, 176p, p-o, 3cp)	Barse	(1910)	Kay, G.A.	50-65	
Carroll, L.	Through the Looking Glass (1st, 8vo, 235p, red/gilt, 8cp, pep)	Lippincott	(1929)	Kay, G.A.	30-50	*
Leet, F.R.	To the Circus the Children Go (ob folio, wraps, color)	Saalfield	1931	Kay, G.A.	35-50	*
Addington, S.	Tommy Tingle-Tangle (1st, sq8vo, ibds, 39p, color, pep)	Volland	(1927)	Kay, G.A.	60-85	

AUTHOR	TITLE	PUBLISHER	DATE	ARTIST	PRICE	LC
Kay, G.A.	Us Kids at the Circus (1st, 8vo, ibds, 120p, color, pep)	Volland	(1927)	Kay, G.A.	60-80	*
Kay, G.A.	When the Sandman Comes (1st, 8vo, 183p, p-o, pep, 4cp)	Moffat	1916	Kay, G.A.	50-70	
Coatsworth, E.	Cat & the Captain (1st, 16mo, 95p, green cl, 3cp)	MacMillan	1927	Kaye, G.	35-50	*
Balch, Glenn	Brave Riders (1st {std}, sm8vo, 191p, green cl, b/w)	Crowell	(1959)	Keats, E.J.	25-45	*
Clymer, E.L.	Chester (1st, sm8vo, 141p, red cl, fp b/w)	Dodd	1954	Keats, E.J.	30-45	*
Eberle, I.	Grasses (1st, 8vo, green cl, 56p, brown illus)	Walck	1960	Keats, E.J.	35-60	*
Pine, Tillie S.	Indians Knew (1st, sm4to, teal cl, 32p, 2-color, pep)	Whittlesey	(1957)	Keats, E.J.	65-90	*
Lansing, Eliz.	Jubilant for Sure (1st {std}, 8vo, green cl, 148p, fp b/w)	Crowell	(1954)	Keats, E.J.	65-90	R*
Cherr, Pat	My Dog is Lost! (1st, lg8vo, beige cl, [48]p, 1-color)	Crowell	(1960)	Keats, E.J.	35-50	*
Murphey, E.A.	Nihal (1st, lg8vo, aqua cl, 39p, fp 2-color)	Crowell	(1960)	Keats, E.J.	45-65	*
Cheney, Cora	Peg-Legged Pirate of Sulu (1st {std}, sm8vo, 109p, b/w, cep)	Knopf	1960	Keats, E.J.	30-50	*
Lansing, Eliz.	Sure Thing for Shep (1st {std}, sm8vo, red cl, 177p, b/w)	Coward	(1956)	Keats, E.J.	35-50	*
Albee, George	Three Young Kings (1st {std}, 4to, 47p, yel cl, 1-color, pep)	Watts	1956	Keats, E.J.	45-60	*
Williams, Jay	Tournament of the Lions (1st, 8vo, black/gilt, 120p, 5 fp b/w)	Walck	1960	Keats, E.J.	35-50	*
Carpenter, Frances	Wonder Tales of Dogs & Cats (1st, 8vo, yellow cl, 255p, fp b/w)	Doubleday	(1955)	Keats, E.J.	35-50	*
Coatsworth, E.	Kitten Stand (1st, 8vo, ipcb, [28]p, color, pep)	Grosset/Dunlap	(1945)	Keeler, K.	35-50	*
Gates, J.S.	April Fool Doll (1st, 4to, 152p, red cl, p-o)	Bobbs-Merrill	(1909)	Keep, V.	50-70	
Gates, J.S.	Little Girl Blue Lives in the Woods... (1st, 16mo, 53p, 4cp)	Houghton	1910	Keep, V.	45-70	
Gates, J.S.	Little Girl Blue Plays I-Spy (1st, 16mo, 61p, color)	Houghton	1913	Keep, V.	45-60	*
Gates, J.S.	Little Red, White, Blue (1st, 4to, 118p, 9pl)	Bobbs-Merrill	(1906)	Keep, V.	50-65	
Goss, F.C.	Little St. Sunshine (1st, 8vo, green/gilt, 153p)	Bowen-Merrill	1902	Keep, V.	30-45	*
Gates, J.S.	Live Doll's House Party (1st, sm4to, red cl, 102p, p-o, 8pl)	Bobbs-Merrill	(1906)	Keep, V.	60-75	
Gates, J.S.	Live Doll's Play Days (1st, sm4to, p-o, red cl, 109p)	Bobbs-Merrill	(1908)	Keep, V.	60-75	
Gates, J.S.	Live Dolls in Fairyland (1st, 4to, p-o, 136p, 6cp)	Bobbs-Merrill	(1911)	Keep, V.	60-80	
Gates, J.S.	Live Dolls in Wonderland (1st, 8vo, 149p, p-o, 5pl)	Bobbs-Merrill	(1912)	Keep, V.	60-75	
Krag, M.A.	Martha-Jane: Nursery Nonsense (1st, ob4to, [24]p)	Bowen-Merrill	1897	Keep, V.	120-170	
Gates, J.S.	Story of the Live Dolls (1st, sm4to, 103p, p-o, b/w)	Bowen-Merrill	1901	Keep, V.	60-80	
Gates, J.S.	Story of the Lost Doll (1st, sm4to, red cl, p-o, 10pl)	Bobbs-Merrill	(1905)	Keep, V.	50-70	
Gates, J.S.	Story of the Three Dolls (1st, sm4to, red cl, 148p, p-o, 9pl)	Bobbs-Merrill	(1905)	Keep, V.	70-100	
Page, T.N.	Two Prisoners (1st, 8vo, 82p, teg, gilt, 5cp)	R.H. Russell	1903	Keep, V.	25-40	
Wheeler, Candace	Doubledarling & Dreamspinner (1st, 8vo, 167p blue cl, p-o, 11cp)	Fox Duffield	1905	Keith, D.W.	70-100	
Aesopus	Aesop's Fables (1st, 4to, 71p, color)	Duell/Sloan	(1944)	Kelen, E.	35-50	*
Mitchell, J.A.	Amos Judd (1st, 8vo, teg, 252p, 8cp)	Scribner	1901	Keller, A.I.	20-25	
Overton, G.	Anne Carmel (1st, sm8vo, 335p, teg, 6pl)	MacMillan	1903	Keller, A.I.	20-35	*
Chambers, Rbt.	Barbarians (1st, 8vo, 353p, 4pl)	Appleton	1917	Keller, A.I.	20-30	
Parrish, R.	Bob Hampton of Placer (1st, 8vo, 383p, 4cp)	McClurg	1906	Keller, A.I.	20-30	
Smith, F.H.	Caleb West, Master Diver (1st, 8vo, green cl, 378p, 6pl by...)	Houghton	1898	Keller, A.I.	25-45	
Dickens, C.	Christmas Carol (1st, 8vo, 130p, blue/gilt, teg, 8cp)	McKay	(1914)	Keller, A.I.	30-45	
Locke, Wm. J.	Fortunate Youth (1st, sm8vo, 352p, green/gilt, 8pl by...)	NY: J. Lane	1914	Keller, A.I.	30-45	*
Longfellow, H.W.	Hanging of the Crane (1st, 8vo, teg, p-o, 10cp)	Houghton	1907	Keller, A.I.	35-50	
Harte, Bret	Her Letter (1st, lg8vo, p-o, green/gilt, teg, unpag, col, pep)	Houghton	1905	Keller, A.I.	35-50	
Wilkins, M.E.	Jerome, A Poor Man (1st, 12mo, 506p)	Harper	1897	Keller, A.I.	30-45	
Hough, E.	Law of the Land (1st, 8vo, 416p, tan cl, 5pl)	Bobbs-Merrill	(1904)	Keller, A.I.	25-40	
Irving, W.	Legend of Sleepy Hollow (1st, sm8vo, 92p, p-o, pep, 14pl)	Bobbs-Merrill	(1906)	Keller, A.I.	75-100	
Nicholson, M.	Lords of High Decision (1st, 8vo, 503p, 4cp)	Doubleday/Page	1909	Keller, A.I.	20-30	*
Barnes, James	Loyal Traitor (1st, 12mo, 306p, 21pl)	Harper	1897	Keller, A.I.	25-40	*
Farnol, J.	Money Moon (1st, 4to, p-o, teg, 385p, 22pl)	Dodd	1911	Keller, A.I.	40-60	
Mitchell, S.W.	Red City (1st, 8vo, 421p, p-o, 10pl)	Century	1908	Keller, A.I.	20-30	
Nesbit, E.	Red House (1st AM, 12mo, 274p, green cl)	Harper	1902	Keller, A.I.	70-110	
Smith, F.H.	Romance of an Old Fashioned Gentleman (1st, 8vo, 213p, teg, 5cp)	Scribner	1907	Keller, A.I.	20-30	
Lindsey, Wm.	Severed Mantle (1st, lg8vo, 452p, 7cp)	Houghton	1909	Keller, A.I.	20-35	
Watson, H.B.M.	The Adventurers (1st, sm8vo, 298p, 20pl)	Harper	1899	Keller, A.I.	30-45	*
Dixon, Thomas	The Clansman (1st, 8vo, 374p, red cl, b/w)	Doubleday/Page	1905	Keller, A.I.	30-45	
Lowell, J.R.	The Courtin' (1st, 8vo, teg, bds/gilt, unpag, color, pep)	Houghton	1909	Keller, A.I.	30-45	
Wister, O.	The Virginian (1st, 8vo, 504p, tan cloth, 8pl)	MacMillan	1902	Keller, A.I.	150-200	
Green, A.K.	Woman in the Alcove (1st, 12mo, beige/gilt, 372p, 5pl)	Bobbs-Merrill	(1906)	Keller, A.I.	20-35	
O'Day, James	Daddy Long Legs Fun Songs (lg4to, ibds, color)	Chi: Witmark	1900	Keller, E.	120-180	
Boylan, G.D.	Yama Yama Land (1st, sq8vo, 200p, p-o, color)	Reilly/Britton	(1909)	Keller, E.	80-100	
Stockton, Frank	Kate Bonnet (1st, 8vo, 420p, b/w pl)	Appleton	1902	Keller/Potter	30-45	
Turner, Josie	Elsie Dinsmore on the Loose (1st, sm8vo, 166p)	Cape/Smith	(1930)	Kelley, E.	30-45	*
Kelly, R.T.	Egypt (1st, 8vo, gilt, teg, 246p, 75cp)	L: A&C Black	1902	Kelly, R.T.	65-90	
Stevenson, R.L.	Treasure Island (1st, lg8vo, 241p, col frn)	Sears	(1926)	Kelsey, C.W.	25-40	*
Disney, W.	Disney's Perri (1st, folio, ibds, [24]p, color, pep, GGB)	Simon/Schuster	(1957)	Kelsey, D.	100-140	*
Lincoln, J.	Cape Cod Ballads (1st [1st bk.], 8vo, yellow/gilt, 198p)	NJ: Brandt	1902	Kemble, E.W.	100-150	
Kemble, E.W.	Comical Coons (1st UK, ob4to, ibds, unpag, b/w)	L: Kegan Paul	1898	Kemble, E.W.	280-350	
Kemble, E.W.	Coon Alphabet (1st, sm4to, ibds, b/w)	R.H. Russell	1898	Kemble, E.W.	250-400	
Harris, J.C.	Daddy Jake the Runaway (1st, 8vo, 145p, cream bds, 19 b/w, cep)	Century	(1889)	Kemble, E.W.	120-165	*
Harris, J.C.	Daddy Jake the Runaway (1st UK, sq4to, 145p, b/w)	L: T.F. Unwin	1890	Kemble, E.W.	100-150	
Marquis, Don	Danny's Own Story (1st, 8vo, green cl, 333p, p-o, 16pl)	Doubleday/Page	1912	Kemble, E.W.	100-150	
Pratt, L.	Ezekiel Expands (1st, 8vo, 228p)	Houghton	1914	Kemble, E.W.	50-85	
Dunbar, P.L.	Folks from Dixie (1st, 12mo, 263p, 8pl)	Dodd	1898	Kemble, E.W.	150-185	
Dunbar, P.L.	Heart of Happy Hollow (1st, sm8vo, 309p, 6pl)	Dodd	1904	Kemble, E.W.	150-180	

AUTHOR	TITLE	PUBLISHER	DATE	ARTIST	PRICE	LC
Kemble, E.W.	Kemble's Coons (1st, ob4to, ibds, 31pl, b/w)	R.H. Russell	1896	Kemble, E.W.	225-350	
Kemble, E.W.	Kemble's Pickaninnies (1st, lg ob4to, 31pl, b/w)	R.H. Russell	1901	Kemble, E.W.	250-400	*
Kemble, E.W.	Kemble's Sketch Book (1st, lg ob8vo, tan buckram, 30pl)	R.H. Russell	1899	Kemble, E.W.	180-240	
Dix, D.	Mirandy (1st, 8vo, brown cl, 256p, 21pl)	Hearst	1914	Kemble, E.W.	35-50	
Dunne, F.P.	Mr. Dooley's Philosophy (1st, 12mo, red cl, 263p, b/w by…)	R.H. Russell	1900	Kemble, E.W.	25-40	
Harris, J.C.	On the Plantation (1st, 8vo, orange/gilt, 233p, b/w)	Appleton	1892	Kemble, E.W.	140-185	
Riley, J.W.	Poems Here at Home (1st, 8vo, green cl, 187p, teg, b/w)	Century	1893	Kemble, E.W.	50-80	
Brown, K.	Putter Perkins (1st, 12mo, green cl, 121p, 10pl)	Houghton	1923	Kemble, E.W.	30-50	*
Dunbar, P.L.	Strength of Gideon (1st, 8vo, 362p, gilt, 6pl)	Dodd	1900	Kemble, E.W.	180-265	
Kemble, E.W.	The Blackberries… (1st, ob4to, ibds, [36]p, 16cp)	R.H. Russell	1897	Kemble, E.W.	280-450	
Carleton, H.G.	Thompson Street Poker Club (1st, 8vo, 48p, ibds, 11 fp b/w)	White & Allen	1888	Kemble, E.W.	80-100	*
Edwards, Harry S.	Two Runaways (1st, 8vo, 246p, b/w pl)	Century	(1889)	Kemble, E.W.	45-65	*
Johnson, R.M.	Widow Guthrie (1st, sm8vo, blue/gilt, 309p, 6pl, cep)	Appleton	1890	Kemble, E.W.	30-45	*
Porter, G.S.	At the Foot of the Rainbow (1st, 8vo, 258p, yellow cl, 4cp)	Outing	1907	Kemp, O.	400-600	
Sewell, Anna	Black Beauty (1st, 8vo, 224p, blue/gilt, 24cp)	L: J.M. Dent	1915	Kemp-Welch, L.	100-130	
Fletcher, J.S.	Making of Matthais (1st, sm8vo, AEG, 141p, blue/gilt, b/w)	L: J. Lane	1898	Kemp-Welch, L.	30-50	
Nesbit, E.	Pussy & Doggy Tales (1st, 12mo, 132p, b/w)	L: J.M. Dent	1899	Kemp-Welch, L.	140-200	*
Kempson, F.C.	Sad Fate of Erica's Blackamoor (1st, ob folio, ibds, [40]p)	L: E. Arnold	1903	Kempson, F.C.	140-175	
Willett, Edward	Cat's Cradle Rhymes for Children (sm4to, ibds, 60p, fp color)	Worthington	1881	Kendrick, C.	75-130	*
Egan, Constance	Epaminondas & the Lettuces (1st, 16mo, 62p, brown bds)	L: Collins	[1938]	Kennedy, A.E.	50-70	*
Egan, Constance	Epaminondas & the Puppy (1st, 12mo, unpag, pep, color)	L: Collins	1959	Kennedy, A.E.	90-130	*
Egan, Constance	Epaminondas Helps in the Garden (1st, 16mo, 62p, blue bds)	L: Collins	[1937]	Kennedy, A.E.	50-70	*
Baum, L.F.	Army Alphabet (1st, lg4to, ibds, 29cp)	Geo. Hill	1900	Kennedy, H.	700-1000	
Baum, L.F.	Navy Alphabet (1st, lg4to, ibds, unpag, color)	Geo. Hill	1900	Kennedy, H.	700-1000	
Costello, C.J.	Old Mother Hubbard (4to, pict cl, color)	Chi: Jamieson	(1902)	Kennedy, H.O.	100-160	
Alcott, L.M.	Silver Pitchers (1st, 8vo, 365p, 8pl)	Little/Brown	1908	Kennedy, J.W.	30-45	
Aldington, R.	All Men are Enemies (1st {std}, 8vo, 574p, b/w, DJ)	Doubleday/Dor.	1933	Kent, R.	50-70	
Squires, F.	Architec-tonics (1st {1st bk.}, 12mo, gilt, 172p, col frn)	Comstock Co.	1914	Kent, R.	160-200	R
Pushkin, A.	Ballad of Yukon Jake (1st, 12mo, 36p, 2pl, pcb)	Coward	1928	Kent, R.	60-75	
Chappell, G.S.	Basket of Poses (1st, 4to, pcb, p-o, 109p, b/w)	A.& C. Boni	1924	Kent, R.	80-100	
Untermeyer, L.	Book of Noble Thoughts (1st, 8vo, 121p, ibds, 1-color, dep)	A.A. Group	(1946)	Kent, R.	30-50	
Voltaire, J.F.	Candide (1st, 8vo, 111p, maroon/gilt)	Random	1930	Kent, R.	45-60	*
Alexander, L.M.	Candy (1st, 8vo, cloth, 310p, 5pl, pep, DJ)	Dodd	1934	Kent, R.	60-80	
Chaucer, G.	Canterbury Tales (1st, lg8vo, 627p, b/w, DJ)	Garden City	1934	Kent, R.	60-80	
Robinson, S.	City Child (1st, 12mo, red/gilt, 64p, DJ)	Farrar/Rine.	1931	Kent, R.	65-80	
Rich, Edwin G.	Hans the Eskimo (1st, 8vo, 287p, blue cl, p-o, b/w)	Houghton	1934	Kent, R.	25-40	*
Kent, R.	It's Me O Lord… (1st, lg8vo, gilt, 617p, b/w)	Dodd	(1955)	Kent, R.	35-50	*
Melville, Herman	Moby Dick (1st, sm8vo, 822p, black/silver, DJ)	Random	1930	Kent, R.	90-120	
Kent, R.	N by E (1st, 8vo, white cl, 281p, DJ)	Brewer/Warren	1930	Kent, R.	80-100	
Kent, R.	Northern Christmas (1st, 12mo, [32]p, ipcb, 1-color, DJ)	A.A. Group	(1941)	Kent, R.	50-70	
Kent, R.	On Earth Peace… (1st, 12mo, [24]p, ibds, 1-color)	A.A. Group	(1942)	Kent, R.	35-50	
Shephard, E.	Paul Bunyon (1st, 8vo, 234p, fp b/w)	Harcourt	(1924)	Kent, R.	80-100	
Kent, R.	Rockwellkentiana (1st {std}, 4to, col frn, blue cl, DJ)	Harcourt	1933	Kent, R.	75-100	
Chappell, G.S.	Rollo in Society (1st, 16mo, p-o, 178p)	Putnam	1922	Kent, R.	60-85	R
Allen, R.B.	Saga of Gisli (1st {std}, lg8vo, 148p, uncut, b/w, DJ)	Harcourt	(1936)	Kent, R.	85-120	
Kent, R.	Salamina (1st {std}, 8vo, blue/silver, 336p, 23pl)	Harcourt	1935	Kent, R.	80-130	R
Kent, R.	This is my Own (1st {std}, 8vo, cream cl, 393p, DJ)	Duell/Sloan	(1940)	Kent, R.	100-140	
Kent, R.	Voyaging: Southward… (1st, 4to, yellow cl, 184p, pep)	Putnam	1924	Kent, R.	70-100	
Kent, R.	Wilderness (1st, 4to, teg, 217p, grey/gilt, pep)	Putnam	1920	Kent, R.	100-165	
Norris, C.G.	Zest (1st {std}, 8vo, 445p, pict cl, frn by…)	Doubleday/Dor.	1933	Kent, R.	35-50	
Smith, Wm. J.	Boy Blue's Book of Beasts (1st {std}, 8vo, 58p, fp 1-color, cep)	Little/Brown	(1957)	Kepes, J.A.	65-80	R*
Kepes, J.A.	Five Little Monkeys (1st {1st bk}, lg sq8vo, 32p, col, pep, CH)	Houghton	1952	Kepes, J.A.	70-100	*
Miller, Mary B.	Give a Guess (1st, 8vo, blue cl, [32]p, 1-color, dep)	Pantheon	1957	Kepes, J.A.	50-80	R*
Smith, Wm. J.	Laughing Time (1st {std}, 8vo, 54p, yellow cl, fp 1-color, cep)	Little/Brown	(1955)	Kepes, J.A.	65-80	R*
Smith, Wm. J.	Puptents & Pebbles (1st {std}, 4to, yellow cl, 32p, color, pep)	Little/Brown	(1959)	Kepes, J.A.	60-90	R*
McLeod, Emilie	Seven Remarkable Bears (1st, sq8vo, 46p, blue cl, fp 2-col, pep)	Houghton	1954	Kepes, J.A.	45-70	*
Kepes, J.A.	Two Little Birds & Three (1st, 8vo, 62p, blue cl, fp 1-color)	Houghton	1960	Kepes, J.A.	60-90	R*
Burgess, T.	Mother West Wind's Children (1st, 12mo, 243p, 7pl)	Little/Brown	1911	Kerr, G.	70-110	*
Burgess, T.	Mother West Wind's Neighbors (1st, 12mo, tan cl, 223p, 6pl)	Little/Brown	1913	Kerr, G.	70-110	
Baum, L.F.	Baum's American Fairy Tales (1st, 4to, [223]p, p-o, 16cp)	Bobbs-Merrill	(1908)	Kerr, G.F.	600-850	
Dunham, Curtis	Bobbie in Bugaboo Land (1st, lg8vo, grey cl, 215p, 11 pl)	Bobbs-Merrill	(1907)	Kerr, G.F.	90-120	*
Dunham, Curtis	Golden Goblin (1st, lg8vo, ipcb, 190p, 8cp)	Bobbs-Merrill	(1906)	Kerr, G.F.	80-100	
Burgess, T.	Mother West Wind's Animal Friends (1st, 12mo, 221p, 6pl)	Little/Brown	1912	Kerr, G.F.	100-135	
Burgess, T.	Old Mother West Wind (1st, 12mo, 169p, 7pl, PPP)	Little/Brown	(1910)	Kerr, G.F.	150-200	
Schlein, M.	Fast is Not a Ladybug (1st, sm8vo, ipcb, [34]p, 1-color, pep)	W.R. Scott	(1953)	Kessler, L.	30-45	*
Schlein, M.	Heavy is a Hippopotamus (1st, sm8vo, ipcb, unpag, 1-color, pep)	W.R. Scott	1954	Kessler, L.	50-80	R*
Schlein, M.	It's About Time (1st, sm8vo, [41]p)	W.R. Scott	1955	Kessler, L.	30-45	*
Ketchum, J.	Stick-in-the-Mud (1st, sm8vo, unpag, green cl, pep, 1-color)	W.R. Scott	(1953)	Ketchum, F.	30-50	*
Leacock, S.B.	Nonsense Novels (1st, 8vo, 176p, grey bds, gilt, 8 color)	L: Bodley Head	1921	Kettelwell, J.	65-90	
Fuller, O.M.	Book of Dragons (1st, 4to, green cl, 181p, 4cp, DJ)	McBride	1931	Key, A.	65-80	
Key, A.	Red Eagle (1st, 4to, 95p, ibds, pep, color)	Volland	(1930)	Key, A.	70-90	
Kidd, Will	Dickydidos (1st, folio, 94p, ibds, 22cp)	L: Richards	[1903]	Kidd, Will	250-400	*

ILLUSTRATOR: 72

AUTHOR	TITLE	PUBLISHER	DATE	ARTIST	PRICE	LC
Forrester, I.L.	Us Fellers (1st, 4to, blue cl, p-o, 150p, 7cp)	Jacobs	(1907)	Kilvert, C.	45-60	*
Wharton, E.	Fruit of the Tree (1st, 12mo, 633p, red/gilt, 3pl)	Scribner	1907	Kimball, A.	90-120	
Parrish, R.	Love Under Fire (1st, 8vo, 400p, 5cp)	McClurg	1911	Kimball, A.	20-30	*
Parrish, R.	My Lady of the South (1st, 8vo, 360p, tan cl, 4cp)	McClurg	1909	Kimball, A.	20-25	
Smith, F.H.	Wood Fire in No.3 (1st, sm8vo, 298p, teg, uncut, 9cp)	Scribner	1905	Kimball, A.	20-30	
Hichens, R.	Flames (1st, 8vo, 523p, pcb, cvr by...)	H. Stone	1897	Kimbrough, F.R.	45-60	
Magruder, Julia	Miss Ayr of Virginia (1st, 8vo, green cl, 395p, cvr by..)	H. Stone	1896	Kimbrough, F.R.	60-80	
Fort, Chas.	LO! (1st, 8vo, 411p, 12 illus, DJ)	NY: Kendall	(1931)	King, Alex.	100-150	
McEvoy, Joseph P.	Slams of Life... (1st, sm4to, 127p, uncut, 10 fp b/w)	Volland	(1919)	King, Frank	65-80	*
N/A	A Carol: Good King Wenceslas (4to, [26]p, wraps, p-o, 12 ticp)	L: L.B. Hill	[1920]	King, J.	300-450	
N/A	Arabian Nights (1st, 8vo, 501p, cvr by...)	L: Routledge	1904	King, J.	120-160	
Arcambeau, E.	Book of Bridges (1st, 4to, 149p, green cl, p-o, 18cp)	L: Gowans/Gray	1911	King, J.	270-320	
King, J.M.	City of the West (1st, 8vo, wraps, 27p, 24 ticp)	L: Foulis	1910	King, J.	150-200	*
Milton, J.	Comus (1st, 12mo, 83p, teg, gilt, 9pl)	L: Routledge	1906	King, J.	240-320	
Morris, Wm.	Defense of Guenevere (1st, 8vo, teg, 310p, red/gilt, 24pl)	L: J. Lane	1904	King, J.	280-350	
King, J.M.	Dwellings/Old World Town (8vo, 51p, wraps, 24 b/w)	L: Gowans/Gray	1909	King, J.	100-160	
Grimm Bros.	Fairy Tales (1st, 8vo, 511p, cvr by....)	L: Routledge	(1904)	King, J.	100-120	
Andersen, H.C.	Fairy Tales & Stories (2nd, 8vo, 572p, cvr by...)	L: Routledge	[1905]	King, J.	80-100	
Drummond, F.	Fringes of Paradise (1st, 12mo, ipcb, 48p, 4cp)	L: F. Muller	(1935)	King, J.	50-65	
King, J.M.	Grey City of the North (1st, 8vo, 51p, wraps, 26pl)	L: Foulis	(1910)	King, J.	130-200	
Evans, S.	High History of the Holy Grail (1st, 8vo, gilt, teg, 379p, 22pl)	L: Dent	1903	King, J.	450-600	
Wilde, O.	House of Pomegranates (1st, 4to, teg, 162p, gilt, 16 ticp, pep)	L: Methuen	(1915)	King, J.	600-800	
Wilde, O.	House of Pomegranates (1st AM, 4to, teg, 162p, gilt 16ticp, pep)	Brentano's	[1915]	King, J.	550-750	
King, J.M.	How Cinderella/Go to the Ball (1st, 8vo, 57p, teg, 16 ticp)	L: Foulis	(1924)	King, J.	300-500	
Keats, J.	Isabella... (1st, 12mo, 42p, wraps, uncut, 5cp)	L: Foulis	1907	King, J.	70-100	
Buchanan, G.	Jeptha (1st {1st illus bk.}, 8vo, blue/gilt, 130p, 5pl)	L: A. Gardner	[1903]	King, J.	220-350	
Hogg, J.	Kilmeny (1st, 16mo, 31p, 5cp)	L: Foulis	1911	King, J.	130-160	
King, J.M.	Legends of Flowers (1st, sm8vo, teg, p-o, 168p)	L: Foulis	1909	King, J.	100-140	
Hawtrey	Life of St. Mary Magdalen (1st, 12mo, gilt, 285p, cvr by...)	L: J. Lane	1904	King, J.	80-120	
King, J.M.	Little White Town of Never Weary (1st, 4to, 155p, 4 ticp, cep)	L: Harrap	(1917)	King, J.	300-450	
Marion	Mummy's Bedtime Story Book (1st, lg4to, ibds, 56p, pep, 12cp)	L: C. Palmer	(1920)	King, J.	400-600	
Shelley	Poems of Shelley (1st, 16mo, 244p, teg, purple/gilt, 8cp)	L: Jack	(1907)	King, J.	80-120	
Spencer, W.	Poems of Spencer (1st, 16mo, purple/gilt, 290p, teg, 8cp)	L: Jack	(1906)	King, J.	100-150	
Hogg, J.	Songs of Ettrick Shepherd (1st, 12mo, 151p, teg, 7 ticp)	L: Foulis	(1912)	King, J.	100-150	
Stowe, H.B.	Uncle Tom's Cabin (1st, 8vo, 529p, gilt, cvr by...)	L: Routledge	1904	King, J.	145-180	
Berry, E.	Careers of Cynthia (1st, sm8vo, red cl, 320p, 9 fp b/w)	Harcourt	(1932)	King, R.	25-40	*
Berry, E.	Illustrations of Cynthia (1st {std}, 8vo, 205p, 8 fp b/w)	Harcourt	(1931)	King, R.	20-30	*
Terhune, A.P.	The Woman (1st, 12mo, 341p, b/w pl)	Bobbs-Merrill	(1912)	King, W.B.	25-40	*
Kinney, T.& M.	Dance: Its Place in Art & Life (1st, 8vo, 334p, col frn)	Stokes	1914	Kinneys	30-45	
Bennett, R.A.	For the White Christ (1st, 8vo, p-o, 474p, 4cp)	McClurg	1906	Kinneys	20-30	
Taylor, C.B.	Nicanor, Teller of Tales (1st, 8vo, p-o, 422p, pep, 5cp)	McClurg	1906	Kinneys	20-30	
Parrish, R.	Prisoners of Chance (1st, 8vo, yellow cl, 423p, 4cp)	McClurg	1908	Kinneys	25-40	
Doyle, A.C.	Sir Nigel (1st AM, 8vo, 346p, 6pl)	McClure	1906	Kinneys	70-90	
Parrish, R.	When Wilderness was King (1st, 8vo, 388p, uncut, 6cp, dep)	McClurg	1904	Kinneys	20-30	
Kipling, R.	Kim (1st AM, 4to, teg, 460p, uncut, 10 tipl)	Doubleday/Page	1901	Kipling, J.L.	180-220	
Kipling, R.	Second Jungle Book (1st, 8vo, 238p, blue/gilt, AEG)	L: MacMillan	1895	Kipling, J.L.	180-250	
Kipling, R.	Tales of the Punjab (1st, 8vo, 359p, black/gilt, 5pl)	L: MacMillan	1894	Kipling, J.L.	160-220	
Kipling, R.	Just So Stories... (1st, sq4to, red cl, 249p, 22pl)	L: MacMillan	1902	Kipling, R.	200-250	
Kipling, R.	Just So Stories... (1st AM, lg8vo, green cl, 249p, b/w)	Doubleday/Page	1902	Kipling, R.	180-250	R
Berlic-Mazuranic	Croation Tales of Long Ago (1st, 8vo, 259p, 10 ticp)	L: T.F. Unwin	1924	Kirin, V.	150-185	
Craik, D.	Adventures of a Brownie (1st, 4to, teg, 281p, p-o, 14 ticp)	Lippincott	1922	Kirk, M.L.	80-100	
Carroll, L.	Alice/Wonderland (1st, 8vo, 247p, grey/gilt, 12cp)	Stokes	(1904)	Kirk, M.L.	140-200	
N/A	All Shakespeare's Tales (1st, lg8vo, p-o, 453p, 11cp)	Stokes	(1911)	Kirk, M.L.	70-100	
Perry, S.G.	Angel of Christmas (1st, 12mo, p-o, 4cp)	Stokes	1917	Kirk, M.L.	25-40	
Montgomery, L.M.	Anne's House of Dreams (1st, 8vo, 346p, p-o, col frn)	Stokes	(1917)	Kirk, M.L.	90-140	
MacDonald, Geo.	Back of the North Wind (1st, 8vo, 352p, gilt, pep, teg, 12cp)	Lippincott	1909	Kirk, M.L.	75-100	
De La Rame, L.	Bimbi (1st, 8vo, 212p, red/gilt, 8cp)	Lippincott	1910	Kirk, M.L.	35-50	*
Chaucer, G.	Canterbury Pilgrims (1st, 4to, p-o, 310p, 12cp)	Stokes	(1914)	Kirk, M.L.	65-80	
Stevenson, R.L.	Child's Garden of Verses (1st, 8vo, 191p, teg, gilt, 8cp)	Lippincott	1919	Kirk, M.L.	80-120	
Irving, W.	Child's Rip Van Winkle (1st, 8vo, 39p, red cl, p-o, 12cp)	Stokes	(1908)	Kirk, M.L.	70-100	
Hume, F.	Chronicles of Fairy-Land (1st, 8vo, 191p, teg, gilt, pep, 8cp)	Lippincott	1911	Kirk, M.L.	90-145	
Spyri, J.	Cornelli... (1st {Gift ed.}, 4to, teg, 275p, p-o, pep, 14 ticp)	Lippincott	1921	Kirk, M.L.	65-90	
Molesworth, M.	Cuckoo Clock (1st, 8vo, teg, red/gilt, 283p, pep, 8cp)	Lippincott	1914	Kirk, M.L.	35-50	*
Dowd, E.	Doodles (1st, sm8vo, 347p, grey cl, col frn)	Houghton	1915	Kirk, M.L.	35-50	
Spyri, J.	Dora (1st, 8vo, red/gilt, 216p, 8cp)	Lippincott	(1924)	Kirk, M.L.	30-45	*
Montgomery, L.M.	Emily Climbs (1st, sm8vo, green cl, 312p, col frn & p-o by)	Stokes	1925	Kirk, M.L.	70-100	
Montgomery, L.M.	Emily of New Moon (1st, sm8vo, 351p, col frn & p-o by...)	Stokes	1923	Kirk, M.L.	70-100	
Montgomery, L.M.	Emily's Quest (1st, sm8vo, 310p, green cl, p-o & col frn by...)	Stokes	1927	Kirk, M.L.	65-80	*
Andersen, H.C.	Fairy Tales (1st, 8vo, 219p, teg, pep, cp)	Lippincott	1911	Kirk, M.L.	100-140	
Lounsberry, A.	Frank & Bessie's Forester (1st, sm8vo, 191p, p-o & frn by...)	Stokes	(1912)	Kirk, M.L.	30-45	
Spyri, J.	Gritli's Chldren (1st {Gift ed.}, 4to, 264p, p-o, teg, 14cp pep)	Lippincott	(1924)	Kirk, M.L.	70-100	
Swift, J.	Gulliver's Travels (1st, 8vo, 221p, col frn, cp)	Lippincott	1918	Kirk, M.L.	60-75	*

AUTHOR	TITLE	PUBLISHER	DATE	ARTIST	PRICE	LC
Spyri, J.	Heidi (1st, 8vo, 318p, 8cp)	Lippincott	1915	Kirk, M.L.	25-40	*
Spyri, J.	Heidi (1st {Gift ed.}, sm4to, gilt, 318p, teg, 14 ticp, pep)	Lippincott	1919	Kirk, M.L.	80-120	
Longfellow, H.W.	Hiawatha (1st, sm4to, 313p, p-o, 11cp)	Stokes	(1910)	Kirk, M.L.	70-100	
Tennyson, A.	Idylls of the King (1st, 4to, black cl, p-o, 394p, 12 ticp, pep)	Stokes	(1912)	Kirk, M.L.	80-120	
Gellibrand, E.	J. Cole (1st, 8vo, 86p, beige cl, 4cp)	Lippincott	1917	Kirk, M.L.	30-45	
Perry, S.G.	Kind Adventure (1st, 12mo, 318p, green cl, p-o, 4cp)	Stokes	(1914)	Kirk, M.L.	45-60	
Noseworthy, F.	Land of Play (1st, 4to, 128p, p-o, blue cl, 10cp)	Cupples	(1911)	Kirk, M.L.	70-100	
Ogden, Ruth	Little Pierre & Big Peter (1st, 8vo, p-o, 367p, 5cp, pep)	Stokes	(1915)	Kirk, M.L.	50-75	
Spyri, J.	Mazli (1st {Gift ed.}, sm4to, 320p, teg, p-o, 14cp, pep)	Lippincott	(1923)	Kirk, M.L.	80-100	
Spyri, J.	Moni the Goat Boy (1st, 12mo, red cl, 72p, 4cp)	Lippincott	1916	Kirk, M.L.	35-50	*
Ingelow, J.	Mopsa the Fairy (1st, lg8vo, teg, 257p, 10cp, pep)	Lippincott	1910	Kirk, M.L.	80-100	
De La Rame, M.	Nurnberg Stove (1st, 12mo, 96p, 4cp)	Lippincott	1916	Kirk, M.L.	20-35	
Collodi, C.	Pinocchio (1st {Gift ed.}, lg8vo, 234p, p-o, teg, 14 ticp)	Lippincott	1920	Kirk, M.L.	100-140	
MacDonald, Geo.	Princess & Curdie (1st, 8vo, 305p, gilt, 12cp)	Lippincott	1908	Kirk, M.L.	70-100	
MacDonald, Geo.	Princess & Goblin (1st, 8vo, red/gilt, 305p, teg, pep, 12cp)	Lippincott	1907	Kirk, M.L.	80-120	
Montgomery, L.M.	Rainbow Valley (1st, sm8vo, 341p, col frn & p-o by...)	Stokes	1919	Kirk, M.L.	70-100	
Montgomery, L.M.	Rilla of Ingleside (1st, sm8vo, 370p, col frn)	Stokes	(1921)	Kirk, M.L.	80-100	
Burnett, F.H.	Secret Garden (1st, 8vo, p-o, teg, 375p, gilt, 4cp)	Stokes	(1911)	Kirk, M.L.	300-500	
Darton, H.	Story o/t Canterbury Pilgrims (1st, 4to, p-o, 310p, pep, 10cp)	Stokes	(1914)	Kirk, M.L.	80-120	
Longfellow, H.W.	Story of Evangeline (1st, 4to, p-o, 260p, 11cp)	Stokes	(1913)	Kirk, M.L.	100-140	*
Carroll, L.	Through the Looking Glass (1st, 8vo, gilt, p-o, 271p, 12cp)	Stokes	(1905)	Kirk, M.L.	200-300	
Spyri, J.	Vinzi (1st, 8vo, 296p, red cl, 8cp)	Lippincott	1923	Kirk, M.L.	20-30	*
Kingsley, C.	Water Babies (1st, 8vo, teg, 316p, 8cp, pep)	Lippincott	1917	Kirk, M.L.	70-100	
Sedberry, J.H.	Under the Flag of the Cross (1st, 8vo, blue/gilt, 10pl)	C.M. Clark	1908	Kirkpatrick, W.	65-90	
Hudson, W.H.	Disappointed Squirrel (1st, 4to, p-o, 144p, 8 ticp, pep)	Doran	(1925)	Kirmse, M.	50-75	
Atkinson, E.	Greyfriars Bobby (1st, lg8vo, red cl, 269p, uncut, 4pl)	Harper	1929	Kirmse, M.	25-40	*
Terhune, A.P.	Heart of a Dog (1st, 8vo, 249p, 8 ticp)	Doran	(1924)	Kirmse, M.	25-40	
Terhune, A.P.	My Friend the Dog (1st {std}, lg8vo, gilt, 317p, 8 ticp, pep)	Harper	1926	Kirmse, M.	25-45	*
Eberle, I.	Our Oldest Friends (1st, sm8vo, 146p, 1-color)	Holiday House	(1942)	Kirmse, M.	20-30	*
L'Hommedieu, D.	Scampy the Little Black Cocker (1st, sm4to, ibds, 62p, pep, col)	Lippincott	(1939)	Kirmse, M.	60-90	*
Wyss, J.D.	Swiss Family Robinson (8vo, green bds, 291p, gilt, 6cp, 8pl)	Nister/Dutton	[1900]	Kley, H.	65-80	
Thompson, Kay	Eloise (1st {std}, 4to, 65p, white cloth, color, pep)	Simon-Schuster	1955	Knight, H.	100-150	*
Thompson, Kay	Eloise at Christmastime (1st {std}, 4to, red ibds, [52]p, col)	Random	(1958)	Knight, H.	120-160	
Thompson, Kay	Eloise in Moscow (1st {std}, 4to, [66]p, ibds, pep, color)	Simon/Schuster	1959	Knight, H.	120-165	
Thompson, Kay	Eloise in Paris (1st {std}, 4to, red pcb, [65]p, pep)	Simon/Schuster	1957	Knight, H.	130-165	
MacDonald, Betty	Hello, Mrs. Piggle-Wiggle (1st {std}, 8vo, green cl, 119p, col)	Lippincott	(1957)	Knight, H.	60-110	*
Gendel, Evelyn	Tortoise & Turtle (1st {std}, 4to, ibds, [64]p, color, pep)	Simon/Schuster	1960	Knight, H.	35-50	*
Gury, Jeremy	Wonderful World of Aunt Tuddy (1st {std}, 4to, ibds, color)	Random	(1958)	Knight, H.	45-70	*
Haines, Alice C.	Boys (1st, lg ob4to, ibds, 8cp)	Stokes	(1905)	Knipe, E.B.	80-120	
Knipe, A.A.	Cavalier Maid (1st, 8vo, 255p, 6pl)	MacMillan	1919	Knipe, E.B.	25-40	
Chambers, Rbt.	Forest-Land (1st, 4to, ipcb, 118p, 8cp, pep)	Appleton	1905	Knipe, E.B.	70-100	
Haines, Alice C.	Girls (1st, lg4to, ipcb, 4cp)	Stokes	(1905)	Knipe, E.B.	80-100	
Knipe, A.A.	Luck of Denewood (1st, 8vo, brown cl, b/w)	Century	1921	Knipe, E.B.	30-45	
Knipe, E.B.	May Flower Maid (1st, 8vo, 297p, blue cl, 4pl)	Century	1920	Knipe, E.B.	30-45	
Knipe, A.A.	Remember Rhymes (1st, 4to, brown/gilt, 80p, 4cp, pep)	Penn	1914	Knipe, E.B.	75-100	
Olmstead, M.	Land of Never Was (1st, sm4to, p-o, 148p, 12cp, pep)	Jacobs	(1908)	Knipe, H.A.	60-90	
Olmstead, M.	Land of Really True (1st, sm4to, p-o, 187p, 12cp, pep)	Jacobs	(1909)	Knipe, H.A.	40-65	
Sabin, E.H.	Magical Man of Mirth (1st, 8vo, p-o, 233p, 8cp, pep)	Jacobs	(1910)	Knipe, H.A.	50-65	
Sabin, E.H.	Queen of the City of Mirth (1st, 8vo, p-o, 164p, 8cp)	Jacobs	(1911)	Knipe, H.A.	50-80	
Asbjornsen, P.C.	Norse Fairy Tales (1st, sm8vo, 463p, 8cp, 20pl, pep)	L: Freemantle	1910	Knowles, H.& R.	200-300	
Lagerlof, Selma	Christ Legends (1st, 8vo, 244p, blue cl, b/w)	L: E. Matthews	1930	Knowles, H.J.	45-60	*
Pedley, M.	Land of Goodness Knows Where (1st, 8vo, 117p, col frn, b/w)	L: Newnes	(1923)	Knowles, H.J.	90-135	
Knowles, H.	Peeps into Fairyland (1st, lg4to, 89p, tan/gilt, 6cp, pep)	L: Butterworth	(1924)	Knowles, H.J.	500-700	
Mother Goose	Mother Goose Rhymes (1st, 8vo, 199p, b/w)	Baker/Tayler	1911	Knowles, M.	80-120	*
Mother Goose	Mother Goose Rhymes (1st, 8vo, 206p, cp)	NY: Noble	1917	Knowles, M.	70-110	R*
Lee, H.	Legends from Fairyland (1st, 8vo, 276p, blue/gilt, 17pl, pep)	L: Chatto	1907	Knowles, R.L.	180-240	
Asbjornsen, P.C.	Norse Fairy Tales (16mo, ibds, 8cp)	L: Routledge	[1920]	Knowles, R.L.	160-200	
Mason, E.	Old-World Love Stories (1st, 8vo, 282p, gilt, teg, 8 ticp)	L: J.M. Dent	1913	Knowles, R.L.	150-200	
Kennedy, M.	Forest Beyond the Woodlands (1st, 8vo, 152p, pcb, 14pl)	Knopf	1921	Knowlton, V.	30-45	*
Bontemps, A.	Slappy Hooper... (1st, ob8vo, 44p, color, pep)	Houghton	1946	Koering, U.	45-70	*
Bacheller, I.	Charge It (1st, 12mo, p-o, 192p, b/w)	Harper	1912	Koerner	20-35	
Snow, Jack	Magical Mimics in Oz (1st, 8vo, grey cl, p-o, 243p)	Reilly/Lee	(1946)	Kramer, F.	260-400	
Snow, Jack	Shaggy Man of Oz (1st, 4to, grey cl, p-o, 254p)	Reilly/Lee	(1949)	Kramer, F.	280-400	
Kraus, Robert	I, Mouse (1st, 12mo, ibds, 32p, b/w)	Harper	(1958)	Kraus, R.	30-50	*
Carroll, L.	Alice/Wonderland (1st, 8vo, 150p, color)	Random	(1946)	Kredel F.	45-70	*
Roosevelt, Eleanor	Christmas (1st {std}, 24mo, ibds, 42p, 8 fp b/w, dep)	Knopf	1940	Kredel, F.	30-45	
Grimm Bros.	Fairy Tales (1st, 8vo, 363p, 10cp, cep)	Grosset/Dunlap	(1945)	Kredel, F.	60-90	R*
Steele, Wm. O.	Golden Root (1st {std}, sm8vo, 76p)	Aladdin	1951	Kredel, F.	25-40	*
Wheeler, Opal	H.M.S. Pinafore (1st {std}, 4to, 96p, color, DJ)	Dutton	1946	Kredel, F.	25-40	
Hoffman, H.	Slovenly Peter (1st {std}, lg8vo, ibds, [30]p, color)	Harper	1935	Kredel, F.	100-140	*
Lamb, C.	Tales from Shakespeare (1st, 8vo, 296p, color, pep)	Garden City	1939	Kredel, F.	25-45	*
Gurko, Leo	Tom Paine, Freedom's Apostle (1st {std}, 8vo, 213p, b/w, NH)	Crowell	(1957)	Kredel, F.	45-60	*

AUTHOR	TITLE	PUBLISHER	DATE	ARTIST	PRICE	LC
Snedeker, C.D.	White Isle (1st {std}, sm8vo, 271p, pep, b/w pl)	Doubleday/Dor.	1940	Kredel, F.	20-35	*
Boyle, Kay	Youngest Camel (1st {std}, 8vo, 96p, beige cl, 6cp)	Little/Brown	1939	Kredel, F.	20-35	
Schmidt, S.L.	Secret of Silver Peak (1st, sm8vo, 334p, rust cl, b/w)	Random	(1938)	Kreis, H.	25-40	*
Fyleman, R.	Katy Kruse Play Book (1st AM, 4to, p-o, 32p, 12cp)	McKay	(1930)	Kruse, K.	120-165	*
Fyleman, R.	Katy Kruse Play Book (1st, 4to, ibds, p-o, 32p, 12cp)	L: Harrap	(1930)	Kruse, K.	120-165	*
Farjeon, E.	Perfect Zoo (1st, ob4to, red cl, p-o, 31p, 12cp)	McKay	(1929)	Kruse, K.	120-160	
Scott, Sally	Benjie & his Family (1st {std}, 8vo, yellow cl, [62]p, fp b/w)	Harcourt	(1952)	Krush, B.	25-40	*
Scott, Sally	Rip & Royal (1st {std}, 8vo, 58p, tan cl, b/w)	Harcourt	(1950)	Krush, B.	25-45	*
Scott, Sally	What Susan Wanted (1st {std}, sm8vo, pink cl, 36p, fp b/w)	Harcourt	(1956)	Krush, B.	30-50	*
Norton, Mary	Borrowers Afield (1st AM {std}, 8vo, 215p, green cl, b/w, DJ)	Harcourt	(1955)	Krush, B.& J.	50-80	
Norton, Mary	Borrowers Afloat (1st AM {std}, 8vo, 191p, b/w, DJ)	Harcourt	(1959)	Krush, B.& J.	50-80	
Enright, E.	Gone-Away Lake (1st {std}, 8vo, 192p, green cl, b/w, NH)	Harcourt	(1957)	Krush, B.& J.	45-60	*
Untermeyer, L.	Magic Circle (1st, sm8vo, 288p, fp b/w)	Harcourt	(1952)	Krush, B.& J.	30-45	*
Sorensen, Virginia	Miracles on Maple Hill (1st {std}, 8vo, 180p, b/w, NM)	Harcourt	(1956)	Krush, B.& J.	50-85	R*
Kramer, N. (ed.)	Storybook (1st, lg8vo, 160p, b/w, cep)	J. Messner	(1955)	Krush, B.& J.	30-45	*
Norton, Mary	The Borrowers (1st AM {std}, 8vo, 180p, blue cl, b/w, DJ)	Harcourt	(1953)	Krush, B.& J.	50-80	
Chambers, M.C.	Boy Heroes of Chapultepec (1st {std}, 8vo, 182p, 1-color, pep)	Winston	(1953)	Krush, J.	25-40	*
Scott, Sally	Chica (1st {std}, 8vo, 114p, rust cl, fp b/w)	Harcourt	(1954)	Krush, J.	25-45	*
Trease, G.	Secret Fiord (1st AM {std}, sm8vo, 241p)	Harcourt	(1950)	Krush, J.	25-45	*
Trease, G.	Trumpets in the West (1st AM {std}, sm8vo, 239p)	Harcourt	(1947)	Krush, J.	30-45	*
Kjelgaard, J.A.	Big Red (1st, 8vo, 231p, tan cl, b/w, pep)	Holiday House	(1945)	Kuhn, B.	20-30	*
Kunhardt, D.	Junket is Nice (1st, sm ob4to, ibds, [63]p, 1-color)	Harcourt	1933	Kunhardt, D.	65-100	*
Kunhardt, D.	Lucky Mrs. Ticklefeather (1st, sm ob4to, ibds, [63]p, 1-color)	Harcourt	1935	Kunhardt, D.	65-100	*
Kunhardt, D.	Now Open the Box (1st, sm ob4to, [61]p, ipcb, color)	Harcourt	1934	Kunhardt, D.	65-100	*
Kunhardt, D.	Wise Old Aard-Vark (1st, ob4to, ibds, 62p, 1-color)	Viking	1936	Kunhardt, D.	100-150	
Rockwood, Roy	Through Space to Mars (1st, sm8vo, 248p, blue cl, 4pl)	Cupples	(1910)	Kuser, G.M.	65-90	*
Andersen, H.C.	Fairy Tales (1st, lg8vo, 367p, 24cp)	Penn	(1930)	Kutcher, B.	45-60	*
Wilde, O.	House of Pomegranates (1st, 8vo, black/gilt, 180p, 16pl, pep)	Dodd	1925	Kutcher, B.	45-60	
Moore, T.	Lalla Rookh (1st, 4to, 179p, red/gilt, uncut, 16pl, pep)	MacVeagh/Dial	1930	Kutcher, B.	45-60	
Shakespeare, Wm.	Venus & Adonis (1st, 4to, red cl, 112p, pep, 12cp)	Macveagh/Dial	1930	Kutcher, B.	30-45	*
Clement, Marg.	Flowers of Chivalry (1st, 4to, ipcb, 72p, color, cep)	Doubleday/Dor.	1934	L'Hardy, G.& P.	50-85	*
Atkins, E.H.	Pot of Gold (1st, 8vo, p-o, 164p, 4cp, 6pl, cep)	Stokes	1930	LaDow, St. C.	45-60	*
Bowman, J.C.	John Henry... (1st, 8vo, t.e. red, 288p, 2cp, 12pl)	Whitman	1942	LaGrone, R.	30-45	
N/A	Tales of Hoffman (4to, 207p, 10cp)	L: Harrap	(1932)	Laboccetta, M.	120-160	
Baker, C.	Magic Image from India (1st, 4to, 163p, 5cp)	Stern	1909	Lachman, H.B.	65-90	*
Laird, Rowena	Stuffy (1st, sm4to, [32]p, p-o, color)	Wm. Morrow	1945	Laird, R.	25-40	
Dodge, Louis	Everychild (1st, 4to, 284p, 6cp, pep, uncut, SC)	Scribner	1921	Laite, B.F.	50-70	*
Hewlett, P.	Grandmother's Fairy Tales (1st, 4to, 116p, 8cp)	L: Heinemann	1915	Lalan, M.	100-140	
Lamb, Tom	Jolly Kid Alphabet (1st, lg ob4to, ibds, color)	Volland	[1930]	Lamb, T.	200-300	
Higgins, Alice	Runaway Rhymes (1st, 8vo, 127p, red bds, gilt, pep, 14 fp col)	Volland	(1931)	Lamb, T.	65-80	
Lamb, Tom	Tale of Bingo (1st, 8vo, ibds, 120p, color)	Volland	(1927)	Lamb, T.	65-80	*
Lambert, H.G.C.	Peter Pixie at Play (4to, ibds, p-o, 6cp, pep)	L: Gale	[1910]	Lambert, M.	165-220	*
Saint-Exupery, A.	Flight to Arras (1st AM, 8vo, 255p, 13pl, pep)	Reynal/Hitch.	(1942)	Lamotte, B.	65-80	*
LeFevre, A.	Puzzling Pair (1st, sq8vo, 144p, b/w)	Revell	1898	Lance, E.	20-30	*
Kjelgaard, J.A.	Snow Dog (1st, 8vo, 236p, olive cl, b/w, pep)	Holiday House	(1948)	Landau, J.	20-25	*
Dawson, Coningsby	Little House (1st, 8vo, pcb, p-o, 127p, 8pl, pep)	NY: J. Lane	1920	Langdale, S.	25-40	*
Graham, E.	Night Adventures of Alexis (sm4to, 34p, 9cp)	L: Faber/Gwyer	1925	Langlands, W.	40-65	*
Langley, Noel	Tale/Land of Green Ginger (1st AM, lg4to, 143p, green cl, col)	Wm. Morrow	1938	Langley, N.	140-175	*
Crawford, P.	Hello, the Boat! (1st, 8vo, 227p, tan cl, pep, NH)	Holt	(1938)	Laning, E.	45-65	*
Potter, B.	Wag by Wall (1st {std}, 12mo, [30]p, buckram, p-o, t-i frn)	Horn Book	1944	Lankes, J.J.	100-165	
Wells, H.G.	When the Sleeper Wakes (1st AM, 8vo, red/gilt, 328p, 3pl)	Harper	1899	Lanos, H.	180-220	
Gates, Doris	Blue Willow (1st, 8vo, 172p, blue cl, 10pl, pep, DJ, NH)	Viking	1940	Lantz, P.	50-80	
Holdridge, Betty	Island Boy (1st, 8vo, 110p, green cl, 1-color, pep)	Holiday House	(1942)	Lantz, P.	20-35	*
Means, F.C.	Knock at the Door, Emmy (1st, 8vo, 240p, tan cl, b/w)	Houghton	1956	Lantz, P.	30-45	*
Clark, A.N.	Little Navajo Bluebird (1st, 8vo, 143p)	Viking	1943	Lantz, P.	30-45	*
Edmonds, W.D.	Matchlock Gun (1st {std}, sm4to, 50p, dp color, pep, NM)	Dodd	1941	Lantz, P.	65-110	
Andersen, H.C.	Ugly Duckling (1st AM, ob4to, ibds, 54p, 24 fp color)	MacMillan	1955	Larsen, J.	50-75	*
Flack, M.	I See a Kitty (1st, sq12mo, ibds, [16]p, color)	Garden City	1943	Larsson, K.	25-40	*
Flack, M.	Pedro (1st, 8vo, blue cl, 96p, dp color, pep, DJ)	MacMillan	1940	Larsson, K.	45-60	
Flack, M.	Up in The Air (1st, lg8vo, blue cl, [40]p, color)	MacMillan	1935	Larsson, K.	25-40	
Sears, P.M.	Downy Woodpecker (1st, 8vo, 43p, 2-color, cep)	Holiday House	(1953)	Latham, B.	25-40	*
Black, I.S.	Dusty & his Friends (1st, sm8vo, [56]p)	Holiday House	(1950)	Latham, B.	20-30	*
Fiedler, Jean	Green Thumb Story (1st, sm8vo, 38p, red cl, 2-color, pep)	Holiday House	1952	Latham, B.	20-25	*
Conklin, Gladys	I Like Caterpillars (1st, sm4to, yellow cl, [26]p, color)	Holiday House	(1958)	Latham, B.	25-45	*
Black, I.S.	Maggie, Mischievous Magpie (1st, sm8vo, [61]p, grn cl, b/w, cep)	Holiday House	(1949)	Latham, B.	35-60	R*
Marcher, M.W.	Monarch Butterfly (1st, 8vo, 42p, green cl, 2-color)	Holiday House	(1954)	Latham, B.	30-50	R*
Duplaix, L.	Pedro, Nina & Perrito (1st, lg4to, [48]p, ibds, fp color, pep)	Harper	1939	Latham, B.	80-100	*
Sears, P.M.	Tree Frog (1st, 8vo, 45p, green cl, 2-color)	Holiday House	(1954)	Latham, B.	35-50	R*
LeFevre, A.	Odd One (1st, sq8vo, uncut, 142p)	Revell	1898	Lathbury, M.	30-45	*
Lathbury, M.A.	April Skies (1st, 4to, ibds, [25]p, 12 chromos)	Worthington	1889	Lathbury, M.A.	100-145	
Lathrop, D.	Angel in the Woods (1st {std}, 8vo, red cl, [48]p, fp b/w, cep)	MacMillan	1947	Lathrop, D.	40-60	
Fish, H.D.	Animals of the Bible (1st, 4to, [65]p, gilt, CM)	Stokes	1937	Lathrop, D.	120-165	

AUTHOR	TITLE	PUBLISHER	DATE	ARTIST	PRICE	LC
Fish, H.D.	Animals of the Bible (1st UK, 4to, aqua/gilt, [66]p, pep)	L: OUP	1938	Lathrop, D.	100-135	
Cabot, E.	Balloon Moon (1st, 8vo, 99p, blue/gilt, col frn, fp b/w)	Holt	(1927)	Lathrop, D.	50-80	
De La Mare, W.	Bells & Grass (1st AM, 8vo, p-o, 144p, b/w, pep, DJ)	Viking	1942	Lathrop, D.	60-85	
Lathrop, D.	Bouncing Betsy (1st, ob4to, [41]p, 16pl, DJ)	MacMillan	1936	Lathrop, D.	60-80	
Field, R.	Branches Green (1st, 8vo, green cl, 66p, 12 b/w, DJ)	MacMillan	1934	Lathrop, D.	70-90	
Lathrop, D.	Colt from Moon Mountain (1st, 8vo, [62]p, b/w, pep, DJ)	MacMillan	1941	Lathrop, D.	140-175	
De La Mare, W.	Crossings... (1st, lg8vo, 170p, teg, blue/gilt, col frn)	Knopf	1923	Lathrop, D.	70-120	
Lathrop, D.	Dog in the Tapestry Garden (1st, sm4to, red cl, b/w)	MacMillan	1942	Lathrop, D.	30-55	*
De La Mare, W.	Down-Adown-Derry (1st, 4to, 190p, blue/gilt, teg, 3cp, 32pl)	L: Constable	(1922)	Lathrop, D.	100-145	
De La Mare, W.	Down-Adown-Derry (1st AM, 8vo, 195p, gilt, uncut, col frn)	Holt	1922	Lathrop, D.	70-100	R
De La Mare, W.	Dutch Cheese (1st {std}, 4to, 75p, green/gilt, 4cp)	Knopf	1931	Lathrop, D.	70-100	
Farjeon, E.	Fair of St. James (1st, 8vo, 310p, green/gilt, b/w)	Stokes	1932	Lathrop, D.	50-80	
Lathrop, D.	Fairy Circus (1st {1st bk.}, ob8vo, gilt, 67p, 8cp, 12pl, NH)	MacMillan	1931	Lathrop, D.	140-200	
Mukerji, D.G.	Fierce Face (1st {std}, 8vo, 77p, green cl, pep, DJ)	Dutton	1936	Lathrop, D.	80-115	
Lathrop, D.	Follow the Brook (1st {std}, sm4to, blue cl, 40p, fp b/w)	MacMillan	(1960)	Lathrop, D.	35-60	*
Snedeker, C.D.	Forgotten Daughter (1st {std}, 8vo, 309p, col frn, 3pl, pep, NH)	Doubleday/Dor.	1933	Lathrop, D.	60-85	
Burlingame, E.W.	Grateful Elephant (1st, 4to, 172p, col frn, 10pl)	Yale U. Press	1923	Lathrop, D.	85-120	
Fleuron, S.	Grim: Story of a Pike (1st, sm8vo, green cl, 186p, 4pl)	Knopf	1921	Lathrop, D.	45-65	
Mandal, S.R.	Happy Flute (1st, lg8vo, 54p, tan cl, 10 fp b/w, pep, DJ)	Stokes	1939	Lathrop, D.	80-100	
Lathrop, D.	Hide and Go Seek (1st, 4to, grey cl, unpag, fp b/w, pep, DJ)	MacMillan	1938	Lathrop, D.	65-90	
Field, R.	Hitty... (1st, sq8vo, 207p, p-o, 3cp, NM, PPPa)	MacMillan	1929	Lathrop, D.	100-135	
Lathrop, D.	Let Them Live (1st {std}, 8vo, orang cl, 80p, b/w, cep, DJ)	MacMillan	1951	Lathrop, D.	45-60	
MacDonald, Geo.	Light Princess (1st, 12mo, 133p, col frn, 12pl, pep)	MacMillan	1926	Lathrop, D.	85-100	
Hudson, W.H.	Little Boy Lost (1st, 4to, teg, 187p, gilt, uncut, pep, 8cp)	Knopf	1920	Lathrop, D.	120-160	
Andersen, H.C.	Little Mermaid (1st, 4to, blue/gilt, [48]p, 6 fp col, pep)	MacMillan	1939	Lathrop, D.	120-150	
Lathrop, D.	Little White Goat (1st, ob4to, 59p, col frn, 15pl, pep)	MacMillan	1933	Lathrop, D.	80-120	
Lathrop, D.	Littlest Mouse (1st {std}, sm8vo, ibds, 32p, b/w)	MacMillan	(1955)	Lathrop, D.	25-45	*
Howes, E.	Long Bright Land (1st, 8vo, 207p, grn/gilt, col frn, 12pl, pep)	Little/Brown	1929	Lathrop, D.	65-80	
Lathrop, D.	Lost Merry-Go-Round (1st, sq4to, 104p, col frn, 10pl, pep)	MacMillan	1934	Lathrop, D.	80-100	
Canfield, Dorothy	Made-to-Order Stories (1st, sm8vo, 263p, col frn)	Harcourt	(1925)	Lathrop, D.	35-50	*
Ingelow, J.	Mopsa the Fairy (1st, 8vo, p-o, 259p, uncut, col frn, 12pl pep)	Harper	1927	Lathrop, D.	75-120	
De La Mare, W.	Mr. Bumps & His Monkey (1st, sq8vo, 69p, 7 fp color, DJ)	Winston	(1942)	Lathrop, D.	80-120	
Lathrop, D.	Presents for Lupe (1st, sq4to, orang cl, [40]p, color, dep, DJ)	MacMillan	1940	Lathrop, D.	50-75	
MacDonald, Geo.	Princess & Curdie (1st, 8vo, p-o, 265p, gilt, col frn, 12pl pep)	MacMillan	1927	Lathrop, D.	85-130	
Lathrop, D.	Puffy & Seven Leaf Clover (1st {std}, 8vo, 34p, 2-color, cep)	MacMillan	(1954)	Lathrop, D.	35-50	*
Lathrop, D.	Puppies for Keeps (1st {std}, ob4to, brown cl, [40]p, color, DJ)	MacMillan	1943	Lathrop, D.	75-90	
Conkling, H.	Silverhorn (1st, 8vo, p-o, 159p, col frn, fp b/w, pep)	Stokes	1924	Lathrop, D.	70-90	
Lathrop, D.	Skittle-Skattle Monkey (1st, lg8vo, red cl, [48]p, b/w, DJ)	MacMillan	1945	Lathrop, D.	70-100	
Lathrop, D.	Snail Who Ran (1st, 16mo, green cl, 57p, col frn)	Stokes	1934	Lathrop, D.	45-60	
Hawthorne, N.	Snow Image (1st, 16mo, blue cl, 69p, dp color, pep)	MacMillan	1930	Lathrop, D.	40-60	
Teasdale, S.	Stars Tonight (1st, 8vo, blue cl, 49p, col frn, 14 fp b/w)	MacMillan	1930	Lathrop, D.	45-60	
Various	Sung Under the Silver Umbrella (1st, lg8vo, 211p, red cl, b/w)	MacMillan	1935	Lathrop, D.	35-50	*
Gate, E.M.	Tales/Enchanted Isles (1st, sq8vo, 118p, green cl, col frn, b/w)	Yale U. Press	1926	Lathrop, D.	60-80	
De La Mare, W.	Three Mulla Mulgars (1st, 8vo, blue/gilt, 275p, 8cp, pep)	Knopf	1919	Lathrop, D.	120-165	
De La Mare, W.	Three Mulla Mulgars (1st UK, 4to, 12pl)	L: Duckworth	1921	Lathrop, D.	80-120	
Robida, A.	Treasure of Corcassone (1st {std}, 8vo, 213p, col frn, 7pl, pep)	Longmans	1928	Lathrop, D.	40-60	
Lathrop, D.	Who Goes There? (1st, ob4to, [40]p, 16 fp b/w, pep)	MacMillan	1935	Lathrop, D.	65-100	
Robinson, Gertrude	Chee-Chee's Brother (1st {std}, sm4to, grn cl, 40p, fp b/w, pep)	Dutton	(1937)	Latimer, G.M.	25-45	*
Lattimore, Eleanor	Lost Leopard (1st, ob8vo, orange cl, 104p, 8cp, pep)	Harcourt	(1935)	Lattimore, E.	30-45	
Schmidt, S.L.	Ranching on Eagle Eye (1st {std}, 12mo, 374p, pep)	McBride	(1936)	Laune, P.	25-40	*
Annixter, Jane	The Runner (1st, 8vo, 220p, red cl, pep)	Holiday House	(1956)	Laune, P.	20-30	*
Demuth, Averil	Trudi and Hansel (1st, 8vo, silver cl, 174p, fp color, pep)	Winston	(1938)	Lavrin, Nora	25-40	
Lawrence, C.H.	Santa Claus in Toyland (1st, 4to, 96p, ibds, 8cp, 12pl)	Reilly/Britton	(1915)	Lawrence, C.H.	120-175	
Macleod, F.	Hills of Ruel (1st AM, 4to, teg, 92p, pep, 8 ticp)	Duffield	1921	Lawrence, M.H.	80-100	
Lawson, L.	Christmas Roses (lg8vo, [31]p, ibds, 10 chromos, pep)	Nister/Dutton	[1880]	Lawson, L.	145-200	
Spyri, J.	Heidi (1st, 8vo, 219p, color)	Dent/Dutton	(1909)	Lawson, L.	25-40	*
Moore, C.C.	Night Before Christmas (8vo, [24]p, pep, 12 chromos)	L: Nister	[1885]	Lawson, L.	100-150	*
Mack, R.E.	Old Father Santa Claus (4to, ibds, [40]p, 14 chromos)	Nister/Dutton	[1885]	Lawson, L.	180-265	
Mack, R.E.	Under the Mistletoe (lg8vo, ibds, [40]p, 14 chromos)	Nister/Dutton	(1890)	Lawson, L.	100-160	
Dickens, C.	Boots of the Holly Tree Inn (8vo, red/gilt, pep, 44p, col frn)	Harper	1928	Lawson, M.A.	30-45	*
Malkus, A.S.	Caravans to Sante Fe (1st {std}, 12mo, 289p, b/w)	Harper	1928	Lawson, M.A.	30-45	*
Lawson, Marie A.	Dragon John (1st, 8vo, 51p, green cl, 2-color, dep)	Viking	1943	Lawson, M.A.	25-45	*
Moore, Colleen	Enchanted Castle (1st, 4to, 63p, ibds, 6 fp 1-color, cep)	Garden City	1935	Lawson, M.A.	30-50	
Lawson, Marie A.	Hail Columbia (1st {std}, 4to, 387p, 7cp, 14 2-color, pep)	Doubleday/Dor.	1931	Lawson, M.A.	35-50	*
Montgomery, L.M.	Mistress Pat (1st, 12mo, 338p, col frn)	Stokes	1935	Lawson, M.A.	45-65	*
Lawson, Marie A.	Sea is Blue (1st, 8vo, 126p, pep, 11pl)	Viking	1946	Lawson, M.A.	30-45	*
Jewett, E.M.	Told on the King's Highway (1st, 8vo, 246p, b/w, pep)	Viking	1943	Lawson, M.A.	30-45	*
Gray, Eliz. J.	Adam of the Road (1st, lg8vo, 317p, green cl, 23pl, pep, NM)	Viking	1942	Lawson, R.	65-100	R
Gray, Eliz. J.	Adam of the Road (1st UK, 8vo, 174p, b/w)	L: A&C Black	1943	Lawson, R.	30-45	*
Aesopus	Aesop's Fables (1st, lg4to, brown/gilt, 134p, pep)	Heritage Press	(1941)	Lawson, R.	70-100	*
Lawson, R.	At that Time (1st, 8vo, 127p, b/w, DJ)	Viking	1947	Lawson, R.	40-60	
Lawson, R.	Ben & Me (1st {std}, sq8vo, 114p, brown cl, pep, DJ)	Little/Brown	1939	Lawson, R.	100-140	

AUTHOR	TITLE	PUBLISHER	DATE	ARTIST	PRICE	LC
Bates, Helen D.	Betsy Ross (1st, 8vo, 127p, b/w, DJ)	Whittlesey	1936	Lawson, R.	30-45	
Lawson, R.	Captain Kidd's Cat (1st {std}, 8vo, 151p, green cl, b/w, DJ)	Little/Brown	(1956)	Lawson, R.	50-75	
Lawson, R.	Country Colic (1st {std}, sq8vo, 70p, beige cl, b/w, pep)	Little/Brown	1944	Lawson, R.	30-50	
Sterne, Emma G.	Drums of Monmouth (1st, 8vo, 287p, aqua cl, uncut, b/w, pep)	Dodd	1935	Lawson, R.	30-45	*
Lawson, R.	Edward, Hoppy & Joe (1st {std}, 8vo, 122p, fp b/w, pep)	Knopf	(1952)	Lawson, R.	50-75	
Lawson, R.	Fabulous Flight (1st {std}, 8vo, 152p, green cl, b/w, pep)	Little/Brown	1949	Lawson, R.	40-60	
Fish, H.D.	Four & Twenty Blackbirds (1st, 4to, 104p, 1-color, pep, CH)	Stokes	1937	Lawson, R.	100-150	
Mason, A.	From the Horn of the Moon (1st {std}, 8vo, 259p, blue cl, b/w)	Doubleday/Dor.	1931	Lawson, R.	35-50	
Brewton, John	Gaily We Parade (1st, sm4to, 218p, pep, b/w)	MacMillan	1940	Lawson, R.	45-65	*
Coatsworth, E.	Golden Horseshoe (1st, 8vo, 151p, gilt, pep, 14pl)	MacMillan	1935	Lawson, R.	45-60	
Lawson, R.	Great Wheel (1st, 8vo, 188p, pep, b/w, green cl, DJ, NH)	Viking	(1957)	Lawson, R.	70-100	*
Robinson, Tom P.	Greylock & the Robins (1st, sm4to, 32p, ibds, color)	Viking	1946	Lawson, R.	70-100	
Marquand, John	Haven's End (1st, 8vo, 341p, uncut, b/w)	Little/Brown	1933	Lawson, R.	45-60	*
Bianco, M.W.	Hurdy-Gurdy Man (1st, sq12mo, 56p, ibds, cep, b/w, DJ)	OUP	(1933)	Lawson, R.	80-110	
Lawson, R.	I Discover Columbus (1st {std}, 8vo, blue cl, 113p, pep, DJ)	Little/Brown	1941	Lawson, R.	50-65	
Barnes, Ruth A.	I Hear America Singing (1st, 8vo, 346p, 1-color, pep)	Winston	(1937)	Lawson, R.	35-50	*
Chester, Geo. R.	Little Prince Toofat (1st, sq4to, 71p, col frn, cp)	McCann	(1922)	Lawson, R.	160-200	R
Teal, Val	Little Woman Wanted Noise (1st, 8vo, [40]p, orang cl, b/w, pep)	Rand/McNally	(1943)	Lawson, R.	80-120	*
Lawson, R.	McWhinney's Jaunt (1st {std}, sq8vo, 77p, cloth, b/w, DJ)	Little/Brown	1951	Lawson, R.	45-70	
Sterne, Emma G.	Miranda is a Princess (1st, 8vo, 221p, yellow cl, b/w, pep)	Dodd	1937	Lawson, R.	45-65	*
Atwater, R.	Mr. Popper's Penguins (1st {std}, 8vo, 138p, 1-col, pep, DJ, NH)	Little/Brown	1938	Lawson, R.	70-100	R
Lawson, R.	Mr. Revere & I (1st {std}, 8vo, 152p, b/w, pep)	Little/Brown	(1953)	Lawson, R.	70-90	R
Lawson, R.	Mr. Twigg's Mistake (1st {std}, 8vo, 143p, aqua cl, pep, DJ)	Little/Brown	1947	Lawson, R.	65-80	
Lawson, R.	Mr. Wilmer (1st {std}, 8vo, 218p, beige cl, b/w, DJ)	Little/Brown	1945	Lawson, R.	50-80	
Farjeon, E.	One Foot in Fairyland (1st, 8vo, 261p, gilt, b/w, cep, DJ)	Stokes	1938	Lawson, R.	80-100	
Ring, B.	Peik (1st, 8vo, cloth, 268p, 15 fp b/w, cep)	Little/Brown	1932	Lawson, R.	50-70	
Godolphin, M.	Pilgrims' Progress (1st, 4to, red cl, b/w, 120p, DJ)	Stokes	1939	Lawson, R.	65-80	
Forester, C.S.	Poo Poo & the Dragons (1st {std}, 8vo, 142p, green cl, b/w, pep)	Little/Brown	1942	Lawson, R.	165-220	
Twain, M.	Prince & the Pauper (1st, 8vo, 274p, p-o, gilt, color, pep)	Winston	(1937)	Lawson, R.	45-65	
Lang, A.	Prince Prigio (1st {std}, sq8vo, green cl, 108p, b/w, pep, DJ)	Little/Brown	1942	Lawson, R.	65-80	
Lawson, R.	Rabbit Hill (1st, 8vo, 128p, pep, DJ, NM)	Viking	1944	Lawson, R.	90-130	R
Lawson, R.	Robbut: Tale of Tails (1st, 4to, ibds, 94p, pep, DJ)	Viking	1948	Lawson, R.	75-100	
Mason, A.	Roving Lobster (1st {std}, 8vo, 132p, green cl, 10 fp b/w, cep)	Doubleday/Dor.	1931	Lawson, R.	65-100	
Gale, Eliz.	Seven Beads of Wampum (1st, 8vo, 298p, pep)	Putnam	(1936)	Lawson, R.	50-85	*
Hall, Wm.	Shoelace Robin (1st, 8vo, ipcb, [20]p, 1-color, pep)	Crowell	1945	Lawson, R.	45-60	*
Haines, Wm.	Slim (1st, 8vo, 414p, 6 fp b/w, pep)	Little/Brown	1934	Lawson, R.	35-50	
Lawson, R.	Smeller Martin (1st, sm4to, green cl, 157p, fp b/w, DJ)	Viking	1950	Lawson, R.	40-60	
Leaf, M.	Story of Ferdinand (1st, 8vo, ibds, [68]p, b/w, pep, DJ)	Viking	1936	Lawson, R.	380-550	R
Bowie, W.R.	Story of Jesus for Young People (1st, 8vo, 125p, blue cl, 6cp)	Scribner	1937	Lawson, R.	50-70	
Leaf, M.	Story of Simpson & Sampson (1st, sq4to, [64]p, blue cl, b/w pep)	Viking	1941	Lawson, R.	65-100	*
White, T.H.	Sword in the Stone (1st AM, sm8vo, 311p, gilt, pep by....)	Putnam	1939	Lawson, R.	80-130	*
Stratton, Clarence	Swords & Statues (1st, 8vo, 254p, col frn, gilt, 7 b/w)	Winston	(1937)	Lawson, R.	65-80	*
Lawson, R.	They Were Strong & Good (1st, lg4to, unpag, fp b/w, pep, CM)	Viking	1940	Lawson, R.	80-120	
Lawson, R.	Tough Winter (1st, 8vo, 128p, blue/silver, pep, DJ)	Viking	1954	Lawson, R.	65-80	
Tarn, W.W.	Treasure of Isle of Mist (1st, 8vo, 184p, pep, b/w)	Putnam	(1934)	Lawson, R.	30-45	*
Young, Ella	Unicorn with Silver Shoes (1st {std}, 8vo, gilt, 214p, 9pl, pep)	Longmans	1932	Lawson, R.	50-75	R
Lawson, R.	Watchwords of Liberty (1st {std}, 4to, 115p, b/w, pep, DJ)	Little/Brown	1943	Lawson, R.	50-65	
Leaf, M.	Wee Gillis (1st, 4to, ipcb, [76]p, 33 fp b/w, pep, CH)	Viking	1938	Lawson, R.	70-100	R
Mason, A.	Wee Men of Ballywooden (1st {std}, lg8vo, 266p, pep, 4pl)	Doubleday/Dor.	1930	Lawson, R.	100-145	
Mason, A.	Wee Men of Ballywooden (1st {this pub}, 8vo, p-o, 266p, 4pl pep)	Garden City	(1937)	Lawson, R.	45-65	
Cormack, M.	Wind of the Vikings (1st, 8vo, 259p, tan cl, 6 fp b/w, pep)	Appleton/Cen.	1937	Lawson, R.	30-50	*
Dixon, Charles	Fifteen Hundred Miles an Hour (1st, 8vo, blue/gilt, AEG, 6pl)	L: Bliss Sands	1895	Layard, A.	50-75	
Haggard, H.R.	People of the Mist (1st, 8vo, 343p, blue/gilt, 16pl)	L: Longmans	1894	Layard, A.	70-120	
Malory, T.	King Arthur... (1st, 12mo, 64p, green wraps, fp b/w)	Penn	1908	LeFanu, B.	35-50	*
Hawthorne, N.	Wonder Tales (1st, 12mo, 62p, b/w)	Penn	1908	LeFanu, B.	20-30	*
LeMair, H.W.	Auntie's Little Rhyme Book (ob12mo, ibds, 26p, 10 color)	Augener/McKay	[1918]	LeMair, H.W.	120-165	
LeMair, H.W.	Baby's Little Rhyme Book (ob 12mo, ibds, 10 color)	L: Augener	[1920]	LeMair, H.W.	130-165	
Stevenson, R.L.	Child's Garden of Verses (1st, ob4to, p-o, 89p, gilt, 12cp, pep)	McKay	(1926)	LeMair, H.W.	200-300	
Stevenson, R.L.	Child's Garden of Verses (1st UK, ob4to, ibds, pep, 71p, 12cp)	L: Harrap	(1931)	LeMair, H.W.	200-275	
Elkin, R.H.	Children's Corner (1st AM, ob8vo, p-o, gilt, 15 ticp)	McKay	[1915]	LeMair, H.W.	160-200	
LeMair, H.W.	Daddy's Little Rhyme Book (ob 12mo, ibds, 10 color)	L: Augener	[1920]	LeMair, H.W.	130-165	
Milne, A.A.	Gallery of Children (1st, lg4to, p-o, 105p, 12cp)	L: Stan. Paul	(1925)	LeMair, H.W.	180-265	
Milne, A.A.	Gallery of Children (1st AM, 4to, 105p, p-o, gilt, 12cp)	McKay	(1925)	LeMair, H.W.	120-165	
LeMair, H.W.	Granny's Little Rhyme Book (ob12mo, 26p, ibds, 12 color)	L: Augener	(1912)	LeMair, H.W.	120-165	
Elkin, R.H.	Little People (ob4to, red/gilt, p-o, 16 fp color)	McKay/Augener	[1920]	LeMair, H.W.	140-220	
Moffat, A.	Little Songs/Long Ago (1st, ob4to, 64p, p-o, 32 fp color)	L: Augener	(1912)	LeMair, H.W.	140-170	
LeMair, H.W.	Mother's Little Rhyme Book (ob 16mo, ibds)	McKay	[n.d.]	LeMair, H.W.	100-130	
LeMair, H.W.	Nursie's Little Rhyme Book. (ob12mo, ibds, 26p, 10 color)	Augener/McKay	[1915]	LeMair, H.W.	120-165	
Elkin, R.H.	Old Dutch Nursery Rhymes (1st, ob4to, p-o, 31p, color)	L: Augener	(1917)	LeMair, H.W.	160-200	
Moffat, A.	Our Old Nursery Rhymes (1st, ob4to, 63p, p-o, 30 fp color)	L: Augener	1911	LeMair, H.W.	150-200	
Inayat, N.	Twenty Jakata Tales (1st AM, lg8vo, 138p, gilt, col frn, 19pl)	McKay	(1939)	LeMair, H.W.	80-120	
Inayat, N.	Twenty Jataka Tales (1st, 8vo, blue cl, 138p, col frn, 19pl)	L: Harrap	(1939)	LeMair, H.W.	120-165	

AUTHOR	TITLE	PUBLISHER	DATE	ARTIST	PRICE	LC
LeWitt, J.	The Vegetabull (1st {std}, 4to, ibds, [32]p)	Harcourt	1956	LeWitt, J.	30-50	*
Jackson, Joseph	Christmas Flower (1st {std}, 8vo, 31p, ibds, 1-color, pep)	Harcourt	(1951)	Lea, Tom	30-50	*
Leaf, M.	Gordon the Goat (1st {std}, 8vo, green cl, 48p, color)	Lippincott	(1944)	Leaf, M.	30-45	*
Newbolt, H.	Taken From the Enemy (1st, 8vo, teg, 170p, p-o, 8cp)	L: Chatto	1911	Leake, G.	25-45	
Lang, A.	Gold of Fairnilee (1st, 4to, teg, 86p, uncut, 13cp)	L: Arrowsmith	1888	Leamann, E.A.	100-150	*
Lebeck, O.	Diary of Terwilliger Jellico (1st, lg8vo, ibds, [48]p, col, pep)	Grosset/Dunlap	1935	Lebeck, O.	35-50	
Baum, L.F.	Wizard of Oz (1st, ob8vo, [56]p, ibds, color, pep)	Grosset/Dunlap	1939	Lebeck, O.	70-125	*
Criss, Mildred	Malou (1st {std}, 8vo, blue cl, 280p, uncut, col frn, 4 fp b/w)	Doubleday/Dor.	1929	Lederer, C.	20-35	*
McNeer, May	Tales/Crescent Moon (1st, lg8vo, 306p, blue/silver, color, pep)	Farrar/Rine.	(1930)	Lederer, C.	35-50	
McNeer, May	Tinka Minka & Linka (1st, 8vo, 30p, yellow cl, cep, fp color)	Knopf	1931	Lederer, C.	30-45	*
Koch, Dorothy	Gone is My Goose (1st, lg8vo, green cl, [27]p, 1-color, cep)	Holiday House	(1956)	Lee, Doris	25-40	*
Thurber, J.	Great Quillow (1st, lg sq8vo, 54p, p-o, yellow cl, color, DJ)	Harcourt	(1944)	Lee, Doris	70-120	
Stong, Phil	Hired Man's Elephant (1st, 8vo, 149p, beige cl, b/w)	Dodd	1939	Lee, Doris	25-40	*
Pease, L.	Dollies in Happy-Land (1st, lg8vo, pict cl, [45]p, color)	Whitman	(1914)	Lee, E.D.	80-120	
Mother Goose	Ella D. Lee Mother Goose (1st, 4to, 280p, 24cp, pep)	Donohue	(1918)	Lee, E.D.	100-145	
Lee, E.D.	Ever Living Fairy Tales (lg8vo, green cl, p-o, 18cp)	(NY)	1924	Lee, E.D.	40-60	*
Grimm Bros.	Fairy Tales (4to, 229p, p-o, 24cp, pep)	Donohue	(1920)	Lee, E.D.	85-120	*
Andersen, H.C.	Fairy Tales (4to, 245p, 16cp, pep)	Donohue	(1926)	Lee, E.D.	65-80	
McGovern, Mary H.	Fifty Famous Fairy Tales (1st, sm4to, 254p, cp)	Whitman	(1917)	Lee, E.D.	50-85	*
Pease, L.	Four & Twenty Dollies (1st, sm sq4to, 94p, ibds, color)	Hamming	(1914)	Lee, E.D.	65-80	
Keys, Leonora	Happy Dollies (lg8vo, [46]p, color, cloth)	Whitman	(1914)	Lee, E.D.	80-100	
Gordon, Eliz.	Lorraine & Little People of Spring (1st, sm8vo, 64p, color)	Rand/McNally	(1918)	Lee, E.D.	30-45	*
Keys, Leonora	Play Dollies (sm4to, 38p, ibds, color)	Whitman	(1927)	Lee, E.D.	75-100	*
Lang, A.	Red Fairy Book (1st, 8vo, 399p, p-o, 7cp)	Macrae-Smith	[1925]	Lee, M.V.	50-70	
Kauffmann, R.	Spanish Dollars (1st, 8vo, p-o, 7pl)	Penn	1925	Lee, M.V.	20-30	
Richards, L.E.	Merry-Go-Round (1st, 8vo, 113p, bds, p-o, b/w)	Appleton/Cent.	1935	Lefferts, W.E.	25-40	*
Quick, Herbert	Virginia of the Air Lanes (1st, 8vo, blue cl, 424p, 5pl)	Bobbs-Merrill	(1909)	Leigh, W.R.	45-60	*
Wilder, T.N.	Bridge/San Luis Rey (1st, 8vo, 139p, red cl, color)	Longmans	(1935)	Leighton, C.	70-100	
Symington, E.H.	By Light of Sun (1st, 8vo, 196p, fp woodcuts by...)	Putnam	1941	Leighton, C.	35-50	*
Leighton, C.	Country Matters (1st, 4to, 159p, 70 wood engravings)	MacMillan	1937	Leighton, C.	50-80	R*
Leighton, C.	Farmer's Year... (1st, ob folio, 54p, pep, 12 fp woodcuts)	L: Collins	1933	Leighton, C.	120-165	*
Nathan, Rbt.	Fiddler in Barly (1st, 8vo, 137p, 6 woodcuts)	L: Heinemann	1927	Leighton, C.	50-75	*
Leighton, C.	Four Hedges... (1st, lg8vo, 167p, blue cl, wood engravings)	MacMillan	1935	Leighton, C.	35-50	
Auslander, Jos.	Letters to Women... (1st {std}, 8vo, 85p, frn & b/w illus)	Harper	1929	Leighton, C.	45-60	*
Brailsford, M.	Making of William Penn (1st, 8vo, 367p, t-i frn by...)	Longmans	1930	Leighton, C.	30-45	
Farjeon, E.	Perkin the Pedlar (1st, sm4to, blue cl, 205p, 8cp)	L: Faber	(1932)	Leighton, C.	65-80	*
Hardy, T.	Return of the Native (1st, 8vo, 484p)	L: MacMillan	1929	Leighton, C.	45-60	*
Tomlinson, H.M.	Sea & the Jungle (1st, 8vo, 343p, green ipcb, woodcuts)	L: Duckworth	1930	Leighton, C.	45-60	*
Leighton, C.	Sometime Never (1st, lg8vo, 178p, b/w, DJ)	MacMillan	1939	Leighton, C.	45-60	
Leighton, C.	Southern Harvest (1st UK, 4to, 123p)	L: Gollancz	1943	Leighton, C.	45-70	*
Roberts, E.M.	Time of Man (1st, 8vo, 397p, p-o)	Viking	1945	Leighton, C.	35-50	
Holme, C.	Trumpet in the Dust (1st, 8vo, 255p, 6 woodcuts)	L: Nicholson	1934	Leighton, C.	65-80	*
Shakespeare, Wm.	Under the Greenwood Tree (1st, 4to, 236p, wood engravings)	L: MacMillan	1940	Leighton, C.	45-60	*
Leighton, C.	Where Land Meets Sea (1st, 4to, 202p, 4 fp b/w)	Rinehart	(1954)	Leighton, C.	30-50	
Bronte, E.J.	Wuthering Heights (1st {std}, 4to, 325p, 12pl, DJ)	Random	1931	Leighton, C.	60-85	
Daudet, A.	Letters from my Mill (1st, 8vo, 236p, tan/gilt, 10cp)	Dodd	1893	Lemaire, M.	30-45	
Meredith, O.	Lucille (1st, 8vo, teg, 12cp by...)	Stokes	(1897)	Lemaire, M.	60-85	
Andersen, H.C.	Fairy Tales (1st, lg8vo, 219p, b/w)	L: E. Arnold	1893	Lemann, E.A.	80-100	
Andersen, H.C.	Snow Queen (1st, lg8vo, 232p, 35 illus, AEG)	L: E. Arnold	1894	Lemann, E.A.	80-100	
Hazard, R.H.	House on Stilts (1st, 8vo, red cl, 346p, 4pl)	Dillingham	(1910)	Lemon, J.A.	25-40	
Locke, Wm. J.	Christmas Mystery (1st, 8vo, 35p, orang cl, 6cp)	L: J. Lane	1922	Lendon, W.W.	30-50	*
Locke, Wm. J.	Story of the Three Wise Men (1st, 8vo, 38p, gilt, 6cp)	L: J. Lane	1922	Lendon, W.W.	35-50	
Lenski, L.	A-Going to the Westward (1st, 8vo, 370p, uncut, b/w, pep)	Stokes	1937	Lenski, L.	45-60	*
Lenski, L.	Alphabet People (1st {std}, lg8vo, 190p, p-o, blue cl, col, pep)	Harper	1928	Lenski, L.	60-90	
Lenski, L.	Arabella & Her Aunts (1st, sq12mo, p-o, 115p, 5cp, cep, DJ)	Stokes	1932	Lenski, L.	100-135	
Lenski, L.	Bayou Suzette (1st {std}, 8vo, 207p, map, fp b/w, pep)	Stokes	1943	Lenski, L.	45-60	*
Lenski, L.	Benny & His Penny (1st, ob4to, blue cl, [32]p, color)	Knopf	1931	Lenski, L.	65-80	*
Lovelace, M.H.	Betsy-Tacy (1st, 8vo, 112p, pink cl, b/w, pep)	Crowell	1940	Lenski, L.	30-45	*
Lenski, L.	Blue Ridge Billy (1st {std}, 8vo, 203p, b/w, pep)	Lippincott	(1946)	Lenski, L.	30-45	
Lenski, L.	Blueberry Corners (1st, 8vo, blue/gilt, 209p, b/w, pep)	Stokes	1940	Lenski, L.	35-50	*
Adams, K.	Book of Enchantment Tales (1st, 4to, 23p, pep, 4cp)	Dodd	1928	Lenski, L.	50-80	
Adams, K.	Book of Princess Stories (1st, 4to, blue/gilt, 223p, 4cp, pep)	Dodd	1927	Lenski, L.	50-80	
Lenski, L.	Bound Girl of Cobble Hill (1st, 8vo, 292p, uncut, b/w, dep)	Stokes	1938	Lenski, L.	30-45	
Hutchinson, V.	Candle-Light Stories (1st, 4to, 146p, 6cp, pep)	Minton Balch	1928	Lenski, L.	70-100	
Hutchinson, V.	Chimney Corner Fairy Tales (1st, 4to, 183p, 6cp, pep)	Minton Balch	1926	Lenski, L.	70-100	
Lenski, L.	Cotton in My Sack (1st {std}, lg8vo, 191p, dp b/w, pep)	Lippincott	(1949)	Lenski, L.	35-50	
Lenski, L.	Cowboy Small (1st, 8vo, tan cl, [48]p, color, pep)	OUP	(1949)	Lenski, L.	45-65	
Bulla, Clyde R.	Donkey Cart (1st, 8vo, yellow cl, 89p, b/w, pep)	Crowell	(1946)	Lenski, L.	35-50	*
Grahame, K.	Dream Days (1st, 8vo, 192p, color, pep)	L: J. Lane	1922	Lenski, L.	70-100	*
Lenski, L.	Easter Rabbit's Parade (1st, lg8vo, ipcb, [31]p, color, pep)	OUP	(1936)	Lenski, L.	50-75	
Stong, Phil	Edgar: The 7:58 (1st, sm8vo, 101p, pep, b/w)	Farrar/Rine.	1938	Lenski, L.	35-50	*
Hutchinson, V.	Fireside Poems (1st, 4to, 147p, 5cp, pep)	Minton Balch	1930	Lenski, L.	65-90	

ILLUSTRATOR: 78

AUTHOR	TITLE	PUBLISHER	DATE	ARTIST	PRICE	LC
Hutchinson, V.	Fireside Stories (1st, 8vo, 150p, 6cp, pep)	Minton Balch	1927	Lenski, L.	60-90	
Barksdale, L.	First Thanksgiving (1st {std}, sm8vo, 57p, 6cp)	Knopf	1942	Lenski, L.	30-55	
Whitehead, R.	Five & Ten (1st, 8vo, red cl, [41]p, color, pep)	Houghton	1943	Lenski, L.	45-60	
Grahame, K.	Golden Age (1st [1st bk.], 8vo, uncut, 199p, 4 ticp)	L: J. Lane	1921	Lenski, L.	75-100	
Becker, May L.	Golden Tales of Far West (1st, sm8vo, 304p, decor by...)	Dodd	1935	Lenski, L.	35-50	*
Becker, May L.	Golden Tales of Prairie States (1st, sm8vo, 355p, decor by...)	Dodd	1932	Lenski, L.	35-50	*
Lenski, L.	Gooseberry Garden (1st {std}, ob8vo, ipcb, [32]p, color)	Harper	1934	Lenski, L.	60-80	*
Lenski, L.	Grandmother Tippytoe (1st, sm4to, p-o, 104p, 8cp)	Stokes	1931	Lenski, L.	45-60	
Birch, V.	Green-Faced Toad (1st, lg8vo, 107p, green cl, 8cp)	Stokes	1923	Lenski, L.	70-100	
Emerson, C.	Hat Tub Tale... (1st {std}, 8vo, 185p, blue cl, uncut, b/w, pep)	Dutton	1928	Lenski, L.	30-45	*
Lenski, L.	Indian Captive (1st, 8vo, 269p, pep, color, DJ, NH)	Stokes	1941	Lenski, L.	50-85	
Lenski, L.	Jack Horner's Pie (1st, lg8vo, 83p, color)	Harper	1927	Lenski, L.	35-50	
Lenski, L.	Johnny Goes to the Fair (1st, 8vo, [32]p, yellow cl, color)	Minton Balch	1932	Lenski, L.	40-60	*
Piper, W. (ed.)	Jolly Rhymes of Mother Goose (1st, 12mo, [118]p, col frn)	Platt/Munk	(1932)	Lenski, L.	45-60	*
Lenski, L.	Judy's Journey (1st {std}, 8vo, 212p, b/w, pep)	Lippincott	1947	Lenski, L.	30-45	
LaRue, M.G.	Letter to Popsey (1st, sq8vo, [28]p, ibds, color, pep)	Grosset/Dunlap	1942	Lenski, L.	35-50	*
Lenski, L.	Little Airplane (1st, sq8vo, [48]p, 1-color, pep)	OUP	(1938)	Lenski, L.	35-50	
Piper, W. (ed.)	Little Engine that Could (1st, sm8vo, unpag, p-o, color, pep)	Platt/Munk	(1930)	Lenski, L.	50-70	
Lenski, L.	Little Family (1st {std}, sq12mo, ibds, unpag, color, dep)	Doubleday/Dor.	1932	Lenski, L.	30-50	
Lenski, L.	Little Fire Engine (1st, ob8vo, red/gilt, [46]p, 1-color)	OUP	1946	Lenski, L.	45-60	
Lenski, L.	Little Girl of 1900 (1st, 8vo, 218p, p-o, col frn, 9pl, pep)	Stokes	1928	Lenski, L.	65-90	R*
Phillips, E.C.	Little Rag Doll (1st, 8vo, p-o, 173p, 4cp, pep)	Houghton	1930	Lenski, L.	50-70	
Mother Goose	Lois Lenski's Mother Goose (1st, sm8vo, 83p, 2-color)	Harper	(1936)	Lenski, L.	80-120	*
Lenski, L.	Mamma Hattie's Girl (1st {std}, 8vo, 182p, pep, b/w, DJ)	Lippincott	(1953)	Lenski, L.	35-50	
Meigs, C.	Mother Makes Christmas (1st, sq8vo, ibds, [28]p, pep, 14 color)	Grosset/Dunlap	1940	Lenski, L.	45-60	*
Emerson, C.	Mr. Nip & Mr. Tuck (1st {std}, 8vo, 173p, aqua/gilt, b/w, dep)	Dutton	1930	Lenski, L.	30-45	*
Phillips, E.C.	Name for Obed (1st, lg8vo, 117p, 1-color, pep, DJ)	Houghton	1941	Lenski, L.	50-70	
Lenski, L.	Now It's Fall (1st, ob12mo, [48]p, color, DJ)	OUP	(1948)	Lenski, L.	40-60	
Lenski, L.	Ocean-Born Mary (1st, sm8vo, 388p, pep, b/w)	Stokes	1939	Lenski, L.	45-60	*
Thompson, Dorothy	Once on Christmas (1st, 16mo, ipcb, [44]p, pep, b/w)	NY: OUP	1938	Lenski, L.	20-30	
Lovelace, M.H.	Over the Big Hill (1st, 8vo, 171p, b/w, pep)	Crowell	1942	Lenski, L.	25-40	
Colum, P.	Peep-Show Man (1st, 12mo, blue cl, 65p, 4cp, pep)	MacMillan	1924	Lenski, L.	40-60	
Lenski, L.	Phebe Fairchild... (1st, 8vo, 316p, rust/gilt, b/w, dep, NH)	Stokes	1936	Lenski, L.	45-65	
Collodi, C.	Pinocchio (1st, 4to, yellow bds, [65]p, 7 fp color)	Random	(1946)	Lenski, L.	65-100	
Lenski, L.	Prairie School (1st {std}, 8vo, 196p, b/w)	Lippincott	(1951)	Lenski, L.	30-45	*
Robins, E.	Prudence & Peter... (1st, sm8vo, 244p, grey cl, p-o)	Wm. Morrow	(1928)	Lenski, L.	35-50	
Lenski, L.	Puritan Adventure (1st {std}, 8vo, 223p, color, DJ)	Lippincott	1944	Lenski, L.	30-45	*
Chidsey, A.	Rustam Lion of Persia (1st, 8vo, 271p, blue cl, b/w, pep)	Minton Balch	1930	Lenski, L.	30-45	
Powers, Tom	Scotch Circus (1st, 8vo, [96]p, 7 fp color)	Houghton	1934	Lenski, L.	45-60	
Lenski, L.	Skipping Village (1st, 4to, 179p, blue cl, 4cp, 3pl, pep)	Stokes	1927	Lenski, L.	50-75	
Bulla, Clyde R.	Songs of Mr. Small (1st, 4to, 40p, color, DJ)	NY: OUP	1954	Lenski, L.	40-60	
Lenski, L.	Spinach-Boy (1st, 12mo, 91p, p-o, 6cp, pep, DJ)	Stokes	1930	Lenski, L.	50-65	
Lenski, L.	Spring is Here (1st, ob12mo, [48]p, yellow cl, color, cep, DJ)	OUP	(1945)	Lenski, L.	50-80	
Lenski, L.	Strawberry Girl (1st {std}, 8vo, 194p, green/gilt, dep, DJ, NM)	Lippincott	(1945)	Lenski, L.	65-90	R
Lenski, L.	Sugarplum House (1st {std}, ob8vo, ipcb, [91]p, color)	Harper	1935	Lenski, L.	50-70	
Lenski, L.	Surprise for Mother (1st, sq12mo, 91p, yellow cl, col frn, b/w)	Stokes	1934	Lenski, L.	35-50	
Lenski, L.	Susie Mauiar (1st, ob8vo, unpag, color, dep)	NY: OUP	(1939)	Lenski, L.	45-60	*
Lenski, L.	Texas Tomboy (1st {std}, 4to, 180p)	Lippincott	(1950)	Lenski, L.	45-65	*
Adams, K.	There Were Giants (1st, 8vo, 234p, green cl, 4pl, pep)	Dodd	1929	Lenski, L.	30-45	
Judson, C.I.	They Came from France (1st, 8vo, red cl, 245p, fp b/w, pep)	Houghton	1943	Lenski, L.	30-45	*
Lofting, H.	Twilight of Magic (1st, 8vo, p-o, 303p, col frn, b/w, pep)	Stokes	1930	Lenski, L.	60-90	
Lenski, L.	Two Brothers/Animal Friends (1st, ob12mo, 122p, p-o, col, pep)	Stokes	1929	Lenski, L.	80-120	*
Lenski, L.	Two Brothers/Baby Sister (1st, ob12mo, 121p, p-o, 12cp, pep)	Stokes	1930	Lenski, L.	80-120	
Lenski, L.	Washington Picture Book (1st, ob4to, ibds, [32]p, color, pep)	Coward	1930	Lenski, L.	70-120	
Bulla, Clyde R.	We Are thy Children (1st {std}, ob4to, [32]p)	Crowell	1952	Lenski, L.	65-80	*
Mother Goose	Mother Goose Rhymes (1st, 4to, p-o, [120]p, 8cp, pep)	Platt/Munk	(1931)	Lenski/Eulalie	40-65	
Piper, W. (ed.)	Stories Children Love (lg4to, green cl, p-o, [71]p, color)	Platt/Munk	(1932)	Lenski/Eulalie	45-60	
Weil, Ann	Silver Fawn (1st {std}, 8vo, 228p, 1-color, pep)	Bobbs-Merrill	(1939)	Leon, E.	25-45	*
Peck, H.T.	Hilda and the Wishes (1st, sm8vo, 240p, 8pl)	Dodd	1907	Leonard, M.E.	30-50	*
Sautriax [Rabelais]	Gargantua (1st, ob folio, 52p, ibds, 6cp)	Duffield	1921	Leroy, Adrien	120-170	*
Buchan, J.	Lake of Gold (1st AM, 8vo, 189p, green cl, b/w, pep, DJ)	Houghton	1941	Levenson, S.	40-60	
Bangs, J.K.	Alice in Blunderland (1st, 12mo, 124p, brown cl, p-o, b/w)	Doubleday/Page	1907	Levering, A.	45-60	
Carryl, G.W.	Grimm's Tales Made Gay (1st, sq8vo, green cl, 142p, b/w)	Houghton	(1902)	Levering, A.	100-145	R
Ade, G.	In Pastures New (1st, 12mo, 309p, red cl, b/w)	McClure	1906	Levering, A.	25-40	
Bangs, J.K.	Jack & the Check Book (1st, 8vo, 236p, green cl, b/w)	Harper	1911	Levering, A.	35-50	
Ade, G.	Knocking the Neighbors (1st, 12mo, 229p, brown cl, 15pl)	Doubleday/Page	1912	Levering, A.	45-65	R
Bangs, J.K.	Molly & The Unwiseman (1st, 8vo, 198p, 8pl)	Coates	1902	Levering, A.	35-50	*
Bangs, J.K.	Olympian Nights (1st, 12mo, red/gilt, 224p, 16pl)	Harper	1902	Levering, A.	45-60	
Blake, Wm.	Songs of Experience (1st, 8vo, 83p, green cl, uncut)	L: D. Nutt	1899	Levetus, C.	80-100	
Blake, Wm.	Songs of Innocence (1st, 24mo, 118p, designs by...)	L: Wells/Gard.	1899	Levetus, C.	70-90	*
Kunos, I	Turkish Fairy Tales... (1st, lg8vo, 275p, teg, 9pl)	L: Lawrence	1896	Levetus, C.	70-90	
Greene, S.P.M.	Power Lot (1st, 8vo, teg, 396p, 5pl)	Baker/Taylor	1906	Levy, A.O.	20-25	

AUTHOR	TITLE	PUBLISHER	DATE	ARTIST	PRICE	LC
Burroughs, Marg.	Jasper the Drummin' Boy (1st, lg8vo, 63p, fp b/w)	Viking	1947	Lewin, T.	70-95	*
Field, R.	Calico Bush (1st, lg8vo, 213p, p-o, color, DJ, NH)	MacMillan	1931	Lewis, A.	45-70	
Field, R.	Hepatica Hawks (1st, 8vo, 239p, blue cl, 6pl, NH)	MacMillan	1932	Lewis, A.	40-65	
Brooks, C.S.	Journeys to Baghdad (1st, 8vo, bds, p-o, 140p, teg, 27 woodcuts)	Yale U. Press	1915	Lewis, A.	35-50	*
Stevens, J.	Paul Bunyon (1st, 8vo, 245p, woodcuts)	Knopf	(1925)	Lewis, A.	25-40	
Kipling, R.	With the Night Mail (1st, 8vo, teg, blue cl, 77p, pep, 4cp)	Doubleday/Page	1909	Leyendecker, F.X.	150-180	
Morris, M.	Bryn Mawr Stories (1st, 8vo, teg, green/gilt, cvr by...)	Jacobs	(1901)	Leyendecker, J.C.	100-135	
Hudson, C.	Crimson Conquest (1st, 8vo, 454p, cvr by...)	McClurg	1907	Leyendecker, J.C.	40-60	
Lorimer, G.H.	False Gods (1st, 8vo, p-o, 91p, 4pl)	Appleton	1906	Leyendecker, J.C.	50-65	
Brown, A.G.	Fireside Battles (1st, 8vo, teg, 327p, 8pl)	Laird & Lee	1900	Leyendecker, J.C.	65-80	*
Craig, Alexander	Ionia... (1st, 8vo, grey buckram, 301p, 6pl)	E.A. Weeks	1898	Leyendecker, J.C.	85-130	
Boylan, G.D.	Kiss of Glory (1st, sm8vo, 298p, col frn & cvr by...)	Dillingham	(1902)	Leyendecker, J.C.	35-50	*
Williams, E.	Ridolfo (1st, 8vo, p-o, 406p, 4cp)	McClurg	1906	Leyendecker, J.C.	60-80	
Catherwood, Mary	Spanish Peggy (1st, 8vo, uncut, teg, 85p, red cl, p-o, b/w)	H. Stone	1899	Leyendecker, J.C.	80-100	
Morris, G.	Voice in the Rice (1st, 12mo, 158p, 6cp)	Dodd	1910	Leyendecker, J.C.	50-65	
Chambers, Rbt.	Iole (1st, sm8vo, 142p, p-o, 2pl by...)	Appleton	1905	Leyendeckers	25-40	
Collodi, C.	Adventures of Pinocchio (1st {std}, sm8vo, 280p, col frn)	Doubleday/Dor.	1930	Liddell, M.	50-80	*
Liddell, Mary	Little Machinery (1st, 4to, 62p, ibds, color)	Doubleday/Page	(1926)	Liddell, M.	90-130	
Patri, Angelo	Pinocchio in America (1st {std}, 8vo, 255p, col frn, 17pl, pep)	Doubleday/Dor.	1928	Liddell, M.	50-75	
Perera, Lydia	Frisky (1st, sm8vo, [46]p, red cl, color, cep)	Holiday House	1955	Liebman, O.	20-30	*
Baruch, D.W.	Funny Little Boy (1st, sq12mo, [36]p, color, pep)	Lothrop/Lee	1936	Lietta	25-40	*
Lindsay, N.	Magic Pudding (1st AM, 12mo, orange cl, [159]p, b/w)	Farrar/Rine.	[1936]	Lindsay, N.	40-60	
Cooke, G.M.	Doings of the Dollivers (1st, 12mo, 174p, 7pl)	Sturgis	1910	Linnell, H.	35-50	*
Shakespeare, Wm.	Merchant of Venice (sm4to, cloth, gilt, 143p, 16 ticp)	L: Hodder	[1920]	Linton, J.	60-85	
Lionni, L.	Inch by Inch (1st, sq4to, ipcb, unpag, color, pep, CH)	Obolensky	(1960)	Lionni, L.	70-110	R*
Lionni, L.	Little Blue & Little Yellow (1st, sq8vo, ibds, unpag, color)	Obolensky	(1959)	Lionni, L.	70-100	R*
Lipman, M.	The Chatterlings (1st, lg8vo, 96p, ibds, color, pep)	Volland	(1928)	Lipman, M.	50-80	R
Andersen, H.C.	Tumble-Bug (1st, lg8vo, green cl, 166p, pep, fp 1-color)	Harcourt	(1940)	List, H.	30-45	*
N/A	Arabian Nights (1st, sm8vo, 420p, cp)	Jacobs	(1918)	Lister, W.H.	20-30	*
Jewett, J.H.	Con the Wizard (1st AM, narrow 12mo, 123p, ibds, 8cp)	Stokes	(1905)	Little, E.R.	45-60	
Farjeon, E.	Singing Games for Children (1st, 8vo, 71p)	Dent/Dutton	[1919]	Littlejohns, J.	45-60	*
Grimm Bros.	Hansel & Gretel (1st, 12mo, [32]p, color)	Rand/McNally	1937	Livings, B.	30-45	*
Bianco, M.W.	Franzi & Gizi (1st, 4to, p-o, [56]p, fp color, pep)	J. Messner	1941	Loeffler, G.	30-45	*
Lofting, H.	Dr. Dolittle & Green Canary (1st {std}, 8vo, 276p, col frn, pep)	Lippincott	(1950)	Lofting, H.	70-100	
Lofting, H.	Dr. Dolittle & Secret Lake (1st {std}, 8vo, 366p pep, p-o colfrn)	Lippincott	(1948)	Lofting, H.	70-100	
Lofting, H.	Dr. Dolittle in the Moon (1st, 8vo, p-o, 307p, col frn, pep)	Stokes	(1928)	Lofting, H.	65-100	
Lofting, H.	Dr. Dolittle in the Moon (1st UK, 8vo, 319p, 2cp, pep)	L: J. Cape	(1929)	Lofting, H.	60-90	
Lofting, H.	Dr. Dolittle's Birthday Book (1st, sq12mo, gilt, col frn, dep)	Stokes	(1935)	Lofting, H.	60-90	
Lofting, H.	Dr. Dolittle's Caravan (1st {std}, 8vo, p-o, col frn, pep)	Stokes	(1926)	Lofting, H.	70-100	
Lofting, H.	Dr. Dolittle's Circus (1st, 8vo, 379p, p-o, col frn, pep)	Stokes	1924	Lofting, H.	70-100	
Lofting, H.	Dr. Dolittle's Garden (1st, 8vo, 327p, p-o, col frn, pep)	Stokes	(1927)	Lofting, H.	70-90	
Lofting, H.	Dr. Dolittle's Post Office (1st, 8vo, 359p, p-o, col frn, pep)	Stokes	(1923)	Lofting, H.	70-100	
Lofting, H.	Dr. Dolittle's Puddleby Advens (1st {std} 8vo, 241p, pep, colfrn)	Lippincott	(1952)	Lofting, H.	50-70	*
Lofting, H.	Dr. Dolittle's Return (1st, 8vo, p-o, 273p, col frn, b/w, pep)	Stokes	1933	Lofting, H.	65-90	
Lofting, H.	Dr. Dolittle's Zoo (1st, 8vo, grey cl, p-o, 338p, col frn, pep)	Stokes	(1925)	Lofting, H.	70-100	
Lofting, H.	Gub Gub's Book (1st, 8vo, 185p, p-o, 2cp, 6pl, pep)	Stokes	(1932)	Lofting, H.	70-120	
Lofting, H.	Noisy Nora (1st, 16mo, [53]p, pink cl, p-o, pep, color)	Stokes	(1929)	Lofting, H.	90-135	*
Lofting, H.	Porridge Poetry (1st, ob8vo, [96]p, p-o, yellow cl)	Stokes	(1924)	Lofting, H.	80-120	
Lofting, H.	Story of Dr. Dolittle (1st, 8vo, p-o, 180p, col frn, PPP)	Stokes	1920	Lofting, H.	85-120	
Lofting, H.	Story of Mrs. Tubbs (1st, sm ob8vo, p-o, [95]p, color)	Stokes	(1923)	Lofting, H.	85-125	
Lofting, H.	Tommy, Tilly & Mrs. Tubbs (1st UK, ob12mo, 72p, ibds, 2 col)	L: J. Cape	(1937)	Lofting, H.	85-120	
Lofting, H.	Voyages of Doctor Dolittle (1st, 12mo, p-o, 364p, 2cp, pep, NM)	Stokes	1922	Lofting, H.	100-170	
Mother Goose	Mother Goose (1st, lg4to, 113p, color, pep)	Saalfield	(1938)	Lohman, F.D.	65-80	*
Oursler, Fulton	String of Blue Beads (1st {std}, 12mo, ibds, [32]p, color)	Doubleday	1956	Lonette, R.	25-40	*
Crothers, S.M.	Miss Muffet's Christmas Party (1st, 8vo, blue/gilt, 106p, pep)	Houghton	1902	Long, O.M.	30-45	
Long, O.M.	The Lollipops (1st, ob8vo, ipcb, [28]p, b/w)	R.H. Russell	1901	Long, O.M.	100-140	*
Kilbourne, C.E.	Baby Elephant & Zoo Man (1st, 8vo, p-o, color, pep)	Penn	1911	Longstreet, H.	70-110	*
Kilbourne, C.E.	Baby Ostrich & Mr. Wise Owl (1st, 16mo, ipcb, p-o, 82p, col, pep)	Penn	1915	Longstreet, H.	80-120	R*
Kilbourne, C.E.	Baby Reindeer & Silver Fox (1st, 16mo, ipcb, p-o, 82p, col, pep)	Penn	1916	Longstreet, H.	70-100	R*
Barzini, Luigi	Little Match Man (1st, lg8vo, 164p, p-o, 5cp, pep)	Penn	1917	Longstreet, H.	35-50	*
Mother Goose	Familiar Rhymes of Mother Goose (1st, 8vo, 30cp, pcb)	L: Nister	1888	Loomis, C.B.	180-260	
Loomis, C.B.	Little Maud & her Mama (1st, 16mo, 43p, brown cl, 4pl)	Doubleday/Page	1909	Loomis, C.B.	30-45	*
Deutsch, B.	Tales of Faraway Folk (1st, 8vo, yellow cl, 68p, b/w, pep)	Harper	(1952)	Lorentowicz, I.	25-45	*
Loud, Marian V.	Picnic on a Pyramid (1st, 8vo, 114p, grey cl, 4pl)	Saalfield	1904	Loud, M.V.	30-45	*
Love, E.	Rocking Island (1st, lg8vo, p-o, 182p, purple cl, 6cp)	Nelson	(1927)	Love, E.	30-45	
MacMunn, G.F.	Armies of India (1st, 8vo, blue/gilt, 224p, teg, 72cp)	L: A&C Black	1911	Lovett, A.C.	60-100	
Schlein, M.	Big Cheese (1st, sm4to, white cl, [48]p, 2-color)	W.R. Scott	1958	Low, J.	30-45	*
Keiser, R.	God Returns to Vuelta Abajo (1st, lg8vo, 149p, rust cl, p-o)	W.R. Scott	(1936)	Low, J.	70-100	R*
Hawley, H.E.	Story of a Little Tin Soldier (1st, 4to, p-o, 64p, 6cp)	Cupples	(1914)	Low, L.	50-70	
Hawley, H.E.	Timothy Toddlekin (1st, 4to, red cl, 64p, p-o, 6cp, 6pl)	Cupples	(1914)	Low, L.	40-65	
Hawley, H.E.	Woodland Party (1st, 4to, p-o, 49p, 6cp)	Cupples	(1913)	Low, L.	50-70	
Mabie, H.W.	In Arcady (1st, 8vo, 128p, teg, green/gilt, 4pl, pep)	Dodd	1903	Low, W.H.	30-45	

AUTHOR	TITLE	PUBLISHER	DATE	ARTIST	PRICE	LC
Stockton, Frank	Bicycle of Cathay (1st, sm8vo, 240p, 32pl)	Harper	1900	Lowell, O.	30-45	
Kipling, R.	Brushwood Boy (1st, 8vo, blue cl, teg, uncut, 119p, b/w, pep)	Doub./McClure	1899	Lowell, O.	100-165	
White, W.A.	Court of Boyville (1st, 8vo, 358p, buckram, PPP)	Doub./McClure	1899	Lowell, O.	120-160	
Webster, J.	Jerry Junior (1st, 8vo, green cl, p-o, 282p, 15pl)	Century	1907	Lowell, O.	20-25	
Powell, R.S.	Phyllis in Bohemia (1st, 12mo, teg, 233p, 3pl)	H. Stone	1897	Lowell, O.	45-60	
Creswick, Paul	Greypaws... (1st, 8vo, 64p, 5pl)	L: Partridge	[1909]	Lucas, K.	50-65	*
Chesterton, G.K.	Innocence of Father Brown (1st, 8vo, 334p, red/gilt, 8pl)	L: Cassell	1911	Lucas, S.S.	180-220	
Ludins, Ryah	Wonder Rock (1st, ob8vo, [40]p, ibds, 2-color)	Coward	1931	Ludins, R.	35-50	*
Selsam, M.E.	A Time for Sleep (1st, sm8vo, [57]p)	W.R. Scott	1953	Ludwig, H.	25-40	*
Selsam, M.E.	All About Eggs (1st, sm8vo, [62]p, 3-color)	W.R. Scott	1952	Ludwig, H.	30-45	*
Kelly, Eric P.	At the Sign/Golden Compass (1st, 8vo, grn/gilt, 195p, 11pl, pep)	MacMillan	1938	Lufkin, R.	20-30	*
Lide, A.A.	Ood-Le-Uk: Wanderer (1st, sm8vo, 265p, col frn, pep, NH)	Little/Brown	1930	Lufkin, R.	30-55	*
Bontemps, A.	Story of the Negro (1st, 8vo, 239p, b/w, NH)	Knopf	1948	Lufkin, R.	70-100	*
Kelly, Eric P.	Treasure Mountain (1st, 8vo, 211p, green cl, pep, b/w)	MacMillan	1937	Lufkin, R.	25-40	*
Arnold, E.	Voyage of Ithobal (1st, 8vo, teg, blue cl, 8pl)	Dillingham	1901	Lumley, A.	20-25	
France, A.	Honey-Bee (1st, lg8vo, red cl, 172p, uncut, teg, 12cp, pep)	L: J. Lane	1911	Lundborg, F.	45-60	
White, S.E.	The Mountains (1st, 8vo, 282p, teg, col frn, 15pl)	McClure	1904	Lungren, F.H.	30-45	
White, S.E.	The Pass (1st, 8vo, 194p, blue cl, 15pl)	Outing	1906	Lungren, F.H.	25-40	
Lupprian, H.	Honey Land (1st, 4to, [30]p, ibds, color)	McLoughlin	1927	Lupprian, H.	80-120	
Bonner, M.G.	Hundred Trips to Storyland (1st, 8vo, 327p, orang cl, 7cp, pep)	Macaulay	(1930)	Lupprian, H.	45-65	*
Harrison, Eliz.	In the Story World (1st, 12mo, 204p, gilt, dep, fp b/w)	M. Bradley	(1931)	Lupprian, H.	25-40	
Bannerman, H.	Little Black Sambo (12mo, ibds, color)	McLoughlin	(1938)	Lupprian, H.	90-140	
Hulbert, H.B.	Omjee, The Wizard... (1st, lg8vo, 156p, black cl, color, pep)	M. Bradley	(1925)	Lupprian, H.	35-50	
Bailey, C.S.	Read Aloud Stories (1st, 8vo, 215p, red/gilt, 6cp, pep)	M. Bradley	(1929)	Lupprian, H.	25-40	*
Harraden, B.	New Book of the Fairies (1st, 8vo, 190p, gilt, 10pl)	L: Griffith	[1891]	Lupton, E.D.	65-80	*
Lyall, M.M.	Cubies' ABC (1st, ob8vo, p-o, 56p, color)	Putnam	1913	Lyall, E.H.	170-230	
Lang, A. (tr.)	Johnny Nut & Golden Goose (1st, 4to, 45p, teg, blu/glt, b/w, cep)	L: Longmans	1887	Lynen, A.	80-120	
Tripp, Paul	Tale of Tubby the Tuba (1st, ob8vo, ibds, [26]p, color, pep)	Vanguard Pr.	(1948)	Maas, G.	65-90	*
Rourke, C.	Davy Crockett (1st, 8vo, green cl, 276p, 8pl, NH)	Harcourt	(1934)	MacDonald, J.	40-65	*
Rossetti, D.G.	Blessed Damozel (1st, 8vo, 54p, gilt, teg, uncut)	L: Duckworth	1898	MacDougall, W.B.	85-120	
N/A	Book of Ruth (1st AM, 4to, tan/gilt, 16 designs by...)	Dodd	1896	MacDougall, W.B.	150-200	
Armour, M. (ed.)	Eerie Book (1st, lg8vo, teg, 211p, uncut, 15pl)	L: Shiells	1898	MacDougall, W.B.	150-225	
Armour, M.	Fall of the Nibelungs (1st, 8vo, 16pl)	L: Dent	1897	MacDougall, W.B.	170-240	
Keats, J.	Isabella... (1st, 4to, teg, gilt, 8pl)	L: Kegan Paul	1898	MacDougall, W.B.	150-200	
Omar Khayyam	Rubaiyat... (1st, 4to, uncut, green/gilt, 43p, b/w)	L: MacMillan	1898	MacDougall, W.B.	100-165	
Armour, M.	Shadow of Love (1st, 8vo, 124p)	L: Duckworth	1898	MacDougall, W.B.	65-80	*
Brown, Dr. John	Jeems the Door Keeper (1st, 16mo, teg, uncut, 105p, 8 ticp)	L: Foulis	1912	MacGoun, H.C.P.	50-65	
Brown, Dr. John	Little Book of Children (12mo, 57p, ibds, teg, gilt, 8cp)	L: Foulis	1923	MacGoun, H.C.P.	30-45	*
Parry, E.A.	Butterscotia... (1st, 8vo, blue/gilt, uncut, 170p, map, 6pl)	L: D. Nutt	1896	MacGregor, A.	150-220	
Parry, E.A.	First Book of Krab (1st, lg8vo, green cl, 132p, uncut)	L: D. Nutt	1897	MacGregor, A.	120-170	
Parry, E.A.	Katawampus: Its Treatment & Cure (1st, 8vo, green cl, 96p, b/w)	L: D. Nutt	1895	MacGregor, A.	100-145	
Smedley, C.	Wizards of Ryetown (1st, 12mo, gilt, 273p, b/w)	Holt	1905	MacGregor, A.	50-70	
Fezandie, Clement	Through the Earth (1st, 8vo, tan cl, 238p, 15pl by...)	Century	1898	MacKay, W.A.	60-85	
N/A	Aladdin & his Wonderful Lamp (1st, 4to, [17]p, cloth, color, DJ)	MacMillan	1935	MacKinstry, E.	70-100	
Field, R.	Eliza & the Elves (1st, 8vo, green/gilt, 96p, 2cp, pep)	MacMillan	1926	MacKinstry, E.	65-85	
MacKinstry, E.	Fairy Alphabet (1st, lg8vo, 59p, ibds, 26pl, DJ)	Viking	1933	MacKinstry, E.	80-120	
Andersen, H.C.	Fairy Tales (1st {std}, 4to, 253p, p-o, color, pep, DJ)	Coward	(1933)	MacKinstry, E.	70-100	
Noyes, A.	Forty Singing Seamen (1st, 8vo, ipcb, 124p, 6cp, pep)	Stokes	(1930)	MacKinstry, E.	45-60	
Colum, P.	Legend of St. Columbia (1st, lg8vo, green cl, 156p, b/w)	MacMillan	1935	MacKinstry, E.	40-65	
Johnson, Burgess	Little Book/Necessary Nonsense (1st {std}, 16mo, 81p, b/w, dep)	Harper	1929	MacKinstry, E.	25-40	*
Field, R.	Magic Pawnshop (1st, 8vo, ibds, 125p, color, DJ)	Dutton	(1927)	MacKinstry, E.	50-80	
Moore, C.C.	Night Before Christmas (1st, 4to, ibds, [26]p, color)	Dutton	1928	MacKinstry, E.	80-130	R
Isben, H.	Peer Gynt (1st {std}, 4to, green bds, p-o, 286p, pep, 10cp)	Doubleday/Dor.	1929	MacKinstry, E.	60-80	
MacDonald, Geo.	Princess & Goblin (1st, lg8vo, 271p, 4cp)	Doubleday/Dor.	1928	MacKinstry, E.	60-85	
MacKinstry, E.	Puck in Pasture (1st {std}, 8vo, ibds, 79p, pep, b/w)	Doubleday/Page	1925	MacKinstry, E.	35-50	
White, Hervey	Snake Gold (1st, 12mo, 220p, decor by...)	MacMillan	1926	MacKinstry, E.	25-40	*
Wiggin, K.D.	Tales of Laughter (1st, lg8vo, 331p, black cl, 8cp)	Doubleday/Page	1926	MacKinstry, E.	60-85	
MacKaye, P.	Tall Tales/Kentucky Mountains (1st, 8vo, ipcb, p-o, col frn 185p)	Doran	(1926)	MacKinstry, E.	30-45	*
Kilmer, J.	Trees (1st, 8vo, [24]p, ipcb, color, DJ)	Doran	(1925)	MacKinstry, E.	45-65	
Geister, E.	What Shall We Play? (1st, lg8vo, 175p, ibds, p-o, col frn, cep)	Doran	(1924)	MacKinstry, E.	40-65	
D'Aulnoy	White Cat... (1st, 4to, ibds, p-o, 8cp, pep, DJ)	MacMillan	1928	MacKinstry, E.	85-110	
Sefton, H.L.	Dream Imp & Others (1st, 4to, 96p, red/gilt, 10cp)	L: Bickers	[1912]	MacQuigg, G.E.	120-180	
Stevenson, R.L.	Dr. Jekyll & Mr. Hyde (1st, lg8vo, gilt, teg, 189p, 8pl)	Scott-Thaw	1904	Macauley, C.R.	70-100	*
Bangs, J.K.	Emblemland (1st, 8vo, 164p, blue/gilt, fp b/w)	R.H. Russell	1902	Macauley, C.R.	60-85	*
Macauley, C.R.	Fantasma Land (1st, brown/gilt, 8vo, 204p, b/w)	Bobbs-Merrill	(1904)	Macauley, C.R.	60-85	
Adams, S.H.	Flying Death (1st, 12mo, brown cl, 239p, 4pl)	McClure	1908	Macauley, C.R.	30-45	
Harper, Vincent	Mortgage on the Brain (1st, 8vo, brown/gilt, 293p, 4pl)	Doubleday/Page	1905	Macauley, C.R.	25-40	*
Conrad, J.	Romance (1st AM, 8vo, 428p, 8pl)	McClure	1904	Macauley, C.R.	120-165	
Tarn, W.W.	Treasure of Isle of Mist (1st, 8vo, grn/gilt, 163p, fp 1-color)	L: P. Allan	1919	Macdonald, S.	45-65	
Mitchell, J.A.	Drowsy (1st [1], 8vo, blue/gilt, 301p, 19pl)	Stokes	(1917)	Macdonall, A.	30-45	
Pope, J.	Bobbity Flop (1st, ob8vo, unpag)	L: Blackie	[1912]	Macgregor, A.J.	50-70	*
Pope, J.	Bunny Book (1st, 4to, [36]p, ibds, color)	L: Blackie	(1909)	Macgregor, A.J.	50-70	*

AUTHOR	TITLE	PUBLISHER	DATE	ARTIST	PRICE	LC
Woodhouse, S.C.	Crude Ditties (1st, 16mo, 103p, tan cl, 24 fp color)	Swan/Dutton	1903	Macgregor, A.J.	80-100	*
Cullen, Countee	My Lives & How I Lost Them (1st {std}, 8vo, orang cl, 160p, b/w)	Harper	(1942)	Macguire, R.R.	80-120	*
Dawson, Forbes	Sensational Trance (1st, 8vo, 178p, red cl, 20pl)	L: Downey	1895	Mackenzie, F.	80-100	
Ransome, A.	Aladdin & his Wonderful Lamp (1st, 4to, [128]p, cloth, 12 ticp)	L: J. Nisbet	[1919]	Mackenzie, T.	280-400	
Ransome, A.	Aladdin & his Wonderful Lamp (1st AM, sm4to, [128]p, 12ticp pep)	Brentano's	[1920]	Mackenzie, T.	120-165	
N/A	Ali Baba & Aladdin (1st, 4to, 128p, ibds, 8cp)	L: Harrap	1918	Mackenzie, T.	160-200	
Chaundler, C.	Arthur & His Knights (1st AM, lg8vo, 311p, 8 ticp, pep)	Stokes	[1923]	Mackenzie, T.	100-165	
Stephens, J.	Crock of Gold (1st, sm4to, 227p, red/gilt, 12cp)	L: MacMillan	1926	Mackenzie, T.	80-100	
Flecker, J.E.	Hassan (1st, 4to, 155p, teg, red/gilt, 12 ticp, pep)	L: Heinemann	1924	Mackenzie, T.	100-150	
Stapp, E.B.	Uncle Peter-Heathen (1st, 8vo, 285p, 10cp)	McKay	(1912)	Macy, H.	20-30	
Collodi, C.	Pinocchio (1st, 4to, ibds, 96p, cvr & col frn by...)	Saalfield	(1939)	Madsen, E.	75-100	*
Joseph, A.W.	Sondo: A Liberian Boy (1st, 4to, ibds, pep, 32p, fp b/w)	Whitman	(1936)	Magnie, B.	50-70	
Langford, George	Stories/First American Animals (1st, lg8vo, p-o, 242p, 5cp)	Boni/Liveright	(1923)	Mahon, Ty	45-60	*
Mallison, C.	Wooster-Poosters (1st, ob4to, p-o, 88p, 15cp, pep)	Stokes	(1931)	Mallison, C.	90-140	
Dalgliesh, A.	America Builds Homes (1st, sq8vo, ibds, [84]p, color, DJ)	Scribner	(1938)	Maloy, L.	30-45	
Maloy, L.	Arabella of the Merry-Go-Round (1st, sm ob4to, 64p, color)	Scribner	1935	Maloy, L.	25-40	
Dalgliesh, A.	Long Live the King! (1st, sq8vo, ipcb, 76p, color, dep)	Scribner	1937	Maloy, L.	25-40	
Johnson, Richard	Saint George & the Dragon (1st, lg8vo, [30]p, pep)	Scribner	1941	Maloy, L.	25-40	*
Maloy, L.	Tea Party in Plumpudding Street (1st, lg8vo, ibds, [54]p, 1-col)	Grosset/Dunlap	(1946)	Maloy, L.	25-40	
Maloy, L.	Wooden Shoes in America (1st, ob4to, [72]p, color)	Scribner	(1940)	Maloy, L.	35-50	*
Madison, J.	Sweethearts Always (2nd, 8vo, 210p, green/gilt, 8cp)	Reilly/Britton	1907	Manning, F.S.	65-80	
Meigs, C.	Wind in the Chimney (1st, 8vo, 144p, blue cl, col frn, 8pl, cep)	MacMillan	1934	Mansfield, L.	20-30	
Haines, Alice C.	Little Japs at Home (1st, lg4to, ibds, [26]p, 4cp)	Stokes	(1905)	Mar, Alice	170-240	
March, Eleanor	Little White Barbara (1st, 24mo, green cl, [91]p, color)	L: Richards	1902	March, E.	180-220	
Mighels, P.V.	Furnace of Gold (1st, sm8vo, 402p, p-o, 12pl)	D. Fitzgerald	(1910)	Marchand, J.	20-30	
Garland, H.	Money Magic (1st, 8vo, pcb, 354p, 8pl)	Harper	1907	Marchand, J.	30-45	
Thompson, R.P.	King Kojo (1st, 8vo, red cl, p-o, 239p, 8cp, pep)	McKay	(1938)	Marge	170-250	*
Bontemps, A.	Drums at Dusk (1st {std}, sm8vo, 226p, black cl, b/w, cep)	MacMillan	1939	Margenta	50-70	*
Browne, Frances	Granny's Wonderful Chair (24mo, gilt, 166p, AEG, 12cp)	L: H. Frowde	1908	Margetson, W.H.	85-140	
Clark, J.M.	Legends/King Arthur & his Knights (8vo, 307p, AEG, 6cp, pep)	L: Nister	[1899]	Margetson, W.H.	70-100	*
Andersen, H.C.	The Nightingale (1st {std}, 12mo, 20p, color, pep)	Harper	1937	Marine, E.	35-50	*
Moodey, M.M.	Here Comes the Peddler! (1st, lg8vo, ipcb, [32]p, b/w, cep)	Holiday House	(1947)	Markham, K.	20-30	*
DeSelincourt, Hugh	Oxford From Within (1st, 4to, 180p, blue/gilt, 12cp)	L: Chatto	1910	Markino, Y.	80-100	
Kalashnikoff, N.	Toyon: Dog of the North (1st {std}, 8vo, 246p, uncut, b/w)	Harper	(1950)	Markovia, A.	20-30	*
Smith, G.	Loveable Tales/Janey, Josey & Joe (1st, 4to, grn cl, 157p, 16cp)	Harper	1902	Mars, E.	65-100	
Smith, G.	Peter & Ellen (1st, lgsq8vo, 15cp)	Harper	1903	Mars, E.	65-80	*
Smith, G.	Roggie & Reggie Stories (1st, lgsq8vo, 15cp)	Harper	1900	Mars, E.	65-80	*
Speare, Eliz. G.	Calico Captive (1st, 8vo, red cl, 274p, b/w)	Houghton	1957	Mars, W.T.	25-40	*
Kalnay, Francis	Richest Boy in the World (1st {std}, 8vo, 92p, grn cl, fp b/w)	Harcourt	(1959)	Mars, W.T.	30-45	*
Lamb, C.	Adventures of Ulysses (1st, 4to, 117p, uncut, 16cp, cep)	R.H. Russell	1902	Mars/Squire	140-185	*
Stevenson, R.L.	Child's Garden of Verses (1st, lg sq4to, ibds, 115p, 12cp)	R.H. Russell	(1900)	Mars/Squire	165-220	
Stevenson, R.L.	Child's Garden of Verses (1st {this pub.}, 8vo, 94p, cp)	Rand/McNally	(1902)	Mars/Squire	65-80	
Hobart, G.V.	Li'l Verses for Li'l Fellers (1st, 4to, 121p, 7cp, 8pl)	R.H. Russell	1903	Mars/Squire	80-130	*
Kingsley, C.	The Heroes (1st, sm4to, blue cl, 186p, uncut, 24cp)	R.H. Russell	1901	Mars/Squire	180-225	R*
Marshall, H.	Scenery of London (1st, 8vo, 223p, gilt, teg, 75cp)	L: A&C Black	1905	Marshall, H.	50-90	
Gordon, Eliz.	Sheaf of Roses (1st, 8vo, [72]p, ipcb, color)	Rand/McNally	(1915)	Martin, F.W.	35-50	*
Adrian, M.	Fiddler Crab (1st, 8vo, 40p, aqua cl, 2-color)	Holiday House	(1953)	Martinez, J.	20-25	*
Voight, V.F.	House in Robin Lane (1st, sm8vo, 220p, yellow, cl, b/w)	Holiday House	(1951)	Martinez, J.	20-25	*
Moore, C.C.	Night Before Christmas (1st, 4to, ipcb, [18]p, color)	Whitman	1940	Masden, E.	25-45	
Mother Goose	Masha's Stuffed Mother Goose (1st {std}, 4to, 64p, color)	Garden City	1946	Masha	50-70	
Granville, A.	Fallen Race (1st, 8vo, blue/gilt, 352p, 5pl)	F.T. Neely	(1892)	Mason, E.	200-250	
Inman, H.E.	Gobbo Bobo (1st, 8vo, 477p, gilt, AEG, b/w)	L: Warne	1900	Mason, E.A.	85-110	*
Hall, A.W. (ed.)	Icelandic Fairy Tales (1st, 12mo, 317p, gilt, 8pl)	L: Warne	1897	Mason, E.A.	70-110	
Inman, H.E.	One-Eyed Griffin... (1st, 12mo, 353p, teg, gilt, 4pl, dep)	L: Warne	1897	Mason, E.A.	100-130	
Inman, H.E.	Owl King... (1st, 12mo, 353p, teg, 4pl, dep)	L: Warne	1897	Mason, E.A.	100-130	
Hendry, Hamish	Holidays & Happy Days (1st, 8vo, teg, 120p, 24cp)	L: Richards	1901	Mason, E.F.	85-130	
Steele, R. (tr.)	Renaud of Montauban (1st, 8vo, 284p, gilt, uncut 10 fp b/w)	L: G. Allen	1897	Mason, F.	70-95	
Steele, R.	Story of Alexander (1st, 8vo, 226p, uncut, 6pl)	L: D. Nutt	1894	Mason, F.	60-80	
Balch, Glenn	Hide-Rack Kidnapped (1st, sm8vo, 302p, dp pl)	Crowell	1939	Mason, G.F.	20-30	*
Harben, Wm. N.	Mam' Linda (1st, 12mo, 387p, green/gilt, 8pl)	Harper	1907	Masters, F.B.	30-45	
Merwin, S.	Road Builders (1st, 8vo, 313p, 10pl)	MacMillan	1905	Masters, F.B.	25-40	
Kozisek, Josef	Forest Story (1st, 4to, ibds, [58]p, color, pep)	MacMillan	1929	Mates, R.	120-165	*
Kozisek, Josef	Magic Flutes (1st, ob folio, [56]p, ibds, color)	L: Longmans	1929	Mates, R.	200-300	
Sedlacek, H.	Nursery Rhymes/Bohemia (1st AM, lg4to, [24]p, ibds, color, pep)	McBride	1929	Mates, R.	75-100	
Mother Goose	Mother Goose: Her Rhymes (lg8vo, blue cl, 142p, 6 ticp, pep)	Saalfield	(1915)	Matthews, H.B.	90-120	
Maud, C.	Wagner's Heroes (1st, 8vo, 285p, black/silver, 7pl)	L: E. Arnold	1896	Maud, W.T.	45-65	
Kipling, R.	East of Suez (1st, 4to, 72p, blue/gilt, 10cp)	L: MacMillan	1931	Maxwell, D.	80-100	
Maxwell, D.	Excursions in Color (1st, 8vo, 89 illus, 118p)	L: Cassell	1927	Maxwell, D.	70-120	
Maxwell, G.S.	Just Beyond London (1st, 8vo, 18pl)	L: Methuen	1927	Maxwell, D.	70-100	
Maxwell, D.	New Lights O'London (1st, lg8vo, 65 illus)	L: H. Jenkins	1926	Maxwell, D.	65-90	
Kipling, R.	Sea & Sussex (1st AM {std}, sm4to, 94p, teg, blue cl, 24 ticp)	Doubleday/Page	1926	Maxwell, D.	80-120	
Kipling, R.	Sea & Sussex (1st, 4to, 94p, blue/gilt, teg, 24 ticp)	L: MacMillan	1926	Maxwell, D.	120-165	

ILLUSTRATOR: 82

AUTHOR	TITLE	PUBLISHER	DATE	ARTIST	PRICE	LC
Kipling, R.	Songs of the Sea (1st, 4to, 99p, blue cl, 12cp)	L: MacMillan	1927	Maxwell, D.	65-80	
Milne, J.	Travels in Hope (1st, 4to, 190p, blue cl, 22cp)	L: Hodder	[1926]	Maxwell, D.	75-110	
Maxwell, D.	Wembley in Colour (1st, 4to, bds, 112p, 37cp)	L: Longmans	1924	Maxwell, D.	65-80	
Carroll, L.	Alice/Wonderland (1st, 12mo, 198p, col frn, gilt)	L: Routledge	[1907]	Maybank, T.	100-145	
Drayton, Michael	Court of Faery (8vo, teg, gilt, 8pl)	L: Routledge	1906	Maybank, T.	80-135	*
Herbertson, A.	Teddy & Trots in Wonderland (1st, 8vo, 254p, 27 illus)	L: Ward Lock	1910	Maybank, T.	70-100	*
Mayer, Henry	Adventures of a Japanese Doll (1st, ob4to, 127p, ibds, 30cp)	L: Richards	1901	Mayer, H.	200-300	
Mayer, Henry	In Laughland (1st, folio, [58]p)	R.H. Russell	1899	Mayer, H.	250-400	*
Mayer, Henry	Trip to Toyland (lg ob4to, ibds, 127p, 30 fp color)	L: Richards	1900	Mayer, H.	200-300	
Collodi, C.	Story of a Puppet (1st {Engl.trans.}, 8vo, grn/gilt, 232p, teg)	L: T. F. Unwin	1892	Mazzanti, C.	800-1000	
Laboulaye, E.R.	Laboulaye's Fairy Book (1st, lg8vo, 199p, p-o, 12cp, DJ)	Harper	(1920)	McCandlish, E.	60-80	
Voight, V.F.	Zeke & the Fisher-Cat (1st, 8vo, 201p, red cl, b/w, pep)	Holiday House	(1953)	McChesney, H.	20-30	*
Blodgett, M.F.	When Christmas Came Too Early (1st, 12mo, 107p, 6cp)	Little/Brown	1912	McClellan, R.	30-45	*
McCloskey, R.	Blueberries for Sal (1st, ob4to, 54p, fp 1-color, CH)	Viking	1948	McCloskey, R.	60-90	*
Robertson, Keith	Henry Reed, Inc. (1st, 8vo, 239p, b/w)	Viking	(1958)	McCloskey, R.	30-60	R*
McCloskey, R.	Homer Price (1st, lg8vo, 149p, blue cloth, sepia)	Viking	1943	McCloskey, R.	60-100	R*
Sawyer, R.S.	Journey Cake, Ho! (1st, 4to, 45p, 2-color, pep, DJ, CH)	Viking	1953	McCloskey, R.	65-100	R
White, Anne H.	Junket (1st, 8vo, 184p, b/w, DJ)	Viking	1955	McCloskey, R.	40-65	*
McCloskey, R.	Lentil (1st {1st bk.}, lg4to, beige cl, fp b/w, [61]p, pep)	Viking	1940	McCloskey, R.	85-130	R
McCloskey, R.	Make Way for Ducklings (1st, lg4to, [70]p, 1-color, pep, CM)	Viking	1941	McCloskey, R.	100-170	R
Bishop, C.H.	Man Who Lost his Head (1st, ob4to, ibds, pep, [53]p, b/w)	Viking	1942	McCloskey, R.	35-60	*
McCloskey, R.	One Morning in Maine (1st, lg4to, 64p, grey cl, pep, DJ, CH)	Viking	1952	McCloskey, R.	100-140	
McCloskey, R.	Time of Wonder (1st, lg4to, 63p, blue cl, color, CM)	Viking	(1957)	McCloskey, R.	70-100	*
Davis, Rbt.	Tree Toad (1st, 8vo, 276p, b/w)	Stokes	1942	McCloskey, R.	30-50	*
Robinson, Tom P.	Trigger John's Son (1st, 8vo, 284p, b/w, DJ)	Viking	1949	McCloskey, R.	45-60	
Malcolmson, A.	Yankee Doodle's Cousins (1st, 4to, 267p, red cl, fp b/w, pep)	Houghton	1941	McCloskey, R.	75-120	R*
Crissey, F.	Country Boy (1st, 8vo, 300p, uncut, gilt, 14pl by...)	Revell	(1903)	McClure, G.M.	40-60	*
Knowles, R.E.	Dawn at Shanty Bay (1st, 8vo, green/gilt, 156p, col frn, dep)	Revell	(1907)	McClure, G.M.	30-45	
Stewart, Mary	Once Upon a Time Tales (1st, 8vo, 275p, pep, 8cp)	Revell	(1912)	McClure, G.M.	40-60	*
Barr, A.	Souls of Passage (1st, sm8vo, 327p, 6pl)	Dodd	1901	McConnell, E.	20-25	*
Sewell, Daisy	About Fairies.... (1st, sq8vo, ibds, 76p, 5cp)	L: Allenson	[1930]	McConnell, J.	100-140	
Sewell, Daisy	Visions in Fairyland (1st, sq8vo, ibds, 69p, 3cp)	L: Allenson	[1930]	McConnell, J.	100-150	
Newbolt, H.	Drake's Drum... (1st, 4to, green cl, 143p, 12cp)	L: Hodder	[1914]	McCormick, A.D.	65-100	
Hudson, W.H.	Little Boy Lost (1st, 8vo, buckram, 201p, b/w pl)	L: Duckworth	1905	McCormick, A.D.	140-185	
MacGregor, M.	Romance of the Netherlands (1st, 8vo, teg, 344p, uncut, 12cp)	Jack/Stokes	[1910]	McCormick, A.D.	50-65	
Poe, E.A.	Tales of Mystery... (1st, 8vo, 416p)	L: A. Pearson	1905	McCormick, A.D.	65-80	*
McCoy, N.	Jupie the Wise Old Owl (1st, 8vo, cloth, 95p, 3cp, pep)	MacMillan	1931	McCoy, N.	20-35	
Stevenson, R.L.	Child's Garden of Verses (1st, 8vo, 127p, color)	Whitman	(1930)	McCracken, J.	25-40	*
Gordon, Eliz.	Lorraine & Little People of Summer (1st, sm8vo, 64p, color)	Rand/McNally	(1920)	McCracken, J.	30-45	*
Browning, R.	Pied Piper of Hamelin (1st, sm4to, p-o, [64]p, color, pep)	Whitman	1927	McCracken, J.	45-70	
Garnett, L.A.	The Merrymakers (1st, sm4to, ipcb, 80p, 8 fp color)	Rand/McNally	(1918)	McCracken, J.	45-65	
Pratt, Ella	Happy Children (1st, lg4to, 64p, ibds, 8cp)	Crowell	(1896)	McCullough, Wm.	130-165	*
Pyle/Porter	Theodora (1st, 12mo, 271p, 4pl)	Little/Brown	1907	McCullough, Wm.	30-45	*
Ade, G.	Artie (1st {1st bk.}, 12mo, 192p, teg, blue cl)	H. Stone	1896	McCutcheon, J.T.	50-85	
McCutcheon, J.T.	Congressman Pumphrey (1st, 8vo, 126p, b/w)	Bobbs-Merrill	(1907)	McCutcheon, J.T.	20-30	*
Kiser, S.E.	Love Sonnets/Office Boy (1st, 16mo, ibds, 42p)	Chi: Forbes	1902	McCutcheon, J.T.	25-40	*
Ade, G.	People You Know (1st, 12mo, blue cl, 224p, b/w)	R.H. Russell	1903	McCutcheon, J.T.	35-50	
Ade, G.	Pink Marsh (1st, sm8vo, green cl, 197p, teg, uncut)	H. Stone	1897	McCutcheon, J.T.	50-70	
Crissey, F.	Tattlings of a Retired Politician (1st, lg8vo, teg, 487p)	Chi: Thompson	1904	McCutcheon, J.T.	25-40	
Lippmann, J.M.	Jock O'Dreams (1st, 8vo, 211p, gilt, b/w)	Roberts	1891	McDermott, J.	30-45	*
McDougall, Walt	Rambillicus Book (1st, lg8vo, 239p, 20pl)	Jacobs	(1903)	McDougall, W.H.	65-80	*
McGaw, Jessie B.	How Medicine Man Cured Paleface Women (1st, ob4to, [62]p, 1-col)	W.R. Scott	(1956)	McGaw, J.B.	35-50	*
McGinley, Phyllis	On the Contrary (1st {std}, sm8vo, 119p, b/w)	Doubleday/Dor.	1934	McGinley, P.	25-40	*
Topelius, Z.	Canute Whistlewinks... (1st {std}, 8vo, 272p, orang cl, 5cp, dep)	NY: Longmans	1927	McIntosh, F.	40-60	
Coatsworth, E.	Sun's Diary (1st, sq8vo, ibds, [98]p, b/w, cep)	MacMillan	1929	McIntosh, F.	65-80	R
N/A	Cinderella (1st, ob4to, [14]p, color)	McLoughlin	1943	McKean, E.C.	45-60	*
N/A	Goldilocks & Three Bears (1st, ob4to, [14]p, color)	McLoughlin	1943	McKean, E.C.	35-65	*
Sewell, Anna	Black Beauty (1st, 4to, 244p, p-o, gilt, col frn)	Sears	(1926)	McMann, J.S.	35-50	*
Carroll, L.	Alice... & Through... (8vo, 255p, beige cl, 16 fp color)	Platt/Peck	(1900)	McManus, B.	100-165	*
Carroll, L.	Alice... & Through... (1st, lg8vo, 255p, yellow cl, 12cp)	A. Wessels	(1900)	McManus, B.	120-170	*
Carroll, L.	Alice/Wonderland (1st, 4to, 255p, yellow/gilt, 16cp)	Wessels	(1899)	McManus, B.	120-165	R
Carroll, L.	Alice/Wonderland (sm8vo, green/gilt, 8pl)	L: Ward Lock	[1901]	McManus, B.	60-90	
Ervin, M.C.	As Told by the Typewriter Girl (1st, 8vo, 245p)	Herrick	(1898)	McManus, B.	50-75	
Miltoun, F.	Automobilist Abroad (1st, 8vo, 381p, p-o, col frn)	Page	1907	McManus, B.	25-40	
McManus, B.	Bachelor Ballads (1st, 8vo, beige cl, 159p, color)	New Amsterdam	1898	McManus, B.	50-75	
Mansfield, R.	Blown Away (1st, 8vo, 180p, cvr by...)	Page	1897	McManus, B.	50-80	
McManus, B.	Calendar of Omar Khayaam (4to, ibds, dep, color)	Page	1904	McManus, B.	70-100	*
Miltoun, F.	Castles & Chateaux of Touraine (1st, 8vo, 347p, 39pl)	Page	1906	McManus, B.	35-50	
Raymond, W.	Charity Chance (1st, 12mo, 256p, cvr by..)	Dodd	1896	McManus, B.	20-25	*
Porter, Rose	Charm of Birds (1st, 12mo, 206p, teg, cvr by...)	Herrick	(1897)	McManus, B.	35-50	
Watts, Isaac	Childhood Songs of Long Ago (1st, 8vo, 87p, 20pl, pep)	Herrick	(1897)	McManus, B.	60-80	
Hawthorne, N.	In Colonial Days (1st, 8vo, 104p, beige/gilt, cvr by...)	Page	1906	McManus, B.	20-35	

AUTHOR	TITLE	PUBLISHER	DATE	ARTIST	PRICE	LC
Clemens, W.M.	Ken of Kipling (1st, 12mo, 141p, orange cl)	New Amsterdam	1899	McManus, B.	40-70	
McManus, B.	Little Dutch Cousin (1st, 12mo, 99p, 6pl)	Page	1906	McManus, B.	20-35	*
McManus, B.	Little French Cousin (1st, sm8vo, 116p, 6pl)	Page	1905	McManus, B.	20-35	*
McManus, B.	Little Hindu Cousin (1st, sm8vo, 103p, 6pl)	Page	1907	McManus, B.	20-35	*
McManus, B.	Little Scotish Cousin (1st, sm8vo, 95p, 6pl)	Page	1906	McManus, B.	20-35	*
Nixon-Roulet	Little Spanish Cousin (1st, sm8vo, 125p, 6pl)	Page	1906	McManus, B.	20-35	*
Mother Goose	Mother Goose Nursery Rhymes (1st {this pub}, sq8vo, 136p, b/w)	Platt/Peck	(1912)	McManus, B.	70-90	
Miltoun, F.	Rambles on the Riviera (1st, 8vo, teg, 434p, 32pl)	Page	1906	McManus, B.	30-45	
Omar Khayyam	Rubaiyat... (1st, 8vo, 25p, 12 illus)	L: A. Moring	1903	McManus, B.	65-90	*
Omar Khayyam	Rubaiyat... (1st {this pub}, 12mo, 159p, color)	Page	1907	McManus, B.	35-50	*
Fezandie, Clement	Through the Earth (1st, 8vo, tan cl, 238p, cvr by...)	Century	1898	McManus, B.	60-85	
Carroll, L.	Through the Looking Glass (1st, lg8vo, 139p, grey/gilt, 12cp)	Mansfield/Wes.	1899	McManus, B.	120-160	
N/A	Told in the Twilight (1st, 8vo, tan cloth, 9pl)	Herrick	(1898)	McManus, B.	65-80	
Mother Goose	True Mother Goose (1st, lg8vo, 138p)	Chi: Lamson	1896	McManus, B.	100-165	R*
Mother Goose	True Mother Goose (1st, lg8vo, 138p, b/w)	Mansfield/Wes.	1899	McManus, B.	80-150	*
Mother Goose	True Mother Goose (1st {this pub.}, 4to, 136p)	Wessels	1901	McManus, B.	80-100	
Hall, Tom	When Cupid Calls (1st, sm8vo, teg, 116p)	Herrick	1898	McManus, B.	20-35	*
Roberts, C.G.D.	Young Acadian (1st, 12mo, 139p, 6pl)	Page	1907	McManus, B.	25-40	*
McNagny, B.	Noah's Nightmare (1st, 4to, p-o, [67]p, 30cp)	Bobbs-Merrill	(1926)	McNagny, B.	50-80	
Pollard, J.	Boston Tea Party (1st, 8vo, ipcb, [32]p, color)	Dodd	1882	McVickar, H.W.	75-90	
Plummer, M.W.	Chronicles of the Cid (1st, 12mo, 155p, 10pl)	Holt	1910	McVickar, H.W.	50-80	*
James, Henry	Daisy Miller (1st, 8vo, stripe cl, 133p, b/w)	Harper	1892	McVickar, H.W.	90-130	
Holmes, O.W.	Grandmother's Story/Bunker Hill Battle (1st, 8vo, 32p, col, dep)	Dodd	(1883)	McVickar, H.W.	45-70	*
Bangs, J.K.	Mr. Bonaparte of Corsica (1st, 12mo, 265p, gilt)	Harper	1895	McVickar, H.W.	30-45	
N/A	Our Amateur Circus (1st, ob8vo, black/gilt, color)	Harper	1892	McVickar, H.W.	120-165	
Munroe, K.	Blue Dragon (1st, 12mo, 268p, grey cl, 7pl)	Harper	1904	Mears, W.E.	30-45	
Smith, G.	Doris & Julie (1st, lg sq8vo, 167p, 14cp)	Harper	1901	Mears, W.E.	65-80	*
Barnes, James	Son of Light Horse (1st, 12mo, 242p, 8pl)	Harper	1904	Mears, W.E.	20-35	*
Roche, J.J.	Sorrows of Sap'ed (1st, 8vo, uncut, 195p, p-o, 8cp)	Harper	1904	Mears, W.E.	20-30	
Garland, H.	Tyranny of the Dark (1st, 8vo, blue/gilt, 438p, 8pl)	Harper	1905	Mears, W.E.	25-40	
Grover, E.O.	Overall Boys in Switzerland (1st, 8vo, beige cl, 160p, pep)	Rand/McNally	(1916)	Melcher, B.C.	65-80	
Grover, E.O.	Sonbonnet Babies in Holland (1st, 8vo, map, 150p, color, pep)	Rand/McNally	(1915)	Melcher, B.C.	65-100	
Grover, E.O.	Sunbonnet Babies ABC Book... (1st, 4to, p-o, 64p, pep, color)	Rand/McNally	(1929)	Melcher, B.C.	75-100	
Grover, E.O.	Sunbonnet Babies in Mother Goose Land (1st, lg8vo, 115p, color)	Rand/McNally	(1927)	Melcher, B.C.	80-120	
Grover, E.O.	Sunbonnet Babies in Italy (1st, 8vo, 187p, color, pep)	Rand/McNally	(1922)	Melcher/McCracken	60-100	*
Farley, Walter	Blood Bay Colt (1st {std}, 8vo, 307p, fp b/w)	Random	(1950)	Menasco, M.	25-40	*
Menpes, M.	Brittany (1st, 8vo, gilt, 254p, teg, 75cp)	L: A&C Black	1912	Menpes, M.	65-100	
Blake, A.H.	China (1st, sm4to, 138p, blue/gilt, 16cp)	L: A&C Black	1909	Menpes, M.	60-90	
Menpes, M.	Japan (1st, lg8vo, 207p, teg, blue/gilt, 75cp)	L: A&C Black	1905	Menpes, M.	65-100	
Menpes, M.	Rembrandt (1st, 4to, 50p, teg, gilt, 16cp)	L: A&C Black	1905	Menpes, M.	70-110	
Menpes, D.	World Pictures (1st AM, 8vo, 332p, color)	R.H. Russell	1902	Menpes, M.	70-100	*
Menpes, M.	World's Children (1st, 8vo, teg, 246p, blue/gilt, 100cp)	L: A&C Black	1903	Menpes, M.	80-130	
Jacberns, R.	Crab Cottage (1st, 12mo, 285p, cep)	L: Chambers	1905	Menzies, J.	50-70	
Gilbert, Wm.	Magic Mirror (1st, 8vo, 253p, purple/gilt, p-o, teg, 20cp)	L: MacLaren	1908	Menzies, J.	65-90	
Syrett, Netta	Rachel & the Seven Wonders (1st, 8vo, 172p, p-o, 5cp, pep)	Stokes	(1923)	Mercer, J.	70-90	
Reed, H.L.	Brenda's Ward (1st, 8vo, 340p, 6pl)	Little/Brown	1906	Merrill, F.	20-30	
Richards, L.E.	Captain January (1st, sq8vo, teg, 133p, gilt, b/w)	Estes	1893	Merrill, F.	45-65	*
Bynner, E.L.	Chase of the Meteor... (1st, 8vo, 209p, gilt, 10b/w)	Little/Brown	1891	Merrill, F.	50-70	
Dickens, C.	Christmas Carol (8vo, AEG, blue cl)	Putnam	1907	Merrill, F.	30-50	
Otis, James	Fighting for the Empire (1st, 8vo, 466p, 8pl)	Estes	(1900)	Merrill, F.	35-50	
Johnston, A.F.	Giant Scissors (1st, 8vo, 201p, blue/gilt, teg, 8cp)	Page	1906	Merrill, F.	25-40	
Wattles, W.D.	Hell-Fire Harrison (1st, sm8vo, green cl, 6cp)	Page	1910	Merrill, F.	20-25	
Hawthorne, N.	In Colonial Days (1st, 8vo, 104p, beige/gilt, cp)	Page	1906	Merrill, F.	20-35	
Atkinson, E.	Johnny Apple-Seed (1st, sm8vo, 340p, b/w)	Harper	1915	Merrill, F.	20-30	*
Johnston, A.F.	Mary Ware of Texas (1st, 8vo, pict cl, 8pl)	Page	1910	Merrill, F.	25-40	
Dix, B.M.	Merrylips (1st, 8vo, 307p, 8pl, PPPa)	MacMillan	1906	Merrill, F.	35-50	*
Vaile, C.M.	Orcutt Girls (8vo, 316p, green cl)	Wilde	(1896)	Merrill, F.	20-25	
Irving, W.	Rip Van Winkle (1st, lg4to, 49p, b/w pl)	S.E. Cassino	1888	Merrill, F.	90-140	*
Peattie, E.W.	Edda & the Oak (1st, sq8vo, 134p, p-o)	Rand/McNally	(1911)	Merrill, K.	30-45	*
Wynne, Annette	Treasure Things (1st, 12mo, [39]p, ibds, pep, color)	Volland	(1922)	Merritt, E.	45-70	*
Eastwick, I.O.	Fairies & Suchlike (1st {std}, sq8vo, 63p, ipcb, 1-color, pep)	Dutton	1946	Merwin, D.	35-50	*
Turner, N.B.	Magpie Lane (1st, sm8vo, 88p, orang cl, silhouettes, dep)	Harcourt	(1927)	Merwin, D.	25-45	*
Shakespeare, Wm.	Romeo & Juliet (1st, 4to, purple cl, 8 ticp)	L: Batsford	1936	Messel, O.	70-100	*
Longfellow, H.W.	Golden Legend (1st, 4to, green/gilt, teg, 153p, 25 ticp)	L: Hodder	[1910]	Meteyard, S.	120-165	
Longfellow, H.W.	Golden Legend (1st AM, 4to, 153p, gilt, 25 ticp)	Doran	[1912]	Meteyard, S.	100-140	
Stevenson, R.L.	Ebb-Tide (1st, 16mo, 204p, gilt, ^Evr by...)	Stone/Kimball	1894	Meteyard, T.B.	70-110	
Hovey, R.	Marriage of Guenevere (1st, 8vo, 179p, cvr by...)	H. Stone	1895	Meteyard, T.B.	65-90	R
Carman, B.	Winter Holiday (1st, 12mo, 43p, cvr by...)	Small/Maynard	1899	Meteyard, T.B.	45-60	
Nesbit, W.D.	Jolly Kid Book (1st, ob4to, ibds, [12]p, color)	Volland	(1926)	Meyers, M.H.	120-170	
Michael, A.C.	Artist in Spain (1st, 4to, rust cl, 205p, 20 ticp)	L: Hodder	[1920]	Michael, A.C.	50-70	
Stevenson, R.L.	Catriona (1st, 8vo, 357p, 4cp)	L: Cassell	(1915)	Michael, A.C.	45-60	*
Haggard, H.R.	Child of the Storm (1st AM, 8vo, red cl, 335p, 3pl)	NY: Longmans	1913	Michael, A.C.	50-70	*

AUTHOR	TITLE	PUBLISHER	DATE	ARTIST	PRICE	LC
Dickens, C.	Christmas Carol (1st, 4to, red/gilt, 116p, pep, 9 ticp)	L: Hodder	[1911]	Michael, A.C.	80-140	R
Haggard, H.R.	Ivory Child (1st, 8vo, 344p, col frn, 3pl)	L: Cassell	(1916)	Michael, A.C.	70-95	
Dorrington, A.	Radium Terrors (1st, sm8vo, red/gilt, 361p, 4pl)	Doubleday/Page	1912	Michael, A.C.	30-50	
Wells, H.G.	War in the Air (1st, 8vo, blue/gilt, 389p, uncut, 16pl)	L: G. Bell	1908	Michael, A.C.	260-350	
Mighels, P.V.	Chatwit the Man-Talk Bird (1st, 8vo, blue cl, 265p, b/w)	Harper	1906	Mighels, P.	20-35	*
Dalgliesh, A.	Along Janet's Road (1st, sm8vo, 208p, gilt, pep, decor by...)	Scribner	1946	Milhous, K.	30-45	*
Milhous, Kath.	Appolonia's Valentine (1st, 4to, red cl, [32]p, color, DJ)	Scribner	(1954)	Milhous, K.	70-120	R*
Hunt, M.L.	Billy Button's Buttered Biscuit (1st, 12mo, 56p, color, cep)	Stokes	1941	Milhous, K.	20-35	*
Dalgliesh, A.	Book for Jennifer (1st, 8vo, 114p, uncut, 10cp)	Scribner	1940	Milhous, K.	50-70	
Milhous, Kath.	Corporal Keeperupper (1st, sm8vo, 62p, ipcb, color)	Scribner	1943	Milhous, K.	25-40	*
Milhous, Kath.	Egg Tree (1st, sm4to, [32]p, aqua cl, color, DJ, CM)	Scribner	(1950)	Milhous, K.	100-135	
Milhous, Kath.	First Christmas Crib (1st, 12mo, ibds, 47p, color)	Scribner	1944	Milhous, K.	20-25	*
Dalgliesh, A.	Happily Ever After (1st, 4to, 60p, 7 fp color, DJ)	Scribner	(1939)	Milhous, K.	70-90	
Milhous, Kath.	Herodia the Lovely Puppet (1st, 8vo, 193p, red cl, pep, 7cp)	Scribner	1942	Milhous, K.	60-100	R*
Dalgliesh, A.	Little Angel (1st, 8vo, 70p, color, pep, DJ)	Scribner	1943	Milhous, K.	35-50	
Milhous, Kath.	Lovina (1st, ob4to, [48]p, red cl, color)	Scribner	(1940)	Milhous, K.	30-45	*
Sherwood, L.	Old Abe, American Eagle (1st, 8vo, 60p, ibds, color, DJ)	Scribner	1946	Milhous, K.	25-40	
Dalgliesh, A.	Once On a Time (1st, sm4to, 70p, 10 fp color)	Scribner	(1938)	Milhous, K.	30-45	*
Hunt, M.L.	Peter Piper's Pickled Peppers (1st, 16mo, 62p, cep, 4cp)	Stokes	1942	Milhous, K.	25-40	*
Dalgliesh, A.	Silver Pencil (1st, 8vo, 235p, blue/gilt, pep, NH)	Scribner	1944	Milhous, K.	50-70	
Milhous, Kath.	Snow Over Bethlehem (1st, 8vo, 98p, pep, 3 dp color)	Scribner	1945	Milhous, K.	25-40	*
Ewing, J.H.	The Brownies (1st, 12mo, ibds, 50p, color, DJ)	Scribner	1946	Milhous, K.	30-45	
Dalgliesh, A.	Wings Around South America (1st, 4to, 158p, fp color, cep)	Scribner	1941	Milhous, K.	30-45	
Milius, W.	Here Comes Daddy (1st, ob8vo, ipcb, [22]p, color)	W.R. Scott	1944	Milius, W.	35-50	*
Nesbit, E.	Book of Dragons (1st, 8vo, teg, 290p, blue/gilt, 16 b/w by...)	L: Harper	1901	Millar, H.R.	400-500	
N/A	Diamond Fairy Book (1st, 8vo, 310p, gilt, AEG, b/w, dep)	L: Hutchinson	(1897)	Millar, H.R.	100-165	
Millar, H.R.	Dreamland Express (1st AM, ob4to, 56p, ibds, 14cp)	Dodd	(1927)	Millar, H.R.	85-125	
Nesbit, E.	Enchanted Castle (1st AM, 12mo, 297p, 8pl)	Harper	1908	Millar, H.R.	180-220	*
Nesbit, E.	Enchanted Castle (1st, 8vo, 352p, red/gilt, 46pl)	L: T.F. Unwin	1908	Millar, H.R.	160-250	
Kinglake, A.W.	Eothen (1st, sm8vo, 341p, teg, uncut, blue cl, b/w)	L: Newnes	1898	Millar, H.R.	60-80	
Quiller-Couch, A.	Fairy Tales from Far & Near (1st, 12mo, teg, 192p)	L: Cassell	1895	Millar, H.R.	100-140	*
Gower, M.L.	Fighting Six (1st, 8vo, 250p, b/w)	Harcourt	(1929)	Millar, H.R.	25-40	*
Nesbit, E.	Five Children and It (1st, 8vo, 301p, teg, red/gilt, 46pl)	L: T.F. Unwin	1902	Millar, H.R.	120-200	*
N/A	Golden Fairy Book (1st, lg8vo, 312p, AEG, b/w, gilt)	L: Hutchinson	[1890]	Millar, H.R.	100-150	
Nesbit, E.	Harding's Luck (1st, 8vo, gilt, 16 b/w, teg)	L: Hodder	1909	Millar, H.R.	200-300	
Nesbit, E.	Harding's Luck (1st AM, 12mo, green cl, 308p, 16pl)	Stokes	(1910)	Millar, H.R.	150-230	
Nesbit, E.	House of Arden (1st, 8vo, 349p, teg, red/gilt, 33pl)	L: T.F. Unwin	1908	Millar, H.R.	250-320	
Nesbit, E.	House of Arden (1st AM, 12mo, 349p, gilt, 33pl)	Dutton	1909	Millar, H.R.	180-250	
Nesbit, E.	Magic City (1st, 12mo, red/gilt, teg, 333p, 26pl)	L: MacMillan	1910	Millar, H.R.	200-300	
Nesbit, E.	Magic World (1st, 12mo, teg, 280p, red/gilt, 24pl)	L: MacMillan	1912	Millar, H.R.	250-350	
Stevenson, R.L.	Merry Men (1st, 8vo, 266p)	L: MacMillan	1928	Millar, H.R.	30-45	*
Kennedy, H.A.	New World Fairy Book (1st, 8vo, 354p, gilt, teg, uncut, b/w)	L: Dent	1904	Millar, H.R.	70-100	*
Molesworth, M.	Peterkin (1st, sm8vo, 198p, orange cloth, 8pl)	L: MacMillan	1902	Millar, H.R.	35-50	
Nesbit, E.	Phoenix & the Carpet (1st, lg8vo, blue/gilt, 321p, col frn, teg)	L: Newnes	(1904)	Millar, H.R.	250-350	
Kipling, R.	Puck of Pook's Hill (1st, 8vo, 306p, gilt, b/w pl)	L: MacMillan	1906	Millar, H.R.	100-145	
Various	Ruby Fairy Book (1st, 8vo, gilt, b/w)	L: Hutchinson	(1900)	Millar, H.R.	70-100	
Marryat, Fred.	Snarleyyow (1st, sm8vo, 405p, blue/gilt, AEG)	L: MacMillan	1897	Millar, H.R.	45-60	
Nesbit, E.	Story of the Amulet (1st, 12mo, teg, 374p, red/gilt, 48pl)	L: T.F. Unwin	1906	Millar, H.R.	140-180	
Hugo, V.	Story of the Bold Pecopin (1st, sm4to, 92p, gilt, 8pl)	L: Smith Elder	1902	Millar, H.R.	65-80	*
Harraden, B.	Untold Tales of the Past (1st, 8vo, 273p, teg, gilt, b/w)	L: Blackwood	1897	Millar, H.R.	60-75	
Nesbit, E.	Wet Magic (1st, 12mo, teg, red/gilt, 274p, 12pl)	L: T. Laurie	(1913)	Millar, H.R.	135-180	
Nesbit, E.	Wonderful Garden... (1st, 8vo, teg, 402p, red/gilt, 26 b/w)	L: MacMillan	1911	Millar, H.R.	200-250	
Nesbit, E.	Five Children (1st, 8vo, 306p, col frn)	Coward	1930	Millar/Blam	70-100	*
Shannon, Monica	California Fairy Tales (1st {std}, sm8vo, 298p, cp)	Doubleday/Page	1926	Millard, C.E.	45-60	*
Shannon, Monica	Eyes for the Dark (1st {std}, 8vo, 311p, 4cp, 15pl)	Doubleday/Dor.	1928	Millard, C.E.	30-45	*
Retner, Beth	Tired Trolly Car (1st {std}, 8vo, 158p, green cl, 4cp, dep)	Doubleday/Page	1926	Millard, C.E.	20-30	*
Sewell, Anna	Black Beauty (1st, 8vo, 96p)	Saalfield	(1905)	Miller, H.L.	30-45	*
Lapen, F.	Brownyboo (4to, ibds, cp)	Saalfield	(1908)	Miller, H.L.	75-100	
Raiker, A.M.	Dulcibella & the Fairies (1st, 4to, green bds, 54p, p-o, 13cp)	L: C. Faulkner	(1919)	Miller, H.T.	180-250	
Saunders, Phyllis	Flame Flower (1st, lg8vo, purple cl, 127p, p-o, 4cp)	L: Butterworth	1922	Miller, H.T.	100-150	
De La Mare, W.	Lucy (1st, 8vo, 40p, ipcb, p-o, b/w)	L: Blackwell	(1927)	Miller, H.T.	45-65	R*
Fyleman, R.	Rose Fyleman Fairy Book (1st, 4to, 102p, blue/gilt, 12 ticp)	L: Methuen	1923	Miller, H.T.	120-160	
Brown, M.W.	Wonderful Story (1st, 4to, ibds, 92p, color, pep, BGB)	Simon/Schuster	(1948)	Miller, J.P.	35-50	*
Ciardi, John	Scrappy the Pup (1st {std}, 4to, blue cl, unpag, 1-color, cep)	Lippincott	(1960)	Miller, Jane	65-80	*
Sorensen, Virginia	Curious Missie (1st {std}, 8vo, 208p)	Harcourt	(1953)	Miller, M.	30-45	*
Lang, L.B.	Red Book of Heroes (1st, 8vo, 368p, red/gilt, AEG, 8cp)	L: Longmans	1909	Mills, A.W.	120-180	
Milne-Home, M.P.	Mama's Black Nurse Stories (1st, 8vo, 131p, grey/gilt, 6 fp b/w)	L: Blackwood	1890	Milne-Home, M.P.	65-80	
Baker, K.W.	Garden of the Plynck (1st, 4to, ibds, 112p, col frn, b/w)	Yale U. Press	(1920)	Minard, F.	65-100	*
Nicholson, M.	Reversible Santa Claus (1st, 8vo, blue cl, 176p, 4cp, dep)	Houghton	1917	Minard, F.H.	20-35	*
Barrie, J.M.	Peter Pan (1st, 8vo, 27p, color)	Grosset/Dunlap	1942	Miss Elliott	25-40	*
Ransome, A.	Old Peter's Russian Tales (1st {this pub}, 8vo, 309p, 7cp)	L: Nelson	1935	Mitrokhin, D.	65-80	*
Allen, Phil S.	Begging Bear (1st, lg ob4to, 60p, p-o, 20cp)	Reilly/Lee	(1932)	Moe, L.M.	100-150	

AUTHOR	TITLE	PUBLISHER	DATE	ARTIST	PRICE	LC
Moe, Louis M.	Kylle Kluk (1st AM, ob4to, [24]p, orang cl, 11 fp color)	NY: Laidlaw	[1931]	Moe, L.M.	120-185	*
Moe, Louis M.	Peter Kroak (1st AM, ob4to, [17]p, p-o, 8 fp color, cep)	Whitman	1932	Moe, L.M.	130-180	*
Moe, Louis M.	Vain Pussy Cat (1st, ob4to, ipcb, [32]p, b/w, pep)	Coward	(1929)	Moe, L.M.	120-185	*
Moeschlin, Elsa	Little Boy with Big Apples (1st, 4to, ibds, [23]p, color)	Coward	[1932]	Moeschlin, E.	85-120	
Moeschlin, Elsa	Red Horse (1st AM, 4to, ibds, [20]p, color, cep)	Coward	[1929]	Moeschlin, E.	70-100	
Rasmussen, K.	People of the Frozen North (1st UK, 4to, 358p, 12cp)	L: Trubner	1908	Moltke, H.	100-140	
Stapp, E.B.	Bread & Lasses (1st, 8vo, 94p, 6pl)	(DeMoines)	1902	Monahan, P.J.	25-45	
England, G.A.	Flying Legion (1st, 8vo, 394p, frn by...)	McClurg	1920	Monahan, P.J.	35-60	*
London, J.	Smoke Bellew (1st, 8vo, blue cl, 385p, 8pl)	Century	1912	Monahan, P.J.	165-220	
Van Dyke, H.	Story of the Other Wise Man (8vo, gold cl, 87p, designs by...)	Harper	(1907)	Monetti, E.	70-100	
Herbertson, A.	Busy Broom (1st, 4to, unpag, color)	L: Cassell	[1910]	Monsell, J.R.	65-80	
Darwin, Bernard	Elves & Princes (1st, 8vo, 199p)	L: Duckworth	1913	Monsell, J.R.	120-165	*
Grimm Bros.	Fairy Tales (1st, 8vo, 336p, 16cp)	L: Cassell	1908	Monsell, J.R.	80-120	*
Monsell, J.R.	Hooded Crow (1st, 8vo, unpag, yellow cl, color)	L: Blackwell	(1926)	Monsell, J.R.	60-80	*
MacKenzie, C.	Kensington Rhymes (1st, 4to, pcb, 9cp)	(London)	(1913)	Monsell, J.R.	80-100	
Monsell, J.R.	Pink Knight (1st, 16mo, 95p, 24cp)	L: Richards	1901	Monsell, J.R.	85-120	
Thackeray, Wm.	Rose & the Ring (1st AM, 4to, red/gilt, 128p, 12 ticp, pep)	Crowell	[1911]	Monsell, J.R.	80-115	
Thackeray, Wm.	Rose & the Ring (1st, sq8vo, 128p, gilt, teg, 12 ticp, pep)	L: Kegan Paul	1911	Monsell, J.R.	100-145	
De La Mare, W.	Three Mulla Mulgars (1st, 8vo, teg, green/gilt, 312p, 2cp)	L: Duckworth	1910	Monsell, J.R.	160-220	
Williams, Orlando	Three Naughty Children (1st, 4to, 110p)	L: Duckworth	1922	Monsell, J.R.	50-70	*
Housman, L.	What-O'Clock Tales (1st, 8vo, 225p, 14 fp b/w)	L: Blackwell	(1932)	Monsell, J.R.	45-60	*
Moon, G.	Arrow of Tee-May (1st {std}, sm8vo, 284p, col frn, b/w, pep)	Doubleday/Dor.	1931	Moon, C.	30-45	
Moon, G.	Book of Nah-Wee (1st {std}, sm sq4to, 59p, ibds, color, pep)	Doubleday/Dor.	1932	Moon, C.	30-45	
Moon, G.	Chi-Wee and Loki (1st {std}, 8vo, 208p, tan cl, col frn, 18pl)	Doubleday/Page	1926	Moon, C.	30-45	
Moon, G.	Daughter of Thunder (1st, sm8vo, 184p, col frn, pep)	MacMillan	1942	Moon, C.	25-40	
Moon, G.	Far-Away Desert (1st {std}, sm8vo, 261p, color, pep)	Doubleday/Dor.	1932	Moon, C.	30-45	
Moon, G.	Indian Legends in Rhyme (1st, sm4to, p-o, 54p, cp)	Stokes	(1917)	Moon, C.	100-130	
Moon, G.	Lost Indian Magic (1st, sm8vo, 301p, p-o, 8cp, pep)	Stokes	1918	Moon, C.	30-50	*
Moon, G.	Magic Trail (1st {std}, sm8vo, 234p, col frn, 13pl, pep)	Doubleday/Dor.	1929	Moon, C.	40-60	
Moon, G.	Missing Katchina (1st {std}, 8vo, 286p, col frn, b/w, pep)	Doubleday/Dor.	1930	Moon, C.	30-45	*
Moon, G.	Nadita (1st {std}, 8vo, 274p, col frn, 16pl, pep)	Doubleday/Dor.	1927	Moon, C.	30-45	
Moon, C.	Painted Moccasins (1st, 8vo, 318p, green/gilt, col frn, pep)	Stokes	1931	Moon, C.	30-45	
Moon, G.	Runaway Papoose (1st {std}, 8vo, 264p, col frn, b/w, pep, NH)	Doubleday/Dor.	1928	Moon, C.	35-50	
Moon, G.	Singing Sands (1st {std}, 8vo, 245p, col frn, b/w)	Doubleday/Dor.	1936	Moon, C.	25-40	
Moon, G.	Solita (1st {std}, 8vo, tan cl, 241p, col frn, b/w, pep)	Doubleday/Dor.	1938	Moon, C.	30-45	
Moon, G.	Tita of Mexico (1st, sm8vo, 213p, col frn, 4pl, pep)	Stokes	1934	Moon, C.	30-45	*
Moon, G.	White Indian (1st {std}, sm8vo, 221p, col frn, b/w, pep)	Doubleday/Dor.	1937	Moon, C.	25-45	*
Moon, G.	Wongo & the Wise Old Crow (1st, 8vo, 188p, pep, gilt, col frn)	Reilly/Lee	(1923)	Moon, C.	45-60	*
Grahame, K.	Golden Age (1st, sm4to, 243p, uncut, 19cp)	L: J. Lane	1914	Moony, R.J.E.	90-135	
Bannerman, H.	Little Black Sambo (sm4to, [22]p, color)	Grosset/Dunlap	(1942)	Moore, Robert	45-65	*
Moorepark, C.	Alphabet of Animals (1st, 4to, ibds, 105p, b/w)	L: Blackie	1899	Moorepark, C.	160-200	
Norman	Elfin Rhymes (1st AM, sm4to, unpag, 40 color)	Stokes	(1900)	Moorepark, C.	120-200	
Norman	Elfin Rhymes (1st, 4to, unpag, 40 color)	L: Gay & Bird	1900	Moorepark, C.	150-240	*
Morris, Alice T.	Old Friends/New Fables (1st AM, 4to, p-o, 52p, 21 ticp)	Dodge	[1916]	Moorepark, C.	150-180	
Morris, Alice T.	Old Friends/New Fables (1st, 4to, 51p, p-o, 21 ticp)	L: Blackie	1916	Moorepark, C.	165-180	
Gilby/Cuming	George Moorland... (1st, 8vo, 290p, teg, 50cp)	L: A&C Black	1907	Moorland, G.	70-100	
Aesopus	Animals of Aesop (1st, lg8vo, 210p, color)	D. Estes	1900	Mora, J.J.	65-80	*
Andersen, H.C.	Fairy Tales (1st, sm4to, 188p, 24pl)	D. Estes	(1902)	Mora, J.J.	160-220	
Sawyer, R.S.	Tonio Antonia (1st, 8vo, 132p, red/gilt, 8 fp b/w, pep)	Viking	1934	Mora, L.	25-40	*
Tucker, E.S.	Children of Colonial Days (1st, lg4to, [50]p, 12cp)	Stokes	1894	Moran, E.P.	150-220	*
Tucker, E.S.	Rhymes & Stories of Olden Times (1st, lg4to, ibds, [26]p, 6cp)	Stokes	1894	Moran, E.P.	120-165	*
Carlson, N.S.	Alphonse, that Bearded One (1st {std}, 8vo, blue cl, 78p, b/w)	Harcourt	(1954)	Mordvinoff, N.	50-80	R*
Lipkind, Wm.	Christmas Bunny (1st {std}, 4to, [49]p, green cl, color, pep)	Harcourt	(1953)	Mordvinoff, N.	65-90	R*
Carlson, N.S.	Evangeline, Pigeon of Paris (1st {std}, 8vo, red cl, 70p fp b/w)	Harcourt	(1960)	Mordvinoff, N.	35-50	*
Lipkind, Wm.	Finders Keepers (1st {std}, 4to, [32]p, pep, 28 color, CM)	Harcourt	(1951)	Mordvinoff, N.	80-100	*
Stone, Wm. S.	Pepe was the Saddest Bird (1st {std}, 8vo, [62]p, ipcb, b/w)	Knopf	1944	Mordvinoff, N.	65-90	R*
Stone, Wm. S.	Ship of Flame (1st {std}, lg4to, 164p, bds, col frn, b/w)	Knopf	1945	Mordvinoff, N.	70-120	R*
Lipkind, Wm.	Sleepyhead (1st {std}, 4to, green cl, [38]p, 2-color, pep)	Harcourt	(1957)	Mordvinoff, N.	45-65	*
Stone, Wm. S.	Thunder Island (1st {std}, sm8vo, 194p, 7cp)	Knopf	(1942)	Mordvinoff, N.	30-50	*
Lipkind, Wm.	Two Reds (1st {std}, 4to, [48]p, color, pep, CH)	Harcourt	(1950)	Mordvinoff, N.	80-120	R*
Boylan, G.D.	Kids of Many Colors (1st, 8vo, tan cl, 156p, color)	Chi: Jamieson	(1901)	Morgan, Ike	100-150	*
N/A	Night Before Christmas & Jingles (sq8vo, 48p, p-o, 12cp by...)	Hurst	(1908)	Morgan, Ike	130-165	*
Reed, Myrtle	Pickaback Songs (1st, 4to, [70]p, ibds, pep, color)	Putnam	1903	Morgan, Ike	300-400	
Boylan, G.D.	Steps to Nowhere (1st, 4to, 230p, p-o, blue cl, 8cp)	Baker/Taylor	1910	Morgan, Ike	100-150	
Baum, L.F.	Woggle-Bug Book (1st, folio, [48]p, wraps, color)	Reilly/Britton	1905	Morgan, Ike	2500	
Boylan, G.D.	Young Folks Uncle Tom's Cabin (1st, 4to, ipcb, 166p, 16 fp b/w)	Jamieson	1901	Morgan, Ike	165-220	*
Wells, Carolyn	Folly in Fairyland (1st, sm8vo, 261p, 12pl)	Altemus	(1901)	Morgan, W.	45-60	
Evans, F.G.	Puffin, Puma & Co. (1st AM, sm4to, ibds, 96p)	MacMillan	1929	Morrow, G.	20-25	
Means, F.C.	Borrowed Brother (1st, 8vo, blue cl, 239p, b/w)	Houghton	1958	Morse, D.B.	25-40	*
Caudill, R.	Tree of Freedom (1st, 8vo, 279p, green cl, pep, DJ, NH)	Viking	1949	Morse, D.B.	35-50	
Morse, L.B.	Road to Nowhere (1st, sm8vo, 236p)	Harper	1900	Morse, E.	45-60	*
Carroll, L.	Alice... & Through... (1st, 8vo, yellow cl, 317p, col frn, 8pl)	L: Clowes	[1935]	Morton-Sale, J.	35-50	*

AUTHOR	TITLE	PUBLISHER	DATE	ARTIST	PRICE	LC
Farjeon, E.	Cherrystones (1st AM {std}, 12mo, red/gilt, 58p, fp b/w)	Lippincott	(1944)	Morton-Sale, J.	25-40	
Farjeon, E.	Martin Pippin/Daisy-Field (1st AM {std}, 8vo, 320p, col frn)	Stokes	1938	Morton-Sale, J.	50-65	*
Griggs, Mary	Yellow Cat (1st, 8vo, 110p, yellow cl, 6 doub pg cp)	L: H. Milford	(1936)	Morton-Sale, J.	65-80	*
Bailey, T.	Star in the Well (1st, sm8vo, 46p, wraps, color decor by...)	Volland	(1928)	Moschcowitz, P.	45-60	*
Harris, J.C.	Wally Wandroon... (1st, lg8vo, 294p, 31pl)	McClure	1903	Mosley, K.	120-160	
France, A.	CLIO (1st, sm8vo, teg, 7 color illus.)	Paris: Calmann	1900	Mucha, A.	450-600	
Blackmore, R.D.	Fringilla (1st, 8vo, 128p, 8pl)	L: Matthews	1895	Muckley, L.F.	350	
Wyss, J.D.	Swiss Family Robinson (lg4to, 96p, color)	Saalfield	(1940)	Muheim, H.	25-50	*
Schultz, J.W.	Gold Dust (1st, 8vo, 243p, b/w, DJ)	Houghton	1934	Mulford, S.	35-50	
Porter, E.	Pollyanna (1st, 8vo, 310p, pink/gilt, 8pl, PPP)	Page	1913	Mulford, S.	100-160	
Porter, E.	Pollyanna (1st UK, 8vo, 310p, 8pl)	L: I. Pitman	1913	Mulford, S.	90-120	
Lamb, C.	Tales from Shakespeare (1st, 8vo, 242p, ticp)	L: Scott	1915	Mulliner, M.	100-130	
Sawyer, R.S.	Primrose Ring (1st, 12mo, 186p, b/w, pl)	Harper	(1915)	Munsell, F.	20-35	*
Collodi, C.	Adventures of Pinocchio (1st AM, lg4to, 404p, cp, DJ)	MacMillan	(1925)	Mussino, A.	180-250	
N/A	Just Because of You (1st, 12mo, ibds, color)	Volland	(1925)	Myers, M.H.	35-50	*
Bailey, A.C.	Skating Gander (1st, 8vo, ibds, 93p, color, pep)	Volland	(1927)	Myers, M.H.	35-50	
Wilde, O.	Fisherman & his Soul (1st, 4to, 212p, gilt, 15 ticp)	Farrar/Rine.	(1929)	Nadejen, T.	100-165	
Zeitlin, I.	Gessar-Khan (1st, 4to, 203p, gilt, 40 color)	Doran	(1927)	Nadejen, T.	40-70	
Zeitlin, I.	King's Pleasure (1st {std}, lg8vo, 230p, blue/gilt, 17cp, cep)	Harper	1929	Nadejen, T.	50-70	
Adams, J.D.	Mountains are Free (1st {std}, 8vo, gilt, 250p, 10pl, NH)	Dutton	(1930)	Nadejen, T.	50-70	*
Mirza, Y.B.	Myself when Young (1st {std}, 8vo, 260p, col frn)	Doubleday/Dor.	1929	Nadejen, T.	30-45	*
Zeitlin, I.	Skazki (1st, 4to, 335p, black/gilt, teg, pep, 24 ticp)	Doran	(1926)	Nadejen, T.	65-90	
De La Mare, W.	Stories from the Bible (1st, lg8vo, 393p, pep, 9cp)	Cosmopolitan	1929	Nadejen, T.	45-60	*
Ryder, Arthur	Twenty-Two Goblins (1st, 8vo, 220p, 20cp)	L: Dent	1917	Nahl, Perham	65-90	*
Nash, Ogden	Christmas that Almost Wasn't (1st {std}, 8vo, 63p, 8 fp color)	Little/Brown	(1957)	Nash, L.	40-65	*
Drinkwater, J.	Cotswold Characters (1st, 12mo, bds, 54p, DJ)	Yale U. Press	1921	Nash, P.	140-200	R
Nash, Dorothy	Moon Baby (4to, ibds, p-o, 87p, 9 ticp)	L: Jarrolds	[1905]	Nash/Rudge	100-150	*
Nast, Thomas	Christmas Drawings/Human Race (1st, 4to, [67]p, fp b/w)	Harper	1890	Nast, Thos.	180-260	*
Irving, W.	Rip Van Winkle (sq4to, [11]p, wraps, 6 chromos)	McLoughlin	[1880]	Nast, Thos.	180-265	
N/A	Yankee Doodle (4to, wraps, 6 chromos by...)	McLoughlin	[1872]	Nast, Thos.	150-200	
Dimmick, R.C.	Bogie Man (1st, lg8vo, ibds, [71]p, fp b/w)	Winston	(1906)	Neale, M.B.	55-85	*
Craik, D.	Adventures of a Brownie (1st, 16mo, 57p, p-o)	Reilly/Britton	(1912)	Neill, J.R.	35-60	
Sewell, Anna	Black Beauty (sm8vo, red cl, 58p, p-o, color)	Reilly/Britton	1908	Neill, J.R.	65-90	
Thompson, R.P.	Captain Salt in Oz (1st, 8vo, 306p, blue cl, p-o, b/w, pep)	Reilly/Lee	(1936)	Neill, J.R.	230-300	
Benoit, C.F.	Children's Stories that Never Grow Old (12mo, 312p, yellow cl)	Reilly/Britton	(1908)	Neill, J.R.	65-80	
Dickens, C.	Christmas Carol (12mo, ipcb, p-o)	Reilly/Britton	1915	Neill, J.R.	50-65	
Hancock, H.I.	Chuggins (1st, sm8vo, 96p, col frn, 4pl)	Altemus	(1904)	Neill, J.R.	30-50	*
N/A	Cinderella (16mo, ibds, p-o)	Reilly/Britton	1908	Neill, J.R.	80-100	
Douglas, A.M.	Clover's Princess (1st, 16mo, p-o, 95p, blue/gilt, 6pl)	Altemus	(1904)	Neill, J.R.	50-70	
Thompson, R.P.	Cowardly Lion of Oz (1st [1], lg8vo, 291p, p-o, pep, 12cp)	Reilly/Lee	(1923)	Neill, J.R.	250-400	
Thompson, R.P.	Curious Cruise of Captain Santa (1st, sq8vo, 124p, p-o, color)	Reilly/Lee	(1926)	Neill, J.R.	250-350	
Baum, L.F.	Dorothy & Wizard of Oz (1st [1], 8vo, p-o, 256p, pep, 16cp)	Reilly/Britton	(1908)	Neill, J.R.	600-800	
Baum, L.F.	Emerald City of Oz (1st [1], 8vo, 296p, p-o, 16 ticp, pep)	Reilly/Britton	(1910)	Neill, J.R.	650-800	R
Longfellow, H.W.	Evangeline (1st, 8vo, teg, p-o, 172p)	Reilly/Britton	(1909)	Neill, J.R.	70-95	
Andersen, H.C.	Fairy Tales (1st, lg8vo, p-o, 180p, blue/gilt, 2cp)	Cupples	(1923)	Neill, J.R.	70-90	
N/A	Foolish Fox (1st, 16mo, ibds, p-o, 92p, color)	Altemus	(1904)	Neill, J.R.	40-60	R
Bangs, J.K.	From Pillar to Post (1st, 8vo, 339p, b/w)	Century	1916	Neill, J.R.	35-50	*
Johnston, A.F.	Georgina of the Rainbows (1st, sm8vo, 348p, b/w pl)	NY: Britton	(1916)	Neill, J.R.	40-60	*
Thompson, R.P.	Giant Horse of Oz (1st, lg8vo, 283p, p-o, brown cl, pep, 12cp)	Reilly/Lee	(1928)	Neill, J.R.	240-320	
Baum, L.F.	Gingerbread Man (1st, sm4to, ibds, 62p, col frn)	Reilly/Britton	(1917)	Neill, J.R.	200-275	
Baum, L.F.	Glinda of Oz (1st [1], lg8vo, grey cl, p-o, 279p, 12cp, pep)	Reilly/Lee	(1920)	Neill, J.R.	350-500	R
Thompson, R.P.	Gnome King of Oz (1st, lg8vo, 282p, p-o, green cl, pep, 12cp)	Reilly/Lee	(1927)	Neill, J.R.	250-400	
Thompson, R.P.	Grampa in Oz (1st, lg8vo, 271p, 12cp, p-o)	Reilly/Lee	(1924)	Neill, J.R.	200-300	
Thompson, R.P.	Handy Mandy in Oz (1st, 4to, 246p, blue cl, p-o, pep)	Reilly/Lee	(1937)	Neill, J.R.	280-400	
Grimm Bros.	Hansel & Gretel (1st, 12mo, red bds, 58p, p-o, color)	Reilly/Britton	(1908)	Neill, J.R.	70-100	
Longfellow, H.W.	Hiawatha (1st, 8vo, p-o, b/w pl)	Reilly/Britton	(1909)	Neill, J.R.	70-100	
Thompson, R.P.	Hungry Tiger of Oz (1st, 8vo, p-o, 261p, 12cp, pep)	Reilly/Lee	(1926)	Neill, J.R.	230-300	
Johnston, A.F.	It Was the Road to Jericho (1st {std}, 8vo, [41]p, gilt, pep)	Britton	(1919)	Neill, J.R.	40-60	
Thompson, R.P.	Jack Pumpkinhead of Oz (1st, 8vo, 252p p-o, 12cp, pep)	Reilly/Lee	(1929)	Neill, J.R.	260-320	
Baum, L.F.	John Dough & the Cherub (1st [1], 8vo, tan cl, 315p, col, pep)	Reilly/Britton	(1906)	Neill, J.R.	600-800	
Thompson, R.P.	Kabumpo in Oz (1st, lg8vo, blue cl, 297p, p-o, 12cp, pep)	Reilly/Lee	(1922)	Neill, J.R.	250-400	
Bannerman, H.	Little Black Sambo (sq8vo, ibds, 28p, color)	Reilly/Britton	(1908)	Neill, J.R.	100-165	
N/A	Little Red Riding Hood (12mo, ibds, 57p, fp color)	Reilly/Britton	(1908)	Neill, J.R.	80-100	*
Baum, L.F.	Little Wizard Stories/Oz (1st [1], 8vo, p-o, 152p, 42cp)	Reilly/Britton	(1914)	Neill, J.R.	350-450	
Thompson, R.P.	Lost King of Oz (1st, 8vo, p-o, 280p, 12cp, pep)	Reilly/Lee	(1925)	Neill, J.R.	200-240	
Baum, L.F.	Lost Princess of Oz (1st [1], 8vo, 312p, p-o, 12cp, pep)	Reilly/Britton	(1917)	Neill, J.R.	700-800	
Baum, L.F.	Lucky Bucky in Oz (1st, 8vo, p-o, blue cl, pep, 289p)	Reilly/Lee	(1942)	Neill, J.R.	165-220	
Hartwell (ed.)	Magic Bed (1st, 12mo, 109p, b/w pl)	Altemus	(1906)	Neill, J.R.	60-90	*
Baum, L.F.	Magic Cloak... (1st [1], 8vo, 58p, ibds)	Reilly/Britton	(1916)	Neill, J.R.	450-600	
James, Hart.	Magic Jaw Bone (1st, 12mo, 107p, 2-color)	Altemus	(1906)	Neill, J.R.	50-70	
Baum, L.F.	Magic of Oz (1st [1], lg8vo, [266]p, p-o, green cl, 12cp)	Reilly/Lee	(1919)	Neill, J.R.	400-600	
Jenks, Tudor	Magician for One Day (1st, 24mo, brown ipcb, 107p, color)	Altemus	(1905)	Neill, J.R.	50-85	*

AUTHOR	TITLE	PUBLISHER	DATE	ARTIST	PRICE	LC
Baum, L.F.	Marvelous Land of Oz (1st [1], lg8vo, 287p, green cl, 16cp, pep)	Reilly/Britton	1904	Neill, J.R.	700-850	
Warwick, Charles	Mirabeau & the French Revolution (1st, 8vo, 483p, 15pl)	Lippincott	1905	Neill, J.R.	45-60	*
Mother Goose	Mother Goose Nursery Tales (12mo, 91p, green cl, p-o, color)	Altemus	(1904)	Neill, J.R.	75-90	*
Thompson, R.P.	Ojo in Oz (1st, 8vo, p-o, 304p, red cl, 12cp, pep)	Reilly/Lee	(1933)	Neill, J.R.	200-265	
Baum, L.F.	Ozma of Oz (1st [1], 8vo, 270p, tan cl, color, pep)	Reilly/Britton	(1907)	Neill, J.R.	500-750	
Thompson, R.P.	Ozoplanning/Wizard of Oz (1st, lg8vo, 272p, p-o, yellow cl, pep)	Reilly/Lee	(1939)	Neill, J.R.	250-350	
Baum, L.F.	Patchwork Girl of Oz (1st [1], 8vo, 341p, green cl, color, pep)	Reilly/Britton	(1913)	Neill, J.R.	500-750	
Grabo, C.H.	Peter & the Princess (1st, sm4to, teg, gilt, p-o, 243p, 8cp pep)	Reilly/Lee	(1920)	Neill, J.R.	200-300	
Thompson, R.P.	Pirates in Oz (1st [1], 8vo, green cl, p-o, 280p, 12cp, pep)	Reilly/Lee	(1931)	Neill, J.R.	280-400	
Thompson, R.P.	Purple Prince of Oz (1st [1], lg8vo, p-o, 281p, 12cp, pep)	Reilly/Lee	(1932)	Neill, J.R.	320-450	
Jenks, Tudor	Rescue Syndicate (1st, 24mo, ipcb, 110p, b/w, pep)	Altemus	(1905)	Neill, J.R.	50-80	*
Baum, L.F.	Rinkitink in Oz (1st [1], 8vo, blue cl, 314p, p-o, 12cp, pep)	Reilly/Britton	(1916)	Neill, J.R.	550-700	
Baum, L.F.	Road to Oz (1st [1], 8vo, green cl, b/w, p-o, 261p, pep)	Reilly/Britton	(1909)	Neill, J.R.	400-600	
N/A	Robber Kitten (1st, 16mo, 96p, gilt, color)	Altemus	(1904)	Neill, J.R.	65-80	
Baum, L.F.	Royal Book of Oz (1st [1], 8vo, 312p, grey cl, 12cp, pep)	Reilly/Lee	(1921)	Neill, J.R.	220-300	
Baum, L.F.	Scarecrow of Oz (1st [1], lg8vo, green cl, p-o, 288p, 12cp, pep)	Reilly/Britton	(1915)	Neill, J.R.	400-600	
Baum, L.F.	Sea Fairies (1st [1], 8vo, p-o, 240p, green cl, 12pl, pep)	Reilly/Britton	(1911)	Neill, J.R.	400-550	
Thompson, R.P.	Silver Princess of Oz (1st, lg8vo, 255p, orang cl, p-o, b/w, pep)	Reilly/Lee	(1938)	Neill, J.R.	300-400	
Baum, L.F.	Sky Island (1st, lg8vo, blue cl, p-o, [288]p, 12cp, pep)	Reilly/Britton	(1912)	Neill, J.R.	400-600	
Whittier, J.G.	Snowbound (1st, 8vo, p-o, 123p, green cl, 12pl, pep)	Reilly/Britton	(1909)	Neill, J.R.	50-70	
Thompson, R.P.	Speedy in Oz (1st, lg8vo, p-o, 298p, blue cl, 12cp, pep)	Reilly/Lee	(1934)	Neill, J.R.	280-400	
Potter, B.	Story of Peter Rabbit (1st, 24mo, p-o, ibds)	Reilly/Britton	(1911)	Neill, J.R.	75-100	
Poe, E.A.	The Raven (1st, sm8vo, 110p, b/w pl, pep)	Reilly/Britton	(1910)	Neill, J.R.	80-120	*
Baum, L.F.	Tik-Tok of Oz (1st [1], lg8vo, 272p, blue cl, p-o, pep, 12cp)	Reilly/Britton	(1914)	Neill, J.R.	650-800	
Jenks, Tudor	Timothy's Magical Afternoon (1st, 24mo, ipcb, 98p, b/w, pep)	Altemus	(1905)	Neill, J.R.	65-80	
Baum, L.F.	Tin Woodman of Oz (1st [1], 8vo, red cl, 288p, 12cp, pep)	Reilly/Britton	(1918)	Neill, J.R.	400-600	
Andersen, H.C.	Ugly Duckling (1st, 16mo, bds, p-o, 57p, color)	Reilly/Britton	(1912)	Neill, J.R.	60-80	
Wright, H.B.	Uncrowned King (1st, 16mo, green cl, 118p, 5pl)	Book Supp. Co.	1910	Neill, J.R.	60-80	
Harris, Credo	Where Souls of Men are Calling (1st, 12mo, 298p, col frn by...)	Britton	(1918)	Neill, J.R.	30-50	*
Thompson, R.P.	Wishing Horse of Oz (1st, 4to, grey cl, 298p, p-o, 12cp)	Reilly/Lee	(1935)	Neill, J.R.	275-400	
Thompson, R.P.	Yellow Knight of Oz (1st, 8vo, 275p, grey cl, p-o, 12cp, pep)	Reilly/Lee	(1930)	Neill, J.R.	220-285	
Iogolevitch, Paul	Young Russian Corporal (1st, sm8vo, 327p, frn & b/w by...)	Harper	1919	Neill, J.R.	45-60	*
Allen, Phil S.	King Arthur & his Knights (1st, sm4to, 455p, black cl, p-o, 8cp)	Rand/McNally	(1924)	Neill/Schaeffer	50-70	*
Baring-Gould, S.	Amazing Adventures (1st, ob folio, 53p, color)	L: Skeffington	[1903]	Neilson, H.B.	140-200	*
N/A	Droll Doings (1st, 4to, [64]p, red cl, 40 color)	L: Blackie	[1905]	Neilson, H.B.	120-170	*
Hamer, S.H.	Jungle School (1st, 4to, 64p, color)	L: Cassell	1900	Neilson, H.B.	50-70	*
Hamer, S.H.	Micky Magee's Menagerie (1st, lg8vo, 100p)	L: Cassell	1897	Neilson, H.B.	45-60	*
Farrow, G.E.	Pixie Pickles (1st, lg4to, ibds, 46p, 20 pl)	L: Skeffington	[1908]	Neilson, H.B.	145-200	
N/A	Intimations of Immortality... (4to, 12cp)	L: J.M. Dent	[1913]	Neilson-Gray	100-150	
Burglon, N.	Ghost Ship (1st, sm8vo, 275p, blue cl, 8pl, pep)	Little/Brown	1936	Nelson, A.R.	20-30	*
Farjeon, E.	Wonders of Herodotus (1st, 8vo, 176p)	L: Nelson	1937	Nelson, E.	35-50	*
Van Dyne, Edith	Aunt Jane's Nieces (1st, 12mo, p-o, 325p, 6pl)	Reilly/Britton	(1906)	Nelson, E.A.	200-300	
Van Dyne, Edith	Aunt Jane's Nieces Abroad (1st, 12mo, green cl, p-o, 5pl)	Reilly/Britton	(1906)	Nelson, E.A.	160-220	
Akers, Floyd	Boy Fortune Hunters in China (1st [1], 12mo, brown cl, frn by)	Reilly/Britton	(1909)	Nelson, E.A.	160-220	*
Akers, Floyd	Boy Fortune Hunters in Egypt (1st [1], 12mo, 291p, 3pl)	Reilly/Britton	(1908)	Nelson, E.A.	180-250	
Akers, Floyd	Boy Fortune Hunters/South Seas (1st, 8vo, 263p, tan cl, frn by)	Reilly/Britton	(1911)	Nelson, E.A.	200-300	
Henderson, L.R.	Magic Aeroplane (1st, lg4to, ibds, 96p, 6cp)	Reilly/Britton	(1911)	Nelson, E.A.	160-220	
Wiggin & Smith	Talking Beasts... (1st, 8vo, 391p, p-o, col frn, pl)	Doubleday/Page	1911	Nelson, H.	25-40	*
North, S.	So Red the Nose (1st, sm8vo, pink cl, [72]p, fp b/w)	Farrar/Rine.	(1935)	Nelson, R.C.	25-40	*
Grimm Bros.	Goose Girl (1st, 16mo, tan cl, 165p, 3cp, 10 fp b/w, dep)	MacMillan	1929	Nerman, E.R.	45-60	*
Andersen, H.C.	The Swineherd (folio, ibds, unpag, color, pep)	Knopf	[1924]	Nerman, E.R.	50-65	
Andersen, H.C.	Thumbelina (1st, 16mo, 79p, fp color, pep)	MacMillan	1928	Nerman, E.R.	35-50	*
Coatsworth, E.	Lonely Maria (1st, 8vo, yellow cl, [38]p, 2-color)	Pantheon	(1960)	Ness, E.M.	45-60	*
Pope, Eliz. M.	Sherwood Ring (1st, 8vo, tan cl, 266p, fp b/w)	Houghton	1958	Ness, E.M.	50-80	R*
Gibbons, Mary	Story of Ophelia (1st {std}, 4to, ibds, [32]p, color)	Doubleday	1954	Ness, E.M.	50-70	*
Ogburn, Charlton	The Bridge (1st, 8vo, cloth, 68p, fp 2-color)	Houghton	1957	Ness, E.M.	50-80	*
Harper, Wilhelmina	Brownie of the Circus (1st {std}, 8vo, 107p, color, pep)	McKay	(1941)	Neville, V.	35-50	*
Webber, Frank M.	Peter Painter's Merry-Go-Round (1st {std}, sm4to, ibds, [32]p)	McKay	(1946)	Neville, V.	40-65	*
Newberry, C.T.	April's Kittens (1st {std}, 4to, [32]p, gilt, color, pep, CH)	Harper	1940	Newberry, C.T.	70-115	*
Newberry, C.T.	Babette (1st {std}, lg8vo, 32p, pep, color)	Harper	1937	Newberry, C.T.	50-70	*
Newberry, C.T.	Barkis (1st {std}, sm ob4to, 31p, color, pep, CH)	Harper	1938	Newberry, C.T.	70-120	*
Newberry, C.T.	Cousin Toby (1st {std}, 8vo, [32]p, yellow bds, pep)	Harper	1939	Newberry, C.T.	70-100	
Newberry, C.T.	Herbert the Lion (1st, ob4to, [41]p, pep, color)	Brewer/Warren	1931	Newberry, C.T.	80-120	*
Newberry, C.T.	Herbert the Lion (1st {thus}-{std}, ob4to, ibds 64]p, pep, col)	Harper	1939	Newberry, C.T.	70-100	*
Newberry, C.T.	Kitten's ABC (1st {std}, lg4to, ibds, [36]p, color, DJ)	Harper	(1946)	Newberry, C.T.	70-100	
Newberry, C.T.	Lambert's Bargain (1st {std}, 4to, 31p, b/w, pep, DJ)	Harper	1941	Newberry, C.T.	50-80	
Newberry, C.T.	Marshmallow (1st {std}, lg ob4to, [31]p, color, CH)	Harper	(1942)	Newberry, C.T.	70-120	
Newberry, C.T.	Mittens (1st {std}, sm4to, ibds, [28]p, pep, CH)	Harper	1936	Newberry, C.T.	40-60	*
Newberry, C.T.	Pandora (1st {std}, folio, ibds, p-o, [35]p, b/w)	Harper	(1944)	Newberry, C.T.	70-100	
Newberry, C.T.	T-Bone the Baby-Sitter (1st, ob4to, [30]p, color, CH)	Harper	1950	Newberry, C.T.	65-100	*
Ramsden, G.	Smile Within a Tear (1st, sm8vo, 251p, blue/gilt, 8pl)	L: Hutchinson	1897	Newcombe, B.	50-80	
Newell, D.	American Animals (1st, 8vo, blue cl, 80p, 10cp, pep)	Volland	(1929)	Newell, D.	60-80	

ILLUSTRATOR: 88

AUTHOR	TITLE	PUBLISHER	DATE	ARTIST	PRICE	LC
Stockton, Frank	Afield & Afloat (1st, 8vo, teg, 422p, 12pl)	Scribner	1900	Newell, P.	35-50	
Carroll, L.	Alice/Wonderland (1st, 8vo, vellum/gilt, 193p, teg, 40pl)	Harper	1901	Newell, P.	120-160	
Bangs, J.K.	Bikey the Skycycle (1st, 8vo, blue/gilt, 321p, col frn, 7pl)	NY: Riggs	1902	Newell, P.	35-50	
Reed, Myrtle	Book of Clever Beasts (1st, 8vo, p-o, 231p, col frn, 8pl)	Putnam	1904	Newell, P.	70-100	
Cobb, I.	Cobb's Anatomy (1st, 8vo, tan pcb, 141p, 17pl, pep)	Doran	(1912)	Newell, P.	35-50	
Cobb, I.	Cobb's Bill of Fare (1st, 8vo, tan, pcb, 148p, 15pl, pep)	Doran	(1913)	Newell, P.	35-50	
Garnett, L.A.	Creature Songs (1st, lg4to, 30p, p-o, green/gilt, 10pl)	NY: Ditson	(1912)	Newell, P.	140-200	
Bangs, J.K.	Enchanted Typewriter (1st, 12mo, 171p, uncut, 10pl)	Harper	1899	Newell, P.	40-60	
Carryl, G.W.	Fables for the Frivolous (1st, 8vo, 120p, teg, gilt, 6pl)	Harper	1898	Newell, P.	60-85	
Carryl, G.W.	Far from Maddening Girls (1st, 8vo, 185p, 8pl)	McClure	1904	Newell, P.	45-70	
N/A	Favorite Fairy Tales (1st, 8vo, 355p, gilt, teg, 16pl)	Harper	1907	Newell, P.	170-220	
Harris, A.V.	Favorites from Fairyland (1st, 8vo, blue cl, 130p, 6pl)	Harper	1911	Newell, P.	100-165	
Stockton, Frank	Great Stone of Sardis (1st, 8vo, 230p, teg, uncut, gilt, 52pl)	Harper	1898	Newell, P.	60-85	R
Newell, P.	Hole Book (1st, 4to, p-o, [51]p, blue cloth, 24 fp color, PPP)	Harper	(1908)	Newell, P.	200-300	R
Bangs, J.K.	House Boat on the Styx (1st, 16mo, green/gilt, 171p, 23pl)	Harper	1896	Newell, P.	35-50	
Carroll, L.	Hunting of the Snark (1st, lg8vo, ibds, teg, 248p, 40pl)	Harper	1903	Newell, P.	120-160	
Stone, S.B.	Kingdom of Why (1st, 8vo, green cl, 275p, p-o, 9pl)	Bobbs-Merrill	(1913)	Newell, P.	120-150	
Wells, Carolyn	Merry-Go-Round (1st, sm8vo, gilt, 152p, 11pl)	R.H. Russell	1901	Newell, P.	150-180	
Carryl, G.W.	Mother Goose for Grownups (1st, lg8vo, teg, 125p, 3pl by...)	Harper	1900	Newell, P.	100-125	
Wells, Carolyn	Mother Goose's Menagerie (1st, 8vo, tan cl, 111p, 12cp)	Noyes/Platt	1901	Newell, P.	170-225	
Bangs, J.K.	Mr. Munchausen (1st, sm8vo, 180p, tan cl, 15cp)	Noyes	1901	Newell, P.	35-50	
Irwin, W.	Nautical Lays of a Landsman (1st, sm8vo, 135p, 5pl, dep)	Dodd	1904	Newell, P.	45-60	
Johnson, Clifton	Parson's Devil (1st, 8vo, 296p, green cl, 4pl)	Crowell	(1927)	Newell, P.	65-90	
Browne, P.E.	Peace at any Price (1st, 8vo, brown pcb, 70p, p-o, 6pl)	Appleton	1916	Newell, P.	70-100	*
Bailey, C.S.	Peter Newell's Mother Goose (1st, 8vo, 265p, 20pl)	Holt	1905	Newell, P.	85-120	
Newell, P.	Peter Newell's Pictures & Rhymes (1st, ob8vo, tan cl, p-o, 50pl)	Harper	1899	Newell, P.	170-250	
Bangs, J.K.	Pursuit of the House Boat (1st, 12mo, 204p, 24pl)	Harper	1897	Newell, P.	35-50	
Towne, C.H.	Rise & Fall of Prohibition (1st, sm8vo, blue/gilt, 220p, 4pl)	MacMillan	1923	Newell, P.	50-80	
Newell, P.	Rocket Book (1st, lg8vo, [48]p, p-o, 23 fp color)	Harper	(1912)	Newell, P.	180-260	R
Bell, L.	Runaway Equator (1st, 8vo, 118p, p-o, 16pl)	Stokes	(1911)	Newell, P.	130-200	
Browne, P.E.	Scars & Stripes (1st, 8vo, gilt, 208p, frn by..)	Doran	(1917)	Newell, P.	25-45	*
Newell, P.	Shadow Show (1st, ob8vo, ipcb, 72p, color)	Century	1896	Newell, P.	250-300	
Newell, P.	Slant Book (1st, 8vo, [47]p, ibds, 22 fp color)	Harper	(1910)	Newell, P.	200-300	R
Crane, S.	The Monster... (1st, 8vo, 188p, orange/gilt, 25pl)	Harper	1899	Newell, P.	170-220	
Cooke, G.M.	Their First Formal Call (1st, 8vo, 55p, p-o, gilt, 14pl)	Harper	1906	Newell, P.	65-90	
Carroll, L.	Through the Looking Glass (1st, lg8vo, bds, teg, 211p, 40pl)	Harper	1902	Newell, P.	100-145	
Lee, Al	Tommy Toodles (1st, 8vo, p-o, blue cl, 192p, 26pl)	Harper	1896	Newell, P.	160-200	
Newell, P.	Topsys & Turveys (1st, ob4to, bds, p-o, 31cp)	Century	1893	Newell, P.	250-350	
Newell, P.	Topsys & Turvys Number 2 (1st, oblg8vo, ipcb)	Century	(1894)	Newell, P.	200-300	
Crane, S.	Whilomville Stories (1st, 8vo, green/gilt, 198p, 34pl)	Harper	1900	Newell, P.	180-230	
Wilkins, M.E.	Wind in the Rose Bush (1st, 8vo, green/gilt, 237p, 8pl)	Doubleday/Page	1903	Newell, P.	50-70	
Mother Goose	Mother Goose Stories (folio, ibds, 76p, 14 fp color)	L: Collins	[1928]	Newton, Ruth	50-70	
Mother Goose	Mother Goose (1st, lg4to, [28]p, 12 fp color, pep)	Whitman	(1934)	Newton/Horn	80-100	*
Means, F.C.	Emmy & the Blue Door (1st, 8vo, yellow cl, 217p, b/w)	Houghton	1959	Nicholas, F.	20-30	*
Colby, J.P.	Jim the Cat (1st {std}, lg8vo, yellow cl, 46p, fp b/w)	Little/Brown	(1957)	Nichols, M.C.	30-45	
Dickens, C.	Christmas Carol (1st AM, 8vo, 78p, 4cp)	Stokes	[1913]	Nichols, S.B.	35-50	*
Wilde, O.	Happy Prince (1st, 8vo, p-o, 204p, gilt, 8cp)	Stokes	(1913)	Nichols, S.B.	60-80	
Noyes, Alfred	Sherwood (1st, 8vo, 225p, black/gilt, p-o, 4cp)	Stokes	1911	Nichols, S.B.	30-45	*
Kipling, R.	Almanac of 12 Sports (1st, 4to, ibds, unpag, 12cp)	L: Heinemann	1898	Nicholson, W.	350-450	
Kipling, R.	Almanac of 12 Sports (1st AM, 4to, ipcb, 12cp)	R.H. Russell	1898	Nicholson, W.	200-300	
Nicholson, Wm.	An Alphabet (1st AM, 4to, ibds, 26cp)	R.H. Russell	1898	Nicholson, W.	400-550	
Nicholson, Wm.	An Alphabet (1st, lg4to, ipcb, 26cp)	L: Heinemann	1898	Nicholson, W.	400-600	
Nicholson, Wm.	Book of Blokes (1st, sm8vo, 30p, green/gilt)	L: Faber	[1929]	Nicholson, W.	350-500	
Nicholson, Wm.	Clever Bill (1st, ob4to, yellow ipcb, 21cp)	L: Heinemann	[1926]	Nicholson, W.	400-600	
Nicholson, Wm.	Clever Bill (1st AM, ob sm4to, yel bds, 23p, color)	Doubleday/Dor.	[1927]	Nicholson, W.	350-500	
Rook, Clarence	Hooligan Nights (1st, 8vo, 289p, rust cl, col frn by...)	L: Richards	1899	Nicholson, W.	50-80	*
Davies, W.B.	Hour of Magic (1st, 12mo, pcb, 34p)	L: J. Cape	(1922)	Nicholson, W.	100-150	
Nicholson, Wm.	London Types (1st AM, lg4to, ibds, 28p, 12cp)	R.H. Russell	1898	Nicholson, W.	220-300	
Nicholson, Wm.	London Types (1st, folio, ipcb, 12cp)	L: Heinemann	1898	Nicholson, W.	350-400	
Sassoon, S.	Memoirs of a Fox Hunting Man (1st AM, lg8vo, 296p, 7pl)	Coward	1929	Nicholson, W.	80-110	
Dunne, F.P.	Mr. Dooley's Philosophy (1st, 8vo, red cl, col frn by...)	R.H. Russell	1900	Nicholson, W.	25-40	
Nicholson, Wm.	Pirate Twins (1st AM, ob8vo, 28p, ibds, color)	Coward	(1929)	Nicholson, W.	250-400	
Nicholson, Wm.	Pirate Twins (1st, ob4to, ibds, 32p, color)	L: Faber	(1929)	Nicholson, W.	300-500	
Gay, J.	Polly: An Opera (1st, lg8vo, blue bds, 107p, 8cp)	L: Heinemann	1923	Nicholson, W.	70-100	
Hardy, T.	Selected Poems of... (pcb, teg, frn by...)	L: P.L. Warner	1926	Nicholson, W.	140-200	
Waugh, A.	Square Book of Animals (1st, sq4to, [14]p, ibds, 12cp)	L: Heinemann	1900	Nicholson, W.	350-500	
Waugh, A.	Square Book of Animals (1st AM, sq4to, [14]p, ibds, 12cp)	R.H. Russell	1900	Nicholson, W.	280-400	R
Pugh, E.	Tony Drum (1st, sm8vo, 225p, tan cl, 10cp)	Holt	1898	Nicholson, W.	70-100	
Davies, W.H.	True Travellers (1st, 8vo, 53p, grey bds)	L: J. Cape	1923	Nicholson, W.	120-160	
Williams, M.	Velveteen Rabbit (1st, lg8vo, 19p, ipcb, 7cp, pep)	L: Heinemann	1922	Nicholson, W.	450-600	
Williams, M.	Velveteen Rabbit (1st AM, 8vo, ibds, 33p, 7cp, pep)	Doran	[1922]	Nicholson, W.	350-500	
Asbjornsen, P.C.	East o/t Sun/West o/t Moon (1st, 4to, gilt, 206p, pep, 25 ticp)	L: Hodder	(1914)	Nielsen, K.	600-800	

AUTHOR	TITLE	PUBLISHER	DATE	ARTIST	PRICE	LC
Asbjornsen, P.C.	East o/t Sun/West o/t Moon (1st AM, 4to, 205p, p-o, 25 ticp pep)	Doran	[1914]	Nielsen, K.	450-600	
Asbjornsen, P.C.	East o/t Sun/West o/t Moon (8vo, 204p, p-o, cp, pep, later)	Garden City	[1930]	Nielsen, K.	75-100	
Andersen, H.C.	Fairy Tales (1st, 4to, 197p, green/gilt, 12 ticp, pep)	L: Hodder	(1924)	Nielsen, K.	800-1000	
Andersen, H.C.	Fairy Tales (1st AM, 4to, p-o, 281p, pep, 12 ticp)	Doran	(1924)	Nielsen, K.	400-600	
Andersen, H.C.	Fairy Tales (1st {this pub}, 4to, p-o, 272p, 8cp)	Garden City	(1932)	Nielsen, K.	75-100	
Grimm Bros.	Hansel & Gretel (1st AM, 4to, red cl, p-o, gilt, 310p, 12cp)	Doran	(1925)	Nielsen, K.	250-350	
Quiller-Couch, A.	In Powder & Crinoline (1st, 4to, 164p, ibds, teg, gilt, 24 ticp)	L: Hodder	[1913]	Nielsen, K.	650-850	
Wilson, Romer	Red Magic... (1st, sm8vo, red/gilt, 368p, 8cp)	L: J. Cape	(1930)	Nielsen, K.	400-600	
Wilson, Romer	Red Magic... (1st AM, 8vo, 368p, black cl, uncut, 8cp)	Harcourt	(1931)	Nielsen, K.	350-500	
Quiller-Couch, A.	Twelve Dancing Princesses (1st AM, 8vo, 244p, 16 ticp, pep)	Doran	[1913]	Nielsen, K.	320-400	
Quiller-Couch, A.	Twelve Dancing Princesses (sm4to, 244p, col frn, cp)	Doubleday/Dor.	1930	Nielsen, K.	85-100	
Nightingale, M.	Tony-O'-Dreams (lg8vo, p-o, 160p, 8cp)	L: Simpkin	1919	Nightingale, M.	60-90	*
Bain, R.N.	Russian Fairy Tales (1st, 4to, teg, p-o, 283p, 16pl)	L: Harrap	1915	Nisbet, N.L.	150-200	
Bailey, M.	Seven Peas in the Pod (1st, 8vo, 201p, 4cp)	L: Harrap	(1921)	Nixon, K.	60-80	
Browne, E.G.	Puck's Broom (1st AM, sm8vo, 237p, red/gilt, 4cp)	Moffat	1923	Nixon, K.I.	25-45	*
Woole, R.	Animal Legends of Many Lands (4to, gilt, 144p, 12cp)	Tuck/McKay	[1915]	Noble, E.	85-140	
Pycraft, W.P.	Animal Why Book (1st AM, sm4to, 90p, p-o, 31 ticp)	Stokes	[1910]	Noble, E.	150-200	*
Davidson, G.	Helpers Without Hands (sm4to, p-o, bds, 118p, 32cp)	L: Wells/Gard.	(1914)	Noble, E.	150-200	
Pycraft, W.P.	Pads, Paws & Claws (1st, 4to, ibds, 123p, p-o, 32 ticp)	L: Wells/Gard.	(1911)	Noble, E.	150-185	
Ewing, J.H.	Jacanapes (1st, 12mo, 72p, col frn, 4 fp b/w, dep)	McLoughlin	(1906)	Noble-Ives, S.	30-45	*
Noble-Ives, S.	Key to Betsy's Heart (1st, 12mo, 225p, green cl, 4pl)	MacMillan	1916	Noble-Ives, S.	20-30	
Otis, James	Old Ben (1st, 12mo, ipcb, 188p, 7pl)	Harper	1911	Noble-Ives, S.	25-40	
Noble-Ives, S.	Songs of the Shining Way (1st, 8vo, tan ipcb, 45p, fp b/w)	R.H. Russell	1899	Noble-Ives, S.	65-80	*
Noble-Ives, S.	Story of the Teddy the Bear (1st, lg4to, [42]p, ibds, 5cp)	McLoughlin	[1907]	Noble-Ives, S.	80-130	
Stevenson, R.L.	Child's Garden of Verses (1st, lg8vo, 243p, col frn, b/w, pep)	Sears	(1926)	Noe, Eva	25-40	*
Dalgliesh, A.	Fourth of July Story (1st, 4to, [30]p, fp color)	Scribner	(1956)	Nonnast, M.	30-50	*
Parrish, R.	Don MacGrath (1st, 8vo, 269p, b/w pl)	McClurg	1910	Norton, J.W.	25-40	
Dow, E.C.	Diary of a Birthday Doll (1st, 8vo, 88p, 6cp)	Stern	1908	Nosworthy, F.	70-100	
Sawyer, E.A.	Elsa's Gift Home (1st, 8vo, 229p, 6pl)	Page	1911	Nosworthy, F.	20-30	*
Nuckel, O.	Destiny... (1st AM, sm4to, 190p, red cl, woodcuts)	Farrar/Rine.	(1930)	Nuckel, O.	45-70	
Metcalf, S.	Annabel (2nd, 8vo, 213p, green cl, 3pl)	Reilly/Britton	(1912)	Nuyttens, J.P.	170-240	
Peattie, E.W.	Azalea at Sunset Gap (1st, sm8vo, tan cl, 286p, 4pl)	Reilly/Britton	(1914)	Nuyttens, J.P.	25-40	*
Mitchell, Lebbeus	Bobby in Search of/Birthday (1st, 8vo, pcb, 64p, p-o, gilt, b/w)	Volland	1916	Nuyttens, J.P.	35-50	
Van Dyne, Edith	Flying Girl (1st [1], sm8vo, red cl, 232p, 4pl)	Reilly/Britton	(1911)	Nuyttens, J.P.	200-265	
Van Dyne, Edith	Flying Girl & her Chum (1st, 12mo, 313p, red cl, 4pl)	Reilly/Britton	(1912)	Nuyttens, J.P.	180-220	
Baum, L.F.	Phoebe Daring... (1st, 8vo, 298p, grey cl, 4pl)	Reilly/Britton	(1912)	Nuyttens, J.P.	180-250	
Nyce, Vera	Adventures of Greyfur Family (1st, 16mo, 76p, 24cp)	Lippincott	(1917)	Nyce, Helen	45-60	*
Nyce, Vera	Greyfur's Neighbors (1st, 16mo, 76p, 24cp)	Lippincott	(1917)	Nyce, Helen	45-60	*
Tappan, E.M.	Prince from Nowhere... (1st, sm8vo, 206p, blue cl, 8cp)	Houghton	1928	Nystrom, J.	25-40	*
Mendel, F.E.	Little Polish Cousin (1st, 12mo, 147p, 6pl)	Page	1912	O'Brien, H.	25-40	*
Bacon, J.D.	Biography of a Boy (1st, 8vo, 322p, blue cl, 14pl)	Harper	1910	O'Neill, R.	50-80	
Wilson, H.L.	Boss of the Little Arcady (1st, 8vo, green cl, 371p, 4pl)	Lothrop/Lee	1905	O'Neill, R.	30-50	
Burnham, C.L.	Clever Betsy (1st, 8vo, red/gilt, 402p, 3pl)	Houghton	1910	O'Neill, R.	25-45	
Brainerd, E.H.	For Love of Mary Ellen (1st, 12mo, 43p, tan cl, 4pl)	Harper	1912	O'Neill, R.	30-45	
O'Neill, Rose	Garda (1st {std}, 8vo, blue cloth, 305p, pep, DJ)	Doubleday/Dor.	1929	O'Neill, R.	35-50	
O'Neill, Rose	Goblin Woman (1st {std}, 8vo, 345p, b/w, pep)	Doubleday/Dor.	1930	O'Neill, R.	40-60	
Fillmore, P.H.	Hickory Limb (1st, 8vo, green cl, 70p, p-o, 4pf)	J. Lane	1910	O'Neill, R.	45-60	
O'Neill, Rose	Kewpie Kutouts (1st, 4to, bds, p-o, 48p, pep, color)	Stokes	(1914)	O'Neill, R.	700-1000	*
O'Neill, Rose	Kewpie Primer (1st, sq8vo, pict cloth, 118p, color, cep)	Stokes	(1916)	O'Neill, R.	280-400	
O'Neill, Rose	Kewpies & Dotty Darling (1st, 4to, p-o, tan bds, 88p, pep)	Stokes	(1912)	O'Neill, R.	250-400	
O'Neill, Rose	Kewpies & Runaway Baby (1st {std}, 8vo, 111p, red cl, col, cep)	Doubleday/Dor.	1928	O'Neill, R.	180-250	
O'Neill, Rose	Kewpies: Their Book (1st, lg4to, tan bds, p-o, 80p, dep)	Stokes	(1913)	O'Neill, R.	300-450	
O'Neill, Rose	Lady in the White Veil (1st, 12mo, blue cl, 350p, 5pl)	Harper	1909	O'Neill, R.	50-80	*
Wilson, H.L.	Lions of the Lord (1st, 8vo, p-o, 520p, 6pl)	Lothrop	(1903)	O'Neill, R.	30-45	
Fillmore, P.H.	Little Question of Ladies' Rights (1st, 12mo, 79p, p-o, b/w)	J. Lane	1916	O'Neill, R.	35-50	
O'Neill, Rose	Loves of Edwy (1st, sm8vo, tan cl, 432p, b/w)	Lothrop	(1904)	O'Neill, R.	50-70	
O'Neill, Rose	Master-Mistress (1st, 8vo, maroon bds, 227p, 9pl)	Knopf	1922	O'Neill, R.	50-75	
Lee, A.	Round Rabbit (1st, 12mo, brown cl, 52p, 6pl)	Copeland & Day	1898	O'Neill, R.	200-300	
Wilson, H.L.	The Seeker (1st, 8vo, green cl, 341p, b/w)	Doubleday/Page	1904	O'Neill, R.	25-40	
O'Neill, G.	Tomorrow's House (1st, sq8vo, purple cl, 159p, b/w, pep)	Dutton	1930	O'Neill, R.	65-90	
Vorse, M.H.	Very Little Person (1st, 8vo, 163p, green/gilt, 8pl)	Houghton	1911	O'Neill, R.	35-50	*
Stevenson, R.L.	Child's Garden of Verses (1st, sm8vo, 131p, cp, pep)	Chi: Flanagan	(1908)	O'Reilly, E.D.	40-65	*
Kingsley, C.	Westward Ho! (1st, lg8vo, 604p, p-o, 14cp, pep)	Jacobs	[1920]	Oakley, T.	60-80	
Rives, A.	Damsel Errant (1st, 12mo, teg, 211p, uncut, 4pl)	Lippincott	1898	Oakley, V.	80-100	*
Skinner, C.M.	Do-Nothing Days (1st, 12mo, 219p, teg, frn by...)	Lippincott	1899	Oakley, V.	80-100	
Longfellow, H.W.	Evangeline (1st, 8vo, 143p, teg, gilt, 5cp by...)	Houghton	1897	Oakley, V.	180-230	
King, C.	From School to Battlefield (1st, 8vo, beige cl, 322p, 6pl)	Lippincott	1899	Oakley, V.	90-120	
Gale, N.	June Romance (1st, 12mo, teg, blue cl, 193p, b/w)	Stone/Kimball	1899	Oakley, V.	75-90	
Walford, L.B	Little Legacy (1st, 12mo, blue cl, 344p, teg, frn by...)	H. Stone	1899	Oakley, V.	70-90	
Spofford, H.P.	Maid He Married (1st, 8vo, blue cl, 210p, teg)	Stone/Kimball	1899	Oakley, V.	80-95	
Otis, James	Princess & Joe Potter (1st, sq8vo, 249p, 7pl)	Estes	(1898)	Oakley, V.	100-150	
Thanet, O.	Slave to Duty (1st, 12mo, 221p, teg, frn by...)	H. Stone	1898	Oakley, V.	60-80	

AUTHOR	TITLE	PUBLISHER	DATE	ARTIST	PRICE	LC
Skinner, C.M.	With Feet to the Earth (1st, 12mo, 231p, teg, frn by...)	Lippincott	1899	Oakley, V.	90-120	
Whitehorn, A.L.	Wonder Tales of Old Japan (1st, 8vo, 173p, p-o, 12cp)	L: Jack	1911	Obata, S.	70-90	*
Whitehorn, A.L.	Wonder Tales of Old Japan (1st AM, 8vo, 173p, teg, p-o, 12cp)	Stokes	(1912)	Obata, S.	60-90	*
Williston, T.P.	Japanese Fairy Tales (1st, sm8vo, blue cl, 88p, 8 fp color, pep)	Rand/McNally	(1904)	Ogawa, S.	45-65	
Ogden, Ruth	Little Queen of Hearts (1st, 8vo, 232p, 15 fp b/w, gilt)	Stokes	(1893)	Ogden, H.A.	35-50	*
Ogden, Ruth	Loyal Little Redcoat (1st, 4to, 217p, gilt, b/w, PPPa)	Stokes	1890	Ogden, H.A.	65-80	
Fryer, Alfred C.	Fairy Tales/Harz Mountains (1st, lg8vo, 206p, gilt, b/w)	L: D. Nutt	1908	Ogders, A.M.	65-80	*
Gilly Bear	Adventures of Peterkin (1st, lg8vo, 153p, brown/gilt, 12cp)	NY: S. Gabriel	(1916)	Ohrenschall, H.	65-80	
Gilly Bear	Tom Tit Tales (1st, 4to, 155p, purple/gilt, 12cp)	NY: S. Gabriel	(1915)	Ohrenschall, H.	60-80	
Gordon, H.C.	Golden Key (1st, 8vo, 223p, col frn, 5 fp b/w)	L: J. Murray	(1932)	Oldfield, M.	30-45	*
Olds, Eliz.	Big Fire (1st, ob8vo, red cl, [32]p, color, pep)	Houghton	1945	Olds, E.	35-50	*
Olds, Eliz.	Feather Mountain (1st, lg ob8vo, aqua cl, 27p, color, pep, CH)	Houghton	1951	Olds, E.	65-90	*
Olds, Eliz.	Riding the Rails (1st, ob8vo, 43p, color, dep)	Houghton	1948	Olds, E.	35-50	*
Fish, H.D.	Butterfly Land (1st AM, ob4to, [15]p, p-o, 7cp)	Stokes	1931	Olfers, S.	130-180	
Fish, H.D.	When the Root Children Wake Up (1st AM, 4to, [22]p, 9cp, pep)	Stokes	1930	Olfers, S.	100-150	
Gratacap, L.P.	New Northland (1st, sm8vo, 391p, blue/gilt, 16pl)	NY: T. Benton	1915	Operti, A.	45-60	*
Aesopus	Aesop's Fables (1st, 8vo, 318p, color)	Lippincott	1916	Opper, F.	45-60	*
Mother Goose	Mother Goose's Nursery Rhymes (1st, sm8vo, 320p, col frn, b/w)	Lippincott	1900	Opper, F.	50-80	*
Coatsworth, E.	Toast to the King (1st, 8vo, 159p, pep)	Coward	(1940)	Orr, F.	25-40	*
Mother Goose	Mother Goose Nursery Rhymes (4to, ibds, 128p, 16cp)	L: Jack	[1915]	Orr, J.	150-180	
N/A	Arabian Nights (1st, lg8vo, teg, 294p, gilt, 15cp)	L: Harrap	1913	Orr, M.S.	80-100	
N/A	Arabian Nights (1st AM, 8vo, 294p, 15cp)	Holt	1913	Orr, M.S.	65-80	
Grimm Bros.	Fairy Tales (1st, 8vo, 333p)	L: Harrap	1914	Orr, M.S.	65-80	*
Andersen, H.C.	Fairy Tales (1st, 8vo, 309p, cream cl, 8cp)	L: Harrap	1925	Orr, M.S.	50-75	*
Kingsley, C.	Hereward the Wake (1st, 8vo, 196p, pcb, p-o, 8cp)	L: Jack	[1910]	Orr, M.S.	65-80	*
Mother Goose	Mother Goose (1st AM, 8vo, 255p, 16cp)	McKay	(1915)	Orr, M.S.	80-120	*
Mother Goose	Mother Goose (1st, 4to, teg, 255p, 16cp)	L: Harrap	(1915)	Orr, M.S.	160-200	
Orr, M.S.	The Alphabet (1st, 4to, ibds, 60p, 26cp)	L: J.M. Dent	1931	Orr, M.S.	140-185	
Stevenson, R.L.	Treasure Island (1st, 8vo, red/gilt, 252p, 10cp)	L: Muller	1934	Orr, M.S.	80-120	
N/A	World's Fairy Book (1st, lg8vo, 256p, 12cp)	L: Harrap	(1930)	Orr, M.S.	100-130	
N/A	Two Jolly Mariners (ob4to, ibds, 24cp)	L: Blackie	[1917]	Orr, S.	150-185	
Ort, Jane	Mr. Mogo Mouse (1st, sm8vo, ibds, 39p, color, pep)	Volland	(1930)	Ort, J.	35-50	
Browning, R.	Men and Women (1st, sm8vo, green/gilt, teg, 312p, 15pl)	L: Dent	1903	Ospovat, H.	60-80	
Arnold, M.	Poems (1st, 12mo, brown/gilt, 374p, teg, uncut, 18pl)	J. Lane	1900	Ospovat, H.	40-65	
Shakespeare, Wm.	Songs (1st, 12mo, 140p, uncut, green/gilt, teg, 11pl)	J. Lane	1901	Ospovat, H.	50-65	
Muller, M.	Memories... (1st, 8vo, 135p, teg, gilt, p-o, 8pl)	McClurg	1902	Ostertag, B.	35-50	
Forsythe, C.	Old Songs for Young Americans (1st, ob4to, green cl, color)	Doubleday/Page	1901	Ostertag, B.	80-120	
Adams, J.D.	Vaino: Boy of New Finland (1st, 8vo, 273p, pep, NH)	Dutton	1929	Ostman, L.	40-65	*
Blanchard, A.E.	Little Girl's Summer Holidays (1st, sm8vo, 5cp)	Jacobs	(1911)	Otis, E.	25-40	*
Outhwaite, I.	Blossom: A Fairy Story (1st, 4to, p-o, blue cl, 94p, 8cp, pep)	L: A&C Black	(1928)	Outhwaite, I.R.	500-700	
Outhwaite, I.	Bunny & Brownie (1st UK, 4to, 99p, blue cl, 8 color, p-o, pep)	L: A&C Black	(1930)	Outhwaite, I.R.	450-600	
Daskein, Tarella	Chimney Town (1st, lg8vo, 238p, blue cl, color)	L: A&C Black	1934	Outhwaite, I.R.	100-140	*
Outhwaite, G.	Enchanted Forest (1st, 4to, 93p, gilt, pep, 16 ticp)	L: A&C Black	1921	Outhwaite, I.R.	500-700	
Outhwaite, I.	Fairyland (1st, lg4to, blue cl, 128p, 15cp, pep)	L: A&C Black	(1931)	Outhwaite, I.R.	650-900	
Danks, B.M.	Janet & the Fairies (sm8vo, 64p, 4cp)	L: A&C Black	(1937)	Outhwaite, I.R.	160-200	
Outhwaite, I.	Little Fairy Sister (2nd, 4to, 91p, 8cp, pep)	L: A&C Black	1929	Outhwaite, I.R.	180-260	
Outhwaite, I. & A.	Little Green Road to Fairyland (1st, 4to, 103p, bds, p-o, 8cp)	L: A&C Black	1922	Outhwaite, I.R.	300-450	
Outhwaite, I. & A.	Little Green Road to Fairyland (1st AM, 4to, pep, 102p, 8cp)	Dutton	[1922]	Outhwaite, I.R.	200-300	
Outhwaite, I.	Sixpence to Spend (4to, bds, 5 ticp)	(Sydney)	1935	Outhwaite, I.R.	350-500	
Nash, Ogden	Musical Zoo (1st {std}, 4to, 47p, cloth, b/w, DJ)	Little/Brown	1947	Owen, Frank	40-65	
Grimm Bros.	Robber Bridegroom (1st lg4to, p-o, 39p, pep, 8 ticp)	L: A&C Black	1922	Owen, H.S.	120-175	
Carroll, L.	Alice... & Through... (1st, 8vo, ibds, 284p, 2-color, pep)	Whitman	(1955)	Paflin, R.	30-50	*
Moore, C.C.	Night Before Christmas (1st, 8vo, ibds, [16]p, color)	Dutton	(1944)	Paflin, R.	25-40	
Andersen, H.C.	Tales from Andersen (1st {std}, lg8vo, 78p, color)	Dutton	1946	Paflin, R.	65-80	*
Grimm Bros.	Tales from Grimm (1st {std}, lg8vo, 78p, color)	Dutton	1945	Paflin, R.	65-80	*
Goldsmith, O.	Vicar of Wakefield (1st, 8vo, AEG, 224p, green cl)	L: Nister	[1898]	Paget, H.M.	50-70	
Doyle, A.C.	Desert Drama (1st AM, 8vo, 277p, tan cl, 32pl)	Lippincott	1898	Paget, S.	70-100	
Doyle, A.C.	Memoirs of Sherlock Holmes (1st, 8vo, AEG, blue cl, 279p)	L: G. Newnes	1904	Paget, S.	350-500	
N/A	Arabian Nights (1st, 8vo, 328p, 5cp)	Nister/Dutton	[1907]	Paget, W.	65-90	*
Stevenson, R.L.	Master of Ballantrae (1st, 8vo, 349p, 12cp)	L: Cassell	1911	Paget, W.	35-50	*
Smeaton, O.	Mystery of the Pacific (1st, 8vo, 335p, red/gilt, 8pl)	L: Blackie	1899	Paget, W.	60-85	
Jameson, Anna	Shakespeare's Heroines (lg8vo, 308p, gilt, AEG, 6cp, pep)	L: Nister	[1900]	Paget, W.	65-90	
Lamb, C.	Tales from Shakespeare (lg8vo, AEG, 319p, gilt, 6cp, pep)	L: Nister	[1901]	Paget, W.	80-100	
Stevenson, R.L.	Treasure Island (1st, 12mo, 388p)	Scribner	1900	Paget, W.	45-60	*
Henty, G.A.	Treasure of the Incas (1st, 8vo, green/gilt, 8pl)	L: Blackie	1903	Paget, W.	35-50	*
Paget-Fredericks, J.	Green-Pipes (1st {1st bk.}, folio, 50p, green/gilt, 6cp)	MacMillan	1929	Paget-Fredericks	80-100	
Paget-Fredericks, J.	Miss Pert's Christmas Tree (1st, lg4to, red/gilt, 24p, 6cp, pep)	MacMillan	1929	Paget-Fredericks	60-85	r
Millay, Edna St. V.	Princess Marries the Page (1st {std}, lg8vo, 50p, bds, col frn)	Harper	1932	Paget-Fredericks	70-100	R*
Asbjornsen, P.C.	Fifteen Norse Tales (1st, 8vo, 180p)	L: Nelson	1931	Pailthorpe, D.	50-65	*
Palazzo, T.	Charley the Horse (1st, sq4to, 56p, color, pep)	Viking	1950	Palazzo, T.	45-60	*
Palazzo, T.	Federico the Flying Squirrel (1st, 4to, 54p, ipcb, color, pep)	Viking	1951	Palazzo, T.	45-60	*
Kjelgaard, J.A.	Forest Patrol (1st, sm8vo, 293p, rust cl, fp b/w)	Holiday House	(1941)	Palazzo, T.	30-45	*

AUTHOR	TITLE	PUBLISHER	DATE	ARTIST	PRICE	LC
Palazzo, T.	Giant Nursery Book (1st, lg4to, 188p)	Garden City	1957	Palazzo, T.	45-65	*
Palazzo, T.	Great Othello (1st, ob4to, 48p, blue cl, 1-color)	Viking	1952	Palazzo, T.	40-65	*
Mother Goose	Mother Goose Nursery Almanac (1st {std}, folio, ibds, 88p, col)	Garden City	1960	Palazzo, T.	70-120	*
Graham, Al	Mouse with a Small Guitar (1st, 8vo, 35p, grey cl, color, pep)	Welch Pub. Co.	(1947)	Palazzo, T.	35-60	R*
Liers, Emil	Otter's Story (1st, 8vo, blue cl, 191p, fp b/w)	Viking	1953	Palazzo, T.	45-65	R*
N/A	Story of Noah's Ark (1st, 4to, ibds, [88]p, color)	Garden City	(1955)	Palazzo, T.	40-65	*
White, Anne H.	Story of Seraphina (1st, 4to, 128p, orang cl, b/w)	Viking	1951	Palazzo, T.	30-50	*
Palazzo, T.	Susie the Cat (1st, 4to, 50p, ipcb, color, pep)	Viking	1949	Palazzo, T.	35-50	*
Graham, Al	Timothy Turtle (1st, lg4to, [30]p, pep, CH)	Welch Pub. Co.	(1946)	Palazzo, T.	70-100	*
Bontemps, A.	We Have Tomorrow (1st, sm8vo, 131p, photos by...)	Houghton	1945	Palfi, M.	45-70	*
Omar Khayyam	Rubaiyat... (1st, 4to, 128p, gilt, 12 ticp)	L: L.B. Hill	[1925]	Palmer, D.M.	145-200	
Burgess, T.	Tales from Storyteller's House (1st {std}, sq8vo, 195p, 8cp)	Little/Brown	1937	Palmer, L.	60-75	
Burgess, T.	While the Story Log Burns (1st {std}, 8vo, 195p, 8cp, DJ)	Little/Brown	1938	Palmer, L.	60-90	
Austin, Mary H.	California: Land of the Sun (1st, lg8vo, 178p, gilt, 32 ticp)	L: A&C Black	1914	Palmer, S.	120-165	
Palmer, S.	Surrey (1st, 8vo, blue/gilt, 252p, teg, 75p)	L: A&C Black	1906	Palmer, S.	70-100	
Sewell, Anna	Black Beauty (1st, 8vo, p-o, 261p, color)	Dodge	(1907)	Pancoast, C.W.	35-50	*
Pancoast, M.H.	Rejuvenation/Mama & Papa Goose (1st, lg4to, ipcb, [84]p, color)	NY: Britton	(1916)	Pancoast, M.H.	150-230	*
N/A	Arabian Nights (1st, sm8vo, 371p, col frn, b/w)	MacMillan	1923	Pape, Eric	30-50	
Andersen, H.C.	Fairy Tales & Stories (1st, 8vo, 214p, gilt, col frn, pep)	L: MacMillan	1921	Pape, Eric	65-80	
Austin, Mary	Isidro (1st, 8vo, 425p, green/gilt, dep, 4cp)	Houghton	1905	Pape, Eric	50-70	
Irving, W.	Rip Van Winkle (1st, 12mo, blue cl, 183p, 4cp, fp b/w, pep)	MacMillan	1925	Pape, Eric	35-50	*
Groesbeck, T.	The Incas (1st, 4to, green/gilt, 71p, teg, uncut, 14pl)	Putnam	1896	Pape, Eric	65-80	*
Wells, H.G.	War in the Air (1st AM, 8vo, 395p, grey/gilt, uncut, 20pl)	MacMillan	1908	Pape, Eric	240-300	
France, A.	At the Sign o/t Reine Padauque (1st, 4to, 275p, gilt, 12pl, pep)	L: J. Lane	1922	Pape, F.	35-50	
MacDonald, Geo.	Back of the North Wind (1st AM, 8vo, blue cl, p-o, 12 fp color)	Caldwell	[1911]	Pape, F.	65-90	*
MacDonald, Geo.	Back of the North Wind (1st, 8vo, 391p, p-o, 12cp)	L: Blackie	1911	Pape, F.	95-130	
N/A	Book of Psalms (1st, sm folio, teg, gilt, 282p, 24cp)	L: Hutchinson	(1912)	Pape, F.	100-150	
Buckley, E.F.	Children of the Dawn (1st, 8vo, 348p, gilt, 24pl)	L: Wells/Gard.	1908	Pape, F.	70-120	
Buckley, E.F.	Children of the Dawn (1st AM, 8vo, 348p)	Stokes	(1909)	Pape, F.	45-65	*
Andersen, H.C.	Fairy Tales (1st, sm8vo, 324p, cp)	Nister/Dutton	[1910]	Pape, F.	65-90	*
Stawell, Mrs. R.	Fairy of Old Spain... (1st AM, 8vo, beige/gilt, 134p, 6cp)	Dutton	1912	Pape, F.	65-110	
Underdown, E.	Gateway to Spenser (1st, 8vo, 399p, 16cp)	L: Nelson	[1911]	Pape, F.	65-80	*
Wilson, R.	Indian Story Book (1st, 8vo, 272p, blue/gilt, 16cp)	L: MacMillan	1914	Pape, F.	90-110	
Blackmore, R.D.	Lorna Doone (1st, 4to, blue cl, col frn)	L: J. Lane	1933	Pape, F.	65-80	
Rowsell, M.	Pedlar & His Dog (8vo, green cl, p-o, 156p, 4cp)	L: Blackie	[1912]	Pape, F.	40-60	
Bunyan, J.	Pilgrim's Progress (1st, lg8vo, 315p, green/gilt, 12cp)	L: J.M. Dent	1910	Pape, F.	90-140	
Rix, H.	Prince Pimpernel (1st, 8vo, 141p, 8cp)	L: Duckworth	1909	Pape, F.	80-120	
France, A.	Revolt of the Angels (1st AM, 8vo, 357p, black/gilt, 12 tipl)	Dodd/Lane	1924	Pape, F.	50-65	
France, A.	Revolt of the Angels (1st, 8vo, 357p, 12 tipl)	L: J. Lane	1924	Pape, F.	80-100	
Wilson, R.	Russian Story Book (1st, 8vo, 307p, gilt, 16cp)	L: Methuen	1916	Pape, F.	60-80	
Grove, F.	Story Without an End (1st, 8vo, 165p, teg, gilt, 8 ticp)	L: Duckworth	(1912)	Pape, F.	65-80	
Lamb, C.	Tales from Shakespeare (1st, 8vo, 308p, teg, gilt, 12cp)	L: Warne	1923	Pape, F.	70-85	
France, A.	Thais (1st, 4to, black/gilt, 247p, 12pl, pep)	L: Bodley Head	1926	Pape, F.	50-70	
France, A.	Well of St. Clare (1st, 8vo, black bds, 302p, gilt, 12pl)	L: J. Lane	(1928)	Pape, F.	45-65	
Spielmann, M.H.	Love Family (1st, 8vo, ibds, 63p, 12cp)	L: G. Allen	(1908)	Park, C.M.	90-130	*
Bates, H.E.	Down the River (1st AM, 4to, 151p, wood engravings, DJ)	Holt	1937	Parker, A.M.	35-50	
Power, Rhoda	How it Happened (1st, 8vo, beige cl, 188p, 12pl)	(Cambridge)	1930	Parker, A.M.	45-60	*
Bates, H.E.	Through the Woods (1st AM, 4to, 142p, engravings)	MacMillan	1936	Parker, A.M.	30-50	
N/A	Jack & the Beanstalk (1st, 24mo, ibds, [39]p, decor by...)	Holiday House	(1935)	Parker, Arvilla	60-90	R*
Parker, B.	Cinderella at the Zoo (4to, ibds, 16 chromos)	L: Chambers	[1900]	Parker, B.	300-450	
Parker, B.	Lays of the Grays (ob 4to, ibds, color)	L: Chambers	[1910]	Parker, B.	250-400	
Perry, Nora	Flock of Girls & Boys (1st, sm8vo, 323p, grey/gilt, 9pl)	Little/Brown	1895	Parker, C.T.	30-45	
Parker, B.	Arctic Orphans (ob folio, ibds, color, pep)	L: Chambers	[1910]	Parker, N.	400-600	
Parker, B.	Funny Bunnies (ob folio, ibds, 12cp)	L: Chambers	[1905]	Parker, N.	250-400	*
Parker, B.	History of the Hoppers (lg4to, ibds, color)	Chambers/Stoke	[1908]	Parker, N.	250-350	
Parker, B.& N.	Larder Lodge (lg ob4to, ibds, 14 fp color)	L: Chambers	[1910]	Parker, N.	240-350	
Parkes, W.T.	Spook Ballads (1st, 12mo, 246p, brown/gilt, b/w, cep)	L: Simpkin	1895	Parkes, W.T.	50-65	
Byron, May	Sambo & Susanna (ob4to, ibds, 24 color, [french fold paper])	L: Blackie	[1905]	Parkinson, E.	300-500	
Parrish, A.& D.	Floating Island (1st {std}, lg8vo, p-o, 265p, 13pl, NH)	Harper	(1930)	Parrish, A.	60-85	R
Parrish, Anne	Story of Appleby Capple (1st, lg4to, 184p, pep, b/w, NH)	Harper	(1950)	Parrish, A.	50-80	*
Parrish, A.& D.	Dream Coach (1st, 8vo, 143p, blue/gilt, fp b/w, pep, NH)	MacMillan	1924	Parrish, A.& D.	45-65	
Parrish, A.& D.	Knee-High to a Grasshopper (1st, 8vo, yellow cl, 209p, b/w, pep)	MacMillan	1923	Parrish, A.& D.	35-50	
N/A	Arabian Nights (1st, lg8vo, 339p, teg, p-o, 12cp, pep, SC)	Scribner	1909	Parrish, M.	160-200	R
Read, Opie	Bolanyo (1st, 12mo, tan cl, teg, 309p, uncut, cvr by...)	Way/Williams	1897	Parrish, M.	200-320	
Scudder, Horace E.	Children's Book (8vo, p-o by...)	Houghton	1909	Parrish, M.	50-70	*
Grahame, K.	Dream Days (1st, sq8vo, teg, 228p, gilt, 9pl, pep)	L: J. Lane	(1902)	Parrish, M.	130-170	
Rayner, E.	Free to Serve (2nd, 8vo, 434p, cover art by..)	Copeland & Day	1897	Parrish, M.	125-165	
Carryl, G.W.	Garden of Years (1st, 8vo, 129p, uncut, teg, dep, frn by...)	Putnam	1904	Parrish, M.	60-85	R
Grahame, K.	Golden Age (1st, 8vo, red/gilt, 252p, teg, 19pl, pep)	J. Lane	1900	Parrish, M.	120-165	
Grahame, K.	Golden Age (2nd, 8vo, 252p, 18pl)	J. Lane	1904	Parrish, M.	65-85	
Palgrave, F.	Golden Treasury/Songs & Lyrics (1st, 4to, p-o, 373p, pep, 8cp)	Duffield	1911	Parrish, M.	160-200	
Longfellow, H.W.	Hiawatha (1st, red/gilt, 8vo, teg, 242p, p-o by...)	Houghton	1911	Parrish, M.	300-500	

AUTHOR	TITLE	PUBLISHER	DATE	ARTIST	PRICE	LC
Irving, W.	History of New York (1st, lg4to, bds, teg, p-o, 299p, 8pl)	R.H. Russell	1900	Parrish, M.	250-350	
Irving, W.	History of New York (1st {this format}, 4to, 299p, bds, 8 ticp)	Dodd	1915	Parrish, M.	200-250	
Wharton, E.	Italian Villas... (1st, 4to, teg, 270p, gilt, 15cp)	Scribner	1904	Parrish, M.	300-450	
Saunders, L.	Knave of Hearts (1st {hardback}, folio, 46p, p-o, color, pep)	Scribner	1925	Parrish, M.	800-1000	
Hawthorne, H.	Lure of the Garden (1st, 4to, teg, uncut, 259p, dep, 1cp by...)	Century	1911	Parrish, M.	100-140	
Baum, L.F.	Mother Goose in Prose (1st [1], 4to, gilt, 265p, cloth, 12pl)	Way/Williams	(1897)	Parrish, M.	7000	R
Baum, L.F.	Mother Goose in Prose (1st UK, lg4to, tan cl, 265p)	L: Duckworth	(1898)	Parrish, M.	5000	
Baum, L.F.	Mother Goose in Prose (3rd, sq8vo, 265p, 12pl)	Bobbs-Merrill	(1905)	Parrish, M.	500-700	
Jackson, G.E.	Peterkin (1st, lg8vo, p-o, 75p, col frn by...)	Duffield	1912	Parrish, M.	120-165	*
Field, E.	Poems of Childhood (1st, 4to, p-o, teg, 199p, 8cp, pep, SC)	Scribner	1904	Parrish, M.	140-200	
Field, E.	Poems of Childhood (1st UK, 8vo, 199p, red/gilt, teg, pep, 8cp)	L: J. Lane	1904	Parrish, M.	140-185	
Schauffer, R.H.	Romantic America (1st, 4to, 339p, gilt, teg, col frn by...)	Century	1913	Parrish, M.	80-125	
Skinner, A.M.	Topaz Story Book (1st, 12mo, 381p, col frn by...)	Duffield	1917	Parrish, M.	100-150	*
Stein, E.	Troubadour Tales (1st, sm8vo, 165p, gilt, frn by...)	Bobbs-Merrill	(1903)	Parrish, M.	85-120	
Smith, A.C.	Turquoise Cup (1st, 8vo, blue bds, 209p, frn by...)	Scribner	1903	Parrish, M.	70-100	
Skinner, A.M.	Turquoise Story Book (1st, sm8vo, blue cl, frn by...)	Duffield	1918	Parrish, M.	100-140	
Hawthorne, N.	Wonder Book... (1st, 4to, p-o, 358p, blue/gilt, pep, 10cp)	Duffield	1910	Parrish, M.	160-200	
Winsor, F.	Space Child's Mother Goose (1st {std}, 8vo, [88]p, b/w, pep)	Simon/Schuster	1958	Parry, M.	30-45	*
Coburn, Grace	Heroes & Wizards (1st, 8vo, 246p, col frn, 8 fp b/w)	L: Nelson	1939	Parsons, J.	25-40	*
Blake, Wm.	Songs of Innocence (1st, 4to, 42p, 12cp)	L: Medici	1927	Parsons, J.	60-80	
Dobson, Austin	Proverbs in Porcelain (1st, sq8vo, teg, 112p, uncut, b/w)	L: Kegan Paul	1893	Partridge, B.	50-75	
Browning, R.	Rabbi Ben Ezra... (1st, 4to, 84p, 12 ticp)	L: Hodder	(1915)	Partridge, B.	80-100	
France, A.	Golden Tales of Anatole France (1st {this fmt}, 4to, 352p)	Dodd	1927	Patterson, M.	40-65	
Costantino, Joan	Pepito at Capistrano (1st, lg8vo, p-o, 32p, color)	Whitman	1943	Patton, L.	20-30	*
N/A	Aucassin & Nicolette (1st, 4to, 120p, p-o, teg, 13 ticp)	L: Harrap	[1917]	Paul, E.	120-170	
N/A	Aucassin & Nicolette (1st AM, 4to, p-o, unpag, 13 ticp)	Brentano's	[1917]	Paul, E.	90-130	
West, M.	Clair De Lune (1st, lg4to, 140p, teg, brown/gilt, 8 ticp, pep)	L: Harrap	[1913]	Paul, E.	140-180	
Gaskell, Mrs.	Cranford (1st, sm8vo, 247p, teg, 24cp)	L: Chapman	[1911]	Paul, E.	40-60	
Lindsey, Wm.	Curtain of Forgetfulness (1st, lg8vo, 31p, 11 ticp)	Houghton	1923	Paul, E.	65-100	
Monro, W.D.	India's Gods & Heroes (1st AM, 8vo, uncut, 237p, 16cp)	Crowell	(1910)	Paul, E.	60-80	
Davis, F.H.	Myths & Legends of Japan (1st, 432p, gilt, 32cp)	L: Harrap	1912	Paul, E.	70-90	
Spence, L.	Myths of Babylonia & Assyria (1st AM, 4to, teg, 411p, 8cp)	Stokes	[1915]	Paul, E.	75-100	
Dante	New Life (1st, 4to, 168p, teg, color)	L: Harrap	[1916]	Paul, E.	80-120	
N/A	Romance of Tristam & Isoude (4to, color)	Brentano's	[1910]	Paul, E.	50-75	*
Cunnington, S.	Stories from Dante (1st, p-o, 8vo, 355p, gilt, 16cp)	L: Harrap	1911	Paul, E.	75-90	
Bishop, C.H.	Augustus (1st, sm4to, [32]p, ipcb, color, pep)	Viking	1945	Paull, G.	25-45	*
Hunt, M.L.	Benjie's Hat (1st, 8vo, 119p, orange cl, pep, b/w)	Stokes	1938	Paull, G.	20-30	*
Bailey, C.S.	Children of the Handcrafts (1st, lg8vo, 192p, b/w, dep)	Viking	1935	Paull, G.	30-45	
Bailey, C.S.	Country-Stop (1st, 8vo, 128p, dep, 8 fp color)	Viking	1942	Paull, G.	35-50	*
Coatsworth, E.	Dancing Tom (1st, sq12mo, tan cl, [49]p, 1-color)	MacMillan	1938	Paull, G.	30-45	*
Coatsworth, E.	Forgotten Island (1st, sm8vo, 65p, tan cl, b/w)	Grosset/Dunlap	(1942)	Paull, G.	25-45	*
Hunt, M.L.	Little Girl with Seven Names (1st, 8vo, 63p, b/w, pep)	Stokes	1936	Paull, G.	25-40	*
Coatsworth, E.	Little Haymakers (1st {std}, sm8vo, tan cl, 79p, fp b/w)	MacMillan	1949	Paull, G.	25-40	*
Bianco, M.W.	Street of Little Shops (1st {std}, 8vo, 111p, uncut, cep, 8cp)	Doubleday/Dor.	1932	Paull, G.	50-85	R*
Bailey, C.S.	Tops & Whistles (1st, lg8vo, 193p, 20 fp b/w, pep)	Viking	1937	Paull, G.	25-40	*
Harper, Wilhelmina	Uncle Sam's Story Book (1st {std}, lg8vo, 144p, color)	McKay	(1944)	Paull, G.	30-45	*
Hunt, M.L.	Wonderful Baker (1st {std}, 8vo, blue cl, 47p, b/w, dep)	Lippincott	(1950)	Paull, G.	25-40	*
Maeterlinck, M.	Children's Blue Bird (1st, 4to, p-o, 182p, teg, 19pl)	Dodd	1913	Paus, H.	60-85	
Maeterlinck, M.	Tyltyl (1st, 4to, blue/gilt, p-o, 159p, 8 ticp, pep)	Dodd	1920	Paus, H.	90-135	
Maeterlinck, M.	Tyltyl (1st UK, sm4to, p-o, 159p, blue/gilt, 8 ticp)	L: Methuen	(1921)	Paus, H.	70-100	
Henry, A.H.	By Order of the Prophet (1st, 8vo, orang cl, 402p, 5pl)	Revell	1902	Paxon, E.S.	25-40	
Garth, Mary	What Happened to Hannah (4to, p-o, color)	L: Goschen	1913	Payne, Irene	50-70	*
Beaumont, C.W.	Sea Magic... (1st, 8vo, 120p, pcb, gilt, color)	L: Bodley Head	(1928)	Payne, W.	45-60	*
Grahame, K.	Wind in the Willows (1st, 8vo, 247p, blue/gilt, teg, color)	L: Methuen	(1927)	Payne, W.	100-145	
Mendes, C.	Fairy Spinning Wheel (1st, sq8vo, 146p, 14 fp b/w)	Badger	1898	Peabody, M.L.	100-130	*
Stringer, A.J.	Loom of Destiny (1st, 12mo, 208p, blue/silver, cvr by...)	Small	1899	Peabody, M.L.	45-75	*
Stevenson, R.L.	Dr. Jekyll & Mr. Hyde (1st, 8vo, gilt, 12 fp b/w)	Folio Society	1948	Peake, M.	70-100	
Grimm Bros.	Household Tales (1st, sm4to, 303p, yellow cl, 6 fp color)	L: Eyre/Spotts	(1946)	Peake, M.	125-185	
Carroll, L.	Hunting of the Snark (1st, 8vo, red cl, 46p, b/w)	L: Chatto	1941	Peake, M.	130-200	*
Judah, Aaron	Pot of Gold (1st, 8vo, 62p, red cloth, b/w)	L: Faber	1959	Peake, M.	45-60	*
Laing, Allan M.	Prayers & Graces (1st, sq12mo, 64p, blue/gilt, 30 b/w)	L: Gollancz	1944	Peake, M.	70-100	
Collis, Maurice	Quest for Sita (1st AM, 8vo, blue/gilt, uncut, 31 fp b/w)	NY: J. Day	1947	Peake, M.	80-100	*
N/A	Rhymes without Reason (1st, sm4to, yellow cl, 16 fp color)	L: Eyre/Spotts	1944	Peake, M.	90-130	*
N/A	Ride a Cock-Horse (1st, 4to, 29p, ibds, color)	L: Chatto	1940	Peake, M.	300-450	
Peake, M.	Shapes & Sounds (1st, 8vo, 23p, ibds)	L: Chatto	1941	Peake, M.	200-300	
Stevenson, R.L.	Treasure Island (1st, 8vo, gilt, 20 fp b/w)	L: Eyre/Spotts	1949	Peake, M.	80-120	*
Hole, Christina	Witchcraft in England (1st, 8vo, 167p, maroon/gilt, fp b/w)	L: Batsford	1945	Peake, M.	90-125	*
Hole, Christina	Witchcraft in England (1st AM, lg8vo, 168p, fp b/w)	Scribner	1947	Peake, M.	70-100	*
Stacpoole, H.D.	Poppyland (1st, 4to, 219p, blue/gilt, 17cp, pep)	L: Bodley Head	1914	Pearce, L.	120-180	
Dana, R.H.	Two Years Before the Mast (1st, 8vo, 415p, 15cp)	L: MacMillan	1915	Pears, Charles	25-40	*
Ash, Fenton	By Airship to Ophir (1st, 8vo, 320p, red/gilt, 3 color)	L: J.F. Shaw	(1911)	Pearse, A.	70-100	*
Stables, Gordon	City at the Pole (1st, 8vo, blue cl, 8pl)	L: J. Nisbet	1906	Pearse, A.	50-75	

AUTHOR	TITLE	PUBLISHER	DATE	ARTIST	PRICE	LC
Heward, C.	Ameliaranne & Green Umbrella (1st AM, 8vo, 109p, p-o, col, pep)	Jacobs	(1920)	Pearse, S.B.	60-80	
Heward, C.	Ameliaranne & the Monkey (1st AM, 8vo, p-o, [63]p, color, pep)	McKay	(1929)	Pearse, S.B.	50-65	
Morris, Ethel.	Ameliaranne Bridesmaid (1st, 8vo, ibds, unpag, p-o, color)	L: Harrap	(1946)	Pearse, S.B.	30-45	
Heward, C.	Ameliaranne Camps Out (1st, 4to, ibds, unpag)	L: Harrap	(1939)	Pearse, S.B.	50-75	
Heward, C.	Ameliaranne Cinema Star (1st, 12mo, tan bds, p-o, unpag)	L: Harrap	(1929)	Pearse, S.B.	50-75	
Gilmour, Marg.	Ameliaranne Gives a Concert (1st, 8vo, unpag)	L: Harrap	1944	Pearse, S.B.	50-70	*
Heward, C.	Ameliaranne Gives a Party (1st, 8vo, ibds, pep, 28 color)	L: Harrap	(1938)	Pearse, S.B.	50-75	
Heward, C.	Ameliaranne Goes Touring (1st, 4to, ibds, unpag, pep, color)	L: Harrap	(1941)	Pearse, S.B.	50-75	
Heward, C.	Ameliaranne Keeps Shop (1st, 8vo, ibds, [128]p, color, pep)	McKay	(1928)	Pearse, S.B.	45-60	
Gilmour, Marg.	Ameliaranne at the Circus (1st, 12mo, p-o, [63]p, color)	L: Harrap	(1931)	Pearse, S.B.	40-65	*
Heward, C.	Ameliaranne at the Farm (1st, 8vo, [58]p, ibds, pep)	L: Harrap	1937	Pearse, S.B.	45-60	
Heward, C.	Ameliaranne at the Farm (1st AM, 8vo, [58]p, p-o, color)	McKay	(1937)	Pearse, S.B.	45-70	
Gilmour, Marg.	Ameliaranne at the Seaside (1st, 8vo, unpag)	L: Harrap	1935	Pearse, S.B.	50-65	*
Thompson, K.L.	Ameliaranne at the Zoo (1st AM, 8vo, p-o)	McKay	[1920]	Pearse, S.B.	45-60	
Joan, Natalie	Ameliaranne in Town (1st, 12mo, unpag, color)	L: Harrap	1930	Pearse, S.B.	35-50	*
Morris, Ethel.	Ameliaranne's Moving-Day (1st, 8vo, unpag)	L: Harrap	1950	Pearse, S.B.	45-60	*
Nathan, J.	Ameliaranne/Big Treasure (1st AM, 8vo, red cl, p-o, color)	McKay	[1932]	Pearse, S.B.	45-60	
Farjeon, E.	Ameliaranne/Magic Ring (1st AM, 8vo, [63]p, p-o, color, pep)	McKay	[1933]	Pearse, S.B.	40-60	
Heward, C.	Twins & Tabiffa (1st, 8vo, 121p, p-o, blue cl, color, pep)	Jacobs	(1923)	Pearse, S.B.	40-60	
Carroll, L.	Alice/Wonderland (1st Canadian, blue bds, 8 color)	Musson	1908	Pease, B.C.	200-300	
Carroll, L.	Alice/Wonderland (1st {this pub}, 4to, ibds, 164p, 8cp)	L: Coker	[1915]	Pease, B.C.	100-140	
Cooke, E.V.	Biography of Our Baby (1st, lg8vo, white/gilt, [60]p, color)	Dodge	(1906)	Pease, B.C.	165-200	
Stevenson, R.L.	Child's Garden of Verses (1st, 8vo, blue cl, 110p, 21pl)	Dodge	(1905)	Pease, B.C.	90-130	
Cooke, E.V.	Chronicles of a Little Tot (1st, 8vo, 119p, 3cp)	Dodge	(1905)	Pease, B.C.	160-220	
Cooke, E.V.	Told to the Little Tot (1st, 8vo, 132p, p-o, teg, 10cp)	Dodge	(1906)	Pease, B.C.	160-200	*
Leet, F.R.	Animal Caravan (1st, lg4to, 60p, ibds, 12 fp color)	Saalfield	(1930)	Peat, F.B.	40-65	
Shankland, Frank	Bird Book (1st, 4to, ibds, 8 fp color)	Saalfield	(1931)	Peat, F.B.	40-60	
Stevenson, R.L.	Child's Garden of Verses (4to, ibds, 89p, 7cp, pep)	Saalfield	(1940)	Peat, F.B.	40-60	
Dickens, C.	Christmas Carol (1st, 8vo, 249p, blue/gilt, 7cp)	Saalfield	(1929)	Peat, F.B.	50-70	
Peat, F.E.	Christmas Carols (1st, folio, ibds, 45p, gilt, pep)	Saalfield	(1937)	Peat, F.B.	45-60	
N/A	Cinderella (sm folio, 16p, wraps, 8cp)	Harter	(1931)	Peat, F.B.	40-55	
Lefevre, F.	Cock, Mouse & Little Red Hen (ob folio, wraps, color)	Saalfield	1931	Peat, F.B.	50-80	
Dauzet, M.	Forest Friends (1st, sq4to, 18p, ibds, fp color, pep)	Saalfield	1940	Peat, F.B.	40-60	
N/A	Gingerbread Boy (folio, wraps, 16 color)	Whitman	(1941)	Peat, F.B.	40-60	
Grimm Bros.	Hansel & Gretel (folio, wraps, color)	Harter	1932	Peat, F.B.	45-60	
Leet, F.R.	Hop, Skip & Jump (4to, ibds, 34p, 6cp, DJ)	Saalfield	1936	Peat, F.B.	65-80	
Mayol, L.B.	Jiji Lou (1st, 4to, p-o, 142p, blue cl, 8 fp color, dep)	Saalfield	1928	Peat, F.B.	50-65	
N/A	Kittens (1st, folio, [12]p, wraps, 6cp)	Saalfield	1937	Peat, F.B.	45-60	
Bannerman, H.	Little Black Sambo (folio, wraps, 8cp)	Harter	(1931)	Peat, F.B.	120-165	
Bannerman, H.	Little Black Sambo (1st, 8vo, [20]p, color)	Saalfield	(1932)	Peat, F.B.	100-130	
Goldsmith, O.	Little Goody Two-Shoes (1st, 8vo, [40]p, ibds, pep, color)	Saalfield	(1929)	Peat, F.B.	45-60	
N/A	Little Housekeepers (folio, wraps, 8cp)	Saalfield	1934	Peat, F.B.	45-60	
Barnaby, H.T.	Long-Eared Bat (1st, 4to, ibds, unpag, 4cp)	Saalfield	(1929)	Peat, F.B.	70-90	*
Peat, F.B.	Magnificent Squeak (1st, 8vo, ibds, 42p, color)	Saalfield	(1929)	Peat, F.B.	45-60	
Mother Goose	Mother Goose (1st, lg4to, ipcb, [60]p, p-o, 8cp)	Saalfield	(1929)	Peat, F.B.	85-100	
Mother Goose	Mother Goose: Best Known Rhymes (1st, lg4to, ibds, [34]p, color)	Saalfield	1933	Peat, F.B.	70-100	
Mother Goose	Mother Goose: Her Rhymes & Riddles (1st, 4to, [16]p, color)	Saalfield	1939	Peat, F.B.	65-80	*
Moore, C.C.	Night Before Christmas (folio, wraps, unpag, color)	Saalfield	(1932)	Peat, F.B.	45-70	
N/A	Picture & Rhyme Book (folio, wraps, 20 color)	Saalfield	1941	Peat, F.B.	60-80	
N/A	Picture Story Book (folio, [18]p, wraps, shape bk., 12 color)	Saalfield	1929	Peat, F.B.	40-60	
Leet, F.R.	Purr & Meow (1st, 4to, ibds, 60p, 12cp)	Saalfield	(1931)	Peat, F.B.	50-70	
Treffinger, C.	Rag Doll Jane (1st, lg4to, ibds, 12cp)	Saalfield	(1930)	Peat, F.B.	65-80	
Wurth, A.	Rag Doll Susie... (1st, lg sq8vo, [16]p, ibds, 6 color, pep)	Saalfield	1939	Peat, F.B.	65-80	
Peat, F.B.	Rags (1st, lg4to, [12]p, wraps, color)	Saalfield	1929	Peat, F.B.	50-65	
McNeil, Marion	Round the Mulberry Bush (1st, 4to, ibds, 32p, 8cp)	Saalfield	1933	Peat, F.B.	50-70	
Peat, F.B.	Stories Children Like (1st, lg4to, [34]p, ibds, 8cp)	Saalfield	1933	Peat, F.B.	45-60	
Mayol, L.B.	Story of a Happy Doll (4to, ibds, 142p, 1cp, DJ)	Saalfield	1928	Peat, F.B.	35-50	
Field, E.	Sugar-Plum Tree (1st, 4to, ipcb, 38p, 12cp)	Saalfield	1930	Peat, F.B.	50-65	
Potter, B.	Tale of Peter Rabbit (lg4to, wraps, 8 color)	Harter	1931	Peat, F.B.	70-90	
N/A	Three Little Kittens (1st, 4to, ipcb, [16]p, color, dep)	Saalfield	1940	Peat, F.B.	35-60	*
N/A	Three Little Pigs (folio, wraps, 16p, color)	Saalfield	1933	Peat, F.B.	40-65	
Semple, D.	Tommy & Jane & the Birds (1st, 8vo, p-o, 94p, color, pep)	Saalfield	(1929)	Peat, F.B.	45-75	
DuBois, Theodora	Travelling Toys (1st, lg8vo, 201p, p-o, 4cp, pep)	Penn	1934	Peat, F.B.	50-85	
Clinton, A.L.	Treasure Book/Best Stories (1st, 4to, 92p, ibds, 10cp)	Saalfield	(1933)	Peat, F.B.	45-60	
Andersen, H.C.	Ugly Duckling (1st, lg8vo, [40]p, ibds, 5cp, pep)	Saalfield	1931	Peat, F.B.	50-80	
Hawthorne, N.	Wonder Book (1st, 12mo, 234p, color)	Saalfield	(1929)	Peat, F.B.	30-45	*
Field, E.	Wynken, Blynken & Nod (1st, folio, wraps, 12p, color)	Saalfield	1930	Peat, F.B.	40-60	
LaRue, M.G.	Good-Time Book (1st, 12mo, 111p, 2-color, cep)	MacMillan	1931	Peck, A.G.	25-40	*
Warde, M.	Holiday Book (1st, 8vo, 208p, 5pl)	Little/Brown	1925	Peck, A.M.	20-30	
Newell, Hope	Steppin & Family (1st, 8vo, 198p, color, pep)	NY: OUP	(1942)	Peck, A.M.	65-80	*
Brown, K.H.	Hallowell Partnership (1st, 8vo, 241p, 4pl)	Scribner	1912	Peck, C.E.	20-30	*
Bacon, J.D.	In the Border Country (1st, 8vo, 130p, 5cp)	Doubleday/Page	1909	Peck, C.E.	25-40	

AUTHOR	TITLE	PUBLISHER	DATE	ARTIST	PRICE	LC
Sterling, S.H.	Lady of King Arthur's Court (1st, 8vo, teg, 262p, p-o, 5cp)	Jacobs	(1907)	Peck, C.E.	45-70	
Sterling, S.H.	Shakespeare's Sweetheart (1st, 8vo, p-o, teg, 282p, 5pl)	Jacobs	(1905)	Peck, C.E.	25-45	
Greene, S.P.M.	Deacon Lysander (1st, 12mo, teg, 223p, red/gilt, 4pl)	Baker/Taylor	(1904)	Peck, H.J.	25-40	
Means, F.C.	Ranch and Ring (1st, sm8vo, tan cl, 260p, pep)	Houghton	1932	Peck, H.J.	20-35	*
Norton, Mary	Magic Bed-Knob (1st {1st bk}, 4to, ibds, [48]p, fp color, pep)	Hyperion Press	(1943)	Peirce, W.	65-90	*
Staunton, S.	Daughters of Destiny (1st [1], 8vo, p-o, gilt, 319p, 8cp)	Reilly/Britton	(1906)	Peirce/DeLay	170-220	
Thompson, Maurice	Rosalynde's Lovers (1st, 8vo, p-o, 249p, 11pl, dep)	Bowen-Merrill	1901	Peirson, G.	20-25	
Wharton, E.	Italian Backgrounds (1st, 8vo, 214p, 12pl by...)	Scribner	1905	Peixotto, E.C.	75-100	
Penfield, E.	Big Book of Horses & Goats (1st, ob folio, [24]p, color)	R.H. Russell	1901	Penfield, E.	200-300	*
Bangs, J.K.	Dreamers, A Club (1st, 16mo, brown/gilt, 247p, b/w)	Harper	1899	Penfield, E.	30-45	
Penfield, E.	Holland Sketches (1st, sm4to, 147p, ibds, 34 ticp, pep)	Scribner	1907	Penfield, E.	120-165	
Bangs, J.K.	Peeps at People (1st, 12mo, 184p, gilt, 36pl)	Harper	1899	Penfield, E.	30-50	
Williamson, C.& N.	Princess Passes (1st, 12mo, green cl, 369p, 12 pl by...)	Holt	1905	Penfield, E.	25-40	
Penfield, E.	Spanish Sketches (1st, sm4to, 146p, yellow bds, 27 ticp, pep)	Scribner	1911	Penfield, E.	120-160	
Bangs, J.K.	The Bicyclers (1st, 16mo, 176p, blue/gilt, 4pl)	Harper	1896	Penfield, E.	30-50	
Pennell, J.	Adventures of an Illustrator (1st, folio, buckram, 372p)	Little/Brown	1925	Pennell, J.	65-80	
Hay, J.	Castilion Days (1st, 8vo, teg, green cl)	Houghton	1903	Pennell, J.	40-60	
James, Henry	English Hours (1st AM, lg8vo, cloth, 336p)	Houghton	1905	Pennell, J.	60-80	
Pennell, J.	French Cathedrals (1st, 4to, 424p)	Century	1910	Pennell, J.	45-65	
James, Henry	Italian Hours (1st AM, 8vo, 504p, teg, uncut, 32cp)	Houghton	1909	Pennell, J.	80-130	
Pennell, J.	Jew at Home (1st, 12mo, red cl, 105p, b/w)	Appleton	1892	Pennell, J.	80-125	
James, Henry	Little Tour in France (1st, 8vo, teg, 345p, b/w)	Houghton	1900	Pennell, J.	80-120	
Pennell, E.R.	Our House (1st, 8vo, ipcb, 373p, 10pl)	Houghton	1912	Pennell, J.	35-65	*
Pennell, J.	Our Philadelphia (1st, 4to, red/gilt, 552p, teg)	Lippincott	1914	Pennell, J.	50-80	
Pennell, J.	Pictures of Panama Canal (1st, 4to, brown cl, p-o, 28pl)	Lippincott	1912	Pennell, J.	50-80	
Pennell, J.	Play in Provence (1st, 8vo, tan cl, teg, uncut, 202p, b/w)	Century	1892	Pennell, J.	35-50	
Crawford, F.M.	Salve Venetia (1st, 8vo, 2 volumes, gilt)	MacMillan	1905	Pennell, J.	45-60	
Irving, W.	The Alhambra (1st, 12mo, green/gilt, AEG, 436p, b/w, cep)	L: MacMillan	1896	Pennell, J.	45-65	
Pennell, E.R.	To Gypsyland (1st UK, sm8vo, pink cl, 240p, b/w)	L: T.F. Unwin	1893	Pennell, J.	35-50	
Pennell, J.	Wonder of Work (1st, 4to, brown cl, p-o, 52pl)	Lippincott	1916	Pennell, J.	65-90	
Eustis, C.	Cooking in Old Creole Days (1st, 8vo, ipcb, 112p, 8pl)	R.H. Russell	1903	Pennington, H.	80-120	R*
Biddle, A.	Second Froggy Fairy Book (1st, 8vo, 90p, col frn, 11 fp b/w)	Drexel Biddle	1898	Pennock, A.	80-120	
Irving, W.	Rip Van Winkle (1st, 8vo, 127p, b/w)	Stokes	1933	Perard, V.	20-35	*
Fox, F.M.	Wildling Princess (1st, 8vo, 79p, gilt, pep, 10cp)	Volland	(1929)	Perkins, J.E.	70-100	
Aesopus	Aesop's Fables (1st, lg8vo, p-o, 111p, 12cp)	Stokes	(1908)	Perkins, L.F.	70-110	
Perkins, L.F.	American Twins of the Revolution (1st, 8vo, 208p, pep, b/w)	Houghton	1926	Perkins, L.F.	30-45	*
Perkins, L.F.	Belgian Twins (1st, 8vo, brown cl, 198p, b/w)	Houghton	1917	Perkins, L.F.	25-45	
Perkins, L.F.	Book of Joys (1st, lg8vo, 212p, green cl, uncut, p-o, 5cp)	McClurg	1907	Perkins, L.F.	50-75	
Perkins, L.F.	Cave Twins (1st, 8vo, 164p, b/w)	Houghton	1916	Perkins, L.F.	35-50	*
Pease, L.	Child You Used to Be (1st, 8vo, 198p, 10pl)	McClurg	1909	Perkins, L.F.	45-65	*
Perkins, L.F.	Chinese Twins (1st, 8vo, yellow cl, 166p, col frn, b/w)	Houghton	1935	Perkins, L.F.	25-40	
Baker, C.	Coquo & the King's Children (1st, 8vo, 250p, brown/gilt, 6 col)	McClurg	1902	Perkins, L.F.	25-40	
Perkins, L.F.	Cornelia (1st, sm8vo, 202p, 8pl)	Houghton	1919	Perkins, L.F.	30-45	*
Perkins, L.F.	Dutch Twins (1st, 8vo, 190p, b/w, PPPa)	Houghton	1911	Perkins, L.F.	45-60	
Brown, J.	Enchanted Peacock (1st, 4to, p-o, 4cp, 4pl)	Rand/McNally	(1911)	Perkins, L.F.	65-80	
Blakeley, E.S.	Fairy Starlight (1st, 12mo, lavender cl, 213p, b/w)	McClurg	1896	Perkins, L.F.	65-90	*
Shimer, E.D.	Fairy Stories... (1st, sm8vo, 277p, b/w)	L.A. & N.	1920	Perkins, L.F.	45-60	*
Perkins, L.F.	Filipino Twins (1st, 8vo, 150p, b/w)	Houghton	1923	Perkins, L.F.	30-45	
Harrison, E.O.	Flaming Sword... (1st, 4to, blue/silver, 133p, 4cp)	McClurg	1908	Perkins, L.F.	50-80	
Perkins, L.F.	French Twins (1st, 8vo, blue cl, 202p, b/w)	Houghton	1918	Perkins, L.F.	35-50	
Wade, B.E.	Garden in Pink (1st, lg8vo, p-o, blue cl, 12pl)	McClurg	1905	Perkins, L.F.	30-50	
Perkins, L.F.	Indian Twins (1st, 8vo, 203p, b/w)	Houghton	1930	Perkins, L.F.	35-50	*
Perkins, L.F.	Irish Twins (1st, 8vo, 206p, b/w)	Houghton	1913	Perkins, L.F.	35-50	*
Perkins, L.F.	Italian Twins (1st, lg8vo, green cl, 149p, b/w, pep)	Houghton	1920	Perkins, L.F.	30-45	
Perkins, L.F.	Japanese Twins (1st, 8vo, 178p, beige cl, b/w, pep)	Houghton	1912	Perkins, L.F.	30-45	
English, T.D.	Little Giant... (1st, 4to, 150p, t.e. yellow, 4 fp b/w)	McClurg	1904	Perkins, L.F.	65-80	
Warren, Maude L.	Little Pioneers (1st, 12mo, 253p, b/w, pep)	Rand/McNally	(1916)	Perkins, L.F.	25-40	*
Van Sickle, J.H.	Magic Key (1st, 12mo, blue cl, 270p, 10 fp b/w)	Houghton	(1931)	Perkins, L.F.	25-40	*
Perkins, L.F.	Mexican Twins (1st, 8vo, 186p, b/w)	Houghton	1915	Perkins, L.F.	30-45	
Shakespeare, Wm.	MidSummer Night's Dream (1st, 4to, p-o, 93p, 12cp, pep)	Stokes	(1907)	Perkins, L.F.	100-165	
Harrison, E.O.	Moon Princess (1st, 4to, blue cl, 6cp)	McClurg	1905	Perkins, L.F.	70-85	
Mother Goose	Mother Goose Book (ob4to, red cl, p-o, 11cp)	Whitman	(1915)	Perkins, L.F.	85-125	
Perkins, L.F.	Mr. Chick... (1st, ob4to, 117p, p-o, orange cl, fp b/w)	Houghton	1926	Perkins, L.F.	35-55	
Perkins, E.E.	News from Notown (1st, 4to, 108p, b/w)	Houghton	1919	Perkins, L.F.	35-50	
Perkins, L.F.	Pickaninny Twins (1st, 8vo, 152p, tan cl, b/w, pep)	Houghton	1931	Perkins, L.F.	90-140	
Harrison, E.O.	Prince Silverwings... (1st, 4to, blue/silver, 313p, 4cp)	McClurg	1902	Perkins, L.F.	65-90	
Perkins, L.F.	Puritan Twins (1st, 8vo, 179p, pep, b/w)	Houghton	1921	Perkins, L.F.	25-40	
N/A	Robin Hood (1st, lg8vo, olive cl, 115p, 12cp)	Stokes	(1906)	Perkins, L.F.	75-90	
Perkins, L.F.	Spartan Twins (1st, 12mo, 161p, b/w)	Houghton	1920	Perkins, L.F.	30-45	
Harrison, E.O.	Star Fairies (1st, 4to, 128p, 6cp)	McClurg	1903	Perkins, L.F.	70-90	
Perkins, L.F.	Swiss Twins (1st, 8vo, 132p, brown cl, b/w, pep)	Houghton	1922	Perkins, L.F.	30-45	
Hawthorne, N.	Wonder Book... (1st, lg8vo, p-o, 125p, 12cp)	Stokes	(1908)	Perkins, L.F.	60-80	

AUTHOR	TITLE	PUBLISHER	DATE	ARTIST	PRICE	LC
D'Aulnoy	Fairy Tales (1st, 8vo, 535p, teg, gilt, b/w by...)	L: Lawrence	1892	Peters, C.	180-250	
Bartug, C.M.	Mother Goose Etiquette Rhymes (1st, ob8vo, 32p, blue cl, pep)	Whitman	1941	Peters, M.	45-65	*
Wheeler, P.	Albanian Wonder Tales (1st {std}, 8vo, 282p, col frn, b/w, pep)	Doubleday/Dor.	1936	Petershams	65-80	*
Petershams	America's Stamps... (1st, 4to, 144p, 3 fp color, DJ)	MacMillan	1947	Petershams	30-45	
Petersham, M.	American ABC (1st, lg8vo, [56]p, gilt, color, cep, CH)	MacMillan	1941	Petershams	80-120	
Petershams	Ark/Father Noah & Mother Noah (1st {std}, sq4to, ibds, col, pep)	Doubleday/Dor.	1930	Petershams	70-100	R*
Petersham, M.	Auntie & Celia Jane & Miki (1st {std}, 4to, ibds, [64]p, col, NH)	Doubleday/Dor.	1932	Petershams	80-120	*
LaRue, M.G.	Billy Bang Book (1st, 12mo, 176p, 2-color)	MacMillan	1927	Petershams	30-55	*
Franklin, B.	Bird in the Hand (1st {std}, 4to, blue cl, [36]p, color, cep)	MacMillan	(1951)	Petershams	35-50	*
Petersham, M.	Box with Red Wheels (1st, sm4to, [32]p, color)	MacMillan	(1949)	Petershams	50-80	*
Petershams	Boy Who Had no Heart (1st {std}, sm4to, red cl, [30]p, color)	MacMillan	(1955)	Petershams	45-60	
Lamprey, L.	Children of Ancient Britain (1st, 12mo, 222p, fp b/w)	Little/Brown	1921	Petershams	35-50	*
Miller, E.C.	Children of Mountain Eagle (1st {std}, sm8vo, 328p, 3cp, pep)	Doubleday/Dor.	1927	Petershams	30-45	*
Petersham, M.	Christ Child (1st {std}, 4to, ibds, [62]p, color, pep)	Doubleday/Dor.	(1931)	Petershams	45-70	
Petersham, M.	Circus Baby (1st, 4to, ibds, [32]p, color)	MacMillan	(1950)	Petershams	65-100	
Bowen, W.A.	Enchanted Forest (1st, 12mo, 197p, color, pep)	MacMillan	1920	Petershams	45-60	*
Adams, S.W.	Five Little Friends (1st, 12mo, 139p, color)	MacMillan	1922	Petershams	45-65	*
Barringer, M.	Four & Lena (1st {std}, 8vo, 216p, black cl, 6cp, pep)	Doubleday/Dor.	1938	Petershams	35-50	
Petersham, M.	Get-A-Way & Harry Janos (1st, 4to, ibds, p-o, [64]p, 14cp)	Viking	1933	Petershams	70-100	
Spyri, J.	Heidi (1st, 8vo, blue cl, p-o, 319p, 4cp, pep)	Garden City	1932	Petershams	35-50	
Kelly, Eric P.	In Clean Hay (1st {std}, 8vo, ibds, 31p, color, cep)	MacMillan	1953	Petershams	25-40	*
Petershams	Jesus' Story (1st, sm8vo, 119p, 6 fp color, cep, DJ)	MacMillan	1942	Petershams	40-60	
Johnson, E.F.	Little Book of Prayers (1st, 12mo, unpag, 1-color, pep, DJ)	Viking	1941	Petershams	45-65	
LaRue, M.G.	Little Indians (1st, sm8vo, 170p, color)	MacMillan	1930	Petershams	40-60	*
Coolidge, F.	Little Ugly Face (1st, sm8vo, 181p, 2-color)	MacMillan	1925	Petershams	25-45	*
Lamprey, L.	Long Ago People (1st, 12mo, 222p, fp b/w)	Little/Brown	1921	Petershams	35-50	*
Queen Marie	Magic Doll of Roumania (1st, 8vo, p-o, 319p, 10cp)	Stokes	1929	Petershams	85-120	
Barringer, M.	Martin the Goose Boy (1st {std}, 8vo, 188p, black cl, 8cp, pep)	Doubleday/Dor.	1932	Petershams	45-60	
Petersham, M.	Miki (1st {std}, 4to, [63]p, ibds, color, pep)	Doubleday/Dor.	1929	Petershams	50-80	
Petersham, M.	Miki & Mary... (1st, 4to, ibds, [64]p, color, pep, DJ)	Viking	1934	Petershams	70-100	
Mason, Miriam E.	Miss Posy Longlegs (1st {std}, 8vo, 54p, 1-color, DJ)	MacMillan	(1955)	Petershams	30-45	*
Petersham, M.	Moses (1st, lg8vo, blue cl, [32]p, color, pep, DJ)	Winston	1938	Petershams	50-70	
Miller, O.B.	Nursery Friends from France (1st, 4to, 190p, p-o, color)	Book House	(1925)	Petershams	35-50	
Ayer, Jean	Picnic Book (1st, 12mo, 46p, color, wraps)	MacMillan	1934	Petershams	30-45	*
Collodi, C.	Pinocchio (1st, 8vo, p-o, blue cl, 323p, 4cp, pep)	Garden City	1932	Petershams	65-90	
Clark, M.	Poppy Seed Cakes (1st {std}, sm sq8vo, 154p, 16cp, pep)	Doubleday/Page	1924	Petershams	70-120	R*
Miller, E.C.	Pran of Albania (1st {std}, 8vo, 257p, col frn, pep, NH)	Doubleday/Dor.	1929	Petershams	60-95	
Irving, W.	Rip Van Winkle & Sleepy Hollow (1st, 8vo, 105p, 1-color, pep)	MacMillan	(1951)	Petershams	50-85	*
Petersham, M.	Rooster Crows (1st, sm4to, [64]p, tan cl, color, cep, CM)	MacMillan	1945	Petershams	75-110	R
Sandburg, C.	Rootabaga Pigeons (1st, 8vo, blue cl, 218p, col frn)	Harcourt	(1923)	Petershams	70-100	
Sandburg, C.	Rootabaga Stories (1st, 8vo, 230p, blue cl, col frn, PPP)	Harcourt	(1922)	Petershams	70-110	
Petersham, M.	Ruth (1st, sm4to, blue/gilt, [32]p, pep, 8 fp color)	Winston	1938	Petershams	35-50	
Petershams	Silver Mace (1st {std}, 4to, ibds, 38p, fp color)	MacMillan	(1956)	Petershams	45-60	
Petersham, M.	Stories from the Old Testament (1st, lg8vo, [128]p, color, pep)	Winston	1938	Petershams	35-50	
Petersham, M.	Story Book of Clothes (1st, 12mo, 31p, p-o, yellow cl, color)	Winston	1933	Petershams	25-40	
Petersham, M.	Story Book of Cotton (1st, sq8vo, [32]p, p-o, color)	Winston	1939	Petershams	25-40	
Mason, Miriam E.	Susannah: Pioneer Cow (1st, 8vo, yellow cl, 151p, 1-color, cep)	MacMillan	1941	Petershams	45-60	*
Miller, O.B.	Tales Told in Holland (1st, 4to, 190p, p-o, pep, gilt, color)	Book House	(1926)	Petershams	45-60	
Lamb, C.	Tales from Shakespeare (1st, sm8vo, 375p, blue cl, 4cp, pep)	MacMillan	1923	Petershams	45-60	
Various	Told Under the Christmas Tree (1st {std}, 8vo, 304p, b/w)	MacMillan	1948	Petershams	35-50	*
Tyler, Anna C.	Twenty-Four Unusual Stories (1st, 12mo, 328p, fp b/w)	Harcourt	1921	Petershams	45-60	*
LaRue, M.G.	Under the Story Tree (1st, 12mo, 139p, color)	MacMillan	1923	Petershams	40-60	*
Clement, Marg.	Where Was Bobby? (1st {std}, 8vo, 151p, 19cp, pep)	Doubleday/Dor.	1928	Petershams	35-50	*
Snowden, J.H.	Wonderful Night (1st, 12mo, blue cl, 95p, p-o, designs by...)	MacMillan	1919	Petershams	20-30	*
Miller, E.C.	Young Trajan (1st {std}, 8vo, 232p, black cl, pep, col frn)	Doubleday/Dor.	1931	Petershams	25-40	*
LaRue, M.G.	Zip the Toy Mule (1st, sm4to, 46p, 6cp, pep)	MacMillan	1932	Petershams	40-60	
Peterson, Barbara	Whitefoot Mouse (1st, 8vo, 52p, red cl, 2-color, pep)	Holiday House	(1959)	Peterson, R.F.	20-25	*
Byron, May	Teddy Bear Book (sq8vo, ibds, 12cp)	L: H. Frowde	[1911]	Petherick, R.	200-300	
Peto, Gladys	China Cow (1st, 4to, p-o, 129p, black/gilt, 8cp)	Houghton	[1926]	Peto, G.	70-100	
Hunt, Enid	Fine Lady Upon a White Horse (4to, gilt, 120p, 8cp)	Dodge	[1929]	Peto, G.	70-100	
Peto, Gladys	Gladys Peto's Children's Book (lg8vo, ibds, 7cp)	L: Routledge	[1930]	Peto, G.	65-90	*
Lyons, A. Neil	Simple Simon... (1st, 8vo, 344p, red/gilt, 8pl)	L: J. Lane	1914	Peto, G.	35-50	
Peto, Gladys	Twilight Stories (1st, 4to, ibds, unpag, 8cp)	L: J.F. Shaw	[1932]	Peto, G.	85-120	*
Norwood, Edwin P.	Adventures of Diggeldy Dan (1st, 8vo, p-o, 240p, 8cp)	Little/Brown	1922	Peyton, A.C.	20-35	*
Norwood, Edwin P.	Davy Winkle in Circusland (1st, 8vo, 202p, tan cl, col frn)	Little/Brown	1926	Peyton, A.C.	25-40	
Norwood, Edwin P.	In the Land of Diggeldy Dan (1st, 8vo, p-o, 226p, 8cp)	Little/Brown	1923	Peyton, A.C.	20-35	*
Porter, G.S.	Laddie (1st, 8vo, 602p, blue cl, col frn, 3pl)	Doubleday/Page	1913	Pfeifer	35-50	
Phillips, C.	Gallery of Girls (1st, 4to, p-o, unpag, green cl, 39cp)	Century	1911	Phillips, C.	250-350	
Atherton, G.	Gorgeous Isle (1st, 8vo, 223p, orang cl, 4cp, pep)	Doubleday/Page	1908	Phillips, C.	35-50	
Sinclair, M.	Immortal Moment (1st, 8vo, 315p, white cl, 4pl)	Doubleday/Page	1908	Phillips, C.	30-45	
Michelson, M.	Michael Thwaites's Wife (1st, 8vo, red cl, 402p, 3cp)	Doubleday/Page	1909	Phillips, C.	20-25	
Nicholson, M.	Siege of the Seven Suitors (1st, 8vo, green cl, 401p, col frn)	Houghton	1910	Phillips, C.	20-25	

AUTHOR	TITLE	PUBLISHER	DATE	ARTIST	PRICE	LC
Phillips, C.	Young Man's Fancy (1st, 4to, unpag, gilt, 19cp)	Bobbs-Merrill	(1912)	Phillips, C.	200-300	
Phillips, J.C.	Plantation Sketches (1st, ob folio, brown ibds, b/w)	R.H. Russell	1899	Phillips, J.C.	200-300	
Kingsley, C.	Water Babies (1st, 12mo, 295p, b/w)	Rand/McNally	(1900)	Phillips, M.E.	25-45	*
Phipps, Mary	All About Patsy (1st {std}, 8vo, red cl, 136p, 16cp, 38pl, pep)	Doubleday/Dor.	1930	Phipps, M.	85-135	
Phipps, Mary	Liza Jane & the Kinkies (1st, 4to, ibds, [90]p, color, pep)	Sears	(1929)	Phipps, M.	150-220	*
Merryman, M.P.	Quack! Said Jerusha (1st, 8vo, ibds, [50]p, 1-color, pep)	Sears	(1930)	Phipps, M.	45-60	
Pierson, C.D.	Tales of a Poultry Farm (1st, 8vo, 195p, gilt, 9pl)	L: J. Murray	1904	Pierson, C.D.	45-60	*
Hodder, W.R.	Daughter of the Dawn (1st, 8vo, green cl, 333p, 12pl)	L: Jarrold	1903	Piffard, H.	45-65	*
Burnett, F.H.	Little Princess (1st UK, 8vo, 302p, p-o, 8cp)	L: Warne	(1905)	Piffard, H.	80-125	
Tracy, Louis	Lost Provinces (1st, 8vo, 380p, olive/gilt, 12pl)	L: C. Pearson	1898	Piffard, H.	45-60	*
Terry, R.R.	Old Rhymes with New Tunes (1st, 4to, ibds, 32p, b/w)	Longmans	1912	Pippet, G.	45-60	*
Molesworth, M.	Magic Nuts (1st, 8vo, 194p, orange/gilt, 7pl)	L: MacMillan	1898	Pitman, R.M.M.	45-60	
Molesworth, M.	Ruby Ring (1st, 8vo, 213p, orange cl, 8pl)	L: MacMillan	1904	Pitman, R.M.M.	35-50	*
Fouque, La Motte	Undine (1st, 8vo, blue/gilt, 204p, teg, 19pl)	L: MacMillan	1897	Pitman, R.M.M.	70-100	
Cooper, Page	Amigo, Circus Horse (1st {std}, 8vo, 238p, yel cl, uncut, b/w)	World Pub. Co.	(1955)	Pitz, H.C.	30-45	*
Aspden, Don	Barney's Barges (1st, 8vo, 192p, green cl, fp b/w, pep)	Holiday House	(1944)	Pitz, H.C.	20-30	*
Macleod, Mary	Book of King Arthur (1st {std}, 8vo, blue cl, 324p, color)	Lippincott	(1949)	Pitz, H.C.	30-50	*
Means, F.C.	Bowlful of Stars (1st, 8vo, green cl, 247p, b/w, pep)	Houghton	1934	Pitz, H.C.	25-40	*
Fenner, P.R.	Demons & Dervishes (1st {std}, 8vo, red cl, 183p, fp b/w, pep)	Knopf	(1946)	Pitz, H.C.	30-45	*
Finger, C.J.	Dog at His Heel (1st, 8vo, 304p, orange cl, dp color, pep)	Winston	(1936)	Pitz, H.C.	30-45	*
Coblentz, C.C.	Falcon of Eric the Red (1st {std}, 8vo, 211p, dp pl)	Longmans	1942	Pitz, H.C.	30-45	*
Fenner, P.R.	Giants & Witches (1st {std}, 8vo, red cl, 208p, fp b/w, pep)	Knopf	1943	Pitz, H.C.	35-50	*
Davis, Rbt.	Hudson Bay Express (1st, 8vo, 262p, blue cl, b/w)	Holiday House	(1942)	Pitz, H.C.	20-30	*
Scott, Walter	Ivanhoe (1st, 8vo, red cl, 469p, uncut, 6pl)	Sears	(1928)	Pitz, H.C.	25-40	*
Bennett, John	Master Skylark (1st, 4to, blue cl, 322p, p-o, 8cp, pep)	Century	1922	Pitz, H.C.	25-40	
Fenner, P.R.	Princesses & Peasant Boys (1st {std}, 8vo, 188p, b/w, pep)	Knopf	1944	Pitz, H.C.	25-40	*
Meigs, C.	Trade Wind (1st, 8vo, 309p, black cl, p-o, 8cp, pep)	Little/Brown	1927	Pitz, H.C.	30-45	*
Kingsley, C.	Westward Ho! (1st, 12mo, 342p, col frn, b/w)	MacMillan	1930	Pitz, H.C.	35-50	*
Fenner, P.R.	Yankee Doodle (1st {std}, 8vo, red cl, 214p, uncut, fp b/w)	Knopf	1951	Pitz, H.C.	25-45	*
Coatsworth, E.	You Shall Have a Carriage (1st {std}, 8vo, 138p, pep)	MacMillan	1941	Pitz, H.C.	25-40	*
Bianco, M.W.	Bright Morning (1st, 8vo, 143p, b/w, dep, DJ)	Viking	1942	Platt, M.	25-40	
Johnson, A.E.	Below Zero (lg4to, cloth, 12cp)	L: Hodder	[1910]	Pocock, N.	50-80	
Grimm Bros.	Fairy Tales (1st AM, 4to, blue/gilt, 346p, 23 ticp)	Doran	[1913]	Pocock, N.	80-125	
Grimm Bros.	Fairy Tales (1st, lg8vo, 346p, 23 ticp)	L: Hodder	(1913)	Pocock, N.	100-165	*
Grimm Bros.	Fairy Tales (8vo, green cl, 337p, 8cp, pep, rprnt)	Garden City	[1930]	Pocock, N.	45-60	
Defoe, D.	Robinson Crusoe (lg8vo, 352p, tan cl, 24 ticp)	L: Hodder	[1910]	Pocock, N.	70-100	
Olcott, F.J. (ed.)	Adventures of Haroun Er Raschid (1st, 8vo, 363p, gilt, col frn)	Holt	1923	Pogany, W.	45-60	*
Colum, P.	Adventures of Odysseus (1st, 8vo, 254p, 8cp, pep)	MacMillan	1918	Pogany, W.	50-70	
Farrow, G.E.	Adventures of a Dodo (1st, 8vo, gilt, 245p, 70 b/w, pep)	L: T.F. Unwin	(1907)	Pogany, W.	180-260	
Carroll, L.	Alice/Wonderland (1st, 8vo, purple/gilt, 192p, pep, b/w)	Dutton	(1929)	Pogany, W.	140-200	
Heine, H.	Atta Troll (1st, 12mo, 185p, grey bds, gilt, pep, b/w)	L: Sidgwick	1913	Pogany, W.	120-165	
Heine, H.	Atta Troll (1st AM, 12mo, 185p, bds, gilt, 3pl)	Huebsch	(1914)	Pogany, W.	100-130	
Olcott, F.J.	Bible Stories to Read & Tell (1st, 8vo, blue cl, 465p, 8cp)	Houghton	1916	Pogany, W.	45-65	
Stacpoole, H.D.	Blue Lagoon (1st, 8vo, blue/gilt, 326p, 13 ticp)	L: T.F. Unwin	1910	Pogany, W.	150-180	
Bartruse, G.	Children in Japan (1st, lg8vo, [32]p, bds, p-o, 16cp)	McBride	1915	Pogany, W.	160-200	
Colum, P.	Children of Odin (1st, sm8vo, 282p, 4cp)	MacMillan	1920	Pogany, W.	30-45	
Elias, E. (ed.)	Cinderella (1st, sm4to, red bds, p-o, 8 dp color)	McBride	1915	Pogany, W.	160-230	
Ambrose, B.A.	Coppa Hamba (1st, 4to, [82]p, orange cl, 3cp, fp b/w, pep)	Suttonhouse	1936	Pogany, W.	100-150	*
Gask, Lilian	Fairies & Christmas Child (1st AM, lg8vo, p-o, 261p, 8cp, pep)	Crowell	(1912)	Pogany, W.	180-240	
Gask, Lilian	Fairies & the Christmas Child (1st, 8vo, 260p)	L: Harrap	[1912]	Pogany, W.	65-80	*
Newman, I.	Fairy Flowers (1st, 4to, ibds, 160p, 15 ticp, pep)	L: H. Milford	(1926)	Pogany, W.	160-200	
Newman, I.	Fairy Flowers (1st AM, 8vo, ibds, 196p, 15 ticp, pep)	Holt	(1926)	Pogany, W.	130-180	
Newman, I.	Fairy Flowers (sm4to, 160p, bds, 15 ticp)	NY: OUP	1929	Pogany, W.	100-130	
Goethe	Faust (1st, 4to, red/gilt, teg, 205p, 31 ticp)	L: Hutchinson	1908	Pogany, W.	200-300	
Newman, I.	Flowers Facts & Fables (1st, 4to, 141p, ibds, 7cp, cep)	NY: Snellgrove	1937	Pogany, W.	80-100	
Gask, Lilian	Folk Tales of Many Lands (1st AM, 8vo, p-o, uncut, 8cp)	Crowell	(1910)	Pogany, W.	100-150	
Gask, Lilian	Folk Tales of Many Lands (1st, 8vo, red/gilt, 287p, p-o, 8cp)	L: Harrap	1910	Pogany, W.	125-165	
Kunos, I.	Forty-Four Turkish Tales (1st, 4to, tan cl, teg, 363p, 16 ticp)	L: Harrap	(1913)	Pogany, W.	180-260	
Colum, P.	Frenzied Prince (1st {std}, sm4to, 196p, 10 fp color, pep, DJ)	McKay	(1943)	Pogany, W.	65-80	
Thomas, Marg. L.	Geo. Washington Lincoln Goes Around/World (1st, 8vo, p-o, 205p)	NY: T. Nelson	(1927)	Pogany, W.	65-100	*
Fable, L.	Gingerbread Man (1st, 4to, [32]p, p-o, bds, 8cp)	McBride	1915	Pogany, W.	100-130	
Robertson, W.G.	Golden Book of Sonnets (1st, 8vo, vellum)	L: Harrap	1903	Pogany, W.	130-180	
Pushkin, A.	Golden Cockerel (1st, folio, red/gilt, 46p, 12cp, pep, DJ)	NY: Nelson	1938	Pogany, W.	100-145	
Colum, P.	Golden Fleece (1st, sq8vo, 290p, gilt, 8cp, pep, NH)	MacMillan	1921	Pogany, W.	45-60	
Swift, J.	Gulliver's Travels (1st, 8vo, 296p, blue/gilt, 12cp, pep)	MacMillan	1917	Pogany, W.	80-100	
Harmon, M.	How Santa Found the Cobbler's Shop (1st, 4to, [46]p, color, pep)	Suttonhouse	1936	Pogany, W.	90-150	*
Pogany, Nebby	Hungarian Fairy Book (1st, 8vo, 287p, blue/gilt, col frn)	L: T.F. Unwin	(1913)	Pogany, W.	130-165	
Burton, R.	Kasidah of Haji Abdu El-Yezdi (1st, lg4to, p-o, 129p, 12pl)	McKay	(1931)	Pogany, W.	65-100	
Colum, P.	King of Ireland's Son (1st, 8vo, green/gilt, 316p, 4cp)	Holt	1916	Pogany, W.	70-100	*
Colum, P.	King of Ireland's Son (1st UK, 8vo, 316p, 4cp)	L: Harrap	1920	Pogany, W.	70-100	
Colum, P.	King of Ireland's Son (1st {this pub.}, sq8vo, 316p, 4cp)	MacMillan	1921	Pogany, W.	25-40	
Newman, I.	Legend of the Lilac (1st, 4to, ibds, [23]p, 4cp)	Whitman	1926	Pogany, W.	45-60	

AUTHOR	TITLE	PUBLISHER	DATE	ARTIST	PRICE	LC
Newman, I.	Legend of the Tulip... (1st, 4to, [24]p, ibds, 5cp)	Whitman	(1926)	Pogany, W.	45-70	
Arnold, E.	Light of Asia (1st, 4to, black/silver, p-o, 182p, 12pl)	McKay	(1932)	Pogany, W.	100-150	
Mother Goose	Little Mother Goose (1st, sm4to, bds, p-o, [30]p, 16cp)	McBride	1915	Pogany, W.	180-250	
Crownfield, Gertrude	Little Tailor of Windy Way (1st, sm8vo, 132p, 4cp)	MacMillan	1917	Pogany, W.	25-40	*
Flanders, H.H.	Looking Out of Jimmie (1st, 8vo, 94p, gilt, pep, uncut, b/w)	Dutton	(1927)	Pogany, W.	40-60	*
Pogany, Nebby	Magyar Fairy Tales (1st {std}, 8vo, green/gilt, 268p, b/w, pep)	Dutton	(1930)	Pogany, W.	100-150	R
Olcott, F.J. (ed.)	More Tales/Arabian Nights (1st, sm8vo, 274p, red/gilt, 12cp)	Holt	1915	Pogany, W.	100-135	
Huffard, G.T.	My Poetry Book (1st AM, lg8vo, 504p, blue/gilt, 6cp, pep)	Winston	(1934)	Pogany, W.	30-50	
Huffard, G.T.	My Poetry Book (1st, lg8vo, blue cl, 6cp)	(London)	1934	Pogany, W.	45-60	
Wagner, R.	Parsifal (1st, 4to, [192]p, grey/gilt, 16 ticp, pep)	L: Harrap	(1912)	Pogany, W.	200-300	
Wagner, R.	Parsifal (1st AM, 4to, maroon/gilt, teg, 16 ticp, pep)	Crowell	(1912)	Pogany, W.	220-300	
Pogany, Elaine	Peterkin (1st, 4to, ibds, [75]p, 14 fp color, pep)	McKay	1940	Pogany, W.	100-165	
Mother Goose	Pogany's Mother Goose (1st, 4to, [152]p, teg, gilt, col, pep)	Nelson	(1928)	Pogany, W.	140-200	
Johnson, Margaret	Polly & the Wishing Ring (1st, 12mo, 123p, 4cp)	MacMillan	1918	Pogany, W.	30-45	*
Banks, Helen M.	Polly's Garden (1st, sm8vo, 96p, grey cl, 4cp)	MacMillan	1918	Pogany, W.	25-40	*
Coleridge, S.T.	Rime of the Ancient Mariner (1st AM, lg4to, gilt, 20 ticp, pep)	Crowell	(1910)	Pogany, W.	200-300	
Coleridge, S.T.	Rime of the Ancient Mariner (1st, lg4to, gilt, teg, pep, 20 ticp)	L: Harrap	(1910)	Pogany, W.	250-400	
Coleridge, S.T.	Rime/Ancient Mariner (1st {this fmt}, sm4to, teg, gilt, 20 ticp)	Doran	[1915]	Pogany, W.	120-165	
Capes, B.	Romance of Lohengrin (1st, 8vo, blue/gilt, 271p, 14pl)	L: Dean	1905	Pogany, W.	160-220	
Omar Khayyam	Rubaiyat... (1st, 4to, ibds, teg, gilt, 24 ticp)	L: Harrap	(1909)	Pogany, W.	250-320	
Omar Khayyam	Rubaiyat... (1st AM, 4to, ibds, teg, 96p, 24 ticp)	Crowell	(1909)	Pogany, W.	165-220	
Omar Khayyam	Rubaiyat... (lg8vo, 96p, green/gilt, 12 ticp, reprint)	Crowell	[1920]	Pogany, W.	70-100	
Omar Khayyam	Rubaiyat... (4to, 171p, later ed.)	L: Harrap	(1930)	Pogany, W.	70-100	*
Garrard, P.	Running Away with Nebby (1st {std}, sm4to, 144p, 6cp, 11pl, pep)	McKay	(1944)	Pogany, W.	65-80	
Arnold, E.	Song Celestial (1st, 4to, 135p, black/silver, p-o, 18pl)	McKay	(1934)	Pogany, W.	85-120	
Browning, E.B.	Sonnetts from the Portuguese (1st, 8vo, 96p, 8 ticp)	Crowell	(1936)	Pogany, W.	50-65	
Bryant, S.C.	Stories to Tell the Littlest Ones (1st, 12mo, 178p, 6cp)	L: Harrap	1918	Pogany, W.	80-130	
Tagore, R.	Stray Birds (1st, 8vo, 84p, col frn by...)	L: MacMillan	1917	Pogany, W.	30-50	
Wagner, R.	Tale of Lohengrin (1st AM, grey/gilt, 4to, teg, 8 ticp)	Crowell	(1913)	Pogany, W.	200-350	
Wagner, R.	Tale of Lohengrin (1st, 4to, brown/gilt, 8 ticp, pep)	L: Harrap	(1913)	Pogany, W.	240-350	
Olcott, F.J. (ed.)	Tales of the Persian Genii (1st, 8vo, gilt, pep, 225p, 4cp)	Houghton	(1917)	Pogany, W.	45-70	
Olcott, F.J. (ed.)	Tales of the Persian Genii (1st UK, 8vo, grey cl, 225p, 4cp)	L: Harrap	1919	Pogany, W.	70-90	
Hawthorne, N.	Tanglewood Tales (12mo, red cl, 320p, 4cp, 24pl, pep)	L: T.F. Unwin	[1910]	Pogany, W.	100-130	
Wagner, R.	Tannhauser (1st, 4to, unpag, grey/gilt, 22 ticp)	L: Harrap	(1911)	Pogany, W.	180-240	
Wagner, R.	Tannhauser (1st AM, 4to, black/gilt, unpag, 22 ticp)	Brentano's	[1911]	Pogany, W.	140-200	
Schwimmer, R.	Tisza Tales (1st {std}, 8vo, 225p, blue/gilt, 8cp, pep, DJ)	Doubleday/Dor.	1928	Pogany, W.	85-100	
Edgar, M.G.	Treasury of Verse... (1st AM, lg8vo, 261p, teg, gilt, pep, 8cp)	Crowell	(1908)	Pogany, W.	100-150	
Newman, I.	Wee Miss Violet... (1st, 4to, ibds, unpag, 4cp)	Whitman	(1926)	Pogany, W.	35-60	*
Jenkyn-Thomas, W.	Welsh Fairy Book (1st AM, 8vo, blue/gilt, col frn, 303p)	Stokes	[1907]	Pogany, W.	90-145	*
Jenkyn-Thomas, W.	Welsh Fairy Book (1st, 8vo, 312p, blue cl, col frn, 9pl)	L: T.F. Unwin	(1907)	Pogany, W.	180-275	
Various	Wimp & the Woodle (1st, 4to, blue/gilt bds, 180p, 7cp, pep)	Suttonhouse	1935	Pogany, W.	130-180	R
Young, Gerald	Witches' Kitchen (1st, sm4to, p-o, 223p, gilt, 8cp)	L: Harrap	(1910)	Pogany, W.	150-200	
Young, Gerald	Witches' Kitchen (1st AM, 8vo, 223p, teg, p-o, 8cp, pep)	Crowell	(1911)	Pogany, W.	100-165	*
Hawthorne, N.	Wonder Book... (1st AM, lg8vo, gilt, 320p, 4cp, pep)	Jacobs	(1909)	Pogany, W.	100-165	
Holbrook, Florence	Hiawatha Alphabet (1st, 4to, 30p, p-o, fp color)	Rand/McNally	(1910)	Pohl, H.D.	65-90	*
Garrett, H.	Angelo, the Naughty One (1st, 4to, ipcb, 40p, color, pep)	Viking	1944	Politi, L.	50-85	
Parish, Helen R.	At the Palace Gates (1st, sm4to, ipcb, 64p, fp 2-color, pep)	Viking	1949	Politi, L.	45-70	*
Politi, L.	Boat for Peppe (1st, 4to, cloth, [38]p, color, DJ)	Scribner	1950	Politi, L.	65-80	
Politi, L.	Butterflies Come (1st, sm4to, yellow cl, unpag, color)	Scribner	(1957)	Politi, L.	30-50	*
Dalgliesh, A.	Columbus Story (1st, 4to, [30]p, dp color)	Scribner	(1955)	Politi, L.	70-100	R*
Perez, Luis	El Coyote the Rebel (1st {std}, sm8vo, orange cl, 233p, b/w)	Holt	(1947)	Politi, L.	35-50	*
Politi, L.	Juanita (1st, sm4to, [31]p, color, CH)	Scribner	1948	Politi, L.	65-100	*
Sawyer, R.S.	Least One (1st, lg8vo, 89p, 2-color, pep, DJ)	Viking	1936	Politi, L.	35-50	
Politi, L.	Little Leo (1st, 4to, [30]p, color, DJ)	Scribner	1951	Politi, L.	75-100	
Politi, L.	Little Pancho (1st {1st book}, 16mo, [40]p, ibds, color, pep)	Viking	1938	Politi, L.	65-100	
Clark, A.N.	Looking for Something (1st, 8vo, 53p, dp color, pep)	Viking	1952	Politi, L.	25-40	
Clark, A.N.	Magic Money (1st, sm4to, 121p, red cl, pep, fp 1-color)	Viking	1950	Politi, L.	25-45	*
Politi, L.	Mission Bell (1st, ob8vo, [32]p, blue cl, color)	Scribner	1953	Politi, L.	30-45	*
Politi, L.	Pedro, Angel of Olvera Street (1st, 8vo, [32]p, color, CH)	Scribner	1946	Politi, L.	60-95	*
Politi, L.	Song of the Swallows (1st, 4to, [32]p, color, CM)	Scribner	1949	Politi, L.	70-100	R
Politi, L.	St. Francis & the Animals (1st, 8vo, beige cl, unpag, color)	Scribner	1957	Politi, L.	25-40	*
Henius, F.	Stories from the Americas (1st, lg8vo, orang cl, 115p, fp b/w)	Scribner	1944	Politi, L.	45-60	*
Brown, A.F.	Lonesomest Doll (1st, sm8vo, ibds, 76p, 4pl)	Houghton	1901	Pollak, E.	30-50	*
Johnson, C.	Fir-Tree Fairy Book (1st, 8vo, 333p, color, pep)	Little/Brown	1912	Popini, A.	45-60	*
Stokley, E.	Bubbleloon (1st, sm4to, 201p, blue/gilt, 6 ticp, pep)	Doran	(1926)	Porter, J.E.	65-90	
King, C.	Tonio, Son of Sierras (1st, 12mo, 338p, 4cp, 4pl)	Dillingham	(1906)	Post, C.J.	20-30	
Tietjens, E.& J.	Jaw Breaker's Alphabet (1st, ob4to, ibds, [111]p, b/w, dep)	A.& C. Boni	1930	Post, H.	60-80	*
Mother Goose	Mother Goose in Holland (1st, 4to, 90p, color, pep)	Jacobs	(1912)	Post, M.A.	70-100	*
Potter, B.	Appley Dapply's Nursery Rhymes (1st, 16mo, p-o [52]p, ibds, 15cp)	L: Warne	[1917]	Potter, B.	450-600	
Potter, B.	Cecily Parsley's Nursery Rhymes (1st, 16mo orang bds, p-o, 15cp)	L: Warne	(1922)	Potter, B.	400-600	
Potter, B.	Fairy Caravan (1st, 8vo, green/gilt, p-o, 225p, 6cp)	McKay	(1929)	Potter, B.	280-400	
Potter, B.	Ginger & Pickles (1st, 8vo, 52p, bds, p-o, 10cp, pep)	L: Warne	1909	Potter, B.	450-600	

AUTHOR	TITLE	PUBLISHER	DATE	ARTIST	PRICE	LC
Potter, B.	Pie & Patty Pan (1st, 12mo, 52p, p-o, bds, 10cp)	L: Warne	1905	Potter, B.	385-500	
Potter, B.	Roly Poly Pudding (1st, lg8vo, 69p, p-o, 18cp)	L: Warne	1908	Potter, B.	375-500	
Potter, B.	Story of Miss Moppet (1st, 16mo, bds, p-o, 14cp)	L: Warne	1906	Potter, B.	400-600	
Potter, B.	Tailor of Gloucester (1st, 16mo, green bds, 85p, p-o, 27cp)	L: Warne	1903	Potter, B.	500-650	
Lane, Marg.	Tale of Beatrix Potter (1st, 8vo, 162p, 4cp, 16 b/w)	Warne	(1946)	Potter, B.	85-100	
Potter, B.	Tale of Benjamin Bunny (1st, 16mo, 85p, p-o, tan bds, col, pep)	L: Warne	1904	Potter, B.	400-500	
Potter, B.	Tale of Flopsy Bunnies (1st, sm8vo, 85p, bds, p-o, 27cp, pep)	L: Warne	1909	Potter, B.	450-600	
Potter, B.	Tale of Jemima Puddle Duck (1st, sq16mo, grey bds, p-o, 85p)	L: Warne	1908	Potter, B.	450-600	
Potter, B.	Tale of Johnny Town Mouse (1st, 16mo, 85p, bds, p-o)	L: Warne	1918	Potter, B.	380-500	
Potter, B.	Tale of Little Pig Robinson (1st, 8vo, p-o, 141p, gilt, 6cp)	L: Warne	(1930)	Potter, B.	250-400	
Potter, B.	Tale of Little Pig Robinson (1st AM, 8vo, p-o, 141p, 6cp, pep)	McKay	(1930)	Potter, B.	200-300	
Potter, B.	Tale of Mr. Jeremy Fisher (1st, 24mo, red bds, 85p, p-o, color)	L: Warne	1906	Potter, B.	400-650	
Potter, B.	Tale of Mr. Tod (1st, 16mo, grey bds, p-o, 94p, color)	L: Warne	1912	Potter, B.	400-600	
Potter, B.	Tale of Mrs. Tiggy-Winkle (1st, 16mo, grey bds, 85p, p-o, col)	L: Warne	1905	Potter, B.	450-600	
Potter, B.	Tale of Mrs. Tittlemouse (1st, 24mo, bds, 85p, p-o, 27p)	L: Warne	1910	Potter, B.	380-550	
Potter, B.	Tale of Peter Rabbit (1st {trade}, 16mo, 97p, grey bds, p-o 31cp)	L: Warne	(1902)	Potter, B.	600-800	
Potter, B.	Tale of Peter Rabbit (1st {this pub}, 16mo, 127p, grn cl, 31cp)	Altemus	1904	Potter, B.	200-300	R*
Potter, B.	Tale of Pigling Bland (1st, 16mo, 94p, bds, p-o, 15cp, pep)	L: Warne	1913	Potter, B.	380-500	
Potter, B.	Tale of Squirrel Nutkin (1st, 16mo, grey bds, p-o, 27cp)	L: Warne	1903	Potter, B.	350-500	
Potter, B.	Tale of Timmy Tiptoes (1st, sq16mo, 85p, brown bds, p-o, color)	L: Warne	1911	Potter, B.	350-500	
Potter, B.	Tale of Tom Kitten (1st, 16mo, green bds, 85p, p-o, pep, color)	L: Warne	1907	Potter, B.	400-550	
Potter, B.	Tale of Two Bad Mice (1st, 16mo, bds, p-o, 85p, color, pep)	L: Warne	1904	Potter, B.	450-650	
DeJong, Meindert	Big Goose & Little White Duck (1st {std}, 8vo, 160p, 8cp, pep)	Harper	1938	Potter, E.	30-55	*
Hunt, M.L.	Such a Kind World (1st, sq8vo, [28]p, color)	Grosset/Dunlap	1947	Potter, E.	25-40	*
Laboulaye, E.R.	Laboulaye's Fairy Book (1st, sm8vo, 363p, black cl, p-o, b/w)	Harper	(1925)	Potter, E.E.	30-50	*
Childs, M.F.	De Namin ob De Twins (1st, 8vo, teg, 139p, 7pl)	Dodge	1908	Potthast, E.	70-110	
Stuart, Ruth M.	George Washington Jones (1st, 12mo, 147p, 5pl)	Altemus	(1903)	Potthast, E.	30-50	
Stuart, Ruth M.	Holly & Pizen (1st, 12mo, 216p, 7pl)	Century	1899	Potthast, E.	50-70	*
Stuart, Ruth M.	Napoleon Jackson (1st, sm8vo, 132p, red/gilt, 8pl)	Century	1902	Potthast, E.	40-60	
Praeger, S.R.	Adventures of Three Bold Bears (ob4to, ibds, 48p)	L: Longmans	1897	Praeger, S.R.	100-165	
Aesopus	Aesop's Fables (1st AM, 16mo, gilt, p-o, 47p, 24cp)	Jack/Dutton	[1910]	Praeger, S.R.	60-80	*
Nesbit, E.	As Happy as a King (1st, ob8vo, unpag)	L: Marcus Ward	[1896]	Praeger, S.R.	80-100	*
Praeger, S.R.	Little Twin Dragon (1st, 60p, ob4to, ibds)	L: Longmans	1900	Praeger, S.R.	100-165	
Stevenson, R.L.	Child's Garden of Verses (1st, 4to, 76p, color, pep)	Graham	(1930)	Pratt, J.C.	30-50	*
Cromie, Rbt.	From the Cliffs of Croaghaun (1st AM, 8vo, blue/gilt, 343p, 2pl)	Saalfield	1904	Praut, V.	30-45	
Barrie, J.M.	My Lady Nicotine (1st {this pub}, 8vo, teg, 276p)	J. Knight	1896	Prendergast, M	85-130	
Brady, L.E.	Green Forest Fairy Book (1st, 8vo, 271p, 8cp)	Little/Brown	1920	Preston, A.B.	65-100	
Sandwell, H.B.	Valley of Color Days (1st, 8vo, tan cl, 299p, 6cp, pep)	Little/Brown	1924	Preston, A.B.	45-60	
Byron, May	Adventures of Trooper Peek-A-Boo (1st, 8vo, unpag)	L: Hodder	[1916]	Preston, C.	50-70	*
Byron, May	Barbara Peek-A-Boo's Holiday (1st, 4to, unpag)	L: Hodder	[1914]	Preston, C.	80-100	*
Preston, Tom	Peek-A-Boo Twins (1st, 4to, tan bds, p-o, 12cp)	L: H. Frowde	(1915)	Preston, C.	200-300	
Byron, May	Peek-a-Boos at the Zoo (1st, sq4to, ibds, unpag, p-o, 12cp)	L: H. Frowde	[1915]	Preston, C.	165-225	
Byron, May	Peek-a-Boos in Town (1st, ob folio, ibds, unpag, 12 fp col)	L: H. Frowde	[1915]	Preston, C.	180-250	
Byron, May	Peek-a-Boos in Winter (ob folio, ibds, 18cp)	L: H. Frowde	[1910]	Preston, C.	280-400	
Byron, May	William & Woggs (sq8vo, bds, p-o, 6cp)	L: H. Frowde	[1910]	Preston, C.	100-130	*
Lardner, R.	Big Town (1st, sm8vo, 244p, green cl, b/w pl)	Bobbs-Merrill	(1921)	Preston, M.W.	80-100	
Lardner, R.	Gullible's Travels (1st, sm8vo, blue cl, 255p, col frn)	Bobbs-Merrill	(1917)	Preston, M.W.	100-125	
Butler, E.P.	Incubator Baby (1st, 12mo, 111p, 4cp)	Funk/Wagnalls	1906	Preston, M.W.	20-30	
Wodehouse, P.G.	Piccadilly Jim (1st, sm8vo, 363p, orange cl, 8cp)	Dodd	1917	Preston, M.W.	250-400	
Stone, Eugenia	Secret of the Bog (1st, sm8vo, 217p, b/w, cep)	Holiday House	(1948)	Price, C.	20-30	*
Goldberg, M.	Wait for the Rain (1st, sm8vo, [43]p, blue cl, b/w, cep)	Holiday House	(1952)	Price, C.	20-25	*
Kiviat, Esther	Paji (1st {std}, sm4to, 56p, color, DJ)	McGraw-Hill	(1946)	Price, H.	45-60	
Widdemer, M.	Binkie and Bell Dolls (1st, 8vo, tan cl, 146p, p-o, 8cp, pep)	Penn	1923	Price, H.L.	45-70	*
Larrimore, L.	Blossoming of Patricia-The-Less (1st, lg8vo, 253p, p-o, 4cp)	Penn	1924	Price, H.L.	45-60	
Alcott, L.M.	Eight Cousins (1st, 8vo, 278p, 6cp)	Little/Brown	1927	Price, H.L.	20-35	
Allee, M.H.	Judith Lankester (1st, sm8vo, 241p, b/w, pep)	Houghton	1930	Price, H.L.	20-30	*
Franchi, A.	Little Lead Soldier (1st, lg8vo, p-o, 186p, 5cp)	Penn	1919	Price, H.L.	35-50	
Campbell, Ruth	Runaway Smalls (1st, 4to, ibds, 73p, b/w)	Penn	1923	Price, H.L.	25-40	
Allee, M.H.	Susanna & Tristram (1st, sm8vo, 220p, b/w, pep)	Houghton	1929	Price, H.L.	25-40	*
McNeely, M.H.	Winning Out (1st {std}, 12mo, 308p, b/w)	Longmans	1931	Price, H.L.	30-45	*
Singmaster, Elsie	Young Ravenals (1st, 12mo, 214p, blue cl, 9pl)	Houghton	1932	Price, H.L.	20-35	*
Bonner, M.G.	Magic Clock (1st, 8vo, yellow cl, 187p, 8cp)	Macaulay	(1931)	Price, L.	50-75	
Bonner, M.G.	Magic Journeys (1st, 4to, orange cl, 286p, 16cp)	Macaulay	(1928)	Price, L.	60-80	
Bonner, M.G.	Magic Map (1st, 4to, 238p, 17cp)	Macaulay	(1927)	Price, L.	60-80	
Bonner, M.G.	Magic Music Shop (1st, folio, orang cl, 95p, color, pep)	Macaulay	(1929)	Price, L.	70-100	
Price, Luxor	The Quoks (1st UK, lg4to, 62p, ibds, color)	L: Chambers	(1924)	Price, L.	180-300	
Price, Luxor	The Quoks (1st, 4to, [63]p, p-o, red cl, color)	Stokes	1924	Price, L.	150-220	
Price, M.E.	Angora Twinnies (4to, wraps, [12]p, shape book, color)	Stecher	1919	Price, M.E.	45-60	
Price, M.E.	Betty Fairy Book (folio, [14]p, wraps, shape book, color)	Stecher	1915	Price, M.E.	65-80	
Price, M.E.	Child's Book of Myths (1st, 4to, blue cl, p-o, 112p, 6cp)	Rand/McNally	(1924)	Price, M.E.	50-80	
Price, M.E.	Down Comes the Wilderness (1st {std}, sm8vo, 212p, b/w, pep)	Harper	1937	Price, M.E.	20-35	*
Price, M.E.	Enchantment Tales for Children (1st, 4to, 118p, p-o, col, pep)	Rand/McNally	(1926)	Price, M.E.	50-80	

AUTHOR	TITLE	PUBLISHER	DATE	ARTIST	PRICE	LC
Grimm Bros.	Hansel & Gretel (folio, shape bk, [12]p, wraps, color)	Stecher	1916	Price, M.E.	40-65	
Price, M.E.	Land of Nod (folio, wraps, [12]p, shape book, color)	Stecher	1916	Price, M.E.	45-60	
Price, M.E.	Legends o/t Seven Seas (1st {std}, 8vo, 168p, gilt col frn, pep)	Harper	1929	Price, M.E.	30-45	
Price, M.E.	Manger Babe (folio, [14]p, wraps, shape bk., color)	Stecher	1916	Price, M.E.	45-60	
Price, M.E.	Monkey-Do (1st {std}, 8vo, 149p, b/w, pep)	Harper	1934	Price, M.E.	20-35	*
Price, M.E.	Mota & the Monkey Tree (1st {std}, 8vo, 146p, pep)	Harper	1935	Price, M.E.	25-40	*
Mother Goose	Mother Goose Bk. of Rhymes (narrow folio, wraps, color)	Stecher	1927	Price, M.E.	45-60	
Price, M.E.	Myths & Enchantment Tales (1st, 8vo, 100p, color)	Rand/McNally	(1935)	Price, M.E.	30-45	*
Moore, C.C.	Night Before Christmas (folio, wraps {shape bk}, color)	NY: Stecher	(1917)	Price, M.E.	35-50	
Bates, Kath. L.	Once Upon a Time (1st, lg4to, p-o, blue cl, 128p, color, pep)	Rand/McNally	(1921)	Price, M.E.	50-70	
N/A	Three Bears (12mo, 63p, color)	Rand/McNally	(1937)	Price, M.E.	30-45	*
Price, M.E.	Visit to Santa Claus (sm4to, wraps, color)	Stecher	[1915]	Price, M.E.	35-50	
Dalgliesh, A.	West Indian Play Days (1st, 12mo, 174p, col frn, b/w, pep)	Rand/McNally	(1926)	Price, M.E.	30-45	*
Price, M.E.	Windy Shore (1st {std}, 4to, brown cl, 181p, col frn, 18pl, pep)	Harper	1930	Price, M.E.	35-50	
Stevenson, R.L.	Treasure Island (1st, 8vo, 342p, color)	Grosset/Dunlap	(1947)	Price, N.	25-45	*
Lamb, C.	Tales from Shakespeare (1st AM, 4to, 324p, gilt, teg, 20cp)	Scribner	[1905]	Price, N.M.	70-95	
Harrington, J.W.	Adventures of Admiral Frog (1st, lg8vo, ipcb, fp 1-color)	R.H. Russell	1902	Price, W.B.	100-180	*
Carroll, L.	Alice... & Through... (1st, 8vo, 319p, gilt, p-o, 4cp, pep)	Winston	(1923)	Prittie, E.J.	50-85	
Fryer, J.E.	Bible Story Book (1st, lg8vo, blue cl, p-o, 352p, 4cp)	Winston	(1924)	Prittie, E.J.	50-70	
Sewell, Anna	Black Beauty (1st, lg8vo, green/gilt, p-o, 293p, 4cp, pep)	Winston	(1927)	Prittie, E.J.	30-45	
Grimm Bros.	Fairy Tales (1st, 8vo, 310p, cp)	Winston	(1922)	Prittie, E.J.	50-75	*
Swift, J.	Gulliver's Travels (1st, 8vo, 274p, cp, pep)	Winston	(1930)	Prittie, E.J.	25-40	
Holmes, Mabel D.	Joan of Arc (1st, sm4to, 300p, gilt, p-o, 4cp, pep)	Winston	(1930)	Prittie, E.J.	30-50	
Fryer, J.E.	Mary Frances Story Book (1st, lg8vo, p-o, 328p, pep)	Winston	(1921)	Prittie, E.J.	120-185	
Fillebrown, R.H.	Rhymes/Happy Childhood (1st, lg8vo, 119p, p-o, 3cp, pep)	Winston	(1908)	Prittie, E.J.	40-65	
Mother Goose	Golden Mother Goose (1st, folio, ibds, 96p, color, GGB)	Simon/Schuster	(1948)	Provensen, A.& M.	70-120	*
Kelly, Eric P.	Blacksmith of Vilno (1st, 8vo, 184p, green cl, 3cp)	MacMillan	1930	Pruszynska, A.	30-45	*
Kelly, Eric P.	Gold Star of Halich (1st, 8vo, green cl, 215p, 3cp, fp b/w)	MacMillan	1931	Pruszynska, A.	35-50	*
Kelly, Eric P.	Trumpeter of Krakow (1st, 8vo, 218p, blue cl, 3cp, NM)	MacMillan	1928	Pruszynska, A.	65-90	*
Nesbit, E.	These Little Ones (1st, 8vo, 210p, teg, 10pl)	L: G. Allen	1909	Pryse, S.	140-200	
Holmes, O.W.	Autocrat at Breakfast Table (1st, 8vo, teg, 2vols, gilt, 15pl)	Houghton	1894	Pyle, H.	120-165	
Van Dyke, H.	Blue Flower (1st, 8vo, 298p, blue/gilt, teg, 3cp by...)	Scribner	1909	Pyle, H.	20-35	
Pyle, H.	Book of American Spirit (1st {std}, lg4to, 344p, ibds, p-o, 23cp)	Harper	1923	Pyle, H.	140-200	
Pyle, H.	Book of Pirates (1st, lg4to, 247p, bds, gilt, p-o, 11cp, 25pl)	Harper	1921	Pyle, H.	150-200	
Pyle, H.	Champions of the Round Table (1st, lg8vo, tan/gilt, 328p, b/w)	Scribner	1905	Pyle, H.	180-220	
Cabell, J.B.	Chivalry (1st, 8vo, red cl, teg, 224p, 12cp, dep)	Harper	1909	Pyle, H.	90-125	
Holmes, O.W.	Dorothy Q. (1st, 8vo, grey cl, t.e. silver, 131p, b/w)	Houghton	1893	Pyle, H.	70-90	
Petersen, H.	Dulcibel (1st, 12mo, grey cl, 402p, teg, p-o, 3cp)	Winston	1907	Pyle, H.	40-65	
Van Dyke, H.	First Christmas Tree (1st, 8vo, olive/gilt, 76p, teg, 4pl)	Scribner	1897	Pyle, H.	60-95	
Cabell, J.B.	Gallantry (1st, 8vo, teg, grey cl, 334p, 4 ticp, pep)	Harper	1907	Pyle, H.	100-145	
Pyle, H.	Garden Behind the Moon (1st, 12mo, green/gilt, 192p, 10pl)	Scribner	1895	Pyle, H.	130-170	
Wilson, W.	George Washington (1st, 8vo, 333p, teg, 20pl)	Harper	1897	Pyle, H.	65-100	
Abbott, C.	Howard Pyle: A Chronicle (1st, sm4to, 249p, grey bds, 6cp)	Harper	1925	Pyle, H.	120-150	
Janvier, T.A.	In Old New York (1st, 12mo, 285p, rust/gilt, b/w by...)	Harper	1894	Pyle, H.	40-65	
Forman, J.M.	Island of Enchantment (1st, 8vo, blue/gilt, teg, 106p, 4cp, dep)	Harper	1905	Pyle, H.	70-95	
Tennyson, A.	Lady of Shalott (1st, lg8vo, [64]p, blue/gilt, AEG, color, dep)	Dodd	(1881)	Pyle, H.	350-450	
Cabell, J.B.	Line of Love (1st, 8vo, p-o, teg, 291p, uncut, 10cp)	Harper	1905	Pyle, H.	85-120	
Markham, E.	Man With the Hoe... (1st, 12mo, 114p, gilt, teg, b/w)	Doub./McClure	1900	Pyle, H.	80-100	
Pyle, H.	Men of Iron (1st, 8vo, 328p, red cl, teg, 15pl)	Harper	1892	Pyle, H.	140-200	
Pyle, H.	Merry Advens./Robin Hood (1st 4to, leather/gilt, 296p, 23fp b/w)	Scribner	1883	Pyle, H.	600-850	
Pyle, H.	Modern Aladdin (1st, 8vo, 205p, blue/gilt, b/w)	Harper	1892	Pyle, H.	100-130	
Deland, M.	Old Chester Tales (1st [1], 12mo, 360p, green cl, 16pl)	Harper	1899	Pyle, H.	65-80	
Holmes, O.W.	One-Hoss Shay (1st [new ed.], 12mo, teg, gilt, 12cp)	Houghton	1905	Pyle, H.	85-120	
Pyle, H.	Otto of the Silver Hand (1st, lg8vo, olive/gilt, 173p, PPP)	Scribner	1888	Pyle, H.	180-250	
Pyle, H.	Pepper and Salt (1st, 4to, tan/gilt, 121p, b/w)	Harper	1886	Pyle, H.	280-400	
Pyle, H.	Price of Blood (1st, 12mo, ipcb, 98p, 6cp, A.E. red)	Badger	1899	Pyle, H.	150-220	
Pyle, H.	Rose of Paradise (1st, 12mo, green/gilt, 231p, 8pl)	Harper	1888	Pyle, H.	100-150	
Pyle, H.	Ruby of Kishmoor (1st, 8vo, teg, 74p, gilt, 10cp)	Harper	1908	Pyle, H.	80-120	
Goodwin, M.W.	Sir Christopher... (1st, 12mo, 411p, frn by...)	Little/Brown	1901	Pyle, H.	25-40	
Cabell, J.B.	Soul of Melicent (1st, 8vo, 216p, gilt, p-o, 4cp)	Stokes	(1913)	Pyle, H.	90-130	
Twain, M.	St. Joan of Arc (1st, lg8vo, black/gilt, 32p, p-o, 4 ticp, pep)	Harper	(1919)	Pyle, H.	70-100	
Pyle, H.	Stolen Treasure (1st, 12mo, 253p, orange cl, p-o, 8pl)	Harper	1907	Pyle, H.	90-120	
Howells, W.D.	Stops of Various Quills (1st, 8vo, teg, gilt, designs by...)	Harper	1895	Pyle, H.	60-85	
Brooks, E.S.	Storied Holidays (1st, 8vo, 271p, cloth)	Lothrop	[1887]	Pyle, H.	150-180	
Pyle, H.	Story of Jack Ballister's Fortunes (1st, 8vo, 420p, 14pl)	Century	1895	Pyle, H.	150-200	
Pyle, H.	Story of King Arthur... (1st, lg8vo, tan/gilt, 313p, b/w, cep)	Scribner	1903	Pyle, H.	140-200	
Baldwin, J.	Story of Seigfried (1st, 8vo, red/gilt, 306p, teg, PPP)	Scribner	1882	Pyle, H.	150-200	
Pyle, H.	Story of Sir Lancelot (1st, lg8vo, 340p, tan/gilt, b/w)	Scribner	1907	Pyle, H.	160-200	
Baldwin, J.	Story of the Golden Age (1st, 8vo, 286p, uncut, PPP)	Scribner	1887	Pyle, H.	180-230	
Pyle, H.	Story of the Grail (1st, sm4to, 258p, tan/gilt, b/w)	Scribner	1910	Pyle, H.	150-200	R
Seitz, D.	The Bucaneers (1st, 8vo, p-o, teg, 52p, frn by...)	Harper	1912	Pyle, H.	50-80	
Doyle, A.C.	The Parasite (1st AM, 12mo, 143p, 4pl)	Harper	1895	Pyle, H.	70-100	

AUTHOR	TITLE	PUBLISHER	DATE	ARTIST	PRICE	LC
Pyle, H.	Twilight Land (1st, 8vo, 438p, gilt, b/w)	Harper	1895	Pyle, H.	120-165	
Pyle, H.	Wonder Clock (1st, tall 8vo, grey cl, 318p, b/w)	Harper	1888	Pyle, H.	200-300	
Pyle, H.	Yankee Doodle (1st, 4to, 31p, ibds, 8 fp color)	Dodd	1881	Pyle, H.	350-500	
Reed, H.L.	Amy in Acadia (1st, 8vo, 344p, blue cl, 6pl)	Little/Brown	1905	Pyle, Kath.	35-50	
Pyle, Kath.	As the Goose Flies (1st, 8vo, 183p, gilt, 6pl)	Little/Brown	1901	Pyle, Kath.	40-60	
Sewell, Anna	Black Beauty (1st, lg8vo, p-o, 239p, 4cp, 13pl, pep)	Dodd	1923	Pyle, Kath.	80-120	
Pyle, Kath.	Black-Eyed Puppy (1st, 8vo, 89p, p-o, 12cp)	Dutton	1923	Pyle, Kath.	45-60	
White, E.O.	Blue Aunt (1st, 8vo, 144p, col frn & cvr by…)	Houghton	1918	Pyle, Kath.	30-50	
White, E.O.	Borrowed Sister (1st, 8vo, 150p, green cl, p-o, 4pl)	Houghton	1906	Pyle, Kath.	50-70	
Pyle, Kath.	Careless Jane (1st, sm8vo, green cl, 110p, b/w)	Dutton	(1902)	Pyle, Kath.	45-65	*
Pyle, Kath.	Charlemagne & his Knights (1st, sm4to, gilt, 302p, col frn, 7pl)	Lippincott	(1932)	Pyle, Kath.	45-60	
Pyle, Kath.	Christmas Angel (1st, 12mo, green/gilt, teg, 136p, 6pl)	Little/Brown	1900	Pyle, Kath.	65-85	
Pyle, Kath.	Counterpane Fairy (1st, 8vo, green/gilt, uncut, teg, 191p)	Dutton	1898	Pyle, Kath.	70-90	*
Halkett, S.	Elf King's Flowers (1st, 4to, 79p, ibds, col frn, pep)	Dutton	(1924)	Pyle, Kath.	35-50	
Sholl, A.	Faery Tales of Weir (1st, 8vo, 172p, purple/gilt, col frn, pep)	Dutton	(1918)	Pyle, Kath.	65-90	
Pyle, Kath.	Fairy Tales from Far & Near (1st, 8vo, green cl, 274p, 7cp)	Little/Brown	1922	Pyle, Kath.	50-80	
Pyle, Kath.	Fairy Tales from India (1st, 4to, 229p, red/gilt, 12cp, pep)	Lippincott	1926	Pyle, Kath.	60-85	
Pyle, Kath.	Fairy Tales from Many Lands (1st, 8vo, 316p, col frn)	Dutton	(1911)	Pyle, Kath.	60-80	*
Blodgett, M.F.	Giant's Ruby (1st, 8vo, 292p, blue cl, 6pl)	Little/Brown	1903	Pyle, Kath.	70-100	
Browne, Frances	Granny's Wonderful Chair (1st, 4to, 211p, red/gilt, 6cp, pep)	Dutton	(1916)	Pyle, Kath.	80-100	
Thomas, E.M.	In Sunshine Land (1st, 8vo, tan/silver, 152p, b/w pl, cep)	Houghton	1894	Pyle, Kath.	50-70	
Pyle, Kath.	In the Green Forest (1st, lg8vo, green cl, 171p, 5pl)	Little/Brown	1902	Pyle, Kath.	50-70	
Morgan, H.	Island Impossible (1st, 12mo, 206p, 5pl)	Little/Brown	1899	Pyle, Kath.	50-80	*
Pyle, Kath.	Katherine Pyle's Bk/Fairy Tales (1st, 8vo, 338p, col frn, 28pl)	Dutton	(1925)	Pyle, Kath.	100-150	
Pyle, Kath.	Lazy Matilda… (1st, 8vo, 173p, blue cl, b/w)	Dutton	(1921)	Pyle, Kath.	30-45	*
Pyle, Kath.	Mother's Nursery Tales (1st, 8vo, gilt, 376p, 7cp)	Dutton	(1918)	Pyle, Kath.	100-145	
Pyle, Kath.	Nancy Rutledge (1st, 8vo, 206p, 6pl)	Little/Brown	1906	Pyle, Kath.	45-60	
White, E.O.	Only Child (1st, 8vo, 167p, grey cl, p-o, 4pl)	Houghton	1905	Pyle, Kath.	30-50	
Pyle, Kath.	Rabbit Witch (1st, ob4to, 81p, cloth)	Dutton	(1895)	Pyle, Kath.	100-135	
Pyle, Kath.	Six Little Ducklings (1st, 8vo, green cl, p-o, 99p, 24pl, pep)	Dodd	1915	Pyle, Kath.	85-120	
Pyle, Kath.	Tales from Greek Mythology (1st, 8vo, blue cl, 312p, 12pl)	Lippincott	1928	Pyle, Kath.	50-70	
Pyle, Kath.	Tales from Norse Mythology (1st, sm4to, 256p, 8cp, pep)	Lippincott	1930	Pyle, Kath.	45-65	
Pyle, Kath.	Tales of Folk & Fairies (1st, 8vo, blue cl, 288p, 6cp)	Little/Brown	1919	Pyle, Kath.	60-80	
Pyle, Kath.	Tales of Two Bunnies (1st, 8vo, 87p, red cl, b/w, pep)	Dutton	(1913)	Pyle, Kath.	65-100	
Pyle, Kath.	Tales of Wonder & Magic (1st, 8vo, green cl, 314p, 8cp)	Little/Brown	1920	Pyle, Kath.	65-80	*
LeBaron, G.	Twixt You & Me (1st, 8vo, 296p, decorations by…)	Little/Brown	1898	Pyle, Kath.	35-50	*
Pyle, Kath.	Two Little Mice (1st, 8vo, 108p, 16pl)	Dodd	1917	Pyle, Kath.	50-70	
White, E.O.	When Molly was Six (1st, 8vo, 133p, cloth, 3pl)	Houghton	1894	Pyle, Kath.	35-50	
Pyle, Kath.	Wonder Tales Retold (1st, 8vo, green/gilt, 322p, 8cp)	Little/Brown	1916	Pyle, Kath.	50-70	
Collodi, C.	Pinocchio's Advens. in Wonderland (12m^E, 212p, 4cp)	J. Marsh	(1898)	Quentin, R.	180-250	
Girv^En, B.	Mr. Piccolo (1st, 8vo, 247p)	L: G. Allen	1911	Quick, H.	25-45	*
Girvin, B.	Pam & Billy (1st, 8vo, 209p, col frn, 12pl)	L: G. Allen	1910	Quick, H.	35-50	*
Browning, R.	Pied Piper of Hamelin (1st, folio, red/gilt, unpag, b/w)	L: Quilter	1898	Quilter, H.	130-165	
Allee, M.H.	Little American Girl (1st, 8vo, 237p, b/w, pep)	Houghton	1938	Quinn, P.	20-35	*
Schlein, M.	Four Little Foxes (1st, sm4to, ipcb, unpag, color, pep)	W.R. Scott	1953	Quintanilla, L.	45-70	*
Garis, H.	Uncle Wiggily's Automobile (8vo, 184p, color)	Platt/Munk	(1939)	Rache, A.	20-30	*
Garis, H.	Uncle Wiggily's Happy Days (1st, sm4to, 211p, col frn)	Platt/Munk	(1947)	Rache, A.	30-45	
Aesopus	Aesop's Fables (1st, sm4to, green/gilt, 223p, 13cp, pep)	L: Heinemann	1912	Rackham, A.	250-400	
Aesopus	Aesop's Fables (1st AM, sq8vo, 224p, p-o, 13cp)	Doubleday/Page	1912	Rackham, A.	200-300	
Aesopus	Aesop's Fables (8vo, gilt, p-o, t.e. red, 13cp)	Garden City	(1939)	Rackham, A.	65-80	
Carroll, L.	Alice/Wonderland (1st, 8vo, green/gilt, 161p, 13cp, pep)	L: Heinemann	(1907)	Rackham, A.	200-300	
Carroll, L.	Alice/Wonderland (1st AM, 8vo, p-o, 162p, 13cp, pep)	Doubleday/Page	[1907]	Rackham, A.	200-300	
Gosse (intro)	Allies' Fairy Book (1st, 8vo, blue/gilt, 12cp)	L: Heinemann	(1916)	Rackham, A.	240-320	
Kenyon, C.R.	Argonauts of the Amazon (1st, 8vo, blue/gilt, 305p, 6pl)	L: Chambers	1901	Rackham, A.	200-250	
Rackham, A.	Arthur Rackham Fairy Book (1st, lg8vo, red cl, 287p, 8cp, pep)	L: Harrap	(1933)	Rackham, A.	170-250	
Browne, Maggie	Book of Betty Barber (1st AM, sq8vo, teg, p-o, 130p, 6cp)	Badger	[1910]	Rackham, A.	300-400	
Browne, Maggie	Book of Betty Barber (1st, 8vo, brown cl, teg, p-o, 129p, 6cp)	L: Duckworth	(1910)	Rackham, A.	280-400	*
Irving, W.	Bracebridge Hall (1st, 2 vols, 8vo, teg, 5pl by…)	Putnam	1896	Rackham, A.	120-160	
Various	Brains & Bravery (1st, 8vo, 398p, green/gilt, 8pl)	L: Chambers	1903	Rackham, A.	150-200	*
Weyman, S.J.	Castle Inn (1st, 8vo, blue/gilt, 371p, frn by…)	L: Smith Elder	1898	Rackham, A.	120-145	
Lever, Chas.	Charles O'Malley… (1st, 8vo, 628p, uncut, red/gilt, 16pl)	L: Service	1897	Rackham, A.	140-170	
Dickens, C.	Christmas Carol (1st, 8vo, olive/gilt, 147p, 12cp, pep)	L: Heinemann	(1915)	Rackham, A.	120-165	
Dickens, C.	Christmas Carol (1st AM, 8vo, 146p, purple/gilt, 12cp, pep)	Lippincott	(1915)	Rackham, A.	90-140	
N/A	Cinderella (1st AM, 4to, ibds, 100p, DJ)	Lippincott	(1919)	Rackham, A.	200-250	
Evans, C.S.	Cinderella (1st, 4to, 110p, cream bds, ti-col frn, dp b/w, pep)	L: Heinemann	(1919)	Rackham, A.	225-280	
Walton, Isaac	Complete Angler (1st AM, sm4to, 224p, gilt, teg, 12cp, pep)	McKay	[1931]	Rackham, A.	140-200	
Walton, Isaac	Complete Angler (1st, 4to, teg, 12cp)	L: Harrap	[1931]	Rackham, A.	220-265	
Milton, J.	Comus (1st AM, 4to, teg, green/gilt, 76p, 24 ticp, pep)	Doubleday/Page	[1921]	Rackham, A.	175-235	
Burns, Rbt.	Cotter's Saturday Night (1st, 12mo, ibds, 17p, frn by..)	L: Hewetson	(1908)	Rackham, A.	120-165	
Phillpotts, E.	Dish of Apples (1st, sm4to, lavender cl, 75p, 3 ticp, pep)	Hodder	[1921]	Rackham, A.	180-220	
Hope, A.	Dolly Dialogues (1st, AM, 12mo, 195p, uncut, teg, frn by…)	Holt	1894	Rackham, A.	80-100	
Hawkins, A.H.	Dolly Dialogues (1st, sm sq8vo, 111p, wraps)	(London)	1894	Rackham, A.	175-250	

AUTHOR	TITLE	PUBLISHER	DATE	ARTIST	PRICE	LC
Steele, F.A.	English Fairy Tales (1st AM, 8vo, red/gilt, 363p, 16cp, pep)	MacMillan	1918	Rackham, A.	180-260	
Burney, Fanny	Evelina... (1st, sm8vo, teg, blue cl, 16 b/w, 416p)	L: Newnes	1898	Rackham, A.	175-230	
Rackham, A.	Fairy Book (1st, 8vo, 111p, blue/gilt, 11cp)	Doubleday/Page	1923	Rackham, A.	140-180	
Grimm Bros.	Fairy Tales (1st, sm8vo, 464p, col frn, pep)	L: Freemantle	1900	Rackham, A.	100-170	*
Grimm Bros.	Fairy Tales (1st, sm4to, 325p, gilt, 40 ticp, pep)	L: Constable	1909	Rackham, A.	750-1000	
Grimm Bros.	Fairy Tales (1st AM, 4to, ibds, gilt, 325p, 40 ticp)	Doubleday/Page	1909	Rackham, A.	480-700	
Andersen, H.C.	Fairy Tales (1st, 4to, 287p, teg, uncut, 12cp, pep)	L: Harrap	(1932)	Rackham, A.	250-320	
Andersen, H.C.	Fairy Tales (1st AM, lg8vo, teg, 288p, 12cp, pep)	McKay	(1932)	Rackham, A.	185-240	
N/A	Faithful Friends (4to, pict red cl, 6pl by...)	L: Blackie	[1913]	Rackham, A.	250-300	
Martineau, H.	Feats on the Fjord (1st, 16mo, blue cl, teg, 237p, col frn)	L: Dent	1899	Rackham, A.	150-200	
Martineau, H.	Feats on the Fjord (1st AM, 12mo, p-o, 128p, 8cp)	Dutton	[1914]	Rackham, A.	80-120	
Rossetti, C.	Goblin Market (1st AM, 8vo, p-o, red cl, 4cp, pep)	Lippincott	[1933]	Rackham, A.	100-140	
Rossetti, C.	Goblin Market (1st, 8vo, wraps, 43p, 4cp, pep)	L: Harrap	(1933)	Rackham, A.	180-250	
Gates, Eleanor	Good Night (1st, 8vo, 53p, bds, 5cp)	Crowell	(1907)	Rackham, A.	350-500	
Niebuhr	Greek Heroes (12mo, p-o, teg, blue/gilt, 4cp)	L: Cassell	1910	Rackham, A.	250	
Greene, Mrs.	Grey House on the Hill (1st, sm8vo, red cl, 205p, 8cp)	L: Nelson	[1903]	Rackham, A.	180-225	
Merriman, H.S.	Grey Lady (1st, 8vo, blue/gilt, 342p, 11pl)	L: Smith Elder	1897	Rackham, A.	160-225	
Swift, J.	Gulliver's Travels (1st, 8vo, 291p, gilt, teg, 12 ticp, pep)	L: Dent	1909	Rackham, A.	250-300	
Swift, J.	Gulliver's Travels (1st AM, 8vo, teg, 291p, 12 ticp, pep)	Dent/Dutton	1909	Rackham, A.	180-240	
Grimm Bros.	Hansel & Gretel (1st, lg8vo, blue/gilt, 159p, 20 ticp)	L: Constable	(1920)	Rackham, A.	185-250	
Grimm Bros.	Hansel & Gretel (1st AM, lg8vo, 159p, 20 ticp)	Dutton	(1920)	Rackham, A.	160-240	R
Ford, Julia E.	Imagina (1st, lg8vo, 178p, blue/gilt, 2 fp color)	Duffield	1914	Rackham, A.	150-200	
Ingoldsby, T.	Ingoldsby Legends (1st, 8vo, teg, 638p, green/gilt, 12cp, pep)	L: Dent	1898	Rackham, A.	165-220	
Ingoldsby, T.	Ingoldsby Legends (1st AM, 4to, teg, green/gilt, 24 ticp, pep)	Dent/Dutton	1907	Rackham, A.	250-400	
Stephens, J.	Irish Fairy Tales (1st, 8vo, 318p, green/gilt, 16cp)	L: MacMillan	1920	Rackham, A.	200-300	
Ruskin, J.	King of the Golden River (1st AM, 8vo, red cl, 47p, p-o, 4cp)	Lippincott	(1932)	Rackham, A.	120-180	
Ruskin, J.	King of the Golden River (1st, 8vo, wraps, 47p, 4cp, pep)	L: Harrap	(1932)	Rackham, A.	165-220	
N/A	Land of Enchantment (1st, 4to, 144p, olive/gilt, 14pl)	L: Cassell	1907	Rackham, A.	220-265	
Irving, W.	Legend of Sleepy Hollow (1st AM sm4to, 102p, teg, p-o, 8cp, pep)	McKay	(1928)	Rackham, A.	145-200	
Irving, W.	Legend of Sleepy Hollow (1st, 4to, teg, 102p, 8cp, pep)	L: Harrap	(1928)	Rackham, A.	240-300	
Grimm Bros.	Little Brother/Little Sister (1st, 4to, gilt 251p, 12 ticp, pep)	L: Constable	(1917)	Rackham, A.	260-400	
Grimm Bros.	Little Brother/Little Sister (1st AM, 4to, 251p, 12 ticp)	Dodd	(1917)	Rackham, A.	200-265	
Barrie, J.M.	Little White Bird (8vo, teg, 242p, 2pl by...)	L: Hodder	1912	Rackham, A.	220-300	
Barrie, J.M.	Little White Bird (1st AM, 8vo, 286p, teg, uncut, 2pl by...)	Scribner	1912	Rackham, A.	140-185	
Brown, A.F.	Lonesomest Doll (1st, 8vo, 81p, tan cl, 4pl)	Houghton	(1928)	Rackham, A.	200-260	
Shakespeare, Wm.	MidSummer Night's Dream (1st, lg8vo, 134p, grey/gilt, 40 ticp)	L: Heinemann	1908	Rackham, A.	350-500	
Merriman, H.S.	Money Spinner (1st, sm8vo, 242p, gilt, 12pl)	L: Smith Elder	1896	Rackham, A.	200-300	
Mother Goose	Mother Goose (1st AM, 4to, p-o, 262p, 13cp)	Century	1913	Rackham, A.	220-300	R
Mother Goose	Mother Goose (1st, sm4to, grey cl, 159p, 13 ticp, pep)	L: Heinemann	(1913)	Rackham, A.	300-400	R
Moore, C.C.	Night Before Christmas (1st AM, 8vo, p-o, 37p, 4cp, pep)	Lippincott	[1931]	Rackham, A.	140-185	
Nisbet, J.	Our Forests & Woodlands (1st, 8vo, teg, gilt, 340p, pep)	L: J.M. Dent	1900	Rackham, A.	140-180	
Isben, H.	Peer Gynt (1st AM, 4to, 255p, orange cl, 12cp)	Lippincott	[1936]	Rackham, A.	120-180	
Isben, H.	Peer Gynt (1st, 4to, brown/gilt, 12cp, pep)	(London)	(1936)	Rackham, A.	150-200	
Drury, W.P.	Peradventure of Private Pagett (1st, 12mo, orang cl, 242p, 8pl)	L: Chapman	1904	Rackham, A.	200-300	*
Barrie, J.M.	Peter Pan... (1st AM, lg8vo, 125p, green/gilt, 50 ticp)	Scribner	1906	Rackham, A.	350-500	
Barrie, J.M.	Peter Pan... (1st, sm4to, 125p, red/gilt, 50 ticp)	L: Hodder	1906	Rackham, A.	450-600	
Browning, R.	Pied Piper of Hamelin (1st AM, 8vo, 45p, p-o, 4cp, pep, DJ)	Lippincott	[1934]	Rackham, A.	140-185	
Browning, R.	Pied Piper of Hamelin (1st, 8vo, wraps, 4cp, pep, DJ)	L: Harrap	(1934)	Rackham, A.	230-285	
Bianco, M.W.	Poor Cecco (1st AM, 4to, blue/gilt, 175p, 7 ticp, pep)	Doran	(1925)	Rackham, A.	100-150	R
Kipling, R.	Puck of Pook's Hill (1st AM, 8vo, grn/gilt, teg, 277p, 4cp)	Doubleday/Page	1906	Rackham, A.	100-140	
Rackham, A.	Rackham's Book of Pictures (1st, 4to, grey/gilt, 44 ticp)	L: Heinemann	(1913)	Rackham, A.	300-400	
Cholmondeley, M.	Red Pottage (1st, 8vo, 202p, tan wraps, 8pl)	L: Newnes	1904	Rackham, A.	375-550	
Wagner, R.	Rhinegold & the Valkyrie (1st AM, lg8vo, 160p, 34 ticp, pep)	Doubleday/Page	1910	Rackham, A.	240-300	
Wagner, R.	Rhinegold & the Valkyrie (1st, 4to, 160p, gilt, 34 ticp, pep)	L: Heinemann	1910	Rackham, A.	300-400	
Irving, W.	Rip Van Winkle (1st AM, 4to, green/gilt, 51 ticp)	Doubleday/Page	1905	Rackham, A.	250-350	
Irving, W.	Rip Van Winkle (1st, 4to, 57p, green/gilt, 51 ticp, dep)	L: Heinemann	1905	Rackham, A.	350-450	
Fay, E.	Road to Fairyland (1st AM, 8vo, grey cl, 218p, col frn by..)	Putnam	(1926)	Rackham, A.	145-200	
Pollard, A.	Romance of King Arthur (1st AM, lg8vo, 517p, green/gilt, 16cp)	MacMillan	1917	Rackham, A.	170-240	
Wagner, R.	Seigfried... (1st, sm4to, 182p, tan/gilt, 30 ticp, pep)	L: Heinemann	1911	Rackham, A.	260-320	
Wagner, R.	Siegfried... (1st AM, sm4to, 182p, blue/gilt bds, 30 ticp)	Doubleday/Page	1911	Rackham, A.	220-275	
Evans, C.S.	Sleeping Beauty (1st, 4to, ibds, 110p, 1 ticp, 4 dp color)	L: Heinemann	(1920)	Rackham, A.	180-250	
Ford, Julia E.	Snickerty Nick (1st, lg8vo, 78p, blue cl, 3cp)	Moffat	1919	Rackham, A.	165-250	
Grimm Bros.	Snowdrop... (1st, lg8vo, 165p, blue/gilt, 20 ticp)	L: Constable	(1920)	Rackham, A.	180-220	
Grimm Bros.	Snowdrop.... (1st AM, lg8vo, 165p, teg, 20 ticp)	Dutton	(1920)	Rackham, A.	150-180	
N/A	Some British Ballads (1st, 4to, 170p, blue/gilt, 16 ticp, pep)	L: Constable	1919	Rackham, A.	160-200	
Starkie, Walter	Spanish Raggle-Taggle (1st, 8vo, 488p, red/gilt, frn by...)	L: J. Murray	(1934)	Rackham, A.	35-50	
Swinburne, A.C.	Springtide of Life (1st AM, 4to, 132p, green cl, 8cp, pep)	Lippincott	1918	Rackham, A.	165-220	
Swinburne, A.C.	Springtide of Life (1st, 4to, green/gilt, 133p, 8cp, pep)	L: Heinemann	(1918)	Rackham, A.	200-250	
Haydon, A.L.	Stories of King Arthur (1st, 12mo, 94p, p-o, red/gilt, 4cp by)	L: Cassell	1910	Rackham, A.	140-200	*
Berlyn, A.	Sunrise-Land (1st, 8vo, 345p, grey cloth)	L: Jarrolds	1894	Rackham, A.	200-300	
Brown, M.	Surprising Advens. of Tuppy & Tue (1st, sm8vo, 190p, 4cp)	L: Cassell	1904	Rackham, A.	350-420	
Lamb, C.	Tales from Shakespeare (1st, 8vo, 304p, gilt, teg, 12cp, pep)	L: Dent	1909	Rackham, A.	250-320	

AUTHOR	TITLE	PUBLISHER	DATE	ARTIST	PRICE	LC
Lamb, C.	Tales from Shakespeare (1st AM, 8vo, 304p, teg, 12cp, pep)	Dutton	1909	Rackham, A.	200-260	
Poe, E.A.	Tales of Mystery... (1st AM, 4to, gilt, 318p, 12cp, pep)	Lippincott	[1935]	Rackham, A.	200-280	
Poe, E.A.	Tales of Mystery... (1st, 4to, 318p, gilt, 12cp, pep)	L: Harrap	(1935)	Rackham, A.	240-300	
Irving, W.	Tales of a Traveller (1st, 2vols, lg8vo, white/gilt, 5pl by...)	Putnam	1895	Rackham, A.	100-135	
Shakespeare, Wm.	The Tempest (1st, sm4to, olive/gilt, 185p, 20 ticp)	L: Heinemann	1926	Rackham, A.	250-400	
Fouque, La Motte	Undine (1st, sm4to, 136p, blue/gilt, 15 ticp, pep)	L: Heinemann	1909	Rackham, A.	265-320	
Fouque, La Motte	Undine (1st AM, 4to, 136p, grey/gilt, 15 ticp, pep)	Doubleday/Page	1909	Rackham, A.	185-225	
Goldsmith, O.	Vicar of Wakefield (1st AM, 4to, gilt, 232p, teg, 12cp, pep)	McKay	[1929]	Rackham, A.	100-130	
Goldsmith, O.	Vicar of Wakefield (1st, 4to, uncut, gilt, 232p, 12cp, pep)	L: Harrap	(1929)	Rackham, A.	220-260	
Harbour, H.	Where Flies the Flag (1st, 12mo, 286p, gilt, 6cp)	L: Collins	(1904)	Rackham, A.	160-220	
Morley, C.	Where the Blue Begins (1st AM, 4to, blue/gilt, teg, 227p, 4cp)	Doubleday/Page	(1925)	Rackham, A.	125-160	
Dewar, G.A.B.	Wild Life/Hampshire Highlands (1st, 8vo, teg, grn/gilt, b/w, pep)	L: J.M. Dent	1899	Rackham, A.	200-350	
Grahame, K.	Wind in the Willows (1st {this pub}, lg8vo, 190p, 12cp, box)	Heritage Press	(1940)	Rackham, A.	100-130	
Hawthorne, N.	Wonder Book... (1st AM, 4to, red/gilt, 16 ticp, 8cp)	Doran	[1922]	Rackham, A.	200-260	
Hawthorne, N.	Wonder Book... (1st, 4to, 207p, red/gilt, 16 ticp, 8cp, pep)	L: Hodder	[1922]	Rackham, A.	240-300	
Fitzgerald, S.	Zankiwank & Bletherwitch (1st AM, 8vo, 188p, gilt, b/w)	Stokes	(1896)	Rackham, A.	450-600	
Fitzgerald, S.	Zankiwank & Bletherwitch (1st, 8vo, teg, green/gilt, 188p)	L: J.M. Dent	1896	Rackham, A.	600-800	
Larned, W.T.	American Indian Fairy Tales (1st, 8vo, ibds, [88]p, color, pep)	Volland	(1921)	Rae, J.	85-120	
Gillmore, Inez H.	Angel Island (1st, 8vo, blue cl, 351p, 2pl)	Holt	1914	Rae, J.	100-120	
Rae, J.	Big Family (1st, ob4to, p-o, 50p)	Dodd	1916	Rae, J.	50-70	*
Gordon, Eliz.	Buddy Jim... (1st, 8vo, ibds, [93]p, color)	Volland	(1922)	Rae, J.	40-65	
N/A	Children at Play in Many Lands (1st, lg ob4to, [16]p, color)	Volland	1922	Rae, J.	100-150	*
N/A	Christmas Story from Saint Mark (1st, 24mo, ibds, unpag, color)	Volland	(1921)	Rae, J.	45-60	*
Rowland, H.	Countess Diane (1st, 8vo, 149p, uncut, p-o, 5cp, pep)	Dodd	1908	Rae, J.	35-50	
Cox, F.T.	Epic of Ebenezer (1st, 12mo, ibds, 72p)	Dodd	1912	Rae, J.	20-30	
LaFontaine, J.	Fables in Rhyme for Little Folks (1st, 8vo, ibds, color)	Volland	(1918)	Rae, J.	70-100	
Larned, W.T.	Fairy Tales From France (1st, lg8vo, ibds, [93]p, color, pep)	Volland	(1920)	Rae, J.	70-90	
Mills, W.J.	Girl I Left Behind Me (1st, 4to, 90p, teg, p-o, 11cp, pep)	Dodd	1910	Rae, J.	70-90	
Rae, J.	Granny Goose (1st, lg4to, 44p, ibds, 21 fp color, pep)	Volland	(1926)	Rae, J.	160-220	
Rae, J.	Grasshopper Green/Meadow Mice (1st, 12mo, ibds, [40]p, color)	Volland	(1922)	Rae, J.	65-80	
Grimm Bros.	Grimm's Animal Stories (1st, 4to, green cl, p-o, 9cp)	Duffield	(1911)	Rae, J.	185-300	
Viele, H.K.	Heartbreak Hill (1st, 12mo, 330p, grey cl, p-o, 6cp, pep)	Duffield	1908	Rae, J.	25-40	*
Snyder, F.	Lovely Garden (1st, 12mo, ibds, [38]p, color)	Volland	(1919)	Rae, J.	65-80	
Rae, J.	Lucy Locket... (1st, 8vo, 120p, ibds, color)	Volland	(1928)	Rae, J.	65-80	
Meigs, C.	Master Simon's Garden (1st, 8vo, 320p, blue cl, col frn, pep)	MacMillan	1929	Rae, J.	50-70	R
Marryat, Fred.	Masterman Ready (1st, sm4to, 403p, p-o, 6cp)	Harper	1928	Rae, J.	30-45	
Gordon, Eliz.	More Really So Stories (1st, 8vo, ibds, 95p, color, pep)	Volland	(1929)	Rae, J.	65-85	
Wister, O.	Mother (1st, 8vo, 95p, p-o, uncut, 3cp, 4pl, dep)	Dodd	1907	Rae, J.	30-45	
Klein, C.	Music Master (1st, 8vo, 341p, p-o, 4cp)	Dodd	1909	Rae, J.	30-45	
Rae, J.	New Adventures of Alice (1st, lg8vo, ibds, 158p gilt, 12cp, pep)	Volland	(1917)	Rae, J.	120-165	
Dorrington, A.	Our Lady of Darkness (1st, 12mo, 371p, red/gilt, 4pl)	Macaulay	1910	Rae, J.	45-60	*
Meigs, C.	Pool of Stars (1st, 8vo, 203p, blue cl, pep, col frn)	MacMillan	1929	Rae, J.	20-30	*
Martin, J.	Prayers for Little Men & Women (1st, 8vo, 96p, gilt, 6 ticp)	Harper	1912	Rae, J.	50-65	
Gordon, Eliz.	Really So Stories (1st, lg8vo, ibds, 96p, 11cp, pep)	Volland	(1924)	Rae, J.	60-85	
Belasco, D.	Return of Peter Grimm (1st, 8vo, 344p, p-o, 3cp)	Dodd	1912	Rae, J.	25-40	
Masefield, J.	Reynard the Fox (1st, lg8vo, ibds, [94]p, color, pep)	Volland	(1925)	Rae, J.	65-80	
Gates, J.S.	Story of the Mince Pie (1st, 8vo, 164p, p-o, 16cp)	Dodd	1916	Rae, J.	65-80	*
Barbour, R.H.	Story the Dogie Told to Me (1st, sm8vo, p-o, 182p)	Dodd	1914	Rae, J.	30-45	*
Peck, T.A.	Sword of Dundee (1st, sm8vo, 398p, p-o, 7pl)	Duffield	1908	Rae, J.	30-45	*
Churchill, W.	The Crossing... (1st, 8vo, green/gilt, 296p, 10pl)	MacMillan	1930	Rae, J.	30-45	
Mee, J.	Three Little Frogs (1st, 8vo, ibds, color)	Volland	(1924)	Rae, J.	50-75	
Mills, W.J.	Through the Gates of Old Romance (1st, sm8vo, 283p, teg, b/w)	Lippincott	1903	Rae, J.	30-45	
Robins, E.	Under the Southern Cross (1st, 8vo, teg, p-o, 234p, 4cp, pep)	Stokes	(1907)	Rae, J.	30-45	
Mills, W.J.	Van Rensselaers of Old Manhattan (1st, 8vo, p-o, 215p, 5cp)	Stokes	(1907)	Rae, J.	30-45	
Rae, J.	Why: Reflections for Children (1st, 4to, blue cl, p-o)	Dodd	1910	Rae, J.	85-100	
Hutton, W.H.	Hampton Court (1st, sm4to, 244p, blue bds, gilt, b/w)	L: Nimmo	1897	Railton, H.	50-70	
Hood, Thos.	Haunted House (1st, 12mo, AEG, green/gilt, b/w)	L: Lawrence	1896	Railton, H.	35-50	
Tilney, F.C.	Robin Hood & his Merry Outlaws (12mo, grn/gilt, 128p, p-o, 8cp)	Dent/Dutton	[1899]	Railton, I.	30-50	*
Brereton, F.S.	Boy of the Dominion (1st, 8vo, 367p, gilt, 6cp)	L: Blackie	1913	Rainey, W.	35-50	
MacGregor, M.	Story of France (1st AM, lg8vo, 508p, 20cp)	Stokes	[1920]	Rainey, W.	35-50	
Twain, M.	Eve's Diary (1st, 8vo, 109p, red cloth, b/w)	Harper	1906	Ralph, L.	100-150	
Burgess, G.	Heart Line (1st, sm8vo, 584p, p-o, b/w)	Bobbs-Merrill	(1907)	Ralph, L.	35-50	
Davis, M.E.M.	Moons of Balbanca (1st, 8vo, 180p, 6pl)	Houghton	1908	Rand, A.	40-65	
Booth, M.B.	Twilight Fairy Tales (1st, 8vo, 273p, gilt, teg, 16cp)	Putnam	1906	Rand, Amy	65-95	
Rand, Ann	Sparkle & Spin (1st {std}, sm4to, blue cl, [30]p, color, dep)	Harcourt	(1957)	Rand, P.	60-85	R*
Van Derveer, H.	Little Slam Bang (1st, 8vo, 38p, color)	Volland	(1928)	Ransom, F.C.	35-50	*
Brown, M.W.	Fish with a Deep Sea Smile (1st {std}, 8vo, 128p, color, cep)	Dutton	(1938)	Rauch, R.	45-65	
Wedgwood, Henry A.	Bird Talisman (1st, 8vo, 70p, geilt, pep, 8cp)	L: Faber	1939	Raverat, G.	45-60	*
Shippen, K.B.	Men, Microscopes & Living Things (1st, 8vo, grn cl, fp b/w, NH)	Viking	1955	Ravielli, A.	50-80	R*
Cross, L.	Book of Old Sun Dials (1st, 8vo, ibds, 102p)	L: Foulis	(1915)	Rawlings, A.	50-85	
Mitford, M.R.	Our Village (1st, lg8vo, green/gilt, 256p, teg, 16 ticp)	L: MacMillan	1910	Rawlings, A.	80-100	
Kjelgaard, J.A.	Buckskin Brigade (1st, 8vo, 310p)	Holiday House	(1947)	Ray, R.	20-25	*

AUTHOR	TITLE	PUBLISHER	DATE	ARTIST	PRICE	LC
Kjelgaard, J.A.	Chip the Dam Builder (1st, sm8vo, 233p, b/w, pep)	Holiday House	(1950)	Ray, R.	20-25	*
Kjelgaard, J.A.	Fire-Hunter (1st, 8vo, 217p, tan cl, b/w, pep)	Holiday House	(1951)	Ray, R.	20-25	*
Adrian, M.	Garden Spider (1st, sm8vo, 38p, blue cl, 2-color, pep)	Holiday House	(1951)	Ray, R.	20-25	*
Coblentz, C.C.	Sequoya (1st {std}, sm8vo, 199p, decor by...)	Longmans	1946	Ray, R.	25-45	*
Hornibrook, I.	Scout of Today (1st, 8vo, 290p, 5pl)	Houghton	1913	Reading, J.	20-30	*
London, J.	Children of the Frost (1st, sm8vo, 261p, blue cl, 8pl)	MacMillan	1902	Reay, R.M.	350-500	
Smith, G.	Arabella & Araminta Stories (1st, sq8vo, 103p, 15pl, PPPa)	(Boston)	1895	Reed, E.	350-500	*
Smith, G.	Arabella & Araminta Stories (8vo, 103p, 15pl, pep, later)	Small	1903	Reed, E.	90-140	
Blodgett, M.F.	Fairy Tales (1st, sm4to, yellow cl, 204p, teg, 12pl, pep)	Chi: Lamson	1896	Reed, E.	375-500	
Cabot, C.S.	Football Grandma (1st, 8vo, 79p, tan cl, b/w, pep by...)	Small	1905	Reed, E.	35-50	*
Moulton, L.C.	In Childhood's Country (1st, 8vo, tan cl, 69p, uncut, 9pl, pep)	Copeland & Day	1896	Reed, E.	180-250	
Bolton, C.K.	Love Story/Ursula Wolcott (1st, 12mo, 31p, designs by..)	Chi: Lamson	1895	Reed, E.	100-165	*
Dickens, C.	Christmas Carol (1st, 12mo, 148p, ipcb, uncut, color)	Holiday House	(1940)	Reed, P.	45-60	*
N/A	Seven Voyages of Sinbad (1st, 12mo, 71p, ipcb, color)	Holiday House	1939	Reed, P.	60-90	R*
Goldsmith, O.	Deserted Village (1st, ob4to, 59p, vellum/gilt, 14cp, pep)	L: Gowans/Gray	1907	Reid, S.	100-160	
Noyes, A. (ed.)	Magic Casement (1st, 8vo, 391p, gilt, b/w)	L: Chapman	(1908)	Reid, S.	35-50	
Gowans, Adam I.	Treasury of English Verse (1st, 8vo, 303p, green cl, 50pl)	L: Gowans/Gray	1907	Reid, S.	70-100	*
Krauss, Ruth	Good Man & his Good Wife (1st, 8vo, [32]p, fp 2-color)	Harper	1944	Reinhardt, A.	30-45	*
Burnett, F.H.	Pretty Sister of Jose (1st [1], 12mo, 127p, gilt, 12pl)	Scribner	1889	Reinhart, C.S.	80-120	
Smith, F.H.	Tom Grogan (1st, 12mo, 246p, teg, 19pl)	Houghton	1896	Reinhart, C.S.	25-40	
Gray, Eliz. J.	Fair Adventure (1st, sm8vo, 298p, pep)	Viking	1940	Reischer, A.K.	20-30	*
Gianakoulis, T.P.	Fairy Tales of Modern Greece (1st {std}, 8vo, 126p, pep)	Dutton	1930	Reiss, H.	45-65	*
Linderman, F.B.	Blackfeet Indians (1st, lg4to, 65p, ibds, 49 color)	(St. Paul)	1935	Reiss, W.	140-200	
Locke, A.	New Negro (1st, 8vo, 445p, col frn, b/w, DJ)	A.& C. Boni	1925	Reiss, W.	180-250	
Seawell, M.E.	House of Egremont (1st, 8vo, 515p)	Scribner	1900	Relyea, C.M.	15-20	
Hughes, Rupert	Lakerim Athletic Club (1st, sm8vo, 286p, 20pl, PPPa)	Century	1898	Relyea, C.M.	70-100	*
Richmond, Grace S.	On Christmas Day in the Evening (1st, 8vo, 76p, white bds, 4cp)	Doubleday/Page	1910	Relyea, C.M.	25-40	*
Barbour, R.H.	On Your Mark (1st, 8vo, 267p, p-o, 4cp)	Appleton	1904	Relyea, C.M.	20-25	
Riley, J.W.	Rubaiyat of Doc Sifers (1st, 12mo, teg, 211p, green/gilt, b/w)	Century	1897	Relyea, C.M.	45-70	R
Janvier, T.A.	Aztec Treasure House (1st, 8vo, 446p, grey/gilt, 19pl, PPPa)	Harper	1890	Remington, F.	80-125	
Lewis, A.H.	Black Lion Inn (1st, 8vo, 380p, 16pl)	R.H. Russell	1903	Remington, F.	70-85	
Garland, H.	Book of American Indian (1st {std}, 4to, bds, 274p, p-o, 4cp)	Harper	1923	Remington, F.	160-200	
Bigelow, P.	Borderland of Czar & Kaiser (1st, 8vo, 343p, gilt, 50pl)	Harper	1895	Remington, F.	60-80	
Fitzhugh, P.K.	Boy's Book of Scouts (1st, 8vo, 317p, 3pl by...)	Crowell	(1917)	Remington, F.	65-90	*
Remington, F.	Crooked Trails (1st, sm4to, 150p, tan cloth)	Harper	1898	Remington, F.	180-250	
Davis, R.H.	Cuba in War Time (1st, 12mo, 143p, brown bds, 24pl)	R.H. Russell	1897	Remington, F.	180-220	
King, C.	Daughter of the Sioux (1st, 8vo, 306p, teg, p-o, 4pl)	Hobart	1903	Remington, F.	50-70	
Morris, F.	Deal in Wheat... (1st, 12mo, red/gilt, teg, 272p)	Doubleday/Page	1903	Remington, F.	45-70	
Remington, F.	Done in the Open (1st, folio, [90]p, ibds, 70 b/w)	R.H. Russell	1902	Remington, F.	250-400	
Remington, F.	Drawings (1st, ob folio, ibds, 60pl)	R.H. Russell	1897	Remington, F.	650-900	
Decker, K.	Evangelina Cisneros (1st, 8vo, teg, uncut, 257p, 4pl by...)	Continental	1898	Remington, F.	40-60	
Custer, E.B.	Following The Guidon (1st, 8vo, 341p, 2pl by...)	Harper	1890	Remington, F.	50-75	
Remington, F.	Frontier Sketches (1st, ob4to, pcb, 15pl)	Werner	1898	Remington, F.	350-500	
Longfellow, H.W.	Hiawatha (1st, 8vo, suede/gilt, 242p, teg, 23pl)	Houghton	1891	Remington, F.	220-300	
Longfellow, H.W.	Hiawatha (lg8vo, p-o, 193p, 9pl by...)	Riverside	1908	Remington, F.	100-140	
Longfellow, H.W.	Hiawatha (1st, 8vo, teg, red cl, 242p, b/w illus by...)	Houghton	1911	Remington, F.	300-500	
Wister, O.	Jimmyjohn Boss (1st, 8vo, 333p, 5pl by...)	Harper	1900	Remington, F.	50-70	
Remington, F.	John Ermine/Yellowstone (1st, 8vo, 271p, teg, 7pl)	MacMillan	1902	Remington, F.	120-165	
Wister, O.	Journey in Search of Christmas (1st Canadian, 8vo, 93p)	(Toronto)	1904	Remington, F.	50-75	
Wister, O.	Journey in Search of Christmas (1st, 8vo, teg, gilt, 93p, 3pl)	Harper	1904	Remington, F.	70-85	
Remington, F.	Men with The Bark On (1st, sm8vo, 209p, tan cl, 32pl)	Harper	1900	Remington, F.	130-165	
Inman, H.E.	Old Santa Fe Trail (1st, 8vo, 493p, teg, 8pl)	MacMillan	1897	Remington, F.	150-185	
Ralph, J.	On Canada's Frontier (1st, 8vo, 325p, 60 illus by...)	Harper	1892	Remington, F.	70-100	
Whitney, Casper	On Snow-Shoes/Barren Grounds (1st, 8vo, teg, 324p, blue cl, b/w)	Harper	1896	Remington, F.	75-115	
Parkman, F.	Oregon Trail (1st, 8vo, 411p, 10pl)	Little/Brown	1892	Remington, F.	140-200	
Remington, F.	Pony Tracks (1st {1st bk.}, 8vo, tan/gilt, 269p, 70 illus)	Harper	1895	Remington, F.	350-500	
Roosevelt, T.	Ranch Life... (1st, 4to, tan/gilt, 180p, AEG, b/w)	Century	(1888)	Remington, F.	165-200	
Wister, O.	Red Men & White (1st, 8vo, 280p, 17 illus)	Harper	1896	Remington, F.	60-80	
Dodge, T.A.	Riders/Many Lands (1st, 8vo, brown/gilt, teg, 406p)	Harper	1894	Remington, F.	100-130	
Whitney, Casper	Sporting Pilgrimage (1st, lg8vo, red cl, 379p)	Harper	1894	Remington, F.	50-70	
Remington, F.	Stories of Peace & War (1st, 12mo, blue cl, 98p, 2pl)	Harper	1899	Remington, F.	80-120	
Remington, F.	Sundown Leflare (1st, 12mo, brown/gilt, 115p, 12pl)	Harper	1899	Remington, F.	130-170	
Custer, E.B.	Tenting on the Plains (1st, 702p, 11 b/w, gilt)	Webster	1887	Remington, F.	135-160	
Wister, O.	The Virginian (1st, red cl, p-o, 506p, teg, 10pl by...)	MacMillan	1911	Remington, F.	250-300	*
King, C.	To the Front (1st, 8vo, ibds, 260p, 4pl)	Harper	1908	Remington, F.	60-80	*
Remington, F.	Way of an Indian (1st, 12mo, red cl, 251p, p-o, 14pl)	Fox Duffield	1906	Remington, F.	100-150	
Hough, E.	Way to the West (1st, sm8vo, grey cl, 446p, 6pl)	Bobbs-Merrill	(1903)	Remington, F.	60-80	
Davis, R.H.	West From a Car Window (1st, 8vo, red cl, 242p)	Harper	1892	Remington, F.	90-135	
Bigelow, P.	White Man's Africa (1st, 8vo, 271p, 3pl by...)	Harper	1900	Remington, F.	50-80	
Lewis, A.H.	Wolfville (1st, 12mo, red cl, 337p, 18pl)	Stokes	(1897)	Remington, F.	90-130	
Lewis, A.H.	Wolfville Days (1st, 8vo, 311p, frn by...)	Stokes	(1902)	Remington, F.	50-70	
King, C.	Apache Princess (1st, 12mo, 328p, p-o, teg, 6pl)	Hobart	1903	Remington/Deming	35-50	

AUTHOR	TITLE	PUBLISHER	DATE	ARTIST	PRICE	LC
Rey, H.A.	Anybody at Home? (1st, ob8vo, [24]p, color)	Houghton	1942	Rey, H.A.	50-85	*
Rey, M.E.	Billy's Picture (1st, sm4to, ibds, [22]p, color)	Harper	(1948)	Rey, H.A.	65-90	*
Rey, H.A.	Cecily G. & the 9 Monkeys (1st AM, lg4to, 31p, color)	Houghton	1942	Rey, H.A.	70-100	*
Rey, H.A.	Curious George (1st, lg8vo, [55]p, color, pep)	Houghton	1941	Rey, H.A.	80-120	*
Rey, H.A.	Curious George Takes a Job (1st, 4to, 47p, color, pep)	Houghton	1947	Rey, H.A.	75-100	*
Brown, M.W.	Don't Frighten the Lion (1st {std}, sq4to, [26]p, p-o, 1-col)	Harper	(1942)	Rey, H.A.	70-100	*
Gilbert, P.T.	Egbert & his Marvelous Adventures (1st {std}, sm8vo, 103p, b/w)	Harper	(1944)	Rey, H.A.	35-50	*
Rey, H.A.	Elizabite (1st {std}, sq4to, ipcb, [32]p, color)	Harper	(1942)	Rey, H.A.	60-90	*
Rey, H.A.	Humpty Dumpty... (1st {std}, ob4to, [23]p, color)	Harper	(1943)	Rey, H.A.	80-120	*
Payne, E.	Katy No-Pocket (1st, 4to, [32]p, color, pep)	Houghton	1944	Rey, H.A.	45-65	*
Zolotow, C.	Park Book (1st {std}, sm ob4to, [32]p, color, pep)	Harper	(1944)	Rey, H.A.	100-150	R*
Brown, M.W.	Polite Penguin (1st {std}, sm4to, green cl, 31p, 2-color, pep)	Harper	(1941)	Rey, H.A.	50-80	*
Rey, M.E.	Pretzel (1st {std}-[1st bk.], 4to, [30]p, cloth, color)	Harper	(1944)	Rey, H.A.	70-100	*
Rey, M.E.	Pretzel & the Puppies (1st, lg8vo, ibds, [30]p, color)	Harper	(1946)	Rey, H.A.	35-60	*
Rey, H.A.	Raffy & the 9 Monkeys (1st, lg4to, 31p, ibds, color)	L: Chatto	1939	Rey, H.A.	90-135	
Rey, M.E.	Spotty (1st, sm4to, [30]p, ibds, p-o, color)	Harper	(1945)	Rey, H.A.	35-50	*
Rey, H.A.	Tit for Tat (1st {std}, sq4to, ipcb, [30]p, color)	Harper	(1942)	Rey, H.A.	60-100	*
Waldstein, H.F.	We Three Kings (1st {std}, ob4to, [23]p, color)	Harper	(1944)	Rey, H.A.	80-120	*
Dickens, C.	David Copperfield (1st, 4to, gilt, 572p, 20 ticp, pep)	Westminster Pr	(1911)	Reynolds, F.	160-225	
Dickens, C.	Mr. Pickwick... (4to, red/gilt, 21 ticp)	(NY & Lon)	[1911]	Reynolds, F.	165-200	
Dickens, C.	Old Curiosity Shop (1st, 4to, 359p, teg, red/gilt, 21 ticp)	L: Hodder	[1912]	Reynolds, F.	165-220	
Dickens, C.	Posthumous Papers/Pickwick Club (1st, 4to, gilt, 534p, 20 ticp)	Westminster Pr	(1912)	Reynolds, F.	150-200	
Bunyan, J.	Life & Death of Mr. Badman (1st, folio, ibds, teg, 12pl)	R.H. Russell	1900	Rhead Bros.	120-160	
Bunyan, J.	Life & Death of Mr. Badman (1st UK, folio, 143p, teg, 12pl)	L: Heinemann	1900	Rhead Bros.	100-150	
Bunyan, J.	Pilgrim's Progress (1st, folio, 184p, ibds, b/w)	Century	1898	Rhead Bros.	100-150	
Bunyan, J.	Pilgrim's Progress (1st UK, folio, gilt, 201p)	L: A. Pearson	[1898]	Rhead Bros.	120-160	
Aesopus	Aesop's Fables (1st, 8vo, 194p, color)	Harper	(1927)	Rhead, L.	25-40	*
N/A	Arabian Nights' Entertainment (1st, 8vo, 430p, p-o, 4cp, pep)	Harper	(1916)	Rhead, L.	35-60	
Conner, Ralph	Black Rock (1st, tan cl, 8vo, 322p, 8pl by...)	Revell	1900	Rhead, L.	20-35	
Craik, D.	Fairy Book (1st, 8vo, 403p, col frn)	Harper	(1922)	Rhead, L.	35-50	*
Grimm Bros.	Fairy Tales (1st, 8vo, 443p, b/w)	Harper	(1917)	Rhead, L.	35-50	*
Andersen, H.C.	Fairy Tales & Wonder Stories (1st, lg8vo, 442p, b/w, dep)	Harper	1914	Rhead, L.	65-90	*
Swift, J.	Gulliver's Travels (1st, 8vo, 350p, b/w, pep)	Harper	1913	Rhead, L.	30-45	*
Spyri, J.	Heidi (1st, lg8vo, 333p, col frn, 23pl, p-o)	Harper	(1925)	Rhead, L.	25-40	*
Morris, Wm.	History of Over Sea (1st, 4to, 28p, ipcb)	R.H. Russell	1902	Rhead, L.	120-160	
Tennyson, A.	Idylls of the King (1st, lg4to, [114]p, uncut, 24 woodcuts)	R.H. Russell	1898	Rhead, L.	100-145	
Stevenson, R.L.	Kidnapped (1st, 8vo, 301p, col frn, b/w, pep)	Harper	(1921)	Rhead, L.	25-45	*
Sudermann, H.	Magda (1st, 12mo, 161p, red/gilt, cvr by...)	Chi: Lamson	1896	Rhead, L.	70-100	
Brown, Alice	Meadow Grass (1st, 12mo, olive cl, 315p, cvr by...)	Copeland & Day	1895	Rhead, L.	65-90	
N/A	Psalms of David (1st, lg8vo, red cl, 16pl)	Revell	1900	Rhead, L.	65-100	
Rhead, Louis	Robin Hood (1st, 4to, p-o, b/w)	Harper	1912	Rhead, L.	65-80	
Wyss, J.D.	Swiss Family Robinson (1st, lg8vo, 602p, red cl, p-o)	Harper	1909	Rhead, L.	45-65	*
Lamb, C.	Tales from Shakespeare (1st, 8vo, 366p, b/w)	Harper	(1918)	Rhead, L.	25-45	*
Cooper, J.F.	The Deerslayer (1st, 8vo, black cl, p-o, 556p, 4cp)	Harper	(1926)	Rhead, L.	35-50	
Hughes, Thos.	Tom Brown's School Days (1st, 8vo, 376p, pict cl)	Harper	1911	Rhead, L.	50-65	
Stevenson, R.L.	Treasure Island (1st, 8vo, 288p, 35pl, pep)	Harper	(1915)	Rhead, L.	35-50	*
Grimm Bros.	Hansel & Gretel (1st, sq12mo, [60]p, color)	McLoughlin	(1943)	Rice, A.	30-50	*
Russell, W.	Bending of the Twig (1st, 297p, p-o, cvr by...)	Dodd	1903	Richards, A.M.	20-35	
Richards, A.M.	New Alice/Old Wonderland (1st, 8vo, 309p, teg, red/gilt, b/w)	Lippincott	1895	Richards, A.M.	120-180	
Crockett, S.R.	Red Axe (1st, 8vo, 421p)	L: Smith Elder	1898	Richards, F.	25-40	*
Bangs, J.K.	Idiot at Home (1st, 12mo, 314p, teg, uncut)	Harper	1900	Richards, F.T.	35-50	*
Bangs, J.K.	The Idiot (1st, 12mo, 115p, 8pl)	Harper	1895	Richards, F.T.	30-45	
Lindsay, V.	Johnny Appleseed (1st, 12mo, green cl, 144p, color)	MacMillan	1928	Richards, G.	45-70	
Andersen, H.C.	Steadfast Tin Soldier (1st, sq12mo, ibds, unpag, color)	MacMillan	1927	Richards, G.M.	45-65	
Alcott, L.M.	Eight Cousins (1st, sm8vo, 292p, 8pl)	Little/Brown	1904	Richards, H.R.	25-40	
Bailey, A.W.	Roberta and her Brothers (1st, 8vo, 310p, 4pl)	Little/Brown	1906	Richards, H.R.	20-30	*
Alcott, L.M.	Rose in Bloom (1st, 8vo, teg, 344p, 8pl)	Little/Brown	1904	Richards, H.R.	25-40	
Vredenburg, E.	Golden Locks & Pretty Frocks (8vo, ibds, p-o, 12cp)	L: R. Tuck	(1914)	Richardson, A.	160-200	*
Richardson, E.	Doors... (1st, 8vo, 160p, 12cp)	L: Headley	[1909]	Richardson, E.	120-160	*
Richardson, E.	Songs of Near & Far Away (1st, 4to, tan cl, 80p, color)	L: Cassell	1900	Richardson, E.	100-150	*
Richardson, E.	Sun-Moon & Stars... (1st, 4to, green cl, unpag, b/w)	L: Bodley Head	1899	Richardson, E.	100-150	
Collodi, C.	Adventures of Pinocchio (8vo, 259p, p-o, 8cp)	Winston	(1920)	Richardson, F.	40-65	
Lear, E.	Alphabet Book (1st, ob8vo, ibds, [55]p, color)	Reilly/Britton	(1915)	Richardson, F.	75-120	
Richardson, F.	Book for Children (1st, ob4to, 107p, pep, p-o, 35cp)	Donohue	(1938)	Richardson, F.	80-100	
Richardson, F.	Book of Drawings (1st, sm folio, [106]p, b/w, grey bds)	Lakeside Pr.	1899	Richardson, F.	350-500	
Asbjornsen, P.C.	East o/t Sun/West o/t Moon (1st, 12mo, 218p, 9cp)	Row/Peterson	(1912)	Richardson, F.	50-80	*
Andersen, H.C.	Fairy Tales (1st, 8vo, p-o, 276p, black/gilt, pep, 4cp)	Winston	(1926)	Richardson, F.	40-60	
N/A	Gingerbread Boy (ob12mo, 32p, bds, p-o)	Winston	(1918)	Richardson, F.	35-50	
Green, Allen A.	Good Fairy & the Bunnies (1st, ob4to, ibds, 140p, 11cp)	McClurg	1906	Richardson, F.	200-300	
Herben, B.S.	Jack O'Health, Peg O'Joy (1st, 12mo, 39p, 10cp)	Scribner	(1921)	Richardson, F.	65-85	
Faulkner, Georgene	Little Peachling... (1st, 4to, 91p, orange cl, color, pep)	Volland	(1928)	Richardson, F.	60-80	
Mother Goose	Mother Goose (4to, 108p, cp)	Donohue	(1915)	Richardson, F.	70-85	

AUTHOR	TITLE	PUBLISHER	DATE	ARTIST	PRICE	LC
Mother Goose	Mother Goose (1st, lg4to, grey/gilt, [119]p, p-o, color)	Volland	(1915)	Richardson, F.	130-185	
Mother Goose	Mother Goose (1st, folio, ibds, color)	Volland	(1921)	Richardson, F.	100-150	
Chambers, Rbt.	Mountain-Land (1st, lg8vo, ibds, 122p, 8cp)	Appleton	1906	Richardson, F.	70-100	
Various	Old Old Tales Retold (1st, ob4vo, [108]p, blue/gilt, color, pep)	Volland	(1923)	Richardson, F.	100-170	
Collodi, C.	Pinocchio (1st, 8vo, 167p, gilt, p-o, 21cp, pep)	Winston	(1923)	Richardson, F.	70-120	*
Baum, L.F.	Queen Zixi of Ix (1st [1], 8vo, 303p, green cl, 16cp)	Century	1905	Richardson, F.	400-500	
Stockton, Frank	Queen's Museum (1st, 4to, 219p, gilt, p-o, teg, 10cp, pep, SC)	Scribner	1906	Richardson, F.	130-180	
Lang, A.	Red Fairy Book (1st, 8vo, 386p, gilt, p-o, 4cp)	Winston	(1930)	Richardson, F.	35-50	
Olcott, F.J.	Red Indian Fairy Book (1st, 8vo, 338p, col frn, 5pl)	Houghton	1917	Richardson, F.	65-80	
Fry, J.H.	Revolt Against Beauty (1st, 8vo, 212p, designs by...)	Putnam	1934	Richardson, F.	25-40	*
Faulkner, Georgene	Road to Enchantment (1st, 8vo, 312p, p-o, 8cp)	Sears	(1929)	Richardson, F.	80-120	
Faulkner, Georgene	Squeaky & the Scare Box (1st, 8vo, [32]p, ibds, 4cp, pep)	Grosset/Dunlap	(1931)	Richardson, F.	50-80	
Faulkner, Georgene	Story Lady's Christmas Stories (1st, 8vo, 93p, red cl, 5cp, pep)	Sears	(1927)	Richardson, F.	30-45	*
Faulkner, Georgene	Story Lady's Italian Tales (1st, 8vo, 95p, gilt, uncut, pep, 5cp)	Chi: Daughaday	(1916)	Richardson, F.	65-80	*
Faulkner, Georgene	White Elephant (1st, 8vo, ibds, 92p, 10 fp color, pep)	Volland	(1929)	Richardson, F.	65-85	R
Hawthorne, N.	Wonder Book... (1st, 8vo, p-o, 403p, red/gilt, 4cp, pep)	Winston	(1930)	Richardson, F.	35-50	
Forbush, Wm. B.	Wonder Book/Myths & Legends (lg8vo, blue cl, p-o, 3cp, 11 b/w)	Winston	(1928)	Richardson, F.	20-30	*
Krauss, Ruth	Great Duffy (1st, sm4to, [32]p, color)	Harper	(1946)	Richter	30-45	*
Wilde, O.	House of Pomegranates (1st, lg8vo, gilt, 158p, uncut)	L: Osgood	1891	Ricketts, C.	400-600	
Symonds, J.A.	In the Key of Blue (1st, 8vo, 302p, blue/gilt, cvr by...)	L: Matthews	1893	Ricketts, C.	125-200	
Shaw, G.B.	St. Joan (1st, folio, ibds, 182p, p-o, teg, 16 ticp)	L: Constable	(1924)	Ricketts, C.	180-250	
Wilde, O.	Woman of No Importance (1st, pink/gilt, cvr by...)	L: J. Lane	1894	Ricketts, C.	260	
Tomlins, W.	Child's Garden of Song (1st, lg8vo, 72p, red/gilt, color)	McClurg	1895	Ricketts, E.	100-150	
Akers, Floyd	Boy Fortune Hunters in Yucatan (1st, 8vo, 343p, tan cl, frn by)	Reilly/Britton	(1910)	Rieman, G.A.	200-300	
Brett, Edna P.	Circus Day... (1st, 12mo, 64p, 8 fp color, ibds)	Rand/McNally	1922	Riley, G.C.	20-30	
Hawes, C.B.	Dark Frigate (1st, 8vo, yellow cl, 247p, b/w, PPP, NM)	Atl. Month Pr.	(1923)	Ripley, A.L.	65-95	
Donaldson, Lois	Runzel-Punzel (1st, 8vo, yellow cl, p-o, 16p, color, cep)	Whitman	1933	Ritter, M.	45-60	
Walter, E.D.	Bugs (1st, lg4to, wraps, [16]p, color)	Whitman	1931	Roberts, H.M.	35-50	
Farrow, G.E.	Mysterious Voyage (1st, 8vo, 160p, 32 illus)	L: Partridge	[1910]	Roberts, K.M.	45-60	*
Robertson, W.G.	Baby's Day Book (1st, lg8vo, 127p, grey cl, col frn, b/w)	L: J. Lane	1908	Robertson, W.G.	145-200	
Robertson, W.G.	Gold, Frankincense & Myrrh (1st, 4to, blue cl, 152p, 12cp)	L: J. Lane	1907	Robertson, W.G.	185-265	
Scott-Gatty	I Wonder Why? (lg4to, 72p, bds, p-o, 16 ticp)	L: Collins	1920	Robertson, W.G.	130-170	
Robertson, W.G.	Masque of May Morning (1st, 4to, green cl, 62p, 12cp)	L: J. Lane	1904	Robertson, W.G.	180-250	
Chesterton, G.K.	Napoleon of Notting Hill (1st, 8vo, uncut, 301p, 8pl)	L: J. Lane	1904	Robertson, W.G.	150-185	
Cheatham, G.	Nursery Garland (1st, lg4to, ibds, 171p, 14cp)	Schirmer	(1917)	Robertson, W.G.	130-165	
N/A	Old English Songs & Dances (1st, sm folio, [62]p, ibds, color)	L: Longmans	1902	Robertson, W.G.	250-450	
N/A	Old English Songs & Dances (folio, ibds, color)	L: Hamish	[1910]	Robertson, W.G.	200-300	
Ewing, J.H.	Old Fashioned Fairy Tales (1st, 12mo, 125p, 8cp, pep)	L: G. Bell	(1919)	Robertson, W.G.	120-160	
Robertson, W.G.	Pinkie & the Fairies (1st, 12mo, 146p, 6 fp b/w)	L: Heinemann	1909	Robertson, W.G.	120-160	
Grahame, K.	Wind in the Willows (1st AM, 8vo, grn/glt, 302p, teg, frn by...)	Scribner	1908	Robertson, W.G.	350-500	
Grahame, K.	Wind in the Willows (1st, 8vo, 302p, teg, blue/gilt, frn by)	L: Methuen	(1908)	Robertson, W.G.	500-700	
Robertson, W.G.	Yen of Songs/Baby in a Garden (1st, 8vo, 111p)	L: J. Lane	1906	Robertson, W.G.	130-165	*
Andersen, H.C.	Andersen in German (1st, 8vo, 219p, beige cl, b/w)	L: J.M. Dent	1902	Robinson Bros.	200-285	
Andersen, H.C.	Fairy Tales (1st, 12mo, 539p, col frn, pl)	L: Dent	1899	Robinson Bros.	120-170	*
Andersen, H.C.	Fairy Tales (1st {this fmt}, 16mo, 312p, 12 b/w)	L: Dent	1901	Robinson Bros.	100-140	*
Bell, J.J.	Jack of All Trades (1st, 4to, brown cl, 64p, 32cp)	L: J. Lane	1900	Robinson Bros.	245-300	
Sage, B.	Rhymes of If & Why (1st, 4to, 31p, ibds, 4cp)	Duffield	1927	Robinson, B.	70-90	
Various	Adventures of Odysseus (1st, 8vo, 227p, green/gilt, teg, 13pl)	Dutton	(1900)	Robinson, C.	165-220	
Aesopus	Aesop's Fables (1st {1st bk}, 16mo, [60]p, red/gilt, teg, pep)	L: J.M. Dent	1895	Robinson, C.	150-200	
Carroll, L.	Alice/Wonderland (1st, sm4to, teg, gilt, 179p, 8cp)	L: Cassell	(1907)	Robinson, C.	400-600	
Carroll, L.	Alice/Wonderland (lg8vo, [new ed.], 8cp)	L: Cassell	1928	Robinson, C.	120-165	
Copeland, W.	Awful Airship (1st, ob16mo, 62p, 30cp)	L: Blackie	[1906]	Robinson, C.	200-280	
Pope, J.	Babes & Beasts (1st, 8vo, ibds, unpag, color)	L: Blackie	[1912]	Robinson, C.	150-220	*
Pope, J.	Babes & Birds (1st, 8vo, ibds, unpag, 17cp)	L: Blackie	[1910]	Robinson, C.	170-240	
Pope, J.	Babes & Birds (1st AM, 8vo, ibds, 17cp)	Caldwell	[1910]	Robinson, C.	150-220	
Copeland, W.	Babes & Blossoms (1st AM, sm8vo, ipcb, 16cp)	Caldwell	[1908]	Robinson, C.	165-230	
Copeland, W.	Babes & Blossoms (1st, 8vo, ibds, [66]p, 16cp, pep)	L: Blackie	(1908)	Robinson, C.	180-275	
Pope, J.	Baby Scouts (1st, ob 16mo, unpag)	L: Blackie	[1911]	Robinson, C.	125-160	*
Bridgman, Clare	Bairn's Coronation Book (24mo, 120p, 44cp)	L: Dent	[1902]	Robinson, C.	80-120	
France, A.	Bee (1st, 8vo, grey bds, [128]p, teg, 17 ticp)	L: Dent	1912	Robinson, C.	200-300	
Jerrold, W.C.	Big Book of Fables (1st, lg8vo, 293p, teg, red cl, 28cp, pep)	L: Blackie	1912	Robinson, C.	265-340	
Jerrold, W.C.	Big Book of Fairy Tales (1st AM, 4to, 344p, 12cp)	Caldwell	(1911)	Robinson, C.	200-300	
Jerrold, W.C.	Big Book of Fairy Tales (1st, 4to, 344p, gilt, AEG, 12cp)	L: Blackie	1911	Robinson, C.	280-350	
Jerrold, W.C.	Big Book of Nursery Rhymes (1st, 4to, red/gilt, 320p, AEG, 18cp)	L: Blackie	[1903]	Robinson, C.	275-400	
Robinson, C.	Black Bunnies (1st, 16mo, blue/gilt, silhouettes)	L: Blackie	(1907)	Robinson, C.	250-400	*
Copeland, W.	Black Cat Book (1st, 8vo, unpag)	L: Blackie	[1905]	Robinson, C.	100-140	*
N/A	Black Doggies (16mo, red cloth, silhouttes)	L: Blackie	[1907]	Robinson, C.	250-350	
Bridgman, Clare	Book of Days for Little Ones (1st, 12mo, 3cp)	L: Dent	1901	Robinson, C.	100-140	
Bridgman, Clare	Book of Shops (1st, sq12mo, 120p, color)	L: Dent	1902	Robinson, C.	120-170	
Copeland, W.	Book of the Zoo (1st, 16mo, 120p)	L: Dent	1902	Robinson, C.	75-100	*
Stables, Gordon	Boy's Book of Battleships (lg4to, ibds, 16 color)	L: Blackie	[1909]	Robinson, C.	120-165	
Stevenson, A.M.	Bridget's Fairies (1st, sm8vo, p-o, 131p, b/w)	L: R.T.S.	(1919)	Robinson, C.	130-200	

AUTHOR	TITLE	PUBLISHER	DATE	ARTIST	PRICE	LC
Arkwright, R.	Brownikins & Other Fancies (1st, 4to, p-o, [82]p, 5 ticp, pep)	L: Wells/Gard.	[1910]	Robinson, C.	250-350	
Setoun, G.	Child World (1st, 8vo, AEG, 174p, uncut, 14pl)	L: J. Lane	1896	Robinson, C.	130-180	
Morris, Alice T.	Child's Book of Empire (1st, 4to, unpag)	L: Blackie	[1914]	Robinson, C.	150-200	*
Sharp, E.	Child's Christmas (1st, lg8vo, 227p, orang/gilt, AEG, 38 color)	L: Blackie	(1906)	Robinson, C.	180-245	
Sharp, E.	Child's Christmas (1st AM, lg8vo, 227p, color, pep)	Caldwell	[1907]	Robinson, C.	165-220	
Stevenson, R.L.	Child's Garden of Verses (1st UK, 8vo, 136p, AEG, gilt, b/w)	L: J. Lane	1895	Robinson, C.	150-185	
Stevenson, R.L.	Child's Garden of Verses (1st, 8vo, teg, uncut, gilt, 137p)	Scribner	1895	Robinson, C.	220-260	R
Stevenson, R.L.	Child's Garden of Verses (1st {col ed}, 8vo, glt, teg, 8cp, pep)	L: Bodley Head	(1908)	Robinson, C.	180-220	
Rhys, Grace (ed.)	Children's Garland of Verse (8vo, 296p, 8cp)	L: J.M. Dent	1921	Robinson, C.	130-180	*
Wallis, I.H.	Cloud Kingdom (1st, 12mo, green/gilt, 174p, teg, 18pl)	L: J. Lane	(1905)	Robinson, C.	165-250	
Marc, E.	Doris & David All Alone (1st, 8vo, 259p, red cl, 4cp, pep)	L: Hutchinson	(1922)	Robinson, C.	80-100	
Cesaresco, E.	Fairies' Fountain (1st, 8vo, 268p, blue/gilt, col frn, 15pl)	L: Fairbanks	1908	Robinson, C.	180-225	
Grimm Bros.	Fairy Tales (1st, 8vo, 356p, gilt, p-o, pep, 4cp)	L: Nister	[1910]	Robinson, C.	190-265	
Perrault, C.	Fairy Tales (1st, 12mo, p-o, 128p, 8cp)	L: Dent	(1913)	Robinson, C.	90-125	
Copeland, W.	Farm Book (1st, 16mo, 120p)	Dent/Dutton	1901	Robinson, C.	65-80	*
Jerrold, D.	Fireside Saints (1st, 12mo, teg, 109p, gilt, col frn, b/w, pep)	L: Blackie	1903	Robinson, C.	70-100	
Mord, W.	Four Champions/Great Britain & Ireland (1st, 4to, ibds, 16cp)	L: T.F. Unwin	[1905]	Robinson, C.	220-300	
Handasyde	Four Gardens (1st AM, 8vo, 161p, purple/gilt, 8cp, pep)	Lippincott	1912	Robinson, C.	80-100	
Wilde, O.	Happy Prince (1st, 4to, teg, gilt, 134p, 12 ticp, dep)	L: Duckworth	(1913)	Robinson, C.	600-800	
Wilde, O.	Happy Prince (1st AM, 4to, 134p, gilt, teg, 12 ticp, pep)	Putnam	(1913)	Robinson, C.	400-600	
MacGregor, B.	King Longbeard (1st, 8vo, 262p, blue/gilt, 12pl)	L: J. Lane	1898	Robinson, C.	180-220	
Rand, W.B.	Lilliput Lyrics (1st, 8vo, 330p, gilt, col frn, b/w)	L: J. Lane	1899	Robinson, C.	70-100	
Tynan, Kath.	Little Book of Courtesies (1st, 12mo, teg, 57p, gilt, col frn)	L: Dent	1906	Robinson, C.	70-100	
Dearmer, P.	Little Lives of the Saints (1st, 12mo, 144p, green cl, dep)	L: Wells/Gard.	1900	Robinson, C.	70-100	*
Field, E.	Lullaby Land (1st, 8vo, teg, 229p, gilt)	Scribner	1897	Robinson, C.	120-180	
Field, E.	Lullaby Land (1st UK, sm8vo, 229p, gilt, AEG)	L: J. Lane	1898	Robinson, C.	120-160	
Copeland, W.	Mad Motor (1st, ob24mo, ibds, color)	L: Blackie	(1906)	Robinson, C.	170-200	
Lowry, H.D.	Make-Believe (1st, 8vo, 177p, teg, green/gilt)	L: J. Lane	1896	Robinson, C.	90-140	
Fielding-Hall, H.	Margaret's Book (1st AM, 4to, 283p, teg, gilt, 12 ticp)	Stokes	(1913)	Robinson, C.	180-260	
Fielding-Hall, H.	Margaret's Book (1st, 4to, AEG, red/gilt, 283p, 12 ticp)	L: Hutchinson	(1913)	Robinson, C.	240-350	
Coleridge, C.R.	Minstrel Dick (1st, 8vo, 288p, 3pl)	L: Wells/Gard.	1896	Robinson, C.	50-80	*
Mother Goose	Mother Goose Nursery Rhymes (1st, 8vo, 159p)	L: Collins	[1928]	Robinson, C.	70-100	*
Burn, J.H.	Mother's Book of Song (1st, 8vo, 216p, blue/gilt, teg, b/w)	L: Wells/Gard.	[1902]	Robinson, C.	130-180	
Bell, J.J.	New Noah's Ark (1st, 4to, brown cl, 64p, color)	L: J. Lane	1899	Robinson, C.	200-240	
Jerrold, W.C.	Nonsense Nonsense! (1st, 4to, [68]p, ibds, 30cp)	L: Blackie	1902	Robinson, C.	275-400	
Milne, A.A.	Once On a Time (1st AM, 8vo, 358, col frn, pep)	Putnam	1922	Robinson, C.	100-140	
Milne, A.A.	Once On a Time (1st, 12mo, gilt, 269p, col frn, pep)	L: Hodder	[1922]	Robinson, C.	150-180	
Thurston, E.T.	Open Window (1st, lg8vo, 287p, blue/gilt, 4cp)	L: Chapman	1913	Robinson, C.	85-130	
Castle, A.& E.	Our Sentimental Garden (1st AM, 8vo, gilt, 304p, 8 ticp, pep)	Lippincott	1914	Robinson, C.	100-165	
Castle, A.& E.	Our Sentimental Garden (1st, lg8vo, 304p, gilt, 8 ticp, pep)	L: Heinemann	(1914)	Robinson, C.	140-200	
Stacpoole, H.D.	Pierrette (1st, 8vo, 294p, teg, b/w)	L: J. Lane	1900	Robinson, C.	80-100	
N/A	Prince Ahmed/Fairy Perie Banou (1st, 8vo, 118p, bds, p-o, 5cp)	L: Gay/Hancock	(1915)	Robinson, C.	125-160	
Nella	Prince Babillon (1st, 8vo, 131p, uncut, gilt, color)	Kennerley	[1910]	Robinson, C.	120-165	
Spicer, M.D.	Rainbows (1st, 8vo, 44p, white cl, p-o, b/w)	L: A. Melrose	1913	Robinson, C.	80-100	
Canton, Wm.	Reign of King Herla (1st, 8vo, AEG, 367p, col frn)	L: J.M. Dent	(1900)	Robinson, C.	100-150	
N/A	Reign of King Oberon (1st, 8vo, 338p, col frn, pep)	L: Dent	(1902)	Robinson, C.	100-140	
Gibbon, J.M.	Reign of Old King Cole (8vo, pict cl, 338p)	Dutton	(1911)	Robinson, C.	140-170	
Irving, W.	Rip Van Winkle (lg8vo, 68p, col frn, cp)	Stokes	[1915]	Robinson, C.	90-160	*
Jerrold, W.C.	Road, Rail & Sea (1st, 4to, ibds, unpag, 10cp)	L: Blackie	[1906]	Robinson, C.	180-250	
Omar Khayyam	Rubaiyat... (32mo, leather, teg, 86p, 3 ticp)	L: Collins	[1910]	Robinson, C.	65-80	
Omar Khayyam	Rubaiyat... (1st, 4to, 56p, 4 ticp)	L: Collins	[1929]	Robinson, C.	100-160	*
Unknown	Rule Britannia (4to, ibds, 66p, 8 fp color)	L: Hodder	[1916]	Robinson, C.	200-300	
Radcliffe, W.	Saint's Garden (1st, sm8vo, 150p, green/gilt, 8pl)	L: SPCK	1927	Robinson, C.	100-140	
Burnett, F.H.	Secret Garden (1st, 8vo, green/gilt, 306p, 8cp, pep)	L: Heinemann	1911	Robinson, C.	400-600	
Shelley, P.B.	Sensitive Plant (1st AM, 4to, 127p, gilt, teg, 18 ticp)	Heinn/Lipp.	(1911)	Robinson, C.	220-350	
Shelley, P.B.	Sensitive Plant (1st, 4to, teg, 127p, gilt, 18 ticp)	L: Heinemann	(1911)	Robinson, C.	280-400	
Bridgman, Clare	Shopping Day (1st, 16mo, 120p)	Dent/Dutton	1902	Robinson, C.	65-80	*
Baring-Gould, S.	Siegfried (1st, 8vo, red/gilt, 351p, col frn, 10 fp b/w)	L: Dean	1904	Robinson, C.	120-185	
Robinson, C.	Silly Submarine (1st, ob16mo, ibds, 30 color, pep)	L: Blackie	(1906)	Robinson, C.	170-220	
Fouque, La Motte	Sintram and his Companions (1st, 12mo, 12pl)	L: Dent	1900	Robinson, C.	140-200	
Unknown	Soldiers of the King (4to, 66p, ibds, 8cp)	L: Hodder	[1916]	Robinson, C.	200-300	
Shakespeare, Wm.	Songs & Sonnets (1st, lg8vo, 240p, blue/gilt, 12 ticp, pep)	L: Duckworth	(1915)	Robinson, C.	240-320	
Shakespeare, Wm.	Songs & Sonnets (1st AM, 4to, 240p, blue/gilt, 12 ticp, pep)	McKay	[1915]	Robinson, C.	180-275	
Maunder, I.	Songs of Happy Children (12mo, 10p, b/w)	L: Clark	[1908]	Robinson, C.	50-70	
Blake, Wm.	Songs of Innocence (1st, 12mo, 56p, teg, gilt, 7cp)	L: Dent	(1911)	Robinson, C.	180-200	
Matheson, Annie	Songs of Love & Praise (1st, 8vo, unpag, designs by...)	L: J.M. Dent	1907	Robinson, C.	65-80	*
Sharp, E.	Story o/t Weathercock (1st AM, 4to, 258p, teg, red/gilt, 16cp)	Caldwell	[1907]	Robinson, C.	160-225	
Sharp, E.	Story o/t Weathercock (1st, 4to, 258p, red/gilt, AEG, 16cp, pep)	L: Blackie	(1907)	Robinson, C.	200-280	
Garstin, N.	Suitors of Aprille (1st, 8vo, teg, 212p, 19pl)	L: J. Lane	1900	Robinson, C.	100-160	
Gullick, M.E.	Teddy's Year with the Fairies (1st, lg8vo, 176p, ibds, 3cp, pep)	L: R.T.S.	(1920)	Robinson, C.	120-170	*
Meynell, A.	The Children (1st, 12mo, gilt, 96p, title page by...)	L: J. Lane	1897	Robinson, C.	70-100	
Minnion, W.J.	Topsy Turvey (1st, 4to, 72p)	L: Connoisseur	1913	Robinson, C.	140-200	*

AUTHOR	TITLE	PUBLISHER	DATE	ARTIST	PRICE	LC
Syrett, Netta	Vanishing Princess (1st, 8vo, 93p)	L: D. Nutt	[1910]	Robinson, C.	90-130	*
Girvin/Cosens	Wee Men (1st, 12mo, p-o, 160p, 4cp)	L: Hutchinson	[1923]	Robinson, C.	140-180	
Sharp, E.	What Happened at Christmas (1st, 4to, unpag)	L: Blackie	[1915]	Robinson, C.	130-170	*
Dunbar, J.	Young Hopeful (1st, 8vo, 78p, blue/gilt, b/w)	L: H. Jenkins	1932	Robinson, C.	80-100	*
Maeterlinck, M.	Blue Bird (1st AM, 4to, teg, blue/gilt, 211p, 25 ticp)	Dodd	1911	Robinson, F.C.	120-165	
Trine, Ralph W.	In Tune with the Infinite (1st, 8vo, ibds, 254p, 8 ticp)	L: Foulis	(1926)	Robinson, F.C.	70-100	*
Webling, P.	Saints & their Stories (1st, 8vo, grey cl, 312p, 7 ticp, pep)	L: J. Nisbet	[1914]	Robinson, F.C.	70-100	
Chesterton, G.K.	St. Francis of Assissi (1st, sm8vo, 185p, brwn/gilt, p-o, 7 ticp)	L: Hodder	[1926]	Robinson, F.C.	70-100	
Carroll, L.	Alice/Wonderland (1st, 8vo, 201p, blue/gilt, 6cp)	L: C.H. Kelly	(1916)	Robinson, G.	120-170	
Carroll, L.	Alice/Wonderland (1st AM, lg8vo, p-o, 48p, 4cp)	NY: S. Gabriel	(1916)	Robinson, G.	90-140	*
Andersen, H.C.	Fairy Tales (1st, 8vo, p-o, 513p, 12cp)	L: Chambers	[1917]	Robinson, G.	120-165	
Byron, May	Little Brown Rooster (1st, 4to, p-o, orange cl, 6cp)	Nelson	1928	Robinson, G.	50-80	
Malone, H.	Lost Fairy Tales (1st, 8vo, gilt, 288p, 8cp)	L: C.H. Kelly	(1915)	Robinson, G.	65-85	
Leigh, M.C.	Love Songs & Verses (1st, sm4to, 65p, teg, 4pl)	L: Humphreys	1913	Robinson, G.	50-90	
DeJong, Meindert	Cat that Walked a Week (1st {std}, 8vo, grey cl, 148p, 13 fp bw)	Harper	1943	Robinson, J.	30-45	*
Weil, Ann	Very First Day (1st, sm8vo, red cl, [32]p, 1-color)	Appleton/Cent.	(1946)	Robinson, J.	25-40	*
Smith, G.	Little Girl & Phillip (1st, lg sq8vo, 187p, 8cp)	Harper	1902	Robinson, R.	40-65	*
Sill, L.M.	Sunnyfield (1st, 8vo, 228p, 4pl)	Harper	1909	Robinson, R.	25-40	
Jackson, G.E.	Wee Winkles & her Friends (1st, 8vo, 155p, 8pl)	Harper	1907	Robinson, R.	35-50	*
Carroll, L.	Alice/Wonderland (8vo, 190p, red/gilt, 30pl by...)	L: Collins	[1910]	Robinson, T.H.	100-135	
Haydon, A.L.	Book of Robin Hood (8vo, green cl, 263p, 12cp)	L: Warne	[1931]	Robinson, T.H.	45-60	
Macy, S.B.	Book of the Kingdom (1st, 4to, 388p, col frn)	L: Longmans	1912	Robinson, T.H.	70-100	*
Canton, Wm.	Child's Book of Saints (1st [new ed.], 8vo, 257p, 19pl)	L: J.M. Dent	1902	Robinson, T.H.	50-75	*
Gaskell, Mrs.	Cranford (1st, 8vo, 316p, b/w)	L: Bliss Sands	1896	Robinson, T.H.	35-50	*
N/A	Fairy Tales/Arabian Nights (1st, 12mo, 287p, col frn, 12pl)	L: Dent	1899	Robinson, T.H.	65-80	*
Oxenham, E.J.	Goblin Island (1st, 8vo, 316p, p-o, col frn)	L: Collins	[1907]	Robinson, T.H.	50-80	*
Creswick, Paul	Hastings the Pirate (1st, 8vo, 303p)	Nister/Dutton	(1902)	Robinson, T.H.	45-60	*
Boult, K.F.	Heroes of the Norselands (1st, 8vo, 211p, 9pl)	L: Dent	1903	Robinson, T.H.	45-60	*
Creswick, Paul	In Alfred's Days (sm8vo, teg, uncut, 304p, 18pl)	L: Nister	[1900]	Robinson, T.H.	40-60	
Various	Legends from River & Mountain (1st, 8vo, 328p, b/w)	L: G. Allen	1896	Robinson, T.H.	75-100	
Pollard, E.F.	Little Chief (1st, sm8vo, teg, uncut, 236p, 6pl)	L: Nister	(1901)	Robinson, T.H.	30-45	
Rinder, F.	Old World Japan (1st, 8vo, blue cl, teg, uncut, 195p, 15pl)	L: G. Allen	1895	Robinson, T.H.	65-90	
Creswick, Paul	Robin Hood & his Adventures (1st, 8vo, 312p, 4cp)	Nister/Dutton	(1902)	Robinson, T.H.	50-70	
Omar Khayyam	Rubaiyat... (1st, 8vo, 147p, AEG, grey cl, color)	Nister/Dutton	[1907]	Robinson, T.H.	70-100	
Hawthorne, N.	Scarlet Letter (1st, 8vo, AEG, blue bds, 8pl)	L: Bliss Sands	1897	Robinson, T.H.	65-90	
Sterne, Laurence	Sentimental Journey/France & Italy (1st, 12mo, blue/gilt, AEG)	L: Bliss Sands	1897	Robinson, T.H.	65-80	
Wyss, J.D.	Swiss Family Robinson (1st AM, 4to, red cl, 25 ticp)	Hodder	[1913]	Robinson, T.H.	80-120	
Wyss, J.D.	Swiss Family Robinson (1st, sm4to, 431p, teg, red/gilt, 25 ticp)	L: H. Milford	[1913]	Robinson, T.H.	100-150	
Wyss, J.D.	Swiss Family Robinson (8vo, 436p, color, pep)	Garden City	(1931)	Robinson, T.H.	30-50	*
Marsh, Lewis	Tales of the Homeland (1st, 8vo, buckram, 199p, 6cp)	L: Hodder	[1911]	Robinson, T.H.	65-80	*
Kingsley, C.	The Heroes (1st, 8vo, AEG, 296p, 6cp, pep)	L: Nister	[1899]	Robinson, T.H.	70-100	
Spenser, Edmund	Una & Red Cross Knight (1st, 8vo, 264p)	L: J.M. Dent	1905	Robinson, T.H.	50-65	*
Creswick, Paul	Under the Black Raven (1st, 8vo, 303p, teg, b/w pl)	Nister/Dutton	[1901]	Robinson, T.H.	45-60	*
Aguilar, G.	Vale of Cedars (1st, 8vo, 428p, uncut, teg, col frn, 11pl, pep)	L: Dent	1902	Robinson, T.H.	50-70	
Robinson, W.H.	Absurdities (1st, lg4to, ibds, fp b/w illus)	L: Hutchinson	[1934]	Robinson, W.H.	120-165	
Cervantes	Adventures of Don Quixote (1st, 8vo, 532p, teg, uncut, b/w, pep)	Dent/Dutton	1902	Robinson, W.H.	100-140	
Robinson, W.H.	Adventures of Uncle Lubin (1st, sm4to, 117p, col frn)	L: Richards	1902	Robinson, W.H.	450-600	
Robinson, W.H.	Adventures of Uncle Lubin (sm4to, ibds, 7 b/w, later, DJ)	L: Chatto	(1934)	Robinson, W.H.	150-200	
Robinson, W.H.	Bill the Minder (1st AM, 4to, p-o, 254p, gilt, 16 ticp)	Holt	1912	Robinson, W.H.	300-450	
Robinson, W.H.	Bill the Minder (1st, 4to, green/gilt, 255p, p-o, 16 ticp)	L: Constable	1912	Robinson, W.H.	400-600	
Robinson, W.H.	Book of Goblins (1st, 4to, 239p, blue/gilt, 7cp)	L: Hutchinson	(1934)	Robinson, W.H.	300-425	
Robinson, W.H.	Child's Arabian Nights (2nd, 4to, ibds, 84p, 12cp)	L: Richards	1904	Robinson, W.H.	500-700	
Kipling, R.	Collected Verse of... (1st, 4to, red/gilt, 392p, teg, 17 ticp)	Doubleday/Page	1910	Robinson, W.H.	180-260	
Shakespeare, Wm.	Comedy of the Twelfth Night (1st, 4to, green/gilt, 40 ticp)	L: Hodder	[1908]	Robinson, W.H.	200-300	
Andersen, H.C.	Danish Fairy Tales (1st {1st bk.}, 8vo, red/gilt, 332p, 16pl)	L: Bliss Sands	1897	Robinson, W.H.	200-250	
Kipling, R.	Dead King (1st, 8vo, 48p, wraps, designs by...)	L: Hodder	[1910]	Robinson, W.H.	120-170	
Cervantes	Don Quixote (8vo, red/gilt, 614p, 16 b/w)	Dodd	1925	Robinson, W.H.	70-90	
Andersen, H.C.	Fairy Tales (1st AM, 4to, red/gilt, 16 ticp)	Holt	1913	Robinson, W.H.	200-250	
Andersen, H.C.	Fairy Tales (1st, 4to, red/gilt, 289p, 16 ticp)	L: Constable	1913	Robinson, W.H.	280-400	
Andersen, H.C.	Fairy Tales (4to, 320p, red/gilt, 16 ticp)	L: Hodder	[1913]	Robinson, W.H.	160-200	
Andersen, H.C.	Fairy Tales (1st {this pub}, sm4to, 355p, color)	Houghton	1931	Robinson, W.H.	65-80	*
Rouse, W.H.D.	Giant Crab (1st, 8vo, 134p, 7pl)	L: D. Nutt	1897	Robinson, W.H.	180-240	
Robinson, W.H.	Humours of Golf (1st AM, 4to, ibds, 50p, b/w)	Dodd	1923	Robinson, W.H.	100-165	
Robinson, W.H.	Hunlikely! (1st, 4to, ibds, 24pl)	L: Duckworth	(1916)	Robinson, W.H.	130-170	
Hunter, N.	Incredible Advens/Professor Brawnestawm (1st, lg8vo, col frn)	L: Bodley Head	1933	Robinson, W.H.	150-250	
Robinson, W.H.	Jamboree of Laughter (4to, 24p, wraps)	Jones	(1920)	Robinson, W.H.	100-125	
O'Cluny, Thomas	Merry Multifleet/Mounting Multicorps (1st, 8vo, 206p, 16 illus)	L: J.M. Dent	1904	Robinson, W.H.	100-130	*
Shakespeare, Wm.	MidSummer Night's Dream (1st, lg4to, 187p, gilt, 12 ticp)	L: Constable	1914	Robinson, W.H.	320-450	
Shakespeare, Wm.	MidSummer Night's Dream (1st AM, 4to, 187p, teg, gilt, 12 ticp)	Holt	1914	Robinson, W.H.	280-360	
Carse, R.	Monarchs of Merry England (1st, 4to, 52p, p-o, 10cp)	L: T.F. Unwin	1904	Robinson, W.H.	250-300	
Perrault, C.	Old Time Stories (1st AM, 4to, 200p, p-o, gilt, 6 ticp)	Dodd	(1921)	Robinson, W.H.	200-300	
Perrault, C.	Old-Time Stories (1st, 4to, red/gilt, 200p, 6 ticp)	L: Constable	1921	Robinson, W.H.	280-400	

AUTHOR	TITLE	PUBLISHER	DATE	ARTIST	PRICE	LC
De La Mare, W.	Peacock Pie (1st, 8vo, 178p, green/gilt, col frn)	L: Constable	(1916)	Robinson, W.H.	100-130	
De La Mare, W.	Peacock Pie (1st AM, 8vo, green/gilt, 178p, col frn)	Holt	[1917]	Robinson, W.H.	70-120	
Bunyan, J.	Pilgrim's Progress (1st, 8vo, 284p, red cl, 24pl)	L: Bliss Sands	1897	Robinson, W.H.	125-165	*
Robinson, W.H.	Railway Ribaldry (1st, 4to, [96]p, wraps, 88 fp b/w)	G.W. Railway	1935	Robinson, W.H.	160-200	
Robinson, W.H.	Some Frightful War Pictures (1st, folio, [54]p, 24 fp b/w, pep)	L: Duckworth	(1915)	Robinson, W.H.	180-250	
Kipling, R.	Song of the English (1st AM, 4to, red/gilt, 30 ticp)	Doubleday/Page	(1909)	Robinson, W.H.	250-350	
Kipling, R.	Song of the English (1st, lg4to, 91p, 30 ticp)	L: Hodder	(1909)	Robinson, W.H.	250-400	
Kelman, J.H.	Stories from Chaucer (1st, 12mo, 114p, p-o, gilt, 8cp)	L: Jack	[1906]	Robinson, W.H.	120-165	
N/A	Stories from the Odyssey (16mo, 118p, brown/gilt, p-o)	L: Jack	[1910]	Robinson, W.H.	70-100	*
Hope, A.R.	Tales For Toby (1st, 8vo, 207p, 5pl)	L: Dent	1900	Robinson, W.H.	100-130	
Lamb, C.	Tales from Shakespeare (1st, 8vo, red cl, 296p, 16pl)	L: Sands	[1902]	Robinson, W.H.	130-170	*
Rouse, W.H.D.	Talking Thrush (8vo, 8pl, cvr by...)	L: Dent	1902	Robinson, W.H.	170-230	
Munro, E.S.	Topsy-Turvey Tales (1st, lg8vo, 180p, 6cp, 16 b/w)	L: J. Lane	1923	Robinson, W.H.	150-220	
Robinson, W.H.	Uncle Lubin (1st AM, 8vo, green cl, b/w)	Brentano's	1902	Robinson, W.H.	450-600	*
Kingsley, C.	Water Babies (1st, 8vo, 319p, green/gilt, 8cp)	L: Constable	1915	Robinson, W.H.	350-500	
Kingsley, C.	Water Babies (1st AM, 8vo, green cl, p-o, 320p, 8cp)	Houghton	(1915)	Robinson, W.H.	240-300	
Unknown	Wonders of Wilmington (lg4to, ibds, 5pl)	Hull	[n.d.]	Robinson, W.H.	300	
N/A	Tales from Arabian Nights (1st, 8vo, 128p, p-o, 8cp)	L: Dent	(1914)	Robinson/Curtis	100-130	*
Macy, S.B.	From Slavery to Freedom (4to, 299p, green/gilt, 8cp, pep)	L: Longmans	1910	Robinson/Sarg	160-220	
Dyer, Kate G.	Turky Trott & Black Santa (1st, 4to, [39]p, orang cl, col frn)	Platt/Munk	(1942)	Robson, J.	70-100	
May, Eliz.	Flower Babies (1st, 4to, [100]p, ibds, color)	Saalfield	(1905)	Rockwell, I.M.	145-200	*
Twain, M.	Adventures of Huckleberry Finn (1st, 4to, 346p, 8 ticp, box)	Heritage Press	(1940)	Rockwell, N.	80-100	
Twain, M.	Adventures of Tom Sawyer (1st, 4to, 284p, 8 ticp, box)	Heritage Press	(1937)	Rockwell, N.	80-100	
Barbour, R.H.	Hitting the Line (1st, sm8vo, 322p, 5cp)	Appleton	1917	Rockwell, N.	75-100	*
Barbour, R.H.	Lucky Seventh (1st, sm8vo, 310p, 4cp)	Appleton	1915	Rockwell, N.	70-100	*
Jackson, G.E.	Maid of Middies' Haven (1st, 12mo, 299p, 4pl)	McBride	1912	Rockwell, N.	150-200	*
Barbour, R.H.	Purple Pennant (1st, sm8vo, 322p, cp)	Appleton	1916	Rockwell, N.	100-150	*
Tomlinson, E.	Scouting with Daniel Boone (1st, 8vo, 303p, green cl, 8pl)	Doubleday/Page	1914	Rockwell, N.	100-140	
Barbour, R.H.	Secret Play (1st, 8vo, 335p, 4cp)	Appleton	1915	Rockwell, N.	100-150	*
Claudy, C.H.	Tell Me Why Stories (1st, lg8vo, tan cl, 154p, 8cp)	McBride	1912	Rockwell, N.	600-800	*
Sawyer, R.S.	This Way to Christmas (1st, 12mo, 165p, gilt, frn by...)	Harper	(1916)	Rockwell, N.	45-60	*
Phelps, E.S.	Avery... (1st, 12mo, 238p)	Houghton	1902	Rogers, B.	20-30	
Warner, C.D.	Backlog Studies (1st, 12mo, 257p, title page by...)	Houghton	1899	Rogers, B.	25-40	
Bellamy, W.	Century of Charades (1st, 16mo, 100p)	Houghton	1901	Rogers, B.	25-40	
Chestnutt, Charles	Conjure Woman (1st, sm8vo, 229p, green cl, designs by...)	Houghton	1899	Rogers, B.	300-400	
Todd, M.L.	Corona & Coronet (1st, 8vo, teg, 383p)	Houghton	1898	Rogers, B.	30-45	
Brown, Alice	Day of His Youth (1st, 12mo, green/gilt, 143p)	Houghton	1897	Rogers, B.	35-50	R
James, Henry	English Hours (1st AM, lg8vo, 336p, design by...)	Houghton	1905	Rogers, B.	125-150	
Crothers, S.M.	Gentle Reader (1st, 12mo, 321p)	Houghton	1903	Rogers, B.	20-30	
Smith, F.H.	Gondola Days (1st, 12mo, 205p, red/gilt)	Houghton	1897	Rogers, B.	25-40	
Aldrich, T.B.	Judith of Bethulia (1st, 8vo, green/gilt, 98p, teg)	Houghton	1904	Rogers, B.	25-40	
Hearn, L.	Kwaidan... (1st, 12mo, 240p, teg, uncut, designs by..)	Houghton	1904	Rogers, B.	100-120	
Fiske, J.	Life Everlasting (1st, 12mo, 87p)	Houghton	1901	Rogers, B.	20-30	
Sherman, F.D.	Little Folk Lyrics (1st, 8vo, 140p)	Houghton	1897	Rogers, B.	30-45	
Peattie, E.W.	Mountain Woman (1st, 12mo, 251p, teg, cvr by...)	Way/Williams	1896	Rogers, B.	85-125	
Smith, F.H.	Other Fellow (1st, 8vo, teg, 218p)	Houghton	1899	Rogers, B.	25-40	
Crothers, S.M.	Pardoner's Wallet (1st, 12mo, 287p, teg)	Houghton	1905	Rogers, B.	20-30	
Drachman, Holger	Paul & Virginia/Northern Zone (1st, 8vo, gilt, teg, cvr by...)	Way/Williams	1896	Rogers, B.	90-120	
Sherwood, M.	Prince Por Quoi (1st, 12mo, 211p)	Houghton	1907	Rogers, B.	20-35	
Johnston, M.	Prisoners of Hope (1st, 8vo, 378p)	Houghton	1899	Rogers, B.	30-45	
James, Henry	Question of Our Speech (1st, 8vo, gilt, teg, 115p, uncut)	Houghton	1905	Rogers, B.	100-140	
Hearn, L.	Romance of the Milky Way (1st, 12mo, 209p, t.e. yellow)	Houghton	1905	Rogers, B.	85-100	
Aldrich, T.B.	Sea Turn (1st, 8vo, grey cl, 300p)	Houghton	1902	Rogers, B.	20-35	
Muir, J.	Stickeen... (1st, 12mo, tan cl, [73]p, designs, PPPa)	Houghton	1909	Rogers, B.	100-165	
Brown, Alice	Tiverton Tales (1st, 8vo, green/gilt, 339p, designs by..)	Houghton	1899	Rogers, B.	20-25	
Parker, Gilbert	When Valmond Came to Pontiac (1st, 12mo, teg, green/gilt, 222p)	Stone/Kimball	1895	Rogers, B.	60-90	
New, C.M.	Woman Reigns (1st, 16mo, 112p, teg, cvr by...)	Bowen-Merrill	1895	Rogers, B.	20-30	*
Porter, G.S.	Daughter of the Land (1st, 8vo, 475p, green cl, col frn)	Doubleday/Page	1918	Rogers, F.	30-45	
Porter, G.S.	Michael O'Halloran (1st, 8vo, 560p, green cl, 4pl, pep)	Doubleday/Page	1915	Rogers, F.	45-60	
Miller, Leo E.	Adrift on the Amazon (1st, 8vo, 263p, olive cl, 4pl)	Scribner	1923	Rogers, W.A.	25-40	*
Munroe, K.	Copper Princess (1st, 12mo, 237p, 12pl)	Harper	1898	Rogers, W.A.	30-50	*
Munroe, K.	Fur-Seal's Tooth (1st, 12mo, 267p, green cl, b/w)	Harper	1894	Rogers, W.A.	60-80	
Otis, James	Jenny Wren's Boarding House (1st, 8vo, blue cl, 173p, PPP)	Estes	(1893)	Rogers, W.A.	130-170	
Pool, M.L.	Mrs. Gerald (1st, 8vo, 339p, orange/silver, 13pl)	Harper	1896	Rogers, W.A.	20-40	
Munroe, K.	Ready Rangers (1st, 8vo, 334p, red cl, 6pl)	Lothrop	(1897)	Rogers, W.A.	35-50	*
Otis, James	Tim & Tip (1st, 16mo, 179p, 13 fp b/w, dep)	Harper	1883	Rogers, W.A.	70-100	R*
Otis, James	Toby Tyler... (1st, sq8vo, 265p, brown/gilt, 21 fp b/w, PPP)	Harper	1881	Rogers, W.A.	140-200	
Bishop, C.H.	All Alone (1st, 4to, unpag, b/w, pep, NH)	Viking	1953	Rojankovsky, F.	45-60	
Lida	Bruin the Brown Bear (1st {std}, 4to, ibds, [32]p, color, pep)	Harper	1937	Rojankovsky, F.	35-50	
Fritz, Jean	Cabin Faced West (1st, 8vo, blue cl, 124p, b/w)	Coward	(1958)	Rojankovsky, F.	25-40	*
Brown, M.W.	Children's Year (1st {std}, ob12mo, [26]p, ipcb, pep, color)	Harper	1937	Rojankovsky, F.	40-70	*
Lida	Cuckoo (1st {std}, sm sq4to, ibds, [32]p, pep, color)	Harper	1942	Rojankovsky, F.	45-60	*

AUTHOR	TITLE	PUBLISHER	DATE	ARTIST	PRICE	LC
Averill, Esther	Daniel Boone (1st AM {std}, 4to, ipcb, 58p, color)	Harper	(1945)	Rojankovsky, F.	60-80	
Kipling, R.	Elephant's Child (1st, 8vo, ibds, [28]p, color)	Garden City	(1942)	Rojankovsky, F.	25-40	*
N/A	Favorite Fairy Tales (1st, folio, ibds, [28]p, color, GGB)	Simon/Schuster	(1949)	Rojankovsky, F.	45-60	*
Averill, Esther	Flash: Story of a Horse (1st UK, 4to, ibds, 32p, color)	L: Faber	(1934)	Rojankovsky, F.	90-130	*
Averill, Esther	Flash: Story of a Horse (1st AM, narrow 4to, 32p, color, ibds)	Smith/Haas	(1934)	Rojankovsky, F.	70-100	*
Langstaff, John	Frog Went A-Courtin' (1st {std}, lg4to, [32]p, color, pep, CM)	Harcourt	(1955)	Rojankovsky, F.	80-130	R*
Werner, Elsa	Golden Bible (1st {std}, folio, 124p, ibds, color, GGB)	Simon/Schuster	(1946)	Rojankovsky, F.	25-40	
N/A	Great Big Animal Book (1st, folio, ibds, color, GGB)	Simon/Schuster	1950	Rojankovsky, F.	35-50	
Kipling, R.	How the Leopard Got his Spots (1st, lg8vo, ibds, [28]p, color)	Garden City	(1942)	Rojankovsky, F.	35-50	*
Kipling, R.	How the Rhinoceros Got his Skin (1st, lg8vo, ibds, [31]p, col)	Garden City	(1942)	Rojankovsky, F.	35-50	*
Koch, Dorothy	I Play at the Beach (1st, lg8vo, blue cl, [28]p, color, pep)	Holiday House	1955	Rojankovsky, F.	35-50	*
Rand, Ann	Little River (1st {std}, ob4to, ibds, [32]p, color, pep)	Harcourt	(1959)	Rojankovsky, F.	40-65	
Kalashnikoff, N.	My Friend Yakub (1st, sm8vo, 249p, b/w)	Scribner	(1953)	Rojankovsky, F.	25-40	
McGinley, Phyllis	Name for Kitty (1st, sm8vo, ibds, [28]p, color, LGB)	Simon/Schuster	(1948)	Rojankovsky, F.	20-30	*
Andersen, H.C.	Old Man is Always Right (1st {std}, sq8vo, ibds, 28p)	Harper	(1940)	Rojankovsky, F.	40-65	
Lida	Plouf the Little Wild Duck (1st, sq4to, ibds, [40]p, color, pep)	Harper	1936	Rojankovsky, F.	45-60	*
Lida	Pompom (1st, sq4to, ibds, [38]p, color, pep, DJ)	Harper	1936	Rojankovsky, F.	50-70	
Averill, Esther	Powder (1st AM, 4to, ibds, 29p, color)	Smith/Haas	(1933)	Rojankovsky, F.	75-110	*
Lida	Scuff the Seal (1st {std}, sq4to, ibds, [32]p, color, pep)	Harper	1937	Rojankovsky, F.	45-70	*
Lida	Spiky the Hedgehog (1st {std}, 4to, ibds, unpag, color, pep)	Harper	1938	Rojankovsky, F.	50-70	
Mother Goose	Tall Bk./Mother Goose (1st {std}, lg4to, 120p, ibds, color, pep)	Harper	(1942)	Rojankovsky, F.	65-90	*
N/A	Tall Book of Nursery Tales (1st, 8vo, ibds, color, DJ)	A.& W. Guild	(1944)	Rojankovsky, F.	60-80	*
Lida	The Kingfisher (1st {std}, sm sq4to, ibds, [32]p, pep, color)	Harper	1940	Rojankovsky, F.	45-60	
Prishvin, M.	Treasure Trove of the Sun (1st, 4to, 80p, color, pep)	Viking	1952	Rojankovsky, F.	50-80	R*
Andersen, H.C.	Ugly Duckling (1st, 8vo, ibds, [32]p, color)	Grosset/Dunlap	(1945)	Rojankovsky, F.	25-45	
Reynier, M.	Wild Animals at Home (sq4to, wraps, [16]p, color)	A.& W. Guild	(1934)	Rojankovsky, F.	30-45	
Celli, Rose	Wild Animals/Little Ones (1st AM, 4to, [16]p, wraps, 12 color)	A.& W. Guild	(1933)	Rojankovsky, F.	35-50	
Raymond, E.	The Whirligig (1st, 12mo, 351p, 6pl)	Penn	1905	Rollins, R.	30-50	*
Cowper, Wm.	Diverting History/John Gilpin (1st, ob4to [36]p, gilt, bds, 8cp)	L: Routledge	[1888]	Rosa, H.	100-150	
Embry, Margaret	Blue-Nosed Witch (1st, 8vo, 45p, yellow cl, b/w, pep)	Holiday House	(1955)	Rose, C.	20-30	*
Eaton, J.	Leader by Destiny (1st, 8vo, 402p, blue/gilt, 19pl, DJ, NH)	Harcourt	(1938)	Rose, J.M.	40-65	
Wright, E.B.	Saturday Flight (1st, ob8vo, [20]p, color)	W.R. Scott	1944	Rose, R.	30-45	*
Ovington, Mary W.	Hazel (1st, sm8vo, 162p, b/w)	NY: Crisis Pub	(1913)	Roseland, H.	80-100	*
Lightfoot, B.H.	Jolly Jack Horner (1st, 8vo, p-o, 4 color)	Whitman	(1916)	Rosenkrans, E.	30-50	
Paine, A.B.	Great White Way (1st, 8vo, blue cl, teg, 327p, 6pl)	J.F. Taylor	1901	Rosenmeyer, B.J.	80-100	
Daskam, J.	Imp & The Angel (1st, 8vo, 168p, tan cl, 8pl)	Scribner	1901	Rosenmeyer, B.J.	30-50	*
Russell, W.C.	Two Captains (1st UK, 8vo, 372p, cloth, b/w)	L: Sampson	1897	Rosenmeyer, B.J.	65-80	
Martin, J.	Children's Munchausen (1st, lg8vo, p-o, 8cp)	Houghton	1921	Ross, G.	30-45	
Irving, W.	Christmas Dinner (1st, 8vo, ipcb, 22p, b/w)	W. Rudge	1929	Ross, G.	45-75	R
Cooke, E.V.	Impertinent Poems (1st, 8vo, p-o, teg, uncut, 103p, 11cp)	Dodge	(1907)	Ross, G.	30-50	
Kirkwood, E.B.	Animal Children (1st, 8vo, yellow ipcb, p-o, 96p, pep, color)	Volland	(1913)	Ross, M.T.	90-140	
Gordon, Eliz.	Bird Children (1st, lg8vo, 96p, ibds, color, pep)	Volland	(1912)	Ross, M.T.	85-140	
Gordon, Eliz.	Butterfly Babies' Book (1st, 8vo, 78p, ibds, color)	Rand/McNally	(1914)	Ross, M.T.	70-100	
Scott, A.M.	Flower Babies' Book (8vo, 78p, ibds, color)	Rand/McNally	(1914)	Ross, M.T.	60-80	
Gordon, Eliz.	Flower Children (1st, 8vo, ibds, [92]p, color, pep)	Volland	(1910)	Ross, M.T.	100-140	
Gordon, Eliz.	I Wonder Why? (1st, sm8vo, 72p, color)	Rand/McNally	(1916)	Ross, M.T.	40-65	
Gordon, Eliz.	Lorraine & the Little People (1st, 12mo, ibds, 73p, color)	Rand/McNally	(1915)	Ross, M.T.	70-90	
Sandler, M.C.	Mamma's Angel Child (1st, 8vo, ibds, p-o, 115p, color)	Rand/McNally	(1915)	Ross, M.T.	90-140	
Gordon, Eliz.	Mother Earth's Children (1st, 8vo, 95p, ibds, color, pep)	Volland	(1914)	Ross, M.T.	70-100	
Gordon, Eliz.	Some Smiles (1st, 12mo, ibds, [29]p, color)	Wilde	(1911)	Ross, M.T.	35-50	
Scott, A.M.	Year with the Fairies (1st, lg4to, ibds, [100]p, color, pep)	Volland	(1914)	Ross, M.T.	120-145	
Bailey, A.C.	Katrina & Jan (1st, 8vo, ibds, unpag, color, pep)	Volland	(1923)	Rosse, H.	45-60	*
Olcott, F.J. (ed.)	Wonder Tales/Pirate Isles (1st, 12mo, 256p, orang cl, col frn)	NY: Longmans	1927	Rosse, H.	35-50	*
Olcott, F.J.	Wonder Tales/Windmill Lands (1st, 8vo, 238p, col frn, pep, DJ)	L: Longmans	1926	Rosse, H.	45-70	
Rossetti, C.	Pageant & other Poems (1st, 8vo, 198p, blue/gilt)	MacMillan	1881	Rossetti, D.G.	90-130	
LeBlanc, G.	Children's Blue Bird (1st, sq8vo, 172p, 12cp)	L: Methuen	1913	Rothenstein, A.	70-100	
Aesopus	Aesop's Fables (1st, 8vo, 162p, color)	Lippincott	(1949)	Rounds, G.	35-50	*
Rounds, Glen	Blind Colt (1st, lg8vo, blue cl, [80]p, color)	Holiday House	(1941)	Rounds, G.	35-50	*
Sears, P.M.	Firefly (1st, sm8vo, 37p, green cl, 2-color, pep)	Holiday House	1956	Rounds, G.	25-40	*
Black, I.S.	Flipper: Sea Lion (1st, sm8vo, [50]p, color, pep)	Holiday House	1940	Rounds, G.	30-45	*
Kjelgaard, J.A.	Haunt Fox (1st, sm8vo, 220p, brown cl, b/w, pep)	Holiday House	(1954)	Rounds, G.	45-60	R*
Rounds, Glen	Lumbercamp (1st, sm8vo, wood bds, 116p, b/w, pep)	Holiday House	1937	Rounds, G.	25-40	*
Rounds, Glen	Ol' Paul, Mighty Logger (1st, 12mo, beige cl, 132p, b/w, pep)	Holiday House	1936	Rounds, G.	45-65	R*
Webb, W.P.	Uncle Swithin's Inventions (1st, lg8vo, 114p, fp b/w, pep)	Holiday House	(1947)	Rounds, G.	20-35	*
Rounds, Glen	Whitey & Jinglebob (1st, sq8vo, [28]p, ibds, pep, color)	Grosset/Dunlap	(1946)	Rounds, G.	35-50	*
Rounds, Glen	Whitey & the Blizzard (1st, sm8vo, blue cl, 31p, b/w, cep)	Holiday House	(1952)	Rounds, G.	25-45	*
Rounds, Glen	Whitey Looks for a Job (1st, lg8vo, [28]p, ibds, color)	Grosset/Dunlap	(1944)	Rounds, G.	35-50	*
Rounds, Glen	Whitey's First Roundup (1st, lg8vo, [28]p, ibds, color)	Grosset/Dunlap	(1942)	Rounds, G.	35-50	*
Rounds, Glen	Whitey's Sunday Horse (1st, lg8vo, [28]p, ibds, color)	Grosset/Dunlap	1943	Rounds, G.	45-60	*
Rountree, H.	Adventures of Mabel (1st AM, sm4to, 223p, 8cp)	Dodd	1916	Rountree, H.	50-70	
Aesopus	Aesop's Fables (1st, 8vo, 340p, green cl, p-o, 48cp, pep)	L: Ward Lock	[1920]	Rountree, H.	120-180	*
Aesopus	Aesop's Fables (8vo, red cl, 340p, 30cp, reprint, pep)	L: Ward Lock	[1924]	Rountree, H.	75-100	

AUTHOR	TITLE	PUBLISHER	DATE	ARTIST	PRICE	LC
Carroll, L.	Alice... & Through... (4to, 143p, green/gilt, 8 ticp)	L: Collins	[1928]	Rountree, H.	200-265	
Carroll, L.	Alice/Wonderland (1st, sq12mo, 160p, gilt, p-o, 8cp)	L: Nelson	1908	Rountree, H.	70-100	*
Jeffries, R.	Bevis... (1st, 8vo, ibds, 8cp)	L: Duckworth	1913	Rountree, H.	65-90	
Towers, Alton	Billy Bunce... (1st, 4to, ibds, unpag, 17cp)	L: A. Cooke	(1907)	Rountree, H.	200-300	
Dumas, A.	Dumas Fairy Tale Book (8vo, 290p, grey cl, 4cp)	L: Warne	1924	Rountree, H.	65-80	*
Hamer, S.H.	Enchanted Wood (1st, 8vo, 100p, 8cp)	L: Duckworth	1909	Rountree, H.	65-80	*
Hamer, S.H.	Enchanted Wood (1st AM, 12mo, 101p, p-o, 8cp)	Estes	[1910]	Rountree, H.	50-70	
Hamer, S.H.	Forest Foundling (1st AM, sm4to, p-o, 109p, 8cp)	Estes	[1909]	Rountree, H.	70-90	R
Hamer, S.H.	Forest Foundling (1st, sm4to, 109p, 8cp)	L: Duckworth	1909	Rountree, H.	80-100	*
Hamer, S.H.	Four Glass Balls (1st, 8vo, 109p, color)	L: Duckworth	1911	Rountree, H.	65-80	*
Hamer, S.H.	Magic Wand (lg8vo, 88p, cloth, 12cp)	Estes	[1908]	Rountree, H.	70-100	
Bayne, C. (ed.)	My Book/Best Fairy Tales (1st AM, sm4to, blue/gilt, 368p, 16cp)	Funk/Wagnalls	[1915]	Rountree, H.	85-130	
Bayne, C. (ed.)	My Book/Best Fairy Tales (1st, 4to, blue/gilt, 368p, 16cp)	L: Cassell	(1915)	Rountree, H.	170-220	
Rountree, H.	Peter Pink-Eye (1st AM, 8vo, p-o, 85p, 8cp)	Estes	(1908)	Rountree, H.	45-70	
St. Mars, F.	Pinion & Paw (1st, sm8vo, green cl, 296p, 12pl)	L: Chambers	1919	Rountree, H.	45-60	*
Doyle, A.C.	Poison Belt (1st, 8vo, 199p, blue/gilt, uncut, 16pl)	L: Hodder	(1913)	Rountree, H.	165-220	*
Nesbit, E.	Pug Peter (1st, 4to, 64p, teg, blue cloth, color)	L: A. Cooke	(1905)	Rountree, H.	200-260	
Hamer, S.H.	Quackles Junior (1st, sm4to, ibds, 4cp)	L: Cassell	1903	Rountree, H.	40-65	
Rountree, H.	Sonny Jim (4to, ibds, unpag, 14 color)	L: A. Cooke	[n.d.]	Rountree, H.	150-200	
Steedman, Amy	Stories from Grimm... (16mo, 116p, p-o, 8cp)	Jack/Dutton	[1908]	Rountree, H.	50-75	
Hamer, S.H.	Story of the Ring (1st AM, 8vo, 53p, 4cp)	Dodd	1907	Rountree, H.	50-70	*
Hamer, S.H.	Story of the Ring (1st, 8vo, 53p, 4cp)	L: Cassell	1907	Rountree, H.	60-80	*
Wyss, J.D.	Swiss Family Robinson (1st, 8vo, 307p, grey/gilt, 12cp)	L: A&C Black	(1907)	Rountree, H.	65-90	*
Wyss, J.D.	Swiss Family Robinson (1st AM, 12mo, 307p, cp)	MacMillan	1926	Rountree, H.	30-50	*
Hamer, S.H.	The Dolomites (1st, lg8vo, 305p, 16cp)	L: Methuen	1910	Rountree, H.	90-120	*
Hamer, S.H.	The Dolomites (1st AM, sm4to, 305p, 16cp)	NY: J. Lane	1910	Rountree, H.	85-110	*
Hamer, S.H.	Transformations of the Truefitts (1st, 4to, 77p, 4cp)	L: Cassell	1908	Rountree, H.	70-100	*
Harris, J.C.	Uncle Remus (1st, folio, [111]p, 12cp)	L: Nelson	[1906]	Rountree, H.	350-500	
Harris, J.C.	Uncle Remus... (sm8vo, 8cp, later)	L: Nelson	[1930]	Rountree, H.	80-120	
Deardon, H.	Wonderful Adventure (1st UK, 4to, ibds, 52p, b/w)	L: Heinemann	1929	Rountree, H.	35-50	*
Hamer, S.H.	Wonderful Isles (1st, sm4to, 107p, 8cp)	L: Duckworth	1908	Rountree, H.	65-80	*
Hamer, S.H.	Wonderful Isles (1st AM, sm4to, p-o, 107p, 8cp)	Estes	[1908]	Rountree, H.	40-60	
Verne, Jules	Antarctic Mystery (1st AM, 8vo, 336p, red/silver, 17pl)	Lippincott	1899	Roux, G.	350-400	R
Krauss, Ruth	Bears (1st, 4to, [23]p, ibds, 2-color)	Harper	(1948)	Rowand, P.	40-60	*
Rowand, Phyllis	Day After Yesterday (1st {std}, 8vo, 54p, green cl, fp 2-color)	Little/Brown	(1953)	Rowand, P.	30-45	*
Krauss, Ruth	Growing Story (1st, 4to, [32]p, color)	Harper	(1947)	Rowand, P.	45-60	*
Krauss, Ruth	Monkey Day (1st, lg4to, ibds, [26]p, fp 1-color)	Harper	(1957)	Rowand, P.	40-65	
Rowand, Phyllis	Watch the Birdie! (1st, lg8vo, ipcb, [40]p, 1-color)	W.R. Scott	1947	Rowand, P.	30-50	*
Stevenson, R.L.	Kidnapped (1st, 12mo, 387p, b/w)	MacMillan	(1930)	Rowe, C.	25-40	*
Seton, E.T.	Preacher of Cedar Mountain (1st, 8vo, 426p, gilt, frn by...)	Doubleday/Page	1917	Rowe, C.	25-40	*
Sabin, E.L.	Range & Trail (1st, 8vo, 445p, 8pl)	Crowell	(1910)	Rowe, C.	35-60	
Seltzer, C.A.	Range Riders (1st, 8vo, 310p)	Outing	1911	Rowe, C.	30-45	
Sinclair, B.W.	Raw Gold (1st, sm8vo, 311p, 4pl)	Dillingham	1908	Rowe, C.	35-50	
Raine, W.M.	Wyoming (1st, sm8vo, 353p, 4pl)	Dillingham	1908	Rowe, C.	35-50	
Baker, Edna D.	Child is Born (1st, folio, ibds, 60p, color, pep)	Reilly/Lee	(1932)	Royt, M.	30-45	*
Mother Goose	Mother Goose: Her Own Book (1st, folio, [55]p, color, pep)	Reilly/Lee	(1932)	Royt, M.	100-160	*
Lewis, Claudia	Straps the Cat (1st, 12mo, 141p, rust cl, fp b/w)	W.R. Scott	(1957)	Ruhtenberg, C.	35-50	*
Nash, Ogden	Cricket of Carador (1st {std}-{1st bk}, 8vo, 165p, col frn, pep)	Doubleday/Page	1925	Rule, C.	50-75	
Mother Goose	Littlefolks' Mother Goose (1st, lg4to, 158p, p-o, b/w, pep)	Sears	(1926)	Rule, C.	35-50	*
Kirk, V.	Mickey & the Monkeys (1st, 4to, 175p, col frn, b/w, pep)	Viking	1927	Rule, C.	35-50	
Collodi, C.	Pinocchio (1st, sm4to, 236p, p-o, orange cl, pep)	Sears	(1926)	Rule, C.	35-50	*
Craddock, Harry	Savoy Cocktail Book (1st, 8vo, 287p, pcb, gilt, color)	L: Constable	1930	Rumbold, G.	160-200	
Rumbold, G.	Wayside Book... (1st, 8vo, 175p, ibds, color)	L: Methuen	1934	Rumbold, G.	65-80	*
Parry, E.A.	Scarlet Herring (1st, 8vo, 253p, uncut, green/gilt, b/w, AEG)	L: Smith Elder	1899	Rusden, A.D.	65-80	
Marshall, Helen L.	New Mexican Boy (1st, 8vo, 85p, 9 fp color, cep)	Holiday House	(1940)	Rush, O.	20-25	*
Strahorn, C.A.	15 Thousand Miles by Stage (1st, 8vo, 673p, teg, 4cp)	Putnam	1911	Russell, C.M.	130-170	
Jennings, A.	Beating Back (1st, 8vo, 355p, 3pl by...)	Appleton	1914	Russell, C.M.	60-80	*
Freeman, H.C.	Brief History of Butte Montana (1st, 123p, 4 illus by..)	(Chicago)	1900	Russell, C.M.	100-120	*
Brummitt, S.W.	Brother Van (1st, sm8vo, 171p, pict cl, 2 illus by...)	(NY)	(1919)	Russell, C.M.	40-65	*
Steedman, C.	Bucking the Sagebrush (1st, 8vo, 270p, map, teg, 9pl)	Putnam	1904	Russell, C.M.	130-170	
Bower, B.M.	Chip of the Flying-U (1st, 12mo, 264p, red cl, 3cp)	Dillingham	(1906)	Russell, C.M.	35-50	
MacKay, M.	Cow Range & Hunting Trail (1st, 8vo, gilt, 243p, 3pl by...)	Putnam	1925	Russell, C.M.	85-100	
Davis, Duke	Flashlights from Mountain & Plain (1st, sm8vo, 266p, 4cp)	(New Jersey)	1911	Russell, C.M.	100-150	
Russell, C.M.	Good Medicine (1st, 4to, 162p, tan cl, col frn)	Doubleday/Dor.	(1930)	Russell, C.M.	100-150	
Parker, F.	Hope Hathaway (1st, 8vo, 408p, green cl, 9pl)	C.M. Clark	1904	Russell, C.M.	80-100	
Beacom, John	How the Buffalo Lost his Crown (1st, ob folio, 7pl)	Forest/Stream	1894	Russell, C.M.	1200	
Linderman, F.B.	Indian Old-Man Stories (1st, sm4to, p-o, 169p, 9cp, SC)	Scribner	1920	Russell, C.M.	140-200	
Linderman, F.B.	Indian Why Stories (1st, 8vo, maroon cl, p-o, 236p, 8cp, SC)	Scribner	1915	Russell, C.M.	150-200	
Bower, B.M.	Lure of the Dim Trails (1st, 8vo, red cl, 210p, 3cp)	Dillingham	(1907)	Russell, C.M.	35-50	
Bower, B.M.	Range Dwellers (1st, 12mo, 356p, 3cp)	Street & Smith	(1907)	Russell, C.M.	150-200	*
Coburn, W.D.	Rhymes of the Roundup Camp (1st, 12mo, 138p, 7 b/w)	Ridgley Pr.	1899	Russell, C.M.	200-300	
Coburn, W.D.	Rhymes of the Roundup Camp (sm8vo, teg, 137p, 7pl)	Putnam	1903	Russell, C.M.	100-140	*

AUTHOR	TITLE	PUBLISHER	DATE	ARTIST	PRICE	LC
Hamilton, W.	Sixty Years on the Plains (1st, 8vo, 244p, p-o, 6pl)	Forest/Stream	1905	Russell, C.M.	150-200	
Hough, E.	Story of the Cowboy (1st, 8vo, 349p, 6pl by...)	Appleton	1897	Russell, C.M.	120-165	
Hough, E.	Story of the Cowboy (1st UK, 8vo)	(London)	1897	Russell, C.M.	100-150	
Wister,^EO.	The Virginian (1st, red cl, p-o, 506p, teg, 42 illus by...)	MacMillan	1911	Russell, C.M.	250-300	*
Vaughn, R.	Then & Now (1st, 8vo, 461p, black/gilt, 8pl)	(Minneap)	1900	Russell, C.M.	200-250	
Russell, C.M.	Trails Plowed Under (1st {std}, 4to, 210p, 5 dp cp)	Doubleday/Page	1927	Russell, C.M.	100-160	
Bower, B.M.	Uphill Climb (1st, 8vo, 283p, 4pl)	Little/Brown	1913	Russell, C.M.	60-85	*
Deihl, E.G.	Teddy Bear that Prowled the Night (4to, ibds, 24p, color)	NY: S. Gabriel	(1924)	Russell, L.M.	70-100	*
Bannerman, H.	Little Black Sambo (4to, wraps)	NY: S. Gabriel	1948	Russell, M.L.	60-95	
Birdsall, K.N.	Jacks of All Trades (1st, 8vo, 236p, 6cp)	Appleton	1902	Russell, W.	25-40	*
Shiel, M.P.	Lord of the Sea (1st AM, 8vo, 474p, blue cl, frn by...)	Stokes	(1901)	Russell, W.	100-150	
Habberton, J.	Tiger & the Insect (1st, 8vo, ipcb, 235p, uncut, 9pl)	R.H. Russell	1902	Russell, W.	30-45	
Housman, L.	Angels & Ministers (1st, 8vo, 139p)	L: J. Cape	1922	Rutherston, A.	30-45	*
Colvile, Kath.	Jason & the Princess (1st AM, sm8vo, blue cl, 86p, 4cp)	Houghton	(1926)	Rutherston, A.	30-45	*
Edey, B.O.	Six Giants & a Griffin (1st, 4to, 46p, 6pl)	R.H. Russell	1903	Ruyl, B.B.	140-200	*
Ewing, J.H.	Jacanapes (1st, 12mo, 60p, blue cl, b/w)	J. Knight	1895	Sacker, A.	30-45	*
Robinson, E.	Loyal Little Maid (12mo, 79p, b/w illus)	J. Knight	1897	Sacker, A.	20-30	
Sleight, C.L.	Prince of the Pin Elves (1st, 8vo, 159p, b/w)	Page	1897	Sacker, A.	50-65	
Saint, L.B.	Knight of the Cross (1st, 8vo, 220p, uncut, p-o, teg, 7 ticp)	Jacobs	(1914)	Saint, L.B.	20-30	
Saint-Exupery, A.	Little Prince (1st AM, sq8vo, 91p, color)	Reynal/Hitch.	(1943)	Saint-Exupery, A.	100-145	*
Godden, Rumer	Doll's House (1st AM, sm8vo, 125p, yellow, cl, 4cp, DJ)	Viking	1948	Saintsbury, Dana	45-70	
Lord Brabourne	Friends & Foes from Fairy Land (1st AM, yellow cl)	Little/Brown	1886	Sambourne, L.	90-135	
Andersen, H.C.	Three Tales/Hans Andersen (lg sq8vo, 79p, blue/gilt, 22 b/w)	L: MacMillan	1910	Sambourne, L.	70-120	
Kingsley, C.	Water Babies (1st, 8vo, 371p, blue/gilt, AEG, b/w, cep)	L: MacMillan	1885	Sambourne, L.	75-120	
Kingsley, C.	Water Babies (1st [new ed.], 8vo, blue/gilt, 330p, b/w)	L: MacMillan	1894	Sambourne, L.	85-120	
Bianco, M.W. (ed.)	Rufus the Fox (1st, folio, ibds, [44]p, color)	Harper	1937	Samivel	65-80	*
Lide, A.A.	Aztec Drums (1st {std}, sm8vo, 142p, blue cl, fp b/w, pep)	Longmans	1931	Sanchez, C.M.	20-30	*
Belpre, Pura	Perez & Martina (1st, ob4to, 79p, 16cp, pep)	Warne	(1932)	Sanchez, C.M.	70-100	*
Lide, A.A.	Princess of Yucatan (1st {std}, 12mo, tan cl, 187p, b/w, pep)	Longmans	1939	Sanchez, C.M.	25-40	*
Lederer, J.	Fafan in China (1st, 8vo, 137p, green cl, b/w, pep)	Holiday House	(1939)	Sanderson, W.	20-25	*
Blodgett, M.F.	At the Queen's Mercy (1st, 8vo, 261p, teg, uncut, 5pl)	Chi: Lamson	1897	Sandham, H.	60-80	*
Burnett, F.H.	Editha's Burglar (1st [2], 12mo, blue/gilt, 64p, 13pl)	J. Marsh	1888	Sandham, H.	50-70	
Jackson, H.H.	Father Junipero... (1st, sm8vo, 159p, b/w)	Little/Brown	1902	Sandham, H.	30-45	
Lummis, C.F.	Gold Fish of Gran Chimu (1st, 12mo, gilt, 126p, teg, 7pl)	Bos: Lamson	1896	Sandham, H.	90-140	
Baylor, F.C.	Juan & Juanita (1st, 8vo, green/gilt, 276p, b/w, pep, PPP)	Ticknor	1888	Sandham, H.	180-250	*
Jacobs, Violet	Golden Heart (1st AM, 171p, green/gilt, p-o, 16pl)	Doubleday/Page	1905	Sandheim, M.	45-60	*
Rossetti, C.	Prince's Progress (1st, 8vo, 146p, teg, b/w)	L: A. Melrose	[1900]	Sandheim, M.	75-90	
Sandys, Ruth	Numerous Names Nimbly Narrated (1st, lg4to, ibds, unpag, col)	L: H. Milford	(1930)	Sandys, R.	150-200	
Johnson, L.R.	Teddy-Bear ABC (1st, sq8vo, [55]p, color, pep)	Caldwell	(1907)	Sanford, M.L.	180-300	*
Boyd, Eliz. M.	All About David (1st, lg8vo, 117p, pep, b/w)	Winston	(1940)	Sarg, T.	25-40	*
Pezet, A.W.	Aristokia (1st, 8vo, 214p, blue/gilt, 8pl)	Century	1919	Sarg, T.	25-45	*
MacPherson, J.F.	Children For Ever (1st, 8vo, 352p, 16 color)	L: J. Long	1908	Sarg, T.	100-145	*
Lefevre, F.	Cock, Mouse & Little Red Hen (1st AM, 8vo, 103p, 24cp)	Jacobs	(1907)	Sarg, T.	145-220	
Lefevre, F.	Cock, Mouse & Little Red Hen (1st, 8vo, 103p, 24cp)	L: Richards	1907	Sarg, T.	200-300	
Cobb, I.	Fibble, D.D. (1st, 8vo, 279p, blue cl, p-o, b/w, pep)	Doran	(1916)	Sarg, T.	30-50	
Wells, Carveth	Jungle Man & his Animals (1st {this pub}, 4to, 68p, ibds, 7cp)	McBride	(1925)	Sarg, T.	150-200	
Wells, Carveth	Jungle Man & his Animals (1st, lg4to, ibds, 68p, 12cp)	Duffield	1925	Sarg, T.	160-200	*
Mitchell G.W.	Kernel Cob & Little Miss Sweetclover (1st, 8vo, [96]p, col, pep)	Volland	(1918)	Sarg, T.	80-120	*
Hellman, Sam	Low Bridge & Punk Pungs (1st, 12mo, 111p, b/w pl)	Little/Brown	1924	Sarg, T.	30-45	*
White, W.A.	Martial Advens. of Henry & Me (1st, 8vo, 340p, red cl, 25 b/w)	MacMillan	1918	Sarg, T.	20-30	*
Collodi, C.	Pinocchio (1st, 4to, red cl, 122p, pep, 6cp)	Platt/Munk	(1940)	Sarg, T.	80-120	
Lefevre, F.	Soldier Boy (1st, sm8vo, [64]p, orang cl, color, pep)	Greenberg	(1926)	Sarg, T.	50-70	
Mills, G.R.	Talking Dolls (1st, 4to, [96]p, color, pep)	Greenberg	(1930)	Sarg, T.	65-80	*
Potter, M.C.	The Gigglequicks (1st, 12mo, ibds, color)	Volland	(1918)	Sarg, T.	85-120	*
Sarg, Tony	Tony Sarg's Alphabet (1st UK, sm4to, [30]p, ibds, color, DJ)	(London)	(1930)	Sarg, T.	80-120	
Sarg, Tony	Tony Sarg's Book of Animals (4to, green ibds, color)	Greenberg	(1925)	Sarg, T.	75-110	
Sarg, Tony	Tony Sarg's Book of Tricks (1st, 4to, ibds, [96]p, color, pep)	Greenberg	(1928)	Sarg, T.	70-100	
Sarg, Tony	Tony Sarg's New York (1st, lg4to, [60]p, 24cp)	Greenberg	1926	Sarg, T.	70-120	
Moses, M. (ed)	Treasury of Plays/Children (1st, 8vo, 550p, col frn, 8pl, pep)	Little/Brown	1921	Sarg, T.	50-80	
O'Malley, F.W.	War-Whirl in Washington (1st, 8vo, 298p, grey cl, 16pl)	Century	1918	Sarg, T.	35-50	
Sarg, Tony	Where is Tommy? (1st, ob4to, [20]p, ipcb, color)	Greenberg	(1932)	Sarg, T.	35-50	
Macy, S.B.	From Slavery to Freedom (4to, 299p, green/gilt, 8cp, pep)	L: Longmans	1910	Sarg/Robinson	160-220	
Stevens, F.	Adventures in Hiveland (1st, 8vo, 227p, green/gilt, b/w)	L: Hutchinson	1903	Sargent, L.A.	120-180	
N/A	Puss in Boots (1st, 16mo, [59]p, fp color)	McLoughlin	(1941)	Sari	20-30	*
Pollard, J.	Elfin-Land (1st, lg ob4to, [40]p, ibds, chromos, dep)	G.W. Harlan	(1882)	Saterlee, W.	140-200	
Moore, F.F.	Impudent Comedian (1st, 8vo, green cl, 274p, 10pl)	H. Stone	1897	Sauber, R.	45-70	
Malot, H.	Adventures of Remi (1st, lg8vo, p-o, 492p, gilt, pep, 8cp)	Rand/McNally	(1925)	Schaeffer, M.	30-45	*
Meader, S.W.	Black Bucaneer (1st, lg8vo, black/gilt, 269p, 8cp)	Harcourt	(1920)	Schaeffer, M.	30-45	*
Dumas, A.	Count of Monte Cristo (4to, black/gilt, p-o, 8cp, pep)	Dodd	(1920)	Schaeffer, M.	35-50	
Bullen, F.T.	Cruise of the Cachalot (1st, lg8vo, 301p, 8cp, pep)	Dodd	1926	Schaeffer, M.	30-50	
Knipe, A.A.	Everybody's Washington (1st, 4to, 282p, uncut, p-o, 7cp, pep)	Dodd	1931	Schaeffer, M.	30-45	
Masefield, J.	Jim Davis (1st, 8vo, blue/gilt, p-o, 226p, 8cp)	Stokes	1924	Schaeffer, M.	30-45	*

AUTHOR	TITLE	PUBLISHER	DATE	ARTIST	PRICE	LC
Hugo, V.	Les Miserables (sm4to, black cl, 585p, 11cp)	Dodd	[1925]	Schaeffer, M.	40-60	
Blackmore, R.D.	Lorna Doone (1st, 8vo, p-o, 646p, black/gilt, 8cp, pep)	Dodd	(1930)	Schaeffer, M.	30-50	
Melville, Herman	Moby Dick (1st, lg8vo, p-o, 540p, black/gilt, teg, 12cp, pep)	Dodd	1922	Schaeffer, M.	45-60	
Melville, Herman	Omoo (1st, 4to, teg, 299p, black cl, 8cp, pep)	Dodd	1924	Schaeffer, M.	35-50	
Dumas, A.	Three Musketeers (1st, lg8vo, black/gilt, 555p, 8cp)	Dodd	[1929]	Schaeffer, M.	40-60	
Scott, Michael	Tom Cringle's Log (1st, 4to, black/gilt, 384p, p-o, 7cp, pep)	Dodd	1927	Schaeffer, M.	40-60	
Melville, Herman	Typee (sm4to, black cl, 283p, 8cp, pep)	Dodd	(1923)	Schaeffer, M.	35-50	
Tracy, Louis	Wings of the Morning (1st, lg8vo, black/gilt, 320p, teg, 12cp)	E.J. Clode	(1924)	Schaeffer, M.	30-45	
Tracy, Louis	Wings of the Morning (lg8vo, 319p, cp)	Winston	[1927]	Schaeffer, M.	30-45	
Andersen, H.C.	Fir Tree (1st, 4to, [24]p, color)	Grosset/Dunlap	(1948)	Schlesinger, A.	35-50	*
Grimm Bros.	Three Tales from Grimm (1st AM, sm4to, pink cl, color)	MacMillan	1938	Schlotter, B.	90-140	
Burnham, C.L.	Jewel's Story Book (1st, 12mo, 343p, green cl, 6pl, pep)	Houghton	1904	Schmitt, A.	20-25	
Nulets, L.E.	Stories of the Little Fishes (1st, 8vo, 288p, 6pl)	Page	1905	Schneider, S.	20-30	*
Kauffmann, R.	Barbary Bo... (1st, 8vo, p-o, 261p, 5pl)	Penn	1929	Schoonover, F.	25-45	
Paine, R.D.	Blackbeard Buccaneer (1st, 8vo, 309p, p-o, 6pl)	Penn	1922	Schoonover, F.	30-45	
Fraser, W.A.	Blood Lilies (1st, 8vo, 262p, 6pl)	Scribner	1903	Schoonover, F.	25-40	
Van Dyke, H.	Broken Soldier & Maid of France (1st, 8vo, 66p, blu/glt, 2 ticp)	Harper	(1919)	Schoonover, F.	30-45	
Carter, Russell	Crimson Cutlass (1st, 8vo, 302p, col frn, pep)	Penn	(1933)	Schoonover, F.	20-30	*
McIlwraith, J.N.	Curious Career of Roderick Campbell (1st, 8vo, 287p, 4pl)	Houghton	1901	Schoonover, F.	20-35	
Munroe, K.	Flamingo Feather (1st, lg8vo, p-o, 222p, 10cp)	Harper	(1915)	Schoonover, F.	45-70	
Swan, O.	Frontier Days (1st, 4to, 512p, 3cp by...)	Macrae-Smith	(1928)	Schoonover, F.	50-70	
Lee, J.	Happy Island (1st, 8vo, 330p, frn by...)	Century	1910	Schoonover, F.	20-25	
Scott, Walter	Ivanhoe (1st, 4to, 515p, p-o, blue/gilt, 10cp, pep)	Harper	1922	Schoonover, F.	50-70	
Tomlinson, E.	Jersey Boy in the Revolution (1st, 8vo, 428p, 4pl)	Houghton	1899	Schoonover, F.	30-45	
Madison, L.F.	Joan of Arc (1st, 4to, 389p, p-o, blue/gilt, 8cp, pep)	Penn	1918	Schoonover, F.	45-70	
Frith, Henry	King Arthur & his Knights (1st, 8vo, black cl, p-o, 406p, 4cp)	Garden City	1932	Schoonover, F.	40-65	
Madison, L.F.	Lafayette (1st, 4to, p-o, 371p, blue cl, 8cp, pep)	Penn	1921	Schoonover, F.	50-75	
Parker, Gilbert	Lane that Had No Turning (1st, lg8vo, 215p, teg, uncut, 5pl)	Doubleday/Page	1902	Schoonover, F.	30-50	
Madison, L.F.	Lincoln (1st, tall 8vo, p-o, 368p, 8cp, pep)	Penn	1928	Schoonover, F.	50-70	
Parrish, R.	Maid of the Forest (1st, 8vo, 427p, 5cp)	McClurg	1913	Schoonover, F.	25-40	
Cummings, E.	Marmaduke of Tennessee (1st, 8vo, 371p, 5pl)	McClurg	1914	Schoonover, F.	25-40	
Seltzer, C.A.	Range Boss (1st, 8vo, 333p, 4pl)	McClurg	1916	Schoonover, F.	25-40	
Schultz, J.W.	Seizer of Eagles (1st, 8vo, 230p, brown cl, 4pl)	Houghton	1922	Schoonover, F.	25-40	*
Voss, R.	Sigurd Eckdel's Bride (1st, 8vo, 235p, 4pl)	Little/Brown	1900	Schoonover, F.	25-40	
Schultz, J.W.	Skull Head the Terrible (1st, 8vo, 208p, brown cl, 4pl, pep)	Houghton	1929	Schoonover, F.	25-40	*
Marsh, Geo.	Sled Trails/White Waters (1st, 8vo, 298p, p-o, 10pl)	Penn	1929	Schoonover, F.	25-40	
Glasgow, E.	The Deliverance (1st, 8vo, 543p, red/gilt, 4cp)	Doubleday/Page	1904	Schoonover, F.	30-45	
Johnston, M.	To Have & to Hold (1st {this format}, lg8vo, 331p, 5cp)	Houghton	1931	Schoonover, F.	45-60	
Marsh, Geo.	Toilers of the Trails (1st, sm4to, p-o, 245p, col frn, 8pl)	Penn	1921	Schoonover, F.	30-50	
Madison, L.F.	Washington (1st, 4to, blue/gilt, p-o, 399p, 8cp, pep)	Penn	1925	Schoonover, F.	50-70	
Mott, L.	White Darkness (1st, sm8vo, blue cl, 308p, 3pl by...)	Outing	1907	Schoonover, F.	30-45	
Watson, V.	With Cortes the Conqueror (1st, 4to, p-o, 332p, 8cp, pep)	Penn	1917	Schoonover, F.	50-80	
Holland, R.S.	Yankee Ships in Pirate Waters (1st, lg8vo, p-o, 317p, 5cp, pep)	Macrae-Smith	(1931)	Schoonover, F.	35-50	
Schreiber, G.	Bambino the Clown (1st, 4to, 30p, ipcb, color, pep, CH)	Viking	1947	Schreiber, G.	70-100	
Sauer, J.L.	Light at Tern Rock (1st, 4to, 62p, pep, brown illus, NH)	Viking	1951	Schreiber, G.	65-100	R*
Bishop, C.H.	Pancakes-Paris (1st, sm4to, 63p, grey cl, pep, NH)	Viking	1947	Schreiber, G.	45-65	
Bragdon, Elspeth	That Jud! (1st, 8vo, ivory cl, 126p, fp b/w)	Viking	(1957)	Schreiber, G.	30-45	*
White, S.E.	Daniel Boone (1st {std}, 8vo, 308p, blue cl, p-o, 5pl, PPP)	Doubleday/Page	1922	Schuyler, R.	75-100	R
Schwartz, Eliz. R.	Cottontail Rabbit (1st, 8vo, 45p, olive cl, 2-color, cep)	Holiday House	(1957)	Schwartz, C.	25-40	*
Scott, F.E.	Kindergarten Limericks (1st, 4to, [59]p, 27cp)	Hurst	(1915)	Scott, A.O.	140-200	*
N/A	Cinderella (1st, 24mo, [41]p, ipcb, 2-color)	Holiday House	[1938]	Scott, H.	45-60	*
Andersen, H.C.	Thumbelina (1st, sq32mo, ipcb, [60]p, color, dep)	Holiday House	(1939)	Scott, H.	50-70	R*
Jahn, Mary L.	Yelly (1st, lg ob4to, [32]p, color, pep)	NY: OUP	(1941)	Scott, H.	45-60	*
Mitchell, Edith	Betty, Bobby & Bubbles (1st, 12mo, ibds, [40]p, pep, color)	Volland	(1921)	Scott, J.L.	40-60	*
Stevenson, R.L.	Child's Garden of Verses (1st, 12mo, ipcb, [52]p, color, pep)	Whitman	1947	Scott, J.L.	25-40	*
Merryman, M.P.	Daddy Domino (1st {std}, 8vo, ibds, 6 fp color)	Volland	(1929)	Scott, J.L.	65-100	
Graham, Mary N.	Fifty Songs for Boys & Girls (1st, ob4to, 60p, color)	Whitman	(1935)	Scott, J.L.	70-100	*
N/A	Happy Day Begins (lg sq4to, wraps, [12]p, color)	Saalfield	1931	Scott, J.L.	45-60	
Bowman, J.	Happy all Day Through (1st, lg ob4to, ibds, color)	Volland	(1917)	Scott, J.L.	60-80	
O'Donnell, T.C.	Ladder of Ricketty Rungs (1st, 8vo, ibds, unpag, color, pep)	Volland	(1923)	Scott, J.L.	50-70	
Muter, Gladys N.	Little Bim the Circus Boy (1st, ob folio, color)	Volland	(1924)	Scott, J.L.	120-175	*
Bonner, M.G.	Miss Angelina Adorable (1st, 8vo, cloth, [102]p, color)	M. Bradley	(1928)	Scott, J.L.	30-45	
Bonner, M.G.	Mrs. Cucumber Green (1st, 8vo, 108p, pep, color)	M. Bradley	(1927)	Scott, J.L.	20-30	*
Dauzet, M.	One Happy Day (lg sq4to, ibds, [16]p, color, pep)	Saalfield	1939	Scott, J.L.	30-45	*
Thompson, R.P.	Princess of Cozytown (1st, lg8vo, ibds, [96]p, color, pep)	Volland	(1922)	Scott, J.L.	130-180	
Addington, S.	Pudding Lane People (1st, lg8vo, p-o, 183p, 4cp, pep)	Little/Brown	1926	Scott, J.L.	25-45	
Scott, J.L.	Round the World We Sail (1st, sq4to, ibds, [16]p, color, pep)	Saalfield	1939	Scott, J.L.	35-50	
Chamberlin, E.C.	Shoes, Ships & Sealing Wax (1st, 8vo, 123p, ibds, color)	Saalfield	(1928)	Scott, J.L.	20-30	
Bonner, M.G.	Story Teller's Holiday (1st, lg4to, [64]p, red cl, p-o)	McLoughlin	(1938)	Scott, J.L.	85-130	
Trimpey, Alice	Story of My Dolls (1st, 4to, 76p, ibds, b/w, pep)	Whitman	1935	Scott, J.L.	60-85	*
Gordon, Eliz.	Turned-Intos (1st, 8vo, ipcb, unpag, color, pep)	Volland	(1920)	Scott, J.L.	65-80	
Gordon, Eliz.	Wild Flower Children (1st, 8vo, ibds, [84]p, color, pep)	Volland	(1918)	Scott, J.L.	100-150	

AUTHOR	TITLE	PUBLISHER	DATE	ARTIST	PRICE	LC
Sewell, Anna	Black Beauty (1st, 8vo, 295p, 12cp)	Jacobs	(1910)	Scrivener, M.	45-65	*
N/A	Golden Goose (1st, sq16mo, ibds, [42]p, color)	MacMillan	1928	Seaman, M.L.	50-80	
Cullen, Countee	Lost Zoo (1st {std}, 8vo, 72p, yellow cl, 16cp, pep)	Harper	(1940)	Sebree, C.	100-165	*
Seccombe, Lieut.	Good Old Story/Cinderella (1st AM, sm4to, 48p, gilt, 12cp)	NY: Armstrong	(1882)	Seccombe, Lieut.	100-150	*
Dalgliesh, A.	Gulliver Joins the Army (1st, sm8vo, 96p, b/w)	Scribner	1942	Segner, E.	20-30	*
Ponset, Marie	Fairy Tale Book (1st, folio, ibds, 156p, color, GGB)	Simon/Schuster	(1958)	Segur, A.	120-180	*
DeJong, Meindert	Along Came a Dog (1st, 8vo, 172p, b/w, NH)	Harper	(1958)	Sendak, M.	120-170	R*
Eidinoff, M.L.	Atomics for the Millions (1st, 8vo, 281p, blue cl, b/w, DJ)	Whittlesey	(1947)	Sendak, M.	380-500	
Krauss, Ruth	Birthday Party (1st, ob12mo, ipcb, [23]p, dep, color)	Harper	1957	Sendak, M.	130-180	R*
Krauss, Ruth	Charlotte & White Horse (1st, 16mo, ibds, [20]p, color, dep)	Harper	(1955)	Sendak, M.	120-170	
Sendak, Jack	Circus Girl (1st, lg8vo, beige cl, [30]p, color)	Harper	1957	Sendak, M.	120-165	R*
Hauff, Wilhelm	Dwarf Long-Nose (1st, sq8vo, ipcb, 61p, 2-color, pep)	Random	(1960)	Sendak, M.	130-170	R*
Minarik, E.H.	Father Bear Comes Home (1st, 8vo, ibds, 62p, color)	Harper	(1959)	Sendak, M.	100-160	*
DeRegniers, B.S.	Giant Story (1st, 4to, unpag, grey cl, color)	Harper	(1953)	Sendak, M.	130-200	*
Sendak, Jack	Happy Rain (1st, sm4to, 40p, blue cl, 8 fp b/w)	Harper	(1956)	Sendak, M.	160-250	R*
Krauss, Ruth	Hole is to Dig (1st, 12mo, [48]p, ibds, green pep, DJ)	Harper	(1952)	Sendak, M.	200-300	R
DeJong, Meindert	House of Sixty Fathers (1st, 8vo, 189p, tan cl, b/w, NH)	Harper	(1956)	Sendak, M.	120-165	R*
DeJong, Meindert	Hurry Home, Candy (1st, 8vo, 244p, green cl, b/w, NH)	Harper	(1953)	Sendak, M.	120-165	R*
Krauss, Ruth	I Want to Paint My Bathroom Blue (1st, 8vo, ibds, [22]p col, cep)	Harper	1956	Sendak, M.	120-170	R*
Krauss, Ruth	I'll Be You and You Be Me (1st, 4to, ibds, pep, [38]p, b/w)	Harper	(1954)	Sendak, M.	130-170	R
Sendak, M.	Kenny's Window (1st, lg sq8vo, tan cl, 1-color, unpag)	Harper	(1956)	Sendak, M.	130-170	R
Minarik, E.H.	Little Bear (1st, 8vo, 63p, ibds, color)	Harper	(1957)	Sendak, M.	120-170	R
DeJong, Meindert	Little Cow & the Turtle (1st, 8vo, 178p, b/w, DJ)	Harper	(1955)	Sendak, M.	180-250	
Sawyer, R.S.	Maggie Rose: Her Birthday Christmas (1st {std}, 12mo, 151p, b/w)	Harper	1952	Sendak, M.	130-175	*
Ayme, Marcel	Magic Pictures (1st {std}, 8vo, blue cl, 117p, b/w)	Harper	(1954)	Sendak, M.	120-175	
Udry, J.M.	Moon Jumpers (1st, 4to, ibds, [31]p, 7 dp color, CH)	Harper	(1959)	Sendak, M.	250-400	*
MacDonald, Betty	Mrs. Piggle-Wiggle's Farm (1st {std}, 8vo, 128p, b/w)	Lippincott	(1954)	Sendak, M.	120-180	
Minarik, E.H.	No Fighting! No Biting! (1st, 8vo, 62p, b/w)	Harper	1958	Sendak, M.	120-165	*
Krauss, Ruth	Open House for Butterflies (1st, 16mo, ibds, [46]p, pep, b/w)	Harper	(1960)	Sendak, M.	130-170	R
Andersen, H.C.	Seven Tales (1st, 8vo, 128p, blue/gilt, 5cp, fp b/w)	Harper	1959	Sendak, M.	100-160	*
DeJong, Meindert	Shadrach (1st {std}, 8vo, rust cl, 182p, b/w, NH)	Harper	(1953)	Sendak, M.	100-165	R*
Sendak, M.	Sign on Rosie's Door (1st, 8vo, grey cl, 47p, color)	Harper	(1960)	Sendak, M.	120-165	*
Ritchie, Jean	Singing Family of the Cumberlands (1st, 8vo, grn cl, 282p, b/w)	NY: OUP	1955	Sendak, M.	120-170	*
DeJong, Meindert	Singing Hill (1st, 8vo, 180p, b/w, DJ)	Harper	(1962)	Sendak, M.	65-80	
Krauss, Ruth	Somebody Else's Nut Tree (1st, 4to, ibds, 43p, fp b/w)	Harper	(1958)	Sendak, M.	120-165	*
Tripp, E.	Tin Fiddle (1st, ob4to, pink cl, unpag, brown illus, cep)	NY: OUP	1954	Sendak, M.	160-200	R
Sendak, M.	Very Far Away (1st, 8vo, green cl, cep, 52p, color)	Harper	(1957)	Sendak, M.	120-165	R*
Krauss, Ruth	Very Special House (1st, 4to, ibds, [22]p, 1-color, CH)	Harper	(1953)	Sendak, M.	140-200	R*
DeRegniers, B.S.	What Can You Do with a Shoe? (1st, ob4to, ipcb, unpag, 1-color)	Harper	(1955)	Sendak, M.	160-220	*
Joslin, Sesyle	What Do You Say, Dear? (1st, ob8vo, unpag, CH)	W.R. Scott	1958	Sendak, M.	120-170	*
DeJong, Meindert	Wheel on the School (1st, 8vo, 298p, b/w, uncut, DJ, NM)	Harper	(1954)	Sendak, M.	145-200	R
Ayme, Marcel	Wonderful Farm (1st {std}, 8vo, 182p, red cl, b/w)	Harper	(1951)	Sendak, M.	140-180	R
Nash, Ogden	You Can't Get There from Here (1st {std}, 12mo, gilt, 190p, b/w)	Little/Brown	(1957)	Sendak, M.	90-140	
Daringer, H.F.	Adopted Jane (1st, sm8vo, 225p, fp b/w)	Harcourt	(1947)	Seredy, K.	25-45	*
Thompson, B.J.	Bible Children... (1st {std}, sm4to, ibds, [32]p, color, DJ)	Dodd	(1937)	Seredy, K.	35-50	
Daugherty, Sonia	Broken Song (1st, sm8vo, 270p, b/w)	Nelson	1934	Seredy, K.	25-45	*
Brink, C.R.	Caddie Woodlawn (1st, 8vo, 270p, b/w, cep, DJ, NM)	MacMillan	1935	Seredy, K.	70-95	
Thompson, B.J.	Candle Burns for France (1st, 12mo, 80p, col frn, DJ)	Bruce	(1946)	Seredy, K.	35-50	
Seredy, K.	Chestry Oak (1st, 8vo, 236p, red cl, fp b/w)	Viking	1948	Seredy, K.	30-50	*
Sawyer, R.S.	Christmas Anna Angel (1st, 8vo, 48p, color, pep, DJ, CH)	Viking	1944	Seredy, K.	65-90	
Gaggin, E.R.	Ear for Uncle Emil (1st, 8vo, 238p, 83 b/w, pep)	Viking	1939	Seredy, K.	25-40	*
Bailey, C.S.	Finnigan II - His Nine Lives (1st, tall 4to, red cl, 95p, pep)	Viking	1953	Seredy, K.	45-60	*
Seredy, K.	Good Master (1st, sq8vo, 211p, b/w, pep, DJ, NH)	Viking	1935	Seredy, K.	65-90	R
Harper, Wilhelmina	Gunniwolf... (1st {std}, 8vo, green/gilt, 104p, fp color, pep)	McKay	(1936)	Seredy, K.	65-80	*
Seredy, K.	Gypsy (1st, lg4to, 62p, cloth, 29pl, DJ)	Viking	1951	Seredy, K.	85-100	
LaRue, M.G.	Hoot-Owl (1st, 12mo, blue cl, 207p, 2-color, pep)	MacMillan	1936	Seredy, K.	30-45	*
Seredy, K.	Listening (1st, 8vo, gilt, 157p, pep, 18pl)	Viking	1936	Seredy, K.	30-45	*
Gates, Doris	Little Vic (1st, 8vo, 160p, tan cl, b/w, pep)	Viking	1951	Seredy, K.	25-40	*
Brink, C.R.	Mademoiselle Misfortune (1st, 8vo, 267p, 12 fp b/w, cep)	MacMillan	1936	Seredy, K.	30-50	*
Daringer, H.F.	Mary Montgomery, Rebel (1st, 8vo, green cl, 222p, b/w, DJ)	Harcourt	(1948)	Seredy, K.	35-50	*
Hunt, M.L.	Michel's Island (1st, sm4to, 265p, pep, b/w)	Stokes	1940	Seredy, K.	25-40	*
Seredy, K.	Open Gate (1st, 8vo, blue cl, 280p, fp b/w, pep, DJ)	Viking	1943	Seredy, K.	35-50	
Seredy, K.	Philomena (1st, tall 8vo, 95p, cloth, b/w, pep)	Viking	1955	Seredy, K.	30-45	
Harper, Wilhelmina	Selfish Giant... (1st, lg8vo, 86p, 6cp, DJ)	McKay	(1935)	Seredy, K.	50-65	
Seredy, K.	Singing Tree (1st, 8vo, 247p, color, 32 fp b/w, pep, NH)	Viking	1939	Seredy, K.	45-65	*
Mason, Miriam E.	Smiling Hill Farm (1st, 8vo, 311p, pep, b/w)	Ginn	(1937)	Seredy, K.	25-45	*
Seredy, K.	Tree for Peter (1st, lg8vo, 102p, cloth, brown illus)	Viking	1941	Seredy, K.	35-50	*
Seredy, K.	White Stag (1st, lg8vo, 95p, gilt, b/w, pep, DJ, NM)	Viking	1937	Seredy, K.	100-145	
Seredy, K.	White Stag (1st UK, 4to, cloth, 94p, b/w, DJ)	L: Harrap	(1938)	Seredy, K.	35-50	
Barnes, Nancy	Wonderful Year (1st, 8vo, 185p, NH)	J. Messner	(1946)	Seredy, K.	45-60	*
Gray, Eliz. J.	Young Walter Scott (1st, 8vo, 239p, pep, port. frn, NH)	Viking	1935	Seredy, K.	50-70	*
Seton, E.T.	Animal Heroes (1st, 8vo, green/gilt, 362p, teg, 19pl)	Scribner	1905	Seton, E.T.	50-80	

AUTHOR	TITLE	PUBLISHER	DATE	ARTIST	PRICE	LC
Seton, E.T.	Biography of a Grizzly (1st, sq8vo, 167p, 12 tipl, cep)	Century	1900	Seton, E.T.	70-90	
Seton, E.T.	Biography of a Silver Fox (1st, sm8vo, blue cl, 209p, 10pl)	Century	1909	Seton, E.T.	50-65	
Seton, E.T.	Bird Portraits (1st, lg4to, 40p, green cl, 20pl)	Ginn	1901	Seton, E.T.	120-160	
Stickney, J.H.	Bird World (1st, 8vo, 214p, green cl, 10pl by...)	Ginn & Co.	1898	Seton, E.T.	80-120	*
Seton, E.T.	Book of Woodcraft (1st, lg8vo, 567p, green/gilt, b/w)	Doubleday/Page	1912	Seton, E.T.	30-45	
Wright, M.O.	Four-Footed Americans... (1st, sm8vo, 432p, b/w)	MacMillan	1898	Seton, E.T.	65-80	
Seton, E.T.	Krag & Johnny Bear (1st, sm8vo, 141p, b/w pl)	Scribner	1902	Seton, E.T.	60-90	
Seton, E.T.	Lives of the Hunted (1st, 8vo, 360p, green/gilt, teg, b/w)	Scribner	1901	Seton, E.T.	65-80	
Seton, E.T.	Monarch the Big Bear... (1st, 8vo, 214p, blue cl, p-o)	Scribner	1904	Seton, E.T.	40-60	
Seton, G.	Nimrod's Wife (1st, 8vo, 406p, 18pl)	Doubleday/Page	1907	Seton, E.T.	45-70	
Seton, E.T.	Rolf in the Woods (1st, lg8vo, 437p, green/gilt, 12pl)	Doubleday/Page	1911	Seton, E.T.	35-50	
Seton, E.T.	Studies/Art Anatomy/Animals (1st, folio, green/gilt, 49pl)	L: MacMillan	1896	Seton, E.T.	350-500	
Grinnell, G.B.	Trail & Camp Fire (1st, 8vo, 353p, b/w)	Forest/Stream	1897	Seton, E.T.	180-250	
Seton, E.T.	Trail of the Sandhill Stag (1st, 8vo, teg, 93p, gilt, col frn)	Scribner	1899	Seton, E.T.	70-90	
Seton, E.T.	Two Little Savages (1st, 8vo, grey/gilt, 552p, 29pl)	Doubleday/Page	1903	Seton, E.T.	65-80	
Seton, E.T.	Wild Animal Play for Children (1st, sm8vo, green cl, 79p, b/w)	Doubleday/Page	1900	Seton, E.T.	90-120	
Seton, E.T.	Wild Animals I Have Known (1st, 8vo, teg, 359p, PPP)	Scribner	1898	Seton, E.T.	90-130	
Seton, E.T.	Wild Animals at Home (1st, 8vo, 226p, gilt, b/w)	Doubleday/Page	1913	Seton, E.T.	50-70	
Seton, G.	Woman Tenderfoot (1st, 8vo, 361p, teg, b/w)	Doubleday/Page	1900	Seton, E.T.	50-70	
Seton, E.T.	Woodmyth & Fable (1st, 8vo, 181p, red/gilt)	Century	1905	Seton, E.T.	70-100	
Seuss, Dr.	500 Hats/Bartholomew Cubbins (1st, 4to, ibds, [47]p, pep, col)	Vanguard Pr.	(1938)	Seuss, Dr.	130-185	
Seuss, Dr.	And to Think/I Saw It/Mulberry Street (1st, 4to, [32]p, ibds pep)	Vanguard Pr.	1937	Seuss, Dr.	250-350	R*
Seuss, Dr.	Bartholomew & the Oobleck (1st, lg4to, [48]p, red ibds, CH)	Random	(1950)	Seuss, Dr.	200-300	*
Abingdon, Alex	Boners (1st, sq16mo, 102p, b/w)	Viking	1931	Seuss, Dr.	100-130	*
Seuss, Dr.	Cat in the Hat (1st, sm4to, 61p, ipcb, color, pep)	Random	(1957)	Seuss, Dr.	250-400	R*
Seuss, Dr.	Cat in the Hat Comes Back (1st {std}, 4to, 61p, color, pep)	Random	(1958)	Seuss, Dr.	250-350	
Seuss, Dr.	Green Eggs & Ham (1st, lg8vo, 62p)	Random	1960	Seuss, Dr.	120-170	*
Seuss, Dr.	Happy Birthday to You! (1st, lg4to, [57]p, ibds, color)	Random	(1959)	Seuss, Dr.	200-300	*
Seuss, Dr.	Horton Hatches the Egg (1st {std}, sq4to, [55]p, ibds, color)	Random	(1940)	Seuss, Dr.	180-240	*
Seuss, Dr.	Horton Hears a Who! (1st, 4to, unpag, ibds, color, pep)	Random	(1954)	Seuss, Dr.	150-200	*
Seuss, Dr.	How the Grinch Stole Christmas (1st, lg4to, ibds, unpag, color)	Random	1957	Seuss, Dr.	250-350	
Seuss, Dr.	If I Ran the Circus (1st, lg4to, ibds, pep, unpag)	Random	(1956)	Seuss, Dr.	200-350	*
Seuss, Dr.	If I Ran the Zoo (1st, lg4to, ibds, [56]p, color, pep, CH)	Random	(1950)	Seuss, Dr.	200-300	*
Sullivan, Frank	In One Ear (1st, 8vo, red/gilt, 169p, frn by...)	Viking	1933	Seuss, Dr.	65-90	*
Seuss, Dr.	King's Stilts (1st, lg4to, [48]p, red epps, color)	Random	(1939)	Seuss, Dr.	300-400	*
Seuss, Dr.	McElligot's Pool (1st, 4to, [56]p, green cl, color, CH)	Random	(1947)	Seuss, Dr.	220-300	
Abingdon, Alex	More Boners (1st, 16mo, 89p, b/w)	Viking	1931	Seuss, Dr.	100-130	*
Abingdon, Alex	Omnibus Boners (1st, 16mo, b/w)	Viking	1931	Seuss, Dr.	90-120	*
Seuss, Dr.	On Beyond Zebra (1st, 4to, unpag)	Random	(1955)	Seuss, Dr.	200-250	*
Seuss, Dr.	One Fish Two Fish Red Fish Blue Fish (1st, lg8vo, 62p, ipcb, col)	Random	1960	Seuss, Dr.	120-180	*
Seuss, Dr.	Scrambled Eggs Supper (1st, lg4to, ibds, [52]p, color, pep)	Random	(1953)	Seuss, Dr.	200-300	
Seuss, Dr.	Seven Lady Godivas (1st {std}, 4to, [80]p, 1-color, pep, DJ)	Random	(1939)	Seuss, Dr.	240-350	
Seuss, Dr.	Thidwick/Big-Hearted Moose (1st, 4to, blue cl, [40]p, color)	Random	(1948)	Seuss, Dr.	220-320	
Seuss, Dr.	Yertle the Turtle (1st, 4to, ibds, unpag, 2-color, pep)	Random	(1958)	Seuss, Dr.	200-250	*
Corelli, M.	Devil's Motor (1st, 4to, 42p, red/gilt, 6 ticp)	L: Hodder	[1910]	Severn, A.	90-135	
Sewell, A.A.	Ballad of the Prince (1st, lg4to, unpag, 12pl)	R.H. Russell	1900	Sewell, A.A.	180-250	*
Sewell, H.	ABC for Everyday (1st, 4to, ipcb, [28]p, pep, 2-color)	MacMillan	1930	Sewell, H.	100-140	R*
White, E.O.	Ann Frances (1st, 8vo, 126p, blue cl, 7cp, cep)	Houghton	1935	Sewell, H.	30-45	
Coatsworth, E.	Away Goes Sally (1st, lg8vo, 122p, p-o, b/w, pep)	MacMillan	1934	Sewell, H.	45-70	R
Crowley, Maude	Azor (1st, sm8vo, 54p, b/w)	NY: OUP	1948	Sewell, H.	30-45	*
Crowley, Maude	Azor & the Haddock (1st, sm8vo, 63p, grey cl, b/w)	NY: OUP	1949	Sewell, H.	30-45	*
Brink, C.R.	Baby Island (1st, sm8vo, 172p, pep, 6cp)	MacMillan	1937	Sewell, H.	30-45	*
Dalgliesh, A.	Bears on Hemlock Mountain (1st, 8vo, unpag, 1-color, NH)	Scribner	(1952)	Sewell, H.	50-85	*
Kristofferson, E.M.	Bee in Her Bonnet (1st, 8vo, 168p, b/w, pep)	Crowell	1944	Sewell, H.	20-35	
Sewell, H.	Belinda the Mouse (1st, sq12mo, grey cl, [61]p, color, DJ)	OUP	(1944)	Sewell, H.	35-50	
Coatsworth, E.	Big Green Umbrella (1st, sq8vo, ibds, [28]p, color, pep)	Grosset/Dunlap	(1944)	Sewell, H.	45-60	*
Sewell, H.	Birthdays for Robin (1st, sq12mo, [46]p, grey cl, fp 3-color)	MacMillan	1943	Sewell, H.	30-45	*
Sewell, H.	Blue Barns (1st, sq4to, [46]p, DJ)	MacMillan	1933	Sewell, H.	65-100	R
Sayers, F.C.	Blue Bonnets for Lucinda (1st, sq8vo, ibds, [30]p, color, pep)	Viking	1934	Sewell, H.	35-50	
Molnar, F.	Blue-Eyed Lady (1st, 4to, blue cl, 46p, color, pep, DJ)	Viking	1942	Sewell, H.	35-50	
Ward, Marion	Boat Children of Canton (1st {std}, 4to, 92p, color, pep)	McKay	(1944)	Sewell, H.	20-35	*
Bulfinch, T.	Book of Myths (1st, lg8vo, 126p, color, DJ)	MacMillan	1942	Sewell, H.	50-75	
Seaman, Louise	Brave Bantam (1st, 8vo, green cl, 48p, b/w, pep)	MacMillan	1946	Sewell, H.	25-40	*
Falkberget, J.	Broomstick & Snowflake (1st, 8vo, blue cl, 88p, b/w, cep)	MacMillan	1933	Sewell, H.	35-50	*
Cautley, Marg.	Building a House in Sweeden (1st, sq8vo, 40p, fp brown illus)	MacMillan	1931	Sewell, H.	30-50	
Tippett, James S.	Christmas Magic (1st, 16mo, ibds, [40]p, fp color, pep)	Grosset/Dunlap	(1944)	Sewell, H.	30-50	*
Smith, Susan C.	Christmas Tree in the Woods (1st, sq12mo, [38]p, color, pep)	Minton Balch	(1932)	Sewell, H.	30-50	*
N/A	Cinderella (1st, 4to, blue cl, [17]p, color, DJ)	MacMillan	1934	Sewell, H.	85-100	R
Evers, Alf	Colonel's Squad (1st {std}, 8vo, blue/gilt, 200p, b/w)	MacMillan	1952	Sewell, H.	25-40	*
Langer, S.K.	Cruise of the Little Dipper (1st, 12mo, 176p, gilt, 5cp, pep)	NY: Norcross	(1923)	Sewell, H.	90-140	
Hughes, Langston	Dream Keeper (1st {std}, 8vo, 77p, blue/silver, b/w)	Knopf	1932	Sewell, H.	380-500	R
Coatsworth, E.	Fair American (1st, 8vo, 132p, p-o, pep, 14pl)	MacMillan	1940	Sewell, H.	30-50	

AUTHOR	TITLE	PUBLISHER	DATE	ARTIST	PRICE	LC
Wilder, L.I.	Farmer Boy (1st {std}, 8vo, 230p, col frn, b/w, dep)	Harper	1933	Sewell, H.	70-100	R*
Sewell, H.	First Bible (1st, 4to, blue/gilt, 110p, 13pl, pep)	OUP	1934	Sewell, H.	70-120	
Coatsworth, E.	Five Bushel Farm (1st, lg8vo, 152p, pep, p-o, b/w, DJ)	MacMillan	1939	Sewell, H.	35-50	*
Sewell, H.	Head for Happy (1st, ob4to, [56]p, cloth, p-o, pep, DJ)	MacMillan	1931	Sewell, H.	70-100	
Evers, Alf	In the Beginning (1st, 8vo, aqua cl, [30]p, 2-color, dep)	MacMillan	1954	Sewell, H.	45-60	R*
Sewell, H.	Jimmy & Jemima (1st, 8vo, [47]p, cloth, p-o, color)	MacMillan	1940	Sewell, H.	35-50	
Milne, A.A.	Magic Hill (1st {this pub}, 4to, 40p, ibds, 8 fp color)	Grosset/Dunlap	(1937)	Sewell, H.	70-120	
Miller, M.B.	Menagerie (1st, sq8vo, 124p, col frn, 8pl, pep)	MacMillan	1928	Sewell, H.	30-50	
Sewell, H.	Ming & Mehitable (1st, 16mo, yellow cl, [60]p, dep, color)	MacMillan	1936	Sewell, H.	35-50	*
Rhys, Mimpsy	Mr. Hermit Crab (1st, 8vo, green cl, 190p, col frn, 6pl, pep)	MacMillan	1929	Sewell, H.	30-45	*
Cregan, M.	Old John (1st, 8vo, 183p, 11pl, pep, DJ)	MacMillan	1936	Sewell, H.	35-50	
Kunhardt, D.	Once there was a Little Boy (1st, lg8vo, 66p, color)	Viking	1946	Sewell, H.	30-50	*
Sewell, H.	Peggy & the Pony (1st, sq8vo, blue cl, [47]p, 2-color, DJ)	OUP	(1936)	Sewell, H.	45-70	
Sewell, H.	Peggy & the Pup (1st, sq8vo, [46]p, beige cl, fp 2-color)	OUP	(1941)	Sewell, H.	30-50	*
Jones, V.M.	Peter & Gretchen/Old Nuremberg (1st, 4to, p-o, 96p, color, pep)	Whitman	1935	Sewell, H.	35-50	
Collodi, C.	Pinocchio (1st, sm8vo, rust cl, 282p, 13 fp b/w)	Appleton/Cent.	(1935)	Sewell, H.	30-50	*
Milne, A.A.	Princess & the Apple Tree (1st, 4to, 40p, 8 fp color)	Grosset/Dunlap	1937	Sewell, H.	65-100	*
Noble, T.T.	Round of Carols (1st {std}, 4to, red/gilt, 72p, b/w, pep, DJ)	OUP	1935	Sewell, H.	35-50	
Potter, M.C.	Sally Gabble & the Fairies (1st, 12mo, 87p, col frn, b/w, DJ)	MacMillan	1929	Sewell, H.	70-90	
Sayers, F.C.	Tag-Along Tooloo (1st, 8vo, 87p, pep, 8 fp color)	Viking	1941	Sewell, H.	25-40	*
Farjeon, E.	Ten Saints (1st AM {std}, 8vo, 124p, 10 fp color, pep)	NY: OUP	1936	Sewell, H.	50-75	
Dalgliesh, A.	Thanksgiving Story (1st, 4to, red cl, unpag, fp color, CH)	Scribner	(1954)	Sewell, H.	65-80	R*
Sewell, H.	Three Tall Tales (1st, sq4to, ibds, [40]p, color)	MacMillan	1947	Sewell, H.	50-80	*
White, E.O.	Where is Adelaide? (1st, 8vo, 155p, orange cl, b/w, dep)	Houghton	1933	Sewell, H.	20-30	
Coatsworth, E.	White Horse (1st {std}, 8vo, 164p, p-o, 14 fp b/w, pep, DJ)	MacMillan	1942	Sewell, H.	40-65	
Coatsworth, E.	Wonderful Day (1st {std}, 8vo, yellow cl, 126p, p-o, pep)	MacMillan	1946	Sewell, H.	35-60	*
Sewell, H.	Words to the Wise (1st, ob8vo, [64]p, 1-color, tan cl, dep)	Dodd	(1932)	Sewell, H.	30-50	*
Wilder, L.I.	By the Shores of Silver Lake (1st {std}, 8vo, 260p, col frn, NH)	Harper	1939	Sewell/Boyle	100-140	R*
Wilder, L.I.	Little House in Big Woods (1st {1st bk}, 8vo, 176p, col frn, NH)	Harper	1932	Sewell/Boyle	100-135	*
Wilder, L.I.	Little House o/t Prairie (1st {std}, sq8vo, 200p, col frn, dep)	Harper	1935	Sewell/Boyle	150-200	R*
Wilder, L.I.	Little Town o/t Prairie (1st {std}, 8vo, 288p, col frn, dep, NH)	Harper	(1941)	Sewell/Boyle	100-140	R*
Wilder, L.I.	Long Winter (1st {std}, 8vo, 325p, col frn, dep, NH)	Harper	1940	Sewell/Boyle	100-140	R*
Wilder, L.I.	On the Banks of Plum Creek (1st {std}, 8vo, 239p, col frn, NH)	Harper	1937	Sewell/Boyle	100-145	*
Wilder, L.I.	These Happy Golden Years (1st {std}, 8vo, 299p, col frn, NH)	Harper	(1943)	Sewell/Boyle	100-150	R*
Carson, Norma B.	Children's Own Story Book (1st, sm4to, yellow cl, 160p, col)	Reilly/Britton	(1916)	Sewsmith, H.	45-60	*
Morse, Eliz.	Siamese Cat (1st, sm8vo, 62p, b/w)	Dutton	(1929)	Seymour, Ruth	25-40	*
Smith, Thorne	Lazy Bear Lane (1st {std}, 8vo, 240p, green cl, pep, b/w, DJ)	Doubleday/Dor.	1931	Shanks, G.	120-165	
Wilde, O.	House of Pomegranates (1st, 8vo, 158p, gilt, uncut, dep, 4pl)	L: McIlvanie	1891	Shannon, C.	650-900	
Bontemps, A.	Golden Slippers (1st {std}, 8vo, 220p, b/w pl)	Harper	(1941)	Sharon, H.B.	45-65	*
Steele, F.A.	Adventures of Akbar (1st AM, 8vo, 204p, gilt, 8cp)	Stokes	(1913)	Shaw, B.	50-70	
Steele, F.A.	Adventures of Akbar (1st, 8vo, 204p, gilt, 8cp)	L: Heinemann	1913	Shaw, B.	60-80	
Sidgwick (ed.)	Ballads & Lyrics of Love (1st, lg8vo, teg, 178p, uncut, 10cp)	L: Chatto	1908	Shaw, B.	65-90	
Reade, C.	Cloister & Hearth (1st, 4to, 663p, violet/gilt, teg, 20cp)	L: Chatto	1909	Shaw, B.	50-70	
Tennyson, A.	Geraint & Enid (1st, 16mo, blue/gilt, 4cp)	L: Jack	[n.d.]	Shaw, B.	70-90	
Hope, L.	India's Love Lyrics (1st, lg8vo, 181p, 8cp)	Dodd	1902	Shaw, B.	75-100	
Sidgwick (ed.)	Legendary Ballads (1st, lg8vo, 180p, red/gilt, teg, 10cp)	L: Chatto	1908	Shaw, B.	60-90	
Hadden, C.	Operas of Richard Wagner (1st, 8vo, gilt, teg, 246p, 24cp)	L: Jack	1908	Shaw, B.	60-75	
Bunyan, J.	Pilgrim's Progress (sm4to, gilt, 393p, teg, 29cp)	L: Jack	[1910]	Shaw, B.	45-60	
MacGregor, M.	Pilgrim's Progress told to Children (24mo, p-o, 8cp)	L: Jack	[1910]	Shaw, B.	25-40	
Garnett (ed.)	Poems by Robert Browning (1st, 8vo, 377p, gilt, b/w)	L: Bell	1900	Shaw, B.	60-80	
Poe, E.A.	Selected Tales of Mystery (1st AM, 4to, 334p, teg, 16cp)	Lippincott	1909	Shaw, B.	70-125	*
Lamb, C.	Tales from Shakespeare (1st, sm8vo, 363p, gilt, teg, 24pl)	L: G. Bell	1903	Shaw, B.	50-70	
Jacobs (ed.)	Tales/Boccaccio (1st, sq8vo, teg, 117p, 20pl)	L: G. Allen	1899	Shaw, B.	80-100	
Scott, Wm. R.	Apple that Jack Ate (1st, sm ob4to, ipcb, [25]p, color, dep)	W.R. Scott	1951	Shaw, C.G.	30-45	*
Brown, M.W.	Black and White (1st, 4to, ibds, [32]p, fp b/w)	Harper	1944	Shaw, C.G.	85-100	
Shaw, C.G.	Blue Guess Book (1st, 8vo, ipcb, [48]p, color)	W.R. Scott	(1942)	Shaw, C.G.	45-65	
McCullough, J.G.	Dark is Dark (1st, lg8vo, [34]p, ibds, color, cep)	W.R. Scott	1947	Shaw, C.G.	35-50	*
Shaw, C.G.	Giant of Central Park (1st, lg8vo, ipcb, [64]p, fp b/w)	W.R. Scott	(1940)	Shaw, C.G.	35-50	*
Shaw, C.G.	Guess Book (1st, 8vo, [48]p, ipcb, color)	W.R. Scott	(1941)	Shaw, C.G.	35-50	*
Scott, Wm. R.	This is the Milk that Jack Drank (1st, ob4to, ipcb, [24]p, col)	W.R. Scott	1944	Shaw, C.G.	45-65	*
Scott, Wm. R.	Water that Jack Drank (1st, ob4to, ipcb, [24]p, color, pep)	W.R. Scott	1950	Shaw, C.G.	50-65	*
Brown, M.W.	Winter Noisy Book (1st, sm4to, [42]p, ipcb, pep, color)	W.R. Scott	1947	Shaw, C.G.	45-60	
Staunton, S.	Fate of a Crown (1st, 8vo, 306p, red/gilt, 6pl)	Reilly/Britton	(1905)	Sheffer, G.C.	300-400	*
Tietjens, E.	Boy of the South Seas (1st, 8vo, 193p, 20 fp b/w, pep, NH)	Coward	(1931)	Sheldon, M.	45-60	*
Stevenson, R.L.	Child's Garden of Verses (12mo, 96p, cloth)	Donohue	(1916)	Sheldon, M.	35-50	
Tarry, Ellen	Janie Belle (1st, 4to, [30]p, ibds, fp brown illus)	Garden City	1940	Sheldon, M.	70-100	
Jones, Paul	Alphabet of Aviation (1st, 4to, blue cl, 28 fp color)	Macrae-Smith	(1928)	Shenton, E.	130-165	*
Meader, S.W.	Boy with a Pack (1st, 8vo, 297p, brown cl, b/w, pep, NH)	Harcourt	(1939)	Shenton, E.	30-50	*
Kalashnikoff, N.	Jumper (1st, 8vo, blue/silver, 224p, b/w)	Scribner	1944	Shenton, E.	25-40	*
DeJong, Meindert	Little Stray Dog (1st {std}, 8vo, 51p, b/w)	Harper	(1943)	Shenton, E.	30-50	*
Kalashnikoff, N.	The Defender (1st, 8vo, 136p, tan cl, 8 fp b/w, NH)	Scribner	1951	Shenton, E.	60-85	L
Lucas, E.V.	As the Bee Sucks (1st, 8vo, 169p, pink cl, b/w)	L: Methuen	(1937)	Shepard, E.H.	40-65	*

AUTHOR	TITLE	PUBLISHER	DATE	ARTIST	PRICE	LC
Grahame, K.	Bertie's Escapade (1st, sm8vo, 41p, grey cl, b/w)	Lippincott	(1949)	Shepard, E.H.	45-70	R
Jeffries, R.	Bevis... (1st, 8vo, 519p, DJ)	L: J. Cape	1932	Shepard, E.H.	45-60	
Drinkwater, J.	Christmas Poems (1st, sq8vo, orange wraps, uncut, 6 b/w)	L: Sidgwick	1931	Shepard, E.H.	60-85	
Milne, A.A.	Christopher Robin Birthday Bk. (1st, 16mo, 215p, orang/gilt, b/w)	L: Methuen	(1930)	Shepard, E.H.	180-240	
Milne, A.A.	Christopher Robin Story Book (1st AM, 8vo, 171p, b/w)	Dutton	(1929)	Shepard, E.H.	120-180	
Milne, A.A.	Christopher Robin Verses (1st, 8vo, 210p, blue/gilt, 12cp)	L: Methuen	(1932)	Shepard, E.H.	160-220	
Milne, A.A.	Christopher Robin Verses (1st AM {std}, 8vo, 210p, 12cp)	Dutton	(1932)	Shepard, E.H.	130-185	*
Chalmers, Patrick	Cricket in the Cage (1st, 8vo, 77p, gilt)	L: A&C Black	1933	Shepard, E.H.	35-50	*
Grahame, K.	Dream Days (1st AM, 8vo, 172p, gilt, pep)	Dodd	1931	Shepard, E.H.	35-50	
Milne (intro)	Fun & Fantasy (1st, lg4to, ibds, color)	L: Methuen	1927	Shepard, E.H.	120-170	
Farjeon, E.	Glass Slipper (1st, 8vo, 175p, b/w, DJ)	L: OUP	1955	Shepard, E.H.	45-60	
Farjeon, E.	Glass Slipper (1st AM, 8vo, 187p, red cl, b/w, DJ)	Viking	1956	Shepard, E.H.	30-45	
Grahame, K.	Golden Age (1st, 12mo, 166p, beige/gilt, t.e. pink, b/w, DJ)	L: J. Lane	(1928)	Shepard, E.H.	100-150	
Grahame, K.	Golden Age (1st AM, sm8vo, 170p, b/w, pep)	Dodd	1929	Shepard, E.H.	65-80	
Housman, L.	Golden Sovereign (1st, 8vo, green/gilt, 349p)	L: J. Cape	1937	Shepard, E.H.	50-65	
Housman, L.	Gracious Majesty (1st, 8vo, 222p)	L: J. Cape	1941	Shepard, E.H.	45-60	*
Dickens, C.	Holly Tree... (1st AM, sm4to, green cloth, 192p, 30pl)	Scribner	(1925)	Shepard, E.H.	45-65	
Milne, A.A.	House at Pooh Corner (1st [1], 12mo, 178p, teg, pink/gilt, pep)	L: Methuen	(1928)	Shepard, E.H.	280-400	
Fraser-Simson, H.	Hums of Pooh (1st AM, lg4to, 67p)	Dutton	(1930)	Shepard, E.H.	65-80	*
Walpole, H.	Jeremy (1st AM, 8vo, 304p, col frn, b/w, pep)	Doran	(1919)	Shepard, E.H.	35-50	*
Milne, A.A.	King's Breakfast (1st, lg8vo, bds, 17p, b/w, DJ)	L: Methuen	(1925)	Shepard, E.H.	120-160	
Agnew, G.	Let's Pretend (1st, 12mo, 63p, blue/gilt, teg, pep)	L: J. Saville	1927	Shepard, E.H.	70-85	
Green, Roger L.	Modern Fairy Stories (1st {std}, 8vo, 270p, 8cp)	Dutton	(1955)	Shepard, E.H.	65-80	*
Struther, J.	Modern Struwwelpeter (1st, 8vo, bds, color)	L: Methuen	1936	Shepard, E.H.	70-90	
Milne, A.A.	More Very Young Songs (1st, folio, 40p, bds, b/w)	L: Methuen	(1928)	Shepard, E.H.	130-180	
Lucas, E.V.	Mr. Punch's Country Songs (1st, lg4to, 92p, ibds, b/w)	L: Methuen	1928	Shepard, E.H.	65-90	*
Milne, A.A.	Now We Are Six (1st AM, 8vo, buckram, 103p, gilt)	Dutton	(1927)	Shepard, E.H.	180-250	
Milne, A.A.	Now We Are Six (1st, 12mo, 103p, maroon/gilt, teg, pep)	L: Methuen	(1927)	Shepard, E.H.	250-350	
Milne, A.A.	Old Sailor (1st AM, lg8vo, ipcb, [23]p, 1-color, pep)	Dutton	(1947)	Shepard, E.H.	80-120	*
Lucas, E.V.	Playtime & Company (1st, 4to, ibds, b/w, 95p, pep, DJ)	L: Methuen	(1925)	Shepard, E.H.	100-165	
Grahame, K.	Reluctant Dragon (1st, 8vo, [57]p, cloth, b/w, DJ)	Holiday House	(1938)	Shepard, E.H.	50-80	
Goulden, S.	Royal Reflections (1st, 8vo, ibds, b/w, DJ)	L: Methuen	1936	Shepard, E.H.	45-60	
Farjeon, E.	Silver Curlew (1st, 8vo, 192p, b/w)	L: OUP	1953	Shepard, E.H.	45-60	*
Milne, A.A.	Sneezles (1st AM, lg sq8vo, ibds, [23]p, pep)	Dutton	(1947)	Shepard, E.H.	70-100	*
Milne, A.A.	Songs from Now We are Six (1st, sm folio, 33p, bds, p-o, b/w)	L: Methuen	(1927)	Shepard, E.H.	150-200	
Struther, J.	Sycamore Square... (1st, 8vo, green/gilt, 63p, b/w)	L: Methuen	(1932)	Shepard, E.H.	45-60	
Milne, A.A.	Teddy Bear... (1st AM, lg4to, bds, p-o, 43p)	Dutton	(1926)	Shepard, E.H.	130-165	
Milne, A.A.	Teddy Bear... (1st, lg4to, bds, p-o, 43p)	L: Methuen	(1926)	Shepard, E.H.	120-165	
Milne, A.A.	Very Young Verses (1st, sm8vo, 88p, blue cl, 6pl)	L: Methuen	(1929)	Shepard, E.H.	100-140	*
Milne, A.A.	When We Were Very Young (1st AM, 12mo, 100p, gilt)	Dutton	(1924)	Shepard, E.H.	140-195	*
Milne, A.A.	When We Were Very Young (1st, 12mo, 100p, gilt, AEG)	L: Methuen	(1924)	Shepard, E.H.	420-600	
Grahame, K.	Wind in the Willows (1st, 8vo, green/gilt, 312p, b/w, pep)	L: Methuen	(1931)	Shepard, E.H.	150-200	
Grahame, K.	Wind in the Willows (1st AM, 8vo, blue/gilt, b/w, pep)	Scribner	1933	Shepard, E.H.	85-100	
Milne, A.A.	Winnie-the-Pooh (1st AM, 12mo, 158p, b/w)	Dutton	(1926)	Shepard, E.H.	200-280	
Milne, A.A.	Winnie-the-Pooh (1st, 12mo, 158p, gilt, teg, pep)	L: Methuen	(1926)	Shepard, E.H.	250-400	
Travers, P.L.	Mary Poppins (1st AM, 12mo, 206p, blue cl, b/w, pep, DJ)	Reynal/Hitch.	(1934)	Shepard, M.	200-320	R
Travers, P.L.	Mary Poppins Comes Back (1st AM, 12mo, 268p, green cl, b/w, pep)	Reynal/Hitch.	(1935)	Shepard, M.	130-165	
Travers, P.L.	Mary Poppins Comes Back (1st, sm8vo, 303p, beige cl, b/w, DJ)	L: Lovat/Dicks	(1935)	Shepard, M.	250-350	
Travers, P.L.	Mary Poppins in the Park (1st AM {std}, 12mo, 235p, b/w, dep)	Harcourt	(1952)	Shepard, M.	70-100	*
Travers, P.L.	Mary Poppins Opens the Door (1st AM, sm8vo, 239p, grey cl, b/w)	Reynal/Hitch.	(1943)	Shepard/Sims	70-115	*
Harris, J.C.	Nights with Uncle Remus (1st, 8vo, 367p, b/w)	L: A. Moring	[1907]	Shepherd, J.A.	180-250	*
Rostand, E.	Story of Chanticleer (1st AM, 8vo, 144p, 12cp)	Stokes	(1913)	Shepherd, J.A.	50-70	
Rostand, E.	Story of Chanticleer (1st, 8vo, 144p, cloth, 12cp)	L: Heinemann	1913	Shepherd, J.A.	65-80	
Cuming, E.W.D.	Three Jovial Puppies (1st, lg4to, bds, 36p, p-o, color)	L: Blackie	[1908]	Shepherd, J.A.	85-120	
Cuming, E.W.D.	Wonders in Monsterland (1st, 12mo, 257p, col frn, cp)	Longmans/Allen	1902	Shepherd, J.A.	100-150	*
N/A	Zig Zag Fables (1st, ob4to, 36p, ibds, color)	L: Wells/Gard.	1897	Shepherd, J.A.	150-200	
Daley, C.F.	Sundials (1st, 4to, ibds, 12cp)	Worthington	(1891)	Shepley, A.B.	100-150	
Wiggin, K.D.	Diary of a Goose Girl (1st, 12mo, 117p, tan cl, b/w)	Houghton	1902	Shepperson, C.	25-40	
Wells, H.G.	First Men in the Moon (1st UK, 8vo, 342p, blue/gilt, 14pl)	L: G. Newnes	1901	Shepperson, C.	300-450	*
Tracy, Louis	Final War (1st, sq8vo, 372p, grey/gilt, 16pl)	L: C. Pearson	1896	Sherie, E.F.	25-40	*
MacMillan, C.	Canadian Wonder Tales (1st, 4to, 199p, 17cp, pep)	L: J. Lane	1918	Sheringham, G.	70-100	
Beerbohm, M.	Happy Hypocrite (1st, 4to, 70p, white/gilt, uncut, 24cp, dep)	L: J. Lane	(1915)	Sheringham, G.	90-130	
Sheridan, R.B.	The Duenna (1st, lg8vo, 105p, grey cl, 12cp)	L: Constable	1925	Sheringham, G.	50-70	
Crawford, P.	Walking on Gold (1st, sm8vo, 284p, dp b/w, pep)	J. Messner	(1940)	Sherman, R.	20-30	*
Black, I.S.	Big Puppy & Little Puppy (1st, 8vo, yellow cl, [33]p, b/w, pep)	Holiday House	1960	Sherman, T.	20-30	*
Schlein, M.	Little Rabbit the High Jumper (1st, 8vo, [46]p, 2-color)	W.R. Scott	1957	Sherman, T.	30-50	*
Selsam, M.E.	Nature Detective (1st, ob8vo, [48]p, color)	W.R. Scott	1958	Sherman, T.	25-40	*
Sherwood, E.H.	Bobbie Bubbles (1st, sq8vo, 78p, ibds, color)	Rand/McNally	(1916)	Sherwood, E.H.	70-90	*
Sherwood, E.H.	Jack Jingling in Jungleland (1st, sm ob4to, 80p, ibds, fp color)	Rand/McNally	(1918)	Sherwood, E.H.	80-125	
Schlein, M.	Elephant Herd (1st, lg8vo, ipcb, [40]p, 1-color, cep)	W.R. Scott	1954	Shimin, S.	30-50	*
Schneider, H.	How Big is Big? (1st {this fmt.}, 4to, [40]p, color)	W.R. Scott	1950	Shimin, S.	25-45	*
Krumgold, Joseph	Onion John (1st {std}, 8vo, 248p, b/w, NM)	Crowell	(1959)	Shimin, S.	50-90	*

AUTHOR	TITLE	PUBLISHER	DATE	ARTIST	PRICE	LC
Brown, M.W.	Young Kangaroo (1st, 8vo, 42p, color)	W.R. Scott	(1955)	Shimin, S.	45-70	*
Bannerman, H.	Little Black Sambo (1st, 8vo, 63p, col frn, color)	Whitman	(1925)	Shinn, C.X.	65-90	*
Dickens, C.	Christmas Carol (1st {std}, sm4to, red/gilt, teg, pep, 12 col)	Winston	1938	Shinn, E.	90-120	R*
Dickens, C.	David Copperfield (1st {std}, 8vo, 423p, color)	Winston	(1948)	Shinn, E.	35-50	*
Wilde, O.	Happy Prince (1st, 4to, blue/gilt, teg, 148p, pep, 12cp)	Winston	(1940)	Shinn, E.	50-80	*
Dickens, C.	Life of Our Lord (1st, sm4to, 125p, gilt, 12 color)	Garden City	(1939)	Shinn, E.	30-45	
Moore, C.C.	Night Before Christmas (1st, 4to, [24]p, ibds, color)	Winston	(1942)	Shinn, E.	35-50	
Irving, W.	Rip Van Winkle (1st, lg4to, [40]p, color, pep)	Garden City	(1939)	Shinn, E.	65-90	*
N/A	Sermon on the Mount (1st, 4to, unpag, 18cp, DJ)	Winston	1946	Shinn, E.	25-40	
Howells, W.D.	Flight of Pony Baker (1st, sm8vo, red/silver, 223p, 8pl, PPP)	Harper	1902	Shinn, F.S.	100-165	R
Rice, Alice H.	Lovey Mary (1st, 8vo, teg, uncut, 236p, 24pl)	Century	1903	Shinn, F.S.	20-30	
Hurd, E.T.	Hurry Hurry (1st, 8vo, ipcb, 45p, 1-color, cep)	W.R. Scott	(1938)	Shipman, M.D.	35-50	*
Shirk, J.C.	Mr. Baxter's Dandelion Garden (1st {std}, 4to, 58p, fp b/w, dep)	Dutton	1940	Shirk, J.C.	25-40	*
Spyri, J.	Heidi (1st, 12mo, 305p, p-o, gilt, 7 fp color)	Macrae-Smith	(1925)	Shoemaker, E.C.	20-30	
Montgomery, L.M.	Magic for Marigold (1st, sm8vo, 328p, p-o, col frn)	Stokes	1929	Shoemaker, E.C.	65-90	
Bond, Gladys B.	Blue Chimney (1st, sm8vo, 164p, red cl, b/w, pep)	Holiday House	(1959)	Shortall, L.	25-40	*
Robinson, M.L.	Skipper Riley: Terrier Dog (1st, 8vo, blue cl, 90p, b/w)	Random	(1955)	Shortall, L.	25-40	*
Russell, W.C.	Lady Maud (8vo, 312p, b/w pl)	Fenno	(1896)	Shute, A.B.	20-30	*
Richardson, W.C.F.	India Rubber Jack (1st, 16mo, blue cl, [124]p, 28 color)	L: Swan/Sonn.	[1902]	Sichel, G.	100-140	
DeMille, W.M.C.	Forest Ring (1st, lg8vo, 180p, gilt, p-o, 10cp)	Doran	(1914)	Sichel, H.	50-70	*
Bancroft, Alberta	Goblins of Haubeck (1st, 12mo, 117p, green/gilt, pep, col frn)	McBride	1925	Sichel, H.	20-30	*
Burnett, F.H.	Good Wolf (1st, 8vo, 125p, 5cp)	Moffat	1908	Sichel, H.	30-45	
Olcott, F.J. (ed.)	Wonder Tales/Goblin Hills (1st {std}, 12mo, 268p, col frn, pep)	NY: Longmans	1930	Sichel, H.	35-50	*
Robbins, Ruth	Baboushka & Three Kings (1st, sq12mo, ipcb, [28]p, col, pep, CM)	Parnassus Pr.	(1960)	Sidjakov, N.	65-100	R*
Towne, Rbt. D.	Teddy Bears in Hot Water (1st, sm8vo, ibds, unpag, color)	Reilly/Britton	(1907)	Sieber, C.A.	70-100	
Towne, Rbt. D.	Teddy Bears in a Smashup (1st, 12mo, [16]p, color)	Reilly/Britton	(1907)	Sieber, C.A.	65-90	*
Towne, Rbt. D.	Teddy Bears on a Lark (1st, 12mo, [16]p, color)	Reilly/Britton	(1907)	Sieber, C.A.	65-80	
Siegel, Wm.	Around the World in a Mailbag (1st, 4to, ibds, [30]p, col, pep)	McBride	1932	Siegel, W.	35-50	*
McNeely, M.H.	Jumping-Off Place (1st {std}, sm8vo, 308p, b/w, pep, NH)	Longmans	1929	Siegel, W.	45-60	*
Sime, Sidney H.	Bogey Beasts (1st, 4to, ibds)	L: Goodwin	(1923)	Sime, S.H.	250-400	
Lord Dunsany	Book of Wonder (1st, 8vo, 98p, brown pcb, p-o, 10pl)	L: Heinemann	1912	Sime, S.H.	60-85	*
Lord Dunsany	Gods of Pegana (1st, 8vo, 94p, grey bds, uncut, 8pl)	L: E. Matthews	1905	Sime, S.H.	50-80	*
Lord Dunsany	Sword of Welleran (1st, 4to, 243p, green/gilt, teg, 10pl)	L: G. Allen	1908	Sime, S.H.	70-90	
Lord Dunsany	Time & the Gods (1st AM, 8vo, bds, 179p, p-o, 10pl)	J.W. Luce	1913	Sime, S.H.	50-75	
Shakespeare, Wm.	Hamlet (1st, lg4to, 165p, gilt, 30 ticp)	L: Hodder	[1900]	Simmonds, W.G.	125-160	
Simmons, H.B.	Jingle Jangle Rhyme Book (1st, ob4to, ibds, 18cp)	Stokes	1898	Simmons, H.B.	150-220	*
Simon, Ellen	Critter Book (1st, ob4to, [48]p, color)	Holiday House	(1940)	Simon, E.	35-60	*
Stone, C.R.	Inga of Porcupine Mine (1st, sm8vo, 212p, blue cl, b/w)	Holiday House	(1942)	Simon, E.	20-25	*
Judson, C.I.	Railway Engineer (1st, 8vo, 171p, b/w pl, pep)	Scribner	(1941)	Simon, E.M.	25-40	*
Krauss, Ruth	Backward Day (1st, 8vo, [31]p, color)	Harper	1950	Simont, M.	25-45	*
Krauss, Ruth	Big World & Little House (1st, 4to, ibds, [41]p, color, pep)	NY: Schuman	1949	Simont, M.	50-70	R
DeJong, Meindert	Billy & the Unhappy Bull (1st {std}, 8vo, 206p, brown cl, b/w)	Harper	(1946)	Simont, M.	35-50	*
Owen, Ruth	Castle in Silver Wood (1st, 8vo, 181p, blue cl, col frn, pep)	Dodd	1939	Simont, M.	30-45	*
Cooke, Alistair	Christmas Eve (1st AM {std}, 8vo, 56p, bds, 1-color)	Knopf	(1952)	Simont, M.	35-50	
Alger, Leclaire	Dougal's Wish (1st {std}, 8vo, 244p, rust cl, fp b/w)	Harper	1942	Simont, M.	30-45	*
Trent, R.	First Christmas (1st, 12mo, ipcb, [32]p, color, pep)	Harper	1948	Simont, M.	35-50	*
Brown, M.W.	First Story (1st, 4to, [31]p, ibds, 1-color, pep)	Harper	(1947)	Simont, M.	50-85	
Fritz, Jean	Fish Head (1st, sm4to, tan cl, [38]p, fp 3-color, pep)	Coward	(1954)	Simont, M.	45-70	*
Vinton, Iris	Flying Ebony (1st, sm8vo, 289p, olive cl, b/w)	Dodd	1947	Simont, M.	30-45	*
DeJong, Meindert	Good Luck Duck (1st, lg8vo, yellow cl, 57p, color, pep)	Harper	(1950)	Simont, M.	35-50	*
Krauss, Ruth	Happy Day (1st, lg4to, [33]p, CH)	Harper	1949	Simont, M.	70-110	
Powell, Miriam	Jareb (1st {std}, sm8vo, grey cl, 241p, b/w, cep)	Crowell	(1952)	Simont, M.	30-45	*
Simont, M.	Lovely Summer (1st, sm4to, blue cl, [46]p, b/w)	Harper	(1952)	Simont, M.	25-40	*
Simont, M.	Mimi (1st, 8vo, beige cl, 55p, b/w)	Harper	(1954)	Simont, M.	45-60	*
Walsh, Chad	Nellie & her Flying Crocodile (1st {std}, 8vo, 179p, b/w)	Harper	(1956)	Simont, M.	30-45	*
Liggett, Thos.	Pigeon, Fly Home! (1st, 8vo, 189p, tan cl, b/w, pep)	Holiday House	(1956)	Simont, M.	20-30	*
Sterne, Emma G.	Pirate of Chatham Square (1st, 8vo, 213p, b/w, pep)	Dodd	1939	Simont, M.	20-30	*
Simont, M.	Plumber Out of the Sea (1st, lg8vo, ipcb, 39p, 2-color, pep)	Harper	(1955)	Simont, M.	35-50	*
Simont, M.	Polly's Oats (1st, sm4to, [46]p, fp b/w)	Harper	(1951)	Simont, M.	30-45	*
Leach, Maria	Rainbow Bk./American Folk Tales (1st {std}, 4to, 318p, color)	World Pub. Co.	(1958)	Simont, M.	30-50	*
Jackson, Charlotte	Sarah Deborah's Day (1st, lg8vo, ipcb, 74p, 2-color)	Dodd	1941	Simont, M.	35-50	*
Ladas, Alexis	Seal that Couldn't Swim (1st {std}, lg8vo, 55p, blue cl, 3-col)	Little/Brown	(1959)	Simont, M.	25-45	*
Deutsch, B.	The Welcome (1st {std}, sm8vo, 197p, blue cl, 9 fp b/w)	Harper	(1942)	Simont, M.	45-60	R*
Thurber, J.	Thirteen Clocks (1st, 8vo, ibds, 124p, color, pep)	Simon/Schuster	(1950)	Simont, M.	65-80	R
Gipson, Fred B.	Trail-Driving Rooster (1st, 8vo, grey cl, 79p, b/w)	Harper	(1955)	Simont, M.	30-45	*
Udry, J.M.	Tree is Nice (1st, 4to, ibds, [30]p, fp color, CM)	Harper	1956	Simont, M.	70-100	R*
Thurber, J.	Wonderful O. (1st {std}, 8vo, bds, 72p, 2-color, dep, DJ)	Simon/Schuster	(1957)	Simont, M.	50-70	
N/A	Aucassin & Nicolette (1st, narrow 12mo, 106p, color)	Holiday House	1936	Simpson, M.	60-85	R*
Perrault, C.	Once Upon a Time (1st, 4to, 115p)	L: O'Connor	1922	Sinclair, H.	70-120	*
Byron, May	Teddy Bearoplane (sm4to, ibds, 12cp)	NY: Hodder	[1909]	Sinclair, J.R.	130-200	
Skaar, G.M.	All About Dogs, Dogs, Dogs (1st, sq8vo, wraps, unpag, color)	W.R. Scott	1947	Skaar, G.M.	45-60	*
Skaar, G.M.	Nothing But Cats, Cats, Cats (1st, ob8vo, wraps, [20]p, color)	W.R. Scott	1947	Skaar, G.M.	45-60	*

AUTHOR	TITLE	PUBLISHER	DATE	ARTIST	PRICE	LC
Skaar, G.M.	Very Little Dog (1st, ob8vo, [20]p, ipcb, 2-color)	W.R. Scott	1949	Skaar, G.M.	35-50	*
Skaar, G.M.	What Do they Say! (1st, ob8vo, ibds, [20]p, color)	W.R. Scott	1950	Skaar, G.M.	30-50	*
Wiig, Hanna	Tale of Tiny Tutak (1st AM, 16mo, unpag, color, pep)	Lippincott	[1957]	Skauge, S.	25-40	*
Jerome, J.K.	Told After Supper (1st, 12mo, 169p, teg, uncut)	Field & Tuer	1891	Skeaping, K.M.	65-90	
Marshall, H.E.	Empire Story (8vo, 493p, 8cp, maps)	Stokes	(1908)	Skelton, J.R.	40-60	
England, G.A.	Air Trust (8vo, red/gilt, 4pl)	P. Wagner	(1915)	Sloan, J.	130-165	
Bergengren, R.W.	Gentlemen & All Merry Companions (1st, 12mo, 247p)	Bos: Brimmer	1922	Sloan, J.	35-50	*
England, G.A.	Golden Blight (1st, 8vo, 350p, brown/gilt, 5pl)	H.K. Fly	(1916)	Sloan, J.	65-80	*
Crane, S.	Great Battles of the World (1st, 8vo, red/gilt, 278p, 7pl)	Lippincott	1901	Sloan, J.	180-250	
Daly, T.A.	Madrigali (1st, sm8vo, 169p, gilt, frn by...)	McKay	(1912)	Sloan, J.	30-45	*
Gaboriau, Emile	Within an Inch of His Life (1st AM, 8vo, teg, 608p, gilt, 4pl)	Scribner	1913	Sloan, J.	70-100	*
Slobodkin, L.	Adventures of Arab (1st, lg8vo, 128p, color, cep)	MacMillan	1946	Slobodkin, L.	30-45	
Slobodkin, L.	Big Circus April 1st (1st {std}, sm8vo, 90p, cep, DJ)	MacMillan	(1953)	Slobodkin, L.	25-40	
Slobodkin, L.	Bixxy & the Secret Message (1st {std}, 8vo, 94p, b/w, pep)	MacMillan	1949	Slobodkin, L.	20-30	*
Slobodkin, L.	Dinny & Danny (1st {std}, 4to, [30]p, color, pep)	MacMillan	(1951)	Slobodkin, L.	30-45	*
Eberle, I.	Evie & Cooky (1st, 8vo, 122p, 1-color, pep)	Knopf	(1957)	Slobodkin, L.	20-30	*
Eberle, I.	Evie & Wonderful Kangaroo (1st, 8vo, 128p, 1-color, pep)	Knopf	(1955)	Slobodkin, L.	20-30	*
Slobodkin, L.	Gogo: French Seagull (1st {std}, 4to, [46]p, fp color)	MacMillan	(1960)	Slobodkin, L.	35-50	*
Estes, Eleanor	Hundred Dresses (1st, sm4to, 80p, red cl, color, NH)	Harcourt	(1944)	Slobodkin, L.	65-90	
Slobodkin, L.	Hustle & Bustle (1st, ob lg8vo, [36]p, 1-color)	MacMillan	1948	Slobodkin, L.	25-45	*
Blanck, Jacob	Jonathan & the Rainbow (1st, 4to, ibds, 48p, color)	Houghton	1948	Slobodkin, L.	45-65	*
Blanck, Jacob	King & Noble Blacksmith (1st, sm4to, yellow cl, 48p, color)	Houghton	1950	Slobodkin, L.	45-60	
Dickens, C.	Magic Fishbone (1st, 4to, ibds, 36p, color)	Vanguard Pr.	(1953)	Slobodkin, L.	50-80	R
Slobodkin, L.	Magic Michael (1st, ob8vo, red cl, unpag, color, cep)	MacMillan	(1944)	Slobodkin, L.	25-40	*
Thurber, J.	Many Moons (1st, 4to, red cl, [47]p, color, pep, DJ, CM)	Harcourt	(1943)	Slobodkin, L.	125-160	R
Estes, Eleanor	Middle Moffat (1st, 8vo, 317p, p-o, b/w, pep, NH)	Harcourt	(1942)	Slobodkin, L.	60-85	
Slobodkin, L.	Mr. Mushroom (1st {std}, sq16mo, ipcb, [32]p, color)	MacMillan	(1950)	Slobodkin, L.	25-40	*
Slobodkin, L.	Mr. Petersand's Cats & Kittens (1st {std}, 8vo, 63p, col, cep)	MacMillan	(1954)	Slobodkin, L.	25-40	*
Baker, Nina B.	Peter the Great (1st, 8vo, 310p, fp b/w)	Vanguard Pr.	(1943)	Slobodkin, L.	30-45	*
McSpadden, J.W.	Robin Hood & his Merry Outlaws (1st, 8vo, 285p)	World	1946	Slobodkin, L.	45-60	*
Estes, Eleanor	Rufus M. (1st, 8vo, 320p, red cl, b/w, pep, NH)	Harcourt	(1943)	Slobodkin, L.	60-80	
Slobodkin, L.	Seaweed Hat (1st, 8vo, [48]p, color)	MacMillan	1947	Slobodkin, L.	30-45	*
Slobodkin, L.	Space Ship Returns to Apple Tree (1st {std}, 8vo, 128p, b/w)	MacMillan	(1958)	Slobodkin, L.	25-45	*
Slobodkin, L.	Space Ship Under Apple Tree (1st {std}, 8vo, 116p, blue cl, b/w)	MacMillan	(1952)	Slobodkin, L.	25-45	*
Estes, Eleanor	Sun, Wind & Mr. Todd (1st, 4to, [92]p, brown cl, 1-color, pep)	Harcourt	(1943)	Slobodkin, L.	40-60	*
Estes, Eleanor	The Moffats (1st [1st bk.], 8vo, pink cl, 290p, b/w, pep)	Harcourt	(1941)	Slobodkin, L.	50-80	R*
Hunt, M.L.	Young Man of the House (1st {std}, 8vo, 171p, 10 fp b/w)	Lippincott	(1944)	Slobodkin, L.	25-40	*
Slobodkina, E.	Caps for Sale (1st, 8vo, [43]p, color, pep)	W.R. Scott	1940	Slobodkina, E.	35-50	*
Brown, M.W.	Little Cowboy (1st, lg8vo, ipcb, [33]p, color, pep)	W.R. Scott	(1948)	Slobodkina, E.	50-80	*
Brown, M.W.	Little Farmer (1st, sm4to, [38]p, ipcb, color)	W.R. Scott	1948	Slobodkina, E.	50-80	*
Brown, M.W.	Little Fireman (1st, 8vo, ibds, [34]p, color, cep, p-o)	W.R. Scott	(1938)	Slobodkina, E.	60-80	*
Brown, M.W.	Sleepy ABC (1st, lg8vo, ibds, unpag, color, dep)	Lothrop/Lee	1953	Slobodkina, E.	50-80	*
Slobodkina, E.	Wonderful Feast (1st, sq8vo, ipcb, [26]p, color)	Lothrop/Lee	1955	Slobodkina, E.	40-60	*
Brown, M.W.	When the Wind Blew (1st {std}-[1st Bk], lg8vo, unpag, ibds, col)	Harper	1937	Slocum, R.	80-130	*
Howells, W.D.	Coast of Bohemia (1st, 12mo, red cl, 340p, 8pl)	Harper	1893	Small, F.O.	45-60	
Porter, Jane	Biffy Buffalo (1st, 8vo, 63p, color, pep)	Wm. Morrow	1942	Smalley, J.	35-50	*
Smalley, J.	Do You Know about Fishes? (1st, ob8vo, 45p, color, pep)	Wm. Morrow	(1936)	Smalley, J.	50-70	*
Smalley, J.	Do You Know? (1st, ob8vo, 44p, color, pep)	Wm. Morrow	(1934)	Smalley, J.	50-70	*
Benet, W.R.	Flying King of Kurio (1st, 8vo, 289p, 4cp, pep)	Doran	(1926)	Smalley, J.	30-50	
Smalley, J.	How It All Began (1st, 8vo, ibds, 94p, color)	Wm. Morrow	(1932)	Smalley, J.	50-80	
Smalley, J.	Now and Then... (1st, 8vo, 91p, ibds, color, pep)	Wm. Morrow	(1931)	Smalley, J.	65-110	
Smalley, J.	Plum to Plum Jam (1st, 8vo, 87p, ibds, color, pep)	Wm. Morrow	(1929)	Smalley, J.	70-100	
Smalley, J.	Rice to Rice Pudding (1st, smsq8vo, 85p, ibds, color, pep)	Wm. Morrow	(1928)	Smalley, J.	70-90	
Twain, M.	Dog's Tale (1st AM, 8vo, 36p, 4cp)	Harper	1904	Smedley, W.T.	100-140	
James, Henry	Julia Bride (1st, 8vo, 83p, teg, 4pl)	Harper	1909	Smedley, W.T.	80-100	
Bangs, J.K.	Rebellious Heroine (1st, 12mo, yellow/gilt, 8pl)	Harper	1896	Smedley, W.T.	30-45	
Anderson, Rbt. G.	Half-Past Seven Stories (1st, lg8vo, p-o, 251p, 16cp)	Putnam	(1922)	Smith, D.H.	30-45	*
Baring-Gould, S.	Book of Ghosts (1st, 8vo, 383p)	L: Methuen	1904	Smith, D.M.	50-70	*
Aubrey, Frank	Queen of Atlantis... (1st AM, 8vo, red/gilt, 391p, 8pl)	Lippincott	1900	Smith, D.M.	120-165	
Cocke, Sarah J.	Bypaths in Dixie (1st, 8vo, blue/gilt, 317p, 7pl)	Dutton	(1911)	Smith, Duncan	45-60	*
Aesopus	Aesop's Fables (1st, 8vo, 172p, teg, brown/gilt, 6pl)	Century	1911	Smith, E.B.	100-150	
Smith, E.B.	After they Came Out of the Ark (1st, ob4to, ibds, 48p, 22cp)	Putnam	(1918)	Smith, E.B.	150-200	
Mother Goose	Boyd Smith Mother Goose (1st, 4to, red/gilt, 223p, 20cp)	Putnam	(1919)	Smith, E.B.	180-220	
Smith, E.B.	Chicken World (1st, ob4to, ibds, [28]p, color)	Putnam	1910	Smith, E.B.	130-170	
Marryat, Fred.	Children of the New Forest (1st, 8vo, 397p, p-o, 8cp)	Holt	1911	Smith, E.B.	65-80	
Marryat, Fred.	Children of the New Forest (8vo, 397p, p-o, 8cp)	L: Constable	1914	Smith, E.B.	45-60	
Smith, E.B.	Circus & All About It (1st, 4to, p-o, 62p, 16cp, pep)	Stokes	(1909)	Smith, E.B.	180-240	
Brown, A.F.	Curious Book of Birds (1st, 8vo, gilt, 191p, 8pl)	Houghton	1903	Smith, E.B.	45-70	
Smith, E.B.	Early Life of Mr. Man... (1st, ob4to, ibds, 56p, 23cp, pep)	Houghton	1914	Smith, E.B.	140-200	
Oxley, J.M.	Family on Wheels (1st AM, sm8vo, 219p, 4pl)	Crowell	(1905)	Smith, E.B.	30-45	*
Pine, F.W. (ed.)	Franklin's Autobiography (1st, lg8vo, green cl, 341p, 10cp)	Holt	1916	Smith, E.B.	50-70	
Smith, E.B.	Fun in the Radio World (1st, ob4to, [30]p, p-o, 12cp, pep)	Stokes	1923	Smith, E.B.	140-200	

AUTHOR	TITLE	PUBLISHER	DATE	ARTIST	PRICE	LC
Holbrook, Florence	Hiawatha Primer (1st, 8vo, green cl, 148p, 8cp)	Houghton	1898	Smith, E.B.	70-85	
Brown, A.F.	In the Days of Giants (1st, 12mo, 259p, 6pl)	Houghton	1902	Smith, E.B.	80-100	
Smith, E.B.	In the Land of Make-Believe (1st, ob4to, ibds, [28]p, 12cp, pep)	Holt	(1916)	Smith, E.B.	180-250	R*
Scott, Walter	Ivanhoe (1st, 8vo, red cl, 676p, teg, 16cp)	Houghton	1913	Smith, E.B.	75-120	
Brown, A.F.	John of the Woods (1st, sm8vo, 189p, 15pl)	Houghton	1909	Smith, E.B.	35-50	
Austin, Mary	Land of Little Rain (1st, 8vo, green/gilt, 281p, p-o, teg)	Houghton	1903	Smith, E.B.	240-350	
Cooper, J.F.	Last of the Mohicans (1st, 8vo, p-o, 523p, 8cp)	Holt	(1910)	Smith, E.B.	65-90	
Smith, E.B.	Lions 'n' Elephants & Everything (1st, ob4to, [32]p, ibds, 12cp)	Putnam	(1929)	Smith, E.B.	185-250	
Adams, A.	Log of a Cowboy (1st, 8vo, 387p, gilt, 6pl, map, PPPa)	Houghton	1903	Smith, E.B.	80-120	
Smith, E.B.	My Village (1st [1st bk], 12mo, teg, 325p)	Scribner	1896	Smith, E.B.	80-100	
Harris, J.C.	Plantation Pageants (1st, sq8vo, green cl, 247p, 20pl, cep)	Houghton	1899	Smith, E.B.	140-200	R
Harris, J.C.	Plantation Pageants (1st UK, 12mo, 247p, 20 fp b/w)	L: Constable	1899	Smith, E.B.	80-120	
Smith, E.B.	Pocahontas & Captain Smith (1st, ob4to, ibds, unpag, color, pep)	Houghton	1906	Smith, E.B.	140-200	
Smith, E.B.	Railroad Book (1st, ob4to, [28]p, p-o, 12cp, pep)	Houghton	1913	Smith, E.B.	160-225	R
Defoe, D.	Robinson Crusoe (1st, 8vo, blue/gilt, 435p, p-o, 12cp)	Houghton	1909	Smith, E.B.	60-80	
Smith, E.B.	Seashore Book (1st, ob4to, [30]p, ibds, 12cp, pep)	Houghton	1912	Smith, E.B.	150-200	R
Anderson, Rbt. G.	Seven O'Clock Stories (1st, lg8vo, 180p, gilt, p-o, 20cp, pep)	Putnam	(1920)	Smith, E.B.	130-160	
Smith, E.B.	So Long Ago (1st, lg4to, green cl, 36p, 17cp, DJ)	Houghton	1944	Smith, E.B.	70-100	
Smith, E.B.	Story of Noah's Ark (1st, ob4to, ibds, [56]p, p-o, 26cp, pep)	Houghton	1905	Smith, E.B.	140-200	
Phelps, E.S.	Supply at St. Agatha's (1st, 8vo, 38p, uncut, teg, 2pl by...)	Houghton	1896	Smith, E.B.	30-50	
Harris, J.C.	Tales of Home Folks/Peace & War (1st, 8vo, 417p, 4pl, cep)	Houghton	1898	Smith, E.B.	80-100	
Knibbs, H.H.	Tang of Life (1st, sm8vo, 393p, 4cp)	Houghton	1918	Smith, E.B.	35-50	
Adams, A.	Texas Matchmaker (1st, 12mo, 355p, 6pl)	Houghton	1904	Smith, E.B.	80-120	
Austin, Mary	The Flock (1st, 8vo, 266p, frn by...)	Houghton	1906	Smith, E.B.	40-60	
Austin, Mary	The Ford (1st, sm8vo, 440p, 4pl)	Houghton	1917	Smith, E.B.	50-70	
Adams, A.	The Outlet (1st, 8vo, 371p, brown/gilt, 6pl)	Houghton	1905	Smith, E.B.	60-80	
Dana, R.H.	Two Years Before the Mast (1st, lg8vo, 553p, p-o, 10cp, pep)	Houghton	1911	Smith, E.B.	70-90	
Meigs, C.	Willow Whistle (1st, ob4to, 144p, yellow cl, col frn, 10pl)	MacMillan	1931	Smith, E.B.	65-90	R
N/A	Aucassin & Nicolette (1st, lg4to, 69p, gilt, 17pl)	L: Melrose	1914	Smith, E.L.	100-150	
Russell, R.H.	Delft Cat (1st, 16mo, 71p, uncut, b/w)	R.H. Russell	1896	Smith, F.B.	65-100	*
Smith, F.B.	Real Latin Quarter (1st, 8vo, 204p, b/w)	Funk/Wagnalls	1901	Smith, F.B.	30-45	
Smith, F.H.	Charcoals of New & Old New York (1st, 4to, 142p, bds, 23 tipl)	Doubleday/Page	1912	Smith, F.H.	80-100	
Smith, F.H.	Day at Laguerre's... (1st, 8vo, tan cl, 190p)	Houghton	1892	Smith, F.H.	85-100	
Smith, F.H.	In Dickens' London (1st, 4to, bds, 199p, teg, 22 tipl)	Scribner	1914	Smith, F.H.	65-80	
Smith, F.H.	Old Lines & New in Black & White (1st, ob folio, p-o, 12pl)	Houghton	1886	Smith, F.H.	80-100	
Smith, F.H.	Outdoor Sketching (1st, sm8vo, pcb, 145p, 3pl)	Scribner	1915	Smith, F.H.	25-45	
Mother Goose	Mother Goose: Her Book (1st, lg8vo, 48p, color, pep)	Duffield	(1906)	Smith, H.L.	50-80	*
Ade, G.	True Bills (1st, 16mo, 154p, b/w)	Harper	1904	Smith, H.L.	30-50	
Dickens, C.	David Copperfield (1st, 12mo, 506p, b/w pl)	MacMillan	1925	Smith, H.S.	25-40	*
Asbjornsen, P.C.	Tales from the Field (1st AM, 8vo, 403p, gilt, 11pl)	Putnam	1896	Smith, J. Moyr	50-80	
Daldorne, Evan	Wooing of the Water-Witch (1st, 8vo, gilt, 132p, AEG)	Holt	1880	Smith, J. Moyr	90-145	*
MacDonald, Geo.	Back of the North Wind (1st, 4to, p-o, teg, 342p, 8cp, pep)	McKay	1919	Smith, J.W.	130-180	
Whitney, H.H.	Bed-Time Book (1st, lg4to, ipcb, 31p, 6cp, pep)	Duffield	1907	Smith, J.W.	280-400	
Long, J.L.	Billy Boy (1st, 8vo, blue cl, 74p, teg, p-o, uncut, 4pl, pep)	Dodd	1906	Smith, J.W.	160-220	
Franchot, A.W.	Bobs, King of Fortunate Isle (1st, 8vo, 210p, blue cl, col frn)	Dutton	(1928)	Smith, J.W.	35-50	*
Humphrey, Mabel	Book of the Child (1st, folio, ibds, 3cp by...)	Stokes	(1903)	Smith, J.W.	600-750	
Smith, N.A.	Boys & Girls of Bookland (1st, lg4to, p-o, 100p, 11cp, cep)	Cosmopolitan	1923	Smith, J.W.	130-165	
Smith, N.A.	Boys & Girls of Bookland (lg4to, 100p, brown pcb, 11cp, later)	McKay	(1924)	Smith, J.W.	100-150	
Reed, H.L.	Brenda's Summer at Rockley (1st, 8vo, blue/gilt, 376p, 5pl)	Little/Brown	1901	Smith, J.W.	180-220	
Reed, H.L.	Brenda, Her School & her Club (1st, sm8vo, 328p, gilt, 5pl)	Little/Brown	1900	Smith, J.W.	140-180	
Skinner, A.M.	Child's Book of Country Stories (1st, lg8vo, 265p, p-o, 4cp)	Duffield	1925	Smith, J.W.	165-200	
Skinner, A.M.	Child's Book of Country Stories (1st {this pub}, 8vo, p-o, 4cp)	Dial	1935	Smith, J.W.	80-100	
Skinner, A.M.	Child's Book of Modern Stories (1st, lg8vo, gilt p-o, 340p, 8cp)	Duffield	1920	Smith, J.W.	140-185	
Skinner, A.M.	Child's Book of Modern Stories (4to, gilt, 341p, 8cp)	Dial	1935	Smith, J.W.	70-100	
Smith, J.W.	Child's Book of Old Verses (1st, lg8vo, p-o, teg, 124p, 10cp)	Duffield	1910	Smith, J.W.	160-240	
Coussens, P.W.	Child's Book of Stories (1st, lg8vo, gilt, 463p, 10cp, pep)	Duffield	1911	Smith, J.W.	260-320	
Stevenson, R.L.	Child's Garden/Verses (1st, 4to, p-o, 125p, teg uncut, 12cp, SC)	Scribner	1905	Smith, J.W.	160-230	
Toogood, C.C.	Child's Prayer (1st, lg8vo, [16]p, blue/gilt, col frn)	McKay	(1925)	Smith, J.W.	35-50	*
Crothers, S.M.	Children of Dickens (1st, 4to, p-o, 259p, 10cp, pep, SC)	Scribner	1925	Smith, J.W.	85-120	
Cox, F.T.	Chronicles of Rhoda (1st, 12mo, 287p, red/gilt, 2cp)	Small	(1909)	Smith, J.W.	80-120	
Chabot, Adrien	Dancing-Master (1st, 12mo, teg, green cl, 139p, 4pl)	Lippincott	1901	Smith, J.W.	120-170	*
Dickens, C.	Dickens' Children (1st, lg8vo, [48]p, gilt, p-o, teg, 10cp)	Scribner	1912	Smith, J.W.	150-200	
Higgins, A.C.	Dream Blocks (1st, lg8vo, p-o, 47p, beige cl, 15cp, pep)	Duffield	1908	Smith, J.W.	300-450	
Longfellow, H.W.	Evangeline (1st, 8vo, 143p, teg, gilt, 5cp by...)	Houghton	1897	Smith, J.W.	180-230	
Chapin, A.A.	Everyday & Nowaday Fairy Book (lg4to, 160p, ibds, 8cp)	L: Coker	[1920]	Smith, J.W.	180-250	
Chapin, A.A.	Everyday Fairy Book (1st, 4to, 160p, p-o, 7cp)	Dodd	1915	Smith, J.W.	250-320	
Chapin, A.A.	Everyday Fairy Book (1st UK, 4to, 160p, p-o, 7cp)	L: Harrap	1917	Smith, J.W.	185-250	
Keyes, A.M.	Five Senses (1st, 8vo, ivory cl, 252p, 5cp)	Moffat	1911	Smith, J.W.	250-320	
Goodwin, M.W.	Head of a Hundred (1st, 12mo, green/gilt, 225p, teg, 2pl by...)	Little/Brown	1897	Smith, J.W.	70-90	
Goodwin, M.W.	Head of a Hundred (1st {new ed}, 12mo, 221p, red/glt, 2pl)	Little/Brown	1900	Smith, J.W.	75-100	
Spyri, J.	Heidi (1st, lg8vo, 380p, teg, p-o, blue cl, 10cp, pep)	McKay	1922	Smith, J.W.	120-160	
Burnett, F.H.	In the Closed Room (1st, 8vo, green/gilt, teg, 130p, 8cp, dep)	McClurg	1904	Smith, J.W.	70-100	

AUTHOR	TITLE	PUBLISHER	DATE	ARTIST	PRICE	LC
Mother Goose	J.W. Smith Mother Goose (1st, ob4to, 173p, p-o, 12cp, 5pl, pep)	Dodd	(1914)	Smith, J.W.	280-450	
Bell, L.P.	Kitchen Fun (1st, sm4to, ibds, 27p, cvr by...)	Harter	1932	Smith, J.W.	45-65	
Skinner, A.M.	Little Child's Book of Stories (1st, lg8vo, 258p, gilt 8cp, pep)	Duffield	1922	Smith, J.W.	150-220	*
Taylor, M.I.	Little Mistress Goodhope (1st, 12mo, gilt, p-o, 186p, col frn)	McClurg	1902	Smith, J.W.	180-260	
Mother Goose	Little Mother Goose (1st, ob8vo, p-o, 176p, gilt, 12cp)	Dodd	(1918)	Smith, J.W.	180-225	
Alcott, L.M.	Little Women (1st, 8vo, p-o, 617p, green/gilt, 8cp, pep)	Little/Brown	1915	Smith, J.W.	140-180	
Shelby, A.B.	Lullaby Book (1st, 8vo, blue/gilt, 183p, col frn by...)	Duffield	1921	Smith, J.W.	50-75	
Mother Goose	Mother Goose (1st, 12mo, 173p, black cl, p-o, 12cp)	Dodd	1914	Smith, J.W.	400-600	
Moore, C.C.	Night Before Christmas (1st, ob8vo, [32]p, ibds, 12cp, pep)	Houghton	(1912)	Smith, J.W.	185-250	
Chapin, A.A.	Nowadays Fairy Book (1st, lg4to, ibds, 159p, 6 ticp)	Dodd	1911	Smith, J.W.	280-400	
Alcott, L.M.	Old-Fashioned Girl (1st, sm8vo, green/gilt, teg, 371p, 12pl)	Little/Brown	1902	Smith, J.W.	90-130	
MacDonald, Geo.	Princess & Goblin (1st, 4to, gilt, p-o, teg, 203p, 8cp, pep)	McKay	1920	Smith, J.W.	140-200	
Sill, S.C.	Reminiscences/Chest of Drawers (1st, sm8vo, [40]p, AEG, 6pl)	Lippincott	1900	Smith, J.W.	70-110	
Sage, B.	Rhymes of Real Children (1st, sq4to, 32p, ibds, 6cp)	Fox/Duffield	1903	Smith, J.W.	275-400	
Wells, Carolyn	Seven Ages of Childhood (1st, sm4to, gilt, 56p, p-o, 7cp, pep)	Moffat	1909	Smith, J.W.	280-400	
Richards, L.E.	Silver Crown (1st, 8vo, 105p, teg, grey/gilt, cvr by...)	Little/Brown	1906	Smith, J.W.	45-60	
Stuart, Ruth M.	Sonny's Father (1st, 12mo, teg, 240p, uncut, 2pl by...)	Century	1910	Smith, J.W.	60-90	
Bacon, J.D.	Ten to Seventeen (1st, sm8vo, 261p, green cl, p-o, 3pl by...)	Harper	1908	Smith, J.W.	35-60	*
McCall, S.	Truth Dexter (1st, 8vo, 375p, blue cloth, frn by...)	Little/Brown	1903	Smith, J.W.	30-50	
Skinner, A.W.	Very Little Child's Bk. of Stories (1st, lg8vo, 232p, gilt, 8cp)	Duffield	1923	Smith, J.W.	150-220	*
Kingsley, C.	Water Babies (1st {this format}, 12mo, 270p, p-o, 8cp, pep)	Dodd	1916	Smith, J.W.	120-165	*
Kingsley, C.	Water Babies (1st, sm4to, p-o, gilt, 362p, 12cp, pep)	Dodd	(1916)	Smith, J.W.	300-400	
Kingsley, C.	Water Babies (1st UK, 4to, 240p, gilt, 12 ticp)	L: Boots	[1918]	Smith, J.W.	250-300	
Stewart, M.	Way to Wonderland (1st, lg8vo, 144p, gilt, 194p, p-o, 6cp, pep)	Dodd	(1917)	Smith, J.W.	170-240	
Stewart, M.	Way to Wonderland (1st UK, lg8vo, 144p, blue/gilt, 6 ticp, pep)	L: Hodder	[1918]	Smith, J.W.	220-300	
Underwood, P.	When Christmas Comes Around (1st, 4to, ipcb, 26p, 6cp, pep)	Duffield	1915	Smith, J.W.	500-800	
Smith, M.P.W.	Young Puritans in Captivity (1st, 8vo, grey cl, 323p, 6pl, dep)	Little/Brown	1899	Smith, J.W.	100-160	
Farjeon, E.	Westwoods (1st, sm8vo, ibds, [44]p, b/w, pep)	A.& W. Guild	(1935)	Smith, M.	25-40	
Mother Goose	Mother Goose Song Book (1st, ob4to, 100p, color)	Garden City	(1948)	Smith, Marion F.	70-120	*
Smith, Pamela C.	Annancy Stories (1st, folio)	R.H. Russell	1899	Smith, Pamela	150-200	*
Smith, Pamela C.	Golden Vanity & Green Bed (1st, folio, p-o, green cl, 12cp)	Doub./McClure	1899	Smith, Pamela	200-270	
Smith, R.G.	Ancient Tales/Japan (1st, 8vo, teg, 361p, color)	L: A&C Black	1908	Smith, R.G.	70-120	
Brown, Alice	Secret of the Clan (1st, 8vo, blue/gilt, 314p, 12pl)	MacMillan	1912	Smith, S.K.	25-40	
Beaman, E.H.	Ozmar the Mystic (1st, 8vo, 378p, blue/gilt, 12pl)	L: Bliss Sands	1896	Smith, Thomas	45-65	*
Smith, Wallace	Little Tigress (1st, 8vo, 209p, teg, 15pl)	Putnam	1923	Smith, Wallace	25-40	*
Gomme, Alice B.	Children's Singing Games (1st, ob4to, ibds, b/w)	L: D. Nutt	1894	Smith, Winifred	100-165	*
Carr, A.V.	Fairy of the Rhone (1st, 12mo, 69p, woodcuts)	Page	1901	Smith, Winifred	30-45	*
Buck, Pearl S.	Water-Buffalo Children (1st, 8vo, ipcb, 59p)	NY: J. Day	(1943)	Smith, Wm. A.	45-70	*
Jackson, G.E.	By Love's Sweet Rule (1st, 12mo, 320p, b/w)	Winston	1906	Smith, Wuanita	25-45	*
Unknown	Christmas Letter (1st, 12mo, 85p, 13pl)	Cupples	1902	Smith, Wuanita	40-60	
Blanchard, A.E.	Four Corners (1st, sm8vo, 387p, green cl, 5pl)	Jacobs	(1906)	Smith, Wuanita	25-45	*
Grimm Bros.	Golden Bird (1st, sm8vo, 116p, color, pep)	Jacobs	(1922)	Smith, Wuanita	50-70	*
Curtis, A.T.	Grandpa's Little Girls & Friends (1st 12mo, p-o, 190p, 5pl, pep)	Penn	1910	Smith, Wuanita	25-40	
Curtis, A.T.	Grandpa's Little Girls at School (1st, 12mo, 195p, p-o, 5pl)	Penn	1908	Smith, Wuanita	25-40	
Swift, J.	Gulliver's Travels (1st, sm8vo, 370p, cp)	Jacobs	[1923]	Smith, Wuanita	25-40	*
Byrne, M.A.	One Too Many (1st, 8vo, green cl, 191p, 4pl)	Saalfield	(1912)	Smith, Wuanita	30-45	*
Lefferts, S.T.	Pansy Wedding (1st, sq16mo, 86p, color, pep)	Cupples	(1909)	Smith, Wuanita	50-80	*
Lefferts, S.T.	Patriotic Jubilee (1st, sq16mo, 84p, color, pep)	Cupples	(1910)	Smith, Wuanita	50-80	*
Grimm Bros.	Snow White... (1st, sm8vo, 115p, col frn, cp, pep)	Jacobs	(1922)	Smith, Wuanita	45-60	*
Franchot, A.W.	Bugs, Wings & other Things (1st, 8vo, 99p, green/gilt, 7cp, pep)	Dutton	(1918)	Smith/Cady	150-180	
Barrows, M.	Ezra the Elephant (1st, sq8vo, ibds, [44]p, color, pep)	Grosset/Dunlap	1934	Smock, N.S.	25-40	*
Biggers, E.D.	Love Insurance (1st, 12mo, 402p, brown cl, 8pl)	Bobbs-Merrill	(1914)	Snapp, F.	35-60	
Biggers, E.D.	Seven Keys to Baldpate (1st, 8vo, blue/gilt, b/w)	Bobbs-Merrill	(1913)	Snapp, F.	50-75	
LaPrade, E.	Alice in Orchestralia (1st, sm8vo, 171p, b/w)	Doubleday/Page	1925	Snell, C.	25-40	
Mother Goose	Mother Goose (1st, 4to, 380p, color, pep)	Whitman	(1941)	Snow, D.J.	30-45	*
Nash, Ogden	Happy Days (1st, 8vo, 161p, p-o, b/w)	Simon/Schuster	1933	Soglow, Otto	70-100	*
Brooks, Gwen.	Bronzeville Boys & Girls (1st, 8vo, grey cl, 40p, b/w, cep)	Harper	(1956)	Solbert, R.	100-160	R*
Merrill, Jean	Shan's Lucky Knife (1st, sm4to, [48]p, 2-color)	W.R. Scott	1960	Solbert, R.	25-40	
Carroll, L.	Alice/Wonderland (1st, sq8vo, 192p, red cl, 6 ticp)	L: Headley	(1911)	Soper, G.	100-150	
Carroll, L.	Alice/Wonderland (1st AM, sq8vo, 192p, teg, 192p, 6 ticp, pep)	Baker/Taylor	(1911)	Soper, G.	90-140	
Carroll, L.	Alice/Wonderland (lg8vo, 192p, red cl, 6 ticp)	Small	[1911]	Soper, G.	80-125	
N/A	Arabian Nights (1st, 8vo, 295p, 6cp)	L: Allen/Unwin	(1913)	Soper, G.	60-80	
Grimm Bros.	Fairy Tales (1st AM, 8vo, 278p, cp)	Doran	(1924)	Soper, G.	45-60	*
Lamb, C.	Tales from Shakespeare (lg8vo, 14cp, DJ)	Doran	[1924]	Soper, G.	45-70	
Hawthorne, N.	Tanglewood Tales (1st, 8vo, 242p, 6cp, pep)	L: G. Allen	1912	Soper, G.	100-140	
Kingsley, C.	The Heroes (sm4to, 6cp)	Doran	(1920)	Soper, G.	35-50	
Kingsley, C.	Water Babies (lg8vo, teg, 4cp)	Baker/Taylor	(1910)	Soper, G.	35-50	
Miller, Warren	Goings on at Little Wishful (1st {std}, ob4to, [30]p, 2-col, cep)	Little/Brown	(1959)	Sorel, E.	50-80	R*
Miller, Warren	King Carlo of Capri (1st {std}, lg8vo, [32]p, 2-color, pep)	Harcourt	(1958)	Sorel, E.	50-80	R*
Miller, Warren	Pablo Paints a Picture (1st {std}, ob4to, [28]p, 1-color, pep)	Little/Brown	(1959)	Sorel, E.	45-70	*
Perrault, C.	Story of Blue-Beard (1st, 8vo, green cl, 61p)	L: Lawrence	1895	Southall, J.E.	65-80	*
Carroll, L.	Alice/Wonderland (1st, 8vo, teg, p-o, gilt, 166p, 12cp, pep)	L: Chatto	1907	Sowerby, M.	200-300	

AUTHOR	TITLE	PUBLISHER	DATE	ARTIST	PRICE	LC
Carroll, L.	Alice/Wonderland (1st AM, 8vo, p-o, 165p, 12cp)	Duffield	1908	Sowerby, M.	180-240	
Carroll, L.	Alice/Wonderland (1st {this fmt}, sq12mo, 157p, p-o, 8cp)	L: H. Frowde	1913	Sowerby, M.	65-90	
Sowerby, Githa	Bonnie Book (1st, 8vo, p-o, 12cp)	L: OUP	(1919)	Sowerby, M.	65-100	
Stevenson, R.L.	Child's Garden of Verses (1st, 4to, blue/gilt, teg, 12ticp, pep)	L: Chatto	1908	Sowerby, M.	140-170	
Stevenson, R.L.	Child's Garden of Verses (1st AM, 4to, 125p, teg, 12cp, pep)	Scribner	1908	Sowerby, M.	120-160	
Sowerby, M.	Childhood (1st AM, lg8vo, 44p, p-o, 12cp)	Duffield	1907	Sowerby, M.	90-125	
N/A	Cinderella (4to, ipcb, teg, 62p, gilt, 12 ticp)	L: Hodder	[1915]	Sowerby, M.	90-120	
Sowerby, Githa	Dainty Book (1st, sq8vo, ibds, unpag, 12cp)	Hodder	[1915]	Sowerby, M.	65-80	*
Grimm Bros.	Fairy Tales (1st, 4to, 255p, 12cp)	L: Richards	1909	Sowerby, M.	100-135	*
Grimm Bros.	Fairy Tales (1st AM, 8vo, 255p, 12cp, dep)	Stokes	(1910)	Sowerby, M.	80-120	*
Sowerby, Githa	Gay Book (1st {this pub.}, 8vo, [29]p, ibds, 12 fp color)	A.& W. Guild	(1935)	Sowerby, M.	30-45	
Joan, Natalie	Glad Book (1st, 8vo, ibds, 12 fp color)	L: H. Milford	(1921)	Sowerby, M.	80-120	
Sowerby, Githa	Glad Book (1st {this pub}, 8vo, [29]p, ibds, 12 fp color)	A.& W. Guild	(1935)	Sowerby, M.	30-45	
Sowerby, Githa	Little Stories/Little People (1st, lg8vo, 72p)	L: H. Frowde	(1910)	Sowerby, M.	65-80	*
Sowerby, Githa	Merry Book (smsq4to, white bds, 12cp)	L: Hodder	[1908]	Sowerby, M.	60-85	
Sowerby, Githa	Poems of Childhood (1st, 4to, teg, ibds, gilt, 12 ticp)	L: H. Frowde	(1912)	Sowerby, M.	130-165	
Sowerby, Githa	The Bumbletoes (1st, 12mo, ibds, 60p, 12cp)	L: Chatto	1907	Sowerby, M.	70-100	*
Strang, H.	What Baby Reads (1st AM, 12mo, bds, gilt, p-o, [32]p, 6cp)	NY: Hodder	[1910]	Sowerby, M.	50-70	*
Sowerby, Githa	Wise Book (1st AM, 12mo, ipcb, 13cp)	Dent/Dutton	1906	Sowerby, M.	65-80	
Sowerby, Githa	Yesterday's Children (1st, 4to, p-o, 12cp)	Duffield	1909	Sowerby, M.	70-100	
Mason, Francis E.	Daddy Gander (1st, 4to, ibds, [90]p, color)	F.E. Mason	(1900)	Spedon	50-70	*
Lyall, Edna	Autobiography of a Slander (1st, 8vo, blue/gilt, 146p, AEG)	L: Longmans	1892	Speed, L.	50-80	
Holland, R. (ed.)	King Arthur & Knights of Rountable (1st, 8vo, 360p, p-o, 7cp pep)	Jacobs	(1919)	Speed, L.	50-65	
Knowles, J. (arr.)	King Arthur & his Knights (1st, 8vo, 340p, 8cp)	L: Warne	(1912)	Speed, L.	65-80	
Sperry, A.	All Sail Set (1st, sm4to, 175p, pep, b/w, NH)	Winston	(1935)	Sperry, A.	45-60	*
Judson, C.I.	Boat Builder (1st, 8vo, tan cl, 121p, fp b/w, pep)	Scribner	1940	Sperry, A.	30-45	*
Carter, Russell	Brothers of the Frontier (1st, sm8vo, 205p, tan cl, b/w)	Appleton/Cent.	1938	Sperry, A.	25-40	*
Sperry, A.	Call it Courage (1st, lg8vo, 95p, beige cl, 1-color, pep, NM)	MacMillan	1940	Sperry, A.	50-85	R*
Sperry, A.	Coconut: Wonder Tree (1st, 8vo, blue cl, [47]p, 1-color, pep)	MacMillan	1942	Sperry, A.	25-40	*
Hewes, A.D.	Codfish Musket (1st {std}, 8vo, 390p, pep, NH)	Doubleday/Dor.	1936	Sperry, A.	40-65	
Heal, Edith	Dogie Boy (1st, sm4to, 79p, brown cl, pep, 11 fp color)	Whitman	1943	Sperry, A.	30-45	
Sperry, A.	Frozen Fire (1st {std}, 8vo, 192p, green cl, b/w)	Doubleday	(1956)	Sperry, A.	20-30	*
Follett, H.T.	House Afire! (1st, 8vo, 102p, pep)	Scribner	1941	Sperry, A.	30-45	*
Pease, Howard	Jungle River (1st {std}, sm8vo, 295p, col frn, pep)	Doubleday/Dor.	1938	Sperry, A.	30-45	*
Coryell, Hubert	Klondike Gold (1st, 8vo, 319p, blue cl, pep, b/w)	MacMillan	1938	Sperry, A.	35-50	*
Sperry, A.	Little Eagle: A Navaho Boy (1st, 4to, 102p, color, pep, DJ)	Winston	(1938)	Sperry, A.	35-50	
Follett, H.T.	Magic Portholes (1st, lg8vo, 321p, orange cl, fp b/w, pep)	MacMillan	1932	Sperry, A.	30-45	*
Follett, H.T.	Ocean Outposts (1st, 4to, 133p, maps by...)	Scribner	1942	Sperry, A.	30-45	*
Sperry, A.	One Day with Manu (1st [1st bk.], 8vo, ibds, [64]p, color, pep)	Winston	(1933)	Sperry, A.	50-80	*
Sperry, A.	One Day with Tuktu (1st, sm4to, blue/gilt, 10 dp color, pep)	Winston	1935	Sperry, A.	25-40	
Sperry, A.	Rain Forest (1st, 8vo, 190p, green cl, pep, 1-color)	MacMillan	1947	Sperry, A.	30-45	*
Means, F.C.	Shuttered Windows (1st, 8vo, 206p, 8pl)	Houghton	1938	Sperry, A.	45-60	*
Follett, H.T.	Stars to Steer By (1st, sm8vo, blue cl, 257p, fp b/w)	MacMillan	1934	Sperry, A.	30-45	*
Sperry, A.	Storm Canvas (1st {std}, 8vo, pep, 301p, col frn)	Winston	(1944)	Sperry, A.	25-40	
Longfellow, H.W.	Story of Hiawatha (1st, 4to, ibds, [68]p, color)	Random	(1951)	Sperry, A.	35-50	*
Stone, Wm. S.	Teri Taro from Bora Bora (1st {std}, sm8vo, 133p, 8cp, pep)	Knopf	1940	Sperry, A.	30-45	*
Pease, Howard	Thunderbolt House (1st {std}, sm8vo, 287p, b/w, pep)	Doubleday/Dor.	1944	Sperry, A.	20-40	*
Sperry, A.	Wagons Westward (1st, 8vo, 276p, orang cl, pep, b/w)	Winston	1936	Sperry, A.	30-45	*
Bowman, J.C.	Winabojo (1st, 8vo, 296p, orang cl, col frn, 12pl, pep)	Whitman	1941	Sperry, A.	30-45	*
Jackson, Jesse	Anchor Man (1st {std}, 8vo, 142p, red cl, fp b/w)	Harper	1947	Spiegel, D.	50-80	*
Jackson, Jesse	Call Me Charley (1st {std}, 8vo, 156p, b/w)	Harper	(1945)	Spiegel, D.	45-60	*
Bishop, C.H.	King's Day (1st, lg8vo, [47]p, ipcb, fp b/w, cep)	Coward	1940	Spiegel, D.	25-45	*
Humphrey, Mabel	Bright Days... (lg4to, 36p, ibds, 12cp)	Stokes	1901	Spiegle, F.	125-180	
Spilka, A.	Whom Shall I Marry? (1st, 8vo, pink cl, [33]p, 1-color)	Holiday House	1960	Spilka, A.	25-40	*
Chisholm, L.	Golden Staircase (1st, lg8vo, 361p, uncut, gilt, teg, 16cp)	L: Jack	(1906)	Spooner, M.D.	65-80	
Steedman, Amy	Margot/Golden Fish (8vo, 96p, AEG, p-o, 8cp)	L: Jack	(1911)	Spooner, M.D.	40-65	
Steedman, Amy	Our Island Saints (1st AM, 8vo, teg, 178p, 8 ticp)	Putnam	(1912)	Spooner, M.D.	40-70	
Williams, W.H.	Fairy Tales from Folk Lore (1st, 12mo, 288p, b/w)	Moffat	1908	Squire, M.H.	35-50	
Williston, T.P.	Hindu Stories (1st, 8vo, 111p, p-o, brown cl, color, pep)	Rand/McNally	(1925)	Squire, M.H.	35-50	*
Andersen, H.C.	Ugly Duckling (1st, sm4to, 24p, ibds, 3 fp color)	Moffat	1905	Squire, M.H.	100-165	R*
Kelly, E.M.	When I was Little (1st, 8vo, p-o, 96p, color)	Rand/McNally	(1915)	Squire, M.H.	50-75	
Carroll, L.	Alice/Wonderland (1st, 4to, gilt, teg, 6cp)	McClurg	1915	St. John, J.A.	150-200	
St. John, J.A.	Face in the Pool (1st, lg4to, 156p, grey/gilt, 4cp)	McClurg	1905	St. John, J.A.	100-145	
Mason, Edith H.	Great Plan (1st, 8vo, green/white, 308p, 5pl)	McClurg	1913	St. John, J.A.	60-80	
Munroe, K.	White Conquerors (1st, 12mo, 326p, uncut, gilt, 8pl)	Harper	1893	Stacey, W.S.	35-50	
Swift, J.	Gulliver's Travels (1st, sm8vo, 64p)	Chi: Rockwell	1931	Stahl, B.	45-65	*
Marais, Josef	Koos the Hottentot (1st {std}, 8vo, ibds, 182p, color)	Knopf	1945	Stahlhut, H.	60-80	R
Atkey, B.	Easy Money (1st, 8vo, p-o, 311p)	Estes	(1908)	Stampa, G.L.	20-30	
Carroll, L.	Alice... & Through... (1st, 8vo, 246p, 8 color)	Dutton	(1954)	Stanley, D.	35-50	*
Norton, Mary	Borrowers Afloat (1st, sm8vo, 176p, blue cl, col frn, DJ)	L: Dent	(1959)	Stanley, Diana	70-90	
Crew, A.	Mary & her Kitchen Garden (1st, lg8vo, 52p, p-o, 9cp, pep)	Doran	(1917)	Stanley, L.W.	35-50	*
Mijatovich, M.	Serbian Fairy Tales (1st, 8vo, gilt, 204p, 8cp)	L: Heinemann	(1917)	Stanley, S.	70-90	

AUTHOR	TITLE	PUBLISHER	DATE	ARTIST	PRICE	LC
Mijatovich, M.	Serbian Fairy Tales (1st AM, 8vo, black cl, 204p, 8cp)	McBride	1918	Stanley, S.	65-80	
Parker, Gilbert	March of the White Guard (1st, 12mo, 133p, b/w)	Fenno	1902	Starkweather, W.	20-30	
Harrison, T.M.	Modern Arms and a Feudal Throne (1st, 8vo, 376p, green cl, 4pl)	Fenno	1904	Starkweather, W.	35-50	*
Disney, W.	Bongo (1st {std}, folio, [26]p, ibds, color, GGB)	Simon/Schuster	(1947)	Starr, E.	70-100	*
Swift, J.	Gulliver's Travels (1st, 8vo, 235p, 8cp, pep)	L: Sidgwick	(1912)	Staynes, P.A.	30-50	*
Swift, J.	Gulliver's Travels (1st AM, 8vo, 235p, 8cp, pep)	Holt	(1912)	Staynes, P.A.	30-45	*
Mother Goose	Baby's Mother Goose (1st, sq16mo, [16]p, color, pep)	Grosset/Dunlap	1938	Stearns, S.	45-65	*
Andersen, H.C.	Favorite Fairy Tales (1st, lg8vo, [33]p, color)	Wilcox/Follett	(1946)	Stearns, S.	50-80	*
N/A	Jack & the Beanstalk (1st, 12mo, [31]p, color)	NY: Sully	(1920)	Stecher, W.F.	30-50	*
Steedman, Amy	Madonna of the Goldfinch (1st, 8vo, 194p, uncut, 8 ticp)	L: Jack	[1917]	Steedman, E.M.	50-75	
Davis, R.H.	Scarlet Car (1st, 8vo, tan cl, 166p, uncut, 12pl)	Scribner	1907	Steele, F.D.	25-40	
Steig, Wm.	About People (1st {std}, 8vo, 105p, b/w)	Random	(1939)	Steig, Wm.	65-90	*
Steig, Wm.	Agony in the Kindergarten (1st {std}, lg8vo, b/w)	Duell/Sloan	(1950)	Steig, Wm.	70-100	*
Steig, Wm.	All Embarrassed (1st {std}, 8vo, 101p, b/w)	Duell/Sloan	(1944)	Steig, Wm.	40-65	*
Steig, Wm.	Dreams of Glory (1st {std}, lg8vo, 147p, b/w)	Knopf	(1953)	Steig, Wm.	35-50	*
Fenner, P.R.	Giggle Box (1st {std}, lg8vo, yellow cl, 144p, uncut, b/w, pep)	Knopf	1950	Steig, Wm.	35-60	*
Cuppy, Will	How to Become Extinct (1st, sm8vo, 181p, cream cl, b/w)	Farrar/Rine.	(1941)	Steig, Wm.	30-45	*
Steig, Wm.	Lonely Ones (1st {std}, 8vo, 102p, ibds, fp b/w)	Duell/Sloan	(1942)	Steig, Wm.	50-85	*
Steig, Wm.	Persistent Faces (1st {std}, 8vo, brown cl, [186]p, b/w)	Duell/Sloan	(1945)	Steig, Wm.	45-60	*
Steig, Wm.	Rejected Lovers (1st {std}, 8vo, 152p, b/w)	Knopf	1951	Steig, Wm.	40-65	*
Steig, Wm.	Small Fry (1st, ob12mo, [128]p, b/w)	Duell/Sloan	(1944)	Steig, Wm.	45-70	*
Steig, Wm.	Till Death Do Us Part (1st {std}, 8vo, [128]p, b/w)	Duell/Sloan	(1947)	Steig, Wm.	45-70	*
Alcott, L.M.	Little Women (lg8vo, green cl, p-o, 475p, 8cp)	Garden City	1932	Stein, H.	25-40	
Coatsworth, E.	Sword of the Wilderness (1st, 8vo, 160p, b/w, pep)	MacMillan	1936	Stein, H.	20-35	*
Steiner, C.	Kiki & Muffy (1st {std}, ob8vo, ibds, [26]p, 2-color, cep)	Doubleday/Dor.	1943	Steiner, C.	35-50	
Steiner, C.	Kiki Dances (1st {std}, sm4to, ibds, [32]p, color)	Doubleday	(1949)	Steiner, C.	45-70	
Steiner, C.	Patsy's Pet (1st {std}, sm ob4to, ibds, [30]p, color)	Doubleday	1955	Steiner, C.	35-50	
N/A	Cinderella (1st, lg8vo, [16]p, color, pep)	Grosset/Dunlap	(1939)	Stenberg-Masolle	35-50	*
Deland, M.	An Encore (1st {std}, 8vo, teg, 79p, 3pl)	Harper	1907	Stephens, A.B.	30-45	
Deland, M.	Around Old Chester (1st, 8vo, p-o, 6pl)	Harper	1915	Stephens, A.B.	30-50	
Walcott, E.A.	Blindfolded (1st, 8vo, tan cl, 400p, 8pl)	Bobbs-Merrill	(1906)	Stephens, A.B.	20-35	
Reed, H.L.	Brenda's Cousin at Radcliffe (1st, 8vo, 318p, 5pl)	Little/Brown	1902	Stephens, A.B.	30-45	*
Robinson, E.	Captain of the Old School (1st, 8vo, grey cl, 15pl)	Little/Brown	1901	Stephens, A.B.	30-45	
Laughlin, C.E.	Felicity (1st, 8vo, green/gilt, 426p, 4cp)	Scribner	1907	Stephens, A.B.	25-40	
Abbott, C.C.	Freedom of the Fields (1st, 8vo, 233p, frn by...)	Lippincott	1898	Stephens, A.B.	35-50	
Kingsley, F.M.	Glass House (1st, sm8vo, 312p, 4pl)	Dodd	1909	Stephens, A.B.	25-40	*
Ray, A.C.	Hearts & Creeds (1st, 8vo, 320p, 4pl)	Little/Brown	1906	Stephens, A.B.	25-40	
Martin, H.R.	His Courtship (1st, 8vo, uncut, 322p, 4pl)	McClure	1907	Stephens, A.B.	25-40	*
Gilson, R.R.	In the Morning Glow (1st, 8vo, p-o, 16pl)	Harper	1904	Stephens, A.B.	30-50	
Ray, A.C.	Janet: Her Winter in Quebec (1st, 12mo, 370p, 4pl)	Little/Brown	1914	Stephens, A.B.	20-30	*
Gilson, R.R.	Katrina (1st, 8vo, green cl, 316p, teg, 6cp)	Baker/Taylor	(1906)	Stephens, A.B.	30-45	
Alcott, L.M.	Little Women (8vo, 617p, teg, 15pl)	Little/Brown	1914	Stephens, A.B.	25-45	
Green, A.K.	Mayor's Wife (1st, sm8vo, 389p, p-o)	Bobbs-Merrill	(1907)	Stephens, A.B.	20-30	
Gilson, R.R.	Mother & Father (1st, 8vo, teg, 63p, green cl, b/w)	Harper	1903	Stephens, A.B.	45-65	
Wiggin, K.D.	Mother Carey's Chickens (1st, 8vo, green cl, 356p, 10pl)	Houghton	1911	Stephens, A.B.	40-65	
Ray, A.C.	Nathalie's Sister (1st, 12mo, 290p, 6pl)	Little/Brown	1904	Stephens, A.B.	30-45	*
Deland, E.D.	Oakleigh (1st, 12mo, green cl, 233p, 19pl)	Harper	1896	Stephens, A.B.	30-45	
Wiggin, K.D.	Old Peabody Pew (1st, 8vo, grey cl, teg, 143p, 6pl, pep)	Houghton	1907	Stephens, A.B.	30-45	
Sidney, Marg.	Our Davie Pepper (1st, 16mo, 492p, green/gilt, 6pl)	Lothrop/Lee	(1916)	Stephens, A.B.	25-45	
Ray, A.C.	Sidney: Summer on St. Lawrence (1st, 12mo, 332p, blue/gilt, 4pl)	Little/Brown	1905	Stephens, A.B.	30-45	
Dyer, R.O.	Sleepy-Time Story Book (1st, sm8vo, 147p, gilt, pep, col frn)	Lothrop/Lee	(1915)	Stephens, A.B.	30-45	*
Brown, Alice	Story of Thyrza (1st, 8vo, gilt, 326p, col frn)	Houghton	1909	Stephens, A.B.	25-40	
Taylor, S.	Story of a Little Poet (1st, 8vo, green cl, 8pl)	Little/Brown	1901	Stephens, A.B.	25-40	
Cutting, M.S.	Suburban Whirl (1st, 12mo, green cl, uncut, 202p, 7pl)	McClure	1907	Stephens, A.B.	20-30	
Warner, A.	Susan Clegg... (1st, 12mo, 279p, grey cl, 4pl)	Little/Brown	1907	Stephens, A.B.	20-30	
Cutting, M.S.	The Wayfarers (1st, 8vo, 374p, 16pl)	McClure	1908	Stephens, A.B.	20-35	
Blanchard, A.E.	Three Pretty Maids (1st, 12mo, 243p, b/w plates)	Lippincott	1897	Stephens, A.B.	25-40	*
Abbott, C.C.	Travels in a Treetop (1st, 12mo, 215p, frn by...)	Lippincott	1898	Stephens, A.B.	35-50	
Henry, O.	Trimmed Lamp (1st, 12mo, 260p, frn by...)	McClure	1907	Stephens, A.B.	65-80	
Alcott, L.M.	Under the Lilacs (1st, 8vo, 302p, green cl, teg, 8pl)	Little/Brown	1905	Stephens, A.B.	50-70	*
Deland, M.	Way to Peace (1st, 8vo, grey cl, teg, uncut, 93p, 7pl, dep)	Harper	1910	Stephens, A.B.	30-45	
Deland, M.	Where Laborers are Few (1st, 8vo, 86p, 3pl)	Harper	1909	Stephens, A.B.	30-45	
Various	Whole Family (1st, 8vo, blue/gilt, 12pl)	Harper	1908	Stephens, A.B.	50-70	
Pidgin, C.F.	Blennerhassett (1st, 8vo, blue cl, teg, 12pl)	C.M. Clark	1901	Stephens, C.H.	20-30	
Stockton, Frank	Captain Chap (1st, sm8vo, 298p, tan cl, 6pl)	Lippincott	1897	Stephens, C.H.	35-50	
Sabin, E.L.	Gold Seekers of '49 (1st, sm8vo, 335p, tan cl, col frn, 4pl by)	Lippincott	1915	Stephens, C.H.	50-80	R*
Tilton, D.	Miss Petticoats (1st, 8vo, tan cl, teg, 7cp)	C.M. Clark	1902	Stephens, C.H.	15-25	
Bannerman, H.	Story of Little Black Sambo (ob12mo, 32p, ibds, color)	Winston	(1930)	Stephenson, E.	70-100	*
Cadby, C.	Brownies in Switzerland (1st AM, lg8vo, p-o, 127p, 6cp)	Macaulay	(1924)	Stephensons	45-75	*
N/A	Arabian Nights (1st, 4to, 308p, black cl, p-o, 16cp, pep)	Penn	(1928)	Sterrett, V.	200-280	
DeSegur, S.	Old French Fairy Tales (1st, lg4to, 279p, gilt, p-o, 8cp, pep)	Penn	(1920)	Sterrett, V.	200-280	
Hawthorne, N.	Tanglewood Tales (1st, lg4to, p-o, 261p, gilt, pep, 10cp)	Penn	(1921)	Sterrett, V.	200-280	

AUTHOR	TITLE	PUBLISHER	DATE	ARTIST	PRICE	LC
Yonge, C.M.	Little Duke (1st, 8vo, 240p, red/gilt, 4cp)	Duffield	1923	Stevens, B.	30-45	
Boult, E.M.	Romance of Cinderella (1st, 4to, 146p, color)	R.H. Russell	1902	Stevens, B.	160-250	*
Carter, R.G.	White Plume of Navarre (1st, 8vo, p-o, 192p, color)	Volland	(1928)	Stevens, B.	45-75	*
Uncle Frank	Uncle Frank's Visit to Fairy-Land (1st, 12mo, 244p, b/w)	Doub./McClure	1897	Stevens, W.D.	70-100	*
Wister, O.	Dragon of Wantley (1st, 8vo, teg, blue/gilt, 149p, b/w)	Lippincott	1892	Stewardson, J.	80-125	R
Grierson, E.W.	Children's Tales/Scottish Ballads (1st, 4to, 326p, teg, 12cp)	L: A&C Black	1906	Stewart, A.	120-160	*
McSpadden, J.W.	Robin Hood/his Merry Outlaws (1st, 8vo, grn cl, 320p, teg, 12cp)	Crowell	1923	Stewart, A.	35-50	*
N/A	Homes in the Wilderness (1st, 8vo, 74p, p-o, maps)	W.R. Scott	(1939)	Stewart, M.W.	35-50	*
Moodie, S.	Roughing It in the Bush (1st, 8vo, 568p, uncut, teg, ticp)	L: G. Bell	1913	Stewart, R.	50-70	
Pyle, Kath.	Childhood (1st, sm4to, ibds, 46p, 21cp)	Dutton	(1904)	Stilwell, S.	140-200	
Welsh, Richard	Kiddie-Kar Book (lg ob4to, ibds, p-o, 9cp)	Lippincott	(1920)	Stilwell, S.	180-250	*
Martin, E.S.	Lucid Intervals (1st, 8vo, 263p, teg, blue cl, 6pl)	Harper	1900	Stilwell, S.	45-60	
Martin, E.S.	Luxury of Children (1st, 8vo, 213p, green/gilt, p-o, teg, 8cp)	Harper	1904	Stilwell, S.	60-80	
Stilwell, S.	Musical Tree (1st, 4to, tan cloth, color)	Penn	1925	Stilwell, S.	65-85	
Dodge, M.M.	Rhymes & Jingles (1st, 8vo, gilt, teg, uncut, 222p, b/w)	Scribner	1904	Stilwell, S.	75-100	
Reed, L.	Sausages & Sundials (1st, 4to, 131p, ibds, b/w)	L: Jarrolds	[1927]	Stimpson, M.	30-45	
Stokes, Vernon	Blobbs at the Sea Side (folio, ibds, 11 chromos)	L: Chambers	[1908]	Stokes, V.	240-300	
N/A	Cinderella (lg8vo, [33]p, color)	Wilcox/Follett	(1948)	Stolberg, D.	30-45	*
Kissin, Rita	Pete the Pelican (1st, 8vo, 31p, p-o, b/w, pep)	Lippincott	(1937)	Stolper, J.	45-65	*
McGinley, Phyllis	All Around the Town (1st {std}, 4to, [63]p, fp color, CH)	Lippincott	(1948)	Stone, H.	60-85	*
Krauss, Ruth	Bundle Book (1st, lg ob8vo, ipcb, unpag, pep, color, DJ)	Harper	(1951)	Stone, H.	35-50	
Lockridge, Frances	Cats & People (1st {std}, 8vo, 286p, b/w)	Lippincott	(1950)	Stone, H.	25-45	*
Burton, Earl	Exciting Adventures of Waldo (1st, sm4to, 64p, grey cl, fp col)	Whittlesey	(1945)	Stone, H.	45-60	*
McGinley, Phyllis	Horse Who Lived Upstairs (1st {std}, sm4to, [48]p, color)	Lippincott	(1944)	Stone, H.	40-70	*
Koch, Dorothy	Let it Rain (1st, 4to, [27]p, green cl, color, cep)	Holiday House	(1959)	Stone, H.	30-50	*
Stirling, Monica	Little Ballet Dancer (1st, lg8vo, ipcb, 61p, 2-color, pep)	Lothrop	1952	Stone, H.	25-40	*
Tate, Eliz.	Little Flower Girl (1st, lg8vo, aqua cl, [40]p, 3-color, pep)	Lothrop/Lee	(1956)	Stone, H.	45-60	*
Bennett, Anna E.	Little Witch (1st {std}, [1st bk.], 8vo, 127p, grn cl, b/w, DJ)	Lippincott	(1953)	Stone, H.	45-60	
McGinley, Phyllis	Lucy McLockett (1st, sm4to, [32]p, color)	Lippincott	(1959)	Stone, H.	45-70	*
McGinley, Phyllis	Most Wonderful Doll in the World (1st, 8vo, 61p, color, CH)	Lippincott	(1950)	Stone, H.	50-90	*
McGinley, Phyllis	Plain Princess (1st {std}, sm8vo, 62p, color)	Lippincott	(1945)	Stone, H.	30-45	*
Brown, M.W.	Pussycat's Christmas (1st, sq8vo, yellow cl, [32]p, color, dep)	Crowell	1949	Stone, H.	50-70	*
Weiss, Edna S.	Sally Saucer (1st, 8vo, 179p, yellow cl, b/w)	Houghton	1956	Stone, H.	20-30	*
Burton, Earl & L.	Taffy & Joe (1st, sm4to, green cl, 60p, dp col frn, b/w)	Whittlesey	1947	Stone, H.	40-60	*
Simon, Norma	Tree For Me (1st, 8vo, green cl, [26]p, 1-color, dep)	Lippincott	(1956)	Stone, H.	30-45	*
Goldberg, M.	Twirly Skirt (1st, 8vo, 45p, green cl, fp b/w, pep)	Holiday House	1954	Stone, H.	40-65	R*
Kennedy, Mary	Violets are Blue (1st, 8vo, 154p, blue cl, fp b/w)	Lothrop/Lee	(1951)	Stone, H.	25-40	*
Stewart, Anna B.	Young Miss Burney (1st {std}, 8vo, green/gilt, 270p, b/w)	Lippincott	1947	Stone, H.	25-40	*
Jackson, H.H.	Ramona (1st, 8vo, col frn, 447p, DJ)	Little/Brown	1932	Stoops, H.M.	25-40	
Means, F.C.	Tangled Waters (1st, sm8vo, 212p, col frn)	Houghton	1936	Stoops, H.M.	20-35	*
Stevenson, R.L.	Child's Garden of Verses (1st, 8vo, 115p, 8cp)	Scribner	1909	Storer, E.	40-65	
Field, E.	Christmas Tales/Christmas Verse (1st, 4to, 119p, gilt, 8cp, SC)	Scribner	1912	Storer, F.	70-100	
Van Deeser	How to Find Happyland (1st, p-o, AEG, 122p)	Putnam	1907	Storer, F.	45-60	
Gilbert, P.T.	Elmer Buys a Circus (1st, 8vo, ibds, 71p, b/w)	Grosset/Dunlap	(1941)	Stossel, A.	20-25	*
Stevenson, R.L.	Kidnapped (1st, 8vo, 343p, 8cp)	L: Cassell	1913	Stott, W.R.S.	45-60	*
Strang, W.	Book of Giants (1st, 8vo, 56p, 12pl)	(London)	1898	Strang, W.	150-200	
Bunyan, J.	Pilgrim's Progress (1st, 4to, teg, uncut, black/gilt)	L: Nimmo	1895	Strang, W.	80-100	
N/A	Sinbad the Sailor (1st, 8vo, 279p)	L: Lawrence	1896	Strang/Clark	50-75	*
Davidson (ed.)	Ali Baba & the Forty Thieves (folio, ibds, 9 fp color)	L: Blackie	[1900]	Stratton, H.	60-80	
N/A	Arabian Nights (folio, unpag)	L: Blackie	(1906)	Stratton, H.	70-100	*
N/A	Arabian Nights (8vo, 352p, 29cp)	L: Blackie	[1910]	Stratton, H.	45-75	*
Campbell, W.D.	Beyond the Border (1st AM, 8vo, AEG, 456p)	R.H. Russell	1898	Stratton, H.	75-120	
Lang, Jean	Book of Myths (1st, 8vo, 340p, 20cp)	L: Jack	1914	Stratton, H.	80-120	
Andersen, H.C.	Fairy Tales (1st, 4to, white/gilt, AEG, 320p, col frn, b/w)	L: G. Newnes	1899	Stratton, H.	160-220	
Andersen, H.C.	Fairy Tales (1st AM, 4to, blue/gilt, AEG, 320p, b/w, cep)	NY: Truslove	1899	Stratton, H.	130-180	*
Andersen, H.C.	Fairy Tales (1st AM, 8vo, green/gilt, 28cp)	Dodge	[1905]	Stratton, H.	160-200	
Andersen, H.C.	Fairy Tales (4to, ibds, [86]p, 24cp)	L: Blackie	[1905]	Stratton, H.	65-80	*
Grimm Bros.	Fairy Tales (1st, 8vo, 336p, 20cp)	L: Blackie	1905	Stratton, H.	100-150	
Andersen, H.C.	Fairy Tales (8vo, 380p, color)	L: Blackie	[1908]	Stratton, H.	70-100	*
Andersen, H.C.	Fairy Tales (sm8vo, 441p, col frn, dep)	Lippincott	(1908)	Stratton, H.	35-60	*
Grimm Bros.	Grimm's & Andersen's Fairy Tales (1st, folio, [176]p, col, cep)	L: Blackie	[1906]	Stratton, H.	180-250	R*
Herbertson, A.	Heroic Legends (1st, 8vo, 253p, AEG, gilt, 16cp, cep)	L: Blackie	1908	Stratton, H.	100-145	
Sylva, C.	Lily of Life (1st, 4to, gilt, teg, 146p, p-o, 18 ticp)	L: Hodder	[1910]	Stratton, H.	350-450	
Dearmer, M.	Playmate, A Christmas Mystery (1st, 8vo, 31p, 4 illus)	L: A. Mowbray	1910	Stratton, H.	65-90	*
MacDonald, Geo.	Princess & Curdie (1st, 8vo, 304p, blue/gilt, 31 b/w, cep)	L: Blackie	1900	Stratton, H.	120-150	
MacDonald, Geo.	Princess & Goblin (1st AM, 8vo, 308p, teg, blue/gilt, p-o, 12cp)	Caldwell	[1911]	Stratton, H.	135-180	
MacDonald, Geo.	Princess & Goblin (1st, 8vo, teg, 308p, p-o, gilt, 12cp)	L: Blackie	1911	Stratton, H.	165-200	
Gomme, G.L.	Princess's Story Book (1st, sm8vo, gilt, teg, 443p, 23pl)	L: Constable	1901	Stratton, H.	75-125	*
Thomson, C.L.	Selections from LeMorte Darthur (1st, 8vo, 240p)	L: H. Marshall	1902	Stratton, H.	50-75	*
Gale, N.	Songs for Little People (1st, 8vo, teg, 110p, uncut, gilt, 8pl)	L: Constable	1896	Stratton, H.	100-165	
Andersen, H.C.	Tales from Andersen (8vo, 194p)	L: Constable	1896	Stratton, H.	100-130	*
Hewes, A.D.	Sword of Roland Arnot (1st, 8vo, red cl, 206p, 4cp, DJ)	Houghton	1939	Strayer, P.	30-45	

AUTHOR	TITLE	PUBLISHER	DATE	ARTIST	PRICE	LC
Kipling, R.	Tales of India (1st, lg8vo, p-o, 320p, black cl, 5cp)	Rand/McNally	(1935)	Strayer, P.	40-65	
Hall, E.C.	Aunt Jane of Kentucky (1st, 12mo, 283p)	Little/Brown	1907	Strong, B.	20-30	
Burgess, T.	Bride's Primer (1st, lg4to, ipcb, [62]p, 24 fp color)	NY: Phelps	(1905)	Strothmann, F.	250-450	R*
Twain, M.	Extracts from Adam's Diary (1st, 8vo, red cl, 89p)	Harper	1904	Strothmann, F.	80-110	
Wells, Carolyn	In the Reign of Queen Dick (1st, 8vo, tan cl, 229p, 8pl)	Appleton	1904	Strothmann, F.	30-50	
Twain, M.	Jumping Frog (1st, 8vo, 65p, 11pl)	Harper	1903	Strothmann, F.	70-100	
Gulliver, L.	Over the Nonsense Road (1st, 8vo, 234p, orang cl, 8cp)	Appleton	1910	Strothmann, F.	50-80	
Hoover, B.R.	Pa Flickinger's Folks (1st, 12mo, grey cl, 274p, 10pl)	Harper	1909	Strothmann, F.	40-60	
Wells, Carolyn	Rubaiyat of a Motor Car (1st, 12mo, [60]p, ibds, 14cp)	Dodd	1906	Strothmann, F.	45-60	*
Pattee, F.L.	House/Black Ring (1st, 8vo, 324p, cvr by...)	Holt	1905	Stuart, B.	20-25	*
Underhill, A.F.	Goochy Goggles... (1st, sm4to, [93]p, ibds, color)	McLoughlin	(1926)	Sturges, K.	50-80	*
Miller, O.B.	Little Pictures of Japan (1st, 4to, 191p, p-o, pep, color)	Book House	(1925)	Sturges, K.	40-60	
Chamberlin, E.C.	Omar the Discontented Cat (1st, 12mo, [39]p, ipcb, pep, color)	Volland	(1925)	Sturges, K.	35-50	*
Alden, R.M.	Why the Chimes Rang (1st, 4to, 148p, orang cl, p-o, 8cp)	Bobbs-Merrill	(1924)	Sturges, K.	45-60	*
Sturges, L.B.	Runaway Toys (1st, 12mo, [64]p, black cl, p-o, color)	Rand/McNally	(1920)	Sturges, L.B.	70-100	*
Sturges, L.B.	Toys of Nuremberg (1st, sm8vo, p-o, [80]p, color)	Rand/McNally	(1915)	Sturges, L.B.	50-70	
Ford, Lauren	Ageless Story (1st, sq4to, blue/gilt, [40]p, color, CH)	Dodd	1939	Suba, S.	65-80	*
Petry, Ann	Drugstore Cat (1st, lg8vo, 87p, red cl, fp b/w, pep)	Crowell	1949	Suba, S.	50-75	*
Grimm Bros.	Favorite Fairy Tales told in Germany (1st {std}, lg8vo, 83p)	Little/Brown	(1959)	Suba, S.	45-60	*
Moses, H.S.	Here Comes the Circus (1st, lg8vo, 47p, color)	Houghton	1941	Suba, S.	45-60	*
Fox, F.M.	Little Cat/Could Not Sleep (1st {std}, ob4to, [31]p, pep, color)	Dutton	1941	Suba, S.	65-80	*
Morrow, Eliz.	My Favorite Age (1st, sm8vo, 220p, green cl, fp b/w, cep)	MacMillan	1943	Suba, S.	25-40	*
Morrow, Eliz.	Pint of Judgment (1st {std}, 24mo, ibds, 43p, dep)	Knopf	(1939)	Suba, S.	25-40	*
Otto, M.G.	Roly-Poly Snowman (1st {std}, 8vo, blue cl, 83p, fp b/w)	Holt	(1954)	Suba, S.	30-50	*
Herzog, E.	Tinkers of Turntable (1st, 8vo, grey cl, 125p, b/w)	W.R. Scott	(1940)	Suba, S.	30-45	*
Tennyson, A.	Dream of Fair Women (1st AM, lg8vo, 197p, gilt, b/w)	Page/Richards	1900	Sullivan, E.J.	65-90	
Borrow, G.	Lavengro (1st, 8vo, teg, green/gilt, 655p, 12 ticp, cep)	L: Foulis	(1914)	Sullivan, E.J.	45-60	
Tennyson, A.	Maud (1st, sm4to, 103p, uncut, 8cp, DJ)	L: MacMillan	1922	Sullivan, E.J.	60-75	
Wells, H.G.	Modern Utopia (1st, 8vo, red/gilt, teg, 393p, 7pl)	L: Chapman	1905	Sullivan, E.J.	170-250	
Marryat, Fred.	Newton Foster (1st, 12mo, 393p, blue/gilt, 40 b/w, pep)	L: MacMillan	1897	Sullivan, E.J.	45-60	
Omar Khayyam	Rubaiyat... (1st, 4to, red/gilt, unpag, teg, uncut, col frn)	L: Methuen	1913	Sullivan, E.J.	100-140	
Omar Khayyam	Rubaiyat... (1st AM, 4to, red/gilt, unpag, teg, col frn)	Dutton	(1913)	Sullivan, E.J.	80-130	
Carlyle, T.	Sartor Resartus (1st, sm8vo, AEG, 352p, blue/gilt, b/w, dep)	L: G. Bell	1898	Sullivan, E.J.	85-120	
Fouque, La Motte	Sintram and his Companions (1st, 8vo, 193p, olive cl, teg, 20pl)	L: Methuen	(1908)	Sullivan, E.J.	70-90	
Sheridan, R.B.	The Rivals (1st, 8vo, 365p, b/w)	(London)	1896	Sullivan, E.J.	60-90	
Goldsmith, O.	Vicar of Wakefield (1st AM, 4to, 345p, blue/gilt, 16cp)	Holt	1914	Sullivan, E.J.	90-140	
Goldsmith, O.	Vicar of Wakefield (1st, 4to, 345p, green/gilt, teg, 16cp)	L: Constable	1914	Sullivan, E.J.	120-165	
Porter, G.S.	Her Father's Daughter (1st, 8vo, 486p, pep, col frn by...)	Doubleday/Page	1921	Summers, D.G.	45-70	
Dix, D.	Fables of the Elite (1st, 12mo, teg, 261p, b/w pl)	Fenno	1902	Swinnerton	40-65	*
Defoe, D.	Robinson Crusoe (8vo, 472p, teg, bds, 16 fp color)	L: J.M. Dent	(1945)	Symington, J.A.	85-130	*
Scott, Michael	Tom Cringle's Log (1st, 8vo, 569p, AEG, blue/gilt, 42 b/w)	L: MacMillan	1895	Symington, J.A.	35-50	
Andersen, H.C.	Fairy Tales (1st, sm8vo, 343p, color)	Grosset/Dunlap	(1945)	Szyk, A.	35-50	*
Szyk, Arthur	New Order (1st, 4to, 8 fp color, DJ)	Putnam	(1941)	Szyk, A.	100-165	
Omar Khayyam	Rubaiyat... (sm4to, blue ibds, [40]p, 8cp)	Heritage Press	1946	Szyk, A.	45-70	
Kipling, R.	Captains Courageous (1st AM, 8vo, grn/gilt, 323p, teg, b/w)	Century	1897	Taber, I.W.	140-170	
Bradley-Birt, F.	Bengal Fairy Tales (1st, lg8vo, 209p, 6 color)	L: J. Lane	1920	Tagore, A.N.	80-100	
Omar Khayyam	Rubaiyat... (1st, 8vo, 63p, 7 ticp)	L: L.B. Hill	(1920)	Tagore, A.N.	100-130	*
Black, I.S.	Barbara's Birthday (1st, 8vo, 44p, color)	W.R. Scott	1946	Takis, N.	45-65	*
Sykes, M.	Poe's Run.... (1st, 8vo, teg, green cl, 84p, b/w)	Cannon Pr.	1904	Tarkington, B.	35-50	
Carroll, L.	Alice/Wonderland (1st, sm4to, p-o, 340p, blue/gilt, 48cp, pep)	L: Ward Lock	1916	Tarrant, M.	180-250	
Carroll, L.	Alice/Wonderland (1st AM, lg8vo, p-o, 332p, 48cp, pep)	Platt/Peck	1916	Tarrant, M.	150-200	
Carroll, L.	Alice/Wonderland (4to, 175p, ibds, 24cp, later)	L: Ward Lock	[1929]	Tarrant, M.	140-180	
Farjeon, E.	Alphabet of Magic (1st, 8vo, 57p)	L: Medici	1928	Tarrant, M.	45-65	*
Hayes, Nancy M.	Book of Games (1st, 8vo, ibds, 144p, p-o, dep, 24cp)	L: Ward Lock	1920	Tarrant, M.	125-200	
Golding, Harry	Book of the Clock (1st, 8vo, p-o, 140p, 27cp)	L: Ward Lock	1920	Tarrant, M.	75-100	
Andersen, H.C.	Fairy Stories (1st, sm4to, 340p, blue cl, p-o, 48cp)	L: Ward Lock	1917	Tarrant, M.	140-200	
Andersen, H.C.	Fairy Tales (4to, ibds, 176p, 24cp)	L: Ward Lock	[1920]	Tarrant, M.	80-120	
Tarrant, M.	Joan in Flowerland (1st, 8vo, 60p, blue cl, 16cp, DJ)	L: Warne	(1935)	Tarrant, M.	85-120	
Adcock, Marion	Littlest One (1st, 4to, 41p, ibds, 4cp)	L: Harrap	1914	Tarrant, M.	60-80	
Adcock, Marion	Littlest One (1st AM, 8vo, ibds, p-o, 4cp)	Stokes	[1915]	Tarrant, M.	45-70	*
Webb, M. St. John	Littlest One Again (1st, 4to, p-o, bds, 4cp)	L: Harrap	1926	Tarrant, M.	65-90	
Herbertson, A.	Lucy-Mary (1st, 8vo, 203p)	L: Blackie	1910	Tarrant, M.	45-60	*
Webb, M. St. John	Magic Lamplighter (1st, 8vo, 167p, 7cp, pep)	L: Medici	1926	Tarrant, M.	45-60	
Rhys, Grace (ed.)	Magic Wood Beyond the World (8vo, ibds, 4cp)	L: Harrap	1931	Tarrant, M.	40-65	
Tarrant, M.	Margaret Tarrant's Christmas Garland (1st, sq8vo, 125p, 19 ticp)	Hale-Cushman	(1942)	Tarrant, M.	45-60	*
Mother Goose	Mother Goose (1st, 4to, 16cp, DJ)	L: Coker	(1920)	Tarrant, M.	100-120	
Mother Goose	Mother Goose Nursery Rhymes (1st, 4to, 176p, 24cp)	L: Ward Lock	[1929]	Tarrant, M.	80-100	*
Peacocke, I.M.	My Friend Phil (1st, 8vo, p-o, 320p, 6cp)	L: Ward Lock	1915	Tarrant, M.	50-70	*
N/A	Nursery Rhymes (1st, 8vo, 340p, blue/gilt, p-o, 44cp, pep)	L: Ward Lock	[1920]	Tarrant, M.	100-140	*
Golding, Harry	Our Animal Friends (4to, ibds, 176p, 24cp)	L: Ward Lock	[1920]	Tarrant, M.	65-80	*
Cole, Frank (ed.)	Picture Birthday Book/Boys & Girls (16mo, gilt, 12cp)	L: Harrap	(1915)	Tarrant, M.	50-75	
Browning, R.	Pied Piper of Hamelin (1st, 8vo, green/gilt, teg, 8cp)	L: J.M. Dent	1912	Tarrant, M.	50-80	

AUTHOR	TITLE	PUBLISHER	DATE	ARTIST	PRICE	LC
N/A	Rhymes of Old Times (1st, 8vo, 107p, teg, 16 ticp)	L: Medici	1925	Tarrant, M.	50-70	
Webb, M. St. John	Sea-Shore Fairies (1st, 16mo, tan bds, p-o, 6 fp color)	L: Mod.Art.Soc	(1925)	Tarrant, M.	85-120	
Webb, M. St. John	Seed Fairies (1st, 12mo, 39p, bds, p-o, 6 ticp, pep)	L: Mod.Art Soc	[1923]	Tarrant, M.	100-140	
Stevenson, R.L.	Songs with Music/Child's Garden/Verses (1st, 4to, 55p, pcb, 12cp)	L: Jack	[1915]	Tarrant, M.	75-100	
Kingsley, C.	Water Babies (1st, 8vo, 284p, p-o, teg, 12cp)	L: Dent	1908	Tarrant, M.	70-100	
Webb, M. St. John	Wild Fruit Fairies (1st, 12mo, 41p, ibds, 6cp)	L: Medici	1932	Tarrant, M.	65-80	
Golding, Harry	Willie Winkie... (16mo, 96p, ibds, 24 fp color)	L: Ward Lock	[1920]	Tarrant, M.	65-80	
Golding, Harry	Zoo Days (2nd, lg8vo, p-o, 48cp)	L: Ward Lock	[1920]	Tarrant, M.	30-50	
Scott, Walter	Quentin Durward (1st, lg8vo, uncut, 499p, 16cp)	Dodd	1923	Tarrant, P.	30-45	*
Mother Goose	Mother Goose (1st, 4to, 224p, ibds, 12pl)	L: Harrap	1932	Tawse, S.	80-100	
Porter, E.	Pollyanna (1st {this pub.}, 8vo, 255p, 8pl)	L: Harrap	1938	Tawse, S.	45-60	*
Kingsley, C.	The Heroes (1st, 8vo, 221p, 8cp)	L: A&C Black	1915	Tawse, S.	35-50	*
Stranathan, May	Silhouette Stories (1st, 8vo, 198p, brown cl, 14 fp bw)	Moffat	1921	Taylor, E.C.	30-45	*
Ransome, A.	Bohemia in London (1st AM, 8vo, 284p, teg, uncut, 16pl)	Dodd	1907	Taylor, F.	40-60	*
Montgomery, L.M.	Anne of the Island (1st, sm8vo, 326p, col frn & p-o)	Page	1915	Taylor, H.W.	90-140	*
Porter, E.	Pollyanna Grows Up (1st, 8vo, 308p, 8pl)	L.C. Page	1915	Taylor, H.W.	60-100	*
Smith, Harriet L.	Pollyanna of the Orange Blossoms (1st, 8vo, p-o, 313p, 6pl)	Page	1924	Taylor, H.W.	25-40	*
Smith, Harriet L.	Pollyanna's Jewels (1st, 8vo, 328p, blue cl, p-o, 6pl)	Page	(1925)	Taylor, H.W.	25-40	*
Lewis, A.H.	Sandburrs (1st, 8vo, 318p, 16pl)	Stokes	(1900)	Taylor, H.W.	40-65	
Taylor, Paul B.	Tippletappleteven Town (1st, sq8vo, [12]p, ibds, color, pep)	Holt	(1931)	Taylor, P.B.	65-90	*
Sidney, Marg.	Five Little Peppers Midway (1st, 16mo, 512p, gilt, 20pl)	D. Lothrop	(1890)	Taylor, W.L.	60-80	
Maunder, I.	Plain Princess (1st, 4to, 95p, brown cl, 14pl, dep)	L: Longmans	1905	Taylor/Baxter	80-120	
Andersen, H.C.	Fairy Tales (1st, 4to, 56p, color)	Duell/Sloan	(1946)	Taylor/Day	35-50	*
N/A	Three Bears (1st, sm4to, [18]p, color, pep)	Grosset/Dunlap	(1938)	Tedder, E.	25-40	*
Andersen, H.C.	Fairy Tales (1st AM, lg4to, 524p, gilt, 85pl)	Century	1900	Tegner, H.	225-300	
Andersen, H.C.	Fairy Tales (1st, 4to, 2 volumes, bds, gilt, b/w)	L: Heinemann	1900	Tegner, H.	300-400	
Wyatt, Horace	Malice in Kulturland (1st AM, 12mo, 84p, b/w)	Dutton	(1917)	Tell, W.	50-80	*
Uttley, Alison	Hare & the Easter Egg (1st, sq12mo, 80p, grn bds, 16 fp color)	L: Collins	(1952)	Tempest, M.	35-50	
Uttley, Alison	Knot Squirrel Tied (1st, 8vo, 101p, grey pcb, p-o, 23 col)	L: Collins	1937	Tempest, M.	45-60	
Uttley, Alison	Little Grey Rabbit & Weasels (1st, 80p, pcb, p-o, color, pep)	L: Collins	1947	Tempest, M.	45-60	
Uttley, Alison	Little Grey Rabbit's Christmas (1st, sq8vo, 104p, ibds, color)	L: Collins	1939	Tempest, M.	50-70	
Evans, Myfanwy	No Rubbish Here (1st, 4to, green ibds, 34p, color)	L: Collins	(1936)	Tempest, M.	70-100	*
Kaye, M.	Potter Pinner Meadow (1st, sq4to, 40p, ibds)	L: Collins	(1930)	Tempest, M.	50-70	
Uttley, Alison	Story of Fuzzypeg the Hedgehog (1st, 8vo, 98p, 23cp, pep)	L: Heinemann	1932	Tempest, M.	65-80	*
Uttley, Alison	Wise Owl's Story (1st, sm8vo, 108p, ipcb, p-o, pep)	L: Collins	1935	Tempest, M.	45-65	
Hewes, A.D.	Boy of the Lost Crusade (1st, 8vo, p-o, 279p, gilt, 4cp, pep)	Houghton	1923	Tenggren, G.	30-50	
Rihbany, A.M.	Christ Story for Boys & Girls (1st, 8vo, gilt, p-o, 239p, 4cp)	Houghton	(1923)	Tenggren, G.	45-60	
D'Aulnoy	D'Aulnoy's Fairy Tales (1st, 4to, gilt, teg, p-o, 457p, 9cp pep)	McKay	1923	Tenggren, G.	120-170	
Woodruff, E.	Dickey Bird (1st, lg4to, black cl, 16p, 6 ticp, pep)	M. Bradley	(1928)	Tenggren, G.	250-320	
Andersen, H.C.	Fairy Tales (1st, sm8vo, 224p, tan cl, 13 fp b/w)	Appleton/Cent.	(1935)	Tenggren, G.	35-50	*
Jackson, K.& B.	Farm Stories (1st {std}, folio, ibds, 91p, color, GGB)	Simon/Schuster	(1946)	Tenggren, G.	70-100	
N/A	Good Dog Book (1st, 8vo, blue cl, 264p, p-o, 5cp)	Houghton	1924	Tenggren, G.	40-60	
Spyri, J.	Heidi (1st, 8vo, 356p, blue cl, p-o, 4cp)	Houghton	1923	Tenggren, G.	50-90	
Muller, C.	How they Carried the Goods (1st, 4to, 318p, 4cp, 9pl)	Sears	(1932)	Tenggren, G.	35-50	
Baylor, F.C.	Juan & Juanita (1st, 8vo, 300p, blue cl, p-o, 4cp, pep)	Houghton	1926	Tenggren, G.	60-85	
Bannerman, H.	Little Black Sambo (1st, sm8vo, [42]p, color)	Simon/Schuster	(1948)	Tenggren, G.	50-80	*
Andersen, H.C.	Little Match Girl (1st, 4to, ibds, [24]p, pep, fp color)	Grosset/Dunlap	(1944)	Tenggren, G.	35-50	*
Mother Goose	Mother Goose (1st, 4to, 136p, color, pep)	Little/Brown	1940	Tenggren, G.	65-80	
Rodgers, C.	Pirate's Loot (1st, 8vo, yellow cl, 282p, 30 fp 1-color)	Sears	(1931)	Tenggren, G.	45-65	
Lowrey, J.S.	Poky Little Puppy (1st, 12mo, [42]p, ibds, color, LGB)	Simon/Schuster	1942	Tenggren, G.	35-50	
Lang, A.	Red Fairy Book (1st, 4to, 285p, p-o, teg, red cl, 8cp, pep)	McKay	(1924)	Tenggren, G.	160-250	
Henderson, G.	Ring of the Nibelung (1st, 8vo, 218p, beige cl, col frn, b/w)	Knopf	1932	Tenggren, G.	40-65	
Schrank, J.	Seldom & the Golden Cheese (1st, 8vo, blue cl, uncut, 8pl, pep)	Dodd	1933	Tenggren, G.	45-65	
Wheeler, Opal	Sing for America (1st {std}, 4to, 127p, ibds, color, pep)	Dutton	(1944)	Tenggren, G.	40-65	
Wheeler, Opal	Sing for Christmas (1st {std}, 4to, ibds, 127p, 12cp, pep, DJ)	Dutton	1943	Tenggren, G.	70-100	
Campbell, Ruth	Small Fry/Winged Horse (1st, 8vo, ibds, 28p, 10cp, pep)	Volland	(1927)	Tenggren, G.	50-85	
Woodruff, E.	Stories from the Magic World (4to, 130p, color)	McLoughlin	(1938)	Tenggren, G.	140-220	
Dike, H.	Stories of Great Metropolitan Operas (1st, lg8vo, 247p, 12cp)	Random	(1943)	Tenggren, G.	30-45	
Tenggren, G.	Tenggren's Story Book (1st {std}, lg4to, ibds, color, pep, GGB)	Simon/Schuster	1944	Tenggren, G.	75-110	
Hawthorne, N.	Wonder Book... (1st, 8vo, p-o, gilt, 421p, 4cp)	Houghton	1923	Tenggren, G.	30-50	
Girvin, B.	Girl Scout (1st, 8vo, 319p, color)	L: H. Frowde	1913	Tenison, N.	25-45	*
Stanley, H.M.	London Street Arabs (1st, 4to, green cl, 28pl)	L: Cassell	1890	Tennant, D.	40-65	
Carroll, L.	Alice... & Through... (1st [combined], 12mo, 383p, green cl)	L: MacMillan	1887	Tenniel, J.	200-300	
Carroll, L.	Alice... & Through... (8vo, teg, 351p, b/w)	Altemus	1895	Tenniel, J.	85-135	*
Carroll, L.	Alice... & Through... (4to, blue/gilt, col frn, b/w)	McLoughlin	[1910]	Tenniel, J.	100-160	*
Carroll, L.	Alice... & Through... (1st [color ed.], 8vo, 292p, gilt, 16cp)	L: MacMillan	1911	Tenniel, J.	160-250	
Carroll, L.	Alice... & Through... (1st {this pub}, 4to, p-o, 59p, cep, col)	Platt/Munk	(1938)	Tenniel, J.	85-120	*
Carroll, L.	Alice... Through... & Hunting (1st, 8vo, 351p, teg, uncut, b/w)	Boni/Liveright	1925	Tenniel, J.	100-150	*
Carroll, L.	Alice/Wonderland (sm4to, tan cl, 160p, 4cp)	Altemus	(1897)	Tenniel, J.	65-90	*
Carroll, L.	Alice/Wonderland (1st, 12mo, 179p, color)	NY: McKibbin	1899	Tenniel, J.	70-100	*
Carroll, L.	Alice/Wonderland (16mo, ibds, p-o, 126p, 30cp, pep)	Altemus	[1900]	Tenniel, J.	70-100	
Carroll, L.	Alice/Wonderland (32mo, 127p, 32 color)	L: MacMillan	1903	Tenniel, J.	70-120	*

AUTHOR	TITLE	PUBLISHER	DATE	ARTIST	PRICE	LC
Carroll, L.	Alice/Wonderland (sm8vo, ibds, 202p, pep)	Caldwell	[1904]	Tenniel, J.	70-120	*
Carroll, L.	Alice/Wonderland (1st, 12mo, ipcb, [56]p, 8 fp color)	McLoughlin	(1940)	Tenniel, J.	70-100	*
Carroll, L.	Nursery Alice (1st, 4to, ibds, 56p, 20 color, cep)	L: MacMillan	1890	Tenniel, J.	600-800	
Carroll, L.	Through the Looking Glass (12mo, 175p, grey/gilt, 4 chromos)	DeWolfe/Fiske	1898	Tenniel, J.	130-180	
Carroll, L.	Through the Looking Glass (1st {this pub}, 4to, 96p, color)	Whittlesey	(1946)	Tenniel, J.	35-50	*
Carroll, L.	Alice... & Through... (1st {this pub}, sm8vo, 317p, col frn)	Collier	1903	Tenniel/Stevens	65-90	*
Winfrey, Guy	Bunny Bearskin (1st, 8vo, ibds, color, pep)	M. Bradley	(1926)	Tessin, L.	70-100	
Winfrey, Guy	Pussy Purr-Mew (1st, 8vo, ibds, color, pep)	M. Bradley	(1927)	Tessin, L.	80-120	
Thackeray, L.	Light Side of Egypt (1st, ob4to, ibds, unpag, 36cp)	L: A&C Black	1908	Thackeray, L.	80-125	
Porter, G.S.	Magic Garden (1st {std}, sm8vo, 272p, pep, designs by...)	Doubleday/Page	1927	Thayer, L.	100-130	
Comstock, H.T.	Princess Rags & Tatters (1st, 12mo, grey cl, 112p, 4cp)	Doubleday/Page	1912	Thayer, L.	30-45	
Woolf, Rose	Children's Stories/Arabian Nights (1st, lg8vo, 144p, 10cp)	L: R. Tuck	[1914]	Theaker, H.G.	65-90	*
Kato, N. (tr.)	Children's Stories/Japanese Fairy Tales... (1st, 4to, ibds, 10cp)	L: R. Tuck	[1918]	Theaker, H.G.	80-125	
Cervantes	Don Quixote (1st, lg8vo, 340p, 48cp)	L: Ward Lock	[1910]	Theaker, H.G.	50-75	*
Grimm Bros.	Fairy Tales (1st, sm4to, 344p, 48cp)	L: Ward Lock	1920	Theaker, H.G.	70-100	*
Grimm Bros.	Fairy Tales (sm4to, ibds, 175p, 16cp, reprint)	L: Ward Lock	[1925]	Theaker, H.G.	65-80	
Ingoldsby, T.	Ingoldsby Legends (1st, 8vo, a.e. blue, 546p, 16cp)	L: MacMillan	1911	Theaker, H.G.	80-120	
Winder, Blanche	King Arthur & his Knights (8vo, 128p, 48cp)	L: Ward Lock	[1910]	Theaker, H.G.	70-100	*
Winter, B. (ed.)	Stories of King Arthur (1st, 8vo, green cl, p-o, 340p, 48cp)	L: Ward Lock	[1925]	Theaker, H.G.	65-80	
Kingsley, C.	Water Babies (1st, 8vo, 340p, grey cl, p-o, 48cp, pep)	L: Ward Lock	1916	Theaker, H.G.	90-140	
Richards, Dorothy	Adventures in an Old Shoe House (1st, 12mo, ibds, 6cp)	L: Faber	(1948)	Thomas, E.	35-50	
Richards, Dorothy	Roma Rabbit's Picnic (1st, 12mo, ibds, 6cp)	L: Faber	(1947)	Thomas, E.	35-50	
Stowe, H.B.	Uncle Tom's Cabin (1st, 8vo, 529p, gilt, illus by...)	L: Routledge	1904	Thomas, G.	145-180	
Warner, A.	The Panther (1st, 8vo, teg, uncut, 91p)	Small	1908	Thomas, P.K.	20-25	*
Crockett, D.	Adventures of Davy Crockett (1st, 8vo, black cl, 258p, p-o, 3cp)	Scribner	1934	Thomason, J.	45-70	*
Thomason, J.W.	Fix Bayonets (1st, lg8vo, 245p, bds, col frn)	Scribner	1926	Thomason, J.W.	35-60	
Page, T.N.	Two Little Confederates (1st, sm4to, 189p, gilt, p-o, col frn)	Scribner	1932	Thomason, J.W.	60-85	
Reed, H.L.	Brenda's Bargain (1st, 8vo, 251p, 6pl)	Little/Brown	1903	Thompson, E.B.	30-45	
Ray, A.C.	Nathalie's Chum (1st, 8vo, 289p, 6pl)	Little/Brown	1902	Thompson, E.B.	30-50	
LeBaron, G.	Twixt You & Me (1st, 8vo, 296p, 5pl by...)	Little/Brown	1898	Thompson, E.B.	35-50	*
Bingham, C.	Airship in Animal Land (ob4to, ibds, 8 chromos)	L: Nister	[1910]	Thompson, G.H.	250-400	*
Lang, A.	Story of the Golden Fleece (1st, 8vo, 93p, 6pl)	Altemus	(1903)	Thompson, M.	65-80	*
Carroll, L.	Three Sunsets... (1st, sq8vo, green/gilt, AEG, 68p, 12 fp b/w)	L: MacMillan	1898	Thomson, E.G.	280-350	*
Barrie, J.M.	Admirable Crichton (1st, 4to, 235p, gilt, 21 ticp)	L: Hodder	[1914]	Thomson, H.	125-165	
Shakespeare, Wm.	As You Like It (1st, 4to, ibds, 143p, gilt, 40 ticp)	L: Hodder	[1909]	Thomson, H.	130-165	
Dobson, Austin	Ballad of Beau Brocade (1st, 8vo, 89p, uncut, gilt, teg, b/w)	L: Kegan Paul	1892	Thomson, H.	60-85	
N/A	Coridon's Song (1st, 12mo, green/gilt, AEG, 163p, b/w, cep)	L: MacMillan	1894	Thomson, H.	90-135	
Gaskell, Mrs.	Cranford (1st {color ed.}, 12mo, teg, gilt, 298p, 40cp)	L: MacMillan	1898	Thomson, H.	65-90	
Burney, Fanny	Evelina... (1st, 8vo, 477p, gilt, b/w)	L: MacMillan	(1903)	Thomson, H.	50-75	
Gwynn, S.L.	Fair Hills of Ireland (1st, 8vo, 416p)	L: MacMillan	1906	Thomson, H.	50-70	*
Thackeray, Wm.	History of Henry Esmond (1st, AEG, 50 illus)	L: MacMillan	1905	Thomson, H.	50-80	
Spielmann, M.H.	Hugh Thomson: His Art (1st, lg8vo, 269p, gilt, 12cp)	L: A&C Black	1931	Thomson, H.	85-125	
Thomson, Hugh	Jack the Giant Killer (1st, sq8vo, [32]p, wraps, 16 color)	L: MacMillan	1898	Thomson, H.	170-300	
Allen, J.L.	Kentucky Cardinal Aftermath (1st AM, 8vo, 276p, teg)	MacMillan	1900	Thomson, H.	60-80	
Peacock, T.L.	Maid Marian.... (1st, AEG, 12mo, 321p, blue bds, dep)	L: MacMillan	1895	Thomson, H.	60-80	
Shakespeare, Wm.	Merry Wives of Windsor (1st, 4to, teg, gilt, 172p, 40 ticp)	L: Heinemann	1910	Thomson, H.	180-250	
Shakespeare, Wm.	Merry Wives of Windsor (1st AM, 4to, red/gilt, teg, 40 ticp)	Stokes	(1910)	Thomson, H.	160-220	
Spielmann, M.H.	My Son & I (1st, 8vo, red/gilt, teg, 307p, uncut, col frn, 9pl)	L: G. Allen	1908	Thomson, H.	60-85	
Austen, J.	Northanger Abbey (1st, 8vo, AEG, red cloth, b/w)	L: MacMillan	1897	Thomson, H.	70-90	
N/A	Old English Songs (1st, sm8vo, 163p, AEG, green/gilt)	L: MacMillan	1894	Thomson, H.	50-75	
Mitford, M.R.	Our Village (1st, sm8vo, AEG, green/gilt, b/w, cep)	L: MacMillan	1893	Thomson, H.	50-65	
Reade, C.	Peg Woffington (1st AM, 12mo, green/gilt, 298p, AEG)	Doub./McClure	1899	Thomson, H.	50-70	
Reade, C.	Peg Woffington (1st, 12mo, 298p, green/gilt, AEG, b/w)	L: G. Allen	1899	Thomson, H.	65-80	
Browning, R.	Pied Piper of Hamelin (1st, 8vo, 64p, uncut, 12pl)	L: Heinemann	1893	Thomson, H.	80-120	
Austen, J.	Pride & Prejudice (1st, 12mo, 476p, AEG, grn/gilt, b/w, cep)	L: G. Allen	1894	Thomson, H.	65-90	
Barrie, J.M.	Quality Street (1st, 4to, 198p, blue/gilt, 22 ticp, pep)	L: Hodder	[1913]	Thomson, H.	130-200	
Hawthorne, N.	Scarlet Letter (1st, 4to, uncut, 296p, gilt, teg, 31 ticp)	L: Methuen	(1920)	Thomson, H.	160-220	
Hawthorne, N.	Scarlet Letter (1st AM, 4to, ibds, 31 ticp)	Doran	(1920)	Thomson, H.	150-200	
Eliot, Geo.	Scenes from Clerical Life (1st, 12mo, 429p, grn/gilt, AEG, 16cp)	L: MacMillan	1906	Thomson, H.	50-90	
Sheridan, R.B.	School for Scandal (1st, 4to, gilt, teg, 196p, 25 ticp)	L: Hodder	(1911)	Thomson, H.	140-200	
Goldsmith, O.	She Stoops to Conquer (1st, 4to, 198p, gilt, 25 ticp)	L: Hodder	(1912)	Thomson, H.	120-160	
Dobson, Austin	Story of Rosina (1st, sm8vo, AEG, 120p, gilt, 28pl, cep)	L: Kegan Paul	1895	Thomson, H.	65-80	
Edgeworth, M.	Tales from.... (1st AM, 8vo, brown/gilt, teg, 412p, uncut, b/w)	Stokes	(1903)	Thomson, H.	85-100	
Somerville, Wm.	The Chase (1st, lg sq8vo, 87p, gilt, teg, b/w)	L: Redway	1896	Thomson, H.	65-85	
Dickens, C.	The Chimes (1st, 8vo, 137p, red/gilt, 7 ticp, pep)	L: Hodder	[1912]	Thomson, H.	140-180	
Molesworth, M.	This & That (1st, 12mo, 212p, orange/gilt, 8pl)	L: MacMillan	1899	Thomson, H.	50-65	
Goldsmith, O.	Vicar of Wakefield (1st, 8vo, 305p, AEG, gilt, b/w)	L: MacMillan	1890	Thomson, H.	60-80	
Malory, T.	King Arthur... (1st, 12mo, 335p, cp)	MacMillan	1916	Thomson, R.	35-50	*
Bradley, A.G.	Highways & Byways/North Wales (1st, 8vo, 474p, b/w)	L: MacMillan	1898	Thomson/Pennell	65-80	*
Terhune, A.P.	Columbia Stories (1st {1st bk.}, sm8vo, 214p, b/w)	Dillingham	1897	Thornburgh, F.	35-60	*
Henry, M.	Boy & a Dog (1st, sm4to, [42]p, 2-color, pep)	Wilcox/Follett	1944	Thorne, D.	30-50	*
Garner, Elvira	Little Cat Lost (1st, sq4to, [28]p, 2-color, pep)	J. Messner	(1943)	Thorne, D.	35-50	*

AUTHOR	TITLE	PUBLISHER	DATE	ARTIST	PRICE	LC
Henry, M.	Little Fellow (1st, 4to, [64]p, color)	Winston	(1945)	Thorne, D.	35-50	
Orton, Ruth	Pepito the Colt (1st, ob4to, ibds, 36p, b/w, pep)	Houghton	1933	Thorne, D.	40-65	*
Terhune, A.P.	Real Tales of Real Dogs (1st, lg4to, 92p, b/w)	Saalfield	(1935)	Thorne, D.	30-45	*
Salten, Felix	Rennie the Rescuer (1st {std}, 8vo, 326p, cloth, b/w)	Bobbs-Merrill	1940	Thorne, D.	35-50	
Terhune, A.P.	True Dog Stories (1st, 12mo, 60p, b/w)	Saalfield	1936	Thorne, D.	25-40	*
Farjeon, E.	Heroes & Heroines (1st AM, lg8vo, 79p, fp color, DJ)	Dutton	[1933]	Thornycroft, R.	45-65	
Farjeon, E.	Italian Peepshow (1st, 8vo, p-o, 146p, 12 fp color, pep)	Stokes	1926	Thornycroft, R.	30-45	*
Farjeon, E.	Kings & Queens (1st, 8vo, 79p, ibds, 38cp, DJ)	L: Gollancz	(1932)	Thornycroft, R.	50-65	
Farjeon, E.	Kings & Queens (1st AM, 8vo, 79p, color, DJ)	Dutton	1932	Thornycroft, R.	45-60	
Farjeon, E.	Kings & Queens (sm4to, red cl, 86p, 40 fp color)	Dent/Dutton	(1940)	Thornycroft, R.	30-50	*
Farjeon, E.	Kings & Queens (sm4to, ibds, 86p, 40 color, DJ)	Lippincott	[1940]	Thornycroft, R.	30-50	
Farjeon, E.	Nuts & May (1st, 4to, p-o, 263p, color)	L: Collins	1926	Thornycroft, R.	70-120	*
Walton, Isaac	Complete Angler (4to, 25pl)	L: Hodder	[1911]	Thorpe, J.	130-170	
Thurber, J.	Further Fables/Our Time (1st {std}, 8vo, 174p, bds, gilt, b/w)	Simon/Schuster	1956	Thurber, J.	45-65	*
Hawes, Eliz.	Men Can Take It (1st {std}, 8vo, blue cl, 275p, 14pl)	Random	(1939)	Thurber, J.	65-80	*
Thurber, J.	Owl in the Attic (1st {std}, 8vo, 151p, yellow cl, b/w)	Harper	1931	Thurber, J.	100-130	R*
Thurston, C.B.	Discontented Stuffed Cat (1st, 4to, ibds, b/w)	Saalfield	(1910)	Thurston, C.B.	65-80	*
Thurston, C.B.	Jingle of a Jap (1st, lg8vo, [64]p, p-o, color, pep)	Caldwell	(1906)	Thurston, C.B.	70-120	*
Vetsch, Earnest	New Story/Little Black Sambo (12mo, grey bds, color)	Whitman	1926	Thurston, C.B.	90-120	
Gibson, Katherine	Zauberlinda: Wise Witch (1st, 4to, 256p, blue cl, 1-color, pep)	Chi: R. Smith	(1901)	Tibbitts, M.	100-150	*
N/A	ABC Dogs (folio, ibds, [32]p, color, pep)	NY: W. Funk	1940	Tice, C.	120-180	
Chilvers, H.A.	Out of the Crucible (1st, 8vo, 273p, 16 illus)	L: Cassell	1929	Timlin, W.M.	100-130	*
Timlin, W.M.	Ship that Sailed to Mars (1st, lg4to, 48p, ibds, 48 ticp)	L: Harrap	(1923)	Timlin, W.M.	900-1100	
N/A	Old Woman & her Pig (1st, 24mo, [41]p)	Holiday House	[1937]	Tinker, J.H.	25-40	*
Collodi, C.	Pinocchio (1st [Gift ed.], 4to, 284p, 10cp)	Lippincott	(1930)	Tinker, J.H.	65-80	*
Thackeray, Wm.	Rose & the Ring (4to, 161p, p-o, color)	Brentano's	[1920]	Tinker, J.H.	65-80	
Tittle, W.	Colonial Holidays (1st, sm4to, 73p, p-o, 22cp)	Doubleday/Page	1910	Tittle, W.	60-80	
Tittle, W.	First Nantuckett Tea-Party (1st, 4to, tan cl, p-o, 23cp)	Doubleday/Page	1907	Tittle, W.	45-70	
Tittle, W.	My Country (1st, lg4to, ipcb, color)	Tandy-Thomas	(1909)	Tittle, W.	65-100	*
Beach, R.	The Net (1st, 8vo, p-o, 4pl)	Harper	1912	Tittle, W.	20-35	
Sewell, Anna	Black Beauty (1st, sm8vo, 200p, 22 illus)	Hovendon	1894	Toaspern, H.	45-60	*
Adams, V.M.	Captain Joe & the Eskimo (1st, lg8vo, ipcb, [40]p, 1-color)	W.R. Scott	1943	Tobey, B.	65-80	*
Goldberg, M.	Lunch Box Story (1st, sm8vo, red cl, [30]p, b/w)	Holiday House	1951	Tobias, B.	20-30	*
Judson, C.I.	Mr. Justice Holmes (1st, sm4to, 192p, NH)	Follett	(1956)	Todd, R.	65-80	*
Tolkien, J.R.R.	The Hobbit (1st AM, sm8vo, 310p, beige cl, 4cp, pep, DJ)	Houghton	1938	Tolkien, J.R.R.	350-500	
N/A	Book of Job (1st, 4to, teg, 102p, gilt, 8 ticp)	L: C. Palmer	1916	Tongue, M.C.	85-130	
Bontemps, A.	Lonesome Boy (1st, 8vo, blue cl, 28p, fp b/w, cep)	Houghton	1955	Topolski, F.	45-65	*
DuBois, Theodora	Banjo the Crow (1st, sm4to, 142p, pep, b/w)	Houghton	1943	Torrey, H.	30-45	*
Gall, Alice	Little Black Ant (1st, 8vo, 128p, pep)	OUP	(1936)	Torrey, H.	25-40	*
Morrow, Eliz.	Shannon (1st {std}, 24mo, ipcb, 68p, fp b/w)	MacMillan	1941	Torrey, H.	25-45	*
Thompson, B.J.	Golden Trumpets (1st, sm8vo, 163p, blue/gilt, 2-color)	MacMillan	1927	Torrey, H.M.	25-40	
Carroll, L.	Alice/Wonderland (1st, 4to, green cl, 64p, p-o, 15 fp col, pep)	Random	1955	Torrey, M.	65-80	*
Torrey, M.	Artie & the Princess (1st, lg8vo, 107p, green cl, 5cp, pep)	Howell/Soskin	(1945)	Torrey, M.	20-35	*
Philbrook, Eliz.	Far From Marlborough Street (1st, sm8vo, 302p, b/w)	Viking	1944	Torrey, M.	30-45	*
Torrey, M.	Merriweathers (1st, 8vo, 254p)	Viking	1949	Torrey, M.	30-45	*
Torrey, M.	Penny (1st, tall 8vo, 126p, color)	Howell/Soskin	1944	Torrey, M.	25-40	
Gates, Doris	Sarah's Idea (1st, 8vo, orange cl, 146p, fp b/w, pep)	Viking	1938	Torrey, M.	20-35	*
Gates, Doris	Sensible Kate (1st, 8vo, yellow cl, 189p, b/w, pep, DJ)	Viking	1943	Torrey, M.	30-45	
Wheeler, Opal	Sing Mother Goose (1st {std}, 4to, 102p, ibds, color, CH)	Dutton	1945	Torrey, M.	65-90	*
Wheeler, Opal	Sing in Praise (1st {std}, 4to, 94p, ibds, color, pep, CH)	Dutton	1946	Torrey, M.	50-85	*
Torrey, M.	Three Little Chipmunks (1st, 4to, ipcb, [40]p, color, pep)	Grosset/Dunlap	(1947)	Torrey, M.	30-45	*
Gates, Doris	Trouble for Jerry (1st, 8vo, 179p, rust cl, fp b/w, pep)	Viking	1944	Torrey, M.	25-40	*
Tousey, S.	Bob & the Railroad (1st {std}, 8vo, ibds, 53p, pep, color)	Doubleday/Dor.	1941	Tousey, S.	30-45	*
Tousey, S.	Buffalo Bill (1st, 8vo, [36]p, map, ibds, color, pep)	Rand/McNally	1938	Tousey, S.	25-40	
Tousey, S.	Chinky Joins the Circus (1st {std}, lg ob8vo, [56]p, ibds, col)	Doubleday/Dor.	1938	Tousey, S.	25-40	
Tousey, S.	Chinky: Banker Pony (1st {std}, ob8vo, ibds, [56]p, color, pep)	Doubleday/Dor.	1937	Tousey, S.	35-50	
Tousey, S.	Cowboy Tommy (1st {std}, ob8vo, ibds, [56]p, pep, color)	Doubleday/Dor.	1932	Tousey, S.	30-45	
Tousey, S.	Cowboy Tommy's Roundup (1st {std}, ob8vo, [56]p, pep, color)	Doubleday/Dor.	1934	Tousey, S.	35-50	*
Tousey, S.	Cowboys of America (1st, 8vo, [36]p, ibds, color)	Rand/McNally	1937	Tousey, S.	25-40	
Tousey, S.	Daniel Boone (1st, 8vo, [36]p, map, color)	Rand/McNally	1939	Tousey, S.	30-45	*
Tousey, S.	Davy Crockett (1st, sm4to, 48p, cloth, p-o, color)	Whitman	1948	Tousey, S.	25-40	
Tousey, S.	Dick & the Canal Boat (1st {std}, lg8vo, [41]p, ipcb, color)	Doubleday/Dor.	1943	Tousey, S.	25-40	
Tousey, S.	Fisherman Tommy (1st, 4to, 47p, pep, color)	Houghton	1940	Tousey, S.	30-45	*
Tousey, S.	Indians & Cowboys (1st, 8vo, [76]p, color, pep)	Rand/McNally	(1940)	Tousey, S.	25-40	
Tousey, S.	Indians of the Plains (1st, 8vo, ipcb, [36]p, 1-color)	Rand/McNally	1940	Tousey, S.	30-45	*
Tousey, S.	Jerry & Pony Express (1st {std}, ob8vo, [56]p, pep, color)	Doubleday/Dor.	1936	Tousey, S.	30-45	*
Tousey, S.	Little Bear's Pinto Pony (1st, lg8vo, 29p, col frn)	Whitman	1943	Tousey, S.	25-40	
Tousey, S.	Lumberjack Bill (1st, 4to, blue cl, 47p, color, pep)	Houghton	1943	Tousey, S.	35-50	*
Tousey, S.	Steamboat Billy (1st {std}, ob8vo, ibds, [56]p, color, pep)	Doubleday/Dor.	1935	Tousey, S.	45-60	*
Norris, June	Dotzie the Dancey Duck (1st, sq8vo, ibds, color)	Volland	(1927)	Tower, L.	45-60	*
Norris, June	Katherine the Komical Kow (1st, 12mo, ibds, color, pep)	Volland	(1926)	Tower, L.	50-70	
Kipling, R.	Brushwood Boy (1st AM {this artist}, 8vo, 73p, p-o, teg, 12cp)	Doubleday/Page	1907	Townsend, F.H.	50-80	

AUTHOR	TITLE	PUBLISHER	DATE	ARTIST	PRICE	LC
Kipling, R.	Brushwood Boy (1st, 8vo, 91p, grey/gilt, teg, 12cp)	L: MacMillan	1907	Townsend, F.H.	60-95	
Barclay, F.	Following of the Star (1st, lg8vo, teg, 8pl by...)	Putnam	1911	Townsend, F.H.	35-50	*
Peacock, T.L.	Gryll Grange (1st, sm8vo, 292p, AEG, b/w)	L: MacMillan	1896	Townsend, F.H.	45-65	
Marryat, Fred.	King's Own (1st, 12mo, AEG, 429p, 40pl, pep)	L: MacMillan	1896	Townsend, F.H.	45-65	
Peacock, T.L.	Maid Marian/Crotchet Castle (1st, 12mo, AEG, gilt, 321p, dep)	L: MacMillan	1895	Townsend, F.H.	65-80	
Peacock, T.L.	Melincourt... (1st, 8vo, 326p, AEG, blue bds, 40 illus)	L: MacMillan	1896	Townsend, F.H.	65-80	
Peacock, T.L.	Misfortunes of Elphin & Rhododaphne (1st, 8vo, 262p)	L: MacMillan	1897	Townsend, F.H.	50-75	*
Kipling, R.	They (1st AM, 8vo, 80p, p-o, teg, uncut, 15cp)	Doubleday/Page	1906	Townsend, F.H.	60-80	
Kipling, R.	They (1st {this format}, red/gilt, teg, 27cp)	L: MacMillan	1925	Townsend, F.H.	35-50	
Rankin, L.S.	Gentling of Jonathan (1st, 8vo, 223p, green cl, b/w, pep)	Viking	1950	Townsend, L.	30-50	*
Farjeon, E.	Joan's Door (1st, 8vo, 127p)	L: Collins	(1926)	Townsend, W.	30-45	*
Baring-Gould, S.	Gladys of the Stewponey (1st, 8vo, 319p)	L: Methuen	1897	Townsend/Munns	45-60	*
Uttley, Alison	Moonshine & Magic (1st, 8vo, 208p, cloth, 8cp)	L: Faber	1932	Townshend, W.	30-45	
Gordon, H.C.	Paradoc to the Rescue (1st, 8vo, 206p)	L: J. Murray	(1939)	Tozer, K.	30-45	*
Raine, W.M.	Daughter of Raasay (1st [1st bk.], 12mo, 311p, b/w pl)	Stokes	(1902)	Travis, S.	100-150	*
Wilson, A.E.	Devota (1st, 8vo, teg, p-o, 122p, red/gilt, dep)	Dillingham	(1907)	Travis, S.	20-30	
Kastner, Erich	Animal's Conference (1st AM, 4to, ibds, [62]p, color)	McKay	(1949)	Trier, W.	65-90	*
Kastner, Erich	Emil & the Detectives (1st {std}, 8vo, 224p, yellow cl, color)	Doubleday/Dor.	1930	Trier, W.	80-100	*
Kastner, Erich	Emil & the Three Twins (1st UK, 8vo, 251p, ibds, 8 illus)	L: Cape	1935	Trier, W.	65-80	
Kastner, Erich	Flying Classroom (1st UK, 8vo, 223p, ibds, 10 illus)	L: Cape	1934	Trier, W.	65-80	
Kastner, Erich	Puss in Boots (1st AM, 4to, ibds, 66p, color)	J. Messner	1957	Trier, W.	25-40	*
Forster, F.J.	On the Road to Make-Believe (1st, 4to, 128p, p-o, color)	Rand/McNally	(1924)	Trippe, U.	45-65	*
Forster, F.J.	Tippytoes... (1st, 4to, 96p, color)	Rand/McNally	(1926)	Trippe, U.	35-50	*
Sawyer, R.S.	Enchanted Schoolhouse (1st, lg8vo, green cl, 128p, fp b/w, pep)	Viking	1956	Troy, H.	20-35	*
Sawyer, R.S.	Year of the Christmas Dragon (1st, lg8vo, red cl, 88p, b/w, pep)	Viking	(1960)	Troy, H.	25-45	*
Baker, Augusta	Golden Lynx (1st {std}, 8vo, 160p, red cl, fp b/w)	Lippincott	(1960)	Troyer, J.	40-65	*
Baker, Augusta	Talking Tree (1st {std}, 8vo, 255p, maroon cl, b/w)	Lippincott	(1955)	Troyer, J.	40-65	*
Parrish, R.	Last Voyage of the Donna Isabel (1st, 8vo, blue cl, 366p, 4cp)	McClurg	1908	True, A.	20-35	
Browne, Frances	Granny's Wonderful Chair (1st, 8vo, gilt, 213p, 8cp)	McClure	1904	Truman, Edith	30-50	
N/A	Book of Pets (lg4to, ibds, 12cp by,...)	Gardner/Dar.	1897	Tucker, E.S.	350-500	
Tucker, E.S.	Bubbles (4to, 12p, ibds, 6cp)	Worthington	(1892)	Tucker, E.S.	75-120	
Tucker, E.S.	Cup of Tea (ob4to, 22p, ibds, chromos)	Worthington	1892	Tucker, E.S.	120-165	
Tucker, E.S.	Favorite Pets (1st, 4to, ibds, 12cp)	Stokes	1893	Tucker, E.S.	100-130	
Tucker, E.S.	Royal Little People (1st, 4to, unpag, ibds, 12cp)	Stokes	(1895)	Tucker, E.S.	100-150	
Tudor, T.	1 Is One (1st, ob4to, unpag, pep, pink cl, color, CH)	NY: OUP	1956	Tudor, T.	100-145	*
Tudor, T.	A is for Annabelle (1st, ob4to, unpag, grn/gilt, 27 color, pep)	NY: OUP	1954	Tudor, T.	100-150	*
Tudor, T.	Alexander the Gander (1st, 24mo, green cl, [47]p, color, pep)	OUP	(1939)	Tudor, T.	150-200	*
Tudor, T.	Amanda & the Bear (1st, 12mo, unpag, p-o, blue cl, color, dep)	NY: OUP	1951	Tudor, T.	90-135	*
Tudor, T.	Around the Year (1st, lg ob8vo, [54]p, cloth, color)	NY: OUP	1957	Tudor, T.	100-150	
Tudor, T.	Becky's Birthday (1st, 4to, yellow cl, color)	Viking	(1960)	Tudor, T.	120-165	*
McCready, T.L.	Biggity Bantam (1st, 8vo, yellow cl, 49p, color, cep)	Ariel	(1954)	Tudor, T.	70-110	
Stevenson, R.L.	Child's Garden of Verses (1st, 8vo 118p, grn cl, p-o, 15cp, pep)	OUP	1947	Tudor, T.	150-180	
Tudor, T.	County Fair (1st, 24mo, [47]p, red/white, pep, color, DJ)	L: OUP	1940	Tudor, T.	120-150	
Tudor, T.	Doll's Christmas (1st, sq12mo, red cl, [29]p, pep, p-o, color)	NY: OUP	1950	Tudor, T.	120-160	
Tudor, T.	Dorcas Porcas (1st, 24mo, [35]p, orang cl, color, DJ)	NY: OUP	(1942)	Tudor, T.	250-400	
Tudor, T.	Edgar Allan Crow (1st, sq12mo, p-o, unpag, fp color, DJ)	OUP	1953	Tudor, T.	180-220	
Andersen, H.C.	Fairy Tales (1st, 8vo, blue cl, 273p, 10 fp color, DJ)	NY: OUP	(1945)	Tudor, T.	145-200	
N/A	First Graces (1st, 16mo, blue cl, 47p, p-o, color, pep)	NY: OUP	1955	Tudor, T.	100-140	
N/A	First Prayers (1st, 16mo, 48p, blue cl, p-o, color)	NY: OUP	(1952)	Tudor, T.	90-130	
McCready, T.L.	Increase Rabbit (1st, sm8vo, yellow cl, unpag, color, pep)	Ariel	(1958)	Tudor, T.	70-110	*
Ewing, J.H.	Jacanapes (1st, sm8vo, green cl, 62p, color, pep)	OUP	1948	Tudor, T.	100-130	
Tudor, T.	Linsey Woolsey (1st, sq24mo, [43]p, yellow bds, color)	NY: OUP	1946	Tudor, T.	160-200	*
Mother Goose	Mother Goose (1st, sm sq8vo, green cl, 87p, color, pep, CH)	NY: OUP	(1944)	Tudor, T.	200-350	
McCready, T.L.	Mr. Stubbs (1st, sm8vo, 48p, red cl, color, pep)	Ariel	(1956)	Tudor, T.	70-110	*
McCready, T.L.	Pekin White (1st, sm8vo, green cl, 49p, color, pep)	Ariel	(1955)	Tudor, T.	70-110	*
Tudor, T.	Pumpkin Moonshine (1st, 24mo, blue cl, [41]p, color, pep)	OUP	(1938)	Tudor, T.	160-240	*
Tudor, T.	Snow Before Christmas (1st, sq12mo, [37]p, pep, p-o, color)	NY: OUP	(1941)	Tudor, T.	100-165	
Tudor, T.	Tale for Easter (1st, sq12mo, [33]p, dep, p-o, color)	NY: OUP	(1941)	Tudor, T.	90-130	*
Tudor, T.	Thistly B. (1st, sq12mo, [27]p, red bds, p-o, color)	NY: OUP	1949	Tudor, T.	130-165	*
Tudor, T.	White Goose (1st, sq12mo, grey cl, p-o, [27]p, color)	OUP	(1943)	Tudor, T.	140-175	
Tunis, Edwin	Oars & Sails (1st {std}, lg4to, 78p, ivory cl, b/w)	World Pub. Co.	(1952)	Tunis, E.	80-130	R*
Rogerson, Sidney	Both Sides of the Road (1st, 4to, red cl, 183p, 23cp)	L: Collins	1949	Tunnicliffe, C.F.	45-60	
Hawkins, Q.	Aunt-Sitter (1st, 8vo, 35p, yellow cl, b/w, pep)	Holiday House	(1958)	Turkle, B.	20-30	*
Eaton, S.	Prince Domino & Muffles (1st, sq8vo, p-o, 146p, 7cp)	Stern	1910	Twelvetrees, C.	100-150	
Coonley, L.A.	Singing Verses for Children (1st, ob4to, 80p, gilt)	MacMillan	1897	Tyler, A.K.	65-100	
Hurst, Edward H.	Mystery Island (1st, 8vo, 313p, uncut, gilt, col frn by...)	Page	1907	Tyng, G.	20-25	*
Black, I.S.	This is the Bread that Betsy Ate (1st, ob4to, [26]p, color)	W.R. Scott	1945	Ullman, A.	40-65	*
Parrish, R.	Air Pilot (1st, 8vo, 318p, 3cp)	McClurg	1913	Underwood, C.F.	25-45	
Underwood, C.F.	American Types (1st, 4to, p-o, red cl, 16cp)	Stokes	(1912)	Underwood, C.F.	70-100	
Chamberlain, Esth.	Coast of Chance (1st, 8vo, tan/gilt, 465p, 4pl)	Bobbs-Merrill	(1908)	Underwood, C.F.	20-25	*
N/A	Comin' Thro the Rye (1st, lg8vo, p-o, 6cp)	Bobbs-Merrill	(1909)	Underwood, C.F.	30-45	
N/A	Famous Love Songs (1st, lg8vo, blue cl, p-o, 17cp)	Bobbs-Merrill	(1909)	Underwood, C.F.	50-65	

AUTHOR	TITLE	PUBLISHER	DATE	ARTIST	PRICE	LC
Barbour, R.H.	Golden Heart (1st, 8vo, 219p, teg, p-o, 5cp, pep)	Lippincott	1910	Underwood, C.F.	20-30	
Nesbit, E.	Incomplete Amorist (1st AM, 12mo, p-o, 356p, 8pl)	Doubleday/Page	1906	Underwood, C.F.	70-100	*
N/A	Love Songs Old & New (1st, sm4to, p-o, unpag, 18cp)	Bobbs-Merrill	(1909)	Underwood, C.F.	70-90	
Seawell, M.E.	Loves of Lady Arabella (1st, 8vo, p-o, 244p, 12cp)	Bobbs-Merrill	(1906)	Underwood, C.F.	20-25	
Bianco, M.W.	Adventures of Andy (1st, sm4to, 227p, 8cp, pep)	Doran	(1927)	Underwood, L.	50-80	*
Ungerer, Tomi	Crictor (1st, 4to, green ibds, 32p, 2-color)	Harper	(1958)	Ungerer, T.	65-90	R*
Ungerer, Tomi	Emile (1st, 4to, 32p, ibds, 2-color)	Harper	(1960)	Ungerer, T.	60-80	*
Ungerer, Tomi	Mellops Go Diving for Treasure (1st, 8vo, ibds, unpag, 2-color)	Harper	(1957)	Ungerer, T.	50-80	*
Ungerer, Tomi	Mellops Go Flying (1st, ob8vo, ibds, [32]p, 2-color)	Harper	(1957)	Ungerer, T.	60-100	R*
Selsam, M.E.	Seeds & More Seeds (1st, 8vo, ibds, 60p, 2-color)	Harper	(1959)	Ungerer, T.	25-40	*
Twain, M.	$30000 Bequest (1st, sm8vo, 522p, red cl, 8pl)	Harper	1906	Unknown	100-140	
Nesbit, W.D.	A Friend or Two (1st, 16mo, ibds, color)	Volland	(1915)	Unknown	65-80	*
N/A	Aladdin (1st, sq4to, wraps, [15]p, chromos)	McLoughlin	1898	Unknown	35-60	*
Girvin, B.	Alice & the White Rabbit (1st, 8vo, 160p, 33 illus)	L: Partridge	(1909)	Unknown	65-80	*
Farrow, G.E.	All About the Wallypug (1st, folio, unpag)	L: R. Tuck	[1904]	Unknown	100-150	*
Baum, L.F. (intro)	Animal ABC (1st, 24mo, ibds, 124p, color)	Reilly/Britton	1905	Unknown	90-130	
Altsheler, J.A.	Apache Gold (1st, sm8vo, 382p, cp)	Appleton	1913	Unknown	30-45	*
Streamer, Col. D.	Baby's Baedeker (1st, 8vo, 56p, uncut, ibds, 9pl)	R.H. Russell	1902	Unknown	70-100	*
Cobb, I.	Back Home (1st, 8vo, cloth, 348p, 10pl)	Doran	(1912)	Unknown	45-60	
Alcott, L.M.	Candy Country (1st, 12mo, 52p, 3pl)	Little/Brown	(1900)	Unknown	60-80	R*
Alcott, L.M.	Christmas Dream (1st, 12mo, green cl, 55p)	Little/Brown	(1901)	Unknown	50-70	*
Howells, W.D.	Christmas Every Day... (1st, 8vo, 150p, rust cl, 14 b/w)	Harper	1893	Unknown	35-50	R*
Huntington, I.M.	Christmas Party for Santa Claus (1st, 8vo, 102p, 6cp)	Rand/McNally	(1912)	Unknown	65-90	*
Hughes, R.	Colonel Crockett's Cooperative Christmas (1st, sm8vo, 66p, 6cp)	Jacobs	(1906)	Unknown	20-30	
Pyrnelle, L.C.	Diddie, Dumps & Tot (1st, 12mo, green cl, 217p, 12pl, PPP)	Harper	1882	Unknown	250-320	
Muter, Gladys N.	Duck's Adventure (1st, sm sq4to, color)	Volland	(1927)	Unknown	45-60	*
Cain, Neville	Fairies' Circus (1st, lg4to, ibds, [16]p, calligraphy, color)	R.H. Russell	1903	Unknown	100-160	*
Cain, Neville	Fairies' Menagerie (1st, lg4to, ibds, [16]p, color)	R.H. Russell	1903	Unknown	100-150	*
Grimm Bros.	Fairy Tales (1st, 24mo, 127p, ibds, color)	Reilly/Britton	1905	Unknown	60-85	
N/A	Father Tuck's Bird ABC (4to, wraps, [14]p, 4cp)	L: R. Tuck	1895	Unknown	70-100	
Barbour, R.H.	Finkler's Field (1st, 8vo, 226p, 4cp)	Appleton	1911	Unknown	35-50	
Stockton, Frank	Floating Prince... (1st, 8vo, 199p, PPP, b/w)	Scribner	1881	Unknown	100-165	*
Altsheler, J.A.	Free Rangers (1st, 8vo, 365p, 4cp)	Appleton	1909	Unknown	25-40	*
Nesbit, W.D.	Friend O'Mine (1st, 12mo)	Volland	(1912)	Unknown	35-60	*
Brine, M.D.	Funnyland Boys (1st, sm8vo, 54p, ipcb, col frn, b/w)	Drexel Biddle	1903	Unknown	60-100	*
Stuart, Ruth M.	Gobolinks (1st, ob8vo, ibds, 73p, b/w)	Century	1896	Unknown	80-120	
Atkinson, E.	Greyfriars Bobby (1st, 12mo, 291p, frontis, PPPa)	Harper	1912	Unknown	45-60	*
Cutler, Carl	Greyhounds of the Sea (1st {std}, 4to, 592p, 8cp, photos)	Putnam	1930	Unknown	35-50	
Seegmiller, W.	Hand Clasp (1st, narrow 16mo)	Volland	(1911)	Unknown	40-65	*
Spyri, J.	Heidi (1st {this pub}, 12mo, red cl, 338p, b/w pl)	Crowell	(1902)	Unknown	25-40	*
Wharton, A.H.	Heirlooms in Miniatures (1st, 8vo, 259p, uncut, teg)	Lippincott	1898	Unknown	20-30	
Peirce, G.	How Percival Caught the Python (1st, sq24mo, [89]p, color)	Holiday House	(1937)	Unknown	30-50	*
Peirce, G.	How Percival Caught the Tiger (1st, sq24mo, [89]p, color)	Holiday House	(1936)	Unknown	30-50	*
Copley, F.B.	Impeachment/President Israels (1st, 12mo, blue/gilt, 124p, 3pl)	NY: MacMillan	1913	Unknown	25-45	
Warren, I.R.	In Cupid's Court (1st, 12mo, 79p, white/gilt, fp b/w)	R.H. Russell	1900	Unknown	65-80	*
Wodehouse, P.G.	Intrusion of Jimmy (1st, sm8vo, 314p, black/gilt, p-o, col frn)	NY: Watt	(1910)	Unknown	300-400	
Scott, Walter	Ivanhoe (1st, sm8vo, 346p, 4cp)	Appleton	1910	Unknown	20-35	*
Whittier, J.G.	Jack in the Pulpit (1st, sq8vo, color)	NY: S. Tilton	1883	Unknown	70-90	*
Hardy, T.	Jude the Obscure (1st AM, 8vo, 488p)	Harper	1896	Unknown	150	
Gordon, Eliz.	Just You (1st, sq16mo, ipcb, color, pep)	Volland	(1920)	Unknown	50-70	*
Nesbit, W.D.	Land of Make-Believe (1st, 8vo, green cl, 98p, 5pl)	Harper	1907	Unknown	30-50	*
Bailey, C.S.	Li'l Hannibal (1st, 8vo, [24]p, color, pep)	Platt/Munk	(1938)	Unknown	45-65	*
Blanchard, A.E.	Little Miss Mouse (1st, sm8vo, 230p, p-o, 5cp, pep)	Jacobs	(1906)	Unknown	25-40	
Gordon, A.C.	Maje: A Love Story (1st, 12mo, ipcb, uncut, 119p, 4pl)	Scribner	1914	Unknown	35-50	*
Chambers, Rbt.	Maker of Moons (1st, 8vo, blue cl, 401p)	Putnam	1896	Unknown	75-100	
Bangs, J.K.	Mantel-Piece Minstrels (1st, 12mo, 84p, pcb)	R.H. Russell	1896	Unknown	35-60	
Cawein, M.J.	Message of the Lilies (1st, narrow 8vo, pcb, color, pep)	Volland	(1913)	Unknown	65-90	R*
Spyri, J.	Moni the Goat Boy (1st, 12mo, 43p, 3pl)	Crowell	(1914)	Unknown	20-30	*
Gugu	Mother Duck's Children (sq4to, 48p, ibds, color)	R.H. Russell	1900	Unknown	150-200	
LeGallienne, R.	Mr. Sun & Mrs. Moon (1st, folio, bds, [62]p, 12pl)	R.H. Russell	1902	Unknown	185-230	R
Van Valkenburgh, H.	Myself & I (1st, 12mo, [36]p, color)	Volland	(1918)	Unknown	30-50	*
Gielow, M.S.	Old Plantation Days (1st, sm8vo, 183p, b/w)	R.H. Russell	1902	Unknown	100-150	*
Bowen, Wm.	Old Tobacco Shop (1st, 8vo, 236p, green/gilt cl, p-o, NH)	MacMillan	1921	Unknown	50-70	
Gates, J.S.	One Day in Betty's Life (1st, ob4to, [56]p, 2-color)	Bobbs-Merrill	(1913)	Unknown	90-130	*
Rossetti, D.G.	Pictures & Poems (1st, folio, [54]p, 13 tipl)	R.H. Russell	1899	Unknown	250-375	*
Collodi, C.	Pinocchio's Advens/Wonderland (1st AM, sm8vo, green/gilt, 212p)	J. Marsh	(1898)	Unknown	300-400	R*
Wright, Henrietta	Princess Liliwinkins (1st, 8vo, 220p, 9pl)	Harper	1889	Unknown	50-65	*
Gordon, A.L.	Racing Rhymes (1st, 12mo, 146p, uncut, b/w)	R.H. Russell	1901	Unknown	65-80	*
Bangs, J.K.	Real Thing... (1st, sm8vo, 135p, brown/gilt, uncut, 4pl)	Harper	1909	Unknown	25-40	
Asbjornsen, P.C.	Round the Yule Log (1st, lg8vo, 316p)	L: Sampson	1881	Unknown	65-90	*
Nesbit, W.D.	Sermons in Song (1st, 12mo, 96p)	Volland	(1929)	Unknown	30-50	*
Kipling, R.	Seven Seas (1st {illus ed}, 8vo, teg, uncut, 209p, 8pl)	Appleton	1905	Unknown	45-70	*

AUTHOR	TITLE	PUBLISHER	DATE	ARTIST	PRICE	LC
Cawein, M.J.	So Many Ways (1st, 12mo, pcb, gilt, [12]p, color)	Volland	(1911)	Unknown	65-90	R*
Wharton, A.H.	Social Life/Early Republic (1st, 8vo, 346p, teg, uncut)	Lippincott	1902	Unknown	25-40	
Kipling, R.	Soldier Tales (1st, 8vo, AEG, 172p, blue/gilt, 21pl)	L: MacMillan	1896	Unknown	100-140	
Foley, James W.	Some One Like You (1st, 16mo, ibds, color, pep)	Volland	(1916)	Unknown	65-80	*
Malloch, D.	Someone to Care (1st, sq16mo, color, ibds)	Volland	(1920)	Unknown	30-45	*
Lovelace, R.	Songs & Sonnets (1st, 8vo, 57p, uncut, 1-color)	R.H. Russell	1901	Unknown	65-100	*
Kjelgaard, J.A.	Stormy (1st, 8vo, 190p, grey cl, pep)	Holiday House	(1959)	Unknown	20-25	*
Dopp, K.E.	Story of the Early Sea People (1st, 8vo, 224p, b/w)	Rand/McNally	(1912)	Unknown	25-40	*
Ade, G.	Sultan of Sulu (1st, 12mo, 127p, b/w)	R.H. Russell	1903	Unknown	45-60	*
N/A	Tales & Talks About Animals (4to, 29cp, pcb, p-o)	Caldwell	[1901]	Unknown	50-80	*
Brown, A.F.	Tales of the Red Children (1st, sm8vo, 125p, tan cl, b/w)	Appleton	1909	Unknown	25-40	*
Sutton, Adah L.	Teddy Bears (1st, 4to, 154p, ibds, 6cp)	Saalfield	1907	Unknown	220-350	
Richards, L.E.	The Piccolo (1st, lg8vo, 121p, pict cl)	Estes	(1906)	Unknown	25-40	*
Evers, Helen	This Little Pig (1st, ob4to, [32]p, ibds, color, pep)	Farrar/Rine.	(1932)	Unknown	40-60	*
Foley, James W.	Through All the Years (1st, sq16mo, pep, unpag, color)	Volland	(1920)	Unknown	30-45	*
Moerleim, G.	Trip Around the World (1st, 4to, AEG, red/gilt, 100 chromos)	Burgheim	1880	Unknown	150-200	
Pritchard, M.T.	Upward Path (1st, sm8vo, 255p)	Harcourt	(1920)	Unknown	65-80	*
Burnett, F.H.	Way to the House of Santa Claus (1st, ob lg4to, p-o, [25]p, col)	Harper	1916	Unknown	80-120	*
Meigs, C.	Windy Hill (1st, 8vo, 210p, frontis, NH)	MacMillan	1921	Unknown	30-45	*
Bianco, M.W.	Winterbound (1st, 8vo, blue cl, 234p, pep, NH)	Viking	1936	Unknown	45-60	*
Henty, G.A.	Yuletide Yarns (1st AM, sm8vo, beige cl, 370p, teg)	Longmans	1899	Unknown	45-60	*
Yates, Eliz.	Amos Fortune, Free Man (1st {std}, 8vo, 181p, b/w, NM)	Aladdin	1950	Unwin, N.S.	80-120	R*
Tregarthen, Enys	Doll Who Came Alive (1st, sq12mo, 75p, fp 3-color)	NY: J. Day	(1942)	Unwin, N.S.	45-65	*
Nesbit, E.	Five of Us & Madeline (1st, 8vo, 310p, red cl)	L: T.F. Unwin	1925	Unwin, N.S.	100-150	
Unwin, Nora S.	Lucy & Little Red Horse (1st, 4to, bds, p-o, gilt, 8 fp color)	L: A. Moring	(1943)	Unwin, N.S.	45-60	
Snedeker, C.D.	Luke's Quest (1st {std}, sm8vo, blue cl, 208p, uncut, b/w)	Doubleday	1947	Unwin, N.S.	25-40	*
Yates, Eliz.	Mountain Born (1st, 8vo, 118p, brown cl, b/w, pep, NH)	Coward	(1943)	Unwin, N.S.	40-65	*
Yates, Eliz.	Once in the Year (1st, 8vo, red cl, p-o, [64]p, 1-color)	Coward	(1947)	Unwin, N.S.	30-45	
Barrie, J.M.	Peter Pan (1st, 8vo, 242p, pink cl, fp b/w)	Scribner	1950	Unwin, N.S.	30-45	*
Barrie, J.M.	Peter Pan (1st UK, 8vo, red/gilt, 23 b/w illus, DJ)	L: Hodder	1951	Unwin, N.S.	45-60	
MacDonald, Geo.	Princess & Curdie (1st, 8vo, 240p)	MacMillan	(1954)	Unwin, N.S.	25-45	*
MacDonald, Geo.	Princess & Goblin (1st, 8vo, olive cl, 249p, 1-color, pep)	MacMillan	(1951)	Unwin, N.S.	30-45	*
Goudge, Eliz.	Reward of Faith (1st AM, 8vo, blue cl, 186p, b/w)	Coward	(1950)	Unwin, N.S.	30-45	*
Brown, A.F.	Fresh Posies (1st, sq8vo, p-o, 4cp)	Houghton	1908	Upjohn, A.M.	35-50	*
Byrne, M.	House of the Red Fox (1st, sq12mo, 116p, 8pl)	Stokes	(1907)	Upjohn, A.M.	30-45	*
Jewett, J.H.	Little Christmas (1st, 8vo, 113p, ibds, 8cp)	Stokes	(1906)	Upjohn, A.M.	35-50	*
Burnham, C.L.	Quest Flower (1st, 8vo, red/gilt, 4cp)	Houghton	1908	Upjohn, A.M.	45-60	
Jewett, J.H.	Snuggy Bedtime Stories (1st, ob12mo, 126p, ibds, 8cp)	Stokes	(1906)	Upjohn, A.M.	45-70	
Byrne, M.	Would-Be Witch (1st, sq12mo, 127p, 8pl)	Stokes	(1906)	Upjohn, A.M.	30-45	*
Upton, F.	Adventures of Borbee & Wisp (1st, sq4to, ibds, [67]p, 31 color)	L: Longmans	1908	Upton, F.	250-350	
Upton, B.	Adventures of Two Dutch Dolls (1st, ob4to, 64p, ibds, 29cp)	Longmans	1898	Upton, F.	300-400	
Alden, W.L.	Among the Freaks (1st, 195p, 45 illus)	Longmans	1896	Upton, F.	120-160	
Upton, F.	Golliwogg at Sea-Side (1st, ob4to, ibds, 63p)	L: Longmans	1898	Upton, F.	240-320	
Upton, B.	Golliwogg in Holland (1st, ob4to, ibds, 31 fp color, dep)	L: Longmans	1904	Upton, F.	250-350	R
Upton, B.	Golliwogg in War! (1st, ob4to, 65p, ibds, color)	L: Longmans	1899	Upton, F.	280-400	
Upton, F.	Golliwogg's Air-Ship (ob4to, ipcb, 65p)	L: Longmans	1902	Upton, F.	230-320	
Upton, F.	Golliwogg's Auto Go Cart (1st, ob4to, ibds, 66p)	L: Longmans	1901	Upton, F.	200-300	
Upton, B.	Golliwogg's Bicycle Club (1st, ob4to, ibds)	L: Longmans	1896	Upton, F.	240-285	
Upton, B.	Golliwogg's Christmas (1st, ob4to, 62p, ipcb, 31 fp color)	L: Longmans	1907	Upton, F.	185-225	
Upton, B.	Golliwogg's Circus (1st, ob4to, ibds, 31 fp color)	L: Longmans	1903	Upton, F.	250-350	R
Upton, B.	Golliwogg's Desert Island (1st, ob4to, ibds, 64p, color)	L: Longmans	1906	Upton, F.	180-230	
Upton, B.	Golliwogg's Fox Hunt (1st, ob4to, ipcb, 32 fp color)	Longmans	1905	Upton, F.	200-240	
Upton, B.	Golliwogg's Polar Advens. (ob4to, 63p, ibds, color)	L: Longmans	1900	Upton, F.	160-200	
Brine, M.D.	Little Miss Toodledums (1st, 8vo, b/w pl)	Dutton	1893	Upton, F.	60-85	*
Brine, M.D.	Poor Sally/her Christmas (1st, 8vo, 182p, b/w pl)	Dutton	1898	Upton, F.	80-120	*
Upton, B.	Two Dutch Dolls & Golliwogg (1st, ob4to, ibds, 64p, dep)	Longmans	1895	Upton, F.	240-320	
Upton, F.	Vege-Men's Revenge (1st, ob4to, ibds, 63p, color)	L: Longmans	1897	Upton, F.	280-375	
Van Doren, M.	Transparent Tree (1st, 4to, ipcb, 87p, 2-color, pep)	Holt	(1940)	Van Doren, M.	65-90	R*
Moore, Ann C.	Nicholas (1st, 12mo, red/gilt, 331p, col frn, pep, NH)	Putnam	1924	Van Everan, J.	60-80	
Moore, Ann C.	Nicholas & Golden Goose (1st, 12mo, 259p, blue/gilt, color, pep)	Putnam	1932	Van Everan, J.	25-40	*
Davis, M.G.	Truce of the Wolf (1st, sm4to, uncut, 125p, fp b/w, dep, NH)	Harcourt	(1931)	Van Everan, J.	35-50	*
Andersen, H.C.	Ugly Duckling (1st, 4to, unpag, color)	L: D. Nutt	1894	Van Hoytems, T.	70-100	*
Van Loon, H.W.	Elephant Up a Tree (1st, 8vo, 206p, 3cp)	Simon/Schuster	1933	Van Loon, H.	25-40	
Van Loon, H.W.	Folk Songs of Many Lands (1st, 4to, ibds, 96p)	Simon/Schuster	1938	Van Loon, H.	25-45	*
Van Loon, H.W.	History with a Match (1st, 4to, 126p, p-o, color)	McKay	1917	Van Loon, H.	45-70	*
Van Loon, H.W.	Message of the Bells (1st, 12mo, ibds, gilt, pep, 16p, color)	(Garden City)	(1942)	Van Loon, H.	45-60	*
Van Loon, H.W.	Story of Mankind (1st, lg8vo, 479p, color, NM, PPPa)	Boni/Liveright	(1921)	Van Loon, H.	50-80	
Van Loon, H.W.	Wilbur the Hat (1st, 4to, ibds, 110p, p-o, color, pep)	H.B. Liveright	(1925)	Van Loon, H.	80-100	
Mother Goose	Tiny Book of Nursery Rhymes (1st, 12mo, ipcb, 61p, color, pep)	Harter	(1934)	Van Nortwick, C.	35-50	*
Van Stockum, H.	Andries (1st, 8vo, 192p, grey cl, 1 dp color, fp b/w)	Viking	1942	Van Stockum, H.	30-45	*
Van Stockum, H.	Angel's Alphabet (1st, lg8vo, [64]p, ipcb, fp b/w)	Viking	1948	Van Stockum, H.	30-45	*
Coblentz, C.C.	Beggar's Penny (1st {std}, 8vo, 269p, map)	Longmans	1943	Van Stockum, H.	25-45	*

AUTHOR	TITLE	PUBLISHER	DATE	ARTIST	PRICE	LC
Coblentz, C.C.	Bells of Leyden Sing (1st {std}, 8vo, 259p, pep, b/w)	Longmans	1944	Van Stockum, H.	25-45	*
Van Stockum, H.	Cottage at Bantry Bay (1st, 8vo, 252p, pep)	Viking	1938	Van Stockum, H.	25-40	*
Van Stockum, H.	Day on Skates (1st {std}, ob4to, 40p, 8cp, pep, NH)	Harper	1934	Van Stockum, H.	50-80	*
Van Stockum, H.	France on the Run (1st, 8vo, 303p, pep)	Viking	1939	Van Stockum, H.	30-45	*
Van Stockum, H.	Gerrit & the Organ (1st, 8vo, 178p, col frn, fp b/w)	Viking	1943	Van Stockum, H.	25-40	*
Van Stockum, H.	Pageen (1st, 8vo, 268p, b/w, pep)	Viking	1941	Van Stockum, H.	30-45	*
Van Stockum, H.	Patsy & the Pup (1st, sm8vo, 82p, ipcb, fp b/w)	Viking	1950	Van Stockum, H.	30-45	*
Van Stockum, H.	The Mitchells (1st, 8vo, 246p)	Viking	1945	Van Stockum, H.	25-40	*
MacDonald, Geo.	Fairy Fleet (1st, 8vo, [52]p, pattern cl, 1-color)	Holiday House	1936	Van Veen, S.	50-85	R*
Wellman, M.W.	Rebel Mail Runner (1st, sm8vo, 221p, red cl, b/w, pep)	Holiday House	(1954)	Van Veen, S.	20-30	*
Adams, Darwin	Adventures of Monte & Molly (1st, 4to, blue cl, 152p, cp)	Macaulay	(1938)	Van Zelm, L.F.	75-100	*
Keeler, D.B.	Memoirs of Simple Simon (1st, 4to, [56]p, color)	R.H. Russell	(1901)	Vandevort, C.S.	120-170	*
Abbot, A.B.	Frigate's Namesake (1st, 8vo, 204p, blue cl, 17pl)	Century	1901	Varian, G.	25-40	*
Hammond, H.	Further Fortunes of Pinkey Perkins (1st, sm8vo, 391p, 22pl)	Century	1906	Varian, G.	30-45	
Hawes, C.B.	Great Quest (1st, 8vo, 359p, 5pl, NH)	Little/Brown	(1921)	Varian, G.	40-65	*
Murai, G.	Kibun Daizin (1st, sm8vo, 164p, 12pl)	Century	1904	Varian, G.	30-45	*
Schultz, J.W.	Lone Bull's Mistake (1st, 8vo, 207p, p-o, 4pl)	Houghton	1918	Varian, G.	35-50	
Hammond, H.	Pinkey Perkins, Just a Boy (1st, 8vo, 327p, b/w, PPPa)	Century	1905	Varian, G.	80-130	*
Schultz, J.W.	Plumed Snake Medicine (1st, 8vo, 244p, p-o, 4pl)	Houghton	1924	Varian, G.	40-60	*
Scott, Walter	Quentin Durward (1st, sm8vo, 348p, 4cp)	Appleton	1910	Varian, G.	20-35	*
Schultz, J.W.	Quest of the Fish-Dog Skin (1st, 8vo, tan cl, p-o, 4pl)	Houghton	1913	Varian, G.	45-60	
Serviss, G.P.	Second Deluge (1st, sm8vo, 399p, aqua cl, 4pl)	McBride	1912	Varian, G.	150-200	
London, J.	Tales/Fish Patrol (1st, 8vo, teg, 243p, map, 7pl)	MacMillan	1905	Varian, G.	220-280	
Kennan, G.	Tragedy of Pelee (1st, 8vo, 257p, 7pl)	Outlook	1902	Varian, G.	30-45	
Stevenson, R.L.	Treasure Island (1st, sm8vo, 306p, 7cp, fp b/w)	Scribner	1918	Varian, G.	50-85	*
Schultz, J.W.	With the Indians in the Rockies (1st, 8vo, p-o, 227p, 6pl)	Houghton	1912	Varian, G.	40-60	*
Farjeon, B.L.	Lucy & their Majesties (1st, 8vo, 332p, tan cl, 20pl)	Century	1904	Varian/Cory	30-45	
N/A	All About Story Book (1st, sq4to, 63p, orange/gilt, color)	Cupples	(1929)	Various	70-100	*
Baum, L.F.	American Fairy Tales (1st, 8vo, [205]p, teg, cloth, b/w)	Geo. Hill	1901	Various	700-1000	*
N/A	Arabian Nights (1st, 4to, 472p, green cl, b/w)	L: Newnes	1899	Various	100-120	*
N/A	Arabian Nights (1st, lg8vo, 435p)	L: Constable	(1908)	Various	65-80	*
N/A	Arabian Nights (8vo, 435p, col frn)	Dodge	(1910)	Various	20-35	*
Smith, F.H.	Arm-Chair at the Inn (1st, sm8vo, green cl, uncut, 357p)	Scribner	1912	Various	25-40	
Wharton, T.I.	Bobbo and other Fancies (1st, 8vo, 182p, uncut, b/w)	Harper	1897	Various	25-40	
Baring-Gould, S.	Book of Nursery Songs & Rhymes (1st, 8vo, teg, 16pl)	L: Methuen	1895	Various	180-240	
Baring-Gould, S.	Book of Nursery Songs & Rhymes (2nd, 8vo, b/w)	L: Methuen	1906	Various	140-200	
Baring-Gould, S.	Book of Pictured Carols (1st, 8vo, uncut, 75p)	L: G. Allen	1893	Various	120-165	
Wharton, E.	Book of the Homeless (1st, 4to, 155p, bds, 8cp, 13pl)	Scribner	1916	Various	120-165	
Towers, Alton	Bunny & Bobbie (1st, 4to, unpag)	Cooke/Stokes	[1907]	Various	70-100	*
Stephens, R.N.	Captain Ravenshaw (1st, 12mo, teg, blue/gilt, 369p)	Page	1901	Various	30-45	
Squire, C.	Celtic Myth & Legend (1st, 8vo, 450p, gilt, 4cp)	L: Gresham	[1910]	Various	80-135	
Riis, J.A.	Children of the Tenements (1st, 8vo, green cl, 387p, 8pl)	MacMillan	1903	Various	65-80	
N/A	Children's Bible (1st, 4to, black cl, p-o, 15cp)	Scribner	1922	Various	60-80	
Longfellow, H.W.	Children's Longfellow (1st, 4to, 324p, p-o, 8cp)	Houghton	1908	Various	40-65	*
Fox, John Jr.	Christmas Eve on Lonesome (1st, sm8vo, 234p, teg, 8cp)	Scribner	1904	Various	20-30	
Thackeray, Wm.	Chronicle of the Drum (1st, 4to, AEG, 70p, brown cl, 32pl)	Scribner	1882	Various	125-165	
Chesterton, G.K.	Club of Queer Trades (1st, 8vo, 270p, 6pl)	Harper	1905	Various	45-60	*
Masson, T.	Corner In Women (1st, 8vo, teg, ipcb, gilt, 332p, b/w)	Moffat	1905	Various	30-50	
Gates, Eleanor	Cupid the Cowpunch (1st, sm8vo, 316p, p-o, 8pl)	McClure	1907	Various	35-60	
Swan, O.	Deep Water Days (1st, lg8vo, 506p, p-o, 11cp, pep)	Macrae-Smith	(1929)	Various	50-70	
Ralph, J.	Dixie... (1st, 4to, 411p, gilt, b/w)	Harper	1896	Various	50-70	
Carleton, K.	Dorothy/Motor Girl (1st, 8vo, 386p, 33pl)	Century	1911	Various	20-25	
Freeman, M.E.	Fair Lavina... (1st, 12mo, 308p, lavender/gilt, 8pl)	Harper	1907	Various	20-35	
Craik, D.	Fairy Book (1st, 8vo, 416p, gilt, teg, 32cp)	L: Nelson	(1913)	Various	160-185	
Djurklou, Baron G.	Fairy Tales from Sweedish (1stUK, 8vo, gilt, 178p, 20 fp b/w)	L: Heinemann	1901	Various	120-170	
Piper, W. (ed.)	Famous Rhymes/Mother Goose (4to, blue/gilt, p-o, color)	Platt/Munk	(1923)	Various	35-60	*
Asquith, C. (ed.)	Flying Carpet (1st, 4to, 200p, cloth, 4 ticp)	Scribner	(1925)	Various	30-45	
Underdown, E.	Gateway to Romance (1st, 4to, 299p, teg, 16cp)	L: Nelson	[1909]	Various	80-100	
Bangs, J.K.	Ghosts I Have Met (1st, 16mo, 191p, uncut, 23pl)	Harper	1898	Various	40-65	
Bangs, J.K.	Half-Hours with Jimmie-Boy (1st, 8vo, green cl, 212p, b/w)	R.H. Russell	1893	Various	50-65	
Stuart, Ruth M.	Haunted Photograph (1st, 12mo, gilt, 168p, 10pl)	Century	1911	Various	50-80	
N/A	Ideal Heads (1st, folio, brown/gilt, AEG, 20cp)	Sunshine	1890	Various	250-400	
Thaxter, Cellia	Idyls and Pastorals (1st, 8vo, AEG, 58p, gilt, 24pl)	D. Lothrop	(1886)	Various	80-100	*
Glave, E.J.	In Savage Africa (1st, lg8vo, 247p, grey cl, b/w)	R.H. Russell	(1892)	Various	100-160	*
Stuart, Ruth M.	In Simkinsville (1st, 8vo, 244p, 8pl)	Harper	1897	Various	30-50	
Kipling, R.	Indian Tales (1st AM, 8vo, 750p, 16pl)	Caldwell	(1899)	Various	80-120	
N/A	King Albert's Book (1st, 4to, 187p, pcb, 17 ticp)	L: Hodder	(1914)	Various	100-165	
Hamilton, M.	Kingdoms Curious (1st, 8vo, 248p, tan/gilt, 8pl)	L: Heinemann	1905	Various	120-160	
Dodge, M.M.	Land of Pluck (1st, 8vo, 313p, gilt, teg, b/w)	Century	1894	Various	45-60	
Toland, M.B.M.	Legend Laymone (1st, 4to, 61p, gilt, teg, 10pl, dep)	Lippincott	1890	Various	65-80	*
Kemble, E.W.	Life's Book of Animals (1st, ob4to, 80p, buckram, b/w)	Doub./McClure	1898	Various	75-100	
N/A	Little Bright Eyes (1st, sm4to, unpag, ipcb)	Juvenile Pub.	1890	Various	40-60	

AUTHOR	TITLE	PUBLISHER	DATE	ARTIST	PRICE	LC
Spielmann, M.H.	Littledom Castle (1st, sm8vo, 377p, gilt, col & b/w, teg)	L: Routledge	1903	Various	400-550	
N/A	Lovely Woman (1st, 4to, p-o, 9cp)	Bobbs-Merrill	(1910)	Various	100-150	
N/A	Merry Children's Nursery Rhymes (1st, 4to, ipcb, t-i frn)	L: Nister	[1890]	Various	75-100	
Waylett, Richard	Mixed Pickles (1st, 12mo, ibds, 48p, p-o, 10cp)	L: Gale	[1916]	Various	30-50	
Munkittrick, R.K.	Moon Prince & Other Nabobs (1st, sm8vo, 340p, aqua/gilt, b/w)	Harper	1893	Various	45-65	*
Loomis, C.B.	More Cheerful Americans (1st, 8vo, green cl, 284p)	Holt	1904	Various	25-40	
Brine, M.D.	Mother & Baby (1st, 4to, uncut, 48p, 14pl)	R.H. Russell	1901	Various	160-200	*
Staver, M.W.	New & True (1st, sm4to, 136p, green/gilt, 4pl, dep)	Lee & Shepard	1892	Various	180-230	*
Parker, Gilbert	Northern Lights (1st, 12mo, green/gilt, 352p, 16pl)	Harper	1909	Various	30-45	
McCook, Henry C.	Old Farm Fairies (1st, 8vo, 392p, woodcuts)	L: Hodder	1895	Various	65-90	*
Bates, Clara D.	On the Tree Top (1st, 4to, [90]p, ibds, 4cp)	D. Lothrop	(1891)	Various	80-120	
Brown, Alice	One-Footed Fairy (1st, 8vo, p-o, yellow cl, 182p, 12pl)	Houghton	1911	Various	50-80	*
LeGallienne, R.	Perseus & Andromeda (1st, 8vo, teg, gilt, p-o, uncut, 53p, 6pl)	R.H. Russell	1902	Various	80-130	R*
Hiatt, C.	Picture Posters (1st, 8vo, 367p, 151pl)	L: G. Bell	1895	Various	350-450	
Pollard, Percival	Posters in Miniature (1st, 8vo, [255]p, 250pl)	R.H. Russell	1896	Various	200-300	
N/A	Queen Mab's Fairy Realm (1st, 8vo, AEG, 310p, gilt, 27pl, pep)	L: G. Newnes	1901	Various	170-220	
Spielmann, M.H.	Rainbow Book (1st, 8vo, 289p, teg, red/gilt, 16pl)	L: Chatto	1909	Various	140-180	
Carson, Thos.	Ranching Sport/Travel (1st AM, 8vo, 319p, teg)	Scribner	(1912)	Various	65	
Davis, R.H.	Ranson's Folly (1st, 8vo, red/gilt, teg, 345p, uncut, 16pl)	Scribner	1902	Various	30-50	
Brady, C.T.	Reuben James (1st, 8vo, 158p, pict cl, b/w)	Appleton	1900	Various	20-30	*
Fyleman, R.	Round the Mulberry Bush (1st, 4to, 192p, red cl, 6cp)	Dodd	(1928)	Various	40-65	
Asquith, C. (ed.)	Sails of Gold (1st AM, 4to, 166p, ticp)	Scribner	(1927)	Various	30-45	*
Whittier, J.G.	Snowbound (lg8vo, teg, 96p)	Houghton	1906	Various	25-50	
Chisholm, L.	Staircase of Stories (1st, sm4to, 527p, p-o, 31cp)	L: Jack	(1919)	Various	75-120	*
Tileston, M.W.	Sugar & Spice/All that's Nice (1st, 12mo, red/gilt, 239p, b/w)	Little/Brown	(1910)	Various	30-45	*
Layard, George S.	Suppressed Plates... (1st, 8vo, 254p, gilt, b/w)	L: A&C Black	1907	Various	130-165	
Molesworth, M.	Tales Told in the Twilight (1st, 8vo, 152p, color)	Nister/Dutton	[1911]	Various	65-80	*
Johnston, M.	To Have & to Hold (1st, 8vo, green cl, 403p, 8pl)	Houghton	1900	Various	30-50	
Harris, J.C.	Told by Uncle Remus (1st, 12mo, gilt, p-o, teg, 295p, uncut)	McClure	1905	Various	160-220	
Willcox, L.C.	Torch: Book of Poems for Boys (1st, sm4to, 514p, gilt, 7cp)	Harper	1924	Various	50-75	
Asquith, C. (ed.)	Treasure Cave (1st, 4to, 144p, 5 ticp)	Scribner	(1928)	Various	30-45	
Asquith, C. (ed.)	Treasure Ship (1st, 4to, 198p, 4 ticp)	Scribner	(1926)	Various	30-45	
Lang, A.	True Story Book (1st, 8vo, blue/gilt, 337p, AEG, 9pl, cep)	L: Longmans	1893	Various	150-220	
Dodge, M.M.	When Life is Young (1st, 12mo, teg, 255p)	Century	1894	Various	30-45	
N/A	Yours Truly (ob folio, ibds, b/w)	(NY)	1907	Various	80-130	
Wilde, O.	Ballad of Redding Gaol (1st, 4to, bds, 124p, 16pl)	Dutton	1928	Vassos, J.	70-100	
Vassos, R.	Contempo (1st, lg4to, [50]p, woodcuts)	Dutton	1929	Vassos, J.	100-140	
Gray, T.	Elegy in a Country Church Yard (1st, 4to, 75p, ibds, 18pl)	Dutton	(1931)	Vassos, J.	65-80	
Wilde, O.	Harlot's House (1st, sm4to, ibds, 105p, 16pl, DJ)	Dutton	1929	Vassos, J.	100-140	
Vassos, R.	Humanities (1st, lg4to, 140p, 24 fp b/w)	Dutton	1935	Vassos, J.	85-120	
Coleridge, S.T.	Kubla Kahn (1st {std}, 4to, unpag, gilt, 13 fp brown illus)	Dutton	1933	Vassos, J.	100-140	
Wilde, O.	Salome... (1st, 8vo, bds, 57p, 13pl)	Dutton	(1927)	Vassos, J.	100-140	
Vassos, R.	Ultimo (1st, lg8vo, [52]p, ibds, 22pl)	Dutton	1930	Vassos, J.	90-130	
Bergengren, R.W.	Susan & the Butterbees (1st {std}, sm8vo, 175p, b/w, pep)	Longmans	1947	Vaughan, A.	25-40	*
Mother Goose	Mother Goose (1st, 12mo, [52]p, 2-color)	Whitman	1950	Vaughn, E.F.	30-50	*
Riley, J.W.	Book of Joyous Children (1st, 8vo, teg, 176p, uncut)	Scribner	1902	Vawter, J.W.	30-50	
Riley, J.W.	Boys of the Old Glee Club (1st, tall 8vo, unpag, 13pl)	Bobbs-Merrill	(1907)	Vawter, J.W.	50-80	R
Riley, J.W.	Defective Santa Claus (1st, 12mo, green/gilt, 77p, b/w)	Bobbs-Merrill	(1904)	Vawter, J.W.	50-80	R
Burdette, R.J.	Smiles Yoked with Sighs (1st, 8vo, 180p, green/gilt)	Bowen-Merrill	(1901)	Vawter, J.W.	20-30	
Riley, J.W.	Riley Fairy Tales (1st, sm4to, [33]p, p-o, color)	Bobbs-Merrill	(1923)	Vawter, W.	50-75	*
Nesbit, W.D.	Trail to Boyland (1st, 8vo, tan/gilt, uncut, 163p, 5pl)	Bobbs-Merrill	(1904)	Vawter, W.	30-45	*
Omar Khayyam	Rubaiyat... (folio, brown/gilt, unpag, 56pl)	Houghton	1884	Vedder, E.	300-450	
Stowe, H.B.	Uncle Tom's Cabin (1st, 8vo, 508p, 8cp)	L: A&C Black	1904	Vedder, S.H.	70-100	*
VerBeck, F.	Acrobatic Animals (1st, lg ob4to, ibds, [58]p, b/w)	R.H. Russell	1899	VerBeck, F.	160-200	
Macvane, E.	Adventures of Joujou (1st, sq8vo, 302p, teg, p-o, 15cp, pep)	Lippincott	1906	VerBeck, F.	50-65	
Paine, A.B.	Arkansas Bear (1st, 8vo, 118p, b/w)	R.H. Russell	1898	VerBeck, F.	230-400	*
Hay, Helen	Beasts & Birds (1st, lg4to, ibds, 15 fp illus)	R.H. Russell	1900	VerBeck, F.	200-300	
VerBeck, F.	Book of Bears (1st, lg4to, ibds, [85]p, color)	Lippincott	1906	VerBeck, F.	180-240	
Heaton, J.L.	Book of Lies (1st, 12mo, black/silver, 175p, b/w)	NY: Morse	1896	VerBeck, F.	70-100	*
MacManus, Seumas	Donegal Fairy Stories (1st, sm8vo, 256p, 34pl)	McClure	1900	VerBeck, F.	45-60	*
Willard, C.D.	Fall of Ulysses (1st, 8vo, grey pcb, gilt, unpag, 4cp, dep)	Doran	1912	VerBeck, F.	60-85	*
VerBeck, F.	Hand-Book of Golf for Bears (1st, lg8vo, ipcb, [59]p, 1-color)	R.H. Russell	1900	VerBeck, F.	350-500	*
Bannerman, H.	Little Black Sambo & Baby Elephant (24mo, 62p, 30 col, pep)	Platt/Munk	1925	VerBeck, F.	50-75	
Bannerman, H.	Little Black Sambo Story Book (1st, sm4to, 63p, col frn)	Altemus	(1930)	VerBeck, F.	130-180	R*
Bannerman, H.	Little Black Sambo Story Book (4to, 63p, ipcb, color)	Platt/Munk	(1935)	VerBeck, F.	120-165	
Baum, L.F.	Magical Monarch of Mo (1st [1], lg8vo, [237]p, p-o, 12cp)	Bobbs-Merrill	(1903)	VerBeck, F.	500-750	
Baum, L.F.	New Wonderland (1st [1], 4to, [189]p, cloth, 16cp, pep)	R.H. Russell	1900	VerBeck, F.	3000	
Rion, H.	Smiling Road (1st, 8vo, green cl, 191p, 10pl)	E.J. Clode	(1910)	VerBeck, F.	25-40	*
VerBeck, F.	The Dumpies (1st, ob4to, 119p)	R.H. Russell	1897	VerBeck, F.	100-150	
VerBeck, F.	Three Bears (1st, sm folio, [60]p)	R.H. Russell	(1899)	VerBeck, F.	300-500	*
VerBeck, F.	VerBeck's Bears in Mother Goose-Land (4to, gilt, bds, 3cp)	L: H. Milford	[1900]	VerBeck, F.	200-300	
Velvin, E.	Rataplan.... (1st, sm8vo, red/gilt, 328p, p-o, 12cp)	Altemus	(1902)	Verbeek, G.	50-85	*

AUTHOR	TITLE	PUBLISHER	DATE	ARTIST	PRICE	LC
Spyri, J.	Heidi (1st, lg4to, 284p, ibds, col frn)	Whitman	(1934)	Vernon, E.	30-45	*
Vickers, V.C.	Google Book (1st, lg4to, p-o, 24cp)	L: Medici	(1931)	Vickers, V.C.	130-180	
Faure, G.	Gardens of Rome (lg4to, p-o, 100p, cp)	Brentano's	1920	Vignal, P.	70-100	
Mills, E.A.	Animal Trainer (1st, ob8vo, 31p, p-o, 6cp)	Duffield	1910	Vimar, A.	60-85	
Guizow, P.	Animals in the Ark (1st, ob8vo, p-o, 31p, 7cp)	Duffield	(1909)	Vimar, A.	65-90	
Von Gottschalck, O.	Innocent Industries (1st, lg4to, ibds, [50]p, b/w)	R.H. Russell	1903	Von Gottschalck	145-200	*
Gail, Otto W.	By Rocket to the Moon (1st AM, 8vo, black cl, 303p, te red, 8pl)	Sears	(1931)	Von Grunberg, R.	60-85	
Carroll, L.	Alice/Wonderland (1st, 8vo, 48p, color)	Barse/Hopkins	[1910]	Von Hofsten, H.	45-80	*
Sewell, Anna	Black Beauty (1st, sm8vo, 45p, 6cp, pep)	Brewer/Barse	(1907)	Von Hofsten, H.	25-40	*
Montgomery, F.T.	Cats & Kitts (1st, 8vo, 63p, p-o, 6cp)	Brewer/Barse	(1908)	Von Hofsten, H.	60-80	*
Stevenson, R.L.	Child's Garden of Verses (12mo, ibds, 92p)	Barse	(1910)	Von Hofsten, H.	35-50	
Dickens, C.	Christmas Carol (1st, sm8vo, 48p, 6cp, pep)	Brewer/Barse	(1907)	Von Hofsten, H.	25-40	*
Montgomery, F.T.	Horses & Colts (1st, 8vo, red cl, p-o)	Barse	(1911)	Von Hofsten, H.	30-45	*
Mother Goose	Mother Goose Jungle Book (1st, 4to, 63p, color)	Madison Co.	1903	Von Hofsten, H.	60-100	*
Stowe, H.B.	Uncle Tom's Cabin (brown cl, p-o, 12mo, 46p, 6 color)	Barse	[1915]	Von Hofsten, H.	50-70	*
Hubbard, R.	Queer Person (1st {std}, 8vo, 336p, doub. plates, pep, NH)	Doubleday/Dor.	1930	Von Schmidt, H.	50-85	*
Carr, Mary J.	Peggy & Paul & Laddy (1st, sm8vo, 207p, brown cl, b/w, pep)	Crowell	(1936)	Voute, Kathleen	20-25	*
Hay, Timothy	Horses (1st {std}, sm ob4to, [32]p, ipcb, fp b/w)	Harper	(1944)	Wag	70-110	*
Hamill, K.F.	Rhymes for Wee Sweethearts (1st, lg8vo, 181p, p-o, 5cp)	Jacobs	(1906)	Wager-Smith	40-70	
McNeil, E.	Dickon Bend-The-Bow (1st, sm4to, 126p, color, pep)	Saalfield	1903	Wagner, Rob.	65-80	*
Hunt, B.S.	Stories of Little Brown Koko (1st, 4to, bds, 96p)	Am. Colortype	1940	Wagstaff, D.	65-100	
Wahn, J.& G.	Edgar, Runaway Elephant (1st, 4to, ipcb, [38]p, color)	W.R. Scott	(1941)	Wahn, J.& G.	65-80	*
Hurrell, M.I.	Adventures of Friskers & His Friends (1st, 12mo, 159p, 16cp)	L: R. Culley	[1907]	Wain, L.	100-160	*
Wain, L.	Big Dogs, Little Dogs, Cats & Kittens (1st, folio, color, gilt)	L/NY: R. Tuck	[1900]	Wain, L.	250-400	*
Pope, J.	Cat Scouts (1st, sm4to, ibds, [48]p, p-o, 6cp)	L: Blackie	[1912]	Wain, L.	350-500	
Byron, May	Cat's Cradle (1st, sm4to, ibds, [48]p, color)	L: Blackie	[1908]	Wain, L.	350-500	
Woodhouse, S.C.	Cats at School (1st, 4to, french fold, 21cp)	L: Routledge	[1911]	Wain, L.	375-550	*
Grimalkin	Cats! Cats! Cats! (4to, blue cl, 47p, color)	L: Sands	[1901]	Wain, L.	350-500	
Wain, L.	Daddy Cat (1st AM, sm4to, 36p, ibds, color)	Dodge	[1915]	Wain, L.	250-400	*
Bingham, C.	Dandy Lion (4to, ibds, t-i col frn, b/w)	L: Nister	[1900]	Wain, L.	100-140	
Bingham, C.	Funny Favorites (1st, sm4to, [44]p, ibds, tip-in col frn)	L: Nister	[1907]	Wain, L.	200-300	
Wain, L.	Funny Frolics (sm4to, [32]p, ibds, color frn)	L: Nister	[1900]	Wain, L.	140-175	
N/A	In Cat & Dog Land (lg4to, 36p, ibds, 12pl)	L: R. Tuck	[1900]	Wain, L.	200-275	
Braine/Floyd	In Nurseryland (1st, 4to, ibds, [48]p, color)	L: R. Tuck	[1900]	Wain, L.	450-600	
Bingham, C.	Jingles, Jokes & Funny Folks (sm4to, wraps, b/w)	McLoughlin	[1910]	Wain, L.	75-120	*
Bingham, C.	Kittenland (sm folio, ipcb, 8cp)	L: Collins	(1903)	Wain, L.	300-400	
Watson, E.	Lament of Billy Villy (lg sq8vo, wraps, 8cp)	L: R. Tuck	[1890]	Wain, L.	200-300	
Crommelin, May	Little Soldiers (1st, 4to, 94p, 39 color)	L: Hutchinson	[1916]	Wain, L.	300-500	*
Wain, L.	Louis Wain's Baby Picture Book (1st, 4to, ibds, unpag, b/w)	L: Clarke	1903	Wain, L.	200-300	
Wain, L.	Louis Wain's Cats & Dogs (1st, lg4to, ibds)	L: R. Tuck	(1903)	Wain, L.	500-600	*
Wain, L.	Louis Wain's Children's Book (1st, 4to, ibds, 17pl)	L: Hutchinson	(1923)	Wain, L.	300-500	
Wain, L.	Louis Wain's Father Christmas (8vo, ibds, p-o, 5 ticp)	L: J.F. Shaw	(1912)	Wain, L.	350-500	
N/A	Merry Times (sm folio, 14p, wraps, 12 fp color)	L: R. Tuck	[1900]	Wain, L.	150-200	*
Drummond, Henry	Monkey that Would Not Kill (1st, 8vo, 115p, gilt, 16 fp b/w)	L: Hodder	1898	Wain, L.	180-250	*
Drummond, Henry	Monkey that Would Not Kill (1st AM, 12mo, 115p, cloth, 16pl)	Dodd	1898	Wain, L.	180-250	*
Owen, M.A.	Old Rabbit the Voodoo (1st, 8vo, blue cl)	L: T.F. Unwin	1893	Wain, L.	60-85	
Father Tuck	Pa Cats, Ma Cats... (1st, lg4to, [36]p, gilt, 12cp)	L: R. Tuck	[1901]	Wain, L.	300-400	
Morley, Charles	Peter, a Cat O' One Tail (1st AM, 8vo, 110p, ibds, b/w)	Putnam	1892	Wain, L.	200-300	
Bingham, C.	Ping Pong (ob narrow 4to, wraps, 6cp)	L: R. Tuck	[1903]	Wain, L.	350-500	
Wain, L.	Pussies & Puppies (1st, 4to, ibds, 96p, color & b/w)	L: Partridge	[1899]	Wain, L.	280-400	
Wain, L.	Somebody's Pussies (4to, ibds, 13cp)	L: R. Tuck	[1920]	Wain, L.	800-1000	
Duppa, C.M.	Stories of a Lowly Life (1st, lg8vo, 95p, uncut, red/gilt)	L: MacMillan	1898	Wain, L.	100-140	
Bingham, C.	To Nursery Land (4to, 56p, 16 color, green cl)	L: R. Tuck	[1900]	Wain, L.	250-350	
Woodhouse, S.C.	Two Cats at Large (1st, 4to, ibds, 24 fp color)	L: Routledge	[1910]	Wain, L.	500-700	*
Johnson, Burgess	Bashful Ballads (1st, 8vo, teg, 145p, b/w)	Harper	1911	Walker, A.B.	20-35	
Macleod, Mary	Book of King Arthur (1st AM, 8vo, 417p, pl)	Stokes	[1900]	Walker, A.G.	65-90	*
Macleod, Mary	King Arthur & Noble Knights (1st, 8vo, 418p, gilt, 35 fp b/w)	L: Wells/Gard.	(1900)	Walker, A.G.	100-140	
MacDonald, Geo.	Lost Princess (1st, 8vo, 258p, blue/gilt, 6pl)	L: Wells/Gard.	(1895)	Walker, A.G.	125-160	
Macleod, Mary	Red Cross Knight & Sir Guyan (1st, 8vo, 128p)	L: Wells/Gard.	1908	Walker, A.G.	35-50	*
Colum, P.	Boy Apprenticed to an Enchanter (1st, sm8vo, 168p, b/w)	MacMillan	1920	Walker, D.S.	30-50	
Colum, P.	Boy Who Knew what the Birds Said (1st, 12mo, 178p, b/w)	MacMillan	1918	Walker, D.S.	30-45	
Colum, P.	Children Who Followed/Piper (1st, sm8vo, 152p, col frn)	MacMillan	1922	Walker, D.S.	45-60	
Ingraham, C.	Cottontail & Wishing-Fairy (1st, lg8vo, pcb, 39p, p-o, 2cp, pep)	Brentano's	(1921)	Walker, D.S.	80-120	*
Walker, D.S.	Dream Boats (1st, lg8vo, 219p, 4cp, 16pl, pep, DJ)	Doubleday/Page	1918	Walker, D.S.	120-165	
Ingraham, C.	Elephant & Wishing Fairy (1st, lg8vo, bds, unpag, p-o, 2cp, pep)	Brentano's	(1921)	Walker, D.S.	80-120	
Andersen, H.C.	Fairy Tales (1st, sm4to, p-o, gilt, 267p, 12cp)	Doubleday/Page	1914	Walker, D.S.	140-170	
Andersen, H.C.	Fairy Tales (1st UK, lg8vo, 268p, p-o, 12cp, pep)	L: Harrap	(1914)	Walker, D.S.	170-220	
Stewart, Anna B.	Gentlest Giant (1st {1st bk.}, 4to, 142p, blue bds, color)	NY: Wayne	1915	Walker, D.S.	100-120	
Stewart, Anna B.	Gentlest Giant (1st {this pub.}, 8vo, blue cl, 148p, uncut, dep)	McBride	1929	Walker, D.S.	30-50	*
Colum, P.	Girl Who Sat by the Ashes (1st, 8vo, 175p, col frn)	MacMillan	1919	Walker, D.S.	30-45	
Olcott, F.J.	Go! Champions of Light (1st, 8vo, 226p, b/w, pep, DJ)	Revell	(1933)	Walker, D.S.	40-60	
Hutchinson, W.M.L.	Golden Porch (1st, 8vo, 302p, purple cl, pep, col frn, fp b/w)	NY: Longmans	1925	Walker, D.S.	50-70	

AUTHOR	TITLE	PUBLISHER	DATE	ARTIST	PRICE	LC
Ingelow, J.	Mopsa the Fairy (1st, 8vo, 259p, blue cl, col frn, pep)	MacMillan	1927	Walker, D.S.	80-120	
Hutchinson, W.M.L.	Orpheus with his Lute (1st, 8vo, 300p, col frn, b/w, pep)	NY: Longmans	1926	Walker, D.S.	50-75	*
Ingraham, C.	Peacock & Wishing-Fairy (1st, lg8vo, p-o, pcb, [42]p, 2cp, pep)	Brentano's	(1921)	Walker, D.S.	85-140	*
Teasdale, S.	Rainbow Gold (1st, 8vo, 267p, blue/gilt, col frn, b/w, pep)	MacMillan	1922	Walker, D.S.	45-60	
Walker, D.S.	Sally's ABC (1st, 4to, [58]p, buckram, 2-color, pep, DJ)	Harcourt	1929	Walker, D.S.	120-160	
Colum, P.	Six Who were Left in a Shoe (1st, sq8vo, ibds, unpag, col, pep)	Volland	(1923)	Walker, D.S.	50-65	
Garrott, H.	Snythergen (1st, 8vo, blue/gilt, 157p, 4cp, 16pl, pep)	McBride	1923	Walker, D.S.	50-80	
Garrott, H.	Squiffer (1st {std}, 8vo, 226p, green/gilt, uncut, 4cp, pep)	McBride	1924	Walker, D.S.	70-90	
MacKay, H.	Stories for Pictures (1st, 8vo, ibds, uncut, teg, 168p, 8cp pep)	Duffield	1912	Walker, D.S.	70-100	
Andersen, H.C.	Thumbelisa... (1st, lg8vo, [80]p, p-o, 3cp)	Doubleday/Page	1923	Walker, D.S.	65-80	*
Ingraham, C.	Wishing Fairy's Animal Friends (1st, lg8vo, 141p, p-o, 8cp, pep)	Brentano's	(1921)	Walker, D.S.	100-160	
Ingraham, C.	Zebra & the Wishing Fairy (1st, lg8vo, [45]p, color, pep)	Brentano's	(1921)	Walker, D.S.	85-140	*
Carroll, L.	Alice/Wonderland (1st, 8vo, blue/gilt, AEG, p-o, 152p, 8cp)	L: J. Lane	(1907)	Walker, W.H.	180-220	
Carroll, L.	Alice/Wonderland (sm8vo, uncut, 152p, 8cp)	L/NY: J. Lane	[1911]	Walker, W.H.	75-100	*
Young, C.	Night-Caps for the Babies (1st, 8vo, 126p, 8cp)	L: J. Lane	(1907)	Walker, W.H.	60-85	
Uncle Milton	Bennie & Jennie (obsm4to, ibds, cp)	Cupples	1907	Wall, B.	65-80	
Parry, David M.	Scarlet Empire (1st, 8vo, red/gilt, 400p, 10pl)	Bobbs-Merrill	(1906)	Wall, H.C.	65-90	
Johnston, H.	Pioneers in Canada (1st, 8vo, 328p, gilt, 8cp)	L: Blackie	1912	Wall-Cousins, E.	30-50	
Bowman, J.C.	Mystery Mountain (1st, 8vo, 293p, blue cl, 4cp, 10pl, pep)	Whitman	1940	Wallower, L.	30-45	*
Andersen, H.C.	Fairy Tales (1st AM, sm4to, blue/gilt, teg, 431p, uncut, 24cp)	Stokes	[1911]	Walton, C.	140-220	R*
Andersen, H.C.	Fairy Tales (1st, 4to, black/gilt, teg, 431p, 24cp, pep)	L: Jack	1911	Walton, C.	200-300	
Cooper, J.F.	The Pathfinder (1st, 8vo, blue cl, p-o, 430p, 6cp, pep)	Minton Balch	1928	Ward, E.F.	35-50	
Lear, E.	Duck & the Kangaroo (1st, 12mo, [56]p, pep, color)	Western Prntg.	(1932)	Ward, Keith	45-60	*
Gaggin, E.R.	Jolly Animals (1st, sq4to, p-o, 110p, 7 fp color, pep)	Rand/McNally	(1930)	Ward, Keith	80-120	*
Bannerman, H.	Little Black Sambo (1st, folio, [16]p)	Whitman	(1935)	Ward, Keith	70-100	*
Barrows, M.	Muggins Mouse (1st, folio, ibds, 60p, color)	Reilly/Lee	1932	Ward, Keith	50-90	*
Moore, C.C.	Night Before Christmas (4to, [16]p, wraps, color)	Whitman	(1935)	Ward, Keith	35-50	*
Lear, E.	Owl & the Pussycat (1st, ob8vo, [56]p, color, pep)	Whitman	(1932)	Ward, Keith	30-45	*
Judson, C.I.	People Who Work Near our House (1st, sm8vo, 48p, color)	Rand/McNally	(1942)	Ward, Keith	35-50	*
Judson, C.I.	People Who Work in Country & City (1st, sm4to, 94p, color)	Rand/McNally	(1943)	Ward, Keith	35-50	*
Turner, N.B.	Ray Coon to the Rescue (1st, 8vo, 80p, ipcb, b/w, pep)	Rand/McNally	(1931)	Ward, Keith	45-70	*
N/A	Story of Little Red Hen (1st, folio, red ipcb, [16]p, b/w)	Whitman	(1935)	Ward, Keith	85-120	*
Meyer, Edith P.	Tim Chick (1st, sm sq4to, 42p, p-o, color)	Rand/McNally	1932	Ward, Keith	35-50	*
North, S.	Zipper ABC Book (1st, 12mo, ipcb, [59]p, 2-color)	Rand/McNally	(1937)	Ward, Keith	50-70	*
Holbrook, S.	America's Ethan Allen (1st, lg8vo, 95p, color, DJ, CH)	Houghton	1949	Ward, L.	55-80	
Forbes, Esther	America's Paul Revere (1st, 4to, 46p, color, red cl, DJ)	Houghton	1946	Ward, L.	45-60	
Scribner, Grace	American Pilgrimage (1st, 12mo, 89p, 4 woodcuts)	Vanguard Pr.	(1927)	Ward, L.	45-60	*
Rowe, Dorothy	Begging Dear (1st, sm8vo, 109p, tan cl, 8cp, pep)	MacMillan	1928	Ward, L.	30-50	*
Ward, Lynd	Biggest Bear (1st, 4to, 84p, beige cl, b/w, CM)	Houghton	1952	Ward, L.	70-115	*
Halle, L.J.	Birds Against Men (1st, 8vo, 228p, b/w)	Viking	1938	Ward, L.	35-50	*
Peattie, D.C.	Book of Hours (1st, 8vo, 246p, 202p, b/w, cvr by...)	Putnam	1937	Ward, L.	35-50	*
Knight, R.A.	Brave Companions (1st {std}, 8vo, blue cl, 215p, col frn)	Doubleday	1945	Ward, L.	30-45	*
Robinson, M.L.	Bright Island (1st, 8vo, 268p, silver cl, b/w, pep, DJ, NH)	Random	(1937)	Ward, L.	50-70	
Coatsworth, E.	Cat Who Went to Heaven (1st, lg8vo, red cl, 57p, b/w, NM)	MacMillan	1930	Ward, L.	65-80	R
Marryat, Fred.	Children of the New Forest (1st, 8vo, 322p, green cl, 10 fp b/w)	MacMillan	1930	Ward, L.	35-50	
Howard, A.W.	Ching-Li & the Dragons (1st, 4to, blue/silver, 55p, 10pl)	MacMillan	1931	Ward, L.	45-65	
Dawson, Carley	Dragon Run (1st, 8vo, 282p)	Houghton	1955	Ward, L.	30-45	*
Goethe	Faust (1st, 8vo, 262p, 6pl, DJ)	Cape/Smith	(1930)	Ward, L.	80-100	
Brinig, M.	Flutter of an Eyelid (1st, 12mo, 310p)	Farrar/Rine.	1933	Ward, L.	30-45	*
Sauer, J.L.	Fog Magic (1st, 8vo, grey cl, 107p, pep, NH)	Viking	1943	Ward, L.	60-100	R*
Shelley, M.W.	Frankenstein... (1st, 8vo, 259p, 15 b/w)	Smith/Haas	1934	Ward, L.	120-165	
Henry, M.	Gaudenzia (1st {A}, sm4to, 237p, red/gilt, 7 fp color, pep)	Rand/McNally	(1960)	Ward, L.	30-50	*
Ward, Lynd	God's Man (1st, 8vo, woodcuts, pep, 293p, cep)	Cape/Smith	(1929)	Ward, L.	100-140	
McNeer, May	Golden Flash (1st, 8vo, 227p, pep, color)	Viking	1947	Ward, L.	30-45	
Faulkner, Wm.	Green Bough (1st, 8vo, green cl, 67p, title page by...)	Smith/Haas	1933	Ward, L.	150-250	*
Laing, A.K.	Haunted Omnibus (1st, 8vo, 848p, fp b/w)	Farrar/Rine.	(1937)	Ward, L.	40-65	*
Waugh, A.	Hot Countries (1st, 8vo, 304p, gilt, b/w)	Farrar/Rine.	(1930)	Ward, L.	45-60	
Swift, H.H.	House by the Sea (1st, 8vo, 245p, blue cl, 8pl, pep, DJ)	Harcourt	(1938)	Ward, L.	35-50	
Powys, L.	Impassioned Clay (1st {std}, 8vo, bds, 120p, tp-in frn, DJ)	Longmans	1931	Ward, L.	100-130	
Ward, H.F.	In Place of Profit (1st, 8vo, green cl, 460p, gilt, woodcuts)	Scribner	1933	Ward, L.	35-50	
McNeer, May	John Wesley (1st, lg8vo, 96p, color, DJ)	Abingdon	(1951)	Ward, L.	25-40	
Forbes, Esther	Johnny Tremain (1st, 8vo, 256p, cloth, col frn, pep, DJ, NM)	Houghton	1943	Ward, L.	70-100	R
Peattie, D.C.	Journey into America (1st, 8vo, 276p, color, pep)	Houghton	1943	Ward, L.	25-40	*
Genevoix, M.	Last Hunt (1st {std}, 8vo, p-o, 281p, 10 fp brown illus, pep)	Random	(1940)	Ward, L.	30-50	
Swift, H.H.	Little Blacknose (1st, 8vo, 149p, color, pep, DJ, NH)	Harcourt	1929	Ward, L.	40-65	
Rideout, H.	Lola the Bear (1st, 8vo, 159p, gilt, col frn, 3pl, DJ)	Duffield	1928	Ward, L.	40-60	
Ward, Lynd	Mad-Man's Drum (1st, 8vo, ipcb, [257]p, woodcuts, cep)	Cape/Smith	(1930)	Ward, L.	120-160	
Cowen, Wm. J.	Man with Four Lives (1st, sm8vo, 277p, b/w pl)	Farrar/Rine.	(1934)	Ward, L.	30-45	*
Jones, J.O. (ed.)	Many Mansions... (1st, lg8vo, 134p, color, DJ)	Viking	1947	Ward, L.	30-45	
McNeer, May	Martin Luther (1st, lg8vo, 95p, rust cl, pep, color, DJ)	Abingdon	(1953)	Ward, L.	45-65	R
Wilhelmson, C.	Midsummer Night (1st, 8vo, uncut, 305p, 10pl)	Farrar/Rine.	1930	Ward, L.	70-90	
Waugh, A.	Most Women (1st, 8vo, gilt, 323p, woodcuts)	Farrar/Rine.	(1931)	Ward, L.	30-50	*

AUTHOR	TITLE	PUBLISHER	DATE	ARTIST	PRICE	LC
Dawson, Carley	Mr. Wicker's Window (1st, 8vo, 272p)	Houghton	1952	Ward, L.	25-40	*
Swift, H.H.	North Star Shining (1st, 4to, 44p, 8 fp color)	Wm. Morrow	(1947)	Ward, L.	70-90	*
Hicks, G.	One of Us (1st, 8vo, [64]p, 30 b/w illus, DJ)	Equinox	(1935)	Ward, L.	50-70	
Emblen, Don L.	Palomino Boy (1st, 8vo, blue cl, 189p, pep, decor by...)	Viking	1948	Ward, L.	25-40	*
Howard, F.M.	Porpoise of Pirate Bay (1st, 8vo, 152p, 8 fp b/w, pep)	Random	(1938)	Ward, L.	30-45	
McNeer, May	Prince Bantam (1st, sm4to, 229p, aqua cl, col frn, 15 fp b/w)	MacMillan	1929	Ward, L.	35-50	
Robinson, M.L.	Runner of the Mountain Tops (1st {std}, 8vo, blue/gilt, DJ, NH)	Random	(1939)	Ward, L.	50-85	
Clark, A.N.	Santiago (1st, 8vo, 189p, color, pep, DJ)	Viking	1955	Ward, L.	25-40	
Madariaga, S.	Sir Bob (1st {std}, 8vo, 202p, b/w)	Harcourt	(1930)	Ward, L.	30-45	*
Saint-Exupery, A.	Southern Mail (1st AM, sm8vo, 253p, 1-color lithos by...)	Smith/Haas	1933	Ward, L.	65-85	*
Hewes, A.D.	Spice & Devil's Cave (1st, sm8vo, 331p, gilt, pep, DJ, NH)	Knopf	1930	Ward, L.	60-80	
McNeer, May	Stop Tim! (1st, ob8vo, ibds, [39]p, 2-color, pep)	Farrar/Rine.	1930	Ward, L.	45-60	
Robinson, M.L.	Strong Wings (1st {std}, 8vo, 249p, blue cl, b/w)	Random	(1951)	Ward, L.	25-40	*
Wyss, J.D.	Swiss Family Robinson (1st, 8vo, 388p, 9cp)	Grosset/Dunlap	(1949)	Ward, L.	40-65	*
Medary, Marj.	Topgallant: A Herring Gull (1st {std}, 8vo, 159p, p-o, pep, b/w)	Smith/Haas	(1935)	Ward, L.	30-50	*
Rowe, Dorothy	Traveling Shops (1st, sm8vo, yellow cl, 109p, col frn, pep)	MacMillan	1929	Ward, L.	25-45	*
Ward, Lynd	Vertigo (1st, 8vo, 231p, woodcuts)	Random	1937	Ward, L.	85-120	
McNeer, May	Waif Maid (1st, 8vo, p-o, 212p, col frn, woodcuts, cep)	MacMillan	1930	Ward, L.	35-50	
Colum, P.	White Sparrow (1st, sq8vo, 46p, grey cl, pep, DJ)	MacMillan	1933	Ward, L.	45-60	
Ward, Lynd	Wild Pilgrimage (1st, lg8vo, [95]p, p-o, woodcuts)	Smith/Haas	1932	Ward, L.	130-160	
Baruch, D.W.	I Like Animals (1st {std}, 16mo, ipcb, 48p, b/w, dep)	Harper	1933	Waterall, C.P.	20-35	*
Nesbit, E.	Cat Tales (1st, 12mo, 62p, grey cl, cp)	Nister/Dutton	[1904]	Watkin, I.	120-160	*
Seeger, E.	Pageant of Chinese History (1st {std}, 8vo, 386p, b/w, pep, NH)	Longmans	1934	Watkins, B.	45-60	*
Carmichael, Phil	Man from the Moon (1st, 8vo, 296p, blue cl, 8cp)	L: Richards	1909	Watkins, F.	90-135	*
Swift, J.	Gulliver's Travels (1st, smvo, 306p, color)	Grosset/Dunlap	(1947)	Watson, A.	35-50	*
Watson, N.D.	Fairy Tale Picture Book (1st {std}, lg4to, 91p, color)	Garden City	1957	Watson, A.A.	50-80	*
Muehl, L.B.	My Name Is... (1st, sm8vo, tan cl, [55]p, 2-color)	Holiday House	(1959)	Watson, A.A.	20-35	*
DeJong, Meindert	Wheels Over the Bridge (1st {std}, 8vo, 219p, pep, 10pl)	Harper	(1941)	Watson, A.A.	25-40	*
Fyleman, R.	Adventure Club (1st, 8vo, 80p, blue/gilt, 10 b/w)	L: Methuen	1925	Watson, A.H.	35-50	*
Fyleman, R.	Adventure Club (1st AM, 8vo, p-o, 138p, col frn, b/w)	Doran	(1926)	Watson, A.H.	25-40	*
Strang, H.	Big Book of Fairy Stories (1st, 8vo, 191p, ibds, 4cp, pep)	L: H. Milford	(1929)	Watson, A.H.	70-100	
Milne, A.A.	Gallery of Children (1st AM {this fmt}, 12mo, 125p, b/w, DJ)	McKay	[1939]	Watson, A.H.	65-100	
De La Mare, W.	Told Again (1st, 8vo, 320p, blue/gilt, 8cp)	L: Blackwell	1927	Watson, A.H.	60-80	
De La Mare, W.	Told Again (1st AM, 8vo, 248p, color)	Knopf	1927	Watson, A.H.	35-65	*
Paine, A.B.	Tent Dwellers (1st, 8vo, uncut, 272p, b/w)	Outing	1908	Watson, H.	30-45	
Weatherly, F.E.	Out of Town (1st, 8vo, 64p, ibds, 12 chromos)	Dutton	(1884)	Watt, L.	70-130	
Weston, J.L.	Sir Gleges/Sir Libeaus Desconus (1st AM, 12mo, 77p)	New Amsterdam	1902	Watts, C.	40-60	
Waugh, D.	Among the Leaves & Grasses (1st sm4to, orang cl, 93p, color)	Holt	1931	Waugh, D.	65-100	
Waugh, F.	Clan of Munes (1st, ob4to, blue cl, 58p, 8 fp color)	Scribner	1916	Waugh, F.	250-400	R
Waugh, Ida	Ideal Heads (1st, folio, brown/gilt, [51]p, AEG, 20 chromos)	Sunshine Co.	1890	Waugh, I.	150-230	*
Neally, A.	Baby Days... (1st, 4to, bds)	Dutton	1890	Waugh, Ida	150-200	
Waugh, Ida	Becky Longnose... (4to, wraps, 8cp)	McLoughlin	(1882)	Waugh, Ida	50-65	
Mathews, J.	Belle's Pink Boots (1st, AEG, green/gilt, 16cp)	Dutton	1881	Waugh, Ida	100-165	
Blanchard, A.E.	Bonny Bairns (1st, 4to, 48p, ibds, 25cp)	Worthington	(1888)	Waugh, Ida	165-220	
N/A	Christmas Card (8vo, wraps, 8cp)	Dutton	1883	Waugh, Ida	60-90	
Newbery, F.E.	Everyday Honor (1st, 12mo, 429p, b/w)	Jacobs	1898	Waugh, Ida	20-35	*
Marshall, Mrs.	Girl Ranchers of San Coulee (1st, 12mo, 322p, 4pl)	Penn	1897	Waugh, Ida	30-50	
Elmslie, T.C.	His Lordship's Puppy (1st, sm8vo, 205p, 4pl)	Penn	1901	Waugh, Ida	25-40	
N/A	Holly Berries (1st, 4to, 48p, ibds)	Dutton	(1881)	Waugh, Ida	70-100	
Waugh, Ida	Ida Waugh's Alphabet Book (1st, 4to, ibds, 26 illus)	Lippincott	1888	Waugh, Ida	100-145	
Blanchard, A.E.	Janet's College Career (1st, 8vo, 365p, 5pl)	Jacobs	(1904)	Waugh, Ida	20-30	*
Waugh, Ida	Little Chicks/Baby Tricks (1st, 4to, ibds, 44p)	Dutton	1885	Waugh, Ida	100-120	
Gould, E.L.	Little Polly Prentiss (1st, sm8vo, 192p, 5pl)	Penn	1902	Waugh, Ida	25-40	
Blanchard, A.E.	Mammy's Baby (4to, [16]p, ipcb, chromos)	Worthington	(1890)	Waugh, Ida	120-165	
Blanchard, A.E.	My Own Dolly (1st, 8vo, ipcb, 64p, 15cp)	Dutton	1882	Waugh, Ida	100-150	
Waugh, Ida	Over the Hills (1st, 4to, ibds, [48]p, color)	McLoughlin	(1882)	Waugh, Ida	120-165	
Lippmann, J.M.	Sweet P's (1st, 8vo, 192p, 5pl, pep)	Penn	1902	Waugh, Ida	25-40	
Blanchard, A.E.	Tangles & Curls (1st, 4to, [16]p, ibds, 9pl)	Worthington	1888	Waugh, Ida	100-120	
Blanchard, A.E.	Tell Me a Story (1st, lg sq8vo, [15]p, ibds, 10 fp color)	Worthington	1888	Waugh, Ida	120-165	
Blanchard, A.E.	Twenty Little Maidens (1st, lg8vo, 160p, 18pl)	Lippincott	1893	Waugh, Ida	45-65	*
Marshall, C.	Two Wyoming Girls (1st, 12mo, 329p)	Penn	1899	Waugh, Ida	25-40	*
Lovell, L.	Walcott Twins (1st, 8vo, 211p, 5pl)	Penn	1900	Waugh, Ida	25-40	
Blanchard, A.E.	Wee Babies (1st, 4to, ibds, unpag, color)	Dutton	1882	Waugh, Ida	85-100	
Fleckenstein, A.	Prince of Gravas... (1st, 8vo, 270p, grey/gilt, 3pl)	Jacobs	1898	Waugh, J.	35-65	
Stevenson, R.L.	Child's Garden of Verses (1st, 4to, p-o, 140p, color, pep)	Whitman	(1917)	Weage, J.W.	50-70	*
Weaver, A.V.	Frawg (1st, ob12mo, p-o, 128p, color, pep)	Stokes	1930	Weaver, A.V.	100-165	*
Baker, C.	Court Jester (1st, 8vo, 259p, b/w pl)	Bobbs-Merrill	(1906)	Webb, M.E.	20-30	*
Converse, F.	House of Prayer (1st, 12mo, 276p, teg, uncut, 8pl)	L: Dent	1908	Webb, M.E.	25-40	
Washburne, M.F.	Old Fashioned Fairy Tales (1st, 8vo, brown/gilt, 102p, 3cp, pep)	Rand/McNally	(1909)	Webb, M.E.	65-90	*
Webber, I.E.	Anywhere in the World (1st, sm8vo, ipcb, 64p, color)	W.R. Scott	(1947)	Webber, I.E.	30-45	*
Webber, I.E.	Bits that Grow Big (1st, sm8vo, ipcb, 64p, 2-color)	W.R. Scott	(1949)	Webber, I.E.	30-50	*
Webber, I.E.	It Looks Like This (1st, 8vo, [40]p, b/w)	W.R. Scott	1949	Webber, I.E.	25-40	*

AUTHOR	TITLE	PUBLISHER	DATE	ARTIST	PRICE	LC
Webber, I.E.	Thanks to Trees (1st, sm8vo, grey cl, 60p, 3-color, pep)	W.R. Scott	(1952)	Webber, I.E.	30-45	*
Webber, I.E.	Travelers All (1st, sm8vo, [32]p, color)	W.R. Scott	1944	Webber, I.E.	30-50	*
Webber, I.E.	Up Above & Down Below (1st, sm8vo, ibds, [31]p, color)	W.R. Scott	(1943)	Webber, I.E.	30-50	*
Mukerji, D.G.	Master Monkey (1st {std}, 8vo, aqua/gilt, 261p, pep, 5pl)	Dutton	(1932)	Weber, F.	30-50	*
Webster, J.	Daddy Long Legs (1st, 12mo, blue cl, 304p, b/w, PPP)	Century	1912	Webster, J.	45-60	
Mother Goose	Mother Goose Rhymes (1st, 12mo, [62]p, color)	Rand/McNally	(1942)	Wedde, J.	35-50	*
Weeden, Mrs. H.	Bandanna Ballads (1st, 8vo, green/gilt, uncut, 90p, 24pl)	Doub./McClure	1899	Weeden, H.	70-120	
Grimm Bros.	Fairy Tales (1st, 8vo, 511p, red cl, 4cp)	L: Routledge	(1904)	Wehnert, E.H.	100-120	
Mother Goose	Mother Goose (1st, 12mo, [53]p, wraps, color)	Whitman	1944	Weihs, E.	30-50	*
N/A	Wonderful Kittens (sq4to, ibds, 5cp)	Worthington	1883	Weir, H.	130-180	
Dalgliesh, A.	Adam & the Golden Cock (1st, sm8vo, 64p, grey cl, 1-color)	Scribner	(1959)	Weisgard, L.	30-50	*
Carroll, L.	Alice... & Through... (1st, 4to, 159p, ibds, 24 fp color, pep)	Harper	(1949)	Weisgard, L.	75-120	*
Davis, L.R.	Americans Every One (1st {std}, sm8vo, 123p, color)	Doubleday/Dor.	1942	Weisgard, L.	30-45	*
MacDonald, Golden	Big Dog, Little Dog (1st, lg sq8vo, [36]p, red cl, b/w, dep)	Doubleday/Dor.	(1943)	Weisgard, L.	35-50	*
N/A	Cinderella (1st, 4to, ibds, [32]p, color, pep)	Garden City	1938	Weisgard, L.	65-80	*
Weisgard, L.	Clean Pig (1st, ob4to, [34]p, fp brown illus, pep)	Scribner	1952	Weisgard, L.	30-45	*
Brown, M.W.	Country Noisy Book (1st, 8vo, [44]p, bds, color, pep)	W.R. Scott	(1940)	Weisgard, L.	65-90	
Dalgliesh, A.	Courage of Sarah Noble (1st, 8vo, 52p, 7 fp illus, NH)	Scribner	(1954)	Weisgard, L.	45-60	*
Kramer, N. (ed.)	Cozy Hour Story Book (1st, 4to, 63p, yellow cl, color, pep)	Random	1960	Weisgard, L.	30-50	*
Brown, M.W.	Dark Wood o/t Golden Birds (1st, 8vo, ibds, unpag, 2-color, pep)	Harper	(1950)	Weisgard, L.	75-110	R*
Howard, Eliz.	Dorinda (1st, sm8vo, 303p, beige cl, fp b/w, pep)	Lothrop/Lee	(1944)	Weisgard, L.	20 5-40	
Mother Goose	Family Mother Goose (1st, 12mo)	Harper	(1951)	Weisgard, L.	65-80	*
Brown, M.W.	Golden Bunny (1st, folio, ibds, [25]p, color, pep, GGB)	Simon/Schuster	(1953)	Weisgard, L.	35-60	R*
Brown, M.W.	Golden Egg Book (1st, folio, ibds, [28]p, color, GGB)	Simon/Schuster	(1947)	Weisgard, L.	35-50	
Davis, L.R.	Grab Bag (1st {std}, sm8vo, 312p, b/w, pep)	Doubleday/Dor.	1941	Weisgard, L.	20-35	*
Brown, M.W.	Important Book (1st, 4to, [21]p, color)	Harper	1949	Weisgard, L.	70-100	*
Zolotow, C.	Indian, Indian (1st, sm8vo, ibds, unpag, color, LGB)	Simon/Schuster	(1952)	Weisgard, L.	20-35	*
Brown, M.W.	Indoor Noisy Book (1st, 8vo, ipcb, [44]p, color)	W.R. Scott	(1942)	Weisgard, L.	50-80	*
Brown, M.W.	Little Chicken (1st {std}, ob8vo, cloth, [39]p, color)	Harper	(1943)	Weisgard, L.	30-50	
Brown, M.W.	Little Frightened Tiger (1st {std}, ob4to, ibds, unpag, color)	Doubleday	1953	Weisgard, L.	50-70	
MacDonald, Golden	Little Island (1st {std}, ob4to, [42]p, ibds, color, pep, CM)	Doubleday	1946	Weisgard, L.	100-150	R*
MacDonald, Golden	Little Lost Lamb (1st {std}, 4to, 48p, ibds, color, pep, CH)	Doubleday	1945	Weisgard, L.	70-120	
Cavanah, F.	Louis of New Orleans (1st, lg8vo, ipcb, 36p, color, pep)	McKay	(1941)	Weisgard, L.	35-50	*
Weisgard, L.	Mr. Peaceable Paints (1st, ob4to, [32]p, cloth, dp color)	Scribner	1956	Weisgard, L.	35-50	
Brown, M.W.	Nibble Nibble (1st, 4to, [64]p, 1-color)	W.R. Scott	(1959)	Weisgard, L.	45-60	*
Moore, C.C.	Night Before Christmas (1st, lg4to, ibds, [28]p, color, pep)	Grosset/Dunlap	1949	Weisgard, L.	65-90	*
Brown, M.W.	Night and Day (1st {std}, 4to, cloth, [32]p, color)	Harper	(1942)	Weisgard, L.	65-90	
Brown, M.W.	Noisy Bird Book (1st, 8vo, ibds, [41]p, color)	W.R. Scott	1943	Weisgard, L.	50-80	*
Brown, M.W.	Noisy Book (1st, sq8vo, [42]p, ibds, color, pep)	W.R. Scott	(1939)	Weisgard, L.	60-80	
Brown, M.W.	Noon Balloon (1st, 4to, ibds, unpag, color, pep)	Harper	1952	Weisgard, L.	45-60	
Cavanah, F.	Pedro of Santa Fe (1st, lg8vo, ipcb, [35]p, 3-color, pep)	McKay	(1941)	Weisgard, L.	30-45	*
Weisgard, L.	Pelican Here, Pelican There (1st, 4to, [30]p, 6 dp color, pep)	Scribner	1948	Weisgard, L.	35-50	R*
Reno, E.W.	Pick the Vegetables (1st, 4to, wraps, unpag)	Lothrop/Lee	1944	Weisgard, L.	65-90	*
Lacey, Marion	Picture Book of Musical Instruments (1st, 4to, ibds, 55p, b/w)	Lothrop/Lee	(1942)	Weisgard, L.	35-60	*
Brown, M.W.	Poodle & the Sheep (1st {std}, ob8vo, [55]p, ibds, 1-color, pep)	Dutton	1941	Weisgard, L.	45-70	
Reno, E.W.	Pup Called Cinderella (1st {std}, 8vo, [32]p, ibds, 1-col, b/w)	Bobbs-Merrill	(1939)	Weisgard, L.	30-45	*
Brown, M.W.	Pussy Willow (1st, lg4to, [25]p, color, pep, GGB)	Simon/Schuster	1951	Weisgard, L.	35-55	
Brown, M.W.	Quiet Noisy Book (1st, 4to, ipcb, [34]p, pep, color)	Harper	1950	Weisgard, L.	70-100	R*
Tresselt, A.R.	Rain Drop Splash (1st, 4to, [29]p, ipcb, color, pep, CH)	Lothrop/Lee	(1946)	Weisgard, L.	60-90	*
MacDonald, Golden	Red Light Green Light (1st {std}, ob4to, ibds, [40]p, col, cep)	Doubleday/Dor.	(1944)	Weisgard, L.	70-100	R*
Jackson, Charlotte	Round the Afternoon (1st, 4to, blue cl, [63]p, pep, color)	Dodd	1946	Weisgard, L.	30-45	*
Brown, M.W.	Seashore Noisy Book (1st, 8vo, ibds, [42]p, color, pep)	W.R. Scott	(1941)	Weisgard, L.	40-65	
Rawlings, M.K.	Secret River (1st, 8vo, [57]p, b/w, brown pages, NH)	Scribner	(1955)	Weisgard, L.	70-100	R*
Weisgard, L.	Silly Willy Nilly (1st, sm4to, [32]p, 8 fp color)	Scribner	1953	Weisgard, L.	50-80	R*
Nathan, Robert	Snowflake & the Starfish (1st {std}, 8vo, 68p, fp 2-color)	Knopf	(1959)	Weisgard, L.	30-45	
Weisgard, L.	Suki/Siamese Pussy (1st, sm4to, [32]p, color, DJ)	NY: Nelson	1937	Weisgard, L.	50-70	
Brown, M.W.	Summer Noisy Book (1st, 4to, ibds, color)	Harper	1951	Weisgard, L.	80-120	
Martin, Pat. M.	Sylvester Jones & Voice in the Forest (1st, 4to, [32]p, 2-color)	Lothrop/Lee	(1958)	Weisgard, L.	30-45	*
Bro, Marguerite	Three & Domingo (1st {std}, sm8vo, 127p)	Doubleday	1953	Weisgard, L.	30-45	*
Eberle, I.	Through the Harbor from Everywhere (1st {std}, 8vo, 158p, pep)	Bobbs-Merrill	(1938)	Weisgard, L.	30-45	*
Williams, Gwen M.	Timid Timothy... (1st, sm ob8vo, ibds, [68]p, color)	W.R. Scott	1944	Weisgard, L.	25-40	*
Weisgard, L.	Treasures to See (1st {std}, sm4to, [32]p, rust cl, color)	Harcourt	(1956)	Weisgard, L.	50-85	R*
Shakespeare, Wm.	Under the Greenwood Tree (4to, black/gilt, 51p, color)	NY: OUP	[1940]	Weisgard, L.	45-65	*
Bulla, Clyde R.	Valentine Cat (1st, 4to, unpag, pink cl, 2-color)	Crowell	(1959)	Weisgard, L.	30-45	*
Chambers, M.C.	Water-Carrier's Secrets (1st, 8vo, 157p, 29 fp 1-color, pep)	OUP	(1942)	Weisgard, L.	25-40	*
Weisgard, L.	Who Dreams of Cheese? (1st, 4to, black cl, [32]p, color)	Scribner	1950	Weisgard, L.	60-85	R*
Schlein, M.	Big Talk (1st, sq8vo, olive cl, [36]p, 2-color, pep)	W.R. Scott	1955	Weiss, H.	30-50	*
Rice, Alice H.	Captain June (1st, 8vo, blue cl, 120p, 8pl)	Century	1907	Weldon, C.D.	20-35	
Bunner, H.C.	Three Operettas (1st, ob4to, 163p)	Harper	1897	Weldon/Taylor	100-165	*
Carroll, L.	Alice... & Through... (1st, 4to, 236p, gilt, p-o, col frn)	Sears	(1926)	Welling, G.	100-165	*
Spyri, J.	Heidi (1st, 4to, 243p, col frn, 1-color)	Sears	(1926)	Welling, G.	20-30	*
Wells, H.G.	Adventures of Tommy (1st AM, 4to, red cl, [46]p, p-o, color)	Stokes	1929	Wells, H.G.	100-145	

AUTHOR	TITLE	PUBLISHER	DATE	ARTIST	PRICE	LC
Wells, H.G.	Adventures of Tommy (1st, lg4to, 45p, bds, color)	L: Harrap	(1929)	Wells, H.G.	180-220	
English, James W.	Tailbone Patrol (1st, 8vo, 186p, grey cl, fp b/w, pep)	Holiday House	(1955)	Wells, P.	20-30	*
Wells, Rhea	Beppo the Donkey (1st {std}, 12mo, 135p, color, pep)	Doubleday/Dor.	1930	Wells, Rhea	30-45	*
Wells, Rhea	Coco the Goat (1st {std}, sm8vo, 135p, dp color, pep)	Doubleday/Dor.	1929	Wells, Rhea	25-40	*
Wells, Rhea	Zeke the Raccoon (1st, sm8vo, green cl, 159p, 8cp, pep)	Viking	1933	Wells, Rhea	25-40	*
Wharton, E.	House of Mirth (1st, 8vo, teg, uncut, 533p, 8pl)	Scribner	1905	Wenzell, A.B.	90-120	
Asbjornsen, P.C.	Fairy Tales from the Far North (1st, 8vo, 303p, b/w pl)	L: D. Nutt	1897	Werenskiold, E.	100-150	
Asbjornsen, P.C.	Fairy Tales from the Far North (1st AM, 8vo, 303p, b/w)	A.C. Armstrong	1897	Werenskiold, E.	80-120	*
Buck, Pearl S.	Johnny Jack & his Beginnings (1st, 8vo, 47p, green cl, 1-color)	NY: J. Day	(1954)	Werth, K.	40-65	*
Kay, Helen	One Mitten Lewis (1st, 4to, ibds, [32]p, color)	Lothrop/Lee	(1955)	Werth, K.	40-60	*
Fenner, P.R.	Stories of the Sea (1st {std}, lg8vo, beige cl, 178p, b/w)	Knopf	1953	Werth, K.	25-40	*
McGinley, Phyllis	Year Without a Santa Claus (1st, sm4to, tan cl, [32]p, color)	Lippincott	1957	Werth, K.	25-40	*
Spyri, J.	New Year's Carol (1st, 12mo, 34p, col frn)	Houghton	(1924)	Wesson, G.E.	25-40	*
Perez-Guerra, A.	Poppy, Adventures of a Fairy (1st, lg8vo, ibds, 80p, pep)	Rand/McNally	(1931)	West, B.	80-120	*
Omar Khayyam	Rubaiyat... (1st, 8vo, 159p, 8cp)	L: Kegan Paul	(1923)	Weston, H.	45-65	*
Evans, F.A.	Alice's Adventures in Pictureland (1st, sm4to, 192p, b/w pl)	Dodge	(1900)	Wheelan, A.R.	100-165	*
Terhune, Anice	Chinese Child's Day (1st, lg4to, 33p, ibds, 15 color)	NY: Schirmer	[1910]	Wheelan, A.R.	100-150	
Terhune, Anice	Dutch Ditties for Children (1st, lg4to, 31p, ibds, 15 color)	NY: Schirmer	[1910]	Wheelan, A.R.	80-125	
McElhone, N.K.	Secrets of the Elves (green cloth, p-o)	Devin-Adair	1913	Wheelan, A.R.	120-180	
McElhone, N.K.	Surprise Book (1st, lg ob4to, yellow cl, 33pl)	Stokes	1901	Wheelan, A.R.	120-180	
Broadwood, Lucy	English Nursery Rhymes (lg4to, color)	L: A&C Black	(1916)	Wheeler, D.M.	100-150	
Swift, J.	Gulliver's Travels (1st, 8vo, 414p, 12cp)	L: Routledge	1895	Wheeler, E.J.	35-60	*
Ewing, J.H.	Flat Iron for a Farthing (1st, 12mo, 235p, 8cp)	L: G. Bell	1908	Wheelhouse, M.V.	30-45	*
Alcott, L.M.	Good Wives (1st UK, 12mo, 316p, 8cp)	L: G. Bell	1911	Wheelhouse, M.V.	25-40	
Baldwin, May	Holly House & Ridges Row (1st, 8vo, 339p, red/gilt, 12cp)	L: Chambers	1908	Wheelhouse, M.V.	45-60	
Ewing, J.H.	Jan of the Windmill (1st, 12mo, 307p, 8cp, pep)	L: G. Bell	1917	Wheelhouse, M.V.	35-50	*
Ewing, J.H.	Mrs. Overtheway's Rememberances... (1st, 8vo, teg, 8cp)	L: G. Bell	1909	Wheelhouse, M.V.	30-45	
MacDonald, Geo.	Ronald Bannerman's Boyhood (12mo, 335p, teg, p-o, gilt, 12cp)	L: Blackie	[1910]	Wheelhouse, M.V.	85-120	
Ewing, J.H.	Six to Sixteen (1st, 12mo, green cl, 237p, teg, 8cp)	L: G. Bell	1910	Wheelhouse, M.V.	25-40	
Lucas, E.V.	The Slowcoach (1st, 8vo, brown cl, 284p, 16cp, pep)	L: Wells/Gard.	[1912]	Wheelhouse, M.V.	35-60	
Phillips, M.E.	Tommy Tregennis (lg8vo, teg, 209p, 7cp)	L: Constable	1914	Wheelhouse, M.V.	50-85	*
Ewing, J.H.	We & the World (1st, 12mo, rust cl, 315p, teg, 8cp)	L: G. Allen	1910	Wheelhouse, M.V.	25-40	
Price, Eleanor C.	Adventures of King Arthur (1st, 8vo, 153p, 6cp, p-o)	L: Coker	1931	Wheelwright, R.	35-50	*
N/A	Hunchback of Notre-Dame (1st, 424p, 16cp)	Dodd	1928	Wheelwright, R.	45-60	*
Sterling, S.H.	Robin Hood & his Merry Men (8vo, brown cl, 118p, 7cp)	L: Coker	[1933]	Wheelwright, R.	30-45	*
Black, I.S.	Spoodles, Puppy Who Learned (1st, ob8vo, [48]p, ipcb, 1-color)	W.R. Scott	(1948)	Whistle, J.	35-50	*
Pennell, E.R.	Life of J.M. Whistler (4to, 2 volumes, bds, b/w)	Lippincott	1909	Whistler, J.M.	70-90	
Cary, E.L.	Works of J.M. Whistler (1st, lg8vo, bds, 302p, uncut, 31pl)	Moffat	1907	Whistler, J.M.	85-110	
De La Mare, W.	Desert Islands & Robinson Crusoe (1st {std}, 4to, 285p, b/w)	L: Faber	1930	Whistler, R.	70-100	*
De La Mare, W.	Desert Islands & Robinson Crusoe (1st AM, lg8vo, 299p, b/w)	Farrar/Rine.	1930	Whistler, R.	50-80	*
Andersen, H.C.	Fairy Tales & Legends (1st, 8vo, gilt, 470p, a.e. red, 10 b/w)	L: Cobden	(1935)	Whistler, R.	150-200	R
Andersen, H.C.	Fairy Tales & Legends (1st AM, 8vo, 470p, b/w)	NY: OUP	1936	Whistler, R.	80-120	*
De La Mare, W.	Lord Fish (1st, 8vo, mauve/gilt, 289p, 3cp, pep)	L: Faber	[1933]	Whistler, R.	60-80	
White, C.	Flip Flop Show (folio, bds, color)	Donohue	(1909)	White, C.	65-80	
Meigs, C.	Kingdom of the Winding Road (1st, sm8vo, blue cl, 238p, 6cp)	MacMillan	1915	White, F.	40-65	
N/A	Peter Pan's ABC (4to, ibds, p-o, gilt, 25cp)	L: H. Frowde	[1912]	White, F.	180-260	
Herr, Charoltte	Brownie Robinson Crusoe (1st, 8vo, 163p, p-o, 8cp)	Dodd	1920	White, O.A.	30-45	*
White, T.H.	Sword in the Stone (1st, 8vo, 339p, black cl, b/w)	L: Collins	1938	White, T.H.	120-160	
White, T.H.	Sword in the Stone (1st AM, sm8vo, 311p, blue/gilt, b/w)	Putnam	1939	White, T.H.	80-130	*
White, T.H.	Witch in the Wood (1st AM, 8vo, blue/gilt bds, 270p, b/w)	Putnam	1939	White, T.H.	100-150	
Frank, Mabel L.	Child's Day in Song (1st, lg4to, ibds, 31p, 12cp)	Schirmer	(1916)	Whitelaw, N.	65-80	*
Rhys, E. (ed.)	English Fairy Book (1st, 8vo, 318p)	L: T.F. Unwin	1912	Whitney, F.C.	50-75	*
Gray, Eliz. J.	Penn (1st, 8vo, red cl, 298p, maps, b/w, pep, DJ, NH)	Viking	1938	Whitney, G.G.	45-60	
Randolph, Althea	Bouquet of Rhymes for Children (1st, folio, ibds, 6cp)	Bonnell/Silver	(1909)	Whitney, I.	120-180	*
Spyri, J.	Heidi (1st, 8vo, 433p, pep, 12cp)	Crowell	(1927)	Whittemore, C.	25-40	*
Almond, Linda S.	Mary Redding Takes Charge (1st, sm8vo, 310p, col frn, cp)	Crowell	(1926)	Whittemore, C.	20-25	*
Moore, C.C.	Visit from Saint Nicholas (1st, 16mo, 53p, gilt, pep, color)	MacMillan	1925	Whittemore, C.	40-65	R*
Wodehouse, P.G.	Mike (1st, 8vo, 339p, olive cl, 12pl)	L: A&C Black	1909	Whitwell, T.M.R.	1000	
Wodehouse, P.G.	Psmith in the City (1st, 8vo, 266p, blue cl, 12pl)	L: A&C Black	1910	Whitwell, T.M.R.	800-1000	
Farjeon, E.	Old Nurse's Stocking Basket (1st AM, 8vo, 154p, col frn, b/w)	Stokes	1931	Whydale, E.H.	30-45	
Aflalo, F.G.	Fisherman's Weather (1st, 8vo, teg, gilt, 256p, 8cp)	L: A&C Black	1906	Whymper, C.	50-80	
Wiederseim, G.	Baby's Day (1st, 4to, ibds, 11 fp color)	Stokes	1910	Wiederseim, G.	140-200	
Wiederseim, G.	Dolly Drake (1st, 4to, ibds, [16]p, color, shape bk.)	Stokes	(1909)	Wiederseim, G.	100-150	*
Wiederseim, G.	Ducky Daddles (folio, shape bk, 16p, ibds, color)	Stokes	(1911)	Wiederseim, G.	120-200	
Wiederseim, G.	Fido (shape book, folio, ibds, 16p, color)	Stokes	(1910)	Wiederseim, G.	130-200	
Hays, M.G.	Kaptin Kiddo & Puppo (ob4to, ibds, color)	L: Chambers	1910	Wiederseim, G.	600-800	
Hays, M.G.	Kiddie Land (1st, 4to, [52]p, tan bds, p-o, 6cp, pep)	Jacobs	(1910)	Wiederseim, G.	250-350	
Hays, M.G.	Kiddie Rhymes (1st, 4to, [52]p, ibds, p-o, 7cp, pep)	Jacobs	(1911)	Wiederseim, G.	250-350	*
Hays, M.G.	Little Pets Book (1st, 4to, ibds, 6cp)	Jacobs	(1911)	Wiederseim, G.	200-300	
Wiederseim, G.	Little Sunbeam's Book (wraps)	Hurst	(1918)	Wiederseim, G.	50-70	
Bangs, J.K.	Molly & Unwiseman Abroad (1st, 8vo, p-o, 262p, teg, 10cp)	Lippincott	1910	Wiederseim, G.	100-180	
Mother Goose	Nursery Rhymes from Mother Goose (1st, lg4to, [48]p, color)	Scribner	1907	Wiederseim, G.	150-200	*

AUTHOR	TITLE	PUBLISHER	DATE	ARTIST	PRICE	LC
Hays, M.G.	Rosy Childhood (1st, 4to, ibds, 6 fp color, pep)	Jacobs	(1911)	Wiederseim, G.	160-240	*
Hays, M.G.	Vegetable Verselets (1st, 12mo, 60p, ibds, 20 fp 1-color)	Lippincott	1911	Wiederseim, G.	150-220	R*
Coblentz, C.C.	Animal Pioneers (1st, 8vo, green cl, 241p, b/w)	Little/Brown	1936	Wiese, K.	25-45	*
Ross, M.I.	Back of Time (1st {std}, sm8vo, 271p, pep, b/w)	Harper	1932	Wiese, K.	25-45	*
Salten, Felix	Bambi... (1st AM {std}, 12mo, 293p, green/gilt, b/w, pep)	Simon/Schuster	1928	Wiese, K.	85-125	R
DeJong, Meindert	Bells of the Harbor (1st {std}, 8vo, 289p, pep, b/w)	Harper	1941	Wiese, K.	25-40	*
Harris, Leila	Blackfellow Bundi... (1st, lg8vo, 63p, pep, p-o, color)	Whitman	1939	Wiese, K.	35-50	
Holton, Priscila	Blue Junk (1st {std}, sm8vo, 178p, blue cl, b/w, pep)	Longmans	1931	Wiese, K.	45-65	*
Reely, Mary	Blue Mittens (1st, 8vo, 153p, green cl, b/w, pep)	E.M. Hale	1935	Wiese, K.	30-45	*
Wiese, K.	Buddy the Bear (1st, 4to, ibds, color, [32]p, pep, DJ)	Coward	1936	Wiese, K.	70-90	
Ratzesberger, A.	Camel Bells (1st, 4to, ipcb, 80p, color, pep)	Whitman	1935	Wiese, K.	30-50	*
Harris, M.V.	Carnival Time (1st, 4to, p-o, 64p)	Whitman	1938	Wiese, K.	30-45	*
LaRue, M.G.	Cats for the Tooseys (1st, lg4to, 40p, ipcb, b/w)	Nelson	1939	Wiese, K.	50-80	*
Lau, Josephine	Cheeky: A Prairie Dog (1st, 8vo, 62p, color, pep)	Whitman	1937	Wiese, K.	25-40	*
Williams, Herschel	Children of the Clouds (1st, lg8vo, 224p, col frn, 10 b/w, pep)	NY: Nelson	1929	Wiese, K.	30-45	
Wiese, K.	Chinese Ink Stick (1st {std}, 8vo, 199p, 4cp, pep, DJ)	Doubleday/Dor.	1929	Wiese, K.	50-65	
Brooks, W.R.	Clockwork Twin (1st {std}, 8vo, 241p, 7 fp b/w, pep)	Knopf	1937	Wiese, K.	75-90	
Hunt, M.L.	Corn-Belt Billy (1st, lg8vo, ibds, [26]p, pep, color)	Grosset/Dunlap	(1942)	Wiese, K.	30-45	*
O'Brien, Jack	Corporal Corey (1st, lg8vo, gilt, 276p, col frn)	Winston	(1936)	Wiese, K.	25-40	*
Stong, Phil	Cowhand Goes to Town (1st {std}, 4to, ibds, 85p, color)	Dodd	1939	Wiese, K.	30-45	
Lowell, Joan	Cradle of the Deep (1st, 8vo, 261p, pep, b/w)	Simon/Schuster	1929	Wiese, K.	30-50	*
Rankin, L.S.	Daughter of the Mountains (1st, lg8vo, 191p, fp b/w, pep, NH)	Viking	1948	Wiese, K.	50-70	R
DeJong, Meindert	Dirk's Dog Bello (1st {std}, 8vo, 296p, color, pep)	Harper	1939	Wiese, K.	35-50	
Terhune, A.P.	Dogs (1st, 4to, ipcb, 60p, col frn, fp b/w)	Saalfield	(1940)	Wiese, K.	30-45	*
Grey, Zane	Don: Story of Lion Dog (1st {std}, 12mo, 69p, col frn, 4pl, pep)	Harper	1928	Wiese, K.	45-60	*
Ratzesberger, A.	Donkey Beads (1st, lg8vo, 62p, p-o, pep, color)	Whitman	1938	Wiese, K.	30-45	*
Kellock, Harold	Down in the Grass (1st, 12mo, 247p, uncut, col frn, 25 fp b/w)	Coward	1929	Wiese, K.	30-45	*
Gall, Alice	Each in his Way (1st {std}, 8vo, 180p, brown bds, p-o, b/w, pep)	OUP	(1937)	Wiese, K.	25-40	
Wiese, K.	Ella the Elephant (1st, 4to, p-o, [31]p, 2-color, pep)	Coward	1931	Wiese, K.	35-50	
Stong, Phil	Farm Boy... (1st {std}, 4to, col frn, 80p, pep)	Doubleday/Dor.	1934	Wiese, K.	30-45	*
Bishop, C.H.	Ferryman (1st, ob lg8vo, [64]p, ipcb, 1-color, pep)	Coward	1941	Wiese, K.	35-50	*
Wiese, K.	Fish in the Air (1st, ob4to, ipcb, [32]p, color, pep, CH)	Viking	1948	Wiese, K.	65-110	R*
Bishop, C.H.	Five Chinese Brothers (1st, lg ob8vo, ipcb, [52]p, 1-col, pep)	Coward	(1938)	Wiese, K.	35-50	
Brooks, W.R.	Freddy & Men from Mars (1st {std}, 8vo, 246p, pep, b/w)	Knopf	1954	Wiese, K.	60-80	*
Brooks, W.R.	Freddy & Mr. Camphor (1st {std}, 8vo, 244p, green cl, b/w, pep)	Knopf	1944	Wiese, K.	50-70	
Brooks, W.R.	Freddy the Magician (1st {std}, 8vo, red cl, 258p, b/w)	Knopf	1947	Wiese, K.	50-70	
Brooks, W.R.	Freddy the Pied Piper (1st {std}, 8vo, 253p, b/w)	Knopf	1946	Wiese, K.	50-70	*
Brooks, W.R.	Freddy's Cousin Weedly (1st {std}, sm8vo, 283p, b/w, pep)	Knopf	1940	Wiese, K.	45-65	*
Pease, E.F.	Gay Pippo (1st, 4to, p-o, 80p, color, pep)	Whitman	1936	Wiese, K.	30-50	
Morley, C.	Goldfish Under the Ice (1st {std}, sm8vo, 69p, 14 b/w, cep)	Doubleday/Dor.	1932	Wiese, K.	30-45	
Osborne, N.C.	Good Wind & Good Water (1st, sm8vo, 248p, red cl, b/w, pep)	Viking	1934	Wiese, K.	25-40	*
North, S.	Greased Lightning (1st, 4to, [93]p, color, pep)	Winston	(1940)	Wiese, K.	35-50	*
Stong, Phil	High Water (1st {std}, 4to, ibds, 79p, color)	Dodd	1937	Wiese, K.	35-50	*
Harper, T.A.	His Excellency & Peter (1st {std}, 8vo, 313p, col frn, pep uncut)	Doubleday/Dor.	1930	Wiese, K.	20-30	
Lewis, Eliz. F.	Ho-Ming, Girl of New China (1st, 8vo, 266p, gilt, pep, 4cp)	Winston	1934	Wiese, K.	20-25	*
Stong, Phil	Honk! the Moose (1st {std}, sm4to, ibds, 80p, color, pep, NH)	Dodd	1935	Wiese, K.	65-90	R*
Waldeck, T.	Jamba the Elephant (1st, 8vo, 224p, b/w)	Viking	1942	Wiese, K.	20-25	*
Kahmann, C.	Jasper the Gypsy Dog (1st, 8vo, yellow cl, 93p, b/w, pep)	J. Messner	(1938)	Wiese, K.	30-45	*
DeLeeuw, Hendrik	Java Jungle Tales (1st {std}, 8vo, 311p, col frn, pep)	Doubleday/Dor.	1933	Wiese, K.	30-45	*
Medary, Marj.	Joan & the Three Deer (1st {std}, 8vo, 160p, b/w)	Random	(1939)	Wiese, K.	30-45	*
Wiese, K.	Joe Buys Nails (1st {std}, ob8vo, ibds, [54]p, color)	Doubleday/Dor.	1931	Wiese, K.	45-60	
Williams, Herschel	Jolly Old Whistle (1st, lg8vo, 187p, purple cl, col frn)	Nelson	1927	Wiese, K.	30-45	
Wiese, K.	Karoo the Kangaroo (1st {1st bk.}, sm4to, [35]p, color, pep)	Coward	1929	Wiese, K.	45-65	
Black, I.S.	Kip: Young Rooster (1st, 12mo, [68]p, purple cl, b/w)	Holiday House	(1939)	Wiese, K.	25-45	*
Treffinger, C.	Li Lun: Lad of Courage (1st, 8vo, 93p, grn cl, 1-color, pep, NH)	Abingdon/Coke.	(1947)	Wiese, K.	40-65	*
Wiese, K.	Liang & Lo (1st {std}, ob4to, [56]p, color, pep)	Doubleday/Dor.	1930	Wiese, K.	45-65	*
Voight, V.F.	Lions in the Barn (1st, sm8vo, 95p, yellow cl, b/w, pep)	Holiday House	1955	Wiese, K.	20-30	*
Kunhardt, D.	Little Ones (1st, sm4to, red cl, 78p, color, DJ)	Viking	1935	Wiese, K.	35-50	
Peary, M.A.	Little Tooktoo (1st, 8vo, ibds, 62p, pep, 5cp)	Wm. Morrow	(1930)	Wiese, K.	40-65	*
North, S.	Midnight & Jeremiah (1st {std}, 8vo, 125p, tan cl, color, pep)	Winston	(1943)	Wiese, K.	35-50	*
Tompkins, Jane	Moo-Wee: The Musk-Ox (1st, 8vo, blue cl, 103p, 11 fp b/w, pep)	Stokes	1938	Wiese, K.	25-40	
Pauli, Hertha	Most Beautiful House... (1st {std}, 8vo, 114p, color, DJ)	Knopf	1949	Wiese, K.	20-30	
Robinson, Tom P.	Mr. Red Squirrel (1st, sm4to, ibds, [32]p, color, pep)	Viking	1943	Wiese, K.	30-45	*
Stafford, M.A.	Muskox: Little Tootoo's Friend (1st, 8vo, 64p, color, pep)	Wm. Morrow	(1931)	Wiese, K.	45-65	*
Graham, Stephen	New York Nights (1st, 8vo, 288p, bds, 14 b/w)	Doran	(1927)	Wiese, K.	35-50	*
Baker, O.	Panther Magic (1st, 8vo, gilt, 312p, 8cp, pep)	Dodd	1928	Wiese, K.	25-40	*
Wiese, K.	Parrot Dealer (1st {std}, 8vo, 239p, pep)	Coward	(1932)	Wiese, K.	30-45	*
Peck, Leigh	Pecos Bill & Lightning (1st, sm4to, 68p, color)	Houghton	1940	Wiese, K.	25-40	*
Hahn, E.	Picture Story of China (1st, 4to, 52p, DJ)	Reynal/Hitch.	(1946)	Wiese, K.	40-60	
Collodi, C.	Pinocchio (1st, 8vo, red/gilt, p-o, 239p, 6cp, pep)	T. Nelson	1928	Wiese, K.	50-75	*
Tomkins, J.	Polar Bear Twins (1st, 8vo, 106p, cloth, b/w)	Stokes	1937	Wiese, K.	25-40	
Mackall, L.	Poodle-Oodle on Doodle Farm (1st, ob12mo, p-o, 137p, color, pep)	Stokes	1929	Wiese, K.	35-50	

AUTHOR	TITLE	PUBLISHER	DATE	ARTIST	PRICE	LC
Stong, Phil	Positive Pete (1st, sm4to, ibds, 64p, color, pep, DJ)	Dodd	1947	Wiese, K.	35-50	
Hawkins, Q.	Puppy for Keeps (1st, 8vo, [28]p, b/w, pep)	Holiday House	(1943)	Wiese, K.	20-25	*
Tompkins, Jane	Raccoon Twins (1st, 8vo, 126p, orange cl, b/w, pep)	Stokes	1942	Wiese, K.	25-45	*
Kent, Louise A.	Red Rajah (1st, sm8vo, 290p, blue cl, 6 fp b/w, pep)	Houghton	1933	Wiese, K.	25-40	*
Tompkins, Jane	Red Squirrel Twins (1st {std}, 8vo, tan cl, 123p, b/w)	Stokes	(1950)	Wiese, K.	25-40	*
Beecroft, John	Rocco Came In (1st, 4to, red cl, [30]p, fp color)	Dodd	1959	Wiese, K.	20-30	*
Voight, V.F.	Rolling Show (1st, 8vo, 188p, red cl, b/w, cep)	Holiday House	1956	Wiese, K.	20-30	*
Gilfillan, A.B.	Sheep (1st, 8vo, 272p, b/w)	Little/Brown	1929	Wiese, K.	20-35	
O'Brien, Jack	Silver Chief (1st, 8vo, 218p, col frn)	Winston	(1933)	Wiese, K.	20-30	
O'Brien, Jack	Silver Chief to the Rescue (1st, 8vo, silver cl, 235p, col frn)	Winston	(1937)	Wiese, K.	25-40	
Russell, Arthur	Snowy for Luck (1st, 8vo, p-o, 128p, col frn, pep)	Whitman	1934	Wiese, K.	20-35	*
Flack, M.	Story about Ping (1st, lg8vo, ipcb, [32]p, color)	Viking	1933	Wiese, K.	120-160	R
Brooks, W.R.	Story of Freginald (1st, 4to, 249p, pep, beige cl, 10 fp b/w)	Knopf	1936	Wiese, K.	50-70	*
Brown, M.W.	Streamlined Pig (1st {std}, ob4to, [32]p, color, pep)	Harper	1938	Wiese, K.	50-80	
Bro, Marguerite	Su-Mei's Golden Year (1st {std}, 8vo, 246p, beige cl, b/w)	Doubleday	1950	Wiese, K.	30-45	*
Tschiffely, A.F.	Tale of Two Horses (1st AM, 8vo, 220p, pep, b/w)	Simon/Schuster	1935	Wiese, K.	30-45	*
Kuh, Charlotte	The Deliveryman (1st, 16mo, ibds, [42]p, color)	MacMillan	1929	Wiese, K.	30-50	*
Kuh, Charlotte	The Engineer (1st, 16mo, [42]p, ibds, color)	MacMillan	1929	Wiese, K.	30-50	*
Kuh, Charlotte	The Fireman (1st, 16mo, [42]p, ibds, color)	MacMillan	1929	Wiese, K.	30-50	
Kuh, Charlotte	The Motorman (1st, 16mo, [42]p, ibds, color)	MacMillan	1929	Wiese, K.	35-50	*
Kuh, Charlotte	The Policeman (1st, 16mo, [42]p, ibds, color)	MacMillan	1929	Wiese, K.	45-60	*
N/A	Three Little Kittens (1st, 16mo, [42]p, ibds, color)	MacMillan	1928	Wiese, K.	35-50	
Black, I.S.	Toby: A Curious Cat (1st, 8vo, rust cl, [63]p, b/w, cep)	Holiday House	1948	Wiese, K.	25-45	*
Bridges, Wm.	Toco Toucan (1st {std}, 8vo, [32]p, color)	Harper	(1940)	Wiese, K.	20-40	*
Hawkins, Q.	Too Many Dogs (1st, 8vo, [57]p, olive cl, fp b/w, pep)	Holiday House	(1946)	Wiese, K.	20-25	*
Lang, Don	Tramp: The Sheep Dog (1st, sq8vo, [28]p, ibds, color, pep)	Grosset/Dunlap	1943	Wiese, K.	25-45	*
Davis, L.R.	Very Special Pet (1st, 8vo, ibds, [28]p, color)	Grosset/Dunlap	1944	Wiese, K.	30-45	*
Hall, Wm.	Walking Hat (1st {std}, 4to, ibds, [32]p, color)	Knopf	(1950)	Wiese, K.	40-65	
Lewis, Eliz. F.	When the Typhoon Blows (1st, 8vo, 273p, orange cl, col frn, pep)	Winston	(1942)	Wiese, K.	25-40	*
Weber, Lenora M.	Wind on the Prairie (1st, 8vo, 276p, pep, col frn, b/w)	Little/Brown	1929	Wiese, K.	25-40	*
Grey, Zane	Wolf-Tracker (1st, 12mo, orange cl, 98p, col frn, b/w, pep)	Harper	1930	Wiese, K.	50-80	*
Eldridge, E.J.	Yen-Foh, a Chinese Boy (1st, 8vo, 29p, color, pep)	Whitman	1935	Wiese, K.	30-50	*
Lide, A.A.	Yinka-Tu the Yak (1st, 4to, ibds, 63p, color, pep)	Viking	1938	Wiese, K.	35-50	
Wiese, K.	You Can Write Chinese (1st, ob4to, ibds, [64]p, color, CH)	Viking	1945	Wiese, K.	80-120	*
Lewis, Eliz. F.	Young Fu/Upper Yangtze (1st, 8vo, 265p, black cl, 4cp, pep, NM)	Winston	1932	Wiese, K.	50-85	R
Stong, Phil	Young Settler (1st {std}, sm4to, ibds, 80p, 20 fp color, pep)	Dodd	1938	Wiese, K.	30-60	*
McGinley, Phyllis	Blunderbus (1st {std}, 4to, 47p, yellow cl, 1-color)	Lippincott	(1951)	Wiesner, Wm.	30-45	*
Wightman, F.P.	Jingle Jangle Jumbly Lays... (1st, lg4to, [26]p, color)	NY: Blanchard	1899	Wightman, F.P.	200-300	*
Baum, L.F.	Last Egyptian (1st, 12mo, blue cl, p-o, 287p, 8cp)	Stern	1908	Wightman, F.P.	200-300	
Wightman, F.P.	Little Leather Breeches (1st, 4to, wraps, [48]p, color)	J.F. Taylor	1899	Wightman, F.P.	85-125	*
Bibbins, R.M.	Mammy 'mongst the Wild Nations (1st, sm8vo, 305p, 8pl)	Stokes	(1904)	Wightman, F.P.	50-80	*
Eaton, S.	Teddy-B & Teddy-G/Bear Detectives (1st, 4to, bds, p-o, 15cp)	Stern	1909	Wightman, F.P.	250-325	
Eaton, S.	Teddy-B & Teddy-G/Bear Detectives (4to, ipcb, 152p, p-o, 15cp)	Barse	(1909)	Wightman, F.P.	180-250	
Carruth, H.	Voyage of the Rattletrap (1st, 12mo, gilt, 207p, b/w, PPPa)	Harper	1897	Wilder, H.M.	65-90	*
Spielmann, M.H.	Child of the Air (1st, 8vo, blue cl, 125p, pep)	L: Duckworth	1910	Wilhelm, C.	50-80	
Voight, V.F.	Apple Tree Cottage (1st, sm8vo, green cl, b/w, cep)	Holiday House	(1949)	Wilkin, E.	20-25	*
Buntain, R.J.	Birthday Story (1st, sm8vo, unpag)	Holiday House	(1953)	Wilkin, E.	20-30	*
Dalgliesh, A.	Choosing Book (1st, 16mo, [56]p, red cl, color)	MacMillan	1932	Wilkin, E.B.	30-45	*
Robinson, M.L.	Robin & Angus (1st, 8vo, green cl, 186p, col frn, fp b/w)	MacMillan	1931	Wilkin, E.B.	20-35	*
Morley, C.	Don't Open Until Christmas (1st {std}, sm8vo, ibds, 26p, b/w)	Doubleday/Dor.	1931	Willard, H.	20-35	*
Morrow, Eliz.	Rabbit's Nest (1st {std}, 24mo, 43p, ipcb, 1-color, pep)	MacMillan	1940	Willard, H.	35-50	*
Kingsley, C.	Water Babies (1st, 8vo, 104p, b/w)	Saalfield	(1905)	Williams, C.B.	30-45	*
Naylor, James B.	Witch Crow & Barney Bylow (1st, sm4to, ipcb, 118p, 6cp)	Saalfield	1906	Williams, C.B.	35-50	*
Dixon, Thomas	Leopard's Spots (1st, 8vo, red cl, 465p, 8pl)	Doubleday/Page	1902	Williams, C.D.	30-45	
Long, J.L.	Seffy (1st, sm8vo, 144p, green/gilt, 8pl)	Bobbs-Merrill	(1905)	Williams, C.D.	25-40	
Dixon, Thomas	The Traitor (1st, 8vo, red cl, 331p, 4cp)	Doubleday/Page	1907	Williams, C.D.	25-40	
Bacon, J.D.	Luck/O'Lady Joan (1st, sm8vo, 58p, frn by)	F.G. Browne	1913	Williams, C.E.	20-30	*
Williams, Emery	Alphabet of Indians (1st, folio, ipcb, [57]p, fp 1-color)	R.H. Russell	1900	Williams, E.	250-400	*
Sewell, Anna	Black Beauty (1st, 8vo, 234p, col frn)	Saalfield	(1930)	Williams, F.W.	20-35	*
Bannerman, H.	Little Black Sambo (sq8vo, ibds, [42]p, color)	Saalfield	[1920]	Williams, F.W.	100-165	*
Williams, C.A.	ABC of Animals (1st, 4to, 17p, color, cep)	Stokes	(1911)	Williams, G.A.	80-130	*
Williams, C.A.	Bettijak Book (4to, p-o, color)	Stokes	(1914)	Williams, G.A.	180-220	
Sweetser, K.D.	Book of Indian Braves (1st, lg8vo, 183p, p-o, col frn)	Harper	1913	Williams, G.A.	45-60	
Williams, G.A.	Boy's Book of Indians & Wild West (1st, ob4to, p-o, 47p, 11cp)	Stokes	1911	Williams, G.A.	70-100	
Sweetser, K.D.	Boys & Girls from George Eliot (1st, lg8vo, 212p, 8pl)	Duffield	1906	Williams, G.A.	45-60	*
Dickens, C.	Christmas Carol (1st, sm4to, 198p, col frn, 9pl)	Baker/Taylor	(1905)	Williams, G.A.	60-85	*
Dickens, C.	Holly Tree Inn (1st, sm4to, 139p, 9pl, col frn)	Baker/Taylor	(1907)	Williams, G.A.	40-65	
Williams, C.A.	Magic Book (1st, 4to, 64p, color)	Stokes	(1912)	Williams, G.A.	80-120	*
Williams, C.A.	Mammy's Lil'l Chillums (1st, sm4to, [63]p, ibds, fp color)	Stokes	(1904)	Williams, G.A.	160-200	R
Dickens, C.	Mr. Pickwick's Christmas (1st, 4to, p-o, AEG, 149p, 6cp)	Baker/Taylor	(1906)	Williams, G.A.	45-65	
Williams, C.A.	Stories that Glue Told (1st, ob folio, [36]p, ibds, color)	Stokes	1907	Williams, G.A.	100-150	*
Williams, C.A.	Story Book of Silhouettes (ob folio, ibds, b/w)	Stokes	(1914)	Williams, G.A.	130-200	

AUTHOR	TITLE	PUBLISHER	DATE	ARTIST	PRICE	LC
Sweetser, K.D.	Ten Boys from Dickens (1st, lg8vo, 223p, uncut, b/w pl)	R.H. Russell	1901	Williams, G.A.	50-80	
Sweetser, K.D.	Ten Girls from Dickens (1st, 8vo, 236p, p-o, uncut, 11pl)	Baker/Taylor	1902	Williams, G.A.	45-65	
Dickens, C.	The Chimes (1st, lg8vo, p-o, 210p, col frn, 9pl)	Baker/Taylor	(1908)	Williams, G.A.	35-50	*
LeGallienne, R.	Wagner's Tristan & Isolde (1st, 4to, black/gilt, 7cp)	Stokes	(1909)	Williams, G.A.	100-130	
Williams, Garth	Adventures of Benjamin Pink (1st, 8vo, 151p, green cl, b/w)	Harper	(1951)	Williams, Garth	30-45	*
Hoban, Russell	Bedtime for Frances (1st, 4to, unpag)	Harper	(1960)	Williams, Garth	65-80	*
White, E.B.	Charlotte's Web (1st {std}, 8vo, 184p, b/w, pep, NH)	Harper	(1952)	Williams, Garth	85-100	R
Williams, Garth	Chicken Book (1st, ob8vo, [31]p, color)	Howell/Soskin	(1946)	Williams, Garth	65-80	*
Selden, George	Cricket in Times Square (1st, lg8vo, 151p, fp b/w, NH)	Ariel	(1960)	Williams, Garth	45-65	*
Werner, Jane	Elves & Fairies (1st, sm folio, ibds, 76p, color, pep, GGB)	Simon/Schuster	(1951)	Williams, Garth	160-200	
Stolz, Mary S.	Emmett's Pig (1st, 8vo, ibds, 61p, 2-color)	Harper	(1959)	Williams, Garth	40-65	*
Carlson, N.S.	Family Under the Bridge (1st, 8vo, 99p, green cl, 11 fp b/w, NH)	Harper	(1958)	Williams, Garth	65-100	R*
LeGallienne, Eva	Flossie & Bossie (1st {std}, sm8vo, 210p, 30 fp b/w, DJ)	Harper	(1949)	Williams, Garth	50-85	R
Lindquist, Jennie	Golden Name Day (1st, 8vo, blue cl, 247p, pep, b/w, NH)	Harper	(1955)	Williams, Garth	65-90	R*
Carlson, N.S.	Happy Orpheline (1st, sm4to, blue cl, 96p, fp b/w)	Harper	(1957)	Williams, Garth	30-45	*
Brown, M.W.	Little Fur Family (1st {this format}, 8vo, [37]p, b/w)	Harper	1946	Williams, Garth	80-130	
Wilder, L.I.	Little House on the Prairie (1st, 8vo, DJ)	Harper	(1953)	Williams, Garth	50-80	R*
Lindquist, Jennie	Little Silver House (1st, sm8vo, 213p, green cl, b/w)	Harper	(1959)	Williams, Garth	35-50	*
Brown, M.W.	Mister Dog (1st, sm8vo, unpag, ibds, color, LGB)	Simon/Schuster	(1952)	Williams, Garth	20-30	*
Williams, Garth	Rabbit's Wedding (1st, 4to, ibds, unpag, color)	Harper	(1958)	Williams, Garth	75-120	
Sharp, M.	Rescuers: A Fantasy (1st {std}, 8vo, blue cl, 149p, b/w, DJ)	Little/Brown	(1959)	Williams, Garth	100-165	*
White, E.B.	Stuart Little (1st {std}, 8vo, tan cl, b/w, 131p, pep, DJ)	Harper	(1945)	Williams, Garth	100-135	R
Werner, Jane	Tall Book of Make-Believe (1st, narrow 4to, ibds, 92p, col, pep)	Harper	(1950)	Williams, Garth	60-100	*
Brown, M.W.	Three Little Animals (1st, 4to, ibds, [30]p, color)	Harper	(1956)	Williams, Garth	80-130	R*
Brown, M.W.	Wait Till the Moon is Full (1st, sm4to, ibds, [32]p, 1-color)	Harper	(1948)	Williams, Garth	65-100	*
King, Ben	Jane Jones.... (1st, 8vo, 94p, 16cp)	Chi: Forbes	1909	Williams, J.A.	65-100	*
Parker, L.N.	Pomander Walk (1st, lg8vo, 267p, 16pl)	J. Lane	1911	Williams, J.A.	45-70	*
Emerson, W.G.	Smoky God (1st, 8vo, 186p, blue cl, 11pl)	Chi: Forbes	1908	Williams, J.A.	35-50	*
Marshall, B.G.	Cedric the Forester (1st, 8vo, 278p, 18pl, NH)	Appleton	1921	Williams, J.S.	30-55	*
Sawyer, R.S.	Doctor Danny (1st, sm8vo, 410p, ibds, pep, 8pl)	Harper	1918	Williams, J.S.	20-40	*
MacDonell, Anne	Italian Fairy Book (8vo, gilt, 307p, col frn, 17 fp b/w, pep)	Stokes	[1911]	Williams, M.M.	65-80	
Sawyer, E.A.	Christmas Maker's Club (1st, 8vo, 275p, 6pl)	Page	1908	Williamson	20-30	*
Canfield, D.	Understood Betsy (1st, 8vo, 271p, green cl, 11pl, PPP)	Holt	1917	Williamson, A.C.	70-100	
Henderson, B.	Wonder Tales of Ancient Wales (1st, 8vo, gilt, 166p, teg, 8cp)	L: P. Allan	(1921)	Williamson, D.	80-130	*
Almond, Linda S.	Peter Rabbit & the Little Girl (1st, 24mo, 58p, col frn)	Altemus	(1930)	Willis, B.G.	30-45	*
N/A	Peter Rabbit Story Book (lg8vo, 62p, col frn)	Platt/Munk	(1935)	Willis, B.G.	70-100	*
Willoughby, Rachel	Tunes for Tiny Troubadours (1st, lg4to, ibds, 31p, color)	Putnam	(1936)	Willoughby, W.	65-80	*
Harland, H.	Cardinal's Snuff-Box (1st, 8vo, red/gilt, 263p, teg)	J. Lane	1903	Wilmshurst, G.	25-40	
Annixter, Jane	Buffalo Chief (1st, 8vo, 219p, red cl, pep by...)	Holiday House	(1958)	Wilson, C.B.	25-40	*
Davis, Rbt.	Gid Granger (1st, sm8vo, 179p, tan cl, fp b/w)	Holiday House	(1945)	Wilson, C.B.	20-35	*
Neyhart, L.	Henry's Lincoln (1st, lg8vo, 49p, ipcb, 9 fp b/w, pep)	Holiday House	(1945)	Wilson, C.B.	35-50	R*
Kjelgaard, J.A.	Rebel Siege (1st, 8vo, 221p)	Holiday House	(1943)	Wilson, C.B.	20-25	*
Harrison, E.O.	Glittering Festival (1st, 4to, 176p, gilt, p-o, 4cp)	McClurg	1911	Wilson, C.P.	70-90	
Judson, C.I.	Good-Night Stories (1st, 12mo, pict cl, 131p, b/w)	McClurg	1916	Wilson, C.P.	20-35	*
Smith, Laura R.	Pixie in the House (1st, sm8vo, 123p, pep)	McClurg	1915	Wilson, C.P.	25-40	*
Peltier, F.	Through the Rainbow (1st, 8vo, blue cl, p-o, 117p, 7cp)	Revell	(1917)	Wilson, C.P.	25-40	
Schneider, N.	While Susie Sleeps (1st, sm4to, [32]p, color)	W.R. Scott	(1948)	Wilson, D.	45-60	*
Wilson, E.H.	Flyaway Flippety (1st {std}, lg8vo, 104p, pep, 14cp)	Harper	1932	Wilson, E.H.	25-40	*
Wilson, Edward A.	Pirate's Treasure (1st, 8vo, ibds, color)	Volland	(1926)	Wilson, E.H.	35-50	*
Mother Goose	Everychild's Mother Goose (1st, 12mo, 308p, 64 fp 1-color)	MacMillan	1918	Wilson, E.R.	50-80	*
Chester, Geo. R.	The Jingo (1st, 8vo, grey/gilt, 394p, 10pl)	Bobbs-Merrill	(1912)	Wilson, F.V.	30-45	*
N/A	Daniel in the Lion's Den (1st, 16mo, brown cl, 100p, 19cp)	L: Richards	1903	Wilson, P.	70-100	
Gask, Lilian	Legends of our Little Brothers (1st, 8vo, 268p, 15pl)	L: Harrap	1912	Wilson, P.	45-60	*
Gask, Lilian	Legends of our Little Brothers (1st AM, 8vo, p-o, 268p, 15pl)	Crowell	(1912)	Wilson, P.	35-50	
Fletcher, J.S.	Life in Arcadia (1st, sm8vo, 265p, green/gilt, cvr by...)	L: J. Lane	1896	Wilson, P.	50-70	
Porter, G.S.	Jesus of the Emerald (1st, lg8vo, [44]p, white bds, col frn)	Doubleday/Page	1923	Winchell, E.	350-500	
Brown, A.F.	Kisington Town (1st, 8vo, p-o, 213p, 5pl)	Houghton	1915	Winckler, R.	25-40	*
Lippmann, J.M.	Dearie Dot/The Dog (1st, sm8vo, 194p, 5pl)	Penn	1903	Winner, M.F.	20-30	*
Lent, Henry B.	Bus Driver (1st, sq16mo, [42]p, color, pep)	MacMillan	1937	Winslow, E.	30-45	*
Lent, Henry B.	The Captain (1st, sq16mo, [42]p, color, pep)	MacMillan	1937	Winslow, E.	30-45	*
Malot, H.	Adventures of Perrine (1st, lg8vo, 284p, black cl, p-o 5cp, pep)	Rand/McNally	(1932)	Winter, M.	45-65	
Craik, D.	Adventures of a Brownie (1st, 8vo, p-o, 128p, color)	Rand/McNally	(1923)	Winter, M.	50-65	
Aesopus	Aesop for Children (1st, 4to, p-o, 112p, color, pep)	Rand/McNally	(1919)	Winter, M.	65-90	
Carroll, L.	Alice... & Through... (1st, lg8vo, 242p, p-o, 14cp, pep)	Rand/McNally	(1916)	Winter, M.	130-200	
Evans, Lawton	America First (1st, 8vo, 447p, p-o, pep, col frn, 9pl)	M. Bradley	1920	Winter, M.	35-50	*
N/A	Arabian Nights (1st, lg8vo, 293p, p-o, 16cp, pep)	Rand/McNally	(1914)	Winter, M.	60-80	
Winter, M.	Billy Popgun (1st, 4to, ibds, p-o, 61p, 8cp, pep)	Houghton	1912	Winter, M.	150-200	
Olcott, F.J.	Book of Elves & Fairies (1st, 8vo, 303p, p-o, 3cp by...)	Houghton	1918	Winter, M.	75-100	
Olcott, F.J.	Book of Elves & Fairies (1st UK, 8vo, 303p, 3cp by...)	L: Harrap	1919	Winter, M.	70-100	*
Dickens, C.	Christmas Carol (1st, 12mo, 157p, tan cl, 12pl)	Rand/McNally	(1912)	Winter, M.	35-50	*
Barton, O.R.	Cloud Boat Stories (1st, 8vo, 138p, blue cl, p-o, 4cp)	Houghton	1917	Winter, M.	40-70	
Hinkle, T.C.	Dr. Rabbit & Ki-Yi Coyote (1st, sm8vo, 106p, yellow bds, color)	Rand/McNally	(1918)	Winter, M.	40-65	*

AUTHOR	TITLE	PUBLISHER	DATE	ARTIST	PRICE	LC
Snell, Roy	Eskimo Island & Penguin Land (1st, 8vo, 128p, cloth, p-o by...)	Whitman	1928	Winter, M.	20-30	
Grimm Bros.	Fairy Tales (1st, 8vo, 275p, p-o, 12cp)	Rand/McNally	(1913)	Winter, M.	50-70	
Andersen, H.C.	Fairy Tales (1st, 4to, 286p, p-o, 15cp, pep)	Rand/McNally	(1916)	Winter, M.	70-120	
Bigham, M.A.	Goober Village (1st, sm8vo, 184p, color)	Rand/McNally	(1936)	Winter, M.	25-40	*
Swift, J.	Gulliver's Travels (1st, lg8vo, 344p, gilt, p-o, 12cp, pep)	Rand/McNally	(1912)	Winter, M.	65-100	
Loveland, Mrs. S.	Illustrated Bible Story Book (1st, lg4to, 126p, p-o, 12cp, pep)	Rand/McNally	(1923)	Winter, M.	45-70	
Scott, Walter	Ivanhoe (1st, lg8vo, p-o, 637p, blue/gilt, 14cp, pep)	Rand/McNally	(1918)	Winter, M.	45-70	
Townsend, R.	Journey to the Garden Gate (1st, 4to, p-o, gilt, 127p, 8cp, pep)	Houghton	1919	Winter, M.	50-80	
Stevenson, R.L.	Kidnapped (1st, sm8vo, 262p, cp)	Rand/McNally	(1916)	Winter, M.	65-90	*
N/A	Land of Don't-Want-To (lg8vo, 212p, blue cl, p-o, 10cp)	Rand/McNally	(1923)	Winter, M.	45-60	
Gill, Frances	Little Days (1st, 8vo, ibds, [51]p, col frn)	Houghton	1917	Winter, M.	65-80	
Hardy, M.E.	Little King/Princess True (1st, 8vo, 182p, 4pl)	Rand/McNally	(1912)	Winter, M.	65-80	
DeWolf, W.L.	Mardo's Animal Rhymes (1st, sq8vo, 44p, 4cp)	Rand/McNally	(1916)	Winter, M.	45-65	
Deihl, E.G.	Mother Brown Earth's Children (1st, 8vo, 111p, pep, p-o by...)	Whitman	(1927)	Winter, M.	30-45	*
Harris, J.C.	Nights with Uncle Remus (1st, lg8vo, gilt, p-o, 328p, 12cp)	Houghton	(1917)	Winter, M.	100-165	
Kellogg, V.	Nuova or the New Bee (1st, 8vo, 150p, col frn, 14pl, pep)	Houghton	1920	Winter, M.	50-70	
Spiegelberg, F.	Princess Goldenhair... (1st, 8vo, 176p, p-o, color)	Rand/McNally	(1915)	Winter, M.	65-80	*
Spiegelberg, F.	Princess Goldenhair... (8vo, 176p, green cl, p-o, 8cp)	World	(1932)	Winter, M.	50-70	
Mother Goose	Real Mother Goose (4to, p-o, 33cp)	Rand/McNally	(1928)	Winter, M.	75-90	
Garis, H.	Rick & Ruddy in Camp (1st, sm8vo, 254p, tan cl, 4pl)	M. Bradley	1921	Winter, M.	25-40	*
Defoe, D.	Robinson Crusoe (1st, lg8vo, 382p, p-o, 16cp, pep)	Rand/McNally	(1914)	Winter, M.	45-70	
Hinkle, T.C.	Snowy Tail: Champion Jack Rabbit (1st, 12mo, ibds, 64p)	Rand/McNally	(1921)	Winter, M.	40-65	*
Faulkner, Georgene	Story Lady's Nursery Tales (1st, 8vo, 241p, p-o, 8cp, pep)	Sears	(1927)	Winter, M.	65-80	*
Wyss, J.D.	Swiss Family Robinson (1st, 8vo, 441p, 14cp, pep)	Rand/McNally	(1916)	Winter, M.	45-80	*
Hawthorne, N.	Tanglewood Tales (1st, lg8vo, p-o, gilt, 283p, 10cp, pep)	Rand/McNally	(1913)	Winter, M.	70-120	
Hawthorne, N.	Tanglewood Tales (1st UK, lg8vo, 283p, blue/gilt, 10cp)	L: Duckworth	1914	Winter, M.	70-100	
Dumas, A.	Three Musketeers (1st, 8vo, 545p, p-o, 8cp)	Rand/McNally	(1923)	Winter, M.	50-80	
Austin, Mary	Trail Book (1st, 8vo, 304p)	Houghton	1918	Winter, M.	35-50	
Stevenson, R.L.	Treasure Island (1st, 8vo, 258p, p-o, cp, pep)	Rand/McNally	(1915)	Winter, M.	65-90	*
Barrows, M.	Who's Who in the Zoo (1st, folio, 60p, p-o, pep, 25 fp color)	Reilly/Lee	(1932)	Winter, M.	100-140	*
Hawthorne, N.	Wonder Book... (1st, lg8vo, p-o, 254p, 8cp)	Rand/McNally	(1913)	Winter, M.	70-110	
Olcott, F.J.	Wonderful Garden (1st, 12mo, 483p, p-o, 4cp)	Houghton	1919	Winter, M.	40-65	
Donahey, M.D.	Magical House of Zur (1st, 4to, 124p, p-o, 6cp)	Barse	(1914)	Wireman, E.	50-70	
Dow, E.C.	Proud Roxana (1st, lg8vo, 130p, p-o, 6cp)	Stern	1909	Wireman, E.	80-125	
Wiggin, K.D.	Birds' Christmas Carol (1st, 8vo, 91p, green cl, col frn)	Houghton	1912	Wireman, K.	35-50	
N/A	Children's Story Garden (1st, 8vo, 247p, blue cl, col frn, 9pl)	Lippincott	1920	Wireman, K.	30-50	
Blaisdell, M.F.	Pretty Polly Flinders (1st, sm sq8vo, green cl, 188p, 4cp)	Little/Brown	1914	Wireman, K.	25-40	*
Almond, Linda S.	Little Glad Heart (1st, sm8vo, 317p, 6pl)	Page	1922	Withington, E.R.	20-25	*
Baruch, D.W.	Blimps & Such (1st, 4to, 80p, ibds, col frn, b/w, DJ)	Harper	1932	Wolcott, E.T.	50-85	
Lownsbery, Eloise	Out of the Flame (1st {std}, sm8vo, 352p, pep, b/w, NH)	NY: Longmans	1931	Wolcott, E.T.	30-45	*
Doyle, A.C.	Adventures of Gerard (1st AM, 8vo, 297p, uncut, 16pl)	McClure	1903	Wollen, W.B.	60-85	
Wood, Esther	Great Sweeping Day (1st {std}, 12mo, 158p, pep)	Longmans	1936	Wood, E.	20-35	*
Wood, Esther	Pedro's Coconut Skates (1st {std}, sm8vo, 191p, pep)	Longmans	1938	Wood, E.	20-35	*
Horn, M.D.	Farm on the Hill (1st, 4to, 78p, blue cl, 8cp, pep, DJ)	Scribner	1936	Wood, Grant	125-160	
Hallock, G.T.	Boy Who Was (1st {std}, sm4to, 153p, ipcb, 10cp, pep, NH)	Dutton	(1928)	Wood, H.	45-70	*
Hallock, G.T.	Petersham's Hill (1st, sm8vo, green cl, 132p, 5 fp b/w, pep)	Dutton	(1927)	Wood, H.	30-45	*
N/A	Bedtime Story Book (lg4to, wraps, 16cp)	L: Birn Bros.	(1943)	Wood, Lawson	60-80	
N/A	Old Nursery Rhymes (4to, 142p, beige cl, 24cp)	L: Nelson	[1931]	Wood, Lawson	150-200	
Hinkson, H.A.	Splendid Knight (1st, 8vo, 262p, grey cl, b/w)	L: F.V. White	1905	Wood, Lawson	75-120	*
Tracy, Louis	The Invaders (1st, 8vo, maroon cl, 428p, 4pl)	L: C. Pearson	1901	Wood, Lawson	65-80	*
Wood, M. & H.	Something Perfectly Silly (1st, sq8vo, ibds, [66]p, color, pep)	Knopf	1930	Wood, M.& H.	80-120	*
Jewett, S.O.	Deephaven (1st, 8vo, 305p, teg)	Houghton	1894	Woodbury, C.& M.	70-90	
Crawford, P.	Secret Brother (1st, sm8vo, 238p, b/w)	Holt	(1941)	Woodbury, M.J.	20-35	*
Lang, A.	Book of Dreams & Ghosts (1st, 8vo, 303p, gilt, teg, cvr by...)	L: Longmans	1897	Woodroffe, P.	50-70	
Mourat, Joseph	Humpty Dumpty & other Songs (1st, sq4to, ibds, 32p, 7 fp b/w)	L: Blackwell	1920	Woodroffe, P.	180-220	
Shakespeare, Wm.	The Tempest (1st, 4to, gilt, teg, 130p, 20 ticp, pep)	L: Chapman	1908	Woodroffe, P.	150-200	
Moorat, Joseph	Thirty Old-Time Nursery Songs (1st, lg4to, 32p, ibds, col, pep)	L: Jack	[1895]	Woodroffe, P.	165-250	
Moorat, Joseph	Ye Booke of Nursery Rhymes (1st, lg ob4to, [47]p, ipcb, b/w)	L: G. Bell	(1895)	Woodroffe, P.	140-200	
Moorat, Joseph	Ye Second Book of Nursery Rhymes (1st, ob4to, ipcb, 54p, b/w)	L: G. Allen	1896	Woodroffe, P.	100-150	
Woodruff, H.S.	Mis' Beauty (1st, 12mo, 163p, p-o, 5cp)	A. Harriman	1911	Woodruff, H.	70-100	*
Smith, G.	Wonderful Stories of Jane & John (1st, 8vo, 74p, 10cp)	H. Stone	1899	Woods, A.	100-150	*
King-Hall, E.	Adventures in Toyland (1st, 4to, blue/gilt, AEG, 152p, 8cp)	L: Blackie	[1897]	Woodward, A.B.	150-200	
Carroll, L.	Alice/Wonderland (1st, 8vo, 161p, 8cp)	L: Bell	1914	Woodward, A.B.	70-100	
N/A	Banbury Cross... (1st, 8vo, unpag, red cl, 29pl)	L: Dent	1893	Woodward, A.B.	45-65	*
Sewell, Anna	Black Beauty (1st, 8vo, 224p, 8cp)	L: Bell	1931	Woodward, A.B.	45-60	
Jerrold, W.C.	Bon-Mots/Eighteenth Century (1st, 16mo, 195p)	L: Dent	1897	Woodward, A.B.	35-50	*
Morris, Alice T.	Elephant's Apology (1st, sm8vo, AEG, 152p, blue/gilt, b/w, cep)	L: Blackie	1899	Woodward, A.B.	80-120	
Unknown	Eric Prince of Lorlonia (1st, 8vo, gilt, AEG, 182p, 8cp)	L: MacMillan	1895	Woodward, A.B.	100-145	
Molesworth, M.	House that Grew (1st, 12mo, 206p, orange/gilt, 7pl)	L: MacMillan	1900	Woodward, A.B.	65-80	
Ewing, J.H.	Lob Lie-by-the-Fire (1st, sq8vo, teg, 189p, 8cp)	L: Bell	1909	Woodward, A.B.	40-60	
Clark, Mary S.	Lost Legends/Nursery Songs (1st, 12mo, 278p, red cl, uncut, 8cp)	L: G. Bell	1920	Woodward, A.B.	70-90	
Gatty, M.	Parables from Nature (1st, 8vo, green cl, 210p, 8pl)	L: G. Bell	1910	Woodward, A.B.	50-65	

AUTHOR	TITLE	PUBLISHER	DATE	ARTIST	PRICE	LC
Barrie, J.M.	Peter Pan (1st, .sq8vo, blue cl, 73p, 16 illus, pep)	S. Burdett	(1916)	Woodward, A.B.	60-80	
Barrie, J.M.	Peter Pan Picture Book (1st, lg8vo, 62p, p-o, 28cp, pep)	L: G. Bell	1907	Woodward, A.B.	170-240	
Gilbert, W.S.	Pinafore Picture Book (1st, 4to, 131p, blue cl, 16cp)	L: G. Bell	1908	Woodward, A.B.	70-120	
Braine, S.E.	Princess of Hearts (1st, 8vo, AEG, 172p, green/gilt, col frn)	L: Blackie	1899	Woodward, A.B.	120-165	
Hendry, Hamish	Red Apple & Silver Bells (1st, 8vo, 151p, AEG, red/silver, 20pl)	L: Blackie	[1897]	Woodward, A.B.	50-75	*
Sharp, E.	Round the World to Wympland (1st, 8vo, 235p, 8pl)	L: J. Lane	1902	Woodward, A.B.	70-100	*
Gilbert, W.S.	Story of the Mikado (1st, sm4to, ibds, 114p, 6cp)	L: O'Conner	1921	Woodward, A.B.	45-60	
Braine, S.E.	To Tell the King the Sky is Falling (1st, 8vo, 171p, b/w)	L: Blackie	(1896)	Woodward, A.B.	45-60	
Morris, Alice T.	Troubles of Tatters (1st, lg8vo, 155p, b/w)	L: Blackie	1898	Woodward, A.B.	70-100	
Kingsley, C.	Water Babies (1st, 8vo, 256p)	L: Blackie	1909	Woodward, A.B.	50-75	*
Dalgliesh, A.	Blue Teapot (1st, 8vo, 73p, col frn, pep)	MacMillan	1931	Woodward, H.	30-45	
Wasson, V.P.	Chosen Baby (1st {A}, ob8vo, blue cl, [48]p, color, pep)	Carrick/Evans	(1939)	Woodward, H.	45-60	*
Wasson, V.P.	Chosen Baby (1st {this pub.}, 8vo, 46p, color)	Lippincott	(1950)	Woodward, H.	30-45	*
Dalgliesh, A.	Christmas (1st, 8vo, 232p, col frn, b/w, pep)	Scribner	1934	Woodward, H.	35-50	
Coatsworth, E.	Country Neighborhood (1st {std} 8vo, 181p, decor by...)	MacMillan	1944	Woodward, H.	25-40	*
Davis, L.R.	Danny's Luck (1st, ob4to, ipcb, 43p, 2-color, pep)	Doubleday	1953	Woodward, H.	45-60	*
Woodward, H.	Everyday Children (1st, sq12mo, ipcb, [48]p, 1-color, pep)	NY: OUP	(1935)	Woodward, H.	25-45	*
Wright, Isa L.	Having Fun (1st, 12mo, 124p, color)	Houghton	(1929)	Woodward, H.	30-45	*
Stone, Amy	Here's Juggins (1st, sm8vo, 162p, blue cl, 6cp, pep)	Lothrop/Lee	1936	Woodward, H.	25-45	*
Stone, Amy	P-Penny & his Little Red Cart (1st, sm8vo, 165p, color, pep)	Lothrop/Lee	1934	Woodward, H.	30-45	*
Dalgliesh, A.	Relief's Rocker (1st, 8vo, 62p)	MacMillan	1932	Woodward, H.	20-35	*
Davis, L.R.	Roger & the Fox (1st {std}, ob4to, [43]p, ipcb, dep, color, CH)	Doubleday	1947	Woodward, H.	60-100	*
Davis, L.R.	Round Robin (1st, 8vo, 147p, b/w)	Scribner	1943	Woodward, H.	20-35	*
Dalgliesh, A.	Roundabout (1st, 8vo, 64p, b/w, pep)	MacMillan	1934	Woodward, H.	30-45	*
Davis, L.R.	Summer is Fun (1st {std}, sm ob4to, ibds, 48p, color)	Doubleday	1951	Woodward, H.	30-45	*
Davis, L.R.	Wild Birthday Cake (1st {std}, ob4to, [50]p, ibds, pep, col, CH)	Doubleday	1949	Woodward, H.	70-120	*
Bryant, B.M.	Yammy Buys a Bicycle (1st, 8vo, 168p, pep, 5cp)	Whitman	1940	Woodward, H.	30-45	*
N/A	Golden Ship... (1st, 8vo, 98p, green bds, gilt, b/w)	(London)	1900	Woodward/Bell	120-160	*
Worm, Piet	3 Little Horses (1st, narrow 4to, red bds, 62p, pep)	Random	(1954)	Worm, P.	65-80	*
Worthington, Eliz.	Lullabies of Many Lands (ibds, 24 color)	Caldwell	(1908)	Worthington, E.	70-100	
Dixon, Thomas	Fall of a Nation (1st, 8vo, red/gilt, 362p, 6pl)	Appleton	1916	Wrenn, Chas.	20-30	
Claudy, C.H.	Tell Me Why Stories (1st {this fmt}, 8vo, blue cl, 209p, 8cp)	McBride	1914	Wrenn, T.	20-30	*
Farrow, G.E.	Adventures in Wallypug-Land (1st, AEG, 8vo, gilt, 186p, 17pl)	L: Methuen	1898	Wright, A.	100-140	
Farrow, G.E.	Adventures in Wallypug-Land (1st AM, 8vo, blue cl, AEG, b/w)	New Amsterdam	1899	Wright, A.	70-100	*
Farrow, G.E.	Baker Minor & Dragon (1st, lg8vo, blue/gilt, AEG, 210p, b/w)	L: A. Pearson	1902	Wright, A.	90-110	*
Farrow, G.E.	Little Panjandrum's Dodo (1st, 8vo, 210p, gilt, b/w)	L: Skeffington	1899	Wright, A.	60-80	
Farrow, G.E.	Mandarin's Kite (1st, 8vo, 154p)	L: Skeffington	1900	Wright, A.	50-75	*
Farrow, G.E.	New Panjandrum (1st, 8vo, 199p, gilt, AEG, b/w)	L: A. Pearson	1902	Wright, A.	80-100	
Lowe, S.E.	New Story of Peter Rabbit (16mo, tan bds, 8cp)	Whitman	1926	Wright, A.	70-100	*
Farrow, G.E.	Professor Philanderpan (1st, 8vo, 216p, green/gilt, AEG, b/w)	L: A. Pearson	1904	Wright, A.	50-80	*
Low, Frances H.	Queen Victoria's Dolls (1st, 4to, [86]p, gilt, ae yellow, 34cp)	L: Newnes	1894	Wright, A.	100-165	
Herbertson, A.	Sing Song Stories (4to, ibds, 111p, p-o, 3cp by...)	L: H. Milford	[1922]	Wright, A.	85-130	
Farrow, G.E.	Wallypug Birthday Book (1st, sq8vo, gilt, AEG, 143p, 12cp)	L: Routledge	1904	Wright, A.	150-220	
Farrow, G.E.	Wallypug Tales (1st, sm folio, grey ibds, unpag, color)	L: R. Tuck	[1904]	Wright, A.	200-260	
Farrow, G.E.	Wallypug at Play (folio, ibds, 12 chromos)	L: R. Tuck	[1895]	Wright, A.	350-500	
Farrow, G.E.	Wallypug in Fogland (1st, 8vo, 207p, blue/gilt, AEG, b/w)	L: A. Pearson	1904	Wright, A.	100-160	*
Farrow, G.E.	Wallypug in London (1st, 8vo, 174p, b/w)	L: Methuen	1898	Wright, A.	80-120	
Farrow, G.E.	Wallypug in the Moon (1st AM, 8vo, 256p, AEG, blue/gilt, b/w)	Lippincott	1905	Wright, A.	100-130	
Farrow, G.E.	Wallypug in the Moon (1st, 8vo, AEG, 256p, grey/gilt)	L: A. Pearson	1905	Wright, A.	100-150	*
Rippey, Sarah C.	Goody-Naughty Book (1st, 12mo, tan cl, p-o, [62]p, color)	Rand/McNally	(1913)	Wright, B.F.	30-45	
Mother Goose	Jolly Mother Goose (1st, folio, [66]p, p-o, 19cp)	Rand/McNally	(1916)	Wright, B.F.	80-125	
Jackson, L.F.	Peter Patter Book (1st, 4to, 110p, color)	Rand/McNally	(1918)	Wright, B.F.	45-75	
Mother Goose	Real Mother Goose (1st, lg4to, [132]p, color, pep)	Rand/McNally	(1916)	Wright, B.F.	80-130	*
Mother Goose	Real Mother Goose (lg4to, 134p, color)	Rand/McNally	(1941)	Wright, B.F.	45-65	*
Rippey, Sarah C.	Sunny-Sulky Book (1st, sm8vo, p-o, 12cp)	Rand/McNally	(1915)	Wright, B.F.	35-60	
Hunt, M.L.	Boy Who Had no Birthday (1st, 8vo, orange cl, 259p, fp b/w)	Stokes	1935	Wright, C.	20-30	*
Hunt, M.L.	Lucinda: Little Girl of 1860 (1st, sm8vo, 233p, blue cl, b/w)	Stokes	1934	Wright, C.	20-30	*
Bailey, C.S.	Stories & Rhymes for a Child (1st, 8vo, 194p, col frn, p-o, 5pl)	M. Bradley	1909	Wright, C.	20-30	*
Wright, F.	New Zealand (1st, 8vo, gilt, teg, 241p, 75cp)	L: A&C Black	1908	Wright, F.	70-120	
Barske, C.	King Cotton (1st, folio, ipcb, 23p, color)	A.& W. Guild	1938	Wright, G.	65-90	
Mabie, H.W.	Norse Stories (1st, 8vo, green/gilt, 250p, 10cp)	Dodd	1901	Wright, G.	65-90	
Rice, Alice H.	Romance of Billy-Goat Hill (1st, 12mo, green/gilt, 404p, 8pl)	Century	1912	Wright, G.	20-30	
Kingsley, C.	Water Babies (1st, lg8vo, 231p, cp, pep)	A. Wessels	1900	Wright, G.	65-90	*
Goldsmith, O.	Vicar of Wakefield (1st, 8vo, green/gilt, 260p, teg, 13cp)	L: A&C Black	1903	Wright, J.M.	80-120	*
Robinson, M.L.	All by Ourselves (1st, sm8vo, 254p, decor by...)	Dutton	(1924)	Wright, M.S.	20-30	*
Paine, A.B.	Beacon Prize Medals (1st, 12mo, 325p, 6pl)	Baker/Taylor	1899	Wright/Huestis	35-50	*
Donaldson, J.W.	Arthur Pendragon of Britain (1st, 8vo, 542p, uncut, 4pl, pep)	Putnam	(1943)	Wyeth, Andrew	70-100	*
White, S.E.	Arizona Nights (1st, 8vo, gilt, p-o, 351p, 7cp)	McClure	1907	Wyeth, N.C.	45-70	
Mulford, C.	Bar 20 (1st, 8vo, 382p, 2pl by...)	Outing	1907	Wyeth, N.C.	45-60	
Parrish, R.	Beth Norvell (1st, 8vo, 341p, tan cl, col frn by...)	McClurg	1907	Wyeth, N.C.	30-45	
Stevenson, R.L.	Black Arrow (1st, 4to, teg, p-o, 328p, 14cp, pep, SC)	Scribner	1916	Wyeth, N.C.	150-200	
Malory, T.	Boy's King Arthur (1st, 4to, p-o, teg, 321p, 14cp, pep, SC)	Scribner	1917	Wyeth, N.C.	140-200	

AUTHOR	TITLE	PUBLISHER	DATE	ARTIST	PRICE	LC
Lanier, S.	Boy's King Arthur (1st UK, 4to, 321p, 14cp)	L: Hodder	[1918]	Wyeth, N.C.	130-180	*
Pier, A.S.	Boys of St. Timothy's (1st, 12mo, 284p, 3pl, PPPa)	Scribner	1904	Wyeth, N.C.	65-90	
Sabatini, Rafael	Captain Blood (1st, 12mo, black cl, 356p, col frn by...)	Houghton	1922	Wyeth, N.C.	25-40	*
Longfellow, H.W.	Courtship of Miles Standish (1st, sm4to, 148p, p-o, 8cp, pep)	Houghton	1920	Wyeth, N.C.	145-200	
Connolly, J.B.	Crested Seas (1st, 8vo, 311p, gilt, teg, 2pl by..)	Scribner	1907	Wyeth, N.C.	30-45	
Stevenson, R.L.	David Balfour (1st, 4to, p-o, 356p, 12cp, pep, SC)	Scribner	1924	Wyeth, N.C.	100-150	
Boyd, J.	Drums (1st, 4to, p-o, 409p, 17cp, pep, SC)	Scribner	1928	Wyeth, N.C.	100-165	
Hewes, A.D.	Glory of the Seas (1st {std}, 8vo, 315p, blue cl, col frn, NH)	Knopf	1933	Wyeth, N.C.	35-50	*
Longfellow, H.W.	Hiawatha (1st, 8vo, red/gilt, teg, 242p, frn by...)	Houghton	1911	Wyeth, N.C.	300-500	
Connolly, J.B.	Hiker Joy (1st, 12mo, red/gilt, uncut, 244p, 4pl)	Scribner	1920	Wyeth, N.C.	25-40	
Rollins, P.A.	Jinglebob (1st, 4to, black cl, 263p, p-o, 4cp, pep, SC)	Scribner	1930	Wyeth, N.C.	200-300	
Stevenson, R.L.	Kidnapped (1st, 4to, map, teg, 289p, 14cp, pep, SC)	Scribner	1913	Wyeth, N.C.	180-300	
Stevenson, R.L.	Kidnapped (1st UK, 4to, green cl, p-o, 14cp)	L: Cassell	(1913)	Wyeth, N.C.	160-200	
Boyles, K.	Langford of the Three Bars (1st, 8vo, 278p, 4cp)	McClurg	1907	Wyeth, N.C.	50-70	
Doyle, A.C.	Last Galley (1st AM, 12mo, red cl, 321p, col frn by...)	Doubleday/Page	1911	Wyeth, N.C.	100-160	
Cooper, J.F	Last of the Mohicans (1st, 4to, 370p, p-o, 14cp, pep, SC)	Scribner	1919	Wyeth, N.C.	150-200	
Bulfinch, T.	Legends of Charlemagne (1st, 4to, teg, p-o, 273p, 8cp, pep)	Cosmopolitan	1924	Wyeth, N.C.	180-220	
Stewart, E.P.	Letters of a Woman Homesteader (1st, 12mo, 282p, 6pl)	Houghton	1914	Wyeth, N.C.	55-85	
Fox, John Jr.	Little Shepherd of Kingdom Come (1st, 4to, 322p, p-o, 14cp, SC)	Scribner	1931	Wyeth, N.C.	180-225	
Johnston, M.	Long Roll (1st, 8vo, 683p, grey cl, 4cp, pep)	Houghton	1911	Wyeth, N.C.	30-45	
Van Dyke, H.	Lost Boy (1st, 16mo, 69p, green/gilt, 3pl by...)	Harper	1914	Wyeth, N.C.	20-30	
Thoreau, H.D.	Men of Concord (1st, 4to, 255p, green/silver, 10cp, pep, DJ)	Houghton	1936	Wyeth, N.C.	145-180	
Verne, Jules	Michael Strogoff (1st, 4to, p-o, 397p, 9cp, pep, SC)	Scribner	1927	Wyeth, N.C.	150-200	
Verne, Jules	Mysterious Island (1st, sm4to, 493p, gilt, p-o, 14cp, pep, SC)	Scribner	1918	Wyeth, N.C.	165-220	
Twain, M.	Mysterious Stranger (1st, 4to, 151p, gilt, teg, p-o, 7cp)	Harper	(1916)	Wyeth, N.C.	100-150	
Spearman, Frank	Nan of Music Mountain (1st, 12mo, green cl, 430p, 4cp)	Scribner	1916	Wyeth, N.C.	30-45	
Palmer, G. (tr)	Odyssey of Homer (1st, 4to, red/gilt, 314p, p-o, 16cp, pep)	Houghton	1929	Wyeth, N.C.	160-220	
Parkman, F.	Oregon Trail (1st, 8vo, 364p, p-o, 5cp, pep)	Little/Brown	1925	Wyeth, N.C.	125-165	
Cadman, S.P.	Parables of Jesus (1st, 4to, p-o, 163p, purple cl, pep, 8cp)	McKay	(1931)	Wyeth, N.C.	450-600	
Hay, J.	Pike County Ballads (1st, 8vo, p-o, 47p, 6cp, pep)	Houghton	(1912)	Wyeth, N.C.	90-140	
Matthews, B.	Poems of American Patriotism (1st, 4to, p-o, 14cp, pep, SC)	Scribner	1922	Wyeth, N.C.	200-300	
Irving, W.	Rip Van Winkle (1st, lg8vo, 86p, teg, gilt, p-o, 8cp, pep)	McKay	(1921)	Wyeth, N.C.	160-220	
N/A	Robin Hood (1st, lg8vo, green/gilt, p-o, teg, 362p, 8cp, pep)	McKay	1917	Wyeth, N.C.	140-200	
Defoe, D.	Robinson Crusoe (1st, 4to, teg, p-o, 368p, 13cp, pep)	Cosmopolitan	1920	Wyeth, N.C.	145-200	
Marriott, C.	Sally Castleton, Southerner (1st, 8vo, uncut 312p, col frn, 5pl)	Lippincott	1913	Wyeth, N.C.	65-80	
Wiggin, K.D.	Scottish Chiefs (1st, 4to, p-o, gilt, 503p, 17cp, pep, SC)	Scribner	1921	Wyeth, N.C.	150-200	
Merwin, S.	Silk (1st, 12mo, 266p, red/gilt, pep, col frn by...)	Houghton	1923	Wyeth, N.C.	35-50	
Wiggin, K.D.	Susanna & Sue (1st, 8vo, 225p, teg, p-o, color, dep)	Houghton	1909	Wyeth, N.C.	60-80	
Cheney, W.	The Challenge (1st, 12mo, 386p, red cl, 4pl)	Bobbs-Merrill	(1906)	Wyeth, N.C.	20-35	
Cooper, J.F.	The Deerslayer (1st, 4to, p-o, 462p, 9cp, pep, SC)	Scribner	1925	Wyeth, N.C.	140-200	
Andrews, M.S.	The Militants (1st, 12mo, 379p, teg, 2pl by...)	Scribner	1907	Wyeth, N.C.	45-60	
White, S.E.	The Riverman (1st, 8vo, p-o, 368p, 12pl)	McClure	1908	Wyeth, N.C.	50-70	
Baldwin, J.	The Sampo (1st, 8vo, green cl, 368p, 4cp)	Scribner	1912	Wyeth, N.C.	60-80	
Lewis, A.H.	The Throwback (1st, 12mo, 347p, green cl, 4cp)	Outing	1906	Wyeth, N.C.	35-50	
Rawlings, M.K.	The Yearling (1st {Pulitzer ed.}, sm4to, 400p, 14cp, DJ)	Scribner	1939	Wyeth, N.C.	100-140	
Rawlings, M.K.	The Yearling (1st {this fmt}, 4to, 400p, p-o, 12cp, pep, SC)	Scribner	1940	Wyeth, N.C.	140-200	
Stevenson, R.L.	Treasure Island (1st, 4to, p-o, gilt, teg, 273p, 14cp, pep, SC)	Scribner	1911	Wyeth, N.C.	220-300	
Roberts, K.	Trending into Maine (1st, lg8vo, 382p, tan cl, 14cp, pep)	Little/Brown	1938	Wyeth, N.C.	70-100	
Quick, Herbert	Vandemark's Folly (1st, 12mo, 420p, 8pl)	Bobbs-Merrill	(1922)	Wyeth, N.C.	30-50	
Long, J.L.	War (1st, 12mo, red cl, 371p, 4cp)	Bobbs-Merrill	(1913)	Wyeth, N.C.	50-85	
Kingsley, C.	Westward Ho! (1st, 4to, 413p, p-o, 14cp, pep, SC)	Scribner	1920	Wyeth, N.C.	150-220	
Spearman, Frank	Whispering Smith (1st, 12mo, red cl, 421p, 4cp)	Scribner	1906	Wyeth, N.C.	30-45	
Doyle, A.C.	White Company (1st, 4to, 363p, teg, p-o, 13cp, pep)	Cosmopolitan	1922	Wyeth, N.C.	160-200	
Coatsworth, E.	Cricket & the Emperor's Son (1st, sq8vo, dep, 112p, b/w)	MacMillan	1932	Yap, W.	45-60	*
Buck, Pearl S.	Stories for Little Children (1st, ob8vo, [48]p, 10 fp 2-color)	NY: J. Day	(1940)	Yap, W.	70-100	R*
Chrisman, A.B.	Treasures Long Hidden (1st {std}, 8vo, blue cl, 302p, b/w, pep)	Dutton	1941	Yap, W.	25-45	*
Yashima, Taro	Crow Boy (1st, lg4to, 37p, brown cl, color, DJ, CH)	Viking	1955	Yashima, T.	75-100	
Kubota, H.	Golden Footprints (1st {std}, 8vo, 50p, blue cl, 1-color, pep)	World Pub. Co.	(1960)	Yashima, T.	80-120	R*
Yashima, M.& T.	Plenty to Watch (1st, sm4to, 39p, color)	Viking	1954	Yashima, T.	70-110	R*
Yashima, Taro	Umbrella (1st, ob4to, 32p, pep, fp color, CH)	Viking	(1958)	Yashima, T.	70-100	R*
Yashima, Taro	Village Tree (1st, 4to, grey cl, 34p, fp color, dep)	Viking	1953	Yashima, T.	65-100	R*
Jewett, E.M.	Which was Witch? (1st, sm8vo, 160p, yellow cl, b/w, pep)	Viking	1953	Yashima, T.	50-90	R*
Colum, P.	Big Tree of Bunlahy (1st, 8vo, 166p, col frn, DJ, NH)	MacMillan	1933	Yeats, J.B.	80-100	
Colum, P.	Boy in Eirinn (1st, 8vo, 255p, blue/gilt, col frn, 4pl)	Dutton	(1913)	Yeats, J.B.	100-140	*
Colum, P.	Boy in Eirinn (1st UK, bds, 255p, 6pl)	L: Dent	1915	Yeats, J.B.	150-185	
N/A	Irish Fairy Tales (1st, 12mo, 236p, 2pl)	L: T.F. Unwin	1892	Yeats, J.B.	250-320	
Lynch, Patricia	Turf-Cutter's Donkey (1st, sm8vo, green cl, 245p, 5cp, dep)	Dutton	1935	Yeats, J.B.	80-120	*
Thompson, Maurice	Alice of Old Vincennes (1st [1], 8vo, 419p, green/gilt, 6pl)	Bobbs-Merrill	(1900)	Yohn, F.C.	25-40	
Smith, F.H.	Colonel Carter's Christmas (1st, 8vo, teg, gilt, 159p, 8cp)	Scribner	1903	Yohn, F.C.	20-30	
London, J.	Daughter of the Snows (1st, 12mo, 334p, 4cp)	Lippincott	1902	Yohn, F.C.	200-300	
Burnett, F.H.	Dawn of To-Morrow (1st, 12mo, brown/gilt, 156p, 8cp)	Scribner	1906	Yohn, F.C.	25-40	
Fox, John Jr.	Heart of the Hills (1st, 8vo, red/gilt, 396p, 7pl)	Scribner	1913	Yohn, F.C.	20-30	

AUTHOR	TITLE	PUBLISHER	DATE	ARTIST	PRICE	LC
Nicholson, M.	Hoosier Chronicle (1st, 8vo, 606p, brown/gilt, 4cp)	Houghton	1912	Yohn, F.C.	20-30	
Fox, John Jr.	In Happy Valley (1st, 8vo, 229p, red/gilt, 8pl)	Scribner	1917	Yohn, F.C.	25-40	
Lytton, E.B.	Last Days of Pompeii (1st, 4to, p-o, 425p, 9cp, pep, SC)	Scribner	1926	Yohn, F.C.	60-75	
Wiggin, K.D.	New Chronicles of Rebecca (1st, 12mo, p-o, 278p, 8pl)	Houghton	1907	Yohn, F.C.	25-40	
Parrish, R.	Sword of the Old Frontier (1st, 8vo, 407p, tan cl, 4cp)	McClurg	1905	Yohn, F.C.	20-35	
Fox, John Jr.	Trail of the Lonesome Pine (1st, 12mo, teg, uncut, 422p)	Scribner	1908	Yohn, F.C.	25-40	
Dalrymple, Leona	Uncle Noah's Christmas Inspiration (1st, 12mo, 124p, pep, 4cp)	McBride	1912	Yohn, F.C.	30-50	*
Young, Evelyn	Wu & Lu & Li (1st, sq12mo, [31]p, green cl, color)	NY: OUP	(1939)	Young, E.	35-50	
Pease, J.V.D.	Nimbo (1st, 8vo, p-o, 64p, cp)	Whitman	(1934)	Young, E.M.	30-45	*
Bigham, M.A.	Bad Little Rabbit (1st, sq12mo, 155p, color)	Little/Brown	1927	Young, F.L.	25-40	*
Lindsay, M.M.	Bobby & the Big Road (1st, sm8vo, 112p, blue cl, 16cp)	Lothrop/Lee	(1920)	Young, F.L.	25-45	*
Lindsay, M.M.	Little Missy (1st, sq8vo, 188p, 8cp)	Lothrop/Lee	(1922)	Young, F.L.	30-45	*
Smith, E.	Song Devices & Jingles (1st, lgsq8vo, 65p, 6cp)	Lothrop/Lee	(1920)	Young, F.L.	25-40	*
Lindsay, M.M.	Story-Teller (1st, sm sq8vo, 117p, 12cp)	Lothrop/Lee	(1915)	Young, F.L.	30-45	*
Kingsley, C.	Water Babies (1st, 12mo, 280p)	Ginn & Co.	(1916)	Young, F.L.	25-40	*
Poulsson, E.	What Happened to Inger Johanne (1st, 8vo, grey cl, 283p, color)	Lothrop/Lee	(1919)	Young, F.L.	25-40	*
Grimm Bros.	Fairy Tales (1st, sm4to, 253p, color)	Whitman	(1941)	Young, Goldy	30-45	*
Uttley, Alison	Adventures of Peter & Judy in Bunnyland (4to, ibds, 39p, 8cp)	L: Collins	[1935]	Young, L.	130-200	*
Young, Lillian E.	Advens. of Tommy Cat the Sailor (1st, sm4to, 165p, 20 fp color)	Sears	(1928)	Young, L.E.	35-50	*
Young, Lillian E.	Pussy Willow's Naughty Kittens (1st, 4to, p-o, 54p)	Funk/Wagnalls	(1924)	Young, L.E.	35-50	*
Dickens, C.	Christmas Carol (1st, 4to, ibds, 74p, 11 fp color, pep)	Grosset/Dunlap	(1939)	Young, W.M.	35-50	
Baum, Frank J.	Laughing Dragon of Oz (1st [Big-Little bk.], sq32mo, 425p, ibds)	Whitman	(1934)	Youngren, M.	200-300	*
Sherman, S.	Critical Woodcuts (1st, 8vo, 348p, 15 fp b/w, DJ)	Scribner	1926	Zadig, B.	45-60	
Watanna, O.	Japanese Blossom (1st, 8vo, 263p, uncut, teg, 4cp, dep)	Harper	1906	Ziegler, L.W.	25-40	
Barr, A.	Thyra Varrick (1st, sm8vo, green cl, 343p, 12pl)	J.F. Taylor	1903	Ziegler, L.W.	20-30	
DeRegniers, B.S.	Snow Party (1st {std}, sm4to, unpag)	Pantheon	(1959)	Zimnik, R.	65-100	R*
Streatfield, N.	Party Shoes (1st AM {std}, 8vo, 333p, grey cl, fp b/w)	Random	(1947)	Zinkeisen, A.	25-40	
Barnes, James	Yankee Ships & Yankee Sailors (1st, sm8vo, 281p, 13pl)	MacMillan	1897	Zogbaum, R.F.	25-40	*
King, C.	Cadet Days (1st, sm8vo, 293p, blue/gilt, PPP)	Harper	1894	Zogbaum, R.F.	90-120	
Zogbaum, R.F.	Horse, Foot & Dragons (1st, sm4to, 176p, teg, b/w)	Harper	1888	Zogbaum, R.F.	180-250	
Zogbaum, R.F.	Junior Officer o/t Watch (1st, 8vo, 311p, 4pl)	Appleton	1908	Zogbaum, R.F.	25-40	*
Davis, Reb. H.	Kent Hampden (1st, 8vo, 152p, 4pl)	Scribner	1892	Zogbaum, R.F.	30-45	*
Barnes, J.	Ships & Sailors (1st, ob folio, 124p, ibds, 12cp)	Stokes	1898	Zogbaum, R.F.	140-200	
Munroe, K.	Son of Satsuma (1st, 8vo, 306p, 8pl)	Scribner	1901	Zogbaum, R.F.	30-55	
Forsyth, G.A.	Thrilling Days/Army Life (1st, sm8vo, 196p, 16pl)	Harper	1900	Zogbaum, R.F.	50-75	*
Barker, Mrs. S.	Feathered & Four-Footed Friends (1st, sq8vo, 96p, 24cp)	L: Routledge	1993	Zwecker, J.B.	70-100	*
Fryer, J.E.	Mary Frances Garden Book (1st, lg8vo, p-o, gilt, 378p, col, pep)	Winston	(1916)	Zwirner, W.	120-185	

Section 3

Title Cross-Reference

AUTHOR	TITLE		AUTHOR	TITLE
Twain, M.	$30000 Bequest		Harrington, J.W.	Adventures of Admiral Frog
Tudor, T.	1 Is One		Steele, F.A.	Adventures of Akbar
N/A	100 Best Fairy Tales		Pickard, W.B.	Adventures of Alcassin
Ingpen, R.	1000 Poems for Children		Bianco, M.W.	Adventures of Andy
Strahorn, C.A.	15 Thousand Miles by Stage		Slobodkin, L.	Adventures of Arab
Crespi, P.	170 Cats		Austin, Cyril F.	Adventures of Benjamin & Christabel
Verne, Jules	20 Thousand Leagues...		Williams, Garth	Adventures of Benjamin Pink
Johnson, J.P.	20 Years of Hus'ling		Burgess, T.	Adventures of Bobby Coon
Worm, Piet	3 Little Horses		Upton, F.	Adventures of Borbee & Wisp
Corbett, E.T.	3 Wise Old Couples		Burgess, T.	Adventures of Buster Bear
Bonner, M.G.	365 Bedtime Stories		Stockton, Frank	Adventures of Captain Horn
Disney, W.	40 Big Pages of Mickey Mouse		Burgess, T.	Adventures of Chatterer the Red Squirrel
Fyleman, R.	40 Good-Night Tales		Crockett, D.	Adventures of Davy Crockett
Beerbohm, M.	50 Caracitures		Norwood, Edwin P.	Adventures of Diggeldy Dan
Dali, S.	50 Secrets...		Cervantes	Adventures of Don Quixote
Seuss, Dr.	500 Hats of Bartholomew Cubbins		Mitchell, S.W.	Adventures of Francois
Greenaway, K.	A Apple Pie		Hurrell, M.I.	Adventures of Friskers & His Friends
N/A	A Carol: Good King Wenceslas		Doyle, A.C.	Adventures of Gerard
Nesbit, W.D.	A Friend or Two		Burgess, T.	Adventures of Grandfather Frog
Beerbohm, M.	A Survey		Nyce, Vera	Adventures of Greyfur Family
Selsam, M.E.	A Time for Sleep		Bickley, F.L.	Adventures of Harlequin
Tudor, T.	A is for Annabelle		Olcott, F.J. (ed.)	Adventures of Haroun Er Raschid
Lenski, L.	A-Going to the Westward		Molesworth, M.	Adventures of Herr Baby
Falls, C.B.	ABC Book		Twain, M.	Adventures of Huckleberry Finn
Gag, W.	ABC Bunny		N/A	Adventures of Jack
N/A	ABC Dogs		Burgess, T.	Adventures of Jerry Muskrat
Disney, W.	ABC Mickey Mouse Alphabet Book		Burgess, T.	Adventures of Jimmy Skunk
Frisbie, W.A.	ABC Mother Goose		Burgess, T.	Adventures of Johnny Chuck
Sewell, H.	ABC for Everyday		Macvane, E.	Adventures of Joujou
Williams, C.A.	ABC of Animals		Price, Eleanor C.	Adventures of King Arthur
DeBrunhoff, J.	ABC of Babar		Flagg, J.M.	Adventures of Kitty Cobb
Harris, J.C.	Aaron in the Wildwoods		Hope, A.	Adventures of Lady Ursula
Choate, F.	Abby in the Gobi		Rountree, H.	Adventures of Mabel
Sewell, Daisy	About Fairies....		Disney, W.	Adventures of Mickey Mouse Bk. # 2
Hunt, Clara W.	About Harriet		Adams, Darwin	Adventures of Monte & Molly
Davis, R.H.	About Paris		Ardley, Pat	Adventures of Mr. Horace Hedgehog
Steig, Wm.	About People		Burgess, T.	Adventures of Mr. Mocker
Wilson, E.H.	About Ricco		Mitchell, Muriel M.	Adventures of Nip & Tuck
D'Aulaire, I.& E.	Abraham Lincoln		Colum, P.	Adventures of Odysseus
Daugherty, J.	Abraham Lincoln		Various	Adventures of Odysseus
Foster, Genevieve	Abraham Lincoln's World		Burgess, T.	Adventures of Ol' Mistah Buzzard
Crane, Thos.	Abroad		Burgess, T.	Adventures of Old Mr. Toad
Farrow, G.E.	Absurd Ditties		Malot, H.	Adventures of Perrine
Robinson, W.H.	Absurdities		Uttley, Alison	Adventures of Peter & Judy in Bunnyland
Parsons, F.T.	According to Season...		Beskow, E.	Adventures of Peter & Lotta
VerBeck, F.	Acrobatic Animals		Burgess, T.	Adventures of Peter Cottontail
Credle, Ellis	Across the Cotton Patch		Gilly Bear	Adventures of Peterkin
Burton, J.B.	Across the Salt Seas		Collodi, C.	Adventures of Pinocchio
Dante	Ad Astra		Burgess, T.	Adventures of Poor Mrs. Quack
Dalgliesh, A.	Adam & the Golden Cock		Burgess, T.	Adventures of Prickly Porky
Eliot, Geo.	Adam Bede		Burgess, T.	Adventures of Reddy Fox
Gray, Eliz. J.	Adam of the Road		Malot, H.	Adventures of Remi
Barrie, J.M.	Admirable Crichton		Burgess, T.	Adventures of Sammy Jay
Sherman, Fanny J.	Admiral Wags of USS Lexington		Fox, F.M.	Adventures of Sonny Bear
Carryl, C.E.	Admiral's Caravan		Praeger, S.R.	Adventures of Three Bold Bears
Daringer, H.F.	Adopted Jane		Twain, M.	Adventures of Tom Sawyer
Miller, Leo E.	Adrift on the Amazon		Wells, H.G.	Adventures of Tommy
Fyleman, R.	Adventure Club		Young, Lillian E.	Adventures of Tommy Cat the Sailor
Finger, C.J.	Adventure Under Sapphire Skies		Byron, May	Adventures of Trooper Peek-A-Boo
Thanet, O.	Adventure in Photography		Upton, B.	Adventures of Two Dutch Dolls
Donahey, M.D.	Adventure of a Happy Dolly		Lamb, C.	Adventures of Ulysses
Collodi, C.	Adventures Every Child Should Know		Burgess, T.	Adventures of Uncle Billy Possum
Kay, G.A.	Adventures in Geography		Robinson, W.H.	Adventures of Uncle Lubin
Stevens, F.	Adventures in Hiveland		Craik, D.	Adventures of a Brownie
King-Hall, E.	Adventures in Toyland		Farrow, G.E.	Adventures of a Dodo
Farrow, G.E.	Adventures in Wallypug-Land		Mayer, Henry	Adventures of a Japanese Doll
Groth, Eleanor	Adventures in a Dishpan		McKenna, Dolores	Adventures of a Wee Mouse
Richards, Dorothy	Adventures in an Old Shoe House		Pennell, J.	Adventures of an Illustrator
Putnam, Nina W.	Adventures in the Open		O'Dyer, Ruth	Adventures of the Ink Spots

AUTHOR	TITLE	AUTHOR	TITLE
Donahey, Wm.	Adventures of the Teenie Weenies	N/A	All Shakespeare's Tales
Kay, G.A.	Adventures on our Street	Lang, L.B.	All Sorts of Stories Book
Arnold, E.	Adzuma	Daugherty, Sonia	All Things New
Brookfield, A.	Aesop's Fables for Little Readers	Field, R.	All Through the Night
White, Richardson	Aesop's Fables in Rhyme	Robinson, M.L.	All by Ourselves
Wiggin, K.D.	Affair at the Inn	James, Will	All in the Day's Riding
Stockton, Frank	Afield & Afloat	Flagg, J.M.	All in the Same Boat
Meriwether, L.	Afloat & Ashore on the Mediterranean	Fischer, Marj.	All on a Summer's Day
Smith, E.B.	After they Came Out of the Ark	McKown, G.	All the Days Were Antonia's
Ford, Lauren	Ageless Story	Sharp, E.	All the Way to Fairyland
Biggers, E.D.	Agony Column	Lucas, E.V.	All the World Over
Steig, Wm.	Agony in the Kindergarten	Riley, J.W.	All the Year Round
Lent, Henry B.	Air Pilot	Mack, R.E.	All-Around the Clock
Parrish, R.	Air Pilot	Housman, L.	All-Fellows & Cloak of Friendship
England, G.A.	Air Trust	Housman, L.	All-Fellows...
Murray, Gilbert	Airplane Spider	Hall, G.	Allegretto
Bingham, C.	Airship in Animal Land	Gosse (intro)	Allies' Fairy Book
Malmberg, Bertil	Ake & his World	Elliott, H.	Alliterative Alphabet...
N/A	Aladdin [MOST TITLES]	Cowie, John	Alliterative Anomalies/Infants & Invalids
Ransome, A.	Aladdin & his Wonderful Lamp	Kipling, R.	Almanac of 12 Sports
Crane, W.	Aladdin's Picture Book	DeJong, Meindert	Along Came a Dog
Wheeler, P.	Albanian Wonder Tales	Dalgliesh, A.	Along Janet's Road
Tudor, T.	Alexander the Gander	Wallace, Susan A.	Along the Bosphorus
N/A	Ali Baba & Aladdin	Saunders, M.	Alpatok
Davidson (ed.)	Ali Baba & the Forty Thieves	Lear, E.	Alphabet Book
N/A	Ali Baba & the Forty Thieves	Lenski, L.	Alphabet People
Ratzesberger, A.	Ali Hassan of Hamadan	Field, R.	Alphabet for Boys & Girls
Singer, Caroline	Ali Lives in Iran	Moorepark, C.	Alphabet of Animals
Bagnold, Enid	Alice & Thomas & Jane	Jones, Paul	Alphabet of Aviation
Donahey, Wm.	Alice & the Teenie Weenies	Herford, O.	Alphabet of Celebrities
Girvin, B.	Alice & the White Rabbit	Williams, Emery	Alphabet of Indians
Bangs, J.K.	Alice in Blunderland	Farjeon, E.	Alphabet of Magic
Bradley, Mary H.	Alice in Elephantland	Carlson, N.S.	Alphonse, that Bearded One
Bradley, Mary H.	Alice in Jungleland	Flemwell, G.	Alpine Flowers & Gardens
LaPrade, E.	Alice in Orchestralia	Edwards, G.W.	Alsace-Lorraine
Carroll, L.	Alice in Wonderland [ALL TITLES]	Menotti, G-C.	Amahl & Night Visitors
Carroll, L.	Alice in Wonderland & Through Looking Glass	Tudor, T.	Amanda & the Bear
Hope, E.	Alice in the Delighted States	Farnol, J.	Amateur Gentleman
Thompson, Maurice	Alice of Old Vincennes	Baring-Gould, S.	Amazing Adventures
Evans, F.A.	Alice's Adventures in Pictureland	Heward, C.	Ameliaranne & Green Umbrella
Coatsworth, E.	Alice-All-by-Herself	Heward, C.	Ameliaranne & the Monkey
Kingsbury, H.O.	All Aboard for Wonderland	Morris, Ethel.	Ameliaranne Bridesmaid
Duvoisin, R.	All Aboard!	Heward, C.	Ameliaranne Camps Out
Gruelle, J.	All About Cinderella	Heward, C.	Ameliaranne Cinema Star
Boyd, Eliz. M.	All About David	Gilmour, Marg.	Ameliaranne Gives a Concert
Skaar, G.M.	All About Dogs, Dogs, Dogs	Heward, C.	Ameliaranne Gives a Party
Selsam, M.E.	All About Eggs	Heward, C.	Ameliaranne Goes Touring
N/A	All About Hansel & Gretel	Heward, C.	Ameliaranne Keeps Shop
Bannerman, H.	All About Little Black Sambo	Gilmour, Marg.	Ameliaranne at the Circus
Sterne, Emma G.	All About Little Boy Blue	Heward, C.	Ameliaranne at the Farm
Drinkwater, J.	All About Me	Gilmour, Marg.	Ameliaranne at the Seaside
Gruelle, J.	All About Mother Goose	Thompson, K.L.	Ameliaranne at the Zoo
Phipps, Mary	All About Patsy	Joan, Natalie	Ameliaranne in Town
Sterne, Emma G.	All About Peter Pan	Morris, Ethel.	Ameliaranne's Moving-Day
Potter, B.	All About Peter Rabbit	Nathan, J.	Ameliaranne & the Big Treasure
N/A	All About Red Riding Hood	Farjeon, E.	Ameliaranne & the Magic Ring
N/A	All About Story Book	Tooze, Ruth	America
Farrow, G.E.	All About the Wallypug	Baity, E.C.	America Before Man
Bishop, C.H.	All Alone	Dalgliesh, A.	America Builds Homes
Dyer, W.A.	All Around Robin Hood's Barn	Evans, Lawton	America First
Flack, M.	All Around Town	Johnson, Gerald W.	America is Born
Hofman, Caroline	All Around the Sun-Dial	Holbrook, S.	America's Ethan Allen
McGinley, Phyllis	All Around the Town	Forbes, Esther	America's Paul Revere
Steig, Wm.	All Embarrassed	Petershams	America's Stamps...
Zion, Gene	All Falling Down	Petersham, M.	American ABC
Behn, Harry	All Kinds of Time	Deming, T.O.	American Animal Life
Aldington, R.	All Men are Enemies	Newell, D.	American Animals
Collins, C.	All Round the Farm	Fisher, H.	American Beauties
Sperry, A.	All Sail Set	Twain, M.	American Claimant

AUTHOR	TITLE	AUTHOR	TITLE
Tracy, Louis	American Emperor	Mills, E.A.	Animal Trainer
Baum, L.F.	American Fairy Tales	Pycraft, W.P.	Animal Why Book
Field, R.	American Folk & Fairy Tales	Eaton, A.T.	Animal's Christmas
Christy, H.C.	American Girl	Kastner, Erich	Animal's Conference
Fisher, H.	American Girl	Fallon, Sara W.	Animal-Alphabet Book
Larned, W.T.	American Indian Fairy Tales	D'Aulaire, I.& E.	Animals Everywhere
Scribner, Grace	American Pilgrimage	Blaisdell, E.W.	Animals at the Fair
Gibbs, Geo.	American Sea Fights	Anderson, R.C.	Animals in Social Captivity
Palmer, Winthrop	American Songs for Children	Guizow, P.	Animals in the Ark
N/A	American Stage of Today	Aesopus	Animals of Aesop
Perkins, L.F.	American Twins of the Revolution	Fish, H.D.	Animals of the Bible
Underwood, C.F.	American Types	N/A	Animals on the Farm
Gibson, C.D.	Americans	Hall, Rosalys	Animals to Africa
Baity, E.C.	Americans Before Columbus	Bacon, P.	Animosities
Davis, L.R.	Americans Every One	Anderson, A.	Ann Anderson's Fairy Book
Cooper, Page	Amigo, Circus Horse	White, E.O.	Ann Frances
King, Marian	Amnon, Lad of Palestine	Allee, M.H.	Ann's Surprising Summer
Hill, W.E.	Among Us Cats	Fatio, Louise	Anna the Horse
Pierson, C.D.	Among the Farmyard People	Metcalf, S.	Annabel
Pierson, C.D.	Among the Forest People	Galt, J.	Annals of the Parish
Alden, W.L.	Among the Freaks	Smith, Pamela C.	Annancy Stories
Waugh, D.	Among the Leaves & Grasses	Overton, G.	Anne Carmel
Pierson, C.D.	Among the Meadow People	Montgomery, L.M.	Anne of Avonlea
Pierson, C.D.	Among the Night People	Montgomery, L.M.	Anne of Green Gables
Pierson, C.D.	Among the Pond People	Montgomery, L.M.	Anne of Ingleside
Yates, Eliz.	Amos Fortune, Free Man	Montgomery, L.M.	Anne of the Island
Mitchell, J.A.	Amos Judd	Chambers, Rbt.	Anne's Bridge
Reed, H.L.	Amy in Acadia	Montgomery, L.M.	Anne's House of Dreams
Nicholson, Wm.	An Alphabet	Hurd, E.T.	Annie Moran
Deland, M.	An Encore	Lucas, E.V.	Another Book of Verses for Children
Sherlock, Philip	Anansi the Spider Man	Cox, P.	Another Brownie Book
Titus, Eve	Anatole & the Cat	Ets, Marie H.	Another Day
Jackson, Jesse	Anchor Man	Perry, Nora	Another Flock of Girls
Smith, R.G.	Ancient Tales of Japan	Ely, H.R.	Another Hardy Garden Book
Krumgold, Joseph	And Now Miguel	Wade, B.E.	Ant Ventures
Brady, C.T.	And Thus He Came	Verne, Jules	Antarctic Mystery
Williams, Eleanor	And a Good Fat Hen	Michelson, M.	Anthony Overman
Seuss, Dr.	And to Think I Saw It on Mulberry Street	Bourget, P.	Antigone
Bangs, J.K.	Andiron Tales	Rey, H.A.	Anybody at Home?
Van Stockum, H.	Andries	Brink, C.R.	Anything Can Happen on a River
Daugherty, J.	Andy & the Lion	Webber, I.E.	Anywhere in the World
Gillmore, Inez H.	Angel Island	Altsheler, J.A.	Apache Gold
Lathrop, D.	Angel in the Woods	King, C.	Apache Princess
Perry, S.G.	Angel of Christmas	Eichenberg, Fritz	Ape in a Cape
Van Stockum, H.	Angel's Alphabet	Steedman, Amy	Apple Pie...
Rogers, Eliz.	Angela of Angel Court	Bianco, M.W.	Apple Tree
Fox, F.M.	Angeline Goes Traveling	Voight, V.F.	Apple Tree Cottage
Garrett, H.	Angelo, the Naughty One	Buff, M. & C.	Apple and the Arrow
Housman, L.	Angels & Ministers	Scott, Wm. R.	Apple that Jack Ate
Price, M.E.	Angora Twinnies	Potter, B.	Appley Dapply's Nursery Rhymes
Flack, M.	Angus & the Cat	Milhous, Kath.	Appolonia's Valentine
Flack, M.	Angus & the Ducks	Kyle, Anne D.	Apprentice of Florence
Flack, M.	Angus Lost	Russell, M.	April Baby's Book of Tunes
Baum, L.F. (intro)	Animal ABC	Gates, J.S.	April Fool Doll
N/A	Animal Alphabet	Lathbury, M.A.	April Skies
Beard, D.	Animal Book & Campfire Stories	Newberry, C.T.	April's Kittens
Leet, F.R.	Animal Caravan	Smith, G.	Arabella & Araminta Stories
Kirkwood, E.B.	Animal Children	Lenski, L.	Arabella & Her Aunts
Seeger, Ruth C.	Animal Folk Songs for Children	Maloy, L.	Arabella of the Merry-Go-Round
Deming, T.O.	Animal Folk of Wood & Plain	N/A	Arabian Nights
Byron, May	Animal Frolics	Davidson, G.	Arabian Nights Retold for Children
Seton, E.T.	Animal Heroes	Austin, Margot	Archie Angel
Ipcar, D.	Animal Hide & Seek	Squires, F.	Architec-tonics
Corbet, K.& S.	Animal Land Where there are No People	Marquis, Don	Archy Does His Part
Woole, R.	Animal Legends of Many Lands	Parker, B.	Arctic Orphans
Coblentz, C.C.	Animal Pioneers	Seton, E.T.	Arctic Prairies
Lang, A.	Animal Story Book	Kenyon, C.R.	Argonauts of the Amazon
Toon, G.E.	Animal Story Book	Cooper, F.T.	Argosy of Fables
Cobb, L.M.	Animal Tales of Old North State	Pezet, A.W.	Aristokia

AUTHOR	TITLE	AUTHOR	TITLE
White, S.E.	Arizona Nights	Beskow, E.	Aunt Brown's Birthday
Derrick, Freda	Ark Book	Beskow, E.	Aunt Green.../Aunt Lavender
Petershams	Ark of Father Noah & Mother Noah	Hall, E.C.	Aunt Jane of Kentucky
Paine, A.B.	Arkansas Bear	Van Dyne, Edith	Aunt Jane's Nieces
Read, Opie	Arkansas Planter	N/A	Aunt Louisa's Choice Present
Smith, F.H.	Arm-Chair at the Inn	Hawkins, Q.	Aunt-Sitter
Boyajian, Z.C.	Armenian Legends & Poems	Petersham, M.	Auntie & Celia Jane & Miki
Armfield, C.	Armfield's Animal Book	LeMair, H.W.	Auntie's Little Rhyme Book
MacMunn, G.F.	Armies of India	Hardy, A.S.	Aurelie
Baum, L.F.	Army Alphabet	Bangs, J.K.	Autobiography of Methuselah
Downey, Fairfax	Army Mule	Lyall, Edna	Autobiography of a Slander
Deland, M.	Around Old Chester	Holmes, O.W.	Autocrat at Breakfast Table
Bennett, Rowena B.	Around a Toadstool Table	Miltoun, F.	Automobilist Abroad
N/A	Around the House	Tresselt, A.R.	Autumn Harvest
Siegel, Wm.	Around the World in a Mailbag	Linnell, O.	Autumn Songs with Music
Tudor, T.	Around the Year	Disney, W.	Ave Maria
Moon, G.	Arrow of Tee-May	Phelps, E.S.	Avery...
Grant, Rbt.	Art of Living	Deland, M.	Awakening of Helena Richie
Konody, P.G.	Art of Walter Crane	Coatsworth, E.	Away Goes Sally
Blake, Wm.	Art of William Blake	Kahl, V.	Away Went Wolfgang
Herford, O.	Artful Antics	Copeland, W.	Awful Airship
Chaundler, C.	Arthur & His Knights	Peattie, E.W.	Azalea at Sunset Gap
Holland, Josiah G.	Arthur Bonnicastle	Crowley, Maude	Azor
Moulton, L.C.	Arthur O'Shaughnessy	Lide, A.A.	Aztec Drums
Donaldson, J.W.	Arthur Pendragon of Britain	Janvier, T.A.	Aztec Treasure House
Ade, G.	Artie	Gilbert, W.S.	Bab Ballads
Torrey, M.	Artie & the Princess	DeBrunhoff, J. or L.	Babar [ALL TITLES]
Michael, A.C.	Artist in Spain	Pope, J.	Babes & Beasts
Aldin, C.	Artist's Models	Pope, J.	Babes & Birds
Nesbit, W.D.	As Children Do	Copeland, W.	Babes & Blossoms
Nesbit, E.	As Happy as a King	Bancroft, L.	Babes in Birdland
Artzybasheff, B.	As I See	MacDonough, G.	Babes in Toyland
Hanemann, H.W.	As Is	Thomas, E.M.	Babes of the Nations
Ervin, M.C.	As Told by the Typewriter Girl	Humphrey, M.	Babes of the Year
Shakespeare, Wm.	As You Like It	Newberry, C.T.	Babette
Lucas, E.V.	As the Bee Sucks	MacDonald, L.	Babies' Classics
Pyle, Kath.	As the Goose Flies	Robbins, Ruth	Baboushka & Three Kings
Chambers, Rbt.	Ashes of Empire	Brown, M.W.	Baby Animals
Flack, M.	Ask Mr. Bear	Williamson, H.	Baby Bear
Stockton, Frank	Associate Hermits	Drayton, G.	Baby Bears & their Wishing Rings
Means, F.C.	Assorted Sisters	Corbett, B.	Baby Days
Herford, O.	Astonishing Tale of a Pen & Ink Puppet	Neally, A.	Baby Days...
Misch, Rbt. J.	At Daddy's Office	Kilbourne, C.E.	Baby Elephant & Zoo Man
Holloway, J.	At Flower Farm	Tucker, E.S.	Baby Folk
Ainslie, K.	At Great Aunt Martha's	Ostrander, Fannie	Baby Goose: His Adventures
N/A	At Home	Simon, Norma	Baby House
McCullough, J.G.	At Our House	Brink, C.R.	Baby Island
Lawson, R.	At that Time	Kilbourne, C.E.	Baby Ostrich & Mr. Wise Owl
Culbertson, A.V.	At the Big House	Kilbourne, C.E.	Baby Reindeer & Silver Fox
Means, F.C.	At the End of Nowhere	Pope, J.	Baby Scouts
Justus, May	At the Foot of Windy Low	Cone, H.G.	Baby Sweethearts
Porter, G.S.	At the Foot of the Rainbow	Grant, J.C.	Baby Weems
Colum, P.	At the Gateways of the Day	Tucker, E.S.	Baby and Me!
Parish, Helen R.	At the Palace Gates	N/A	Baby's Animal Book
Blodgett, M.F.	At the Queen's Mercy	Streamer, Col. D.	Baby's Baedeker
Sharp, E.	At the Relton Arms	Kaplan, A.O.	Baby's Biography
Kelly, Eric P.	At the Sign of the Golden Compass	N/A	Baby's Birthday Book
France, A.	At the Sign of the Reine Padauque	Taylor, I.S.	Baby's Book
Burgess, T.	At the Smiling Pool	Crane, W.	Baby's Bouquet
Rives, A.	Athelwold	Wiederseim, G.	Baby's Day
Coatsworth, E.	Atlas & Beyond	Robertson, W.G.	Baby's Day Book
Eidinoff, M.L.	Atomics for the Millions	LeMair, H.W.	Baby's Little Rhyme Book
Heine, H.	Atta Troll	Crane, W.	Baby's Opera
Jacberns, R.	Attic Boarders	Crane, W.	Baby's Own Aesop
Ross, R.	Aubrey Beardsley	N/A	Baby's Record
Symons, A.	Aubrey Beardsley	McManus, B.	Bachelor Ballads
N/A	Aucassin & Nicolette	Spurr, H.A.	Bachelor Ballads
Bishop, C.H.	Augustus	Fisher, H.	Bachelor Belles
Stuart, Ruth M.	Aunt Amity's Silver Wedding	Grant, Rbt.	Bachelor's Christmas

AUTHOR	TITLE	AUTHOR	TITLE
Cobb, I.	Back Home	Hogan, Inez	Bear Twins
Wood, E.	Back Home	Krauss, Ruth	Bears
Ross, M.I.	Back of Time	Dalgliesh, A.	Bears on Hemlock Mountain
MacDonald, Geo.	Back of the North Wind	Tarkington, B.	Beasley's Christmas Party
Gorham, Maurice	Back to the Local	Morrow, Eliz.	Beast, Bird & Fish
Warner, C.D.	Backlog Studies	Hay, Helen	Beasts & Birds
Krauss, Ruth	Backward Day	DeBosschere, J.	Beasts & Men
Belloc, H.	Bad Child's Book of Beasts	Ets, Marie H.	Beasts & Nonsense
Brown, M.W.	Bad Little Duckhunter	Waddell, H.	Beasts & Saints
Bigham, M.A.	Bad Little Rabbit	Jennings, A.	Beating Back
Nash, Ogden	Bad Parents' Garden of Verse	Wells, Carolyn	Beauties
Wheelwright, J.	Bad Penny	Saunders, M.	Beautiful Joe's Paradise
Ardizzone, E.	Baggage to the Enemy	Dowson, Ernest	Beauty & the Beast
Bridgman, Clare	Bairn's Coronation Book	N/A	Beauty & the Beast
Farrow, G.E.	Baker Minor & Dragon	Waugh, Ida	Becky Longnose...
Davis, M.G.	Baker's Dozen	Tudor, T.	Becky's Birthday
Evarts, Hal G.	Bald Face & other Animal Stories	Norton, Mary	Bed-Knob & Broomstick
Darling, E.B.	Baldy of Nome	Whitney, H.H.	Bed-Time Book
Dobson, Austin	Ballad of Beau Brocade	Wetmore, C.H.	Bedtime Stories
Wilde, O.	Ballad of Redding Gaol	N/A	Bedtime Story Book
Bacon, P.	Ballad of Tangle Street	Hoban, Russell	Bedtime for Frances
Pushkin, A.	Ballad of Yukon Jake	Kristofferson, E.M.	Bee in Her Bonnet
Sidney, Marg.	Ballad of the Lost Hare	France, A.	Bee...
Sewell, A.A.	Ballad of the Prince	London, J.	Before Adam
Sidgwick (ed.)	Ballads & Lyrics of Love	Gay, J.	Beggar's Opera
Thackeray, Wm.	Ballads & Songs	Coblentz, C.C.	Beggar's Penny
Stevens, D.K.	Ballads of the Be-Ba-Boes	Allen, Phil S.	Begging Bear
Streatfield, N.	Ballet Shoes	Rowe, Dorothy	Begging Dear
Lee, V.	Ballet of the Nations	Burne-Jones, E.	Beginning of the World
Cabot, E.	Balloon Moon	Morris, C.L.	Behind Moroccan Walls
McEvoy, Joseph P.	Bam Bam Clock	Young, Martha	Behind the Dark Pines
Salten, Felix	Bambi...	Shirk, J.C.	Bela the Juggler
Schreiber, G.	Bambino the Clown	Perkins, L.F.	Belgian Twins
Hader, B.& E.	Banana Tree House	Forestier, A.	Belgium
N/A	Banbury Cross...	Stokes, H.	Belgium
Weeden, Mrs. H.	Bandanna Ballads	Sewell, H.	Belinda the Mouse
Bancroft, L.	Bandit Jim Crow	Mathews, J.	Belle's Pink Boots
Culbertson, A.V.	Banjo Talks	De La Mare, W.	Bells & Grass
DuBois, Theodora	Banjo the Crow	Angelo, V.	Bells of Bleeker Street
Mulford, C.	Bar 20	Coblentz, C.C.	Bells of Leyden Sing
Davis, R.H.	Bar Sinister	DeJong, Meindert	Bells of the Harbor
Byron, May	Barbara Peek-A-Boo's Holiday	Gruelle, J.	Beloved Belindy
Black, I.S.	Barbara's Birthday	Locke, Wm. J.	Beloved Vagabond
Hartog, C.	Barbara's Song Book	Johnson, A.E.	Below Zero
Whitson, J.H.	Barbara, Woman of the West	Lawson, R.	Ben & Me
Chambers, Rbt.	Barbarians	King, Ben	Ben King's Southland Melodies
Kauffmann, R.	Barbary Bo...	Waterman (ed.)	Ben King's Verse
Newberry, C.T.	Barkis	Russell, W.	Bending of the Twig
Sears, P.M.	Barn Swallow	Bradley-Birt, F.	Bengal Fairy Tales
Johnson, Crockett	Barnaby	D'Aulaire, I.& E.	Benjamin Franklin
Bennett, John	Barnaby Lee	Scott, Sally	Benjie & his Family
Austin, Margot	Barney's Adventure	Hunt, M.L.	Benjie's Hat
Aspden, Don	Barney's Barges	Uncle Milton	Bennie & Jennie
Quilp, J.	Baron Verdigris	Lenski, L.	Benny & His Penny
Seuss, Dr.	Bartholomew & the Oobleck	Hurd, E.T.	Benny the Bulldozer
Crane, W.	Bases of Design	May, Rbt.	Benny the Bunny Liked Beans
Johnson, Burgess	Bashful Ballads	Wells, Rhea	Beppo the Donkey
Herford, O.	Bashful Earthquake	Gray, Eliz. J.	Beppy Marlowe of Charles Town
Titus, Eve	Basil of Baker Street	Chittenden, W.L.	Bermuda Verses
Chappell, G.S.	Basket of Poses	Grahame, K.	Bertie's Escapade
Nesbit, E.	Bastable Children	Kingman, Lee	Best Christmas
Dickens, C.	Battle of Life	MacGrath, H.	Best Man
Barlow, J.	Battle of the Frogs & Mice	Bryant, S.C.	Best Stories to Tell Children
Lenski, L.	Bayou Suzette	Cradock, H.C.	Best Teddy Bear in the World
Herbertson, A.	Be-Wee the Gnome...	Bemelmans, L.	Best of Times
Paine, A.B.	Beacon Prize Medals	Parrish, R.	Beth Norvell
Freeman, Don	Beady Bear	Housman, L.	Bethlehem
Culbertson, P.	Bear Facts	Bates, Helen D.	Betsy Ross
DuBois, W.P.	Bear Party	Eaton, J.	Betsy's Napoleon

AUTHOR	TITLE	AUTHOR	TITLE
Lovelace, M.H.	Betsy-Tacy	MacDonald, Greville	Billy Barnicoat
Hunt, M.L.	Better Known as Johnny Appleseed	Denslow, W.W.	Billy Bounce
Andrews, M.S.	Better Treasure	Long, J.L.	Billy Boy
Williams, C.A.	Bettijak Book	Towers, Alton	Billy Bunce...
N/A	Bettina's Bonnet	Gordon, Eliz.	Billy Bunny's Fortune
Anderson, A.	Betty Book	Hader, B.& E.	Billy Butter
Price, M.E.	Betty Fairy Book	Hunt, M.L.	Billy Button's Buttered Biscuit
Jewett, S.O.	Betty Leicester's Christmas	Burgess, T.	Billy Mink
Seawell, M.E.	Betty at Fort Blizzard	Winter, M.	Billy Popgun
Fox, F.M.	Betty of.Mackinaw	Montgomery, F.T.	Billy Whiskers at the Fair
Russell, D.	Betty's Diary	Montgomery, F.T.	Billy Whiskers in the South
Mitchell, Edith	Betty, Bobby & Bubbles	Montgomery, F.T.	Billy Whiskers' Kids
McCutcheon, G.B.	Beverly of Graustark	Rey, M.E.	Billy's Picture
Jeffries, R.	Bevis...	De La Rame, L.	Bimbi
Campbell, W.D.	Beyond the Border	Widdemer, M.	Binkie and Bell Dolls
Brown, Palmer	Beyond the Pawpaw Trees	Cooke, E.V.	Biography of Our Baby
Weston, C.	Bhimsa the Dancing Bear	Bacon, J.D.	Biography of a Boy
Lardner, R.	Bib Ballads	Seton, E.T.	Biography of a Grizzly
Thompson, B.J.	Bible Children...	Seton, E.T.	Biography of a Silver Fox
Olcott, F.J.	Bible Stories to Read & Tell	Field, R.	Bird Began to Sing
Fryer, J.E.	Bible Story Book	Shankland, Frank	Bird Book
Stockton, Frank	Bicycle of Cathay	Gordon, Eliz.	Bird Children
Porter, Jane	Biffy Buffalo	Harrison, G.	Bird Diary
Disney, W.	Big Bad Wolf & Little Red Riding Hood	Seton, E.T.	Bird Portraits
Helle, A.	Big Beasts & Little Beasts	Wedgwood, Henry A.	Bird Talisman
Jerrold, W.C.	Big Book of Fables	Stickney, J.H.	Bird World
Strang, H.	Big Book of Fairy Stories	Hallock, G.T.	Bird in the Bush
Jerrold, W.C.	Big Book of Fairy Tales	Franklin, B.	Bird in the Hand
Penfield, E.	Big Book of Horses & Goats	Lemonnier	Birds & Beasts
Jerrold, W.C.	Big Book of Nursery Rhymes	Halle, L.J.	Birds Against Men
Fiedler, Jean	Big Brother Danny	Hudson, W.H.	Birds in Town & Village
Schlein, M.	Big Cheese	Porter, G.S.	Birds of the Bible
Slobodkin, L.	Big Circus April 1st	Wiggin, K.D.	Birds' Christmas Carol
Hader, B.& E.	Big City	Allen, D.	Birth of the Opal
MacDonald, Golden	Big Dog, Little Dog	Barker, Mrs. S.	Birthday Book for Children
Wain, L.	Big Dogs, Little Dogs, Cats & Kittens	Krauss, Ruth	Birthday Party
Credle, Ellis	Big Doin's on Razorback Ridge	Buntain, R.J.	Birthday Story
Rae, J.	Big Family	North, S.	Birthday of Little Jesus
Baruch, D.W.	Big Fellow at Work	Wilde, O.	Birthday of the Infanta
Olds, Eliz.	Big Fire	Sewell, H.	Birthdays for Robin
DeJong, Meindert	Big Goose & Little White Duck	Foster, Genevieve	Birthdays of Freedom
Coatsworth, E.	Big Green Umbrella	Harris, J.C.	Bishop & Boogerman
Bishop, C.H.	Big Loop	Webber, I.E.	Bits that Grow Big
Shippen, K.B.	Big Mose	Fitzgerald, J.	Bixby of Boston
Hogan, Inez	Big Ones	Slobodkin, L.	Bixxy & the Secret Message
Black, I.S.	Big Puppy & Little Puppy	Brown, Paul	Black & White
Anderson, C.W.	Big Red	Stevenson, R.L.	Black Arrow
Kjelgaard, J.A.	Big Red	Hains, T.J.	Black Barque
Brown, M.W.	Big Red Barn	Anderson, C.W.	Black Bay & Chestnut
Duncan, Eula G.	Big Road Walker	Sewell, Anna	Black Beauty
Hader, B.& E.	Big Snow	Meader, S.W.	Black Bucaneer
Jones, E.O.	Big Susan	Robinson, C.	Black Bunnies
Schlein, M.	Big Talk	Copeland, W.	Black Cat Book
Lardner, R.	Big Town	N/A	Black Doggies
Buff, Mary	Big Tree	Bell, Thelma H.	Black Face
Colum, P.	Big Tree of Bunlahy	Berry, E.	Black Folk Tales
Krauss, Ruth	Big World & Little House	DeAngeli, M.	Black Fox of Lorne
James, Will	Big-Enough	Isham, F.S.	Black Friday
Ward, Lynd	Biggest Bear	Lewis, A.H.	Black Lion Inn
McCracken, H.	Biggest Bear on Earth	Ash, Fenton	Black Opal
McCready, T.L.	Biggity Bantam	Conner, Ralph	Black Rock
Lowell, J.R.	Biglow Papers	Stigand, C.H.	Black Tales for White Children
Bangs, J.K.	Bikey the Skycycle	Lippincott, J.W.	Black Wings
Lindgren, Astrid	Bill Bergson Lives Dangerously	Brown, M.W.	Black and White
Brennan, G.H.	Bill Truetell...	Pyle, Kath.	Black-Eyed Puppy
Robinson, W.H.	Bill the Minder	Paine, R.D.	Blackbeard Buccaneer
Anderson, C.W.	Billy & Blaze	Linderman, F.B.	Blackfeet Indians
DeJong, Meindert	Billy & the Unhappy Bull	Harris, Leila	Blackfellow Bundi...
LaRue, M.G.	Billy Bang Book	Bigham, M.A.	Blackie, His Friends & Enemies

AUTHOR	TITLE	AUTHOR	TITLE
Cowham, Hilda	Blacklegs....	Dimmick, R.C.	Bogie Man
Rickert, Edith	Blacksmith & the Birds	Ransome, A.	Bohemia in London
Kelly, Eric P.	Blacksmith of Vilno	Read, Opie	Bolanyo
Burgess, T.	Blacky the Crow	Irving, W.	Bold Dragon
Anderson, C.W.	Blaze & the Gypsies	Brown, C.	Bold Robin
Anderson, C.W.	Blaze Finds the Trail	Jerrold, W.C.	Bon-Mots of the Eighteenth Century
Pidgin, C.F.	Blennerhassett	Jerrold, W.C.	Bon-Mots...
Rossetti, D.G.	Blessed Damozel	Cable, G.W.	Bonaventure
Baruch, D.W.	Blimps & Such	Abingdon, Alex	Boners
Rounds, Glen	Blind Colt	Norton, Mary	Bonfires & Broomsticks
Walcott, E.A.	Blindfolded	Disney, W.	Bongo
Stokes, Vernon	Blobbs at the Sea Side	Sowerby, Githa	Bonnie Book
Farley, Walter	Blood Bay Colt	Cone, H.G.	Bonnie Little People
Fraser, W.A.	Blood Lilies	Blanchard, A.E.	Bonny Bairns
Outhwaite, I.	Blossom: A Fairy Story	Veale, E.	Bonny Birds
Larrimore, L.	Blossoming of Patricia-The-Less	Richardson, F.	Book for Children
Crawford, P.	Blot: Little City Cat	Dalgliesh, A.	Book for Jennifer
Mansfield, R.	Blown Away	N/A	Book for Little People
Ewing, J.H.	Blue & Red....	Beardsley, Aubrey	Book of 50 Drawings
Coblentz, C.C.	Blue & Silver Necklace	Garland, H.	Book of American Indian
White, E.O.	Blue Aunt	Pyle, H.	Book of American Spirit
Sewell, H.	Blue Barns	Southwold, S.	Book of Animal Tales
Crane, W.	Blue Beard's Picture Book	Dugdale, F.E.	Book of Baby Beasts
Maeterlinck, M.	Blue Bird	Dugdale, F.E.	Book of Baby Birds
Sayers, F.C.	Blue Bonnets for Lucinda	Dugdale, F.E.	Book of Baby Dogs
Clark, A.N.	Blue Canyon Horse	Dugdale, F.E.	Book of Baby Pets
Coblentz, C.C.	Blue Cat of Castle Town	O'Sullivan, V.	Book of Bargains
Bond, Gladys B.	Blue Chimney	VerBeck, F.	Book of Bears
Bemelmans, L.	Blue Danube	Browne, Maggie	Book of Betty Barber
Munroe, K.	Blue Dragon	Nicholson, Wm.	Book of Blokes
Lang, A.	Blue Fairy Book	Arcambeau, E.	Book of Bridges
Van Dyke, H.	Blue Flower	Sparrow, W.S.	Book of Bridges
Burgess, G.	Blue Goops & Red	Francis, J.G.	Book of Cheerful Cats
Fox, John Jr.	Blue Grass & Rhododendron	Mabie, H.W.	Book of Christmas
Shaw, C.G.	Blue Guess Book	Beeching (ed.)	Book of Christmas Verse
Holton, Priscila	Blue Junk	Reed, Myrtle	Book of Clever Beasts
Stacpoole, H.D.	Blue Lagoon	Holling, H.C.	Book of Cowboys
Reely, Mary	Blue Mittens	Bridgman, Clare	Book of Days for Little Ones
Housman, L.	Blue Moon	Masefield, J.	Book of Discoveries
Lewis, B.	Blue Mountain	Nesbit, E.	Book of Dogs
Lang, A.	Blue Poetry Book	Fuller, O.M.	Book of Dragons
Johnson, Crockett	Blue Ribbon Puppies	Nesbit, E.	Book of Dragons
Lenski, L.	Blue Ridge Billy	Frost, A.B.	Book of Drawings
Dalgliesh, A.	Blue Teapot	Richardson, F.	Book of Drawings
Gates, Doris	Blue Willow	Lang, A.	Book of Dreams & Ghosts
Molnar, F.	Blue-Eyed Lady	Olcott, F.J.	Book of Elves & Fairies
Embry, Margaret	Blue-Nosed Witch	Adams, K.	Book of Enchantment Tales
McCloskey, R.	Blueberries for Sal	Aesopus	Book of Fables
Lenski, L.	Blueberry Corners	Owen, Dora	Book of Fairy Poetry
Thompson, Mary W.	Blueberry Muffin	Baring-Gould, S.	Book of Fairy Tales
McGinley, Phyllis	Blunderbus	Humphrey, M.	Book of Fairy Tales
Judson, C.I.	Boat Builder	N/A	Book of Fairy Tales
Ward, Marion	Boat Children of Canton	Terhune, A.P.	Book of Famous Dogs
Politi, L.	Boat for Peppe	Barker, C.M.	Book of Flower Fairies
Flack, M.	Boats on the River	Hayes, Nancy M.	Book of Games
Andrews, M.S.	Bob & the Guides	Baring-Gould, S.	Book of Ghosts
Tousey, S.	Bob & the Railroad	Strang, W.	Book of Giants
Parrish, R.	Bob Hampton of Placer	Lawless, E.	Book of Gilly
Sherwood, E.H.	Bobbie Bubbles	Weatherly, F.E.	Book of Gnomes
Dunham, Curtis	Bobbie in Bugaboo Land	Robinson, W.H.	Book of Goblins
Pope, J.	Bobbity Flop	Herbertson, A.	Book of Happy Gnomes
Wharton, T.I.	Bobbo and other Fancies	Peattie, D.C.	Book of Hours
Lindsay, M.M.	Bobby & the Big Road	Sweetser, K.D.	Book of Indian Braves
Baruch, D.W.	Bobby Goes Riding	Holling, H.C.	Book of Indians
Mitchell, Lebbeus	Bobby in Search of a Birthday	N/A	Book of Job
McConnell, Marg.	Bobo the Barrage Balloon	Riley, J.W.	Book of Joyous Children
Franchot, A.W.	Bobs, King of Fortunate Isle	Perkins, L.F.	Book of Joys
Aldin, C.	Bobtail Puppy Book	Macleod, Mary	Book of King Arthur
Sime, Sidney H.	Bogey Beasts	Heaton, J.L.	Book of Lies

AUTHOR	TITLE	AUTHOR	TITLE
MacFall, H.	Book of Lovat	Chambers, M.C.	Boy Heroes of Chapultepec
Various	Book of Modern Ballads	Gordon, Pat	Boy Jones
Bulfinch, T.	Book of Myths	Garland, H.	Boy Life on the Prairie
Lang, Jean	Book of Myths	Riley, J.W.	Boy Lives on our Farm
Moon, G.	Book of Nah-Wee	Burgess, T.	Boy Scouts in a Trappers Camp
N/A	Book of New Fairy Tales	Burgess, T.	Boy Scouts in a Woodcraft Camp
English, Doug	Book of Nimble Beasts	Brenner, A.	Boy Who Could Do Anything
Untermeyer, L.	Book of Noble Thoughts	Hunt, M.L.	Boy Who Had no Birthday
N/A	Book of Nursery Rhymes	Petershams	Boy Who Had no Heart
Baring-Gould, S.	Book of Nursery Songs & Rhymes	Colum, P.	Boy Who Knew what the Birds Said
Nichols, B.	Book of Old Ballads	Addington, S.	Boy Who Lived in Pudding Lane
Edwards, G.W.	Book of Old English Love Songs	Hallock, G.T.	Boy Who Was
Culver, H.	Book of Old Ships	Jacberns, R.	Boy and a Secret
Cross, L.	Book of Old Sun Dials	Colum, P.	Boy in Eirinn
Dearmer, M.	Book of Penny Toys	Tietjens, E.	Boy of the Desert
N/A	Book of Pets	Brereton, F.S.	Boy of the Dominion
Baring-Gould, S.	Book of Pictured Carols	Hewes, A.D.	Boy of the Lost Crusade
Pyle, H.	Book of Pirates	Tietjens, E.	Boy of the South Seas
Lang, A.	Book of Princes & Princesses	Meader, S.W.	Boy with a Pack
Adams, K.	Book of Princess Stories	Coatsworth, E.	Boy with a Parrot
N/A	Book of Psalms	Stables, Gordon	Boy's Book of Battleships
Haydon, A.L.	Book of Robin Hood	Williams, G.A.	Boy's Book of Indians & Wild West
Lang, A.	Book of Romance	Fitzhugh, P.K.	Boy's Book of Scouts
N/A	Book of Ruth	Lanier, S.	Boy's King Arthur
Brown, A.F.	Book of Saints & Friendly Beasts	Malory, T.	Boy's King Arthur
Lang, L.B.	Book of Saints & Heroes	Lanier, S.	Boy's Mabinogian
Kay, G.A.	Book of Seven Wishes	Otis, James	Boy's Revolt
Bridgman, Clare	Book of Shops	Howells, W.D.	Boy's Town
Lucas, E.V.	Book of Shops	Cavanah, F.	Boyhood Adventures of Our Presidents
Morris, K.	Book of Three Dragons	Haines, Alice C.	Boys
Reid, K.E.J.	Book of Wedding Days	Sweetser, K.D.	Boys & Girls from George Eliot
Lord Dunsany	Book of Wonder	Smith, N.A.	Boys & Girls of Bookland
Jacobs, J.	Book of Wonder Voyages	Raymond, E.	Boys & Girls of Brantham
Seton, E.T.	Book of Woodcraft	Smith, G.	Boys of Marmiton Prairie
Humphrey, Mabel	Book of the Child	Taylor, B.	Boys of Other Countries
Golding, Harry	Book of the Clock	Pier, A.S.	Boys of St. Timothy's
Newbolt, H.	Book of the Happy Warrior	Riley, J.W.	Boys of the Old Glee Club
Wharton, E.	Book of the Homeless	Irving, W.	Bracebridge Hall
Macy, S.B.	Book of the Kingdom	Various	Brains & Bravery
Peabody, J.	Book of the Little Past	Field, R.	Branches Green
Hoffman, A.S.	Book of the Sagas	Seaman, Louise	Brave Bantam
Copeland, W.	Book of the Zoo	Knight, R.A.	Brave Companions
Singer, Caroline	Boomba Lives in Africa	Anglund, J.W.	Brave Cowboy
Bangs, J.K.	Booming of Acre Hill	Austin, Margot	Brave John Henry
Dickens, C.	Boots of the Holly Tree Inn	Balch, Glenn	Brave Riders
Binney, I.	Boppet, Please Stop It	Allen, F.M.	Brayhard
Bigelow, P.	Borderland of Czar & Kaiser	Eells, E.S.	Brazilian Fairy Book
Henry, M.	Born to Trot	Stapp, E.B.	Bread & Lasses
Means, F.C.	Borrowed Brother	Page, T.N.	Bred in the Bone
White, E.O.	Borrowed Sister	Singmaster, Elsie	Bred in the Bone
Norton, Mary	Borrowers Afield	N/A	Breman Band
Norton, Mary	Borrowers Afloat	Reed, H.L.	Brenda's Bargain
Chisholm, A.M.	Boss of Wind River	Reed, H.L.	Brenda's Cousin at Radcliffe
Wilson, H.L.	Boss of the Little Arcady	Reed, H.L.	Brenda's Summer at Rockley
Pollard, J.	Boston Tea Party	Reed, H.L.	Brenda's Ward
Rogerson, Sidney	Both Sides of the Road	Reed, H.L.	Brenda, Her School & her Club
Lathrop, D.	Bouncing Betsy	Blackburn, H.	Breton Folk
Lenski, L.	Bound Girl of Cobble Hill	N/A	Briar Rose Book of Old Fairy Tales
Randolph, Althea	Bouquet of Rhymes for Children	Harrison, B.	Bric-a-Brac Stories
Littlewood, L.	Bower Book of Simple Poems....	Burgess, T.	Bride's Primer
Means, F.C.	Bowlful of Stars	Balch, F.H.	Bridge of the Gods
Burgess, T.	Bowser the Hound	Wilder, T.N.	Bridge/San Luis Rey
May, Charles P.	Box Turtle Lives in Armor	Stevenson, A.M.	Bridget's Fairies
Petersham, M.	Box with Red Wheels	Bridgman, L.J.	Bridgman's Kewts
Henry, M.	Boy & a Dog	Freeman, H.C.	Brief History of Butte Montana
Colum, P.	Boy Apprenticed to an Enchanter	Long, W.J.	Brier-Patch Philosophy
Smith, Wm. J.	Boy Blue's Book of Beasts	DeAngeli, M.	Bright April
Brooks, Noah	Boy Emigrants	Humphrey, Mabel	Bright Days...
Akers, Floyd	Boy Fortune Hunters [ALL TITLES]	Rhoads, Dorothy	Bright Feather

AUTHOR	TITLE	AUTHOR	TITLE
Robinson, M.L.	Bright Island	Lippincott, J.W.	Bun, a Wild Rabbit
Colum, P.	Bright Islands	Krauss, Ruth	Bundle Book
Bianco, M.W.	Bright Morning	Holmes, O.W.	Bunker Hill Battle
Tempski, Armine	Bright Spurs	Gee, John	Bunnie Bear
Henry, M.	Brighty of the Grand Canyon	Towers, Alton	Bunny & Bobbie
Piper, W.	Brimful Book	Outhwaite, I.	Bunny & Brownie
Allen, G.	British Barbarians	Winfrey, Guy	Bunny Bearskin
Glover, C.	British Fairy & Folk Tales	Pope, J.	Bunny Book
Menpes, M.	Brittany	Clayton, J.	Bunny Brothers
Farnol, J.	Broad Highway	Jewett, J.H.	Bunny Stories
Montgomery, R.G.	Broken Fang	Aldin, C.	Bunnyborough
Van Dyke, H.	Broken Soldier & Maid of France	Lent, Henry B.	Bus Driver
Daugherty, Sonia	Broken Song	Coggins, Herbert	Busby & Co.
Vance, Louis J.	Bronze Bell	Finger, C.J.	Bushrangers
Brooks, Gwen.	Bronzeville Boys & Girls	Artzybasheff, B.	Busiest Man in Town
Baring-Gould, S.	Broom-Squire	Burgess, T.	Buster Bear's Twins
Falkberget, J.	Broomstick & Snowflake	Herbertson, A.	Busy Broom
De La Mare, W.	Broomsticks & other Fairy Tales	Belloc, H.	But Softly - We are Observed
Bryant, S.C.	Brother Rabbit	Clarkson, L.	Buttercup's Visit...
Brummitt, S.W.	Brother Van	Politi, L.	Butterflies Come
Green, L.M.	Brother of the Birds	Gordon, Eliz.	Butterfly Babies' Book
Carter, Russell	Brothers of the Frontier	Fish, H.D.	Butterfly Land
Lang, A.	Brown Fairy Book	McCutcheon, G.B.	Butterfly Man
Cox, P.	Brownie Clown of Brownie Town	Parry, E.A.	Butterscotia...
Benson, A.B.	Brownie Primer	Robinson, Tom P.	Buttons
Herr, Charoltte	Brownie Robinson Crusoe	Davis, L.R.	Buttonwood Island
Cox, P.	Brownie Year Book	Ash, Fenton	By Airship to Ophir
Harper, Wilhelmina	Brownie of the Circus	Symington, E.H.	By Light of Sun
Chaffee, Allen	Brownie: Engineer of Beaver Brook	Jackson, G.E.	By Love's Sweet Rule
Cox, P.	Brownies & Prince Florimel	Cable, G.W.	By Low Hill
White, Roma	Brownies & Rose-Leaves	Henry, A.H.	By Order of the Prophet
Banta, N.M.	Brownies & the Goblins	Gail, Otto W.	By Rocket to the Moon
Adshead, Gladys	Brownies - Hush!	Wilder, L.I.	By the Shores of Silver Lake
Cox, P.	Brownies Abroad	Pratt, C.S.	Bye O' Baby Ballads
Cox, P.	Brownies Around the World	Byng, Douglas	Byng Ballads
Cox, P.	Brownies Through the Union	Cocke, Sarah J.	Bypaths in Dixie
Cox, P.	Brownies at Home	Armstrong, Leroy	Byrd Flam in Town
Cox, P.	Brownies in Fairyland	France, A.	CLIO
Cadby, C.	Brownies in Switzerland	Fritz, Jean	Cabin Faced West
Cox, P.	Brownies in the Philippines	Hurd, E.T.	Caboose
Cox, P.	Brownies: Their Book	Armer, L.A.	Cactus
Arkwright, R.	Brownikins & Other Fancies	Brink, C.R.	Caddie Woodlawn
Lapen, F.	Brownyboo	King, C.	Cadet Days
Lida	Bruin the Brown Bear	Miller, A.D.	Calderon's Prisoner
Kipling, R.	Brushwood Boy	Cady, H.	Caleb Cottontail
Morris, M.	Bryn Mawr Stories	Smith, F.H.	Caleb West, Master Diver
Chater, M.	Bubble Ballads	Benet, Laura	Caleb's Luck
Stokley, E.	Bubbleloon	McManus, B.	Calendar of Omar Khayaam
Tucker, E.S.	Bubbles	Field, R.	Calico Bush
Mulford, C.	Buck Peters, Ranchman	Speare, Eliz. G.	Calico Captive
Steedman, C.	Bucking the Sagebrush	Thompson, C.M.	Calico Cat
Kjelgaard, J.A.	Buckskin Brigade	Burton, V.L.	Calico the Wonder Horse
Gordon, Eliz.	Buddy Jim...	Shannon, Monica	California Fairy Tales
Wiese, K.	Buddy the Bear	James, G.W.	California, Romantic & Beautiful
Beskow, E.	Buddy's Advens. in the Blueberry Patch	Austin, Mary H.	California: Land of the Sun
D'Aulaire, I.& E.	Buffalo Bill	Jackson, Jesse	Call Me Charley
Tousey, S.	Buffalo Bill	Sperry, A.	Call it Courage
Annixter, Jane	Buffalo Chief	London, J.	Call of the Wild
Steele, Wm. O.	Buffalo Knife	Ratzesberger, A.	Camel Bells
Gorey, Edward	Bug Book	Gruelle, Justin	Camel with Wrinkled Knees
Bascom, L.R.	Bugaboo Men	White, S.E.	Camp & Trail
Walter, E.D.	Bugs	MacMillan, C.	Canadian Wonder Tales
Franchot, A.W.	Bugs, Wings & other Things	Voltaire, J.F.	Candide
Cautley, Marg.	Building a House in Sweeden	Thompson, B.J.	Candle Burns for France
Heath, J.F.	Built-Upon House	Durston, G.R.	Candle Light
Frost, A.B.	Bull Calf	Means, F.C.	Candle in the Mist
Kidd, Dudley	Bull of the Kraal	Hutchinson, V.	Candle-Light Stories
Brown, M.W.	Bumble Bugs & Elephants	Dunbar, P.L.	Candle-Lightin' Time
N/A	Bumps & Thumps	Alexander, L.M.	Candy

AUTHOR	TITLE	AUTHOR	TITLE
Alcott, L.M.	Candy Country	Wiggin, K.D.	Cathedral Courtship
Godden, Rumer	Candy Floss	Aldin, C.	Cathedrals & Abbey Churches of England
Chaucer, G.	Canterbury Pilgrims	Stevenson, R.L.	Catriona
Chaucer, G.	Canterbury Tales	Tucker, E.S.	Cats & Kittens
Wilde, O.	Canterville Ghost	Montgomery, F.T.	Cats & Kitts
Topelius, Z.	Canute Whistlewinks...	Lockridge, Frances	Cats & People
Thoreau, H.D.	Cape Cod	Rowand, Phyllis	Cats Who Stayed for Dinner
Lincoln, J.	Cape Cod Ballads	Woodhouse, S.C.	Cats at School
Slobodkina, E.	Caps for Sale	LaRue, M.G.	Cats for the Tooseys
Sabatini, Rafael	Captain Blood	Downey, Fairfax	Cats of Destiny
Stockton, Frank	Captain Chap	Grimalkin	Cats! Cats! Cats!
Richards, L.E.	Captain January	Belloc, H.	Cautionary Tales for Children
Crosby, E.	Captain Jinks, Hero	Knipe, A.A.	Cavalier Maid
Adams, V.M.	Captain Joe & the Eskimo	Perkins, L.F.	Cave Twins
Rice, Alice H.	Captain June	Byron, May	Cecil Aldin's Happy Family
Lawson, R.	Captain Kidd's Cat	Byron, May	Cecil Aldin's Merry Party
Madison, L.F.	Captain Kitty Colonial	Helm, C.	Cecily
Merington, M.	Captain Lettarblair	Rey, H.A.	Cecily G. & the 9 Monkeys
Davis, R.H.	Captain Macklin	Potter, B.	Cecily Parsley's Nursery Rhymes
Cooney, Barbara	Captain Pottle's House	Marshall, B.G.	Cedric the Forester
Torjesen, Eliz.	Captain Ramsay's Daughter	Campbell, J.	Celtic Dragon Myth
Stephens, R.N.	Captain Ravenshaw	Jacobs, J.	Celtic Fairy Tales
Thompson, R.P.	Captain Salt in Oz	Squire, C.	Celtic Myth & Legend
Robinson, E.	Captain of the Old School	Thomson, C.L.	Celtic Wonder World
Kipling, R.	Captains Courageous	Bouve, E.T.	Centuries Apart
Veale, E.	Captivating Stories about Animals	Bellamy, W.	Century of Charades
Page, T.N.	Captured Santa Claus	Pyle, H.	Champions of the Round Table
Malkus, A.S.	Caravans to Sante Fe	Morse, Eliz.	Chang of the Siamese Jungle
Harland, H.	Cardinal's Snuff-Box	Chaucer, G.	Chanticleer & the Fox
Berry, E.	Careers of Cynthia	Smith, F.H.	Charcoals of New & Old New York
Pyle, Kath.	Careless Jane	Bacheller, I.	Charge It
Beerbohm, M.	Caricatures of 25 Gentlemen	Wallace, Lew	Chariot Race of Ben-Hur
Frost, A.B.	Carlo	Raymond, W.	Charity Chance
Barnes, Nancy	Carlota	Pyle, Kath.	Charlemagne & his Knights
Merimee, P.	Carmen	Hawksley, E.D.	Charles Dickens Birthday Book
Harris, M.V.	Carnival Time	Lever, Chas.	Charles O'Malley...
Mills, W.J.	Caroline of Courtlandt Street	Palazzo, T.	Charley the Horse
Krauss, Ruth	Carrot Seed	Krauss, Ruth	Charlotte & White Horse
Latham, Jean L.	Carry On, Mr. Bowditch	White, E.B.	Charlotte's Web
Dobias, D.F.	Casey Joins the Circus	Porter, Rose	Charm of Birds
Hay, J.	Castilion Days	Futrelle, J.	Chase of the Golden Plate
Buchanan, T.	Castle Comedy	Bynner, E.L.	Chase of the Meteor...
Weyman, S.J.	Castle Inn	Seawell, M.E.	Chateau of Montplaisir
Bemelmans, L.	Castle Number Nine	Lansdale, M.	Chateaux of Touraine
Owen, Ruth	Castle in Silver Wood	Mighels, P.V.	Chatwit the Man-Talk Bird
Donahey, M.D.	Castle of Grumpy Grouch	Ford, P.L.	Checked Love Affair
Miltoun, F.	Castles & Chateaux of Touraine	Robinson, Gertrude	Chee-Chee's Brother
Coatsworth, E.	Cat & the Captain	Lau, Josephine	Cheeky: A Prairie Dog
Hader, B.& E.	Cat & the Kitten	Brown, Palmer	Cheerful
Bacon, P.	Cat Calls	Marks, J.	Cheerful Cricket...
Abdullah, Achmed	Cat Had Nine Lives	Gruelle, J.	Cheery Scarcrow
Pope, J.	Cat Scouts	Jones, Idwal	Chef's Holiday
Nesbit, E.	Cat Tales	Farjeon, E.	Cherrystones
Lockridge, Frances	Cat Who Rode Cows	Clymer, E.L.	Chester
Coatsworth, E.	Cat Who Went to Heaven	Seredy, K.	Chestry Oak
Campbell, Ruth	Cat Whose Whiskers Slipped	Moon, G.	Chi-Wee and Loki
Hurd, E.T.	Cat from Telegraph Hill	Scott, Sally	Chica
Seuss, Dr.	Cat in the Hat	Mitchell, E.	Chickabiddy Stories
Hoffmann, Eleanor	Cat of Paris	Williams, Garth	Chicken Book
Hecht, Ben	Cat that Jumped Out of the Story	N/A	Chicken Little & Little Half Chick
DeJong, Meindert	Cat that Walked a Week	Smith, E.B.	Chicken World
Byron, May	Cat's Cradle	Mukerji, D.G.	Chief of the Herd
Willett, Edward	Cat's Cradle Rhymes for Children	Magruder, Julia	Child Amy
Burgess, G.	Cat's Elegy	Weedon, L.L.	Child Characters from Dickens
Johnson, M.	Cat's Fairy Land...	Earle, A.M.	Child Life in Colonial Days
Ainslie, K.	Catharine Susan & Me Goes Abroad	Stein, E.	Child Songs of Cheer
Ainslie, K.	Catharine Susan & Me's Coming Out	Setoun, G.	Child World
Ainslie, K.	Catharine Susan in Hot Water	Pease, L.	Child You Used to Be
Ainslie, K.	Catharine Susan's Little Holiday	Baker, Edna D.	Child is Born

AUTHOR	TITLE	AUTHOR	TITLE
Spielmann, M.H.	Child of the Air	Lee, Frank H.	Children's King Arthur
Littlewood, S.R.	Child of the Sea	Longfellow, H.W.	Children's Longfellow
Haggard, H.R.	Child of the Storm	Martin, J.	Children's Munchausen
Banks, C.E.	Child of the Sun	Routledge, Wm.	Children's Musical Cinderella
Towers, Alton	Child's Aesop	Carson, Norma B.	Children's Own Story Book
Robinson, W.H.	Child's Arabian Nights	Gould, F.J.	Children's Plutarch
Skinner, A.M.	Child's Book of Country Stories	Hoffman, A.S.	Children's Shakespeare
Morris, Alice T.	Child's Book of Empire	Nesbit, E.	Children's Shakespeare
Skinner, A.M.	Child's Book of Modern Stories	Gomme, Alice B.	Children's Singing Games
Price, M.E.	Child's Book of Myths	Benoit, C.F.	Children's Stories that Never Grow Old
Smith, J.W.	Child's Book of Old Verses	Woolf, Rose	Children's Stories from Arabian Nights
Canton, Wm.	Child's Book of Saints	Kato, N. (tr.)	Children's Stories/Japanese Fairy Tales...
Coussens, P.W.	Child's Book of Stories	N/A	Children's Story Garden
Canton, Wm.	Child's Book of Warriors	Grierson, E.W.	Children's Tales/Scottish Ballads
Sharp, E.	Child's Christmas	Harris, J.C.	Children's Uncle Remus
De La Mare, W.	Child's Day	Brown, M.W.	Children's Year
Frank, Mabel L.	Child's Day in Song	Hutchinson, V.	Chimney Corner Fairy Tales
Manning, W.	Child's Dream of the Zoo	Daskein, Tarella	Chimney Town
Tomlins, W.	Child's Garden of Song	Stilwell, Alison	Chin Ling & Chinese Cricket
Stevenson, R.L.	Child's Garden of Verses	Blake, A.H.	China
Brown, M.W.	Child's Good Morning	Peto, Gladys	China Cow
Brown, M.W.	Child's Good Night Book	Headland, I.T.	Chinese Boy & Girl
Dearmer, M.	Child's Life of Christ	Terhune, Anice	Chinese Child's Day
Toogood, C.C.	Child's Prayer	Wiese, K.	Chinese Ink Stick
Herford, O.	Child's Primer of Natural History	Headland, I.T.	Chinese Mother Goose Rhymes
Irving, W.	Child's Rip Van Winkle	Perkins, L.F.	Chinese Twins
Peattie, D.C.	Child's Story of the World	Howard, A.W.	Ching-Li & the Dragons
Pyle, Kath.	Childhood	Tousey, S.	Chinky Joins the Circus
Sowerby, M.	Childhood	Tousey, S.	Chinky: Banker Pony
Watts, Isaac	Childhood Songs of Long Ago	Bower, B.M.	Chip of the Flying-U
N/A	Children All	Kjelgaard, J.A.	Chip the Dam Builder
MacPherson, J.F.	Children For Ever	Bellew, F.P.	Chip's Dogs
Colum, P.	Children Who Followed the Piper	Tileston, M.W.	Chiquita
N/A	Children at Play in Many Lands	Cabell, J.B.	Chivalry
Bartruse, G.	Children in Japan	Watson, H.B.M.	Chloris of the Island
Burke, Thos. (ed.)	Children in Verse	Adams, M.M.	Choir Visible
Lamprey, L.	Children of Ancient Britain	Burton, V.L.	Choo-Choo
Tucker, E.S.	Children of Colonial Days	Holling, H.C.	Choo-Me-Shoo
Crothers, S.M.	Children of Dickens	Averill, Naomi	Choochee: Story of an Eskimo Boy
Miller, E.C.	Children of Mountain Eagle	Faulkner, John	Chooky
Colum, P.	Children of Odin	Dalgliesh, A.	Choosing Book
Piper, W.	Children of Other Lands	Wasson, V.P.	Chosen Baby
Thomas, E.M.	Children of Spring	Petersham, M.	Christ Child
Peary, J.	Children of the Arctic	Lagerlof, Selma	Christ Legends
Williams, Herschel	Children of the Clouds	Rihbany, A.M.	Christ Story for Boys & Girls
Schwatka, Fred	Children of the Cold	Abbott, Lyman	Christ's Secret of Happiness
Buckley, E.F.	Children of the Dawn	Whyte, A.G.	Christabel's Fairyland
London, J.	Children of the Frost	Dalgliesh, A.	Christmas
Boston, Lucy	Children of the Green Knowe	Roosevelt, Eleanor	Christmas
Bailey, C.S.	Children of the Handcrafts	Pyle, Kath.	Christmas Angel
Mirza, Y.B.	Children of the Housetops	Sawyer, R.S.	Christmas Anna Angel
Marryat, Fred.	Children of the New Forest	Lipkind, Wm.	Christmas Bunny
Robinson, E.A.	Children of the Night	Duvoisin, R.	Christmas Cake
D'Aulaire, I.& E.	Children of the North Lights	N/A	Christmas Card
Humphrey, M.	Children of the Revolution	Dickens, C.	Christmas Carol
Bronson, W.S.	Children of the Sea	Peat, F.E.	Christmas Carols
Burglon, N.	Children of the Soil	Molesworth, M.	Christmas Child
Riis, J.A.	Children of the Tenements	Irving, W.	Christmas Day
Deming, T.O.	Children of the Wild	Irving, W.	Christmas Dinner
Stevens, Thos.	Children of the World from A to Z	Nast, Thomas	Christmas Drawings/Human Race
N/A	Children's Bible	Alcott, L.M.	Christmas Dream
LeBlanc, G.	Children's Blue Bird	Cooke, Alistair	Christmas Eve
Maeterlinck, M.	Children's Blue Bird	Lewis, Cecil D.	Christmas Eve
Scudder, Horace E.	Children's Book	Fox, John Jr.	Christmas Eve on Lonesome
Barker, C.M.	Children's Book of Hymns	Howells, W.D.	Christmas Every Day...
Bone, Gertrude	Children's Children	Jackson, Joseph	Christmas Flower
Elkin, R.H.	Children's Corner	Fatio, Louise	Christmas Forest
Cox, P.	Children's Funny Book	Turner, Thyra	Christmas House...
Rhys, Grace (ed.)	Children's Garland of Verse	Unknown	Christmas Letter

AUTHOR	TITLE	AUTHOR	TITLE
Tippett, James S.	Christmas Magic	Holling, H.C.	Claws of the Thunderbird
Sawyer, E.A.	Christmas Maker's Club	Weisgard, L.	Clean Pig
Locke, Wm. J.	Christmas Mystery	Meigs, C.	Clearing Weather
Kelly, Eric P.	Christmas Nightingale	Burnham, C.L.	Clever Betsy
Huntington, I.M.	Christmas Party for Santa Claus	Nicholson, Wm.	Clever Bill
Drinkwater, J.	Christmas Poems	Housman, L.	Cloak of Friendship
Hall, Wm.	Christmas Pony	Brooks, W.R.	Clockwork Twin
Foley, James W.	Christmas Prayer	Reade, C.	Cloister & Hearth
Veale, E.	Christmas Pudding	DeBosschere, J.	Closed Door
Burgess, T.	Christmas Reindeer	Barton, O.R.	Cloud Boat Stories
Lawson, L.	Christmas Roses	Wallis, I.H.	Cloud Kingdom
Bonte, W.	Christmas Stocking Rhymes	Douglas, A.M.	Clover's Princess
Dickens, C.	Christmas Stories from Dickens	Willson, Dixie	Clown Town
Mencken, H.L.	Christmas Story	Chesterton, G.K.	Club of Queer Trades
N/A	Christmas Story from Saint Mark	Howells, W.D.	Coast of Bohemia
DeBosschere, J.	Christmas Tales of Flanders	Chamberlain, Esth.	Coast of Chance
Field, E.	Christmas Tales/Christmas Verse	Cobb, I.	Cobb's Anatomy
Field, R.	Christmas Time	Cobb, I.	Cobb's Bill of Fare
Enright, E.	Christmas Tree for Lydia	Lefevre, F.	Cock, Mouse & Little Red Hen
Smith, Susan C.	Christmas Tree in the Woods	Hader, B.& E.	Cock-a-Doodle-Doo
Duvoisin, R.	Christmas Whale	Dearmer, M.	Cockyolly Bird
Irving, W.	Christmas at Bracebridge Hall	Hamp, S.F.	Coco Bolo
Brown, M.W.	Christmas in the Barn	Wells, Rhea	Coco the Goat
Nash, Ogden	Christmas that Almost Wasn't	Ehrlich, Bettina	Cocolo Comes to America
Molesworth, M.	Christmas-Tree Land	Ehrlich, Bettina	Cocolo's Home
Milne, A.A.	Christopher Robin Birthday Bk.	Sperry, A.	Coconut: Wonder Tree
Milne, A.A.	Christopher Robin Story Book	Hewes, A.D.	Codfish Musket
Milne, A.A.	Christopher Robin Verses	Disney, W.	Cold-Blooded Penguin
Christy, H.C.	Christy Girl	Seabrook, Katie	Colette & Baba in Timbuctoo
Thackeray, Wm.	Chronicle of the Drum	Kipling, R.	Collected Verse of...
Harris, J.C.	Chronicles of Aunt Minervy Ann	Goodloe, A.C.	College Girls
Montgomery, L.M.	Chronicles of Avonlea	Hall, E.G.	College on Horseback
Hume, F.	Chronicles of Fairy-Land	Smith, F.H.	Colonel Carter's Christmas
Cox, F.T.	Chronicles of Rhoda	Hughes, R.	Colonel Crockett's Cooperative Christmas
Cooke, E.V.	Chronicles of a Little Tot	Evers, Alf	Colonel's Squad
Plummer, M.W.	Chronicles of the Cid	Fesenden, L.D.	Colonial Dame
Kalnay, Francis	Chucaro, Wild Pony of Pampa	Earle, A.M.	Colonial Days in Old New York
Hader, B.& E.	Chuck-a-Luck & his Reindeer	Tittle, W.	Colonial Holidays
Hancock, H.I.	Chuggins	Chesterton, G.K.	Coloured Lands
Freeman, Don	Chuggy & Blue Caboose	Lathrop, D.	Colt from Moon Mountain
Pool, M.L.	Chums	Terhune, A.P.	Columbia Stories
Brown, E.P.	Ciderville Folks	Crane, W.	Columbia's Courtship
Elias, E. (ed.)	Cinderella	D'Aulaire, I.& E.	Columbus
Evans, C.S.	Cinderella	Dalgliesh, A.	Columbus Story
N/A	Cinderella	Serviss, G.P.	Columbus of Space
Perrault, C.	Cinderella	Farjeon, E.	Come Christmas
Parker, B.	Cinderella at the Zoo	De La Mare, W.	Come Hither
N/A	Cinderella's Picture Book	Disney, W.	Come Play with Donald Duck
Henry, M.	Cinnabar: One O'Clock Fox	Miller, O.B.	Come Play with Me
Hueffer, F.M.	Cinque Ports...	Disney, W.	Come Play with Mickey Mouse
Smith, E.B.	Circus & All About It	Woods, M.	Come Unto these Yellow Sands
Willson, Dixie	Circus ABC	Chalmers, Mary	Come for a Walk with Me
Petersham, M.	Circus Baby	Hope, A.	Comedies of Courtship
Hutchinson, V.	Circus Comes to Town	Goldsmith, O.	Comedies of...
Brett, Edna P.	Circus Day...	Shakespeare, Wm.	Comedy of the Twelfth Night
Sendak, Jack	Circus Girl	Cox, P.	Comic Yarns
Fenner, P.R.	Circus Parade	Kemble, E.W.	Comical Coons
Brown, Paul	Circus School	N/A	Comin' Thro the Rye
Streatfield, N.	Circus Shoes	Everson, Howard	Coming of the Dragon Ships
Conger, Marion	Circus Time	Mulford, C.	Coming of Cassidy
Randolph, Jane	Circus in Peter's Closet	Van Dyke, H.	Companionable Books
Finney, C.	Circus of Dr. Lao	Walton, Isaac	Complete Angler
Robinson, S.	City Child	Chaucer, G.	Complete Poetical Works of...
DeBosschere, J.	City Curious	Milton, J.	Comus
Flagg, J.M.	City People	Jewett, J.H.	Con the Wizard
Stables, Gordon	City at the Pole	Emanuel, W.	Conceited Puppy...
King, J.M.	City of the West	Herford, O.	Confessions of a Caricaturist
West, M.	Clair De Lune	Butler, E.P.	Confessions of a Daddy
Waugh, F.	Clan of Munes	Davis, R.H.	Congo & Coasts of Africa

AUTHOR	TITLE	AUTHOR	TITLE
McCutcheon, J.T.	Congressman Pumphrey	Tousey, S.	Cowboy Tommy
Chestnutt, Charles	Conjure Woman	James, Will	Cowboys North & South
White, S.E.	Conjuror's House	Tousey, S.	Cowboys of America
D'Aulaire, I.& E.	Conquest of the Atlantic	Stong, Phil	Cowhand Goes to Town
Crawford, M.	Constantinople	Molesworth, M.	Cozy Corner Stories
Van Millingen	Constantinople	Kramer, N. (ed.)	Cozy Hour Story Book
Vassos, R.	Contempo	Burnett, F.H.	Cozy Lion
Eustis, C.	Cooking in Old Creole Days	Jacberns, R.	Crab Cottage
Kemble, E.W.	Coon Alphabet	Lowell, Joan	Cradle of the Deep
Ambrose, B.A.	Coppa Hamba	Gaskell, Mrs.	Cranford
Munroe, K.	Copper Princess	Brown, Paul	Crazy Quilt
DeAngeli, M.	Copper-Toed Boots	Garnett, L.A.	Creature Songs
Gaze, H.	Coppertop	Colum, P.	Creatures
Baker, C.	Coquo & the King's Children	Gramatky, H.	Creeper's Jeep
N/A	Coridon's Song	Connolly, J.B.	Crested Seas
Rhoads, Dorothy	Corn Grows Ripe	Hader, B.& E.	Cricket
Hunt, M.L.	Corn-Belt Billy	Coatsworth, E.	Cricket & the Emperor's Son
Perkins, L.F.	Cornelia	Selden, George	Cricket in Times Square
Spyri, J.	Cornelli...	Chalmers, Patrick	Cricket in the Cage
Masson, T.	Corner In Women	Nash, Ogden	Cricket of Carador
Masson, T.	Corner in Women	Dickens, C.	Cricket on the Hearth
Todd, M.L.	Corona & Coronet	Ungerer, Tomi	Crictor
O'Brien, Jack	Corporal Corey	Hudson, C.	Crimson Conquest
Milhous, Kath.	Corporal Keeperupper	Carter, Russell	Crimson Cutlass
Ward, Mrs. H.	Coryston Family	Lang, A.	Crimson Fairy Book
Deming, T.O.	Cosel: With Geronimo on His Last Raid	Sherman, S.	Critical Woodcuts
Earle, A.M.	Costumes of Colonial Times	Simon, Ellen	Critter Book
Joan, Natalie	Cosy-Time Tales	Berlic-Mazuranic	Croation Tales of Long Ago
Drinkwater, J.	Cotswold Characters	Baring-Gould, S.	Crock of Gold
Van Stockum, H.	Cottage at Bantry Bay	Stephens, J.	Crock of Gold
Burns, Rbt.	Cotter's Saturday Night	Deutsch, B. (tr.)	Crocodile
Beckenbaugh, G.	Cotton Tails	Mother Goose	Crooked Man
Housman, L.	Cotton Woolleena	Remington, F.	Crooked Trails
Lenski, L.	Cotton in My Sack	De La Mare, W.	Crossings...
Ingraham, C.	Cottontail & Wishing-Fairy	Yashima, Taro	Crow Boy
Schwartz, Eliz. R.	Cottontail Rabbit	Sheldon, Chas.	Crucifixion of Philip Strong
MacDonald, Greville	Count Billy	Woodhouse, S.C.	Crude Ditties
Dumas, A.	Count of Monte Cristo	Layard, George S.	Cruikshank's Portraits of Himself
Pyle, Kath.	Counterpane Fairy	Grego, J.	Cruikshank's Water Colours
Rowland, H.	Countess Diane	Stoddard, C.W.	Cruise Under the Crescent
Crissey, F.	Country Boy	Jerrold, A.	Cruise in the Acorn
Heyward, DuBose	Country Bunny & Little Gold Shoes	Bullen, F.T.	Cruise of the Cachalot
Lawson, R.	Country Colic	Langer, S.K.	Cruise of the Little Dipper
Disney, W.	Country Cousin	London, J.	Cruise of the Snark
Dyer, W.A.	Country Cousins	Sargant, Alice	Crystal Ball
Leighton, C.	Country Matters	Rowe, Nellie	Crystal Locket
Coatsworth, E.	Country Neighborhood	Manners, R.	Cuba & other Verse
Brown, M.W.	Country Noisy Book	Davis, R.H.	Cuba in War Time
DuChaillu, Paul	Country of the Dwarfs	Burgess, T.	Cubby Finds an Open Door
Bailey, C.S.	Country-Stop	Lyall, M.M.	Cubies' ABC
Fox, F.M.	County Christmas	Lida	Cuckoo
Tudor, T.	County Fair	Burglon, N.	Cuckoo Calls
Dalgliesh, A.	Courage of Sarah Noble	Molesworth, M.	Cuckoo Clock
Finger, C.J.	Courageous Companions	Hinkson, K.T.	Cuckoo Songs
Baker, C.	Court Jester	Tucker, E.S.	Cup of Tea
White, W.A.	Court of Boyville	Gates, Eleanor	Cupid the Cowpunch
Drayton, Michael	Court of Faery	Herford, O.	Cupid's Almanac
Frost, W.H.	Court of King Arthur	Clay/Herford	Cupid's Cyclopedia
Longfellow, H.W.	Courtship of Miles Standish	Brown, A.F.	Curious Book of Birds
Martin, E.S.	Cousin Anthony & I	McIlwraith, J.N.	Curious Career of Roderick Campbell
Newberry, C.T.	Cousin Toby	Thompson, R.P.	Curious Cruise of Captain Santa
Sackett, Rose M.	Cousin from Clare	Rey, H.A.	Curious George
Meigs, C.	Covered Bridge	Cook, Bernadine	Curious Little Kitten
James, Will	Cow Country	Sorensen, Virginia	Curious Missie
MacKay, M.	Cow Range & Hunting Trail	Earle, A.M.	Curious Punishments...
Courlander, H.	Cow-Tail Switch	Lindsey, Wm.	Curtain of Forgetfulness
Thompson, R.P.	Cowardly Lion of Oz	Freeman, Don	Cyrano the Crow
Carr, R.V.	Cowboy Lyrics	D'Aulnoy	D'Aulnoy's Fairy Tales
Lenski, L.	Cowboy Small	Wain, L.	Daddy Cat

AUTHOR	TITLE	AUTHOR	TITLE
Ewing, J.H.	Daddy Darwin's Dovecoat	Brown, M.W.	David's Little Indian
Merryman, M.P.	Daddy Domino	Jones, E.O.	David: Bible Story with Pictures
Hankins, Maude M.	Daddy Gander	Rourke, C.	Davy Crockett
Mason, Francis E.	Daddy Gander	Tousey, S.	Davy Crockett
Harris, J.C.	Daddy Jake the Runaway	Norwood, Edwin P.	Davy Winkle in Circusland
Webster, J.	Daddy Long Legs	Knowles, R.E.	Dawn at Shanty Bay
O'Day, James	Daddy Long Legs Fun Songs	Burnett, F.H.	Dawn of To-Morrow
Stuart, Ruth M.	Daddy'Do-Funny's Wisdom Jingles	Rowand, Phyllis	Day After Yesterday
Bonner, M.G.	Daddy's Bedtime Fairy Stories	Smith, F.H.	Day at Laguerre's...
LeMair, H.W.	Daddy's Little Rhyme Book	Foster, M.B.	Day in a Child's Life
Brown, Paul	Daffy Taffy	Lowrey, J.S.	Day in the Jungle
Sowerby, Githa	Dainty Book	Brown, Alice	Day of His Youth
N/A	Daisy Days	McCutcheon, G.B.	Day of the Dog
Denton, C.J.	Daisy Dells	Van Stockum, H.	Day on Skates
James, Henry	Daisy Miller	Endres, Ernest	Day with The Gnomes
Ruskin, John (ed.)	Dame Wiggin of Lee	Cowan, James	Daybreak...
Rives, A.	Damsel Errant	Van Dyke, H.	Days Off
Charlot, J.	Dance of Death	Dyer, R.O.	Daytime Story Book
Choate, F.	Dance of the Hours	Childs, M.F.	De Namin ob De Twins
Disney, W.	Dance of the Hours	Greene, S.P.M.	Deacon Lysander
Monroe, H.	Dance of the Seasons	Brown, M.W.	Dead Bird
Kinney, T.& M.	Dance: Its Place in Art & Life	Kipling, R.	Dead King
Buff, Mary	Dancing Cloud	Morris, F.	Deal in Wheat...
Farr, Florence	Dancing Faun	MacDonald, Geo.	Dealings with Fairies
Coatsworth, E.	Dancing Tom	Zion, Gene	Dear Garbage Man
Eichenberg, Fritz	Dancing in the Moon	Haslewood, C.	Dear Old Nursery Rhymes
Chabot, Adrien	Dancing-Master	Crosby, P.	Dear Sooky
Bingham, C.	Dandy Lion	Lippmann, J.M.	Dearie Dot/The Dog
N/A	Dandy-Andy Book	N/A	Death & Burial of Poor Cock Robin
Averill, Esther	Daniel Boone	Malory, T.	Death of King Arthur
Daugherty, J.	Daniel Boone	Herford, O.	Deb's Dictionary
Tousey, S.	Daniel Boone	Wilkins, M.E.	Decorative Plaques
White, S.E.	Daniel Boone	Moore, N.H.	Deeds of Daring...
N/A	Daniel in the Lion's Den	McMahon, J.	Deenie Folks/Friends of Theirs
Stroebe, C. (ed.)	Danish Fairy Book	Burglon, N.	Deep Silver
Andersen, H.C.	Danish Fairy Tales	Anderson, C.W.	Deep Through the Heart
Gillilan, S.	Danny & Fanny	Swan, O.	Deep Water Days
Held, John	Danny Decoy	Jewett, S.O.	Deephaven
Henderson, D.	Danny the Dream Man	Riley, J.W.	Defective Santa Claus
Davis, L.R.	Danny's Luck	Morris, Wm.	Defense of Guenevere
Marquis, Don	Danny's Own Story	Kelly, F.	Delafield Affair
Nesbit, E.	Daphne of Fitzroy Street	Russell, R.H.	Delft Cat
Thornley (tr.)	Daphnis & Chloe	Dooley, Mrs.	Dem Good Ole Times
Baum, L.F.	Daring Twins	Fenner, P.R.	Demons & Dervishes
Hawes, C.B.	Dark Frigate	Graham, H.	Deportmental Ditties
James, Will	Dark Horse	Coatsworth, E.	Desert Dan
Malkus, A.S.	Dark Star of Itza	Doyle, A.C.	Desert Drama
Brown, M.W.	Dark Wood of the Golden Birds	Grey, Zane	Desert Gold
McCullough, J.G.	Dark is Dark	De La Mare, W.	Desert Islands & Robinson Crusoe
Buff, Mary	Dash and Dart	Goldsmith, O.	Deserted Village
McCutcheon, G.B.	Daughter of Anderson Crow	Rhodes, E.M.	Desire of the Moth
Crowley, Mary C.	Daughter of New France	Nuckel, O.	Destiny...
Raine, W.M.	Daughter of Raasay	Boyle, V.F.	Devil Tales
Moon, G.	Daughter of Thunder	Corelli, M.	Devil's Motor
Hodder, W.R.	Daughter of the Dawn	Hurd, E.T.	Devil's Tail
Porter, G.S.	Daughter of the Land	Aubrey, Frank	Devil-Tree of El Dorado
Rankin, L.S.	Daughter of the Mountains	Wilson, A.E.	Devota
Waller, M.E.	Daughter of the Rich	Sowers, P.A.	Dhan of the Pearl Country
Eaton, J.	Daughter of the Seine	N/A	Diamond Fairy Book
King, C.	Daughter of the Sioux	Wesselhoeft, Lily	Diamond King....
London, J.	Daughter of the Snows	Cramer, M.	Diamond Princess
Crary, M.	Daughter of the Stars	N/A	Diamonds & Toads
Staunton, S.	Daughters of Destiny	Lebeck, O.	Diary of Terwilliger Jellico
Dalgliesh, A.	Davenports & Cherry Pie	Dow, E.C.	Diary of a Birthday Doll
Dalgliesh, A.	Davenports are at Dinner	Wiggin, K.D.	Diary of a Goose Girl
Stevenson, R.L.	David Balfour	Dunham, E.	Diary of a Mouse
Dickens, C.	David Copperfield	Tousey, S.	Dick & the Canal Boat
Totheroh, D.	David Hotfoot	N/A	Dick Whittington & his Cat
Bergengren, R.W.	David the Dreamer	Dickens, C.	Dickens' Children

AUTHOR	TITLE	AUTHOR	TITLE
Prentiss, L.E.	Dickens' Year Book	Disney, W.	Donald Duck [ALL TITLES]
Woodruff, E.	Dickey Bird	Peedie, J.M.	Donald in Numberland
McNeil, E.	Dickon Bend-The-Bow	Disney, W.	Donald's Lucky Day
Kidd, Will	Dickydidos	Disney, W.	Donald's Penguin
Pyrnelle, L.C.	Diddie, Dumps & Tot	Remington, F.	Done in the Open
Everson, Dale	Different Dog	MacManus, Seumas	Donegal Fairy Stories
Brown, M.W.	Diggers	Ratzesberger, A.	Donkey Beads
Morris, A.A.	Digging in Yucatan	Bulla, Clyde R.	Donkey Cart
Henry, M.	Dilly-Dally Sally	Bemelmans, L.	Donkey Inside
Hader, B.& E.	Ding Dong Bell	Duvoisin, R.	Donkey-Donkey
Young, Percy	Ding Dong Bell	Dowd, E.	Doodles
Campbell, Lang	Dinky Ducklings	Morris, Wm.	Doom of King Acrisius
Slobodkin, L.	Dinny & Danny	DeAngeli, M.	Door in the Wall
DeJong, Meindert	Dirk's Dog Bello	Coatsworth, E.	Door to the North
Hudson, W.H.	Disappointed Squirrel	Richardson, E.	Doors...
Thurston, C.B.	Discontented Stuffed Cat	Housman, L.	Doorway in Fairyland
Riley, J.W.	Discouraging Model	Disney, W.	Dopey: He Don't Talk None
Lang, A.	Disentanglers	Spyri, J.	Dora
Phillpotts, E.	Dish of Apples	Tudor, T.	Dorcas Porcas
Mowbray, John	Dismal Jimmy of the Fourth	Howard, Eliz.	Dorinda
Lamb, C.	Dissertation Upon a Roast Pig	Marc, E.	Doris & David All Alone
Crawford, F.M.	Diva's Ruby	Smith, G.	Doris & Julie
Cowper, Wm.	Diverting History of John Gilpin	Atwater, R.	Doris & the Trolls
Watts, Isaac	Divine & Moral Songs for Children	Baum, L.F.	Dorothy & Wizard of Oz
Ralph, J.	Dixie...	Holmes, O.W.	Dorothy Q.
Smalley, J.	Do You Know about Fishes?	Major, C.	Dorothy Vernon of Haddon Hall
Smalley, J.	Do You Know?	Goldsmith, Milton	Dorothy's Dolls...
Skinner, C.M.	Do-Nothing Days	Calhoun, M.E.	Dorothy's Rabbit Stories
Shannon, Monica	Dobry	Carleton, K.	Dorothy/Motor Girl
Sawyer, R.S.	Doctor Danny	Baum, L.F.	Dot & Tot in Merryland
Cable, G.W.	Doctor Seiver	Clayton, John	Dot in Dreamland
MacLaren, Ian	Doctor of the Old School	Norris, June	Dotzie the Dancey Duck
Fischer, Marj.	Dog Cantbark	Hunt, M.L.	Double Birthday Present
Emanuel, W.	Dog Day	Twain, M.	Double-Barrelled Detective Story
Black, I.S.	Dog Doctor	Wheeler, Candace	Doubledarling & Dreamspinner
Finger, C.J.	Dog at His Heel	Gorey, Edward	Doubtful Guest
Lathrop, D.	Dog in the Tapestry Garden	Alger, Leclaire	Dougal's Wish
Selden, George	Dog that Could Swim Underwater	Yonge, C.M.	Dove in the Eagle's Nest
Twain, M.	Dog's Tale	Price, M.E.	Down Comes the Wilderness
Heal, Edith	Dogie Boy	Cloud, V.W.	Down Durley Land
Terhune, A.P.	Dogs	Thwaites, R.G.	Down Historic Waterways
Aldin, C.	Dogs of Character	Gaggin, E.R.	Down Ryton Water
Downey, Fairfax	Dogs of Destiny	Eickemeyer, R.	Down South
Emanuel, W.	Dogs of War	Donahey, M.D.	Down Spider Web Lane
Cooke, G.M.	Doings of the Dollivers	Kellock, Harold	Down in the Grass
Howard, H.	Doings of the Dollymites	Bates, H.E.	Down the River
Bates, Clara D.	Doll Rosy's Days	Colmont, Marie	Down the River
Tregarthen, Enys	Doll Who Came Alive	Donahey, Wm.	Down the River with the Teenie Weenies
Bianco, P.	Doll in the Window	Credle, Ellis	Down, Down the Mountain
Tudor, T.	Doll's Christmas	De La Mare, W.	Down-Adown-Derry
Godden, Rumer	Doll's House	Snedeker, C.D.	Downright Dencey
Hunter, Richard	Dollies	Sears, P.M.	Downy Woodpecker
Pease, L.	Dollies in Happy-Land	Chalmers, Patrick	Dozen Dogs or So
Gordon, Eliz.	Dolly & Molly at Seashore	Lofting, H.	Dr. Dolittle [ALL TITLES]
Gordon, Eliz.	Dolly & Molly at the Circus	Stevenson, R.L.	Dr. Jekyll & Mr. Hyde
Herbertson, A.	Dolly Book	Deland, M.	Dr. Lavendar's People
Hawkins, A.H.	Dolly Dialogues	Hinkle, T.C.	Dr. Rabbit & Ki-Yi Coyote
Hope, A.	Dolly Dialogues	Malkus, A.S.	Dragon Fly of Zuni
Wiederseim, G.	Dolly Drake	Lawson, Marie A.	Dragon John
Peck, Leigh	Don Coyote	Dawson, Carley	Dragon Run
Byron	Don Juan	Wister, O.	Dragon of Wantley
Parrish, R.	Don MacGrath	Gannett, R.S.	Dragons of Blueland
Cervantes	Don Quixote	Barnes, James	Drake & his Yeomen
Hughes, Rich. A.	Don't Blame Me!	Newbolt, H.	Drake's Drum...
D'Aulaire, I.& E.	Don't Count Your Chicks	Rogers, Cameron	Drake's Quest
Brown, M.W.	Don't Frighten the Lion	Browning, R.	Dramatis Personae...
Morley, C.	Don't Open Until Christmas	Brown, Paul	Draw Horses: It's Fun & Easy
Hawkins, Q.	Don't Run, Apple!	Christy, H.C.	Drawings
Grey, Zane	Don: Story of Lion Dog	Gibson, C.D.	Drawings

AUTHOR	TITLE	AUTHOR	TITLE
Remington, F.	Drawings	Stevenson, R.L.	Ebb-Tide
Shay, F.	Drawn from the Wood	N/A	Ecclesiasticus...
Beerbohm, M.	Dreadful Dragon of Hay Hill	Peattie, E.W.	Edda & the Oak
Hobbes, J.O.	Dream & the Business	Gruelle, J.	Eddie Elephant
Haldane, W.A.	Dream Bag	Tudor, T.	Edgar Allan Crow
Higgins, A.C.	Dream Blocks	Wahn, J.& G.	Edgar, Runaway Elephant
Walker, D.S.	Dream Boats	Stong, Phil	Edgar: The 7:58
Brown, M.W.	Dream Book	Horton, George	Edge of Hazard
Parrish, A.& D.	Dream Coach	Fullylove, J.	Edinburgh
Grahame, K.	Dream Days	Burnett, F.H.	Editha's Burglar
Sefton, H.L.	Dream Imp & Others	Dulac, E.	Edmund Dulac's Fairy Book
Hughes, Langston	Dream Keeper	Gibson, C.D.	Education of Mr. Pipp
Sackville, M.	Dream Pedlar	Austin, Cyril F.	Edward Buttoneye & his Advens.
Tennyson, A.	Dream of Fair Women	Lawson, R.	Edward, Hoppy & Joe
Arthur, Lady	Dream of Little Hazy Cream	Lucas, E.V.	Edwin A. Abbey
Queen Marie	Dreamer of Dreams	Armour, M. (ed.)	Eerie Book
Bangs, J.K.	Dreamers, A Club	Austin, Margot	Effelli
Lippmann, J.M.	Dreamland	Gilbert, P.T.	Egbert & his Marvelous Adventures
Millar, H.R.	Dreamland Express	Milhous, Kath.	Egg Tree
Ault, N.	Dreamland Shores	Kelly, R.T.	Egypt
Woodward, C.S.	Dreams & Fables	Jewett, E.M.	Egyptian Tales of Magic
Steig, Wm.	Dreams of Glory	Alcott, L.M.	Eight Cousins
Charlip, R.	Dress Up & Let's Have a Party	Gibson, C.D.	Eighty Drawings including Weaker Sex
James, Will	Drifting Cowboy	MacDonald, Zillah	Eileen's Adventures in Wonderland
Howlett, E.	Driving Lessons	Perez, Luis	El Coyote the Rebel
N/A	Droll Doings	Waters, R.J.	El Estranjero
Mitchell, J.A.	Drowsy	Gray, T.	Elegy in a Country Church Yard
Petry, Ann	Drugstore Cat	Goldsmith, O.	Elegy of the Glory of Her Sex...
Fortesque, J.W.	Drummer's Coat	Ingraham, C.	Elephant & Wishing Fairy
Boyd, J.	Drums	Schlein, M.	Elephant Herd
Bontemps, A.	Drums at Dusk	Hogan, Inez	Elephant Twins
Sterne, Emma G.	Drums of Monmouth	Van Loon, H.W.	Elephant Up a Tree
Cooke, M.B.	Dual Alliance	Morris, Alice T.	Elephant's Apology
Lear, E.	Duck & the Kangaroo	Kipling, R.	Elephant's Child
Muter, Gladys N.	Duck's Adventure	Aristophanes	Eleven Comedies
Wiederseim, G.	Ducky Daddles	Beskow, E.	Elf Children of the Woods
Toon, G.E.	Ducky Dee	Halkett, S.	Elf King's Flowers
Petersen, H.	Dulcibel	Buff, M. & C.	Elf Owl
Raiker, A.M.	Dulcibella & the Fairies	O'Neill, M.	Elf-Errant
Sedgwick, Anne D.	Dull Miss Archinard	Norman	Elfin Rhymes
Dumas, A.	Dumas Fairy Tale Book	Harrison, F.	Elfin Song
Brenner, Anita	Dumb Juan & the Bandits	Pollard, J.	Elfin-Land
Disney, W.	Dumbo of the Circus	DeAngeli, M.	Elin's Amerika
Black, I.S.	Dusty & his Friends	DuBois, W.P.	Elisabeth the Cow Ghost
Baker, O.	Dusty Star	Field, R.	Eliza & the Elves
De La Mare, W.	Dutch Cheese	Rey, H.A.	Elizabite
Terhune, Anice	Dutch Ditties for Children	Wiese, K.	Ella the Elephant
Robbins, Louis	Dutch Doll Ditties	Gannett, R.S.	Elmer & the Dragon
Perkins, L.F.	Dutch Twins	Gilbert, P.T.	Elmer Buys a Circus
Hauff, Wilhelm	Dwarf Long-Nose	Disney, W.	Elmer Elephant
Underhill (ed.)	Dwarf's Tailor...	Thompson, Kay	Eloise
King, J.M.	Dwellings/Old World Town	Thompson, Kay	Eloise in Moscow
Farrow, G.E.	Dwindleberry Zoo	Thompson, Kay	Eloise in Paris
Gall, Alice	Each in his Way	Sawyer, E.A.	Elsa's Gift Home
Cabell, J.B.	Eagle's Shadow	Turner, Josie	Elsie Dinsmore on the Loose
Gaggin, E.R.	Ear for Uncle Emil	Werner, Jane	Elves & Fairies
Taylor, Una	Early Italian Love Stories	Darwin, Bernard	Elves & Princes
Smith, E.B.	Early Life of Mr. Man...	Bangs, J.K.	Emblemland
Sandburg, C.	Early Moon	Baum, L.F.	Emerald City of Oz
Morris, Wm.	Early Poems of...	Cary, E.L.	Emerson, Poet & Thinker
N/A	Early Work of Aubrey Beardsley	Kastner, Erich	Emil & the Detectives
A.E.	Earth Breath	Kastner, Erich	Emil & the Three Twins
Roberts, C.G.D.	Earth's Enigmas	Ungerer, Tomi	Emile
Kipling, R.	East of Suez	Montgomery, L.M.	Emily Climbs
Asbjornsen, P.C.	East of the Sun & West of the Moon	Montgomery, L.M.	Emily of New Moon
Friedrich, Priscilla	Easter Bunny that Overslept	Montgomery, L.M.	Emily's Quest
Lenski, L.	Easter Rabbit's Parade	Austen, J.	Emma
Duvoisin, R.	Easter Treat	Stolz, Mary S.	Emmett's Pig
Atkey, B.	Easy Money	Means, F.C.	Emmy & the Blue Door

AUTHOR	TITLE	AUTHOR	TITLE
Glendon, George	Emperor of the Air	Twain, M.	Extracts from Adam's Diary
Whishaw, F.	Emperor's Englishman	Shannon, Monica	Eyes for the Dark
Andersen, H.C.	Emperor's New Clothes	Garner, Elvira	Ezekiel
Marshall, H.E.	Empire Story	Pratt, L.	Ezekiel Expands
Willson, Dixie	Empty Elephant	Garner, Elvira	Ezekiel Travels
Dalgliesh, A.	Enchanted Book	Barrows, M.	Ezra the Elephant
Lummis, C.F.	Enchanted Burro	Stevenson, R.L.	Fables
Moore, Colleen	Enchanted Castle	Carryl, G.W.	Fables for the Frivolous
Nesbit, E.	Enchanted Castle	Bourke, S.T.E.	Fables in Feathers
Bowen, W.A.	Enchanted Forest	LaFontaine, J.	Fables in Rhyme for Little Folks
Outhwaite, G.	Enchanted Forest	Aesopus	Fables of Aesop
Molesworth, M.	Enchanted Garden: Fairy Stories	LaFontaine, J.	Fables of Jean De La Fontaine
Baum, L.F.	Enchanted Island of Yew	Brown, M.W. (ed.)	Fables of La Fontaine
Chisholm, L.	Enchanted Land	LaFontaine, J.	Fables of La Fontaine
Brown, J.	Enchanted Peacock	Dix, D.	Fables of the Elite
Sawyer, R.S.	Enchanted Schoolhouse	Fabre	Fabre's Book of Insects
Bangs, J.K.	Enchanted Typewriter	Stawell, R. (ed.)	Fabre's Book of Insects
Hamer, S.H.	Enchanted Wood	Lawson, R.	Fabulous Flight
Price, M.E.	Enchantment Tales for Children	St. John, J.A.	Face in the Pool
Barlow, J.	End of Elfintown	Sholl, A.	Faery Tales of Weir
Higgins, V.M.	Endless Story	Lederer, J.	Fafan in China
Hurd, E.T.	Engine, Engine No. 9	Gray, Eliz. J.	Fair Adventure
Hartland, Edwin	English Fairy & Folk Tales	Coatsworth, E.	Fair American
Rhys, E. (ed.)	English Fairy Book	Fisher, H.	Fair Americans
Jacobs, J.	English Fairy Tales	Vernede, R.E.	Fair Dominion
Rhys, E. (ed.)	English Fairy Tales	Gwynn, S.L.	Fair Hills of Ireland
Steele, F.A.	English Fairy Tales	Freeman, M.E.	Fair Lavina...
James, Henry	English Hours	N/A	Fair Women from Vogue
Broadwood, Lucy	English Nursery Rhymes	Farjeon, E.	Fair of St. James
Greenaway, K.	English Spelling Book	Sherwood, M.	Fairchild Family
Kinglake, A.W.	Eothen	Fyleman, R.	Fairies & Chimneys
Bryant, S.C.	Epaminondas & his Auntie	Gask, Lilian	Fairies & Christmas Child
Egan, Constance	Epaminondas & the Lettuces	Eastwick, I.O.	Fairies & Suchlike
Egan, Constance	Epaminondas & the Puppy	Gask, Lilian	Fairies & the Christmas Child
Egan, Constance	Epaminondas Helps in the Garden	Molesworth, M.	Fairies Afield
Cox, F.T.	Epic of Ebenezer	Stawell, Mrs. R.	Fairies I Have Met
Unknown	Eric Prince of Lorlonia	Anthony, E. & J.	Fairies Up-to-Date
Farrow, G.E.	Escape of the Mullingong	Molesworth, M.	Fairies of Sorts
Snell, Roy	Eskimo Island & Penguin Land	Cain, Neville	Fairies' Circus
DeMontaigne	Essays	Cesaresco, E.	Fairies' Fountain
Lamb, C.	Essays of Elia	Cain, Neville	Fairies' Menagerie
Butt, G.	Esther...	MacKinstry, E.	Fairy Alphabet
Andrews, M.S.	Eternal Masculine	Craik, D.	Fairy Book
Benton, T.H.	Europe After 8:15	Rackham, A.	Fairy Book
Decker, K.	Evangelina Cisneros	Potter, B.	Fairy Caravan
Longfellow, H.W.	Evangeline	Spofford, H.P.	Fairy Changeling
Carlson, N.S.	Evangeline, Pigeon of Paris	Lathrop, D.	Fairy Circus
Twain, M.	Eve's Diary	Hughes, Rupert	Fairy Detective
Spyri, J.	Eveli	Godden, Rumer	Fairy Doll
Burney, Fanny	Evelina...	MacDonald, Geo.	Fairy Fleet
Lee, E.D.	Ever Living Fairy Tales	Campbell, A.M.	Fairy Flights in Cloudland
Green, M.M.	Everybody Eats	Newman, I.	Fairy Flowers
Green, M.M.	Everybody has a House	Comstock, E.B.	Fairy Frolics
Egan, M.F.	Everybody's Saint Francis	Dulac, E.	Fairy Garland
Knipe, A.A.	Everybody's Washington	Rhys, Grace (ed.)	Fairy Gifts
Dodge, Louis	Everychild	Leamy, Edmund	Fairy Minstrel of Glenmalure
Chapin, A.A.	Everyday & Nowaday Fairy Book	Richards, L.E.	Fairy Operettas
Woodward, H.	Everyday Children	Fyleman, R.	Fairy Queen
Chapin, A.A.	Everyday Fairy Book	N/A	Fairy Ship
Newbery, F.E.	Everyday Honor	Artzybasheff, B.	Fairy Shoemaker
Gibson, C.D.	Everyday People	Mendes, C.	Fairy Spinning Wheel
N/A	Everyman & other Plays	Blakeley, E.S.	Fairy Starlight
Eberle, I.	Evie & Cooky	Andersen, H.C.	Fairy Stories
Eberle, I.	Evie & Wonderful Kangaroo	Shimer, E.D.	Fairy Stories...
Ruding, W.	Evil Motherhood	Ponset, Marie	Fairy Tale Book
Eastman, Charlotte	Evolution of Dodd's Sister	N/A	Fairy Tale Omnibus
Burton, Earl	Exciting Adventures of Waldo	Watson, N.D.	Fairy Tale Picture Book
Maxwell, D.	Excursions in Color	Larned, W.T.	Fairy Tales From France
Herford, O.	Excuse it Please	Catrevas, C.	Fairy Tales for Little People

AUTHOR	TITLE	AUTHOR	TITLE
Mutt, E.	Fairy Tales from Baltic Shores	Minarik, E.H.	Father Bear Comes Home
Brentano, C.M.	Fairy Tales from Brentano	Baum, L.F.	Father Goose's Yearbook
Christie, E.R.	Fairy Tales from England	Baum, L.F.	Father Goose: His Book
Pyle, Kath.	Fairy Tales from Far & Near	Jackson, H.H.	Father Junipero...
Quiller-Couch, A.	Fairy Tales from Far & Near	N/A	Father Tuck's Bird ABC
Christie, E.R.	Fairy Tales from Finland	Gardiner, A.	Father's Gone A-Whaling
Williams, W.H.	Fairy Tales from Folk Lore	Goethe	Faust
Pyle, Kath.	Fairy Tales from India	Salten, Felix	Favorite Animal Stories
Pyle, Kath.	Fairy Tales from Many Lands	Andersen, H.C.	Favorite Fairy Tales
Martens, F.	Fairy Tales from Orient	N/A	Favorite Fairy Tales
Djurklou, Baron G.	Fairy Tales from Sweedish	Osbourne, M. (ed.)	Favorite Fairy Tales
Asbjornsen, P.C.	Fairy Tales from the Far North	Grimm Bros.	Favorite Fairy Tales told in Germany
N/A	Fairy Tales in Other Lands	Douglas, B.	Favorite French Fairy Tales
Dulac, E.	Fairy Tales of Allied Nations	Mother Goose	Favorite Nursery Rhymes
Curtin, J.S.	Fairy Tales of Eastern Europe	Tucker, E.S.	Favorite Pets
Gianakoulis, T.P.	Fairy Tales of Modern Greece	Harris, A.V.	Favorites from Fairyland
Stephan, A.C.	Fairy Tales of a Parrot	N/A	Favourite Fairy Tales
Andersen, H.C.	Fairy Tales, Stories & Legends	Root, Charlet	Feast of Lamps
Dixon, E. (ed.)	Fairy Tales from Arabian Nights	Olds, Eliz.	Feather Mountain
N/A	Fairy Tales from Arabian Nights	Barker, Mrs. S.	Feathered & Four-Footed Friends
Fryer, Alfred C.	Fairy Tales/Harz Mountains	Martineau, H.	Feats on the Fiord
Westerman, J.M.E.	Fairy Tales/Wonderland	Molesworth, M.	February Boys
Kay, G.A.	Fairy Who Believed in Human Beings	Palazzo, T.	Federico the Flying Squirrel
Stawell, Mrs. R.	Fairy of Old Spain...	Brown, Marcia	Felice
Carr, A.V.	Fairy of the Rhone	Long, J.L.	Felice
Wesselhoeft, Lily	Fairy-Folk of Blue Hill	Laughlin, C.E.	Felicity
Rhys, E. (ed.)	Fairy-Gold	Howells, W.D.	Fennel & Rue
Horwitz, C.N.	Fairy-Lure	Leaf, M.	Ferdinand the Bull
Outhwaite, I.	Fairyland	Hankins, Maude M.	Fermentations of Eliza
N/A	Faithful Friends	Bishop, C.H.	Ferryman
Coblentz, C.C.	Falcon of Eric the Red	Cobb, I.	Fibble, D.D.
Willard, C.D.	Fall of Ulysses	Lefevre, F.	Fiddle Diddle Dee
Dixon, Thomas	Fall of a Nation	Adrian, M.	Fiddler Crab
Armour, M.	Fall of the Nibelungs	Nathan, Rbt.	Fiddler in Barly
Granville, A.	Fallen Race	Wiederseim, G.	Fido
Lorimer, G.H.	False Gods	Hawkes, Clarence	Field & Forest Friends
Carlson, N.S.	Family Under the Bridge	Housman, L.	Field of Clover
Oxley, J.M.	Family on Wheels	Armstrong, M.	Fieldbook of Western Wilderness
N/A	Famous Animal Tales	Mukerji, D.G.	Fierce Face
N/A	Famous Love Songs	Oxley, J.M.	Fife & Drum in Louisburg
Piper, W. (ed.)	Famous Rhymes of Mother Goose	Bemelmans, L.	Fifi
Francoise	Fanchette & Jeannot	Dixon, Charles	Fifteen Hundred Miles an Hour
Stockton, Frank	Fanciful Tales	Asbjornsen, P.C.	Fifteen Norse Tales
Holt, Ardern	Fancy Dresses Described	Sousa, J.P.	Fifth String
Taylor, Deems	Fantasia	McGovern, Mary H.	Fifty Famous Fairy Tales
Macauley, C.R.	Fantasma Land	Graham, Mary N.	Fifty Songs for Boys & Girls
Philbrook, Eliz.	Far From Marlborough Street	Disney, W.	Figaro and Cleo
Carryl, G.W.	Far from Maddening Girls	Gower, M.L.	Fighting Six
Moon, G.	Far-Away Desert	Otis, James	Fighting for the Empire
Hurd, E.T.	Faraway Christmas	Perkins, L.F.	Filipino Twins
Handforth, T.	Faraway Meadow	Tracy, Louis	Final War
Copeland, W.	Farm Book	Lipkind, Wm.	Finders Keepers
Stong, Phil	Farm Boy...	Hunt, Enid	Fine Lady Upon a White Horse
Jackson, K.& B.	Farm Stories	Poulsson, E.	Finger Plays for Nursery & Kindergarten
Housman, L.	Farm in Fairyland	Barbour, R.H.	Finkler's Field
Horn, M.D.	Farm on the Hill	Bailey, C.S.	Finnigan II - His Nine Lives
Wilder, L.I.	Farmer Boy	Andersen, H.C.	Fir Tree
Burgess, T.	Farmer Brown's Boy Becomes Curious	Johnson, C.	Fir-Tree Fairy Book
Bridgman, L.J.	Farmer Fox	Porter, G.S.	Fire Bird
Tolkien, J.R.R.	Farmer Giles of Ham	Brown, Paul	Fire! The Mascot
Hader, B.& E.	Farmer in the Dell	Kjelgaard, J.A.	Fire-Hunter
Leighton, C.	Farmer's Year...	Sears, P.M.	Firefly
Munkittrick, R.K.	Farming	Bailey, C.S.	Firelight Stories
Shute, H.A.	Farming It	Brown, A.G.	Fireside Battles
Aldin, C.	Farmyard Puppies	Hutchinson, V.	Fireside Poems
Bontemps, A.	Fast Sooner Hound	Jerrold, D.	Fireside Saints
Schlein, M.	Fast is Not a Ladybug	Repplier, A.	Fireside Sphinx
Maurois, Andre	Fatapoufs & Thinifers	Hutchinson, V.	Fireside Stories
Staunton, S.	Fate of a Crown	Sewell, H.	First Bible

AUTHOR	TITLE	AUTHOR	TITLE
Parry, E.A.	First Book of Krab	Bicknell, A.G.	Flower Folk
Trent, R.	First Christmas	Murray, Hilda	Flower Legends for Children
Wallace, Lew	First Christmas	Andersen, H.C.	Flower Maiden
Milhous, Kath.	First Christmas Crib	Gordon, H.C.	Flower Name Fancies
Van Dyke, H.	First Christmas Tree	Herrick, R.	Flower Poems
N/A	First Graces	Barker, C.M.	Flower Songs of the Seasons
Wells, H.G.	First Men in the Moon	Crane, W.	Flower Wedding
Tittle, W.	First Nantuckett Tea-Party	Meynell, A.	Flower of the Mind
N/A	First Prayers	Ranking, B.M.	Flowers & Fancies
Austin, Margot	First Prize for Danny	Newman, I.	Flowers Facts & Fables
Brown, M.W.	First Story	Crane, W.	Flowers from Shakespeare's Garden
Barksdale, L.	First Thanksgiving	Clement, Marg.	Flowers of Chivalry
Fritz, Jean	Fish Head	Skelding, S.	Flowers of Dell & Bower
Wiese, K.	Fish in the Air	Skelding, S.	Flowers of Glade & Garden
Brown, M.W.	Fish with a Deep Sea Smile	Ryan, M.E.	Flute of the Gods
Wilde, O.	Fisherman & his Soul	Brinig, M.	Flutter of an Eyelid
Tousey, S.	Fisherman Tommy	Freeman, Don	Fly High, Fly Low
Van Dyke, H.	Fisherman's Luck	Clarkson, L.	Fly-Away Fairies
Aflalo, F.G.	Fisherman's Weather	Wilson, E.H.	Flyaway Flippety
Myers, Grace	Fishing Cat	Asquith, C. (ed.)	Flying Carpet
Whitehead, R.	Five & Ten	Kastner, Erich	Flying Classroom
Allison, J.M.	Five Black Cousins...	Adams, S.H.	Flying Death
Coatsworth, E.	Five Bushel Farm	Vinton, Iris	Flying Ebony
Nesbit, E.	Five Children	Van Dyne, Edith	Flying Girl
Bishop, C.H.	Five Chinese Brothers	Harper, Wilhelmina	Flying Hoofs
North, S.	Five Little Bears	Riley, J.W.	Flying Islands of the Night
Adams, S.W.	Five Little Friends	Benet, W.R.	Flying King of Kurio
Kepes, J.A.	Five Little Monkeys	England, G.A.	Flying Legion
Sidney, Marg.	Five Little Peppers Midway	DuBois, W.P.	Flying Locomotive
Gay, Romney	Five Little Playmates	Roberts, G.E.	Flying Plover
Keyes, A.M.	Five Senses	Sauer, J.L.	Fog Magic
Nesbit, E.	Five of Us & Madeline	Hauser, Heinrich	Folding Father
Thomason, J.W.	Fix Bayonets	Van Loon, H.W.	Folk Songs of Many Lands
Saunders, Phyllis	Flame Flower	Day, L.B.	Folk Tales of Bengal
Hichens, R.	Flames	Gask, Lilian	Folk Tales of Many Lands
Steele, Wm. O.	Flaming Arrows	DeBosschere, J.	Folk Tales of Flanders
Harrison, E.O.	Flaming Sword...	Pardee, L.C.	Folk of the Woods
Munroe, K.	Flamingo Feather	Dunbar, P.L.	Folks from Dixie
Pratt, Marg.	Flash of Washington Square	Lathrop, D.	Follow the Brook
Averill, Esther	Flash: Story of a Horse	Tresselt, A.R.	Follow the Road
Davis, Duke	Flashlights from Mountain & Plain	Schneider, H.	Follow the Sunset
Ewing, J.H.	Flat Iron for a Farthing	Tresselt, A.R.	Follow the Wind
Leighton (ed.)	Fleur & Blanchefleur	Custer, E.B.	Following The Guidon
Howells, W.D.	Flight of Pony Baker	Barclay, F.	Following of the Star
Hopkins, H.M.	Flight of Rosy Dawn	Wells, Carolyn	Folly for the Wise
Saint-Exupery, A.	Flight to Arras	Wells, Carolyn	Folly in Fairyland
Phillpotts, E.	Flint Heart	Wells, Carolyn	Folly in the Forest
James, Will	Flint Spears	N/A	Foolish Fox
White, C.	Flip Flop Show	Cabot, C.S.	Football Grandma
Black, I.S.	Flipper: Sea Lion	Brainerd, E.H.	For Love of Mary Ellen
Parrish, A.& D.	Floating Island	Bailey, C.S.	For the Children's Hour
Stockton, Frank	Floating Prince...	Bennett, R.A.	For the White Christ
Perry, Nora	Flock of Girls & Boys	Kennedy, M.	Forest Beyond the Woodlands
Credle, Ellis	Flop-Eared Hound	Hamer, S.H.	Forest Foundling
Crane, W.	Flora's Feast...	Dauzet, M.	Forest Friends
De La Mare, W.	Flora: A Book of Drawings	Major, C.	Forest Hearth
Crane, W.	Floral Fantasy	Hewlett, M.	Forest Lovers
LeGallienne, Eva	Flossie & Bossie	Kjelgaard, J.A.	Forest Patrol
May, Eliz.	Flower Babies	Armer, L.A.	Forest Pool
Scott, A.M.	Flower Babies' Book	DeMille, W.M.C.	Forest Ring
Armfield, C.	Flower Book	Kozisek, Josef	Forest Story
Coybee, E.	Flower Book	Edwards, G.W.	Forest of Arden
Gordon, Eliz.	Flower Children	Chambers, Rbt.	Forest-Land
Judson, C.I.	Flower Fairies	Colum, P.	Forge in the Forest
Whittemore	Flower Fairies	Greene, Jean	Forgetful Elephant
Barker, C.M.	Flower Fairies of Autumn	Snedeker, C.D.	Forgotten Daughter
Barker, C.M.	Flower Fairies of Spring	Coatsworth, E.	Forgotten Island
Barker, C.M.	Flower Fairies of Summer	Lucas, E.V.	Forgotten Tales of Long Ago
Barker, C.M.	Flower Fairy Alphabet	Locke, Wm. J.	Fortunate Youth

AUTHOR	TITLE	AUTHOR	TITLE
Seawell, M.E.	Fortunes of Fifi	Perera, Lydia	Frisky
Smith, F.H.	Fortunes of Oliver Horn	Langstaff, John	Frog Went A-Courtin'
Noyes, A.	Forty Singing Seamen	Tresselt, A.R.	Frog in the Well
Kunos, I.	Forty-Four Turkish Tales	Doubleday, R.	From Cattle-Ranch To College
Munroe, K.	Forward March	Bangs, J.K.	From Pillar to Post
Barringer, M.	Four & Lena	King, C.	From School to Battlefield
Fish, H.D.	Four & Twenty Blackbirds	Dalton, Agnes M.	From Sioux to Susan
Pease, L.	Four & Twenty Dollies	Macy, S.B.	From Slavery to Freedom
Lucas, E.V.	Four & Twenty Toilers	Cromie, Rbt.	From the Cliffs of Croaghaun
Mord, W.	Four Champions/Great Britain & Ireland	Mason, A.	From the Horn of the Moon
Blanchard, A.E.	Four Corners	Finger, C.J.	Frontier Ballads
N/A	Four Feet by Two	Hanson, J.M.	Frontier Ballads
Hogan, Erlin	Four Funny Men	Swan, O.	Frontier Days
Handasyde	Four Gardens	Cox, P.	Frontier Humor
Hamer, S.H.	Four Glass Balls	Remington, F.	Frontier Sketches
Leighton, C.	Four Hedges...	Alcott, L.M.	Frost King
Schlein, M.	Four Little Foxes	Sperry, A.	Frozen Fire
Yeats, W.B.	Four Plays for Dancers	Wharton, E.	Fruit of the Tree
Molesworth, M.	Four Winds Farm	Milne (intro)	Fun & Fantasy
Wright, M.O.	Four-Footed Americans...	Bonte, W.	Fun & Nonsense
Deming, T.O.	Four-Footed Wilderness People	Quigg, Jane	Fun for Freddy
Enright, E.	Four-Story Mistake	Smith, E.B.	Fun in the Radio World
Banta, N.M.	Four-and-Forty Fairies	Parker, B.	Funny Bunnies
Dalgliesh, A.	Fourth of July Story	N/A	Funny Bunny ABC
Brown, M.W.	Fox Eyes	Bingham, C.	Funny Favorites
Caldecott, R.	Fox Jumps Over the Parson's Gate	Veale, E.	Funny Foxes
Travers, P.L.	Fox at the Manger	Wain, L.	Funny Frolics
Hurd, E.T.	Fox in a Box	Gruelle, J.	Funny Little Book
D'Aulaire, I.& E.	Foxie	Baruch, D.W.	Funny Little Boy
Van Stockum, H.	France on the Run	N/A	Funny Little Darkies
Seawell, M.E.	Francezka	Gag, W.	Funny Thing
Brooks, E.C.	Francisco...	Kreymborg, A.	Funnybone Alley
Abbott, J.	Franconia Stories	Campbell, L.	Funnyfeathers
Lounsberry, A.	Frank & Bessie's Forester	Brine, M.D.	Funnyland Boys
Sparrow, W.S.	Frank Brangwyn: His Work	Wallace, D.	Fur Trail Adventures
Shelley, M.W.	Frankenstein...	Smith, Lawrence B.	Fur or Feather
Calkins, E.	Franklin Booth	Munroe, K.	Fur-Seal's Tooth
Pine, F.W. (ed.)	Franklin's Autobiography	Mighels, P.V.	Furnace of Gold
Bianco, M.W.	Franzi & Gizi	Terhune, A.P.	Further Adventures of Lad
Weaver, A.V.	Frawg	Lagerlof, Selma	Further Adventures of Nils
Porter, G.S.	Freckles	Montgomery, L.M.	Further Chronicles of Avonlea
Brooks, W.R.	Freddy & Men from Mars	Brisley, J.L.	Further Doings of Milly-Molly-Mandy
Brooks, W.R.	Freddy & Mr. Camphor	Thurber, J.	Further Fables of Our Time
Brooks, W.R.	Freddy the Magician	Hammond, H.	Further Fortunes of Pinkey Perkins
Brooks, W.R.	Freddy the Pied Piper	Carroll, L.	Further Nonsense Prose...
Brooks, W.R.	Freddy's Cousin Weedly	Justus, May	Gabby Gaffer
Harris, J.C.	Free Joe...	Austin, Margot	Gabriel Churchkitten
Altsheler, J.A.	Free Rangers	Merriam, Eve	Gaggle of Geese
Rayner, E.	Free to Serve	Brewton, John	Gaily We Parade
Abbott, C.C.	Freedom of the Fields	Humphrey, M.	Gallant Little Patriots
Boswell, H.	French Canada	Cabell, J.B.	Gallantry
Pennell, J.	French Cathedrals	Milne, A.A.	Gallery of Children
Ashley, D.	French Fairy Tales	Phillips, C.	Gallery of Girls
Perkins, L.F.	French Twins	Parry, E.A.	Gamble Gold
Colum, P.	Frenzied Prince	Kendall, Carol	Gammage Cup
Brown, A.F.	Fresh Posies	Seabrook, Katie	Gao of the Ivory Coast
Byron, May	Friday & Saturday...	O'Neill, Rose	Garda
Montefiore	Friend & Foe	Judson, C.I.	Garden Adventures of Tommy Tittlemouse
Nesbit, W.D.	Friend O'Mine	Pyle, H.	Garden Behind the Moon
Anglund, J.W.	Friend is Someone Who Likes You	Paquin, S.S.	Garden Fairies
Pace, Mildred M.	Friend of Animals	Adrian, M.	Garden Spider
Gruelle, J.	Friendly Fairies	Jepson, Edgar	Garden at 19
Hader, B.& E.	Friendly Phoebe	Wade, B.E.	Garden in Pink
Lord Brabourne	Friends & Foes from Fairy Land	Fisher, H.	Garden of Girls
Porter, G.S.	Friends In Feathers	Huntington, I.M.	Garden of Hearts' Delight
Kay, G.A.	Friends of Jimmy	Carryl, G.W.	Garden of Years
Abbot, A.B.	Frigate's Namesake	Hooker, F.	Garden of the Lost Key
Drummond, F.	Fringes of Paradise	Baker, K.W.	Garden of the Plynck
Blackmore, R.D.	Fringilla	Chambers, Rbt.	Garden-Land

AUTHOR	TITLE	AUTHOR	TITLE
Faure, G.	Gardens of Rome	Colum, P.	Girl Who Sat by the Ashes
Sautriax [Rabelais]	Gargantua	Kelly, Eric P.	Girl Who Would Be Queen
Alcott, L.M.	Garland for Girls	Stockton, Frank	Girl at Cobhurst
Fyleman, R.	Garland of Roses	Hardy, M.E.	Girl of the Forest
Best, H.	Garram the Hunter	Warren, C.	Girl of the Governor
Duplaix, G.	Gaston & Josephine	Porter, G.S.	Girl of the Limberlost
Burglon, N.	Gate Swings In	Haines, Alice C.	Girls
Chaucer, G.	Gateway to Chaucer	Hutt, H.	Girls
Underdown, E.	Gateway to Romance	France, A.	Girls & Boys
Underdown, E.	Gateway to Spenser	Molesworth, M.	Girls & I
Clarkson, L.	Gathering of the Lillies	Berry, E.	Girls in Africa
Henry, M.	Gaudenzia	Miller, Mary B.	Give a Guess
Francoise	Gay ABC	Joan, Natalie	Glad Book
Sowerby, Githa	Gay Book	Sowerby, Githa	Glad Book
Aldin, C.	Gay Dog	Peto, Gladys	Gladys Peto's Children's Book
Mukerji, D.G.	Gay Neck	Baring-Gould, S.	Gladys of the Stewponey
Pease, E.F.	Gay Pippo	Kingsley, F.M.	Glass House
Chambers, Rbt.	Gay Rebellion	Baring, M.	Glass Mender
Crothers, S.M.	Gentle Reader	Farjeon, E.	Glass Slipper
Bergengren, R.W.	Gentlemen & All Merry Companions	Goodrich, A.	Gleam O'Dawn
Stewart, Anna B.	Gentlest Giant	Caldecott, R.	Gleanings from the Graphic
Rankin, L.S.	Gentling of Jonathan	Ingold, John	Glimpses from Wonderland
Thomas, Marg. L.	Geo. Washington Lincoln Goes Around World	Miller, J.R.	Glimpses of Heavenly Life
Alsop, Reese F.	George & his Horse	Baum, L.F.	Glinda of Oz
Gilby/Cuming	George Moorland...	Harrison, E.O.	Glittering Festival
D'Aulaire, I.& E.	George Washington	Hewes, A.D.	Glory of the Seas
Foster, Genevieve	George Washington	Thompson, R.P.	Gnome King of Oz
Wilson, W.	George Washington	Olcott, F.J.	Go! Champions of Light
Stuart, Ruth M.	George Washington Jones	Credle, Ellis	Goat that Went to School
Foster, Genevieve	George Washington's World	Inman, H.E.	Gobbo Bobo
Johnston, A.F.	Georgina of the Rainbows	Sherratt, J.L.	Goblin Gobblers
Tennyson, A.	Geraint & Enid	Oxenham, E.J.	Goblin Island
Van Stockum, H.	Gerrit & the Organ	Rossetti, C.	Goblin Market
Zeitlin, I.	Gessar-Khan	O'Neill, Rose	Goblin Woman
Petersham, M.	Get-A-Way & Harry Janos	Gaze, H.	Goblin's Glen
Mukerji, D.G.	Ghond the Hunter	Bancroft, Alberta	Goblins of Haubeck
Burglon, N.	Ghost Ship	Stuart, Ruth M.	Gobolinks
Eames, G.T.	Ghost Town Cowboy	Keiser, M.	God Returns to Vuelta Abajo
Bulla, Clyde R.	Ghost Town Treasure	Ward, Lynd	God's Man
Bangs, J.K.	Ghosts I Have Met	Johnson, J.W.	God's Trombones
Rouse, W.H.D.	Giant Crab	Syrett, Netta	Godmother's Garden
Thompson, R.P.	Giant Horse of Oz	Williamson, H.	Gods & Mortals in Love
Palazzo, T.	Giant Nursery Book	France, A.	Gods are Athirst
DuBois, W.P.	Giant Otto	Lord Dunsany	Gods of Pegana
Johnston, A.F.	Giant Scissors	Slobodkin, L.	Gogo: French Seagull
DeRegniers, B.S.	Giant Story	Miller, Warren	Goings on at Little Wishful
Shaw, C.G.	Giant of Central Park	White, S.E.	Gold
Blodgett, M.F.	Giant's Ruby	Schultz, J.W.	Gold Dust
Fenner, P.R.	Giants & Witches	Lummis, C.F.	Gold Fish of Gran Chimu
Gibson, C.D.	Gibson Book	Sabin, E.L.	Gold Seekers of '49
Davis, Rbt.	Gid Granger	Kelly, Eric P.	Gold Star of Halich
Henry, O.	Gift of the Magi	Harris-Burland, J.	Gold Worshipers
Ostrander, Fannie	Gift of the Magic Staff	Lang, A.	Gold of Fairnilee
Fenner, P.R.	Giggle Box	Robertson, W.G.	Gold, Frankincense & Myrrh
Boyajian, Z.C.	Gilgamesh: Dream of Eternal Quest	Grahame, K.	Golden Age
Elkin, Ben	Gillespie & the Guards	Gregory, Lady	Golden Apple
Vincent, Kitty	Gin & Ginger	Aldington, W.	Golden Asse/Lucius Apuleius
Potter, B.	Ginger & Pickles	Bemelmans, L.	Golden Basket
Estes, Eleanor	Ginger Pye	Werner, Elsa	Golden Bible
N/A	Gingerbread Boy	Grimm Bros.	Golden Bird
Tietjens, E.	Gingerbread Boy	England, G.A.	Golden Blight
Baum, L.F.	Gingerbread Man	Brickdale, E.	Golden Book of Famous Women
Fable, L.	Gingerbread Man	Warner, J. (ed.)	Golden Book of Poetry
Burnett, F.H.	Giovanni & the Other	Robertson, W.G.	Golden Book of Sonnets
Hogan, Inez	Giraffe Twins	N/A	Golden Book of Songs & Ballads
Phillpotts, E.	Girl & The Faun	Brown, M.W.	Golden Bunny
Mills, W.J.	Girl I Left Behind Me	Pushkin, A.	Golden Cockerel
Marshall, Mrs.	Girl Ranchers of San Coulee	Brown, M.W.	Golden Egg Book
Girvin, B.	Girl Scout	N/A	Golden Fairy Book

AUTHOR	TITLE	AUTHOR	TITLE
McNeer, May	Golden Flash	Krauss, Ruth	Good Man & his Good Wife
Colum, P.	Golden Fleece	Seredy, K.	Good Master
Kubota, H.	Golden Footprints	Russell, C.M.	Good Medicine
Angelo, V.	Golden Gate	Gates, Eleanor	Good Night
Dunham, Curtis	Golden Goblin	Palmer, Eliz.	Good Old Clipsy
Grimm Bros.	Golden Goose	Seccombe, Lieut.	Good Old Story of Cinderella
N/A	Golden Goose	Girvin, B.	Good Queen Bees
Barbour, R.H.	Golden Heart	Osborne, N.C.	Good Wind & Good Water
Jacobs, Violet	Golden Heart	Alcott, L.M.	Good Wives
Coatsworth, E.	Golden Horseshoe	Burnett, F.H.	Good Wolf
Locke, Wm. J.	Golden Journey of Mr. Paradyne	Riley, J.W.	Good-Bye Jim
Gordon, H.C.	Golden Key	Chan, Chih-Yi	Good-Luck Horse
Longfellow, H.W.	Golden Legend	Judson, C.I.	Good-Night Stories
Vredenburg, E.	Golden Locks & Pretty Frocks	Smith, Laura R.	Good-Night Stories
Baker, Augusta	Golden Lynx	LaRue, M.G.	Good-Time Book
Lindquist, Jennie	Golden Name Day	Brown, M.W.	Goodnight Moon
Robinson, W.	Golden Palace/Neverland	Crane, W.	Goody Two Shoes...
Hutchinson, W.M.L.	Golden Porch	Rippey, Sarah C.	Goody-Naughty Book
Allen, F.W.	Golden Road	Vickers, V.C.	Google Book
Montgomery, L.M.	Golden Road	Burgess, G.	Goop Directory of Juvenile Offenders
Steele, Wm. O.	Golden Root	Burgess, G.	Goop Tales Alphabetically Told
N/A	Golden Ship...	Burgess, G.	Goops & How to be Them
Bontemps, A.	Golden Slippers	Ostrander, Fannie	Goose Family Tales
Housman, L.	Golden Sovereign	Grimm Bros.	Goose Girl
Chisholm, L.	Golden Staircase	Shannon, Monica	Goose Grass Rhymes
Anderson, A.	Golden Story Book	Lenski, L.	Gooseberry Garden
Finger, C.J.	Golden Tales from Far Away	Page, T.N.	Gordon Keith
France, A.	Golden Tales of Anatole France	Leaf, M.	Gordon the Goat
Becker, May L.	Golden Tales of Far West	Atherton, G.	Gorgeous Isle
Becker, May L.	Golden Tales of Prairie States	Davis, L.R.	Grab Bag
Disney, W.	Golden Touch	Housman, L.	Gracious Majesty
Hawthorne, N.	Golden Touch	Addington, S.	Grammar Town
Palgrave, F.	Golden Treasury of Songs & Lyrics	Thompson, R.P.	Grampa in Oz
Thompson, B.J.	Golden Trumpets	Burgess, T.	Grandfather Frog Gets a Ride
Smith, Pamela C.	Golden Vanity & Green Bed	Geller, J.J.	Grandfather's Follies
Richards, L.E.	Golden Windows	Lenski, L.	Grandmother Tippytoe
Capuana, L.	Golden-Feather	Bouten, E.G.	Grandmother's Doll
Singleton, E.	Goldenrod Fairy Book	Hewlett, P.	Grandmother's Fairy Tales
Morley, C.	Goldfish Under the Ice	Holmes, O.W.	Grandmother's Story of Bunker Hill Battle
N/A	Goldilocks	Heward, C.	Grandpa & the Tiger
Humphrey, M.	Golf Girl	Curtis, A.T.	Grandpa's Little Girls & Friends
Van Sutphen, W.	Golfer's Alphabet	Curtis, A.T.	Grandpa's Little Girls at School
Upton, F.	Golliwogg at Sea-Side	Rae, J.	Granny Goose
Upton, B.	Golliwogg in Holland	LeMair, H.W.	Granny's Little Rhyme Book
Upton, B.	Golliwogg in War!	Browne, Frances	Granny's Wonderful Chair
Upton, F.	Golliwogg's Air-Ship	Caldecott, R.	Graphic Pictures
Upton, F.	Golliwogg's Auto Go Cart	Eberle, I.	Grasses
Upton, B.	Golliwogg's Bicycle Club	Rae, J.	Grasshopper Green & Meadow Mice
Upton, B.	Golliwogg's Christmas	Burlingame, E.W.	Grateful Elephant
Upton, B.	Golliwogg's Circus	Adrian, M.	Gray Squirrel
Upton, B.	Golliwogg's Desert Island	Lippincott, J.W.	Gray Squirrel
Fisher, Murray	Golliwogg's Dream... Little Folks	Leonard, Nellie	Graymouse Family
Upton, B.	Golliwogg's Fox Hunt	North, S.	Greased Lightning
Upton, B.	Golliwogg's Polar Advens.	Grant, Gordon	Greasy Luck
Smith, F.H.	Gondola Days	Aldin, C.	Great Adventure
Knott, M.O.	Gone Away with O'Malley	Addington, S.	Great Adventure of Mrs. Santa Claus
Rollins P.A.	Gone Haywire	Otto, M.G.	Great Aunt Victoria's House
Gag, W.	Gone is Gone	Crane, S.	Great Battles of the World
Koch, Dorothy	Gone is My Goose	McFarlane, A.E.	Great Bear Island
Enright, E.	Gone-Away Lake	N/A	Great Big Animal Book
Bigham, M.A.	Goober Village	Means, F.C.	Great Day in the Morning
Underhill, A.F.	Goochy Goggles...	Krauss, Ruth	Great Duffy
DeMonvel, M.B.	Good Children & Bad	Ewing, J.H.	Great Emergency
N/A	Good Dog Book	Dickens, C.	Great Expectations
Green, Allen A.	Good Fairy & the Bunnies	DuBois, W.P.	Great Geppy
Sampson, Martin	Good Giant	Machen, Arthur	Great God Pan/Inmost Light
Stoddard, Ann	Good Little Dog	Shippen, K.B.	Great Heritage
Eames, G.T.	Good Luck Colt	Cooper, Page	Great Horse Stories
DeJong, Meindert	Good Luck Duck	Burgess, T.	Great Joke on Jimmy Skunk

AUTHOR	TITLE
Begbie, H.	Great Men
Palazzo, T.	Great Othello
Parrish, R.	Great Plains
Mason, Edith H.	Great Plan
Hawes, C.B.	Great Quest
Thurber, J.	Great Quillow
Gray, Maxwell	Great Refusal
Anderson, I.	Great Sea Horse
Stockton, Frank	Great Stone of Sardis
Wood, Esther	Great Sweeping Day
Lawson, R.	Great Wheel
Paine, A.B.	Great White Way
Dudley, A.T.	Great Year
Gasquet, A.	Greater Abbeys of England
Niebuhr	Greek Heroes
Hader, B.& E.	Green & Gold...
Housman, L.	Green Arras
Faulkner, Wm.	Green Bough
White, E.O.	Green Door
Seuss, Dr.	Green Eggs & Ham
Birnbaum, A.	Green Eyes
Lang, A.	Green Fairy Book
Brady, L.E.	Green Forest Fairy Book
Judson, C.I.	Green Ginger Jar
Aydelotte, Dora	Green Gravel
Beauclerk, H.	Green Lacquer Pavillion
Hudson, W.H.	Green Mansions
Chambers, Rbt.	Green Mouse
Fiedler, Jean	Green Thumb Story
Chapman, W.G.	Green Timber Trails
James, G.	Green Willow...
Birch, V.	Green-Faced Toad
Paget-Fredericks, J.	Green-Pipes
Greenaway, K.	Greenaway's Babies
Beim, Lorraine	Gregori's Lamb
Bannon, L.	Gregorio & the White Llama
Dahl, Ronald	Gremlins
Grishina, N.G.	Gresha/Clay Pig
King, J.M.	Grey City of the North
Lang, A.	Grey Fairy Book
Greene, Mrs.	Grey House on the Hill
Merriman, H.S.	Grey Lady
Atkinson, E.	Greyfriars Bobby
Nyce, Vera	Greyfur's Neighbors
Cutler, Carl	Greyhounds of the Sea
Robinson, Tom P.	Greylock & the Robins
Creswick, Paul	Greypaws...
Molesworth, M.	Grim House
Fleuron, S.	Grim: Story of a Pike
Grimm Bros.	Grimm's Animal Stories
Carryl, G.W.	Grimm's Tales Made Gay
Spyri, J.	Gritli's Chldren
Clymer, E.L.	Grocery Mouse
Gag, W.	Growing Pains
Krauss, Ruth	Growing Story
Austin, Margot	Growl Bear
Vorse, M.E.	Grubby Gets Clean
Peacock, T.L.	Gryll Grange
Lofting, H.	Gub Gub's Book
Coolidge, S.	Guernsey Lily
Bridgman, L.J.	Guess
Shaw, C.G.	Guess Book
Mitchell, L.S.	Guess What's in the Grass
Nye, Edgar W.	Guest at the Ludlow
Tennyson, A.	Guinevere...
Lardner, R.	Gullible's Travels
Dalgliesh, A.	Gulliver Joins the Army
Gulliver, L.	Gulliver's Bird Book
Swift, J.	Gulliver's Travels

AUTHOR	TITLE
DeBosschere, J.	Gulliver's Travels in Lilliput
Harper, Wilhelmina	Gunniwolf...
MacDonald, Geo.	Gutta-Percha Willie
Davidson, G.	Gyp's Hour of Bliss
Seredy, K.	Gypsy
Wheeler, Opal	H.M.S. Pinafore
Horgan, Paul	Habit of Empire
Buff, M. & C.	Hah-Nee of the Cliff Dwellers
Lawson, Marie A.	Hail Columbia
Morier, J.	Hajji Baba of Ispahan
MacGrath, H.	Half a Rogue
Singer, Caroline	Half the World is Isfahan
Barbour, R.H.	Half-Back
Bangs, J.K.	Half-Hours with Jimmie-Boy
Anderson, Rbt. G.	Half-Past Seven Stories
Brown, K.H.	Hallowell Partnership
Shakespeare, Wm.	Hamlet
Hutton, W.H.	Hampton Court
Seegmiller, W.	Hand Clasp
VerBeck, F.	Hand-Book of Golf for Bears
Davis, M.G.	Handsome Donkey
Lover, S.	Handy Andy
Thompson, R.P.	Handy Mandy in Oz
Armfield, M.	Hanging Garden...
Longfellow, H.W.	Hanging of the Crane
Dodge, M.M.	Hans Brinker
Kristoffersen, E.M.	Hans Christian Elsinore
Rich, Edwin G.	Hans the Eskimo
Grimm Bros.	Hansel & Gretel
Bemelmans, L.	Hansi
Ludmann, Oscar	Hansi the Stork
Dalgliesh, A.	Happily Ever After
Aldin, C.	Happy Annual
Whitlock, Brand	Happy Average
Seuss, Dr.	Happy Birthday to You!
Pratt, Ella	Happy Children
Krauss, Ruth	Happy Day
N/A	Happy Day Begins
Herford, O.	Happy Days
Nash, Ogden	Happy Days
Keys, Leonora	Happy Dollies
Mandal, S.R.	Happy Flute
Gerson, V.	Happy Heart Family
Gordon, Eliz.	Happy Home Children
Beerbohm, M.	Happy Hypocrite
Lee, J.	Happy Island
Burgess, T.	Happy Jack
Fatio, Louise	Happy Lion
Carlson, N.S.	Happy Orpheline
Bemelmans, L.	Happy Place
Jepson, Edgar	Happy Pollyooly
Wilde, O.	Happy Prince
Sendak, Jack	Happy Rain
Dalgliesh, A.	Happy School Year
Bowman, J.	Happy all Day Through
Wister, A.L.	Happy-Go-Lucky
Wells, Carolyn	Happychaps
Nesbit, E.	Harding's Luck
Uttley, Alison	Hare & the Easter Egg
Wilde, O.	Harlot's House
Johnson, Crockett	Harold & the Purple Crayon
Johnson, Crockett	Harold's Circus
McKinley, C.F.	Harriett
Zion, Gene	Harry the Dirty Dog
Harper, Wilhelmina	Harvest Feast
Flecker, J.E.	Hassan
Creswick, Paul	Hastings the Pirate
Beskow, E.	Hat House
Emerson, C.	Hat Tub Tale...

AUTHOR	TITLE	AUTHOR	TITLE
Wheeler, P.	Hathoo of the Elephants	Petrovitch, W.	Heroes & Legends of Serbians
Kjelgaard, J.A.	Haunt Fox	Coburn, Grace	Heroes & Wizards
Belloc, H.	Haunted House	Deutsch, B.	Heroes of the Kalevala
Hood, Thos.	Haunted House	Boult, K.F.	Heroes of the Norselands
Dickens, C.	Haunted Man	Kingsley, C.	Heroes of Greek Fairy Tales
Laing, A.K.	Haunted Omnibus	Herbertson, A.	Heroic Legends
Stuart, Ruth M.	Haunted Photograph	Herrick, R.	Herrick's Poems
Hunt, M.L.	Have You Seen Tom Thumb?	Hunt, Marigold	Hester & the Gnomes
Marquand, John	Haven's End	Means, F.C.	Hetty of the Grande Deluxe
Wright, Isa L.	Having Fun	Tarry, Ellen	Hezekiah Horton
Ovington, Mary W.	Hazel	Brown, Paul	Hi Guy the Cinderella Horse
Barker, D.O.	He Leadeth Me...	Marino, Josef	Hi! Ho! Pinocchio
Sewell, H.	Head for Happy	Thomas, Dorothy	Hi-Po the Hippo
Goodwin, M.W.	Head of a Hundred	Disney, W.	Hiawatha
Anderson, C.W.	Heads Up & Heels Down	Longfellow, H.W.	Hiawatha
Burgess, G.	Heart Line	Holbrook, Florence	Hiawatha Alphabet
Dunbar, P.L.	Heart of Happy Hollow	Holbrook, Florence	Hiawatha Primer
Castle, A.	Heart of Lady Ann	Fillmore, P.H.	Hickory Limb
Thanet, O.	Heart of Toil	Dali, S.	Hidden Faces
Terhune, A.P.	Heart of a Dog	Brown, M.W.	Hidden House
Pickett, G.E.	Heart of a Soldier	Miller, Leo E.	Hidden People
Fox, John Jr.	Heart of the Hills	Jewett, E.M.	Hidden Treasure of Glaston
Wilkins, M.E.	Heart's Highway	Cosgrove, R.R.	Hidden Valley of Oz
Viele, H.K.	Heartbreak Hill	Coolidge, D.	Hidden Water
Ray, A.C.	Hearts & Creeds	Lathrop, D.	Hide and Go Seek
Barbour, R.H.	Hearts Content	Balch, Glenn	Hide-Rack Kidnapped
Clarkson, L.	Heartsease & Happy Days	Anderson, C.W.	High Courage
Maxwell, Wm.	Heavenly Tenants	Evans, S.	High History of the Holy Grail
Schlein, M.	Heavy is a Hippopotamus	Parker, D.	High Society
Spyri, J.	Heidi	Stong, Phil	High Water
Yonge, C.M.	Heir of Redclyffe	Finger, C.J.	Highwaymen...
Wharton, A.H.	Heirlooms in Miniatures	Bradley, A.G.	Highways & Byways of North Wales
Edgeworth, M.	Helen	Graham, T.	Hike & the Aeroplane
Wattles, W.D.	Hell-Fire Harrison	Connolly, J.B.	Hiker Joy
Breakenridge, W.	Helldorado	Peck, H.T.	Hilda and the Wishes
Gipson, M.	Hello Peter	Montgomery, R.G.	Hill Ranch
MacDonald, Betty	Hello, Mrs. Piggle-Wiggle	Sharp, E.	Hill that Fell Down
Crawford, P.	Hello, the Boat!	Macleod, F.	Hills of Ruel
Davidson, G.	Helpers Without Hands	N/A	Hind in the Wood
Kay, G.A.	Helping the Weatherman	Jacobs, H.	Hindu Fairy Tales
Brock, Emma	Hen that Kept House	Williston, T.P.	Hindu Stories
DeAngeli, M.	Henner's Lydia	Stong, Phil	Hired Man's Elephant
Brown, Marcia	Henry Fisherman	Martin, H.R.	His Courtship
Hutt, H.	Henry Hutt Picture Book	Harper, T.A.	His Excellency & Peter
Robertson, Keith	Henry Reed, Inc.	Elmslie, T.C.	His Lordship's Puppy
Lynch, M.B.	Henry the Navigator	Ford, P.L.	His Version of It
Neyhart, L.	Henry's Lincoln	Johnson, Ben	His Volpone
Field, R.	Hepatica Hawks	N/A	History of Ali Baba
Porter, G.S.	Her Father's Daughter	N/A	History of Cinderella
Daskam, J.	Her Fiance	Cervantes	History of Don Quixote...
Harte, Bret	Her Letter	Thackeray, Wm.	History of Henry Esmond
Roche, J.J.	Her Majesty the King	Irving, W.	History of New York
Newberry, C.T.	Herbert the Lion	Morris, Wm.	History of Over Sea
Gramatky, H.	Hercules	Ellis, F.S.	History of Reynard the Fox
Stoddard, Ann	Here Bingo!	Parker, B.	History of the Hoppers
Milius, W.	Here Comes Daddy	Van Loon, H.W.	History with a Match
Parks, G.T.	Here Comes Daddy	Barbour, R.H.	Hitting the Line
Moses, H.S.	Here Comes the Circus	Field, R.	Hitty...
Moodey, M.M.	Here Comes the Peddler!	Lewis, Eliz. F.	Ho-Ming, Girl of New China
Stone, Amy	Here's Juggins	Davis, L.R.	Hobby Horse Hill
Lecky, E.	Here, There, Everywhere	Newell, P.	Hole Book
Kingsley, C.	Hereward the Wake	Krauss, Ruth	Hole is to Dig
Herford, O.	Herford Aesop	Warde, M.	Holiday Book
Homer, A.N.	Hernani the Jew	Patch, E.M.	Holiday Hill
Brenner, A.	Hero by Mistake	Cady, H.	Holiday Time on Butternut Hill
Barton, W.E.	Hero in Homespun	Hendry, Hamish	Holidays & Happy Days
Milhous, Kath.	Herodia the Lovely Puppet	Jungman, B.	Holland
King, G.	Herodotus	Penfield, E.	Holland Sketches
Farjeon, E.	Heroes & Heroines	Paine, A.B.	Hollow Tree

AUTHOR	TITLE	AUTHOR	TITLE
Stuart, Ruth M.	Holly & Pizen	Preston, Hayter	House of Vanities
N/A	Holly Berries	Nicholson, M.	House of a Thousand Candles
Baldwin, May	Holly House & Ridges Row	Ryan, M.E.	House of the Dawn
Dickens, C.	Holly Tree Inn	Byrne, M.	House of the Red Fox
Dickens, C.	Holly Tree...	Hazard, R.H.	House on Stilts
Hichens, R.	Holy Land	Molesworth, M.	House that Grew
Earle, A.M.	Home Life in Colonial Days	Bianco, M.W.	House that Grew Smaller
Herrick, F.H.	Home Life of Wild Birds	Denslow, W.W.	House that Jack Built
Nye, Harry	Home is If You Find It	N/A	House that Jack Built
Gramatky, H.	Homer & the Circus Train	Tappan, E.M.	House with the Silver Door
McCloskey, R.	Homer Price	Coatsworth, E.	House-Boat Summer
N/A	Homes in the Wilderness	Pattee, F.L.	House/Black Ring
Porter, G.S.	Homing With Birds	Grimm Bros.	Household Stories
Disney, W.	Honest John & Giddy	Grimm Bros.	Household Tales
Willson, Dixie	Honey Bear	Manning, A.	Household/Sir Thomas Moore
Lupprian, H.	Honey Land	Goudey, Alice E.	Houses from the Sea
Paltenghi, M.	Honey on a Raft	Long, W.J.	How Animals Talk
Paltenghi, M.	Honey the City Bear	Schneider, H.	How Big is Big?
France, A.	Honey-Bee	King, J.M.	How Cinderella was Able to Go to the Ball
Stong, Phil	Honk! the Moose	Brainerd, E.H.	How Could You, Jean?
Farnol, J.	Honorable Mr. Tawnish	McBride, Mary M.	How Dear to My Heart
Monsell, J.R.	Hooded Crow	Tyrell, Eleanor	How I Tamed the Wild Squirrels
Rook, Clarence	Hooligan Nights	Smalley, J.	How It All Began
Nicholson, M.	Hoosier Chronicle	Linderman, F.B.	How It Came About Stories
Dreiser, T.	Hoosier Holiday	Monrad, Jean	How Many Kisses Good Night?
Eggleston, E.	Hoosier Schoolboy	McGaw, Jessie B.	How Medicine Man Cured Paleface Women
LaRue, M.G.	Hoot-Owl	Peirce, G.	How Percival Caught the Python
N/A	Hop O' My Thumb	Peirce, G.	How Percival Caught the Tiger
Eberle, I.	Hop, Skip & Fly	Harmon, M.	How Santa Found the Cobbler's Shop
Leet, F.R.	Hop, Skip & Jump	Reid, Sydney	How Sing Found the World is Round
Mulford, C.	Hopalong Cassidy	Power, Rhoda	How it Happened
Parker, F.	Hope Hathaway	Beacom, John	How the Buffalo Lost his Crown
Lewis, C.S.	Horse & his Boy	Jones, W.	How the Derrick Works
McGinley, Phyllis	Horse Who Lived Upstairs	Seuss, Dr.	How the Grinch Stole Christmas
Bannon, L.	Horse on a Houseboat	Kipling, R.	How the Leopard Got his Spots
Eames, G.T.	Horse to Remember	Kipling, R.	How the Rhinoceros Got his Skin
Twain, M.	Horse's Tale	Leonard, M.F.	How the Two Ends Met
Zogbaum, R.F.	Horse, Foot & Dragons	Muller, C.	How they Carried the Goods
Hay, Timothy	Horses	Cuppy, Will	How to Become Extinct
Montgomery, F.T.	Horses & Colts	Van Deeser	How to Find Happyland
James, Will	Horses I've Known	Parsons, F.T.	How to Know the Ferns
Anderson, C.W.	Horses are Folks	Krehbiel, H.	How to Listen to Music
Downey, Fairfax	Horses of Destiny	Krauss, Ruth	How to Make an Earthquake
Seuss, Dr.	Horton Hatches the Egg	Abbott, C.	Howard Pyle: A Chronicle
Seuss, Dr.	Horton Hears a Who!	Twain, M.	Huckleberry Finn
Riley, J.W.	Host of Children	Davis, Rbt.	Hudson Bay Express
Waugh, A.	Hot Countries	Dix, B.M.	Hugh Gwyeth: Roundhead Cavalier
Davies, W.B.	Hour of Magic	Spielmann, M.H.	Hugh Thomson: His Art
Maeterlinck, M.	Hours of Gladness	Cooke, G.M.	Huldah
Follett, H.T.	House Afire!	Vassos, R.	Humanities
Bangs, J.K.	House Boat on the Styx	Berry, E.	Humbo the Hippo
Means, F.C.	House Under the Hill	Hood, Thos.	Humerous Poems
Pemberton, Max	House Under the Sea	Robinson, W.H.	Humours of Golf
Sandoz, M.	House Without Windows	Flack, M.	Humphrey
Milne, A.A.	House at Pooh Corner	Chapin, A.A.	Humpty Dumpty
Swift, H.H.	House by the Sea	Mourat, Joseph	Humpty Dumpty & other Songs
Justus, May	House in No-End Hollow	Rey, H.A.	Humpty Dumpty...
Voight, V.F.	House in Robin Lane	N/A	Humpty-Dumpty
Barbour, R.H.	House in the Hedge	Williamson, H.	Humpy, Son of the Sands
Nesbit, E.	House of Arden	Fraser-Simson, H.	Hums of Pooh
Wolf, A.S.	House of Cards	N/A	Hunchback of Notre-Dame
Seawell, M.E.	House of Egremont	Estes, Eleanor	Hundred Dresses
Cradock, H.C.	House of Fancy	Aesopus	Hundred Fables of Aesop
Peake, Elmore E.	House of Hawley	LaFontaine, J.	Hundred Fables of La Fontaine
Housman, L.	House of Joy	Bonner, M.G.	Hundred Trips to Storyland
Wharton, E.	House of Mirth	Lilly, Jean	Hundred Tuftys
Wilde, O.	House of Pomegranates	Pogany, Nebby	Hungarian Fairy Book
Converse, F.	House of Prayer	Thompson, R.P.	Hungry Tiger of Oz
DeJong, Meindert	House of Sixty Fathers	Robinson, W.H.	Hunlikely!

AUTHOR	TITLE	AUTHOR	TITLE
Carroll, L.	Hunting of the Snark	Clement, Marg.	In France
Bianco, M.W.	Hurdy-Gurdy Man	Fox, John Jr.	In Happy Valley
DeJong, Meindert	Hurry Home, Candy	Mayer, Henry	In Laughland
Hurd, E.T.	Hurry Hurry	Zolotow, C.	In My Garden
Buff, M. & C.	Hurry, Scurry & Flurry	Clark, A.N.	In My Mother's House
McCutcheon, G.B.	Husbands of Edith	Adams, W.I.L.	In Nature's Image
Slobodkin, L.	Hustle & Bustle	Braine/Floyd	In Nurseryland
Lawson, R.	I Discover Columbus	Janvier, T.A.	In Old New York
Gaines, M.L.	I Heah de Voices Callin'	Sullivan, Frank	In One Ear
Barnes, Ruth A.	I Hear America Singing	Ade, G.	In Pastures New
Baruch, D.W.	I Like Animals	Ward, H.F.	In Place of Profit
Baruch, D.W.	I Like Automobiles	Quiller-Couch, A.	In Powder & Crinoline
Conklin, Gladys	I Like Caterpillars	Gosse, E.	In Russet & Silver
Musselman, M.M.	I Married a Redhead	Glave, E.J.	In Savage Africa
Koch, Dorothy	I Play at the Beach	Day, L.G.	In Shadow Town
Flack, M.	I See a Kitty	Stuart, Ruth M.	In Simkinsville
Flagg, J.M.	I Should Say So	Thomas, E.M.	In Sunshine Land
Beistle, A.S.	I Spy	Michelson, M.	In The Bishop's Carriage
Brenner, A.	I Want to Fly	Nesbit, W.D.	In Tumbledown Town
Krauss, Ruth	I Want to Paint My Bathroom Blue	Trine, Ralph W.	In Tune with the Infinite
Gordon, Eliz.	I Wonder Why?	Gray, P.L.	In a Car of Gold
Scott-Gatty	I Wonder Why?	LeFanu, J.S.	In a Glass Darkly
Krauss, Ruth	I'll Be You and You Be Me	Anglund, J.W.	In a Pumpkin Shell
Kraus, Robert	I, Mouse	Evers, Alf	In the Beginning
Hall, A.W. (ed.)	Icelandic Fairy Tales	N/A	In the Beginning...
Waugh, Ida	Ida Waugh's Alphabet Book	McCutcheon, G.B.	In the Bishop's Carriage
N/A	Ideal Heads	Bacon, J.D.	In the Border Country
Waugh, Ida	Ideal Heads	Poulsson, E.	In the Child's World
Crane, W.	Ideals in Art	Burnett, F.H.	In the Closed Room
Bangs, J.K.	Idiot at Home	Brown, A.F.	In the Days of Giants
Wells, Carolyn	Idle Idyls	Paine, A.B.	In the Deep Woods
Bacon, J.D.	Idyll on All Fool's Day	Harrison, F.	In the Fairy Ring
Tennyson, A.	Idylls of the King	Quick, Herbert	In the Fairyland of America
Thaxter, Cellia	Idyls and Pastorals	Ets, Marie H.	In the Forest
Lathbury, M.A.	Idyls of the Months	Schultz, J.W.	In the Great Apache Forest
Hubbell, R.S.	If I Could Fly	Pyle, Kath.	In the Green Forest
Seuss, Dr.	If I Ran the Circus	Symonds, J.A.	In the Key of Blue
Seuss, Dr.	If I Ran the Zoo	Norwood, Edwin P.	In the Land of Diggeldy Dan
Kingman, Lee	Ilenka	Smith, E.B.	In the Land of Make-Believe
Moore, M.	Illegitimate Sonnets	Ward, G.	In the Miz
Loveland, Mrs. S.	Illustrated Bible Story Book	Gilson, R.R.	In the Morning Glow
Berry, E.	Illustrations of Cynthia	Wells, Carolyn	In the Reign of Queen Dick
Ford, Julia E.	Imagina	McIntyre, J.T.	In the Rockies with Kit Carson
Kempis	Imitation of Christ	James, Will	In the Saddle with Uncle Bill
Storm, T.	Immensee	Harrison, Eliz.	In the Story World
Sinclair, M.	Immortal Moment	Miller, Leo E.	In the Tiger's Lair
Daskam, J.	Imp & The Angel	Hart, Ruby	In the Woods
Powys, L.	Impassioned Clay	Ware, R.D.	In the Woods/On the Shore
Copley, F.B.	Impeachment of President Israels	Lionni, L.	Inch by Inch
Cooke, E.V.	Impertinent Poems	Burnand (ed.)	Incompleat Angler
Brown, M.W.	Important Book	Nesbit, E.	Incomplete Amorist
Carpenter, John	Improving Songs for Anxious Children	McCready, T.L.	Increase Rabbit
Moore, F.F.	Impudent Comedian	Hunter, N.	Incredible Advens./Professor Brawnestawm
Godden, Rumer	Impunity Jane	Butler, E.P.	Incubator Baby
Robinson, Tom P.	In & Out	Lamb, Dean I.	Incurable Filibuster
Rowland, E.E.	In & Out of the Nursery	Crane, W.	India Impressions
France, A.	In ALL France	Richardson, W.C.F.	India Rubber Jack
Creswick, Paul	In Alfred's Days	Monro, W.D.	India's Gods & Heroes
Mabie, H.W.	In Arcady	Hope, L.	India's Love Lyrics
Mills, E.A.	In Beaver World	Brereton, F.S.	Indian & Scout
Bangs, J.K.	In Camp with a Tin Soldier	Eastman, C.A.	Indian Boyhood
N/A	In Cat & Dog Land	Haines, Alice C.	Indian Boys & Girls
Page, Marg.	In Childhood Land	Lenski, L.	Indian Captive
Moulton, L.C.	In Childhood's Country	Deming, T.O.	Indian Child Life
Kelly, Eric P.	In Clean Hay	N/A	Indian Fairy Book
Hawthorne, N.	In Colonial Days	MacKenzie, D.A.	Indian Fairy Stories
Warren, I.R.	In Cupid's Court	Jacobs, J. (ed.)	Indian Fairy Tales
Smith, F.H.	In Dickens' London	Moon, G.	Indian Legends in Rhyme
Chisholm, L.	In Fairyland	Mackenzie, D.	Indian Myth & Legend

AUTHOR	TITLE	AUTHOR	TITLE
Linderman, F.B.	Indian Old-Man Stories	Lenski, L.	Jack Horner's Pie
Wilson, R.	Indian Story Book	Sherwood, E.H.	Jack Jingling in Jungleland
Clarkson, L.	Indian Summer	Herben, B.S.	Jack O'Health, Peg O'Joy
Kipling, R.	Indian Tales	Thompson, R.P.	Jack Pumpkinhead of Oz
Perkins, L.F.	Indian Twins	Whittier, J.G.	Jack in the Pulpit
Linderman, F.B.	Indian Why Stories	Grinnell, G.B.	Jack in the Rockies
Zolotow, C.	Indian, Indian	Bell, J.J.	Jack of All Trades
Tousey, S.	Indians & Cowboys	N/A	Jack the Giant Killer
Pine, Tillie S.	Indians Knew	Thomson, Hugh	Jack the Giant Killer
Tousey, S.	Indians of the Plains	Grinnell, G.B.	Jack/Young Ranchman
Deming, T.O.	Indians of the Wigwams	Ingoldsby, T.	Jackdaw of Rheims
Brown, M.W.	Indoor Noisy Book	Hill, Wm.	Jackie Boy in Rainbowland
Lide, A.A.	Inemak: Little Greenlander	Birdsall, K.N.	Jacks of All Trades
Unknown	Infernal Marriage	Marryat, Fred.	Jacob Faithful
Stone, C.R.	Inga of Porcupine Mine	Henderson, J.	Jamaica
Ingoldsby, T.	Ingoldsby Legends	Hader, B.& E.	Jamaica Johnny
Dixon, Maynard	Injun Babies	Waldeck, T.	Jamba the Elephant
Chesterton, G.K.	Innocence of Father Brown	Robinson, W.H.	Jamboree of Laughter
Von Gottschalck, O.	Innocent Industries	Alger, Leclaire	Jan & Wonderful Mouth-Organ
N/A	Intimations of Immortality...	Ewing, J.H.	Jan of the Windmill
Wodehouse, P.G.	Intrusion of Jimmy	McCutcheon, G.B.	Jane Cable
Meigs, C.	Invincible Louisa	King, Ben	Jane Jones....
Gilbert, W.S.	Iolanthe...	Montgomery, L.M.	Jane of Lantern Hill
Chambers, Rbt.	Iole	Allee, M.H.	Jane's Island
Erskine, P.	Iona	Bergengren, R.W.	Jane, Joseph & John
Craig, Alexander	Ionia...	Danks, B.M.	Janet & the Fairies
Gibbings, Rbt.	Iorana!	Blanchard, A.E.	Janet's College Career
Burrows, Eliz.	Irene of Tundra Towers	Ray, A.C.	Janet: Her Winter in Quebec
Graves, A.P.	Irish Fairy Book	Fox, F.M.	Janey
N/A	Irish Fairy Tales	Tarry, Ellen	Janie Belle
Stephens, J.	Irish Fairy Tales	Menpes, M.	Japan
Perkins, L.F.	Irish Twins	Watanna, O.	Japanese Blossom
Barlow, J.	Irish Ways	Williston, T.P.	Japanese Fairy Tales
Beach, R.	Iron Trail	Perkins, L.F.	Japanese Twins
Krauss, Ruth	Is This You?	Marryat, Fred.	Japhet...
Green, M.M.	Is it Hard? Is it Easy?	Chambers, Rbt.	Japonette
Keats, J.	Isabella...	Arnold, E.	Japonica
Austin, Mary	Isidro	Powell, Miriam	Jareb
Holdridge, Betty	Island Boy	DeAngeli, M.	Jared's Island
Thaxter, Cellia	Island Garden	Colvile, Kath.	Jason & the Princess
Morgan, H.	Island Impossible	Burroughs, Marg.	Jasper the Drummin' Boy
Forman, J.M.	Island of Enchantment	Kahmann, C.	Jasper the Gypsy Dog
Colum, P.	Island of the Mighty	Jaufre	Jaufre the Knight & Fair Brunissende
Singmaster, Elsie	Isle of Que	DeLeeuw, Hendrik	Java Jungle Tales
Webber, I.E.	It Looks Like This	Tietjens, E.& J.	Jaw Breaker's Alphabet
Freeman, Don	It Shouldn't Happen	DeMonvel, M.B.	Jeanne d' Arc
Johnston, A.F.	It Was the Road to Jericho	Francoise	Jeanne-Marie Counts her Sheep
Schlein, M.	It's About Time	Brown, Dr. John	Jeems the Door Keeper
Kent, R.	It's Me O Lord...	Kennedy, Mary	Jenny
Andersen, H.C.	It's Perfectly True...	Otis, James	Jenny Wren's Boarding House
Hurd, E.T.	It's Snowing	Dolbier, Maurice	Jenny: Bus that Nobody Loved
Deutsch, B.	It's a Secret!	Buchanan, G.	Jeptha
Wharton, E.	Italian Backgrounds	Walpole, H.	Jeremy
MacDonell, Anne	Italian Fairy Book	Evans, Eva K.	Jerome Anthony
James, Henry	Italian Hours	Wilkins, M.E.	Jerome, A Poor Man
Farjeon, E.	Italian Peepshow	Tousey, S.	Jerry & Pony Express
Perkins, L.F.	Italian Twins	Addington, S.	Jerry Juddikins
Wharton, E.	Italian Villas...	Webster, J.	Jerry Junior
Scott, Walter	Ivanhoe	Burgess, T.	Jerry Muskrat Wins Respect
Haggard, H.R.	Ivory Child	Burgess, T.	Jerry Muskrat at Home
Gellibrand, E.	J. Cole	Hurd, E.T.	Jerry the Jeep
Ewing, J.H.	Jacanapes	Tomlinson, E.	Jersey Boy in the Revolution
Denslow, W.W.	Jack & the Bean Stalk	Bunner, H.C.	Jersey Street & Jersey Lane
Tennyson, H.	Jack & the Bean Stalk	Porter, G.S.	Jesus of the Emerald
N/A	Jack & the Beanstalk	Petershams	Jesus' Story
Bangs, J.K.	Jack & the Check Book	Pennell, J.	Jew at Home
Grinnell, G.B.	Jack Among the Indians	Evans, F.A.	Jewel Story Book
N/A	Jack Frost Arrives on Butternut Hill	Winter, A.A.	Jewel Weed
Grant, Rbt.	Jack Hall	Burnham, C.L.	Jewel's Story Book

AUTHOR	TITLE	AUTHOR	TITLE
Johnston, I.M.	Jeweled Toad	Williams, Herschel	Jolly Old Whistle
Friedlander, G.	Jewish Fairy Book	Smith, G.	Jolly Polly Stories
Sacher-Masoch, L.	Jewish Tales	Piper, W. (ed.)	Jolly Rhymes of Mother Goose
Downey, Fairfax	Jezebel the Jeep	Nathan, Rbt.	Jonah...
Mayol, L.B.	Jiji Lou	Blanck, Jacob	Jonathan & the Rainbow
Masefield, J.	Jim Davis	Surtees, R.S.	Jorrock's on 'Unting
Colby, J.P.	Jim the Cat	Coyle, Kath.	Josephine
Disney, W.	Jiminy Cricket	Cradock, H.C.	Josephine & Her Dolls
Sewell, H.	Jimmy & Jemima	Cradock, H.C.	Josephine Dolly Book
Miller, Jane	Jimmy the Groceryman	Cradock, H.C.	Josephine Keeps House
Treffinger, C.	Jimmy's Shoes	Cradock, H.C.	Josephine Keeps School
Wister, O.	Jimmyjohn Boss	Cradock, H.C.	Josephine is Busy
Van Dresser, J.	Jimsey	Cradock, H.C.	Josephine's Birthday
Dana, M.P.	Jingle Book	Cradock, H.C.	Josephine's Happy Family
Wells, Carolyn	Jingle Book	Cradock, H.C.	Josephine's Pantomime
Wightman, F.P.	Jingle Jangle Jumbly Lays...	Reid, Sydney	Josey & the Chipmunk
Simmons, H.B.	Jingle Jangle Rhyme Book	Sawyer, R.S.	Journey Cake, Ho!
Thurston, C.B.	Jingle of a Jap	Astor, J.J.	Journey in Other Worlds
Rollins, P.A.	Jinglebob	Wister, O.	Journey in Search of Christmas
Bingham, C.	Jingles, Jokes & Funny Folks	Peattie, D.C.	Journey into America
N/A	Jo & Uncle George Kritters	Blanchard, A.E.	Journey of Joy
Alcott, L.M.	Jo's Boys...	Rahr, Ruth	Journey of the Toys
Elliott, K.M.	Jo-Yo's Idea	Townsend, R.	Journey to the Garden Gate
Medary, Marj.	Joan & the Three Deer	Seegmiller, W.	Journeys in Storyland
Gemmill, J.	Joan Wanted a Kitty	Brooks, C.S.	Journeys to Baghdad
Tarrant, M.	Joan in Flowerland	Bianco, P.	Joy & the Christmas Angel
DeMonvel, M.B.	Joan of Arc	Francis, J.G.	Joyous Aztecs
Holmes, Mabel D.	Joan of Arc	Lindsay, M.M.	Joyous Guests
Madison, L.F.	Joan of Arc	Lindsay, M.M.	Joyous Travelers
Farjeon, E.	Joan's Door	Baylor, F.C.	Juan & Juanita
Lippmann, J.M.	Jock O'Dreams	Politi, L.	Juanita
Johns, Rowland	Jock the King's Pony	Lansing, Eliz.	Jubilant for Sure
Rosman, A.G.	Jock the Scot	Hardy, T.	Jude the Obscure
Wiese, K.	Joe Buys Nails	Sinclair, M.	Judgement of Eve
London, J.	John Barleycorn	Allee, M.H.	Judith Lankester
Baum, L.F.	John Dough & the Cherub	Aldrich, T.B.	Judith of Bethulia
Remington, F.	John Ermine of Yellowstone	Lenski, L.	Judy's Journey
Stockton, Frank	John Gayther's Garden...	James, Henry	Julia Bride
Johnson, A.E.	John Hassall, R.I.	Tyman, Loretta	Julio
Adams, F.U.	John Henry Smith	Berry, E.	Juma of the Hills
Bowman, J.C.	John Henry...	Meredith, G.	Jump to Glory Jane
Cable, G.W.	John March, Southerner	Kalashnikoff, N.	Jumper
Page, T.N.	John Marvel, Assistant	Twain, M.	Jumping Frog
McNeer, May	John Wesley	McNeely, M.H.	Jumping-Off Place
Hunt, M.L.	John of Pudding Lane	Howard, Janet	Jumpy the Kangaroo
Brown, A.F.	John of the Woods	Gale, N.	June Romance
Laughlin, E.O.	Johnnie	Kipling, R.	Jungle Book
Credle, Ellis	Johnny & his Mule	Wells, Carveth	Jungle Man & his Animals
Atkinson, E.	Johnny Apple-Seed	Pease, Howard	Jungle River
Lindsay, V.	Johnny Appleseed	Hamer, S.H.	Jungle School
Zwilgmeyer, D.	Johnny Blossom	Zogbaum, R.F.	Junior Officer of the Watch
Brooke, L.L.	Johnny Crow's Garden	White, Anne H.	Junket
Brooke, L.L.	Johnny Crow's New Garden	Kunhardt, D.	Junket is Nice
Brooke, L.L.	Johnny Crow's Party	McCoy, N.	Jupie the Wise Old Owl
Lenski, L.	Johnny Goes to the Fair	Aldin, C.	Just Among Friends
Buck, Pearl S.	Johnny Jack & his Beginnings	N/A	Just Because of You
Hurd, E.T.	Johnny Littlejohn	Maxwell, G.S.	Just Beyond London
Gruelle, J.	Johnny Mouse & Wishing Stick	DeAngeli, M.	Just Like David
Lang, A. (tr.)	Johnny Nut & Golden Goose	Beistle, A.S.	Just Peggy
Forbes, Esther	Johnny Tremain	Beim, Lorraine	Just Plain Maggie
Gaggin, E.R.	Jolly Animals	Loomis, C.B.	Just Rhymes
Cox, P.	Jolly Chinee	Kipling, R.	Just So Stories...
Lightfoot, B.H.	Jolly Jack Horner	Gordon, Eliz.	Just You
Amend, Ottillie	Jolly Jungle Jingles	Croll, Pauline	Just for You
Lamb, Tom	Jolly Kid Alphabet	Henry, M.	Justin Morgan had a Horse
Nesbit, W.D.	Jolly Kid Book	Thompson, R.P.	Kabumpo in Oz
Pease, E.F.	Jolly Little Clown	Hogan, Inez	Kangaroo Twins
Kay, G.A.	Jolly Old Shadow Man	Hays, M.G.	Kaptin Kiddo & Puppo
N/A	Jolly Old Sports	Scott, Gabriel	Kari

AUTHOR	TITLE	AUTHOR	TITLE
Wiese, K.	Karoo the Kangaroo	Horne, Richard H.	King Penguin
Burton, R.	Kasidah of Haji Abdu El-Yezdi	Fitzhugh, P.K.	King Time
Siebe, Josephine	Kasperle's Adventures	Hough, E.	King of Gee Whiz
Parry, E.A.	Katawampus: Its Treatment & Cure	Colum, P.	King of Ireland's Son
Stockton, Frank	Kate Bonnet	Ayers, Ray F.	King of Kinkiddie...
Spielmann, M.H.	Kate Greenaway	Cooney, Barbara	King of Wreck Island
Norris, June	Katherine the Komical Kow	Lummis, C.F.	King of the Broncos
Carter, C.F.	Katooticut	Ruskin, J.	King of the Golden River
Gilson, R.R.	Katrina	About, E.	King of the Mountains
Bailey, A.C.	Katrina & Jan	Tracy, Edward B.	King of the Stallions
Gale, Eliz.	Katrina Van Ost & Silver Rose	Henry, M.	King of the Wind
Burton, V.L.	Katy & the Big Snow	Milne, A.A.	King's Breakfast
Fyleman, R.	Katy Kruse Dolly Book	Bishop, C.H.	King's Day
Fyleman, R.	Katy Kruse Play Book	Farrow, G.E.	King's Gardens
Payne, E.	Katy No-Pocket	Hinkson, H.A.	King's Liege
Bradford, Marg.	Keep Singing, Keep Humming	Marryat, Fred.	King's Own
Porter, G.S.	Keeper of the Bees	Zeitlin, I.	King's Pleasure
Irving, W.	Keeping of Christmas...	Seuss, Dr.	King's Stilts
King, Marian	Kees	N/A	Kingdom & Power & Glory
Parrish, R.	Keith of the Border	Stone, S.B.	Kingdom of Why
Clemens, W.M.	Ken of Kipling	Rosenthal, L.	Kingdom of the Pearl
Scott, Walter	Kenilworth	Meigs, C.	Kingdom of the Winding Road
Sendak, M.	Kenny's Window	Hamilton, M.	Kingdoms Curious
MacKenzie, C.	Kensington Rhymes	Farjeon, E.	Kings & Queens
Davis, Reb. H.	Kent Hampden	Wilkinson, F.	Kings & Queens
Allen, J.L.	Kentucky Cardinal Aftermath	Enright, E.	Kintu: A Congo Adventure
Mitchell G.W.	Kernel Cob & Little Miss Sweetclover	Black, I.S.	Kip: Young Rooster
O'Neill, Rose	Kewpie [ALL TITLES]	Lamb, Harold	Kirdy
Evans, Eva K.	Key Corner	Brown, A.F.	Kisington Town
Cheney, Cora	Key of Gold	Boylan, G.D.	Kiss of Glory
Noble-Ives, S.	Key to Betsy's Heart	Bell, L.P.	Kitchen Fun
Murai, G.	Kibun Daizin	Coatsworth, E.	Kitten Stand
Embry, Margaret	Kid Sister	Winlow, Clara V.	Kitten that Grew Too Fat
Hays, M.G.	Kiddie Land	Newberry, C.T.	Kitten's ABC
Hays, M.G.	Kiddie Rhymes	Herford, O.	Kitten's Garden of Verses
Welsh, Richard	Kiddie-Kar Book	Bingham, C.	Kittenland
Stevenson, R.L.	Kidnapped	N/A	Kittens
Ballantyne, Joan	Kidnappers at Coombe	Grover, E.O.	Kittens & Cats
Boylan, G.D.	Kids of Many Colors	Schlein, M.	Kittens, Cubs & Babies
Steiner, C.	Kiki & Muffy	Coryell, Hubert	Klondike Gold
Steiner, C.	Kiki Dances	Saunders, L.	Knave of Hearts
Montgomery, R.G.	Kildee House	Parrish, A.& D.	Knee-High to a Grasshopper
Hogg, J.	Kilmeny	Saint, L.B.	Knight of the Cross
Montgomery, L.M.	Kilmeny of the Orchard	Barr, A.	Knight of the Nets
Kipling, R.	Kim	Fitch, Wm. C.	Knighting of the Twins
Bailey, A.C.	Kimo	Colt, Terry S.	Knights, Goats & Battleships
Cable, G.W.	Kincaid's Battery	Alden, R.M.	Knights of the Silver Shield
Perry, S.G.	Kind Adventure	Coatsworth, E.	Knock at the Door
Scott, F.E.	Kindergarten Limericks	Means, F.C.	Knock at the Door, Emmy
Roberts, C.G.D.	Kindred of the Wild	Ade, G.	Knocking the Neighbors
Blanck, Jacob	King & Noble Blacksmith	Uttley, Alison	Knot Squirrel Tied
N/A	King Albert's Book	Buff, M. & C.	Kobi, a Boy of Switzerland
N/A	King Arthur & His Knights	Marais, Josef	Koos the Hottentot
Holland, R. (ed.)	King Arthur & Knights of Rountable	Linderman, F.B.	Kootenai Why Stories
Macleod, Mary	King Arthur & Noble Knights	Seton, E.T.	Krag & Johnny Bear
Allen, Phil S.	King Arthur & his Knights	Bruce, M.	Kris & Kristina
Frith, Henry	King Arthur & his Knights	Miller, O.T.	Kristy's Rainy Day Picnic
Knowles, J. (arr.)	King Arthur & his Knights	Aunt Jo	Kritters of Kitchen Kingdom
Malory, T.	King Arthur & his Knights	Coleridge, S.T.	Kubla Kahn
Winder, Blanche	King Arthur & his Knights	Shipman, Neil	Kurly Kew & Tree-Princess
Gilbert, Henry	King Arthur's Knights	Hearn, L.	Kwaidan....
MacGregor, M.	King Arthur's Knights	Moe, Louis M.	Kylle Kluk
Forbes, Eliz. S.	King Arthur's Wood	Fort, Chas.	LO!
Malory, T.	King Arthur...	Shirley (ed.)	La Fontaine's Fables
Miller, Warren	King Carlo of Capri	Laboulaye, E.R.	Laboulaye's Fairy Book
Barske, C.	King Cotton	Brink, C.R.	Lad with a Whistle
Gordon, Eliz.	King Gumdrop...	O'Donnell, T.C.	Ladder of Ricketty Rungs
Thompson, R.P.	King Kojo	Porter, G.S.	Laddie
MacGregor, B.	King Longbeard	Gaskell, C.M.	Lady Anne's Fairy Tales

AUTHOR	TITLE	AUTHOR	TITLE
Baker, M.	Lady Arabella's Birthday Party	Frazer, Lilly	Leaves from The Golden Bough
Lockhart, C.	Lady Doc	Sawyer, R.S.	Leerie
Walker, M.	Lady Hollyhock & her Friends	Stolz, Mary S.	Leftover Elf
Jamison, C.V.	Lady Jane	Toland, M.B.M.	Legend Laymone
Barbour, R.H.	Lady Laughter	DuMaurier, G.	Legend of Camelot
Russell, W.C.	Lady Maud	Irving, W.	Legend of Sleepy Hollow
Burgess, G.	Lady Mechante	Colum, P.	Legend of St. Columbia
Ainslie, K.	Lady Tabitha and Us	Newman, I.	Legend of the Lilac
O'Neill, Rose	Lady in the White Veil	Newman, I.	Legend of the. Tulip...
Sterling, S.H.	Lady of King Arthur's Court	Sidgwick (ed.)	Legendary Ballads
Burnett, F.H.	Lady of Quality	Steedman, Amy	Legends & Stories of Italy for Children
Tennyson, A.	Lady of Shalott	Crane, W.	Legends for Lionel
Wilkinson, F.	Lady of the Flag-Flowers	Lee, H.	Legends from Fairyland
Scott, Walter	Lady of the Lake	Various	Legends from River & Mountain
Madison, L.F.	Lafayette	Bulfinch, T.	Legends of Charlemagne
Buchan, J.	Lake of Gold	King, J.M.	Legends of Flowers
Hughes, Rupert	Lakerim Athletic Club	Gask, Lilian	Legends of our Little Brothers
Moore, T.	Lalla Rookh	Irving, W.	Legends of the Alhambra
Newberry, C.T.	Lambert's Bargain	Price, M.E.	Legends of the Seven Seas
Watson, E.	Lament of Billy Villy	Janvier, T.A.	Legends of the City of Mexico
Yonge, C.M.	Lances of Lynwood	Clark, J.M.	Legends of King Arthur & his Knights
Gates, J.S.	Land of Delight	D'Aulaire, I.& E.	Leif the Lucky
N/A	Land of Don't-Want-To	Morrow, W.C.	Lentala of the South Seas
Blake, Wm.	Land of Dreams	McCloskey, R.	Lentil
N/A	Land of Enchantment	Dixon, Thomas	Leopard's Spots
Pedley, M.	Land of Goodness Knows Where	Hugo, V.	Les Miserables
Yeats, W.B.	Land of Hearts Desire	Lathrop, D.	Let them Live
Austin, Mary	Land of Little Rain	Koch, Dorothy	Let it Rain
Nesbit, W.D.	Land of Make-Believe	Schneider, N.	Let's Find Out
Olmstead, M.	Land of Never Was	Drayton, G.	Let's Go to the Zoo
Price, M.E.	Land of Nod	Crawford, P.	Let's Go!
Daglish, A. (ed.)	Land of Nursery Rhyme	Marshall, Peter	Let's Keep Christmas
Noseworthy, F.	Land of Play	Schneider, N.	Let's Look Inside your House
Dodge, M.M.	Land of Pluck	Schneider, H.	Let's Look Under the City
Lummis, C.F.	Land of Poco Tiempo	Agnew, G.	Let's Pretend
Olmstead, M.	Land of Really True	MacHarg, Wm. B.	Let's Pretend...
Burnett, F.H.	Land of the Blue Flower	LaRue, M.G.	Letter to Popsey
Parker, Gilbert	Lane that Had No Turning	Daudet, A.	Letters from my Mill
Boyles, K.	Langford of the Three Bars	Stewart, E.P.	Letters of a Woman Homesteader
Greenaway, K.	Language of Flowers	Auslander, Jos.	Letters to Women...
Parker, B.& N.	Larder Lodge	Treffinger, C.	Li Lun: Lad of Courage
Lewis, C.S.	Last Battle	Dunbar, P.L.	Li'L' Gal
Lytton, E.B.	Last Days of Pompeii	Bailey, C.S.	Li'l Hannibal
Baum, L.F.	Last Egyptian	Hobart, G.V.	Li'l Verses for Li'l Fellers
Lamb, C.	Last Essays of Elia	Wiese, K.	Liang & Lo
Doyle, A.C.	Last Galley	N/A	Liberty Belles
Caldecott, R.	Last Graphic Pictures	Joan, Natalie	Lie-Down Stories
Genevoix, M.	Last Hunt	Baum, L.F.	Life & Adventures of Santa Claus
Chalmers, Patrick	Last Muster	Morris, Wm.	Life & Death of Jason
Browning, R.	Last Ride Together	Bunyan, J.	Life & Death of Mr. Badman
Parrish, R.	Last Voyage of the Donna Isabel	Douglas, R.B.	Life & Times of Madame Du Barry
Eggleston, G.C.	Last of the Flatboats	Bemelmans, L.	Life Class
Cooper, J.F	Last of the Mohicans	Fiske, J.	Life Everlasting
Crowninshield, Mrs.	Lattitude 19	Dixon, Thomas	Life Worth Living
Baum, Frank J.	Laughing Dragon of Oz	Fletcher, J.S.	Life in Arcadia
Smith, Wm. J.	Laughing Time	Pennell, E.R.	Life of J.M. Whistler
Herford, O.	Laughing Willow	Banks, Helen W.	Life of Jesus Retold for Children
Edmondson, N.M.	Lavender Garden	Dickens, C.	Life of Nicholas Nickleby
Borrow, G.	Lavengro	Dickens, C.	Life of Our Lord
Hough, E.	Law of the Land	Hawtrey	Life of St. Mary Magdalen
Macaulay, T.B.	Lays of Ancient Rome	Maeterlinck, M.	Life of the Bee
Parker, B.	Lays of the Grays	Kemble, E.W.	Life's Book of Animals
Catherwood, Mary	Lazarre	MacDonald, Geo.	Light Princess
Smith, Thorne	Lazy Bear Lane	Thackeray, L.	Light Side of Egypt
Pyle, Kath.	Lazy Matilda...	Sauer, J.L.	Light at Tern Rock
Malory, T.	Le Morte D'Arthur	Arnold, E.	Light of Asia
Eaton, J.	Leader by Destiny	Crowninshield, Mrs.	Light-House Children Abroad
Sawyer, R.S.	Least One	Hay, I.	Lighter Side of School Life
Unknown	Leather Bottel	Burgess, T.	Lightfoot the Deer

AUTHOR	TITLE	AUTHOR	TITLE
Lang, A.	Lilac Fairy Book	Upham, Eliz.	Little Brown Bear
Rand, W.B.	Lilliput Lyrics	Farrow, D.P.	Little Brown Hen
Sylva, C.	Lily of Life	Nicholson, M.	Little Brown Jug at Kildare
Madison, L.F.	Lincoln	Upham, Eliz.	Little Brown Monkey
Daugherty, J.	Lincoln's Gettysburg Address	Byron, May	Little Brown Rooster
Crane, W.	Line & Form	Holling, H.C.	Little Buffalo Boy
Cabell, J.B.	Line of Love	MacDonald, E.R.	Little Canadian Cousin
Tudor, T.	Linsey Woolsey	Brown, Marcia	Little Carousel
DuBois, W.P.	Lion	Garner, Elvira	Little Cat Lost
Davis, R.H.	Lion & the Unicorn	Fox, F.M.	Little Cat that Could Not Sleep
Williamson, H.	Lion Cub: Jungle Tale	Brown, M.W.	Little Chicken
Hoffmann, Eleanor	Lion of Barbary	Waugh, Ida	Little Chicks/Baby Tricks
Lewis, C.S.	Lion, Witch & the Wardrobe	Pollard, E.F.	Little Chief
Bacon, P.	Lion-Hearted Kitten	Jones, J.O.	Little Child
Hader, B.& E.	Lions & Tigers & Elephants Too	Skinner, A.M.	Little Child's Book of Stories
Smith, E.B.	Lions 'n' Elephants & Everything	Jewett, J.H.	Little Christmas
Voight, V.F.	Lions in the Barn	Fyleman, R.	Little Christmas Book
Wilson, H.L.	Lions of the Lord	Crawford, F.M.	Little City of Hope
Seredy, K.	Listening	Johnston, A.F.	Little Colonel
Thacher, L.W.	Listening Child	Sage, A.C.	Little Colonial Dame
Gorey, Edward	Listing Attic	Humphrey, Mabel	Little Continentals
Lenski, L.	Little Airplane	DeJong, Meindert	Little Cow & the Turtle
Allee, M.H.	Little American Girl	Brown, M.W.	Little Cowboy
Dalgliesh, A.	Little Angel	Kyser, Halsa A.	Little Cumsee in Dixie
Brady, C.T.	Little Angel from Canyon Creek	Gill, Frances	Little Days
Taylor, Jane	Little Ann...	Bannerman, H.	Little Degchie Head
Keen, R.H.	Little Ape...	Gerson, V.	Little Dignity
Hader, B.& E.	Little Appaloosa	Field, R.	Little Dog Toby
Mitchell, G.W.	Little Babs	Yonge, C.M.	Little Duke
Stirling, Monica	Little Ballet Dancer	McManus, B.	Little Dutch Cousin
Minarik, E.H.	Little Bear	Ransom, Will	Little Dutchy...
Tousey, S.	Little Bear's Pinto Pony	Sperry, A.	Little Eagle: A Navaho Boy
Tucker, E.S.	Little Belles & Beaux	Williamson, H.	Little Elephant
Pool, M.L.	Little Bermuda	Piper, W. (ed.)	Little Engine that Could
Warren, C.	Little Betty Marigold	Skariatina, I.	Little Era in Old Russia
Holling, H.C.	Little Big-Bye-and-Bye	Outhwaite, I.	Little Fairy Sister
Muter, Gladys N.	Little Bim the Circus Boy	Lenski, L.	Little Family
Hogan, Inez	Little Black & White Lamb	Brown, M.W.	Little Farmer
Gall, Alice	Little Black Ant	Henry, M.	Little Fellow
Bannerman, H.	Little Black Bobtail	Brown, M.W.	Little Fir Tree
Bannerman, H.	Little Black Mingo	Lenski, L.	Little Fire Engine
Bannerman, H.	Little Black Quasha	Brown, M.W.	Little Fireman
Bannerman, H.	Little Black Quibba	Cook, Bernadine	Little Fish that Got Away
Bannerman, H.	Little Black Sambo	Brown, M.W.	Little Fisherman
Bannerman, H.	Little Black Sambo Story Book	Tate, Eliz.	Little Flower Girl
Swift, H.H.	Little Blacknose	Sherman, F.D.	Little Folk Lyrics
Andre, R.	Little Blossoms	Frees, Harry W.	Little Folks of Animal Land
Lionni, L.	Little Blue & Little Yellow	Piper, W.	Little Folks of Other Lands
Auston, C.	Little Blue Rabbit	Davies, M.C.	Little Freckled Person
N/A	Little Book of Bores	McManus, B.	Little French Cousin
Brown, Dr. John	Little Book of Children	Lida	Little French Farm
Bangs, J.K.	Little Book of Christmas	Brown, M.W.	Little Frightened Tiger
Tynan, Kath.	Little Book of Courtesies	Brown, M.W.	Little Fur Family
Field, R.	Little Book of Days	Morgenstern, Eliz.	Little Gardeners
Johnson, E.F.	Little Book of Prayers	Fox, F.M.	Little Giant's Neighbours
Johnson, Burgess	Little Book of Necessary Nonsense	English, T.D.	Little Giant...
Farjeon, E.	Little Bookroom	Fisher, H.	Little Gift Book
Harris, Isobel	Little Boy Brown	Smith, G.	Little Girl & Phillip
Hudson, W.H.	Little Boy Lost	Gates, J.S.	Little Girl Blue Lives in the Woods...
Duvoisin, R.	Little Boy Who was Drawing	Gates, J.S.	Little Girl Blue Plays I-Spy
Moeschlin, Elsa	Little Boy with Big Apples	Mockler, G.	Little Girl from Next Door
Brown, M.W.	Little Brass Band	Lenski, L.	Little Girl of 1900
Deming, T.O.	Little Braves	Hunt, M.L.	Little Girl with Seven Names
N/A	Little Bright Eyes	Blanchard, A.E.	Little Girl's Summer Holidays
Grimm Bros.	Little Brother & Little Sister	Almond, Linda S.	Little Glad Heart
Williams, Michael	Little Brother Francis of Assisi	Goldsmith, O.	Little Goody Two-Shoes
Deming, T.O.	Little Brothers of the West	Jewett, J.H.	Little Governor of Fableland
Hyde, Eliz.	Little Brothers to the Scouts	Emerson, C.D.	Little Green Car
Gruelle, J.	Little Brown Bear	McNeil, Marion	Little Green Cart

AUTHOR	TITLE	AUTHOR	TITLE
Outhwaite, I. & A.	Little Green Road to Fairyland	Miller, O.B.	Little Pictures of Japan
Uttley, Alison	Little Grey Rabbit & Weasels	Ogden, Ruth	Little Pierre & Big Peter
Uttley, Alison	Little Grey Rabbit's Christmas	Brown, M.W.	Little Pig's Picnic...
Tucker, E.S.	Little Grown-Ups	Disney, W.	Little Pigs' Picnic
Scripps, H.J.	Little Handfull	Warren, Maude L.	Little Pioneers
Coatsworth, E.	Little Haymakers	Mendel, F.E.	Little Polish Cousin
Humphrey, M.	Little Heroes & Heroines	Gould, E.L.	Little Polly Prentiss
Behn, Harry	Little Hill	Smith, G.	Little Precious
McManus, B.	Little Hindu Cousin	Saint-Exupery, A.	Little Prince
Ogden, Ruth	Little Homespun	Chester, Geo. R.	Little Prince Toofat
Malloch, D.	Little Hop Skipper	Burnett, F.H.	Little Princess
Greene, G.	Little Horse Bus	Charskaya, L.A.	Little Princess Nina
Burton, V.L.	Little House	Ogden, Ruth	Little Queen of Hearts
Dawson, Coningsby	Little House	Fillmore, P.H.	Little Question of Ladies' Rights
Wilder, L.I.	Little House in Big Woods	Schlein, M.	Little Rabbit the High Jumper
Bouvet, M.	Little House in Pimlico	Phillips, E.C.	Little Rag Doll
Wilder, L.I.	Little House on the Prairie	Hofman, Caroline	Little Red Balloon
N/A	Little Housekeepers	Sawyer, R.S.	Little Red Horse
Burnett, F.H.	Little Hunchback Zia	Deming, T.O.	Little Red People
Deming, T.O.	Little Indian Folk	Denslow, W.W.	Little Red Riding Hood
LaRue, M.G.	Little Indians	N/A	Little Red Riding Hood
MacDonald, Golden	Little Island	Gates, J.S.	Little Red, White, Blue
Haines, Alice C.	Little Japs at Home	Jamieson, M.M.	Little Redskins
Credle, Ellis	Little Jeems Henry	Seegmiller, W.	Little Rhymes for Little Readers
Burgess, T.	Little Joe Otter	Rand, Ann	Little River
Bannerman, H.	Little Kettle-Head	Van Dyke, H.	Little Rivers
Hardy, M.E.	Little King & Princess True	McManus, B.	Little Scotish Cousin
Craik, D.	Little Lame Prince	France, A.	Little Sea-Dogs
Housman, L.	Little Land	Fox, John Jr.	Little Shepherd of Kingdom Come
Franchi, A.	Little Lead Soldier	Lindquist, Jennie	Little Silver House
Wightman, F.P.	Little Leather Breeches	Little, F.	Little Sister Snow
Walford, L.B	Little Legacy	Van Derveer, H.	Little Slam Bang
Politi, L.	Little Leo	Stoddard, W.O.	Little Smoke
Dearmer, P.	Little Lives of the Saints	Crommelin, May	Little Soldiers
Burnett, F.H.	Little Lord Fauntleroy	Humphrey, M.	Little Soldiers & Sailors
MacDonald, Golden	Little Lost Lamb	Moffat, A.	Little Songs from Long Ago
Robinson, M.L.	Little Lucia's School	Nixon-Roulet	Little Spanish Cousin
Liddell, Mary	Little Machinery	Burnett, F.H.	Little St. Elizabeth
Bouvet, M.	Little Marjorie's Love Story	Goss, F.C.	Little St. Sunshine
Andersen, H.C.	Little Match Girl	Greene, G.	Little Steam Roller
Barzini, Luigi	Little Match Man	Hader, B.& E.	Little Stone House
Loomis, C.B.	Little Maud & her Mama	Sowerby, Githa	Little Stories for Little People
Cory, F.	Little Me	DeJong, Meindert	Little Stray Dog
Alcott, L.M.	Little Men	Wiederseim, G.	Little Sunbeam's Book
Tucker, E.S.	Little Men & Maids	Gruelle, J.	Little Sunny Stories
Low, Frances H.	Little Men in Scarlet	Gropper, Wm.	Little Tailor
Andersen, H.C.	Little Mermaid	Crownfield, Gertrude	Little Tailor of Windy Way
Butler, E.C.	Little Mexican Cousin	Smith, Wallace	Little Tigress
Blanchard, A.E.	Little Miss Mouse	Ardizzone, E.	Little Tim & Brave Sea Captain
Molesworth, M.	Little Miss Peggy	Peary, M.A.	Little Tooktoo
Brine, M.D.	Little Miss Toodledums	Gramatky, H.	Little Toot
Lindsay, M.M.	Little Missy	James, Henry	Little Tour in France
Taylor, M.I.	Little Mistress Goodhope	Hader, B.& E.	Little Town
Smith, G.	Little Mother & Georgie	Wilder, L.I.	Little Town on the Prairie
Joan, Natalie	Little Mothers	Hogan, Inez	Little Toy Airplane
Harris, J.C.	Little Mr. Thimblefinger	Greene, G.	Little Train
Cheever, H.A.	Little Mr. Van Vere of China	Lyle, G.M.	Little Travellers in Wales
Clark, A.N.	Little Navajo Bluebird	Baldwin, Clara	Little Tuck
Ets, Marie H.	Little Old Automobile	Praeger, S.R.	Little Twin Dragon
Barnum, Jay H.	Little Old Truck	Coolidge, F.	Little Ugly Face
Kunhardt, D.	Little Ones	Harris, J.C.	Little Union Scout
Politi, L.	Little Pancho	Gates, Doris	Little Vic
Farrow, G.E.	Little Panjandrum's Dodo	Wells, H.G.	Little Wars
Faulkner, Georgene	Little Peachling	Frost, F.	Little Whistler
Elkin, R.H.	Little People	March, Eleanor	Little White Barbara
Choate, F.	Little People of the Hills	Barrie, J.M.	Little White Bird
Malet, Lucas	Little Peter	Hader, B.& E.	Little White Foot
Hays, M.G.	Little Pets Book	Lathrop, D.	Little White Goat
Hunter, Richard	Little Pickles	Goudge, Eliz.	Little White Horse

AUTHOR	TITLE	AUTHOR	TITLE
King, J.M.	Little White Town of Never Weary	Thompson, R.P.	Lost King of Oz
Lang, A.	Little Wildrose	Clark, Mary S.	Lost Legends/Nursery Songs
Disney, W.	Little Wise Hen	Lattimore, Eleanor	Lost Leopard
Bennett, Anna E.	Little Witch	Lathrop, D.	Lost Merry-Go-Round
Baum, L.F.	Little Wizard Stories/Oz	Burnett, F.H.	Lost Prince
Teal, Val	Little Woman Wanted Noise	Gordon, H.C.	Lost Princess
Alcott, L.M.	Little Women	MacDonald, Geo.	Lost Princess
Bianco, M.W.	Little Wooden Doll	Queen Marie	Lost Princess
Dalgliesh, A.	Little Wooden Farmer	Baum, L.F.	Lost Princess of Oz
Spielmann, M.H.	Littledom Castle	Tracy, Louis	Lost Provinces
Webb, E. & D.	Littlest Fairy	McNeil, E.	Lost Treasure Cave
Coatsworth, E.	Littlest House	Bancroft, Alberta	Lost Village
Lathrop, D.	Littlest Mouse	Cullen, Countee	Lost Zoo
Adcock, Marion	Littlest One	DuChaillu, Paul	Lost in the Jungle
Webb, M. St. John	Littlest One Again	Ashmore, M.	Lost, Stolen & Strayed
Tucker, E.S.	Littlest Ones	Cavanah, F.	Louis of New Orleans
Massey, Jeanne	Littlest Witch	Becker, May L.	Louisa Alcott's People
Turpin, Edna	Littling of Gaywood	De La Mare, W.	Love
Gates, J.S.	Live Doll's House Party	DeBosschere, J.	Love Books of Ovid
Gates, J.S.	Live Doll's Play Days	Spielmann, M.H.	Love Family
Gates, J.S.	Live Dolls in Fairyland	Ford, P.L.	Love Finds the Way
Gates, J.S.	Live Dolls in Wonderland	Biggers, E.D.	Love Insurance
Burgess, G.	Lively City O'Ligg	Wither, G.	Love Song
Seton, E.T.	Lives of the Hunted	Leigh, M.C.	Love Songs & Verses
Phipps, Mary	Liza Jane & the Kinkies	N/A	Love Songs Old & New
Ewing, J.H.	Lob Lie-by-the-Fire	Kiser, S.E.	Love Sonnets of an Office Boy
Adams, A.	Log of a Cowboy	Bolton, C.K.	Love Story of Ursula Wolcott
Bangs, J.K.	Lohengrin	Parrish, R.	Love Under Fire
Rideout, H.	Lola the Bear	Potter, M.K.	Love in Art
Stanley, H.M.	London Street Arabs	Bunner, H.C.	Love in Old Cloathes
Nicholson, Wm.	London Types	Anglund, J.W.	Love is a Special Way of Feeling
Gorham, Maurice	Londoners	Beauclerk, H.	Love of the Foolish Angel
Schultz, J.W.	Lone Bull's Mistake	Herrick, R.	Love's Dilemmas
James, Will	Lone Cowboy...	Smith, G.	Loveable Tales of Janey, Josey & Joe
Eaton, J.	Lone Journey	Snyder, F.	Lovely Garden
Lyle, E.P.	Lone Star	Simont, M.	Lovely Summer
Coatsworth, E.	Lonely Maria	N/A	Lovely Woman
Steig, Wm.	Lonely Ones	Gibbings, Rbt.	Lovely is The Lee
Bontemps, A.	Lonesome Boy	Clay, J.C.	Lovers' Mother Goose
Brown, A.F.	Lonesomest Doll	O'Neill, Rose	Loves of Edwy
Lamprey, L.	Long Ago People	Seawell, M.E.	Loves of Lady Arabella
Howes, E.	Long Bright Land	Crockett, S.R.	Loves of Miss Ann
Sawyer, R.S.	Long Christmas	Rice, Alice H.	Lovey Mary
Dalgliesh, A.	Long Live the King!	Milhous, Kath.	Lovina
Johnston, M.	Long Roll	Hellman, Sam	Low Bridge & Punk Pungs
Wilder, L.I.	Long Winter	Carman, B.	Low Tide/Grand Pre
Barnaby, H.T.	Long-Eared Bat	Robinson, E.	Loyal Little Maid
Burgess, T.	Longlegs the Heron	Ogden, Ruth	Loyal Little Redcoat
Anglund, J.W.	Look Out the Window	Barnes, James	Loyal Traitor
Bianco, P.	Look-Inside Easter Egg	Willson, J.	Lucian's Wonderland...
James, Will	Look-See with Uncle Bill	Martin, E.S.	Lucid Intervals
Flanders, H.H.	Looking Out of Jimmie	Meredith, O.	Lucille
Clark, A.N.	Looking for Something	Hunt, M.L.	Lucinda: Little Girl of 1860
Stringer, A.J.	Loom of Destiny	Bacon, J.D.	Luck O'Lady Joan
Gramatky, H.	Loopy	Knipe, A.A.	Luck of Denewood
De La Mare, W.	Lord Fish	Nodier, C.	Luck of the Bean Rows
Shiel, M.P.	Lord of the Sea	Darling, E.B.	Luck of the Trail
D'Aulaire, I.& E.	Lord's Prayer	Baum, L.F.	Lucky Bucky in Oz
Nicholson, M.	Lords of High Decision	Kunhardt, D.	Lucky Mrs. Ticklefeather
Scoville, S.	Lords of the Wild	Barbour, R.H.	Lucky Seventh
Bindloss, H.	Lorimer of the Northwest	Knipe, E.& A.	Lucky Sixpence
Blackmore, R.D.	Lorna Doone	De La Mare, W.	Lucy
Gordon, Eliz.	Lorraine & Little People of Spring	Unwin, Nora S.	Lucy & Little Red Horse
Gordon, Eliz.	Lorraine & Little People of Summer	Hughes, Shirley	Lucy & Tom's Day
Gordon, Eliz.	Lorraine & the Little People	Farjeon, B.L.	Lucy & their Majesties
Van Dyke, H.	Lost Boy	Ardizzone, E.	Lucy Brown & Mr. Grimes
Badger, J.E.	Lost City	Rae, J.	Lucy Locket...
Malone, H.	Lost Fairy Tales	McGinley, Phyllis	Lucy McLockett
Moon, G.	Lost Indian Magic	Molloy, Anne	Lucy's Christmas

AUTHOR	TITLE	AUTHOR	TITLE
Harrison, Ada	Lucy's Village	Molesworth, M.	Magic Nuts
Herbertson, A.	Lucy-Mary	Field, R.	Magic Pawnshop
Snedeker, C.D.	Luke's Quest	Ayme, Marcel	Magic Pictures
Strettell, A.	Lullabies of Many Lands	Follett, H.T.	Magic Portholes
Worthington, Eliz.	Lullabies of Many Lands	Lindsay, N.	Magic Pudding
Shelby, A.B.	Lullaby Book	D'Aulaire, I.& E.	Magic Rug
Field, E.	Lullaby Land	Dolbier, Maurice	Magic Shop
Bridgman, Betty	Lullaby for Eggs	Blodgett, M.F.	Magic Slippers
Rounds, Glen	Lumbercamp	Grishina, N.G.	Magic Squirrel
Tousey, S.	Lumberjack Bill	Wade, B.E.	Magic Stone
Goldberg, M.	Lunch Box Story	Buffano, R.	Magic Strings...
Bower, B.M.	Lure of the Dim Trails	Eells, E.S.	Magic Tooth
Hawthorne, H.	Lure of the Garden	Moon, G.	Magic Trail
Fraser, C.L.	Lute of Love	Buchan, J.	Magic Walking Stick
Austin, Margot	Lutie	Hamer, S.H.	Magic Wand
Martin, E.S.	Luxury of Children	Browne, E.G.	Magic Whistle
Dulac, E.	Lyrics Pathetic & Humorous...	Rhys, Grace (ed.)	Magic Wood Beyond the World
Shakespeare, Wm.	Macbeth	Nesbit, E.	Magic World
Copeland, W.	Mad Motor	Montgomery, L.M.	Magic for Marigold
MacDonald, Ray	Mad Scientist	Baum, L.F.	Magic of Oz
Ward, Lynd	Mad-Man's Drum	Donahey, M.D.	Magical House of Zur
Wesselhoeft, Lily	Madam Mary of the Zoo	Gruelle, J.	Magical Land of Noom
Flaubert, G.	Madame Bovary	Sabin, E.H.	Magical Man of Mirth
Long, J.L.	Madame Butterfly	Brink, C.R.	Magical Melons
Tarbell, Ida M.	Madame Roland	Snow, Jack	Magical Mimics in Oz
Canfield, Dorothy	Made-to-Order Stories	Baum, L.F.	Magical Monarch of Mo
Bemelmans, L.	Madeline	Jenks, Tudor	Magician for One Day
Bemelmans, L.	Madeline & the Gypsies	Lewis, C.S.	Magician's Nephew
Bemelmans, L.	Madeline's Rescue	Disney, W.	Magnificent Mr. Toad
Brink, C.R.	Mademoiselle Misfortune	Peat, F.B.	Magnificent Squeak
Steedman, Amy	Madonna of the Goldfinch	Turner, N.B.	Magpie Lane
Daly, T.A.	Madrigali	Pogany, Nebby	Magyar Fairy Tales
Sudermann, H.	Magda	Haggard, H.R.	Mahatma & the Hare
Sawyer, R.S.	Maggie Rose: Her Birthday Christmas	Spofford, H.P.	Maid He Married
Black, I.S.	Maggie, Mischievous Magpie	Peacock, T.L.	Maid Marian/Crotchet Castle
Henderson, L.R.	Magic Aeroplane	Jackson, G.E.	Maid of Middies' Haven
Hartwell (ed.)	Magic Bed	Parrish, R.	Maid of the Forest
Norton, Mary	Magic Bed-Knob	Chambers, Rbt.	Maid-at-Arms
Williams, C.A.	Magic Book	Fisher, H.	Maidens Fair
Dolbier, Maurice	Magic Bus	Thoreau, H.D.	Maine Woods
Noyes, A. (ed.)	Magic Casement	Musson, B.	Maisie & her Dog Skip in Fairyland
Corkey, E.	Magic Circle	N/A	Maisie-Daisie Book
Untermeyer, L.	Magic Circle	Gordon, A.C.	Maje: A Love Story
Higgins, V.M.	Magic Circus	McCloskey, R.	Make Way for Ducklings
Nesbit, E.	Magic City	Lowry, H.D.	Make-Believe
Baum, L.F.	Magic Cloak...	Tucker, E.S.	Make-Believe Men & Women
Bonner, M.G.	Magic Clock	Chambers, Rbt.	Maker of Moons
MacDonald, Geo.	Magic Crook	LeGallienne, R.	Maker of Rainbows
Queen Marie	Magic Doll of Roumania	Fletcher, J.S.	Making of Matthais
Black, Dorothy	Magic Egg	Brailsford, M.	Making of William Penn
Dickens, C.	Magic Fishbone	Wyatt, Horace	Malice in Kulturland
Kozisek, Josef	Magic Flutes	Malory, T.	Malory's King Arthur
Porter, G.S.	Magic Garden	Criss, Mildred	Malou
Milne, A.A.	Magic Hill	Harben, Wm. N.	Mam' Linda
Housman, L.	Magic Horse	Gregory, L.F.	Mama Nelly & I
Baker, C.	Magic Image from India	Milne-Home, M.P.	Mama's Black Nurse Stories
Marchioness/London	Magic Ink Spot	Lenski, L.	Mamma Hattie's Girl
De La Mare, W.	Magic Jacket	Sandler, M.C.	Mamma's Angel Child
James, Hart.	Magic Jaw Bone	Bibbins, R.M.	Mammy 'mongst the Wild Nations
Bonner, M.G.	Magic Journeys	Blanchard, A.E.	Mammy's Baby
Van Sickle, J.H.	Magic Key	Williams, C.A.	Mammy's Lil'l Chillums
Webb, M. St. John	Magic Lamplighter	Attwood, Wm.	Man Who Could Grow Hair
Buff, Mary	Magic Maize	Krasilovsky, P.	Man Who Didn't Wash his Dishes
Bonner, M.G.	Magic Map	Godfrey, Hollis	Man Who Ended War
D'Aulaire, I.& E.	Magic Meadow	Bishop, C.H.	Man Who Lost his Head
Slobodkin, L.	Magic Michael	Markham, E.	Man With the Hoe...
Gilbert, Wm.	Magic Mirror	Lockhart, C.	Man from Bitter Roots
Clark, A.N.	Magic Money	McCutcheon, G.B.	Man from Brodneys
Bonner, M.G.	Magic Music Shop	Tarkington, B.	Man from Home

AUTHOR	TITLE
Carmichael, Phil	Man from the Moon
Bateson, C.	Man in the Camelot Cloak
Rinehart, M.R.	Man in the Lower Ten
Sage, J.	Man in the Manhole & Fix-It-Men
N/A	Man in the Moon
Otto, M.G.	Man in the Moon
Lawrence, J.	Man in the Moon Stories...
Thanet, O.	Man of the Hour
MacGrath, H.	Man on the Box
Cowen, Wm. J.	Man with Four Lives
Farrow, G.E.	Mandarin's Kite
Price, M.E.	Manger Babe
Sylvester, C.	Manny & Co.
Bangs, J.K.	Mantel-Piece Minstrels
Austin, Margot	Manuel's Kite String
Bannon, L.	Manuela's Birthday in Old Mexico
Crespi, P.	Manuelito of Costa Rica
Jones, J.O. (ed.)	Many Mansions...
Thurber, J.	Many Moons
Deming, T.O.	Many Snows Ago
Edwards, Harry S.	Marbeau Cousins
Angelo, V.	Marble Fountain
Gruelle, J.	Marcella Stories
Parker, Gilbert	March of the White Guard
Lee, M.	Marcos...
DeWolf, W.L.	Mardo's Animal Rhymes
Tarrant, M.	Margaret Tarrant's Christmas Garland
Colcock, A.T.	Margaret Tudor
Fielding-Hall, H.	Margaret's Book
Steedman, Amy	Margot/Golden Fish
Greenaway, K.	Marigold Garden
Forbes, Helen	Mario's Castle
Dwiggins, W.	Marionette in Motion
Mills, W.H.	Marionettes, Masks & Shadows
Aldrich, T.B.	Marjorie Daw
Beard, P.	Marjorie's Little Doll School
Hawkins, Q.	Mark, Mark, Shut the Door!
Frederic, H.	Market Place
Cummings, E.	Marmaduke of Tennessee
Hovey, R.	Marriage of Guenevere
Castle, E.	Marshfield the Observer
Newberry, C.T.	Marshmallow
Krag, M.A.	Martha-Jane: Nursery Nonsense
White, W.A.	Martial Advens. of Henry & Me
Bishop, C.H.	Martin DePorres, Hero
Masefield, J.	Martin Hyde
McNeer, May	Martin Luther
Farjeon, E.	Martin Pippin/Apple Orchard
Farjeon, E.	Martin Pippin/Daisy-Field
Barringer, M.	Martin the Goose Boy
Baum, L.F.	Marvelous Land of Oz
Molesworth, M.	Mary
Crew, A.	Mary & her Kitchen Garden
Fryer, J.E.	Mary Frances [ALL TITLES]
Denslow, W.W.	Mary Had a Little Lamb
Daringer, H.F.	Mary Montgomery, Rebel
Meyer, L.R.	Mary North
Travers, P.L.	Mary Poppins [ALL TITLES]
Almond, Linda S.	Mary Redding Takes Charge
Johnston, A.F.	Mary Ware of Texas
Daugherty, Sonia	Mashinka's Secret
Crane, W.	Masque of Days
Hewlett, M.	Masque of Dead Florentines
Robertson, W.G.	Masque of May Morning
Ewing, J.H.	Master Fritz
Baum, L.F.	Master Key
Mukerji, D.G.	Master Monkey
Meigs, C.	Master Simon's Garden
Bennett, John	Master Skylark

AUTHOR	TITLE
Stevenson, R.L.	Master of Ballantrae
Brooks, E.S.	Master of Strong Hearts
O'Neill, Rose	Master-Mistress
Marryat, Fred.	Masterman Ready
Bindloss, H.	Masters of the Wheat-Lands
Edmonds, W.D.	Matchlock Gun
Tennyson, A.	Maud
Rossetti, C.	Maude: Prose & Verse
Bare, A.E.	Maui's Summer
Burgess, G.	Maxims of Methuselah
N/A	May & November Correspondence
Knipe, E.B.	May Flower Maid
Jordan, E.	May Iverson...
Johnston, A.F.	May Ware, Little Colonel's Chum
Burton, V.L.	Maybelle the Cable Car
Gratacap, L.P.	Mayor of New York
Green, A.K.	Mayor's Wife
Spyri, J.	Mazli
Seuss, Dr.	McElligot's Pool
Lawson, R.	McWhinney's Jaunt
Ainslie, K.	Me & Catharine Susan Earns Honest Penny
Webb, R.	Me & Lawson
Ainslie, K.	Me and Catharine Susan
Lyman, E.B.	Me'ow Jones
Brown, Alice	Meadow Grass
King, C.	Medal of Honor
Gray, Eliz. J.	Meggy McIntosh
Handforth, T.	Mei Li
Peacock, T.L.	Melincourt...
Ungerer, Tomi	Mellops Go Diving for Treasure
Ungerer, Tomi	Mellops Go Flying
Davis, L.R.	Melody, Mutton, Bone & Slam
Wister, O.	Members of the Family
Doyle, A.C.	Memoirs of Sherlock Holmes
Keeler, D.B.	Memoirs of Simple Simon
Daskam, J.	Memoirs of a Baby
DeSegur, S.	Memoirs of a Donkey
Sassoon, S.	Memoirs of a Fox Hunting Man
Horne, Richard H.	Memoirs of a London Doll
Galsworthy, J.	Memories
Muller, M.	Memories...
Hawes, Eliz.	Men Can Take It
Browning, R.	Men and Women
Thoreau, H.D.	Men of Concord
Pyle, H.	Men of Iron
Remington, F.	Men with The Bark On
Shippen, K.B.	Men, Microscopes & Living Things
Miller, M.B.	Menagerie
Shakespeare, Wm.	Merchant of Venice
Bacon, P.	Mercy & the Mouse
Gray, Eliz. J.	Meredith's Ann
Andersen, H.C.	Mermaid & other Tales
Brown, J.	Mermaid's Gift
Bowen, W.A.	Merrimeg
Torrey, M.	Merriweathers
Aldin, C.	Merry & Bright
Pyle, H.	Merry Adventures of Robin Hood
Sowerby, Githa	Merry Book
Hurd, C.	Merry Chase
N/A	Merry Children's Nursery Rhymes
McGinley, Phyllis	Merry Christmas, Happy New Year
Brown, Alice	Merry Links
Stevenson, R.L.	Merry Men
O'Cluny, Thomas	Merry Multifleet/Mounting Multicorps
Gaze, H.	Merry Piper
Duplaix, G.	Merry Shipwreck
N/A	Merry Times
Shakespeare, Wm.	Merry Wives of Windsor
Richards, L.E.	Merry-Go-Round

AUTHOR	TITLE	AUTHOR	TITLE
Wells, Carolyn	Merry-Go-Round	Johnston, A.F.	Miss Santa Claus of the Pullman
Brown, Paul	Merrylegs	Robertson, Keith	Missing Brother
Dix, B.M.	Merrylips	Moon, G.	Missing Katchina
Van Loon, H.W.	Message of the Bells	Belloc, H.	Missing Masterpiece
Cawein, M.J.	Message of the Lilies	Farrow, G.E.	Missing Prince
Byrne, D.	Messer. Marco Polo	Politi, L.	Mission Bell
Rosseau, Victor	Messiah of the Cylinder	Thanet, O.	Missionary Sheriff
Carus, Helena	Metten of Tyre	Brown, M.W.	Mister Dog
Blichfeldt, E.H.	Mexican Journey	Montgomery, R.G.	Mister Jim
Perkins, L.F.	Mexican Twins	Ets, Marie H.	Mister Penny
D'Harnoncourt, R.	Mexicana	White, T.H.	Mistress Masham's Repose
Porter, G.S.	Michael O'Halloran	Montgomery, L.M.	Mistress Pat
Verne, Jules	Michael Strogoff	Barclay, F.	Mistress of Shenstone
Michelson, M.	Michael Thwaites's Wife	Henry, M.	Misty of Chincoteague
Hunt, M.L.	Michel's Island	Newberry, C.T.	Mittens
Brown, Paul	Mick & Mac	Holberg, R.	Mitty on Mr. Syrup's Farm
Disney, W.	Mickey & the Beanstalk	Waylett, Richard	Mixed Pickles
Kirk, V.	Mickey & the Monkeys	Melville, Herman	Moby Dick
Disney, W.	Mickey Mouse [ALL TITLES]	Weedon, L.L.	Model Menagerie
Branley, Frank	Mickey's Magnet	Falls, C.B.	Modern ABC Book
Hamer, S.H.	Micky Magee's Menagerie	Pyle, H.	Modern Aladdin
Sharp, E.	Micky...	Harrison, T.M.	Modern Arms and a Feudal Throne
Shakespeare, Wm.	MidSummer Night's Dream	Green, Roger L.	Modern Fairy Stories
Estes, Eleanor	Middle Moffat	Miller, A.D.	Modern Obstacle
Hader, B.& E.	Midget & Bridget	Wadsworth, W.	Modern Story Book
North, S.	Midnight & Jeremiah	Struther, J.	Modern Struwwelpeter
Masefield, J.	Midnight Folk	Belloc, H.	Modern Traveller
Seawell, M.E.	Midshipman Paulding	Wells, H.G.	Modern Utopia
Wilhelmson, C.	Midsummer Night	Defoe, D.	Moll Flanders
Hader, B.& E.	Mighty Hunter	Bangs, J.K.	Molly & The Unwiseman
Wodehouse, P.G.	Mike	Bangs, J.K.	Molly & Unwiseman Abroad
Burton, V.L.	Mike Mulligan & his Steam Shovel	Jacobs, Joseph	Molly Whuppie
Aspden, Don	Mike of Company D.	Berry, E.	Mom Du Jos...
Sauer, J.L.	Mike's House	Marcher, M.W.	Monarch Butterfly
Petersham, M.	Miki	Seton, E.T.	Monarch the Big Bear...
Kingman, Lee	Mikko's Fortune	Carse, R.	Monarchs of Merry England
Johnston, A.F.	Mildred's Inheritance	Garland, H.	Money Magic
Brainerd, E.S.	Millicent in Dreamland	Parker, Gilbert	Money Master
Gag, W.	Millions of Cats	Farnol, J.	Money Moon
Ward, Mrs. H.	Milly & Olly	Merriman, H.S.	Money Spinner
Simont, M.	Mimi	Spyri, J.	Moni the Goat Boy
Sewell, H.	Ming & Mehitable	Bourget, P.	Monica
Holling, H.C.	Minn of the Mississippi	Krauss, Ruth	Monkey Day
Jones, E.O.	Minnie the Mermaid	Hall, G.	Monkey Shines
Coleridge, C.R.	Minstrel Dick	Williamson, H.	Monkey Tale
Warwick, Charles	Mirabeau & the French Revolution	Christopher, Anne	Monkey Twins
Sorensen, Virginia	Miracles on Maple Hill	Hogan, Inez	Monkey Twins, They Saw it All
Sterne, Emma G.	Miranda is a Princess	Drummond, Henry	Monkey that Would Not Kill
Dix, D.	Mirandy	Price, M.E.	Monkey-Do
Makower, S.	Mirror of Music	D'Arcy, Ella	Monochromes
Woodruff, H.S.	Mis' Beauty	Herford, B.	Monologues
Ingoldsby, T.	Misadventures at Margate	Haggard, H.R.	Montezuma's Daughter
Hoffmann, Eleanor	Mischief in Fez	Tompkins, Jane	Moo-Wee: The Musk-Ox
Bacon, P.	Mischief in Mayfield	Heath, J.F.	Mooky & Tooky
Peacock, T.L.	Misfortunes of Elphin & Rhododaphne	Greener, Leslie	Moon Ahead
Graham, H.	Misrepresentative Women	Clark, G.O.	Moon Babies
Bonner, M.G.	Miss Angelina Adorable	Nash, Dorothy	Moon Baby
Magruder, Julia	Miss Ayr of Virginia	Udry, J.M.	Moon Jumpers
Hurd, Marian K.	Miss Billy: Neighborhood Story	Munkittrick, R.K.	Moon Prince & Other Nabobs
Allen, G.	Miss Cayley's Adventures	Harrison, E.O.	Moon Princess
Bailey, C.S.	Miss Hickory	Hopkins, H.C.	Moon-Boat
De La Mare, W.	Miss Jemima	White, Roma	Moonbeams/Brownies
Orr, Aileen	Miss Manners	Beard, D.	Moonblight
Molesworth, M.	Miss Mouse & her Boys	Davis, M.E.M.	Moons of Balbanca
Crothers, S.M.	Miss Muffet's Christmas Party	Housman, L.	Moonshine & Clover
Paget-Fredericks, J.	Miss Pert's Christmas Tree	Uttley, Alison	Moonshine & Magic
Tilton, D.	Miss Petticoats	Freeman, Don	Mop Top
MacGregor, Ellen	Miss Pickerell Goes to Mars	Ainslie, K.	Mops Versus Tails
Mason, Miriam E.	Miss Posy Longlegs	Ingelow, J.	Mopsa the Fairy

AUTHOR	TITLE	AUTHOR	TITLE
Belloc, H.	Moral Alphabet	Irwin, V.	Mountain of Jade
Beerbohm, M.	More	Chambers, Rbt.	Mountain-Land
Drinkwater, J.	More About Me	Adams, J.D.	Mountains are Free
Tyrell, Eleanor	More About the Squirrels	Godden, Rumer	Mouse House
Gerson, V.	More Adventures of Happy Heart Family	Eager, E.M.	Mouse Manor
Herford, O.	More Animals	Graham, Al	Mouse with a Small Guitar
Belloc, H.	More Beasts for Worse Children	Godden, Rumer	Mousewife
Abingdon, Alex	More Boners	Rigby, D.	Moustachio
Jacobs, J.	More Celtic Fairy Tales	Means, F.C.	Moved-Outers
Loomis, C.B.	More Cheerful Americans	Austin, Margot	Moxie & Hanty & Bunty
Jacobs, J.	More English Fairy Tales	Francoise	Mr. & Mrs. So and So
Ade, G.	More Fables	Shirk, J.C.	Mr. Baxter's Dandelion Garden
Caldecott, R.	More Graphic Pictures	Shippen, K.B.	Mr. Bell Invents the Telephone
Bigham, M.A.	More Mother Goose Village Stories	Farmiloe, Edith	Mr. Biddle & the Dragon
Shay, F.	More Pious Friends	Hader, B.& E.	Mr. Billy's Gun
Gordon, Eliz.	More Really So Stories	Bangs, J.K.	Mr. Bonaparte of Corsica
Olcott, F.J. (ed.)	More Tales from Arabian Nights	De La Mare, W.	Mr. Bumps & His Monkey
Milne, A.A.	More Very Young Songs	Sutton, Adah L.	Mr. Bunny - His Book
Eaton, S.	More about Teddy B. & Teddy G.	Perkins, L.F.	Mr. Chick...
Ross, M.I.	Morgan's Fourth Son	Lefferts, S.T.	Mr. Cinnamon Bear
Stuart, Ruth M.	Moriah's Mourning	Paine, A.B.	Mr. Crow & the Whitewash
Porter, G.S.	Morning Face	Dunne, F.P.	Mr. Dooley's Philosophy
Forrest, A.S.	Morocco	Beistle, A.S.	Mr. Heinie
Harper, Vincent	Mortgage on the Brain	Rhys, Mimpsy	Mr. Hermit Crab
Petersham, M.	Moses	Evans, Eva K.	Mr. Jones & Mr. Finnigan
Shippen, K.B.	Moses	Judson, C.I.	Mr. Justice Holmes
Pauli, Hertha	Most Beautiful House...	Mitchell, S.W.	Mr. Kris Kringle
Waugh, A.	Most Women	Carruth, H.	Mr. Milo Bush
McGinley, Phyllis	Most Wonderful Doll in the World	Ort, Jane	Mr. Mogo Mouse
Price, M.E.	Mota & the Monkey Tree	Bangs, J.K.	Mr. Munchausen
Wister, O.	Mother	Slobodkin, L.	Mr. Mushroom
Brine, M.D.	Mother & Baby	Emerson, C.	Mr. Nip & Mr. Tuck
Gilson, R.R.	Mother & Father	Weisgard, L.	Mr. Peaceable Paints
Deihl, E.G.	Mother Brown Earth's Children	Seaman, Louise	Mr. Peck's Pets
Wiggin, K.D.	Mother Carey's Chickens	Ets, Marie H.	Mr. Penny's Race Horse
Gugu	Mother Duck's Children	Slobodkin, L.	Mr. Petersand's Cats & Kittens
Gordon, Eliz.	Mother Earth's Children	Girvin, B.	Mr. Piccolo
Mother Goose	Mother Goose [MAJORITY OF TITLES]	Dickens, C.	Mr. Pickwick's Christmas
Warren, M.R.	Mother Goose & her Friends	Dickens, C.	Mr. Pickwick...
Bartug, C.M.	Mother Goose Etiquette Rhymes	Atwater, R.	Mr. Popper's Penguins
Byington, Eloise	Mother Goose Fun	Lucas, E.V.	Mr. Punch's Country Songs
Jordan, N.	Mother Goose Handicraft	Harris, J.C.	Mr. Rabbit at Home
Gruelle, Justin	Mother Goose Parade	Paine, A.B.	Mr. Rabbit's Wedding
Bigham, M.A.	Mother Goose Village	Robinson, Tom P.	Mr. Red Squirrel
Whitney, A.D.T.	Mother Goose for Grown Folks	Lawson, R.	Mr. Revere & I
Carryl, G.W.	Mother Goose for Grownups	McCready, T.L.	Mr. Stubbs
Baum, L.F.	Mother Goose in Prose	LeGallienne, R.	Mr. Sun & Mrs. Moon
Wells, Carolyn	Mother Goose's Menagerie	Ets, Marie H.	Mr. T.W. Anthony Woo
Cavally, Fred. L.	Mother Goose's Teddy Bears	Sayers, F.C.	Mr. Tidy Paws
Bridgman, L.J.	Mother Goose/Wild Beast Show	Darwin, Bernard	Mr. Tootleoo & Co.
Muter, Gladys N.	Mother Let Me Do It	Lawson, R.	Mr. Twigg's Mistake
Warren, I.R.	Mother Love	Dawson, Carley	Mr. Wicker's Window
Meigs, C.	Mother Makes Christmas	Lawson, R.	Mr. Wilmer
Long, W.J.	Mother Nature	DeMusset, Paul	Mr. Wind & Madam Rain
Fox, F.M.	Mother Nature's Little Ones	Bancroft, L.	Mr. Woodchuck
Burgess, T.	Mother West Wind Why Stories	Merryman, M.P.	Mr. Wubbles Bubbles
Burgess, T.	Mother West Wind's Animal Friends	Stockton, Frank	Mrs. Cliff's Yacht
Burgess, T.	Mother West Wind's Children	Bonner, M.G.	Mrs. Cucumber Green
Burgess, T.	Mother West Wind's Neighbors	Dodworth, D.	Mrs. Doodlepunk Trades Work
Bridgman, L.J.	Mother Wild Beast/Wild Beast Show	Pool, M.L.	Mrs. Gerald
Burn, J.H.	Mother's Book of Song	Addison, J.	Mrs. John Vernon
LeMair, H.W.	Mother's Little Rhyme Book	Howes, E.	Mrs. Kindbush
Pyle, Kath.	Mother's Nursery Tales	Stimson, F.J.	Mrs. Knollys...
Porter, G.S.	Moths of the Limberlost	Lamb, C.	Mrs. Leicester's School
Wharton, E.	Motor-Flight through France	Goldsmith, O.	Mrs. Mary Blaize
Barnum, Jay H.	Motorcycle Dog	Ewing, J.H.	Mrs. Overtheway's Rememberances
Yates, Eliz.	Mountain Born	Thayer, Jane	Mrs. Perrywinkle's Pets
MacLeod	Mountain Lovers	Burgess, T.	Mrs. Peter Rabbit
Peattie, E.W.	Mountain Woman	MacDonald, Betty	Mrs. Piggle-Wiggle

AUTHOR	TITLE	AUTHOR	TITLE
Aldin, C.	Mrs. Tickler's Caravan	Mabie, H.W.	Myths Every Child Should Know
Garnett, L.A.	Muffin Shop	Spence, L.	Myths of Babylonia & Assyria
Barrows, M.	Muggins Mouse	Kent, R.	N by E
Hogan, Inez	Mule Twins	Moon, G.	Nadita
Marion	Mummy's Bedtime Story Book	Haskell, H.	Nadya Makes her Bow
Harper, T.A.	Mushroom Boy	McGinley, Phyllis	Name for Kitty
Klein, C.	Music Master	Phillips, E.C.	Name for Obed
Porter, G.S.	Music of the Wild	Hamlin, M.S.	Nan in the City
Stilwell, S.	Musical Tree	Spearman, Frank	Nan of Music Mountain
Nash, Ogden	Musical Zoo	Hamlin, M.S.	Nan's Chicopee Children
Gray, W.C.	Musings/Campfire & Wayside	Fox, F.M.	Nancy Davenport
Stafford, M.A.	Muskox: Little Tootoo's Friend	Pyle, Kath.	Nancy Rutledge
Santos-Dumont	My Air-Ships	Hoyt, E.	Nancy's Country Christmas
Cather, W.	My Antonia	Gates, J.S.	Nanette Goes to Visit Grandmother
DuChaillu, Paul	My Apingi Kingdom	Fox, F.M.	Nannette
Bayne, C. (ed.)	My Book of Best Fairy Tales	Hall, A.G.	Nansen
Brown, V.	My Brother	Stuart, Ruth M.	Napoleon Jackson
Ames, Evelyn	My Brother Bird	Chesterton, G.K.	Napoleon of Notting Hill
Finta, Alex.	My Brothers & I	Hogan, Inez	Nappy Chooses a Pet
Sturgis, E.B.	My Busy Days	Ray, A.C.	Nathalie's Chum
Tittle, W.	My Country	Ray, A.C.	Nathalie's Sister
Stawell, Mrs. R.	My Days with the Fairies	Selsam, M.E.	Nature Detective
Maeterlinck, M.	My Dog	Irwin, W.	Nautical Lays of a Landsman
Tarry, Ellen	My Dog Rinty	Darling, E.B.	Navarre of the North
Cherr, Pat	My Dog is Lost!	Baum, L.F.	Navy Alphabet
Malcolm, F.	My Fairyland	Beach, R.	Ne'er-Do-Well
Gannett, R.S.	My Father's Dragon	Hichens, R.	Near East
Morrow, Eliz.	My Favorite Age	Burgess, T.	Neatness of Bobby Coon
James, Will	My First Horse	DeMorgan, M.	Necklace of Princess Fiorimonde
Alexander, L.C.	My Five Tigers	McCutcheon, G.B.	Nedra
O'Hara, Mary	My Friend Flicka	Mattheson, J.	Needle in the Haystack
Peacocke, I.M.	My Friend Phil	Walsh, Chad	Nellie & her Flying Crocodile
Kalashnikoff, N.	My Friend Yakub	Costello, F.H.	Nelson's Yankee Boy
Terhune, A.P.	My Friend the Dog	Aesopus	Never-Grow-Old Stories
N/A	My High School Days	Staver, M.W.	New & True
Bouvet, M.	My Lady	Rae, J.	New Adventures of Alice
Farnol, J.	My Lady Caprice	Richards, A.M.	New Alice in Old Wonderland
Barrie, J.M.	My Lady Nicotine	Harraden, B.	New Book of the Fairies
Mathews, F.A.	My Lady Peggy Goes to Town	Belloc, H.	New Cautionary Tales
Parrish, R.	My Lady of the South	Wiggin, K.D.	New Chronicles of Rebecca
Brady, C.T.	My Lady's Slipper	Barnum, Jay H.	New Fire Engine
Cullen, Countee	My Lives & How I Lost Them	Shippen, K.B.	New Found World
Muehl, L.B.	My Name Is...	King, Eliz.	New House that Jack Built
Blanchard, A.E.	My Own Dolly	Schmidt, S.L.	New Land
Lang, A.	My Own Fairy Book	Dante	New Life
Credle, Ellis	My Pet Peepelo	Maxwell, D.	New Lights O'London
N/A	My Picture Scrap Book	Marshall, Helen L.	New Mexican Boy
Huffard, G.T.	My Poetry Book	Meigs, C.	New Moon
Burnett, F.H.	My Robin	Locke, A.	New Negro
George, Jean C.	My Side of the Mountain	Bell, J.J.	New Noah's Ark
Spielmann, M.H.	My Son & I	Gratacap, L.P.	New Northland
Bates, H.E.	My Uncle Silas	Szyk, Arthur	New Order
Gruelle, J.	My Very Own Fairy Stories	Bancroft, Hubert H.	New Pacific
Smith, E.B.	My Village	Farrow, G.E.	New Panjandrum
Brown, M.W.	My World	Flack, M.	New Pet
Van Valkenburgh, H.	Myself & I	Untermeyer, L.	New Songs for New Voices
Mirza, Y.B.	Myself when Young	Lowe, S.E.	New Story of Peter Rabbit
Verne, Jules	Mysterious Island	Bannerman, H.	New Story of Little Black Sambo
Twain, M.	Mysterious Stranger	Vetsch, Earnest	New Story of Little Black Sambo
Farrow, G.E.	Mysterious Voyage	Nesbit, E.	New Treasure Seekers
Hurst, Edward H.	Mystery Island	Baum, L.F.	New Wizard of Oz
Bowman, J.C.	Mystery Mountain	Baum, L.F.	New Wonderland
Jewett, E.M.	Mystery at Boulder Point	Kennedy, H.A.	New World Fairy Book
Bacon, P.	Mystery at East Hatchett	Spyri, J.	New Year's Carol
Lenotre, Therese	Mystery of Dog Flip	Graham, Stephen	New York Nights
Smeaton, O.	Mystery of the Pacific	Wright, F.	New Zealand
Herford, O.	Mythological Zoo	Perkins, E.E.	News from Notown
Price, M.E.	Myths & Enchantment Tales	Maeterlinck, M.	News of Spring
Davis, F.H.	Myths & Legends of Japan	Marryat, Fred.	Newton Foster

AUTHOR	TITLE		AUTHOR	TITLE
Molesworth, M.	Next-Door House		Milne, A.A.	Now We Are Six
Lewis, E.W.	Next-Door Morelands		Smalley, J.	Now and Then...
Messer, C.J.	Next-Night Stories		Chapin, A.A.	Nowadays Fairy Book
Brown, M.W.	Nibble Nibble		Sandys, Ruth	Numerous Names Nimbly Narrated
Taylor, C.B.	Nicanor, Teller of Tales		Kellogg, V.	Nuova or the New Bee
Moore, Ann C.	Nicholas		De La Rame, M.	Nurnberg Stove
Ardizzone, E.	Nicholas & Fast Moving Diesel		Molesworth, M.	Nurse Heatherdale's Story
Moore, Ann C.	Nicholas & Golden Goose		Flower, Esther	Nurse Nora...
Hogan, Inez	Nicodemus & his Little Sister		DeAngeli, M.	Nursery & Mother Goose Rhymes
Hogan, Inez	Nicodemus & the Goose		Carroll, L.	Nursery Alice
Hogan, Inez	Nicodemus & the Houn' Dog		Miller, O.B.	Nursery Friends from France
Hogan, Inez	Nicodemus Laughs		Cheatham, G.	Nursery Garland
Coatsworth, E.	Night & the Cat		Lang, A.	Nursery Rhyme Book
Graham, E.	Night Adventures of Alexis		N/A	Nursery Rhyme Picture Book
Denslow, W.W.	Night Before Christmas		Fraser, C.L.	Nursery Rhymes
Moore, C.C.	Night Before Christmas		N/A	Nursery Rhymes
N/A	Night Before Christmas & Jingles		Sedlacek, H.	Nursery Rhymes/Bohemia
Black, I.S.	Night Cat		Farjeon, E.	Nursery Rhymes/London Town
Machray, R.	Night Side of London		Disney, W.	Nursery Stories from Silly Symphony
Brown, M.W.	Night and Day		Anderson, A.	Nursery Zoo
Bedford, F.D.	Night of Wonders		LeMair, H.W.	Nursie's Little Rhyme Book
Freeman, Don	Night the Lights Went Out		Browne, Edgar G.	Nutcracker & Mouse King
Young, C.	Night-Caps for the Babies		Hoffman, H.	Nutcracker & Mouse King
Clark, G.O	Nightmare Land		Disney, W.	Nutcracker Suite
Harris, J.C.	Nights with Uncle Remus		Dumas, A.	Nutcracker of Nuremberg
Murphey, E.A.	Nihal		Farjeon, E.	Nuts & May
D'Aulaire, I.& E.	Nils		Haskell, H.E.	O-Heart-San
Pease, J.V.D.	Nimbo		Deland, E.D.	Oakleigh
Seton, G.	Nimrod's Wife		N/A	Oaktree Fairy Book
Ets, Marie H.	Nine Days to Christmas		Tunis, Edwin	Oars & Sails
Fenton, Edward	Nine Lives		Gorey, Edward	Object Lesson
Nesbit, E.	Nine Unlikely Tales for Children		Beerbohm, M.	Observations
Angelo, V.	Nino		Follett, H.T.	Ocean Outposts
Hurd, E.T.	Nino & his Fish		Lenski, L.	Ocean-Born Mary
Freeman, L.C.	Nip & Tuck		LeGallienne, R.	October Vagabonds
Saunders, M.	Nita		LeFevre, A.	Odd One
Minarik, E.H.	No Fighting! No Biting!		Burt, Mary E.	Odysseus, Hero of Ithaca
N/A	No Place Like Home		N/A	Odyssey of Homer
Dobbs, Rose	No Room		Palmer, G. (tr)	Odyssey of Homer
Evans, Myfanwy	No Rubbish Here		Daugherty, J.	Of Courage Undaunted...
Brown, Paul	No Trouble at All		Bacon, P.	Off With Their Heads!
Fish	Noah's Ark Book		Nesbit, W.D.	Oh Skin-nay!
McNagny, B.	Noah's Nightmare		Ainslie, K.	Oh! Poor Amelia Jane!
Malot, H.	Nobody's Boy		Thompson, R.P.	Ojo in Oz
Brown, M.W.	Noisy Bird Book		Rounds, Glen	Ol' Paul, Mighty Logger
Brown, M.W.	Noisy Book		D'Aulaire, I.& E.	Ola
Lofting, H.	Noisy Nora		Sherwood, L.	Old Abe, American Eagle
Jerrold, W.C.	Nonsense Nonsense!		Otis, James	Old Ben
Leacock, S.B.	Nonsense Novels		Bulla, Clyde R.	Old Charlie
Lear, E.	Nonsense Songs		Deland, M.	Old Chester Tales
Leaf, M.	Noodle		Irving, W.	Old Christmas
Brown, M.W.	Noon Balloon		Irving, W.	Old Christmas Day
Freeman, Don	Norman the Doorman		LeGallienne, R.	Old Country House
Asbjornsen, P.C.	Norse Fairy Tales		Cable, G.W.	Old Creole Days
Mabie, H.W.	Norse Stories		Dickens, C.	Old Curiosity Shop
Swift, H.H.	North Star Shining		Elkin, R.H.	Old Dutch Nursery Rhymes
Sinclair, B.W.	North of Fifty-Three		Irving, W.	Old English Christmas
Austen, J.	Northanger Abbey		Baring-Gould, S.	Old English Fairy Tales
Kent, R.	Northern Christmas		Mansion, Horace	Old English Nursery Songs
Parker, Gilbert	Northern Lights		Harwood, E.	Old English Sing-Games
Long, W.J.	Northern Trails		N/A	Old English Songs
Stroebe, C. (ed.)	Norwegian Fairy Book		N/A	Old English Songs & Dances
Zolotow, C.	Not a Little Monkey		N/A	Old Fairy Tales
Skaar, G.M.	Nothing But Cats, Cats, Cats		Vredenberg, E.	Old Fairy Tales
Gag, W.	Nothing at All		McCook, Henry C.	Old Farm Fairies
Craig, E.G.	Nothing...		Irving, W.	Old Fashioned Christmas Day
Lenski, L.	Now It's Fall		Ewing, J.H.	Old Fashioned Fairy Tales
Kunhardt, D.	Now Open the Box		Washburne, M.F.	Old Fashioned Fairy Tales
Baer, Howard	Now This, Now That		Maeterlinck, M.	Old Fashioned Flowers

AUTHOR	TITLE	AUTHOR	TITLE
Fyleman, R.	Old Fashioned Girls	Montgomery, F.T.	On a Lark to the Planets
Lucas, E.V.	Old Fashioned Tales	Wilder, L.I.	On the Banks of Plum Creek
Mack, R.E.	Old Father Santa Claus	McGinley, Phyllis	On the Contrary
DeSegur, S.	Old French Fairy Tales	Burgess, T.	On the Green Meadows
Anderson, A.	Old French Nursery Songs	Harris, J.C.	On the Plantation
Morris, Alice T.	Old Friends/New Fables	Forster, F.J.	On the Road to Make-Believe
Deland, M.	Old Garden	Bates, Clara D.	On the Tree Top
Page, T.N.	Old Gentlemen of the Black Stock	Sandoz, M.	On the Verge
Burgess, T.	Old Granny Fox	Bates, Clara D.	On the Way to Wonderland
Boylan, G.D.	Old House	Atkinson, Brooks	Once Around the Sun
Eastman, C.A.	Old Indian Days	Dalgliesh, A.	Once On a Time
Aldin, C.	Old Inns	Milne, A.A.	Once On a Time
Cregan, M.	Old John	Dunbar, A.	Once There was a Prince
Smith, F.H.	Old Lines & New in Black & White	Willson, Dixie	Once Upon a Monday
De La Mare, W.	Old Lion	Austin, Margot	Once Upon a Springtime
Andersen, H.C.	Old Man is Always Right	Bates, Kath. L.	Once Upon a Time
Strang, H.	Old Man of the Mountain	Perrault, C.	Once Upon a Time
Aldin, C.	Old Manor Houses	Stewart, Mary	Once Upon a Time Tales
Costello, C.J.	Old Mother Hubbard	Gere, Frances K.	Once Upon a Time in Egypt
Denslow, W.W.	Old Mother Hubbard	Yates, Eliz.	Once in the Year
N/A	Old Mother Hubbard	Thompson, Dorothy	Once on Christmas
Burgess, T.	Old Mother West Wind	Kelsey, A.	Once the Hodja
Farjeon, E.	Old Nurse's Stocking Basket	Kunhardt, D.	Once there was a Little Boy
N/A	Old Nursery Rhymes	Evans, Lawton	Once to Every Man
Various	Old Old Tales Retold	Gates, J.S.	One Day in Betty's Life
Wiggin, K.D.	Old Peabody Pew	Sperry, A.	One Day with Manu
Ransome, A.	Old Peter's Russian Tales	Sperry, A.	One Day with Tuktu
Molesworth, M.	Old Pincushion	Seuss, Dr.	One Fish Two Fish Red Fish Blue Fish
Gielow, M.S.	Old Plantation Days	Farjeon, E.	One Foot in Fairyland
Eliot, T.S.	Old Possum's Book of Practical Cats	Dauzet, M.	One Happy Day
Owen, M.A.	Old Rabbit the Voodoo	Burnett, F.H.	One I Knew Best of All
Terry, R.R.	Old Rhymes with New Tunes	Kay, Helen	One Mitten Lewis
Reed, Myrtle	Old Rose and Silver	McCloskey, R.	One Morning in Maine
Milne, A.A.	Old Sailor	Zolotow, C.	One Step, Two
Inman, H.E.	Old Santa Fe Trail	Duvoisin, R.	One Thousand Christmas Beards
Hurd, E.T.	Old Silversides	Byrne, M.A.	One Too Many
Forsythe, C.	Old Songs for Young Americans	Von Hutten, B.	One Way Out
N/A	Old Songs in French & English	Hicks, G.	One of Us
Wahlenberg, A.	Old Swedish Fairy Tales	Cone, H.G.	One, Two, Three, Four
Riley, J.W.	Old Sweetheart of Mine	Inman, H.E.	One-Eyed Griffin...
N/A	Old Time Rhymes	Brown, Alice	One-Footed Fairy
Perrault, C.	Old Time Stories	Holmes, O.W.	One-Hoss Shay
Bowen, Wm.	Old Tobacco Shop	Berry, E.	One-String Fiddle
Bennett, A.	Old Wives' Tale	Krumgold, Joseph	Onion John
Hader, B.& E.	Old Woman & Crooked Sixpence	White, E.O.	Only Child
N/A	Old Woman & her Pig	Lide, A.A.	Ood-Le-Uk: Wanderer
Rinder, F.	Old World Japan	Van Dyke, J.C.	Opal Sea
Gipson, Fred B.	Old Yeller	Beistle, A.S.	Open Daily
Tucker, E.S.	Old Youngsters	Seredy, K.	Open Gate
Alcott, L.M.	Old-Fashioned Girl	Krauss, Ruth	Open House for Butterflies
Perrault, C.	Old-Time Stories	Thurston, E.T.	Open Window
Mason, E.	Old-World Love Stories	Levy, N.	Opera Guyed
Johnston, A.F.	Ole Mammy's Torment	Hadden, C.	Operas of Richard Wagner
Ets, Marie H.	Oley, the Sea Monster	Lang, A.	Orange Fairy Book
Lang, A.	Olive Fairy Book	N/A	Oranges & Lemons
Durant, Nancy M.	Oliver & the Crying Chip	Barbour, R.H.	Orchard Princess
Beskow, E.	Ollie's Ski Trip	Chambers, Rbt.	Orchard-Land
Bangs, J.K.	Olympian Nights	Vaile, C.M.	Orcutt Girls
Chamberlin, E.C.	Omar the Discontented Cat	Parkman, F.	Oregon Trail
Hulbert, H.B.	Omjee, The Wizard...	Molesworth, M.	Oriel Window
Abingdon, Alex	Omnibus Boners	N/A	Oriental Fairy Tales
Melville, Herman	Omoo	Taylor, A.& J.	Original Poems
Seuss, Dr.	On Beyond Zebra	Martin, Chas. M.	Orphans of the Range
Ralph, J.	On Canada's Frontier	Riley, J.W.	Orphant Annie Book
Richmond, Grace S.	On Christmas Day in the Evening	Gruelle, J.	Orphant Annie Story Book
Kent, R.	On Earth Peace...	Hutchinson, W.M.L.	Orpheus with his Lute
Page, T.N.	On Newfound River	Colum, P.	Orpheus: Myths of the World
Whitney, Casper	On Snow-Shoes in Barren Grounds	Nesbit, E.	Oswald Bastable & Others
Barbour, R.H.	On Your Mark	Smith, F.H.	Other Fellow

AUTHOR	TITLE	AUTHOR	TITLE
Liers, Emil	Otter's Story	Greenaway, K.	Painting Book
Lewis, Cecil D.	Otterbury Incident	Kiviat, Esther	Paji
DuBois, W.P.	Otto at Sea	Molesworth, M.	Palace in the Garden
DuBois, W.P.	Otto in Texas	Cox, P.	Palmer Cox Brownie Primer
Pyle, H.	Otto of the Silver Hand	Emblen, Don L.	Palomino Boy
Garnett, L.M.	Ottoman Wonder Tales	Girvin, B.	Pam & Billy
N/A	Our Amateur Circus	Tempski, Armine	Pam's Paradise Ranch
Golding, Harry	Our Animal Friends	Marzials	Pan Pipes
Cory, F.	Our Baby Book	Byington, Eloise	Pancake Brownies
France, A.	Our Children	Bishop, C.H.	Pancakes-Paris
Sidney, Marg.	Our Davie Pepper	Gay, Zhenya	Pancho & His Burro
Nisbet, J.	Our Forests & Woodlands	Newberry, C.T.	Pandora
Disney, W.	Our Friend the Atom	Broughton, P.	Pandy
Maeterlinck, M.	Our Friend the Dog	Caldecott, R.	Panjandrum Picture Book
Ewing, J.H.	Our Garden	Lefferts, S.T.	Pansy Wedding
Christy, H.C.	Our Girls	Beard, P.	Pantalette Doll
Pennell, E.R.	Our House	Stokely, E.K.	Pantaloon
Steedman, Amy	Our Island Saints	Baker, O.	Panther Magic
Dorrington, A.	Our Lady of Darkness	Seawell, M.E.	Papa Bouchard
Parish, Helen R.	Our Lady of Guadalupe	Gruelle, J.	Paper Dragon
Hazelton, Mary	Our Little African Cousin	Gatty, M.	Parables from Nature
Kaberry, C.J.	Our Little Neighbors	Cadman, S.P.	Parables of Jesus
Gibson, C.D.	Our Neighbors	Bianco, P.	Paradise Square
Moffat, A.	Our Old Nursery Rhymes	Gordon, H.C.	Paradoc to the Rescue
Eberle, I.	Our Oldest Friends	Crothers, S.M.	Pardoner's Wallet
Pennell, J.	Our Philadelphia	Whiteing, R.	Paris of Today
Castle, A.& E.	Our Sentimental Garden	Zolotow, C.	Park Book
Mitford, M.R.	Our Village	Wiese, K.	Parrot Dealer
Field, H.	Our Western Archipelago	Wagner, R.	Parsifal
Weatherly, F.E.	Out of Town	Bemelmans, L.	Parsley
Chilvers, H.A.	Out of the Crucible	Johnson, Clifton	Parson's Devil
Lownsbery, Eloise	Out of the Flame	Davis, Rbt.	Partners of Powder Hole
Smith, F.H.	Outdoor Sketching	Streatfield, N.	Party Shoes
Chambers, Rbt.	Outdoorland	Evarts, Hal G.	Passing of the Old West
Thompson, J.M.	Over Indian & Animal Trails	Page, T.N.	Passtime Stories
Lovelace, M.H.	Over the Big Hill	Southwart, Eliz.	Password to Fairyland
Waugh, Ida	Over the Hills	Bjornson, B.	Pastor Sang
Cook, Hartley K.	Over the Hills & Far Away	Disney, W.	Pastoral
Gulliver, L.	Over the Nonsense Road	Bannerman, H.	Pat & the Spider
Haynes, L.M.	Over the Rainbow Bridge	Montgomery, L.M.	Pat of Silver Bush
Gibbings, Rbt.	Over the Reefs	Baum, L.F.	Patchwork Girl of Oz
Grover, E.O.	Overall Boys	Field, R.	Patchwork Plays
Bigham, M.A.	Overheard in Fairyland	Lefferts, S.T.	Patriotic Jubilee
Herford, O.	Overheard in a Garden	Van Stockum, H.	Patsy & the Pup
Lear, E.	Owl & the Pussycat	Anderson, A.	Patsy Book
Inman, H.E.	Owl King...	Ames, E.M.	Patsy for Keeps
Thurber, J.	Owl in the Attic	Steiner, C.	Patsy's Pet
DeSelincourt, Hugh	Oxford From Within	Bannon, L.	Patty Paints a Picture
Baum, L.F.	Ozma of Oz	Drachman, Holger	Paul & Virginia/Northern Zone
Beaman, E.H.	Ozmar the Mystic	Shephard, E.	Paul Bunyon
Thompson, R.P.	Ozoplanning/Wizard of Oz	Stevens, J.	Paul Bunyon
Stone, Amy	P-Penny & his Little Red Cart	Ardizzone, E.	Paul, Hero of the Fire
Hamilton, Eliz.	P-Zoo	Vance, Marguerite	Paula
Father Tuck	Pa Cats, Ma Cats...	Stevenson, R.L.	Pavilion on the Links
Hoover, B.R.	Pa Flickinger's Folks	Browne, P.E.	Peace at any Price
Miller, Warren	Pablo Paints a Picture	Coatsworth, E.	Peaceable Kingdom
Holling, H.C.	Paddle to the Sea	Ingraham, C.	Peacock & Wishing-Fairy
Wister, O.	Padre Ignacio	De La Mare, W.	Peacock Pie
Davis, Rbt.	Padre Porko	Johnston, R.M.	Pearce Amerson's Will
Pycraft, W.P.	Pads, Paws & Claws	West, Paul	Pearl & Pumpkin
Grahame, K.	Pagan Papers	Lide, A.A.	Pearls of Fortune
Rossetti, C.	Pageant & other Poems	Blodgett, M.F.	Peasblossom
Seeger, E.	Pageant of Chinese History	Bowman, J.C.	Pecos Bill
Van Stockum, H.	Pageen	Peck, Leigh	Pecos Bill & Lightning
Washburn, C.C.	Pages/Book of Paris	Disney, W.	Peculiar Penguins
Holling, H.C.	Pagoo	Hunt, M.L.	Peddler's Clock
Behn, Harry	Painted Cave	Rowsell, M.	Pedlar & His Dog
Moon, C.	Painted Moccasins	Shepard, O.	Pedlar's Progress
Morrow, Eliz.	Painted Pig	Flack, M.	Pedro

AUTHOR	TITLE	AUTHOR	TITLE
Cavanah, F.	Pedro of Santa Fe	Donahey, M.D.	Peter & Prue...
Wood, Esther	Pedro's Coconut Skates	Barrie, J.M.	Peter & Wendy
Politi, L.	Pedro, Angel of Olvera Street	Grabo, C.H.	Peter & the Princess
Duplaix, L.	Pedro, Nina & Perrito	Prokofieff, S.	Peter & the Wolf
Duplaix, G.	Pee-Gloo	Austin, Margot	Peter Churchmouse
Preston, Tom	Peek-A-Boo Twins	DuBois, W.P.	Peter Graves
Byron, May	Peek-a-Boos at the Zoo	Moe, Louis M.	Peter Kroak
Byron, May	Peek-a-Boos in Town	Van Sinderen, A.	Peter Makebelieve
Byron, May	Peek-a-Boos in Winter	Bailey, C.S.	Peter Newell's Mother Goose
Various	Peep into Cat-Land	Newell, P.	Peter Newell's Pictures & Rhymes
Castle, Jane	Peep-Lo	Webber, Frank M.	Peter Painter's Merry-Go-Round
Colum, P.	Peep-Show Man	Colby, J.P.	Peter Paints the U.S.A.
Sylva, C.	Peeping Pansy	Barrie, J.M.	Peter Pan
Bangs, J.K.	Peeps at People	Herford, O.	Peter Pan Alphabet
Knowles, H.	Peeps into Fairyland	Barrie, J.M.	Peter Pan Picture Book
Cox-McCormack, N.	Peeps: Really Truly Sunshine Fairy	N/A	Peter Pan's ABC
Isben, H.	Peer Gynt	Barrie, J.M.	Peter Pan...
DeLeeuw, Hendrik	Peewee the Mousedeer	Jackson, L.F.	Peter Patter Book
Reade, C.	Peg Woffington	Phillips, E.C.	Peter Peppercorn
Cheney, Cora	Peg-Legged Pirate of Sulu	Rountree, H.	Peter Pink-Eye
Cradock, H.C.	Peggy & Joan	Brown, Marcia	Peter Piper's Alphabet
Carr, Mary J.	Peggy & Paul & Laddy	Hunt, M.L.	Peter Piper's Pickled Peppers
Sewell, H.	Peggy & the Pony	Lambert, H.G.C.	Peter Pixie at Play
Sewell, H.	Peggy & the Pup	Bradley, W.	Peter Poodle...
Lewis, A.H.	Peggy O'Neal	Huntington, I.M.	Peter Pumpkin in Wonderland
Marshall, A.	Peggy in Toyland	Field, L.A.	Peter Rabbit & his Pa
Cook, W.	Peggy's Travels	Hudson, Alma	Peter Rabbit & the Fairies
Potter, M.K.	Peggy's Trial	Almond, Linda S.	Peter Rabbit & the Little Girl
Ring, B.	Peik	Almond, Linda S.	Peter Rabbit & the Tinybits
McCready, T.L.	Pekin White	N/A	Peter Rabbit Story Book
Lear, E.	Pelican Chorus	Hudson, Alma	Peter Rabbit in Mother Goose Land
Weisgard, L.	Pelican Here, Pelican There	Chamisso, A.	Peter Schlemihl
Herford, O.	Pen & Inklings	Baker, Nina B.	Peter the Great
Wiggin, K.D.	Penelope's Irish Experiences	Gay, Romney	Peter's Adventure
Gray, Eliz. J.	Penn	Kingman, Lee	Peter's Long Walk
Torrey, M.	Penny	Kay, G.A.	Peter, Patter & Pixie
Graves, Rbt.	Penny Fiddle	Morley, Charles	Peter, a Cat O' One Tail
Berry, E.	Penny-Whistle	Lyman, Betty K.	Peter-Pan Twins are Glad to Help
Tarkington, B.	Penrod	Grishina, N.G.	Peter-Pea
Tarkington, B.	Penrod Jashper	Jackson, G.E.	Peterkin
Judson, C.I.	People Who Work Near our House	Molesworth, M.	Peterkin
Judson, C.I.	People Who Work in Country & City	Pogany, Elaine	Peterkin
Ade, G.	People You Know	Hallock, G.T.	Petersham's Hill
Field, R.	People from Dickens	DeAngeli, M.	Petite Suzanne
London, J.	People of the Abyss	Duvoisin, R.	Petunia
Rasmussen, K.	People of the Frozen North	Christopher, Anne	Petunia Be Keerful
Haggard, H.R.	People of the Mist	Duvoisin, R.	Petunia Takes a Trip
Stone, Wm. S.	Pepe was the Saddest Bird	Duvoisin, R.	Petunia's Christmas
Costantino, Joan	Pepito at Capistrano	MacDonald, Geo.	Phantastes
Orton, Ruth	Pepito the Colt	Lippincott, J.W.	Phantom Deer
Reynolds, B.L.	Pepper	Cradock, C.E.	Phantoms of the Foot-Bridge
Pyle, H.	Pepper and Salt	Lenski, L.	Phebe Fairchild...
Davis, Rbt.	Pepperfoot of Thursday Market	Wells, Carolyn	Phenomenal Fauna
Brown, M.W.	Peppermint Family	Seredy, K.	Philomena
Spyri, J.	Peppino	Baum, L.F.	Phoebe Daring...
Drury, W.P.	Peradventure of Private Pagett	Eberle, I.	Phoebe-Belle
Belpre, Pura	Perez & Martina	Nesbit, E.	Phoenix & the Carpet
Farjeon, E.	Perfect Zoo	Powell, R.S.	Phyllis in Bohemia
Thompson, R.P.	Perhappsy Chaps	Wodehouse, P.G.	Piccadilly Jim
Steele, Wm. O.	Perilous Road	Burnett, F.H.	Piccino...
Farjeon, E.	Perkin the Pedlar	Reno, E.W.	Pick the Vegetables
LeGallienne, R.	Perseus & Andromeda	Reed, Myrtle	Pickaback Songs
Steig, Wm.	Persistent Faces	Perkins, L.F.	Pickaninny Twins
Steele, R.	Perverse Widow	Gilman, Eliz. L.	Picnic Adventures
Freeman, Lydia	Pet of the Met	Ayer, Jean	Picnic Book
Wells, Carolyn	Pete & Polly Stories	DeBrunhoff, L.	Picnic at Babar's
Kissin, Rita	Pete the Pelican	Loud, Marian V.	Picnic on a Pyramid
Smith, G.	Peter & Ellen	N/A	Picture & Rhyme Book
Jones, V.M.	Peter & Gretchen of Old Nuremberg	Cole, Frank (ed.)	Picture Birthday Book for Boys & Girls

AUTHOR	TITLE	AUTHOR	TITLE
Hader, B.& E.	Picture Book of the States	Sorensen, Virginia	Plain Girl
Lacey, Marion	Picture Book of Musical Instruments	Maunder, I.	Plain Princess
Gimmage, Peter	Picture Book of Ships	McGinley, Phyllis	Plain Princess
Hader, B.& E.	Picture Book of Travel	Young, Martha	Plantation Bird Legends
Dulac, E.	Picture Book of French Red Cross	Peterkin, Julia	Plantation Christmas
Hiatt, C.	Picture Posters	Harris, J.C.	Plantation Pageants
N/A	Picture Story Book	Phillips, J.C.	Plantation Sketches
Hahn, E.	Picture Story of China	Shepperd, E.	Plantation Songs for My Lady's Banjo
Bealer, A.W.	Picture-Skin Story	Perry, Bliss	Plated City
Rossetti, D.G.	Pictures & Poems	Allen, W.B.	Play Away
Shuldham, E.	Pictures from Birdland	Keys, Leonora	Play Dollies
Fisher, H.	Pictures in Color	Pennell, J.	Play in Provence
Pennell, J.	Pictures of Panama Canal	Ets, Marie H.	Play with Me
Gibson, C.D.	Pictures of People	Ray, A.C.	Playground Toni
Stonier, G.W.	Pictures on the Pavement	Eager, E.M.	Playing Possum
Potter, B.	Pie & Patty Pan	Dearmer, M.	Playmate, A Christmas Mystery
Browning, R.	Pied Piper of Hamelin	Davidson, John	Plays by...
Addington, S.	Pied Piper of Pudding Lane	Yeats, W.B.	Plays/Irish Theatre
Kingman, Lee	Pierre Pidgeon	Lucas, E.V.	Playtime & Company
Stacpoole, H.D.	Pierrette	Johnson, Burgess	Pleasant Tragedies of Childhood
Stacpoole, H.D.	Pierrot!	Yashima, M.& T.	Plenty to Watch
Gask, Lilian	Pig Tales	Lida	Plouf the Little Wild Duck
Credle, Ellis	Pig-O-Wee	Davis, L.R.	Plow Penny Mystery
Liggett, Thos.	Pigeon, Fly Home!	Pierson, C.D.	Plucky Allens
Butler, Chas.	Pigs is Pigs	Corrin, S.	Plucky Sailor & Postage Stamp
Bennett, John	Pigtail of Ah Lee Ben Loo	Coatsworth, E.	Plum Daffy Adventure
Hay, J.	Pike County Ballads	Smalley, J.	Plum to Plum Jam
Bunyan, J.	Pilgrim's Progress	Simont, M.	Plumber Out of the Sea
MacGregor, M.	Pilgrim's Progress told to Children	Schultz, J.W.	Plumed Snake Medicine
Godolphin, M.	Pilgrims' Progress	Disney, W.	Pluto & the Puppy
Heward, C.	Pillow Stories	D'Aulaire, I.& E.	Pocahontas
Beard, P.	Pillow-Time Tales	Smith, E.B.	Pocahontas & Captain Smith
Greene, H.P.	Pilot & Other Stories	Brown, A.F.	Pocket Full of Posies
Gilbert, W.S.	Pinafore Picture Book	Field, R.	Pocket-Handkerchief Park
Choate, F.	Pinafores & Pantalets	Ault, L.& N.	Podgy Book of Tales
Bingham, C.	Ping Pong	Sykes, M.	Poe's Run....
St. Mars, F.	Pinion & Paw	Arnold, M.	Poems
Lang, A.	Pink Fairy Book	Yeats, W.B.	Poems
Monsell, J.R.	Pink Knight	Riley, J.W.	Poems Here at Home
Ade, G.	Pink Marsh	Dobson, L.	Poems by Dobson, Locker & Praed
Chapin, F.	Pinkey & the Plumed Knight	Garnett (ed.)	Poems by Robert Browning
Hammond, H.	Pinkey Perkins, Just a Boy	Matthews, B.	Poems of American Patriotism
Estes, Eleanor	Pinkey Pye	Dunbar, P.L.	Poems of Cabin & Field
Robertson, W.G.	Pinkie & the Fairies	Field, E.	Poems of Childhood
Nelson, M.W.	Pinky Finds a Home	Sowerby, Githa	Poems of Childhood
Willson, Dixie	Pinky-Pup & Empty Elephant	Whitman, W.	Poems of Leaves & Grass
Collodi, C.	Pinocchio [MOST TITLES]	Hall, A.V.	Poems of a South African
Disney, W.	Pinocchio Picture Book	Beerbohm, M.	Poet's Corner
Patri, Angelo	Pinocchio in America	Herrick, R.	Poetry of...
Morrow, Eliz.	Pint of Judgment	Baker, Geo.	Point Lace & Diamonds
Judson, C.I.	Pioneer Girl	Martin, Pat. M.	Pointed Brush
Johnston, H.	Pioneers in Canada	Field, R.	Pointed People
Brown, Paul	Piper's Pony	Doyle, A.C.	Poison Belt
Mother Goose	Piper's Son	Lowrey, J.S.	Poky Little Puppy
Boylan, G.D.	Pipes of Clovis	Tomkins, J.	Polar Bear Twins
Sousa, J.P.	Pipetown Sandy	Chambers, Rbt.	Police!
Browning, R.	Pippa Passes	Bancroft, L.	Policeman Blue Jay
Frisbie, W.A.	Pirate Frog...	Brown, M.W.	Polite Penguin
Nicholson, Wm.	Pirate Twins	Begbie, H.	Political Struwwelpeter
Sterne, Emma G.	Pirate of Chatham Square	Johnson, Margaret	Polly & the Wishing Ring
Rodgers, C.	Pirate's Loot	Field, R.	Polly Patchwork
Wilson, Edward A.	Pirate's Treasure	Emery, Carlyle	Polly Through the Crystal
Fraser, C.L.	Pirates	Emery, Carlyle	Polly Through the Mountains
Thompson, R.P.	Pirates in Oz	Banks, Helen M.	Polly's Garden
Banning, Kendall	Pirates!	Simont, M.	Polly's Oats
Fischer, Hans	Pitschi	Gay, J.	Polly: An Opera
Farrow, G.E.	Pixie Pickles	Porter, E.	Pollyanna
Smith, Laura R.	Pixie in the House	Smith, Harriet L.	Pollyanna of the Orange Blossoms
Harrison, F.	Pixy Book	Smith, Harriet L.	Pollyanna's Jewels

AUTHOR	TITLE	AUTHOR	TITLE
Brown, Paul	Polo	McNeer, May	Prince Bantam
Parker, L.N.	Pomander Walk	Jones, H.	Prince Boo Hoo & Little Smuts
Nesbit, E.	Pomander of Verse	Lewis, C.S.	Prince Caspian
Stockton, Frank	Pomona's Travels	Eaton, S.	Prince Domino & Muffles
Lida	Pompom	Kelly, James P.	Prince Izon
Brown, Paul	Pony Farm	Bancroft, L.	Prince Mud-Turtle
Remington, F.	Pony Tracks	Rix, H.	Prince Pimpernel
Lansing, Eliz.	Pony that Ran Away	Sherwood, M.	Prince Por Quoi
Forester, C.S.	Poo Poo & the Dragons	Lang, A.	Prince Prigio
Brown, M.W.	Poodle & the Sheep	Lang, A.	Prince Ricardo of Pantouflia
Mackall, L.	Poodle-Oodle on Doodle Farm	Harrison, E.O.	Prince Silverwings...
Van Housen, Nita	Poogie & Sibella	Bouvet, M.	Prince Tip-Top
Meigs, C.	Pool of Stars	Donahey, M.D.	Prince Without a Country
Bianco, M.W.	Poor Cecco	Tappan, E.M.	Prince from Nowhere...
Dostoievsky, F.	Poor Folk	Fleckenstein, A.	Prince of Gravas...
Daugherty, J.	Poor Richard	Kyle, Anne D.	Prince of the Pale Mountains
Brine, M.D.	Poor Sally/her Christmas	Sleight, C.L.	Prince of the Pin Elves
Artzybasheff, B.	Poor Shaydullah	Rossetti, C.	Prince's Progress
Jacberns, R.	Poor Uncle Harry	MacDonald, Geo.	Princess & Curdie
Bontemps, A.	Popo & Fifina	MacDonald, Geo.	Princess & Goblin
Duplaix, G.	Popo the Hippopotamus	Otis, James	Princess & Joe Potter
Austin, Margot	Poppet	Milne, A.A.	Princess & the Apple Tree
Clark, M.	Poppy Seed Cakes	Hamer, S.H.	Princess & the Dragon
Bulla, Clyde R.	Poppy Seeds	Housman, L.	Princess Badoura
Perez-Guerra, A.	Poppy, Adventures of a Fairy	Fyleman, R.	Princess Comes to Our Town
Stacpoole, H.D.	Poppyland	Disney, W.	Princess Elizabeth Gift Book
Howard, F.M.	Porpoise of Pirate Bay	Hofman, Caroline	Princess Finds a Playmate
Lofting, H.	Porridge Poetry	Spiegelberg, F.	Princess Goldenhair...
Downey, Fairfax	Portrait of an Era	Gilbert, W.S.	Princess Ida
Lindsay, M.M.	Posey & the Pedlar	Orcutt, Wm. D.	Princess Kallisto
Stong, Phil	Positive Pete	Wright, Henrietta	Princess Liliwinkins
Cable, G.W.	Posson Jane...	Millay, Edna St. V.	Princess Marries the Page
Pollard, Percival	Posters in Miniature	Lang, A.	Princess Nobody
Dickens, C.	Posthumous Papers of Pickwick Club	Williamson, C.& N.	Princess Passes
Belloc, H.	Postmaster-General	Watson, V.	Princess Pocahontas
Atkins, E.H.	Pot of Gold	Comstock, H.T.	Princess Rags & Tatters
Judah, Aaron	Pot of Gold	Maugham, W.S.	Princess September & Nightingale
Crane, W.	Pothooks & Perseverance	Magruder, Julia	Princess Sonia
Arnold, E.	Potiphar's Wife	Harris-Burland, J.	Princess Thora
Kaye, M.	Potter Pinner Meadow	DeVries, P.J.C.	Princess Who Grew
Averill, Esther	Powder	Thompson, R.P.	Princess of Cozytown
Greene, S.P.M.	Power Lot	Braine, S.E.	Princess of Hearts
Disney, W.	Practical Pig	Lide, A.A.	Princess of Yucatan
Lenski, L.	Prairie School	Knatchbull-Hugessen	Princess with Pea-Green Nose
Barton, W.E.	Prairie Schooner	Gomme, G.L.	Princess's Story Book
Garland, H.	Prairie Songs...	Fenner, P.R.	Princesses & Peasant Boys
Miller, E.C.	Pran of Albania	Sparrow, W.S.	Prints & Drawings of Frank Brangwyn
Farjeon, E.	Prayer for Little Things	Parrish, R.	Prisoners of Chance
Field, R.	Prayer for a Child	Johnston, M.	Prisoners of Hope
Laing, Allan M.	Prayers & Graces	Johnson, E.G.	Private Memoirs of Madame Roland
Hawkins, Q.	Prayers & Graces for Small Children	Pemberton, Max	Pro Patria
Martin, J.	Prayers for Little Men & Women	Farrow, G.E.	Professor Philanderpan
Seton, E.T.	Preacher of Cedar Mountain	LeGallienne, R.	Prose Fancies
Brock, Emma	Present for Auntie	Dow, E.C.	Proud Roxana
Lathrop, D.	Presents for Lupe	Dobson, Austin	Proverbs in Porcelain
Emmet, R.	Pretty Peggy...	Robins, E.	Prudence & Peter...
Bingham, C.	Pretty Pets	Curtis, G.W.	Prue & I
Blaisdell, M.F.	Pretty Polly Flinders	N/A	Psalms of David
Burnett, F.H.	Pretty Sister of Jose	Wodehouse, P.G.	Psmith in the City
Rey, M.E.	Pretzel	MacKinstry, E.	Puck in Pasture
Pyle, H.	Price of Blood	Kipling, R.	Puck of Pook's Hill
Ackerman, A.W.	Price of Peace	Browne, E.G.	Puck's Broom
Austen, J.	Pride & Prejudice	Addington, S.	Pudding Lane People
Sawyer, R.S.	Primrose Ring	Brown, Paul	Puff Ball
Wodehouse, P.G.	Prince & Betty	Evans, F.G.	Puffin, Puma & Co.
Yonge, C.M.	Prince & the Page	Lathrop, D.	Puffy & Seven Leaf Clover
Twain, M.	Prince & the Pauper	Nesbit, E.	Pug Peter
N/A	Prince Ahmed & Fairy Perie Banou	Tudor, T.	Pumpkin Moonshine
Nella	Prince Babillon	Otto, M.G.	Pumpkin, Ginger & Spice

AUTHOR	TITLE	AUTHOR	TITLE
Gate, E.M.	Punch & Robinetta	Morrow, Eliz.	Rabbit's Nest
Reno, E.W.	Pup Called Cinderella	Plimpton, Geo.	Rabbit's Umbrella
Lathrop, D.	Puppies for Keeps	Williams, Garth	Rabbit's Wedding
Waylett, Richard	Puppy Tales	Tompkins, Jane	Raccoon Twins
Hawkins, Q.	Puppy for Keeps	Litsey, E.C.	Race of the Swift
Smith, Wm. J.	Puptents & Pebbles	Syrett, Netta	Rachel & the Seven Wonders
Lenski, L.	Puritan Adventure	Gordon, A.L.	Racing Rhymes
Perkins, L.F.	Puritan Twins	Burnett, F.H.	Racketty-Packetty House
Hudson, W.H.	Purple Land	Rackham, A.	Rackham's Book of Pictures
McCutcheon, G.B.	Purple Parasol	Hopkins, N.M.	Racoon Lake Mystery
Barbour, R.H.	Purple Pennant	Dorrington, A.	Radium Terrors
Thompson, R.P.	Purple Prince of Oz	Rey, H.A.	Raffy & the 9 Monkeys
Leet, F.R.	Purr & Meow	Hays, M.G.	Rag Animals ABC
Bangs, J.K.	Pursuit of the House Boat	Treffinger, C.	Rag Doll Jane
Kastner, Erich	Puss in Boots	Wurth, A.	Rag Doll Susie...
N/A	Puss in Boots	Rippey, Sarah C.	Raggedies in Fairy Land
N/A	Puss in Boots	Gruelle, J.	Raggedy Andy [ALL TITLES]
Perrault, C.	Puss in Boots	Gruelle, J.	Raggedy Ann [ALL TITLES]
Wain, L.	Pussies & Puppies	Riley, J.W.	Raggedy Man
Nesbit, E.	Pussy & Doggy Tales	Peat, F.B.	Rags
Winfrey, Guy	Pussy Purr-Mew	Smith, E.B.	Railroad Book
Brown, M.W.	Pussy Willow	Swift, H.H.	Railroad to Freedom
Young, Lillian E.	Pussy Willow's Naughty Kittens	Nesbit, E.	Railway Children
Taggart, M.A.	Pussy-Cat Town	Judson, C.I.	Railway Engineer
Anthony, Edward	Pussycat Princess	Robinson, W.H.	Railway Ribaldry
Brown, M.W.	Pussycat's Christmas	Tresselt, A.R.	Rain Drop Splash
Brown, K.	Putter Perkins	Sperry, A.	Rain Forest
LeFevre, A.	Puzzling Pair	Spielmann, M.H.	Rainbow Book
Morris, Wm.	Pygmalion & the Image	Leach, Maria	Rainbow Book of American Folk Tales
Merryman, M.P.	Quack! Said Jerusha	Miers, E.S.	Rainbow Book of American History
Hamer, S.H.	Quackles Junior	Fyleman, R.	Rainbow Cat
Hubbell, R.S.	Quacky Doodles...	Teasdale, S.	Rainbow Gold
Barrie, J.M.	Quality Street	Hall, A.V.	Rainbow Houses for Boys & Girls
Smith, C.M.	Queen Bee	Montgomery, L.M.	Rainbow Valley
N/A	Queen Mab's Fairy Realm	Hader, B.& E.	Rainbow's End
Burnett, F.H.	Queen Silver-Bell	Spicer, M.D.	Rainbows
Crane, W.	Queen Summer	Means, F.C.	Rains Will Come
Wetmore, C.H.	Queen Tiny's Little People	Mukerji, D.G.	Rama, Hero of India
Low, Frances H.	Queen Victoria's Dolls	McDougall, Walt	Rambillicus Book
Greenaway, K.	Queen Victoria's Jubilee Garland	Miltoun, F.	Rambles on the Riviera
Baum, L.F.	Queen Zixi of Ix	Jackson, H.H.	Ramona
Aubrey, Frank	Queen of Atlantis...	Roosevelt, T.	Ranch Life...
Caldecott, R.	Queen of Hearts	Chittenden, W.L.	Ranch Verses
Harte, Bret	Queen of Pirate Isle	Means, F.C.	Ranch and Ring
Sabin, E.H.	Queen of the City of Mirth	Carson, Thos.	Ranching Sport & Travel
Mack, R.E.	Queen of the Meadow	Schmidt, S.L.	Ranching on Eagle Eye
Stockton, Frank	Queen's Museum	Sabin, E.L.	Range & Trail
Baker, C.	Queen's Page	Seltzer, C.A.	Range Boss
Girvin, B.	Queer Cousin Claude	Bower, B.M.	Range Dwellers
Cox, P.	Queer People	Seltzer, C.A.	Range Riders
Hubbard, R.	Queer Person	Davis, R.H.	Ranson's Folly
Cox, P.	Queerie Queers with Hands, Wings & Claws	Pope, A.	Rape of the Lock
Scott, Walter	Quentin Durward	Velvin, E.	Rataplan....
Burnham, C.L.	Quest Flower	Sinclair, B.W.	Raw Gold
Collis, Maurice	Quest for Sita	Turner, N.B.	Ray Coon to the Rescue
Wallace, E.K.	Quest of the Dream	Bailey, C.S.	Read Aloud Stories
Schultz, J.W.	Quest of the Fish-Dog Skin	Munroe, K.	Ready Rangers
LeGallienne, R.	Quest of the Golden Girl	Smith, F.B.	Real Latin Quarter
Greenslet, F.	Quest of the Holy Grail	Andersen, H.C.	Real Princess
DuBois, W.E.B.	Quest of the Silver Fleece	Higgins, V.M.	Real Story of a Real Doll
James, Henry	Question of Our Speech	Terhune, A.P.	Real Tales of Real Dogs
Brown, M.W.	Quiet Noisy Book	Bangs, J.K.	Real Thing...
Bemelmans, L.	Quito Express	Ames, Mrs. E.	Really & Truly
N/A	Quiver of Love	Brownell, Eliz.	Really Babies
Bangs, J.K.	R. Holmes & Co.	Gordon, Eliz.	Really So Stories
Browning, R.	Rabbi Ben Ezra	Zion, Gene	Really Spring
Lawson, R.	Rabbit Hill	Judson, C.I.	Reaper Man
Pyle, Kath.	Rabbit Witch	Ciardi, John	Reason for the Pelican
Procter, E.H.	Rabbit's Day in Town	Donnell, A.H.	Rebecca Mary

AUTHOR	TITLE	AUTHOR	TITLE
Wellman, M.W.	Rebel Mail Runner	Washburne, Heluiz	Rhaman: Boy of Kashmir
Kjelgaard, J.A.	Rebel Siege	Wagner, R.	Rhinegold & the Valkyrie
Bangs, J.K.	Rebellious Heroine	Allan, M.B.	Rhyme Garden
Raymond, W.M.	Rebels of the New South	Harrison, F.	Rhyme of a Run...
Molesworth, M.	Rectory Children	Browning, E.B.	Rhyme of the Duchess May
Hendry, Hamish	Red Apple & Silver Bells	Carroll, L.	Rhyme? And Reason?
Crockett, S.R.	Red Axe	Dodge, M.M.	Rhymes & Jingles
Bronson, E.B.	Red Blooded	Tucker, E.S.	Rhymes & Stories of Olden Times
Lang, A.	Red Book of Animal Stories	De La Mare, W.	Rhymes & Verses
Lang, L.B.	Red Book of Heroes	Chute, Marchette	Rhymes About the City
Mitchell, S.W.	Red City	Chute, Marchette	Rhymes About the Country
Macleod, Mary	Red Cross Knight & Sir Guyan	Fairmont, E.	Rhymes for Kindly Children
Key, A.	Red Eagle	Snyder, F.	Rhymes for Kindly Children
Lang, A.	Red Fairy Book	Hamill, K.F.	Rhymes for Wee Sweethearts
Roberts, Theodore	Red Feathers	Allingham, W.	Rhymes for the Young Folks
Deming, T.O.	Red Folk & Wild Folk	March, Mary E.	Rhymes of Early Jungle Folk
Roberts, C.G.D.	Red Fox	Sage, B.	Rhymes of If & Why
Moeschlin, Elsa	Red Horse	N/A	Rhymes of Old Times
Nesbit, E.	Red House	Sage, B.	Rhymes of Real Children
Olcott, F.J.	Red Indian Fairy Book	Brill, Geo. R.	Rhymes of the Golden Age
MacDonald, Golden	Red Light Green Light	Coburn, W.D.	Rhymes of the Roundup Camp
Wilson, Romer	Red Magic...	N/A	Rhymes without Reason
Wister, O.	Red Men & White	Fillebrown, R.H.	Rhymes/Happy Childhood
Deming, T.O.	Red People of the Wooded Country	Gordon, H.C.	Rhymes/Red Triangle
Cholmondeley, M.	Red Pottage	Mitchison, Naomi	Rib of the Green Umbrella
Aldin, C.	Red Puppy Book	Smalley, J.	Rice to Rice Pudding
Kent, Louise A.	Red Rajah	Kalnay, Francis	Richest Boy in the World
Lippincott, J.W.	Red Roan Pony	Garis, H.	Rick & Ruddy
Lang, A.	Red Romance Book	Bialk, Elisa	Ride 'Em Peggy!
Weil, Ann	Red Sails to Capri	N/A	Ride a Cock-Horse
Kyle, Anne D.	Red Sky over Rome	Courlander, H.	Ride with the Sun
Tompkins, Jane	Red Squirrel Twins	Dean, G.M.	Riders of the Gabilans
Lang, A.	Red True Story Book	Grey, Zane	Riders of the Purple Sage
Mitchell, L.S.	Red, White & Blue Auto	Dodge, T.A.	Riders of Many Lands
Pool, M.L.	Red-Bridge Neighborhood	Olds, Eliz.	Riding the Rails
Lloyd, J.U.	Red-Head	Williams, E.	Ridolfo
Canton, Wm.	Reign of King Herla	Elliott, K.M.	Riema...
N/A	Reign of King Oberon	Masefield, J.	Right Royal
Gibbon, J.M.	Reign of Old King Cole	Lloyd, J.U.	Right Side of the Car
Hader, B.& E.	Reindeer Trail	Montgomery, L.M.	Rilla of Ingleside
Steig, Wm.	Rejected Lovers	Coleridge, S.T.	Rime of the Ancient Mariner
Pancoast, M.H.	Rejuvenation of Mama & Papa Goose	Jackson, L.F.	Rimskittle's Book
Dalgliesh, A.	Relief's Rocker	Brooke, L.L.	Ring O' Roses
Grahame, K.	Reluctant Dragon	Henderson, G.	Ring of the Nibelung
Francis, P.W.	Remarkable Adventures of Little Boy Pip	Baum, L.F.	Rinkitink in Oz
Wright, Isa L.	Remarkable Tale of a Whale	Scott, Sally	Rip & Royal
Menpes, M.	Rembrandt	Irving, W.	Rip Van Winkle
Knipe, A.A.	Remember Rhymes	Towne, C.H.	Rise & Fall of Prohibition
Sill, S.C.	Reminiscences of Old Chest of Drawers	Hyde, F.	Ritz Carltons
Bronson, E.B.	Reminiscences of a Ranchman	Frey, N.A.	River Horse
Paltenghi, M.	Remus Goes to Town	Boston, Lucy	River at Green Knowe
Steele, R. (tr.)	Renaud of Montauban	Stuart, Ruth M.	River's Children
Salten, Felix	Rennie the Rescuer	Chambers, Rbt.	River-Land
Jenks, Tudor	Rescue Syndicate	Merwin, S.	Road Builders
Sharp, M.	Rescuers: A Fantasy	Johnston, A.F.	Road of the Loving Heart
Henderson, L.L.	Resolute	Faulkner, Georgene	Road to Enchantment
Flack, M.	Restless Robin	Fay, E.	Road to Fairyland
Belasco, D.	Return of Peter Grimm	Morse, L.B.	Road to Nowhere
Hardy, T.	Return of the Native	Baum, L.F.	Road to Oz
Horgan, Paul	Return of the Weed	Jerrold, W.C.	Road, Rail & Sea
Dalgliesh, A.	Reuben & his Red Wheelbarrow	Hare, K.	Roads & Vagabonds
Brady, C.T.	Reuben James	Grimm Bros.	Robber Bridegroom
Marvel, I.	Reveries of a Bachelor	Disney, W.	Robber Kitten
Nicholson, M.	Reversible Santa Claus	N/A	Robber Kitten
Fry, J.H.	Revolt Against Beauty	Lawson, R.	Robbut: Tale of Tails
France, A.	Revolt of the Angels	Spearman, Frank	Robert Kimberly
Goudge, Eliz.	Reward of Faith	Raymond, M.T.	Roberta Goes Adventuring
Kipling, R.	Rewards & Fairies	Bailey, A.W.	Roberta and her Brothers
Masefield, J.	Reynard the Fox	Robinson, M.L.	Robin & Angus

AUTHOR	TITLE	AUTHOR	TITLE
Robinson, M.L.	Robin & Tito	Davies, Maria T.	Rose of Old Harpeth
N/A	Robin Hood	Pyle, H.	Rose of Paradise
Rhead, Louis	Robin Hood	Bemelmans, L.	Rosebud
Creswick, Paul	Robin Hood & his Adventures	Humphrey, M.	Rosebud Stories
Sterling, S.H.	Robin Hood & his Merry Men	Hutt, H.	Rosebuds
McSpadden, J.W.	Robin Hood & his Merry Outlaws	Casserley, A.T.	Roseen
McSpadden, J.W.	Robin Hood & his Merry Outlaws	Amber	Rosemary & Rue
Tilney, F.C.	Robin Hood & his Merry Outlaws	Lustig, Sonia	Roses of the Winds
Gilbert, Henry	Robin Hood...	N/A	Rosie-Posie Book
Tappan, E.M.	Robin Hood: His Book	Beerbohm, M.	Rossetti & his Circle
Defoe, D.	Robinson Crusoe	Molesworth, M.	Rosy
Beecroft, John	Rocco Came In	Hays, M.G.	Rosy Childhood
Newell, P.	Rocket Book	Aldin, C.	Rough & Tumble
Cheney, Cora	Rocking Chair Buck	Moodie, S.	Roughing It in the Bush
Love, E.	Rocking Island	Christie, G.F.	Round De Ole Plantation
Kent, R.	Rockwellkentiana	Girvin, B.	Round Fairyland with Alice
Holling, H.C.	Rocky Billy	Girvin, B.	Round Fairyland with Alice & White Rabbit
Kingman, Lee	Rocky Summer	Lee, A.	Round Rabbit
Davis, L.R.	Roger & the Fox	Davis, L.R.	Round Robin
Smith, G.	Roggie & Reggie Stories	Noble, T.T.	Round of Carols
Austen, J.	Rogues in Porcelain	Jackson, Charlotte	Round the Afternoon
Seton, E.T.	Rolf in the Woods	Bennet, H.	Round the Hearth
Quiller-Couch, A.	Roll Call of Honor	Fyleman, R.	Round the Mulberry Bush
Sawyer, R.S.	Roller Skates	McNeil, Marion	Round the Mulberry Bush
Wells, A.R.	Rollicking Rhymes for Youngsters	Farrow, G.E.	Round the World ABC
Voight, V.F.	Rolling Show	Scott, J.L.	Round the World We Sail
Chappell, G.S.	Rollo in Society	Sharp, E.	Round the World to Wympland
Potter, B.	Roly Poly Pudding	Addington, S.	Round the Year on Pudding Lane
Otto, M.G.	Roly-Poly Snowman	Asbjornsen, P.C.	Round the Yule Log
Richards, Dorothy	Roma Rabbit's Picnic	Dalgliesh, A.	Roundabout
Conrad, J.	Romance	Charles, R.H.	Roundabout Turn
Rice, Alice H.	Romance of Billy-Goat Hill	Mason, A.	Roving Lobster
Boult, E.M.	Romance of Cinderella	Blumberg, F.B.	Rowena Teena Tot & Blackberries
Pollard, A.	Romance of King Arthur	Schackne, S.	Rowena the Skating Cow
Capes, B.	Romance of Lohengrin	Baum, L.F.	Royal Book of Oz
Champney, E.W.	Romance of Old Japan	Nesbit, E.	Royal Children of English History
LeGallienne, R.	Romance of Perfume	Tucker, E.S.	Royal Little People
N/A	Romance of Tristam & Isoude	Cresswell, B.	Royal Progress of King Pepito
LeGallienne, R.	Romance of Zion Chapel	Goulden, S.	Royal Reflections
Loti, P.	Romance of a Child	Riley, J.W.	Rubaiyat of Doc Sifers
Wiggin, K.D.	Romance of a Christmas Card	Wells, Carolyn	Rubaiyat of a Motor Car
Smith, F.H.	Romance of an Old Fashioned Gentleman	Herford, O.	Rubaiyat of a Persian Kitten
Hearn, L.	Romance of the Milky Way	Omar Khayyam	Rubaiyat...
MacGregor, M.	Romance of the Netherlands	Various	Ruby Fairy Book
Ponsat, Georges	Romance of the River	Molesworth, M.	Ruby Ring
Aldin, C.	Romance of the Road	Pyle, H.	Ruby of Kishmoor
Crane, W.	Romance of the Three R's	King, B.	Ruffs & Pompons
Schauffer, R.H.	Romantic America	Sechrist, Eliz. H.	Rufie Had a Monkey!
Finger, C.J.	Romantic Rascals	Estes, Eleanor	Rufus M.
Hawthorne, H.	Romantic Rebel	Bianco, M.W. (ed.)	Rufus the Fox
Shakespeare, Wm.	Romeo & Juliet	Unknown	Rule Britannia
MacDonald, Geo.	Ronald Bannerman's Boyhood	White, S.E.	Rules of the Game
Sharp, D.L.	Roof & Meadow	Holling, H.C.	Rum-Tum-Tummy...
Eaton, S.	Roosevelt Bears	Gaster, Moses	Rumanian Legends & Fairy Tales
Angelo, V.	Rooster Club	Calmour, A.C.	Rumbo Rhymes...
Petersham, M.	Rooster Crows	Hawthorne, J.	Rumpty-Dudget's Tower
Sandburg, C.	Rootabaga Country	Paltenghi, M.	Rumpus Rabbit
Sandburg, C.	Rootabaga Pigeons	Riley, J.W.	Runaway Boy
Sandburg, C.	Rootabaga Stories	Brown, M.W.	Runaway Bunny
Archer, J.C.	Rosalina	Smith, Laura R.	Runaway Bunny
Thompson, Maurice	Rosalynde's Lovers	Tarry, Ellen	Runaway Elephant
Thackeray, Wm.	Rose & the Ring	Bell, L.	Runaway Equator
Strang, H.	Rose Book of the Fairies	Disney, W.	Runaway Lamb at County Fair
McCabe, O.	Rose Fairies	Moon, G.	Runaway Papoose
Strang, H.	Rose Fairy Book	Higgins, Alice	Runaway Rhymes
Fyleman, R.	Rose Fyleman Fairy Book	Campbell, Ruth	Runaway Smalls
Alcott, L.M.	Rose In Bloom	Hogan, Inez	Runaway Toys
Russell, W.C.	Rose Island	Sturges, L.B.	Runaway Toys
Alcott, L.M.	Rose in Bloom	Robinson, M.L.	Runner of the Mountain Tops

AUTHOR	TITLE
Garrard, P.	Running Away with Nebby
Donaldson, Lois	Runzel-Punzel
Johnson, A.E.	Russian Ballet
Dole, N.H.	Russian Fairy Book
Bain, R.N.	Russian Fairy Tales
Wilson, R.	Russian Story Book
Bilibin, I.	Russian Wonder Tales
Chidsey, A.	Rustam Lion of Persia
McNeely, M.H.	Rusty Ruston
Petersham, M.	Ruth
Streamer, Col. D.	Ruthless Rhymes for Heartless Homes
Brown, M.W.	SHHhhh... Bang!
Housman, L.	Sabrina Warham
Kempson, F.C.	Sad Fate of Erica's Blackamoor
Bontemps, A.	Sad-Faced Boy
Allen, R.B.	Saga of Gisli
Dalgliesh, A.	Sailor Sam
Asquith, C. (ed.)	Sails of Gold
Johnson, Richard	Saint George & the Dragon
Radcliffe, W.	Saint's Garden
Webling, P.	Saints & their Stories
Gay, Zhenya	Sakimura
Kent, R.	Salamina
Perry, Bliss	Salem Kittredge...
Marriott, C.	Sally Castleton, Southerner
Potter, M.C.	Sally Gabble & the Fairies
Weiss, Edna S.	Sally Saucer
Walker, D.S.	Sally's ABC
Wilde, O.	Salome...
Harte, Bret	Salomy Jane
Anderson, C.W.	Salute
Crawford, F.M.	Salve Venetia
Bontemps, A.	Sam Patch...
Fitzgerald, Hugh	Sam Steele's Advens. in Panama
Fitzgerald, Hugh	Sam Steele's Advens. on Land & Sea
Byron, May	Sambo & Susanna
Bannerman, H.	Sambo & the Twins
Justus, May	Sammy
Ault, L.& N.	Sammy & the Snarlywink
Ainslie, K.	Sammy Goes a Hunting
Crowninshield, Mrs.	San Isidro
Keats, Mark	Sancho & Stubborn Mule
Wharton, E.	Sanctuary
James, Will	Sand
Lewis, A.H.	Sandburrs
Dodge, Louis	Sandman's Forest
Dodge, Louis	Sandman's Mountain
Frees, Harry W.	Sandman: His Animal Stories
Gray, Eliz. J.	Sandy
Davis, M.G.	Sandy's Kingdom
Hogan, Inez	Sandy, Skip & Man in the Moon
Singer, Caroline	Santa Claus Comes to America
Lawrence, C.H.	Santa Claus in Toyland
Page, T.N.	Santa Claus' Partner
Janvier, T.A.	Santa Fe's Partner
Clark, A.N.	Santiago
Burnett, F.H.	Sara Crew...
Jackson, Charlotte	Sarah Deborah's Day
Garner, Elvira	Sarah Faith Anderson
Robinson, M.L.	Sarah's Daikin
Gates, Doris	Sarah's Idea
Carlyle, T.	Sartor Resartus
Wright, E.B.	Saturday Flight
Corbett, Scott	Sauce for the Gander
Reed, L.	Sausages & Sundials
Craddock, Harry	Savoy Cocktail Book
Gilbert, W.S.	Savoy Operas
DeKoven, R.	Sawdust Doll
Fraser, W.A.	Sazada Tales

AUTHOR	TITLE
Dall, A.R.	Scamper...
L'Hommedieu, D.	Scampy the Little Black Cocker
Denslow, W.W.	Scarecrow & the Tin Man
Baum, L.F.	Scarecrow of Oz
Davis, R.H.	Scarlet Car
Parry, David M.	Scarlet Empire
Parry, E.A.	Scarlet Herring
Hawthorne, N.	Scarlet Letter
Meigs, C.	Scarlet Oak
London, J.	Scarlet Plague
Aldin, C.	Scarlet to M.F.H.
Browne, P.E.	Scars & Stripes
Howland, E.	Scary-Ann & the Cookie Man
Marshall, H.	Scenery of London
Eliot, Geo.	Scenes from Clerical Life
Atkinson, J.C.	Scenes in Fairyland
Arnold, M.	Scholar-Gypsy
Bruce, J.	School Days
Emerson, C.D.	School Days in Disneyville
Hobbes, J.O.	School for Saints
Sheridan, R.B.	School for Scandal
Strain, E.H.	School in Fairyland
Goldman, J.M.	School in Our Village
James, Will	Scorpion: Good Bad Horse
Powers, Tom	Scotch Circus
Wiggin, K.D.	Scottish Chiefs
Hornibrook, I.	Scout of Today
Tomlinson, E.	Scouting with Daniel Boone
Seuss, Dr.	Scrambled Eggs Supper
Boyle, E.	Scrap Basket Sam
Ciardi, John	Scrappy the Pup
Lida	Scuff the Seal
Kipling, R.	Sea & Sussex
Tomlinson, H.M.	Sea & the Jungle
Baum, L.F.	Sea Fairies
Herford, O.	Sea Legs
Beaumont, C.W.	Sea Magic...
Henry, M.	Sea Star: Orphan of Chincoteague
Aldrich, T.B.	Sea Turn
London, J.	Sea Wolf
Enright, E.	Sea is All Around
Lawson, Marie A.	Sea is Blue
Eberle, I.	Sea-Horse Adventure
Larken, E.P.	Sea-Prince
Webb, M. St. John	Sea-Shore Fairies
Holling, H.C.	Seabird
Ladas, Alexis	Seal that Couldn't Swim
King, Marian	Sean & Sheela
Smith, E.B.	Seashore Book
Brown, M.W.	Seashore Noisy Book
Slobodkin, L.	Seaweed Hat
Beardsley, Aubrey	Second Book of 50 Drawings
Beerbohm, M.	Second Childhood of John Bull
Serviss, G.P.	Second Deluge
Biddle, A.	Second Froggy Fairy Book
Kipling, R.	Second Jungle Book
Crawford, P.	Second Shift
Stuart, Ruth M.	Second Wooing of Salina Sue
Crawford, P.	Secret Brother
Trease, G.	Secret Fiord
Burnett, F.H.	Secret Garden
Barbour, R.H.	Secret Play
Rawlings, M.K.	Secret River
Roberts, C.G.D.	Secret Trails
Grant, Gordon	Secret Voyage
Schmidt, S.L.	Secret of Silver Peak
Clark, A.N.	Secret of the Andes
Stone, Eugenia	Secret of the Bog
Brown, Alice	Secret of the Clan

AUTHOR	TITLE	AUTHOR	TITLE
Jones, J.O.	Secrets	Timlin, W.M.	Ship that Sailed to Mars
McElhone, N.K.	Secrets of the Elves	Morrow, Honore	Ship's Monkey
Frasconi, Antonio	See & Say	Collins, Dale	Shipmates Down Under
Webb, M. St. John	Seed Fairies	Barnes, J.	Ships & Sailors
Selsam, M.E.	Seeds & More Seeds	Grant, Gordon	Ships Under Sail
Bridgman, L.J.	Seem-So's	Gay, J.	Shire Colt
Long, J.L.	Seffy	Bronte, C.	Shirley
Wagner, R.	Seigfried...	Spyri, J.	Shirley Temple in Heidi
Schultz, J.W.	Seizer of Eagles	Hall, Wm.	Shoelace Robin
Schrank, J.	Seldom & the Golden Cheese	Chamberlin, E.C.	Shoes, Ships & Sealing Wax
Thomson, C.L.	Selections from LeMorte Darthur	Molloy, Anne	Shooting Star Farm
Harper, Wilhelmina	Selfish Giant...	Bridgman, Clare	Shopping Day
Dawson, Forbes	Sensational Trance	Waterstone, S.S.	Short Stories of Musical Melodies
Austen, J.	Sense & Sensibility	Rossetti, C.	Shorter Poems of...
Gates, Doris	Sensible Kate	Gorham, Maurice	Showmen & Suckers
Shelley, P.B.	Sensitive Plant	Means, F.C.	Shuttered Windows
Sterne, Laurence	Sentimental Journey through France & Italy	Morse, Eliz.	Siamese Cat
Barrie, J.M.	Sentimental Tommy	Hunt, M.L.	Sibby Botherbox
Coblentz, C.C.	Sequoya	Harper, T.A.	Siberian Gold
Mijatovich, M.	Serbian Fairy Tales	Abbott, E.H.	Sick-a-Bed-Lady
N/A	Sermon on the Mount	Metcalfe, F.	Side Show Studies
Nesbit, W.D.	Sermons in Song	Ray, A.C.	Sidney: Summer on St. Lawrence
Owen, C.D.	Seth Way	Aanrud, Hans.	Sidsel Longskirt & Solve Suntrap
Wells, Carolyn	Seven Ages of Childhood	Nicholson, M.	Siege of the Seven Suitors
Gale, Eliz.	Seven Beads of Wampum	Baring-Gould, S.	Siegfried
Darton (ed.)	Seven Champions of Christendom	Wagner, R.	Siegfried...
Fox, F.M.	Seven Christmas Candles	Sendak, M.	Sign on Rosie's Door
Galt, Tom	Seven Days from Sunday	Voss, R.	Sigurd Eckdel's Bride
Biggers, E.D.	Seven Keys to Baldpate	Eliot, Geo.	Silas Marner
Seuss, Dr.	Seven Lady Godivas	Stranathan, May	Silhouette Stories
Gilmour, Marg.	Seven Little Spillikins	Merwin, S.	Silk
Anderson, Rbt. G.	Seven O'Clock Stories	N/A	Silly Hare
Bailey, M.	Seven Peas in the Pod	Robinson, C.	Silly Submarine
McLeod, Emilie	Seven Remarkable Bears	Weisgard, L.	Silly Willy Nilly
Kipling, R.	Seven Seas	Lovell, Dorothy A.	Silvanus Goes to Sea
Artzybasheff, B.	Seven Simeons	Blyton, E.	Silver & Gold
Andersen, H.C.	Seven Tales	Hunter, Richard	Silver Bubbles...
N/A	Seven Voyages of Sinbad	Lewis, C.S.	Silver Chair
Tarkington, B.	Seventeen	O'Brien, Jack	Silver Chief
Lindsey, Wm.	Severed Mantle	Richards, L.E.	Silver Crown
Newman, I.	Shades of Blue	Farjeon, E.	Silver Curlew
Harris, J.C.	Shadow Between his Shoulder Blades	Weil, Ann	Silver Fawn
Means, F.C.	Shadow Over Wide Ruin	Beach, R.	Silver Horde
Newell, P.	Shadow Show	Petershams	Silver Mace
Armour, M.	Shadow of Love	Wilson, Romer	Silver Magic
Hornung, E.W.	Shadow of the Rope	Brown, Palmer	Silver Nutmeg
Schmidt, S.L.	Shadow over Winding Ranch	Dalgliesh, A.	Silver Pencil
Belloc, H.	Shadowed!	Alcott, L.M.	Silver Pitchers
DeJong, Meindert	Shadrach	Thompson, R.P.	Silver Princess of Oz
Snow, Jack	Shaggy Man of Oz	Bialk, Elisa	Silver Purse
Jameson, Anna	Shakespeare's Heroines	Sawyer, R.S.	Silver Sixpence
Sterling, S.H.	Shakespeare's Sweetheart	Barfield, O.	Silver Trumpet
Merrill, Jean	Shan's Lucky Knife	Conkling, H.	Silverhorn
Morrow, Eliz.	Shannon	Hawkes, Clarence	Silversheene: King of Sled Dogs
Schlein, M.	Shapes	N/A	Simple Addition
Peake, M.	Shapes & Sounds	Herford, O.	Simple Jography
Shiel, M.P.	Shapes in the Fire	Denslow, W.W.	Simple Simon
Burglon, N.	Shark Hole	Lyons, A. Neil	Simple Simon...
Baker, O.	Shasta of the Wolves	N/A	Sinbad the Sailor
Hutt, H.	She Loves Me	Wheeler, Opal	Sing Mother Goose
Goldsmith, O.	She Stoops to Conquer	Rossetti, C.	Sing Song
Gordon, Eliz.	Sheaf of Roses	Herbertson, A.	Sing Song Stories
Gilfillan, A.B.	Sheep	Gag, Flavia	Sing a Song of Seasons
Chrisman, A.B.	Shen of the Sea	Wheeler, Opal	Sing for America
Spenser, Edmund	Shepheard's Calander	Wheeler, Opal	Sing for Christmas
Noyes, Alfred	Sherwood	Wheeler, Opal	Sing in Praise
Pope, Eliz. M.	Sherwood Ring	Broadbent, H.	Sing-A-Song
Van Vrooman, M.	Shine	Rossetti, C.	Sing-Song
Stone, Wm. S.	Ship of Flame	Ritchie, Jean	Singing Family of the Cumberlands

AUTHOR	TITLE	AUTHOR	TITLE
Farjeon, E.	Singing Games for Children	Neidlinger, W.H.	Small Songs for Small Singers
DeJong, Meindert	Singing Hill	Lawson, R.	Smeller Martin
Hough, E.	Singing Mouse Stories	Ramsden, G.	Smile Within a Tear
Moon, G.	Singing Sands	Burdette, R.J.	Smiles Yoked with Sighs
Somervell, A.	Singing Time	Mason, Miriam E.	Smiling Hill Farm
Seredy, K.	Singing Tree	Aikins, Ruth	Smiling Princess
Coonley, L.A.	Singing Verses for Children	Rion, H.	Smiling Road
Lady Frazer	Singing Wood	Dalgliesh, A.	Smiths & Rusty
Fouque, La Motte	Sintram and his Companions	London, J.	Smoke Bellew
Madariaga, S.	Sir Bob	Herford, O.	Smoker's Yearbook
Goodwin, M.W.	Sir Christopher...	Emerson, W.G.	Smoky God
Weston, J.L.	Sir Gleges/Sir Libeaus Desconus	Goudge, Eliz.	Smoky House
Doyle, A.C.	Sir Nigel	James, Will	Smoky the Cow Horse
Crockett, S.R.	Sir Toady Crusoe	Kneeland, C.A.	Smuggler's Island
Crane, W.	Sirens Three	Lathrop, D.	Snail Who Ran
Fox, F.M.	Sister Sally	White, Hervey	Snake Gold
Goudge, Eliz.	Sister of the Angels	Marryat, Fred.	Snarleyyow
Puner, Helen	Sitter Who Didn't Sit	Brown, M.W.	Sneakers
Edey, B.O.	Six Giants & a Griffin	Milne, A.A.	Sneezles
Pyle, Kath.	Six Little Ducklings	Ford, Julia E.	Snickerty Nick
Wilkins, M.E.	Six Trees	Gag, W.	Snippy & Snappy
Colum, P.	Six Who were Left in a Shoe	Peary, J.	Snow Baby
Ewing, J.H.	Six to Sixteen	Tudor, T.	Snow Before Christmas
Outhwaite, I.	Sixpence to Spend	Compton, M.	Snow Bird & Water Tiger...
Hamilton, W.	Sixty Years on the Plains	Kjelgaard, J.A.	Snow Dog
Bailey, A.C.	Skating Gander	Hawthorne, N.	Snow Image
Daley, C.F.	Skating Party	Bird, M.H.	Snow Man's Christmas
Zeitlin, I.	Skazki	Milhous, Kath.	Snow Over Bethlehem
Caldecott, R.	Sketch Book	DeRegniers, B.S.	Snow Party
Gibson, C.D.	Sketches in Egypt	Andersen, H.C.	Snow Queen
Bianco, M.W.	Skin Horse	N/A	Snow White & Rose Red
Vorse, M.E.	Skinny Gets Fat	Disney, W.	Snow White & Seven Dwarfs
DeAngeli, M.	Skippack School	Grimm Bros.	Snow White & Seven Dwarfs
Brown, Marcia	Skipper John's Cook	Grimm Bros.	Snow White...
Robinson, M.L.	Skipper Riley: Terrier Dog	Whittier, J.G.	Snowbound
Welles, W.	Skipping Along	Grimm Bros.	Snowdrop...
Lenski, L.	Skipping Village	Nathan, Robert	Snowflake & the Starfish
Lathrop, D.	Skittle-Skattle Monkey	Hinkle, T.C.	Snowy Tail: Champion Jack Rabbit
Bennett, R.	Skookum & Sandy	Russell, Arthur	Snowy for Luck
Schultz, J.W.	Skull Head the Terrible	Jewett, J.H.	Snuggy Bedtime Stories
Parker, A.C.	Skunny Wundy	Garrott, H.	Snythergen
Teilhet, Darwin	Skwee-Gee	Smith, E.B.	So Long Ago
Hurd, E.T.	Sky High	Cawein, M.J.	So Many Ways
Baum, L.F.	Sky Island	North, S.	So Red the Nose
McEvoy, Joseph P.	Slams of Life...	Gibson, C.D.	Social Ladder
Newell, P.	Slant Book	Page, T.N.	Social Life in Old Virginia
Bontemps, A.	Slappy Hooper...	Wharton, A.H.	Social Life in the Early Republic
Crane, W.	Slateandpencilvania	Best, A.	Sojo: Story of Little Lazy Bones
Thanet, O.	Slave to Duty	Lefevre, F.	Soldier Boy
Marsh, Geo.	Sled Trails/White Waters	Kipling, R.	Soldier Tales
Evans, C.S.	Sleeping Beauty	Lloyd, N.	Soldier of the Valley
N/A	Sleeping Beauty	Ewing, J.H.	Soldier's Children
Perrault, C.	Sleeping Beauty	Davis, R.H.	Soldiers of Fortune
N/A	Sleeping Beauty Picture Book	Unknown	Soldiers of the King
Quiller-Couch, A.	Sleeping Beauty...	Moon, G.	Solita
Estes, Eleanor	Sleeping Giant	Stuart, Ruth M.	Solomon Crow's Christmas Pockets
N/A	Sleeping Partners	N/A	Some British Ballads
Brown, M.W.	Sleepy ABC	Robinson, W.H.	Some Frightful War Pictures
Zolotow, C.	Sleepy Book	N/A	Some Old Nursery Tales
Various	Sleepy-Song Book	Foley, James W.	Some One Like You
Booth, M.B.	Sleepy-Time Stories	Gordon, Eliz.	Some Smiles
Dyer, R.O.	Sleepy-Time Story Book	Krauss, Ruth	Somebody Else's Nut Tree
Lipkind, Wm.	Sleepyhead	Cowham, Hilda	Somebody's Baby
Haines, Wm.	Slim	Wain, L.	Somebody's Pussies
Hoffman, H.	Slovenly Peter	Malloch, D.	Someone to Care
Bemelmans, L.	Small Bear	Bullard, Marion	Somersaulting Rabbit
Steig, Wm.	Small Fry	Wood, M. & H.	Something Perfectly Silly
Campbell, Ruth	Small Fry/Winged Horse	Brown, Palmer	Something for Christmas
Jones, J.O.	Small Rain	Leighton, C.	Sometime Never

AUTHOR	TITLE
Barnes, James	Son of Light Horse
Munroe, K.	Son of Satsuma
London, J.	Son of the Sun
Mirza, Y.B.	Son of the Sword
Best, H.	Son of the White Man
Grover, E.O.	Sonbonnet Babies in Holland
Joseph, A.W.	Sondo: A Liberian Boy
Arnold, E.	Song Celestial
Smith, E.	Song Devices & Jingles
Malcolmson, A.	Song of Robin Hood
N/A	Song of Songs...
Barr, A.	Song of a Single Note
Porter, G.S.	Song of the Cardinal
Kipling, R.	Song of the English
Havighurst, Walt.	Song of the Pines
St. Francis/Assisi	Song of the Sun
Politi, L.	Song of the Swallows
Shakespeare, Wm.	Songs
Lovelace, R.	Songs & Sonnets
Shakespeare, Wm.	Songs & Sonnets
Aldrich, A.R.	Songs about Life, Love & Death
Gale, N.	Songs for Little People
Farjeon, E.	Songs for Music....
Belloc, H.	Songs from Bad Child's Bk./Beasts
Milne, A.A.	Songs from Now We are Six
N/A	Songs of Bryn Mawr College
De La Mare, W.	Songs of Childhood
Ramal, W.	Songs of Childhood
Hogg, J.	Songs of Ettrick Shepherd
Blake, Wm.	Songs of Experience
Baum, L.F.	Songs of Father Goose
Maunder, I.	Songs of Happy Children
Blake, Wm.	Songs of Innocence
Matheson, Annie	Songs of Love & Praise
Bulla, Clyde R.	Songs of Mr. Small
Richardson, E.	Songs of Near & Far Away
Christy, H.C.	Songs of Sentiment
Kipling, R.	Songs of the Sea
Noble-Ives, S.	Songs of the Shining Way
Stevenson, R.L.	Songs with Music/Child's Garden/Verses
Broadwood, Lucy	Songs from Alice in Wonderland
Thomas, E.M.	Songs/Jingles/Rhymes
Browning, E.B.	Sonnetts from the Portuguese
Bigham, M.A.	Sonny Elephant
Rountree, H.	Sonny Jim
Cory, F.	Sonny Sayings
Stuart, Ruth M.	Sonny's Father
Stuart, Ruth M.	Sonny, A Christmas Guest
Sowers, P.A.	Sons of the Dragon
Elliott, K.M.	Soomoon, Boy of Bali
DeSegur, S.	Sophie...
Moran, Jim	Sophocles the Hyena
Disney, W.	Sorcerer's Apprentice
Roche, J.J.	Sorrows of Sap'ed
Dolson, Hildegarde	Sorry to Be So Cheerful
Cabell, J.B.	Soul of Melicent
Barr, A.	Souls of Passage
Douglas, N.	South Wind
Leighton, C.	Southern Harvest
Saint-Exupery, A.	Southern Mail
Todd, Ruthven	Space Cat
Winsor, F.	Space Child's Mother Goose
Slobodkin, L.	Space Ship Returns to Apple Tree
Slobodkin, L.	Space Ship Under Apple Tree
Freeman, Don	Space Witch
Kauffmann, R.	Spanish Dollars
Catherwood, Mary	Spanish Peggy
Starkie, Walter	Spanish Raggle-Taggle
Penfield, E.	Spanish Sketches
Brown, Paul	Sparkie & Puff Ball
Rand, Ann	Sparkle & Spin
Grishina, N.G.	Sparrow House
Cammack, K.	Spartan Primer
Perkins, L.F.	Spartan Twins
Thompson, R.P.	Speedy in Oz
Hurd, E.T.	Speedy...
Hewes, A.D.	Spice & Devil's Cave
Eberle, I.	Spice on the Wind
Housman, L.	Spikenard
Lida	Spiky the Hedgehog
N/A	Spin Top Spin
Lenski, L.	Spinach-Boy
Malkus, A.S.	Spindle Imp
Boyles, K.	Spirit Trail
Van Dyke, H.	Spirit of Christmas
Atherton, G.	Splendid Idle Forties
Hinkson, H.A.	Splendid Knight
Quiller-Couch, A.	Splendid Spur
Black, I.S.	Spoodles, Puppy Who Learned
Parkes, W.T.	Spook Ballads
Whitney, Casper	Sporting Pilgrimage
Rey, M.E.	Spotty
Finger, C.J.	Spreading Stain
Burnett, F.H.	Spring Cleaning
Mockler, G.	Spring Fairies & Sea Fairies
Linnell, O.	Spring Songs with Music
Lenski, L.	Spring is Here
Swinburne, A.C.	Springtide of Life
Hader, B.& E.	Spunky
Waugh, A.	Square Book of Animals
Faulkner, Georgene	Squeaky & the Scare Box
Garrott, H.	Squiffer
DuBois, W.P.	Squirrel Hotel
Stockton, Frank	Squirrel Inn
Hader, B.& E.	Squirrely of Willow Hill
Politi, L.	St. Francis & the Animals
Chesterton, G.K.	St. Francis of Assisi
Stevenson, R.L.	St. Ives
Shaw, G.B.	St. Joan
Twain, M.	St. Joan of Arc
Earle, A.M.	Stage Coach & Tavern Days
Chisholm, L.	Staircase of Stories
Harrison, E.O.	Star Fairies
Brown, A.F.	Star Jewels...
Dewey, K.F.	Star People
D'Aulaire, I.& E.	Star Spangled Banner
Bailey, T.	Star in the Well
Bianco, P.	Starlit Journey
Teasdale, S.	Stars Tonight
Follett, H.T.	Stars to Steer By
Bacon, P.	Starting from Scratch
Andersen, H.C.	Steadfast Tin Soldier
Unknown	Stealers of Light
Tousey, S.	Steamboat Billy
Sabin, E.H.	Stella's Adventure in Starland
Newell, Hope	Steppin & Family
Boylan, G.D.	Steps to Nowhere
Stevenson, R.L.	Stevenson Song Book
Ketchum, J.	Stick-in-the-Mud
Muir, J.	Stickeen...
Burglon, N.	Sticks Across the Chimney
Barnes, Madeline	Stirabout Stories
Pyle, H.	Stolen Treasure
Brown, Marcia	Stone Soup
McNeer, May	Stop Tim!
Hader, B.& E.	Stop, Look & Listen
Howells, W.D.	Stops of Various Quills
Brooks, E.S.	Storied Holidays

AUTHOR	TITLE	AUTHOR	TITLE
Andersen, H.C.	Stories & Fairy Tales	Wells, Carolyn	Story of Betty
Bailey, C.S.	Stories & Rhymes for a Child	Perrault, C.	Story of Blue-Beard
Peat, F.B.	Stories Children Like	Watson, Eliz.	Story of Bread
Piper, W. (ed.)	Stories Children Love	McNeer, May	Story of California
Welch, C.	Stories Children Love	Disney, W.	Story of Casey Jr.
McSpadden, J.W.	Stories From Wagner	Rhoads, Dorothy	Story of Chan Yuc
N/A	Stories Merry & Wise	Rostand, E.	Story of Chanticleer
Morrison, M.W.	Stories True & Fancies New	Francoise	Story of Colette
Buck, Pearl S.	Stories for Little Children	Johnston, A.F.	Story of Dago
MacKay, H.	Stories for Pictures	Terhune, A.P.	Story of Damon & Pythias
Housman, L. (ed.)	Stories from Arabian Nights	Lofting, H.	Story of Dr. Dolittle
N/A	Stories from Aunt Judy	Longfellow, H.W.	Story of Evangeline
Kelman, J.H.	Stories from Chaucer	Leaf, M.	Story of Ferdinand
Underdown, E.	Stories from Chaucer	Nesbit, E.	Story of Five Rebellious Dolls
Cunnington, S.	Stories from Dante	MacGregor, M.	Story of France
Dawson, L.H. (ed.)	Stories from Faerie Queen	Brooks, W.R.	Story of Freginald
Disney, W.	Stories from Fantasia	Uttley, Alison	Story of Fuzzypeg the Hedgehog
Steedman, Amy	Stories from Grimm...	Longfellow, H.W.	Story of Hiawatha
Henius, F.	Stories from the Americas	Godden, Rumer	Story of Holly & Ivy
De La Mare, W.	Stories from the Bible	Pyle, H.	Story of Jack Ballister's Fortunes
Farrar, Evelyn	Stories from the Bible	Bowie, W.R.	Story of Jesus for Young People
Woodruff, E.	Stories from the Magic World	Brooks, Edward	Story of King Arthur
N/A	Stories from the Odyssey	Pyle, H.	Story of King Arthur...
Petersham, M.	Stories from the Old Testament	N/A	Story of Little Red Hen
Basile, G.	Stories from the Pentamerone	Welch, D.	Story of Louise
Andersen, H.C.	Stories from...	Van Loon, H.W.	Story of Mankind
Dike, H.	Stories of Great Metropolitan Operas	Disney, W.	Story of Minnie Mouse
Clay, Beatrice	Stories of King Arthur	De La Mare, W.	Story of Miss Jemima
Cutler, U.W.	Stories of King Arthur	Potter, B.	Story of Miss Moppet
Haydon, A.L.	Stories of King Arthur	Feuillet, O.	Story of Mr. Punch
Winter, B. (ed.)	Stories of King Arthur	Lofting, H.	Story of Mrs. Tubbs
Hunt, B.S.	Stories of Little Brown Koko	Trimpey, Alice	Story of My Dolls
Remington, F.	Stories of Peace & War	McClintock, M.	Story of New England
Duppa, C.M.	Stories of a Lowly Life	N/A	Story of Noah's Ark
Nulets, L.E.	Stories of the Little Fishes	Smith, E.B.	Story of Noah's Ark
Fenner, P.R.	Stories of the Sea	Gibbons, Mary	Story of Ophelia
Williams, C.A.	Stories that Glue Told	Hader, B.	Story of Pancho
Bryant, S.C.	Stories to Tell the Littlest Ones	Potter, B.	Story of Peter Rabbit
Andersen, H.C.	Stories...	Spyri, J.	Story of Rico
Langford, George	Stories/First American Animals	Baldwin, J.	Story of Roland
Tompkins, Jane	Storks Fly Home	Dobson, Austin	Story of Rosina
Zolotow, C.	Storm Book	Baldwin, J.	Story of Seigfried
Sperry, A.	Storm Canvas	White, Anne H.	Story of Seraphina
Kjelgaard, J.A.	Stormy	Baldwin, J.	Story of Siegfried
N/A	Story Book	N/A	Story of Simple Simon
Petersham, M.	Story Book of Clothes	Leaf, M.	Story of Simpson & Sampson
Petersham, M.	Story Book of Cotton	Sterling, M.B.	Story of Sir Galahad
Williams, C.A.	Story Book of Silhouettes	Pyle, H.	Story of Sir Lancelot
Cooke, E.V.	Story Club	Brown, Alice	Story of Thyrza
Montgomery, L.M.	Story Girl	Disney, W.	Story of Timothy's House
Faulkner, Georgene	Story Lady's Christmas Stories	Ets, Marie H.	Story of a Baby
Faulkner, Georgene	Story Lady's Italian Tales	Mayol, L.B.	Story of a Happy Doll
Faulkner, Georgene	Story Lady's Nursery Tales	Taylor, S.	Story of a Little Poet
Bonner, M.G.	Story Teller's Holiday	Hawley, H.E.	Story of a Little Tin Soldier
Austin, S.	Story Without an End	Collodi, C.	Story of a Puppet
Grove, F.	Story Without an End	Hamblen, H.E.	Story of a Yankee Boy
Flack, M.	Story about Ping	Connolly, J.	Story of an Old Fashioned Doll
Darton, H.	Story of the Canterbury Pilgrims	Nesbit, E.	Story of the Amulet
Sharp, E.	Story of the Weathercock	Hugo, V.	Story of the Bold Pecopin
Waterloo, S.	Story of AB	Hough, E.	Story of the Cowboy
Harris, J.C.	Story of Aaron	Dopp, K.E.	Story of the Early Sea People
Lambert, C.	Story of Alaska	N/A	Story of the Firemen
Steele, R.	Story of Alexander	Peattie, D.C.	Story of the First Men
Peattie, D.C.	Story of America	Baldwin, J.	Story of the Golden Age
Peattie, D.C.	Story of Ancient Civilization	Lang, A.	Story of the Golden Fleece
Parrish, Anne	Story of Appleby Capple	Pyle, H.	Story of the Grail
DeBrunhoff, J.	Story of Babar	Gilchrist, Marie	Story of the Great Lakes
Stuart, Ruth M.	Story of Babette	Gates, J.S.	Story of the Live Dolls
Hare, C.	Story of Bayard	Gates, J.S.	Story of the Lost Doll

AUTHOR	TITLE	AUTHOR	TITLE
Camp, Ruth O.	Story of the Markets	Tresselt, A.R.	Sun Up
Gilbert, W.S.	Story of the Mikado	James, Will	Sun Up, Tales of the Cow Camps
Gates, J.S.	Story of the Mince Pie	Coatsworth, E.	Sun's Diary
McClintock, M.	Story of the Mississippi	Del Rio, A.M.	Sun, Moon & a Rabbit
Bontemps, A.	Story of the Negro	Estes, Eleanor	Sun, Wind & Mr. Todd
Van Dyke, H.	Story of the Other Wise Man	Beskow, E.	Sun-Egg
Halstead	Story of the Philippines	Richardson, E.	Sun-Moon & Stars...
Hamer, S.H.	Story of the Ring	Grover, E.O.	Sunbonnet Babies [ALL TITLES]
Housman, L.	Story of the Seven Young Goslings	Hogate, E.C.	Sunbonnets & Overalls...
Grant, Gordon	Story of the Ship	Daley, C.F.	Sundials
McNeer, May	Story of the South-West	Remington, F.	Sundown Leflare
Bannerman, H.	Story of the Teasing Monkey	Various	Sung Under the Silver Umbrella
Noble-Ives, S.	Story of the Teddy the Bear	Berry, E.	Sunhelmet Sue
Hader, B.& E.	Story of the Three Bears	Adams, W.I.L.	Sunlight & Shadow
Gates, J.S.	Story of the Three Dolls	Putnam, Nina W.	Sunny Bunny
Locke, Wm. J.	Story of the Three Wise Men	Molesworth, O.	Sunny Land Stories
Nesbit, E.	Story of the Treasure Seekers	Miller, O.B.	Sunny Rhymes/Happy Children
Barbour, R.H.	Story the Dogie Told to Me	Magruder, Julia	Sunny Southerner
Grey, Sydney	Story-Land	Rippey, Sarah C.	Sunny-Sulky Book
Lindsay, M.M.	Story-Teller	Sill, L.M.	Sunnyfield
Kramer, N. (ed.)	Storybook	Berlyn, A.	Sunrise-Land
Stockton, Frank	Storyteller's Pack	Hutchinson, W.M.L.	Sunset of the Heroes
Lang, A.	Strange Story Book	Gates, J.S.	Sunshine Annie
Streatfield, N.	Stranger in Primrose Lane	Bemelmans, L.	Sunshine...
Lewis, Claudia	Straps the Cat	Phelps, E.S.	Supply at St. Agatha's
Lenski, L.	Strawberry Girl	Baxter, Betty	Supposin'
Tagore, R.	Stray Birds	Layard, George S.	Suppressed Plates...
Parsons, G.	Stream of History	Lansing, Eliz.	Sure Thing for Shep
Brown, M.W.	Streamlined Pig	McElhone, N.K.	Surprise Book
Fischer, Marj.	Street Fair	Lenski, L.	Surprise for Mother
Bianco, M.W.	Street of Little Shops	Kennedy, M.	Surprise to the Children
Chambers, Rbt.	Streets of Ascalon	Steward, R.	Surprising Advens. of Man in the Moon
Dunbar, P.L.	Strength of Gideon	Crockett, S.R.	Surprising Advens. of Sir Toady Lion
Oursler, Fulton	String of Blue Beads	Brown, M.	Surprising Advens. of Tuppy & Tue
Berry, E.	Strings to Adventure	Palmer, S.	Surrey
Lloyd, J.U.	Stringtown on the Pike	Bergengren, R.W.	Susan & the Butterbees
Williamson, H.	Stripey	Hunt, M.L.	Susan Beware!
Barr, Rbt.	Strong Arm	Warner, A.	Susan Clegg...
Cable, G.W.	Strong Hearts	Leonard, M.F.	Susan Grows Up
Robinson, M.L.	Strong Wings	Wiggin, K.D.	Susanna & Sue
Begbie, H.	Struwwelpeter Alphabet	Allee, M.H.	Susanna & Tristram
White, E.B.	Stuart Little	Field, R.	Susanna B. & William C.
Molesworth, M.	Studies & Stories	Mason, Miriam E.	Susannah: Pioneer Cow
Van Dyke, J.C.	Studies in Pictures	Lenski, L.	Susie Mauiar
Seton, E.T.	Studies/Art Anatomy/Animals	Palazzo, T.	Susie the Cat
De La Mare, W.	Stuff & Nonsense	Wahlenberg, A.	Sweedish Fairy Tales
Frost, A.B.	Stuff & Nonsense	Lippmann, J.M.	Sweet P's
N/A	Stuffed Owl	Calhoun, Mary	Sweet Papootie Doll
Laird, Rowena	Stuffy	Bouvet, M.	Sweet William
Bro, Marguerite	Su-Mei's Golden Year	Crockett, S.R.	Sweetheart Travellers
Kenward, James	Suburban Child	Madison, J.	Sweethearts Always
Cutting, M.S.	Suburban Whirl	Meigs, C.	Swift Rivers
Coleman, O.	Successful Houses	Wyss, J.D.	Swiss Family Robinson
Pratt, Marg.	Successful Secretary	Perkins, L.F.	Swiss Twins
Hunt, M.L.	Such a Kind World	Kuhns, O.	Switzerland
Gag, Asta	Sue & Sew-and-Sew	White, T.H.	Sword in the Stone
Tileston, M.W.	Sugar & Spice & All That's Nice	Bulla, Clyde R.	Sword in the Tree
Bancroft, L.	Sugar-Loaf Mountain	Norton, A.	Sword is Drawn
Field, E.	Sugar-Plum Tree	Peck, T.A.	Sword of Dundee
Lenski, L.	Sugarplum House	Hewes, A.D.	Sword of Roland Arnot
Duncan, N.	Suitable Child	Lord Dunsany	Sword of Welleran
Garstin, N.	Suitors of Aprille	Parrish, R.	Sword of the Old Frontier
Weisgard, L.	Suki the Siamese Pussy	Coatsworth, E.	Sword of the Wilderness
Ade, G.	Sultan of Sulu	Stratton, Clarence	Swords & Statues
DeAngeli, M.	Summer Day with Ted & Nina	Singmaster, Elsie	Swords of Steel
Brown, M.W.	Summer Noisy Book	Hewes, A.D.	Swords on the Sea
Zion, Gene	Summer Snowman	Struther, J.	Sycamore Square...
Barker, C.M.	Summer Songs with Music	Martin, Pat. M.	Sylvester Jones & Voice in the Forest
Davis, L.R.	Summer is Fun	Gardiner, Linda	Sylvia in Flowerland

AUTHOR	TITLE	AUTHOR	TITLE
Armfield, C.	Sylvia's Travels	Jacobs-Bond, C.	Tales of Little Cats
Carroll, L.	Sylvie & Bruno	Jacobs-Bond, C.	Tales of Little Dogs
Newberry, C.T.	T-Bone the Baby-Sitter	Hayman, D. (ed.)	Tales of Longfellow
Jacberns, R.	Tabitha Smallways, Schoolgirl	Poe, E.A.	Tales of Mystery...
McKenney, John	Tackroom Tattles	Crockett, S.R.	Tales of Our Coast
Burton, Earl & L.	Taffy & Joe	Perrault, C.	Tales of Past Times...
Sayers, F.C.	Tag-Along Tooloo	Lang, A.	Tales of Troy & Greece
English, James W.	Tailbone Patrol	Pyle, Kath.	Tales of Two Bunnies
Brooke, L.L.	Tailor & the Crow	Pyle, Kath.	Tales of Wonder & Magic
Potter, B.	Tailor of Gloucester	Carpenter, Frances	Tales of a Chinese Grandmother
Newbolt, H.	Taken From the Enemy	Pierson, C.D.	Tales of a Poultry Farm
Tudor, T.	Tale for Easter	Irving, W.	Tales of a Traveller
Swinburne, A.C.	Tale of Balen	Bouvet, M.	Tales of an Old Chateau
Lane, Marg.	Tale of Beatrix Potter	Marsh, Lewis	Tales of the Fairies
Potter, B.	Tale of Benjamin Bunny	Marsh, Lewis	Tales of the Homeland
Lamb, Tom	Tale of Bingo	Hudson, W.H.	Tales of the Pampas
Potter, B.	Tale of Flopsy Bunnies	Olcott, F.J. (ed.)	Tales of the Persian Genii
Potter, B.	Tale of Jemima Puddle Duck	Kipling, R.	Tales of the Punjab
Gordon, Eliz.	Tale of Johnny Mouse	Brown, A.F.	Tales of the Red Children
Potter, B.	Tale of Johnny Town Mouse	Doucet, J.	Tales of the Spinner
Potter, B.	Tale of Little Pig Robinson	Jacobs (ed.)	Tales/Boccaccio
Wagner, R.	Tale of Lohengrin	McNeer, May	Tales/Crescent Moon
Potter, B.	Tale of Mr. Jeremy Fisher	Gate, E.M.	Tales/Enchanted Isles
Potter, B.	Tale of Mr. Tod	Lang, A.	Tales/Fairy Court
Potter, B.	Tale of Mrs. Tiggy-Winkle	London, J.	Tales/Fish Patrol
Potter, B.	Tale of Mrs. Tittlemouse	Carpenter, Frances	Tales/Russian Grandmother
Potter, B.	Tale of Peter Rabbit	Wiggin & Smith	Talking Beasts...
Potter, B.	Tale of Pigling Bland	Donahey, M.D.	Talking Bird & Wonderful Wishes
Potter, B.	Tale of Squirrel Nutkin	Carlson, N.S.	Talking Cat...
Potter, B.	Tale of Timmy Tiptoes	Mills, G.R.	Talking Dolls
Wiig, Hanna	Tale of Tiny Tutak	Rouse, W.H.D.	Talking Thrush
Potter, B.	Tale of Tom Kitten	Baker, Augusta	Talking Tree
Farjeon, E.	Tale of Tom Tiddler	Pratt, Marg.	Talking Typewriter
Tripp, Paul	Tale of Tubby the Tuba	Werner, Jane	Tall Book of Make-Believe
Potter, B.	Tale of Two Bad Mice	N/A	Tall Book of Nursery Tales
Dickens, C.	Tale of Two Cities	MacKaye, P.	Tall Tales/Kentucky Mountains
Bemelmans, L.	Tale of Two Glimps	Watanna, O.	Tama
Tschiffely, A.F.	Tale of Two Horses	Brown, Marcia	Tamarindo!
Beskow, E.	Tale of Wee Little Old Woman	Lynde, F.	Taming/Red Butte Western
McKay (ed.)	Tale of the Cauldron	Bryson, C.L.	Tan & Teckle
Langley, Noel	Tale/Land of Green Ginger	Knibbs, H.H.	Tang of Life
N/A	Tales & Talks About Animals	Gray, Eliz. J.	Tangle Garden
Hope, A.R.	Tales For Toby	Young, Ella	Tangle-Coated Horse
Warren, M.R.	Tales Told by Gander	Carroll, L.	Tangled Tale
Miller, O.B.	Tales Told in Holland	Means, F.C.	Tangled Waters
Molesworth, M.	Tales Told in the Twilight	Blanchard, A.E.	Tangles & Curls
Gould, F.C.	Tales Told in the Zoo	Hawthorne, N.	Tanglewood Tales
Finger, C.J.	Tales Worth Telling	Wagner, R.	Tannhauser
Porter, G.S.	Tales You Won't Believe	Molesworth, M.	Tapestry Room
Farjeon, E.	Tales from Chaucer	Harris, J.C.	Tar-Baby
Pyle, Kath.	Tales from Greek Mythology	Lang, A.	Tartan Tales
Grimm Bros.	Tales from Grimm	Burroughs, E.R.	Tarzan Twins
Pyle, Kath.	Tales from Norse Mythology	Crissey, F.	Tattlings of a Retired Politician
Lamb, C.	Tales from Shakespeare	Flack, M.	Tatuk, Arctic Boy
Finger, C.J.	Tales from Silver Lands	Shannon, Monica	Tawnymore
Piper, W. (ed.)	Tales from Storyland	Field, R.	Taxis & Toadstools
Burgess, T.	Tales from Storyteller's House	Maloy, L.	Tea Party in Plumpudding Street
Chesson	Tales from Tennyson	Jerome, J.K.	Tea-Table Talk
Armfield, C.	Tales from Timbuktu	Gibson, Lydia	Teacup Whale
Bowman, J.C.	Tales from a Finnish Tupa	DeAngeli, M.	Ted & Nina Go to the Grocery Store
Asbjornsen, P.C.	Tales from the Field	DeAngeli, M.	Ted & Nina Have/Happy Rainy Day
Gate, E.M.	Tales from the Secret Kingdom	Herbertson, A.	Teddy & Trots in Wonderland
Edgeworth, M.	Tales from....	Byron, May	Teddy Bear Book
Deutsch, B.	Tales of Faraway Folk	Deihl, E.G.	Teddy Bear that Prowled the Night
Pyle, Kath.	Tales of Folk & Fairies	Milne, A.A.	Teddy Bear...
N/A	Tales of Hoffman	Byron, May	Teddy Bearoplane
Harris, J.C.	Tales of Home Folks/Peace & War	Sutton, Adah L.	Teddy Bears
Kipling, R.	Tales of India	Towne, Rbt. D.	Teddy Bears Come to Life
Wiggin, K.D.	Tales of Laughter	Towne, Rbt. D.	Teddy Bears in Hot Water

AUTHOR	TITLE	AUTHOR	TITLE
Towne, Rbt. D.	Teddy Bears in a Smashup	Kalashnikoff, N.	The Defender
Towne, Rbt. D.	Teddy Bears on a Lark	Glasgow, E.	The Deliverance
Towne, Rbt. D.	Teddy Bears on a Tobaggon	Kuh, Charlotte	The Deliveryman
Folkard, C.	Teddy Tail of the Daily Mail	Hamer, S.H.	The Dolomites
Gullick, M.E.	Teddy's Year with the Fairies	Sheridan, R.B.	The Duenna
Eaton, S.	Teddy-B & Teddy-G, Bear Detectives	VerBeck, F.	The Dumpies
Johnson, L.R.	Teddy-Bear ABC	Kuh, Charlotte	The Engineer
Donahey, Wm.	Teenie Weenie Days	Lent, Henry B.	The Farmer
Donahey, Wm.	Teenie Weenie Neighbors	Kuh, Charlotte	The Fireman
Donahey, Wm.	Teenie Weenie Town	Austin, Mary	The Flock
Donahey, Wm.	Teenie Weenies Under the Rose Bush	Downer, M.L.	The Flower
Donahey, Wm.	Teenie Weenies in Wonderland	Gerry, M.S.	The Flowers
Day, M.	Tell 'Em Again Tales	Austin, Mary	The Ford
Claudy, C.H.	Tell Me Why Stories	White, S.E.	The Forest
Blanchard, A.E.	Tell Me a Story	London, J.	The Game
Ashley, Fred	Temple of Fire	DuBois, W.P.	The Giant
Lever, Chas.	Templelogue Lever	Potter, M.C.	The Gigglequicks
Flaubert, G.	Temptation of St. Anthony	Cable, G.W.	The Grandissimes
Sweetser, K.D.	Ten Boys from Dickens	Farmer, J.E.	The Grenadier
Sweetser, K.D.	Ten Girls from Dickens	Porter, G.S.	The Harvester
Norman	Ten Little Boer Boys	Grahame, K.	The Headswoman
Farjeon, E.	Ten Saints	Kingsley, C.	The Heroes
Bacon, J.D.	Ten to Seventeen	Bemelmans, L.	The Highworld
Tenggren, G.	Tenggren's Story Book	Tolkien, J.R.R.	The Hobbit
Johnson, O.	Tennessee Shad	Dalgliesh, A.	The Hollyberrys
Cary, E.L.	Tennyson	Bangs, J.K.	The Idiot
Paine, A.B.	Tent Dwellers	Groesbeck, T.	The Incas
Whittier, J.G.	Tent on the Beach	Tracy, Louis	The Invaders
Custer, E.B.	Tenting on the Plains	Chester, Geo. R.	The Jingo
Stone, Wm. S.	Teri Taro from Bora Bora	Lear, E.	The Jumblies
Courlander, H.	Terrapin's Pot of Sense	Cooney, Barbara	The Kellyhorns
Bacon, P.	Terrible Nuisance	Lida	The Kingfisher
Johnson, Crockett	Terrible Terrifying Toby	Goldoni, C.	The Liar
Adams, A.	Texas Matchmaker	Gorham, Maurice	The Local
Lenski, L.	Texas Tomboy	Long, O.M.	The Lollipops
France, A.	Thais	Van Dyke, H.	The Mansion
Webber, I.E.	Thanks to Trees	DuMaurier, G.	The Martian
Dalgliesh, A.	Thanksgiving Story	Sandoz, M.	The Maze
Davis, Rbt.	That Girl of Pierre's	Bonney, T.G.	The Mediterranean
Bragdon, Elspeth	That Jud!	Garnett, L.A.	The Merrymakers
Baldwin, May	That Little Limb	Dawson, A.J.	The Message
Watson, H.B.M.	The Adventurers	Gilbert, W.S.	The Mikado
Irving, W.	The Alhambra	Andrews, M.S.	The Militants
Orr, M.S.	The Alphabet	Lyle, E.P.	The Missourian
McCutcheon, G.B.	The Alternative	Van Stockum, H.	The Mitchells
Bingham, D.	The Bastille	Estes, Eleanor	The Moffats
Poe, E.A.	The Bells...	Crane, S.	The Monster...
Bangs, J.K.	The Bicyclers	Kuh, Charlotte	The Motorman
Kemble, E.W.	The Blackberries...	White, S.E.	The Mountains
Norton, Mary	The Borrowers	Thurston, K.C.	The Mystics
Bourman, C.	The Bridge	Beach, R.	The Net
Ogburn, Charlton	The Bridge	Andersen, H.C.	The Nightingale
Ewing, J.H.	The Brownies	Dixon, Thomas	The One Woman
Seitz, D.	The Bucaneers	Fraser, W.A.	The Outcasts
Sowerby, Githa	The Bumbletoes	Adams, A.	The Outlet
Lent, Henry B.	The Captain	Warner, A.	The Panther
Harrison, Mrs. B.	The Carlyles	Doyle, A.C.	The Parasite
Cable, G.W.	The Cavalier	White, S.E.	The Pass
Cheney, W.	The Challenge	Cooper, J.F.	The Pathfinder
Somerville, Wm.	The Chase	Phillips, H.W.	The Pets
Lipman, M.	The Chatterlings	Richards, L.E.	The Piccolo
Meynell, A.	The Children	Molloy, Anne	The Pigeoneers
Dickens, C.	The Chimes	Bonner, G.	The Pioneer
Dixon, Thomas	The Clansman	Nicholson, M.	The Poet
Phillips, D.G.	The Cost	Kuh, Charlotte	The Policeman
Lowell, J.R.	The Courtin'	Tennyson, A.	The Princess
Churchill, W.	The Crossing...	Price, Luxor	The Quoks
Aldington (tr.)	The Decameron...	Hurd, C.	The Race
Cooper, J.F.	The Deerslayer	Poe, E.A.	The Raven

AUTHOR	TITLE	AUTHOR	TITLE
Sheridan, R.B.	The Rivals	Thurber, J.	Thirteen Clocks
White, S.E.	The Riverman	Chaundler, C.	Thirteenth Orphan
London, J.	The Road	Moorat, Joseph	Thirty Old-Time Nursery Songs
Barclay, F.	The Rosary	Molesworth, M.	This & That
Riley, J.W.	The Rose	Herford, O.	This Giddy Globe
Kelly, A.	The Rosebud....	Evers, Helen	This Little Pig
Cary, E.L.	The Rossettis	Bone, Gertrude	This Old Man
Hader, B.& E.	The Runaways	Sawyer, R.S.	This Way to Christmas
Annixter, Jane	The Runner	De La Mare, W.	This Year: Next Year
McElrath, F.	The Rustler	Kent, R.	This is my Own
Baldwin, J.	The Sampo	Black, I.S.	This is the Bread that Betsy Ate
Enright, E.	The Saturdays	Scott, Wm. R.	This is the Milk that Jack Drank
Wilson, H.L.	The Seeker	Jones, J.O. (ed.)	This is the Way
Waterloo, S.	The Seekers	Woodcock, L.	This is the Way the Animals Walk
McCutcheon, G.B.	The Sherrods	Tudor, T.	Thistly B.
Hader, B.& E.	The Skyrocket	Carleton, H.G.	Thompson Street Poker Club
Lucas, E.V.	The Slowcoach	Anderson, C.W.	Thoroughbreds
Wilde, O.	The Spinx	Kingsley, F.M.	Those Brewster Children
Cooper, J.F.	The Spy	Carruth, F.W.	Those Dale Girls
Lent, Henry B.	The Storekeeper	Bro, Marguerite	Three & Domingo
Maeterlinck, M.	The Swarm	Dorey, J.	Three & the Moon
Andersen, H.C.	The Swineherd	N/A	Three Bears
Shakespeare, Wm.	The Tempest	VerBeck, F.	Three Bears
Coolidge, D.	The Texican	Asbjornsen, P.C.	Three Billy Goats Gruff
Lewis, A.H.	The Throwback	N/A	Three Billy Goats Gruff
Aldredge, Edna	The Timbertoes	Black, Marg.	Three Brothers & a Lady
Dixon, Thomas	The Traitor	Ewing, J.H.	Three Christmas Trees
Powys, L.	The Twelve Months	Gag, W.	Three Gay Tales from Grimm
Shirley, E.	The Twins	Kyne, P.B.	Three Godfathers
Grant, Rbt.	The Undercurrent	Boggs, R.S.	Three Golden Oranges
Johnson, O.	The Varmint	Andersen, H.C.	Three Hanses
LeWitt, J.	The Vegetabull	Caldecott, R.	Three Jovial Huntsmen
Magruder, Julia	The Violet	Cuming, E.W.D.	Three Jovial Puppies
Wister, O.	The Virginian	Brown, M.W.	Three Little Animals
Colum, P.	The Voyagers	Torrey, M.	Three Little Chipmunks
Cutting, M.S.	The Wayfarers	Mee, J.	Three Little Frogs
Parker, Gilbert	The Weavers	N/A	Three Little Kittens
Deutsch, B.	The Welcome	Benstead, V. (adap)	Three Little Pigs
Raymond, E.	The Whirligig	Disney, W.	Three Little Pigs
Aldin, C.	The Widow	N/A	Three Little Pigs
Terhune, A.P.	The Woman	Jerome, J.K.	Three Men on Wheels
Stein, Gertrude	The World's Round	De La Mare, W.	Three Mulla Mulgars
Nesbit, E.	The Wouldbegoods	Dumas, A.	Three Musketeers
Rawlings, M.K.	The Yearling	James, Will	Three Mustangeers
Miller, E.	The Yoke	Williams, Orlando	Three Naughty Children
Streatfield, N.	Theater Shoes	March, Eleanor	Three Naughty Elves
DeAngeli, M.	Thee, Hannah!	Bunner, H.C.	Three Operettas
Cooke, G.M.	Their First Formal Call	Disney, W.	Three Orphan Kittens
Perry, F.F.	Their Hearts' Desire	DuBois, W.P.	Three Policemen
Vaughn, R.	Then & Now	Blanchard, A.E.	Three Pretty Maids
Enright, E.	Then There were Five	Brown, Paul	Three Rings: A Circus Book
Pyle/Porter	Theodora	De La Mare, W.	Three Royal Monkeys
MacGregor, Ellen	Theodore Turtle	Kelly, Eric P.	Three Sides of Agiochook
Udry, J.M.	Theodore's Parents	Austin, Margot	Three Silly Kittens
Snedeker, C.D.	Theras & his Town	Elliott, K.M.	Three Sneezes...
Weston, C.	There & Then	Carroll, L.	Three Sunsets...
Adams, K.	There Were Giants	Sewell, H.	Three Tall Tales
Whitman, W.	There was a Child Went Forth	Molesworth, M.	Three Witches
Wilder, L.I.	These Happy Golden Years	Albee, George	Three Young Kings
Nesbit, E.	These Little Ones	Southwold, S.	Three by Candlelight
Kipling, R.	They	Dalgliesh, A.	Three from Greenways
Judson, C.I.	They Came from France	Forsyth, G.A.	Thrilling Days/Army Life
Worth, Kath.	They Loved to Laugh	Foley, James W.	Through All the Years
Duvoisin, R.	They Put Out to Sea	Bernard, F.S.	Through Cloud Mountain
Lawson, R.	They Were Strong & Good	Stevens, F.	Through Merrie England
Seuss, Dr.	Thidwick the Big-Hearted Moose	Van Dyke, H.	Through South America
Enright, E.	Thimble Summer	Rockwood, Roy	Through Space to Mars
Beerbohm, M.	Things New & Old	Marks, J.	Through Welsh Doorways
Clark, A.N.	Third Monkey	Fezandie, Clement	Through the Earth

AUTHOR	TITLE	AUTHOR	TITLE
Mills, W.J.	Through the Gates of Old Romance	Reeves, James	Titus in Trouble
Eberle, I.	Through the Harbor from Everywhere	Brown, Alice	Tiverton Tales
Donahey, M.D.	Through the Little Green Door	Trent, R.	To Church We Go
Carroll, L.	Through the Looking Glass	Pennell, E.R.	To Gypsyland
Disney, W.	Through the Picture Frame	Johnston, M.	To Have & to Hold
Peltier, F.	Through the Rainbow	Brock, Emma	To Market! To Market!
Bates, H.E.	Through the Woods	Bingham, C.	To Nursery Land
Andersen, H.C.	Thumbelina	Braine, S.E.	To Tell the King the Sky is Falling
Andersen, H.C.	Thumbelisa...	Wellman, M.W.	To Unknown Lands
Baker, O.	Thunder Boy	Leet, F.R.	To the Circus the Children Go
Stone, Wm. S.	Thunder Island	King, C.	To the Front
Greer, Blanche	Thunder's Tail	Coatsworth, E.	Toast to the King
Pease, Howard	Thunderbolt House	Gay, Romney	Toby & Sue
Edwards, G.W.	Thus Think and Smoke Tobacco	Syrett, Netta	Toby & the Odd Beasts
Barr, A.	Thyra Varrick	Otis, James	Toby Tyler...
Bennett, R.A.	Thyra: Romance of the Polar Pit	Black, I.S.	Toby: A Curious Cat
Bangs, J.K.	Tiddledywink Tales	Bridges, Wm.	Toco Toucan
Bangs, J.K.	Tiddledywink's Poetry Book	Whitney, Elinor	Tod of the Fens
Habberton, J.	Tiger & the Insect	Marsh, Geo.	Toilers of the Trails
Courlander, H.	Tiger's Whisper	Jerome, J.K.	Told After Supper
Baum, L.F.	Tik-Tok of Oz	De La Mare, W.	Told Again
Steig, Wm.	Till Death Do Us Part	Various	Told Under the Blue Umbrella
Gray, Eliz. J.	Tilly-Tod	Various	Told Under the Christmas Tree
Ardizzone, E.	Tim & Charlotte	Various	Told Under the Magic Umbrella
Ardizzone, E.	Tim & Lucy Go to Sea	Harris, J.C.	Told by Uncle Remus
Otis, James	Tim & Tip	Muter, Gladys N.	Told in Our Neighborhood
Ames, Mrs. E.	Tim & the Dusty Man	N/A	Told in the Twilight
Ardizzone, E.	Tim All Alone	Weatherly, F.E.	Told in the Twilight
Meyer, Edith P.	Tim Chick	Jewett, E.M.	Told on the King's Highway
Flack, M.	Tim Tadpole...	Cooke, E.V.	Told to the Little Tot
Ardizzone, E.	Tim in Danger	Hughes, Thos.	Tom Brown's School Days
Ardizzone, E.	Tim to the Rescue	Scott, Michael	Tom Cringle's Log
Lord Dunsany	Time & the Gods	Smith, F.H.	Tom Grogan
Aldin, C.	Time I Was Dead	Gurko, Leo	Tom Paine, Freedom's Apostle
Wells, H.G.	Time Machine	Twain, M.	Tom Sawyer Abroad
Woodward, H.	Time Was	Denslow, W.W.	Tom Thumb
Roberts, E.M.	Time of Man	Gilly Bear	Tom Tit Tales
McCloskey, R.	Time of Wonder	N/A	Tom the Piper's Son
Cady, H.	Time to Get Up	Lyons, A. Neil	Tom, Dick & Harriet
Disney, W.	Timid Elmer	Semple, D.	Tommy & Jane & the Birds
Williams, Gwen M.	Timid Timothy...	Burgess, T.	Tommy & the Wishing Stone
Whitney, Elinor	Timothy & the Blue Cart	Gay, Romney	Tommy Grows Wise
Hawley, H.E.	Timothy Toddlekin	Gates, J.S.	Tommy Sweet Tooth
Graham, Al	Timothy Turtle	Hader, B.& E.	Tommy Thatcher Goes to Sea
Mason, Miriam E.	Timothy has Ideas	Addington, S.	Tommy Tingle-Tangle
Benet, W.R.	Timothy's Angels	Lee, Al	Tommy Toodles
Jenks, Tudor	Timothy's Magical Afternoon	Phillips, M.E.	Tommy Tregennis
Tripp, E.	Tin Fiddle	Page, T.N.	Tommy Trot's Visit to Santa Claus
Baum, L.F.	Tin Woodman of Oz	Lofting, H.	Tommy, Tilly & Mrs. Tubbs
Stockton, Frank	Ting-a-Ling	Anderson, C.W.	Tomorrow's Champion
McNeer, May	Tinka Minka & Linka	O'Neill, G.	Tomorrow's House
Syrett, Netta	Tinkelly Winkle	Coatsworth, E.	Tonio & the Stranger
Grant, V.	Tinker Tim the Toy Maker	Sawyer, R.S.	Tonio Antonia
Herzog, E.	Tinkers of Turntable	King, C.	Tonio, Son of Sierras
Herbertson, A.	Tinkler Johnny	Pugh, E.	Tony Drum
Mother Goose	Tiny Book of Nursery Rhymes	Nightingale, M.	Tony-O'-Dreams
Thomas, E.M.	Tiny Folk of Sunny Days	D'Aulaire, I.& E.	Too Big
Thomas, E.M.	Tiny Folk of Wintery Days	Carmer, Carl	Too Many Cherries
Humphrey, M.	Tiny Toddlers	Hawkins, Q.	Too Many Dogs
Gleaves, Suzanne	Tip & Dip	Hader, B.& E.	Tooky...
Taylor, Paul B.	Tippletappleteven Town	Skinner, A.M.	Topaz Story Book
Forster, F.J.	Tippytoes...	Medary, Marj.	Topgallant: A Herring Gull
Retner, Beth	Tired Trolly Car	Brunefille, G.	Topo...
Richards, L.E.	Tirra Lirra	Bailey, C.S.	Tops & Whistles
Spyri, J.	Tiss - A Little Alpine Waif	Minnion, W.J.	Topsy Turvey
Schwimmer, R.	Tisza Tales	Duplaix, G.	Topsy Turvey Circus
Rey, H.A.	Tit for Tat	Anderson, B.	Topsy Turvey's Pigtails
Moon, G.	Tita of Mexico	Munro, E.S.	Topsy-Turvey Tales
Ferrer, Melchor	Tito's Hats	Newell, P.	Topsys & Turveys

AUTHOR	TITLE	AUTHOR	TITLE
Newell, P.	Topsys & Turvys Number 2	Simon, Norma	Tree For Me
Willcox, L.C.	Torch: Book of Poems for Boys	Sears, P.M.	Tree Frog
McElravy, May F.	Tortilla Girl	Davis, Rbt.	Tree Toad
Gendel, Evelyn	Tortoise & Turtle	Seredy, K.	Tree for Peter
Disney, W.	Tortoise & the Hare	Holling, H.C.	Tree in the Trail
Anderson, C.W.	Touch of Greatness	Udry, J.M.	Tree is Nice
Lawson, R.	Tough Winter	Caudill, R.	Tree of Freedom
Hurd, E.T.	Toughy & his Trailer Truck	Beston, Henry	Tree that Ran Away
Williams, Jay	Tournament of the Lions	Kilmer, J.	Trees
Coatsworth, E.	Toutou in Bondage	Ames, Mrs. E.	Tremendous Twins
Gay, Zhenya	Town Cats	Roberts, K.	Trending into Maine
Kalashnikoff, N.	Toyon: Dog of the North	Robinson, Tom P.	Trigger John's Son
Sturges, L.B.	Toys of Nuremberg	DuMaurier, G.	Trilby
Carruth, H.	Track's End	Henry, O.	Trimmed Lamp
Meigs, C.	Trade Wind	Moerleim, G.	Trip Around the World
Russell, W.C.	Tragedy of Ida Noble	Phillips, J.	Trip to Fairyland
Kennan, G.	Tragedy of Pelee	Ash, Frank	Trip to Mars
Bourget, P.	Tragic Idyll	Mayer, Henry	Trip to Toyland
Field, M.	Tragic Mary	Crane, W.	Triplets
Grinnell, G.B.	Trail & Camp Fire	Montgomery, R.G.	Troopers Three
Austin, Mary	Trail Book	Greenaway, K.	Trot's Journey
Brininstool, E.A.	Trail Dust of a Maverick	Stein, E.	Troubadour Tales
Watson, Virginia	Trail of Courage	Morris, C.	Trouble Woman
Service, Rbt.	Trail of Ninety-Eight	Gates, Doris	Trouble for Jerry
Fox, John Jr.	Trail of the Lonesome Pine	Morris, Alice T.	Troubles of Tatters
Seton, E.T.	Trail of the Sandhill Stag	Kossak-Szczucka	Troubles of a Gnome
Nesbit, W.D.	Trail to Boyland	Jacberns, R.	Troublesome Dog
Gipson, Fred B.	Trail-Driving Rooster	Quiller-Couch, A.	Troublesome Ursula
Russell, C.M.	Trails Plowed Under	Davis, M.G.	Truce of the Wolf
Kuh, Charlotte	Train, a Boat & an Island	Demuth, Averil	Trudi and Hansel
Lang, Don	Tramp: The Sheep Dog	Hendrich, Paula	Trudy's First Day at Camp
Smith, Susan C.	Tranquilina's Paradise	Ade, G.	True Bills
Kingsley, F.M.	Transfiguration of Miss Philura	Terhune, A.P.	True Dog Stories
Hamer, S.H.	Transformations of the Truefitts	Fox, F.M.	True Monkey Stories
Van Doren, M.	Transparent Tree	Bacon, P.	True Philosopher
Webber, I.E.	Travelers All	Gask, Lilian	True Stories/Big Game & Jungles
Rowe, Dorothy	Traveling Shops	Lang, A.	True Story Book
Eaton, S.	Travelling Bears [ALL TITLES]	Chapin, A.A.	True Story of Humpty Dumpty
Sackville, M.	Travelling Companions...	Davies, W.H.	True Travellers
DuBois, Theodora	Travelling Toys	Austin, Margot	Trumpet
Milne, J.	Travels in Hope	Holme, C.	Trumpet in the Dust
Abbott, C.C.	Travels in a Treetop	Kelly, Eric P.	Trumpeter of Krakow
DeBrunhoff, J.	Travels of Babar	Trease, G.	Trumpets in the West
Bright, Rbt.	Travels of Ching	Lang, A.	Trusty John...
Stevenson, R.L.	Travels with a Donkey in the Cevennes	McCall, S.	Truth Dexter
Quiller-Couch, A.	Treasure Book of Children's Verse	Raymond, W.	Tryphena In Love...
Clinton, A.L.	Treasure Book/Best Stories	Barnes, Madeline	Tub-Time Tales
Asquith, C. (ed.)	Treasure Cave	Comstock, E.B.	Tuck-Me-In Stories
Holder, Charles F.	Treasure Divers	Hood, Thos.	Tucker & Little Bo Peep
Proudfit, I.B.	Treasure Hunter	Willson, Dixie	Tuffy Good Luck
Stevenson, R.L.	Treasure Island	Garis, H.	Tuftoo the Clown
Kelly, Eric P.	Treasure Mountain	Austin, Margot	Tumble Bear
Asquith, C. (ed.)	Treasure Ship	Carlton, M.	Tumble Down Pictures
Wynne, Annette	Treasure Things	Andersen, H.C.	Tumble-Bug
Prishvin, M.	Treasure Trove of the Sun	Willoughby, Rachel	Tunes for Tiny Troubadours
Lamprey, L.	Treasure Valley	Lynch, Patricia	Turf-Cutter's Donkey
Robida, A.	Treasure of Corcassone	Kunos, I	Turkish Fairy Tales...
Boston, Lucy	Treasure of Green Knowe	Dyer, Kate G.	Turky Trott & Black Santa
Tarn, W.W.	Treasure of Isle of Mist	Beardsley, Alice	Turn-Around Book
Henty, G.A.	Treasure of the Incas	Clark, Mary S.	Turnaside Cottage
Chrisman, A.B.	Treasures Long Hidden	Gordon, Eliz.	Turned-Intos
Weisgard, L.	Treasures to See	Smith, A.C.	Turquoise Cup
Zistel, E.	Treasury of Cat Stories	Skinner, A.M.	Turquoise Story Book
Gowans, Adam I.	Treasury of English Verse	Campbell, Ruth	Turtle Whose Snap Unfastened
Pourrat, Henry	Treasury of French Tales	Quiller-Couch, A.	Twelve Dancing Princesses
Moses, M. (ed)	Treasury of Plays/Children	Bishop, C.H.	Twenty & Ten
Edgar, M.G.	Treasury of Verse...	Smith, M.S.	Twenty Centuries of Paris
Edgar, M.G.	Treasury of Verse/School & Home	Inayat, N.	Twenty Jakata Tales
Rhead, G.W.	Treatment of Drapery in Art	Inayat, N.	Twenty Jataka Tales

AUTHOR	TITLE	AUTHOR	TITLE
Blanchard, A.E.	Twenty Little Maidens	Sedberry, J.H.	Under the Flag of the Cross
Tyler, Anna C.	Twenty-Four Unusual Stories	Munroe, K.	Under the Great Bear
DuBois, W.P.	Twenty-One Balloons	Shakespeare, Wm.	Under the Greenwood Tree
Ryder, Arthur	Twenty-Two Goblins	Alcott, L.M.	Under the Lilacs
Booth, M.B.	Twilight Fairy Tales	Mack, R.E.	Under the Mistletoe
Pyle, H.	Twilight Land	Bull, C.L.	Under the Roof of the Jungle
Peto, Gladys	Twilight Stories	Isham, F.S.	Under the Rose
Beard, P.	Twilight Tales	Brown, A.F.	Under the Rowan Tree
Lofting, H.	Twilight of Magic	Robins, E.	Under the Southern Cross
Hogan, Inez	Twin Kids	LaRue, M.G.	Under the Story Tree
Bancroft, L.	Twinkle & Chubbins	Greenaway, K.	Under the Window
Bancroft, L.	Twinkle's Enchantment	Canfield, D.	Understood Betsy
Heward, C.	Twins & Tabiffa	Wilson, E.	Undertaker's Garland
Holling, H.C.	Twins Who Flew Around the World	Fouque, La Motte	Undine
Goldberg, M.	Twirly Skirt	Young, Ella	Unicorn with Silver Shoes
LeBaron, G.	Twixt You & Me	White, Anne H.	Uninvited Donkey
Lenski, L.	Two Brothers & Animal Friends	Van Dyke, H.	Unknown Quantity
Lenski, L.	Two Brothers & Baby Sister	Grant, Rbt.	Unleavened Bread
Russell, W.C.	Two Captains	Herr, Charlotte	Unselfish Pig
Woodhouse, S.C.	Two Cats at Large	Gorey, Edward	Unstrung Harp
Upton, B.	Two Dutch Dolls & Golliwogg	Wing, Paul	Unsuccessful Elf
Hader, B.& E.	Two Funny Clowns	Harraden, B.	Untold Tales of the Past
Sage, A.C.	Two Girls/Old New Jersey	Webber, I.E.	Up Above & Down Below
N/A	Two Jolly Mariners	Flack, M.	Up in The Air
Kepes, J.A.	Two Little Birds & Three	DeAngeli, M.	Up the Hill
Page, T.N.	Two Little Confederates	Bower, B.M.	Uphill Climb
Johnston, A.F.	Two Little Knights of Kentucky	Pritchard, M.T.	Upward Path
Pyle, Kath.	Two Little Mice	Forrester, I.L.	Us Fellers
Burnett, F.H.	Two Little Pilgrim's Progress	Kay, G.A.	Us Kids at the Circus
Buckland, J.	Two Little Runaways	Moe, Louis M.	Vain Pussy Cat
Seton, E.T.	Two Little Savages	Adams, J.D.	Vaino: Boy of New Finland
Brown, M.W.	Two Little Trains	Aguilar, G.	Vale of Cedars
Molesworth, M.	Two Little Waifs	Crane, W.	Valentine & Orson
Edmonds, W.D.	Two Logs Crossing	Littlewood, S.R.	Valentine & Orson
Page, T.N.	Two Prisoners	Bulla, Clyde R.	Valentine Cat
Lipkind, Wm.	Two Reds	Atherton, G.	Valiant Runaways
Edwards, Harry S.	Two Runaways	Rives, H.E.	Valiants of Virginia
Tarkington, B.	Two Vanrevels	Sandwell, H.B.	Valley of Color Days
Marshall, C.	Two Wyoming Girls	London, J.	Valley of the Moon
Dana, R.H.	Two Years Before the Mast	Davis, R.H.	Van Bibber & Others
Beim, Lorraine	Two is a Team	Mills, W.J.	Van Rensselaers of Old Manhattan
Brown, Gladys	Two-Bow Bill	Quick, Herbert	Vandemark's Folly
Maeterlinck, M.	Tyltyl	Carden, Priscilla	Vanilla Village
Melville, Herman	Typee	Syrett, Netta	Vanishing Princess
Garland, H.	Tyranny of the Dark	Thackeray, Wm.	Vanity Fair
Molesworth, M.	US: An Old Fashioned Story	Daugherty, Sonia	Vanka's Donkey
Andersen, H.C.	Ugly Duckling	Upton, F.	Vege-Men's Revenge
Vassos, R.	Ultimo	Hays, M.G.	Vegetable Verselets
Yashima, Taro	Umbrella	Williams, M.	Velveteen Rabbit
Spenser, Edmund	Una & Red Cross Knight	Coffin, J.H.	Vendor of Dreams
Sinclair, M.	Uncanny Stories	Shakespeare, Wm.	Venus & Adonis
James, Will	Uncle Bill...	VerBeck, F.	VerBeck's Bears in Mother Goose-Land
Courlander, H.	Uncle Bouqui of Haiti	Siberiak, M.	Verotchka's Tales
Uncle Frank	Uncle Frank's Visit to Fairy-Land	Hay, Helen	Verses/Jock & Joan
Robinson, W.H.	Uncle Lubin	Ward, Lynd	Vertigo
Dalrymple, Leona	Uncle Noah's Christmas Inspiration	Sendak, M.	Very Far Away
Stapp, E.B.	Uncle Peter-Heathen	Weil, Ann	Very First Day
Harris, J.C.	Uncle Remus [ALL TITLES]	Skinner, A.W.	Very Little Child's Book of Stories
Harper, Wilhelmina	Uncle Sam's Story Book	Skaar, G.M.	Very Little Dog
Webb, W.P.	Uncle Swithin's Inventions	Vorse, M.H.	Very Little Person
Stowe, H.B.	Uncle Tom's Cabin	Donnell, A.H.	Very Small Person
Mason, W.	Uncle Walt	Krauss, Ruth	Very Special House
Garis, H.	Uncle Wiggily [ALL TITLES]	Davis, L.R.	Very Special Pet
Wright, H.B.	Uncrowned King	Rosvall, T.D.	Very Stupid Folk
Brigham, S.J.	Under Blue Skies	Milne, A.A.	Very Young Verses
Beardsley, Aubrey	Under The Hill	Goldsmith, O.	Vicar of Wakefield
Mabie, H.W.	Under The Trees	Yashima, Taro	Village Tree
Creswick, Paul	Under the Black Raven	Spyri, J.	Vinzi
Page, T.N.	Under the Crust	Clarkson, L.	Violet Among the Lilies

AUTHOR	TITLE	AUTHOR	TITLE
Underwood, P.	When Christmas Comes Around	Moon, G.	White Indian
Hall, Tom	When Cupid Calls	Snedeker, C.D.	White Isle
Shetter, S.C.	When Grandma Was a Little Girl	Aldin, C.	White Kitten Book
Harland, M.	When Grandmamma Was 14	Bigelow, P.	White Man's Africa
Hall, Tom	When Hearts are Trumps	Burnett, F.H.	White People
Denslow, W.W.	When I Grow Up	Carter, R.G.	White Plume of Navarre
Kelly, E.M.	When I was Little	Aldin, C.	White Puppy Book
Bowie, W.R.	When Jesus was Born	Reed, Myrtle	White Shield
Dodge, M.M.	When Life is Young	Tresselt, A.R.	White Snow, Bright Snow
Carpenter, John	When Little Boys Sing	Colum, P.	White Sparrow
Knobel, E.	When Little Thoughts Go Rhyming	Seredy, K.	White Stag
Dunbar, P.L.	When Malindy Sings	Heilberg, N.	White-Ear & Peter
White, E.O.	When Molly was Six	Peterson, Barbara	Whitefoot Mouse
Almond, Linda S.	When Peter Rabbit Went a-Fishing	Burgess, T.	Whitefoot the Wood Mouse
Almond, Linda S.	When Peter Rabbit Went to School	Rounds, Glen	Whitey & Jinglebob
Singmaster, Elsie	When Sarah Saved the Day	Rounds, Glen	Whitey & the Blizzard
Hurd, Marian K.	When She Came Home from College	Rounds, Glen	Whitey Looks for a Job
Parker, Gilbert	When Valmond Came to Pontiac	Rounds, Glen	Whitey's First Roundup
Milne, A.A.	When We Were Very Young	Rounds, Glen	Whitey's Sunday Horse
Parrish, R.	When Wilderness was King	Adelson, L.	Who Blew that Whistle?
Schlein, M.	When Will the World be Mine?	Weisgard, L.	Who Dreams of Cheese?
Warner, A.	When Woman Proposes	Lathrop, D.	Who Goes There?
Nesbit, W.D.	When a Feller Needs a Friend	Hawkins, Q.	Who Wants an Apple
Rinehart, M.R.	When a Man Marries	Johnson, Crockett	Who's Upside Down?
Turner, N.B.	When it Rained Cats & Dogs	Murphy, Ruby B.	Who's Who in Mother Goose Land
Fish, H.D.	When the Root Children Wake Up	Barrows, M.	Who's Who in the Zoo
Kay, G.A.	When the Sandman Comes	Morton, J.B.	Who's Who in the Zoo
Wells, H.G.	When the Sleeper Wakes	Rich, Edwin G.	Who-So Stories
Lewis, Eliz. F.	When the Typhoon Blows	Various	Whole Family
Brown, M.W.	When the Wind Blew	Spilka, A.	Whom Shall I Marry?
Harbour, H.	Where Flies the Flag	Daskam, J.	Whom the Gods Destroyed
Harland, M.	Where Ghosts Walk	N/A	Whose Little Kitty are You?
Brown, M.W.	Where Have You Been?	Burgess, G.	Why Be a Goop?
Deland, M.	Where Laborers are Few	Ainslie, K.	Why Was He Late?
Leighton, C.	Where Land Meets Sea	Alden, R.M.	Why the Chimes Rang
Harris, Credo	Where Souls of Men are Calling	Flagg, J.M.	Why they Married
Clement, Marg.	Where Was Bobby?	Rae, J.	Why: Reflections for Children
White, E.O.	Where is Adelaide?	Fyleman, R.	Widdy-Widdy-Wurkey
Charlip, R.	Where is Everybody?	Eberle, I.	Wide Fields
Sarg, Tony	Where is Tommy?	Warner, S.	Wide, Wide World
Williams, I.A.	Where the Bee Sucks	Gibson, C.D.	Widow & Her Friends
Morley, C.	Where the Blue Begins	Johnson, R.M.	Widow Guthrie
Pyle, Kath.	Where the Wind Blows	Chestnutt, Charles	Wife of His Youth
Jewett, E.M.	Which was Witch?	Rice, Ethel	Wiggle & Waggle
Hader, B.	Whiffy McMann	Deming, T.O.	Wigwam Children
Schneider, N.	While Susie Sleeps	Eastman, C.A.	Wigwam Evenings
Riley, J.W.	While the Heart Beats Young	Van Loon, H.W.	Wilbur the Hat
Burgess, T.	While the Story Log Burns	Cook, W.W.	Wilby's Dan
Crane, S.	Whilomville Stories	Seton, E.T.	Wild Animal Play for Children
Miller, O.B.	Whisk Away on a Sunbeam	Seton, E.T.	Wild Animals I Have Known
Means, F.C.	Whispering Girl	Reynier, M.	Wild Animals at Home
Spearman, Frank	Whispering Smith	Seton, E.T.	Wild Animals at Home
Debenham, M.H.	Whispering Winds & Tales they Told	Celli, Rose	Wild Animals/Little Ones
Jones, Idwal	Whistler's Van	Davis, L.R.	Wild Birthday Cake
Averill, Naomi	Whistling-Two-Teeth	Gordon, Eliz.	Wild Flower Children
D'Aulnoy	White Cat...	Chaffee, Allen	Wild Folk
Doyle, A.C.	White Company	Webb, M. St. John	Wild Fruit Fairies
Munroe, K.	White Conquerors	Squier, E-L.	Wild Heart
Garis, H.	White Crystals	Fleuron, S.	Wild Horses of Iceland
Hawkes, Clarence	White Czar...	Dewar, G.A.B.	Wild Life/Hampshire Highlands
Mott, L.	White Darkness	Ward, Lynd	Wild Pilgrimage
Thurber, J.	White Deer	Andersen, H.C.	Wild Swans
Faulkner, Georgene	White Elephant	Daugherty, J.	Wild Wild West
Ogburn, Charlton	White Falcon	Kent, R.	Wilderness
London, J.	White Fang	Lippincott, J.W.	Wilderness Champion
Franchot, A.W.	White Giant & Black Giant	Steele, Wm. O.	Wilderness Journey
Tudor, T.	White Goose	Annixter, Paul	Wilderness Ways
Robinson, Gertrude	White Heron Feather	Singleton, E.	Wildflower Fairy Book
Coatsworth, E.	White Horse	Fox, F.M.	Wildling Princess

AUTHOR	TITLE	AUTHOR	TITLE
Austin, Margot	Willamette Way	Davis, M.G.	With Cap & Bells
Byron, May	William & Woggs	Watson, V.	With Cortes the Conqueror
Flack, M.	William & his Kitten	Skinner, C.M.	With Feet to the Earth
Cary, E.L.	William Morris	McNeil, E.	With Kit Carson in the Rockies
Crane, W.	William Morris to Whistler	Field, E.	With Trumpet & Drum
Austin, Margot	William's Shadow	Habberton, J.	With the Dream Maker
Lea, John	Willie Wimple's Adventures	Schultz, J.W.	With the Indians in the Rockies
Golding, Harry	Willie Winkie...	Kipling, R.	With the Night Mail
Brown, M.W.	Willie's Adventures	Gaboriau, Emile	Within an Inch of His Life
Brown, M.W.	Willie's Walk to Grandmama	Behn, Harry	Wizard in the Well
Meigs, C.	Willow Whistle	Baum, L.F.	Wizard of Oz
Flack, M.	Willy Nilly	Smedley, C.	Wizards of Ryetown
Hurd, E.T.	Willy's Farm	Baum, L.F.	Woggle-Bug Book
Travers, Georgia	Wily Woodchucks	Lippincott, J.W.	Wolf King
Various	Wimp & the Woodle	McCleery, Wm.	Wolf Story
Bowman, J.C.	Winabojo	Morris, Wm.	Wolf's Head & the Queen
Eliot, E.C.	Wind Boy	Grey, Zane	Wolf-Tracker
Allen, Marian	Wind in the Chimney	Lewis, A.H.	Wolfville
Meigs, C.	Wind in the Chimney	Lewis, A.H.	Wolfville Folks
Wilkins, M.E.	Wind in the Rose Bush	New, C.M.	Woman Reigns
Grahame, K.	Wind in the Willows	Seton, G.	Woman Tenderfoot
Cormack, M.	Wind of the Vikings	Allen, G.	Woman Who Did
Weber, Lenora M.	Wind on the Prairie	Green, A.K.	Woman in the Alcove
Chrisman, A.B.	Wind that Wouldn't Blow	Wilde, O.	Woman of No Importance
Saint-Exupery, A.	Wind, Sand & Stars	Malory, T.	Women of Morte Darthur
DeMorgan, M.	Windfairies...	Hawthorne, N.	Wonder Book
Preston, Hayter	Windmills	Thompson, R.P.	Wonder Book
Meigs, C.	Windy Hill	Hawthorne, N.	Wonder Book & Tanglewood Tales
Behn, Harry	Windy Morning	Darton, F.J.	Wonder Book of Beasts
Price, M.E.	Windy Shore	Hawthorne, N.	Wonder Book...
Bradley, Mary H.	Wine of Astonishment	Forbush, Wm. B.	Wonder Book/Myths & Legends
Brown, Anna R.	Wine-Press	Pyle, H.	Wonder Clock
Berry, E.	Winged Girl of Knossos	Hall, A.N.	Wonder Hill
Dalgliesh, A.	Wings Around South America	Ludins, Ryah	Wonder Rock
D'Aulaire, I.& E.	Wings for Per	Young, Ella	Wonder Smith & His Son
Dalgliesh, A.	Wings for the Smiths	Bailey, C.S.	Wonder Stories
Daugherty, Sonia	Wings of Glory	N/A	Wonder Stories of Herodotus
Tracy, Louis	Wings of the Morning	Hawthorne, N.	Wonder Tales
Putnam, Nina W.	Winkle, Twinkle & Lollypop	Pyle, Kath.	Wonder Tales Retold
Milne, A.A.	Winnie-the-Pooh	Jewett, E.M.	Wonder Tales from Tibet
McNeely, M.H.	Winning Out	Henderson, B.	Wonder Tales of Ancient Wales
Bindloss, H.	Winston of the Prairie	Carpenter, Frances	Wonder Tales of Dogs & Cats
Carman, B.	Winter Holiday	Whitehorn, A.L.	Wonder Tales of Old Japan
Brown, M.W.	Winter Noisy Book	Olcott, F.J.	Wonder Tales/Baltic Wizards
Haggard, H.R.	Winter Pilgrimmage	Olcott, F.J. (ed.)	Wonder Tales/Goblin Hills
Thomas, E.M.	Winter Swallow...	Olcott, F.J. (ed.)	Wonder Tales/Pirate Isles
Shakespeare, Wm.	Winter's Tale	Olcott, F.J.	Wonder Tales/Windmill Lands
Bianco, M.W.	Winterbound	Pennell, J.	Wonder of Work
Sowerby, Githa	Wise Book	Bradley, W.	Wonderbox Stories
Hofman, Caroline	Wise Gray Cat	Deardon, H.	Wonderful Adventure
DeSegur, S.	Wise Little Donkey	Lagerlof, Selma	Wonderful Adventures of Nils
Disney, W.	Wise Little Hen	Hunt, M.L.	Wonderful Baker
Herr, Charlotte	Wise Mamma Goose	Knevels, G.	Wonderful Bed
Kunhardt, D.	Wise Old Aard-Vark	Coatsworth, E.	Wonderful Day
Uttley, Alison	Wise Owl's Story	Bailey, C.S.	Wonderful Days
Hader, B.& E.	Wish on the Moon	Montgomery, F.T.	Wonderful Electric Elephant
Byington, Eloise	Wishbone Children	Ayme, Marcel	Wonderful Farm
Bigham, M.A.	Wishing Fairies	Slobodkina, E.	Wonderful Feast
Ingraham, C.	Wishing Fairy's Animal Friends	Olcott, F.J.	Wonderful Garden
Thompson, R.P.	Wishing Horse of Oz	Nesbit, E.	Wonderful Garden...
Naylor, James B.	Witch Crow & Barney Bylow	Gannett, R.S.	Wonderful House-Boat-Train
Estes, Eleanor	Witch Family	Hamer, S.H.	Wonderful Isles
Harris, J.C.	Witch Wolf...	N/A	Wonderful Kittens
White, T.H.	Witch in the Wood	Meigs, C.	Wonderful Locomotive
Gordon, Pat	Witch of Scrapfaggot Green	Davidson, John	Wonderful Mission/Earl Lavender
Brook, Arthur	Witch's Hollow	Snowden, J.H.	Wonderful Night
Hole, Christina	Witchcraft in England	Thurber, J.	Wonderful O.
Wells, A.R.	Witchery Ways	Bischoff, Ilse	Wonderful Poodle
Young, Gerald	Witches' Kitchen	Smith, G.	Wonderful Stories of Jane & John

AUTHOR	TITLE	AUTHOR	TITLE
Brown, M.W.	Wonderful Story	Seuss, Dr.	Yertle the Turtle
Disney, W.	Wonderful Tar Baby	Sowerby, Githa	Yesterday's Children
Gay, Zhenya	Wonderful Things!	Lide, A.A.	Yinka-Tu the Yak
Dickerson	Wonderful Wishes of Jackie & Jean	Gilbert, W.S.	Yoeman of the Guard
Baum, L.F.	Wonderful Wizard of Oz	DeAngeli, M.	Yonie Wondernose
Gury, Jeremy	Wonderful World of Aunt Tuddy	Wiese, K.	You Can Write Chinese
Barnes, Nancy	Wonderful Year	Bontemps, A.	You Can't Eat a Possum
Cuming, E.W.D.	Wonders in Monsterland	Nash, Ogden	You Can't Get There from Here
Farjeon, E.	Wonders of Herodotus	Coatsworth, E.	You Shall Have a Carriage
Unknown	Wonders of Wilmington	Roberts, C.G.D.	Young Acadian
Moon, G.	Wongo & the Wise Old Crow	Hough, E.	Young Alaskans
Smith, F.H.	Wood Fire in No.3	Dalgliesh, A.	Young Aunts
Long, W.J.	Wood-Folk Comedies	James, Will	Young Cowboy
Craig, E.G.	Woodcuts & Some Words	N/A	Young Folks Birthday Book
Nodier, C.	Woodcutter's Dog	Boylan, G.D.	Young Folks Uncle Tom's Cabin
Higgins, V.M.	Woodcutter's Son	Lewis, Eliz. F.	Young Fu of the Upper Yangtze
Maloy, L.	Wooden Shoes in America	Dunbar, J.	Young Hopeful
Gruelle, J.	Wooden Willie	Brown, M.W.	Young Kangaroo
Hawley, H.E.	Woodland Party	LeGallienne, R.	Young Lives
Seton, E.T.	Woodmyth & Fable	Carr, Mary J.	Young Mac of Fort Vancouver
Wallace, Lew	Wooing of Malkatoon	Hunt, M.L.	Young Man of the House
Daldorne, Evan	Wooing of the Water-Witch	Phillips, C.	Young Man's Fancy
Mallison, C.	Wooster-Poosters	Stewart, Anna B.	Young Miss Burney
Sewell, H.	Words to the Wise	Cradock, C.E.	Young Mountaineers
Cary, E.L.	Works of J.M. Whistler	Stables, Wm. G.	Young Peggy McQueen
Beerbohm, M.	Works of...	Baker, C.	Young People in Old Places
Menpes, D.	World Pictures	Smith, M.P.W.	Young Puritans in Captivity
Hogan, Inez	World Round	Smith, M.P.W.	Young Puritans/Old Hadley
Tunis, John R.	World Series	Singmaster, Elsie	Young Ravenals
Earl of Birkenhead	World in 2030	Iogolevitch, Paul	Young Russian Corporal
Bemelmans, L.	World of Bemelmans	Stong, Phil	Young Settler
Menpes, M.	World's Children	Miller, E.C.	Young Trajan
Jefferson, C.E.	World's Christmas Tree	Ashford, Daisy	Young Visitors
N/A	World's Fairy Book	Gray, Eliz. J.	Young Walter Scott
Eddison, E.R.	Worm Ouroboros	Boyle, Kay	Youngest Camel
Byrne, M.	Would-Be Witch	Sharp, E.	Youngest Girl in the School
Gatti, Attilio	Wrath of Moto	N/A	Yours Truly
Leighton, Rbt.	Wreck of the Golden Fleece	Strong, R.	Yoyo's Animal Friends
Young, Evelyn	Wu & Lu & Li	Henty, G.A.	Yuletide Yarns
Bronte, E.J.	Wuthering Heights	Fitzgerald, S.	Zankiwank & Bletherwitch
Sharp, E.	Wymps & other Fairy Tales	Gibson, Katherine	Zauberlinda: Wise Witch
Field, E.	Wynken, Blynken & Nod	Ingraham, C.	Zebra & the Wishing Fairy
Raine, W.M.	Wyoming	Ovington, Mary W.	Zeke
Wood, J.S.	Yale Yarns	Voight, V.F.	Zeke & the Fisher-Cat
Boylan, G.D.	Yama Yama Land	Wells, Rhea	Zeke the Raccoon
Bryant, B.M.	Yammy Buys a Bicycle	Nicholson, M.	Zelda Dameron
Fenner, P.R.	Yankee Doodle	DeBrunhoff, J.	Zephir's Holidays
N/A	Yankee Doodle	Norris, C.G.	Zest
Pyle, H.	Yankee Doodle	N/A	Zig Zag Fables
Malcolmson, A.	Yankee Doodle's Cousins	LaRue, M.G.	Zip the Toy Mule
Loomis, C.B.	Yankee Enchantments	Montgomery, F.T.	Zip: Advens. of a Frisky Fox Terrier
Barnes, James	Yankee Ships & Yankee Sailors	North, S.	Zipper ABC Book
Holland, R.S.	Yankee Ships in Pirate Waters	Channing, Blanche	Zodiac Stories
Shapiro, I.	Yankee Thunder	Turner, N.B.	Zodiac Town
Moorat, Joseph	Ye Booke of Nursery Rhymes	Farrow, G.E.	Zoo Babies
Moorat, Joseph	Ye Second Book of Nursery Rhymes	Golding, Harry	Zoo Days
McGinley, Phyllis	Year Without a Santa Claus	Harshberger, K.	Zoological Soliloquies
Sawyer, R.S.	Year of the Christmas Dragon	Perkins, Marlin	Zooparade
Scott, A.M.	Year with the Fairies	Beerbohm, M.	Zuleika Dobson
Walters, L.	Year's at the Spring		
Dawe, W.C.	Yellow & White		
Griggs, Mary	Yellow Cat		
Dwight, G.	Yellow Cat & Friends		
Lang, A.	Yellow Fairy Book		
Thompson, R.P.	Yellow Knight of Oz		
Field, R.	Yellow Ship		
Jahn, Mary L.	Yelly		
Robertson, W.G.	Yen of Songs/Baby in a Garden		
Eldridge, E.J.	Yen-Foh, a Chinese Boy		

Librarians -- Researchers -- Reference Specialists

Available in Mid-1996

A Companion Guide featuring...

Library of Congress Card Catalog Numbers
and
LC Internal Call Numbers

Intended to provide additional information for books listed in the Price Guide & Bibliographic Checklist for Children's & Illustrated Books, the new reference work will be sorted according to author, and will list internal Library of Congress (LC) call numbers and the LC card catalog numbers for the majority of American-published books in the price guide. Also, you'll know instantly which books are not in the LC collection. All such books will feature the National Union Catalog (NUC) volume reference and the number of copies located through NUC.

You'll have this valuable information available at your fingertips for quick reference whenever you need it!

SEND FOR FREE DETAILS AT ANY TIME!

Just drop a postcard or quick note in the mail to receive free details on this upcoming work just as soon as it's completed.

Also...

Interested in multiple copies of the price guide? Discounts of up to 50% are possible on as few as 21 copies of the guide (your choice of how many hardback and paperback in each order). Just send a postcard or note requesting info, and a detailed multiple-copy price schedule will be sent free of charge.

Please mail all correspondence to:

E. Lee Baumgarten
PO Box 2876
Martinsburg, WV 25401